MW01045250

~ THE ~
COMPLETE
54-BOOK
APOCRYPHA

2022 EDITION

With the Deuterocanon, 1–3 Enoch, Giants, Jasher, Jubilees, Pseudepigrapha, & the Apostolic Fathers

Literal Standard Version

© 2022 by Covenant Press

of the Covenant Christian Coalition

www.ccc.one

PREFACE TO THE 2022 EDITION

The 2022 edition of *The Complete Apocrypha* follows many of the same translation principles and formatting practices as the *Literal Standard Version of The Holy Bible* (LSV), published in 2020. You can consult the preface and introduction to the LSV for more information about the translation and formatting style of this 2022 edition. In general, this 54-book collection is a highly literal, word-for-word (formal equivalence) translation, formatted with justified text blocks in the manner of the original manuscripts. The caesura mark is used in lieu of line breaks in poetic portions of the text. Unlike the LSV Bible, the Tetragrammaton is not used (except in a handful of specific cases that demand its use), but where a reference to the Divine Name is likely, the all-uppercase title LORD can be found for distinction.

This library of apocryphal works is not Scripture but is the definitive collection of very early extra-biblical writings in the Judeo-Christian tradition. As such, this collection was meticulously collated and excludes writings foreign to the traditional Judeo-Christian stream of theological thought, such as Gnostic and Ebionite texts. The 2022 edition is an exhaustively-inclusive repository of the works generally thought to fall within *common Judeo-Christian thought*, and for that reason Gnostic works like the Gospel of Thomas are not well-suited for inclusion here.

Opinions of the apocryphal works vary, but they generally fall into either of two extremes: the first is the view that these works are inherently heretical because of their absence from the Protocanon and must be censored and condemned at all costs; the second is the view that traditional religious authorities, Jewish and Christian alike, are responsible for a massive coverup of divine revelation by excluding many of these texts from the canon, and that these works should be regarded as hidden Scripture. Both views are a sort of knee-jerk reaction to a more nuanced reality. On the one hand, we can have total confidence in the protocanonical 66 books of the Bible, and the deuterocanonical books have always held a sort of secondary or "limbo" status. The Muratorian Canon of the 2nd century demonstrates as much, and early collators and translators like Jerome fought against the full inclusion of the Deuterocanon. Even in the early years of the Reformation we see a hesitancy toward these texts—Luther did not consider these works equal to Scripture (although he did consider them worthy of study); likewise, the 1611 King James Version consigned the intertestamental Deuterocanon to an essentially appendix status, demoted with the title *Apocrypha* ("hidden" or "obscure" writings).

There are good reasons not to consider these texts equal to Scripture: first, they are scarcely if ever quoted in the protocanonical books, and the handful of possible quotations and allusions are highly controversial. Second, the Old Testament and intertestamental apocryphal texts appear to have been written much later than the 39 protocanonical books (and often in Greek rather than Hebrew); likewise, the apocryphal New Testament texts and Apostolic Fathers are generally thought to have been written decades, even many decades, after the core 27 books of the New Testament. Third, manuscripts are scarcer and show much greater historical redaction than the protocanonical books. Fourth, a number of the supposed pseudepigraphical works show a tendency toward perfectionist soteriology (i.e., an aversion or ignorance toward the Old and New Testament system of atoning, substitutionary sacrifice and the imputation of righteousness). And fifth, some of the narratives describe very fanciful and exaggerated descriptions that generally seem out-of-sync with the biblical tradition—Abraham conversing with death personified, Jacob's sons utilizing superpowers to conquer Canaan, Solomon binding demons to build the Temple, Isaiah flying through and describing each level of Heaven, and so forth.

On the other hand, there is little doubt the biblical writers had at least some familiarity with these texts or perhaps the oral traditions on which they were based. Jude seemingly quotes from Enoch. Paul mentions names found only in some of the apocryphal literature. Jesus celebrated the Feast of Dedication (Hanukkah), a festival established according to the accounts found in 1 and 2 Maccabees. The debate over the Apocrypha often belies simpler conclusions: some apocryphal texts are simply historical accounts (e.g., Maccabees); other apocryphal texts were not necessarily written to add to Scripture, but rather as entertaining stories—*fictions even*—in a similar vein to what contemporary Jewish and Christian writers do; still others may contain kernels of primordial oral traditions harkening back to real sayings and accounts between God and man. The apocryphal books are not to be revered as Scripture, but they do help us understand the history, traditions, and thinking at the time much of the Bible was written.

This edition is based on and greatly expands the bestselling 2018 edition, but is its own translation (© 2022), featuring 54 books and an additional section of apocryphal fragments. This is the largest Apocrypha collection ever published which includes all of the deuterocanonical books, the Apostolic Fathers, and most of the non-Gnostic pseudepigrapha. In order to collate and translate this definitive Apocrypha collection, it was necessary to establish some key parameters regarding what to include and what to exclude. As mentioned beforehand, any blatantly Gnostic or Ebionite texts were excluded since these fall outside the purview of orthodox Jewish and Christian belief. All included books had to have been composed prior to the third century AD, or, at the very least, have scholarly support for at least some core portion of the text to fit that criterion. Jasher and the Testament of Solomon are perhaps the most debatable in this collection. It is widely agreed that their present forms show undeniable medieval redaction, but there was likely some simpler, primordial form of Solomon, and a growing number of researchers suppose that at least some portion of Jasher (*Sefer haYashar*) was based on an ancient text or oral tradition.

KEY FACTS

LANGUAGES: Like the Bible, which was originally composed in Hebrew, Aramaic, and Greek, the apocryphal works were also likely written in those languages. However, there are not always extant manuscripts in those languages remaining, so the translation-base, in addition to Hebrew, Aramaic, and Greek, also includes Syriac (a dialect of Aramaic), Coptic, Ethiopic, and Slavonic.

LONGEST BOOK: The Book of Jasher, also called Sefer haYashar, while containing fewer chapters than 1 Enoch (91 vs. 108), is considerably the longest book in this complete collection. It is a midrash exploring biblical history in great detail, from the creation of mankind all the way to the death of Joshua and the conquest of Canaan.

SHORTEST BOOK: The likely pseudepigraphical Prayer of Manasseh, with its 15 short verses, is attributed to King Manasseh of Judah. It is considered apocryphal by most Christians, but is included in many Bibles, usually as an appendix.

DATES OF COMPOSITION: Secular scholarship generally assigns the works in this collection to the third century BC through the third century AD, although some works likely underwent considerable medieval redaction, including the Testament of Solomon and the Book of Jasher.

WHAT IS INCLUDED: Almost all the notable Jewish and Christian extra-biblical religious texts from these early centuries are included in this collection except for those that would be widely considered heretical or unorthodox works (e.g., Gnostic, Ebionite, or Arian).

NUMBERS: 54 books plus all the additions to Esther, Psalms, and Daniel, 1,541 chapters (incl. psalms, odes, visions, commandments, similitudes, and fragments), and 24,444 verses.

INTRODUCTION FROM THE 2018 EDITION

The Deuterocanon, more commonly known as *Apocrypha*, is the collection of writings often sandwiched between the Old and New Testaments. These books are considered by some Christian denominations to be canonical or semi-canonical. While Protestants largely reject the books as spurious or even heretical, and the Roman and Orthodox churches accept them as canonical, it may be wise to recognize that historic Christianity has held to more of a middle ground, including by Reformers such as Martin Luther and early Catholic writers like Jerome. There has always been a distinction between protocanonical books of the Bible and the deuterocanonical books— the former being near-universally attested to as God-breathed by the Church and the latter often questioned for their canonicity. At the same time, the deuterocanonical books are held in higher regard than the truly heretical Gnostic works that were written after the advent of Christianity.

While it is unwise to hold the apocryphal Deuterocanon to the same God-breathed standard as the 66 books of the Bible, we hold, as Martin Luther did, to their value as possibly true and good to read, but unverified:

> *"Apocrypha, that are books which are not considered equal to the*
> *Holy Scriptures, but are useful and good to read."*

Because certain books of the Roman Catholic Deuterocanon do not rise to the level of Holy Scripture, we must reject their canonicity, but that rejection does not exclude their profitability for reading as enlightening works that closely mirror Scripture and inform us about ancient, biblical history. They are lower than Scripture, but not spurious or inherently heretical. The Constitution of the CCC states:

> *"The Bible is the final authority for all matters of life, faith, and doctrine and in its*
> *original Hebrew, Greek, and Aramaic form is completely infallible. The Bible says that*
> *the heart is deceitful above all else (Jer. 17:9) and the understanding of mankind*
> *corrupted (1 Cor. 1:20; 3:19), so God's word must inform and ultimately decide all*
> *questions of truth and doctrine. The CCC rejects the deuterocanonical books,*
> *otherwise known as Apocrypha, because the ancient Jewish canons excluded them,*
> *Jesus excludes the time period in which they were written in Luke 11:50–51, no*
> *references can be found to them in the New Testament, and early Christians like*
> *Jerome fought against their inclusion. However, the Bible mentions and makes allusion*
> *to several books that are not in the current Protestant canon such as Jasher, Enoch,*
> *and the Wars of the Lord. The true canon begins with Genesis, ends with Revelation,*
> *excludes the Apocrypha, and likely includes several of these other referenced books,*
> *although it is not clear that the current translations of Jasher, Enoch, and others are*
> *accurate translations of the original writings and therefore their authority is in dispute.*
> *For this reason only the sixty-six books of the Protestant canon are considered*
> *authoritative and divinely inspired, although the study of Jasher, Enoch, and other*
> *books that are explicitly mentioned or referenced in Scripture is not precluded, so long*
> *as the studier recognizes their current unverifiable state."*

With this basic foundation laid, we can now appreciate the deuterocanonical books for what they are: valuable historical and biblical commentaries with perhaps bits of real Scripture intertwined, but not works on which to formulate doctrine. Lastly, it should be noted that the book transliterated "Jasher" is the one most in question in this collection. It was written no later than the mid-sixteenth century AD, but there is debate regarding whether this is in fact the original *Jasher* referenced in the Bible, or, if it is a later, spurious work.

THE GOOD NEWS OF SALVATION

In accordance with the Scriptures, Christ the Messiah, the Son of the living God, became human, incarnate in the person of Jesus of Nazareth, lived a morally perfect and sinless life, died for our sins on the Cross as a substitutionary sacrifice, was buried in a tomb, and was raised bodily from the dead on the third day. Everyone who hears and accepts this message of salvation, believing in their heart that God raised the Christ from the dead, will be pardoned of all their sins, given the gift of the Holy Spirit, and granted everlasting life in perpetual union with God. Salvation is found in Christ alone by grace alone through faith alone and not by works.

BOOKS OF THE APOCRYPHA

BOOKS OF THE APOCRYPHA CONTINUED ON NEXT PAGE →

NEW TESTAMENT

APPENDIX

ADDITIONS TO THE BIBLE

APOCRYPHAL ESTHER

The Septuagint (LXX) version of Esther contains a number of sections not found in the Hebrew version of the text (chs. 11–16). These Greek chapters are canonical in a variety of traditions.

CHAPTER 11

[1] In the fourth year of the reign of Ptolemy and Cleopatra, Dositheus, who said he was a priest, and of the Levitical race, and Ptolemy his son brought this letter of Purim, which they said Lysimachus the son of Ptolemy had interpreted in Jerusalem. [2] In the second year of the reign of Artaxerxes the great, in the first day of the month of Nisan, Mordecai the son of Jair, the son of Semei, the son of Cis, of the tribe of Benjamin: [3] a Jew who dwelt in the city of Shushan, a great man and among the first of the king's court, had a dream. [4] Now he was of the number of the captives, whom Nebuchadnezzar king of Babylon had carried away from Jerusalem with Jehoiachin king of Judah: [5] And this was his dream: Behold, there were voices, and tumults, and thunders, and earthquakes, and a disturbance on the earth. [6] And behold, two great dragons came forth ready to fight against one another. [7] And at their cry all nations were stirred up to fight against the nation of the just. [8] And that was a day of darkness and danger, of tribulation and distress, and great fear on the earth. [9] And the nation of the just was troubled fearing their own evils and was prepared for death. [10] And they cried to God: and as they were crying, a little fountain grew into a very great river, and abounded into many waters. [11] The light and the sun rose up, and the humble were exalted, and they devoured the glorious. [12] And when Mordecai had seen this, and arose out of his bed, he was thinking what God would do: and he kept it fixed in his mind, desirous to know what the dream should signify.

CHAPTER 12

[1] And he abode at that time in the king's court with Bagatha and Thara, the king's eunuchs, who were porters of the palace. [2] And when he understood their designs, and had diligently searched into their projects, he learned that they went about to lay violent hands on King Artaxerxes, and he told the king thereof. [3] Then the king had them both examined, and after they had confessed, commanded them to be put to death. [4] But the king made a record of what was done: and Mordecai also committed the memory of the thing to writing. [5] And the king commanded him to abide in the court of the palace, and gave him presents for the information. [6] But Haman, the son of Amadathi the Bugite, was in great honor with the king, and sought to hurt Mordecai and his people, because of the two eunuchs of the king who were put to death.

CHAPTER 13

[1] And this was the copy of the letter: Artaxerxes the great king who reigns from India to Ethiopia, to the princes and governors of the one hundred and twenty-seven provinces that are subject to his empire, greetings. [2] Whereas I reigned over many nations, and had brought all the world under my dominion, I was not willing to abuse the greatness of my power, but to govern my subjects with clemency and leniency, that they might live quietly without any terror, and might enjoy peace, which is desired by all men. [3] But when I asked my counselors how this might be accomplished, one that excelled the rest in wisdom and fidelity, and was second after the king, Haman by name, [4] he told me that there was a people scattered through the whole world, which used new laws, and acted against the customs of all nations, despised the commands of kings, and violated by their opposition the concord of all nations. [5] For what reason having learned this, and seeing one nation in opposition to all mankind using perverse laws, and going against our commands, and disturbing the peace and concord of the provinces subject to us, [6] we have commanded that all whom Haman will mark out, who is chief over all the provinces, and second after the king, and whom we honor as a father, will be utterly destroyed by their enemies, with their wives and children, and that none will have pity on them, on the fourteenth day of the twelfth month Adar of this present year: [7] that these wicked men going down to Hades in one day, may restore to our empire the peace which they had disturbed. [8] But Mordecai implored the LORD, remembering all His works, [9] and said, "O LORD, LORD, almighty King, for all things are in Your power, and there is none that can resist Your will, if You determine to save Israel. [10] You have made the heavens and earth, and all things that are under the cover of Heaven. [11] You are Lord of all, and there is none that can resist Your majesty. [12] You know all things, and You know that it was not out of pride and contempt, or any desire of glory, that I refused to worship the proud Haman, [13] (for I would willingly and readily for the salvation of Israel have kissed even the steps of his feet,) [14] but I feared lest I should transfer the honor of my God to a man, and lest I should adore anyone except my God. [15] And now, O LORD, O King, O God of Abraham, have mercy on Your people, because our enemies resolve to destroy us, and extinguish Your inheritance. [16] Do not despise Your portion, which You have redeemed for Yourself

out of Egypt. [17] Hear my supplication, and be merciful to Your lot and inheritance, and turn our mourning into joy, that we may live and praise Your Name, O LORD, and do not shut the mouths of them that sing to You." [18] And all Israel with like mind and supplication cried to the LORD, because they saw certain death hanging over their heads.

CHAPTER 14

[1] Queen Esther also, fearing the danger that was at hand, had recourse to the LORD. [2] And when she had laid away her royal apparel, she put on garments suitable for weeping and mourning: instead of various precious ointments, she covered her head with ashes and dung, and she humbled her body with fasts: and all the places in which before she was accustomed to rejoice, she filled with her torn hair. [3] And she prayed to the LORD, the God of Israel, saying, "O my LORD, who alone are our King, help me, a desolate woman, and who has no other helper but You. [4] My danger is in my hands. [5] I have heard from my father that You, O LORD, took Israel from among all nations, and our fathers from all their predecessors, to possess them as a perpetual inheritance, and You have done to them as You have promised. [6] We have sinned in Your sight, and therefore You have delivered us into the hands of our enemies: [7] For we have worshiped their gods. You are just, O LORD. [8] And now they are not content to oppress us with most hard bondage, but attributing the strength of their hands to the power of their idols, [9] they design to change Your promises, and destroy Your inheritance, and shut the mouths of them that praise You, and extinguish the glory of Your temple and altar, [10] that they may open the mouths of nations, and praise the strength of idols, and magnify a carnal king forever. [11] Do not give, O LORD, Your scepter to them that are nothing, lest they laugh at our ruin, but turn their counsel on themselves, and destroy him that has begun to rage against us. [12] Remember, O LORD, and show Yourself to us in the time of our tribulation, and give me boldness, O LORD, King of gods, and of all power: [13] give me a well-ordered speech in my mouth in the presence of the lion, and turn his heart to the hatred of our enemy, that both he himself may perish, and the rest that consent to him. [14] But deliver us by Your hand, and help me, who has no other helper, but You, O LORD, who has the knowledge of all things. [15] And You know that I hate the glory of the wicked, and abhor the bed of the uncircumcised, and of every stranger. [16] You know my necessity, that I abominate the sign of my pride and glory, which is on my head in the days of my public appearance, and detest it as a menstruous rag, and do not wear it in the days of my silence, [17] and that I have not eaten at Haman's table, nor has the king's banquet pleased me, and that I have not drunk the wine of the drink offerings: [18] And that Your handmaid has never rejoiced, since I was brought here to this day, but in You, O LORD, the God of Abraham. [19] O God, who is mighty above all, hear the voice of them that have no other hope, and deliver us from the hand of the wicked, and deliver me from my fear."

CHAPTER 15

[1] And he [(Mordecai)] commanded her to go to the king, and petition for her people, and for her country. [2] "Remember," [he said,] "the days of your low estate, how you were brought up by my hand, because Haman—the second after the king—has spoken against us to [put us to] death. [3] And you [must] call on the LORD, and speak to the king for us, and deliver us from death." [4] And on the third day she laid away the garments she wore, and put on her glorious apparel. [5] And glittering in royal robes, after she had called on God the Ruler and Savior of all, she took two maids with her, [6] and she leaned on one of them, as if for delicateness and excessive tenderness she were not able to bear up her own body. [7] And the other maid followed her lady, bearing up her train flowing on the ground. [8] But she with a rosy color in her face, and with gracious and bright eyes, hid a mind full of anguish, and exceeding great fear. [9] So going in she passed through all the doors in order, and stood before the king, where he sat on his royal throne, clothed with his royal robes, and glittering with gold, and precious stones, and he was terrible to behold. [10] And when he had lifted up his countenance, and with burning eyes had shown the wrath of his heart, the queen sunk down, and her color turned pale, and she rested her weary head on her handmaid. [11] And God changed the king's spirit into mildness, and all in haste and in fear he leaped from his throne, and holding her up in his arms, until she came to herself, caressed her with these words: [12] "What is the matter, Esther? I am your brother, do not fear. [13] You will not die, for this law is not made for you, but for all others. [14] Come near then, and touch the scepter." [15] And as she held her peace, he took the golden scepter, and laid it on her neck, and kissed her, and said, "Why do you not speak to me?" [16] She answered, "I saw you, my lord, as a messenger of God, and my heart was troubled for fear of your majesty. [17] For you, my lord, are very admirable, and your face is full of graces." [18] And while she was speaking, she fell down again, and was almost in a swoon. [19] But the king was troubled, and all his servants comforted her.

CHAPTER 16

[1] The great King Artaxerxes, from India to Ethiopia, to the governors and princes of one hundred and twenty-seven provinces, which obey our command, sends greetings. [2] Many have abused to pride the goodness of princes, and the honor that has been bestowed on them: [3] and not only endeavor to oppress the king's subjects, but not bearing the glory that is

given them, take in hand to practice also against them that gave it. [4] Neither are they content not to return thanks for benefits received, and to violate in themselves the laws of humanity, but they think they can also escape the justice of God who sees all things. [5] And they break out into such great madness, as to endeavor to undermine by lies such as observe diligently the offices committed to them, and do all things in such manner as to be worthy of all men's praise, [6] while, with crafty fraud, they deceive the ears of princes that are well meaning, and judge of others by their own nature. [7] Now this is proved both from ancient histories, and by the things which are done daily, how the good designs of kings are depraved by the evil suggestions of certain men. [8] For what reason we must provide for the peace of all provinces. [9] Neither must you think, if we command different things, that it comes from the levity of our mind, but that we give sentence according to the quality and necessity of times, as the profit of the commonwealth requires. [10] Now that you may more plainly understand what we say, I, Haman, the son of Amadathi, a Macedonian both in mind and country, and having nothing of the Persian blood, but with his cruelty staining our goodness, was received, being a stranger by us: [11] and found our humanity so great toward him, that he was called our father, and was worshiped by all as the next man after the king, [12] but he was so far puffed up with arrogancy, as to go about to deprive us of our kingdom and life. [13] For with certain new and unheard-of devices he has sought the destruction of Mordecai, by whose fidelity and good services our life was saved, and of Esther the partner of our kingdom, with all their nation, [14] thinking that after they were slain, he might work treason against us left alone without friends, and might transfer the kingdom of the Persians to the Macedonians. [15] But we have found that the Jews, who were by that most wicked man appointed to be slain, are in no fault at all, but to the contrary, use just laws, [16] and are the children of the highest and the greatest, and the ever-living God, by whose benefit the kingdom was given both to our fathers and to us, and is kept to this day. [17] For what reason, know that those letters which he sent in our name are void and of no effect. [18] For which crime both he himself that devised it, and all his relatives hang on gallows, before the gates of this city Shushan—not us, but God repaying him as he deserved. [19] But this edict, which we now send, will be published in all cities, that the Jews may freely follow their own laws. [20] And you will aid them that they may kill those who had prepared themselves to kill them, on the thirteenth day of the twelfth month, which is called Adar. [21] For the Almighty God has turned this day of sadness and mourning into joy to them. [22] For what reason you will also count this day among other festival days, and celebrate it with all joy, that it may be known also in times to come, [23] that all they who faithfully obey the Persians, receive a worthy reward for their fidelity, but they that are traitors to their kingdom, are destroyed for their wickedness. [24] And let every province and city, that will not be partaker of this solemnity, perish by the sword and by fire, and be destroyed in such manner as to be made unpassable, both to men and beasts, for an example of contempt, and disobedience.

APOCRYPHAL PSALMS

Psalm 151 is a short psalm found in most copies of the Septuagint but not in the Hebrew Bible. The Greek title given to this psalm indicates that it is supernumerary. It is also included in some manuscripts of the Peshitta. The psalm concerns the story of David and Goliath. The Eastern Orthodox Church, as well as the Coptic Orthodox Church, Armenian Apostolic Church, and the Armenian Catholic Church accept Psalm 151 as deuterocanonical. Psalms 152–155 are found extant in two Syriac manuscripts and appear to have been composed in the pre-Christian era. Psalms 154 and 155 have also been found in Hebrew in the Dead Sea Scrolls.

I. THIS PSALM IS ASCRIBED TO DAVID AND IS OUTSIDE THE NUMBER. WHEN HE SLEW GOLIATH IN A DUEL.

PSALM 151

[1] I was the youngest among my brothers, || And a youth in my father's house. [2] I used to feed my father's flock, || And I found a lion and a wolf, || And slew them and tore them. [3] My hands made an organ, || And my fingers fashioned a harp. [4] Who will show me my Lord? He, my Lord, has become my God. [5] He sent His messenger and took me away from my father's flock, || And anointed me with the oil of anointing. [6] My brothers, the fair and the tall, || In them the LORD had no pleasure. [7] And I went forth to meet the Philistine, || And he cursed me by his idols. [8] But I drew his sword and cut off his head, || And took away the reproach from the sons of Israel.

II. THE PRAYER OF HEZEKIAH WHEN ENEMIES SURROUNDED HIM.

PSALM 152

[1] With a loud voice glorify God; In the assembly of many proclaim His glory. [2] Amid the multitude of the upright glorify His praise; And speak of His glory with the righteous. [3] Join your soul to the good and to the perfect, || To glorify the Most High. [4] Gather yourselves together to make known His strength; And do not be slow in showing forth His deliverance and His glory to all babies. [5] That the honor of the LORD may be known, wisdom has been given; And to tell of His works it has been made known to men: [6] To make known to babies His strength, || And to make them that lack understanding [[or heart]] to comprehend His glory; [7] Who are far from His entrances and distant from His gates: [8] Because the Lord of Jacob is exalted, || And His glory is on all His works. [9] And a man who glorifies the Most High, in

him will He take pleasure; As in one who offers fine meal, || And as in one who offers male goats and calves; [10] And as in one who makes fat the altar with a multitude of burnt-offerings; And as the smell of incense from the hands of the just. [11] From your upright gates will be heard His voice, || And from the voice of the upright admonition. [12] And in their eating will be satisfying in truth, || And in their drinking, when they share together. [13] Their dwelling is in the law of the Most High, || And their speech is to make known His strength. [14] How far from the wicked is speech of Him, || And from all transgressors to know Him! [15] Behold, the eye of the LORD takes pity on the good, || And to them that glorify Him will He multiply mercy, || And from the time of evil will He deliver their soul. [16] Blessed is the LORD, who has delivered the wretched from the hand of the wicked; Who raises up a horn out of Jacob and a judge of the nations out of Israel; [17] That He may prolong His dwelling in Zion, || And may adorn our age in Jerusalem.

III. WHEN THE PEOPLE OBTAINED PERMISSION FROM CYRUS TO RETURN HOME.

PSALM 153

[1] O LORD, I have cried to You; Listen to me. [2] I have lifted up my hands to Your holy dwelling-place; Incline Your ear to me. [3] And grant me my request; Do not withhold my prayer from me. [4] Build up my soul, and do not destroy it; And do not lay it bare before the wicked. [5] Them that repay evil things—turn [them] away from me, O judge of truth. [6] O LORD, do not judge me according to my sins, || Because no flesh is innocent before You. [7] Make plain to me, O LORD, Your law, || And teach me Your judgments; [8] And many will hear of Your works, || And the nations will praise Your honor. [9] Remember me and do not forget me; And do not lead me into things that are too hard for me. [10] Make the sins of my youth pass from me, || And my discipline—do not let them remember [it] against me. [11] Cleanse me, O LORD, from the evil leprosy, || And let it no longer come to me. [12] Dry up its roots from me, || And do not let its leaves sprout within me. [13] Great are You, O LORD; Therefore, my request will be fulfilled from before You. [14] To whom will I complain that he may give to me? And what can the strength of men add [to me]? [15] From before You, O LORD, is my confidence; I cried to the LORD and He heard me, and healed the breaking of my heart. [16] I slumbered and slept; I dreamed and was helped, and the LORD sustained me. [17] They severely pained my heart; I will return thanks because the LORD delivered me. [18] Now I will rejoice in their shame; I have hoped in You, and I will not be

ashamed. [19] Give You honor for all time—even forever and ever! [20] Deliver Israel, Your chosen one, || And them of the house of Jacob Your proved one.

IV. Spoken by David when he was contending with the lion and the wolf which took a sheep from his flock.

PSALM 154

[1] O God, O God, come to my aid; Help me and save me; Deliver my soul from the slayer. [2] Will I go down to Sheol by the mouth of the lion? Or will the wolf confound me? [3] Was it not enough for them that they lay in wait for my father's flock, || And tore in pieces a sheep of my father's drove, || But they were also wishing to destroy my soul? [4] Have pity, O Lord, and save Your holy one from destruction; That he may rehearse Your glories in all his times, || And may praise Your great Name: [5] When You have delivered him from the hands of the destroying lion and of the ravening wolf, || And when You have rescued my captivity from the hands of the wild beasts. [6] Quickly, O my Lord, send a deliverer from before You, || And draw me out of the gaping pit, || Which imprisons me in its depths.

V. Spoken by David when returning thanks to God, who had delivered him from the lion and the wolf and he had slain both of them.

PSALM 155

[1] Praise the Lord, all you nations; Glorify Him, and bless His Name— [2] Who rescued the soul of His chosen one from the hands of death, || And delivered His holy one from destruction, [3] And saved me from the nets of Sheol, || And my soul from the pit that cannot be fathomed. [4] Because, before my deliverance could go forth from before Him, || I was well nearly torn in two pieces by two wild beasts. [5] But He sent His messenger, || And shut up from me the gaping mouths, || And rescued my life from destruction. [6] My soul will glorify Him and exalt Him, || Because of all His kindnesses which He has done and will do to me.

APOCRYPHAL DANIEL

The Septuagint (LXX) version of Daniel contains three sections not found in the Hebrew version of the text. These are known as "The Prayer of Azariah and Song of the Three Holy Children" (often placed as vv. 3:24–90), "Susanna and the Elders" (Ch. 13), and "Bel and the Dragon" (Ch. 14). All three are included in the LSV, with "The Prayer of Azariah" versified as 3B:1–68, which can be read between verses 3:23 and 3:24 of the standard text of *Daniel*. This particular book is an account of the prayer of Azariah (Abednego) while in the midst of the fire and the song that he and his two other companions sung in praise to God while in the furnace. "Susanna and the Elders" portrays the lovely and virtuous wife Susanna as sexually accosted by two conniving elders. They falsely accuse her of adultery, but the prophet Daniel cross-examines them, exposing them as liars, and then they are put to death. "Bel and the Dragon" recounts Daniel's confrontation with the followers of the false god Bel during the reign of King Cyrus of Persia, which results in their execution. Later in the narrative Daniel slays a much-revered dragon and is thrust into a lion's den as a result. God intervenes to deliver him.

SECTION 1:
THE PRAYER OF AZARIAH AND SONG OF THE THREE HOLY CHILDREN

CHAPTER 3B

[1] They walked in the midst of the fire, praising God, and blessing the LORD. [2] Then Azariah stood and prayed like this—opening his mouth in the midst of the fire, he said: [3] "Blessed are You, O LORD, You God of our fathers! Your Name is worthy to be praised and glorified forevermore; [4] For You are righteous in all the things that You have done. Yes, all Your works are true. Your ways are right, and all Your judgments are truth. [5] In all the things that You have brought on us, and on the holy city of our fathers, Jerusalem, ‖ You have executed true judgments. For according to truth and justice You have brought all these things on us because of our sins. [6] For we have sinned and committed iniquity in departing from You. [7] In all things we have trespassed, and not obeyed Your commands or kept them. We have not done as You have commanded us, that it might go well with us. [8] Therefore all that You have brought on us, and everything that You have done to us, ‖ You have done in true judgment. [9] You delivered us into the hands of lawless enemies, most hateful rebels, ‖ And to an unjust king who is the most wicked in all the world. [10] And now we cannot open our mouth. Shame and reproach have come on Your servants and those who worship You. [11] Do not utterly deliver us up, for Your Name's sake. Do not annul Your covenant. [12] Do not cause Your mercy to depart from us, ‖ For the sake of Abraham who is loved by You, ‖ And for the sake of Isaac Your servant, and Israel Your holy one, [13] To whom You promised that You would multiply their offspring as the stars of the sky, ‖ And as the sand that is on the seashore. [14] For we, O LORD, have become less than any nation, ‖ And are kept under this day in all the world because of our sins. [15] There is not at this time prince, or prophet, or leader, or burnt-offering, ‖ Or sacrifice, or oblation, or incense, or place to offer before You, and to find mercy. [16] Nevertheless, in a contrite heart and a humble spirit let us be accepted, [17] Like the burnt-offerings of rams and bullocks, and like tens of thousands of fat lambs—So let our sacrifice be in Your sight this day, that we may wholly go after You, ‖ For they will not be ashamed who put their trust in You. [18] And now we follow You with all our heart. We fear You and seek Your face. [19] Do not put us to shame; but deal with us after Your kindness, ‖ And according to the multitude of Your mercy. [20] Deliver us also according to Your marvelous works, and give glory to Your Name, O LORD. Let all those who harm Your servants be confounded. [21] Let them be ashamed of all their power and might, and let their strength be broken. [22] Let them know that You are the LORD, the only God, ‖ And [are] glorious over the whole world." [23] The king's servants who put them in did not stop making the furnace hot with naphtha, pitch, tinder, and small wood, [24] so that the flame streamed out forty-nine cubits above the furnace. [25] It spread and burned those Chaldeans whom it found around the furnace. [26] But the Messenger of the LORD came down into the furnace together with Azariah and his fellows, and He struck the flame of the fire out of the furnace, [27] and made the midst of the furnace as it had been a moist whistling wind, so that the fire did not touch them at all. It neither hurt nor troubled them. [28] Then the three, as out of one mouth, praised, glorified, and blessed God in the furnace, saying, [29] "Blessed are You, O LORD, You God of our fathers, ‖ To be praised and exalted above all forever! [30] Blessed is Your glorious and holy Name, ‖ To be praised and exalted above all forever! [31] Blessed are You in the temple of Your holy glory, ‖ To be praised and glorified above all forever! [32] Blessed are You who see the depths and sit on the cherubim, ‖ To be praised and exalted above all forever. [33] Blessed are You on the throne of Your kingdom, ‖ To be praised and extolled above all forever! [34] Blessed are You in the expanse of Heaven, ‖ To be praised and glorified

forever! ³⁵ O all you works of the LORD, bless the LORD! Praise and exalt Him above all forever! ³⁶ O you heavens, bless the LORD! Praise and exalt Him above all forever! ³⁷ O you messengers of the LORD, bless the LORD! Praise and exalt Him above all forever! ³⁸ O all you waters that are above the sky, bless the LORD! Praise and exalt Him above all forever! ³⁹ O all you powers of the LORD, bless the LORD! Praise and exalt Him above all forever! ⁴⁰ O you sun and moon, bless the LORD! Praise and exalt Him above all forever! ⁴¹ O you stars of the heavens, bless the LORD! Praise and exalt Him above all forever! ⁴² O every shower and dew, bless the LORD! Praise and exalt Him above all forever! ⁴³ O all you winds, bless the LORD! Praise and exalt Him above all forever! ⁴⁴ O you fire and heat, bless the LORD! Praise and exalt Him above all forever! ⁴⁵ O you winter and summer, bless the LORD! Praise and exalt Him above all forever! ⁴⁶ O you dews and storms of snow, bless the LORD! Praise and exalt Him above all forever! ⁴⁷ O you nights and days, bless the LORD! Praise and exalt Him above all forever! ⁴⁸ O you light and darkness, bless the LORD! Praise and exalt Him above all forever! ⁴⁹ O you cold and heat, bless the LORD! Praise and exalt Him above all forever! ⁵⁰ O you frost and snow, bless the LORD! Praise and exalt Him above all forever! ⁵¹ O you lightnings and clouds, bless the LORD! Praise and exalt Him above all forever! ⁵² O let the earth bless the LORD! Let it praise and exalt Him above all forever! ⁵³ O you mountains and hills, bless the LORD! Praise and exalt Him above all forever! ⁵⁴ O all you things that grow on the earth, bless the LORD! Praise and exalt Him above all forever! ⁵⁵ O sea and rivers, bless the LORD! Praise and exalt Him above all forever! ⁵⁶ O you springs, bless the LORD! Praise and exalt Him above all forever! ⁵⁷ O you whales and all that move in the waters, bless the LORD! Praise and exalt Him above all forever! ⁵⁸ O all you birds of the air, bless the LORD! Praise and exalt Him above all forever! ⁵⁹ O all you beasts and cattle, bless the LORD! Praise and exalt Him above all forever! ⁶⁰ O you children of men, bless the LORD! Praise and exalt Him above all forever! ⁶¹ O let Israel bless the LORD! Praise and exalt Him above all forever. ⁶² O you priests of the LORD, bless the LORD! Praise and exalt Him above all forever! ⁶³ O you servants of the LORD, bless the LORD! Praise and exalt Him above all forever! ⁶⁴ O you spirits and souls of the righteous, bless the LORD! Praise and exalt Him above all forever! ⁶⁵ O you who are holy and humble of heart, bless the LORD! Praise and exalt Him above all forever! ⁶⁶ O Hananiah, Mishael, and Azariah, bless the LORD! Praise and exalt Him above all forever; For He has rescued us from Hades and saved us from the hand of death! He has delivered us out of the midst of the furnace and burning flame. He has delivered us out of the midst of the fire. ⁶⁷ O give thanks to the LORD, for He is good; For His mercy is forever. ⁶⁸ O all you who worship the LORD, bless the God of gods, praise Him, and give Him thanks; for His mercy is forever!"

SECTION 2:
SUSANNA AND THE ELDERS

CHAPTER 13

¹ A man lived in Babylon, and his name was Jehoiakim. ² He took a wife, whose name was Susanna, the daughter of Hilkiah, a very fair woman, and one who feared the LORD. ³ Her parents were also righteous and taught their daughter according to the Law of Moses. ⁴ Now Jehoiakim was a great rich man, and had a fair garden joining to his house. The Jews used to come to him, because he was more honorable than all others. ⁵ The same year two of the elders of the people were appointed to be judges, such as the LORD spoke of, that wickedness came from Babylon from elders who were judges, who were supposed to govern the people. ⁶ These were often at Jehoiakim's house. All that had any suits in law came to them. ⁷ When the people departed away at noon, Susanna went into her husband's garden to walk. ⁸ The two elders saw her going in every day, and walking; and they were inflamed with lust for her. ⁹ They perverted their own mind and turned away their eyes, that they might not look to Heaven, nor remember just judgments. ¹⁰ And although they both were wounded with lust for her yet dared not show the other his grief. ¹¹ For they were ashamed to declare their lust, that they desired to have to do with her. ¹² Yet they watched jealously from day to day to see her. ¹³ The one said to the other, "Let us go home, now; for it is dinner time." ¹⁴ So when they had gone out, they parted company, and turning back again, they came to the same place. After they had asked one another the cause, they acknowledged their lust. Then they appointed a time both together, when they might find her alone. ¹⁵ It happened, as they watched on an opportune day, she went in as before with only two maids, and she desired to wash herself in the garden; for it was hot. ¹⁶ There was nobody there except the two elders who had hid themselves and watched her. ¹⁷ Then she said to her maids, "Bring me oil and washing balls, and shut the garden doors, that I may wash myself." ¹⁸ They did as she asked them, and shut the garden doors, and went out themselves at the side doors to fetch the things that she had commanded them. They did not see the elders, because they were hidden. ¹⁹ Now when the maids had gone out, the two elders rose up, and ran to her, saying, ²⁰ "Behold, the garden doors are shut, that no man can see us, and we are in love with you. Therefore, consent to us, and lie with us. ²¹ If you will not, we will testify against you, that a young man was with you; therefore, you sent your maids away from you." ²² Then Susanna sighed, and said, "I am trapped; for if I do this thing, it is

death to me. If I do not do it, I cannot escape your hands. ²³ It is better for me to fall into your hands, and not do it, than to sin in the sight of the LORD." ²⁴ With that Susanna cried with a loud voice; and the two elders cried out against her. ²⁵ Then one of them ran and opened the garden doors. ²⁶ So when the servants of the house heard the cry in the garden, they rushed in at the side door, to see what had happened to her. ²⁷ But when the elders had told their tale, the servants were greatly ashamed; for there was never such a report made of Susanna. ²⁸ It came to pass on the next day, when the people assembled to her husband Jehoiakim, the two elders came full of their wicked intent against Susanna to put her to death, ²⁹ and said before the people, "Send for Susanna, the daughter of Hilkiah, Jehoiakim's wife." So they sent; ³⁰ and she came with her father and mother, her children, and all her relatives. ³¹ Now Susanna was a very delicate woman, and beautiful to behold. ³² These wicked men commanded her to be unveiled, for she was veiled, that they might be filled with her beauty. ³³ Therefore her friends and all who saw her wept. ³⁴ Then the two elders stood up in the midst of the people and laid their hands on her head. ³⁵ She, weeping, looked up toward Heaven; for her heart trusted in the LORD. ³⁶ The elders said, "As we walked in the garden alone, this woman came in with two maids, shut the garden doors, and sent the maids away. ³⁷ Then a young man, who was hidden there, came to her and lay with her. ³⁸ And we, being in a corner of the garden, saw this wickedness and ran to them. ³⁹ And when we saw them together, we could not hold the man; for he was stronger than we, and opened the doors, and leapt out. ⁴⁰ But having taken this woman, we asked who the young man was, but she would not tell us. We testify these things." ⁴¹ Then the assembly believed them, as those who were elders of the people and judges; so they condemned her to death. ⁴² Then Susanna cried out with a loud voice, and said, "O perpetual God, You know the secrets, and know all things before they happen, ⁴³ You know that they have testified falsely against me. Behold, I must die, even though I never did such things as these men have maliciously invented against me." ⁴⁴ The LORD heard her voice. ⁴⁵ Therefore when she was led away to be put to death, God raised up the holy spirit of a young youth, whose name was Daniel. ⁴⁶ He cried with a loud voice, "I am clear from the blood of this woman!" ⁴⁷ Then all the people turned them toward him, and said, "What do these words that you have spoken mean?" ⁴⁸ So he, standing in the midst of them, said, "Are you all such fools, you sons of Israel, that without examination or knowledge of the truth you have condemned a daughter of Israel? ⁴⁹ Return again to the place of judgment; for these have testified falsely against her." ⁵⁰ Therefore all the people turned again in haste, and the elders said to him, "Come, sit down among us, and show it to us, seeing God has given you the honor

of an elder." ⁵¹ Then Daniel said to them, "Put them far apart from each another, and I will examine them." ⁵² So when they were put apart from one another, he called one of them, and said to him, "O you who have become old in wickedness, now your sins have returned which you have committed before, ⁵³ in pronouncing unjust judgment, condemning the innocent, and letting the guilty go free; although the LORD says, You will not kill the innocent and righteous. ⁵⁴ Now then, if you saw her, tell me, under which tree did you see them companying together?" He answered, "Under a mastick tree." ⁵⁵ And Daniel said, "You have certainly lied against your own head; for even now the messenger of God has received the sentence of God and will cut you in two." ⁵⁶ So he put him aside, and commanded to bring the other, and said to him, "O you seed of Canaan, and not of Judah, beauty has deceived you, and lust has perverted your heart. ⁵⁷ Thus you have dealt with the daughters of Israel, and they for fear were intimate with you; but the daughter of Judah would not tolerate your wickedness. ⁵⁸ Now therefore, tell me, under which tree did you take them being intimate together?" He answered, "Under an evergreen oak tree." ⁵⁹ Then Daniel said to him, "You have also certainly lied against your own head; for the messenger of God waits with the sword to cut you in two, that he may destroy you." ⁶⁰ With that, all the assembly cried out with a loud voice, and blessed God, who saves those who hope in him. ⁶¹ Then they arose against the two elders, for Daniel had convicted them of false testimony out of their own mouth. ⁶² According to the Law of Moses they did to them in such sort as they maliciously intended to do to their neighbor. They put them to death, and the innocent blood was saved the same day. ⁶³ Therefore Hilkiah and his wife praised God for their daughter Susanna, with Jehoiakim her husband, and all the relatives, because there was no dishonesty found in her. ⁶⁴ And from that day out, Daniel was held in high regard in the sight of the people.

SECTION 3:
BEL AND THE DRAGON

CHAPTER 14
¹ King Astyages was gathered to his fathers, and Cyrus the Persian received his kingdom. ² Daniel lived with the king and was honored above all his friends. ³ Now the Babylonians had an idol, called Bel, and every day twelve great measures of fine flour, forty sheep, and six firkins of wine were spent on him. ⁴ And the king honored it and went daily to worship it; but Daniel worshiped his own God. The king said to him, "Why do you not worship Bel?" ⁵ He said, "Because I may not honor idols made with hands, but only the living God, who has created the sky and the earth, and has sovereignty over all flesh."

[6] Then the king said to him, "Do you not think that Bel is a living god? Do you not see how much he eats and drinks every day?" [7] Then Daniel laughed, and said, "O king, do not be deceived; for this is just clay inside, and brass outside, and never ate or drank anything." [8] So the king was angry, and called for his priests, and said to them, "If you do not tell me who this is who devours these expenses, you will die. [9] But if you can show me that Bel devours them, then Daniel will die; for he has spoken blasphemy against Bel." Daniel said to the king, "Let it be according to your word." [10] Now there were seventy priests of Bel, besides their wives and children. The king went with Daniel into Bel's temple. [11] So Bel's priests said, "Behold, we will leave; but you, O king, set out the meat, and mix the wine and set it out, shut the door securely, and seal it with your own signet. [12] When you come in the morning, if you do not find that Bel has eaten everything, we will suffer death, or else Daniel, who speaks falsely against us." [13] They were not concerned, for under the table they had made a secret entrance, whereby they entered in continually, and consumed those things. [14] It happened, when they had gone out, the king set the meat before Bel. Now Daniel had commanded his servants to bring ashes, and they scattered them all over the temple in the presence of the king alone. Then they went out, shut the door, sealed it with the king's signet, and so departed. [15] Now in the night, the priests came with their wives and children, as they usually did, and ate and drank it all. [16] In the morning, the king arose, and Daniel with him. [17] The king said, "Daniel, are the seals whole?" He said, "Yes, O king, they are whole." [18] And as soon as he had opened the door, the king looked at the table, and cried with a loud voice, "You are great, O Bel, and with you is no deceit at all!" [19] Then Daniel laughed, and held the king that he should not go in, and said, "Behold now the pavement, and mark well whose footsteps these are." [20] The king said, "I see the footsteps of men, women, and children." Then the king was angry, [21] and took the priests with their wives and children, who showed him the secret doors, where they came in, and consumed the things that were on the table. [22] Therefore the king killed them, and delivered Bel into Daniel's power, who overthrew him and his temple. [23] In that same place there was a great dragon, which the people of Babylon worshiped. [24] The king said to Daniel, "Will you also say that this is of brass? Behold, he lives, eats, and drinks. You cannot say that he is no living god. Therefore, worship him." [25] Then Daniel said, "I will worship the LORD my God; for He is a living God. [26] But allow me, O king, and I will kill this dragon without sword or staff." The king said, "I allow you." [27] Then Daniel took pitch, fat, and hair, and melted them together, and made lumps of them. He put these in the dragon's mouth, so the dragon ate and burst apart. Daniel said, "Behold, these are the gods you all worship." [28] When the people of Babylon heard that, they took great indignation, and conspired against the king, saying, "The king has become a Jew. He has pulled down Bel, slain the dragon, and put the priests to the sword." [29] So they came to the king, and said, "Deliver Daniel to us, or else we will destroy you and your house." [30] Now when the king saw that they trapped him, being constrained, the king delivered Daniel to them. [31] They cast him into the lion's den, where he was six days. [32] There were seven lions in the den, and they had been giving them two carcasses and two sheep every day, which then were not given to them, intending that they would devour Daniel. [33] Now there was in Jewry the prophet Habakkuk, who had made stew, and had broken bread into a bowl. He was going into the field to bring it to the reapers. [34] But the messenger of the LORD said to Habakkuk, "Go, carry the dinner that you have into Babylon—to Daniel in the lions' den." [35] Habakkuk said, "Lord, I never saw Babylon. I do not know where the den is." [36] Then the messenger of the LORD took him by the crown and lifted him up by the hair of his head, and with the blast of his breath set him in Babylon over the den. [37] Habakkuk cried, saying, "O Daniel, Daniel, take the dinner which God has sent you." [38] Daniel said, "You have remembered me, O God! You have not forsaken those who love you!" [39] So Daniel arose and ate; and the messenger of God immediately set Habakkuk in his own place again. [40] On the seventh day, the king came to mourn for Daniel. When he came to the den, he looked in, and behold, Daniel was sitting. [41] Then the king cried with a loud voice, saying, "Great are You, O LORD, You God of Daniel, and there is no other besides You!" [42] So he drew him out, and cast those that were the cause of his destruction into the den; and they were devoured in a moment before his face.

UNIVERSAL DEUTEROCANON

TOBIT

The Book of Tobit, named after its principal character, combines Jewish piety and morality with folklore in a fascinating story that has enjoyed wide popularity in both Jewish and Christian circles. Prayers, psalms, and words of wisdom, as well as the skillfully constructed story itself, provide valuable insights into the faith and the religious milieu of its unknown author. The book was probably written early in the 2nd century BC; it is not known where.

CHAPTER 1

[1] The scroll of the words of Tobit, the son of Tobiel, the son of Ananiel, the son of Aduel, the son of Gabael, of the seed of Asiel, of the tribe of Naphtali; [2] who in the days of Enemessar king of the Assyrians was carried away captive out of Thisbe, which is on the right side of Kedesh Naphtali in Galilee above Asher. [3] I, Tobit, walked in the ways of truth and righteousness all the days of my life, and I did many kind acts to my countrymen and my nation, who went with me into the land of the Assyrians, to Nineveh. [4] When I was in my own country, in the land of Israel, while I was yet young, all the tribe of my father Naphtali fell away from the house of Jerusalem, which was chosen out of all the tribes of Israel, that all the tribes should sacrifice there, and the temple of the habitation of the Most High was hallowed and built therein for all ages. [5] All the tribes which fell away together sacrificed to the heifer Ba'al, and so did the house of my father Naphtali. [6] I alone went often to Jerusalem at the feasts, as it has been ordained to all Israel by a perpetual decree, having the first-fruits and the tenths of my increase, and that which was first shorn; and I gave them to the priests at the altar, the sons of Aaron. [7] I gave a tenth part of all my increase to the sons of Levi, who ministered at Jerusalem. A second tenth part I sold away, and went, and spent it each year at Jerusalem. [8] A third tenth I gave to them to whom it was appropriate, as Deborah my father's mother had commanded me, because I was left an orphan by my father. [9] When I became a man, I took as wife Anna of the seed of our own family. With her, I became the father of Tobias. [10] When I was carried away captive to Nineveh, all my countrymen and my family ate of the bread of the nations; [11] but I kept myself from eating, [12] because I remembered God with all my soul. [13] So the Most High gave me grace and favor in the sight of Enemessar, and I was his purchasing agent. [14] And I went into Media and left ten talents of silver in trust with Gabael, the brother of Gabrias, at Rages of Media. [15] And when Enemessar was dead, Sennacherib his son reigned in his place. In his time,

the highways were troubled, and I could no longer go into Media. [16] In the days of Enemessar, I did many kind acts to my countrymen: I gave my bread to the hungry, [17] and my garments to the naked. If I saw any of my race dead, and thrown out on the wall of Nineveh, I buried him. [18] If Sennacherib the king killed any, when he came fleeing from Judea, I buried them privately; for in his wrath he killed many; and the bodies were sought for by the king and were not found. [19] But one of the Ninevites went and showed to the king concerning me, how I buried them, and hid myself; and when I knew that I was sought for to be put to death, I withdrew myself for fear. [20] And all my goods were forcibly taken away, and there was nothing left to me, save my wife Anna and my son Tobias. [21] No more than fifty-five days passed before two of his sons killed him, and they fled into the mountains of Ararat. And Esarhaddon his son reigned in his place; and he appointed Ahikar, my brother Anael's son, over all the accounts of his kingdom, and over all his affairs. [22] Ahikar requested me, and I came to Nineveh. Now Ahikar was cupbearer, keeper of the signet, steward, and overseer of the accounts. Esarhaddon appointed him next to himself, but he was my brother's son.

CHAPTER 2

[1] Now when I had come home again, and my wife Anna was restored to me, and my son Tobias, in the Celebration of Pentecost, which is the holy celebration of the seven weeks, there was a good dinner prepared [for] me, and I sat down to eat. [2] I saw abundance of meat, and I said to my son, "Go and bring whatever poor man you find of our countrymen, who is mindful of the LORD. Behold, I wait for you." [3] Then he came, and said, "Father, one of our race is strangled, and has been cast out in the marketplace." [4] Before I had tasted anything, I sprang up, and took him up into a chamber until the sun had set. [5] Then I returned, washed myself, ate my bread in heaviness, [6] and remembered the prophecy of Amos, as he said, "Your feasts will be turned into mourning, and all your mirth into lamentation." [7] So I wept: and when the sun had set, I went and dug a grave, and buried him. [8] My neighbors mocked me, and said, "He is no longer afraid to be put to death for this matter; and yet he fled away. Behold, he buries the dead again." [9] The same night I returned from burying him, and slept by the wall of my courtyard, being polluted; and my face was uncovered. [10] I did not know that there were sparrows in the wall. My eyes were open, and the sparrows dropped warm dung into my eyes, and white films came over my eyes. I went to the physicians, and they did not help me; but Ahikar nourished me,

until I went into Elymais. [11] My wife Anna wove cloth in the women's chambers, [12] and sent the work back to the owners. They on their part paid her wages, and also gave her a kid. [13] But when it came to my house, it began to cry, and I said to her, "Where did this kid come from? Is it stolen? Give it back to the owners; for it is not lawful to eat anything that is stolen." [14] But she said, "It has been given to me for a gift more than the wages." I did not believe her, and I asked her to return it to the owners; and I was ashamed of her. But she answered and said to me, "Where are your alms and your righteous deeds? Behold, you and all your works are known."

CHAPTER 3

[1] I was grieved and wept, and prayed in sorrow, saying, [2] "O LORD, You are righteous, || And all Your works and all Your ways are mercy and truth, || And You judge true and righteous judgment forever. [3] Remember me and look at me. Do not take vengeance on me for my sins and my ignorance, || And the sins of my fathers who sinned before You. [4] For they disobeyed Your commands. You gave us as plunder, for captivity, for death, || And for a proverb of reproach to all the nations among whom we are dispersed. [5] Now Your judgments are many and true; That You should deal with me according to my sins and the sins of my fathers; Because we did not keep Your commands, || For we did not walk in truth before You. [6] Now deal with me according to that which is pleasing in Your sight. Command my spirit to be taken from me, || That I may be released, and become earth. For it is more profitable for me to die rather than to live, || Because I have heard false reproaches, || And there is much sorrow in me. Command that I be released from my distress, now, || And go to the agelong place. Do not turn Your face away from me." [7] The same day it happened to Sarah, the daughter of Raguel, in Ecbatana of Media, that she also was reproached by her father's maidservants; [8] because that she had been given to seven husbands, and Asmodeus the evil spirit killed them, before they had lain with her. And they said to her, "Do you not know that you strangle your husbands? You have already had seven husbands, and you have not borne the name of any of them. [9] Why do you scourge us? If they are dead, go your ways with them. Let us never see either son or daughter from you." [10] When she heard these things, she was grieved exceedingly, so that she thought about hanging herself. Then she said, "I am the only daughter of my father. If I do this, it will be a reproach to him, and I will bring down his old age with sorrow to the grave." [11] Then she prayed by the window, and said, "Blessed are You, O LORD my God, || And blessed is Your holy and honorable Name forever! Let all Your works praise You forever! [12] And now, LORD, I have set my eyes and my face toward You. [13] Command that I be released from the

earth, || And that I no longer hear reproach. [14] You know, LORD, that I am pure from all sin with man, [15] And that I never polluted my name or the name of my father, || In the land of my captivity. I am the only daughter of my father, || And he has no child that will be his heir, nor brother near him, || Nor son belonging to him, that I should keep myself for a wife to him. Seven husbands of mine are dead already. Why should I live? If it does not please You to kill me, || Command some regard to be had of me, and pity taken of me, || And that I hear no more reproach." [16] The prayer of both was heard before the glory of the great God. [17] Raphael, also, was sent to heal them both, to scale away the white films from Tobit's eyes, and to give Sarah the daughter of Raguel for a wife to Tobias the son of Tobit, and to bind Asmodeus the evil spirit; because it belonged to Tobias that he should inherit her. At that very time, Tobit returned and entered into his house, and Sarah the daughter of Raguel came down from her upper chamber.

CHAPTER 4

[1] In that day Tobit remembered the money which he had left in trust with Gabael in Rages of Media, [2] and he said to himself, I have asked for death; why do I not call my son Tobias, that I may explain to him about the money before I die? [3] And he called him, and said, "My child, if I die, bury me. Do not despise your mother. Honor her all the days of your life, and do that which is pleasing to her, and do not grieve her. [4] Remember, my child, that she has seen many dangers for you, when you were in her womb. When she is dead, bury her by me in one grave. [5] My child, be mindful of the LORD our God all your days, and do not let your will be set to sin and to transgress His commands: do righteousness all the days of your life, and do not follow the ways of unrighteousness. [6] For if you do what is true, your deeds will prosperously succeed for you, and for all those who do righteousness. [7] Give alms from your possessions. When you give alms, do not let your eye be envious. Do not turn your face away from any poor man, and the face of God will not be turned away from you. [8] As your possessions are, give alms of it according to your abundance. If you have little, do not be afraid to give alms according to that little; [9] for you lay up a good treasure for yourself against the day of necessity; [10] because kindness delivers from death, and does not allow you to come into darkness. [11] Alms is a good gift in the sight of the Most High for all that give it. [12] Beware, my child, of all whoredom, and take first a wife of the seed of your fathers. Do not take a strange wife, who is not of your father's tribe; for we are the descendants of the prophets. Remember, my child, that Noah, Abraham, Isaac, and Jacob, our fathers from antiquity, all took wives of their countrymen, and were blessed in their children, and their seed will inherit the land. [13] And now, my child, love your

TOBIT

relatives, and do not scorn your countrymen and the sons and the daughters of your people in your heart, to take a wife of them; for in scornfulness is destruction and much trouble, and in naughtiness is decay and great lack; for naughtiness is the mother of famine. ¹⁴ Do not let the wages of any man who works for you wait with you but give it to him out of hand. If you serve God, you will be rewarded. Take heed to yourself, my child, in all your works, and be discreet in all your behavior. ¹⁵ And what you yourself hate, do to no man. Do not drink wine to drunkenness, and do not let drunkenness go with you on your way. ¹⁶ Give of your bread to the hungry, and of your garments to those who are naked. Give alms from all your abundance. Do not let your eye be envious when you give alms. ¹⁷ Pour out your bread on the burial of the just and give nothing to sinners. ¹⁸ Ask counsel of every man who is wise, and do not despise any counsel that is profitable. ¹⁹ Bless the Lord your God at all times and ask of Him that your ways may be made straight, and that all your paths and counsels may prosper; for every nation has no counsel; but the Lord Himself gives all good things, and He humbles whom He will, as He will. And now, my child, remember my commands, and do not let them be blotted out of your mind. ²⁰ And now I explain to you about the ten talents of silver, which I left in trust with Gabael the son of Gabrias at Rages of Media. ²¹ And do not fear, my child, because we are made poor. You have much wealth, if you fear God, and depart from all sin, and do that which is pleasing in His sight."

CHAPTER 5

¹ Then Tobias answered and said to him, "Father, I will do all things, whatever you have commanded me. ² But how could I receive the money, since I do not know him?" ³ He gave him the handwriting, and said to him, "Seek a man who will go with you, and I will give him wages, while I yet live; and go and receive the money." ⁴ He went to seek a man and found Raphael who was a messenger; ⁵ and he did not know it. He said to him, "Can I go with you to Rages of Media? Do you know those places well?" ⁶ The messenger said to him, "I will go with you. I know the way well. I have lodged with our brother Gabael." ⁷ Tobias said to him, "Wait for me, and I will tell my father." ⁸ He said to him, "Go, and do not wait." And he went in and said to his father, "Behold, I have found someone who will go with me." But he said, "Call him to me, that I may know of what tribe he is, and whether he is a trustworthy man to go with you." ⁹ So he called him, and he came in, and they saluted one another. ¹⁰ And Tobit said to him, "Brother, of what tribe and of what family are you? Tell me." ¹¹ He said to him, "Do you seek a tribe and a family, or a hired man which will go with your son?" And Tobit said to him, "I want to know, brother, your relatives and your name." ¹² And he said, "I am Azariah, the son of Ananias the great, of your relatives." ¹³ And he said to him, "Welcome, brother. Do not be angry with me, because I sought to know your tribe and family. You are my brother, of an honest and good lineage; for I knew Ananias and Jathan, the sons of Shemaiah the great, when we went together to Jerusalem to worship, and offered the firstborn, and the tenths of our increase; and they did not go astray in the error of our countrymen. My brother, you are of a great stock. ¹⁴ But tell me, what wages will I give you? A drachma a day, and those things that are necessary for you, as to my son? ¹⁵ And moreover, if you both return safe and sound, I will add something to your wages." ¹⁶ And so they agreed. And he said to Tobias, "Prepare yourself for the journey. May God prosper you." So, his son prepared what was needful for the journey, and his father said to him, "Go with this man; but God, who dwells in Heaven, will prosper your journey. May His messenger go with you." Then they both departed, and the young man's dog went with them. ¹⁷ But Anna his mother wept, and said to Tobit, "Why have you sent our child away? Is he not the staff of our hand, in going in and out before us? ¹⁸ Do not be greedy to add money to money; but let it be as refuse compared to our child. ¹⁹ For what the Lord has given us to live is enough for us." ²⁰ Tobit said to her, "Do not worry, my sister. He will return safe and sound, and your eyes will see him. ²¹ For a good messenger will go with him. His journey will be prospered, and he will return safe and sound." ²² So she stopped weeping.

CHAPTER 6

¹ Now as they went on their journey, they came at evening to the River Tigris, and they lodged there. ² But the young man went down to wash himself, and a fish leaped out of the river, and would have swallowed up the young man. ³ But the messenger said to him, "Grab the fish!" So the young man grabbed the fish, and hauled it up onto the land. ⁴ And the messenger said to him, "Cut the fish open, and take the heart, the liver, and the bile, and keep them with you." ⁵ And the young man did as the messenger commanded him; but they roasted the fish and ate it. And they both went on their way, until they drew near to Ecbatana. ⁶ The young man said to the messenger, "Brother Azariah, of what use is the heart, the liver, and the bile of the fish?" ⁷ He said to him, "About the heart and the liver: If a demon or an evil spirit troubles anyone, we must burn those and make smoke of them before the man or the woman, and the affliction will flee. ⁸ But as for the bile, it is good to anoint a man that has white films in his eyes, and he will be healed." ⁹ But when they drew near to Rages, ¹⁰ the messenger said to the young man, "Brother, today we will lodge with Raguel. He is your relative. He has an only daughter named Sarah. I will speak about her, that she should be given to you for a wife. ¹¹ For her

inheritance belongs to you, and you only are of her relatives. ¹²The maid is fair and wise. And now hear me, and I will speak to her father. When we return from Rages we will celebrate the marriage; for I know that Raguel may in no way marry her to another according to the Law of Moses, or else he would be liable to death, because it belongs to you to take the inheritance, rather than any other." ¹³Then the young man said to the messenger, "Brother Azariah, I have heard that this maid has been given to seven men, and that they all perished in the bride-chamber. ¹⁴Now I am the only son of my father, and I am afraid, lest I go in and die, even as those before me. For a demon loves her, which harms no man, but those which come to her. Now I fear lest I die and bring my father's and my mother's life to the grave with sorrow because of me. They have no other son to bury them." ¹⁵But the messenger said to him, "Do not you remember the words which your father commanded you, that you should take a wife of your own relatives? Now hear me, brother; for she will be your wife. Do not worry about the demon; for this night she will be given you as wife. ¹⁶And when you come into the bride-chamber, you will take the ashes of incense, and will lay on them some of the heart and liver of the fish and will make smoke with them. ¹⁷The demon will smell it, and flee away, and never come again anymore. But when you go near to her, both of you rise up, and cry to God who is merciful. He will save you and have mercy on you. Do not be afraid, for she was prepared for you from the beginning; and you will save her, and she will go with you. And I suppose that you will have children with her." When Tobias heard these things, he loved her, and his soul was strongly joined to her.

CHAPTER 7

¹They came to Ecbatana and arrived at the house of Raguel. But Sarah met them; and she greeted them, and they her. Then she brought them into the house. ²Raguel said to Edna his wife, "This young man really resembles Tobit my cousin!" ³And Raguel asked them, "Where are you two from, countrymen?" They said to him, "We are of the sons of Naphtali, who are captives in Nineveh." ⁴He said to them, "Do you know Tobit our brother?" They said, "We know him." Then he said to them, "Is he in good health?" ⁵They said, "He is both alive, and in good health." Tobias said, "He is my father." ⁶And Raguel sprang up, and kissed him, wept, ⁷blessed him, and said to him, "You are the son of an honest and good man." When he had heard that Tobit had lost his sight, he was grieved, and wept; ⁸and Edna his wife and Sarah his daughter wept. They received them gladly; and they killed a ram of the flock and served them meat. But Tobias said to Raphael, "Brother Azariah, speak of those things of which you talked about in the way, and let the matter be finished." ⁹So he communicated

the thing to Raguel. Raguel said to Tobias, "Eat, drink, and make merry: ¹⁰for it belongs to you to take my child. However, I will tell you the truth. ¹¹I have given my child to seven men of our countrymen, and whenever they came in to her, they died in the night. But for the present be merry." And Tobias said, "I will taste nothing here, until you all make a covenant and enter into that covenant with me." ¹²Raguel said, "Take her to yourself from now on according to custom. You are her relative, and she is yours. The merciful God will give all good success to you." ¹³And he called his daughter Sarah, and took her by the hand, and gave her to be wife of Tobias, and said, "Behold, take her to yourself after the Law of Moses, and lead her away to your father." And he blessed them. ¹⁴He called Edna his wife, then took a scroll, wrote a contract, and sealed it. ¹⁵Then they began to eat. ¹⁶And Raguel called his wife Edna, and said to her, "Sister, prepare the other chamber, and bring her in there." ¹⁷She did as he asked her, and brought her in there. She wept, and she received the tears of her daughter, and said to her, ¹⁸"Be comforted, my child. May the Lord of the heavens and earth give you favor for this your sorrow. Be comforted, my daughter."

CHAPTER 8

¹When they had finished their supper, they brought Tobias in to her. ²But as he went, he remembered the words of Raphael, and took the ashes of the incense, and put the heart and the liver of the fish on them and made smoke with them. ³When the demon smelled that smell, it fled into the uppermost parts of Egypt, and the messenger bound him. ⁴But after they were both shut in together, Tobias rose up from the bed, and said, "Sister, arise, and let us pray that the LORD may have mercy on us." ⁵And Tobias began to say, "Blessed are You, O God of our fathers, || And blessed is Your holy and glorious Name forever. Let the heavens bless You, and all Your creatures. ⁶You made Adam and gave him Eve his wife for a helper and support. From them came the seed of men. You said, It is not good that the man should be alone. Let Us make him a helper like him. ⁷And now, O LORD, I do not take this my sister for lust, but in truth. Command that I may find mercy and grow old with her." ⁸She said with him, "Amen." And they both slept that night. ⁹Raguel arose, and went and dug a grave, ¹⁰saying, "Lest he also should die." ¹¹And Raguel came into his house, ¹²and said to Edna his wife, "Send one of the maidservants, and let them see if he is alive. If not, we will bury him, and no man will know it." ¹³So the maidservant opened the door, and went in, and found them both sleeping, ¹⁴and came out, and told them that he was alive. ¹⁵Then Raguel blessed God, saying, "Blessed are You, O God, with all pure and holy blessing! Let Your saints bless You, and all Your creatures! Let all Your messengers and Your chosen ones bless You forever!

[16] Blessed are You, because You have made me glad; and it has not happened to me as I suspected; but You have dealt with us according to Your great mercy. [17] Blessed are You, because You have had mercy on two that were the only begotten children of their parents. Show them mercy, O LORD. Fulfill their life in health with gladness and mercy." [18] He commanded his servants to fill the grave. [19] He kept the wedding feast for them fourteen days. [20] Before the days of the wedding feast were finished, Raguel swore to him that he should not depart until the fourteen days of the wedding feast were fulfilled; [21] and that then he should take half of his goods and go in safety to his father; "and the rest," he said, "when my wife and I die."

CHAPTER 9

[1] And Tobias called Raphael, and said to him, [2] "Brother Azariah, take a servant and two camels with you, and go to Rages of Media to Gabael, and receive the money for me, and bring him to the wedding feast, [3] because Raguel has sworn that I must not depart. [4] My father counts the days; and if I wait long, he will be very grieved." [5] So Raphael went on his way, and lodged with Gabael, and gave him the handwriting; so he brought out the bags with their seals, and gave them to him. [6] Then they rose up early in the morning together and came to the wedding feast. Tobias blessed his wife.

CHAPTER 10

[1] Tobit his father counted every day. When the days of the journey were expired, and they did not come, [2] he said, "Is he perhaps detained? Or is Gabael perhaps dead, and there is no one to give him the money?" [3] He was very grieved. [4] But his wife said to him, "The child has perished, seeing he waits long." She began to mourn him, and said, [5] "I care about nothing, my child, since I have let you go, the light of my eyes." [6] Tobit said to her, "Hold your peace. Do not worry. He is in good health." [7] And she said to him, "Hold your peace. Do not deceive me. My child has perished." And she went out every day into the way by which they went, and ate no bread in the daytime, and did not stop mourning her son Tobias for whole nights, until the fourteen days of the wedding feast were expired, which Raguel had sworn that he should spend there. Then Tobias said to Raguel, "Send me away, for my father and my mother no longer look to see me." [8] But his father-in-law said to him, "Stay with me, and I will send to your father, and they will declare to him how things go with you." [9] Tobias said, "No. Send me away to my father." [10] Raguel arose, and gave him Sarah his wife, and half his goods, servants and cattle and money; [11] and he blessed them, and sent them away, saying, "The God of Heaven will prosper you, my children, before I die." [12] And he said to his daughter, "Honor your father-in-law and your mother-in-law. They are now your parents. Let me hear a good report of you." Then he kissed her. Edna said to Tobias, "May the Lord of Heaven restore you, dear brother, and grant to me that I may see your children of my daughter Sarah, that I may rejoice before the LORD. Behold, I commit my daughter to you in special trust. Do not cause her grief."

CHAPTER 11

[1] After these things Tobias also went his way, blessing God because He had prospered his journey; and he blessed Raguel and Edna his wife. Then he went on his way until they drew near to Nineveh. [2] Raphael said to Tobias, "Do you not know, brother, how you left your father? [3] Let us run forward before your wife and prepare the house. [4] But take in your hand the bile of the fish." So they went their way, and the dog went after them. [5] Anna sat looking around toward the path for her son. [6] She saw him coming, and said to his father, "Behold, your son is coming with the man that went with him!" [7] Raphael said, "I know, Tobias, that your father will open his eyes. [8] Therefore anoint his eyes with the bile, and being pricked with it, he will rub, and will make the white films fall away. Then he will see you." [9] Anna ran to him, and fell on the neck of her son, and said to him, "I have seen you, my child! I am ready to die." They both wept. [10] Tobit went toward the door and stumbled; but his son ran to him, [11] and took hold of his father. He rubbed the bile on his father's eyes, saying, "Cheer up, my father." [12] When his eyes began to hurt, he rubbed them. [13] Then the white films peeled away from the corners of his eyes; and he saw his son and fell on his neck. [14] He wept, and said, "Blessed are You, O God, || And blessed is Your Name forever! Blessed are all Your holy messengers! [15] For You scourged and had mercy on me. Behold, I see my son Tobias." And his son went in rejoicing and told his father the great things that had happened to him in Media. [16] Tobit went out to meet his daughter-in-law at the gate of Nineveh, rejoicing, and blessing God. Those who saw him go marveled, because he had received his sight. [17] Tobit gave thanks before them, because God had shown mercy on him. When Tobit came near to Sarah his daughter-in-law, he blessed her, saying, "Welcome, daughter! Blessed is God who has brought you to us and blessed are your father and your mother." And there was joy among all his relatives who were at Nineveh. [18] Ahikar and Nasbas his brother's son came. [19] Tobias' wedding feast was kept seven days with great gladness.

CHAPTER 12

[1] And Tobit called his son Tobias, and said to him, "See, my child, that the man which went with you have his wages, and you must give him more." [2] And he said to him, "Father, it is no harm to me to give

him the half of those things which I have brought; ³ for he has led me for you in safety, and he cured my wife, and brought my money, and likewise cured you." ⁴ The old man said, "It is due to him." ⁵ And he called the messenger, and said to him, "Take half of all that you all have brought." ⁶ Then he called them both privately, and said to them, "Bless God, and give Him thanks, and magnify Him, and give Him thanks in the sight of all that live, for the things which He has done with you. It is good to bless God and exalt His Name, showing out with honor the works of God. Do not be slack to give Him thanks. ⁷ It is good to keep close the secret of a king, but to reveal gloriously the works of God. Do good, and evil will not find you. ⁸ Good is prayer with fasting, kindness, and righteousness. A little with righteousness is better than much with unrighteousness. It is better to give alms than to lay up gold. ⁹ Kindness delivers from death, and it purges away all sin. Those who give alms and do righteousness will be filled with life; ¹⁰ but those who sin are enemies to their own life. ¹¹ Surely I will keep nothing closed from you. I have said, It is good to keep close the secret of a king, but to reveal gloriously the works of God. ¹² And now, when you prayed, and Sarah your daughter-in-law, I brought the memorial of your prayer before the Holy One. When you buried the dead, I was with you likewise. ¹³ And when you did not delay to rise up, and leave your dinner, that you might go and cover the dead, your good deed was not hidden from me. I was with you. ¹⁴ And now God sent me to heal you and your daughter-in-law Sarah. ¹⁵ I am Raphael, one of the seven holy messengers, which present the prayers of the saints, and go in before the glory of the Holy One." ¹⁶ And they were both troubled and fell on their faces; for they were afraid. ¹⁷ And he said to them, "Do not be afraid. You will all have peace; but bless God forever. ¹⁸ For I did not come of any favor of my own, but by the will of your God. Therefore, bless Him forever. ¹⁹ All these days I appeared to you, I did not eat or drink, but you all saw a vision. ²⁰ Now give God thanks, because I ascend to Him that sent me. Write in a scroll all the things which have been done." ²¹ Then they rose up and saw him no longer. ²² They confessed the great and wonderful works of God, and how the messenger of the LORD had appeared to them.

CHAPTER 13

¹ And Tobit wrote a prayer for rejoicing, and said, "Blessed is God who lives forever! Blessed is His kingdom! ² For He scourges and shows mercy. He leads down to the grave and brings up again. There is no one that will escape His hand. ³ Give thanks to Him before the nations, all you sons of Israel! For He has scattered us among them. ⁴ Declare His greatness there. Extol Him before all the living; because He is our Lord, and God is our Father forever. ⁵ He will scourge us for our iniquities, ‖ And will again show

mercy, ‖ And will gather us out of all the nations among whom you are all scattered. ⁶ If you turn to Him with your whole heart and with your whole soul, ‖ To do truth before Him, ‖ Then He will turn to you, ‖ And will not hide His face from you. See what He will do with you. Give Him thanks with your whole mouth. Bless the Lord of righteousness. Exalt the perpetual King. I give Him thanks in the land of my captivity, ‖ And show His strength and majesty to a nation of sinners. Turn, you sinners, and do righteousness before Him. Who can tell if He will accept you and have mercy on you? ⁷ I exalt my God. My soul exalts the King of Heaven and rejoices in His greatness. ⁸ Let all men speak and let them give Him thanks in Jerusalem. ⁹ O Jerusalem, the holy city, He will scourge you for the works of your sons, ‖ And will again have mercy on the sons of the righteous. ¹⁰ Give thanks to the LORD with goodness, ‖ And bless the perpetual King, ‖ That His dwelling place may be built in you again with joy, ‖ And that He may make glad in you those who are captives, ‖ And love in you forever those who are miserable. ¹¹ Many nations will come from afar to the Name of the LORD God with gifts in their hands, ‖ Even gifts to the King of Heaven. Generations of generations will praise you and sing songs of rejoicing. ¹² All those who hate you are cursed. All those who love you forever will be blessed. ¹³ Rejoice and be exceedingly glad for the sons of the righteous; For they will be gathered together and will bless the Lord of the righteous. ¹⁴ Oh blessed are those who love you. They will rejoice for your peace. Blessed are all those who sorrowed for all your scourges; Because they will rejoice for you when they have seen all your glory. They will be made glad forever. ¹⁵ Let my soul bless God the great King. ¹⁶ For Jerusalem will be built with sapphires, emeralds, and precious stones; Your walls and towers and battlements with pure gold. ¹⁷ The streets of Jerusalem will be paved with beryl, carbuncle, and stones of Ophir. ¹⁸ All her streets will say, Hallelujah! And give praise, saying, Blessed is God, who has exalted you forever!"

CHAPTER 14

¹ Then Tobit finished giving thanks. ² He was fifty-eight years old when he lost his sight. After eight years, he received it again. He gave alms and he feared the LORD God more and more and gave thanks to Him. ³ Now he grew very old; and he called his son with the six sons of his son, and said to him, "My child, take your sons. Behold, I have grown old, and am ready to depart out of this life. ⁴ Go into Media, my child, for I surely believe all the things which Jonah the prophet spoke of Nineveh, that it will be overthrown, but in Media there will rather be peace for a season. Our countrymen will be scattered in the earth from the good land. Jerusalem will be desolate, and the house of God in it will be burned up and will

be desolate for a time. ⁵ God will again have mercy on them, and bring them back into the land, and they will build the house, but not like to the former house, until the times of that age are fulfilled. Afterward they will return from the places of their captivity and build up Jerusalem with honor. The house of God will be built in it forever with a glorious building, even as the prophets spoke concerning it. ⁶ And all the nations will turn to fear the Lᴏʀᴅ God in truth and will bury their idols. ⁷ All the nations will bless the Lᴏʀᴅ, and His people will give thanks to God, and the Lᴏʀᴅ will exalt His people; and all those who love the Lᴏʀᴅ God in truth and righteousness will rejoice, showing mercy to our countrymen. ⁸ And now, my child, depart from Nineveh, because those things which the prophet Jonah spoke will surely come to pass. ⁹ But you must keep the law and the ordinances, and show yourself merciful and righteous, that it may be well with you. ¹⁰ Bury me decently, and your mother with me. Do not stay at Nineveh. See, my child, what Nadab did to Ahikar that nourished him, how out of

light he brought him into darkness, and all the repayment that he made him. Ahikar was saved, but the other had his repayment, and he went down into darkness. Manasseh gave alms and escaped the snare of death which he set for him; but Nadab fell into the snare and perished. ¹¹ And now, my children, consider what kindness does, and how righteousness delivers." While he was saying these things, he gave up the spirit in the bed; but he was one hundred fifty-eight years old. Tobias buried him magnificently. ¹² When Anna died, he buried her with his father. But Tobias departed with his wife and his sons to Ecbatana to Raguel his father-in-law, ¹³ and he grew old in honor, and he buried his father-in-law and mother-in-law magnificently, and he inherited their possessions, and his father Tobit's. ¹⁴ He died at Ecbatana of Media, being one hundred twenty-seven years old. ¹⁵ Before he died, he heard of the destruction of Nineveh, which Nebuchadnezzar and Ahasuerus took captive. Before his death, he rejoiced over Nineveh.

JUDITH

The Book of Judith relates the story of God's deliverance of the Jewish people. This was accomplished "by the hand of a female"—a constant motif (cf. 8:33; 9:9, 10; 12:4; 13:4, 14, 15; 15:10; 16:5) meant to recall the "hand" of God in the Exodus narrative (cf. Ex. 15:6). The work may have been written around 100 BC. There are four Greek recensions of Judith (Septuagint codices Vaticanus, Sinaiticus, Alexandrinus, and Basiliano-Vaticanus), four ancient translations (Old Latin, Syriac, Sahidic, and Ethiopic), and some late Hebrew versions, apparently translated from the Vulgate. Despite Jerome's claim to have translated an Aramaic text, no ancient Aramaic or Hebrew manuscripts have been found. The oldest extant text of Judith is the preservation of 15:1–7 inscribed on a third-century AD potsherd. Whatever the reasons, the rabbis did not count Judith among their scriptures, and the Reformers adopted that position.

CHAPTER 1

¹ In the twelfth year of the reign of Nebuchadnezzar, who reigned over the Assyrians in Nineveh, the great city, in the days of Arphaxad, who reigned over the Medes in Ecbatana, ² and built around Ecbatana walls of hewn stones three cubits broad and six cubits long, and made the height of the wall seventy cubits, and its breadth fifty cubits; ³ and set its towers at its gates, one hundred cubits high, and its breadth in the foundation was sixty cubits; ⁴ and made its gates, even gates that were raised to the height of seventy cubits, and their breadth forty cubits, for his mighty army to go out of, and the setting in array of his footmen— ⁵ even in those days King Nebuchadnezzar made war with King Arphaxad in the great plain. This plain is on the borders of Ragau. ⁶ There came to meet him all that lived in the hill country, and all that lived by Euphrates, Tigris, and Hydaspes, and in the plain of Arioch the king of the Elymaeans. Many nations of the sons of Chelod assembled themselves to the battle. ⁷ And Nebuchadnezzar king of the Assyrians sent to all who lived in Persia, and to all who lived westward, to those who lived in Cilicia, Damascus, Libanus, and Antilibanus, and to all who lived along the seacoast, ⁸ and to those among the nations that were of Carmel and Gilead, and to the higher Galilee and the great plain of Esdraelon, ⁹ and to all who were in Samaria and its cities, and beyond Jordan to Jerusalem, Betane, Chellus, Kadesh, the river of Egypt, Tahpanhes, Rameses, and all the land of Goshen, ¹⁰ until you come above Tanis and Memphis, and to all that lived in Egypt, until you come to the borders of Ethiopia. ¹¹ All those who lived in all the land made light of the command of Nebuchadnezzar king of the Assyrians and did not go with him to the war; for they were not afraid of him, but he was before them as one man. They turned away his messengers from their presence without effect, and with disgrace. ¹² And Nebuchadnezzar was exceedingly angry with all this land, and he swore by his throne and kingdom, that he would surely be avenged on all the coasts of Cilicia, Damascus, and Syria, that he would kill with his sword all the inhabitants of the land of Moab, and the children of Ammon, all Judea, and all that were in Egypt, until you come to the borders of the two seas. ¹³ And he set the battle in array with his army against King Arphaxad in the seventeenth year; and he prevailed in his battle, and turned to flight all the army of Arphaxad, with all his horses and all his chariots. ¹⁴ He became master of his cities, and he came even to Ecbatana, and took the towers, plundered its streets, and turned its beauty into shame. ¹⁵ He took Arphaxad in the mountains of Ragau, struck him through with his darts, and utterly destroyed him, to this day. ¹⁶ He returned with them to Nineveh, he and all his company of various nations, an exceedingly great multitude of men of war, and there he took his ease and banqueted, he and his army, for one hundred twenty days.

CHAPTER 2

¹ In the eighteenth year, the twenty-second day of the first month, there was talk in the house of Nebuchadnezzar king of the Assyrians, that he should be avenged on all the land, even as he spoke. ² He called together all his servants and all his great men, and communicated with them his secret counsel, and concluded the afflicting of all the land out of his own mouth. ³ They decreed to destroy all flesh which did not follow the word of his mouth. ⁴ It came to pass, when he had ended his counsel, Nebuchadnezzar king of the Assyrians called Holofernes the chief captain of his army, which was next after himself, and said to him, ⁵ "The great king, the lord of all the earth, says: Behold, you will go out from my presence, and take with you men who trust in their strength, to one hundred twenty thousand footmen and twelve thousand horses with their riders. ⁶ And you will go out against all the west country, because they disobeyed the command of my mouth. ⁷ You will declare to them that they should prepare earth and water, because I will go out in my wrath against them and will cover the whole face of the earth with the feet of my army, and I will give them as plunder to them. ⁸ Their slain will fill their valleys and brooks, and the river will be filled with their dead until it overflows.

⁹ I will lead them captives to the utmost parts of all the earth. ¹⁰ But you will go out and take all their coasts for me first. If they will yield themselves to you, then you must reserve them for me until the day of their reproof. ¹¹ As for those who are disobedient, your eye will not spare; but you will give them up to be slain and to be plundered in all your land. ¹² For as I live, and by the power of my kingdom, I have spoken, and I will do this with my hand. ¹³ Moreover, you will not transgress anything of the commands of your lord, but you will surely accomplish them, as I have commanded you. You will not defer to do them." ¹⁴ So Holofernes went out from the presence of his lord, and called all the governors, the captains, and officers of the army of Asshur. ¹⁵ He counted chosen men for the battle, as his lord had commanded him, to one hundred twenty thousand, with twelve thousand archers on horseback. ¹⁶ He arranged them as a great multitude is ordered for the war. ¹⁷ He took camels and donkeys and mules for their baggage, an exceedingly great multitude, and sheep and oxen and goats without number for their provision, ¹⁸ and great store of rations for every man, and exceedingly much gold and silver out of the king's house. ¹⁹ He went out, he and all his army, on their journey, to go before King Nebuchadnezzar, and to cover all the face of the earth westward with their chariots, horsemen, and chosen footmen. ²⁰ A great company of various nations went out with them like locusts, and like the sand of the earth. For they could not be counted by reason of their multitude. ²¹ And they departed out of Nineveh three days' journey toward the plain of Bectileth and encamped from Bectileth near the mountain which is at the left hand of the upper Cilicia. ²² And he took all his army, his footmen, horsemen, and chariots, and went away from there into the hill country, ²³ and destroyed Put and Lud, and plundered all the children of Rasses and the children of Ishmael, which were along the wilderness to the south of the land of the Chellians. ²⁴ And he went over Euphrates, and went through Mesopotamia, and broke down all the high cities that were on the River Arbonai, until you come to the sea. ²⁵ And he took possession of the borders of Cilicia, and killed all that resisted him, and came to the borders of Japheth, which were toward the south, opposite Arabia. ²⁶ He surrounded all the children of Midian, and set their tents on fire, and plundered their sheepfolds. ²⁷ He went down into the plain of Damascus in the days of wheat harvest, and set all their fields on fire, and utterly destroyed their flocks and herds, and plundered their cities, laid their plains waste, and struck all their young men with the edge of the sword. ²⁸ And the fear and the dread of him fell on those who lived on the seacoast, on those who were in Sidon and Tyre, those who lived in Sur and Ocina, and all who lived in Jemnaan. Those who lived in Azotus and Ashkelon feared him exceedingly.

CHAPTER 3

¹ And they sent to him messengers with words of peace, saying, ² "Behold, we the servants of Nebuchadnezzar the great king lie before you. Use us as it is pleasing in your sight. ³ Behold, our dwellings, and all our country, and all our fields of wheat, and our flocks and herds, and all the sheepfolds of our tents, lie before your face. Use them as it may please you. ⁴ Behold, even our cities and those who dwell in them are your servants. Come and deal with them as it is good in your eyes." ⁵ So the men came to Holofernes and declared to him according to these words. ⁶ He came down toward the seacoast, he and his army, and set garrisons in the high cities, and took out of them chosen men for allies. ⁷ They received him, they and all the country around them, with garlands and dances and timbrels. ⁸ He cast down all their borders and cut down their sacred groves. It had been given to him to destroy all the gods of the land, that all the nations would worship Nebuchadnezzar only, and that all their tongues and their tribes would call on him as god. ⁹ Then he came toward Esdraelon near to Dotaea, which is opposite the great ridge of Judea. ¹⁰ He encamped between Geba and Scythopolis. He was there a whole month, that he might gather together all the baggage of his army.

CHAPTER 4

¹ The sons of Israel that lived in Judea heard all that Holofernes the chief captain of Nebuchadnezzar king of the Assyrians had done to the nations, and how he had plundered all their temples and destroyed them utterly. ² They were exceedingly afraid before him, and were troubled for Jerusalem, and for the temple of the LORD their God; ³ because they had newly come up from the captivity, and all the people of Judea were recently gathered together; and the vessels, the altar, and the house were sanctified after being profaned. ⁴ And they sent into every coast of Samaria, to Konae, to Beth-Horon, Belmaim, Jericho, to Choba, Aesora, and to the Valley of Salem; ⁵ and they occupied beforehand all the tops of the high mountains, fortified the villages that were in them, stored supplies for the provision of war; for their fields were newly reaped. ⁶ Jehoiakim the chief priest, who was in those days at Jerusalem, wrote to those who lived in Bethulia, and Betomesthaim, which is opposite Esdraelon toward the plain that is near to Doesaim, ⁷ charging them to seize on the ascents of the hill country; because by them was the entrance into Judea, and it was easy to stop them from approaching, since the approach was narrow, with space for two men at the most. ⁸ And the sons of Israel did as Jehoiakim the chief priest had commanded them, as did the senate of all the people of Israel, which lived at Jerusalem. ⁹ And every man of Israel cried to God with great earnestness, and with great earnestness they humbled their souls. ¹⁰ They, their wives, their children, their cattle, and every sojourner, hireling,

JUDITH

and servant bought with their money put sackcloth on their loins. ¹¹ Every man and woman of Israel, and the little children, and the inhabitants of Jerusalem, fell before the temple, and cast ashes on their heads, and spread out their sackcloth before the LORD. They put sackcloth around the altar. ¹² They cried to the God of Israel earnestly with one consent, that He would not give their children as prey, their wives as plunder, the cities of their inheritance to destruction, and the sanctuary to being profaned and being made a reproach, for the nations to rejoice at. ¹³ The LORD heard their voice and looked at their affliction. The people continued fasting many days in all Judea and Jerusalem before the sanctuary of the LORD Almighty. ¹⁴ And Jehoiakim the chief priest, and all the priests that stood before the LORD, and those who ministered to the LORD, had their loins dressed in sackcloth, and offered the continual burnt-offering, the vows, and the free gifts of the people. ¹⁵ They had ashes on their hats. They cried to the LORD with all their power, that He would look on all the house of Israel for good.

CHAPTER 5

¹ Holofernes, the chief captain of the army of Asshur, was told that the sons of Israel had prepared for war, had shut up the passages of the hill country, had fortified all the tops of the high hills, and had laid impediments in the plains. ² Then he was exceedingly angry, and he called all the princes of Moab, and the captains of Ammon, and all the governors of the seacoast, ³ and he said to them, "Tell me now, you sons of Canaan, who are these people who dwell in the hill country? What are the cities that they inhabit? How large is their army? Where is their power and their strength? What king is set over them, to be the leader of their army? ⁴ Why have they turned their backs, that they should not come and meet me, more than all that dwell in the west?" ⁵ Then Achior, the leader of all the children of Ammon, said to him, "Let my lord now hear a word from the mouth of your servant, and I will tell you the truth concerning these people who dwell in this hill country, near to the place where you dwell. No lie will come out of the mouth of your servant. ⁶ These people are descended from the Chaldeans. ⁷ They sojourned before this in Mesopotamia, because they did not want to follow the gods of their fathers, which were in the land of the Chaldeans. ⁸ They departed from the way of their parents, and worshiped the God of Heaven, the God whom they knew. Their parents cast them out from the face of their gods, and they fled into Mesopotamia, and sojourned there many days. ⁹ Then their God commanded them to depart from the place where they sojourned, and to go into the land of Canaan. They lived there, and prospered with gold and silver, and with exceedingly much cattle. ¹⁰ Then they went down into Egypt, for a famine covered all the land of Canaan. They sojourned there until they had grown up. They became a great multitude there, so that one could not count the population of their nation. ¹¹ Then the king of Egypt rose up against them, and dealt subtly with them, and brought them low, making them labor in brick, and made them slaves. ¹² They cried to their God, and He struck all the land of Egypt with incurable plagues; so the Egyptians cast them out of their sight. ¹³ God dried up the Red Sea before them, ¹⁴ and brought them into the way of Sinai Kadesh-Barnea, and they cast out all that lived in the wilderness. ¹⁵ They lived in the land of the Amorites, and they destroyed by their strength everyone in Heshbon. Passing over Jordan, they possessed all the hill country. ¹⁶ They cast out before them the Canaanite, the Perizzite, the Jebusite, the Shechemite, and all the Girgashites, and they lived in that country many days. ¹⁷ And while they did not sin before their God, they prospered, because God who hates iniquity was with them. ¹⁸ But when they departed from the way which He appointed them, they were destroyed in many severe battles, and were led captives into a land that was not theirs. The temple of their God was cast to the ground, and their cities were taken by their adversaries. ¹⁹ And now they have returned to their God and have come up from the dispersion where they were dispersed, and have possessed Jerusalem, where their sanctuary is, and are seated in the hill country; for it was desolate. ²⁰ And now, my lord and master, if there is any error in this people, and they sin against their God, we will consider what this thing is in which they stumble, and we will go up and overcome them. ²¹ But if there is no lawlessness in their nation, let my lord now pass by, lest their Lord defend them, and their God be for them, and we will be a reproach before all the earth." ²² It came to pass, when Achior had finished speaking these words, all the people standing around the tent murmured. The great men of Holofernes, and all that lived by the seaside and in Moab, said that he should kill him. ²³ For, they said, "We will not be afraid of the sons of Israel, because, behold, they are a people that has no power nor might to make the battle strong. ²⁴ Therefore now we will go up, and they will be a prey to be devoured by all your army, Lord Holofernes."

CHAPTER 6

¹ And when the disturbance of the men that were around the council had ceased, Holofernes the chief captain of the army of Asshur said to Achior and to all the children of Moab before all the people of the foreigners, ² "And who are you, Achior, and the hirelings of Ephraim, that you have prophesied among us as today, and have said that we should not make war with the race of Israel, because their God will defend them? And who is God but Nebuchadnezzar? ³ He will send out his might and

~ 32 ~

will destroy them from the face of the earth, and their God will not deliver them; but we his servants will strike them as one man. They will not sustain the might of our horses. ⁴For with them we will burn them up. Their mountains will be drunken with their blood. Their plains will be filled with their dead bodies. Their footsteps will not stand before us, but they will surely perish, says King Nebuchadnezzar, lord of all the earth; for he said, The words that I have spoken will not be in vain. ⁵But you, Achior, hireling of Ammon, who have spoken these words in the day of your iniquity, will see my face no longer from this day, until I am avenged of the race of those that came out of Egypt. ⁶And then the sword of my army, and the multitude of those who serve me, will pass through your sides, and you will fall among their slain when I return. ⁷Then my servants will bring you back into the hill country and will set you in one of the cities of the ascents. ⁸You will not perish until you are destroyed with them. ⁹And if you hope in your heart that they will not be taken, do not let your countenance fall. I have spoken it, and none of my words will fall to the ground." ¹⁰Then Holofernes commanded his servants who waited in his tent to take Achior, and bring him back to Bethulia, and deliver him into the hands of the sons of Israel. ¹¹So his servants took him and brought him out of the camp into the plain, and they moved from the midst of the plains into the hill country and came to the springs that were under Bethulia. ¹²When the men of the city saw them on the top of the hill, they took up their weapons, and went out of the city against them to the top of the hill. Every man that used a sling kept them from coming up and cast stones against them. ¹³They took cover under the hill, bound Achior, cast him down, left him at the foot of the hill, and went away to their lord. ¹⁴But the sons of Israel descended from their city, and came to him, untied him, led him away into Bethulia, and presented him to the rulers of their city; ¹⁵which were in those days Ozias the son of Micah, of the tribe of Simeon, and Chabris the son of Gothoniel, and Charmis the son of Melchiel. ¹⁶Then they called together all the elders of the city; and all their young men ran together, with their women, to the assembly. They set Achior in the midst of all their people. Then Ozias asked him what had happened. ¹⁷He answered and declared to them the words of the council of Holofernes, and all the words that he had spoken in the midst of the princes of the children of Asshur, and all the great words that Holofernes had spoken against the house of Israel. ¹⁸Then the people fell down and worshiped God, and cried, saying, ¹⁹"O LORD God of Heaven, behold their arrogance, and pity the low estate of our race. Look on the face of those who are sanctified to You this day." ²⁰They comforted Achior and praised him exceedingly. ²¹Then Ozias took him out of the assembly into his house and made a feast for the elders. They called on the God of Israel for help all that night.

CHAPTER 7

¹The next day Holofernes commanded all his army and all the people who had come to be his allies, that they should move their camp toward Bethulia, take beforehand the ascents of the hill country, and make war against the sons of Israel. ²Every mighty man of them moved that day. The army of their men of war was one hundred seventy thousand footmen, plus twelve thousand horsemen, besides the baggage, and the men that were on foot among them: an exceedingly great multitude. ³They encamped in the valley near Bethulia, by the fountain. They spread themselves in breadth over Doesaim even to Belmaim, and in length from Bethulia to Cyamon, which is near Esdraelon. ⁴But the sons of Israel, when they saw the multitude of them, were troubled exceedingly, and everyone said to his neighbor, "Now these men will lick up the face of all the earth. Neither the high mountains, nor the valleys, nor the hills will be able to bear their weight." ⁵Every man took up his weapons of war, and when they had kindled fires on their towers, they remained and watched all that night. ⁶But on the second day Holofernes led out all his cavalry in the sight of the sons of Israel which were in Bethulia, ⁷viewed the ascents to their city, and searched out the springs of the waters, seized on them, and set garrisons of men of war over them. Then he departed back to his people. ⁸All the rulers of the children of Esau, all the leaders of the people of Moab, and the captains of the seacoast came to him and said, ⁹"Let our lord now hear a word, that there not be losses in your army. ¹⁰For this people of the sons of Israel do not trust in their spears, but in the height of the mountains wherein they dwell, for it is not easy to come up to the tops of their mountains. ¹¹And now, my lord, do not fight against them as men fight who join battle, and there will not so much as one man of your people perish. ¹²Remain in your camp and keep every man of your army safe. Let your servants get possession of the water spring, which flows from the foot of the mountain, ¹³because all the inhabitants of Bethulia get their water from there. Then thirst will kill them, and they will give up their city. Then we and our people will go up to the tops of the mountains that are near, and will encamp on them, to watch that not one man gets out of the city. ¹⁴They will be consumed with famine, they and their wives and their children. Before the sword comes against them, they will be laid low in the streets where they dwell. ¹⁵And you will pay them back with evil, because they rebelled, and did not meet your face in peace." ¹⁶Their words were pleasing in the sight of Holofernes and in the sight of all his servants; and he ordered them to do as they had spoken. ¹⁷And the army of the children of

Ammon moved, and with them five thousand of the children of Asshur, and they encamped in the valley. They seized the waters and the springs of the waters of the sons of Israel. ¹⁸ The children of Esau went up with the children of Ammon and encamped in the hill country near Doesaim. They sent some of them toward the south, and toward the east, near Ekrebel, which is near Chusi, that is on the brook Mochmur. The rest of the army of the Assyrians encamped in the plain and covered all the face of the land. Their tents and baggage were pitched on it in a great crowd. They were an exceedingly great multitude. ¹⁹ The sons of Israel cried to the Lord their God, for their spirit fainted; for all their enemies had surrounded them. There was no way to escape out from among them. ²⁰ All the army of Asshur remained around them, their footmen and their chariots and their horsemen, thirty-four days. All their vessels of water ran dry for all the inhabitants of Bethulia. ²¹ The cisterns were emptied, and they had no water to drink their fill for one day; for they rationed drink by measure. ²² Their young children were discouraged. The women and the young men fainted for thirst. They fell down in the streets of the city, and in the passages of the gates. There was no longer any strength in them. ²³ All the people, including the young men, the women, and the children, were gathered together against Ozias, and against the rulers of the city. They cried with a loud voice, and said before all the elders, ²⁴ "God be judge between all of you and us, because you have done us great wrong, in that you have not spoken words of peace with the children of Asshur. ²⁵ Now we have no helper; but God has sold us into their hands, that we should be laid low before them with thirst and great destruction. ²⁶ And now summon them and deliver up the whole city as prey to the people of Holofernes, and to all his army. ²⁷ For it is better for us to be made a plunder to them. For we will be servants, and our souls will live, and we will not see the death of our babies before our eyes, and our wives and our children fainting in death. ²⁸ We take to witness against you the heavens and the earth, and our God and the Lord of our fathers, who punishes us according to our sins and the sins of our fathers. Do what we have said today!" ²⁹ And there was great weeping of all with one consent in the midst of the assembly; and they cried to the Lord God with a loud voice. ³⁰ And Ozias said to them, "Brothers, be of good courage! Let us endure five more days, during which the Lord our God will turn His mercy toward us; for He will not forsake us utterly. ³¹ But if these days pass, and no help comes to us, I will do what you say." ³² Then he dispersed the people, every man to his own camp; and they went away to the walls and towers of their city. He sent the women and children into their houses. They were brought very low in the city.

CHAPTER 8

¹ In those days Judith heard about this. She was the daughter of Merari, the son of Ox, the son of Joseph, the son of Oziel, the son of Elkiah, the son of Ananias, the son of Gideon, the son of Raphaim, the son of Ahitub, the son of Elihu, the son of Eliab, the son of Nathanael, the son of Salamiel, the son of Salasadai, the son of Israel. ² Her husband was Manasseh, of her tribe and of her family. He died in the days of barley harvest. ³ For he stood over those who bound sheaves in the field, and the heat came on his head, and he fell on his bed, and died in his city Bethulia. So they buried him with his fathers in the field which is between Doesaim and Balamon. ⁴ Judith was a widow in her house three years and four months. ⁵ She made herself a tent on the roof of her house and put on sackcloth on her loins. The garments of her widowhood were on her. ⁶ And she fasted all the days of her widowhood, except the eves of the Sabbaths, the Sabbaths, the eves of the new moons, the new moons, and the feasts and joyful days of the house of Israel. ⁷ She was of an attractive countenance, and exceedingly beautiful to behold. Her husband Manasseh had left her gold, silver, menservants, maidservants, cattle, and lands. She remained on those lands. ⁸ No one said anything evil about her; for she feared God exceedingly. ⁹ She heard the evil words of the people against the governor, because they fainted for lack of water; and Judith heard all the words that Ozias spoke to them, how he swore to them that he would deliver the city to the Assyrians after five days. ¹⁰ So she sent her maid, who was over all things that she had, to summon Ozias, Chabris, and Charmis, the elders of her city. ¹¹ They came to her, and she said to them, "Hear me now, O you rulers of the inhabitants of Bethulia, for your word that you have spoken before the people this day is not right. You have set the oath which you have pronounced between God and you and have promised to deliver the city to our enemies, unless within these days the Lord turns to help you. ¹² Now who are you that you have tempted God this day, and stand in the place of God among the children of men? ¹³ Now try the Lord Almighty, and you will never know anything. ¹⁴ For you will not find the depth of the heart of man, and you will not perceive the things that he thinks. How will you search out God, who has made all these things, and know His mind, and comprehend His purpose? No, my countrymen, do not provoke the Lord our God to anger! ¹⁵ For if He has not decided to help us within these five days, He has power to defend us in such time as He will, or to destroy us before the face of our enemies. ¹⁶ But do not pledge the counsels of the Lord our God! For God is not as man, that He should be threatened; neither as the son of man, that He should be turned by entreaty. ¹⁷ Therefore let us wait for the salvation that comes from Him and call on Him to help us. He will hear

our voice, if it pleases Him. [18] For there arose none in our age, neither is there any of us today, tribe, or countrymen, or family, or city, which worship gods made with hands, as it was in the former days; [19] for this reason our fathers were given to the sword, and for plunder, and fell with a great fall before our enemies. [20] But we know no other god besides Him. Therefore, we hope that He will not despise us, nor any of our race. [21] For if we are taken so, all Judea will sit on the ground, and our sanctuary will be plundered; and He will require our blood for profaning it. [22] And the slaughter of our countrymen, and the captivity of the land, and the desolation of our inheritance, He will turn on our heads among the nations, wherever we will be in bondage. We will be an offense and a reproach before those who take us for a possession. [23] For our bondage will not be ordered to favor; but the LORD our God will turn it to dishonor. [24] And now, countrymen, let us show an example to our countrymen, because their soul hangs on us, and the sanctuary, the house, and the altar rest on us. [25] Besides all this, let us give thanks to the LORD our God, who tries us, even as He did our fathers also. [26] Remember all the things which He did to Abraham, and all the things in which He tried Isaac, and all the things which happened to Jacob in Mesopotamia of Syria, when he kept the sheep of Laban his mother's brother. [27] For He has not tried us in the fire, as He did them, to search out their hearts, neither has He taken vengeance on us; but the LORD does scourge them that come near to Him, to admonish them." [28] And Ozias said to her, "All that you have spoken, you have spoken with a good heart. There is no one who will deny your words. [29] For this is not the first day wherein your wisdom is manifested; but from the beginning of your days all the people have known your understanding, because the disposition of your heart is good. [30] But the people were exceedingly thirsty and compelled us to do as we spoke to them, and to bring an oath on ourselves, which we will not break. [31] And now pray for us, because you are a godly woman, and the LORD will send us rain to fill our cisterns, and we will faint no more." [32] Then Judith said to them, "Hear me, and I will do a thing, which will go down to all generations among the children of our race. [33] You will all stand at the gate tonight. I will go out with my maid. Within the days after which you said that you would deliver the city to our enemies, the LORD will visit Israel by my hand. [34] But you will not inquire of my act; for I will not declare it to you, until the things are finished that I will do." [35] Then Ozias and the rulers said to her, "Go in peace. May the LORD God be before you, to take vengeance on our enemies." [36] So they returned from the tent and went to their stations.

CHAPTER 9

[1] But Judith fell on her face, and put ashes on her head, and uncovered the sackcloth with which she was clothed. The incense of that evening was now being offered at Jerusalem in the house of God, and Judith cried to the LORD with a loud voice, and said, [2] "O LORD God of my father Simeon, into whose hand You gave a sword to take vengeance on the strangers who loosened the belt of a virgin to defile her, uncovered the thigh to her shame, and profaned the womb to her reproach; for You said, It will not be so; and they did so. [3] Therefore You gave their rulers to be slain, and their bed, which was ashamed for her who was deceived, to be dyed in blood, and struck the servants with their masters, and the masters on their thrones; [4] and gave their wives for a prey, and their daughters to be captives, and all their spoils to be divided among Your dear children; which were moved with zeal for You, and abhorred the pollution of their blood, and called on You for aid. O God, O my God, hear me who am also a widow. [5] For You did the things that were before those things, and those things, and such as come after; and You planned the things which are now, and the things which are to come. The things which You planned came to pass. [6] Yes, the things which You determined stood before You, and said, Behold, we are here; for all Your ways are prepared, and Your judgment is with foreknowledge. [7] For behold, the Assyrians are multiplied in their power. They are exalted with horse and rider. They were proud of the strength of their footmen. They have trusted in shield, spear, bow, and sling. They do not know that You are the LORD who breaks the battles. The LORD is Your Name. [8] Break their strength in Your power and bring down their force in Your wrath; for they intend to profane Your sanctuary, and to defile the dwelling place where Your glorious Name rests, and to destroy the horn of Your altar with the sword. [9] Look at their pride and send Your wrath on their heads. Give into my hand, which am a widow, the might that I have conceived. [10] Strike by the deceit of my lips the servant with the prince, and the prince with his servant. Break down their arrogance by the hand of a woman. [11] For Your power stands not in multitude, nor Your might in strong men, but You are a God of the afflicted. You are a helper of the minorities, a helper of the weak, a protector of the forsaken, a Savior of those who are without hope. [12] Yes, yes, God of my father, and God of the inheritance of Israel, Lord of the heavens and of the earth. Creator of the waters, King of every creature, hear my prayer. [13] Make my speech and deceit to be their wound and stripe, who intend hard things against Your covenant, Your holy house, the top of Zion, and the house of the possession of Your children. [14] Make every nation and tribe of Yours to know that You are God, the God of all power and

might, and that there is none other that protects the race of Israel but You."

CHAPTER 10

[1] It came to pass, when she had ceased to cry to the God of Israel, and had finished saying all these words, [2] that she rose up where she had fallen down, called her maid, and went down into the house that she used to live in on the Sabbath days and on her feast days. [3] She pulled off the sackcloth which she had put on, took off the garments of her widowhood, washed her body all over with water, anointed herself with rich ointment, braided the hair of her head, and put a tiara on it. She put on her garments of gladness, which she used to wear in the days of the life of Manasseh her husband. [4] She took sandals for her feet, and put her chains around her, and her bracelets, her rings, her earrings, and all her jewelry, and decked herself bravely, to deceive the eyes of all men who would see her. [5] She gave her maid a leather container of wine and a flask of oil, and filled a bag with parched corn, lumps of figs, and fine bread. She packed all her vessels together and laid them on her. [6] They went out to the gate of the city of Bethulia, and found Ozias and the elders of the city, Chabris and Charmis standing by it. [7] But when they saw her, that her countenance was altered, and her apparel was changed, they wondered at her beauty very exceedingly, and said to her, [8] "May the God of our fathers give you favor and accomplish your purposes to the glory of the sons of Israel, and to the exaltation of Jerusalem." Then she worshiped God, [9] and said to them, "Command that they open the gate of the city for me, and I will go out to accomplish the things you spoke with me about." And they commanded the young men to open to her, as she had spoken, [10] and they did so. Then Judith went out, she, and her handmaid with her. The men of the city watched her until she had gone down the mountain, until she had passed the valley, and they could see her no longer. [11] They went straight onward in the valley. The watch of the Assyrians met her; [12] and they took her, and asked her, "Of what people are you? Where are you coming from? Where are you going?" She said, "I am a daughter of the Hebrews. I am fleeing away from their presence, because they are about to be given to you to be consumed. [13] I am coming into the presence of Holofernes the chief captain of your army, to declare words of truth. I will show him a way that he can go and win all the hill country, and there will not be lacking of his men one person, nor one life." [14] Now when the men heard her words, and considered her countenance, the beauty thereof was exceedingly marvelous in their eyes. They said to her, [15] "You have saved your life, in that you have hurried to come down to the presence of our master. Now come to his tent. Some of us will guide you until they deliver you into his hands. [16] But when you stand before him, do not be afraid in your heart, but declare to him according to your words; and he will treat you well." [17] They chose out of them one hundred men, and appointed them to accompany her and her maid; and they brought them to the tent of Holofernes. [18] And there was great excitement throughout all the camp, for her coming was reported among the tents. They came and surrounded her as she stood outside Holofernes' tent, until they told him about her. [19] They marveled at her beauty and marveled at the sons of Israel because of her. Each one said to his neighbor, "Who would despise this people, that have among them such women? For it is not good that one man of them be left, seeing that, if they are let go, they will be able to deceive the whole earth." [20] Those who lay near Holofernes, and all his servants, went out and brought her into the tent. [21] And Holofernes was resting on his bed under the canopy, which was woven with purple, gold, emeralds, and precious stones. [22] And they told him about her; and he came out into the space before his tent, with silver lamps going before him. [23] But when Judith had come before him and his servants, they all marveled at the beauty of her countenance. She fell down on her face, and bowed down to him, but his servants raised her up.

CHAPTER 11

[1] Holofernes said to her, "Woman, take courage. Do not be afraid in your heart; for I never hurt anyone who has chosen to serve Nebuchadnezzar, the king of all the earth. [2] And now, if your people who dwell in the hill country had not slighted me, I would not have lifted up my spear against them; but they have done these things to themselves. [3] And now tell me why you fled from them and came to us; for you have come to save yourself. Take courage! You will live tonight, and hereafter; [4] for there is no one that will wrong you, but all will treat you well, as is done to the servants of King Nebuchadnezzar my lord." [5] And Judith said to him, "Receive the words of your servant, and let your handmaid speak in your presence, and I will declare no lie to my lord this night. [6] If you will follow the words of your handmaid, God will bring the thing to pass perfectly with you; and my lord will not fail to accomplish his purposes. [7] As Nebuchadnezzar king of all the earth lives, and as his power lives, who has sent you for the preservation of every living thing, not only do men serve him by you, but also the beasts of the field, the cattle, and the birds of the sky will live through your strength, in the time of Nebuchadnezzar and of all his house. [8] For we have heard of your wisdom and the subtle plans of your soul. It has been reported in all the earth that you only are brave in all the kingdom, mighty in knowledge, and wonderful in feats of war. [9] And now as concerning the matter which Achior spoke in your council, we have heard his words; for the men of Bethulia saved him, and he declared to

JUDITH

them all that he had spoken before you. [10]Therefore, O lord and master, do not neglect his word; but lay it up in your heart, for it is true; for our race will not be punished, neither will the sword prevail against them, unless they sin against their God. [11]And now, that my lord not be defeated and frustrated of his purpose, and that death may fall on them, their sin has overtaken them, with which they will provoke their God to anger, whenever they do wickedness. [12]Since their food failed them, and all their water was scant, they took counsel to lay hands on their cattle, and determined to consume all those things which God charged them by his laws that they should not eat. [13]They are resolved to spend the first-fruits of the corn, and the tenths of the wine and the oil, which they had sanctified and reserved for the priests who stand before the face of our God in Jerusalem; which things it is not fitting for any of the people so much as to touch with their hands. [14]They have sent some to Jerusalem, because they also that dwell there have done this thing, to bring them permission from the council of elders. [15]It will be, when word comes to them and they do it, they will be given to you to be destroyed the same day. [16]Therefore I, your servant, knowing all this, fled away from their presence. God sent me to work things with you, at which all the earth will be astonished, even as many as hear it. [17]For your servant is religious and serves the God of Heaven day and night. Now, my lord, I will stay with you, and your servant will go out by night into the valley. I will pray to God, and He will tell me when they have committed their sins. [18]Then I will come and show it also to you. Then you will go out with all your army, and there will be none of them that will resist you. [19]And I will lead you through the midst of Judea, until you come to Jerusalem. I will set your seat in the midst of it. You will drive them as sheep that have no shepherd, and a dog will not so much as open his mouth before you; for these things were told me according to my foreknowledge, and were declared to me, and I was sent to tell you." [20]Her words were pleasing in the sight of Holofernes and of all his servants. They marveled at her wisdom, and said, [21]"There is not such a woman from one end of the earth to the other, for beauty of face and wisdom of words." [22]Holofernes said to her, "God did well to send you before the people, that might would be in our hands, and destruction among those who slighted my lord. [23]And now you are beautiful in your countenance, and wise in your words. If you will do as you have spoken, your God will be my God, and you will dwell in the house of King Nebuchadnezzar and will be renowned through the whole earth."

CHAPTER 12

[1]He commanded that she should be brought in where his silver vessels were set and asked that his servants should prepare some of his own meats for her, and that she should drink from his own wine. [2]And Judith said, "I will not eat of it, lest there be an occasion of stumbling, but provision will be made for me of the things that have come with me." [3]And Holofernes said to her, "But if the things that are with you should fail, from where will we be able to give you more like it? For there is none of your race with us." [4]And Judith said to him, "As your soul lives, my lord, your servant will not spend those things that are with me, until the LORD works by my hand the things that He has determined." [5]Then Holofernes' servants brought her into the tent, and she slept until midnight. Then she rose up toward the morning watch, [6]and sent to Holofernes, saying, "Let my lord now command that they allow your servant to go out to pray." [7]Holofernes commanded his guards that they should not stop her. She stayed in the camp three days and went out every night into the Valley of Bethulia and washed herself at the fountain of water in the camp. [8]And when she came up, she implored the LORD God of Israel to direct her way to the raising up of the children of His people. [9]She came in clean, and remained in the tent, until she ate her food toward evening. [10]It came to pass on the fourth day, that Holofernes made a feast for his own servants only and called none of the officers to the banquet. [11]And he said to Bagoas the eunuch, who had charge over all that he had, "Go now, and persuade this Hebrew woman who is with you that she come to us and eat and drink with us. [12]For behold, it is a shame for our person, if we will let such a woman go, not having had her company; for if we do not draw her to ourselves, she will laugh us to scorn." [13]Bagoas went from the presence of Holofernes, and came in to her, and said, "Let this fair lady not fear to come to my lord, and to be honored in his presence, and to drink wine and be merry with us, and to be made this day as one of the daughters of the children of Asshur, which wait in the house of Nebuchadnezzar." [14]Judith said to him, "Who am I, that I should contradict my lord? For whatever would be pleasing in his eyes, I will do speedily, and this will be my joy to the day of my death." [15]She arose and decked herself with her apparel and all her woman's attire; and her servant went and laid fleeces on the ground for her next to Holofernes, which she had received from Bagoas for her daily use, that she might sit and eat on them. [16]Judith came in and sat down, and Holofernes' heart was ravished with her. His soul was moved, and he exceedingly desired her company. He was watching for a time to deceive her, from the day that he had seen her. [17]Holofernes said to her, "Drink now, and be merry with us." [18]Judith said, "I will drink now, my lord, because my life is magnified in me this day more than all the days since I was born." [19]Then she took and ate and drank before him what her servant had prepared. [20]Holofernes took great delight in her,

and drank exceedingly much wine, more than he had drunk at any time in one day since he was born.

CHAPTER 13

¹ But when the evening had come, his servants hurried to depart. Bagoas shut the tent outside and dismissed those who waited from the presence of his lord. They went away to their beds; for they were all weary, because the feast had been long. ² But Judith was left alone in the tent, with Holofernes lying alone on his bed; for he was drunk with wine. ³ Judith had said to her servant that she should stand outside her bedchamber, and wait for her to come out, as she did daily; for she said she would go out to her prayer. She spoke to Bagoas according to the same words. ⁴ All went away from her presence, and none was left in the bedchamber, small or great. Judith, standing by his bed, said in her heart, O LORD God of all power, look in this hour on the works of my hands for the exaltation of Jerusalem. ⁵ For now is the time to help Your inheritance, and to do the thing that I have purposed to the destruction of the enemies which have risen up against us. ⁶ She came to the rail of the bed, which was at Holofernes' head, and took down his scimitar from there. ⁷ She drew near to the bed, took hold of the hair of his head, and said, "Strengthen me, O LORD God of Israel, this day." ⁸ She struck twice on his neck with all her might, and took away his head from him, ⁹ tumbled his body down from the bed, and took down the canopy from the pillars. After a little while she went out and gave Holofernes' head to her maid; ¹⁰ and she put it in her bag of food. They both went out together to prayer, according to their custom. They passed through the camp, circled around that valley, and went up to the mountain of Bethulia, and came to its gates. ¹¹ Judith said far off to the watchmen at the gates, "Open, open the gate, now. God is with us, even our God, to show His power yet in Israel, and His might against the enemy, as He has done even this day." ¹² It came to pass, when the men of her city heard her voice, they hurried to go down to the gate of their city, and they called together the elders of the city. ¹³ They all ran together, both small and great, for it was strange to them that she had come. They opened the gate and received them, making a fire to give light, and surrounded them. ¹⁴ She said to them with a loud voice, "Praise God! Praise Him! Praise God, who has not taken away His mercy from the house of Israel but has destroyed our enemies by my hand tonight!" ¹⁵ Then she took the head out of the bag and showed it, and said to them, "Behold, the head of Holofernes, the chief captain of the army of Asshur, and behold, the canopy, in which he laid in his drunkenness. The LORD struck him by the hand of a woman. ¹⁶ And as the LORD lives, who preserved me in my way that I went, my countenance deceived him to his destruction, and he did not commit sin with me, to defile and shame me." ¹⁷ All the people were exceedingly amazed, and bowed themselves, and worshiped God, and said with one accord, "Blessed are You, O our God, which have this day brought to nothing the enemies of Your people." ¹⁸ Ozias said to her, "Blessed are you, daughter, in the sight of the Most High God, above all the women on the earth; and blessed is the LORD God, who created the heavens and the earth, who directed you to cut off the head of the prince of our enemies. ¹⁹ For your hope will not depart from the heart of men that remember the strength of God forever. ²⁰ May God turn these things to you for a perpetual praise, to visit you with good things, because you did not spare your life by reason of the affliction of our race, but avenged our fall, walking a straight way before our God." And all the people said, "Amen! Amen!"

CHAPTER 14

¹ Judith said to them, "Hear me now, my countrymen, and take this head, and hang it on the battlement of your wall. ² It will be, so soon as the morning appears, and the sun comes up on the earth, you will each take up his weapons of war, and every valiant man of you go out of the city. You will set a captain over them, as though you would go down to the plain toward the watch of the children of Asshur; but you men will not go down. ³ These will take up their full armor and will go into their camp and rouse up the captains of the army of Asshur. They will run together to Holofernes' tent. They will not find him. Fear will fall on them, and they will flee before your face. ⁴ You men, and all that inhabit every coast of Israel, will pursue them and overthrow them as they go. ⁵ But before you do these things, summon Achior the Ammonite to me, that he may see and know him that despised the house of Israel, and that sent him to us, as it were to death." ⁶ And they called Achior out of the house of Ozias; but when he came and saw the head of Holofernes in a man's hand in the assembly of the people, he fell on his face, and his spirit failed. ⁷ But when they had recovered him, he fell at Judith's feet, and bowed down to her, and said, "Blessed are you in every tent of Judah, and in every nation, which hearing your name will be troubled. ⁸ Now tell me all the things that you have done in these days." And Judith declared to him in the midst of the people all the things that she had done, from the day that she went out until the time that she spoke to them. ⁹ But when she finished speaking, the people shouted with a loud voice, and made a joyful noise in their city. ¹⁰ But when Achior saw all the things that the God of Israel had done, he believed in God exceedingly, and circumcised the flesh of his foreskin, and was joined to the house of Israel, to this day. ¹¹ But as soon as the morning arose, they hanged the head of Holofernes on the wall, and every man took up his weapons, and they went out by bands to the ascents of the mountain.

12 But when the children of Asshur saw them, they sent word to their leaders; but they went to their captains and tribunes, and to each of their rulers. 13 They came to Holofernes' tent, and said to him that was over all that he had, "Wake our lord up, now; for the slaves have been bold to come down against us to battle, that they may be utterly destroyed." 14 Bagoas went in and knocked at the outer door of the tent; for he supposed that he was sleeping with Judith. 15 But when no one listened to him, he opened it, and went into the bedchamber, and found him cast on the threshold dead, and his head had been taken from him. 16 He cried with a loud voice, with weeping and groaning and a mighty cry, and tore his garments. 17 He entered into the tent where Judith lodged, and he did not find her. He leaped out to the people, and cried aloud, 18 "The slaves have dealt treacherously! One woman of the Hebrews has brought shame on the house of King Nebuchadnezzar; for behold, Holofernes lies on the ground, and his head is not on him!" 19 But when the rulers of the army of Asshur heard the words, they tore their coats, and their soul was troubled exceedingly. There was a cry and an exceedingly great noise in the midst of the camp.

CHAPTER 15

1 When those who were in the tents heard, they were amazed at what happened. 2 Trembling and fear fell on them, and no man dared stay anymore in the sight of his neighbor, but rushing out with one accord, they fled into every way of the plain and of the hill country. 3 Those who had encamped in the hill country around Bethulia fled away. And then the sons of Israel, everyone who was a warrior among them, rushed out on them. 4 Ozias sent to Betomasthaim, Bebai, Chobai, and Chola, and to every coast of Israel, to tell about the things that had been accomplished, and that all should rush on their enemies to destroy them. 5 But when the sons of Israel heard, they all fell on them with one accord, and struck them to Chobai. Yes, and in like manner also they of Jerusalem and of all the hill country came (for men had told them about what happened in their enemies' camp), and those who were in Gilead and in Galilee fell on their flank with a great slaughter, until they were past Damascus and its borders. 6 The rest of the people who lived at Bethulia fell on the camp of Asshur, and plundered them, and were enriched exceedingly. 7 The sons of Israel returned from the slaughter and got possession of that which remained. The villages and the cities that were in the hill country and in the plain country, took many spoils; for there was an exceedingly great supply. 8 Jehoiakim the chief priest, and the elders of the sons of Israel who lived in Jerusalem, came to see the good things which the LORD had showed to Israel, and to see Judith, and to salute her. 9 When they came to her, they all blessed her with one accord, and said to her, "You are the exaltation of Jerusalem! You are the great glory of Israel! You are the great rejoicing of our race! 10 You have done all these things by your hand. You have done with Israel the things that are good, and God is pleased with it. Blessed are you with the Almighty LORD forever." And all the people said, "Amen!" 11 And the people plundered the camp for the space of thirty days: and they gave Holofernes' tent to Judith, along with all his silver cups, his beds, his bowls, and all his furniture. She took them, and placed them on her mule, and prepared her wagons, and heaped them on it. 12 And all the women of Israel ran together to see her; and they blessed her and made a dance among them for her. She took branches in her hand and distributed them to the women who were with her. 13 Then they made themselves garlands of olive, she and those who were with her, and she went before all the people in the dance, leading all the women. All the men of Israel followed in their armor with garlands, and with songs in their mouths.

CHAPTER 16

1 And Judith began to sing this song of thanksgiving in all Israel, and all the people sang with loud voices this song of praise. 2 Judith said, "Begin a song to my God with timbrels. Sing to my Lord with cymbals. Make melody to Him with psalm and praise. Exalt Him and call on His Name. 3 For the LORD is the God that crushes battles. For in His armies in the midst of the people, || He delivered me out of the hand of those who persecuted me. 4 Asshur came out of the mountains from the north. He came with tens of thousands of his army. Its multitude stopped the torrents. Their horsemen covered the hills. 5 He said that he would burn up my borders, || Kill my young men with the sword, || Throw my nursing children to the ground, || Give my infants up as prey, || And make my virgins a plunder. 6 The Almighty LORD brought them to nothing by the hand of a woman. 7 For their mighty one did not fall by young men, || Neither did sons of the Titans strike him. Tall giants did not attack him, || But Judith the daughter of Merari made him weak with the beauty of her countenance. 8 For she put off the apparel of her widowhood || For the exaltation of those who were distressed in Israel. She anointed her face with ointment, || Bound her hair in a tiara, || And took a linen garment to deceive him. 9 Her sandal ravished his eye. Her beauty took his soul prisoner. The scimitar passed through his neck. 10 The Persians quaked at her daring. The Medes were daunted at her boldness. 11 Then my lowly ones shouted aloud. My weak ones were terrified and trembled for fear. They lifted up their voice, and they fled. 12 The sons of ladies pierced them through and wounded them as fugitives' children. They perished by the battle of my Lord. 13 I will sing to my God a new song: O LORD, You are great and glorious, || Marvelous in strength, invincible. 14 Let all Your

JUDITH

creation serve You; For You spoke, and they were made. You sent out Your Spirit, ‖ And it built them. There is no one who can resist Your voice. ¹⁵ For the mountains will be moved from their foundations with the waters, ‖ And the rocks will melt as wax at your presence, ‖ But You are yet merciful to those who fear You. ¹⁶ For all sacrifice is little for a sweet savor, ‖ And all the fat is very little for a whole burnt-offering to You; But he who fears the LORD is great continually. ¹⁷ Woe to the nations who rise up against my race! The LORD Almighty will take vengeance on them in the Day of Judgment, ‖ To put fire and worms in their flesh; And they will weep and feel their pain forever." ¹⁸ Now when they came to Jerusalem, they worshiped God. When the people were purified, they offered their whole burnt-offerings, their free will offerings, and their gifts. ¹⁹ Judith dedicated all Holofernes' stuff, which the people had given her, and gave the canopy, which she had taken for herself out of his bedchamber, for a gift to the LORD. ²⁰ And the people continued feasting in Jerusalem before the sanctuary for three months, and Judith remained with them. ²¹ But after these days, everyone departed to his own inheritance. Judith went away to Bethulia, and remained in her own possession, and was honorable in her time in all the land. ²² Many desired her, and no man knew her all the days of her life, from the day that Manasseh her husband died and was gathered to his people. ²³ She increased in greatness exceedingly; and she grew old in her husband's house, to one hundred five years, and let her maid go free. Then she died in Bethulia. They buried her in the cave of her husband Manasseh. ²⁴ The house of Israel mourned for her seven days. She distributed her goods before she died to all those who were nearest relatives to Manasseh her husband, and to those who were nearest of her own relatives. ²⁵ There was no one that made the sons of Israel afraid anymore in the days of Judith, nor a long time after her death.

WISDOM

Otherwise known as Wisdom of Solomon

The Book of Wisdom was written as late as fifty years before the coming of Christ. Its author, whose name is not known to us, was probably a member of the Jewish community at Alexandria, in Egypt. He wrote in Greek, in a style patterned on that of Hebrew verse. At times he speaks in the person of Solomon, placing his teachings on the lips of the wise king of Hebrew tradition in order to emphasize their value.

CHAPTER 1

¹ Love righteousness, all you who are judges of the earth. Think of the LORD with a good mind. Seek Him in singleness of heart, ² Because He is found by those who do not tempt Him and is manifested to those who trust Him. ³ For crooked thoughts separate from God. His Power convicts when it is tested and exposes the foolish, ⁴ Because wisdom will not enter into a soul that devises evil, || Nor dwell in a body that is enslaved by sin. ⁵ For a holy spirit of discipline will flee deceit, || And will depart from thoughts that are without understanding, || And will be ashamed when unrighteousness has come in. ⁶ For wisdom is a spirit who loves man, || And she will not hold a blasphemer guiltless for his lips; Because God is [the] witness of his innermost self, || And is [the] true overseer of his heart, and a hearer of his tongue: ⁷ Because the Spirit of the LORD has filled the world, || And that which holds all things together knows what is said. ⁸ Therefore no one who utters unrighteous things will be unseen; Neither will justice, when it convicts, pass him by. ⁹ For in his counsels the ungodly will be searched out, || And the sound of his words will come to the LORD to bring his lawless deeds to conviction; ¹⁰ Because a jealous ear listens to all things, || And the noise of murmurings is not hidden. ¹¹ Beware then of unprofitable murmuring and keep your tongue from slander, || Because no secret utterance will go on its way void, || And a lying mouth destroys a soul. ¹² Do not court death in the error of your life; And do not draw destruction on yourselves by the works of your hands, ¹³ Because God did not make death; Neither does He delight when the living perish. ¹⁴ For He created all things that they might have being. The generative powers of the world are wholesome, || And there is no poison of destruction in them, || Nor does Hades have royal dominion on earth; ¹⁵ For righteousness is immortal, ¹⁶ But ungodly men, by their hands and their words, summon death; Deeming him a friend, they wear themselves out [for him]. They made a covenant with him, || Because they are worthy to belong with him.

CHAPTER 2

¹ For they said within themselves, with unsound reasoning, "Our life is short and sorrowful. There is no healing when a man comes to his end, || And no one was ever known who was released from Hades, ² Because we were born by mere chance, || And hereafter we will be as though we had never been; Because the breath in our nostrils is smoke, || And reason is a spark kindled by the beating of our heart, ³ Which being extinguished, the body will be turned into ashes, || And the spirit will be dispersed as thin air. ⁴ Our name will be forgotten in time. No one will remember our works. Our life will pass away as the traces of a cloud, || And will be scattered as is a mist, when it is chased by the rays of the sun and overcome by its heat. ⁵ For our allotted time is the passing of a shadow, and our end does not retreat, || Because it is securely sealed, and no one turns it back. ⁶ Come therefore and let us enjoy the good things that exist. Let us use the creation earnestly as in our youth. ⁷ Let us fill ourselves with costly wine and perfumes || And let no Spring flower pass us by. ⁸ Let us crown ourselves with rosebuds before they wither. ⁹ Let none of us go without his share in our proud revelry. Let us leave signs of mirth everywhere, || Because this is our portion, and this is our lot. ¹⁰ Let us oppress the righteous poor. Let us not spare the widow, || Nor give reverence to the gray hair of the old man. ¹¹ But let our strength be a law of righteousness; For that which is weak is proven useless. ¹² But let us lie in wait for the righteous man, || Because he annoys us, is contrary to our works, reproaches us with sins against the law, and charges us with sins against our training. ¹³ He professes to have knowledge of God and calls himself a child of the LORD. ¹⁴ He became to us a reproof of our thoughts. ¹⁵ He is grievous to us even to look at, || Because his life is unlike other men's, and his paths are strange. ¹⁶ We were regarded by him as worthless metal, || And he abstains from our ways as from uncleanness. He calls the latter end of the righteous happy. He boasts that God is his father. ¹⁷ Let us see if his words are true. Let us test what will happen at the end of his life. ¹⁸ For if the righteous man is God's son, He will uphold him, || And He will deliver him out of the hand of his adversaries. ¹⁹ Let us test him with outrage and torture, || That we may find out how gentle he is and test his patience. ²⁰ Let us condemn him to a shameful death, || For he will be overseen according to his words." ²¹ So they reasoned, and they were led astray; For their wickedness blinded them, ²² And they did not know the mysteries of God, || Neither did they hope for wages of holiness, || Nor did they discern that there is a prize for blameless souls.

WISDOM

²³ Because God created man for incorruption ‖ And made Him an image of His own perpetuity; ²⁴ But death entered into the world by the envy of the Devil, ‖ And those who belong to him experience it.

CHAPTER 3

¹ But the souls of the righteous are in the hand of God, ‖ And no torment will touch them. ² In the eyes of the foolish they seemed to have died. Their departure was considered affliction, ³ And their travel away from us ruin; But they are in peace. ⁴ For even if they are punished in the sight of men, ‖ Their hope is full of immortality. ⁵ Having borne a little disciplining, they will receive great good, ‖ Because God tested them and found them worthy of Himself. ⁶ He tested them like gold in the furnace, ‖ And He accepted them as a whole burnt-offering. ⁷ In the time of their visitation they will shine. They will run back and out like sparks among stubble. ⁸ They will judge nations and have dominion over peoples. The LORD will reign over them forever. ⁹ Those who trust Him will understand truth. The faithful will live with Him in love, ‖ Because grace and mercy are with His chosen ones. ¹⁰ But the ungodly will be punished even as they reasoned, ‖ Those who neglected righteousness and revolted from the LORD; ¹¹ For he who despises wisdom and discipline is miserable. Their hope is void and their toils unprofitable. Their works are useless. ¹² Their wives are foolish and their children are wicked. ¹³ Their descendants are cursed, ‖ Because the barren woman who is undefiled is happy—she who has not conceived in transgression. She will have fruit in the visitation of souls. ¹⁴ So is the eunuch which has done no lawless deed with his hands, ‖ Nor imagined wicked things against the LORD; For a precious gift will be given to him for his faithfulness—a special favor, and a delightful inheritance in the LORD's sanctuary. ¹⁵ For good labors have fruit of great renown. The root of understanding cannot fail. ¹⁶ But children of adulterers will not come to maturity. The seed of an unlawful bed will vanish away. ¹⁷ For if they live long, they will not be esteemed, ‖ And in the end, their old age will be without honor. ¹⁸ If they die quickly, they will have no hope, ‖ Nor consolation in the day of decision. ¹⁹ For the end of an unrighteous generation is always grievous.

CHAPTER 4

¹ It is better to be childless with virtue, ‖ For immortality is in the memory of virtue, ‖ Because it is recognized both before God and before men. ² When it is present, people imitate it. They long after it when it has departed. Throughout all time it marches crowned in triumph—Victorious in the competition for the prizes that are undefiled. ³ But the multiplying brood of the ungodly will be of no profit, ‖ And their illegitimate offshoots will not take deep root, ‖ Nor will they establish a sure hold. ⁴ For even if they grow branches and flourish for a season, ‖ Standing unsure, they will be shaken by the wind. They will be uprooted by the violence of winds. ⁵ Their branches will be broken off before they come to maturity. Their fruit will be useless—Never ripe to eat and fit for nothing. ⁶ For unlawfully conceived children are witnesses of wickedness against parents when they are investigated. ⁷ But a righteous man, even if he dies before his time, will be at rest. ⁸ For honorable old age is not that which stands in length of time, ‖ Nor is its measure given by number of years, ⁹ But understanding is gray hair to men, ‖ And an unspotted life is ripe old age. ¹⁰ Being found well-pleasing to God, he was loved; While living among sinners he was transported. ¹¹ He was caught away, lest evil should change his understanding, ‖ Or guile deceive his soul. ¹² For the witchcraft of worthlessness obscures the things which are good, ‖ And the whirl of desire perverts an innocent mind. ¹³ Being made perfect quickly, he filled a long time; ¹⁴ For his soul was pleasing to the LORD. Therefore, he hurried out of the midst of wickedness. ¹⁵ But as for the peoples seeing and not understanding, ‖ They are not considering this: that grace and mercy are with His chosen, ‖ And that He visits His holy ones. ¹⁶ But a righteous man who is dead will condemn the ungodly who are living, ‖ And youth that is quickly perfected will condemn the many years of an unrighteous man's old age. ¹⁷ For the ungodly will see a wise man's end, ‖ And will not understand what the LORD planned for him, and why He safely kept him. ¹⁸ They will see, and they will despise; But the LORD will laugh them to scorn. After this, they will become a dishonored carcass and a reproach among the dead forever, ¹⁹ Because He will dash them speechless to the ground ‖ And will shake them from the foundations. They will lie utterly waste. They will be in anguish and their memory will perish. ²⁰ They will come with cowardly fear when their sins are counted. Their lawless deeds will convict them to their face.

CHAPTER 5

¹ Then the righteous man will stand in great boldness ‖ Before the face of those who afflicted him, ‖ And those who make his labors of no account. ² When they see him, they will be troubled with terrible fear, ‖ And will be amazed at the marvel of salvation. ³ They will speak among themselves converting, ‖ And for distress of spirit they will groan, ‖ "This was he whom we used to hold in derision, as an allegory of reproach. ⁴ We fools considered his life madness, and his end without honor. ⁵ How was he counted among sons of God? How is his lot among saints? ⁶ Truly we went astray from the way of truth. The light of righteousness did not shine for us. The sun did not rise for us. ⁷ We took our fill of the paths of lawlessness and destruction. We traveled through

trackless deserts, || But we did not know the LORD's way. **⁸**What did our arrogance profit us? What good have riches and boasting brought us? **⁹**Those things all passed away as a shadow, || Like a message that runs by, **¹⁰**Like a ship passing through the billowy water, || Which, when it has gone by, there is no trace to be found, || No pathway of its keel in the billows. **¹¹**Or it is like when a bird flies through the air [and] no evidence of its passage is found, || But the light wind, lashed with the stroke of its pinions, || And torn apart with the violent rush of the moving wings, is passed through. Afterward no sign of its coming remains. **¹²**Or it is like when an arrow is shot at a mark [and] the parted air closes up again immediately, || So that men do not know where it passed through. **¹³**So we also, as soon as we were born, ceased to be; And we had no sign of virtue to show, but we were utterly consumed in our wickedness." **¹⁴**Because the hope of the ungodly man is like chaff carried by the wind, || And as foam vanishing before a tempest; And [it] is scattered like smoke by the wind, || And passes by as the remembrance of a guest that waits but a day. **¹⁵**But the righteous live forever. Their reward is in the LORD, || And the care for them with the Most High. **¹⁶**Therefore they will receive the crown of royal dignity || And the diadem of beauty from the LORD's hand; Because He will cover them with His right hand, || And He will shield them with His arm. **¹⁷**He will take His jealousy as complete armor || And will make the whole creation His weapons to punish His enemies: **¹⁸**He will put on righteousness as a breastplate || And will wear impartial judgment as a helmet. **¹⁹**He will take holiness as an invincible shield. **²⁰**He will sharpen stern wrath for a sword. The world will go with Him to fight against His frenzied enemies. **²¹**Shafts of lightning will fly with true aim. They will leap to the mark from the clouds, as from a well-drawn bow. **²²**Hailstones full of wrath will be hurled from an engine of war. The water of the sea will be angered against them. Rivers will sternly overwhelm them. **²³**A mighty blast will encounter them. It will winnow them away like a tempest. So lawlessness will make all the land desolate. Their evildoing will overturn the thrones of princes.

CHAPTER 6

¹Hear therefore, you kings, and understand. Learn, you judges of the ends of the earth. **²**Give ear, you rulers who have dominion over many people, || And [who] make your boast in multitudes of nations, **³**Because your dominion was given to you from the LORD, || And your sovereignty from the Most High. He will search out your works and will inquire about your plans; **⁴**Because, being officers of His kingdom, you did not judge rightly, || Nor did you keep law, nor did you walk according to God's counsel. **⁵**He will come on you awfully and swiftly, || Because a stern judgment comes on those who are in high places. **⁶**For

the man of low estate may be pardoned in mercy, || But mighty men will be mightily tested. **⁷**For the Sovereign Lord of all will not be impressed with anyone, || Neither will He show deference to greatness; Because it is He who made both small and great, and cares about them all; **⁸**But the scrutiny that comes on the powerful is strict. **⁹**Therefore, my words are to you, O princes, || That you may learn wisdom and not fall away. **¹⁰**For those who have kept the things that are holy in holiness will be made holy. Those who have been taught them will find what to say in defense. **¹¹**Therefore set your desire on my words. Long for them, and you princes will be instructed. **¹²**Wisdom is radiant and does not fade away, || And is easily seen by those who love her || And found by those who seek her. **¹³**She anticipates those who desire her, making herself known. **¹⁴**He who rises up early to seek her will not have difficulty, || For he will find her sitting at his gates. **¹⁵**For to think on her is perfection of understanding, || And he who watches for her will quickly be free from care; **¹⁶**Because she herself goes around, seeking those who are worthy of her, || And in their paths she appears to them graciously, || And in every purpose she meets them. **¹⁷**For her true beginning is desire for instruction; And desire for instruction is love. **¹⁸**And love is observance of her laws. To give heed to her laws confirms immortality. **¹⁹**Immortality brings closeness to God. **²⁰**So then, desire for wisdom promotes to a kingdom. **²¹**If, therefore, you delight in thrones and scepters—you princes of peoples— Honor wisdom, that you may reign forever. **²²**But what wisdom is, and how she came into being, I will declare. I will not hide mysteries from you; But I will explore from her first beginning; [I will] bring the knowledge of her into clear light, || And I will not pass by the truth. **²³**Indeed, I will not go with consuming envy, || Because envy will have no fellowship with wisdom. **²⁴**But a multitude of wise men is salvation to the world, || And an understanding king is stability for his people. **²⁵**Therefore be instructed by my words, and you will profit.

CHAPTER 7

¹I myself am also mortal, like everyone else, || And am a descendant of one formed first and born of the earth. **²**I [was] molded into flesh in the time of ten months in my mother's womb, || Being compacted in blood from the seed of man and pleasure that came with sleep. **³**I also, when I was born, drew in the common air, and fell on the related earth, || Uttering, like all, for my first voice, the same cry. **⁴**I was nursed with care in swaddling clothes. **⁵**For no king had any other first beginning; **⁶**But all men have one entrance into life, and a common departure. **⁷**For this reason I prayed, and understanding was given to me. I asked, and a spirit of wisdom came to me. **⁸**I preferred her before scepters and thrones. I considered riches

WISDOM

nothing in comparison to her. [9] Neither did I liken to her any priceless gem, ‖ Because all gold in her presence is a little sand, ‖ And silver will be considered as clay before her. [10] I loved her more than health and beauty, ‖ And I chose to have her rather than light, ‖ Because her bright shining is never laid to sleep. [11] All good things came to me with her, ‖ And innumerable riches are in her hands. [12] And I rejoiced over them all because wisdom leads them, ‖ Although I did not know that she was their mother. [13] As I learned without guile, I impart without grudging. I do not hide her riches. [14] For she is a treasure for men that does not fail, ‖ And those who use it obtain friendship with God, ‖ Commended by the gifts which they present through discipline. [15] But may God grant that I may speak His judgment, ‖ And to conceive thoughts worthy of what has been given me; Because He is one who guides even wisdom and who corrects the wise. [16] For both we and our words are in His hand, ‖ With all understanding and skill in various crafts. [17] For He Himself gave me an unerring knowledge of the things that are, ‖ To know the structure of the universe and the operation of the elements; [18] The beginning, end, and middle of times; The alternations of the solstices and the changes of seasons; [19] The circuits of years and the positions of stars; [20] The natures of living creatures and the raging of wild beasts; The violence of winds and the thoughts of men; The diversities of plants and the virtues of roots. [21] All things that are either secret or manifest I learned, [22] For wisdom, that is the architect of all things, taught me. For there is a spirit in her that is quick to understand, ‖ Holy, unique, manifold, subtle, freely moving, clear in utterance, ‖ Unpolluted, distinct, unharmed, loving what is good, keen, unhindered, [23] Beneficent, loving toward man, steadfast, sure, free from care, all-powerful, all-surveying, ‖ And penetrating through all spirits that are quick to understand, pure, most subtle: [24] For wisdom is more mobile than any motion. Yes, she pervades and penetrates all things by reason of her purity. [25] For she is a breath of the power of God, ‖ And a clear effluence of the glory of the Almighty. Therefore, nothing defiled can find entrance into her. [26] For she is a reflection of continuous light, ‖ An unspotted mirror of the working of God, ‖ And an image of His goodness. [27] She, being one, has power to do all things. Remaining in herself, she renews all things. From generation to generation passing into holy souls, ‖ She makes friends of God and prophets. [28] For God loves nothing as much as one who dwells with wisdom. [29] For she is fairer than the sun, and above all the constellations of the stars. She is better than light. [30] For daylight yields to night, but evil does not prevail against wisdom.

CHAPTER 8

[1] But she reaches from one end to the other with full strength and orders all things well. [2] I loved her and sought her from my youth. I sought to take her for my bride. I became enamored by her beauty. [3] She glorifies her noble birth by living with God. The Sovereign Lord of all loves her. [4] For she is initiated into the knowledge of God, ‖ And she chooses His works. [5] But if riches are a desired possession in life, ‖ What is richer than wisdom, which makes all things? [6] And if understanding works, ‖ Who more than wisdom is an architect of the things that exist? [7] If a man loves righteousness, the fruits of wisdom's labor are virtues, ‖ For she teaches soberness, understanding, righteousness, and courage. There is nothing in life more profitable for people than these. [8] And if anyone longs for wide experience, ‖ She knows the things of old, and infers the things to come. She understands subtleties of speeches and interpretations of dark sayings. She foresees signs and wonders, and the issues of seasons and times. [9] Therefore I determined to take her to live with me, ‖ Knowing that she is one who would give me good counsel, ‖ And encourage me in cares and grief. [10] Because of her, I will have glory among multitudes, ‖ And honor in the sight of elders, though I am young. [11] I will be found keen when I give judgment. I will be admired in the presence of rulers. [12] When I am silent, they will wait for me. When I open my lips, they will heed what I say. If I continue speaking, they will put their hands on their mouths. [13] Because of her, I will have immortality, ‖ And leave behind a continuous memory to those who come after me. [14] I will govern peoples. Nations will be subjected to me. [15] Dreaded monarchs will fear me when they hear of me. Among the people, I will show myself to be good and courageous in war. [16] When I come into my house, I will find rest with her. For conversation with her has no bitterness, ‖ And living with her has no pain, but gladness and joy. [17] When I considered these things in myself ‖ And thought in my heart how immortality is in kinship to wisdom, [18] And in her friendship is good delight, ‖ And in the labors of her hands is wealth that does not fail, ‖ And understanding is in her companionship, ‖ And great renown in having fellowship with her words, ‖ I went around seeking how to take her to myself. [19] Now I was a clever child and received a good soul. [20] Or rather, being good, I came into an undefiled body. [21] But perceiving that I could not otherwise possess wisdom unless God gave her to me—Yes, and to know and understand by whom the grace is given—I pleaded with the LORD and implored Him, and with my whole heart I said:

CHAPTER 9

[1] "O God of the fathers, and Lord of mercy, who made all things by Your word; [2] And by Your wisdom You formed man, that he should have dominion over the

WISDOM

creatures that were made by You, ³ And rule the world in holiness and righteousness, and execute judgment in uprightness of soul; ⁴ Give me wisdom—her who sits by You on Your thrones. Do not reject me from among Your servants, ⁵ Because I am Your servant and the son of Your handmaid, ‖ A weak and short-lived man, with little power to understand judgment and laws. ⁶ For even if a man is perfect among the sons of men, ‖ If the wisdom that comes from You is not with him, he will count for nothing. ⁷ You chose me to be king of Your people, ‖ And a judge for Your sons and daughters. ⁸ You gave a command to build a sanctuary on Your holy mountain, ‖ And an altar in the city where You pitch Your tent—A copy of the holy tent which You prepared from the beginning. ⁹ Wisdom is with You and knows Your works, ‖ And was present when You were making the world, ‖ And understands what is pleasing in Your eyes, ‖ And what is right according to Your commands. ¹⁰ Send her from the holy heavens and ask her to come from the throne of Your glory, ‖ That being present with me she may work, ‖ And I may learn what pleases You well. ¹¹ For she knows all things and understands, ‖ And she will guide me soberly in my actions. She will guard me in her glory. ¹² So my works will be acceptable. I will judge Your people righteously, ‖ And I will be worthy of my father's throne. ¹³ For what man will know the counsel of God? Or who will conceive what the LORD wills? ¹⁴ For the thoughts of mortals are unstable, and our plans are prone to fail. ¹⁵ For a corruptible body weighs down the soul. The earthy frame lies heavy on a mind that is full of cares. ¹⁶ We can hardly guess the things that are on earth, ‖ And we find the things that are close at hand with labor; But who has traced out the things that are in the heavens? ¹⁷ Who gained knowledge of Your counsel, ‖ Unless You gave wisdom, and sent Your Holy Spirit from the highest? ¹⁸ It was so that the ways of those who are on earth were corrected, ‖ And men were taught the things that are pleasing to You. They were saved through wisdom."

CHAPTER 10

¹ Wisdom guarded to the end the first formed father of the world, ‖ Who was created alone, and delivered him out of his own transgression, ² And gave him strength to get dominion over all things. ³ But when an unrighteous man fell away from her in his anger, ‖ He perished himself in the rage with which he killed his brother. ⁴ When for his cause the earth was drowning with a flood, ‖ Wisdom again saved it, guiding the righteous man's course by a poor piece of wood. ⁵ Moreover, when nations consenting together in wickedness had been confounded, ‖ Wisdom knew the righteous man, and preserved him blameless to God, ‖ And kept him strong when his heart yearned toward his child. ⁶ While the ungodly were perishing, wisdom delivered a righteous man, ‖ When he fled

from the fire that descended out of Heaven on [the] five cities— ⁷ To whose wickedness a smoking waste still witnesses, ‖ And plants bearing fair fruit that does not ripen, ‖ A disbelieving soul has a memorial: a standing pillar of salt. ⁸ For having passed wisdom by, ‖ Not only were they disabled from recognizing the things which are good, ‖ But they also left behind them for their life a monument of their folly, ‖ To the end that where they stumbled, they might fail even to be unseen; ⁹ But wisdom delivered those who waited on her out of troubles. ¹⁰ When a righteous man was a fugitive from a brother's wrath, ‖ Wisdom guided him in straight paths. She showed him God's Kingdom and gave him knowledge of holy things. She prospered him in his toils and multiplied the fruits of his labor. ¹¹ When in their covetousness men dealt harshly with him, ‖ She stood by him and made him rich. ¹² She guarded him from enemies, ‖ And she kept him safe from those who lay in wait. Over his severe conflict, she watched as judge, ‖ That he might know that godliness is more powerful than everyone. ¹³ When a righteous man was sold, ‖ Wisdom did not forsake him, but she delivered him from sin. She went down with him into a dungeon, ¹⁴ And in bonds she did not depart from him, ‖ Until she brought him the scepter of a kingdom, and authority over those that dealt unjustly with him. She also showed those who had mockingly accused him to be false and gave him continuous glory. ¹⁵ Wisdom delivered a holy people and a blameless seed from a nation of oppressors. ¹⁶ She entered into the soul of a servant of the LORD ‖ And withstood terrible kings in wonders and signs. ¹⁷ She rendered to holy men a reward of their toils. She guided them along a marvelous way ‖ And became to them a covering in the daytime, ‖ And a flame of stars through the night. ¹⁸ She brought them over the Red Sea and led them through much water; ¹⁹ But she drowned their enemies, and she cast them up from the bottom of the deep. ²⁰ Therefore the righteous plundered the ungodly, ‖ And they sang praise to Your holy Name, O LORD, ‖ And extolled with one accord Your hand that fought for them, ²¹ Because wisdom opened the mouth of the mute, ‖ And made the tongues of babies to speak clearly.

CHAPTER 11

¹ She prospered their works in the hand of a holy prophet. ² They traveled through a desert without inhabitant, ‖ And they pitched their tents in trackless regions. ³ They withstood enemies and repelled enemies. ⁴ They thirsted, and they called on You, ‖ And water was given to them out of the flinty rock, ‖ And healing of their thirst out of the hard stone. ⁵ For by what things their enemies were punished, ‖ By these they in their need were benefited. ⁶ When enemies were troubled with clotted blood instead of a river's ever-flowing fountain, ⁷ To rebuke the decree for the slaying of babies, You gave them abundant

~ 45 ~

water beyond all hope, ⁸ Having shown by the thirst which they had suffered how You punished the adversaries. ⁹ For when they were tried, although disciplined in mercy, ‖ They learned how the ungodly were tormented, being judged with wrath. ¹⁰ For You tested these as a father admonishing them; But You searched out those as a stern king condemning them. ¹¹ Yes, and whether they were far off or near, they were equally distressed; ¹² For a double grief seized them, ‖ And a groaning at the memory of things past. ¹³ For when they heard that through their own punishments the others benefited, ‖ They recognized the LORD. ¹⁴ For him who long before was thrown out and exposed they stopped mocking. In the end of what happened, they marveled, ‖ Having thirsted in another manner than the righteous. ¹⁵ But in return for the senseless imaginings of their unrighteousness, ‖ Wherein they were led astray to worship irrational reptiles and wretched vermin, ‖ You sent on them a multitude of irrational creatures for vengeance, ¹⁶ That they might learn that by what things a man sins, by these he is punished. ¹⁷ For Your all-powerful hand that created the world out of formless matter ‖ Did not lack means to send on them a multitude of bears, fierce lions, ¹⁸ Or newly-created and unknown wild beasts, full of rage, ‖ Either breathing out a blast of fiery breath, or belching out smoke, ‖ Or flashing dreadful sparks from their eyes, ¹⁹ Which had power not only to consume them by their violence, ‖ But to destroy them even by the terror of their sight. ²⁰ Yes, and without these they might have fallen by a single breath, ‖ Being pursued by justice, and scattered abroad by the breath of Your power; But You arranged all things by measure, number, and weight. ²¹ For to be greatly strong is Yours at all times. Who could withstand the might of Your arm? ²² Because the whole world before You is as a grain in a balance, ‖ And as a drop of dew that comes down on the earth in the morning. ²³ But You have mercy on all men, ‖ Because You have power to do all things, ‖ And You overlook the sins of men to the end that they may convert. ²⁴ For You love all things that are ‖ And abhor none of the things which You made; For You never would have formed anything if You hated it. ²⁵ How would anything have endured unless You had willed it? Or that which was not called by You, how would it have been preserved? ²⁶ But You spare all things, because they are Yours, ‖ O Sovereign LORD—You lover of lives.

CHAPTER 12

¹ For Your incorruptible Spirit is in all things— ² Why [indeed] You convict little by little those who fall from the right way, ‖ And, putting them in remembrance by the things wherein they sin, You admonish them, ‖ That escaping from their wickedness they may believe in You, O LORD. ³ For truly the old inhabitants of Your holy land, ⁴ Hating them because they practiced detestable works of enchantments and unholy rites— ⁵ Merciless slaughters of children and sacrificial banquets of men's flesh and of blood— ⁶ Allies in an impious fellowship, and murderers of their own helpless babies, ‖ It was Your counsel to destroy [them] by the hands of our fathers, ⁷ That the land which in Your sight is most precious of all might receive a worthy colony of God's servants. ⁸ Nevertheless, You even spared these as men, ‖ And You sent hornets as forerunners of Your army, ‖ To cause them to perish little by little; ⁹ Not that You were unable to subdue the ungodly under the hand of the righteous in battle, ‖ Or by terrible beasts, or by a stern word to make away with them at once; ¹⁰ But judging them little by little, You gave them a chance to convert, ‖ Not being ignorant that their nature by birth was evil, their wickedness inborn, ‖ And that their manner of thought would never be changed. ¹¹ For they were a cursed seed from the beginning. It was not through fear of any that You left them unpunished for their sins. ¹² For who will say, "What have You done?" Or "Who will withstand Your judgment?" Who will accuse You for the perishing of nations which You caused? Or who will come and stand before You as an avenger for unrighteous men? ¹³ For there is not any God besides You that cares for all, ‖ That You might show that You did not judge unrighteously. ¹⁴ No king or prince will be able to look You in the face ‖ For those whom You have punished. ¹⁵ But being righteous, You rule all things righteously, ‖ Deeming it a thing alien from Your power to condemn one that does not deserve to be punished. ¹⁶ For Your strength is the beginning of righteousness, ‖ And Your sovereignty over all makes You to forbear all. ¹⁷ For when men do not believe that You are perfect in power, ‖ You show Your strength, ‖ And in dealing with those who think this, ‖ You confuse their boldness. ¹⁸ But You, being sovereign over strength, ‖ Judge in gentleness and govern us with great forbearance; For the power is Yours whenever You desire it. ¹⁹ But You taught Your people by such works as these, ‖ How the righteous must be a lover of men. You made Your sons to have good hope, ‖ Because You give conversion when men have sinned. ²⁰ For if on those who were enemies of Your servants, ‖ And due to death, You took vengeance with so great deliberation and indulgence, ‖ Giving them times and opportunities when they might escape from their wickedness— ²¹ With how much greater carefulness You judged Your sons, ‖ To whose fathers You gave oaths and covenants of good promises! ²² Therefore, while You discipline us, ‖ You scourge our enemies ten thousand times more, ‖ To the intent that we may ponder Your goodness when we judge, ‖ And when we are judged may look for mercy. ²³ Why also the unrighteous that lived in folly of life, ‖ You tormented through their own

abominations. [24] For truly they went very far astray in the ways of error, || Taking as gods those animals which even among their enemies were held in dishonor, || Deceived like foolish babies. [25] Therefore, as to unreasoning children, || You sent Your judgment to mock them. [26] But those who would not be admonished by a mocking correction as of children, || Will experience a judgment worthy of God. [27] For through the sufferings they were indignant of, || Being punished in these creatures which they supposed to be gods, || They saw and recognized as the true God Him whom they refused to know. Therefore, the result of condemnation also came on them.

CHAPTER 13

[1] For truly all men who had no perception of God were vain by nature || And did not gain power to know Him who exists from the good things that are seen. They did not recognize the Architect from His works. [2] But they thought that either fire, or wind, or swift air, || Or circling stars, or raging water, or luminaries of the heavens were gods that rule the world. [3] If it was through delight in their beauty that they took them to be gods, || Let them know how much better their Sovereign LORD is than these, || For the first Author of beauty created them. [4] But if it was through astonishment at their power and influence, || Then let them understand from them how much more powerful He who formed them is. [5] For from the greatness of the beauty of created things, || Mankind forms the corresponding image of their Maker. [6] But yet for these men there is but small blame, || For they too perhaps go astray while they are seeking God and desiring to find Him. [7] For they diligently search while living among His works, || And they trust their sight that the things that they look at are beautiful. [8] But again even they are not to be excused. [9] For if they had power to know so much, || That they should be able to explore the world, || How is it that they did not find the Sovereign LORD sooner? [10] But they [were] miserable—And their hopes [were] in dead things—Who called them gods which are works of men's hands: Gold and silver, skillfully made, and likenesses of animals, || Or a useless stone, the work of an ancient hand; [11] Yes, and if some woodcutter, having sawn down a tree that is easily moved, || Skillfully strips away all its bark, and fashioning it in attractive form, || Makes a useful vessel to serve his life's needs. [12] Burning the scraps from his handiwork to cook his food, he eats his fill. [13] Taking a discarded scrap which served no purpose, || A crooked piece of wood and full of knots, || He carves it with the diligence of his idleness, || And shapes it by the skill of his idleness. He shapes it in the image of a man, [14] Or makes it like some paltry animal, || Smearing it with something red, || Painting it red, and smearing over every stain in it. [15] Having made a worthy chamber for it, || He sets it in a wall, securing it with iron. [16] He plans for it that it may not fall down, || Knowing that it is unable to help itself; For it is truly an image, and needs [his] help. [17] When he makes his prayer concerning goods and his marriage and children, || He is not ashamed to speak to that which has no life. [18] Yes, for health, he calls on that which is weak. For life, he implores that which is dead. For aid, he supplicates that which has no experience. For a good journey, he asks that which cannot so much as move a step. [19] And for profit in business and good success of his hands, || He asks ability from that which has hands with no ability.

CHAPTER 14

[1] Again, one preparing to sail, and about to journey over raging waves, || Calls on a piece of wood more rotten than the vessel that carries him. [2] For the hunger for profit planned it, || And wisdom was the craftsman who built it. [3] Your providence, O Father, guides it along, || Because even in the sea You gave a way, || And in the waves a sure path, [4] Showing that You can save out of every danger, || That even a man without skill may put to sea. [5] It is Your will that the works of Your wisdom should not be idle. Therefore, men also entrust their lives to a little piece of wood, || And passing through the surge on a raft come safely to land. [6] For in the old time also, when proud giants were perishing, || The hope of the world, taking refuge on a raft, || Your hand guided the seed of generations of the race of men. [7] For blessed is [the] wood through which comes righteousness; [8] But the idol made with hands is accursed—Itself and he that made it; Because his was the working, || And the corruptible thing was called a god; [9] For both the ungodly and his ungodliness are alike hateful to God; [10] For the deed will truly be punished together with him who committed it. [11] Therefore there will also be a visitation among the idols of the nation, || Because, though formed of things which God created, || They were made an abomination, stumbling blocks to the souls of men, || And a snare to the feet of the foolish. [12] For the devising of idols was the beginning of fornication, || And the invention of them the corruption of life. [13] For they did not exist from the beginning, || And they will not exist forever. [14] For by the vain pride of men they entered into the world, || And therefore a speedy end was planned for them. [15] For a father worn with untimely grief, making an image of the child quickly taken away, || Now honored him as a god which was then a dead man, || And delivered to those that were under him mysteries and solemn rites. [16] Afterward the ungodly custom, in process of time grown strong, was kept as a law, || And the engraved images received worship by the commands of princes. [17] And when men could not honor them in presence because they lived far off, imagining the likeness from afar, || They made a visible image of the king whom they honored, || That

by their zeal they might flatter the absent as if present. ¹⁸ But worship was raised to a yet higher pitch, ‖ Even by those who did not know him, urged forward by the ambition of the architect; ¹⁹ For he, wishing perhaps to please one in authority, ‖ Used his art to force the likeness toward a greater beauty. ²⁰ So the multitude, allured by reason of the grace of his handiwork, ‖ Now consider an object of devotion him that a little while before was honored as a man. ²¹ And this became an ambush, because men, in bondage either to calamity or to tyranny, ‖ Invested stones and stocks with the incommunicable Name. ²² Afterward it was not enough for them to go astray concerning the knowledge of God, ‖ But also, while they live in a great war of ignorance, they call a multitude of evils peace. ²³ For either slaughtering children in solemn rites, ‖ Or celebrating secret mysteries, ‖ Or holding frantic revels of strange ordinances, ²⁴ No longer do they guard either life or purity of marriage, ‖ But one brings on another: Either death by treachery, or anguish by adultery. ²⁵ And all things confusedly are filled with blood and murder, ‖ Theft and deceit, corruption, faithlessness, tumult, perjury, ²⁶ Confusion about what is good, forgetfulness of favors, ingratitude for benefits, ‖ Defiling of souls, confusion of sex, disorder in marriage, adultery and wantonness. ²⁷ For the worship of idols that may not be named ‖ Is a beginning, and cause, and end of every evil. ²⁸ For their worshipers either make merry to madness, ‖ Or prophesy lies, or live unrighteously, or lightly commit perjury. ²⁹ For putting their trust in lifeless idols, when they have sworn a wicked oath, ‖ They do not expect to suffer harm. ³⁰ But for both, the just doom will pursue them, ‖ Because they had evil thoughts of God by giving heed to idols ‖ And swore unrighteously in deceit through contempt for holiness. ³¹ For it is not the power of them by whom men swear, ‖ But it is the just penalty for those who sin that always visits the transgression of the unrighteous.

CHAPTER 15

¹ But You, our God, are gracious and true, ‖ Patient, and ordering all things in mercy. ² For even if we sin, we are Yours, knowing Your dominion; But we will not sin, knowing that we have been accounted Yours. ³ For to be acquainted with You is perfect righteousness, ‖ And to know Your dominion is the root of immortality. ⁴ For we were not led astray by any evil plan of men's, ‖ Nor yet by painters' fruitless labor, a form stained with varied colors, ⁵ The sight of which leads fools into lust. Their desire is for the breathless form of a dead image. ⁶ Lovers of evil things, and worthy of such hopes, ‖ Are those who make, desire, and worship them. ⁷ For a potter, kneading soft earth, laboriously molds each article for our service. He fashions out of the same clay both the vessels that minister to clean uses, ‖ And those of a

contrary sort, all in like manner. What will be the use of each article of either sort—the potter is the judge. ⁸ Also, laboring to an evil end, he molds a vain god out of the same clay, ‖ He who, having but a little while before been made of earth, ‖ After a short span goes his way to the earth out of which he was taken, ‖ When he is required to render back the soul which was lent him. ⁹ However, he has anxious care, not because his powers must fail, ‖ Nor because his span of life is short; But he compares himself with goldsmiths and silversmiths, ‖ And he imitates molders in brass, ‖ And esteems it glory that he molds counterfeits. ¹⁰ His heart is ashes. His hope is of less value than earth. His life is of less honor than clay; ¹¹ Because he was ignorant of Him who molded him, ‖ And of Him that inspired into him an active soul ‖ And breathed into him a vital spirit. ¹² But he accounted our life to be a game, ‖ And our lifetime a festival for profit; For, he says, one must get gain however one can, even if it is by evil. ¹³ For this man knows that he sins beyond all others, ‖ Making brittle vessels and graven images out of earthly matter. ¹⁴ But most foolish and more miserable than a baby, ‖ Are the enemies of Your people, who oppressed them; ¹⁵ Because they even considered all the idols of the nations to be gods, ‖ Which have neither the use of eyes for seeing, nor nostrils for drawing breath, ‖ Nor ears to hear, nor fingers for handling, and their feet are helpless for walking. ¹⁶ For a man made them, and one whose own spirit is borrowed molded them; For no one has power as a man to mold a god like to himself. ¹⁷ But, being mortal, he makes a dead thing by the work of lawless hands; For he is better than the objects of his worship, ‖ Since he indeed had life, but they never did. ¹⁸ Yes, and they worship the creatures that are most hateful, ‖ For, being compared as to lack of sense, these are worse than all others; ¹⁹ Neither, as seen beside other creatures, are they beautiful, so that one should desire them, ‖ But they have escaped both the praise of God and His blessing.

CHAPTER 16

¹ For this reason, they were deservedly punished through creatures like those which they worship ‖ And tormented through a multitude of vermin. ² Instead of this punishment, You, giving benefits to Your people, ‖ Prepared quails for food, a delicacy to satisfy the desire of their appetite, ³ To the end that Your enemies, desiring food, ‖ Might for the hideousness of the creatures sent among them, ‖ Loathe even the necessary appetite; But these, Your people, having suffered lack for a short time, ‖ Might even partake of delicacies. ⁴ For it was necessary that inescapable lack should come on those oppressors, ‖ But that to these it should only be showed how their enemies were tormented. ⁵ For even when terrible raging of wild beasts came on Your people, ‖ And they were perishing by the bites of crooked serpents,

|| Your wrath did not continue to the uttermost; ⁶But for admonition they were troubled for a short time, || Having a token of salvation to put them in remembrance of the command of Your law; ⁷For he who turned toward it was not saved because of that which was seen, || But because of You, the Savior of all. ⁸Yes, and in this You persuaded our enemies || That You are He who delivers out of every evil. ⁹For the bites of locusts and flies truly killed them. No healing for their life was found, || Because they were worthy to be punished by such things. ¹⁰But Your children were not overcome by the very teeth of venomous dragons, || For Your mercy passed by where they were and healed them. ¹¹For they were bitten to put them in remembrance of Your oracles, || And were quickly saved, lest, falling into deep forgetfulness, || They should become unable to respond to Your kindness. ¹²For truly it was neither herb nor mollifying plaster that cured them, || But Your word, O LORD, which heals all things. ¹³For You have authority over life and death, || And You lead down to the gates of Hades and lead up again. ¹⁴But though a man kills by his wickedness, || He cannot retrieve the spirit that has departed or release the imprisoned soul. ¹⁵But it is not possible to escape Your hand; ¹⁶For ungodly men, refusing to know You, || Were scourged in the strength of Your arm, || Pursued with strange rains, and hails, and relentless storms, || And utterly consumed with fire. ¹⁷For, what was most marvelous, || In the water which quenches all things, the fire burned hotter; For the world fights for the righteous. ¹⁸For at one time the flame lost its fierceness, || That it might not burn up the creatures sent against the ungodly, || But that these themselves as they looked might see || That they were chased through the judgment of God. ¹⁹At another time even in the midst of water it burns above the power of fire, || That it may destroy the produce of an unrighteous land. ²⁰Instead of these things, You gave Your people messengers' food to eat, || And You provided ready-to-eat bread for them from Heaven without toil, || Having the virtue of every pleasant flavor, || And agreeable to every taste. ²¹For Your nature showed Your sweetness toward Your children, || While that bread, serving the desire of the eater, changed itself according to every man's choice. ²²But snow and ice endured fire, and did not melt, || That people might know that fire was destroying the fruits of the enemies, || Burning in the hail and flashing in the rains; ²³And that this fire again, in order that righteous people may be nourished, || Has even forgotten its own power. ²⁴For the creation, ministering to You its Maker, || Strains its force against the unrighteous for punishment || And slackens it on behalf of those who trust in You, for kindness. ²⁵Therefore at that time also, converting itself into all forms, || It ministered to Your all-nourishing bounty, according to the desire of those who had need, ²⁶That Your sons, whom You loved, O LORD, || Might learn that it is not the growth of crops that nourishes a man, || But that Your word preserves those who trust You. ²⁷For that which was not marred by fire, || When it was simply warmed by a faint sunbeam melted away, ²⁸That it might be known that we must rise before the sun to give You thanks || And must plead with You at the dawning of the light; ²⁹For the hope of the unthankful will melt as the winter's hoarfrost || And will flow away as water that has no use.

CHAPTER 17

¹For Your judgments are great, and hard to interpret; Therefore, undisciplined souls went astray. ²For when lawless men had supposed that they held a holy nation in their power, || They, prisoners of darkness, and bound in the chains of a long night, || Kept close beneath their roofs, [and] lay exiled from the perpetual providence. ³For while they thought that they were unseen in [their] secret sins, || They were divided from one another by a dark curtain of forgetfulness, || Stricken with terrible awe, and very troubled by apparitions. ⁴For neither did the dark recesses that held them guard them from fears, || But terrifying sounds rang around them, || And dismal phantoms appeared with unsmiling faces. ⁵And no force of fire prevailed to give light, || Neither were the brightest flames of the stars strong enough to illuminate that gloomy night; ⁶But only the glimmering of a self-kindled fire appeared to them, full of fear. In terror, they considered the things which they saw || To be worse than that sight, on which they could not gaze. ⁷The mockeries of their magic arts were powerless now, || And a shameful rebuke of their boasted understanding: ⁸For those who promised to drive away terrors and disorders from a sick soul, || These were sick with a ludicrous fearfulness. ⁹For even if no troubling thing frightened them, || Yet, scared with the creeping of vermin and hissing of serpents, ¹⁰They perished trembling in fear, || Refusing even to look at the air, which could not be escaped on any side. ¹¹For wickedness, condemned by a witness within, is a cowardly thing, || And, being pressed hard by conscience, has always added forecasts of the worst. ¹²For fear is nothing else but a surrender of the help which reason offers; ¹³And from within, the expectation of being less || Makes of greater account the ignorance of the cause that brings the torment. ¹⁴But they, all through the night which was powerless indeed, || And which came on them out of the recesses of powerless Hades, || Sleeping the same sleep, ¹⁵Now were haunted by monstrous apparitions, || And now were paralyzed by their soul's surrendering; For sudden and unexpected fear came on them. ¹⁶So then, whoever it might be, sinking down in his place, || Was kept captive, shut up in that prison which was not barred with iron; ¹⁷For whether he was a farmer, or a shepherd, or a laborer whose

toils were in the wilderness, || He was overtaken, and endured that inevitable necessity; For they were all bound with one chain of darkness. ¹⁸ Whether there was a whistling wind, || Or a melodious sound of birds among the spreading branches, || Or a measured fall of water running violently, ¹⁹ Or a harsh crashing of rocks hurled down, || Or the swift course of animals bounding along unseen, || Or the voice of wild beasts harshly roaring, || Or an echo rebounding from the hollows of the mountains, || All these things paralyzed them with terror. ²⁰ For the whole world was illuminated with clear light, || And was occupied with unhindered works, ²¹ While over them alone was spread a heavy night, || An image of the darkness that should afterward receive them; But to themselves, they were heavier than darkness.

CHAPTER 18

¹ But there was great light for Your holy ones. Their enemies, hearing their voice but not seeing their form, || Counted it a happy thing that they too had suffered, ² Yet for that they do not hurt them, || Though wronged by them before, they are thankful; And because they had been at variance with them, they begged for pardon. ³ Whereas You provided a burning pillar of fire to be a guide for Your people's unknown journey, || And a harmless sun for their glorious exile. ⁴ For the Egyptians well deserved to be deprived of light and imprisoned by darkness, || They who had imprisoned Your children, through whom the incorruptible light of the Law was to be given to the race of men. ⁵ After they had taken counsel to kill the babies of the holy ones, || And when a single child had been abandoned and saved to convict them of their sin, || You took their multitude of children away from them, || And destroyed all their army together in a mighty flood. ⁶ Our fathers were made aware of that night beforehand, || That, having sure knowledge, they might be cheered by the oaths which they had trusted. ⁷ Salvation of the righteous and destruction of the enemies was expected by Your people. ⁸ For as You took vengeance on the adversaries, || By the same means, calling us to Yourself, You glorified us. ⁹ For holy children of good men offered sacrifice in secret, || And with one consent they took on themselves the covenant of the divine law, || That they would partake alike in the same good things and the same perils, || The fathers already leading the sacred songs of praise. ¹⁰ But the discordant cry of the enemies echoed back, || And a pitiful voice of lamentation for children was spread abroad. ¹¹ Both servant and master were punished with the same just doom, || And the commoner suffering the same as king; ¹² Yes, they all together, under one form of death, had corpses without number. For the living were not even sufficient to bury them, || Since at a single stroke, their most cherished offspring was consumed. ¹³ For while they were disbelieving all things by reason of the enchantments, || On the destruction of the firstborn they confessed the people to be God's son. ¹⁴ For while peaceful silence wrapped all things, || And night in her own swiftness was in mid-course, ¹⁵ Your all-powerful word leapt from Heaven out of the royal thrones—A stern warrior, into the midst of the doomed land, ¹⁶ Bearing Your authentic command as a sharp sword; And standing, it filled all things with death, || And while it touched the heavens it stood on the earth. ¹⁷ Then immediately apparitions in dreams troubled them terribly, || And unexpected fears came on them. ¹⁸ And each—one thrown here half dead, another there—Made known why he was dying; ¹⁹ For the dreams, disturbing them, forewarned them of this, || That they might not perish without knowing why they were afflicted. ²⁰ But experience of death also touched the righteous, || And a multitude were destroyed in the wilderness; However, the wrath did not last long. ²¹ For a blameless man hurried to be their champion, || Bringing the weapon of his own ministry: Prayer and the atoning sacrifice of incense. He withstood the indignation, and set an end to the calamity, || Showing that he was your servant. ²² And he overcame the anger, || Not by strength of body, not by force of weapons, || But he subdued him who was punishing by word, || By bringing to remembrance oaths and covenants made with the fathers. ²³ For when the dead had already fallen in heaps on one another, || Standing between, he stopped the wrath, || And cut off the way to the living. ²⁴ For the whole world was on his long robe, || And the glories of the fathers were on the engraving of the four rows of precious stones, || And Your majesty was on the diadem of his head. ²⁵ The destroyer yielded to these, and they feared; For it was enough only to test the wrath.

CHAPTER 19

¹ But indignation without mercy came on the ungodly to the end; For God also foreknew their future, ² How, having changed their minds to let Your people go, || And having sped them eagerly on their way, || They would change their minds and pursue them. ³ For while they were yet in the midst of their mourning, || And lamenting at the graves of the dead, || They drew on themselves another counsel of folly, || And pursued as fugitives those whom they had begged to leave and driven out. ⁴ For the doom which they deserved was drawing them to this end, || And it made them forget the things that had happened to them, || That they might fill up the punishment which was yet lacking to their torments, ⁵ And that Your people might journey on by a marvelous road, || But they themselves might find a strange death. ⁶ For the whole creation, each part in its diverse kind, || Was made new again, complying with Your commands, || That Your servants might be kept unharmed. ⁷ Then the cloud that overshadowed the camp was seen, || And

dry land rising up out of what had been water, || Out of the Red Sea an unhindered highway, || And a grassy plain out of the violent surge, [8] By which they passed over with all their army, || These who were covered with Your hand, having seen strange marvels. [9] For like horses they roamed at large, || And they skipped about like lambs, || Praising You, O LORD, who was their deliverer. [10] For they still remembered the things that happened in the time of their sojourning, || How instead of bearing cattle, the land brought out lice, || And instead of fish, the river spewed out a multitude of frogs. [11] But afterward, they also saw a new kind of birds, || When, led on by desire, they asked for luxurious delicacies; [12] For, to comfort them, quails came up for them from the sea. [13] Punishments came on the sinners, || Not without the signs that were given beforehand by the force of the thunders; For they justly suffered through their own wickedness, || For the hatred which they practiced toward guests was grievous indeed. [14] For whereas the others did not receive the strangers when they came to them, || The Egyptians made slaves of guests who were their benefactors. [15] And not only so, but God will visit the men of Sodom another way, || Since they received as enemies those who were aliens; [16] Whereas these first welcomed with feastings, || And then afflicted with dreadful toils—Those who had already shared with them in the same rights. [17] And moreover, they were stricken with loss of sight, || Even as were those others at the righteous man's doors, || When, being surrounded with yawning darkness, || They each looked for the passage through his own door. [18] For as the notes of a lute vary the character of the rhythm, || Even so the elements— Changing their order with one another, continuing always in its sound, || As may clearly be conjectured from the sight of the things that have happened. [19] For creatures of the dry land were turned into creatures of the waters, || And creatures that swim moved on the land. [20] Fire kept the mastery of its own power in water, || And water forgot its quenching nature. [21] On the contrary, flames did not consume flesh of perishable creatures that walked among them, || Neither did they melt the ice-like grains of ambrosial food that were apt to melt. [22] For in all things, O LORD, You magnified Your people, || And You glorified them and did not lightly regard them, || Standing by their side in every time and place.

SIRACH

Otherwise known as Ecclesiasticus

The Wisdom of Ben Sira derives its title from the author, "Yeshua [Jesus], son of Eleazar, son of Sira" (50:27). This seems to be the earliest title of the book. The designation Liber Ecclesiasticus, meaning "Church Book," appended to some Greek and Latin manuscripts, is perhaps due to the extensive use the church made of this book in presenting moral teaching to catechumens and to the faithful. The author, a sage who lived in Jerusalem, was thoroughly imbued with love for the wisdom tradition, and also for the law, priesthood, Temple, and divine worship. Written in Hebrew in the early years of the 2nd century BC, the book was finished by approximately 175.

CHAPTER 1

¹ All wisdom comes from the LORD and is with Him forever. ² Who can count the sand of the seas, || The drops of rain, and the days of [the] age? ³ Who will search out the height of the sky, || The breadth of the earth, the deep, and wisdom? ⁴ Wisdom has been created before all things, || And the understanding of prudence from perpetuity. ⁵ . . . ⁶ To whom has the root of wisdom been revealed? Who has known her shrewd counsels? ⁷ . . . ⁸ There is one wise, greatly to be feared, sitting on His throne: The LORD. ⁹ He created her. He saw and measured her. He poured her out on all His works. ¹⁰ She is with all flesh according to His gift. He gave her freely to those who love Him. ¹¹ The fear of the LORD is glory, || Exultation, and gladness, and a crown of rejoicing. ¹² The fear of the LORD will delight the heart, || And will give gladness, joy, and length of days. ¹³ Whoever fears the LORD, || It will go well with him at the end. He will be blessed in the day of his death. ¹⁴ To fear the LORD is the beginning of wisdom. It was created together with the faithful in the womb. ¹⁵ She laid a perpetual foundation with men. She will be trusted among their offspring. ¹⁶ To fear the LORD is the fullness of wisdom. She inebriates men with her fruits. ¹⁷ She will fill all her house with desirable things, || And her storehouses with her produce. ¹⁸ The fear of the LORD is the crown of wisdom, || Making peace and perfect health to flourish. ¹⁹ He both saw and measured her. He rained down skill and knowledge of understanding || And exalted the honor of those who hold her fast. ²⁰ To fear the LORD is the root of wisdom. Her branches are length of days. ²¹ . . . ²² Unjust wrath can never be justified, || For the sway of his wrath is his downfall. ²³ A man that is patient will resist for a season, || And afterward gladness will spring up to him. ²⁴ He will hide his words for a season, || And the lips of many will tell of his understanding. ²⁵ An allegory of knowledge is in the treasures of wisdom; But godliness is an abomination to a sinner. ²⁶ If you desire wisdom, keep the commands || And the LORD will give her to you freely; ²⁷ For the fear of the LORD is wisdom and instruction. Faith and humility are His good pleasure. ²⁸ Do not disobey the fear of the LORD. Do not come to Him with a double heart. ²⁹ Do not be a hypocrite in the mouths of men. Keep watch over your lips. ³⁰ Do not exalt yourself, || Lest you fall and bring dishonor on your soul. The LORD will reveal your secrets || And will cast you down in the midst of the congregation, || Because you did not come to the fear of the LORD || And your heart was full of deceit.

CHAPTER 2

¹ My son, if you come to serve the LORD, || Prepare your soul for temptation. ² Set your heart correctly, || Constantly endure, || And do not hurry in time of calamity. ³ Cling to Him, and do not depart, || That you may be increased at your latter end. ⁴ Accept whatever is brought on you || And be patient when you suffer humiliation. ⁵ For gold is tried in the fire, || And acceptable men in the furnace of humiliation. ⁶ Put your trust in Him, || And He will help you. Make your ways straight || And set your hope on Him. ⁷ All you who fear the LORD, || Wait for His mercy. Do not turn aside, lest you fall. ⁸ All you who fear the LORD, || Put your trust in Him, || And your reward will not fail. ⁹ All you who fear the LORD, || Hope for good things, || And for continuous gladness and mercy. ¹⁰ Look at the generations of old, and see: Who ever put his trust in the LORD, and was ashamed? Or who remained in His fear, and was forsaken? Or who called on Him, and He despised him? ¹¹ For the LORD is full of compassion and mercy. He forgives sins and saves in time of affliction. ¹² Woe to fearful hearts, to faint hands, || And to the sinner that goes two ways! ¹³ Woe to the faint heart! For it does not believe. Therefore, it will not be defended. ¹⁴ Woe to you who have lost your patience! And what will you all do when the LORD visits you? ¹⁵ Those who fear the LORD will not disobey His words. Those who love Him will keep His ways. ¹⁶ Those who fear the LORD will seek His good pleasure. Those who love Him will be filled with the Law. ¹⁷ Those who fear the LORD will prepare their hearts || And will humble their souls in His sight. ¹⁸ We will fall into the hands of the LORD, || And not into the hands of men; For as His majesty is, so also is His mercy.

CHAPTER 3

[1] Hear me, your father, O my children, || And do what you hear, that you all may be saved. [2] For the LORD has given the father glory concerning the children || And has confirmed the judgment of the mother concerning the sons. [3] He who honors his father will make atonement for sins. [4] He that gives glory to his mother is as one who lays up treasure. [5] Whoever honors his father will have joy in his own children. He will be heard in the day of his prayer. [6] He who gives glory to his father will have length of days. He who listens to the LORD will bring rest to his mother, [7] And will serve under his parents, as to masters. [8] Honor your father in deed and word, || That a blessing may come on you from him. [9] For the blessing of the father establishes the houses of children, || But the curse of the mother roots out the foundations. [10] Do not glorify yourself in the dishonor of your father, || For your father's dishonor is no glory to you. [11] For the glory of a man is from the honor of his father, || And a mother in dishonor is a reproach to her children. [12] My son, help your father in his old age, || And do not grieve him as long as he lives. [13] If he fails in understanding, have patience with him. Do not dishonor him in your full strength. [14] For the relieving of your father will not be forgotten. Instead of sins it will be added to build you up. [15] In the day of your affliction it will remember you; As fair weather on ice, so will your sins also melt away. [16] He who forsakes his father is as a blasphemer. He who provokes his mother is cursed by the LORD. [17] My son, go on with your business in humility; So you will be loved by an acceptable man. [18] The greater you are, humble yourself [all] the more, || And you will find favor before the LORD. [19] . . . [20] For the power of the LORD is great, || And He is glorified by those who are lowly. [21] Do not seek things that are too hard for you, || And do not search out things that are above your strength. [22] Think about the things that have been commanded you, || For you have no need of the things that are secret. [23] Do not be overly busy in your superfluous works, || For more things are showed to you than men can understand. [24] For the conceit of many has led them astray. Evil opinion has caused their judgment to slip. [25] There is no light without eyes. There is no wisdom without knowledge. [26] A stubborn heart will do badly at the end. He who loves danger will perish in it. [27] A stubborn heart will be burdened with troubles. The sinner will heap sin on sins. [28] The calamity of the proud is no healing, || For a weed of wickedness has taken root in him. [29] The heart of the prudent will understand an allegory. A wise man desires the ear of a listener. [30] Water will quench a flaming fire; Kindness will make atonement for sins. [31] He who repays with kind acts is mindful of that which comes afterward. In the time of his falling, he will find a support.

CHAPTER 4

[1] My son, do not deprive the poor of his living. Do not make the needy eyes wait long. [2] Do not make a hungry soul sorrowful || Or provoke a man in his distress. [3] Do not add more trouble to a heart that is provoked. Do not put off giving to him who is in need. [4] Do not reject a suppliant in his affliction. Do not turn your face away from a poor man. [5] Do not turn your eye away from one who asks. Give no occasion to a man to curse you. [6] For if he curses you in the bitterness of his soul, || He who made him will hear his supplication. [7] Endear yourself to the assembly. Bow your head to a great man. [8] Incline your ear to a poor man. Answer him with peaceful words in humility. [9] Deliver him who is wronged from the hand of him that wrongs him; Do not be faint-hearted in giving judgment. [10] Be as a father to the fatherless, || And like a husband to their mother. So you will be as a son of the Most High, || And He will love you more than your mother does. [11] Wisdom exalts her sons || And takes hold of those who seek her. [12] He who loves her loves life. Those who seek her early will be filled with gladness. [13] He who holds her fast will inherit glory. Where he enters, the LORD will bless. [14] Those who serve her minister to the Holy One. The LORD loves those who love her. [15] He who gives ear to her will judge the nations. He who heeds her will dwell securely. [16] If he trusts her, he will inherit her, || And his generations will possess her. [17] For at the first she will walk with him in crooked ways, || And will bring fear and dread on him, || And torment him with her discipline, || Until she may trust his soul, and try him by her judgments. [18] Then she will return him again to the straight way, || And will gladden him, and reveal to him her secrets. [19] If he goes astray, she will forsake him, || And hand him over to his fall. [20] Observe the opportunity and beware of evil. Do not be ashamed of your soul. [21] For there is a shame that brings sin, || And there is a shame that is glory and grace. [22] Do not show partiality against your soul. Do not revere any man to your falling. [23] Do not refrain from speaking when it is for safety. Do not hide your wisdom for the sake of seeming fair. [24] For wisdom will be known by speech, || And instruction by the word of the tongue. [25] Do not speak against the truth and be shamed for your ignorance. [26] Do not be ashamed to confess your sins. Do not fight the river's current. [27] Do not lay yourself down for a fool to tread on. Do not be partial to one that is mighty. [28] Strive for the truth to death, || And the LORD God will fight for you. [29] Do not be hasty with your tongue, || Or slack and negligent in your deeds. [30] Do not be like a lion in your house, || Or suspicious of your servants. [31] Do not let your hand be stretched out to receive || And closed when you should repay.

CHAPTER 5

¹ Do not set your heart on your goods. Do not say, "They are sufficient for me." ² Do not follow your own mind and your strength ‖ To walk in the desires of your heart. ³ Do not say, "Who will have dominion over me?" For the LORD will surely take vengeance on you. ⁴ Do not say, "I sinned, and what happened to me?" For the LORD is patient. ⁵ Do not be so confident of atonement that you add sin on sins. ⁶ Do not say, "His compassion is great. He will be pacified for the multitude of my sins," ‖ For mercy and wrath are with Him, ‖ And His indignation will rest on sinners. ⁷ Do not wait to turn to the LORD. Do not put off from day to day; For the wrath of the LORD will suddenly come on you, ‖ And you will perish in the time of vengeance. ⁸ Do not set your heart on unrighteous gains, ‖ For you will profit nothing in the day of calamity. ⁹ Do not winnow with every wind. Do not walk in every path. This is what the sinner who has a double tongue does. ¹⁰ Be steadfast in your understanding. Let your speech be consistent. ¹¹ Be swift to hear and answer with patience. ¹² If you have understanding, answer your neighbor; But if not, put your hand over your mouth. ¹³ Glory and dishonor is in talk. A man's tongue may be his downfall. ¹⁴ Do not be called a whisperer. Do not lie in wait with your tongue; For shame is on the thief, ‖ And an evil condemnation is on him who has a double tongue. ¹⁵ Do not be ignorant in a great or small matter.

CHAPTER 6

¹ Do not become an enemy instead of a friend; For an evil name will inherit shame and reproach. So it is with the sinner who has a double tongue. ² Do not exalt yourself in the counsel of your soul, ‖ That your soul is not torn in pieces as a bull. ³ You will eat up your leaves, destroy your fruit, ‖ And leave yourself as a dry tree. ⁴ A wicked soul will destroy him who has it ‖ And will make him a laughing-stock to his enemies. ⁵ Sweet words will multiply a man's friends. A gracious tongue will multiply courtesies. ⁶ Let those that are at peace with you be many, ‖ But your advisers one of one thousand. ⁷ If you want to gain a friend, get him in a time of testing, ‖ And do not be in a hurry to trust him. ⁸ For there is a friend just for an occasion. He will not continue in the day of your affliction. ⁹ And there is a friend who turns into an enemy. He will discover strife to your reproach. ¹⁰ And there is a friend who is a companion at the table, ‖ But he will not continue in the day of your affliction. ¹¹ In your prosperity he will be as yourself ‖ And will be bold over your servants. ¹² If you are brought low, he will be against you, ‖ And will hide himself from your face. ¹³ Separate yourself from your enemies and beware of your friends. ¹⁴ A faithful friend is a strong defense. He who has found him has found a treasure. ¹⁵ There is nothing that can be taken in exchange for a faithful friend. His excellency is beyond price. ¹⁶ A faithful friend is a life-saving medicine. Those who fear the LORD will find Him. ¹⁷ He who fears the LORD directs his friendship properly; For as he is, so is his neighbor also. ¹⁸ My son, gather instruction from your youth up. Even when you have gray hair you will find wisdom. ¹⁹ Come to her as one who plows and sows ‖ And wait for her good fruit; For your toil will be little in her tillage, ‖ And you will soon eat of her fruit. ²⁰ How exceedingly harsh she is to the unlearned! He who is without understanding will not remain in her. ²¹ She will rest on him as a mighty stone of trial. He will not hesitate to cast her from him. ²² For wisdom is according to her name. She is not manifest to many. ²³ Give ear, my son, and accept my judgment. Do not refuse my counsel. ²⁴ Bring your feet into her chains, ‖ And your neck into her chain. ²⁵ Put your shoulder under her and bear her. Do not be grieved with her bonds. ²⁶ Come to her with all your soul. Keep her ways with your whole power. ²⁷ Search and seek, and she will be made known to you. When you get hold of her, do not let her go. ²⁸ For at the end you will find her rest; And she will be turned into gladness for you. ²⁹ Her chains will be to you for a covering of strength, ‖ And her chains for a robe of glory. ³⁰ For there is a golden ornament on her, ‖ And her bonds [are] a purple ribbon. ³¹ You will put her on as a robe of glory ‖ And will put her on as a crown of rejoicing. ³² My son, if you are willing, you will be instructed. If you will yield your soul, you will be prudent. ³³ If you love to hear, you will receive. If you incline your ear, you will be wise. ³⁴ Stand in the multitude of the elders. Attach yourself to whoever is wise. ³⁵ Be willing to listen to every godly discourse. Do not let the proverbs of understanding escape you. ³⁶ If you see a man of understanding, get to him early. Let your foot wear out the steps of his doors. ³⁷ Let your mind dwell on the ordinances of the LORD ‖ And meditate continually on His commands. He will establish your heart ‖ And your desire for wisdom will be given to you.

CHAPTER 7

¹ Do no evil, so no evil will overtake you. ² Depart from wrong, and it will turn away from you. ³ My son, do not sow on the furrows of unrighteousness, ‖ And you will not reap them sevenfold. ⁴ Do not seek preeminence from the LORD, ‖ Nor the seat of honor from the king. ⁵ Do not justify yourself in the presence of the LORD, ‖ And do not display your wisdom before the king. ⁶ Do not seek to be a judge, ‖ Lest you not be able to take away iniquities, ‖ Lest perhaps you fear the person of a mighty man ‖ And lay a stumbling block in the way of your uprightness. ⁷ Do not sin against the multitude of the city. Do not cast yourself down in the crowd. ⁸ Do not commit a sin twice, ‖ For even in one you will not be unpunished. ⁹ Do not say, "He will look on the multitude of my gifts. When I

SIRACH

make an offering to the Most High God, He will accept it." **10** Do not be faint-hearted in your prayer. Do not neglect to give alms. **11** Do not laugh a man to scorn when he is in the bitterness of his soul, ‖ For there is one who humbles and exalts. **12** Do not devise a lie against your brother or do the same to a friend. **13** Do not love to make any manner of lie, for that is not a good habit. **14** Do not babble in the multitude of elders. Do not repeat your words in your prayer. **15** Do not hate hard labor or farm work, which the Most High has created. **16** Do not number yourself among the multitude of sinners. Remember that wrath will not wait. **17** Humble your soul greatly, ‖ For the punishment of the ungodly man is fire and the worm. **18** Do not exchange a friend for something, ‖ Neither a true brother for the gold of Ophir. **19** Do not deprive yourself of a wise and good wife, ‖ For her grace is worth more than gold. **20** Do not abuse a servant who works faithfully, ‖ Or a hireling who gives you his life. **21** Let your soul love a wise servant. Do not defraud him of liberty. **22** Do you have cattle? Look after them. If they are profitable to you, let them stay by you. **23** Do you have children? Correct them and bow their necks from their youth. **24** Do you have daughters? Take care of their bodies, ‖ And do not be overly indulgent toward them. **25** Give your daughter in marriage, ‖ And you will have accomplished a great matter. Give her to a man of understanding. **26** Do you have a wife after your mind? Do not cast her out. But do not entrust yourself to one who is hateful. **27** Give glory to your father with your whole heart, ‖ And do not forget the birth pangs of your mother. **28** Remember that you were born of them. What will you repay them for the things that they have done for you? **29** Fear the LORD with all your soul; Also revere His priests. **30** With all your strength love Him who made you. Do not forsake His ministers. **31** Fear the LORD and honor the priest. Give him his portion, even as it is commanded you: The first-fruits, the trespass offering, the gift of the shoulders, ‖ The sacrifice of sanctification, and the first-fruits of holy things. **32** Also stretch out your hand to the poor man, ‖ That your blessing may be perfected. **33** A gift has grace in the sight of every living man. Do not withhold grace for a dead man. **34** Do not be lacking to those who weep, ‖ And mourn with those who mourn. **35** Do not be slow to visit a sick man, ‖ For by such things you will gain love. **36** In all your words, remember eternity, ‖ And you will never sin.

CHAPTER 8

1 Do not contend with a mighty man, lest perhaps you fall into his hands. **2** Do not strive with a rich man, lest perhaps he overpowers you; For gold has destroyed many and turned away the hearts of kings. **3** Do not contend with a talkative man. Do not heap wood on his fire. **4** Do not jest with a rude man, lest your ancestors be dishonored. **5** Do not reproach a man

when he turns from sin. Remember that we are all worthy of punishment. **6** Do not dishonor a man in his old age; For some of us are also growing old. **7** Do not rejoice over one who is dead. Remember that we all die. **8** Do not neglect the discourse of the wise. Be conversant with their proverbs; For from them you will learn instruction ‖ And how to minister to great men. **9** Do not miss the discourse of the aged, ‖ For they also learned from their fathers, ‖ Because from them you will learn understanding, ‖ And [how] to give an answer in time of need. **10** Do not kindle the coals of a sinner, ‖ Lest you be burned with the flame of his fire. **11** Do not rise up from the presence of an insolent man, ‖ Lest he lie in wait as an ambush for your mouth. **12** Do not lend to a man who is mightier than yourself; And if you lend, be as one who has lost. **13** Do not be a guarantee above your power. If you are a guarantee, think as one who will have to pay. **14** Do not go to law with a judge; For according to his honor they will give judgment for him. **15** Do not go in the way with a rash man, ‖ Lest he be burdensome to you; For he will do according to his own will, ‖ And you will perish with his folly. **16** Do not fight with a wrathful man. Do not travel with him through the desert, ‖ For blood is as nothing in his sight. Where there is no help, he will overthrow you. **17** Do not take counsel with a fool, ‖ For he will not be able to conceal the matter. **18** Do no secret thing before a stranger, ‖ For you do not know what it will cause. **19** Do not open your heart to every man. Do not let him return you a favor.

CHAPTER 9

1 Do not be jealous over the wife of your bosom, ‖ And do not teach her an evil lesson against yourself. **2** Do not give your soul to a woman, ‖ That she should set her foot on your strength. **3** Do not go to meet a woman who plays the prostitute, ‖ Lest perhaps you fall into her snares. **4** Do not use the company of a woman who is a singer, ‖ Lest perhaps you be caught by her attempts. **5** Do not gaze at a maid, ‖ Lest perhaps you be trapped in her penalties. **6** Do not give your soul to prostitutes, ‖ That you may not lose your inheritance. **7** Do not look around you in the streets of the city, ‖ Neither wander in its solitary places. **8** Turn your eye away from a beautiful woman, ‖ And do not gaze at another's beauty. Many have been led astray by the beauty of a woman; And with this, affection is kindled as a fire. **9** Do not sit at all with a woman who has a husband, ‖ Or revel with her at the wine, ‖ Lest perhaps your soul turns away to her, ‖ And with your spirit you slide into destruction. **10** Do not forsake an old friend; For the new is not comparable to him. A new friend is like new wine: If it becomes old, you will drink it with gladness. **11** Do not envy the glory of a sinner; For you do not know what his overthrow will be. **12** Do not delight in the delights of the ungodly. Remember, they will not go to the grave unpunished.

¹³ Keep yourself far from the man who has power to kill, ‖ And you will have no suspicion of the fear of death. If you come to him, commit no fault, ‖ Lest he takes your life away. Surely know that you go about in the midst of snares ‖ And walk on the battlements of a city. ¹⁴ As well as you can, aim to know your neighbors, ‖ And take counsel with the wise. ¹⁵ Let your conversation be with men of understanding. Let all your discourse be in the Law of the Most High. ¹⁶ Let just men be companions at your table. Let your glorying be in the fear of the LORD. ¹⁷ A work is commended because of the hand of the artisan; So he who rules the people will be considered wise for his speech. ¹⁸ A talkative man is dangerous in his city. He who is headlong in his speech will be hated.

CHAPTER 10

¹ A wise judge will instruct his people. The government of a man of understanding will be well ordered. ² As is the judge of his people, ‖ So are his ministers. As the city's ruler is, ‖ So are all those who dwell in it. ³ An uninstructed king will destroy his people. A city will be established through the understanding of the powerful. ⁴ The authority of the earth is in the LORD's hand. In due time, He will raise up over it one who is profitable. ⁵ A man's prosperity is in the LORD's hand. He will lay his honor on the person of the scribe. ⁶ Do not be angry with your neighbor for every wrong. Do nothing by works of violence. ⁷ Pride is hateful before the LORD and men. Unrighteousness is abhorrent in the judgment of both. ⁸ Sovereignty is transferred from nation to nation ‖ Because of iniquities, deeds of violence, and greed for money. ⁹ Why are dirt and ashes proud? Because in life, my body decays. ¹⁰ A long disease mocks the physician. He is a king today, and tomorrow he will die. ¹¹ For when a man is dead, ‖ He will inherit creeping things, and beasts, and worms. ¹² It is the beginning of pride when a man departs from the LORD. His heart has departed from Him who made him. ¹³ For the beginning of pride is sin. He who keeps it will pour out abomination. For this reason, the LORD brought strange calamities on them ‖ And utterly overthrew them. ¹⁴ The LORD cast down the thrones of rulers ‖ And set the meek in their place. ¹⁵ The LORD plucked up the roots of nations ‖ And planted the lowly in their place. ¹⁶ The LORD overthrew the lands of nations ‖ And destroyed them to the foundations of the earth. ¹⁷ He took some of them away ‖ And destroyed them and made their memorial to cease from the earth. ¹⁸ Pride has not been created for men, ‖ Nor wrathful anger for the offspring of women. ¹⁹ What manner of seed has honor? The seed of man, those who fear the LORD. What manner of seed has no honor? The seed of man, those who transgress the commands. ²⁰ In the midst of countrymen he who rules them has honor. Those who fear the LORD have honor in his eyes. ²¹ . . . ²² The rich man, the honorable, and the poor ‖ All glory in the fear of the LORD. ²³ It is not right to dishonor a poor man who has understanding. It is not fitting to glorify a man who is a sinner. ²⁴ The great man, the judge, and the mighty man will be glorified. There is not one of them greater than he who fears the LORD. ²⁵ Free men will minister to a wise servant. A man who has knowledge will not complain. ²⁶ Do not flaunt your wisdom in doing your work. Do not glorify yourself in the time of your distress. ²⁷ Better is he who labors and abounds in all things, ‖ Than he who glorifies himself and lacks bread. ²⁸ My son, glorify your soul in humility, ‖ And esteem yourself honor according to your true worth. ²⁹ Who will justify him who sins against his own soul? Who will glorify him who dishonors his own life? ³⁰ A poor man is glorified for his knowledge. A rich man is glorified for his riches. ³¹ But he who is glorified in poverty, how much more in riches? He who is dishonored in riches, how much more in poverty?

CHAPTER 11

¹ The wisdom of the lowly will lift up his head ‖ And make him sit in the midst of great men. ² Do not commend a man for his beauty. Do not abhor a man for his outward appearance. ³ The bee is little among flying creatures, ‖ But what it produces is the best of confections. ⁴ Do not boast about the clothes you wear, ‖ And do not exalt yourself in the day of honor; For the LORD's works are wonderful, ‖ And His works are hidden among men. ⁵ Many kings have sat down on the ground, ‖ But one who was never thought of has worn a crown. ⁶ Many mighty men have been greatly disgraced. Men of renown have been delivered into other men's hands. ⁷ Do not blame before you investigate. Understand first, and then rebuke. ⁸ Do not answer before you have heard. Do not interrupt while someone else is speaking. ⁹ Do not argue about a matter that does not concern you. Do not sit with sinners when they judge. ¹⁰ My son, do not be busy about many matters; For if you meddle much, ‖ You will not be unpunished. If you pursue, you will not overtake, ‖ And you will not escape by fleeing. ¹¹ There is one who toils, labors, and makes haste, ‖ And is even more behind. ¹² There is one who is sluggish, and needs help, lacking in strength, and who abounds in poverty, ‖ But the LORD's eyes looked on him for good, ‖ And He raised him up from his low condition, ¹³ And lifted up his head so that many marveled at him. ¹⁴ Good things and evil, life and death, ‖ Poverty and riches, are from the LORD. ¹⁵ . . . ¹⁶ . . . ¹⁷ The LORD's gift remains with the godly. His good pleasure will prosper forever. ¹⁸ One grows rich by his diligence and self-denial, ‖ And this is the portion of his reward: ¹⁹ When he says, "I have found rest, and now I will eat of my goods!" He does not know how much time will pass ‖ Until he leaves them to others and dies. ²⁰ Be steadfast in your covenant ‖

And be doing it and grow old in your work. ²¹ Do not marvel at the works of a sinner, ‖ But trust the LORD and stay in your labor; For it is an easy thing in the sight of the LORD ‖ To swiftly and suddenly make a poor man rich. ²² The LORD's blessing is in the reward of the godly. He makes his blessing flourish in an hour that comes swiftly. ²³ Do not say, "What use is there of me? What further good things can be mine?" ²⁴ Do not say, "I have enough. What harm could happen to me now?" ²⁵ In the day of good things, ‖ Evil things are forgotten. In the day of evil things, ‖ A man will not remember things that are good. ²⁶ For it is an easy thing in the sight of the LORD ‖ To reward a man in the day of death according to his ways. ²⁷ The affliction of an hour causes delights to be forgotten. In the end, a man's deeds are revealed. ²⁸ Call no man happy before his death. A man will be known in his children. ²⁹ Do not bring every man into your house, ‖ For many are the plots of a deceitful man. ³⁰ Like a decoy partridge in a cage, ‖ So is the heart of a proud man. Like a spy, he looks for your weakness. ³¹ For he lies in wait to turn things that are good into evil ‖ And assigns blame in things that are praiseworthy. ³² From a spark of fire, a heap of many coals is kindled, ‖ And a sinful man lies in wait for blood. ³³ Take heed of an evildoer, for he plans wicked things, ‖ Lest perhaps he ruins your reputation forever. ³⁴ Receive a stranger into your house, ‖ And he will distract you with arguments and estrange you from your own.

CHAPTER 12

¹ If you do good, know to whom you do it, ‖ And your good deeds will have thanks. ² Do good to a godly man, and you will find a reward—If not from him, then from the Most High. ³ No good will come to him who continues to do evil, ‖ Nor to him who gives no alms. ⁴ Give to the godly man, ‖ And do not help the sinner. ⁵ Do good to one who is lowly. Do not give to an ungodly man. Keep back his bread, and do not give it to him, ‖ Lest he subdue you with it; For you would receive twice as much evil ‖ For all the good you would have done to him. ⁶ For the Most High also hates sinners ‖ And will repay vengeance to the ungodly. ⁷ Give to the good man, and do not help the sinner. ⁸ A man's friend will not be fully tried in prosperity. His enemy will not be hidden in adversity. ⁹ In a man's prosperity, his enemies are grieved. In his adversity, even his friend leaves. ¹⁰ Never trust your enemy, ‖ For his wickedness is like corrosion in copper. ¹¹ Though he humbles himself and walks bowed down, ‖ Still be careful and beware of him. You will be to him as one who has wiped a mirror, ‖ To be sure it does not completely tarnish. ¹² Do not set him next to you, ‖ Lest he overthrow you and stand in your place. Do not let him sit on your right hand, ‖ Lest he seek to take your seat, ‖ And at the last you acknowledge my words, ‖ And be pricked with my sayings. ¹³ Who will pity a charmer that is bitten by a snake, ‖ Or any who come near wild beasts? ¹⁴ Even so, who will pity him who goes to a sinner, ‖ And is associated with him in his sins? ¹⁵ For a while he will stay with you, ‖ And if you falter, he will not stay. ¹⁶ The enemy will speak sweetly with his lips, ‖ And in his heart plan to throw you into a pit. The enemy may weep with his eyes, ‖ But if he finds opportunity, he will want more blood. ¹⁷ If adversity meets you, ‖ You will find him there before you. Pretending to help you, he will trip you. ¹⁸ He will shake his head, clap his hands, ‖ Whisper much, and change his countenance.

CHAPTER 13

¹ He who touches pitch will be defiled. He who has fellowship with a proud man will become like him. ² Do not take up a burden above your strength. Have no fellowship with one who is mightier and richer than yourself. What fellowship would the earthen pot have with the kettle? The kettle will strike, ‖ And the pot will be dashed in pieces. ³ The rich man does a wrong and threatens. The poor is wronged and apologizes. ⁴ If you are profitable, ‖ He will make merchandise of you. If you are in lack, ‖ He will forsake you. ⁵ If you own something, ‖ He will live with you. He will drain you bare and will not be sorry. ⁶ Does he need you? Then he will deceive you, ‖ Smile at you, and give you hope. He will speak kindly to you and say, "What do you need?" ⁷ He will shame you by his meats ‖ Until he has made you bare twice or three times, ‖ And in the end he will laugh you to scorn. Afterward he will see you, ‖ Will forsake you, and shake his head at you. ⁸ Beware that you are not deceived ‖ And brought low in your mirth. ⁹ If a mighty man invites you, be reserved, ‖ And he will invite you more. ¹⁰ Do not press him, lest you be thrust back. Do not stand far off, lest you be forgotten. ¹¹ Do not try to speak with him as an equal, ‖ And do not believe his many words; For he will test you with much talk ‖ And will examine you in a smiling manner. ¹² He who does not keep secrets to himself is unmerciful. He will not hesitate to harm and to bind. ¹³ Keep them to yourself and be careful, ‖ For you walk in danger of falling. ¹⁴ . . . ¹⁵ Every living creature loves its own kind, ‖ And every man loves his neighbor. ¹⁶ All flesh associates with their own kind. A man will stick to people like himself. ¹⁷ What fellowship would the wolf have with the lamb? So is the sinner to the godly. ¹⁸ What peace is there between a hyena and a dog? What peace is there between a rich man and the poor? ¹⁹ Wild donkeys are the prey of lions in the wilderness; Likewise, poor men are feeding grounds for the rich. ²⁰ Lowliness is an abomination to a proud man; Likewise, a poor man is an abomination to the rich. ²¹ When a rich man is shaken, ‖ He is supported by his friends, ‖ But when one of low degree is down, ‖ He is pushed away even by his friends. ²² When a rich man falls, there are

many helpers. He speaks things not to be spoken, || And men justify him. A man of low degree falls, and men rebuke him. He utters wisdom and is not listened to. ²³ A rich man speaks, and all keep silence. They extol what he says to the clouds. A poor man speaks, and they say, "Who is this?" If he stumbles, they will help to overthrow him. ²⁴ Riches are good if they have no sin. Poverty is evil in the mouth of the ungodly. ²⁵ The heart of a man changes his countenance, || Whether it is for good or for evil. ²⁶ A cheerful countenance is a sign of a prosperous heart. Devising proverbs takes strenuous thinking.

CHAPTER 14

¹ Blessed is the man who has not slipped with his mouth || And does not suffer from sorrow for sins. ² Blessed is he whose soul does not condemn him, || And who has not given up hope. ³ Riches are not appropriate for a stingy person. What would an envious man do with money? ⁴ He who gathers by denying himself gathers for others. Others will revel in his goods. ⁵ If one is mean to himself, || To whom will he be good? He will not enjoy his possessions. ⁶ There is none more evil than he who is stingy with himself. This is a punishment for his wickedness. ⁷ Even if he does good, he does it in forgetfulness. In the end, he reveals his wickedness. ⁸ A miser is evil. He turns away and disregards souls. ⁹ A covetous man's eye is not satisfied with his portion. Wicked injustice dries up his soul. ¹⁰ A miser begrudges bread, || And it is lacking at his table. ¹¹ My son, according to what you have, treat yourself well, || And bring worthy offerings to the LORD. ¹² Remember that death will not wait, || And that the covenant of Hades has not been shown to you. ¹³ Do good to your friend before you die. According to your ability, reach out and give to him. ¹⁴ Do not defraud yourself of a good day. Do not let the portion of a good desire pass you by. ¹⁵ Will you not leave your labors to another, || And your toils be divided by lot? ¹⁶ Give, take, and treat yourself well, || Because there is no seeking of luxury in Hades. ¹⁷ All flesh grows old like a garment, || For the covenant from the beginning is, "You must die." ¹⁸ Like the leaves flourishing on a thick tree—Some it sheds, and some grow—So also are the generations of flesh and blood: One comes to an end and another is born. ¹⁹ Every work rots and falls away, || And its builder will depart with it. ²⁰ Blessed is the man who meditates on wisdom, || And who reasons by his understanding. ²¹ He who considers her ways in his heart || Will also have knowledge of her secrets. ²² Go after her like one who tracks || And lie in wait in her ways. ²³ He who pries in at her windows || Will also listen at her doors. ²⁴ He who lodges close to her house || Will also fasten a nail in her walls. ²⁵ He will pitch his tent near at hand to her || And will lodge in a lodging where good things are. ²⁶ He will set his children under her shelter || And will rest under her branches. ²⁷ By her he will be covered from heat || And will lodge in her glory.

CHAPTER 15

¹ He who fears the LORD will do this. He who has possession of the Law will obtain her. ² As a mother, she will meet him || And receive him as a wife married in her virginity. ³ She will feed him with bread of understanding || And give him water of wisdom to drink. ⁴ He will be stayed on her and will not be moved. He will rely on her and will not be confounded. ⁵ She will exalt him above his neighbors. She will open his mouth in the midst of the congregation. ⁶ He will inherit joy, a crown of gladness, and a perpetual name. ⁷ Foolish men will not obtain her. Sinners will not see her. ⁸ She is far from pride. Liars will not remember her. ⁹ Praise is not attractive in the mouth of a sinner; For it was not sent to him from the LORD. ¹⁰ For praise will be spoken in wisdom; The LORD will prosper it. ¹¹ Do not say, "It is through the LORD that I fell away"; For you will not do the things that He hates. ¹² Do not say, "It is He that caused me to err"; For He has no need of a sinful man. ¹³ The LORD hates every abomination; And those who fear Him do not love them. ¹⁴ He Himself made man from the beginning || And left him in the hand of his own counsel. ¹⁵ If you will, you will keep the commands. To be faithful is good pleasure. ¹⁶ He has set fire and water before you. You will stretch out your hand to whichever you desire. ¹⁷ Before man is life and death. Whichever he likes, it will be given to him. ¹⁸ For great is the wisdom of the LORD. He is mighty in power and sees all things. ¹⁹ His eyes are on those who fear Him. He knows every work of man. ²⁰ He has not commanded any man to be ungodly. He has not given any man license to sin.

CHAPTER 16

¹ Do not desire a multitude of unprofitable children, || Neither delight in ungodly sons. ² If they multiply, do not delight in them || Unless the fear of the LORD is in them. ³ Do not trust in their life. Do not rely on their condition. For one is better than one thousand, || And to die childless than to have ungodly children. ⁴ For from one who has understanding, a city will be populated, || But a race of wicked men will be made desolate. ⁵ I have seen many such things with my eyes. My ear has heard mightier things than these. ⁶ In the congregation of sinners, a fire will be kindled. In a disobedient nation, wrath is kindled. ⁷ He was not pacified toward the giants of ancient time, || Who revolted in their strength. ⁸ He did not spare Lot's neighbors, || Whom He abhorred for their pride. ⁹ He did not pity the people of perdition || Who were taken away in their sins, ¹⁰ Or in like manner, the six hundred thousand footmen || Who were gathered together in the hardness of their hearts. ¹¹ Even if there is one stiff-necked person, || It is a marvel if he will

be unpunished, || For mercy and wrath are both with Him who is mighty to forgive, || And He pours out wrath. ¹² As His mercy is great, || So is His correction also. He judges a man according to his works. ¹³ The sinner will not escape with plunder. The perseverance of the godly will not be frustrated. ¹⁴ He will make room for every work of mercy. Each man will receive according to his works. ¹⁵ The LORD made the king of Egypt so stubborn || That he would not acknowledge the LORD, || In order that the world might know the LORD's works. ¹⁶ He shows His mercy to all creation; He has divided His light from darkness with a plumb line. ¹⁷ Do not say, "I will be hidden from the LORD," || And "Who will remember me from on high?" I will not be known among so many people, || For what is my soul in a boundless creation? ¹⁸ Behold, the Heaven—the Heaven of heavens—The deep, and the earth, will be moved when He visits. ¹⁹ The mountains and the foundations of the earth together || Are shaken with trembling when He looks at them. ²⁰ No heart will think about these things. Who could comprehend His ways? ²¹ Like a tempest which no man can see, || Yes, the majority of His works are hidden. ²² Who will declare His works of righteousness? Who will endure them? For His covenant is far off. ²³ He who is lacking in understanding thinks about these things. An unwise and erring man thinks follies. ²⁴ My son, listen to me, learn knowledge, || And heed my words with your heart. ²⁵ I will impart instruction with precision || And declare knowledge exactly. ²⁶ In the judgment of the LORD are His works from the beginning. From the making of them He determined their parts. ²⁷ He arranged His works for all time, || And their beginnings to their generations. They are not hungry or weary, || And they do not cease from their works. ²⁸ No one thrusts aside his neighbor. They will never disobey His word. ²⁹ After this the LORD also looked at the earth || And filled it with His blessings. ³⁰ All manner of living things covered its face, || And into it is their return.

CHAPTER 17

¹ The LORD created mankind out of the earth || And turned them back to it again. ² He gave them days by number, and a set time, || And gave them authority over the things that are on it. ³ He endowed them with strength appropriate for them || And made them according to His own image. ⁴ He put the fear of man on all flesh || And gave him dominion over beasts and birds. ⁵ The LORD gave them the five senses, || But He also gave them a sixth—intelligence, || And a seventh—reason, || Which enables them to interpret what comes to them through the senses. ⁶ He gave them counsel, tongue, eyes, ears, || And heart to have understanding. ⁷ He filled them with the knowledge of wisdom || And showed them good and evil. ⁸ He set His eye on their hearts, || To show them the majesty of His works. ⁹ And He allowed them to take pride

forever in His marvelous deeds. ¹⁰ And they will praise the Name of His holiness, || That they may declare the majesty of His works. ¹¹ He added to them knowledge || And gave them a law of life for a heritage. ¹² He made a perpetual covenant with them || And showed them His judgments. ¹³ Their eyes saw the majesty of His glory. Their ears heard the glory of His voice. ¹⁴ He said to them, "Beware of all unrighteousness." So He gave them command—Each man concerning his neighbor. ¹⁵ Their ways are ever before Him. They will not be hidden from His eyes. ¹⁶ From childhood on they tend to be evil; Their heart is like stone, || And they do not seem to be able to make it more human. ¹⁷ He divided the nations of the whole earth. For every nation He appointed ¡a ruler, || But Israel is the LORD's portion. ¹⁸ Israel is His firstborn, || Whom He disciplines as He brings him up. He gives him the light of His love and never neglects him. ¹⁹ All their works are as clear as the sun before Him. His eyes are continually on their ways. ²⁰ Their iniquities are not hidden from Him. All their sins are before the LORD. ²¹ But the LORD is gracious and knows His creatures; So He has spared them rather than abandon them. ²² With Him the kindness of a man is as a signet. He will keep the bounty of a man as the apple of the eye. ²³ Afterward He will rise up, and repay them, || And render their repayment on their head. ²⁴ However, to those who convert He grants a return. He comforts those who are losing patience. ²⁵ Return to the LORD and forsake sins. Make your prayer before His face offend less. ²⁶ Turn to the Most High again || And turn away from iniquity. Greatly hate the abominable thing. ²⁷ Who will give praise to the Most High in Hades, || In place of those who live and return thanks? ²⁸ Thanksgiving perishes from the dead, || As from one who does not exist. He who is in life and health will praise the LORD. ²⁹ How great is the mercy of the LORD, || And His forgiveness to those who turn to Him! ³⁰ For all things cannot be in men, || Because the son of man is not immortal. ³¹ What is brighter than the sun? Yet even this fails. An evil man thinks about flesh and blood. ³² He looks on the power of the height of Heaven, || While all men are earth and ashes.

CHAPTER 18

¹ He who lives forever created all things in common. ² The LORD alone will be justified || And there is no other besides Him. ³ He guides the world with His hand, || And everything obeys Him. He is the King of all things, || And His power separates what is holy from what is not. ⁴ He has given power to declare His works to no one. Who could trace out His mighty deeds? ⁵ Who could measure the strength of His majesty? Who could also proclaim His mercies? ⁶ As for the wondrous works of the LORD, || It is not possible to take from them nor add to them, || Neither is it possible to explore them. ⁷ When a man has

finished, || Then he is just at the beginning. When he ceases, || Then he will be in perplexity. ⁸ What is mankind, and what purpose do they serve? What is their good, and what is their evil? ⁹ The number of man's days at the most are one hundred years. ¹⁰ As a drop of water from the sea, and a pebble from the sand, || So are a few years in the day [[or time]] of [the] age. ¹¹ For this reason the LORD was patient over them || And poured out His mercy on them. ¹² He saw and perceived their end, || That it is evil. Therefore, He multiplied His forgiveness. ¹³ The mercy of a man is on his neighbor; But the mercy of the LORD is on all flesh: Reproving, disciplining, teaching, and bringing back, || As a shepherd does his flock. ¹⁴ He has mercy on those who accept disciplining, || And that diligently seek after His judgments. ¹⁵ My son, add no blemish to your good deeds, || And no grief of words in any of your giving. ¹⁶ Does the dew not relieve the scorching heat? So a word is better than a gift. ¹⁷ Behold, is a word not better than a gift? Both are with a gracious man. ¹⁸ A fool is ungracious and abusive. The gift of an envious man consumes the eyes. ¹⁹ Learn before you speak. Take care of your health before you are sick. ²⁰ Before judgment examine yourself, || And in the hour of visitation you will find forgiveness. ²¹ Humble yourself before you become sick. In the time of sins, show conversion. ²² Let nothing hinder you to pay your vow in due time. Do not wait until death to be justified. ²³ Before you make a vow, prepare yourself. Do not be like a man who tempts the LORD. ²⁴ Think about the wrath coming in the days of the end, || And the time of vengeance, when He turns away His face. ²⁵ In the days of fullness remember the time of hunger. Remember poverty and lack in the days of wealth. ²⁶ From morning until evening, the time changes. All things are speedy before the LORD. ²⁷ A wise man is cautious in everything. In days of sinning, he will beware of offense. ²⁸ Every man of understanding knows wisdom. He will give thanks to him who found her. ²⁹ They who were of understanding in sayings || Also became wise themselves and poured out apt proverbs. ³⁰ Do not go after your lusts. Refrain yourself from your appetites. ³¹ If you give fully to your soul the delight of her desire, || She will make you the laughing-stock of your enemies. ³² Do not make merry in much luxury, || Neither be tied to the expense thereof. ³³ Do not be made a beggar by banqueting on borrowing || When you have nothing in your purse.

CHAPTER 19

¹ A workman who is a drunkard will not become rich. He who despises small things will fall little by little. ² Wine and women will make men of understanding fall away. And he who joins with prostitutes will be more reckless. ³ Moths and worms will have him as their heritage. A reckless soul will be taken away. ⁴ He who is hasty to trust is shallow-minded. He who sins will offend against his own soul. ⁵ He who makes merry in his heart will be condemned: ⁶ He who hates talk has less wickedness. ⁷ Never repeat what is told you, || And you will not be lacking. ⁸ Whether it is of friend or enemy, do not tell it. Unless it is a sin to you, do not reveal it. ⁹ For he has heard you and observed you, || And when the time comes, he will hate you. ¹⁰ Have you heard a word? Let it die with you. Be of good courage: it will not burst you. ¹¹ A fool will travail in pain with a word, || As a woman in labor with a child. ¹² As an arrow that sticks in the flesh of the thigh, || So is a word in a fool's belly. ¹³ Reprove a friend: It may be [that] he did not do it. If he did something, || It may be [that] he may not do it again. ¹⁴ Reprove your neighbor: It may be [that] he did not say it. If he has said it, || It may be [that] he may not say it again. ¹⁵ Reprove a friend: For many times there is slander. Do not trust every word. ¹⁶ There is one who slips, and not from the heart. Who is he who has not sinned with his tongue? ¹⁷ Reprove your neighbor before you threaten him; And give place to the Law of the Most High; And do not be angry. ¹⁸ Fearing the LORD is the first step toward His accepting you; He will love you if you are wise. ¹⁹ Learn the LORD's commands. It is a discipline that gives life. Those who do what pleases Him || Enjoy the fruit of the tree of immortality. ²⁰ All wisdom is the fear of the LORD. In all wisdom is the doing of the Law || And what the knowledge of His omnipotence means. ²¹ If a servant refuses to obey his master, but later does obey, || The master is still angry. ²² The knowledge of wickedness is not wisdom. The prudence of sinners is not counsel. ²³ There is a wickedness, and it is abomination. There is a fool lacking in wisdom. ²⁴ Better is one who has small understanding, and fears, || Than one who has much prudence, and transgresses the Law. ²⁵ There is an exquisite subtlety, and it is unjust. And there is one who perverts favor to gain a judgment. ²⁶ There is one who does wickedly, || Who hangs down his head with mourning, || But inwardly he is full of deceit, ²⁷ Bowing his face down, || And making [it seem] as if he were deaf of one ear. Where he is not known, || He will be beforehand with you. ²⁸ And if for lack of power he is hindered from sinning, || If he finds opportunity, he will do mischief. ²⁹ A man will be known by his look; One who has understanding will be known by his face when you meet him. ³⁰ A man's attire, grinning laughter, || And gait show what he is.

CHAPTER 20

¹ There is a reproof that is not timely; And there is a man who keeps silent and is wise. ² How good it is to reprove, rather than to be angry. He who confesses will be kept back from hurt. ³ Admit when you are wrong, || And you will avoid embarrassment. ⁴ As is the lust of a eunuch to deflower a virgin, || So is he who executes judgments with violence. ⁵ There is one

who keeps silent and is found wise; And there is one who is hated for his much talk. ⁶There is one who keeps silent, ‖ For he has no answer to make; And there is one who keeps silent, as knowing his time. ⁷A wise man will be silent until his time has come, ‖ But the braggart and fool will miss his time. ⁸He who uses many words will be abhorred. He who takes authority for himself will be hated in it. ⁹There is a prosperity that a man finds in misfortunes; And there is a gain that turns to loss. ¹⁰There is a gift that will not profit you; And there is a gift [that] pays back double. ¹¹There is an abasement because of glory; And there is one who has lifted up his head from a low estate. ¹²There is one who buys much for a little and pays for it again sevenfold. ¹³He who is wise in words will make himself beloved; But the pleasantries of fools will be wasted. ¹⁴The gift of a fool will not profit you; For his eyes are many instead of one. ¹⁵He will give little and insult much. He will open his mouth like a crier. Today he will lend, ‖ And tomorrow he will ask for it back. Such a one is a hateful man. ¹⁶The fool will say, "I have no friend, ‖ And I have no thanks for my good deeds. They who eat my bread are of evil tongue." ¹⁷How often, and of how many, will he be laughed to scorn! ¹⁸A slip on a pavement is better than a slip with the tongue. So the fall of the wicked will come speedily. ¹⁹A man without grace is a tale out of season. It will be continually in the mouth of the ignorant. ²⁰An allegory from a fool's mouth will be rejected; For he will not speak it in its season. ²¹There is one who is hindered from sinning through lack. When he rests, he will not be troubled. ²²There is one who destroys his soul through bashfulness. By a foolish countenance, he will destroy it. ²³There is one who for bashfulness makes promises to his friend; And he makes him his enemy for nothing. ²⁴A lie is a foul blot in a man. It will be continually in the mouth of the ignorant. ²⁵A thief is better than a man who is continually lying, ‖ But they will both inherit destruction. ²⁶The disposition of a liar is dishonor. His shame is with him continually. ²⁷He who is wise in words will advance himself. And one who is prudent will please great men. ²⁸He who tills his land will raise his heap high. He who pleases great men will get pardon for iniquity. ²⁹Presents and gifts blind the eyes of the wise, ‖ And as a muzzle on the mouth, turn away reproofs. ³⁰Wisdom that is hidden, and treasure that is out of sight—What profit is in them both? ³¹Better is a man who hides his folly ‖ Than a man who hides his wisdom.

CHAPTER 21

¹My son, have you sinned? Add no more to it; And ask forgiveness for your past sins. ²Flee from sin as from the face of a serpent; For if you draw near, it will bite you. Its teeth are lion's teeth, slaying men's souls. ³All iniquity is as a two-edged sword. Its stroke has no healing. ⁴Terror and violence will lay waste riches.

So the house of an arrogant man will be laid waste. ⁵Supplication from a poor man's mouth reaches to the ears of God, ‖ And his judgment comes speedily. ⁶One who hates reproof is in the path of the sinner. He who fears the LORD will turn again in his heart. ⁷He who is mighty in tongue is known far away, ‖ But the man of understanding knows when he slips. ⁸He who builds his house with other men's money ‖ Is like one who gathers stones for his own tomb. ⁹The congregation of wicked men is as a bundle of tow ‖ With a flame of fire at the end of them. ¹⁰The way of sinners is paved with stones, ‖ And at the end of it is the pit of Hades. ¹¹He who keeps the Law becomes master of its intent. The end of the fear of the LORD is wisdom. ¹²He who is not clever will not be instructed. There is a cleverness which makes bitterness abound. ¹³The knowledge of a wise man will be made to abound as a flood, ‖ And his counsel as a fountain of life. ¹⁴The inward parts of a fool are like a broken vessel. He will hold no knowledge. ¹⁵If a man of knowledge hears a wise word, ‖ He will commend it and add to it. The wanton man hears it, and it displeases him, ‖ So he puts it away behind his back. ¹⁶The discourse of a fool is like a burden in the way, ‖ But grace will be found on the lips of the wise. ¹⁷The mouth of the prudent man will be sought for in the congregation. They will ponder his words in their heart. ¹⁸As a house that is destroyed, ‖ So is wisdom to a fool. The knowledge of an unwise man is talk without sense. ¹⁹Instruction is as chains on the feet of an unwise man, ‖ And as shackles on the right hand. ²⁰A fool lifts up his voice with laughter, ‖ But a clever man smiles quietly. ²¹Instruction is to a prudent man as an ornament of gold, ‖ And as a bracelet on his right arm. ²²The foot of a fool rushes into a house, ‖ But a man of experience will be ashamed of entering. ²³A foolish man peers into the door of a house, ‖ But a man who is instructed will stand outside. ²⁴It is a lack of instruction in a man to listen at a door, ‖ But a prudent man will be grieved with the disgrace. ²⁵The lips of strangers will be grieved at these things, ‖ But the words of prudent men will be weighed in the balance. ²⁶The heart of fools is in their mouth, ‖ But the mouth of wise men is their heart. ²⁷When the ungodly curses Satan, ‖ He curses his own soul. ²⁸A whisperer defiles his own soul ‖ And will be hated wherever he travels.

CHAPTER 22

¹A slothful man is compared to a stone that is defiled. Everyone will hiss at him in his disgrace. ²A slothful man is compared to the filth of a dunghill. Every man who takes it up will shake out his hand. ³An uninstructed child is a disgrace to his father, ‖ And a foolish daughter is born to his loss. ⁴A prudent daughter will inherit a husband of her own. She who brings shame is the grief of her father. ⁵She who is bold brings shame on father and husband. She will be

SIRACH

despised by both of them. ⁶Unseasonable discourse is as music in mourning, || But stripes and correction are wisdom in every season. ⁷He who teaches a fool is as one who glues a potsherd together, || Even as one who wakes a sleeper out of a deep sleep. ⁸He who teaches a fool is as one who teaches a man who slumbers. In the end he will say, "What is it?" ⁹Children who are brought up well || Do not show the humble origin of their parents. ¹⁰Children who are not brought up well, || Who are arrogant and conceited, || Are a stain on the noblest family. ¹¹Weep for the dead, for he lacks light. Weep for a fool, for he lacks understanding. Weep more sweetly for the dead, because he has found rest, || But the life of the fool is worse than death. ¹²Mourning for the dead lasts seven days, || But for a fool and an ungodly man, all the days of his life. ¹³Do not talk much with a foolish man, || And do not go to one that has no understanding: Beware of him, lest you have trouble and be defiled in his onslaught. Turn away from him, and you will find rest, || And you will not be wearied in his madness. ¹⁴What would be heavier than lead? What is its name, but a fool? ¹⁵Sand, salt, and a mass of iron are easier to bear || Than a man without understanding. ¹⁶Timber girded and bound into a building || Will not be released with shaking. So a heart established in due season on well advised counsel || Will not be afraid. ¹⁷A heart settled on a thoughtful understanding || Is as an ornament of plaster on a polished wall. ¹⁸Fences set on a high place || Will not stand against the wind; So a fearful heart in the imagination of a fool || Will not stand against any fear. ¹⁹He who pricks the eye will make tears fall. He who pricks the heart makes it show feeling. ²⁰Whoever casts a stone at birds scares them away. He who insults a friend will dissolve friendship. ²¹If you have drawn a sword against a friend, do not despair, || For there may be a way back. ²²If you have opened your mouth against a friend, do not be afraid, || For there may be reconciliation, || Unless it is for insulting, arrogance, disclosing of a secret, or a treacherous blow—For any friend will flee these things. ²³Gain trust with your neighbor in his poverty, || That in his prosperity you may have gladness. Stay steadfast to him in the time of his affliction, || That you may be heir with him in his inheritance. ²⁴Before fire is the vapor and smoke of a furnace, || So insults precede bloodshed. ²⁵I will not be ashamed to shelter a friend. I will not hide myself from his face: ²⁶If any evil happens to me because of him, || Everyone that hears it will beware of him. ²⁷Who will set a watch over my mouth, || And a seal of shrewdness on my lips, || That I do not fall from it, || And that my tongue does not destroy me?

CHAPTER 23

¹O Lord, Father and Master of my life, || Do not abandon me to their counsel. Do not let me fall by them. ²Who will set scourges over my thought, || And a discipline of wisdom over my heart, || That they do not spare me for my errors, || And not overlook their [[or my]] sins? ³Otherwise my errors might be multiplied, || And my sins abound, || [And] I fall before my adversaries, || And my enemy rejoice over me. ⁴O Lord, Father and God of my life, || Do not give me haughty eyes, ⁵And turn evil desire away from me. ⁶Let neither gluttony nor lust overtake me. Do not give me over to a shameless mind. ⁷Listen, my children, to the discipline of the mouth. He who keeps it will not be taken. ⁸The sinner will be overpowered through his lips. By them, the insulter and the arrogant will stumble. ⁹Do not accustom your mouth to an oath, || And do not be accustomed to naming the Holy One, ¹⁰For as a servant who is continually scourged will not lack a bruise, || So he also who swears and continually utters the Name || Will not be cleansed from sin. ¹¹A man of many oaths will be filled with iniquity. The scourge will not depart from his house. If he offends, his sin will be on him. If he disregards it, he has sinned doubly. If he has sworn in vain, he will not be justified, || For his house will be filled with calamities. ¹²There is a manner of speech that is clothed with death. Do not let it be found in the heritage of Jacob, || For all these things will be far from the godly, || And they will not wallow in sins. ¹³Do not accustom your mouth to gross rudeness, || For it involves sinful speech. ¹⁴Remember your father and your mother, || For you sit in the midst of great men, || That you are not forgetful before them, || And become a fool by your custom; So you may wish that you had not been born, || And curse the day of your nativity. ¹⁵A man who is accustomed to words of reproach || Will not be corrected all the days of his life. ¹⁶Two sorts of people multiply sins, || And the third will bring wrath: A hot mind, as a burning fire, || Will not be quenched until it is consumed; A fornicator, in the body of his flesh, || Will never cease until he has burned out the fire. ¹⁷All bread is sweet to a fornicator. He will not cease until he dies. ¹⁸A man who goes astray from his own bed, || Says in his heart, "Who sees me? Darkness is around me, and the walls hide me. No one sees me. Of whom am I afraid? The Most High will not remember my sins." ¹⁹The eyes of men are his terror. He does not know that the eyes of the Lord || Are ten thousand times brighter than the sun, || Seeing all the ways of men, || And looking into secret places. ²⁰All things were known to Him before they were created, || And also after they were completed. ²¹This man will be punished in the streets of the city. He will be seized where he least expects it. ²²So also is a wife who leaves her husband || And brings in an heir by a stranger. ²³For first, she was disobedient in the Law of the Most High. Second, she trespassed against her own husband. Third, she played the adulteress in whoredom, || And brought in children by a stranger. ²⁴She will be brought out into the congregation. Her punishment will extend to her

children. ²⁵ Her children will not take root. Her branches will bear no fruit. ²⁶ She will leave her memory for a curse. Her reproach will not be blotted out. ²⁷ And those who are left behind ‖ Will know that there is nothing better than the fear of the LORD, ‖ And nothing sweeter than to heed the commands of the LORD.

CHAPTER 24

¹ Wisdom will praise her own soul ‖ And will proclaim her glory in the midst of her people. ² She will open her mouth in the congregation of the Most High ‖ And proclaim her glory in the presence of His power. ³ "I came out of the mouth of the Most High ‖ And covered the earth as a mist. ⁴ I lived in high places, ‖ And my throne is in the pillar of the cloud. ⁵ Alone I surrounded the circuit of Heaven ‖ And walked in the depth of the abyss. ⁶ In the waves of the sea, and in all the earth, ‖ And in every people and nation, I got a possession. ⁷ With all these I sought rest. In whose inheritance will I lodge? ⁸ Then the Creator of all things gave me a command. He who created me made my dwelling place to rest, ‖ And said, Let your dwelling place be in Jacob, ‖ And your inheritance in Israel. ⁹ He created me from the beginning before the world. For all ages, I will not cease to exist. ¹⁰ In the holy Dwelling Place, I ministered before Him. So I was established in Zion. ¹¹ In the beloved city, likewise He gave me rest. In Jerusalem was my domain. ¹² I took root in a people that was glorified, ‖ Even in the portion of the LORD's own inheritance. ¹³ I was exalted like a cedar in Lebanon, ‖ And like a cypress tree on the mountains of Hermon. ¹⁴ I was exalted like a palm tree on the seashore, ‖ And as rose plants in Jericho, ‖ And as a fair olive tree in the plain. I was exalted as a plane tree. ¹⁵ As cinnamon and as palathus, ‖ I have given a scent to perfumes. As choice myrrh, I spread abroad a pleasant fragrance, ‖ As galbanum, onyx, stacte, ‖ And as the smell of frankincense in the Dwelling Place. ¹⁶ As the terebinth, I stretched out my branches. My branches are branches of glory and grace. ¹⁷ As the vine, I put out grace. My flowers are the fruit of glory and riches. ¹⁸ I am the mother of beautiful love, ‖ Of fear, knowledge, and holy hope. Since I am perpetual, ‖ I am given to all my children, who are named by Him. ¹⁹ Come to me, all you who desire me, ‖ And be filled with my fruits. ²⁰ For my memorial is sweeter than honey, ‖ And my inheritance [is sweeter] than the honeycomb. ²¹ Those who eat me will be hungry for more. Those who drink me will be thirsty for more. ²² He who obeys me will not be ashamed. Those who work in me will not sin." ²³ All these things are the Scroll of the Covenant of the Most High God, ‖ The Law which Moses commanded us for an inheritance for the assemblies of Jacob. ²⁴ Always be strong in the LORD; Stay with Him, so that He may make you strong. There is no God but the LORD

Almighty, ‖ And no savior except Him. ²⁵ It is He who makes wisdom abundant, ‖ As Pishon, and as Tigris in the days of first-fruits. ²⁶ He makes understanding as full as [the] Euphrates, ‖ And as [the] Jordan in the days of harvest, ²⁷ Who makes instruction shine out as the light, ‖ As [the] Gihon in the days of vintage. ²⁸ The first man did not know her perfectly. In like manner, the last has not explored her. ²⁹ For her thoughts are filled from the sea, ‖ And her counsels from the great deep. ³⁰ "I came out as a canal stream from a river, ‖ And as an irrigation ditch into a garden. ³¹ I said, I will water my garden, ‖ And will drench my garden bed. Behold, my stream became a river, ‖ And my river became a sea. ³² I will yet bring instruction to light as the morning ‖ And will make these things clear from far away. ³³ I will continue to pour out doctrine like prophecy ‖ And leave it to generations of ages. ³⁴ Behold that I have not labored for myself only, ‖ But for all those who diligently seek her."

CHAPTER 25

¹ In three things I was beautified ‖ And stood up beautiful before the LORD and men: The concord of relatives, ‖ And friendship of neighbors, ‖ And a woman and her husband that walk together in agreement. ² But three sorts [of men] my soul hates, ‖ And I am greatly offended at their life: A poor man that is arrogant, ‖ And a rich man that is a liar, ‖ [And] an old man that is an adulterer lacking understanding. ³ In [your] youth you have not gathered, ‖ And how should you find in your old age? ⁴ How beautiful a thing is judgment for gray hairs, ‖ And for elders to know counsel! ⁵ How beautiful is the wisdom of old men, ‖ And thought and counsel to men that are in honor! ⁶ Much experience is the crown of old men; And their glorying is the fear of the LORD. ⁷ There are nine things that I have thought of, ‖ And in my heart counted happy; And the tenth I will utter with my tongue: A man that rejoices in his children; A man that lives and looks on the fall of his enemies; ⁸ Happy is he that dwells with a wife of understanding; And he that has not slipped with his tongue; And he that has not served a man that is unworthy of him; ⁹ Happy is he that has found prudence; And he that speaks in the ears of those who listen. ¹⁰ How great is he that has found wisdom! Yet there is none above him that fears the LORD. ¹¹ The fear of the LORD passes all things: He that holds it—To whom will he be likened? ¹² Fearing the LORD is the first step toward loving Him, ‖ And faith is the first step toward loyalty to Him. ¹³ [Give me] any plague but the plague of the heart; And any wickedness but the wickedness of a woman; ¹⁴ Any calamity, but a calamity from those who hate me; And any vengeance, but the vengeance of enemies. ¹⁵ There is no head above the head of a serpent; And there is no wrath above the wrath of an enemy. ¹⁶ I would rather dwell with a lion and a dragon, ‖ Than keep house with a wicked woman.

¹⁷ The wickedness of a woman changes her look ‖ And darkens her countenance as a bear does. ¹⁸ Her husband will sit at meat among his neighbors, ‖ And when he hears it he sighs bitterly. ¹⁹ All malice is but little to the malice of a woman: Let the portion of a sinner fall on her. ²⁰ [As] the going up a sandy way [is] to the feet of the aged, ‖ So is a wife full of words to a quiet man. ²¹ Do not throw yourself on the beauty of a woman; And do not desire a woman for her beauty. ²² There is anger, and impudence, and great reproach, ‖ If a woman supports her husband. ²³ A wicked woman is a dejection of heart, ‖ And sadness of countenance, and a wounded heart: A woman that will not make her husband happy ‖ Is [as] hands that hang down, and palsied knees. ²⁴ From a woman [was] the beginning of sin; And because of her we all die. ²⁵ Do not give water an outlet; Neither [give] freedom of speech to a wicked woman. ²⁶ If she does not go as you would have her, ‖ Cut her off from your flesh.

CHAPTER 26

¹ Happy is the husband of a good wife; And the number of his days will be doubled. ² A brave woman rejoices her husband; And he will fulfill his years in peace. ³ A good wife is a good portion: She will be given in the portion of such as fear the LORD. ⁴ Whether a man is rich or poor, ‖ A good heart [makes] a cheerful countenance at all times. ⁵ Of three things my heart was afraid; And concerning the fourth kind I made supplication: The slander of a city, ‖ And the assembly of a multitude, ‖ And a false accusation: All these are more grievous than death. ⁶ A grief of heart and sorrow is a woman that is jealous of [another] woman, ‖ And the scourge of a tongue communicating to all. ⁷ A wicked woman is [as] a yoke of oxen shaken to and fro: He that takes hold of her is as one that grasps a scorpion. ⁸ A drunken woman [causes] great wrath; And she will not cover her own shame. ⁹ The whoredom of a woman is in the lifting up of her eyes; And it will be known by her eyelids. ¹⁰ Keep strict watch on a headstrong daughter, ‖ Lest she finds liberty for herself, and uses it. ¹¹ Look well after an impudent eye; And do not marvel if it trespasses against you. ¹² She will open her mouth as a thirsty traveler, ‖ And drink of every water that is near: She will sit down at every post ‖ And open her quiver against [any] arrow. ¹³ The grace of a wife will delight her husband; And her knowledge will fatten his bones. ¹⁴ A silent woman is a gift of the LORD; And there is nothing worth so much as a well-instructed soul. ¹⁵ A modest woman is grace on grace; And there is no price worthy of a continent soul. ¹⁶ As the sun when it arises in the highest places of the LORD, ‖ So is the beauty of a good wife in the ordering of a man's house. ¹⁷ As the lamp that shines on the holy candlestick, ‖ So is the beauty of the face in ripe age. ¹⁸ As the golden pillars are on a base of silver, ‖ So are beautiful feet with the breasts of one that is steadfast.

¹⁹ My child, stay healthy while you are young, ‖ And do not give your strength to strangers. ²⁰ Search the whole land for a fertile field, ‖ And plant it with your own seed, ‖ Trusting your own good stock. ²¹ Then your children will survive ‖ And grow up confident of their good family. ²² A prostitute is like spit; A married woman who has affairs brings death to her lovers. ²³ A lawless man will get a godless wife, as he deserves, ‖ But a man who honors the LORD will have a devout wife. ²⁴ A shameless wife enjoys making a disgrace of herself, ‖ But a modest wife will act modestly even alone with her husband. ²⁵ A self-willed woman is a dog, ‖ But a woman with a sense of decency honors the LORD. ²⁶ A wife who honors her husband will seem wise to everyone; But if she dishonors him by her overbearing attitude, ‖ Everyone will know that she is ungodly. The husband of a good wife is fortunate, ‖ Because he will live twice as long. ²⁷ A loud-mouthed, talkative woman is like a trumpet sounding the signal for attack, ‖ And any man who has such a wife will spend his life at war. ²⁸ For two things my heart is grieved; And for the third anger comes on me: A man of war that suffers for poverty; And men of understanding that are counted as refuse; One that turns back from righteousness to sin—The LORD will prepare him for the sword. ²⁹ A merchant will hardly keep himself from wrongdoing; And a huckster will not be acquitted of sin.

CHAPTER 27

¹ Many have sinned for a thing indifferent; And he that seeks to multiply [gain] will turn his eye away. ² A nail will stick fast between the joining of stones; And sin will thrust itself in between buying and selling. ³ Unless [a man] holds on diligently in the fear of the LORD, ‖ His house will soon be overthrown. ⁴ In the shaking of a sieve, the refuse remains; So is the filth of man in his reasoning. ⁵ The furnace will prove the potter's vessels; And the trial of a man is in his reasoning. ⁶ The fruit of a tree declares the farming thereof; So is the utterance of the thought of the heart of a man. ⁷ Praise no man before [you hear him] reason; For this is the trial of men. ⁸ If you follow righteousness, you will obtain her, ‖ And put her on, as a long robe of glory. ⁹ Birds will return to their like; And truth will return to those who practice her. ¹⁰ The lion lies in wait for prey; So does sin for those who work iniquity. ¹¹ The discourse of a godly man is always wisdom, ‖ But the foolish man changes as the moon. ¹² Among men void of understanding observe the opportunity; But continually stay among the thoughtful. ¹³ The discourse of fools is an offense; And their laughter is in the wantonness of sin. ¹⁴ The talk of a man of many oaths will make the hair stand upright; And their strife makes one stop his ears. ¹⁵ The strife of the proud is a shedding of blood; And their reviling of each other is a grievous thing to hear.

SIRACH

¹⁶ He that reveals secrets destroys credit || And will not find a friend to his mind. ¹⁷ Love a friend and keep faith with him, || But if you reveal his secrets, || You will not pursue after him; ¹⁸ For as a man has destroyed his enemy, || So have you destroyed the friendship of your neighbor. ¹⁹ And as a bird which you have released out of your hand, || So have you let your neighbor go, || And you will not catch him again: ²⁰ Do not pursue him, for he has gone far away, || And has escaped as a gazelle out of the snare. ²¹ For a wound may be bound up, || And after reviling there may be a reconcilement; But he that reveals secrets has lost hope. ²² One that winks with the eye contrives evil things; And no man will remove him from it. ²³ When you are present, he will speak sweetly, || And will admire your words; But afterward he will writhe his mouth || And set a trap [for you] in your words. ²⁴ I have hated many things, || But nothing like him; And the LORD will hate him. ²⁵ One that casts a stone on high casts it on his own head; And a deceitful stroke will open wounds. ²⁶ He that digs a pit will fall into it; And he that sets a snare will be taken therein. ²⁷ He that does evil things, they will roll on him, || And he will not know from where they have come to him. ²⁸ Mockery and reproach are from the arrogant; And vengeance, as a lion, will lie in wait for him. ²⁹ They that rejoice at the fall of the godly || Will be taken in a snare; And anguish will consume them before they die. ³⁰ Wrath and anger, these are also abominations; And a sinful man will possess them.

CHAPTER 28

¹ He that takes vengeance will find vengeance from the LORD; And he will surely make firm his sins. ² Forgive your neighbor the hurt that he has done [you]; And then your sins will be pardoned when you pray. ³ Man cherishes anger against man; And does he [then] seek healing from the LORD? ⁴ On a man like himself he has no mercy; And does he [then] make supplication for his own sins? ⁵ He being himself flesh nourishes wrath: Who will make atonement for his sins? ⁶ Remember your last end, || And cease from enmity: [Remember] corruption and death, || And remain in the commands. ⁷ Remember the commands || And do not be angry with your neighbor; And [remember] the covenant of the Highest, || And wink at ignorance. ⁸ Abstain from strife, and you will diminish your sins, || For a passionate man will kindle strife; ⁹ And a man that is a sinner will trouble friends || And will make debate among those who are at peace. ¹⁰ As is the fuel of the fire, so will it burn; And as the stoutness of the strife is, [so] will it burn; As is the strength of the man, [so] will be his wrath; And as is his wealth, [so] he will exalt his anger. ¹¹ A contention begun in haste kindles a fire; And a hasty fighting sheds blood. ¹² If you blow a spark, it will burn; And if you spit on it, it will be quenched: And both these will come out of your mouth. ¹³ Curse the whisperer and double-tongued, || For he has destroyed many that were at peace. ¹⁴ A third person's tongue has shaken many || And dispersed them from nation to nation; And it has pulled down strong cities || And overthrown the houses of great men. ¹⁵ A third person's tongue has cast out brave women || And deprived them of their labors. ¹⁶ He that listens to it will not find rest, || Nor will he dwell quietly. ¹⁷ The stroke of a whip makes a mark in the flesh; But the stroke of a tongue will break bones. ¹⁸ Many have fallen by the edge of the sword: Yet not so many as those who have fallen because of the tongue. ¹⁹ Happy is he that is sheltered from it, || Who has not passed through the wrath thereof; Who has not drawn its yoke, || And has not been bound with its bands. ²⁰ For the yoke thereof is a yoke of iron, || And the bands thereof are bands of brass. ²¹ The death thereof is an evil death; And Hades would be better than it. ²² It will not have rule over godly men; And they will not be burned in its flame. ²³ They that forsake the LORD will fall into it; And it will burn among them and will not be quenched: It will be sent out on them as a lion; And as a leopard it will destroy them. ²⁴ See to it that you hedge around your possession with thorns; Bind up your silver and your gold; ²⁵ And make a balance and a weight for your words; And make a door and a bar for your mouth. ²⁶ Take heed lest you slip therein; Lest you fall before one that lies in wait.

CHAPTER 29

¹ He that shows mercy will lend to his neighbor; And he that strengthens him with his hand keeps the commands. ² Lend to your neighbor in time of his need; And pay your neighbor again in due season. ³ Confirm your word and keep faith with him; And at all seasons you will find what you need. ⁴ Many have reckoned a loan as a windfall || And have given trouble to those that helped them. ⁵ Until he has received, he will kiss a man's hands; And for his neighbor's money he will speak submissively: And when payment is due, he will prolong the time, || And return words of heaviness, and complain of the times. ⁶ If he prevails, he will hardly receive the half; And he will count it as a windfall: If not, he has deprived him of his money, || And he has gotten him for an enemy without cause: He will pay him with cursing and railing; And he will pay him disgrace for honor. ⁷ Many on account of [men's] ill-dealing have turned away; They have feared to be defrauded for nothing. ⁸ However, be patient with a man in poor estate; And do not let him wait for [your] kindness. ⁹ Help a poor man for the command's sake; And according to his need, do not send him away empty. ¹⁰ Lose [your] money for a brother and a friend; And do not let it rust under the stone to be lost. ¹¹ Bestow your treasure according to the commands of the Most High, || And it will profit you more than gold. ¹² Shut up alms in your store-chambers, || And it will deliver you out of

SIRACH

all affliction: ¹³ It will fight for you against your enemy ‖ Better than a mighty shield and a ponderous spear. ¹⁴ A good man will be a guarantee for his neighbor; And he that has lost shame will fail him. ¹⁵ Do not forget the good offices of your guarantor; For he has given his life for you. ¹⁶ A sinner will overthrow the good estate of his guarantor; ¹⁷ And he that is of an unthankful mind will fail him that delivered him. ¹⁸ Suretyship has undone many that were prospering ‖ And shaken them as a wave of the sea: It has driven mighty men from their homes; And they wandered among strange nations. ¹⁹ A sinner that falls into suretyship, ‖ And undertakes contracts for work, ‖ Will fall into lawsuits. ²⁰ Help your neighbor according to your power ‖ And take heed to yourself that you do not fall [the same way]. ²¹ The chief thing for life is water, and bread, ‖ And a garment, and a house to cover shame. ²² Better is the life of a poor man under a shelter of logs, ‖ Than sumptuous fare in another man's house. ²³ With little or with much, be well satisfied. ²⁴ It is a miserable life to go from house to house: And where you are a sojourner, ‖ You will not [dare to] open your mouth. ²⁵ You will entertain, and give to drink, and have no thanks: And in addition to this, you will hear bitter words. ²⁶ "Come here, you sojourner, furnish a table, ‖ And if you have anything in your hand, feed me with it. ²⁷ Go out, you sojourner, from the face of honor; My brother has come to be my guest; I have need of my house." ²⁸ These things are grievous to a man of understanding: The scolding of [the] household, ‖ And the reproaching of the money-lender.

CHAPTER 30

¹ He that loves his son will continue to lay stripes on him, ‖ That he may rejoice in him in the end. ² He that disciplines his son will profit from him ‖ And will boast of him among his acquaintance. ³ He that teaches his son will provoke his enemy to jealousy; And he will rejoice in him before friends. ⁴ His father dies and is as though he had not died; For he has left one behind him like himself. ⁵ In his life, he saw and rejoiced [in him]; And when he died, he did not sorrow: ⁶ He left behind him an avenger against his enemies, ‖ And one to repay kindness to his friends. ⁷ He that makes too much of his son will bind up his wounds; And his heart will be troubled at every cry. ⁸ An unbroken horse becomes stubborn; And a son left at large becomes headstrong. ⁹ Pamper your child, and he will make you afraid: Play with him, and he will grieve you. ¹⁰ Do not laugh with him, lest you have sorrow with him; And you will gnash your teeth in the end. ¹¹ Give him no liberty in his youth, ‖ And do not wink at his follies. ¹² Bow his neck down in his youth ‖ And beat him on the sides while he is a child, ‖ Lest he wax stubborn, and be disobedient to you; And there will be sorrow to your soul. ¹³ Discipline your son, and take pains with him, ‖ Lest his

shameless behavior be an offense to you. ¹⁴ Better is a poor man, being sound and strong of constitution, ‖ Than a rich man that is plagued in his body. ¹⁵ Health and a good constitution are better than all gold; And a strong body than wealth without measure. ¹⁶ There is no riches better than health of body; And there is no gladness above the joy of the heart. ¹⁷ Death is better than a bitter life, ‖ And perpetual rest than a continual sickness. ¹⁸ Good things poured out on a mouth that is closed ‖ Are [as] messes of meat laid on a grave. ¹⁹ What does an offering profit an idol? For neither will it eat nor smell; So is he that is afflicted of the LORD, ²⁰ Seeing with his eyes and groaning, ‖ As a eunuch embracing a virgin and groaning. ²¹ Do not give your soul over to sorrow; And do not afflict yourself in your own counsel. ²² Gladness of heart is the life of a man; And the joyfulness of a man is length of days. ²³ Love your own soul and comfort your heart: And remove sorrow far from you; For sorrow has destroyed many, ‖ And there is no profit therein. ²⁴ Envy and wrath shorten [a man's] days; And care brings old age before the time. ²⁵ A cheerful and good heart ‖ Will have a care of his meat and diet.

CHAPTER 31

¹ Wakefulness that comes of riches consumes the flesh, ‖ And the anxiety thereof puts away sleep. ² Wakeful anxiety will crave slumber; And in a severe disease sleep will be broken. ³ A rich man toils in gathering money together; And when he rests, he is filled with his good things. ⁴ A poor man toils in lack of substance; And when he rests, he becomes needy. ⁵ He that loves gold will not be justified; And he that follows destruction will himself have his fill [of it]. ⁶ Many have been given over to ruin for the sake of gold; And their perdition meets them face to face. ⁷ It is a stumbling block to those who sacrifice to it; And every fool will be taken with that. ⁸ Blessed is the rich who is found without blemish, ‖ And who does not go after gold. ⁹ Who is he? And we will call him blessed; For he has done wonderful things among his people. ¹⁰ Who has been tried by it, and found perfect? Then let him glory. Who has had the power to transgress, and has not transgressed? And to do evil, and has not done it? ¹¹ His goods will be made sure, ‖ And the congregation will declare his alms. ¹² Do you sit at a great table? Do not be greedy on it, ‖ And do not say, "There are many things on it." ¹³ Remember that an evil eye is a wicked thing: What has been created more evil than an eye? Therefore, it sheds tears from every face. ¹⁴ Do not stretch your hand wherever it looks ‖ And do not thrust yourself with it into the dish. ¹⁵ Consider your neighbor's [liking] by your own; And be discreet in every point. ¹⁶ Eat, as [becomes] a man, ‖ Those things which are set before you; And do not eat greedily, lest you be hated. ¹⁷ Be first to leave off for manners' sake; And do not be insatiable, lest you offend. ¹⁸ And if you sit among

many, || Do not reach out your hand before them. [19] How sufficient to a well-mannered man is a very little, || And he does not breathe hard on his bed. [20] Healthy sleep comes of moderate eating; He rises early, and his wits are with him: The pain of wakefulness, and colic, and griping, || Are with an insatiable man. [21] And if you have been forced to eat, || Rise up in the midst thereof, and you will have rest. [22] Hear me, my son, and do not despise me, || And at the end you will find my words [true]: In all your works be quick, || And no disease will come to you. [23] Him that is liberal of his meat the lips will bless; And the testimony of his excellence will be believed. [24] The city will murmur at he who is stingy with his meat; And the testimony of his stinginess will be sure. [25] Do not show yourself valiant in wine, || For wine has destroyed many. [26] The furnace proves the temper [of steel] by dipping; So does wine [prove] hearts in the quarreling of the proud. [27] Wine is as good as life to men, || If you drink it in its measure: What life is there to a man that is without wine? And it has been created to make men glad. [28] Wine drunk in season, to satisfy, || Is joy of heart and gladness of soul: [29] Wine drunk abundantly is bitterness of soul, || With provocation and conflict. [30] Drunkenness increases the rage of a fool to his hurt; It diminishes strength and adds wounds. [31] Do not rebuke your neighbor at a banquet of wine, || Neither set him at nothing in his mirth; Do not speak a word of reproach to him, || And do not press on him by asking back [a debt].

CHAPTER 32

[1] Have they made you ruler [of a feast]? Do not be lifted up; Be among them as one of them; Take thought for them, and so sit down. [2] And when you have done all your office, take your place, || That you may be gladdened on their account, || And receive a crown for your well ordering. [3] Speak, you that are the elder, || For it is suitable for you, [but] with sound knowledge; And do not hinder music. [4] Do not pour out talk where there is a performance of music, || And do not display your wisdom out of season. [5] [As] a signet of carbuncle in a setting of gold, || [So] is a concert of music in a banquet of wine. [6] [As] a signet of emerald in a work of gold, || [So] is a strain of music with pleasant wine. [7] Speak, young man, if there is need of you; [Yet] scarcely if you be twice asked. [8] Sum up your speech, many things in few words; Be as one that knows and yet holds his tongue. [9] [If you be] among great men, || Do not behave as their equal; And when another is speaking, || Do not make much babbling. [10] Lightning speeds before thunder; And before a modest man favor will go out. [11] Rise up on time and do not be the last; Get home quickly and do not loiter: [12] Take your pastime there and do what is in your heart; And do not sin by proud speech: [13] And for these things bless Him that made you || And gives you to drink freely of His good

things. [14] He that fears the LORD will receive [His] discipline; And those who seek [Him] early will find favor. [15] He that seeks the Law will be filled with that, || But the hypocrite will stumble at that. [16] They that fear the LORD will find judgment || And will kindle righteous acts as a light. [17] A sinful man shuns reproof || And will find a judgment according to his will. [18] A man of counsel will not neglect a thought; A strange and proud man will not crouch in fear, || Even after he has done a thing by himself without counsel. [19] Do nothing without counsel; And when you have once done [it], || Do not convert [from it]. [20] Do not go in a way of conflict; And do not stumble in stony places. [21] Do not be confident in a smooth way. [22] And beware of your own children. [23] In every work trust your own soul; For this is the keeping of the commands. [24] He that believes the Law gives heed to the command; And he that trusts in the LORD will suffer no loss.

CHAPTER 33

[1] No evil will happen to him that fears the LORD, || But in temptation He will once again deliver him. [2] A wise man will not hate the Law; But he that is a hypocrite therein is as a ship in a storm. [3] A man of understanding will put his trust in the Law; And the Law is faithful to him, || As when one asks at the oracle. [4] Prepare [your] speech, and so will you be heard; Bind up instruction and make your answer. [5] The heart of a fool is [as] a cartwheel; And his thoughts like a rolling axle-tree. [6] A stallion horse is as a mocking friend; He neighs under everyone that sits on him. [7] Why does one day excel [over] another, || When all the light of every day in the year is of the sun? [8] By the knowledge of the LORD they were distinguished; And He varied seasons and feasts: [9] Some of them He exalted and hallowed, || And some of them He has made ordinary days. [10] And all men are from the ground, || And Adam was created of earth. [11] In the abundance of His knowledge the LORD distinguished them || And made their ways various: [12] Some of them He blessed and exalted, || And some of them He hallowed and brought near to Himself; Some of them He cursed and brought low, || And overthrew them from their place. [13] As the clay of the potter in his hand, || All his ways are according to his good pleasure; So men are in the hand of Him that made them, || To render to them according to His judgment. [14] Good is the opposite of evil, || And life is the opposite of death; So the sinner is the opposite of the godly. [15] And so look on all the works of the Most High: Two and two, one against another. [16] And I awoke last, as one that gleans after the grape gatherers: By the blessing of the LORD I got before them, || And filled my winepress as one that gathers grapes. [17] Consider that I did not labor for myself alone, || But for all those who seek instruction. [18] Hear me, you great men of the people, || And listen with your ears, you rulers of the congregation. [19] To son

and wife, to brother and friend, ‖ Do not give power over yourself while you live; And do not give your goods to another, ‖ Lest you convert and make supplication for them [again]. ²⁰ While you yet live, and breath is in you, ‖ Do not give yourself over to anybody. ²¹ For it is better that your children should supplicate you, ‖ Than that you should look to the hand of your sons. ²² In all your works keep the upper hand; Do not bring a stain on your honor. ²³ In the day that you end the days of your life, ‖ And in the time of death, distribute your inheritance. ²⁴ Fodder, a stick, and burdens, for a donkey; Bread, and discipline, and work, for a servant. ²⁵ Set your servant to work, and you will find rest: Leave his hands idle, and he will seek liberty. ²⁶ Yoke and thong will bow the neck: And for an evil servant there are racks and tortures. ²⁷ Send him to labor, that he may not be idle; For idleness teaches much mischief. ²⁸ Set him to work, as is fit for him; And if he does not obey, make his chains heavy. ²⁹ And do not be excessive toward any; And do nothing without judgment. ³⁰ If you have a servant, let him be as yourself, ‖ Because you have bought him with blood. ³¹ If you have a servant, treat him as yourself, ‖ For you will have need of him as your own soul: If you treat him ill, and he departs and runs away, ‖ Which way will you go to seek him?

CHAPTER 34

¹ Vain and false hopes are for a man void of understanding; And dreams give wings to fools. ² As one that catches at a shadow, ‖ And follows after the wind, ‖ So is he that sets his mind on dreams. ³ The vision of dreams is [as] this thing against that, ‖ The likeness of a face near a face. ⁴ Of an unclean thing what will be cleansed? And of that which is false what will be true? ⁵ Divinations, and soothsayings, and dreams, are vain: And the heart has fantasies, as a woman's in travail. ⁶ If they are not sent from the Most High in [your] visitation, ‖ Do not give your heart to them. ⁷ For dreams have led many astray: And they have failed by putting their hope in them. ⁸ Without lying the Law will be accomplished; And wisdom is perfection to a faithful mouth. ⁹ A well-instructed man knows many things; And he that has much experience will declare understanding. ¹⁰ He that has no experience knows few things, ‖ But he that has wandered will increase [his] skill. ¹¹ In my wandering I have seen many things; And my understanding is more than my words. ¹² I was often in danger even to death; And I was preserved because of these things. ¹³ The spirit of those that fear the LORD will live; For their hope is on Him that saves them. ¹⁴ Whoever fears the LORD will not be afraid ‖ And will not play the coward; For He is his hope. ¹⁵ Blessed is the soul of him that fears the LORD: To whom does he give heed? And who is his stay? ¹⁶ The eyes of the LORD are on those who love Him, ‖ A mighty protection and strong stay, ‖ A cover from the hot blast, and a cover from the noonday, ‖ A guard from stumbling, and a help from falling. ¹⁷ He raises up the soul, and enlightens the eyes: He gives healing, life, and blessing. ¹⁸ He that sacrifices of a thing wrongfully gotten—His offering is made in mockery; And the mockeries of wicked men are not well-pleasing. ¹⁹ The Most High has no pleasure in the offerings of the ungodly; Neither is He pacified for sins by the multitude of sacrifices. ²⁰ [As] one that kills the son before his father's eyes ‖ Is he that brings a sacrifice from the goods of the poor. ²¹ The bread of the needy is the life of the poor: He that deprives him thereof is a man of blood. ²² [As] one that slays his neighbor ‖ Is he that takes away his living; And [as] a shedder of blood ‖ Is he that deprives a hireling of his hire. ²³ One building, and another pulling down— What profit have they had but toil? ²⁴ One praying, and another cursing—Whose voice will the LORD listen to? ²⁵ He that washes himself after [touching] a dead body, and touches it again—What profit does he have in his washing? ²⁶ Even so a man fasting for his sins, and going again, and doing the same—Who will listen to his prayer? And what profit does he have in his humiliation?

CHAPTER 35

¹ He that keeps the Law multiplies offerings; He that takes heed to the commands sacrifices a peace offering. ² He that returns a favor offers fine flour; And he that gives alms sacrifices a thank offering. ³ To depart from wickedness is a thing pleasing to the LORD; And to depart from unrighteousness is an atoning sacrifice. ⁴ See that you do not appear in the presence of the LORD empty. ⁵ For all these things [are to be done] because of the command. ⁶ The offering of the righteous makes the altar fat; And the sweet savor thereof [is] before the Most High. ⁷ The sacrifice of a righteous man is acceptable; And the memorial thereof will not be forgotten. ⁸ Glorify the LORD with a good eye, ‖ And do not limit the first-fruits of your hands. ⁹ In every gift show a cheerful countenance ‖ And dedicate your tithe with gladness. ¹⁰ Give to the Most High according as He has given; And as your hand has found, [give] with a good eye. ¹¹ For the LORD rewards, ‖ And He will reward you sevenfold. ¹² Do not think to corrupt with gifts, ‖ For He will not receive them: And do not set your mind on an unrighteous sacrifice, ‖ For the LORD is judge, ‖ And with Him is no respect of persons. ¹³ He will not accept any person against a poor man; And He will listen to the prayer of him that is wronged. ¹⁴ He will in no way despise the supplication of the fatherless; Nor the widow, when she pours out her tale. ¹⁵ Do the tears of the widow not run down her cheek? And is her cry not against him that has caused them to fall? ¹⁶ He that serves [God] according to His good pleasure will be accepted, ‖ And his supplication will reach to the clouds. ¹⁷ The prayer of the humble pierces the

clouds; And until it comes near, he will not be comforted; And he will not depart, until the Most High will visit; And He will judge righteously and execute judgment. ¹⁸ And the LORD will not be slack, || Neither will He be patient toward them, || Until He has crushed the loins of the unmerciful; And He will repay vengeance to the heathen, || Until He has taken away the multitude of the arrogant, || And broken in pieces the scepters of the unrighteous; ¹⁹ Until He has rendered to [every] man according to his doings, || And [to] the works of men according to their plans; Until He has judged the cause of His people; And He will make them to rejoice in His mercy. ²⁰ Mercy is seasonable in the time of His afflicting [them], || As clouds of rain in the time of drought.

CHAPTER 36

¹ Have mercy on us, O LORD the God of all, and behold; ² And send Your fear on all the nations: ³ Lift up Your hand against the strange nations; And let them see Your mighty power. ⁴ As You were sanctified in us before them, || So be magnified in them before us. ⁵ And let them know You, as we also have known You, || That there is no God but only You, O God. ⁶ Show new signs and work various wonders; Glorify Your hand and Your right arm. ⁷ Raise up indignation, and pour out wrath; Take away the adversary, and destroy the enemy. ⁸ Hasten the time and remember the oath; And let them declare Your mighty works. ⁹ Let him that escapes be devoured by the rage of fire; And may those who harm Your people find destruction. ¹⁰ Crush the heads of the rulers of the enemies, || That say, "There is none but us." ¹¹ Gather all the tribes of Jacob together, || And take them for Your inheritance, as from the beginning. ¹² O LORD, have mercy on the people that is called by Your Name, || And on Israel, whom You did liken to a firstborn. ¹³ Have compassion on the city of Your sanctuary: Jerusalem, the place of Your rest. ¹⁴ Fill Zion; exalt Your oracles || And [fill] Your people with Your glory. ¹⁵ Give testimony to those that were Your creatures in the beginning || And raise up the prophecies that have been in Your Name. ¹⁶ Give reward to those who wait for You: And men will put their trust in Your prophets. ¹⁷ Listen, O LORD, to the prayer of Your suppliants, || According to the blessing of Aaron concerning Your people; And all those who are on the earth will know || That You are the LORD, the perpetual God. ¹⁸ The belly will eat any meat; Yet one meat is better than another. ¹⁹ The mouth tastes meats taken in hunting; So does an understanding heart false speeches. ²⁰ A contrary heart will cause heaviness: And a man of experience will reward him. ²¹ A woman will receive any man; But one daughter is better than another. ²² The beauty of a woman cheers the countenance; And a man desires nothing so much. ²³ If there is mercy and meekness on her tongue, || Her husband is not like the sons of men. ²⁴ He that gets a wife enters on a possession: A help appropriate for him, and a pillar of rest. ²⁵ Where no hedge is, the possession will be laid waste; And he that has no wife will mourn as he wanders up and down. ²⁶ For who will trust a nimble robber || Who skips from city to city? Even so, [who will trust] a man that has no nest, || And [who] lodges wherever he finds himself at nightfall?

CHAPTER 37

¹ Every friend will say, "I am also his friend," || But there is a friend who is only a friend in name. ² Is there not a grief in it even to death, || When a companion and friend is turned to enmity? ³ O wicked imagination, from where did you come, || Rolling in to cover the dry land with deceitfulness? ⁴ There is a companion who rejoices in the gladness of a friend, || But in time of affliction will be against him. ⁵ There is a companion who for the belly's sake labors with his friend, || [But] in the face of battle will take up the buckler. ⁶ Do not forget a friend in your soul; And do not be unmindful of him in your riches. ⁷ Every counselor extols counsel; But there is [one] who counsels for himself. ⁸ Let your soul beware of a counselor || And know beforehand what his interest is, || For he will take counsel for himself; Lest he casts the lot on you, ⁹ And says to you, "Your way is good": And he will stand near you, || To see what will happen to you. ¹⁰ Take no counsel with one that looks suspiciously at you; And hide your counsel from such as are jealous of you. ¹¹ [Take no counsel] with a woman about her rival; Neither with a coward about war; Nor with a merchant about exchange; Nor with a buyer about selling; Nor with an envious man about thankfulness; Nor with an unmerciful man about kindness; Nor with a sluggard about any kind of work; Nor with a hireling in your house about finishing [his work]; Nor with an idle servant about much business: Give no heed to these in any matter of counsel, ¹² But rather be continually with a godly man, || Whom you will have known to be a keeper of the commands, || Who in his soul is as your own soul, || And who will grieve with you, if you will miscarry. ¹³ And make the counsel of your heart to stand; For there is none more faithful to you than it. ¹⁴ For a man's soul is sometimes accustomed to bring him tidings—More than seven watchmen that sit up high on a watchtower. ¹⁵ And above all this, entreat the Most High, || That He may direct your way in truth. ¹⁶ Let reason be the beginning of every work, || And let counsel go before every action. ¹⁷ As a token of the changing of the heart, ¹⁸ Four manner of things rise up: Good and evil, life and death; And that which rules over them continually is the tongue. ¹⁹ There is one that is shrewd [and] the instructor of many, || And yet is unprofitable to his own soul. ²⁰ There is [one] that is subtle in words and is hated; He will be destitute of all food: ²¹ For grace was not given to him

from the LORD, || Because he is deprived of all wisdom. ²² There is one that is wise to his own soul, || And the fruits of his understanding are trustworthy in the mouth. ²³ A wise man will instruct his own people, || And the fruits of his understanding are trustworthy. ²⁴ A wise man will be filled with blessing, || And all those who see him will call him happy. ²⁵ The life of man is counted by days, || And the days of Israel are innumerable. ²⁶ The wise man will inherit confidence among his people, || And his name will live forever. ²⁷ My son, prove your soul in your life, || And see what is evil for it, and do not give that to it. ²⁸ For all things are not profitable for all men, || Neither does every soul have pleasure in everything. ²⁹ Do not be insatiable in any luxury, || And do not be greedy in the things that you eat. ³⁰ For in multitude of meats there will be disease, || And gorging will come near to colic. ³¹ Because of gorging many have perished; But he that takes heed will prolong his life.

CHAPTER 38

¹ Honor a physician according to your need [of him] || With the honors due to him; For the LORD has truly created him. ² For from the Most High comes healing; And from the king he will receive a gift. ³ The skill of the physician will lift up his head; And in the sight of great men he will be admired. ⁴ The LORD created medicines out of the earth; And a prudent man will have no disgust at them. ⁵ Was water not made sweet with wood, || That the virtue thereof might be known? ⁶ And He gave men skill, || That they might be glorified in His marvelous works. ⁷ With them He heals [a man and] takes away his pain. ⁸ With these the apothecary will make a confection; And his works will not be brought to an end; And from him is peace on the face of the earth. ⁹ My son, in your sickness do not be negligent; But pray to the LORD, and He will heal you. ¹⁰ Put away wrongdoing, || And order your hands correctly, || And cleanse your heart from all manner of sin. ¹¹ Give a sweet savor, and a memorial of fine flour; And make fat your offering, as one that is not. ¹² Then give place to the physician, || For the LORD has truly created him; And do not let him go from you, for you have need of him. ¹³ There is a time when in their very hands is the issue for good. ¹⁴ For they will also implore the LORD, || That He may prosper them in [giving] relief and in healing for the maintenance of life. ¹⁵ He that sins before his Maker, || Let him fall into the hands of the physician. ¹⁶ My son, let your tears fall over the dead, || And as one that suffers grievously begin lamentation; And wind up his body according to his due, || And do not neglect his burial. ¹⁷ Make bitter weeping, and make passionate wailing, || And let your mourning be according to his merit—For one day or two, || Lest you be spoken evil of: And so be comforted for your sorrow. ¹⁸ For of sorrow comes death, || And sorrow of heart will bow down the strength. ¹⁹ In calamity sorrow also remains: And the poor man's life is grievous to the heart. ²⁰ Do not give your heart to sorrow. Put it away, remembering the latter end. ²¹ Do not forget it, || For there is no returning again: You will not profit him, || And you will hurt yourself. ²² Remember the sentence on him; For so yours will also be; Yesterday for me, and today for you. ²³ When the dead is at rest, || Let his remembrance rest; And be comforted for him, || When his spirit departs from him. ²⁴ The wisdom of the scribe comes by opportunity of leisure; And he that has little business will become wise. ²⁵ How will he become wise that holds the plow, || That glories in the shaft of the goad, || That drives oxen, and is occupied in their labors, || And whose discourse is of the stock of bulls? ²⁶ He will set his heart on turning his furrows; And his wakefulness is to give his heifers their fodder. ²⁷ So is every craftsman and master workman, || That passes his time by night as by day; They that cut gravings of signets, || And his diligence is to make great variety; He will set his heart to preserve likeness in his portraiture || And will be wakeful to finish his work. ²⁸ So is the smith sitting by the anvil and considering the unworked iron: The vapor of the fire will waste his flesh; And in the heat of the furnace he will wrestle [with his work]: The noise of the hammer will be ever in his ear, || And his eyes are on the pattern of the vessel; He will set his heart on perfecting his works, || And he will be wakeful to adorn them perfectly. ²⁹ So is the potter sitting at his work, || And turning the wheel around with his feet, || Who is always anxiously set at his work, || And all his handiwork is by number; ³⁰ He will fashion the clay with his arm || And will bend its strength in front of his feet; He will apply his heart to finish the glazing; And he will be wakeful to make clean the furnace. ³¹ All these put their trust in their hands; And each becomes wise in his own work. ³² Without these a city will not be inhabited, || And men will not sojourn nor walk up and down [therein]. ³³ They will not be sought for in the council of the people, || And in the assembly, they will not mount on high; They will not sit on the seat of the judge, || And they will not understand the covenant of judgment: Neither will they declare instruction and judgment; And where allegories are, they will not be found. ³⁴ But they will maintain the fabric of the world; And in the handiwork of their craft is their prayer.

CHAPTER 39

¹ Not so he that has applied his soul || And meditates in the Law of the Most High; He will seek out the wisdom of all the ancients || And will be occupied in prophecies. ² He will keep the discourse of the men of renown || And will enter in amidst the subtleties of allegories. ³ He will seek out the hidden meaning of proverbs || And be conversant in the dark sayings of allegories. ⁴ He will serve among great men || And

appear before him that rules. He will travel through the land of strange nations; For he has tried good things and evil among men. ⁵He will apply his heart to return early to the LORD that made him, ‖ And will make supplication before the Most High, ‖ And will open his mouth in prayer, ‖ And will make supplication for his sins. ⁶If the great LORD wills, ‖ He will be filled with the spirit of understanding: He will pour out the words of his wisdom, ‖ And in prayer give thanks to the LORD. ⁷He will direct his counsel and knowledge, ‖ And in His secrets he will meditate. ⁸He will show out the instruction which he has been taught ‖ And will glory in the Law of the covenant of the LORD. ⁹Many will commend his understanding; And so long as the world endures, ‖ It will not be blotted out: His memorial will not depart, ‖ And his name will live from generation to generation. ¹⁰Nations will declare his wisdom, ‖ And the congregation will tell out his praise. ¹¹If he continues, he will leave a greater name than one thousand, ‖ And if he dies, he adds to that. ¹²Yet more I will utter, which I have thought on; And I am filled as the moon at the full. ¹³Listen to me, you holy children, ‖ And bud out as a rose growing by a brook of water: ¹⁴And give a sweet savor as frankincense, ‖ And put out flowers as a lily; Spread abroad a sweet smell, ‖ And sing a song of praise; Bless the LORD for all His works. ¹⁵Magnify His Name, and give utterance to His praise ‖ With the songs of your lips, and with harps; And so will you say when you utter [His praise]: ¹⁶"All the works of the LORD are exceedingly good, ‖ And every command will be [accomplished] in his season." ¹⁷None can say, "What is this? What is that?" For in his season they will all be sought out. At His word the waters stood as a heap, ‖ And the receptacles of waters at the word of His mouth. ¹⁸At His command all His good pleasure is [done]; And there is none that will hinder His salvation. ¹⁹The works of all flesh are before Him; And it is not possible to be hid from His eyes. ²⁰He sees from age to age; And there is nothing wonderful before Him. ²¹None can say, "What is this? What is that?" For all things are created for their uses. ²²His blessing covered the dry land as a river ‖ And saturated it as a flood. ²³As He has made the waters salty, ‖ So the heathen will inherit His wrath. ²⁴His ways are plain to the holy, ‖ So are they stumbling blocks to the wicked. ²⁵Good things are created from the beginning for the good, ‖ So are evil things for sinners. ²⁶The chief of all things necessary for the life of man ‖ Are water, and fire, and iron, and salt, ‖ And flour of wheat, and honey, and milk, ‖ The blood of the grape, and oil, and clothing. ²⁷All these things are for good to the godly; So to the sinners they will be turned into evil. ²⁸There are winds that are created for vengeance, ‖ And in their fury their scourges lay on heavily; In the time of consummation they pour out their strength ‖ And will appease the wrath of Him that made them. ²⁹Fire, and hail, and famine, and death—All these are created for vengeance— ³⁰Teeth of wild beasts, and scorpions and adders, ‖ And a sword punishing the ungodly to destruction. ³¹They will rejoice in His command, ‖ And will be made ready on earth when there is need; And in their seasons they will not transgress [His] word. ³²Therefore, I was resolved from the beginning, ‖ And I considered [this, and] left it in writing; ³³All the works of the LORD are good: And He will supply every need in its season. ³⁴And none can say, "This is worse than that," ‖ For they will all be well approved in their season. ³⁵And now with all your heart and mouth ‖ Sing praises and bless the Name of the LORD.

CHAPTER 40

¹Great travail is created for every man, ‖ And a heavy yoke is on the sons of Adam, ‖ From the day of their coming out from their mother's womb, ‖ Until the day for their burial in the mother of all things. ²The expectation of things to come, and the day of death, ‖ [Trouble] their thoughts, and [cause] fear of heart— ³From him that sits on a lofty throne, ‖ Even to him that is humbled in earth and ashes; ⁴From him that wears purple and a crown, ‖ Even to him that is clothed with a hempen gown. ⁵[There is] wrath, and jealousy, and trouble, and disquiet, ‖ And fear of death, and anger, and strife; And in the time of rest on his bed ‖ His night sleep changes his knowledge. ⁶Little or nothing is his resting, ‖ And afterward in his sleep, as in a day of keeping watch, ‖ He is troubled in the vision of his heart, ‖ As one that has escaped from the front of battle. ⁷In the very time of his deliverance he awakens, ‖ And marvels that the fear is nothing. ⁸[It is so] with all flesh, from man to beast, ‖ And on sinners sevenfold more. ⁹Death, and bloodshed, and strife, and sword, ‖ Calamities, famine, suffering, and the scourge— ¹⁰All these things were created for the wicked, ‖ And because of them the flood came. ¹¹All things that are of the earth return to the earth again, ‖ And [all things that are] of the waters return into the sea. ¹²All bribery and injustice will be blotted out; And good faith will stand forever. ¹³The goods of the unjust will be dried up like a river, ‖ And like a great thunder in rain will go off in noise. ¹⁴In opening his hands, [a man] will be made glad; So will transgressors utterly fail. ¹⁵The children of the ungodly will not put out many branches; And [they are as] unclean roots on a sheer rock. ¹⁶The sedge [that grows] on every water and bank of a river ‖ Will be plucked up before all grass. ¹⁷Bounty is as a garden of blessings, ‖ And kindness endures forever. ¹⁸The life of one that labors, and is content, will be made sweet; And he that finds a treasure is above both. ¹⁹Children and the building of a city establish a name; And a blameless wife is counted above both. ²⁰Wine and music make the heart rejoice; And the love of wisdom is above both. ²¹The pipe and the lute

make pleasant melody; And a pleasant tongue is above both. ²² Your eye will desire grace and beauty; And above both—the green blade of corn. ²³ A friend and a companion never meet wrongly; And a wife with her husband is above both. ²⁴ Brothers and help are for a time of affliction; And kindness is a deliverer above both. ²⁵ Gold and silver will make the foot stand sure; And counsel is esteemed above them both. ²⁶ Riches and strength will lift up the heart; And the fear of the LORD is above both: There is nothing lacking in the fear of the LORD, ‖ And there is no need to seek help therein. ²⁷ The fear of the LORD is as a garden of blessing ‖ And [it] covers a man above all glory. ²⁸ My son, do not lead a beggar's life; It is better to die than to beg. ²⁹ A man that looks to the table of another, ‖ His life is not to be counted for a life; He will pollute his soul with another man's meats, ‖ But a man wise and well-instructed will beware thereof. ³⁰ In the mouth of the shameless, begging will be sweet; And in his belly a fire will be kindled.

CHAPTER 41

¹ O death, how bitter is the remembrance of you ‖ To a man that is at peace in his possessions, ‖ To the man that has nothing to distract him, ‖ And [who] has prosperity in all things, ‖ And who still has strength to receive meat! ² O death, your sentence is acceptable to a man that is needy, ‖ And that fails in strength, that is in extreme old age, ‖ And is distracted about all things, and is perverse, and has lost patience! ³ Do not be afraid of the sentence of death; Remember those who have been before you, ‖ And that come after: This is the sentence from the LORD over all flesh. ⁴ And why do you refuse, ‖ When it is the good pleasure of the Most High? Whether it be ten, or one hundred, or one thousand years, ‖ There is no inquisition of life in the grave. ⁵ The children of sinners are abominable children, ‖ And they frequent the dwellings of the ungodly. ⁶ The inheritance of sinners' children will perish, ‖ And a perpetual reproach will be with their posterity. ⁷ Children will complain of an ungodly father, ‖ Because they will be reproached for his sake. ⁸ Woe to you, ungodly men, ‖ Which have forsaken the Law of the Most High God! ⁹ If you are born, you will be born to a curse; If you die, a curse will be your portion. ¹⁰ All things that are of the earth will go back to the earth; So the ungodly will go from a curse to perdition. ¹¹ The mourning of men is about their bodies, ‖ But the name of sinners being evil will be blotted out. ¹² Have regard for your name, ‖ For it continues with you longer than one thousand great treasures of gold. ¹³ A good life has its number of days; And a good name continues forever. ¹⁴ My children, keep instruction in peace, ‖ But wisdom that is hid, and a treasure that is not seen, ‖ What profit is in them both? ¹⁵ Better is a man that hides his foolishness ‖ Than a man that hides his wisdom. ¹⁶ Why show reverence to my word, ‖ For it

is not good to retain every kind of shame; And not all things are approved by all in good faith. ¹⁷ Be ashamed of whoredom before father and mother, ‖ And of a lie before a prince and a mighty man; ¹⁸ Of an offense before a judge and ruler; Of iniquity before the congregation and the people; Of unjust dealing before a partner and friend; ¹⁹ And of theft in regard of the place where you sojourn, ‖ And in regard of the truth of God and His covenant; And of leaning with your elbow at meat; And of vulgarity in the matter of giving and taking; ²⁰ And of silence before those who salute you; And of looking on a woman that is a prostitute; ²¹ And of turning your face away from a relative; Of taking away a portion or a gift; And of gazing on a woman that has a husband; ²² Of being over-busy with his maid—And do not come near her bed; Of scolding speeches before friends; And after you have given, do not scold; ²³ Of repeating and speaking what you have heard; And of revealing of secrets. ²⁴ So you will be truly modest and find favor in the sight of every man.

CHAPTER 42

¹ Do not be ashamed of these things, ‖ And accept no man's person to sin [by it]: ² Of the Law of the Most High, and His covenant; And of judgment to do justice to the ungodly; ³ Of reckoning with a partner and with travelers; And of a gift from the heritage of friends; ⁴ Of exactness of balance and weights; And of getting much or little; ⁵ Of indifferent selling of merchants; And of much correction of children; And of making the side of an evil servant to bleed. ⁶ Keeping a seal is good where an evil wife is; And where many hands are, shut [things] closed. ⁷ Whatever you hand over, ‖ Let it be by number and weight; And in giving and receiving, ‖ Let all be in writing. ⁸ [Do not be ashamed] to instruct the unwise and foolish, ‖ And one of extreme old age that contends with those that are young; And so you will be well instructed indeed, ‖ And approved in the sight of every living man. ⁹ A daughter is a secret cause of wakefulness to a father; And the care for her puts away sleep in her youth, ‖ Lest she pass the flower of her age; And when she is married, ‖ Lest she should be hated; ¹⁰ In her virginity, ‖ Lest she should be defiled ‖ And be with child in her father's house; And when she has a husband, ‖ Lest she should transgress; And when she is married, ‖ Lest she should be barren. ¹¹ Keep a strict watch over a headstrong daughter, ‖ Lest she makes you a laughing-stock to your enemies, ‖ A byword in the city and notorious among the people, ‖ And shame you before the multitude. ¹² Do not look on everybody in regard of beauty ‖ And do not sit in the midst of women; ¹³ For from garments comes a moth, ‖ And from a woman a woman's wickedness. ¹⁴ Better is the wickedness of a man ‖ Than a pleasant-dealing woman, ‖ And a woman which puts you to shameful reproach. ¹⁵ I will now

make mention of the works of the LORD || And will declare the things that I have seen: In the words of the LORD are His works. ¹⁶ The sun that gives light looks on all things; And the work of the LORD is full of His glory. ¹⁷ The LORD has not given power to the saints || To declare all His marvelous works, || Which the Almighty LORD firmly settled, || That whatever exists might be established in His glory. ¹⁸ He searches out the deep, and the heart, || And He has understanding of their cunning plans; For the Most High knows all knowledge, || And He looks into the signs of the world, ¹⁹ Declaring the things that are past, || And the things that will be, || And revealing the traces of hidden things. ²⁰ No thought escapes Him; There is no word hidden from Him. ²¹ He has ordered the mighty works of His wisdom—[He] who is from age to age: Nothing has been added to them, || Nor diminished from them; And He had no need of any counselor. ²² How desirable are all His works! One may behold [this] even to a spark. ²³ All these things live and remain forever in all manner of uses, || And they are all obedient. ²⁴ All things are double—one against another: And He has made nothing imperfect. ²⁵ One thing establishes the good things of another; And who will be filled with beholding His glory?

CHAPTER 43

¹ The pride of the height is the expanse in its clearness, || The appearance of Heaven, in the spectacle of its glory. ² The sun when he appears, || Bringing tidings as he goes out, || Is a marvelous instrument, the work of the Most High: ³ At his noon he dries up the country, || And who will stand against his burning heat? ⁴ A man blowing a furnace is in works of heat, || [But] the sun [is] three times more: Burning up the mountains, || Breathing out fiery vapors, || And sending out bright beams—he dims the eyes. ⁵ Great is the LORD that made him; And at His word he hastens his course. ⁶ The moon is also in all things for her season, || For a declaration of times, and a sign of the world. ⁷ From the moon is the sign of the feast day—A light that wanes when she has come to the full. ⁸ The month is called after her name, || Increasing wonderfully in her changing; An instrument of the army on high, || Shining out in the expanse of Heaven; ⁹ The beauty of Heaven, the glory of the stars, || An ornament giving light in the highest places of the LORD. ¹⁰ At the word of the Holy One they will stand in due order, || And they will not faint in their watches. ¹¹ Look on the rainbow and praise Him that made it— Exceedingly beautiful in the brightness thereof. ¹² It encircles the Heaven around with a circle of glory; The hands of the Most High have stretched it. ¹³ By His command He makes the snow to fall speedily || And swiftly sends the lightnings of His judgment. ¹⁴ By reason thereof the treasure-houses are opened; And clouds fly out as birds. ¹⁵ By His mighty power He makes the clouds strong, || And the hailstones are broken small: ¹⁶ And at His appearing the mountains will be shaken, || And at His will the south wind will blow. ¹⁷ The voice of His thunder makes the earth to travail; So does the northern storm and the whirlwind. As birds flying down, He sprinkles the snow; And as the lighting of the locust is the falling down thereof: ¹⁸ The eye will marvel at the beauty of its whiteness, || And the heart will be astonished at the raining of it. ¹⁹ He also pours the hoarfrost on the earth as salt; And when it is congealed, it is [as] points of thorns. ²⁰ The cold north wind will blow, || And the ice will be congealed on the water: It will lodge on every gathering of water, || And the water will put it on as [if] it were a breastplate. ²¹ It will devour the mountains, and burn up the wilderness, || And consume the green herb as fire. ²² A mist coming speedily is the healing of all things; A dew coming after heat will bring cheerfulness. ²³ By His counsel He has stilled the deep, || And planted islands therein. ²⁴ They that sail on the sea tell of the danger thereof; And when we hear it with our ears, we marvel. ²⁵ Therein are also those strange and wondrous works, || A variety of all that has life—the race of sea-monsters. ²⁶ By reason of Him his end has success, || And by His word all things consist. ²⁷ We may say many things, || Yet we will not attain [to them]; And the sum of our words is, "He is all." ²⁸ How will we have strength to glorify Him? For He Himself is the great one above all His works. ²⁹ The LORD is terrible and exceedingly great; And His power is marvelous. ³⁰ When you glorify the LORD, || Exalt Him as much as you can; For even yet He will exceed: And when you exalt Him, put out your full strength: Do not be weary, for you will never attain. ³¹ Who has seen Him, that he may declare Him? And who will magnify Him as He is? ³² Many things are hidden greater than these; For we have seen but a few of His works. ³³ For the LORD made all things; And He gave wisdom to the godly.

CHAPTER 44

¹ Let us now praise famous men, || And our fathers that became the father of us. ² The LORD manifested [in them] great glory, || [Even] His mighty power from the beginning: ³ Such as bore rule in their kingdoms, || And were men renowned for their power, || Giving counsel by their understanding; Such as have brought tidings in prophecies; ⁴ Leaders of the people by their counsels, || And by their understanding [men of] learning for the people—Wise [were] their words in their instruction; ⁵ Such as sought out musical tunes, || And set out verses in writing; ⁶ Rich men furnished with ability, || Living peaceably in their habitations: ⁷ All these were honored in their generations, || And were a glory in their days. ⁸ There is of them, that have left a name behind them, || To declare their praises. ⁹ And there are some which have no memorial, || Who have perished as though they had not been || And have

become as though they had not been born—And their children after them. ¹⁰But these were men of mercy, || Whose righteous deeds have not been forgotten. ¹¹A good inheritance will remain with their seed continually; Their children [are] within the covenants. ¹²Their seed stands fast, || And their children for their sakes. ¹³Their seed will remain forever, || And their glory will not be blotted out. ¹⁴Their bodies were buried in peace, || And their name lives to all generations. ¹⁵Peoples will declare their wisdom, || And the congregation tells out their praise. ¹⁶Enoch pleased the Lord, and was translated, || [Being] an example of conversion to all generations. ¹⁷Noah was found perfect [and] righteous; In the season of wrath, he was taken in exchange [for the world]; Therefore a remnant was left to the earth when the flood came. ¹⁸Perpetual covenants were made with him, || That all flesh should no longer be blotted out by a flood. ¹⁹Abraham was a great father of a multitude of nations; And there was none found like him in glory, ²⁰Who kept the Law of the Most High || And was taken into covenant with Him: In his flesh he established the covenant; And when he was tested, he was found faithful. ²¹Therefore He assured him by an oath, || That the nations should be blessed in his seed; That He would multiply him as the dust of the earth, || And exalt his seed as the stars, || And cause them to inherit from sea to sea, || And from the River to the utmost part of the earth. ²²In Isaac He also established likewise, for his father Abraham's sake, || The blessing of all men, and the covenant: ²³And He made it rest on the head of Jacob; He acknowledged him in His blessings, || And gave to him by inheritance, and divided his portions; He parted them among [the] twelve tribes.

CHAPTER 45

¹And He brought out of him a man of mercy, || Which found favor in the sight of all flesh; A man beloved of God and men—Even Moses, whose memorial is blessed. ²He made him like to the glory of the saints || And magnified him in the fears of his enemies. ³By his words He caused the wonders to cease; He glorified him in the sight of kings; He gave him command for his people || And showed him part of His glory. ⁴He sanctified him in his faithfulness and meekness; He chose him out of all flesh. ⁵He made him to hear His voice, || And led him into the thick darkness, || And gave him commands face to face—Even the law of life and knowledge, || That he might teach Jacob the covenant, || And Israel His judgments. ⁶He exalted Aaron, a holy man like to him, || Even his brother, of the tribe of Levi. ⁷He established a perpetual covenant for him || And gave him the priesthood of the people; He beautified him with attractive ornaments || And girded him around with a robe of glory. ⁸He clothed him with the perfection of exultation, || And strengthened him with apparel of

honor: The linen trousers, the long robe, and the ephod. ⁹And He compassed him with pomegranates of gold, || And with many bells around—To send out a sound as he went, || To make a sound that might be heard in the temple, || For a memorial to the children of his people— ¹⁰With a holy garment, || With gold, and blue, and purple, the work of the embroiderer, || With an oracle of judgment, || With the Lights and Perfections; ¹¹With twisted scarlet, the work of the craftsman, || With precious stones graven like a signet, || In a setting of gold, the work of the jeweler, || For a memorial engraved in writing, || After the number of the tribes of Israel; ¹²With a crown of gold on the miter, || Having graven on it, as on a signet, Holiness, || An ornament of honor, a work of might, || The desires of the eyes, attractive and beautiful. ¹³There have never been any such before him; No stranger put them on, || But his sons only, and his offspring perpetually. ¹⁴His sacrifices will be wholly consumed every day—twice continually. ¹⁵Moses consecrated him and anointed him with holy oil: It was to him for a perpetual covenant, || And to his seed, all the days of Heaven, || To minister to Him, and also to execute the priest's office, || And to bless His people in His Name. ¹⁶He chose him out of all living to offer sacrifice to the Lord, || Incense, and a sweet savor, for a memorial, || To make reconciliation for Your people. ¹⁷He gave His commands to him—Authority in the covenants of judgments, || To teach Jacob the testimonies, || And to enlighten Israel in His law. ¹⁸Strangers gathered themselves together against him, || And envied him in the wilderness, || [Even] Dathan and Abiram with their company, || And the congregation of Korah, with wrath and anger. ¹⁹The Lord saw it, and it displeased Him; And in the wrath of His anger they were destroyed: He did wonders on them, || To consume them with flaming fire. ²⁰And He added glory to Aaron and gave him a heritage: He divided to him the first-fruits of the increase; [And] first he prepared bread in abundance: ²¹For they will eat the sacrifices of the Lord, || Which He gave to him and to his seed. ²²However, in the land of the people he will have no inheritance, || And he has no portion among the people; For He Himself is your portion [and] inheritance. ²³And Phinehas the son of Eleazar is the third in glory, || In that he was zealous in the fear of the Lord, || And stood fast in the good forwardness of his soul when the people turned away, || And he made reconciliation for Israel. ²⁴Therefore there was a covenant of peace established for him, || [That he should be] leader of the saints and of His people; That he and his seed should have the dignity of the priesthood forever. ²⁵Also [He made] a covenant with David the son of Jesse, of the tribe of Judah; The inheritance of the king is his alone from son to son; So the inheritance of Aaron is also to his seed. ²⁶[God] give you wisdom in your heart to judge His people in righteousness, || That their good things may not be abolished, || And [that] their glory [may endure] for all their generations.

CHAPTER 46

¹ Joshua the son of Nun was valiant in war || And was the successor of Moses in prophecies: Who according to his name was made great for the saving of God's chosen ones, || To take vengeance of the enemies that rose up against them, || That he might give Israel their inheritance. ² How he was glorified in lifting up his hands, || And in stretching out his sword against the cities! ³ Who before him so stood fast? For the Lord Himself brought his enemies to him. ⁴ Did the sun not go back by his hand? And did one day not become as two? ⁵ He called on the Most High [and] Mighty One, || When his enemies pressed him around; And the great Lord heard him. ⁶ With hailstones of mighty power || He caused war to break violently on the nation, || And in the going down he destroyed those who resisted, || That the nations might know his armor, || How that he fought in the sight of the Lord; For he followed after the Mighty One. ⁷ Also in the time of Moses he did a work of mercy—He and Caleb the son of Jephunneh, || In that they withstood the adversary, || Hindered the people from sin, || And stilled the murmuring of wickedness. ⁸ And of six hundred thousand people on foot, || They two alone were preserved to bring them into the heritage, || Even into a land flowing with milk and honey. ⁹ Also the Lord gave strength to Caleb, || And it remained with him to his old age, || So that he entered on the height of the land, || And his seed obtained it for a heritage: ¹⁰ That all the sons of Israel might see || That it is good to walk after the Lord. ¹¹ Also the judges, everyone by His Name—All whose hearts did not go whoring, || And who did not turn away from the Lord—May their memorial be blessed, ¹² May their bones again flourish out of their place, || And may the name of those who have been honored be renewed on their children. ¹³ Samuel, the prophet of the Lord, beloved of his Lord, || Established a kingdom, and anointed princes over His people. ¹⁴ By the Law of the Lord he judged the congregation, || And the Lord visited Jacob. ¹⁵ By his faithfulness he was proved to be a prophet, || And by his words he was known to be faithful in vision. ¹⁶ Also when his enemies pressed around him, || He called on the Lord, the Mighty One, || With the offering of the sucking lamb. ¹⁷ And the Lord thundered from Heaven, || And made His voice to be heard with a mighty sound. ¹⁸ And He utterly destroyed the rulers of the Tyrians, || And all the princes of the Philistines. ¹⁹ Also before the time of his long sleep || He made protestations in the sight of the Lord and [His] anointed: "I have not taken any man's goods, so much as a sandal": And no man did accuse him. ²⁰ And after he fell asleep, he prophesied, || And showed the king his end, || And lifted up his voice

from the earth in prophecy, || To blot out the wickedness of the people.

CHAPTER 47

¹ And after him, Nathan rose up to prophesy in the days of David. ² As is the fat when it is separated from the peace offering, || So was David [separated] from the sons of Israel. ³ He played with lions as with kids, || And with bears as with lambs of the flock. ⁴ In his youth did he not kill a giant, || And take away reproach from the people, || When he lifted up his hand with a sling stone, || And beat down the boasting of Goliath? ⁵ For he called on the Most High Lord; And He gave him strength in his right hand, || To kill a man mighty in war, || To exalt the horn of His people. ⁶ So they glorified him for [his] tens of thousands, || And praised him for the blessings of the Lord, || In that there was given to him a diadem of glory. ⁷ For he destroyed the enemies on every side, || And brought to nothing the Philistines his adversaries, || [And] broke their horn in pieces to this day. ⁸ In every work of his || He gave thanks to the Holy One Most High with words of glory; With his whole heart he sang praise || And loved Him that made him. ⁹ He also set singers before the altar, || So as to make sweet melody by their music. ¹⁰ He gave beauty to the feasts, || And set in order the seasons to perfection, || While they praised His holy Name, || And the sanctuary sounded from early morning. ¹¹ The Lord took away his sins, || And exalted his horn forever, || And gave him a covenant of kings, || And a throne of glory in Israel. ¹² After him, [his] son rose up—a man of understanding; And for his sake he lived at large. ¹³ Solomon reigned in days of peace; And God gave to him rest around, || That he might set up a house for His Name || And prepare a sanctuary forever. ¹⁴ How wise you were made in your youth || And filled as a river with understanding! ¹⁵ Your soul covered the earth, || And you filled it with dark allegories. ¹⁶ Your name reached to the isles far off; And you were beloved for your peace. ¹⁷ For your songs, and proverbs, and allegories, || And for your interpretations, the countries marveled at you. ¹⁸ By the Name of the Lord God, which is called the God of Israel, || You gathered gold as tin and multiplied silver as lead. ¹⁹ You bowed your loins to women, || And in your body you were brought into subjection. ²⁰ You blemished your honor and profaned your seed, || To bring wrath on your children; And I was grieved for your folly, ²¹ So that the sovereignty was divided, || And out of Ephraim a disobedient kingdom ruled. ²² But the Lord will never forsake His mercy; And He will not destroy any of His works, || Nor blot out the posterity of His chosen ones; And the seed of him that loved Him He will not take away; And He gave a remnant to Jacob, || And to David a root out of him. ²³ And [so] rested Solomon with his fathers; And of his seed he left behind him Rehoboam—[Even] the

foolishness of the people, || And one that lacked understanding, || Who made the people to revolt by his counsel. Also Jeroboam the son of Nebat, || Who made Israel to sin, and gave to Ephraim a way of sin. ²⁴ And their sins were multiplied exceedingly, || To remove them from their land. ²⁵ For they sought out all manner of wickedness, || Until vengeance should come on them.

CHAPTER 48

¹ Also there arose Elijah the prophet as fire, || And his word burned like a torch: ² Who brought a famine on them, || And by his zeal made them few in number. ³ By the word of the Lᴏʀᴅ he shut up the Heaven: Three times he so brought down fire. ⁴ How you were glorified, O Elijah, in your wondrous deeds! And who will [have] glory like to you? ⁵ Who raised up a dead man from death, || And from the place of the dead, by the word of the Most High; ⁶ Who brought down kings to destruction, || And honorable men from their bed; ⁷ Who heard rebuke in Sinai, || And judgments of vengeance in Horeb; ⁸ Who anointed kings for retribution, || And prophets to succeed after him; ⁹ Who was taken up in a tempest of fire, || In a chariot of fiery horses; ¹⁰ Who was recorded for reproofs in their seasons, || To pacify anger, before it broke out into wrath; To turn the heart of the father to the son, || And to restore the tribes of Jacob. ¹¹ Blessed are those who saw you, || And those who have been beautified with love; For we also will surely live. ¹² [It was] Elijah who was wrapped in a tempest, || And Elisha was filled with his spirit; And in [all] his days he was not moved by [the fear of] any ruler, || And no one brought him into subjection. ¹³ Nothing was too high for him; And when he was laid on sleep his body prophesied. ¹⁴ As in his life he did wonders, || So in death his works were marvelous. ¹⁵ For all this the people did not convert, || And they did not depart from their sins, || Until they were carried away as a plunder from their land || And were scattered through all the earth; And the people were left very few in number, || And a ruler [was left] in the house of David. ¹⁶ Some of them did that which was pleasing [to God], || [And] some multiplied sins. ¹⁷ Hezekiah fortified his city || And brought in water into the midst of them: He dug the sheer rock with iron || And built up wells for waters. ¹⁸ In his days Sennacherib came up, || And sent Rabshakeh, and departed; And he lifted up his hand against Zion || And boasted great things in his arrogance. ¹⁹ Then their hearts and their hands were shaken, || And they were in pain, as women in travail; ²⁰ And they called on the Lᴏʀᴅ, who is merciful, || Spreading out their hands to Him: And the Holy One heard them speedily out of Heaven, || And delivered them by the hand of Isaiah. ²¹ He struck the camp of the Assyrians, || And His messenger utterly destroyed them. ²² For Hezekiah did that which was pleasing to the Lᴏʀᴅ || And was strong in the ways of his father David, || Which Isaiah the prophet commanded, || Who was great and faithful in his vision. ²³ In his days the sun went backward; And he added life to the king. ²⁴ He saw by an excellent spirit what should come to pass at the end; And he comforted those who mourned in Zion. ²⁵ He showed the things that should be to the end of time, || And the hidden things before they came.

CHAPTER 49

¹ The memorial of Josiah is like the composition of incense || Prepared by the work of the apothecary: It will be sweet as honey in every mouth, || And as music at a banquet of wine. ² He behaved himself uprightly in the conversion of the people || And took away the abominations of iniquity. ³ He set his heart right toward the Lᴏʀᴅ; In the days of wicked men, || He made godliness to prevail. ⁴ Except David, and Hezekiah, and Josiah, all committed trespass; For they forsook the Law of the Most High; The kings of Judah failed. ⁵ For they gave their power to others, || And their glory to a strange nation. ⁶ They set the chosen city of the sanctuary on fire, || And made her streets desolate, [as it was written] by the hand of Jeremiah. ⁷ For they mistreated him; And yet he was sanctified in the womb to be a prophet, || To root out, and to afflict, and to destroy; [And] in like manner to build and to plant. ⁸ [It was] Ezekiel who saw the vision of glory, || Which [God] showed him on the chariot of the cherubim. ⁹ For truly he remembered the enemies in storm, || And to do good to those who directed their ways correctly. ¹⁰ Also of the twelve prophets || May the bones flourish again out of their place. And he comforted Jacob and delivered them by confidence of hope. ¹¹ How will we magnify Zerubbabel? And he was as a signet on the right hand: ¹² So was Jesus the son of Josedek: Who in their days built the house, || And exalted a people holy to the Lᴏʀᴅ, prepared for continuous glory. ¹³ Also of Nehemiah the memorial is great: Who raised up for us the walls that were fallen, || And set up the gates and bars, and raised up our homes again. ¹⁴ No man was created on the earth such as was Enoch; For he was taken up from the earth. ¹⁵ Neither was there a man born like to Joseph, || A governor of his countrymen, a support of the people: Yes, his bones were visited. ¹⁶ Shem and Seth were glorified among men; And above every living thing in the creation is Adam.

CHAPTER 50

¹ [It was] Simon, the son of Onias, the great priest, || Who in his life repaired the house, || And in his days strengthened the temple: ² And by him was built from the foundation the height of the double [wall], || The lofty underworks of the enclosure of the temple: ³ In his days the cistern of waters was diminished, || The brazen vessel in compass as the sea. ⁴ [It was] he that

took thought for his people that they should not fall || And fortified the city against besieging; ⁵ How glorious was he when the people gathered around him || At his coming out of the sanctuary— ⁶ As the morning star in the midst of a cloud, || As the moon at the full; ⁷ As the sun shining out on the temple of the Most High, || And as the rainbow giving light in clouds of glory; ⁸ As the flower of roses in the days of new [fruits], || As lilies at the water spring, || As the shoot of the frankincense tree in the time of summer; ⁹ As fire and incense in the censer, || As a vessel all of beaten gold, || Adorned with all manner of precious stones; ¹⁰ As an olive tree budding out fruits, || And as a cypress growing high among the clouds. ¹¹ When he took up the robe of glory, || And put on the perfection of exultation, || In the ascent of the holy altar, || He made the precinct of the sanctuary glorious. ¹² And when he received the portions out of the priests' hands, || Himself also standing by the hearth of the altar, || His countrymen as a garland around him, || He was as a young cedar in Libanus; And as stems of palm trees compassed around him, ¹³ And all the sons of Aaron in their glory, || And the LORD's offering in their hands, || Before all the congregation of Israel. ¹⁴ And finishing the service at the altars, || That he might adorn the offering of the Most High, the Almighty, ¹⁵ He stretched out his hand to the cup, || And poured out the cup of the grape; He poured out at the foot of the altar || A sweet smelling savor to the Most High, the King of all. ¹⁶ Then the sons of Aaron shouted, || They sounded the trumpets of beaten work, || They made a great noise to be heard, || For a remembrance before the Most High. ¹⁷ Then all the people hurried together || And fell down on the earth on their faces to worship their Lord—The Almighty, God Most High. ¹⁸ The singers also praised Him with their voices; In the whole house sweet melody was made. ¹⁹ And the people implored the LORD Most High, || In prayer before Him that is merciful, || Until the worship of the LORD should be ended; And so, they accomplished His service. ²⁰ Then he went down and lifted up his hands || Over the whole congregation of the sons of Israel, || To give blessing to the LORD with his lips, || And to glory in His Name. ²¹ And he bowed himself down in worship the second time, || To declare the blessing from the Most High. ²² And now bless the God of all, who everywhere does great things, || Who exalts our days from the womb, || And deals with us according to His mercy. ²³ May He grant us joyfulness of heart, || And that peace may be in our days in Israel for the days of [the] age: ²⁴ To entrust His mercy with us; And let Him deliver us in His time! ²⁵ With two nations is my soul vexed, || And the third is no nation: ²⁶ They that sit on the mountain of Samaria, and the Philistines, || And that foolish people that dwells in Shechem. ²⁷ I have written in this scroll the instruction of understanding and knowledge, || I, Jesus, the son of Sirach Eleazar, of Jerusalem, || Who

out of his heart poured out wisdom. ²⁸ Blessed is he that will be exercised in these things; And he that lays them up in his heart will become wise. ²⁹ For if he does them, he will be strong for all things; For the light of the LORD is his guide.

CHAPTER 51

A PRAYER OF JESUS THE SON OF SIRACH. ¹ I will give thanks to You, O LORD, O King, || And will praise You, O God my Savior: I give thanks to Your Name, ² For You were my protector and helper, || And You delivered my body out of destruction, || And out of the snare of a slanderous tongue, || From lips that forge lies, || And were my helper before those who stood by; ³ And You delivered me, || According to the abundance of Your mercy, and [greatness] of Your Name, || From the gnashing [of teeth] ready to devour, || Out of the hand of such as sought my life, || Out of the manifold afflictions which I had; ⁴ From the choking of a fire on every side, || And out of the midst of fire which I did not kindle; ⁵ Out of the depth of the belly of the grave, || And from an unclean tongue, and from lying words— ⁶ The slander of an unrighteous tongue to the king. My soul drew near even to death, || And my life was near to the grave beneath. ⁷ They compassed me on every side, || And there was none to help [me]. I was looking for the help of men, and it was not. ⁸ And I remembered Your mercy, O LORD, || And Your working which has been from perpetuity, || How You deliver those who wait for You, || And save them out of the hand of the enemies. ⁹ And I lifted up my supplication from the earth || And prayed for deliverance from death. ¹⁰ I called on the LORD, the Father of my Lord, || That He would not forsake me in the days of affliction, || In the time when there was no help against the proud. ¹¹ I will praise Your Name continually || And will sing praise with thanksgiving; And my supplication was heard: ¹² For You saved me from destruction, || And delivered me from the evil time. Therefore, I will give thanks and praise to You, || And bless the Name of the LORD. ¹³ When I was yet young, before I went abroad, || I sought wisdom openly in my prayer. ¹⁴ Before the temple I asked for her, || And I will seek her out even to the end. ¹⁵ From [her] flower, as from the ripening grape, || My heart delighted in her; My foot trod in uprightness, || From my youth I tracked her out. ¹⁶ I bowed my ear down a little, and received her, || And found for myself much instruction. ¹⁷ I profited in her: To Him that gives me wisdom I will give glory. ¹⁸ For I purposed to practice her, || And I was zealous for that which is good; And I will never be put to shame. ¹⁹ My soul has wrestled in her, || And in my doing I was exact: I spread out my hands to the Heaven above || And mourned my ignorance of her. ²⁰ I set my soul properly to her, || And in pureness I found her. I got myself a heart [joined] with her from the beginning: Therefore, I will not be forsaken. ²¹ My inward part was also troubled to seek her: Therefore, I have gotten a good possession. [22] The LORD gave me a tongue for my reward; And I will praise Him with that. [23] Draw near to me, you unlearned, || And lodge in the house of instruction. [24] Say, "Why are you lacking in these things, || And your souls are very thirsty?" [25] I opened my mouth, and spoke, || "Get her for yourselves without money. [26] Put your neck under the yoke, || And let your soul receive instruction: She is hard at hand to find. [27] Behold with your eyes, how that I labored but a little, || And found for myself much rest. [28] Get instruction with a great sum of silver || And gain much gold by her. [29] May your soul rejoice in His mercy, || And may you not be put to shame in praising Him. [30] Work your work before the time comes, || And in His time, He will give you your reward."

1 BARUCH

Called Baruch by most, but 1 Baruch in the LSV for distinction, the opening verses ascribe the book to the well-known assistant to Jeremiah (Jer. 32:12; 36:4, 32; 45:1). It is a collection of four very different compositions, ending with a work entitled "The Letter of Jeremiah," which circulated separately in major manuscripts of the Greek tradition. The original language was likely Hebrew, but only the Greek and other versions have been preserved. The setting is Babylon, where Baruch reads his scroll to King Jechoniah (Jehoiachin) and the exiles; they react by sending gifts and the scroll to Jerusalem (1:1–14), presumably by the hand of Baruch (1:7). No certain date can be given for the book, but it may have been edited in final form during the last two centuries BC.

CHAPTER 1

¹ These are the words of the scroll, which Baruch the son of Neriah, the son of Mahseiah, the son of Zedekiah, the son of Hasadiah, the son of Hilkiah, wrote in Babylon, ² in the fifth year, [and] in the seventh day of the month, at the time the Chaldeans took Jerusalem, and burned it with fire. ³ And Baruch read the words of this scroll in the hearing of Jehoiachin the son of Jehoiakim king of Judah, and in the hearing of all the people that came to [hear] the scroll, ⁴ and in the hearing of the mighty men, and of the kings' sons, and in the hearing of the elders, and in the hearing of all the people, from the least to the greatest, even of all those who lived at Babylon by the River Sud. ⁵ And they wept, and fasted, and prayed before the LORD; ⁶ they also made a collection of money according to every man's power: ⁷ and they sent [it] to Jerusalem to Jehoiakim the [high] priest, the son of Hilkiah, the son of Salom, and to the priests, and to all the people which were found with him at Jerusalem, ⁸ at the same time when he took the vessels of the house of the LORD, that had been carried out of the temple, to return [them] into the land of Judah, the tenth day of the [month] Sivan, [namely,] silver vessels, which Zedekiah the son of Josiah king of Judah had made, ⁹ after Nebuchadnezzar king of Babylon had carried away Jehoiachin, and the princes, and the captives, and the mighty men, and the people of the land, from Jerusalem, and brought them to Babylon. ¹⁰ And they said: "Behold, we have sent you money; therefore buy with the money burnt-offerings, and sin offerings, and incense, and prepare an oblation, and offer on the altar of the LORD our God; ¹¹ and pray for the life of Nebuchadnezzar king of Babylon, and for the life of his son Belshazzar, that their days may be as the days of Heaven above the earth: ¹² and the LORD will give us strength, and lighten our eyes, and we will live under the shadow of Nebuchadnezzar king of Babylon, and under the shadow of his son Belshazzar, and we will serve them many days, and find favor in their sight. ¹³ Pray for us also to the LORD our God, for we have sinned against the LORD our God; and to this day the wrath of the LORD and His indignation is not turned from us. ¹⁴ And you will read this scroll which we have sent to you, to make confession in the house of the LORD, on the day of the feast and on the days of the solemn assembly." ¹⁵ And you will say: To the LORD our God [belongs] righteousness, but to us confusion of face, as at this day, to the men of Judah, and to the inhabitants of Jerusalem, ¹⁶ and to our kings, and to our princes, and to our priests, and to our prophets, and to our fathers: ¹⁷ for that we have sinned before the LORD, ¹⁸ and disobeyed Him, and have not listened to the voice of the LORD our God, to walk in the commands of the LORD that He has set before us: ¹⁹ since the day that the LORD brought our fathers out of the land of Egypt, to this present day, we have been disobedient to the LORD our God, and we have dealt unadvisedly in not listening to His voice. ²⁰ Why the plagues cleaved to us, and the curse, which the LORD commanded Moses His servant [to pronounce] in the day that He brought our fathers out of the land of Egypt, to give us a land that flows with milk and honey, as at this day. ²¹ Nevertheless, we did not listen to the voice of the LORD our God, according to all the words of the prophets, whom He sent to us, ²² but we walked—every man—in the imagination of his own wicked heart, to serve strange gods, and to do that which is evil in the sight of the LORD our God.

CHAPTER 2

¹ Therefore the LORD has made good His word, which He pronounced against us, and against our judges that judged Israel, and against our kings, and against our princes, and against the men of Israel and Judah, ² to bring on us great plagues, such as never happened under the whole Heaven, as it came to pass in Jerusalem, according to the things that are written in the Law of Moses; ³ That we should eat—every man—the flesh of his own son, and every man the flesh of his own daughter. ⁴ Moreover, He has given them to be in subjection to all the kingdoms that are around us, to be a reproach and a desolation among all the surrounding people, where the LORD has scattered them. ⁵ So were they cast down, and not exalted, because we sinned against the LORD our God, in not listening to His voice. ⁶ To the LORD our God [belongs] righteousness, but to us and to our fathers confusion of face, as at this day. ⁷ [For] all these

plagues have come on us, which the LORD has pronounced against us. [8] Yet we have not entreated the favor of the LORD, in turning everyone from the thoughts of his wicked heart. [9] Therefore the LORD has kept watch over the plagues, and the LORD has brought [them] on us; for the LORD is righteous in all His works which He has commanded us. [10] Yet we have not listened to His voice, to walk in the commands of the LORD that He has set before us. [11] And now, O LORD, You God of Israel, that have brought Your people out of the land of Egypt with a mighty hand, and with signs, and with wonders, and with great power, and with a high arm, and have gotten Yourself a Name, as at this day: [12] O LORD our God, we have sinned, we have been ungodly, we have dealt unrighteously in all Your ordinances. [13] Let Your wrath turn from us, for we are but a few left among the heathen, where You have scattered us. [14] Hear our prayer, O LORD, and our petition, and deliver us for Your own sake, and give us favor in the sight of them which have led us away captive, [15] that all the earth may know that You are the LORD our God, because Israel and his posterity is called by Your Name. [16] O LORD, look down from Your holy house, and consider us: incline Your ear, O LORD, and hear: [17] open Your eyes, and behold, for the dead that are in the grave, whose breath is taken from their bodies, will give to the LORD neither glory nor righteousness: [18] but the soul that is greatly vexed, which goes stooping and feeble, and the eyes that fail, and the hungry soul, will give You glory and righteousness, O LORD. [19] For we do not present our supplication before You, O LORD our God, for the righteousness of our fathers, and of our kings. [20] For You have sent Your wrath and Your indignation on us, as You have spoken by Your servants the prophets, [saying,] [21] "The LORD says, Bow your shoulders to serve the king of Babylon, and remain in the land that I gave to your fathers. [22] But if you will not hear the voice of the LORD, to serve the king of Babylon, [23] I will cause to cease out of the cities of Judah, and from the region near Jerusalem, the voice of mirth, and the voice of gladness, the voice of the bridegroom, and the voice of the bride: and the whole land will be desolate without inhabitant." [24] But we would not listen to Your voice, to serve the king of Babylon: therefore You have made good Your words that You spoke by Your servants the prophets, [namely,] that the bones of our kings, and the bones of our fathers, should be taken out of their places. [25] And behold, they are cast out to the heat by day, and to the frost by night, and they died in great miseries by famine, by sword, and by pestilence. [26] And the house which is called by Your Name have You laid [waste], as at this day, for the wickedness of the house of Israel and the house of Judah. [27] Yet, O LORD our God, You have dealt with us after all Your kindness, and according to all Your great mercy, [28] as You spoke by Your servant Moses in the day when You commanded him to write Your law before the sons of Israel, saying, [29] "If you will not hear My voice, surely this very great multitude will be turned into a small [number] among the nations, where I will scatter them. [30] For I know that they will not hear Me, because it is a stiff-necked people, but in the land of their captivity they will take it to heart, [31] and will know that I am the LORD their God: and I will give them a heart, and ears to hear: [32] and they will praise Me in the land of their captivity, and think on My Name, [33] and will return from their stiff neck, and from their wicked deeds, for they will remember the way of their fathers, which sinned before the LORD. [34] And I will bring them again into the land which I swore to their fathers, to Abraham, to Isaac, and to Jacob, and they will be lords of it: and I will increase them, and they will not be diminished. [35] And I will make a perpetual covenant with them to be their God, and they will be My people: and I will no longer remove My people Israel out of the land that I have given them."

CHAPTER 3

[1] O LORD Almighty, You God of Israel, the soul in anguish, the troubled spirit, cries to You. [2] Hear, O LORD, and have mercy; for You are a merciful God: yes, have mercy on us, because we have sinned before You. [3] For You sit [as king] forever, and we perish forevermore. [4] O LORD Almighty, You God of Israel, hear now the prayer of the dead Israelites, and of the children of them which were sinners before You, that did not listen to the voice of You their God, for this reason these plagues cleaved to us. [5] Do not remember the iniquities of our fathers, but remember Your power and Your Name [now] at this time. [6] For You are the LORD our God, and You, O LORD, will we praise. [7] For this reason You have put Your fear in our hearts, to the intent that we should call on Your Name, and we will praise You in our captivity, for we have called to mind all the iniquity of our fathers, that sinned before You. [8] Behold, we are yet this day in our captivity, where You have scattered us, for a reproach and a curse, and to be subject to penalty, according to all the iniquities of our fathers, which departed from the LORD our God. [9] Hear, O Israel, the commands of life: give ear to understand wisdom. [10] How is it, O Israel, that you are in your enemies' land, that you have become old in a strange country, that you are defiled with the dead, [11] that you are counted with those who [go down] into the grave? [12] You have forsaken the fountain of wisdom. [13] [For] if you had walked in the way of God, you should have dwelled in peace forever. [14] Learn where is wisdom, where is strength, where is understanding; that you may also know where is length of days, and life, where is the light of the eyes, and peace. [15] Who has found out her place? And who has come into her treasuries?

¹⁶ Where are the princes of the heathen, and such as ruled the beasts that are on the earth; ¹⁷ those who had their pastime with the birds of the air, and those who hoarded up silver and gold, wherein men trust; and of whose getting there is no end? ¹⁸ For those who made in silver, and were so careful, and whose works are past finding out, ¹⁹ they are vanished and gone down to the grave, and others have come up in their steads. ²⁰ Younger men have seen the light and lived on the earth, but the way of knowledge they have not known, ²¹ neither did they understand the paths thereof, neither have their children embraced it: they are far off from their way. ²² It has not been heard of in Canaan, neither has it been seen in Teman. ²³ The sons also of Agar that seek understanding, which are in the land, the merchants of Merran and Teman, and the authors of fables, and the searchers out of understanding; none of these have known the way of wisdom or remembered her paths. ²⁴ O Israel, how great is the house of God! And how large is the place of His possession! ²⁵ [It is] great, and has no end; high, and unmeasurable. ²⁶ There were the giants born that were famous of old, great of stature, [and] expert in war. ²⁷ God did not choose these, nor did He give the way of knowledge to them; ²⁸ so they perished, because they had no wisdom, they perished through their own foolishness. ²⁹ Who has gone up into Heaven, and taken her, and brought her down from the clouds? ³⁰ Who has gone over the sea, and found her, and will bring her for choice gold? ³¹ There is none that knows her way, nor any that comprehends her path. ³² But He that knows all things knows her, He found her out with His understanding: He that prepared the earth forevermore has filled it with four-footed beasts: ³³ He that sends out the light, and it goes; He called it, and it obeyed Him with fear: ³⁴ and the stars shone in their watches, and were glad when He called them, they said, "Here we are." They shone with gladness to Him that made them. ³⁵ This is our God, [and] there will none other be accounted of in comparison of Him. ³⁶ He has found out all the way of knowledge, and has given it to His servant Jacob, and to Israel that is beloved of Him. ³⁷ Afterward she appeared on earth and was conversant with men.

CHAPTER 4

¹ This is the scroll of the commands of God, and the law that endures forever: All those who hold it fast [are appointed] to life; but such as leave it will die. ² Turn, O Jacob, and take hold of it: walk toward her shining in the presence of the light thereof. ³ Do not give your glory to another, nor the things that are profitable to you to a strange nation. ⁴ O Israel, happy are we, for the things that are pleasing to God are made known to us. ⁵ Be of good cheer, my people, the memorial of Israel. ⁶ You were sold to the nations, [but] not for destruction: because you moved God to wrath, you were delivered to your adversaries. ⁷ For

you provoked Him that made you by sacrificing to demons, and not to God. ⁸ You forgot the perpetual God that brought you up; you also grieved Jerusalem that nursed you. ⁹ For she saw the wrath that has come on you from God, and said, "Listen, you [women] that dwell about Zion, for God has brought on me great mourning; ¹⁰ for I have seen the captivity of my sons and daughters, which the Perpetual has brought on them. ¹¹ For with joy I nourished them, but sent them away with weeping and mourning. ¹² Let no man rejoice over me, a widow, and forsaken of many, for the sins of my children I am left desolate, because they turned away from the law of God, ¹³ and had no regard to His statutes, neither did they walk in the ways of God's commands, nor trod in the paths of discipline in His righteousness. ¹⁴ Let those who dwell about Zion come, and remember the captivity of my sons and daughters, which the Perpetual has brought on them. ¹⁵ For He has brought a nation on them from far, a shameless nation, and of a strange language, who neither gave reverence to old man, nor pitied child. ¹⁶ And they have carried away the dear beloved sons of the widow and left her that was alone desolate of her daughters. ¹⁷ But I—how can I help you? ¹⁸ For He that brought these plagues on you will deliver you from the hand of your enemies. ¹⁹ Go your way, O my children, go your way, for I am left desolate. ²⁰ I have put off the garment of peace and put on myself the sackcloth of my petition: I will cry to the Perpetual as long as I live. ²¹ Be of good cheer, O my children, cry to God, and He will deliver you from the power and hand of the enemies. ²² For I have trusted in the Perpetual, that He will save you; and joy has come to me from the Holy One, because of the mercy which will soon come to you from your continuous Savior. ²³ For I sent you out with mourning and weeping, but God will give you to me again with joy and gladness forever. ²⁴ For like as now those who dwell about Zion have seen your captivity, so they will shortly see your salvation from our God, which will come on you with great glory, and brightness of the Perpetual. ²⁵ My children, suffer patiently the wrath that has come on you from God, for your enemy has persecuted you; but shortly you will see his destruction, and will tread on their necks. ²⁶ My delicate ones have gone rough ways; they were taken away as a flock carried off by the enemies. ²⁷ Be of good cheer, O my children, and cry to God, for you will be remembered of Him that has brought [these things] on you. ²⁸ For as it was your mind to go astray from God, return and seek Him ten times more. ²⁹ For He that brought these plagues on you will bring you continuous joy again with your salvation." ³⁰ Be of good cheer, O Jerusalem, for He that called you by name will comfort you. ³¹ Miserable are those who afflicted you and rejoiced at your fall. ³² Miserable are the cities which your children served; miserable is she that received your sons. ³³ For as she rejoiced at your fall, and was glad of your ruin, so she will be grieved for her own desolation. [34] And I will take away her exultation in her great multitude, and her boasting will be turned into mourning. [35] For fire will come on her from the Perpetual, long to endure; and she will be inhabited of devils for a great time. [36] O Jerusalem look around you toward the east and behold the joy that comes to you from God. [37] Behold, your sons come, whom you sent away, they come gathered together from the east to the west at the word of the Holy One, rejoicing in the glory of God.

CHAPTER 5

[1] Put off, O Jerusalem, the garment of your mourning and affliction, and put on the beauty of the glory that [comes] from God forever. [2] Cast about you the robe of the righteousness which [comes] from God; set a diadem on your head of the glory of the Perpetual. [3] For God will show your brightness to every [region] under Heaven. [4] For your name will be called of God forever, THE PEACE OF RIGHTEOUSNESS, and, THE GLORY OF GODLINESS. [5] Arise, O Jerusalem, and stand on the height, and look around you toward the east, and behold your children gathered from the going down of the sun to the rising thereof at the word of the Holy One, rejoicing that God has remembered them. [6] For they went from you on foot, being led away of their enemies, but God brings them in to you, borne on high with glory, as [on] a royal throne. [7] For God has appointed that every high mountain, and the perpetual hills, should be made low, and the valleys filled up, to make plain the ground, that Israel may go safely in the glory of God. [8] Moreover the woods and every sweet-smelling tree have overshadowed Israel by the command of God. [9] For God will lead Israel with joy in the light of His glory with the mercy and righteousness that comes from Him.

CHAPTER 6

[1] A COPY OF A LETTER, WHICH JEREMIAH SENT TO THEM WHICH WERE TO BE LED CAPTIVES INTO BABYLON BY THE KING OF THE BABYLONIANS, TO CERTIFY THEM, AS IT WAS COMMANDED HIM OF GOD. [2] Because of the sins which you have committed before God, you will be led away captives to Babylon by Nebuchadnezzar king of the Babylonians. [3] So when you come to Babylon, you will remain there many years, and for a long season, even for seven generations: and after that I will bring you out peaceably from there. [4] But now you will see in Babylon gods of silver, and of gold, and of wood, borne on shoulders, which cause the nations to fear. [5] Beware, therefore, that you in no way become like to the strangers, neither let fear take hold on you because of them, when you see the multitude before them and behind them, worshiping them. [6] But say in your hearts, "O LORD, we must worship You." [7] For My messenger is with you, and I Myself care for your souls. [8] For their tongue is polished by the workman, and they themselves are overlaid with gold

and with silver; yet they are but false and cannot speak. [9] And taking gold, as it were for a virgin that loves to be happy, they make crowns for the heads of their gods: [10] and sometimes also the priests carry from their gods gold and silver and bestow it on themselves; [11] and will even give thereof to the common prostitutes: and they deck them as men with garments, [even] the gods of silver, and gods of gold, and of wood. [12] Yet these gods cannot save themselves from rust and moths, though they are covered with purple raiment. [13] They wipe their faces because of the dust of the temple, which is thick on them. [14] And he that cannot put to death one that offends against him holds a scepter, as though he were judge of a country. [15] He also has a dagger in his right hand, and an axe, but cannot deliver himself from war and robbers. [16] Whereby they are not known to be gods: therefore, do not fear them. [17] For like as a vessel that a man uses is worth nothing when it is broken, even so it is with their gods: when they are set up in the temples their eyes are full of dust through the feet of those who come in. [18] And as the courts are made sure on every side on him that offends the king, as being committed to suffer death, [even so] the priests make fast their temples with doors, with locks, and bars, lest they are carried off by robbers. [19] They light the candles, yes, more than for themselves, of which they cannot see one. [20] They are as one of the beams of the temple; and men say their hearts are eaten out, when things creeping out of the earth devour both them and their raiment: [21] they do not feel it when their faces are blackened through the smoke that comes out of the temple: [22] bats, swallows, and birds land on their bodies and heads; and in like manner the cats also. [23] Whereby you may know that they are no gods: therefore, do not fear them. [24] Notwithstanding the gold with which they are beset to make them beautiful, except one wipe off the rust, they will not shine, for not even when they were molten did they feel it. [25] Things wherein there is no breath are bought at any cost. [26] Having no feet, they are borne on shoulders, whereby they declare to men that they are worth nothing. [27] They also that serve them are ashamed, for if they fall to the ground at any time, they cannot rise up again of themselves; neither, if they are bowed down, can they make themselves straight, but the offerings are set before them, as if they were dead men. [28] And the things that are sacrificed to them, their priests sell and spend; and in like manner their wives also lay up part thereof in salt; but to the poor and to the impotent they will give nothing thereof. [29] The menstruous woman and the woman in childbirth touch their sacrifices, knowing, therefore, by these things, that they are not gods, [and so] do not fear them. [30] For how can they be called gods? Because women set meat before the gods of silver, gold, and wood. [31] And in their temples the priests sit on seats, having their clothes torn, and their heads and beards shaven, and nothing on their heads. [32] They roar and cry before their gods, as men do at the feast when one is dead. [33] The priests also take off garments from them and clothe their wives and children in addition. [34] Whether it be evil that one does to them, or good, they are not able to repay it: they can neither set up a king, nor put him down. [35] In like manner, they can neither give riches nor money; though a man makes a vow to them, and does not keep it, they will never exact it. [36] They can save no man from death, neither deliver the weak from the mighty. [37] They cannot restore a blind man to his sight, nor deliver any that is in distress. [38] They can show no mercy to the widow, nor do good to the fatherless. [39] They are like the stones that are [hewn] out of the mountain, [these gods] of wood, and that are overlaid with gold and with silver. Those who minister to them will be confounded. [40] How should a man then think or say that they are gods, when even the Chaldeans themselves dishonor them? [41] Who if they will see one mute that cannot speak, they bring him, and entreat him to call on Bel, as though he were able to understand. [42] Yet they cannot perceive this themselves and forsake them, for they have no understanding. [43] The women also with cords around them sit in the ways, burning bran for incense, but if any of them, drawn by some that passes by, lies with him, she reproaches her fellow, that she was not thought as worthy as herself, nor her cord broken. [44] Whatever is done among them is false. How should a man then think or say that they are gods? [45] They are fashioned by carpenters and goldsmiths—they can be nothing else than the workmen will have them to be. [46] And they themselves that fashioned them can never continue long; how then should the things that are fashioned by them? [47] For they have left lies and reproaches to those who come after. [48] For when there comes any war or plague on them, the priests consult with themselves, where they may be hidden with them. [49] How then can men not understand that they are not gods, which can neither save themselves from war, nor from plague? [50] For seeing they are but of wood, and overlaid with gold and with silver, it will be known hereafter that they are false; [51] and it will be manifest to all nations and kings that they are no gods, but the works of men's hands, and that there is no work of God in them. [52] Who then may not know that they are no gods? [53] For neither can they set up a king in a land, nor give rain to men. [54] Neither can they judge their own cause, nor redress a wrong, being unable, for they are as crows between the heavens and earth. [55] For even when fire falls on the house of gods of wood, or overlaid with gold or with silver, their priests will flee away, and escape, but they themselves will be burned apart like beams. [56] Moreover they cannot withstand any king or enemies. How should a man then allow or think that they are gods? [57] Neither are those gods of wood, and overlaid with silver or with gold, able to escape either from thieves or robbers. [58] Whose gold, and silver, and garments with which they are clothed, they that are strong will take from them, and go away with [them]; neither will they be able to help themselves. [59] Therefore it is better to be a king that shows his manhood, or else a vessel in a house profitable for that of which the owner will have need, than such false gods; or even a door in a house, to keep the things safe that are therein, than such false gods; or a pillar of wood in a palace, than such false gods. [60] For sun, and moon, and stars, being bright and sent to do their offices, are obedient. [61] Likewise also, the lightning when it glitters is fair to see; and after the same manner the wind also blows in every country. [62] And when God commands the clouds to go over the whole world, they do as they are told. [63] And the fire sent from above to consume mountains and woods does as it is commanded, but these are to be likened to them neither in show nor power. [64] Why a man should neither think nor say that they are gods, seeing they are neither able to judge causes, nor to do good to men. [65] Knowing, therefore, that they are not gods, do not fear them. [66] For they can neither curse nor bless kings; [67] neither can they show signs in the heavens among the nations, nor shine as the sun, nor give light as the moon. [68] The beasts are better than they, for they can get under a covert and help themselves. [69] In no way then is it manifest to us that they are gods. Therefore, do not fear them. [70] For as a scarecrow in a garden of cucumbers that keeps nothing, so are their gods of wood, and overlaid with gold and with silver. [71] Likewise also, their gods of wood, and overlaid with gold and with silver, are like to a white thorn in an orchard, that every bird sits on; as also to a dead body that is cast out into the dark. [72] And you will know them to be no gods by the bright purple that rots on them: And they themselves afterward will be consumed and will be a reproach in the country. [73] Better therefore is the just man that has no idols, for he will be far from reproach.

1 MACCABEES

The name Maccabee, probably meaning "hammer," is actually applied in the Books of Maccabees to only one man, Judas, third son of the priest Mattathias and first leader of the revolt against the Seleucid kings who persecuted the Jews (1 Mc. 2:4, 66; 2 Mc. 8:5, 16; 10:1, 16). Traditionally the name has come to be extended to the brothers of Judas, his supporters, and even to other Jewish heroes of the period, such as the seven brothers (2 Mc. 7). First Maccabees was written about 100 BC in Hebrew, but the original has not come down to us. Instead, we have an early, pre-Christian, Greek translation full of Hebrew idioms. The author, probably a Jew, is unknown. He was familiar with the traditions and sacred books of his people and had access to much reliable information on their recent history (from 175 to 134 BC). He may well have played some part in it himself in his youth. His purpose in writing is to record the deliverance of Israel that God worked through the family of Mattathias (5:62)—especially through his three sons, Judas, Jonathan, and Simon, and his grandson, John Hyrcanus.

CHAPTER 1

¹ It came to pass, after that Alexander the Macedonian, the son of Philip, who came out of the land of Chittim, and struck Darius king of the Persians and Medes, [it came to pass,] after he had struck him, that he reigned in his stead, in former time, over Greece. ² And he fought many battles, and won many strongholds, and killed the kings of the earth, ³ and went through to the ends of the earth and took spoils of a multitude of nations. And the earth was quiet before him, and he was exalted, and his heart was lifted up, ⁴ and he gathered together an exceedingly strong army, and ruled over countries and nations and principalities, and they became tributary to him. ⁵ And after these things he fell sick, and perceived that he should die. ⁶ And he called his servants, which were honorable, which had been brought up with him from his youth, and he divided to them his kingdom, while he was yet alive. ⁷ And Alexander reigned twelve years, and he died. ⁸ And his servants bare rule, each one in his place. ⁹ And they did all put diadems on themselves after that he was dead, and so did their sons after them many years: and they multiplied evils in the earth. ¹⁰ And there came out of them a sinful root, Antiochus Epiphanes, son of Antiochus the king, who had been a hostage at Rome, and he reigned in the one hundred and thirty-seventh year of the kingdom of the Greeks. ¹¹ In those days came there out of Israel transgressors of the law, and persuaded many, saying, let us go and make a covenant with the nations that are around us; for since we were parted from them many evils have befallen us. ¹² And the saying was good in their eyes. ¹³ And certain of the people were forward [here in] land went to the king, and he gave them license to do after the ordinances of the nations. ¹⁴ And they built a place of exercise in Jerusalem according to the laws of the nations; ¹⁵ and they made themselves uncircumcised, and forsook the holy covenant, and joined themselves to the nations, and sold themselves to do evil. ¹⁶ And the kingdom was well ordered in the sight of Antiochus, and he thought to reign over Egypt, that he might reign over the two kingdoms. ¹⁷ And he entered into Egypt with a great multitude, with chariots, and with elephants, and with horsemen, and with a great navy; ¹⁸ and he made war against Ptolemy king of Egypt; and Ptolemy was put to shame before him and fled; and many fell wounded to death. ¹⁹ And they got possession of the strong cities in the land of Egypt; and he took the spoils of Egypt. ²⁰ And Antiochus, after he had struck Egypt, returned in the one hundred and forty-third year, and went up against Israel and Jerusalem with a great multitude, ²¹ and entered presumptuously into the sanctuary, and took the golden altar, and the candlestick of the light, and all that pertained to that, ²² and the table of the Bread of the Presentation, and the cups to pour with, and the bowls, and the golden censers, and the veil, and the crowns, and the adorning of gold which was on the face of the temple, and he peeled it all off. ²³ And he took the silver and the gold and the precious vessels; and he took the hidden treasures which he found. ²⁴ And when he had taken all, he went away into his own land, and he made a great slaughter, and spoke very presumptuously. ²⁵ And there came great mourning on Israel, in every place where they were; ²⁶ and the rulers and elders groaned, the virgins and young men were made feeble, and the beauty of the women was changed. ²⁷ Every bridegroom took up lamentation, she that sat in the marriage chamber was in heaviness. ²⁸ And the land was moved for the inhabitants thereof, and all the house of Jacob was clothed with shame. ²⁹ And after two full years the king sent a chief collector of tribute to the cities of Judah, and he came to Jerusalem with a great multitude. ³⁰ And he spoke words of peace to them in subtlety, and they gave him credence: and he fell on the city suddenly, and struck it very severely, and destroyed much people out of Israel. ³¹ And he took the spoils of the city, and set it on fire, and pulled down the houses thereof and the walls thereof on every side. ³² And they led captive the women and the children, and the cattle they took in possession. ³³ And they built the city of David with a great and strong

wall, with strong towers, and it became to them a citadel. ³⁴ And they put there a sinful nation, transgressors of the law, and they strengthened themselves therein. ³⁵ And they stored up arms and food, and gathering together the spoils of Jerusalem, they laid them up there, and they became a severe snare: ³⁶ and it became a place to lie in wait in against the sanctuary, and an evil adversary to Israel continually. ³⁷ And they shed innocent blood on every side of the sanctuary and defiled the sanctuary. ³⁸ And the inhabitants of Jerusalem fled because of them; and she became a habitation of strangers, and she became strange to those who were born in her, and her children forsook her. ³⁹ Her sanctuary was laid waste like a wilderness, her feasts were turned into mourning, her Sabbaths into reproach, her honor into contempt. ⁴⁰ According to her glory, so was her dishonor multiplied, and her high estate was turned into mourning. ⁴¹ And King Antiochus wrote to his whole kingdom, that all should be one people, ⁴² and that each should forsake his own laws. And all the nations agreed according to the word of the king; ⁴³ and many of Israel consented to his worship, and sacrificed to the idols, and profaned the Sabbath. ⁴⁴ And the king sent letters by the hand of messengers to Jerusalem and the cities of Judah, that they should follow laws strange to the land, ⁴⁵ and should forbid whole burnt-offerings and sacrifice and drink offerings in the sanctuary; and should profane the Sabbaths and feasts, ⁴⁶ and pollute the sanctuary and those who were holy; ⁴⁷ that they should build altars, and temples, and shrines for idols, and should sacrifice swine's flesh and unclean beasts: ⁴⁸ and that they should leave their sons uncircumcised, that they should make their souls abominable with all manner of uncleanness and profanation; ⁴⁹ so that they might forget the law, and change all the ordinances. ⁵⁰ And whoever will not do according to the word of the king, he will die. ⁵¹ According to all these words wrote he to his whole kingdom; and he appointed overseers over all the people, and he commanded the cities of Judah to sacrifice, city by city. ⁵² And from the people were gathered together to them many, everyone that had forsaken the law; and they did evil things in the land; ⁵³ and they made Israel to hide themselves in every place of refuge which they had. ⁵⁴ And on the fifteenth day of Kislev, in the one hundred and forty-fifth year, they built an abomination of desolation on the altar, and in the cities of Judah on every side they built [idol] altars. ⁵⁵ And at the doors of the houses and in the streets they burned incense. ⁵⁶ And they tore in pieces the scrolls of the law which they found and set them on fire. ⁵⁷ And wherever was found with any a scroll of the Covenant, and if any consented to the law, the king's sentence delivered him to death. ⁵⁸ So did they in their might to Israel, to those that were found month by month in the cities. ⁵⁹ And on the twenty-fifth day of the month they sacrificed on the [idol] altar [of God]. ⁶⁰ And the women that had circumcised their children they put to death according to the command. ⁶¹ And they hanged their babies about their necks, and [destroyed] their houses, and those who had circumcised them. ⁶² And many in Israel were fully resolved and confirmed in themselves not to eat unclean things. ⁶³ And they chose to die, that they might not be defiled with the meats, and that they might not profane the holy covenant: and they died. ⁶⁴ And there came exceedingly great wrath on Israel.

CHAPTER 2

¹ In those days Mattathias rose up, the son of John, the son of Simeon, a priest of the sons of Joarib, from Jerusalem; and he lived at Modin. ² And he had five sons, John, who was surnamed Gaddis; ³ Simon, who was called Thassi; ⁴ Judas, who was called Maccabaeus; ⁵ Eleazar, who was called Avaran; Jonathan, who was called Apphus. ⁶ And he saw the blasphemies that were committed in Judah and in Jerusalem, ⁷ and he said, "Woe is me! Why was I born to see the destruction of my people, and the destruction of the holy city, and to dwell there, when it was given into the hand of the enemy, the sanctuary into the hand of aliens? ⁸ Her temple is become as a man that was glorious: ⁹ her vessels of glory are carried away into captivity, her infants are slain in her streets, her young men with the sword of the enemy. ¹⁰ What nation has not inherited her palaces, and gotten possession of her spoils? ¹¹ Her adorning is all taken away; instead of a free woman she is become a bond woman: ¹² and behold, our holy things and our beauty and our glory are laid waste, and the nations have profaned them. ¹³ Why should we live any longer?" ¹⁴ And Mattathias and his sons tore their clothes, and put on sackcloth, and mourned exceedingly. ¹⁵ And the king's officers, that were enforcing the apostasy, came into the city Modin to sacrifice. ¹⁶ And many of Israel came to them, and Mattathias and his sons were gathered together. ¹⁷ And the king's officers answered and spoke to Mattathias, saying, "You are a ruler and an honorable and great man in this city, and strengthened with sons and relatives: ¹⁸ now therefore, come first and do the command of the king, as all the nations have done, and the men of Judah, and those who remain in Jerusalem: and you and your house will be in the number of the king's friends, and you and your sons will be honored with silver and gold and many gifts." ¹⁹ And Mattathias answered and said with a loud voice, "If all the nations that are in the house of the king's dominion listen to him, to each one fall away from the worship of his fathers, and have made choice to follow his commands, ²⁰ yet I and my sons and my relatives will walk in the covenant of our fathers. ²¹ Heaven forbid that we should forsake the law and the ordinances. ²² We will not listen to the king's

words, to go aside from our worship, on the right hand, or on the left." [23] And when he had left speaking these words, there came a Jew in the sight of all to sacrifice on the altar which was at Modin, according to the king's command. [24] And Mattathias saw it, and his zeal was kindled, and his reins trembled, and he showed out his wrath according to judgment, and ran, and killed him on the altar. [25] And the king's officer, who compelled men to sacrifice, he killed at that time, and pulled down the altar. [26] And he was zealous for the law, even as Phinehas did to Zimri the son of Salu. [27] And Mattathias cried out in the city with a loud voice, saying, "Whoever is zealous for the law, and maintains the covenant, let him come out after me." [28] And he and his sons fled into the mountains and forsook all that they had in the city. [29] Then many that sought after justice and judgment went down into the wilderness, to dwell there, [30] they, and their sons, and their wives, and their cattle; because evils were multiplied on them. [31] And it was told the king's officers, and the forces that were in Jerusalem, the city of David, that certain men, who had broken the king's command, were gone down into the secret places in the wilderness; [32] and many pursued after them, and having overtaken them, they encamped against them, and set the battle in array against them on the Sabbath day. [33] And they said to them, so far, "Come out, and do according to the word of the king, and you will live." [34] And they said, "We will not come out, neither will we do the word of the king, to profane the Sabbath day." [35] And they hurried to give them battle. [36] And they did not answer them, neither did they cast a stone at them, nor stopped up the secret places, [37] saying, "Let us die all in our innocence: the heavens and earth witness over us, that you put us to death without trial." [38] And they rose up against them in battle on the Sabbath, and they died, they and their wives and their children, and their cattle, to the number of one thousand souls. [39] And Mattathias and his friends knew it, and they mourned over them exceedingly. [40] And one said to another, "If we all do as our countrymen have done, and fight not against the nations for our lives and our ordinances, they will now quickly destroy us from off the earth." [41] And they took counsel on that day, saying, "Whoever will come against us to battle on the Sabbath day, let us fight against him, and we will in no way all die, as our countrymen died in the secret places." [42] Then were gathered together to them a company of Hasidaeans, mighty men of Israel, everyone that offered himself willingly for the law. [43] And all those who fled from the evils were added to them and became a stay to them. [44] And they mustered an army, and struck sinners in their anger, and lawless men in their wrath: and the rest fled to the nations for safety. [45] And Mattathias and his friends went around and pulled down the altars; [46] and they circumcised by force the children that were uncircumcised, as many as they found in the coasts of Israel. [47] And they pursued after the sons of pride, and the work prospered in their hand. [48] And they rescued the law out of the hand of the nations, and out of the hand of the kings, neither suffered they the sinner to triumph. [49] And the days of Mattathias drew near that he should die, and he said to his sons, "Now have pride and rebuke gotten strength, and a season of overthrow, and wrath of indignation. [50] And now, my children, be zealous for the law, and give your lives for the covenant of your fathers. [51] And call to remembrance the deeds of our fathers which they did in their generations; and receive great glory and a perpetual name. [52] Was not Abraham found faithful in temptation, and it was reckoned to him for righteousness? [53] Joseph in the time of his distress kept the command and became lord of Egypt. [54] Phinehas our father, for that he was zealous exceedingly, obtained the covenant of a perpetual priesthood. [55] Joshua for fulfilling the word became a judge in Israel. [56] Caleb for bearing witness in the congregation obtained a heritage in the land. [57] David for being merciful inherited the throne of a kingdom forever and ever. [58] Elijah, for that he was exceedingly zealous for the law, was taken up into Heaven. [59] Hananiah, Azariah, Mishael, believed, and were saved out of the flame. [60] Daniel for his innocence was delivered from the mouth of lions. [61] And so consider you from generation to generation, that none that put their trust in him will lack for strength. [62] And do not be afraid of the words of a sinful man; for his glory will be dung and worms. [63] Today he will be lifted up, and tomorrow he will in no way be found, because he is returned to his dust, and his thought is perished. [64] And you, my children, be strong, and show yourselves men in behalf of the law; for therein will you obtain glory. [65] And behold, Simon your brother, I know that he is a man of counsel; give ear to him always: he will be a father to you. [66] And Judas Maccabaeus, he has been strong and mighty from his youth: he will be your captain and will fight the battle of the people. [67] And take to yourself all the doers of the law and avenge the wrong of your people. [68] Render a repayment to the nations and take heed to the commands of the law." [69] And he blessed them and was gathered to his fathers. [70] And he died in the one hundred and forty-sixth year, and his sons buried him in the tombs of his fathers at Modin, and all Israel made great lamentation for him.

CHAPTER 3

[1] And his son Judas, who was called Maccabaeus, rose up in his stead. [2] And all his countrymen helped him, and so did all those who cleaved to his father, and they fought with gladness the battle of Israel. [3] And he got his people great glory, and put on a breastplate as a giant, and girded his warlike harness about him, and set battles in array, protecting the army with his sword. [4] And he was like a lion in his deeds, and as a

lion's whelp roaring for prey. ⁵ And he pursued the lawless, seeking them out, and he burned up those that troubled his people. ⁶ And the lawless shrunk for fear of him, and all the workers of lawlessness were severely troubled, and salvation prospered in his hand. ⁷ And he angered many kings, and made Jacob glad with his acts, and his memorial is blessed forever. ⁸ And he went around among the cities of Judah, and destroyed the ungodly out of the land, and turned away wrath from Israel: ⁹ and he was renowned to the utmost part of the earth, and he gathered together such as were ready to perish. ¹⁰ And Apollonius gathered the nations together, and a great army from Samaria, to fight against Israel. ¹¹ And Judas perceived it, and he went out to meet him, and struck him, and killed him: and many fell wounded to death, and the rest fled. ¹² And they took their spoils, and Judas took the sword of Apollonius, and with that he fought all his days. ¹³ And Seron, the commander of the army of Syria, heard it said that Judas had gathered a gathering and a congregation of faithful men with him, and of such as went out to war; ¹⁴ And he said, I will make myself a name and get me glory in the kingdom; and I will fight against Judas and those who are with him, that set at nothing the word of the king. ¹⁵ And there went up with him also a mighty army of the ungodly to help him, to take vengeance on the sons of Israel. ¹⁶ And he came near to the going up of Bethhoron, and Judas went out to meet him with a small company. ¹⁷ But when they saw the army coming to meet them, they said to Judas, "What? Will we be able, being a small company, to fight against so great and strong a multitude? And we for our part are faint, having tasted no food this day." ¹⁸ And Judas said, "It is an easy thing for many to be shut up in the hands of a few; and with Heaven it is all one, to save by many or by few: ¹⁹ for victory in battle stands not in the multitude of an army; but strength is from Heaven. ²⁰ They come to us in fullness of insolence and lawlessness, to destroy us and our wives and our children, for to plunder us: ²¹ but we fight for our lives and our laws. ²² And he himself will defeat them before our face, but as for you, do not be afraid of them." ²³ Now when he had left off speaking, he leapt suddenly on them, and Seron and his army were defeated before him. ²⁴ And they pursued them in the going down of Bethhoron to the plain, and there fell of them about eight hundred men; but the residue fled into the land of the Philistines. ²⁵ And the fear of Judas and his countrymen, and the dread of them, began to fall on the nations around them: ²⁶ and his name came near even to the king, and every nation told of the battles of Judas. ²⁷ But when King Antiochus heard these words, he was full of indignation: and he sent and gathered together all the forces of his realm, an exceedingly strong army. ²⁸ And he opened his treasury, and gave his forces pay for a year, and commanded them to be ready for every need. ²⁹ And he saw that the money failed from his treasures, and that the tributes of the country were small, because of the dissension and plague which he had brought on the land, to the end that he might take away the laws which had been from the first days; ³⁰ and he feared that he should not have enough as at other times for the charges and the gifts which he gave previously with a liberal hand, and he abounded above the kings that were before him. ³¹ And he was exceedingly perplexed in his mind, and he determined to go into Persia, and to take the tributes of the countries, and to gather much money. ³² And he left Lysias, an honorable man, and one of the seed royal, to be over the affairs of the king from the River Euphrates to the borders of Egypt, ³³ and to bring up his son Antiochus, until he came again. ³⁴ And he delivered to him the half of his forces, and the elephants, and gave him charge of all the things that he would have done, and concerning those who lived in Judea and in Jerusalem, ³⁵ that he should send an army against them, to root out and destroy the strength of Israel, and the remnant of Jerusalem, and to take away their memorial from the place; ³⁶ And that he should make strangers to dwell on all their coasts, and should divide their land to them by lot. ³⁷ And the king took the half that remained of the forces, and removed from Antioch, from his royal city, the one hundred and forty-seventh year; and he passed over the River Euphrates and went through the upper countries. ³⁸ And Lysias chose Ptolemy the son of Dorymenes, and Nicanor, and Gorgias, mighty men of the king's friends; ³⁹ and with them he sent forty thousand footmen, and seven thousand horse, to go into the land of Judah, and to destroy it, according to the word of the king. ⁴⁰ And they removed with all their army and came and pitched near to Emmaus in the plain country. ⁴¹ And the merchants of the country heard the fame of them, and took silver and gold exceedingly much, with chains, and came into the camp to take the sons of Israel for servants: and there were added to them the forces of Syria and of the land of the Philistines. ⁴² And Judas and his countrymen saw that evils were multiplied, and that the forces were encamping in their borders; and they took knowledge of the king's words which he had commanded, to destroy the people and make an end of them; ⁴³ and they said each man to his neighbor, "Let us raise up the ruin of our people, and let us fight for our people and the holy place." ⁴⁴ And the congregation was gathered together, that they might be ready for battle, and that they might pray, and ask for mercy and compassion. ⁴⁵ And Jerusalem was without inhabitant as a wilderness, there was none of her offspring that went in or went out; and the sanctuary was trodden down, and the sons of strangers were in the citadel, the nations lodged therein; and joy was taken away from Jacob, and the pipe and the harp ceased. ⁴⁶ And they gathered themselves together, and came to Mizpeh, near Jerusalem; for in Mizpeh was there a place of prayer previously for Israel. ⁴⁷And they fasted that day, and put on sackcloth, and [put] ashes on their heads, and tore their clothes, ⁴⁸and laid open the Scroll of the Law, concerning which the nations were accustomed to inquire, seeking the likenesses of their idols. ⁴⁹And they brought the priests' garments, and the first-fruits, and the tithes: and they stirred up the Nazarites, who had accomplished their days. ⁵⁰And they cried aloud toward Heaven, saying, "What will we do with these men, and where will we carry them away? ⁵¹And your holy place is trodden down and profaned, and your priests are in heaviness and brought low. ⁵²And behold, the nations are assembled together against us to destroy us: you know what things they imagine against us. ⁵³How will we be able to stand before them, except you be our help?" ⁵⁴And they sounded with the trumpets and cried with a loud voice. ⁵⁵And after this Judas appointed leaders of the people, captains of thousands, and captains of hundreds, and captains of fifties, and captains of tens. ⁵⁶And he said to those who were building houses, and were betrothing wives, and were planting vineyards, and were fearful, that they should return, each man to his own house, according to the law. ⁵⁷And the army removed and encamped on the south side of Emmaus. ⁵⁸And Judas said, "Gird yourselves, and be valiant men, and be in readiness against the morning, that you may fight with these nations, that are assembled together against us to destroy us, and our holy place: ⁵⁹for it is better for us to die in battle, than to look on the evils of our nation and the holy place. ⁶⁰Nevertheless, as may be the will in Heaven, so will he do."

CHAPTER 4

¹And Gorgias took five thousand footmen, and one thousand chosen horse, and the army removed by night, ²that it might fall on the army of the Jews and strike them suddenly: and the men of the citadel were his guides. ³And Judas heard thereof, and removed, he and the valiant men, that he might strike the king's army which was at Emmaus, ⁴while as yet the forces were dispersed from the camp. ⁵And Gorgias came into the camp of Judas by night and found no man; and he sought them in the mountains; for he said, "These men flee from us." ⁶And as soon as it was day, Judas appeared in the plain with three thousand men: however, they did not have the armor and swords they desired. ⁷And they saw the camp of the nations strong [and] fortified, and horsemen compassing it around; and these were expert in war. ⁸And Judas said to the men that were with him, "Do not fear their multitude, neither be afraid of their onset. ⁹Remember how our fathers were saved in the Red Sea, when Pharaoh pursued them with an army. ¹⁰And now let us cry to Heaven, if He will have us, and will remember the covenant of our fathers, and destroy this army before our face today: ¹¹and all the nations will know that there is one who redeems and saves Israel." ¹²And the strangers lifted up their eyes and saw them coming near them: ¹³and they went out of the camp to battle. And those who were with Judas sounded their trumpets, ¹⁴and joined battle, and the nations were defeated, and fled into the plain. ¹⁵But all the furthest back fell by the sword: and they pursued them to Gazara, and to the plains of Idumaea and Azotus and Jamnia, and there fell of them about three thousand men. ¹⁶And Judas and his army returned from pursuing after them, ¹⁷and he said to the people, "Do not be greedy of the spoils, inasmuch as there is a battle before us; ¹⁸and Gorgias and his army are near to us in the mountain. But stand you now against our enemies, and fight against them, and afterward take the spoils with boldness." ¹⁹While Judas was yet making an end of these words, there appeared a part of them looking out from the mountain: ²⁰and they saw that their army had been put to flight, and that the Jews were burning the camp; for the smoke that was seen declared what was done. ²¹But when they perceived these things, they were severely afraid; and perceiving also the army of Judas in the plain ready for battle, ²²they fled—all of them—into the land of the Philistines. ²³And Judas returned to plunder the camp, and they got much gold, and silver, and blue, and sea purple, and great riches. ²⁴And they returned home, and sang a song of thanksgiving, and gave praise to Heaven; because [His mercy] is good, because His mercy endures forever. ²⁵And Israel had a great deliverance that day. ²⁶But the strangers, as many as had escaped, came and told Lysias all the things that had happened: ²⁷but when he heard thereof, he was confounded and discouraged, because neither had such things as he desired been done to Israel, nor had such things as the king commanded him come to pass. ²⁸And in the next year he gathered together sixty thousand chosen footmen, and five thousand horse, that he might subdue them. ²⁹And they came into Idumaea and encamped at Bethsura; and Judas met them with ten thousand men. ³⁰And he saw that the army was strong, and he prayed and said, "Blessed are You, O Savior of Israel, who quelled the onset of the mighty man by the hand of Your servant David, and delivered the army of the Philistines into the hands of Jonathan the son of Saul, and of his armor bearer: ³¹shut up this army in the hand of Your people Israel, and let them be ashamed for their army and their horsemen: ³²give them faintness of heart, and cause the boldness of their strength to melt away, and let them quake at their destruction: ³³cast them down with the sword of those who love You, and let all that know Your Name praise You with thanksgiving." ³⁴And they joined battle; and there fell of the army of Lysias about five thousand men, and they fell down near them. ³⁵But when Lysias saw that

his array was put to flight, and the boldness that had come on those who were with Judas, and how they were ready either to live or to die nobly, he removed to Antioch, and gathered together hired soldiers, that he might come again into Judea with even a greater company. ³⁶ But Judas and his countrymen said, "Behold, our enemies are defeated: let us go up to cleanse the holy place, and to dedicate it afresh." ³⁷ And all the army was gathered together, and they went up to Mount Zion. ³⁸ And they saw the sanctuary laid desolate, and the altar profaned, and the gates burned up, and shrubs growing in the courts as in a forest or as on one of the mountains, and the priests' chambers pulled down; ³⁹ and they tore their clothes, and made great lamentation, and put ashes on their heads, ⁴⁰ and fell on their faces to the ground, and blew with the solemn trumpets, and cried toward Heaven. ⁴¹ Then Judas appointed certain men to fight against those that were in the citadel, until he should have cleansed the holy place. ⁴² And he chose blameless priests, such as had pleasure in the law: ⁴³ and they cleansed the holy place and bare out the stones of defilement into an unclean place. ⁴⁴ And they took counsel concerning the altar of burnt-offerings, which had been profaned, what they should do with it: ⁴⁵ and there came into their mind a good counsel, that they should pull it down, lest it should be a reproach to them, because the nations had defiled it: and they pulled down the altar, ⁴⁶ and laid up the stones in the mountain of the house in a convenient place, until there should come a prophet to give an answer concerning them. ⁴⁷ And they took whole stones according to the law and built a new altar after the fashion of the former; ⁴⁸ and they built the holy place, and the inner parts of the house; and they hallowed the courts. ⁴⁹ And they made the holy vessels new, and they brought the candlestick, and the altar of burnt-offerings and of incense, and the table, into the temple. ⁵⁰ And they burned incense on the altar, and they lighted the lamps that were on the candlestick, and they gave light in the temple. ⁵¹ And they set loaves on the table, and spread out the veils, and finished all the works which they made. ⁵² And they rose up early in the morning, on the twenty-fifth day of the ninth month, which is the month Kislev, in the one hundred and forty-eighth year, ⁵³ and offered sacrifice according to the law on the new altar of burnt-offerings which they had made. ⁵⁴ At what time and on what day the nations had profaned it, even on that [day] was it dedicated afresh, with songs and harps and lutes, and with cymbals. ⁵⁵ And all the people fell on their faces, and worshiped, and gave praise to Heaven, which had given them good success. ⁵⁶ And they kept the dedication of the altar eight days, and offered burnt-offerings with gladness, and sacrificed a sacrifice of deliverance and praise. ⁵⁷ And they decked the forefront of the temple with crowns of gold and small shields, and dedicated afresh the gates and the priests' chambers, and made doors for them. ⁵⁸ And there was exceedingly great gladness among the people, and the reproach of the nations was turned away. ⁵⁹ And Judas and his countrymen and the whole congregation of Israel ordained, that the days of the dedication of the altar should be kept in their seasons from year to year by the space of eight days, from the twenty-fifth day of the month Kislev, with gladness and joy. ⁶⁰ And at that season they built up Mount Zion with high walls and strong towers around, lest perhaps the nations should come and tread them down, as they had done previously. ⁶¹ And he set there a force to keep it, and they fortified Bethsura to keep it; that the people might have a stronghold near Idumaea.

CHAPTER 5

¹ And it came to pass, when the surrounding nations heard that the altar was built, and the sanctuary dedicated as previously, they were exceedingly angry. ² And they took counsel to destroy the race of Jacob that was in the midst of them, and they began to kill and destroy among the people. ³ And Judas fought against the children of Esau in Idumaea at Akrabattine, because they besieged Israel: and he struck them with a great slaughter, and brought down their pride, and took their spoils. ⁴ And he remembered the wickedness of the children of Baean, who were to the people a snare and a stumbling block, lying in wait for them in the ways. ⁵ And they were shut up by him in the towers; and he encamped against them, and destroyed them utterly, and burned with fire the towers of the place, with all that were therein. ⁶ And he passed over to the children of Ammon, and found a mighty band, and much people, with Timotheus for their leader. ⁷ And he fought many battles with them, and they were defeated before his face; and he struck them, ⁸ and got possession of Jazer, and the villages thereof, and returned again into Judea. ⁹ And the nations that were in Gilead gathered themselves together against the Israelites that were on their borders, to destroy them. And they fled to the stronghold of Dathema, ¹⁰ and sent letters to Judas and his countrymen, saying, "The nations that are around us are gathered together against us to destroy us: ¹¹ and they are preparing to come and get possession of the stronghold whereto we have fled for refuge, and Timotheus is the leader of their army. ¹² Now therefore come and deliver us from their hand, for many of us are fallen. ¹³ And all our countrymen that were in the land of Tubias have been put to death; and they have carried into captivity their wives and their children and their stuff; and they destroyed there about one thousand men." ¹⁴ While the letters were yet being read, behold, there came other messengers from Galilee with their clothes torn, bringing a report in this way, ¹⁵ saying that there were gathered together against them those of Ptolemais, and of Tyre, and of

Sidon, and all Galilee of the nations to consume them. [16] Now when Judas and the people heard these words, there assembled together a great congregation, to consult what they should do for their countrymen, that were in suffering, and were assaulted of them. [17] And Judas said to Simon his brother, "Choose out men, and go and deliver your countrymen that are in Galilee, but my brother Jonathan and I will go into the land of Gilead." [18] And he left Joseph the son of Zechariah, and Azariah, as leaders of the people, with the remnant of the army, in Judea, for to keep it. [19] And he gave command to them, saying, "Take you the charge of this people, and fight no battle with the nations until that we come again." [20] And to Simon were divided three thousand men to go into Galilee, but to Judas eight thousand men [to go] into the land of Gilead. [21] And Simon went into Galilee, and fought many battles with the nations, and the nations were defeated before him. [22] And he pursued them to the gate of Ptolemais; and there fell of the nations about three thousand men, and he took their spoils. [23] And they took to them those that were in Galilee, and in Arbatta, with their wives and their children, and all that they had, and brought them into Judea with great gladness. [24] And Judas Maccabaeus and his brother Jonathan passed over Jordan, and went three days' journey in the wilderness; [25] and they met with the Nabathaeans, and these met them in a peaceful manner, and told them all things that had befallen their countrymen in the land of Gilead: [26] and how that many of them were shut up in Bosora, and Bosor, and Alema, Casphor, Maked, and Carnaim; all these cities are strong and great: [27] and how that they were shut up in the rest of the cities of the land of Gilead, and that tomorrow they have appointed to encamp against the strongholds, and to take them, and to destroy all these men in one day. [28] And Judas and his army turned suddenly by the way of the wilderness to Bosora; and he took the city and killed all the males with the edge of the sword, and took all their spoils, and burned the city with fire. [29] And he left from there by night and went until he came to the stronghold. [30] And the morning came, and they lifted up their eyes, and behold, much people which could not be counted, bearing ladders and engines of war, to take the stronghold; and they were fighting against them. [31] And Judas saw that the battle was begun, and that the cry of the city went up to Heaven, with trumpets and a great sound, [32] and he said to the men of his army, "Fight this day for your countrymen." [33] And he went out behind them in three companies, and they sounded with their trumpets, and cried out in prayer. [34] And the army of Timotheus perceived that it was Maccabaeus, and they fled from before him: and he struck them with a great slaughter; and there fell of them on that day about eight thousand men. [35] And he turned away to Mizpeh and fought against it, and took it, and killed all the males thereof, and took the spoils thereof, and burned it with fire. [36] From there he left, and took Casphor, Maked, Bosor, and the other cities of the land of Gilead. [37] Now after these things Timotheus gathered another army and encamped near Raphon beyond the brook. [38] And Judas sent men to spy on the army; and they brought him word, saying, "All the nations that are around us are gathered together to them, an exceedingly great army. [39] And they have hired Arabians to help them, and are encamping beyond the brook, ready to come against you to battle." And Judas went to meet them. [40] And Timotheus said to the captains of his army, when Judas and his army drew near to the brook of water, "If he passes over first to us, we will not be able to withstand him; for he will mightily prevail against us: [41] but if he be afraid, and encamp beyond the river, we will cross over to him, and prevail against him." [42] Now when Judas came near to the brook of water, he caused the scribes of the people to remain by the brook, and gave command to them, saying, "Permit no man to encamp, but let all come to the battle." [43] And he crossed over the first against them, and all the people after him: and all the nations were defeated before his face, and cast away their arms, and fled to the temple at Carnaim. [44] And they took the city, and burned the temple with fire, together with all that were therein. And Carnaim was subdued, neither could they stand any longer before the face of Judas. [45] And Judas gathered together all Israel, those who were in the land of Gilead, from the least to the greatest, and their wives, and their children, and their stuff, an exceedingly great army, that they might come into the land of Judah. [46] And they came as far as Ephron, and this same city was great, [and it was] in the way as they should go, exceedingly strong: they could not turn away from it on the right hand or on the left but must necessarily pass through the midst of it. [47] And they of the city shut them out and stopped up the gates with stones. [48] And Judas sent to them with words of peace, saying, "We will pass through your land to go into our own land, and none will do you any harm, we will only pass by on our feet." And they would not open to him. [49] And Judas commanded proclamation to be made in the army, that each man should encamp in the place where he was. [50] And the men of the army encamped and fought against the city all that day and all that night, and the city was delivered into his hands; [51] and he destroyed all the males with the edge of the sword, and razed the city, and took the spoils thereof, and passed through the city over those who were slain. [52] And they went over Jordan into the great plain near Bethshan. [53] And Judas gathered together those that lagged behind, and encouraged the people all the way through, until he came into the land of Judah. [54] And they went up to Mount Zion with gladness and joy, and offered whole burnt-offerings, because not so much as one of them was slain until they returned in peace. [55] And in the days when Judas and Jonathan were in the land of Gilead, and Simon his brother in Galilee before Ptolemais, ⁵⁶ Joseph the son of Zechariah, and Azariah, rulers of the army, heard of their exploits and of the war, what things they had done; ⁵⁷ and they said, "Let us also get us a name, and let us go fight against the nations that are around us." ⁵⁸ And they gave charge to the men of the army that was with them and went toward Jamnia. ⁵⁹ And Gorgias and his men came out of the city to meet them in battle. ⁶⁰ And Joseph and Azariah were put to flight and were pursued to the borders of Judea; and there fell on that day of the people of Israel about two thousand men. ⁶¹ And there was a great overthrow among the people, because they did not listen to Judas and his countrymen, thinking to do some exploit. ⁶² But they were not of the seed of those men, by whose hand deliverance was given to Israel. ⁶³ And the man Judas and his countrymen were glorified exceedingly in the sight of all Israel, and of all the nations, wherever their name was heard of; ⁶⁴ and men gathered together to them, acclaiming them. ⁶⁵ And Judas and his countrymen went out and fought against the children of Esau in the land toward the south; and he struck Hebron and the villages thereof, and pulled down the strongholds thereof, and burned the towers thereof. ⁶⁶ And he left to go into the land of the Philistines, and he went through Samaria. ⁶⁷ In that day certain priests, desiring to do exploits there, were slain in battle, when he went out to battle unadvisedly. ⁶⁸ And Judas turned toward Azotus, to the land of the Philistines, and pulled down their altars, and burned the carved images of their gods with fire, and took the plunder of their cities, and returned into the land of Judah.

CHAPTER 6

¹ And King Antiochus was journeying through the upper countries; and he heard it said that in Elymais in Persia there was a city renowned for riches, for silver and gold; ² and that the temple which was in it was exceedingly rich, and that therein were golden shields, and breastplates, and arms, which Alexander, son of Philip, the Macedonian king, who reigned first among the Greeks, left behind there. ³ And he came and sought to take the city, and to pillage it; and he was not able, because the thing was known to them of the city, ⁴ and they rose up against him to battle: and he fled, and left from there with great heaviness, to return to Babylon. ⁵ And there came one bringing him tidings into Persia, that the armies, which went against the land of Judah, had been put to flight; ⁶ and that Lysias went first with a strong army, and was put to shame before them; and that they had waxed strong by reason of arms and power, and with store of spoils, which they took from the armies that they had cut off; ⁷ and that they had pulled down the abomination which he had built on the altar that was in Jerusalem; and that they had compassed about the sanctuary with high walls, as before, and Bethsura, his city. ⁸ And it came to pass, when the king heard these words, he was astonished and moved exceedingly: and he laid down on his bed, and fell sick for grief, because it had not befallen him as he looked for. ⁹ And he was there many days, because great grief was renewed on him, and he made account that he should die. ¹⁰ And he called for all his friends, and said to them, "Sleep departs from my eyes, and my heart fails for care. ¹¹ And I said in my heart, To what suffering am I come, and how great a flood is it, wherein I now am! For I was gracious and beloved in my power. ¹² But now I remember the evils which I did at Jerusalem, and that I took all the vessels of silver and gold that were therein and sent out to destroy the inhabitants of Judah without a cause. ¹³ I perceive that on this account these evils have come on me, and behold, I perish through great grief in a strange land." ¹⁴ And he called for Philip, one of his Friends, and set him over all his kingdom, ¹⁵ and gave him his diadem, and his robe, and his signet ring, to the end he should bring Antiochus his son, and nourish him up that he might be king. ¹⁶ And King Antiochus died there in the one hundred and forty-ninth year. ¹⁷ And Lysias knew that the king was dead, and he set up Antiochus his son to reign, whom he had nourished up being young, and he called his name Eupator. ¹⁸ And those who were in the citadel shut up Israel around the sanctuary, and sought always their hurt, and the strengthening of the nations. ¹⁹ And Judas thought to destroy them and called all the people together to besiege them. ²⁰ And they were gathered together, and besieged them in the one hundred and fiftieth year, and he made mounds to shoot from, and engines of war. ²¹ And there came out some of those who were shut up, and there were joined to them certain ungodly men of Israel. ²² And they went to the king, and said, "How long will you not execute judgment, and avenge our countrymen? ²³ We were willing to serve your father, and to walk after his words, and to follow his commands; ²⁴ and for this reason the children of our people besieged the citadel and were alienated from us; but as many of us as they could descend on they killed and plundered our inheritances. ²⁵ And not against us only did they stretch out their hand, but also against all their borders. ²⁶ And behold, they are encamped this day against the citadel at Jerusalem, to take it: and they have fortified the sanctuary and Bethsura. ²⁷ And if you are not beforehand with them quickly, they will do greater things than these, and you will not be able to control them." ²⁸ And when the king heard this, he was angry, and gathered together all his friends, [even the] rulers of his army, and those who were over the horse. ²⁹ And there came to him from other kingdoms, and from isles of the sea, bands of hired soldiers. ³⁰ And the number of his forces was one hundred thousand footmen, and twenty thousand horsemen, and thirty-two elephants trained for war. ³¹ And they

went through Idumaea, and encamped against Bethsura, and fought against it many days, and made engines of war; and they [of Bethsura] came out, and burned them with fire, and fought valiantly. ³² And Judas left from the citadel, and encamped at Bethzacharias, near the king's camp. ³³ And the king rose early in the morning and sent his army at full speed along the road to Bethzacharias, and his forces made them ready to battle, and sounded with the trumpets. ³⁴ And they showed the elephants the blood of grapes and mulberries, that they might prepare them for the battle. ³⁵ And they divided the beasts among the phalanxes, and they set by each elephant one thousand men armed with coats of mail, and helmets of brass on their heads; and for each beast were appointed five hundred chosen horsemen. ³⁶ These were ready beforehand, wherever the beast was; and wherever the beast went, they went with him; they did not depart from him. ³⁷ And towers of wood were on them, strong [and] covered, one on each beast, girded fast on him with cunning contrivances; and on each [beast] were thirty-two valiant men that fought on them, beside his Indian ³⁸ (and the residue of the horsemen he set on this side and that side at the two parts of the army), striking terror [into the enemy], and protected by the phalanxes. ³⁹ Now when the sun shone on the shields of gold and brass, the mountains shone with them, and blazed like torches of fire. ⁴⁰ And a part of the king's army was spread on the high mountains, and some on the low ground, and they went on firmly and in order. ⁴¹ And all that heard the noise of their multitude, and the marching of the multitude, and the rattling of the arms, did quake, for the army was exceedingly great and strong. ⁴² And Judas and his army drew near for battle, and there fell of the king's army six hundred men. ⁴³ And Eleazar, who was [called] Avaran, saw one of the beasts armed with royal breastplates, and he was higher than all the beasts, and the king seemed to be on him; ⁴⁴ and he gave himself to deliver his people, and to get himself a perpetual name; ⁴⁵ and he ran on him courageously into the midst of the phalanx, and killed on the right hand and on the left, and they separated apart from him on this side and on that. ⁴⁶ And he crept under the elephant, and thrust him from beneath, and killed him; and the [elephant] fell to the earth on him, and he died there. ⁴⁷ And they saw the strength of the kingdom, and the fierce onset of the army, and turned away from them. ⁴⁸ But they of the king's army went up to Jerusalem to meet them, and the king encamped toward Judea, and toward Mount Zion. ⁴⁹ And he made peace with them of Bethsura; and he came out of the city, because they had no food there to endure the siege, because it was a Sabbath to the land. ⁵⁰ And the king took Bethsura and appointed a garrison there to keep it. ⁵¹ And he encamped against the sanctuary many days; and set there mounds to shoot from, and engines of war, and instruments for casting fire and stones, and pieces to cast darts, and slings. ⁵² And they also made engines against their engines and fought for many days. ⁵³ But there was no food in the sanctuary, because it was the seventh year, and those who fled for safety into Judea from among the nations had eaten up the residue of the store; ⁵⁴ and there were but a few left in the sanctuary, because the famine prevailed against them, and they were scattered, each man to his own place. ⁵⁵ And Lysias heard it said that Philip, whom Antiochus the king, while he was yet alive, appointed to nourish up his son Antiochus, that he might be king, ⁵⁶ had returned from Persia and Media, and with him the forces that went with the king, and that he was seeking to take the government to himself. ⁵⁷ And he hurried, and gave consent to depart; and he said to the king and the leaders of the army and to the men, "We decay daily, and our food is scant, and the place where we encamp is strong, and the affairs of the kingdom lie on us: ⁵⁸ now therefore let us give the right hand to these men, and make peace with them and with all their nation, ⁵⁹ and covenant with them, that they will walk after their own laws, as previously, for because of their laws which we abolished they were angered, and did all these things." ⁶⁰ And the saying pleased the king and the princes, and he sent to them to make peace; and they accepted thereof. ⁶¹ And the king and the princes swore to them: immediately they came out from the stronghold. ⁶² And the king entered into Mount Zion; and he saw the strength of the place and set at nothing the oath which he had sworn and gave command to pull down the wall around. ⁶³ And he left in haste, and returned to Antioch, and found Philip master of the city; and he fought against him and took the city by force.

CHAPTER 7

¹ In the one hundred and fiftieth year, Demetrius the son of Seleucus came out from Rome and went up with a few men to a city by the sea and reigned there. ² And it came to pass, when he would go into the house of the kingdom of his fathers, that the army laid hands on Antiochus and Lysias, to bring them to him. ³ And the thing was known to him, and he said, "Do not show me their faces." ⁴ And the army killed them. And Demetrius sat on the throne of his kingdom. ⁵ And there came to him all the lawless and ungodly men of Israel; and Alcimus was their leader, desiring to be chief priest; ⁶ and they accused the people to the king, saying, "Judas and his countrymen have destroyed all your friends, and have scattered us from our own land. ⁷ Now therefore send a man whom you trust and let him go and see all the havock which he has made of us, and of the king's country, and [how] he has punished them and all that helped them." ⁸ And the king chose Bacchides, one of the king's friends, who was ruler in the country beyond the river, and

was a great man in the kingdom, and faithful to the king. ⁹ And he sent him, and that ungodly Alcimus, and made sure to him the chief priesthood, and he commanded him to take vengeance on the sons of Israel. ¹⁰ And they went and came with a great army into the land of Judah, and he sent messengers to Judas and his countrymen with words of peace deceitfully. ¹¹ And they gave no heed to their words; for they saw that they were come with a great army. ¹² And there were gathered together to Alcimus and Bacchides a company of scribes, to seek for justice. ¹³ And the Hasidaeans were the first among the sons of Israel that sought peace of them; ¹⁴ for they said, "One that is a priest of the seed of Aaron has come with the forces, and he will do us no wrong." ¹⁵ And he spoke with them words of peace, and swore to them, saying, "We will seek the hurt neither of you nor your friends." ¹⁶ And they gave him credence: and he laid hands on sixty men of them, and killed them in one day, according to the word which [the psalmist] wrote, ¹⁷ "The flesh of your saints [they cast out, and] their blood they shed around Jerusalem; And there was no man to bury them." ¹⁸ And the fear and the dread of them fell on all the people, for they said, "There is neither truth nor judgment in them; for they have broken the covenant and the oath which they swore." ¹⁹ And Bacchides left from Jerusalem and encamped in Bezeth; and he sent and took away many of the deserters that were with him, and certain of the people, and he killed them, and [cast them] into the great pit. ²⁰ And he made sure the country to Alcimus and left with him a force to aid him; and Bacchides went away to the king. ²¹ And Alcimus strove for his chief priesthood. ²² And there were gathered to him all those who troubled their people, and they got the mastery of the land of Judah and did great hurt in Israel. ²³ And Judas saw all the mischief that Alcimus and his company had done among the sons of Israel, [even] above the nations, ²⁴ and he went out into all the surrounding coasts of Judea and took vengeance on the men that had deserted from him, and they were restrained from going out into the country. ²⁵ But when Alcimus saw that Judas and his company waxed strong and knew that he was not able to withstand them, he returned to the king, and brought evil accusations against them. ²⁶ And the king sent Nicanor, one of his honorable princes, a man that hated Israel and was their enemy, and commanded him to destroy the people. ²⁷ And Nicanor came to Jerusalem with a great army; and he sent to Judas and his countrymen deceitfully with words of peace, saying, ²⁸ "Let there be no battle between me and you; I will come with a few men, that I may see your faces in peace." ²⁹ And he came to Judas, and they saluted one another peaceably. And the enemies were ready to take away Judas by violence. ³⁰ And the thing was known to Judas, that he came to him with deceit, and he was severely afraid of him, and would see his face

no longer. ³¹ And Nicanor knew that his counsel was discovered; and he went out to meet Judas in battle beside Capharsalama; ³² and there fell of Nicanor's side about five hundred men, and they fled into the city of David. ³³ And after these things Nicanor went up to Mount Zion: and there came some of the priests out of the sanctuary, and some of the elders of the people, to salute him peaceably, and to show him the whole burned sacrifice that was being offered for the king. ³⁴ And he mocked them, and laughed at them, and entreated them shamefully, and spoke haughtily, ³⁵ and swore in a rage, saying, "Unless Judas and his army are now delivered into my hands, it will be that, if I come again in peace, I will burn up this house"; and he went out in a great rage. ³⁶ And the priests entered in and stood before the altar and the temple; and they wept, and said, ³⁷ "You chose this house to be called by Your Name, to be a house of prayer and supplication for Your people: ³⁸ take vengeance on this man and his army, and let them fall by the sword: remember their blasphemies, and do not allow them to live any longer." ³⁹ And Nicanor went out from Jerusalem, and encamped in Bethhoron, and there met him the army of Syria. ⁴⁰ And Judas encamped in Adasa with three thousand men: and Judas prayed and said, ⁴¹ "When those who came from the king blasphemed, your messenger went out, and struck among them one hundred and eighty-five thousand. ⁴² Even so defeat this army before us today and let all the rest know that he has spoken wickedly against Your sanctuary and judge him according to his wickedness." ⁴³ And on the thirteenth day of the month Adar the armies joined battle: and Nicanor's army was defeated, and he himself was the first to fall in the battle. ⁴⁴ Now when his army saw that Nicanor was fallen, they cast away their arms, and fled. ⁴⁵ And they pursued after them a day's journey from Adasa until you come to Gazara, and they sounded an alarm after them with the solemn trumpets. ⁴⁶ And they came out of all the surrounding villages of Judea and closed them in; and these turned them back on those, and they all fell by the sword, and there was not one of them left. ⁴⁷ And they took the spoils, and the plunder, and they struck off Nicanor's head, and his right hand, which he stretched out so haughtily, and brought them, and hanged them up beside Jerusalem. ⁴⁸ And the people were exceedingly glad, and they kept that day as a day of great gladness. ⁴⁹ And they ordained to keep this day year by year, the thirteenth day of Adar. ⁵⁰ And the land of Judah had rest a little while.

CHAPTER 8

¹ And Judas heard of the fame of the Romans, that they are valiant men, and have pleasure in all that join themselves to them and make friends with all such as come to them, ² and that they are valiant men. And they told him of their wars and exploits which they do among the Gauls, and how that they conquered them,

and brought them under tribute; [3] and what things they did in the land of Spain, that they might become masters of the mines of silver and gold which were there; [4] and how that by their policy and persistence they conquered all the place (and the place was exceedingly far from them), and the kings that came against them from the uttermost part of the earth, until they had defeated them, and struck them very severely; and how the rest give them tribute year by year: [5] and Philip, and Perseus, king of Chittim, and those who lifted up themselves against them, did they defeat in battle, and conquered them: [6] Antiochus also, the great king of Asia, who came against them to battle, having one hundred and twenty elephants, with horse, and chariots, and an exceedingly great army, and he was defeated by them, [7] and they took him alive, and appointed that both he and such as reigned after him should give them a great tribute, and should give hostages, and a parcel [of land], [8] the country of India, and Media, and Lydia, and of the attractive of their countries; and they took them from him, and gave them to King Eumenes: [9] and how they of Greece took counsel to come and destroy them; [10] and the thing was known to them, and they sent against them a captain, and fought against them, and many of them fell down wounded to death, and they made captive their wives and their children, and plundered them, and conquered their land, and pulled down their strongholds, and plundered them, and brought them into bondage to this day: [11] and the residue of the kingdoms and of the isles, as many as rose up against them at any time, they destroyed and made them to be their servants; [12] but with their friends and such as relied on them they stayed friends; and they conquered the kingdoms that were near and those that were far off, and all that heard of their fame were afraid of them: [13] moreover, whoever they will to help and to make kings, these do they make kings; and whoever they will, do they depose; and they are exalted exceedingly: [14] and for all this none of them ever put on a diadem, neither did they clothe themselves with purple, to be magnified by it: [15] and how they had made for themselves a senate house, and day by day three hundred and twenty men sat in council, always consulting for the people, to the end they might be well ordered: [16] and how they commit their government to one man year by year, that he should rule over them, and be lord over all their country, and all are obedient to that one, and there is neither envy nor emulation among them. [17] And Judas chose Eupolemus the son of John, the son of Accos, and Jason the son of Eleazar, and sent them to Rome, to establish friendship and alliance with them, [18] and that they should take the yoke from them; for they saw that the kingdom of the Greeks kept Israel in bondage. [19] And they went to Rome (and the way was exceedingly long), and they entered into the senate house, and answered and said, [20] Judas, who is also [called] Maccabaeus, and his countrymen, and the people of the Jews, have sent us to you, to make a confederacy and peace with you, and that we might be registered your allies and friends. [21] And the thing was well-pleasing in their sight. [22] And this is the copy of the writing which they wrote back again on tablets of brass, and sent to Jerusalem, that it might be with them there for a memorial of peace and confederacy: [23] "Good success be to the Romans, and to the nation of the Jews, by sea and by land forever: the sword also and the enemy be far from them. [24] But if war arise for Rome first, or any of their allies in all their dominion, [25] the nation of the Jews will help them as allies, as the occasion will prescribe to them, with all their heart: [26] and to those who make war on them they will not give, neither supply, food, arms, money, or ships, as it has seemed good to Rome, and they will keep their ordinances without taking anything therefore. [27] In the same manner, moreover, if war comes first on the nation of the Jews, the Romans will help them as allies with all their soul, as the occasion will prescribe to them: [28] and to those who are allies [with their enemies] there will not be given food, arms, money, or ships, as it has seemed good to Rome; and they will keep these ordinances, and that without deceit. [29] According to these words have the Romans made a covenant with the people of the Jews. [30] But if hereafter the one party and the other will take counsel to add or diminish anything, they will do it at their pleasure, and whatever they will add or take away will be established. [31] And as touching the evils which King Demetrius does to them, we have written to him, saying, Why have you made your yoke heavy on our friends and allies the Jews? [32] If, therefore, they plead anymore against you, we will do them justice, and fight with you by sea and by land."

CHAPTER 9

[1] And Demetrius heard that Nicanor was fallen with his forces in battle, and he sent Bacchides and Alcimus again into the land of Judah a second time, and the right wing [of his army] with them: [2] and they went by the way that leads to Gilgal, and encamped against Mesaloth, which is in Arbela, and got possession of it, and destroyed many people. [3] And the first month of the one hundred and fifty-second year they encamped against Jerusalem: [4] and they left, and went to Berea, with twenty thousand footmen and two thousand horses. [5] And Judas was encamped at Elasa, and three thousand chosen men with him: [6] and they saw the multitude of the forces, that they were many, and they feared exceedingly: and many slipped away out of the army; there were not left of them more than eight hundred men. [7] And Judas saw that his army slipped away, and that the battle pressed on him, and he was severely troubled in heart, for that he had no time to gather them together, and he waxed faint. [8] And he said to those who were left, "Let us

arise and go up against our adversaries, if perhaps we may be able to fight with them." ⁹ And they would have dissuaded him, saying, "We will in no way be able, but let us rather save our lives now: let us return again, [we] and our countrymen, and fight against them, but we are few." ¹⁰ And Judas said, "Do not let it be so that I should do this thing, to flee from them: and if our time has come, let us die in a manly way for our countrymen's sake, and not leave a cause of reproach against our glory." ¹¹ And the army went from the camp, and stood to encounter them, and the horse was parted into two companies, and the slingers and the archers went before the army, and all the mighty men that fought in the front of the battle. ¹² But Bacchides was in the right wing; and the phalanx drew near on the two parts, and they blew with their trumpets. ¹³ And the men of Judas' side, even they sounded with their trumpets, and the earth shook with the shout of the armies, and the battle was joined, and continued from morning until evening. ¹⁴ And Judas saw that Bacchides and the strength of his army were on the right side, and there went with him all that were brave in heart, ¹⁵ and the right wing was defeated by them, and he pursued after them to Mount Azotus. ¹⁶ And those who were on the left wing saw that the right wing was defeated, and they turned and followed on the footsteps of Judas and of those that were with him: ¹⁷ and the battle waxed severe, and many on both parts fell wounded to death. ¹⁸ And Judas fell, and the rest fled. ¹⁹ And Jonathan and Simon took Judas their brother and buried him in the tomb of his fathers at Modin. ²⁰ And they mourned him, and all Israel made great lamentation for him, and mourned many days, and said, ²¹ "How is the mighty fallen, the savior of Israel!" ²² And the rest of the acts of Judas, and his wars, and the valiant deeds which he did, and his greatness, they are not written; for they were exceedingly many. ²³ And it came to pass after the death of Judas, that the lawless put out their heads in all the coasts of Israel, and all those who did iniquity rose up ²⁴ (in those days there was an exceedingly great famine), and the country went over with them. ²⁵ And Bacchides chose out the ungodly men and made them lords of the country. ²⁶ And they sought out and searched for the friends of Judas, and brought them to Bacchides, and he took vengeance on them, and used them despitefully. ²⁷ And there was great suffering in Israel, such as was not since the time that no prophet appeared to them. ²⁸ And all the friends of Judas were gathered together, and they said to Jonathan, ²⁹ Since your brother Judas has died, we have no man like him to go out against our enemies, and Bacchides, and among them of our nation that hate us. ³⁰ Now therefore, we have chosen you this day to be our prince and leader in his stead, that you may fight our battles. ³¹ And Jonathan took the governance on him at that time and rose up in the stead of his brother Judas. ³² And Bacchides knew it, and he sought to kill him. ³³ And Jonathan, and Simon his brother, and all that were with him, knew it; and they fled into the wilderness of Tekoah, and encamped by the water of the pool Asphar. ³⁴ And Bacchides knew it on the Sabbath day, and came, he and all his army, over Jordan. ³⁵ And [Jonathan] sent his brother, a leader of the multitude, and implored his friends the Nabathaeans, that they might leave with them their baggage, which was much. ³⁶ And the children of Jambri came out of Medaba, and took John, and all that he had, and went their way with it. ³⁷ But after these things they brought word to Jonathan and Simon his brother, that the children of Jambri were making a great marriage and were bringing the bride from Nadabath with a great train, a daughter of one of the great nobles of Canaan. ³⁸ And they remembered John their brother, and went up, and hid themselves under the covert of the mountain: ³⁹ and they lifted up their eyes, and saw, and behold, a great ado and much baggage: and the bridegroom came out, and his friends and his countrymen, to meet them with timbrels, and minstrels, and many weapons. ⁴⁰ And they rose up against them from their ambush, and killed them, and many fell wounded to death, and the remnant fled into the mountain, and they took all their spoils. ⁴¹ And the marriage was turned into mourning, and the voice of their minstrels into lamentation. ⁴² And they avenged fully the blood of their brother and turned back to the marsh of Jordan. ⁴³ And Bacchides heard it, and he came on the Sabbath day to the banks of Jordan with a great army. ⁴⁴ And Jonathan said to his company, "Let us stand up now and fight for our lives, for it is not [with us] today, as yesterday and the day before. ⁴⁵ For behold, the battle is before us and behind us; moreover, the water of the Jordan is on this side and on that side, and marsh and wood; and there is no place to escape. ⁴⁶ Now therefore, cry to Heaven, that you may be delivered out of the hand of your enemies." ⁴⁷ And the battle was joined, and Jonathan stretched out his hand to strike Bacchides, and he turned away back from him. ⁴⁸ And Jonathan and those who were with him leapt into the Jordan and swam over to the other side: and they did not pass over Jordan against them. ⁴⁹ And there fell of Bacchides' company that day about one thousand men; ⁵⁰ and he returned to Jerusalem. And they built strong cities in Judea, the stronghold that was in Jericho, and Emmaus, and Bethhoron, and Bethel, and Timnath, Pharathon, and Tephon, with high walls and gates and bars. ⁵¹ And in them he set a garrison, to vex Israel. ⁵² And he fortified the city Bethsura, and Gazara, and the citadel, and put forces in them, and store of food. ⁵³ And he took the sons of the chief men of the country for hostages and put them in ward in the citadel at Jerusalem. ⁵⁴ And in the one hundred and fifty-third year, in the second month, Alcimus commanded to pull down the wall of the inner court of the sanctuary; he pulled down also the works of the prophets; ⁵⁵ and he began to pull down. At that time was Alcimus stricken, and his works were hindered; and his mouth was stopped, and he was taken with a palsy, and he could no longer speak anything and give order concerning his house. ⁵⁶ And Alcimus died at that time with great torment. ⁵⁷ And Bacchides saw that Alcimus was dead, and he returned to the king: and the land of Judah had rest two years. ⁵⁸ And all the lawless men took counsel, saying, "Behold, Jonathan and they of his part are dwelling at ease, and in security: now therefore we will bring Bacchides, and he will lay hands on them all in one night." ⁵⁹ And they went and consulted with him. ⁶⁰ And he went, and came with a great army, and sent letters privily to all his allies that were in Judea, that they should lay hands on Jonathan and those that were with him: and they could not, because their counsel was known to them. ⁶¹ And [those who were of Jonathan's part] laid hands on about fifty of the men of the country, that were authors of the wickedness, and he killed them. ⁶² And Jonathan, and Simon, and those who were with him, got them away to Bethbasi, which is in the wilderness, and he built up that which had been pulled down thereof, and they made it strong. ⁶³ And Bacchides knew it, and he gathered together all his multitude, and sent word to those who were of Judea. ⁶⁴ And he went and encamped against Bethbasi, and fought against it many days, and made engines of war. ⁶⁵ And Jonathan left his brother Simon in the city, and went out into the country, and he went with a few men. ⁶⁶ And he struck Odomera and his relatives, and the children of Phasiron in their tent. ⁶⁷ And they began to strike them, and to go up with their forces. And Simon and those who were with him went out of the city, and set on fire the engines of war, ⁶⁸ and fought against Bacchides, and he was defeated by them, and they afflicted him severely; for his counsel was in vain, and his inroad. ⁶⁹ And they were very angry with the lawless men that gave him counsel to come into the country, and they killed many of them. And he took counsel to depart into his own land. ⁷⁰ And Jonathan had knowledge thereof, and sent ambassadors to him, to the end that they should make peace with him, and that he should restore to them the captives. ⁷¹ And he accepted the thing, and did according to his words, and swore to him that he would not seek his hurt all the days of his life. ⁷² And he restored to him the captives which he had taken previously out of the land of Judah, and he returned and departed into his own land, and came not anymore into their borders. ⁷³ And the sword ceased from Israel. And Jonathan lived at Michmash; and Jonathan began to judge the people; and he destroyed the ungodly out of Israel.

CHAPTER 10

¹ And in the one hundred and sixtieth year, Alexander Epiphanes, the son of Antiochus, went up and took possession of Ptolemais: and they received him, and he reigned there. ² And King Demetrius heard thereof, and he gathered together exceedingly great forces, and went out to meet him in battle. ³ And Demetrius sent letters to Jonathan with words of peace, so as to magnify him. ⁴ For he said, "Let us go beforehand to make peace with them, before he makes peace with Alexander against us: ⁵ for he will remember all the evils that we have done against him, and to his countrymen and to his nation." ⁶ And he gave him authority to gather together forces, and to provide arms, and that he should be his ally: and he commanded that they should deliver up to him the hostages that were in the citadel. ⁷ And Jonathan came to Jerusalem and read the letters in the audience of all the people, and of those who were in the citadel: ⁸ and they were severely afraid, when they heard that the king had given him authority to gather together an army. ⁹ And they of the citadel delivered up the hostages to Jonathan, and he restored them to their parents. ¹⁰ And Jonathan lived in Jerusalem and began to build and renew the city. ¹¹ And he commanded those who did the work to build the walls and Mount Zion around with square stones for defense; and they did so. ¹² And the strangers, that were in the strongholds which Bacchides had built, fled away; ¹³ and each man left his place, and departed into his own land. ¹⁴ Only at Bethsura were there left certain of those that had forsaken the law and the commands; for it was a place of refuge to them. ¹⁵ And King Alexander heard all the promises which Demetrius had sent to Jonathan: and they told him of the battles and the valiant deeds which he and his countrymen had done, and of the toils which they had endured; ¹⁶ And he said, "Will we find such another man? And now we will make him our friend and ally." ¹⁷ And he wrote letters, and sent them to him, according to these words, saying, ¹⁸ "King Alexander to his brother Jonathan, greetings: ¹⁹ We have heard of you, that you are a mighty man of valor, and meet to be our friend. ²⁰ And now we have appointed you this day to be chief priest of your nation, and to be called the king's friend (and he sent to him a purple robe and a crown of gold), and to take our part, and to keep friendship with us." ²¹ And Jonathan put on the holy garments in the seventh month of the one hundred and sixtieth year, at the Celebration of Shelters, and he gathered together forces, and provided arms in abundance. ²² And Demetrius heard these things, and he was grieved, and said, ²³ "What is this that we have done, that Alexander has been beforehand with us in establishing friendship with the Jews, to strengthen himself? ²⁴ I also will write to them words of encouragement and of honor and of gifts, that they may be with me to aid me." ²⁵ And he sent to them according to these words: "King Demetrius to the nation of the Jews, greetings: ²⁶ Forasmuch as you have kept your covenants with us, and continued in

our friendship, and have not joined yourselves to our enemies, we have heard of this, and are glad. ²⁷ And now continue still to keep faith with us, and we will repay to you good things in return for your dealings with us, ²⁸ and will grant you many immunities, and give you gifts. ²⁹ And now I free you, and release all the Jews, from the tributes, and from the customs of salt, and from the crowns. ³⁰ And instead of the third part of the seed, and instead of the half of the fruit of the trees, which falls to me to receive, I release it from this day and from now on, so that I will not take it from the land of Judah, and from the three governments which are added to that from the country of Samaria and Galilee, from this day out and for all time. ³¹ And let Jerusalem be holy and free, and her borders; the tenths and the tolls [also]. ³² I yield up also my authority over the citadel which is at Jerusalem, and give it to the chief priest, that he may appoint in it such men as he will choose to keep it. ³³ And every soul of the Jews, that has been carried captive from the land of Judah into any part of my kingdom, I set at liberty without price; and let all remit the tributes of their cattle also. ³⁴ And all the feasts, and the Sabbaths, and new moons, and appointed days, and three days before a feast, and three days after a feast, let them all be days of immunity and release for all the Jews that are in my kingdom. ³⁵ And no man will have authority to exact from any of them, or to trouble them concerning any matter. ³⁶ And let there be enrolled among the king's forces about thirty thousand men of the Jews, and pay will be given to them, as belongs to all the king's forces. ³⁷ And of them some will be placed in the king's great strongholds, and some of them will be placed over the affairs of the kingdom, which are of trust: and let those that are over them, and their rulers, be of themselves, and let them walk after their own laws, even as the king has commanded in the land of Judah. ³⁸ And the three governments that have been added to Judea from the country of Samaria, let them be added to Judea, that they may be reckoned to be under one, that they may not obey other authority than the chief priest's. ³⁹ As for Ptolemais, and the land pertaining to that, I have given it as a gift to the sanctuary that is at Jerusalem, for the expenses that befit the sanctuary. ⁴⁰ And I give every year fifteen thousand shekels of silver from the king's revenues from the places that are convenient. ⁴¹ And all the overplus, which those who manage the king's affairs paid not in as in the first years, they will give from now on toward the works of the house. ⁴² And besides this, the five thousand shekels of silver, which they received from the uses of the sanctuary from the revenue year by year, this is also released, because it pertains to the priests that minister. ⁴³ And whoever will flee to the temple that is at Jerusalem, and [be found] within all the borders thereof, whether one owes money to the king, or any other matter, let them

go free, and all that they have in my kingdom. ⁴⁴ And for the building and renewing of the works of the sanctuary the expense will be given also out of the king's revenue. ⁴⁵ And for the building of the walls of Jerusalem, and the fortifying thereof around, will the expense be given also out of the king's revenue, and for the building of the walls in Judea." ⁴⁶ Now when Jonathan and the people heard these words, they gave no credence to them, nor received them, because they remembered the great evil which he had done in Israel, and that he had afflicted them very severely. ⁴⁷ And they were well pleased with Alexander, because he was the first that spoke words of peace to them, and they were allies with him always. ⁴⁸ And King Alexander gathered together great forces and encamped near Demetrius. ⁴⁹ And the two kings joined battle, and the army of Alexander fled; and Demetrius followed after him and prevailed against them. ⁵⁰ And he strengthened the battle exceedingly until the sun went down: and Demetrius fell that day. ⁵¹ And Alexander sent ambassadors to Ptolemy king of Egypt according to these words, saying, ⁵² "Forasmuch as I am returned to my kingdom, and am set on the throne of my fathers, and have gotten the dominion, and have overthrown Demetrius, and have gotten possession of our country; ⁵³ yes, I joined the battle with him, and he and his army were defeated by us, and we sat on the throne of his kingdom: ⁵⁴ now also let us make friends with one another, and give me now your daughter to wife: and I will be joined with you, and will give both you and her gifts worthy of you." ⁵⁵ And Ptolemy the king answered, saying, "Happy is the day wherein you returned into the land of your fathers, and sat on the throne of their kingdom. ⁵⁶ And now I will do to you as you have written, but meet me at Ptolemais, that we may see one another; and I will join with you, even as you have said." ⁵⁷ And Ptolemy went out of Egypt, himself and Cleopatra his daughter, and came to Ptolemais in the one hundred and sixty-second year: ⁵⁸ and King Alexander met him, and he bestowed on him his daughter Cleopatra, and celebrated her wedding at Ptolemais with great pomp, as the manner of kings is. ⁵⁹ And King Alexander wrote to Jonathan, that he should come to meet him. ⁶⁰ And he went with pomp to Ptolemais, and met the two kings, and gave them and their friends silver and gold, and many gifts, and found favor in their sight. ⁶¹ And there were gathered together against him certain pernicious fellows out of Israel, men that were transgressors of the law, to complain against him: and the king gave no heed to them. ⁶² And the king commanded, and they took off Jonathan's garments, and clothed him in purple: and so they did. ⁶³ And the king made him sit with him, and said to his princes, "Go out with him into the midst of the city, and make proclamation, that no man complains against him of any matter, and let no man trouble him for any manner of cause." ⁶⁴ And it came to pass, when those who complained against him saw his glory according as [the herald] made proclamation, and [saw] him clothed in purple, they all fled away. ⁶⁵ And the king gave him honor, and wrote him among his chief friends, and made him a captain, and governor of a province. ⁶⁶ And Jonathan returned to Jerusalem with peace and gladness. ⁶⁷ And in the one hundred and sixty-fifth year came Demetrius, son of Demetrius, out of Crete into the land of his fathers: ⁶⁸ and King Alexander heard thereof, and he grieved exceedingly, and returned to Antioch. ⁶⁹ And Demetrius appointed Apollonius, who was over Coele-Syria, and he gathered together a great army, and encamped in Jamnia, and sent to Jonathan the chief priest, saying, ⁷⁰ "You alone lift up yourself against us, but I am had in derision and in reproach because of you. And why do you vaunt your power against us in the mountains? ⁷¹ Now therefore, if you trust in your forces, come down to us into the plain, and there let us try the matter together; for with me is the power of the cities. ⁷² Ask and learn who I am, and the rest that help us; and they say your foot cannot stand before our face; for your fathers have been twice put to flight in their own land. ⁷³ And now you will not be able to withstand the horse and such an army as this in the plain, where is neither stone nor flint, nor place to flee to." ⁷⁴ Now when Jonathan heard the words of Apollonius, he was moved in his mind, and he chose out ten thousand men, and went out from Jerusalem, and Simon his brother met him for to help him. ⁷⁵ And he encamped against Joppa: and they of the city shut him out, because Apollonius had a garrison in Joppa: ⁷⁶ and they fought against it. And they of the city were afraid and opened to him: and Jonathan became master of Joppa. ⁷⁷ And Apollonius heard, and he gathered an army of three thousand horses, and a great army, and went to Azotus as though he were on a journey, and immediately drew onward into the plain, because he had a multitude of horse, and trusted therein. ⁷⁸ And he pursued after him to Azotus, and the armies joined battle. ⁷⁹ And Apollonius had left one thousand horses behind them privily. ⁸⁰ And Jonathan knew that there was an ambush behind him. And they compassed round his army, and cast their darts at the people, from morning until evening: ⁸¹ but the people stood still, as Jonathan commanded them: and their horses were wearied. ⁸² And Simon drew out his army and joined battle with the phalanx (for the horsemen were spent), and they were defeated by him, and fled. ⁸³ And the horsemen were scattered in the plain, and they fled to Azotus, and entered into Beth-Dagon, their idol's temple, to save themselves. ⁸⁴ And Jonathan burned Azotus, and the surrounding cities, and took their spoils; and the temple of Dagon, and those who fled into it, he burned with fire. ⁸⁵ And those who had fallen by the sword, with those who were burned, were about eight thousand men. ⁸⁶ And from there Jonathan left, and encamped against Ashkelon, and they of the city came out to meet him with great pomp. ⁸⁷ And Jonathan, with those who were on his side, returned to Jerusalem, having many spoils. ⁸⁸ And it came to pass, when King Alexander heard these things, he honored Jonathan yet more; ⁸⁹ and he sent to him a buckle of gold, as the use is to give to such as are of the relatives of the kings: and he gave him Ekron and all the coasts thereof for a possession.

CHAPTER 11

¹ And the king of Egypt gathered together great forces, as the sand which is by the seashore, and many ships, and sought to make himself master of Alexander's kingdom by deceit, and to add it to his own kingdom. ² And he went out into Syria with words of peace, and they of the cities opened to him, and met him; For King Alexander's command was that they should meet him, because he was his father-in-law. ³ Now as he entered into the cities of Ptolemais, he set his forces for a garrison in each city. ⁴ But when he came near to Azotus, they showed him the temple of Dagon burned with fire, and Azotus and the pasture lands thereof pulled down, and the bodies cast abroad, and those who had been burned, whom he burned in the war, for they had made heaps of them in his way. ⁵ And they told the king what things Jonathan had done, that they might cast blame on him: and the king held his peace. ⁶ And Jonathan met the king with pomp at Joppa, and they saluted one another, and they slept there. ⁷ And Jonathan went with the king as far as the river that is called Eleutherus and returned to Jerusalem. ⁸ But King Ptolemy became master of the cities on the seacoast, to Selucia which is by the sea, and he devised evil plans concerning Alexander. ⁹ And he sent ambassadors to King Demetrius, saying, "Come! Let us make a covenant with one another, and I will give you my daughter whom Alexander has, and you will reign over your father's kingdom; ¹⁰ for I have changed my mind that I gave my daughter to him, for he sought to kill me." ¹¹ And he cast blame on him, because he coveted his kingdom. ¹² And taking his daughter from him, he gave her to Demetrius, and was estranged from Alexander, and their enmity was openly seen. ¹³ And Ptolemy entered into Antioch and put on himself the diadem of Asia; and he put two diadems on his head, the diadem of Egypt and that of Asia. ¹⁴ But King Alexander was in Cilicia at that season, because they of those parts were in revolt. ¹⁵ And Alexander heard of it, and he came against him in war: and Ptolemy led out [his army, and] met him with a strong force, and put him to flight. ¹⁶ And Alexander fled into Arabia, that he might be sheltered there; but King Ptolemy was exalted. ¹⁷ And Zabdiel the Arabian took off Alexander's head and sent it to Ptolemy. ¹⁸ And King Ptolemy died the third day after,

and those who were in his strongholds were slain by those who were in the strongholds. ¹⁹And Demetrius reigned in the one hundred and sixty-seventh year. ²⁰In those days Jonathan gathered together them of Judea, to take the citadel that was at Jerusalem: and he made many engines of war against it. ²¹And certain that hated their own nation, men that transgressed the law, went to the king, and reported to him that Jonathan was besieging the citadel. ²²And he heard, and was angered; but when he heard it, he set out immediately, and came to Ptolemais, and wrote to Jonathan, that he should not besiege it, and that he should meet him and speak with him at Ptolemais with all speed. ²³But when Jonathan heard this, he commanded to besiege it [still]: and he chose certain of the elders of Israel and of the priests, and put himself in peril, ²⁴and taking silver and gold and raiment and various presents besides, went to Ptolemais to the king. And he found favor in his sight. ²⁵And certain lawless men of those who were of the nation made complaints against him, ²⁶and the king did to him even as his predecessors had done to him and exalted him in the sight of all his friends, ²⁷and confirmed to him the chief priesthood, and all the other honors that he had before, and gave him preeminence among his chief friends. ²⁸And Jonathan requested of the king, that he would make Judea free from tribute, and the three provinces, and the country of Samaria; and promised him three hundred talents. ²⁹And the king consented and wrote letters to Jonathan concerning all these things after this manner: ³⁰"King Demetrius to his brother Jonathan, and to the nation of the Jews, greetings: ³¹The copy of the letter which we wrote to Lasthenes our countryman concerning you, we have written also to you, that you may see it. ³²King Demetrius to Lasthenes his father, greetings: ³³We have determined to do good to the nation of the Jews, who are our friends, and observe what is just toward us, because of their good will toward us. ³⁴We have confirmed therefore to them the borders of Judea, and also the three governments of Aphaerema and Lydda and Ramathaim ([these] were added to Judea from the country of Samaria), and all things pertaining to them, for all such as do sacrifice in Jerusalem, instead of the king's dues which the king received of them yearly previously from the produce of the earth and the fruits of trees. ³⁵And as for the other things that pertain to us from now on, of the tenths and the tolls that pertain to us, and the salt pits, and the crowns that pertain to us, all these we will bestow on them. ³⁶And not one of these things will be annulled from this time out and forever. ³⁷Now therefore, be careful to make a copy of these things, and let it be given to Jonathan, and let it be set up on the holy mount in an appropriate and conspicuous place." ³⁸And King Demetrius saw that the land was quiet before him, and that no resistance was made to him, and he sent away all his forces, each man to his own place, except the foreign forces, which he had raised from the isles of the nations: and all the forces of his fathers hated him. ³⁹Now Tryphon was of those who previously had been of Alexander's part, and he saw that all the forces murmured against Demetrius, and he went to Imalcue the Arabian, who was nourishing up Antiochus the young child of Alexander, ⁴⁰and pressed severely on him that he should deliver him to him, that he might reign in his father's stead: and he told him all that Demetrius had done, and the hatred with which his forces hated him; and he dwelt there many days. ⁴¹And Jonathan sent to King Demetrius, that he should cast out of Jerusalem them of the citadel, and those who were in the strongholds; for they fought against Israel continually. ⁴²And Demetrius sent to Jonathan, saying, "I will not only do this for you and your nation, but I will greatly honor you and your nation, if I find fair occasion. ⁴³Now therefore you will do well, if you send me men who will fight for me; for all my forces are revolted." ⁴⁴And Jonathan sent him three thousand valiant men to Antioch: and they came to the king, and the king was glad at their coming. ⁴⁵And they of the city gathered themselves together into the midst of the city, to the number of one hundred and twenty thousand men, and they were inclined to kill the king. ⁴⁶And the king fled into the court of the palace, and they of the city seized the passages of the city and began to fight. ⁴⁷And the king called the Jews to help him, and they were gathered together to him all at once, and they dispersed themselves in the city, and killed that day to the number of one hundred thousand. ⁴⁸And they set the city on fire, and got many spoils that day, and saved the king. ⁴⁹And they of the city saw that the Jews had made themselves masters of the city as they would, and they waxed faint in their hearts, and they cried out to the king with supplication, saying, ⁵⁰"Give us your right hand, and let the Jews cease from fighting against us and the city." ⁵¹And they cast away their arms and made peace; and the Jews were glorified in the sight of the king, and before all that were in his kingdom; and they returned to Jerusalem, having many spoils. ⁵²And King Demetrius sat on the throne of his kingdom, and the land was quiet before him. ⁵³And he lied in all that he spoke, and estranged himself from Jonathan, and did not repay him according to the benefits with which he had repaid him and afflicted him exceedingly. ⁵⁴Now after this, Tryphon returned, and with him the young child Antiochus; and he reigned and put on a diadem. ⁵⁵And there were gathered to him all the forces which Demetrius had sent away with disgrace, and they fought against him, and he fled and was put to the rout. ⁵⁶And Tryphon took the elephants and became master of Antioch. ⁵⁷And the young Antiochus wrote to Jonathan, saying, "I confirm to you the chief priesthood, and appoint you over the four governments, and to be one of the king's friends." [58] And he sent to him golden vessels and furniture for the table, and gave him leave to drink in golden vessels, and to be clothed in purple, and to have a golden buckle. [59] And his brother Simon he made captain from the Ladder of Tyre to the borders of Egypt. [60] And Jonathan went out and took his journey beyond the river and through the cities; and all the forces of Syria gathered themselves to him for to be his allies. And he came to Ashkelon, and they of the city met him honorably. [61] And he departed from there to Gaza, and they of Gaza shut him out; and he laid siege to it, and burned the pasture lands thereof with fire, and plundered them. [62] And they of Gaza made request to Jonathan, and he gave them his right hand, and took the sons of their princes for hostages, and sent them away to Jerusalem; and he passed through the country as far as Damascus. [63] And Jonathan heard that Demetrius' princes were come to Kedesh, which is in Galilee, with a great army, purposing to remove him from his office; [64] and he went to meet them, but Simon his brother he left in the country. [65] And Simon encamped against Bethsura, and fought against it many days, and shut it up: [66] and they made request to him that he would give them his right hand, and he gave it to them; and he put them out from there, and took possession of the city, and set a garrison over it. [67] And Jonathan and his army encamped at the water of Gennesareth, and early in the morning they got them to the plain of Hazor. [68] And behold, an army of strangers met him in the plain, and they laid an ambush for him in the mountains, but themselves met him face to face. [69] But those who lay in ambush rose out of their places and joined battle; and all those who were of Jonathan's side fled: [70] not one of them was left, except Mattathias, the son of Absalom, and Judas the son of Chalphi, captains of the forces. [71] And Jonathan tore his clothes, and put earth on his head, and prayed. [72] And he turned again to them in battle, and put them to the rout, and they fled. [73] And they of his side that fled saw it, and returned to him, and pursued with him to Kedesh to their camp, and they encamped there. [74] And there fell of the strangers on that day about three thousand men: and Jonathan returned to Jerusalem.

CHAPTER 12

[1] And Jonathan saw that the time served him, and he chose men, and sent them to Rome, to confirm and renew the friendship that they had with them. [2] And to the Spartans, and to other places, he sent letters after the same manner. [3] And they went to Rome, and entered into the senate house, and said, "Jonathan the chief priest, and the nation of the Jews, have sent us, to renew for them the friendship and the confederacy, as in former time." [4] And they gave them letters to the men in every place, that they should bring them on their way to the land of Judah in peace. [5] And this is the copy of the letters which Jonathan wrote to the Spartans: [6] "Jonathan the chief priest, and the senate of the nation, and the priests, and the rest of the people of the Jews, to their countrymen the Spartans, greetings: [7] Even before this time were letters sent to Onias the chief priest from Arius, who was reigning among you, to signify that you are our countrymen, as the copy written below shows. [8] And Onias entreated honorably the man that was sent, and received the letters, wherein declaration was made of confederacy and friendship. [9] Therefore we also, albeit we need none of these things, having for our encouragement the holy scrolls which are in our hands, [10] have determined to send that we might renew our brotherhood and friendship with you, to the end that we should not become estranged from you altogether, for a long time has passed since you sent to us. [11] We therefore, at all times without ceasing, both in our feasts, and on the other convenient days, remember you in the sacrifices which we offer, and in our prayers, as it is right and appropriate to be mindful of countrymen: [12] and moreover are glad for your glory. [13] But as for ourselves, many afflictions and many wars have encompassed us, and the kings that are around us have fought against us. [14] We were not inclined therefore to be troublesome to you, and to the rest of our allies and friends, in these wars; [15] for we have the help which is from Heaven to help us, and we have been delivered from our enemies, and our enemies have been brought low. [16] We chose, therefore, Numenius the son of Antiochus, and Antipater the son of Jason, and have sent them to the Romans, to renew the friendship that we had with them, and the former confederacy. [17] We commanded them, therefore, to go also to you, and to salute you, and to deliver you our letters concerning the renewing [of friendship] and our brotherhood. [18] And now you will do well if you give us an answer to that. [19] And this is the copy of the letters which they sent to Onias: [20] Arius, king of the Spartans, to Onias the chief priest, greetings: [21] It has been found in writing, concerning the Spartans and the Jews, that they are countrymen, and that they are of the stock of Abraham: [22] and now, since this has come to our knowledge, you will do well to write to us of your prosperity. [23] And we moreover write on our part to you, that your cattle and goods are ours, and ours are yours. We command, therefore, that they make report to you concerning this." [24] And Jonathan heard that Demetrius' princes were returned to fight against him with a greater army than before, [25] and he went from Jerusalem, and met them in the country of Hamath; for he gave them no respite to set foot in his country. [26] And he sent spies into his camp, and they came again, and reported to him that they were appointed in such and such a way to fall on them in the night season. [27] But as soon as the sun was down, Jonathan commanded his men to watch, and to be in arms, that all the night long they

might be ready for battle: and he put out sentinels around the camp. ²⁸ And the adversaries heard that Jonathan and his men were ready for battle, and they feared, and trembled in their hearts, and they kindled fires in their camp, ²⁹ but Jonathan and his men did not know it until the morning; for they saw the lights burning. ³⁰ And Jonathan pursued after them and overtook them not; for they were gone over the River Eleutherus. ³¹ And Jonathan turned toward the Arabians, who are called Zabadaeans, and struck them, and took their spoils. ³² And he came out from there, and came to Damascus, and took his journey through all the country. ³³ And Simon went out, and took his journey as far as Ashkelon, and the strongholds that were near to it. And he turned toward Joppa and took possession of it; ³⁴ for he had heard that they were determined to deliver the stronghold to the men of Demetrius; and he set a garrison there to keep it. ³⁵ And Jonathan returned, and called the elders of the people together; and he took counsel with them to build strongholds in Judea, ³⁶ and to make the walls of Jerusalem higher, and to raise a great mound between the citadel and the city, for to separate it from the city, that so it might be all alone, that men might neither buy nor sell. ³⁷ And they were gathered together to build the city, and there fell down part of the wall of the brook that is on the east side, and he repaired that which is called Chaphenatha. ³⁸ And Simon also built Adida in the plain country, and made it strong, and set up gates and bars. ³⁹ And Tryphon sought to reign over Asia and to put on himself the diadem, and to stretch out his hand against Antiochus the king. ⁴⁰ And he was afraid lest perhaps Jonathan should not permit him, and lest he should fight against him; and he sought a way how to take him, that he might destroy him. And he went and came to Bethshan. ⁴¹ And Jonathan came out to meet him with forty thousand men chosen for battle and came to Bethshan. ⁴² And Tryphon saw that he came with a great army, and he was afraid to stretch out his hand against him: ⁴³ and he received him honorably, and commended him to all his friends, and gave him gifts, and commanded his forces to be obedient to him, as to himself. ⁴⁴ And he said to Jonathan, "Why have you put all this people to trouble, seeing there is no war between us? ⁴⁵ And now send them away to their homes but choose for yourself a few men who will be with you, and come you with me to Ptolemais, and I will give it up to you, and the rest of the strongholds and the rest of the forces, and all the king's officers: and I will return and depart; for this is the cause of my coming." ⁴⁶ And he put his trust in him, and did even as he said, and sent away his forces, and they departed into the land of Judah. ⁴⁷ But he reserved to himself three thousand men, of whom he left two thousand in Galilee, but one thousand went with him. ⁴⁸ Now as soon as Jonathan entered into Ptolemais, they of Ptolemais shut the gates, and laid hands on him; and

all those who came in with him they killed with the sword. ⁴⁹ And Tryphon sent forces and horsemen into Galilee, and into the great plain, to destroy all Jonathan's men. ⁵⁰ And they perceived that he was taken and had perished, and those who were with him; and they encouraged one another, and went on their way close together, prepared to fight. ⁵¹ And those who followed on them saw that they were ready to fight for their lives and turned back again. ⁵² And they all came in peace into the land of Judah, and they mourned for Jonathan, and those who were with him, and they were severely afraid; and all Israel mourned with a great mourning. ⁵³ And all the nations that were around them sought to destroy them utterly, for they said, "They have no ruler, nor any to help them: now therefore, let us fight against them and take away their memorial from among men."

CHAPTER 13

¹ And Simon heard that Tryphon had gathered together a mighty army to come into the land of Judah and destroy it utterly. ² And he saw that the people trembled and were in great fear; and he went up to Jerusalem, and gathered the people together; ³ and he encouraged them, and said to them, "You yourselves know all the things that I, and my countrymen, and my father's house, have done for the laws and the sanctuary, and the battles and the distresses which we have seen: ⁴ by reason of this all my countrymen have perished for Israel's sake, and I am left alone. ⁵ And now be it far from me, that I should spare my own life in any time of affliction; for I am not better than my countrymen. ⁶ However, I will take vengeance for my nation, and for the sanctuary, and for our wives and children, because all the nations are gathered to destroy us of very [great] hatred." ⁷ And the spirit of the people revived, as soon as they heard these words. ⁸ And they answered with a loud voice, saying, "You are our leader instead of Judas and Jonathan your brother. ⁹ Fight our battles, and all that you will say to us, that will we do." ¹⁰ And he gathered together all the men of war, and hurried to finish the walls of Jerusalem, and he fortified it around. ¹¹ And he sent Jonathan the son of Absalom, and with him a great army, to Joppa; and he cast out those who were therein and dwelt there in it. ¹² And Tryphon left from Ptolemais with a mighty army to enter into the land of Judah, and Jonathan was with him in ward. ¹³ But Simon encamped at Adida, near the plain. ¹⁴ And Tryphon knew that Simon was risen up instead of his brother Jonathan, and meant to join battle with him, and he sent ambassadors to him, saying, ¹⁵ "It is for money which Jonathan your brother owed to the king's treasure, by reason of the offices which he had, that we hold him fast. ¹⁶ And now send one hundred talents of silver, and two of his sons for hostages, that when he is set at liberty he may not revolt from us, and we will set him at liberty." ¹⁷ And Simon knew

that they spoke to him deceitfully; and he sent the money and the children, lest perhaps he should procure to himself great hatred of the people, [18] and they should say, "Because I did not send him the money and the children, he perished." [19] And he sent the children and the hundred talents. And he dealt falsely and did not set Jonathan at liberty. [20] And after this Tryphon came to invade the land, and destroy it, and he went around by the way that leads to Adora: and Simon and his army marched near him to every place, wherever he went. [21] Now they of the citadel sent to Tryphon ambassadors, hastening him to come to them through the wilderness, and to send them food. [22] And Tryphon made ready all his horse to come: and on that night there fell a very great snow, and he came not by reason of the snow. And he left and came into the country of Gilead. [23] But when he came near to Bascama, he killed Jonathan, and he was buried there. [24] And Tryphon returned and went away into his own land. [25] And Simon sent, and took the bones of Jonathan his brother, and buried him at Modin, the city of his fathers. [26] And all Israel made great lamentation over him and mourned for him many days. [27] And Simon built [a monument] on the tomb of his father and his relatives, and raised it aloft to the sight, with polished stone behind and before. [28] And he set up seven pyramids, one near another, for his father, and his mother, and his four relatives. [29] And for these he made cunning devices, setting around them great pillars, and on the pillars he fashioned all manner of arms for a perpetual memory, and beside the arms ships carved, that they should be seen of all that sail on the sea. [30] This is the tomb which he made at Modin, and [it is there] to this day. [31] Now Tryphon dealt deceitfully with the young King Antiochus, and killed him, [32] and reigned in his stead, and put the diadem of Asia on himself, and brought a great calamity on the land. [33] And Simon built the strongholds of Judea, and fenced them about with high towers, and great walls, and gates, and bars; and he laid up food in the strongholds. [34] And Simon chose men, and sent to King Demetrius, to the end he should give the country an immunity, because all that Tryphon did was to plunder. [35] And King Demetrius sent to him according to these words, and answered him, and wrote a letter to him, after this manner: [36] "King Demetrius to Simon the chief priest and friend of kings, and to the elders and nation of the Jews, greetings: [37] The golden crown, and the palm branch, which you sent, we have received: and we are ready to make a steadfast peace with you, yes, and to write to our officers, to grant immunities to you. [38] And whatever things we confirmed to you, they are confirmed; and the strongholds, which you have built, let them be your own. [39] As for any oversights and faults committed to this day, we forgive them, and the crown which you owed us: and if there were any other toll exacted in Jerusalem, let it be exacted no longer.

[40] And if there are any among you appropriate to be enrolled in our court, let them be enrolled, and let there be peace between us." [41] In the one hundred and seventieth year was the yoke of the heathen taken away from Israel. [42] And the people began to write in their instruments and contracts, "In the first year of Simon, the great chief priest and captain and leader of the Jews." [43] In those days he encamped against Gazara and compassed it around with armies; and he made an engine of siege, and brought it up to the city, and struck a tower, and took it. [44] And those who were in the engine leaped out into the city; and there was a great uproar in the city: [45] and they of the city tore their clothes and went up on the walls with their wives and children, and cried with a loud voice, making request to Simon to give them his right hand. [46] And they said, "Do not deal with us according to our wickedness, but according to your mercy." [47] And Simon was reconciled to them and did not fight against them: and he put them out of the city, and cleansed the houses wherein the idols were, and so entered into it with singing and giving praise. [48] And he put all uncleanness out of it and placed in it such men as would keep the law, and made it stronger than it was before, and built therein a dwelling place for himself. [49] But they of the citadel in Jerusalem were hindered from going out, and from going into the country, and from buying and selling; and they hungered exceedingly, and a great number of them perished through famine. [50] And they cried out to Simon, that he should give them his right hand; and he gave it to them: and he put them out from there, and he cleansed the citadel from its pollutions. [51] And he entered into it on the twenty-third day of the second month, in the one hundred and seventy-first year, with praise and palm branches, and with harps, and with cymbals, and with lutes, and with hymns, and with songs: because a great enemy was destroyed out of Israel. [52] And he ordained that they should keep that day every year with gladness. And the hill of the temple that was by the citadel he made stronger than before, and there he lived, himself and his men. [53] And Simon saw that John his son was a [valiant] man, and he made him leader of all his forces: and he lived in Gazara.

CHAPTER 14

[1] And in the one hundred and seventy-second year, King Demetrius gathered his forces together, and went into Media, to get himself help, that he might fight against Tryphon. [2] And Arsaces, the king of Persia and Media, heard that Demetrius had come into his borders, and he sent one of his princes to take him alive: [3] and he went and struck the army of Demetrius, and took him, and brought him to Arsaces; and he put him in ward. [4] And the land had rest all the days of Simon: and he sought the good of his nation; and his authority and his glory was well-

pleasing to them all his days. ⁵ And amid all his glory he took Joppa for a haven and made it an entrance for the isles of the sea; ⁶ and he enlarged the borders of his nation and got possession of the country; ⁷ and he gathered together a great number of captives, and got the dominion of Gazara, and Bethsura, and the citadel, and he took away from it its uncleanness; and there was none that resisted him. ⁸ And they tilled their land in peace, and the land gave her increase, and the trees of the plains their fruit. ⁹ The ancient men sat in the streets, they communed—all of them—together of good things, and the young men put on glorious and warlike apparel. ¹⁰ He provided food for the cities, and furnished them with all manner of munition, until the name of his glory was named to the end of the earth. ¹¹ He made peace in the land, and Israel rejoiced with great joy; ¹² and each man sat under his vine and his fig tree, and there was none to make them afraid; ¹³ and there ceased in the land any that fought against them: and the kings were defeated in those days. ¹⁴ And he strengthened all those of his people that were brought low: the law he searched out, and every lawless and wicked person he took away. ¹⁵ He glorified the sanctuary, and the vessels of the temple he multiplied. ¹⁶ And it was heard at Rome that Jonathan was dead, and even to Sparta, and they were exceedingly sorry. ¹⁷ But as soon as they heard that his brother Simon was made chief priest in his stead, and ruled the country, and the cities therein, ¹⁸ they wrote to him on tablets of brass, to renew with him the friendship and the confederacy which they had confirmed with Judas and Jonathan his relatives; ¹⁹ and they were read before the congregation at Jerusalem. ²⁰ And this is the copy of the letters which the Spartans sent: "The rulers of the Spartans, and the city, to Simon the chief priest, and to the elders, and the priests, and the residue of the people of the Jews, our countrymen, greetings: ²¹ The ambassadors that were sent to our people made report to us of your glory and honor: and we were glad for their coming, ²² and we registered the things that were spoken by them in the public records after this manner: Numenius son of Antiochus, and Antipater son of Jason, the Jews' ambassadors, came to us to renew the friendship they had with us." ²³ And it pleased the people to entertain the men honorably, and to put the copy of their words in the public records, to the end that the people of the Spartans might have a memorial thereof: moreover, they wrote a copy of these things to Simon the chief priest. ²⁴ After this Simon sent Numenius to Rome with a great shield of gold of one-thousand-pound weight, in order to confirm the confederacy with them. ²⁵ But when the people heard these things, they said, "What thanks will we give to Simon and his sons? ²⁶ For he and his countrymen and the house of his father have made themselves strong and have chased away in fight the enemies of Israel from them, and confirmed liberty to Israel." ²⁷ And they wrote on tablets of brass, and set them on pillars in Mount Zion: and this is the copy of the writing: "On the eighteenth day of Elul, in the one hundred and seventy-second year, and this is the third year of Simon the chief priest, ²⁸ in Asaramel, in a great congregation of priests and people and princes of the nation, and of the elders of the country, was it notified to us: ²⁹ Forasmuch as oftentimes there have been wars in the country, but Simon the son of Mattathias, the son of the sons of Joarib, and his countrymen, put themselves in danger, and withstood the enemies of their nation, that their sanctuary and the law might be established, and glorified their nation with great glory: ³⁰ and Jonathan assembled their nation together, and became their chief priest, and was gathered to his people: ³¹ and their enemies purposed to invade their country, that they might destroy their country utterly, and stretch out their hands against their sanctuary: ³² then rose up Simon, and fought for his nation, and spent much of his own substance, and armed the valiant men of his nation, and gave them wages: ³³ and he fortified the cities of Judea, and Bethsura that lies on the borders of Judea, where the arms of the enemies were previously, and set there a garrison of Jews: ³⁴ and he fortified Joppa which is on the sea, and Gazara which is on the borders of Azotus, wherein the enemies lived previously, and placed Jews there, and set therein all things convenient for their restoration: ³⁵ and the people saw the faith of Simon, and the glory which he thought to bring to his nation, and they made him their leader and chief priest, because he had done all these things, and for the justice and the faith which he kept to his nation, and for that he sought by all means to exalt his people: ³⁶ and in his days things prospered in his hands, so that the nations were taken away out of their country, and they also that were in the city of David, those who were in Jerusalem, who had made themselves a citadel, out of which they issued, and polluted all things around the sanctuary, and did great hurt to its purity; ³⁷ and he placed Jews therein, and fortified it for the safety of the country and the city, and made high the walls of Jerusalem: ³⁸ and King Demetrius confirmed to him the chief priesthood according to these things, ³⁹ and made him one of his friends, and honored him with great honor; ⁴⁰ for he had heard it said that the Jews had been called by the Romans friends and allies and countrymen, and that they had met the ambassadors of Simon honorably; ⁴¹ and that the Jews and the priests were well pleased that Simon should be their leader and chief priest forever, until there should arise a faithful prophet; ⁴² and that he should be captain over them, and should take charge of the sanctuary, to set them over their works, and over the country, and over the arms, and over the strongholds; and that he should take charge of the sanctuary, ⁴³ and that he should be obeyed by all, and that all instruments in the country should be written in his name, and that he should be clothed in purple, and wear gold; ⁴⁴ and that it should not be lawful for any of the people or of the priests to set at nothing any of these things, or to deny the words that he should speak, or to gather an assembly in the country without him, or to be clothed in purple, or wear a buckle of gold; ⁴⁵ but whoever should do otherwise, or set at nothing any of these things, he should be liable to punishment." ⁴⁶ All the people consented to ordain for Simon that he should do according to these words; ⁴⁷ and Simon accepted this, and consented to be chief priest, and to be captain and governor of the Jews and of the priests, and to be protector of all. ⁴⁸ And they commanded to put this writing on tablets of brass, and to set them up within the precinct of the sanctuary in a conspicuous place; ⁴⁹ and moreover to put the copies thereof in the treasury, to the end that Simon and his sons might have them.

CHAPTER 15

¹ And Antiochus son of Demetrius the king sent letters from the isles of the sea to Simon the priest and governor of the Jews, and to all the nation; ² and the contents thereof were after this manner: "King Antiochus to Simon the chief priest and governor, and to the nation of the Jews, greetings: ³ Forasmuch as certain pernicious fellows have made themselves masters of the kingdom of our fathers, but my purpose is to claim the kingdom, that I may restore it as it was before; and moreover I have raised a multitude of foreign soldiers, and have prepared ships of war; ⁴ moreover I am inclined to land in the country, that I may punish those who have destroyed our country, and those who have made many cities in the kingdom desolate: ⁵ Now therefore, I confirm to you all the exactions which the kings that were before me remitted to you, and whatever gifts besides they remitted to you: ⁶ and I give you leave to coin money for your country with your own stamp, ⁷ but that Jerusalem and the sanctuary should be free: and all the arms that you have prepared, and the strongholds that you have built, which you have in your possession, let them remain to you: ⁸ and everything owing to the king, and the things that will be owing to the king from now on and forevermore, let them be remitted to you: ⁹ moreover, when we will have established our kingdom, we will glorify you and your nation and the temple with great glory, so that your glory will be made manifest in all the earth." ¹⁰ In the one hundred and seventy-fourth year Antiochus went out into the land of his fathers; and all the forces came together to him, so that there were few men with Tryphon. ¹¹ And King Antiochus pursued him, and he came, as he fled, to Dor, which is by the sea: ¹² for he knew that troubles were come on him all at once, and that his forces had forsaken him. ¹³ And Antiochus encamped against Dor, and with him one hundred and twenty thousand men of war, and eight thousand

horses. ¹⁴ And he compassed the city around, and the ships joined in the attack from the sea; and he vexed the city by land and sea, and suffered no man to go out or in. ¹⁵ And Numenius and his company came from Rome, having letters to the kings and to the countries, wherein were written these things: ¹⁶ "Lucius, consul of the Romans, to King Ptolemy, greetings: ¹⁷ The Jews' ambassadors came to us as our friends and allies, to renew the old friendship and confederacy, being sent from Simon the chief priest, and from the people of the Jews: ¹⁸ moreover they brought a shield of gold of one thousand pounds. ¹⁹ It pleased us therefore to write to the kings and to the countries, that they should not seek their hurt, nor fight against them, and their cities, and their country, nor be allies with such as fight against them. ²⁰ Moreover it seemed good to us to receive the shield from them. ²¹ If, therefore, any pernicious fellows have fled from their country to you, deliver them to Simon the chief priest, that he may take vengeance on them according to their law." ²² And he wrote the same things to Demetrius the king, and to Attalus, and to Arathes, and to Arsaces, ²³ and to all the countries, and to Sampsames, and to the Spartans, and to Delos, and to Myndos, and to Sicyon, and to Caria, and to Samos, and to Pamphylia, and to Lycia, and to Halicarnassus, and to Rhodes, and to Phaselis, and to Cos, and to Side, and to Aradus, and Gortyna, and Cnidus, and Cyprus, and Cyrene. ²⁴ But they wrote this copy to Simon the chief priest. ²⁵ But Antiochus the king encamped against Dor the second day, bringing his forces up to it continually, and making engines of war, and he shut up Tryphon from going in or out. ²⁶ And Simon sent him two thousand chosen men to fight on his side; and silver, and gold, and instruments of war in abundance. ²⁷ And he would not receive them but set at nothing all the covenants which he had made with him previously and was estranged from him. ²⁸ And he sent to him Athenobius, one of his friends, to commune with him, saying, "You hold possession of Joppa and Gazara, and the citadel that is in Jerusalem, cities of my kingdom. ²⁹ The borders thereof you have wasted, and done great hurt in the land, and gotten the dominion of many places in my kingdom. ³⁰ Now therefore, deliver up the cities which you have taken, and the tributes of the places of which you have gotten dominion without the borders of Judea: ³¹ or else give me for them five hundred talents of silver; and for the harm that you have done, and the tributes of the cities, other five hundred talents: or else we will come and subdue you." ³² And Athenobius the king's friend came to Jerusalem; and he saw the glory of Simon, and the cupboard of gold and silver vessels, and his great attendance, and he was amazed; and he reported to him the king's words. ³³ And Simon answered, and said to him, "We have neither taken other men's land, nor have we possession of that which pertains to others, but of the inheritance of our fathers; however, it was had in possession of our enemies wrongfully for a certain time. ³⁴ But we, having opportunity, hold fast the inheritance of our fathers. ³⁵ But as touching Joppa and Gazara, which you demand, they did great harm among the people throughout our country, we will give one hundred talents for them." And he did not answer him a word, ³⁶ but returned in a rage to the king, and reported to him these words, and the glory of Simon, and all that he had seen: and the king was exceedingly angry. ³⁷ But Tryphon embarked on board a ship and fled to Orthosia. ³⁸ And the king appointed Cendebaeus chief captain of the seacoast and gave him forces of foot and horse: ³⁹ and he commanded him to encamp before Judea, and he commanded him to build up Kidron, and to fortify the gates, and that he should fight against the people, but the king pursued Tryphon. ⁴⁰ And Cendebaeus came to Jamnia, and began to provoke the people, and to invade Judea, and to take the people captive, and to kill them. ⁴¹ And he built Kidron, and set horsemen there, and forces of foot, to the end that issuing out they might make excursions on the ways of Judea, according as the king commanded him.

CHAPTER 16

¹ And John went up from Gazara and told his father Simon what Cendebaeus was doing. ² And Simon called his two oldest sons, Judas and John, and said to them, I and my countrymen and my father's house have fought the battles of Israel from our youth, even to this day; and things have prospered in our hands, that we should deliver Israel oftentimes. ³ But now I am old, and you moreover, by [His] mercy, are of a sufficient age: be instead of me and my brother and go out and fight for our nation; but let the help which is from Heaven be with you. ⁴ And he chose out of the country twenty thousand men of war and horsemen, and they went against Cendebaeus, and slept at Modin. ⁵ And rising up in the morning, they went into the plain, and behold, a great army came to meet them, of footmen and horsemen: and there was a brook between them. ⁶ And he encamped near them, he and his people: and he saw that the people were afraid to pass over the brook, and he passed over first, and the men saw him, and passed over after him. ⁷ And he divided the people and [set] the horsemen in the midst of the footmen, but the enemies' horsemen were exceedingly many. ⁸ And they sounded with the trumpets; and Cendebaeus and his army were put to the rout, and there fell of them many wounded to death, but those who were left fled to the stronghold: ⁹ at that time was Judas, John's brother, wounded, but John pursued after them, until he came to Kidron, which [Cendebaeus] had built; ¹⁰ and they fled to the towers that are in the fields of Azotus; and he burned it with fire; and there fell of them about two thousand men. And he returned into Judea in peace. ¹¹ And Ptolemy the son of Abubus had been appointed captain for the plain of Jericho, and he had much silver and gold; ¹² for he was the chief priest's son-in-law. ¹³ And his heart was lifted up, and he was inclined to make himself master of the country, and he took counsel deceitfully against Simon and his sons, to make away with them. ¹⁴ Now Simon was visiting the cities that were in the country, and taking care for the good ordering of them; and he went down to Jericho, himself and Mattathias and Judas his sons, in the one hundred and seventy-seventh year, in the eleventh month, which is the month Sebat: ¹⁵ and the son of Abubus received them deceitfully into the little stronghold that is called Dok, which he had built, and made them a great banquet, and hid men there. ¹⁶ And when Simon and his sons had drunk freely, Ptolemy and his men rose up, and took their arms, and came in on Simon into the banqueting place, and killed him, and his two sons, and certain of his servants. ¹⁷ And he committed a great iniquity, and repaid evil for good. ¹⁸ And Ptolemy wrote these things, and sent to the king, that he should send him forces to aid him, and should deliver him, their country, and the cities. ¹⁹ And he sent others to Gazara to make away with John: and to the captains of thousands, he sent letters to come to him, that he might give them silver and gold and gifts. ²⁰ And others he sent to take possession of Jerusalem, and the mount of the temple. ²¹ And one ran before to Gazara and told John that his father and countrymen were perished, and he has sent to kill you also. ²² And when he heard, he was severely amazed; and he laid hands on the men that came to destroy him and killed them; for he perceived that they were seeking to destroy him. ²³ And the rest of the acts of John, and of his wars, and of his valiant deeds which he did, and of the building of the walls which he built, and of his doings, ²⁴ behold, they are written in the chronicles of his chief priesthood, from the time that he was made chief priest after his father.

2 MACCABEES

2 Maccabees is a deuterocanonical book which focuses on the Maccabean Revolt against Antiochus IV Epiphanes and concludes with the defeat of the Seleucid empire general Nicanor in 161 BC by Judas Maccabeus, the hero of the work. Unlike 1 Maccabees, 2 Maccabees was written in Koine Greek, probably in Alexandria, Egypt, circa 124 BC. It presents a revised version of the historical events recounted in the first seven chapters of 1 Maccabees, adding material from the Pharisaic tradition, including prayer for the dead and a resurrection on Judgment Day. Jews and Protestants reject most of the doctrinal issues present in the work, while Catholics and Eastern Orthodox consider the work to be deuterocanonical.

CHAPTER 1

¹ The countrymen, the Jews that are in Jerusalem and those who are in the country of Judea, send greetings to the countrymen, the Jews that are throughout Egypt, and [wish them] good peace: ² and may God do good to you, and remember His covenant with Abraham, and Isaac, and Jacob, His faithful servants; ³ and give you all a heart to worship Him and do His pleasure with a great heart and a willing soul; ⁴ and open your heart in His law and in His statutes, and make peace, ⁵ and listen to your requests, and be reconciled with you, and not forsake you in an evil time. ⁶ And now we here are praying for you. ⁷ In the reign of Demetrius, in the one hundred [and] sixty-ninth year, we the Jews have [already] written to you in the suffering and in the extremity that has come on us in these years, from the time that Jason and his company revolted from the holy land and the kingdom, ⁸ and set the gate on fire, and shed innocent blood: and we implored the LORD, and were heard; and we offered sacrifice and meal [offering, and] we lighted the lamps, and we set out the Bread of the Presentation. ⁹ And now [see] that you keep the days of the Celebration of Shelters of the month Kislev. ¹⁰ [Written] in the one hundred eighty-eighth year. They that are in Jerusalem and those who are in Judea and the senate and Judas, to Aristobulus, King Ptolemy's teacher, who is also of the stock of the anointed priests, and to the Jews that are in Egypt, send greetings and health. ¹¹ Having been saved by God out of great perils, as men arrayed against a king, we thank Him greatly. ¹² For He cast out into Persia those who arrayed themselves [against us] in the holy city. ¹³ For when the prince had come, [and] the army with him that seemed irresistible, they were cut to pieces in the temple of Nanaea by the treachery of Nanaea's priests. ¹⁴ For Antiochus, on the pretense

that he would marry her, came into the place, he and his friends that were with him, that they might take a great part of the treasures in name of a dowry. ¹⁵ And when the priests of Nanaea's temple had set the treasures out, and he had come there with a small company within the wall of the precincts, they shut to the temple when Antiochus had come in: ¹⁶ and opening the secret door of the paneled ceiling, they threw stones and struck down the prince, and they hewed [him and his company] in pieces, and struck off their heads, and cast them to those that were without. ¹⁷ Blessed [be] our God in all things, who gave [for a prey] those who had committed impiety. ¹⁸ Whereas we are now about to keep the purification of the temple in the [month] Kislev, on the twenty-fifth day, we thought it necessary to certify you thereof, that you also may keep [the] Celebration of Shelters, and [a memorial] of the fire [which was given] when Nehemiah offered sacrifices, after he had built both the temple and the altar. ¹⁹ For indeed when our fathers were about to be led into the land of Persia, the godly priests of that time took of the fire of the altar and hid it privily in the hollow of a well that was without water, wherein they made [it] sure, so that the place was unknown to all men. ²⁰ Now after many years, when it pleased God, Nehemiah, having received a charge from the king of Persia, sent in quest of the fire the descendants of the priests that hid it. When they declared to us that they had found no fire, but thick water, ²¹ he commanded them to draw out thereof and bring [to him]: and when the sacrifices had been offered, Nehemiah commanded the priests to sprinkle with the water both the wood and the things laid immediately. ²² And when it was done, and some time had passed, and the sun shone out, which before was hid with clouds, there was kindled a great blaze, so that all men marveled. ²³ And the priests made a prayer while the sacrifice was consuming, both the priests and all [others], Jonathan leading and the rest answering, as Nehemiah did. ²⁴ And the prayer was after this manner: "O LORD, LORD God, the Creator of all things, who are terrible and strong and righteous and merciful, who alone are King and gracious, ²⁵ who alone supplies [every need], who alone are righteous, and almighty, and continuous, You that save Israel out of all evil, who made the fathers [your] chosen, and sanctified them: ²⁶ accept the sacrifice for all Your people Israel, and guard Your own portion, and consecrate it. ²⁷ Gather together our dispersion, set at liberty those who are in bondage among the heathen, look on those who are despised and abhorred, and let the heathen know that You are our God. ²⁸ Torment those who oppress us and in arrogance shamefully entreat us. ²⁹ Plant Your people in Your holy place, even as Moses said." ³⁰ And immediately the priests sang the hymns. ³¹ And as soon as the sacrifice was consumed, then Nehemiah commanded to pour [on] great stones the water that was left. ³² And when this was done, a flame was kindled; but when the light from the altar shone near it, [all] was consumed. ³³ And when the matter became known, and it was told the king of the Persians, that, in the place where the priests that were led away had hid the fire, there appeared the water, with which also Nehemiah and those who were with him purified the sacrifice, ³⁴ then the king, enclosing [the place], made it sacred, after he had proved the matter. ³⁵ And when the king would show favor to any, he would take [from them] many presents and give them some of [this water]. ³⁶ And Nehemiah and those who were with him called this thing Nephthar, which is by interpretation, "Cleansing"; but most men call it Nephthai.

CHAPTER 2

¹ It is also found in the records, that Jeremiah the prophet commanded those who were carried away to take of the fire, as has been signified [above]: ² and how that the prophet charged those who were carried away, having given them the law, that they should not forget the statutes of the LORD, neither be led astray in their minds, when they saw images of gold and silver, and the adornment thereof. ³ And with other such words exhorted he them, that the law should not depart from their heart. ⁴ And it was [contained] in the writing, that the prophet, being warned of God, commanded that the Dwelling Place and the Ark should follow with him, when he went out into the mountain where Moses went up and saw the heritage of God. ⁵ And Jeremiah came and found a chamber in the rock, and there he brought in the Dwelling Place, and the Ark, and the altar of incense; and he made fast the door. ⁶ And some of those that followed with him came there that they might mark the way and could not find it. ⁷ But when Jeremiah perceived it, he blamed them, saying, "Yes, and the place will be unknown until God gathers the people again together, and mercy comes: ⁸ and then will the LORD disclose these things, and the glory of the LORD will be seen, and the cloud." As also it was shown with Moses; as also Solomon implored that the place might be consecrated greatly, ⁹ and it was also declared that he, having wisdom, offered a sacrifice of dedication, and of the finishing of the temple; [so we would have it now.] ¹⁰ As Moses prayed to the LORD, and fire came down out of Heaven and consumed the sacrifice, even so prayed Solomon also, and the fire came down and consumed the burnt-offerings ¹¹ (and Moses said, "Because the sin offering had not been eaten, it was consumed in like manner [with the rest]"); ¹² and Solomon kept the eight days. ¹³ And the same things were related both in the public archives and in the records that concern Nehemiah; and how he, founding a library, gathered together the scrolls about the kings and prophets, and the [scrolls] of David, and letters of kings about sacred gifts. ¹⁴ And in like manner Judas also gathered together for us all those [writings] that had been scattered by reason of the war that befell, and they are [still] with us. ¹⁵ If, therefore, you have need thereof, send some to fetch them to you. ¹⁶ Seeing then that we are about to keep the purification, we write to you; you will therefore do well if you keep the days. ¹⁷ Now God, who saved all His people, and restored the heritage to all, and the kingdom, and the priesthood, and the hallowing, ¹⁸ even as He promised through the law—in God we have hope, that He will quickly have mercy on us, and gather [us] together out of all the earth to the holy place, for He delivered us out of great evils, and purified the place. ¹⁹ Now the things concerning Judas Maccabaeus and his countrymen, and the purification of the great temple, and the dedication of the altar, ²⁰ and further the wars against Antiochus Epiphanes, and Eupator his son, ²¹ and the manifestations that came from Heaven to those that vied with one another in courageous deeds for the religion of the Jews; so that, being but a few, they rescued the whole country, and chased the barbarous multitudes, ²² and recovered again the temple renowned all the world over, and freed the city, and restored the laws which were like to be overthrown, seeing the LORD became gracious to them with all forbearance: ²³ [these things, I say,] which have been declared by Jason of Cyrene in five scrolls, we will determine to abridge in one work. ²⁴ For having in view the confused mass of the numbers, and the difficulty which awaits those who would enter into the narratives of the history, by reason of the abundance of the matter, ²⁵ we were careful that they who choose to read may be attracted, and that they who wish well [to our cause] may find it easy to recall [what we have written, and] that all readers may have profit. ²⁶ And although to us, who have taken on us the painful labor of the abridgement, the task is not easy, but [matter] of sweat and watching ²⁷ (even as it is no light thing to him that prepares a banquet, and seeks the benefit of others); yet for the sake of the gratitude of the many we will gladly endure the painful labor, ²⁸ leaving to the historian the exact handling of every particular, and again having no strength to fill in the outlines of our abridgement. ²⁹ For as the master builder of a new house must care for the whole structure, and again he that undertakes to decorate and paint it must seek out the things fit for the adorning thereof; even so I think it is also with us. ³⁰ To occupy the ground, and to indulge in long discussions, and to be curious in particulars, becomes the first author of the history: ³¹ but to strive after brevity of expression, and to avoid a labored fullness in the treatment, is to be granted to him that would bring a writing into a new form.

³²Here then let us begin the narration, only adding so much to that which has been already said; for it is a foolish thing to make a long prologue to the history, and to abridge the history [itself].

CHAPTER 3

¹When the holy city was inhabited with all peace, and the laws were kept very well, because of the godliness of Onias the chief priest, and his hatred of wickedness, ²it came to pass that even the kings themselves did honor the place and glorify the temple with the noblest presents; ³insomuch that even Seleucus the king of Asia of his own revenues bare all the costs belonging to the services of the sacrifices. ⁴But one Simon of the tribe of Benjamin, having been made guardian of the temple, fell out with the chief priest about the ruling of the market in the city. ⁵And when he could not overcome Onias, he got him to Apollonius [the son] of Thraseus, who at that time was governor of Coele-Syria and Phoenicia: ⁶and he brought him word how that the treasury in Jerusalem was full of untold sums of money, so that the multitude of the funds was innumerable, and that they did not pertain to the account of the sacrifices, but that it was possible that these should fall under the king's power. ⁷And when Apollonius met the king, he informed him of the money of which he had been told; and the king appointed Heliodorus, who was his chancellor, and sent him with a command to accomplish the removal of the previously mentioned money. ⁸So out with Heliodorus took his journey, under a color of visiting the cities of Coele-Syria and Phoenicia, but in fact to execute the king's purpose. ⁹And when he had come to Jerusalem and had been courteously received by the chief priest of the city, he laid before [the man] account of the information which had been given [him and] declared why he had come; and he inquired if in truth these things were so. ¹⁰And the chief priest explained to him that there were [in the treasury] deposits of widows and orphans, ¹¹and moreover some [money] belonging to Hyrcanus the [son] of Tobias, a man in very high place, and [that the case] was not as that impious Simon falsely alleged; and that in all there were four hundred talents of silver and two hundred of gold; ¹²and that it was altogether impossible that wrong should be done to them that had put trust in the holiness of the place, and in the majesty and inviolable sanctity of the temple, honored over all the world. ¹³But Heliodorus, because of the king's commands given him, said that in any case this [money] must be confiscated for the king's treasury. ¹⁴So having appointed a day, he entered in to direct the inquiry concerning these matters; and there was no small distress throughout the whole city. ¹⁵And the priests, prostrating themselves before the altar in their priestly garments, and [looking] toward Heaven, called on him that gave the law concerning deposits, that he should preserve these [treasures] safe for those that had deposited them. ¹⁶And whoever saw the mien of the chief priest was wounded in mind; for his countenance and the change of his color betrayed the distress of his soul. ¹⁷For a terror and a shuddering of the body had come over the man, whereby the pain that was in his heart was plainly shown to those who looked on him. ¹⁸And those who were in the houses rushed flocking out to make a universal supplication, because the place was like to come into contempt. ¹⁹And the women, girded with sackcloth under their breasts, thronged the streets, and the virgins that were kept in ward ran together, some to the gates, others to the walls, and some looked out through the windows. ²⁰And all, stretching out their hands toward Heaven, made their solemn supplication. ²¹Then it would have pitied a man to see the multitude prostrating themselves all mixed together, and the expectation of the chief priest in his severe distress. ²²While therefore they called on the Almighty Lord to keep the things entrusted [to them] safe and sure for those that had entrusted them, ²³Heliodorus went on to execute that which had been decreed. ²⁴But when he was already present there with his guards near the treasury, the Sovereign of spirits and of all authority caused a great apparition, so that all that had presumed to come [in] with him, stricken with dismay at the power of God, fainted and were severely afraid. ²⁵For there was seen by them a horse with a terrible rider on him, and adorned with beautiful trappings, and he rushed fiercely and struck at Heliodorus with his forefeet, and it seemed that he that sat on the horse had complete armor of gold. ²⁶Two others also appeared to him, young men notable in their strength, and beautiful in their glory, and splendid in their apparel, who stood by him on either side, and scourged him unceasingly, inflicting on him many severe stripes. ²⁷And when he had fallen suddenly to the ground, and great darkness had come over him, [his guards] caught him up and put him into a litter, ²⁸and carried him, him that had just now entered with a great train and all his guard into the previously mentioned treasury, himself now brought to utter helplessness, manifestly made to recognize the sovereignty of God. ²⁹And so, while he, through the working of God, speechless and deprived of all hope and deliverance, lay prostrate, ³⁰they blessed the Lord, that made marvelous his own place; and the temple, which a little before was full of terror and alarm, was filled with joy and gladness after the Almighty Lord appeared. ³¹But quickly certain of Heliodorus' familiar friends implored Onias to call on the Most High, and grant life to him who lay quite at the last gasp. ³²And the chief priest, secretly fearing lest the king might come to think that some treachery toward Heliodorus had been perpetrated by the Jews, brought a sacrifice for the deliverance of the man. ³³But as the chief priest was making the atoning sacrifice, the same young men appeared again to

Heliodorus, arrayed in the same garments; and they
stood and said, "Give Onias the chief priest great
thanks, for his sake the LORD has granted you life;
34 and do you, since you have been scourged from
Heaven, publish to all men the sovereign majesty of
God." And when they had spoken these words, they
vanished out of sight. 35 So Heliodorus, having offered
a sacrifice to the LORD and vowed great vows to him
that had saved his life, and having graciously received
Onias, returned with his army to the king. 36 And he
testified to all men the works of the great God which
he had seen with his eyes. 37 And when the king asked
Heliodorus, what manner of man was fit to be sent yet
once again to Jerusalem, he said, 38 "If you have any
enemy or conspirator against the state, send him
there, and you will receive him back well scourged, if
he even escapes with his life; because of a truth there
is about the place a power of God. 39 For He that has
His dwelling in Heaven Himself has His eyes on that
place and helps it; and those who come to hurt it He
strikes and destroys." 40 And such was the history of
Heliodorus and the keeping of the treasury.

CHAPTER 4

1 But the previously mentioned Simon, he who had
given information of the money, and [had betrayed]
his country, slandered Onias, [saying] that it was he
who had incited Heliodorus, and made himself the
author of these evils. 2 And him that was the
benefactor of the city, and the guardian of his fellow
countrymen, and a zealot for the laws, he dared to call
a conspirator against the state. 3 But when the growing
enmity [between them] waxed so great, that even
murders were perpetrated through one of Simon's
trusted followers, 4 Onias, seeing the danger of the
contention, and that Apollonius [the son] of
Menestheus, the governor of Coele-Syria and
Phoenicia, was increasing Simon's malice, 5 went
himself to the king, not to be an accuser of his fellow-
citizens, but looking to the good of all the people,
both public and private; 6 for he saw that without the
king's providence it was impossible for the state to
obtain peace anymore, and that Simon would not
cease from his madness. 7 But when Seleucus was
deceased, and Antiochus, who was called Epiphanes,
succeeded to the kingdom, Jason the brother of Onias
supplanted [his brother] in the chief priesthood,
8 having promised to the king at an audience three
hundred and sixty talents of silver, and [out] of
another fund eighty talents; 9 and besides this, he
undertook to assign one hundred and fifty more, if it
might be allowed him through the king's authority to
set him up a [Greek] place of exercise and [form] a
body of youths [to be trained therein, and] to register
the inhabitants of Jerusalem as [citizens] of Antioch.
10 And when the king had given assent, and he had
gotten possession of the office, he out with brought
over them of his own race to the Greek fashion. 11 And
setting aside the royal ordinances of special favor to
the Jews, granted by the means of John the father of
Eupolemus, who went on the delegation to the
Romans for friendship and alliance, and seeking to
overthrow the lawful modes of life, he brought in new
customs forbidden by the law: 12 for he eagerly
established a [Greek] place of exercise under the
citadel itself; and caused the noblest of the young men
to wear the [Greek] cap. 13 And so there was an
extreme of hellenization, and an advance of an alien
religion, by reason of the exceeding profaneness of
Jason, that ungodly man and no chief priest; 14 so that
the priests had no longer any zeal for the services of
the altar, but despising the sanctuary, and neglecting
the sacrifices, they hastened to enjoy that which was
unlawfully provided in the palaestra, after the
summons of the discus; 15 making of no account the
honors of their fathers, and thinking the glories of the
Greeks best of all. 16 By reason of which severe
calamity beset them; and the men whose ways of
living they earnestly followed, and to whom they
desired to be made like in all things, these became
their enemies and punished them. 17 For it is not a light
thing to do impiously against the laws of God, but
these things the time following will declare. 18 Now
when certain games that came every fifth year were
kept at Tyre, and the king was present, 19 the vile Jason
sent sacred envoys, as being Antiochians of
Jerusalem, bearing three hundred drachmas of silver
to the sacrifice of Hercules, which even the bearers
thereof thought not right to use for [any] sacrifice,
because it was not fit, but to expend on another
charge. 20 And though in the purpose of the sender this
[money was for] the sacrifice of Hercules, yet on
account of present circumstances it went to the
equipment of the galleys. 21 Now when Apollonius the
[son] of Menestheus was sent into Egypt for the
enthronement of [Ptolemy] Philometor as king,
Antiochus, learning that [Ptolemy] had shown
himself ill affected toward the state, took thought for
the security of his realm; for that reason, going [by
sea] to Joppa, he traveled on to Jerusalem. 22 And
being magnificently received by Jason and the city,
he was brought in with torches and shouting. This
done, he afterward led his army down into Phoenicia.
23 Now after a space of three years Jason sent
Menelaus, the previously mentioned Simon's brother,
to bear the money to the king, and to make reports
concerning some necessary matters. 24 But he, being
commended to the king, and having glorified himself
by the display of his authority, got the chief
priesthood for himself, outbidding Jason by three
hundred talents of silver. 25 And having received the
royal mandates he came [to Jerusalem], bringing
nothing worthy the chief priesthood, but having the
passion of a cruel tyrant, and the rage of a savage
beast. 26 And whereas Jason, who had supplanted his
own brother, was supplanted by another and driven as

a fugitive into the country of the Ammonites, ²⁷ Menelaus had possession of the office, but of the money that had been promised to the king nothing was duly paid, and that though Sostratus the governor of the citadel demanded it ²⁸ (for to him pertained the gathering of the revenues); for this reason they were both called by the king to his presence. ²⁹ And Menelaus left his own brother Lysimachus for his deputy in the chief priesthood; and Sostratus [left] Crates, who was over the Cyprians. ³⁰ Now while such was the state of things, it came to pass that they of Tarsus and Mallus made insurrection, because they were to be given as a present to Antiochis, the king's concubine. ³¹ The king therefore came [to Cilicia] in all haste to settle matters, leaving for his deputy Andronicus, a man of high rank. ³² And Menelaus, supposing that he had gotten a favorable opportunity, presented to Andronicus certain vessels of gold belonging to the temple, which he had stolen: other [vessels] also he had already sold into Tyre and the surrounding cities. ³³ And when Onias had sure knowledge [of this], he sharply reproved him, having withdrawn himself into a sanctuary at Daphne, that lies by Antioch. ³⁴ For that reason, Menelaus, taking Andronicus apart, begged him to kill Onias. And coming to Onias, and being persuaded to use treachery, and being received as a friend, Andronicus gave him his right hand with oaths [of fidelity, and], though he was suspected, persuaded him to come out of the sanctuary; and out with he dispatched him without regard of justice. ³⁵ For this reason, not only Jews, but many also of the other nations, had indignation and displeasure at the unjust murder of the man. ³⁶ And when the king had come back again from the places in Cilicia, the Jews that were in the city pleaded before him [against Andronicus] (the Greeks also joining with them in hatred of the wickedness), urging that Onias had been wrongfully slain. ³⁷ Antiochus therefore was heartily sorry, and was moved to pity, and wept, because of the sober and well-ordered life of him that was dead; ³⁸ and being inflamed with passion, out with he stripped off Andronicus' purple robe, and tore off his under garments, and when he had led him round through the whole city to that very place where he had committed impiety against Onias, there he put the murderer out of the way, the LORD rendering to him the punishment he had deserved. ³⁹ Now when many sacrileges had been committed in the city by Lysimachus with the consent of Menelaus, and when the report of them was spread abroad outside, the people gathered themselves together against Lysimachus, after many vessels of gold had been already dispersed. ⁴⁰ And when the multitudes were rising against [him, and] were filled with anger, Lysimachus armed about three thousand men, and with unrighteous violence began [the conflict], one Hauran, a man far gone in years and no less also in madness, leading [the attack].

⁴¹ But when they perceived the assault of Lysimachus, some caught up stones, others logs of wood, and some took handfuls of the ashes that lay near, and they flung them all pell-mell on Lysimachus and those who were with him; ⁴² by reason of which they wounded many of them, and some they struck to the ground, and all [of them] they forced to flee, but the author of the sacrilege himself they killed beside the treasury. ⁴³ But touching these matters there was an accusation laid against Menelaus. ⁴⁴ And when the king had come to Tyre, the three men that were sent by the senate pleaded the cause before him. ⁴⁵ But Menelaus, seeing himself now defeated, promised much money to Ptolemy the [son] of Dorymenes, that he might win over the king. ⁴⁶ After which Ptolemy taking the king aside into a cloister, as it were to take the air, brought him to be of another mind: ⁴⁷ and him that was the cause of all the evil, Menelaus, he discharged from the accusations; but these hapless men, who, if they had pleaded even before Scythians, would have been discharged uncondemned, them he sentenced to death. ⁴⁸ Soon then did those who were spokesmen for the city and the families [of Israel] and the holy vessels suffer that unrighteous penalty. ⁴⁹ For this reason even certain Tyrians, moved with hatred of the wickedness, provided magnificently for their burial. ⁵⁰ But Menelaus through the covetous dealings of those who were in power remained still in his office, growing in wickedness, as a great conspirator against his fellow-citizens.

CHAPTER 5

¹ Now about this time Antiochus made his second inroad into Egypt. ² And it [so] befell that throughout all the city, for the space of almost forty days, there appeared in the midst of the sky horsemen in swift motion, wearing robes inworked with gold and [carrying] spears, equipped in troops for battle; ³ and drawing of swords; and [on the other side] squadrons of horse in array; and encounters and pursuits of both [armies]; and shaking of shields, and multitudes of lances, and casting of darts, and flashing of golden trappings, and girding on of all sorts of armor. ⁴ For that reason, all men implored that the vision might have been given for good. ⁵ But when a false rumor had arisen that Antiochus was deceased, Jason took not less than one thousand men, and suddenly made an assault on the city; and those who were on the wall being routed, and the city being now at length well near taken, Menelaus took refuge in the citadel. ⁶ But Jason slaughtered his own citizens without mercy, not considering that good success against countrymen is the greatest ill success, but supposing himself to be setting up trophies over enemies, and not over fellow countrymen. ⁷ The office [however] he did not get, but, receiving shame as the end of his conspiracy, he passed again a fugitive into the country of the Ammonites. ⁸ At the last therefore he met with a

miserable end: having been shut up at the court of Aretas the prince of the Arabians, fleeing from city to city, pursued of all men, hated as an apostate from the laws, and held in abomination as the butcher of his country and his fellow-citizens, he was cast out into Egypt; [9] and he that had driven many from their own country into strange lands perished [himself] in a strange land, having crossed the sea to the Lacedaemonians, as thinking to find shelter [there] because they were related; [10] and he that had cast out a multitude unburied had none to mourn for him, nor had he any funeral at all, or place in the tomb of his fathers. [11] Now when tidings came to the king concerning that which was done, he thought that Judea was in revolt; after which setting out from Egypt in a furious mind, he took the city by force of arms, [12] and commanded his soldiers to cut down without mercy such as came in their way, and to kill such as went up on the houses; [13] and there was killing of young and old, making away of boys, women, and children, slaying of virgins and infants. [14] And in all the three days [of the slaughter] there were destroyed eighty thousand, [where of] forty thousand [were slain] in close combat, and no fewer were sold than slain. [15] But not content with this, he presumed to enter into the most holy temple of all the earth, having Menelaus for his guide (him that had proved himself a traitor both to the laws and to his country), [16] even taking the sacred vessels with his polluted hands, and dragging down with his profane hands the offerings that had been dedicated by other kings to the augmentation and glory and honor of the place. [17] And Antiochus was lifted up in mind, not seeing that because of the sins of those who lived in the city the Sovereign LORD had been provoked to anger a little, and therefore His eye was [then] turned away from the place. [18] But had it not so been that they were already bound by many sins, this man, even as Heliodorus who was sent by Seleucus the king to view the treasury, would, so soon as he pressed forward, have been scourged and turned back from his daring deed. [19] However, the LORD did not choose the nation for the place's sake, but the place for the nation's sake. [20] For that reason, also the place itself, having shared in the calamities that befell the nation, did afterward share in [its] benefits; and the [place] which was forsaken in the wrath of the Almighty was, at the reconciliation of the great Sovereign, restored again with all glory. [21] As for Antiochus, when he had carried away out of the temple one thousand and eight hundred talents, he departed in all haste to Antioch, thinking in his arrogance to make the land navigable and the sea passable by foot, because his heart was lifted up. [22] And moreover he left governors to afflict the race: at Jerusalem, Philip, by race a Phrygian, and in character more barbarous than him that set him there; [23] and at Gerizim, Andronicus; and besides these, Menelaus, who worse than all the rest exalted himself against his fellow-citizens. And having a malicious mind toward the Jews—his citizens, [24] he sent that lord of pollutions Apollonius with an army of twenty-two thousand, commanding him to kill all those that were of full age, and to sell the women and the younger men. [25] And he, coming to Jerusalem, and playing the man of peace, waited until the holy day of the Sabbath, and finding the Jews at rest from work, he commanded his men to parade in arms. [26] And he put to the sword all those who came out to the spectacle; and running into the city with the armed men he killed great multitudes. [27] But Judas, who is also Maccabaeus, with nine others or thereabout, withdrew himself, and with his company kept himself alive in the mountains after the manner of wild beasts; and they continued feeding on such poor herbs as grew there, that they might not be partakers of the pollution.

CHAPTER 6

[1] And not long after this the king sent out an old man of Athens to compel the Jews to depart from the laws of their fathers, and not to live after the laws of God; [2] and also to pollute the sanctuary in Jerusalem, and to call it by the name of Jupiter Olympius, and [to call] the [sanctuary] in Gerizim by the name of Jupiter the Protector of strangers, even as they were that lived in the place. [3] But severe and utterly grievous was the visitation of this evil. [4] For the temple was filled with riot and reveling by the heathen, who dallied with prostitutes, and had to do with women within the sacred precincts, and moreover brought inside things that were not befitting; [5] and the place of sacrifice was filled with those abominable things which had been prohibited by the laws. [6] And a man could neither keep the Sabbath, nor observe the feasts of the fathers, nor so much as confess himself to be a Jew. [7] And on the day of the king's birth every month they were led along with bitter constraint to eat of the sacrifices; and when the Festival of Bacchus came, they were compelled to go in procession in honor of Bacchus, wearing wreaths of ivy. [8] A decree went out to the neighboring Greek cities, by the suggestion of Ptolemy, that they should observe the same conduct against the Jews and should make them eat of the sacrifices; [9] and that they should kill such as did not choose to go over to the Greek rites. So the present misery was for all to see: [10] for two women were brought up for having circumcised their children; and these, when they had led them publicly around the city, with the babies hung from their breasts, they cast down headlong from the wall. [11] And others, that had run together into the caves nearby to keep the seventh day secretly, being betrayed to Philip, were all burned together, because they hesitated to defend themselves, from regard to the honor of that most solemn day. [12] I implore, therefore, those that read this scroll, that they not be discouraged because of the

calamities, but account that these punishments were not for the destruction, but for the disciplining of our race. [13] For indeed that those who act impiously are not left alone any long time, but immediately meet with retribution, is a sign of great beneficence. [14] For in the case of the other nations the Sovereign LORD does with patience forbear, until that He punishes them when they have attained to the full measure of [their] sins; but not so judged He as touching us, [15] that He may not take vengeance on us afterward, when we come to the height of our sins. [16] For that reason, He never withdraws His mercy from us; but though He chastens with calamity, yet He does not forsake His own people. [17] However, let this that we have spoken suffice to put [you] in remembrance; but after [these] few words we must come to the narrative. [18] Eleazar, one of the principal scribes, a man already well stricken in years, and of a noble countenance, was compelled to open his mouth to eat swine's flesh. [19] But he, welcoming death with renown rather than life with pollution, advanced of his own accord to the instrument of torture, but first spat out [the flesh], [20] [coming forward] as men should come that are resolute to repel such things as not [even] for the natural love of life is it lawful to taste. [21] But those who had the charge of that forbidden sacrificial feast took the man aside, for the acquaintance which of old times they had with him, and privately implored him to bring flesh of his own providing, such as was befitting for him to use, and to make as if he did eat of the flesh from the sacrifice, as had been commanded by the king; [22] that by so doing he might be delivered from death, and for his ancient friendship with them might be treated kindly. [23] But he, having formed a high resolve, and one that became his years, and the dignity of old age, and the gray hairs which he had reached with honor, and his excellent education from a child, or rather [that became] the holy laws of God's ordaining, declared his mind accordingly, bidding them quickly send him to Hades. [24] "For it does not become our years to deceive," [he said,] "that [through this] many of the young should suppose that Eleazar, the man of eighty years and ten, had gone over to an alien religion; [25] and [so] they, by reason of my deception, and for the sake of this brief and momentary life, should be led astray because of me, and [so] I get to myself a pollution and a stain of my old age. [26] For even if for the present time I will remove from myself the punishment of men, yet I will not escape the hands of the Almighty, either living or dead. [27] For that reason, by courageously parting with my life now, I will show myself worthy of my old age, [28] and leave behind a noble example to the young to die willingly and nobly a glorious death for the reverend and holy laws." And when he had said these words, he went immediately to the instrument of torture. [29] And when they changed the good will they bore toward him a little before into

ill will, because these words of his were, as they thought, sheer madness, [30] and when he was at the point to die with the stripes, he groaned aloud and said, "To the LORD, who has the holy knowledge, it is manifest that, whereas I might have been delivered from death, I endure severe pains in my body by being scourged; but in soul I gladly suffer these things for my fear of Him." [31] So this man also died after this manner, leaving his death for an example of nobleness and a memorial of virtue, not only to the young but also to the great body of his nation.

CHAPTER 7

[1] And it came to pass that seven brothers also with their mother were at the king's command taken and shamefully handled with scourges and cords, to compel them to taste of the abominable swine's flesh. [2] But one of them made himself the spokesman and said, "What would you ask and learn of us? For we are ready to die rather than transgress the laws of our fathers." [3] And the king fell into a rage and commanded to heat pans and cauldrons: [4] and when these were heated, he commanded to cut out the tongue of him that had been their spokesman, and to scalp him, and to cut off his extremities, the rest of his brothers and his mother looking on. [5] And when he was utterly maimed, [the king] commanded to bring him to the fire, being yet alive, and to fry him in the pan. And as the vapor of the pan spread far, they and their mother also exhorted one another to die nobly, saying, [6] "The LORD God sees, and in truth is entreated for us, as Moses declared in his song, which witnesses against [the people] to their faces, saying, And He will be treated for His servants." [7] And when the first had died after this manner, they brought the second to the mocking; and they pulled off the skin of his head with the hair and asked him, "Will you eat, before your body is punished in every limb?" [8] But he answered in the language of his fathers and said to them, "No." Therefore he also underwent the next torture in succession, as the first had done. [9] And when he was at the last gasp, he said, "You—miscreant—release us out of this present life, but the King of the world will raise us up, who have died for His laws, to a continuous renewal of life." [10] And after him the third was made a laughingstock. And when he was required, he quickly put out his tongue, and stretched out his hands courageously, [11] and nobly said, "From Heaven I possess these; and for His laws' sake I treat these with contempt; and from Him I hope to receive these back again": [12] insomuch that the king himself and those who were with him were astonished at the young man's soul, for he regarded the pain as nothing. [13] And when he too was dead, they shamefully handled and tortured the fourth in like manner. [14] And having come near to death he said, "It is good to die at the hands of men and look for the hopes which are [given] by God, that we will be

raised up again by Him; for as for you, you will have no resurrection to life." [15] And next after him they brought the fifth, and shamefully handled him. [16] But he looked toward the king and said, "Because you have authority among men, though you are [yourself] corruptible, you do what you will; yet do not think that our race has been forsaken of God; [17] but hold on your way, and behold His sovereign majesty, how it will torture you and your seed." [18] And after him they brought the sixth. And when he was at the point to die he said, "Do not be vainly deceived, for we suffer these things for our own doings, as sinning against our own God: marvelous things have come to pass; [19] but do not think that you will be unpunished, having determined to fight against God." [20] But above all was the mother marvelous and worthy of honorable memory; for when she looked on seven sons perishing within the space of one day, she bare [the sight] with good courage for the hopes [that she had set] on the LORD. [21] And she exhorted each one of them in the language of their fathers, filled with a noble temper and stirring up her womanish thought with manly passion, saying to them, [22] "I do not know how you came into my womb, neither was it I that bestowed on you your spirit and your life, and it was not I that brought into order the first elements of each one of you. [23] Therefore the Creator of the world, who fashioned the generation of man and devised the generation of all things, in mercy gives back to you again both your spirit and your life, as you now treat yourselves with contempt for His laws' sake." [24] But Antiochus, thinking himself to be despised, and suspecting the reproachful voice, while the youngest was yet alive did not only make his appeal [to him] by words, but also at the same time promised with oaths that he would enrich him and raise him to high estate, if he would turn from the [customs] of his fathers, and that he would take him for his friend and entrust him with affairs. [25] But when the young man would in no way give heed, the king called to him his mother, and exhorted her that she would counsel the youth to save himself. [26] And when he had exhorted her with many words, she undertook to persuade her son. [27] But bending toward him, laughing the cruel tyrant to scorn, she spoke this in the language of her fathers: "My son, have pity on me that carried you nine months in my womb, and gave you suck three years, and nourished and brought you up to this age, and sustained you. [28] I implore you, my child, to lift your eyes to the Heaven and the earth, and to see all things that are in it, and so to recognize that God made them not of things that were, and [that] the race of men in this way comes into being. [29] Do not be afraid of this butcher, but, proving yourself worthy of your brothers, accept your death, that in the mercy [of God] I may receive you again with your brothers." [30] But before she had yet ended speaking, the young man said, "Whom do you wait for? I do not obey the command of the king, but I listen to the command of the law that was given to our fathers through Moses. [31] But you, that have devised all manner of evil against the Hebrews, will in no way escape the hands of God. [32] For we are suffering because of our own sins; [33] and if for rebuke and disciplining our living Lord has been angered a little while, yet He will again be reconciled with His own servants. [34] But you, O unholy man and of all most vile, do not be vainly lifted up in your wild pride with uncertain hopes, raising your hand against the heavenly children; [35] for not yet have you escaped the judgment of the Almighty God that sees [all things]. [36] For these our brothers, having endured a short pain that brings continuous life, have now died under God's covenant; but you, through the judgment of God, will receive in just measure the penalties of your arrogance. [37] But I, as my brothers, give up both body and soul for the laws of our fathers, calling on God that He may speedily become gracious to the nation; and that you amidst trials and plagues may confess that He alone is God; [38] and that in me and my brothers you may stay the wrath of the Almighty, which has been justly brought on our whole race." [39] But the king, falling into a rage, handled him worse than all the rest, being exasperated at his mocking. [40] So he also died pure [from pollution], putting his whole trust in the LORD. [41] And last of all, after her sons, the mother died. [42] Let it then suffice to have said so much concerning the sacrificial feasts and the [king's] exceeding barbarities.

CHAPTER 8

[1] But Judas, who is also [called] Maccabaeus, and those who were with him, making their way privily into the villages, called to them their countrymen; and taking to them such as had continued in the Jews' religion, gathered together as many as six thousand. [2] And they called on the LORD, [imploring Him] to look on the people that was oppressed by all; and to also have compassion on the sanctuary that had been profaned by the ungodly men; [3] and to have pity on the city also that was suffering ruin and ready to be made level with the ground; and to listen to the blood that cried to Him; [4] and to remember also the lawless slaughter of the innocent infants, and the blasphemies that had been committed against His Name; and to show His hatred of wickedness. [5] And when Maccabaeus had trained his men for service, the heathen at once found him irresistible, for that the wrath of the LORD was turned into pity. [6] And coming unawares he set fire to cities and villages. And in winning back the most important positions, putting to flight no small number of the enemies, [7] he especially took advantage of the nights for such assaults. And his courage was loudly talked of everywhere. [8] But when Philip saw the man gaining ground little by little, and increasing more and more in his prosperity, he wrote to Ptolemy, the governor of Coele-Syria and

Phoenicia, that he should support the king's cause. [9] And [Ptolemy] quickly appointed Nicanor the [son] of Patroclus, one of the king's chief friends, and sent him, in command of no fewer than twenty thousand of all nations, to destroy the whole race of Judea; and with him he joined Gorgias also, a captain and one that had experience in matters of war. [10] And Nicanor undertook by [the sale of the] captive Jews to make up for the king the tribute of two thousand talents which he was to pay to the Romans. [11] And immediately he sent to the cities on the seacoast, inviting them to buy Jewish slaves, promising to allow ninety slaves for a talent, not expecting the judgment that was to follow on him from the Almighty. [12] But tidings came to Judas concerning the inroad of Nicanor; and when he communicated to those who were with him the presence of the army, [13] those who were cowardly and distrustful of the judgment of God ran away and left the country. [14] And others sold all that was left over to them, and in addition implored the LORD to deliver those who had been sold [as slaves] by the impious Nicanor before he ever met them; [15] and, if not for their own sakes, yet for the covenants made with their fathers, and because he had called them by his reverend and glorious name. [16] And Maccabaeus gathered his men together, six thousand in number, and exhorted them not to be stricken with dismay at the enemy, nor to fear the great multitude of the heathen who came wrongfully against them; but to contend nobly, [17] setting before their eyes the outrage that had been lawlessly perpetrated on the holy place, and the shameful handling of the city that had been turned to mockery, and further the overthrow of the mode of life received from their ancestors. [18] "For they," he said, "trust to arms, and in addition to deeds of daring; but we trust on the Almighty God, since He is able at a beckoning to cast down those who are coming against us, and even the whole world." [19] And moreover He recounted to them the help given from time to time in the days of their ancestors, both the [help given] in the days of Sennacherib, how that one hundred and eighty-five thousand perished, [20] and the [help given] in the land of Babylon, even the battle that was fought against the Gauls, how that they came to the engagement eight thousand in all, with four thousand Macedonians, and [how that,] the Macedonians being hard-pressed, the six thousand destroyed the one hundred and twenty thousand, because of the help which they had from Heaven, and took great plunder. [21] And when he had with these words made them of good courage, and ready to die for the laws and their country, he divided his army into four parts; [22] appointing his relatives to be leaders with himself of the several bands—Simon, and Joseph, and Jonathan—giving each the command of fifteen hundred men, [23] and moreover Eleazer also: [then,] having read aloud the sacred scroll, and having

given as a watchword, THE HELP OF GOD, leading the first band himself, he joined battle with Nicanor. [24] And, since the Almighty fought on their side, they killed of the enemy above nine thousand, and wounded and disabled the greater part of Nicanor's army and compelled all to flee: [25] and they took the money of those that had come there to buy them. And after they had pursued them for some distance, they returned, being constrained by the time of the day; [26] for it was the day before the Sabbath, and for this reason they made no effort to chase them far. [27] And when they had gathered the arms of the enemy together, and had stripped off their spoils, they occupied themselves about the Sabbath, blessing and thanking the LORD exceedingly, who had saved them to this day, for that He had caused a beginning of mercy to distill on them. [28] And after the Sabbath, when they had given of the spoils to the maimed, and to the widows and orphans, the residue they distributed among themselves and their children. [29] And when they had accomplished these things, and had made a common supplication, they implored the merciful LORD to be wholly reconciled with His servants. [30] And having had an encounter with the forces of Timotheus and Bacchides, they killed above twenty thousand of them, and made themselves masters of strongholds exceedingly high, and divided very much plunder, giving the maimed and orphans and widows, and moreover the aged also, an equal share with themselves. [31] And when they had gathered the arms of the enemy together, they stored them all up carefully in the most important positions, and the residue of the spoils they carried to Jerusalem. [32] And they killed the phylarch of Timotheus' forces, a most unholy man, and one who had done the Jews much hurt. [33] And as they celebrated [the] victory in the city of their fathers, they burned those that had set the sacred gates on fire, and [among them] Callisthenes, who had fled into an outhouse; and [so] they received the suitable reward of their impiety. [34] And the three times-accursed Nicanor, who had brought the thousand merchants to buy the Jews [for slaves], [35] being through the help of the LORD humbled by them who in his eyes were held to be of least account, put off his glorious apparel, and [passing] through the midland, shunning all company like a fugitive slave, arrived at Antioch, having, [as he thought,] had the greatest possible good fortune, though his army was destroyed. [36] And he that had taken on himself to make tribute sure for the Romans by the captivity of the men of Jerusalem published abroad that the Jews had One who fought for them, and that because this was so the Jews were invulnerable, because they followed the laws ordained by Him.

CHAPTER 9

[1] Now about that time it befell that Antiochus had returned in disorder from the region of Persia. [2] For he

had entered into the city called Persepolis, and he determined to rob a temple and to hold down the city. After which there was an onset of the multitudes, and [Antiochus and his men] turned to make defense with arms; and it came to pass that Antiochus was put to flight by the people of the country and broke up his camp with disgrace. ³ And while he was at Ecbatana, news was brought him what had happened to Nicanor and the forces of Timotheus. ⁴ And being lifted up by his passion he thought to make the Jews suffer even for the evildoing of those that had put him to rout. For that reason, the judgment from Heaven even now accompanying him, he gave order to his charioteer to drive without ceasing and dispatch the journey; for so he arrogantly spoke: I will make Jerusalem a common graveyard of Jews, when I come there. ⁵ But the All-seeing Lord, the God of Israel, struck him with a fatal and invisible stroke; and as soon as he had ceased speaking this word, an incurable pain of the bowels seized him, and bitter torments of the inner parts; ⁶ and that most justly, for he had tormented other men's bowels with many and strange sufferings. ⁷ But he in no way ceased from his rude insolence; no, still more was he filled with arrogance, breathing fire in his passion against the Jews, and commanding to hasten the journey. But it came to pass moreover that he fell from his chariot as it rushed along, and having a grievous fall was racked in all the members of his body. ⁸ And he that but now supposed himself to have the waves of the sea at his bidding, so vainglorious was he beyond the condition of a man, and that thought to weigh the heights of the mountains in a balance, was now brought to the ground and carried in a litter, showing to all that the power was manifestly God's; ⁹ so that out of the body of the impious man worms swarmed, and while he was still living in anguish and pains, his flesh fell off, and by reason of the stench all the army turned with loathing from his corruption. ¹⁰ And the man that a little before supposed himself to touch the stars of the heavens, no one could endure to carry for his intolerable stench. ¹¹ Therefore he began in great part to cease from his arrogance, being broken [in spirit, and] to come to knowledge under the scourge of God, his pains increasing every moment. ¹² And when he himself could not stand his own smell, he said these words: "It is right to be subject to God, and that one who is mortal should not be inclined arrogantly." ¹³ And the vile man vowed to the Sovereign LORD, who now no longer would have pity on him, saying concerning this ¹⁴ that the holy city, to which he was going in haste, to lay it even with the ground and to make it a common graveyard, he would declare free; ¹⁵ and as touching the Jews, whom he had decided not even to count worthy of burial, but to cast them out to the beasts with their infants, for the birds to devour, he would make them all equal to citizens of Athens; ¹⁶ and the holy sanctuary, which before he had

plundered, he would adorn with excellent offerings, and would restore all the sacred vessels many times multiplied, and out of his own revenues would defray the charges that were required for the sacrifices; ¹⁷ and, besides all this, that he would become a Jew, and would visit every inhabited place, publishing abroad the might of God. ¹⁸ But when his sufferings did in no way cease, for the judgment of God had come on him in righteousness, having given up all hope of himself, he wrote to the Jews the letter written below, having the nature of a supplication, to this effect: ¹⁹ "To the worthy Jews, his fellow-citizens, Antiochus, king and general, wishes much joy and health and prosperity. ²⁰ May you and your children fare well; and your affairs will be to your mind. Having my hope in Heaven, ²¹ I remembered with affection your honor and good will [toward me]. Returning out of the region of Persia, and being taken with a ghastly sickness, I deemed it necessary to take thought for the common safety of all, ²² not despairing of myself, but having great hope to escape from the sickness. ²³ But considering that my father also, at what time he led an army into the upper country, appointed his successor, ²⁴ to the end that, if anything fell out contrary to expectation, or if any unwelcome tidings were brought, they [that remained] in the country, knowing to whom the state had been left, might not be troubled; ²⁵ and, besides all this, observing how that the princes that are borderers and neighbors to my kingdom watch opportunities, and look for the future event, I have appointed my son Antiochus [to be] king, whom I often committed and commended to most of you, when I was hastening to the upper provinces; and I have written to him what is written below. ²⁶ I exhort you therefore and implore you, having in your remembrance the benefits done to you in common and separately, to preserve each of you your present good will toward me and my son. ²⁷ For I am persuaded that he, in gentleness and kindness, will follow my purpose and treat you with indulgence." ²⁸ So the murderer and blasphemer, having endured the most intense sufferings, even as he had dealt with other men, ended his life among the mountains by a most piteous fate in a strange land. ²⁹ And Philip his foster brother carried the body [home]; and then, fearing the son of Antiochus, he went himself to Ptolemy Philometor in Egypt.

CHAPTER 10

¹ And Maccabaeus and those who were with him, the LORD leading them on, recovered the temple and the city; ² and they pulled down the altars that had been built in the marketplace by the aliens, and also sacred enclosures. ³ And having cleansed the sanctuary they made another altar of sacrifice; and striking stones and taking fire out of them, they offered sacrifices, after two years, and [burned] incense, and [lighted] lamps, and set out the Bread of the Presentation. ⁴ And

when they had done these things, they fell prostrate and implored the Lord that they might no longer fall into such evils; but that, if ever they should sin, they might be disciplined by Him with forbearance, and not be delivered to blaspheming and barbarous heathen. ⁵ Now on the same day that the sanctuary was profaned by aliens, on that very day it came to pass that the cleansing of the sanctuary was made, even on the twenty-fifth day of the same month, which is Kislev. ⁶ And they kept eight days with gladness in the manner [of the Celebration] of Shelters, remembering how that not long before, during the Celebration of Shelters, they were wandering in the mountains and in the caves after the manner of wild beasts. ⁷ For that reason, bearing wands wreathed with leaves, and fair boughs, and palms also, they offered up hymns of thanksgiving to him that had prosperously brought to pass the cleansing of his own place. ⁸ They ordained also with a common statute and decree, for all the nation of the Jews, that they should keep these days every year. ⁹ And such was the end of Antiochus, who was called Epiphanes. ¹⁰ But now we will declare what came to pass under Antiochus [named] Eupator, who proved himself a [true] son of that ungodly man and will gather up briefly the successive evils of the wars. ¹¹ For this man, when he succeeded to the kingdom, appointed one Lysias—chancellor, and supreme governor of Coele-Syria and Phoenicia. ¹² For Ptolemy that was called Macron, setting an example of observing justice toward the Jews because of the wrong that had been done to them, endeavored to conduct his dealings with them on peaceful terms. ¹³ After which being accused by the king before Eupator, and hearing himself called traitor at every turn, because he had abandoned Cyprus which Philometor had entrusted to him, and had withdrawn himself to Antiochus [called] Epiphanes, and failing to uphold the honor of his office, he took poison and made away with himself. ¹⁴ But Gorgias, when he was made governor of the district, maintained a force of mercenaries, and at every turn kept up war with the Jews. ¹⁵ And together with him the Idumaeans also, being masters of important strongholds, harassed the Jews; and receiving to them those that had taken refuge [there] from Jerusalem, they determined to keep up war. ¹⁶ But Maccabaeus and his men, having made solemn supplication and having implored God to fight on their side, rushed on the strongholds of the Idumaeans; ¹⁷ and assaulting them vigorously they made themselves masters of the positions, and kept off all that fought on the wall, and killed those that fell in their way, and killed no fewer than twenty thousand. ¹⁸ And because no less than nine thousand were fled into two towers exceedingly strong and having all things [needed] for a siege, ¹⁹ Maccabaeus, having left Simon and Joseph, and Zacchaeus besides and those who were with him, a force sufficient to besiege them, departed himself to places where he

was most needed. ²⁰ But Simon and those who were with him, yielding to covetousness, were bribed by certain of those that were in the towers, and receiving seventy thousand drachmas let some of them slip away. ²¹ But when word was brought to Maccabaeus of what was done, he gathered the leaders of the people together, and accused [those men] of having sold their countrymen for money, by setting their enemies free [to fight] against them. ²² So he killed these men for having turned traitors, and out with took possession of the two towers. ²³ And prospering with his arms in all things he took in hand, he destroyed in the two strongholds more than twenty thousand. ²⁴ Now Timotheus, who had been before defeated by the Jews, having gathered together foreign forces in great multitudes, and having collected the horsemen which belonged to Asia, not a few, came as though he would take Judea by force of arms. ²⁵ But as he drew near, Maccabaeus and his men sprinkled earth on their heads and girded their loins with sackcloth, in supplication to God, ²⁶ and falling down on the step in front of the altar, implored Him to become gracious to them, and be an enemy to their enemies and an adversary to their adversaries, as the law declares. ²⁷ And rising from their prayer they took up their arms and advanced some distance from the city; and when they had come near to their enemies they halted. ²⁸ And when the dawn was now spreading, the two [armies] joined battle; the one part having this, besides [their] virtue, for a pledge of success and victory, that they had fled to the Lord for refuge, the others making their passion their leader in the strife. ²⁹ But when the battle waxed strong, there appeared out of Heaven to their adversaries five men on horses with bridles of gold, [in] splendid [array]; and two of them, leading on the Jews, ³⁰ and taking Maccabaeus in the midst of them, and covering him with their own armor, guarded him from wounds, while on the adversaries they shot out arrows and thunderbolts; by reason of which they were blinded and thrown into confusion, and were cut to pieces, filled with bewilderment. ³¹ And there were slain twenty thousand and five hundred, beside six hundred horsemen. ³² But Timotheus himself fled into a stronghold called Gazara, a fortress of exceeding strength, Chaereas being in command there. ³³ But Maccabaeus and his men were glad and laid siege to the fortress twenty-four days. ³⁴ And those who were within, trusting to the strength of the place, blasphemed exceedingly, and hurled out impious words. ³⁵ But at dawn of the twenty-fifth day certain young men of the company of Maccabaeus, inflamed with passion because of the blasphemies, assaulted the wall with masculine force and with furious passion, and cut down whoever came in their way. ³⁶ And others climbing up in like manner, while [the besieged] were distracted with them [that had made their way] within, set fire to the towers, and kindling fires burned the blasphemers alive; while others broke open the gates, and, having given entrance to the rest of the band, occupied the city. ³⁷ And they killed Timotheus, who was hidden in a cistern, and his brother Chaereas, and Apollophanes. ³⁸ And when they had accomplished these things, they blessed the LORD with hymns and thanksgiving, Him who does great benefits to Israel, and gives them the victory.

CHAPTER 11

¹ Now after a very short time, Lysias, the king's guardian and countryman and chancellor, being severely displeased for the things that had come to pass, ² collected about eighty thousand [footmen] and all his horsemen and came against the Jews, thinking to make the city a place for Greeks to dwell in, ³ and to levy tribute on the temple, as of the other sacred places of the nations, and to put up the chief priesthood to sale every year; ⁴ holding in no account the might of God, but puffed up with his tens of thousands of footmen, and his thousands of horsemen, and his eighty elephants. ⁵ And coming into Judea and drawing near to Bethsuron, which was a strong place and distant from Jerusalem about five leagues, he pressed it hard. ⁶ But when Maccabaeus and his men learned that he was besieging the strongholds, they and all the people with lamentations and tears made supplication to the LORD to send a good messenger to save Israel. ⁷ And Maccabaeus himself took up arms first and exhorted the others to put themselves in danger together with him and help their countrymen; and they went out with him very willingly. ⁸ And as they were there, close to Jerusalem, there appeared at their head one on horseback in white apparel, brandishing weapons of gold. ⁹ And they all together praised the merciful God and were yet more strengthened in heart: being ready to assail not men only but the wildest beasts, and walls of iron, ¹⁰ they advanced in array, having Him that is in Heaven to fight on their side, for the LORD had mercy on them. ¹¹ And hurling [themselves] like lions on the enemy, they killed of them eleven thousand [footmen] and sixteen hundred horsemen and forced all [the rest] to flee. ¹² But the greater part of them escaped wounded [and] naked; and Lysias also himself escaped by shameful flight. ¹³ But as he was a man not void of understanding, weighing with himself the defeat which had befallen him, and considering that the Hebrews could not be overcome, because the Almighty God fought on their side, he sent again [to them], ¹⁴ and persuaded them to come to terms on condition that all their rights were acknowledged, and [promised] that he would also persuade the king to become their friend. ¹⁵ And Maccabaeus gave consent on all the conditions which Lysias proposed to him, being careful of the [common] good; for whatever [requests] Maccabaeus delivered in writing to Lysias concerning the Jews the king allowed. ¹⁶ For the letters written to the Jews from Lysias were to this effect: "Lysias to the people of the Jews, greetings. ¹⁷ John and Absalom, who were sent from you, having delivered the petition written below, made request concerning the things signified therein. ¹⁸ Whatever things therefore had need to be brought before the king I declared [to him, and] what things were possible he allowed. ¹⁹ If then you will preserve your good will toward the state, henceforward I will also endeavor to contribute to [your] good. ²⁰ And on this behalf, I have given order in detail, both to these men and to those [that are sent] from me, to confer with you. ²¹ Farewell. [Written] in the one hundred [and] forty-eighth year, on the twenty-fourth day of the [month] Dioscorinthius." ²² And the king's letter was in these words: "King Antiochus to his brother Lysias, greetings. ²³ Seeing that our father passed to the gods having the wish that the subjects of his kingdom should be undisturbed and give themselves to the care of their own affairs, ²⁴ we, having heard that the Jews do not consent to our father's purpose to turn them to the [customs] of the Greeks, but choose rather their own manner of living, and make request that the [customs] of their law be allowed to them— ²⁵ choosing therefore that this nation also should be free from disturbance, we determine that their temple be restored to them, and that they live according to the customs that were in the days of their ancestors. ²⁶ You will therefore do well to send [messengers] to them and give them the right hand [of friendship], that they, knowing our mind, may be of good heart, and gladly occupy themselves with the conduct of their own affairs." ²⁷ And to the nation the king's letter was after this manner: "King Antiochus to the senate of the Jews and to the other Jews, greetings. ²⁸ If you fare well, we have our desire: we ourselves are also in good health. ²⁹ Menelaus informed us that your desire was to return home and follow your own business. ³⁰ They therefore that depart home up to the thirtieth day of Xanthicus will have [our] friendship, with full permission ³¹ that the Jews use their own [proper] meats and [observe their own] laws, even as formerly; and none of them will be in any way molested for the things that have been ignorantly done. ³² Moreover I have sent Menelaus also, that he may encourage you. ³³ Farewell. [Written] in the one hundred [and] forty-eighth year, on the fifteenth day of Xanthicus." ³⁴ And the Romans also sent to them a letter in these words: "Quintus Memmius [and] Titus Manius, ambassadors of the Romans, to the people of the Jews, greetings. ³⁵ In regard to the things which Lysias the king's countryman granted you, we also give consent. ³⁶ But as for the things which he judged should be referred to the king, send one out with, after you have advised thereof, that we may publish such [decrees] as befit your case; for we are on our way to Antioch. ³⁷ For that reason, send some with speed, that we also may

learn what is your mind. [38] Farewell. [Written] in the one hundred [and] forty-eighth year, on the fifteenth day of Xanthicus."

CHAPTER 12

[1] So when these covenants had been made, Lysias departed to the king, and the Jews went about their farming. [2] But [certain] of the governors of districts, Timotheus, and Apollonius the [son] of Gennaeus, and Hieronymus also, and Demophon, and besides them, Nicanor the governor of Cyprus would not permit them to enjoy tranquility and live in peace. [3] And men of Joppa perpetrated this great impiety: they invited the Jews that lived among them to go with their wives and children into the boats which they had provided, as though they had no ill will toward them; [4] and when the Jews, relying on the common decree of the city, accepted [the invitation], as men desiring to live in peace and suspecting nothing, they took them out to sea and drowned them—not less than two hundred. [5] But when Judas heard of the cruelty done to his fellow-countrymen, giving command to the men that were with him [6] and calling on God the righteous Judge, he came against the murderers of his countrymen, and set the haven on fire by night, and burned the boats, and put to the sword those that had fled there. [7] But when the town was closed [against him], he withdrew, intending to come again to root out the whole community of the men of Joppa. [8] But learning that the men of Jamnia were inclined to do in like manner to the Jews that sojourned among them, [9] he fell on the Jamnites also by night, and set fire to the haven together with the fleet, so that the glare of the light was seen at Jerusalem, two hundred and forty furlongs distant. [10] Now when they had drawn off nine furlongs from there, as they marched against Timotheus, [an army] of Arabians attacked him, no fewer than five thousand [footmen] and five hundred horsemen. [11] And when a severe battle had been fought, and Judas and his company by the help of God had good success, the nomads being overcome implored Judas to grant them friendship, promising to give [him] cattle, and to help his people in all other ways. [12] So Judas, thinking that they would indeed be profitable in many things, agreed to live in peace with them; and receiving pledges of friendship they departed to their tents. [13] And he also fell on a certain city, Gephyrun, strong and fenced about with walls, and inhabited by a mixed multitude of various nations; and it was named Caspin. [14] But those who were within, trusting to the strength of the walls and to their store of provisions, behaved themselves rudely toward Judas and those who were with him, railing, and furthermore blaspheming and speaking impious words. [15] But Judas and his company, calling on the great Sovereign of the world, who without rams and cunning engines of war hurled down Jericho in the times of Joshua, rushed wildly against the wall; [16] and having taken the city by the will of God, they made unspeakable slaughter, insomuch that the adjoining lake, which was two furlongs broad, appeared to be filled with the deluge of blood. [17] And when they had drawn off seven hundred and fifty furlongs from there, they made their way to Charax, to the Jews that are called Tubieni. [18] And they did not find Timotheus in occupation of that district, for he had then departed from the district without accomplishing anything, but had left behind a garrison, and that a very strong one, in a certain post. [19] But Dositheus and Sosipater, who were of Maccabaeus' captains, went out and destroyed those that had been left by Timotheus in the stronghold, above ten thousand men. [20] And Maccabaeus, ranging his own army by bands, set these two over the bands, and marched in haste against Timotheus, who had with him one hundred and twenty thousand footmen and two thousand and five hundred horsemen. [21] But when Timotheus heard of the inroad of Judas, he at once sent away the women and the children and also the baggage into the [fortress] called Carnion; for the place was hard to besiege and difficult of access by reason of the narrowness of the approaches on all sides. [22] But when the band of Judas, who led the van, appeared in sight, and when terror came on the enemy and fear, because the manifestation of him who sees all things came on them, they fled a main, carried this way and that, so that they were often hurt of their own men, and pierced with the points of their swords. [23] And Judas continued in hot pursuit, putting the wicked wretches to the sword, and he destroyed as many as thirty thousand men. [24] But Timotheus himself, falling in with the company of Dositheus and Sosipater, implored them with much crafty guile to let him go with his life, because he had in [his power] the parents of many [of them] and the relatives of some: otherwise, [he said,] little regard will be shown to these. [25] So when he had with many words confirmed the agreement to restore them without harm, they let him go that they might save their relatives. [26] And [Judas], marching against Carnion and the temple of Atergatis, killed twenty-five thousand persons. [27] And after he had put these to flight and destroyed them, he also marched against Ephron, a strong city, wherein were multitudes of people of all nations; and stalwart young men placed on the walls made a vigorous defense; and there were great stores of engines and darts there. [28] But calling on the Sovereign who with might breaks in pieces the strength of the enemy, they got the city into their hands, and killed as many as twenty-five thousand of those who were within. [29] And setting out from there they marched in haste against Scythopolis, which is distant from Jerusalem six hundred furlongs. [30] But when the Jews that were settled there testified of the good will that the Scythopolitans had shown toward them, and of their

2 MACCABEES

kindly bearing [toward them] in the times of their misfortune, ³¹ they gave thanks, and further exhorted them to remain well-affected toward the race for the future; and they went up to Jerusalem, the Celebration of Weeks being close to hand. ³² But after the [festival] called Pentecost they marched in haste against Gorgias the governor of Idumaea: ³³ and he came out with three thousand footmen and four hundred horsemen. ³⁴ And when they had set themselves in array, it came to pass that a few of the Jews fell. ³⁵ And a certain Dositheus, one of Bacenor's company, who was on horseback and a strong man, pressed hard on Gorgias, and taking hold of his cloak drew him along by main force; and while he was inclined to take the accursed man alive, one of the Thracian horsemen bore down on him and disabled his shoulder, and so Gorgias escaped to Marisa. ³⁶ And when those who were with Esdris had been fighting long and were wearied out, Judas called on the LORD to show Himself, fighting on their side and leading the van of the battle; ³⁷ and [then] in the language of his fathers he raised the battle-cry joined with hymns, and rushing unawares on the troops of Gorgias put them to flight. ³⁸ And Judas gathering his army came to the city of Adullam; and as the seventh day was coming on, they purified themselves according to the custom, and kept the Sabbath there. ³⁹ And on the day following, at which time it had become necessary, Judas and his company came to take up the bodies of those who had fallen, and in company with their countrymen to bring them back to the tombs of their fathers. ⁴⁰ But under the garments of each one of the dead they found consecrated signs of the idols of Jamnia, which the law forbids the Jews to have anything to do with; and it became clear to all that it was for this reason that they had fallen. ⁴¹ All therefore, blessing the [works] of the LORD, the righteous Judge, who makes manifest the things that are hid, ⁴² went themselves to supplication, imploring that the sin committed might be wholly blotted out. And the noble Judas exhorted the multitude to keep themselves from sin, for so much as they had seen before their eyes what things had come to pass because of the sin of those who had fallen. ⁴³ And when he had made a collection—man by man—to the sum of two thousand drachmas of silver, he sent to Jerusalem to offer a sacrifice for sin, doing therein right well and honorably, in that he took thought for a resurrection. ⁴⁴ For if he were not expecting that those who had fallen would rise again, it was superfluous and idle to pray for the dead. ⁴⁵ (And if [he did it] looking to an honorable memorial of gratitude laid up for those who die in godliness, holy and godly was the thought.) For that reason, he made the atoning sacrifice for those who had died, that they might be released from their sin.

CHAPTER 13

¹ In the one hundred and forty-ninth year, tidings were brought to Judas and his company that Antiochus Eupator was coming with [great] multitudes against Judea, ² and with him Lysias his guardian and chancellor, each having a Greek force, one hundred and ten thousand footmen, and five thousand and three hundred horsemen, and twenty-two elephants, and three hundred chariots armed with scythes. ³ And Menelaus also joined himself with them, and with great deception encouraged Antiochus, not for the saving of his country, but because he thought that he would be set over the government. ⁴ But the King of kings stirred up the passion of Antiochus against the wicked wretch; and when Lysias informed him that this man was the cause of all the evils, [the king] commanded to bring him to Beroea, and to put him to death after the manner of that place. ⁵ Now there is in that place a tower of fifty cubits high, full of ashes, and it had all around it a gallery descending sheer on every side into the ashes. ⁶ Here him that is guilty of sacrilege or has attained a preeminence in any other evil deeds, they all push forward into destruction. ⁷ By such a fate it befell the breaker of the law, Menelaus, to die, without obtaining so much as [a grave in] the earth, and that right justly; ⁸ for since he had perpetrated many sins against the altar, whose fire and whose ashes were holy, in ashes he received his death. ⁹ Now the king, infuriated in spirit, was coming with intent to inflict on the Jews the very worst of the sufferings that had befallen [them] in his father's time. ¹⁰ But when Judas heard of these things, he gave charge to the multitude to call on the LORD day and night, [imploring Him,] if ever at any other time, so now to help those who were at the point to be deprived of the law and their country and the holy temple, ¹¹ and not to permit the people that had been but now a little while revived to fall into the hands of those profane heathen. ¹² So when they had all done the same thing together, imploring the merciful Lord with weeping, and fasting, and prostration for three days without ceasing, Judas exhorted them and commanded they should join him. ¹³ And having gone apart with the elders, he resolved that, before the king's army should enter into Judea and make themselves masters of the city, they should go out and try the matter [in fight] by the help of God. ¹⁴ And committing the decision to the Lord of the world and exhorting those who were with him to contend nobly even to death for laws, temple, city, country, commonwealth, he pitched his camp by Modin. ¹⁵ And given out to his men the watchword, VICTORY IS GOD'S, with a chosen body of the bravest young men he fell on [the camp] by night [and penetrated] to the king's tent and killed [of] the army as many as two thousand men and brought down the mightiest elephant with him that was in the tower on him. ¹⁶ And at last they filled the army with terror and alarm and

departed with good success. [17] And this had been accomplished when the day was but now dawning, because of the LORD's protection that gave Judas help. [18] But the king, having had a taste of the exceeding boldness of the Jews, made attempts by stratagem on their positions; [19] and [on] a strong fortress of the Jews at Bethsura, he advanced, was turned back, failed, was defeated, [20] and Judas carried such things as were necessary to those who were within. [21] But Rhodocus, from the Jewish ranks, made known to the enemy the secrets [of his countrymen]. He was sought out, and taken, and shut up in prison. [22] The king treated with them in Bethsura the second time, gave his hand, took theirs, departed, attacked the forces of Judas, was given a worse [outcome], [23] heard that Philip, who had been left as chancellor in Antioch, had become reckless, was confounded, made to the Jews an overture [of peace], submitted himself, and swore to acknowledge all their rights, came to terms with them and offered sacrifice, honored the sanctuary and the place, [24] showed kindness and graciously received Maccabaeus, left Hegemonides governor from Ptolemais even to the Gerrenians, [25] [and] came to Ptolemais. The men of Ptolemais were displeased at the treaty, for they had exceedingly great indignation [against the Jews]: they desired to annul the articles of the agreement. [26] Lysias came forward to speak, made the best defense that was possible, persuaded, pacified, made them well-affected, [and] departed to Antioch. This was the issue of the inroad and departure of the king.

CHAPTER 14

[1] Now after a space of three years tidings were brought to Judas and his company that Demetrius the [son] of Seleucus, having sailed into the haven of Tripolis with a mighty army and a fleet, [2] had gotten possession of the country, having made away with Antiochus and his guardian Lysias. [3] But one Alcimus, who had formerly been chief priest, and had willfully polluted himself in the times when there was no mingling [with the nations], considering that there was no deliverance for him in any way, nor any more access to the holy altar, [4] came to King Demetrius in about the one hundred [and] fifty-first year, presenting to him a crown of gold and a palm, and beside these some of the festal olive boughs of the temple. And for that day he held his peace; [5] but having gotten opportunity to further his own madness, being called by Demetrius into a meeting of his council and asked how the Jews stood affected and what they purposed, he answered to that. [6] Those of the Jews that he called Hasidaeans, whose leader is Judas Maccabaeus, keep up war, and are seditious, not suffering the kingdom to find tranquility. [7] For that reason, having laid aside my ancestral glory, I mean the chief priesthood, I have now come here; [8] first, for the genuine care I have for the things that

concern the king, and secondly, because I also have regard to my own fellow-citizens; for, through the unadvised dealing of those of whom I spoke before, our whole race is in no small misfortune. [9] But do you, O king, having informed yourself of these things separately, take thought both for our country and for our race, which is surrounded [by enemies], according to the gracious kindness with which you receive all? [10] For as long as Judas remains alive, it is impossible that the state should find peace. [11] And when he had spoken such words as these, at once the rest of the [king's] friends, having ill will against Judas, inflamed Demetrius yet more. [12] And then appointing Nicanor, who had been master of the elephants, and making him governor of Judea, he sent him out, [13] giving him written instructions to make away with Judas himself and to scatter those who were with him, and to set up Alcimus as chief priest of the great temple. [14] And those in Judea that had [before] driven Judas into exile thronged to Nicanor in flocks, supposing that the misfortunes and calamities of the Jews would be successes to themselves. [15] But when [the Jews] heard of Nicanor's inroad and the assault of the heathen, they sprinkled earth [on their heads] and made solemn supplication to him who had established His own people forevermore, and who always, making manifest His presence, upholds [those who are] His own portion. [16] And when the leader had given [his] commands, he immediately set out from there, and joined battle with them at a village [called] Lessau. [17] But Simon, the brother of Judas, had encountered Nicanor, yet not until late, having received a check by reason of the sudden consternation caused by his adversaries. [18] Nevertheless Nicanor, hearing of the manliness of those who were with Judas, and their courage in fighting for their country, shrank from bringing the matter to the decision of the sword. [19] For that reason, he sent Posidonius, and Theodotus, and Mattathias to give and receive pledges of friendship. [20] So when these proposals had been long considered, and the leader had made the troops acquainted with them, and it appeared that they were all of like mind, they consented to the covenants. [21] And they appointed a day on which to meet together by themselves. And a litter was borne forward from each [army]; they set chairs of state; [22] Judas stationed armed men ready in convenient places, lest perhaps there should suddenly be treachery on the part of the enemy; they held such conference as was suitable. [23] Nicanor waited in Jerusalem, and did nothing to cause disturbance, but dismissed the flocks of people that had gathered together. [24] And he kept Judas always in his presence; he had gained a hearty affection for the man; [25] he urged him to marry and beget children; he married, settled quietly, took part in common life. [26] But Alcimus, perceiving the good will that was between them, and having gotten possession of the covenants

2 MACCABEES

that had been made, came to Demetrius and told him that Nicanor was ill-affected toward the state, for he had appointed that conspirator against his kingdom, Judas, to be his successor. 27 And the king, falling into a rage, and being exasperated by the false accusations of that most wicked man, wrote to Nicanor, signifying that he was displeased at the covenants, and commanding him to send Maccabaeus prisoner to Antioch in all haste. 28 And when this message came to Nicanor, he was confounded, and was severely troubled at the thought of annulling the articles that had been agreed on, the man having done no wrong; 29 but because there was no dealing against the king, he watched his time to execute this purpose by stratagem. 30 But Maccabaeus, when he perceived that Nicanor was behaving more harshly in his dealings with him, and that he had become ruler in his customary bearing, understanding that this harshness came not of good, gathered together not a few of his men, and concealed himself from Nicanor. 31 But the other, when he became aware that he had been bravely defeated by the stratagem of Judas, came to the great and holy temple, while the priests were offering the usual sacrifices, and commanded them to deliver the man up. 32 And when they declared with oaths that they had no knowledge where the man was whom he sought, 33 he stretched out his right hand toward the sanctuary and swore this oath: "If you will not deliver up to me Judas as a prisoner, I will lay this temple of God even with the ground, and will break down the altar, and I will erect here a temple to Bacchus for all to see." 34 And having said this, he departed. But the priests, stretching out their hands toward Heaven, called on Him that ever fights for our nation, in these words: 35 "You, O Lord of the universe, who in Yourself have need of nothing, was well pleased that a sanctuary of Your habitation should be set among us; 36 so now, O holy Lord of all hallowing, keep undefiled forever this house that has been lately cleansed." 37 Now information was given to Nicanor against one Razis, an elder of Jerusalem, as being a lover of his countrymen and a man of very good report, and one called "Father of the Jews" for his good will [toward them]. 38 For in the former times when there was no mingling [with the nations] he had been accused of [cleaving to the] Jews' religion, and had endangered body and life with all earnestness for the religion of the Jews. 39 And Nicanor, wishing to make evident the ill will that he bore to the Jews, sent above five hundred soldiers to take him; 40 for he thought by taking him to inflict a calamity on them. 41 But when the troops were on the point of taking the tower, and were forcing the door of the court, and commanded to bring fire and burn the doors, he being surrounded on every side, fell on his sword, 42 choosing rather to die nobly than to fall into the hands of the wicked wretches, and suffer outrage unworthy of his own nobleness: 43 but since he missed his stroke through the excitement of the struggle, and the crowds were now rushing within the door, he ran bravely up to the wall and cast himself down courageously among the crowds. 44 But as they quickly gave back, a space was made, and he fell on the middle of his side. 45 And having yet breath within him, and being inflamed with passion, he rose up, and though his blood gushed out in streams and his wounds were grievous, he ran through the crowds, and standing on a steep rock, 46 when as his blood was now well near spent, he drew out his bowels [through the wound, and] taking them in both his hands he shook them at the crowds; and calling on Him who is Lord of the life and the spirit to restore these again, he thus died.

CHAPTER 15

1 But Nicanor, hearing that Judas and his company were in the region of Samaria, resolved to set on them with all security on the day of rest. 2 And when the Jews that were compelled to follow him said, "Do not destroy so savagely and barbarously, but give due glory to the day which He that sees all things has honored and hallowed above [other days]"; 3 then the three times-accursed wretch asked if there were a Sovereign in Heaven that had commanded to keep the Sabbath day. 4 And when they declared, "There is the LORD, living Himself [as the] Sovereign in Heaven, who commanded [us] to observe the seventh day"; 5 then the other says, "I also am a sovereign on the earth, who [now] command to take up arms and execute the king's business." Nevertheless, he did not prevail to execute his cruel purpose. 6 And Nicanor, bearing himself haughtily in all vain pride, had determined to set up a monument of complete victory over Judas and all those who were with him: 7 but Maccabaeus still trusted unceasingly, with all hope that he should obtain help from the LORD. 8 And he exhorted his company not to be fearful at the inroad of the heathen, but, keeping in mind the help which of old they had oftentimes received from Heaven, so now also to look for the victory which would come to them from the Almighty; 9 and comforting them out of the Law and the Prophets, and in addition, putting them in mind of the conflicts that they had maintained, he made them more eager [for the battle]. 10 And when he had roused their spirit, he gave them [his] commands, at the same time pointing out the disloyalty of the heathen and their breach of their oaths. 11 And arming each one of them, not so much with the sure defense of shields and spears as with the encouragement [that lies] in good words, and moreover relating to them a dream worthy to be believed, he made them all exceedingly glad. 12 And the vision of that [dream] was this: [He saw] Onias, him that was chief priest, a noble and good man, reverend in bearing, yet gentle in manner and well-spoken, and exercised from a child in all points of

virtue, with outstretched hands invoking [blessings] on the whole body of the Jews: [13] there on [he saw] a man appear, of venerable age and exceeding glory, and wonderful and most majestic was the dignity around him: [14] and Onias answered and said, "This is the lover of the countrymen, he who prays much for the people and the holy city, Jeremiah the prophet of God": [15] and Jeremiah stretching out his right hand delivered to Judas a sword of gold, and in giving it addressed [him], saying, [16] "Take the holy sword, a gift from God, with which you will strike down the adversaries." [17] And being encouraged by the words of Judas, which were of a lofty strain, and able to incite to virtue and to stir the souls of the young to manly courage, they determined not to carry on a campaign, but nobly to bear down on [the enemy, and] fighting hand to hand with all courage bring the matter to an issue, because the city and the sanctuary and the temple were in danger. [18] For their fear for wives and children, and furthermore for relatives and countrymen, was in less account with them; but greatest and first was their fear for the consecrated sanctuary. [19] And they also that were shut up in the city were in no light distress, being troubled because of the encounter in the open ground. [20] And when all were now waiting for the decision of the issue, and the enemy had already joined battle, and the army had been set in array, and the elephants brought back to a convenient post, and the horsemen drawn on the flank, [21] Maccabaeus, perceiving the presence of the troops, and the various arms with which they were equipped, and the savageness of the elephants, holding up his hands to Heaven called on the LORD that works wonders, recognizing that [success] comes not by arms, but that, according as [the LORD] will judge, He gains the victory for those who are worthy. [22] And calling on [God], he said after this manner: "You, O Sovereign LORD, sent Your messenger in the time of Hezekiah king of Judea, and he killed of the army of Sennacherib as many as one hundred and eighty-five thousand; [23] so now also, O Sovereign of the heavens, send a good messenger before us to bring terror and trembling: [24] through the greatness of Your arm let them be stricken with dismay that have come here against Your holy people with blasphemy." And as he ended with these words, [25] Nicanor and his company advanced with trumpets and victory songs;

[26] but Judas and his company joined battle with the enemy with invocation and prayers. [27] And contending with their hands, and praying to God with their hearts, they killed no less than thirty-five thousand men, being made exceedingly glad by the manifestation of God. [28] And when the engagement was over, and they were returning again with joy, they recognized Nicanor lying dead in full armor; [29] and there arose a shout and tumult, and then they blessed the Sovereign [LORD] in the language of their fathers. [30] And he that in all things was in body and soul the foremost champion of his fellow-citizens, he that kept through life the good will of his youth toward his countrymen, commanded to cut off Nicanor's head, and his hand with the shoulder, and bring them to Jerusalem. [31] And when he had arrived there, and had called his countrymen together and set the priests before the altar, he sent for those who were in the citadel; [32] and showing the head of the vile Nicanor, and the hand of that profane man, which with proud brags he had stretched out against the holy house of the Almighty, [33] and cutting out the tongue of the impious Nicanor, he said that he would give it by pieces to the birds, and hang up the rewards of his madness near the sanctuary. [34] And they all, [looking up] to Heaven, blessed the LORD who had manifested Himself, saying, "Blessed is He that has preserved His own place undefiled." [35] And he hanged Nicanor's head and shoulder from the citadel, a sign, evident to all and manifest, of the help of the LORD. [36] And they all ordained with a common decree in no way to let this day pass undistinguished, but to mark with honor the thirteenth day of the twelfth month (it is called Adar in the Syrian tongue), the day before the day of Mordecai. [37] This then having been the issue of the attempt of Nicanor, and the city having from those times been held by the Hebrews, I will also here make an end of my scroll. [38] And if [I have written] well and to the point in my story, this is what I myself desired; but if meanly and indifferently, this is all I could attain to. [39] For as it is distasteful to drink wine alone and in like manner again [to drink] water [alone], while the mingling of wine with water at once gives full pleasantness to the flavor; so also, the fashioning of the language delights the ears of those who read the story. And here will be the end.

ORTHODOX DEUTEROCANON

1 ESDRAS

Otherwise known as 3 Esdras

1 Esdras, also called Greek Esdras, Greek Ezra, or 3 Esdras, is an ancient Greek version of the biblical Book of Ezra in use among the early church, and many modern Christians with varying degrees of canonicity. First Esdras is substantially the same as Masoretic Ezra. As part of the Septuagint translation of the Old Testament, it is regarded as deuterocanonical in the churches of the East, but apocryphal in the West. First Esdras is found in Origen's Hexapla. Greek and related versions of the Bible include both Esdras A (English title: 1 Esdras) and Esdras B (Ezra–Nehemiah) in parallel.

CHAPTER 1

¹ Josiah held the Passover in Jerusalem to his Lord and offered the Passover [on] the fourteenth day of the first month; ² having set the priests according to their daily courses, being arrayed in their vestments, in the temple of the LORD. ³ And he spoke to the Levites, the temple-servants of Israel, that they should make themselves holy to the LORD, to set the holy Ark of the LORD in the house that King Solomon the son of David had built, ⁴ [and he said,] "You will no longer have need to bear it on your shoulders: now therefore, serve the LORD your God, and minister to His people Israel, and prepare after your fathers' houses and relatives, ⁵ according to the writing of David, king of Israel, and according to the magnificence of his son Solomon: and standing in the holy place according to the several divisions of the families of you the Levites, who [minister] in the presence of your countrymen the sons of Israel, ⁶ offer the Passover in order, and make the sacrifices ready for your countrymen, and keep the Passover according to the command of the LORD, which was given to Moses." ⁷ And to the people which were present Josiah gave thirty thousand lambs and kids, and three thousand calves: these things were given of the king's substance, according as he promised, to the people, and to the priests and Levites. ⁸ And Hilkiah, and Zechariah, and Esyelus, the rulers of the temple, gave to the priests for the Passover two thousand [and] six hundred sheep, and three hundred calves. ⁹ And Jeconias, and Samaias, and his brother Nathanael, and Sabias, and Ochielus, and Joram, captains over thousands, gave to the Levites for the Passover five thousand sheep, and seven hundred calves. ¹⁰ And when these things were done, the priests and Levites, having the unleavened bread, stood in agreeable order according to the countrymen, ¹¹ and according to the several divisions by fathers' houses, before the people, to offer to the LORD, as it is written in the Scroll of Moses: and so [they] did [in] the morning. ¹² And they roasted the Passover with fire, as pertains: and they boiled the sacrifices in the brazen vessels and cauldrons with a good savor, ¹³ and set them before all the people; and afterward they prepared for themselves, and for their relatives the priests, the sons of Aaron. ¹⁴ For the priests offered the fat until night: and the Levites prepared for themselves, and for their relatives the priests, the sons of Aaron. ¹⁵ The holy singers also, the sons of Asaph, were in their order, according to the appointment of David, Asaph, Zechariah, and Eddinus, who was of the king's retinue. ¹⁶ Moreover, the gatekeepers were at every gate; none had need to depart from his daily course, for their relatives the Levites prepared for them. ¹⁷ So were the things that belonged to the sacrifices of the LORD accomplished in that day, in holding the Passover, ¹⁸ and offering sacrifices on the altar of the LORD, according to the command of King Josiah. ¹⁹ So the sons of Israel, which were present at that time, held the Passover and the Celebration of Unleavened Bread [for] seven days. ²⁰ And such a Passover was not held in Israel since the time of the prophet Samuel. ²¹ Yes, all the kings of Israel had not held such a Passover as Josiah, and the priests, and the Levites, and the Jews, with all Israel that were present in their dwelling place at Jerusalem. ²² In the eighteenth year of the reign of Josiah this Passover was held. ²³ And the works of Josiah were upright before his Lord with a heart full of godliness. ²⁴ Moreover, the things that came to pass in his days have been written in times past, concerning those that sinned, and did wickedly against the LORD above every people and kingdom, and how they grieved Him exceedingly, so that the words of the LORD were confirmed against Israel. ²⁵ Now after all these acts of Josiah, it came to pass that Pharaoh the king of Egypt came to raise war at Carchemish on [the] Euphrates: and Josiah went out against him. ²⁶ But the king of Egypt sent to him, saying, "What have I to do with you, O king of Judea? ²⁷ I am not sent out from the LORD God against you; for my war is on [the] Euphrates: and now the LORD is with me, yes, the LORD is with me hastening me forward. Depart from me and do not be against the LORD." ²⁸ However, Josiah did not turn back to his chariot, but undertook to fight with him, not regarding the words of the prophet Jeremiah [spoken] by the mouth of the LORD, ²⁹ but he joined battle with him in the plain of Megiddo, and the princes came down against King Josiah. ³⁰ Then the king said to his servants, "Carry me away out of the battle; for I am very weak. And immediately his servants carried him away out of the

1 ESDRAS

army." ³¹ Then he got up on his second chariot; and being brought back to Jerusalem he died and was buried in the tomb of his fathers. ³² And in all Jewry they mourned for Josiah; and the prophet Jeremiah lamented for Josiah, and the chief men with the women made lamentation for him, to this day: and this was given out for an ordinance to be done continually in all the nation of Israel. ³³ These things are written in the Scroll of the Histories of the Kings of Judea, and each of the acts that Josiah did, and his glory, and his understanding in the Law of the LORD, and the things that he had done before, and the things now [recited], are reported in the Scroll of the Kings of Israel and Judah. ³⁴ And the people took Joachaz, the son of Josiah, and made him king instead of his father Josiah, when he was twenty-three years old. ³⁵ And he reigned in Judah and in Jerusalem three months: and then the king of Egypt deposed him from reigning in Jerusalem. ³⁶ And he set a tax on the people of one hundred talents of silver and one talent of gold. ³⁷ The king of Egypt also made King Jehoiakim, his brother, king of Judea and Jerusalem. ³⁸ And Jehoiakim bound the nobles, but he apprehended his brother Zarakes and brought him up out of Egypt. ³⁹ Jehoiakim was twenty-five years old when he began to reign in Judea and Jerusalem; and he did that which was evil in the sight of the LORD. ⁴⁰ And Nebuchadnezzar the king of Babylon came up against him, and bound him with a chain of brass, and carried him to Babylon. ⁴¹ Nebuchadnezzar also took of the holy vessels of the LORD, and carried them away, and set them up in his own temple at Babylon. ⁴² But those things that are reported of him, and of his uncleanness and impiety, are written in the Chronicles of the Kings. ⁴³ And his son Jehoiakim reigned in his stead; for when he was made king he was eighteen years old; ⁴⁴ and he reigned three months and ten days in Jerusalem; and did that which was evil before the LORD. ⁴⁵ So after a year Nebuchadnezzar sent and caused him to be brought to Babylon with the holy vessels of the LORD, ⁴⁶ and he made Zedekiah king of Judea and Jerusalem when he was twenty-one years old; and he reigned eleven years: ⁴⁷ and he also did that which was evil in the sight of the LORD and did not care for the words that were spoken by the prophet Jeremiah from the mouth of the LORD. ⁴⁸ And after King Nebuchadnezzar had made him to swear by the Name of the LORD, he renounced it, and rebelled; and hardening his neck and his heart, he transgressed the laws of the LORD, the God of Israel. ⁴⁹ Moreover, the governors of the people and of the priests did many things wickedly, and surpassed all the pollutions of all nations, and defiled the temple of the LORD, which was sanctified in Jerusalem. ⁵⁰ And the God of their fathers sent by His messenger to call them back, because He had compassion on them and on His dwelling place. ⁵¹ But they mocked His messengers; and in the day when the LORD spoke [to them], they scoffed at His prophets, ⁵² so much so that He, being angry with His people for their great ungodliness, commanded to bring up the kings of the Chaldeans against them, ⁵³ who killed their young men with the sword, around their holy temple, and spared neither young man nor maid, old man nor child; but He delivered all into their hands. ⁵⁴ And they took all the holy vessels of the LORD, both great and small, with the vessels of the Ark of the LORD, and the king's treasures, and carried them away to Babylon. ⁵⁵ And they burned the house of the LORD, and broke down the walls of Jerusalem, and burned the towers thereof with fire. ⁵⁶ And as for her glorious things, they never ceased until they had brought them all to nothing; and the people that were not slain with the sword he carried to Babylon, ⁵⁷ and they were servants to him and to his children, until the Persians reigned, to fulfill the word of the LORD by the mouth of Jeremiah: ⁵⁸ "Until the land has enjoyed her Sabbaths, the whole time of her desolation she will keep Sabbath, to fulfill seventy years."

CHAPTER 2

¹ In the first year of Cyrus king of the Persians, that the word of the LORD by the mouth of Jeremiah might be accomplished, ² the LORD stirred up the spirit of Cyrus king of the Persians, and he made proclamation through all his kingdom, and also by writing, ³ saying, "Cyrus king of the Persians says: The Lord of Israel, the Most High LORD, has made me king of the whole world, ⁴ and commanded me to build Him a house at Jerusalem that is in Judea. ⁵ If, therefore, there are any of you that are of His people, let the LORD, even his Lord, be with him, and let him go up to Jerusalem that is in Judea, and build the house of the LORD of Israel: He is the LORD that dwells in Jerusalem. ⁶ Of such therefore as dwell in various places, let those who are in his own place help each one with gold, and with silver, ⁷ with gifts, also with horses and cattle, besides the other things which have been added by vow for the temple of the LORD which is in Jerusalem." ⁸ Then the chief of the families of Judah and of the tribe of Benjamin stood up; the priests also, and the Levites, and all they whose spirit the LORD had stirred to go up, to build the house for the LORD which is in Jerusalem. ⁹ And those who lived around them helped them in all things with silver and gold, with horses and cattle, and with very many gifts that were vowed of a great number whose minds were stirred up. ¹⁰ King Cyrus also brought out the holy vessels of the LORD, which Nebuchadnezzar had carried away from Jerusalem, and had set up in his temple of idols. ¹¹ Now when Cyrus king of the Persians had brought them out, he delivered them to his treasurer Mithradates, ¹² and they were delivered by him to Sanabassar the governor of Judea. ¹³ And this was the number of them: one thousand golden cups, one thousand cups of silver, twenty-nine censers of silver,

thirty vials of gold, and of silver—two thousand four hundred and ten, and other vessels—one thousand. [14] So all the vessels of gold and of silver were brought up, even five thousand four hundred and sixty-nine, [15] and were carried back by Sanabassar, together with them of the captivity, from Babylon to Jerusalem. [16] But in the time of Artaxerxes king of the Persians, Belemus, and Mithradates, and Tabellius, and Rathumus, and Beeltethmus, and Samellius the scribe, with the others that were in commission with them, dwelling in Samaria and other places, wrote to him against those who lived in Judea and Jerusalem the following letter: [17] "To King Artaxerxes our Lord, Your servants, Rathumus the recorder, and Samellius the scribe, and the rest of their council, and the judges that are in Coele-Syria and Phoenicia. [18] Be it now known to our lord the king, that the Jews that have come up from you to us, having come to Jerusalem, are building that rebellious and wicked city, and are repairing its marketplaces and walls, and are laying the foundation of a temple. [19] Now if this city is built and the walls [thereof] are finished, they will not only refuse to give tribute, but will even stand up against kings. [20] And forasmuch as the things pertaining to the temple are now in hand, we think it suitable not to neglect such a matter, [21] but to speak to our lord the king, to the intent that, if it be your pleasure, search may be made in the scrolls of your fathers: [22] and you will find in the chronicles what is written concerning these things, and will understand that that city was rebellious, troubling both kings and cities, [23] and that the Jews were rebellious, and always raised wars therein of former time; for this reason even this city was laid waste. [24] For that reason, now we declare to you, O lord the king, that if this city is built again, and the walls thereof set up anew, you will from now on have no passage into Coele-Syria and Phoenicia." [25] Then the king wrote back again to Rathumus the recorder, and Beeltethmus, and Samellius the scribe, and to the rest that were in commission, and lived in Samaria, and Syria, and Phoenicia, after this manner: [26] "I have read the letter which you have sent to me; therefore, I commanded to make search, and it has been found that that city of former time has made insurrection against kings; [27] and the men were given to rebellion and war therein; and that fierce and mighty kings were in Jerusalem, who reigned and exacted tribute in Coele-Syria and Phoenicia. [28] Now therefore, I have commanded to hinder those men from building the city, and heed to be taken that there is nothing done contrary to this [order]; [29] and that those wicked doings proceed no further to the annoyance of kings. [30] Then King Artaxerxes, his letters being read, Rathumus, and Samellius the scribe, and the rest that were in commission with them, removing in haste to Jerusalem with horsemen and a multitude of people in battle array, began to hinder the builders; and the building of the temple in Jerusalem ceased until the second year of the reign of Darius king of the Persians.

CHAPTER 3

[1] Now King Darius made a great feast to all his subjects, and to all that were born in his house, and to all the princes of Media and of Persia, [2] and to all the local governors, and captains, and governors that were under him, from India to Ethiopia, in the one hundred [and] twenty-seven provinces. [3] And when they had eaten and drunken, and being satisfied were gone home, then Darius the king went into his bedchamber, and slept, and awoke out of his sleep. [4] Then the three young men of the bodyguard, that kept the king's person, spoke to one another: [5] "Let each of us say one thing which will be strongest; and he whose sentence will seem wiser than the others, to him Darius the king will give great gifts, and great honors in token of victory: [6] as, to be clothed in purple, to drink in gold, and to sleep on gold, and a chariot with bridles of gold, and a turban of fine linen, and a chain around his neck; [7] and he will sit next to Darius because of his wisdom, and will be called cousin of Darius." [8] And then they each wrote his sentence, and set to their seals, and laid [the writing] under [the] pillow of King Darius, [9] and said, "When the king is risen, some will give him the writing; and of whose side the king and the three princes of Persia will judge that his sentence is the wisest, to him will the victory be given, as it is written." [10] The first wrote, "WINE IS THE STRONGEST." [11] The second wrote, "THE KING IS STRONGEST." [12] The third wrote, "WOMEN ARE STRONGEST, BUT ABOVE ALL THINGS TRUTH BEARS AWAY THE VICTORY." [13] Now when the king was risen up, they took the writing, and gave it to him, and so he read it: [14] and sending out he called all the princes of Persia and of Media, and the local governors, and the captains, and the governors, and the chief officers, [15] and he sat down in the royal seat of judgment, and the writing was read before them. [16] And he said, "Call the young men, and they will explain their own sentences." So they were called, and came in. [17] And they said to them, "Declare to us your mind concerning the things you have written." Then began the first, who had spoken of the strength of wine, [18] and said, "O lords, how exceedingly strong is wine! It causes all men to err that drink it: [19] it makes the mind of the king and of the fatherless child to be all one; of the bondman and of the freeman, of the poor man and of the rich; [20] it also turns every thought into cheer and mirth, so that a man remembers neither sorrow nor debt; [21] and it makes every heart rich, so that a man remembers neither king nor local governor; and it makes all things to speak by talents; [22] and when they are in their cups, they forget their love both to friends and relatives, and a little after draw their swords, [23] but when they awake from their wine, they do not remember what they

have done. ²⁴ O lords, is not wine the strongest, seeing that it enforces to do so?" And when he had so spoken, he held his peace.

CHAPTER 4

¹ Then the second, that had spoken of the strength of the king, began to say, ² "O lords, do men not excel in strength, that bear rule over the sea and land, and all things in them? ³ But yet is the king stronger: and he is their lord and has dominion over them; and in whatever he commands them they obey him. ⁴ If he commands them to make war—the one against the other—they do it; and if he sends them out against the enemies, they go, and overcome mountains, walls, and towers. ⁵ They kill and are slain, and [still] do not transgress the king's command: if they get the victory, they bring everything to the king, as well as the plunder, as everything else. ⁶ Likewise for those that are not soldiers, and have nothing to do with wars, but are farming, when they have again reaped that which they had sown, they bring it to the king, and compel one another to pay tribute to the king. ⁷ And he is but one man: if he commands to kill, they kill; if he commands to spare, they spare; ⁸ if he commands to strike, they strike; if he commands to make desolate, they make desolate; if he commands to build, they build; ⁹ if he commands to cut down, they cut down; if he commands to plant, they plant. ¹⁰ So all his people and his armies obey him: furthermore, he lies down, he eats and drinks, and takes his rest, ¹¹ and these keep watch around him, neither may anyone depart and do his own business, neither do they disobey him in [anything]. ¹² O lords, how should the king not be strongest, seeing that in such sort he is obeyed? And he held his peace. ¹³ Then the third, who had spoken of women and of truth (this was Zerubbabel), began to speak. ¹⁴ "O lords, is not the king great, and men are many, and wine is strong? Who is it then that rules them, or has the lordship over them? Are they not women? ¹⁵ Women have borne the king and all the people that bear rule by sea and land. ¹⁶ Even from them they came: and they nourished them up that planted the vineyards, from where the wine comes. ¹⁷ These also make garments for men; these bring glory to men; and without women men cannot be. ¹⁸ Yes, and if men have gathered together gold, and silver, and any other attractive thing, and see a woman which is attractive in favor and beauty, ¹⁹ they let all those things go, and stare after her, and even with open mouth fix their eyes fast on her; and they have all [the] more desire for her than for gold or silver, or any other attractive thing. ²⁰ A man leaves his own father that brought him up, and his own country, and joins with his wife. ²¹ And with his wife he ends his days, and remembers neither father, nor mother, nor country. ²² By this also you must know that women have dominion over you: do you not labor and toil, and give and bring all to women?

²³ Yes, a man takes his sword, and goes out to make excursions, and to rob and to steal, and to sail on the sea and on rivers; ²⁴ and looks on a lion and walks in the darkness; and when he has stolen, plundered, and robbed, he brings it to his love. ²⁵ For that reason, a man loves his wife better than father or mother. ²⁶ Yes, there are many that have run out of their wits for women and become bondmen for their sakes. ²⁷ Many have also perished, have stumbled, and sinned, for women. ²⁸ And now do you not believe me? Is the king not great in his power? Do all regions not fear to touch him? ²⁹ Yet I saw him and the king's concubine Apame, the daughter of the illustrious Barticus, sitting at the right hand of the king, ³⁰ and taking the crown from the king's head, and setting it on her own head; yes, she struck the king with her left hand: ³¹ and immediately the king stared and gazed on her with open mouth. If she laughed on him, he also laughed, but if she took any displeasure at him, he was glad to flatter, that she might be reconciled to him again. ³² O lords, how can it be but women should be strong, seeing they do so?" ³³ Then the king and the nobles looked on one another, so he began to speak concerning truth. ³⁴ "O lords, are women not strong? Great is the earth, high is the Heaven, swift is the sun in his course, for he encircles the heavens around, and fetches his course again to his own place in one day. ³⁵ Is He not great that makes these things? Therefore, great is truth, and stronger than all things. ³⁶ All the earth calls on truth, and the Heaven blesses her; all works shake and tremble, but with her is no unrighteous thing. ³⁷ Wine is unrighteous, the king is unrighteous, women are unrighteous, all the children of men are unrighteous, and all such works of theirs are unrighteous; and there is no truth in them; in their unrighteousness also, they will perish. ³⁸ But truth remains and is strong forever; she lives and conquers forevermore. ³⁹ With her there is no accepting of persons or rewards; but she does the things that are just, and [refrains] from all unrighteous and wicked things; and all men do well like of her works. ⁴⁰ Neither is any unrighteousness in her judgment; and she is the strength, and the kingdom, and the power, and the majesty, of all ages. Blessed is the God of truth." ⁴¹ And with that he held his tongue. And all the people then shouted, and said, "Great is truth, and strong above all things." ⁴² Then the king said to him, "Ask what you will more than is appointed in writing, and we will give it to you, inasmuch as you are found wisest; and you will sit next to me, and will be called my cousin." ⁴³ Then he said to the king, "Remember your vow, which you vowed to build Jerusalem, in the day when you came to your kingdom, ⁴⁴ and to send away all the vessels that were taken out of Jerusalem, which Cyrus set apart, when he vowed to destroy Babylon, and vowed to send them there again. ⁴⁵ You also vowed to build up the temple, which the Edomites burned when Judea was made desolate by

1 ESDRAS

the Chaldeans. ⁴⁶ And now, O lord the king, this is that which I require, and which I desire of you, and this is the princely generosity that will proceed from you: I pray therefore that you make good the vow, the performance of which you have vowed to the King of Heaven with your own mouth." ⁴⁷ Then Darius the king stood up, and kissed him, and wrote letters for him to all the treasurers, and governors, and captains, and local governors, that they should safely bring on their way both him, and all those that should go up with him to build Jerusalem. ⁴⁸ He also wrote letters to all the governors that were in Coele-Syria and Phoenicia, and to them in Libanus, that they should bring cedar wood from Libanus to Jerusalem, and that they should build the city with him. ⁴⁹ Moreover, he wrote for all the Jews that should go out of his realm up into Jewry, concerning their freedom, that no officer, no governor, no local governor, nor treasurer, should forcibly enter into their doors; ⁵⁰ and that all the country which they occupied should be free to them without tribute; and that the Edomites should give over the villages of the Jews which they then held: ⁵¹ and that there should be yearly given twenty talents to the building of the temple, until the time that it were built; ⁵² and ten more talents yearly, for burnt-offerings to be presented on the altar every day, as they had a command to offer seventeen: ⁵³ and that all those who should come from Babylonia to build the city should have their freedom—they as well as their posterity, and all the priests that came. ⁵⁴ He also wrote [to give them] their charges, and the priests' vestments wherein they minister; ⁵⁵ and for the Levites he wrote that their charges should be given them until the day that the house were finished, and Jerusalem built up. ⁵⁶ And he commanded to give to all that kept the city lands and wages. ⁵⁷ He also sent away all the vessels from Babylon that Cyrus had set apart; and all that Cyrus had given in command, he also charged to be done, and sent to Jerusalem. ⁵⁸ Now when this young man had gone out, he lifted up his face to Heaven toward Jerusalem, and praised the King of Heaven, ⁵⁹ and said, "From You comes victory, from You comes wisdom, and Yours is the glory, and I am Your servant. ⁶⁰ Blessed are You, who have given me wisdom: and to You I give thanks, O LORD of our fathers." ⁶¹ And so he took the letters, and went out, and came to Babylon, and told it [to] all his countrymen. ⁶² And they praised the God of their fathers, because He had given them freedom and liberty ⁶³ to go up, and to build Jerusalem, and the temple which is called by His Name: and they feasted with instruments of music and gladness [for] seven days.

CHAPTER 5

¹ After this the chiefs of fathers' houses were chosen to go up according to their tribes, with their wives, and sons, and daughters, with their menservants and maidservants, and their cattle. ² And Darius sent one thousand horsemen with them, until they had brought them back to Jerusalem safely, and with musical instruments, tabrets, and flutes. ³ And all their countrymen played, and he made them go up together with them. ⁴ And these are the names of the men which went up, according to their families among their tribes, after their several divisions. ⁵ The priests, the sons of Phinehas, the sons of Aaron: Jesus the son of Josedek, the son of Saraias, and Jehoiakim the son of Zerubbabel, the son of Salathiel, of the house of David, of the lineage of Phares, of the tribe of Judah; ⁶ who spoke wise sentences before Darius the king of Persia in the second year of his reign, in the month Nisan, which is the first month. ⁷ And these are they of Jewry that came up from the captivity, where they lived as strangers, whom Nebuchadnezzar the king of Babylon had carried away to Babylon. ⁸ And they returned to Jerusalem, and to the other parts of Jewry, every man to his own city, who came with Zerubbabel, with Jesus, Nehemiah, and Zerahiah, Resaias, Eneneus, Mardocheus, Beelsarus, Aspharsus, Reelias, Roimus, and Baana, their leaders. ⁹ The number of them of the nation, and their leaders: the sons of Phoros, two thousand one hundred and seventy-two; the sons of Saphat, four hundred and seventy-two; ¹⁰ the sons of Ares, seven hundred and fifty-six; ¹¹ the sons of Phaath-Moab, of the sons of Jesus and Joab, two thousand eight hundred and twelve; ¹² the sons of Elam, one thousand two hundred and fifty-four; the sons of Zathui, nine hundred and forty-five; the sons of Chorbe, seven hundred and five; the sons of Bani, six hundred and forty-eight; ¹³ the sons of Bebai, six hundred and twenty-three; the sons of Astad, one thousand three hundred and twenty-two; ¹⁴ the sons of Adonikam, six hundred and sixty-seven; the sons of Bagoi, two thousand and sixty-six; the sons of Adinu, four hundred and fifty-four; ¹⁵ the sons of Ater, of Ezekias, ninety-two; the sons of Kilan and Azetas, sixty-seven; the sons of Azaru, four hundred and thirty-two; ¹⁶ the sons of Annis, one hundred and one; the sons of Arom, of the sons of Bassai, three hundred and twenty-three; the sons of Arsiphurith, one hundred and twelve; ¹⁷ the sons of Baiterus, three thousand and five; the sons of Bethlomon, one hundred and twenty-three; ¹⁸ they of Netophas, fifty-five; they of Anathoth, one hundred and fifty-eight; they of Bethasmoth, forty-two; ¹⁹ they of Kariathiarius, twenty-five; they of Caphira and Beroth, seven hundred and forty-three; ²⁰ the Chadiasai and Ammidioi, four hundred and twenty-two; they of Kirama and Gabbe, six hundred and twenty-one; ²¹ they of Macalon, one hundred and twenty-two; they of Betolion, fifty-two; the sons of Niphis, one hundred and fifty-six; ²² the sons of Calamolalus and Onus, seven hundred and twenty-five; the sons of Jerechu, three hundred and forty-five; ²³ the sons of Sanaas, three thousand three

hundred and thirty. [24] The priests: the sons of Jeddu, the son of Jesus, among the sons of Sanasib, nine hundred and seventy-two; the sons of Emmeruth, one thousand and fifty-two; [25] the sons of Phassurus, one thousand two hundred and forty-seven; the sons of Charme, one thousand and seventeen. [26] The Levites: the sons of Jesus, and Kadmiel, and Bannas, and Sudias, seventy-four. [27] The holy singers: the sons of Asaph, one hundred and twenty-eight. [28] The gatekeepers: the sons of Salum, the sons of Atar, the sons of Tolman, the sons of Dacubi, the sons of Ateta, the sons of Sabi, in all one hundred and thirty-nine. [29] The temple servants: the sons of Esau, the sons of Asipha, the sons of Tabaoth, the sons of Keras, the sons of Sua, the sons of Phaleas, the sons of Labana, the sons of Aggaba. [30] The sons of Acud, the sons of Uta, the sons of Ketab, the sons of Accaba, the sons of Subai, the sons of Anan, the sons of Cathua, the sons of Geddur, [31] the sons of Jairus, the sons of Daisan, the sons of Noeba, the sons of Chaseba, the sons of Gazera, the sons of Ozias, the sons of Phinoe, the sons of Asara, the sons of Basthai, the sons of Asana, the sons of Maani, the sons of Naphisi, the sons of Acub, the sons of Achipha, the sons of Asur, the sons of Pharakim, the sons of Basaloth, [32] the sons of Meedda, the sons of Cutha, the sons of Charea, the sons of Barchus, the sons of Serar, the sons of Thomei, the sons of Nasi, the sons of Atipha. [33] The sons of the servants of Solomon: the sons of Assaphioth, the sons of Pharida, the sons of Jeeli, the sons of Lozon, the sons of Isdael, the sons of Saphuthi, [34] the sons of Agia, the sons of Phacareth, the sons of Sabie, the sons of Sarothie, the sons of Masias, the sons of Gas, the sons of Addus, the sons of Subas, the sons of Apherra, the sons of Barodis, the sons of Saphat, the sons of Allon. [35] All the temple-servants, and the sons of the servants of Solomon, were three hundred and seventy-two. [36] These came up from Thermeleth, and Thelersas, Charaathalan leading them, and Allar; [37] and they could not show their families, nor their stock, how they were of Israel: the sons of Dalan the son of Ban, the sons of Nekodan, six hundred and fifty-two. [38] And of the priests, those who usurped the office of the priesthood and were not found: the sons of Obdia, the sons of Akkos, the sons of Jaddus, who married Augia one of the daughters of Zorzelleus, and was called after his name. [39] And when the description of the relatives of these men was sought in the register, and was not found, they were removed from executing the office of the priesthood: [40] for Nehemiah and Attharias said to them that they should not be partakers of the holy things, until there arose up a chief priest wearing Lights and Perfections. [41] So all those of Israel, from twelve years old [and upward], besides menservants and maidservants, were in [number forty] and two thousand three hundred and sixty. [42] Their menservants and handmaids were seven thousand three hundred and thirty-seven; the minstrels and singers, two hundred and forty-five; [43] four hundred and thirty-five camels, seven thousand and thirty-six horses, two hundred and forty-five mules, five thousand five hundred and twenty-five beasts of burden. [44] And certain of the chief men of their families, when they came to the temple of God that is in Jerusalem, vowed to set up the house again in its own place according to their ability, [45] and to give into the holy treasury of the works one thousand pounds of gold, five thousand of silver, and one hundred priestly vestments. [46] And the priests, and the Levites, and those who were of the people lived in Jerusalem and the country; the holy singers also, and the gatekeepers, and all Israel in their villages. [47] But when the seventh month was at hand, and when the sons of Israel were each in his own place, they all came together with one consent into the broad place before the first porch which is toward the east. [48] Then Jesus the son of Josedek arose, and his relatives the priests, and Zerubbabel the son of Salathiel, and his relatives, and they made the altar of the God of Israel ready, [49] to offer burned sacrifices on it, according as it is expressly commanded in the Scroll of Moses the man of God. [50] And certain [ones] were gathered to them out of the other nations of the land, and they erected the altar on its own place, because all the nations of the land were at enmity with them and oppressed them; and they offered sacrifices according to the time and burnt-offerings to the LORD, both morning and evening. [51] They also held the Celebration of Shelters, as it is commanded in the Law, and [offered] sacrifices daily, as was suitable; [52] and after that, the continual oblations, and the sacrifices of the Sabbaths, and of the new moons, and of all the consecrated feasts. [53] And all those who had made any vow to God began to offer sacrifices to God from the new moon of the seventh month, although the temple of God was not yet built. [54] And they gave money to the masons and carpenters, and meat and drink, [55] and carts to them of Sidon and Tyre, that they should bring cedar trees from Libanus, and transport them in floats to the haven of Joppa, according to the command which was written for them by Cyrus king of the Persians. [56] And in the second year after his coming to the temple of God at Jerusalem, in the second month, Zerubbabel the son of Salathiel, and Jesus the son of Josedek, and their relatives, and the Levitical priests, and all those who had come to Jerusalem out of the captivity commenced: [57] and they laid the foundation of the temple of God on the new moon of the second month, in the second year after they had come to Jewry and Jerusalem. [58] And they appointed the Levites from twenty years old over the works of the LORD. Then Jesus arose, and his sons and relatives, and his brother Kadmiel, and the sons of Jesus, Emadabun, and the sons of Joda the son of Iliadun, and their sons and relatives, all the Levites, started the undertaking with one accord, laboring to advance the works in the house of God. So the builders built the temple of the LORD. ⁵⁹ And the priests stood arrayed in their vestments with musical instruments and trumpets, and the Levites, the sons of Asaph, with their cymbals, ⁶⁰ singing songs of thanksgiving, and praising the LORD, after the order of David king of Israel. ⁶¹ And they sang aloud, praising the LORD in songs of thanksgiving, because His goodness and His glory are forever in all Israel. ⁶² And all the people sounded trumpets, and shouted with a loud voice, singing songs of thanksgiving to the LORD for the rearing up of the house of the LORD. ⁶³ Also of the Levitical priests, and of the heads of their families, the ancients who had seen the former house, came to the building of this with lamentation and great weeping. ⁶⁴ But many with trumpets and joy [shouted] with a loud voice, ⁶⁵ insomuch that the people did not hear the trumpets for the weeping of the people; for the multitude sounded marvelously, so that it was heard far off. ⁶⁶ For that reason, when the enemies of the tribe of Judah and Benjamin heard it, they came to know what that noise of trumpets should mean. ⁶⁷ And they perceived that those who were of the captivity built the temple to the LORD, the God of Israel. ⁶⁸ So they went to Zerubbabel and Jesus, and to the chief men of the families, and said to them, "We will build together with you. ⁶⁹ For we likewise, as you, obey your Lord, and sacrifice to Him from the days of Asbasareth the king of the Assyrians, who brought us here." ⁷⁰ Then Zerubbabel, and Jesus, and the chief men of the families of Israel said to them, "It is not for you to build the house to the LORD our God. ⁷¹ We ourselves alone will build to the LORD of Israel, according as Cyrus the king of the Persians has commanded us." ⁷² But the heathen of the land lying heavy on the inhabitants of Judea, and holding them constricted, hindered their building; ⁷³ and by their secret plots, and popular persuasions, and commotions, hindered the finishing of the building all the time that King Cyrus lived; so they were hindered from building for the space of two years, until the reign of Darius.

CHAPTER 6

¹ Now in the second year of the reign of Darius, Haggai and Zechariah, the [grand]son of Iddo, the prophets, prophesied to the Jews in Jewry and Jerusalem; in the Name of the LORD, the God of Israel, [they prophesied] to them. ² Then Zerubbabel the son of Salathiel and Jesus the son of Josedek stood up and began to build the house of the LORD at Jerusalem, the prophets of the LORD being with them, and helping them. ³ At the same time, Sisinnes the governor of Syria and Phoenicia came to them, with Sathrabuzanes and his companions, and said to them, ⁴ "By whose appointment do you build this house and this roof, and perform all the other things? And who

are the builders that perform these things?" ⁵ Nevertheless, the elders of the Jews obtained favor, because the LORD had visited the captivity; ⁶ and they were not hindered from building, until such time as communication was made to Darius concerning them, and his answer signified. ⁷ The copy of the letter which Sisinnes, governor of Syria and Phoenicia, and Sathrabuzanes, with their companions, the rulers in Syria and Phoenicia, wrote and sent to Darius: ⁸ "To King Darius, greetings: Let all things be known to our lord the king, that having come into the country of Judea, and having entered into the city of Jerusalem, we found in the city of Jerusalem the elders of the Jews that were of the captivity ⁹ building a house to the LORD, great [and] new, of hewn and costly stones, with timber laid in the walls. ¹⁰ And those works are done with great speed, and the work goes on prosperously in their hands, and it is accomplished with all glory and diligence. ¹¹ Then we asked these elders, saying, By whose command do you build this house, and lay the foundations of these works? ¹² Therefore, to the intent that we might give knowledge to you by writing who were the chief doers, we questioned them, and we required of them the names in writing of their principal men. ¹³ So they gave us this answer: We are the servants of the LORD which made the heavens and earth. ¹⁴ And as for this house, it was built many years ago by a great and mighty king of Israel and was completed. ¹⁵ But when our fathers sinned against the LORD of Israel, who is in Heaven, and provoked Him to wrath, He gave them over into the hands of Nebuchadnezzar king of Babylon, king of the Chaldeans; ¹⁶ and they pulled down the house, and burned it, and carried the people away [as] captives to Babylon. ¹⁷ But in the first year that Cyrus reigned over the country of Babylon, King Cyrus wrote [an edict] to build up this house. ¹⁸ And the holy vessels of gold and of silver, that Nebuchadnezzar had carried away out of the house at Jerusalem, and had set up in his own temple, those Cyrus the king brought out again out of the temple in Babylonia, and they were delivered to Zerubbabel and to Sanabassarus the governor, ¹⁹ with command that he should carry away all these vessels and put them in the temple at Jerusalem; and that the temple of the LORD should be built in its place. ²⁰ Then Sanabassarus, having come here, laid the foundations of the house of the LORD which is in Jerusalem; and from that time to this being still a building, it is not yet fully ended. ²¹ Now therefore, if it seems good, O king, let search be made among the royal archives of our lord the king that are in Babylon: ²² and if it is found that the building of the house of the LORD which is in Jerusalem has been done with the consent of King Cyrus, and it seems good to our lord the king, let him signify to us thereof." ²³ Then King Darius commanded to seek among the archives that were laid up at Babylon: and so at Ekbatana the palace, which is in the country of Media, there was found a scroll where these things were recorded: ²⁴ "In the first year of the reign of Cyrus, King Cyrus commanded to build up the house of the LORD which is in Jerusalem, where they sacrifice with continual fire: ²⁵ whose height will be sixty cubits, and the breadth sixty cubits, with three rows of hewn stones, and one row of new wood of that country; and the expenses thereof to be given out of the house of King Cyrus; ²⁶ and that the holy vessels of the house of the LORD, both gold and silver, that Nebuchadnezzar took out of the house at Jerusalem, and carried away to Babylon, should be restored to the house at Jerusalem, and be set in the place where they were before." ²⁷ And also, he commanded that Sisinnes the governor of Syria and Phoenicia, and Sathrabuzanes, and their companions, and those which were appointed rulers in Syria and Phoenicia, should be careful not to meddle with the place, but permit Zerubbabel, the servant of the LORD, and governor of Judea, and the elders of the Jews, to build that house of the LORD in its place. ²⁸ "And I also command to have it built up whole again; and that they look diligently to help those that be of the captivity of Judea, until the house of the LORD is finished; ²⁹ and that out of the tribute of Coele-Syria and Phoenicia a portion be carefully given these men for the sacrifices of the LORD, [that is,] to Zerubbabel the governor, for bullocks, and rams, and lambs; ³⁰ and also corn, salt, wine, and oil—and that continually every year without further question, according as the priests that are in Jerusalem will signify to be daily spent, ³¹ that drink offerings may be made to the Most High God for the king and for his children, and that they may pray for their lives. ³² And that command [will] be given that whoever will transgress, yes, or neglect anything written here, out of his own [house] will a tree be taken, and he [will] be hanged on it, and all his goods seized for the king. ³³ May the LORD therefore, whose Name is there called on, utterly destroy every king and nation that will stretch out his hand to hinder or damage that house of the LORD in Jerusalem. ³⁴ I, Darius the king, have ordained that according to these things it [will] be done with diligence."

CHAPTER 7

¹ Then Sisinnes the governor of Coele-Syria and Phoenicia, and Sathrabuzanes, with their companions, following the commands of King Darius, ² very carefully oversaw the holy works, assisting the elders of the Jews and rulers of the temple. ³ And so the holy works prospered, while Haggai and Zechariah the prophets prophesied. ⁴ And they finished these things by the command of the LORD, the God of Israel, and with the consent of Cyrus, Darius, and Artaxerxes, kings of the Persians. ⁵ [And so] the house was finished by the twenty-third [[or third]] day of the month Adar, in the sixth year of King Darius. ⁶ And the sons of Israel, the priests, and the Levites, and the others that were of the captivity, that were added [to them], did according to the things [written] in the Scroll of Moses. ⁷ And for the dedication of the temple of the LORD they offered one hundred bullocks, two hundred rams, [and] four hundred lambs; ⁸ [and also] twelve male goats for the sin of all Israel, according to the number of the twelve princes of the tribes of Israel. ⁹ The priests and the Levites also stood arrayed in their vestments, according to their relatives, for the services of the LORD, the God of Israel, according to the Scroll of Moses: and the gatekeepers at every gate. ¹⁰ And the sons of Israel that came out of the captivity held the Passover [on] the fourteenth day of the first month, when the priests and the Levites were sanctified together, ¹¹ and all those who were of the captivity; for they were sanctified. For the Levites were all sanctified together, ¹² and they offered the Passover for all those of the captivity, and for their relatives the priests, and for themselves. ¹³ And the sons of Israel that came out of the captivity ate, even all those who had separated themselves from the abominations of the heathen of the land and sought the LORD. ¹⁴ And they kept the Celebration of Unleavened Bread seven days, making merry before the LORD, ¹⁵ for that He had turned the counsel of the king of Assyria toward them, to strengthen their hands in the works of the LORD, the God of Israel.

CHAPTER 8

¹ And after these things, when Artaxerxes the king of the Persians reigned, Ezra came, the son of Seraiah, the son of Azariah, the son of Hilkiah, the son of Salem, ² the son of Zadok, the son of Ahitob, the son of Amariah, the son of Ozias, the son of Memeroth, the son of Zerahiah, the son of Savias, the son of Boccas, the son of Abisne, the son of Phinehas, the son of Eleazar, the son of Aaron, the chief priest. ³ This Ezra went up from Babylon, as being a ready scribe in the Law of Moses that was given by the God of Israel. ⁴ And the king honored him, for he found grace in his sight in all his requests. ⁵ There also went up with him certain of the sons of Israel, and of the priests, and Levites, and holy singers, and gatekeepers, and temple servants, to Jerusalem, ⁶ in the seventh year of the reign of Artaxerxes, in the fifth month, this was the king's seventh year; for they went from Babylon on the new moon of the first month, and came to Jerusalem, according to the prosperous journey which the LORD gave them for His sake. ⁷ For Ezra had very great skill, so that he omitted nothing of the law and commands of the LORD but taught all Israel the ordinances and judgments. ⁸ Now the commission, which was written from Artaxerxes the king, came to Ezra the priest and reader of the Law of the LORD, of which this that follows is a copy: ⁹ "King Artaxerxes to Ezra the priest and reader of the Law of

the Lord, greetings: [10]Having determined to deal graciously, I have given order that such of the nation of the Jews, and of the priests and Levites, and of those within our realm, as are willing and desirous, should go with you to Jerusalem. [11]Therefore, as many as have a mind [to this purpose], let them depart with you, as it has seemed good both to me and my seven friends the counselors, [12]that they may look to the affairs of Judea and Jerusalem, agreeably to that which is in the Law of the Lord, [13]and carry the gifts to the Lord of Israel to Jerusalem, which my friends and I have vowed; and that all the gold and silver that can be found in the country of Babylonia for the Lord in Jerusalem, [14]with that also which is given of the people for the temple of the Lord their God that is at Jerusalem, be collected: even the gold and silver for bullocks, rams, and lambs, and things pertaining to that, [15]to the end that they may offer sacrifices to the Lord on the altar of the Lord their God, which is in Jerusalem— [16]and whatever you and your relatives are inclined to do with gold and silver, that perform, according to the will of your God. [17]And the holy vessels of the Lord, which are given to you for the use of the temple of your God, which is in Jerusalem, [18]and anything else you will remember for the use of the temple of your God, you will give it out of the king's treasury. [19]And I, King Artaxerxes, have also commanded the keepers of the treasures in Syria and Phoenicia, that whatever Ezra the priest and reader of the Law of the Most High God will send for, they should give it to him with all diligence, [20]to the sum of one hundred talents of silver, likewise also of wheat even to one hundred measures, and one hundred firkins of wine, and salt in abundance. [21]Let all things be diligently performed after the Law of God—to the Most High God—that wrath does not come on the kingdom of the king and his sons. [22]I also command you that no tax, nor any other imposition, be laid on any of the priests, or Levites, or holy singers, or gatekeepers, or temple servants, or any that have employment in this temple, and that no man have authority to impose anything on them. [23]And you, Ezra, according to the wisdom of God, ordain judges and justices, that they may judge in all Syria and Phoenicia all those that know the law of your God; and you will teach those that do not know it. [24]And whoever will transgress the law of your God, and of the king, will be punished diligently, whether it be by death, or other punishment, by penalty of money, or by imprisonment." [25]Then Ezra the scribe said, "Blessed is the only Lord, the God of my fathers, who has put these things into the heart of the king, to glorify His house that is in Jerusalem, [26]and has honored me in the sight of the king, and his counselors, and all his friends and nobles. [27]Therefore, I was encouraged by the help of the Lord my God and gathered together out of Israel men to go up with me. [28]And these are the chiefs, according to their families and the several divisions thereof, that went up with me from Babylon in the reign of King Artaxerxes: [29]of the sons of Phinehas, Gerson; of the sons of Ithamar, Gamael; of the sons of David, Attus the son of Sechenias; [30]of the sons of Phoros, Zechariah, and with him were counted one hundred and fifty men; [31]of the sons of Phaath-Moab, Eliehoenai the son of Zerahiah, and with him two hundred men; [32]of the sons of Zathoes, Sechenias the son of Jezelus, and with him three hundred men; of the sons of Adin, Obeth the son of Jonathan, and with him two hundred and fifty men; [33]of the sons of Elam, Jesias son of Gotholia, and with him seventy men; [34]of the sons of Saphatias, Zerahiah son of Michael, and with him seventy men; [35]of the sons of Joab, Obadiah son of Jehiel, and with him two hundred and twelve men; [36]of the sons of Banias, Salimoth son of Josaphias, and with him one hundred and sixty men; [37]of the sons of Babi, Zechariah son of Bebai, and with him twenty-eight men; [38]of the sons of Azgad, Joannes son of Hakkatan, and with him one hundred and ten men; [39]of the sons of Adonikam, the last, and these are the names of them—Eliphalat, Jeuel, and Shemaiah, and with them seventy men; [40]of the sons of Bigvai, Uthi the son of Istalcurus, and with him seventy men. [41]And I gathered them together to the river called Theras; and there we pitched our tents three days, and I surveyed them. [42]But when I had found there none of the priests and Levites, [43]then I sent to Eleazar, and Iduel, and Maasmas, [44]and Elnathan, and Samaias, and [Jarib], Nathan, Ennatan, Zechariah, and Mosollamus, principal men and men of understanding. [45]And I commanded those who should go to [Iddo], Loddeus the captain, who was in the place of [Casiphia], the treasury; [46]and I commanded them that they should speak to Loddeus, and to his relatives, and to the treasurers in that place, to send us such men as might execute the priests' office in the house of our Lord. [47]And by the mighty hand of our Lord they brought to us men of understanding of the sons of Mooli the son of Levi, the son of Israel, Asebebias, and his sons, and his relatives, who were eighteen, [48]and Asebias, and Annuus, and Osaias his brother, of the sons of Chanuneus, and their sons were twenty men; [49]and of the temple-servants whom David and the principal men had appointed for the servants of the Levites, two hundred and twenty temple-servants, the catalogue of all their names was shown. [50]And there I vowed a fast for the young men before our Lord, to desire of Him a prosperous journey both for us and for our children, and [for the] cattle that were with us: [51]for I was ashamed to ask of the king footmen, and horsemen, and conduct for protection against our adversaries. [52]For we had said to the king that the power of our Lord would be with those who seek Him, to support them in all ways. [53]And again we implored our Lord as touching these things and found Him favorable [to us]. ⁵⁴ Then I separated twelve men of the chiefs of the priests: Eserebias, and Assamias, and ten men of their relatives with them; ⁵⁵ and I weighed them the silver, and the gold, and the holy vessels of the house of our Lord, which the king, and his counselors, and the nobles, and all Israel, had given. ⁵⁶ And when I had weighed it, I delivered to them six hundred and fifty talents of silver, and silver vessels of one hundred talents, and one hundred talents of gold, ⁵⁷ and twenty golden vessels, and twelve vessels of brass, even of fine brass, glittering like gold. ⁵⁸ And I said to them, "You are holy to the LORD and the vessels are holy—both—and the gold and the silver are a vow to the LORD, the Lord of our fathers. ⁵⁹ Watch and keep them until you deliver them to the chiefs of the priests and Levites, and to the principal men of the families of Israel, in Jerusalem, in the chambers of the house of our Lord." ⁶⁰ So the priests and the Levites, who received the silver, and the gold, and the vessels which were in Jerusalem, brought them into the temple of the LORD. ⁶¹ And from the River Theras we departed [on] the twelfth day of the first month, until we came to Jerusalem, by the mighty hand of our Lord which was on us: and the LORD delivered us from [assault by] the way, from every enemy, and so we came to Jerusalem. ⁶² And when we had been there three days, the silver and gold was weighed and delivered in the house of our Lord on the fourth day to Marmoth the priest, the son of Urias. ⁶³ And with him was Eleazar the son of Phinehas, and with them were Josabdus the son of Jesus and Moeth the son of Sabannus, the Levites: all [was delivered to them] by number and weight. ⁶⁴ And all the weight of them was written up the same hour. ⁶⁵ Moreover, those who had come out of the captivity offered sacrifices to the LORD, the God of Israel, even twelve bullocks for all Israel, [and] ninety-six rams, ⁶⁶ seventy-two lambs, goats for a peace offering—twelve; all of them a sacrifice to the LORD. ⁶⁷ And they delivered the king's commands to the king's stewards, and to the governors of Coele-Syria and Phoenicia; and they honored the people and the temple of the LORD. ⁶⁸ Now when these things were done, the principal men came to me, and said, ⁶⁹ "The nation of Israel, and the princes, and the priests, and the Levites, have not put away the strange people of the land, nor the uncleanness of the nations—of the Canaanites, Hittites, Perizzites, Jebusites, and the Moabites, Egyptians, and Edomites. ⁷⁰ For both they and their sons have married with their daughters, and the holy seed is mixed with the strange people of the land; and from the beginning of this matter the rulers and the nobles have been partakers of this iniquity." ⁷¹ And as soon as I had heard these things, I tore my clothes and my holy garment, and plucked the hair from off my head and beard, and sat myself down sad and full of heaviness. ⁷² So all those who were moved at the word of the LORD, the God of Israel, assembled to me, while I mourned for the iniquity, but I sat still full of heaviness until the evening sacrifice. ⁷³ Then rising up from the fast with my clothes and my holy garment torn, and bowing my knees, and stretching out my hands to the LORD, ⁷⁴ I said, "O LORD, I am ashamed and confounded before Your face, ⁷⁵ for our sins are multiplied above our heads, and our errors have reached up to Heaven, ⁷⁶ ever since the time of our fathers; and we are in great sin, even to this day. ⁷⁷ And for our sins and our fathers' we with our relatives, and our kings, and our priests were given up to the kings of the earth, to the sword, and to captivity, and for a prey with shame, to this day. ⁷⁸ And now in some measure mercy has been shown to us from You, O LORD, that a root and a name should be left for us in the place of Your sanctuary, ⁷⁹ and to discover a light for us in the house of the LORD our God, and to give us food in the time of our servitude. ⁸⁰ Yes, when we were in bondage, we were not forsaken of our Lord, but He made us gracious before the kings of Persia, so that they gave us food, ⁸¹ and glorified the temple of our Lord, and raised up the desolate Zion, to give us a sure dwelling in Jewry and Jerusalem. ⁸² And now, O LORD, what will we say, having these things? For we have transgressed Your commands, which You gave by the hand of Your servants the prophets, saying, ⁸³ The land, which you enter into to possess as a heritage, is a land polluted with the pollutions of the strangers of the land, and they have filled it with their uncleanness. ⁸⁴ Therefore now, you will not join your daughters to their sons, neither will you take their daughters to your sons, ⁸⁵ neither will you seek to have peace with them forever, that you may be strong, and eat the good things of the land, and that you may leave it for an inheritance to your children forevermore. ⁸⁶ And all that has befallen [us] is done to us for our wicked works and great sins, for You, O LORD, made our sins light, ⁸⁷ and gave to us such a root, [but] we have turned back again to transgress Your law, in mingling ourselves with the uncleanness of the heathen of the land. ⁸⁸ You were not angry with us to destroy us, until You had left us neither root, seed, nor name. ⁸⁹ O LORD of Israel, You are true, for we are left a root to this day. ⁹⁰ Behold, now we are before You in our iniquities, for we cannot stand any longer before You by reason of these things." ⁹¹ And as Ezra made his confession in his prayer, weeping and lying flat on the ground before the temple, there gathered to him from Jerusalem a very great crowd of men, and women, and children, for there was great weeping among the multitude. ⁹² Then Jehoiachin the son of Jeelus, one of the sons of Israel, called out, and said, "O Ezra, we have sinned against the LORD God, we have married strange women of the heathen of the land, and now is all Israel aloft. ⁹³ Let us make an oath to the LORD herein, that we will put away all our wives, which [we have taken] of the strangers, with their children, ⁹⁴ like as seems good to you, and to as many as obey the Law of the LORD. ⁹⁵ Arise and execute this, for this matter pertains to you, and we will be with you to do valiantly." ⁹⁶ So Ezra arose, and took an oath of the chief of the priests and Levites of all Israel to do after these things; and [so] they swore.

CHAPTER 9

¹ Then Ezra, rising from the court of the temple, went to the chamber of Jonas the son of Eliasib, ² and lodged there, and ate no bread nor drank water, mourning for the great iniquities of the multitude. ³ And there was made proclamation in all Jewry and Jerusalem to all those who were of the captivity, that they should be gathered together at Jerusalem, ⁴ and that whoever did not meet there within two or three days, according as the elders that bore rule appointed, their cattle should be seized to the use of the temple, and himself cast out from the multitude of those who were of the captivity. ⁵ And in three days all those of the tribe of Judah and Benjamin were gathered together at Jerusalem: this was the ninth month, on the twentieth day of the month. ⁶ And all the multitude sat together trembling in the broad place before the temple because of the present foul weather. ⁷ So Ezra arose and said to them, "You have transgressed the Law and married strange wives to increase the sins of Israel. ⁸ And now make confession and give glory to the LORD, the God of our fathers, ⁹ and do His will, and separate yourselves from the heathen of the land, and from the strange women." ¹⁰ Then the whole multitude cried, and said with a loud voice, "Just as you have spoken, so we will do. ¹¹ But forasmuch as the multitude is great, and it is foul weather, so that we cannot stand outside, this indeed is not a work of one day or two, seeing our sin in these things is spread far: ¹² therefore, let the rulers of the multitude stay, and let all those of our habitations that have strange wives come at the time appointed, ¹³ and with them the rulers and judges of every place, until we turn the wrath of the LORD away from us for this matter." ¹⁴ [Then] Jonathan the son of Azael and Ezekias the son of Thocanus took the matter on them accordingly; and Mosollamus, and Levis, and Sabbateus were assessors to them. ¹⁵ And those who were of the captivity did according to all these things. ¹⁶ And Ezra the priest chose principal men for himself of their families, all by name: and on the new moon of the tenth month, they were shut in together to examine the matter. ¹⁷ So their cause that held strange wives was brought to an end by the new moon of the first month. ¹⁸ And there were found of the priests that had come together and had strange wives, ¹⁹ of the sons of Jesus the son of Josedek, and his relatives: Mathelas, and Eleazar, and Joribus, and Joadanus. ²⁰ And they gave their hands to put away their wives, and to [offer] rams to make reconciliation for their error. ²¹ And of the sons of Emmer: Ananias, and Zabdeus,

and Manes, and Sameus, and Hiereel, and Azariah. ²² And of the sons of Phaisur: Elionas, Massias, Ishmael, and Nathanael, and Ocidelus, and Saloas. ²³ And of the Levites: Jozabdus, and Semeis, and Colius, who was called Calitas, and Patheus, and Judas, and Jonas. ²⁴ Of the holy singers: Eliasibus [and] Bacchurus. ²⁵ Of the gatekeepers: Sallumus and tolbanes. ²⁶ Of Israel, of the sons of Phoros: Hiermas, and Ieddias, and Melchias, and Maelus, and Eleazar, and Asibas, and Banneas. ²⁷ Of the sons of Ela: Matthanias, Zechariah, and Jezrielus, and Oabdius, and Hieremoth, and Aedias. ²⁸ And of the sons of Zamoth: Eliadas, Eliasimus, Othonias, Jarimoth, and Sabathus, and Zardeus. ²⁹ Of the sons of Bebai: Joannes, and Ananias, and Jozabdus, and Ematheis. ³⁰ Of the sons of Mani: Olamus, Mamuchus, Jedeus, Jasubas, and Jasaelus, and Hieremoth. ³¹ And of the sons of Addi: Naathus, and Moossias, Laccunus, and Naidus, and Matthanias, and Sesthel, Balnuus, and Manasseas. ³² And of the sons of Annas: Elionas, and Aseas, and Melchias, and Sabbeus, and Simon Chosameus. ³³ And of the sons of Asom: Maltanneus, and Mattathias, and Sabanneus, Eliphalat, and Manasseh, and Semei. ³⁴ And of the sons of Baani: Jeremias, Momdis, Ismaerus, Juel, Mamdai, and Pedias, and Anos, Carabasion, and Enasibus, and Mamnitamenus, Eliasis, Bannus, Eliali, someis, Selemias, Nathanias. And of the sons of Ezora: Scsis, Ezril, Azaelus, Samatus, Zambri, Josephus. ³⁵ And of the sons of Nooma: Mazitias, Zabadeas, Edos, Juel, Banaias. ³⁶ All these had taken strange wives, and they put them away with their children. ³⁷ And the priests and Levites, and those who were of Israel, lived in Jerusalem, and in the country, on the new moon of the seventh month, and the sons of Israel in their habitations. ³⁸ And the whole multitude were gathered together with one accord into the broad place before the porch of the temple toward the east; ³⁹ and they said to Ezra the priest and reader, "Bring the Law of Moses, that was given of the LORD, the God of Israel." ⁴⁰ So Ezra the chief priest brought the Law to the whole multitude of both men and women, and to all the priests, to hear the Law on the new moon of the seventh month. ⁴¹ And he read in the broad place before the porch of the temple from morning to midday, before both men and women; and all the multitude gave heed to the Law. ⁴² And Ezra the priest and reader of the Law stood up on the pulpit of wood, which was made [for that purpose]. ⁴³ And there stood up by him Mattathias, Sammus, Ananias, Azariah, Urias, Ezekias, Ba'alsamus, on the right hand; ⁴⁴ and on his left hand: Phaldeus, Misael, Melchias, Lothasubus, Nabarias, [and] Zechariah. ⁴⁵ Then Ezra took the Scroll of the Law before the multitude and sat honorably in the first place before all. ⁴⁶ And when he opened the Law, they all stood straight up. So Ezra blessed the LORD God Most High, the God of armies, Almighty. ⁴⁷ And all the people answered, "Amen";

and lifting up their hands they fell to the ground and worshiped the LORD. [48] Also Jesus, Annus, Sarabias, Iadinus, Jacubus, Sabateus, Auteas, Maiannas, and Calitas, Azariah, and Jozabdus, and Ananias, Phalias, the Levites, taught the Law of the LORD, and read the Law of the LORD to the multitude, in addition, making them to understand it. [49] Then Attharates said to Ezra the chief priest and reader, and to the Levites that taught the multitude, even to all, [50] "This day is holy to the LORD"—now they all wept when they heard the Law— [51] "go then, and eat the fat, and drink the sweet, and send portions to those who have nothing, [52] for the day is holy to the LORD; and do not be sorrowful, for the LORD will bring you to honor." [53] So the Levites published all things to the people, saying, "This day is holy; do not be sorrowful." [54] Then they went their way, everyone to eat, and drink, and make merry, and to give portions to those who had nothing, and to make great cheer, [55] because they understood the words wherein they were instructed, and for which they had been assembled.

2 ESDRAS

Otherwise known as 4 Esdras

2 Esdras (also called 4 Esdras, Latin Esdras, or Latin Ezra) is the name of an apocalyptic book in many English versions of the Bible. Its authorship is ascribed to Ezra, a scribe and priest of the 5th century BC, although modern scholarship places its composition between 70 and 218 AD. It is reckoned among the apocrypha by Roman Catholics, Protestants, and most Eastern Orthodox Christians. Although 2 Esdras was preserved in Latin as an appendix to the Vulgate and passed down as a unified book, it is generally considered to be a tripartite work.

CHAPTER 1

¹ The second scroll of the prophet Ezra, the son of Saraias, the son of Azariah, the son of Hilkiah, the son of Salemas, the son of Zadok, the son of Ahitob, ² the son of Achias, the son of Phinehas, the son of Eli, the son of Amariah, the son of Aziei, the son of Marimoth, the son of Arna, the son of Ozias, the son of Borith, the son of Abissei, the son of Phinehas, the son of Eleazar, ³ the son of Aaron, of the tribe of Levi, which was captive in the land of the Medes, in the reign of Artaxerxes king of the Persians. ⁴ And the word of the LORD came to me, saying, ⁵ "Go your way, and show My people their sinful deeds, and their children their wickedness which they have done against Me, that they may tell their children's children, ⁶ because the sins of their fathers are increased in them, for they have forgotten Me, and have done sacrifice to strange gods. ⁷ Did I not bring them out of the land of Egypt, out of the house of bondage? But they have provoked Me to wrath and have despised My counsels. ⁸ Shake then the hair of your head, and cast all evils on them, for they have not been obedient to My law, but it is a rebellious people. ⁹ How long will I forbear them, to whom I have done so much good? ¹⁰ I have overthrown many kings for their sakes; I have struck down Pharaoh with his servants and all his army. ¹¹ I have destroyed all the nations before them, and in the east, I have scattered the people of two provinces, even of Tyre and Sidon, and have slain all their adversaries. ¹² Therefore, speak to them, saying, ¹³ The LORD says, Of a truth I brought you through the sea, and where there was no path I made highways for you; I gave you Moses for a leader, and Aaron for a priest. ¹⁴ I gave you light in a pillar of fire, and I have done great wonders among you; yet you have forgotten Me, says the LORD." ¹⁵ The LORD Almighty says, "The quails were for a token to you; I gave you a camp for your protection, nevertheless you murmured there: ¹⁶ and you did not triumph in My Name for the destruction of your enemies, but ever to this day you yet murmur. ¹⁷ Where are the benefits that I have done for you? When you were hungry and thirsty in the wilderness, did you not cry to Me, ¹⁸ saying, Why have You brought us into this wilderness to kill us? It had been better for us to have served the Egyptians, than to die in this wilderness. ¹⁹ I had pity on your mourning and gave you manna for food; you ate messengers' bread. ²⁰ When you were thirsty, did I not cleave the rock, and waters flowed out to your fill? For the heat I covered you with the leaves of the trees. ²¹ I divided fruitful lands among you; I cast out the Canaanites, the Perizzites, and the Philistines, before you: what will I yet do more for you?" Says the LORD. ²² The LORD Almighty says, "When you were in the wilderness, at the bitter river, being thirsty, and blaspheming My Name, ²³ I did not give you fire for your blasphemies, but cast a tree in the water, and made the river sweet. ²⁴ What will I do to you, O Jacob? You, Judah, would not obey Me: I will turn Myself to other nations, and I will give My Name to them, that they may keep my statutes. ²⁵ Seeing you have forsaken Me, I will also forsake you; when you ask me to be merciful to you, I will have no mercy on you. ²⁶ Whenever you will call on Me, I will not hear you, for you have defiled your hands with blood, and your feet are swift to commit manslaughter. ²⁷ You have not as it were forsaken Me, but your own selves," says the LORD. ²⁸ The LORD Almighty says, "Have I not pleaded with you as a father his sons, as a mother her daughters, and a nurse her young babies, ²⁹ that you would be My people, and I should be your God; that you would be My children, and I should be your Father? ³⁰ I gathered you together, as a hen [gathers] her chickens under her wings, but now, what will I do to you? I will cast you out from My presence. ³¹ When you offer oblations to Me, I will turn My face from you, for your solemn feast days, your new moons, and your circumcisions of the flesh, I have rejected. ³² I sent My servants the prophets to you, whom you have taken and slain, and torn their bodies in pieces, whose blood I will require [of your hands]," says the LORD. ³³ The LORD Almighty says, "Your house is desolate, I will cast you out as the wind does stubble. ³⁴ And your children will not be fruitful; for they have neglected My command to you and done that which is evil before Me. ³⁵ I will give your houses to a people that will come, which having not heard of Me, yet believe Me; they to whom I have showed no signs will do that which I have commanded. ³⁶ They have seen no prophets, yet they will call their former estate to remembrance. ³⁷ I take to witness the grace of the people that will come, whose little ones rejoice

with gladness: and though they do not see Me with bodily eyes, yet in spirit they will believe the thing that I say. [38] And now, O father, behold with glory; and see the people that come from the east, [39] to whom I will give for leaders: Abraham, Isaac, and Jacob, Hosea, Amos, and Micah, Joel, Obadiah, and Jonah, [40] Nahum, and Habakkuk, Zephaniah, Haggai, Zechariah, and Malachi, which is also called the Messenger of the LORD."

CHAPTER 2

[1] The LORD says, "I brought this people out of bondage, and I gave them My commands by My servants the prophets; whom they would not hear but set My counsels at nothing. [2] The mother that bears them says to them, Go your way, O my children; for I am a widow and forsaken. [3] I brought you up with gladness, and with sorrow and heaviness I have lost you; for you have sinned before the LORD God and done that which is evil before me. [4] But what will I now do to you? For I am a widow and forsaken: go your way, O my children, and ask mercy of the LORD. [5] As for Me, O father, I call on you for a witness over the mother of [these] children, because they would not keep My covenant, [6] that you bring them to confusion, and their mother to a plunder, that there may be no offspring of them. [7] Let them be scattered abroad among the heathen, let their names be blotted out of the earth; for they have despised My covenant. [8] Woe to you, Asshur, you that hide the unrighteous with you! O you wicked nation, remember what I did to Sodom and Gomorrah, [9] whose land lies in clods of pitch and heaps of ashes: even so I will also do to those who have not listened to Me," says the LORD Almighty. [10] The LORD says to Ezra, "Tell My people that I will give them the kingdom of Jerusalem, which I would have given to Israel. [11] I will also take their glory, and give these the continuous dwelling places, which I had prepared for them. [12] They will have the Tree of Life for an ointment of sweet savor; they will neither labor, nor be weary. [13] Ask, and you will receive: pray for few days for you, that they may be shortened: the kingdom is already prepared for you: watch. [14] Take the heavens and earth to witness, take them to witness; for I have given up the evil, and created the good; for I live," says the LORD. [15] "Mother, embrace your children; I will bring them out with gladness like a dove; establish their feet; for I have chosen you," says the LORD. [16] "And I will raise those who are dead up again from their places and bring them out from their tombs; for I have known My Name in them. [17] Do not be afraid, you mother of the children, for I have chosen you," says the LORD. [18] "For your help I will send My servants Isaiah and Jeremiah, after whose counsel I have sanctified and prepared for you twelve trees laden with various fruits, [19] and as many springs flowing with milk and honey, and seven mighty mountains, after which there grow roses and lilies, whereby I will fill your children with joy. [20] Do right to the widow, judge the fatherless, give to the poor, defend the orphan, clothe the naked, [21] heal the broken and the weak, do not laugh a lame man to scorn, defend the maimed, and let the blind man come to the sight of My glory. [22] Keep the old and young within your walls. [23] Wherever you find the dead, set a sign on them and commit them to the grave, and I will give you the first place in My resurrection. [24] Stay still, O My people, and take your rest, for your quietness will come. [25] Nourish your children, O you good nurse, and establish their feet. [26] As for the servants whom I have given you, not one of them will perish, for I will require them from among your number. [27] Do not be careful excessively, for when the day of suffering and anguish comes, others will weep and be sorrowful, but you will be merry and have abundance. [28] The nations will envy you, but they will be able to do nothing against you," says the LORD. [29] "My hands will cover you, so that your children do not see Gehenna. [30] Be joyful, O you mother, with your children; for I will deliver you," says the LORD. [31] "Remember your children that sleep, for I will bring them out of the secret places of the earth and show mercy to them, for I am merciful," says the LORD Almighty. [32] "Embrace your children until I come and proclaim mercy to them, for My wells run over, and My grace will not fail." [33] I, Ezra, received a charge from the LORD on Mount Horeb, that I should go to Israel; but when I came to them, they would have none of me, and rejected the command of the LORD. [34] And therefore I say to you, O you nations that hear and understand: look for your Shepherd; He will give you continuous rest; for He is near at hand who will come in the end of the world. [35] Be ready to the rewards of the kingdom, for the continuous light will shine on you forevermore. [36] Flee the shadow of this world, receive the joyfulness of your glory: I call to witness my Savior openly. [37] O receive that which is given to you of the LORD, and be joyful, giving thanks to Him that has called you to heavenly kingdoms. [38] Arise, and stand, and behold the number of those that are sealed in the celebration of the LORD; [39] those who withdrew themselves from the shadow of the world have received glorious garments of the LORD. [40] Look on your number, O Zion, and make up the reckoning of those of you that are clothed in white, which have fulfilled the Law of the LORD. [41] The number of your children, whom you long for, is fulfilled: implore the power of the LORD, that your people, which have been called from the beginning, may be hallowed. [42] I, Ezra, saw on Mount Zion a great multitude, whom I could not number, and they all praised the LORD with songs. [43] And in the midst of them there was a young Man of a high stature, taller than all the rest, and on each of their heads He set crowns and was more exalted. I marveled greatly

at this. ⁴⁴So I asked the Messenger, and said, "What are these, my Lord?" ⁴⁵He answered and said to me, "These are those who have put off the mortal clothing, and put on the immortal, and have confessed the Name of God: now they are crowned, and receive palms." ⁴⁶Then I said to the Messenger, "What young Man is He that sets crowns on them, and gives them palms in their hands?" ⁴⁷So He answered and said to me, "It is the Son of God, whom they have confessed in the world." Then I began to greatly commend those who stood so stiffly for the Name of the LORD. ⁴⁸Then the Messenger said to me, "Go your way, and tell My people what manner of things, and how great wonders of the LORD God you have seen."

CHAPTER 3

¹In the thirty years after the ruin of the city, I, Salathiel (also called Ezra), was in Babylon, and lay troubled on my bed, and my thoughts came up over my heart: ²for I saw the desolation of Zion, and the wealth of those who lived at Babylon. ³And my spirit was severely moved, so that I began to speak words full of fear to the Most High, and said, ⁴"O LORD that bears rule, did You not speak at the beginning, when You fashioned the earth, and that Yourself alone, and commanded the dust? ⁵And it gave You Adam, a body without a soul? Yet it was the workmanship of Your hands, and You breathed into him the breath of life, and he was made living before You. ⁶And You led him into paradise, which Your right hand planted, before the earth ever came forward. ⁷And You gave to him Your one command, which he transgressed, and immediately You appointed death for him and in his generations; and there were born of him nations and tribes, peoples and relatives, out of number. ⁸And every nation walked after their own will, and did ungodly things before You, and despised [Your commands, and] You did not forbid them. ⁹Nevertheless, again in [the] process of time You brought the flood on those that lived in the world and destroyed them. ¹⁰And it came to pass, that the same fortune befell them; like as death was to Adam, so was the flood to these. ¹¹Nevertheless, one of them You left—Noah with his household, [even] all the righteous men [that came] of him. ¹²And it came to pass, that when those who lived on the earth began to multiply, they also multiplied children, and peoples, and many nations, and again began to be more ungodly than the first. ¹³And it came to pass, when they did wickedly before You, You chose one from among them, whose name was Abraham; ¹⁴and You loved him, and only to him did You show the end of the times secretly by night, ¹⁵and made a perpetual covenant with him, promising him that You would never forsake his seed. ¹⁶And to him You gave Isaac, and to Isaac You gave Jacob and Esau. And You set Jacob apart for Yourself, but put [him] by Esau: and Jacob became a great multitude. ¹⁷And it came to

pass, that when You led his seed out of Egypt, You brought them up to Mount Sinai. ¹⁸You also bowed the heavens, and shook the earth, and moved the whole world, and made the depths to tremble, and troubled the [course of that] age. ¹⁹And Your glory went through four gates: of fire, and of earthquake, and of wind, and of cold, that You might give the Law to the seed of Jacob, and the command to the generation of Israel. ²⁰And yet You did not take away from them [their] wicked heart, that Your law might bring out fruit in them. ²¹For the first Adam bearing a wicked heart transgressed, and was overcome; [and not only him,] but also all of them that are born of him. ²²Therefore disease was made permanent; and the Law was in the heart of the people along with the wickedness of the root; so the good departed away, and that which was wicked dwelt still. ²³So the times passed away, and the years were brought to an end: then You raised up a servant, called David, ²⁴whom You commanded to build a city to Your Name, and to offer oblations to You therein of Your own. ²⁵When this was done [for] many years, then those who inhabited the city did evil, ²⁶in all things doing even as Adam and all his generations had done; for they also bore a wicked heart: ²⁷and so You gave Your city over into the hands of Your enemies. ²⁸And then I said in my heart, Are their deeds any better that inhabit Babylon? And does she therefore have dominion over Zion? ²⁹For it came to pass when I came here, that I also saw impieties without number, and my soul saw many evildoers in this thirtieth year, so that my heart failed me. ³⁰For I have seen how You permit them sinning, and have spared the ungodly doers, and have destroyed Your people, and have preserved Your enemies; and You have not signified to any how Your way may be comprehended. ³¹Are the deeds of Babylon better than those of Zion? ³²Or is there any other nation that knows You besides Israel? Or what tribes have so believed Your covenants as these [tribes of] Jacob? ³³And yet their reward does not appear, and their labor has no fruit, for I have gone here and there through the nations, and I see that they abound [in wealth, and] do not think on Your commands. ³⁴Therefore, weigh our iniquities in the balance now, and also theirs that dwell in the world, and so it will be found which way the scale inclines. ³⁵Or when was it that they which dwell on the earth have not sinned in Your sight? Or what nation has so kept Your commands? ³⁶You will find that men [who may be reckoned] by name have kept Your precepts; but nations You will not find."

CHAPTER 4

¹And the messenger that was sent to me, whose name was Uriel, gave me an answer, ²and said to me, "Your heart has utterly failed you in [regard to] this world, and do you think to comprehend the way of the Most High?" ³Then I said, "Yes my Lord." And he

answered me, and said, "I have been sent to show you three ways, and to set out three similitudes before you: ⁴ of which if you can declare me one, I also will show you the way that you desire to see, and I will teach you why the heart is wicked." ⁵ And I said, "Speak, my Lord." Then he said to me, "Go forth, weigh me a weight of fire, or measure me a measure of wind, or call me again the day that is past." ⁶ Then I answered and said, "Who of the sons [of men] is able to do this, that you should ask me of such things?" ⁷ And he said to me, "If I had asked you, saying, How many dwellings are there in the heart of the sea? Or how many springs are there at the fountain head of the deep? Or how many ways are above the expanse? Or which are the exits of Hades? Or which are the paths of paradise? ⁸ Perhaps you would say to me, I never went down into the deep, nor as yet into Hades, neither did I ever climb up into Heaven. ⁹ Nevertheless, now I have asked you but only of the fire and wind, and of the day, things you have experienced, and without which you cannot be, and yet you have given me no answer about them." ¹⁰ Moreover, he said to me, "Your own things, that are grown up with you, you cannot know; ¹¹ how then can you comprehend the way of the Most High? And how can he that is already worn out with the corrupted world understand incorruption?" ¹² And when I heard these things I fell on my face, and said to him, "It would be better that we were not here at all, than that we should come here and live in the midst of ungodliness, and suffer, and not know why." ¹³ He answered me, and said, "The woods of the trees of the field went out, and took counsel together, ¹⁴ and said, Come! Let us go and make war against the sea, that it may depart away before us, and that we may make ourselves more woods. ¹⁵ The waves of the sea also in like manner took counsel together, and said, Come! Let us go up and subdue the wood of the plain, that we may make ourselves another country there also. ¹⁶ The counsel of the wood was in vain, for the fire came and consumed it; ¹⁷ likewise also, the counsel of the waves of the sea, for the sand stood up and stopped them. ¹⁸ If you were judge now between these two, whom would you justify, or whom condemn?" ¹⁹ I answered and said, "It is a foolish counsel that they both have taken, for the ground is given to the wood, and the place of the sea [is given] to bear his waves." ²⁰ Then he answered me, and said, "You have given a right judgment, and why do you not judge in your own case? ²¹ For just as the ground is given to the wood, and the sea to his waves, even so those who dwell on the earth may understand nothing but that which is on the earth: and he [only that dwells] above the heavens [may understand the] things that are above the height of the heavens." ²² Then I answered and said, "I implore you, O Lord, why is the power of understanding given to me? ²³ For it was not in my mind to be curious of the ways above, but of such things as pass by us daily, because Israel is given up as a reproach to the heathen, and the people whom you have loved is given over to ungodly nations, and the Law of our forefathers is made of no effect, and the written covenants are nowhere [regarded], ²⁴ and we pass away out of the world as grasshoppers, and our life is as a vapor, neither are we worthy to obtain mercy. ²⁵ What will He then do for His Name whereby we are called? Of these things have I asked." ²⁶ Then he answered me, and said, "If you are [alive] you will see, and if you live long, you will marvel, for the world hastens quickly to pass away. ²⁷ For it is not able to bear the things that are promised to the righteous in the times [to come], for this world is full of sadness and infirmities. ²⁸ For the evil of which you asked me is sown, but the gathering thereof has not yet come. ²⁹ If, therefore, that which is sown has not reaped, and if the place where the evil is sown has not passed away, there cannot come the field where the good is sown. ³⁰ For a grain of evil seed was sown in the heart of Adam from the beginning, and how much wickedness has it brought out to this time! And how much will it yet bring out until the time of threshing comes! ³¹ Now ponder [this] by yourself: how great a fruit of wickedness a grain of evil seed has brought out. ³² When the ears which are without number will be sown, how great a floor they will fill!" ³³ Then I answered and said, "How long? And when will these things come to pass? Why are our years few and evil?" ³⁴ And he answered me, and said, "You do not hasten more than the Most High, for your haste is for your own self, but He that is above hastens on behalf of many. ³⁵ Did the souls of the righteous not ask questions of these things in their chambers, saying, How long are we here? When does the fruit of the threshing time of our reward come?" ³⁶ And to them Jeremiel the chief-messenger gave answer, and said, "When the number is fulfilled of those who are like to you. For He has weighed the world in the balance; ³⁷ and by measure He has measured the times, and by number He has counted the seasons; and He will not move nor stir them until the said measure is fulfilled." ³⁸ Then I answered and said, "O Lord that bears rule, yet even we are all full of impiety: ³⁹ and for our sakes perhaps it is that the threshing time of the righteous is kept back, because of the sins of those who dwell on the earth." ⁴⁰ So he answered me, and said, "Go your way to a woman with child, and ask of her when she has fulfilled her nine months, if her womb may keep the birth any longer within her." ⁴¹ Then I said, "No, Lord, that it cannot." And he said to me, "In the grave the chambers of souls are like the womb: ⁴² for like as a woman that travails hurries to escape the anguish of the travail, even so do these places hasten to deliver those things that are committed to them from the beginning. ⁴³ Then it will be shown to you concerning those things which you desire to see." ⁴⁴ Then I answered and said, "If I have found favor in your sight, and if it is possible, and if I am therefore suitable, ⁴⁵ show me this also, whether there are more to come than are past, or whether the greater part has [already] gone over us. ⁴⁶ For what is gone I know, but what is still to come I do not know." ⁴⁷ And he said to me, "Stand up on the right side, and I will expound the similitude to you." ⁴⁸ So I stood, and saw, and behold, a hot burning oven passed by before me: and it happened, that when the flame was gone by, I looked, and behold, the smoke remained still. ⁴⁹ After this there passed by before me a watery cloud and it sent down much rain with a storm; and when the stormy rain was past, the drops remained therein still. ⁵⁰ Then he said to me, "Consider with yourself; as the rain is more than the drops, and the fire is greater than the smoke, so the quantity which is past did exceed more; but the drops and the smoke remained still." ⁵¹ Then I prayed, and said, "Will I live until that time? Or who will be alive in those days?" ⁵² He answered me, and said, "As for the signs of which you asked me, I may tell you of them in part, but as touching your life, I am not sent to show you; for I do not know it."

CHAPTER 5

¹ "Nevertheless, as concerning the signs, behold, the days will come, that they which dwell on earth will be taken with great amazement, and the way of truth will be hidden, and the land will be barren of faith. ² But iniquity will be increased above that which you now see, or that you have heard of long ago. ³ And the land, that you now see to have rule, will be waste and untrodden, and men will see it desolate. ⁴ But if the Most High grants you to live, you will see that which is after the third [kingdom] to be troubled; and the sun will suddenly shine out in the night, and the moon in the day; ⁵ and blood will drop out of wood, and the stone will give his voice, and the peoples will be troubled; and their goings will be changed; ⁶ and he will rule, whom those who dwell on the earth do not look for, and the birds will take their flight away together; ⁷ and the Sodomite sea will cast out fish, and make a noise in the night, which many have not known, but all will hear the voice thereof. ⁸ There will also be chaos in many places, and the fire will often be sent out, and the wild beasts will change their places, and women will bring out monsters; ⁹ and salt waters will be found in the sweet, and all friends will destroy one another; then sense will hide itself, and understanding withdraw itself into its chamber; ¹⁰ and it will be sought of [by] many, and will not be found; and unrighteousness and incontinency will be multiplied on earth. ¹¹ One land will also ask another, and say, Has righteousness—has a man that does righteousness—gone through you? And it will say, No. ¹² And it will come to pass at that time that men will hope, but will not obtain: they will labor, but their ways will not prosper. ¹³ To show you such signs I

have [taken] leave; and if you will pray again, and weep as now, and fast [for] seven days, you will hear yet greater things than these." ¹⁴ Then I awoke, and an extreme trembling went through my body, and my mind was troubled, so that it fainted. ¹⁵ So the messenger that had come to talk with me held me, comforted me, and set me up on my feet. ¹⁶ And in the second night it came to pass, that Phaltiel the captain of the people came to me, saying, "Where have you been? And why is your countenance sad? ¹⁷ Or do you not know that Israel is committed to you in the land of their captivity? ¹⁸ Get up then, and eat some bread, and do not forsake us, as the shepherd [that leaves the flock] in the hands of cruel wolves." ¹⁹ Then I said to him, "Go your ways from me, and do not come near me for seven days, and then you will come to me." And he heard what I said and went from me. ²⁰ And so I fasted seven days, mourning and weeping, just as Uriel the messenger commanded me. ²¹ And after seven days, so it was, that the thoughts of my heart were very grievous to me again, ²² and my soul recovered the spirit of understanding, and I began to speak words before the Most High again, ²³ and said, "O LORD that bears rule, of all the woods of the earth, and of all the trees thereof, You have chosen one vine for Yourself; ²⁴ and of all the lands of the world You have chosen one country for Yourself; and of all the flowers of the world You have chosen one lily for Yourself; ²⁵ and of all the depths of the sea You have filled one river for Yourself; and of all built cities You have hallowed Zion for Yourself; ²⁶ and of all the birds that are created You have named one dove for Yourself; and of all the cattle that are made You have provided one sheep for Yourself; ²⁷ and among all the multitudes of peoples You have gotten one people for Yourself; and to this people, whom You loved, You gave a law that is approved of all. ²⁸ And now, O LORD, why have You given this one people over to many, and have dishonored the one root above others, and have scattered Your only one among many? ²⁹ And they which denied Your promises have trodden them down that believed Your covenants. ³⁰ If You hate Your people so much, they should be punished with Your own hands." ³¹ Now when I had spoken these words, the Messenger that came to me a previous night was sent to me, ³² and said to me, "Hear Me, and I will instruct you; listen to Me, and I will tell you more." ³³ And I said, "Speak, my Lord." Then He said to me, "You are severely troubled in mind for Israel's sake: do you [love] that people better than He that made them?" ³⁴ And I said, "No, Lord, but I have spoken in great grief, for my reins torment me every hour, while I labor to comprehend the way of the Most High, and to seek out part of His judgment." ³⁵ And he said to me, "You cannot." And I said, "Why, Lord, or for what purpose was I born? Or why was my mother's womb not then my grave, that I might not have seen the travail of Jacob, and the wearisome toil of the stock of Israel?" ³⁶ And He said to me, "Number to Me those who have not yet come, gather together to Me the drops that are scattered abroad, make for Me the flowers green again that are withered, ³⁷ open to Me the chambers that are closed, and bring out to Me the winds that in them are shut up, or show Me the image of a voice: and then I will declare to you the travail that you asked to see." ³⁸ And I said, "O LORD that bears rule, who may know these things, but He that does not have his dwelling with men? ³⁹ As for me, I am unwise: how may I then speak of these things of which You asked me?" ⁴⁰ Then He said to me, "Just as you can do none of these things that I have spoken of, even so you cannot find out My judgment, or the end of the love that I have promised to My people." ⁴¹ And I said, "But, behold, O LORD, You have made the promise to those who are in the end: and what will they do that have been before us, or we [that are now], or those who will come after us?" ⁴² And He said to me, "I will liken My judgment to a ring: just as there is no slackness of those who are last, even so there is no swiftness of those who are first." ⁴³ So I answered and said, "Could You not make them [to be] at once that have been made, and that are now, and that are still to come; that You might show Your judgment sooner?" ⁴⁴ Then He answered me, and said, "The creature may not hasten above the Creator; neither may the world hold them at once that will be created therein." ⁴⁵ And I said, "How have You said to Your servant that You will surely make alive at once the creature that You have created? If, therefore, they will be alive at once, and the creature will sustain them, even so it might now also support them to be present at once." ⁴⁶ And He said to me, "Ask the womb of a woman, and say to her, If you bring out ten children, why [do you do it] several times? Pray instead to bring out ten children at once." ⁴⁷ And I said, "She cannot, but must do it by distance of time." ⁴⁸ Then He said to me, "Even so have I given the womb of the earth to those that are sown therein in their several times. ⁴⁹ For just as a young child may not bring out, neither may she that has grown old [bring out] any more, even so—I have disposed the world which I created." ⁵⁰ And I asked, and said, "Seeing You have now showed me the way, I will speak before You: Is our mother, of whom You have told me, still young? Or does she now draw near to age?" ⁵¹ He answered me, and said, "Ask a woman that bears children, and she will tell you. ⁵² Say to her, Why are they whom you have now not brought out like those that were before, but of less stature? ⁵³ And she will also answer you, They that are born in the strength of youth are of one fashion, and those who are born in the time of age, when the womb fails, are otherwise. ⁵⁴ Therefore, also consider yourself, how that you are of less stature than those that were before you. ⁵⁵ And so are those who come after you less than you, as [born] of the creature which now begins to be

old and is past the strength of youth." ⁵⁶ Then I said, "Lord, I implore You, if I have found favor in Your sight, show Your servant by whom You visit Your creature."

CHAPTER 6

¹ And He said to me, "In the beginning, when the earth was made, before the portals of the world were fixed, or the gatherings of the winds ever blew, ² before the voices of the thunder sounded, and before the flashes of the lightning shone, or the foundations of paradise were ever laid, ³ before the fair flowers were seen, or the powers of the earthquake were ever established, before the innumerable army of messengers were gathered together, ⁴ or the heights of the air were ever lifted up, before the measures of the expanse were named, or the footstool of Zion was ever established, ⁵ and before the present years were sought out, and or the imaginations of those who now sin were ever estranged, before they were sealed that have gathered faith for a treasure— ⁶ then I considered these things, and they were all made through Me alone, and through none other: as by Me they will also be ended, and by none other." ⁷ Then I answered and said, "What will be the separating apart of the times? Or when will be the end of the first, and the beginning of it that follows?" ⁸ And He said to me, "From Abraham to Abraham, inasmuch as Jacob and Esau were born of him, for Jacob's hand held the heel of Esau from the beginning. ⁹ For Esau is the end of this world, and Jacob is the beginning of it that follows. ¹⁰ The beginning of a man is his hand, and the end of a man is his heel; between the heel and the hand do not seek anything else, Ezra." ¹¹ I answered then and said, "O LORD that bears rule, If I have found favor in Your sight, ¹² I implore You, show Your servant the end of Your signs, of which You showed me part the last night." ¹³ So He answered and said to me, "Stand up on your feet, and you will hear a mighty sounding voice; ¹⁴ and if the place you stand on is greatly moved, ¹⁵ when it speaks, do not be afraid, for the word is of the end, and the foundations of the earth will understand, ¹⁶ that the speech is of them: they will tremble and be moved, for they know that their end must be changed." ¹⁷ And it happened, that when I had heard it I stood up on my feet, and listened, and behold, there was a voice that spoke, and the sound of it was like the sound of many waters. ¹⁸ And it said, "Behold, the days come, and it will be that when I draw near to visit those who dwell on the earth, ¹⁹ and when I will make inquisition of those who have done hurt unjustly with their unrighteousness, and when the affliction of Zion will be fulfilled, ²⁰ and when the seal will be set on the world that is to pass away, then I will show these signs: the scrolls will be opened before the expanse, and all will see together; ²¹ and the children of a year old will speak with their voices, [and] the women with child will bring out untimely

children at three or four months, and they will live, and dance; ²²and suddenly the sown places will appear unsown, [and] the full storehouses will suddenly be found empty; ²³and the trumpet will give a sound, which when every man hears, they will be suddenly afraid. ²⁴At that time friends will make war against one another like enemies, and the earth will stand in fear with those that dwell therein; the springs of the springs will stand still, so that for three hours they will not run. ²⁵And it will be that whoever remains after all these things that I have told you of, he will be saved, and will see My salvation and the end of My world. ²⁶And they will see the men that have been taken up, who have not tasted death from their birth: and the heart of the inhabitants will be changed and turned into another meaning. ²⁷For evil will be blotted out, and deceit will be quenched; ²⁸and faith will flourish, and corruption will be overcome, and the truth, which has been so long without fruit, will be declared." ²⁹And when He talked with me, behold, little by little the place I stood on rocked to and fro. ³⁰And He said to me, "These things I came to show you this night. ³¹If, therefore, you will pray yet again, and fast [for] seven more days, I will yet tell you greater things than these. ³²For your voice has surely been heard before the Most High, for the Mighty has seen your righteous dealing; He has also previously seen your chastity, which you have had ever since your youth. ³³And therefore He has sent Me to show you all these things, and to say to you, Be of good comfort, and do not fear. ³⁴And do not be hasty in [regard of the] former times, to think vain things, that you may not hasten in the latter times." ³⁵And it came to pass after this, that I wept again, and fasted [for] seven days in like manner, that I might fulfill the three weeks which He told me. ³⁶And in the eighth night my heart was vexed within me again, and I began to speak before the Most High. ³⁷For my spirit was greatly set on fire, and my soul was in distress. ³⁸And I said, "O LORD, of a truth You spoke at the beginning of the creation, on the first day, and said this: Let the heavens and earth be made; and Your word perfected the work. ³⁹And then the Spirit was fluttering, and darkness and silence were on every side; the sound of man's voice was not yet [heard]. ⁴⁰Then You commanded a ray of light to be brought out of Your treasures, that Your works might then appear. ⁴¹On the second day again You made the spirit of the expanse and commanded it to separate apart, and to make a division between the waters, that the one part might go up, and the other remain beneath. ⁴²On the third day You commanded that the waters should be gathered together in the seventh part of the earth: six parts You dried up, and You keep them, to the intent that of these some being both planted and tilled might serve before You. ⁴³For as soon as Your word went out the work was done. ⁴⁴For immediately there came out great and innumerable

fruit, and manifold pleasures for the taste, and flowers of inimitable color, and aromas of most exquisite smell: and this was done the third day. ⁴⁵On the fourth day You commanded that the sun should shine, and the moon give her light, and the stars should be in their order: ⁴⁶and You gave them a charge to do service to man that was to be made. ⁴⁷On the fifth day You said to the seventh part, where the water was gathered together, that it should bring out living creatures—birds and fishes: and so it came to pass, ⁴⁸that the mute water—and without life—brought out living things as it was told, that the peoples might therefore praise Your wondrous works. ⁴⁹Then You preserved two living creatures, the one You called Behemoth, and the other you called Leviathan; ⁵⁰and You separated the one from the other; for the seventh part, namely, where the water was gathered together, might not hold them both. ⁵¹To Behemoth You gave one part, which was dried up on the third day, that he should dwell in it, wherein are one thousand hills, ⁵²but to Leviathan You gave the seventh part, namely, the moist; and You have kept them to be devoured of whom You will, and when. ⁵³But on the sixth day You gave command to the earth, that it should bring out cattle, beasts, and creeping things before You: ⁵⁴and over these [is] Adam, whom You ordain lord over all the works that You have made; of him we all come— the people whom You have chosen. ⁵⁵I have spoken all this before You, O LORD, because You have said that You have made this world for our sakes. ⁵⁶As for the other nations, which also come of Adam, You have said that they are nothing, and are like to spittle: and You have likened the abundance of them to a drop that falls from a vessel. ⁵⁷And now, O LORD, behold [how] these nations, which are regarded as nothing, are lords over us, and devour us. ⁵⁸But we Your people, whom You have called Your firstborn, Your only begotten, and Your fervent lover, are given into their hands. ⁵⁹If the world is now made for our sakes, why do we not possess our world for an inheritance? How long will this endure?"

CHAPTER 7

¹And when I had made an end of speaking these words, there was sent to me the Messenger which had been sent to me the nights before, ²and He said to me, "Get up, Ezra, and hear the words that I have come to tell you." ³And I said, "Speak, my Lord." Then He said to me, "There is a sea set in a wide place, that it might be broad and vast. ⁴But the entrance thereof will be set in a narrow place so as to be like a river; ⁵whoever then should desire to go into the sea to look on it, or to rule it, if he did not go through the narrow, how could he come into the broad? ⁶Another thing also: there is a city built and set in a plain country, and full of all good things; ⁷but the entrance thereof is narrow and is set in a dangerous place to fall, having a fire on the right hand, and on the left a deep

water; [8] and there is only one path between them both, even between the fire and the water, [so small] that there could [be] but one man [who could] go there at once. [9] If this city is now given to a man for an inheritance, if the heir does not pass the danger before him, how will he receive his inheritance?" [10] And I said, "It is so, Lord." Then He said to me, "Even so is Israel's portion also. [11] Because for their sakes I made the world; and when Adam transgressed My statutes, then was decreed that [which] now is done. [12] Then the entrances of this world were made narrow, and sorrowful, and toilsome: they are but few and evil, full of perils, and charged with great toils. [13] For the entrances of the greater world are wide, and sure, and bring out fruit of immortality. [14] If then those who live do not enter these narrow and vain things, they can never receive those that are laid up for them. [15] Now therefore, why do you disquiet yourself, seeing you are but a corruptible man? And why are you moved, whereas you are but mortal? [16] And why have you not considered in your mind that which is to come, rather than that which is present?" [17] Then I answered and said, "O LORD that bears rule, behold, You have ordained in Your law that the righteous should inherit these things, but that the ungodly should perish. [18] The righteous will therefore suffer narrow things, and hope for wide, but those who have done wickedly have suffered the narrow things, and yet will not see the wide." [19] And He said to me, "You are not a judge above God, neither have you understanding above the Most High. [20] Yes, rather let many that now are perish, than that the Law of God which is set before them be despised. [21] For God strictly commanded such as came, even as they came, what they should do to live, and what they should observe to avoid punishment. [22] Nevertheless, they were not obedient to Him, but spoke against Him and imagined for themselves vain things, [23] and framed cunning plans of wickedness, and said, moreover, of the Most High, that He is not, and did not know His ways, [24] but they despised His law and denied His covenants; they have not been faithful to His statutes and have not performed His works. [25] Therefore, Ezra, for the empty are empty things, and for the full are the full things. [26] For behold, the time will come, and it will be, when these signs of which I told you before will come to pass: that the bride will appear, even the city coming out, and she will be seen that now is withdrawn from the earth. [27] And whoever is delivered from the previously mentioned evils will see My wonders. [28] For My Son the Christ will be revealed with those that are with Him and will rejoice with those who remain four hundred years. [29] After these years My Son the Christ will die, and all those that have the breath of life. [30] And the world will be turned into the primordial silence [for] seven days, just as in the first beginning, so that no man will remain. [31] And after seven days, the world that has not yet awaken will be raised up,

and that which is corruptible will die. [32] And the earth will restore those that are asleep in her, and so will the dust those that dwell therein in silence, and the secret places will deliver those souls that were committed to them. [33] And the Most High will be revealed on the seat of judgment, and compassion will pass away, and patience will be withdrawn, [34] but only judgment will remain, truth will stand, and faith will wax strong; [35] and the work will follow, and the reward will be shown, and good deeds will awake, and wicked deeds will not sleep. [36] And the pit of torment will appear, and near it will be the place of rest; and the furnace will be shown, and near it the paradise of delight. [37] And then the Most High will say to the nations that are raised from the dead: See and understand whom you have denied, or whom you have not served, or whose commands you have despised. [38] Look on this side and on that: here is delight and rest, and there fire and torments. He will speak this to them in the Day of Judgment: [39] this is a day that has neither sun, nor moon, nor stars, [40] neither cloud, nor thunder, nor lightning, neither wind, nor water, nor air, neither darkness, nor evening, nor morning, [41] neither summer, nor spring, nor heat, nor winter, neither frost, nor cold, nor hail, nor rain, nor dew, [42] neither noon, nor night, nor dawn, neither shining, nor brightness, nor light, save only the splendor of the glory of the Most High, whereby all will see the things that are set before them, [43] for it will endure as it were a week of years. [44] This is My judgment and the ordinance thereof; but only to you have I showed these things." [45] And I answered, I said even then, "O LORD, and I say now: blessed are those who are now alive and keep the [statutes] ordained of You. [46] But as touching them for whom my prayer was made, [what will I say]? For who is there of those who are alive that has not sinned, and who of the sons [of men] that has not transgressed Your covenant? [47] And now I see that the world to come will bring delight to few, but torments to many. [48] For an evil heart has grown up in us, which has led us astray from these [statutes, and] has brought us into corruption and into the ways of death, has showed us the paths of perdition, and removed us far from life—and that, not a few only, but well near all that have been created." [49] And He answered me, and said, "Listen to Me, and I will instruct you; and I will admonish you yet again: [50] for this reason the Most High has not made one world, but two. [51] For whereas you have said that the just are not many, but few, and the ungodly abound, hear [the answer] to that. [52] If you have exceedingly few choice stones, will you set for yourself near them, according to their number, [things of] lead and clay?" [53] And I said, "Lord, how will this be?" [54] And He said to me, "Not only this, but ask the earth, and she will tell you; entreat her, and she will declare to you. [55] For you will say to her, You bring out gold, and silver, and brass, and iron also, and lead, and clay; [56] but silver is more abundant than gold, and brass than silver, and iron than brass, lead than iron, and clay than lead. ⁵⁷ Therefore judge which things are precious and to be desired, what is abundant or what is rare." ⁵⁸ And I said, "O LORD that bears rule, that which is plentiful is of less worth, for that which is more rare is more precious." ⁵⁹ And He answered me, and said, "Weigh within yourself the things that you have thought, for he that has what is hard to get rejoices over him that has what is plentiful. ⁶⁰ So also is the judgment which I have promised, for I will rejoice over the few that will be saved, inasmuch as these are those who have made My glory now to prevail, and of whom My Name is now named. ⁶¹ And I will not grieve over the multitude of those who perish; for these are those who are now like to vapor and have become as flame and smoke; they are set on fire and burn hotly and are quenched." ⁶² And I answered and said, "O you earth, why have you brought out, if the mind is made out of dust, like as all other created things? ⁶³ For it were better that the dust itself had been unborn, so that the mind might not have been made from it. ⁶⁴ But now the mind grows with us, and by reason of this we are tormented, because we perish and know it. ⁶⁵ Let the race of men lament and the beasts of the field be glad; let all that are born lament, but let the four-footed beasts and the cattle rejoice. ⁶⁶ For it is far better with them than with us; for they do not look for judgment, neither do they know of torments or of salvation promised to them after death. ⁶⁷ For what does it profit us, that we will be preserved alive, but yet be afflicted with torment? ⁶⁸ For all that are born are defiled with iniquities, and are full of sins, and laden with offenses; ⁶⁹ and if after death we were not to come into judgment, perhaps it had been better for us." ⁷⁰ And He answered me, and said, "When the Most High made the world, and Adam and all those who came of him, He first prepared the judgment and the things that pertain to the judgment. ⁷¹ And now understand from your own words, for you have said that the mind grows with us. ⁷² Therefore, they that dwell on the earth will be tormented for this reason, that having understanding, they have done iniquity, and receiving commands, have not kept them, and having obtained a law, they dealt unfaithfully with that which they received. ⁷³ What then will they have to say in the judgment, or how will they answer in the last times? ⁷⁴ For how great a time has the Most High been patient with those who inhabit the world, and not for their sakes, but because of the times which He has foreordained!" ⁷⁵ And I answered and said, "If I have found grace in Your sight, O LORD, show this to Your servant also, whether after death, even now when each of us gives up his soul, we will be kept in rest until those times come, in which You will renew the creation, or whether we will be tormented immediately." ⁷⁶ And He answered me, and said, "I will show you this also, but do not join yourself with those who are scorners, nor count yourself with those who are tormented. ⁷⁷ For you have a treasure of [good] works laid up with the Most High, but it will not be shown to you until the last times. ⁷⁸ For concerning death the teaching is: When the determinate sentence has gone out from the Most High that a man should die, as the spirit leaves the body to return again to Him who gave it, it adores the glory of the Most High first of all. ⁷⁹ And if it is one of those that have been scorners and have not kept the way of the Most High, and that have despised His law, and that hate those who fear God, ⁸⁰ these spirits will not enter into habitations, but will wander and be in torments immediately, ever grieving and sad, in seven ways. ⁸¹ The first way, because they have despised the Law of the Most High. ⁸² The second way, because they cannot now make a good returning that they may live. ⁸³ The third way, they will see the reward laid up for those who have believed the covenants of the Most High. ⁸⁴ The fourth way, they will consider the torment laid up for themselves in the last days. ⁸⁵ The fifth way, they will see the dwelling places of the others guarded by messengers, with great quietness. ⁸⁶ The sixth way, they will see how some of them will immediately pass into torment. ⁸⁷ The seventh way, which is more grievous than all the previously mentioned ways, because they will pine away in confusion, and be consumed with shame, and will be withered up by fears, seeing the glory of the Most High before whom they have sinned while living, and before whom they will be judged in the last times. ⁸⁸ Now this is the order of those who have kept the ways of the Most High, when they will be separated from the corruptible vessel. ⁸⁹ In the time that they lived therein they painfully served the Most High, and were in danger every hour, that they might keep the Law of the Lawgiver perfectly. ⁹⁰ Here then is the teaching concerning them: ⁹¹ First of all, they will see with great joy the glory of Him who takes them up, for they will have rest in seven orders. ⁹² The first order, because they have labored with great effort to overcome the evil thought which was fashioned together with them, that it might not lead them astray from life into death. ⁹³ The second order, because they see the perplexity in which the souls of the ungodly wander, and the punishment that awaits them. ⁹⁴ The third order, they see the witness which He that fashioned them bears concerning them, that while they lived they kept the Law which was given them in trust. ⁹⁵ The fourth order, they understand the rest which, being gathered in their chambers, they now enjoy with great quietness, guarded by messengers, and the glory that awaits them in the last days. ⁹⁶ The fifth order, they rejoice, [seeing] how they have now escaped from that which is corruptible, and how they will inherit that which is to come, while they see moreover the narrowness and the painfulness from which they have been delivered, and the large room which they will receive with joy and immortality. [97] The sixth order, when it is showed to them how their face will shine as the sun, and how they will be made like to the light of the stars, being from now on incorruptible. [98] The seventh order, which is greater than all the previous orders, because they will rejoice with confidence, and because they will be bold without confusion, and will be glad without fear, for they hasten to behold the face of Him whom in their lifetime they served, and from whom they will receive [their] reward in glory. [99] This is the order of the souls of the just, as from now on is announced to them, and announced are the ways of torture which those who would not give heed will suffer from now on." [100] And I answered and said, "Will time therefore be given to the souls after they are separated from the bodies, that they may see what You have spoken to me?" [101] And He said, "Their freedom will be for seven days, that for seven days they may see the things that you have been told, and afterward they will be gathered together in their habitations." [102] And I answered and said, "If I have found favor in Your sight, show further to me Your servant whether in the Day of Judgment the just will be able to intercede for the ungodly or to entreat the Most High for them, [103] whether fathers for children, or children for parents, or relatives for relatives, or countrymen for countrymen, or friends for those who are most dear." [104] And He answered me, and said, "Since you have found favor in My sight, I will show you this also: the Day of Judgment is a day of decision, and displays to all the seal of truth; even as now a father does not send his son, or a son his father, or a master his slave, or a friend him that is most dear, that in his stead he may be sick, or sleep, or eat, or be healed, [105] so never will anyone pray for another in that day, neither will one lay a burden on another, for then everyone will bear his own righteousness or unrighteousness." [106] And I answered and said, "How do we now find that first Abraham prayed for the people of Sodom, and Moses for the fathers that sinned in the wilderness, [107] and Joshua after him for Israel in the days of Achar, [108] and Samuel in the days of Saul, and David for the plague, and Solomon for those who [should worship] in the sanctuary, [109] and Elijah for those that received rain, and for the dead, that he might live, [110] and Hezekiah for the people in the days of Sennacherib, and many for many? [111] If, therefore now, when corruption is grown up, and unrighteousness increased, the righteous have prayed for the ungodly, why will it not be so then also?" [112] He answered me, and said, "This present world is not the end; the full glory does not remain therein. Therefore, they who were able have prayed for the weak, [113] but the Day of Judgment will be the end of this time, and the beginning of the immortality to come, wherein corruption has passed away,

[114] intemperance is at an end, infidelity is cut off, but righteousness has grown, and truth has sprung up. [115] Then no man will be able to have mercy on him that is cast in judgment, nor to thrust down him that has gotten the victory." [116] I answered then and said, "This is my first and last saying, that it had been better that the earth had not given Adam: or else, when it had given [him], to have restrained him from sinning. [117] For what profit is it for all that are in this present time to live in heaviness, and after death to look for punishment? [118] O you Adam! What have you done? For though it was you that sinned, the evil is not fallen on you alone, but on all of us that come of you. [119] For what profit is it to us, if there is promised us an immortal time, whereas we have done the works that bring death? [120] And that there has been promised us a continuous hope, whereas we have become most miserably vain? [121] And that there are reserved habitations of health and safety, whereas we have lived wickedly? [122] And that the glory of the Most High will defend them which have led a pure life, whereas we have walked in the most wicked ways of all? [123] And that there will be showed a paradise, whose fruit endures without decay, wherein is abundance and healing, but we will not enter into it, [124] for we have walked in unpleasant places? [125] And that the faces of them which have used abstinence will shine above the stars, whereas our faces will be blacker than darkness? [126] For while we lived and committed iniquity, we did not consider what we should have to suffer after death." [127] Then He answered and said, "This is the condition of the battle, which man that is born on the earth will fight; [128] that, if he is overcome, he will suffer as you have said, but if he gets the victory, he will receive the thing that I say. [129] For this is the way of which Moses spoke to the people while he lived, saying, Choose life, that you may live. [130] Nevertheless, they did not believe him, nor yet the prophets after him, no, nor Me which have spoken to them, [131] so that there will not be such heaviness in their destruction, as there will be joy over those who are persuaded to salvation." [132] I answered then and said, "I know, Lord, that the Most High is now called merciful, in that He has mercy on them which have not yet come into the world; [133] and compassionate, in that He has compassion on those that turn to His law; [134] and patient, for that He long endures those that have sinned, as His creatures; [135] and bountiful, for that He is ready to give rather than to exact; [136] and of great mercy, for that He multiplies more and more mercies to those who are present, and that are past, and also to them which are to come [137] (for if He did not multiply [His mercies], the world would not continue with those who dwell therein); [138] and one that forgives, for if He did not forgive of His goodness, that they which have committed iniquities might be eased of them, the ten-thousandth part of men would not remain living;

139 and a judge, [for] if He did not pardon those who were created by His word, and blot out the multitude of offenses, 140 there would perhaps be very few left in an innumerable multitude."

CHAPTER 8

1 And He answered me, and said, "The Most High has made this world for many, but the world to come for few. 2 I will now tell you a similitude, Ezra: [just] as when you ask the earth, it will say to you that it gives very much mold of which earthen vessels are made, and little dust that gold comes of, even so is the course of the present world. 3 There are many created, but few will be saved." 4 And I answered and said, "Swallow down understanding then, O my soul, and let [my heart] devour wisdom. 5 For you have come here without your will and depart when you would not, for there is given to you no more space than only to live a short time. 6 O LORD, You that are over us, permit Your servant, that we may pray before You, and give us seed to our heart, and culture to our understanding, that there may come fruit of it, whereby each one will live that is corrupt, who bears the likeness of a man. 7 For You are alone, and we are all one workmanship of Your hands, just as You have said. 8 Forasmuch as You give life to the body that is fashioned now in the womb, and give it members, Your creature is preserved in fire and water, and [for] nine months Your workmanship endures Your creature which is created in her. 9 But that which keeps and that which is kept will both be kept by Your keeping: and when the womb gives up again that which has grown in it, 10 You have commanded that out of the parts of the body, that is to say, out of the breasts, be given milk, which is the fruit of the breasts, 11 that the thing which is fashioned may be nourished for a time, and afterward You will order it in Your mercy. 12 Yes, You have brought it up in Your righteousness, and nurtured it in Your law, and corrected it with Your judgment. 13 And You will mortify it as Your creature and give it life as Your work. 14 If, therefore, You will lightly and suddenly destroy him which with so great labor was fashioned by Your command, to what purpose was he made? 15 Now therefore, I will speak; touching man in general, You know best; but touching Your people [I will speak], for whose sake I am sorry; 16 and for Your inheritance, for whose cause I mourn; and for Israel, for whom I am heavy; and for the seed of Jacob, for whose sake I am troubled; 17 therefore I will begin to pray before You for myself and for them, for I see the falls of us that dwell in the land, 18 but I have heard the swiftness of the judgment which is to come. 19 Therefore hear my voice, and understand my saying, and I will speak before You." The beginning of the words of Ezra, before he was taken up. And he said, 20 "O LORD, You who remain forever, whose eyes are exalted, and whose chambers are in the air;

21 whose throne is inestimable; whose glory may not be comprehended; before whom the army of messengers stand with trembling, 22 at whose bidding they are changed to wind and fire; whose word is sure, and sayings constant; whose ordinance is strong, and command fearful; 23 whose look dries up the depths, and whose indignation makes the mountains to melt away, and whose truth bears witness: 24 hear, O LORD, the prayer of Your servant, and give ear to the petition of Your handiwork; 25 attend to my words, for so long as I live I will speak, and so long as I have understanding I will answer. 26 Do not look on the sins of Your people, but on those who have served You in truth. 27 Do not regard the doings of those who deal wickedly, but of those who have kept Your covenants in affliction. 28 Do not think on those that have walked ungenuine before You, but remember them which have willingly known Your fear. 29 Do not let it be Your will to destroy them which have lived like cattle, but look on those who have clearly taught Your law. 30 Take no indignation at them which are deemed worse than beasts, but love those who have always put their trust in Your glory. 31 For we and our fathers have passed our lives in ways that bring death, but You, because of us sinners, are called merciful. 32 For if You have a desire to have mercy on us, then You will be called merciful, to us, namely, that have no works of righteousness. 33 For the just, which have many [good] works laid up with You, will for their own deeds receive reward. 34 For what is man that You should take displeasure at him? Or what is a corruptible race that You should be so bitter toward it? 35 For in truth there is no man among those who are born, but he [who] has dealt wickedly; and among them that have lived there is none which have not done wrong. 36 For in this, O LORD, Your righteousness and Your goodness will be declared, if You are merciful to them which have no store of good works." 37 Then He answered me, and said, "You have spoken some things correctly, and according to your words so it will come to pass. 38 For indeed, I will not think on the fashioning of them which have sinned, or their death, their judgment, or their destruction, 39 but I will rejoice over the framing of the righteous, their pilgrimage also, and the salvation and the reward that they will have. 40 Therefore, just as I have spoken, so it will be. 41 For as the farmer sows much seed on the ground, and plants many trees, and yet not all that is sown will come up in due season, neither will all that is planted take root: even so those who are sown in the world will not all be saved." 42 I answered then and said, "If I have found favor, let me speak before You. 43 Forasmuch as the farmer's seed, if it does not come up, seeing that it has not received Your rain in due season, or if it is corrupted through too much rain, so perishes, 44 likewise man, which is formed with Your hands, and is called Your own image, because he is made like [You], for whose sake You have formed all

things, even him you have made like to the farmer's seed. ⁴⁵ Do not be angry with us, but spare Your people, and have mercy on Your inheritance; for You have mercy on Your own creation." ⁴⁶ Then He answered me, and said, "Things present are for those who now are, and things to come for such as will be hereafter. ⁴⁷ For you come far short that you should be able to love My creature more than Me. But you have brought yourself full near to the unrighteous—never! ⁴⁸ Yet in this you will be admirable to the Most High: ⁴⁹ in that you have humbled yourself, as it is appropriate for you, and have not judged yourself [worthy to be] among the righteous, so as to be much glorified. ⁵⁰ For many grievous miseries will fall on those who in the last times dwell in the world, because they have walked in great pride. ⁵¹ But understand for yourself, and of such as are like you—seek out the glory. ⁵² For to you paradise is opened, the Tree of Life planted, the time to come is prepared, bounty is made ready, a city is built, and rest is allowed, goodness is perfected, wisdom being perfect beforehand. ⁵³ The root [of evil] is sealed up from you, weakness is done away from you, and [death] is hidden; Hades and corruption have fled into forgetfulness; ⁵⁴ sorrows have passed away, and in the end, the treasure of immortality is shown. ⁵⁵ Therefore, do not ask any more questions concerning the multitude of them that perish. ⁵⁶ For when they had received liberty, they despised the Most High, thought scorn of His law, and forsook His ways. ⁵⁷ Moreover, they have trodden down His righteous, ⁵⁸ and said in their heart that there is no God; yes, and that knowing they must die. ⁵⁹ For as the things previously stated you will receive, so thirst and pain which are prepared [they will receive], for the Most High did not will that men should come to nothing, ⁶⁰ but they which are created have themselves defiled the Name of Him that made them and were unthankful to Him which prepared life for them. ⁶¹ And therefore My judgment is now at hand, ⁶² which I have not showed to all men, but to you, and a few like you." Then I answered and said, ⁶³ "Behold, O LORD, now You have showed me the multitude of the wonders, which You will do in the last times, but at what time, You have not showed me."

CHAPTER 9

¹ And He answered me, and said, "Measure diligently within yourself: and when you see that a certain part of the signs are past, which have been told to you beforehand, ² then you will understand that it is the very time wherein the Most High will visit the world which was made by Him. ³ And when there will be seen in the world earthquakes, disquietude of peoples, plans of nations, wavering of leaders, disquietude of princes, ⁴ then you will understand that the Most High spoke of these things from the days that were previously from the beginning. ⁵ For just as of all that

is made in the world, the beginning is evident and the end manifest, ⁶ so also are the times of the Most High: the beginnings are manifest in wonders and mighty works, and the end in effects and signs. ⁷ And everyone that will be saved, and will be able to escape by his works, or by faith, whereby he has believed, ⁸ will be preserved from the stated perils, and will see My salvation in My land, and within My borders, which I have sanctified for Myself from the beginning. ⁹ Then those which have now abused My ways will be amazed, and those who have despitefully cast them away will dwell in torments. ¹⁰ For as many as in their life have received benefits, and yet have not known Me, ¹¹ and as many as have scorned My law while they still had liberty, and, when conversion was open to them, did not understand, but despised [it], ¹² must know [it] after death by torment. ¹³ And therefore, no longer be curious how the ungodly will be punished, but inquire how the righteous will be saved, they whose the world [is, and] for whom the world [was created]." ¹⁴ And I answered and said, ¹⁵ "I have said before, and now speak, and will speak it also hereafter, that there are more of them which perish, than of those which will be saved: ¹⁶ just as a wave is greater than a drop." ¹⁷ And He answered me, saying, "Just as the field is, so also the seed; and as the flowers are, such are the colors also; and such as the work is, such is the judgment [on it] also; and as is the farmer, so is his threshing floor also. For there was a time in the world, ¹⁸ even then when I was preparing for those who now live, before the world was made for them to dwell in; and then no man spoke against Me— ¹⁹ there was not any; but now they which are created in this world that is prepared, both with a table that does not fail, and a law which is unsearchable, are corrupted in their manners. ²⁰ So I considered My world, and behold, it was destroyed, and My earth, and behold, it was in peril, because of the plans that had come into it. ²¹ And I saw, and spared them, but not greatly, and saved Myself a grape out of a cluster, and a plant out of a great forest. ²² Let the multitude which was born in vain perish then; and let My grape be saved, and My plant; for I have made them perfect with great labor. ²³ Nevertheless, if you will cease yet seven more days, (however you will not fast in them, ²⁴ but will go into a field of flowers, where no house is built, and eat only of the flowers of the field; and you will taste no flesh, and will drink no wine, but [will eat] flowers only;) ²⁵ and pray to the Most High continually, then I will come and talk with you." ²⁶ So I went my way, just as He commanded me, into the field which is called Ardat; and there I sat among the flowers, and ate of the herbs of the field, and its meat satisfied me. ²⁷ And it came to pass after seven days that I lay on the grass, and my heart was vexed again just as before; ²⁸ and my mouth was opened, and I began to speak before the LORD Most High, and said, ²⁹ "O

LORD, You showed Yourself among us, to our fathers in the wilderness, when they went out of Egypt, and when they came into the wilderness, where no man treads and which bears no fruit; ³⁰ and You said, Hear Me, Israel; and mark My words, O seed of Jacob. ³¹ For behold, I sow My law in you, and it will bring out fruit in you, and you will be glorified in it forever. ³² But our fathers, which received the Law, did not keep it, and did not observe the statutes: and the fruit of the Law did not perish, neither could it, for it was Yours; ³³ yet those who received it perished, because they did not keep the thing that was sown in them. ³⁴ And behold, it is a custom that when the ground has received seed, or the sea a ship, or any vessel meat or drink, and when it comes to pass that that which is sown, or that which is launched, ³⁵ or the things which have been received, should come to an end, these come to an end, but the receptacles remain: yet with us it has not happened so. ³⁶ For we that have received the Law will perish by sin, and also our heart which received it. ³⁷ Notwithstanding, the Law does not perish, but remains in its honor." ³⁸ And when I spoke these things in my heart, I looked around me with my eyes, and on the right side I saw a woman, and behold, she mourned and wept with a loud voice, and was greatly grieved in mind, and her clothes were torn, and she had ashes on her head. ³⁹ Then I let my thoughts go wherein I was occupied, and I turned to her, ⁴⁰ and said to her, "Why do you weep? And why are you grieved in your mind?" ⁴¹ And she said to me, "Leave me alone, my lord, that I may mourn myself, and add to my sorrow, for I am severely vexed in my mind, and brought very low." ⁴² And I said to her, "What ails you? Tell me." ⁴³ She said to me, "I, your servant, was barren, and had no child, though I had a husband [for] thirty years. ⁴⁴ And every hour and every day these thirty years I made my prayer to the Most High day and night. ⁴⁵ And it came to pass after thirty years, that God heard me, your handmaid, and looked on my low estate, and considered my trouble, and gave me a son: and I rejoiced in him greatly— me, and my husband, and all my neighbors—and we gave great honor to the Mighty. ⁴⁶ And I nourished him with great travail. ⁴⁷ So when he grew up, and I came to take a wife for him, I made him a feast day."

CHAPTER 10

¹ "And so it came to pass, that when my son had entered into his wedding chamber, he fell down and died. ² Then we all overthrew the lights, and all my neighbors rose up to comfort me: and I remained quiet to the second day at night. ³ And it came to pass when they had all ceased to comfort me, to the end I might be quiet, then I arose by night, and fled, and came here into this field, as you see. ⁴ And now I do not purpose to return into the city, but to stay here, and neither to eat nor drink, but to continually mourn and fast until I die." ⁵ Then I left the meditations wherein

I was, and answered her in anger, and said, ⁶ "You foolish woman above all others! Do you not see our mourning, and what has happened to us? ⁷ How Zion, the mother of us all, is full of sorrow, and greatly humbled. ⁸ It is right to mourn very severely now, seeing we all mourn, and to be sorrowful, seeing we are all in sorrow, but you mourn for one son. ⁹ For ask the earth, and she will tell you that it is she which should mourn for so many that grow on her. ¹⁰ For out of her all had their beginnings, and others will come; and behold, almost all of them walk into destruction, and the multitude of them is utterly rooted out. ¹¹ Who then should make more mourning: she that has lost so great a multitude, or you which are grieved but for one? ¹² But if you say to me, My lamentation is not like the earth's, for I have lost the fruit of my womb, which I brought out with pains, and bore with sorrows, ¹³ but [it is with the] earth after the manner of the earth—the multitude present in it is gone, as it came: ¹⁴ then I say to you, just as you have brought out with sorrow, even so the earth has also given her fruit, namely, man, ever since the beginning to Him that made her. ¹⁵ Now therefore, keep your sorrow to yourself, and bear with a good courage the adversities which have befallen you. ¹⁶ For if you will acknowledge the decree of God to be just, you will both receive your son in time, and will be praised among women. ¹⁷ Go your way then into the city to your husband." ¹⁸ And she said to me, "I will not do that. I will not go into the city, but I will die here." ¹⁹ So I proceeded to speak further to her, and said, ²⁰ "Do not do that, but permit yourself to be prevailed on by reason of the adversities of Zion; and be comforted by reason of the sorrow of Jerusalem. ²¹ For you see that our sanctuary is laid waste, our altar broken down, our temple destroyed; ²² our lute is brought low, our song is put to silence, our rejoicing is at an end; the light of our candlestick is put out, the Ark of our covenant is plundered, our holy things are defiled, and the name that is called on us is profaned; our freemen are despitefully treated, our priests are burned, our Levites have gone into captivity, our virgins are defiled, and our wives ravished; our righteous men carried away, our little ones betrayed, our young men are brought into bondage, and our strong men have become weak; ²³ and, what is more than all, the seal of Zion—for she has now lost the seal of her honor, and is delivered into the hands of those who hate us. ²⁴ Therefore, shake off your great heaviness, and put away from yourself the multitude of sorrows, that the Mighty may be merciful to you again, and the Most High may give you rest, even ease from your travails." ²⁵ And it came to pass, while I was talking with her, behold, her face suddenly shined exceedingly, and her countenance radiated like lightning, so that I was terrified of her, and wondered what this might be; ²⁶ and behold, she suddenly made a great [and] very fearful cry, so that the earth shook at the noise. [27] And I looked, and behold, the woman appeared to me no longer, but there [where she was] a city was built, and a place showed itself from large foundations. Then I was afraid, and cried with a loud voice, and said, [28] "Where is Uriel the messenger, who came to me at the first? For he has caused me to fall into this great trance, and my end is turned into corruption, and my prayer to rebuke." [29] And as I was speaking these words, behold, the messenger who had come to me at the first came to me, and he looked on me; [30] and behold, I lay as one that had been dead, and my understanding was taken from me; and he took me by the right hand, and comforted me, and set me on my feet, and said to me, [31] "What ails you? And why are you so disquieted? And why is your understanding troubled, and the thoughts of your heart?" [32] And I said, "Because you have forsaken me: yet I did according to your words, and went into the field, and behold, I have seen, and yet see, that which I am not able to express." [33] And he said to me, "Stand up like a man, and I will advise you." [34] Then I said, "Speak, my Lord; only do not forsake me, lest I die without hope. [35] For I have seen and heard that [which] I do not understand. [36] Or is my sense deceived, or my soul in a dream? [37] Now therefore, I implore you to show your servant concerning this vision." [38] And he answered me, and said, "Hear me, and I will inform you, and tell you concerning the things of which you are afraid. For the Most High has revealed many secret things to you. [39] He has seen that your way is right, for that you continually mourn for your people and make great lamentation for Zion. [40] Therefore, this is the meaning of the vision: [41] the woman which appeared to you a little while ago—whom you saw mourning, and began to comfort her, [42] but now you no longer see the likeness of the woman, but there appeared to you a city in building, [43] and whereas she told you of the death of her son—this is the solution: [44] this woman, whom you saw, is Zion, whom you now see as a city built. [45] And whereas she said to you that she has been barren [for] thirty years, [it is] because there were three thousand years in the world wherein there was no offering as yet offered in her. [46] And it came to pass after three thousand years, that Solomon built the city and offered offerings: then it was that the barren [woman] bore a son. [47] And whereas she told you that she nourished him with travail: that was the dwelling in Jerusalem. [48] And whereas she said to you, My son coming into his marriage chamber died, and that misfortune befell her: this was the destruction that came to Jerusalem. [49] And behold, you saw her likeness, how she mourned for her son, and you began to comfort her for what has befallen her: these were the things to be opened to you. [50] For now the Most High, seeing that you are grieved, and suffer from your whole heart for her, has showed you the brightness of her glory, and the attractiveness of her beauty: [51] and therefore I commanded you to remain in the field where no house was built, [52] for I knew that the Most High would show this to you. [53] Therefore I commanded you to come into the field where no foundation of any building was. [54] For in the place wherein the city of the Most High was to be shown, the work of no man's building could stand. [55] Therefore, do not fear, nor let your heart be frightened, but go your way in, and see the beauty and greatness of the building, as much as your eyes are able to see, [56] and then you will hear as much as your ears may comprehend. [57] For you are blessed above many, and are called by name with the Most High, like as but few. [58] But tomorrow at night you will remain here; [59] and so the Most High will show you those visions in dreams, of what the Most High will do to those who dwell on the earth in the last days." So I slept that night and another, just as he commanded me.

CHAPTER 11

[1] And it came to pass the second night that I saw a dream, and behold, there came up from the sea an eagle which had twelve feathered wings and three heads. [2] And I saw, and behold, she spread her wings over all the earth, and all the winds of the sky blew on her, and the clouds were gathered together against her. [3] And I saw, and out of her wings there grew [other] wings near them; and they became little wings and small. [4] But her heads were at rest: the head in the midst was greater than the other heads yet rested with them. [5] Moreover, I saw, and behold, the eagle flew with her wings, to reign over the earth, and over those who dwell therein. [6] And I saw how all things under Heaven were subject to her, and no man spoke against her, no, not one creature on earth. [7] And I saw, and behold, the eagle rose on her talons, and uttered her voice to her wings, saying, [8] "Do not watch all at once: everyone sleep in his own place, and watch by course; [9] but let the heads be preserved for the last." [10] And I saw, and behold, the voice did not go out of her heads, but from the midst of her body. [11] And I counted her wings that were near the other, and behold, there were eight of them. [12] And I saw, and behold, on the right side there arose one wing, and it reigned over all the earth; [13] and so it was, that when it reigned, the end of it came and it did not appear, so that the place thereof appeared no longer; and following [it], the next rose up and reigned, and it ruled a great time; [14] and it happened, that when it reigned, the end of it also came, so that it appeared no longer, just as the first. [15] And behold, there came a voice to it, and said, [16] "Hear—you that have borne rule over the earth all this time; this I proclaim to you, before you will appear no longer: [17] none after you will attain to your time, neither to the half thereof." [18] Then the third arose, and had the rule as the others before, and it also appeared no longer. [19] So it went with all the wings,

one after another, as that each one bore rule, and then appeared no longer. [20] And I saw, and behold, in process of time the wings that followed were set up on the right side, that they might also rule; and some of them ruled, but within a while they appeared no longer; [21] some of them also rose up, but did not rule. [22] After this I saw, and behold, the twelve wings appeared no longer, nor two of the little wings, [23] and there was no longer left on the eagle's body, but the three heads that rested, and six little wings. [24] And I saw, and behold, two little wings divided themselves from the six, and remained under the head that was on the right side, but four remained in their place. [25] And I saw, and behold, these wings under thought to set themselves up, and to have the rule. [26] And I saw, and behold, there was one set up, but within a while it appeared no longer. [27] A second also, and it was gone sooner than the first. [28] And I saw, and behold, the two that remained also thought in themselves to reign: [29] and while they so thought, behold, there awakened one of the heads that were at rest, [namely, it] that was in the midst; for that was greater than the two [other] heads. [30] And I saw how it joined the two [other] heads with it. [31] And behold, the head was turned with those who were with it, and it ate up the two wings under that thought to have reigned. [32] But this head held the whole earth in possession, and bore rule over those that dwell therein with much oppression; and it had the governance of the world more than all the wings that had been. [33] And after this I saw, and behold, the head that was in the midst also suddenly appeared no longer, just as the wings. [34] But there remained the two heads, which also in like manner reigned over the earth, and over those that dwell therein. [35] And I saw, and behold, the head on the right side devoured it that was on the left side. [36] Then I heard a voice, which said to me, "Look before you, and consider the thing that you see." [37] And I saw, and behold, as it were a lion roused out of the wood roaring; and I heard how that he sent out a man's voice to the eagle, and spoke, saying, [38] "Hear! I will talk with you, and the Most High will say to you, [39] Are you not it that remains of the four beasts, whom I made to reign in My world, that the end of My times might come through them? [40] And the fourth came, and overcame all the beasts that were past, and held the world in governance with great trembling, and the whole circle of the earth with grievous oppression; and for such a long time he lived on the earth with deceit. [41] And you have judged the earth, but not with truth. [42] For you have afflicted the meek, you have hurt the peaceful, you have hated those who speak truth, you have loved liars, and destroyed the dwellings of those who brought out fruit, and cast down the walls of such as did you no harm. [43] Therefore your insolent dealing has come up to the Most High, and your pride to the Mighty. [44] The Most High has also looked on His times, and behold,

they are ended, and His ages are fulfilled. [45] And therefore, appear no longer you eagle, nor your horrible wings, nor your evil little wings, nor your cruel heads, nor your hurtful talons, nor all your vain body, [46] that all the earth may be refreshed, and be eased, being delivered from your violence, and that she may hope for the judgment and mercy of Him that made her."

CHAPTER 12

[1] And it came to pass while the lion spoke these words to the eagle, I saw, [2] and behold, the head that remained appeared no longer, and the two wings which went over to it arose and set themselves up to reign, and their kingdom was small, and full of uproar. [3] And I saw, and behold, they appeared no longer, and the whole body of the eagle was burned, so that the earth was in great fear: then I awoke by reason of great ecstasy of mind, and from great fear, and said to my spirit, [4] "Behold, you have done this to me, in that you search out the ways of the Most High. [5] Behold, I am yet weary in my mind, and very weak in my spirit; nor is there the least strength in me, because of the great fear with which I was frightened this night. [6] Therefore, I will now implore the Most High, that He will strengthen me to the end." [7] And I said, "O LORD that bears rule, if I have found favor in Your sight, and if I am justified with You above many others, and if my prayer has indeed come up before Your face, [8] strengthen me then and show me, Your servant, the interpretation and plain meaning of this fearful vision, that You may perfectly comfort my soul. [9] For You have judged me worthy to show me the end of time and the last times." [10] And He said to me, "This is the interpretation of this vision which you saw: [11] the eagle, whom you saw come up from the sea, is the fourth kingdom which appeared in vision to your brother Daniel. [12] But it was not expounded to him, as I now expound it to you or have expounded it. [13] Behold, the days come that there will rise up a kingdom on earth, and it will be feared above all the kingdoms that were before it. [14] Twelve kings will reign in it, one after another, [15] of which the second will begin to reign and will have a longer time than [any of the] twelve. [16] This is the interpretation of the twelve wings, which you saw. [17] And whereas you heard a voice which spoke, not going out from the heads, but from the midst of the body thereof, this is the interpretation: [18] that after the time of that kingdom there will arise no small contentions, and it will stand in peril of falling; nevertheless, it will not then fall, but will be restored again to its first estate. [19] And whereas you saw the eight wings under sticking to her wings, this is the interpretation: [20] that there will arise eight kings in it, whose times will be but small, and their years swift. [21] And two of them will perish when the middle time approaches; four will be kept for awhile until the time of the ending

thereof will approach; but two will be kept to the end. ²² And whereas you saw three heads resting, this is the interpretation: ²³ in the last days thereof, the Most High will raise up three kingdoms, and renew many things therein, and they will bear rule over the earth, ²⁴ and over those that dwell therein, with much oppression, above all those that were before them. Therefore they are called the heads of the eagle. ²⁵ For these are those who will accomplish her wickedness, and that will finish her last end. ²⁶ And whereas you saw that the great head appeared no longer, [it signifies] that one of them will die on his bed, and yet with pain. ²⁷ But for the two that remained, the sword will devour them. ²⁸ For the sword of the one will devour him that was with him, but he will also fall by the sword in the last days. ²⁹ And whereas you saw two wings under passing over to the head that is on the right side, ³⁰ this is the interpretation: these are they whom the Most High has kept to His end; this is the small kingdom and full of trouble, as you saw. ³¹ And the lion, whom you saw rising up out of the wood, and roaring, and speaking to the eagle, and rebuking her for her unrighteousness, and all her words which you have heard: ³² this is the Anointed One, whom the Most High has kept to the end of days, who will spring up out of the seed of David, and He will come and speak to them, and reprove them for their wickedness and unrighteousness, and will heap up before them their contemptuous dealings. ³³ For at the first He will set them alive in His judgment, and when He has reproved them, He will destroy them. ³⁴ For He will deliver the rest of My people with mercy, those that have been preserved throughout My borders, and He will make them joyful until the coming of the end, even the Day of Judgment, of which I have spoken to you from the beginning. ³⁵ This is the dream that you saw, and this is the interpretation thereof: ³⁶ and you alone have been chosen to know the secret of the Most High. ³⁷ Therefore, write all these things that you have seen in a scroll and put them in a secret place, ³⁸ and you will teach them to the wise of your people, whose hearts you know are able to comprehend and keep these secrets. ³⁹ But wait here yourself yet seven more days, that there may be showed to you whatever it pleases the Most High to show you." And He departed from me. ⁴⁰ And it came to pass, when all the people saw that the seven days were past, and I had not come into the city again, they gathered themselves all together, from the least to the greatest, and came to me, and spoke to me, saying, ⁴¹ "How have we offended you? And what evil have we done against you that you have utterly forsaken us, and sit in this place? ⁴² For of all the prophets you alone are left to us, as a cluster of the vintage, and as a lamp in a dark place, and as a haven for a ship saved from the tempest. ⁴³ Are the evils which have come to us not sufficient? ⁴⁴ If you will forsake us, how much better

had it been for us if we had also been consumed in the burning of Zion! ⁴⁵ For we are not better than those who died there." And they wept with a loud voice. And I answered them, and said, ⁴⁶ "Be of good comfort, O Israel; and do not be sorrowful, you house of Jacob: ⁴⁷ for the Most High has you in remembrance, and the Mighty has not forgotten you forever. ⁴⁸ As for me, I have not forsaken you, neither have I departed from you, but have come into this place to pray for the desolation of Zion, and that I might seek mercy for the low estate of your sanctuary. ⁴⁹ And now go your way, every man to his own house, and after these days I will come to you." ⁵⁰ So the people went their way into the city, just as I said to them, ⁵¹ but I sat in the field seven days, as [the messenger] commanded me; and in those days I ate only of the flowers of the field and had my meat of the herbs.

CHAPTER 13

¹ And it came to pass after seven days, I dreamed a dream by night: ² and behold, there arose a wind from the sea, that it moved all the waves thereof. ³ And I saw, and behold, this wind caused to come up from the midst of the sea as it were the likeness of a Man, and I saw, and behold, that Man flew with the clouds of Heaven; and when He turned His countenance to look, all things trembled that were seen under Him. ⁴ And whenever the voice went out of His mouth, all those that heard His voice burned, just as the wax melts when it feels the fire. ⁵ And after this I saw, and behold, there was gathered together a multitude of men, out of number, from the four winds of the sky, to make war against the Man that came out of the sea. ⁶ And I saw, and behold, He carved Himself a great mountain, and flew on it. ⁷ But I sought to see the region or place where the mountain was graven, and I could not. ⁸ And after this I saw, and behold, all they which were gathered together to fight against Him were severely afraid, and yet dared fight. ⁹ And behold, as He saw the assault of the multitude that came, He neither lifted up His hand, nor held spear, nor any instrument of war, ¹⁰ but only I saw how that He sent out of His mouth as it had been a flood of fire, and out of His lips a flaming breath, and out of His tongue He cast out sparks of the storm. ¹¹ And these were all mixed together: the flood of fire, the flaming breath, and the great storm; and they fell on the assault of the multitude which was prepared to fight, and burned all of them up, so that suddenly nothing of [the] innumerable multitude was to be seen, but only dust of ashes and smell of smoke. When I saw this, I was amazed. ¹² Afterward I saw the same Man come down from the mountain, and call to Himself another multitude which was peaceful. ¹³ And many people came to Him, of which some were glad, some were sorry, some of them were bound, and some brought of those who were offered. Then through

great fear I awakened, and prayed to the Most High, and said, [14] "You have showed Your servant these wonders from the beginning, and have counted me worthy that You should receive my prayer: [15] and now show me, moreover, the interpretation of this dream. [16] For as I conceive in my understanding, woe to those who will be left in those days! And much more, woe to those who are not left! [17] For those who were not left will be in heaviness, [18] understanding the things that are laid up in the latter days, but not attaining to them. [19] But also woe to them that are left, for this reason; for they will see great perils and many necessities, just as these dreams declare. [20] Yet it is better for one to be in peril and to come into these things, than to pass away as a cloud out of the world, and not to see the things that will happen in the last days." And He answered to me, and said, [21] "I will tell you the interpretation of the vision, and I will also open to you the things of which you have made mention. [22] Whereas you have spoken of those who are left behind, this is the interpretation: [23] He that will endure the peril in that time will keep those who have fallen into danger, even such as have works and faith toward the Almighty. [24] Therefore, know that they which are left behind are more blessed than those who are dead. [25] These are the interpretations of the vision: whereas you saw a Man coming up from the midst of the sea, [26] this is He whom the Most High has kept a great season, which by His own self will deliver His creature; and He will order those who are left behind. [27] And whereas you saw that out of His mouth there came wind, and fire, and storm, [28] and whereas He held neither spear, nor any instrument of war, but destroyed the assault of that multitude which came to fight against Him, this is the interpretation: [29] behold, the days come when the Most High will begin to deliver those who are on the earth. [30] And there will come astonishment of mind on those who dwell on the earth. [31] And one will think to war against another—city against city, place against place, people against people, and kingdom against kingdom. [32] And it will be, when these things will come to pass, and the signs will happen which I showed you before, then My Son will be revealed, whom you saw [as] a Man ascending. [33] And it will be, when all the nations hear His voice, every man will leave his own land and the battle they have against one another. [34] And an innumerable multitude will be gathered together, as you saw, desiring to come and to fight against Him. [35] But He will stand on the top of Mount Zion. [36] And Zion will come, and will be shown to all men, being prepared and built, just as you saw the mountain graven without hands. [37] And He, My Son, will rebuke the nations which have come for their wickedness, [with plagues] that are like to a tempest; [38] and He will taunt them to their face with their evil thoughts, and the torments with which they will be tormented, which are likened to a flame; and He will destroy them without labor by the Law, which is likened to fire. [39] And whereas you saw that He gathered to Himself another multitude that was peaceful: [40] these are the ten tribes, which were led away out of their own land in the time of Hoshea the king, whom Salmananser the king of the Assyrians led away captive, and he carried them beyond the River, and they were carried into another land. [41] But they took this counsel among themselves, that they would leave the multitude of the heathen, and go out into a further country, where mankind never lived, [42] that they might keep their statutes there, which they had not kept in their own land. [43] And they entered by the narrow passages of the River Euphrates. [44] For the Most High then performed signs for them, and held back the springs of the River until they had passed over. [45] For through that country there was a great way to go, namely, of a year and a half: and the same region is called Arzareth. [46] Then they lived there until the latter time; and now when they begin to come again, [47] the Most High holds back the springs of the River again, that they may go through: therefore you saw the multitude gathered together with peace. [48] But those that are left behind of your people are those who are found within My holy border. [49] It will be, therefore, when He will destroy the multitude of the nations that are gathered together, He will defend the people that remain. [50] And then He will show them very many wonders." [51] Then I said, "O LORD that bears rule, show me this: why I have seen the Man coming up from the midst of the sea." [52] And He said to me, "Just as one can neither seek out nor know what is in the deep of the sea, even so can no man on earth see My Son, or those that are with Him, but in the time of His day. [53] This is the interpretation of the dream which you saw, and for this you only are enlightened herein. [54] For you have forsaken your own [ways, and] applied your diligence to Mine, and have sought out My law. [55] You have ordered your life in wisdom and have called understanding your mother. [56] And therefore I have showed you this; for there is a reward laid up with the Most High; and it will be, after another three days I will speak other things to you and declare to you mighty and wondrous things." [57] Then I went out and passed into the field, greatly giving praise and thanks to the Most High because of His wonders, which He did from time to time, [58] and because He governs the time, and such things as fall in their seasons. And there I sat three days.

CHAPTER 14

[1] And it came to pass on the third day, I sat under an oak, and behold, there came a voice out of a bush near me, and said, "Ezra, Ezra." [2] And I said, "Here I am, Lord." And I stood up on my feet. [3] Then He said to me, "In the bush I manifestly revealed Myself, and talked with Moses when My people were in bondage in Egypt: [4] and I sent him, and he led My people out

of Egypt; and I brought him up to [the] mountain of Sinai, where I kept him near Me for many days, ⁵ and told him many wondrous things, and showed him the secrets of the times, and the end of the seasons, and commanded him, saying, ⁶ You will publish these words openly, and these you will hide. ⁷ And now I say to you, ⁸ lay up in your heart the signs that I have showed, and the dreams that you have seen, and the interpretations which you have heard: ⁹ for you will be taken away from men, and from now on you will remain with My Son, and with such as are like you, until the times are ended. ¹⁰ For the world has lost its youth, and the times begin to wax old. ¹¹ For the world is divided into twelve parts, and ten parts of it are already gone, even the half of the tenth part: ¹² and there remains of it two parts after the middle of the tenth part. ¹³ Now therefore, set your house in order, and reprove your people, comfort the lowly among them, and instruct such of them as are wise, and now renounce the life that is corruptible, ¹⁴ and let go from the mortal thoughts, cast yourself away from the burdens of man, put off now your weak nature, ¹⁵ and lay aside the thoughts that are most grievous to you, and hasten to depart from these times. ¹⁶ For yet worse evils than those which you have seen happen will be done hereafter. ¹⁷ For see how much the world will be weaker through age—so much the more will evils increase on those who dwell therein. ¹⁸ For the truth will withdraw itself further off, and falsehood will be hard at hand; for now the eagle which you saw in [the] vision hastens to come." ¹⁹ Then I answered and said, "I will speak before You, O Lord. ²⁰ Behold, I will go, as You have commanded me, and reprove the people that now are, but those who will be born afterward, who will admonish them? For the world is set in darkness, and those who dwell therein are without light. ²¹ For Your law is burned, therefore no man knows the things that You have done, or the works that will be done. ²² But if I have found favor before You, send the Holy Spirit to me, and I will write all that has been done in the world since the beginning, even the things that were written in Your law, that men may be able to find the path, and that they which would live in the latter days may live." ²³ And He answered me and said, "Go your way, gather the people together, and say to them that they may not seek you for forty days. ²⁴ But prepare many tablets, and take with you Sarea, Dabria, Selemia, Ethanus, and Asiel, these five, which are ready to write swiftly; ²⁵ and come here, and I will light a lamp of understanding in your heart, which will not be put out until the things which you will write are ended. ²⁶ And when you have done this, some things you will publish openly, and some things you will deliver in secret to the wise. Tomorrow at this hour you will begin to write." ²⁷ Then I went out, as He commanded me, and gathered all the people together, and said, ²⁸ "Hear these words, O Israel. ²⁹ At the beginning our fathers were strangers in Egypt, and they were delivered from there, ³⁰ and received the law of life, which they did not keep, which you also have transgressed after them. ³¹ Then the land, even the land of Zion, was given to you for a possession, but you yourselves, and your fathers, have done unrighteousness, and have not kept the ways which the Most High commanded you. ³² And forasmuch as He is a righteous judge, He took from you for awhile the thing that He had given to you. ³³ And now you are here, and your relatives are among you. ³⁴ Therefore, if [it] so be that you will rule over your own understanding, and instruct your hearts, you will be kept alive, and after death you will obtain mercy. ³⁵ For after death the judgment will come when we will live again; and then the names of the righteous will be manifest, and the works of the ungodly will be declared. ³⁶ Therefore, let no man come to me now, nor seek after me these forty days." ³⁷ So I took the five men as He commanded me, and we went out into the field and remained there. ³⁸ And it came to pass on the next day that, behold, a voice called me, saying, "Ezra, open your mouth, and drink what I give you to drink." ³⁹ Then I opened my mouth, and behold, there was given to me a full cup, which was full as it were with water, but the color of it was like fire. ⁴⁰ And I took it and drank. And when I had drunk of it, my heart uttered understanding, and wisdom grew in my breast, for my spirit retained its memory; ⁴¹ and my mouth was opened and no longer shut. ⁴² The Most High gave understanding to the five men, and they wrote by course the things that were told them, in characters which they did not know, and they sat [for] forty days. Now they wrote in the daytime, and at night they ate bread. ⁴³ As for me, I spoke in the day, and I did not hold my tongue by night. ⁴⁴ So in forty days ninety-four scrolls were written. ⁴⁵ And it came to pass, when the forty days were fulfilled, that the Most High spoke to me, saying, "The first that you have written publish openly, and let the worthy and unworthy read it, ⁴⁶ but keep the seventy last, that you may deliver them to such as are wise among your people, ⁴⁷ for in them is the spring of understanding, the fountain of wisdom, and the stream of knowledge." ⁴⁸ And I did so.

CHAPTER 15

¹ "Behold, speak in the ears of My people the words of prophecy, which I will put in your mouth," says the Lord; ² "and cause them to be written in paper, for they are faithful and true. ³ Do not be afraid of their imaginations against you, do not let the unbelief of them that speak against you trouble you. ⁴ For all the unbelievers will die in their unbelief. ⁵ Behold," says the Lord, "I bring calamities on the whole earth: sword, and famine, and death, and destruction. ⁶ For wickedness has prevailed over every land, and their hurtful works have come to the full. ⁷ Therefore," says

the LORD, [8]"I will no longer hold My peace as touching their wickedness, which they profanely commit, neither will I permit them in these things, which they wickedly practice. Behold, the innocent and righteous blood cries to Me, and the souls of the righteous cry out continually. [9]I will surely avenge them," says the LORD, "and will receive to Myself all the innocent blood from among them. [10]Behold, My people are led as a flock to the slaughter: I will not permit them to now dwell in the land of Egypt, [11]but I will bring them out with a mighty hand and with a high arm, and will strike Egypt with plagues, as previously, and will destroy all the land thereof. [12]Let Egypt mourn, and the foundations thereof, for the plague of the discipline and the punishment that God will bring on it. [13]Let the farmers that till the ground mourn, for their seeds will fail and their trees will be laid waste through the blasting, and hail, and a terrible storm. [14]Woe to the world and those who dwell therein! [15]For the sword and their destruction draws near, and nation will rise up against nation to battle with weapons in their hands. [16]For there will be sedition among men; and waxing strong against one another, they will not regard their king nor the chief of their great ones, in their might. [17]For a man will desire to go into a city and will not be able. [18]For because of their pride the cities will be troubled, the houses will be destroyed, and men will be afraid. [19]A man will have no pity on his neighbor but will make an assault on their houses with the sword, and plunder their goods, because of the lack of bread, and for great suffering. [20]Behold," says God, "I call together all the kings of the earth, to stir up those who are from the rising of the sun, from the south, from the east, and Libanus, to turn themselves against one another, and repay the things that they have done to them. [21]Just as they yet do this day to My chosen, so I will do also, and repay in their bosom." The LORD God says: [22]"My right hand will not spare the sinners, and My sword will not cease over those who shed innocent blood on the earth. [23]And a fire has gone out from His wrath, and has consumed the foundations of the earth, and the sinners, like the straw that is kindled. [24]Woe to those who sin and do not keep My commands!" says the LORD. [25]"I will not spare them. Go your way, you rebellious children, do not defile My sanctuary. [26]For the LORD knows all those who trespass against Him, therefore He has delivered them to death and destruction. [27]For now the calamities have come on the whole earth, and you will remain in them, for God will not deliver you, because you have sinned against Him. [28]Behold, a horrible vision, and the appearance thereof from the east! [29]And the nations of the dragons of Arabia will come out with many chariots, and from the day that they set out the hissing of them is carried over the earth, so that all they which will hear them may also fear and tremble. [30]Also the Carmonians raging in wrath will go out as the wild

boars of the wood, and they will come with great power and join battle with them, and will waste a portion of the land of the Assyrians with their teeth. [31]And then the dragons will have the upper hand, remembering their nature; and if they will turn themselves, conspiring together in great power to persecute them, [32]then these will be troubled, and keep silence through their power, and will turn and flee. [33]And from the land of the Assyrians the ambusher in wait will besiege them, and consume one of them, and on their army will be fear and trembling, and sedition against their kings. [34]Behold, clouds from the east and from the north to the south, and they are very horrible to look on—full of wrath and storm. [35]They will dash one against another, and they will pour out a plentiful storm on the earth, even their own storm; and there will be blood from the sword to the horse's belly, [36]and to the thigh of man, and to the camel's hock. [37]And there will be fearfulness and great trembling on earth: and they that see that wrath will be afraid, and trembling will take hold on them. [38]And after this there will be stirred up great storms from the south, and from the north, and another part from the west. [39]And strong winds will arise from the east, and will shut it up, even the cloud which He raised up in wrath; and the storm that was to cause destruction by the east wind will be violently driven toward the south and west. [40]And great clouds, indeed mighty and full of wrath, will be lifted up—and the storm—that they may destroy all the earth, and those who dwell therein; and they will pour out over every high and eminent one a terrible storm, [41][with] fire, and hail, and flying swords, and many waters, that all plains may be full, and all rivers, with the abundance of those waters. [42]And they will break down the cities and walls, mountains and hills, trees of the wood, and grass of the meadows, and their corn. [43]And they will go on steadfastly to Babylon and destroy her. [44]They will come to her and surround her; they will pour out the storm and all wrath on her; then the dust and smoke will rise up to the sky, and all those who are around her will mourn her. [45]And those who remain will do service to those who have put her in fear. [46]And you, Asia, that are partaker in the beauty of Babylon, and in the glory of her person: [47]woe to you, you wretch, because you have made yourself like to her; you have decked your daughters in whoredom, that they might please and glory in your lovers, which have always desired you to commit whoredom with! [48]You have followed her that is hateful in all her works and inventions: therefore," says God, [49]"I will send evils on you: widowhood, poverty, famine, sword, and pestilence, to waste your houses to destruction and death. [50]And the glory of your power will be dried up as a flower, when the heat will arise that is sent over you. [51]You will be weakened as a poor woman with stripes, and as one disciplined with wounds, so that you will not be able to receive your mighty ones and [your] lovers. [52] Would I with jealousy have so proceeded against you," says the LORD, [53] "if you had not always slain My chosen, exalting the stroke of your hands, and saying over their dead, when you were drunken, [54] Set out the beauty of your countenance? [55] The reward of a prostitute will be in your bosom, therefore you will receive repayment. [56] Just as you will do to My chosen," says the LORD, "even so God will do to you, and will deliver you into mischief. [57] And your children will die of hunger, and you will fall by the sword, and your cities will be broken down, and all yours will perish by the sword in the field. [58] And those who are in the mountains will die of hunger, and eat their own flesh, and drink [their own] blood, for great hunger of bread, and thirst of water. [59] You, unhappy above all, will come and will receive calamities again. [60] And in the passage, they will rush on the idle city, and will destroy some portion of your land, and mar part of your glory, and will again return to Babylon that was destroyed. [61] And you will be cast down by them as stubble, and they will be to you as fire, [62] and will devour you, and your cities, your land, and your mountains; they will burn up all your woods and your fruitful trees with fire. [63] They will carry your children away captive, and will plunder your wealth, and mar the glory of your face."

CHAPTER 16

[1] "Woe to you, Babylon and Asia! Woe to you, Egypt and Syria! [2] Gird yourselves with sackcloth and garments of hair, and mourn your children, and lament; for your destruction is at hand. [3] A sword is sent on you, and who is he that may turn it back? [4] A fire is sent on you, and who is he that may quench it? [5] Calamities are sent on you, and who is he that may drive them away? [6] May one drive away a hungry lion in the wood? Or may one quench the fire in stubble, when it has once begun to burn? [7] May one turn again the arrow that is shot of a strong archer? [8] The LORD God sends the evils, and who will drive them away? [9] A fire will go out from His wrath, and who is he that may quench it? [10] He will cast lightning, and who will not fear? He will thunder, and who will not tremble? [11] The LORD will threaten, and who will not be utterly broken in pieces at His presence? [12] The earth quakes, and the foundations thereof; the sea arises with waves from the deep, and the waves of it will be troubled, and also the fishes thereof, at the presence of the LORD, and before the glory of His power: [13] for strong is His right hand that bends the bow; His arrows that He shoots are sharp, and will not miss, when they begin to be shot into the ends of the world. [14] Behold, the calamities are sent out, and will not return again, until they come on the earth. [15] The fire is kindled, and will not be put out, until it consumes the foundations of the earth. [16] Just as an arrow which is shot by a mighty archer does not return backward, even so the

calamities that are sent out on earth will not return again. [17] Woe is me! Woe is me! Who will deliver me in those days? [18] The beginning of sorrows, and the great mourning; the beginning of famine, and many will perish; the beginning of wars, and the powers will stand in fear; the beginning of calamities, and all will tremble! What will they do in [all] this when the calamities will come? [19] Behold, famine and plague, suffering and anguish! They are sent as scourges for amendment. [20] But for all these things they will not turn them from their wickedness, nor be always mindful of the scourges. [21] Behold, food will be so cheap on earth that they will think themselves to be in a good case, and even then, calamities will grow on earth: sword, famine, and great confusion. [22] For many of those who dwell on earth will perish of famine; and the other, that escape the famine, will the sword destroy. [23] And the dead will be cast out as dung, and there will be no man to comfort them, for the earth will be left desolate, and the cities thereof will be cast down. [24] There will be no farmer left to till the earth, and to sow it. [25] The trees will give fruit, and who will gather them? [26] The grapes will ripen, and who will tread them? For in [all] places there will be a great forsaking. [27] for one man will desire to see another, or to hear his voice. [28] For of a city there will be ten left, and two of the field, which have hidden themselves in the thick groves, and in the clefts of the rocks. [29] As in an orchard of olives on every tree there are left three or four olives, [30] or as when a vineyard is gathered there are some clusters left by those who diligently seek through the vineyard; [31] even so in those days there will be three or four left by those who search their houses with the sword. [32] And the earth will be left desolate, and the fields thereof will be for briers, and her ways and all her paths will bring out thorns, because no sheep will pass through there. [33] The virgins will mourn, having no bridegrooms; the women will mourn, having no husbands; their daughters will mourn, having no helpers. [34] In the wars their bridegrooms will be destroyed, and their husbands will perish of famine. [35] Now hear these things, and understand them, you servants of the LORD. [36] Behold, the word of the LORD, receive it: do not disbelieve the things of which the LORD speaks. [37] Behold, the calamities draw near, and are not slack. [38] Just as a woman with child in the ninth month, when the hour of her delivery draws near, within two or three hours sorrowful pains surround her womb, and when the child comes out from the womb, there will be no waiting for [even] a moment: [39] even so the calamities will not be slack to come on the earth, and the world will groan, and sorrows will take hold of it on every side. [40] O My people, hear My word: make ready for the battle, and in those calamities be even as pilgrims on the earth. [41] He that sells, let him be as he that flees away; and he that buys, as one that will lose; [42] he that occupies merchandise, as he that has no profit by it; and he that builds, as he that will not dwell therein; [43] he that sows, as if he should not reap; so also he that prunes [the vines], as he that will not gather the grapes; [44] those who marry, as those who will get no children; and those who do not marry, as the widowed. [45] Because of this, those who labor labor in vain; [46] for strangers will reap their fruits, and plunder their goods, overthrow their houses, and take their children captive, for in captivity and famine they will beget their children; [47] and those who traffic traffic to become a plunder—the more they deck their cities, their houses, their possessions, and their own persons, [48] the more I will hate them for their sins," says the LORD. [49] "Just as a rightly honest and virtuous woman hates a prostitute, [50] so righteousness will hate iniquity when she decks herself, and will accuse her to her face when He comes that will defend him that diligently searches out every sin on earth. [51] Therefore, do not be like them, nor do the works thereof. [52] For yet a little while, and iniquity will be taken away out of the earth, and righteousness will reign over us. [53] Do not let the sinner say that he has not sinned, for he will burn coals of fire on his head, which says, I have not sinned before God and His glory. [54] Behold, the LORD knows all the works of men, their imaginations, their thoughts, and their hearts— [55] [He] who said, Let the earth be made, and it was made; [and,] Let the heaven be made, and it was made; [56] and at His word the stars were established, and He knows the number of the stars; [57] who searches the deep, and the treasures thereof; He has measured the sea, and what it contains; [58] who has shut the sea in the midst of the waters, and with His word He has hanged the earth on the waters; [59] who spreads out the sky like a vault; He has established it on the waters; [60] who has made springs of water in the desert, and pools on the tops of the mountains, to send out rivers from the height to water the earth; [61] who framed man and put a heart in the midst of the body, and gave him breath, life, and understanding— [62] yes, the Spirit of God Almighty. He who made all things, and searches out hidden things in hidden places, [63] surely He knows your imagination, and what you think in your hearts. Woe to those who sin and would gladly hide their sin! [64] Because of this, the LORD will exactly search out all your works, and He will put you all to shame. [65] And when your sins are brought out before men, you will be ashamed, and your own iniquities will stand as your accusers in that day. [66] What will you do? Or how will you hide your sins before God and His messengers? [67] Behold, God is the judge—fear Him: depart from your sins, and forget your iniquities, to no longer meddle with them forever, so God will lead you out, and deliver you from all suffering. [68] For behold, the burning wrath of a great multitude is kindled over you, and they will take away certain of you, and feed you with that which is slain to idols. [69] And those who consent to them will be held in derision and in reproach and will be trodden under their foot. [70] For there will be in various places, and in the next cities, a great insurrection on those that fear the LORD. [71] They will be like mad men, sparing none, but spoiling and destroying those who still fear the LORD. [72] For they will waste and take away their goods and cast them out of their houses. [73] Then the trial of My chosen ones will be manifested, even as the gold that is tried in the fire. [74] Hear, O you My chosen ones," says the LORD: "behold, the days of suffering are at hand, and I will deliver you from them. [75] Do not be afraid, neither doubt; for God is your guide. [76] And you who keep My commands and precepts," says the LORD God, "do not let your sins weigh you down, and do not let your iniquities lift themselves up. [77] Woe to those who are fast bound with their sins, and covered with their iniquities, like as a field is fast bound with bushes, and the path thereof covered with thorns, that no man may travel through! [78] It is even shut off and given up to be consumed by fire."

3 MACCABEES

The book of 3 Maccabees is found in most Orthodox Bibles as a part of the deuterocanon. Catholics consider it to be an example of pseudepigrapha and do not regard it as canonical. Protestants, with the exception of the Moravian Brothers who include it in the Apocrypha of the Czech Kralice Bible and Polish Gdańsk Bible, likewise regard it as non-canonical. Despite the title, the book has nothing to do with the Maccabees or their revolt against the Seleucid Empire, as described in 1 Maccabees and 2 Maccabees. Instead, it tells the story of persecution of the Jews under Ptolemy IV Philopator (222–205 BC), some decades before the Maccabean uprising. The name of the book apparently comes from the similarities between this book and the stories of the martyrdom of Eleazar and the Maccabean youths in 2 Maccabees; the chief priest Shimon is also mentioned.

CHAPTER 1

[1] When Philopator learned from those who came back that Antiochus had made himself master of the places which belonged to himself, he sent orders to all his footmen and horsemen, took his sister Arsinoe with him, and marched out as far as the parts of Raphia, where Antiochus and his forces encamped. [2] And one Theodotus, intending to carry out his design, took with him the bravest of the armed men who had been previously committed to his trust by Ptolemy, and got through at night to the tent of Ptolemy, to kill him on his own responsibility, and so to end the war. [3] But Dositheus, called the son of Drimulus, by birth a Jew, afterward a renegade from the laws and observances of his country, carried Ptolemy away, and made an obscure person lie down in his place in the tent. It befell this man to receive the fate which was meant for the other. [4] A fierce battle then took place, and the men of Antiochus prevailing, Arsinoe continually went up and down the ranks, and with disheveled hair, with tears and pleadings, begged the soldiers to fight courageously for themselves, their children, and wives; and promised that if they proved conquerors, she would give them each two minas of gold. [5] It then happened that their enemies were defeated in hand-to-hand encounter, and that many of them were taken prisoners. [6] Having vanquished this attempt, the king then decided to proceed to the neighboring cities and encourage them. [7] By doing this, and by making donations to their temples, he inspired his subjects with confidence. [8] The Jews sent some of their council and of their elders to him. The greetings, gifts of welcome, and commendations of the past, bestowed by them, filled him with the greater eagerness to visit their city. [9] Having arrived at Jerusalem, sacrificed, and offered thank-offerings to the greatest God, and done whatever else was suitable to the sanctity of the place, and entered the inner court, [10] he was so struck with the magnificence of the place, and so wondered at the orderly arrangements of the temple, that he considered entering the sanctuary itself. [11] And when they told him that this was not permissible, none of the nation, no, nor even the priests in general, but only the supreme chief priest of all, and he only once in a year, being allowed to go in, he would by no means give way. [12] Then they read the Law to him; but he persisted in obtruding himself, exclaiming that he should be allowed, and saying, "Be it that they were deprived of this honor, I should not be." [13] And he put the question, "Why, when he entered all the temples, did none of the priests who were present forbid him?" [14] He was thoroughly answered by someone, that he did wrong to boast of this. [15] "Well; since I have done this," he said, "be the cause what it may, will I not enter with or without your consent?" [16] And when the priests fell down in their sacred vestments imploring the greatest God to come and help in time of need, and to avert the violence of the fierce aggressor, and when they filled the temple with lamentations and tears, [17] then those who had been left behind in the city were scared, and rushed out, uncertain of the event. [18] Virgins, who had been shut up within their chambers, came out with their mothers, scattering dust and ashes on their heads, and filling the streets with outcries. [19] Women, but recently separated off, left their bridal chambers, left the reserve that suited them, and ran around the city in a disorderly manner. [20] Newborn babies were deserted by the mothers or nurses who waited on them; some here, some there— in houses, or in fields; these now, with a zeal which could not be checked, swarmed into the most high temple. [21] Manifold prayers were offered up by those who assembled in this place, on account of the unholy attempt of the king. [22] Along with these there were some of the citizens who took courage, and would not submit to his obstinacy, and his intention of carrying out his purpose. [23] Calling out to arms, and to die bravely in defense of the law of their fathers, they created a great uproar in the place, and were with difficulty brought back by the aged and the elders to the station of prayer which they had occupied before. [24] During this time, the multitude kept on praying. [25] The elders who surrounded the king tried in many ways to divert his arrogant mind from the design which he had formed. [26] He, in his hardened mood, insensible to all persuasion, was going onward with the view of carrying out this design. [27] Yet even his own officers, when they saw this, joined the Jews in

an appeal to Him who has all power, to aid in the present crisis, and not to wink at such overconfident lawlessness. [28] Such was the frequency and the vehemence of the cry of the assembled crowd, that an indescribable noise ensued. [29] Not the men only, but the very walls and floor seemed to sound out—all things preferring dissolution rather than to see the place defiled.

CHAPTER 2

[1] Then the chief priest Simon bowed his knees near the holy place, and spread out his hands in reverent form, and uttered the following supplication: [2] "O LORD, LORD, King of the heavens, and Ruler of the whole creation, Holy among the holy, sole Governor, Almighty, give ear to us who are oppressed by a wicked and profane one, who celebrates in his confidence and strength. [3] It is You, the Creator of all, the Lord of the universe, who are a righteous Governor, and judge all who act with pride and insolence. [4] It was You who destroyed the former workers of unrighteousness, among whom were the giants, who trusted in their strength and daring, by covering them with a measureless flood. [5] It was You who made the Sodomites, those workers of exceeding iniquity, men notorious for their vices, an example to following generations, when You covered them with fire and brimstone. [6] You made Your power known when You caused the bold Pharaoh, the enslaver of Your people, to pass through the ordeal of many and diverse afflictions. [7] And You rolled the depths of the sea over him, when he made pursuit with chariots, and with a multitude of followers, and gave a safe passage to those who put their trust in You, the Lord of the whole creation. [8] These saw and felt the works of Your hands, and praised You, the Almighty. [9] You, O King, when You created the limitless and measureless earth, chose out this city: You made this place sacred to Your Name, albeit You need nothing. You glorified it with Your illustrious presence, after constructing it to the glory of Your great and honorable Name. [10] And You promised, out of love, to the people of Israel, that should we fall away from You, and become afflicted, and then come to this house and pray, You would hear our prayer. [11] Truly You are faithful and true. [12] And when You often aided our fathers when hard-pressed, and in low estate, and delivered them out of great dangers, [13] see now, holy King, how through our many and great sins we are borne down, and made subject to our enemies, and have become weak and powerless. [14] We being in this low condition, this bold and profane man seeks to dishonor this, Your holy place, consecrated out of the earth to the Name of Your Majesty. [15] Your dwelling place, the Heaven of heavens, is indeed unapproachable to men. [16] But since it seemed good to You to exhibit Your glory among Your people Israel, You sanctified this place. [17] Do not punish us by

means of the uncleanness of their men, nor discipline us by means of their profanity, lest the lawless ones should boast in their rage, and exult in exuberant pride of speech, and say, [18] We have trampled on the holy house, as idolatrous houses are trampled on. [19] Blot out our iniquities, and do away with our errors, and show forth Your compassion in this hour. [20] Let Your mercies quickly go before us. Grant us peace, that the cast down and brokenhearted may praise You with their mouth." [21] At that time God, who sees all things, who is beyond all Holy among the holy, heard that prayer, so suitable, and scourged the man greatly uplifted with scorn and insolence. [22] Shaking him to and fro as a reed is shaken with the wind, He cast him on the pavement, powerless, with limbs paralyzed, by a righteous judgment deprived [him] of the faculty of speech. [23] His friends and bodyguards, beholding the swift repayment which had suddenly overtaken him, struck with exceeding terror, and fearing that he would die, speedily removed him. [24] When in [the] course of time he had come to himself, this severe check caused no conversion within him, but he departed with bitter threats. [25] He proceeded to Egypt, grew worse in wickedness through his aforementioned companions in wine, who were lost to all goodness; [26] and not satisfied with countless acts of impiety, his audacity so increased that he raised evil reports there, and many of his friends, watching his purpose attentively, joined in furthering his will. [27] His purpose was to indict a public stigma on our race; for that reason, he erected a pillar at the tower-porch, and caused the following inscription to be engraved on it: [28] "THE ENTRANCE TO THEIR TEMPLE IS TO BE REFUSED TO ALL THOSE WHO WILL NOT SACRIFICE; ALL THE JEWS ARE TO BE REGISTERED AMONG THE COMMON PEOPLE; THOSE WHO RESIST ARE TO BE FORCIBLY SEIZED AND PUT TO DEATH; [29] THOSE WHO ARE SO REGISTERED, ARE TO BE MARKED ON THEIR PERSONS BY THE IVY-LEAF SYMBOL OF DIONYSUS, AND TO BE SET APART WITH THESE LIMITED RIGHTS." [30] To do away with the appearance of hating them all, he had it written underneath: "IF ANY OF THEM SHOULD CHOOSE TO ENTER THE COMMUNITY OF THOSE INITIATED IN THE RITES, THESE SHOULD HAVE EQUAL RIGHTS WITH THE ALEXANDRIANS." [31] Some of those who were over the city, therefore, abhorring any approach to the city of piety, unhesitatingly gave in to the king, and expected to derive some great honor from a future connection with him. [32] A nobler spirit, however, prompted the majority to cling to their religious observances, and by paying money that they might live unmolested, these sought to escape the registration. [33] Cheerfully looking forward to future aid, they abhorred their own apostates, considering them to be national enemies, and were debarring them from the common usages of social intercourse.

CHAPTER 3

[1] On discovering this, so incensed was the wicked king that he no longer confined his rage to the Jews in Alexandria. Laying his hand more heavily on those who lived in the country, he gave orders that they should be quickly collected into one place, and most cruelly deprived of their lives. [2] While this was going on, an invidious rumor was uttered abroad by men who had banded together to injure the Jewish race. The purport of their charge was that the Jews kept them away from the ordinances of the law. [3] Now, while the Jews always maintained a feeling of unwavering loyalty toward the kings, [4] yet, as they worshiped God, and observed His law, they made certain distinctions, and avoided certain things. Hence some persons held them in revulsion; [5] although, as they adorned their conversation with works of righteousness, they had established themselves in the good opinion of the world. [6] What all the rest of mankind said, was, however, made of no account by the foreigners, [7] who said much of the exclusiveness of the Jews with regard to their worship and meats; they alleged that they were unsociable men, hostile to the king's interests, refusing to associate with him or his troops. By this way of speaking, they brought much odium on them. [8] Nor was this unexpected uproar and sudden conflux of people unobserved by the Greeks who lived in the city, concerning men who had never harmed them: yet to aid them was not in their power, since there was oppression all around, but they encouraged them in their troubles, and expected a favorable turn of affairs. [9] He who knows all things, will not, [they said,] disregard so great a people. [10] Some of the neighbors, friends, and fellow dealers of the Jews, even called them secretly to an interview, pledged them their assistance, and promised to do their very utmost for them. [11] Now the king, elated with his prosperous fortune, and not regarding the superior power of God, but thinking to persevere in his present purpose, wrote the following letter to the prejudice of the Jews: [12] "King Ptolemy Philopator, to the commanders and soldiers in Egypt, and in all places, health and happiness! [13] I am right [and] well; and so, too, are my affairs. [14] Since our Asiatic campaign, the particulars of which you know, and which by the aid of the gods, not lightly given, and by our own vigor, has been brought to a successful issue according to our expectation, [15] we resolved, not with strength of spear, but with gentleness and much humanity, as it were to nurse the inhabitants of Coele-Syria and Phoenicia, and to be their willing benefactors. [16] So, having bestowed considerable sums of money on the temples of the several cities, we proceeded even as far as Jerusalem, and went up to honor the temple of these wretched beings who never cease from their folly. [17] To outward appearance they received us willingly, but belied that appearance by their deeds. When we were eager to enter their temple, and to honor it with the most beautiful and exquisite gifts, [18] they were so carried away by their old arrogance, as to forbid us the entrance; while we, out of our forbearance toward all men, refrained from exercising our power on them. [19] And so, exhibiting their enmity against us, they alone among the nations lift up their heads against kings and benefactors, as men unwilling to submit to anything reasonable. [20] We then, having endeavored to make allowance for the madness of these persons, and on our victorious return treating all people in Egypt courteously, acted in a manner which was befitting. [21] Accordingly, bearing no ill-will against their countrymen [at Jerusalem], but rather remembering our connection with them, and the numerous matters with sincere heart from a remote period entrusted to them, we wished to venture a total alteration of their state, by giving them the rights of citizens of Alexandria, and to admit them to the continuous rites of our solemnities. [22] All this, however, they have taken in a very different spirit. With their innate malignity, they have spurned the fair offer; and constantly inclining to evil, [23] have rejected the inestimable rights. Not only so, but by using speech, and by refraining from speech, they abhor the few among them who are heartily disposed toward us, ever deeming that their ignoble course of procedure will force us to do away with our reform. [24] Having then received certain proofs that these [Jews] bear us every sort of ill-will, we must look forward to the possibility of some sudden tumult among ourselves, when these impious men may turn traitors and barbarous enemies. [25] As soon, therefore, as the contents of this letter become known to you, in that same hour we order those [Jews] who dwell among you, with wives and children, to be sent to us, vilified and abused, in chains of iron, to undergo a death, cruel and ignominious, suitable to disaffected men. [26] For by the punishment of them in one body we perceive that we have found the only means of establishing our affairs for the future on a firm and satisfactory basis. [27] Whoever will shield a Jew, whether it be old man, child, or nursing baby, will with his whole house be tortured to death. [28] Whoever will inform against the [Jews], besides receiving the property of the person charged, will be presented with two thousand drachmas from the royal treasury, will be made free, and will be crowned. [29] Whatever place will shelter a Jew, will, when he is hunted out, be put under the ban of fire, and be forever rendered useless to every living being for all time to come." [30] Such was the purport of the king's letter.

CHAPTER 4

[1] Wherever this decree was received, the people kept up a revelry of joy and shouting, as if their long-pent-up, hardened hatred, was now to show itself openly.

² The Jews suffered great throes of sorrow and wept much, while their hearts, all things around being lamentable, were set on fire as they mourned the sudden destruction which was decreed against them. ³ What home, or city, or place at all inhabited, or what streets were there, which their condition did not fill with wailing and lamentation? ⁴ They were sent out unanimously by the generals in the several cities, with such stern and pitiless feeling, that the exceptional nature of the infliction moved even some of their enemies. These influenced by sentiments of common humanity, and reflecting on the uncertain issue of life, shed tears at this miserable expulsion of theirs. ⁵ A multitude of aged, gray-haired old men, were driven along with halting [and] bending feet, urged onward by the impulse of a violent, shameless force to quick speed. ⁶ Girls who had entered the bridal chamber quite lately, to enjoy the partnership of marriage, exchanged pleasure for misery, and with dust scattered on their myrrh-anointed heads, were hurried along unveiled, and, in the midst of outlandish insults, set up a lamentable cry with one accord instead of the marriage hymn. ⁷ Bound, and exposed to public gaze, they were violently hurried on board ship. ⁸ The husbands of these, in the prime of their youthful vigor, wore halters around their necks instead of crowns; instead of feasting and youthful celebration, they spent the rest of their nuptial days in wailing, and saw only the grave at hand. ⁹ They were dragged along by unyielding chains, like wild beasts; of these, some had their necks thrust into the benches of the rowers, while the feet of others were enclosed in hard chains. ¹⁰ The planks of the deck above them blocked out the light, and shut out the day on every side, so that they might be treated like traitors during the whole voyage. ¹¹ They were accordingly transported in this vessel, and at the end of it arrived at Schedia. The king had ordered them to be cast into the vast hippodrome, which was built in front of the city. This place was well adapted by its situation to expose them to the gaze of all those coming into the city, and of those who went from the city into the country. So they could hold no communication with his forces, no, [and] were deemed unworthy of any civilized accommodation. ¹² When this was done, the king, hearing that their relatives in the city often went out and lamented the melancholy distress of these victims, ¹³ was full of rage, and commanded that they should be carefully subjected to the same (and not one bit milder) treatment. ¹⁴ The whole nation was now to be registered. Every individual was to be specified by name, not for that hard servitude of labor which we have shortly before mentioned, but that he might expose them to the previously mentioned tortures; and finally, in the short space of a day, might eradicate them by his cruelties. ¹⁵ The registering of these men was carried on cruelly, zealously, assiduously, from the rising of the sun to its going down, and was not brought to an end in forty days. ¹⁶ The king was filled with great and constant joy, and celebrated banquets before the temple idols. His erring heart, far from the truth, and his profane mouth, gave glory to idols, deaf and incapable of speaking or aiding, and uttered unworthy speech against the greatest God. ¹⁷ At the end of the above-mentioned interval of time, the registrars brought word to the king that the multitude of the Jews was too great for registration, ¹⁸ inasmuch as there were many still left in the land, of whom some were in inhabited houses, and others were scattered around in various places, so that all the commanders in Egypt were insufficient for the work. ¹⁹ The king threatened them, and charged them with taking bribes, in order to contrive the escape of the Jews, but was clearly convinced of the truth of what had been said. ²⁰ They said, and proved, that paper and pens had failed them for the carrying out of their purpose. ²¹ Now this was an active interference of the unconquerable providence which assisted the Jews from Heaven.

CHAPTER 5

¹ Then he called Hermon, who had charge of the elephants. Full of rage, altogether fixed in his furious design, ² he commanded him, with a quantity of unmixed wine and handfuls of incense [infused] to drug the elephants early on the following day. These five hundred elephants were, when infuriated by the copious draughts of frankincense, to be led up to the execution of death on the Jews. ³ The king, after issuing these orders, went to his feasting and gathered together all those of his friends and of the army who hated the Jews the most. ⁴ The master of the elephants, Hermon, fulfilled his commission punctually. ⁵ The underlings appointed for the purpose went out about evening and bound the hands of the miserable victims, and took other precautions for their security at night, thinking that the whole race would perish together. ⁶ The heathen believed the Jews to be destitute of all protection, for chains bound them around. ⁷ They invoked the Almighty LORD, and ceaselessly implored with tears their merciful God and Father, Ruler of all, Lord of every power, ⁸ to overthrow the evil purpose which had gone out against them, and to deliver them by extraordinary manifestation from that death which was in store for them. ⁹ Their litany so earnest went up to Heaven. ¹⁰ Then Hermon, who had filled his merciless elephants with copious draughts of mixed wine and frankincense, came early to the palace to certify the kind thereof. ¹¹ He, however, who has sent His good creature sleep from all time, by night or by day, so gratifying whom He wills, now diffused a portion thereof on the king. ¹² By this sweet and profound influence of the LORD he was held fast, and so his unjust purpose was quite frustrated, and his unflinching resolve greatly falsified. ¹³ But the Jews,

having escaped the hour which had been fixed, praised their holy God, and again begged Him who is easily reconciled to display the power of His powerful hand to the overconfident nations. ¹⁴The middle of the tenth hour had well near arrived, when the person who sent invitations, seeing the guests who were invited present, came and shook the king. ¹⁵He gained his attention with difficulty, and hinting that the mealtime was getting past, talked the matter over with him. ¹⁶The king listened to this, and then turning aside to his drinking, commanded the guests to sit down before him. ¹⁷This done, he asked them to enjoy themselves, and to indulge in mirth at this somewhat late hour of the banquet. ¹⁸Conversation grew on, and the king sent for Hermon, and inquired of him, with fierce denunciations, why the Jews had been allowed to outlive that day. ¹⁹Hermon explained that he had done his bidding over night; and in this he was confirmed by his friends. ²⁰The king, then, with a barbarity exceeding that of Phalaris, said that they might thank his sleep of that day: "Lose no time, and get the elephants ready against tomorrow, as you did before, for the destruction of these accursed Jews." ²¹When the king said this, the company present were glad, and approved; and then each man went to his own home. ²²Nor did they employ the night in sleep, so much as in contriving cruel mockeries for those deemed miserable. ²³The morning cock had just crowed, and Hermon, having harnessed the brutes, was stimulating them in the great colonnade. ²⁴The city crowds were collected together to see the hideous spectacle and waited impatiently for the dawn. ²⁵The Jews, breathless with momentary suspense, stretched out their hands, and prayed to the greatest God, in mournful strains, to quickly help them again. ²⁶The sun's rays were not yet shed abroad, and the king was waiting for his friends, when Hermon came to him, calling him out, and saying that his desires could now be realized. ²⁷The king, receiving him, was astonished at his unusual exit, and overwhelmed with a spirit of oblivion about everything, inquired [regarding] the object of this earnest preparation. ²⁸But this was the working of that Almighty God who had made him forget all his purpose. ²⁹Hermon and all his friends pointed out the preparation of the animals. "They are ready, O king, according to your own strict injunction." ³⁰The king was filled with fierce anger at these words, for, by the providence of God regarding these things, his mind had become entirely confused. He looked hard at Hermon, and threatened him as follows: ³¹"Your parents or your children, were they here, should have been furnished [as] a large meal for these wild beasts—not these innocent Jews, who my forefathers and I have loyally served. ³²Had it not been for familiar friendship, and the claims of your office, your life should have gone for theirs. ³³Hermon, being threatened in this unexpected and alarming manner, was troubled in

visage, and depressed in countenance. ³⁴The friends, too, slipped out one by one, and dismissed the assembled multitudes to their respective occupations. ³⁵The Jews, having heard of these events, praised the glorious God and King of kings, because they too had obtained this help from Him. ³⁶Now the king arranged another banquet after the same manner and proclaimed an invitation to mirth. ³⁷And he summoned Hermon to his presence, and said, with threats, "How often, O wretch, must I repeat my orders to you about these same persons? ³⁸Once more, arm the elephants for the extermination of the Jews tomorrow." ³⁹His countrymen, who were reclining with him, wondered at his instability, and so expressed themselves: ⁴⁰"O king, how long do you make trial of us, as of men deprived of reason? This is the third time that you have ordered their destruction. When the thing is to be done, you change your mind, and recall your instructions. ⁴¹For this reason the feeling of expectation causes tumult in the city: it swarms with factions and is continually at the point of being plundered." ⁴²The king, just like another Phalaris, a prey to thoughtlessness, made no account of the changes which his own mind had undergone, issuing in the deliverance of the Jews. He swore a fruitless oath, and firmly determined to send them to Hades, crushed by the knees and feet of the elephants. ⁴³He would also invade Judea, and level its towns with fire and the sword, and destroy that temple which the heathen might not enter, and prevent sacrifices from ever being offered up there. ⁴⁴Joyfully his friends broke up, together with his countrymen, and, trusting in his determination, arranged their forces in guard at the most convenient places of the city. ⁴⁵And the master of the elephants urged the beasts into an almost maniacal state, drenched them with incense and wine, and decked them with frightful instruments. ⁴⁶About early morning, when the city was now filled with an immense number of people at the hippodrome, he entered the palace and called the king to the business at hand. ⁴⁷The king's heart teemed with impious rage, and he rushed out with the mass, along with the elephants. With feelings unsoftened, and eyes pitiless, he longed to gaze at the hard and wretched doom of the above-mentioned [Jews]. ⁴⁸But the [Jews], when the elephants went out at the gate, followed by the armed force; and when they saw the dust raised by the throng, and heard the loud cries of the crowd, ⁴⁹thought that they had come to the last moment of their lives, to the end of what they had tremblingly expected. They gave way, therefore, to lamentations and moans; they kissed each other; those related to each other hung around one another's necks: fathers around their sons, mothers [around] their daughters; other women held their infants to their breasts, which drew what seemed their last milk. ⁵⁰Nevertheless, when they reflected on the help previously granted them from Heaven, they prostrated themselves with one accord, even removed the sucking children from the breasts, [51] and sent up an exceedingly great cry asking the Lord of all power to reveal Himself and have mercy on those who now lay at the gates of Hades.

CHAPTER 6

[1] And Eleazar, an illustrious priest of the country, who had attained to length of days, and whose life had been adorned with virtue, caused the elders who were around him to cease to cry out to the holy God, and prayed this: [2] "O King, mighty in power, Most High, Almighty God, who regulates the whole creation with Your tender mercy, [3] look on the seed of Abraham, on the children of the sanctified Jacob, Your sanctified inheritance, O Father, now being wrongfully destroyed as strangers in a strange land. [4] You destroyed Pharaoh, with his army of chariots, when that lord of this same Egypt was uplifted with lawless daring and a loud-sounding tongue. Shedding the beams of Your mercy on the race of Israel, You overwhelmed him with his proud army. [5] When Sennacherib, the grievous king of the Assyrians, exulting in his countless army, had subdued the whole land with his spear, and was lifting himself against Your holy city, with boastings [too] grievous to be endured, You, O LORD, demolished him and showed Your might to many nations. [6] When the three friends in the land of Babylon of their own will exposed their lives to the fire rather than serve vain things, You sent a moist coolness through the fiery furnace and brought the fire on all their adversaries. [7] It was You who, when Daniel was hurled—through slander and envy—as a prey to lions down below, brought him back up to [the] light unharmed. [8] When Jonah was pining away in the belly of the sea-bred monster, You looked on him, O Father, and restored him to the sight of his own. [9] And now, You who hate insolence; You who abound in mercy; You who are the protector of all things: appear quickly to those of the race of Israel, who are insulted by abhorred, lawless nations. [10] If our life has been stained with iniquity during our exile, deliver us from the hand of the enemy, and destroy us, O LORD, by the death which You prefer. [11] Do not let the vain-minded congratulate vain idols at the destruction of Your beloved, saying, "Neither did their God deliver them." [12] You, who are All-powerful and Almighty, O Perpetual One, behold! Have mercy on us who are being withdrawn from life, like traitors, by the unreasoning insolence of lawless men. [13] Let the heathen cower before Your invincible might today, O glorious One, who has all power to save the race of Jacob. [14] The whole band of infants and their parents implore You with tears. [15] Let it be shown to all the nations that You are with us, O LORD, and have not turned Your face away from us; but as You said that You would not forget them even in the land of their enemies, so fulfill this saying, O LORD. [16] Now,

at the time that Eleazar had ended his prayer, the king came along to the hippodrome, with the wild beasts, and with his tumultuous power. [17] When the Jews saw this, they uttered a loud cry to Heaven, so that the adjacent valleys resounded, and caused an irrepressible lamentation throughout the army. [18] Then the all-glorious, all-powerful, and true God, displayed His holy countenance, and opened the gates of Heaven, from which two messengers, dreadful of form, came down and were visible to all but the Jews. [19] And they stood opposite and filled the enemies' army with confusion and cowardice, and bound them with immoveable chains. [20] And a cold shudder came over the person of the king, and oblivion paralyzed the vehemence of his spirit. [21] They turned the animals back on the armed forces which followed them, and the animals trod them down and destroyed them. [22] The king's wrath was converted into compassion, and he wept at his own machinations. [23] For when he heard the cry, and saw them all on the verge of destruction, he angrily threatened his friends with tears, saying, [24] "You have governed badly, and have exceeded tyrants in cruelty; and me, your benefactor, you have labored to deprive of my dominion and my life at once, by secretly devising measures injurious to the kingdom. [25] Who has gathered here, unreasonably removing each from his home, those who, in fidelity to us, had held the fortresses of the country? [26] Who has so consigned to unmerited punishments those who in good will toward us from the beginning have in all things surpassed all nations, and who often have engaged in the most dangerous undertakings? [27] Loose, loose the unjust bonds; send them to their homes in peace, and deprecate what has been done. [28] Release the sons of the almighty living God of Heaven, who from our ancestors' times until now has granted a glorious and uninterrupted prosperity to our affairs. [29] He said these things, and they, released the same moment, having now escaped death, praised God their holy Savior. [30] The king then departed to the city, and called his financier to him, and asked him to provide a seven days' quantity of wine and other materials for feasting for the Jews. He decided that they should keep a joyful festival of deliverance in the very place in which they expected to meet with their destruction. [31] Then they who were previously despised and near to Hades, yes, rather advanced into it, partook of the cup of salvation, instead of a grievous and lamentable death. Full of exultation, they parted out the place intended for their fall and burial into banqueting shelters. [32] Ceasing their miserable strain of woe, they took up the subject of their fatherland, singing praise to God, their wonder-working Savior. All groans, all wailing, were laid aside: they formed dances as a sign of serene joy. [33] So also the king—he collected a number of guests for the occasion and returned unceasing thanks with much magnificence for the unexpected deliverance afforded him. ³⁴ Those who had marked them out as for death and for carrion, and had registered them with joy, howled aloud, and were clothed with shame, and had the fire of their rage ingloriously put out. ³⁵ But the Jews, as we just said, instituted a dance, and then gave themselves up to feasting, glad thanksgiving, and psalms. ³⁶ They made a public ordinance to commemorate these things for generations to come, as long as they should be sojourners. Therefore, they established these days as days of mirth, not for the purpose of drinking or luxury, but because God had saved them. ³⁷ They requested the king to send them back to their homes. ³⁸ They were being enrolled from the twenty-fifth of Pachon to the fourth of Epiphi—a period of forty days. The measures taken for their destruction lasted from the fifth of Epiphi until the seventh—that is, three days. ³⁹ The Ruler over all gloriously manifested His mercy during this time and delivered them all together unharmed. ⁴⁰ They feasted on the king's provision up to the fourteenth day, and then asked to be sent away. ⁴¹ The king commended them and wrote the following letter, of magnanimous importance for them, to the commanders of every city:

CHAPTER 7

¹ "King Ptolemy Philopator to the commanders throughout Egypt, and to all who are set over affairs—joy and strength. ² We ourselves and our children are well, and God has directed our affairs as we wish. ³ Certain of our friends vehemently urged us from malice to punish the Jews of our realm in a body, with the infliction of a monstrous punishment. ⁴ They pretended that our affairs would never be in a good state until this took place. Such, they said, was the hatred borne by the Jews to all other people. ⁵ They brought them bound in grievous chains as slaves, no, as traitors. Without inquiry or examination, they endeavored to annihilate them. They buckled themselves with a savage cruelty, worse than Scythian custom. ⁶ For this reason we severely threatened them; yet, with the clemency which we are accustomed to extend to all men, we at length permitted them to live. Finding that the God of Heaven cast a shield of protection over the Jews so as to preserve them, and that He fought for them as a father always fights for his sons, ⁷ and taking into consideration their constancy and fidelity toward us and toward our ancestors, we have, as we should, acquitted them of every sort of charge. ⁸ And we have dismissed them to their various homes, bidding all men everywhere to do them no wrong, or unrighteously revile them about the past. ⁹ Know that

should we conceive any evil design, or in any way aggrieve them, we will ever have as our opposite, not man, but the highest God, the ruler of all might. From Him there will be no escape, as the avenger of such deeds. Farewell." ¹⁰ When they had received this letter, they were not hurried to depart immediately. They petitioned the king to be allowed to inflict fitting punishment on those of their race who had willingly transgressed the holy God, and the Law of God. ¹¹ They alleged that men who had for their bellies' sake transgressed the ordinances of God, would never be faithful to the interests of the king. ¹² The king admitted the truth of this reasoning and commended them. Full power was given them, without warrant or special commission, to destroy those who had transgressed the Law of God boldly in every part of the king's dominions. ¹³ Their priests, then, as it was suitable, saluted him with good wishes, and all the people echoed with the "Hallelujah." They then joyfully departed. ¹⁴ Then they punished and destroyed with ignominy every polluted Jew that fell in their way; ¹⁵ slaying therefore, in that day, more than three hundred men, and esteeming this destruction of the wicked a season of joy. ¹⁶ They themselves having held fast their God to death, and having enjoyed a full deliverance, departed from the city garlanded with sweet-flowered wreaths of every kind. Uttering exclamations of joy, with songs of praise and melodious hymns, they thanked the God of their fathers, the perpetual Savior of Israel. ¹⁷ Having arrived at Ptolemais, called from the specialty of that district Rose-bearing, where the fleet, in accordance with the general wish, waited seven days for them, ¹⁸ they partook of a banquet of deliverance, for the king generously granted them separately the means of securing a return home. ¹⁹ They were accordingly brought back in peace, while they gave utterance to appropriate thanks; and they determined to keep these days during their sojourn as days of joyfulness. ²⁰ These they registered as sacred on a pillar, when they had dedicated the place of their festivity to be one of prayer. They departed unharmed, free, abundant in joy, preserved by the king's command, by land, by sea, and by river, each to his own home. ²¹ They had more weight than before among their enemies, and were honored and feared, and no one in any way robbed them of their goods. ²² Every man received back his own, according to inventory, [from] those who had obtained their goods, giving them up with the greatest terror. For the greatest God made perfect wonders for their salvation. ²³ Blessed is the Redeemer of Israel to [the] age. Amen.

4 MACCABEES

The book of 4 Maccabees is a homily or philosophic discourse praising the supremacy of pious reason over passion. It is not in the Bible for most churches, but is an appendix to the Greek Bible, and in the canon of the Georgian Orthodox Bible. It was included in the 1688 Romanian Orthodox and the eighteenth-century Romanian Catholic Bibles where it was called "Iosip" (Joseph). It is no longer printed in Romanian Bibles today. The book was ascribed to Josephus by Eusebius and Jerome, and this opinion was accepted for many years, leading to its inclusion in many editions of Josephus' works. Scholars have, however, pointed to perceived differences of language and style. The book is generally dated between 20 and 130 AD, likely in the later half of that range.

CHAPTER 1

¹ As I am going to demonstrate a most philosophical proposition, namely, that religious reasoning is absolute master of the passions, I would willingly advise you to give the utmost heed to philosophy. ² For reason is necessary to everyone as a step to science: and it more especially embraces the praise of prudence, the highest virtue. ³ If then reasoning appears to hold the mastery over the passions which stand in the way of temperance, such as gluttony and lust, ⁴ it also surely and manifestly has the rule over the affections which are contrary to justice, such as malice; and of those which are hindrances to manliness, as wrath, and pain, and fear. ⁵ How then is it, perhaps some may say, that reasoning, if it rules the affections, is not also master of forgetfulness and ignorance? They attempt a ridiculous argument. ⁶ For reasoning does not rule over its own affections, but over such as are contrary to justice, and manliness, and temperance, and prudence; and yet over these, so as to withstand, without destroying them. ⁷ I might prove to you, from many other considerations, that religious reasoning is sole master of the passions; ⁸ but I will prove it with the greatest force from the fortitude of Eleazar, and seven brothers, and their mother, who suffered death in defense of virtue. ⁹ For all these, treating pains with contempt even to death, by this contempt, demonstrated that reasoning has command over the passions. ¹⁰ For their virtues, then, it is right that I should commend those men who died with their mother at this time in behalf of rectitude; and for their honors, I may count them happy. ¹¹ For they, winning admiration not only from men in general, but even from the persecutors, for their manliness and endurance, became the means of the destruction of the tyranny against their nation, having conquered the tyrant by their endurance, so that by them their country was purified. ¹² But we may now at once enter on the question, having commenced, as is our custom, with laying down the doctrine, and so proceed to the account of these persons, giving glory to the all-wise God. ¹³ Therefore the question is whether reasoning is absolute master of the passions. ¹⁴ Let us determine, then, what reasoning is, and what passion [is], and how many forms of the passions, and whether reasoning bears sway over all of these. ¹⁵ Reasoning is, then, intellect accompanied by a life of rectitude, putting foremost the consideration of wisdom. ¹⁶ And wisdom is a knowledge of divine and human things, and of their causes. ¹⁷ And this is contained in the education of the Law, by means of which we learn divine things reverently, and human things profitably. ¹⁸ And the forms of wisdom are prudence, and justice, and manliness, and temperance. ¹⁹ The leading one of these is prudence, by whose means, indeed, it is that reasoning bears rule over the passions. ²⁰ Of the passions, pleasure and pain are the two most comprehensive, and they also by nature refer to the soul. ²¹ And there are many attendant affections surrounding pleasure and pain. ²² Before pleasure is lust, and after pleasure, joy. ²³ And before pain is fear, and after pain is sorrow. ²⁴ Wrath is an affection, common to pleasure and to pain, if anyone will pay attention when it comes on him. ²⁵ And there exists in pleasure a malicious disposition, which is the most multiform of all the affections. ²⁶ In the soul it is arrogance, and love of money, and vain pride, and contention, and faithlessness, and the evil eye. ²⁷ In the body it is greediness, and gorging, and solitary gluttony. ²⁸ As pleasure and pain are, therefore, two growths of the body and the soul, so there are many offshoots of these passions. ²⁹ And reasoning, the universal farmer, purging, and pruning these separately, and binding around, and watering, and transplanting, in every way improves the materials of the morals and affections. ³⁰ For reasoning is the leader of the virtues, but it is the sole ruler of the passions. Observe then first, through the very things which stand in the way of temperance, that reasoning is absolute ruler of the passions. ³¹ Now temperance consists of a command over the lusts. ³² But of the lusts, some belong to the soul, others to the body: and over each of these classes the reasoning appears to bear sway. ³³ For where is it, otherwise, that when urged on to forbidden meats, we reject the gratification which would ensue from them? Is it not because reasoning is able to command the appetites? I believe so. ³⁴ Hence it is, then, that when lusting after aquatic animals and birds, and four-footed beasts, and all kinds of food which are

forbidden us by the Law, we withhold ourselves through the mastery of reasoning. [35] For the affections of our appetites are resisted by the temperate understanding, and bent back again, and all the impulses of the body are reined in by reasoning.

CHAPTER 2

[1] And what wonder [is it] if the lusts of the soul, after participation with what is beautiful, are frustrated? [2] On this ground, therefore, the temperate Joseph is praised in that by reasoning he subdued, on reflection, the indulgence of sense. [3] For, although young, and ripe for sexual intercourse, he abrogated by reasoning the stimulus of his passions. [4] And it is not merely the stimulus of sensual indulgence, but that of every desire, that reasoning is able to master. [5] For instance, the Law says, "You will not covet your neighbor's wife, nor anything that belongs to your neighbor." [6] Now, then, since it is the Law which has forbidden us to desire, I will much more easily persuade you that reasoning is able to govern our lusts, just as it does the affections which are impediments to justice. [7] Since in what way is a solitary eater, and a glutton, and a drunkard reclaimed, unless it is clear that reasoning is lord of the passions? [8] Therefore, a man who regulates his course by the Law, even if he is a lover of money, immediately puts force on his own disposition; lending to the needy without interest and cancelling the debt of the incoming Sabbath. [9] And should a man be parsimonious, he is ruled by the Law acting through reasoning, so that he does not glean his harvest crops, nor vintage: and in reference to other points we may perceive that it is reasoning that conquers his passions. [10] For the Law conquers even affection toward parents, not surrendering virtue on their account. [11] And it prevails over marriage love, condemning it when transgressing Law. [12] And it lords it over the love of parents toward their children, for they punish them for vice; and it domineers over the intimacy of friends, reproving them when wicked. [13] And do not think it a strange assertion that reasoning can in behalf of the Law conquer even enmity. [14] It does not allow [one] to cut down the cultivated herbage of an enemy, but preserves it from the destroyers, and collects their fallen ruins. [15] And reason appears to be master of the more violent passions, such as love of power, and empty boasting, and slander. [16] For the temperate understanding repels all these malignant passions, as it does wrath, for it masters even this. [17] So Moses, when angered against Dathan and Abiram, did nothing to them in wrath, but regulated his anger by reasoning. [18] For the temperate mind is able, as I said, to be superior to the passions, and to transfer some, and destroy others. [19] For why else does our most wise father Jacob blame Simeon and Levi for having irrationally slain the whole race of the Shechemites, saying, "Cursed be their anger"? [20] For if reasoning did not possess the power of subduing angry affections, he would not have spoken like this. [21] For at the time when God created man, He implanted within him his passions and moral nature. [22] And at that time He enthroned above all the holy leader mind, through the medium of the senses. [23] And He gave a law to this mind, by living according to which it will maintain a temperate, and just, and good, and manly reign. [24] How [is it] then [that] a man might say that if reasoning is master of the passions, it has no control over forgetfulness and ignorance?

CHAPTER 3

[1] The argument is exceedingly ridiculous, for reasoning does not appear to bear sway over its own affections, but over those of the body, [2] in such a way as that anyone of you may not be able to root out desire, but reasoning will enable you to avoid being enslaved to it. [3] One may not be able to root out anger from the soul, but it is possible to withstand anger. [4] Anyone of you may not be able to eradicate malice, but reasoning has force to work with you to prevent you yielding to malice. [5] For reasoning is not an eradicator, but an antagonist of the passions. [6] And this may be more clearly comprehended from the thirst of King David. [7] For after David had been attacking the Philistines the whole day, he with the soldiers of his nation killed many of them; [8] then when evening came, sweating and very weary, he came to the royal tent, around which the entire army of our ancestors was encamped. [9] Now all the rest of them were at supper, [10] but the king, being very much thirsty, although he had numerous springs, could not by their means quench his thirst, [11] but a certain irrational longing for the water in the enemy's camp grew stronger and fiercer on him, and consumed him with languish. [12] For that reason, his bodyguards being troubled at this longing of the king, two valiant young soldiers, reverencing the desire of the king, put on their armor, and taking a pitcher, got over the ramparts of the enemies: [13] and unperceived by the guardians of the gate, they went throughout the whole camp of the enemy in quest. [14] And having boldly discovered the fountain, they filled out of it the draught for the king. [15] But he, though parched with thirst, reasoned that a draught regarded of equal value to blood, would be terribly dangerous to his soul. [16] For that reason, setting up reasoning in opposition to his desire, he poured out the draught to God. [17] For the temperate mind has power to conquer the pressure of the passions, and to quench the fires of excitement, [18] and to wrestle down the pains of the body, however excessive; and, through the excellency of reasoning, to abominate all the assaults of the passions. [19] But the occasion now invites us to give an illustration of temperate reasoning from history. [20] For at a time when our fathers were in possession of undisturbed peace through obedience to the Law, and were prosperous, so that Seleucus Nicanor, the king of

Asia, both assigned them money for divine service, and accepted their form of government, ²¹ then certain persons, bringing in new things contrary to the general unanimity, fell into calamities in various ways.

CHAPTER 4

¹ For a certain man named Simon, who was in opposition to Onias, who once held the chief priesthood for life, and was an honorable and good man, after slandering him in every way, he could not injure him with the people, went away as an exile, with the intention of betraying his country. ² When coming to Apollonius, the military governor of Syria, and Phoenicia, and Cilicia, he said, ³ "Having good will to the king's affairs, I have come to inform you that infinite private wealth is laid up in the treasuries of Jerusalem which do not belong to the temple but pertain to King Seleucus." ⁴ Apollonius, acquainting himself with the particulars of this, praised Simon for his care of the king's interests, and going up to Seleucus informed him of the treasure; ⁵ and getting authority over it, and quickly advancing into our country with the accursed Simon and a very heavy force, ⁶ he said that he came with the commands of the king that he should take the private money of the treasure. ⁷ And the nation, indignant at this proclamation, and replying to the effect that it was extremely unfair that those who had committed deposits to the sacred treasury should be deprived of them, resisted as well as they could. ⁸ But Apollonius went away with threats into the temple. ⁹ And the priests, with the women and children, having supplicated God to throw His shield over the holy, despised place, ¹⁰ and Apollonius going up with his armed force to the seizure of the treasure, there appeared from Heaven messengers riding on horseback, all radiant in armor, filling them with much fear and trembling. ¹¹ And Apollonius fell half dead on the court which is open to all nations, and extended his hands to Heaven, and implored the Hebrews, with tears, to pray for him, and propitiate the heavenly army. ¹² For he said that he had sinned, so as to be consequently worthy of death; and that if he were saved, he would celebrate to all men the blessedness of the holy place. ¹³ Onias the chief priest, induced by these words, although for other reasons anxious that King Seleucus should not suppose that Apollonius was slain by human device and not by Divine punishment, prayed for him; ¹⁴ and he being unexpectedly saved, departed to manifest to the king what had happened to him. ¹⁵ But on the death of Seleucus the king, his son Antiochus Epiphanes succeeds to the kingdom: a man of arrogant pride and terrible, ¹⁶ who having deposed Onias from the chief priesthood, appointed his brother Jason to be chief priest, ¹⁷ who had made a covenant to pay three thousand six hundred and sixty talents yearly if he would give him this authority. ¹⁸ And he committed the chief priesthood and rulership over the nation to him. ¹⁹ And he both changed the manner of living of the people and perverted their civil customs into all lawlessness, ²⁰ so that he not only erected a gymnasium on the very citadel of our country, but [neglected] the guardianship of the temple. ²¹ At which Divine vengeance being grieved, instigated Antiochus himself against them. ²² For being at war with Ptolemy in Egypt, he heard that on a report of his death being spread abroad, the inhabitants of Jerusalem had exceedingly rejoiced, and he quickly marched against them. ²³ And having subdued them, he established a decree that if any of them lived according to the laws of his country he should die. ²⁴ And when he could by no means destroy by his decrees the obedience to the law of the nation, but saw all his threats and punishments without effect, ²⁵ for even women, because they continued to circumcise their children, were flung down a precipice along with them, knowing beforehand of the punishment. ²⁶ When, therefore, his decrees were disregarded by the people, he himself compelled by means of tortures everyone of this race, by tasting forbidden meats, to renounce the Jewish religion.

CHAPTER 5

¹ The tyrant Antiochus, therefore, sitting in public state with his assessors on a certain lofty place, with his armed troops standing in a circle around him, ² commanded his spear-bearers to seize everyone of the Hebrews, and to compel them to taste swine's flesh, and things offered to idols. ³ And should any of them be unwilling to eat the accursed food, they were to be tortured on the wheel, and so killed. ⁴ And when many had been seized, a foremost man of the assembly, a Hebrew, by name Eleazar, a priest by family, by profession a lawyer, and advanced in years, and for this reason known to many of the king's followers, was brought near to him. ⁵ And Antiochus seeing him, said, ⁶ "I would counsel you, old man, before your tortures begin, to taste the swine's flesh, and save your life; for I feel respect for your age and gray head, which since you have had so long, you appear to me to be no philosopher in retaining the superstition of the Jews. ⁷ For that reason, since nature has conferred on you the most excellent flesh of this animal, do you loathe it? ⁸ It seems senseless not to enjoy what is pleasant, yet not disgraceful; and from notions of sinfulness, to reject the boons of nature. ⁹ And you will be acting, I think, still more senselessly, if you follow vain conceits about the truth. ¹⁰ And you will, moreover, be despising me to your own punishment. ¹¹ Will you not awake from your trifling philosophy, and give up the folly of your notions, and regaining understanding worthy of your age, search into the truth of an expedient course, ¹² and reverencing my kindly admonition, have pity on your

4 MACCABEES

own years? ¹³ For bear in mind that if there is any power which watches over this religion of yours, it will pardon you for all transgressions of the Law which you commit through compulsion." ¹⁴ While the tyrant incited him in this manner to the unlawful eating of flesh, Eleazar begged permission to speak. ¹⁵ And having received power to speak, he began to deliver himself like this: ¹⁶ "We, O Antiochus, who are persuaded that we live under a divine law, consider no compulsion to be so forcible as obedience to that law; ¹⁷ for this reason we consider that we should not in any point transgress the Law. ¹⁸ And indeed, were our law (as you suppose) not truly divine, and if we wrongly think it divine, we should have no right even in that case to destroy our sense of religion. ¹⁹ Do not think eating the unclean, then, a trifling offense. ²⁰ For transgression of the Law, whether in small or great matters, is of equal moment, ²¹ for in either case the Law is equally slighted. ²² But you deride our philosophy, as though we lived irrationally in it. ²³ Yet it instructs us in temperance, so that we are superior to all pleasures and lusts; and it exercises us in manliness, so that we cheerfully undergo every grievance. ²⁴ And it instructs us in justice, so that in all our dealings we render what is due; and it teaches us piety, so that we worship the one [and] only God as is appropriate. ²⁵ For it is that reason we do not eat the unclean; for believing that the Law was established by God, we are convinced that the Creator of the world, in giving His laws, sympathizes with our nature. ²⁶ Those things which are convenient to our souls, He has directed us to eat, but those which are repugnant to them, He has interdicted. ²⁷ But, tyrant-like, you not only force us to break the Law, but also to eat, that you may ridicule us as we so profanely eat; ²⁸ but you will not have this cause of laughter against me, ²⁹ nor will I transgress the sacred oaths of my forefathers to keep the Law. ³⁰ No, not if you pluck out my eyes, and consume my entrails. ³¹ I am not so old, and void of manliness, but that my rational powers are youthful in defense of my religion. ³² Now then, prepare your wheels and kindle a fiercer flame. ³³ I will not so pity my old age, as on my account to break the law of my country. ³⁴ I will not betray you, O law, my instructor! Or forsake you, O beloved self-control! ³⁵ I will not put you to shame, O philosopher reason! Or deny you, O honored priesthood, and science of the law. ³⁶ Mouth! You will not pollute my old age, nor the full stature of a perfect life. ³⁷ My fathers will receive me pure, not having cowered before your compulsion, though to death. ³⁸ For you will tyrannize over the ungodly, but you will not lord it over my thoughts about religion, either by your arguments, or through deeds.

CHAPTER 6

¹ When Eleazar had answered the exhortations of the tyrant in this manner, the spear-bearers came up and violently dragged Eleazar to the instruments of torture. ² And first they stripped the old man, adorned as he was with the beauty of piety. ³ Then tying back his arms and hands, they disdainfully abused him with stripes, ⁴ [while] a herald opposite was crying out, "Obey the commands of the king!" ⁵ But Eleazar, the high-minded and truly noble, as one tortured in a dream, did not regard it at all. ⁶ But raising his eyes on high to Heaven, the old man's flesh was stripped off by the scourges, and his blood streamed down, and his sides were pierced through. ⁷ And falling on the ground, from his body having no power to support the pains, he yet kept his reasoning upright and unbending. ⁸ Then one of the harsh spear-bearers leaped on his belly as he was falling, to force him upright. ⁹ But he endured the pains, and despised the cruelty, and persevered through the indignities; ¹⁰ and like a noble athlete, the old man, when struck, vanquished his torturers. ¹¹ His countenance sweating, and panting for breath, he was admired by the very torturers for his courage. ¹² For that reason, partly in pity for his old age, ¹³ partly from the sympathy of acquaintance, and partly in admiration of his endurance, some of the attendants of the king said, ¹⁴ "Why do you unreasonably destroy yourself, O Eleazar, with these miseries? ¹⁵ We will bring you some meat cooked by yourself, and you can save yourself by pretending that you have eaten swine's flesh." ¹⁶ And Eleazar, as though the advice more painfully tortured him, cried out, ¹⁷ "Do not let us who are children of Abraham be so wickedly advised as by giving way to make use of an inappropriate pretense; ¹⁸ for it were irrational, if having lived up to old age in all truth, and having scrupulously guarded our character for it, we should now turn back, ¹⁹ and ourselves should become a pattern of impiety to the young, as being an example of eating pollution. ²⁰ It would be disgraceful if we should live for some short time—and that scorned by all men for cowardice— ²¹ and be condemned by the tyrant for unmanliness, by not contending to the death for our divine law. ²² For this reason, you, O children of Abraham, die nobly for your religion. ²³ You spear-bearers of the tyrant, why do you linger?" ²⁴ Beholding him so high-minded against misery, and not changing at their pity, they led him to the fire: ²⁵ then with their wickedly contrived instruments they burned him on the fire and poured stinking fluids down into his nostrils. ²⁶ And he being at length burned down to the bones, and about to expire, raised his eyes toward God, and said, ²⁷ "You know, O God, that when I might have been saved, I am slain for the sake of the Law by tortures of fire. ²⁸ Be merciful to Your people and be satisfied with my punishment on their account. ²⁹ Let my blood be a purification for them and take my life in repayment for theirs." ³⁰ Therefore speaking, the holy man departed, noble in his torments, and even to the agonies of death resisted in his reasoning for the sake

of the Law. ³¹ Confessedly, therefore, religious reasoning is master of the passions. ³² For had the passions been superior to reasoning, I would have given them the witness of this mastery. ³³ But now, since reasoning conquered the passions, we befittingly awarded it the authority of first place. ³⁴ And it is but fair that we should allow that the power belongs to reasoning, since it masters external miseries. ³⁵ It would be ridiculous were it not so; and I prove that reasoning has not only mastered pains, but that it is also superior to the pleasures, and withstands them.

CHAPTER 7

¹ The reasoning of our father Eleazar, like a first-rate pilot, steering the vessel of piety in the sea of passions, ² and flouted by the threats of the tyrant, and overwhelmed with the breakers of torture, ³ in no way shifted the rudder of piety until it sailed into the harbor of victory over death. ⁴ A city has never, when besieged, held out against many and various machines as that holy man did when his pious soul was tried with the fiery trial of tortures and racking, [and when] he moved his besiegers through the religious reasoning that shielded him. ⁵ For father Eleazar, projecting his disposition, broke the raging waves of the passions as with a jutting promontory. ⁶ O priest worthy of the priesthood! You did not pollute your sacred teeth, nor make your appetite, which had always embraced the clean and lawful, a partaker of profanity. ⁷ O harmonizer with the Law, and sage devoted to a divine life! ⁸ Of such a character should those be who perform the duties of the Law at the risk of their own blood and defend it with generous sweat by sufferings even to death. ⁹ You, father, have gloriously established our right government by your endurance, and making our past service of much account, prevented its destruction, and, by your deeds, have made the words of philosophy credible. ¹⁰ O aged man of more power than tortures, elder more vigorous than fire, greatest king over the passions, Eleazar! ¹¹ For as father Aaron, armed with a censer, hastening through the consuming fire, vanquished the flame-bearing messenger, ¹² so Eleazar, the descendant of Aaron, wasted away by the fire, did not give up his reasoning. ¹³ And what is most wonderful, though an old man, though the labors of his body were now spent, and his muscles were relaxed, and his sinews worn out, he recovered youth. ¹⁴ By the spirit of reasoning, and the reasoning of Isaac, he rendered the many-headed instrument powerless. ¹⁵ O blessed old age, and venerable gray head, and life obedient to the Law, which the faithful seal of death perfected. ¹⁶ If then an old man, through religion, despised tortures even to death, confessedly religious reasoning is ruler of the passions. ¹⁷ But perhaps some might say, "It is not all who conquer passions, as all do not possess wise reasoning." ¹⁸ But they who have meditated on religion with their whole heart, these alone can master the passions of the flesh— ¹⁹ they who believe that they do not die to God; for as our forefathers Abraham, Isaac, [and] Jacob, they live to God. ²⁰ This circumstance, then, is by no means an objection, that some who have weak reasoning are governed by their passions: ²¹ since what person, walking religiously by the whole rule of philosophy, and believing in God, ²² and knowing that it is a blessed thing to endure all kinds of hardships for virtue, would not, for the sake of religion, master his passion? ²³ For only the wise and brave man is lord over his passions. ²⁴ From where it is that even boys, trained with the philosophy of religious reasoning, have conquered still more bitter tortures:

CHAPTER 8

¹ For when the tyrant was manifestly vanquished in his first attempt, in being unable to force the old man to eat the unclean thing, then indeed, vehemently swayed with passion, he commanded others of the adult Hebrews to be brought, and if they would eat of the unclean thing, to let them go when they had eaten, but if they objected, to torment them more grievously. ² The tyrant having given this charge, seven brothers were brought into his presence, along with their aged mother, handsome, and modest, and well-born, and altogether beautiful. ³ When the tyrant saw them encircling their mother as in a dance, he was pleased at them; and being struck with their appropriate and innocent manner, smiled on them, and calling them near, said, ⁴ "O youths, with favorable feelings I admire the beauty of each of you; and greatly honoring such a numerous a band of brothers, I not only counsel you not to share the madness of the old man who has been tortured before, ⁵ but I beg you to yield and to enjoy my friendship; for I possess the power, not only of punishing those who disobey my commands, but of doing good to those who obey them. ⁶ Put confidence in me, then, and you will receive places of authority in my government if you forsake your national ordinance, ⁷ and, conforming to the Greek mode of life, alter your rule, and revel in youth's delights. ⁸ For if you provoke me by your disobedience, you will compel me to destroy you— everyone—with terrible punishments by tortures. ⁹ Have mercy, then, on your own selves, whom I, although an enemy, pity for your age and attractive appearance. ¹⁰ Will you not reason on this—that if you disobey, there will be nothing left for you but to die in tortures?" ¹¹ So speaking, he ordered the instruments of torture to be brought forward, that great fear might prevail on them to eat unclean meat. ¹² And when the spearman brought forward the wheels, and the racks, and the hooks, and catapults, and cauldrons, pans, and finger-racks, and iron hands and wedges, and bellows, the tyrant continued:

[13] "Fear, young men, and the righteousness which you worship will be merciful to you if you err from compulsion." [14] Now, they having listened to these words of persuasion and seeing the fearful instruments, not only were not afraid, but even answered the arguments of the tyrant, and through their good reasoning destroyed his power. [15] Now let us consider the matter: had any of them been weak-spirited and cowardly among them, what reasoning would they have employed but these? [16] "O wretched that we are, and exceedingly senseless! When the king exhorts us, and calls us to his bounty, should we not obey him? [17] Why do we cheer ourselves with vain counsels, and venture on a disobedience bringing death? [18] Will we not fear, O brothers, the instruments of torture, and weigh the threats of torment, and shun this vainglory and destructive pride? [19] Let us have compassion on our age and relent over the years of our mother. [20] And let us bear in mind that we will be dying as rebels. [21] And Divine Justice will pardon us if we fear the king through necessity. [22] Why withdraw ourselves from a most sweet life, and deprive ourselves of this pleasant world? [23] Let us not oppose necessity, nor seek vainglory by our own excruciation. [24] The Law itself is not forward to put us to death if we dread torture. [25] From where has such angry zeal taken root in us, and such fatal obstinacy approved itself to us, when we might live unmolested by the king?" [26] But nothing of this kind did the young men say or think when about to be tortured. [27] For they were well aware of the sufferings and were masters of the pains. [28] . . . [29] So that as soon as the tyrant had ceased counseling them to eat the unclean, they all with one voice, as from the same heart, said:

CHAPTER 9

[1] "Why do you delay, O tyrant? For we are more ready to die than to transgress the injunctions of our fathers. [2] And we should be disgracing our fathers if we did not obey the Law and take knowledge for our guide. [3] O tyrant, counselor of law-breaking, do not, hating us as you do, pity us more than we pity ourselves. [4] For we account escape to be worse than death. [5] And you think to scare us, by threatening us with death by tortures, as though you had learned nothing by the death of Eleazar. [6] But if aged men of the Hebrews have died in the cause of religion after enduring torture, more rightly should we younger men die, scorning your cruel tortures, which our aged instructor overcame. [7] Make the attempt, then, O tyrant; and if you put us to death for our religion, do not think that you harm us by torturing us. [8] For we through this mistreatment and endurance will bear off the rewards of virtue. [9] But you, for the wicked and despotic slaughter of us, will, from the Divine vengeance, endure continuous torture by fire." [10] When they had so spoken, the tyrant was not only exasperated against them as being refractory, but

enraged with them as being ungrateful. [11] So that, at his bidding, the torturers brought out the oldest of them, and tearing through his tunic, bound his hands and arms on each side with thongs. [12] And when they had labored hard without effect in scourging him, they hurled him on the wheel. [13] And the noble youth, extended on this, became dislocated. [14] And with every member disjointed, he exclaimed in protest: [15] "O most accursed tyrant, and enemy of heavenly justice, and cruel-hearted, I am no murderer, nor sacrilegious man, whom you so mistreated, but a defender of the Divine law." [16] And when the spearmen said, "Consent to eat, that you may be released from your tortures," [17] he answered, "Not so powerful, O accursed ministers, is your wheel, as to stifle my reasoning; cut my limbs, and burn my flesh, and twist my joints. [18] For through all my torments I will convince you that the children of the Hebrews are alone unconquered in behalf of virtue." [19] While he was saying this, they heaped up fuel, and setting fire to it, strained him on the wheel still more. [20] And the wheel was defiled all over with blood, and the hot ashes were quenched by the droppings of gore, and pieces of flesh were scattered around the axles of the machine. [21] And although the framework of his bones was now destroyed, the high-minded and Abrahamic youth did not groan. [22] But, as though transformed by fire into immortality, he nobly endured the racking, saying, [23] "Imitate me, O brothers, [and] never desert your station, nor renounce our courageous brotherhood: fight the holy and honorable fight of religion, [24] by which means our just and paternal Providence, becoming merciful to the nation, will punish the pernicious tyrant." [25] And saying this, the revered youth abruptly closed his life. [26] And when all admired his courageous soul, the spearmen brought forward him who was second in point of age, and having put on iron hands, bound him with pointed hooks to the torture device. [27] And when, on inquiring whether he would eat before he was tortured, they heard his noble sentiment, [28] after they with the iron hands had violently dragged all the flesh from the neck to the chin—the panther-like beasts tore off the very skin of his head, but he, bearing this misery with firmness, said, [29] "How sweet is every form of death for the religion of our fathers!" And he said to the tyrant, [30] "Do you think, most cruel of all tyrants, that you are now tortured more than I, finding your overconfident conception of tyranny conquered by our perseverance in behalf of our religion? [31] For I lighten my suffering by the pleasures which are connected with virtue. [32] But you are tortured with threats for impiety; and you will not escape, most corrupt tyrant, the vengeance of Divine wrath."

CHAPTER 10

[1] Now this one, having endured this praiseworthy death, the third was brought along, and exhorted by

many to taste and save his life. [2] But he cried out and said, "Do you not know that the father of those who are dead, became the father of me also, and that the same mother bore me, and that I was brought up in the same tenets? [3] I do not renounce the noble relationship of my brothers. [4] Now then, whatever instrument of vengeance you have, apply it to my body, for you are not able to touch, even if you wish it, my soul. [5] But they, highly incensed at his boldness of speech, dislocated his hands and feet with racking engines, and wrenching them from their sockets, dismembered him." [6] And they dragged around his fingers, and his arms, and his legs, and his ankles. [7] And not being able by any means to strangle him, they tore off his skin, together with the extreme tips of his fingers and then dragged him to the wheel, [8] around which his vertebral joints were loosened, and he saw his own flesh torn to shreds, and streams of blood flowing from his entrails. [9] And when about to die, he said, [10] "We, O accursed tyrant, suffer this for the sake of Divine education and virtue. [11] But you, for your impiety and blood shedding, will endure indissoluble torments." [12] And having died worthily of his brothers, they dragged forward the fourth, saying, [13] "Do not share the madness of your brothers, but give regard to the king, and save yourself." [14] But he said to them, "You do not have a fire so scorching as to make me play the coward. [15] By the blessed death of my brothers, and the continuous punishment of the tyrant, and the glorious life of the pious, I will not repudiate the noble brotherhood. [16] Invent, O tyrant, tortures, that you may learn, even through them, that I am the brother of those tormented before." [17] When he had said this, the blood-thirsty, and murderous, and unhallowed Antiochus ordered his tongue to be cut out. [18] But he said, "Even if you take away the organ of speech, yet God hears the silent. [19] Behold, my tongue is extended, cut it off; for by that you will not halt my reasoning. [20] We gladly lose our limbs in behalf of God. [21] But God will swiftly find you, since you cut off the tongue—the instrument of divine melody."

CHAPTER 11

[1] And when he had died, disfigured in his torments, the fifth leaped forward, and said, [2] "I do not intend, O tyrant, to get excused from the torment which is in behalf of virtue. [3] But I have come of my own accord, that by my death you may owe heavenly vengeance a punishment for more crimes. [4] O you hater of virtue and of men! What have we done that you so revel in our blood? [5] Does it seem evil to you that we worship the Founder of all things, and live according to His surpassing law? [6] But this is worthy of honors, not torments, [7] had you been capable of the higher feelings of men and possessed the hope of salvation from God. [8] Behold now, being alien from God, you make war against those who are religious toward God." [9] As he said this, the spear-bearers bound him and drew him to the torture device, [10] to which binding him at his knees, and fastening them with iron chains, they bent down his loins on the wedge of the wheel; and his body was then dismembered, scorpion-fashion. [11] With his breath so confined, and his body strangled, he said, [12] "A great favor you bestow on us, O tyrant, by enabling us to manifest our adherence to the Law by means of nobler sufferings." [13] He also being dead, the sixth, quite a youth, was brought out; and on the tyrant asking him whether he would eat and be delivered, he said, [14] "I am indeed younger than my brothers, but I am as old in understanding; [15] for having been born and reared to the same end, we are also bound to die in behalf of the same cause. [16] So that if you think proper to torment us for not eating the unclean, then torment!" [17] As he said this, they brought him to the wheel, [18] extended on which, with limbs racked and dislocated, he was gradually roasted from beneath. [19] And having heated sharp spits, they approached them to his back; and having transfixed his sides, they burned away his entrails. [20] And he, while tormented, said, "O period good and holy, in which, for the sake of religion, we brothers have been called to the contest of pain, and have not been conquered! [21] For religious understanding, O tyrant, is unconquered. [22] Armed with upright virtue, I will also depart with my brothers. [23] I, too, [am] bearing with myself a great Avenger, O inventor of tortures and enemy of the truly pious! [24] We six youths have destroyed your tyranny. [25] For is not your inability to overrule our reasoning, and to compel us to eat the unclean, your destruction? [26] Your fire is cold to us, your devices are painless, and your violence harmless. [27] For the guards not of a tyrant but of a divine law are our defenders: through this we keep our reasoning unconquered."

CHAPTER 12

[1] When he, too, had undergone blessed martyrdom, and died in the cauldron into which he had been thrown, the seventh, the youngest of all, came forward, [2] whom the tyrant pitying, though he had been dreadfully reproached by his brothers, [3] seeing him already encompassed with chains, had him brought nearer, and endeavored to counsel him, saying, [4] "You see the end of the madness of your brothers, for they have died in torture through disobedience; and you, if disobedient, having been miserably tormented, will yourself perish prematurely. [5] But if you obey, you will be my friend, and have a charge over the affairs of the kingdom." [6] And having so exhorted him, he sent for the mother of the boy, that, by condoling with her for the loss of so many sons, he might incline her, through the hope of safety, to render the survivor obedient. [7] And he, after his mother had urged him on in the Hebrew tongue (as we will soon relate), says, [8] "Release me

that I may speak to the king and all his friends." [9] And they, rejoicing exceedingly at the promise of the youth, quickly let him go. [10] And he, running up to the pans, said, [11] "Impious tyrant, and most blasphemous man, were you not ashamed, having received prosperity and a kingdom from God, to kill His servants, and to rack the doers of godliness? [12] For this reason the Divine vengeance is reserving you for continuous fire and torments, which will cling to you for all time. [13] Were you not ashamed, man as you are, yet most savage, to cut out the tongues of men of like feeling and origin, and having so abused to torture them? [14] But they, bravely dying, fulfilled their religion toward God. [15] But you will groan according to your deserts for having slain the champions of virtue without cause." [16] "For this reason," he continued, "I myself, being about to die, [17] will not forsake my brothers. [18] And I call on the God of my fathers to be merciful to my race. [19] But you, both living and dead, He will punish." [20] So having prayed, he hurled himself into the pans, and so expired.

CHAPTER 13

[1] If then the seven brothers despised troubles even to death, it is confessed on all sides that righteous reasoning is absolute master over the passions. [2] For just as if, had they as slaves to the passions eaten of the unholy, we should have said that they had been conquered; [3] now it is not so, but by means of the reasoning which is praised by God, they mastered their passions. [4] And it is impossible to overlook the leadership of reflection, for it gained the victory over both passions and troubles. [5] How then can we avoid, according to these men, mastery of passion through right reasoning, since they did not draw back from the pains of fire? [6] For just as by means of towers projecting in front of harbors men break the threatening waves, and therefore assure a still course to vessels entering port, [7] so that seven-towered right-reasoning of the young men, securing the harbor of religion, conquered the intemperance of passions. [8] For having arranged a holy choir of piety, they encouraged one another, saying, [9] "Brothers, may we die brotherly for the Law. Let us imitate the three young men in Assyria who despised the equally afflicting furnace. [10] Let us not be cowards in the manifestation of piety." [11] And one said, "Courage, brother"; and another, "Nobly endure." [12] And another, "Remember of what stock you are—and by the hand of our father Isaac who endured to be slain for the sake of piety." [13] And one and all, looking on each other serene and confident, said, "Let us sacrifice with all our heart our souls to God who gave them, and employ our bodies for the keeping of the Law. [14] Let us not fear him who thinks he kills, [15] for great is the trial of soul and danger of continuous torment laid up for those who transgress the command of God. [16] Let us therefore arm ourselves in the self-control, which is divine reasoning. [17] If we suffer like this, Abraham, and Isaac, and Jacob will receive us, and all the fathers will commend us." [18] And as each one of the brothers was hauled away, the rest exclaimed, "Do not disgrace us, O brother, nor falsify those who died before you. [19] Now you are not ignorant of the charm of brotherhood, which the Divine and all-wise Providence has imparted through fathers to children and has engendered through the mother's womb." [20] In which these brothers having remained an equal time, and having been formed for the same period, and been increased by the same blood, and having been perfected through the same principle of life, [21] and having been brought out at equal intervals, and having sucked milk from the same springs, their brotherly souls are reared up lovingly together, [22] and increase [all] the more powerfully by reason of this simultaneous rearing, and by daily companionship, and by other education, and exercise in the law of God. [23] Brotherly love being so sympathetically constituted, the seven brothers had a more sympathetic mutual harmony. [24] For being educated in the same law, and practicing the same virtues, and reared up in a just course of life, they increased this harmony with each other. [25] For a like zeal for what is right and honorable increased their fellow-feeling toward each other. [26] For it acting along with religion, made their brotherly feeling more desirable to them. [27] And yet, although nature, and companionship, and virtuous morals increased their brotherly love, those who were left endured to behold their brothers, who were mistreated for their religion [and] tortured even to death.

CHAPTER 14

[1] And more than this, they even urged them on to this mistreatment, so that they not only despised pains themselves, but they even got the better of their affections of brotherly love. [2] O reasoning, more royal than a king and freer than freemen! [3] O sacred and harmonious concord of the seven brothers as concerning piety! [4] None of the seven youths turned cowardly or shrank back from death. [5] But all of them, as though running the road to immortality, hastened on to death through tortures. [6] For just as hands and feet are moved sympathetically with the directions of the soul, so those holy youths agreed to death for religion's sake, as through the immortal soul of religion. [7] O holy seven—harmonious brothers! For as the seven days of creation, about religion, [8] so the youths, circling around the number seven, annulled the fear of torments. [9] We now shudder at the recital of the affliction of those young men, but they not only saw, and not only heard the immediate execution of the threat, but undergoing it, persevered—and that through the pains of fire. [10] And what could be more painful? For the power of fire, being sharp and quick, speedily dissolved their bodies. [11] And do not think it

wonderful that reasoning bore rule over those men in their torments, when even a woman's mind despised more manifold pains. [12] For the mother of those seven youths endured the rackings of each of her children. [13] And consider how comprehensive the love for offspring is, which draws everyone to sympathy of affection, [14] where irrational animals possess a similar sympathy and love for their offspring with men. [15] The tame birds frequenting the roofs of our houses, defend their fledglings. [16] Others build their nests and hatch their young in the tops of mountains, and in the precipices of valleys, and the holes and tops of trees, and keep off the intruder. [17] And if not able to do this, they fly circling around them in agony of affection, calling out in their own note, and save their offspring in whatever manner they are able. [18] But why should we point attention to the sympathy toward children shown by irrational animals? [19] The very bees, at the season of honey-making, attack all who approach, and pierce with their sting, as with a sword, those who draw near their hive, and repel them even to death. [20] But sympathy for her children did not turn away the mother of the young men—[she] who had a spirit related with that of Abraham.

CHAPTER 15

[1] O reasoning of the sons, lord over the passions, and religion more desirable to a mother than progeny! [2] The mother, when two things were set before her—religion and the safety of her seven sons for a time on the conditional promise of a tyrant— [3] rather chose the religion which according to God preserves to continuous life. [4] O in what way can I describe ethically the affections of parents toward their children, the resemblance of soul and of form engrafted into the small type of a child in a wonderful manner, especially through the greater sympathy of mothers with the feelings of those born of them! [5] For by how much mothers are by nature weak in disposition and prolific in offspring, by so much the fonder they are of children. [6] And of all mothers the mother of the seven was the fondest of children, who in seven childbirths had deeply engendered love toward them, [7] and through her many pains undergone in connection with each one, was compelled to feel sympathy with them, [8] yet, through fear of God, she neglected the temporary salvation of her children. [9] Not [only] that, but on account of the excellent disposition to the Law, her maternal affection toward them was increased. [10] For they were both just and temperate, and manly, and high-minded, and fond of their brothers, and so fond of their mother that even to death they obeyed her by observing the Law. [11] And yet, though there were so many circumstances connected with love of children to draw on a mother to sympathy, in the case of none of them were the various tortures able to pervert her principle. [12] But she inclined each one separately and all together to

death for religion. [13] O holy nature and parental feeling, and reward of bringing up children, and unconquerable maternal affection! [14] At the racking and roasting of each one of them, the observant mother was prevented by religion from changing. [15] She saw her children's flesh dissolving around the fire, and their extremities quivering on the ground, and the flesh of their heads dropped forward down to their beards, like masks. [16] O you mother who was tried at this time with bitterer pangs than those of childbirth! [17] O you only woman who has brought out perfect holiness! [18] Your firstborn, expiring, did not sway you; nor the second, looking miserable in his torments; nor the third, breathing out his soul. [19] Nor did you weep when you beheld the eyes of each of them looking sternly on their tortures, and their nostrils foreboding death! [20] When you saw children's flesh heaped on children's flesh that had been torn off, heads decapitated on heads, dead falling on the dead, and a choir of children turned through torture into a burying ground, you did not lament. [21] Not so do siren melodies or songs of swans attract the hearers to listening [as did the] voices of [you] children calling on your mother in the midst of torments! [22] O with what and what manner of torments was the mother herself tortured as her sons were undergoing the wheel and the fires! [23] But religious reasoning, having strengthened her courage in the midst of sufferings, enabled her to forego, for the time, parental love. [24] Although beholding the destruction of seven children, the noble mother, after one embrace, stripped off [her feelings] through faith in God. [25] For just as in a council-room, beholding in her own soul vehement counselors—nature, and parentage, and love of her children, and the racking of her children— [26] she holding two votes, one for the death, the other for the preservation of her children, [27] did not lean to that which would have saved her children for the safety of a brief space. [28] But this daughter of Abraham remembered his holy fortitude. [29] O holy mother of a nation, avenger of the Law, and defender of religion, and prime bearer in the battle of the affections! [30] O you nobler in endurance than males, and more manly than men in perseverance! [31] For as the Ark of Noah, bearing the world in the world-filling flood, bore up against the waves, [32] so you, the guardian of the Law, when surrounded on every side by the flood of passions, and constricted by violent storms which were the torments of those children, nobly bore up against the storms against religion.

CHAPTER 16

[1] If then, even a woman, and that an aged one and the mother of seven children, endured to see her children's torments even to death, confessedly religious reasoning is master even of the passions. [2] I have proved, then, that not only men have obtained

the mastery of their passions, but also that a woman despised the greatest torments. ³And not so fierce were the lions around Daniel, nor the furnace of Mishael burning with most vehement fires as that natural love of children burned within her, when she saw her seven sons tortured. ⁴But with the reasoning of religion, the mother quenched passions so great and powerful. ⁵For we must consider this also: that, had the woman been faint-hearted, as being their other, she would have lamented over them, and perhaps might have spoken like this: ⁶"Ah! Wretched me, and many times miserable, who having born seven sons, have become the mother of none. ⁷O seven useless childbirths, and seven profitless periods of labor, and fruitless giving of suck, and miserable nursing at the breast. ⁸Vainly, for your sakes, O sons, have I endured many pangs, and the more difficult anxieties of rearing. ⁹Aah! Of my children, some of you unmarried, and some who have married to no profit, I will not see your children, nor be congratulated as a grandmother. ¹⁰Ah! That I who had many and fair children, should be a lone widow full of sorrows! ¹¹Nor, should I die, will I have a son to bury me." But with such a lament as this the holy and God-fearing mother mourned none of them. ¹²Nor did she divert any of them from death, nor grieve for them as for the dead. ¹³But as one possessed with an adamantine mind, and as one bringing out again her full number of sons to immortality, she rather with supplication exhorted them to death in behalf of religion. ¹⁴O woman, soldier of God for religion, you, aged and a female, have even conquered a tyrant through endurance; and though but weak, have been found more powerful in deeds and words. ¹⁵For when you were seized along with your children, you stood looking on Eleazar in torments, and said to your sons in the Hebrew tongue, ¹⁶"O sons, the contest is noble to which you are being called as a witness for the nation, [to which] you strive zealously for the laws of your country. ¹⁷For it were disgraceful that this old man should endure pains for the sake of righteousness, and that you who are younger should be afraid of the tortures. ¹⁸Remember that through God you obtained existence and have enjoyed it. ¹⁹And on this second account you should bear every affliction because of God, ²⁰for whom our father Abraham was also forward to sacrifice our progenitor Isaac, and did not shudder at the sight of his own paternal hand descending down with the sword on him. ²¹And the righteous Daniel was cast to the lions; and Hananiah, and Azariah, and Mishael were slung out into a furnace of fire, yet they endured through God. ²²You, then, having the same faith toward God, do not be troubled. ²³For it is unreasonable that they who know religion should not stand up against troubles. ²⁴With these arguments, the mother of seven, exhorting each of her sons, over-persuaded them from transgressing the command of God. ²⁵And

they also saw this, that they who die for God live to God, as Abraham, and Isaac, and Jacob, and all the patriarchs.

CHAPTER 17

¹And some of the spear-bearers said that when she herself was about to be seized for the purpose of being put to death, she threw herself on the pile, rather than that they should touch her person. ²O you mother, who together with seven children destroyed the violence of the tyrant, and rendered his wicked intentions void, and exhibited the nobleness of faith! ³For you, as a house bravely built on the pillar of your children, bore the shock of tortures without swaying. ⁴Be of good cheer, therefore, O holy-minded mother, holding the firm [substance of the] hope of your steadfastness with God. ⁵The moon does not appear with the stars in the sky as gracious as you are: established honorable before God, and fixed in the expanse with your sons who you illuminated with religion to the stars. ⁶For your bearing of children was after the fashion of a child of Abraham. ⁷And, were it lawful for us to paint as on a tablet the religion of your story, the spectators would not shudder at beholding the mother of seven children enduring, for the sake of religion, various tortures even to death. ⁸And it had been a worthy thing to have inscribed on the tomb itself these words as a memorial to those of the nation: ⁹"HERE AN AGED PRIEST, AND AN AGED WOMAN, AND SEVEN SONS, ARE BURIED THROUGH THE VIOLENCE OF A TYRANT, WHO WISHED TO DESTROY THE SOCIETY OF THE HEBREWS. ¹⁰THESE ALSO AVENGED THEIR NATION, LOOKING TO GOD AND ENDURING TORMENTS TO DEATH." ¹¹For it was truly a divine contest which was carried through by them. ¹²For at that time virtue presided over the contest, approving the victory through endurance, namely, immortality [and] continuous life. ¹³Eleazar was the first to contend, and [then] the mother of the seven children entered the contest, and [then] the brothers contended. ¹⁴The tyrant was the opposite; and the world and living men were the spectators. ¹⁵And reverence for God conquered and crowned her own athletes. ¹⁶Who did not admire those champions of true legislation? Who were not astonished? ¹⁷The tyrant himself, and all their council, admired their endurance; ¹⁸through which, also, they now stand beside the divine throne, and live a blessed life. ¹⁹For Moses says, "And all the saints are under Your hands." ²⁰These, therefore, having been sanctified through God, have been honored not only with this honor, but that also by their means the enemy did not overcome our nation, ²¹and that the tyrant was punished, and their country purified. ²²For they became the ransom to the sin of the nation, and the Divine Providence saved Israel, previously afflicted, by the blood of those pious ones, and the propitiatory death. ²³For the tyrant Antiochus, looking to their manly virtue, and to their endurance

in torture, proclaimed that endurance as an example to his soldiers. ²⁴ And they proved to him to be noble and brave for land battles and for sieges; and he conquered and stormed the towns of all his enemies.

CHAPTER 18

¹ O Israeli children, descendants of the seed of Abraham, obey this law, and in every way be religious, ² knowing that religious reasoning is lord of the passions, and those not only inward but outward. ³ When those persons were giving up their bodies to pains for the sake of religion, they were not only admired by men, but were deemed worthy of a divine portion. ⁴ And the nation obtained peace through them, and having renewed the observance of the Law in their country, they drove the enemy out of the land. ⁵ And the tyrant Antiochus was both punished on earth and is punished now [that] he is dead; for when he was quite unable to compel the Israelites to adopt foreign customs and to desert the manner of life of their fathers, ⁶ then, departing from Jerusalem, he made war against the Persians. ⁷ And the righteous mother of the seven children also spoke as follows to her offspring: "I was a pure virgin and did not go beyond my father's house, but I took care of the built-up rib. ⁸ No destroyer of the desert [or] ravisher of the plain injured me; nor did the destructive, deceitful snake make plunder of my pure virginity; and I remained with my husband during the period of my prime. ⁹ And these children of mine, having arrived at maturity, their father died: he was blessed! For having sought out a life of fertility in children, he was not grieved with a period of loss of children. ¹⁰ And he used to teach you, when yet with you, the Law and the Prophets. ¹¹ He used to read to you the slaying of Abel by Cain, and the offering up of Isaac, and the imprisonment of Joseph. ¹² And he used to tell you of the zealous Phinehas; and informed you of Hananiah, and Azariah, and Mishael in the fire. ¹³ And he used to glorify Daniel, who was in the den of lions, and pronounce him blessed. ¹⁴ And he used to put you in mind of the Writing of Isaiah, which says, Even if you pass through the fire, it will not burn you. ¹⁵ He chanted to you David, the hymn-writer, who says, Many are the afflictions of the just. ¹⁶ He declared the proverbs of Solomon, who says, He is a Tree of Life to all those who do His will. ¹⁷ He used to verify Ezekiel, who said, Will these dry bones live? ¹⁸ For he did not forget the song which Moses taught, proclaiming, I will kill, and I will make to live. ¹⁹ This is our life, and the length of our days." ²⁰ O that bitter—and yet not bitter—day when the bitter tyrant of the Greeks, quenching fire with fire in his cruel cauldrons, brought with boiling rage the seven sons of the daughter of Abraham to the torture device, and to all his torments! ²¹ He pierced the balls of their eyes, and cut out their tongues, and put them to death with varied tortures. ²² For this reason divine retribution pursued and will [still] pursue the pernicious wretch. ²³ But the children of Abraham, with their victorious mother, are assembled together to the choir of their father, having received pure and immortal souls from God, ²⁴ to whom be glory forever and ever. Amen.

PRAYER OF MANASSEH

The Prayer of Manasseh (or Manasses) is a short work of 15 verses recording a penitential prayer attributed to King Manasseh of Judah. Most scholars believe that the Prayer of Manasseh was written in Greek in the 1st or 2nd century BC. Another work by the same title, written in Hebrew and containing distinctly different content, was found among the Dead Sea Scrolls.

CHAPTER 1

¹ O LORD Almighty, that are in Heaven, You God of our fathers, of Abraham, and Isaac, and Jacob, and of their righteous seed; ² who have made the heavens and earth, with all the ornament thereof; ³ who have bound the sea by the word of Your command; who have shut up the deep, and sealed it by Your terrible and glorious Name; ⁴ whom all things fear, yes, tremble before Your power; ⁵ for the majesty of Your glory cannot be borne, and the anger of Your threatening toward sinners is importable: ⁶ Your merciful promise is unmeasurable and unsearchable; ⁷ for You are the LORD Most High, of great compassion, patient and abundant in mercy, and relenting of bringing evils on men. ⁸ You, O LORD, according to Your great goodness have promised conversion and forgiveness to those who have sinned against You: and of Your infinite mercies have appointed conversion to sinners, that they may be saved. You, therefore, O LORD, that are the God of the just, have not appointed conversion to the just, to Abraham, and Isaac, and Jacob, which have not sinned against You; but You have appointed conversion to me that am a sinner: ⁹ for I have sinned above the number of the sands of the sea. My transgressions are multiplied, O LORD: my transgressions are multiplied, and I am not worthy to behold and see the height of Heaven for the multitude of my iniquities. ¹⁰ I am bowed down with many iron bands, that I cannot lift up my head by reason of my sins, neither do I have any respite, for I have provoked Your wrath and done that which is evil before You: I did not do Your will, neither did I keep Your commands: I have set up abominations and have multiplied detestable things. ¹¹ Now therefore, I bow the knee of my heart, imploring You of grace. ¹² I have sinned, O LORD, I have sinned, and I acknowledge my iniquities: ¹³ but, I humbly implore You, forgive me, O LORD, forgive me, and do not destroy me with my iniquities. Do not be angry with me forever, by reserving evil for me; neither condemn me into the lower parts of the earth. For You, O LORD, are the God of those who convert; ¹⁴ and in me You will show all Your goodness, for You will save me, that am unworthy, according to Your great mercy. ¹⁵ And I will praise You forever all the days of my life, for all the army of Heaven sings Your praise, and Yours is the glory forever and ever. Amen.

TESTAMENTS OF THE TWELVE PATRIARCHS

The Testaments of the Twelve Patriarchs is an apocryphal work purporting to contain the last words of the twelve sons of Jacob. It is part of the Oskan Armenian Orthodox Bible. Fragments of similar writings were found at Qumran and scholarship maintains that the Testaments were written in Hebrew or Greek, possibly in the 2nd century BC, and reached their final form in the 2nd century AD.

THE TESTAMENT OF REUBEN, THE FIRSTBORN SON OF JACOB AND LEAH

CHAPTER 1

[1] The copy of the Testament of Reuben, even the commands which he gave his sons before he died in the one hundred and twenty-fifth year of his life. [2] Two years after the death of his brother Joseph, when Reuben fell sick, his sons and his sons' sons were gathered together to visit him. [3] And he said to them, "My children, behold, I am dying, and I go the way of my fathers." [4] And seeing his brothers Judah, and Gad, and Asher there, he said to them, "Raise me up, that I may tell to my brothers and to my children what things I have hidden in my heart, for behold, now at length I am passing away." [5] And he arose and kissed them, and said to them, "Hear, my brothers, and my children, give ear to your father Reuben in the commands which I give to you. [6] And behold, I call the God of Heaven to witness against you this day, that you may not walk in the sins of youth and fornication, wherein I was poured out, and defiled the bed of my father Jacob. [7] And I tell you that He struck me with a sore plague in my loins for seven months, and had my father Jacob not prayed for me to the LORD, the LORD would have destroyed me. [8] For I was thirty years old when I worked the evil thing before the LORD, and I was sick to death for seven months. [9] And after this I converted with set purpose of my soul for seven years before the LORD. [10] And I did not drink wine and strong drink, and flesh did not enter into my mouth, and I did not eat pleasant food; but I mourned over my sin, for it was great—such as had not been in Israel."

CHAPTER 2

[1] "And now hear me, my children, what things I saw concerning the seven spirits of deceit, when I converted. [2] Therefore seven spirits are appointed against man, and they are the leaders in the works of youth. [[[3] And seven other spirits are given to him at his creation, that through them should be done every work of man. [4] The first is the spirit of life, with which the constitution [of man] is created. [5] The second is the sense of sight, with which arises desire. The third is the sense of hearing, with which comes teaching. [6] The fourth is the sense of smell, with which tastes are given to draw air and breath. The fifth is the power of speech, with which comes knowledge. [7] The sixth is the sense of taste, with which comes the eating of meats and drinks; and by it strength is produced, for in food is the foundation of strength. [8] The seventh is the power of procreation and sexual intercourse, with which through love of pleasure sins enter in. [9] For what reason it is the last in order of creation, and the first in that of youth, because it is filled with ignorance, and leads the youth as a blind man to a pit, and as a beast to a precipice."

CHAPTER 3

[1] "Besides all these there is an eighth spirit of sleep, with which is brought about the trance of nature and the image of death. With these spirits are mingled the spirits of error.]] [2] First, the spirit of fornication is seated in the nature and in the senses; the second, the spirit of insatiableness, in the belly; [3] the third, the spirit of fighting, in the liver and gall; [4] the fourth is the spirit of groveling and trickery, that through overbearing attention one may [falsely] seem fair; [5] the fifth is the spirit of pride, that one may be boastful and arrogant; [6] the sixth is the spirit of lying, to practice deceits in perdition and jealousy, and concealments from kindred and friends; [7] the seventh is the spirit of injustice, with which are thefts and acts of rapacity, that a man may fulfill the desire of his heart; for injustice works together with the other spirits by the taking of gifts. [8] And with all these the spirit of sleep is joined which is [that] of error and fantasy. And so perishes every young man, darkening his mind from the truth, and not understanding the Law of God, nor obeying the admonitions of his fathers as also befell me in my youth. [9] And now, my children, love the truth, and it will preserve you: hear the words of your father Reuben. [10] Pay no heed to the face of a woman, nor associate with another man's wife, nor meddle with affairs of womankind. [11] For had I not seen Bilhah bathing in a covered place, I would not have fallen into this great iniquity. [12] For my mind, taking in the thought of the woman's nakedness, did not permit me to sleep until I had worked the abominable thing. [13] For while our father Jacob had gone to his father Isaac, when we were in

Eder, near to Ephrath in Beth-Lehem, Bilhah became drunk and was asleep uncovered in her chamber. [14] Therefore, having gone in and beheld [her] nakedness, I worked the impiety without her perceiving it, and leaving her sleeping, I departed. [15] And immediately a messenger of God revealed to my father concerning my impiety, and he came and mourned over me, and touched her no longer."

CHAPTER 4

[1] "Pay no heed, therefore, my children, to the beauty of women, nor set your mind on their affairs; but walk in singleness of heart in the fear of the LORD, and expend labor on good works, and on study, and on your flocks, until the LORD gives you a wife, whom He will, that you do not permit as I did. [2] For until my father's death, I did not have boldness to look in his face, or to speak to any of my brothers, because of the reproach. [3] Even until now, my conscience causes me anguish on account of my impiety. [4] And yet my father comforted me much and prayed for me to the LORD, that the anger of the LORD might pass from me, even as the LORD showed. [5] And from then until now, I have been on my guard and have not sinned. Therefore, my children, I say to you: observe all things, whatever I command you, and you will not sin. [6] For the sin of fornication is a pit to the soul, separating it from God, and bringing it near to idols, because it deceives the mind and understanding, and leads young men into Hades before their time. [7] For fornication has destroyed many, because, though a man may be old or noble, or rich or poor, he brings reproach on himself with the sons of men and derision with Belial. [8] For you heard regarding Joseph how he guarded himself from a woman, and purged his thoughts from all fornication, and found favor in the sight of God and men. [9] For the Egyptian woman did many things to him, and summoned magicians, and offered him love potions, but the purpose of his soul admitted no evil desire. [10] Therefore the God of your fathers delivered him from every evil [and] hidden death. For if fornication does not overcome your mind, neither can Belial overcome you."

CHAPTER 5

[1] "For women are evil, my children; and since they have no power or strength over man, they use schemes by outward attractions, that they may draw him to themselves. [2] And whom they cannot bewitch by outward attractions, they overcome him by craft. [3] For moreover, concerning them, the messenger of the LORD told me, and taught me, that women are overcome by the spirit of fornication more than men, and they plot against men in their heart; and by means of their adornment they first deceive their minds, and by the glance of the eye instill the poison, and then through the accomplished act, they take them captive. [4] For a woman cannot force a man openly, but by a harlot's bearing she deceives him. [5] Flee, therefore, fornication, my children, and command your wives and your daughters, that they do not adorn their heads and faces to deceive the mind, because every woman who uses these schemes has been reserved for continuous punishment; [6] for thus they allured the Watchers who were before the flood; for as these continually beheld them, they lusted after them, and they conceived the act in their mind; for they changed themselves into the shape of men, and appeared to them when they were with their husbands. [7] And the women, lusting in their minds after their forms, gave birth to giants, for the Watchers appeared to them as reaching even to Heaven."

CHAPTER 6

[1] "Beware, therefore, of fornication; and if you wish to be pure in mind, guard your senses from every woman. [2] And likewise command the women not to associate with men, that they may also be pure in mind. [3] For constant meetings, even though the ungodly deed is not worked, are an irremediable disease to them, and to us a destruction of Belial and a continuous reproach. [4] For in fornication there is neither understanding nor godliness, and all jealousy dwells in the lust thereof. [5] Therefore, I say to you then: you will be jealous against the sons of Levi and will seek to be exalted over them, but you will not be able. [6] For God will avenge them, and you will die by an evil death. [7] For God gave the sovereignty to Levi, [[and to Judah with him, and to me also, and to Dan and Joseph, that we should be for rulers;]] [8] therefore I command you to listen to Levi, because he will know the Law of the LORD, and will give ordinances for judgment, and will sacrifice for all Israel until the consummation of the times, as the anointed chief priest, of whom the LORD spoke, [9] I adjure you by the God of Heaven to do truth—each one to his neighbor, and to entertain love—each one for his brother. [10] And draw near to Levi in humbleness of heart, that you may receive a blessing from his mouth. [11] For he will bless Israel and Judah, because the LORD has chosen him to be king over all the nation. [12] And bow down before his seed, for on our behalf it will die in wars, visible and invisible, and will be among you [as] a perpetual king."

CHAPTER 7

[1] And Reuben died, having given these commands to his sons. [2] And they placed him in a coffin until they carried him up from Egypt and buried him in Hebron in the cave where his father was.

TESTAMENTS OF THE TWELVE PATRIARCHS

THE TESTAMENT OF SIMEON, THE SECOND SON OF JACOB AND LEAH

CHAPTER 1

[1] The copy of the words of Simeon, the things which he spoke to his sons before he died, in the one hundred and twentieth year of his life, at which time his brother Joseph died. [2] For when Simeon was sick, his sons came to visit him, and he strengthened himself and sat up and kissed them, and said:

CHAPTER 2

[1] "Listen, my children, to your father Simeon, and I will declare to you what things I have in my heart. [2] I was born of Jacob as my father's second son; and my mother Leah called me Simeon, because the LORD had heard her prayer. [3] Moreover, I became exceedingly strong; I shrank from no achievement, nor was I afraid of anything. [4] For my heart was hard, and my liver was immovable, and my bowels [were] without compassion, [5] because valor has also been given from the Most High to men in soul and body. [6] For in the time of my youth I was jealous in many things of Joseph, because my father loved him beyond all. [7] And I set my mind against him to destroy him, because the prince of deceit sent forth the spirit of jealousy and blinded my mind, so that I did not regard him as a brother, nor did I even spare my father Jacob. [8] But his God and the God of his fathers sent forth His messenger and delivered him out of my hands. [9] For when I went to Shechem to bring ointment for the flocks, and Reuben to Dothan, where our necessities and all our stores were, my brother Judah sold him to the Ishmaelites. [10] And when Reuben heard these things, he was grieved, for he wished to restore him to his father. [11] But on hearing this I was exceedingly angry against Judah in that he let him go away alive, and for five months I continued being wrathful against him. [12] But the LORD restrained me and withheld from me the power of my hands, for my right hand was half withered for seven days. [13] And I knew, my children, that this had befallen me because of Joseph, and I converted and wept; and I implored the LORD God that my hand might be restored, and that I might hold aloof from all pollution, and envy, and from all folly. [14] For I knew that I had devised an evil thing before the LORD and my father Jacob, on account of my brother Joseph, in that I envied him."

CHAPTER 3

[1] "And now, my children, listen to me and beware of the spirit of deceit and envy. [2] For envy rules over the whole mind of a man and permits him neither to eat, nor to drink, nor to do any good thing. [3] But it always suggests [to him] to destroy him that he envies; and so long as he that is envied flourishes, he that envies fades away. [4] Therefore, I afflicted my soul with fasting in the fear of the LORD [for] two years, and I learned that deliverance from envy comes by the fear of God. [5] For if a man flees to the LORD, the evil spirit runs away from him, and his mind is lightened. [6] And henceforward he sympathizes with him whom he envied and forgives those who are hostile to him, and so ceases from his envy."

CHAPTER 4

[1] "And my father asked concerning me, because he saw that I was sad; and I said to him, I am pained in my liver. [2] For I mourned more than all of them, because I was guilty of the selling of Joseph. [3] And when we went down into Egypt, and he bound me as a spy, I knew that I was suffering justly, and I did not grieve. [4] Now Joseph was a good man and had the Spirit of God within him: being compassionate and pitiful, he bore no malice against me, but loved me even as the rest of his brothers. [5] Beware, therefore, my children, of all jealousy and envy, and walk in singleness of soul and with good heart, keeping in mind Joseph, your father's brother, that God may also give you grace and glory, and blessing on your heads, even as you saw in Joseph's case. [6] All his days he did not reproach us concerning this thing, but loved us as his own soul, and glorified us beyond his own sons, and gave us riches, and cattle, and fruits. [7] You also, my children, must love his brother—each one—with a good heart, and the spirit of envy will withdraw from you. [8] For this [[(envy)]] makes the soul savage and destroys the body; it causes anger and war in the mind, and stirs up to deeds of blood, and leads the mind into frenzy, and does not permit prudence to act in men; moreover, it takes away sleep, [[and causes tumult to the soul and trembling to the body]]. [9] For even in sleep, some malicious jealousy, deluding him, gnaws and with wicked spirits disturbs his soul, and causes the body to be troubled, and wakes the mind from sleep in confusion; and as a wicked and poisonous spirit, so it appears to men."

CHAPTER 5

[1] "Therefore Joseph was handsome in appearance and attractive to look on, because no wickedness dwelt in him; for the face manifests some of the trouble of the spirit. [2] And now, my children, make your hearts good before the LORD and your ways straight before men, and you will find grace before the LORD and men. [3] Beware, therefore, of fornication, for fornication is a mother of all evils, separating from God and bringing near to Belial. [4] For I have seen it inscribed in the writing of Enoch that your sons will be corrupted in fornication, [5] and will do harm to the sons of Levi with the sword. But they will not be able to withstand Levi; [6] for he will wage the war of the LORD and will conquer all your hosts. And they will be few in number, divided in Levi and Judah, and there will be

none of you for sovereignty, even as our father also prophesied in his blessings."

CHAPTER 6

[1] "Behold, I have told you all things that I may be acquitted of your sin. [2] Now, if you remove your envy and all stiff-neckedness from yourselves, || My bones will flourish in Israel as a rose, || And my flesh in Jacob as a lily, || And my fragrance will be as the fragrance of Libanus; And holy ones will be multiplied from me as cedars forever, || And their branches will stretch far off. [3] Then the seed of Canaan will perish, || And a remnant will not be to Amalek, || And all the Cappadocians will perish, || And all the Hittites will be utterly destroyed. [4] Then the land of Ham will fail, || And all the people will perish. Then all the earth will rest from trouble, || And all the world under Heaven from war. [5] Then the Mighty One of Israel will glorify Shem, || For the LORD God will appear on earth, || And [He] Himself will save men. [6] Then all the spirits of deceit will be given to be trodden under foot, || And men will rule over wicked spirits. [7] Then I will arise in joy, || And will bless the Most High because of His marvelous works, [[|| Because God has taken a body and eaten with men and saved men.]]"

CHAPTER 7

[1] "And now, my children, obey Levi and Judah, and do not be lifted up against these two tribes, for from them the salvation of God will arise to you. [2] For the LORD will raise up from Levi as it were a Chief Priest, and from Judah as it were a King—[[God and man;]] He will save all [[the nations and]] the race of Israel. [3] Therefore I give you these commands that you may also command your children that they may observe them throughout their generations."

CHAPTER 8

[1] And when Simeon had made an end of commanding his sons, he slept with his fathers, [2] being one hundred and twenty years old. [2] And they laid him in a wooden coffin, to take up his bones to Hebron. [3] And they took them up secretly during a war of the Egyptians. [4] For the Egyptians guarded the bones of Joseph in the tombs of the kings. [5] For the sorcerers told them that on the departure of the bones of Joseph there should be darkness and gloom throughout all the land, and an exceedingly great plague to the Egyptians, so that even with a lamp a man should not recognize his brother.

CHAPTER 9

[1] And the sons of Simeon lamented their father. [2] And they were in Egypt until the day of their departure by the hand of Moses.

THE TESTAMENT OF LEVI, THE THIRD SON OF JACOB AND LEAH

CHAPTER 1

[1] The copy of the words of Levi, the things which he ordained to his sons, according to all that they should do, and what things should befall them until the Day of Judgment. [2] He was sound in health when he called them to himself; for it had been revealed to him that he should die. And when they were gathered together, he said to them:

CHAPTER 2

[1] "I, Levi, was born in Haran, and I came with my father to Shechem. [2] And I was young, about twenty years of age, when, with Simeon, I worked vengeance on Hamor for our sister Dinah. [3] And when I was feeding the flocks in Abel-Maul, the spirit of understanding of the LORD came on me, and I saw all men corrupting their way, and that unrighteousness had built walls for itself, and lawlessness sat on towers. [4] And I was grieving for the race of the sons of men, and I prayed to the LORD that I might be saved. [5] Then there fell on me a sleep, and I beheld a high mountain, and I was on it. [6] And behold, the heavens were opened and a messenger of God said to me, Levi, enter. [7] And I entered from the first heaven, and I saw a great sea hanging there. [8] And further, I saw a second heaven far brighter and more brilliant, for there was a boundless light also therein. [9] And I said to the messenger, Why is this so? And the messenger said to me, Do not marvel at this, for you will see another heaven more brilliant and incomparable. [10] And when you have ascended there, you will stand near the LORD, and will be His minister, and will declare His mysteries to men, and will proclaim concerning Him who will redeem Israel. [11] And by you and Judah the LORD will appear among men, saving every race of men. [12] And from the LORD's portion will be your life, and He will be your field, and vineyard, and fruits, gold, and silver."

CHAPTER 3

[1] "Hear, therefore, regarding the heavens which have been shown to you. The lowest is for this reason gloomy to you, in that it beholds all the unrighteous deeds of men. [2] And it has fire, snow, and ice made ready for the Day of Judgment, in the righteous judgment of God; for in it are all the spirits of the retributions for vengeance on men. [3] And in the second are the hosts of the armies which are ordained for the Day of Judgment, to work vengeance on the spirits of deceit and of Belial. And above them are the holy ones. [4] And in the highest of all dwells the Great Glory, far above all holiness. [5] In [[the heaven next to]] it are the chief-messengers, who minister and make propitiation to the LORD for all the sins of ignorance of the righteous, offering a sweet-smelling

savor to the LORD, a reasonable and a bloodless offering. [7] And [[in the heaven below this]] are the messengers who bear answers to the messengers of the presence of the LORD. [8] And in the heaven next to this are thrones and dominions, in which they always offer praise to God. [9] When, therefore, the LORD looks on us, all of us are shaken; yes, the heavens, and the earth, and the abysses are shaken at the presence of His majesty. [10] But the sons of men, having no perception of these things, sin and provoke the Most High."

CHAPTER 4

[1] "Now, therefore, know that the LORD will execute judgment on the sons of men. Because when the rocks are being split, and the sun quenched, and the waters dried up, and the fire cowering, and all creation troubled, and the invisible spirits melting away, and Hades takes spoils through the visitations of the Most High, men will be unbelieving and persist in their iniquity. On this account they will be judged with punishment. [2] Therefore the Most High has heard your prayer, to separate you from iniquity, and that you should become a son to Him, and a servant, and a minister of His presence. [3] You will light the light of knowledge in Jacob, and you will be as the sun to all the seed of Israel. [4] And a blessing will be given to you and to all your seed until the LORD will visit all the nations in His tender mercies forever. [5] And therefore counsel and understanding have been given to you that you might instruct your sons concerning this, [6] because they that bless Him will be blessed, and they that curse Him will perish."

CHAPTER 5

[1] "And thereon the Messenger opened the gates of Heaven to me, and I saw the holy temple, and the Most High on a throne of glory. [2] And He said to me, Levi, I have given you the blessings of the priesthood until I come and sojourn in the midst of Israel. [3] Then the Messenger brought me down to the earth, and gave me a shield and a sword, and said to me, [4] Execute vengeance on Shechem because of your sister Dinah, and I will be with you because the LORD has sent Me. [5] And I destroyed the sons of Hamor at that time, as it is written in the heavenly tablets. [6] And I said to Him, Please, O Lord, tell me Your Name, that I may call on You in a day of tribulation. [7] And He said, I am the Messenger who intercedes for the nation of Israel that they may not be utterly smitten, for every evil spirit attacks it. [8] And after these things I awoke, and blessed the Most High and the Messenger who intercedes for the nation of Israel and for all the righteous."

CHAPTER 6

[1] "And when I was going to my father, I found a brazen shield—also for what reason the name of the mountain is Aspis, which is near Gebal, to the south of Abila. And I kept these words in my heart. [2] And after this I counseled my father and my brother Reuben to command the sons of Hamor not to be circumcised, [3] for I was zealous because of the abomination which they had worked on my sister. [4] And I slew Shechem first, and Simeon slew Hamor. [5] And after this my brothers came and struck that city with the edge of the sword. [6] And my father heard these things and was angry, and he was grieved in that they had received the circumcision, and after that had been put to death, and in his blessings he looked wrongly on us. [7] For we sinned because we had done this thing against his will, and he was sick on that day. [8] But I saw that the sentence of God was for evil on Shechem, for they sought to do to Sarah and Rebekah as they had done to our sister Dinah, but the LORD prevented them. [9] And they persecuted our father Abraham when he was a stranger, and they vexed his flocks when they were big with young; and Eblaen, who was born in his house, they most shamefully handled. [10] And thus they did to all strangers, taking away their wives by force, and they banished them. [11] But the wrath of the LORD came on them to the uttermost."

CHAPTER 7

[1] "And I said to my father Jacob, By you the LORD will plunder the Canaanites, and will give their land to you and to your seed after you. [2] For from this day forward Shechem will be called a city of imbeciles; for as a man mocks a fool, so we mocked them. [3] Because they had also worked folly in Israel by defiling my sister. [4] And we departed and came to Bethel."

CHAPTER 8

[1] "And there again I saw a vision as the former, after we had spent seventy days there. [2] And I saw seven men in white raiment saying to me, Arise, put on the robe of the priesthood, and the crown of righteousness, and the breastplate of understanding, and the garment of truth, and the plate of faith, and the turban of the head, and the ephod of prophecy. [3] And they carried [these things] separately, and put [them] on me, and said to me, From now on become a priest of the LORD—you and your seed forever. [4] And the first anointed me with holy oil and gave the staff of judgment to me. [5] The second washed me with pure water, and fed me with bread and wine (the most holy things), and clad me with a holy and glorious robe. [6] The third clothed me with a linen vestment like an ephod. [7] The fourth put a girdle around me like to purple. [8] The fifth gave me a branch of rich olive. [9] The sixth placed a crown on my head. [10] The seventh placed a diadem of priesthood on my head and filled my hands with incense that I might serve as priest to the LORD God. [11] And they said to me, Levi, your seed

will be divided into three offices for a sign of the glory of the LORD who is to come: [12] and the first portion will be great; yes, there will be none greater than it; [13] the second will be in the priesthood; [14] and the third will be called by a new name, because a King will arise in Judah, and will establish a new priesthood, after the fashion of the nations [[*or* to all the nations]]. [15] And His presence is beloved, as a prophet of the Most High, of the seed of our father Abraham. [16] Therefore, every desirable thing in Israel will be for you and for your seed, and you will eat everything fair to look on, and your seed will apportion the table of the LORD. [17] And some of them will be high priests, and judges, and scribes, for the holy place will be guarded by their mouth. [18] And when I awoke, I understood that this [dream] was like the first dream. [19] And I also hid this in my heart and did not tell it to any man on the earth."

CHAPTER 9

[1] "And after two days Judah and I went up with our father Jacob to Isaac, our father's father. [2] And my father's father blessed me according to all the words of the visions which I had seen. [3] And he would not come with us to Bethel. And when we came to Bethel, my father saw a vision concerning me, that I should be their priest to God. [4] And he rose up early in the morning, and paid tithes of all to the LORD through me. [5] And so we came to Hebron to dwell there. [6] And Isaac called me continually to put me in remembrance of the Law of the LORD, even as the Messenger of the LORD showed to me. [7] And he taught me the law of the priesthood, of sacrifices, whole burnt-offerings, first-fruits, freewill-offerings, peace-offerings. [8] And each day he was instructing me, and was busy on my behalf before the LORD, and said to me, [9] Beware of the spirit of fornication, for this will continue and will pollute the holy place by your seed. [10] Therefore, take a wife for yourself without blemish or pollution, while you are yet young, and not of the race of strange nations. [11] And before entering into the holy place, bathe; and when you offer the sacrifices, wash; [12] and again, when you finish the sacrifice, wash; of twelve trees having leaves, offer to the LORD as Abraham also taught me. [13] And of every clean beast and bird, offer a sacrifice to the LORD. [14] And of all your first-fruits and of wine, offer the first as a sacrifice to the LORD God; and you will salt every sacrifice with salt."

CHAPTER 10

[1] "Now, therefore, observe whatever I command you, children, for whatever things I have heard from my fathers I have declared to you. [2] And behold, I am clear from your ungodliness and transgression, which you will commit in the end of the ages [[against the Savior of the world, Christ, acting godlessly]], deceiving Israel, and stirring up against it great calamities from the LORD. [3] And you will deal lawlessly together with Israel, so He will not bear with Jerusalem because of your wickedness; but the veil of the temple will be torn, so as not to cover your shame. [4] And you will be scattered as captives among the nations and will be for a reproach and for a curse there. [5] For the house which the LORD will choose will be called Jerusalem, as is contained in the scroll of Enoch the righteous."

CHAPTER 11

[1] "Therefore, when I took a wife, I was twenty-eight years old, and her name was Melcha. [2] And she conceived and bore a son, and I called his name Gershom, for we were sojourners in our land. [3] And I saw concerning him that he would not be in the first rank. [4] And Kohath was born in the thirty-fifth year of my life, toward sunrise. [5] And I saw in a vision that he was standing on high in the midst of all the congregation, [6] therefore I called his name Kohath [[(which is, beginning of majesty and instruction)]]. [7] And she bore me a third son, in the fortieth year of my life; and since his mother bore him with difficulty, I called him Merari (which is, my bitterness), because he was also like to death. [8] And Jochebed was born in Egypt, in my sixty-fourth year, for I was renowned then in the midst of my brothers."

CHAPTER 12

[1] "And Gershom took a wife, and she bore Lomni and Semei to him. [2] And the sons of Kohath: Ambram, Issachar, Hebron, and Ozeel. [3] And the sons of Merari: Mooli and Mouses. [4] And in the ninety-fourth year, Ambram took my daughter Jochebed to himself to be [his] wife, for they were born in one day, he and my daughter. [5] I was eight years old when I went into the land of Canaan, and [was] eighteen years when I slew Shechem, and at nineteen years I became priest, and at twenty-eight years I took a wife, and at forty-eight I went into Egypt. [6] And behold, my children, you are a third generation. [7] In my one hundred and eighteenth year Joseph died."

CHAPTER 13

[1] "And now, my children, I command you: fear the LORD your God with your whole heart and walk in simplicity according to all His law. [2] And also teach your children letters that they may have understanding all their life, reading the Law of God unceasingly. [3] For everyone that knows the Law of the LORD will be honored, ‖ And will not be a stranger wherever he goes. [4] Yes, he will gain many more friends than his parents, ‖ And many men will desire to serve him, ‖ And to hear the Law from his mouth. [5] Work righteousness, therefore, my children, on the earth, ‖ That you may have [it] as a treasure in Heaven. [6] And sow good things in your souls, ‖ That you may find them in your life. But if you sow evil

things, || You will reap every trouble and affliction. [7] Get wisdom in the fear of God with diligence; For though there is a leading into captivity, || And cities and lands are destroyed, || And gold, and silver, and every possession perish, || Nothing can take away the wisdom of the wise, || Save the blindness of ungodliness, and the callousness of sin. [8] For if one keeps oneself from these evil things, || Then even among his enemies wisdom will be a glory to him, || And in a strange country a fatherland, || And in the midst of foes will prove a friend. [9] Whosoever teaches noble things and does them, || Will be enthroned with kings, || As was also my brother Joseph."

CHAPTER 14

[1] "Therefore, my children, I have learned that at the end of the ages you will transgress against the LORD, stretching out hands to wickedness [[against Him]]; and you will become a scorn to all the nations. [2] For our father Israel is pure from the transgressions of the chief priests [[who will lay their hands on the Savior of the world]]. [3] For as the Heaven is purer in the LORD's sight than the earth, so also are you, the lights of Israel, [purer] than all the nations. [4] But if you are darkened through transgressions, what, therefore, will all the nations do living in blindness? Yes, you will bring a curse on our race, because the light of the Law which was given to lighten every man—this you desire to destroy by teaching commandments contrary to the ordinances of God. [5] You will rob the offerings of the LORD, and you will steal choice portions from His portion, eating [them] contemptuously with harlots. [6] And out of covetousness you will teach the commandments of the LORD; you will pollute wedded women, and you will defile the virgins of Jerusalem, and you will be joined with harlots and adulteresses, and you will take the daughters of the nations to be [your] wives, purifying them with an unlawful purification; and your union will be like to Sodom and Gomorrah. [7] And you will be puffed up because of your priesthood, lifting yourselves up against men, and not only so, but also against the commands of God. [8] For you will despise the holy things with jests and laughter."

CHAPTER 15

[1] "Therefore the temple, which the LORD will choose, will be laid waste through your uncleanness, and you will be captives throughout all nations. [2] And you will be an abomination to them, and you will receive reproach and everlasting shame from the righteous judgment of God. [3] And all who hate you will rejoice at your destruction. [4] And if you were not to receive mercy through Abraham, Isaac, and Jacob, our fathers, not one of our seed should be left on the earth.

CHAPTER 16

[1] And now I have learned that for seventy weeks you will go astray, and profane the priesthood, and pollute the sacrifices. [2] And you will make the Law void, and set at nothing the words of the prophets by evil perverseness. [3] And you will persecute righteous men and hate the godly; you will abhor the words of the faithful. [[[4] And a man who renews the Law in the power of the Most High, you will call a deceiver; and at last you will rush [on him] to slay him, not knowing his dignity, taking innocent blood through [the] wickedness on your heads.]] [5] And your holy places will be laid waste even to the ground because of him. [6] And you will have no place that is clean, but you will be a curse and a dispersion among the nations until He will again visit you and in pity will receive you [[through faith and water]]."

CHAPTER 17

[1] "And whereas you have heard concerning the seventy weeks, hear also concerning the priesthood. [2] For in each jubilee there will be a priesthood. And in the first jubilee, the first who is anointed to the priesthood will be great and will speak to God as to a father. And his priesthood will be perfect with the LORD, [[and in the day of his gladness he will arise for the salvation of the world]]. [3] In the second jubilee, he that is anointed will be conceived in the sorrow of beloved ones; and his priesthood will be honored and will be glorified by all. [4] And the third priest will be taken hold of by sorrow. [5] And the fourth will be in pain, because unrighteousness will gather itself against him exceedingly, and all Israel will hate his neighbor—each one. [6] The fifth will be taken hold of by darkness. Likewise also the sixth and the seventh. [7] And in the seventh will be such pollution as I cannot express before men, for they will know it who do these things. [8] Therefore they will be taken captive and become a prey, and their land and their substance will be destroyed. [9] And in the fifth week they will return to their desolate country and will renew the house of the LORD. [10] And in the seventh week they will become priests, [who are] idolaters, adulterers, lovers of money, proud, lawless, lascivious, abusers of children and beasts."

CHAPTER 18

[1] "And after their punishment will have come from the LORD, the priesthood will fail. [2] Then the LORD will raise up a new priest. And to him all the words of the LORD will be revealed; And He will execute a righteous judgment on the earth for a multitude of days. [3] And His star will arise in Heaven as of a King—Lighting up the light of knowledge as the sun [lights] the day, || And He will be magnified in the world. [4] He will shine forth as the sun on the earth, || And will remove all darkness from under Heaven, || And there will be peace in all the earth. [5] The heavens

will exult in His days, || And the earth will be glad, || And the clouds will rejoice, || And the knowledge of the LORD will be poured forth on the earth, || As the water of the seas; And the messengers of the glory of the presence of the LORD will be glad in Him. [6] The heavens will be opened, || And sanctification will come on Him from the temple of glory, || With the Father's voice as from Abraham to Isaac. [7] And the glory of the Most High will be uttered over Him, || And the Spirit of understanding and sanctification will rest on Him [in the water]. [8] For He will give the majesty of the LORD to His sons in truth forevermore; And none will succeed Him for all generations forever. [9] And in His priesthood the nations will be multiplied in knowledge on the earth, || And enlightened through the grace of the LORD: In His priesthood sin will come to an end, || And the lawless will cease to do evil, [[And the just will rest in Him.]] [10] And He will open the gates of paradise, || And will remove the threatening sword against Adam. [11] And He will give to the saints to eat from the Tree of Life, || And the Spirit of holiness will be on them. [12] And Belial will be bound by Him, || And He will give power to His children to tread on the evil spirits. [13] And the LORD will rejoice in His children, || And be well pleased in His beloved ones forever. [14] Then Abraham, and Isaac, and Jacob will exult, || And I will be glad, || And all the saints will clothe themselves with joy."

CHAPTER 19

[1] "And now, my children, you have heard all; therefore, choose for yourselves either the light or the darkness, either the Law of the LORD or the works of Belial." [2] And his sons answered him, saying, [3] "We will walk before the LORD according to His law." And their father said to them, "The LORD is a witness, and His messengers are witnesses, and you are witnesses, and I am a witness, concerning the word of your mouth." [4] And his sons said to him, "We are witnesses." [5] And thus Levi ceased commanding his sons; and he stretched out his feet on the bed, and was gathered to his fathers, after he had lived one hundred and thirty-seven years. [6] And they laid him in a coffin, and afterward they buried him in Hebron, with Abraham, Isaac, and Jacob.

THE TESTAMENT OF JUDAH, THE FOURTH SON OF JACOB AND LEAH

CHAPTER 1

[1] The copy of the words of Judah, what things he spoke to his sons before he died. [2] They gathered themselves together, therefore, and came to him, and he said to them, [3] "Listen, my children, to your father Judah. I was the fourth son born to my father Jacob; and my mother Leah named me Judah, saying, [4] I give thanks to the LORD, because He has given me a fourth

son also. [5] I was swift in my youth, and obedient to my father in everything. And I honored my mother and my mother's sister. [6] And it came to pass, when I became a man, that my father blessed me, saying, You will be a king, prospering in all things."

CHAPTER 2

[1] "And the LORD showed me favor in all my works, both in the field and in the house. [2] I know that I raced a doe, and caught it, and prepared the meat for my father, and he ate. [3] And I used to master the roes in the chase and overtake all that were in the plains. [4] I overtook a wild mare, and caught it, and tamed it. I slew a lion and plucked a kid out of its mouth. [5] I took a bear by its paw and hurled it down the cliff, and it was crushed. I outran the wild boar, and seizing it as I ran, I tore it apart. [6] A leopard in Hebron leaped on my dog, and I caught it by the tail, and hurled it on the rocks, and it was broken in half. [7] I found a wild ox feeding in the fields, and seizing it by the horns, and whirling it around and stunning it, I cast it from myself and slew it."

CHAPTER 3

[1] "And when the two kings of the Canaanites came sheathed in armor against our flocks, and many people with them, I rushed on the king of Hazor single-handedly, [2] and struck him on the greaves, and dragged him down, and so I slew him. And the other, the king of Tappuah, as he sat on his horse, [3] [[I slew, and so I scattered all his people. Achor the king,]] a man of giant stature, I found hurling javelins before and behind as he sat on horseback, and I took up a stone of sixty pounds weight, and hurled it, and struck his horse, and killed it. [4] And I fought with [this] other for two hours; and I cleaved his shield in half, and I chopped off his feet, and killed him. [5] And as I was stripping off his breastplate, behold, nine men, his companions, began to fight with me. [6] And I wound my garment on my hand; and I slung stones at them, and killed four of them, and the rest fled. [7] And my father Jacob slew Beelesath, king of all the kings, a giant in strength—twelve cubits high. [8] And fear fell on them, and they ceased warring against us. [9] Therefore my father was free from anxiety in the wars when I was with my brothers. [10] For he saw in a vision concerning me that a messenger of might followed me everywhere, that I should not be overcome."

CHAPTER 4

[1] "And in the south, there came on us a greater war than that in Shechem; and I joined in battle array with my brothers, and pursued one thousand men, and slew of them two hundred men and four kings. [2] And I went up on the wall, and I slew four mighty men. [3] And so we captured Hazor and took all the spoil."

CHAPTER 5

[1] "On the next day we departed to Aretan, a city strong, and walled, and inaccessible, threatening us with death. [2] But Gad and I approached on the east side of the city, and Reuben and Levi on the west. [3] And they that were on the wall, thinking that we were alone, were drawn down against us. [4] And so my brothers secretly climbed up the wall on both sides by stakes and entered the city while the men did not know it. [5] And we took it with the edge of the sword. And as for those who had taken refuge in the tower, we set fire to the tower and took both it and them. [6] And as we were departing, the men of Tappuah set on our spoil, and delivering it up to our sons, we fought with them as far as Tappuah. [7] And we slew them, and burned their city, and took all that was in it as spoil."

CHAPTER 6

[1] "And when I was at the waters of Kozeba, the men of Jobel came against us to battle. [2] And we fought with them and routed them, and we slew their allies from Shiloh, and we did not leave them power to come in against us. [3] And the men of Makir came on us the fifth day to seize our spoil; and we attacked them and overcame them in fierce battle, for there was a host of mighty men among them, [4] and we slew them before they had gone up the ascent. [5] And when we came to their city, their women rolled stones on us from the brow of the hill on which the city stood, [6] and Simeon and I hid ourselves behind the town, and seized on the heights, and destroyed this city also."

CHAPTER 7

[1] "And the next day it was told to us that the king of the city of Gaash was coming against us with a mighty host. [2] Therefore Dan and I pretended we were Amorites and went into their city as [if] allies. [3] And in the depth of night our brothers came and we opened the gates to them; and we destroyed all the men and their substance, and we took all that was theirs for a prey, and we cast down their three walls. [4] And we drew near to Thamna, where all the substance of the hostile kings was. [5] Then being insulted by them, I was therefore angry, and rushed against them to the summit; and they kept slinging stones and darts against me. [6] And had my brother Dan not aided me, they would have slain me. [7] We came on them, therefore, with wrath, and they all fled; and passing by another way, they implored my father, and he made peace with them. [8] And we did no harm to them, and they became tributary to us, and we restored their spoil to them. [9] And I built Thamna, and my father built Pabael. [10] I was twenty years old when this war occurred. And the Canaanites feared me and my brothers."

CHAPTER 8

[1] "And I had many cattle, and I had Iram the Adullamite for [my] chief herdsman. [2] And when I went to him, I saw Parsaba, king of Adullam, and he spoke to us, and he made us a feast; [3] and when I was heated, he gave me his daughter Bathshua to be [my] wife. [4] She bore me Er, and Onan, and Shelah; and the LORD struck two of them, for Shelah lived, and you are his children."

CHAPTER 9

[1] "And [for] eighteen years my father abode in peace with his brother Esau, and his sons with us, after we had come from Mesopotamia, from Laban. [2] And when eighteen years were fulfilled, in the fortieth year of my life, Esau, the brother of my father, came on us with a mighty and strong people. [3] And Jacob struck Esau with an arrow, and he was taken up wounded on Mount Seir, and as he went, he died at Anoniram, and we pursued after the sons of Esau. [4] Now they had a city with walls of iron and gates of brass; and we could not enter into it, and we encamped around, and besieged it. [5] And when they did not open to us in twenty days, I set up a ladder in the sight of all, and I went up with my shield on my head, sustaining the assault of stones—upwards of three talents weight; [6] and I slew four of their mighty men. And Reuben and Gad slew six others. [7] Then they asked [for] terms of peace from us; and having taken counsel with our father, we received them as tributaries. [8] And they gave us five hundred cors of wheat, five hundred baths of oil, five hundred measures of wine, until the famine, when we went down into Egypt."

CHAPTER 10

[1] "And after these things my son Er took Tamar, from Mesopotamia, a daughter of Aram, to be [his] wife. [2] Now Er was wicked, and he was in need concerning Tamar, because she was not of the land of Canaan. [3] And on the third night a messenger of the LORD struck him. And he had not known her according to the evil craftiness of his mother, for he did not wish to have children by her. [4] In the days of the wedding-feast I gave Onan to her in marriage; and he also in wickedness did not know her, though he spent a year with her. [5] And when I threatened him, he went in to her, but he spilled the seed on the ground, according to the command of his mother, and he also died through wickedness. [6] And I wished to give Shelah to her also, but his mother did not permit it; for she worked evil against Tamar, because she was not of the daughters of Canaan, as she also herself was."

CHAPTER 11

[1] "And I knew that the race of the Canaanites was wicked, but the impulse of youth blinded my mind. [2] And when I saw her pouring out wine, owing to the

intoxication of wine, I was deceived and took her although my father had not counseled [it]. ³ And while I was away, she went and took a wife for Shelah from Canaan. ⁴ And when I knew what she had done, I cursed her in the anguish of my soul. ⁵ And she also died through her wickedness together with her sons."

CHAPTER 12

¹ "And after these things, while Tamar was a widow, she heard after two years that I was going up to shear my sheep, and adorned herself in bridal array, and sat in the city Enaim by the gate. ² For it was a law of the Amorites that she who was about to marry should sit in fornication seven days by the gate. ³ Therefore being drunk with wine, I did not recognize her; and her beauty deceived me, through the fashion of her adorning. ⁴ And I turned aside to her, and said, Let me go in to you. And she said, What will you give me? And I gave her my staff, and my girdle, and the diadem of my kingdom in pledge. ⁵ And I went in to her, and she conceived. And not knowing what I had done, I wished to slay her; but she privily sent my pledges and put me to shame. ⁶ And when I called her, I also heard the secret words which I spoke when lying with her in my drunkenness; ⁷ and I could not slay her, because it was from the LORD. ⁸ For I said, Lest perhaps she did it in subtlety, having received the pledge from another woman. ⁹ But I did not come near her again while I lived, because I had done this abomination in all Israel. ¹⁰ Moreover, they who were in the city said there was no harlot in the gate, because she came from another place, and sat for a while in the gate. ¹¹ And I thought that no one knew that I had gone in to her. ¹² And after this, we came into Egypt to Joseph, because of the famine. And I was forty-six years old, and I lived in Egypt seventy-three years."

CHAPTER 13

¹ "And now I command you, my children, listen to your father Judah, and keep my sayings to perform all the ordinances of the LORD, and to obey the commands of God. ² And do not walk after your lusts, nor in the imaginations of your thoughts in haughtiness of heart; and do not glory in the deeds and strength of your youth, for this is also evil in the eyes of the LORD. ³ Since I also gloried that in wars no beautiful woman's face ever enticed me, and reproved my brother Reuben concerning Bilhah, the wife of my father, the spirits of jealousy and of fornication arrayed themselves against me until I lay with Bathshua the Canaanite, and Tamar, who was espoused to my sons. ⁴ For I said to my father-in-law, I will take counsel with my father, and so I will take your daughter. And he was unwilling, but he showed me a boundless store of gold in his daughter's behalf, for he was a king. ⁵ And he adorned her with gold and pearls and caused her to pour out wine for us at the feast with the beauty of women. ⁶ And the wine turned

my eyes aside, and pleasure blinded my heart. ⁷ And I became enamored, and I laid with her, and transgressed the commandment of the LORD and the commandment of my fathers, and I took her to be [my] wife. ⁸ And the LORD rewarded me according to the imagination of my heart, inasmuch as I had no joy in her children."

CHAPTER 14

¹ "And now, my children, I say to you: do not be drunk with wine, for wine turns the mind away from the truth, and inspires the passion of lust, and leads the eyes into error. ² For the spirit of fornication has wine as a minister to give pleasure to the mind; for these two also take away the mind of man. ³ For if a man drinks wine to drunkenness, it disturbs the mind with filthy thoughts leading to fornication and heats the body to carnal union; and if the occasion of the lust is present, he works the sin, and is not ashamed. ⁴ Such is the inebriated man, my children; for he who is drunken reveres no man. ⁵ For behold, it also made me to err, so that I was not ashamed of the multitude in the city, in that I turned aside to Tamar before the eyes of all, and I worked a great sin, and I uncovered the covering of my sons' shame. ⁶ After I had drunk wine, I did not revere the commandment of God, and I took a woman of Canaan to be [my] wife. ⁷ For the man who drinks wine needs much discretion, my children; and herein is discretion in drinking wine: a man may drink so long as he preserves modesty. ⁸ But if he goes beyond this limit, the spirit of deceit attacks his mind, and it makes the drunkard to talk filthily, and to transgress and not to be ashamed, but even to glory in his shame, and to account himself honorable."

CHAPTER 15

¹ "He that commits fornication is not aware when he suffers loss and is not ashamed when put to dishonor. ² For even though a man is a king and commits fornication, he is stripped of his kingship by becoming the slave of fornication, as I myself also suffered. ³ For I gave my staff, that is, the stay of my tribe; and my girdle, that is, my power; and my diadem, that is, the glory of my kingdom. ⁴ And I indeed converted of these things; I did not eat wine and flesh until my old age, nor did I behold any joy. ⁵ And the messenger of God showed me that women bear rule over king and beggar alike forever. ⁶ And from the king they take away his glory, and from the valiant man his might, and from the beggar even that little which is the stay of his poverty."

CHAPTER 16

¹ "Therefore observe, my children, the right limit in wine; for there are four evil spirits in it: of lust, of hot desire, of profligacy, [and] of shameful gain. ² If you drink wine in gladness, be modest in the fear of God. For if in [your] gladness the fear of God departs, then

drunkenness arises and shamelessness steals in. ³But if you would live soberly, do not touch wine at all, lest you sin in words of outrage, and in fightings and slanders, and transgressions of the commandments of God, and you perish before your time. ⁴Moreover, wine reveals the mysteries of God and men, even as I also revealed the commandments of God and the mysteries of my father Jacob to the Canaanite woman Bathshua, which God commanded me not to reveal. ⁵And wine is a cause both of war and confusion."

CHAPTER 17

¹"And now, I command you, my children, not to love money, nor to gaze on the beauty of women, because for the sake of money and beauty I was led astray to Bathshua the Canaanite. [[²For I know that because of these two things my race will fall into wickedness. ³For they will even mar wise men among my sons and will cause the kingdom of Judah to be diminished, which the LORD gave me because of my obedience to my father. ⁴For I never caused grief to my father Jacob, for all things, whatever he commanded, I did. ⁵And Isaac, the father of my father, blessed me to be king in Israel, and Jacob further blessed me in like manner. ⁶And I know that the kingdom will be established from me."

CHAPTER 18

¹"And I know what evils you will do in the last days.]] ²Beware, therefore, my children, of fornication, and the love of money, and listen to your father Judah. ³For these things withdraw you from the Law of God, || And blind the inclination of the soul, || And teach arrogance, || And do not permit a man to have compassion on his neighbor. ⁴They rob his soul of all goodness, || And oppress him with toils and troubles, || And drive away sleep from him, || And devour his flesh. ⁵And he hinders the sacrifices of God; And he does not remember the blessing of God, || He does not listen to a prophet when he speaks, || And resents the words of godliness. ⁶For he is a slave to two contrary passions, || And cannot obey God, || Because they have blinded his soul, || And he walks in the day as in the night."

CHAPTER 19

¹"My children, the love of money leads to idolatry, because, when led astray through money, men name as gods those who are not gods, and it causes him who has it to fall into madness. ²For the sake of money I lost my children and did not have my conversion and my humiliation; and had the prayers of my father [not] been accepted, I should have died childless. ³But the God of my fathers had mercy on me, because I did it in ignorance. ⁴And the prince of deceit blinded me, and I sinned as a man and as flesh, being corrupted through sins; and I learned my own weakness while thinking myself invincible."

CHAPTER 20

¹"Know, therefore, my children, that two spirits wait on man: the Spirit of truth and the spirit of deceit. ²And in the midst is the spirit of understanding of the mind, to which it belongs to turn wherever it will. ³And the works of truth and the works of deceit are written on the hearts of men, and the LORD knows each one of them. ⁴And there is no time at which the works of men can be hid, for on the heart itself they have been written down before the LORD. ⁵And the Spirit of truth testifies all things and accuses all; and the sinner is burned up by his own heart and cannot raise his face to the Judge."

CHAPTER 21

¹"And now, my children, I command you: love Levi, that you may abide, and do not exalt yourselves against him, lest you be utterly destroyed. ²For the LORD gave the kingdom to me, and the priesthood to him, and He set the kingdom beneath the priesthood. ³He gave the things on the earth to me [and] the things in the heavens to him. ⁴As the Heaven is higher than the earth, so is the priesthood of God higher than the earthly kingdom, unless it falls away through sin from the LORD and is dominated by the earthly kingdom. ⁵For the messenger of the LORD said to me, The LORD chose him rather than you to draw near to Him, and to eat of His table, and to offer Him the first-fruits of the choice things of the sons of Israel, but you will be king of Jacob. ⁶And you will be among them as the sea. For as, on the sea, [both] just and unjust are tossed around—some taken into captivity while some are enriched—so also will every race of men be in you; some will be impoverished, being taken captive, and others will grow rich by plundering the possessions of others. ⁷For the kings will be as sea-monsters; They will swallow men like fishes, || They will enslave the sons and daughters of free men, || They will plunder houses, lands, flocks, money, ⁸And with the flesh of many they will wrongfully feed the ravens and the cranes; And they will advance in evil, uplifted in covetousness, ⁹And there will be false prophets like tempests, || And they will persecute all righteous men."

CHAPTER 22

¹"And the LORD will bring on them divisions against one another. And there will be continual wars in Israel; ²And from among men of another race my kingdom will be brought to an end, || Until the salvation of Israel will come, || Until the appearing of the God of righteousness, || That Jacob [[and all the nations]] may rest in peace. ³And He will guard the might of my kingdom forever; For the LORD swore to me with an oath || That He would not destroy the kingdom from my seed forever."

CHAPTER 23

[1] "Now I have much grief, my children, because of your lewdness, and witchcrafts, and idolatries which you will practice against the kingdom, following them that have familiar spirits, diviners, and demons of error. [2] You will make your daughters singing girls and harlots, and you will mingle in the abominations of the nations. [3] For which things' sake the LORD will bring on you famine and pestilence, death and the sword, besieging by enemies, and revilings of friends, the slaughter of children, the rape of wives, the plundering of possessions, the burning of the temple of God, the laying waste of the land, the enslavement of yourselves among the nations. And they will make some of you eunuchs for their wives, [5] until the LORD visits you, when with perfect heart you convert and walk in all His commandments, and He brings you up from captivity among the nations."

CHAPTER 24

[1] "And after these things a star will arise to you from Jacob in peace, || And a Man will arise [[from my seed]], || Like the Sun of Righteousness, || Walking with the sons of men in meekness and righteousness; And no sin will be found in Him. [2] And the heavens will be open to Him, || To pour out the Spirit, || [Even] the blessing of the Holy Father; [3] And He will pour out the Spirit of grace on you; And you will be to Him sons in truth, || And you will walk in His commandments first and last— [[[4] This Branch of God Most High, || And this Fountain giving life to all.]] [5] Then the scepter of my kingdom will shine forth; And a stem will arise from your root; [6] And a rod of righteousness will grow from it to the nations, || To judge and to save all that call on the LORD."

CHAPTER 25

[1] "And after these things Abraham, and Isaac, and Jacob will arise to life, and my brothers and I will be chiefs of the tribes of Israel: Levi first, I the second, Joseph third, Benjamin fourth, Simeon fifth, Issachar sixth, and so all in order. [2] And the LORD blessed Levi; and the Messenger of the Presence, me; the powers of glory, Simeon; the Heaven, Reuben; the earth, Issachar; the sea, Zebulun; the mountains, Joseph; the Dwelling Place, Benjamin; the luminaries, Dan; Eden, Naphtali; the sun, Gad; the moon, Asher. [3] And you will be the people of the LORD and have one tongue, and there will be no spirit of deceit of Belial there, for he will be cast into the fire forever. [4] And they who have died in grief will arise in joy, || And they who were poor for the LORD's sake will be made rich, || And they who are put to death for the LORD's sake will awake to life. [5] And the deer of Jacob will run in joyfulness, || And the eagles of Israel will fly in gladness; And all the people will glorify the LORD forever."

CHAPTER 26

[1] "Therefore observe, my children, all the Law of the LORD, for there is hope for all them who hold fast to His ways." [2] And he said to them, "Behold, I die before your eyes this day—one hundred and nineteen years old. [3] Let no one bury me in costly apparel, nor tear open my bowels, for this is what they who are kings do; and carry me up to Hebron with you." [4] And Judah, when he had said these things, fell asleep; and his sons did according to everything he commanded them, and they buried him in Hebron, with his fathers.

THE TESTAMENT OF ISSACHAR, THE FIFTH SON OF JACOB AND LEAH

CHAPTER 1

[1] The copy of the words of Issachar. For he called his sons and said to them, [2] "Listen, my children, to your father Issachar; give ear to the words of him who is beloved of the LORD. [3] I was born the fifth son to Jacob, by way of hire for the mandrakes. [4] For my brother Reuben brought in mandrakes from the field, and Rachel met him and took them. And Reuben wept, and at his voice my mother Leah came forth. [5] Now these [mandrakes] were sweet-smelling apples which were produced in the land of Haran below a ravine of water. [6] And Rachel said, I will not give them to you, but they will be to me instead of children. [7] For the LORD has despised me, and I have not borne children to Jacob. Now there were two apples, and Leah said to Rachel, [8] Is it enough for you that you have taken my husband? Will you take these also? [9] And Rachel said to her, You will have Jacob this night for the mandrakes of your son. And Leah said to her, [10] Jacob is mine, for I am the wife of his youth. But Rachel said, Do not boast, and do not vaunt yourself; for he espoused me before you, and he served our father fourteen years for my sake. [11] And had craft not increased on the earth and had the wickedness of men [not] prospered, you would not now see the face of Jacob."

CHAPTER 2

[1] "Then a messenger of the LORD appeared to Jacob, saying, Rachel will bear two children, inasmuch as she has refused company with her husband, and has chosen continency. [2] And had my mother Leah not paid for the two apples for the sake of his company, she would have borne eight sons; for this reason, she bore six, and Rachel bore the two. For on account of the mandrakes the LORD visited her. [3] For He knew that for the sake of children she wished to company with Jacob, and not for lust of pleasure. [4] For also on the next day she again gave up Jacob. Because of the mandrakes, [5] therefore, the LORD listened to Rachel. For though she desired them, she did not eat them, but offered them in the house of the LORD, presenting

them to who was the priest of the Most High at that time.”

CHAPTER 3

¹ “When, therefore, I grew up, my children, I walked in uprightness of heart, and I became a farmer for my father and my brothers, and I brought in fruits from the field according to their season. ² And my father blessed me, for he saw that I walked in rectitude before him. ³ And I was not a busybody in my doings, nor envious and malicious against my neighbor. ⁴ I never slandered anyone, nor did I censure the life of any man, walking as I did in singleness of eye. ⁵ Therefore, when I was thirty-five years old, I took a wife for myself, for my labor wore away my strength, and I never thought on pleasure with women, but owing to my toil, sleep overcame me. ⁶ And my father always rejoiced in my rectitude, because I offered all first-fruits through the priest to the LORD—then to my father also. ⁷ And the LORD increased ten thousandfold His benefits in my hands; and also Jacob, my father, knew that God aided my singleness. ⁸ For on all the poor and oppressed I bestowed the good things of the earth in the singleness of my heart.”

CHAPTER 4

¹ “And now, listen to me, my children, ‖ And walk in singleness of your heart, ‖ For I have seen in it all that is well-pleasing to the LORD. ² The single-[minded] man does not covet gold, ‖ He does not overreach his neighbor, ‖ He does not long after manifold delicacies, ‖ He does not delight in varied apparel. ³ He does not desire to live a long life, ‖ But only waits for the will of God. ⁴ And the spirits of deceit have no power against him, ‖ For he does not look on the beauty of women, ‖ Lest he should pollute his mind with corruption. ⁵ There is no envy in his thoughts; [[No malicious person makes his soul to pine away, ‖]] Nor worry with insatiable desire in his mind. ⁶ For he walks in singleness of soul, ‖ And beholds all things in uprightness of heart, ‖ Shunning eyes [made] evil through the error of the world, ‖ Lest he should see the perversion of any of the commandments of the LORD.”

CHAPTER 5

¹ “Therefore, my children, keep the Law of God, ‖ And get singleness. And walk in guilelessness, ‖ Not playing the busybody with the business of your neighbor, ² But love the LORD and your neighbor, ‖ Have compassion on the poor and weak. ³ Bow down your back to farming, ‖ And toil in labors in all manner of farming, ‖ Offering gifts to the LORD with thanksgiving. ⁴ For the LORD will bless you with the first-fruits of the earth, even as He blessed all the saints from Abel even until now. ⁵ For no other portion is given to you than of the fatness of the earth, whose fruits are raised by toil. ⁶ For our father Jacob blessed me with blessings of the earth and of first-fruits. ⁷ And Levi and Judah were glorified by the LORD even among the sons of Jacob, for the LORD gave them an inheritance: indeed, He gave the priesthood to Levi and the kingdom to Judah. ⁸ And you must therefore obey them and walk in the singleness of your father, [[for it has been given to Gad to destroy the troops that are coming on Israel]].”

CHAPTER 6

¹ “Therefore, my children, know that in the last times Your sons will forsake singleness, ‖ And will cleave to insatiable desire; And leaving guilelessness will draw near to malice; And forsaking the commandments of the LORD, ‖ They will cleave to Belial. ² And leaving farming, ‖ They will follow after their own wicked devices, ‖ And they will be dispersed among the nations, ‖ And will serve their enemies. ³ And, therefore, give these commands to your children, that, if they sin, they may [even] more quickly return to the LORD; ⁴ for He is merciful, and will deliver them, even to bring them back into their land.”

CHAPTER 7

¹ “Behold, therefore, as you see, I am one hundred and twenty-six years old and am not conscious of committing any sin. ² I have not known any woman except my wife; I never committed fornication by the uplifting of my eyes. ³ I did not drink wine to be led astray thereby; I did not covet any desirable thing that was my neighbor’s. ⁴ Guile did not arise in my heart; A lie did not pass through my lips. ⁵ If any man was in distress, ‖ I joined my sighs with his, ‖ And I shared my bread with the poor. I worked godliness, ‖ [And] all my days I kept truth. ⁶ I loved the LORD; Likewise also every man with all my heart. ⁷ So you must also do these things, my children, ‖ And every spirit of Belial will flee from you, ‖ And no deed of wicked men will rule over you; And you will subdue every wild beast ‖ Since you have the God of the heavens and earth with you; [And] walk with men in singleness of heart.” ⁸ And having said these things, he commanded his sons that they should carry him up to Hebron, and bury him there in the cave with his fathers. And he stretched out his feet and died at a good old age; with every limb sound, and with strength unabated, he slept the continuous sleep.

THE TESTAMENT OF ZEBULUN, THE SIXTH SON OF JACOB AND LEAH

CHAPTER 1

¹ The copy of the words of Zebulun, which he enjoined on his sons before he died in the one hundred and fourteenth year of his life, two years after the death of Joseph. ² And he said to them, “Listen to me,

you sons of Zebulun, attend to the words of your father. [3] I, Zebulun, was born [as] a good gift to my parents. For when I was born my father was increased very exceedingly, both in flocks and herds, when with the straked rods he had his portion. [4] I am not conscious that I have sinned all my days, save in thought. [5] Nor yet do I remember that I have done any iniquity, except the sin of ignorance which I committed against Joseph; for I covenanted with my brothers not to tell my father what had been done. [6] But I wept [for] many days in secret on account of Joseph, for I feared my brothers, because they had all agreed that if anyone should declare the secret, he should be slain. [7] But when they wished to kill him, I adjured them much with tears not to be guilty of this sin."

CHAPTER 2

[1] "For Simeon and Gad came against Joseph to kill him, and he said to them with tears: [2] Pity me, my brothers, have mercy on the bowels of our father Jacob. Do not lay your hands on me to shed innocent blood, for I have not sinned against you. [3] And if I have indeed sinned, discipline me with disciplining, my brothers, but do not lay your hand on me for the sake of our father Jacob. [4] And as he spoke these words, wailing as he did so, I was unable to bear his lamentations, and began to weep, and my liver was poured out, and all the substance of my bowels was loosened. [5] And I wept with Joseph, and my heart sounded, and the joints of my body trembled, and I was not able to stand. [6] And when Joseph saw me weeping with him, and them coming against him to slay him, he fled behind me, imploring them. [7] But meanwhile Reuben arose and said, Come, my brothers, let us not slay him, but let us cast him into one of these dry pits, which our fathers dug and found no water. [8] For this reason the LORD forbade that water should rise up in them, in order that Joseph should be preserved. And they did so, until they sold him to the Ishmaelites."

CHAPTER 3

[1] "For I had no share in his price, my children. [2] But Simeon, and Gad, and six other of our brothers took the price of Joseph, and bought sandals for themselves, and their wives, and their children, saying, [3] We will not eat of it, for it is the price of our brother's blood, but we will assuredly tread it under foot, because he said that he would be king over us, and so let us see what will become of his dreams. [4] Therefore it is written in the writing of the Law of Moses that whosoever will not raise up seed to his brother, his sandal should be unloosed, and they should spit in his face. [5] And the brothers of Joseph did not wish that their brother should live, and the LORD loosed from them the sandal which they wore against Joseph their brother. [6] For when they came

into Egypt they were unloosed by the servants of Joseph outside the gate, and so they paid respect to Joseph after the fashion of King Pharaoh. [7] And not only did they pay respect to him, but were also spit on, falling down before him immediately, and so they were put to shame before the Egyptians. [8] For after this the Egyptians heard all the evils that they had done to Joseph."

CHAPTER 4

[1] "And after he was sold, my brothers sat down to eat and drink. [2] But I, through pity for Joseph, did not eat, but watched the pit, since Judah feared lest Simeon, Dan, and Gad should rush off and slay him. [3] But when they saw that I did not eat, they set me to watch him, until he was sold to the Ishmaelites. [4] And when Reuben came and heard that [Joseph] had been sold while he was away, he tore his garments, [and] mourning, said, [5] How will I look on the face of my father Jacob? [6] And he took the money and ran after the merchants, but as he failed to find them, he returned grieving. But the merchants had left the broad road and marched through the Troglodytes by a short cut. [7] But Reuben was grieved and ate no food that day. [8] Therefore Dan came to him and said, Do not weep, neither grieve; for we have found what we can say to our father Jacob. [9] Let us slay a kid of the goats and dip the coat of Joseph in it; [10] and let us send it to Jacob, saying, Know, is this the coat of your son? [11] And they did so. For they stripped off from Joseph his coat when they were selling him and put the garment of a slave on him. [12] Now Simeon took the coat, and would not give it up, for he wished to tear it with his sword, as he was angry that Joseph lived and that he had not slain him. [13] Then we all rose up and said to him, If you do not give up the coat, we will say to our father that you alone did this evil thing in Israel. And so he gave it to them, and they did even as Dan had said."

CHAPTER 5

[1] "And now, my children, I bid you to keep the commands of the LORD, and to show mercy to your neighbors, and to have compassion toward all, not toward men only, but also toward beasts. [2] For all this thing's sake the LORD blessed me, and when all my brothers were sick, I escaped without sickness, for the LORD knows the purposes of each. [3] Therefore, have compassion in your hearts, my children, because even as a man does to his neighbor, even so will the LORD do to him also. [4] For the sons of my brothers were getting sick and dying on account of Joseph, because they did not show mercy in their hearts; but my sons were preserved without sickness, as you know. [5] And when I was in the land of Canaan, by the seacoast, I made a catch of fish for my father Jacob; and when many were drowned in the sea, I continued unharmed."

CHAPTER 6

[1] "I was the first to make a boat to sail on the sea, for the LORD gave me understanding and wisdom therein. [2] And I let down a rudder behind it, and I stretched a sail on another upright piece of wood in the midst. [3] And I sailed therein along the shores, catching fish for the house of my father until we came to Egypt. [4] [[And through compassion I shared my catch with every stranger. And if a man was a stranger, or sick, or aged, I boiled the fish, and dressed them well, and offered them to all men, as every man had need, grieving with and having compassion on them. [5] For this reason the LORD also satisfied me with abundance of fish when catching fish; for he that shares with his neighbor receives manifold more from the LORD.]] [6] For five years I caught fish [[and gave thereof to every man whom I saw, [8] and enough for all the house of my father]]. [7] And in the summer I caught fish, and in the winter I kept sheep with my brothers."

CHAPTER 7

[[[1] "Now I will declare to you what I did: I saw a man in distress through nakedness in wintertime, and had compassion on him, and secretly stole a garment from my father's house, and gave it to him who was in distress. [2] Therefore, my children, from that which God bestows on you, show compassion and mercy without hesitation to all men, and give to every man with a good heart. [3] And if you do not have the means to give to him that needs, have compassion for him in yearnings of mercy. [4] I know that my hand did not find the means to give to him that needed, and I walked with him weeping for seven furlongs, and my bowels yearned toward him in compassion."

CHAPTER 8

[1] "Have, therefore, yourselves also, my children, compassion toward every man with mercy, that the LORD may also have compassion and mercy on you. [2] Because also in the last days God will send His compassion on the earth, and wheresoever He finds yearnings of mercy He dwells in him. [3] For in the degree in which a man has compassion on his neighbors, in the same degree the LORD also has [compassion] on him.]] [4] And when we went down into Egypt, Joseph bore no malice against us. [5] To whom taking heed, you also, my children, must approve yourselves without malice, and love one another; and do not set down in account—each one of you—evil against his brother. [6] For this breaks unity and divides all kindred, and troubles the soul, and wears away the countenance."

CHAPTER 9

[1] "Therefore, observe the waters and know when they flow together—they sweep along stones, trees, [2] earth, and other things. But if they are divided into many streams, the earth swallows them up, and they vanish away. [3] So you will also be if you are divided. [4] Do not be, therefore, divided into two heads, for everything which the LORD made has but one head, and two shoulders, two hands, two feet, and all the remaining members. [5] For I have learned in the writing of my fathers that you will be divided in Israel, and will follow two kings, and will work every abomination. [6] And your enemies will lead you captive, and you will be treated evil among the nations with many infirmities and tribulations. [7] And after these things you will remember the LORD, and convert, [[And He will cause you to return]]; for He is merciful and compassionate. And He does not set down in account evil to the sons of men, because they are flesh, and the spirits of deceit deceive them in all their deeds. [8] And after these things the LORD Himself will arise to you—the Light of righteousness—[[and healing and compassion will be in His wings. He will redeem all the captivity of the sons of men from Belial, and every spirit of deceit will be trodden down]]. And He will bring back all the nations into zeal for Him. And you will return to your land. And you will see Him in Jerusalem, for His Name's sake. [9] And again through the wickedness of your works you will provoke Him to anger, and you will be cast away by Him to the time of consummation."

CHAPTER 10

[1] "And now, my children, do not grieve that I am dying, nor be cast down in that I am coming to my end. [2] For I will rise again in the midst of you, as a ruler in the midst of his sons; and I will rejoice in the midst of my tribe, as many as will keep the Law of the LORD and the commandments of their father Zebulun. [3] But the LORD will bring continuous fire on the ungodly and destroy them throughout all generations. [4] But I am now hastening away to my rest, as my fathers also did. [5] But fear the LORD our God with all your strength all the days of your life." [6] And when he had said these things, he fell asleep at a good old age. [7] And his sons laid him in a wooden coffin. And afterward they carried him up and buried him in Hebron with his fathers.

THE TESTAMENT OF DAN, THE SEVENTH SON OF JACOB AND BILHAH

CHAPTER 1

[1] The copy of the words of Dan, which he spoke to his sons in his last days, in the one hundred and twenty-fifth year of his life. [2] For he called together his family, and said, "Listen to my words, you sons of Dan; and give heed to the words of your father. [3] I have proved in my heart, and in my whole life, that truth with just dealing is good and well pleasing to God, and that lying and anger are evil, because they teach man all wickedness. [4] I confess, therefore, this day to you, my children, that in my heart I resolved

on the death of my brother Joseph, the true and good man. [[⁵ And I rejoiced that he was sold, because his father loved him more than us.]] ⁶ For the spirit of jealousy and vainglory said to me, You yourself are also his son. ⁷ And one of the spirits of Belial stirred me up, saying, Take this sword, and slay Joseph with it, so your father will love you when he is dead. ⁸ Now this is the spirit of anger that persuaded me to crush Joseph as a leopard crushes a kid. ⁹ But the God of my fathers did not permit him to fall into my hands, so that I should find him alone and slay him and cause a second tribe to be destroyed in Israel."

CHAPTER 2

¹ "And now, my children, behold, I am dying, and I tell you of a truth, that unless you keep yourselves from the spirit of lying and of anger, and love truth and longsuffering, you will perish. ² For anger is blindness and does not permit one to see the face of any man with truth. ³ For though it may be a father or a mother, he behaves toward them as enemies; though it may be a brother, he does not know him; though it may be a prophet of the Lord, he disobeys him; though a righteous man, he does not regard him; though a friend, he does not acknowledge him. ⁴ For the spirit of anger encompasses him with the net of deceit, and blinds his eyes, and through lying, darkens his mind, and gives him its own peculiar vision. ⁵ And with which encompasses it—his eyes? With hatred of heart, so as to be envious of his brother."

CHAPTER 3

¹ "For anger is an evil thing, my children, for it troubles even the soul itself. ² And it makes the body of the angry man its own, and it gets the mastery over his soul, and it bestows power on the body that it may work all iniquity. ³ And when the body does all these things, the soul justifies what is done, since it does not see right. ⁴ Therefore he that is wrathful, if he is a mighty man, has a threefold power in his anger: one by the help of his servants; and a second by his wealth, whereby he persuades and overcomes wrongfully; and thirdly, having his own natural power, he thereby works the evil. ⁵ And though the wrathful man may be weak, yet he has a power twofold of that which is by nature, for wrath always aids such in lawlessness. ⁶ This spirit always goes with lying at the right hand of Satan, that with cruelty and lying his works may be worked."

CHAPTER 4

¹ "Therefore, understand the power of wrath, that it is vain. ² For it first of all gives provocation by word; then by deeds it strengthens him who is angry, and with sharp losses disturbs his mind, and so stirs up his soul with great wrath. ³ Therefore, when anyone speaks against you, do not be moved to anger, [[and if any man praises you as holy men, do not be uplifted: do not be moved either to delight or to disgust]]. ⁴ For first it pleases the hearing, and so makes the mind keen to perceive the grounds for provocation; and then being enraged, he thinks that he is justly angry. ⁵ If you fall into any loss or ruin, my children, do not be afflicted, for this very spirit makes [a man] desire that which is perishable in order that he may be enraged through the affliction. ⁶ And if you suffer loss voluntarily, or involuntarily, do not be vexed, for from vexation arises wrath with lying. ⁷ Moreover, a twofold mischief is wrath with lying; and they assist one another in order to disturb the heart; and when the soul is continually disturbed, the Lord departs from it, and Belial rules over it."

CHAPTER 5

¹ "Therefore observe, my children, the commandments of the Lord, and keep His law. Depart from wrath and hate lying, that the Lord may dwell among you and Belial may flee from you. ² Speak truth, each one, with his neighbor; so you will not fall into wrath and confusion, but you will be in peace, having the God of peace, so no war will prevail over you. ³ Love the Lord throughout all your life, and [love] one another with a true heart. ⁴ I know that in the last days you will depart from the Lord, and provoke Levi to anger, and fight against Judah, but you will not prevail against them, for a messenger of the Lord will guide them both; for by them Israel will stand. ⁵ And whenever you depart from the Lord, you will walk in all evil and work the abominations of the nations, going whoring after women of the lawless ones while the spirits of wickedness work in you with all wickedness. [[⁶ For I have read in the scroll of Enoch, the righteous, that your prince is Satan, and that all the spirits of wickedness and pride will conspire to attend constantly on the sons of Levi, to cause them to sin before the Lord. ⁷ And my sons will draw near to Levi, and sin with them in all things. And the sons of Judah will be covetous, plundering other men's goods like lions.]] ⁸ Therefore you will be led away [with them] into captivity, ‖ And you will receive all the plagues of Egypt there, ‖ And all the evils of the nations. ⁹ And so when you return to the Lord you will obtain mercy, ‖ And He will bring you into His sanctuary, ‖ And He will give you peace. ¹⁰ And there will arise to you from the tribe of [[Judah and of]] Levi the Salvation of the Lord; And He will make war against Belial ‖ And execute an everlasting vengeance on our enemies; ¹¹ And He will take the captivity from Belial—[[the souls of the saints]], ‖ And turn disobedient hearts to the Lord, ‖ And give continuous peace to them that call on Him. ¹² And the saints will rest in Eden, ‖ And the righteous will rejoice in the New Jerusalem, ‖ And it will be to the glory of God forever. ¹³ And Jerusalem will no longer endure desolation, ‖ Nor will Israel be led captive, ‖ For the Lord will be in the midst of it [[living among

men]], ‖ And the Holy One of Israel will reign over it [[in humility and in poverty; And he who believes on Him will reign among men in truth]]."

CHAPTER 6

[1] "And now, fear the LORD, my children, and beware of Satan and his spirits. [2] Draw near to God and to the Messenger that intercedes for you, for He is a mediator between God and man, and for the peace of Israel He will stand up against the kingdom of the enemy. [3] Therefore the enemy is eager to destroy all that call on the LORD. [4] For he knows that on the day on which Israel will convert, the kingdom of the enemy will be brought to an end. [5] For this very Messenger of peace will strengthen Israel, that it does not fall into the extremity of evil. [6] And it will be in the time of the lawlessness of Israel that the LORD will not depart from them, but will transform them into a nation that does His will, for none of the messengers will be equal to Him. [7] And His Name will be in every place in Israel and among the nations. [8] Therefore keep yourselves, my children, from every evil work, and cast away wrath and all lying, and love truth and long-suffering. [9] And also impart to your children the things which you have heard from your father [[that the Savior of the nations may receive you, for He is true and long-suffering, meek and lowly, and teaches the Law of God by His works]]. [10] Therefore, depart from all unrighteousness, and cleave to the righteousness of God, and your race will be saved forever. And bury me near my fathers."

CHAPTER 7

[1] And when he had said these things, he kissed them and fell asleep at a good old age. [2] And his sons buried him, and after that they carried up his bones, and placed them near Abraham, and Isaac, and Jacob. [[[3] Nevertheless, Dan prophesied to them that they should forget their God and should be alienated from the land of their inheritance, and from the race of Israel, and from the family of their seed.]]

THE TESTAMENT OF NAPHTALI, THE EIGHTH SON OF JACOB AND BILHAH

CHAPTER 1

[1] The copy of the testament of Naphtali, which he ordained at the time of his death in the one hundred and thirtieth year of his life. [2] When his sons were gathered together in the seventh month, on the first day of the month, while still in good health, he made them a feast of food and wine. [3] And after he was awake in the morning, he said to them, "I am dying"; and they did not believe him. [4] And as he glorified the LORD, he grew strong and said that after yesterday's feast he should die. [5] And he then began to say, "Hear, my children—you sons of Naphtali—hear the words of your father. [6] I was born from Bilhah, and because Rachel dealt craftily, and gave Bilhah in place of herself to Jacob, and she conceived and bore me on Rachel's knees, therefore she called my name Naphtali. [7] For Rachel loved me very much because I was born on her lap; and when I was still young, she was accustomed to kiss me, and say, [8] May I have a brother of yours from my own womb, like to you. [9] From where also Joseph was like to me in all things, according to the prayers of Rachel. Now my mother was Bilhah, daughter of Rotheus, the brother of Deborah, Rebekah's nurse, who was born on one and the same day with Rachel. [10] And Rotheus was of the family of Abraham, a Chaldean, God-fearing, free-born, and noble. [11] And he was taken captive and was bought by Laban; and he gave him his handmaid Euna to be [his] wife, and she bore a daughter and called her name Zilpah after the name of the village in which he had been taken captive. [12] And next she bore Bilhah, saying, My daughter hastens after what is new, for as soon as she was born she seized the breast and hastened to suck it."

CHAPTER 2

[1] "And I was swift on my feet like the deer, and my father Jacob appointed me for all messages, and he gave me his blessing as a deer. [2] For as the potter knows how much the vessel is to contain, and brings clay accordingly, so also the LORD makes the body after the likeness of the spirit, and He implants the spirit according to the capacity of the body. [3] And the one does not fall short of the other by a third part of a hair; for by weight, and measure, and rule was all the creation made. [4] And as the potter knows the use of each vessel, what it is appropriate for, so also the LORD knows the body, how far it will persist in goodness, and when it begins in evil. [5] For there is no inclination or thought which the LORD does not know, for He created every man after His own image. [6] As a man's strength, so also is his work; and as his mind, so also is his skill; and as his purpose, so also is his achievement; and as his heart, so also is his mouth; as his eye, so also is his sleep; as his soul, so also is his word, either in the Law of the LORD or in the works of Belial. [7] And as there is a division between light and darkness, between seeing and hearing, so also is there a division between man and man, and between woman and woman; and it is not to be said that the one is like the other, either in face or in mind. [8] For God made all things good in their order: the five senses in the head (and He joined the neck to the head, also adding the hair to it for comeliness and glory), then the heart for understanding, the belly for excrement, and the stomach for [grinding], the windpipe for taking in [the breath], the liver for wrath, the gall for bitterness, the spleen for laughter, the reins for prudence, the muscles of the loins for power, the lungs for drawing in, the loins for strength, and so forth. [9] So then, my children, let all your works be

done in order with good intent in the fear of God, and do nothing disorderly in scorn or out of its due season. [10] For if you command the eye to hear, it cannot; so neither can you do the works of light while you are in darkness."

CHAPTER 3

[1] "Therefore, do not be eager to corrupt your doings through covetousness or to deceive your souls with vain words, because if you keep silence in purity of heart, you will understand how to hold fast the will of God and to cast away the will of Belial. [2] Sun, and moon, and stars do not change their order; so you also must not change the Law of God in the disorderliness of your doings. [3] The nations went astray, and forsook the LORD, and changed their order, and obeyed stocks and stones, spirits of deceit. [4] But you will not be so, my children, recognizing in the expanse, in the earth, and in the sea, and in all created things, the LORD who made all things, that you do not become as Sodom, which changed the order of nature. [5] In like manner the Watchers also changed the order of their nature, whom the LORD cursed at the flood, on whose account He made the earth without inhabitants and fruitless."

CHAPTER 4

[1] "These things I say to you, my children, for I have read in the writing of Enoch that you yourselves will also depart from the LORD, walking according to all the lawlessness of the nations, and you will do according to all the wickedness of Sodom. [2] And the LORD will bring captivity on you, and there you will serve your enemies, and you will be bowed down with every affliction and tribulation, until the LORD has consumed you all. [3] And after you have become diminished and made few, you will return and acknowledge the LORD your God, and He will bring you back into your land, according to His abundant mercy. [4] And it will be that after they come into the land of their fathers, they will again forget the LORD and become ungodly. [5] And the LORD will scatter them on the face of all the earth, until the Compassion of the LORD will come—a Man working righteousness and working mercy to all of them that are far off, and to them that are near."

CHAPTER 5

[1] "For in the fortieth year of my life, I saw a vision on the Mount of Olives, on the east of Jerusalem, that the sun and the moon were standing still. [2] And behold, Isaac, the father of my father, said to us, Run and lay hold of them, each one according to his strength; and the sun and moon will belong to him that seizes them. [3] And all of us ran together, and Levi laid hold of the sun, and Judah outstripped the others and seized the moon, and both of them were lifted up with them. [4] And when Levi became as [the] sun, behold, a certain young man gave twelve palm branches to him; [5] and Judah was bright as the moon, and under their feet were twelve rays. [[[6] And the two, Levi and Judah, ran, and laid hold of them,]] [7] and a bull on the earth, with two great horns, and an eagle's wings on its back; and we wished to seize him, but could not. [8] But Joseph came, and seized him, and ascended up with him on high. And I saw, for I was there, and behold, a holy writing appeared to us, saying, Assyrians, Medes, Persians, [[Chaldeans,]] [and] Syrians will possess in captivity the twelve tribes of Israel."

CHAPTER 6

[1] "And again after seven days I saw our father Jacob standing by the Sea of Jamnia, and we were with him. [2] And behold, there came a ship sailing by, without sailors or pilot; and there was written on the ship: THE SHIP OF JACOB. [3] And our father said to us, Come, let us embark on our ship. [4] And when he had gone on board, there arose a vehement storm, and a mighty tempest of wind; and our father, who was holding the helm, departed from us. [5] And we, being tossed with the tempest, were borne along over the sea; and the ship was filled with water, [and was] pounded by mighty waves, until it was broken up. [6] And Joseph fled away on a little boat, and we were all divided on nine planks, and Levi and Judah were together. [7] And we were all scattered to the ends of the earth. [8] Then Levi, girt around with sackcloth, prayed for us all to the LORD. [9] And when the storm ceased, the ship reached the land as it were in peace. [10] And our father came, and we all rejoiced with one accord."

CHAPTER 7

[1] "I told these two dreams to my father; and he said to me, These things must be fulfilled in their season, after Israel has endured many things. [2] Then my father says to me, I believe God that Joseph lives, for I see that the LORD always numbers him with you. [3] And he said, weeping, Ah me! My son Joseph, you live, though I do not see you, and you do not see Jacob who begot you. [4] He caused me also, therefore, to weep by these words, and I burned in my heart to declare that Joseph had been sold, but I feared my brothers."

CHAPTER 8

[1] "And behold, my children, I have shown the last times to you, how everything will come to pass in Israel. [2] Therefore, also charge your children that they should be united to Levi and to Judah: For salvation will arise to Israel through them, || And Jacob will be blessed in them. [3] For through their tribes God will appear [dwelling among men] on earth, || To save the race of Israel, || And to gather together the righteous from among the nations. [4] If you work that which is good, my children, || Both men and messengers will bless you; And God will be glorified among the

nations through you, || And the Devil will flee from you, || And the wild beasts will fear you, || And the LORD will love you, || [[And the messengers will cleave to you]]. ⁵ As a man who has trained a child well is kept in kindly remembrance, || So also for a good work there is a good remembrance before God. ⁶ But him that does not [do] that which is good, || Both messengers and men will curse, || And God will be dishonored among the nations through him, || And the Devil will make him as his own peculiar instrument, || And every wild beast will master him, || And the LORD will hate him. ⁷ For the commandments of the Law are twofold, || And through prudence they must be fulfilled. ⁸ For there is a season for a man to embrace his wife, || And a season to abstain from that for his prayer. ⁹ So then, there are two commandments, and unless they are done in due order, they bring very great sin on men. ¹⁰ So it is also with the other commandments. Therefore, be wise in God, my children, and prudent, understanding the order of His commandments and the laws of every word that the LORD may love you."

CHAPTER 9

¹ And when he had charged them with many such words, he exhorted them that they should remove his bones to Hebron, and that they should bury him with his fathers. ² And when he had eaten and drunken with a merry heart, he covered his face and died. ³ And his sons did according to all that their father Naphtali had commanded them.

THE TESTAMENT OF GAD, THE NINTH SON OF JACOB AND ZILPAH

CHAPTER 1

¹ The copy of the testament of Gad, what things he spoke to his sons in the one hundred and twenty-fifth year of his life, saying to them, ² "Listen, my children. I was the ninth son born to Jacob, and I was valiant in keeping the flocks. ³ Accordingly, I guarded the flock at night; and whenever the lion came, or the wolf, or any wild beast against the fold, I pursued it, and overtaking [it], I seized its foot with my hand and hurled it about a stone's throw, and so killed it. ⁴ Now my brother Joseph was feeding the flock with us for upwards of thirty days, and being young, he fell sick by reason of the heat. ⁵ And he returned to Hebron to our father, who made him lie down near him, because he loved him greatly. ⁶ And Joseph told our father that the sons of Zilpah and Bilhah were slaying the best of the flock and eating them against the judgment of Reuben and Judah. ⁷ For he saw that I had delivered a lamb out of the mouth of a bear and put the bear to death, but had slain the lamb, being grieved concerning it that it could not live, and that we had eaten it. ⁸ And regarding this matter, I was angry with Joseph until the day that he was sold, ⁹ and the spirit of hatred was in me, and I did not wish either to hear of Joseph with the ears or see him with the eyes, because he rebuked us to our faces, saying that we were eating of the flock without Judah. For whatever things he told our father, he believed him."

CHAPTER 2

¹ "I now confess my sin, my children, that oftentimes I wished to kill him, because I hated him from my heart. ² Moreover, I hated him even more for his dreams; and I wished to lick him out of the land of the living, even as an ox licks up the grass of the field. ³ Therefore Simeon and I sold him to the Ishmaelites [[for thirty pieces of gold, and ten of them we hid, and showed the twenty to our brothers]] ⁴ And thus we were bent on slaying him through covetousness. ⁵ And the God of my fathers delivered him from my hands, that I should not work lawlessness in Israel."

CHAPTER 3

¹ "And now, my children, listen to the words of truth to work righteousness, and all the Law of the Most High, and do not go astray through the spirit of hatred, for it is evil in all the doings of men. ² Whatever a man does, the hater abominates himself: and though a man works the Law of the LORD, he does not praise Him; though a man fears the LORD, and takes pleasure in that which is righteous, he does not love Him. ³ He disparages the truth, he envies him that prospers, he welcomes evil-speaking, he loves arrogance, for hatred blinds his soul—as I also then looked on Joseph."

CHAPTER 4

¹ "Therefore, beware of hatred, my children, for it even works lawlessness against the LORD Himself. ² For it will not hear the words of His commandments concerning the loving of one's neighbor, and it sins against God. ³ For if a brother stumbles, it immediately delights to proclaim it to all men, and is urgent that he should be judged for it, and be punished, and be put to death. ⁴ And if it is a servant, it stirs him up against his master, and with every affliction it devises against him [that], if it were possible, he can be put to death. ⁵ For hatred also works with envy against them that prosper; so long as it hears of or sees their success, it always languishes. ⁶ For as love would even give life to the dead and would call back them that are condemned to die, so hatred would slay the living, and it would not permit those that had sinned to live. ⁷ For the spirit of hatred works together with Satan, through hastiness of spirit, in all things to men's death; but the spirit of love works together with the Law of God in long-suffering to the salvation of men."

CHAPTER 5

[1] "Therefore hatred is evil, for it constantly mates with lying, speaking against the truth; and it makes small things to be great, and causes the light to be darkness, and calls the sweet bitter, and teaches slander, and kindles wrath, and stirs up war, and violence, and all covetousness; [2] it fills the heart with evils and devilish poison. Therefore, I say these things to you from experience, my children, that you may drive hatred away, which is of the Devil, and cleave to the love of God. Righteousness casts out hatred, humility destroys envy. [3] For he that is just and humble is ashamed to do what is unjust, not being reproved by another, but by his own heart, because the LORD looks on his inclination. [4] He does not speak against a holy man, because the fear of God overcomes hatred. [5] For fearing lest he should offend the LORD, he will not do wrong to any man, even in thought. [6] I learned these things at last, after I had converted concerning Joseph. [7] For true conversion after a godly sort [[destroys ignorance, and]] drives away the darkness, and enlightens the eyes, and gives knowledge to the soul, and leads the mind to salvation. [8] And those things which it has not learned from man, it knows through conversion. [9] For God brought a disease of the liver on me; and had the prayers of my father Jacob not aided me, my spirit would have surely departed. [10] For by what things a man transgresses, by the same he is also punished. [11] Since, therefore, my liver was mercilessly set against Joseph, I too suffered in my liver mercilessly, and was judged for eleven months, for so long a time as I had been angry against Joseph."

CHAPTER 6

[1] "And now, my children, I exhort each one of you to love his brother and put away hatred from your hearts. Love one another in deed, and in word, and in the inclination of the soul. [2] For I spoke peaceably to Joseph in the presence of my father, and when I had gone out, the spirit of hatred darkened my mind, and stirred up my soul to slay him. [3] Therefore love one another from the heart; and if a man sins against you, cast out the poison of hate and speak peaceably to him, and do not hold guile in your soul; and if he confesses and converts, forgive him. [4] But if he denies it, do not get into a passion with him, lest catching the poison from you, he takes to swearing and so you sin doubly. [[5] Do not let another man hear your secrets when engaged in legal strife, lest he comes to hate you, and becomes your enemy, and commits a great sin against you; for oftentimes he addresses you cunningly or busies himself concerning you with wicked intent.]] [6] And though he denies it and yet has a sense of shame when reproved, give over reproving him. [7] For he who denies may convert so as not to wrong you again; yes, he may also honor you, and be at peace with you. [8] And if he is shameless and persists in his wrongdoing, even so forgive him from the heart, and leave the avenging to God."

CHAPTER 7

[1] "If a man prospers more than you, do not be vexed, but also pray for him, that he may have perfect prosperity. [2] For so it is expedient for you. And if he is further exalted, do not be envious of him, remembering that all flesh will die; and offer praise to God, who gives good and profitable things to all men. [3] Seek out the judgments of the LORD and your mind will rest and be at peace. [4] And though a man becomes rich by evil means, even as Esau, the brother of my father, do not be jealous, [5] but wait for the end from the LORD. For if he takes away [from a man] wealth (gotten by evil means), He forgives him if he converts, but the unconverted is reserved for continuous punishment. [6] For the poor man, if free from envy, pleases the LORD in all things—he is blessed beyond all men, because he does not have the travail of vain men. [7] Therefore put away jealousy from your souls and love one another with uprightness of heart."

CHAPTER 8

[1] "Therefore, tell these things to your children, that they may honor Judah and Levi, for the LORD will raise up salvation to Israel from them. [[2] For I know that at the end your children will depart from Him, and will walk in all wickedness, and affliction, and corruption before the LORD.]]" [3] And when he had rested for a little while, he said again, "My children, obey your father, and bury me near to my fathers." [4] And he drew up his feet and fell asleep in peace. [5] And after five years they carried him up to Hebron and laid him with his fathers.

THE TESTAMENT OF ASHER, THE TENTH SON OF JACOB AND ZILPAH

CHAPTER 1

[1] The copy of the Testament of Asher, what things he spoke to his sons in the one hundred and twenty-fifth year of his life. [2] For while he was still in health, he said to them, "Listen, you children of Asher, to your father, and I will declare to you all that is upright in the sight of the LORD. [3] God has given two ways to the sons of men, and two inclinations, and two kinds of action, and two modes [of action], and two issues. [4] Therefore all things are by twos—one over against the other. [5] For there are two ways of good and evil, and with these are the two inclinations in our breasts discriminating them. [6] Therefore if the soul takes pleasure in the good [inclination], all its actions are in righteousness; and if it sins it immediately converts. [7] For, having its thoughts set on righteousness, and casting away wickedness, it immediately overthrows the evil, and uproots the sin. [8] But if it inclines to the

evil inclination, all its actions are in wickedness, and it drives away the good, and cleaves to the evil, and is ruled by Belial; even though it works what is good, he perverts it to evil. [9] For whenever it begins to do good, he forces the issue of the action into evil for him, seeing that the treasure of the inclination is filled with an evil spirit."

CHAPTER 2

[1] "A person may then with words help the good for the sake of the evil, yet the issue of the action leads to mischief. [2] There is a man who shows no compassion on him who serves his turn in evil; and this thing has two aspects, but the whole is evil. [3] And there is a man that loves him that works evil, because he would prefer even to die in evil for his sake; and concerning this it is clear that it has two aspects, but the whole is an evil work. [4] Though indeed he has love, yet he is wicked who conceals what is evil for the sake of the good name, but the end of the action tends to evil. [5] Another steals, does unjustly, plunders, defrauds, and moreover pities the poor: this too has a twofold aspect, but the whole is evil. [6] He who defrauds his neighbor provokes God, and swears falsely against the Most High, and yet pities the poor: he sets the LORD who commands the Law at nothing and provokes [Him], and yet he refreshes the poor. [7] He defiles the soul, and makes the body happy; he kills many, and pities a few: this, too, has a twofold aspect, but the whole is evil. [8] Another commits adultery and fornication, and abstains from meats, and when he fasts, he does evil, and by the power of his wealth overwhelms many; and notwithstanding his excessive wickedness, he does the commandments: this, too, has a twofold aspect, but the whole is evil. [9] Such men are hares—clean, like those that divide the hoof, but in very deed are unclean. [10] For God has thus declared in the tablets of the commandments."

CHAPTER 3

[1] "But do not, my children, wear two faces like to them—of goodness and of wickedness; but cleave to goodness only, for God has His habitation therein, and men desire it. [2] But flee away from wickedness, destroying the [evil] inclination by your good works; [3] for they that are double-faced do not serve God, but their own lusts, so that they may please Belial and men like to themselves."

CHAPTER 4

[1] "For good men, even they that are of single face, though they are thought by them that are double-faced to sin, are just before God. [2] For many in killing the wicked do two works, of good and evil; but the whole is good, because he has uprooted and destroyed that which is evil. [3] One man hates the merciful and unjust man, and the man who commits adultery and fasts: this, too, has a twofold aspect, but the whole work is

good, because he follows the LORD's example, in that he does not accept the seemingly good as the genuine good. [4] Another does not desire to see a good day with them that riot, lest he defile his body and pollute his soul: this, too, is double-faced, but the whole is good. [5] For such men are like to stags and to hinds, because in the manner of wild animals they seem to be unclean, but they are altogether clean, because they walk in zeal for the LORD and abstain from what God also hates and forbids by His commandments, warding off the evil from the good."

CHAPTER 5

[1] "You see, my children, how that there are two in all things—one against the other, and the one is hidden by the other: in wealth [is hidden] covetousness, in conviviality drunkenness, in laughter grief, in wedlock profligacy. [2] Death succeeds to life, dishonor to glory, night to day, and darkness to light; [[and all things are under the day, just things under life, unjust things under death;]] [3] for what reason also, continuous life awaits death. Nor may it be said that truth is a lie, nor right wrong, for all truth is under the light, even as all things are under God. [4] All these things, therefore, I proved in my life, and I did not wander from the truth of the LORD, and I searched out the commandments of the Most High, walking according to all my strength with singleness of face to that which is good."

CHAPTER 6

[1] "Therefore, you also take heed, my children, to the commandments of the LORD, following the truth with singleness of face. [2] For they that are double-faced are guilty of a twofold sin, for they both do the evil thing and they have pleasure in them that do it, following the example of the spirits of deceit, and striving against mankind. [3] Therefore, my children, keep the Law of the LORD and do not give heed to evil as to good, but look to the thing that is really good and keep it in all commandments of the LORD, having your conversation therein, and resting therein. [4] For the latter ends of men show their righteousness [[or unrighteousness]], when they meet the messengers of the LORD and of Satan. [5] For when the soul departs troubled, it is tormented by the evil spirit which it also served in lusts and evil works. [6] But if he is peaceful with joy, he meets the messenger of peace, and he leads him into continuous life."

CHAPTER 7

[1] "Do not become, my children, as Sodom, which sinned against the messengers of the LORD, and perished forever. [2] For I know that you will sin, and be delivered into the hands of your enemies, and your land will be made desolate, and your holy places destroyed, and you will be scattered to the four corners of the earth. [3] And you will be set at nothing

in the dispersion, vanishing away as water ⁴until the Most High will visit the earth, coming Himself [[as a Man, eating and drinking with men, and breaking the head of the dragon in the water. ⁵He will save Israel and all the nations—God speaking in the person of [this] Man. ⁶Therefore you also, my children, tell these things to your children that they do not disobey Him. For I have known that you will assuredly be disobedient, and assuredly act ungodly, not giving heed to the Law of God, but to the commandments of men, being corrupted through wickedness. ⁷And therefore you will be scattered as my brothers Gad and Dan, and you will not know your lands, tribe, and tongue. ⁸But the Lord will gather you together in faith through His tender mercy, and for the sake of Abraham, Isaac, and Jacob.]]"

CHAPTER 8

¹And when he had said these things to them, he commanded them, saying, "Bury me in Hebron." ²And he fell asleep and died at a good old age. And his sons did as he had commanded them, and they carried him up to Hebron and buried him with his fathers.

THE TESTAMENT OF JOSEPH, THE ELEVENTH SON OF JACOB AND RACHEL

CHAPTER 1

¹The copy of the Testament of Joseph. When he was about to die, he called his sons and his brothers together and said to them, ²"My brothers and my children, || Listen to Joseph, the beloved of Israel; Give ear, my sons, to your father. ³I have seen in my life envy and death, || Yet I did not go astray, but persevered in the truth of the Lord. ⁴These brothers of mine hated me, but the Lord loved me; They wished to slay me, but the God of my fathers guarded me; They let me down into a pit, and the Most High brought me up again; ⁵I was sold into slavery, and the Lord of all made me free; I was taken into captivity, and His strong hand aided me; I was beset with hunger, and the Lord Himself nourished me; ⁶I was alone, and God comforted me; I was sick, and the Lord visited me; I was in prison, and my God showed favor to me; In bonds, and He released me; ⁷Slandered, and He pleaded my cause; Bitterly spoken against by the Egyptians, and He delivered me; Envied by my fellow-slaves, and He exalted me."

CHAPTER 2

¹"And this chief captain of Pharaoh entrusted his house to me. ²And I struggled against a shameless woman, urging me to transgress with her, but the God of my father Israel delivered me from the burning flame. ³I was cast into prison, I was beaten, I was mocked, but the Lord granted me to find mercy in the sight of the keeper of the prison. ⁴For the Lord

does not forsake them that fear Him, || Neither in darkness, nor in bonds, nor in tribulations, nor in necessities. ⁵For God is not put to shame as a man, || Nor as the son of man is He afraid, || Nor as one that is earth-born is He [weak or] frightened. ⁶But in all those things He gives protection, || And He comforts in various ways, || [Though] for a short time He departs to try the inclination of the soul. ⁷In ten temptations He showed me approved, || And in all of them I endured; For endurance is a mighty charm, || And patience gives many good things."

CHAPTER 3

¹"How often did the Egyptian woman threaten me with death! How often did she give me over to punishment, and then call me back and threaten me, and when I was unwilling to company with her, she said to me, ²You will be lord of me, and all that is in my house, if you will give yourself to me, and you will be as our master. ³But I remembered the words of my father, and going into my chamber, I wept and prayed to the Lord. ⁴And I fasted in those seven years, and I appeared to the Egyptians as one living delicately, for they that fast for God's sake receive beauty of face. ⁵And if my lord was away from home, I drank no wine; nor for three days did I take my food, but I gave it to the poor and sick. ⁶And I sought the Lord early, and I wept for the Egyptian woman of Memphis, for she troubled me very unceasingly, for she also came to me at night under pretense of visiting me. ⁷And because she had no male child, she pretended to regard me as a son, and so I prayed to the Lord, and she bore a male child. ⁸And for a time she embraced me as a son, and I did not know it; but later, she sought to draw me into fornication. ⁹And when I perceived it, I sorrowed to death; and when she had gone out, I came to myself, and lamented for her many days, because I recognized her guile and her deceit. ¹⁰And I declared the words of the Most High to her, if perhaps she would turn from her evil lust."

CHAPTER 4

¹"Therefore, she often flattered me with words as a holy man, and guilefully in her talk praised my chastity before her husband, while desiring to ensnare me when we were alone. ²For she lauded me openly as chaste, and in secret she said to me, Do not fear my husband, for he is persuaded concerning your chastity. For even should one tell him concerning us, he would not believe [it]. ³Owing to all these things, I lay on the ground, and implored God that the Lord would deliver me from her deceit. ⁴And when she had not prevailed thereby, she came to me again under the plea of instruction, that she might learn the word of God. ⁵And she said to me, If you will that I should leave my idols, lie with me, and I will persuade my husband to depart from his idols, and we will walk in the Law of your Lord. ⁶And I said to her, The Lord

does not will that those who revere Him should be in uncleanness, nor does He take pleasure in them that commit adultery, [7] but in those that approach Him with a pure heart and undefiled lips. [7] But she held her peace, longing to accomplish her evil desire. [8] And I gave myself even more to fasting and prayer, that the LORD might deliver me from her."

CHAPTER 5

[1] "And again, at another time she said to me, If you will not commit adultery, I will kill my husband by poison and take you to be my husband. [2] I therefore, when I heard this, tore my garments, and said to her, Woman, revere God, and do not do this evil deed, lest you be destroyed; [3] for indeed know that I will declare this scheme of yours to all men. [4] She therefore, being afraid, implored that I would not declare this scheme. And she departed, soothing me with gifts, and sending to me every delight of the sons of men."

CHAPTER 6

[1] "And afterward she sent me food mingled with enchantments. [2] And when the eunuch who brought it came, I looked up and beheld a terrible man giving me a sword with the dish, and I perceived that [her] scheme was to deceive me. [3] And when he had gone out, I wept, nor did I taste that or any other of her food. [4] So then after one day she came to me and observed the food, [5] and said to me, Why is it that you have not eaten of the food? And I said to her, It is because you have filled it with deadly enchantments; and how you said, I do not come near to idols, but to the LORD alone. [6] Now therefore know that the God of my father has revealed your wickedness to me by His messenger, and I have kept it to convict you, if perhaps you may see and convert. [7] But that you may learn that the wickedness of the ungodly has no power over them that worship God with chastity, behold, I will take of it and eat before you. And having said so, I prayed thus: The God of my fathers and the Messenger of Abraham, be with me; and [then] I ate. [8] And when she saw this she fell on her face at my feet, weeping; and I raised her up and admonished her. And she promised to do this iniquity no longer."

CHAPTER 7

[1] "But her heart was still set on evil, and she looked around [regarding] how to ensnare me, and sighing deeply, she became downcast, though she was not sick. [2] And when her husband saw her, he said to her, Why is your countenance fallen? And she said to him, I have a pain at my heart, and the groanings of my spirit oppress me; and so he comforted her who was not sick. [3] Then, accordingly seizing an opportunity, she rushed to me while her husband was still outside, and said to me, I will hang myself or cast myself over a cliff if you will not lie with me. [4] And when I saw the spirit of Belial was troubling her, I prayed to the

LORD and said to her, [5] Why, wretched woman, are you troubled and disturbed, blinded through sins? Remember that if you kill yourself, Asteho, the concubine of your husband, your rival, will beat your children, and you will destroy your memorial from off the earth. [6] And she said to me, Behold, then you love me; let this be enough for me: only strive for my life and my children, [7] and I expect that I will also enjoy my desire. But she did not know that I spoke this because of my lord, and not because of her. [8] For if a man has fallen before the passion of a wicked desire and become enslaved by it even as she, whatever good thing he may hear with regard to that passion, he receives it with a view to his wicked desire."

CHAPTER 8

[1] "Therefore, I declare to you, my children, that it was about the sixth hour when she departed from me; and I knelt before the LORD all day, and all the night; and about dawn I arose, weeping and praying for a release from her. [2] At last, then, she laid hold of my garments, forcibly dragging me to have relations with her. [3] Therefore, when I saw that in her madness she was holding fast to my garment, I left it behind, and fled away naked. [4] And holding fast to the garment, she falsely accused me, and when her husband came, he cast me into [the] prison in his house; and on the next day he scourged me and sent me into Pharaoh's prison. [5] And when I was in bonds, the Egyptian woman was oppressed with grief, and she came and heard how I gave thanks to the LORD and sang praises in the abode of darkness, and with glad voice rejoiced, glorifying my God that I was delivered from the lustful desire of the Egyptian woman."

CHAPTER 9

[1] "And often she sent to me, saying, Consent to fulfill my desire, and I will release you from your bonds, and I will free you from the darkness. And not even in thought did I incline to her. [2] For God loves him who in a den of wickedness combines fasting with chastity, rather than the man who in kings' chambers combines luxury with license. And if a man lives in chastity, and also desires glory, and the Most High knows that it is expedient for him, He also bestows this on me. [3] How often, though she were sick, did she come down to me at [the] unwatched times, and listened to my voice as I prayed! [4] And when I heard her groanings I held my peace. [5] For when I was in her house, she was accustomed to bare her arms, and breasts, and legs, that I might lie with her, for she was very beautiful, splendidly adorned in order to deceive me. And the LORD guarded me from her devices."

CHAPTER 10

[1] "You see, therefore, my children, how great things patience works, and prayer with fasting. [2] So you too,

if you follow after chastity and purity with patience and prayer, with fasting in humility of heart, the LORD will dwell among you, because He loves chastity. ³ And wheresoever the Most High dwells, even though envy, or slavery, or slander befalls [a man], the LORD who dwells in him, for the sake of his chastity, not only delivers him from evil, but also exalts him even as me. ⁴ For in every way the man is lifted up, whether in deed, or in word, or in thought. ⁵ My brothers knew how my father loved me, and yet I did not exalt myself in my mind; although I was a child, I had the fear of God in my heart, for I knew that all things would pass away. ⁶ And I did not raise myself [against them] with evil intent, but I honored my brothers; and out of respect for them, even when I was being sold, I refrained from telling the Ishmaelites that I was a son of Jacob, a great and mighty man."

CHAPTER 11

¹ "My children, have the fear of God in all your works before your eyes, and honor your brothers. ² For everyone who does the Law of the LORD will be loved by Him. And when I came to the Indocolpitae with the Ishmaelites, they asked me, saying, Are you a slave? ³ And I said that I was a homeborn slave, that I might not put my brothers to shame. And the eldest of them said to me, You are not a slave, for even your appearance makes it manifest. ⁴ But I said that I was their slave. Now when we came into Egypt, they strove concerning me, which of them should buy me and take me. ⁵ Therefore it seemed good to all that I should remain in Egypt with the merchant of their trade, until they should return bringing merchandise. ⁶ And the LORD gave me favor in the eyes of the merchant, and he entrusted his house to me. ⁷ And God blessed him by my means and increased him in gold, and silver, and in household servants. ⁸ And I was with him three months and five days."

CHAPTER 12

¹ "And about that time the Memphian woman, the wife of Potiphar, came down in a chariot with great pomp, because she had heard from her eunuchs concerning me. ² And she told her husband that the merchant had become rich by means of a young Hebrew, and they say that he had assuredly been stolen out of the land of Canaan. ³ Now therefore, render justice to him, and take the youth away to your house, so the God of the Hebrews will bless you, for grace from Heaven is on him."

CHAPTER 13

¹ "And Potiphar was persuaded by her words, and commanded the merchant to be brought, and said to him, What is this that I hear concerning you, that you steal persons out of the land of Canaan and sell them for slaves? ² But the merchant fell at his feet and

implored him, saying, ³ I implore you, my lord, I do not know what you say. And Potiphar said to him, From where, then, is the Hebrew slave? And he said, The Ishmaelites entrusted him to me until they should return. ⁴ But he did not believe him, but commanded him to be stripped and beaten. ⁵ And when he persisted in this statement, Potiphar said, Let the youth be brought. ⁶ And when I was brought in, I paid respect to Potiphar (for he was third in rank of the officers of Pharaoh). ⁷ And he took me apart from him, and said to me, Are you a slave or free? And I said, A slave. And he said, Whose? ⁸ And I said, The Ishmaelites. And he said, How did you become their slave? ⁹ And I said, They bought me out of the land of Canaan. And he said to me, You truly lie; and immediately he commanded me to be stripped and beaten."

CHAPTER 14

¹ "Now the Memphian woman was looking through a window at me while I was being beaten, for her house was near, and she sent to him, saying, Your judgment is unjust, for you punish a free man who has been stolen, as though he were a transgressor. ² And when I made no change in my statement, though I was beaten, he ordered me to be imprisoned, until, he said, the owners of the boy should come. ³ And the woman said to her husband, For what reason do you detain the captive and well-born youth in bonds, who ought rather to be set at liberty, and be waited on? ⁴ For she wished to see me out of a desire of sin, but I was ignorant concerning all these things. ⁵ And he said to her, It is not the custom of the Egyptians to take that which belongs to others before proof is given. ⁶ This, therefore, he said concerning the merchant; [and he said,] But as for the youth, he must be imprisoned."

CHAPTER 15

¹ "Now after twenty-four days the Ishmaelites came, for they had heard that my father Jacob was mourning much concerning me. ² And they came and said to me, How is it that you said that you were a slave? And behold, we have learned that you are the son of a mighty man in the land of Canaan, and your father still mourns for you in sackcloth and ashes. ³ When I heard this, my bowels were dissolved, and my heart melted, and I greatly desired to weep, but I restrained myself, that I should not put my brothers to shame. And I said to them, I do not know, I am a slave. ⁴ Then, therefore, they took counsel to sell me, that I should not be found in their hands. ⁵ For they feared my father, lest he [should come and] execute on them a grievous vengeance. ⁶ For they had heard that he was mighty with God and with men. ⁷ Then the merchant said to them, Release me from the judgment of Potiphar. ⁸ And they came and requested me, saying, Say that you were bought by us with money, and he will set us free."

CHAPTER 16

[1] "Now the Memphian woman said to her husband, Buy the youth; for I hear, she said, that they are selling him. [2] And she immediately sent a eunuch to the Ishmaelites and asked them to sell me. [3] But since the eunuch would not agree to buy me [at their price], he returned, having made trial of them, and he made known to his mistress that they requested a large price for their slave. [4] And she sent another eunuch, saying, Even though they demand two minas, give [it to] them, do not spare the gold; only buy the boy, and bring him to me. [5] The eunuch therefore went and gave them eighty pieces of gold, and he received me; but he said to the Egyptian woman, I have given one hundred. [6] And though I knew [this], I held my peace, lest the eunuch should be put to shame."

CHAPTER 17

[1] "You see, therefore, my children, what great things I endured that I should not put my brothers to shame. [2] You also, therefore, love one another, and with long-suffering hide one another's faults. [3] For God delights in the unity of brothers, and in the purpose of a heart that takes pleasure in love. [4] And when my brothers came into Egypt, they learned that I had returned their money to them and had not scolded them, and I comforted them. [5] And I loved them more abundantly after the death of my father Jacob; and all things, whatever he commanded, I did very abundantly for them, [6] and I did not allow them to be afflicted in the smallest matter; and I gave all that was in my hand to them. [7] And their children were my children, and my children as their servants; and their life was my life, and all their suffering was my suffering, and all their sickness was my infirmity. [8] My land was their land, and their counsel my counsel. And I did not exalt myself among them in arrogance because of my worldly glory, but I was among them as one of the least."

CHAPTER 18

[1] "Therefore, if you also walk in the commandments of the LORD, my children, He will exalt you there, and will bless you with good things forever and ever. [2] And if anyone seeks to do evil to you, do well to him, and pray for him, and you will be redeemed of the LORD from all evil. [3] Behold, you see that out of my humility and long-suffering I took the daughter of the priest of Heliopolis to be [my] wife. [4] And one hundred talents of gold were given to me with her, and the LORD made them to serve me. [5] And He also gave me beauty as a flower beyond the beautiful ones of Israel; and He preserved me to old age in strength and in beauty, because I was like in all things to Jacob."

CHAPTER 19

[1] "Therefore, hear my vision which I saw: [2] I saw twelve deer feeding. And nine of them were dispersed. Now the three were preserved, but on the following day they were also dispersed. [3] And I saw that the three deer became three lambs, and they cried to the LORD, and He brought them forth into a flourishing and well-watered place, yes, He brought them out of darkness into light. [4] And there they cried to the LORD until there gathered together to them the nine deer, and they became as twelve sheep, and after a short time they increased and became many flocks. [5] And after these things I saw and behold, twelve bulls were sucking one cow, which produced a sea of milk, and there drank thereof the twelve flocks and innumerable herds. [6] And the horns of the fourth bull went up to Heaven and became as a wall for the flocks, and in the midst of the two horns there grew another horn. [7] And I saw a bull calf which surrounded them twelve times, and it became a help to all the bulls. [8] And I saw in the midst of the horns a virgin [[wearing a many-colored garment, and from her]] went forth a lamb; and on his right [[was as it were a lion; and]] all the beasts and all the reptiles rushed [against him], and the lamb overcame them and destroyed them. [9] And the bulls rejoiced because of him, and the cow [and the deer] exulted together with them. [10] And these things must come to pass in their season. Therefore, my children, observe the commandments of the LORD, and honor Levi and Judah; [11] for from them will arise to you [[the Lamb of God, who takes away the sin of the world]]—One who saves [[all the nations and]] Israel. [12] For His kingdom is an everlasting kingdom, which will not pass away; but my kingdom among you will come to an end as a watcher's hammock, which disappears after the summer."

CHAPTER 20

[1] "For I know that after my death the Egyptians will afflict you, but God will avenge you, and will bring you into that which He promised to your fathers. [2] But you will carry up my bones with you; for when my bones are being taken up there, the LORD will be with you in light, and Belial will be in darkness with the Egyptians. [3] And carry your mother Asenath to the Hippodrome and bury her near your mother Rachel." [4] And when he had said these things, he stretched out his feet and died at a good old age. [5] And all Israel mourned for him, and all Egypt, with a great mourning. [6] And when the sons of Israel went out of Egypt, they took the bones of Joseph with them, and they buried him in Hebron with his fathers, and the years of his life were one hundred and ten years.

TESTAMENTS OF THE TWELVE PATRIARCHS

THE TESTAMENT OF BENJAMIN, THE TWELFTH SON OF JACOB AND RACHEL

CHAPTER 1

¹The copy of the words of Benjamin, which he commanded his sons to observe after he had lived one hundred and twenty-five years. ²And he kissed them, and said, "As Isaac was born to Abraham in his old age, so was I also to Jacob. ³And since my mother Rachel died in giving me birth, I had no milk; therefore I was suckled by her handmaid Bilhah. ⁴For Rachel remained barren for twelve years after she had borne Joseph; and she prayed [to] the LORD with fasting [for] twelve days, and she conceived and bore me. ⁵For my father loved Rachel dearly, and prayed that he might see two sons born from her. ⁶Therefore I was called Benjamin, that is, a son of days."

CHAPTER 2

¹"And when I went into Egypt, to Joseph, and my brother recognized me, he said to me, ²What did they tell my father when they sold me? And I said to him, They dabbled your coat with blood and sent it, and said, Do you know whether this is your son's coat? ³And Joseph said to me, Even so, brother, the Canaanite merchants stole me by force, ⁴and it came to pass that as they went on their way they concealed my garment as though a wild beast had met me and slain me. ⁵And so his associates sold me to the Ishmaelites. ⁶And they did not lie in saying this. For he wished to conceal the deeds of my brothers from me. And he called his brothers to himself and said, ⁷Do not tell my father what you have done to me, but tell him as I have told Benjamin. ⁸And let the thoughts among you be such, and do not let these things come to the heart of my father."

CHAPTER 3

¹"Therefore, my children, you must also love the LORD God of the heavens and earth, and keep His commandments, following the example of the good and holy man Joseph. ²And let your mind be to good, even as you know me; for he that has his mind right sees all things rightly. ³Fear the LORD and love your neighbor; and even though the spirits of Belial claim you to afflict you with every evil, yet they will not have dominion over you, even as they did not have [dominion] over my brother Joseph. ⁴How many men wished to slay him, and God shielded him! For he that fears God and loves his neighbor cannot be smitten by the spirit of Belial, being shielded by the fear of God. ⁵Nor can he be ruled over by the device of men or beasts, for he is helped by the LORD through the love which he has toward his neighbor. ⁶For Joseph also implored our father that he would pray for his brothers, that the LORD would not impute to them as sin whatever evil they had done to him. ⁷And thus Jacob cried out: My good child, you have prevailed over the yearnings of your father Jacob. And he embraced him, and kissed him for two hours, saying, ⁸In you the prophecy of Heaven will be fulfilled [[concerning the Lamb of God, and Savior of the world]], and that a blameless One will be delivered up for lawless men, and a sinless One will die for ungodly men [[in the blood of the covenant, for the salvation of the nations and of Israel, and will destroy Belial and his servants]]."

CHAPTER 4

¹"Therefore, my children, do you see the end of the good man? Be followers of his compassion, therefore, with a good mind, that you may also wear crowns of glory. ²For the good man does not have a dark eye, for he shows mercy to all men, even though they are sinners. ³And though they devise with evil intent concerning him, by doing good he overcomes evil, being shielded by God: and he loves the righteous as his own soul. ⁴If anyone is glorified, he does not envy him; if anyone is enriched, he is not jealous; if anyone is valiant, he praises him; he praises the virtuous man; he has mercy on the poor man; he has compassion on the weak; he sings praises to God. ⁵As for him who has the fear of God, he protects him as with a shield; he helps him that loves God; he admonishes and turns back him that rejects the Most High; and he loves him that has the grace of a good spirit as his own soul."

CHAPTER 5

¹"Therefore, if you also have a good mind, then will both wicked men be at peace with you, and the profligate will revere you and turn to good; ²and the covetous will not only cease from their inordinate desire, but even give the objects of their covetousness to them that are afflicted. ³If you do well, even the unclean spirits will flee from you, and the beasts will dread you. For where there is reverence for good works and light in the mind, even darkness flees away from him. ⁴For if anyone does violence to a holy man, he converts; for the holy man is merciful to his reviler and holds his peace. ⁵And if anyone betrays a righteous man, the righteous man prays: though for a little while he is humbled, yet not long after he appears far more glorious, as was my brother Joseph."

CHAPTER 6

¹"The inclination of the good man is not in the power of the deceit of the spirit of Belial, for the messenger of peace guides his soul. ²And he does not gaze passionately on corruptible things, nor gathers together riches through a desire of pleasure. ³He does not delight in pleasure, [[he does not grieve for what is his neighbor's]], he does not satisfy himself with luxuries, he does not err in the uplifting of the eyes; the LORD is his portion. ⁴The good inclination does not receive glory nor dishonor from men, and it does not know any guile, or lie, or fighting, or reviling; for

the LORD dwells in him and lights up his soul, and he always rejoices toward all men. [5] The good mind does not have two tongues, of blessing and of cursing, of insolence and of honor, of sorrow and of joy, of quietness and of confusion, of hypocrisy and of truth, [[of poverty and of wealth]], but it has one disposition, uncorrupt and pure, concerning all men. [6] It has no double sight, nor double hearing, for in everything which he does, or speaks, or sees, he knows that the LORD looks on his soul. [7] And he cleanses his mind that he may not be condemned by men as well as by God. And in like manner, the works of Belial are twofold, and there is no singleness in them."

CHAPTER 7

[1] "Therefore, my children, I tell you: flee the malice of Belial, for he gives a sword to them that obey him. [2] And the sword is the mother of seven evils: first the mind conceives through Belial, and first there is bloodshed; secondly, ruin; thirdly, tribulation; fourthly, exile; fifthly, scarcity; sixthly, panic; seventhly, destruction. [3] Therefore Cain was also delivered over to seven vengeances by God, for in every hundred years the LORD brought one plague on him. [4] And when he was two hundred years old, he began to suffer, and in the nine-hundredth year he was destroyed. For on account of his brother Abel, he was judged with all the evils—but Lamech with seventy times seven. [5] Because those who are like Cain in envy and hatred of brothers, will be punished with the same judgment forever."

CHAPTER 8

[1] "And you, my children, must flee evildoing, envy, and hatred of brothers, and cleave to goodness and love. [2] He that has a pure mind in love does not look after a woman with a view to fornication, for he has no defilement in his heart, because the Spirit of God rests on him. [3] For as the sun is not defiled by shining on dung and mire, but rather dries up both and drives away the evil smell, so also the pure mind, though encompassed by the defilements of earth, rather cleanses [them] and is not itself defiled."

CHAPTER 9

[1] "And I believe that there will also be evildoings among you, according to the words of Enoch the righteous—that you will commit fornication with the fornication of Sodom, and will perish, all except a few, and will renew wanton deeds with women; and the Kingdom of the LORD will not be among you, for He will immediately take it away. [2] Nevertheless, the temple of God will be in your portion, and the last [temple] will be more glorious than the first. And the twelve tribes will be gathered together there, and all the nations, until the Most High will send forth His salvation in the visitation of an only begotten Prophet.

[[[3] And He will enter into the temple, and there the LORD will be treated with outrage, and He will be lifted up on a tree. [4] And the veil of the temple will be torn, and the Spirit of God will pass on to the nations as fire poured forth. [5] And He will ascend from Hades and will pass from earth into Heaven. And I know how lowly He will be on earth, and how glorious in Heaven.]]"

CHAPTER 10

[1] "Now when Joseph was in Egypt, I longed to see his figure and the form of his countenance, and through the prayers of my father Jacob I saw him while awake in the daytime, even his entire figure exactly as he was. [2] And when he had said these things, he said to them, Therefore, my children, know that I am dying. [3] Therefore, do truth and righteousness, each one to his neighbor, and judgment to confirmation, and keep the Law of the LORD and His commandments. [4] For I leave you these things instead of an inheritance. Therefore, you must also give them to your children for an everlasting possession, for so did both Abraham, and Isaac, and Jacob. [5] For they gave us all these things for an inheritance, saying, Keep the commandments of God until the LORD will reveal His salvation to all nations. [6] And then you will see Enoch, Noah, and Shem, and Abraham, and Isaac, and Jacob, rising on the right hand in gladness. [7] Then we will also rise, each one over our tribe, worshiping the King of Heaven [[who appeared on earth in the form of a Man in humility. And as many as believe on Him will rejoice with Him on the earth]]. [8] Then all men will also rise, some to glory and some to shame. And the LORD will judge Israel first, for their unrighteousness, [[for when He appeared as God in the flesh to deliver them they did not believe Him]]. [9] And then He will judge all the nations, [[as many as did not believe Him when He appeared on earth]]. [10] And He will convict Israel through the chosen ones of the nations, even as He reproved Esau through the Midianites, who deceived their brothers, [[so that they fell into fornication, and idolatry; and they were alienated from God]], therefore becoming children in the portion of them that fear the LORD. [11] If you therefore, my children, walk in holiness according to the commandments of the LORD, you will again dwell securely with me, and all Israel will be gathered to the LORD."

CHAPTER 11

[1] "And I will no longer be called a ravening wolf on account of your ravages, but [[a worker of the LORD, distributing food to them that work what is good. [2] And there will rise up from my seed in the latter times One]] beloved of the LORD, [[hearing His voice on the earth,]] and a doer of the good pleasure of His will, [[enlightening all the nations with new knowledge, even the light of knowledge, bursting in

on Israel for salvation, and tearing away from them like a wolf, and giving to the synagogue of the nations. [3] Until the consummation of the age He will be in the synagogues of the nations, and among their rulers, as a strain of music in the mouth of all. [4] And He will be inscribed in the holy scrolls, both His work and His word, and He will be [the] Chosen One of God forever. [5] And through them He will go to and fro as my father Jacob, saying, He will fill up that which lacks of your tribe]]."

CHAPTER 12

[1] And when he finished his words, he said, "I command you, my children, carry up my bones out of Egypt, and bury me at Hebron, near my fathers." [2] So Benjamin died one hundred and twenty-five years old, at a good old age, and they placed him in a coffin. [3] And in the ninety-first year from the entrance of the sons of Israel into Egypt, they and their brothers secretly brought up the bones of their fathers during the Canaanite war, and they buried them in Hebron by the feet of their fathers. [4] And they returned from the land of Canaan and dwelt in Egypt until the day of their departure from the land of Egypt.

JUBILEES

The Book of Jubilees, sometimes called Lesser Genesis (Leptogenesis), is an ancient Jewish religious work of 50 chapters, considered canonical by the Ethiopian Orthodox Church as well as Beta Israel (Ethiopian Jews), where it is known as the Book of Division. Jubilees is considered one of the pseudepigrapha by Protestant, Roman Catholic, and Eastern Orthodox Churches. It is also not considered canonical within Judaism outside of Beta Israel. It is generally dated to the 2nd century BC and its primary purpose seems to be in promoting the use of a 364-day calendar in Israel (a year equally divided into 52 weeks of seven days each). With no intercalary method given, the year would not synchronize with the seasons in the longterm. The book also reimagines some of the history of Genesis and introduces a concept foreign to Judeo-Christianity in which certain sins are unatonable.

THIS IS THE HISTORY OF THE DIVISION OF THE DAYS OF THE LAW AND OF THE TESTIMONY, OF THE EVENTS OF THE YEARS, OF THEIR PERIODS OF SEVEN, OF THEIR JUBILEES THROUGHOUT ALL THE YEARS OF THE WORLD, AS THE LORD SPOKE TO MOSES ON MOUNT SINAI WHEN HE WENT UP TO RECEIVE THE TABLETS OF THE LAW AND OF THE COMMAND, ACCORDING TO THE VOICE OF GOD AS HE SAID TO HIM, "GO UP TO THE TOP OF THE MOUNTAIN."

CHAPTER 1

¹ And it came to pass in the first year of the exodus of the sons of Israel out of Egypt, in the third month, on the sixteenth day of the month, that God spoke to Moses, saying, "Come up to Me on the mountain, and I will give you two tablets of stone, of the Law and of the command, which I have written, that you may teach them." ² And Moses went up into the mountain of God, and the glory of the LORD abode on Mount Sinai, and a cloud overshadowed it [for] six days. ³ And He called to Moses on the seventh day out of the midst of the cloud, and the appearance of the glory of the LORD was like a flaming fire on the top of the mountain. ⁴ And Moses was on the mountain [for] forty days and forty nights, and God taught him the earlier and the later history of the division of all the days of the Law and of the Testimony. ⁵ And He said, "Incline your heart to every word which I will speak to you on this mountain and write them in a scroll in order that their generations may see how I have not forsaken them for all the evil which they have worked in transgressing the covenant which I establish between Me and you for their generations this day on Mount Sinai. ⁶ And thus it will come to pass when all

these things come on them, that they will recognize that I am more righteous than they in all their judgments and in all their actions, and they will recognize that I have truly been with them. ⁷ And write for yourself all these words which I declare to you this day, for I know their rebellion and their stiff neck, before I bring them into the land of which I swore to their fathers, to Abraham, and to Isaac, and to Jacob, saying, To your seed I will give a land flowing with milk and honey. ⁸ And they will eat and be satisfied, and they will turn to strange gods, to [gods] which cannot deliver them from any of their tribulation: and this witness will be heard for a witness against them. ⁹ For they will forget all My commands, [even] all that I command them, and they will walk after the nations, and after their uncleanness, and after their shame, and will serve their gods, and these will prove to them an offense, and a tribulation, and an affliction, and a snare. ¹⁰ And many will perish, and they will be taken captive, and will fall into the hands of the enemy, because they have forsaken My ordinances and My commands, and the festivals of My covenant, and My Sabbaths, and My holy place which I have hallowed for Myself in their midst, and My Dwelling Place, and My sanctuary, which I have hallowed for Myself in the midst of the land, that I should set My Name on it, and that it should dwell [there]. ¹¹ And they will make to themselves high places, and groves, and graven images, and they will worship, each his own [graven image], so as to go astray, and they will sacrifice their children to demons, and to all the works of the error of their hearts. ¹² And I will send witnesses to them that I may witness against them, but they will not hear, and will slay the witnesses also, and they will persecute those who seek the Law, and they will abrogate and change everything so as to work evil before My eyes. ¹³ And I will hide My face from them, and I will deliver them into the hand of the nations for captivity, and for a prey, and for devouring, and I will remove them from the midst of the land, and I will scatter them among the nations. ¹⁴ And they will forget all My law, and all My commands, and all My judgments, and will go astray as to new moons, and Sabbaths, and festivals, and jubilees, and ordinances. ¹⁵ And after this they will turn to Me from among the nations with all their heart, and with all their soul, and with all their strength, and I will gather them from among all the nations, and they will seek Me, so that I will be found by them when they seek Me with all their heart and with all their soul. ¹⁶ And I will disclose to them abounding peace with righteousness, and I will remove them—the plant of uprightness—with all My heart and with all My soul, and they will be for a blessing and not for a curse, and they will be the head and not the tail. [17] And I will build My sanctuary in their midst, and I will dwell with them, and I will be their God and they will be My people in truth and righteousness. [18] And I will not forsake them nor fail them; for I am the LORD their God." [19] And Moses fell on his face and prayed and said, "O LORD my God, do not forsake Your people and Your inheritance, so that they should wander in the error of their hearts, and do not deliver them into the hands of their enemies, the nations, lest they should rule over them and cause them to sin against You. [20] Let Your mercy, O LORD, be lifted up on Your people, and create an upright spirit in them, and do not let the spirit of Belial rule over them to accuse them before You, and to ensnare them from all the paths of righteousness, so that they may perish from before Your face. [21] But they are Your people and Your inheritance, which You have delivered with Your great power from the hands of the Egyptians: create in them a clean heart and a holy spirit, and do not let them be ensnared in their sins from now on [and] forever." [22] And the LORD said to Moses, "I know their contrariness, and their thoughts, and their stubbornness, and they will not be obedient until they confess their own sin and the sin of their fathers. [23] And after this they will turn to Me in all uprightness and with all [their] heart and with all [their] soul, and I will circumcise the foreskin of their heart and the foreskin of the heart of their seed, and I will create in them a holy spirit, and I will cleanse them so that they will not turn away from Me from that day [and] continuously. [24] And their souls will cleave to Me and to all My commands, and they will fulfill My commands, and I will be their Father and they will be My children. [25] And they will all be called children of the living God, and every messenger and every spirit will know, yes, they will know that these are My children, and that I am their Father in uprightness and righteousness, and that I love them. [26] And write down for yourself all these words which I declare to you on this mountain, the first and the last, which will come to pass in all the divisions of the days in the Law, and in the Testimony, and in the periods of seven, and the jubilees continuously, until I descend and dwell with them forever." [27] And He said to the Messenger of the Presence, "Write for Moses from the beginning of creation until My sanctuary has been built among them for all ages. [28] And the LORD will appear to the eyes of all, and all will know that I am the God of Israel and the Father of all the children of Jacob, and King on Mount Zion for all ages. And Zion and Jerusalem will be holy." [29] And the Messenger of the Presence who went before the camp of Israel took the tablets of the divisions of the years—from the time of the creation—of the Law, and of the Testimony of the periods of seven, of the jubilees, according to the individual years, according to all the number of the jubilees [according to the individual years], from the day of the [new] creation when the heavens and the earth will be renewed and all their creation according to the powers of the heavens, and according to all the creation of the earth, until the sanctuary of the LORD will be made in Jerusalem on Mount Zion, and all the luminaries are renewed for healing, and for peace, and for blessing for all the chosen of Israel, and that thus it may be from that day and to all the days of the earth.

CHAPTER 2

[1] And the Messenger of the Presence spoke to Moses according to the word of the LORD, saying, Write the complete history of the creation, how in six days the LORD God finished all His works and all that He created, and kept Sabbath on the seventh day and hallowed it for all ages, and appointed it as a sign for all His works. [2] For on the first day He created the heavens which are above, and the earth, and the waters, and all the spirits which serve before Him— the messengers of the presence, and the messengers of sanctification, and the messengers [[of the spirit of fire, and the messengers]] of the spirit of the winds, and the messengers of the spirit of the clouds, and of darkness, and of snow, and of hail, and of hoarfrost, and the messengers of the voices, and of the thunder, and of the lightning, and the messengers of the spirits of cold, and of heat, and of winter, and of spring, and of autumn, and of summer, and of all the spirits of His creatures which are in the heavens and on the earth, [He created] the abysses and the darkness, evening [and night], and the light, dawn and day, which He has prepared in the knowledge of His heart. [3] And we immediately saw His works, and praised Him, and lauded before Him on account of all His works; for He created seven great works on the first day. [4] And on the second day He created the expanse in the midst of the waters, and the waters were divided on that day—half of them went up above and half of them went down below the expanse [that was] in the midst over the face of the whole earth. And this was the only work [God] created on the second day. [5] And on the third day He commanded the waters to pass from off the face of the whole earth into one place, and the dry land to appear. [6] And the waters did so as He commanded them, and they retired from off the face of the earth into one place outside of this expanse, and the dry land appeared. [7] And on that day, He created for them all the seas according to their separate gathering-places, and all the rivers, and the gatherings of the waters in the mountains and on all the earth, and all the lakes, and all the dew of the earth, and the seed which is sown, and all sprouting things, and fruit-bearing trees, and trees of the wood, and the Garden of Eden, in Eden, and all [plants after their kind]. These four great works God created on the third day. [8] And on the fourth day He created the sun,

and the moon, and the stars, and set them in the expanse of the heavens, to give light on all the earth, and to rule over the day and the night, and divide the light from the darkness. ⁹ And God appointed the sun to be a great sign on the earth for days, and for Sabbaths, and for months, and for feasts, and for years, and for Sabbaths of years, and for jubilees, and for all seasons of the years. ¹⁰ And it divides the light from the darkness [and] for prosperity, that all things may prosper which shoot and grow on the earth. These three kinds He made on the fourth day. ¹¹ And on the fifth day He created great sea monsters in the depths of the waters, for these were the first things of flesh that were created by His hands, the fish and everything that moves in the waters, and everything that flies—the birds and all their kind. ¹² And the sun rose above them to prosper [them], and above everything that was on the earth, everything that shoots out of the earth, and all fruit-bearing trees, and all flesh. These three kinds He created on the fifth day. ¹³ And on the sixth day He created all the animals of the earth, and all cattle, and everything that moves on the earth. ¹⁴ And after all this He created man, a man and a woman He created them, and gave him dominion over all that is on the earth, and in the seas, and over everything that flies, and over beasts and over cattle, and over everything that moves on the earth, and over the whole earth, and over all this He gave him dominion. And these four kinds He created on the sixth day. ¹⁵ And there were altogether twenty-two kinds. ¹⁶ And He finished all His work on the sixth day—all that is in the heavens and on the earth, and in the seas and in the abysses, and in the light and in the darkness, and in everything. ¹⁷ And He gave us a great sign, the Sabbath day, that we should work six days, but keep Sabbath on the seventh day from all work. ¹⁸ And all the messengers of the presence, and all the messengers of sanctification, these two great classes—He has bidden us to keep the Sabbath with Him in the heavens and on earth. ¹⁹ And He said to us, "Behold, I will separate a people to Myself from among all the peoples, and these will keep the Sabbath day, and I will sanctify them to Myself as My people and will bless them; as I have sanctified the Sabbath day and sanctify [it] to Myself, even so will I bless them, and they will be My people and I will be their God. ²⁰ And I have chosen the seed of Jacob from among all that I have seen, and have written him down as My firstborn son, and have sanctified him to Myself forever and ever; and I will teach them the Sabbath day, that they may keep Sabbath thereon from all work." ²¹ And thus He created therein a sign in accordance with which they should keep Sabbath with us on the seventh day, to eat and to drink, and to bless Him who has created all things as He has blessed and sanctified to Himself a peculiar people above all peoples, and that they should keep Sabbath together with us. ²² And He caused His commands to

ascend as a sweet savor acceptable before Him all the days. ²³ There [were] twenty-two heads of mankind from Adam to Jacob, and twenty-two kinds of work were made until the seventh day; this is blessed and holy; and the former is also blessed and holy; and this one serves with that one for sanctification and blessing. ²⁴ And to these [(Jacob and his seed)] it was granted that they should always be the blessed and holy ones of the first testimony and law, even as He had sanctified and blessed the Sabbath day on the seventh day. ²⁵ He created the heavens, and earth, and everything that He created in six days, and God made the seventh day holy for all His works; therefore, He commanded on its behalf that whoever does any work thereon will die, and that he who defiles it will surely die. ²⁶ For that reason, command the sons of Israel to observe this day that they may keep it holy and not do any work thereon, and not to defile it, as it is holier than all other days. ²⁷ And whoever profanes it will surely die, and whoever does any work thereon will surely die forever, that the sons of Israel may observe this day throughout their generations, and not be rooted out of the land; for it is a holy day and a blessed day. ²⁸ And everyone who observes it and keeps Sabbath thereon from all his work will be holy and blessed throughout all days like to us. ²⁹ Declare and say to the sons of Israel the law of this day, both that they should keep Sabbath thereon, and that they should not forsake it in the error of their hearts; [and] that it is not lawful to do any work thereon which is unseemly, to do their own pleasure thereon, and that they should not prepare anything thereon to be eaten or drunk, and [that it is not lawful] to draw water or bring in or take out thereon through their gates any burden, which they had not prepared for themselves on the sixth day in their dwellings. ³⁰ And they will not bring in nor take out from house to house on that day; for that day is more holy and blessed than any jubilee day of the jubilees: on this we kept Sabbath in the heavens before it was made known to any flesh to keep Sabbath thereon on the earth. ³¹ And the Creator of all things blessed it, but He did not sanctify all peoples and nations to keep Sabbath thereon, but Israel alone: them alone He permitted to eat and drink and to keep Sabbath thereon on the earth. ³² And the Creator of all things blessed this day which He had created for a blessing, and a sanctification, and a glory above all days. ³³ This law and testimony was given to the sons of Israel as a law forever to their generations.

CHAPTER 3

¹ And on the six days of the second week we brought, according to the word of God, to Adam all the beasts, and all the cattle, and all the birds, and everything that moves on the earth, and everything that moves in the water, according to their kinds, and according to their types: the beasts on the first day; the cattle on the second day; the birds on the third day; and all that

which moves on the earth on the fourth day; and that which moves in the water on the fifth day. ² And Adam named them all by their respective names, and as he called them, so was their name. ³ And on these five days Adam saw all these, male and female, according to every kind that was on the earth, but he was alone and found no helpmate for him. ⁴ And the LORD said to us, "It is not good that the man should be alone: let us make a helpmate for him." ⁵ And the LORD our God caused a deep sleep to fall on him, and he slept, and He took for the woman one rib from among his ribs, and this rib was the origin of the woman from among his ribs, and He built up the flesh in its stead, and built the woman. ⁶ And He awoke Adam out of his sleep and on awaking he rose on the sixth day, and He brought her to him, and he knew her, and said to her, "This is now bone of my bones and flesh of my flesh; she will be called Woman, because she was taken from Man." ⁷ Therefore man and wife will be one, and therefore a man will leave his father and his mother, and cleave to his wife, and they will be one flesh. ⁸ In the first week Adam was created, and the rib—his wife; in the second week He showed her to him: and for this reason, the command was given to keep in their defilement, for a male seven days, and for a female twice seven days. ⁹ And after Adam had completed forty days in the land where he had been created, we brought him into the Garden of Eden to till and keep it, but they brought his wife in on the eightieth day, and after this she entered into the Garden of Eden. ¹⁰ And for this reason the command is written on the heavenly tablets in regard to her that gives birth: "If she bears a male, she will remain in her uncleanness seven days according to the first week of days, and thirty-three days she will remain in the blood of her purifying, and she will not touch any hallowed thing, nor enter into the sanctuary, until she accomplishes these days which [are prescribed] in the case of a male child. ¹¹ But in the case of a female child she will remain in her uncleanness two weeks of days, according to the first two weeks, and sixty-six days in the blood of her purification, and they will be in all eighty days." ¹² And when she had completed these eighty days, we brought her into the Garden of Eden, for it is holier than all the earth besides, and every tree that is planted in it is holy. ¹³ Therefore, there was ordained regarding her who bears a male or a female child the statute of those days that she should touch no hallowed thing, nor enter into the sanctuary until these days for the male or female child are accomplished. ¹⁴ This is the law and testimony which was written down for Israel, in order that they should observe [it] all the days. ¹⁵ And in the first week of the first jubilee, Adam and his wife were in the Garden of Eden for seven years tilling and keeping it, and we gave him work and we instructed him to do everything that is suitable for tillage. ¹⁶ And he tilled [the garden], and was naked and did not know it, and was not ashamed, and he protected the garden from the birds, and beasts, and cattle, and gathered its fruit, and ate, and put aside the residue for himself and for his wife. ¹⁷ And after the completion of the seven years, which he had completed there, seven years exactly, and in the second month, on the seventeenth day [of the month], the serpent came and approached the woman, and the serpent said to the woman, "Has God commanded you, saying, you will not eat of every tree of the garden?" ¹⁸ And she said to it, "Of all the fruit of the trees of the garden God has said to us, Eat; but of the fruit of the tree which is in the midst of the garden God has said to us, You will not eat thereof, neither will you touch it, lest you die." ¹⁹ And the serpent said to the woman, "You will not surely die, for God knows that on the day you will eat thereof, your eyes will be opened, and you will be as gods, and you will know good and evil." ²⁰ And the woman saw the tree that it was agreeable and pleasant to the eye, and that its fruit was good for food, and she took thereof and ate. ²¹ And when she had first covered her shame with fig-leaves, she gave thereof to Adam and he ate, and his eyes were opened, and he saw that he was naked. ²² And he took fig-leaves and sewed [them] together, and made an apron for himself, and covered his shame. ³² And God cursed the serpent and was angry with it forever. ²⁴ And He was angry with the woman because she listened to the voice of the serpent and ate; and He said to her, "I will greatly multiply your sorrow and your pains; in sorrow you will bring out children, and your return will be to your husband [[or Man]], and he [[or He]] will rule over you." ²⁵ And He also said to Adam, "Because you have listened to the voice of your wife, and have eaten of the tree of which I commanded you that you should not eat thereof, the ground is cursed for your sake: it will bring out thorns and thistles to you, and you will eat your bread in the sweat of your face, until you return to the earth from where you were taken; for earth you are, and to earth you will return." ²⁶ And He made coats of skin for them, and clothed them, and sent them out from the Garden of Eden. ²⁷ And on that day on which Adam went out from the garden, he offered as a sweet savor an offering: frankincense, galbanum, and stacte, and spices in the morning with the rising of the sun from the day when he covered his shame. ²⁸ And on that day the mouth of all beasts, and of cattle, and of birds, and of whatever walks, and of whatever moves was closed, so that they could no longer speak, for they had all spoken with one another with one lip and with one tongue. ²⁹ And He sent out of the Garden of Eden all flesh that was in the Garden of Eden, and all flesh was scattered according to its kinds, and according to its types to the places which had been created for them. ³⁰ And to man alone did He give [the means] to cover his shame, of all the beasts and cattle. ³¹ On this account, it is prescribed on the heavenly tablets as touching all those who know the judgment of the Law, that they should cover their shame, and should not uncover themselves as the nations uncover themselves. ³² And on the new moon of the fourth month, Adam and his wife went out from the Garden of Eden, and they dwelt in the land of 'Eldâ, in the land of their creation. ³³ And Adam called the name of his wife Eve. ³⁴ And they had no son until the first jubilee, and after this he knew her. ³⁵ Now he tilled the land as he had been instructed in the Garden of Eden.

CHAPTER 4

¹ And in the third week in the second jubilee she gave birth to Cain, and in the fourth she gave birth to Abel, and in the fifth she gave birth to her daughter 'Âwân. ² And in the first [year] of the third jubilee, Cain slew Abel because [God] accepted the sacrifice of Abel and did not accept the offering of Cain. ³ And he slew him in the field: and his blood cried from the ground to Heaven, complaining because he had slain him. ⁴ And the LORD reproved Cain because of Abel, because he had slain him, and he made him a fugitive on the earth because of the blood of his brother, and he cursed him on the earth. ⁵ And on this account, it is written on the heavenly tablets: "Cursed is he who strikes his neighbor treacherously, and let all who have seen and heard it say so; and the man who has seen and not declared [it], let him be accursed as the other." And for this reason, we announce when we come before the LORD our God all the sin which is committed in the heavens and on earth, and in light and in darkness, and everywhere. ⁷ And Adam and his wife mourned for Abel four weeks of years, and in the fourth year of the fifth week they became joyful, and Adam knew his wife again, and she bore him a son, and he called his name Seth, for he said, "God has raised up a second seed to us on the earth instead of Abel, for Cain slew him." ⁸ And in the sixth week he begot his daughter 'Azûrâ. ⁹ And Cain took his sister 'Âwân to be his wife and she bore him Enoch at the close of the fourth jubilee. And in the first year of the first week of the fifth jubilee, houses were built on the earth, and Cain built a city, and called its name after the name of his son Enoch. ¹⁰ And Adam knew his wife Eve and she bore nine more sons. ¹¹ And in the fifth week of the fifth jubilee Seth took his sister 'Azûrâ to be his wife, and in the fourth [year of the sixth week] she bore him Enos. ¹² He began to call on the Name of the LORD on the earth. ¹³ And in the seventh jubilee in the third week Enos took his sister Nôâm to be his wife, and she bore him a son in the third year of the fifth week, and he called his name Kenan. ¹⁴ And at the close of the eighth jubilee Kenan took his sister Mûalêlêth to be his wife, and she bore him a son in the ninth jubilee, in the first week in the third year of this week, and he called his name Mahalalel. ¹⁵ And in the second week of the tenth jubilee Mahalalel took to himself Dînâh to be [his] wife, the daughter of Barâkî'êl, the daughter of his father's brother, and she bore him a son in the third week in the sixth year, and he called his name Jared, for in his days the messengers of the LORD descended on the earth, those who are named the Watchers, that they should instruct the children of men, and that they should do judgment and uprightness on the earth. ¹⁶ And in the eleventh jubilee Jared took to himself a wife, and her name was Bâraka, the daughter of Râsûjâl, a daughter of his father's brother, in the fourth week of this jubilee, and she bore him a son in the fifth week, in the fourth year of the jubilee, and he called his name Enoch. ¹⁷ And he was the first among men that are born on earth who learned writing, and knowledge, and wisdom, and who wrote down the signs of the heavens according to the order of their months in a scroll, that men might know the seasons of the years according to the order of their separate months. ¹⁸ And he was the first to write a testimony, and he testified to the sons of men among the generations of the earth, and recounted the weeks of the jubilees, and made known to them the days of the years, and set in order the months, and recounted the Sabbaths of the years as we made [them] known to him. ¹⁹ And what was and what will be he saw in a vision of his sleep, as it will happen to the children of men throughout their generations until the Day of Judgment; he saw and understood everything, and wrote his testimony, and placed the testimony on earth for all the children of men and for their generations. ²⁰ And in the twelfth jubilee, in the seventh week thereof, he took to himself a wife, and her name was Ednî, the daughter of Dânêl, the daughter of his father's brother, and in the sixth year in this week she bore him a son and he called his name Methuselah. ²¹ And he was moreover with the messengers of God these six jubilees of years, and they showed him everything which is on earth and in the heavens, the rule of the sun, and he wrote down everything. ²² And he testified to the Watchers who had sinned with the daughters of men, for these had begun to unite themselves [with them], so as to be defiled with the daughters of men, and Enoch testified against [them] all. ²³ And he was taken from among the children of men, and we conducted him into the Garden of Eden in majesty and honor, and behold, there he wrote down the condemnation and judgment of the world, and all the wickedness of the children of men. ²⁴ And on account of it [God] brought the waters of the flood on all the land of Eden; for there he was set as a sign and that he should testify against all the children of men, that he should recount all the deeds of the generations until the day of condemnation. ²⁵ And he burned the incense of the sanctuary, [even] sweet spices, acceptable before the LORD on the mountain. ²⁶ For the LORD has four places on the earth: the Garden of Eden, and the mountain of the

East, and this mountain on which you are this day, Mount Sinai, and Mount Zion [which] will be sanctified in the new creation for a sanctification of the earth; through it the earth will be sanctified from all [its] guilt and its uncleanness throughout the generations of the world. [27] And in the fourteenth jubilee Methuselah took to himself a wife, Ednâ the daughter of 'Âzrîâl, the daughter of his father's brother, in the third week, in the first year of this week, and he begot a son and called his name Lamech. [28] And in the fifteenth jubilee in the third week Lamech took to himself a wife, and her name was Bêtênôs, the daughter of Bârâkî'îl, the daughter of his father's brother, and in this week she bore him a son and he called his name Noah, saying, "This one will comfort me for my trouble, and all my work, and for the ground which the LORD has cursed." [29] And at the close of the nineteenth jubilee, in the seventh week in the sixth year thereof, Adam died, and all his sons buried him in the land of his creation, and he was the first to be buried in the earth. [30] And he lacked seventy years of one thousand years; for one thousand years are as one day in the testimony of the heavens and therefore it was written concerning the Tree of Knowledge: "On the day that you eat thereof you will die." For this reason, he did not complete the years of this day, for he died during it. [31] At the close of this jubilee Cain was killed after him in the same year, for his house fell on him and he died in the midst of his house, and he was killed by its stones, for with a stone he had killed Abel, and by a stone he was killed in righteous judgment. [32] For this reason it was ordained on the heavenly tablets: "With the instrument with which a man kills his neighbor with the same he will be killed; after the manner that he wounded him, in like manner they will deal with him." [33] And in the twenty-fifth jubilee Noah took to himself a wife, and her name was 'Ĕmzârâ, the daughter of Râkê'êl, the daughter of his father's brother, in the first year in the fifth week: and in the third year thereof she bore him Shem, in the fifth year thereof she bore him Ham, and in the first year in the sixth week she bore him Japheth.

CHAPTER 5

[1] And it came to pass when the children of men began to multiply on the face of the earth and daughters were born to them, that the messengers of God saw them on a certain year of this jubilee, that they were beautiful to look on; and they took wives [for] themselves of all whom they chose, and they bore sons to them and they were giants. [2] And lawlessness increased on the earth and all flesh corrupted its way—men, and cattle, and beasts, and birds, and everything that walks on the earth alike—all of them corrupted their ways and their orders, and they began to devour each other, and lawlessness increased on the earth, and every imagination of the thoughts of all men was evil continually. [3] And God looked on the earth, and behold it was corrupt, and all flesh had corrupted its orders, and all that were on the earth had worked all manner of evil before His eyes. [4] And He said that He would destroy man and all flesh on the face of the earth which He had created. [5] But Noah found grace before the eyes of the LORD. [6] And against the messengers whom He had sent on the earth, He was exceedingly angry, and He gave command to root them out of all their dominion, and He commanded us to bind them in the depths of the earth, and behold, they are bound in the midst of them and are [kept] separate. [7] And a command went out against their sons from before His face that they should be smitten with the sword and be removed from under the heavens. [8] And He said, "My Spirit will not always abide on man, for they are also flesh and their days will be one hundred and twenty years." [9] And He sent His sword into their midst that each should slay his neighbor, and they began to slay each other until they all fell by the sword and were destroyed from the earth. [10] And their fathers were witnesses [of their destruction], and after this they were bound in the depths of the earth forever, until the day of the great condemnation, when judgment is executed on all those who have corrupted their ways and their works before the LORD. [11] And He destroyed all from their places, and there was not left [even] one of them whom He did not judge according to all their wickedness. [12] And He made for all His works a new and righteous nature, so that they should not sin in their whole nature forever but should be all righteous—each in his kind always. [13] And the judgment of all is ordained and written on the heavenly tablets in righteousness—even [the judgment of] all who depart from the path which is ordained for them to walk in; and if they do not walk therein, judgment is written down for every creature and for every kind. [14] And there is nothing in the heavens or on earth, or in light or in darkness, or in Sheol or in the depth, or in the place of darkness [which is not judged]; and all their judgments are ordained, and written, and engraved. [15] In regard to all He will judge, the great according to his greatness, and the small according to his smallness, and each according to his way. [16] And He is not one who will regard the person [of any], nor is He one who will receive gifts, if He says that He will execute judgment on each: if one gave everything that is on the earth, He will not regard the gifts or the person [of any], nor accept anything at his hands, for He is a righteous judge. [17] And of the sons of Israel it has been written and ordained [that] if they turn to Him in righteousness, He will forgive all their transgressions and pardon all their sins. [18] It is written and ordained that He will show mercy to all who turn from all their guilt once each year. [19] And as for all those who corrupted their ways and their thoughts before the

flood, no man's person was accepted save that of Noah alone; for his person was accepted in behalf of his sons, whom [God] saved from the waters of the flood on his account; for his heart was righteous in all his ways, according as it was commanded regarding him, and he had not departed from anything that was ordained for him. [20] And the LORD said that He would destroy everything which was on the earth, both men, and cattle, and beasts, and birds of the air, and that which moves on the earth. [21] And He commanded Noah to make himself an ark, that he might save himself from the waters of the flood. [22] And Noah made the Ark in all respects as He commanded him, in the twenty-seventh jubilee of years, in the fifth week in the fifth year [[on the new moon of the first month]]. [1307 A.M.] [23] And he entered in the sixth [year] thereof [1308 A.M.], in the second month, on the new moon of the second month, until the sixteenth; and he entered, and all that we brought to him, into the Ark, and the LORD closed it from outside on the seventeenth evening. [24] And the LORD opened seven floodgates of [the] heavens, and the mouths of the fountains of the great deep—seven mouths in number. [25] And the floodgates began to pour down water from the heavens forty days and forty nights, and the fountains of the deep also sent up waters, until the whole world was full of water. [26] And the waters increased on the earth: the waters rose fifteen cubits above all the high mountains, and the Ark was lifted up above the earth, and it moved on the face of the waters. [27] And the water prevailed on the face of the earth five months—one hundred and fifty days. [28] And the Ark went and rested on the top of Lûbâr, one of the mountains of Ararat. [29] And [on the new moon] in the fourth month the fountains of the great deep were closed and the floodgates of the heavens were restrained; and on the new moon of the seventh month all the mouths of the abysses of the earth were opened, and the water began to descend into the deep below. [30] And on the new moon of the tenth month the tops of the mountains were seen, and on the new moon of the first month the earth became visible. [31] And the waters disappeared from above the earth in the fifth week in the seventh year [1309 A.M.] thereof, and on the seventeenth day in the second month the earth was dry. [32] And on the twenty-seventh thereof he opened the Ark, and sent out from it beasts, and cattle, and birds, and every moving thing.

CHAPTER 6

[1] And on the new moon of the third month he went out from the Ark and built an altar on that mountain. [2] And he made atonement for the earth and took a kid and made atonement by its blood for all the guilt of the earth; for everything that had been on it had been destroyed, save those that were in the Ark with Noah. [3] And he placed the fat thereof on the altar, and he took an ox, and a goat, and a sheep and kids, and salt,

and a turtle-dove, and the young of a dove, and placed a burnt sacrifice on the altar, and poured an offering mingled with oil thereon, and sprinkled wine and scattered frankincense over everything, and caused an attractive savor to arise, acceptable before the LORD. [4] And the LORD smelled the attractive savor, and He made a covenant with him that there should not be a flood to destroy the earth anymore; that all the days of the earth, seed-time and harvest, should never cease; cold and heat, and summer and winter, and day and night should not change their order, nor cease forever. [5] "And you: increase and multiply on the earth, and become many on it, and be a blessing on it. The fear of you and the dread of you I will inspire in everything that is on earth and in the sea. [6] And behold, I have given to you all beasts, and all winged things, and everything that moves on the earth, and the fish in the waters, and all things for food; as the green herbs, I have given you all things to eat. [7] But flesh, with the life thereof, with the blood, you will not eat; for the life of all flesh is in the blood, lest your blood of your lives be required. At the hand of every man, at the hand of every [beast], I will require the blood of man. [8] Whoever sheds man's blood by man his blood will be shed, for in the image of God He made man. [9] And you: increase and multiply on the earth." [10] And Noah and his sons swore that they would not eat any blood that was in any flesh, and he made a covenant before the LORD God forever throughout all the generations of the earth in this month. [11] On this account He spoke to you that you should make a covenant with the sons of Israel in this month on the mountain with an oath, and that you should sprinkle blood on them because of all the words of the covenant, which the LORD made with them forever. [12] And this testimony is written concerning you that you should observe it continually, so that you should not eat on any day any blood of beasts, or birds, or cattle during all the days of the earth, and the man who eats the blood of beast, or of cattle, or of birds during all the days of the earth, he and his seed will be rooted out of the land. [13] And command the sons of Israel to eat no blood, so that their names and their seed may continually be before the LORD our God. [14] And for this law there is no limit of days, for it is forever. They will observe it throughout their generations, so that they may continue supplicating on your behalf with blood before the altar; every day and at the time of morning and evening they will seek forgiveness on your behalf perpetually before the LORD that they may keep it and not be rooted out. [15] And He gave a sign to Noah and his sons that there should not be a flood on the [whole] earth again. [16] He set His bow in the cloud for a sign of the perpetual covenant that there should not again be a flood on the earth to destroy it all the days of the earth. [17] For this reason it is ordained and written on the heavenly tablets that they should celebrate the Celebration of Weeks in this month once a year, to renew the covenant every year. [18] And this whole festival was celebrated in Heaven from the day of creation until the days of Noah—twenty-six jubilees and five weeks of years: and Noah and his sons observed it for seven jubilees and one week of years, until the day of Noah's death, and from the day of Noah's death his sons did away with [it] until the days of Abraham, and they ate blood. [19] But Abraham observed it, and Isaac, and Jacob, and his children observed it up to your days, and in your days the sons of Israel forgot it until you celebrated it anew on this mountain. [20] And command the sons of Israel to observe this festival in all their generations for a command to them: one day in the year in this month they will celebrate the festival. [21] For it is the Celebration of Weeks and the Celebration of First-Fruits: this feast is twofold and of a double nature. According to what is written and engraved concerning it, celebrate it. [22] For I have written in the scroll of the first law, in that which I have written for you, that you should celebrate it in its season, one day in the year, and I explained to you its sacrifices that the sons of Israel should remember and should celebrate it throughout their generations in this month, one day in every year. [23] And on the new moon of the first month, and on the new moon of the fourth month, and on the new moon of the seventh month, and on the new moon of the tenth month are the days of remembrance, and the days of the seasons in the four divisions of the year. These are written and ordained as a testimony forever. [24] And Noah ordained them for himself as feasts for the generations forever, so that they have thereby become a memorial to him. [25] And on the new moon of the first month he was commanded to make for himself an ark, and on that [day] the earth became dry, and he opened [the Ark], and saw the earth. [26] And on the new moon of the fourth month the mouths of the depths of the abysses beneath were closed. And on the new moon of the seventh month all the mouths of the abysses of the earth were opened, and the waters began to descend into them. [27] And on the new moon of the tenth month the tops of the mountains were seen, and Noah was glad. [28] And on this account, he ordained them for himself as feasts for a memorial forever, and thus they are ordained. [29] And they placed them on the heavenly tablets; each had thirteen weeks; from one to another—their memorial, from the first to the second, and from the second to the third, and from the third to the fourth. [30] And all the days of the command will be fifty-two weeks of days, and [these will make] the entire year complete. [31] Thus it is engraved and ordained on the heavenly tablets. And there is no neglecting [this command] for a single year or from year to year. [32] And command the sons of Israel that they observe the years according to this reckoning—three hundred and sixty-four days, and [these] will constitute a complete year, and they will not disturb its time from its days and from its feasts; for everything will fall out in them according to their testimony, and they will not leave out any day nor disturb any feasts. [33] But if they neglect and do not observe them according to His command, then they will disturb all their seasons, and the years will be dislodged from this [order], and they will neglect their ordinances. [34] And all the sons of Israel will forget, and will not find the path of the years, and will forget the new moons, and seasons, and Sabbaths, and they will go wrong as to all the order of the years. [35] For I know and from now on will declare it to you, and it is not of My own devising, for the scroll [lies] written before Me, and on the heavenly tablets the division of days is ordained, lest they forget the feasts of the covenant and walk according to the feasts of the nations after their error and after their ignorance. [36] For there will be those who will assuredly make observations of the moon—how [it] disturbs the seasons and comes in from year to year ten days too soon. [37] For this reason the years will come on them when they will disturb [the order] and make an abominable [day] the day of testimony, and an unclean day a feast day, and they will confound all the days, the holy with the unclean, and the unclean day with the holy; for they will go wrong as to the months, and Sabbaths, and feasts, and jubilees. [38] For this reason I command and testify to you that you may testify to them; for after your death your children will disturb [them], so that they will not make the year three hundred and sixty-four days only, and for this reason they will go wrong as to the new moons, and seasons, and Sabbaths, and festivals, and they will eat all kinds of blood with all kinds of flesh.

CHAPTER 7

[1] And in the seventh week in the first year thereof, in this jubilee, Noah planted vines on the mountain on which the Ark had rested, named Lûbâr, one of the Ararat Mountains, and they produced fruit in the fourth year, and he guarded their fruit, and gathered it in this year in the seventh month. [2] And he made wine from that and put it into a vessel, and kept it until the fifth year, until the first day, on the new moon of the first month. [3] And he celebrated with joy the day of this feast, and he made a burnt sacrifice to the LORD—one young ox, and one ram, and seven sheep, each a year old, and a kid of the goats, that he might make atonement thereby for himself and his sons. [4] And he prepared the kid first and placed some of its blood on the flesh that was on the altar which he had made, and all the fat he laid on the altar where he made the burnt sacrifice, and the ox, and the ram, and the sheep, and he laid all their flesh on the altar. [5] And he placed all their offerings mingled with oil on it, and afterward he sprinkled wine on the fire which he had previously made on the altar, and he placed incense on the altar

and caused a sweet savor to ascend acceptable before the LORD his God. ⁶ And he rejoiced and drank of this wine—he and his children with joy. ⁷ And it was evening, and he went into his tent, and being drunken, he lay down and slept, and was uncovered in his tent as he slept. ⁸ And Ham saw his father Noah naked and went out and told his two brothers outside. ⁹ And Shem took his garment and arose, he and Japheth, and they placed the garment on their shoulders and went backward and covered the shame of their father, and their faces were backward. ¹⁰ And Noah awoke from his sleep and knew all that his younger son had done to him, and he cursed his son and said, "Cursed be Canaan; he will be an enslaved servant to his brothers." ¹¹ And he blessed Shem and said, "Blessed is the LORD God of Shem, and Canaan will be his servant. ¹² God will enlarge Japheth, and God will dwell in the dwelling of Shem, and Canaan will be his servant." ¹³ And Ham knew that his father had cursed his younger son, and he was displeased that he had cursed his son, and he parted from his father, he and his sons with him—Cush, and Mizraim, and Put, and Canaan. ¹⁴ And he built a city for himself and called its name after the name of his wife Nê'êlâtamâ'ûk. ¹⁵ And Japheth saw it, and became envious of his brother, and he too built a city for himself, and he called its name after the name of his wife 'Adâtanêsês. ¹⁶ And Shem dwelt with his father Noah, and he built a city close to his father on the mountain, and he too called its name after the name of his wife Sêdêqêtêlĕbâb. ¹⁷ And behold, these three cities are near Mount Lûbâr: Sêdêqêtêlĕbâb, fronting the mountain on its east, and Na'êlâtamâ'ûk on the south, [and] 'Adatanêsês toward the west. ¹⁸ And these are the sons of Shem: Elam, and Asshur, and Arphaxad (this [son] was born two years after the flood), and Lud, and Aram. ¹⁹ The sons of Japheth: Gomer, and Magog, and Madai, and Javan, Tubal, and Meshech, and Tiras. These are the sons of Noah. ²⁰ And in the twenty-eighth jubilee Noah began to prescribe on his sons' sons the ordinances and commands, and all the judgments that he knew, and he exhorted his sons to observe righteousness, and to cover the shame of their flesh, and to bless their Creator, and honor father and mother, and love their neighbor, and guard their souls from fornication, and uncleanness, and all iniquity. ²¹ For owing to these three things the flood came on the earth, namely, owing to the fornication wherein the Watchers against the law of their ordinances went whoring after the daughters of men, and took wives [for] themselves of all which they chose: and they made the beginning of uncleanness. ²² And they begot sons, the Nâphîdîm, and they were all different, and they devoured one another: and the Giants slew the Nâphîl, and the Nâphîl slew the Eljô, and the Eljô mankind, and one man another. ²³ And everyone sold himself to work iniquity and to shed much blood, and the earth was filled with iniquity. ²⁴ And after this they sinned against the beasts, and birds, and all that moves and walks on the earth: and much blood was shed on the earth, and every imagination and desire of men they imagined [was] vanity and evil continually. ²⁵ And the LORD destroyed everything from off the face of the earth; because of the wickedness of their deeds, and because of the blood which they had shed in the midst of the earth He destroyed everything. ²⁶ "And we were left, you and I, my sons, and everything that entered with us into the Ark, and behold, I see your works before me that you do not walk in righteousness; for you have begun to walk in the path of destruction, and you are parting from one another, and are envious of one another, and [so it is] that you are not in harmony, my sons, each with his brother. ²⁷ For I see and behold [that] the demons have begun [their] seductions against you and against your children, and now I fear on your behalf that after my death you will shed the blood of men on the earth, and that you, too, will be destroyed from the face of the earth. ²⁸ For whoever sheds man's blood, and whoever eats the blood of any flesh, will all be destroyed from the earth. ²⁹ And there will not be left any man that eats blood or that sheds the blood of man on the earth, nor will there be left to him any seed or descendants living under the heavens; for they will go into Sheol, and they will descend into the place of condemnation. And into the darkness of the deep they will all be removed by a violent death. ³⁰ No blood will be seen on you of all the blood there will be all the days in which you have killed any beasts, or cattle, or whatever flies on the earth; and work a good work for your souls by covering that which has been shed on the face of the earth. ³¹ And you will not be like him who eats with blood, but guard yourselves that none may eat blood before you: cover the blood, for thus I have been commanded to testify to you and your children, together with all flesh. ³² And do not permit the soul to be eaten with the flesh, that your blood, which is your life, may not be required at the hand of any flesh that sheds [it] on the earth. ³³ For the earth will not be clean from the blood which has been shed on it; for [only] through the blood of him that shed it will the earth be purified throughout all its generations. ³⁴ And now, my children, listen: work judgment and righteousness that you may be planted in righteousness over the face of the whole earth, and your glory [will be] lifted up before my God, who saved me from the waters of the flood. ³⁵ And behold, you will go and build cities for yourselves, and plant in them all the plants that are on the earth, and moreover all fruit-bearing trees. ³⁶ For three years the fruit of everything that is eaten will not be gathered: and in the fourth year its fruit will be accounted holy, acceptable before the Most High God, who created the heavens, and earth, and all things. Let them offer in abundance the first of the wine and oil [as] first-fruits on the altar of the LORD, who receives it, and let the servants of the house of the LORD eat what is left before the altar which receives [it]. [37] And in the fifth year make the release so that you release it in righteousness and uprightness, and you will be righteous, and all that you plant will prosper. [38] For thus did Enoch, the father of your father command Methuselah, his son, and Methuselah his son Lamech, and Lamech commanded me all the things which his fathers commanded him. [39] And I also will give you command, my sons, as Enoch commanded his son in the first jubilees: while still living, the seventh in his generation, he commanded and testified to his son and to his sons' sons until the day of his death."

CHAPTER 8

[1] In the twenty-ninth jubilee, in the first week, in the beginning thereof, Arphaxad took to himself a wife and her name was Râsû'ĕjâ, [the daughter of Sûsân,] the daughter of Elam, and she bore him a son in the third year in this week, and he called his name Kâinâm. [2] And the son grew, and his father taught him writing, and he went to seek for himself a place where he might seize for himself a city. [3] And he found a writing which former [generations] had carved on the rock, and he read what was thereon, and he transcribed it and sinned owing to it; for it contained the teaching of the Watchers in accordance with which they used to observe the omens of the sun, and moon, and stars in all the signs of the heavens. [4] And he wrote it down and said nothing regarding it; for he was afraid to speak to Noah about it lest he should be angry with him on account of it. [5] And in the thirtieth jubilee, in the second week, in the first year thereof, he took to himself a wife, and her name was Mêlkâ, the daughter of Madai, the son of Japheth, and in the fourth year he begot a son, and called his name Shelah, for he said, "Truly I have been sent." [6] [And in the fourth year he was born], and Shelah grew up and took to himself a wife, and her name was Mû'ak, the daughter of Kêsêd, his father's brother, in the thirty-first jubilee, in the fifth week, in the first year thereof. [7] And she bore him a son in the fifth year thereof, and he called his name Eber: and he took to himself a wife, and her name was 'Azûrâd, the daughter of Nêbrôd, in the thirty-second jubilee, in the seventh week, in the third year thereof. [8] And in the sixth year thereof, she bore him a son, and he called his name Peleg, for in the days when he was born the children of Noah began to divide the earth among themselves; for this reason he called his name Peleg. [9] And they divided [it] secretly among themselves and told it to Noah. [10] And it came to pass in the beginning of the thirty-third jubilee that they divided the earth into three parts, for Shem, and Ham, and Japheth, according to the inheritance of each, in the first year in the first week, when one of us, who had been sent, was with them. [11] And he called his sons, and they drew near to him, they and their children, and he divided the earth into the lots, which his three sons were to take in possession, and they reached out their hands, and took the writing out of the bosom of their father Noah. [12] And there came out on the writing as Shem's lot the middle of the earth which he should take as an inheritance for himself and for his sons, for the perpetual generations, from the middle of the mountain range of Râfâ, from the mouth of the water from the River Tînâ, and his portion goes toward the west through the midst of this river, and it extends until it reaches the water of the abysses, out of which this river goes out and pours its waters into the sea Mê'at, and this river flows into the Great Sea. And all that is toward the north is Japheth's, and all that is toward the south belongs to Shem. [13] And it extends until it reaches Kârâsô: this is in the bosom of the tongue which looks toward the south. [14] And his portion extends along the Great Sea, and it extends in a straight line until it reaches the west of the tongue which looks toward the south; for this sea is called the tongue of the Egyptian Sea. [15] And it turns from here toward the south toward the mouth of the Great Sea on the shore of [its] waters, and it extends to the west to 'Afrâ and it extends until it reaches the waters of the River Gihon, and to the south of the waters of Gihon, to the banks of this river. [16] And it extends toward the east until it reaches the Garden of Eden, to the south thereof, [to the south] and from the east of the whole land of Eden and of the whole east [thereof], it turns to the east, and proceeds until it reaches the east of the mountain named Râfâ, and it descends to the bank of the mouth of the River Tînâ. [17] This portion came out by lot for Shem and his sons, that they should possess it forever to his generations forevermore. [18] And Noah rejoiced that this portion came out for Shem and for his sons, and he remembered all that he had spoken with his mouth in prophecy; for he had said, "Blessed is the LORD God of Shem, and may the LORD dwell in the dwelling of Shem." [19] And he knew that the Garden of Eden is the Holy of Holies and the dwelling of the LORD, and Mount Sinai—the center of the desert, and Mount Zion—the center of the navel of the earth: these three were created as holy places facing each other. [20] And he blessed the God of gods who had put the word of the LORD into his mouth, and [blessed] the LORD forevermore. [21] And he knew that a blessed portion and a blessing had come to Shem and his sons to the generations forever—the whole land of Eden and the whole land of the Red Sea, and the whole land of the east, and India, and on the Red Sea and the mountains thereof, and all the land of Bashan, and all the land of Lebanon and the islands of Kaftûr, and all the mountains of Sanîr and 'Amânâ, and the mountains of Asshur in the north, and all the land of Elam, Asshur, and Bâbêl, and Sûsân, and Mâ'ĕdâi, and all the mountains of Ararat, and all the region beyond the sea, which is beyond the mountains of Asshur toward

the north, a blessed and spacious land, and all that is in it is very good. ²² And for Ham came out the second portion, beyond the Gihon toward the south to the right of the Garden, and it extends toward the south and it extends to all the mountains of fire, and it extends toward the west to the Sea of 'Atêl and it extends toward the west until it reaches the Sea of Mâ'ûk—that [sea] into which everything which is not destroyed descends. ²³ And it goes out toward the north to the limits of Gâdîr, and it goes out to the coast of the waters of the sea to the waters of the Great Sea until it draws near to the River Gihon and goes along the River Gihon until it reaches the right of the Garden of Eden. ²⁴ And this is the land which came out for Ham as the portion which he was to occupy forever for himself and his sons to their generations forever. ²⁵ And for Japheth came out the third portion beyond the River Tînâ to the north of the outflow of its waters, and it extends northeastward to the whole region of Gog and to all the country east thereof. ²⁶ And it extends northward to the north, and it extends to the mountains of Qêlt toward the north, and toward the Sea of Mâ'ûk, and it goes out to the east of Gâdîr as far as the region of the waters of the sea. ²⁷ And it extends until it approaches the west of Fârâ, and it returns toward 'Afêrâg, and it extends eastward to the waters of the Sea of Mê'at. ²⁸ And it extends to the region of the River Tînâ in a northeasterly direction until it approaches the boundary of its waters toward the mountain Râfâ, and it turns toward the north. ²⁹ This is the land which came out for Japheth and his sons as the portion of his inheritance which he should possess for himself and his sons, for their generations forever: five great islands, and a great land in the north. ³⁰ But it is cold, and the land of Ham is hot, and the land of Shem is neither hot nor cold, but it is of blended cold and heat.

CHAPTER 9

¹ And Ham divided among his sons, and the first portion came out for Cush toward the east, and to the west of him for Mizraim, and to the west of him for Put, and to the west of him [and to the west thereof] on the sea for Canaan. ² And Shem also divided among his sons, and the first portion came out for Elam and his sons, to the east of the River Tigris until it approaches the east, the whole land of India, and on the Red Sea on its coast, and the waters of Dêdân, and all the mountains of Mebrî and 'Êlâ, and all the land of Sûsân and all that is on the side of Pharnâk to the Red Sea and the River Tînâ. ³ And for Asshur came out the second portion, all the land of Asshur, and Nineveh, and Shinar, and to the border of India, and it ascends and skirts the river. ⁴ And for Arphaxad came out the third portion, all the land of the region of the Chaldees to the east of the Euphrates, bordering on the Red Sea, and all the waters of the desert close to the tongue of the sea which looks toward Egypt, all

the land of Lebanon, and Sanîr, and 'Amânâ to the border of the Euphrates. ⁵ And for Aram there came out the fourth portion, all the land of Mesopotamia between the Tigris and the Euphrates to the north of the Chaldees to the border of the mountains of Asshur and the land of 'Arârâ. ⁶ And there came out for Lud the fifth portion, the mountains of Asshur and all pertaining to them until it reaches the Great Sea, and until it reaches the east of his brother Asshur. ⁷ And Japheth also divided the land of his inheritance among his sons. ⁸ And the first portion came out for Gomer to the east from the north side to the River Tînâ; and in the north there came out for Magog all the inner portions of the north until it reaches to the Sea of Mê'at. ⁹ And for Madai came out as his portion that he should possess from the west of his two brothers to the islands, and to the coasts of the islands. ¹⁰ And for Javan came out the fourth portion, every island and the islands which are toward the border of Lud. ¹¹ And for Tubal there came out the fifth portion in the midst of the tongue which approaches toward the border of the portion of Lud to the second tongue, to the region beyond the second tongue to the third tongue. ¹² And for Meshech came out the sixth portion, all the region beyond the third tongue until it approaches the east of Gâdîr. ¹³ And for Tiras there came out the seventh portion: four great islands in the midst of the sea, which reach to the portion of Ham [[and the islands of Kamâtûrî came out by lot for the sons of Arphaxad as his inheritance]]. ¹⁴ And thus the sons of Noah divided to their sons in the presence of their father Noah, and he bound them all by an oath, invoking a curse on everyone that sought to seize the portion which had not fallen [to him] by his lot. ¹⁵ And they all said, "So be it; so be it," for themselves and their sons forever throughout their generations until the Day of Judgment, on which the LORD God will judge them with a sword and with fire, for all the unclean wickedness of their errors, with which they have filled the earth with transgression, and uncleanness, and fornication, and sin.

CHAPTER 10

¹ And in the third week of this jubilee the unclean demons began to lead the children of the sons of Noah astray, and to make [them] to err, and destroy them. ² And the sons of Noah came to their father Noah, and they told him concerning the demons which were leading astray, and blinding, and slaying his sons' sons. ³ And he prayed before the LORD his God, and said, "God of the spirits of all flesh, || Who has shown mercy to me, || And has saved me and my sons from the waters of the flood, || And has not caused me to perish as you did the sons of perdition, || For Your grace has been great toward me, || And great has been Your mercy to my soul: Let Your grace be lifted up on my sons, || And do not let wicked spirits rule over them || Lest they should destroy them from the earth.

[4] But bless me and my sons, || That we may increase, and multiply, and replenish the earth. [5] And You know how Your Watchers, || The fathers of these spirits, acted in my day: And as for these spirits which are living, || Imprison them and hold them fast in the place of condemnation, || And do not let them bring destruction on the sons of Your servant, my God; For these are malevolent, and created in order to destroy. [6] And do not let them rule over the spirits of the living, || For You alone can exercise dominion over them. And do not let them have power over the sons of the righteous || From now on and forevermore." [7] And the LORD our God commanded us to bind all. [8] And the chief of the spirits, Mastêmâ, came and said, "LORD, Creator, let some of them remain before me, and let them listen to my voice, and do all that I will say to them; for if some of them are not left to me, I will not be able to execute the power of my will on the sons of men; for these are for corruption and leading astray before my judgment, for great is the wickedness of the sons of men." [9] And He said, "Let the tenth part of them remain before him, and let nine parts descend into the place of condemnation." [10] And He commanded that one of us should teach Noah all their medicines; for He knew that they would not walk in uprightness, nor strive in righteousness. [11] And we did according to all His words: we bound all the malevolent evil ones in the place of condemnation, and a tenth part of them we left that they might be subject before Satan on the earth. [12] And we explained to Noah all the medicines of their diseases, together with their seductions, how he might heal them with herbs of the earth. [13] And Noah wrote down all things in a scroll as we instructed him concerning every kind of medicine. Thus, the evil spirits were precluded from [hurting] the sons of Noah. [14] And he gave all that he had written to Shem, his eldest son, for he loved him exceedingly above all his sons. [15] And Noah slept with his fathers and was buried on Mount Lûbâr in the land of Ararat. [16] Nine hundred and fifty years he completed in his life—nineteen jubilees, and two weeks, and five years. [17] And in his life on earth he excelled the children of men, save Enoch because of the righteousness wherein he was perfect. For Enoch's office was ordained for a testimony to the generations of the world, so that he should recount all the deeds of generation to generation, until the Day of Judgment. [18] And in the thirty-third jubilee, in the first year in the second week, Peleg took to himself a wife, whose name was Lômnâ, the daughter of Sînâ'ar, and she bore him a son in the fourth year of this week, and he called his name Reu, for he said, "Behold, the children of men have become evil through the wicked purpose of building for themselves a city and a tower in the land of Shinar." [19] For they departed from the land of Ararat eastward to Shinar, for in his days they built the city and the tower, saying, "Go forth; let us ascend thereby into the heavens." [20] And they began to build, and in the fourth week they made brick with fire, and the bricks served them for stone, and the clay with which they cemented them together was asphalt, which comes out of the sea and out of the fountains of water in the land of Shinar. [21] And they built it; forty-three years they were building it; its breadth was two hundred and three bricks, and the height [of a brick] was the third of one; its height amounted to five thousand and four hundred and thirty-three cubits and two palms, and [the extent of one wall was] thirteen stadia [[and of the other thirty stadia]]. [22] And the LORD our God said to us, "Behold, they are one people, and they begin to do [this], and now nothing will be withheld from them. Go forth; let us go down and confound their language that they may not understand one another's speech, and they may be dispersed into cities and nations, and one purpose will no longer abide with them until the Day of Judgment." [23] And the LORD descended, and we descended with Him to see the city and the tower which the children of men had built. [24] And He confounded their language, and they no longer understood one another's speech, and then they ceased to build the city and the tower. [25] For this reason the whole land of Shinar is called Babel, because the LORD confounded all the language of the children of men there, and from there they were dispersed into their cities, each according to his language and his nation. [26] And the LORD sent a mighty wind against the tower and overthrew it on the earth, and behold, it was between Asshur and Babylon in the land of Shinar, and they called its name "Overthrow." [27] In the fourth week, in the first year, in the beginning thereof, in the thirty-fourth jubilee, they were dispersed from the land of Shinar. [28] And Ham and his sons went into the land which he was to occupy, which he acquired as his portion in the land of the south. [29] And Canaan saw the land of Lebanon to the river of Egypt that it was very good, and he did not go into the land of his inheritance to the west [that is to] the sea, and he dwelt in the land of Lebanon, eastward and westward from the border of Jordan and from the border of the sea. [30] And his father Ham, and his brothers Cush and Mizraim, said to him, "You have settled in a land which is not yours, and which did not fall to us by lot: do not do so; for if you do so, you and your sons will fall in the land and [be] accursed through sedition; for by sedition you have settled, and by sedition your children will fall, and you will be rooted out forever. [31] Do not dwell in the dwelling of Shem, for to Shem and to his sons did it come by their lot. [32] Cursed are you and cursed will you be beyond all the sons of Noah, by the curse by which we bound ourselves by an oath in the presence of the Holy Judge, and in the presence of our father Noah." [33] But he did not listen to them and dwelt in the land of Lebanon from Hamath to the entering of Egypt—he and his sons until this day. [34] And for this

reason that land is named Canaan. ³⁵ And Japheth and his sons went toward the sea and dwelt in the land of their portion, and Madai saw the land of the sea and it did not please him, and he begged [for] a [portion] from Elam, and Asshur, and Arphaxad, his wife's brother, and he dwelt in the land of Media, near to his wife's brother, until this day. ³⁶ And he called his dwelling-place and the dwelling-place of his sons Media, after the name of their father Madai.

CHAPTER 11

¹ And in the thirty-fifth jubilee, in the third week, in the first year thereof, Reu took to himself a wife, and her name was 'Ôrâ, the daughter of 'Ûr, the son of Kêsêd, and she bore him a son, and he called his name Sêrôḫ, in the seventh year of this week in this jubilee. ² And the sons of Noah began to war on each other, to take captive and to slay each other, and to shed the blood of men on the earth, and to eat blood, and to build strong cities, and walls, and towers, and individuals [began] to exalt themselves above the nation, and to found the beginnings of kingdoms, and to go to war—people against people, and nation against nation, and city against city, and all [began] to do evil, and to acquire arms, and to teach their sons war, and they began to capture cities, and to sell menservants and maidservants. ³ And 'Ûr, the son of Kêsêd, built the city of 'Arâ of the Chaldees, and called its name after his own name and the name of his father. ⁴ And they made molten images for themselves, and they each worshiped the idol, the molten image which they had made for themselves, and they began to make graven images and unclean statues, and malevolent spirits assisted and seduced [them] into committing transgression and uncleanness. ⁵ And the prince Mastêmâ exerted himself to do all this, and he sent out other spirits, those which were put under his hand, to do all manner of wrong and sin, and all manner of transgression, to corrupt and destroy, and to shed blood on the earth. ⁶ For this reason he called the name of Sêrôḫ, Serug, for everyone turned to do all manner of sin and transgression. ⁷ And he grew up and dwelt in Ur of the Chaldees, near to the father of his wife's mother, and he worshiped idols, and he took to himself a wife in the thirty-sixth jubilee, in the fifth week, in the first year thereof, and her name was Mêlkâ, the daughter of Kâbêr, the daughter of his father's brother. ⁸ And she bore him Nahor in the first year of this week, and he grew and dwelt in Ur of the Chaldees, and his father taught him the research of the Chaldees to divine and portend, according to the signs of the heavens. ⁹ And in the thirty-seventh jubilee, in the sixth week, in the first year thereof, he took to himself a wife, and her name was 'Îjâskâ, the daughter of Nêstâg of the Chaldees. ¹⁰ And she bore him Terah in the seventh year of this week. ¹¹ And the prince Mastêmâ sent ravens and birds to devour the seed which was sown in the land, in order to destroy the land, and rob the children of men of their labors. Before they could plow in the seed, the ravens picked [it] from the surface of the ground. ¹² And for this reason he called his name Terah, because the ravens and the birds reduced them to destitution and devoured their seed. ¹³ And the years began to be barren, owing to the birds, and they devoured all the fruit of the trees from the trees: it was only with great effort that they could save a little of all the fruit of the earth in their days. ¹⁴ And in this thirty-ninth jubilee, in the second week in the first year, Terah took to himself a wife, and her name was 'Êdnâ, the daughter of 'Abrâm, the daughter of his father's sister. ¹⁵ And in the seventh year of this week she bore him a son, and he called his name Abram, by the name of the father of his mother, for he had died before his daughter had conceived a son. ¹⁶ And the child began to understand the errors of the earth, that all went astray after graven images and after uncleanness, and his father taught him writing, and he was two weeks of years old, and he separated himself from his father that he might not worship idols with him. ¹⁷ And he began to pray to the Creator of all things that He might save him from the errors of the children of men, and that his portion should not fall into error after uncleanness and vileness. ¹⁸ And the seed-time came for the sowing of seed on the land, and they all went out together to protect their seed against the ravens, and Abram went out with those that went, and the child was a youth of fourteen years. ¹⁹ And a cloud of ravens came to devour the seed, and Abram ran to meet them before they settled on the ground and cried to them before they settled on the ground to devour the seed, and said, "Do not descend! Return to the place where you came!" And they proceeded to turn back. ²⁰ And he caused the clouds of ravens to turn back that day seventy times, and of all the ravens throughout all the land where Abram was there settled there not so much as one. ²¹ And all who were with him throughout all the land saw him cry out, and all the ravens turn back, and his name became great in all the land of the Chaldees. ²² And there came to him this year all those that wished to sow, and he went with them until the time of sowing ceased: and they sowed their land, and that year they brought enough grain home and ate and were satisfied. ²³ And in the first year of the fifth week Abram taught those who made implements for oxen, the craftsmen in wood, and they made a vessel above the ground, facing the frame of the plow, in order to put the seed thereon, and the seed fell down from that on the share of the plow, and was hidden in the earth, and they no longer feared the ravens. ²⁴ And after this manner they made [vessels] above the ground on all the frames of the plows, and they sowed and tilled all the land, according as Abram commanded them, and they no longer feared the birds.

CHAPTER 12

[1] And it came to pass in the sixth week, in the seventh year thereof, that Abram spoke to his father Terah, saying, "Father!" And he said, "Behold, here I am, my son." [2] And he said, "What help and profit do we have from those idols which you worship, and before which you bow yourself? [3] For there is no spirit in them, for they are mute forms, and a misleading of the heart. Do not worship them: [4] worship the God of Heaven, who causes the rain and the dew to descend on the earth, and does everything on the earth, and has created everything by His word, and all life is from before His face. [5] Why do you worship things that have no spirit in them? For they are the work of [men's] hands, and you bear them on your shoulders, and you have no help from them, but they are a great cause of shame to those who make them, and a misleading of the heart to those who worship them: do not worship them." [6] And his father said to him, "I also know it, my son, but what will I do with a people who have made me to serve before them? [7] And if I tell them the truth, they will slay me, for their soul cleaved to them to worship them and honor them. Keep silent, my son, lest they slay you." [8] And he spoke these words to his two brothers, and they were angry with him and he kept silent. [9] And in the fortieth jubilee, in the second week, in the seventh year thereof, Abram took to himself a wife, and her name was Sarai, the daughter of his father, and she became his wife. [10] And his brother Haran took to himself a wife in the third year of the third week, and she bore him a son in the seventh year of this week, and he called his name Lot. [11] And his brother Nahor took to himself a wife. [12] And in the sixtieth year of the life of Abram, that is, in the fourth week, in the fourth year thereof, Abram arose by night, and burned the house of the idols, and he burned all that was in the house, and no man knew it. [13] And they arose in the night and sought to save their gods from the midst of the fire. [14] And Haran tried to save them, but the fire flamed over him, and he was burned in the fire, and he died in Ur of the Chaldees before his father Terah, and they buried him in Ur of the Chaldees. [15] And Terah went out from Ur of the Chaldees, he and his sons, to go into the land of Lebanon and into the land of Canaan, and he dwelt in the land of Haran, and Abram dwelt with his father Terah in Haran [for] two weeks of years. [16] And in the sixth week, in the fifth year thereof, Abram sat up throughout the night on the new moon of the seventh month to observe the stars from the evening to the morning, in order to see what the nature of the year would be with regard to the rains, and he was alone as he sat and observed. [17] And a word came into his heart and he said, "All the signs of the stars, and the signs of the moon and of the sun are all in the hand of the LORD. Why do I search [them] out? [18] If He desires, He causes it to rain, morning and evening; and if He desires, He withholds it, and all things are in His hand." [19] And he prayed that night and said, "My God, God Most High, You alone are my God, and I have chosen You and Your dominion. And You have created all things, and all things that exist are the work of Your hands. [20] Deliver me from the hands of evil spirits who have sway over the thoughts of men's hearts, and do not let them lead me astray from You, my God. And establish me and my seed forever so that we do not go astray from now and forevermore." [21] And he said, "Will I return to Ur of the Chaldees who seek my face that I may return to them, or am I to remain here in this place? The right path before You—prosper it in the hands of Your servant that he may fulfill [it] and that I may not walk in the deceitfulness of my heart, O my God." [22] And he made an end of speaking and praying, and behold, the word of the LORD was sent to him through me, saying, "Go forth from your country, and from your relatives, and from the house of your father to a land which I will show you, and I will make you a great and numerous nation. [23] And I will bless you, and I will make your name great, and you will be blessed in the earth, and all [the] families of the earth will be blessed in you, and I will bless them that bless you, and curse them that curse you. [24] And I will be God to you and your son, and to your son's son, and to all your seed: do not fear, from now and to all generations of the earth I am your God." [25] And the LORD God said, "Open his mouth and his ears that he may hear and speak with his mouth, with the language which has been revealed," for it had ceased from the mouths of all the children of men from the day of the overthrow [of Babel]. [26] And I opened his mouth, and his ears, and his lips, and I began to speak with him in Hebrew in the tongue of the creation. [27] And he took the scrolls of his fathers, and these were written in Hebrew, and he transcribed them, and he began from then on to study them, and I made known to him that which he could not [understand], and he studied them during the six rainy months. [28] And it came to pass in the seventh year of the sixth week that he spoke to his father and informed him that he would leave Haran to go into the land of Canaan to see it and [then] return to him. [29] And his father Terah said to him, "Go in peace; may the perpetual God make your path straight, and the LORD [[be with you, and]] protect you from all evil, and grant grace, mercy, and favor to you before those who see you, and may none of the children of men have power over you to harm you; go in peace. [30] And if you see a land pleasant to your eyes to dwell in, then arise and take me to you, and take Lot, the son of your brother Haran, with you as your own son: the LORD be with you. [31] And leave your brother Nahor with me until you return in peace, and we all go with you together."

CHAPTER 13

¹ And Abram journeyed from Haran, and he took his wife Sarai, and Lot, his brother Haran's son, to the land of Canaan, and he came into Asshur, and proceeded to Shechem, and dwelt near a lofty oak. ² And he saw, and behold, the land was very pleasant from the entering of Hamath to the lofty oak. ³ And the LORD said to him, "To you and to your seed I will give this land." ⁴ And he built an altar there, and he offered a burnt sacrifice thereon to the LORD, who had appeared to him. ⁵ And he left from there to the mountain [with] Bethel on the west and Ai on the east and pitched his tent there. ⁶ And he saw, and behold, the land was very wide and good, and everything grew thereon—vines, and figs, and pomegranates, oaks, and hollies, and terebinths, and oil trees, and cedars, and cypresses, and date trees, and all trees of the field, and there was water on the mountains. ⁷ And he blessed the LORD who had led him out of Ur of the Chaldees and had brought him to this land. ⁸ And it came to pass in the first year, in the seventh week, on the new moon of the first month, that he built an altar on this mountain, and called on the Name of the LORD: "You, the perpetual God, are my God." ⁹ And he offered a burnt sacrifice to the LORD on the altar that He should be with him and not forsake him all the days of his life. ¹⁰ And he left from there and went toward the south, and he came to Hebron, and Hebron was built at that time, and he dwelt there two years, and he went into the land of the south, to Bealoth, and there was a famine in the land. ¹¹ And Abram went into Egypt in the third year of the week, and he dwelt in Egypt five years before his wife was torn away from him. ¹² Now Tanis [(Zoan)] in Egypt was at that time built—seven years after Hebron. ¹¹ And it came to pass when Pharaoh seized Sarai, the wife of Abram, that the LORD plagued Pharaoh and his house with great plagues because of Sarai, Abram's wife. ¹⁴ And Abram was very glorious by reason of possessions in sheep, and cattle, and donkeys, and horses, and camels, and menservants, and maidservants, and in exceeding silver and gold. And Lot also, his brother's son, was wealthy. ¹⁵ And Pharaoh gave back Sarai, the wife of Abram, and he sent him out of the land of Egypt, and he journeyed to the place where he had pitched his tent at the beginning, to the place of the altar, with Ai on the east and Bethel on the west, and he blessed the LORD his God who had brought him back in peace. ¹⁶ And it came to pass in the forty-first jubilee, in the third year of the first week, that he returned to this place and offered a burnt sacrifice there, and called on the Name of the LORD, and said, "You, the Most High God, are my God forever and ever." ¹⁷ And in the fourth year of this week Lot parted from him, and Lot dwelt in Sodom, and the men of Sodom were sinners exceedingly. ¹⁸ And it grieved him in his heart that his brother's son had parted from him, for he had no children. ¹⁹ In that year, when Lot was taken captive, the LORD said to Abram after Lot had parted from him, in the fourth year of this week: "Lift up your eyes from the place where you are dwelling—northward, and southward, and westward, and eastward. ²⁰ For all the land which you see I will give to you and to your seed forever, and I will make your seed as the sand of the sea: though a man may number the dust of the earth, yet your seed will not be numbered. ²¹ Arise, walk in the length of it and the breadth of it, and see it all; for to your seed I will give it." And Abram went to Hebron and dwelt there. ²² And in this year Chedorlaomer, king of Elam, and Amraphel, king of Shinar, and Arioch, king of Sêllâsar and Têrgâl, king of nations, came and slew the king of Gomorrah, and the king of Sodom fled, and many fell through wounds in the Valley of Siddim, by the Salt Sea. ²³ And they took Sodom, and Adam, and Zeboim captive, and they took Lot captive also, the son of Abram's brother, and all his possessions, and they went to Dan. ²⁴ And one who had escaped came and told Abram that his brother's son had been taken captive and [Abram] armed his household servants. ²⁵ For Abram, and for his seed, a tenth of the first-fruits to the LORD, and the LORD ordained it as an ordinance forever that they should give it to the priests who served before Him, that they should possess it forever. ²⁶ And to this law there is no limit of days; for He has ordained it for the generations forever that they should give to the LORD the tenth of everything, of the seed, and of the wine, and of the oil, and of the cattle, and of the sheep. ²⁷ And He gave [it] to His priests to eat and to drink with joy before Him. ²⁸ And the king of Sodom came to him and bowed himself before him, and said, "Our Lord Abram, give to us the souls which you have rescued, but let the plunder be yours." ²⁹ And Abram said to him, "I lift up my hands to the Most High God, that from a thread to a shoe-strap I will not take anything that is yours, lest you should say, I have made Abram rich—save only what the young men have eaten, and the portion of the men who went with me—Aner, Eschol, and Mamre. These will take their portion."

CHAPTER 14

¹ After these things, in the fourth year of this week, on the new moon of the third month, the word of the LORD came to Abram in a dream, saying, "Do not fear, Abram; I am your defender, and your reward will be exceedingly great." ² And he said, "Lord YHWH, what will You give me, seeing I go childless, and the son of Mâsêq, the son of my handmaid, is the Demmesek Eliezer: he will be my heir, and to me You have not given seed." ³ And He said to him, "This [man] will not be your heir, but one that will come out of your own bowels, he will be your heir." ⁴ And He brought him out abroad, and said to him, "Look

toward the heavens and number the stars, if you are able to number them." [5] And he looked toward the heavens and beheld the stars. And He said to him, "So will your seed be." [6] And he believed in the LORD, and it was counted to him for righteousness. [7] And He said to him, "I am the LORD that brought you out of Ur of the Chaldees, to give you the land of the Canaanites to possess it forever; and I will be God to you and to your seed after you." [8] And he said, "Lord YHWH, whereby will I know that I will inherit [it]?" [9] And He said to him, "Take Me a heifer of three years, and a goat of three years, and a sheep of three years, and a turtle-dove, and a pigeon." [10] And he took all these in the middle of the month; and he dwelt at the oak of Mamre, which is near Hebron. [11] And he built an altar there and sacrificed all these; and he poured their blood on the altar, and divided them in the midst, and laid them over against each other, but he did not divide the birds. [12] And birds came down on the pieces, and Abram drove them away, and did not permit the birds to touch them. [13] And it came to pass, when the sun had set, that an ecstasy fell on Abram, and behold, a horror of great darkness fell on him, and it was said to Abram: "Know for sure that your seed will be a stranger in a land [that is] not theirs, and they will bring them into bondage, and afflict them four hundred years. [14] And the nation to whom they will be in bondage I will also judge, and after that they will come out from there with much substance. [15] And you will go to your fathers in peace and be buried in a good old age. [16] But in the fourth generation they will return here, for the iniquity of the Amorites is not yet full." [17] And he awoke from his sleep, and he arose, and the sun had set; and there was a flame, and behold, a furnace was smoking, and a flame of fire passed between the pieces. [18] And on that day the LORD made a covenant with Abram, saying, "To your seed I will give this land, from the river of Egypt to the great river, the River Euphrates—the Kenites, the Kenizzites, the Kadmonites, the Perizzites, and the Rephaim, the Phakorites, and the Hivites, and the Amorites, and the Canaanites, and the Girgashites, and the Jebusites." [19] And the day passed, and Abram offered the pieces, and the birds, and their fruit-offerings, and their drink-offerings, and the fire devoured them. [20] And on that day we made a covenant with Abram, according as we had covenanted with Noah in this month; and Abram renewed the festival and ordinance for himself forever. [21] And Abram rejoiced and made all these things known to his wife Sarai; and he believed that he would have seed, but she did not bear. [22] And Sarai advised her husband Abram and said to him, "Go in to Hagar, my Egyptian maid: it may be that I will build up seed to you by her." [23] And Abram listened to the voice of his wife Sarai and said to her, "Do [so]." And Sarai took Hagar, her maid, the Egyptian, and gave her to her husband Abram to be his wife.

[24] And he went in to her, and she conceived and bore him a son, and he called his name Ishmael, in the fifth year of this week; and this was the eighty-sixth year in the life of Abram.

CHAPTER 15

[1] And in the fifth year of the fourth week of this jubilee, in the third month, in the middle of the month, Abram celebrated the Celebration of the First-Fruits of the grain harvest. [2] And he offered new offerings on the altar, the first-fruits of the produce, to the LORD: a heifer, and a goat, and a sheep on the altar as a burnt sacrifice to the LORD; their fruit-offerings and their drink-offerings he offered on the altar with frankincense. [3] And the LORD appeared to Abram and said to him, "I am God Almighty; approve yourself before Me and be perfect. [4] And I will make My covenant between Me and you, and I will multiply you exceedingly." [5] And Abram fell on his face, and God talked with him, and said, [6] "Behold, My ordinance is with you, and you will be the father of many nations. [7] Neither will your name be called Abram anymore, but your name from now on, even forever, will be Abraham. For I have made you the father of many nations. [8] And I will make you very great, and I will make you into nations, and kings will come out from you. [9] And I will establish My covenant between Me and you, and your seed after you, throughout their generations, for a perpetual covenant, so that I may be a God to you, and to your seed after you. [10] [[And I will give to you and to your seed after you]] the land where you have been a sojourner, the land of Canaan, that you may possess it forever, and I will be their God." [11] And the LORD said to Abraham, "And as for you: keep My covenant, you and your seed after you, and circumcise every male among you, and circumcise your foreskins, and it will be a token of a perpetual covenant between Me and you. [12] And you will circumcise the child on the eighth day, every male throughout your generations—him that is born in the house, or whom you have bought with money from any stranger, whom you have acquired who is not of your seed. [13] He that is born in your house will surely be circumcised, and those whom you have bought with money will be circumcised, and My covenant will be in your flesh for a perpetual ordinance. [14] And the uncircumcised male who is not circumcised in the flesh of his foreskin on the eighth day, that soul will be cut off from his people, for he has broken My covenant." [15] And God said to Abraham, "As for Sarai your wife, her name will no longer be called Sarai, but Sarah will be her name. [16] And I will bless her, and give you a son by her, and I will bless him, and he will become a nation, and kings of nations will proceed from him." [17] And Abraham fell on his face, and rejoiced, and said in his heart, "Will a son be born to him that is one hundred years old, and will Sarah,

who is ninety years old, bring out?" [18] And Abraham said to God, "O that Ishmael might live before you!" [19] And God said, "Yes, and Sarah will also bear you a son, and you will call his name Isaac, and I will establish My covenant with him, a perpetual covenant, and for his seed after him. [20] And as for Ishmael, I have also heard you, and behold, I will bless him, and make him great, and multiply him exceedingly, and he will beget twelve princes, and I will make him a great nation. [21] But I will establish My covenant with Isaac, whom Sarah will bear to you, in these days, in the next year." [22] And He left off speaking with him, and God went up from Abraham. [23] And Abraham did according as God had said to him, and he took his son Ishmael, and all that were born in his house, and whom he had bought with his money, every male in his house, and circumcised the flesh of their foreskin. [24] And on the same day Abraham was circumcised, indeed, all the men of his house and all those whom he had bought with money from the children of the stranger were circumcised with him. [25] This law is for all the generations forever, and there is no circumcision of the days, and no omission of one day out of the eight days, for it is a perpetual ordinance, ordained and written on the heavenly tablets. [26] And everyone that is born, the flesh of whose foreskin is not circumcised on the eighth day, does not belong to the children of the covenant which the LORD made with Abraham, but to the children of destruction; nor is there, moreover, any sign on him that he is the LORD's, but [he is destined] to be destroyed and slain from the earth, and to be rooted out of the earth, for he has broken the covenant of the LORD our God. [27] For all the messengers of the presence and all the messengers of sanctification have been so created from the day of their creation, and before the messengers of the presence and the messengers of sanctification, He has sanctified Israel, that they should be with Him and with His holy messengers. [28] And command the sons of Israel and let them observe the sign of this covenant for their generations as a perpetual ordinance, and they will not be rooted out of the land. [29] For the command is ordained for a covenant, that they should observe it forever among all the sons of Israel. [30] For Ishmael, and his sons, and his brothers, and Esau, the LORD did not cause to approach Him, and He did not choose them because they are the children of Abraham, because He knew them, but He chose Israel to be His people. [31] And He sanctified it and gathered it from among all the children of men; for there are many nations and many peoples, and all are His, and over all He has placed spirits in authority to lead them astray from Him. [32] But over Israel He did not appoint any messenger or spirit, for He alone is their ruler, and He will preserve them and require them at the hand of His messengers and His spirits, and at the hand of all His powers in order that He may preserve them and bless them, and that they may be His and He may be theirs from now on and forever. [33] And now I announce to you that the sons of Israel will not keep true to this ordinance, and they will not circumcise their sons according to all this law, for in the flesh of their circumcision they will omit this circumcision of their sons, and all of them, sons of Belial, will leave their sons uncircumcised as they were born. [34] And there will be great wrath from the LORD against the sons of Israel, because they have forsaken His covenant and turned aside from His word, and provoked and blasphemed, inasmuch as they do not observe the ordinance of this law, for they have treated their members like the nations, so that they may be removed and rooted out of the land. And there will no longer be pardon or forgiveness to them for all the sin of this continuous error.

CHAPTER 16

[1] And on the new moon of the fourth month we appeared to Abraham, at the oak of Mamre, and we talked with him, and we announced to him that a son would be given to him by his wife Sarah. [2] And Sarah laughed, for she heard that we had spoken these words with Abraham, and we admonished her, and she became afraid, and denied that she had laughed on account of the words. [3] And we told her the name of her son, as his name [(Isaac)] is ordained and written in the heavenly tablets, [4] and [that] when we returned to her at a set time, she would have conceived a son. [5] And in this month the LORD executed His judgments on Sodom, and Gomorrah, and Zeboim, and all the region of the Jordan, and He burned them with fire and brimstone, and destroyed them until this day, even as I have declared to you all their works, that they are sinners and exceedingly wicked, and that they defile themselves and commit fornication in their flesh, and work uncleanness on the earth. [6] And, in like manner, God will execute judgment on the places where they have done according to the uncleanness of the Sodomites, like to the judgment of Sodom. [7] But we saved Lot, for God remembered Abraham and sent him out from the midst of the overthrow. [8] And he and his daughters committed sin on the earth, such as had not been on the earth since the days of Adam until his time, for the man lay with his daughters. [9] And behold, it was commanded and engraved concerning all his seed, on the heavenly tablets, to remove them and root them out, and to execute judgment on them like the judgment of Sodom, and to leave no seed of the man on earth on the day of condemnation. [10] And in this month Abraham moved from Hebron and departed and dwelt between Kadesh and Shur in the mountains of Gerar. [11] And in the middle of the fifth month he moved from there and dwelt at the Well of the Oath. [12] And in the middle of the sixth month the LORD visited Sarah and did to her as He had spoken, and she

conceived. [13] And she bore a son in the third month, and in the middle of the month, at the time of which the LORD had spoken to Abraham, on the festival of the first-fruits of the harvest, Isaac was born. [14] And Abraham circumcised his son on the eighth day: he was the first that was circumcised according to the covenant which is ordained forever. [15] And in the sixth year of the fourth week we came to Abraham, to the Well of the Oath, and we appeared to him [[as we had told Sarah that we should return to her, and she would have conceived a son. [16] And we returned in the seventh month, and found Sarah with child before us,]] and we blessed him, and we announced to him all the things which had been decreed concerning him: that he should not die until he should beget six more sons, and should see [them] before he died, but [that] in Isaac should his name and seed be called, [17] and [that] all the seed of his sons should be nations, and be reckoned with the nations, but from the sons of Isaac one should become a holy seed and should not be reckoned among the nations. [18] For he should become the portion of the Most High, and all his seed had fallen into the possession of God, that it should be to the LORD a people for [His] possession above all nations and that it should become a kingdom, and priests, and a holy nation. [19] And we went our way, and we announced to Sarah all that we had told him, and they both rejoiced with exceedingly great joy. [20] And he built an altar there to the LORD who had delivered him, and who was making him rejoice in the land of his sojourning, and he celebrated a festival of joy in this month [for] seven days, near the altar which he had built at the Well of the Oath. [21] And he built shelters for himself and for his servants on this festival, and he was the first to celebrate the Celebration of Shelters on the earth. [22] And during these seven days he brought each day to the altar a burnt-offering to the LORD: two oxen, two rams, seven sheep, one male goat, for a sin-offering, that he might atone for himself and for his seed thereby. [23] And as a thank-offering: seven rams, seven kids, seven sheep, and seven male goats, and their fruit-offerings and their drink-offerings; and he burned all the fat thereof on the altar, a chosen offering to the LORD for a sweet-smelling savor. [24] And morning and evening he burned fragrant substances: frankincense, and galbanum, and stacte, and nard, and myrrh, and spice, and costum; all these seven he offered crushed, mixed together in equal parts, [and] pure. [25] And he celebrated this feast during seven days, rejoicing with all his heart and with all his soul, he and all those who were in his house; and there was no stranger with him, nor any that was uncircumcised. [26] And he blessed his Creator who had created him in his generation, for He had created him according to His good pleasure, for He knew and perceived that from him would arise the Plant of Righteousness for the continuous generations, and from him a holy Seed, so that it should become like Him who had made all things. [27] And he blessed and rejoiced, and he called the name of this festival the Festival of the LORD, a joy acceptable to the Most High God. [28] And we blessed him forever, and all his seed after him throughout all the generations of the earth, because he celebrated this festival in its season, according to the testimony of the heavenly tablets. [29] For this reason it is ordained on the heavenly tablets concerning Israel that they will celebrate the Celebration of Shelters [for] seven days with joy, in the seventh month, acceptable before the LORD—a statute forever throughout their generations every year. [30] And to this there is no limit of days, for it is ordained forever regarding Israel that they should celebrate it and dwell in shelters, and set wreaths on their heads, and take leafy boughs, and willows from the brook. [31] And Abraham took branches of palm trees, and the fruit of attractive trees, and every day going around the altar with the branches seven times [a day] in the morning, he praised and gave thanks to his God for all things in joy.

CHAPTER 17

[1] And in the first year of the fifth week Isaac was weaned in this jubilee, and Abraham made a great banquet in the third month, on the day his son Isaac was weaned. [2] And Ishmael, the son of Hagar the Egyptian, was before the face of his father Abraham, in his place, and Abraham rejoiced and blessed God because he had seen his sons and had not died childless. [3] And he remembered the words which He had spoken to him on the day on which Lot had parted from him, and he rejoiced because the LORD had given him seed on the earth to inherit the earth, and he blessed the Creator of all things with all his mouth. [4] And Sarah saw Ishmael playing and dancing and Abraham rejoicing with great joy, and she became jealous of Ishmael and said to Abraham, "Cast out this bondwoman and her son, for the son of this bondwoman will not be heir with my son Isaac." [5] And the thing was grievous in Abraham's sight, because of his maidservant and because of his son, that he should drive them from him. [6] And God said to Abraham, "Do not let it be grievous in your sight, because of the child and because of the bondwoman; in all that Sarah has said to you, listen to her words and do [them], for in Isaac will your name and seed be called. [7] But as for the son of this bondwoman, I will make him a great nation, because he is of your seed." [8] And Abraham rose up early in the morning and took bread and a bottle of water and placed them on the shoulders of Hagar and the child and sent her away. [9] And she departed and wandered in the wilderness of Beersheba, and the water in the bottle was spent, and the child thirsted, and was not able to go on, and fell down. [10] And his mother took him and cast him under an olive tree, and went and sat her

down over against him, at the distance of a bow-shot; for she said, "Let me not see the death of my child," and as she sat, she wept. [11] And a messenger of God, one of the holy ones, said to her, "Why do you weep, Hagar? Arise, take the child, and hold him in your hand, for God has heard your voice, and has seen the child." [12] And she opened her eyes, and she saw a well of water, and she went and filled her bottle with water, and she gave her child to drink, and she arose and went toward the wilderness of Paran. [13] And the child grew and became an archer, and God was with him; and his mother took a wife [for] him from among the daughters of Egypt. [14] And she bore him a son, and he called his name Nebaioth, for she said, "The LORD was near to me when I called on Him." [15] And it came to pass in the seventh week, in the first year thereof, in the first month in this jubilee, on the twelfth of this month, there were voices in Heaven regarding Abraham, that he was faithful in all that He told him, and that he loved the LORD, and that in every affliction he was faithful. [16] And the prince Mastêmâ came and said before God, "Behold, Abraham loves his son Isaac, and he delights in him above all other things; command him to offer him as a burnt-offering on the altar, and You will see if he will do this command, and You will know if he is faithful in everything wherein You try him." [17] And the LORD knew that Abraham was faithful in all his afflictions, for He had tried him through his country and with famine, and had tried him with the wealth of kings, and had tried him again through his wife, when she was torn [from him], and with circumcision, and had tried him through Ishmael and Hagar, his maidservant, when he sent them away. [18] And in everything wherein He had tried him, he was found faithful, and his soul was not impatient, and he was not slow to act, for he was faithful and a lover of the LORD.

CHAPTER 18

[1] And God said to him, "Abraham, Abraham"; and he said, "Behold, [here] I am." [2] And He said, "Take your beloved son whom you love, [even] Isaac, and go to the high country, and offer him on one of the mountains which I will point out to you." [3] And he rose early in the morning and saddled his donkey, and took his two young men with him, and his son Isaac, and cleaved the wood of the burnt-offering, and he went to the place on the third day, and he saw the place far off. [4] And he came to a well of water, and he said to his young men, "Abide here with the donkey, and the youth and I will go [over there], and when we have worshiped we will come again to you." [5] And he took the wood of the burnt-offering and laid it on his son Isaac, and he took in his hand the fire and the knife, and both of them went together to that place. [6] And Isaac said to his father, "Father"; and he said, "Here I am, my son." And he said to him, "Behold the

fire, and the knife, and the wood, but where is the sheep for the burnt-offering, father?" [7] And he said, "God will provide for Himself a sheep for a burnt-offering, my son." And he drew near to the place of the mount of God. [8] And he built an altar, and he placed the wood on the altar, and bound his son Isaac, and placed him on the wood which was on the altar, and stretched out his hand to take the knife to slay his son Isaac. [9] And I stood before him, and before the prince of the Mastêmâ, and the LORD said, "Command him not to lay his hand on the youth, nor to do anything to him, for I have shown that he fears the LORD." [10] And I called to him from Heaven, and said to him, "Abraham! Abraham!" And he was terrified and said, "Behold, [here] I am." [11] And I said to him, "Do not lay your hand on the youth, neither do anything to him, for now I have shown that you fear the LORD, and have not withheld your son, your firstborn [[or only]] son, from Me." [12] And the prince of the Mastêmâ was put to shame, and Abraham lifted up his eyes and looked, and behold, a single ram was caught by his horns, and Abraham went and took the ram and offered it for a burnt-offering in the place of his son. [13] And Abraham called that place "The LORD has seen," so that it is said, "[in the mount] the LORD has seen": that is Mount Zion. [14] And the LORD called Abraham by his name a second time from Heaven, as He caused us to appear to speak to him in the Name of the LORD. [15] And He said, "By Myself I have sworn, says the LORD, because you have done this thing, and have not withheld your son, your beloved son, from Me, that in blessing I will bless you, and in multiplying I will multiply your seed as the stars of the heavens, and as the sand which is on the seashore. And your Seed will inherit the cities of its enemies, [16] and in your Seed all nations of the earth will be blessed; because you have obeyed My voice, and I have shown to all that you are faithful to Me in all that I have said to you: go in peace." [17] And Abraham went to his young men, and they arose and went together to Beersheba, and Abraham dwelt by the Well of the Oath. [18] And he celebrated this festival every year [for] seven days with joy, and he called it the Festival of the LORD according to the seven days during which he went and returned in peace. [19] And accordingly it has been ordained and written on the heavenly tablets regarding Israel and its seed that they should observe this festival [for] seven days with the joy of festival.

CHAPTER 19

[1] And in the first year of the first week, in the forty-second jubilee, Abraham returned and dwelt opposite Hebron, that is Kirjath-Arba, two weeks of years. [2] And in the first year of the third week of this jubilee the days of the life of Sarah were accomplished, and she died in Hebron. [3] And Abraham went to mourn over her and bury her, and we tried him [to see] if his spirit was patient and he was not indignant in the

words of his mouth, and he was found patient in this and was not disturbed. ⁴ For in patience of spirit he conversed with the children of Heth, to the intent that they should give him a place in which to bury his dead. ⁵ And the LORD gave him grace before all who saw him, and he implored in gentleness the sons of Heth, and they gave him the land of the double cave over against Mamre, that is Hebron, for four hundred pieces of silver. ⁶ And they implored him, saying, "We will give it to you for nothing," but he would not take it from their hands for nothing, for he gave the price of the place, the money in full, and he bowed down before them twice; and after this he buried his dead in the double cave. ⁷ And all the days of the life of Sarah were one hundred and twenty-seven years, that is, two jubilees and four weeks and one year: these are the days of the years of the life of Sarah. ⁸ This is the tenth trial with which Abraham was tried, and he was found faithful, patient in spirit. ⁹ And he said not a single word regarding the rumor in the land, how that God had said that He would give it to him and to his seed after him, and he begged [for] a place there to bury his dead, for he was found faithful and was recorded on the heavenly tablets as the friend of God. ¹⁰ And in the fourth year thereof he took a wife for his son Isaac and her name was Rebekah [[the daughter of Bethuel, the son of Nahor, the brother of Abraham,]] the sister of Laban and daughter of Bethuel; and Bethuel was the son of Mêlcâ, who was the wife of Nahor, the brother of Abraham. ¹¹ And Abraham took to himself a third wife—and her name was Keturah—from among the daughters of his household servants, for Hagar had died before Sarah. ¹² And she bore him six sons: Zimram, and Jokshan, and Medan, and Midian, and Ishbak, and Shuah, in the two weeks of years. ¹³ And in the sixth week, in the second year thereof, Rebekah bore to Isaac two sons, Jacob and Esau, and Jacob was a smooth and upright man, and Esau was fierce, a man of the field, and hairy, and Jacob dwelt in tents. ¹⁴ And the youths grew, and Jacob learned to write, but Esau did not learn, for he was a man of the field and a hunter, and he learned war, and all his deeds were fierce. ¹⁵ And Abraham loved Jacob, but Isaac loved Esau. ¹⁶ And Abraham saw the deeds of Esau, and he knew that in Jacob should his name and seed be called; and he called Rebekah and gave command regarding Jacob, for he knew that she [too] loved Jacob much more than Esau. ¹⁷ And he said to her, "My daughter, watch over my son Jacob, for he will be in my stead on the earth, and for a blessing in the midst of the children of men, and for the glory of the whole seed of Shem. ¹⁸ For I know that the LORD will choose him to be a people for possession to Himself, above all peoples that are on the face of the earth. ¹⁹ And behold, my son Isaac loves Esau more than Jacob, but I see that you truly love Jacob. ²⁰ Add still further to your kindness to him, and let your eyes be on him in love, for he will

be a blessing to us on the earth from now on and to all generations of the earth. ²¹ Let your hands be strong and let your heart rejoice in your son Jacob, for I have loved him far beyond all my sons. He will be blessed forever, and his seed will fill the whole earth. ²² If a man can number the sand of the earth, his seed will also be numbered. ²³ And all the blessings with which the LORD has blessed me and my seed will belong to Jacob and his seed always. ²⁴ And in his seed my name will be blessed, and the name of my fathers: Shem, and Noah, and Enoch, and Mahalalel, and Enos, and Seth, and Adam. ²⁵ And these will serve to lay the foundations of the heavens, and to strengthen the earth, and to renew all the luminaries which are in the expanse." ²⁶ And he called Jacob before the eyes of his mother Rebekah, and kissed him, and blessed him, and said, ²⁷ "Jacob, my beloved son, whom my soul loves, may God bless you from above the expanse, and may He give you all the blessings with which He blessed Adam, and Enoch, and Noah, and Shem; and all the things of which He told me, and all the things which He promised to give me, may He cause to cleave to you and to your seed forever, according to the days of Heaven above the earth. ²⁸ And the spirits of Mastêmâ will not rule over you or over your seed to turn you from the LORD, who is your God from now on and forever. ²⁹ And may the LORD God be a father to you—and you [being] the firstborn son—and to the people always. Go in peace, my son." ³⁰ And they both went out together from Abraham. ³¹ And Rebekah loved Jacob with all her heart and with all her soul, very much more than Esau, but Isaac loved Esau much more than Jacob.

CHAPTER 20

¹ And in the forty-second jubilee, in the first year of the seventh week, Abraham called Ishmael, and his twelve sons, and Isaac and his two sons, and the six sons of Keturah, and their sons. ² And he commanded them that they should observe the way of the LORD, that they should work righteousness, and each love his neighbor, and act on this manner among all men, that they should each so walk with regard to them as to do judgment and righteousness on the earth, ³ [and] that they should circumcise their sons according to the covenant which He had made with them, and not deviate to the right hand or the left of all the paths which the LORD had commanded us, and that we should keep ourselves from all fornication and uncleanness. ⁴ "And if any woman or maid may commit fornication among you, burn her with fire, and do not let them commit fornication with her after their eyes and their heart; and do not let them take to themselves wives from the daughters of Canaan, for the seed of Canaan will be rooted out of the land." ⁵ And he told them of the judgment of the giants, and the judgment of the Sodomites, how they had been judged on account of their wickedness, and had died

on account of their fornication, and uncleanness, and mutual corruption through fornication. ⁶"And guard yourselves from all fornication and uncleanness, and from all pollution of sin, lest you make our name a curse, and your whole life a hissing, and all your sons be destroyed by the sword, and you become accursed like Sodom, and all your remnant as the sons of Gomorrah. ⁷I implore you, my sons: love the God of Heaven, and cleave to all His commands. And do not walk after their idols, and after their uncleanness, ⁸and do not make for yourselves molten or graven gods, for they are vanity, and there is no spirit in them, for they are [the] work of [men's] hands, and all who trust in them, trust in nothing. Do not serve them, nor worship them, ⁹but serve the Most High God, and worship Him continually. And hope for His countenance always, and work uprightness and righteousness before Him, that He may have pleasure in you and grant you His mercy, and send rain on you morning and evening, and bless all your works which you have worked on the earth, and bless your bread and your water, and bless the fruit of your womb and the fruit of your land, and the herds of your cattle, and the flocks of your sheep. ¹⁰And you will be for a blessing on the earth, and all nations of the earth will desire you, and bless your sons in my name, that they may be blessed as I am." ¹¹And he gave to Ishmael, and to his sons, and to the sons of Keturah, gifts, and sent them away from his son Isaac, and he gave everything to his son Isaac. ¹²And Ishmael and his sons, and the sons of Keturah and their sons, went together and dwelt from Paran to the entering in of Babylon in all the land which is toward the east facing the desert. ¹³And these mingled with each other, and their name was called Arabs, and Ishmaelites.

CHAPTER 21

¹And in the sixth year of the seventh week of this jubilee, Abraham called his son Isaac and commanded him, saying, "I have become old, and I do not know the day of my death, and am full of my days. ²And behold, I am one hundred and seventy-five years old, and throughout all the days of my life I have remembered the LORD and sought with all my heart to do His will, and to walk uprightly in all His ways. ³My soul has hated idols, [[and I have despised those that served them, and I have given my heart and spirit]] that I might observe to do the will of Him who created me. ⁴For He is the living God, and He is holy and faithful, and He is righteous beyond all, and there is with Him no accepting of [men's] persons and no accepting of gifts, for God is righteous and executes judgment on all those who transgress His commands and despise His covenant. ⁵And you, my son, observe His commands, and His ordinances, and His judgments, and do not walk after the abominations, and after the graven images, and after the molten images. ⁶And eat no blood at all of animals, or cattle,

or of any bird which flies in the heavens. ⁷And if you slay a victim as an acceptable peace-offering, slay it, and pour out its blood on the altar, and all the fat of the offering offer on the altar with fine flour [and the meat-offering] mingled with oil, with its drink-offering—offer them all together on the altar of burnt-offering; it is a sweet savor before the LORD. ⁸And you will offer the fat of the sacrifice of thank-offerings on the fire which is on the altar, and the fat which is on the belly, and all the fat on the innards and the two kidneys, and all the fat that is on them, and on the loins and liver you will remove together with the kidneys. ⁹And offer all these for a sweet savor acceptable before the LORD, with its meat-offering and with its drink-offering, for a sweet savor, the bread of the offering to the LORD, ¹⁰and eat its meat on that day and on the second day, and do not let the sun go down on it on the second day until it is eaten, and let nothing be left over for the third day, for it is not acceptable; and let it no longer be eaten, and all who eat thereof will bring sin on themselves, for thus I have found it written in the scrolls of my forefathers, and in the words of Enoch, and in the words of Noah. ¹¹And on all your oblations you will scatter salt, and do not let the salt of the covenant be lacking in all your oblations before the LORD. ¹²And as regards the wood of the sacrifices, beware lest you bring [other] wood for the altar in addition to these: cypress, dêfrân, sagâd, pine, fir, cedar, savin, palm, olive, myrrh, laurel, and citron, juniper, and balsam. ¹³And of these kinds of wood lay on the altar under the sacrifice, such as have been tested as to their appearance, and do not lay any split or dark wood [on it], [but] hard and clean, without fault—a sound and new growth; and do not lay old wood [on it], for there is no longer fragrance in it as before. ¹⁴Besides these kinds of wood, there is no other that you will place [on the altar], for the fragrance is dispersed, and the smell of its fragrance does not go up to Heaven. ¹⁵Observe this command and do it, my son, that you may be upright in all your deeds. ¹⁶And at all times be clean in your body, and wash yourself with water before you approach to offer on the altar, and wash your hands and your feet before you draw near to the altar; and when you are done sacrificing, wash your hands and your feet again. ¹⁷And let no blood appear on you nor on your clothes; be on your guard, my son, against blood, be on your guard exceedingly; cover it with dust. ¹⁸And do not eat any blood, for it is the soul; eat no blood whatsoever. ¹⁹And take no gifts for the blood of man, lest it be shed with impunity, without judgment, for it is the blood that is shed that causes the earth to sin, and the earth cannot be cleansed from the blood of man save by the blood of him who shed it. ²⁰And take no present or gift for the blood of man, blood for blood, that you may be accepted before the LORD, the Most High God—for He is the defense of the good—and that you may be preserved from all evil, and that He may save you from every kind of death. ²¹ I see, my son, that all the works of the children of men are sin and wickedness, and all their deeds are uncleanness, and an abomination, and a pollution, and there is no righteousness with them. ²² Beware, lest you should walk in their ways, and tread in their paths, and sin a sin to death before the Most High God. Otherwise He will [[hide His face from you, and]] give you back into the hands of your transgression, and root you out of the land, and your seed likewise from under Heaven, and your name and your seed will perish from the whole earth. ²³ Turn away from all their deeds and all their uncleanness, and observe the ordinance of the Most High God, and do His will, and be upright in all things. ²⁴ And He will bless you in all your deeds and will raise up from you the plant of righteousness through all the earth, throughout all generations of the earth, and my name and your name will not be forgotten under Heaven forever. ²⁵ Go, my son, in peace. May the Most High God, my God and your God, strengthen you to do His will, and may He bless all your seed and the residue of your seed for the generations forever, with all righteous blessings, that you may be a blessing on all the earth." ²⁶ And he went out from him rejoicing.

CHAPTER 22

¹ And it came to pass in the first week, in the forty-fourth jubilee, in the second year, that is, the year in which Abraham died, that Isaac and Ishmael came from the Well of the Oath to celebrate the Celebration of Weeks—that is, the celebration of the first-fruits of the harvest—to their father Abraham, and Abraham rejoiced because his two sons had come. ² For Isaac had many possessions in Beersheba, and Isaac was accustomed to go and see his possessions and to return to his father. ³ And in those days Ishmael came to see his father, and they both came together, and Isaac offered a sacrifice for a burnt-offering, and presented it on the altar of his father which he had made in Hebron. ⁴ And he offered a thank-offering and made a feast of joy before his brother Ishmael: and Rebekah made new cakes from the new grain and gave them to her son Jacob to take them to his father Abraham, from the first-fruits of the land, that he might eat and bless the Creator of all things before he died. ⁵ And Isaac, too, sent by the hand of Jacob to Abraham a best thank-offering, that he might eat and drink. ⁶ And he ate, and drank, and blessed the Most High God who has created the heavens and earth, who has made all the fat things of the earth and given them to the children of men that they might eat, and drink, and bless their Creator. ⁷ "And now I give thanks to you, my God, because You have caused me to see this day: behold, I am one hundred and seventy-five years [old], an old man and full of days, and all my days have been peace to me. ⁸ The sword of the adversary has not overcome me in all that You have given me and my children all the days of my life until this day. ⁹ My God, may Your mercy and Your peace be on Your servant and on the seed of his sons, that they may be to You a chosen nation and an inheritance from among all the nations of the earth from now on and to all the days of the generations of the earth—to all the ages." ¹⁰ And he called Jacob and said, "My son Jacob, may the God of all bless you and strengthen you to do righteousness and His will before Him, and may He choose you and your seed that you may become a people for His inheritance according to His will always. And my son Jacob: draw near and kiss me." ¹¹ And he drew near and kissed him, and he said, "Blessed is my son Jacob, and all the sons of God Most High, to all the ages. May God give to you [the] Seed of righteousness; and may He sanctify some of your sons in the midst of the whole earth. May nations serve you, and all the nations bow themselves before your Seed. ¹² Be strong in the presence of men, and exercise authority over all the seed of Seth. Then your ways and the ways of your sons will be justified, so that they will become a holy nation. ¹³ May the Most High God give you all the blessings with which He has blessed me and with which He blessed Noah and Adam. May they rest on the sacred head of your Seed from generation to generation forever. ¹⁴ And may He cleanse you from all unrighteousness and impurity, that you may be forgiven of all [your] transgressions [and] your sins of ignorance. And may He strengthen you and bless you. And may you inherit the whole earth; ¹⁵ and may He renew His covenant with you, that you may be to Him a nation for His inheritance for all the ages, and that He may be to you and to your seed a God in truth and righteousness throughout all the days of the earth. ¹⁶ And my son Jacob: remember my words and observe the commands of your father Abraham: separate yourself from the nations, and do not eat with them, and do not do according to their works, and do not become their associate, for their works are unclean, and all their ways are a pollution, and an abomination, and uncleanness. ¹⁷ They offer their sacrifices to the dead, and they worship evil spirits, and they eat over the graves, and all their works are vanity and nothingness. ¹⁸ They have no heart to understand, and their eyes do not see what their works are, and how they err in saying to a piece of wood, You are my God; and to a stone, You are my lord and you are my deliverer. [[And they have no heart.]] ¹⁹ And as for you, my son Jacob: may the Most High God help you, and the God of Heaven bless you and remove you from their uncleanness and from all their error. ²⁰ Beware, my son Jacob, of taking a wife from any seed of the daughters of Canaan, for all his seed is to be rooted out of the earth. ²¹ For, owing to the transgression of Ham, Canaan erred, and all his seed will be destroyed from off the earth and all the residue thereof, and none springing from him will be

saved on the Day of Judgment. ²²And as for all the worshipers of idols and the profane: there will be no hope for them in the land of the living and there will be no remembrance of them on the earth, for they will descend into Sheol, and they will go into the place of condemnation; as the children of Sodom were taken away from the earth, so will all those who worship idols be taken away. ²³Do not fear, my son Jacob, and do not be dismayed, O son of Abraham: may the Most High God preserve you from destruction, and may He deliver you from all the paths of error. ²⁴I have built this house for myself that I might put my name on it in the earth: [[it is given to you and to your seed forever]], and it will be named the House of Abraham; it is given to you and to your seed forever, for you will build my house and establish my name before God forever: your seed and your name will stand throughout all generations of the earth." ²⁵And he ceased commanding him and blessing him. ²⁶And the two lay together on one bed, and Jacob slept in the bosom of Abraham, his father's father, and he kissed him seven times, and his affection and his heart rejoiced over him. ²⁷And he blessed him with all his heart and said, "The Most High God, the God of all and Creator of all, who brought me out from Ur of the Chaldees that He might give me this land to inherit it forever, and that I might establish a holy Seed—blessed is the Most High forever." ²⁸And he blessed Jacob and said [to God], "My son, over whom with all my heart and my affection I rejoice, may Your grace and Your mercy be lifted up on him and on his seed always. ²⁹And do not forsake him, nor set him at nothing from now on and to the days of [all] ages, and may Your eyes be opened on him and on his seed, that You may preserve him, and bless him, and may sanctify him as a nation for Your inheritance; ³⁰and bless him with all Your blessings from now on and to all the days of [the] ages, and renew Your covenant and Your grace with him and with his seed according to all Your good pleasure to all the generations of the earth."

CHAPTER 23

¹And he placed two of Jacob's fingers on his eyes, and he blessed the God of gods, and he covered his face, and stretched out his feet, and slept the continuous sleep, and was gathered to his fathers. ²And notwithstanding all this, Jacob was lying in his bosom, and did not know that Abraham, his father's father, was dead. ³And Jacob awoke from his sleep, and behold, Abraham was cold as ice, and he said, "Father! Father!" But there was none that spoke, and he knew that he was dead. ⁴And he arose from his bosom and ran and told his mother Rebekah; and Rebekah went to Isaac in the night and told him; and they went together, and Jacob with them, and a lamp was in his hand, and when they had gone in they found Abraham lying dead. ⁵And Isaac fell on the face of his father, and wept, and kissed him. ⁶And the voices were heard in the house of Abraham, and his son Ishmael arose, and went to his father Abraham, and wept over his father Abraham—he and all the house of Abraham—and they wept with a great weeping. ⁷And his sons Isaac and Ishmael buried him in the double cave near his wife Sarah, and they wept for him forty days, all the men of his house, and Isaac and Ishmael, and all their sons, and all the sons of Keturah in their places, and the days of weeping for Abraham were ended. ⁸And he lived three jubilees and four weeks of years—one hundred and seventy-five years—and completed the days of his life, being old and full of days. ⁹For the days of the forefathers, of their life, were nineteen jubilees; and after the flood they began to grow less than nineteen jubilees, and to decrease in jubilees, and to grow old quickly, and to be full of their days by reason of manifold tribulation and the wickedness of their ways, with the exception of Abraham. ¹⁰For Abraham was perfect in all his deeds with the LORD, and well-pleasing in righteousness all the days of his life; and behold, he did not complete four jubilees in his life when he had grown old by reason of the wickedness [in the world] and was full of his days. ¹¹And all the generations which will arise from this time until the Day of the Great Judgment will grow old quickly before they complete two jubilees, and their knowledge will forsake them by reason of their old age. ¹²And in those days, if a man lives [for] a jubilee and a half of years, they will say regarding him: "He has lived long, and the greater part of his days are pain, and sorrow, and tribulation, and there is no peace, ¹³for calamity follows on calamity, and wound on wound, and tribulation on tribulation, and evil tidings on evil tidings, and sickness on sickness, and all evil judgments such as these, with one another—sickness, and overthrow, and snow, and frost, and ice, and fever, and chills, and torpor, and famine, and death, and sword, and captivity, and all kinds of calamities and pains." ¹⁴And all these will come on an evil generation, which transgresses on the earth: their works are uncleanness, and fornication, and pollution, and abominations. ¹⁵Then they will say, "The days of the forefathers were many, [even] to one thousand years, and were good, but behold, the days of our life, if a man has lived many, are sixty years and ten, and, if he is strong, eighty years, and those [are] evil and there is no peace in the days of this evil generation." ¹⁶And in that generation the sons will convict their fathers and their elders of sin and unrighteousness, and of the words of their mouth and the great wickedness which they perpetrate, and concerning their forsaking the covenant which the LORD made between them and Him, that they should observe and do all His commands, and His ordinances, and all His laws, without departing either to the right hand or to the left. ¹⁷For all have done evil,

and every mouth speaks iniquity, and all their works are an uncleanness and an abomination, and all their ways are pollution, uncleanness, and destruction. [18] Behold, the earth will be destroyed on account of all their works, and there will be no seed of the vine and no oil, for their works are altogether faithless, and they will all perish together: beasts, and cattle, and birds, and all the fish of the sea, on account of the children of men. [19] And they will strive with one another, the young with the old, and the old with the young, the poor with the rich, and the lowly with the great, and the beggar with the prince, on account of the Law and the Covenant, for they have forgotten command, and covenant, and feasts, and months, and Sabbaths, and jubilees, and all judgments. [20] And they will stand [[with bows and]] swords, and war to turn them back into the way, but they will not return until much blood has been shed on the earth by one another. [21] And those who have escaped will not return from their wickedness to the way of righteousness, but they will all exalt themselves to deceit and wealth, that they may each take all that is his neighbor's, but not in truth and not in righteousness, and they will defile the Holy of Holies with their uncleanness and the corruption of their pollution. [22] And a great punishment will befall the deeds of this generation from the LORD, and He will give them over to the sword, and to judgment, and to captivity, and to be plundered and devoured. [23] And He will wake up against them the sinners of the nations who have neither mercy nor compassion, and who will respect the person of none, neither old nor young, nor anyone, for they are more wicked and strong to do evil than all the children of men. And they will use violence against Israel and transgression against Jacob, and much blood will be shed on the earth, and there will be none to gather and none to bury. [24] In those days they will cry aloud, and call and pray that they may be saved from the hand of the sinners, the nations, but none will be saved. [25] And the heads of the children will be white with grey hair, and a child of three weeks will appear old like a man of one hundred years, and their stature will be destroyed by tribulation and oppression. [26] And in those days the children will begin to study the laws, and to seek the commands, and to return to the path of righteousness. [27] And the days will begin to grow many and increase among those children of men [until] their days draw near to one thousand years, and to a greater number of years than were the number of the days [before]. [28] And there will be no old man nor one who is not satisfied with his days, for all will be [as] children and youths. [29] And they will complete all their days and live in peace and in joy, and there will be no adversary, nor any evil destroyer, for all their days will be days of blessing and healing, [30] and at that time the LORD will heal His servants, and they will rise up and see great peace, and drive out their adversaries. And the righteous will see and be thankful, and rejoice with joy forever and ever, and will see all their judgments and all their curses on their enemies. [31] And their bones will rest in the earth, and their spirits will have much joy, and they will know that it is the LORD who executes judgment and shows mercy to hundreds, and thousands, and to all that love Him. [32] And you, Moses, write down these words, for thus are they written, and they record [them] on the heavenly tablets for a testimony for the generations forever.

CHAPTER 24

[1] And it came to pass after the death of Abraham, that the LORD blessed his son Isaac, and he arose from Hebron and went and dwelt at the Well of the Vision in the first year of the third week of this jubilee [for] seven years. [2] And in the first year of the fourth week a famine began in the land, besides the first famine which had been in the days of Abraham. [3] And Jacob prepared lentil stew, and Esau came from the field hungry. And he said to his brother Jacob, "Give me of this red stew." And Jacob said to him, "Sell your birthright to me and I will give you bread and also some of this lentil stew." [4] And Esau said in his heart: "I will die; of what profit to me is this birthright?" And he said to Jacob, "I give it to you." [5] And Jacob said, "Swear to me, this day," and he swore to him. [6] And Jacob gave his brother Esau bread and stew, and he ate until he was satisfied, and Esau despised his birthright; for this reason Esau's name was called Edom on account of the red stew which Jacob gave him for his birthright. [7] And Jacob became the elder, and Esau was brought down from his dignity. [8] And the famine was over the land, and Isaac departed to go down into Egypt in the second year of this week, and he went to the king of the Philistines, to Gerar, to Abimelech. [9] And the LORD appeared to him and said to him, "Do not go down into Egypt; dwell in the land that I will tell you of, and sojourn in this land, and I will be with you and bless you. [10] For to you and to your seed I will give all this land, and I will establish My oath which I swore to your father Abraham, and I will multiply your seed as the stars of the heavens, and I will give to your seed all this land. [11] And in your Seed will all the nations of the earth be blessed, because your father obeyed My voice, and kept My charge, and My commands, and My laws, and My ordinances, and My covenant; and now obey My voice and dwell in this land." [12] And he dwelt in Gerar three weeks of years. [13] And Abimelech charged concerning him, and concerning all that was his, saying, "Any man that will touch him or anything that is his will surely die." [14] And Isaac waxed strong among the Philistines, and he got many possessions: oxen, and sheep, and camels, and donkeys, and a great household. [15] And he sowed in the land of the

Philistines and brought in a hundredfold, and Isaac became exceedingly great, and the Philistines envied him. ¹⁶ Now all the wells which the servants of Abraham had dug during the life of Abraham, the Philistines had stopped them after the death of Abraham and filled them with earth. ¹⁷ And Abimelech said to Isaac, "Go from us, for you are much mightier than us"; and Isaac departed from there in the first year of the seventh week and sojourned in the valleys of Gerar. ¹⁸ And they dug the wells of water again which the servants of his father Abraham had dug, and which the Philistines had closed after the death of his father Abraham, and he called their names as his father Abraham had named them. ¹⁹ And the servants of Isaac dug a well in the valley, and found living water, and the shepherds of Gerar strove with the shepherds of Isaac, saying, "The water is ours"; and Isaac called the name of the well "Perversity," because they had been perverse with us. ²⁰ And they dug a second well, and they strove for that also, and he called its name "Enmity." And he arose from there and they dug another well, and for that they did not strive, and he called the name of it "Room," and Isaac said, "Now the LORD has made room for us, and we have increased in the land." ²¹ And he went up from there to the Well of the Oath in the first year of the first week, in the forty-fourth jubilee. ²² And the LORD appeared to him that night, on the new moon of the first month, and said to him, "I am the God of your father Abraham; do not fear, for I am with you, and will bless you and will surely multiply your seed as the sand of the earth, for the sake of my servant Abraham." ²³ And he built an altar there, which his father Abraham had first built, and he called on the Name of the LORD, and he offered sacrifice to the God of his father Abraham. ²⁴ And they dug a well and they found living water. ²⁵ And the servants of Isaac dug another well and did not find water, and they went and told Isaac that they had not found water, and Isaac said, "I have sworn this day to the Philistines and this thing has been announced to us." ²⁶ And he called the name of that place the "Well of the Oath," for there he had sworn to Abimelech, and his friend Ahuzzath, and Phicol, the prefect of his host. ²⁷ And Isaac knew that day that under constraint he had sworn to them to make peace with them. ²⁸ And on that day Isaac cursed the Philistines and said, "Cursed are the Philistines to the day of wrath and indignation from the midst of all nations; may God make them a derision, and a curse, and an object of wrath and indignation in the hands of the sinners—the nations—and in the hands of the Kittim. ²⁹ And whoever escapes the sword of the enemy and the Kittim, may the righteous nation root out in judgment from under Heaven, for they will be the enemies, and enemies of my children, throughout their generations on the earth. ³⁰ And no remnant will be left to them, nor one that will be saved on the day of the wrath of judgment, for destruction, and rooting out, and expulsion from the earth is the whole seed of the Philistines [reserved], and there will no longer be left for these Caphtorim a name or a seed on the earth. ³¹ For though he ascends into Heaven, from there he will be brought down, and though he makes himself strong on earth, from there he will be dragged out, and though he hides himself among the nations, even from there he will be rooted out, and though he descends into Sheol, there also will his condemnation be great, and there also he will have no peace. ³² And if he goes into captivity, by the hands of those that seek his life they will slay him on the way, and neither name nor seed will be left to him on all the earth, for he will depart into a continuous curse." ³³ And thus is it written and engraved concerning him on the heavenly tablets, to do to him on the Day of Judgment, so that he may be rooted out of the earth.

CHAPTER 25

¹ And in the second year of this week, in this jubilee, Rebekah called her son Jacob and spoke to him, saying, "My son, do not take a wife for yourself of the daughters of Canaan, as your brother Esau, who took two wives of the daughters of Canaan for himself, and they have embittered my soul with all their unclean deeds, for all their deeds are fornication and lust, and there is no righteousness with them, for [their deeds] are evil. ² And I, my son, love you exceedingly, and my heart and my affection bless you every hour of the day and watch of the night. ³ And now, my son, listen to my voice, and do the will of your mother, and do not take a wife for yourself of the daughters of this land, but only of the house of my father, and of my father's relatives; you will take a wife of the house of my father, and the Most High God will bless you, and your children will be a righteous generation and a holy seed." ⁴ And then Jacob spoke to his mother Rebekah, and said to her, "Behold, mother, I am nine weeks of years old, and I neither know nor have I touched any woman, nor have I betrothed myself to any, nor even think of taking a wife for myself of the daughters of Canaan. ⁵ For I remember, mother, the words of our father Abraham, for he commanded me not to take a wife of the daughters of Canaan, but to take a wife for myself from the seed of my father's house and from my relatives. ⁶ I have heard before that daughters have been born to your brother Laban, and I have set my heart on them to take a wife from among them. ⁷ And for this reason I have guarded myself in my spirit against sinning or being corrupted in all my ways throughout all the days of my life, for with regard to lust and fornication, my father Abraham gave me many commands. ⁸ And despite all that he has commanded me, these twenty-two years my brother has striven with me, and spoken frequently to me, and said, My brother, take a sister of my two wives to be [your] wife; but I refuse to do as he has

done. ⁹ I swear before you, mother, that all the days of my life I will not take a wife for myself from the daughters of the seed of Canaan, and I will not act wickedly as my brother has done. ¹⁰ Do not fear, mother; be assured that I will do your will, and walk in uprightness, and not corrupt my ways forever." ¹¹ And immediately she lifted up her face to Heaven, and extended the fingers of her hands, and opened her mouth, and blessed the Most High God who had created the heavens and the earth, and she gave Him thanks and praise. ¹² And she said, "Blessed is the LORD God, and may His holy Name be blessed forever and ever, who has given me Jacob as a pure son and a holy seed; for He is Yours, and his seed will be Yours continually and throughout all the generations forevermore. ¹³ Bless him, O LORD, and place in my mouth the blessing of righteousness, that I may bless him." ¹⁴ And at that hour, when the Spirit of righteousness descended into her mouth, she placed both her hands on the head of Jacob, and said, ¹⁵ "Blessed are You, LORD of righteousness and God of the ages. And may He bless you beyond all the generations of men. May He give you, my son, the path of righteousness, and reveal righteousness to your seed. ¹⁶ And may He make your sons many during your life, and may they arise according to the number of the months of the year. And may their sons become many and great beyond the stars of the heavens, and their numbers be more than the sand of the sea. ¹⁷ And may He give them this excellent land— as He said He would give it to Abraham and to his seed after him always—and may they hold it as a possession forever. ¹⁸ And may I see [born] to you, my son, blessed children during my life, and a blessed and holy seed may all your seed be. ¹⁹ And as you have refreshed your mother's spirit during my life, the womb of her that bore you blesses you, and my breasts bless you, and my mouth and my tongue praise you greatly. ²⁰ Increase and spread over the earth, and may your seed be perfect in the joy of the heavens and earth forever; and may your seed rejoice, and on the great day of peace may it have peace. ²¹ And may your name and your seed endure to all the ages, and may the Most High God be their God, and may the God of righteousness dwell with them, and by them may His sanctuary be built to all the ages. ²² Blessed is he that blesses you, and all flesh that curses you falsely—may it be cursed." ²³ And she kissed him and said to him, "May the Lord of the world love you just as the heart of your mother and her affection rejoices in you and blesses you." And she ceased from blessing.

CHAPTER 26

¹ And in the seventh year of this week Isaac called Esau, his elder son, and said to him, "I am old, my son, and behold, my eyes are dim in seeing, and I do not know the day of my death. ² And now take your hunting weapons, your quiver and your bow, and go out to the field, and hunt and catch me [game], my son, and make me savory meat, such as my soul loves, and bring it to me that I may eat, and that my soul may bless you before I die." ³ But Rebekah heard Isaac speaking to Esau. ⁴ And Esau went out early to the field to hunt, and catch, and bring home to his father. ⁵ And Rebekah called her son Jacob and said to him, "Behold, I heard your father Isaac speak to your brother Esau, saying, Hunt for me, and make me savory meat, and bring [it] to me that I may eat and bless you before the LORD before I die. ⁶ And now, my son, obey my voice in that which I command you: go to your flock and fetch me two good kids of the goats, and I will make them savory meat for your father, such as he loves, and you will bring [it] to your father that he may eat and bless you before the LORD before he die, and that you may be blessed." ⁷ And Jacob said to his mother Rebekah, "Mother, I will not withhold anything which my father would eat, and which would please him: only I fear, my mother, that he will recognize my voice and wish to touch me. ⁸ And you know that I am smooth, and my brother Esau is hairy, and I will appear before his eyes as an evildoer, and will do a deed which he had not commanded me, and he will be angry with me, and I will bring a curse on myself, and not a blessing." ⁹ And his mother Rebekah said to him, "Your curse be on me, my son, only obey my voice." ¹⁰ And Jacob obeyed the voice of his mother Rebekah, and went and fetched two good and fat kids of the goats, and brought them to his mother, and his mother made them [savory meat] such as he loved. ¹¹ And Rebekah took the attractive raiment of her elder son Esau, which was with her in the house, and she clothed her younger son Jacob [with them], and she put the skins of the kids on his hands and on the exposed parts of his neck. ¹² And she gave the meat and the bread which she had prepared into the hand of her son Jacob. ¹³ And Jacob went in to his father and said, "I am your son: I have done according as you commanded me. Arise, and sit, and eat of that which I have caught, father, that your soul may bless me." ¹⁴ And Isaac said to his son, "How have you found [game] so quickly, my son?" ¹⁵ And Jacob said, "Because [the LORD] your God caused me to find [it]." ¹⁶ And Isaac said to him, "Come near, that I may feel you, my son, if you are my son Esau or not." ¹⁷ And Jacob went near to his father Isaac, and he felt him, and said, ¹⁸ "The voice is Jacob's voice, but the hands are the hands of Esau," and he did not discern him, because it was a dispensation from Heaven to remove his power of perception, and Isaac did not discern, for his hands were as hairy as [his brother] Esau's, so that he blessed him. ¹⁹ And he said, "Are you my son Esau?" and he said, "I am your son," and he said, "Bring [it] near to me that I may eat of that which you have caught, my son, that my soul may bless you." ²⁰ And he brought [it] near to him, and he

ate, and he brought him wine and he drank. ²¹ And his father Isaac said to him, "Come near and kiss me, my son." And he came near and kissed him. ²² And he smelled the smell of his raiment, and he blessed him, and said, "Behold, the smell of my son is as the smell of a [full] field which the LORD has blessed. ²³ And may the LORD give you of the dew of the heavens and of the dew of the earth, and plenty of corn and oil: Let nations serve you ‖ And peoples bow down to you. ²⁴ Be lord over your brothers ‖ And let your mother's sons bow down to you; And may all the blessings with which the LORD has blessed me and blessed my father Abraham ‖ Be imparted to you and to your seed forever. Cursed is he that curses you, ‖ And blessed is he that blesses you." ²⁵ And it came to pass as soon as Isaac had made an end of blessing his son Jacob and Jacob had gone out from his father Isaac, he hid himself, and his brother Esau came in from his hunting. ²⁶ And he also made savory meat, and brought [it] to his father, and said to his father, "Let my father arise and eat of my venison that your soul may bless me." ²⁷ And his father Isaac said to him, "Who are you?" And he said to him, "I am your firstborn, your son Esau: I have done as you have commanded me." ²⁸ And Isaac was very greatly astonished, and said, "Who is he that has hunted, and caught, and brought [it] to me? And I have eaten of all before you came and have blessed him: [and] he will be blessed, and all his seed forever." ²⁹ And it came to pass when Esau heard the words of his father Isaac that he cried with an exceedingly great and bitter cry, and said to his father, "Bless me, me also, father!" ³⁰ And he said to him, "Your brother came with guile, and has taken away your blessing." And he said, "Now I know why his name is named Jacob: behold, he has supplanted me these two times; he took away my birthright, and now he has taken away my blessing." ³¹ And he said, "Have you not reserved a blessing for me, father?" And Isaac answered and said to Esau, "Behold, I have made him your lord, and I have given all his brothers to him for servants, and I have strengthened him with plenty of corn, and wine, and oil: and what now will I do for you, my son?" ³² And Esau said to his father Isaac, "Have you but one blessing, O father? Bless me, [even] me also, father!" And Esau lifted up his voice and wept. ³³ And Isaac answered and said to him, "Behold, your dwelling will be far from the dew of the earth, and far from the dew of the heavens from above. ³⁴ And you will live by your sword, and you will serve your brother. And it will come to pass when you become great, and shake his yoke from off your neck, you will sin a complete sin to death, and your seed will be rooted out from under Heaven." ³⁵ And Esau kept threatening Jacob because of the blessing with which his father blessed him, and he said in his heart, "May the days of mourning for my father now come, so that I may slay my brother Jacob."

CHAPTER 27

¹ And the words of her elder son Esau were told to Rebekah in a dream, and Rebekah sent and called her younger son Jacob, and said to him, ² "Behold, your brother Esau will take vengeance on you so as to kill you. ³ Now, therefore, my son, obey my voice, and arise and flee to my brother Laban, to Haran, and tarry with him a few days until your brother's anger turns away, and he removes his anger from you, and forgets all that you have done; then I will send and fetch you from there." ⁴ And Jacob said, "I am not afraid; if he wishes to kill me, I will kill him." ⁵ But she said to him, "Let me not be deprived of both my sons on one day." ⁶ And Jacob said to his mother Rebekah, "Behold, you know that my father has become old and does not see because his eyes are dull, and if I leave him it will be evil in his eyes, because I leave him and go away from you, and my father will be angry, and will curse me. I will not go; when he sends me, then only will I go." ⁷ And Rebekah said to Jacob, "I will go in and speak to him, and he will send you away." ⁸ And Rebekah went in and said to Isaac, "I loathe my life because of the two daughters of Heth, whom Esau has taken to himself as wives; and if Jacob takes a wife from among the daughters of the land such as these, for what further purpose do I live? For the daughters of Canaan are evil." ⁹ And Isaac called Jacob and blessed him, and admonished him, and said to him, ¹⁰ "Do not take a wife for yourself of any of the daughters of Canaan; arise and go to Mesopotamia, to the house of Bethuel, your mother's father, and take a wife for yourself from there of the daughters of Laban, your mother's brother. ¹¹ And may God Almighty bless you, and increase and multiply you, that you may become a company of nations, and give you the blessings of my father Abraham—to you and to your seed after you—that you may inherit the land of your sojournings and all the land which God gave to Abraham. Go, my son, in peace." ¹² And Isaac sent Jacob away, and he went to Mesopotamia, to Laban the son of Bethuel the Syrian, the brother of Rebekah, Jacob's mother. ¹³ And it came to pass after Jacob had arisen to go to Mesopotamia that the spirit of Rebekah was grieved after her son, and she wept. ¹⁴ And Isaac said to Rebekah, "My sister, do not weep on account of my son Jacob, for he goes in peace, and in peace he will return. ¹⁵ The Most High God will preserve him from all evil and will be with him, for He will not forsake him all his days, ¹⁶ for I know that his ways will be prospered in all things wherever he goes, until he returns to us in peace and we see him in peace. ¹⁷ Do not fear on his account, my sister, for he is on the upright path and he is a perfect man: and he is faithful and will not perish. Do not weep." ¹⁸ And Isaac comforted Rebekah on account of her son Jacob and blessed him. ¹⁹ And Jacob went from the Well of the Oath to go to Haran on the first year of the second

week, in the forty-fourth Jubilee, and he came to Luz on the mountains, that is, Bethel, on the new moon of the first month of this week, and he came to the place at evening and turned from the way to the west of the road that night: and he slept there, for the sun had set. ²⁰ And he took one of the stones of that place and laid it [at his head] under the tree, and he was journeying alone, and he slept. ²¹ And he dreamt that night, and behold, a ladder [was] set up on the earth, and the top of it reached to Heaven, and behold, the messengers of the LORD ascended and descended on it: and behold, the LORD stood on it. ²² And He spoke to Jacob and said, "I am the LORD God of your father Abraham and the God of Isaac; the land on which you are sleeping, to you I will give it, and to your seed after you. ²³ And your seed will be as the dust of the earth, and you will increase to the west and to the east, to the north and the south, and in you and in your Seed all the families of the nations will be blessed. ²⁴ And behold, I will be with you, and will keep you wherever you go, and I will bring you into this land again in peace, for I will not leave you until I do everything that I told you of." ²⁵ And Jacob awoke from his sleep, and said, "Truly this place is the house of the LORD, and I did not know it." And he was afraid and said, "This place is dreadful, which is none other than the house of God, and this is the gate of Heaven." ²⁶ And Jacob arose early in the morning and took the stone which he had put under his head and set it up as a pillar for a sign, and he poured oil on the top of it. And he called the name of that place Bethel, but the name of the place was Luz at the first. ²⁷ And Jacob vowed a vow to the LORD, saying, "If the LORD will be with me, and will keep me in this way that I go, and give me bread to eat and raiment to put on, so that I come to my father's house again in peace, then the LORD will be my God, and this stone which I have set up as a pillar for a sign in this place will be the LORD's house, and of all that You give me, I will give the tenth to You, my God."

CHAPTER 28

¹ And he went on his journey, and came to the land of the east, to Laban, the brother of Rebekah, and he was with him, and served him for his daughter Rachel [for] one week. ² And in the first year of the third week he said to him, "Give me my wife, for whom I have served you seven years"; and Laban said to Jacob, "I will give you your wife." ³ And Laban made a feast, and took his elder daughter Leah, and gave [her] to Jacob as a wife, and gave her his handmaid Zilpah for a handmaid, and Jacob did not know, for he thought that she was Rachel. ⁴ And he went in to her, and behold, she was Leah; and Jacob was angry with Laban, and said to him, "Why have you dealt thus with me? Did I not serve you for Rachel and not for Leah? Why have you wronged me? Take your daughter, and I will go, for you have done evil to me."

⁵ For Jacob loved Rachel more than Leah, for Leah's eyes were weak, but her form was very attractive, but Rachel had beautiful eyes and a beautiful and very attractive form. ⁶ And Laban said to Jacob, "It is not so done in our country, to give the younger before the elder." And it is not right to do this, for thus it is ordained and written in the heavenly tablets that no one should give his younger daughter before the elder—but he gives the elder one first and after her the younger—and the man who does so, they set down guilt against him in Heaven, and none is righteous that does this thing, for this deed is evil before the LORD. ⁷ And command the sons of Israel that they do not do this thing; let them neither take nor give the younger before they have given the elder, for it is very wicked. ⁸ And Laban said to Jacob, "Let the seven days of the celebration of this one pass by, and I will give you Rachel, that you may serve me another seven years, that you may pasture my sheep as you did in the former week." ⁹ And on the day when the seven days of the celebration of Leah had passed, Laban gave Rachel to Jacob, that he might serve him another seven years, and he gave to Rachel Bilhah, the sister of Zilpah, as a handmaid. ¹⁰ And he served yet another seven years for Rachel, for Leah had been given to him for nothing. ¹¹ And the LORD opened the womb of Leah, and she conceived and bore Jacob a son, and he called his name Reuben, on the fourteenth day of the ninth month, in the first year of the third week. ¹² But the womb of Rachel was closed, for the LORD saw that Leah was hated and Rachel loved. ¹³ And again Jacob went in to Leah, and she conceived, and bore Jacob a second son, and he called his name Simeon, on the twenty-first of the tenth month, and in the third year of this week. ¹⁴ And again Jacob went in to Leah, and she conceived, and bore him a third son, and he called his name Levi, in the new moon of the first month, in the sixth year of this week. ¹⁵ And again Jacob went in to her, and she conceived, and bore him a fourth son, and he called his name Judah, on the fifteenth of the third month, in the first year of the fourth week. ¹⁶ And on account of all this, Rachel envied Leah, for she did not bear, and she said to Jacob, "Give me children"; and Jacob said, "Have I withheld from you the fruits of your womb? Have I forsaken you?" ¹⁷ And when Rachel saw that Leah had borne four sons to Jacob—Reuben, and Simeon, and Levi, and Judah—she said to him, "Go in to my handmaid Bilhah, and she will conceive, and bear a son to me." ¹⁸ And he went in to her, and she conceived, and bore him a son, and he called his name Dan, on the ninth of the sixth month, in the sixth year of the third week. ¹⁹ And Jacob went in again to Bilhah a second time, and she conceived, and bore Jacob another son, and Rachel called his name Naphtali, on the fifth of the seventh month, in the second year of the fourth week. ²⁰ And when Leah saw that she had become sterile and did not bear, she envied [Rachel]

and she also gave her handmaid Zilpah to Jacob to be [his] wife, and she conceived, and bore a son, and Leah called his name Gad, on the twelfth of the eighth month, in the third year of the fourth week. [21] And he went in again to her, and she conceived, and bore him a second son, and Leah called his name Asher, on the second of the eleventh month, in the fifth year of the fourth week. [22] And Jacob went in to Leah, and she conceived, and bore a son, and she called his name Issachar, on the fourth of the fifth month, in the fourth year of the fourth week, and she gave him to a nurse. [23] And Jacob went in again to her, and she conceived, and bore two [children], a son and a daughter, and she called the name of the son Zebulun, and the name of the daughter Dinah, in the seventh of the seventh month, in the sixth year of the fourth week. [24] And the LORD was gracious to Rachel, and opened her womb, and she conceived, and bore a son, and she called his name Joseph, on the new moon of the fourth month, in the sixth year in this fourth week. [25] And in the days when Joseph was born, Jacob said to Laban, "Give me my wives and sons, and let me go to my father Isaac, and let me make myself a house, for I have completed the years in which I have served you for your two daughters, and I will go to the house of my father." [26] And Laban said to Jacob, "Tarry with me for your wages, and pasture my flock for me again, and take your wages." [27] And they agreed with one another that he should give him as his wages those of the lambs and kids which were born black, and spotted, and white; [these] were to be his wages. [28] And all the sheep brought out spotted, and speckled, and black, variously marked, and they brought out again lambs like themselves, and all that were spotted were Jacob's and those which were not were Laban's. [29] And Jacob's possessions multiplied exceedingly, and he possessed oxen, and sheep, and donkeys, and camels, and menservants, and maidservants. [30] And Laban and his sons envied Jacob, and Laban took back his sheep from him, and he observed him with evil intent.

CHAPTER 29

[1] And it came to pass when Rachel had borne Joseph, that Laban went to shear his sheep, for they were distant from him a three days' journey. [2] And Jacob saw that Laban was going to shear his sheep, and Jacob called Leah and Rachel, and spoke kindly to them that they should come with him to the land of Canaan. [3] For he told them how he had seen everything in a dream, even all that He had spoken to him that he should return to his father's house, and they said, "To every place where you go we will go with you." [4] And Jacob blessed the God of his father Isaac, and the God of Abraham, his father's father, and he arose and mounted his wives and his children, and took all his possessions and crossed the river, and came to the land of Gilead, and Jacob hid his intention from Laban and did not tell him. [5] And in the seventh year of the fourth week Jacob turned [his face] toward Gilead in the first month, on the twenty-first thereof. And Laban pursued after him and overtook Jacob in the mountain of Gilead in the third month, on the thirteenth thereof. [6] And the LORD did not permit him to injure Jacob, for He appeared to him in a dream by night. And Laban spoke to Jacob, [7] and on the fifteenth of those days Jacob made a feast for Laban and for all who came with him, and Jacob swore to Laban that day, and Laban also to Jacob, that neither should cross the mountain of Gilead to the other with evil purpose. [8] And he made a heap there for a witness; for that reason the name of that place is called "The Heap of Witness," after this heap. [9] But before [that] they used to call the land of Gilead the land of the Rephaim, for it was the land of the Rephaim, and the Rephaim were born [there]—giants whose height was ten, nine, eight, [and] down to seven cubits. [10] And their habitation was from the land of the children of Ammon to Mount Hermon, and the seats of their kingdom were Karnaim, and Ashtaroth, and Edrei, and Mîsûr, and Beon. [11] And the LORD destroyed them because of the evil of their deeds, for they were very malevolent, and the Amorites dwelt in their stead, wicked and sinful, and there is no people today which has worked to the measure of all their sins, and they have no more length of life on the earth. [12] And Jacob sent Laban away, and he departed into Mesopotamia, the land of the east, and Jacob returned to the land of Gilead. [13] And he passed over the Jabbok in the ninth month, on the eleventh thereof. And on that day his brother Esau came to him, and he was reconciled to him, and departed from him to the land of Seir, but Jacob dwelt in tents. [14] And in the first year of the fifth week in this jubilee he crossed the Jordan, and dwelt beyond the Jordan, and he pastured his sheep from the sea of the heap to Bethshan, and to Dothan, and to the forest of Akrabbim. [15] And he sent to his father Isaac of all his substance: clothing, and food, and meat, and drink, and milk, and butter, and cheese, and some dates of the valley; [16] and also to his mother Rebekah four times a year, between the times of the months, between plowing and reaping, and between autumn and the rain [season], and between winter and spring, to the tower of Abraham. [17] For Isaac had returned from the Well of the Oath and gone up to the tower of his father Abraham, and he dwelt there apart from his son Esau. [18] For in the days when Jacob went to Mesopotamia, Esau took to himself Mahalath, the daughter of Ishmael, to be [his] wife, and he gathered together all the flocks of his father and his wives, and went up and dwelt on Mount Seir, and left his father Isaac at the Well of the Oath alone. [19] And Isaac went up from the Well of the Oath and dwelt in the tower of his father Abraham on the mountains of Hebron, [20] and there Jacob sent all that he sent to his father and his mother from time to

time—all they needed—and they blessed Jacob with all their heart and with all their soul.

CHAPTER 30

[1] And in the first year of the sixth week he went up to Salem, to the east of Shechem, in peace, in the fourth month. [2] And there they carried off Dinah, the daughter of Jacob, into the house of Shechem, the son of Hamor, the Hivite, the prince of the land, and he lay with her and defiled her, and she was a little girl, a child of twelve years. [3] And he implored his father and her brothers that she might be given to him to be [his] wife. And Jacob and his sons were angry because of the men of Shechem, for they had defiled their sister Dinah, and they spoke to them with evil intent, and dealt deceitfully with them, and deceived them. [4] And Simeon and Levi came stealthily to Shechem, and executed judgment on all the men of Shechem, and slew all the men whom they found in it, and left not a single one remaining in it: they slew all in torments because they had dishonored their sister Dinah. [5] And thus do not let it be done again from now on that a daughter of Israel is defiled, for judgment is ordained in Heaven against them that they should destroy with the sword all the men of the Shechemites because they had worked shame in Israel. [6] And the LORD delivered them into the hands of the sons of Jacob that they might exterminate them with the sword, and execute judgment on them, and that it might not thus be done again in Israel that a virgin of Israel should be defiled. [7] And if there is any man in Israel who wishes to give his daughter or his sister to any man who is of the seed of the nations, he will surely die, and they will stone him with stones, for he has worked shame in Israel; and they will burn the woman with fire, because she has dishonored the name of the house of her father, and she will be rooted out of Israel. [8] And do not let an adulteress be found, and no uncleanness, in Israel, throughout all the days of the generations of the earth, for Israel is holy to the LORD, and every man who has defiled [it] will surely die: they will stone him with stones. [9] For thus it has been ordained and written in the heavenly tablets regarding all the seed of Israel: he who defiles [it] will surely die, and he will be stoned with stones. [10] And to this law there is no limit of days, and no forgiveness, nor any atonement, but the man who has defiled his daughter will be rooted out in the midst of all Israel, because he has given of his seed to Moloch, and worked impiously so as to defile it. [11] And you, Moses, command the sons of Israel and exhort them not to give their daughters to the nations, and not to take any of the daughters of the nations for their sons, for this is abominable before the LORD. [12] For this reason I have written for you in the words of the Law all the deeds of the Shechemites, which they worked against Dinah, and how the sons of Jacob spoke, saying, "We will not give our daughter to a man who is uncircumcised, for that would be a reproach to us." [13] And it is a reproach to Israel to those who give and to those who take the daughters of the nations, for this is unclean and abominable to Israel. [14] And Israel will not be free from this uncleanness if it has a wife of the daughters of the nations or has given any of its daughters to a man who is of any of the nations. [15] For there will be plague on plague, and curse on curse, and every judgment, and plague, and curse will come [on him] if he does this thing, or hides his eyes from those who commit uncleanness, or those who defile the sanctuary of the LORD, or those who profane His holy Name, [for] the whole nation will be judged together for all the uncleanness and desecration of this [man]. [16] And there will be no respect of persons, and no receiving at his hands of fruits, and offerings, and burnt-offerings, and fat, nor the fragrance of sweet savor, so as to accept it: and likewise for every man or woman in Israel who defiles the sanctuary. [17] For this reason I have commanded you, saying, "Testify this testimony to Israel: see how the Shechemites and their sons fared, how they were delivered into the hands of two sons of Jacob, and they slew them under tortures, and it was [reckoned] to them for righteousness, and it is written down to them for righteousness. [18] And the seed of Levi was chosen for the priesthood, and to be Levites, that they might minister before the LORD, as we, continually, and that Levi and his sons may be blessed forever, for he was zealous to execute righteousness, and judgment, and vengeance on all those who arose against Israel. [19] And so they inscribe as a testimony in his favor on the heavenly tablets blessing and righteousness before the God of all; [20] and we remember the righteousness which the man fulfilled during his life, at all periods of the year; until one thousand generations they will [still] record it, and it will come to him and to his descendants after him, and he has been recorded on the heavenly tablets as a friend and a righteous man. [21] All this account I have written for you and have commanded you to say to the sons of Israel, that they should not commit sin, nor transgress the ordinances, nor break the covenant which has been ordained for them, [but] that they should fulfill it and be recorded as friends. [22] But if they transgress and work uncleanness in every way, they will be recorded on the heavenly tablets as adversaries, and they will be destroyed out of the Scroll of Life, and they will be recorded in the scroll of those who will be destroyed and with those who will be rooted out of the earth. [23] And on the day when the sons of Jacob slew Shechem, a writing was recorded in their favor in Heaven that they had executed righteousness, and uprightness, and vengeance on the sinners, and it was written for a blessing. [24] And they brought their sister Dinah out of the house of Shechem, and they took everything captive that was in Shechem: their sheep, and their

oxen, and their donkeys, and all their wealth, and all their flocks; and they brought them all to their father Jacob. ²⁵ And he reproached them because they had put the city to the sword, for he feared those who dwelt in the land, the Canaanites and the Perizzites. ²⁶ And the dread of the LORD was on all the cities which are around Shechem, and they did not rise to pursue after the sons of Jacob, for terror had fallen on them."

CHAPTER 31

¹ And on the new moon of the month Jacob spoke to all the people of his house, saying, "Purify yourselves and change your garments, and let us arise and go up to Bethel, where I vowed a vow to Him on the day when I fled from the face of my brother Esau, because He has been with me and has brought me into this land in peace, and put away the strange gods that are among you." ² And they gave up the strange gods, and that which was in their ears and which was on their necks, and the idols which Rachel stole from her father Laban she wholly gave to Jacob. And he burned and broke them to pieces, and destroyed them, and hid them under an oak which is in the land of Shechem. ³ And he went up on the new moon of the seventh month to Bethel. And he built an altar at the place where he had slept, and he set up a pillar there, and he sent word to his father Isaac to come to him to his sacrifice, and to his mother Rebekah. ⁴ And Isaac said, "Let my son Jacob come, and let me see him before I die." ⁵ And Jacob went to his father Isaac and to his mother Rebekah, to the house of his father Abraham, and he took two of his sons with him, Levi and Judah, and he came to his father Isaac and to his mother Rebekah. ⁶ And Rebekah came out from the tower to the front of it to kiss Jacob and embrace him, for her spirit had revived when she heard: "Behold, your son Jacob has come!" And she kissed him. ⁷ And she saw his two sons, and she recognized them, and said to him, "Are these your sons, my son?" and she embraced them, and kissed them, and blessed them, saying, "In you the seed of Abraham will become illustrious, and you will prove a blessing on the earth." ⁸ And Jacob went in to his father Isaac, to the chamber where he lay, and his two sons were with him, and he took the hand of his father, and stooping down, he kissed him, and Isaac clung to the neck of his son Jacob and wept on his neck. ⁹ And the darkness left the eyes of Isaac, and he saw the two sons of Jacob, Levi and Judah, and he said, "Are these your sons, my son? For they are like you." ¹⁰ And he said to him that they were truly his sons: "And you have truly seen that they are truly my sons." ¹¹ And they came near to him, and he turned and kissed them, and embraced them both together. ¹² And the spirit of prophecy came down into his mouth, and he took Levi by his right hand and Judah by his left. ¹³ And he turned to Levi first, and began to bless him first, and

said to him, "May the God of all, the very Lord of all the ages, ‖ Bless you and your children throughout all the ages. ¹⁴ And may the LORD give greatness and great glory to you and to your seed, ‖ And cause you and your seed, from among all flesh, to approach Him ‖ To serve in His sanctuary as the messengers of the presence and as the holy ones. [Even] as they, may the seed of your sons be for glory, and greatness, and holiness, ‖ And may He make them great to all the ages. ¹⁵ And they will be princes and judges, ‖ And chiefs of all the seed of the sons of Jacob; They will speak the word of the LORD in righteousness, ‖ And they will judge all His judgments in righteousness. And they will declare My ways to Jacob, ‖ And My paths to Israel. The blessing of the LORD will be given in their mouths ‖ To bless all the seed of the beloved. ¹⁶ Your mother has called your name Levi, ‖ And justly has she called your name; You will be joined to the LORD, ‖ And be the companion of all the sons of Jacob; Let His table be yours ‖ And you and your sons will eat thereof; And may your table be full to all generations, ‖ And your food will not fail to all the ages. ¹⁷ And let all who hate you fall down before you, ‖ And let all your adversaries be rooted out and perish; And blessed is he that blesses you ‖ And cursed is every nation that curses you." ¹⁸ And to Judah he said, "May the LORD give you strength and power ‖ To tread down all that hate you; You will be a prince—you and one of your sons, ‖ Over the sons of Jacob; May your name and the name of your sons ‖ Go out and traverse every land and region. Then the nations will fear before your face, ‖ And all the nations [[or peoples]] will quake. ¹⁹ In you will be the help of Jacob, ‖ And in you will be found the salvation of Israel. ²⁰ And when you sit on the throne of the honor of your righteousness, ‖ There will be great peace for all the seed of the sons of the beloved, ‖ And he that blesses you will be blessed; And all that hate you, and afflict you, and curse you ‖ Will be rooted out and destroyed from the earth and accursed." ²¹ And turning, he kissed him again and embraced him, and greatly rejoiced, for he had seen the sons of his son Jacob in exceeding truth. ²² And he went out from between his feet and fell down and worshiped him. And he blessed them. And [Jacob] rested there with his father Isaac that night, and they ate and drank with joy. ²³ And he made the two sons of Jacob sleep—the one on his right hand and the other on his left, and it was counted to him for righteousness. ²⁴ And Jacob told his father everything during the night, how the LORD had shown him great mercy, and how He had prospered [him in] all his ways and protected him from all evil. ²⁵ And Isaac blessed the God of his father Abraham who had not withdrawn His mercy and His righteousness from the sons of His servant Isaac. ²⁶ And in the morning, Jacob told his father Isaac the vow which he had vowed to the LORD, and the vision which he had seen, and that he had built an altar, and that everything was ready for the sacrifice to be made before the LORD as he had vowed, and that he had come to set him on a donkey. [27] And Isaac said to his son Jacob, "I am not able to go with you, for I am old and not able to bear the way: go, my son, in peace, for I am one hundred and sixty-five years [old] this day; I am no longer able to journey. Set your mother [on a donkey] and let her go with you. [28] And I know, my son, that you have come on my account, and may this day be blessed on which you have seen me alive, and I also have seen you, my son. [29] May you prosper and fulfill the vow which you have vowed, and do not put off your vow, for you will be called to account as touching the vow. Now, therefore, make sure to perform it, and may He be pleased who has made all things, to whom you have vowed the vow." [30] And he said to Rebekah, "Go with your son Jacob"; and Rebekah went with her son Jacob, and Deborah with her, and they came to Bethel. [31] And Jacob remembered the prayer with which his father had blessed him and his two sons, Levi and Judah, and he rejoiced and blessed the God of his fathers Abraham and Isaac. [32] And he said, "Now I know that I have a continuous hope, and my sons also, before the God of all"; and thus it is ordained concerning the two; and they record it as a perpetual testimony to them on the heavenly tablets how Isaac blessed them.

CHAPTER 32

[1] And he stayed that night at Bethel, and Levi dreamed that they had ordained and made him the priest of the Most High God, him and his sons forever; and he awoke from his sleep and blessed the LORD. [2] And Jacob rose early in the morning, on the fourteenth of this month, and he gave a tithe of all that came with him, both of men and cattle, both of gold and every vessel and garment, yes, he gave tithes of all. [3] And in those days Rachel became pregnant with her son Benjamin. And Jacob counted his sons from him upwards and Levi fell to the portion of the LORD, and his father clothed him in the garments of the priesthood and filled his hands. [4] And on the fifteenth of this month, he brought to the altar fourteen oxen from among the cattle, and twenty-eight rams, and forty-nine sheep, and seven lambs, and twenty-one kids of the goats as a burnt-offering on the altar of sacrifice, well pleasing for a sweet savor before God. [5] This was his offering, in consequence of the vow which he had vowed that he would give a tenth, with their fruit-offerings and their drink-offerings. [6] And when the fire had consumed it, he burned incense on the fire over the fire, and for a thank-offering two oxen, and four rams, and four sheep, four male goats, and two sheep of a year old, and two kids of the goats; and thus he did daily for seven days. [7] And he, and all his sons, and his men were eating [this] with joy there for seven days and were blessing and thanking the LORD who had delivered him out of all his tribulation and had given him his vow. [8] And he tithed all the clean animals, and made a burnt sacrifice, but he did [not] give the unclean animals to his son Levi, and he gave him all the souls of the men. [9] And Levi discharged the priestly office at Bethel before his father Jacob in preference to his ten brothers, and he was a priest there, and Jacob gave his vow: thus he tithed the tithe to the LORD again and sanctified it, and it became holy to Him. [10] And for this reason it is ordained on the heavenly tablets as a law for the tithing the tithe again to eat before the LORD from year to year in the place where it is chosen that His Name should dwell, and to this law there is no limit of days forever. [11] This ordinance is written that it may be fulfilled from year to year in eating the second tithe before the LORD in the place where it has been chosen, and nothing will remain over from it from this year to the year following. [12] For in its year the seed will be eaten until the days of the gathering of the seed of the year, and the wine until the days of the wine, and the oil until the days of its season. [13] And all that is left thereof and becomes old, let it be regarded as polluted: let it be burned with fire, for it is unclean. [14] And thus let them eat it together in the sanctuary and do not let them permit it to become old. [15] And all the tithes of the oxen and sheep will be holy to the LORD, and will belong to His priests, which they will eat before Him from year to year, for thus it is ordained and engraved regarding the tithe on the heavenly tablets. [16] And on the following night, on the twenty-second day of this month, Jacob resolved to build that place, and to surround the court with a wall, and to sanctify it and make it holy forever, for himself and his children after him. [17] And the LORD appeared to him by night, and blessed him, and said to him, "Your name will not be called Jacob, but Israel they will name your name." [18] And He said to him again, "I am the LORD who created the heavens and the earth, and I will increase you and multiply you exceedingly, and kings will come out from you, and they will judge everywhere, wherever the foot of the sons of men has trodden. [19] And I will give to your seed all the earth which is under the heavens, and they will judge all the nations according to their desires, and after that, they will get possession of the whole earth and inherit it forever." [20] And He finished speaking with him, and He went up from him, and Jacob looked until He had ascended into Heaven. [21] And he saw in a vision of the night, and behold, a messenger descended from Heaven with seven tablets in his hands, and he gave them to Jacob, and he read them and knew all that was written therein which would befall him and his sons throughout all the ages. [22] And he showed him all that was written on the tablets and said to him, "Do not build this place, and do not make it a perpetual sanctuary, and do not dwell here, for this is not the place. Go to the house of your

father Abraham and dwell with your father Isaac until the day of the death of your father. ²³ For in Egypt you will die in peace, and you will be buried in this land with honor in the tomb of your fathers, with Abraham and Isaac. ²⁴ Do not fear, for as you have seen and read it, thus it will all be; and write down everything as you have seen and read." ²⁵ And Jacob said, "Lord, how can I remember all that I have read and seen?" And he said to him, "I will bring all things to your remembrance." ²⁶ And he went up from him, and he awoke from his sleep, and he remembered everything which he had read and seen, and he wrote down all the words which he had read and seen. ²⁷ And he celebrated there yet another day, and he sacrificed thereon according to all that he sacrificed on the former days, and called its name "Addition," for this day was added, and the former days he called "The Feast." ²⁸ And thus it was manifested that it should be, and it is written on the heavenly tablets, for that reason it was revealed to him that he should celebrate it and add it to the seven days of the feast. ²⁹ And its name was called "Addition," because that it was recorded among the days of the feast days, according to the number of the days of the year. ³⁰ And in the night, on the twenty-third of this month, Rebekah's nurse Deborah died, and they buried her beneath the city under the oak of the river, and he called the name of this place, "The river of Deborah," and the oak, "The oak of the mourning of Deborah." ³¹ And Rebekah went and returned to her house, to his father Isaac, and Jacob sent by her hand rams, and sheep, and male goats that she should prepare a meal for his father such as he desired. ³² And he went after his mother until he came to the land of Kabrâtân, and he dwelt there. ³³ And Rachel bore a son in the night and called his name "Son of my sorrow," for she suffered in giving him birth, but his father called his name Benjamin, on the eleventh of the eighth month, in the first of the sixth week of this jubilee. ³⁴ And Rachel died there, and she was buried in the land of Ephrath, the same is Beth-Lehem, and Jacob built a pillar on the grave of Rachel, on the road above her grave.

CHAPTER 33

¹ And Jacob went and dwelt to the south of Magdalâdrâ'êf. And he went to his father Isaac, he and his wife Leah, on the new moon of the tenth month. ² And Reuben saw Bilhah, Rachel's maid, the concubine of his father, bathing in water in a secret place, and he loved her. ³ And he hid himself at night, and he entered the house of Bilhah [at night], and he found her sleeping alone on a bed in her house. ⁴ And he lay with her, and she awoke and saw, and behold, Reuben was lying with her in the bed, and she uncovered the border of her covering and seized him, and cried out, and discovered that it was Reuben. ⁵ And she was ashamed because of him, and released her hand from him, and he fled. ⁶ And she lamented exceedingly because of this thing and did not tell it to anyone. ⁷ And when Jacob returned and sought her, she said to him, "I am not clean for you, for I have been defiled as regards you, for Reuben has defiled me, and has lain with me in the night, and I was asleep, and did not discover [it] until he uncovered my skirt and slept with me." ⁸ And Jacob was exceedingly angry with Reuben because he had lain with Bilhah, because he had uncovered his father's skirt. ⁹ And Jacob did not approach her again because Reuben had defiled her. And as for any man who uncovers his father's skirt: his deed is exceedingly wicked, for he is abominable before the LORD. ¹⁰ For this reason it is written and ordained on the heavenly tablets that a man should not lie with his father's wife, and should not uncover his father's skirt, for this is unclean: they will surely die together, the man who lies with his father's wife and the woman also, for they have worked uncleanness on the earth. ¹¹ And there will be nothing unclean before our God in the nation which He has chosen for Himself as a possession. ¹² And again, it is written a second time: "Cursed is he who lies with the wife of his father, for he has uncovered his father's shame"; and all the holy ones of the LORD said, "So be it; so be it." ¹³ And you, Moses, command the sons of Israel that they observe this word, for it [entails] a punishment of death; and it is unclean, and there is no atonement forever to atone for the man who has committed this, but he is to be put to death and slain, and stoned with stones, and rooted out from the midst of the people of our God. ¹⁴ For to no man who does so in Israel is it permitted to remain alive a single day on the earth, for he is abominable and unclean. ¹⁵ And do not let them say, "Life and forgiveness were granted to Reuben after he had lain with his father's concubine, and to her also though she had a husband, and her husband Jacob, his father, was still alive." ¹⁶ For until that time there had not been revealed the ordinance, and judgment, and law in its completeness for all, but in your days [it has been revealed] as a law of seasons and of days, and a continuous law for the perpetual generations. ¹⁷ And for this law there is no consummation of days, and no atonement for it, but they must both be rooted out in the midst of the nation: on the day on which they committed it they will slay them. ¹⁸ And you, Moses, write [it] down for Israel that they may observe it, and do according to these words, and not commit a sin to death, for the LORD our God is judge, who does not respect persons and does not accept gifts. ¹⁹ And tell them these words of the covenant, that they may hear and observe, and be on their guard with respect to them, and not be destroyed and rooted out of the land; for an uncleanness, and an abomination, and a contamination, and a pollution are all they who commit it on the earth before our God. ²⁰ And there is no greater sin than the fornication which they commit

on earth, for Israel is a holy nation to the LORD its God, and a nation of inheritance, and a priestly and royal nation, and for [His own] possession; and no such uncleanness will appear in the midst of the holy nation. ²¹ And in the third year of this sixth week Jacob and all his sons went and dwelt in the house of Abraham, near his father Isaac and his mother Rebekah. ²² And these were the names of the sons of Jacob: the firstborn Reuben, Simeon, Levi, Judah, Issachar, Zebulun—the sons of Leah; and the sons of Rachel: Joseph and Benjamin; and the sons of Bilhah: Dan and Naphtali; and the sons of Zilpah: Gad and Asher; and Dinah, the daughter of Leah, the only daughter of Jacob. ²³ And they came and bowed themselves to Isaac and Rebekah, and when they saw them, they blessed Jacob and all his sons, and Isaac rejoiced exceedingly, for he saw the sons of Jacob, his younger son, and he blessed them.

CHAPTER 34

¹ And in the sixth year of this week, of this forty-fourth jubilee, Jacob sent his sons to pasture their sheep, and his servants with them, to the pastures of Shechem. ² And the seven kings of the Amorites assembled themselves together against them, to slay them, hiding themselves under the trees, and to take their cattle as a prey. ³ And Jacob, and Levi, and Judah, and Joseph were in the house with their father Isaac, for his spirit was sorrowful, and they could not leave him; and Benjamin was the youngest, and for this reason remained with his father. ⁴ And there came the king[s] of Tâphû, and the king[s] of 'Arêsa, and the king[s] of Sêragân, and the king[s] of Sêlô, and the king[s] of Gâ'as, and the king of Bêthôrôn, and the king of Ma'anîsâkîr, and all those who dwell in these mountains [and] who dwell in the woods in the land of Canaan. ⁵ And they announced this to Jacob, saying, "Behold, the kings of the Amorites have surrounded your sons, and plundered their herds." ⁶ And he arose from his house—he, and his three sons, and all the servants of his father, and his own servants—and he went against them with six thousand men who carried swords. ⁷ And he slew them in the pastures of Shechem, and pursued those who fled, and he slew them with the edge of the sword, and he slew 'Arêsa, and Tâphû, and Sêragân, and Sêlô, and Ma'anîsâkîr, and Gâ'as, and he recovered his herds. ⁸ And he prevailed over them, and imposed tribute on them that they should pay him tribute, five fruit products of their land, and he built Rôbêl and Tamnâtârês, ⁹ and he returned in peace, and made peace with them, and they became his servants until the day that he and his sons went down into Egypt. ¹⁰ And in the seventh year of this week he sent Joseph from his house to the land of Shechem to learn about the welfare of his brothers, and he found them in the land of Dothan. ¹¹ And they dealt treacherously with him, and formed a plot against him to slay him,

but changing their minds, they sold him to Ishmaelite merchants, and they brought him down into Egypt, and they sold him to Potiphar, the eunuch of Pharaoh, the chief of the cooks, priest of the city of 'Êlêw. ¹² And the sons of Jacob slaughtered a kid, and dipped the coat of Joseph in the blood, and sent [it] to their father Jacob on the tenth of the seventh month. ¹³ And he mourned all that night, for they had brought it to him in the evening, and he became feverish with mourning for his death, and he said, "An evil beast has devoured Joseph"; and all the members of his house were grieving and mourning with him that whole day. ¹⁴ And his sons and his daughter rose up to comfort him, but he refused to be comforted for his son. ¹⁵ And on that day, Bilhah heard that Joseph had perished, and she died mourning [for] him, and she was living in Qafrâtêf and Dinah also, his daughter, died after Joseph had perished. And these three mournings came on Israel in one month. ¹⁶ And they buried Bilhah over against the tomb of Rachel, and Dinah also, his daughter, they buried there. ¹⁷ And he mourned for Joseph one year, and did not cease, for he said, "Let me go down to the grave mourning for my son." ¹⁸ For this reason it is ordained for the sons of Israel that they should afflict themselves on the tenth of the seventh month—on the day that the news which made him weep for Joseph came to Jacob his father—that they should make atonement for themselves thereon with a young goat on the tenth of the seventh month, once a year, for their sins, for they had grieved the affection of their father regarding his son Joseph. ¹⁹ And this day has been ordained that they should grieve thereon for their sins, and for all their transgressions, and for all their errors, so that they might cleanse themselves on that day once a year. ²⁰ And after Joseph perished, the sons of Jacob took wives for themselves. The name of Reuben's wife is 'Adâ; and the name of Simeon's wife is 'Adîbâ'a, a Canaanite; and the name of Levi's wife is Mêlkâ, of the daughters of Aram, of the seed of the sons of Terah; and the name of Judah's wife, Bêtasû'êl, a Canaanite; and the name of Issachar's wife, Hêzaqâ; and the name of Zebulun's wife, Nî'îmân; and the name of Dan's wife, 'Êglâ; and the name of Naphtali's wife, Rasû'û, of Mesopotamia; and the name of Gad's wife, Mâka; and the name of Asher's wife, 'Îjônâ; and the name of Joseph's wife, Asenath, the Egyptian; and the name of Benjamin's wife, 'Îjasaka. ²¹ And Simeon converted, and took a second wife from Mesopotamia as his brothers.

CHAPTER 35

¹ And in the first year of the first week of the forty-fifth jubilee, Rebekah called her son Jacob and commanded him regarding his father and regarding his brother, that he should honor them all the days of his life. ² And Jacob said, "I will do everything as you have commanded me, for this thing will be honor and

greatness to me, and righteousness before the LORD, that I should honor them. ³And you, mother, also know from the time I was born until this day, all my deeds and all that is in my heart, that I always think good concerning all. ⁴And how should I not do this thing which you have commanded me, that I should honor my father and my brother! ⁵Tell me, mother, what perversity have you seen in me and I will turn away from it, and mercy will be on me." ⁶And she said to him, "My son, I have not seen in you all my days anything perverse, but [only] upright deeds. And yet I will tell you the truth, my son: I will die this year, and I will not survive this year in my life, for I have seen in a dream the day of my death, that I should not live beyond one hundred and fifty-five years; and behold, I have completed all the days of my life which I am to live." ⁷And Jacob laughed at the words of his mother, because his mother had said to him that she should die; and she was sitting opposite to him in possession of her strength, and she was not weak in her strength, for she went in and out and saw, and her teeth were strong, and no ailment had touched her all the days of her life. ⁸And Jacob said to her, "Blessed am I, mother, if my days approach the days of your life, and my strength remains with me thus as your strength: and you will not die, for you are idly jesting with me regarding your death." ⁹And she went in to Isaac and said to him, "One petition I make to you: make Esau swear that he will not injure Jacob, nor pursue him with enmity, for you know that Esau's thoughts are perverse from his youth, and there is no goodness in him, for he desires to kill him after your death. ¹⁰And you know all that he has done since the day his brother Jacob went to Haran until this day, how he has forsaken us with his whole heart and has done evil to us; he has taken your flocks to himself and carried off all your possessions from before your face. ¹¹And when we implored and entreated him for what was our own, he did as a man who was taking pity on us. ¹²And he is bitter against you because you blessed Jacob, your perfect and upright son; for there is no evil but only goodness in him, and since he came from Haran to this day, he has not robbed us of anything, for he always brings us everything in its season, and rejoices with all his heart when we take at his hands, and he blesses us, and has not parted from us since he came from Haran until this day, and he continually remains at home with us, honoring us." ¹³And Isaac said to her, "I, too, know and see the deeds of Jacob who is with us, how that he honors us with all his heart, but I formerly loved Esau more than Jacob, because he was the firstborn, but now I love Jacob more than Esau, for he has done manifold evil deeds, and there is no righteousness in him, for all his ways are unrighteousness and violence. ¹⁴And now my heart is troubled because of all his deeds, and neither he nor his seed is to be saved, for they are those who will be destroyed from the earth, and who

will be rooted out from under the heavens, for he has forsaken the God of Abraham and gone after his wives, and after their uncleanness, and after their error—he and his children. ¹⁵And you command me to make him swear that he will not slay his brother Jacob; even if he swears, he will not abide by his oath, and he will not do good but only evil. ¹⁶But if he desires to slay his brother Jacob, he will be given into Jacob's hands, and he will not escape from his hands. ¹⁷And do not fear on account of Jacob, for the guardian of Jacob is great, and powerful, and honored, and praised more than the guardian of Esau." ¹⁸And Rebekah sent and called Esau, and he came to her, and she said to him, "I have a petition, my son, to make to you, and do you promise to do it, my son?" ¹⁹And he said, "I will do everything that you say to me, and I will not refuse your petition." ²⁰And she said to him, "I ask you that the day I die, you will take me in and bury me near Sarah, your father's mother, and that you and Jacob will love each other, and that neither will desire evil against the other, but mutual love only, and [so] you will prosper, my sons, and be honored in the midst of the land, and no enemy will rejoice over you, and you will be a blessing and a mercy in the eyes of all those that love you." ²¹And he said, "I will do all that you have told me, and I will bury you on the day you die near Sarah, my father's mother, as you have desired, that her bones may be near your bones. ²²And I will also love my brother Jacob above all flesh, for I have no brother in all the earth but him only; and this is no great merit for me if I love him, for he is my brother, and we were sown together in your body, and together we came out from your womb, and if I do not love my brother, whom will I love? ²³And I, myself, beg you to exhort Jacob concerning me and concerning my sons, for I know that he will assuredly be king over me and my sons, for on the day my father blessed him he made him the higher and me the lower. ²⁴And I swear to you that I will love him, and not desire evil against him all the days of my life, but good only." And he swore to her regarding all this matter. ²⁵And she called Jacob before the eyes of Esau and gave him command according to the words which she had spoken to Esau. ²⁶And he said, "I will do your pleasure; believe me that no evil will proceed from me or from my sons against Esau, and I will be first in nothing save in love only." ²⁷And she and her sons ate and drank that night, and she died—three jubilees and one week and one year old—on that night, and her two sons, Esau and Jacob, buried her in the double cave near Sarah, their father's mother.

CHAPTER 36

¹And in the sixth year of this week Isaac called his two sons, Esau and Jacob, and they came to him, and he said to them, "My sons, I am going the way of my fathers, to the continuous house where my fathers are.

² For that reason, bury me near my father Abraham, in the double cave in the field of Ephron the Hittite, where Abraham purchased a tomb to bury in; in the tomb which I dug for myself, bury me there. ³ And this I command you, my sons, that you practice righteousness and uprightness on the earth, so that the LORD may bring on you all that the LORD said that He would do to Abraham and to his seed. ⁴ And, my sons, love one another—your brother—as a man who loves his own soul, and let each seek in what [way] he may benefit his brother, and act together on the earth; and let them love each other as their own souls. ⁵ And concerning the question of idols, I command and admonish you to reject them, and hate them, and not to love them, for they are full of deception for those that worship them and for those that bow down to them. ⁶ Remember, my sons, the LORD God of your father Abraham, and how I also worshiped Him and served Him in righteousness and in joy, that He might multiply you and increase your seed as the stars of the heavens in multitude and establish you on the earth as the plant of righteousness which will not be rooted out to all the generations forever. ⁷ And now I will make you swear a great oath—for there is no oath which is greater than it, by the glorious, and honored, and great, and splendid, and wonderful, and mighty Name, which created the heavens, and the earth, and all things together—that you will fear Him and worship Him, ⁸ and that each will love his brother with affection and righteousness, and that neither will desire evil against his brother from now on and forever, all the days of your life, so that you may prosper in all your deeds and not be destroyed. ⁹ And if either of you devises evil against his brother, know that from now on everyone that devises evil against his brother will fall into his hand, and will be rooted out of the land of the living, and his seed will be destroyed from under the heavens. ¹⁰ But on the day of turbulence, and execration, and indignation, and anger, with flaming devouring fire as He burned Sodom, so likewise He will burn his land, and his city, and all that is his, and he will be blotted out of the scroll of the discipline of the children of men, and not be recorded in the Scroll of Life, but in that which is appointed to destruction, and he will depart into continuous execration, so that their condemnation may always be renewed in hate, and in execration, and in wrath, and in torment, and in indignation, and in plagues, and in disease forever. ¹¹ I say and testify to you, my sons, according to the judgment which will come on the man who wishes to injure his brother." ¹² And he divided all his possessions between the two on that day, and he gave the larger portion to him that was the firstborn, and the tower and all that was around it, and all that Abraham possessed at the Well of the Oath. ¹³ And he said, "I will give this larger portion to the firstborn." ¹⁴ And Esau said, "I have sold to Jacob and given my birthright to Jacob; let it be given to him, and I have not a single word to say regarding it, for it is his." ¹⁵ And Isaac said, "May a blessing rest on you, my sons, and on your seed this day, for you have given me rest, and my heart is not pained concerning the birthright, lest you should work wickedness on account of it. ¹⁶ May the Most High God bless the man that works righteousness—him and his seed forever." ¹⁷ And he ended commanding them and blessing them, and they ate and drank together before him, and he rejoiced because there was one mind between them, and they went out from him, and rested that day, and slept. ¹⁸ And Isaac slept on his bed that day rejoicing; and he slept the continuous sleep and died one hundred and eighty years old. He completed twenty-five weeks and five years; and his two sons Esau and Jacob buried him. ¹⁹ And Esau went to the land of Edom, to the mountains of Seir, and dwelt there. ²⁰ And Jacob dwelt in the mountains of Hebron, in the tower of the land of the sojournings of his father Abraham, and he worshiped the LORD with all his heart and according to the visible commands according as He had divided the days of his generations. ²¹ And his wife Leah died in the fourth year of the second week of the forty-fifth jubilee, and he buried her in the double cave near his mother Rebekah, to the left of the grave of Sarah, his father's mother. ²² And all her sons and his sons came to mourn over his wife Leah with him, and to comfort him regarding her, for he was lamenting her. ²³ For he loved her exceedingly after her sister Rachel died, for she was perfect and upright in all her ways and honored Jacob, and all the days that she lived with him he did not hear from her mouth a harsh word, for she was gentle, and peaceable, and upright, and honorable. ²⁴ And he remembered all her deeds which she had done during her life, and he lamented her exceedingly, for he loved her with all his heart and with all his soul.

CHAPTER 37

¹ And on the day that Isaac the father of Jacob and Esau died, the sons of Esau heard that Isaac had given the portion of the elder to his younger son Jacob and they were very angry. ² And they strove with their father, saying, "Why has your father given Jacob the portion of the elder and passed over you, although you are the elder and Jacob the younger?" ³ And he said to them, "Because I sold my birthright to Jacob for a small mess of lentils; and on the day my father sent me to hunt, and catch, and bring him something that he should eat and bless me, he came with guile and brought my father food and drink, and my father blessed him and put me under his hand. ⁴ And now our father has caused us to swear—me and him—that we will not mutually devise evil, either against his brother, and that we will each continue in love and in peace with his brother and not make our ways

corrupt." ⁵ And they said to him, "We will not listen to you to make peace with him, for our strength is greater than his strength, and we are more powerful than he; we will go against him and slay him, and destroy him and his sons. And if you will not go with us, we will do harm to you also. ⁶ And now listen to us: let us send to Aram, and Philistia, and Moab, and Ammon, and let us choose for ourselves chosen men who are ardent for battle, and let us go against him and do battle with him, and let us exterminate him from the earth before he grows strong." ⁷ And their father said to them, "Do not go and do not make war with him lest you fall before him." ⁸ And they said to him, "This, too, is exactly your mode of action from your youth until this day, and you are putting your neck under his yoke. We will not listen to these words." ⁹ And they sent to Aram and to 'Adurâm, to the friend of their father, and they hired along with them one thousand fighting men, chosen men of war. ¹⁰ And there came to them from Moab and from the children of Ammon those who were hired, one thousand chosen men; and from Philistia, one thousand chosen men of war; and from Edom and from the Horites, one thousand chosen fighting men; and from the Kittim, mighty men of war. ¹¹ And they said to their father, "Go out with them and lead them, else we will slay you." ¹² And he was filled with wrath and indignation on seeing that his sons were forcing him to go before [them] to lead them against his brother Jacob. ¹³ But afterward he remembered all the evil which lay hidden in his heart against his brother Jacob, and he did not remember the oath which he had sworn to his father and to his mother that he would devise no evil all his days against his brother Jacob. ¹⁴ And notwithstanding all this, Jacob did not know that they were coming against him to battle, and he was mourning for his wife Leah until they approached very near to the tower with four thousand warriors and chosen men of war. ¹⁵ And the men of Hebron sent to him, saying, "Behold, your brother has come against you, to fight you, with four thousand girt with the sword, and they carry shields and weapons"; for they loved Jacob more than Esau. So they told him, for Jacob was a more liberal and merciful man than Esau. ¹⁶ But Jacob would not believe [it] until they came very near to the tower. ¹⁷ And he closed the gates of the tower; and he stood on the battlements, and spoke to his brother Esau, and said, "Noble is the comfort with which you have come to comfort me for my wife who has died. Is this the oath that you swore to your father and again to your mother before they died? You have broken the oath, and on the moment that you swore to your father you were condemned." ¹⁸ And then Esau answered and said to him, "Neither the children of men nor the beasts of the earth have any oath of righteousness which in swearing they have sworn forever, but every day they devise evil against one another, and how each may slay his adversary and enemy. ¹⁹ And you hate me and my children forever. And there is no observing the tie of brotherhood with you. ²⁰ Hear these words which I declare to you, If the boar can change its skin and make its bristles as soft as wool, or if it can cause horns to sprout out on its head like the horns of a stag or of a sheep, then I will observe the tie of brotherhood with you. [[And if the breasts separated themselves from their mother; for you have not been a brother to me.]] ²¹ And if the wolves make peace with the lambs so as not to devour or do them violence, and if their hearts are toward them for good, then there will be peace in my heart toward you. ²² And if the lion becomes the friend of the ox and makes peace with him, and if he is bound under one yoke with him and plows with him, then I will make peace with you. ²³ And when the raven becomes white as the râzâ, then know that I have loved you and will make peace with you. You will be rooted out, and your sons will be rooted out, and there will be no peace for you." ²⁴ And when Jacob saw that he was [so] evilly disposed toward him with [all] his heart and with all his soul as to slay him, and that he had come springing like the wild boar which comes on the spear that pierces and kills it, and does not recoil from it, ²⁵ then he spoke to his own and to his servants that they should attack him and all his companions.

CHAPTER 38

¹ And after that, Judah spoke to his father Jacob, and said to him, "Bend your bow, father, and send out your arrows, and cast down the adversary, and slay the enemy; and may you have the power, for we will not slay your brother, for he is such as you, and he is like you: let us give him [this] honor." ² Then Jacob bent his bow, and sent out the arrow, and struck his brother Esau [[on his right breast]], and slew him. ³ And again he sent out an arrow and struck 'Adôrân the Aramaean, on the left breast, and drove him backward and slew him. ⁴ And then the sons of Jacob went out—they and their servants—dividing themselves into companies on the four sides of the tower. ⁵ And Judah went out in front, and Naphtali and Gad with him, and fifty servants with him on the south side of the tower, and they slew all they found before them, and not one individual of them escaped. ⁶ And Levi, and Dan, and Asher went out on the east side of the tower, and fifty [men] with them, and they slew the fighting men of Moab and Ammon. ⁷ And Reuben, and Issachar, and Zebulun went out on the north side of the tower, and fifty men with them, and they slew the fighting men of the Philistines. ⁸ And Simeon, and Benjamin, and Enoch, Reuben's son, went out on the west side of the tower, and fifty [men] with them, and they slew of Edom and of the Horites four hundred men, stout warriors; and six hundred fled, and four of the sons of Esau fled with them, and left their father lying slain, as he had fallen on the hill

which is in 'Adûrâm. ⁹ And the sons of Jacob pursued after them to the mountains of Seir. And Jacob buried his brother on the hill which is in 'Adûrâm, and he returned to his house. ¹⁰ And the sons of Jacob pressed hard on the sons of Esau in the mountains of Seir and bowed their necks so that they became servants of the sons of Jacob. ¹¹ And they sent to their father [to inquire] whether they should make peace with them or slay them. ¹² And Jacob sent word to his sons that they should make peace, and they made peace with them, and placed the yoke of servitude on them, so that they always paid tribute to Jacob and to his sons. ¹³ And they continued to pay tribute to Jacob until the day that he went down into Egypt. ¹⁴ And the sons of Edom have not gotten rid of the yoke of servitude which the twelve sons of Jacob had imposed on them until this day. ¹⁵ And these are the kings that reigned in Edom, in the land of Edom, before any king reigned over the sons of Israel: ¹⁶ and Bâlâq, the son of Beor, reigned in Edom, and the name of his city was Danâbâ; ¹⁷ and Bâlâq died, and Jobab, the son of Zârâ of Bôsêr, reigned in his stead; ¹⁸ and Jobab died, and 'Asâm, of the land of Têmân, reigned in his stead; ¹⁹ and 'Asâm died, and 'Adâth, the son of Barad, who slew Midian in the field of Moab, reigned in his stead, and the name of his city was Avith; ²⁰ and 'Adâth died, and Salman, from 'Amâsêqâ, reigned in his stead; ²¹ and Salman died, and Saul of Râ'abôth [by the] river, reigned in his stead; ²² and Saul died, and Ba'êlûnân, the son of Achbor, reigned in his stead; ²³ and Ba'êlûnân, the son of Achbor, died, and 'Adâth reigned in his stead, and the name of his wife was Maiṭabîth, the daughter of Mâṭarat, the daughter of Mêtabêdzâ'ab. ²⁴ These are the kings who reigned in the land of Edom.

CHAPTER 39

¹ And Jacob dwelt in the land of his father's sojournings in the land of Canaan. ² These are the generations of Jacob. And Joseph was seventeen years old when they took him down into the land of Egypt, and Potiphar, [[a eunuch of Pharaoh,]] the chief cook [[or chief executioner]] bought him. ³ And he set Joseph over all his house, and the blessing of the LORD came on the house of the Egyptian on account of Joseph, and the LORD prospered him in all that he did. ⁴ And the Egyptian committed everything into the hands of Joseph, for he saw that the LORD was with him, and that the LORD prospered him in all that he did. ⁵ And Joseph's appearance was handsome, and his appearance was very beautiful, and his master's wife lifted up her eyes and saw Joseph, and she loved him, and implored him to lie with her. ⁶ But he did not surrender his soul, and he remembered the LORD and the words which his father Jacob used to read from among the words of Abraham, that no man should commit fornication with a woman who has a husband, that the punishment of death has been ordained in the heavens for him before the Most High God, and the sin will be continually recorded against him in the perpetual scrolls before the LORD. ⁷ And Joseph remembered these words and refused to lie with her. ⁸ And she implored him for a year, but he refused and would not listen. ⁹ But she embraced him and held him fast in the house in order to force him to lie with her, and she closed the doors of the house and held him fast, but he left his garment in her hands, and broke through the door, and fled outside from her presence. ¹⁰ And the woman saw that he would not lie with her, and she accused him in the presence of his lord, saying, "Your Hebrew servant, whom you love, sought to force me so that he might lie with me; and it came to pass when I lifted up my voice, that he fled and left his garment in my hands when I held him, and he broke through the door." ¹¹ And the Egyptian saw the garment of Joseph and the broken door, and heard the words of his wife, and cast Joseph into prison into the place where the prisoners were kept whom the king imprisoned. ¹² And he was there in the prison, and the LORD gave Joseph favor in the sight of the chief of the prison guards and compassion before him, for he saw that the LORD was with him, and that the LORD made all that he did to prosper. ¹³ And he committed all things into his hands, and the chief of the prison guards knew of nothing that was with him, for Joseph did everything, and the LORD perfected it. ¹⁴ And he remained there two years. And in those days Pharaoh, king of Egypt, was angry against his two eunuchs, against the chief butler and against the chief baker, and he put them in ward in the house of the chief cook, in the prison where Joseph was kept. ¹⁵ And the chief of the prison guards appointed Joseph to serve them; and he served before them. ¹⁶ And they both dreamed a dream, the chief butler and the chief baker, and they told it to Joseph. ¹⁷ And as he interpreted [the dreams] to them, so it befell them, and Pharaoh restored the chief butler to his office, and he slew the [chief] baker, as Joseph had interpreted to them. ¹⁸ But the chief butler forgot Joseph in the prison, although he had informed him what would befall him, and did not remember to inform Pharaoh how Joseph had told him, for he forgot.

CHAPTER 40

¹ And in those days Pharaoh dreamed two dreams in one night concerning a famine which was to be in all the land, and he awoke from his sleep and called all the interpreters of dreams that were in Egypt, and magicians, and told them his two dreams, and they were not able to declare [the interpretation]. ² And then the chief butler remembered Joseph and spoke of him to the king, and he brought him out from the prison, and he told his two dreams before him. ³ And he said before Pharaoh that his two dreams were one, and he said to him, "Seven years of plenty will come over all the land of Egypt, and after that, seven years

of famine—such a famine as has not been in all the land. ⁴ And now let Pharaoh appoint overseers in all the land of Egypt, and let them store up food in every city throughout the days of the years of plenty, and there will be food for the seven years of famine, and the land will not perish through the famine, for it will be very severe." ⁵ And the LORD gave Joseph favor and mercy in the eyes of Pharaoh, and Pharaoh said to his servants, "We will not find such a wise and discreet man as this man, for the Spirit of the LORD is with him." ⁶ And he appointed him the second in all his kingdom and gave him authority over all Egypt, and caused him to ride in the second chariot of Pharaoh. ⁷ And he clothed him with flax garments, and he put a gold chain on his neck, and [a herald] proclaimed before him "'Êl 'Êl wa' Abîrĕr," and he placed a ring on his hand, and made him ruler over all his house, and magnified him, and said to him, "Only on the throne will I be greater than you." ⁸ And Joseph ruled over all the land of Egypt, and all the princes of Pharaoh, and all his servants, and all who did the king's business loved him, for he walked in uprightness, for he was without pride and arrogance, and he had no respect of persons, and did not accept gifts, but he judged all the people of the land in uprightness. ⁹ And the land of Egypt was at peace before Pharaoh because of Joseph, for the LORD was with him, and gave him favor and mercy for all his generations before all those who knew him and those who heard concerning him, and Pharaoh's kingdom was well ordered, and there was no adversary and no evil person [therein]. ¹⁰ And the king called Joseph's name Sĕphânṭîphâns and gave Joseph the daughter of Potiphar to be [his] wife, the daughter of the priest of Heliopolis, the chief cook [[or chief executioner]]. ¹¹ And on the day that Joseph stood before Pharaoh, he was thirty years old. ¹² And in that year Isaac died. And it came to pass as Joseph had said in the interpretation of his two dreams, according as he had said it, there were seven years of plenty over all the land of Egypt, and the land of Egypt produced abundantly, one measure [producing] eighteen hundred measures. ¹³ And Joseph gathered food into every city until they were full of corn until they could no longer count and measure it for its multitude.

CHAPTER 41

¹ And in the forty-fifth jubilee, in the second week, [and] in the second year, Judah took a wife for his firstborn Er named Tamar, from the daughters of Aram. ² But he hated [her] and did not lie with her, because his mother was of the daughters of Canaan, and he wished to take a wife [for] himself of the countrymen of his mother, but his father Judah would not permit him. ³ And this Er, the firstborn of Judah, was wicked, and the LORD slew him. ⁴ And Judah said to his brother Onan, "Go in to your brother's wife and perform the duty of a husband's brother to her, and raise up seed to your brother." ⁵ And Onan knew that the seed would not be his, [but] his brother's only, and he went into the house of his brother's wife, and spilled the seed on the ground, and he was wicked in the eyes of the LORD, and He slew him. ⁶ And Judah said to his daughter-in-law Tamar, "Remain in your father's house as a widow until my son Shelah is grown up, and I will give you to him to be [his] wife." ⁷ And he grew up, but Bêdsû'êl, the wife of Judah, did not permit her son Shelah to marry. And Bêdsû'êl, the wife of Judah, died in the fifth year of this week. ⁸ And in the sixth year Judah went up to shear his sheep at Timnah. And they told Tamar, "Behold, your father-in-law goes up to Timnah to shear his sheep." ⁹ And she put off her widow's clothes, and put on a veil, and adorned herself, and sat in the gate adjoining the way to Timnah. ¹⁰ And as Judah was going along, he found her, and thought her to be a harlot, and he said to her, "Let me come in to you"; and she said to him, "Come in," and he went in. ¹¹ And she said to him, "Give me my hire"; and he said to her, "I have nothing in my hand except my ring that is on my finger, and my necklace, and my staff which is in my hand." ¹² And she said to him, "Give them to me until you send me my hire"; and he said to her, "I will send a kid of the goats to you"; and he gave them to her, [and he went in to her,] and she conceived by him. ¹³ And Judah went to his sheep, and she went to her father's house. ¹⁴ And Judah sent a kid of the goats by the hand of his shepherd, an Adullamite, and he did not find her; and he asked the people of the place, saying, "Where is the harlot who was here?" And they said to him, "There is no harlot here with us." ¹⁵ And he returned, and informed him, and said to him that he had not found her; "I asked the people of the place, and they said to me, There is no harlot here." And he said, "Let her keep [them] lest we become a cause of derision." ¹⁶ And when she had completed three months, it was manifest that she was with child, and they told Judah, saying, "Behold, your daughter-in-law Tamar is with child by whoredom." ¹⁷ And Judah went to the house of her father, and said to her father and her brothers, "Bring her out, and let them burn her, for she has worked uncleanness in Israel." ¹⁸ And it came to pass when they brought her out to burn her that she sent to her father-in-law the ring, and the necklace, and the staff, saying, "Discern whose these are, for I am with child by him." ¹⁹ And Judah acknowledged [them] and said, "Tamar is more righteous than I am. And therefore, let them not burn her." ²⁰ And for that reason she was not given to Shelah, and he did not approach her again. ²¹ And after that she bore two sons, Perez and Zerah, in the seventh year of this second week. ²² And immediately the seven years of fruitfulness of which Joseph spoke to Pharaoh were accomplished. ²³ And Judah acknowledged that the deed which he had done was evil, for he had lain with his daughter-in-law, and he esteemed it hateful in his

eyes, and he acknowledged that he had transgressed and gone astray, for he had uncovered the skirt of his son, and he began to lament and to supplicate before the LORD because of his transgression. [24] And we told him in a dream that it was forgiven him because he supplicated earnestly, and lamented, and did not commit it again. [25] And he received forgiveness because he turned from his sin and from his ignorance, for he greatly transgressed before our God; and everyone that acts this way, everyone who lies with his mother-in-law, let them burn him with fire that he may burn therein, for there is uncleanness and pollution on them; let them burn them with fire. [26] And you command the sons of Israel that there is no uncleanness among them, for everyone who lies with his daughter-in-law or with his mother-in-law has worked uncleanness; let them burn the man who has lain with her with fire, and likewise the woman, and he will turn away wrath and punishment from Israel. [27] And to Judah we said that his two sons had not lain with her, and for this reason his seed was established for a second generation and would not be rooted out. [28] For in singleness of eye he had gone and sought for punishment, namely, according to the judgment of Abraham, which he had commanded his sons, Judah had sought to burn her with fire.

CHAPTER 42

[1] And in the first year of the third week of the forty-fifth jubilee the famine began to come into the land, and the rain refused to be given to the earth, for none fell whatsoever. [2] And the earth grew barren, but in the land of Egypt there was food, for Joseph had gathered the seed of the land in the seven years of plenty and had preserved it. [3] And the Egyptians came to Joseph that he might give them food, and he opened the storehouses where the grain of the first year was, and he sold it to the people of the land for gold. [4] [[Now the famine was very severe in the land of Canaan]], and Jacob heard that there was food in Egypt, and he sent his ten sons that they should procure food for him in Egypt, but he did not send Benjamin; and they arrived [in Egypt] among those that went [there.] [5] And Joseph recognized them, but they did not recognize him, and he spoke to them and questioned them, and he said to them, "Are you not spies, and have you not come to explore the approaches of the land?" And he put them in ward. [6] And after that, he set them free again, and detained Simeon alone, and sent off his nine brothers. [7] And he filled their sacks with corn, and he put their gold in their sacks, and they did not know. [8] And he commanded them to bring their younger brother, for they had told him their father was living and [also] their younger brother. [9] And they went up from the land of Egypt and they came to the land of Canaan; and they told their father all that had befallen them, and how the lord of the country had spoken roughly

to them and had seized Simeon until they should bring Benjamin. [10] And Jacob said, "You have bereaved me of my children! Joseph is not, and Simeon is also not, and you will take Benjamin away. Your wickedness has come on me." [11] And he said, "My son will not go down with you lest perhaps he falls sick, for their mother gave birth to two sons, and one has perished, and you will also take this one from me. If perhaps he took a fever on the road, you would bring down my old age with sorrow to death." [12] For he saw that their money had been returned to each man in his sack, and for this reason he feared to send him. [13] And the famine increased and became severe in the land of Canaan, and in all lands except in the land of Egypt, for many of the children of the Egyptians had stored up their seed for food from the time when they saw Joseph gathering seed together, and putting it in storehouses, and preserving it for the years of famine. [14] And the people of Egypt fed themselves thereon during the first year of their famine. [15] But when Israel saw that the famine was very severe in the land and there was no deliverance, he said to his sons, "Go again, and procure food for us that we do not die." [16] And they said, "We will not go; unless our youngest brother goes with us, we will not go." [17] And Israel saw that if he did not send him with them, they should all perish by reason of the famine. [18] And Reuben said, "Give him into my hand, and if I do not bring him back to you, slay my two sons instead of his soul." And he said to him, "He will not go with you." [19] And Judah came near and said, "Send him with me, and if I do not bring him back to you, let me bear the blame before you all the days of my life." [20] And he sent him with them in the second year of this week, on the first day of the month, and they came to the land of Egypt with all those who went, and [they had] presents in their hands: stacte, and almonds, and terebinth nuts, and pure honey. [21] And they went and stood before Joseph, and he saw his brother Benjamin, and he knew him, and said to them, "Is this your youngest brother?" And they said to him, "It is he." And he said, "The LORD be gracious to you, my son!" [22] And he sent him into his house, and he brought Simeon out to them, and he made a feast for them, and they presented the gift to him which they had brought in their hands. [23] And they ate before him and he gave them all a portion, but the portion of Benjamin was seven times larger than that of any of theirs. [24] And they ate, and drank, and arose, and remained with their donkeys. [25] And Joseph devised a plan whereby he might learn their thoughts as to whether thoughts of peace prevailed among them, and he said to the steward who was over his house: "Fill all their sacks with food, and return their money to them into their vessels, and my cup, the silver cup out of which I drink, put it in the sack of the youngest, and send them away."

CHAPTER 43

[1] And he did as Joseph had told him and filled all their sacks for them with food, and put their money in their sacks, and put the cup in Benjamin's sack. [2] And early in the morning they departed, and it came to pass that, when they had gone from there, Joseph said to the steward of his house, "Pursue them, run and seize them, saying, For good you have repaid me with evil; you have stolen from me the silver cup out of which my lord drinks. And bring back their youngest brother to me, and fetch [him] quickly before I go out to my seat of judgment." [3] And he ran after them and said to them according to these words. [4] And they said to him, "God forbid that your servants should do this thing, and steal from the house of your lord any utensil, and also the money which we found in our sacks the first time, we, your servants, brought back from the land of Canaan. [5] How then should we steal any utensil? Behold, here we are and our sacks; search, and wherever you find the cup in the sack of any man among us, let him be slain, and we and our donkeys will serve your lord." [6] And he said to them, "Not so; the man with whom I find [it], him only will I take as a servant, and you will return to your house in peace." [7] And as he was searching in their vessels, beginning with the eldest and ending with the youngest, it was found in Benjamin's sack. [8] And they tore their garments, and loaded their donkeys, and returned to the city, and came to the house of Joseph, and they all bowed themselves on their faces to the ground before him. [9] And Joseph said to them, "You have done evil." And they said, "What will we say and how will we defend ourselves? Our lord has discovered the transgression of his servants; behold, we are the servants of our lord, and our donkeys also." [10] And Joseph said to them, "I also fear the LORD; as for you, go to your homes and let your brother be my servant, for you have done evil. Do you not know that a man delights in his cup as I with this cup? And yet you have stolen it from me." [11] And Judah said, "O my lord, please let your servant speak a word in my lord's ear; your servant's mother bore two brothers to our father; one went away and was lost, and has not been found, and he alone is left of his mother, and your servant, our father, loves him, and his life is also bound up with the life of this [youth]. [12] And it will come to pass, when we go to your servant, our father, and the youth is not with us, that he will die, and we will bring down our father with sorrow to death. [13] Now rather let me, your servant, abide instead of the boy as a bondsman to my lord, and let the youth go with his brothers, for I became a guarantee for him at the hand of your servant, our father, and if I do not bring him back, your servant will bear the blame to our father forever." [14] And Joseph saw that they were all in accord in goodness with one another, and he could not refrain himself, and he told them that he was Joseph. [15] And he conversed with them in the Hebrew tongue and fell on their neck and wept. But they did not recognize him, and they began to weep. [16] And he said to them, "Do not weep over me, but hurry and bring my father to me; and you see that it is my mouth that speaks, and the eyes of my brother Benjamin see. [17] For behold, this is the second year of the famine, and there are still five years without harvest, or fruit, of trees, or plowing. [18] Come down quickly, you and your households, so that you do not perish through the famine, and do not be grieved for your possessions, for the LORD sent me before you to set things in order that many people might live. [19] And tell my father that I am still alive, and you, behold, you see that the LORD has made me as a father to Pharaoh, and ruler over his house and over all the land of Egypt. [20] And tell my father of all my glory, and all the riches and glory that the LORD has given Me." [21] And by the command of the mouth of Pharaoh he gave them chariots and provisions for the way, and he gave them all many-colored raiment[s] and silver. [22] And to their father he sent raiment, and silver, and ten donkeys which carried corn, and he sent them away. [23] And they went up and told their father that Joseph was alive and was measuring out corn to all the nations of the earth, and that he was ruler over all the land of Egypt. [24] And their father did not believe it, for he was beside himself in his mind, but when he saw the wagons which Joseph had sent, the life of his spirit revived, and he said, "It is enough for me if Joseph lives; I will go down and see him before I die."

CHAPTER 44

[1] And Israel took his journey from Haran from his house on the new moon of the third month, and he went on the way of the Well of the Oath, and he offered a sacrifice to the God of his father Isaac on the seventh of this month. [2] And Jacob remembered the dream that he had seen at Bethel, and he feared to go down into Egypt. [3] And while he was thinking of sending word to Joseph to come to him, and that he would not go down, he remained there seven days, if perhaps he should see a vision as to whether he should remain or go down. [4] And he celebrated the harvest festival of the first-fruits with old grain, for in all the land of Canaan there was not [even] a handful of seed, for the famine was over all the beasts, and cattle, and birds, and also over man. [5] And on the sixteenth [day] the LORD appeared to him, and said to him, "Jacob, Jacob"; and he said, "Here I am." And He said to him, "I am the God of your fathers, the God of Abraham and Isaac; do not fear to go down into Egypt, for I will make of you a great nation there. [6] I will go down with you, and I will bring you up [again], and you will be buried in this land, and Joseph will put his hands on your eyes. Do not fear; go down into Egypt." [7] And his sons rose up, and his sons' sons, and they placed their father and their possessions on wagons. [8] And Israel rose up from the Well of the Oath on the

sixteenth [day] of this third month, and he went to the land of Egypt. [9] And Israel sent Judah before him to his son Joseph to examine the land of Goshen, for Joseph had told his brothers that they should come and dwell there that they might be near him. [10] And this was the excellent [land] in the land of Egypt, and near to him, for all [of them] and also for the cattle. [11] And these are the names of the sons of Jacob who went into Egypt with their father Jacob: [12] Reuben, the firstborn of Israel; and these are the names of his sons: Enoch, and Pallu, and Hezron, and Carmi—five. [13] Simeon and his sons; and these are the names of his sons: Jemuel, and Jamin, and Ohad, and Jachin, and Zohar, and Shaul, the son of the Zephathite woman—seven. [14] Levi and his sons; and these are the names of his sons: Gershon, and Kohath, and Merari—four. [15] Judah and his sons; and these are the names of his sons: Shela, and Perez, and Zerah—four. [16] Issachar and his sons; and these are the names of his sons: Tola, and Phûa, and Jâsûb, and Shimron—five. [17] Zebulun and his sons; and these are the names of his sons: Sered, and Elon, and Jahleel—four. [18] And these are the sons of Jacob, and their sons, whom Leah bore to Jacob in Mesopotamia—six, and their one sister, Dinah. And all the souls of the sons of Leah, and their sons, who went with their father Jacob into Egypt, were twenty-nine, and their father Jacob being with them, they were thirty. [19] And the sons of Zilpah, Leah's handmaid, the wife of Jacob, whom she bore to Jacob: Gad and Asher. [20] And these are the names of their sons who went with him into Egypt: the sons of Gad: Ziphion, and Haggi, and Shuni, and Ezbon, [and Eri,] and Areli, and Arodi—eight. [21] And the sons of Asher: Imnah, and Ishvah, [and Ishvi], and Beriah, and Serah, their one sister—six. [22] All the souls were fourteen, and all those of Leah were forty-four. [23] And the sons of Rachel, the wife of Jacob: Joseph and Benjamin. [24] And there were born to Joseph in Egypt, before his father came into Egypt, those whom Asenath, daughter of Potiphar priest of Heliopolis, bore to him: Manasseh and Ephraim—three. [25] And the sons of Benjamin: Bela, and Becher, and Ashbel, Gera, and Naaman, and Ehi, and Rosh, and Muppim, and Huppim, and Ard—eleven. [26] And all the souls of Rachel were fourteen. [27] And the sons of Bilhah, the handmaid of Rachel, the wife of Jacob, whom she bore to Jacob, were Dan and Naphtali. [28] And these are the names of their sons who went with them into Egypt: and the sons of Dan were Hushim, and Sâmôn, and Asûdî, and 'Îjâka, and Salômôn—six. [29] And they died the year in which they entered into Egypt, and there was left to Dan Hushim alone. [30] And these are the names of the sons of Naphtali: Jahziel, and Guni, and Jezer, and Shallum, and 'Îv. [31] And 'Îv, who was born after the years of famine, died in Egypt. [32] And all the souls of Rachel were twenty-six. [33] And all the souls of Jacob which went into Egypt were seventy souls. These are his children

and his children's children, seventy in all; but five died in Egypt before Joseph and had no children. [34] And in the land of Canaan two sons of Judah died, Er and Onan, and they had no children, and the sons of Israel buried those who perished, and they were reckoned among the seventy nations.

CHAPTER 45

[1] And Israel went into the country of Egypt, into the land of Goshen, on the new moon of the fourth month, in the second year of the third week of the forty-fifth jubilee. [2] And Joseph went to meet his father Jacob, to the land of Goshen, and he fell on his father's neck and wept. [3] And Israel said to Joseph, "Now let me die since I have seen you, and now may the LORD God of Israel be blessed, the God of Abraham and the God of Isaac who has not withheld His mercy and His grace from His servant Jacob. [4] It is enough for me that I have seen your face while I am yet alive; yes, the vision which I saw at Bethel is true. Blessed is the LORD my God forever and ever and blessed is His Name." [5] And Joseph and his brothers ate bread before their father and drank wine, and Jacob rejoiced with exceedingly great joy because he saw Joseph eating with his brothers and drinking before him, and he blessed the Creator of all things who had preserved him and had preserved his twelve sons for him. [6] And Joseph had given to his father and to his brothers as a gift the right of dwelling in the land of Goshen, and in Rameses, and all the surrounding region, which he ruled over before Pharaoh. And Israel and his sons dwelt in the land of Goshen, the best part of the land of Egypt; and Israel was one hundred and thirty years old when he came into Egypt, [7] and Joseph nourished his father, and his brothers, and also their possessions with as much bread as they needed for the seven years of the famine. [8] And the land of Egypt suffered by reason of the famine, and Joseph acquired all the land of Egypt for Pharaoh in return for food, and he got possession of the people, and their cattle, and everything for Pharaoh. [9] And the years of the famine were accomplished, and Joseph gave seed and food to the people in the land that they might sow in the eighth year, for the river had overflowed all the land of Egypt. [10] For in the seven years of the famine it had not overflowed and had irrigated only a few places on the banks of the river, but now it overflowed, and the Egyptians sowed the land, and it bore much corn that year. [11] And this was the first year of the fourth week of the forty-fifth jubilee. [12] And Joseph took the fifth part of the corn of the harvest for the king and left four parts for them for food and for seed, and Joseph made it an ordinance for the land of Egypt until this day. [13] And Israel lived in the land of Egypt [for] seventeen years, and all the days which he lived were three jubilees, one hundred and forty-seven years, and he died in the fourth year of the fifth week of the forty-fifth jubilee. [14] And Israel blessed his sons

before he died and told them everything that would befall them in the land of Egypt; and he made known to them what would come on them in the last days, and blessed them, and gave two portions to Joseph in the land. ¹⁵ And he slept with his fathers, and he was buried in the double cave in the land of Canaan, near his father Abraham in the grave which he dug for himself in the double cave in the land of Hebron. ¹⁶ And he gave all his scrolls and the scrolls of his fathers to his son Levi that he might preserve them and renew them for his children until this day.

CHAPTER 46

¹ And it came to pass that after Jacob died, the sons of Israel multiplied in the land of Egypt, and they became a great nation, and they were of one accord in heart, so that brother loved brother and every man helped his brother, and they increased abundantly and multiplied exceedingly [for] ten weeks of years, all the days of the life of Joseph. ² And there was no adversary nor any evil all the days of the life of Joseph which he lived after his father Jacob, for all the Egyptians honored the sons of Israel all the days of the life of Joseph. ³ And Joseph died being one hundred and ten years old; he lived seventeen years in the land of Canaan, and he was a servant [for] ten years, and [he was] in prison [for] three years, and he was under the king [for] eighty years, ruling all the land of Egypt. ⁴ And he died, and all his brothers, and all that generation. ⁵ And he commanded the sons of Israel before he died that they should carry his bones with them when they went out from the land of Egypt. ⁶ And he made them swear regarding his bones, for he knew that the Egyptians would not again bring out and bury him in the land of Canaan, for Mâkamârôn, king of Canaan, while dwelling in the land of Assyria, fought in the valley with the king of Egypt and slew him there, and pursued after the Egyptians to the gates of 'Êrmôn. ⁷ But he was not able to enter, for another, a new king, had become king of Egypt, and he was stronger than he, and he returned to the land of Canaan, and the gates of Egypt were closed, and none went out and none came into Egypt. ⁸ And Joseph died in the forty-sixth jubilee, in the sixth week, in the second year, and they buried him in the land of Egypt, and his brothers died after him. ⁹ And the king of Egypt went out to war with the king of Canaan in the forty-seventh jubilee, in the second week, in the second year, and the sons of Israel brought out all the bones of the children of Jacob save the bones of Joseph, and they buried them in the field in the double cave in the mountain. ¹⁰ And most [of them] returned to Egypt, but a few of them remained in the mountains of Hebron, and your father Amram remained with them. ¹¹ And the king of Canaan was victorious over the king of Egypt, and he closed the gates of Egypt. ¹² And he devised an evil scheme against the sons of Israel of afflicting them; and he said to the people of Egypt, ¹³ "Behold, the people of the sons of Israel have increased and multiplied more than we. Come and let us deal wisely with them before they become too many, and let us afflict them with slavery before war comes on us and before they, too, fight against us, otherwise they will join themselves to our enemies; and get them out of our land, for their hearts and faces are toward the land of Canaan." ¹⁴ And he set taskmasters over them to afflict them with slavery; and they built strong cities for Pharaoh, Pithom and Raamses, and they built all the walls and all the fortifications which had fallen in the cities of Egypt. ¹⁵ And they made them serve with rigor, and the more they dealt evilly with them, the more they increased and multiplied. ¹⁶ And the people of Egypt despised the sons of Israel.

CHAPTER 47

¹ And in the seventh week, in the seventh year, in the forty-seventh jubilee, your father went out from the land of Canaan, and you were born in the fourth week, in the sixth year thereof, in the forty-eighth jubilee; this was the time of tribulation on the sons of Israel. ² And Pharaoh, king of Egypt, issued a command regarding them that they should cast all their male children which were born into the river. ³ And they cast them in for seven months until the day that you were born. And your mother hid you for three months, and they told [the Egyptians] regarding her. ⁴ And she made an ark for you, and covered it with pitch and asphalt, and placed it in the flags on the bank of the river, and she placed you in it [for] seven days, and your mother came by night and suckled you, and by day your sister Miriam guarded you from the birds. ⁵ And in those days Tharmuth, the daughter of Pharaoh, came to bathe in the river, and she heard your voice crying, and she told her maidens to bring you out, and they brought you to her. ⁶ And she took you out of the ark, and she had compassion on you. ⁷ And your sister said to her, "Will I go and call to you one of the Hebrew women to nurse and suckle this baby for you?" And she said, "Go." ⁸ And she went and called your mother Jochebed, and she gave her wages, and she nursed you. ⁹ And afterward, when you were grown up, they brought you to the daughter of Pharaoh, and you became her son, and your father Amram taught you writing, and after you had completed three weeks, they brought you into the royal court. ¹⁰ And you were three weeks of years at court until the time when you went out from the royal court and saw an Egyptian striking your friend who was of the sons of Israel, and you slew him and hid him in the sand. ¹¹ And on the second day you found two of the sons of Israel striving together, and you said to him who was doing the wrong: "Why do you strike your brother?" ¹² And he was angry and indignant, and said, "Who made you a prince and a judge over us? Do you think to kill me as you killed

the Egyptian yesterday?" And you were afraid and fled on account of these words.

CHAPTER 48

[1] And in the sixth year of the third week of the forty-ninth jubilee you departed and dwelt in the land of Midian [for] five weeks and one year. And you returned into Egypt in the second week, in the second year, in the fiftieth jubilee. [2] And you yourself know what He spoke to you on Mount Sinai, and what prince Mastêmâ desired to do with you when you were returning into Egypt on the way when you met him at the lodging-place. [3] Did he not, with all his power, seek to slay you and deliver the Egyptians out of your hand when he saw that you were sent to execute judgment and vengeance on the Egyptians? [4] And I delivered you out of his hand, and you performed the signs and wonders which you were sent to perform in Egypt against Pharaoh, and against all his house, and against his servants and his people. [5] And the LORD executed a great vengeance on them for Israel's sake, and struck them through blood and frogs, lice and biting flies, and malignant boils breaking out in blisters, and their cattle by death, and by hailstones, thereby He destroyed everything that grew for them, and by locusts which devoured the residue which had been left by the hail, and by darkness, and [by the death] of the firstborn of men and animals, and on all their idols the LORD took vengeance and burned them with fire. [6] And everything was sent through your hand, that you should declare [these things] before they were done, and you spoke with the king of Egypt before all his servants and before his people. [7] And everything took place according to your words; ten great and terrible judgments came on the land of Egypt that you might execute vengeance on it for Israel. [8] And the LORD did everything for Israel's sake, and according to His covenant, which He had ordained with Abraham that He would take vengeance on them as they had brought them into bondage by force. [9] And the prince of the Mastêmâ stood up against you and sought to cast you into the hands of Pharaoh, and he helped the Egyptian sorcerers, and they stood up and worked before you. [10] We indeed permitted them to work the evils, but we did not allow the remedies to be worked by their hands. [11] And the LORD struck them with malignant ulcers, and they were not able to stand, for we destroyed them so that they could not perform a single sign. [12] And notwithstanding all [these] signs and wonders, the prince of the Mastêmâ was not put to shame because he took courage and cried to the Egyptians to pursue after you with all the powers of the Egyptians, with their chariots, and with their horses, and with all the hosts of the peoples of Egypt. [13] And I stood between the Egyptians and Israel, and we delivered Israel out of his hand, and out of the hand of his people, and the LORD brought them through the midst of the sea as if it were dry land. [14] And all the peoples whom he brought to pursue after Israel, the LORD our God cast them into the midst of the sea, into the depths of the abyss beneath the sons of Israel, even as the people of Egypt had cast their children into the river. He took vengeance on one million of them, and one thousand strong and energetic men were destroyed on account of one suckling of the children of your people which they had thrown into the river. [15] And on the fourteenth day, and on the fifteenth, and on the sixteenth, and on the seventeenth, and on the eighteenth, the prince of the Mastêmâ was bound and imprisoned behind the sons of Israel that he might not accuse them. [16] And on the nineteenth [day] we let them loose that they might help the Egyptians and pursue the sons of Israel. [17] And He hardened their hearts and made them stubborn, and the device was devised by the LORD our God that He might strike the Egyptians and cast them into the sea. [18] And on the fourteenth [day] we bound him that he might not accuse the sons of Israel on the day when they asked the Egyptians for vessels and garments, vessels of silver, and vessels of gold, and vessels of bronze, in order to despoil the Egyptians in return for the bondage in which they had forced them to serve. [19] And we did not lead out the sons of Israel from Egypt empty-handed.

CHAPTER 49

[1] Remember the command which the LORD commanded you concerning the Passover, that you should celebrate it in its season on the fourteenth of the first month, that you should kill it before it is evening, and that they should eat it by night on the evening of the fifteenth from the time of the setting of the sun. [2] For on this night—the beginning of the festival and the beginning of the joy—you were eating the Passover in Egypt, when all the powers of Mastêmâ had been let loose to slay all the firstborn in the land of Egypt, from the firstborn of Pharaoh to the firstborn of the captive maidservant in the mill, and to the cattle. [3] And this is the sign which the LORD gave them: into every house on the lintels of which they saw the blood of a lamb of the first year, into [that] house they should not enter to slay, but should pass by [it], that all those should be saved that were in the house because the sign of the blood was on its lintels. [4] And the powers of the LORD did everything according as the LORD commanded them, and they passed by all the sons of Israel, and the plague did not come on them to destroy any soul from among them, either of cattle, or man, or dog. [5] And the plague was very grievous in Egypt, and there was no house in Egypt where there was not someone dead, and weeping, and lamentation. [6] And all Israel was eating the flesh of the Passover lamb, and drinking the wine, and was lauding and blessing, and giving thanks to the LORD God of their fathers, and was ready to go

out from under the yoke of Egypt and from the evil bondage. ⁷ And remember this day all the days of your life and observe it from year to year all the days of your life, once a year, on its day, according to all the law thereof, and do not adjourn [it] from day to day, or from month to month. ⁸ For it is a perpetual ordinance and engraved on the heavenly tablets regarding all the sons of Israel that they should observe it every year, on its day, once a year, throughout all their generations; and there is no limit of days, for this is ordained forever. ⁹ And the man who is free from uncleanness and does not come to observe it on occasion of its day so as to bring an acceptable offering before the LORD, and to eat and to drink before the LORD on the day of its festival, that man who is clean and close at hand will be cut off, because he did not offer the oblation of the LORD in its appointed season; he will take the guilt on himself. ¹⁰ Let the sons of Israel come and observe the Passover on the day of its fixed time, on the fourteenth day of the first month, between the evenings, from the third part of the day to the third part of the night, for two portions of the day are given to the light, and a third part to the evening. ¹¹ That is that which the LORD commanded you that you should observe it between the evenings. ¹² And it is not permissible to slay it during any period of the light, but during the period bordering on the evening, and let them eat it at the time of the evening until the third part of the night, and whatever is leftover of all its flesh from the third part of the night and onwards, let them burn it with fire. ¹³ And they will not cook it with water, nor will they eat it raw, but roast on the fire: they will eat it with diligence, its head with the inwards thereof and its feet they will roast with fire, and not break any bone thereof, for no bone of the sons of Israel will be crushed. ¹⁴ For this reason the LORD commanded the sons of Israel to observe the Passover on the day of its fixed time, and they will not break a bone thereof, for it is a festival day, and a day commanded, and there may be no passing over from day to day, and month to month, but on the day of its festival let it be observed. ¹⁵ And command the sons of Israel to observe the Passover throughout their days, every year, once a year on the day of its fixed time, and it will come for a memorial well pleasing before the LORD, and no plague will come on them to slay or to strike in that year in which they celebrate the Passover in its season in every respect according to His command. ¹⁶ And they will not eat it outside the sanctuary of the LORD, but before the sanctuary of the LORD, and all the people of the congregation of Israel will celebrate it in its appointed season. ¹⁷ And every man who has come on its day will eat it in the sanctuary of your God before the LORD from twenty years old and upward, for thus it is written and ordained that they should eat it in the sanctuary of the LORD. ¹⁸ And when the sons of Israel come into the land which they are to possess, into the land of Canaan, and set up the Dwelling Place of the LORD in the midst of the land in one of their tribes until the sanctuary of the LORD has been built in the land, let them come and celebrate the Passover in the midst of the Dwelling Place of the LORD, and let them slay it before the LORD from year to year. ¹⁹ And in the days when the house has been built in the Name of the LORD in the land of their inheritance, they will go there and slay the Passover in the evening, at sunset, at the third part of the day. ²⁰ And they will offer its blood on the threshold of the altar and will place its fat on the fire which is on the altar, and they will eat its flesh roasted with fire in the court of the house which has been sanctified in the Name of the LORD. ²¹ And they may not celebrate the Passover in their cities, nor in any place except before the Dwelling Place of the LORD, or before His house where His Name has dwelt; and they will not go astray from the LORD. ²² And you, Moses: command the sons of Israel to observe the ordinances of the Passover, as it was commanded to you; declare to them every year and the day of its days, and the festival of unleavened bread, that they should eat unleavened bread [for] seven days, [and] that they should observe its festival, and that they bring an oblation every day during those seven days of joy before the LORD on the altar of your God. ²³ For you celebrated this festival when you went out from Egypt until you entered into the wilderness of Shur, for you completed it on the shore of the sea.

CHAPTER 50

¹ And after this law I made known to you the days of the Sabbaths in the wilderness of Zin, which is between Elim and Sinai. ² And I told you of the Sabbaths of the land on Mount Sinai, and I told you of the jubilee years in the Sabbaths of years, but the year thereof I have not told you until you enter the land which you are to possess. ³ And the land will also keep its Sabbaths while they dwell on it, and they will know the jubilee year. ⁴ For that reason I have ordained for you the year-weeks, and the years, and the jubilees: there are forty-nine jubilees from the days of Adam until this day, and one week and two years, and there are yet forty years more for learning the commands of the LORD, until they pass over into the land of Canaan, crossing the Jordan to the west. ⁵ And the jubilees will pass by, until Israel is cleansed from all guilt of fornication, and uncleanness, and pollution, and sin, and error, and dwells with confidence in all the land, and there will no longer be an adversary or any evil one, and the land will be clean from that time forevermore. ⁶ And behold, the command regarding the Sabbaths—I have written [them] down for you and all the judgments of its laws. ⁷ Six days you will labor, but on the seventh day is the Sabbath of the LORD your God. In it you will do no manner of work—you, and your sons, and your

menservants, and your maidservants, and all your cattle, and the sojourner who is also with you. [8] And the man that does any work on it will die: whoever desecrates that day, whoever lies with [his] wife, or whoever says he will do something on it, that he will set out on a journey thereon in regard to any buying or selling, and whoever draws water thereon which he had not prepared for himself on the sixth day, and whoever takes up any burden to carry it out of his tent or out of his house will die. [9] You will do no work whatsoever on the Sabbath day except [to utilize] what you have prepared for yourselves on the sixth day, so as to eat, and drink, and rest, and keep Sabbath from all work on that day, and to bless the LORD your God who has given you a day of festival, and a holy day; and a day of the holy kingdom for all Israel is this day among their days forever. [10] For great is the honor which the LORD has given to Israel that they should eat, and drink, and be satisfied on this festival day, and rest thereon from all labor which belongs to the labor of the children of men, except burning frankincense and bringing oblations and sacrifices before the LORD for days and for Sabbaths. [11] Only this work will be done on the Sabbaths in the sanctuary of the LORD your God, that they may atone for Israel with sacrifice continually from day to day for a memorial well-pleasing before the LORD, and that He may always receive them from day to day according as you have been commanded. [12] And every man who does any work thereon, or goes on a journey, or tills [his] farm, whether in his house or any other place, and whoever lights a fire, or rides on any beast, or travels by ship on the sea, and whoever strikes or kills anything, or slaughters a beast or a bird, or whoever catches an animal, or a bird, or a fish, or whoever fasts or makes war on the Sabbaths: [13] the man who does any of these things on the Sabbath will die, so that the sons of Israel will observe the Sabbaths according to the commands regarding the Sabbaths of the land, as it is written in the tablets, which He gave into My hands that I should write out for you—the laws of the seasons and the seasons according to the division of their days. The account of the division of the days is completed.

1 ENOCH

The Book of Enoch (also called 1 Enoch) is an ancient Jewish religious work, ascribed by tradition to Enoch, the great-grandfather of Noah. Enoch contains unique material on the origins of supernatural demons and giants, why some messengers fell from Heaven, an explanation of why the Great Flood was morally necessary, and prophetic exposition of the thousand-year reign of the Messiah. It is wholly extant only in the Ge'ez language, with Aramaic fragments from the Dead Sea Scrolls and a few Greek and Latin fragments. Jude 1:14–15 is a direct quote of Enoch 1:9 (see also 1 Enoch 60:8). Enoch is composed of five sections.

SECTION 1:
THE BOOK OF THE WATCHERS

CHAPTER 1

¹ THE WORDS OF THE BLESSING OF ENOCH, WITH WHICH HE BLESSED THE CHOSEN ONES AND RIGHTEOUS, WHO WILL BE LIVING IN THE DAY OF TRIBULATION, WHEN ALL THE WICKED AND GODLESS ARE TO BE REMOVED. ² And he took up his allegory and spoke—Enoch a righteous man, whose eyes were opened by God, saw the vision of the Holy One in the heavens, which the messengers showed me, and from them I heard everything, and from them I understood as I saw, but not for this generation, but for a remote one which is to come. ³ Concerning the chosen ones, I spoke and took up my allegory concerning them: The Holy Great One will come out from His dwelling, ⁴ And the perpetual God will tread on the earth, [even] on Mount Sinai, ‖ And appear in the strength of His might from the Heaven of heavens. ⁵ And all will be smitten with fear, ‖ And the Watchers will quake, ‖ And great fear and trembling will seize them to the ends of the earth. ⁶ And the high mountains will be shaken, ‖ And the high hills will be made low ‖ And will melt like wax before the flame, ⁷ And the earth will be wholly split apart, ‖ And all that is on the earth will perish, ‖ And there will be a judgment on all [men]. ⁸ But with the righteous He will make peace, ‖ And will protect the chosen ones, ‖ And mercy will be on them. And they will all belong to God, ‖ And they will be prospered, ‖ And they will all be blessed. And He will help them all, ‖ And light will appear to them, ‖ And He will make peace with them. ⁹ And behold, He comes with myriads of His holy ones to execute judgment on all, ‖ And to destroy all the ungodly, ‖ And to convict all flesh of all the works of their ungodliness which they have ungodly committed, ‖ And of all the hard things which ungodly sinners have spoken against Him.

CHAPTER 2

¹ Observe everything that takes place in the heavens, how they do not change their orbits, and the luminaries which are in the heavens, how they all rise and set in order, each in its season, and do not transgress against their appointed order. ² Behold the earth and give heed to the things which take place on it from first to last, how steadfast they are, how none of the things on earth change, but all the works of God appear to you. ³ Behold the summer and the winter, how the whole earth is filled with water, and clouds, and dew, and rain lie on it.

CHAPTER 3

¹ Observe and see how [in the winter] all the trees seem as though they had withered and shed all their leaves, ² except fourteen trees, which do not lose their foliage but retain the old foliage from two to three years until the new comes.

CHAPTER 4

¹ And again, observe the days of summer, how the sun is above the earth—over against it. ² And you seek shade and shelter by reason of the heat of the sun, and the earth also burns with growing heat, and so you cannot tread on the earth, or on a rock by reason of its heat.

CHAPTER 5

¹ Observe how the trees cover themselves with green leaves and bear fruit; for what reason, take heed and know with regard to all His works and recognize how He that lives forever has made them so. ² And all His works go on like this from year to year forever, and all the tasks which they accomplish for Him, and their tasks do not change, but according as God has ordained so it is done. ³ And behold how the sea and the rivers accomplish [their tasks] in like manner and do not change their tasks from His commands. ⁴ But you have not been steadfast, ‖ Nor done the commands of the LORD, ‖ But you have turned away and spoken proud and hard words ‖ With your impure mouths against His greatness. O you hard-hearted! You will find no peace. ⁵ Therefore you will execrate your days, ‖ And the years of your life will perish, ‖ And the years of your destruction will be multiplied in continuous execration, ‖ And you will find no mercy. ⁶ In those days you will make your names a continuous execration to all the righteous, ‖ And by you will all who curse, curse, ‖ And all the sinners and godless will imprecate by you, ‖ And for you, the godless, there will be a curse. And all the [righteous] will rejoice, ‖ And there will be forgiveness of sins, ‖ And every mercy, and peace, and forbearance: There

1 ENOCH

will be salvation to them, an excellent light. And for all of you sinners there will be no salvation, || But a curse will abide on all of you. ⁷But for the chosen ones there will be light, and joy, and peace, || And they will inherit the earth. ⁸And then wisdom will be bestowed on the chosen ones, || And they will all live and never again sin, || Either through ungodliness or through pride, || But they who are wise will be humble. ⁹And they will not transgress again, || Nor will they sin all the days of their life, || Nor will they die of [the divine] anger or wrath, || But they will complete the number of the days of their life. And their lives will be increased in peace, || And the years of their joy will be multiplied, || In continuous gladness and peace, all the days of their life.

CHAPTER 6

¹And it came to pass when the children of men had multiplied that in those days were born to them beautiful and attractive daughters. ²And the messengers, the children of the heavens, saw and lusted after them, and said to one another, "Come, let us choose wives [for] ourselves from among the children of men and beget children [for] ourselves." ³And Semjaza, who was their leader, said to them, "Indeed, I fear you will not agree to do this deed, and I alone will have to pay the penalty of a great sin." ⁴And they all answered him and said, "Let us all swear an oath, and all bind ourselves by mutual imprecations not to abandon this plan but to do this thing." ⁵Then they all swore together and bound themselves by mutual imprecations on it. ⁶And they were two hundred in all who descended in the days of Jared on the summit of Mount Hermon, and they called it Mount Hermon, because they had sworn and bound themselves by mutual imprecations on it. ⁷And these are the names of their leaders: their leader Semjaza, [and] Araklba, Rameel, Kokablel, Tamlel, Ramlel, Danel, Ezeqeel, Baraqijal, Asael, Armaros, Batarel, Ananel, Zaqiel, Samsapeel, Satarel, Turel, Jomjael, [and] Sariel. ⁸These are their chiefs of tens.

CHAPTER 7

¹And all the others took wives to themselves together with them, and each chose one for himself, and they began to go in to them and to defile themselves with them, and they taught them charms and enchantments, and the cutting of roots, and made them acquainted with plants. ²And they became pregnant, and they bore great giants, whose height was [[three thousand ells]], ³who consumed all the acquisitions of men. And when men could no longer sustain them, ⁴the giants turned against them and devoured mankind. ⁵And they began to sin against birds, and beasts, and reptiles, and fish, and to devour one another's flesh, and drink the blood. ⁶Then the earth laid accusation against the lawless ones.

CHAPTER 8

¹And Azazel taught men to make swords, and knives, and shields, and breastplates, and made known to them the metals of the earth and the craft of working them, and bracelets, and ornaments, and the use of antimony, and the beautifying of the eyelids, and all kinds of costly stones, and all coloring tinctures. ²And there arose much godlessness, and they committed fornication, and they were led astray, and became corrupt in all their ways. ³Semjaza taught enchantments and root-cuttings, 'Armaros the resolving of enchantments, Baraqijal [taught] astrology, Kokabel the constellations, Ezeqeel the knowledge of the clouds, Araqiel the signs of the earth, Shamsiel the signs of the sun, and Sariel the course of the moon. And as men perished, they cried, and their cry went up to Heaven.

CHAPTER 9

¹And then Michael, Uriel, Raphael, and Gabriel looked down from Heaven and saw much blood being shed on the earth, and all lawlessness being worked on the earth. ²And they said to one another, "The earth made without inhabitant cries the voice of their crying up to the gates of Heaven." ³And now to you, the holy ones of Heaven, the souls of men make their suit, saying, "Bring our cause before the Most High." ⁴And they said to the Lord of the ages, "Lord of lords, God of gods, King of kings, and God of the ages, the throne of Your glory stands to all the generations of the ages, and Your Name [is] holy, and glorious, and blessed to all the ages! ⁵You have made all things and have power over all things: and all things are naked and open in Your sight, and You see all things, and nothing can hide itself from You. ⁶You see what Azazel has done, who has taught all unrighteousness on earth and revealed the perpetual secrets which were [preserved] in Heaven, which men were striving to learn— ⁷and Semjaza, to whom You have given authority to bear rule over his associates. ⁸And they have gone to the daughters of men on the earth, and have slept with the women, and have defiled themselves, and revealed to them all kinds of sins. ⁹And the women have borne giants, and the whole earth has thereby been filled with blood and unrighteousness. ¹⁰And now, behold, the souls of those who have died are crying and making their suit to the gates of Heaven, and their lamentations have ascended, and they cannot cease because of the lawless deeds which are worked on the earth. ¹¹And You know all things before they come to pass, and You see these things and You permit them, and You do not say to us what we are to do to them in regard to these."

CHAPTER 10

¹Then the Most High uttered, the Holy and Great One spoke, and sent Uriel to the son of Lamech, and said

to him: [2] "Go to Noah and tell him in My Name: Hide yourself! And reveal to him the end that is approaching, that the whole earth will be destroyed, and a deluge is about to come on the whole earth and will destroy all that is on it. [3] And now instruct him that he may escape and his seed may be preserved for all the generations of the world." [4] And again, the LORD said to Raphael, "Bind Azazel hand and foot and cast him into the darkness, and make an opening in the desert, which is in Dudael, and cast him therein. [5] And place rough and jagged rocks over him, and cover him with darkness, and let him abide there forever, and cover his face that he may not see light. [6] And on the Day of the Great Judgment he will be cast into the fire. [7] And heal the earth which the messengers have corrupted, and proclaim the healing of the earth, that they may heal the plague, and that all the children of men may not perish through all the secret things that the Watchers have disclosed and have taught their sons. [8] And the whole earth has been corrupted through the works that were taught by Azazel: to him ascribe all sin." [9] And to Gabriel the LORD said, "Proceed against the bastards and the reprobates, and against the children of fornication, and destroy the children of the Watchers from among men. Send them against one another that they may destroy each other in battle, for they will not have length of days. [10] And no request that they make of you will be granted to their fathers on their behalf, for they hope to live a continuous life, and that each one of them will live five hundred years." [11] And the LORD said to Michael, "Go, bind Semjaza and his associates who have united themselves with women so as to have defiled themselves with them in all their uncleanness. [12] And when their sons have slain one another, and they have seen the destruction of their beloved ones, bind them fast for seventy generations in the valleys of the earth, until the day of their judgment and of their consummation, until the judgment that is forever and ever is consummated. [13] In those days they will be led off to the abyss of fire, and to the torment and the prison in which they will be confined forever. [14] And whoever will be condemned and destroyed will from then on be bound together with them to the end of all generations. [15] And destroy all the spirits of the reprobate and the children of the Watchers, because they have wronged mankind. [16] Destroy all wrong from the face of the earth and let every evil work come to an end; and let the plant of righteousness and truth appear: and it will prove a blessing; the works of righteousness and truth will be planted in truth and joy forevermore. [17] And then all the righteous will escape and will live until they beget thousands of children, and they will complete all the days of their youth and their old age in peace. [18] And then the whole earth will be tilled in righteousness and will all be planted with trees and be full of blessing. [19] And all desirable trees will be planted on it, and they will plant vines on it, and the vine which they plant thereon will yield wine in abundance. And as for all the seed which is sown thereon, each measure [of it] will bear one thousand, and each measure of olives will yield ten presses of oil. [20] And you will cleanse the earth from all oppression, and from all unrighteousness, and from all sin, and from all godlessness: and destroy all the uncleanness that is worked on the earth from off the earth. [21] And all the children of men will become righteous, and all nations will offer adoration and will praise Me, and all will worship Me. [22] And the earth will be cleansed from all defilement, and from all sin, and from all punishment, and from all torment, and I will never again send [them] on it from generation to generation and forever."

CHAPTER 11

[1] "And in those days I will open the store chambers of blessing which are in the heavens, so as to send them down on the earth over the work and labor of the children of men. [2] And truth and peace will be associated together throughout all the days of the world and throughout all the generations of men."

CHAPTER 12

[1] Before these things Enoch was hidden, and no one of the children of men knew where he was hidden, and where he dwelt, and what had become of him. [2] And his activities had to do with the Watchers, and his days were with the holy ones. [3] And I, Enoch, was blessing the Lord of majesty and the King of the ages, and the Watchers called me—Enoch the scribe—and said to me, [4] "Enoch, you scribe of righteousness, go, declare to the Watchers of the heavens who have left the high Heaven, the holy perpetual place, and have defiled themselves with women, and have done as the children of earth do, and have taken wives to themselves: [5] You have worked great destruction on the earth, and you will have no peace nor forgiveness of sin; [6] and inasmuch as they delight themselves in their children, they will see the murder of their beloved ones, and they will lament over the destruction of their children, and will make supplication continuously; but you will not attain mercy and peace."

CHAPTER 13

[1] And Enoch went and said, "Azazel, you will have no peace: a severe sentence has gone out against you to put you in bonds, [2] and you will not have toleration nor request granted to you, because of the unrighteousness which you have taught, and because of all the works of godlessness, and unrighteousness, and sin which you have shown to men." [3] Then I went and spoke to them all together, and they were all afraid, and fear and trembling seized them. [4] And they implored me to draw up a petition for them that they

might find forgiveness, and to read their petition in the presence of the Lord of Heaven. [5] For from that point forward they could not speak [with Him] nor lift up their eyes to Heaven for shame of their sins for which they had been condemned. [6] Then I wrote out their petition, and the prayer in regard to their spirits and their deeds individually, and in regard to their requests that they should have forgiveness and length. [7] And I went off and sat down at the waters of Dan, in the land of Dan, to the south of the west of Hermon, [and there] I read their petition until I fell asleep. [8] And behold, a dream came to me, and visions fell down on me, and I saw visions of discipline, and a voice came bidding me to tell it to the sons of Heaven and reprimand them. [9] And when I awoke, I came to them, and they were all sitting gathered together, weeping in 'Abelsjail, which is between Lebanon and Seneser, with their faces covered. [10] And I recounted before them all the visions which I had seen in sleep, and I began to speak the words of righteousness, and to reprimand the heavenly Watchers.

CHAPTER 14

[1] The Scroll of the Words of Righteousness, and of the reprimand of the perpetual Watchers in accordance with the command of the Holy Great One in that vision. [2] I saw in my sleep what I will now say with a tongue of flesh and with the breath of my mouth, which the Great One has given to men to converse with and understand with the heart. [3] As He has created and given to man the power of understanding, the word of wisdom, so He has also created me and given me the power of reprimanding the Watchers, the children of Heaven. [4] I wrote out your petition, and in my vision it appeared like this, that your petition will not be granted to you throughout all the days of the age, and that judgment has been finally passed on you: yes, [your petition] will not be granted to you. [5] And from now on you will not ascend into Heaven for all ages, and in bonds of the earth the decree has gone out to bind you for all the days of the world. [6] And you will have seen the destruction of your beloved sons beforehand and you will have no pleasure in them, but they will fall before you by the sword. [7] And your petition on their behalf will not be granted, nor yet on your own, even though you weep, and pray, and speak all the words contained in the writing which I have written. [8] And the vision was shown to me like this: behold, in the vision clouds invited me and a mist summoned me, and the course of the stars and the lightnings sped toward me, and the winds in the vision caused me to fly and lifted me upward and bore me into Heaven. [9] And I went in until I drew near to a wall which is built of crystals and surrounded by tongues of fire: and it began to frighten me. [10] And I went into the tongues of fire and drew near to a large house which was built of crystals: and the walls of the house were like a tessellated floor [made] of crystals, and its groundwork was of crystal. [11] Its ceiling was like the path of the stars and the lightnings, and between them were fiery cherubim, and their heaven was [as clear as] water. [12] A flaming fire surrounded the walls, and its portals blazed with fire. [13] And I entered into that house, and it was hot as fire and cold as ice: [14] there were no delights of life therein; fear covered me, and trembling took hold of me. [15] And as I quaked and trembled, I fell on my face. And I beheld a vision, and behold, there was a second house, greater than the former, and the entire portal stood open before me, and it was built of flames of fire. [16] And in every respect it so excelled in splendor, and magnificence, and extent that I cannot describe to you its splendor and its extent. [17] And its floor was of fire, and above it were lightnings and the path of the stars, and its ceiling was also flaming fire. [18] And I looked and saw a lofty throne therein: its appearance was as crystal, and the wheels thereof as the shining sun, and there was the vision of cherubim. [19] And from underneath the throne came streams of flaming fire so that I could not look thereon. [20] And the Great Glory sat thereon, and His raiment shone more brightly than the sun and was whiter than any snow. [21] None of the messengers could enter and behold His face by reason of the magnificence and glory, and no flesh could behold Him. [22] The flaming fire was around Him, and a great fire stood before Him, and none around could draw near Him: myriads of myriads [stood] before Him, yet He needed no counselor. [23] And the most holy ones who were near to Him did not leave by night nor depart from Him. [24] And until then I had been prostrate on my face, trembling: and the Lord called me with His own mouth, and said to me, "Come here, Enoch, and hear My word." [25] And one of the holy ones came to me and waked me, and He made me rise up and approach the door, and I bowed my face downwards.

CHAPTER 15

[1] And He answered and said to me, and I heard His voice: "Do not fear, Enoch, you righteous man and scribe of righteousness: approach here and hear My voice. [2] And go, say to the Watchers of the heavens, who have sent you to intercede for them: You should intercede for men, and not men for you! [3] Why have you left the high, holy, and perpetual Heaven, and lain with women, and defiled yourselves with the daughters of men, and taken wives to yourselves, and done like the children of earth, and begotten giants [as your] sons? [4] And though you were holy [and] spiritual, living the continuous life, you have defiled yourselves with the blood of women, and have begotten [children] with the blood of flesh, and, as the children of men, have lusted after flesh and blood as those who die and perish also do. [5] Therefore I have

1 ENOCH

also given them wives that they might impregnate them, and beget children by them, that nothing might be wanting to them on earth. ⁶ But you were formerly spiritual, living the continuous life, and immortal for all generations of the world. ⁷ And, therefore, I have not appointed wives for you; for as for the spiritual ones of the heavens, their dwelling is in the heavens. ⁸ And now the giants, who are produced from the spirits and flesh, will be called evil spirits on the earth, and their dwelling will be on the earth. ⁹ Evil spirits have proceeded from their bodies, because they are born from men and their beginning and primal origin is from the holy Watchers; they will be evil spirits on earth, and they will be called evil spirits. ¹⁰ [[As for the spirits of Heaven, their dwelling will be in Heaven, but as for the spirits of the earth which were born on the earth, their dwelling will be on the earth.]] ¹¹ And the spirits of the giants afflict, oppress, destroy, attack, do battle, and work destruction on the earth, and cause trouble: they take no food, but nevertheless hunger and thirst, and cause offenses. ¹² And these spirits will rise up against the children of men and against the women, because they have proceeded from them."

CHAPTER 16

¹ From the days of the slaughter, and destruction, and death of the giants—from the souls of whose flesh the spirits, having gone out, will destroy without incurring judgment—they will therefore destroy until the Day of the Consummation, the Great Judgment in which the age will be consummated over the Watchers and the godless; yes, [it] will be wholly consummated. ² And now as to the Watchers who have sent you to intercede for them, who had previously been in Heaven, [say to them]: ³ "You have been in Heaven, but all the mysteries had not yet been revealed to you, and you knew worthless ones, and you have made these known to the women in the hardness of your hearts, and through these mysteries women and men work much evil on earth." ⁴ Therefore, say to them: "You have no peace."

CHAPTER 17

¹ And they took and brought me to a place in which those who were there were like flaming fire, and they appeared as men when they wished. ² And they brought me to the place of darkness, and to a mountain the point of whose summit reached to Heaven. ³ And I saw the places of the luminaries, and the treasuries of the stars and of the thunder, and in the uttermost depths where there were a fiery bow, and arrows, and their quiver, and a fiery sword and all the lightnings. ⁴ And they took me to the living waters, and to the fire of the west, which receives every setting of the sun. ⁵ And I came to a river of fire in which the fire flows like water and discharges itself into the Great Sea toward the west. ⁶ I saw the great

rivers and came to the great river and to the great darkness and went to the place where no flesh walks. ⁷ I saw the mountains of the darkness of winter and the place from where all the waters of the deep flow. ⁸ I saw the mouths of all the rivers of the earth and the mouth of the deep.

CHAPTER 18

¹ I saw the treasuries of all the winds: I saw how He had furnished the whole creation and the firm foundations of the earth with them. ² And I saw the cornerstone of the earth: I saw the four winds which bear [the earth and] the expanse of the heavens. ³ And I saw how the winds stretch out the vaults of the heavens and have their station between the heavens and earth: these are the pillars of the heavens. ⁴ I saw the winds of the heavens which turn and bring the circumference of the sun and all the stars to their setting. ⁵ I saw the winds on the earth carrying the clouds. I saw the paths of the messengers. ⁶ I saw at the end of the earth the expanse of the heavens above. And I proceeded and saw a place which burns day and night, where there are seven mountains of magnificent stones: three toward the east and three toward the south. ⁷ And as for those toward the east: [one] was of colored stone, and one of pearl, and one of jacinth; and those toward the south [were] of red stone. ⁸ But the middle one reached to the heavens like the throne of God, of alabaster, and the summit of the throne was of sapphire. ⁹ And I saw a flaming fire. ¹⁰ And beyond these mountains is a region at the end of the great earth: there the heavens were completed. ¹¹ And I saw a deep abyss with columns of heavenly fire, and among them I saw columns of fire fall, which were beyond measure alike toward the height and toward the depth. ¹² And beyond that abyss I saw a place which had no expanse of the heavens above, and no firmly founded earth beneath it: there was no water on it, and no birds, but it was a waste and horrible place. ¹³ I saw seven stars there like great burning mountains, and to me, when I inquired regarding them, ¹⁴ the messenger said, "This place is the end of the heavens and earth: this has become a prison for the stars and the host of Heaven. ¹⁵ And the stars which roll over the fire are they which have transgressed the command of the LORD in the beginning of their rising, because they did not come out at their appointed times. ¹⁶ And He was angry with them and bound them until the time when their guilt should be consummated for ten thousand years."

CHAPTER 19

¹ And Uriel said to me, "The messengers who have connected themselves with women will stand here, and their spirits assuming many different forms are defiling mankind and will lead them astray into sacrificing to demons as gods; [[they will stand here]] until the Day of the Great Judgment in which they

will be judged until they are made an end of. ² And also, the women of the messengers who went astray will become sirens." ³ And only I, Enoch, saw the vision, the ends of all things: and no man will see as I have seen.

CHAPTER 20

¹ And these are the names of the holy messengers who watch: ² Uriel, one of the holy messengers, who is over the world and over Tartarus; ³ Raphael, one of the holy messengers, who is over the spirits of men; ⁴ Raguel, one of the holy messengers who takes vengeance on the world of the luminaries; ⁵ Michael, one of the holy messengers, namely, he that is set over the best part of mankind and over chaos; ⁶ Saraqael, one of the holy messengers, who is set over the spirits who sin in the spirit; ⁷ Gabriel, one of the holy messengers, who is over Paradise, and the serpents, and the cherubim; ⁸ Remiel, one of the holy messengers, whom God set over those who rise.

CHAPTER 21

¹ And I proceeded to where things were chaotic, ² and I saw something horrible there: I saw neither a heaven above nor a firmly founded earth, but a chaotic and horrible place. ³ And there I saw seven stars of the heavens bound together in it, like great mountains and burning with fire. ⁴ Then I said, "For what sin are they bound, and on what account have they been cast in here?" ⁵ Then Uriel, one of the holy messengers who was with me, and was chief over them, spoke and said, "Enoch, why do you ask, and why are you eager for the truth? ⁶ These are of the number of the stars of the heavens which have transgressed the command of the LORD and are bound here until ten thousand years, the time entailed by their sins, are consummated." ⁷ And from there I went to another place, which was still more horrible than the former, and I saw a horrible thing: a great fire there which burned and blazed, and the place was cleft as far as the abyss, being full of great descending columns of fire: I could see neither its extent or magnitude, nor could I conjecture. ⁸ Then I said, "How fearful is the place and how terrible to look on!" ⁹ Then Uriel answered me, one of the holy messengers who was with me, and said to me, "Enoch, why do you have such fear and fright?" And I answered, "Because of this fearful place, and because of the spectacle of the pain." ¹⁰ And he said to me, "This place is the prison of the messengers, and they will be imprisoned here forever."

CHAPTER 22

¹ And then I went to another place—the mountain of hard rock. ² And there were four hollow places in it, deep, and wide, and very smooth. O how smooth the hollow places are, and deep and dark to look at! ³ Then Raphael answered, one of the holy messengers who was with me, and said to me, "These hollow places have been created for this very purpose, that the spirits of the souls of the dead should assemble therein, yes, that all the souls of the children of men should assemble here. ⁴ And these places have been made to receive them until the day of their judgment and until their appointed period, until the Great Judgment [comes] on them." ⁵ I saw [the spirit of] a dead man making suit, and his voice went out to Heaven and made suit. ⁶ And I asked Raphael, the messenger who was with me, and I said to him, "This spirit which makes suit, whose is it, whose voice goes out and makes suit to Heaven?" ⁷ And he answered me, saying, "This is the spirit which went out from Abel, whom his brother Cain slew, and he makes his suit against him until his seed is destroyed from the face of the earth, and his seed is annihilated from among the seed of men." ⁸ Then I asked regarding it, and regarding all the hollow places: "Why is one separated from the other?" ⁹ And he answered me and said to me, "These three have been made that the spirits of the dead might be separated. And such a division has been made [for] the spirits of the righteous, in which there is the bright spring of water. ¹⁰ And such has been made for sinners when they die and are buried in the earth and judgment has not been executed on them in their lifetime. ¹¹ Here their spirits will be set apart in this great pain until the Great Day of Judgment; and [there will be] punishment and torment of those who are cursed forever, and retribution for their spirits. ¹² There He will bind them forever. And such a division has been made for the spirits of those who make their suit, who make disclosures concerning their destruction, when they were slain in the days of the sinners. ¹³ Such has been made for the spirits of men who were not righteous but sinners, who were complete in transgression, and they will be companions of the transgressors, but their spirits will not be slain in the Day of Judgment nor will they be raised from there." ¹⁴ Then I blessed the Lord of Glory and said, "Blessed is my Lord, the Lord of righteousness, who rules forever."

CHAPTER 23

¹ From there I went to another place to the west of the ends of the earth. ² And I saw a burning fire which ran without resting and did not cease from its course day or night, but [ran] regularly. ³ And I asked, saying, "What is this which does not rest?" ⁴ Then Raguel, one of the holy messengers who was with me, answered me and said to me, "This course of fire which you have seen is the fire in the west which persecutes all the luminaries of the heavens."

CHAPTER 24

¹ And from there I went to another place of the earth, and he showed me a mountain range of fire which burned day and night. ² And I went beyond it and saw

seven magnificent mountains, all differing from each other, and the stones [thereof] were magnificent and beautiful, magnificent as a whole, of glorious appearance and fair exterior: three toward the east, one founded on the other, and three toward the south, one on the other, and deep rough ravines, not one of which joined with any other. ³ And the seventh mountain was in the midst of these, and it excelled them in height, resembling the seat of a throne: and fragrant trees encircled the throne. ⁴ And among them was a tree such as I had never yet smelled, neither was any among them nor were others like it: it had a fragrance beyond all fragrance, and its leaves, and blooms, and wood do not wither forever, and its fruit is beautiful, and its fruit resembles the dates of a palm. ⁵ Then I said, "O how beautiful and fragrant this tree is! And its leaves are fair, and its blooms [are] very delightful in appearance!" ⁶ Then Michael, one of the holy and honored messengers who was with me and was their leader, answered.

CHAPTER 25

¹ And he said to me, "Enoch, why do you ask me regarding the fragrance of the tree, and why do you wish to learn the truth?" ² Then I answered him, saying, "I wish to know about everything, but especially about this tree." ³ And he answered, saying, "This high mountain which you have seen, whose summit is like the throne of God, is His throne, where the Holy Great One, the Lord of Glory, the perpetual King will sit when He will come down to visit the earth with goodness. ⁴ And as for this fragrant tree, no mortal is permitted to touch it until the Great Judgment when He will take vengeance on all and bring [everything] to its consummation forever. ⁵ It will then be given to the righteous and holy. Its fruit will be for food to the chosen ones: it will be transplanted to the holy place, to the temple of the LORD, the perpetual King. ⁶ Then they will rejoice with joy and be glad, ‖ And they will enter into the holy place; And its fragrance will be in their bones, ‖ And they will live a long life on earth, ‖ Such as your fathers lived: And in their days no sorrow, or plague, ‖ Or torment, or calamity will touch them." ⁷ Then I blessed the God of Glory, the perpetual King, who has prepared such things for the righteous, and has created them and promised to give to them.

CHAPTER 26

¹ And I went from there to the middle of the earth, and I saw a blessed place in which there were trees with branches abiding and blooming. ² And there I saw a holy mountain, and underneath the mountain to the east there was a stream and it flowed toward the south. ³ And I saw another mountain higher than this toward the east, and between them a deep and narrow ravine: in it also ran a stream underneath the mountain. ⁴ And to the west thereof there was another mountain, lower than the former and of small elevation, and a deep and dry ravine between them: and another deep and dry ravine was at the extremities of the three mountains. ⁵ And all the ravines were deep and narrow, [being formed] of hard rock, and trees were not planted on them. ⁶ And I marveled at the rocks, and I marveled at the ravine, yes, I marveled very much.

CHAPTER 27

¹ Then I said, "For what purpose is this blessed land, which is entirely filled with trees, and this accursed valley between?" ² Then Uriel, one of the holy messengers who was with me, answered and said, "This accursed valley is for those who are accursed forever. Here all the accursed will be gathered together who utter unseemly words with their lips against the LORD and speak hard things of His glory. Here they will be gathered together, and here will be their place of judgment. ³ In the last days there will be the spectacle of righteous judgment on them in the presence of the righteous forever: here the merciful will bless the Lord of Glory, the perpetual King. ⁴ In the days of judgment over the former, they will bless Him for the mercy in accordance with which He has assigned them [their lot]." ⁵ Then I blessed the Lord of Glory and set out His glory and lauded Him gloriously.

CHAPTER 28

¹ And then I went toward the east, into the midst of the mountain range of the desert, and I saw a wilderness and it was solitary, full of trees and plants. ² And water gushed out from above. ³ Rushing like a copious watercourse [which flowed] toward the northwest, it caused clouds and dew to ascend on every side.

CHAPTER 29

¹ And then I went to another place in the desert and approached to the east of this mountain range. ² And there I saw aromatic trees exhaling the fragrance of frankincense and myrrh, and the trees were also similar to the almond tree.

CHAPTER 30

¹ And beyond these, I went far to the east, and I saw another place, a valley [full] of water. ² And therein there was a tree, the color of fragrant trees such as the mastic. ³ And on the sides of those valleys I saw fragrant cinnamon. And beyond these I proceeded to the east.

CHAPTER 31

¹ And I saw other mountains, and among them were groves of trees, and nectar flowed out from them, which is called sarara and galbanum. ² And beyond these mountains I saw another mountain to the east of the ends of the earth, on which were aloe-trees, and

all the trees were full of stacte, being like almond-trees. ³ And when one burned it, it smelled sweeter than any refreshing fragrance.

CHAPTER 32

¹ And after these fragrant odors, as I looked toward the north over the mountains, I saw seven mountains full of choice nard, and fragrant trees, and cinnamon, and pepper. ² And then I went over the summits of all these mountains, far toward the east of the earth, and passed above the Erythraean Sea, and went far from it and passed over the messenger Zotiel. ³ And I came to the Garden of Righteousness and saw beyond those trees many large trees growing there and of attractive fragrance, large, very beautiful and glorious, and the Tree of Wisdom of which they eat and know great wisdom. ⁴ That tree is in height like the fir, and its leaves are like [those of] the Carob tree, and its fruit is like the clusters of the vine, very beautiful, and the fragrance of the tree penetrates far. ⁵ Then I said, "How beautiful is the tree, and how attractive is its look!" ⁶ Then Raphael, the holy messenger, who was with me, answered me and said, "This is the Tree of Wisdom, of which your ancient father and your ancient mother, who were before you, have eaten, and they learned wisdom, and their eyes were opened, and they knew that they were naked, and they were driven out of the garden."

CHAPTER 33

¹ And from there I went to the ends of the earth and saw great beasts there, and each differed from the other, and also birds differing in appearance, and beauty, and voice—the one differing from the other. ² And to the east of those beasts I saw the ends of the earth on which the heavens rest, and the portals of the heavens open. ³ And I saw how the stars of the heavens come out, and I counted the portals out of which they proceed, and wrote down all their outlets, of each individual star by itself, according to their number and their names, their courses and their positions, and their times and their months, as Uriel, the holy messenger who was with me, showed me. ⁴ He showed all things to me and wrote them down for me. He also wrote their names, and their laws, and their companies for me.

CHAPTER 34

¹ And from there I went toward the north to the ends of the earth, and there I saw a great and glorious device at the ends of the whole earth. ² And here I saw three portals of heaven open in the heavens: north winds proceed through each of them. When they blow there is cold, hail, frost, snow, dew, and rain. ³ And out of one portal they blow for good, but when they blow through the other two portals, it is with violence and affliction on the earth, and they blow with violence.

CHAPTER 35

¹ And from there I went toward the west, to the ends of the earth, and saw three portals of heaven open there such as I had seen in the east, the same number of portals, and the same number of outlets.

CHAPTER 36

¹ And from there I went to the south, to the ends of the earth, and saw three portals of heaven open there: and then there came dew, rain, and wind. ² And from there I went to the east, to the ends of the heavens, and saw the three eastern portals of heaven open here, and small portals [were] above them. ³ Through each of these small portals the stars of the heavens pass and run their course to the west on the path which is shown to them. ⁴ And as often as I saw, I always blessed the Lord of Glory, and I continued to bless the Lord of Glory who has worked great and glorious wonders, to show the greatness of His work to the messengers, and to spirits, and to men, that they might praise His work and all His creation, that they might see the work of His might, and praise the great work of His hands, and bless Him forever.

SECTION 2:
THE BOOK OF ALLEGORIES OF ENOCH

CHAPTER 37

¹ THE SECOND VISION WHICH HE SAW, THE VISION OF WISDOM, WHICH ENOCH THE SON OF JARED, THE SON OF MAHALALEL, THE SON OF CAINAN, THE SON OF ENOS, THE SON OF SETH, THE SON OF ADAM, SAW. ² And this is the beginning of the words of wisdom which I lifted up my voice to speak and say to those which dwell on earth: "Hear, you men of ancient time, and see, you that come after, the words of the Holy One which I will speak before the Lord of Spirits." ³ It were better to declare [them only] to the men of ancient time, but even from those that come after we will not withhold the beginning of wisdom. ⁴ Until the present day such wisdom has never been given by the Lord of Spirits as I have received according to my insight, according to the good pleasure of the Lord of Spirits by whom the lot of continuous life has been given to me. ⁵ Now three allegories were imparted to me, and I lifted up my voice and recounted them to those that dwell on the earth.

CHAPTER 38

¹ THE FIRST ALLEGORY. When the congregation of the righteous will appear, and sinners will be judged for their sins, and will be driven from the face of the earth, ² and when the Righteous One will appear before the eyes of the righteous, whose chosen works hang on the Lord of Spirits, and light will appear to the righteous and the chosen ones who dwell on the earth, where then will be the dwelling of the sinners, and where the resting-place of those who have denied

the Lord of Spirits? It had been good for them if they had not been born. ³ When the secrets of the righteous will be revealed and the sinners judged, and the godless driven from the presence of the righteous and chosen ones, ⁴ from that time those that possess the earth will no longer be powerful and exalted, and they will not be able to behold the face of the holy, for the Lord of Spirits has caused His light to appear on the face of the holy, righteous, and chosen ones. ⁵ Then the kings and the mighty will perish and be given into the hands of the righteous and holy. ⁶ And from then on none will seek for themselves mercy from the Lord of Spirits, for their life is at an end.

CHAPTER 39

¹ [[And it will come to pass in those days that chosen ones and holy children will descend from the high Heaven, and their seed will become one with the children of men. ² And in those days Enoch received scrolls of zeal and wrath, and scrolls of disquiet and expulsion.]] "And mercy will not be accorded to them," says the Lord of Spirits. ³ And in those days a whirlwind carried me off from the earth and set me down at the end of the heavens. ⁴ And there I saw another vision, the dwelling-places of the holy, and the resting-places of the righteous. ⁵ Here my eyes saw their dwellings with His righteous messengers, and their resting-places with the holy. And they petitioned, and interceded, and prayed for the children of men, and righteousness flowed before them as water, and mercy like dew on the earth; so it is among them forever and ever. ⁶ And in that place my eyes saw the Chosen One of righteousness and of faith, and I saw His dwelling-place under the wings of the Lord of Spirits. And righteousness will prevail in His days, and the righteous and chosen ones will be without number before Him forever and ever. ⁷ And all the righteous and chosen ones before Him will be strong as fiery lights, and their mouth will be full of blessing, and their lips extol the Name of the Lord of Spirits, and righteousness will never fail before Him. ⁸ I wished to dwell there, and my spirit longed for that dwelling-place; and my portion has been there until now, for so it has been established concerning me before the Lord of Spirits. ⁹ In those days I praised and extolled the Name of the Lord of Spirits with blessings and praises, because He has destined me for blessing and glory according to the good pleasure of the Lord of Spirits. ¹⁰ For a long time my eyes regarded that place, and I blessed Him and praised Him, saying, "Blessed is He, and may He be blessed from the beginning and forevermore. ¹¹ And before Him there is no ceasing. He knows before the world was created what is forever and what will be from generation to generation. ¹² Those who do not sleep bless You: they stand before Your glory and bless, praise, and extol, saying, HOLY, HOLY, HOLY, is the Lord of Spirits: He fills the earth with spirits."

And here my eyes saw all those who do not sleep: they stand before Him, and bless, and say, "Blessed are You and blessed is the Name of the LORD forever and ever." And my face was changed, for I could no longer behold.

CHAPTER 40

¹ And after that I saw thousands of thousands and ten thousand times ten thousand, I saw a multitude beyond number and reckoning, who stood before the Lord of Spirits. ² And on the four sides of the Lord of Spirits I saw four presences, different from those that do not sleep, and I learned their names, for the messenger that went with me made their names known to me and showed me all the hidden things. ³ And I heard the voices of those four presences as they uttered praises before the Lord of Glory. ⁴ The first voice blesses the Lord of Spirits forever and ever. ⁵ And the second voice I heard blessing the Chosen One and the chosen ones who hang on the Lord of Spirits. ⁶ And the third voice I heard pray and intercede for those who dwell on the earth and supplicate in the Name of the Lord of Spirits. ⁷ And I heard the fourth voice fending off the devils and forbidding them to come before the Lord of Spirits to accuse them who dwell on the earth. ⁸ After that I asked the messenger of peace who went with me, who showed me everything that is hidden: "Who are these four presences which I have seen and whose words I have heard and written down?" ⁹ And he said to me, "This first is Michael, the merciful and long-suffering; and the second, who is set over all the diseases and all the wounds of the children of men, is Raphael; and the third, who is set over all the powers, is Gabriel; and the fourth, who is set over the conversion to hope of those who inherit continuous life, is named Phanuel." ¹⁰ And these are the four messengers of the Lord of Spirits and the four voices I heard in those days.

CHAPTER 41

¹ And after that I saw all the secrets of the heavens, and how the kingdom is divided, and how the actions of men are weighed in the balance. ² And there I saw the mansions of the chosen ones and the mansions of the holy, and there my eyes saw all the sinners which deny the Name of the Lord of Spirits being driven from there and being dragged off: and they could not abide because of the punishment which proceeds from the Lord of Spirits. ³ And there my eyes saw the secrets of the lightning and of the thunder, and the secrets of the winds, how they are divided to blow over the earth, and the secrets of the clouds and dew, and there I saw from where they proceed in that place and from where they saturate the dusty earth. ⁴ And there I saw closed chambers out of which the winds are divided: the chamber of the hail and winds, the chamber of the mist, and of the clouds, and the cloud

1 ENOCH

thereof hovers over the earth from the beginning of the world. ⁵ And I saw the chambers of the sun and moon, from where they proceed and where they come again, and their glorious return, and how one is superior to the other, and their stately orbit, and how they do not leave their orbit, and they add nothing to their orbit and they take nothing from it, and they keep faith with each other in accordance with the oath by which they are bound together. ⁶ And first the sun goes out and traverses his path according to the command of the Lord of Spirits, and mighty is His Name forever and ever. ⁷ And after that I saw the hidden and the visible path of the moon, and she accomplishes the course of her path in that place by day and by night—the one holding a position opposite to the other before the Lord of Spirits. And they give thanks and praise and do not rest, for their thanksgiving is rest to them. ⁸ For the sun often changes for a blessing or a curse, and the course of the path of the moon is light to the righteous and darkness to the sinners in the Name of the LORD, who made a separation between the light and the darkness, and divided the spirits of men, and strengthened the spirits of the righteous, in the name of His righteousness. ⁹ For no messenger hinders and no power is able to hinder, for He appoints a judge for them all and He judges them all before Him.

CHAPTER 42

¹ Wisdom found no place where she might dwell; then a dwelling-place was assigned to her in the heavens. ² Wisdom went out to make her dwelling among the children of men and found no dwelling-place: Wisdom returned to her place and took her seat among the messengers. ³ And unrighteousness went out from her chambers; whom she did not seek she found and dwelt with them, as rain in a desert and dew on a thirsty land.

CHAPTER 43

¹ And I saw other lightnings and the stars of the heavens, and I saw how He called them all by their names and they listened to Him. ² And I saw how they are weighed in a righteous balance according to their proportions of light. [I saw] the width of their spaces, and the day of their appearing, and how their revolution produces lightning; and [I saw] their revolution according to the number of the messengers, and [how] they keep faith with each other. ³ And I asked the messenger who went with me, who showed me what was hidden: "What are these?" ⁴ And he said to me, "The Lord of Spirits has showed you their allegorical meaning: these are the names of the holy who dwell on the earth and believe in the Name of the Lord of Spirits forever and ever."

CHAPTER 44

¹ I also saw another phenomenon in regard to the lightnings: how some of the stars arise and become lightnings and cannot part with their new form.

CHAPTER 45

¹ AND THIS IS THE SECOND ALLEGORY CONCERNING THOSE WHO DENY THE NAME OF THE DWELLING OF THE HOLY ONES AND THE LORD OF SPIRITS. ² And they will not ascend into the heavens, and they will not come on the earth: such will be the lot of the sinners who have denied the Name of the Lord of Spirits, who are therefore preserved for the day of suffering and tribulation. ³ On that day My Chosen One will sit on the throne of glory and will try their works, and their places of rest will be innumerable. And their souls will grow strong within them when they see My chosen ones, and those who have called on My glorious Name. ⁴ Then I will cause My Chosen One to dwell among them. And I will transform Heaven and make it a continuous blessing and light, and I will transform the earth and make it a blessing, ⁵ and I will cause My chosen ones to dwell on it, but the sinners and evildoers will not set foot thereon. ⁶ For I have provided and satisfied My righteous ones with peace and have caused them to dwell before Me, but for the sinners there is judgment impending with Me, so that I will destroy them from the face of the earth.

CHAPTER 46

¹ And there I saw One who had a head of days, and His head was white like wool, and another being was with Him whose countenance had the appearance of a Man, and His face was full of graciousness, like one of the holy messengers. ² And I asked the messenger who went with me and showed me all the hidden things, concerning that Son of Man, who He was, and from where He was, [and] why He went with the Head of Days? ³ And he answered and said to me, "This is the Son of Man who has righteousness, with whom dwells righteousness, and who reveals all the treasures of that which is hidden, because the Lord of Spirits has chosen Him, and whose lot has the preeminence before the Lord of Spirits in uprightness forever. ⁴ And this Son of Man whom you have seen || Will raise up the kings and the mighty from their seats, [[|| And the strong from their thrones,]] || And will loosen the reins of the strong || And break the teeth of the sinners. ⁵ [[And He will put down the kings from their thrones and kingdoms,]] || Because they do not extol and praise Him, nor humbly acknowledge from where the kingdom was bestowed on them. ⁶ And He will put down the countenance of the strong || And will fill them with shame. And darkness will be their dwelling, || And worms will be their bed, || And they will have no hope of rising from their beds, || Because they do not extol the Name of the Lord of Spirits. ⁷ [[And they raise their hands

~ 260 ~

against the Most High,]] || And tread on the earth and dwell on it. And all their deeds manifest unrighteousness, || And their power rests on their riches, || And their faith is in the gods which they have made with their hands, || And they deny the Name of the Lord of Spirits, [8] And they persecute the houses of His congregations, || And the faithful who hang on the Name of the Lord of Spirits."

CHAPTER 47

[1] And in those days the prayer of the righteous and the blood of the righteous will have ascended from the earth before the Lord of Spirits. [2] In those days the holy ones who dwell above in the heavens will unite with one voice, and supplicate, and pray, [[and praise,]] and give thanks, and bless the Name of the Lord of Spirits on behalf of the blood of the righteous which has been shed, and that the prayer of the righteous may not be in vain before the Lord of Spirits, that judgment may be done to them, and that they may not have to suffer forever. [3] In those days I saw the Head of Days when He seated himself on the throne of His glory, and the scrolls of the living were opened before Him, and all His host which is in Heaven above and His counselors stood before Him, [4] And the hearts of the holy were filled with joy, because the number of the righteous had been offered, and the prayer of the righteous had been heard, and the blood of the righteous had been required before the Lord of Spirits.

CHAPTER 48

[1] And in that place I saw the fountain of righteousness which was inexhaustible, and many fountains of wisdom were around it. And all the thirsty drank of them, and were filled with wisdom, and their dwellings were with the righteous, and holy, and chosen ones. [2] And at that hour that Son of Man was named in the presence of the Lord of Spirits, and His Name before the Head of Days. [3] Yes, before the sun and the signs were created, before the stars of the heavens were made, His Name was named before the Lord of Spirits. [4] He will be a staff to the righteous on which to stay themselves and not fall, and He will be the light of the nations, and the hope of those who are troubled of heart. [5] All who dwell on earth will fall down and worship before Him and will praise, and bless, and celebrate the Lord of Spirits with song. [6] And for this reason He has been chosen and hidden before Him, before the creation of the world and forevermore. [7] And the wisdom of the Lord of Spirits has revealed Him to the holy and righteous, for He has preserved the lot of the righteous, because they have hated and despised this world of unrighteousness and have hated all its works and ways in the Name of the Lord of Spirits; for they are saved in His Name, and it has been in regard to their life according to His good pleasure. [8] In these days the

kings of the earth and the strong who possess the land will have become downcast in countenance because of the works of their hands, for on the day of their anguish and affliction they will not [be able to] save themselves. [9] And I will give them over into the hands of My chosen ones as straw in the fire, so they will burn before the face of the holy. They will sink as lead in the water before the face of the righteous, and no trace of them will be found anymore. [10] And on the day of their affliction there will be rest on the earth, and they will fall before them and not rise again, and there will be no one to take them with his hands and raise them, for they have denied the Lord of Spirits and His Anointed. The Name of the Lord of Spirits be blessed.

CHAPTER 49

[1] For wisdom is poured out like water, and glory does not fail before Him forevermore. [2] For He is mighty in all the secrets of righteousness, and unrighteousness will disappear as a shadow and have no continuance, because the Chosen One stands before the Lord of Spirits, and His glory is forever and ever, and His might to all generations. [3] And in Him dwells the Spirit of wisdom, and the Spirit which gives insight, and the Spirit of understanding and of might, and the Spirit of those who have fallen asleep in righteousness. [4] And He will judge the secret things, and none will be able to utter a lying word before Him, for He is the Chosen One before the Lord of Spirits according to His good pleasure.

CHAPTER 50

[1] And in those days a change will take place for the holy and chosen ones, and the light of days will abide on them, and glory and honor will turn to the holy, on the day of affliction on which evil will have been treasured up against the sinners. [2] And the righteous will be victorious in the Name of the Lord of Spirits, and He will cause the others to witness [this] that they may convert and forgo the works of their hands. [3] They will have no honor through the Name of the Lord of Spirits, yet they will be saved through His Name, and the Lord of Spirits will have compassion on them, for His compassion is great. [4] And He is also righteous in His judgment, and also in the presence of His glory unrighteousness will not maintain itself: at His judgment the unconverted will perish before Him. [5] "And from now on I will have no mercy on them," says the Lord of Spirits.

CHAPTER 51

[1] And in those days the earth will also give back that which has been entrusted to it, and Sheol will also give back that which it has received, and destruction will give back that which it owes. For in those days the Chosen One will arise, [2] and He will choose the righteous and holy from among them, for the day has

drawn near that they should be saved. ³ And the Chosen One will sit on My throne in those days, and His mouth will pour out all the secrets of wisdom and counsel, for the Lord of Spirits has given [them] to Him and has glorified Him. ⁴ And in those days the mountains will leap like rams, and the hills will also skip like lambs satisfied with milk, and the faces of [all] the messengers in Heaven will be lit up with joy. ⁵ And the earth will rejoice, and the righteous will dwell on it, and the chosen ones will walk thereon.

CHAPTER 52

¹ And after those days in that place where I had seen all the visions of that which is hidden, I had been carried off in a whirlwind and they had borne me toward the west. ² There my eyes saw all the secret things of Heaven that will be, a mountain of iron, and a mountain of copper, and a mountain of silver, and a mountain of gold, and a mountain of soft metal, and a mountain of lead. ³ And I asked the messenger who went with me, saying, "What things are these which I have seen in secret?" ⁴ And he said to me, "All these things which you have seen will serve the dominion of His Anointed that He may be potent and mighty on the earth." ⁵ And that messenger of peace answered, saying to me, "Wait a little, and all the secret things which surround the Lord of Spirits will be revealed to you. ⁶ And these mountains which your eyes have seen—the mountain of iron, and the mountain of copper, and the mountain of silver, and the mountain of gold, and the mountain of soft metal, and the mountain of lead—all these will be in the presence of the Chosen One as wax before the fire, and like the water which streams down from above, and they will become powerless before His feet. ⁷ And it will come to pass in those days that none will be saved, either by gold or by silver, and none will be able to escape. ⁸ And there will be no iron for war, nor will one clothe oneself with a breastplate. Bronze will be of no service, and tin will not be esteemed, and lead will not be desired. ⁹ And all these things will be destroyed from the surface of the earth when the Chosen One will appear before the face of the Lord of Spirits."

CHAPTER 53

¹ My eyes saw a deep valley with open mouths there, and all who dwell on the earth, and sea, and islands will bring gifts, and presents, and signs of homage to Him, but that deep valley will not become full. ² And their hands commit lawless deeds, and the sinners devour all whom they lawlessly oppress, yet the sinners will be destroyed before the face of the Lord of Spirits, and they will be banished from off the face of His earth, and they will perish forever and ever. ³ For I saw all the messengers of punishment abiding [there] and preparing all the instruments of Satan. ⁴ And I asked the messenger of peace who went with me: "For whom are they preparing these

instruments?" ⁵ And he said to me, "They prepare these for the kings and the mighty of this earth, that they may thereby be destroyed. ⁶ And after this the Righteous and Chosen One will cause the house of His congregation to appear: from now on they will no longer be hindered in the Name of the Lord of Spirits. ⁷ And these mountains will not stand as the earth before His righteousness, but the hills will be as a fountain of water, and the righteous will have rest from the oppression of sinners."

CHAPTER 54

¹ And I looked and turned to another part of the earth and saw a deep valley with burning fire there. ² And they brought the kings and the mighty and began to cast them into this deep valley. ³ And there my eyes saw how they made these instruments of theirs iron chains of immeasurable weight. ⁴ And I asked the messenger of peace who went with me, saying, "For whom are these chains being prepared?" And he said to me, "These are being prepared for the hosts of Azazel, so that they may take them and cast them into the abyss of complete condemnation, and they will cover their jaws with rough stones as the Lord of Spirits commanded. ⁶ And Michael, and Gabriel, and Raphael, and Phanuel will take hold of them on that great day, and cast them on that day into the burning furnace, that the Lord of Spirits may take vengeance on them for their unrighteousness in becoming subject to Satan and leading those who dwell on the earth astray." ⁷ And in those days punishment will come from the Lord of Spirits, and He will open all the chambers of waters which are above the heavens, and of the fountains which are beneath the earth. ⁸ And all the waters will be joined with the waters: that which is above the heavens is the masculine, and the water which is beneath the earth is the feminine. ⁹ And they will destroy all who dwell on the earth and those who dwell under the ends of the heavens. ¹⁰ And when they have recognized their unrighteousness which they have worked on the earth, then by these they will perish.

CHAPTER 55

¹ And after that the Head of Days regretted and said, "I have destroyed all who dwell on the earth in vain." ² And He swore by His great Name: "From now on I will not do so to all who dwell on the earth, and I will set a sign in the heavens: and this will be a pledge of good faith between Me and them forever, so long as the heavens are above the earth. And this is in accordance with My command. ³ When I have desired to take hold of them by the hand of the messengers on the day of tribulation and pain because of this, I will cause My discipline and My wrath to abide on them," says God, the Lord of Spirits. ⁴ "You mighty kings who dwell on the earth, you will have to behold My Chosen One, how He sits on the throne of glory and

1 ENOCH

judges Azazel, and all his associates, and all his hosts in the Name of the Lord of Spirits."

CHAPTER 56

¹ And I saw there the hosts of the messengers of punishment going, and they held scourges and chains of iron and bronze. ² And I asked the messenger of peace who went with me, saying, "To whom are these who hold the scourges going?" ³ And he said to me, "To their chosen and beloved ones, that they may be cast into the chasm of the abyss of the valley. ⁴ And then that valley will be filled with their chosen and beloved ones, and the days of their lives will be at an end, and the days of their leading astray will no longer be reckoned. ⁵ And in those days the messengers will return and hurl themselves to the east on the Parthians and Medes: they will stir up the kings, so that a spirit of unrest will come on them, and they will rouse them from their thrones, that they may break out as lions from their lairs, and as hungry wolves among their flocks. ⁶ And they will go up and tread underfoot the land of His chosen ones, [[and the land of His chosen ones will be a threshing-floor and a highway before them,]] ⁷ but the city of my righteous will be a hindrance to their horses. And they will begin to fight among themselves, and their right hand will be strong against themselves, and a man will not know his brother, nor a son his father or his mother, until there is no number of the corpses through their slaughter, and their punishment is not in vain. ⁸ In those days Sheol will open its jaws, and they will be swallowed up therein, and their destruction will be at an end; Sheol will devour the sinners in the presence of the chosen ones."

CHAPTER 57

¹ And it came to pass after this that I saw another host of wagons, and men riding thereon, and coming on the winds from the east, and from the west to the south. ² And the noise of their wagons was heard, and when this turmoil took place the holy ones from Heaven noted it, and the pillars of the earth were moved from their place, and the sound thereof was heard from one end of the heavens to the other, in one day. ³ And they will all fall down and worship the Lord of Spirits. And this is the end of the second allegory.

CHAPTER 58

¹ AND I BEGAN TO SPEAK THE THIRD ALLEGORY CONCERNING THE RIGHTEOUS AND CHOSEN ONES. ² Blessed are you, you righteous and chosen ones, || For your lot will be glorious. ³ And the righteous will be in the light of the sun, || And the chosen ones in the light of continuous life: The days of their life will be unending, || And the days of the holy without number. ⁴ And they will seek the light and find righteousness || With the Lord of Spirits: There will be peace to the righteous in the Name of the Perpetual Lord. ⁵ And after this it will be said to the holy in Heaven || That they should seek out the secrets of righteousness, || The heritage of faith; For it has become bright as the sun on earth, || And the darkness is past. ⁶ And there will be a light that never ends, || And they will not come to a limit of days, || For the darkness will have first been destroyed, || And the light [[of uprightness]] established forever before the Lord of Spirits.

CHAPTER 59

¹ [[In those days my eyes saw the secrets of the lightnings, and of the lights, and the judgments they execute: and they lighten for a blessing or a curse as the Lord of Spirits wills. ² And there I saw the secrets of the thunder, and how when it resounds above in the heavens, the sound thereof is heard, and he caused me to see the judgments executed on the earth, whether they are for well-being and blessing, or for a curse according to the word of the Lord of Spirits. ³ And after that all the secrets of the lights and lightnings were shown to me, and they lighten for blessing and for satisfying.]]

CHAPTER 60

¹ In the five hundredth year, in the seventh month, on the fourteenth day of the month in the life of Enoch, in that allegory I saw how a mighty quaking made the Heaven of heavens to quake, and the host of the Most High, and the messengers—one million and [even] one hundred million—were disquieted with a great disquiet. ² And the Head of Days sat on the throne of His glory, and the messengers and the righteous stood around Him. ³ And a great trembling seized me, and fear took hold of me, and my loins gave way, and my reins were dissolved, and I fell on my face. ⁴ And Michael sent another messenger from among the holy ones and he raised me up, and when he had raised me up my spirit returned, for I had not been able to endure the look of this host, and the commotion and the quaking of Heaven. ⁵ And Michael said to me, "Why are you disquieted with such a vision? The day of His mercy lasted until this day; and He has been merciful and long-suffering toward those who dwell on the earth. ⁶ And when the day, and the power, and the punishment, and the judgment come, which the Lord of Spirits has prepared for those who do not bow to the righteous law, and for those who deny the righteous judgment, and for those who take His Name in vain—that day is prepared: a covenant for the chosen ones, but an inquisition for sinners. When the punishment of the Lord of Spirits will rest on them, it will rest in order that the punishment of the Lord of Spirits may not come in vain, and it will slay the children with their mothers and the children with their fathers. Afterward the judgment will take place according to His mercy and His patience." ⁷ And on that day two monsters were parted: a female monster

named Leviathan, to dwell in the abysses of the ocean over the fountains of the waters, ⁸ but the male is named Behemoth, who occupied with his breast a waste wilderness named Duidain, on the east of the garden where the chosen ones and righteous dwell, where my grandfather was taken up—the seventh from Adam, the first man whom the Lord of Spirits created. ⁹ And I sought the other messenger that he should show me the might of those monsters, how they were parted on one day and cast, the one into the abysses of the sea, and the other onto the dry land of the wilderness. ¹⁰ And he said to me, "You son of man, herein you seek to know what is hidden." ¹¹ And the other messenger who went with me and showed me what was hidden told me what is first and last in the height of Heaven, and beneath the earth in the depth, and at the ends of the heavens, and on the foundation of the heavens; ¹² and the chambers of the winds, and how the winds are divided, and how they are weighed, and [how] the portals of the winds are reckoned, each according to the power of the wind, and the power of the lights of the moon, and according to the power that is fitting, and the divisions of the stars according to their names, and how all the divisions are divided; ¹³ and the thunders according to the places where they fall, and all the divisions that are made among the lightnings that it may lighten, and their host that they may immediately obey. ¹⁴ For the thunder has places of rest [which] are assigned [to it] while it is waiting for its peal; and the thunder and lightning are inseparable, and although not one and undivided, they both go together through the spirit and do not separate. ¹⁵ For when the lightning lightens, the thunder utters its voice, and the spirit enforces a pause during the peal, and divides equally between them; for the treasury of their peals is like the sand, and each one of them as it peals is held in with a bridle, and turned back by the power of the spirit, and pushed forward according to the many quarters of the earth. ¹⁶ And the spirit of the sea is masculine and strong, and according to the might of his strength he draws it back with a rein, and in like manner it is driven forward and disperses amid all the mountains of the earth. ¹⁷ And the spirit of the hoarfrost is his own messenger, and the spirit of the hail is a good messenger. ¹⁸ And the spirit of the snow has forsaken his chambers on account of his strength. There is a special spirit therein, and that which ascends from it is like smoke, and its name is frost. ¹⁹ And the spirit of the mist is not united with them in their chambers, but it has a special chamber, for its course is glorious both in light and in darkness, and in winter and in summer, and a messenger is in its chamber. ²⁰ And the spirit of the dew has its dwelling at the ends of the heavens, and is connected with the chambers of the rain, and its course is in winter and summer: and its clouds and the clouds of the mist are connected, and the one gives to the other. ²¹ And when the spirit of the rain goes out from its chamber, the messengers come and open the chamber and lead it out, and when it is diffused over the whole earth it unites with the water on the earth. ²² For the waters are for those who dwell on the earth, for they are nourishment for the earth from the Most High who is in Heaven. Therefore, there is a measure for the rain, and the messengers take it in charge. ²³ And these things I saw toward the Garden of the Righteous. ²⁴ And the messenger of peace who was with me said to me, "These two monsters, prepared conformably to the greatness of God, will feed."

CHAPTER 61

¹ And I saw in those days how long cords were given to those messengers, and they took wings for themselves and flew, and they went toward the north. ² And I asked the messenger, saying to him, "Why have those [messengers] taken these cords and gone off?" And he said to me, "They have gone to measure." ³ And the messenger who went with me said to me, "These will bring the measures of the righteous and the ropes of the righteous to the righteous, that they may stay themselves on the Name of the Lord of Spirits forever and ever. ⁴ The chosen ones will begin to dwell with the chosen ones, and those are the measures which will be given to faith and which will strengthen righteousness. ⁵ And these measures will reveal all the secrets of the depths of the earth, and those who have been destroyed by the desert, and those who have been devoured by the beasts, and those who have been devoured by the fish of the sea, that they may return and stay themselves on the day of the Chosen One, for none will be destroyed before the Lord of Spirits, and none can be destroyed. ⁶ And all who dwell above in Heaven received a command, and power, and one voice, and one light like to fire. ⁷ And they blessed that One [with] their first words, and extolled and lauded with wisdom, and they were wise in utterance and in the spirit of life. ⁸ And the Lord of Spirits placed the Chosen One on the throne of glory, and He will judge all the works of the holy above in Heaven, and their deeds will be weighed in the balance, ⁹ and when He will lift up His countenance to judge their secret ways according to the word of the Name of the Lord of Spirits, and their path according to the way of the righteous judgment of the Lord of Spirits, then with one voice they will all speak, and bless, and glorify, and extol, and sanctify the Name of the Lord of Spirits. ¹⁰ And He will summon all the host of the heavens, and all the holy ones above, and the host of God, the cherubim, seraphim, and ophanim, and all the messengers of power, and all the messengers of principalities, and the Chosen One, and the other powers on the earth [and] over the water. ¹¹ They will raise one voice on that day and bless, and glorify, and exalt in the Spirit of faith, and in the Spirit of wisdom, and in the Spirit of patience, and in the Spirit of

mercy, and in the Spirit of judgment and of peace, and in the Spirit of goodness, and will all say with one voice: Blessed is He and may the Name of the Lord of Spirits be blessed forever and ever! ¹²All who do not sleep above in Heaven will bless Him: All the holy ones who are in Heaven will bless Him, ‖ And all the chosen ones who dwell in the garden of life, ‖ And every spirit of light ‖ Who is able to bless, and glorify, and extol, and hallow Your blessed Name, ‖ And all flesh will glorify and bless Your Name beyond measure forever and ever. ¹³For great is the mercy of the Lord of Spirits, and He is long-suffering, and all His works and all that He has created He has revealed to the righteous and chosen ones in the Name of the Lord of Spirits."

CHAPTER 62

¹And so the LORD commanded the kings, and the mighty, and the exalted, and those who dwell on the earth, and said, "Open your eyes and lift up your horns if you are able to recognize the Chosen One." ²And the Lord of Spirits seated Him on the throne of His glory, and the Spirit of righteousness was poured out on Him, and the word of His mouth slays all the sinners, and all the unrighteous are destroyed from before His face. ³And all the kings, and the mighty, and the exalted, and those who hold the earth will stand up in that day, and they will see and recognize how He sits on the throne of His glory, and righteousness is judged before Him, and no lying word is spoken before Him. ⁴Then pain will come on them as on a woman in travail when her child enters the mouth of the womb and she has pain in bringing out. ⁵And one portion of them will look on the other, and they will be terrified, and they will be downcast of countenance, and pain will seize them when they see that Son of Man Sitting on the throne of His glory. ⁶And the kings, and the mighty, and all who possess the earth will bless, and glorify, and extol Him who rules over all, who was hidden. ⁷For from the beginning the Son of Man was hidden, and the Most High preserved Him in the presence of His might and revealed Him to the chosen ones. ⁸And the congregation of the chosen and holy ones will be sown, and all the chosen ones will stand before Him on that day. ⁹And all the kings, and the mighty, and the exalted, and those who rule the earth will fall down before Him on their faces, and worship and set their hope on that Son of Man, and petition Him, and supplicate for mercy at His hands. ¹⁰Nevertheless, that Lord of Spirits will so press them that they will have to go out from His presence, and their faces will be filled with shame, and the darkness will grow deeper on their faces. ¹¹And He will deliver them to the messengers for punishment, to execute vengeance on them because they have oppressed His children and His chosen ones, ¹²and they will be a spectacle for the righteous and for His chosen ones: they will rejoice over them, because the wrath of the Lord of Spirits rests on them, and His sword is drunk with their blood. ¹³And the righteous and chosen ones will be saved on that day, and they will never again see the face of the sinners and unrighteous. ¹⁴And the Lord of Spirits will abide over them, and they will eat, and lie down, and rise up with that Son of Man forever and ever. ¹⁵And the righteous and chosen ones will have risen from the earth and ceased to be of downcast countenance. And they will have been clothed with garments of glory, ¹⁶and these will be the garments of life from the Lord of Spirits: and your garments will not grow old, nor your glory pass away before the Lord of Spirits.

CHAPTER 63

¹In those days the mighty and the kings who possess the earth will implore [Him] to grant them a little respite from His messengers of punishment to whom they were delivered, that they might fall down and worship before the Lord of Spirits and confess their sins before Him. ²And they will bless and glorify the Lord of Spirits and say, "Blessed is the Lord of Spirits and the Lord of kings, ‖ And the Lord of the mighty and the Lord of the rich, ‖ And the Lord of Glory and the Lord of wisdom, ³And splendid in every secret thing is Your power from generation to generation, ‖ And Your glory forever and ever. All Your secrets are deep and innumerable, ‖ And Your righteousness is beyond reckoning. ⁴We have now learned that we should glorify and bless the Lord of kings and Him who is King over all kings." ⁵And they will say, "If only we had rest to glorify, and give thanks, and confess our faith before His glory! ⁶And now we long for a little rest but do not find it; We follow hard on and do not obtain [it]; And light has vanished from before us, ‖ And darkness is our dwelling-place forever and ever, ⁷For we have not believed before Him ‖ Nor glorified the Name of the Lord of Spirits, ‖ But our hope was in the scepter of our kingdom, ‖ And in our glory. ⁸And in the day of our suffering and tribulation ‖ He does not save us, ‖ And we find no respite for confession that our Lord is true in all His works, ‖ And in His judgments and His justice, ‖ And His judgments have no respect of persons. And we pass away from before His face on account of our works, ‖ And all our sins are reckoned up in righteousness." ¹⁰Now they will say to themselves, "Our souls are full of unrighteous gain, but it does not prevent us from descending from the midst thereof into the burden of Sheol." ¹¹And after that their faces will be filled with darkness and shame before that Son of Man, and they will be driven from His presence, and the sword will abide before His face in their midst. ¹²So spoke the Lord of Spirits: "This is the ordinance and judgment with respect to the mighty, and the kings, and the exalted, and those who possess the earth before the Lord of Spirits."

1 ENOCH

CHAPTER 64

[1] And I saw other forms hidden in that place. [2] I heard the voice of the messenger, saying, "These are the messengers who descended to the earth, and revealed what was hidden to the children of men, and seduced the children of men into committing sin."

CHAPTER 65

[1] And in those days Noah saw that the earth had sunk down and its destruction was near. [2] And he arose from there and went to the ends of the earth, and he cried aloud to his grandfather Enoch, [3] and with an embittered voice Noah said three times, "Hear me! Hear me! Hear me!" And I said to him, "Tell me what it is that is falling out on the earth that the earth is in such an evil plight and shaken, lest perhaps I will perish with it?" [4] And there was a great commotion on the earth, and a voice was heard from Heaven, and I fell on my face. [5] And my grandfather Enoch came and stood by me, and said to me, "Why have you cried to me with a bitter cry and weeping? [6] Indeed, a command has gone out from the presence of the LORD concerning those who dwell on the earth that their ruin is accomplished because they have learned all the secrets of the messengers, and all the violence of the devils, and all their powers—the most secret ones— and all the power of those who practice sorcery, and the power of witchcraft, and the power of those who make molten images for the whole earth, [7] and how silver is produced from the dust of the earth, and how soft metal originates in the earth. [8] For lead and tin are not produced from the earth like the first: it is a fountain that produces them, and a messenger stands therein, and that messenger is preeminent." [9] And after that, my grandfather Enoch took hold of me by my hand and raised me up, and said to me, "Go, for I have asked the Lord of Spirits concerning this commotion on the earth." [10] And He said to me, "Because of their unrighteousness their judgment has been determined and will not be withheld by Me forever. Because of the sorceries which they have searched out and learned, the earth and those who dwell on it will be destroyed. [11] And these—they have no place of conversion forever, because they have shown them what was hidden, and they are the damned; but as for you, my son, the Lord of Spirits knows that you are pure and guiltless of this reproach concerning the secrets. [12] And He has destined your name to be among the holy, and will preserve you among those who dwell on the earth, and has destined your righteous Seed both for kingship and for great honors, and from your Seed will proceed a fountain of the righteous and holy without number forever."

CHAPTER 66

[1] And after that he showed me the messengers of punishment who are prepared to come and let loose all the powers of the waters which are beneath in the earth in order to bring judgment and destruction on all who [abide and] dwell on the earth. [2] And the Lord of Spirits gave command to the messengers who were going out, that they should not cause the waters to rise but should hold them in check, for those messengers were over the powers of the waters. [3] And I went away from the presence of Enoch.

CHAPTER 67

[1] And in those days the word of God came to me, and He said to me, "Noah, your lot has come up before Me, a lot without blame, a lot of love and uprightness. [2] And now the messengers are making a wooden [vessel], and when they have completed that task, I will place My hand on it and preserve it, and the seed of life will come out from it, and a change will set in so that the earth will not remain without inhabitant. [3] And I will make your seed firm before Me forever and ever, and I will spread abroad those who dwell with you: it will not be unfruitful on the face of the earth, but it will be blessed and multiply on the earth in the Name of the LORD." [4] And He will imprison those messengers who have shown unrighteousness in that burning valley which my grandfather Enoch had formerly shown to me, in the west among the mountains of gold, and silver, and iron, and soft metal, and tin. [5] And I saw that valley in which there was a great convulsion and a convulsion of the waters. [6] And when all this took place, a smell of sulfur was produced from that fiery molten metal and from the convulsion thereof in that place, and it was connected with those waters, and that valley of the messengers who had led [mankind] astray burned beneath that land. [7] And streams of fire proceed through its valleys where these messengers who had led those who dwell on the earth astray are punished. [8] But in those days those waters will serve for the kings, and the mighty, and the exalted, and those who dwell on the earth, [not] for the healing of the body, but for the punishment of the spirit; now their spirit is full of lust, that they may be punished in their body, for they have denied the Lord of Spirits and see their punishment daily, and yet do not believe in His Name. [9] And in proportion as the burning of their bodies becomes severe, a corresponding change will take place in their spirit forever and ever, for none will utter an idle word before the Lord of Spirits; [10] for the judgment will come on them, because they believe in the lust of their body and deny the Spirit of the LORD. [11] And those same waters will undergo a change in those days, for when those messengers are punished in these waters, these water-springs will change their temperature, and when the messengers ascend, this water of the springs will change and become cold. [12] And I heard Michael answering, and saying, "This judgment with which the messengers are judged is a testimony for the kings and the mighty who possess the earth." [13] Because these waters of judgment

1 ENOCH

minister to the healing of the body of the kings and the lust of their body, therefore, they will not see and will not believe that those waters will change and become a fire which burns forever.

CHAPTER 68

[1] And after that my grandfather Enoch gave me the teaching of all the secrets in the scroll, in the allegories which had been given to him, and he put them together for me in the words of the Scroll of the Allegories. [2] And on that day Michael answered Raphael and said, "The power of the Spirit transports and makes me to tremble because of the severity of the judgment of the secrets, the judgment of the messengers: who can endure the severe judgment which has been executed, and before which they melt away?" [3] And Michael answered again, and said to Raphael, "Who is he whose heart is not softened concerning it, and whose reins are not troubled by this word of judgment [that] has gone out on them because of those who have so led them out?" [4] And it came to pass when he stood before the Lord of Spirits, Michael said this to Raphael: "I will not take their part under the eye of the LORD, for the Lord of Spirits has been angry with them because they do as if they were the LORD. [5] Therefore all that is hidden will come on them forever and ever; for neither messenger nor man will have his portion [in it], but they alone have received their judgment forever and ever."

CHAPTER 69

[1] And after this judgment they will terrify and make them to tremble because they have shown this to those who dwell on the earth. [2] And behold the names of those messengers, [[and these are their names: the first of them is Semjaza, the second Artaqifa, and the third Armen, the fourth Kokabel, the fifth Turael, the sixth Rumjal, the seventh Danjal, the eighth Neqael, the ninth Baraqel, the tenth Azazel, the eleventh Armaros, the twelfth Batarjal, the thirteenth Busasejal, the fourteenth Hananel, the fifteenth Turel, and the sixteenth Simapesiel, the seventeenth Jetrel, the eighteenth Tumael, the nineteenth Turel, the twentieth Rumael, the twenty-first Azazel. [3] And these are the chiefs of their messengers, and their names, and their chief ones over hundreds, and over fifties, and over tens.]] [4] The name of the first Jeqon: that is, the one who led astray [all] the sons of God, and brought them down to the earth, and led them astray through the daughters of men. [5] And the second was named Asbeel: he imparted to the holy sons of God evil counsel and led them astray so that they defiled their bodies with the daughters of men. [6] And the third was named Gadreel: it is he who showed the children of men all the blows of death, and he led Eve astray, and showed the shield, and the coat of mail, and the sword for battle, and all the weapons of death to the children of men; [7] and they have proceeded from his hand against those who dwell on the earth from that day and forevermore. [8] And the fourth was named Penemue: he taught the children of men the bitter and the sweet, and he taught them all the secrets of their wisdom, [9] and he instructed mankind in writing with ink and paper, and thereby many sinned from age to age and until this day, [10] for men were not created for such a purpose, to give confirmation to their good faith with pen and ink. [11] For men were created exactly like the messengers, to the intent that they should continue pure and righteous, and death, which destroys everything, could not have taken hold of them, but through this knowledge of theirs they are perishing, and through this power it is consuming me. [12] And the fifth was named Kasdeja: this is he who showed the children of men all the wicked striking of spirits and demons, and the striking of the embryo in the womb that it may pass away, and the striking of the soul [by] the bites of the serpent, and the striking which befalls through the noontide heat, the son of the serpent named Taba'et. [13] And this is the task of Kasbeel, the chief of the oath which he showed to the holy ones when he dwelt high above in glory, and its name is Biqa. [14] This [messenger] requested Michael to show him the hidden name, that he might enunciate it in the oath, so that those might quake before that name and oath who revealed all that was in secret to the children of men. [15] And this is the power of this oath, for it is powerful and strong, and he placed this oath of Akae in the hand of Michael. [16] And these are the secrets of this oath, and they are strong through his oath: and Heaven was suspended before the world was created—and forever, [17] and through it the earth was founded on the water, and from the secret recesses of the mountains come beautiful waters, from the creation of the world and continuously. [18] And through that oath the sea was created, and at its foundation He set for it the sand against the time of [its] anger, and it does not dare pass beyond it from the creation of the world [and] continuously. [19] And through that oath the depths are made fast, and abide, and do not stir from their place from age to age. [20] And through that oath the sun and moon complete their course and do not deviate from their ordinance from age to age. [21] And through that oath the stars complete their course, and He calls them by their names, and they answer Him from age to age. [22] [[And in like manner the spirits of the water, and of the winds, and of all zephyrs, and [their] paths from all the quarters of the winds. [23] And the voices of the thunder and the light of the lightnings are preserved; and the chambers of the hail, and the chambers of the hoarfrost, and the chambers of the mist, and the chambers of the rain and the dew are preserved. [24] And all these believe and give thanks before the Lord of Spirits, and glorify [Him] with all their power, and their food is in every act of thanksgiving: they thank, and glorify, and extol the Name of the Lord of Spirits

forever and ever.]] ²⁵ And this oath is mighty over them, and their paths are preserved through it, and their course is not destroyed. ²⁶ And there was great joy among them, and they blessed, and glorified, and extolled, because the Name of that Son of Man had been revealed to them. ²⁷ And He sat on the throne of His glory, and the sum of judgment was given to the Son of Man, and He caused the sinners to pass away and be destroyed from off the face of the earth, and those who have led the world astray. ²⁸ They will be bound with chains, and in their gathering place of destruction they will be imprisoned, and all their works will vanish from the face of the earth. ²⁹ And from now on there will be nothing corruptible, for that Son of Man has appeared and has seated Himself on the throne of His glory, and all evil will pass away before His face, and the word of that Son of Man will go out and be strong before the Lord of Spirits.

CHAPTER 70

¹ And it came to pass after this that his name during his lifetime was raised aloft to that Son of Man and to the Lord of Spirits from among those who dwell on the earth. ² And he was raised aloft on the chariots of the Spirit and his name vanished among them. ³ And from that day I was no longer numbered among them: and He set me between the two winds, between the north and the west, where the messengers took the cords to measure for me the place for the chosen ones and righteous. ⁴ And there I saw the first fathers and the righteous who dwell in that place from the beginning.

CHAPTER 71

¹ And it came to pass after this that my spirit was translated, and it ascended into the heavens, and I saw the holy sons of God: they were stepping on flames of fire, their garments were white, and their faces shone like snow. ² And I saw two streams of fire, and the light of that fire shone like hyacinth, and I fell on my face before the Lord of Spirits. ³ And the messenger Michael, [[one of the chief-messengers,]] seized me by my right hand, and lifted me up, and led me out into all the secrets, and he showed me all the secrets of righteousness. ⁴ And he showed me all the secrets of the ends of the heavens, and all the chambers of all the stars, and all the luminaries, from where they proceed before the face of the holy ones. ⁵ And he translated my spirit into the Heaven of heavens, and I saw there as it were a structure built of crystals, and between those crystals, tongues of living fire. ⁶ And my spirit saw the girdle which girt that house of fire, and on its four sides were streams full of living fire, and they girt that house. ⁷ And around were seraphim, cherubim, and ophanim: and these are they who do not sleep, and they guard the throne of His glory. ⁸ And I saw messengers who could not be counted—one million and [even] one hundred million—encircling that house. And Michael, and Raphael, and Gabriel, and Phanuel, and the holy messengers who are above the heavens, go in and out of that house. ⁹ And they came out from that house, and [also] Michael and Gabriel, Raphael and Phanuel, and many holy messengers without number, ¹⁰ and with them the Head of Days, His head white and pure as wool, and His raiment indescribable. ¹¹ And I fell on my face, and my whole body became relaxed, and my spirit was transfigured; and I cried with a loud voice, with the spirit of power, and blessed, and glorified, and extolled. ¹² And these blessings which went out of my mouth were well pleasing before that Head of Days. ¹³ And that Head of Days came with Michael and Gabriel, Raphael and Phanuel, [and] thousands and myriads of messengers without number. ¹⁴ And He came to me and greeted me with His voice, and said to me, "This is the Son of Man who is born to righteousness, and righteousness abides over Him, and the righteousness of the Head of Days does not forsake Him." ¹⁵ And He said to me, "He proclaims peace to you in the name of the world to come, for peace has proceeded from there since the creation of the world, and so it will be to you forever and ever. ¹⁶ And all will walk in His ways since righteousness never forsakes Him: their dwelling-places will be with Him, and their heritage with Him, and they will not be separated from Him forever and ever. And so there will be length of days with that Son of Man, and the righteous will have peace and an upright way in the Name of the Lord of Spirits forever and ever."

SECTION 3:
THE ASTRONOMICAL BOOK

CHAPTER 72

¹ THE SCROLL OF THE COURSES OF THE LUMINARIES OF THE HEAVENS, the relations of each, according to their classes, their dominion and their seasons, according to their names and places of origin, and according to their months, which Uriel, the holy messenger who was with me, who is their guide, showed me; and he showed me all their laws exactly as they are, and how it is with regard to all the years of the world and continuously, until the new creation is accomplished which endures forever. ² And this is the first law of the luminaries: the luminary [named] the Sun has its rising in the eastern portals of heaven, and its setting in the western portals of heaven. ³ And I saw six portals in which the sun rises, and six portals in which the sun sets, and the moon rises and sets in these portals, and the leaders of the stars and those whom they lead: six in the east and six in the west, and all following each other in accurately corresponding order: also, many windows to the right and left of these portals. ⁴ And first there goes out the great luminary named the Sun, and his circumference is

like the circumference of heaven, and he is quite filled with illuminating and heating fire. ⁵The chariot on which he ascends, the wind drives, and the sun goes down from heaven and returns through the north in order to reach the east and is so guided that he comes to the appropriate portal and shines in the face of heaven. ⁶In this way he rises in the first month in the great portal, which is the fourth. ⁷And in that fourth portal from which the sun rises in the first month are twelve window-openings, from which proceed a flame when they are opened in their season. ⁸When the sun rises in heaven, he comes out through that fourth portal [for] thirty mornings in succession, and sets accurately in the fourth portal in the west of heaven. ⁹And during this period the day becomes daily longer and the night nightly shorter to the thirtieth morning. ¹⁰On that day the day is longer than the night by a ninth part, and the day amounts exactly to ten parts and the night to eight parts. ¹¹And the sun rises from that fourth portal, and sets in the fourth, and returns to the fifth portal of the east [for] thirty mornings, and rises from it, and sets in the fifth portal. ¹²And then the day becomes longer by two parts and amounts to eleven parts, and the night becomes shorter and amounts to seven parts. ¹³And it returns to the east and enters into the sixth portal, and rises, and sets in the sixth portal [for] thirty-one mornings on account of its sign. ¹⁴On that day the day becomes longer than the night, and the day becomes double the night, and the day becomes twelve parts, and the night is shortened and becomes six parts. ¹⁵And the sun mounts up to make the day shorter and the night longer, and the sun returns to the east and enters into the sixth portal, and rises from it, and sets [for] thirty mornings. ¹⁶And when thirty mornings are accomplished, the day decreases by exactly one part, and becomes eleven parts, and the night seven. ¹⁷And the sun goes out from that sixth portal in the west, and goes to the east, and rises in the fifth portal for thirty mornings, and sets in the west again in the fifth western portal. ¹⁸On that day the day decreases by two parts and amounts to ten parts and the night to eight parts. ¹⁹And the sun goes out from that fifth portal, and sets in the fifth portal of the west, and rises in the fourth portal for thirty-one mornings on account of its sign, and sets in the west. ²⁰On that day the day is equalized with the night, and the night amounts to nine parts and the day to nine parts. ²¹And the sun rises from that portal, and sets in the west, and returns to the east, and rises [for] thirty mornings in the third portal, and sets in the west in the third portal. ²²And on that day the night becomes longer than the day, and night becomes longer than [the previous] night, and day shorter than [the previous] day until the thirtieth morning, and the night amounts exactly to ten parts and the day to eight parts. ²³And the sun rises from that third portal, and sets in the third portal in the west, and returns to the east, and for thirty

mornings rises in the second portal in the east, and in like manner sets in the second portal in the west of heaven. ²⁴And on that day the night amounts to eleven parts and the day to seven parts. ²⁵And the sun rises on that day from that second portal, and sets in the west in the second portal, and returns to the east into the first portal for thirty-one mornings, and sets in the first portal in the west of heaven. ²⁶And on that day the night becomes longer and amounts to the double of the day: and the night amounts exactly to twelve parts and the day to six. ²⁷And the sun has traversed the divisions of his orbit, and turns again on those divisions of his orbit, and enters that portal [for] thirty mornings, and also sets in the west opposite to it. ²⁸And on that night the night has decreased in length by a ninth part, and the night has become eleven parts and the day seven parts. ²⁹And the sun has returned and entered into the second portal in the east, and returns on those divisions of his orbit for thirty mornings, rising and setting. ³⁰And on that day the night decreases in length, and the night amounts to ten parts and the day to eight. ³¹And on that day the sun rises from that portal, and sets in the west, and returns to the east, and rises in the third portal for thirty-one mornings, and sets in the west of heaven. ³²On that day the night decreases and amounts to nine parts, and the day to nine parts, and the night is equal to the day, and the year is exactly as to its days three hundred and sixty-four. ³³And the length of the day and of the night, and the shortness of the day and of the night arise through the course of the sun [where] these distinctions are made. ³⁴So it comes that its course becomes daily longer, and its course nightly shorter. ³⁵And this is the law and the course of the sun, and his return as often as he returns sixty times and rises—the great luminary, which is named the Sun, forever and ever. ³⁶And that which rises is the great luminary, and is so named according to its appearance, according as the LORD commanded. ³⁷As he rises, so he sets, and does not decrease and does not rest, but runs day and night, and his light is sevenfold brighter than that of the moon, but as regards size, they are both equal.

CHAPTER 73

¹And after this law I saw another law dealing with the smaller luminary, which is named the Moon. ²And her circumference is like the circumference of heaven, and her chariot in which she rides is driven by the wind, and light is given to her in [definite] measure. ³And her rising and setting change every month: and her days are like the days of the sun, and when her light is uniform it amounts to the seventh part of the light of the sun. ⁴And so she rises. And her first phase in the east comes out on the thirtieth morning: and on that day she becomes visible and constitutes for you the first phase of the moon on the thirtieth day, together with the sun in the portal where

the sun rises. ⁵ And the one half of her goes out by a seventh part, and her whole circumference is empty, without light, with the exception of one-seventh part of it, [and] the fourteenth part of her light. ⁶ And when she receives one-seventh part of the half of her light, her light amounts to one-seventh part and the half thereof. ⁷ And she sets with the sun, and when the sun rises, the moon rises with him and receives the half of one part of light, and in that night, in the beginning of her morning, the moon sets with the sun and is invisible that night with the fourteen parts and the half of one of them. ⁸ And she rises on that day with exactly a seventh part, and comes out, and recedes from the rising of the sun, and in her remaining days she becomes bright in the [remaining] thirteen parts.

CHAPTER 74

¹ And I saw another course, a law for her, [and] how according to that law she performs her monthly revolution. ² And Uriel, the holy messenger who is the leader of them all, showed all these to me, and their positions, and I wrote down their positions as he showed them to me, and I wrote down their months as they were, and the appearance of their lights until fifteen days were accomplished. ³ In each seventh part she accomplishes all her light in the east, and in each seventh part accomplishes all her darkness in the west. ⁴ And in certain months she alters her settings, and in certain months she pursues her own peculiar course. ⁵ In two months the moon sets with the sun: in those two middle portals, the third and the fourth. ⁶ She goes out for seven days, and turns around, and returns again through the portal where the sun rises and accomplishes all her light: and she recedes from the sun, and in eight days enters the sixth portal from which the sun goes out. ⁷ And when the sun goes out from the fourth portal, she goes out seven days, until she goes out from the fifth, and turns back again in seven days into the fourth portal and accomplishes all her light: and she recedes and enters into the first portal in eight days. ⁸ And she returns again in seven days into the fourth portal from which the sun goes out. ⁹ So I saw their position—how the moon rose and the sun set in those days. ¹⁰ And if five years are added together the sun has a surplus of thirty days, and all the days which accrue to it for one of those five years, when they are full, amount to three hundred and sixty-four days. ¹¹ And the surplus of the sun and of the stars amounts to six days: in five years six days every year comes to thirty days, and the moon falls behind the sun and stars to the number of thirty days. ¹² And the sun and the stars bring in all the years exactly, so that they do not advance or delay their position by a single day [and] continuously, but complete the years with perfect justice in three hundred and sixty-four days. ¹³ In three years there are one thousand and ninety-two days, and in five years one thousand and eight hundred and twenty days, so that in eight years there are two thousand and nine hundred and twelve days. ¹⁴ For the moon alone the days amount in three years to one thousand and sixty-two days, and in five years she falls fifty days behind: there is [the sum of these five] to be added to [the] one thousand and sixty-two days. ¹⁵ And in five years there are one thousand and seven hundred and seventy days, so that for the moon the days in eight years amount to two thousand and eight hundred and thirty-two days. ¹⁶ [For in eight years she falls behind to the amount of eighty days]; all the days she falls behind in eight years are eighty. ¹⁷ And the year is accurately completed in conformity with their world-stations and the stations of the sun, which rises from the portals through which it rises and sets [for] thirty days.

CHAPTER 75

¹ And the leaders of the heads of the thousands, who are placed over the whole creation and over all the stars, also have to do with the four intercalary days, being inseparable from their office, according to the reckoning of the year, and these render service on the four days which are not reckoned in the reckoning of the year. ² And owing to them men go wrong therein, for those luminaries truly render service on the world-stations, one in the first portal, one in the third portal of heaven, one in the fourth portal, and one in the sixth portal, and the exactness of the year is accomplished through its separate three hundred and sixty-four stations. ³ For the signs, and the times, and the years, and the days the messenger Uriel showed to me, whom the Lord of Glory has set forever over all the luminaries of the heavens, in the heavens and in the world, that they should rule on the face of the heavens and be seen on the earth, and be leaders for the day and the night—the sun, moon, and stars, and all the ministering creatures which make their revolution in all the chariots of the heavens. ⁴ In like manner, Uriel showed me twelve doors open in the circumference of the sun's chariot in the heavens, through which the rays of the sun break out: and from them warmth is diffused over the earth when they are opened at their appointed seasons— ⁵ [[and for the winds and the spirit of the dew when they are opened, standing open in the heavens, at the ends.]] ⁶ As for the twelve portals in the heavens at the ends of the earth, out of which go out the sun, moon, and stars, and all the works of heaven in the east and in the west, ⁷ there are many windows open to the left and right of them, and one window at its [appointed] season produces warmth, corresponding [as these do] to those doors from which the stars come out according as He has commanded them, and wherein they set corresponding to their number. ⁸ And I saw chariots in the heavens, running in the world, above those portals in which revolve the stars that never set. ⁹ And one is

larger than all the rest, and it is that which makes its course through the entire world.

CHAPTER 76

¹ And at the ends of the earth I saw twelve portals open to all the quarters [of the heavens], from which the winds go out and blow over the earth. ² Three of them are open on the face [(the east)] of the heavens, and three in the west, and three on the right [(the south)] of the heavens, and three on the left [(the north)]. ³ And the three first are those of the east, and three are of the north, and three of the south, and three of the west. ⁴ Through four of these come winds of blessing and prosperity, and from those eight come hurtful winds: when they are sent, they bring destruction on all the earth, and on the water on it, and on all who dwell thereon, and on everything which is in the water and on the land. ⁵ And the first wind from those portals, called the East Wind, comes out through the first portal which is in the east, inclining toward the south: desolation, drought, heat, and destruction come out from it. ⁶ And through the second portal in the middle comes what is fitting: and rain, and fruitfulness, and prosperity, and dew come from it. And through the third portal which lies toward the north come cold and drought. ⁷ And after these, the south winds come out through three portals: through the first portal of them inclining to the east a hot wind comes out. ⁸ And through the middle portal next to it, fragrant smells, and dew, and rain, and prosperity, and health come out. ⁹ And through the third portal lying to the west, dew and rain, locusts and desolation come out. ¹⁰ And after these, the north winds: from the seventh portal in the east come dew and rain, locusts and desolation. ¹¹ And from the middle portal, health, and rain, and dew, and prosperity come in a direct direction. And through the third portal in the west come cloud, and hoarfrost, and snow, and rain, and dew, and locusts. ¹² And after these [four] are the west winds: through the first portal adjoining the north, dew, and hoarfrost, and cold, and snow, and frost come out. ¹³ And from the middle portal, dew, and rain, and prosperity, and blessing come out. And through the last portal which adjoins the south, drought, and desolation, and burning, and destruction come out. ¹⁴ And the twelve portals of the four quarters of the heavens are completed with that, and I have shown all their laws, and all their plagues, and all their benefactions to you, my son Methuselah.

CHAPTER 77

¹ And the first quarter is called the East, because it is the first. And the second, the South, because the Most High will descend there—yes, there in quite a special sense will He who is blessed forever descend. ² And the west quarter is named the Diminished, because all the luminaries of the heavens wane and go down there. ³ And the fourth quarter, named the North, is divided into three parts: the first of them is for the dwelling of men; and the second contains seas of water, and the abysses, and forests, and rivers, and darkness, and clouds; and the third part contains the Garden of Righteousness. ⁴ I saw seven high mountains, higher than all the mountains which are on the earth: and there comes out hoarfrost, and days, seasons, and years pass away. ⁵ I saw seven rivers on the earth larger than all the rivers: one of them coming from the west pours its waters into the Great Sea. ⁶ And these two come from the north to the sea and pour their waters into the Erythraean Sea in the east. ⁷ And the remaining four come out on the side of the north to their own sea—two of them to the Erythraean Sea and two into the Great Sea—and discharge themselves there [[or into the desert]]. ⁸ I saw seven great islands in the sea and in the mainland: two in the mainland and five in the Great Sea.

CHAPTER 78

¹ And the names of the sun are the following: the first Orjares, and the second Tomas. ² And the moon has four names: the first name is Asonja, the second Ebla, the third Benase, and the fourth Erae. ³ These are the two great luminaries; their circumference is like the circumference of heaven, and the size of the circumference of both is alike. ⁴ In the circumference of the sun there are seven portions of light which are added to it more than to the moon, and it is transferred in definite measures until the seventh portion of the sun is exhausted. ⁵ And they set and enter the portals of the west, and make their revolution by the north, and come out through the eastern portals on the face of the heavens. ⁶ And when the moon rises, one-fourteenth part appears in the heavens; on the fourteenth day she accomplishes her light. ⁷ And fifteen parts of light are transferred to her until the fifteenth day [when] her light is accomplished, according to the sign of the year, and she becomes fifteen parts, and the moon grows by fourteen parts. ⁸ And in her waning [the moon] decreases on the first day to fourteen parts of her light, on the second to thirteen parts of light, on the third to twelve, on the fourth to eleven, on the fifth to ten, on the sixth to nine, on the seventh to eight, on the eighth to seven, on the ninth to six, on the tenth to five, on the eleventh to four, on the twelfth to three, on the thirteenth to two, on the fourteenth to the half of a seventh, and all her remaining light disappears wholly on the fifteenth. ⁹ And in certain months the month has twenty-nine days and once twenty-eight. ¹⁰ And Uriel showed me another law [regarding] when light is transferred to the moon, and on which side it is transferred to her by the sun. ¹¹ During all the period during which the moon is growing in her light, she is transferring it to herself when opposite to the sun during fourteen days; and when she is illuminated

throughout, her light is fully accomplished in the heavens. [12] And on the first day she is called the new moon, for on that day the light rises on her. [13] She becomes a full moon exactly on the day when the sun sets in the west, and from the east she rises at night, and the moon shines the whole night through until the sun rises over against her and the moon is seen over against the sun. [14] On the side from where the light of the moon comes out, there again she wanes until all the light vanishes and all the days of the month are at an end, and her circumference is empty, void of light. [15] And three months she makes of thirty days, and at her time she makes three months of twenty-nine days each, in which she accomplishes her waning in the first period of time, and in the first portal for one hundred and seventy-seven days. [16] And in the time of her going out she appears for three months [of] thirty days each, and for three months she appears [of] twenty-nine each. [17] At night she appears like a man for twenty days each time, and by day she appears like the heavens, and there is nothing else in her except her light [(the light of day)].

CHAPTER 79

[1] "And now, my son, I have shown you everything, and the law of all the stars of the heavens is completed." [2] And he showed me all the laws of these for every day, and for every season of bearing rule, and for every year, and for its going out, and for the order prescribed to it every month and every week; [3] and the waning of the moon which takes place in the sixth portal; for in this sixth portal her light is accomplished, and after that there is the beginning of the waning; [4] [and the waning] which takes place in the first portal in its season, until one hundred and seventy-seven days are accomplished, reckoned according to weeks—twenty-five [weeks] and two days. [5] She falls behind the sun and the order of the stars exactly five days in the course of one period, and when this place which you see has been traversed. [6] Such is the picture and sketch of every luminary which the chief-messenger Uriel, who is their leader, showed to me.

CHAPTER 80

[1] And in those days the messenger Uriel answered and said to me, "Behold, I have shown you everything, Enoch, and I have revealed everything to you that you should see this sun and this moon, and the leaders of the stars of the heavens and all those who turn them, their tasks, and times, and departures. [2] And in the days of the sinners the years will be shortened, and their seed will be late on their lands and fields, and all things on the earth will alter, and will not appear in their time: And the rain will be kept back, || And the heavens will withhold [it]. [3] And in those times the fruits of the earth will be backward, || And will not grow in their time, || And the fruits of the trees will be withheld in their time. [4] And the moon will alter her order, || And not appear at her time. [5] [[And in those days the sun will be seen, || And he will journey in the evening || On the extremity of the great chariot in the west,]] || And will shine more brightly than accords with the order of light. [6] And many chiefs of the stars || Will transgress the order [prescribed]. And these will alter their orbits and tasks, || And not appear at the seasons prescribed to them. [7] And the whole order of the stars will be concealed from the sinners, || And the thoughts of those on the earth will err concerning them, [[|| And they will be altered from all their ways,]] || Yes, they will err and take them to be gods. [8] And evil will be multiplied on them, || And punishment will come on them so as to destroy all."

CHAPTER 81

[1] And he said to me, "Enoch, observe these heavenly tablets, and read what is written thereon, and mark every individual fact." [2] And I observed the heavenly tablets, and read everything which was written [thereon], and understood everything, and read the scroll of all the deeds of mankind, and of all the children of flesh that will be on the earth to the most remote generations. [3] And thereon I blessed the great LORD, the King of glory, forever, in that He has made all the works of the world, and I extolled the LORD because of His patience, and blessed Him because of the children of men. [4] And after that I said, "Blessed is the man who dies in righteousness and goodness, concerning whom there is no scroll of unrighteousness written, and against whom no Day of Judgment will be found." [5] And those seven holy ones brought me and placed me on the earth before the door of my house, and said to me, "Declare everything to your son Methuselah, and show to all your children that no flesh is righteous in the sight of the LORD, for He is their Creator. [6] One year we will leave you with your son, until you give your [last] commands, that you may teach your children, and record [it] for them, and testify to all your children; and in the second year they will take you from their midst. [7] Let your heart be strong, || For the good will announce righteousness to the good; The righteous will rejoice with the righteous || And will offer congratulations to one another. [8] But the sinners will die with the sinners, || And the apostate goes down with the apostate. [9] And those who practice righteousness || Will die on account of the deeds of men || And be taken away on account of the doings of the godless." [10] And in those days they ceased to speak to me, and I came to my people, blessing the Lord of the world.

CHAPTER 82

[1] And now, my son Methuselah, all these things I am recounting to you and writing down for you! And I have revealed everything to you, and given you

scrolls concerning all these; so preserve, my son Methuselah, the scrolls from your father's hand, and [see] that you deliver them to the generations of the world. ²I have given wisdom to you and to your children, [[‖ And your children that will be to you,]] ‖ That they may give it to their children for generations—This wisdom that surpasses their thought. ³And those who understand it will not sleep, ‖ But will listen with the ear that they may learn this wisdom, ‖ And it will please those that eat thereof better than good food. ⁴Blessed are all the righteous, blessed are all those who walk in the way of righteousness and do not sin as the sinners in the reckoning of all their days in which the sun traverses the heavens, entering into and departing from the portals for thirty days with the heads of thousands of the order of the stars, together with the four which are intercalated, which divide the four portions of the year, which lead them and enter with them four days. ⁵Owing to them, men will be at fault and not reckon them in the whole reckoning of the year: yes, men will be at fault, and not recognize them accurately. ⁶For they belong to the reckoning of the year and are truly recorded [thereon] forever, one in the first portal, and one in the third, and one in the fourth, and one in the sixth, and the year is completed in three hundred and sixty-four days. ⁷And the account thereof is accurate and the recorded reckoning thereof exact, for the luminaries, and months, and festivals, and years, and days, Uriel has shown and revealed to me, to whom the Lord of the whole creation of the world has subjected the host of Heaven. ⁸And he has power over night and day in the heavens to cause the light to give light to men—sun, moon, and stars, and all the powers of the heavens which revolve in their circular chariots. ⁹And these are the orders of the stars, which are set in their places, and in their seasons, and festivals, and months. ¹⁰And these are the names of those who lead them, who watch that they enter at their times, in their orders, in their seasons, in their months, in their periods of dominion, and in their positions. ¹¹Their four leaders who divide the four parts of the year enter first; and after them the twelve leaders of the orders who divide the months; and for the three hundred and sixty [days] there are heads over thousands who divide the days; and for the four intercalary days there are the leaders which split the four parts of the year. ¹²And these heads over thousands are intercalated between leader and leader, each behind a station, but their leaders make the division. ¹³And these are the names of the leaders who divide the four parts of the year which are ordained: Milki'el, Hel'emmelek, and Mel'ejal, and Narel. ¹⁴And the names of those who lead them: Adnar'el, and Ijasusa'el, and 'Elome'el—these three follow the leaders of the orders, and there is one that follows the three leaders of the orders which follow those leaders of stations that divide the four parts of the year. ¹⁵In the beginning of the year Melkejal rises first and rules, who is named Tam'aini and Sun, and all the days of his dominion while he bears rule are ninety-one days. ¹⁶And these are the signs of the days which are to be seen on earth in the days of his dominion: sweat, and heat, and stillness; and all the trees bear fruit, and leaves are produced on all the trees, and the harvest of wheat, and the rose-flowers, and all the flowers which come out in the field, but the trees of the winter season become withered. ¹⁷And these are the names of the leaders which are under them: Berka'el, Zelebs'el, and another who is added, a head of one thousand called Hilujaseph: and the days of the dominion of this [leader] are at an end. ¹⁸The next leader after him is Hel'emmelek, whom one names the Shining Sun, and all the days of his light are ninety-one days. ¹⁹And these are the signs of [his] days on the earth: glowing heat and dryness, and the trees ripen their fruits and produce all their fruits ripe and ready, and the sheep pair and become pregnant, and all the fruits of the earth are gathered in, as well as everything that is in the fields and the winepress: these things take place in the days of his dominion. ²⁰These are the names, and the orders, and the leaders of those heads of thousands: Gida'ljal, Ke'el, and He'el, and the name of the head of one thousand which is added to them, Asfa'el: and the days of his dominion are at an end.

SECTION 4:
THE BOOK OF DREAM VISIONS

CHAPTER 83
¹And now, my son Methuselah, I will show you all my visions which I have seen, recounting them before you. ²I saw two visions before I took a wife, and the one was quite unlike the other: the first when I was learning to write; the second before I took your mother, [when] I saw a terrible vision. ³And I prayed to the LORD regarding them. I had laid myself down in the house of my grandfather Mahalalel [when] I saw in a vision how heaven collapsed and was borne off and fell to the earth. ⁴And when it fell to the earth, I saw how the earth was swallowed up in a great abyss, and mountains were suspended on mountains, and hills sank down on hills, and high trees were torn from their stems, and hurled down, and sunk in the abyss. ⁵And a word suddenly fell into my mouth, and I lifted up [my voice] to cry aloud, and said, "The earth is destroyed!" ⁶And my grandfather Mahalalel waked me as I lay near him, and said to me, "Why do you cry so, my son, and why do you make such lamentation?" ⁷And I recounted to him the whole vision which I had seen, and he said to me, "You have seen a terrible thing, my son, and of grave moment is your dream-vision as to the secrets of all the sin of the earth: it must sink into the abyss and be destroyed with a great destruction. ⁸And now, my son, arise and

make petition to the Lord of Glory, since you are a believer, that a remnant may remain on the earth, and that He may not destroy the whole earth. ⁹ My son, all this will come on the earth from Heaven, and there will be great destruction on the earth." ¹⁰ After that I arose, and prayed, and implored, and sought, and wrote down my prayer for the generations of the world, and I will show everything to you, my son Methuselah. ¹¹ And when I had gone out below and seen the heavens, and the sun rising in the east, and the moon setting in the west, and a few stars, and the whole earth, and everything as He had known it in the beginning, then I blessed the Lord of judgment and extolled Him because He had made the sun to go out from the windows of the east, and he ascended and rose on the face of the heavens, and set out and kept traversing the path shown to him.

CHAPTER 84

¹ And I lifted up my hands in righteousness and blessed the Holy and Great One, and spoke with the breath of my mouth, and with the tongue of flesh, which God has made for the children of the flesh of men, that they should speak with [it], and He gave them breath, and a tongue, and a mouth that they should speak with [them]: ² "Blessed are You, O LORD, ‖ King, great and mighty in Your greatness, ‖ Lord of the whole creation of the heavens, ‖ King of kings and God of the whole world. And Your power, and kingship, and greatness ‖ Abide forever and ever, ‖ And throughout all generations Your dominion; And all the heavens are Your throne forever, ‖ And the whole earth Your footstool forever and ever. ³ For You have made and You rule all things, ‖ And nothing is too hard for You; Wisdom does not depart from the place of Your throne, ‖ Nor turns away from Your presence. And You know, and see, and hear everything, ‖ And there is nothing hidden from You. ⁴ And now the messengers of Your heavens are guilty of trespass, ‖ And Your wrath abides on the flesh of men until the great Day of Judgment. ⁵ And now, O God, and Lord, and Great King, I exceedingly implore You to fulfill my prayer, to leave me a posterity on earth, and not destroy all the flesh of man, and make the earth without inhabitant, so that there should be a continuous destruction. ⁶ And now, my Lord, destroy from the earth the flesh which has aroused Your wrath, but establish the flesh of righteousness and uprightness as a plant of the continuous seed, and do not hide Your face from the prayer of Your servant, O LORD."

CHAPTER 85

¹ And after this I saw another dream, and I will show the whole dream to you, my son. ² And Enoch lifted up [his voice] and spoke to his son Methuselah: "To you, my son, I will speak: hear my words and incline your ear to the dream-vision of your father. ³ Before I

took your mother Edna, I saw in a vision on my bed, and behold, a bull came out from the earth, and that bull was white; and after it a heifer came out, and along with this [heifer] two bulls came out: one of them black and the other red. ⁴ And that black bull gored the red one and pursued him over the earth, and immediately I could no longer see that red bull. ⁵ But that black bull grew, and that heifer went with him, and I saw that many oxen proceeded from him which resembled and followed him. ⁶ And that cow, that first one, went from the presence of that first bull in order to seek that red one, but did not find him, and lamented with a great lamentation over him and sought him. ⁷ And I looked until that first bull came to her and quieted her, and from that time onward she no longer cried. ⁸ And after that, she bore another white bull, and after him she bore many bulls and black cows. ⁹ And I saw in my sleep that white bull likewise grows and becomes a great white bull, and from him proceeded many white bulls, and they resembled him. ¹⁰ And they began to beget many white bulls, which resembled them, one following the other, [even] many."

CHAPTER 86

¹ "And again, I saw with my eyes as I slept, and I saw the heavens above, and behold, a star fell from Heaven, and it arose, and ate, and pastured among those oxen. ² And after that I saw the large and the black oxen, and behold, they all changed their stalls, and pastures, and their cattle, and began to live with each other. ³ And again, I saw in the vision, and looked toward the heavens, and behold, I saw many stars descend and cast themselves down from Heaven to that first star, and they became bulls among those cattle and pastured among them. ⁴ And I looked at them and saw, and behold, they all let out their genitals like horses, and began to cover the cows of the oxen, and they all became pregnant and bore elephants, camels, and donkeys. ⁵ And all the oxen feared them, and were frightened at them, and began to bite with their teeth, and to devour, and to gore with their horns. ⁶ And they began, moreover, to devour those oxen; and behold, all the children of the earth began to tremble and quake before them and to flee from them."

CHAPTER 87

¹ "And again, I saw how they began to gore each other and to devour each other, and the earth began to cry aloud. ² And I raised my eyes again to Heaven, and I saw in the vision, and behold, there came out from Heaven beings who were like white men: and four went out from that place and three with them. ³ And those three that had last come out grasped me by my hand and took me up, away from the generations of the earth, and raised me up to a lofty place, and showed me a tower raised high above the earth, and

all the hills were lower. ⁴ And one said to me, Remain here until you see everything that befalls those elephants, camels, and donkeys, and the stars, and the oxen, and all of them."

CHAPTER 88

¹ "And I saw one of those four who had come out first, and he seized that first star which had fallen from Heaven, and bound it hand and foot, and cast it into an abyss: now that abyss was narrow, and deep, and horrible, and dark. ² And one of them drew a sword and gave it to those elephants, and camels, and donkeys: then they began to strike each other, and the whole earth quaked because of them. ³ And as I was beholding in the vision, one of those four who had come out from Heaven stoned [them], and gathered [them], and took all the great stars whose genitals were like those of horses, and bound them all hand and foot, and cast them in an abyss of the earth."

CHAPTER 89

¹ "And one of those four went to that white bull and instructed him in a secret, without his being terrified: he was born a bull, and became a man, and built a great vessel for himself, and dwelt thereon; and three bulls dwelt with him in that vessel, and they were enclosed inside. ² And again, I raised my eyes toward the heavens and saw a lofty roof with seven water torrents thereon, and those torrents flowed with much water into an enclosure. ³ And I saw again, and behold, fountains were opened on the surface of that great enclosure, and that water began to swell and rise on the surface, and I saw that enclosure until all its surface was covered with water. ⁴ And the water, the darkness, and mist increased on it; and as I looked at the height of that water, that water had risen above the height of that enclosure, and was streaming over that enclosure, and it stood on the earth. ⁵ And all the cattle of that enclosure were gathered together until I saw how they sank, and were swallowed up, and perished in that water. ⁶ But that vessel floated on the water, while all the oxen, and elephants, and camels, and donkeys sank to the bottom with all the animals, so that I could no longer see them, and they were not able to escape, [but] perished and sank into the depths. ⁷ And again, I saw in the vision until those water torrents were removed from that high roof, and the chasms of the earth were leveled up, and other abysses were opened. ⁸ Then the water began to run down into these until the earth became visible, but that vessel settled on the earth, and the darkness retired, and light appeared. ⁹ But that white bull which had become a man came out of that vessel, and the three bulls with him, and one of those three was white like that bull, and one of them was red as blood, and one black: and that white bull departed from them. ¹⁰ And they began to bring out beasts of the field and birds, so that there arose different genera: lions, tigers, wolves, dogs, hyenas, wild boars, foxes, squirrels, swine, falcons, vultures, kites, eagles, and ravens; and a white bull was born among them. ¹¹ And they began to bite one another, but that white bull which was born among them begot a wild donkey and a white bull with it, and the wild donkeys multiplied. ¹² But that bull which was born from him begot a black wild boar and a white sheep; and the former begot many boars, but that sheep begot twelve sheep. ¹³ And when those twelve sheep had grown, they gave up one of them to the donkeys, and those donkeys again gave up that sheep to the wolves, and that sheep grew up among the wolves. ¹⁴ And the LORD brought the eleven sheep to live with it and to pasture with it among the wolves: and they multiplied and became many flocks of sheep. ¹⁵ And the wolves began to fear them, and they oppressed them until they destroyed their little ones, and they cast their young into a river of much water, but those sheep began to cry aloud on account of their little ones, and to complain to their Lord. ¹⁶ And a sheep which had been saved from the wolves fled and escaped to the wild donkeys; and I saw how the sheep lamented, and cried, and implored their Lord with all their might until that Lord of the sheep descended at the voice of the sheep from a lofty abode, and came to them, and pastured them. ¹⁷ And He called that sheep which had escaped the wolves and spoke with it concerning the wolves that it should admonish them not to touch the sheep. ¹⁸ And the sheep went to the wolves according to the word of the LORD, and another sheep met it and went with it, and the two went and entered together into the assembly of those wolves, and spoke with them, and admonished them not to touch the sheep from now on. ¹⁹ And immediately I saw the wolves, and how they oppressed the sheep exceedingly with all their power; and the sheep cried aloud. ²⁰ And the LORD came to the sheep and they began to strike those wolves: and the wolves began to make lamentation, but the sheep became quiet and then ceased to cry out. ²¹ And I saw the sheep until they departed from among the wolves, but the eyes of the wolves were blinded, and those wolves departed in pursuit of the sheep with all their power. ²² And the Lord of the sheep went with them, as their leader, and all His sheep followed Him: and his face was dazzling, and glorious, and terrible to behold. ²³ But the wolves began to pursue those sheep until they reached a sea of water. ²⁴ And that sea was divided, and the water stood on this side and on that before their face, and their Lord led them and placed Himself between them and the wolves. ²⁵ And as those wolves did not yet see the sheep, they proceeded into the midst of that sea, and the wolves followed the sheep, and [those wolves] ran after them into that sea. ²⁶ And when they saw the Lord of the sheep, they turned to flee before His face, but that sea gathered itself together, and became as it had been created, and the water swelled and rose until it covered those

wolves. [27] And I saw until all the wolves who pursued those sheep perished and were drowned. [28] But the sheep escaped from that water and went out into a wilderness, where there was no water and no grass; and they began to open their eyes and to see; and I saw the Lord of the sheep pasturing them and giving them water and grass, and that sheep going and leading them. [29] And that sheep ascended to the summit of that lofty rock, and the Lord of the sheep sent it to them. [30] And after that I saw the Lord of the sheep who stood before them, and His appearance was great, and terrible, and majestic, and all those sheep saw Him and were afraid before His face. [31] And they all feared and trembled because of Him, and they cried to that sheep with them [which was among them]: We are not able to stand before our Lord or to behold Him! [32] And that sheep which led them again ascended to the summit of that rock, but the sheep began to be blinded and to wander from the way which he had showed them, but that sheep was not aware. [33] And the Lord of the sheep was exceedingly wrathful against them, and that sheep discovered it, and went down from the summit of the rock, and came to the sheep, and found the greatest part of them blinded and fallen away. [34] And when they saw it, they feared and trembled at its presence and desired to return to their folds. [35] And that sheep took other sheep with it, and came to those sheep which had fallen away, and began to slay them; and the sheep feared its presence, and so that sheep brought back those sheep that had fallen away, and they returned to their folds. [36] And I saw in this vision until that sheep became a man, and built a house for the Lord of the sheep, and placed all the sheep in that house. [37] And I saw until this sheep which had met that sheep which led them fell asleep: and I saw until all the great sheep perished and little ones arose in their place, and they came to a pasture, and approached a stream of water. [38] Then that sheep, their leader which had become a man, withdrew from them and fell asleep, and all the sheep sought it and cried over it with a great crying. [39] And I saw until they ceased from crying for that sheep and crossed that stream of water, and there arose the two sheep as leaders in the place of those which had led them and fallen asleep. [40] And I saw until the sheep came to an attractive place, and a pleasant and glorious land, and I saw until those sheep were satisfied; and that house stood among them in the pleasant land. [41] And sometimes their eyes were opened, and sometimes blinded, until another sheep arose and led them and brought them all back, and their eyes were opened. [42] And the dogs, and the foxes, and the wild boars began to devour those sheep until the Lord of the sheep raised up a ram from their midst, which led them. [43] And that ram began to butt those dogs, foxes, and wild boars on either side until he had destroyed them all. [44] And that sheep whose eyes were opened saw that ram, which was among the sheep, until it forsook its glory and began to butt those sheep, and trampled on them, and behaved unseemly itself. [45] And the Lord of the sheep sent the lamb to another lamb and raised it to be a ram and leader of the sheep instead of that ram which had forsaken its glory. [46] And it went to it and spoke to it alone, and raised it to be a ram, and made it the prince and leader of the sheep, but during all these things those dogs oppressed the sheep. [47] And the first ram pursued that second ram, and that second ram arose and fled before it, and I saw until those dogs pulled down the first ram. [48] And that second ram arose and led the [little] sheep. And those sheep grew and multiplied, but all the dogs, and foxes, and wild boars feared and fled before it, and that ram butted and killed the wild beasts, and those wild beasts no longer had any power among the sheep and no longer robbed them of anything. [49] And that ram begot many sheep and fell asleep; and a little sheep became ram in its stead and became prince and leader of those sheep. [50] And that house became great and broad, and it was built for those sheep: [and] a great and lofty tower was built on the house for the Lord of the sheep, and that house was low, but the tower was elevated and lofty, and the Lord of the sheep stood on that tower and they offered a full table before Him. [51] And again I saw that those sheep again erred and went many ways, and forsook that house of theirs, and the Lord of the sheep called some from among the sheep and sent them to the sheep, but the sheep began to slay them. [52] And one of them was saved and was not slain, and it sped away and cried aloud over the sheep; and they sought to slay it, but the Lord of the sheep saved it from the sheep, and brought it up to me, and caused it to dwell there. [53] And He sent many other sheep to those sheep to testify to them and lament over them. [54] And after that, I saw that when they forsook the house of the LORD and His tower they fell away entirely, and their eyes were blinded; and I saw how the Lord of the sheep worked much slaughter among them in their herds until those sheep invited that slaughter and betrayed His place. [55] And He gave them over into the hands of the lions, and tigers, and wolves, and hyenas, and into the hand of the foxes, and to all the wild beasts, and those wild beasts began to tear those sheep in pieces. [56] And I saw that He forsook their house and their tower and gave them all into the hand of the lions and into the hand of all the wild beasts to tear and devour them. [57] And I began to cry aloud with all my power, and to appeal to the Lord of the sheep, and to represent to Him in regard to the sheep that they were devoured by all the wild beasts. [58] But He remained unmoved, though He saw it, and rejoiced that they were devoured, and swallowed, and robbed, and He left them to be devoured in the hand of all the beasts. [59] And He called seventy shepherds and cast those sheep to them that they might pasture them, and He spoke to the shepherds and their companions: Let each individual among you pasture the sheep from now on and do everything that I will command you to do. And I will deliver them over to you rightly numbered and tell you which of them are to be destroyed: and destroy them. ⁶⁰ And He gave those sheep over to them. ⁶¹ And He called another and spoke to him: Observe and record everything that the shepherds will do to those sheep, for they will destroy more of them than I have commanded them. ⁶² And every excess and the destruction which will be worked through the shepherds, record—how many they destroy according to My command, and how many according to their own caprice: record against every individual shepherd all the destruction he effects. ⁶³ And read out before Me by number how many they destroy and how many they deliver over for destruction, that I may have this as a testimony against them, and know every deed of the shepherds, that I may comprehend and see what they do, whether or not they abide by My command which I have commanded them. ⁶⁴ But they will not know it, and you will not declare it to them, nor admonish them, but only record against each individual all the destruction which each of the shepherds effect in his time, and lay it all before Me. ⁶⁵ And I saw until those shepherds pastured in their season, and they began to slay and to destroy more than they were commanded, and they delivered those sheep into the hand of the lions. ⁶⁶ And the lions and tigers ate and devoured the greater part of those sheep, and the wild boars ate along with them; and they burned that tower and demolished that house. ⁶⁷ And I became exceedingly sorrowful over that tower because that house of the sheep was demolished, and afterward I was unable to see if those sheep entered that house. ⁶⁸ And the shepherds and their associates delivered those sheep over to all the wild beasts to devour them, and each one of them received a definite number in his time: it was written by the other in a scroll how many of them each one of them destroyed. ⁶⁹ And each one slew and destroyed many more than was prescribed, and I began to weep and lament on account of those sheep. ⁷⁰ And so in the vision I saw how that one who wrote wrote down everyone that was destroyed by those shepherds day by day, and he carried [it] up, and laid [it] down, and actually showed the whole scroll to the Lord of the sheep—[even] everything that they had done, and all that each one of them had made away with, and all that they had given over to destruction. ⁷¹ And the scroll was read before the Lord of the sheep, and He took the scroll from his hand, and read it, and sealed it, and laid it down. ⁷² And then I saw how the shepherds pastured for twelve hours, and behold, three of those sheep turned back, and came, and entered, and began to build up all that had fallen down of that house, but the wild boars tried to hinder them, but they were not able. ⁷³ And they began to build again as before, and they reared up that tower, and it was named the high tower; and they began to place a table again before the tower, but all the bread on it was polluted and not pure. ⁷⁴ And as concerning all this, the eyes of those sheep were blinded so that they did not see, and [the eyes of] their shepherds likewise; and they delivered them in large numbers to their shepherds for destruction, and they trampled the sheep with their feet and devoured them. ⁷⁵ And the Lord of the sheep remained unmoved until all the sheep were dispersed over the field and mingled with them, and they did not save them out of the hand of the beasts. ⁷⁶ And this one who wrote the scroll carried it up, and showed it, and read it before the Lord of the sheep, and implored Him on their account as he showed Him all the doings of the shepherds and gave testimony before Him against all the shepherds. ⁷⁷ And he took the actual scroll, and laid it down beside Him, and departed."

CHAPTER 90

¹ "And I saw until thirty-five shepherds undertook the pasturing [of the sheep] in this manner, and they separately completed their periods as did the first; and others received them into their hands, to pasture them for their period, each shepherd in his own period. ² And after that, I saw in my vision all the birds of the heavens coming: the eagles, the vultures, the kites, the ravens; but the eagles led all the birds, and they began to devour those sheep, and to pick out their eyes, and to devour their flesh. ³ And the sheep cried out because their flesh was being devoured by the birds, and as for me, I looked and lamented in my sleep over that shepherd who pastured the sheep. ⁴ And I saw until those sheep were devoured by the dogs, and eagles, and kites, and they left neither flesh, nor skin, nor sinew remaining on them until only their bones stood there: and their bones also fell to the earth and the sheep became few. ⁵ And I saw until twenty-three had undertaken the pasturing and completed fifty-eight times in their several periods. ⁶ But behold, lambs were borne by those white sheep, and they began to open their eyes and to see, and to cry to the sheep. ⁷ Yes, they cried to them, but they did not listen to what they said to them, but were exceedingly deaf, and their eyes were very exceedingly blinded. ⁸ And I saw in the vision how the ravens flew on those lambs, and took one of those lambs, and dashed the sheep in pieces, and devoured them. ⁹ And I saw until horns grew on those lambs, and the ravens cast down their horns; and I saw until there sprouted a great horn of one of those sheep, and their eyes were opened. ¹⁰ And it looked at them [and their eyes opened], and it cried to the sheep, and the rams saw it, and all ran to it. ¹¹ And notwithstanding all this, those eagles, and vultures, and ravens, and kites still kept tearing the sheep, and swooping down on them, and devouring them: still the sheep remained silent, but the rams lamented and cried out. ¹² And those ravens fought

and battled with it and sought to lay its horn low, but they had no power over it. ¹³ And I saw until the shepherds, and eagles, and those vultures and kites came, and they cried to the ravens that they should break the horn of that ram, and they battled and fought with it, and it battled with them and cried that its help might come. ¹⁴ And I saw until that man, who wrote down the names of the shepherds [and] carried [it] up into the presence of the Lord of the sheep, [[came and helped it and showed it everything: he had come down for the help of that ram.]] ¹⁵ And I saw until the Lord of the sheep came to them in wrath, and all who saw Him fled, and they all fell into His shadow from before His face. ¹⁶ All the eagles, and vultures, and ravens, and kites were gathered together, and there came with them all the sheep of the field, yes, they all came together, and helped each other to break that horn of the ram. ¹⁷ And I saw until that man, who wrote the scroll according to the command of the LORD, opened that scroll concerning the destruction which those twelve last shepherds had worked, and showed before the Lord of the sheep that they had destroyed much more than their predecessors. ¹⁸ And I saw until the Lord of the sheep came to them and took in His hand the staff of His wrath, and struck the earth, and the earth split apart, and all the beasts and all the birds of the heavens fell from among those sheep, and were swallowed up in the earth, and it covered them. ¹⁹ And I saw until a great sword was given to the sheep, and the sheep proceeded against all the beasts of the field to slay them, and all the beasts and the birds of the heavens fled before their face. ²⁰ And I saw until a throne was erected in the pleasant land, and the Lord of the sheep sat Himself thereon, and the other took the sealed scrolls and opened those scrolls before the Lord of the sheep. ²¹ And the LORD called those men, [those] seven first white ones, and commanded that they should bring before Him, beginning with the first star which led the way, all the stars whose genitals were like those of horses, and they brought them all before Him. ²² And He spoke to that man who wrote before Him, being one of those seven white ones, and said to him, Take those seventy shepherds to whom I delivered the sheep, and who taking them on their own authority slew more than I commanded them. ²³ And behold, I saw [that] they were all bound, and they all stood before Him. ²⁴ And the judgment was first held over the stars, and they were judged and found guilty, and went to the place of condemnation, and they were cast into an abyss, full of fire and flaming, and full of pillars of fire. ²⁵ And those seventy shepherds were judged and found guilty, and they were cast into that fiery abyss. ²⁶ And I saw at that time how a similar abyss was opened in the midst of the earth, full of fire, and they brought those blinded sheep, and they were all judged, and found guilty, and cast into this fiery abyss, and they burned; now this abyss was to the right of that house. ²⁷ And I saw those sheep burning and their bones burning. ²⁸ And I stood up to see until they folded up that old house, and carried off all the pillars, and all the beams and ornaments of the house were at the same time folded up with it, and they carried it off and laid it in a place in the south of the land. ²⁹ And I saw until the Lord of the sheep brought a new house greater and loftier than that first and set it up in the place of the first which had been folded up: all its pillars were new, and its ornaments were new and larger than those of the first, the old one which He had taken away, and all the sheep were within it. ³⁰ And I saw all the sheep which had been left, and all the beasts on the earth, and all the birds of the heavens falling down and doing homage to those sheep, and making petition to and obeying them in everything. ³¹ And thereafter those three who were clothed in white and had seized me by my hand, [who had taken me up before], and the hand of that ram also seizing hold of me, they took me up and set me down in the midst of those sheep before the judgment took place. ³² And those sheep were all white, and their wool was abundant and clean. ³³ And all that had been destroyed and dispersed, and all the beasts of the field, and all the birds of the heavens assembled in that house, and the Lord of the sheep rejoiced with great joy because they were all good and had returned to His house. ³⁴ And I saw until they laid down that sword which had been given to the sheep, and they brought it back into the house, and it was sealed before the presence of the LORD, and all the sheep were invited into that house, but it did not hold them. ³⁵ And their eyes were all opened, and they saw the good, and there was not one among them that did not see. ³⁶ And I saw that that house was large, and broad, and very full. ³⁷ And I saw that a white bull was born, with large horns and all the beasts of the field and all the birds of the air feared him and made petition to him all the time. ³⁸ And I saw until all their generations were transformed, and they all became white bulls; and the first among them became a lamb, and that lamb became a great animal and had great black horns on its head; and the Lord of the sheep rejoiced over it and over all the oxen. ³⁹ And I slept in their midst: and I awoke and saw everything. ⁴⁰ This is the vision which I saw while I slept, and I awoke and blessed the Lord of righteousness and gave Him glory. ⁴¹ Then I wept with a great weeping and my tears were unrestrained until I could no longer endure it: when I saw, they flowed on account of what I had seen, for everything will come and be fulfilled, and all the deeds of men in their order were shown to me. ⁴² On that night I remembered the first dream, and I wept because of it, and was troubled because I had seen that vision."

1 ENOCH

CHAPTER 91

[1] "And now, my son Methuselah, call all your brothers to me and gather together all the sons of your mother to me; for the word calls me, and the Spirit is poured out on me, that I may show you everything that will befall you forever." [2] And there on Methuselah went and summoned to himself all his brothers and assembled his relatives. [3] And he spoke to all the children of righteousness and said, "Hear, you sons of Enoch, all the words of your father, and listen to the voice of my mouth; for I exhort you and say to you, beloved: [4] Love uprightness and walk therein. And do not draw near to uprightness with a double heart, || And do not associate with those of a double heart, || But walk in righteousness, my sons. And it will guide you on good paths, || And righteousness will be your companion. [5] For I know that violence must increase on the earth, || And a great discipline will be executed on the earth, || Yes, it will be cut off from its roots, || And its whole structure will be destroyed. [6] And unrighteousness will again be consummated on the earth, || And all the deeds of unrighteousness, and of violence, and transgression || Will prevail in a twofold degree. [7] And when sin, and unrighteousness, and blasphemy, and violence || Increase in all kinds of deeds, || And apostasy, and transgression, and uncleanness increase, || A great discipline will come from Heaven on all these, || And the holy Lord will come out with wrath and discipline || To execute judgment on earth. [8] In those days violence will be cut off from its roots, || And the roots of unrighteousness together with deceit, || And they will be destroyed from under the heavens. [9] And all the idols of the heathen will be abandoned, || And the temples burned with fire, || And they will remove them from the whole earth, || And they will be cast into the judgment of fire || And will perish in wrath and in grievous judgment forever. [10] And the righteous will arise from their sleep, || And wisdom will arise and be given to them. [[And after that the roots of unrighteousness will be cut off, || And the sinners will be destroyed by the sword || [And] will be cut off from the blasphemers in every place, || And those who plan violence and those who commit blasphemy || Will perish by the sword.]] [12] And after that there will be another, the eighth week—That of righteousness— And a sword will be given to it || That a righteous judgment may be executed on the oppressors, || And sinners will be delivered into the hands of the righteous. [13] And at its close they will acquire houses through their righteousness, || And a house will be built for the Great King in glory forevermore, || And all mankind will look to the path of uprightness. [14] And after that, in the ninth week, || The righteous judgment will be revealed to the whole world, || And all the works of the godless will vanish from all the earth, || And the world will be written down for destruction. [15] And after this, in the tenth week, in the seventh part, || There will be the great continuous judgment, || In which He will execute vengeance among the messengers. [16] And the first heaven will depart and pass away, || And a new heaven will appear, || And all the powers of the heavens will give sevenfold light. [17] And after that there will be many weeks without number forever, || And all will be in goodness and righteousness, || And sin will no longer be mentioned forever. [18] And now I tell you, my sons, || And show you the paths of righteousness and the paths of violence. Yes, I will show them to you again || That you may know what will come to pass. [19] And now, listen to me, my sons, || And walk in the paths of righteousness, || And do not walk in the paths of violence, || For all who walk in the paths of unrighteousness will perish forever."

CHAPTER 92

[1] The scroll written by Enoch—[[Enoch indeed wrote this complete doctrine of wisdom, [which is] praised of all men and a judge of all the earth]]—for all my children who will dwell on the earth, and for the future generations who will observe uprightness and peace. [2] Do not let your spirit be troubled on account of the times; For the Holy and Great One has appointed days for all things. [3] And the righteous one will arise from sleep || And walk in the paths of righteousness, || And all his path and conversation || Will be in continuous goodness and grace. [4] He will be gracious to the righteous || And give him continuous uprightness, || And He will give him power || So that he will be [endowed] with goodness and righteousness. And he will walk in perpetual light. [5] And sin will perish in darkness forever || And will no longer be seen from that day forevermore.

CHAPTER 93

[1] And after that, Enoch both gave and began to recount from the scrolls. [2] And Enoch said, "Concerning the children of righteousness, and concerning the chosen ones of the world, and concerning the plant of uprightness, I will speak these things; yes, I, Enoch, will declare [them] to you, my sons, according to that which appeared to me in the heavenly vision, and which I have known through the word of the holy messengers, and have learned from the heavenly tablets." [3] And Enoch began to recount from the scrolls and said, "I was born the seventh in the first week, while judgment and righteousness still endured. [4] And great wickedness will arise after me in the second week, and deceit will have sprung up, and the first end will be in it. And a man will be saved in it; and after it is ended, unrighteousness will grow up, and a law will be made for the sinners. [5] And after that, in the third week, at its close, a man will be

chosen as the plant of righteous judgment, and his posterity will become the plant of righteousness forevermore. ⁶ And after that, in the fourth week, at its close, visions of the holy and righteous will be seen, and a law for all generations and an enclosure will be made for them. ⁷ And after that, in the fifth week, at its close, the house of glory and dominion will be built forever. ⁸ And after that, in the sixth week, all who live in it will be blinded, and the hearts of all of them will godlessly forsake wisdom. And a man will ascend in it; and at its close the house of dominion will be burned with fire, and the whole race of the chosen root will be dispersed. ⁹ And after that, in the seventh week, an apostate generation will arise, and its [wicked] deeds will be many, and all its deeds will be apostate. ¹⁰ And at its close the chosen righteous of the continuous plant of righteousness will be selected to receive sevenfold instruction concerning all His creation. ¹¹ [[For who is there of all the children of men that is able to hear the voice of the Holy One without being troubled? And who can think His thoughts? And who is there that can behold all the works of Heaven? ¹² And how should there be one who could behold Heaven, and who is there that could understand the things of Heaven, and see a soul or a spirit, and could tell thereof, or ascend and see all their ends and think them or do like them? ¹³ And who is there of all men that could know what the breadth and the length of the earth is? And to whom has been shown the measure of all of them? ¹⁴ Or is there anyone who could discern the length of the heavens and how great its height is, and on what it is founded, and how great the number of the stars is, and where all the luminaries rest?]]"

CHAPTER 94

¹ And now I say to you, my sons, love righteousness and walk therein, for the paths of righteousness are worthy of acceptance, but the paths of unrighteousness will suddenly be destroyed and vanish. ² And the paths of violence and death will be revealed to certain men of a generation, and they will hold themselves far from them, and will not follow them. ³ And now I say to you, the righteous: do not walk in the paths of wickedness, nor in the paths of death, and do not draw near to them, lest you be destroyed. ⁴ But seek and choose for yourselves righteousness and a chosen life, and walk in the paths of peace, and you will live and prosper. ⁵ And hold fast my words in the thoughts of your hearts and do not allow them to be effaced from your hearts, for I know that sinners will tempt men to mistreat wisdom, so that no place may be found for her, and no manner of temptation may diminish. ⁶ Woe to those who build unrighteousness and oppression and lay deceit as a foundation, for they will be suddenly overthrown, and they will have no peace. ⁷ Woe to those who build their houses with sin, for they will be overthrown

from all their foundations, and they will fall by the sword. [[And those who acquire gold and silver will suddenly perish in judgment.]] ⁸ Woe to you, you rich, for you have trusted in your riches, and you will depart from your riches, because you have not remembered the Most High in the days of your riches. ⁹ You have committed blasphemy and unrighteousness, and have become ready for the day of slaughter, and the day of darkness, and the Day of the Great Judgment. ¹⁰ So I speak and declare to you: He who has created you will overthrow you, and there will be no compassion for your fall, and your Creator will rejoice at your destruction. ¹¹ And your righteous ones will be a reproach to the sinners and the godless in those days.

CHAPTER 95

¹ Oh that my eyes were [a cloud of] waters that I might weep over you || And pour down my tears as a cloud of waters—So that I might rest from my troubled heart! ² Who has permitted you to practice reproaches and wickedness? And so judgment will overtake you sinners. ³ Do not fear the sinners, you righteous, || For the LORD will deliver them into your hands again, || That you may execute judgment on them according to your desires. ⁴ Woe to you who fulminate anathemas which cannot be reversed: Healing will therefore be far from you because of your sins. ⁵ Woe to you who repay your neighbor with evil, || For you will be repaid according to your works. ⁶ Woe to you, lying witnesses, and to those who weigh out injustice, || For you will suddenly perish. ⁷ Woe to you, sinners, for you persecute the righteous, || For you will be delivered up and persecuted because of injustice, || And its yoke will be heavy on you.

CHAPTER 96

¹ Be hopeful, you righteous, || For the sinners will suddenly perish before you, || And you will have lordship over them according to your desires. ² [[And in the day of the tribulation of the sinners, || Your children will mount and rise as eagles, || And your nest will be higher than the vultures, || And you will ascend and enter the crevices of the earth, || And the clefts of the rock forever as coneys before the unrighteous, || And the sirens will sigh and weep because of you.]] ³ So do not fear, you that have suffered, || For healing will be your portion, || And a bright light will enlighten you, || And you will hear the voice of rest from Heaven. ⁴ Woe to you, you sinners, || For your riches make you appear like the righteous, || But your hearts convict you of being sinners, || And this fact will be a testimony against you for a memorial of [your] evil deeds. ⁵ Woe to you who devour the finest of the wheat, || And drink wine in large bowls, || And tread the lowly underfoot with your might. ⁶ Woe to you who drink water from every fountain, || For you will suddenly be consumed and

wither away, || Because you have forsaken the fountain of life. [7] Woe to you who work unrighteousness, and deceit, and blasphemy: It will be a memorial against you for evil. [8] Woe to you, you mighty, who oppress the righteous with might, || For the day of your destruction is coming. In those days many and good days will come to the righteous—In the day of your judgment.

CHAPTER 97

[1] Believe, you righteous, that the sinners will become a shame and perish in the day of unrighteousness. [2] Be it known to you, [you sinners,] that the Most High is mindful of your destruction, and the messengers of Heaven rejoice over your destruction. [3] What will you do, you sinners, and where will you flee on that Day of Judgment, when you hear the voice of the prayer of the righteous? [4] Yes, you will fare like to them, against whom this word will be a testimony: "You have been companions of sinners." [5] And in those days the prayer of the righteous will reach to the LORD, and for you the days of your judgment will come. [6] And all the words of your unrighteousness will be read out before the Great Holy One, and your faces will be covered with shame, and He will reject every work which is grounded on unrighteousness. [7] Woe to you, you sinners, who live in the midst of [the] ocean and on the dry land, whose remembrance is evil against you. [8] Woe to you who acquire silver and gold in unrighteousness, and say, "We have become rich with riches, and have possessions, and have acquired everything we have desired. [9] And now, let us do what we purposed, for we have gathered silver, and there are many farmers in our houses. And our granaries are brimful as with water, [10] yes, and like water your lies will flow away; for your riches will not abide but speedily ascend from you, for you have acquired it all in unrighteousness, and you will be given over to a great curse.

CHAPTER 98

[1] And now I swear to you—to the wise and to the foolish—for you will have manifold experiences on the earth. [2] For you men will put on more adornments than a woman, and more colored garments than a virgin. They will be poured out as water in royalty, and in grandeur, and in power, and in silver, and in gold, and in purple, and in splendor, and in food. [3] Therefore they will be wanting in doctrine and wisdom, and they will thereby perish together with their possessions, and with all their glory, and their splendor; and in shame, and in slaughter, and in great destitution, their spirits will be cast into the furnace of fire. [4] I have sworn to you, you sinners, as a mountain has not become a slave, and a hill does not become the handmaid of a woman, even so sin has not been sent on the earth, but man has created it of himself, and they who commit it will fall under a great curse. [5] And barrenness has not been given to the woman, but she dies without children on account of the deeds of her own hands. [6] I have sworn to you, you sinners, by the Holy Great One, that all your evil deeds are revealed in the heavens, and that none of your deeds of oppression are covered and hidden. [7] And do not think in your spirit nor say in your heart that you do not know and that you do not see that every sin is recorded every day in Heaven in the presence of the Most High. [8] From now on you know that all your oppression with which you oppress is written down every day until the day of your judgment. [9] Woe to you, you fools, for you will perish through your folly; and you transgress against the wise, and so good fortune will not be your portion. [10] And now, know that you are prepared for the day of destruction. For that reason, do not hope to live, you sinners, but you will depart and die; for you know no ransom; for you are prepared for the Day of the Great Judgment, for the day of tribulation and great shame for your spirits. [11] Woe to you, you obstinate of heart, who work wickedness and eat blood: from where do you have good things to eat, and to drink, and to be filled? From all the good things which the LORD, the Most High, has placed in abundance on the earth. Therefore, you will have no peace. [12] Woe to you who love the deeds of unrighteousness: why do you hope for good for yourselves? Know that you will be delivered into the hands of the righteous, and they will cut off your necks, and slay you, and have no mercy on you. [13] Woe to you who rejoice in the tribulation of the righteous, for no grave will be dug for you. [14] Woe to you who set as nothing the words of the righteous, for you will have no hope of life. [15] Woe to you who write down lying and godless words, for they write down their lies that men may hear them and act godlessly toward [their] neighbor. [16] Therefore, they will have no peace, but will die a sudden death.

CHAPTER 99

[1] Woe to you who work godlessness, and glory in lying and extol them: you will perish, and no happy life will be yours. [2] Woe to them who pervert the words of uprightness, and transgress the perpetual law, and transform themselves into what they were not: they will be trodden underfoot on the earth. [3] In those days make ready, you righteous, to raise your prayers as a memorial, and place them as a testimony before the messengers, that they may place the sin of the sinners for a memorial before the Most High. [4] In those days the nations will be stirred up, and the families of the nations will arise on the day of destruction. [5] And in those days the destitute will go out and carry off their children, and they will abandon them, so that their children will perish through them: yes, they will abandon their children—sucklings, and not return to them, and will have no pity on their

beloved ones. ⁶ And again I swear to you, you sinners, that sin is prepared for a day of unceasing bloodshed. ⁷ And they who worship stones, and grave images of gold, and silver, and wood, and clay, and those who worship impure spirits and demons, and all kinds of idols not according to knowledge, will get no manner of help from them. ⁸ And they will become godless by reason of the folly of their hearts, and their eyes will be blinded through the fear of their hearts and through visions in their dreams. ⁹ They will become godless and fearful through these, for they will have worked all their work in a lie and will have worshiped a stone. Therefore, they will perish in an instant. ¹⁰ But in those days, blessed are all they who accept the words of wisdom, and understand them, and observe the paths of the Most High, and walk in the path of His righteousness, and do not become godless with the godless, for they will be saved. ¹¹ Woe to you who spread evil to your neighbors, for you will be slain in Sheol. ¹² Woe to you who make deceitful and false measures, and who cause bitterness on the earth, for they will thereby be utterly consumed. ¹³ Woe to you who build your houses through the grievous toil of others, and all their building materials are the bricks and stones of sin; I tell you that you will have no peace. ¹⁴ Woe to them who reject the measure and agelong heritage of their fathers and whose souls follow after idols, for they will have no rest. ¹⁵ Woe to them who work unrighteousness, and help oppression, and slay their neighbors until the Day of the Great Judgment. ¹⁶ For He will cast down your glory, and bring affliction on your hearts, and will arouse His fierce indignation, and destroy all of you with the sword; and all the holy and righteous will remember your sins.

CHAPTER 100

¹ And in those days in one place the fathers will be smitten together with their sons and brothers will fall in death with one another until the streams flow with their blood. ² For a man will not withhold his hand from slaying his sons and his sons' sons, and the sinner will not withhold his hand from his honored brother: they will slay one another from dawn until sunset. ³ And the horse will walk up to the breast in the blood of sinners, and the chariot will be submerged to its height. ⁴ In those days the messengers will descend into the secret places and gather together into one place all those who brought down sin, and the Most High will arise on that Day of Judgment to execute great judgment among sinners. ⁵ And He will appoint guardians over all the righteous and holy from among the holy messengers to guard them as the apple of [His] eye, until He makes an end of all wickedness and all sin, and though the righteous sleep a long sleep, they have nothing to fear. ⁶ And [then] the children of the earth will see the wise in security, and will understand all the words of this scroll, and recognize that their riches will not be able to save them in the overthrow of their sins. ⁷ Woe to you, sinners, on the day of strong anguish—you who afflict the righteous and burn them with fire: you will be repaid according to your works. ⁸ Woe to you, you obstinate of heart, who watch in order to devise wickedness: therefore, fear will come on you and there will be none to help you. ⁹ Woe to you, you sinners, on account of the words of your mouth, and on account of the deeds of your hands which your godlessness has worked: you will burn in blazing flames worse than fire. ¹⁰ And now, know that He will inquire from the messengers in Heaven regarding your deeds, [and] from the sun, and from the moon, and from the stars in reference to your sins, because on the earth you execute judgment on the righteous. ¹¹ And He will summon every cloud, and mist, and dew, and rain to testify against you, for they will all be withheld from descending on you because of you, and they will be mindful of your sins. ¹² And now give presents to the rain that it is not withheld from descending on you, nor yet the dew, when it has received gold and silver from you, that it may descend. ¹³ When the hoarfrost and snow with their frigidness, and all the snowstorms with all their plagues fall on you, in those days you will not be able to stand before them.

CHAPTER 101

¹ Observe the heavens, you children of Heaven, and every work of the Most High, and fear Him and work no evil in His presence. ² If He closes the windows of the heavens, and withholds the rain and the dew from descending on the earth on your account, what will you do then? ³ And if He sends His anger on you because of your deeds, you cannot petition Him, for you spoke proud and insolent words against His righteousness: therefore, you will have no peace. ⁴ And do you not see the sailors of the ships, how their ships are tossed to and fro by the waves, and are shaken by the winds, and are in severe trouble? ⁵ And therefore, they fear because all their excellent possessions go on the sea with them, and they have evil forebodings of heart that the sea will swallow them, and they will perish therein. ⁶ Are the entire sea, and all its waters, and all its movements, not the work of the Most High, and has He not set limits to its doings, and confined it throughout by the sand? ⁷ And at His reproof it is afraid and dries up, and all its fish die and all that is in it, but you sinners that are on the earth do not fear Him. ⁸ Has He not made the heavens, and the earth, and all that is therein? Who has given understanding and wisdom to everything that moves on the earth and in the sea? ⁹ Do the sailors of the ships not fear the sea? Yet sinners do not fear the Most High.

CHAPTER 102

¹ In those days when He has brought a grievous fire on you, where will you flee, and where will you find deliverance? And when He launches out His Word against you will you not be frightened and fear? ² And all the luminaries will be frightened with great fear, and all the earth will be frightened, and tremble, and be alarmed. ³ And all the messengers will execute their commands and will seek to hide themselves from the presence of the Great Glory, and the children of earth will tremble and quake; and you sinners will be cursed forever, and you will have no peace. ⁴ Do not fear, you souls of the righteous, and be hopeful, you that have died in righteousness. ⁵ And do not grieve if your soul has descended into Sheol in grief, and that in your life your body did not fare according to your goodness, but wait for the day of the judgment of sinners and for the day of cursing and discipline. ⁶ And yet when you die, the sinners speak over you: "As we die, so the righteous die, and what benefit do they reap for their deeds? ⁷ Behold, so they die even as we, in grief and darkness, and what have they more than we? From now on we are equal. ⁸ And what will they receive and what will they see forever? Behold, they have also died, and from now on and forever they will see no light." ⁹ I tell you, you sinners, you are content to eat and drink, and rob and sin, and strip men naked, and acquire wealth and see good days. ¹⁰ Have you seen the righteous, how their end falls out, that no manner of violence is found in them until their death? ¹¹ "Nevertheless, they perished and became as though they had not been, and their spirits descended into Sheol in tribulation."

CHAPTER 103

¹ Now, therefore, I swear to you, the righteous, by the glory of the Great and Honored and Mighty One in dominion, and by His greatness I swear to you. ² I know a mystery and have read the heavenly tablets, and have seen the holy scrolls, and have found written therein and inscribed regarding them ³ that all goodness, and joy, and glory are prepared for them and written down for the spirits of those who have died in righteousness, and that manifold good will be given to you in reward for your labors, and that your lot is abundantly beyond the lot of the living. ⁴ And the spirits of you who have died in righteousness will live and rejoice, and their spirits will not perish, nor their memorial from before the face of the Great One to all the generations of the world. For that reason, no longer fear their insolence. ⁵ Woe to you, you sinners, when you have died, if you die in the wealth of your sins! And those who are like you say regarding you, "Blessed are the sinners: they have seen all their days. ⁶ And how they have died in prosperity and in wealth and have not seen tribulation or murder in their life. And they have died in honor, and judgment has not been executed on them during their life." ⁷ Know that

their souls will be made to descend into Sheol, and they will be wretched in their great tribulation. ⁸ And your spirits will enter into darkness, and chains, and a burning flame where there is grievous judgment; and the Great Judgment will be for all the generations of the world. Woe to you, for you will have no peace. ⁹ Do not say in regard to the righteous and good who are in life, "In our troubled days we have toiled laboriously, and experienced every trouble, and met with much evil, and been consumed, and have become few and our spirit small. ¹⁰ And we have been destroyed and have not found any to help us even with a word. We have been tortured and have not hoped to see life from day to day. ¹¹ We hoped to be the head and have become the tail. We have toiled laboriously and had no satisfaction in our toil. And we have become the food of the sinners and the unrighteous, and they have laid their yoke heavily on us. ¹² They who hated us have had dominion over us and struck us; and we have bowed our necks to those that hated us, but they did not pity us. ¹³ We desired to get away from them that we might escape and be at rest, but we found no place where we should flee and be safe from them. ¹⁴ And we complained to the rulers in our tribulation and cried out against those who devoured us, but they did not attend to our cries and would not listen to our voice. ¹⁵ And they helped those who robbed us and devoured us and those who made us few; and they concealed their oppression, and they did not remove from us the yoke of those that devoured us, and dispersed us, and murdered us, and they concealed their murder, and did not remember that they had lifted up their hands against us."

CHAPTER 104

¹ I swear to you that the messengers in Heaven remember you for good before the glory of the Great One, and your names are written before the glory of the Great One. ² Be hopeful, for you were previously put to shame through ill and affliction, but now you will shine as the lights of the heavens; you will shine, and you will be seen, and the portals of the heavens will be opened to you. ³ And in your cry, cry for judgment, and it will appear to you, for all your tribulation will be visited on the rulers, and on all who helped those who plundered you. ⁴ Be hopeful and do not cast away your hopes, for you will have great joy as the messengers of Heaven. ⁵ What will you be obliged to do? You will not have to hide on the Day of the Great Judgment, and you will not be found as sinners, and the continuous judgment will be far from you for all the generations of the world. ⁶ And now, do not fear, you righteous, when you see the sinners growing strong and prospering in their ways: do not be companions with them, but keep far from their violence, for you will become companions of the hosts of Heaven. ⁷ And, although you sinners say, "All our sins will not be searched out and written down,"

nevertheless, they will write down all your sins every day. [8] And now I show to you that light and darkness, day and night, see all your sins. [9] Do not be godless in your hearts, and do not lie, and do not alter the words of uprightness, nor charge the words of the Holy Great One with lying, nor take account of your idols, for all your lying and all your godlessness do not issue in righteousness but in great sin. [10] And now I know this mystery, that sinners will alter and pervert the words of righteousness in many ways, and will speak wicked words, and lie, and practice great deceits, and write scrolls concerning their words. [11] But when they write down all my words truthfully in their languages, and do not change or diminish from my words, but write them all down truthfully, all that I first testified concerning them, [12] then—I know another mystery—scrolls will be given to the righteous and the wise to become a cause of joy, and uprightness, and much wisdom. [13] And the scrolls will be given to them, and they will believe in them and rejoice over them, and then all the righteous who have learned from all the paths of uprightness will be repaid.

CHAPTER 105

[1] In those days the LORD commanded [them] to summon and testify to the children of earth concerning their wisdom: "Show [it] to them, for you are their guides and a repayment over the whole earth. [2] For My Son and I will be united with them forever in the paths of uprightness in their lives, and you will have peace. Rejoice, you children of uprightness! Amen."

CHAPTER 106

[1] And after some days my son Methuselah took a wife for his son Lamech, and she became pregnant by him and bore a son. [2] And his body was white as snow and red as the blooming of a rose, and the hair of his head and his long locks were white as wool, and his eyes beautiful. And when he opened his eyes, he lighted up the whole house like the sun, and the whole house was very bright. [3] And he immediately arose in the hands of the midwife, opened his mouth, and conversed with the Lord of Righteousness. [4] And his father Lamech was afraid of him, and fled, and came to his father Methuselah. [5] And he said to him, "I have begotten a strange son, diverse from and unlike man, and resembling the sons of the God of Heaven, and his nature is different, and he is not like us, and his eyes are as the rays of the sun, and his countenance is glorious. [6] And it seems to me that he is not sprung from me but from the messengers, and I fear that a wonder may be worked on the earth in his days. [7] And now, my father, I am here to petition and implore you that you may go to our father Enoch and learn the truth from him, for his dwelling-place is among the messengers." [8] And when Methuselah heard the words of his son, he came to me at the ends of the earth, for he had heard that I was there, and he cried aloud, and I heard his voice, and I came to him. And I said to him, "Behold, here I am, my son, why have you come to me?" [9] And he answered and said, "I have come to you because of a great cause of anxiety, and I have approached because of a disturbing vision. [10] And now, my father, hear me: a son has been born to my son Lamech, the like of whom there is none, and his nature is not like man's nature, and the color of his body is whiter than snow and redder than the bloom of a rose, and the hair of his head is whiter than white wool, and his eyes are like the rays of the sun, and he opened his eyes and immediately lighted up the whole house. [11] And he arose in the hands of the midwife, and opened his mouth, and blessed the Lord of Heaven. [12] And his father Lamech became afraid, and fled to me, and did not believe that he was sprung from him, but that he was in the likeness of the messengers of Heaven; and behold, I have come to you that you may make the truth known to me." [13] And I, Enoch, answered and said to him, "The LORD will do a new thing on the earth, and I have already seen this in a vision, and I make known to you that in the generation of my father Jared some of the messengers of Heaven transgressed the word of the LORD. [14] And behold, they commit sin, and transgress the law, and have united themselves with women, and commit sin with them, and have married some of them, and have begot children by them. And they will produce giants on the earth, not according to the spirit, but according to the flesh, and there will be a great punishment on the earth, and the earth will be cleansed from all impurity. [15] Yes, there will come a great destruction over the whole earth, and there will be a deluge and a great destruction for one year. [16] And this son who has been born to you will be left on the earth, [17] and his three children will be saved with him when all mankind that are on the earth will die. [18] And now, make [it] known to your son Lamech that he who has been born is truly his son and call his name Noah, for he will be left to you, and he and his sons will be saved from the destruction which will come on the earth on account of all the sin and all the unrighteousness which will be consummated on the earth in his days. [19] And after that there will still be more unrighteousness than that which was first consummated on the earth, for I know the mysteries of the holy ones; for He, the LORD, has showed me and informed me, and I have read [them] in the heavenly tablets."

CHAPTER 107

[1] "And I saw written on them that generation on generation will transgress, until a generation of righteousness arises, and transgression is destroyed, and sin passes away from the earth, and all manner of good comes on it. [2] And now, my son, go and make [it] known to your son Lamech that this son which has

been born is truly his son, and that [this] is no lie." [3] And when Methuselah had heard the words of his father Enoch—for he had shown everything to him in secret—he returned and showed [them] to him and called the name of that son Noah, for he will comfort the earth after all the destruction.

CHAPTER 108

[1] Another scroll which Enoch wrote for his son Methuselah and for those who will come after him and keep the Law in the last days. [2] You who have done good will wait for those days until an end is made of those who work evil and an end of the might of the transgressors. [3] And indeed, wait until sin has passed away, for their names will be blotted out of the Scroll of Life and out of the holy scrolls, and their seed will be destroyed forever, and their spirits will be slain, and they will cry and make lamentation in a place that is a chaotic wilderness, and they will burn in the fire, for there is no earth there. [4] And I saw something like an invisible cloud there, for by reason of its depth I could not look over, and I saw a flame of fire blazing brightly, and things like shining mountains circling and sweeping to and fro. [5] And I asked one of the holy messengers who was with me, and said to him, "What is this shining thing? For it is not a heaven but only the flame of a blazing fire, and the voice of weeping, and crying, and lamentation, and strong pain." [6] And he said to me, "[Into] this place which you see here are cast the spirits of sinners, and blasphemers, and of those who work wickedness, and of those who pervert everything that the LORD has spoken through the mouth of the prophets—[even] the things that will be. [7] For some of them are written and inscribed above in Heaven in order that the messengers may read them and know that which will befall the sinners, and the spirits of the humble, and of those who have afflicted their bodies and been repaid by God, and of those who have been put to shame by wicked men, [8] [those] who love God and loved neither gold, nor silver, nor any of the good things which are in the world, but gave their bodies over to torture. [9] Who, since they came into being, did not long after earthly food, but regarded everything as a passing breath, and lived accordingly, and the LORD tried them much, and their spirits were found pure so that they should bless His Name. [10] And I have recounted all the blessings destined for them in the scrolls. And He has assigned them their reward, because they have been found to be such as loved Heaven more than their life in the world, and though they were trodden under [the] foot of wicked men, and experienced abuse and reviling from them, and were put to shame, yet they blessed Me. [11] And now I will summon the spirits of the good who belong to the generation of light, and I will transform those who were born in darkness, who in the flesh were not repaid with such honor as their faithfulness deserved. [12] And I will bring out those who have loved My holy Name in shining light, and I will seat each on the throne of his honor. [13] And they will be resplendent for infinite ages, for righteousness is the judgment of God; for He will give faithfulness to the faithful in the habitation of upright paths. [14] And they will see those who were born in darkness led into darkness, while the righteous will be resplendent. [15] And the sinners will cry aloud and see them resplendent, and they will indeed go where days and seasons are prescribed for them."

JUDEO-CHRISTIAN LEGENDS
AND PSEUDEPIGRAPHA

2 ENOCH

2 Enoch, also called Slavonic Enoch or the Secrets of Enoch, is thought to have been written between the 1st century BC and the 1st century AD. It deals with Enoch's rapture and ascent through the ten heavenly dimensions.

CHAPTER 1

[1] There was a wise man, a great craftsman, and the LORD conceived love for him and received him, that he should behold the uppermost dwellings and be an eyewitness of the wise, and great, and inconceivable, and immutable realm of God Almighty, of the very wonderful, and glorious, and bright, and many-eyed station of the LORD's servants, and of the inaccessible throne of the LORD, and of the degrees and manifestations of the incorporeal hosts, and of the ineffable service of the multitude of the elements, and of the various apparition[s] and inexpressible singing of the host of cherubim, and of the boundless light. [2] At that time he said: When my one hundred and sixty-fifth year was completed, I begot my son Methuselah. [3] After this I also lived two hundred years and completed, of all the years of my life, three hundred and sixty-five years. [4] On the first day of the month I was in my house alone, and was resting on my bed, and slept. [5] And when I was asleep, great distress came up into my heart, and I was weeping with my eyes in sleep, and I could not understand what this distress was, or what would happen to me. [6] And two men appeared to me, exceedingly big, so that I never saw such on earth; their faces were shining like the sun, their eyes were also like a burning light, and fire was coming forth from their lips; with clothing . . . in appearance purple, their wings were brighter than gold, their hands whiter than snow. [7] They were standing at the head of my bed and began to call me by my name. [8] And I arose from my sleep and clearly saw those two men standing in front of me. [9] And I saluted them, and was seized with fear, and the appearance of my face was changed from terror, and those men said to me, [10] "Have courage, Enoch, do not fear; the perpetual God sent us to you, and behold, you will ascend with us into Heaven today, and you will tell your sons and all your household all that they will do without you on earth in your house, and let no one seek you until the LORD returns you to them." [11] And I hurried to obey them, and went out from my house, and made for the doors as it was commanded me, and summoned my sons Methuselah, and Regim, and Gaidad, and made all the marvels those men had told me known to them.

CHAPTER 2

[1] Listen to me, my children: I do not know where I go, or what will befall me; now therefore, my children, I tell you: do not turn from God before the face of the vain, who did not make the heavens and earth, for these will perish and those who worship them, and may the LORD make your hearts confident in the fear of Him. And now, my children, let no one think to seek me until the LORD returns me to you.

CHAPTER 3

[1] It came to pass, when Enoch had told [this to] his sons, that the messengers took him on to their wings and bore him up on to the first heaven and placed him on the clouds. And there I looked, and again I looked higher, and saw the ether, and they placed me on the first heaven and showed me a very great sea, greater than the earthly sea.

CHAPTER 4

[1] They brought the elders and rulers of the stellar orders before my face, and showed me two hundred messengers who rule the stars and their services to the heavens, and fly with their wings, and come around all those who sail.

CHAPTER 5

[1] And here I looked down and saw the treasure-houses of the snow, and the messengers who keep their terrible storehouses, and the clouds from where they come out and into which they go.

CHAPTER 6

[1] They showed me the treasure-house of the dew, like oil of the olive, and the appearance of its form, as of all the flowers of the earth; furthermore, many messengers guarding the treasure-houses of these things, and how they are made to shut and open.

CHAPTER 7

[1] And those men took me and led me up on to the second heaven, and showed me darkness, greater than earthly darkness, and there I saw prisoners hanging, watched, awaiting the great and boundless judgment, and these messengers were dark-looking, more than earthly darkness, and unceasingly making weeping through all hours. [2] And I said to the men who were with me, "For what reason are these unceasingly tortured?" They answered me: "These are God's apostates who did not obey God's commands, but took counsel with their own will, and turned away with their prince who is also fastened on the fifth heaven." [3] And I felt great pity for them, and they saluted me, and said to me, "Man of God, pray for us

to the LORD"; and I answered to them: "Who am I, a mortal man, that I should pray for messengers? Who knows where I go, or what will befall me? Or who will pray for me?"

CHAPTER 8

[1] And those men took me there, and led me up on to the third heaven, and placed me there; and I looked downwards and saw the produce of these places, such as has never been known for goodness. [2] And I saw all the sweet-flowering trees and beheld their fruits, which were sweet-smelling, and all the foods borne by them bubbling with fragrant exhalation. [3] And in the midst of the trees, that of Life, in that place whereon the LORD rests, when He goes up into paradise; and this tree is of ineffable goodness and fragrance and adorned more than every existing thing; and on all sides it is gold-looking, and vermillion, and fire-like in form and covers all, and it has produce from all fruits. [4] Its root is in the garden at the earth's end. [5] And paradise is between corruptibility and incorruptibility. [6] And two springs come out which send forth honey and milk, and their springs send forth oil and wine, and they separate into four parts, and go around with quiet course, and go down into the Paradise of Eden, between corruptibility and incorruptibility. [7] And there they go forth along the earth and have a revolution to their circle even as other elements. [8] And here there is no unfruitful tree, and every place is blessed. [9] And there are three hundred very bright messengers who keep the garden, and with unceasing sweet singing and never-silent voices serve the LORD throughout all days and hours. [10] And I said, "How very sweet this place is!" And those men said to me:

CHAPTER 9

[1] "This place, O Enoch, is prepared for the righteous, who endure all manner of offense from those that exasperate their souls, who avert their eyes from iniquity, and make righteous judgment, and give bread to the hungering, and cover the naked with clothing, and raise up the fallen, and help injured orphans, and who walk without fault before the face of the LORD, and serve Him alone, and for them this place is prepared for continuous inheritance."

CHAPTER 10

[1] And those two men led me up on to the northern side, and showed me a very terrible place there, and there were all manner of tortures in that place: cruel darkness and unilluminated gloom, and there is no light there, but murky fire constantly flaming aloft, and there is a fiery river coming forth, and that whole place is fire everywhere, and everywhere there is frost and ice, thirst and shivering, while the bonds are very cruel, and the messengers fearful and merciless, bearing angry weapons [for] merciless torture, and I

said, [2] "Woe, woe! How very terrible this place is! [3] And those men said to me, "This place, O Enoch, is prepared for those who dishonor God, who practice sin against nature on earth, which is child-corruption after the sodomitic fashion, magic-making, enchantments, and devilish witchcrafts, and who boast of their wicked deeds—stealing, lies, slanders, envy, malice, fornication, murder—and who, cursed, steal the souls of men; who, seeing the poor, take away their goods and themselves wax rich, injuring them for other men's goods; who being able to satisfy the empty, made the hungering to die; being able to clothe, stripped the naked; and who did not know their Creator, and bowed to the soulless and lifeless gods—who cannot see nor hear, vain gods—who also built hewn images and bow down to unclean handiwork; this place is prepared for all these for a continuous inheritance."

CHAPTER 11

[1] Those men took me, and led me up on to the fourth heaven, and showed me all the successive goings, and all the rays of the light of sun and moon. [2] And I measure their goings, and compared their light, and saw that the sun's light is greater than the moon's. [3] Its circle and the wheels on which it goes always, like the wind going past with very marvelous speed, and day and night it has no rest. [4] Its passage and return are accompanied by four great stars, and each star has one thousand stars under it, to the right of the sun's wheel, and by four to the left, each having one thousand stars under it—eight thousand altogether, issuing with the sun continually. [5] And by day, fifteen myriads of messengers attend it, and by night one thousand. [6] And six-winged ones issue with the messengers before the sun's wheel into the fiery flames, and one hundred messengers kindle the sun and set it gleaming.

CHAPTER 12

[1] And I looked and saw other flying elements of the sun, whose names are phoenixes and chalkydri, marvelous and wonderful, with feet and tails in the form of a lion, and a crocodile's head, their appearance is empurpled, like the rainbow; their size is nine hundred measures; their wings are like those of messengers, each has twelve, and they attend and accompany the sun, bearing heat and dew as it is commanded to them from God. [2] Thus the sun revolves and goes, and rises under the heavens, and its course goes under the earth with the light of its rays unceasingly.

CHAPTER 13

[1] Those men bore me away to the east, and placed me at the sun's gates, where the sun goes forth according to the regulation of the seasons, and the circuit of the months of the whole year, and the number of the

hours, day and night. ² And I saw six gates open, each gate having sixty-one stadia and a quarter of one stadium, and I measured them accurately, and understood their size to be so great, through which the sun goes forth, and goes to the west, and is made even, and rises throughout all the months, and turns back again from the six gates according to the succession of the seasons; thus, the period of the whole year is finished after the returns of the four seasons.

CHAPTER 14

¹ And again those men led me away to the western parts and showed me six great gates open corresponding to the eastern gates, opposite to where the sun sets, according to the number of the days— three hundred and sixty-five and a quarter. ² Thus again it goes down to the western gates, and draws away its light, the greatness of its brightness, under the earth; for since the crown of its shining is in Heaven with the LORD, and guarded by four hundred messengers, while the sun goes around [the] wheel under the earth, and stands seven great hours in night, and spends half its course under the earth, when it comes to the eastern approach in the eighth hour of the night, it brings its lights, and the crown of shining, and the sun flames forth more than fire.

CHAPTER 15

¹ Then the elements of the sun, called phoenixes and chalkydri, break into song; therefore, every bird flutters with its wings, rejoicing at the giver of light, and they broke into song at the command of the LORD. ² The giver of light comes to give brightness to the whole world, and the morning guard takes shape, which is the rays of the sun, and the sun of the earth goes out, and receives its brightness to light up the whole face of the earth, and they showed me this calculation of the sun's going. ³ And the gates which it enters, these are the great gates of the calculation of the hours of the year; for this reason, the sun is a great creation, whose circuit lasts twenty-eight years, and begins again from the beginning.

CHAPTER 16

¹ Those men showed me the other course, that of the moon, twelve great gates, crowned from west to east, by which the moon goes in and out of the customary times. ² It goes in at the first gate to the western places of the sun, by the first gates with thirty-one days exactly, by the second gates with thirty-one days exactly, by the third with thirty days exactly, by the fourth with thirty days exactly, by the fifth with thirty-one days exactly, by the sixth with thirty-one days exactly, by the seventh with thirty days exactly, by the eighth with thirty-one days perfectly, by the ninth with thirty-one days exactly, by the tenth with thirty days perfectly, by the eleventh with thirty-one

days exactly, by the twelfth with twenty-eight days exactly. ³ And it goes through the western gates in the order and number of the eastern and accomplishes the three hundred and sixty-five and a quarter days of the solar year, while the lunar year has three hundred fifty-four, and there are twelve days of the solar circle lacking to it, which are the lunar epacts of the whole year. ⁴ Thus, too, the great circle contains five hundred and thirty-two years. ⁵ The quarter of a day is omitted for three years, the fourth fulfills it exactly. ⁶ Therefore they are taken outside of the heavens for three years and are not added to the number of days, because they change the time of the years to two new months toward completion, to two others toward diminution. ⁷ And when the western gates are finished, it returns and goes to the eastern, to the lights, and thus goes around the heavenly circles day and night, lower than all circles, swifter than the heavenly winds, and spirits, and elements, and messengers flying; each messenger has six wings. ⁸ It has a sevenfold course in nineteen years.

CHAPTER 17

¹ I saw armed soldiers in the midst of the heavens serving the LORD with drums and pipes, with unceasing voice, with sweet voice, with sweet and unceasing voice and various singing, which it is impossible to describe, and which astonishes every mind, so wonderful and marvelous is the singing of those messengers, and I was delighted listening to it.

CHAPTER 18

¹ The men took me on to the fifth heaven and placed me [there], and there I saw many countless soldiers called Grigori, of human appearance, and their size was greater than that of great giants, and their faces [were] withered, and the silence of their mouths [was] perpetual, and there was no service on the fifth heaven, and I said to the men who were with me, ² "For what reason are these very withered, and their faces melancholy, and their mouths silent, and for what reason is there no service on this heaven?" ³ And they said to me, "These are the Grigori, who with their prince Satanael rejected the Lord of light, and after them are those who are held in great darkness on the second heaven, and three of them went down on to earth from the LORD's throne, to the place Hermon, and broke through their vows on the shoulder of Mount Hermon, and saw how pleasing the daughters of men are, and took wives to themselves, and polluted the earth with their deeds, who in all times of their age made lawlessness and mixing, and giants are born, and marvelous large men, and great enmity. ⁴ And therefore God judged them with great judgment, and they weep for their brothers, and they will be punished on [the] Great Day of the LORD." ⁵ And I said to the Grigori, "I saw your brothers, and their works, and their great torments, and I prayed for

them, but the LORD has condemned them to be under the earth until the existing heavens and earth will end forever." ⁶And I said, "For what reason do you wait, brothers, and do not serve before the LORD's face, and have not put your services before the LORD's face, lest you utterly anger your Lord?" ⁷And they listened to my admonition, and spoke to the four ranks in Heaven, and behold, as I stood with those two men, four trumpets trumpeted together with great voice, and the Grigori broke into song with one voice, and their voice went up before the LORD pitifully and movingly.

CHAPTER 19

¹And there those men took me and bore me up on to the sixth heaven, and I saw seven bands of messengers there, very bright and very glorious, and their faces shining more than the sun's shining— glistening, and there is no difference in their faces, or behaviour, or manner of dress; and these make the orders, and learn the goings of the stars, and the alteration of the moon, or revolution of the sun, and the good government of the world. ²And when they see evildoing, they make commandments and instruction, and sweet and loud singing, and all songs of praise. ³These are the chief-messengers who are above messengers, [who] measure all life in Heaven and on earth, and the messengers who are appointed over seasons and years, the messengers who are over rivers and sea, and who are over the fruits of the earth, and the messengers who are over every grass, giving food to all, to every living thing, and the messengers who write all the souls of men, and all their deeds, and their lives before the LORD's face; six phoenixes, and six cherubim, and six six-winged ones are in their midst, continually singing with one voice, and it is not possible to describe their singing, and they rejoice before the LORD at His footstool.

CHAPTER 20

¹And those two men lifted me up there on to the seventh heaven, and I saw a very great light there, and fiery troops of great chief-messengers, incorporeal forces, and dominions, orders and governments, cherubim and seraphim, thrones and many-eyed ones, nine regiments, the YAH-favored stations of light, and I became afraid, and began to tremble with great terror, and those men took me, and led me after them, and said to me, ²"Have courage, Enoch, do not fear," and showed me the LORD from afar, sitting on His very high throne. For what is there on the tenth heaven, since the LORD dwells there? ³On the tenth heaven is God, in the Hebrew tongue He is called Aravat. ⁴And all the heavenly troops would come and stand on the ten steps according to their rank, and would bow down to the LORD, and would go to their places again in joy and bliss, singing songs in the boundless light with small and tender voices, gloriously serving Him.

CHAPTER 21

¹And the cherubim and seraphim [are] standing around the throne; the six-winged and many-eyed ones do not depart, standing before the LORD's face, doing His will, and they cover His whole throne, singing with a gentle voice before the LORD's face: "HOLY, HOLY, HOLY, LORD, Ruler of Hosts, the heavens and earth are full of Your glory." ²When I saw all these things, those men said to me, "Enoch, thus far it is commanded us to journey with you," and those men went away from me and thereon I did not see them. ³And I remained alone at the end of the seventh heaven, and became afraid, and fell on my face, and said to myself, "Woe is me! What has befallen me?" ⁴And the LORD sent one of His glorious ones, the chief-messenger Gabriel, and he said to me, "Have courage, Enoch, do not fear; arise before the LORD's face into eternity; arise, come with me." ⁵And I answered him, and said in myself: "My Lord, my soul has departed from me from terror and trembling, and I called to the men who led me up to this place, I relied on them, and it is with them I go before the LORD's face." ⁶And Gabriel caught me up, as a leaf caught up by the wind, and placed me before the LORD's face. ⁷And I saw the eighth heaven, which is called in the Hebrew tongue Muzaloth, changer of the seasons, of drought, and of wet, and of the twelve constellations of the circle of the expanse, which are above the seventh heaven. ⁸And I saw the ninth heaven, which is called in Hebrew Kuchavim, where the heavenly homes of the twelve constellations of the circle of the expanse are.

CHAPTER 22

¹On the tenth heaven, which is called Aravoth, I saw the appearance of the LORD's face, like iron made to glow in fire, and brought out, emitting sparks, and it burns. ²Thus in a moment of eternity I saw the LORD's face, but the LORD's face is ineffable, marvelous and very awful, and very, very terrible. ³And who am I to tell of the LORD's unspeakable being, and of His very wonderful face? And I cannot tell the quantity of His many instructions, and various voices—the LORD's throne is very great and not made with hands—nor the quantity of those standing around Him, troops of cherubim and seraphim, nor their unceasing singing, nor His immutable beauty. And who will tell of the ineffable greatness of His glory? ⁴And I fell prone and bowed down to the LORD, and the LORD said to me with His lips: ⁵"Have courage, Enoch, do not fear; arise and stand before My face into eternity." ⁶And the chief-general Michael lifted me up and led me to before the LORD's face. ⁷And the LORD said to His servants, trying them: "Let Enoch stand before My face into eternity," and the glorious ones bowed down

to the Lord, and said, "Let Enoch go according to Your word." [8] And the Lord said to Michael, "Go and take Enoch from out of his earthly garments, and anoint him with My sweet ointment, and put him into the garments of My glory." [9] And Michael did thus, as the Lord told him. He anointed me, and dressed me, and the appearance of that ointment is more than the great light, and His ointment is like sweet dew, and its smell mild, shining like the sun's ray, and I looked at myself, and I was like one of His glorious ones. [10] And the Lord summoned one of His chief-messengers, Pravuel by name, whose knowledge was quicker in wisdom than the other chief-messengers, who wrote all the deeds of the Lord; and the Lord said to Pravuel, "Bring out the scrolls from My storehouses, and a reed of quick-writing, and give it to Enoch, and deliver to him the choice and comforting scrolls out of your hand."

CHAPTER 23

[1] And he was telling me all the works of Heaven, earth and sea, and all the elements, their passages and goings, and the thunderings of the thunders, the sun and moon, the goings and changes of the stars, the seasons, years, days, and hours, the risings of the wind, the numbers of the messengers, and the formation of their songs, and all human things, the tongue of every human song and life, the commandments, instructions, and sweet-voiced singings, and all things that it is fitting to learn. [2] And Pravuel told me: "All the things that I have told you, we have written. Sit and write all the souls of mankind, however many of them are born, and the places prepared for them to eternity; for all souls are prepared to eternity, before the formation of the world." [3] And [I wrote] all [this for] two periods of thirty days and thirty nights; and I wrote out all things exactly, and wrote three hundred and sixty-six scrolls.

CHAPTER 24

[1] And the Lord summoned me, and said to me, "Enoch, sit down on My left with Gabriel." [2] And I bowed down to the Lord, and the Lord spoke to me: "Enoch, beloved, all that you see, all things that are standing finished, I tell to you even before the very beginning, all that I created from non-being, and visible things from invisible. [3] Hear, Enoch, and take in these words of Mine, for I have not told My secret to My messengers, and I have not told them their rise, nor My endless realm, nor have they understood My creating, which I tell you today. [4] For before all things were visible, I alone used to go around in the invisible things, like the sun from east to west, and from west to east. [5] But even the sun has peace in itself, while I found no peace, because I was creating all things, and I conceived the thought of placing foundations, and of creating visible creation."

CHAPTER 25

[1] "I commanded in the very lowest parts that visible things should come down from invisible, and Adoil came down very great, and I beheld him, and behold, he had a belly of great light. [2] And I said to him, Become undone, Adoil, and let the visible come out of you. [3] And he came undone, and a great light came out. And I was in the midst of the great light, and as there is born light from light, there came forth a great age, and [it] showed all creation, which I had thought to create. [4] And I saw that it was good. [5] And I placed a throne for Myself, and took My seat on it, and said to the light, Go up higher and fix yourself high above the throne, and be a foundation to the highest things. [6] And there is nothing else above the light, and then I bent up and looked up from My throne."

CHAPTER 26

[1] "And I summoned the very lowest a second time, and said, Let Archas come forth hard, and he came forth hard from the invisible. [2] And Archas came forth, hard, heavy, and very red. [3] And I said, Be opened, Archas, and let there be born from you; and [when] he came undone, a very great and very dark age came forth, bearing the creation of all lower things, and I saw that it was good, and said to him, [4] Go down below, and make yourself firm, and be a foundation for the lower things; and it happened, and he went down and fixed himself, and became the foundation for the lower things, and there is nothing else below the darkness."

CHAPTER 27

[1] "And I commanded that there should be taken from light and darkness, and I said, Be thick, and it became thus, and I spread it out with the light, and it became water, and I spread it out over the darkness, below the light, [2] and then I made the waters firm, that is to say, the bottomless, and I made a foundation of light around the water, and created seven circles from inside, and imaged the water like crystal, wet and dry, that is to say, like glass, and the circumcession of the waters and the other elements, [3] and I showed each one of them its road, and the seven stars, each one of them in its heaven, that they go thus, and I saw that it was good. [4] And I separated between light and between darkness, that is to say, in the midst of the water here and there, and I said to the light that it should be the day, and to the darkness, that it should be the night, and there was evening and there was morning the first day."

CHAPTER 28

[1] "And then I made the heavenly circle firm, and made the lower water which is under the heavens collect itself together into one whole, and [made] the chaos become dry, and it became so. [2] Out of the waves I created rock, hard and big, and from the rock I piled

up the dry, and the dry I called Earth, and the midst of the earth I called Abyss, that is to say, the bottomless; I collected the sea in one place and bound it together with a yoke. ³ And I said to the sea, Behold, I give you your perpetual limits, and you will not break loose from your component parts. ⁴ Thus I made the expanse steady. This day I called the first-created [(Sunday)]."

CHAPTER 29

¹ "And for all the heavenly troops I imaged the image and essence of fire, and My eye looked at the very hard, firm rock, and from the gleam of My eye the lightning received its wonderful nature, which is both fire in water and water in fire, and one does not put out the other, nor does the one dry up the other; therefore, the lightning is brighter than the sun, softer than water, and firmer than hard rock. ² And from the rock I cut off a great fire, and from the fire I created the orders of the incorporeal ten troops of messengers, and their weapons are fiery and their raiment a burning flame, and I commanded that each one should stand in his order. ³ And one from out of the order of messengers, having turned away with the order that was under him, conceived an impossible thought: to place his throne higher than the clouds above the earth, that he might become equal in rank to My power. ⁴ And I threw him out from the height with his messengers, and he was continuously flying in the air above the bottomless [pit]."

CHAPTER 30

¹ "On the third day I commanded the earth to make great and fruitful trees grow, and hills, and seed to sow, and I planted Paradise, and enclosed it, and placed flaming messengers as armed guardians, and thus I created renewal. ² Then there came evening, and there came morning—the fourth day [(Wednesday)]. ³ On the fourth day I commanded that there should be great lights on the heavenly circles. ⁴ On the first uppermost circle I placed the stars [and] Kronos [(Saturn)], and on the second Aphrodite [(Venus)], on the third Ares [(Mars)], on the fifth Zeus [(Jupiter)], on the sixth Hermes [(Mercury)], on the lesser seventh the moon, and adorned it with the lesser stars. ⁵ And on the lower I placed the sun for the illumination of day, and the moon and stars for the illumination of night— ⁶ the sun that it should go according to each constellation, twelve, and I appointed the succession of the months and their names and lives, their thunderings, and their hour-markings, how they should succeed. ⁷ Then there came evening, and there came morning—the fifth day [(Thursday)]. ⁸ On the fifth day I commanded the sea, that it should bring forth fishes, and feathered birds of many varieties, and all animals creeping over the earth, going forth over the earth on four legs, and soaring in the air, male and female, and every soul

breathing the breath of life. ⁹ And there came evening, and there came morning—the sixth day [(Friday)]. ¹⁰ On the sixth day I commanded My wisdom to create man from seven consistencies: one, his flesh from the earth; two, his blood from the dew; three, his eyes from the sun; four, his bones from stone; five, his intelligence from the swiftness of the messengers and from cloud; six, his veins and his hair from the grass of the earth; seven, his soul from My breath and from the wind. ¹¹ And I gave him seven natures: to the flesh hearing, the eyes for sight, to the soul smell, the veins for touch, the blood for taste, the bones for endurance, to the intelligence sweetness [(enjoyment)]. ¹² I conceived a cunning saying to say, I created man from invisible and from visible nature, of both are his death, and life, and image; he knows speech like some created thing, small in greatness and again great in smallness, and I placed him on earth, a second messenger, honorable, great and glorious, and I appointed him as ruler to rule on earth and to have My wisdom, and there was none like him of earth of all My existing creatures. ¹³ And I appointed him a name from the four component parts: from east, from west, from south, from north; and I appointed four special stars for him, and I called his name Adam, and showed him the two ways, the light and the darkness, and I told him: ¹⁴ This is good, and that bad, that I should learn whether he has love or hatred toward Me, that it might be clear which in his race love Me. ¹⁵ For I have seen his nature, but he has not seen his own nature; therefore, through not seeing he will sin worse, and I said, After sin what is there but death? ¹⁶ And I put sleep into him, and he fell asleep. And I took a rib from him and created him a wife, that death should come to him by his wife, and I took his last word and called her name mother, that is to say, Eva [(Eve)]."

CHAPTER 31

¹ "Adam has life on earth, and I created a garden in Eden in the east, that he should observe the testament and keep the command. ² I made the heavens open to him, that he should see the messengers singing the song of victory, and the gloomless light. ³ And he was continuously in paradise, and the Devil understood that I wanted to create another world, because Adam was lord on earth, to rule and control it. ⁴ The Devil is the evil spirit of the lower places; as a fugitive from the heavens, he became Satan, as his name was Satanael; thus he became different from the messengers, but his nature did not change his intelligence as far as his understanding of righteous and sinful things. ⁵ And he understood his condemnation and the sin which he had sinned before, therefore he conceived a thought against Adam, in such form he entered and seduced Eve, but did not touch Adam. ⁶ But I cursed ignorance, but what I had blessed previously, those I did not curse: I

did not curse man, nor the earth, nor other creatures, but man's evil fruit, and his works."

CHAPTER 32

¹ "I said to him: Earth you are, and into the earth from where I took you, you will go, and I will not ruin you, but send you from where I took you. ² Then I can receive you again at My second coming. ³ And I blessed all My creatures visible and invisible. And Adam was in paradise [for] five and a half hours. ⁴ And I blessed the seventh day, which is the Sabbath [(Saturday)], on which He rested from all His works."

CHAPTER 33

¹ "And I appointed the eighth day also, that the eighth day should be the first-created after my work, and that the first seven revolve in the form of the seven thousand [years], and that at the beginning of the eighth thousand there should be a time of not-counting—endless, with neither years, nor months, nor weeks, nor days, nor hours. ² And now, Enoch, all that I have told you, all that you have understood, all that you have seen of heavenly things, all that you have seen on earth, and all that I have written in scrolls by My great wisdom, all these things I have devised and created from the uppermost foundation to the lower and to the end, and there is no counselor nor inheritor to My creations. ³ I am self-continuous, not made with hands, and without change. ⁴ My thought is My counselor, My wisdom and My word are prepared, and My eyes observe how all things stand here and tremble with terror. ⁵ If I turn away My face, then all things will be destroyed. ⁶ And apply your mind, Enoch, and know Him who is speaking to you, and take there the scrolls which you yourself have written. ⁷ And I give you Samuel and Raguel, who led you up, and the scrolls, and go down to earth, and tell your sons all that I have told you, and all that you have seen, from the lower heaven up to My throne, and all the troops. ⁸ For I created all forces, and there is none that resists Me or that does not subject himself to Me. For all subject themselves to My monarchy, and labor for My sole rule. ⁹ Give them the scrolls of the handwriting, and they will read them, and will know Me as the Creator of all things, and will understand how there is no other God but Me. ¹⁰ And let them distribute the scrolls of your handwriting—children to children, generation to generation, nations to nations. ¹¹ And I will give you, Enoch, My intercessor, the chief-general Michael, for the handwritings of your fathers Adam, Seth, Enos, Cainan, Mahalaleel, and your father Jared."

CHAPTER 34

¹ "They have rejected My commandments and My yoke; worthless seed has come up, not fearing God, and they would not bow down to Me, but have begun to bow down to vain gods, and denied My unity, and have laden the whole earth with untruths, offenses, abominable lecheries, namely one with another, and all manner of other unclean wickedness, which are disgusting to relate. ² And therefore I will bring down a deluge on the earth and will destroy all men, and the whole earth will crumble together into great darkness."

CHAPTER 35

¹ "Behold, another generation will arise from their seed, much afterward, but of them many will be very insatiate. ² He who raises that generation will reveal to them the scrolls of your handwriting, of your fathers, to them to whom he must point out the guardianship of the world, to the faithful men and workers of My pleasure, who do not acknowledge My Name in vain. ³ And they will tell another generation, and those others, having read, will be glorified thereafter, more than the first."

CHAPTER 36

¹ "Now, Enoch, I give you the term of thirty days to spend in your house, and tell your sons and all your household, that all may hear from My face what is told them by you, that they may read and understand how there is no other God but Me, ² and that they may always keep My commandments, and begin to read and take in the scrolls of your handwriting. ³ And after thirty days I will send My messenger for you, and he will take you from earth and from your sons to Me."

CHAPTER 37

¹ And the LORD called on one of the older messengers, terrible and menacing, and placed him by me, in appearance white as snow, and his hands like ice, having the appearance of great frost, and he froze my face, because I could not endure the terror of the LORD, just as it is not possible to endure a stove's fire, and the sun's heat, and the frost of the air. ² And the LORD said to me, "Enoch, if your face is not frozen here, no man will be able to behold your face."

CHAPTER 38

¹ And the LORD said to those men who first led me up: "Let Enoch go down on to earth with you, and await him until the determined day." ² And they placed me on my bed by night. ³ And Methuselah, expecting my coming, keeping watch by day and by night at my bed, was filled with awe when he heard my coming, and I told him, "Let all my household come together, that I tell them everything."

CHAPTER 39

¹ Oh my children, my beloved ones, hear the admonition of your father, as much as is according to the LORD's will. ² I have been allowed to come to you today, and announce to you, not from my lips, but from the LORD's lips, all that is, and was, and all that

is now, and all that will be until Judgment Day. ³For the LORD has let me come to you; you therefore hear the words of my lips, of a man made big for you, but I am one who has seen the LORD's face: like iron made to glow from fire, it sends forth sparks and burns. ⁴You now look on my eyes, the eyes of a man big with meaning for you, but I have seen the LORD's eyes, shining like the sun's rays and filling the eyes of man with awe. ⁵You see now, my children, the right hand of a man that helps you, but I have seen the LORD's right hand filling Heaven as He helped me. ⁶You see the compass of my work like your own, but I have seen the LORD's limitless and perfect compass, which has no end. ⁷You hear the words of my lips, as I heard the words of the LORD, like great thunder unceasingly with hurling of clouds. ⁸And now, my children, hear the discourses of the father of the earth, how fearful and awful it is to come before the face of the ruler of the earth, how much more terrible and awful it is to come before the face of the ruler of Heaven, the controller of quick and dead, and of the heavenly troops. Who can endure that endless pain?

CHAPTER 40

¹And now, my children, I know all things, for this is from the LORD's lips, and my eyes have seen this from beginning to end. ²I know all things and have written all things into scrolls: the heavens, and their end, and their plenitude, and all the armies and their marchings. ³I have measured and described the stars, the great countless multitude of them. ⁴What man has seen their revolutions and their entrances? For not even the messengers see their number, while I have written all their names. ⁵And I measured the sun's circle, and measured its rays, [and] counted the hours; I also wrote down all things that go over the earth; I have written the things that are nourished, and all seed sown and unsown, which the earth produces, and all plants, and every grass and every flower, and their sweet smells, and their names, and the dwelling-places of the clouds, and their composition, and their wings, and how they bear rain and raindrops. ⁶And I investigated all things and wrote the road of the thunder and of the lightning, and they showed me the keys and their guardians, their rise, the way they go; it is let out gently in measure by a chain, lest by a heavy chain and violence it hurls the angry clouds down and destroys all things on earth. ⁷I wrote the treasure-houses of the snow, and the storehouses of the cold and the frosty airs, and I observed their season's key-holder; he fills the clouds with them and does not exhaust the treasure-houses. ⁸And I wrote the resting-places of the winds and observed and saw how their key-holders bear weighing-scales and measures; first, they put them in one weighing-scale, then in the other, the weights, and they let them out according to measure cunningly over the whole earth, lest by heavy breathing they make the earth to rock.

⁹And I measured out the whole earth, its mountains, and all hills, fields, trees, stones, rivers; I wrote down all existing things: the height from earth to the seventh heaven, and downwards to the very lowest [part of] Hades, and the judgment-place, and the very great, open, and weeping depth. ¹⁰And I saw how the prisoners are in pain, expecting the limitless judgment. ¹¹And I wrote down all those being judged by the judge, and all their judgment, and sentences, and all their works.

CHAPTER 41

¹And I saw all forefathers from all time with Adam and Eve, and I sighed, and broke into tears, and said of the ruin of their dishonor: ²"Woe to me for my infirmity and for that of my forefathers!" And I thought in my heart and said, ³"Blessed is the man who has not been born or who has been born and will not sin before the LORD's face, that he does not come into this place, nor bears the yoke of this place."

CHAPTER 42

¹I saw the key-holders and guards of the gates of Hades standing like great serpents, and their faces like extinguishing lamps, and their eyes of fire, their sharp teeth, and I saw all the LORD's works, how they are right, while some [of] the works of man are good, and others bad, and in their works are known those who lie evilly.

CHAPTER 43

¹I, my children, measured and wrote out every work, and every measure, and every righteous judgment. ²As one year is more honorable than another, so is one man more honorable than another: some for great possessions, some for wisdom of heart, some for particular intellect, some for cunning, one for silence of lip, another for cleanliness, one for strength, another for comeliness, one for youth, another for sharp wit, one for shape of body, another for sensibility. Let it be heard everywhere that there is none better than he who fears God; he will be more glorious in [the] time to come.

CHAPTER 44

¹The LORD, having created man with His hands, in the likeness of His own face, the LORD made him small and great. ²Whoever reviles the ruler's face, and abhors the LORD's face, has despised the LORD's face, and he who vents anger on any man without injury, the LORD's great anger will cut him down; he who spits on the face of man reproachfully will be cut down at the LORD's Great Judgment. ³Blessed is the man who does not direct his heart with malice against any man, and helps the injured and condemned, and raises the broken down, and will do charity to the needy, ⁴because on the Day of the Great Judgment every weight, every measure, and every makeweight

will be as in the market, that is to say, they are hung on scales and stand in the market, and everyone will learn his own measure, and according to his measure will take his reward.

CHAPTER 45

[1] Whoever hastens to make offerings before the LORD's face, the LORD, for His part, will hasten that offering by granting of his work. [2] But whoever increases his lamp before the LORD's face and does not make true judgment, the LORD will not increase his treasure in the realm of the highest. [3] When the LORD demands bread, or candles, or the flesh of beasts, or any other sacrifice, then that is nothing; but God demands pure hearts, and with all that, only tests the heart of man.

CHAPTER 46

[1] Hear, my people, and take in the words of my lips. [2] If anyone brings any gifts to an earthly ruler, and has disloyal thoughts in his heart, and the ruler know this, will he not be angry with him, and will he not refuse his gifts, and will he not give him over to judgment? [3] Or if one man makes himself appear good to another by deceit of tongue, but has evil in his heart, then will the other not understand the treachery of his heart, and himself be condemned, since his untruth was plain to all? [4] And when the LORD will send a great light, then there will be judgment for the just and the unjust, and no one will escape notice there.

CHAPTER 47

[1] And now, my children, lay thought on your hearts; mark well the words of your father, which have all come to you from the LORD's lips. [2] Take these scrolls of your father's handwriting and read them. [3] For the scrolls are many, and in them you will learn all the LORD's works, all that has been from the beginning of creation, and will be until the end of time. [4] And if you will observe my handwriting, you will not sin against the LORD, because there is no other except the LORD, neither in Heaven, nor in earth, nor in the very lowest places, nor in one foundation. [5] The LORD has placed the foundations in the unknown and has spread forth heavens visible and invisible; He fixed the earth on the waters and created countless creatures. [6] And who has counted the water and the foundation of the unfixed, or the dust of the earth, or the sand of the sea, or the drops of the rain, or the morning dew, or the wind's breathings? Who has filled earth, and sea, and the indissoluble winter? [7] "I cut the stars out of fire, and decorated Heaven, and put it in their midst."

CHAPTER 48

[1] So the sun goes along the seven heavenly circles, which are the appointment of one hundred and eighty-two thrones that it goes down on a short day, and again one hundred and eighty-two that it goes down on a big day; and he has two thrones on which he rests, revolving here and there above the thrones of the months, from the seventeenth day of the month Sivan it goes down to the month Thevan, [and] from the seventeenth of Thevan it goes up. [2] And thus it goes close to the earth; then the earth is glad and makes its fruits grow, and when it goes away, then the earth is sad, and trees and all fruits have no florescence. [3] All this He measured with a good measurement of hours, and fixed a measure by His wisdom, of the visible and the invisible. [4] From the invisible He made all things visible, Himself being invisible. [5] Thus I make known to you, my children, and distribute the scrolls to your children, into all your generations, and among the nations who will have the sense to fear God: let them receive them, and may they come to love them more than any food or earthly sweets, and read them, and apply themselves to them. [6] And those who do not understand the LORD, who do not fear God, who do not accept, but reject, who do not receive the scrolls—a terrible judgment awaits these. [7] Blessed is the man who will bear their yoke and will drag them along, for he will be released on the Day of the Great Judgment.

CHAPTER 49

[1] I swear to you, my children, but I swear not by any oath, neither by Heaven nor by earth, nor by any other creature which God created. [2] The LORD said, "There is no curse [[or oath]] in Me, nor injustice, but truth." [3] If there is no truth in men, let them swear by the words, Yes, yes, or else, No, no. [4] And I swear to you, yes, yes, that there has been no man in his mother's womb, except which [was] already [prepared] beforehand, even to each one there is a place prepared for the repose of that soul, and a measure fixed how much it is intended that a man be tried in this world. [5] Yes, children, do not deceive yourselves, for a place has been previously prepared for every soul of man.

CHAPTER 50

[1] I have put every man's work in writing, and none born on earth can remain hidden nor his works remain concealed. I see all things. [2] Now therefore, my children, spend the number of your days in patience and meekness, so that you inherit endless life. [3] Endure every wound, every injury, every evil word and attack for the sake of the LORD. [5] If retaliations befall you, do not return them either to neighbor or enemy, because the LORD will return them for you and be your avenger on the Day of Great Judgment, that there is no avenging here among men. [6] Whoever of you spends gold or silver for his brother's sake, he will receive ample treasure in the world to come. [7] Harm neither widows, nor orphans, nor strangers, lest God's wrath come on you.

CHAPTER 51

[1] Stretch out your hands to the poor according to your strength. [2] Do not hide your silver in the earth. [3] Help the faithful man in affliction, and affliction will not find you in the time of your trouble. [4] And every grievous and cruel yoke that comes on you—bear all for the sake of the LORD, and thus you will find your reward in the Day of Judgment. [5] It is good to go morning, midday, and evening into the LORD's dwelling, for the glory of your Creator, [6] because every breathing thing glorifies Him, and every creature, visible and invisible, returns Him praise.

CHAPTER 52

[1] Blessed is the man who opens his lips in praise of [the] God of Hosts and praises the LORD with his heart. [2] Cursed [is] every man who opens his lips for the bringing into contempt and slander of his neighbor, because he brings God into contempt. [3] Blessed is he who opens his lips blessing and praising God. [4] Cursed is he before the LORD, all the days of his life, who opens his lips to curse and abuse. [5] Blessed is he who blesses all the LORD's works. [6] Cursed is he who brings the LORD's creation into contempt. [7] Blessed is he who looks down and raises the fallen. [8] Cursed is he who looks to and is eager for the destruction of what is not his. [9] Blessed is he who keeps the foundations of his fathers made firm from the beginning. [10] Cursed is he who perverts the decrees of his forefathers. [11] Blessed is he who imparts peace and love. [12] Cursed is he who disturbs those that love their neighbors. [13] Blessed is he who speaks with a humble tongue and heart to all. [14] Cursed is he who speaks peace with his tongue, while in his heart there is no peace but a sword. [15] For all these things will be laid bare in the weighing-scales and in the scrolls on the Day of the Great Judgment.

CHAPTER 53

[1] And now, my children, do not say, "Our father is standing before God and is praying for our sins," for there is no helper there of any man who has sinned. [2] You see how I wrote all works of every man, before his creation, all that is done among all men for all time, and none can tell or relate my handwriting, because the LORD sees all imaginings of man, how they are vain, where they lie in the treasure-houses of the heart. [3] And now, my children, mark well all the words of your father that I tell you, lest you regret, saying, "Why did our father not tell us?"

CHAPTER 54

[1] At that time, not understanding this, let these scrolls which I have given you be for an inheritance of your peace. [2] Hand them to all who want them, and instruct them, that they may see the LORD's very great and marvelous works.

CHAPTER 55

[1] My children, behold, the day of my term and time have approached. [2] For the messengers who will go with me are standing before me and urge me to my departure from you; they are standing here on earth, awaiting what has been told them. [3] For tomorrow I will go up on to Heaven, to the uppermost Jerusalem—to my continuous inheritance. [4] Therefore I command you: before the LORD's face do all His good pleasure.

CHAPTER 56

[1] Methuselah, having answered his father Enoch, said, "What is agreeable to your eyes, father, that I may make before your face, that you may bless our dwellings, and your sons, and that your people may be made glorious through you, and then that you may thus depart as the LORD said?" [2] Enoch answered to his son Methuselah and said, "Hear, child: from the time when the LORD anointed me with the ointment of His glory, there has been no food in me, and my soul does not remember earthly enjoyment, neither do I want anything earthly."

CHAPTER 57

[1] "My child Methuselah, summon all your brothers, and all your household, and the elders of the people, that I may talk to them and depart, as is planned for me." [2] And Methuselah hurried, and summoned his brothers Regim, Riman, Uchan, Chermion, Gaidad, and all the elders of the people before the face of his father Enoch; and he blessed them, and said to them:

CHAPTER 58

[1] Listen to me, my children, today. [2] In those days when the LORD came down on to earth for Adam's sake, and visited all His creatures which He created Himself, after all these He created Adam, and the LORD called all the beasts of the earth, all the reptiles, and all the birds that soar in the air, and brought them all before the face of our father Adam. [3] And Adam gave the names to all things living on earth. [4] And the LORD appointed him ruler over all, and subjected to him all things under his hands, and made them dumb and made them dull that they can be commanded of man, and be in subjection and obedience to him. [5] Thus the LORD also created every man lord over all His possessions. [6] The LORD will not judge a single soul of beast for man's sake, but adjudicates the souls of men to their beasts in this world, for men have a special place. [7] And as every soul of man is according to number, similarly beasts will not perish, nor all souls of beasts which the LORD created, until the Great Judgment, and they will accuse man if he fed them ill.

2 ENOCH

CHAPTER 59

¹ Whoever defiles the soul of beasts, defiles his own soul. ² For man brings clean animals to make sacrifice for sin, that he may have cure of his soul. ³ And if they bring for sacrifice clean animals, and birds, man has a cure—he cures his soul. ⁴ All is given to you for food; bind it by the four feet, that is to make good the cure—he cures his soul. ⁵ But whoever kills beast without wounds, kills his own souls and defiles his own flesh. ⁶ And he who does any beast any injury whatever, in secret, it is evil practice, and he defiles his own soul.

CHAPTER 60

¹ He who works the killing of a man's soul, kills his own soul, and kills his own body, and there is no cure for him for all time. ² He who puts a man in any snare, will stick in it himself, and there is no cure for him for all time. ³ He who puts a man in any vessel, his retribution will not be wanting at the Great Judgment for all time. ⁴ He who works crookedly or speaks evil against any soul will not make justice for himself for all time.

CHAPTER 61

¹ And now, my children, keep your hearts from every injustice, which the LORD hates. Just as a man asks something for his own soul from God, so let him do to every living soul, because I know all things, how in the great time to come there is much inheritance prepared for men, good for the good, and bad for the bad, without number—many. ² Blessed are those who enter the good houses, for in the bad houses there is no peace nor return from them. ³ Hear, my children, small and great: when man puts a good thought in his heart [and] brings gifts from his labors before the LORD's face, but his hands did not make them, then the LORD will turn His face away from the labor of his hand, and that man cannot find the labor of his hands. ⁴ And if his hands made it, but his heart murmurs, and his heart does not cease making murmur unceasingly, he does not have any advantage.

CHAPTER 62

¹ Blessed is the man who in his patience brings his gifts with faith before the LORD's face, because he will find forgiveness of sins. ² But if he takes back his words before the time, there is no conversion for him; and if the time passes and he does not do what is promised of his own will, there is no conversion after death. ³ Because every work which man does before the time is all deceit before men and sin before God.

CHAPTER 63

¹ When man clothes the naked and fills the hungry, he will find reward from God. ² But if his heart murmurs, he commits a double evil: ruin of himself and of that which he gives; and for him there will be no finding of reward on account of that. ³ And if his own heart is filled with his food and his own flesh clothed with his own clothing, he commits contempt, and will forfeit all his endurance of poverty, and will not find reward of his good deeds. ⁴ Every proud and grandiose man, and every false speech clothed in untruth, is hateful to the LORD; it will be cut with the blade of the sword of death, and thrown into the fire, and will burn for all time.

CHAPTER 64

¹ When Enoch had spoken these words to his sons, all people far and near heard how the LORD was calling Enoch. They took counsel together: ² "Let us go and kiss Enoch," and two thousand men came together and came to the place [called] Achuzan where Enoch and his sons were. ³ And the elders of the people, the whole assembly, came and bowed down and began to kiss Enoch and said to him: ⁴ "Our father Enoch, may you be blessed of the LORD, the perpetual ruler, and now bless your sons and all the people, that we may be glorified today before your face. ⁵ For you will be glorified before the LORD's face for all time, since the LORD chose you, rather than all men on earth, and designated you writer of all His creation, visible and invisible, and redeemed of the sins of man, and helper of your household."

CHAPTER 65

¹ And Enoch answered all his people, saying, "Hear, my children: before all creatures were created, the LORD created the visible and invisible things. ² And as much time as there was and went past, understand that after all that, He created man in the likeness of His own form, and put into him eyes to see, and ears to hear, and heart to reflect, and intellect with which to deliberate. ³ And the LORD saw all man's works, and created all His creatures, and divided time: from time He fixed the years, and from the years He appointed the months, and from the months He appointed the days, and of days He appointed seven, ⁴ and in those He appointed the hours, [and] measured them out exactly, that man might reflect on time and count years, months, and hours, their alternation, beginning, and end, and that he might count his own life, from the beginning until death, and reflect on his sin, and write his work, [whether] bad and good, because no work is hidden before the LORD, that every man might know his works, and never transgress all His commandments, and keep my handwriting from generation to generation. ⁵ When all creation visible and invisible, as the LORD created it, will end, then every man goes to the Great Judgment, and then all time will perish, and the years, and from then on there will be neither months, nor days, nor hours; they will adhere together and will not be counted. ⁶ There will be one age, and all the righteous who will escape the

2 ENOCH

LORD's Great Judgment will be collected in the Great Age; the Great Age will begin for the righteous, and they will live continuously, and then there will also be among them neither labor, nor sickness, nor humiliation, nor anxiety, nor need, nor brutality, nor night, nor darkness, but great light. ⁷And they will have a great indestructible wall, and a bright and incorruptible paradise, for all corruptible things will pass away, and there will be continuous life."

CHAPTER 66

¹And now, my children, keep your souls from all injustice, such as the LORD hates. ²Walk before His face with terror and trembling and serve Him alone. ³Bow down to the true God, not to dumb idols, but bow down to His similitude, and bring all just offerings before the LORD's face. The LORD hates what is unjust. ⁴For the LORD sees all things; when man takes thought in his heart, then He counsels the intellects, and every thought is always before the LORD who made the earth firm and put all creatures on it. ⁵If you look to Heaven, the LORD is there; if you take thought of the sea's deep and all under the earth, the LORD is there. ⁶For the LORD created all things. Do not bow down to things made by man, leaving the LORD of all creation, because no work can remain hidden before the LORD's face. ⁷Walk, my children, in long-suffering, in meekness, honesty, in provocation, in grief, in faith, and in truth, in reliance on promises, in sickness, in abuse, in wounds, in temptation, in nakedness, in privation, loving one another, until you go out from this age of ills, that you become inheritors of endless time. ⁸Blessed are the just who will escape the Great Judgment, for they will shine forth more than the sun sevenfold, for in this world the seventh part is taken off from all: light, darkness, food, enjoyment, sorrow, paradise, torture, fire, frost, and other things; he put all down in writing, that you might read and understand.

CHAPTER 67

¹When Enoch had talked to the people, the LORD sent out darkness on to the earth, and there was darkness, and it covered those men standing with Enoch, and they took Enoch up on to the highest Heaven where the LORD is; and He received him and placed him before His face, and the darkness went off from the earth, and light came again. ²And the people did not see and understand how Enoch had been taken, and they glorified God, and they found a roll in which was traced "The Invisible God"; and all went to their dwelling places.

CHAPTER 68

¹Enoch was born on the sixth day of the month Sivan and lived three hundred and sixty-five years. ²He was taken up to Heaven on the first day of the month Sivan and remained in Heaven sixty days. ³He wrote all these signs of all creation, which the LORD created, and wrote three hundred and sixty-six scrolls, and handed them over to his sons, and remained on earth thirty days, and was taken up to Heaven again on the sixth day of the month Sivan, on the very day and hour when he was born. ⁴As every man's nature in this life is dark, so also are his conception, birth, and departure from this life. ⁵At what hour he was conceived, at that hour he was born, and at that hour too he died. ⁶Methuselah and his brothers, all the sons of Enoch, hurried and erected an altar at that place called Achuzan, from which and where Enoch had been taken up to Heaven. ⁷And they took sacrificial oxen, and summoned all people, and sacrificed the sacrifice before the LORD's face. ⁸All people, the elders of the people and the whole assembly, came to the feast and brought gifts to the sons of Enoch. ⁹And they made a great feast, rejoicing and making merry [for] three days, praising God who had given them such a sign through Enoch, who had found favor with Him, ¹⁰and that they should hand it on to their sons from generation to generation, from age to age. Amen.

3 ENOCH

3 Enoch, also called Hebrew Enoch, The Revelation of Metatron, or The Book of the Palaces, was likely written in the 1st or 2nd century AD by either Ishmael ben Elisha ha-Kohen or Rabbi Yishmael ben Elisha. Its Jewish author has an otherworldly experience where he ascends into the heavens and beholds the glorified Enoch (Metatron). Metatron has become the heavenly scribe and among the highest-ranking angels.

CHAPTER 1

[1] Rabbi Ishmael said: When I ascended on high to behold the vision of the Merkaba and had entered the six halls, one within the other, [2] as soon as I reached the door of the Seventh Hall I stood still in prayer before the Holy One, blessed is He, and, lifting up my eyes on high toward the Divine Majesty, I said, [3] "Lord of the Universe, please, that the merit of Aaron, the son of Amram, the lover of peace and pursuer of peace, who received the crown of priesthood from Your Glory on Mount Sinai, be valid for me in this hour, so that Cassiel, the prince, and the messengers with him may not get power over me nor throw me down from the heavens." [4] Immediately the Holy One, blessed is He, sent Metatron to me, his servant the messenger, the Prince of the Presence, and he, spreading his wings, came to meet me with great joy so as to save me from their hand. [5] And he took me by his hand in their sight, saying to me: "Enter in peace before the high and exalted King and behold the picture of the Merkaba." [6] Then I entered the Seventh Hall, and he led me to the camps of Shekinah and placed me before the Holy One, blessed is He, to behold the Merkaba. [7] As soon as the princes of the Merkaba and the flaming seraphim perceived me, they fixed their eyes on me. Trembling and shuddering instantly seized me, and I fell down and was benumbed by the radiant image of their eyes and the splendid appearance of their faces, until the Holy One, blessed is He, rebuked them, saying, [8] "My servants, my seraphim, my cherubim, and my ophanim! Cover your eyes before Ishmael, my son, my friend, my beloved one, and my glory, so he does not tremble or shudder!" [9] Immediately Metatron, the Prince of the Presence, came and restored my spirit and put me on my feet. [10] After that moment there was not strength enough in me to say a song before the Throne of Glory of the glorious King, the mightiest of all kings, the most excellent of all princes, until after the hour had passed. [11] After one hour had passed, the Holy One, blessed is He, opened to me the gates of Shekinah, the gates of Peace, the gates of Wisdom, the gates of Strength, the gates of Power, the gates of Speech, the gates of Song, the gates of Holiness, the gates of Chant. [12] And he enlightened my eyes and my heart by words of psalm, song, praise, exaltation, thanksgiving, extolment, glorification, hymn, and eulogy. And as I opened my mouth, uttering a song before the Holy One, blessed is He, the holy chayyoth beneath and above the Throne of Glory answered and said, "HOLY" and, "Blessed is the glory of the LORD from His place!"

CHAPTER 2

[1] R. Ishmael said: In that hour the eagles of the Merkaba, the flaming ophanim and the seraphim of consuming fire, asked Metatron, saying to him: [2] "Youth! Why permit one born of woman to enter and behold the Merkaba? From which nation, from which tribe is this one? What is his character?" [3] Metatron answered and said to them: "From the nation of Israel whom the Holy One, blessed is He, chose for His people from among seventy tongues, from the tribe of Levi, whom He set aside as a contribution to His Name and from the seed of Aaron whom the Holy One, blessed is He, chose for his servant and put on him the crown of priesthood on Sinai." [4] Immediately they spoke and said, "Indeed, this one is worthy to behold the Merkaba." And they said, "Happy is the people that is in such a case!"

CHAPTER 3

[1] R. Ishmael said: In that hour I asked Metatron, the messenger, the Prince of the Presence: "What is your name?" [2] He answered me: "I have seventy names, corresponding to the seventy tongues of the world, and all of them are based on the name Metatron, Messenger of the Presence; but my King calls me Youth."

CHAPTER 4

[1] R. Ishmael said: I asked Metatron and said to him: "Why are you called by the Name of your Creator, by seventy names? You are greater than all the princes, higher than all the messengers, more beloved than all the servants, honored above all the mighty ones in kingship, greatness, and glory: why do they call you Youth in the high heavens?" [2] He answered and said to me: "Because I am Enoch, the son of Jared. [3] For when the generation of the flood sinned and were confounded in their deeds, saying to God, Depart from us, for we do not desire the knowledge of Your ways, then the Holy One, blessed is He, removed me from their midst to be a witness against them in the high heavens to all the inhabitants of the world, that they may not say: The Merciful One is cruel. What sins had they committed, all those multitudes? Or, let

it be they sinned—what had their sons and their daughters, their mules and their cattle sinned? And likewise, all the animals, domestic and wild, and the birds in the world that God destroyed from the world? [5] Hence the Holy One, blessed is He, lifted me up in their lifetime before their eyes to be a witness against them to the future world. And the Holy One, blessed is He, assigned me for a prince and a ruler among the ministering messengers. [6] In that hour three of the ministering messengers, 'Uzza, 'Azza, and 'Azzael came forth and brought charges against me in the high heavens, saying before the Holy One, blessed is He: Did the Ancient Ones not rightly say before You, Do not create man? The Holy One, blessed is He, answered and said to them: I have made, and I will bear, yes, I will carry and will deliver. [7] As soon as they saw me, they said before Him: Lord of the Universe, what is this one that he should ascend to the height of heights? Is he not one from among the sons of the sons of those who perished in the days of the flood? What is he doing in the Raqia'? [8] Again, the Holy One, blessed is He, answered and said to them: What are you, that you enter and speak in my presence? I delight in this one more than in all of you, and hence he will be a prince and a ruler over you in the high heavens. [9] Immediately all stood up and went out to meet me, prostrated themselves before me, and said, Happy are you and happy is your father, for your Creator favors you. [10] And because I am small and a youth among them in days, months, and years, therefore they call me Youth."

CHAPTER 5

[1] R. Ishmael said: Metatron, the Prince of the Presence, said to me: "From the day when the Holy One, blessed is He, expelled the first Adam from the Garden of Eden and onwards, Shekinah was dwelling on a cherub under the Tree of Life. [2] And the ministering messengers were gathering together and going down from Heaven in parties, from the Raqia in companies, and from the heavens in camps to do His will in the whole world. [3] And the first man and his generation were sitting outside the gate of the Garden to behold the radiant appearance of the Shekinah. [4] For the splendor of the Shekinah traversed the world from one end to the other with a splendor three hundred sixty-five thousand times that of the globe of the sun. And everyone who made use of the splendor of the Shekinah, on him no flies and no gnats rested, neither was he sick nor did he suffer any pain. No demons got power over him, neither were they able to injure him. [5] When the Holy One, blessed is He, went out and went in from the Garden to Eden, from Eden to the Garden, from the Garden to Raqia, and from Raqia to the Garden of Eden, then all and everyone beheld the splendor of His Shekinah and they were not injured, [6] until the time of the generation of Enosh who was the head of all idol worshipers of the world. [7] And what did the generation of Enosh do? They went from one end of the world to the other, and each one brought silver, gold, precious stones, and pearls in heaps like to mountains and hills, making idols out of them throughout all the world. And they erected the idols in every quarter of the world: the size of each idol was one thousand parasangs. [8] And they brought down the sun, the moon, planets, and constellations, and placed them before the idols on their right hand and on their left, to attend them even as they attend the Holy One, blessed is He, as it is written: And all the host of Heaven were standing by Him on His right hand and on His left. [9] What power was in them that they were able to bring them down? They would not have been able to bring them down but for 'Uzza, 'Azza, and 'Azzielis who taught them sorceries whereby they brought them down and made use of them. [10] In that time the ministering messengers brought charges against them before the Holy One, blessed is He, saying before Him: Master of the World! [11] What have You to do with the children of men? As it is written: What is man that You are mindful of him? MAH ADAM is not written here, but MAH ENOSH, for he is the head of the idol worshipers. Why have You left the highest of the high heavens, which are filled with the majesty of Your glory and are high, uplifted, and exalted, and the high and exalted Throne in the Raqia' Araboth on high, and have gone and dwell with the children of men who worship idols and equate You to the idols? [12] Now You are on earth and the idols likewise. What have You to do with the inhabitants of the earth who worship idols? [13] Immediately the Holy One, blessed is He, lifted up His Shekinah from the earth, from their midst. [14] In that moment the ministering messengers came, the troops of hosts and the armies of 'Araboth, in one thousand camps and ten thousand hosts: they fetched trumpets, and took the horns in their hands, and surrounded the Shekinah with all kinds of songs. And He ascended to the high heavens, as it is written: God has gone up with a shout, the LORD with the sound of a trumpet."

CHAPTER 6

[1] R. Ishmael said: Metatron, the messenger, the Prince of the Presence, said to me: "When the Holy One, blessed is He, desired to lift me up on high, He first sent 'Anaphiel H, the prince, and he took me from their midst in their sight and carried me in great glory on a fiery chariot with fiery horses, servants of glory. And he lifted me up to the high heavens together with the Shekinah. [2] As soon as I reached the high heavens, the holy chayyoth, the ophanim, the seraphim, the cherubim, the wheels of the Merkaba, the galgallim, and the ministers of the consuming fire, perceiving my smell from a distance of three hundred sixty-five thousand myriads of parasangs, said, What smell of one born of woman and what taste of a white drop is

this that ascends on high, and behold, he is merely a gnat among those who divide flames of fire? [3] The Holy One, blessed is He, answered and spoke to them: My servants, My hosts, My cherubim, My ophanim, My seraphim! Do not be displeased on account of this! Since all the children of men have denied Me and My great Kingdom and have gone worshiping idols, I have removed My Shekinah from among them and have lifted it up on high. But this one whom I have taken from among them is a chosen one among the inhabitants of the world, and he is equal to all of them in faith, righteousness, and perfection of deed, and I have taken him as a tribute from My world under all the heavens."

CHAPTER 7

[1] R. Ishmael said: Metatron, the messenger, the Prince of the Presence, said to me: "When the Holy One, blessed is He, took me away from the generation of the flood, He lifted me on the wings of the wind of Shekinah to the highest Heaven and brought me into the great palaces of the 'Araboth Raqia' on high, [2] where the glorious Throne of Shekinah, the Merkaba, the troops of anger, the armies of vehemence, the fiery shin'anim, the flaming cherubim, and the burning ophanim, the flaming servants, the flashing chashmallim, and the lightening seraphim are. And He placed me there to attend the Throne of Glory day after day."

CHAPTER 8

[1] R. Ishmael said: Metatron, the Prince of the Presence, said to me: "Before He appointed me to attend the Throne of Glory, the Holy One, blessed is He, opened to me three hundred thousand gates of understanding, three hundred thousand gates of subtlety, three hundred thousand gates of life, three hundred thousand gates of grace and loving-kindness, three hundred thousand gates of love, three hundred thousand gates of instruction, three hundred thousand gates of meekness, three hundred thousand gates of maintenance, three hundred thousand gates of mercy, [and] three hundred thousand gates of fear of Heaven. [2] In that hour the Holy One, blessed is He, added in me wisdom to wisdom, understanding to understanding, subtlety to subtlety, knowledge to knowledge, mercy to mercy, instruction to instruction, love to love, loving-kindness to loving-kindness, goodness to goodness, meekness to meekness, power to power, strength to strength, might to might, brilliance to brilliance, beauty to beauty, splendor to splendor, and I was honored and adorned with all these good and praiseworthy things more than all the children of Heaven."

CHAPTER 9

[1] R. Ishmael said: Metatron, the Prince of the Presence, said to me: "After all these things the Holy One, blessed is He, put His hand on me and blessed me with five hundred thirty-six blessings. [2] And I was raised and enlarged to the size of the length and width of the world. [3] And He caused seventy-two wings to grow on me, thirty-six on each side. And each wing was as the whole world. [4] And He fixed three hundred sixty-five eyes on me: each eye was as the great luminary. [5] And He left no kind of splendor, brilliance, radiance, [or] beauty in of all the lights of the universe that He did not fix on me."

CHAPTER 10

[1] R. Ishmael said: Metatron, the Prince of the Presence, said to me: "All these things the Holy One, blessed is He, made for me: He made me a throne, similar to the Throne of Glory. And He spread a curtain of splendor and brilliant appearance over me—of beauty, grace, and mercy, similar to the curtain of the Throne of Glory; and all kinds of lights in the universe were fixed on it. [2] And He placed it at the door of the Seventh Hall and seated me on it. [3] And the herald went forth into every Heaven, saying, This is My servant Metatron. I have made him into a prince and a ruler over all the princes of My kingdoms and over all the children of Heaven, except the eight great princes, the honored and revered ones who are called LORD, by the Name of their King. [4] And every messenger and every prince who has a word to speak in My presence before Me will go into his presence before him and will speak to him instead. [5] And you observe and fulfill every command that he utters to you in My Name. For I have committed the Prince of Wisdom and the Prince of Understanding to him to instruct him in the wisdom of heavenly things and of earthly things, in the wisdom of this world and of the world to come. [6] Moreover, I have set him over all the treasuries of the palaces of Araboth and over all the stores of life that I have in the high heavens."

CHAPTER 11

[1] R. Ishmael said: Metatron, the messenger, the Prince of the Presence, said to me: "Henceforth, the Holy One, blessed is He, revealed to me all the mysteries of instruction, and all the secrets of wisdom, and all the depths of the Perfect Law; and all living beings' thoughts of heart, and all the secrets of the universe, and all the secrets of creation were revealed to me even as they are revealed to the Maker of creation. [2] And I watched intently to behold the secrets of the depth and the wonderful mystery. Before a man thought, I knew what was in his thought. [3] And there was no thing above on high nor below in the deep hidden from me."

CHAPTER 12

[1] R. Ishmael said: Metatron, the Prince of the Presence, said to me: "By reason of the love with which the Holy One, blessed is He, loved me more

3 ENOCH

than all the children of Heaven, He made me a garment of glory on which were fixed all kinds of lights, and He clad me in it. [2] And He made me a robe of honor on which were fixed all kinds of beauty, splendor, brilliance, and majesty. [3] And He made me a royal crown in which were fixed forty-nine costly stones like to the light of the globe of the sun. [4] For its splendor went forth in the four quarters of the 'Araboth Raqia', and in through the seven heavens, and in the four quarters of the world. And he put it on my head. [5] And He called me THE LESSER YHWH in the presence of all His heavenly household; as it is written: For My Name is in him."

CHAPTER 13

[1] R. Ishmael said: Metatron, the messenger, the Prince of the Presence, the glory of all heavens, said to me: "Because of the great love and mercy with which the Holy One, blessed is He, loved and cherished me more than all the children of Heaven, He wrote with His finger with a flaming style on the crown on my head the letters by which the heavens and earth, the seas and rivers, the mountains and hills, the planets and constellations, the lightnings, winds, earthquakes and voices, the snow and hail, the storm-wind and the tempest were created—the letters by which all the needs of the world and all the orders of creation were created. [2] And every single letter sent forth time after time as it were lightnings, time after time as it were torches, time after time as it were flames of fire, time after time rays like as the rising of the sun, and the moon and the planets."

CHAPTER 14

[1] R. Ishmael said: Metatron, the messenger, the Prince of the Presence, said to me: "When the Holy One, blessed is He, put this crown on my head, [then] all the princes of kingdoms who are in the height of 'Araboth Raqia' and all the hosts of every heaven trembled before me; and even the princes of the elim, the princes of the er'elim, and the princes of the taphsarim, who are greater than all the ministering messengers who minister before the Throne of Glory, shook, feared, and trembled before me when they beheld me. [2] Even Sammael, the prince of the accusers, who is greater than all the princes of kingdoms on high, feared and trembled before me. [3] And even the messenger of fire, and the messenger of hail, and the messenger of the wind, and the messenger of the lightning, and the messenger of anger, and the messenger of the thunder, and the messenger of the snow, and the messenger of the rain, and the messenger of the day, and the messenger of the night, and the messenger of the sun, and the messenger of the moon, and the messenger of the planets, and the messenger of the constellations who rule the world under their hands, feared, and trembled, and were frightened before me when they beheld me. [4] These are the names of the rulers of the world: Gabriel, the messenger of the fire, Baradiel, the messenger of the hail, Ruchiel who is appointed over the wind, Baraqiel who is appointed over the lightnings, Za'amiel who is appointed over the vehemence, Ziqiel who is appointed over the sparks, Zi'iel who is appointed over the commotion, Za'aphiel who is appointed over the storm-wind, Ra'amiel who is appointed over the thunders, Ra'ashiel who is appointed over the earthquake, Shalgiel who is appointed over the snow, Matariel who is appointed over the rain, Shimshiel who is appointed over the day, Lailiel who is appointed over the night, Galgalliel who is appointed over the globe of the sun, 'Ophanniel who is appointed over the globe of the moon, Kokbiel who is appointed over the planets, [and] Rahatiel who is appointed over the constellations. [5] And they all fell prostrate when they saw me. And they were not able to behold me because of the majestic glory and beauty of the appearance of the shining light of the crown of glory on my head."

CHAPTER 15

[1] R. Ishmael said: Metatron, the messenger, the Prince of the Presence, the glory of all heavens, said to me: "As soon as the Holy One, blessed is He, took me in His service to attend the Throne of Glory, and the wheels of the Merkaba, and the needs of Shekinah, my flesh was immediately changed into flames, my sinews into flaming fire, my bones into coals of burning juniper, the light of my eyelids into [the] splendor of lightnings, my eyeballs into firebrands, the hair of my head into hot flames, all my limbs into wings of burning fire, and the whole of my body into glowing fire. [2] And on my right were divisions of fiery flames, on my left firebrands were burning, around me storm-wind and tempest were blowing, and in front of me and behind me was roaring of thunder with earthquake."

CHAPTER 16

[1] R. Ishmael said: Metatron, the messenger, the Prince of the Presence, the glory of all Heaven, said to me: "At first I was sitting on a great throne at the door of the Seventh Hall, and I was judging the children of Heaven, the household on high by authority of the Holy One, blessed is He. And I divided Greatness, Kingship, Dignity, Rulership, Honor and Praise, and Diadem and Crown of Glory to all the princes of kingdoms, while I was presiding in the Celestial Court, and the princes of kingdoms were standing before me, on my right and on my left by authority of the Holy One, blessed is He. [2] But when Acher came to behold the vision of the Merkaba and fixed his eyes on me, he feared and trembled before me and his soul was frightened even to departing from him, because of [the] fear, horror, and dread of me when he beheld me sitting on a throne like a king with all the

ministering messengers standing by me as my servants and all the princes of kingdoms adorned with crowns surrounding me. ³ In that moment he opened his mouth and said, Indeed, there are two Divine Powers in Heaven! ⁴ Immediately Bath Qol, the Divine Voice, went forth from Heaven from before the Shekinah and said, Return, you backsliding children, except Acher! ⁵ Then 'Aniyel, the prince—the honored, glorified, beloved, wonderful, revered, and fearful one—came in commission from the Holy One, blessed is He, and gave me sixty strokes with lashes of fire and made me stand on my feet."

CHAPTER 17

¹ R. Ishmael said: Metatron, the messenger, the Prince of the Presence, the glory of all heavens, said to me: "There are seven princes—the great, beautiful, revered, wonderful, and honored ones—who are appointed over the seven heavens. And they are these: Michael, and Gabriel, Shatqiel, and Baradiel, and Shachaqiel, and Baraqiel, and Sidriel. ² And each of them is the prince of the host of one heaven. And each one of them is accompanied by four hundred ninety-six thousand myriads of ministering messengers. ³ Michael, the great prince, is appointed over the seventh heaven, the highest one, which is in the 'Araboth. Gabriel, the prince of the host, is appointed over the sixth heaven which is in Makon. Shataqiel, prince of the host, is appointed over the fifth heaven which is in Ma'on. Shahaqi'el, prince of the host, is appointed over the fourth heaven which is in Zebul. Badariel, prince of the host, is appointed over the third heaven which is in Shehaqim. Barakiel, prince of the host, is appointed over the second heaven which is in the height of Merom. Pazriel, prince of the host, is appointed over the first heaven which is in Wilon, which is in Shamayim. ⁴ Under them is Galgalliel, the prince who is appointed over the globe of the sun, and with him are ninety-six great and honored messengers who move the sun in Raqia'. ⁵ Under them is 'Ophanniel, the prince who is set over the globe of the moon. And with him are eighty-eight messengers who move the globe of the moon three hundred fifty-four thousand parasangs every night at the time when the moon stands in the east at its turning point. And when is the moon sitting in the east at its turning point? Answer: in the fifteenth day of every month. ⁶ Under them is Rahatiel, the prince who is appointed over the constellations. And he is accompanied by seventy-two great and honored messengers. And why is he called Rahatiel? Because he makes the stars run in their orbits and courses three hundred thirty-nine thousand parasangs every night from the east to the west, and from the west to the east. For the Holy One, blessed is He, has made a tent for all of them: for the sun, the moon, the planets, and the stars in which they travel at night from the west to the east. ⁷ Under them is Kokbiel, the prince who is

appointed over all the planets. And with him are three hundred sixty-five thousand myriads of ministering messengers, great and honored ones who move the planets from city to city and from province to province in the Raqia' of heavens. ⁸ And over them are seventy-two princes of kingdoms on high corresponding to the seventy-two tongues of the world. And all of them are crowned with royal crowns, and clad in royal garments, and wrapped in royal cloaks. And all of them are riding on royal horses and they are holding royal scepters in their hands. And before each one of them, when he is traveling in Raqia', royal servants are running with great glory and majesty; even as on earth they are traveling in chariots with horsemen and great armies, and in glory and greatness, with praise, song, and honor."

CHAPTER 18

¹ R. Ishmael said: Metatron, the messenger, the Prince of the Presence, the glory of all Heaven, said to me: "The messengers of the first heaven, whenever they see their prince, they dismount from their horses and fall on their faces. And the prince of the first heaven, when he sees the prince of the second heaven, he dismounts, removes the crown of glory from his head and falls on his face. And the prince of the second heaven, when he sees the prince of the third heaven, he removes the crown of glory from his head and falls on his face. And the prince of the third heaven, when he sees the prince of the fourth heaven, he removes the crown of glory from his head and falls on his face. And the prince of the fourth heaven, when he sees the prince of the fifth heaven, he removes the crown of glory from his head and falls on his face. And the prince of the fifth heaven, when he sees the prince of the sixth heaven, he removes the crown of glory from his head and falls on his face. And the prince of the sixth heaven, when he sees the prince of the seventh heaven, he removes the crown of glory from his head and falls on his face. ² And the prince of the seventh heaven, when he sees the seventy-two princes of kingdoms, he removes the crown of glory from his head and falls on his face. ³ And the seventy-two princes of kingdoms, when they see the doorkeepers of the First Hall in the 'Araboth Raqia in the highest, they remove the royal crown from their head and fall on their faces. And the doorkeepers of the First Hall, when they see the doorkeepers of the Second Hall, they remove the crown of glory from their head and fall on their faces. And the doorkeepers of the Second Hall, when they see the doorkeepers of the Third Hall, they remove the crown of glory from their head and fall on their faces. And the doorkeepers of the Third Hall, when they see the doorkeepers of the Fourth Hall, they remove the crown of glory from their head and fall on their faces. And the doorkeepers of the Fourth Hall, when they see the doorkeepers of the

Fifth Hall, they remove the crown of glory from their head and fall on their faces. And the doorkeepers of the Fifth Hall, when they see the doorkeepers of the Sixth Hall, they remove the crown of glory from their head and fall on their faces. And the doorkeepers of the Sixth Hall, when they see the doorkeepers of the Seventh Hall, they remove the crown of glory from their head and fall on their faces. ⁴ And the doorkeepers of the Seventh Hall, when they see the four great princes, the honored ones, who are appointed over the four camps of Shekinah, they remove the crowns of glory from their head and fall on their faces. ⁵ And the four great princes, when they see Tag'as, the prince, great and honored with song and praise, at the head of [the] children of Heaven, they remove the crown of glory from their head and fall on their faces. ⁶ And Tag'as, the great and honored prince, when he sees Barattiel, the great prince of three fingers in the height of 'Araboth, the highest Heaven, he removes the crown of glory from his head and falls on his face. ⁷ And Baratiel, the great prince, when he sees Hamon, the great prince, the fearful and honored, pleasant and terrible one who makes all the children of Heaven to tremble, when the time draws near for the saying of the Thrice Holy—as it is written: At the noise of the tumult the peoples are fled; at the lifting up of Yourself the nations are scattered—he removes the crown of the glory from his head and falls on his face. ⁸ And Hamon, the great prince, when he sees Tutresiel, the great prince, he removes the crown of glory from his head and falls on his face. ⁹ And Tutresiel-Yʜᴡʜ, the great prince, when he sees Atrugiel, the great prince, he removes the crown of glory from his head and falls on his face. ¹⁰ And Atrugiel, the great prince, when he sees Na'aririel-Yʜᴡʜ, the great prince, he removes the crown of glory from his head and falls on his face. ¹¹ And Na'aririel-Yʜᴡʜ, the great prince, when he sees Sasnigiel, the great prince, he removes the crown of glory from his head and falls on his face. ¹² And Sasnigiel-Yʜᴡʜ, when he sees Zazriel-Yʜᴡʜ, the great prince, he removes the crown of glory from his head and falls on his face. ¹³ And Zazriel-Yʜᴡʜ, the prince, when he sees Geburatiel-Yʜᴡʜ, the prince, he removes the crown of glory from his head and falls on his face. ¹⁴ And Geburatiel-Yʜᴡʜ, the prince, when he sees 'Araphiel-Yʜᴡʜ, the prince, he removes the crown of glory from his head and falls on his face. ¹⁵ And 'Araphiel-Yʜᴡʜ, the prince, when he sees 'Ashruylu, the prince, who presides in all the sessions of the children of Heaven, he removes the crown of glory from his head and falls on his face. ¹⁶ And Ashruylu-Yʜᴡʜ, the prince, when he sees Gallisur-Yʜᴡʜ, the prince, who reveals all the secrets of the Law, he removes the crown of glory from his head and falls on his face. ¹⁷ And Gallisur-Yʜᴡʜ, the prince, when he sees Zakzakiel-Yʜᴡʜ, the prince who is appointed to write down the merits of Israel on the Throne of Glory, he removes the crown of glory from his head and falls on his face. ¹⁸ And Zakzakiel-Yʜᴡʜ, the great prince, when he sees 'Anaphiel-Yʜᴡʜ, the prince who keeps the keys of the heavenly halls, he removes the crown of glory from his head and falls on his face. Why is he called by the name of 'Anaphiel? Because the bough of his honor and majesty and his crown, and his splendor, and his brilliance cover all the chambers of 'Araboth Raqia on high even as the Maker of the world overshadows them, just as it is written with regard to the Maker of the world: His glory covered the heavens, and the earth was full of His praise—even so do the honor and majesty of 'Anaphiel cover all the glories of 'Araboth the highest. ¹⁹ And when he sees Sother 'Ashiel-Yʜᴡʜ, the prince, the great, fearful, and honored one, he removes the crown of glory from his head and falls on his face. Why is he called Sother 'Ashiel? Because he is appointed over the four heads of the fiery river beside the Throne of Glory; and every single prince who goes out or enters before the Shekinah, only goes out or enters by his permission. For the seals of the fiery river are entrusted to him. And furthermore, his height is seven thousand myriads of parasangs. And he stirs up the fire of the river; and he goes out and enters before the Shekinah to expound what is written concerning the inhabitants of the world, according as it is written: The judgment was set, and the scrolls were opened. ²⁰ And Sother 'Ashiel, the prince, when he sees Shoqed Chozi, the great prince, the mighty, terrible, and honored one, he removes the crown of glory from his head and falls on his face. And why is he called Shoqed Chozi? Because he weighs all the merits of man in a balance in the presence of the Holy One, blessed is He. ²¹ And when he sees Zehanpuryu-Yʜᴡʜ, the great prince, the mighty and terrible one, honored, glorified, and feared in all the heavenly household, he removes the crown of glory from his head and falls on his face. Why is he called Zehanpuryu? Because he rebukes the fiery river and pushes it back to its place. ²² And when he sees 'Azbuga-Yʜᴡʜ, the great prince, glorified, revered, honored, adorned, wonderful, exalted, beloved, and feared among all the great princes who know the mystery of the Throne of Glory, he removes the crown of glory from his head and falls on his face. Why is he called 'Azbuga? Because in the future he will gird the righteous and pious of the world with the garments of life and wrap them in the cloak of life, that they may live a continuous life in them. ²³ And when he sees the two great princes, the strong and glorified ones who are standing above him, he removes the crown of glory from his head and falls on his face. And these are the names of the two princes: Sopheriel-Yʜᴡʜ Wʜᴏ Kɪʟʟs, the great prince, the honored, glorified, blameless, venerable, ancient, and mighty one; and Sopheriel-Yʜᴡʜ Wʜᴏ Mᴀᴋᴇs Aʟɪᴠᴇ, the great prince, the honored, glorified, blameless, ancient, and mighty one. ²⁴ Why is he called Sopheriel-YHWH WHO KILLS? Because he is appointed over the scrolls of the dead, so that everyone, when the day of his death draws near, he writes him in the scrolls of the dead. ²⁵ Why is he called Sopheriel-YHWH WHO MAKES ALIVE? Because he is appointed over the scrolls of the living, so that everyone whom the Holy One, blessed is He, will bring into life, he writes him in the Scroll of the Living, by authority of MAQOM. ²⁶ You might perhaps say: Since the Holy One, blessed is He, is sitting on a throne, they are also sitting when writing. Answer: the Writing teaches us: And all the host of Heaven are standing by Him. ²⁷ It is said, The host of Heaven, in order to show us that even the great princes—like whom there is none in the high heavens—do not fulfill the requests of the Shekinah otherwise than standing. ²⁸ But how is it they are able to write when they are standing? It is like this: one is standing on the wheels of the tempest and the other is standing on the wheels of the storm-wind. ²⁹ The one is clad in kingly garments, the other is clad in kingly garments. The one is wrapped in a mantle of majesty and the other is wrapped in a mantle of majesty. The one is crowned with a royal crown and the other is crowned with a royal crown. The one's body is full of eyes and the other's body is full of eyes. ³⁰ The appearance of one is like to the appearance of lightnings and the appearance of the other is like to the appearance of lightnings. The eyes of the one are like the sun in its might and the eyes of the other are like the sun in its might. The one's height is like the height of the seven heavens and the other's height is like the height of the seven heavens. ³¹ The wings of the one are as many as the days of the year and the wings of the other are as many as the days of the year. The wings of the one extend over the breadth of Raqia' and the wings of the other extend over the breadth of Raqia. ³² The lips of the one are as the gates of the east and the lips of the other are as the gates of the east. The tongue of the one is as high as the waves of the sea and the tongue of the other is as high as the waves of the sea. ³³ From the mouth of the one a flame goes forth and from the mouth of the other a flame goes forth. From the mouth of the one there go forth lightnings and from the mouth of the other there go forth lightnings. ³⁴ From the sweat of the one fire is kindled and from the perspiration of the other fire is kindled. From the one's tongue a torch is burning and from the tongue of the other a torch is burning. ³⁵ On the head of the one there is a sapphire stone and on the head of the other there is a sapphire stone. On the shoulders of the one there is a wheel of a swift cherub and on the shoulders of the other there is a wheel of a swift cherub. ³⁶ One has a burning scroll in his hand, the other has a burning scroll in his hand. The one has a flaming style in his hand, the other has a flaming style in his hand. ³⁷ The length of the scroll is three thousand myriads of parasangs; the size of the style is three thousand myriads of parasangs; the size of every single letter that they write is three hundred sixty-five parasangs."

CHAPTER 19

¹ R. Ishmael said: Metatron, the messenger, the Prince of the Presence, said to me: "Above these three messengers, these great princes, there is one prince, distinguished, honored, noble, glorified, adorned, fearful, valiant, strong, great, magnified, glorious, crowned, wonderful, exalted, blameless, beloved, lordly, high and lofty, ancient and mighty, like to whom there is none among the princes. His name is Rikbiel-YHWH, the great and revered prince who is standing by the Merkaba. ² And why is he called Rikbiel? Because he is appointed over the wheels of the Merkaba, and they are given in his charge. ³ And how many are the wheels? Eight; two in each direction. And there are four winds compassing them around. And these are their names: the Storm-Wind, the Tempest, the Strong Wind, and the Wind of Earthquake. ⁴ And there are four fiery rivers continually running under them, one fiery river on each side. And around them, between the rivers, four clouds are planted, and they are these: clouds of fire, clouds of lamps, clouds of coal, [and] clouds of brimstone, and they are standing beside their wheels. ⁵ And the feet of the chayyoth are resting on the wheels. And between one wheel and the other, earthquake is roaring, and thunder is thundering. ⁶ And when the time draws near for the recital of the Song, then the multitudes of wheels are moved, the multitude of clouds tremble, all the chieftains are made afraid, all the horsemen rage, all the mighty ones are excited, all the hosts are frightened, all the troops are in fear, all the appointed ones hurry away, all the princes and armies are dismayed, all the servants faint, and all the messengers and divisions travail with pain. ⁷ And one wheel makes a sound to be heard to the other, and one cherub to another, one chayya to another, one seraph to another, saying, Extol Him that rides in 'Araboth, by His Name YHWH, and rejoice before Him!"

CHAPTER 20

¹ R. Ishmael said: Metatron, the messenger, the Prince of the Presence, said to me: "Above these there is one great and mighty prince. His name is Chayyliel-YHWH, a noble and revered prince, a glorious and mighty prince, a great and revered prince, a prince before whom all the children of Heaven tremble, a prince who is able to swallow up the whole earth in one moment. ² And why is he called Chayyliel-YHWH? Because he is appointed over the holy chayyoth and strikes the chayyoth with lashes of fire, and glorifies them when they give praise, and glory, and rejoicing, and he causes them to hurry to say

HOLY and BLESSED IS THE GLORY OF YHWH FROM HIS PLACE!"

CHAPTER 21

[1] R. Ishmael said: Metatron, the messenger, the Prince of the Presence, said to me: "Four [are] the chayyoth corresponding to the four winds. Each chayya is as the space of the whole world. And each one has four faces; and each face is as the face of the east. [2] Each one has four wings, and each wing is like the cover of the universe. [3] And each one has faces in the middle of faces and wings in the middle of wings. The size of the faces is as the size of two hundred forty-eight faces, and the size of the wings is as the size of three hundred sixty-five wings. [4] And each one is crowned with two thousand crowns on his head. And each crown is like to the bow in the cloud. And its splendor is like to the splendor of the globe of the sun. And the sparks that go forth from each one are like the splendor of the morning star in the east."

CHAPTER 22 (A)

[1] R. Ishmael said: Metatron, the messenger, the Prince of the Presence, said to me: "Above these there is one prince: noble, wonderful, strong, and praised with all kinds of praise. His name is Kerubiel-YHWH, a mighty prince, full of power and strength, a prince of highness, and with him there is a righteous prince of righteousness, and with him a holy prince of holiness, and with him there is a prince glorified by one thousand hosts, exalted by ten thousand armies. [2] At his wrath the earth trembles, at his anger the camps are moved, from fear of him the foundations are shaken, at his rebuke the 'Araboth trembles. [3] His stature is full of burning coals. The height of his stature is as the height of the seven heavens, the breadth of his stature is as the wideness of the seven heavens, and the thickness of his stature is as the seven heavens. [4] The opening of his mouth is like a lamp of fire. His tongue is a consuming fire. His eyebrows are like to the splendor of the lightning. His eyes are like sparks of brilliance. His countenance is like a burning fire. [5] And there is a crown of holiness on his head on which the Explicit Name is graven— and lightnings go forth from it. And the bow of Shekinah is between his shoulders. And his sword is like to lightning, and on his loins there are arrows like to a flame, and on his armor and shield there is a consuming fire, and on his neck there are coals of burning juniper, and also around him there are coals of burning juniper. [7] And the splendor of Shekinah is on his face, and the horns of majesty on his wheels, and a royal diadem on his skull. [8] And his body is full of eyes. And wings are covering the whole of his high stature. [9] On his right hand a flame is burning, and on his left a fire is glowing; and coals are burning from it. And firebrands go forth from his body. And lightnings are cast forth from his face. With him there

is always thunder on thunder, by his side there is always earthquake on earthquake. [10] And the two princes of the Merkaba are together with him. [11] Why is he called Kerubiel-YHWH, the prince? Because he is appointed over the chariot of the cherubim. And the mighty cherubim are given in his charge. And he adorns the crowns on their heads and polishes the diadem on their skull. [12] He magnifies the glory of their appearance. And he glorifies the beauty of their majesty. And he increases the greatness of their honor. He causes the song of their praise to be sung. He intensifies their beautiful strength. He causes the brilliance of their glory to shine forth. He beautifies their excellent mercy and loving-kindness. He frames the fairness of their radiance. He makes their merciful beauty even more beautiful. He glorifies their upright majesty. He extols the order of their praise, to establish the dwelling place of Him who dwells on the cherubim. [13] And the cherubim are standing by the holy chayyoth, and their wings are raised up to their heads, and Shekinah is resting on them, and the brilliance of the Glory is on their faces, and song and praise [are] in their mouth, and their hands are under their wings, and their feet are covered by their wings, and horns of glory are on their heads, and the splendor of Shekinah on their face, and Shekinah is resting on them, and sapphire stones are around them, and columns of fire [are] on their four sides, and columns of firebrands beside them. [14] There is one sapphire on one side and another sapphire on another side, and under the sapphires there are coals of burning juniper. [15] And one cherub is standing in each direction, but the wings of the cherubim encircle each other above their skulls in glory; and they spread them to sing a song with them to Him that inhabits the clouds and to praise the fearful majesty of the King of kings with them. [16] And Kerubiel-YHWH, the prince who is appointed over them, he arrays them in attractive, beautiful, and pleasant orders, and he exalts them in all manner of exaltation, dignity, and glory. And he hastens them in glory and might to do the will of their Creator every moment. For above their lofty heads continually abides the glory of the High King who dwells on the cherubim."

CHAPTER 22 (B)

[1] R. Ishmael said: Metatron, the Prince of the Presence said to me: "What is the distance between one bridge and another? Twelve myriads of parasangs. Their ascent is myriads of parasangs, and their descent myriads of parasangs. [2] The distance between the rivers of dread and the rivers of fear is twenty-two myriads of parasangs; between the rivers of hail and the rivers of darkness, thirty-six myriads of parasangs; between the chambers of lightnings and the clouds of compassion, forty-two myriads of parasangs; between the clouds of compassion and the Merkaba, eighty-four myriads of parasangs; between

3 ENOCH

the Merkaba and the cherubim, one hundred forty-eight myriads of parasangs; between the cherubim and the ophanim, twenty-four myriads of parasangs; between the ophanim and the chambers of chambers, twenty-four myriads of parasangs; between the chambers of chambers and the holy chayyoth, forty thousand myriads of parasangs; between one wing of the chayyoth and another, twelve myriads of parasangs; and the breadth of each one wing is of that same measure; and the distance between the holy chayyoth and the Throne of Glory is thirty thousand myriads of parasangs. ³ And from the foot of the Throne to the seat there are forty thousand myriads of parasangs. And the Name of Him that sits on it: let the Name be sanctified! ⁴ And the arches of the Bozv are set above the 'Araboth, and they are one million and one hundred million parasangs high. Their measure is after the measure of the 'Irin and Qaddishin, that is, the Watchers and the Holy Ones. As it is written: I have set My bow in the cloud. It is not written here: I will set, but: I have set—already—clouds that surround the Throne of Glory. As His clouds pass by, the messengers of hail turn into burning coal. ⁵ And a fire of the voice goes down from by the holy chayyoth. And because of the breath of that voice, they run to another place, fearing lest it command them to go; and they return lest it injure them from the other side. Therefore, [as it is written:] They run and return. ⁶ And these arches of the bow are more beautiful and radiant than the radiance of the sun during the summer solstice, and they are whiter than a flaming fire, and they are great and beautiful. ⁷ Above the arches of the bow are the wheels of the ophanim. Their height is one million and one hundred million units of measure after the measure of the seraphim and the troops."

CHAPTER 23

¹ R. Ishmael said: Metatron, the messenger, the Prince of the Presence, said to me: "There are numerous winds blowing under the wings of the cherubim. The Fluttering Wind blows there, as it is written: And the Spirit of God was fluttering on the face of the waters. ² The Strong Wind blows there, as it is said: And the LORD caused the sea to go back by a strong east wind all that night. ³ The East Wind blows there, as it is written: The east wind brought the locusts. ⁴ The Wind of Quails blows there, as it is written: And there went forth a wind from the LORD and brought quails. ⁵ The Wind of Jealousy blows there, as it is written: And the wind of jealousy came on him. ⁶ The Wind of Earthquake blows there, as it is written: And after that, the wind of the earthquake, but the LORD was not in the earthquake. ⁷ The Wind of YHWH blows there, as it is written: And He carried me out by the Spirit of the LORD and set me down. ⁸ The Evil Wind blows there, as it is written: And the evil wind departed from him. ⁹ The Wind of Wisdom, and the Wind of Understanding, and the Wind of Knowledge, and the Wind of the Fear of YHWH blow there, as it is written: And the Spirit of the LORD will rest on Him, ‖ The Spirit of wisdom and understanding, ‖ The Spirit of counsel and might, ‖ The Spirit of knowledge and of the fear. ¹⁰ The Wind of Rain blows there, as it is written: The north wind brings forth rain. ¹¹ The Wind of Lightnings blows there, as it is written: He makes lightnings for the rain and brings forth the wind out of His treasuries. ¹² The Wind, Breaking the Rocks, blows there, as it is written: The LORD passed by and a great and strong wind split the mountains and broke in pieces the rocks before the LORD. ¹³ The Wind of Assuagement of the Sea blows there, as it is written: And God made a wind to pass over the earth, and the waters assuaged. ¹⁴ The Wind of Wrath blows there, as it is written: And behold, there came a great wind from the wilderness and [it] struck the four corners of the house and it fell. ¹⁵ The Storm-Wind blows there, as it is written: Storm-wind, fulfilling His word. ¹⁶ And Satan is standing among these winds, for Storm-Wind is nothing else but Satan, and all these winds do not blow but under the wings of the cherubim, as it is written: And He rode on a cherub and flew, yes, and He flew swiftly on the wings of the wind. ¹⁷ And where do all these winds go? The Writing teaches us that they go out from under the wings of the cherubim and descend on the globe of the sun, as it is written: The wind goes toward the south and turns around to the north; it turns around continually in its course and the wind returns again to its circuits. And from the globe of the sun they return and descend on the rivers and the seas, on the mountains and on the hills, as it is written: For behold, He that forms the mountains and creates the wind. ¹⁸ And from the mountains and the hills they return and descend to the seas and the rivers; and from the seas and the rivers they return and descend on the cities and provinces; and from the cities and provinces they return and descend into the Garden, and from the Garden they return and descend to Eden, as it is written: Walking in the Garden in the wind of day. ¹⁹ And in the midst of the Garden they join together and blow from one side to the other and are perfumed with the spices of the Garden even from its remotest parts, until they separate from each other, and, filled with the scent of the pure spices, they bring the fragrance from the remotest parts of Eden and the spices of the Garden to the righteous and godly who in the time to come will inherit the Garden of Eden and the Tree of Life, ²⁰ as it is written: Awake, O north wind; and come you south; blow on my garden, that the spices thereof may flow out. Let my beloved come into his garden and eat his precious fruits."

CHAPTER 24

¹ R. Ishmael said: Metatron, the messenger, the Prince of the Presence, the glory of all Heaven, said to me:

"The Holy One, blessed is He, has numerous chariots: He has the Chariots of the Cherubim, as it is written: And he rode on a cherub and flew. ²He has the Chariots of Wind, as it is written: And he flew swiftly on the wings of the wind. ³He has the Chariots of the Swift Cloud, as it is written: Behold, the LORD rides on a swift cloud. ⁴He has the Chariots of Clouds, as it is written: Behold, I come to you in a cloud. ⁵He has the Chariots of the Altar, as it is written: I saw the LORD standing on the altar. ⁶He has the Chariots of Myriads, as it is written: The chariots of God are myriads, thousands of messengers. ⁷He has the Chariots of the Tent, as it is written: And the LORD appeared in the tent in a pillar of cloud. ⁸He has the Chariots of the Dwelling Place, as it is written: And the LORD spoke to him out of the Dwelling Place. ⁹He has the Chariots of the Propitiatory Covering, as it is written: Then he heard the voice speaking to him from on the propitiatory covering. ¹⁰He has the Chariots of Sapphire Stone, as it is written: And there was under His feet as it were a paved work of sapphire stone. ¹¹He has the Chariots of Eagles, as it is written: I bare you on eagles' wings. (Eagles are not literally meant here but they that fly swiftly as eagles.) ¹²He has the chariots of Shout, as it is written: God has gone up with a shout. ¹³He has the Chariots of 'Araboth, as it is written: Extol Him that rides on the 'Araboth. ¹⁴He has the Chariots of Thick Clouds, as it is written: Who makes the thick clouds His chariot. ¹⁵He has the Chariots of the Chayyoth, as it is written: And the chayyoth ran and returned. They run by permission and return by permission, for Shekinah is above their heads. ¹⁶He has the Chariots of Wheels, as it is written: And He said, Go in between the whirling wheels. ¹⁷He has the Chariots of a Swift Cherub, as it is written: Riding on a swift cherub. And at the time when He rides on a swift cherub, as He sets one of His feet on him, before He sets the other foot on his back, He looks through eighteen thousand worlds at one glance. And He discerns and sees into them all and knows what is in all of them and then he sets down the other foot on him, according as it is written: Around eighteen thousand. From where do we know that He looks through every one of them every day? It is written: He looked down from Heaven on the children of men to see if there were any that understood, that seek after God. ¹⁸He has the Chariots of the Ophanim, as it is written: And the ophanim were full of eyes around. ¹⁹He has the Chariots of His Holy Throne, as it is written: God sits on His holy throne. ²⁰He has the chariots of the Throne of YAH, as it is written: Because a hand is lifted up on the throne of YAH. ²¹He has the Chariots of the Throne of Judgment, as it is written: But the LORD of Hosts will be exalted in judgment. ²²He has the Chariots of the Throne of Glory, as it is written: The throne of glory, set on high from the beginning, is the place of our sanctuary. ²³He has the Chariots of the High and Exalted Throne, as it is written: I saw the LORD sitting on the high and exalted throne."

CHAPTER 25

¹R. Ishmael said: Metatron, the messenger, the Prince of the Presence, said to me: "Above these there is one great prince, revered, high, lordly, fearful, ancient, and strong. 'Ophphanniel-YHWH is his name. ²He has sixteen faces, four faces on each side, one hundred wings on each side. And he has eight thousand four hundred sixty-six eyes, corresponding to the days of the year. Two thousand one hundred and ninety and some say two thousand one hundred sixteen on each side. ³And those two eyes of his face—in each one of them lightnings are flashing, and from each one of them firebrands are burning, and no creature is able to behold them. For anyone who looks at them is burned instantly. ⁴His height is as the distance of two thousand five hundred years' journey. No eye can behold and no mouth can tell the mighty power of his strength except the King of kings, the Holy One, blessed is He, alone. ⁵Why is he called 'Ophphanniel? Because he is appointed over the ophanim and the ophanim are given in his charge. He stands every day, and attends, and beautifies them. And he exalts and orders their apartment, and polishes their standing-place, and makes their dwellings bright, [and] makes their corners even, and cleanses their seats. And he waits on them early and late, by day and by night, to increase their beauty, to make their dignity great, and to make them diligent in praise of their Creator. ⁶And all the ophanim are full of eyes, and they are all full of brightness; seventy-two sapphire stones are fixed on their garments on their right side and seventy-two sapphire stones are fixed on their garments on their left side. ⁷And four carbuncle stones are fixed on the crown of every single one, the splendor of which proceeds in the four directions of 'Araboth even as the splendor of the globe of the sun proceeds in all the directions of the universe. And why is it called Carbuncle? Because its splendor is like the appearance of lightning. And tents of splendor, tents of brilliance, [and] tents of brightness as of sapphire and carbuncle enclose them because of the shining appearance of their eyes."

CHAPTER 26

¹R. Ishmael said: Metatron, the messenger, the Prince of the Presence, said to me: "Above these there is one prince, wonderful, noble, great, honorable, mighty, terrible, a chief, and leader, and a swift scribe, glorified, honored, and beloved. ²He is altogether filled with splendor, full of praise and shining; and he is wholly full of brilliance, of light and of beauty; and the whole of him is filled with goodliness and greatness. ³His countenance is altogether like that of messengers, but his body is like an eagle's body. ⁴His splendor is like to lightnings, his appearance like

firebrands, his beauty like to sparks, his honor like fiery coals, his majesty like electrum, his radiance like the light of the planet Venus. The image of him is like to the Greater Light. His height is as the seven heavens. The light from his eyebrows is like the sevenfold light. ⁵ The sapphire stone on his head is as great as the whole universe and like to the splendor of the very heavens in radiance. ⁶ His body is full of eyes like the stars of the sky, innumerable and unsearchable. Every eye is like the planet Venus. Yet, there are some of them like the Lesser Light and some of them like to the Greater Light. From his ankles to his knees, they are like to stars of lightning; from his knees to his thighs like to the planet Venus; from his thighs to his loins like to the moon; from his loins to his neck like the sun; from his neck to his skull like to the Imperishable Light. ⁷ The crown on his head is like to the splendor of the Throne of Glory. The measure of the crown is the distance of five hundred and two years' journey. There is no kind of splendor, no kind of brilliance, no kind of radiance, no kind of light in the universe but is fixed on that crown. ⁸ The name of that prince is Seraphiel-YHWH. And the crown on his head, its name is the Prince of Peace. And why is he called by the name of Seraphiel-YHWH? Because he is appointed over the seraphim. And the flaming seraphim are given in his charge. And he presides over them by day and by night and teaches them song, praise, proclamation of beauty, might, and majesty, that they may proclaim the beauty of their King in all manner of praise and sanctification. ⁹ How many are the seraphim? Four, corresponding to the four winds of the world. And how many wings does each one of them have? Six, corresponding to the six days of Creation. And how many faces do they have? Each one of them [has] four faces. ¹⁰ The measure of the seraphim and the height of each one of them correspond to the height of the seven heavens. The size of each wing is like the measure of all Raqia'. The size of each face is like that of the face of the east. ¹¹ And each one of them gives forth light like to the splendor of the Throne of Glory, so that not even the holy chayyoth, the honored ophanim, nor the majestic cherubim are able to behold it. For everyone who beholds it, his eyes are darkened because of its great splendor. ¹² Why are they called seraphim? Because they burn the writing tablets of Satan: every day Satan is sitting, together with Sammael, the Prince of Rome, and with Dubbiel, the Prince of Persia, and they write the iniquities of Israel on writing tablets which they hand over to the seraphim in order that they may present them before the Holy One, blessed is He, so that He may destroy Israel from the world. But the seraphim know from the secrets of the Holy One, blessed is He, that He does not desire that this people Israel should perish. What do the seraphim do? Every day they receive them from the hand of Satan and burn them in the burning fire beside the high and exalted Throne in order that they may not come before the Holy One, blessed is He, at the time when He is sitting on the Throne of Judgment, judging the whole world in truth."

CHAPTER 27

¹ R. Ishmael said: Metatron, the messenger of YHWH, the Prince of the Presence, said to me: "Above the seraphim there is one prince, exalted above all the princes, wondrous more than all the servants. His name is Radweriel-YHWH, who is appointed over the treasuries of the scrolls. ² He fetches forth the Case of Writings with the Scroll of Records in it, and brings it before the Holy One, blessed is He. And he breaks the seals of the case, opens it, takes out the scrolls, and delivers them before the Holy One, blessed is He. And the Holy One, blessed is He, receives them from his hand and gives them in his sight to the Scribes that they may read them in the Great House of Judgment in the height of 'Araboth Raqia', before the heavenly household. ³ And why is he called Radweriel? Because out of every word that goes forth from his mouth a messenger is created: and he stands in the singing company of the ministering messengers and utters a song before the Holy One, blessed is He, when the time draws near for the recitation of the Thrice Holy."

CHAPTER 28

¹ R. Ishmael said: Metatron, the messenger, the Prince of the Presence, said to me: "Above all these there are four great princes, Watchers and Holy Ones by name: high, honored, revered, beloved, wonderful, and glorious ones, greater than all the children of Heaven. There is none like to them among all the celestial princes and none their equal among all the servants. For each one of them is equal to all the rest together. ² And their dwelling is beside the Throne of Glory, and their standing place beside the Holy One, blessed is He, so that the brilliance of their dwelling is a reflection of the brilliance of the Throne of Glory. And the splendor of their countenance is a reflection of the splendor of Shekinah. ³ And they are glorified by the glory of the Divine Majesty and praised by the praise of Shekinah. ⁴ And not only that, but the Holy One, blessed is He, does nothing in His world without first consulting them, but after that He does it. As it is written: The sentence is by the decree of the watchers and the demand by the word of the holy ones. ⁵ The watchers are two and the holy ones are two. And how are they standing before the Holy One, blessed is He? It is to be understood that one watcher is standing on one side and the other watcher on the other side, and one holy one is standing on one side and the other on the other side. ⁶ And they always exalt the humble, and they abase to the ground those that are proud, and they exalt to the height those that are humble. ⁷ And

every day, as the Holy One, blessed is He, is sitting on the Throne of Judgment and judges the whole world, and the scrolls of the living and the scrolls of the dead are opened before Him, then all the children of Heaven are standing before Him in fear, dread, awe, and trembling. At that time, when the Holy One, blessed is He, is sitting on the Throne of Judgment to execute judgment, His garment is white as snow, the hair on His head as pure wool, and the whole of His cloak is like the shining light. And He is covered with righteousness all over as with a coat of mail. [8] And those watchers and holy ones are standing before Him like court officers before the judge. And they raise and argue every case and close the case that comes before the Holy One, blessed is He, in judgment, according as it is written: The sentence is by the decree of the watchers and the demand by the word of the holy ones. [9] Some of them argue and others pass the sentence in the Great House of Judgment in 'Araboth. Some of them make the requests from before the Divine Majesty and some close the cases before the Most High. Others finish by going down and executing the sentences on earth below. According as it is written: Behold, a watcher and a holy one came down from Heaven, and cried aloud, and said thus: Hew down the tree, and cut off his branches, shake off his leaves, and scatter his fruit: let the beasts get away from under it, and the birds from his branches. [10] Why are they called watchers and holy ones? By reason that they sanctify the body and the spirit with lashes of fire on the third day of the judgment, as it is written: After two days He will revive us, || On the third [[day]] He will raise us up, || And we will live before Him."

CHAPTER 29

[1] R. Ishmael said: Metatron, the messenger, the Prince of the Presence, said to me: "Each one of them has seventy names corresponding to the seventy tongues of the world. And all of them are based on the Name of the Holy One, blessed is He. And every name is written with a flaming style on the Fearful Crown which is on the head of the high and exalted King. [2] And sparks and lightnings go forth from each one of them. And each one of them is beset with horns of splendor around. From each one lights are shining forth, and each one is surrounded by tents of brilliance so that not even the seraphim and the chayyoth who are greater than all the [other] children of Heaven are able to behold them."

CHAPTER 30

[1] R. Ishmael said: Metatron, the messenger, the Prince of the Presence, said to me: "Whenever the Great House of Judgment is seated in the 'Araboth Raqia' on high there is no opening of the mouth for anyone in the world except those great princes who are called YHWH by the Name of the Holy One, blessed is He.

[2] How many are those princes? Seventy-two princes of the kingdoms of the world besides the Prince of the World who speaks in favor of the world before the Holy One, blessed is He, every day, at the hour when the scroll is opened in which all the doings of the world are recorded, according as it is written: The judgment was set and the scrolls were opened."

CHAPTER 31

[1] R. Ishmael said: Metatron, the messenger, the Prince of the Presence, said to me: "At the time when the Holy One, blessed is He, is sitting on the Throne of Judgment, then Justice is standing on His right, and Mercy on His left, and Truth before His face. [2] And when man enters before Him to judgment, then a staff, as it were, comes forth from the splendor of the Mercy toward him and stands in front of him. Immediately man falls on his face, and all the messengers of destruction fear and tremble before Him, according as it is written: And with mercy will the throne be established, and He will sit on it in truth."

CHAPTER 32

[1] R. Ishmael said: Metatron, the messenger, the Prince of the Presence, said to me: "When the Holy One, blessed is He, opens the Scroll—half of which is fire and half flame—then they go out from before Him in every moment to execute the judgment on the wicked by His sword that is drawn forth out of its sheath and the splendor of which shines like lightning and pervades the world from one end to the other, as it is written: For the LORD will plead by fire and with all flesh by His sword. [2] And all the inhabitants of the world fear and tremble before Him when they behold His sharpened sword like to lightning from one end of the world to the other, and sparks and flashes of the size of the stars of Raqia' going out from it, according as it is written: If I sharpen the lightning of My sword."

CHAPTER 33

[1] R. Ishmael said: Metatron, the messenger, the Prince of the Presence, said to me: "At the time that the Holy One, blessed is He, is sitting on the Throne of Judgment, then the messengers of Mercy are standing on His right, the messengers of Peace are standing on His left, and the messengers of Destruction are standing in front of Him. [2] And one scribe is standing beneath Him, and another scribe above Him. [3] And the glorious seraphim surround the Throne on its four sides with walls of lightnings, and the ophanim surround them with firebrands around the Throne of Glory. And clouds of fire and clouds of flames surround them to the right and to the left; and the holy chayyoth carry the Throne of Glory from below: each one with three fingers. The measure of the fingers of each one is eight hundred thousand and seven

hundred times one hundred, and sixty-six thousand parasangs. ⁴ And underneath the feet of the chayyoth seven fiery rivers are running and flowing. And the breadth of each river is three hundred sixty-five thousand parasangs and its depth is two hundred forty-eight thousand myriads of parasangs. Its length is unsearchable and immeasurable. ⁵ And each river turns around in a bow in the four directions of 'Araboth Raqia', and from there it falls down to Ma'on and is stayed, and from Ma'on to Zebul, from Zebul to Shechaqim, from Shechaqim to Raqia', from Raqia' to Shamayim, and from Shamayim on the heads of the wicked who are in Gehenna, ⁶ as it is written: Behold, a whirlwind of the LORD, even His fury, is gone, yes, a whirling tempest; it will burst on the head of the wicked."

CHAPTER 34

¹ R. Ishmael said: Metatron, the messenger, the Prince of the Presence, said to me: "The hooves of the chayyoth are surrounded by seven clouds of burning coals. The clouds of burning coals are surrounded on the outside by seven walls of flames. The seven walls of flames are surrounded on the outside by seven walls of hailstones. The hailstones are surrounded on the outside by stones of hail. The stones of hail are surrounded on the outside by stones of the wings of the tempest. The stones of the wings of the tempest are surrounded on the outside by flames of fire. The flames of fire are surrounded by the chambers of the whirlwind. The chambers of the whirlwind are surrounded on the outside by the fire and the water. ² Around the fire and the water are those who utter the HOLY. Around those who utter the HOLY are those who utter the BLESSED. Around those who utter the BLESSED are the bright clouds. The bright clouds are surrounded on the outside by coals of burning juniper; and on the outside surrounding the coals of burning juniper there are one thousand camps of fire and ten thousand hosts of flames. And between every camp and every host there is a cloud, so that they may not be burned by the fire."

CHAPTER 35

¹ R. Ishmael said: Metatron, the messenger, the Prince of the Presence, said to me: "The Holy One, blessed is He, has five hundred and six thousand myriads of camps in the height of 'Araboth Raqia'. And each camp is composed of four hundred ninety-six thousand messengers. ² And every single messenger, the height of his stature is as the Great Sea; and the appearance of their countenance as the appearance of the lightning, and their eyes as lamps of fire, and their arms and their feet like in color to polished brass, and the roaring voice of their words like the voice of a multitude. ³ And they are all standing before the Throne of Glory in four rows. And the princes of the army are standing at the head of each row. ⁴ And some

of them utter the HOLY and others utter the BLESSED, some of them run as messengers, others are standing in attendance, according as it is written: One million ministered to Him and one hundred million stood before him, the judgment was set, and the scrolls were opened. ⁵ And in the hour when the time draws near for [them] to say the HOLY, then first there goes forth a whirlwind from before the Holy One, blessed is He, and bursts on the camp of Shekinah and there arises a great commotion among them, as it is written: Behold, the whirlwind of the LORD goes forth with fury—a continuing commotion. ⁶ At that moment one million of them are changed into sparks, one million of them into firebrands, one million into flashes, one million into flames, one million into males, one million into females, one million into winds, one million into burning fires, one million into flames, one million into sparks, one million into chashmals of light, until they take on themselves the yoke of the Kingdom of the heavens, the high and lifted up, of the Creator of them all, with fear, dread, awe, and trembling, with commotion, anguish, terror, and trepidation. Then they are changed again into their former shape to always have the fear of their King before them, as they have set their hearts on saying the Song continually, as it is written: And one cried to another and said, HOLY, HOLY, HOLY."

CHAPTER 36

¹ R. Ishmael said: Metatron, the messenger, the Prince of the Presence, said to me: "At the time when the ministering messengers desire to say the Song, then the fiery stream rises with many thousand[s] of thousands and myriads of myriads of messengers of power and strength of fire and it runs and passes under the Throne of Glory, between the camps of the ministering messengers and the troops of 'Araboth. ² And all the ministering messengers first go down into Nehar di-Nur, and they dip themselves in the fire and dip their tongue and their mouth seven times; and after that they go up and put on the garment of 'Machaqe Samal, and cover themselves with cloaks of chashmal, and stand in four rows beside the Throne of Glory, in all the heavens."

CHAPTER 37

¹ R. Ishmael said: Metatron, the messenger, the Prince of the Presence, said to me: "There are four chariots of Shekinah standing in the seven Halls, and the four camps of Shekinah are standing before each one. Between each camp a river of fire is continually flowing. ² Between each river there are bright clouds surrounding them, and pillars of brimstone are put up between each cloud. Flaming wheels are standing between one pillar and another, surrounding them. And between one wheel and another there are flames of fire around. Between one flame and another there are treasuries of lightnings; behind the treasuries of

lightnings are the wings of the storm wind. Behind the wings of the storm-wind are the chambers of the tempest; behind the chambers of the tempest there are winds, voices, thunders, sparks on sparks, and earthquakes on earthquakes."

CHAPTER 38

[1] R. Ishmael said: Metatron, the messenger, the Prince of the Presence, said to me: "At the time when the ministering messengers utter the Thrice Holy, then all the pillars of the heavens and their sockets tremble, and the gates of the Halls of 'Araboth Raqia' are shaken, and the foundations of Shechaqim and the universe are moved, and the orders of Ma'on and the chambers of Makon quiver, and all the orders of Raqia', and the constellations, and the planets are dismayed, and the globes of the sun and the moon hurry away, and flee out of their courses, and run twelve thousand parasangs, and seek to throw themselves down from the heavens [2] by reason of the roaring voice of their chant, and the noise of their praise, and the sparks and lightnings that go forth from their faces; as it is written: The voice of Your thunder was in the heavens and the lightnings lightened the world, the earth trembled and shook. [3] Until the Prince of the World calls them, saying, Be quiet in your place! Do not fear because of the ministering messengers who sing the Song before the Holy One, blessed is He. As it is written: When the morning stars sang together, || And all the sons of Heaven [[or God]] shouted for joy."

CHAPTER 39

[1] R. Ishmael said: Metatron, the messenger, the Prince of the Presence, said to me: "When the ministering messengers utter the HOLY, then all the explicit names that are graven with a flaming style on the Throne of Glory fly off like eagles, with sixteen wings. And they surround and encircle the Holy One, blessed is He, on the four sides of the place of His Shekinah. [2] And the messengers of the host, and the flaming servants, and the mighty ophanim, and the cherubim of the Shekinah, and the holy chayyoth, and the seraphim, and the er'elim, and the taphsarim and the troops of consuming fire, and the fiery armies, and the flaming hosts, and the holy princes, adorned with crowns, clad in kingly majesty, wrapped in glory, girt with loftiness, fall on their faces three times, saying, Blessed is the name of His glorious Kingdom forever and ever."

CHAPTER 40

[1] R. Ishmael said: Metatron, the messenger, the Prince of the Presence, said to me: "When the ministering messengers say HOLY before the Holy One, blessed is He, in the proper way, then the servants of His Throne, the attendants of His Glory, go forth with great mirth from under the Throne of Glory. [2] And

they all carry in their hands—each one of them—one million and one hundred million crowns of stars, similar in appearance to the planet Venus, and put them on the ministering messengers and the great princes who utter the HOLY. They put three crowns on each one of them: one crown because they say HOLY, another crown because they say HOLY, HOLY, and a third crown because they say HOLY, HOLY, HOLY, is the LORD of Hosts. [3] And in the moment that they do not utter the HOLY in the right order, a consuming fire goes forth from the little finger of the Holy One, blessed is He, and falls down in the midst of their ranks and is divided into four hundred ninety-six thousand parts corresponding to the four camps of the ministering messengers, and consumes them in one moment, as it is written: A fire goes before Him and burns up His adversaries around. [4] After that, the Holy One, blessed is He, opens His mouth, and speaks one word, and creates others in their stead—new ones like them. And each one stands before His Throne of Glory, uttering the HOLY, as it is written: They are new every morning; great is Your faithfulness."

CHAPTER 41

[1] R. Ishmael said: Metatron, the messenger, the Prince of the Presence, said to me: "Come and behold the letters by which the heavens and the earth were created, the letters by which the mountains and hills were created, the letters by which the seas and rivers were created, the letters by which the trees and herbs were created, the letters by which the planets and the constellations were created, the letters by which the globe of the moon and the globe of the sun, Orion, the Pleiades, and all the different luminaries of Raqia' were created, [2] the letters by which the Throne of Glory and the wheels of the Merkaba were created, the letters by which the necessities of the worlds were created, [3] the letters by which wisdom, understanding, knowledge, prudence, meekness, and righteousness were created, by which the whole world is sustained." [4] And I walked by his side, and he took me by his hand, and raised me on his wings, and showed me those letters, all of them, that are graven with a flaming style on the Throne of Glory: and sparks go forth from them and cover all the chambers of 'Araboth.

CHAPTER 42

[1] R. Ishmael said: Metatron, the messenger, the Prince of the Presence, said to me: "Come, and I will show you where the waters are suspended in the highest, where fire is burning in the midst of hail, where lightnings lighten out of the midst of snowy mountains, where thunders are roaring in the celestial heights, where a flame is burning in the midst of the burning fire, and where voices make themselves heard in the midst of thunder and earthquake." [2] Then

I went by his side, and he took me by his hand, and lifted me up on his wings, and showed me all those things. I beheld the waters suspended on high in 'Araboth Raqia', by the Name YAH 'EHYE 'ASHER 'EHYE, that is, YAH, I AM THAT I AM; and [I beheld] their fruits going down from Heaven and watering the face of the world, as it is written: "He waters the mountains from His chambers: the earth is satisfied with the fruit of Your work." ³And I saw fire, and snow, and hailstone that were mingled together within each other and yet were not damaged, by the name 'Esh 'Okela, as it is written: "For the Lord your God is a consuming fire." ⁴And I saw lightnings that were lightening out of mountains of snow and yet were not damaged, by the name YAH Sur 'Olamim, as it is written: "For in YAH, the LORD, the everlasting rock." ⁵And I saw thunders and voices that were roaring in the midst of fiery flames and were not damaged, by the name 'EL-SHADDAI RABBA, as it is written: "I am God Almighty." ⁶And I beheld a flame and a glow that were flaming and glowing in the midst of burning fire, and yet were not damaged, by the name YAD 'AL KES YAH, as it is written: "And he said, For the hand is on the Throne of the LORD." ⁷And I beheld rivers of fire in the midst of rivers of water and they were not damaged, by the name 'OSE SHALOM, as it is written: "He makes peace in His high places." For He makes peace between the fire and the water, between the hail and the fire, between the wind and the cloud, between the earthquake and the sparks.

CHAPTER 43

¹R. Ishmael said: Metatron said to me: "Come, and I will show you where the spirits of the righteous are that have been created and have returned, and the spirits of the righteous that have not yet been created." ²And he lifted me up to his side, took me by his hand, and lifted me up near the Throne of Glory by the place of the Shekinah; and he revealed the Throne of Glory to me, and he showed me the spirits that have been created and had returned: and they were flying above the Throne of Glory before the Holy One, blessed is He. ³After that I went to interpret the following verse of Writing and I found in what is written: "For the spirit clothed itself before me, and the souls I have made"—that means the spirits that have been created in the chamber of creation of the righteous and that have returned before the Holy One, blessed is He; and the words "and the souls I have made" refer to the spirits of the righteous that have not yet been created in the chamber, or Guph.

CHAPTER 44

¹R. Ishmael said: Metatron, the messenger, the Prince of the Presence, said to me: "Come, and I will show you where the spirits of the wicked and the spirits of the intermediate are standing, and the spirits of the

intermediate, where they go down, and the spirits of the wicked, where they go down." ²And he said to me: "The spirits of the wicked go down to Sheol by the hands of two messengers of destruction: their names are Za'aphiel and Simkiel. ³Simkiel is appointed over the intermediate to support them and purify them because of the great mercy of the Prince of the Place. Za'aphiel is appointed over the spirits of the wicked in order to cast them down from the presence of the Holy One, blessed is He, and from the splendor of the Shekinah to Sheol, to be punished in the fire of Gehenna with staves of burning coal." ⁴And I went by his side, and he took me by his hand and showed me all of them with his fingers. ⁵And I beheld the appearance of their faces, and behold, it was as the appearance of children of men, and their bodies like eagles. And not only that, but furthermore the color of the countenance of the intermediate was like pale grey on account of their deeds, for there are stains on them until they have become cleaned from their iniquity in the fire. ⁶And the color of the wicked was like the bottom of a pot on account of the wickedness of their doings. ⁷And I saw the spirits of the Patriarchs—Abraham, Isaac, and Jacob—and the rest of the righteous whom they have brought up out of their graves and who have ascended to Heaven. And they were praying before the Holy One, blessed is He, saying in their prayer: "Lord of the Universe! How long will You sit on Your Throne like a mourner in the days of his mourning with Your right hand behind You and not deliver Your children and reveal Your Kingdom in the world? And for how long will You have no pity on Your children who are made slaves among the nations of the world? Nor on Your right hand that is behind You with which You stretched out the heavens, and the earth, and the heavens of heavens? When will You have compassion?" ⁸Then the Holy One, blessed is He, answered each of them, saying, "Since these wicked sin so and so, and transgress with such and such transgressions against Me, how could I deliver My Great Right Hand in the downfall by their hands?" ⁹In that moment Metatron called me and spoke to me: "My servant! Take the scrolls and read their evil doings!" Immediately I took the scrolls and read their doings and there were to be found thirty-six transgressions written down with regard to each wicked one and besides that they have transgressed all the letters in the Torah, as it is written: "Yes, all Israel has transgressed Your law." It is not written "'al torateka" but, "'et torateka," for they have transgressed from Aleph to Taw; they have transgressed forty statutes for each letter. ¹⁰Immediately Abraham, Isaac, and Jacob wept. Then the Holy One, blessed is He, said to them: "Abraham, My beloved, Isaac, My chosen one, Jacob, My firstborn! How can I now deliver them from among the nations of the world?" And immediately Michael, the prince of Israel, cried and wept with a loud voice and said, "Why do You stand far off, O LORD?"

CHAPTER 45

¹ R. Ishmael said: Metatron said to me: "Come, and I will show you the curtain of the Divine Majesty which is spread before the Holy One, blessed is He, and whereon are graven all the generations of the world and all their doings, both what they have done and what they will do until the end of all generations." ² And I went, and he showed it to me, pointing it out with his fingers like a father who teaches his children the letters of Torah. And I saw each generation, the rulers of each generation, and the heads of each generation, the shepherds of each generation, the oppressors of each generation, the keepers of each generation, the scourgers of each generation, the overseers of each generation, the judges of each generation, the court officers of each generation, the teachers of each generation, the supporters of each generation, the chiefs of each generation, the presidents of academies of each generation, the magistrates of each generation, the princes of each generation, the counselors of each generation, the nobles of each generation, and the men of might of each generation, the elders of each generation, and the guides of each generation. ³ And I saw Adam, his generation, their doings and their thoughts; Noah and his generation, their doings and their thoughts; and the generation of the flood, their doings and their thoughts; Shem and his generation, their doings and their thoughts; Nimrod and the generation of the confusion of tongues, and his generation, their doings and their thoughts; Abraham and his generation, their doings and their thoughts; Isaac and his generation, their doings and their thoughts; Ishmael and his generation, their doings and their thoughts; Jacob and his generation, their doings and their thoughts; Joseph and his generation, their doings and their thoughts; the tribes and their generation, their doings and their thoughts; Amram and his generation, their doings and their thoughts; Moses and his generation, their doings and their thoughts; ⁴ Aaron and Miriam, their works and their doings; the princes and the elders, their works and doings; Joshua and his generation, their works and doings; the judges and their generation, their works and doings; Eli and his generation, their works and doings; Phinehas, their works and doings; Elkanah and his generation, their works and their doings; Samuel and his generation, their works and doings; the kings of Judah with their generations, their works and their doings; the kings of Israel and their generations, their works and their doings; the princes of Israel, their works and their doings; the princes of the nations of the world, their works and their doings; the heads of the councils of Israel, their works and their doings; the heads of the councils in the nations of the world, their generations, their works

and their doings; the rulers of Israel and their generation, their works and their doings; the nobles of Israel and their generation, their works and their doings; the nobles of the nations of the world and their generations, their works and their doings; the men of reputation in Israel, their generation, their works and their doings; the judges of Israel, their generation, their works and their doings; the judges of the nations of the world and their generation, their works and their doings; the teachers of children in Israel, their generations, their works and their doings; the teachers of children in the nations of the world, their generations, their works and their doings; the counselors of Israel, their generation, their works and their doings; the counselors of the nations of the world, their generation, their works and their doings; all the prophets of Israel, their generation, their works and their doings; all the prophets of the nations of the world, their generation, their works and their doings; ⁵ and all the fights and wars that the nations of the world worked against the people of Israel in the time of their kingdom. And I saw Messiah, son of Joseph, and His generation, and their works and their doings that they will do against the nations of the world. And I saw Messiah, son of David, and His generation, and all the fights and wars, and their works and their doings that they will do with Israel both for good and evil. And I saw all the fights and wars that Gog and Magog will fight in the days of Messiah, and all that the Holy One, blessed is He, will do with them in the time to come. ⁶ And all the rest of all the leaders of the generations and all the works of the generations both in Israel and in the nations of the world, both what is done and what will be done hereafter to all generations until the end of time, all were graven on the curtain of MAQOM. And I saw all these things with my eyes; and after I had seen it, I opened my mouth in praise of MAQOM, the Divine Majesty saying thus: "For the King's word has power and who may say to Him: What are You doing? Whosoever keeps the commandments will know no evil thing." And I said, "O LORD, how manifold are Your works!"

CHAPTER 46

¹ R. Ishmael said: Metatron said to me: "Come, and I will show you the space of the stars that are standing in Raqia' night by night in fear of the Almighty and I will show you where they go and where they stand." ² I walked by his side, and he took me by his hand and pointed out all to me with his fingers. And they were standing on sparks of flames around the Merkaba of the Almighty. What did Metatron do? At that moment he clapped his hands and chased them off from their place. Immediately they flew off on flaming wings, rose, and fled from the four sides of the Throne of the Merkaba, and as they flew he told me the names of every single one. As it is written: "He tells the number of the stars, ‖ He gives them all their names," teaching

that the Holy One, blessed is He, has given a name to each one of them. ³ And they all enter in counted order under the guidance of Rahatiel to Raqia' ha-Shamayim to serve the world. And they go out in counted order to praise the Holy One, blessed is He, with songs and hymns, according as it is written: "The heavens declare the glory of God." ⁴ But in the time to come the Holy One, blessed is He, will create them anew, as it is written: "They are new every morning." And they open their mouth and utter a song. Which is the song that they utter? "When I consider Your heavens."

CHAPTER 47

¹ R. Ishmael said: Metatron said to me: "Come, and I will show you the souls of the messengers and the spirits of the ministering servants whose bodies have been burned in the fire of the Almighty that goes forth from His little finger. And they have been made into fiery coals in the midst of the fiery river. But their spirits and their souls are standing behind the Shekinah. ² Whenever the ministering messengers utter a song at a wrong time or as not appointed to be sung, they are burned and consumed by the fire of their Creator and by a flame from their Maker, in the places of the whirlwind, for it blows on them and drives them into the Nehar di-Nur; and there they are made into numerous mountains of burning coal. But their spirit and their soul return to their Creator, and all are standing behind their Master." ³ And I went by his side, and he took me by his hand and showed me all the souls of the messengers and the spirits of the ministering servants who were standing behind the Shekinah on wings of the whirlwind and walls of fire surrounding them. ⁴ At that moment Metatron opened the gates of the walls to me within which they were standing behind the Shekinah, and I lifted up my eyes and saw them, and behold, the likeness of each one was as that of messengers and their wings like birds' wings, made out of flames, the work of burning fire. In that moment I opened my mouth in praise of MAQOM and said, "How great are Your works, O LORD."

CHAPTER 48 (A)

¹ R. Ishmael said: Metatron said to me: "Come, and I will show you the Right Hand of MAQOM, laid behind Him because of the destruction of the holy temple, from which all kinds of splendor and light shine forth and by which the nine hundred fifty-five heavens were created, and whom not even the seraphim and the ophanim are permitted to behold until the day of salvation will arrive." ² And I went by his side, and he took me by his hand and showed me the Right Hand of MAQOM, with all manner of praise, rejoicing, and song: and no mouth can tell its praise, and no eye can behold it, because of its greatness, dignity, majesty, glory, and beauty. ³ And not only that, but all the souls

of the righteous who are counted worthy to behold the joy of Jerusalem, they are standing by it, praising and praying before it three times every day, saying, "Awake, awake, put on strength, O arm of the LORD," according as it is written: "He caused His glorious arm to go at the right hand of Moses." ⁴ In that moment the Right Hand of MAQOM was weeping. And there went forth from its five fingers five rivers of tears, and they fell down into the Great Sea, and shook the whole world, according as it is written: "The earth is utterly broken down, ‖ The earth is clean dissolved, ‖ The earth is utterly moved, ‖ The earth will stagger like a drunken man, ‖ And will be moved to and fro like a lodge," five times corresponding to the fingers of His Great Right Hand. ⁵ But when the Holy One, blessed is He, sees that there is no righteous man in the generation, and no pious man on earth, and no justice in the hands of men, and that there is no man like to Moses, and no intercessor as Samuel who could pray before MAQOM for the salvation and for the deliverance, and for His Kingdom, that it might be revealed in the whole world, and for His Great Right Hand that He put it before Himself again to work great salvation for Israel by it, ⁶ then immediately the Holy One, blessed is He, will remember His own justice, favor, mercy, and grace, and He will deliver His Great Arm by Himself, and His righteousness will support Him, according as it is written: "And He saw that there was no man" (that is, like to Moses who prayed countless times for Israel in the desert and averted the Divine decrees from them) "and He wondered that there was no intercessor"—like to Samuel who entreated the Holy One, blessed is He, and called to Him and He answered him and fulfilled his desire, even if it was not fit in accordance with the Divine plan, according as it is written: "Is it not wheat-harvest today? I will call to the LORD." ⁷ And not only that, but He joined fellowship with Moses in every place, as it is written: "Moses and Aaron among His priests." And again it is written: "Though Moses and Samuel stood before Me, ‖ My own arm brought salvation to Me." ⁸ The Holy One, blessed is He, said in that hour: "How long will I wait for the children of men to work salvation according to their righteousness for My arm? For My own sake and for the sake of My merit and righteousness I will deliver [with] My arm and redeem My children by it from among the nations of the world, as it is written: For My own sake I will do it. For why should My Name be profaned?" ⁹ In that moment the Holy One, blessed is He, will reveal His Great Arm and show it to the nations of the world, for its length is as the length of the world and its breadth is as the width of the world. And the appearance of its splendor is like to the splendor of the sunshine in its might, in the summer solstice. ¹⁰ Immediately Israel will be saved from among the nations of the world. And Messiah will appear to them and He will bring them up to Jerusalem with great joy. And not only that, but they will eat and drink, for they will glorify the Kingdom of Messiah, the house of David, in the four quarters of the world. And the nations of the world will not prevail against them, as it is written: "The LORD has made His holy arm bare ‖ In the eyes of all the nations, ‖ And all the ends of the earth will see ‖ The salvation of our God." And again: "The LORD alone led him, ‖ And there was no strange god with him." [And again:] "And the LORD will be King over all the earth."

CHAPTER 48 (B)

[1] Metatron has seventy names which the Holy One, blessed is He, took from His own Name and put on him. And they are these: (1) YEHOEL YAH, (2) YEHOEL, (3) YOPHIEL, and (4) YOPHPHIEL, and (5) 'APHPHIEL, and (6) MARGEZIEL, (7) GIPPUYEL, (8) PA'AZIEL, (9) 'A'AH, (10) PERIEL, (11) TATRIEL, (12) TABKIEL, (13) 'W, (14) YHWH, (15) DH, (16) WHYH, (17) 'EBED, (18) DIBBURIEL, (19) 'APH'APIEL, (20) SPPIEL, (21) PASPASIEL, (22) SENEGRON, (23) METATRON, (24) SOGDIN, (25) 'ADRIGON, (26) 'ASUM, (27) SAQPAM, (28) SAQTAM, (29) MIGON, (30) MITTON, (31) MOTTRON, (32) ROSPHIM, (33) QINOTH, (34) CHATATYAH, (35) DEGAZYAH, (36) PSPYAH, (37) BSKNYH, (38) MGRG, (39) BARAD, (40) MKRKK, (41) MSPRD, (42) CHSHG, (43) CHSHG, (43) CHSHB, (44) MNRTTT, (45) BSYRYM, (46) MITMON, (47) TITMON, (48) PISQON, (49) SAPHSAPHYAH', (50) ZRCH, (51) ZRCHYAH, (52) B, (53) BEYAH, (54) HBHBEYAH, (55) PELET, (56) PLTYAH, (57) RABRABYAH, (58) CHAS, (59) CHASYAH, (60) TAPHTAPHYAH, (61) TAMTAMYAH, (62) SEHASYAH, (63) IRURYAH, (64) 'AL'ALYAH, (65) BAZRIDYAH, (66) SATSATKYAH, (67) SASDYAH, (68) RAZRAZYAH, (69) BAZRAZYAH, (70) 'ARIMYAH, (71) SBHYAH, (72) SBIBKHYH, (73) SIMKAM, (74) YAHSEYAH, (75) SSBIBYAH, (76) SABKASBEYAH, (77) QELILQALYAH, (78) KIHHH, (79) HHYH, (80) WH, (81) WHYH, (82) ZAKKLKYAH, (83) TUTRISYAH, (84) SURYAH, (85) ZEH, (86) PENIRHYAH, (87) Z'ZI'H, (88) GAL RAZAYYA, (89) MAMLIKYAH, (90) TTYAH, (91) 'EMEQ, (92) QAMYAH, (93) MEKAPPERYAH, (94) PERISHYAH, (95) SEPHAM, (96) GBIR, (97) GIBBORYAH, (98) GOR, (99) GORYAH, (100) ZIW, (101) 'OKBAR, (102) THE LESSER YHWH, after the Name of his Master, "for My Name is in him," (103) RABIBIEL, (104) TUMIEL, (105) SEGANSAKKIEL, THE PRINCE OF WISDOM. [2] And why is he called by the name SAGNESAKIEL? Because all the treasuries of wisdom are committed in his hand. [3] And all of them were opened to Moses on Sinai, so that he learned them during the forty days, while he was standing: the Torah in the seventy aspects of the seventy tongues, the Prophets in the seventy aspects of the seventy tongues, the Writings in the seventy aspects of the seventy tongues, the Halakhas in the seventy aspects of the seventy tongues, the Traditions in the seventy aspects of the seventy tongues, the Haggadahs in the seventy aspects of the seventy tongues, and the Toseftas in the seventy aspects of the seventy tongues. [4] But as soon as the forty days were ended, he forgot all of them in one moment. Then the Holy One, blessed is He, called Yephiphyah, the Prince of the Law, and [through him] they were given to Moses as a gift. As it is written: "And the LORD gave them to me." And after that it remained with him. And from where do we know that it remained in his memory? Because it is written: "Remember the Law of My servant Moses which I commanded to him in Horeb for all Israel, even My statutes and judgments." The Law of Moses: that is, the Teaching; the Prophets and the Writings— [the] statutes: that is, the Halakhas and Traditions; Judgments: that is, the Haggadahs and the Toseftas. And all of them were given to Moses on high on Sinai. [5] These seventy names are a reflection of the Explicit Names on the Merkaba which are graven on the Throne of Glory. For the Holy One, blessed is He, took from His Explicit Names and put seventy names of His on the name of Metatron by which the ministering messengers call the King of the kings of kings, blessed is He, in the high heavens, and twenty-two letters that are on the ring on His finger with which the destinies of the princes of kingdoms on high are sealed in greatness and power and with which the lots of the Messenger of Death are sealed, and the destinies of every nation and tongue. [6] Metatron, the messenger, the Prince of the Presence; the messenger, the Prince of the Wisdom; the messenger, the Prince of the Understanding; the messenger, the Prince of the Kings; the messenger, the Prince of the Rulers; the messenger, the Prince of the Glory; the messenger, the Prince of the High Ones; and of the princes—the exalted, great, and honored ones, in Heaven and on earth—said: [7] "YHWH, the God of Israel, is my witness in this thing, that when I revealed this secret to Moses, then all the hosts in every heaven on high raged against me and said to me: [8] Why do you reveal this secret to a son of man, born of woman, tainted and unclean, a man of a decaying drop—the secret by which the heavens and earth, the sea and the dry land, the mountains and hills, the rivers and springs, Gehenna of fire and hail, the Garden of Eden and the Tree of Life were created; and by which Adam and Eve, and the cattle, and the wild beasts, and the bird of the air, and the fish of the sea, and Behemoth and Leviathan, and the creeping things, the worms, the dragons of the sea, and the creeping things of the deserts, and the Torah, and Wisdom, and Knowledge, and Thought, and the Knowledge of things above, and the fear of Heaven were formed? Why do you reveal this to flesh and blood? Have you obtained authority from

MAQOM? And again: Have you received permission? The Explicit Names went forth from before me with lightnings of fire and flaming chashmallim. ⁹ But they were not appeased until the Holy One, blessed is He, rebuked them and drove them away with rebuke from before Him, saying to them: I delight in, and have set My love on, and have entrusted and committed to Metatron, My servant, alone, for he is one unique among all the children of Heaven." ¹⁰ And Metatron brought them out from his house of treasuries and committed them to Moses, and Moses to Joshua, and Joshua to the elders, and the elders to the prophets, and the prophets to the men of the Great Synagogue, and the men of the Great Synagogue to Ezra, and Ezra the Scribe to Hillel the elder, and Hillel the elder to R. Abbahu, and R. Abbahu to R. Zera, and R. Zera to the men of faith, and the men of faith committed them to give warning and to heal by them all diseases that rage in the world, as it is written: "If you will diligently listen to the voice of the LORD your God and will do that which is right in His eyes, and will give ear to His commandments, and keep all His statutes, I will put none of the diseases on you which I have put on the Egyptians, for I am the LORD that heals you." Ended and finished. Praise be to the Creator of the World.

BOOK OF GIANTS

Once thought to be nothing more than a 3rd century Manichaean corruption of biblical and Jewish legends, a primordial Aramaic form was found among the Dead Sea Scrolls. This much older Book of Giants was composed hundreds of years before Christ's first advent—*at the latest*—and shares Enochian similarities. In this LSV reconstruction of the DSS Book of Giants, instead of presenting each fragmentary section, the narrative is pieced together in a plausible chronological order by chapter, so some fragments are grouped together. The fragment identifiers are listed before each set of verses belonging to that fragment.

[The rebellious Watchers (messengers) descend to earth, bringing secret knowledge and wickedness. Their hybrid offspring are giants.]

CHAPTER 1
[1Q23] ¹ . . . they knew the secrets of . . . ² . . . sin was great in the earth . . . ³ . . . and they killed many . . . ⁴ . . . [they begot] giants . . .

[The messengers observe all the creatures on earth, including human beings.]

CHAPTER 2
[4Q531] ¹ . . . [everything that the] earth produced . . . ² . . . the great fish . . . ³ . . . the sky with all that grew . . . ⁴ . . . [fruit of] the earth and all kinds of grain and all the trees . . . ⁵ . . . beasts and reptiles . . . all creeping things of the earth, ⁶ and they observed all . . . ⁷ . . . every harsh deed and . . . utterance . . . ⁸ . . . male and female, and among humans . . .

[The messengers choose two hundred specimens from each of a variety of creatures on which to perform ungodly acts.]

CHAPTER 3
[1Q23] ¹ . . . [two hundred] donkeys, two hundred mules, two hundred . . . ² . . . rams of the flock, two hundred goats, two hundred . . . ³ . . . [beasts of the] field from every animal, ⁴ from every [bird] . . . ⁵ . . . for interbreeding . . .

[Giants, monsters, and corruption fill the earth as a result of angelic interbreeding.]

CHAPTER 4
[4Q531] ¹ . . . they defiled . . . ² . . . [they begot] giants and monsters . . . ³ . . . they begot, and behold, all [the earth was corrupted] . . . ⁴ . . . with its blood and by

the hand of . . . ⁵ . . . which did not suffice for them and . . . ⁶ . . . and they were seeking to devour many . . . ⁷ . . . the monsters attacked it.

CHAPTER 5
[4Q532] ¹ . . . flesh . . . ² . . . all . . . monsters . . . will be . . . ³ . . . they would arise . . . lacking in true knowledge . . . because . . . ⁴ . . . the earth [grew corrupt] . . . mighty . . . ⁵ . . . they were considering . . . ⁶ . . . from the messengers on . . . ⁷ . . . in the end it will perish and die . . . ⁸ . . . they caused great corruption in the [earth] . . . ⁹ . . . [this did not] suffice to . . . ¹⁰ "They will be . . ."

[The giants are troubled by dreams and visions which hint at a coming judgment on them. In one dream, a stone tablet is drenched in water and emerges with only three names still inscribed (presumably the names of Noah's sons).]

CHAPTER 6
[2Q26] ¹ . . . they drenched the tablet in the water . . . ² . . . the waters went up over the [tablet] . . . ³ . . . they lifted the tablet out from the water of . . .

CHAPTER 7
[4Q530] ¹ . . . [the vision] is for cursing and sorrow. I am the one who confessed . . . ² . . . the whole group of the castaways that I will go to . . . ³ . . . the spirits of the slain, complaining about their killers and crying out . . . ⁴ . . . that we will die together and be made an end of . . . ⁵ . . . much and I will be sleeping, and bread . . . ⁶ . . . for my dwelling; ⁷ the vision and also . . . entered into the gathering of the giants . . . [6Q8] ⁸ . . . Ohya, and he said to Mahway . . . ⁹ " . . . without trembling. Who showed you all this vision, brother?" ¹⁰ . . . "Barakel, my father, was with me." ¹¹ . . . Before Mahway had finished telling what [he had seen] . . . ¹² . . . [said] to him, "Now I have heard wonders! If a barren woman gives birth . . ." [4Q530] ¹³ Thereon Ohya said to Ha[hya], ¹⁴ " . . . [will be destroyed] from on the earth and . . . ¹⁵ . . . [the] earth." ¹⁶ When . . . ¹⁷ . . . they wept before [the giants] . . . ¹⁸ " . . . your strength . . ." ¹⁹ . . . Thereon Ohya [said] to Hahya, ²⁰ . . . Then he answered, "It is not for us, but for Azaiel, ²¹ for he did . . . [the offspring of the] messengers are the giants, ²² [and they would not let all their loved ones] be neglected . . . ²³ . . . [we have] not been cast down; you have strength . . .

BOOK OF GIANTS

[A giant boasts about his strength, but realizes he is not stronger than the faithful messengers of Heaven. One of the speakers is apparently the giant hybrid Gilgamesh from Sumerian myth.]

CHAPTER 8

[4Q531] [1] ". . . I am a giant, and by the mighty strength of my arm and my own great strength . . . [2] . . . anyone mortal, and I have made war against them; [3] but I am not . . . able to stand against them, for my opponents . . . [4] . . . reside in Heaven, and they dwell in the holy places. [5] And not . . . [they] are stronger than me. [6] . . . of the wild beast has come, and they call [me] the wild man." [7] . . . Then Ohya said to him, "I have been forced to have a dream . . . the sleep of my eyes [vanished], to let me see a vision. Now I know that on . . ." [8] . . . Gilgamesh . . .

[Ohya has a dream in which a tree is uprooted, but three roots remain. This is presumably the same message as the dream of the stone tablet.]

CHAPTER 9

[6Q8] [1] . . . three of its roots . . . [2] . . . [while] I was [watching], there came . . . [3] . . . [the roots were moved into] this garden, all of them, and not . . .

[Bothered by the dreams and visions, Ohya suggests the message is actually judgment on another group.]

CHAPTER 10

[4Q530] [1] . . . concerns the death of our souls . . . [2] . . . and all his comrades, [and] Ohya told them what Gilgamesh said to him . . . [3] . . . and it was said . . . ". . . concerning . . . the leader has cursed the potentates." [4] And the giants were glad at his words. Then he turned and left . . .

[Dreamers recount yet more dreams, first to the assembly of monsters, and second to the assembly of giants.]

CHAPTER 11

[4Q530] [1] Thereon two of them had dreams and the sleep of their eye fled from them, [2] and they arose and came to . . . [3] . . . [and recounted] their dreams, and said in the assembly of [the giants and] the monsters, [4] "[In] my dream I was watching this very night, [5] [and within a garden there were] gardeners and they were watering . . . [6] . . . [two hundred trees and] large shoots came out of their root . . . [7] . . . all the water, and the fire burned all [the trees] . . ." [8] . . . They found the giants to tell them [of the dream] . . .

[Mahway is petitioned to seek Enoch for an interpretation of the dream, and then flies to him with the request.]

CHAPTER 12

[4Q530] [1] "[Go to Enoch,] the noted scribe, and he will interpret the dream for us." [2] Thereon his companion Ohya declared [this], and said to the giants, "I too had a dream this night, O giants, and behold, the Ruler of Heaven came down to earth . . . [3] . . . and such is the end of the dream." [4] [Then] all the giants [and monsters] grew afraid and called Mahway. [5] He came to them and the giants pleaded with him and sent him to Enoch . . . [6] They said to him, "Go . . . to you that . . . you have heard his voice." [7] And he said to him, "He will . . . interpret the dreams . . . [8] . . . how long the giants have to live."

CHAPTER 13

[4Q530] [1] . . . [he moved through the air] like strong winds, [2] and flew with his hands like eagles . . . [he left] the inhabited world and passed over Desolation, the great desert . . . [3] . . . and Enoch saw him and hailed him, [4] and Mahway said to him . . . [5] . . . here and there a second time to Mahway . . . [6] "The giants await your words, and all the monsters of the earth. [7] If . . . has been carried . . . from the days of . . . their . . . and they will be added . . . [8] . . . we would know from you their meaning . . . [9] . . . [two hundred] trees that [came down] from Heaven . . ."

[Enoch grants the request and sends Mahway with a stone tablet containing the interpretation.]

CHAPTER 14

[4Q530] [1] The scribe [Enoch] . . . [2] . . . a copy of the second tablet that [Enoch] sent . . . [3] . . . in the very handwriting of Enoch the noted scribe . . . [4] "[In the Name of God the great] and Holy One, to Shemihaza and all [his companions] . . . [5] . . . let it be known to you that not . . . [6] and the things you have done, and that your wives . . . [7] . . . they and their sons and the wives of [their sons] . . . [8] . . . by your licentiousness on the earth, and there has been on you . . . [9] . . . [and the earth is crying out] and complaining about you and the deeds of your children, [10] [and] the harm that you have done to it. [11] . . . until Raphael arrives, behold, destruction [is coming, a great flood, and it will destroy all living things] [12] and whatever is in the deserts and the seas. [13] And the meaning of the matter . . . [14] . . . on you for evil. [15] But now, loosen the bonds binding [you to evil] . . . and pray."

CHAPTER 15

[4Q531] [1] . . . [great fear] seized me and I fell on my face; I heard his voice . . . [2] . . . he dwelt among human beings but he did not learn from them . . .

JASHER

Otherwise known as Sefer haYashar

The Sefer haYashar (first edition 1552) is a Hebrew midrash also known as the Toledot Adam and Dibre ha-Yamim be-'Aruk. The Hebrew title may be transliterated Sefer haYashar, which means "Book of the Correct Record," but it is known in English translation mostly as the Book of Jasher following English tradition. The book is named after the Book of Jasher mentioned in Joshua and 2 Samuel. Although it is presented as the original "Book of Jasher" in the translations such as that of Moses Samuel (1840), it is not accepted as such in rabbinical Judaism, nor does the original Hebrew text make such a claim. However, the writing is of good quality, the chronology largely aligns with the Masoretic account in Genesis, and some scholars believe the midrash may be even older than the 6th century AD.

CHAPTER 1

[1] And God said, "Let Us make man in Our image, after Our likeness," and God created man in His own image. [2] And God formed man from the ground, and He blew into his nostrils the breath of life, and man became a living soul endowed with speech. [3] And the LORD said, "It is not good for man to be alone; I will make a helpmate for him." [4] And the LORD caused a deep sleep to fall on Adam, and he slept, and He took away one of his ribs, and He built flesh on it, and formed it, and brought it to Adam, and Adam awoke from his sleep, and behold, a woman was standing before him. [5] And he said, "This is bone of my bones and it will be called Woman, for this has been taken from Man; and Adam called her name Eve, for she was the mother of all living." [6] And God blessed them and called their names Adam and Eve in the day that He created them, and the LORD God said, "Be fruitful, and multiply, and fill the earth." [7] And the LORD God took Adam and his wife, and He placed them in the Garden of Eden to dress it and to keep it; and He commanded them and said to them, "From every tree of the garden you may eat, but from the Tree of the Knowledge of Good and Evil you will not eat, for in the day that you eat thereof you will surely die." [8] And when God had blessed and commanded them, He went from them, and Adam and his wife dwelt in the garden according to the command which the LORD had commanded them. [9] And the serpent, which God had created with them in the earth, came to them to incite them to transgress the command of God which he had commanded them. [10] And the serpent enticed and persuaded the woman to eat from the Tree of Knowledge, and the woman listened to the voice of the serpent, and she transgressed the word of God, and took from the Tree of the Knowledge of Good and Evil, and she ate, and she took from it, and also gave to her husband and he ate. [11] And Adam and his wife transgressed the command of God which He commanded them, and God knew it, and His anger was kindled against them and He cursed them. [12] And the LORD God drove them that day from the Garden of Eden, to till the ground from which they were taken, and they went and dwelt at the east of the Garden of Eden; and Adam knew his wife Eve and she bore two sons and three daughters. [13] And she called the name of the firstborn Cain, saying, "I have obtained a man from the LORD," and the name of the other she called Abel, for she said, "In vanity we came into the earth, and in vanity we will be taken from it." [14] And the boys grew up and their father gave them a possession in the land; and Cain was a tiller of the ground, and Abel a keeper of sheep. [15] And it was at the expiration of a few years that they brought a comparable offering to the LORD, and Cain brought from the fruit of the ground, and Abel brought from the firstlings of his flock from the fat thereof, and God turned and inclined to Abel and his offering, and a fire came down from the LORD from Heaven and consumed it. [16] And to Cain and his offering the LORD did not turn, and He did not incline to it, for he had brought from the inferior fruit of the ground before the LORD, and Cain was jealous against his brother Abel on account of this, and he sought a pretext to slay him. [17] And some time after, Cain and his brother Abel went into the field one day to do their work; and they were both in the field, Cain tilling and plowing his ground, and Abel feeding his flock; and the flock passed that part which Cain had plowed in the ground, and it severely grieved Cain on this account. [18] And Cain approached his brother Abel in anger, and he said to him, "What is there between me and you, that you come to dwell and bring your flock to feed in my land?" [19] And Abel answered his brother Cain and said to him, "What is there between me and you, that you will eat the flesh of my flock and clothe yourself with their wool? [20] And now therefore, put off the wool of my sheep with which you have clothed yourself, and repay me for their fruit and flesh which you have eaten, and when you will have done this, I will then go from your land as you have said." [21] And Cain said to his brother Abel, "Surely if I slay you this day, who will require your blood from me?" [22] And Abel answered Cain, saying, "Surely God who has made us in the earth will avenge my cause, and He will require my blood from you should you slay me, for the LORD is the judge and arbiter, and it is He who will pay back man according to his evil, and the

JASHER

wicked man according to the wickedness that he may do on earth. ²³ And now, if you should slay me here, surely God knows your secret views, and will judge you for the evil which you declared to do to me this day." ²⁴ And when Cain heard the words which his brother Abel had spoken, behold, the anger of Cain was kindled against his brother Abel for declaring this thing. ²⁵ And Cain hastened and rose up, and took the iron part of his plowing instrument, with which he suddenly struck his brother and slew him, and Cain spilt the blood of his brother Abel on the earth, and the blood of Abel streamed on the earth before the flock. ²⁶ And after this Cain regretted having slain his brother, and he was sadly grieved, and he wept over him, and it exceedingly vexed him. ²⁷ And Cain rose up and dug a hole in the field, wherein he put his brother's body, and he turned the dust over it. ²⁸ And the LORD knew what Cain had done to his brother, and the LORD appeared to Cain and said to him, "Where is your brother Abel that was with you?" ²⁹ And Cain concealed his true motives, and said, "I do not know, am I my brother's keeper?" And the LORD said to him, "What have you done? The voice of your brother's blood cries to Me from the ground where you have slain him. ³⁰ For you have slain your brother, and have concealed your intentions before Me, and imagined in your heart that I did not see you, nor knew all your actions. ³¹ But you did this thing and slew your brother for no reason and because he spoke rightly to you, and now, therefore, cursed are you from the ground which opened its mouth to receive your brother's blood from your hand, and wherein you buried him. ³² And it will be when you will till it, it will no longer give you its strength as in the beginning, for the ground will produce thorns and thistles, and you will be moving and wandering in the earth until the day of your death." ³³ And at that time Cain went out from the presence of the LORD, from the place where he was, and he went moving and wandering in the land toward the east of Eden, he and all belonging to him. ³⁴ And Cain knew his wife in those days, and she conceived and bore a son, and he called his name Enoch, saying, "In that time the LORD began to give him rest and quiet in the earth." ³⁵ And at that time Cain also began to build a city: and he built the city and he called the name of the city Enoch, according to the name of his son, for in those days the LORD had given him rest on the earth, and he did not move about and wander as in the beginning. ³⁶ And Irad was born to Enoch, and Irad begot Mehujael, and Mehujael begot Methusael.

CHAPTER 2

¹ And it was in the one hundred and thirtieth year of the life of Adam on the earth that he knew his wife Eve again, and she conceived and bore a son in his likeness and in his image, and she called his name Seth, saying, "Because God has appointed me another seed in the place of Abel, for Cain has slain him." ² And Seth lived one hundred and five years, and he begot a son; and Seth called the name of his son Enosh, saying, "Because in that time the sons of men began to multiply, and to afflict their souls and hearts by transgressing and rebelling against God." ³ And it was in the days of Enosh that the sons of men continued to rebel and transgress against God, to increase the anger of the LORD against the sons of men. ⁴ And the sons of men went, and they served other gods, and they forgot the LORD who had created them in the earth: and in those days the sons of men made images of brass and iron, wood and stone, and they bowed down and served them. ⁵ And every man made his god and they bowed down to them, and the sons of men forsook the LORD all the days of Enosh and his children; and the anger of the LORD was kindled on account of their works and abominations which they did in the earth. ⁶ And the LORD caused the waters of the River Gihon to overwhelm them, and He destroyed and consumed them, and he destroyed the third part of the earth, and notwithstanding this, the sons of men did not turn from their evil ways, and their hands were yet extended to do evil in the sight of the LORD. ⁷ And in those days there was neither sowing nor reaping in the earth; and there was no food for the sons of men and the famine was very great in those days. ⁸ And the seed which they sowed in those days in the ground became thorns, thistles, and briers; for from the days of Adam this declaration was concerning the earth, of the curse of God, which He cursed the earth on account of the sin which Adam sinned before the LORD. ⁹ And it was when men continued to rebel and transgress against God, and to corrupt their ways, that the earth also became corrupt. ¹⁰ And Enosh lived ninety years and he begot Cainan; ¹¹ And Cainan grew up and he was forty years old, and he became wise and had knowledge and skill in all wisdom, and he reigned over all the sons of men, and he led the sons of men to wisdom and knowledge; for Cainan was a very wise man and had understanding in all wisdom, and with his wisdom he ruled over spirits and demons. ¹² And Cainan knew by his wisdom that God would destroy the sons of men for having sinned on earth, and that the LORD would bring on them the waters of the flood in the latter days. ¹³ And in those days Cainan wrote on tablets of stone what was to take place in time to come, and he put them in his treasures. ¹⁴ And Cainan reigned over the whole earth, and he turned some of the sons of men to the service of God. ¹⁵ And when Cainan was seventy years old, he begot three sons and two daughters. ¹⁶ And these are the names of the children of Cainan: the name of the firstborn Mahalaleel, the second Enan, and the third Mered, and their sisters were Adah and Zillah; these are the five children of Cainan that were born to him. ¹⁷ And Lamech, the son of Methusael, became related to Cainan by marriage,

~ 323 ~

and he took his two daughters for his wives, and Adah conceived and bore a son to Lamech, and she called his name Jabal. ¹⁸ And she again conceived and bore a son, and called his name Jubal; and Zillah, her sister, was barren in those days and had no offspring. ¹⁹ For in those days the sons of men began to trespass against God, and to transgress the commands which He had commanded to Adam, to be fruitful and multiply in the earth. ²⁰ And some of the sons of men caused their wives to drink a draught that would render them barren, in order that they might retain their figures and whereby their beautiful appearance might not fade. ²¹ And when the sons of men caused some of their wives to drink, Zillah drank with them. ²² And the childbearing women appeared abominable in the sight of their husbands as widows, while their husbands lived, for they were only attached to the barren ones. ²³ And in the end of days and years, when Zillah became old, the LORD opened her womb. ²⁴ And she conceived and bore a son, and she called his name Tubal-Cain, saying, "After I had withered away I have obtained him from the Almighty God." ²⁵ And she conceived again and bore a daughter, and she called her name Naamah, for she said, "After I had withered away I have obtained pleasure and delight." ²⁶ And Lamech was old and advanced in years, and his eyes were dim that he could not see, and his son Tubal-Cain was leading him, and it was one day that Lamech went into the field and Tubal Cain his son was with him, and while they were walking in the field, Cain, the son of Adam, advanced toward them; for Lamech was very old and could not see much, and his son Tubal-Cain was very young. ²⁷ And Tubal-Cain told his father to draw his bow, and with the arrows he struck Cain, who was yet far off, and he slew him, for he appeared to them to be an animal. ²⁸ And the arrows entered Cain's body although he was distant from them, and he fell to the ground and died. ²⁹ And the LORD paid back Cain's evil according to his wickedness which he had done to his brother Abel, according to the word of the LORD which He had spoken. ³⁰ And it came to pass when Cain had died, that Lamech and Tubal-Cain went to see the animal which they had slain, and they saw, and behold, their grandfather Cain was fallen dead on the earth. ³¹ And Lamech was very much grieved at having done this, and in clapping his hands together, he struck his son and caused his death. ³² And the wives of Lamech heard what Lamech had done, and they sought to kill him. ³³ And the wives of Lamech hated him from that day, because he slew Cain and Tubal-Cain, and the wives of Lamech separated from him, and would not listen to him in those days. ³⁴ And Lamech came to his wives, and he pressed them to listen to him about this matter. ³⁵ And he said to his wives Adah and Zillah, "Hear my voice, O wives of Lamech, attend to my words, for now you have imagined and said that I slew a man with my wounds, and a child with my stripes, for their having done no violence, but surely know that I am old and grey-headed, and that my eyes are heavy through age, and I did this thing unknowingly." ³⁶ And the wives of Lamech listened to him in this matter, and they returned to him with the advice of their father Adam, but they bore no children to him from that time, knowing that God's anger was increasing in those days against the sons of men, to destroy them with the waters of the flood for their evil doings. ³⁷ And Mahalaleel the son of Cainan lived sixty-five years and he begot Jared, and Jared lived sixty-two years and he begot Enoch.

CHAPTER 3

¹ And Enoch lived sixty-five years and he begot Methuselah; and Enoch walked with God after having begot Methuselah, and he served the LORD, and despised the evil ways of men. ² And the soul of Enoch was wrapped up in the instruction of the LORD, in knowledge and in understanding; and he wisely retired from the sons of men and hid himself from them for many days. ³ And it was at the expiration of many years, while he was serving the LORD and praying before Him in his house, that a messenger of the LORD called to him from Heaven, and he said, "Here I am." ⁴ And he said, "Rise, go out from your house and from the place where you hide yourself, and appear to the sons of men in order that you may teach them the way in which they should go and the work which they must accomplish to enter in the ways of God." ⁵ And Enoch rose up according to the word of the LORD, and went out from his house, from his place and from the chamber in which he was concealed; and he went to the sons of men and taught them the ways of the LORD, and at that time assembled the sons of men and acquainted them with the instruction of the LORD. ⁶ And he ordered it to be proclaimed in all places where the sons of men dwelt, saying, "Where is the man who wishes to know the ways of the LORD and good works? Let him come to Enoch." ⁷ And all the sons of men then assembled to him, for all who desired this thing went to Enoch, and Enoch reigned over the sons of men according to the word of the LORD, and they came and bowed to him and they heard his word. ⁸ And the Spirit of God was on Enoch, and he taught all his men the wisdom of God and His ways, and the sons of men served the LORD all the days of Enoch, and they came to hear his wisdom. ⁹ And all the kings of the sons of men, both first and last, together with their princes and judges, came to Enoch when they heard of his wisdom, and they bowed down to him, and they also required of Enoch to reign over them, to which he consented. ¹⁰ And they assembled one hundred and thirty kings and princes in all, and they made Enoch king over them, and they were all under his power and command. ¹¹ And Enoch taught them wisdom,

JASHER

knowledge, and the ways of the LORD; and he made peace among them, and peace was throughout the earth during the life of Enoch. ¹² And Enoch reigned over the sons of men two hundred and forty-three years, and he did justice and righteousness with all his people, and he led them in the ways of the LORD. ¹³ And these are the generations of Enoch: Methuselah, Elisha, and Elimelech, three sons; and their sisters were Melca and Nahmah, and Methuselah lived eighty-seven years and he begot Lamech. ¹⁴ And it was in the fifty-sixth year of the life of Lamech when Adam died; nine hundred and thirty years old was he at his death, and his two sons, with Enoch and his son Methuselah, buried him with great pomp, as at the burial of kings, in the cave which God had told him. ¹⁵ And in that place all the sons of men made a great mourning and weeping on account of Adam; it has therefore become a custom among the sons of men to this day. ¹⁶ And Adam died because he ate of the Tree of Knowledge—he and his children after him, as the LORD God had spoken. ¹⁷ And it was in the year of Adam's death, which was the two hundred and forty-third year of the reign of Enoch, in that time Enoch resolved to separate himself from the sons of men and to hide himself as at first in order to serve the LORD. ¹⁸ And Enoch did so, but did not entirely hide himself from them, but kept away from the sons of men three days and then went to them for one day. ¹⁹ And during the three days that he was in his chamber, he prayed to, and praised the LORD his God, and the day on which he went and appeared to his subjects he taught them the ways of the LORD, and all they asked him about the LORD he told them. ²⁰ And he did in this manner for many years, and afterward he concealed himself for six days, and appeared to his people one day in seven; and after that once in a month, and then once in a year, until all the kings, princes, and sons of men sought for him, and desired to see the face of Enoch again and to hear his word, but they could not, as all the sons of men were greatly afraid of Enoch, and they feared to approach him on account of the godlike awe that was seated on his countenance; therefore no man could look at him, fearing he might be punished and die. ²¹ And all the kings and princes resolved to assemble the sons of men, and to come to Enoch, thinking that they might all speak to him at the time when he should come out among them, and they did so. ²² And the day came when Enoch went out and they all assembled and came to him, and Enoch spoke to them the words of the LORD and he taught them wisdom and knowledge, and they bowed down before him and they said, "May the king live! May the king live!" ²³ And some time after, when the kings and princes and the sons of men were speaking to Enoch, and Enoch was teaching them the ways of God, behold, a messenger of the LORD then called to Enoch from Heaven, and wished to bring him up to Heaven to make him reign there

over the sons of God, as he had reigned over the sons of men on earth. ²⁴ When at that time Enoch heard this, he went and assembled all the inhabitants of the earth, and taught them wisdom and knowledge, and gave them divine instructions, and he said to them, "I have been required to ascend into Heaven; therefore, I do not know the day of my going. ²⁵ And now, therefore, I will teach you wisdom and knowledge and will give you instruction before I leave you, how to act on earth whereby you may live"; and he did so. ²⁶ And he taught them wisdom and knowledge, and gave them instruction, and he reproved them, and he placed before them statutes and judgments to do on earth, and he made peace among them, and he taught them continuous life, and dwelt with them some time teaching them all these things. ²⁷ And at that time the sons of men were with Enoch, and Enoch was speaking to them, and they lifted up their eyes and the likeness of a great horse descended from Heaven, and the horse paced in the air. ²⁸ And they told Enoch what they had seen, and Enoch said to them, "This horse descends on earth on my account; the time has come when I must go from you and I will no longer be seen by you." ²⁹ And the horse descended at that time and stood before Enoch, and all the sons of men that were with Enoch saw him. ³⁰ And Enoch then again ordered a voice to be proclaimed, saying, "Where is the man who delights to know the ways of the LORD his God? Let him come this day to Enoch before he is taken from us." ³¹ And all the sons of men assembled and came to Enoch that day; and all the kings of the earth with their princes and counselors remained with him that day; and Enoch then taught the sons of men wisdom and knowledge, and gave them divine instruction, and he commanded them to serve the LORD and walk in His ways all the days of their lives, and he continued to make peace among them. ³² And it was after this that he rose up and rode on the horse; and he went out and all the sons of men went after him—about eight hundred thousand men; and they went with him one day's journey. ³³ And the second day he said to them, "Return home to your tents, why will you go? Perhaps you may die"; and some of them went from him, and those that remained went with him six day's journey; and Enoch said to them every day, "Return to your tents, lest you may die"; but they were not willing to return, and they went with him. ³⁴ And on the sixth day some of the men remained and clung to him, and they said to him, "We will go with you to the place where you go; as the LORD lives, only death will separate us." ³⁵ And they urged so much to go with him that he ceased speaking to them; and they went after him and would not return. ³⁶ And when the kings returned, they caused a census to be taken in order to know the number of remaining men that went with Enoch; and it was on the seventh day that Enoch ascended into Heaven in a whirlwind, with horses and chariots of fire. ³⁷ And on the eighth day all the kings that had been with Enoch sent to bring back the number of men that were with Enoch in that place from which he ascended into Heaven. ³⁸ And all those kings went to the place and they found the earth filled with snow there, and on the snow were large stones of snow, and one said to the other, "Come, let us break through the snow and see, perhaps the men that remained with Enoch are dead and are now under the stones of snow," and they searched but could not find him, for he had ascended into Heaven.

CHAPTER 4

¹ And all the days that Enoch lived on earth were three hundred and sixty-five years. ² And when Enoch had ascended into Heaven, all the kings of the earth rose and took his son Methuselah and anointed him, and they caused him to reign over them in the place of his father. ³ And Methuselah acted uprightly in the sight of God, as his father Enoch had taught him, and he likewise during the whole of his life taught the sons of men wisdom, knowledge, and the fear of God, and he did not turn from the good way either to the right or to the left. ⁴ But in the latter days of Methuselah, the sons of men turned from the LORD: they corrupted the earth, they robbed and plundered each other, and they rebelled against God, and they transgressed, and they corrupted their ways, and would not listen to the voice of Methuselah, but rebelled against him. ⁵ And the LORD was exceedingly angry against them, and the LORD continued to destroy the seed in those days, so that there was neither sowing nor reaping in the earth. ⁶ For when they sowed the ground in order that they might obtain food for their support, behold, thorns and thistles were produced which they did not sow. ⁷ And still the sons of men did not turn from their evil ways, and their hands were still extended to do evil in the sight of God, and they provoked the LORD with their evil ways, and the LORD was very angry, and regretted that He had made man. ⁸ And He thought to destroy and annihilate them, and He did so. ⁹ In those days when Lamech the son of Methuselah was one hundred and sixty years old, Seth the son of Adam died. ¹⁰ And all the days that Seth lived were nine hundred and twelve years, and he died. ¹¹ And Lamech was one hundred and eighty years old when he took Ashmua, the daughter of Elisha, the son of his uncle Enoch, and she conceived. ¹² And at that time the sons of men sowed the ground, and a little food was produced, yet the sons of men did not turn from their evil ways, and they trespassed and rebelled against God. ¹³ And the wife of Lamech conceived and bore him a son at that time, at the revolution of the year. ¹⁴ And Methuselah called his name Noah, saying, "The earth was at rest and free from corruption in his days," and his father Lamech called his name Menachem, saying, "This one will comfort us in our works and miserable toil in the earth," which God had cursed. ¹⁵ And the child grew up and was weaned, and he went in the ways of his father Methuselah, perfect and upright with God. ¹⁶ And all the sons of men departed from the ways of the LORD in those days as they multiplied on the face of the earth with sons and daughters, and they taught one another their evil practices and they continued sinning against the LORD. ¹⁷ And every man made a god for himself, and they robbed and plundered every man—his neighbor as well as his relative, and they corrupted the earth, and the earth was filled with violence. ¹⁸ And their judges and rulers went to the daughters of men and took their wives by force from their husbands according to their choice, and the sons of men in those days took from the cattle of the earth, the beasts of the field, and the birds of the air, and taught the mixture of animals of one species with the other, in order with [them] to provoke the LORD; and God saw the whole earth and it was corrupt, for all flesh had corrupted its ways on earth, all men and all animals. ¹⁹ And the LORD said, "I will blot out man that I created from the face of the earth, yes, from man to the birds of the air, together with cattle and beasts that are in the field, for I regret that I made them." ²⁰ And all men who walked in the ways of the LORD died in those days before the LORD brought the evil on man which He had declared, for this was from the LORD, that they should not see the evil which the LORD spoke of concerning the sons of men. ²¹ And Noah found grace in the sight of the LORD, and the LORD chose him and his children to raise up seed from them on the face of the whole earth.

CHAPTER 5

¹ And it was in the eighty-fourth year of the life of Noah that Enoch the son of Seth died; he was nine hundred and five years old at his death. ² And in the one hundred and seventy-ninth year of the life of Noah, Cainan the son of Enosh died, and all the days of Cainan were nine hundred and ten years, and he died. ³ And in the two hundred and thirty-fourth year of the life of Noah, Mahalaleel the son of Cainan died, and the days of Mahalaleel were eight hundred and ninety-five years, and he died. ⁴ And Jared the son of Mahalaleel died in those days, in the three hundred and thirty-sixth year of the life of Noah; and all the days of Jared were nine hundred and sixty-two years, and he died. ⁵ And all who followed the LORD died in those days, before they saw the evil which God declared to do on earth. ⁶ And after the lapse of many years, in the four hundred and eightieth year of the life of Noah, when all those men who followed the LORD had died away from among the sons of men, and only Methuselah was then left, God said to Noah and Methuselah, saying, ⁷ "Speak, and proclaim to the sons of men, saying, Thus says the LORD, return from your evil ways and forsake your works, and the LORD will relent of the evil that He declared to do to you, so that it will not come to pass. ⁸ For thus says the LORD,

Behold, I give you a period of one hundred and twenty years; if you will turn to Me and forsake your evil ways, then I will also turn away from the evil which I told you, and it will not exist, says the LORD." [9] And Noah and Methuselah spoke all the words of the LORD to the sons of men, day after day, constantly speaking to them. [10] But the sons of men would not listen to them, nor incline their ears to their words, and they were stiff-necked. [11] And the LORD granted them a period of one hundred and twenty years, saying, "If they will return, then God will relent of the evil, so as not to destroy the earth." [12] Noah the son of Lamech refrained from taking a wife in those days to beget children, for he said, "Surely now God will destroy the earth, why then will I beget children?" [13] And Noah was a just man, he was perfect in his generation, and the LORD chose him to raise up seed from his seed on the face of the earth. [14] And the LORD said to Noah, "Take a wife for yourself, and beget children, for I have seen you righteous before Me in this generation. [15] And you will raise up seed, and your children with you, in the midst of the earth"; and Noah went and took a wife, and he chose Naamah the daughter of Enoch, and she was five hundred and eighty years old. [16] And Noah was four hundred and ninety-eight years old when he took Naamah for a wife. [17] And Naamah conceived and bore a son, and he called his name Japheth, saying, "God has enlarged me in the earth"; and she conceived again and bore a son, and he called his name Shem, saying, "God has made me a remnant to raise up seed in the midst of the earth." [18] And Noah was five hundred and two years old when Naamah bore Shem, and the boys grew up and went in the ways of the LORD in all that Methuselah and their father Noah taught them. [19] And Lamech the father of Noah died in those days; yet truly he did not go with all his heart in the ways of his father, and he died in the one hundred and ninety-fifth year of the life of Noah. [20] And all the days of Lamech were seven hundred and seventy years, and he died. [21] And all the sons of men who knew the LORD died in that year before the LORD brought evil on them; for the LORD willed them to die, so as not to behold the evil that God would bring on their brothers and relatives, as He had so declared to do. [22] At that time the LORD said to Noah and Methuselah, "Stand out and proclaim to the sons of men all the words that I spoke to you in those days; perhaps they may turn from their evil ways, and I will then relent of the evil and will not bring it." [23] And Noah and Methuselah stood out and said in the ears of the sons of men all that God had spoken concerning them. [24] But the sons of men would not listen, neither would they incline their ears to all their declarations. [25] And it was after this that the LORD said to Noah, "The end of all flesh has come before Me on account of their evil deeds, and behold, I will destroy the earth. [26] So take gopher wood, and go to a certain place, and make a large ark for yourself, and place it in that spot. [27] And thus you will make it three hundred cubits its length, fifty cubits broad, and thirty cubits high. [28] And you will make a door for yourself, open at its side, and to a cubit you will finish above, and cover it within and outside with pitch. [29] And behold, I will bring the flood of waters on the earth, and all flesh will be destroyed from under the heavens—all that is on earth will perish. [30] And you and your household will go and gather two of each of all living things, male and female, and will bring them to the Ark, to raise up seed from them on earth. [31] And gather to yourself all food that is eaten by all the animals, that there may be food for you and for them. [32] And you will choose three maidens for your sons from the daughters of men, and they will be wives to your sons." [33] And Noah rose up, and he made the Ark in the place where God had commanded him, and Noah did as God had ordered him. [34] In his five hundred and ninety-fifth year, Noah commenced to make the Ark, and he made the Ark in five years as the LORD had commanded. [35] Then Noah took the three daughters of Eliakim, son of Methuselah, for wives for his sons, as the LORD had commanded Noah. [36] And it was at that time [that] Methuselah the son of Enoch died; he was nine hundred and sixty years old at his death.

CHAPTER 6

[1] At that time, after the death of Methuselah, the LORD said to Noah, "Go, you with your household, into the Ark; behold, I will gather all the animals of the earth to you—the beasts of the field and the birds of the air—and they will all come and surround the Ark. [2] And you will go and seat yourself by the doors of the Ark, and all the beasts, the animals, and the birds, will assemble and place themselves before you, and such of them as will come and crouch before you, you will take and deliver into the hands of your sons, who will bring them to the Ark, and all that will stand before you you will leave." [3] And the LORD brought this about on the next day, and animals, beasts, and birds came in great multitudes and surrounded the Ark. [4] And Noah went and seated himself by the door of the Ark, and of all flesh that crouched before him, he brought into the Ark, and all that stood before him he left on earth. [5] And a lioness came with her two whelps, male and female, and the three crouched before Noah, and the two whelps rose up against the lioness and struck her and made her flee from her place, and she went away, and they returned to their places, and crouched on the earth before Noah. [6] And the lioness ran away and stood in the place of the lions. [7] And Noah saw this and wondered greatly, and he rose and took the two whelps and brought them into the Ark. [8] And Noah brought into the Ark from all living creatures that were on earth, so that there was none left except which Noah brought into the Ark. [9] Two and two they came to Noah into the Ark,

but from the clean animals and clean birds, he brought seven couples as God had commanded him. [10] And all the animals, and beasts, and birds, were still there, and they surrounded the Ark at every place, and the rain had not descended until seven days after. [11] And on that day, the LORD caused the whole earth to shake, and the sun darkened, and the foundations of the world raged, and the whole earth was moved violently, and the lightning flashed, and the thunder roared, and all the fountains in the earth were broken up, such as was not known to the inhabitants before; and God did this mighty act in order to terrify the sons of men that there might no longer be evil on earth. [12] And still the sons of men would not return from their evil ways, and they increased the anger of the LORD at that time and did not even direct their hearts to all this. [13] And at the end of seven days, in the six hundredth year of the life of Noah, the waters of the flood were on the earth. [14] And all the fountains of the deep were broken up, and the windows of Heaven were opened, and the rain was on the earth forty days and forty nights. [15] And Noah, and his household, and all the living creatures that were with him came into the Ark on account of the waters of the flood, and the LORD shut him in. [16] And all the sons of men that were left on the earth became exhausted through evil on account of the rain, for the waters were coming more violently on the earth, and the animals and beasts were still surrounding the Ark. [17] And the sons of men assembled together, about seven hundred thousand men and women, and they came to Noah at the Ark. [18] And they called to Noah, saying, "Open [the door] for us that we may come to you in the Ark—and why will we die?" [19] And Noah answered them with a loud voice from the Ark, saying, "Have you not all rebelled against the LORD, and said that He does not exist? And therefore, the LORD brought this calamity on you, to destroy and cut you off from the face of the earth. [20] Is this not the thing that I spoke to you of one hundred and twenty years back, and you would not listen to the voice of the LORD, and now you desire to live on earth?" [21] And they said to Noah, "We are ready to return to the LORD; only open [the door] for us that we may live and not die." [22] And Noah answered them, saying, "Behold, now that you see the trouble of your souls, you wish to return to the LORD; why did you not return during these one hundred and twenty years, which the LORD granted you as the determined period? [23] But now you come and tell me this on account of the troubles of your souls; now also the LORD will not listen to you, neither will He give ear to you on this day, so that you will not now succeed in your wishes." [24] And the sons of men approached in order to break into the Ark, to come in on account of the rain, for they could not bear the rain on them. [25] And the LORD sent all the beasts and animals that stood around the Ark, and the beasts overpowered them and drove them from that place,

and every man went his way, and they again scattered themselves on the face of the earth. [26] And the rain was still descending on the earth, and it descended forty days and forty nights, and the waters prevailed greatly on the earth; and all flesh that was on the earth or in the waters died, whether men, animals, beasts, creeping things, or birds of the air, and there only remained Noah and those that were with him in the Ark. [27] And the waters prevailed, and they greatly increased on the earth, and they lifted up the Ark, and it was raised from the earth. [28] And the Ark floated on the face of the waters, and it was tossed on the waters so that all the living creatures within were turned about like stew in a cauldron. [29] And great anxiety seized all the living creatures that were in the Ark, and the Ark was likely to be broken. [30] And all the living creatures that were in the Ark were terrified, and the lions roared, and the oxen lowed, and the wolves howled, and every living creature in the Ark spoke and lamented in its own language, so that their voices reached to a great distance, and Noah and his sons cried and wept in their troubles; they were greatly afraid that they had reached the gates of death. [31] And Noah prayed to the LORD, and cried to Him on account of this, and he said, "O LORD help us, for we have no strength to bear this calamity that has encompassed us, for the waves of the waters have surrounded us, mischievous torrents have terrified us, the snares of death have come before us; answer us, O LORD, answer us! Light up Your countenance toward us and be gracious to us, redeem us and deliver us." [32] And the LORD listened to the voice of Noah, and the LORD remembered him. [33] And a wind passed over the earth, and the waters were still, and the Ark rested. [34] And the fountains of the deep and the windows of the heavens were stopped, and the rain from the heavens was restrained. [35] And the waters decreased in those days, and the Ark rested on the mountains of Ararat. [36] And Noah then opened the windows of the Ark, and Noah still called out to the LORD at that time, and he said, "O LORD who formed the earth, and the heavens, and all that are therein: bring our souls out from this confinement, and from the prison wherein You have placed us, for I am very wearied with sighing." [37] And the LORD listened to the voice of Noah, and said to him, "When you will have completed a full year you will then go out." [38] And at the revolution of the year, when a full year was completed to Noah's dwelling in the Ark, the waters were dried from off the earth, and Noah put off the covering of the Ark. [39] At that time, on the twenty-seventh day of the second month, the earth was dry, but Noah, and his sons, and those that were with him did not go out from the Ark until the LORD told them. [40] And the day came that the LORD told them to go out, and they all went out from the Ark. [41] And they went and returned everyone to his way and to his place, and Noah and his sons dwelt in the land that God had told them, and they served the LORD all their days, and the LORD blessed Noah and his sons on their going out from the Ark. ⁴² And He said to them, "Be fruitful and fill all the earth; become strong, and increase abundantly in the earth, and multiply therein."

CHAPTER 7

¹ And these are the names of the sons of Noah: Japheth, Ham, and Shem; and children were born to them after the flood, for they had taken wives before the flood. ² These are the sons of Japheth: Gomer, Magog, Madai, Javan, Tubal, Meshech, and Tiras, seven sons. ³ And the sons of Gomer were Askinaz, Rephas, and Tegarmah. ⁴ And the sons of Magog were Elichanaf and Lubal. ⁵ And the sons of Madai were Achon, Zeelo, Chazoni, and Lot. ⁶ And the sons of Javan were Elisha, Tarshish, Chittim, and Dudonim. ⁷ And the sons of Tubal were Ariphi, Kesed, and Taari. ⁸ And the sons of Meshech were Dedon, Zaron, and Shebashni. ⁹ And the sons of Tiras were Benib, Gera, Lupirion, and Gilak. These are the sons of Japheth according to their families, and their numbers in those days were about four hundred and sixty men. ¹⁰ And these are the sons of Ham: Cush, Mitzraim, Phut, and Canaan, four sons. And the sons of Cush were Seba, Havilah, Sabta, Raama, and Satecha. And the sons of Raama were Sheba and Dedan. ¹¹ And the sons of Mitzraim were Lud, Anom, and Pathros, Chasloth, and Chaphtor. ¹² And the sons of Phut were Gebul, Hadan, Benah, and Adan. ¹³ And the sons of Canaan were Zidon, Heth, Amori, Gergashi, Hivi, Arkee, Seni, Arodi, Zimodi, and Chamothi. ¹⁴ These are the sons of Ham, according to their families, and their numbers in those days were about seven hundred and thirty men. ¹⁵ And these are the sons of Shem: Elam, Asshur, Arphaxad, Lud, and Aram, five sons. And the sons of Elam were Shushan, Machul, and Harmon. ¹⁶ And the sons of Asshur were Mirus and Mokil. And the sons of Arphaxad were Salah, Anar, and Ashcol. ¹⁷ And the sons of Lud were Pethor and Bizayon. And the sons of Aram were Uz, Chul, Gather, and Mash. ¹⁸ These are the sons of Shem, according to their families, and their numbers in those days were about three hundred men. ¹⁹ These are the generations of Shem: Shem begot Arphaxad, and Arphaxad begot Salah, and Salah begot Eber; and two children were born to Eber, the name of one was Peleg, for in his days the sons of men were divided, and in the latter days, the earth was divided, ²⁰ and the name of the second was Yoktan, meaning that in his day the lives of the sons of men were diminished and lessened. ²¹ These are the sons of Yoktan: Almodad, Shelaf, Chazarmoves, Yerach, Hadurom, Ozel, Diklah, Obal, Abimael, Sheba, Ophir, Havilah, and Jobab; all these are the sons of Yoktan. ²² And his brother Peleg begot Yen, and Yen begot Serug, and Serug begot Nahor, and Nahor begot Terah, and Terah was thirty-eight years old, and he begot Haran

and Nahor. ²³ And Cush, the son of Ham, the son of Noah, took a wife in those days in his old age, and she bore a son, and they called his name Nimrod, saying, "At that time the sons of men again began to rebel and transgress against God," and the child grew up, and his father loved him exceedingly, for he was the son of his old age. ²⁴ And the garments of skin which God made for Adam and his wife (when they went out of the garden) were given to Cush. ²⁵ For after the death of Adam and his wife, the garments were given to Enoch, the son of Jared, and when Enoch was taken up to God, he gave them to his son Methuselah. ²⁶ And at the death of Methuselah, Noah took them and brought them to the Ark, and they were with him until he went out of the Ark. ²⁷ And in their going out, Ham stole those garments from his father Noah, and he took them and hid them from his brothers. ²⁸ And when Ham begot his firstborn Cush, he gave him the garments in secret, and they were with Cush [for] many days. ²⁹ And Cush also concealed them from his sons and brothers, and when Cush had begotten Nimrod, he gave him those garments through his love for him, and Nimrod grew up, and when he was twenty years old, he put on those garments. ³⁰ And Nimrod became strong when he put on the garments, and God gave him might and strength, and he was a mighty hunter in the earth, yes, he was a mighty hunter in the field, and he hunted the animals, and he built altars, and he offered the animals on them before the LORD. ³¹ And Nimrod strengthened himself, and he rose up from among his brothers, and he fought the battles of his brothers against all their surrounding enemies. ³² And the LORD delivered all the enemies of his brothers into his hands, and God prospered him from time to time in his battles, and he reigned on earth. ³³ Therefore it became current in those days, when a man ushered out those that he had trained up for battle, he would say to them, "Like God did to Nimrod, who was a mighty hunter in the earth, and who succeeded in the battles that prevailed against his brothers, that he delivered them from the hands of their enemies, so may God strengthen us and deliver us this day." ³⁴ And when Nimrod was forty years old, at that time there was a war between his brothers and the children of Japheth, so that they were in the power of their enemies. ³⁵ And Nimrod went out at that time, and he assembled all the sons of Cush and their families, about four hundred and sixty men, and he hired also from some of his friends and acquaintances about eighty men, and he gave them their hire, and he went with them to battle, and when he was on the road, Nimrod strengthened the hearts of the people that went with him. ³⁶ And he said to them, "Do not fear, neither be alarmed, for all our enemies will be delivered into our hands, and you may do with them as you please." ³⁷ And all the men that went were about five hundred, and they fought against their enemies, and they destroyed them, and subdued them, and Nimrod placed standing officers over them in their respective places. ³⁸ And he took some of their children as security, and they were all servants to Nimrod and to his brothers, and Nimrod and all the people that were with him turned homeward. ³⁹ And when Nimrod had joyfully returned from battle after having conquered his enemies, all his brothers, together with those who knew him before, assembled to make him king over them, and they placed the regal crown on his head. ⁴⁰ And he set over his subjects and people, princes, judges, and rulers, as is the custom among kings. ⁴¹ And he placed Terah the son of Nahor [as] the prince of his host, and he dignified him and elevated him above all his princes. ⁴² And while he was reigning according to his heart's desire, after having conquered all his surrounding enemies, he advised with his counselors to build a city for his palace, and they did so. ⁴³ And they found a large valley opposite to the east, and they built him a large and extensive city, and Nimrod called the name of the city that he built Shinar, for the LORD had vehemently shaken his enemies and destroyed them. ⁴⁴ And Nimrod dwelt in Shinar, and he reigned securely, and he fought with his enemies, and he subdued them, and he prospered in all his battles, and his kingdom became very great. ⁴⁵ And all nations and tongues heard of his fame, and they gathered themselves to him, and they bowed down to the earth, and they brought him offerings, and he became their lord and king, and they all dwelt with him in the city at Shinar, and Nimrod reigned in the earth over all the sons of Noah, and they were all under his power and counsel. ⁴⁶ And all the earth was of one tongue and words of union, but Nimrod did not go in the ways of the LORD, and he was more wicked than all the men that were before him, from the days of the flood until those days. ⁴⁷ And he made gods of wood and stone, and he bowed down to them, and he rebelled against the LORD, and taught all his subjects and the people of the earth his wicked ways; and his son Mardon was more wicked than his father. ⁴⁸ And everyone that heard of the acts of Mardon the son of Nimrod would say concerning him, "From the wicked goes out wickedness"; therefore, it became a proverb in the whole earth, saying, "From the wicked goes out wickedness," and it was current in the words of men from that time to this. ⁴⁹ And Terah the son of Nahor, prince of Nimrod's host, was in those days very great in the sight of the king and his subjects, and the king and princes loved him, and they elevated him very high. ⁵⁰ And Terah took a wife, and her name was Amthelo the daughter of Cornebo; and the wife of Terah conceived and bore him a son in those days. ⁵¹ Terah was seventy years old when he begot him, and Terah called the name of his son that was born to him Abram, because the king had raised him in those days, and dignified him above all his princes that were with him.

CHAPTER 8

¹ And it was during the night that Abram was born that all the servants of Terah, and all the wise men of Nimrod, and his conjurers came, and ate, and drank in the house of Terah, and they rejoiced with him on that night. ² And when all the wise men and conjurers went out from the house of Terah, they lifted up their eyes toward the heavens that night to look at the stars, and they saw, and behold, one very large star came from the east and ran in the heavens, and he swallowed up the four stars from the four sides of the heavens. ³ And all the wise men of the king and his conjurers were astonished at the sight, and the sages understood this matter, and they knew its meaning. ⁴ And they said to each other, "This only signifies the child that has been born to Terah this night, who will grow up and be fruitful, and multiply, and possess all the earth, he and his children forever, and he and his seed will slay great kings, and inherit their lands." ⁵ And the wise men and conjurers went home that night, and in the morning all these wise men and conjurers rose up early and assembled in an appointed house. ⁶ And they spoke and said to each other, "Behold, the sight that we saw last night is hidden from the king—it has not been made known to him. ⁷ And should this thing get known to the king in the latter days, he will say to us, Why have you concealed this matter from me, and then we will all suffer death; therefore, now let us go and tell the king the sight which we saw, and the interpretation thereof, and we will then remain clear." ⁸ And they did so, and they all went to the king and bowed down to him to the ground, and they said, "May the king live, may the king live. ⁹ We heard that a son was born to Terah the son of Nahor, the prince of your host, and last night we came to his house, and we ate, and drank, and rejoiced with him that night. ¹⁰ And when your servants went out from the house of Terah to go to our respective homes to abide there for the night, we lifted up our eyes to the heavens, and we saw a great star coming from the east, and the same star ran with great speed and swallowed up four great stars from the four sides of the heavens. ¹¹ And your servants were astonished at the sight which we saw, and were greatly terrified, and we made our judgment on the sight, and knew by our wisdom the proper interpretation thereof, that this thing applies to the child that is born to Terah, who will grow up, and multiply greatly, and become powerful, and kill all the kings of the earth, and inherit all their lands, he and his seed forever. ¹² And now our lord and king, behold, we have truly acquainted you with what we have seen concerning this child. ¹³ If it seems good to the king to give his father value for this child, we will slay him before he will grow up, and increase in the land, and his evil increase against us, that we and our children perish through his evil." ¹⁴ And the king heard their words and they seemed good in his sight,

and he sent and called for Terah, and Terah came before the king. ¹⁵ And the king said to Terah, "I have been told that a son was born to you last night, and after this manner was observed in the heavens at his birth. ¹⁶ And now, therefore, give me the child, that we may slay him before his evil springs up against us, and I will give you for his value, your house full of silver and gold." ¹⁷ And Terah answered the king and said to him: "My lord and king, I have heard your words, and your servant will do all that his king desires. ¹⁸ But my lord and king, I will tell you what happened to me last night that I may see what advice the king will give his servant, and then I will answer the king on what he has just spoken"; and the king said, "Speak." ¹⁹ And Terah said to the king, "Ayon, son of Mored, came to me last night, saying, ²⁰ Give to me the great and beautiful horse that the king gave you, and I will give you silver, and gold, and straw, and provender for its value; and I said to him, Wait until I see the king concerning your words, and behold, whatever the king says, that I will do. ²¹ And now my lord and king, behold, I have made this thing known to you, and the advice which my king will give to his servant, that I will follow." ²² And the king heard the words of Terah, and his anger was kindled, and he considered him in the manner of a fool. ²³ And the king answered Terah, and he said to him, "Are you so silly, ignorant, or deficient in understanding to do this thing—to give your beautiful horse for silver and gold or even for straw and provender? ²⁴ Are you so short of silver and gold, that you should do this thing, because you cannot obtain straw and provender to feed your horse? And what is silver and gold to you, or straw and provender, that you should give away that fine horse which I gave you, like which there is none to be had on the whole earth?" ²⁵ And the king left off speaking, and Terah answered the king, saying, "Like to this the king has spoken to his servant; ²⁶ I implore you, my lord and king, what is this which you said to me, saying, Give your son that we may slay him, and I will give you silver and gold for his value; what will I do with silver and gold after the death of my son? Who will inherit me? Surely then at my death, the silver and gold will return to my king who gave it." ²⁷ And when the king heard the words of Terah, and the allegory which he brought concerning the king, it grieved him greatly and he was vexed at this thing, and his anger burned within him. ²⁸ And Terah saw that the anger of the king was kindled against him, and he answered the king, saying, "All that I have is in the king's power; whatever the king desires to do to his servant, that let him do, yes, even my son, he is in the king's power, without value in exchange, he and his two brothers that are older than he." ²⁹ And the king said to Terah, "No, but I will purchase your younger son for a price." ³⁰ And Terah answered the king, saying, "I implore you, my lord and king, to let your servant

speak a word before you, and let the king hear the word of his servant," and Terah said, "Let my king give me three days' time until I consider this matter within myself, and consult with my family concerning the words of my king"; and he pressed the king greatly to agree to this. ³¹ And the king listened to Terah, and he did so, and he gave him three days' time, and Terah went out from the king's presence, and he came home to his family and spoke to them all the words of the king; and the people were greatly afraid. ³² And it was in the third day that the king sent to Terah, saying, "Send me your son for a price as I spoke to you; and should you not do this, I will send and slay all [that] you have in your house, so that you will not even have a dog remaining." ³³ And Terah hastened (as the thing was urgent from the king), and he took a child from one of his servants, which his handmaid had born to him that day, and Terah brought the child to the king and received value for him. ³⁴ And the LORD was with Terah in this matter that Nimrod might not cause Abram's death, and the king took the child from Terah and dashed his head to the ground with all his might, for he thought it had been Abram; and this was concealed from him from that day, and it was forgotten by the king, as it was the will of Providence not to permit Abram's death. ³⁵ And Terah took his son Abram secretly, together with his mother and nurse, and he concealed them in a cave, and he brought them their provisions monthly. ³⁶ And the LORD was with Abram in the cave, and he grew up, and Abram was in the cave ten years, and the king and his princes, soothsayers, and sages thought that the king had killed Abram.

CHAPTER 9

¹ And Haran, the son of Terah, Abram's oldest brother, took a wife in those days. ² Haran was thirty-nine years old when he took her; and the wife of Haran conceived and bore a son, and he called his name Lot. ³ And she conceived again and bore a daughter, and she called her name Milca; and she again conceived and bore a daughter, and she called her name Sarai. ⁴ Haran was forty-two years old when he begot Sarai, which was in the tenth year of the life of Abram; and in those days Abram and his mother and nurse went out from the cave, as the king and his subjects had forgotten the affair of Abram. ⁵ And when Abram came out from the cave, he went to Noah and his son Shem, and he remained with them to learn the instruction of the LORD and His ways, and no man knew where Abram was, and Abram served Noah and his son Shem for a long time. ⁶ And Abram was in Noah's house thirty-nine years, and Abram knew the LORD from three years old, and he went in the ways of the LORD until the day of his death, as Noah and his son Shem had taught him; and all the sons of the earth in those days greatly transgressed against the LORD, and they rebelled against Him, and

they served other gods, and they forgot the LORD who had created them in the earth; and at that time the inhabitants of the earth, each man, made for themselves his god—gods of wood and stone which could neither speak, hear, nor deliver—and the sons of men served them and they became their gods. [7] And the king and all his servants, and Terah with all his household were then the first of those that served gods of wood and stone. [8] And Terah had twelve gods of large size, made of wood and stone, after the twelve months of the year, and he served each one monthly, and every month Terah would bring his meat offering and drink offering to his gods; thus Terah did all the days. [9] And that whole generation was wicked in the sight of the LORD, and they thus made every man his god, but they forsook the LORD who had created them. [10] And there was no man found in those days in the whole earth who knew the LORD (for they each served his own God) except Noah and his household, and all those who were under his counsel knew the LORD in those days. [11] And Abram the son of Terah was waxing great in those days in the house of Noah, and no man knew it, and the LORD was with him. [12] And the LORD gave Abram an understanding heart, and he knew all the works of that generation were vain, and that all their gods were vain and were of no avail. [13] And Abram saw the sun shining on the earth, and Abram said to himself, "Surely now this sun that shines on the earth is God, and I will serve him." [14] And Abram served the sun in that day and he prayed to him, and when evening came, the sun set as usual, and Abram said within himself, "Surely this cannot be God." [15] And Abram still continued to speak within himself, "Who is He who made the heavens and the earth? Who created on earth? Where is He?" [16] And night darkened over him, and he lifted up his eyes toward the west, north, south, and east, and he saw that the sun had vanished from the earth, and the day became dark. [17] And Abram saw the stars and moon before him, and he said, "Surely this is the God who created the whole earth as well as man, and behold, these servants of his are gods around him": and Abram served the moon and prayed to it all that night. [18] And in the morning, when it was light and the sun shone on the earth as usual, Abram saw all the things that the LORD God had made on earth. [19] And Abram said to himself, "Surely these are not gods that made the earth and all mankind, but these are the servants of God," and Abram remained in the house of Noah and there knew the LORD and His ways, and he served the LORD all the days of his life, and all that generation forgot the LORD, and served other gods of wood and stone, and rebelled all their days. [20] And King Nimrod reigned securely, and all the earth was under his control, and all the earth was of one tongue and words of union. [21] And all the princes of Nimrod and his great men took counsel together—Phut, Mitzraim, Cush, and Canaan with their families—and they said to each other, "Come, let us build ourselves a city and a strong tower in it, and its top reaching the heavens, and we will make ourselves famous, so that we may reign over the whole world, in order that the evil of our enemies may cease from us, that we may reign mightily over them, and that we may not become scattered over the earth on account of their wars." [22] And they all went before the king, and they told the king these words, and the king agreed with them in this affair, and he did so. [23] And all the families assembled, consisting of about six hundred thousand men, and they went to seek an extensive piece of ground to build the city and the tower, and they sought in the whole earth and they found none like one valley at the east of the land of Shinar, about two days' walk, and they journeyed there and they dwelt there. [24] And they began to make bricks and burn fires to build the city and the tower that they had imagined to complete. [25] And the building of the tower was a transgression and a sin for them, and they began to build it, and while they were building against the LORD God of Heaven, they imagined in their hearts to war against Him and to ascend into Heaven. [26] And all these people and all the families divided themselves in three parts: the first said, "We will ascend into Heaven and fight against Him"; the second said, "We will ascend to Heaven and place our own gods there and serve them"; and the third part said, "We will ascend to Heaven and strike Him with bows and spears"; and God knew all their works and all their evil thoughts, and He saw the city and the tower which they were building. [27] And when they were building, they built themselves a great city and a very high and strong tower; and on account of its height the mortar and bricks did not reach the builders in their ascent to it until those who went up had completed a full year, and after that, they reached to the builders and gave them the mortar and the bricks; thus it was done daily. [28] And behold, these ascended and others descended the whole day; and if a brick should fall from their hands and get broken, they would all weep over it, and if a man fell and died, none of them would look at him. [29] And the LORD knew their thoughts, and it came to pass when they were building, they cast the arrows toward the heavens, and all the arrows fell on them filled with blood, and when they saw them, they said to each other, "Surely we have slain all those that are in Heaven." [30] For this was from the LORD in order to cause them to err, and in order to destroy them from off the face of the ground. [31] And they built the tower and the city, and they did this thing daily until many days and years were elapsed. [32] And God said to the seventy messengers who stood foremost before Him, to those who were near to Him, saying, "Come, let us descend and confuse their tongues that one man will not understand the language of his neighbor," and they did so to them. [33] And from that day following, they each forgot his neighbor's tongue, and they could not understand to speak in one tongue, and when the builder took lime or stone from the hands of his neighbor which he did not order, the builder would cast it away and throw it on his neighbor [so] that he would die. ³⁴ And they did so many days, and they killed many of them in this manner. ³⁵ And the LORD struck the three divisions that were there, and He punished them according to their works and designs; those who said, "We will ascend to Heaven and serve our gods," became like apes and elephants; and those who said, "We will strike the heavens with arrows," the LORD killed them, one man through the hand of his neighbor; and the third division of those who said, "We will ascend to Heaven and fight against Him," the LORD scattered them throughout the earth. ³⁶ And when those who were left among them knew and understood the calamity which was coming on them, they forsook the building, and they also became scattered on the face of the whole earth. ³⁷ And they ceased building the city and the tower; therefore, He called that place Babel, for there the LORD confounded the language of the whole earth; behold, it was at the east of the land of Shinar. ³⁸ And as to the tower which the sons of men built, the earth opened its mouth and swallowed up one third part thereof, and a fire also descended from Heaven and burned another third, and the other third is left to this day, and it is of that part which was aloft, and its circumference is three days' walk. ³⁹ And many of the sons of men died in that tower—a people without number.

CHAPTER 10

¹ And Peleg the son of Eber died in those days, in the forty-eighth year of the life of Abram son of Terah, and all the days of Peleg were two hundred and thirty-nine years. ² And when the LORD had scattered the sons of men on account of their sin at the tower, behold, they spread out into many divisions, and all the sons of men were dispersed into the four corners of the earth. ³ And all the families each became according to its language, its land, or its city. ⁴ And the sons of men built many cities according to their families in all the places where they went and throughout the earth where the LORD had scattered them. ⁵ And some of them built cities in places from which they were afterward rooted out, and they called these cities after their own names, or the names of their children, or after their particular occurrences. ⁶ And the sons of Japheth the son of Noah went and built themselves cities in the places where they were scattered, and they called all their cities after their names, and the sons of Japheth were divided on the face of the earth into many divisions and languages. ⁷ And these are the sons of Japheth according to their families: Gomer, Magog, Medai, Javan, Tubal, Meshech, and Tiras; these are the sons of Japheth

according to their generations. ⁸ And the children of Gomer, according to their cities, were the Francum who dwell in the land of Franza, by the River Franza, by the River Senah. ⁹ And the children of Rephas are the Bartonim, who dwell in the land of Bartonia by the River Ledah, which empties its waters in the great sea Gihon, that is, Oceanus. ¹⁰ And the children of Togarmah are ten families, and these are their names: Buzar, Parzunac, Balgar, Elicanum, Ragbib, Tarki, Bid, Zebuc, Ongal, and Tilmaz; all these spread and rested in the north and built themselves cities. ¹¹ And they called their cities after their own names, those are they who abide by the rivers Hithlah and Italac to this day. ¹² But the families of Angoli, Balgar, and Parzunac, they dwell by the great river Dubnee; and the names of their cities are also according to their own names. ¹³ And the children of Javan are the Javanim who dwell in the land of Makdonia, and the children of Medai are the Orelum that dwell in the land of Curson, and the children of Tubal are those that dwell in the land of Tuskanah by the River Pashiah. ¹⁴ And the children of Meshech are the Shibashni, and the children of Tiras are Rushash, Cushni, and Ongolis; all these went and built themselves cities; those are the cities that are situated by the sea [of] Jabus by the River Cura, which empties itself in the River Tragan. ¹⁵ And the children of Elishah are the Almanim, and they also went and built themselves cities; those are the cities situated between the mountains of Job and Shibathmo; and of them were the people of Lumbardi who dwell opposite the mountains of Job and Shibathmo, and they conquered the land of Italia and remained there to this day. ¹⁶ And the children of Chittim are the Romim who dwell in the Valley of Canopia by the River Tibreu. ¹⁷ And the children of Dudonim are those who dwell in the cities of the sea [of] Gihon, in the land of Bordna. ¹⁸ These are the families of the children of Japheth, according to their cities and languages, when they were scattered after the tower, and they called their cities after their names and occurrences; and these are the names of all their cities, according to their families, which they built in those days after the tower. ¹⁹ And the sons of Ham were Cush, Mitzraim, Phut, and Canaan, according to their generation and cities. ²⁰ All these went and built themselves cities as they found fit places for them, and they called their cities after the names of their fathers Cush, Mitzraim, Phut, and Canaan. ²¹ And the sons of Mitzraim are the Ludim, Anamim, Lehabim, Naphtuchim, Pathrusim, Casluchim, and Caphturim, seven families. ²² All these dwell by the River Sihor, that is the brook of Egypt, and they built themselves cities and called them after their own names. ²³ And the children of Pathros and Casloch intermarried together, and from them went out the Pelishtim, the Azathim, and the Gerarim, the Githim and the Ekronim, five families in all; these also built themselves cities, and they called their cities after the names of their fathers to this day. ²⁴ And the children of Canaan also built themselves cities, and they called their cities after their names, eleven cities and others without number. ²⁵ And four men from the family of Ham went to the land of the plain; these are the names of the four men: Sodom, Gomorrah, Admah, and Zeboyim. ²⁶ And these men built themselves four cities in the land of the plain, and they called the names of their cities after their own names. ²⁷ And they, and their children, and all belonging to them dwelt in those cities, and they were fruitful, and multiplied greatly, and dwelt peaceably. ²⁸ And Seir the son of Hur, son of Hivi, son of Canaan, went and found a valley opposite to Mount Paran, and he built a city there, and he and his seven sons and his household dwelt there, and he called the city which he built Seir, according to his name; that is the land of Seir to this day. ²⁹ These are the families of the children of Ham, according to their languages and cities, when they were scattered to their countries after the tower. ³⁰ And some of the children of Shem son of Noah, father of all the children of Eber, also went and built themselves cities in the places wherein they were scattered, and they called their cities after their names. ³¹ And the sons of Shem were Elam, Asshur, Arphaxad, Lud, and Aram, and they built themselves cities and called the names of all their cities after their names. ³² And Asshur son of Shem and his children and household went out at that time—a very large body of them—and they went to a distant land that they found, and they met with a very extensive valley in the land that they went to, and they built themselves four cities, and they called them after their own names and occurrences. ³³ And these are the names of the cities which the children of Asshur built: Ninevah, Resen, Calach, and Rehobother; and the children of Asshur dwell there to this day. ³⁴ And the children of Aram also went and built themselves a city, and they called the name of the city Uz after their eldest brother, and they dwell therein; that is the land of Uz to this day. ³⁵ And in the second year after the tower, a man from the house of Asshur, whose name was Bela, went from the land of Ninevah to sojourn with his household wherever he could find a place; and they came until opposite the cities of the plain against Sodom, and they dwelt there. ³⁶ And the man rose up and built a small city there, and called its name Bela after his name; that is the land of Zoar to this day. ³⁷ And these are the families of the children of Shem according to their language and cities, after they were scattered on the earth after the tower. ³⁸ And every kingdom, city, and family of the families of the children of Noah built themselves many cities after this. ³⁹ And they established governments in all their cities in order to be regulated by their orders; so all the families of the children of Noah did forever.

CHAPTER 11

¹ And Nimrod son of Cush was still in the land of Shinar, and he reigned over it and dwelt there, and he built cities in the land of Shinar. ² And these are the names of the four cities which he built, and he called their names after the occurrences that happened to them in the building of the tower. ³ And he called the first Babel, saying, "Because the LORD confounded the language of the whole earth there." And the name of the second he called Erech, because from there God dispersed them. ⁴ And the third he called Eched, saying, "There was a great battle at that place." And the fourth he called Calnah, because his princes and mighty men were consumed there, and they vexed the LORD; they rebelled and transgressed against Him. ⁵ And when Nimrod had built these cities in the land of Shinar, he placed in them the remainder of his people, his princes and his mighty men that were left in his kingdom. ⁶ And Nimrod dwelt in Babel, and he renewed his reign there over the rest of his subjects, and he reigned securely, and the subjects and princes of Nimrod called his name Amraphel, saying that at the tower his princes and men fell through his means. ⁷ And notwithstanding this, Nimrod did not return to the LORD, and he continued in wickedness and teaching wickedness to the sons of men; and his son Mardon was worse than his father and continued to add to the abominations of his father. ⁸ And he caused the sons of men to sin, therefore it is said, "From the wicked goes out wickedness." ⁹ At that time there was war between the families of the children of Ham as they were dwelling in the cities which they had built. ¹⁰ And Chedorlaomer, king of Elam, went away from the families of the children of Ham, and he fought with them and he subdued them, and he went to the five cities of the plain and he fought against them and he subdued them, and they were under his control. ¹¹ And they served him twelve years, and they gave him a yearly tax. ¹² At that time Nahor son of Serug died—in the forty-ninth year of the life of Abram son of Terah. ¹³ And in the fiftieth year of the life of Abram son of Terah, Abram came out from the house of Noah, and went to his father's house. ¹⁴ And Abram knew the LORD, and he went in His ways and instructions, and the LORD his God was with him. ¹⁵ And his father Terah was still captain of the host of King Nimrod in those days, and he still followed strange gods. ¹⁶ And Abram came to his father's house and saw twelve gods standing there in their temples, and the anger of Abram was kindled when he saw these images in his father's house. ¹⁷ And Abram said, "As the LORD lives, these images will not remain in my father's house; so the LORD who created me will do to me if in three days' time I do not break them all." ¹⁸ And Abram went from them and his anger burned within him. And Abram hastened and went from the chamber to his father's outer court, and he found his father sitting in the court, and all his

servants with him, and Abram came and sat before him. ¹⁹ And Abram asked his father, saying, "Father, tell me where is [the] God who created the heavens and earth, and all the sons of men on earth, and who created you and me." And Terah answered his son Abram and said, "Behold, those who created us are all with us in the house." ²⁰ And Abram said to his father, "My lord, please show them to me"; and Terah brought Abram into the chamber of the inner court, and Abram saw, and behold, the whole room was full of gods of wood and stone—twelve great images and others less than they without number. ²¹ And Terah said to his son, "Behold, these are they which made all [that] you see on earth, and which created me and you, and all mankind." ²² And Terah bowed down to his gods, and he then went away from them, and his son Abram went away with him. ²³ And when Abram had gone from them, he went to his mother and sat before her, and he said to his mother, "Behold, my father has shown me those who made the heavens and earth, and all the sons of men. ²⁴ Now, therefore, hasten and fetch a kid from the flock, and make savory meat from it, that I may bring it to my father's gods as an offering for them to eat; perhaps I may thereby become acceptable to them." ²⁵ And his mother did so, and she fetched a kid, and made savory meat thereof, and brought it to Abram, and Abram took the savory meat from his mother and brought it before his father's gods, and he drew near to them that they might eat; and his father Terah did not know of it. ²⁶ And Abram saw on the day when he was sitting among them that they had no voice, no hearing, no motion, and not one of them could stretch out his hand to eat. ²⁷ And Abram mocked them, and said, "Surely the savory meat that I prepared has not pleased them, or perhaps it was too little for them, and for that reason they would not eat; therefore tomorrow I will prepare fresh savory meat, better and more plentiful than this, in order that I may see the result." ²⁸ And it was on the next day that Abram directed his mother concerning the savory meat, and his mother rose and fetched three fine kids from the flock, and she made of them some excellent savory meat, such as her son was fond of, and she gave it to her son Abram; and his father Terah did not know of it. ²⁹ And Abram took the savory meat from his mother and brought it into the chamber before his father's gods; and he came near to them that they might eat, and he placed it before them, and Abram sat before them all day, thinking perhaps they might eat. ³⁰ And Abram viewed them, and behold, they had neither voice nor hearing, nor did one of them stretch out his hand to the meat to eat. ³¹ And in the evening of that day in that house Abram was clothed with the Spirit of God. ³² And he called out and said, "Woe to my father and this wicked generation, whose hearts are all inclined to vanity, who serve these idols of wood and stone which can neither eat, smell, hear, nor speak, who

have mouths without speech, eyes without sight, ears without hearing, hands without feeling, and legs which cannot move; those that made them and that trust in them are like them." ³³ And when Abram saw all these things his anger was kindled against his father, and he hastened and took a hatchet in his hand, and came to the chamber of the gods, and he broke all his father's gods. ³⁴ And when he had finished breaking the images, he placed the hatchet in the hand of the great god which was there before them, and he went out; and his father Terah came home, for he had heard at the door the sound of the striking of the hatchet; so Terah came into the house to know what this was about. ³⁵ And Terah, having heard the noise of the hatchet in the room of images, ran to the room to the images, and he met Abram going out. ³⁶ And Terah entered the room and found all the idols fallen down and broken, and the hatchet in the hand of the largest, which was not broken, and the savory meat which his son Abram had made was still before them. ³⁷ And when Terah saw this his anger was greatly kindled, and he hastened and went from the room to Abram. ³⁸ And he found his son Abram still sitting in the house; and he said to him, "What is this work you have done to my gods?" ³⁹ And Abram answered his father Terah and said, "Not so my lord, for I brought savory meat before them, and when I came near to them with the meat that they might eat, they all at once stretched out their hands to eat before the great one had put out his hand to eat. ⁴⁰ And the large one saw their works that they did before him, and his anger was violently kindled against them, and he went and took the hatchet that was in the house and came to them and broke them all, and behold, the hatchet is yet in his hand as you see." ⁴¹ And Terah's anger was kindled against his son Abram when he spoke this; and Terah said to his son Abram in his anger, "What is this tale that you have told? You speak lies to me. ⁴² Is there spirit, soul, or power in these gods to do all you have told me? Are they not wood and stone, and have I not made them myself, and can you speak such lies, saying that the large god that was with them struck them? It is you that placed the hatchet in his hands, and then say he struck them all." ⁴³ And Abram answered his father and said to him, "And how can you then serve these idols in whom there is no power to do anything? Can those idols in which you trust deliver you? Can they hear your prayers when you call on them? Can they deliver you from the hands of your enemies, or will they fight your battles for you against your enemies, that you should serve wood and stone which can neither speak nor hear? ⁴⁴ And now surely it is not good for you nor for the sons of men that are connected with you to do these things; are you so silly, so foolish, or so short of understanding that you will serve wood and stone, and do after this manner, ⁴⁵ and forget the Lᴏʀᴅ God who made the heavens and earth, and who created you in the earth, and thereby bring a great evil on your souls in this matter by serving stone and wood? ⁴⁶ Did our fathers in days of old not sin in this matter, and the LORD God of the universe brought the waters of the flood on them and destroyed the whole earth? ⁴⁷ And how can you continue to do this and serve gods of wood and stone, who cannot hear, or speak, or deliver you from oppression, thereby bringing down the anger of the God of the universe on you? ⁴⁸ Now therefore, my father, refrain from this and do not bring evil on your soul and the souls of your household." ⁴⁹ And Abram hastened and sprang from before his father, and took the hatchet from his father's largest idol, with which Abram broke it and ran away. ⁵⁰ And Terah, seeing all that Abram had done, hastened to go from his house, and he went to the king, and he came before Nimrod, and stood before him, and he bowed down to the king; and the king said, "What do you want?" ⁵¹ And he said, "I implore you, my lord, to hear me: now fifty years back a child was born to me, and thus he has done to my gods and thus he has spoken; and now therefore, my lord and king, send for him that he may come before you, and judge him according to the law, that we may be delivered from his evil." ⁵² And the king sent three men of his servants, and they went and brought Abram before the king. And Nimrod and all his princes and servants were sitting before him that day, and Terah also sat before them. ⁵³ And the king said to Abram, "What is this that you have done to your father and to his gods?" And Abram answered the king in the words that he spoke to his father, and he said, "The large god that was with them in the house did to them what you have heard." ⁵⁴ And the king said to Abram, "Had they power to speak, and eat, and do as you have said?" And Abram answered the king, saying, "And if there is no power in them why do you serve them and cause the sons of men to err through your follies? ⁵⁵ Do you imagine that they can deliver you or do anything small or great, that you should serve them? And why will you not sense the God of the whole universe, who created you and in whose power it is to kill and keep alive? ⁵⁶ O foolish, simple, and ignorant king, woe to you forever. ⁵⁷ I thought you would teach your servants the upright way, but you have not done this, but have filled the whole earth with your sins and the sins of your people who have followed your ways. ⁵⁸ Do you not know, or have you not heard, that this evil which you do, our ancestors sinned therein in days of old, and the perpetual God brought the waters of the flood on them and destroyed them all, and also destroyed the whole earth on their account? And will you and your people rise up now and do like to this work, in order to bring down the anger of the LORD God of the universe, and to bring calamity on you and the whole earth? ⁵⁹ Now therefore, put away this evil deed which you do, and serve the God of the universe, as your soul is in His hands, and then it will be well with you. ⁶⁰ And if your wicked heart will not listen to my words to cause you to forsake your evil ways, and to serve the perpetual God, then you will die in shame in the latter days— you, your people, and all who are connected with you, hearing your words or walking in your evil ways." ⁶¹ And when Abram had ceased speaking before the king and princes, Abram lifted up his eyes to the heavens, and he said, "The LORD sees all the wicked, and He will judge them."

CHAPTER 12

¹ And when the king heard the words of Abram, he ordered him to be put into prison; and Abram was in prison [for] ten days. ² And at the end of those days the king ordered that all the kings, princes, and governors of different provinces, and the sages, should come before him, and they sat before him, and Abram was still in the house of confinement. ³ And the king said to the princes and sages, "Have you heard what Abram, the son of Terah, has done to his father? Thus he has done to him, and I ordered him to be brought before me, and thus he has spoken; his heart did not misgive him, neither did he stir in my presence, and behold, now he is confined in the prison. ⁴ And therefore decide what judgment is due to this man who reviled the king—who spoke and did all the things that you heard." ⁵ And they all answered the king, saying, "The man who reviles the king should be hanged on a tree; but having done all the things that he said, and having despised our gods, he must therefore be burned to death, for this is the law in this matter. ⁶ If it pleases the king to do this, let him order his servants to kindle a fire both night and day in your brick furnace, and then we will cast this man into it." And the king did so, and he commanded his servants that they should prepare a fire for three days and three nights in the king's furnace, that is in Kasdim; and the king ordered them to take Abram from prison and bring him out to be burned. ⁷ And all the king's servants, princes, lords, governors, and judges, and all the inhabitants of the land, about nine hundred thousand men, stood opposite the furnace to see Abram. ⁸ And all the women and little ones crowded on the roofs and towers to see what was happening with Abram, and they all stood together at a distance; and there was not a man left that did not come on that day to behold the scene. ⁹ And when Abram had come, the conjurers of the king and the sages saw Abram, and they cried out to the king, saying, "Our sovereign lord, surely this is the man whom we know to have been the child at whose birth the great star swallowed the four stars, which we declared to the king now fifty years since. ¹⁰ And behold, now his father has also transgressed your commands and mocked you by bringing you another child, which you killed." ¹¹ And when the king heard their words, he was exceedingly angry, and he

ordered Terah to be brought before him. ¹²And the king said, "Have you heard what the conjurers have spoken? Now tell me truly: what did you do? And if you will speak truth you will be acquitted." ¹³And seeing that the king's anger was so greatly kindled, Terah said to the king, "My lord and king, you have heard the truth, and what the sages have spoken is right." And the king said, "How could you do this thing, to transgress my orders and to give me a child that you did not beget, and to take value for him?" ¹⁴And Terah answered the king, "Because my tender feelings were excited for my son at that time, and I took a son of my handmaid, and I brought him to the king." ¹⁵And the king said, "Who advised you to [do] this? Tell me, do not hide it from me, and then you will not die." ¹⁶And Terah was greatly terrified in the king's presence, and he said to the king, "It was my eldest son Haran who advised me to [do] this"; and Haran was thirty-two years old in those days that Abram was born. ¹⁷But Haran did not advise his father to [do] anything, for Terah said this to the king in order to deliver his soul from the king, for he feared greatly; and the king said to Terah, "Your son Haran who advised you to [do] this will die through fire with Abram; for the sentence of death is on him for having rebelled against the king's desire in doing this thing." ¹⁸And at that time Haran felt inclined to follow the ways of Abram, but he kept it within himself. ¹⁹And Haran said in his heart, "Behold, now the king has seized Abram on account of these things which Abram did, and it will come to pass, that if Abram prevails over the king, I will follow him, but if the king prevails, I will go after the king." ²⁰And when Terah had spoken this to the king concerning his son Haran, the king ordered Haran to be seized with Abram. ²¹And they brought them both, Abram and his brother Haran, to cast them into the fire; and all the inhabitants of the land, and the king's servants, and princes, and all the women, and little ones were there, standing over them that day. ²²And the king's servants took Abram and his brother, and they stripped them of all their clothes excepting their lower garments which were on them. ²³And they bound their hands and feet with linen cords, and the servants of the king lifted them up and cast them both into the furnace. ²⁴And the LORD loved Abram and He had compassion over him, and the LORD came down and delivered Abram from the fire, and he was not burned. ²⁵But all the cords with which they bound him were burned, while Abram remained and walked around in the fire. ²⁶And Haran died when they had cast him into the fire, and he was burned to ashes, for his heart was not perfect with the LORD; and those men who cast him into the fire, the flame of the fire spread over them, and they were burned, and twelve men of them died. ²⁷And Abram walked in the midst of the fire [for] three days and three nights, and all the servants of the king saw him walking in the fire, and they came

and told the king, saying, "Behold, we have seen Abram walking around in the midst of the fire, and even the lower garments which are on him are not burned, but the cord with which he was bound is burned." ²⁸And when the king heard their words his heart fainted and he would not believe them; so he sent other faithful princes to see this matter, and they went, and saw it, and told it to the king; and the king rose to go and see it, and he saw Abram walking to and fro in the midst of the fire, and he saw Haran's body burned, and the king wondered greatly. ²⁹And the king ordered Abram to be taken out from the fire; and his servants approached to take him out and they could not, for the fire was around and the flame ascending toward them from the furnace. ³⁰And the king's servants fled from it, and the king rebuked them, saying, "Hurry and bring Abram out of the fire that you will not die." ³¹And the servants of the king again approached to bring Abram out, and the flames came on them and burned their faces so that eight of them died. ³²And when the king saw that his servants could not approach the fire lest they should be burned, the king called to Abram, "O servant of the God who is in Heaven, go out from amidst the fire and come here before me"; and Abram listened to the voice of the king, and he went out from the fire and came and stood before the king. ³³And when Abram came out, the king and all his servants saw Abram coming before the king with his lower garments on him, for they were not burned, but the cord with which he was bound was burned. ³⁴And the king said to Abram, "How is it that you were not burned in the fire?" ³⁵And Abram said to the king, "The God of the heavens and earth in whom I trust and who has all in His power, He delivered me from the fire into which you cast me." ³⁶And Haran, the brother of Abram, was burned to ashes, and they sought for his body, and they found it consumed. ³⁷And Haran was eighty-two years old when he died in the fire of Kasdim. And the king, princes, and inhabitants of the land, seeing that Abram was delivered from the fire, they came and bowed down to Abram. ³⁸And Abram said to them, "Do not bow down to me, but bow down to the God of the world who made you, and serve Him and go in His ways, for it is He who delivered me from out of this fire, and it is He who created the souls and spirits of all men, and formed man in his mother's womb, and brought him out into the world, and it is He who will deliver those who trust in Him from all pain." ³⁹And this thing seemed very wonderful in the eyes of the king and princes, that Abram was saved from the fire and that Haran was burned; and the king gave Abram many presents and he gave him his two head servants from the king's house; the name of one was Oni and the name of the other was Eliezer. ⁴⁰And all the kings, princes, and servants gave Abram many gifts of silver, and gold, and pearl, and the king and his princes sent him away, and he went in peace.

⁴¹ And Abram went out from the king in peace, and many of the king's servants followed him, and about three hundred men joined him. ⁴² And Abram returned on that day and went to his father's house, he and the men that followed him, and Abram served the LORD his God all the days of his life, and he walked in His ways and followed His law. ⁴³ And from that day forward Abram inclined the hearts of the sons of men to serve the LORD. ⁴⁴ And at that time Nahor and Abram took wives for themselves, the daughters of their brother Haran; the wife of Nahor was Milca and the name of Abram's wife was Sarai. And Sarai, wife of Abram, was barren; she had no offspring in those days. ⁴⁵ And at the expiration of two years from Abram's going out of the fire, that is in the fifty-second year of his life, behold, King Nimrod sat in Babel on the throne, and the king fell asleep and dreamed that he was standing with his troops and hosts in a valley opposite the king's furnace. ⁴⁶ And he lifted up his eyes and saw a man in the likeness of Abram coming out from the furnace, and that he came and stood before the king with his drawn sword, and then sprang to the king with his sword when the king fled from the man, for he was afraid; and while he was running, the man threw an egg on the king's head, and the egg became a great river. ⁴⁷ And the king dreamed that all his troops sank in that river and died, and the king took flight with three men who were before him and he escaped. ⁴⁸ And the king looked at these men and they were clothed in princely dresses as the garments of kings and had the appearance and majesty of kings. ⁴⁹ And while they were running, the river again turned to an egg before the king, and there came out from the egg a young bird which came before the king, and flew at his head, and plucked out the king's eye. ⁵⁰ And the king was grieved at the sight, and he awoke out of his sleep and his spirit was agitated; and he felt a great terror. ⁵¹ And in the morning, the king rose from his couch in fear, and he ordered all the wise men and magicians to come before him when the king related his dream to them. ⁵² And a wise servant of the king, whose name was Anuki, answered the king, saying, "This is nothing else but the evil of Abram and his seed which will spring up against my lord and king in the latter days. ⁵³ And behold, the day will come when Abram, and his seed, and the children of his household will war with my king, and they will strike all the king's hosts and his troops. ⁵⁴ And as to what you have said concerning three men which you saw like to yourself, and which escaped, this means that only you will escape with three kings from the kings of the earth who will be with you in battle. ⁵⁵ And that which you saw of the river which turned to an egg as at first, and the young bird plucking out your eye, this means nothing else but the seed of Abram which will slay the king in latter days. ⁵⁶ This is my king's dream, and this is its interpretation, and the dream is true, and the

interpretation which your servant has given you is right. ⁵⁷ Now therefore, my king, surely you know that it is now fifty-two years since your sages saw this at the birth of Abram, and if my king will permit Abram to live in the earth it will be to the injury of my lord and king, for all the days that Abram lives neither you nor your kingdom will be established, for this was known formerly at his birth; and why will my king not slay him, that his evil may be kept from you in latter days?" ⁵⁸ And Nimrod listened to the voice of Anuki, and he sent some of his servants in secret to go and seize Abram, and bring him before the king to suffer death. ⁵⁹ And Eliezer, Abram's servant whom the king had given him, was at that time in the presence of the king, and he heard what Anuki had advised the king, and what the king had said to cause Abram's death. ⁶⁰ And Eliezer said to Abram, "Hasten, rise up and save your soul, that you may not die through the hands of the king, for thus he saw in a dream concerning you, and thus Anuki interpreted it, and thus also Anuki advised the king concerning you." ⁶¹ And Abram listened to the voice of Eliezer, and Abram hastened and ran for safety to the house of Noah and his son Shem, and he concealed himself there and found a place of safety; and the king's servants came to Abram's house to seek him, but they could not find him, and they searched throughout the country and he was not to be found, and they went and searched in every direction and he was not to be met with. ⁶² And when the king's servants could not find Abram they returned to the king, but the king's anger against Abram was stilled, as they did not find him, and the king drove this matter concerning Abram from his mind. ⁶³ And Abram was concealed in Noah's house for one month until the king had forgotten this matter, but Abram was still afraid of the king; and Terah secretly came to see his son Abram in the house of Noah, and Terah was very great in the eyes of the king. ⁶⁴ And Abram said to his father, "Do you not know that the king thinks to slay me, and to annihilate my name from the earth by the advice of his wicked counselors? ⁶⁵ Now whom have you here and what have you in this land? Arise, let us go together to the land of Canaan, that we may be delivered from his hand, lest you also perish through him in the latter days. ⁶⁶ Do you not know or have you not heard that it is not through love that Nimrod gives you all this honor, but it is only for his benefit that he bestows all this good on you? ⁶⁷ And if he does to you greater good than this, surely these are only vanities of the world, for wealth and riches cannot avail in the day of wrath and anger. ⁶⁸ Now therefore, listen to my voice, and let us arise and go to the land of Canaan, out of the reach of injury from Nimrod; and serve the LORD who created you in the earth and it will be well with you; and cast away all the vain things which you pursue." ⁶⁹ And Abram ceased to speak when Noah and his son Shem answered Terah, saying, "The word which Abram has said to you is true." [70] And Terah listened to the voice of his son Abram, and Terah did all that Abram said, for this was from the LORD that the king should not cause Abram's death.

CHAPTER 13

[1] And Terah took his son Abram and his grandson Lot, the son of Haran, and his daughter-in-law Sarai, the wife of his son Abram, and all the souls of his household and went with them from Ur-Kasdim to go to the land of Canaan. And when they came as far as the land of Haran they remained there, for it was exceedingly good land for pasture, and of sufficient extent for those who accompanied them. [2] And the people of the land of Haran saw that Abram was good and upright with God and men, and that the LORD his God was with him, and some of the people of the land of Haran came and joined Abram, and he taught them the instruction of the LORD and His ways; and these men remained with Abram in his house, and they adhered to him. [3] And Abram remained in the land three years, and at the expiration of three years the LORD appeared to Abram and said to him, "I am the LORD who brought you out from Ur-Kasdim and delivered you from the hands of all your enemies. [4] And now therefore, if you will listen to My voice and keep My commands, My statutes and My laws, then I will cause your enemies to fall before you, and I will multiply your seed like the stars of the heavens, and I will send My blessing on all the works of your hands, and you will lack nothing. [5] Arise now, take your wife and all belonging to you and go to the land of Canaan and remain there, and I will be God to you there, and I will bless you." And Abram rose and took his wife and all belonging to him, and he went to the land of Canaan as the LORD had told him; and Abram was [over] fifty years old when he went from Haran. [6] And Abram came to the land of Canaan and dwelt in the midst of the city, and he pitched his tent there among the children of Canaan, inhabitants of the land. [7] And the LORD appeared to Abram when he came to the land of Canaan, and said to him, "This is the land which I gave to you and to your seed after you forever, and I will make your seed like the stars of the heavens, and I will give all the lands which you see to your seed for an inheritance." [8] And Abram built an altar in the place where God had spoken to him, and Abram called on the Name of the LORD there. [9] At that time, at the end of three years of Abram's dwelling in the land of Canaan, in that year Noah died, which was the fifty-eighth year of the life of Abram; and all the days that Noah lived were nine hundred and fifty years and he died. [10] And Abram dwelt in the land of Canaan, he, his wife, and all belonging to him, and all those that accompanied him, together with those that joined him from the people of the land; but Abram's brother Nahor, and his father Terah, and Lot the son of Haran, and all belonging to them dwelt in Haran.

[11] In the fifth year of Abram's dwelling in the land of Canaan the people of Sodom and Gomorrah and all the cities of the plain revolted from the power of Chedorlaomer, king of Elam, for all the kings of the cities of the plain had served Chedorlaomer for twelve years and given him a yearly tax, but in those days, in the thirteenth year, they rebelled against him. [12] And in the tenth year of Abram's dwelling in the land of Canaan there was war between Nimrod king of Shinar and Chedorlaomer king of Elam, and Nimrod came to fight with Chedorlaomer and to subdue him. [13] For Chedorlaomer was at that time one of the princes of the hosts of Nimrod, and when all the people at the tower were dispersed and those that remained were also scattered on the face of the earth, Chedorlaomer went to the land of Elam and reigned over it and rebelled against his lord. [14] And in those days when Nimrod saw that the cities of the plain had rebelled, he came with pride and anger to war with Chedorlaomer, and Nimrod assembled all his princes and subjects, about seven hundred thousand men, and went against Chedorlaomer, and Chedorlaomer went out to meet him with five thousand men, and they prepared for battle in the Valley of Babel which is between Elam and Shinar. [15] And all those kings fought there, and Nimrod and his people were smitten before the people of Chedorlaomer, and there fell from Nimrod's men about six hundred thousand, and the king's son Mardon fell among them. [16] And Nimrod fled and returned in shame and disgrace to his land, and he was under subjection to Chedorlaomer for a long time, and Chedorlaomer returned to his land and sent princes of his host to the kings that dwelt around him, to Arioch king of Ellasar, and to Tidal king of Goyim, and made a covenant with them, and they were all obedient to his commands. [17] And it was in the fifteenth year of Abram's dwelling in the land of Canaan, which is the seventieth year of the life of Abram, that the LORD appeared to Abram in that year, and He said to him, "I am the LORD who brought you out from Ur-Kasdim to give you this land for an inheritance. [18] Now therefore, walk before Me, and be perfect, and keep My commands, for I will give this land to you and to your seed for an inheritance, from the River Mitzraim to the great river Euphrates. [19] And you will come to your fathers in peace and in good age, and the fourth generation will return here in this land and will inherit it forever"; and Abram built an altar, and he called on the Name of the LORD who appeared to him, and he brought up sacrifices on the altar to the LORD. [20] At that time Abram returned and went to Haran to see his father and mother, and his father's household, and Abram, and his wife, and all belonging to him returned to Haran, and Abram dwelt in Haran [for] five years. [21] And many of the people of Haran, about seventy-two men, followed Abram and Abram taught them the instruction of the LORD and His ways, and he taught them to know the LORD.

²² In those days the LORD appeared to Abram in Haran, and He said to him, "Behold, I spoke to you these twenty years back, saying, ²³ Go out from your land, from your birthplace and from your father's house, to the land which I have shown you to give it to you and to your children, for there in that land I will bless you, and make you a great nation, and make your name great, and in you the families of the earth will be blessed. ²⁴ Now therefore, arise, go out from this place, you, your wife, and all belonging to you, also everyone born in your house and all the souls you have made in Haran, and bring them out with you from here, and rise to return to the land of Canaan." ²⁵ And Abram arose and took his wife Sarai, and all belonging to him, and all that were born to him in his house, and the souls which they had made in Haran, and they came out to go to the land of Canaan. ²⁶ And Abram went and returned to the land of Canaan, according to the word of the LORD. And Lot, the son of his brother Haran, went with him, and Abram was seventy-five years old when he went out from Haran to return to the land of Canaan. ²⁷ And he came to the land of Canaan according to the word of the LORD to Abram, and he pitched his tent and he dwelt in the plain of Mamre, and his brother's son Lot and all belonging to him were with him. ²⁸ And the LORD appeared to Abram again and said, "To your seed I will give this land"; and he built an altar there to the LORD who appeared to him, which is still in the plains of Mamre to this day.

CHAPTER 14

¹ In those days there was a wise man in the land of Shinar who had understanding in all wisdom, and of a beautiful appearance, but he was poor and indigent; his name was Rikayon and he was hard set to support himself. ² And he resolved to go to Egypt, to Oswiris the son of Anom king of Egypt, to show the king his wisdom; for perhaps he might find grace in his sight, to raise him up and give him maintenance; and Rikayon did so. ³ And when Rikayon came to Egypt, he asked the inhabitants of Egypt concerning the king, and the inhabitants of Egypt told him the custom of the king of Egypt, for it was then the custom of the king of Egypt that he went from his royal palace and was seen abroad only one day in the year, and after that the king would return to his palace to remain there. ⁴ And on the day when the king went out, he passed judgment in the land, and everyone having a suit came before the king that day to obtain his request. ⁵ And when Rikayon heard of the custom in Egypt and that he could not come into the presence of the king, he grieved greatly and was very sorrowful. ⁶ And in the evening Rikayon went out and found a house in ruins, formerly a bake house in Egypt, and he remained there all night in bitterness of soul and pinched with hunger, and sleep was removed from his eyes. ⁷ And Rikayon considered within himself what he should do in the town until the king made his appearance, and how he might maintain himself there. ⁸ And he rose in the morning, and walked around, and met in his way those who sold vegetables and various sorts of seed with which they supplied the inhabitants. ⁹ And Rikayon wished to do the same in order to get a maintenance in the city, but he was unacquainted with the custom of the people, and he was like a blind man among them. ¹⁰ And he went and obtained vegetables to sell them for his support, and the rabble assembled around him and ridiculed him, and took his vegetables from him and left him nothing. ¹¹ And he rose up from there in bitterness of soul and went sighing to the bake house in which he had remained all the night before, and he slept there the second night. ¹² And on that night he reasoned within himself again how he could save himself from starvation, and he devised a scheme how to act. ¹³ And he rose up in the morning and acted ingeniously, and went and hired thirty strong men of the rabble, carrying their war instruments in their hands, and he led them to the top of the Egyptian tomb, and he placed them there. ¹⁴ And he commanded them, saying, "Thus says the king, strengthen yourselves and be valiant men, and let no man be buried here until two hundred pieces of silver are given, and then he may be buried"; and those men did according to the order of Rikayon to the people of Egypt the whole of that year. ¹⁵ And in eight months time Rikayon and his men gathered great riches of silver and gold, and Rikayon took a great quantity of horses and other animals, and he hired more men, and he gave them horses and they remained with him. ¹⁶ And when the year came around, at the time the king went out into the town, all the inhabitants of Egypt assembled together to speak to him concerning the work of Rikayon and his men. ¹⁷ And the king went out on the appointed day, and all the Egyptians came before him and cried to him, saying, ¹⁸ "May the king live forever. What is this thing you do in the town to your servants, not to permit a dead body to be buried until so much silver and gold are given? Was there ever the like to this done in the whole earth, from the days of former kings, yes, even from the days of Adam, to this day, that the dead should not be buried, [except] only for a set price? ¹⁹ We know it to be the custom of kings to take a yearly tax from the living, but you do not only do this, but you also exact a tax from the dead day by day. ²⁰ Now, O king, we can no longer bear this, for the whole city is ruined on this account, and do you not know it?" ²¹ And when the king heard all that they had spoken he was very angry and his anger burned within him at this affair, for he had known nothing of it. ²² And the king said, "Who and where is he that dares to do this wicked thing in my land without my command? Surely you will tell me." ²³ And they told him all the works of Rikayon and his men, and the king's anger was aroused, and he ordered Rikayon

and his men to be brought before him. ²⁴ And Rikayon took about one thousand children, sons and daughters, and clothed them in silk and embroidery, and he set them on horses and sent them to the king by means of his men, and he also took a great quantity of silver, and gold, and precious stones, and a strong and beautiful horse as a present for the king, with which he came before the king and bowed down to the earth before him; and the king, his servants, and all the inhabitants of Egypt wondered at the work of Rikayon, and they saw his riches and the present that he had brought to the king. ²⁵ And it greatly pleased the king and he wondered at it; and when Rikayon sat before him, the king asked him concerning all his works, and Rikayon spoke all his words wisely before the king, his servants, and all the inhabitants of Egypt. ²⁶ And when the king heard the words of Rikayon and his wisdom, Rikayon found grace in his sight, and he met with grace and kindness from all the servants of the king and from all the inhabitants of Egypt, on account of his wisdom and excellent speeches, and from that time they loved him exceedingly. ²⁷ And the king answered and said to Rikayon, "Your name will no longer be called Rikayon, but Pharaoh will be your name, since you exacted a tax from the dead"; and he called his name Pharaoh. ²⁸ And the king and his subjects loved Rikayon for his wisdom, and they consulted with all the inhabitants of Egypt to make him prefect under the king. ²⁹ And all the inhabitants of Egypt and its wise men did so, and it was made a law in Egypt. ³⁰ And they made Rikayon Pharaoh prefect under Oswiris king of Egypt, and Rikayon Pharaoh governed over Egypt, daily administering justice to the whole city, but Oswiris the king would judge the people of the land one day in the year when he went out to make his appearance. ³¹ And Rikayon Pharaoh cunningly usurped the government of Egypt, and he exacted a tax from all the inhabitants of Egypt. ³² And all the inhabitants of Egypt greatly loved Rikayon Pharaoh, and they made a decree to call every king that should reign over them and their seed in Egypt, Pharaoh. ³³ Therefore all the kings that reigned in Egypt from that time forward were called Pharaoh to this day.

CHAPTER 15

¹ And in that year there was a heavy famine throughout the land of Canaan, and the inhabitants of the land could not remain on account of the famine for it was very grievous. ² And Abram and all belonging to him rose and went down to Egypt on account of the famine, and when they were at the brook Mitzraim they remained there some time to rest from the fatigue of the road. ³ And Abram and Sarai were walking at the border of the Brook of Mitzraim, and Abram beheld that his wife Sarai was very beautiful. ⁴ And Abram said to his wife Sarai, "Since God has created you with such a beautiful countenance, I am afraid of the Egyptians lest they should slay me and take you away, for the fear of God is not in these places. ⁵ Surely then you will do this: say you are my sister to all that may ask you in order that it may be well with me, and that we may live and not be put to death." ⁶ And Abram commanded the same to all those that came with him to Egypt on account of the famine; also his nephew Lot he commanded, saying, "If the Egyptians ask you concerning Sarai, say she is the sister of Abram." ⁷ And yet with all these orders Abram did not put confidence in them, but he took Sarai, and placed her in a chest, and concealed it among their vessels, for Abram was greatly concerned about Sarai on account of the wickedness of the Egyptians. ⁸ And Abram and all belonging to him rose up from the Brook of Mitzraim and came to Egypt; and they had scarcely entered the gates of the city when the guards stood up to them, saying, "Give tithe to the king from what you have, and then you may come into the town"; and Abram and those that were with him did so. ⁹ And Abram with the people that were with him came to Egypt, and when they came, they brought the chest in which Sarai was concealed and the Egyptians saw the chest. ¹⁰ And the king's servants approached Abram, saying, "What have you here in this chest which we have not seen? Now open the chest and give tithe to the king of all that it contains." ¹¹ And Abram said, "I will not open this chest, but all you demand on it I will give." And Pharaoh's officers answered Abram, saying, "It is a chest of precious stones—give us the tenth thereof." ¹² Abram said, "All that you desire I will give, but you must not open the chest." ¹³ And the king's officers pressed Abram, and they reached the chest and opened it with force, and they saw, and behold, a beautiful woman was in the chest. ¹⁴ And when the officers of the king beheld Sarai, they were struck with admiration at her beauty, and all the princes and servants of Pharaoh assembled to see Sarai, for she was very beautiful. And the king's officers ran and told Pharaoh all that they had seen, and they praised Sarai to the king; and Pharaoh ordered her to be brought, and the woman came before the king. ¹⁵ And Pharaoh beheld Sarai, and she pleased him exceedingly, and he was struck with her beauty, and the king rejoiced greatly on her account, and made presents to those who brought him the tidings concerning her. ¹⁶ And the woman was then brought to Pharaoh's house, and Abram grieved on account of his wife, and he prayed to the LORD to deliver her from the hands of Pharaoh. ¹⁷ And Sarai also prayed at that time and said, "O LORD God, You told my lord Abram to go from his land and from his father's house to the land of Canaan, and You promised to do well with him if he would perform Your commands; now behold, we have done that which You commanded us, and we left our land and our families, and we went to a strange land and to a

people whom we have not known before. ¹⁸ And we came to this land to avoid the famine, and this evil accident has befallen me; now therefore, O LORD God, deliver us and save us from the hand of this oppressor, and do well with me for the sake of Your mercy." ¹⁹ And the LORD listened to the voice of Sarai, and the LORD sent a messenger to deliver Sarai from the power of Pharaoh. ²⁰ And the king came and sat before Sarai, and behold, a messenger of the LORD was standing over them, and he appeared to Sarai and said to her, "Do not fear, for the LORD has heard your prayer." ²¹ And the king approached Sarai and said to her, "What is that man to you who brought you here?" And she said, "He is my brother." ²² And the king said, "It is incumbent on us to make him great, to elevate him and to do to him all the good which you will command us"; and at that time the king sent silver, and gold, and precious stones to Abram in abundance, together with cattle, menservants, and maidservants; and the king ordered Abram to be brought, and he sat in the court of the king's house, and the king greatly exalted Abram on that night. ²³ And the king approached to speak to Sarai, and he reached out his hand to touch her when the messenger struck him heavily, and he was terrified and he refrained from reaching to her. ²⁴ And when the king came near to Sarai, the messenger struck him to the ground, and acted thus to him the whole night, and the king was terrified. ²⁵ And on that night the messenger heavily struck all the servants of the king and his whole household on account of Sarai, and there was a great lamentation that night among the people of Pharaoh's house. ²⁶ And Pharaoh, seeing the evil that befell him, said, "Surely on account of this woman this thing has happened to me," and he removed himself at some distance from her and spoke pleasing words to her. ²⁷ And the king said to Sarai, "Please tell me concerning the man with whom you came here"; and Sarai said, "This man is my husband, and I said to you that he was my brother for I was afraid, lest you should put him to death through wickedness." ²⁸ And the king kept away from Sarai, and the plagues of the messenger of the LORD ceased from him and his household; and Pharaoh knew that he was smitten on account of Sarai, and the king was greatly astonished at this. ²⁹ And in the morning the king called for Abram and said to him, "What is this you have done to me? Why did you say, She is my sister, owing to which I took her to me for a wife, and this heavy plague has therefore come on me and my household? ³⁰ Now therefore, here is your wife, take her and go from our land lest we all die on her account." And Pharaoh took more cattle, menservants and maidservants, and silver and gold, to give to Abram, and he returned his wife Sarai to him. ³¹ And the king took a maiden whom he begot by his concubines, and he gave her to Sarai for a handmaid. ³² And the king said to his daughter, "It is better for you, my daughter,

to be a handmaid in this man's house than to be mistress in my house, after we have beheld the evil that befell us on account of this woman." ³³ And Abram arose, and he and all belonging to him went away from Egypt; and Pharaoh ordered some of his men to accompany him and all that went with him. ³⁴ And Abram returned to the land of Canaan, to the place where he had made the altar, where he at first had pitched his tent. ³⁵ And Lot the son of Haran, Abram's brother, had a heavy stock of cattle, flocks, and herds, and tents, for the LORD was bountiful to them on account of Abram. ³⁶ And when Abram was dwelling in the land, the herdsmen of Lot quarrelled with the herdsmen of Abram, for their property was too great for them to remain together in the land, and the land could not bear them on account of their cattle. ³⁷ And when Abram's herdsmen went to feed their flock, they would not go into the fields of the people of the land, but the cattle of Lot's herdsmen did otherwise, for they were allowed to feed in the fields of the people of the land. ³⁸ And the people of the land saw this occurrence daily, and they came to Abram and quarrelled with him on account of Lot's herdsmen. ³⁹ And Abram said to Lot, "What is this you are doing to me, to make me despicable to the inhabitants of the land, that you order your herdsman to feed your cattle in the fields of other people? Do you not know that I am a stranger in this land among the children of Canaan, and why will you do this to me?" ⁴⁰ And Abram quarrelled daily with Lot on account of this, but Lot would not listen to Abram, and he continued to do the same and the inhabitants of the land came and told Abram. ⁴¹ And Abram said to Lot, "How long will you be to me for a stumbling block with the inhabitants of the land? Now I implore you: let there no longer be quarrelling between us, for we are relatives. ⁴² But please separate from me, go and choose a place where you may dwell with your cattle and all belonging to you, but keep yourself at a distance from me—you and your household. ⁴³ And do not be afraid in going from me, for if anyone does harm to you, let me know and I will avenge your cause from him, only remove from me." ⁴⁴ And when Abram had spoken all these words to Lot, then Lot arose and lifted up his eyes toward the plain of Jordan. ⁴⁵ And he saw that the whole of this place was well watered, and good for man as well as affording pasture for the cattle. ⁴⁶ And Lot went from Abram to that place, and he pitched his tent there and he dwelt in Sodom, and they were separated from each other. ⁴⁷ And Abram dwelt in the plain of Mamre, which is in Hebron, and he pitched his tent there, and Abram remained in that place [for] many years.

CHAPTER 16

¹ At that time Chedorlaomer king of Elam sent to all the neighboring kings, to Nimrod king of Shinar, who was then under his power, and to Tidal king of

Goyim, and to Arioch king of Ellasar, with whom he made a covenant, saying, "Come up to me and assist me, that we may strike all the towns of Sodom and its inhabitants, for they have rebelled against me these thirteen years." ² And these four kings went up with all their camps, about eight hundred thousand men, and they went as they were, and struck every man they found in their road. ³ And the five kings of Sodom and Gomorrah—Shinab king of Admah, Shemeber king of Zeboyim, Bera king of Sodom, Bersha king of Gomorrah, and Bela king of Zoar—went out to meet them, and they all joined together in the Valley of Siddim. ⁴ And these nine kings made war in the Valley of Siddim; and the kings of Sodom and Gomorrah were smitten before the kings of Elam. ⁵ And the Valley of Siddim was full of lime pits and the kings of Elam pursued the kings of Sodom, and the kings of Sodom fled with their camps and fell into the lime pits, and all that remained went to the mountain for safety, and the five kings of Elam came after them and pursued them to the gates of Sodom, and they took all that there was in Sodom. ⁶ And they plundered all the cities of Sodom and Gomorrah, and they also took Lot, Abram's brother's son, and his property, and they seized all the goods of the cities of Sodom, and they went away; and Unic, Abram's servant, who was in the battle, saw this, and told Abram all that the kings had done to the cities of Sodom, and that Lot was taken captive by them. ⁷ And Abram heard this, and he rose up with about three hundred and eighteen men that were with him, and he pursued these kings that night and struck them, and they all fell before Abram and his men, and there was none remaining but the four kings who fled, and they each went his own way. ⁸ And Abram recovered all the property of Sodom, and he also recovered Lot and his property—his wives, and little ones, and all belonging to him—so that Lot lacked nothing. ⁹ And when he returned from striking these kings, he and his men passed the Valley of Siddim where the kings had made war together. ¹⁰ And Bera king of Sodom, and the rest of his men that were with him, went out from the lime pits into which they had fallen, to meet Abram and his men. ¹¹ And Adonizedek king of Jerusalem (the same was Shem) went out with his men to meet Abram and his people with bread and wine, and they remained together in the Valley of Melech. ¹² And Adonizedek blessed Abram, and Abram gave him a tenth from all that he had brought from the spoil of his enemies, for Adonizedek was a priest before God. ¹³ And all the kings of Sodom and Gomorrah who were there, with their servants, approached Abram and begged of him to return them their servants whom he had made captive, and to take to himself all the property. ¹⁴ And Abram answered the kings of Sodom, saying, "As the LORD lives who created the heavens and earth, and who redeemed my soul from all affliction, and who delivered me from my enemies this day, and gave them into my hand, I will not take anything belonging to you, that you may not boast tomorrow, saying, Abram became rich from our property that he saved. ¹⁵ For the LORD my God in whom I trust said to me, You will lack nothing, for I will bless you in all the works of your hands. ¹⁶ And now therefore, behold, here is all belonging to you—take it and go; as the LORD lives I will not take from you from a living soul down to a strap or thread, excepting the expense of the food of those who went out with me to battle, as also the portions of the men who went with me, Anar, Ashcol, and Mamre, they and their men, as well as those who had also remained to watch the baggage, they will take their portion of the spoil." ¹⁷ And the kings of Sodom gave Abram according to all that he had said, and they pressed him to take of whatever he chose, but he would not. ¹⁸ And he sent the kings of Sodom and the remainder of their men away, and he gave them orders about Lot, and they went to their respective places. ¹⁹ And Lot, his brother's son, he also sent away with his property, and he went with them, and Lot returned to his home, to Sodom, and Abram and his people returned to their home to the plains of Mamre, which is in Hebron. ²⁰ At that time the LORD appeared to Abram again, in Hebron, and He said to him, "Do not fear, your reward is very great before Me, for I will not leave you until I will have multiplied you, and blessed you, and made your seed like the stars in the heavens, which cannot be measured nor numbered. ²¹ And I will give to your seed all these lands that you see with your eyes, I will give them to them for an inheritance forever, only be strong and do not fear, walk before Me and be perfect." ²² And in the seventy-eighth year of the life of Abram, in that year Reu the son of Peleg died; and all the days of Reu were two hundred and thirty-nine years, and he died. ²³ And Sarai, the daughter of Haran, Abram's wife, was still barren in those days; she did not bear either son or daughter to Abram. ²⁴ And when she saw that she bore no children, she took her handmaid Hagar, whom Pharaoh had given her, and she gave her to her husband Abram for a wife. ²⁵ For Hagar learned all the ways of Sarai as Sarai taught her; she was not in any way deficient in following her good ways. ²⁶ And Sarai said to Abram, "Behold, here is my handmaid Hagar, go to her that she may bring out on my knees, that I may also obtain children through her." ²⁷ And at the end of ten years of Abram's dwelling in the land of Canaan, which is the eighty-fifth year of Abram's life, Sarai gave Hagar to him. ²⁸ And Abram listened to the voice of his wife Sarai and he took his handmaid Hagar, and Abram came to her and she conceived. ²⁹ And when Hagar saw that she had conceived she rejoiced greatly, and her mistress was despised in her eyes, and she said within herself, "This can only be that I am better before God than my mistress Sarai, for all the days that my mistress has been with my lord, she did not conceive, but the LORD has caused me in so short a time to conceive by him." [30] And when Sarai saw that Hagar had conceived by Abram, Sarai was jealous of her handmaid, and Sarai said within herself, "This is surely nothing else but that she must be better than I am." [31] And Sarai said to Abram, "My wrong be on you, for at the time when you prayed before the LORD for children, why did you not pray on my account that the LORD should give me seed from you? [32] And when I speak to Hagar in your presence, she despises my words, because she has conceived, and you will say nothing to her; may the LORD judge between me and you for what you have done to me." [33] And Abram said to Sarai, "Behold, your handmaid is in your hands, do to her as it may seem good in your eyes"; and Sarai afflicted her, and Hagar fled from her to the wilderness. [34] And [the] Messenger of the LORD found her by a well in the place where she had fled, and He said to her, "Do not fear, for I will multiply your seed, for you will bear a son and you will call his name Ishmael; now then, return to your mistress Sarai, and submit yourself under her hands." [35] And Hagar called the place of that well Beer-lahai-roi, it is between Kadesh and the wilderness of Bered. [36] And Hagar returned to her master's house at that time, and at the end of days Hagar bore a son to Abram, and Abram called his name Ishmael; and Abram was eighty-six years old when he begot him.

CHAPTER 17

[1] And in those days, in the ninety-first year of the life of Abram, the children of Chittim made war with the children of Tubal, for when the LORD had scattered the sons of men on the face of the earth, the children of Chittim went and embodied themselves in the plain of Canopia, and they built themselves cities there and dwelt by the River Tibreu. [2] And the children of Tubal dwelt in Tuscanah, and their boundaries reached the River Tibreu, and the children of Tubal built a city in Tuscanan, and they called the name Sabinah, after the name of Sabinah son of Tubal, their father, and they dwelt there to this day. [3] And it was at that time [that] the children of Chittim made war with the children of Tubal, and the children of Tubal were smitten before the children of Chittim, and the children of Chittim caused three hundred and seventy men to fall from the children of Tubal. [4] And at that time the children of Tubal swore to the children of Chittim, saying, "You will not intermarry among us, and no man will give his daughter to any of the sons of Chittim." [5] For all the daughters of Tubal were attractive in those days, for no women were then found in the whole earth as attractive as the daughters of Tubal. [6] And all who delighted in the beauty of women went to the daughters of Tubal and took wives from them, and the sons of men, kings and princes, who greatly delighted in the beauty of women, took wives in those days

from the daughters of Tubal. [7] And at the end of three years after the children of Tubal had sworn to the children of Chittim not to give them their daughters for wives, about twenty men of the children of Chittim went to take some of the daughters of Tubal, but they found none. [8] For the children of Tubal kept their oaths not to intermarry with them, and they would not break their oaths. [9] And in the days of harvest the children of Tubal went into their fields to get in their harvest, when the young men of Chittim assembled and went to the city of Sabinah, and each man took a young woman from the daughters of Tubal, and they came to their cities. [10] And the children of Tubal heard of it and they went to make war with them, and they could not prevail over them, for the mountain was exceedingly high from them, and when they saw they could not prevail over them they returned to their land. [11] And at the revolution of the year the children of Tubal went and hired about ten thousand men from those cities that were near them, and they went to war with the children of Chittim. [12] And the children of Tubal went to war with the children of Chittim, to destroy their land and to distress them, and in this engagement the children of Tubal prevailed over the children of Chittim, and the children of Chittim, seeing that they were greatly distressed, lifted up the children which they had had by the daughters of Tubal on the wall which had been built, to be before the eyes of the children of Tubal. [13] And the children of Chittim said to them, "Have you come to make war with your own sons and daughters, and have we not been considered your flesh and bones from that time until now?" [14] And when the children of Tubal heard this they ceased to make war with the children of Chittim, and they went away. [15] And they returned to their cities, and the children of Chittim assembled at that time and built two cities by the sea, and they called one Purtu and the other Ariza. [16] And Abram the son of Terah was then ninety-nine years old. [17] At that time the LORD appeared to him and He said to him, "I will make My covenant between me and you, and I will greatly multiply your seed, and this is the covenant which I make between Me and you: that every male child is circumcised—you and your seed after you. [18] At eight days old he will be circumcised, and this covenant will be in your flesh for a perpetual covenant. [19] And now therefore, your name will no longer be called Abram but Abraham, and your wife will no longer be called Sarai but Sarah. [20] For I will bless you both, and I will multiply your seed after you that you will become a great nation, and kings will come out from you."

CHAPTER 18

[1] And Abraham rose and did all that God had ordered him, and he took the men of his household and those bought with his money, and he circumcised them as the LORD had commanded him. [2] And there was not

JASHER

one left whom he did not circumcise, and Abraham and his son Ishmael were circumcised in the flesh of their foreskin; Ishmael was thirteen years old when he was circumcised in the flesh of his foreskin. ³And in the third day Abraham went out of his tent and sat at the door to enjoy the heat of the sun, during the pain of his flesh. ⁴And the LORD appeared to him in the plain of Mamre and sent three of His ministering messengers to visit him, and he was sitting at the door of the tent, and he lifted his eyes and saw, and behold, three men were coming from a distance, and he rose up and ran to meet them, and he bowed down to them, and brought them into his house. ⁵And he said to them, "If I have now found favor in your sight, turn in and eat a morsel of bread"; and he pressed them and they turned in, and he gave them water and they washed their feet, and he placed them under a tree at the door of the tent. ⁶And Abraham ran and took a calf, tender and good, and he hastened to kill it, and gave it to his servant Eliezer to dress. ⁷And Abraham came to Sarah in the tent, and he said to her, "Quickly make ready three measures of fine meal, knead it and make cakes to cover the pot containing the meat," and she did so. ⁸And Abraham hastened and brought before them butter and milk, beef and mutton, and gave it before them to eat before the flesh of the calf was sufficiently done, and they ate. ⁹And when they had finished eating, one of them said to him, "I will return to you according to the time of life, and your wife Sarah will have a son." ¹⁰And afterward the men departed and went their ways, to the places to which they were sent. ¹¹In those days all the people of Sodom and Gomorrah, and of the whole five cities, were exceedingly wicked and sinful against the LORD and they provoked the LORD with their abominations, and they strengthened in aging abominably and scornfully before the LORD, and their wickedness and crimes were great before the LORD in those days. ¹²And they had a very extensive valley in their land, about half a day's walk, and in it there were fountains of water and a great deal of herbage surrounding the water. ¹³And all the people of Sodom and Gomorrah went there four times in the year with their wives, and children, and all belonging to them, and they rejoiced there with timbrels and dances. ¹⁴And in the time of rejoicing they would all rise and lay hold of their neighbor's wives, and some, the virgin daughters of their neighbors, and they enjoyed them, and each man saw his wife and daughter in the hands of his neighbor and did not say a word. ¹⁵And they did so from morning to night, and afterward they returned home—each man to his house and each woman to her tent; so they always did four times in the year. ¹⁶Also when a stranger came into their cities and brought goods which he had purchased with a view to dispose of there, the people of these cities would assemble, men, women, and children, young and old, and go to the man and take his goods by force, giving a little to each man until there was an end to all the goods of the owner which he had brought into the land. ¹⁷And if the owner of the goods quarreled with them, saying, "What is this work which you have done to me?" then they would approach toward him one by one, and each would show him the little which he took and taunt him, saying, "I only took that little which you gave me"; and when he heard this from them all, he would arise and go from them in sorrow and bitterness of soul, when they would all arise and go after him, and drive him out of the city with great noise and tumult. ¹⁸And there was a man from the country of Elam who was leisurely going on the road, seated on his donkey, which carried a fine mantle of varying colors, and the mantle was bound with a cord on the donkey. ¹⁹And the man was on his journey passing through the street of Sodom when the sun set in the evening, and he remained there in order to abide during the night, but no one would let him into his house; and at that time there was a wicked and mischievous man in Sodom, one skillful to do evil, and his name was Hedad. ²⁰And he lifted up his eyes and saw the traveler in the street of the city, and he came to him and said, "From where do you come and to where do you go?" ²¹And the man said to him, "I am traveling from Hebron to Elam where I belong, and as I passed, the sun set and no one would permit me to enter his house, though I had bread, and water, and also straw and provender for my donkey, and am short of nothing." ²²And Hedad answered and said to him, "All that you will want will be supplied by me, but you will not abide in the street all night." ²³And Hedad brought him to his house, and he took off the mantle from the donkey with the cord, and brought them to his house, and he gave the donkey straw and provender while the traveler ate and drank in Hedad's house, and he stayed there that night. ²⁴And in the morning the traveler rose up early to continue his journey, when Hedad said to him, "Wait, comfort your heart with a morsel of bread and then go," and the man did so; and he remained with him, and they both ate and drank together during the day, when the man rose up to go. ²⁵And Hedad said to him, "Behold, now the day is declining, you had better remain all night that your heart may be comforted"; and he pressed him so that he tarried there all night, and on the second day he rose up early to go away, when Hedad pressed him, saying, "Comfort your heart with a morsel of bread and then go," and he remained and ate with him also the second day, and then the man rose up to continue his journey. ²⁶And Hedad said to him, "Behold, now the day is declining, remain with me to comfort your heart and in the morning rise up early and go your way." ²⁷And the man would not remain, but rose and saddled his donkey, and while he was saddling his donkey the wife of Hedad said to her husband, "Behold, this man has remained with us for two days eating and drinking and he has given us nothing, and now will he go away from us without giving anything?" And Hedad said to her, "Be silent." ²⁸ And the man saddled his donkey to go, and he asked Hedad to give him the cord and mantle to tie it on the donkey. ²⁹ And Hedad said to him, "What did you say?" And he said to him, "That you, my lord, will give me the cord and the mantle made with varying colors which you concealed with you in your house to take care of it." ³⁰ And Hedad answered the man, saying, "This is the interpretation of your dream: the cord which you saw means that your life will be lengthened out like a cord, and having seen the mantle colored with all sorts of colors, means that you will have a vineyard in which you will plant trees of all fruits." ³¹ And the traveler answered, saying, "Not so my lord, for I was awake when I gave you the cord and also a mantle woven with different colors, which you took off the donkey to put them away for me"; and Hedad answered and said, "Surely I have told you the interpretation of your dream and it is a good dream, and this is the interpretation thereof. ³² Now the sons of men give me four pieces of silver, which is my charge for interpreting dreams, and of you only I require three pieces of silver." ³³ And the man was provoked at the words of Hedad, and he cried bitterly, and he brought Hedad to Serak, judge of Sodom. ³⁴ And the man laid his cause before Serak the judge, when Hedad replied, saying, "It is not so, but thus the matter stands"; and the judge said to the traveler, "This man Hedad tells you the truth, for he is famed in the cities for the accurate interpretation of dreams." ³⁵ And the man cried at the word of the judge, and he said, "Not so my Lord, for it was in the day that I gave him the cord and mantle which was on the donkey in order to put them away in his house"; and they both disputed before the judge, the one saying, "Thus the matter was," and the other declaring otherwise. ³⁶ And Hedad said to the man, "Give me four pieces of silver that I charge for my interpretations of dreams; I will not make any allowance; and give me the expense of the four meals that you ate in my house." ³⁷ And the man said to Hedad, "Truly I will pay you for what I ate in your house, only give me the cord and mantle which you concealed in your house." ³⁸ And Hedad replied before the judge and said to the man, "Did I not tell you the interpretation of your dream? The cord means that your days will be prolonged like a cord, and the mantle, that you will have a vineyard in which you will plant all kinds of fruit trees. ³⁹ This is the proper interpretation of your dream—now give me the four pieces of silver that I require as a compensation, for I will make you no allowance." ⁴⁰ And the man cried at the words of Hedad and they both quarreled before the judge, and the judge gave orders to his servants, who drove them rashly from the house. ⁴¹ And they went away quarreling from the judge, when the people of Sodom heard them, and they gathered around them and they exclaimed against the stranger, and they drove him rashly from the city. ⁴² And the man continued his journey on his donkey with bitterness of soul, lamenting and weeping. ⁴³ And while he was going along, he wept at what had happened to him in the corrupt city of Sodom.

CHAPTER 19

¹ And the cities of Sodom had four judges for [the] four cities, and these were their names: Serak in the city of Sodom, Sharkad in Gomorrah, Zabnac in Admah, and Menon in Zeboyim. ² And Abraham's servant Eliezer applied different names to them, and he converted Serak to Shakra, Sharkad to Shakrura, Zebnac to Kezobim, and Menon to Matzlodin. ³ And by desire of their four judges the people of Sodom and Gomorrah had beds erected in the streets of the cities, and if a man came to these places, they laid hold of him and brought him to one of their beds, and by force made him to lie in them. ⁴ And as he lay down, three men would stand at his head and three at his feet, and measure him by the length of the bed, and if the man was less than the bed these six men would stretch him at each end, and when he cried out to them, they would not answer him. ⁵ And if he was longer than the bed, they would draw together the two sides of the bed at each end, until the man had reached the gates of death. ⁶ And if he continued to cry out to them, they would answer him, saying, "Thus it will be done to a man that comes into our land." ⁷ And when men heard all these things that the people of the cities of Sodom did, they refrained from coming there. ⁸ And when a poor man came to their land, they would give him silver and gold, and cause a proclamation in the whole city not to give him a morsel of bread to eat, and if the stranger should remain there some days and die from hunger, not having been able to obtain a morsel of bread, then at his death all the people of the city would come and take their silver and gold which they had given to him. ⁹ And those that could recognize the silver or gold which they had given him took it back, and at his death they also stripped him of his garments, and they would fight about them, and he that prevailed over his neighbor took them. ¹⁰ After that they would carry him and bury him under some of the shrubs in the deserts; so they did all the days to anyone that came to them and died in their land. ¹¹ And in the course of time Sarah sent Eliezer to Sodom to see Lot and inquire after his welfare. ¹² And Eliezer went to Sodom, and he met a man of Sodom fighting with a stranger, and the man of Sodom stripped the poor man of all his clothes and went away. ¹³ And this poor man cried to Eliezer and supplicated his favor on account of what the man of Sodom had done to him. ¹⁴ And he said to him, "Why do you act thus to the poor man who came to your land?" ¹⁵ And the man of Sodom answered Eliezer, saying, "Is this man your brother, or have the people

of Sodom made you a judge this day, that you speak about this man?" ¹⁶ And Eliezer strove with the man of Sodom on account of the poor man, and when Eliezer approached to recover the poor man's clothes from the man of Sodom, he hastened and with a stone struck Eliezer in the forehead. ¹⁷ And the blood flowed copiously from Eliezer's forehead, and when the man saw the blood he caught hold of Eliezer, saying, "Give me my hire for having rid you of this bad blood that was in your forehead, for such is the custom and the law in our land." ¹⁸ And Eliezer said to him, "You have wounded me and require me to pay you your hire?" And Eliezer would not listen to the words of the man of Sodom. ¹⁹ And the man laid hold of Eliezer and brought him to Shakra the judge of Sodom for judgment. ²⁰ And the man spoke to the judge, saying, "I implore you my lord, thus this man has done, for I struck him with a stone that the blood flowed from his forehead, and he is unwilling to give me my hire." ²¹ And the judge said to Eliezer, "This man speaks truth to you, give him his hire, for this is the custom in our land"; and Eliezer heard the words of the judge, and he lifted up a stone and struck the judge, and the stone struck on his forehead, and the blood flowed copiously from the forehead of the judge, and Eliezer said, "If this then is the custom in your land, [then] you give to this man what I should have given him, for this has been your decision—you decreed it." ²² And Eliezer left the man of Sodom with the judge, and he went away. ²³ And when the kings of Elam had made war with the kings of Sodom, the kings of Elam captured all the property of Sodom, and they took Lot captive, with his property, and when it was told to Abraham he went and made war with the kings of Elam, and he recovered from their hands all the property of Lot as well as the property of Sodom. ²⁴ At that time the wife of Lot bore him a daughter, and he called her name Paltith, saying, "Because God had delivered him and his whole household from the kings of Elam"; and Paltith daughter of Lot grew up, and one of the men of Sodom took her for a wife. ²⁵ And a poor man came into the city to seek a maintenance, and he remained in the city some days, and all the people of Sodom caused a proclamation of their custom not to give this man a morsel of bread to eat until he dropped dead on the earth, and they did so. ²⁶ And Paltith the daughter of Lot saw this man lying in the streets starved with hunger, and no one would give him anything to keep him alive, and he was just on the point of death. ²⁷ And her soul was filled with pity on account of the man, and she fed him secretly with bread for many days, and the soul of this man was revived. ²⁸ For when she went out to fetch water, she would put the bread in the water pitcher, and when she came to the place where the poor man was, she took the bread from the pitcher and gave it to him to eat; so she did [for] many days. ²⁹ And all the people of Sodom and Gomorrah wondered how this man could bear starvation for so many days. ³⁰ And they said to each other, "This can only be that he eats and drinks, for no man can bear starvation for so many days or live as this man has without even his countenance changing"; and three men concealed themselves in a place where the poor man was stationed to know who it was that brought him bread to eat. ³¹ And Paltith daughter of Lot went out that day to fetch water, and she put bread into her pitcher of water, and she went to draw water by the poor man's place, and she took out the bread from the pitcher and gave it to the poor man and he ate it. ³² And the three men saw what Paltith did to the poor man, and they said to her, "It is you then who have supported him, and therefore he has not starved, nor changed in appearance, nor died like the rest." ³³ And the three men went out of the place in which they were concealed, and they seized Paltith and the bread which was in the poor man's hand. ³⁴ And they took Paltith and brought her before their judges, and they said to them, "Thus did she do, and it is she who supplied the poor man with bread, therefore he did not die all this time; now therefore, declare to us the punishment due to this woman for having transgressed our law." ³⁵ And the people of Sodom and Gomorrah assembled and kindled a fire in the street of the city, and they took the woman and cast her into the fire and she was burned to ashes. ³⁶ And in the city of Admah there was a woman to whom they did the like. ³⁷ For a traveler came into the city of Admah to abide there all night with the intention of going home in the morning, and he sat opposite the door of the house of the young woman's father to remain there, as the sun had set when he had reached that place; and the young woman saw him sitting by the door of the house. ³⁸ And he asked her for a drink of water, and she said to him, "Who are you?" And he said to her, "I was going on the road this day, and reached here when the sun set, so I will abide here all night, and in the morning I will arise early and continue my journey." ³⁹ And the young woman went into the house and fetched the man bread and water to eat and drink. ⁴⁰ And this affair became known to the people of Admah, and they assembled and brought the young woman before the judges that they should judge her for this act. ⁴¹ And the judge said, "The judgment of death must pass on this woman because she transgressed our law, and therefore this is the decision concerning her." ⁴² And the people of those cities assembled and brought out the young woman, and anointed her with honey from head to foot, as the judge had decreed, and they placed her before a swarm of bees which were then in their hives, and the bees flew on her and stung her that her whole body was swelled. ⁴³ And the young woman cried out on account of the bees, but no one took notice of her or pitied her, and her cries ascended to Heaven. ⁴⁴ And the LORD was provoked at this and at all the works of the cities of Sodom, for they had abundance of food, and had tranquility among them, and still would not sustain the poor and the needy, and in those days their evil doings and sins became great before the LORD. ⁴⁵ And the LORD sent for two of the messengers that had come to Abraham's house to destroy Sodom and its cities. ⁴⁶ And the messengers rose up from the door of Abraham's tent after they had eaten and drunk, and they reached Sodom in the evening, and Lot was then sitting in the gate of Sodom, and when he saw them, he rose to meet them, and he bowed down to the ground. ⁴⁷ And he pressed them greatly and brought them into his house, and he gave them victuals which they ate, and they stayed all night in his house. ⁴⁸ And the messengers said to Lot, "Arise, go out from this place, you and all belonging to you, lest you be consumed in the iniquity of this city, for the LORD will destroy this place." ⁴⁹ And the messengers laid hold on the hand of Lot, and on the hand of his wife, and on the hands of his children, and all belonging to him, and they brought him out and set him outside the cities. ⁵⁰ And they said to Lot, "Escape for your life," and he fled and all belonging to him. ⁵¹ Then the LORD rained on Sodom, and on Gomorrah, and on all these cities brimstone and fire from the LORD out of Heaven. ⁵² And he overthrew these cities, all the plain, and all the inhabitants of the cities, and that which grew on the ground; and Ado the wife of Lot looked back to see the destruction of the cities, for her compassion was moved on account of her daughters who remained in Sodom, for they did not go with her. ⁵³ And when she looked back, she became a pillar of salt, and it is yet in that place to this day. ⁵⁴ And the oxen which stood in that place daily licked up the salt to the extremities of their feet, and in the morning it would spring out afresh, and they again licked it up to this day. ⁵⁵ And Lot and two of his daughters that remained with him fled and escaped to the cave of Adullam, and they remained there for some time. ⁵⁶ And Abraham rose up early in the morning to see what had been done to the cities of Sodom; and he looked and beheld the smoke of the cities going up like the smoke of a furnace. ⁵⁷ And Lot and his two daughters remained in the cave, and they made their father drink wine, and they lay with him, for they said there was no man on earth that could raise up seed from them, for they thought that the whole earth was destroyed. ⁵⁸ And they both lay with their father, and they conceived and bore sons, and the firstborn called the name of her son Moab, saying, "From my father I conceived him"; he is the father of the Moabites to this day. ⁵⁹ And the younger also called her son Benami; he is the father of the children of Ammon to this day. ⁶⁰ And after this, Lot and his two daughters went away from there, and he dwelt on the other side of the Jordan with his two daughters and their sons, and the sons of Lot grew up, and they went and took wives [for] themselves from the land of Canaan, and

they begot children, and they were fruitful and multiplied.

CHAPTER 20

¹ And at that time Abraham journeyed from the plain of Mamre, and he went to the land of the Philistines, and he dwelt in Gerar; it was in the twenty-fifth year of Abraham's being in the land of Canaan, and the one hundredth year of the life of Abraham, that he came to Gerar in the land of the Philistines. ² And when they entered the land he said to his wife Sarah, "Say you are my sister to anyone that will ask you in order that we may escape the evil of the inhabitants of the land." ³ And as Abraham was dwelling in the land of the Philistines, the servants of Abimelech, king of the Philistines, saw that Sarah was exceedingly beautiful, and they asked Abraham concerning her, and he said, "She is my sister." ⁴ And the servants of Abimelech went to Abimelech, saying, "A man from the land of Canaan has come to dwell in the land, and he has a sister that is exceedingly attractive." ⁵ And Abimelech heard the words of his servants who praised Sarah to him, and Abimelech sent his officers, and they brought Sarah to the king. ⁶ And Sarah came to the house of Abimelech, and the king saw that Sarah was beautiful, and she pleased him exceedingly. ⁷ And he approached her and said to her, "What is that man to you with whom you came to our land?" And Sarah answered and said, "He is my brother, and we came from the land of Canaan to dwell wherever we could find a place." ⁸ And Abimelech said to Sarah, "Behold, my land is before you: place your brother in any part of this land that pleases you, and it will be our duty to exalt and elevate him above all the people of the land since he is your brother." ⁹ And Abimelech sent for Abraham, and Abraham came to Abimelech. ¹⁰ And Abimelech said to Abraham, "Behold, I have given orders that you will be honored as you desire on account of your sister Sarah." ¹¹ And Abraham went out from the king, and the king's present followed him. ¹² As at evening time, before men lie down to rest, the king was sitting on his throne, and a deep sleep fell on him, and he lay on the throne and slept until morning. ¹³ And he dreamed that a messenger of the LORD came to him with a drawn sword in his hand, and the messenger stood over Abimelech and wished to slay him with the sword, and the king was terrified in his dream, and said to the messenger, "In what have I sinned against you that you come to slay me with your sword?" ¹⁴ And the messenger answered and said to Abimelech, "Behold, you die on account of the woman which you brought to your house last night, for she is a married woman, the wife of Abraham who came to your house; now therefore, return that man his wife, for she is his wife; and should you not return her, know that you will surely die—you and all belonging to you." ¹⁵ And on

JASHER

that night there was a great outcry in the land of the Philistines, and the inhabitants of the land saw the figure of a man standing with a drawn sword in his hand, and he struck the inhabitants of the land with the sword, yes, he continued to strike them. ¹⁶ And the messenger of the LORD struck the whole land of the Philistines on that night, and there was a great confusion on that night and on the following morning. ¹⁷ And every womb was closed, and all their issues, and the hand of the LORD was on them on account of Sarah, wife of Abraham, whom Abimelech had taken. ¹⁸ And in the morning Abimelech rose with terror, and confusion, and with a great dread, and he sent and had his servants called in, and he related his dream to them, and the people were greatly afraid. ¹⁹ And one man standing among the servants of the king answered the king, saying, "O sovereign king, restore this woman to her husband, for he is her husband, for the like happened to the king of Egypt when this man came to Egypt. ²⁰ And he said concerning his wife, She is my sister, for such is his manner of doing when he comes to dwell in the land in which he is a stranger. ²¹ And Pharaoh sent and took this woman for a wife and the LORD brought grievous plagues on him until he returned the woman to her husband. ²² Now therefore, O sovereign king, know what happened last night to the whole land, for there was a very great consternation, and great pain, and lamentation, and we know that it was on account of the woman which you took. ²³ Now, therefore, restore this woman to her husband, lest it should befall us as it did to Pharaoh king of Egypt and his subjects, and that we may not die"; and Abimelech hastened, and called, and had Sarah called for, and she came before him, and he had Abraham called for, and he came before him. ²⁴ And Abimelech said to them, "What is this work you have been doing in saying you are brother and sister, and I took this woman for a wife?" ²⁵ And Abraham said, "Because I thought I should suffer death on account of my wife"; and Abimelech took flocks, and herds, and menservants, and maidservants, and one thousand pieces of silver, and he gave them to Abraham, and he returned Sarah to him. ²⁶ And Abimelech said to Abraham, "Behold, the whole land is before you, dwell in it wherever you will choose." ²⁷ And Abraham and his wife Sarah went out from the king's presence with honor and respect, and they dwelt in the land, even in Gerar. ²⁸ And all the inhabitants of the land of the Philistines and the king's servants were still in pain through the plague which the messenger had inflicted on them the whole night on account of Sarah. ²⁹ And Abimelech sent for Abraham, saying, "Now pray to the LORD your God for your servants, that He may put away this mortality from among us." ³⁰ And Abraham prayed on account of Abimelech and his subjects, and the LORD heard the prayer of Abraham, and He healed Abimelech and all his subjects.

CHAPTER 21

¹ And it was at that time, at the end of a year and four months of Abraham's dwelling in the land of the Philistines in Gerar, that God visited Sarah, and the LORD remembered her, and she conceived and bore a son to Abraham. ² And Abraham called the name of the son which was born to him, which Sarah bore to him, Isaac. ³ And Abraham circumcised his son Isaac at eight days old as God had commanded Abraham to do to his seed after him; and Abraham was one hundred, and Sarah ninety years old, when Isaac was born to them. ⁴ And the child grew up and he was weaned, and Abraham made a great feast on the day that Isaac was weaned. ⁵ And Shem, and Eber, and all the great people of the land, and Abimelech king of the Philistines, and his servants, and Phicol, the captain of his host, came to eat, and drink, and rejoice at the feast which Abraham made on the day of his son Isaac's being weaned. ⁶ Also Terah, the father of Abraham, and Nahor his brother, came from Haran, they and all belonging to them, for they greatly rejoiced on hearing that a son had been born to Sarah. ⁷ And they came to Abraham, and they ate and drank at the feast which Abraham made on the day of Isaac's being weaned. ⁸ And Terah and Nahor rejoiced with Abraham, and they remained with him many days in the land of the Philistines. ⁹ At that time Serug the son of Reu died, in the first year of the birth of Isaac son of Abraham. ¹⁰ And all the days of Serug were two hundred and thirty-nine years, and he died. ¹¹ And Ishmael the son of Abraham had grown up in those days; he was fourteen years old when Sarah bore Isaac to Abraham. ¹² And God was with Ishmael the son of Abraham, and he grew up, and he learned to use the bow and became an archer. ¹³ And when Isaac was five years old, he was sitting with Ishmael at the door of the tent. ¹⁴ And Ishmael came to Isaac and seated himself opposite to him, and he took the bow, and drew it, and put the arrow in it, and intended to slay Isaac. ¹⁵ And Sarah saw the act which Ishmael desired to do to her son Isaac, and it grieved her exceedingly on account of her son, and she sent for Abraham, and said to him, "Cast out this bondwoman and her son, for her son will not be heir with my son, for thus he sought to do to him this day." ¹⁶ And Abraham listened to the voice of Sarah, and he rose up early in the morning, and he took twelve loaves and a bottle of water which he gave to Hagar, and sent her away with her son, and Hagar went with her son to the wilderness, and they dwelt in the wilderness of Paran with the inhabitants of the wilderness, and Ishmael was an archer, and he dwelt in the wilderness a long time. ¹⁷ And afterward he and his mother went to the land of Egypt, and they dwelt there, and Hagar took a wife for her son from Egypt, and her name was Meribah. ¹⁸ And the wife of Ishmael conceived and bore four sons and two daughters, and afterward Ishmael, and his mother, and his wife and children

went and returned to the wilderness. ¹⁹ And they made themselves tents in the wilderness, in which they dwelt, and they continued to travel and then to rest monthly and yearly. ²⁰ And God gave Ishmael flocks, and herds, and tents on account of his father Abraham, and the man increased in cattle. ²¹ And Ishmael dwelt in deserts and in tents, traveling and resting for a long time, and he did not see the face of his father. ²² And some time after, Abraham said to his wife Sarah, "I will go and see my son Ishmael, for I have a desire to see him, for I have not seen him for a long time." ²³ And Abraham rode on one of his camels to the wilderness to seek his son Ishmael, for he heard that he was dwelling in a tent in the wilderness with all belonging to him. ²⁴ And Abraham went to the wilderness, and he reached the tent of Ishmael about noon, and he asked after Ishmael, and he found the wife of Ishmael sitting in the tent with her children, and her husband Ishmael and his mother were not with them. ²⁵ And Abraham asked the wife of Ishmael, saying, "Where has Ishmael gone?" And she said, "He has gone to the field to hunt," and Abraham was still mounted on the camel, for he would not get off to the ground as he had sworn to his wife Sarah that he would not get off from the camel. ²⁶ And Abraham said to Ishmael's wife, "My daughter, give me a little water that I may drink, for I am fatigued from the journey." ²⁷ And Ishmael's wife answered and said to Abraham, "We have neither water nor bread," and she continued sitting in the tent and did not notice Abraham, neither did she ask him who he was. ²⁸ But she was beating her children in the tent, and she was cursing them, and she also cursed her husband Ishmael and reproached him, and Abraham heard the words of Ishmael's wife to her children, and he was very angry and displeased. ²⁹ And Abraham called to the woman to come out to him from the tent, and the woman came and stood opposite to Abraham, for Abraham was still mounted on the camel. ³⁰ And Abraham said to Ishmael's wife, "When your husband Ishmael returns home say to him that a very old man from the land of the Philistines came here to seek you, and thus was his appearance and figure; ³¹ I did not ask him who he was, and seeing you were not here he spoke to me and said, When your husband Ishmael returns, tell him thus this man said, When you come home, put away this nail of the tent which you have placed here, and place another nail in its stead." ³² And Abraham finished his instructions to the woman, and he turned and went off on the camel homeward. ³³ And after that, Ishmael came from the chase—he and his mother—and returned to the tent, and his wife spoke these words to him, ³⁴ "A very old man from the land of the Philistines came to seek you, and thus was his appearance and figure; I did not ask him who he was, and seeing you were not at home he said to me, When your husband comes home tell him, thus says the old man, Put away the nail of the tent

which you have placed here and place another nail in its stead." ³⁵ And Ishmael heard the words of his wife, and he knew that it was his father, and that his wife did not honor him. ³⁶ And Ishmael understood his father's words that he had spoken to his wife, and Ishmael listened to the voice of his father, and Ishmael cast off that woman and she went away. ³⁷ And afterward Ishmael went to the land of Canaan, and he took another wife, and he brought her to his tent to the place where he then dwelt. ³⁸ And at the end of three years Abraham said, "I will again go and see my son Ishmael, for I have not seen him for a long time." ³⁹ And he rode on his camel, and went to the wilderness, and he reached the tent of Ishmael about noon. ⁴⁰ And he asked after Ishmael, and his wife came out of the tent and she said, "He is not here my lord, for he has gone to hunt in the fields, and to feed the camels," and the woman said to Abraham, "Turn in, my lord, into the tent, and eat a morsel of bread, for your soul must be wearied on account of the journey." ⁴¹ And Abraham said to her, "I will not stop for I am in haste to continue my journey, but give me a little water to drink, for I have thirst"; and the woman hastened, and ran into the tent, and she brought out water and bread to Abraham, which she placed before him and she urged him to eat, and he ate and drank, and his heart was comforted, and he blessed his son Ishmael. ⁴² And he finished his meal, and he blessed the LORD, and he said to Ishmael's wife, "When Ishmael comes home say these words to him: ⁴³ A very old man from the land of the Philistines came here and asked after you, and you were not here; and I brought him out bread and water, and he ate and drank, and his heart was comforted. ⁴⁴ And he spoke these words to me: When your husband Ishmael comes home, say to him, The nail of the tent which you have is very good, do not put it away from the tent." ⁴⁵ And Abraham finished commanding the woman, and he rode off to his home, to the land of the Philistines; and when Ishmael came to his tent his wife went out to meet him with joy and a cheerful heart. ⁴⁶ And she said to him, "An old man came here from the land of the Philistines and thus was his appearance, and he asked after you and you were not here, so I brought out bread and water, and he ate and drank, and his heart was comforted. ⁴⁷ And he spoke these words to me: When your husband Ishmael comes home, say to him, The nail of the tent which you have is very good, do not put it away from the tent." ⁴⁸ And Ishmael knew that it was his father, and that his wife had honored him, and the LORD blessed Ishmael.

CHAPTER 22

¹ And Ishmael then rose up and took his wife, and his children, and his cattle, and all belonging to him, and he journeyed from there and he went to his father in the land of the Philistines. ² And Abraham related to

his son Ishmael the transaction with the first wife that Ishmael took, according to what she did. ³ And Ishmael and his children dwelt with Abraham many days in that land, and Abraham dwelt in the land of the Philistines a long time. ⁴ And the days increased and reached twenty six years, and after that, Abraham with his servants and all belonging to him went from the land of the Philistines and removed to a great distance, and they came near to Hebron, and they remained there, and the servants of Abraham dug wells of water, and Abraham and all belonging to him dwelt by the water, and the servants of Abimelech king of the Philistines heard the report that Abraham's servants had dug wells of water in the borders of the land. ⁵ And they came and quarreled with the servants of Abraham, and they robbed them of the great well which they had dug. ⁶ And Abimelech king of the Philistines heard of this affair, and he with Phicol the captain of his host and twenty of his men came to Abraham, and Abimelech spoke to Abraham concerning his servants, and Abraham rebuked Abimelech concerning the well of which his servants had robbed him. ⁷ And Abimelech said to Abraham, "As the LORD lives who created the whole earth, I did not hear of the act which my servants did to your servants until this day." ⁸ And Abraham took seven ewe lambs and gave them to Abimelech, saying, "Please take these from my hands that it may be a testimony for me that I dug this well." ⁹ And Abimelech took the seven ewe lambs which Abraham had given to him, for he had also given him cattle and herds in abundance, and Abimelech swore to Abraham concerning the well, therefore he called that well Beersheba, for there they both swore concerning it. ¹⁰ And they both made a covenant in Beersheba, and Abimelech rose up with Phicol the captain of his host and all his men, and they returned to the land of the Philistines, and Abraham and all belonging to him dwelt in Beersheba, and he was in that land a long time. ¹¹ And Abraham planted a large grove in Beersheba, and he made four gates to it facing the four sides of the earth, and he planted a vineyard in it, so that if a traveler came to Abraham, he entered any gate which was in his road and remained there, and ate, and drank, and satisfied himself, and then departed. ¹² For the house of Abraham was always open to the sons of men that passed and repassed, who came daily to eat and drink in the house of Abraham. ¹³ And any man who had hunger and came to Abraham's house, Abraham would give him bread that he might eat, and drink, and be satisfied, and anyone that came naked to his house he would clothe with garments as he might choose, and give him silver and gold, and make known to him the LORD who had created him in the earth; Abraham did this all his life. ¹⁴ And Abraham, and his children, and all belonging to him dwelt in Beersheba, and he pitched his tent as far as Hebron. ¹⁵ And Abraham's brother Nahor, and

his father, and all belonging to them dwelt in Haran, for they did not come with Abraham to the land of Canaan. ¹⁶ And children were born to Nahor which Milca the daughter of Haran, and sister to Sarah, Abraham's wife, bore to him. ¹⁷ And these are the names of those that were born to him: Uz, Buz, Kemuel, Kesed, Chazo, Pildash, Tidlaf, and Bethuel, being eight sons, these are the children of Milca which she bore to Nahor, Abraham's brother. ¹⁸ And Nahor had a concubine, and her name was Reumah, and she also bore to Nahor: Zebach, Gachash, Tachash, and Maacha, being four sons. ¹⁹ And the children that were born to Nahor were twelve sons besides his daughters, and they also had children born to them in Haran. ²⁰ And the children of Uz the firstborn of Nahor were Abi, Cheref, Gadin, Melus, and their sister Deborah. ²¹ And the sons of Buz were Berachel, Naamath, Sheva, and Madonu. ²² And the sons of Kemuel were Aram and Rechob. ²³ And the sons of Kesed were Anamlech, Meshai, Benon, and Yifi. And the sons of Chazo were Pildash, Mechi, and Opher. ²⁴ And the sons of Pildash were Arud, Chamum, Mered, and Moloch. ²⁵ And the sons of Tidlaf were Mushan, Cushan, and Mutzi. ²⁶ And the children of Bethuel were Sechar, Laban, and their sister Rebekah. ²⁷ These are the families of the children of Nahor that were born to them in Haran; and Aram the son of Kemuel and his brother Rechob went away from Haran, and they found a valley in the land by the River Euphrates. ²⁸ And they built a city there, and they called the name of the city after the name of Pethor the son of Aram, that is Aram Naharayim to this day. ²⁹ And the children of Kesed also went to dwell where they could find a place, and they went and they found a valley opposite to the land of Shinar, and they dwelt there. ³⁰ And they built themselves a city there, and they called the name of the city Kesed after the name of their father, that is the land Kasdim to this day, and the Kasdim dwelt in that land, and they were fruitful and multiplied exceedingly. ³¹ And Terah, father of Nahor and Abraham, went and took another wife in his old age, and her name was Pelilah, and she conceived and bore him a son, and he called his name Zoba. ³² And Terah lived twenty-five years after he begot Zoba. ³³ And Terah died in that year, that is in the thirty-fifth year of the birth of Isaac son of Abraham. ³⁴ And the days of Terah were two hundred and five years, and he was buried in Haran. ³⁵ And Zoba the son of Terah lived thirty years and he begot Aram, Achlis, and Merik. ³⁶ And Aram son of Zoba, son of Terah, had three wives and he begot twelve sons and three daughters; and the LORD gave riches and possessions, and abundance of cattle, and flocks, and herds to Aram the son of Zoba, and the man increased greatly. ³⁷ And Aram the son of Zoba, and his brother, and all his household journeyed from Haran, and they went to dwell where they should find a place, for their property was too great to remain in Haran; for they could not stop in Haran together with their brothers, the children of Nahor. [38] And Aram the son of Zoba went with his brothers, and they found a valley at a distance toward the eastern country, and they dwelt there. [39] And they also built a city there, and they called the name thereof Aram, after the name of their eldest brother; that is Aram Zoba to this day. [40] And Isaac the son of Abraham was growing up in those days, and his father Abraham taught him the way of the LORD to know the LORD, and the LORD was with him. [41] And when Isaac was thirty-seven years old, his brother Ishmael was going around with him in the tent. [42] And Ishmael boasted of himself to Isaac, saying, "I was thirteen years old when the LORD spoke to my father to circumcise us, and I did according to the word of the LORD which He spoke to my father, and I gave my soul to the LORD, and I did not transgress His word which He commanded my father." [43] And Isaac answered Ishmael, saying, "Why do you boast to me about this, about a little bit of your flesh which you took from your body, concerning which the LORD commanded you? [44] As the LORD lives, the God of my father Abraham, if the LORD should say to my father, Now take your son Isaac and bring him up [as] an offering before Me, I would not refrain but I would joyfully accede to it." [45] And the LORD heard the word that Isaac spoke to Ishmael, and it seemed good in the sight of the LORD, and he thought to try Abraham in this matter. [46] And the day arrived when the sons of God came and placed themselves before the LORD, and Satan also came with the sons of God before the LORD. [47] And the LORD said to Satan, "From where do you come?" And Satan answered the LORD and said, "From going to and fro in the earth, and from walking up and down in it." [48] And the LORD said to Satan, "What is your word to Me concerning all the children of the earth?" And Satan answered the LORD and said, "I have seen all the children of the earth who serve You and remember You when they require anything from You. [49] And when You give them the thing which they require from You, they sit at their ease, and forsake You, and they no longer remember You. [50] Have You seen Abraham the son of Terah, who at first had no children, and he served You and erected altars to You wherever he came, and he brought up offerings on them, and he proclaimed Your Name continually to all the children of the earth? [51] And now that his son Isaac is born to him, he has forsaken You; he has made a great feast for all the inhabitants of the land, and he has forgotten the LORD. [52] For amidst all that he has done, he brought You no offering; neither burnt-offering nor peace offering, neither ox, lamb, nor goat of all that he killed on the day that his son was weaned. [53] Even from the time of his son's birth until now, being thirty-seven years, he built no altar before You, nor brought any offering to You, for he saw that You gave what he requested before You, and therefore he forsook You." [54] And the LORD said to Satan, "Have you thus considered My servant Abraham? For there is none like him on earth, a perfect and an upright man before Me, one that fears God and avoids evil; as I live, were I to say to him, Bring up your son Isaac before Me, he would not withhold him from Me, much more if I told him to bring up a burnt-offering before Me from his flock or herds." [55] And Satan answered the LORD and said, "Then speak to Abraham now as You have said, and you will see whether he will not transgress and cast aside Your words this day."

CHAPTER 23

[1] At that time the word of the LORD came to Abraham, and He said to him, "Abraham," and he said, "Here I am." [2] And He said to him, "Now take your son, your only son, whom you love, even Isaac, and go to the land of Moriah, and offer him there for a burnt-offering on one of the mountains which will be shown to you, for there you will see a cloud and the glory of the LORD." [3] And Abraham said within himself, "How will I separate my son Isaac from his mother Sarah in order to bring him up for a burnt-offering before the LORD?" [4] And Abraham came into the tent, and he sat before his wife Sarah, and he spoke these words to her, [5] "My son Isaac has grown up and he has not for some time studied the service of his God; now tomorrow I will go and bring him to Shem and his son Eber, and there he will learn the ways of the LORD, for they will teach him to know the LORD as well as to know that when he prays continually before the LORD, He will answer him; therefore there he will know the way of serving the LORD his God." [6] And Sarah said, "You have spoken well. Go, my lord, and do to him as you have said, but do not remove him at a great distance from me, neither let him remain there too long, for my soul is bound within his soul." [7] And Abraham said to Sarah, "My daughter, let us pray to the LORD our God that He may do good with us." [8] And Sarah took her son Isaac and he remained all that night with her, and she kissed and embraced him, and gave him instructions until morning. [9] And she said to him, "O my son, how can my soul separate itself from you?" And she still kissed him and embraced him, and she gave Abraham instructions concerning him. [10] And Sarah said to Abraham, "O my lord, please take heed of your son, and place your eyes over him, for I have no other son nor daughter but him. [11] O do not forsake him. If he is hungry, give him bread, and if he is thirsty, give him water to drink; do not let him go on foot, neither let him sit in the sun. [12] Neither let him go by himself in the road, neither force him from whatever he may desire, but do to him as he may say to you." [13] And Sarah wept bitterly the whole night on account of Isaac, and she gave him instructions until morning. [14] And in the morning

Sarah selected a very fine and beautiful garment from those garments which she had in the house, that Abimelech had given to her. ¹⁵ And she dressed her son Isaac with that, and she put a turban on his head, and she enclosed a precious stone in the top of the turban, and she gave them provision for the road, and they went out, and Isaac went with his father Abraham, and some of their servants accompanied them to see them off the road. ¹⁶ And Sarah went out with them, and she accompanied them on the road to see them off, and they said to her, "Return to the tent." ¹⁷ And when Sarah heard the words of her son Isaac, she wept bitterly, and her husband Abraham wept with her, and their son wept with them a great weeping; also those who went with them wept greatly. ¹⁸ And Sarah caught hold of her son Isaac, and she held him in her arms, and she embraced him, and continued to weep with him, and Sarah said, "Who knows if after this day I will ever see you again?" ¹⁹ And they still wept together—Abraham, Sarah, and Isaac, and all those that accompanied them on the road wept with them, and afterward Sarah turned away from her son, weeping bitterly, and all her menservants and maidservants returned with her to the tent. ²⁰ And Abraham went with his son Isaac to bring him up as an offering before the LORD as He had commanded him. ²¹ And Abraham took two of his young men with him, Ishmael the son of Hagar and his servant Eliezer, and they went together with them, and while they were walking in the road the young men spoke these words to themselves, ²² and Ishmael said to Eliezer, "Now my father Abraham is going with Isaac to bring him up for a burnt-offering to the LORD, as He commanded him. ²³ Now when he returns he will give all that he possesses to me, to inherit after him, for I am his firstborn." ²⁴ And Eliezer answered Ishmael and said, "Surely Abraham cast you away with your mother and swore that you should not inherit anything of all he possesses, and to whom will he give all that he has, with all his treasures, but to me his servant, who has been faithful in his house, who has served him night and day, and has done all that he desired? To me he will bequeath at his death all that he possesses." ²⁵ And while Abraham was proceeding with his son Isaac along the road, Satan came and appeared to Abraham in the figure of a very aged man, humble and of contrite spirit, and he approached Abraham and said to him, "Are you silly or brutish that you go this day to do this thing to your only son? ²⁶ For God gave you a son in your latter days, in your old age, and will you go and slaughter him this day because he committed no violence, and will you cause the soul of your only son to perish from the earth? ²⁷ Do you not know and understand that this thing cannot be from the LORD? For the LORD cannot do to man such evil on earth to say to him, Go slaughter your child." ²⁸ And Abraham heard this and knew that it was the word of Satan who endeavored to draw him aside from the way of the LORD, but Abraham would not listen to the voice of Satan, and Abraham rebuked him so that he went away. ²⁹ And Satan returned and came to Isaac; and he appeared to Isaac in the figure of a young man, handsome and well-favored. ³⁰ And he approached Isaac and said to him, "Do you not know and understand that your old silly father brings you to the slaughter this day for no reason? ³¹ Now therefore, my son, do not listen nor attend to him, for he is a silly old man, and do not let your precious soul and beautiful figure be lost from the earth." ³² And Isaac heard this, and said to Abraham, "Have you heard, my father, that which this man has spoken? Even thus he has spoken." ³³ And Abraham answered his son Isaac and said to him, "Take heed of him and do not listen to his words, nor attend to him, for he is Satan, endeavoring to draw us aside from the commands of God this day." ³⁴ And Abraham still rebuked Satan, and Satan went from them, and seeing he could not prevail over them, he hid himself from them, and he went and passed before them in the road; and he transformed himself into a large brook of water in the road, and Abraham, and Isaac, and his two young men reached that place, and they saw a brook [as] large and powerful as the mighty waters. ³⁵ And they entered the brook and passed through it, and the waters at first reached their legs. ³⁶ And they went deeper in the brook and the waters reached up to their necks, and they were all terrified on account of the water; and while they were going over the brook, Abraham recognized that place, and he knew that there was no water there before. ³⁷ And Abraham said to his son Isaac, "I know this place in which there was no brook nor water, now therefore, it is this Satan who does all this to us, to draw us aside from the commands of God this day." ³⁸ And Abraham rebuked him and said to him, "The LORD rebuke you, O Satan! Go away from us, for we go by the commands of God." ³⁹ And Satan was terrified at the voice of Abraham, and he went away from them, and the place again became dry land as it was at first. ⁴⁰ And Abraham went with Isaac toward the place that God had told him. ⁴¹ And on the third day Abraham lifted up his eyes and saw the place at a distance which God had told him of. ⁴² And a pillar of fire appeared to him that reached from the earth to the heavens, and a cloud of glory on the mountain, and the glory of the LORD was seen in the cloud. ⁴³ And Abraham said to Isaac, "My son, do you see in that mountain, which we perceive at a distance, that which I see on it?" ⁴⁴ And Isaac answered and said to his father, "I see, and behold, a pillar of fire and a cloud, and the glory of the LORD is seen on the cloud." ⁴⁵ And Abraham knew that his son Isaac was accepted before the LORD for a burnt-offering. ⁴⁶ And Abraham said to Eliezer and to his son Ishmael, "Do you also see that which we see on the mountain which is at a distance?" ⁴⁷ And they answered and said, "We see nothing more than [that] like the other mountains of the earth." And Abraham knew that they were not accepted before the LORD to go with them, and Abraham said to them, "Abide here with the donkey while my son Isaac and I will go to that mount, and worship there before the LORD, and then return to you." ⁴⁸ And Eliezer and Ishmael remained in that place as Abraham had commanded. ⁴⁹ And Abraham took wood for a burnt-offering and placed it on his son Isaac, and he took the fire and the knife, and they both went to that place. ⁵⁰ And when they were going along Isaac said to his father, "Behold, I see the fire and wood here, and where then is the lamb that is to be the burnt-offering before the LORD?" ⁵¹ And Abraham answered his son Isaac, saying, "The LORD has made choice of you, my son, to be a perfect burnt-offering instead of the lamb." ⁵² And Isaac said to his father, "I will do all that the LORD spoke to you with joy and cheerfulness of heart." ⁵³ And Abraham again said to his son Isaac, "Is there any thought or counsel in your heart concerning this, which is not proper? Please tell me, my son; O my son do not conceal it from me." ⁵⁴ And Isaac answered his father Abraham and said to him, "O my father, as the LORD lives and as your soul lives, there is nothing in my heart to cause me to deviate either to the right or to the left from the word that He has spoken to you. ⁵⁵ Neither limb nor muscle has moved or stirred at this, nor is there any thought or evil counsel in my heart concerning this. ⁵⁶ But I am of joyful and cheerful heart in this matter, and I say, Blessed is the LORD who has chosen me to be a burnt-offering before Him this day." ⁵⁷ And Abraham greatly rejoiced at the words of Isaac, and they went on and came together to that place that the LORD had spoken of. ⁵⁸ And Abraham approached to build the altar in that place, and Abraham was weeping, and Isaac took stones and mortar until they had finished building the altar. ⁵⁹ And Abraham took the wood and placed it in order on the altar which he had built. ⁶⁰ And he took his son Isaac and bound him in order to place him on the wood which was on the altar, to slay him for a burnt-offering before the LORD. ⁶¹ And Isaac said to his father, "Bind me securely and then place me on the altar lest I should turn, and move, and break loose from the force of the knife on my flesh and thereof profane the burnt-offering"; and Abraham did so. ⁶² And Isaac still said to his father, "O my father, when you will have slain me and burned me for an offering, take with you that which will remain of my ashes to bring to my mother Sarah, and say to her, This is the sweet-smelling savor of Isaac; but do not tell her this if she should sit near a well or on any high place, lest she should cast her soul after me and die." ⁶³ And Abraham heard the words of Isaac, and he lifted up his voice and wept when Isaac spoke these words; and Abraham's tears gushed down on his son Isaac, and Isaac wept bitterly, and he said to his father, "Hasten you, O my father, and do with me

the will of the LORD our God as He has commanded you." ⁶⁴ And the hearts of Abraham and Isaac rejoiced at this thing which the LORD had commanded them; but the eye wept bitterly while the heart rejoiced. ⁶⁵ And Abraham bound his son Isaac, and placed him on the altar on the wood, and Isaac stretched out his neck on the altar before his father, and Abraham stretched out his hand to take the knife to slay his son as a burnt-offering before the LORD. ⁶⁶ At that time the messengers of mercy came before the LORD and spoke to him concerning Isaac, saying, ⁶⁷ "O LORD, You are a merciful and compassionate King over all that You have created in Heaven and in earth, and You support them all; therefore give ransom and redemption instead of your servant Isaac, and have pity and compassion on Abraham and his son Isaac who are performing Your commands this day. ⁶⁸ Have You seen, O LORD, how Isaac, the son of Your servant Abraham, is bound down to the slaughter like an animal? Now therefore, let Your pity be roused for them, O LORD." ⁶⁹ At that time the LORD appeared to Abraham, and called to him from Heaven, and said to him, "Do not lay your hand on the youth, neither do anything to him, for now I know that you fear God in performing this act, and in not withholding your son, your only son, from Me." ⁷⁰ And Abraham lifted up his eyes and saw, and behold, a ram was caught in a thicket by his horns; that was the ram which the LORD God had created in the earth in the day that he made earth and Heaven. ⁷¹ For the LORD had prepared this ram from that day to be a burnt-offering instead of Isaac. ⁷² And this ram was advancing to Abraham when Satan caught hold of him and entangled his horns in the thicket, that he might not advance to Abraham, in order that Abraham might slay his son. ⁷³ And Abraham, seeing the ram advancing to him and Satan withholding him, fetched him and brought him before the altar, and he loosened his son Isaac from his binding, and he put the ram in his stead, and Abraham killed the ram on the altar, and brought it up as an offering in the place of his son Isaac. ⁷⁴ And Abraham sprinkled some of the blood of the ram on the altar, and he exclaimed and said, "This is in the place of my son, and may this be considered as the blood of my son before the LORD this day." ⁷⁵ And all that Abraham did on this occasion by the altar, he would exclaim and say, "This is in the room of my son, and may it be considered before the LORD in the place of my son this day"; and Abraham finished the whole of the service by the altar, and the service was accepted before the LORD, and was accounted as if it had been Isaac; and the LORD blessed Abraham and his seed on that day. ⁷⁶ And Satan went to Sarah, and he appeared to her in the figure of a very humble and meek old man, and Abraham was yet engaged in the burnt-offering before the LORD. ⁷⁷ And he said to her, "Do you not know all the work that Abraham has made with your only son this day? For he took Isaac, and built an altar, and killed him, and brought him up as a sacrifice on the altar, and Isaac cried and wept before his father, but he did not look at him, neither did he have compassion over him." [78] And Satan repeated these words, and he went away from her, and Sarah heard all the words of Satan, and she imagined him to be an old man from among the sons of men who had been with her son and had come and told her these things. [79] And Sarah lifted up her voice, and wept, and cried out bitterly on account of her son; and she threw herself on the ground, and she cast dust on her head, and she said, "O my son! My son Isaac! O that I had died instead of you this day." And she continued to weep and said, "It grieves me for you, O my son, my son Isaac! O that I had died in your stead this day." [80] And she still continued to weep, and said, "It grieves me for you after I have reared you and have brought you up; now my joy is turned into mourning over you—I that had a longing for you, and cried and prayed to God until I bore you at ninety years old; and now you have served this day for the knife and the fire, to be made an offering. [81] But I console myself with you, my son, in its being the word of the LORD, for you performed the command of your God; for who can transgress the word of our God, in whose hands is the soul of every living creature? [82] You are just, O LORD our God, for all Your works are good and righteous; for I also rejoice with Your word which You commanded, and while my eye weeps bitterly, my heart rejoices." [83] And Sarah laid her head on the bosom of one of her handmaids, and she became as still as a stone. [84] Afterward she rose up and went around making inquiries until she came to Hebron, and she inquired of all those whom she met walking in the road, and no one could tell her what had happened to her son. [85] And she came with her maidservants and menservants to Kirjath-Arba, which is Hebron, and she asked concerning her son, and she remained there while she sent some of her servants to seek where Abraham had gone with Isaac; they went to seek him in the house of Shem and Eber, and they could not find him, and they sought throughout the land and he was not there. [86] And behold, Satan came to Sarah in the shape of an old man, and he came and stood before her, and he said to her, "I spoke falsely to you, for Abraham did not kill his son and he is not dead"; and when she heard the word her joy was so exceedingly violent on account of her son, that her soul went out through joy; she died and was gathered to her people. [87] And when Abraham had finished his service, he returned with his son Isaac to his young men, and they rose up and went together to Beersheba, and they came home. [88] And Abraham sought for Sarah, and could not find her, and he made inquiries concerning her, and they said to him, "She went as far as Hebron to seek you both where you had gone, for thus she was informed." [89] And Abraham and Isaac went to her to Hebron, and when they found that she was dead, they lifted up their voices and wept bitterly over her; and Isaac fell on his mother's face and wept over her, and he said, "O my mother, my mother! How have you left me, and where have you gone? O how, how have you left me!" [90] And Abraham and Isaac wept greatly, and all their servants wept with them on account of Sarah, and they mourned a great and heavy mourning over her.

CHAPTER 24

[1] And the life of Sarah was one hundred and twenty-seven years, and Sarah died; and Abraham rose up from before his dead to seek a burial place to bury his wife Sarah; and he went and spoke to the children of Heth, the inhabitants of the land, saying, [2] "I am a stranger and a sojourner with you in your land; give me possession of a burial place in your land, that I may bury my dead from before me." [3] And the children of Heth said to Abraham, "Behold, the land is before you, in the choice of our tombs bury your dead, for no man will withhold you from burying your dead." [4] And Abraham said to them, "If you are agreeable to this, go and entreat for me to Ephron, the son of Zochar, requesting that he may give me the cave of Machpelah, which is in the end of his field, and I will purchase it from him for whatever he desires for it." [5] And Ephron dwelt among the children of Heth, and they went and called for him, and he came before Abraham, and Ephron said to Abraham, "Behold, your servant will do all [that] you require"; and Abraham said, "No, but I will buy the cave and the field which you have for value, in order that it may be for a possession of a burial place forever." [6] And Ephron answered and said, "Behold, the field and the cave are before you, give whatever you desire"; and Abraham said, "Only at full value will I buy it from your hand, and from the hands of those that go in at the gate of your city, and from the hand of your seed forever." [7] And Ephron and all his brothers heard this, and Abraham weighed four hundred shekels of silver to Ephron in the hands of Ephron and in the hands of all his brothers; and Abraham recorded this transaction, and he recorded it and testified to it with four witnesses. [8] And these are the names of the witnesses: Amigal son of Abishna the Hittite, Adichorom son of Ashunach the Hivite, Abdon son of Achiram the Gomerite, [and] Bakdil the son of Abudish the Zidonite. [9] And Abraham took the scroll of the purchase and placed it in his treasures, and these are the words that Abraham wrote in the scroll, namely that: [10] "THE CAVE AND THE FIELD ABRAHAM BOUGHT FROM EPHRON THE HITTITE, AND FROM HIS SEED, AND FROM THOSE THAT GO OUT OF HIS CITY, AND FROM THEIR SEED FOREVER, ARE TO BE A PURCHASE TO ABRAHAM, AND TO HIS SEED, AND TO THOSE THAT GO OUT FROM HIS LOINS FOR A POSSESSION OF A BURIAL PLACE FOREVER"; and he put a signet to it and testified

to it with witnesses. [11] And the field, and the cave that was in it, and all that place were made sure to Abraham and to his seed after him, from the children of Heth; behold, it is before Mamre in Hebron, which is in the land of Canaan. [12] And after this Abraham buried his wife Sarah there, and that place and all its boundary became to Abraham and to his seed for a possession of a burial place. [13] And Abraham buried Sarah with pomp as observed at the interment of kings, and she was buried in very fine and beautiful garments. [14] And Shem, his sons Eber and Abimelech, together with Anar, Ashcol, and Mamre were at her bier; and all the noblemen of the land followed her bier. [15] And the days of Sarah were one hundred and twenty-seven years and she died, and Abraham made a great and heavy mourning, and he performed the rites of mourning for seven days. [16] And all the inhabitants of the land comforted Abraham and his son Isaac on account of Sarah. [17] And when the days of their mourning passed by, Abraham sent his son Isaac away, and he went to the house of Shem and Eber to learn the ways of the LORD and His instructions, and Abraham remained there three years. [18] At that time Abraham rose up with all his servants, and they went and returned homeward to Beersheba, and Abraham and all his servants remained in Beersheba. [19] And at the revolution of the year Abimelech king of the Philistines died in that year; he was one hundred and ninety-three years old at his death; and Abraham went with his people to the land of the Philistines, and they comforted the whole household and all his servants, and he then turned and went home. [20] And it was after the death of Abimelech that the people of Gerar took his son Benmalich, and he was only twelve years old, and they made him lie in the place of his father. [21] And they called his name Abimelech after the name of his father, for thus it was their custom to do in Gerar, and Abimelech reigned instead of his father Abimelech, and he sat on his throne. [22] And Lot the son of Haran also died in those days, in the thirty-ninth year of the life of Isaac, and all the days that Lot lived were one hundred and forty years and he died. [23] And these are the children of Lot that were born to him by his daughters: the name of the firstborn was Moab, and the name of the second was Benami. [24] And the two sons of Lot went and took wives [for] themselves from the land of Canaan, and they bore children to them, and the children of Moab were Ed, Mayon, Tarsus, and Kanvil—four sons; these are fathers to the children of Moab to this day. [25] And all the families of the children of Lot went to dwell wherever they should settle, for they were fruitful and increased abundantly. [26] And they went and built themselves cities in the land where they dwelt, and they called the names of the cities which they built after their own names. [27] And Nahor the son of Terah, brother to Abraham, died in those days in the fortieth year of the life of Isaac, and all the days

of Nahor were one hundred and seventy-two years and he died and was buried in Haran. [28] And when Abraham heard that his brother was dead, he grieved sadly, and he mourned over his brother many days. [29] And Abraham called for his head servant Eliezer to give him orders concerning his house, and he came and stood before him. [30] And Abraham said to him, "Behold, I am old; I do not know the day of my death, for I am advanced in days; now therefore, rise up, go out, and do not take a wife for my son from this place and from this land, from the daughters of the Canaanites among whom we dwell. [31] But go to my land and to my birthplace, and take a wife for my son from there, and the LORD God of the heavens and earth who took me from my father's house and brought me to this place, and said to me, To your seed I will give this land for an inheritance forever—He will send His messenger before you and prosper your way that you may obtain a wife for my son from my family and from my father's house." [32] And the servant answered his master Abraham and said, "Behold, I go to your birthplace and to your father's house, and will take a wife for your son from there; but if the woman is not willing to follow me to this land, will I take your son back to the land of your birthplace?" [33] And Abraham said to him, "Take heed that you do not bring my son here again, for the LORD before whom I have walked will send His messenger before you and prosper your way." [34] And Eliezer did as Abraham ordered him, and Eliezer swore to Abraham his master on this matter; and Eliezer rose up and took ten camels of the camels of his master, and ten men from his master's servants with him, and they rose up and went to Haran, the city of Abraham and Nahor, in order to fetch a wife for Isaac the son of Abraham; and while they were gone, Abraham sent to the house of Shem and Eber, and they brought his son Isaac from there. [35] And Isaac came home to his father's house, to Beersheba, while Eliezer and his men came to Haran; and they stopped in the city by the watering place, and he made his camels to kneel down by the water, and they remained there. [36] And Eliezer, Abraham's servant, prayed and said, "O God of my master Abraham, please send me good speed this day and show kindness to my master, that You will appoint a wife for my master's son from his family this day." [37] And the LORD listened to the voice of Eliezer for the sake of His servant Abraham, and he happened to meet with the daughter of Bethuel, the son of Milcah, the wife of Nahor, brother to Abraham, and Eliezer came to her house. [38] And Eliezer related to them all his concerns, and that he was Abraham's servant, and they greatly rejoiced at him. [39] And they all blessed the LORD who brought this thing about, and they gave him Rebekah, the daughter of Bethuel, for a wife for Isaac. [40] And the young woman was of very beautiful appearance, she was a virgin, and Rebekah was ten years old in those days. [41] And

Bethuel, and Laban, and his children made a feast on that night, and Eliezer and his men came, and ate, and drank, and rejoiced there on that night. ⁴² And Eliezer rose up in the morning, he and the men that were with him, and he called to the whole household of Bethuel, saying, "Send me away that I may go to my master"; and they rose up and sent away Rebekah and her nurse Deborah, the daughter of Uz, and they gave her silver and gold, menservants and maidservants, and they blessed her. ⁴³ And they sent Eliezer away with his men; and the servants took Rebekah, and he went and returned to his master to the land of Canaan. ⁴⁴ And Isaac took Rebekah, and she became his wife, and he brought her into the tent. ⁴⁵ And Isaac was forty years old when he took Rebekah, the daughter of his uncle Bethuel, for a wife.

CHAPTER 25

¹ And it was at that time that Abraham again took a wife in his old age, and her name was Keturah, from the land of Canaan. ² And she bore to him Zimran, Jokshan, Medan, Midian, Ishbak, and Shuach, being six sons. And the children of Zimran were Abihen, Molich, and Narim. ³ And the sons of Jokshan were Sheba and Dedan, and the sons of Medan were Amida, Joab, Gochi, Elisha, and Nothach. And the sons of Midian were Ephah, Epher, Chanoch, Abida, and Eldaah. ⁴ And the sons of Ishbak were Makiro, Beyodua, and Tator. ⁵ And the sons of Shuach were Bildad, Mamdad, Munan, and Meban; all these are the families of the children of Keturah the Canaanite woman which she bore to Abraham the Hebrew. ⁶ And Abraham sent all these away, and he gave them gifts, and they went away from his son Isaac to dwell wherever they should find a place. ⁷ And all these went to the mountain at the east, and they built themselves six cities in which they dwelt to this day. ⁸ But the children of Sheba and Dedan, children of Jokshan, with their children, did not dwell with their brothers in their cities, and they journeyed and encamped in the countries and wildernesses to this day. ⁹ And the children of Midian, son of Abraham, went to the east of the land of Cush, and they found a large valley there in the eastern country, and they remained there and built a city, and they dwelt therein; that is the land of Midian to this day. ¹⁰ And Midian dwelt in the city which he built—he and his five sons and all belonging to him. ¹¹ And these are the names of the sons of Midian according to their names in their cities: Ephah, Epher, Chanoch, Abida, and Eldaah. ¹² And the sons of Ephah were Methach, Meshar, Avi, and Tzanua. And the sons of Epher were Ephron, Zur, Alirun, and Medin. And the sons of Chanoch were Reuel, Rekem, Azi, Alyoshub, and Alad. ¹³ And the sons of Abida were Chur, Melud, Kerury, Molchi. And the sons of Eldaah were Miker, and Reba, and Malchiyah, and Gabol; these are the names of the Midianites according to their families;

and afterward the families of Midian spread throughout the land of Midian. ¹⁴ And these are the generations of Ishmael the son Abraham, whom Hagar, Sarah's handmaid, bore to Abraham. ¹⁵ And Ishmael took a wife from the land of Egypt, and her name was Ribah, the same is Meribah. ¹⁶ And Ribah bore to Ishmael Nebayoth, Kedar, Adbeel, Mibsam, and their sister Bosmath. ¹⁷ And Ishmael cast away his wife Ribah, and she went from him and returned to Egypt to the house of her father, and she dwelt there, for she had been very bad in the sight of Ishmael and in the sight of his father Abraham. ¹⁸ And afterward Ishmael took a wife from the land of Canaan, and her name was Malchuth, and she bore to him Nishma, Dumah, Masa, Chadad, Tema, Yetur, Naphish, and Kedma. ¹⁹ These are the sons of Ishmael, and these are their names, being twelve princes according to their nations; and afterward the families of Ishmael spread out, and Ishmael took his children and all the property that he had gained, together with the souls of his household and all belonging to him, and they went to dwell where they should find a place. ²⁰ And they went and dwelt near the wilderness of Paran, and their dwelling was from Havilah to Shur, which is before Egypt as you come toward Assyria. ²¹ And Ishmael and his sons dwelt in the land, and they had children born to them, and they were fruitful and increased abundantly. ²² And these are the names of the sons of Nebayoth, the firstborn of Ishmael: Mend, Send, Mayon. And the sons of Kedar were Alyon, Kezem, Chamad, and Eli. ²³ And the sons of Adbeel were Chamad and Jabin. And the sons of Mibsam were Obadiah, Ebedmelech, and Yeush; these are the families of the children of Ribah, the wife of Ishmael. ²⁴ And the sons of Mishma the son of Ishmael were Shamua, Zecaryon, and Obed. And the sons of Dumah were Kezed, Eli, Machmad, and Amed. ²⁵ And the sons of Masa were Melon, Mula, and Ebidadon. And the sons of Chadad were Azur, Minzar, and Ebedmelech. And the sons of Tema were Seir, Sadon, and Yakol. ²⁶ And the sons of Yetur were Merith, Yaish, Alyo, and Pachoth. And the sons of Naphish were Ebed-Tamed, Abiyasaph, and Mir. And the sons of Kedma were Calip, Tachti, and Omir; these were the children of Malchuth the wife of Ishmael according to their families. ²⁷ All these are the families of Ishmael according to their generations, and they dwelt in those lands wherein they had built themselves cities to this day. ²⁸ And Rebekah the daughter of Bethuel, the wife of Abraham's son Isaac, was barren in those days, she had no offspring; and Isaac dwelt with his father in the land of Canaan; and the LORD was with Isaac; and Arphaxad the son of Shem, the son of Noah, died in those days, in the forty-eighth year of the life of Isaac, and all the days that Arphaxad lived were four hundred and thirty-eight years, and he died.

CHAPTER 26

¹ And in the fifty-ninth year of the life of Isaac the son of Abraham, his wife Rebekah was still barren in those days. ² And Rebekah said to Isaac, "Truly I have heard, my lord, that your mother Sarah was barren in her days until my lord Abraham, your father, prayed for her and she conceived by him. ³ Now therefore, stand up, pray also to God and He will hear your prayer and remember us through His mercies." ⁴ And Isaac answered his wife Rebekah, saying, "Abraham has already prayed for me to God to multiply his seed, now therefore, this barrenness must proceed to us from you." ⁵ And Rebekah said to him, "But arise now—you also—and pray that the LORD may hear your prayer and grant me children," and Isaac listened to the words of his wife, and Isaac and his wife rose up and went to the land of Moriah to pray there and to seek the LORD, and when they had reached that place, Isaac stood up and prayed to the LORD on account of his wife because she was barren. ⁶ And Isaac said, "O LORD God of the heavens and earth, whose goodness and mercies fill the earth, You who took my father from his father's house and from his birthplace, and brought him to this land, and said to him, To your seed I will give the land, and You promised him and declared to him, I will multiply your seed as the stars of the heavens and as the sand of the sea: now may Your words be verified which You spoke to my father. ⁷ For You are the LORD our God; our eyes are toward You to give us seed of men, as You promised us, for You are the LORD our God and our eyes are directed toward You alone." ⁸ And the LORD heard the prayer of Isaac the son of Abraham, and the LORD was entreated of him and his wife Rebekah conceived. ⁹ And about seven months later, the children struggled together within her, and it pained her greatly that she was wearied on account of them, and she said to all the women who were then in the land, "Did such a thing happen to you as it has to me?" And they said to her, "No." ¹⁰ And she said to them, "Why am I alone in this among all the women that were on earth?" And she went to the land of Moriah to seek the LORD on account of this; and she went to Shem and his son Eber to make inquiries of them in this matter, and that they should seek the LORD in this thing respecting her. ¹¹ And she also asked Abraham to seek and inquire of the LORD about all that had befallen her. ¹² And they all inquired of the LORD concerning this matter, and they brought her word from the LORD and told her: "Two children are in your womb, and two nations will rise from them; and one nation will be stronger than the other, and the greater will serve the younger." ¹³ And when her days to be delivered were completed, she knelt down, and behold, there were twins in her womb as the LORD had spoken to her. ¹⁴ And the first came out red all over like a hairy garment, and all the people of the land called his name Esau, saying, "That this one was made complete from the womb." ¹⁵ And after that, his brother came, and his hand took hold of Esau's heel; therefore they called his name Jacob. ¹⁶ And Isaac, the son of Abraham, was sixty years old when he begot them. ¹⁷ And the boys grew up to their fifteenth year, and they came among the society of men. Esau was a scheming and deceitful man, and an expert hunter in the field, and Jacob was a perfect and wise man, dwelling in tents, feeding flocks, and learning the instructions of the LORD and the commands of his father and mother. ¹⁸ And Isaac and the children of his household dwelt with his father Abraham in the land of Canaan as God had commanded them. ¹⁹ And Ishmael the son of Abraham went with his children and all belonging to them, and they returned there to the land of Havilah, and they dwelt there. ²⁰ And all the children of Abraham's concubines went to dwell in the land of the east, for Abraham had sent them away from his son, and had given them presents, and they went away. ²¹ And Abraham gave all that he had to his son Isaac, and he also gave him all his treasures. ²² And he commanded him, saying, "Do you not know and understand the LORD is God in Heaven and in earth, and there is no other besides Him? ²³ And it was He who took me from my father's house and from my birthplace, and gave me all the delights on earth; who delivered me from the counsel of the wicked, for I trusted in Him. ²⁴ And He brought me to this place, and He delivered me from Ur-Kasdim; and He said to me, To your seed I will give all these lands, and they will inherit them when they keep My commands, My statutes, and My judgments that I have commanded you, and which I will command them. ²⁵ Now therefore, my son, listen to my voice, and keep the commands of the LORD your God, which I commanded you; do not turn from the right way either to the right or to the left, in order that it may be well with you and your children after you forever. ²⁶ And remember the wonderful works of the LORD, and His kindness that He has shown toward us in having delivered us from the hands of our enemies, and the LORD our God caused them to fall into our hands; and now therefore, keep all that I have commanded you, and do not turn away from the commands of your God, and serve none besides Him in order that it may be well with you and your seed after you. ²⁷ And teach your children and your seed the instructions of the LORD and His commands, and teach them the upright way in which they should go in order that it may be well with them forever." ²⁸ And Isaac answered his father and said to him, "I will do that which my lord has commanded, and I will not depart from the commands of the LORD my God; I will keep all that He commanded me"; and Abraham blessed his son Isaac, and also his children; and Abraham taught Jacob the instruction of the LORD and His ways. ²⁹ And it was at that time that Abraham died, in the fifteenth year of the life of Jacob and Esau, the sons

JASHER

of Isaac, and all the days of Abraham were one hundred and seventy-five years, and he died and was gathered to his people in good old age, old and satisfied with days, and his sons Isaac and Ishmael buried him. ³⁰ And when the inhabitants of Canaan heard that Abraham was dead, they all came with their kings, and princes, and all their men to bury Abraham. ³¹ And all the inhabitants of the land of Haran, and all the families of the house of Abraham, and all the princes and noblemen, and the sons of Abraham by the concubines, all came when they heard of Abraham's death, and they paid back Abraham's kindness, and comforted his son Isaac, and they buried Abraham in the cave which he bought from Ephron the Hittite and his children for the possession of a burial place. ³² And all the inhabitants of Canaan, and all those who had known Abraham, wept for Abraham a whole year, and men and women mourned over him. ³³ And all the little children, and all the inhabitants of the land, wept on account of Abraham, for Abraham had been good to them all, and because he had been upright with God and men. ³⁴ And there did not arise a man who feared God like to Abraham, for he had feared his God from his youth, and had served the LORD, and had gone in all His ways during his life, from his childhood to the day of his death. ³⁵ And the LORD was with him and delivered him from the counsel of Nimrod and his people, and when he made war with the four kings of Elam, he conquered them. ³⁶ And he brought all the children of the earth to the service of God, and he taught them the ways of the LORD, and caused them to know the LORD. ³⁷ And he formed a grove, and he planted a vineyard therein, and he had always prepared meat and drink in his tent for those that passed through the land, that they might satisfy themselves in his house. ³⁸ And the LORD God delivered the whole earth on account of Abraham. ³⁹ And it was after the death of Abraham that God blessed his son Isaac and his children, and the LORD was with Isaac as he had been with his father Abraham, for Isaac kept all the commands of the LORD as his father Abraham had commanded him; he did not turn to the right or to the left from the right path which his father had commanded him.

CHAPTER 27

¹ And Esau at that time, after the death of Abraham, frequently went in the field to hunt. ² And Nimrod king of Babel, the same was Amraphel, also frequently went with his mighty men to hunt in the field, and to walk around with his men in the cool of the day. ³ And Nimrod was observing Esau all the days, for a jealousy was formed in the heart of Nimrod against Esau all the days. ⁴ And on a certain day Esau went in the field to hunt, and he found Nimrod walking in the wilderness with his two men. ⁵ And all his mighty men and his people were with

him in the wilderness, but they removed at a distance from him, and they went from him in different directions to hunt, and Esau concealed himself for Nimrod, and he lurked for him in the wilderness. ⁶ And Nimrod and his men that were with him did not know him, and Nimrod and his men frequently walked around in the field in the cool of the day, and to know where his men were hunting in the field. ⁷ And Nimrod and two of his men that were with him came to the place where they were, when Esau started suddenly from his lurking place, and drew his sword, and hastened, and ran to Nimrod, and cut off his head. ⁸ And Esau fought a desperate fight with the two men that were with Nimrod, and when they called out to him, Esau turned to them and struck them to death with his sword. ⁹ And all the mighty men of Nimrod, who had left him to go to the wilderness, heard the cry at a distance, and they knew the voices of those two men, and they ran to know the cause of it; then they found their king and the two men that were with him lying dead in the wilderness. ¹⁰ And when Esau saw the mighty men of Nimrod coming at a distance, he fled, and thereby escaped; and Esau took the valuable garments of Nimrod, which Nimrod's father had bequeathed to Nimrod, and with which Nimrod prevailed over the whole land, and he ran and concealed them in his house. ¹¹ And Esau took those garments and ran into the city on account of Nimrod's men, and he came to his father's house wearied and exhausted from fight, and he was ready to die through grief when he approached his brother Jacob and sat before him. ¹² And he said to his brother Jacob, "Behold, I will die this day, and why then do I want the birthright?" And Jacob acted wisely with Esau in this matter, and Esau sold his birthright to Jacob, for it was so brought about by the LORD. ¹³ And Esau's portion in the cave of the field of Machpelah, which Abraham had bought from the children of Heth for the possession of a burial ground, Esau also sold to Jacob, and Jacob bought all this from his brother Esau for value given. ¹⁴ And Jacob recorded the whole of this in a scroll, and he testified the same with witnesses, and he sealed it, and the scroll remained in the hands of Jacob. ¹⁵ And when Nimrod the son of Cush died, his men lifted him up and brought him in consternation, and buried him in his city, and all the days that Nimrod lived were two hundred and fifteen years and he died. ¹⁶ And the days that Nimrod reigned over the people of the land were one hundred and eighty-five years; and Nimrod died by the sword of Esau in shame and contempt, and the seed of Abraham caused his death as he had seen in his dream. ¹⁷ And at the death of Nimrod his kingdom became divided into many divisions, and all those parts that Nimrod reigned over were restored to the respective kings of the land, who recovered them after the death of Nimrod, and all the people of the house of Nimrod were enslaved for a long time to all the other kings of the land.

CHAPTER 28

[1] And in those days, after the death of Abraham, in that year the LORD brought a heavy famine in the land, and while the famine was raging in the land of Canaan, Isaac rose up to go down to Egypt on account of the famine, as his father Abraham had done. [2] And that night the LORD appeared to Isaac and said to him, "Do not go down to Egypt, but rise and go to Gerar, to Abimelech king of the Philistines, and remain there until the famine will cease." [3] And Isaac rose up and went to Gerar, as the LORD commanded him, and he remained there a full year. [4] And when Isaac came to Gerar, the people of the land saw that his wife Rebekah was of a beautiful appearance, and the people of Gerar asked Isaac concerning his wife, and he said, "She is my sister," for he was afraid to say she was his wife lest the people of the land should slay him on account of her. [5] And the princes of Abimelech went and praised the woman to the king, but he did not answer them, neither did he attend to their words. [6] But he heard them say that Isaac declared her to be his sister, so the king reserved this within himself. [7] And when Isaac had remained in the land [for] three months, Abimelech looked out at the window, and he saw, and behold, Isaac was sporting with his wife Rebekah, for Isaac dwelt in the outer house belonging to the king, so that the house of Isaac was opposite the house of the king. [8] And the king said to Isaac, "What is this you have done to us in saying of your wife, She is my sister? How easily might one of the great men of the people have lain with her, and you would then have brought guilt on us." [9] And Isaac said to Abimelech, "Because I was afraid lest I die on account of my wife, therefore I said, She is my sister." [10] At that time Abimelech gave orders to all his princes and great men, and they took Isaac and his wife Rebekah and brought them before the king. [11] And the king commanded that they should dress them in princely garments, and make them ride through the streets of the city, and proclaim before them throughout the land, saying, "This is the man and this is his wife; whoever touches this man or his wife will surely die." And Isaac returned with his wife to the king's house, and the LORD was with Isaac and he continued to wax great and lacked nothing. [12] And the LORD caused Isaac to find favor in the sight of Abimelech, and in the sight of all his subjects, and Abimelech acted well with Isaac, for Abimelech remembered the oath and the covenant that existed between his father and Abraham. [13] And Abimelech said to Isaac, "Behold, the whole earth is before you; dwell wherever it may seem good in your sight until you will return to your land"; and Abimelech gave Isaac fields, and vineyards, and the best part of the land of Gerar, to sow, and reap, and eat the fruits of the ground until the days of the famine should have passed by. [14] And Isaac sowed in that land and received a hundredfold in the same year, and the LORD blessed him. [15] And the man waxed great, and he had possession of flocks, and possession of herds, and a great store of servants. [16] And when the days of the famine had passed away, the LORD appeared to Isaac and said to him, "Rise up, go out from this place and return to your land, to the land of Canaan"; and Isaac rose up and returned to Hebron which is in the land of Canaan, he and all belonging to him as the LORD commanded him. [17] And after this, Shelach the son of Arphaxad died in that year, which is the eighteenth year of the lives of Jacob and Esau; and all the days that Shelach lived were four hundred and thirty-three years and he died. [18] At that time Isaac sent his younger son Jacob to the house of Shem and Eber, and he learned the instructions of the LORD, and Jacob remained in the house of Shem and Eber for thirty-two years, and his brother Esau did not go, for he was not willing to go, and he remained in his father's house in the land of Canaan. [19] And Esau was continually hunting in the fields to bring home what he could get—so Esau did all the days. [20] And Esau was a scheming and deceitful man, one who hunted after the hearts of men and persuaded them through deceit, and Esau was a valiant man in the field, and in the course of time went as usual to hunt; and he came as far as the field of Seir, the same is Edom. [21] And he remained in the land of Seir hunting in the field [for] a year and four months. [22] And Esau saw there in the land of Seir the daughter of a man of Canaan, and her name was Jehudith, the daughter of Beeri, son of Epher, from the families of Heth the son of Canaan. [23] And Esau took her for a wife, and he came to her; Esau was forty years old when he took her, and he brought her to Hebron, the land of his father's dwelling place, and he dwelt there. [24] And it came to pass in those days, in the one hundred and tenth year of the life of Isaac, that is in the fiftieth year of the life of Jacob, in that year Shem the son of Noah died; Shem was six hundred years old at his death. [25] And when Shem died Jacob returned to his father, to Hebron, which is in the land of Canaan. [26] And in the fifty-sixth year of the life of Jacob, people came from Haran, and Rebekah was told concerning her brother Laban, the son of Bethuel. [27] For the wife of Laban was barren in those days and bore no children, and also all his handmaids bore none to him. [28] And afterward the LORD remembered Adinah the wife of Laban, and she conceived and bore twin daughters, and Laban called the names of his daughters, the name of the elder Leah, and the name of the younger Rachel. [29] And those people came and told these things to Rebekah, and Rebekah rejoiced greatly that the LORD had visited her brother and that he was given children.

CHAPTER 29

¹ And Isaac the son of Abraham became old and advanced in days, and his eyes became heavy through age; they were dim and could not see. ² At that time Isaac called to his son Esau, saying, "Please get your weapons, your quiver and your bow, rise up and go out into the field, and get me some venison, and make me savory meat, and bring it to me, that I may eat in order that I may bless you before my death, as I have now become old and gray-headed." ³ And Esau did so; and he took his weapon and went out into the field to hunt for venison, as usual, to bring to his father as he had ordered him, so that he might bless him. ⁴ And Rebekah heard all the words that Isaac had spoken to Esau, and she hastened and called her son Jacob, saying, "Thus your father spoke to your brother Esau, and thus I heard; now therefore, hasten and make that which I will tell you. ⁵ Please rise up and go to the flock, and fetch me two fine kids of the goats, and I will get the savory meat for your father, and you will bring the savory meat that he may eat before your brother will have come from the chase, in order that your father may bless you." ⁶ And Jacob hastened and did as his mother had commanded him, and he made the savory meat and brought it before his father before Esau had come from his chase. ⁷ And Isaac said to Jacob, "Who are you, my son?" And he said, "I am your firstborn Esau; I have done as you ordered me, now therefore, please rise up, and eat of my hunt, in order that your soul may bless me as you spoke to me." ⁸ And Isaac rose up, and he ate, and he drank, and his heart was comforted, and he blessed Jacob, and Jacob went away from his father; and as soon as Isaac had blessed Jacob and he had gone away from him, behold, Esau came from his hunt from the field, and he also made savory meat and brought it to his father to eat thereof and to bless him. ⁹ And Isaac said to Esau, "And who was he that has taken venison and brought it to me before you came, and whom did I bless?" And Esau knew that his brother Jacob had done this, and the anger of Esau was kindled against his brother Jacob that he had acted thus toward him. ¹⁰ And Esau said, "Is he not rightly called Jacob? For he has supplanted me twice: he took away my birthright and now he has taken away my blessing"; and Esau wept greatly; and when Isaac heard the voice of his son Esau weeping, Isaac said to Esau, "What can I do, my son? Your brother came with subtlety and took away your blessing"; and Esau hated his brother Jacob on account of the blessing that his father had given him, and his anger was greatly roused against him. ¹¹ And Jacob was very much afraid of his brother Esau, and he rose up and fled to the house of Eber the son of Shem, and he concealed himself there on account of his brother, and Jacob was sixty-three years old when he went out from the land of Canaan from Hebron, and Jacob was concealed in Eber's house [for] fourteen years on account of his brother Esau, and he continued to learn the ways of the LORD and His commands there. ¹² And when Esau saw that Jacob had fled and escaped from him, and that Jacob had cunningly obtained the blessing, then Esau grieved exceedingly, and he was also vexed at his father and mother; and he also rose up, and took his wife, and went away from his father and mother to the land of Seir, and he dwelt there; and Esau saw a woman from among the daughters of Heth there whose name was Bosmath, the daughter of Elon the Hittite, and he took her for a wife in addition to his first wife, and Esau called her name Adah, saying the blessing had at that time passed from him. ¹³ And Esau dwelt in the land of Seir six months without seeing his father and mother, and afterward Esau took his wives, and rose up, and returned to the land of Canaan, and Esau placed his two wives in his father's house in Hebron. ¹⁴ And the wives of Esau vexed and provoked Isaac and Rebekah with their works, for they did not walk in the ways of the LORD, but served their father's gods of wood and stone as their father had taught them, and they were more wicked than their father. ¹⁵ And they went according to the evil desires of their hearts, and they sacrificed and burned incense to the Ba'alim, and Isaac and Rebekah became weary of them. ¹⁶ And Rebekah said, "I am weary of my life because of the daughters of Heth; if Jacob takes a wife from the daughters of Heth such as these, which are of the daughters of the land, what good then is life to me?" ¹⁷ And in those days Adah the wife of Esau conceived and bore him a son, and Esau called the name of the son that was born to him Eliphaz, and Esau was sixty-five years old when she bore him. ¹⁸ And Ishmael the son of Abraham died in those days, in the sixtieth year of the life of Jacob, and all the days that Ishmael lived were one hundred and thirty-seven years and he died. ¹⁹ And when Isaac heard that Ishmael was dead, he mourned for him, and Isaac lamented over him [for] many days. ²⁰ And at the end of fourteen years of Jacob's residing in the house of Eber, Jacob desired to see his father and mother, and Jacob came to the house of his father and mother to Hebron, and in those days Esau had forgotten what Jacob had done to him in having taken the blessing from him in those days. ²¹ And when Esau saw Jacob coming to his father and mother, he remembered what Jacob had done to him, and he was greatly incensed against him, and he sought to slay him. ²² And Isaac the son of Abraham was old and advanced in days, and Esau said, "Now my father's time is drawing near that he must die, and when he will die I will slay my brother Jacob." ²³ And this was told to Rebekah, and she hastened, and sent, and called for her son Jacob, and she said to him, "Arise, go and flee to Haran, to my brother Laban, and remain there for some time until your brother's anger is turned from you and then you will come back." ²⁴ And Isaac called to Jacob and said to him, "Do not take a

wife from the daughters of Canaan, for thus our father Abraham commanded us according to the word of the LORD which He had commanded him, saying, To your seed I will give this land; if your children keep My covenant that I have made with you, then I will also perform to your children that which I have spoken to you and I will not forsake them. ²⁵ Now therefore, my son, listen to my voice, to all that I will command you, and refrain from taking a wife from among the daughters of Canaan; arise, go to Haran, to the house of Bethuel your mother's father, and take a wife for yourself from there from the daughters of your mother's brother Laban. ²⁶ Therefore, take heed lest you should forget the LORD your God and all His ways in the land to which you go, and should get connected with the people of the land, and pursue vanity, and forsake the LORD your God. ²⁷ But when you come to the land serve the LORD there; do not turn to the right or to the left from the way which I commanded you and which you learned. ²⁸ And may the Almighty God grant you favor in the sight of the people of the earth, that you may take a wife there according to your choice, one who is good and upright in the ways of the LORD. ²⁹ And may God give to you and your seed the blessing of your father Abraham, and make you fruitful, and multiply you, and may you become a multitude of people in the land where you go, and may God cause you to return to this land, the land of your father's dwelling, with children and with great riches, with joy and with pleasure." ³⁰ And Isaac finished commanding Jacob and blessing him, and he gave him many gifts, together with silver and gold, and he sent him away; and Jacob listened to his father and mother; he kissed them, and arose, and went to Padan-Aram; and Jacob was seventy-seven years old when he went out from the land of Canaan from Beersheba. ³¹ And when Jacob went away to go to Haran, Esau called to his son Eliphaz, and secretly spoke to him, saying, "Now hasten, take your sword in your hand, and pursue Jacob, and pass before him in the road, and lurk for him, and slay him with your sword in one of the mountains, and take everything belonging to him, and come back." ³² And Eliphaz the son of Esau was an active man and expert with the bow as his father had taught him, and he was a noted hunter in the field and a valiant man. ³³ And Eliphaz did as his father had commanded him, and Eliphaz was thirteen years old at that time, and Eliphaz rose up, and went, and took ten of his mother's brothers with him, and pursued Jacob. ³⁴ And he closely followed Jacob, and he lurked for him in the border of the land of Canaan opposite to the city of Shechem. ³⁵ And Jacob saw Eliphaz and his men pursuing him, and Jacob stood still in the place in which he was going, in order to know what this was, for he did not know the thing; and Eliphaz drew his sword and he went on advancing, he and his men, toward Jacob; and Jacob said to them, "What are you doing that you have come here, and what do you intend that you pursue with your swords?" ³⁶ And Eliphaz came near to Jacob, and he answered and said to him, "Thus my father commanded me, and now therefore, I will not deviate from the orders which my father gave me"; and when Jacob saw that Esau had spoken to Eliphaz to employ force, Jacob then approached and supplicated Eliphaz and his men, saying to him, ³⁷ "Behold all that I have and which my father and mother gave to me: take that to yourselves and go from me, and do not slay me, and may this thing be accounted to you [for] righteousness." ³⁸ And the LORD caused Jacob to find favor in the sight of Eliphaz the son of Esau and his men, and they listened to the voice of Jacob, and they did not put him to death, and Eliphaz and his men took all belonging to Jacob, together with the silver and gold that he had brought with him from Beersheba; they left him nothing. ³⁹ And Eliphaz and his men went away from him and they returned to Esau, to Beersheba, and they told him all that had occurred to them with Jacob, and they gave him all that they had taken from Jacob. ⁴⁰ And Esau was indignant at his son Eliphaz and at his men that were with him, because they had not put Jacob to death. ⁴¹ And they answered and said to Esau, "Because Jacob supplicated us in this matter not to slay him, our pity was excited toward him, and we took all belonging to him and brought it to you; and Esau took all the silver and gold which Eliphaz had taken from Jacob and he put them away in his house." ⁴² At that time when Esau saw that Isaac had blessed Jacob, and had commanded him, saying, "You will not take a wife from among the daughters of Canaan," and that the daughters of Canaan were bad in the sight of Isaac and Rebekah, ⁴³ then he went to the house of his uncle Ishmael, and in addition to his older wives he took Machlath the daughter of Ishmael, the sister of Nebayoth, for a wife.

CHAPTER 30

¹ And Jacob went out, continuing his way to Haran, and he came as far as Mount Moriah, and he tarried there all night near the city of Luz; and on that night the LORD appeared to Jacob there, and He said to him, "I am the LORD God of Abraham and the God of your father Isaac; the land on which you lie I will give to you and your seed. ² And behold, I am with you and will keep you wherever you go, and I will multiply your seed as the stars of the heavens, and I will cause all your enemies to fall before you; and when they will make war with you they will not prevail over you, and I will bring you again to this land with joy, with children, and with great riches." ³ And Jacob awoke from his sleep and he rejoiced greatly at the vision which he had seen; and he called the name of that place Bethel. ⁴ And Jacob rose up from that place quite glad, and when he walked, his feet felt light to

him for joy, and he went from there to the land of the children of the east, and he returned to Haran, and he sat by the shepherd's well. ⁵ And there he found some men going from Haran to feed their flocks, and Jacob made inquiries of them, and they said, "We are from Haran." ⁶ And he said to them, "Do you know Laban, the son of Nahor?" And they said, "We know him, and behold, his daughter Rachel is coming along to feed her father's flock." ⁷ While he was yet speaking with them, Rachel the daughter of Laban came to feed her father's sheep, for she was a shepherdess. ⁸ And when Jacob saw Rachel, the daughter of Laban, his mother's brother, he ran and kissed her, and lifted up his voice and wept. ⁹ And Jacob told Rachel that he was the son of Rebekah, her father's sister, and Rachel ran and told her father, and Jacob continued to cry because he had nothing with him to bring to the house of Laban. ¹⁰ And when Laban heard that his sister's son Jacob had come, he ran and kissed him, and embraced him, and brought him into the house, and gave him bread, and he ate. ¹¹ And Jacob related to Laban what his brother Esau had done to him, and what his son Eliphaz had done to him in the road. ¹² And Jacob resided in Laban's house for one month, and Jacob ate and drank in the house of Laban, and afterward Laban said to Jacob, "Tell me what your wages will be, for how can you serve me for nothing?" ¹³ And Laban had no sons but only daughters, and his other wives and handmaids were still barren in those days; and these are the names of Laban's daughters which his wife Adinah had bore to him: the name of the elder was Leah and the name of the younger was Rachel; and Leah was tender-eyed, but Rachel was beautiful and well-favored, and Jacob loved her. ¹⁴ And Jacob said to Laban, "I will serve you seven years for your younger daughter Rachel"; and Laban consented to this and Jacob served Laban seven years for his daughter Rachel. ¹⁵ And in the second year of Jacob's dwelling in Haran, that is in the seventy-ninth year of the life of Jacob, in that year Eber the son of Shem died; he was four hundred and sixty-four years old at his death. ¹⁶ And when Jacob heard that Eber was dead, he grieved exceedingly, and he lamented and mourned over him [for] many days. ¹⁷ And in the third year of Jacob's dwelling in Haran, Bosmath, the daughter of Ishmael, the wife of Esau, bore a son to him, and Esau called his name Reuel. ¹⁸ And in the fourth year of Jacob's residence in the house of Laban, the LORD visited Laban and remembered him on account of Jacob, and sons were born to him, and his firstborn was Beor, his second was Alib, and the third was Chorash. ¹⁹ And the LORD gave Laban riches and honor, sons and daughters, and the man increased greatly on account of Jacob. ²⁰ And in those days Jacob served Laban in all manner of work, in the house and in the field, and the blessing of the LORD was in all that belonged to Laban in the house and in the field. ²¹ And in the fifth year Jehudith,

the daughter of Beeri, the wife of Esau, died in the land of Canaan, and she had no sons but only daughters. ²² And these are the names of her daughters which she bore to Esau: the name of the elder was Marzith, and the name of the younger was Puith. ²³ And when Jehudith died, Esau rose up and went to Seir to hunt in the field as usual, and Esau dwelt in the land of Seir for a long time. ²⁴ And in the sixth year Esau took for a wife, in addition to his other wives, Aholibamah, the daughter of Zebeon the Hivite, and Esau brought her to the land of Canaan. ²⁵ And Aholibamah conceived and bore three sons to Esau: Yeush, Yaalan, and Korah. ²⁶ And in those days there was a quarrel in the land of Canaan between the herdsmen of Esau and the herdsmen of the inhabitants of the land of Canaan, for Esau's cattle and goods were too abundant for him to remain in the land of Canaan, in his father's house, and the land of Canaan could not bear him on account of his cattle. ²⁷ And when Esau saw that his quarreling increased with the inhabitants of the land of Canaan, he rose up and took his wives, and his sons, and his daughters, and all belonging to him, and the cattle which he possessed, and all his property that he had acquired in the land of Canaan, and he went away from the inhabitants of the land to the land of Seir, and Esau and all belonging to him dwelt in the land of Seir. ²⁸ But from time to time Esau would go and see his father and mother in the land of Canaan, and Esau intermarried with the Horites, and he gave his daughters to the sons of Seir, the Horite. ²⁹ And he gave his elder daughter Marzith to Anah, the son of Zebeon, his wife's brother, and he gave Puith to Azar, the son of Bilhan the Horite; and Esau dwelt in the mountain, he and his children, and they were fruitful and multiplied.

CHAPTER 31

¹ And in the seventh year Jacob's service which he served Laban was completed, and Jacob said to Laban, "Give me my wife, for the days of my service are fulfilled"; and Laban did so, and Laban and Jacob assembled all the people of that place and they made a feast. ² And in the evening Laban came to the house, and afterward Jacob came there with the people of the feast, and Laban extinguished all the lights that were there in the house. ³ And Jacob said to Laban, "Why do you do this thing to us?" And Laban answered, "Such is our custom to act in this land." ⁴ And afterward Laban took his daughter Leah, and he brought her to Jacob, and he came to her and Jacob did not know that she was Leah. ⁵ And Laban gave his daughter Leah his maid Zilpah for a handmaid. ⁶ And all the people at the feast knew what Laban had done to Jacob, but they did not tell the thing to Jacob. ⁷ And all the neighbors came to Jacob's house that night, and they ate, and drank, and rejoiced, and played before Leah on timbrels, and with dances, and they responded before Jacob, "Heleah, Heleah." ⁸ And

Jacob heard their words but did not understand their meaning, but he thought such might be their custom in this land. ⁹ And the neighbors spoke these words before Jacob during the night, and all the lights that were in the house Laban had extinguished that night. ¹⁰ And in the morning, when daylight appeared, Jacob turned to his wife and he saw, and behold, it was Leah that had been lying in his bosom, and Jacob said, "Behold, now I know what the neighbors said last night—Heleah, they said, and I did not know it." ¹¹ And Jacob called to Laban, and said to him, "What is this that you did to me? Surely I served you for Rachel, and why did you deceive me and give me Leah?" ¹² And Laban answered Jacob, saying, "It is not so done in our place to give the younger before the elder; now therefore, if you desire to take her sister likewise, take her to you for the service which you will serve me for another seven years." ¹³ And Jacob did so, and he also took Rachel for a wife, and he served Laban seven more years, and Jacob also came to Rachel, and he loved Rachel more than Leah, and Laban gave her his maid Bilhah for a handmaid. ¹⁴ And when the LORD saw that Leah was hated, the LORD opened her womb, and she conceived and bore Jacob four sons in those days. ¹⁵ And these are their names: Reuben, Simeon, Levi, and Judah, and afterward she stopped bearing. ¹⁶ And at that time Rachel was barren, and she had no offspring, and Rachel envied her sister Leah, and when Rachel saw that she bore no children to Jacob, she took her handmaid Bilhah, and she bore Jacob two sons: Dan and Naphtali. ¹⁷ And when Leah saw that she had stopped bearing, she also took her handmaid Zilpah, and she gave her to Jacob for a wife, and Jacob also came to Zilpah, and she also bore Jacob two sons: Gad and Asher. ¹⁸ And in those days Leah conceived again and bore Jacob two sons and one daughter, and these are their names: Issachar, Zebulun, and their sister Dinah. ¹⁹ And Rachel was still barren in those days, and Rachel prayed to the LORD at that time, and she said, "O LORD God, remember me and visit me, I implore You, for now my husband will cast me off, for I have borne him no children. ²⁰ Now O LORD God, hear my supplication before You, and see my affliction, and give me children like one of the handmaids, that I may no longer bear my reproach." ²¹ And God heard her and opened her womb, and Rachel conceived and bore a son, and she said, "The LORD has taken away my reproach," and she called his name Joseph, saying, "May the LORD add to me another son"; and Jacob was ninety-one years old when she bore him. ²² At that time, Jacob's mother Rebekah sent her nurse Deborah, the daughter of Uz, and two of Isaac's servants to Jacob. ²³ And they came to Jacob, to Haran, and they said to him, "Rebekah has sent us to you that you will return to your father's house to the land of Canaan"; and Jacob listened to them in this which his mother had spoken. ²⁴ At that time, the other seven years which Jacob served Laban for Rachel were completed, and it was at the end of fourteen years that he had dwelt in Haran that Jacob said to Laban, "Give me my wives and send me away that I may go to my land, for behold, my mother sent to me from the land of Canaan that I should return to my father's house." ²⁵ And Laban said to him, "Please not so; if I have found favor in your sight, do not leave me; appoint me your wages and I will give them, and remain with me." ²⁶ And Jacob said to him, "This is what you will give me for wages, that I will pass through all your flock this day and take away from them every lamb that is speckled and spotted and such as are brown among the sheep, and among the goats, and if you will do this thing for me I will return, and feed your flock, and keep them as at first." ²⁷ And Laban did so, and Laban removed from his flock all that Jacob had said and gave them to him. ²⁸ And Jacob placed all that he had removed from Laban's flock in the hands of his sons, and Jacob was feeding the remainder of Laban's flock. ²⁹ And when the servants of Isaac which he had sent to Jacob saw that Jacob would not then return with them to his father, to the land of Canaan, they then went away from him, and they returned home to the land of Canaan. ³⁰ And Deborah remained with Jacob in Haran, and she did not return with the servants of Isaac to the land of Canaan, and Deborah resided with Jacob's wives and children in Haran. ³¹ And Jacob served Laban six years longer, and when the sheep brought out, Jacob removed from them such as were speckled and spotted, as he had determined with Laban, and Jacob did so at Laban's for six years, and the man increased abundantly, and he had cattle, and maidservants, and menservants, camels, and donkeys. ³² And Jacob had two hundred droves of cattle, and his cattle were of large size, and of beautiful appearance, and were very productive, and all the families of the sons of men desired to get some of the cattle of Jacob, for they were exceedingly prosperous. ³³ And many of the sons of men came to procure some of Jacob's flock, and Jacob gave them a sheep for a manservant or a maidservant or for a donkey or a camel, or whatever Jacob desired from them they gave him. ³⁴ And Jacob obtained riches, and honor, and possessions by means of these transactions with the sons of men, and the children of Laban envied him of this honor. ³⁵ And in the course of time he heard the words of Laban's sons, saying, "Jacob has taken away all that was our father's, and of that which was our father's he has acquired all this glory." ³⁶ And Jacob beheld the countenance of Laban and of his children, and behold, it was not toward him in those days as it had been before. ³⁷ And the LORD appeared to Jacob at the expiration of the six years, and said to him, "Arise, go out out of this land, and return to the land of your birthplace and I will be with you." ³⁸ And Jacob rose up at that time, and he mounted his children, and wives, and all belonging to him on camels, and he went out to go to the land of Canaan to his father Isaac. [39] And Laban did not know that Jacob had gone from him, for Laban had been sheep-shearing that day. [40] And Rachel stole her father's images, and she took them, and she concealed them on the camel on which she sat, and she went on. [41] And this is the manner of the images: in taking a man who is the firstborn, and slaying him, and taking the hair off his head, and taking salt and salting the head and anointing it in oil, then taking a small tablet of copper or a tablet of gold and writing the name on it, and placing the tablet under his tongue, and taking the head with the tablet under the tongue and putting it in the house, and lighting up lights before it and bowing down to it. [42] And at the time when they bow down to it, it speaks to them in all matters that they ask of it through the power of the name which is written in it. [43] And some make them in the figures of men, of gold and silver, and go to them in times known to them, and the figures receive the influence of the stars, and tell them future things, and in this manner were the images which Rachel stole from her father. [44] And Rachel stole these images which were her father's in order that Laban might not know through them where Jacob had gone. [45] And Laban came home and asked concerning Jacob and his household, and he was not to be found, and Laban sought his images to know where Jacob had gone, and could not find them, and he went to some other images, and he inquired of them and they told him that Jacob had fled from him to his father's, to the land of Canaan. [46] And Laban then rose up and he took his brothers and all his servants, and he went out and pursued Jacob, and he overtook him in Mount Gilead. [47] And Laban said to Jacob, "What is this you have done to me to flee and deceive me, and lead my daughters and their children as captives taken by the sword? [48] And you did not permit me to kiss them and send them away with joy, and you stole my gods and went away." [49] And Jacob answered Laban, saying, "Because I was afraid lest you would take your daughters by force from me; and now with whomsoever you find your gods he will die." [50] And Laban searched for the images and he examined in all Jacob's tents and furniture but could not find them. [51] And Laban said to Jacob, "We will make a covenant together and it will be a testimony between me and you; if you will afflict my daughters, or will take other wives besides my daughters, even God will be a witness between me and you in this matter." [52] And they took stones and made a heap, and Laban said, "This heap is a witness between me and you," therefore he called the name thereof Gilead. [53] And Jacob and Laban offered a sacrifice on the mount, and they ate there by the heap, and they tarried in the mount all night, and Laban rose up early in the morning, and he wept with his daughters, and he kissed them, and he returned to his place. [54] And he hastened and sent off his son Beor, who was seventeen years old, with Abichorof the son of Uz, the son of Nahor, and ten men were with them. [55] And they hastened, and went, and passed on the road before Jacob, and they came by another road to the land of Seir. [56] And they came to Esau and said to him, "Thus says your brother and relative, your mother's brother Laban, the son of Bethuel, saying, [57] Have you heard what your brother Jacob has done to me, who first came to me naked and bare, and I went to meet him, and brought him to my house with honor, and I made him great, and I gave him my two daughters for wives and also two of my maids? [58] And God blessed him on my account, and he increased abundantly, and had sons, daughters, and maidservants. [59] He also has an immense stock of flocks and herds, camels and donkeys, also silver and gold in abundance; and when he saw that his wealth increased, he left me while I went to shear my sheep, and he rose up and fled in secrecy. [60] And he lifted his wives and children on camels, and he led away all his cattle and property which he acquired in my land, and he lifted up his countenance to go to his father Isaac, to the land of Canaan. [61] And he did not permit me to kiss my daughters and their children, and he led my daughters as captives taken by the sword, and he also stole my gods and he fled. [62] And now I have left him in the mountain of the Brook of Jabuk, him and all belonging to him; he lacks nothing. [63] If it is your wish to go to him, go then and there you will find him, and you can do to him as your soul desires"; and Laban's messengers came and told Esau all these things. [64] And Esau heard all the words of Laban's messengers, and his anger was greatly kindled against Jacob, and he remembered his hatred, and his anger burned within him. [65] And Esau hastened and took his children, and servants, and the souls of his household, being sixty men, and he went and assembled all the children of Seir the Horite and their people, being three hundred and forty men, and took all this number of four hundred men with drawn swords, and he went to Jacob to strike him. [66] And Esau divided this number into several parts, and he took the sixty men of his children, and servants, and the souls of his household as one head and gave them in [the] care of his eldest son Eliphaz. [67] And he gave the remaining heads to the care of the six sons of Seir the Horite, and he placed every man over his generations and children. [68] And the whole of this camp went as it was, and Esau went among them toward Jacob, and he conducted them with speed. [69] And Laban's messengers departed from Esau and went to the land of Canaan, and they came to the house of Rebekah, the mother of Jacob and Esau. [70] And they told her, saying, "Behold, your son Esau has gone against his brother Jacob with four hundred men, for he heard that he was coming, and he has gone to make war with him, and to strike him, and to take all that he has."

71 And Rebekah hastened and sent seventy-two men from the servants of Isaac to meet Jacob on the road, for she said, "Perhaps Esau may make war in the road when he meets him." 72 And these messengers went on the road to meet Jacob, and they met him in the road of the brook on the opposite side of the brook Jabuk, and Jacob said when he saw them, "This camp is destined to me from God," and Jacob called the name of that place Machnayim. 73 And Jacob knew all his father's people, and he kissed them, and embraced them, and came with them, and Jacob asked them concerning his father and mother, and they said they were well. 74 And these messengers said to Jacob, "Your mother Rebekah has sent us to you, saying, I have heard, my son, that your brother Esau has gone out against you on the road with men from the children of Seir the Horite. 75 And therefore, my son, listen to my voice and see with your counsel what you will do, and when he comes up to you, supplicate him, and do not speak rashly to him, and give him a present from what you possess, and from what God has favored | you with. 76 And when he asks you concerning your affairs, conceal nothing from him; perhaps he may turn from his anger against you and you will thereby save your soul—you and all belonging to you—for it is your duty to honor him, for he is your elder brother." 77 And when Jacob heard the words of his mother which the messengers had spoken to him, Jacob lifted up his voice and wept bitterly, and did as his mother then commanded him.

CHAPTER 32

1 And at that time Jacob sent messengers to his brother Esau toward the land of Seir, and he spoke words of supplication to him. 2 And he commanded them, saying, "Thus you will say to my lord, to Esau: Thus says your servant Jacob: Do not let my lord imagine that my father's blessing with which he blessed me has proved beneficial to me. 3 For I have been with Laban these twenty years, and he deceived me and changed my wages ten times, as it has all been already told to my lord. 4 And I served him in his house very laboriously, and afterward God saw my affliction, my labor, and the work of my hands, and He caused me to find grace and favor in His sight. 5 And afterward, through God's great mercy and kindness, I acquired oxen, and donkeys, and cattle, and menservants, and maidservants. 6 And now I am coming to my land and my home, to my father and mother who are in the land of Canaan; and I have sent to let my lord know all this in order to find favor in the sight of my lord, so that he may not imagine that I have obtained wealth of myself, or that the blessing with which my father blessed me has benefited me." 7 And those messengers went to Esau and found him on the borders of the land of Edom going toward Jacob, and four hundred men of the children of Seir the Horite were standing with drawn swords. 8 And the messengers of Jacob told Esau all the words that Jacob had spoken to them concerning Esau. 9 And Esau answered them with pride and contempt, and said to them, "Surely I have heard and truly it has been told to me what Jacob has done to Laban, who exalted him in his house and gave him his daughters for wives, and he begot sons and daughters, and abundantly increased in wealth and riches in Laban's house through his means. 10 And when he saw that his wealth was abundant and his riches great, he fled from Laban's house with all belonging to him, and he led Laban's daughters away from the face of their father, as captives taken by the sword without telling him of it. 11 And not only to Laban has Jacob done this, but he has also done so to me and has twice supplanted me, and will I be silent? 12 Now I have therefore come this day with my camps to meet him, and I will do to him according to the desire of my heart." 13 And the messengers returned and came to Jacob, and said to him, "We came to your brother, to Esau, and we told him all your words, and thus he has answered us, and behold, he comes to meet you with four hundred men. 14 Now then, know and see what you will do and pray before God to deliver you from him." 15 And when he heard the words of his brother which he had spoken to the messengers of Jacob, Jacob was greatly afraid, and he was distressed. 16 And Jacob prayed to the LORD his God, and he said, "O LORD God of my fathers, Abraham and Isaac: You said to me when I went away from my father's house, saying, 17 I am the LORD God of your father Abraham and the God of Isaac; I give this land to you and your seed after you, and I will make your seed as the stars of the heavens, and you will spread out to the four sides of [the] heavens, and in you and in your Seed all the families of the earth will be blessed. 18 And you established Your words and gave to me riches, and children, and cattle—as the utmost wishes of my heart, You gave to Your servant; You gave to me all that I asked from You, so that I lacked nothing. 19 And afterward You said to me, Return to your parents and to your birthplace and I will still do well with you. 20 And now that I have come, and You delivered me from Laban, I will fall into the hands of Esau who will slay me, yes, together with the mothers of my children. 21 Now therefore, O LORD God, please also deliver me from the hands of my brother Esau, for I am greatly afraid of him. 22 And if there is no righteousness in me, do it for the sake of Abraham and my father Isaac. 23 For I know that through kindness and mercy I have acquired this wealth; now therefore, I implore You to deliver me this day with Your kindness and to answer me." 24 And Jacob ceased praying to the LORD, and he divided the people that were with him with the flocks and cattle into two camps, and he gave half to the care of Damesek, the son of Eliezer, Abraham's servant, for a camp, with his children, and the other half he gave to the care of

his brother Elianus the son of Eliezer, to be for a camp with his children. 25 And he commanded them, saying, "Keep yourselves at a distance with your camps, and do not come too near each other, and if Esau comes to one camp and slays it, the other camp at a distance from it will escape him." 26 And Jacob tarried there that night, and during the whole night he gave his servants instructions concerning the forces and his children. 27 And the LORD heard the prayer of Jacob on that day, and the LORD then delivered Jacob from the hands of his brother Esau. 28 And the LORD sent three messengers of the messengers of Heaven, and they went before Esau and came to him. 29 And these messengers appeared to Esau and his people as two thousand men, riding on horses furnished with all sorts of war instruments, and they appeared in the sight of Esau and all his men to be divided into four camps, with four chiefs to them. 30 And one camp went on and they found Esau coming with four hundred men toward his brother Jacob, and this camp ran toward Esau and his people and terrified them, and Esau fell off the horse in alarm, and all his men separated from him in that place, for they were greatly afraid. 31 And the whole of the camp shouted after them when they fled from Esau, and all the warlike men answered, saying, 32 "Surely we are the servants of Jacob, who is the servant of God, and who then can stand against us?" And Esau said to them, "O then, my lord and brother Jacob is your lord, whom I have not seen for these twenty years, and now that I have come to see him this day, do you treat me in this manner?" 33 And the messengers answered him, saying, "As the LORD lives, were Jacob of whom you speak not your brother, we would not have let one remaining from you and your people, but only on account of Jacob we will do nothing to them." 34 And this camp passed from Esau and his men and it went away, and Esau and his men had gone from them about a league when the second camp came toward him with all sorts of weapons, and they also did to Esau and his men as the first camp had done to them. 35 And when they had left it to go on, behold, the third camp came toward him and they were all terrified, and Esau fell off the horse, and the whole camp cried out, and said, "Surely we are the servants of Jacob, who is the servant of God, and who can stand against us?" 36 And Esau again answered them, saying, "O then, Jacob my lord and your lord is my brother, and for twenty years I have not seen his countenance and hearing this day that he was coming, I went this day to meet him, and do you treat me in this manner?" 37 And they answered him, and said to him, "As the LORD lives, were Jacob not your brother as you have said, we would not have left a remnant from you and your men, but on account of Jacob of whom you speak being your brother, we will not meddle with you or your men." 38 And the third camp also passed from them, and he still continued his road with his men toward Jacob, when the fourth camp came toward him, and they also did to him and his men as the others had done. 39 And when Esau beheld the evil which the four messengers had done to him and to his men, he became greatly afraid of his brother Jacob, and he went to meet him in peace. 40 And Esau concealed his hatred against Jacob, because he was afraid of his life on account of his brother Jacob, and because he imagined that the four camps that he had lighted on were Jacob's servants. 41 And Jacob tarried that night with his servants in their camps, and he resolved with his servants to give a present to Esau from all that he had with him, and from all his property; and Jacob rose up in the morning, he and his men, and they chose from among the cattle a present for Esau. 42 And this is the amount of the present which Jacob chose from his flock to give to his brother Esau: and he selected two hundred and forty head from the flocks, and he selected from the camels and donkeys thirty each, and of the herds he chose fifty cows. 43 And he put them all in ten droves, and he placed each sort by itself, and he delivered them into the hands of ten of his servants, each drove by itself. 44 And he commanded them, and said to them, "Keep yourselves at a distance from each other, and put a space between the droves, and when Esau and those who are with him will meet you and ask you, saying, Whose are you, and where do you go, and to whom belongs all this before you, you will say to them, We are the servants of Jacob, and we come to meet Esau in peace, and behold, Jacob comes behind us. 45 And that which is before us is a present sent from Jacob to his brother Esau. 46 And if they will say to you, Why does he delay behind you, from coming to meet his brother and to see his face, then you will say to them, Surely he comes joyfully behind us to meet his brother, for he said, I will appease him with the present that goes to him, and after this I will see his face—perhaps he will accept me." 47 So the whole present passed on in the hands of his servants, and went before him on that day, and he lodged that night with his camps by the border of the Brook of Jabuk, and he rose up in the midst of the night, and he took his wives, and his maidservants, and all belonging to him, and he made them pass over the ford Jabuk that night. 48 And when he made all belonging to him pass over the brook, Jacob was left by himself, and a Man met him, and he wrestled with Him that night until the breaking of the day, and the hollow of Jacob's thigh was out of joint through wrestling with Him. 49 And at the break of day the Man left Jacob there, and He blessed him and went away, and Jacob passed the brook at the break of day, and he halted on his thigh. 50 And the sun rose on him when he had passed the brook, and he came up to the place of his cattle and children. 51 And they went on until midday, and while they were going, the present was passing on before them. 52 And Jacob lifted up his eyes and looked, and behold, Esau was at a distance, coming along with many men, about four hundred, and Jacob was greatly afraid of his brother. ⁵³ And Jacob hastened and divided his children to his wives and his handmaids, and he put his daughter Dinah in a chest, and delivered her into the hands of his servants. ⁵⁴ And he passed before his children and wives to meet his brother, and he bowed down to the ground. He bowed down seven times until he approached his brother, and God caused Jacob to find grace and favor in the sight of Esau and his men, for God had heard the prayer of Jacob. ⁵⁵ And the fear of Jacob and his terror fell on his brother Esau, for Esau was greatly afraid of Jacob for what the messengers of God had done to Esau, and Esau's anger against Jacob was turned into kindness. ⁵⁶ And when Esau saw Jacob running toward him, he also ran toward him, and he embraced him, and he fell on his neck, and they kissed and wept. ⁵⁷ And God put fear and kindness toward Jacob in the hearts of the men that came with Esau, and they also kissed Jacob and embraced him. ⁵⁸ And also Eliphaz, the son of Esau, with his four brothers, sons of Esau, wept with Jacob, and they kissed him and embraced him, for the fear of Jacob had fallen on them all. ⁵⁹ And Esau lifted up his eyes and saw the women with their offspring, the children of Jacob, walking behind Jacob and bowing along the road to Esau. ⁶⁰ And Esau said to Jacob, "Who are these with you, my brother? Are they your children or your servants?" And Jacob answered Esau and said, "They are my children which God has graciously given to your servant." ⁶¹ And while Jacob was speaking to Esau and his men, Esau beheld the whole camp, and he said to Jacob, "From where did you get the whole of the camp that I met last night?" And Jacob said, "To find favor in the sight of my lord, it is that which God graciously gave to your servant." ⁶² And the present came before Esau, and Jacob pressed Esau, saying, "Please take the present that I have brought to my lord," and Esau said, "Why is this my purpose? Keep that which you have to yourself." ⁶³ And Jacob said, "It is incumbent on me to give all this, since I have seen your face, that you still live in peace." ⁶⁴ And Esau refused to take the present, and Jacob said to him, "I implore you, my lord, if I have now found favor in your sight, then receive my present at my hand, for I have therefore seen your face, as though I had seen a godlike face, because you were pleased with me." ⁶⁵ And Esau took the present, and Jacob also gave silver, and gold, and bdellium to Esau, for he pressed him so much that he took them. ⁶⁶ And Esau divided the cattle that were in the camp, and he gave the half to the men who had come with him, for they had come on hire, and the other half he delivered to the hands of his children. ⁶⁷ And the silver, and gold, and bdellium he gave in the hands of his eldest son Eliphaz, and Esau said to Jacob, "Let us remain with you, and we will go slowly along with you until you come to my place with me,

that we may dwell there together." ⁶⁸ And Jacob answered his brother and said, "I would do as my lord speaks to me, but my lord knows that the children are tender, and the flocks and herds with their young who are with me only go slowly, for if they went swiftly they would all die, for you know their burdens and their fatigue. ⁶⁹ Therefore, let my lord pass on before his servant, and I will go on slowly for the sake of the children and the flock, until I come to my lord's place—to Seir." ⁷⁰ And Esau said to Jacob, "I will place with you some of the people that are with me to take care of you in the road, and to bear your fatigue and burden," and he said, "What need is there of that my lord, if I may find grace in your sight? ⁷¹ Behold, I will come to you, to Seir, to dwell there together as you have spoken; go then with your people for I will follow you." ⁷² And Jacob said this to Esau in order to remove Esau and his men from him, so that afterward Jacob might go to his father's house, to the land of Canaan. ⁷³ And Esau listened to the voice of Jacob, and Esau returned with the four hundred men that were with him on their road to Seir, and that day Jacob and all belonging to him went as far as the extremity of the land of Canaan in its borders, and he remained there some time.

CHAPTER 33

¹ And some time after Jacob went away from the borders of the land, he came to the land of Shalem, that is the city of Shechem, which is in the land of Canaan, and he rested in front of the city. ² And he bought a parcel of the field which was there from the children of Hamor, the people of the land, for five shekels. ³ And Jacob built himself a house there, and he pitched his tent there, and he made shelters for his cattle; therefore he called the name of that place Succoth. ⁴ And Jacob remained in Succoth a year and six months. ⁵ At that time some of the women of the inhabitants of the land went to the city of Shechem to dance and rejoice with the daughters of the people of the city, and when they went out, then Rachel and Leah, the wives of Jacob, with their families, also went to behold the rejoicing of the daughters of the city. ⁶ And Dinah, the daughter of Jacob, also went along with them and saw the daughters of the city, and they remained there before these daughters while all the people of the city were standing by them to behold their rejoicings, and all the great people of the city were there. ⁷ And Shechem, the son of Hamor, the prince of the land, was also standing there to see them. ⁸ And Shechem beheld Dinah, the daughter of Jacob, sitting with her mother before the daughters of the city, and the young woman pleased him greatly, and he asked his friends and his people there, saying, "Whose daughter is that sitting among the women, whom I do not know in this city?" ⁹ And they said to him, "Surely this is the daughter of Jacob, the son of Isaac the Hebrew, who has dwelt in this city for some

time, and when it was reported that the daughters of the land were going out to rejoice, she went with her mother and maidservants to sit among them as you see." [10] And Shechem beheld Dinah, the daughter of Jacob, and when he looked at her his soul became fixed on Dinah. [11] And he sent and had her taken by force, and Dinah came to the house of Shechem, and he seized her forcibly, and lay with her, and humbled her, and he loved her exceedingly, and placed her in his house. [12] And they came and told the thing to Jacob, and when Jacob heard that Shechem had defiled his daughter Dinah, Jacob sent twelve of his servants to fetch Dinah from the house of Shechem, and they went and came to the house of Shechem to take Dinah away from there. [13] And when they came, Shechem went out to them with his men and drove them from his house, and he would not permit them to come before Dinah, but Shechem was sitting with Dinah, kissing and embracing her before their eyes. [14] And the servants of Jacob came back and told him, saying, "When we came, he and his men drove us away, and thus Shechem did to Dinah before our eyes." [15] And Jacob knew, moreover, that Shechem had defiled his daughter, but he said nothing, and his sons were feeding his cattle in the field, and Jacob remained silent until their return. [16] And before his sons came home, Jacob sent two maidens from his servants' daughters to take care of Dinah in the house of Shechem and to remain with her, and Shechem sent three of his friends to his father Hamor the son of Chiddekem, the son of Pered, saying, "Get this young woman [for] me for a wife." [17] And Hamor the son of Chiddekem the Hivite came to the house of his son Shechem, and he sat before him, and Hamor said to his son, "Shechem, is there then no woman among the daughters of your people that you will take a Hebrew woman who is not of your people?" [18] And Shechem said to him, "Only her must you get for me, for she is delightful in my sight"; and Hamor did according to the word of his son, for he was greatly beloved by him. [19] And Hamor went out to Jacob to commune with him concerning this matter, and when he had gone from the house of his son Shechem, before he came to Jacob to speak to him, behold, the sons of Jacob had come from the field as soon as they heard the thing that Shechem the son of Hamor had done. [20] And the men were very much grieved concerning their sister, and they all came home fired with anger, before the time of gathering in their cattle. [21] And they came and sat before their father, and they spoke to him kindled with wrath, saying, "Surely death is due to this man and to his household, because the LORD God of the whole earth commanded Noah and his children that man will never rob, nor commit adultery; now behold, Shechem has both ravaged and committed fornication with our sister, and not one of all the people of the city spoke a word to him. [22] Surely you know and understand that the judgment of death is due to Shechem, and to his father, and to the whole city on account of the thing which he has done." [23] And while they were speaking before their father in this matter, behold, Hamor the father of Shechem came to speak to Jacob the words of his son concerning Dinah, and he sat before Jacob and before his sons. [24] And Hamor spoke to them, saying, "The soul of my son Shechem longs for your daughter; please give her to him for a wife and intermarry with us; give us your daughters and we will give you our daughters, and you will dwell with us in our land, and we will be as one people in the land. [25] For our land is very extensive, so dwell and trade therein and get possessions in it, and do therein as you desire, and no one will prevent you by saying a word to you." [26] And Hamor ceased speaking to Jacob and his sons, and behold, his son Shechem had come after him, and he sat before them. [27] And Shechem spoke before Jacob and his sons, saying, "May I find favor in your sight that you will give me your daughter, and whatever you say to me I will do that for her. [28] Ask me for abundance of dowry and gift, and I will give it, and whatever you will say to me I will do that, and whoever he is that will rebel against your orders, he will die; only give me the young woman for a wife." [29] And Simeon and Levi answered Hamor and his son Shechem deceitfully, saying, "All you have spoken to us we will do for you. [30] And behold, our sister is in your house, but keep away from her until we send to our father Isaac concerning this matter, for we can do nothing without his consent. [31] For he knows the ways of our father Abraham, and whatever he says to us we will tell you—we will conceal nothing from you." [32] And Simeon and Levi spoke this to Shechem and his father in order to find a pretext, and to seek counsel what was to be done to Shechem and to his city in this matter. [33] And when Shechem and his father heard the words of Simeon and Levi, it seemed good in their sight, and Shechem and his father came out to go home. [34] And when they had gone, the sons of Jacob said to their father, saying, "Behold, we know that death is due to these wicked ones and to their city, because they transgressed that which God had commanded to Noah, and his children, and his seed after them. [35] And also because Shechem did this thing to our sister Dinah in defiling her, for such vileness will never be done among us. [36] Now therefore, know and see what you will do and seek counsel and pretext [regarding] what is to be done to them, in order to kill all the inhabitants of this city." [37] And Simeon said to them, "Here is a proper suggestion for you: tell them to circumcise every male among them as we are circumcised, and if they do not wish to do this, we will take our daughter from them and go away. [38] And if they consent to do this and will do it, then when they are sunk down with pain, we will attack them with our swords, as on one who is quiet and peaceable, and we will slay every male person among them." ³⁹ And Simeon's advice pleased them, and Simeon and Levi resolved to do to them as it was proposed. ⁴⁰ And on the next morning Shechem and his father Hamor came to Jacob and his sons again to speak concerning Dinah, and to hear what answer the sons of Jacob would give to their words. ⁴¹ And the sons of Jacob spoke deceitfully to them, saying, "We told our father Isaac all your words, and your words pleased him. ⁴² But he spoke to us, saying, Thus his father Abraham commanded him from God, the Lord of the whole earth, that: Any man who is not of his descendants that should wish to take one of his daughters will cause every male belonging to him to be circumcised, as we are circumcised, and then we may give him our daughter for a wife. ⁴³ Now we have made known to you all our ways that our father spoke to us, for we cannot do this of which you spoke to us, to give our daughter to an uncircumcised man, for it is a disgrace to us. ⁴⁴ But herein will we consent to you to give you our daughter, and we will also take your daughters to ourselves, and will dwell among you, and be one people as you have spoken, if you will listen to us, and consent to be like us, to circumcise every male belonging to you, as we are circumcised. ⁴⁵ And if you will not listen to us, to have every male circumcised as we are circumcised, as we have commanded, then we will come to you, and take our daughter from you, and go away." ⁴⁶ And Shechem and his father Hamor heard the words of the sons of Jacob, and the thing pleased them exceedingly, and Shechem and his father Hamor hastened to do the wishes of the sons of Jacob, for Shechem was very fond of Dinah, and his soul was riveted to her. ⁴⁷ And Shechem and his father Hamor hastened to the gate of the city, and they assembled all the men of their city and spoke to them the words of the sons of Jacob, saying, ⁴⁸ "We came to these men, the sons of Jacob, and we spoke to them concerning their daughter, and these men will consent to do according to our wishes, and behold, our land is of great extent for them, and they will dwell in it, and trade in it, and we will be one people; we will take their daughters, and we will give our daughters to them for wives. ⁴⁹ But only on this condition will these men consent to do this thing: that every male among us must be circumcised as they are circumcised, as their God commanded them, and when we will have done according to their instructions to be circumcised, then they will dwell among us, together with their cattle and possessions, and we will be as one people with them." ⁵⁰ And when all the men of the city heard the words of Shechem and his father Hamor, then all the men of their city were agreeable to this proposal, and they obeyed to be circumcised, for Shechem and his father Hamor were greatly esteemed by them, being the princes of the land. ⁵¹ And on the next day, Shechem and his father Hamor rose up early in the morning, and they assembled all

the men of their city into the middle of the city, and they called for the sons of Jacob, who circumcised every male belonging to them on that day and the next. ⁵² And they circumcised Shechem and his father Hamor, and the five brothers of Shechem, and then everyone rose up and went home, for this thing was from the LORD against the city of Shechem, and Simeon's counsel was from the LORD in this matter in order that the LORD might deliver the city of Shechem into the hands of Jacob's two sons.

CHAPTER 34

¹ And the number of all the males that were circumcised were six hundred and forty-five men, and two hundred and forty-six children. ² But Chiddekem, son of Pered, the father of Hamor, and his six brothers, would not listen to Shechem and his father Hamor, and they would not be circumcised, for the proposal of the sons of Jacob was loathsome in their sight, and their anger was greatly roused at this, that the people of the city had not listened to them. ³ And in the evening of the second day they found eight small children who had not been circumcised, for their mothers had concealed them from Shechem, and his father Hamor, and from the men of the city. ⁴ And Shechem and his father Hamor sent to have them brought before them to be circumcised when Chiddekem and his six brothers sprang at them with their swords and sought to slay them. ⁵ And they also sought to slay Shechem and his father Hamor, and they sought to slay Dinah with them on account of this matter. ⁶ And they said to them, "What is this thing that you have done? Are there no women among the daughters of your brothers the Canaanites that you wish to take to yourselves daughters of the Hebrews, whom you did not know before, and will do this act which your fathers never commanded you? ⁷ Do you imagine that you will succeed through this act which you have done? And what will you answer in this affair to your brothers the Canaanites who will come tomorrow and ask you concerning this thing? ⁸ And if your act will not appear just and good in their sight, what will you do for your lives, and me for our lives, in your not having listened to our voices? ⁹ And if the inhabitants of the land and all your brothers, the children of Ham, will hear of your act, saying, ¹⁰ On account of a Hebrew woman, Shechem, and his father Hamor, and all the inhabitants of their city did that with which they had been unacquainted and which their ancestors never commanded them; where then will you fly, or where conceal your shame, all your days before your brothers, the inhabitants of the land of Canaan? ¹¹ Now therefore, we cannot bear up against this thing which you have done, neither can we be burdened with this yoke on us, which our ancestors did not command us. ¹² Behold, tomorrow we will go and assemble all our brothers, the Canaanite brothers who dwell in the land, and we will

all come and strike you and all those who trust in you, that there will not be a remnant left from you or them." [13] And when Hamor and his son Shechem and all the people of the city heard the words of Chiddekem and his brothers, they were terribly afraid for their lives at their words, and they converted of what they had done. [14] And Shechem and his father Hamor answered their father Chiddekem and his brothers, and they said to them, "All the words which you spoke to us are true. [15] Now do not say, nor imagine in your hearts, that on account of the love of the Hebrews we did this thing that our ancestors did not command us. [16] But because we saw that it was not their intention and desire to accede to our wishes concerning their daughter as to our taking her, except on this condition, so we listened to their voices and did this act which you saw in order to obtain our desire from them. [17] And when we will have obtained our request from them, we will then return to them and do to them that which you say to us. [18] We implore you then to wait and tarry until our flesh will be healed and we again become strong, and we will then go together against them, and do to them that which is in your hearts and in ours." [19] And Dinah the daughter of Jacob heard all these words which Chiddekem and his brothers had spoken, and what Hamor, and his son Shechem, and the people of their city had answered them. [20] And she hastened and sent one of her maidens—that her father had sent to take care of her in the house of Shechem—to Jacob her father and to her brothers, saying, [21] "Thus Chiddekem and his brothers advised concerning you, and thus Hamor, and Shechem, and the people of the city answered them." [22] And when Jacob heard these words he was filled with wrath, and he was indignant at them, and his anger was kindled against them. [23] And Simeon and Levi swore and said, "As the LORD lives, the God of the whole earth, by this time tomorrow there will not be a remnant left in the whole city." [24] And twenty young men had concealed themselves who were not circumcised, and these young men fought against Simeon and Levi, and Simeon and Levi killed eighteen of them, and two fled from them and escaped to some lime pits that were in the city, and Simeon and Levi sought for them, but could not find them. [25] And Simeon and Levi continued to go around in the city, and they killed all the people of the city at the edge of the sword, and they left none remaining. [26] And there was a great consternation in the midst of the city, and the cry of the people of the city ascended to Heaven, and all the women and children cried aloud. [27] And Simeon and Levi slew all the city; they did not leave [even one] male remaining in the whole city. [28] And they slew Hamor and his son Shechem at the edge of the sword, and they brought Dinah away from the house of Shechem, and they went from there. [29] And the sons of Jacob went and returned, and came on the slain, and spoiled all their property which was in the city and the field. [30] And while they were taking the spoil, three hundred men stood up, and threw dust at them, and struck them with stones; then Simeon turned to them and he slew them all with the edge of the sword, and Simeon turned before Levi, and came into the city. [31] And they took away their sheep, and their oxen, and their cattle, and also the remainder of the women and little ones, and they led all these away, and they opened a gate, and went out, and came to their father Jacob with vigor. [32] And when Jacob saw all that they had done to the city, and saw the spoil that they took from them, Jacob was very angry at them, and Jacob said to them, "What is this that you have done to me? Behold, I obtained rest among the Canaanite inhabitants of the land, and none of them meddled with me. [33] And now you have done [this] to make me obnoxious to the inhabitants of the land, among the Canaanites and the Perizzites, and I am but of a small number, and they will all assemble against me and slay me when they hear of your work with their brothers, and my household and I will be destroyed." [34] And Simeon, and Levi, and all their brothers with them answered their father Jacob and said to him, "Behold, we live in the land, and will Shechem do this to our sister? Why are you silent at all that Shechem has done? And will he deal with our sister as with a harlot in the streets?" [35] And the number of women whom Simeon and Levi took captives from the city of Shechem, whom they did not slay, was eighty-five who had not known a man. [36] And among them was a young woman of beautiful appearance and well-favored, whose name was Bunah, and Simeon took her for a wife, and the number of the males which they took captives and did not slay was forty-seven men, and the rest they slew. [37] And all the young men and women that Simeon and Levi had taken captives from the city of Shechem were servants to the sons of Jacob and to their children after them until the day of the sons of Jacob going out from the land of Egypt. [38] And when Simeon and Levi had gone out from the city, the two young men that were left, who had concealed themselves in the city, and did not die among the people of the city, rose up, and these young men went into the city and walked around in it, and found the city desolate without man, and only women weeping, and these young men cried out and said, "Behold, this is the evil which the sons of Jacob the Hebrew did to this city in their having destroyed one of the Canaanite cities this day, and they were not afraid of their lives in all the land of Canaan." [39] And these men left the city and went to the city of Tapnach, and they came there and told the inhabitants of Tapnach all that had befallen them, and all that the sons of Jacob had done to the city of Shechem. [40] And the information reached Jashub king of Tapnach, and he sent men to the city of Shechem to see those young men, for the king did not believe them in this account, saying, "How could two men lay waste such a large town as Shechem?" [41] And the messengers of Jashub came back and told him, saying, "We came to the city, and it is destroyed—there is not a man there, only weeping women; neither is any flock or cattle there, for the sons of Jacob took away all that was in the city." [42] And Jashub wondered at this, saying, "How could two men do this thing, to destroy such a large city, and not one man was able to stand against them? [43] For the like has not been from the days of Nimrod, and not even from the remotest time has the like taken place"; and Jashub, king of Tapnach, said to his people, "Be courageous and we will go and fight against these Hebrews, and do to them as they did to the city, and we will avenge the cause of the people of the city." [44] And Jashub, king of Tapnach, consulted with his counselors about this matter, and his advisers said to him, "You will not prevail over the Hebrews alone, for they must be powerful to do this work to the whole city. [45] If two of them laid waste the whole city, and no one stood against them, surely if you will go against them, they will all rise against us and destroy us likewise. [46] But if you will send to all the kings that surround us, and let them come together, then we will go with them and fight against the sons of Jacob; then you will prevail against them." [47] And Jashub heard the words of his counselors, and their words pleased him and his people, and he did so; and Jashub king of Tapnach sent to all the kings of the Amorites that surrounded Shechem and Tapnach, saying, [48] "Go up with me and assist me, and we will strike Jacob the Hebrew and all his sons, and destroy them from the earth, for thus he did to the city of Shechem, and do you not know of it?" [49] And all the kings of the Amorites heard the evil that the sons of Jacob had done to the city of Shechem, and they were greatly astonished at them. [50] And the seven kings of the Amorites assembled with all their armies, about ten thousand men with drawn swords, and they came to fight against the sons of Jacob; and Jacob heard that the kings of the Amorites had assembled to fight against his sons, and Jacob was greatly afraid, and it distressed him. [51] And Jacob exclaimed against Simeon and Levi, saying, "What is this act that you did? Why have you injured me, to bring all the children of Canaan against me to destroy me and my household? For I was at rest, even my household and I, and you have done this thing to me, and provoked the inhabitants of the land against me by your proceedings." [52] And Judah answered his father, saying, "Was it for nothing [that] my brothers Simeon and Levi killed all the inhabitants of Shechem? Surely it was because Shechem had humbled our sister and transgressed the command of our God to Noah and his children, for Shechem took our sister away by force and committed adultery with her. [53] And Shechem did all this evil and not one of the inhabitants of his city interfered with him to say, Why will you do this? Surely my brothers went and struck the city for this [reason], and the LORD delivered it into their hands, because its inhabitants had transgressed the commands of our God. Is it then for nothing that they have done all this? [54] And now why are you afraid or distressed, and why are you displeased at my brothers, and why is your anger kindled against them? [55] Surely our God who delivered the city of Shechem and its people into their hand will also deliver into our hands all the Canaanite kings who are coming against us, and we will do to them as my brothers did to Shechem. [56] Now be tranquil about them and cast away your fears, but trust in the LORD our God, and pray to Him to assist us, and deliver us, and deliver our enemies into our hands." [57] And Judah called to one of his father's servants, "Go now and see where those kings who are coming against us are situated with their armies." [58] And the servant went and looked far off, and went up opposite Mount Sihon, and saw all the camps of the kings standing in the fields, and he returned to Judah and said, "Behold, the kings are situated in the field with all their camps—a people exceedingly numerous, like to the sand on the seashore." [59] And Judah said to Simeon, and Levi, and to all his brothers, "Strengthen yourselves and be sons of valor, for the LORD our God is with us; do not fear them. [60] Stand ready, each man, girt with his weapons of war, his bow and his sword, and we will go and fight against these uncircumcised men; the LORD is our God; He will save us." [61] And they rose up, and each girded on his weapons of war, great and small, eleven sons of Jacob, and all the servants of Jacob with them. [62] And all the servants of Isaac who were with Isaac in Hebron, all came to them equipped in all sorts of war instruments, and the sons of Jacob and their servants, being one hundred and twelve men, went toward these kings, and Jacob also went with them. [63] And the sons of Jacob sent to their father Isaac, the son of Abraham, to Hebron, the same is Kirjath-Arba, saying, [64] "We implore you: pray for us to the LORD our God to protect us from the hands of the Canaanites who are coming against us, and to deliver them into our hands." [65] And Isaac the son of Abraham prayed to the LORD for his sons, and he said, "O LORD God, You promised my father, saying, I will multiply your seed as the stars of the heavens; and You also promised me. And establish Your word now that the kings of Canaan are coming together to make war with my children because they committed no violence. [66] Now therefore, O LORD God, God of the whole earth, please pervert the counsel of these kings that they may not fight against my sons. [67] And impress the hearts of these kings and their people with the terror of my sons and bring down their pride that they may turn away from my sons. [68] And deliver my sons and their servants from them with Your strong hand and outstretched arm, for power and might are in Your hands to do all this." [69] And the sons of Jacob and their servants went toward these kings, and they trusted in the LORD their God, and while they were going, their father Jacob also prayed to the LORD and said, "O LORD God, powerful and exalted God, who has reigned from days of old, from then until now and forever: [70] You are He who stirs up wars and causes them to cease; in Your hand are power and might to exalt and to bring down; O may my prayer be acceptable before You that You may turn to me with Your mercies to impress the hearts of these kings and their people with the terror of my sons, and terrify them and their camps, and deliver all those that trust in You with Your great kindness, for it is You who can bring people under us and reduce nations under our power."

CHAPTER 35

[1] And all the kings of the Amorites came and took their stand in the field to consult with their counselors what was to be done with the sons of Jacob, for they were still afraid of them, saying, "Behold, two of them slew the whole of the city of Shechem." [2] And the LORD heard the prayers of Isaac and Jacob, and He filled the hearts of all these kings' advisers with great fear and terror that they unanimously exclaimed, [3] "Are you silly this day, or is there no understanding in you, that you will fight with the Hebrews, and why will you take a delight in your own destruction this day? [4] Behold, two of them came to the city of Shechem without fear or terror, and they killed all the inhabitants of the city, that no man stood up against them, and how will you be able to fight with them all? [5] Surely you know that their God is exceedingly fond of them, and has done mighty things for them, such as have not been done from days of old, and among all the gods of [the] nations there is none [that] can do like to His mighty deeds. [6] Surely He delivered their father Abraham, the Hebrew, from the hand of Nimrod, and from the hand of all his people who had many times sought to slay him. [7] He also delivered him from the fire in which King Nimrod had cast him, and his God delivered him from it. [8] And who else can do the like? Surely it was Abraham who slew the five kings of Elam when they had touched his brother's son who in those days dwelt in Sodom; [9] and he took his servant that was faithful in his house and a few of his men, and they pursued the kings of Elam in one night, and killed them, and restored to his brother's son all his property which they had taken from him. [10] And surely you know the God of these Hebrews is much delighted with them, and they are also delighted with Him, for they know that He delivered them from all their enemies. [11] And behold, through his love toward his God, Abraham took his only and precious son and intended to bring him up as a burnt-offering to his God, and had it not

been for God who prevented him from doing this, he would then have done it through his love for his God. [12] And God saw all his works, and swore to him, and promised him that He would deliver his sons and all his seed from every trouble that would befall them, because he had done this thing, and through his love for his God stifled his compassion for his child. [13] And have you not heard what their God did to Pharaoh king of Egypt, and to Abimelech king of Gerar, through taking Abraham's wife, who said of her, She is my sister, lest they might slay him on account of her, and think of taking her for a wife? And God did to them and their people all that you heard of. [14] And behold, we ourselves saw with our [own] eyes that Esau, the brother of Jacob, came to him with four hundred men with the intention of slaying him, for he called to mind that he had taken his father's blessing away from him. [15] And he went to meet him when he came from Syria, to strike the mother with the children, and who delivered him from his hands but his God in whom he trusted? He delivered him from the hand of his brother and also from the hands of his enemies, and He will surely protect them again. [16] Who does not know that it was their God who inspired them with strength to do to the town of Shechem the calamity which you heard of? [17] Could it then be with their own strength that two men could destroy such a large city as Shechem had it not been for their God in whom they trusted? He said and did to them all this to slay the inhabitants of the city in their city. [18] And can you then prevail over those who have come out together from your city to fight with the whole of them, even if one thousand times as many more should come to your assistance? [19] Surely you know and understand that you do not come to fight with them, but you come to war with their God who chose them, and you have therefore all come this day to be destroyed. [20] Now therefore, refrain from this calamity which you are endeavoring to bring on yourselves, and it will be better for you not to go to battle with them, although they are but few in numbers, because their God is with them." [21] And when the kings of the Amorites heard all the words of their advisers, their hearts were filled with terror, and they were afraid of the sons of Jacob and would not fight against them. [22] And they inclined their ears to the words of their advisers, and they listened to all their words, and the words of the counselors greatly pleased the kings, and they did so. [23] And the kings turned and refrained from the sons of Jacob, for they dared not approach them to make war with them, for they were greatly afraid of them, and their hearts melted within them from their fear of them. [24] For this proceeded from the LORD to them, for He heard the prayers of His servants Isaac and Jacob, for they trusted in Him; and all these kings returned with their camps on that day, each to his own city, and they did not fight with the sons of Jacob at that time. [25] And the sons of Jacob kept their station that day until evening opposite Mount Sihon, and seeing that these kings did not come to fight against them, the sons of Jacob returned home.

CHAPTER 36

¹ At that time the LORD appeared to Jacob, saying, "Arise, go to Bethel and remain there, and make an altar there to the LORD who appears to you, who delivered you and your sons from affliction." ² And Jacob rose up with his sons and all belonging to him, and they went and came to Bethel according to the word of the LORD. ³ And Jacob was ninety-nine years old when he went up to Bethel, and Jacob, and his sons, and all the people that were with him remained in Bethel in Luz, and he built an altar there to the LORD who appeared to him, and Jacob and his sons remained in Bethel six months. ⁴ At that time Deborah the daughter of Uz, the nurse of Rebekah, who had been with Jacob, died, and Jacob buried her beneath Bethel under an oak that was there. ⁵ And Rebekah the daughter of Bethuel, the mother of Jacob, also died at that time in Hebron, the same is Kirjath-Arba, and she was buried in the cave of Machpelah which Abraham had bought from the children of Heth. ⁶ And the life of Rebekah was one hundred and thirty-three years, and she died; and when Jacob heard that his mother Rebekah was dead, he wept bitterly for his mother, and made a great mourning for her, and for her nurse Deborah beneath the oak, and he called the name of that place Allon-bachuth. ⁷ And Laban the Syrian died in those days, for God struck him because he transgressed the covenant that existed between him and Jacob. ⁸ And Jacob was one hundred years old when the LORD appeared to him, and blessed him, and called his name Israel; and Rachel, the wife of Jacob, conceived in those days. ⁹ And at that time Jacob and all belonging to him journeyed from Bethel to go to his father's house, to Hebron. ¹⁰ And while they were going on the road and there was yet but a little way to come to Ephrath, Rachel bore a son, and she had hard labor, and she died. ¹¹ And Jacob buried her in the way to Ephrath, which is Beth-Lehem, and he set a pillar on her grave which is there to this day; and the days of Rachel were forty-five years and she died. ¹² And Jacob called the name of his son that was born to him, which Rachel bore to him, Benjamin, for he was born to him in the land on the right hand. ¹³ And it was after the death of Rachel that Jacob pitched his tent in the tent of her handmaid Bilhah. ¹⁴ And Reuben was jealous for his mother Leah on account of this, and he was filled with anger, and he rose up in his anger, and went, and entered the tent of Bilhah, and there he removed his father's bed. ¹⁵ At that time the portion of birthright, together with the kingly and priestly offices, was removed from the sons of Reuben, for he had profaned his father's bed, and the birthright was given to Joseph, the kingly office to Judah, and the priesthood to Levi, because Reuben had defiled his father's bed. ¹⁶ And these are the generations of Jacob who were born to him in Padan-Aram, and the sons of Jacob were twelve. ¹⁷ The sons of Leah were Reuben the firstborn, and Simeon, Levi, Judah, Issachar, Zebulun, and their sister Dinah; and the sons of Rachel were Joseph and Benjamin. ¹⁸ The sons of Zilpah, Leah's handmaid, were Gad and Asher; and the sons of Bilhah, Rachel's handmaid, were Dan and Naphtali; these are the sons of Jacob which were born to him in Padan-Aram. ¹⁹ And Jacob, and his sons, and all belonging to him journeyed and came to Mamre, which is Kirjath-Arba, that is in Hebron, where Abraham and Isaac sojourned; and Jacob with his sons and all belonging to him dwelt with his father in Hebron. ²⁰ And his brother Esau, and his sons, and all belonging to him went to the land of Seir and dwelt there, and had possessions in the land of Seir, and the children of Esau were fruitful and multiplied exceedingly in the land of Seir. ²¹ And these are the generations of Esau that were born to him in the land of Canaan, and the sons of Esau were five. ²² And Adah bore to Esau his firstborn Eliphaz, and she also bore Reuel to him; and Aholibamah bore Jeush, Yaalam, and Korah to him. ²³ These are the children of Esau who were born to him in the land of Canaan; and the sons of Eliphaz, the son of Esau, were Teman, Omar, Zepho, Gatam, Kenaz, and Amalek; and the sons of Reuel were Nachas, Zerach, Shamah, and Mizzah; ²⁴ and the sons of Jeush were Timnah, Alvah, [and] Jetheth; and the sons of Yaalam were Alah, Phinor, and Kenaz; ²⁵ and the sons of Korah were Teman, Mibzar, Magdiel, and Eram; these are the families of the sons of Esau according to their chiefdoms in the land of Seir. ²⁶ And these are the names of the sons of Seir the Horite, inhabitants of the land of Seir: Lotan, Shobal, Zibeon, Anah, Dishan, Ezer, and Dishon, being seven sons. ²⁷ And the children of Lotan were Hori, Heman, and their sister Timna (that is Timna who came to Jacob and his sons, and they would not give ear to her, and she went and became a concubine to Eliphaz the son of Esau, and she bore Amalek to him). ²⁸ And the sons of Shobal were Alvan, Manahas, Ebal, Shepho, and Onam; and the sons of Zibeon were Ajah and Anah (this was that Anah who found the Yemim in the wilderness when he fed the donkeys of Zibeon his father. ²⁹ And while he was feeding his father's donkeys, he led them to the wilderness at different times to feed them. ³⁰ And there was a day that he brought them to one of the deserts on the seashore, opposite the wilderness of the people, and while he was feeding them, behold, a very heavy storm came from the other side of the sea and rested on the donkeys that were feeding there, and they all stood still. ³¹ And afterward about one hundred and twenty great and terrible animals came out from the wilderness at the other side of the sea, and they all

came to the place where the donkeys were, and they placed themselves there. ³²And those animals, from their middle downward, were in the shape of the children of men, and from their middle upward, some had the likeness of bears, and some the likeness of the keephas, with tails behind them from between their shoulders reaching down to the earth, like the tails of the ducheephas, and these animals came, and mounted, and rode on these donkeys, and led them away, and they went away to this day. ³³And one of these animals approached Anah and struck him with his tail, and then fled from that place. ³⁴And when he saw this work, he was exceedingly afraid for his life, and he fled and escaped to the city. ³⁵And he related to his sons and brothers all that had happened to him, and many men went to seek the donkeys but could not find them, and Anah and his brothers no longer went to that place from that day following, for they were greatly afraid for their lives). ³⁶And the children of Anah, the son of Seir, were Dishon and his sister Aholibamah, and the children of Dishon were Hemdan, Eshban, Ithran, and Cheran, and the children of Ezer were Bilhan, Zaavan, and Akan, and the children of Dishon were Uz and Aran. ³⁷These are the families of the children of Seir the Horite, according to their chiefdoms in the land of Seir. ³⁸And Esau and his children dwelt in the land of Seir the Horite, the inhabitant of the land, and they had possessions in it, and were fruitful and multiplied exceedingly, and Jacob, and his children, and all belonging to them dwelt with their father Isaac in the land of Canaan as the LORD had commanded their father Abraham.

CHAPTER 37

¹And in the one hundred and fifth year of the life of Jacob, that is the ninth year of Jacob's dwelling with his children in the land of Canaan, he came from Padan-Aram. ²And in those days Jacob journeyed with his children from Hebron, and they went and returned to the city of Shechem, they and all belonging to them, and they dwelt there, for the children of Jacob obtained good and fat pasture land for their cattle in the city of Shechem, the city of Shechem having then been rebuilt, and there were about three hundred men and women in it. ³And Jacob, and his children, and all belonging to him dwelt in the part of the field which Jacob had bought from Hamor the father of Shechem when he came from Padan-Aram before Simeon and Levi had smitten the city. ⁴And all those kings of the Canaanites and Amorites that surrounded the city of Shechem heard that the sons of Jacob had come to Shechem again and dwelt there. ⁵And they said, "Will the sons of Jacob the Hebrew come to the city again and dwell therein after they have smitten its inhabitants and driven them out? Will they now return and also drive out those who are dwelling in the city

or slay them?" ⁶And all the kings of Canaan assembled again, and they came together to make war with Jacob and his sons. ⁷And Jashub king of Tapnach also sent to all his neighboring kings, to Elan king of Gaash, and to Ihuri king of Shiloh, and to Parathon king of Chazar, and to Susi king of Sarton, and to Laban king of Bethchoran, and to Shabir king of Othnay-mah, saying, ⁸"Come up to me and assist me, and let us strike Jacob the Hebrew, and his sons, and all belonging to him, for they have come to Shechem again to possess it and to slay its inhabitants as before." ⁹And all these kings assembled together and came with all their camps—a people exceedingly plentiful like the sand on the seashore—and they were all opposite to Tapnach. ¹⁰And Jashub king of Tapnach went out to them with all his army, and he encamped with them opposite to Tapnach outside the city, and they divided all these kings into seven divisions, being seven camps against the sons of Jacob. ¹¹And they sent a declaration to Jacob and his sons, saying, "Come out to us, all of you, that we may have an interview together in the plain, and revenge the cause of the men of Shechem whom you slew in their city, and you will now return to the city of Shechem again, and dwell therein, and slay its inhabitants as before." ¹²And the sons of Jacob heard this and their anger was exceedingly kindled at the words of the kings of Canaan, and ten of the sons of Jacob hastened and rose up, and each of them girded on his weapons of war; and there were one hundred and two of their servants with them equipped in battle array. ¹³And all these men, the sons of Jacob with their servants, went toward these kings, and their father Jacob was with them, and they all stood on the heap of Shechem. ¹⁴And Jacob prayed to the LORD for his sons, and he spread out his hands to the LORD, and he said, "O God, You are [the] almighty God, You are our Father, You formed us and we are the works of Your hands; please deliver my sons through Your mercy from the hand of their enemies who are coming to fight with them this day and save them from their hand, for in Your hand is power and might to save the few from the many. ¹⁵And give to my sons, Your servants, strength of heart and might to fight with their enemies, to subdue them, and make their enemies fall before them, and do not let my sons and their servants die through the hands of the children of Canaan. ¹⁶But if it seems good in Your eyes to take away the lives of my sons and their servants, take them in Your great mercy through the hands of Your ministers, that they may not perish this day by the hands of the kings of the Amorites." ¹⁷And when Jacob ceased praying to the LORD, the earth shook from its place, and the sun darkened, and all these kings were terrified, and a great consternation seized them. ¹⁸And the LORD listened to the prayer of Jacob, and the LORD impressed the hearts of all the kings and their hosts with the terror and awe of the sons of

Jacob, ¹⁹ for the LORD caused them to hear the voice of chariots, and the voice of mighty horses from the sons of Jacob, and the voice of a great army accompanying them. ²⁰ And these kings were seized with great terror at the sons of Jacob, and while they were standing in their quarters, behold, the sons of Jacob advanced on them with one hundred and twelve men, with a great and tremendous shouting. ²¹ And when the kings saw the sons of Jacob advancing toward them, they were still more panic-stricken, and they were inclined to retreat from before the sons of Jacob as at first, and not to fight with them. ²² But they did not retreat, saying, "It would thus be a disgrace to us to retreat twice from before the Hebrews." ²³ And the sons of Jacob came near and advanced against all these kings and their armies, and they saw, and behold, it was a very mighty people, [as] numerous as the sand of the sea. ²⁴ And the sons of Jacob called to the LORD and said, "Help us, O LORD! Help us and answer us, for we trust in You! And let us not die by the hands of these uncircumcised men who have come against us this day." ²⁵ And the sons of Jacob girded on their weapons of war, and they took in their hands—each man—his shield and his javelin, and they approached to battle. ²⁶ And Judah, the son of Jacob, ran first before his brothers, and ten of his servants with him, and he went toward these kings. ²⁷ And Jashub, king of Tapnach, also came out first with his army before Judah, and Judah saw Jashub and his army coming toward him, and Judah's wrath was kindled, and his anger burned within him, and he approached to battle in which Judah ventured his life. ²⁸ And Jashub and all his army were advancing toward Judah, and he was riding on a very strong and powerful horse, and Jashub was a very valiant man, and covered with iron and brass from head to foot. ²⁹ And while he was on the horse, he shot arrows with both hands from before and behind, as was his manner in all his battles, and he never missed the place to which he aimed his arrows. ³⁰ And when Jashub came to fight with Judah, and was darting many arrows against Judah, the LORD bound the hand of Jashub, and all the arrows that he shot rebounded on his own men. ³¹ And notwithstanding this, Jashub kept advancing toward Judah, to challenge him with the arrows, but the distance between them was about thirty cubits, and when Judah saw Jashub darting out his arrows against him, he ran to him with his wrath-excited might. ³² And Judah took up a large stone from the ground, and its weight was sixty shekels, and Judah ran toward Jashub and struck him on his shield with the stone, [so] that Jashub was stunned with the blow and fell off from his horse to the ground. ³³ And the shield burst apart out of the hand of Jashub, and through the force of the blow sprang to the distance of about fifteen cubits, and the shield fell before the second camp. ³⁴ And the kings that came with Jashub saw at a distance the strength of Judah, the son of Jacob, and what he had done to Jashub, and they were terribly afraid of Judah. ³⁵ And they assembled near Jashub's camp, seeing his confusion, and Judah drew his sword and struck forty-two men of the camp of Jashub, and the whole of Jashub's camp fled before Judah, and no man stood against him, and they left Jashub and fled from him, and Jashub was still prostrate on the ground. ³⁶ And Jashub seeing that all the men of his camp had fled from him, hastened and rose up with terror against Judah, and stood on his legs opposite Judah. ³⁷ And Jashub had a duel with Judah, placing shield toward shield, and Jashub's men all fled, for they were greatly afraid of Judah. ³⁸ And Jashub took his spear in his hand to strike Judah on his head, but Judah had quickly placed his shield to his head against Jashub's spear, so that the shield of Judah received the blow from Jashub's spear, and the shield was split in two. ³⁹ And when Judah saw that his shield was split, he hastily drew his sword and struck Jashub at his ankles and cut off his feet, [so] that Jashub fell on the ground, and the spear fell from his hand. ⁴⁰ And Judah hastily picked up Jashub's spear, with which he severed his head and cast it next to his feet. ⁴¹ And when the sons of Jacob saw what Judah had done to Jashub, they all ran into the ranks of the other kings, and the sons of Jacob fought with the army of Jashub, and the armies of all the kings that were there. ⁴² And the sons of Jacob caused fifteen thousand of their men to fall, and they struck them as if striking at gourds, and the rest fled for their lives. ⁴³ And Judah was still standing by the body of Jashub, and stripped Jashub of his coat of mail. ⁴⁴ And Judah also took off the iron and brass that was around Jashub, and behold, nine men of the captains of Jashub came along to fight against Judah. ⁴⁵ And Judah hastened and took up a stone from the ground, and with it struck one of them on the head, and his skull was fractured, and the body also fell from the horse to the ground. ⁴⁶ And the eight captains that remained, seeing the strength of Judah, were greatly afraid and they fled, and Judah pursued them with his ten men, and they overtook them and slew them. ⁴⁷ And the sons of Jacob were still striking the armies of the kings, and they slew many of them, but those kings daringly kept their stand with their captains, and did not retreat from their places, and they exclaimed against those of their armies that fled from before the sons of Jacob, but none would listen to them, for they were afraid for their lives lest they should die. ⁴⁸ And all the sons of Jacob, after having smitten the armies of the kings, returned and came before Judah, and Judah was still slaying the eight captains of Jashub, and stripping off their garments. ⁴⁹ And Levi saw Elon, king of Gaash, advancing toward him, with his fourteen captains to strike him, but Levi did not know it for certain. ⁵⁰ And Elon with his captains approached nearer, and Levi looked back and saw that battle was given to him in the rear, and

Levi ran with twelve of his servants, and they went and slew Elon and his captains with the edge of the sword.

CHAPTER 38

[1] And Ihuri king of Shiloh came up to assist Elon, and when he approached Jacob, Jacob drew his bow that was in his hand and struck Ihuri with an arrow which caused his death. [2] And when Ihuri king of Shiloh was dead, the four remaining kings fled from their station with the rest of the captains, and they endeavored to retreat, saying, "We have no more strength with the Hebrews after their having killed the three kings and their captains who were more powerful than we are." [3] And when the sons of Jacob saw that the remaining kings had removed from their station, they pursued them, and Jacob also came from the heap of Shechem, from the place where he was standing, and they went after the kings and they approached them with their servants. [4] And the kings and the captains with the rest of their armies, seeing that the sons of Jacob approached them, were afraid for their lives and fled until they reached the city of Chazar. [5] And the sons of Jacob pursued them to the gate of the city of Chazar, and they struck a great striking among the kings and their armies, about four thousand men, and while they were striking the army of the kings, Jacob was occupied with his bow confining himself to striking the kings, and he slew them all. [6] And he slew Parathon king of Chazar at the gate of the city of Chazar, and afterward he struck Susi king of Sarton, and Laban king of Bethchorin, and Shabir king of Machnaymah, and he slew them all with arrows, an arrow to each of them, and they died. [7] And the sons of Jacob seeing that all the kings were dead and that they were broken up and retreating, continued to carry on the battle with the armies of the kings opposite the gate of Chazar, and they still struck about four hundred of their men. [8] And three men of the servants of Jacob fell in that battle, and when Judah saw that three of his servants had died, it grieved him greatly, and his anger burned within him against the Amorites. [9] And all the men that remained of the armies of the kings were greatly afraid for their lives, and they ran and broke the gate of the walls of the city of Chazar, and they all entered the city for safety. [10] And they concealed themselves in the midst of the city of Chazar, for the city of Chazar was very large and extensive, and when all these armies had entered the city, the sons of Jacob ran after them to the city. [11] And four mighty men, experienced in battle, went out from the city and stood against the entrance of the city, with drawn swords and spears in their hands, and they placed themselves opposite the sons of Jacob, and would not permit them to enter the city. [12] And Naphtali ran and came between them, and struck two of them with his sword, and cut off their heads with one stroke. [13] And he turned to the other two, and behold, they had fled, and he pursued them, overtook them, struck them, and slew them. [14] And the sons of Jacob came to the city and saw, and behold, there was another wall to the city, and they sought for the gate of the wall and could not find it, and Judah sprang on the top of the wall, and Simeon and Levi followed him, and they all three descended from the wall into the city. [15] And Simeon and Levi slew all the men who had run into the city for safety, and also the inhabitants of the city with their wives and little ones, they slew with the edge of the sword, and the cries of the city ascended up to Heaven. [16] And Dan and Naphtali sprang on the wall to see what caused the noise of lamentation, for the sons of Jacob felt anxious about their brothers, and they heard the inhabitants of the city speaking with weeping and supplications, saying, "Take all that we possess in the city and go away, only do not put us to death." [17] And when Judah, Simeon, and Levi had ceased striking the inhabitants of the city, they ascended the wall and called to Dan and Naphtali, who were on the wall, and to the rest of their brothers, and Simeon and Levi informed them of the entrance into the city, and all the sons of Jacob came to fetch the spoil. [18] And the sons of Jacob took the spoil of the city of Chazar, the flocks and herds, and the property, and they took all that could be captured, and went away from the city that day. [19] And on the next day the sons of Jacob went to Sarton, for they heard that the men of Sarton who had remained in the city were assembling to fight with them for having slain their king, and Sarton was a very high and fortified city, and it had a deep rampart surrounding the city. [20] And the pillar of the rampart was about fifty cubits and its breadth forty cubits, and there was no place for a man to enter the city on account of the rampart, and the sons of Jacob saw the rampart of the city, and they sought an entrance in it but could not find it. [21] For the entrance to the city was at the rear, and every man that wished to come into the city came by that road and went around the whole city, and afterward he entered the city. [22] And the sons of Jacob seeing [that] they could not find the way into the city, their anger was greatly kindled, and the inhabitants of the city seeing that the sons of Jacob were coming to them were greatly afraid of them, for they had heard of their strength and what they had done to Chazar. [23] And the inhabitants of the city of Sarton could not go out toward the sons of Jacob after having assembled in the city to fight against them, lest they might thereby get into the city, but when they saw that they were coming toward them, they were greatly afraid of them, for they had heard of their strength and what they had done to Chazar. [24] So the inhabitants of Sarton quickly took away the bridge of the road of the city from its place before the sons of Jacob came, and they brought it into the city. [25] And the sons of Jacob came and sought the way into the city and could not find it, and the inhabitants of the

city went up to the top of the wall, and saw, and behold, the sons of Jacob were seeking an entrance into the city. ²⁶ And the inhabitants of the city reproached the sons of Jacob from the top of the wall, and they cursed them, and the sons of Jacob heard the reproaches, and they were greatly incensed, and their anger burned within them. ²⁷ And the sons of Jacob were provoked at them, and they all rose and sprang over the rampart with the force of their strength, and through their might passed the forty cubits' breadth of the rampart. ²⁸ And when they had passed the rampart, they stood under the wall of the city, and they found all the gates of the city enclosed with iron doors. ²⁹ And the sons of Jacob came near to break open the doors of the gates of the city, and the inhabitants did not let them, for from the top of the wall they were casting stones and arrows on them. ³⁰ And the number of the people that were on the wall was about four hundred men, and when the sons of Jacob saw that the men of the city would not let them open the gates of the city, they sprang and ascended the top of the wall, and Judah went up first to the east part of the city. ³¹ And Gad and Asher went up after him to the west corner of the city, and Simeon and Levi to the north, and Dan and Reuben to the south. ³² And the men who were on the top of the wall, the inhabitants of the city, seeing that the sons of Jacob were coming up to them, they all fled from the wall, descended into the city, and concealed themselves in the midst of the city. ³³ And Issachar and Naphtali that remained under the wall approached and broke the gates of the city and kindled a fire at the gates of the city, [so] that the iron melted, and all the sons of Jacob came into the city—they and all their men—and they fought with the inhabitants of the city of Sarton, and struck them with the edge of the sword, and no man stood up before them. ³⁴ And about two hundred men fled from the city, and they all went and hid themselves in a certain tower in the city, and Judah pursued them to the tower, and he broke down the tower, which fell on the men, and they all died. ³⁵ And the sons of Jacob went up the road of the roof of that tower, and they saw, and behold, there was another strong and high tower at a distance in the city, and the top of it reached to [the] heavens, and the sons of Jacob hastened and descended, and went with all their men to that tower, and found it filled with about three hundred men, women, and little ones. ³⁶ And the sons of Jacob struck a great striking among those men in the tower, and they ran away and fled from them. ³⁷ And when Simeon and Levi pursued them, twelve mighty and valiant men came out to them from the place where they had concealed themselves. ³⁸ And those twelve men maintained a strong battle against Simeon and Levi, and Simeon and Levi could not prevail over them, and those valiant men broke the shields of Simeon and Levi, and when one of them struck at Levi's head with his sword, Levi hastily

placed his hand to his head, for he was afraid of the sword, and the sword struck Levi's hand, and it came close to the hand of Levi being cut off. ³⁹ And Levi seized the sword of the valiant man in his hand, and took it forcibly from the man, and he struck at the head of the powerful man with it, and he severed his head. ⁴⁰ And eleven men approached to fight with Levi, for they saw that one of them was killed, and the sons of Jacob fought, but the sons of Jacob could not prevail over them, for those men were very powerful. ⁴¹ And the sons of Jacob seeing that they could not prevail over them, Simeon gave a loud and tremendous shriek, and the eleven powerful men were stunned at the voice of Simeon's shrieking. ⁴² And Judah at a distance knew the voice of Simeon's shouting, and Naphtali and Judah ran with their shields to Simeon and Levi, and found them fighting with those powerful men, unable to prevail over them as their shields were broken. ⁴³ And Naphtali saw that the shields of Simeon and Levi were broken, and he took two shields from his servants and brought them to Simeon and Levi. ⁴⁴ And on that day Simeon, Levi, and Judah fought—all three—against the eleven mighty men until the time of sunset, but they could not prevail over them. ⁴⁵ And this was told to Jacob, and he was severely grieved, and he prayed to the LORD, and he and his son Naphtali went against these mighty men. ⁴⁶ And Jacob approached and drew his bow, and came near to the mighty men, and slew three of their men with the bow, and the remaining eight turned back, and behold, the war waged against them in the front and rear, and they were greatly afraid for their lives, and could not stand before the sons of Jacob, and they fled from before them. ⁴⁷ And in their flight they met Dan and Asher coming toward them, and they suddenly fell on them, and fought with them, and slew two of them, and Judah and his brothers pursued them, and struck the remainder of them, and slew them. ⁴⁸ And all the sons of Jacob returned and walked around the city, searching if they could find any men, and they found about twenty young men in a cave in the city, and Gad and Asher struck them all, and Dan and Naphtali descended on the rest of the men who had fled and escaped from the second tower, and they struck them all. ⁴⁹ And the sons of Jacob struck all the inhabitants of the city of Sarton, but they left the women and little ones in the city and did not slay them. ⁵⁰ And all the inhabitants of the city of Sarton were powerful men: one of them would pursue one thousand, and two of them would not flee from ten thousand of the rest of men. ⁵¹ And the sons of Jacob slew all the inhabitants of the city of Sarton with the edge of the sword, [so] that no man stood up against them, and they left the women in the city. ⁵² And the sons of Jacob took all the spoil of the city, and captured what they desired, and they took flocks, and herds, and property from the city, and the sons of Jacob did to Sarton and its inhabitants as they had done to Chazar and its inhabitants, and they turned and went away.

CHAPTER 39

¹ And when the sons of Jacob went from the city of Sarton, they had gone about two hundred cubits when they met the inhabitants of Tapnach coming toward them, for they went out to fight with them, because they had smitten the king of Tapnach and all his men. ² So all that remained in the city of Tapnach came out to fight with the sons of Jacob, and they thought to retake from them the plunder and the spoil which they had captured from Chazar and Sarton. ³ And the rest of the men of Tapnach fought with the sons of Jacob in that place, and the sons of Jacob struck them, and they fled before them, and they pursued them to the city of Arbelan, and they all fell before the sons of Jacob. ⁴ And the sons of Jacob returned and came to Tapnach to take away the spoil of Tapnach, and when they came to Tapnach they heard that the people of Arbelan had gone out to meet them to save the spoil of their brothers, and the sons of Jacob left ten of their men in Tapnach to plunder the city, and they went out toward the people of Arbelan. ⁵ And the men of Arbelan went out with their wives to fight with the sons of Jacob, for their wives were experienced in battle, and they went out, about four hundred men and women. ⁶ And all the sons of Jacob shouted with a loud voice, and they all ran toward the inhabitants of Arbelan with a great and tremendous voice. ⁷ And the inhabitants of Arbelan heard the noise of the shouting of the sons of Jacob, and their roaring like the noise of lions and like the roaring of the sea and its waves. ⁸ And fear and terror possessed their hearts on account of the sons of Jacob, and they were terribly afraid of them, and they retreated and fled before them into the city, and the sons of Jacob pursued them to the gate of the city, and they came on them in the city. ⁹ And the sons of Jacob fought with them in the city, and all their women were engaged in slinging against the sons of Jacob, and the combat was very severe among them the whole of that day until evening. ¹⁰ And the sons of Jacob could not prevail over them, and the sons of Jacob had almost perished in that battle, and the sons of Jacob cried to the LORD and greatly gained strength toward evening, and the sons of Jacob struck all the inhabitants of Arbelan by the edge of the sword—men, women, and little ones. ¹¹ And also the remainder of the people who had fled from Sarton, the sons of Jacob struck them in Arbelan, and the sons of Jacob did to Arbelan and Tapnach as they had done to Chazar and Sarton, and when the women saw that all the men were dead, they went on the roofs of the city and struck the sons of Jacob by showering down stones like rain. ¹² And the sons of Jacob hastened and came into the city, and seized all the women, and struck them with the edge of the sword, and the sons of Jacob captured all the spoil and plunder, flocks,

and herds, and cattle. ¹³ And the sons of Jacob did to Machnaymah as they had done to Tapnach, to Chazar, and to Shiloh, and they turned from there and went away. ¹⁴ And on the fifth day the sons of Jacob heard that the people of Gaash had gathered against them to battle, because they had slain their king and their captains, for there had been fourteen captains in the city of Gaash, and the sons of Jacob had slain them all in the first battle. ¹⁵ And the sons of Jacob girded on their weapons of war that day, and they marched to battle against the inhabitants of Gaash, and in Gaash there was a strong and mighty people of the people of the Amorites, and Gaash was the strongest and best fortified city of all the cities of the Amorites, and it had three walls. ¹⁶ And the sons of Jacob came to Gaash, and they found the gates of the city locked and about five hundred men standing at the top of the outermost wall, and a people [as] numerous as the sand on the seashore were set in ambush for the sons of Jacob from outside the city, at the rear thereof. ¹⁷ And the sons of Jacob approached to open the gates of the city, and while they were drawing near, behold, those who were set in ambush at the rear of the city came out from their places and surrounded the sons of Jacob. ¹⁸ And the sons of Jacob were enclosed between the people of Gaash, and the battle was both to their front and rear, and all the men that were on the wall were casting from the wall arrows and stones on them. ¹⁹ And Judah, seeing that the men of Gaash were getting too heavy for them, gave a most piercing and tremendous shriek and all the men of Gaash were terrified at the voice of Judah's cry, and men fell from the wall at his powerful shriek, and all those that were from outside and within the city were greatly afraid for their lives. ²⁰ And when the sons of Jacob still came near to break the doors of the city, the men of Gaash threw stones and arrows on them from the top of the wall and made them flee from the gate. ²¹ And the sons of Jacob returned against the men of Gaash who were with them from outside the city, and they struck them terribly, as striking against gourds, and they could not stand against the sons of Jacob, for fright and terror had seized them at the shriek of Judah. ²² And the sons of Jacob slew all those men who were outside the city, and the sons of Jacob still drew near to effect an entrance into the city and to fight under the city walls, but they could not for all the inhabitants of Gaash who remained in the city had surrounded the walls of Gaash in every direction, so that the sons of Jacob were unable to approach the city to fight with them. ²³ And [when] the sons of Jacob came near to one corner to fight under the wall, the inhabitants of Gaash threw arrows and stones on them like showers of rain, and they fled from under the wall. ²⁴ And the people of Gaash who were on the wall, seeing that the sons of Jacob could not prevail over them from under the wall, reproached the sons of Jacob in these words, saying, ²⁵ "What is the matter with you in the battle that you cannot prevail? Can you then do to the mighty city of Gaash and its inhabitants as you did to the cities of the Amorites that were not so powerful? Surely you did those things to those weak ones among us, and slew them in the entrance of the city, for they had no strength when they were terrified at the sound of your shouting. ²⁶ And will you now then be able to fight in this place? Surely you will all die here, and we will avenge the cause of those cities that you have laid waste." ²⁷ And the inhabitants of Gaash greatly reproached the sons of Jacob, and reviled them with their gods, and continued to cast arrows and stones on them from the wall. ²⁸ And Judah and his brothers heard the words of the inhabitants of Gaash and their anger was greatly roused, and Judah was jealous for his God in this matter, and he called out and said, "O LORD, help! Send help to us and our brothers!" ²⁹ And he ran at a distance with all his might, with his drawn sword in his hand, and he sprang from the earth, and by force of his strength mounted the wall, and his sword fell from his hand. ³⁰ And Judah shouted on the wall, and all the men that were on the wall were terrified, and some of them fell from the wall into the city and died, and those who were yet on the wall, when they saw Judah's strength, they were greatly afraid and fled for their lives into the city for safety. ³¹ And some were emboldened to fight with Judah on the wall, and they came near to slay him when they saw there was no sword in Judah's hand, and they thought of casting him from the wall to his brothers, and twenty men of the city came up to assist them, and they surrounded Judah, and they all shouted over him, and approached him with drawn swords, and they terrified Judah, and Judah cried out to his brothers from the wall. ³² And Jacob and his sons drew the bow from under the wall and struck three of the men that were on the top of the wall, and Judah continued to cry, and he exclaimed, "O LORD help us! O LORD deliver us!" And he cried out with a loud voice on the wall, and the cry was heard at a great distance. ³³ And after this cry he again repeated to shout, and all the men who surrounded Judah on the top of the wall were terrified, and they each threw his sword from his hand at the sound of Judah's shouting and his tremor, and they fled. ³⁴ And Judah took the swords which had fallen from their hands, and Judah fought with them and slew twenty of their men on the wall. ³⁵ And about eighty men and women still ascended the wall from the city, and they all surrounded Judah, and the LORD impressed the fear of Judah in their hearts, that they were unable to approach him. ³⁶ And Jacob and all who were with him drew the bow from under the wall, and they slew ten men on the wall, and they fell below the wall near Jacob and his sons. ³⁷ And the people on the wall seeing that twenty of their men had fallen, they still ran toward Judah with drawn swords, but they could

not approach him, for they were greatly terrified at Judah's strength. ³⁸ And when one of their mighty men whose name was Arud approached to strike Judah on the head with his sword, Judah hastily put his shield to his head, and the sword hit the shield, and it was split in two. ³⁹ And this mighty man ran for his life after he had struck Judah, at the fear of Judah, and his feet slipped on the wall and he fell among the sons of Jacob who were below the wall, and the sons of Jacob struck him and slew him. ⁴⁰ And Judah's head pained him from the blow of the powerful man, and Judah had nearly died from it. ⁴¹ And Judah cried out on the wall owing to the pain produced by the blow, when Dan heard him, and his anger burned within him, and he also rose up, and went at a distance, and ran, and sprang from the earth, and mounted the wall with his wrath-excited strength. ⁴² And when Dan came on the wall near to Judah, all the men on the wall who had stood against Judah fled, and they went up to the second wall, and they threw arrows and stones on Dan and Judah from the second wall, and endeavored to drive them from the wall. ⁴³ And the arrows and stones struck Dan and Judah, and they had nearly been killed on the wall, and wherever Dan and Judah fled from the wall, they were attacked with arrows and stones from the second wall. ⁴⁴ And Jacob and his sons were still at the entrance of the city below the first wall, and they were not able to draw their bow against the inhabitants of the city, as they could not be seen by them, being on the second wall. ⁴⁵ And when Dan and Judah could no longer bear the stones and arrows that fell on them from the second wall, they both sprang on the second wall near the people of the city, and when the people of the city who were on the second wall saw that Dan and Judah had come to them on the second wall, they all cried out and descended below between the walls. ⁴⁶ And Jacob and his sons heard the noise of the shouting from the people of the city, and they were still at the entrance of the city, and they were anxious about Dan and Judah who were not seen by them—they being on the second wall. ⁴⁷ And Naphtali went up with his wrath-excited might and sprang on the first wall to see what caused the noise of shouting which they had heard in the city, and Issachar and Zebulun drew near to break the doors of the city, and they opened the gates of the city, and came into the city. ⁴⁸ And Naphtali leaped from the first wall to the second, and came to assist his brothers, and the inhabitants of Gaash who were on the wall, seeing that Naphtali was the third who had come up to assist his brothers, they all fled and descended into the city, and Jacob, and all his sons, and all their young men came into the city to them. ⁴⁹ And Judah, and Dan, and Naphtali descended from the wall into the city and pursued the inhabitants of the city, and Simeon and Levi were from outside the city and did not know that the gate was opened, and they went up from there to the wall and came down to their brothers into the city. ⁵⁰ And the inhabitants of the city had all descended into the city, and the sons of Jacob came to them in different directions, and the battle waged against them from the front and the rear, and the sons of Jacob struck them terribly, and slew about twenty thousand of them—men and women; not one of them could stand up against the sons of Jacob. ⁵¹ And the blood flowed plentifully in the city, and it was like a brook of water, and the blood flowed like a brook to the outer part of the city and reached the desert of Bethchorin. ⁵² And the people of Bethchorin saw at a distance the blood flowing from the city of Gaash, and about seventy men from among them ran to see the blood, and they came to the place where the blood was. ⁵³ And they followed the track of the blood and came to the wall of the city of Gaash, and they saw the blood issue from the city, and they heard the voice of crying from the inhabitants of Gaash, for it ascended to Heaven, and the blood was continuing to flow abundantly like a brook of water. ⁵⁴ And all the sons of Jacob were still striking the inhabitants of Gaash, and were engaged in slaying them until evening—about twenty thousand men and women—and the people of Chorin said, "Surely this is the work of the Hebrews, for they are still carrying on war in all the cities of the Amorites." ⁵⁵ And those people hastened and ran to Bethchorin, and each took his weapons of war, and they cried out to all the inhabitants of Bethchorin, who also girded on their weapons of war to go and fight with the sons of Jacob. ⁵⁶ And when the sons of Jacob had finished striking the inhabitants of Gaash, they walked around the city to strip all the slain, and coming into the innermost part of the city and farther on, they met three very powerful men, and there was no sword in their hand. ⁵⁷ And the sons of Jacob came up to the place where they were, and the powerful men ran away, and one of them had taken Zebulun, who he saw was a young youth and of short stature, and with his might dashed him to the ground. ⁵⁸ And Jacob ran to him with his sword and Jacob struck him below his loins with the sword, and cut him in two, and the body fell on Zebulun. ⁵⁹ And the second one approached and seized Jacob to fell him to the ground, and Jacob turned to him and shouted to him while Simeon and Levi ran and struck him on the hips with the sword and felled him to the ground. ⁶⁰ And the powerful man rose up from the ground with wrath-excited might, and Judah came to him before he had gained his footing, and struck him on the head with the sword, and his head was split, and he died. ⁶¹ And the third powerful man, seeing that his companions were killed, ran from before the sons of Jacob, and the sons of Jacob pursued him in the city; and while the powerful man was fleeing, he found one of the swords of the inhabitants of the city, and he picked it up, and turned to the sons of Jacob, and fought them with that sword. ⁶² And the powerful man ran to Judah to strike him on the head with the sword, and there was no shield in the hand of Judah; and while he was aiming to strike him, Naphtali hastily took his shield and put it to Judah's head, and the sword of the powerful man hit the shield of Naphtali and Judah escaped the sword. ⁶³ And Simeon and Levi ran on the powerful man with their swords and struck at him forcibly with their swords, and the two swords entered the body of the powerful man and divided it in two, lengthwise. ⁶⁴ And the sons of Jacob struck the three mighty men at that time, together with all the inhabitants of Gaash, and the day was about to decline. ⁶⁵ And the sons of Jacob walked around Gaash and took all the spoil of the city; they did not even permit the little ones and women to live, and the sons of Jacob did to Gaash as they had done to Sarton and Shiloh.

CHAPTER 40

¹ And the sons of Jacob led away all the spoil of Gaash and went out of the city by night. ² They were going out marching toward the fortress of Bethchorin, and the inhabitants of Bethchorin were going to the fortress to meet them, and on that night the sons of Jacob fought with the inhabitants of Bethchorin in the fortress of Bethchorin. ³ And all the inhabitants of Bethchorin were mighty men: one of them would not flee from before one thousand men, and they fought on that night on the fortress, and their shouts were heard on that night from afar, and the earth quaked at their shouting. ⁴ And all the sons of Jacob were afraid of those men, as they were not accustomed to fight in the dark, and they were greatly confounded, and the sons of Jacob cried to the LORD, saying, "Give help to us, O LORD! Deliver us that we may not die by the hands of these uncircumcised men." ⁵ And the LORD listened to the voice of the sons of Jacob, and the LORD caused great terror and confusion to seize the people of Bethchorin, and they fought among themselves—the one with the other—in the darkness of night, and struck each other in great numbers. ⁶ And the sons of Jacob, knowing that the LORD had brought a spirit of perverseness among those men, and that each man fought with his neighbor, went out from among the bands of the people of Bethchorin and went as far as the descent of the fortress of Bethchorin, and farther, and they tarried there securely with their young men on that night. ⁷ And the people of Bethchorin fought the whole night—one man with his brother, and the other with his neighbor—and they cried out in every direction on the fortress, and their cry was heard at a distance, and the whole earth shook at their voice, for they were powerful above all the people of the earth. ⁸ And all the inhabitants of the cities of the Canaanites, the Hittites, the Amorites, the Hivites, and all the kings of Canaan, and also those who were on the other side of the Jordan, heard the noise of the shouting on that night. ⁹ And they said, "Surely these are the battles of

the Hebrews who are fighting against the seven cities who came near to them; and who can stand against those Hebrews?" [10] And all the inhabitants of the cities of the Canaanites and all those who were on the other side of the Jordan were greatly afraid of the sons of Jacob, for they said, "Behold, the same will be done to us as was done to those cities, for who can stand against their mighty strength?" [11] And the cries of the Chorinites were very great on that night, and continued to increase; and they struck each other until morning, and [large] numbers of them were killed. [12] And the morning appeared, and all the sons of Jacob rose up at daybreak and went up to the fortress, and they struck those who remained of the Chorinites in a terrible manner, and they were all killed in the fortress. [13] And the sixth day appeared, and all the inhabitants of Canaan saw at a distance all the people of Bethchorin lying dead in the fortress of Bethchorin and scattered around as the carcasses of lambs and goats. [14] And the sons of Jacob led all the spoil which they had captured from Gaash and went to Bethchorin, and they found the city full of people like the sand of the sea, and they fought with them, and the sons of Jacob struck them there until evening time. [15] And the sons of Jacob did to Bethchorin as they had done to Gaash and Tapnach, and as they had done to Chazar, to Sarton, and to Shiloh. [16] And the sons of Jacob took the spoil of Bethchorin and all the spoil of the cities with them, and on that day they went home to Shechem. [17] And the sons of Jacob came home to the city of Shechem and remained outside the city, and then they rested there from the war and tarried there all night. [18] And all their servants, together with all the spoil that they had taken from the cities, they left outside the city, and they did not enter the city, for they said, "Perhaps there may still be more fighting against us, and they may come to besiege us in Shechem." [19] And Jacob, and his sons, and their servants remained on that night and the next day in the portion of the field which Jacob had purchased from Hamor for five shekels, and all that they had captured was with them. [20] And all the plunder which the sons of Jacob had captured was in the portion of the field—immense as the sand on the seashore. [21] And the inhabitants of the land observed them from afar, and all the inhabitants of the land were afraid of the sons of Jacob who had done this thing, for no king from the days of old had ever done the like. [22] And the seven kings of the Canaanites resolved to make peace with the sons of Jacob, for they were greatly afraid for their lives, on account of the sons of Jacob. [23] And on that day, being the seventh day, Japhia king of Hebron sent secretly to the king of Ai, and to the king of Gibeon, and to the king of Shalem, and to the king of Adulam, and to the king of Lachish, and to the king of Chazar, and to all the Canaanite kings who were under their subjection, saying, [24] "Go up with me, and come to me that we may go to the sons of Jacob, and I will make peace with them, and form a treaty with them, lest all your lands be destroyed by the swords of the sons of Jacob as they did to Shechem and the cities around it, as you have heard and seen. [25] And when you come to me, do not come with many men, but let every king bring his three head captains, and every captain bring three of his officers. [26] And all of you come to Hebron, and we will go together to the sons of Jacob and supplicate them that they will form a treaty of peace with us." [27] And all those kings did as the king of Hebron had sent to them, for they were all under his counsel and command, and all the kings of Canaan assembled to go to the sons of Jacob, to make peace with them; and the sons of Jacob returned and went to the portion of the field that was in Shechem, for they did not put confidence in the kings of the land. [28] And the sons of Jacob returned and remained in the portion of the field [for] ten days, and no one came to make war with them. [29] And when the sons of Jacob saw that there was no appearance of war, they all assembled and went to the city of Shechem, and the sons of Jacob remained in Shechem. [30] And at the expiration of forty days, all the kings of the Amorites assembled from all their places and came to Hebron, to Japhia, king of Hebron. [31] And the number of kings that came to Hebron to make peace with the sons of Jacob was twenty-one kings, and the number of captains that came with them was sixty-nine, and their men were one hundred and eighty-nine, and all these kings and their men rested by Mount Hebron. [32] And the king of Hebron went out with his three captains and nine men, and these kings resolved to go to the sons of Jacob to make peace. [33] And they said to the king of Hebron, "Go before us with your men, and speak for us to the sons of Jacob, and we will come after you and confirm your words," and the king of Hebron did so. [34] And the sons of Jacob heard that all the kings of Canaan had gathered together and rested in Hebron, and the sons of Jacob sent four of their servants as spies, saying, "Go and spy on these kings, and search and examine their men whether they are few or many, and if they are but few in number, number them all and come back." [35] And the servants of Jacob went secretly to these kings, and did as the sons of Jacob had commanded them, and on that day they came back to the sons of Jacob, and said to them, "We came to those kings, and they are but few in number, and we numbered them all, and behold, they were two hundred and eighty-eight kings and men." [36] And the sons of Jacob said, "They are but few in number, therefore we will not all go out to them"; and in the morning the sons of Jacob rose up and chose sixty-two of their men, and ten of the sons of Jacob went with them; and they girded on their weapons of war, for they said, "They are coming to make war with us," for they did not know that they were coming to make peace with them. [37] And the sons of Jacob went with their servants to the gate of Shechem, toward those kings, and their father Jacob was with them. [38] And when they had come out, behold, the king of Hebron and his three captains and nine men with him were coming along the road against the sons of Jacob, and the sons of Jacob lifted up their eyes, and saw at a distance Japhia, king of Hebron, with his captains, coming toward them, and the sons of Jacob took their stand at the place of the gate of Shechem, and did not proceed. [39] And the king of Hebron continued to advance, he and his captains, until he came near to the sons of Jacob, and he and his captains bowed down to them to the ground, and the king of Hebron sat with his captains before Jacob and his sons. [40] And the sons of Jacob said to him, "What has befallen you, O king of Hebron? Why have you come to us this day? What do you require from us?" And the king of Hebron said to Jacob, "I implore you, my lord: all the kings of the Canaanites have come to make peace with you this day." [41] And the sons of Jacob heard the words of the king of Hebron, and they would not consent to his proposals, for the sons of Jacob had no faith in him, for they imagined that the king of Hebron had spoken deceitfully to them. [42] And the king of Hebron knew from the words of the sons of Jacob that they did not believe his words, and the king of Hebron approached nearer to Jacob, and said to him, "I implore you, my lord, to be assured that all these kings have come to you on peaceable terms, for they have not come with all their men, neither did they bring their weapons of war with them, for they have come to seek peace from my lord and his sons." [43] And the sons of Jacob answered the king of Hebron, saying, "Send to all these kings, and if you speak truth to us, let them each come before us individually, and if they come to us unarmed, we will then know that they seek peace from us." [44] And Japhia, king of Hebron, sent one of his men to the kings, and they all came before the sons of Jacob, and bowed down to them to the ground, and these kings sat before Jacob and his sons, and they spoke to them, saying, [45] "We have heard all that you did to the kings of the Amorites with your sword and exceedingly mighty arm, so that no man could stand up before you, and we were afraid of you for the sake of our lives, lest it should befall us as it did to them. [46] So we have come to you to form a treaty of peace between us, and now, therefore, contract a covenant of peace and truth with us that you will not meddle with us, inasmuch as we have not meddled with you." [47] And the sons of Jacob knew that they had really come to seek peace from them, and the sons of Jacob listened to them, and formed a covenant with them. [48] And the sons of Jacob swore to them that they would not meddle with them, and all the kings of the Canaanites also swore to them, and the sons of Jacob made them tributary from that day forward. [49] And after this, all the captains of these kings came with their men before Jacob, with presents in their hands for Jacob and his sons, and they bowed down to him to the ground. [50] And these kings then urged the sons of Jacob and begged of them to return all the spoil they had captured from the seven cities of the Amorites, and the sons of Jacob did so, and they returned all that they had captured, the women, the little ones, the cattle, and all the spoil which they had taken, and they sent them off, and they each went away to his city. [51] And all these kings again bowed down to the sons of Jacob, and they sent or brought them many gifts in those days, and the sons of Jacob sent off these kings and their men, and they went peaceably away from them to their cities, and the sons of Jacob also returned to their home, to Shechem. [52] And there was peace from that day forward between the sons of Jacob and the kings of the Canaanites, until the sons of Israel came to inherit the land of Canaan.

CHAPTER 41

[1] And at the revolution of the year the sons of Jacob journeyed from Shechem, and they came to Hebron, to their father Isaac, and they dwelt there, but they fed their flocks and herds daily in Shechem, for there was good and fat pasture there in those days, and Jacob, and his sons, and all their household dwelt in the Valley of Hebron. [2] And it was in those days, in that year, being the one hundred and sixth year of the life of Jacob, in the tenth year of Jacob's coming from Padan-Aram, that Leah the wife of Jacob died; she was fifty-one years old when she died in Hebron. [3] And Jacob and his sons buried her in the cave of the field of Machpelah, which is in Hebron, which Abraham had bought from the children of Heth for the possession of a burial place. [4] And the sons of Jacob dwelt with their father in the Valley of Hebron, and all the inhabitants of the land knew their strength and their fame went throughout the land. [5] And Joseph the son of Jacob, and his brother Benjamin, the sons of Rachel, the wife of Jacob, were yet young in those days, and did not go out with their brothers during their battles in all the cities of the Amorites. [6] And when Joseph saw the strength of his brothers, and their greatness, he praised them and extolled them, but he ranked himself greater than them, and extolled himself above them; and his father Jacob also loved him more than any of his sons, for he was a son of his old age, and through his love toward him he made him a coat of many colors. [7] And when Joseph saw that his father loved him more than his brothers, he continued to exalt himself above his brothers, and he brought to his father evil reports concerning them. [8] And the sons of Jacob, seeing the whole of Joseph's conduct toward them, and that their father loved him more than any of them, hated him and could not speak peaceably to him all the days. [9] And Joseph was seventeen years old, and he was still magnifying himself above his brothers, and thought of raising

himself above them. [10] At that time he dreamed a dream, and he came to his brothers and told them his dream, and he said to them, "I dreamed a dream, and behold, we were all binding sheaves in the field, and my sheaf rose and placed itself on the ground and your sheaves surrounded it and bowed down to it." [11] And his brothers answered him and said to him, "What does this dream that you dreamed mean? Do you imagine in your heart to reign or rule over us?" [12] And he still came, and told the thing to his father Jacob, and Jacob kissed Joseph when he heard these words from his mouth, and Jacob blessed Joseph. [13] And when the sons of Jacob saw that their father had blessed Joseph and had kissed him, and that he loved him exceedingly, they became jealous of him and hated him [even] more. [14] And after this, Joseph dreamed another dream and related the dream to his father in the presence of his brothers, and Joseph said to his father and brothers, "Behold, I have again dreamed a dream, and behold, the sun, and the moon, and the eleven stars bowed down to me." [15] And his father heard the words of Joseph and his dream, and seeing that his brothers hated Joseph on account of this matter, Jacob therefore rebuked Joseph before his brothers on account of this thing, saying, "What does this dream which you have dreamed mean—and this magnifying yourself before your brothers who are older than you are? [16] Do you imagine in your heart that I, and your mother, and your eleven brothers will come and bow down to you, that you speak these things?" [17] And his brothers were jealous of him on account of his words and dreams, and they continued to hate him, and Jacob reserved the dreams in his heart. [18] And one day the sons of Jacob went to feed their father's flock in Shechem, for they were still herdsmen in those days; and while the sons of Jacob were feeding in Shechem that day, they delayed, and the time of gathering in the cattle was passed, and they had not arrived. [19] And Jacob saw that his sons were delayed in Shechem, and Jacob said within himself, "Perhaps the people of Shechem have risen up to fight against them, therefore they have delayed coming this day." [20] And Jacob called his son Joseph and commanded him, saying, "Behold, your brothers are feeding in Shechem this day, and behold, they have not yet come back; now therefore, go and see where they are, and bring word back to me concerning the welfare of your brothers and the welfare of the flock." [21] And Jacob sent his son Joseph to the Valley of Hebron, and Joseph came for his brothers to Shechem, and could not find them, and Joseph went around the field which was near Shechem to see where his brothers had turned, and he missed his road in the wilderness, and did not know which way he should go. [22] And a messenger of the LORD found him wandering in the road toward the field, and Joseph said to the messenger of the LORD, "I seek my brothers; have you not heard where they are feeding?" And the messenger of the LORD said to Joseph, "I saw your brothers feeding here, and I heard them say they would go to feed in Doesan." [23] And Joseph listened to the voice of the messenger of the LORD, and he went to his brothers in Doesan and found them in Doesan feeding the flock. [24] And Joseph advanced to his brothers, and before he had come near to them, they had resolved to slay him. [25] And Simeon said to his brothers, "Behold, the man of dreams is coming to us this day, and now therefore, come and let us kill him and cast him into one of the pits that are in the wilderness, and when his father will seek him from us, we will say an evil beast has devoured him." [26] And Reuben heard the words of his brothers concerning Joseph, and he said to them, "You should not do this thing, for how can we look up to our father Jacob? Cast him into this pit to die there but do not stretch out a hand on him to spill his blood"; and Reuben said this in order to deliver him from their hand, to bring him back to his father. [27] And when Joseph came to his brothers, he sat before them, and they rose on him, and seized him, and struck him to the earth, and stripped the coat of many colors which he had on. [28] And they took him and cast him into a pit, and there was no water in the pit, but serpents and scorpions. And Joseph was afraid of the serpents and scorpions that were in the pit. And Joseph cried out with a loud voice, and the LORD hid the serpents and scorpions in the sides of the pit, and they did no harm to Joseph. [29] And Joseph called out from the pit to his brothers, and said to them, "What have I done to you, and in what have I sinned? Why do you not fear the LORD concerning me? Am I not of your bones and flesh, and is your father Jacob not my father? Why do you do this thing to me this day, and how will you be able to look up to our father Jacob?" [30] And he continued to cry out and call to his brothers from the pit, and he said, "O Judah, Simeon, and Levi, my brothers! Lift me up from the place of darkness in which you have placed me, and come this day to have compassion on me, you children of the LORD, and sons of my father Jacob! And if I have sinned to you, are you not the sons of Abraham, Isaac, and Jacob? If they saw an orphan, they had compassion over him, or one that was hungry, they gave him bread to eat, or one that was thirsty, they gave him water to drink, or one that was naked, they covered him with garments!" [31] And how then will you withhold your pity from your brother, for I am of your flesh and bones, and if I have sinned to you, surely you will do this on account of my father! [32] And Joseph spoke these words from the pit, and his brothers could not listen to him, nor incline their ears to the words of Joseph, and Joseph was crying and weeping in the pit. [33] And Joseph said, "O that my father knew, this day, the act which my brothers have done to me, and the words which they have spoken this day to me." [34] And all his brothers heard his cries and weeping in the pit, and his brothers went and removed themselves from the pit, so that they might not hear the cries of Joseph and his weeping in the pit.

CHAPTER 42

¹ And they went and sat on the opposite side, about the distance of a bow-shot, and they sat there to eat bread, and while they were eating, they held counsel together what was to be done with him, whether to slay him or to bring him back to his father. ² When they were holding the counsel, they lifted up their eyes and saw, and behold, there was a company of Ishmaelites coming at a distance by the road of Gilead, going down to Egypt. ³ And Judah said to them, "What gain will it be to us if we slay our brother? Perhaps God will require him from us; this then is the counsel proposed concerning him, which you will do to him: behold, this company of Ishmaelites going down to Egypt. ⁴ Now therefore, come let us dispose of him to them, and do not let our hand be on him, and they will lead him along with them, and he will be lost among the people of the land, and we will not put him to death with our own hands." And the proposal pleased his brothers, and they did according to the word of Judah. ⁵ And while they were discoursing about this matter, and before the company of Ishmaelites had come up to them, seven trading men of Midian passed by them, and as they passed, they were thirsty, and they lifted up their eyes and saw the pit in which Joseph was confined, and they looked, and behold, every species of bird was on him. ⁶ And these Midianites ran to the pit to drink water, for they thought that it contained water, and on coming before the pit they heard the voice of Joseph crying and weeping in the pit, and they looked down into the pit, and they saw, and behold, there was a youth of handsome appearance and well-favored. ⁷ And they called to him and said, "Who are you and who brought you here? And who placed you in this pit in the wilderness?" And they all helped to raise Joseph up and they drew him out, and brought him up from the pit, and took him, and went away on their journey, and passed by his brothers. ⁸ And these said to them, "Why do you do this, to take our servant from us and to go away? Surely we placed this youth in the pit because he rebelled against us, and you come and bring him up and lead him away; now then, give us back our servant." ⁹ And the Midianites answered and said to the sons of Jacob, "Is this your servant, or does this man attend you? Perhaps you are all his servants, for he is more handsome and well-favored than any of you, and why do you all speak falsely to us? ¹⁰ Now therefore, we will not listen to your words, nor attend to you, for we found the youth in the pit in the wilderness, and we took him; we will therefore go on." ¹¹ And all the sons of Jacob approached them, and rose up to them, and said to them, "Give us back our servant, and why will you all

die by the edge of the sword?" And the Midianites cried out against them, and they drew their swords, and approached to fight with the sons of Jacob. ¹² And behold, Simeon rose up from his seat against them, and sprang on the ground, and drew his sword, and approached the Midianites, and he gave a terrible shout before them, so that his shouting was heard at a distance, and the earth shook at Simeon's shouting. ¹³ And the Midianites were terrified on account of Simeon and the noise of his shouting, and they fell on their faces, and were excessively alarmed. ¹⁴ And Simeon said to them, "I am truly Simeon, the son of the Hebrew Jacob, who has, with my brother alone, destroyed the city of Shechem and the cities of the Amorites; so will God moreover do to me, that if all your brothers, the people of Midian, and also the kings of Canaan, were to come with you, they could not fight against me. ¹⁵ Now therefore, give us back the youth whom you have taken, lest I give your flesh to the birds of the skies and the beasts of the earth." ¹⁶ And the Midianites were more afraid of Simeon, and they approached the sons of Jacob with terror and fright, and with pathetic words, saying, ¹⁷ "Surely you have said that the young man is your servant, and that he rebelled against you, and therefore you placed him in the pit; what then will you do with a servant who rebels against his master? Now therefore, sell him to us, and we will give you all that you require for him"; and the LORD was pleased to do this in order that the sons of Jacob should not slay their brother. ¹⁸ And the Midianites saw that Joseph was of a handsome appearance and well-favored; they desired him in their hearts and were urgent to purchase him from his brothers. ¹⁹ And the sons of Jacob listened to the Midianites and they sold their brother Joseph to them for twenty pieces of silver, and their brother Reuben was not with them, and the Midianites took Joseph and continued their journey to Gilead. ²⁰ They were going along the road, and the Midianites regretted what they had done, in having purchased the young man, and one said to the other, "What is this thing that we have done, in taking this youth from the Hebrews, who is of handsome appearance and well-favored? ²¹ Perhaps this youth is stolen from the land of the Hebrews, and why then have we done this thing? And if he should be sought for and found in our hands, we will die through him. ²² Now surely hardy and powerful men have sold him to us, the strength of one of whom you saw this day; perhaps they stole him from his land with their might and with their powerful arm and have therefore sold him to us for the small value which we gave to them." ²³ And while they were thus discoursing together, they looked, and behold, the company of Ishmaelites which was coming at first, and which the sons of Jacob saw, was advancing toward the Midianites, and the Midianites said to each other, "Come, let us sell this youth to the company of Ishmaelites who are coming toward us, and we will take for him the little that we gave for him, and we will be delivered from his evil." ²⁴ And they did so, and they reached the Ishmaelites, and the Midianites sold Joseph to the Ishmaelites for twenty pieces of silver which they had given for him to his brothers. ²⁵ And the Midianites went on their road to Gilead, and the Ishmaelites took Joseph and they let him ride on one of the camels, and they were leading him to Egypt. ²⁶ And Joseph heard that the Ishmaelites were proceeding to Egypt, and Joseph lamented and wept at this thing that he was to be so far removed from the land of Canaan, from his father, and he wept bitterly while he was riding on the camel, and one of their men observed him, and made him go down from the camel and walk on foot, and notwithstanding this, Joseph continued to cry and weep, and he said, "O my father, my father!" ²⁷ And one of the Ishmaelites rose up and struck Joseph on the cheek, and still he continued to weep; and Joseph was fatigued in the road, and was unable to proceed on account of the bitterness of his soul, and they all struck him and afflicted him in the road, and they terrified him in order that he might cease from weeping. ²⁸ And the LORD saw the ambition of Joseph and his trouble, and the LORD brought down on those men darkness and confusion, and the hand of everyone that struck him became withered. ²⁹ And they said to each other, "What is this thing that God has done to us in the road?" And they did not know that this befell them on account of Joseph. And the men proceeded on the road, and they passed along the road of Ephrath where Rachel was buried. ³⁰ And Joseph reached his mother's grave, and Joseph hastened and ran to his mother's grave, and fell on the grave and wept. ³¹ And Joseph cried aloud on his mother's grave, and he said, "O my mother, my mother! O you who gave birth to me! Awake now, and rise, and see your son—how he has been sold for a slave, and [there is] no one to pity him! ³² O rise and see your son, weep with me on account of my troubles, and see the heart of my brothers! ³³ Arouse my mother, arouse! Awake from your sleep for me and direct your battles against my brothers! O how they have stripped me of my coat, and sold me already twice for a slave, and separated me from my father, and there is no one to pity me! ³⁴ Arouse and lay your cause against them before God, and see whom God will justify in the judgment, and whom He will condemn! ³⁵ Rise, O my mother, rise! Awake from your sleep and see my father—how his soul is with me this day, and comfort him and ease his heart!" ³⁶ And Joseph continued to speak these words, and Joseph cried aloud and wept bitterly on his mother's grave; and he ceased speaking, and from bitterness of heart he became still as a stone on the grave. ³⁷ And Joseph heard a voice speaking to him from beneath the ground, which answered him with bitterness of heart, and with a voice of weeping and praying in these words: ³⁸ "My son, my son Joseph! I have heard the voice of your weeping and the voice of your lamentation; I have seen your tears; I know your troubles, my son, and it grieves me for your sake, and abundant grief is added to my grief. ³⁹ Now therefore, my son, my son Joseph: hope on the LORD, and wait for Him, and do not fear, for the LORD is with you; He will deliver you from all trouble. ⁴⁰ Rise, my son; go down to Egypt with your masters, and do not fear, for the LORD is with you, my son." And she continued to speak like to these words to Joseph, and she was still. ⁴¹ And Joseph heard this, and he wondered greatly at this, and he continued to weep; and after this one of the Ishmaelites observed him crying and weeping on the grave, and his anger was kindled against him, and he drove him from there, and he struck him and cursed him. ⁴² And Joseph said to the men, "May I find grace in your sight to take me back to my father's house, and he will give you abundance of riches." ⁴³ And they answered him, saying, "Are you not a slave, and where is your father? And if you had a father you would not already twice have been sold for a slave for so little value"; and their anger was still roused against him, and they continued to strike him and to punish him, and Joseph wept bitterly. ⁴⁴ And the LORD saw Joseph's affliction, and the LORD again struck these men, and punished them, and the LORD caused darkness to envelope them on the earth, and the lightning flashed, and the thunder roared, and the earth shook at the voice of the thunder and of the mighty wind, and the men were terrified and did not know where they should go. ⁴⁵ And the beasts and camels stood still, and they led them, but they would not go; they struck them, and they crouched on the ground; and the men said to each other, "What is this that God has done to us? What are our transgressions, and what are our sins that this thing has thus befallen us?" ⁴⁶ And one of them answered and said to them, "Perhaps on account of the sin of afflicting this slave this thing has happened to us this day; now therefore, strongly implore him to forgive us, and then we will know on whose account this calamity befalls us, and if God will have compassion over us, then we will know that all this comes to us on account of the sin of afflicting this slave." ⁴⁷ And the men did so, and they supplicated Joseph and pressed him to forgive them, and they said, "We have sinned to the LORD and to you, now therefore, graciously request of your God that He will put away this death from among us, for we have sinned against Him." ⁴⁸ And Joseph did according to their words, and the LORD listened to Joseph, and the LORD put away the plague which He had inflicted on those men on account of Joseph, and the beasts rose up from the ground and they conducted them, and they went on, and the raging storm abated, and the earth became tranquilized, and the men proceeded on their journey to go down to Egypt, and the men knew that this calamity had befallen them on account of

Joseph. ⁴⁹ And they said to each other, "Behold, we know that it was on account of his affliction that this calamity befell us; now therefore, why will we bring this death on our souls? Let us hold counsel what to do to this slave." ⁵⁰ And one answered and said, "Surely he told us to bring him back to his father; now therefore, come, let us take him back, and we will go to the place that he will tell us and take from his family the price that we gave for him, and then we will go away." ⁵¹ And one answered again and said, "Behold, this counsel is very good, but we cannot do so for the way is very far from us, and we cannot go out of our road." ⁵² And one more answered and said to them, "This is the counsel to be adopted, we will not swerve from it; behold, we are going to Egypt this day, and when we will have come to Egypt, we will sell him there at a high price, and we will be delivered from his evil." ⁵³ And this thing pleased the men and they did so, and they continued their journey to Egypt with Joseph.

CHAPTER 43

¹ And when the sons of Jacob had sold their brother Joseph to the Midianites, their hearts were smitten on account of him, and they regretted their acts, and they sought for him to bring him back, but could not find him. ² And Reuben returned to the pit in which Joseph had been put, in order to lift him out, and restore him to his father, and Reuben stood by the pit, and he did not hear a word, and he called out, "Joseph! Joseph!" And no one answered or uttered a word. ³ And Reuben said, "Joseph has died through fright, or some serpent has caused his death"; and Reuben descended into the pit, and he searched for Joseph and could not find him in the pit, and he came out again. ⁴ And Reuben tore his garments and he said, "The child is not there, and how will I reconcile my father concerning him if he is dead?" And he went to his brothers and found them grieving on account of Joseph, and counseling together how to reconcile their father concerning him, and Reuben said to his brothers, "I came to the pit, and behold, Joseph was not there! What then will we say to our father, for my father will only seek the youth from me?" ⁵ And his brothers answered him, saying, "Thus and thus we did, and afterward our hearts struck us on account of this act, and we now sit to seek a pretext how we will reconcile our father to it." ⁶ And Reuben said to them, "What is this you have done to bring down the grey hairs of our father in sorrow to the grave? The thing that you have done is not good." ⁷ And Reuben sat with them, and they all rose up and swore to each other not to tell this thing to Jacob, and they all said, "The man who will tell this to our father or his household, or who will report this to any of the children of the land, we will all rise up against him and slay him with the sword." ⁸ And the sons of Jacob feared each other in this matter, from the youngest to the oldest, and no one spoke a word, and they concealed the thing in their hearts. ⁹ And afterward they sat down to determine and invent something to say to their father Jacob concerning all these things. ¹⁰ And Issachar said to them, "Here is an idea for you, if it seems good in your eyes to do this thing: take the coat which belongs to Joseph, and tear it, and kill a kid of the goats, and dip it in its blood. ¹¹ Then send it to our father, and when he sees it, he will say an evil beast has devoured him; therefore, tear his coat, and behold, his blood will be on his coat, and by your doing this we will be free of our father's murmurings." ¹² And Issachar's advice pleased them, and they listened to him, and they did according to the word of Issachar which he had counseled them. ¹³ And they hastened, and took Joseph's coat, and tore it, and they killed a kid of the goats and dipped the coat in the blood of the kid, and then trampled it in the dust, and they sent the coat to their father Jacob by the hand of Naphtali, and they commanded him to say these words: ¹⁴ "We had gathered in the cattle and had come as far as the road to Shechem and farther when we found this coat on the road in the wilderness dipped in blood and in dust; now therefore, discern whether it is your son's coat or not." ¹⁵ And Naphtali went, and he came to his father, and he gave him the coat, and he spoke to him all the words which his brothers had commanded him. ¹⁶ And Jacob saw Joseph's coat, and he knew it, and he fell on his face to the ground and became as still as a stone, and afterward he rose up and cried out with a loud and weeping voice, and he said, "It is the coat of my son Joseph!" ¹⁷ And Jacob hastened and sent one of his servants to his sons who went to them and found them coming along the road with the flock. ¹⁸ And the sons of Jacob came to their father about evening, and behold, their garments were torn and dust was on their heads, and they found their father crying out and weeping with a loud voice. ¹⁹ And Jacob said to his sons, "Tell me, truthfully, what evil you have suddenly brought on me this day!" And they answered their father Jacob, saying, "We were coming along this day after the flock had been gathered in, and we came as far as the city of Shechem by the road in the wilderness, and we found this coat filled with blood on the ground, and we knew it, and we sent [it] to you [to see] if you could discern it." ²⁰ And Jacob heard the words of his sons and he cried out with a loud voice, and he said, "It is the coat of my son! An evil beast has devoured him! Joseph is torn in pieces, for I sent him this day to see whether it was well with you and well with the flocks, and to bring me word from you again, and he went as I commanded him, and this has happened to him this day while I thought my son was with you." ²¹ And the sons of Jacob answered and said, "He did not come to us, neither have we seen him from the time of our going out from you until now." ²² And when Jacob heard their words, he cried out aloud again, and he rose up and tore his garments, and he put sackcloth

on his loins; then he wept bitterly, and mourned, and lifted up his voice in weeping, and exclaimed and said these words, ²³ "My son Joseph, O my son Joseph! I sent you this day after the welfare of your brothers, and behold, you have been torn in pieces; through my hand this has happened to my son! ²⁴ It grieves me for you, my son Joseph, it grieves me for you! How sweet you were to me during life, and now how exceedingly bitter is your death to me! ²⁵ O that I had died in your stead, my son Joseph, for it grieves me sadly for you my son, O my son, my son! My son Joseph, where are you, and where have you been drawn? Arouse, arouse from your place, and come and see my grief for you, O my son Joseph! ²⁶ Come now and number the tears gushing from my eyes down my cheeks, and bring them up before the LORD, that His anger may turn from me. ²⁷ O my son Joseph, how did you fall by the hand of one by whom no one had fallen from the beginning of the world to this day, for you have been put to death by the striking of an enemy, inflicted with cruelty, but surely I know that this has happened to you on account of the multitude of my sins. ²⁸ Arouse now and see how bitter my trouble is for you my son, although I did not rear you, nor fashion you, nor give you breath and soul, but it was God who formed you, and built your bones, and covered them with flesh, and breathed into your nostrils the breath of life, and then gave you to me. ²⁹ Now truly God who gave you to me has taken you from me, and such then has befallen you." ³⁰ And Jacob continued to speak like to these words concerning Joseph, and he wept bitterly; he fell to the ground and became still. ³¹ And all the sons of Jacob, seeing their father's trouble, regretted what they had done, and they also wept bitterly. ³² And Judah rose up and lifted his father's head from the ground, and placed it on his lap, and he wiped his father's tears from his cheeks, and Judah wept an exceedingly great weeping while his father's head was reclining on his lap, still as a stone. ³³ And the sons of Jacob saw their father's trouble, and they lifted up their voices and continued to weep, and Jacob was yet lying on the ground still as a stone. ³⁴ And all his sons, and his servants, and his servant's children rose up and stood around him to comfort him, and he refused to be comforted. ³⁵ And the whole household of Jacob rose up and mourned a great mourning on account of Joseph and their father's trouble, and the intelligence reached Isaac, the son of Abraham, the father of Jacob, and he wept bitterly on account of Joseph, he and all his household, and he went from the place where he dwelt in Hebron, and his men with him, and he comforted his son Jacob, and he refused to be comforted. ³⁶ And after this, Jacob rose up from the ground, and his tears were running down his cheeks, and he said to his sons, "Rise up and take your swords and your bows, and go out into the field, and seek whether you can find my son's body and bring it to me that I may bury it.

³⁷ Please also seek among the beasts and hunt them, and that which will first come before you, seize [it] and bring it to me—perhaps the LORD will pity my affliction this day; and prepare before you that which tore my son in pieces, and bring it to me, and I will avenge the cause of my son." ³⁸ And his sons did as their father had commanded them, and they rose up early in the morning, and each took his sword and his bow in his hand, and they went out into the field to hunt the beasts. ³⁹ And Jacob was still crying aloud, and weeping, and walking to and fro in the house, and striking his hands together, saying, "My son Joseph! My son Joseph!" ⁴⁰ And the sons of Jacob went into the wilderness to seize the beasts, and behold, a wolf came toward them, and they seized him, and brought him to their father, and they said to him, "This is the first we have found, and we have brought him to you as you commanded us, and we could not find your son's body." ⁴¹ And Jacob took the beast from the hands of his sons, and he cried out with a loud and weeping voice, holding the beast in his hand, and he spoke with a bitter heart to the beast, "Why did you devour my son Joseph, and how did you have no fear of the God of the earth, or of my trouble for my son Joseph? ⁴² And you devoured my son for nothing, because he committed no violence, and thereby rendered me culpable on his account, therefore God will require him that is persecuted." ⁴³ And the LORD opened the mouth of the beast in order to comfort Jacob with its words, and it answered Jacob and spoke these words to him: ⁴⁴ "As God lives who created us in the earth, and as your soul lives, my lord: I did not see your son, neither did I tear him to pieces, but from a distant land I also came to seek my son who went from me this day, and I do not know whether he is living or dead. ⁴⁵ And I came into the field to seek my son this day, and your sons found me, and seized me, and increased my grief, and have brought me before you this day, and I have now spoken all my words to you. ⁴⁶ And now therefore, O son of man, I am in your hands, and do to me this day as it may seem good in your sight, but by the life of God who created me, I did not see your son, nor did I tear him to pieces, neither has the flesh of man entered my mouth all the days of my life." ⁴⁷ And when Jacob heard the words of the beast he was greatly astonished and sent the beast out from his hand, and she went her way. ⁴⁸ And Jacob was still crying aloud and weeping for Joseph day after day, and he mourned for his son many days.

CHAPTER 44

¹ And the sons of Ishmael who had bought Joseph from the Midianites, who had bought him from his brothers, went to Egypt with Joseph, and they came on the borders of Egypt, and when they came near to Egypt, they met four men of the sons of Medan, the son of Abraham, who had gone out from the land of Egypt on their journey. ² And the Ishmaelites said to

them, "Do you desire to purchase this slave from us?" And they said, "Deliver him over to us," and they delivered Joseph over to them, and they beheld him, that he was a very handsome youth and they purchased him for twenty shekels. ³ And the Ishmaelites continued their journey to Egypt and the Medanim also returned to Egypt that day, and the Medanim said to each other, "Behold, we have heard that Potiphar, an officer of Pharaoh, captain of the guard, seeks a good servant who will stand before him to attend him, and to make him overseer over his house and all belonging to him. ⁴ Now therefore, come, let us sell him to him for what we may desire if he is able to give to us that which we will require for him." ⁵ And these Medanim went, and came to the house of Potiphar, and said to him, "We have heard that you seek a good servant to attend you: behold, we have a servant that will please you if you can give to us that which we may desire, and we will sell him to you." ⁶ And Potiphar said, "Bring him before me, and I will see him, and if he pleases me I will give to you that which you may require for him." ⁷ And the Medanim went, and brought Joseph, and placed him before Potiphar, and he saw him, and he pleased him exceedingly, and Potiphar said to them, "Tell me what you require for this youth?" ⁸ And they said, "We desire four hundred pieces of silver for him," and Potiphar said, "I will give it [to] you if you bring me the record of his sale to you, and will tell me his history, for perhaps he may be stolen, for this youth is neither a slave, nor the son of a slave, but I observe in him the appearance of an attractive and handsome person." ⁹ And the Medanim went and brought to him the Ishmaelites who had sold him to them, and they told him, saying, "He is a slave and we sold him to them." ¹⁰ And Potiphar heard the words of the Ishmaelites in his giving the silver to the Medanim, and the Medanim took the silver and went on their journey, and the Ishmaelites also returned home. ¹¹ And Potiphar took Joseph and brought him to his house that he might serve him, and Joseph found favor in the sight of Potiphar, and he placed confidence in him, and made him overseer over his house, and he delivered all that belonged to him over into his hand. ¹² And the LORD was with Joseph and he became a prosperous man, and the LORD blessed the house of Potiphar for the sake of Joseph. ¹³ And Potiphar left all that he had in the hand of Joseph, and Joseph was one that caused things to come in and go out, and everything was regulated by his wish in the house of Potiphar. ¹⁴ And Joseph was eighteen years old, a youth with beautiful eyes and of handsome appearance, and like to him was not in the whole land of Egypt. ¹⁵ At that time, while he was in his master's house going in and out of the house and attending his master, Zelicah, his master's wife, lifted up her eyes toward Joseph and she looked at him, and behold, he was a handsome and well-favored youth. ¹⁶ And she

coveted his beauty in her heart, and her soul was fixed on Joseph, and she enticed him day after day, and Zelicah persuaded Joseph daily, but Joseph did not lift up his eyes to behold his master's wife. ¹⁷ And Zelicah said to him, "How attractive is your appearance and form, truly I have looked at all the slaves, and have not seen so beautiful a slave as you are"; and Joseph said to her, "Surely He who created me in my mother's womb created all mankind." ¹⁸ And she said to him, "How beautiful are your eyes with which you have dazzled all the inhabitants of Egypt, men and women"; and he said to her, "How beautiful they are while we are alive, but should you behold them in the grave, surely you would move away from them." ¹⁹ And she said to him, "How beautiful and pleasing are all your words; please take the harp which is in the house now, and play [it] with your hands, and let us hear your words." ²⁰ And he said to her, "How beautiful and pleasing are my words when I speak the praise of my God and His glory"; and she said to him, "How very beautiful is the hair of your head; behold, the golden comb which is in the house, please take it and curl the hair of your head." ²¹ And he said to her, "How long will you speak these words? Cease to utter these words to me, and rise and attend to your domestic affairs." ²² And she said to him, "There is no one in my house, and there is nothing to attend to but to your words and to your wish"; yet notwithstanding all this, she could not bring Joseph to her, neither did he place his eye on her, but directed his eyes below to the ground. ²³ And Zelicah desired Joseph in her heart, that he should lie with her, and at the time that Joseph was sitting in the house doing his work, Zelicah came and sat before him, and she enticed him daily with her discourse to lie with her, or ever to look at her, but Joseph would not listen to her. ²⁴ And she said to him, "If you will not do according to my words, I will punish you with the punishment of death, and put an iron yoke on you." ²⁵ And Joseph said to her, "Surely God who created man loosens the chains of prisoners, and it is He who will deliver me from your prison and from your judgment." ²⁶ And when she could not prevail over him, to persuade him, and her soul being still fixed on him, her desire threw her into a grievous sickness. ²⁷ And all the women of Egypt came to visit her, and they said to her, "Why are you in this declining state? You that lack nothing—surely your husband is a great and esteemed prince in the sight of the king, should you lack anything of what your heart desires?" ²⁸ And Zelicah answered them, saying, "This day it will be made known to you from where this disorder springs in which you see me," and she commanded her maidservants to prepare food for all the women, and she made a banquet for them, and all the women ate in the house of Zelicah. ²⁹ And she gave them knives to peel the citrons to eat them, and she commanded that they should dress Joseph in costly garments, and that he should appear before them, and Joseph came before their eyes, and all the women looked on Joseph and could not take their eyes from off him, and they all cut their hands with the knives that they had in their hands, and all the citrons that were in their hands were filled with blood. ³⁰ And they did not know what they had done but they continued to look at the beauty of Joseph and did not turn their eyelids from him. ³¹ And Zelicah saw what they had done, and she said to them, "What is this work that you have done? Behold, I gave you citrons to eat and you have all cut your hands." ³² And all the women saw their hands, and behold, they were full of blood, and their blood flowed down on their garments, and they said to her, "This slave in your house has overcome us, and we could not turn our eyelids from him on account of his beauty." ³³ And she said to them, "Surely this happened to you in the moment that you looked at him, and you could not contain yourselves from him; how then can I refrain when he is constantly in my house, and I see him day after day going in and out of my house? How then can I keep from declining or even from perishing on account of this?" ³⁴ And they said to her, "The words are true, for who can see this beautiful form in the house and refrain from him, and is he not your slave and attendant in your house, and why do you not tell him that which is in your heart, and permit your soul to perish through this matter?" ³⁵ And she said to them, "I am daily endeavoring to persuade him, and he will not consent to my wishes, and I promised him everything that is good, and yet I could meet with no return from him; I am therefore in a declining state as you see." ³⁶ And Zelicah became very sick on account of her desire toward Joseph, and she was desperately lovesick on account of him, and all the people of the house of Zelicah and her husband knew nothing of this matter, that Zelicah was sick on account of her love for Joseph. ³⁷ And all the people of her house asked her, saying, "Why are you sick and declining, and lack nothing?" And she said to them, "I do not know this thing which is daily increasing on me." ³⁸ And all the women and her friends came to see her daily, and they spoke with her, and she said to them, "This can only be through the love for Joseph"; and they said to her, "Entice him and seize him secretly, perhaps he may listen to you, and put off this death from you." ³⁹ And Zelicah became worse from her love for Joseph, and she continued to decline until she scarcely had strength to stand. ⁴⁰ And on a certain day Joseph was doing his master's work in the house, and Zelicah came secretly and suddenly fell on him, and Joseph rose up against her, and he was more powerful than her, and he brought her down to the ground. ⁴¹ And Zelicah wept on account of the desire of her heart toward him, and she supplicated him with weeping, and her tears flowed down her cheeks, and she spoke to him in a voice of supplication and in

bitterness of soul, saying, ⁴² "Have you ever heard, seen, or known of so beautiful a woman as I am, or better than myself, who speaks daily to you, fall into a decline through love for you, confer all this honor on you, and still you will not listen to my voice? ⁴³ And if it is through fear of your master lest he punish you, as the king lives, no harm will come to you from your master through this thing; now therefore, please listen to me, and consent for the sake of the honor which I have conferred on you, and put off this death from me, and why should I die for your sake?" And she ceased to speak. ⁴⁴ And Joseph answered her, saying, "Refrain from me, and leave this matter to my master; behold, my master does not know what there is with me in the house, for he has delivered all that belongs to him into my hand, and how will I do these things in my master's house? ⁴⁵ For he has also greatly honored me in his house, and he has also made me overseer over his house, and he has exalted me, and there is no one greater in this house than I am, and my master has kept back nothing from me, excepting you who are his wife. How then can you speak these words to me, and how can I do this great evil and sin to God and to your husband? ⁴⁶ Now therefore, refrain from me, and speak no more such words as these, for I will not listen to your words." But Zelicah would not listen to Joseph when he spoke these words to her, but she daily enticed him to listen to her. ⁴⁷ And it was after this that the brook of Egypt was filled above all its sides, and all the inhabitants of Egypt went out, and also the king and princes went out with timbrels and dances, for it was a great rejoicing in Egypt, and a holiday at the time of the inundation of the sea Sihor, and they went there to rejoice all day long. ⁴⁸ And when the Egyptians went out to the river to rejoice, as was their custom, all the people of the house of Potiphar went with them, but Zelicah would not go with them, for she said, "I am indisposed," and she remained alone in the house, and no other person was with her in the house. ⁴⁹ And she rose up and ascended to her temple in the house, and dressed herself in princely garments, and she placed on her head precious stones of onyx stones, inlaid with silver and gold, and she beautified her face and skin with all sorts of women's purifying liquids, and she perfumed the temple and the house with cassia and frankincense, and she spread myrrh and aloes, and afterward she sat in the entrance of the temple, in the passage of the house through which Joseph passed to do his work, and behold, Joseph came from the field and entered the house to do his master's work. ⁵⁰ And he came to the place through which he had to pass, and he saw all the work of Zelicah, and he turned back. ⁵¹ And Zelicah saw Joseph turning back from her, and she called out to him, saying, "What ails you Joseph? Come to your work, and behold, I will make room for you until you will have passed to your seat." ⁵² And Joseph returned, and came to the house, and passed from there to the place of his seat, and he sat down to do his master's work as usual, and behold, Zelicah came to him and stood before him in princely garments, and the scent from her clothes was spread to a distance. ⁵³ And she hastened and caught hold of Joseph and his garments, and she said to him, "As the king lives, if you will not perform my request you will die this day," and she hastened, and stretched out her other hand, and drew a sword from beneath her garments, and she placed it on Joseph's neck, and she said, "Rise and perform my request, and if not, you die this day." ⁵⁴ And Joseph was afraid of her at her doing this thing, and he rose up to flee from her, and she seized the front of his garments, and in the terror of his flight the garment which Zelicah seized was torn, and Joseph left the garment in the hand of Zelicah, and he fled and got out, for he was in fear. ⁵⁵ And when Zelicah saw that Joseph's garment was torn, and that he had left it in her hand and had fled, she was afraid for her life, lest the report should spread concerning her, and she rose up and acted with cunning, and put off the garments in which she was dressed, and she put on her other garments. ⁵⁶ And she took Joseph's garment, and she laid it beside her, and she went and seated herself in the place where she had sat in her sickness before the people of her house had gone out to the river, and she called a young youth who was then in the house, and she ordered him to call the people of the house to her. ⁵⁷ And when she saw them, she said to them with a loud voice and lamentation, "See what [kind of] a Hebrew your master has brought to me in the house, for he came to lie with me this day! ⁵⁸ For when you had gone out, he came to the house, and seeing that there was no person in the house, he came to me, and caught hold of me, with intent to lie with me. ⁵⁹ And I seized his garments, and tore them, and called out against him with a loud voice, and when I had lifted up my voice, he was afraid for his life, and left his garment before me, and fled." ⁶⁰ And the people of her house spoke nothing, but their wrath was very much kindled against Joseph, and they went to his master and told him the words of his wife. ⁶¹ And Potiphar came home enraged, and his wife cried out to him, saying, "What is this thing that you have done to me in bringing a Hebrew servant into my house, for he came to me this day to sport with me; thus he did to me this day." ⁶² And Potiphar heard the words of his wife, and he ordered Joseph to be punished with severe stripes, and they did so to him. ⁶³ And while they were striking him, Joseph called out with a loud voice, and he lifted up his eyes to Heaven, and he said, "O LORD God, you know that I am innocent of all these things, and why will I die this day through falsehood by the hand of these uncircumcised [and] wicked men whom You know?" ⁶⁴ And while Potiphar's men were beating Joseph, he continued to cry out and weep, and there was a child there eleven months old, and the LORD opened the mouth of the child, and he spoke these words before Potiphar's men who were striking Joseph, saying, ⁶⁵ "What do you want of this man, and why do you do this evil to him? My mother speaks falsely and utters lies; thus was the transaction." ⁶⁶ And the child told them accurately all that happened, and all the words of Zelicah to Joseph day after day he declared to them. ⁶⁷ And all the men heard the words of the child and they wondered greatly at the child's words, and the child ceased to speak and became still. ⁶⁸ And Potiphar was very much ashamed at the words of his son, and he commanded his men not to beat Joseph anymore, and the men ceased beating Joseph. ⁶⁹ And Potiphar took Joseph and ordered him to be brought to justice before the priests, who were judges belonging to the king, in order to judge him concerning this affair. ⁷⁰ And Potiphar and Joseph came before the priests who were the king's judges, and he said to them, "Please decide what judgment is due to a servant, for thus he has done." ⁷¹ And the priests said to Joseph, "Why did you do this thing to your master?" And Joseph answered them, saying, "Not so my lords, thus was the matter"; and Potiphar said to Joseph, "Surely I entrusted into your hands all that belonged to me, and I withheld nothing from you except my wife, and how could you do this evil?" ⁷² And Joseph answered, saying, "Not so my lord; as the LORD lives, and as your soul lives, my lord, the word which you heard from your wife is untrue, for thus was the affair this day. ⁷³ A year has elapsed to me since I have been in your house; have you seen any iniquity in me, or anything which might cause you to demand my life?" ⁷⁴ And the priests said to Potiphar, "Send, please, and let them bring Joseph's torn garment before us, and let us see the tear in it, and if it will be that the tear is in front of the garment, then his face must have been opposite to her and she must have caught hold of him to come to her, and your wife did all that she has spoken with deceit." ⁷⁵ And they brought Joseph's garment before the priests who were judges, and they saw, and behold, the tear was in front of Joseph, and all the judging priests knew that she had pressed him, and they said, "The judgment of death is not due to this slave, for he has done nothing, but his judgment is that he should be placed in the prison-house on account of the report which through him has gone out against your wife." ⁷⁶ And Potiphar heard their words, and he placed him in the prison-house, the place where the king's prisoners are confined, and Joseph was in the house of confinement [for] twelve years. ⁷⁷ And notwithstanding this, his master's wife did not turn from him, and she did not cease from speaking to him day after day to listen to her, and at the end of three months Zelicah continued going to Joseph, to the house of confinement, day by day, and she enticed him to listen to her, and Zelicah said to Joseph, "How long will you remain in this house? But now listen to my voice, and I will bring you out of this house." [78] And Joseph answered her, saying, "It is better for me to remain in this house than to listen to your words to sin against God"; and she said to him, "If you will not perform my wish, I will pluck out your eyes, add chains to your feet, and will deliver you into the hands of them whom you did not know before." [79] And Joseph answered her and said, "Behold, the God of the whole earth is able to deliver me from all that you can do to me, for He opens the eyes of the blind, and loosens those that are bound, and preserves all strangers who are unacquainted with the land." [80] And when Zelicah was unable to persuade Joseph to listen to her, she left off going to entice him; and Joseph was still confined in the house of confinement. [81] And Joseph's father Jacob and all his brothers who were in the land of Canaan still mourned and wept in those days on account of Joseph, for Jacob refused to be comforted for his son Joseph, and Jacob cried aloud, and wept, and mourned all those days.

CHAPTER 45

[1] And it was at that time in that year, which is the year of Joseph's going down to Egypt after his brothers had sold him, that Reuben the son of Jacob went to Timnah and took to himself Eliuram for a wife, the daughter of Avi the Canaanite, and he came to her. [2] And Eliuram the wife of Reuben conceived and bore him Hanoch, Palu, Chetzron, and Carmi, four sons; and his brother Simeon took his sister Dinah for a wife, and she bore to him Memuel, Yamin, Ohad, Jachin, and Zochar, five sons. [3] And afterward he came to Bunah the Canaanite woman, the same is Bunah whom Simeon took captive from the city of Shechem, and Bunah was before Dinah and attended on her, and Simeon came to her, and she bore Saul to him. [4] And at that time Judah went to Adulam, and he came to a man of Adulam, and his name was Hirah, and Judah saw the daughter of a man from Canaan there, and her name was Aliyath, the daughter of Shua, and he took her, and came to her, and Aliyath bore Er, Onan, and Shiloh to Judah, three sons. [5] And Levi and Issachar went to the land of the east, and they took to themselves for wives the daughters of Jobab the son of Yoktan, the son of Eber; and Jobab the son of Yoktan had two daughters; the name of the elder was Adinah, and the name of the younger was Aridah. [6] And Levi took Adinah, and Issachar took Aridah, and they came to the land of Canaan, to their father's house, and Adinah bore Gershon, Kehas, and Merari to Levi, three sons. [7] And Aridah bore Tola, Puvah, Job, and Shomron to Issachar, four sons; and Dan went to the land of Moab and took Aphlaleth, the daughter of Chamudan the Moabite, for a wife, and he brought her to the land of Canaan. [8] And Aphlaleth was barren, she had no offspring, and afterward God remembered Aphlaleth the wife of Dan, and she conceived and bore a son, and she called his name Chushim. [9] And Gad and Naphtali went to Haran and took from there the daughters of Amuram the son of Uz, the son of Nahor, for wives. [10] And these are the names of the daughters of Amuram: the name of the elder was Merimah, and the name of the younger Uzith; and Naphtali took Merimah, and Gad took Uzith, and they brought them to the land of Canaan, to their father's house. [11] And Merimah bore to Naphtali Yachzeel, Guni, Jazer, and Shalem, four sons; and Uzith bore to Gad Zephion, Chagi, Shuni, Ezbon, Eri, Arodi, and Arali, seven sons. [12] And Asher went out and took Adon the daughter of Aphlal, the son of Hadad, the son of Ishmael, for a wife, and he brought her to the land of Canaan. [13] And Adon the wife of Asher died in those days—she had no offspring; and it was after the death of Adon that Asher went to the other side of the river and took for a wife Hadurah the daughter of Abimael, the son of Eber, the son of Shem. [14] And the young woman was of a beautiful appearance, and a woman of sense, and she had been the wife of Malkiel the son of Elam, the son of Shem. [15] And Hadurah bore a daughter to Malkiel, and he called her name Serach, and Malkiel died after this, and Hadurah went and remained in her father's house. [16] And after the death of the wife of Asher he went and took Hadurah for a wife and brought her to the land of Canaan, and he also brought her daughter Serach with them, and she was three years old, and the young woman was brought up in Jacob's house. [17] And the young woman was of a beautiful appearance, and she went in the sanctified ways of the children of Jacob; she lacked nothing, and the LORD gave her wisdom and understanding. [18] And Hadurah the wife of Asher conceived and bore to him Yimnah, Yishvah, Yishvi, and Beriah, four sons. [19] And Zebulun went to Midian and took for a wife Merishah the daughter of Molad, the son of Abida, the son of Midian, and brought her to the land of Canaan. [20] And Merushah bore to Zebulun Sered, Elon, and Yachleel, three sons. [21] And Jacob sent to Aram the son of Zoba, the son of Terah, and he took Mechalia the daughter of Aram for his son Benjamin, and she came to the land of Canaan to the house of Jacob; and Benjamin was ten years old when he took Mechalia the daughter of Aram for a wife. [22] And Mechalia conceived and bore to Benjamin Bela, Becher, Ashbel, Gera, and Naaman, five sons; and afterward Benjamin went and took for a wife Aribath the daughter of Shomron, the son of Abraham, in addition to his first wife, and he was eighteen years old; and Aribath bore to Benjamin Achi, Vosh, Mupim, Chupim, and Ord, five sons. [23] And in those days Judah went to the house of Shem and took Tamar the daughter of Elam, the son of Shem, for a wife for his firstborn Er. [24] And Er came to his wife Tamar, and she became his wife, and when he came to her, he outwardly destroyed his seed, and his work

was evil in the sight of the LORD, and the LORD slew him. [25] And it was after the death of Er, Judah's firstborn, that Judah said to Onan, "Go to your brother's wife and marry her as the next brother and raise up seed to your brother." [26] And Onan took Tamar for a wife and he came to her, and Onan also did like to the work of his brother, and his work was evil in the sight of the LORD, and He slew him also. [27] And when Onan died, Judah said to Tamar, "Remain in your father's house until my son Shiloh will have grown up," and Judah no longer delighted in Tamar to give her to Shiloh, for he said, "Perhaps he will also die like his brothers." [28] And Tamar rose up, and went, and remained in her father's house, and Tamar was in her father's house for some time. [29] And at the revolution of the year, Aliyath the wife of Judah died; and Judah was comforted for his wife, and after the death of Aliyath, Judah went up with his friend Hirah to Timnah to shear their sheep. [30] And Tamar heard that Judah had gone up to Timnah to shear the sheep, and that Shiloh was grown up, and Judah did not delight in her. [31] And Tamar rose up and put off the garments of her widowhood, and she put a veil on her, and she entirely covered herself, and she went and sat in the public thoroughfare, which is on the road to Timnah. [32] And Judah passed and saw her, and he took her and came to her, and she conceived by him, and at the time of being delivered, behold, there were twins in her womb, and he called the name of the first Perez, and the name of the second Zerah.

CHAPTER 46

[1] In those days Joseph was still confined in the prison-house in the land of Egypt. [2] At that time the attendants of Pharaoh were standing before him—the chief of the butlers and the chief of the bakers which belonged to the king of Egypt. [3] And the butler took wine and placed it before the king to drink, and the baker placed bread before the king to eat, and the king drank of the wine and ate of the bread—he and his servants and ministers that ate at the king's table. [4] And while they were eating and drinking, the butler and the baker remained there, and Pharaoh's ministers found many flies in the wine which the butler had brought, and stones of niter were found in the baker's bread. [5] And the captain of the guard placed Joseph as an attendant over Pharaoh's officers, and Pharaoh's officers were in confinement [for] one year. [6] And at the end of the year, they both dreamed dreams in one night in the place of confinement where they were, and in the morning Joseph came to them to attend to them as usual, and he saw them, and behold, their countenances were dejected and sad. [7] And Joseph asked them, "Why are your countenances sad and dejected this day?" And they said to him, "We dreamed a dream, and there is no one to interpret it"; and Joseph said to them, "Please relate your dream to me, and God will give you an answer of peace as you desire." [8] And the butler related his dream to Joseph, and he said, "I saw in my dream, and behold, a large vine was before me, and on that vine I saw three branches, and the vine quickly blossomed and reached a great height, and its clusters were ripened and became grapes. [9] And I took the grapes, and pressed them in a cup, and placed it in Pharaoh's hand, and he drank"; and Joseph said to him, "The three branches that were on the vine are three days. [10] Yet within three days, the king will order you to be brought out and he will restore you to your office, and you will give the king his wine to drink as at first when you were his butler; but let me find favor in your sight [so] that you will remember me before Pharaoh when it will be well with you, and do kindness to me, and get me brought out from this prison, for I was stolen away from the land of Canaan and was sold for a slave in this place. [11] And also that which was told you concerning my master's wife is false, for they placed me in this dungeon for nothing"; and the butler answered Joseph, saying, "If the king deals well with me as at first, as you last interpreted to me, I will do all that you desire and get you brought out of this dungeon." [12] And the baker, seeing that Joseph had accurately interpreted the butler's dream, also approached and related the whole of his dream to Joseph. [13] And he said to him, "In my dream I saw, and behold, [there were] three white baskets on my head, and I looked, and behold, there were all manner of baked meats for Pharaoh in the uppermost basket, and behold, the birds were eating them from off my head." [14] And Joseph said to him, "The three baskets which you saw are three days: yet within three days Pharaoh will take off your head, and hang you on a tree, and the birds will eat your flesh from off you as you saw in your dream." [15] In those days the queen was about to deliver, and on that day she bore a son to the king of Egypt, and they proclaimed that the king had gotten his firstborn son, and all the people of Egypt, together with the officers and servants of Pharaoh, greatly rejoiced. [16] And on the third day of his birth Pharaoh made a feast for his officers and servants, for the hosts of the land of Zoar and of the land of Egypt. [17] And all the people of Egypt and the servants of Pharaoh came to eat and drink with the king at the celebration of his son, and to rejoice at the king's rejoicing. [18] And all the officers of the king and his servants were rejoicing at that time for eight days at the feast, and they made merry with all sorts of musical instruments, with timbrels and with dances in the king's house for eight days. [19] And the butler, to whom Joseph had interpreted his dream, forgot Joseph, and he did not mention him to the king as he had promised, for this thing was from the LORD in order to punish Joseph because he had trusted in man. [20] And after this Joseph remained in the prison-house [for] two years, until he had completed twelve years.

CHAPTER 47

¹ And Isaac the son of Abraham was still living in the land of Canaan in those days; he was very aged—one hundred and eighty years old—and his son Esau, the brother of Jacob, was in the land of Edom, and he and his sons had possessions in it among the children of Seir. ² And Esau heard that his father's time was drawing near to die, and he and his sons and household came to the land of Canaan, to his father's house, and Jacob and his sons went out from the place where they dwelt in Hebron, and they all came to their father Isaac, and they found Esau and his sons in the tent. ³ And Jacob and his sons sat before his father Isaac, and Jacob was still mourning for his son Joseph. ⁴ And Isaac said to Jacob, "Bring your sons to me here and I will bless them"; and Jacob brought his eleven children before his father Isaac. ⁵ And Isaac placed his hands on all the sons of Jacob, and he took hold of them, and embraced them, and kissed them one by one, and Isaac blessed them on that day, and he said to them, "May the God of your fathers bless you and increase your seed like the stars of the heavens for number." ⁶ And Isaac also blessed the sons of Esau, saying, "May God cause you to be a dread and a terror to all that will behold you, and to all your enemies." ⁷ And Isaac called Jacob and his sons, and they all came and sat before Isaac, and Isaac said to Jacob, "The LORD God of the whole earth said to me, To your seed I will give this land for an inheritance if your children keep My statutes and My ways, and I will perform to them the oath which I swore to your father Abraham. ⁸ Now therefore, my son, teach your children and your children's children to fear the LORD, and to go in the good way which will please the LORD your God, for if you keep the ways of the LORD and His statutes, the LORD will also keep His covenant with Abraham to you, and will do well with you and your seed all the days." ⁹ And when Isaac had finished commanding Jacob and his children, he gave up the spirit and died, and was gathered to his people. ¹⁰ And Jacob and Esau fell on the face of their father Isaac, and they wept, and Isaac was one hundred and eighty years old when he died in the land of Canaan, in Hebron, and his sons carried him to the cave of Machpelah, which Abraham had bought from the children of Heth for a possession of a burial place. ¹¹ And all the kings of the land of Canaan went with Jacob and Esau to bury Isaac, and all the kings of Canaan showed Isaac great honor at his death. ¹² And the sons of Jacob and the sons of Esau went around barefooted, walking and lamenting until they reached Kirjath-Arba. ¹³ And Jacob and Esau buried their father Isaac in the cave of Machpelah, which is in Kirjath-Arba in Hebron, and they buried him with very great honor, as at the funeral of kings. ¹⁴ And Jacob and his sons, and Esau and his sons, and all the kings of Canaan made a great and heavy mourning, and they buried him and mourned for him [for] many days. ¹⁵ And at the death of Isaac, he left his cattle, and his possessions, and all belonging to him to his sons; and Esau said to Jacob, "Now behold, all that our father has left we will divide it in two parts, and I will have the choice," and Jacob said, "We will do so." ¹⁶ And Jacob took all that Isaac had left in the land of Canaan, the cattle and the property, and he placed them in two parts before Esau and his sons, and he said to Esau, "Behold, all this is before you, choose for yourself the half which you will take." ¹⁷ And Jacob said to Esau, "Now hear what I will speak to you, saying, The LORD God of the heavens and earth spoke to our fathers Abraham and Isaac, saying, To your seed I will give this land for an inheritance forever. ¹⁸ Now therefore, all that our father has left is before you, and behold, all the land is before you: choose from them what you desire. ¹⁹ If you desire the whole land, take it for you and your children forever, and I will take these riches, and if you desire the riches, take it to you, and I will take this land for me and for my children to inherit it forever." ²⁰ And Nebayoth, the son of Ishmael, was then in the land with his children, and Esau went on that day and consulted with him, saying, ²¹ "Thus Jacob has spoken to me, and thus he has answered me; now give your advice and we will hear." ²² And Nebayoth said, "What is this that Jacob has spoken to you? Behold, all the children of Canaan are dwelling securely in their land, and Jacob says he will inherit it with his seed all the days. ²³ Go now, therefore, and take all your father's riches and leave your brother Jacob in the land as he has spoken." ²⁴ And Esau rose up and returned to Jacob, and he did all that Nebayoth the son of Ishmael had advised; and Esau took all the riches that Isaac had left: the souls, the beasts, the cattle, and the property, and all the riches; he gave nothing to his brother Jacob; and Jacob took all the land of Canaan, from the brook of Egypt to the River Euphrates, and he took it for a perpetual possession, and for his children and for his seed after him forever. ²⁵ Jacob also took from his brother Esau the cave of Machpelah, which is in Hebron, which Abraham had bought from Ephron for a possession of a burial place for him and his seed forever. ²⁶ And Jacob wrote all these things in the scroll of purchase, and he signed it, and he testified all this with four faithful witnesses. ²⁷ And these are the words which Jacob wrote in the scroll, saying, "The land of Canaan and all the cities of the Hittites, the Hivites, the Jebusites, the Amorites, the Perizzites, and the Gergashites—all the seven nations from the river of Egypt to the River Euphrates— ²⁸ and the city of Hebron, Kirjath-Arba, and the cave which is in it, Jacob bought the whole from his brother Esau for value, for a possession and for an inheritance for his seed after him forever." ²⁹ And Jacob took the scroll of purchase, and the signature, [and] the command, and the statutes, and the revealed scroll, and he placed them in an earthen

vessel in order that they should remain for a long time, and he delivered them into the hands of his children. ³⁰ Esau took all that his father had left him after his death from his brother Jacob, and he took all the property, from man and beast, camel and donkey, ox and lamb, silver and gold, stones and bdellium, and all the riches which had belonged to Isaac the son of Abraham; there was nothing left which Esau did not take to himself from all that Isaac had left after his death. ³¹ And Esau took all this, and he and his children went home to the land of Seir the Horite, away from his brother Jacob and his children. ³² And Esau had possessions among the children of Seir, and Esau did not return to the land of Canaan from that day forward. ³³ And the whole land of Canaan became an inheritance to the sons of Israel for a perpetual inheritance, and Esau inherited the mountain of Seir with all his children.

CHAPTER 48

¹ In those days, after the death of Isaac, the LORD commanded and caused a famine on the whole earth. ² At that time Pharaoh king of Egypt was sitting on his throne in the land of Egypt, and he lay in his bed and dreamed dreams, and Pharaoh saw in his dream that he was standing by the side of the river of Egypt. ³ And while he was standing, he saw, and behold, seven fat-fleshed and well-favored cows came up out of the river. ⁴ And seven other cows, lean-fleshed and ill-favored, came up after them, and the seven ill-favored ones swallowed up the well-favored ones, and still their appearance was ill as at first. ⁵ And he awoke, and he slept again, and he dreamed a second time, and he saw, and behold, seven ears of corn came up on one stalk, rank and good, and seven thin ears blasted with the east wind sprang up after them, and the thin ears swallowed up the full ones, and Pharaoh awoke out of his dream. ⁶ And in the morning the king remembered his dreams, and his spirit was sadly troubled on account of his dreams, and the king hastened, and sent and called for all the magicians of Egypt and the wise men, and they came and stood before Pharaoh. ⁷ And the king said to them, "I have dreamed dreams, and there is none to interpret them"; and they said to the king, "Relate your dreams to your servants and let us hear them." ⁸ And the king related his dreams to them, and they all answered and said with one voice to the king, "May the king live forever; and this is the interpretation of your dreams: ⁹ the seven good cows which you saw denote seven daughters that will be born to you in the latter days, and the seven cows which you saw come up after them and swallow them up are for a sign that the daughters which will be born to you will all die in the lifetime of the king. ¹⁰ And that which you saw in the second dream of seven full good ears of corn coming up on one stalk, this is their interpretation: that you will build seven cities for yourself in the latter days

throughout the land of Egypt; and that which you saw of the seven blasted ears of corn springing up after them and swallowing them up while you beheld them with your eyes is for a sign that the cities which you will build will all be destroyed in the latter days, in the lifetime of the king." ¹¹ And when they spoke these words the king did not incline his ear to their words, neither did he fix his heart on them, for the king knew in his wisdom that they did not give a proper interpretation of the dreams; and when they had finished speaking before the king, the king answered them, saying, "What is this thing that you have spoken to me? Surely you have uttered falsehood and spoken lies; now therefore, give the proper interpretation of my dreams that you may not die." ¹² And the king commanded after this, and again he sent and called for other wise men, and they came and stood before the king, and the king related his dreams to them, and they all answered him according to the first interpretation, and the king's anger was kindled and he was very angry, and the king said to them, "Surely you speak lies and utter falsehood in what you have said." ¹³ And the king commanded that a proclamation should be issued throughout the land of Egypt, saying, "It is resolved by the king and his great men that any wise man who knows and understands the interpretation of dreams, and will not come this day before the king, will die. ¹⁴ And the man that will declare to the king the proper interpretation of his dreams, there will be given to him all that he will require from the king." And all the wise men of the land of Egypt came before the king, together with all the magicians and sorcerers that were in Egypt, and in Goshen, in Rameses, in Tachpanches, in Zoar, and in all the places on the borders of Egypt, and they all stood before the king. ¹⁵ And all the nobles, and the princes, and the attendants belonging to the king came together from all the cities of Egypt, and they all sat before the king, and the king related his dreams before the wise men and the princes, and all that sat before the king were astonished at the vision. ¹⁶ And all the wise men who were before the king were greatly divided in their interpretation of his dreams; some of them interpreted them to the king, saying, "The seven good cows are seven kings who will be raised over Egypt from the king's issue. ¹⁷ And the seven bad cows are seven princes who will stand up against them in the latter days and destroy them; and the seven ears of corn are the seven great princes belonging to Egypt who will fall in the hands of the seven less powerful princes of their enemies in the wars of our lord the king." ¹⁸ And some of them interpreted to the king in this manner, saying, "The seven good cows are the strong cities of Egypt, and the seven bad cows are the seven nations of the land of Canaan who will come against the seven cities of Egypt in the latter days and destroy them. ¹⁹ And that which you saw in the second dream of seven good and bad ears of corn is a sign that the government of Egypt will return to your seed again as at first. ²⁰ And in his reign the people of the cities of Egypt will turn against the seven cities of Canaan who are stronger than they are and will destroy them, and the government of Egypt will return to your seed." ²¹ And some of them said to the king, "This is the interpretation of your dreams: the seven good cows are seven queens whom you will take for wives in the latter days, and the seven bad cows denote that those women will all die in the lifetime of the king. ²² And the seven good and bad ears of corn which you saw in the second dream are fourteen children, and it will be in the latter days that they will stand up and fight among themselves, and seven of them will strike the seven that are more powerful." ²³ And some of them said these words to the king, saying, "The seven good cows denote that seven children will be born to you, and they will slay seven of your children's children in the latter days; and the seven good ears of corn which you saw in the second dream are those princes against whom seven other less powerful princes will fight and destroy them in the latter days and avenge your children's cause, and the government will return to your seed again." ²⁴ And the king heard all the words of the wise men of Egypt and their interpretation of his dreams and none of them pleased the king. ²⁵ And the king knew in his wisdom that they did not altogether speak correctly in all these words, for this was from the LORD to frustrate the words of the wise men of Egypt in order that Joseph might go out from the house of confinement, and in order that he should become great in Egypt. ²⁶ And the king saw that none among all the wise men and magicians of Egypt spoke correctly to him, and the king's wrath was kindled, and his anger burned within him. ²⁷ And the king commanded that all the wise men and magicians should go out from before him, and they all went out from before the king with shame and disgrace. ²⁸ And the king commanded that a proclamation be sent throughout Egypt to slay all the magicians that were in Egypt, and not one of them should be permitted to live. ²⁹ And the captains of the guards belonging to the king rose up, and each man drew his sword, and they began to strike the magicians of Egypt, and the wise men. ³⁰ And after this, Merod, chief butler to the king, came and bowed down before the king and sat before him. ³¹ And the butler said to the king, "May the king live forever, and may his government be exalted in the land. ³² You were angry with your servant in those days, now two years past, and placed me in the ward, and I was in the ward for some time, I and the chief of the bakers. ³³ And there was a Hebrew servant with us belonging to the captain of the guard, his name was Joseph, for his master had been angry with him and placed him in the house of confinement, and he attended us there. ³⁴ And some time after, when we were in the ward, we dreamed dreams in one night—

I and the chief of the bakers; we dreamed, each man according to the interpretation of his dream. ³⁵ And we came in the morning and told them to that servant, and he interpreted our dreams to us; he correctly interpreted to each man according to his dream. ³⁶ And it came to pass as he interpreted to us, so was the event; there did not fall to the ground any of his words. ³⁷ And now therefore, my lord and king, do not slay the people of Egypt for nothing; behold, that slave is still confined in the house by the captain of the guard, his master, in the house of confinement. ³⁸ If it pleases the king, let him send for him that he may come before you and he will make the correct interpretation of the dream which you dreamed known to you." ³⁹ And the king heard the words of the chief butler, and the king ordered that the wise men of Egypt should not be slain. ⁴⁰ And the king ordered his servants to bring Joseph before him, and the king said to them, "Go to him and do not terrify him lest he may be confused and will not know [how] to speak properly." ⁴¹ And the servants of the king went to Joseph, and they brought him out of the dungeon hastily, and the king's servants shaved him, and he changed his prison garment and came before the king. ⁴² And the king was sitting on his royal throne in a princely dress girt around with a golden ephod, and the fine gold which was on it sparkled, and the carbuncle, and the ruby, and the emerald, together with all the precious stones that were on the king's head, dazzled the eye, and Joseph greatly wondered at the king. ⁴³ And the throne on which the king sat was covered with gold and silver, and with onyx stones, and it had seventy steps. ⁴⁴ And it was their custom throughout the land of Egypt that every man who came to speak to the king, if he was a prince or one that was estimable in the sight of the king, he ascended to the king's throne as far as the thirty-first step, and the king would descend to the thirty-sixth step, and speak with him. ⁴⁵ If he was one of the common people, he ascended to the third step, and the king would descend to the fourth and speak to him, and their custom was, moreover, that any man who understood to speak in all the seventy languages, he ascended the seventy steps, and went up and spoke until he reached the king. ⁴⁶ And any man who could not complete the seventy, he ascended as many steps as the languages which he knew to speak in. ⁴⁷ And it was customary in those days in Egypt that no one should reign over them, except [one] who understood to speak in the seventy languages. ⁴⁸ And when Joseph came before the king, he bowed down to the ground before the king, and he ascended to the third step, and the king sat on the fourth step and spoke with Joseph. ⁴⁹ And the king said to Joseph, "I dreamed a dream, and there is no interpreter to interpret it properly, and I commanded this day that all the magicians of Egypt and the wise men thereof should come before me, and I related my dreams to them, and no one has properly interpreted them to me. ⁵⁰ And after this I heard this day concerning you that you are a wise man and can correctly interpret every dream that you hear." ⁵¹ And Joseph answered Pharaoh, saying, "Let Pharaoh relate his dreams that he dreamed; surely the interpretations belong to God"; and Pharaoh related his dreams to Joseph, the dream of the cows and the dream of the ears of corn, and the king ceased speaking. ⁵² And Joseph was then clothed with the Spirit of God before the king, and he knew all the things that would befall the king from that day forward, and he knew the proper interpretation of the king's dream, and he spoke before the king. ⁵³ And Joseph found favor in the sight of the king, and the king inclined his ears and his heart, and he heard all the words of Joseph. And Joseph said to the king, "Do not imagine that they are two dreams, for it is only one dream, for that which God has chosen to do throughout the land He has shown to the king in his dream, and this is the proper interpretation of your dream: ⁵⁴ the seven good cows and ears of corn are seven years, and the seven bad cows and ears of corn are also seven years; it is one dream. ⁵⁵ Behold, [during] the seven years that are coming there will be a great plenty throughout the land, and after that the seven years of famine will follow them—a very grievous famine; and all the plenty will be forgotten from the land, and the famine will consume the inhabitants of the land. ⁵⁶ The king dreamed one dream, and the dream was therefore repeated to Pharaoh because the thing is established by God, and God will shortly bring it to pass. ⁵⁷ Now therefore, I will give you counsel and deliver your soul and the souls of the inhabitants of the land from the evil of the famine: seek throughout your kingdom for a very discreet and wise man who knows all the affairs of government and appoint him to superintend over the land of Egypt. ⁵⁸ And let the man whom you place over Egypt appoint officers under him that they gather in all the food of the good years that are coming and let them lay up corn and deposit it in your appointed stores. ⁵⁹ And let them keep that food for the seven years of famine that it may be found for you, and your people, and your whole land, and that you and your land are not cut off by the famine. ⁶⁰ Let all the inhabitants of the land, every man, also be ordered that they gather in the produce of his field, of all sorts of food, during the seven good years, and that they place it in their stores, that it may be found for them in the days of the famine and that they may live on it. ⁶¹ This is the proper interpretation of your dream, and this is the counsel given to save your soul and the souls of all your subjects." ⁶² And the king answered and said to Joseph, "Who says and who knows that your words are correct?" And he said to the king, "This will be a sign for you respecting all my words that they are true and that my advice is good for you: ⁶³ behold, your wife sits on the stool of

delivery this day, and she will bear you a son and you will rejoice with him; when your child will have gone out from his mother's womb, your firstborn son that has been born these two years back will die, and you will be comforted in the child that will be born to you this day." ⁶⁴ And Joseph finished speaking these words to the king, and he bowed down to the king, and he went out, and when Joseph had gone out from the king's presence, those signs which Joseph had spoken to the king came to pass on that day. ⁶⁵ And the queen bore a son on that day and the king heard the glad tidings about his son, and he rejoiced, and when the reporter had gone out from the king's presence, the king's servants found the firstborn son of the king fallen dead on the ground. ⁶⁶ And there was great lamentation and noise in the king's house, and the king heard it, and he said, "What is the noise and lamentation that I have heard in the house?" And they told the king that his firstborn son had died; then the king knew that all Joseph's words that he had spoken were correct, and the king was consoled for his son by the child that was born to him on that day as Joseph had spoken.

CHAPTER 49

¹ After these things the king sent for and assembled all his officers and servants, and all the princes and nobles belonging to the king, and they all came before the king. ² And the king said to them, "Behold, you have seen and heard all the words of this Hebrew man, and all the signs which he declared would come to pass, and not any of his words have fallen to the ground. ³ You know that he has given a proper interpretation of the dream and it will surely come to pass; now therefore, take counsel and know what you will do and how the land will be delivered from the famine. ⁴ Seek now and see whether the same can be found in whose heart there is wisdom and knowledge, and I will appoint him over the land. ⁵ For you have heard what the Hebrew man has advised concerning this to save the land from the famine, and I know that the land will not be delivered from the famine but with the advice of the Hebrew man—him that advised me." ⁶ And they all answered the king and said, "The counsel which the Hebrew has given concerning this is good; now therefore, our lord and king, behold, the whole land is in your hand, do that which seems good in your sight. ⁷ Him whom you choose, and whom you in your wisdom know to be wise and capable of delivering the land with his wisdom, the king will appoint him to be under him over the land." ⁸ And the king said to all the officers: "I have thought that since God has made known to the Hebrew man all that He has spoken, there is none so discreet and wise in the whole land as he is; if it seems good in your sight, I will place him over the land, for he will save the land with his wisdom." ⁹ And all the officers answered the king and said, "But surely it is written in the laws of

Egypt, and it should not be violated, that no man will reign over Egypt, nor be the second to the king, but one who has knowledge in all the languages of the sons of men. [10] Now therefore, our lord and king, behold, this Hebrew man can only speak the Hebrew language, and how then can he be over us—the second under government—a man who does not even know our language? [11] Now please send for him, and let him come before you, and prove him in all things, and do as you see fit." [12] And the king said, "It will be done tomorrow, and the thing that you have spoken is good"; and all the officers came on that day before the king. [13] And on that night the LORD sent one of His ministering messengers, and he came into the land of Egypt to Joseph, and the messenger of the LORD stood over Joseph, and behold, Joseph was lying in the bed at night in his master's house in the dungeon, for his master had put him back into the dungeon on account of his wife. [14] And the messenger roused him from his sleep, and Joseph rose up and stood on his legs, and behold, the messenger of the LORD was standing opposite to him; and the messenger of the LORD spoke with Joseph, and he taught him all the languages of man in that night, and he called his name Jehoseph. [15] And the messenger of the LORD went from him, and Joseph returned and lay on his bed, and Joseph was astonished at the vision which he saw. [16] And it came to pass in the morning that the king sent for all his officers and servants, and they all came and sat before the king, and the king ordered Joseph to be brought, and the king's servants went and brought Joseph before Pharaoh. [17] And the king came out and ascended the steps of the throne, and Joseph spoke to the king in all languages, and Joseph went up to him and spoke to the king until he arrived before the king in the seventieth step, and he sat before the king. [18] And the king greatly rejoiced on account of Joseph, and all the king's officers rejoiced greatly with the king when they heard all the words of Joseph. [19] And the thing seemed good in the sight of the king and the officers, to appoint Joseph to be second to the king over the whole land of Egypt, and the king spoke to Joseph, saying, [20] "Now, you gave me counsel to appoint a wise man over the land of Egypt in order to save the land from the famine with his wisdom; now therefore, since God has made all this known to you, and all the words which you have spoken, there is not a discreet and wise man like you throughout the land. [21] And your name will no longer be called Joseph, but Zaphnath-Paaneah will be your name; you will be second to me, and all the affairs of my government will be according to your word, and at your word my people will go out and come in. [22] Also from under your hand my servants and officers will receive their salary which is given to them monthly, and all the people of the land will bow down to you; only in my throne will I be greater than you." [23] And the king took off his ring from his hand and put it on the hand of Joseph, and the king dressed Joseph in a princely garment, and he put a golden crown on his head, and he put a golden chain on his neck. [24] And the king commanded his servants and they made him ride in the second chariot belonging to the king that went opposite to the king's chariot, and he caused him to ride on a great and strong horse from the king's horses and to be conducted through the streets of the land of Egypt. [25] And the king commanded that all those that played on timbrels, harps, and other musical instruments should go out with Joseph; one thousand timbrels, one thousand mecholoth, and one thousand nebalim went after him, [26] and [also] five thousand men with drawn swords glittering in their hands, and they went marching and playing before Joseph; and twenty thousand of the great men of the king girt with girdles of skin covered with gold marched at the right hand of Joseph, and twenty thousand at his left; and all the women and young girls went on the roofs or stood in the streets playing and rejoicing before Joseph, and they gazed at the appearance of Joseph and at his beauty. [27] And the king's people went before him and behind him, perfuming the road with frankincense, and with cassia, and with all sorts of fine perfume, and they scattered myrrh and aloes along the road, and twenty men proclaimed these words before him throughout the land in a loud voice: [28] "Do you see this man whom the king has chosen to be his second? All the affairs of government will be regulated by him, and he that transgresses his orders or that does not bow down before him to the ground will die, for he rebels against the king and his second." [29] And when the heralds had ceased proclaiming, all the people of Egypt bowed down to the ground before Joseph and said, "May the king live!" Also, "May his second live!" And all the inhabitants of Egypt bowed down along the road, and when the heralds approached them, they bowed down, and they rejoiced with all sorts of timbrels, mechol, and nebal before Joseph. [30] And Joseph lifted up his eyes to Heaven [from] on his horse, and called out and said, "He raises the poor man from the dust; He lifts up the needy from the dunghill. O LORD of Hosts, happy is the man who trusts in You." [31] And Joseph passed throughout the land of Egypt with Pharaoh's servants and officers, and they showed him the whole land of Egypt and all the king's treasures. [32] And Joseph returned and came on that day before Pharaoh, and the king gave to Joseph a possession in the land of Egypt, a possession of fields and vineyards, and the king gave to Joseph three thousand talents of silver and one thousand talents of gold, and onyx stones, and bdellium, and many gifts. [33] And on the next day the king commanded all the people of Egypt to bring offerings and gifts to Joseph, and that he that violated the command of the king should die; and they made a high place in the street of the city, and they spread out garments there, and whoever brought anything to Joseph put it into the high place. ³⁴ And all the people of Egypt cast something into the high place: one man a golden earring, and the other rings and earrings, and different vessels of gold, and silver work, and onyx stones, and bdellium he cast on the high place; everyone gave something of what he possessed. ³⁵ And Joseph took all these and placed them in his treasuries, and all the officers and nobles belonging to the king exalted Joseph, and they gave him many gifts, seeing that the king had chosen him to be his second. ³⁶ And the king sent to Potiphera, the son of Ahiram priest of On, and he took his young daughter Osnath and gave her to Joseph for a wife. ³⁷ And the young woman was very beautiful, a virgin, one whom man had not known, and Joseph took her for a wife; and the king said to Joseph, "I am Pharaoh, and beside you none will dare to lift up his hand or his foot to regulate my people throughout the land of Egypt." ³⁸ And Joseph was thirty years old when he stood before Pharaoh, and Joseph went out from before the king, and he became the king's second in Egypt. ³⁹ And the king gave Joseph one hundred servants to attend him in his house, and Joseph also sent and purchased many servants and they remained in the house of Joseph. ⁴⁰ Joseph then built a very magnificent house for himself like the houses of kings, before the court of the king's palace, and he made a large temple in the house, very elegant in appearance and convenient for his residence; [for] three years Joseph was erecting his house. ⁴¹ And Joseph made a very elegant throne of abundant gold and silver for himself, and he covered it with onyx stones and bdellium, and he made on it the likeness of the whole land of Egypt, and the likeness of the river of Egypt that waters the whole land of Egypt; and Joseph sat securely on his throne in his house and the LORD increased Joseph's wisdom. ⁴² And all the inhabitants of Egypt and Pharaoh's servants and his princes loved Joseph exceedingly, for this thing was from the LORD to Joseph. ⁴³ And Joseph had an army that made war, going out in hosts and troops to the number of forty thousand six hundred men, capable of bearing arms to assist the king and Joseph against the enemy, besides the king's officers, and his servants, and [the] inhabitants of Egypt without number. ⁴⁴ And Joseph gave to his mighty men, and to all his host, shields, and javelins, and caps, and coats of mail, and stones for slinging.

CHAPTER 50

¹ At that time the children of Tarshish came against the sons of Ishmael and made war with them, and the children of Tarshish spoiled the Ishmaelites for a long time. ² And the children of Ishmael were small in number in those days, and they could not prevail over the children of Tarshish, and they were severely oppressed. ³ And the old men of the Ishmaelites sent a record to the king of Egypt, saying, "Please send officers and hosts to your servants to help us fight against the children of Tarshish, for we have been consuming away for a long time." ⁴ And Pharaoh sent Joseph with the mighty men and host which were with him, and also his mighty men from the king's house. ⁵ And they went to the land of Havilah to the children of Ishmael, to assist them against the children of Tarshish, and the children of Ishmael fought with the children of Tarshish, and Joseph struck the Tarshishites, and he subdued all their land, and the children of Ishmael dwell therein to this day. ⁶ And when the land of Tarshish was subdued, all the Tarshishites fled and came on the border of their brothers, the children of Javan, and Joseph returned to Egypt with all his mighty men and host; not one man of them [was] missing. ⁷ And at the revolution of the year, in the second year of Joseph's reigning over Egypt, the LORD gave great plenty throughout the land for seven years as Joseph had spoken, for the LORD blessed all the produce of the earth in those days for seven years, and they ate and were greatly satisfied. ⁸ And at that time Joseph had officers under him, and they collected all the food of the good years, and heaped corn year by year, and they placed it in the treasuries of Joseph. ⁹ And at any time when they gathered the food, Joseph commanded that they should bring the corn in the ears, and also bring with it some of the soil of the field, that it should not spoil. ¹⁰ And Joseph did according to this year by year, and he heaped up corn like the sand of the sea for abundance, for his stores were immense and could not be numbered for abundance. ¹¹ And also all the inhabitants of Egypt gathered all sorts of food in their stores in great abundance during the seven good years, but they did not do to it as Joseph did. ¹² And all the food which Joseph and the Egyptians had gathered during the seven years of plenty was secured for the land in stores for the seven years of famine, for the support of the whole land. ¹³ And each man of the inhabitants of Egypt filled his store and his concealed place with corn to be for support during the famine. ¹⁴ And Joseph placed all the food that he had gathered in all the cities of Egypt, and he closed all the stores and placed sentinels over them. ¹⁵ And Joseph's wife Osnath the daughter of Potiphera bore him two sons, Manasseh and Ephraim, and Joseph was thirty-four years old when he begot them. ¹⁶ And the boys grew up and they went in his ways and in his instructions; they did not deviate from the way which their father taught them, either to the right or left. ¹⁷ And the LORD was with the boys, and they grew up and had understanding and skill in all wisdom and in all the affairs of government, and all the king's officers and his great men of the inhabitants of Egypt exalted the boys, and they were brought up among the king's children. ¹⁸ And the seven years of plenty that were throughout the land were at an end, and the seven years of famine came after them as Joseph had

JASHER

spoken, and the famine was throughout the land. ¹⁹ And all the people of Egypt saw that the famine had commenced in the land of Egypt, and all the people of Egypt opened their stores of corn for the famine prevailed over them. ²⁰ And they found all the food that was in their stores full of vermin and not fit to eat, and the famine prevailed throughout the land, and all the inhabitants of Egypt came and cried before Pharaoh, for the famine was heavy on them. ²¹ And they said to Pharaoh, "Give food to your servants, and why will we die through hunger before your eyes, even we and our little ones?" ²² And Pharaoh answered them, saying, "And why do you cry to me? Did not Joseph command that the corn should be laid up during the seven years of plenty for the years of famine? And why did you not listen to his voice?" ²³ And the people of Egypt answered the king, saying, "As your soul lives, our lord, your servants have done all that Joseph ordered, for your servants also gathered in all the produce of their fields during the seven years of plenty and laid it in the stores to this day. ²⁴ And when the famine prevailed over your servants we opened our stores, and behold, all our produce was filled with vermin and was not fit for food." ²⁵ And when the king heard all that had befallen the inhabitants of Egypt, the king was greatly afraid on account of the famine, and he was very terrified; and the king answered the people of Egypt, saying, "Since all this has happened to you, go to Joseph [and] do whatever he will say to you; do not transgress his commands." ²⁶ And all the people of Egypt went out and came to Joseph, and they said to him, "Give food to us, and why will we die before you through hunger? For we gathered in our produce during the seven years as you commanded, and we put it in store, and thus it has befallen us." ²⁷ And when Joseph heard all the words of the people of Egypt and what had befallen them, Joseph opened all his stores of the produce and he sold it to the people of Egypt. ²⁸ And the famine prevailed throughout the land, and the famine was in all countries, but in the land of Egypt there was produce for sale. ²⁹ And all the inhabitants of Egypt came to Joseph to buy corn, for the famine prevailed over them, and all their corn was spoiled, and Joseph sold it to all the people of Egypt daily. ³⁰ And all the inhabitants of the land of Canaan, and the Philistines, and those beyond the Jordan, and the children of the east, and all the cities of the lands far and near heard that there was corn in Egypt, and they all came to Egypt to buy corn, for the famine prevailed over them. ³¹ And Joseph opened the stores of corn and placed officers over them, and daily they stood and sold to all that came. ³² And Joseph knew that his brothers would also come to Egypt to buy corn, for the famine prevailed throughout the earth. And Joseph commanded all his people that they should cause it to be proclaimed throughout the land of Egypt, saying, ³³ "It is the pleasure of the king, of

his second and of their great men, that any person who wishes to buy corn in Egypt will not send his servants to Egypt to purchase, but his sons, and also any Egyptian or Canaanite who will come from any of the stores from buying corn in Egypt and will go and sell it throughout the land, he will die, for no one will buy but for the support of his household. ³⁴ And any man leading two or three beasts will die, for a man will only lead his own beast." ³⁵ And Joseph placed sentinels at the gates of Egypt and commanded them, saying, "Any person who may come to buy corn, do not allow him to enter until his name, and the name of his father, and the name of his father's father is written down, and whatever is written by day, send their names to me in the evening that I may know their names." ³⁶ And Joseph placed officers throughout the land of Egypt, and he commanded them to do all these things. ³⁷ And Joseph did all these things and made these statutes in order that he might know when his brothers should come to Egypt to buy corn; and Joseph's people caused it to be proclaimed in Egypt daily according to these words and statutes which Joseph had commanded. ³⁸ And all the inhabitants of the east and west country, and of all the earth, heard of the statutes and regulations which Joseph had enacted in Egypt, and the inhabitants of the extreme parts of the earth came and bought corn in Egypt day after day, and then they went away. ³⁹ And all the officers of Egypt did as Joseph had commanded, and all that came to Egypt to buy corn, the gatekeepers would write their names and their fathers' names, and daily bring them before Joseph in the evening.

CHAPTER 51

¹ And afterward Jacob heard that there was corn in Egypt, and he called to his sons to go to Egypt to buy corn, for the famine also prevailed on them, and he called to his sons, saying, ² "Behold, I hear that there is corn in Egypt, and all the people of the earth go there to purchase [some], now therefore, why will you show yourselves satisfied before the whole earth? Also go down to Egypt and buy us a little corn among those that come there that we may not die." ³ And the sons of Jacob listened to the voice of their father, and they rose up to go down to Egypt in order to buy corn among the rest that came there. ⁴ And their father Jacob commanded them, saying, "When you come into the city, do not enter in one gate together on account of the inhabitants of the land." ⁵ And the sons of Jacob went out and they went to Egypt, and the sons of Jacob did everything as their father had commanded them, and Jacob did not send Benjamin, for he said, "Lest an accident might befall him on the road like his brother"; and ten of Jacob's sons went out. ⁶ And while the sons of Jacob were going on the road, they regretted what they had done to Joseph, and they spoke to each other, saying, "We know that our brother Joseph went down to Egypt, and now we will

seek him where we go, and if we find him we will take him from his master for a ransom, and if not, by force, and we will die for him." ⁷ And the sons of Jacob agreed to this thing and strengthened themselves on account of Joseph, to deliver him from the hand of his master, and the sons of Jacob went to Egypt; and when they came near to Egypt they separated from each other, and they came through ten gates of Egypt, and the gatekeepers wrote their names on that day and brought them to Joseph in the evening. ⁸ And Joseph read the names from the hand of the gatekeepers of the city, and he found that his brothers had entered at the ten gates of the city, and at that time Joseph commanded that it should be proclaimed throughout the land of Egypt, saying, ⁹ "Go out, all you store guards, [and] close all the corn stores, and let only one remain open that those who come may purchase from it." ¹⁰ And all the officers of Joseph did so at that time, and they closed all the stores and left only one open. ¹¹ And Joseph gave the written names of his brothers to him that was set over the open store, and he said to him, "Whoever will come to you to buy corn, ask his name, and when men of these names will come before you, seize them and send them," and they did so. ¹² And when the sons of Jacob came into the city, they joined together in the city to seek Joseph before they bought themselves corn. ¹³ And they went to the walls of the harlots, and they sought Joseph in the walls of the harlots for three days, for they thought that Joseph would come in the walls of the harlots, for Joseph was very handsome and well-favored, and the sons of Jacob sought Joseph for three days, and they could not find him. ¹⁴ And the man who was set over the open store sought for those names which Joseph had given him, and he did not find them. ¹⁵ And he sent to Joseph, saying, "These three days have passed, and those men whose names you gave to me have not come"; and Joseph sent servants to seek the men in all Egypt, and to bring them before Joseph. ¹⁶ And Joseph's servants went and came into Egypt and could not find them, and they went to Goshen and they were not there, and then they went to the city of Rameses and could not find them. ¹⁷ And Joseph continued to send sixteen servants to seek his brothers, and they went and spread themselves in the four corners of the city, and four of the servants went into the house of the harlots, and they found the ten men there seeking their brother. ¹⁸ And those four men took them and brought them before him, and they bowed down to him to the ground, and Joseph was sitting on his throne in his temple, clothed with princely garments, and on his head was a large crown of gold, and all the mighty men were sitting around him. ¹⁹ And the sons of Jacob saw Joseph, and his figure, and comeliness, and dignity of countenance seemed wonderful in their eyes, and they again bowed down to him to the ground. ²⁰ And Joseph saw his brothers, and he knew them, but they did not know him, for Joseph was very great in their eyes, therefore they did not know him. ²¹ And Joseph spoke to them, saying, "Where do you come from?" And they all answered and said, "Your servants have come from the land of Canaan to buy corn, for the famine prevails throughout the earth, and your servants heard that there was corn in Egypt, so they have come among the others coming to buy corn for their support." ²² And Joseph answered them, saying, "If you have come to purchase as you say, why do you come through ten gates of the city? It can only be that you have come to spy through the land." ²³ And they all answered Joseph together and said, "Not so my lord, we are right; your servants are not spies, but we have come to buy corn, for your servants are all brothers, the sons of one man in the land of Canaan, and our father commanded us, saying, When you come to the city, do not enter together at one gate on account of the inhabitants of the land." ²⁴ And Joseph answered them again and said, "That is the thing which I spoke to you: you have come to spy through the land! Therefore, you all came through ten gates of the city; you have come to see the nakedness of the land. ²⁵ Surely everyone that comes to buy corn goes his way, and you are already three days in the land, and what do you do in the walls of harlots in which you have been for these three days? Surely spies do like to these things." ²⁶ And they said to Joseph, "Far be it from our lord to speak thus, for we are twelve brothers, the sons of our father Jacob in the land of Canaan, the son of Isaac, the son of Abraham the Hebrew, and behold, the youngest is with our father in the land of Canaan this day, and one is not, for he was lost from us, and we thought perhaps he might be in this land, so we are seeking him throughout the land and have even come to the houses of harlots to seek him there." ²⁷ And Joseph said to them, "And have you then sought him throughout the earth that there only remained Egypt for you to seek him in? And what also should your brother do in the houses of harlots, although he was in Egypt? Have you not said that you are from the sons of Isaac, the son of Abraham, and what will the sons of Jacob do then in the houses of harlots?" ²⁸ And they said to him, "Because we heard that Ishmaelites stole him from us, and it was told to us that they sold him in Egypt, and your servant, our brother, is very handsome and well-favored, so we thought he would surely be in the houses of harlots, therefore your servants went there to seek him and give ransom for him." ²⁹ And Joseph still answered them, saying, "Surely you speak falsely and utter lies to say of yourselves that you are the sons of Abraham; as Pharaoh lives, you are spies! Therefore, you have come to the houses of harlots that you should not be known." ³⁰ And Joseph said to them, "And now if you find him, and his master requires of you a great price, will you give it for him?" And they said, "It will be given." ³¹ And he said to them, "And if his master will not consent to part with him for a great price, what will you do to him on his account?" And they answered him, saying, "If he will not give him to us we will slay him, and take our brother, and go away." ³² And Joseph said to them, "That is the thing which I have spoken to you: you are spies, for you have come to slay the inhabitants of the land, for we heard that two of your brothers struck all the inhabitants of Shechem in the land of Canaan on account of your sister, and you now come to do the same in Egypt on account of your brother. ³³ Only hereby will I know that you are true men: if you will send home one from among you to fetch your youngest brother from your father and to bring him here to me, and by doing this thing I will know that you are right." ³⁴ And Joseph called to seventy of his mighty men, and he said to them, "Take these men and bring them into the ward." ³⁵ And the mighty men took the ten men; they laid hold of them and put them into the ward, and they were in the ward [for] three days. ³⁶ And on the third day Joseph had them brought out of the ward, and he said to them, "Do this for yourselves if you are true men, so that you may live: one of your brothers will be confined in the ward while you go and take home the corn for your household to the land of Canaan, and fetch your youngest brother, and bring him here to me that I may know that you are true men when you do this thing." ³⁷ And Joseph went out from them, and came into the chamber, and wept a great weeping, for his pity was excited for them, and he washed his face, and returned to them again, and he took Simeon from them and ordered him to be bound, but Simeon was not willing to have [this] done so, for he was a very powerful man and they could not bind him. ³⁸ And Joseph called to his mighty men and seventy valiant men came before him with drawn swords in their hands, and the sons of Jacob were terrified at them. ³⁹ And Joseph said to them, "Seize this man and confine him in prison until his brothers come to him," and Joseph's valiant men hastened, and they all laid hold of Simeon to bind him, and Simeon gave a loud and terrible shriek, and the cry was heard at a distance. ⁴⁰ And all the valiant men of Joseph were terrified at the sound of the shriek that they fell on their faces, and they were greatly afraid and fled. ⁴¹ And all the men that were with Joseph fled, for they were greatly afraid for their lives, and only Joseph and his son Manasseh remained there, and Manasseh the son of Joseph saw the strength of Simeon, and he was exceedingly angry. ⁴² And Manasseh, the son of Joseph, rose up to Simeon, and Manasseh struck Simeon [with] a heavy blow, with his fist against the back of his neck, and Simeon was stilled of his rage. ⁴³ And Manasseh laid hold of Simeon, and he violently seized him, and he bound him and brought him into the house of confinement, and all the sons of Jacob were astonished at the act of the youth. ⁴⁴ And Simeon said

to his brothers, "None of you must say that this is the striking of an Egyptian, but it is the striking of the house of my father." ⁴⁵ And after this Joseph ordered him to be called who was set over the storehouse, to fill their sacks with corn as much as they could carry, and to restore every man's money into his sack, and to give them provision for the road, and thus he did to them. ⁴⁶ And Joseph commanded them, saying, "Take heed lest you transgress my orders to bring your brother as I have told you, and it will be when you bring your brother here to me, then I will know that you are true men, and you will traffic in the land, and I will restore your brother to you, and you will return to your father in peace." ⁴⁷ And they all answered and said, "According as our lord speaks, so we will do," and they bowed down to him to the ground. ⁴⁸ And every man lifted his corn on his donkey, and they went out to go to the land of Canaan to their father; and they came to the inn and Levi spread his sack to give provender to his donkey when he saw, and behold, his money in full weight was still in his sack. ⁴⁹ And the man was greatly afraid, and he said to his brothers, "My money is restored, and behold, it is even in my sack," and the men were greatly afraid, and they said, "What is this that God has done to us?" ⁵⁰ And they all said, "And where is the LORD's kindness with our fathers, with Abraham, Isaac, and Jacob, that the LORD has delivered us into the hands of the king of Egypt this day to contrive against us?" ⁵¹ And Judah said to them, "Surely we are guilty sinners before the LORD our God in having sold our brother, our own flesh, and why do you say, Where is the LORD's kindness with our fathers?" ⁵² And Reuben said to them, "Did I not say to you, Do not sin against the youth? And you would not listen to me. Now God requires him from us, and how dare you say, Where is the LORD's kindness with our fathers, while you have sinned to the LORD." ⁵³ And they tarried overnight in that place, and they rose up early in the morning and loaded their donkeys with their corn, and they led them, and went on, and came to their father's house in the land of Canaan. ⁵⁴ And Jacob and his household went out to meet his sons, and Jacob saw, and behold, their brother Simeon was not with them, and Jacob said to his sons, "Where is your brother Simeon whom I do not see?" And his sons told him all that had befallen them in Egypt.

CHAPTER 52

¹ And they entered their house, and every man opened his sack, and they saw, and behold, every man's bundle of money was there, at which they and their father were greatly terrified. ² And Jacob said to them, "What is this that you have done to me? I sent your brother Joseph to inquire after your welfare and you said to me, A wild beast devoured him. ³ And Simeon went with you to buy food and you say the king of Egypt has confined him in prison, and you wish to

take Benjamin to cause his death also and to bring down my grey hairs with sorrow to the grave on account of Benjamin and his brother Joseph. ⁴Now therefore, my son will not go down with you, for his brother is dead and he is left alone, and mischief may befall him by the way in which you go as it befell his brother." ⁵And Reuben said to his father, "You will slay my two sons if I do not bring your son and place him before you"; and Jacob said to his sons, "Abide here and do not go down to Egypt, for my son will not go down with you to Egypt, nor die like his brother." ⁶And Judah said to them, "Refrain from him until the corn is finished, and he will then say, Take your brother down [with you], when he will find his own life and the life of his household in danger from the famine." ⁷And in those days the famine was severe throughout the land, and all the people of the earth went and came to Egypt to buy food, for the famine prevailed greatly among them, and the sons of Jacob remained in Canaan a year and two months until their corn was finished. ⁸And it came to pass after their corn was finished, the whole household of Jacob was pinched with hunger, and all the infants of the sons of Jacob came together and they approached Jacob, and they all surrounded him, and they said to him, "Give bread to us, and why will we all perish through hunger in your presence?" ⁹Jacob heard the words of his son's children, and he wept a great weeping, and his pity was roused for them, and Jacob called to his sons and they all came and sat before him. ¹⁰And Jacob said to them, "And have you not seen how your children have been weeping over me this day, saying, Give bread to us, and there is none? Now therefore, return and buy a little food for us." ¹¹And Judah answered and said to his father, "If you will send our brother with us we will go down and buy corn for you, and if you will not send him then we will not go down, for surely the king of Egypt specifically commanded us, saying, You will not see my face unless your brother is with you, for the king of Egypt is a strong and mighty king, and behold, if we will go to him without our brother we will all be put to death. ¹²Do you not know, and have you not heard, that this king is very powerful and wise, and there is not [one] like him in all the earth? Behold, we have seen all the kings of the earth and we have not seen one like that king, the king of Egypt; surely among all the kings of the earth there is none greater than Abimelech king of the Philistines, yet the king of Egypt is greater and mightier than he, and Abimelech can only be compared to one of his officers. ¹³Father, you have not seen his palace, and his throne, and all his servants standing before him; you have not seen that king on his throne in his pomp and royal appearance, dressed in his kingly robes with a large golden crown on his head; you have not seen the honor and glory which God has given to him, for there is not [one] like him in all the earth. ¹⁴Father, you have not seen the wisdom, the understanding, and the knowledge which God has given in his heart, nor heard his sweet voice when he spoke to us. ¹⁵We do not know, father, who made him acquainted with our names and all that befell us, yet he also asked after you, saying, Is your father still living, and is it well with him? ¹⁶You have not seen the affairs of the government of Egypt regulated by him, without inquiring of Pharaoh, his lord; you have not seen the awe and fear which he impressed on all the Egyptians. ¹⁷And also when we went from him, we threatened to do to Egypt like to the rest of the cities of the Amorites, and we were exceedingly angry against all his words which he spoke concerning us as spies, and now when we will come before him again his terror will fall on us all, and not one of us will be able to speak to him either a small or great thing. ¹⁸Now therefore, father, please send the youth with us, and we will go down and buy you food for our support, and not die through hunger." And Jacob said, "Why have you dealt so ill with me to tell the king you had a brother? What is this thing that you have done to me?" ¹⁹And Judah said to his father Jacob, "Give the youth into my care and we will rise up, and go down to Egypt, and buy corn, and then return, and it will be when we return, if the youth is not with us, then let me bear your blame forever. ²⁰Have you seen all our infants weeping over you through hunger and there is no power in your hand to satisfy them? Now let your pity be roused for them and send our brother with us and we will go. ²¹For how will the LORD's kindness to our ancestors be manifested to you when you say that the king of Egypt will take away your son? As the LORD lives, I will not leave him until I bring him and place him before you; but pray for us to the LORD, that He may deal kindly with us to cause us to be received favorably and kindly before the king of Egypt and his men, for had we not delayed, surely we would have now returned a second time with your son." ²²And Jacob said to his sons, "I trust in the LORD God that He may deliver you and give you favor in the sight of the king of Egypt and in the sight of all his men. ²³Now therefore, rise up, and go to the man, and take a present for him in your hands from what can be obtained in the land, and bring it before him, and may the Almighty God give you mercy before him that he may send your brothers Benjamin and Simeon with you." ²⁴And all the men rose up, and they took their brother Benjamin, and they took a large present of the best of the land in their hands, and they also took a double portion of silver. ²⁵And Jacob strictly commanded his sons concerning Benjamin, saying, "Take heed of him in the way in which you are going, and do not separate yourselves from him in the road, neither in Egypt." ²⁶And Jacob rose up from his sons, and spread out his hands, and prayed to the LORD on account of his sons, saying, "O LORD God of the heavens and earth, remember Your covenant with our father Abraham; remember it with my father Isaac, and deal kindly with my sons, and do not deliver them into the hands of the king of Egypt; please do it, O God, for the sake of Your mercies, and redeem all my children, and rescue them from Egyptian power, and send them their two brothers." ²⁷ And all the wives of the sons of Jacob and their children lifted up their eyes to Heaven, and they all wept before the LORD and cried to Him to deliver their fathers from the hand of the king of Egypt. ²⁸ And Jacob wrote a record to the king of Egypt and gave it into the hand of Judah and into the hands of his sons for the king of Egypt, saying, ²⁹ "From your servant Jacob, son of Isaac, son of Abraham the Hebrew, the prince of God, to the powerful and wise king, the revealer of secrets, king of Egypt, greetings. ³⁰ Be it known to my lord the king of Egypt, the famine was severe on us in the land of Canaan, and I sent my sons to you to buy us a little food from you for our support. ³¹ For my sons surrounded me, and I, being very old, cannot see with my eyes, for my eyes have become very heavy through age, as well as with daily weeping for my son, for Joseph who was lost from before me, and I commanded my sons that they should not enter the gates of the city when they came to Egypt on account of the inhabitants of the land. ³² And I also commanded them to go around Egypt to seek for my son Joseph, [for] perhaps they might find him there, and they did so, and you considered them as spies of the land. ³³ Have we not heard concerning you that you interpreted Pharaoh's dream and spoke truly to him? How then do you not know in your wisdom whether my sons are spies or not? ³⁴ Now therefore, my lord and king, behold, I have sent my son before you as you did speak to my sons; I implore you to put your eyes on him until he is returned to me with his brothers in peace. ³⁵ For do you not know, or have you not heard, that which our God did to Pharaoh when he took my mother Sarah, and what he did to Abimelech king of the Philistines on account of her, and also what our father Abraham did to the nine kings of Elam, how he struck them all with a few men that were with him? ³⁶ And also what my two sons Simeon and Levi did to the eight cities of the Amorites, how they destroyed them on account of their sister Dinah? ³⁷ And also on account of their brother Benjamin they consoled themselves for the loss of his brother Joseph; what will they then do for him when they see the hand of any people prevailing over them for his sake? ³⁸ Do you not know, O king of Egypt, that the power of God is with us, and also that God always hears our prayers and does not forsake us all the days? ³⁹ And when my sons told me of your dealings with them, I did not call to the LORD on account of you, for then you would have perished with your men before my son Benjamin came before you, but I thought that as my son Simeon was in your house, perhaps you might deal kindly with him;

therefore, I did not do this thing to you. ⁴⁰ Now therefore, behold, my son Benjamin comes to you with my sons: take heed of him and put your eyes on him, and then God will place His eyes over you and throughout your kingdom. ⁴¹ Now I have told you all that is in my heart, and behold, my sons are coming to you with their brother; examine the face of the whole earth for their sake and send them back with their brothers in peace." ⁴² And Jacob gave the record to his sons into the care of Judah to give it to the king of Egypt.

CHAPTER 53

¹ And the sons of Jacob rose up and took Benjamin and all of the presents, and they went and came to Egypt, and they stood before Joseph. ² And Joseph beheld his brother Benjamin with them, and he saluted them, and these men came to Joseph's house. ³ And Joseph commanded the superintendent of his house to give [food] to his brothers to eat, and he did so to them. ⁴ And at midday Joseph sent for the men to come before him with Benjamin, and the men told the superintendent of Joseph's house concerning the silver that was returned in their sacks, and he said to them, "It will be well with you, do not fear," and he brought their brother Simeon to them. ⁵ And Simeon said to his brothers, "The lord of the Egyptians has acted very kindly to me; he did not keep me bound, as you saw with your [own] eyes, for when you went out from the city, he let me free and dealt kindly with me in his house." ⁶ And Judah took Benjamin by the hand, and they came before Joseph, and they bowed down to him to the ground. ⁷ And the men gave the present to Joseph and they all sat before him, and Joseph said to them, "Is it well with you? Is it well with your children? Is it well with your aged father?" And they said, "It is well," and Judah took the record which Jacob had sent and gave it into the hand of Joseph. ⁸ And Joseph read the letter and knew his father's writing, and he wished to weep, and he went into an inner room, and he wept a great weeping; then he went out. ⁹ And he lifted up his eyes and beheld his brother Benjamin, and he said, "Is this your brother of whom you spoke to me?" And Benjamin approached Joseph, and Joseph placed his hand on his head and said to him, "May God be gracious to you, my son." ¹⁰ And when Joseph saw his brother, the son of his mother, he wished to weep again, and he entered the chamber, and he wept there, and he washed his face, and went out, and refrained from weeping, and he said, "Prepare food." ¹¹ And Joseph had a cup from which he drank, and it was of silver beautifully inlaid with onyx stones and bdellium, and Joseph struck the cup in the sight of his brothers while they were sitting to eat with him. ¹² And Joseph said to the men, "I know by this cup that Reuben the firstborn, Simeon, and Levi, and Judah, Issachar, and Zebulun are children from one mother; seat

yourselves to eat according to your births." [13] And he also placed the others according to their births, and he said, "I know that this youngest brother of yours has no brother, and I, like him, have no brother: he will therefore sit down to eat with me." [14] And Benjamin went up before Joseph and sat on the throne, and the men beheld the acts of Joseph, and they were astonished at them; and the men ate and drank at that time with Joseph, and he then gave presents to them, and Joseph gave one gift to Benjamin, and Manasseh and Ephraim saw the acts of their father, and they also gave presents to him, and Osnath gave him one present, and there were five presents in the hand of Benjamin. [15] And Joseph brought them out wine to drink, and they would not drink, and they said, "From the day on which Joseph was lost we have not drunk wine, nor eaten any delicacies." [16] And Joseph swore to them, and he pressed them hard, and they drank plentifully with him on that day, and afterward Joseph turned to his brother Benjamin to speak with him, and Benjamin was still sitting on the throne before Joseph. [17] And Joseph said to him, "Have you begotten any children?" And he said, "Your servant has ten sons, and these are their names: Bela, Becher, Ashbal, Gera, Naaman, Achi, Rosh, Mupim, Chupim, and Ord, and I called their names after my brother whom I have not seen." [18] And he ordered them to bring his map of the stars before him, whereby Joseph knew all the times, and Joseph said to Benjamin, "I have heard that the Hebrews are acquainted with all wisdom: do you know anything of this?" [19] And Benjamin said, "Your servant is also knowing in all the wisdom which my father taught me," and Joseph said to Benjamin, "Now look at this instrument and understand where your brother Joseph is in Egypt, who you said went down to Egypt." [20] And Benjamin beheld that instrument with the map of the stars of the heavens, and he was wise and looked therein to know where his brother was, and Benjamin divided the whole land of Egypt into four divisions, and he found that he who was sitting on the throne before him was his brother Joseph, and Benjamin wondered greatly, and when Joseph saw that his brother Benjamin was so much astonished, he said to Benjamin, "What have you seen, and why are you astonished?" [21] And Benjamin said to Joseph, "I can see by this that my brother Joseph sits here with me on the throne," and Joseph said to him, "I am your brother Joseph; do not reveal this thing to your brothers; behold, I will send you with them when they go away, and I will command them to be brought back into the city again, and I will take you away from them. [22] And if they dare their lives and fight for you, then I will know that they have converted from what they did to me, and I will make myself known to them, and if they forsake you when I take you, then you will remain with me, and I will wrangle with them, and they will go away, and I will not become known to them." [23] At that time Joseph commanded his officer to fill their sacks with food, and to put each man's money into his sack, and to put the cup in the sack of Benjamin, and to give them provision for the road, and they did so to them. [24] And on the next day the men rose up early in the morning, and they loaded their donkeys with their corn, and they went out with Benjamin, and they went to the land of Canaan with their brother Benjamin. [25] They had not gone far from Egypt when Joseph commanded him that was set over his house, saying, "Rise, pursue these men before they get too far from Egypt, and say to them, Why have you stolen my master's cup?" [26] And Joseph's officer rose up, and he reached them, and he spoke to them all the words of Joseph; and when they heard this thing they became exceedingly angry, and they said, "He with whom your master's cup will be found will die, and we will also become slaves." [27] And they hastened, and each man brought down his sack from his donkey, and they looked in their bags and the cup was found in Benjamin's bag, and they all tore their garments, and they returned to the city, and they struck Benjamin in the road, continually striking him until he came into the city, and they stood before Joseph. [28] And Judah's anger was kindled, and he said, "This man has only brought me back to destroy Egypt this day." [29] And the men came to Joseph's house, and they found Joseph sitting on his throne, and all the mighty men standing at his right and left. [30] And Joseph said to them, "What is this act that you have done, that you took away my silver cup and went away? But I know that you took my cup in order to know thereby in what part of the land your brother was." [31] And Judah said, "What will we say to our lord, what will we speak, and how will we justify ourselves? God has found the iniquity of all your servants this day, therefore He has done this thing to us this day." [32] And Joseph rose up, and caught hold of Benjamin, and took him from his brothers with violence, and he came to the house and locked the door at them, and Joseph commanded him that was set over his house that he should say to them, "Thus says the king, Go to your father in peace; behold, I have taken the man in whose hand my cup was found."

CHAPTER 54

[1] And when Judah saw the dealings of Joseph with them, Judah approached him and broke open the door, and came with his brothers before Joseph. [2] And Judah said to Joseph, "Do not let it seem grievous in the sight of my lord: may your servant please speak a word before you?" And Joseph said to him, "Speak." [3] And Judah spoke before Joseph, and his brothers were standing there before them; and Judah said to Joseph, "Surely when we first came to our lord to buy food, you considered us as spies of the land, and we brought Benjamin before you, and you still make sport of us this day. [4] Now therefore, let the king hear

my words, and please send our brother that he may go along with us to our father, lest your soul perish this day with all the souls of the inhabitants of Egypt. ⁵ Do you not know what two of my brothers, Simeon and Levi, did to the city of Shechem and to seven cities of the Amorites on account of our sister Dinah, and also what they would do for the sake of their brother Benjamin? ⁶ And I with my strength, who am greater and mightier than both of them, come on you and your land this day if you are unwilling to send our brother. ⁷ Have you not heard what our God who made choice of us did to Pharaoh on account of our mother Sarah, whom he took away from our father, that He struck him and his household with heavy plagues, that even to this day the Egyptians relate this wonder to each other? So will our God do to you on account of Benjamin whom you have taken from his father this day, and on account of the evils which you heap over us in your land this day; for our God will remember His covenant with our father Abraham and bring calamity on you, because you have grieved the soul of our father this day. ⁸ Now therefore, hear my words that I have spoken to you this day and send our brother that he may go away lest you and the people of your land die by the sword, for you cannot all prevail over me." ⁹ And Joseph answered Judah, saying, "Why have you opened your mouth wide and why do you boast over us, saying, Strength is with you? As Pharaoh lives, if I command all my valiant men to fight with you, surely you and these brothers of yours would sink in the mire." ¹⁰ And Judah said to Joseph, "Surely it is fitting [for] you and your people to fear me; as the LORD lives, if I once draw my sword I will not sheathe it again until I will have slain all Egypt this day, and I will commence with you and finish with your master Pharaoh." ¹¹ And Joseph answered and said to him, "Surely strength does not belong to you alone—I am stronger and mightier than you; surely if you draw your sword I will put it to your neck and the necks of all your brothers." ¹² And Judah said to him, "Surely if I open my mouth against you this day I would swallow you up [so] that you are destroyed from off the earth and perish this day from your kingdom." And Joseph said, "Surely if you open your mouth, I have power and might to close your mouth with a stone until you will not be able to utter a word; see how many stones are before us. Truly I can take a stone, and force it into your mouth, and break your jaws." ¹³ And Judah said, "God is witness between us that we have not so far desired to battle with you: only give us our brother and we will go from you"; and Joseph answered and said, "As Pharaoh lives, if all the kings of Canaan came together with you, you should not take him from my hand. ¹⁴ Now therefore, go your way to your father, and your brother will be for a slave to me, for he has robbed the king's house." And Judah said, "What is it to you or to the character of the king? Surely the king

sends out from his house, throughout the land, silver and gold, either in gifts or expenses, and you still talk about your cup which you placed in our brother's bag and say that he has stolen it from you? ¹⁵ God forbid that our brother Benjamin or any of the seed of Abraham should do this thing to steal from you, or from anyone else, whether king, prince, or any man. ¹⁶ Now therefore, cease this accusation lest the whole earth hear your words, saying, For a little silver the king of Egypt wrangled with the men, and he accused them and took their brother for a slave." ¹⁷ And Joseph answered and said, "Take this cup for yourself, and go from me, and leave your brother for a slave, for it is the judgment of a thief to be a slave." ¹⁸ And Judah said, "Why are you not ashamed of your words, to leave our brother and to take your cup? Surely if you give us your cup, or one thousand times as much, we will not leave our brother for the silver which is found in the hand of any man, that we will not die over him." ¹⁹ And Joseph answered, "And why did you forsake your brother and sell him for twenty pieces of silver to this day, and why then will you not do the same to this brother of yours?" ²⁰ And Judah said, "The LORD is witness between me and you that we do not desire your battles; now therefore, give us our brother and we will go from you without quarreling." ²¹ And Joseph answered and said, "If all the kings of the land should assemble, they will not be able to take your brother from my hand"; and Judah said, "What will we say to our father when he sees that our brother does not come with us, and will grieve over him?" ²² And Joseph answered and said, "This is the thing which you will tell to your father, saying, The rope has gone after the bucket." ²³ And Judah said, "Surely you are a king, and why do you speak these things, giving a false judgment? Woe to the king who is like to you." ²⁴ And Joseph answered and said, "There is no false judgment in the word that I spoke on account of your brother Joseph, for all of you sold him to the Midianites for twenty pieces of silver, and you all denied it to your father and said to him, An evil beast has devoured him, Joseph has been torn to pieces." ²⁵ And Judah said, "Behold, the fire of Shem burns in my heart; now I will burn all your land with fire"; and Joseph answered and said, "Surely your sister-in-law Tamar, who killed your sons, extinguished the fire of Shechem." ²⁶ And Judah said, "If I pluck out a single hair from my flesh, I will fill all Egypt with its blood." ²⁷ And Joseph answered and said, "Such is your custom to do as you did to your brother whom you sold, and you dipped his coat in blood and brought it to your father in order that he might say an evil beast devoured him and here is his blood." ²⁸ And when Judah heard this thing he was exceedingly angry and his anger burned within him, and there was a stone before him in that place, the weight of which was about four hundred shekels, and Judah's anger was kindled and he took the stone in one hand, and cast it

JASHER

toward the heavens, and caught it with his left hand.
²⁹ And afterward he placed it under his legs, and he sat on it with all his strength, and the stone was turned into dust from the force of Judah. ³⁰ And Joseph saw the act of Judah and he was very much afraid, but he commanded his son Manasseh and he also did with another stone like to the act of Judah, and Judah said to his brothers, "Do not let any of you say this man is an Egyptian, but by his doing this thing he is of our father's family." ³¹ And Joseph said, "Strength is not given to you alone, for we are also powerful men, and why will you boast over us all?" And Judah said to Joseph, "Please send our brother and do not ruin your country this day." ³² And Joseph answered and said to them, "Go and tell your father an evil beast has devoured him as you said concerning your brother Joseph." ³³ And Judah spoke to his brother Naphtali, and he said to him, "Hurry, go now and number all the streets of Egypt and come and tell me"; and Simeon said to him, "Do not let this thing be a trouble to you; now I will go to the mount, and take up one large stone from the mount, and level it at everyone in Egypt, and kill all that are in it." ³⁴ And Joseph heard all these words that his brothers spoke before him, and they did not know that Joseph understood them, for they imagined that he did not know [how] to speak Hebrew. ³⁵ And Joseph was greatly afraid at the words of his brothers lest they should destroy Egypt, and he commanded his son Manasseh, saying, "Go now, hurry and gather to me all the inhabitants of Egypt, and all the valiant men together, and let them come to me now on horseback, and on foot, and with all sorts of musical instruments," and Manasseh went and did so. ³⁶ And Naphtali went as Judah had commanded him, for Naphtali was lightfooted as one of the swift stags, and he would go on the ears of corn and they would not break under him. ³⁷ And he went and numbered all the streets of Egypt, and found them to be twelve, and he came hastily and told Judah, and Judah said to his brothers, "Hasten, and every man put his sword on his loins, and we will come over Egypt and strike them all, and do not let a remnant remain." ³⁸ And Judah said, "Behold, I will destroy three of the streets with my strength, and you will each destroy one street"; and when Judah was speaking this thing, behold, the inhabitants of Egypt and all the mighty men came toward them with all sorts of musical instruments and with loud shouting. ³⁹ And their number was five hundred cavalry, and ten thousand infantry, and four hundred men who could fight without sword or spear, only with their hands and strength. ⁴⁰ And all the mighty men came with great storming and shouting, and they all surrounded the sons of Jacob and terrified them, and the ground quaked at the sound of their shouting. ⁴¹ And when the sons of Jacob saw these troops, they were greatly afraid for their lives, and Joseph did so in order to terrify the sons of Jacob to become tranquilized.

⁴² And Judah, seeing some of his brothers terrified, said to them, "Why are you afraid while the grace of God is with us?" And when Judah saw all the people of Egypt surrounding them at the command of Joseph to terrify them, only Joseph commanded them, saying, "Do not touch any of them." ⁴³ Then Judah hastened and drew his sword, and uttered a loud and bitter scream, and he struck with his sword, and he sprang on the ground, and he still continued to shout against all the people. ⁴⁴ And when he did this thing, the LORD caused the terror of Judah and his brothers to fall on the valiant men and all the people that surrounded them. ⁴⁵ And they all fled at the sound of the shouting, and they were terrified and fell on one another, and many of them died as they fell, and they all fled from before Judah and his brothers and from before Joseph. ⁴⁶ And while they were fleeing, Judah and his brothers pursued them to the house of Pharaoh, and they all escaped, and Judah sat before Joseph again, and roared at him like a lion, and gave a great and tremendous shriek at him. ⁴⁷ And the shriek was heard at a distance, and all the inhabitants of Succoth heard it, and all Egypt quaked at the sound of the shriek, and also the walls of Egypt and of the land of Goshen fell in from the shaking of the earth, and Pharaoh also fell from his throne on the ground, and also all the pregnant women of Egypt and Goshen miscarried when they heard the noise of the shaking, for they were terribly afraid. ⁴⁸ And Pharaoh sent word, saying, "What is this thing that has happened in the land of Egypt this day?" And they came and told him all the things from beginning to end, and Pharaoh was alarmed, and he wondered and was greatly afraid. ⁴⁹ And his fright increased when he heard all these things, and he sent to Joseph, saying, "You have brought the Hebrews to me to destroy all Egypt; what will you do with that thievish slave? Send him away and let him go with his brothers, and do not let us perish through their evil, even we—you and all Egypt. ⁵⁰ And if you do not desire to do this thing, cast off all my valuable things from yourself, and go with them to their land, if you delight in it, for they will destroy my whole country this day and slay all my people; even all the women of Egypt have miscarried through their screams; see what they have done merely by their shouting and speaking; moreover, if they fight with the sword, they will destroy the land; now therefore, choose that which you desire, whether me or the Hebrews, whether Egypt or the land of the Hebrews." ⁵¹ And they came and told Joseph all the words of Pharaoh that he had said concerning him, and Joseph was greatly afraid at the words of Pharaoh, and Judah and his brothers were still standing before Joseph indignant and enraged, and all the sons of Jacob roared at Joseph like the roaring of the sea and its waves. ⁵² And Joseph was greatly afraid of his brothers and on account of Pharaoh, and Joseph sought a pretext to make himself

known to his brothers, lest they should destroy all Egypt. [53] And Joseph commanded his son Manasseh, and Manasseh went and approached Judah, and placed his hand on his shoulder, and the anger of Judah was stilled. [54] And Judah said to his brothers, "Let no one of you say that this is the act of an Egyptian youth, for this is the work of my father's house." [55] And Joseph, seeing and knowing that Judah's anger was stilled, approached to speak to Judah in the language of mildness. [56] And Joseph said to Judah, "Surely you speak truth and have verified your assertions concerning your strength this day, and may your God who delights in you increase your welfare; but truly tell me why from among all your brothers you wrangle with me on account of the youth, as none of them have spoken one word to me concerning him." [57] And Judah answered Joseph, saying, "Surely you must know that I was security for the youth to his father, saying if I did not bring him to him I should bear his blame forever. [58] Therefore I have approached you from among all my brothers, for I saw that you were unwilling to permit him to go from you; now therefore, may I find grace in your sight that you will send him to go with us, and behold, I will remain as a substitute for him, to serve you in whatever you desire, for wherever you will send me I will go to serve you with great energy. [59] Send me now to a mighty king who has rebelled against you, and you will know what I will do to him and to his land; although he may have cavalry and infantry or an exceedingly mighty people, I will slay them all and bring the king's head before you. [60] Do you not know, or have you not heard, that our father Abraham with his servant Eliezer struck all the kings of Elam with their hosts in one night? They did not leave one remaining. And ever since that day our father's strength was given to us for an inheritance—for us and our seed forever." [61] And Joseph answered and said, "You speak truth, and falsehood is not in your mouth, for it was also told to us that the Hebrews have power and that the LORD their God delights much in them, and who then can stand before them? [62] However, on this condition I will send your brother: if you will bring before me his brother, the son of his mother, of whom you said that he had gone from you down to Egypt; and it will come to pass when you bring his brother to me [that] I will take him in his stead, because not one of you were security for him to your father, and when he will come to me, I will then send with you his brother for whom you have been security." [63] And Judah's anger was kindled against Joseph when he spoke this thing, and his eyes dropped blood with anger, and he said to his brothers, "How does this man seek his own destruction and that of all Egypt this day?" [64] And Simeon answered Joseph, saying, "Did we not tell you at first that we did not know the particular spot to which he went, and whether he was dead or alive, and why does my lord

speak about these things?" [65] And Joseph, observing the countenance of Judah, discerned that his anger began to kindle when he spoke to him, saying, "Bring your other brother to me instead of this brother." [66] And Joseph said to his brothers, "Surely you said that your brother was either dead or lost; now if I should call him this day and he should come before you, would you give him to me instead of his brother?" [67] And Joseph began to speak and call out, "Joseph, Joseph! Come before me this day, and appear to your brothers, and sit before them." [68] And when Joseph spoke this thing before them, they each looked a different way to see from where Joseph would come before them. [69] And Joseph observed all their acts, and said to them, "Why do you look here and there? I am Joseph whom you sold to Egypt; now therefore, do not let it grieve you that you sold me, for God sent me before you as a support during the famine." [70] And his brothers were terrified at him when they heard the words of Joseph, and Judah was exceedingly terrified at him. [71] And when Benjamin heard the words of Joseph he was before them in the inner part of the house, and Benjamin ran to his brother Joseph, and embraced him, and fell on his neck, and they wept. [72] And when Joseph's brothers saw that Benjamin had fallen on his brother's neck and wept with him, they also fell on Joseph and embraced him, and they wept a great weeping with Joseph. [73] And the voice was heard in the house of Joseph that they were Joseph's brothers, and it pleased Pharaoh exceedingly, for he was afraid of them lest they should destroy Egypt. [74] And Pharaoh sent his servants to Joseph to congratulate him concerning his brothers who had come to him, and all the captains of the armies and troops that were in Egypt came to rejoice with Joseph, and all Egypt rejoiced greatly about Joseph's brothers. [75] And Pharaoh sent his servants to Joseph, saying, "Tell your brothers to fetch all belonging to them and let them come to me, and I will place them in the best part of the land of Egypt," and they did so. [76] And Joseph commanded him that was set over his house to bring out gifts and garments to his brothers, and he brought out to them many garments, being robes of royalty, and many gifts, and Joseph divided them among his brothers. [77] And he gave to each of his brothers a change of garments of gold and silver, and three hundred pieces of silver, and Joseph commanded them all to be dressed in these garments, and to be brought before Pharaoh. [78] And Pharaoh, seeing that all of Joseph's brothers were valiant men and of beautiful appearance, greatly rejoiced. [79] And afterward they went out from the presence of Pharaoh to go to the land of Canaan, to their father, and their brother Benjamin was with them. [80] And Joseph rose up and gave eleven chariots from Pharaoh to them, and Joseph gave his chariot to them, on which he rode on the day of his being crowned in Egypt, to fetch his father to Egypt; and Joseph sent to all his brothers' children garments according to their numbers, and one hundred pieces of silver to each of them, and he also sent garments to the wives of his brothers from the garments of the king's wives, and he sent them. [81] And he gave to each of his brothers ten men to go with them to the land of Canaan to serve them, to serve their children and all belonging to them in coming to Egypt. [82] And Joseph sent by the hand of his brother Benjamin ten suits of garments for his ten sons, a portion above the rest of the children of the sons of Jacob. [83] And he sent to each fifty pieces of silver, and ten chariots on the account of Pharaoh, and he sent to his father ten donkeys laden with all the luxuries of Egypt, and ten female donkeys laden with corn, and bread, and nourishment for his father, and to all that were with him as provisions for the road. [84] And he sent to his sister Dinah garments of silver, and gold, and frankincense, and myrrh, and aloes, and women's ornaments in great plenty, and he sent the same from the wives of Pharaoh to the wives of Benjamin. [85] And he gave to all his brothers, also to their wives, all sorts of onyx stones, and bdellium, and from all the valuable things among the great people of Egypt; nothing of all the costly things was left but what Joseph sent of to his father's household. [86] And he sent his brothers away, and they went, and he sent his brother Benjamin with them. [87] And Joseph went out with them to accompany them on the road to the borders of Egypt, and he commanded them concerning his father and his household to come to Egypt. [88] And he said to them, "Do not quarrel on the road, for this thing was from the LORD to keep a great people from starvation, for there will still be five years of famine in the land." [89] And he commanded them, saying, "When you come to the land of Canaan, do not come suddenly before my father in this affair, but act in your wisdom." [90] And Joseph ceased to command them, and he turned and went back to Egypt, and the sons of Jacob went to the land of Canaan with joy and cheerfulness to their father Jacob. [91] And they came to the borders of the land, and they said to each other, "What will we do in this matter before our father, for if we suddenly come to him and tell him the matter, he will be greatly alarmed at our words and will not believe us." [92] And they went along until they came near to their houses, and they found Serach, the daughter of Asher, going out to meet them, and the young girl was very good and subtle, and knew how to play on the harp. [93] And they called to her and she came before them, and she kissed them, and they took her and gave a harp to her, saying, "Go now before our father, and sit before him, and strike on the harp, and speak these words." [94] And they commanded her to go to their house, and she took the harp and hastened before them, and she came and sat near Jacob. [95] And she played well and sang, and uttered in the sweetness of her words, "My uncle Joseph is living, and he rules throughout the land of Egypt, and is not dead." [96] And she continued to repeat and utter these words, and Jacob heard her words, and they were agreeable to him. [97] He listened while she repeated them twice and three times, and joy entered the heart of Jacob at the sweetness of her words, and the Spirit of God was on him, and he knew all her words to be true. [98] And Jacob blessed Serach when she spoke these words before him, and he said to her, "My daughter, may death never prevail over you, for you have revived my spirit; only speak yet before me as you have spoken, for you have gladdened me with all your words." [99] And she continued to sing these words, and Jacob listened and it pleased him, and he rejoiced, and the Spirit of God was on him. [100] While he was still speaking with her, behold, his sons came to him with horses, and chariots, and royal garments, and servants running before them. [101] And Jacob rose up to meet them, and he saw his sons dressed in royal garments, and he saw all the treasures that Joseph had sent to them. [102] And they said to him, "Be informed that our brother Joseph is living, and it is he who rules throughout the land of Egypt, and it is he who spoke to us as we told you." [103] And Jacob heard all the words of his sons, and his heart palpitated at their words, for he could not believe them until he saw all that Joseph had given them, and what he had sent him, and all the signs which Joseph had spoken to them. [104] And they opened out before him and showed him all that Joseph had sent; they gave to each what Joseph had sent him, and he knew that they had spoken the truth, and he rejoiced exceedingly on account of his son. [105] And Jacob said, "It is enough for me that my son Joseph is still living; I will go and see him before I die." [106] And his sons told him all that had befallen them, and Jacob said, "I will go down to Egypt to see my son and his offspring." [107] And Jacob rose up and put on the garments which Joseph had sent him, and after he had washed and shaved his hair, he put the turban on his head which Joseph had sent him. [108] And all the people of Jacob's house and their wives put on the garments which Joseph had sent to them, and they greatly rejoiced at Joseph, that he was still living and that he was ruling in Egypt, [109] and all the inhabitants of Canaan heard of this thing, and they came and rejoiced much with Jacob that he was still living. [110] And Jacob made a feast for them for three days, and all the kings of Canaan and nobles of the land ate, and drank, and rejoiced in the house of Jacob.

CHAPTER 55

[1] And it came to pass after this that Jacob said, "I will go and see my son in Egypt and will then come back to the land of Canaan of which God had spoken to Abraham, for I cannot leave the land of my birthplace." [2] Behold, the word of the LORD came to him, saying, "Go down to Egypt with all your

JASHER

household and remain there; do not fear to go down to Egypt, for I will make you a great nation there." ³ And Jacob said within himself, "I will go and see my son—whether the fear of his God is yet in his heart amidst all the inhabitants of Egypt." ⁴ And the LORD said to Jacob, "Do not fear about Joseph, for he still retains his integrity to serve Me, as will seem good in your sight," and Jacob rejoiced exceedingly concerning his son. ⁵ At that time Jacob commanded his sons and household to go to Egypt according to the word of the LORD to him, and Jacob rose up with his sons and all his household, and he went out from the land of Canaan from Beersheba with joy and gladness of heart, and they went to the land of Egypt. ⁶ And it came to pass when they came near Egypt, Jacob sent Judah before him to Joseph that he might show him a situation in Egypt, and Judah did according to the word of his father, and he hastened, and ran, and came to Joseph, and they assigned a place for them in the land of Goshen for all his household, and Judah returned and came along the road to his father. ⁷ And Joseph harnessed the chariot, and he assembled all his mighty men, and his servants, and all the officers of Egypt in order to go and meet his father Jacob, and Joseph's mandate was proclaimed in Egypt, saying, "All that do not go to meet Jacob will die." ⁸ And on the next day Joseph went out with all Egypt—a great and mighty host, all dressed in garments of fine linen, and purple, and with instruments of silver and gold, and with their instruments of war with them. ⁹ And they all went to meet Jacob with all sorts of musical instruments, with drums and timbrels, scattering myrrh and aloes all along the road, and they all went after this fashion, and the earth shook at their shouting. ¹⁰ And all the women of Egypt went on the roofs of Egypt and on the walls to meet Jacob, and Pharaoh's regal crown was on the head of Joseph, for Pharaoh had sent it to him to put on at the time of his going to meet his father. ¹¹ And when Joseph came within fifty cubits of his father, he descended from the chariot and he walked toward his father, and when all the officers of Egypt and her nobles saw that Joseph had gone on foot toward his father, they also descended and walked on foot toward Jacob. ¹² And when Jacob approached the camp of Joseph, Jacob observed the camp that was coming toward him with Joseph, and it gratified him, and Jacob was astonished at it. ¹³ And Jacob said to Judah, "Who is that man whom I see in the camp of Egypt dressed in kingly robes with a very red garment on him and a royal crown on his head, who has descended from his chariot and is coming toward us?" And Judah answered his father, saying, "He is your son Joseph, the king"; and Jacob rejoiced in seeing the glory of his son. ¹⁴ And Joseph came near to his father and he bowed to his father, and all the men of the camp bowed to the ground with him before Jacob. ¹⁵ And behold, Jacob ran and hastened to his son Joseph, and he fell on his neck and kissed him, and they wept, and Joseph also embraced his father and kissed him, and they wept and all the people of Egypt wept with them. ¹⁶ And Jacob said to Joseph, "Now I will die cheerfully after I have seen your face, that you are still living and with glory." ¹⁷ And the sons of Jacob, and their wives, and their children, and their servants, and all the household of Jacob wept exceedingly with Joseph, and they kissed him and wept greatly with him. ¹⁸ And afterward Joseph and all his people returned home to Egypt, and Jacob, and his sons, and all the children of his household came with Joseph to Egypt, and Joseph placed them in the best part of Egypt, in the land of Goshen. ¹⁹ And Joseph said to his father and to his brothers, "I will go up and tell Pharaoh, saying, My brothers, and my father's household, and all belonging to them have come to me, and behold, they are in the land of Goshen." ²⁰ And Joseph did so and took from his brothers Reuben, Issachar, Zebulun, and his brother Benjamin, and he placed them before Pharaoh. ²¹ And Joseph spoke to Pharaoh, saying, "My brothers, and my father's household, and all belonging to them, together with their flocks and cattle have come to me from the land of Canaan to sojourn in Egypt, for the famine was severe on them." ²² And Pharaoh said to Joseph, "Place your father and brothers in the best part of the land; do not withhold from them anything that is good, and cause them to eat of the fat of the land." ²³ And Joseph answered, saying, "Behold, I have stationed them in the land of Goshen, for they are shepherds; therefore let them remain in Goshen to feed their flocks apart from the Egyptians." ²⁴ And Pharaoh said to Joseph, "Do with your brothers all that they will say to you"; and the sons of Jacob bowed down to Pharaoh, and they went out from him in peace, and afterward Joseph brought his father before Pharaoh. ²⁵ And Jacob came and bowed down to Pharaoh, and Jacob blessed Pharaoh, and he then went out; and Jacob, and all his sons, and all his household dwelt in the land of Goshen. ²⁶ In the second year, that is in the one hundred and thirtieth year of the life of Jacob, Joseph maintained his father, and his brothers, and all his father's household with bread according to their little ones, all the days of the famine; they lacked nothing. ²⁷ And Joseph gave the best part of the whole land to them; they had the best [part] of Egypt all the days of Joseph; and Joseph also gave to them and to the whole of his father's household clothes and garments year by year; and the sons of Jacob remained securely in Egypt all the days of their brother. ²⁸ And Jacob always ate at Joseph's table; Jacob and his sons did not leave Joseph's table day or night, besides what Jacob's children consumed in their houses. ²⁹ And all Egypt ate bread during the days of the famine from the house of Joseph, for all the Egyptians sold all belonging to them on account of the famine. ³⁰ And Joseph purchased all the lands and fields of Egypt for bread on the account of Pharaoh, and Joseph supplied all Egypt with bread all the days of the famine, and Joseph collected all the silver and gold that came to him for the corn which they bought throughout the land, and he accumulated much gold and silver, besides an immense quantity of onyx stones, bdellium, and valuable garments which they brought to Joseph from every part of the land when their money was spent. ³¹ And Joseph took all the silver and gold that came into his hand, about seventy-two talents of gold and silver, and also onyx stones and bdellium in great abundance, and Joseph went and concealed them in four parts, and he concealed one part in the wilderness near the Red Sea, and one part by the River Perath, and the third and fourth part he concealed in the desert opposite to the wilderness of Persia and Media. ³² And he took part of the gold and silver that was left and gave it to all his brothers, and to all his father's household, and to all the women of his father's household, and the rest he brought to the house of Pharaoh, about twenty talents of gold and silver. ³³ And Joseph gave all the gold and silver that was left to Pharaoh, and Pharaoh placed it in the treasury, and the days of the famine ceased after that in the land, and they sowed and reaped in the whole land, and they obtained their usual quantity year by year; they lacked nothing. ³⁴ And Joseph dwelt securely in Egypt, and the whole land was under his advice, and his father and all his brothers dwelt in the land of Goshen and took possession of it. ³⁵ And Joseph was very aged, advanced in days, and his two sons, Ephraim and Manasseh, continually remained in the house of Jacob, together with the children of the sons of Jacob, their brothers, to learn the ways of the LORD and His law. ³⁶ And Jacob and his sons dwelt in the land of Egypt in the land of Goshen, and they took possession in it, and they were fruitful and multiplied in it.

CHAPTER 56

¹ And Jacob lived in the land of Egypt seventeen years, and the days of Jacob and the years of his life were one hundred and forty-seven years. ² At that time Jacob was attacked with that sickness of which he died, and he sent and called for his son Joseph from Egypt, and his son Joseph came from Egypt and Joseph came to his father. ³ And Jacob said to Joseph and to his sons, "Behold, I die, and the God of your ancestors will visit you and bring you back to the land which the LORD swore to give to you and to your children after you; now therefore, when I am dead, bury me in the cave which is in Machpelah in Hebron in the land of Canaan, near my ancestors." ⁴ And Jacob made his sons swear to bury him in Machpelah, in Hebron, and his sons swore to him concerning this thing. ⁵ And he commanded them, saying, "Serve the LORD your God, for He who delivered your fathers will also deliver you from all trouble." ⁶ And Jacob

said, "Call all your children to me," and all the children of Jacob's sons came and sat before him, and Jacob blessed them, and he said to them, "The LORD God of your fathers will grant you one thousand times as much and bless you, and may He give you the blessing of your father Abraham"; and all the children of Jacob's sons went out on that day after he had blessed them. ⁷ And on the next day Jacob called for his sons again, and they all assembled, and came to him, and sat before him, and on that day Jacob blessed his sons before his death: he blessed each man according to his blessing; behold, it is written in the Scroll of the Law of the LORD pertaining to Israel. ⁸ And Jacob said to Judah, "I know, my son, that you are a mighty man for your brothers; reign over them, and your sons will reign over their sons forever. ⁹ Only teach your sons the bow and all the weapons of war in order that they may fight the battles of their brother who will rule over his enemies." ¹⁰ And Jacob commanded his sons again on that day, saying, "Behold, I will be gathered to my people this day; carry me up from Egypt and bury me in the cave of Machpelah as I have commanded you. ¹¹ Nevertheless, please take heed that none of your sons carry me, only yourselves, and this is the manner you will do to me: when you carry my body to go with it to the land of Canaan to bury me, ¹² Judah, Issachar, and Zebulun will carry my bier at the eastern side; Reuben, Simeon, and Gad at the south; Ephraim, Manasseh, and Benjamin at the west; Dan, Asher, and Naphtali at the north. ¹³ Do not let Levi carry with you, for he and his sons will carry the Ark of the Covenant of the LORD with the Israelites in the camp; neither let my son Joseph carry, for as a king so let his glory be; nevertheless, Ephraim and Manasseh will be in their stead. ¹⁴ Thus you will do to me when you carry me away; do not neglect anything of all that I command you; and it will come to pass when you do this to me that the LORD will remember you favorably and your children after you forever. ¹⁵ And you, my sons, each honor his brother and his relative, and command your children and your children's children after you to serve the LORD God of your ancestors all the days ¹⁶ in order that you may prolong your days in the land— you, and your children, and your children's children forever—when you do what is good and upright in the sight of the LORD your God, to go in all His ways. ¹⁷ And you, my son Joseph, please forgive the prongs of your brothers and all their misdeeds in the injury that they heaped on you, for God intended it for you and your children's benefit. ¹⁸ And O, my son, do not leave your brothers to the inhabitants of Egypt, neither hurt their feelings, for behold, I consign them to the hand of God and in your hand to guard them from the Egyptians"; and the sons of Jacob answered their father, saying, "O, our father, all that you have commanded us, so we will do—but may God be with us." ¹⁹ And Jacob said to his sons, "So may God be with you when you keep all His ways; do not turn from His ways either to the right or the left in performing what is good and upright in His sight. ²⁰ For I know that many and grievous troubles will befall you in the latter days in the land—yes, your children and children's children; only serve the LORD and He will save you from all trouble. ²¹ And it will come to pass when you will go after God to serve Him and will teach your children after you, and your children's children, to know the LORD, then the LORD will raise up to you and your children a servant from among your children, and the LORD will deliver you from all affliction through his hand, and bring you out of Egypt, and bring you back to the land of your fathers to inherit it securely." ²² And Jacob ceased commanding his sons and he drew his feet into the bed; he died and was gathered to his people. ²³ And Joseph fell on his father, and he cried out and wept over him, and he kissed him, and he called out in a bitter voice, and he said, "O my father, my father!" ²⁴ And his son's wives and all his household came and fell on Jacob, and they wept over him, and cried in a very loud voice concerning Jacob. ²⁵ And all the sons of Jacob rose up together, and they tore their garments, and they all put sackcloth on their loins, and they fell on their faces, and they cast dust on their heads toward the heavens. ²⁶ And the thing was told to Osnath, Joseph's wife, and she rose up and put on a sack, and she and all the Egyptian women with her came and mourned and wept for Jacob. ²⁷ And also all the people of Egypt who knew Jacob all came on that day when they heard this thing, and all Egypt wept for many days. ²⁸ And also from the land of Canaan women came to Egypt when they heard that Jacob was dead, and they wept for him in Egypt for seventy days. ²⁹ And it came to pass after this that Joseph commanded his servants, the doctors, to embalm his father with myrrh, and frankincense, and all manner of incense and perfume, and the doctors embalmed Jacob as Joseph had commanded them. ³⁰ And all the people of Egypt, and the elders, and all the inhabitants of the land of Goshen wept and mourned over Jacob, and all his sons and the children of his household lamented and mourned over their father Jacob [for] many days. ³¹ And after the days of his weeping had passed away, at the end of seventy days, Joseph said to Pharaoh, "I will go up and bury my father in the land of Canaan as he made me swear, and then I will return." ³² And Pharaoh sent Joseph, saying, "Go up and bury your father as he said, and as he made you swear"; and Joseph rose up with all his brothers to go to the land of Canaan to bury their father Jacob as he had commanded them. ³³ And Pharaoh commanded that it should be proclaimed throughout Egypt, saying, "Whoever does not go up with Joseph and his brothers to the land of Canaan to bury Jacob will die." ³⁴ And all Egypt heard of Pharaoh's proclamation, and they all rose up together, and all the servants of Pharaoh, and the elders of his house, and all the elders of the land of Egypt went up with Joseph, and all the officers and nobles of Pharaoh went up as the servants of Joseph, and they went to bury Jacob in the land of Canaan. ³⁵ And the sons of Jacob carried the bier on which he lay; according to all that their father commanded them, so his sons did for him. ³⁶ And the bier was of pure gold, and it was inlaid around with onyx stones and bdellium; and the covering of the bier was gold-woven work, joined with threads, and over them were hooks of onyx stones and bdellium. ³⁷ And Joseph placed a large golden crown on the head of his father Jacob, and he put a golden scepter in his hand, and they surrounded the bier as was the custom of kings during their lives. ³⁸ And all the troops of Egypt went before him in this array, at first all the mighty men of Pharaoh and the mighty men of Joseph, and after them the rest of the inhabitants of Egypt, and they were all girded with swords and equipped with coats of mail, and the trappings of war were on them. ³⁹ And all the weepers and mourners went at a distance opposite to the bier, going, and weeping, and lamenting, and the rest of the people went after the bier. ⁴⁰ And Joseph and his household went together near the bier barefooted and weeping, and the rest of Joseph's servants went around him; each man had his ornaments on him, and they were all armed with their weapons of war. ⁴¹ And fifty of Jacob's servants went in front of the bier, and they scattered along the road myrrh, and aloes, and all manner of perfume, and all the sons of Jacob that carried the bier walked on the perfumery, and the servants of Jacob went before them scattering the perfume along the road. ⁴² And Joseph went up with a heavy camp, and they did after this manner every day until they reached the land of Canaan, and they came to the threshing floor of Atad, which was on the other side of Jordan, and they mourned an exceedingly great and heavy mourning in that place. ⁴³ And all the kings of Canaan heard of this thing and they all went out, each man from his house—thirty-one kings of Canaan—and they all came with their men to mourn and weep over Jacob. ⁴⁴ And all these kings beheld Jacob's bier, and behold, Joseph's crown was on it, and they also put their crowns on the bier, and encircled it with crowns. ⁴⁵ And all these kings made a great and heavy mourning in that place with the sons of Jacob and Egypt over Jacob, for all the kings of Canaan knew the valor of Jacob and his sons. ⁴⁶ And the report reached Esau, saying, "Jacob died in Egypt, and his sons and all Egypt are carrying him to the land of Canaan to bury him." ⁴⁷ And Esau heard this thing, and he was dwelling in Mount Seir, and he rose up with his sons, and all his people, and all his household, a people exceedingly great, and they came to mourn and weep over Jacob. ⁴⁸ And it came to pass when Esau came, he mourned for his brother Jacob, and all Egypt and all Canaan rose up again and mourned a great mourning with Esau over Jacob in that place. [49] And Joseph and his brothers brought their father Jacob from that place, and they went to Hebron to bury Jacob in the cave by his fathers. [50] And they came to Kirjath-Arba, to the cave, and as they came, Esau stood with his sons against Joseph and his brothers as a hindrance in the cave, saying, "Jacob will not be buried therein, for it belongs to us and to our father." [51] And Joseph and his brothers heard the words of Esau's sons, and they were exceedingly angry, and Joseph approached to Esau, saying, "What is this thing which they have spoken? Surely my father Jacob bought it from you for great riches after the death of Isaac, now twenty-five years ago, and he also bought all the land of Canaan from you, and from your sons, and [from] your seed after you. [52] And Jacob bought it for his sons and his seed after him for an inheritance forever, and why do you speak these things this day?" [53] And Esau answered, saying, "You speak falsely and utter lies, for I did not sell anything belonging to me in all this land as you say, neither did my brother Jacob buy all belonging to me in this land." [54] And Esau spoke these things in order to deceive Joseph with his words, for Esau knew that Joseph was not present in those days when Esau sold all belonging to him in the land of Canaan to Jacob. [55] And Joseph said to Esau, "Surely my father inserted these things with you in the record of purchase, and testified to the record with witnesses, and behold, it is with us in Egypt." [56] And Esau answered, saying to him, "Bring the record—all that you will find in the record, so we will do." [57] And Joseph called to his brother Naphtali, and he said, "Hasten quickly, do not linger, and now run to Egypt and bring all the records—the record of the purchase, the sealed record and the open record, and also all the first records in which all the transactions of the birthright are written; fetch [them]. [58] And you will bring them to us here [so] that we may know from them all the words of Esau and his sons which they spoke this day." [59] And Naphtali listened to the voice of Joseph and he hastened and ran to go down to Egypt, and Naphtali was lighter on foot than any of the stags that were on the wilderness, for he would go on ears of corn without crushing them. [60] And when Esau saw that Naphtali had gone to fetch the records, he and his sons increased their resistance against the cave, and Esau and all his people rose up against Joseph and his brothers to battle. [61] And all the sons of Jacob and the people of Egypt fought with Esau and his men, and the sons of Esau and his people were smitten before the sons of Jacob, and the sons of Jacob slew of Esau's people forty men. [62] And Chushim the son of Dan, the son of Jacob, was with Jacob's sons at that time, but he was about one hundred cubits distant from the place of battle, for he remained with the children of Jacob's sons by Jacob's bier to guard it. [63] And Chushim was mute and deaf, [but] he still understood the voice of consternation among men. [64] And he asked, saying, "Why do you not bury the dead, and what is this great consternation?" And they answered him [with] the words of Esau and his sons; and he ran to Esau in the midst of the battle, and he slew Esau with a sword, and he cut off his head, and it sprang to a distance, and Esau fell among the people of the battle. [65] And when Chushim did this thing the sons of Jacob prevailed over the sons of Esau, and the sons of Jacob buried their father Jacob by force in the cave, and the sons of Esau beheld it. [66] And Jacob was buried in Hebron, in the cave of Machpelah which Abraham had bought from the sons of Heth for the possession of a burial place, and he was buried in very costly garments. [67] And no king had such honor paid him as Joseph paid to his father at his death, for he buried him with great honor like to the burial of kings. [68] And Joseph and his brothers made a mourning of seven days for their father.

CHAPTER 57

[1] And it was after this that the sons of Esau waged war with the sons of Jacob, and the sons of Esau fought with the sons of Jacob in Hebron, and Esau was still lying dead and not buried. [2] And the battle was heavy between them, and the sons of Esau were smitten before the sons of Jacob, and the sons of Jacob slew eighty men of the sons of Esau, and not one died of the people of the sons of Jacob; and the hand of Joseph prevailed over all the people of the sons of Esau, and he took Zepho, the son of Eliphaz, the son of Esau, and fifty of his men captive, and he bound them with chains of iron, and gave them into the hand of his servants to bring them to Egypt. [3] And it came to pass when the sons of Jacob had taken Zepho and his people captive, all those that remained were greatly afraid for their lives from the house of Esau lest they should also be taken captive, and they all fled with Eliphaz the son of Esau and his people, with Esau's body, and they went on their road to Mount Seir. [4] And they came to Mount Seir and they buried Esau in Seir, but they had not brought his head with them to Seir, for it was buried in that place where the battle had been in Hebron. [5] And it came to pass when the sons of Esau had fled from before the sons of Jacob, the sons of Jacob pursued them to the borders of Seir, but they did not slay a single man from among them when they pursued them, for Esau's body which they carried with them excited their confusion, so they fled and the sons of Jacob turned back from them and came up to the place where their brothers were in Hebron, and they remained there on that day and on the next day until they rested from the battle. [6] And it came to pass on the third day, they assembled all the sons of Seir the Horite, and they assembled all the children of the east, a multitude of people like the sand of the sea, and they went and came down to Egypt to fight with Joseph and his brothers in order

to deliver their brothers. [7] And Joseph and all the sons of Jacob heard that the sons of Esau and the children of the east had come on them to battle in order to deliver their brothers. [8] And Joseph, and his brothers, and the strong men of Egypt went out and fought in the city of Rameses, and Joseph and his brothers dealt out a tremendous blow among the sons of Esau and the children of the east. [9] And they slew of them six hundred thousand men, and they slew among them all the mighty men of the children of Seir the Horite; there were only a few of them left, and they also slew a great many of the children of the east and of the children of Esau; and Eliphaz the son of Esau and the children of the east all fled before Joseph and his brothers. [10] And Joseph and his brothers pursued them until they came to Succoth, and they yet slew thirty men of them in Succoth, and the rest escaped and they each fled to his city. [11] And Joseph, and his brothers, and the mighty men of Egypt turned back from them with joy and cheerfulness of heart, for they had smitten all their enemies. [12] And Zepho the son of Eliphaz and his men were still slaves in Egypt to the sons of Jacob, and their pains increased. [13] And when the sons of Esau and the sons of Seir returned to their land, the sons of Seir saw that they had all fallen into the hands of the sons of Jacob and the people of Egypt on account of the battle of the sons of Esau. [14] And the sons of Seir said to the sons of Esau, "You have seen and therefore you know that this camp was on your account, and not one mighty man or an adept in war remains. [15] Now therefore, go out from our land; go from us to the land of Canaan to the land of the dwelling of your fathers; why will your children inherit the effects of our children in latter days?" [16] And the children of Esau would not listen to the children of Seir, and the children of Seir considered to make war with them. [17] And the children of Esau secretly sent to Angeas king of Africa, the same is Dinhabah, saying, [18] "Send some of your men to us and let them come to us, and we will fight together with the children of Seir the Horite, for they have resolved to fight with us to drive us away from the land." [19] And Angeas king of Dinhabah did so, for he was friendly to the children of Esau in those days, and Angeas sent five hundred valiant infantry to the children of Esau, and [also] eight hundred cavalry. [20] And the children of Seir sent to the children of the east and to the children of Midian, saying, "You have seen what the children of Esau have done to us, on whose account we are almost all destroyed, in their battle with the sons of Jacob. [21] Now therefore, come to us and assist us, and we will fight them together, and we will drive them from the land and be avenged of the cause of our brothers who died for their sakes in their battle with their brothers, the sons of Jacob." [22] And all the children of the east listened to the children of Seir, and they came to them—about eight hundred men with drawn swords—and the children of Esau fought with the children of Seir at that time in the wilderness of Paran. [23] And the children of Seir then prevailed over the sons of Esau, and the children of Seir slew on that day of the children of Esau in that battle about two hundred men of the people of Angeas king of Dinhabah. [24] And on the second day the children of Esau came again to fight a second time with the children of Seir, and the battle was severe on the children of Esau this second time, and it troubled them greatly on account of the children of Seir. [25] And when the children of Esau saw that the children of Seir were more powerful than they were, some men of the children of Esau turned and assisted the children of Seir, their enemies. [26] And there fell yet of the people of the children of Esau in the second battle fifty-eight men of the people at Angeas king of Dinhabah. [27] And on the third day the children of Esau heard that some of their brothers had turned from them to fight against them in the second battle; and the children of Esau mourned when they heard this thing. [28] And they said, "What will we do to our brothers who turned from us to assist the children of Seir, our enemies?" And the children of Esau sent to Angeas king of Dinhabah again, saying, [29] "Send other men to us again that with them we may fight with the children of Seir, for they have already twice been heavier than we were." [30] And Angeas again sent to the children of Esau about six hundred valiant men, and they came to assist the children of Esau. [31] And in ten days' time the children of Esau again waged war with the children of Seir in the wilderness of Paran, and the battle was very severe on the children of Seir, and the children of Esau prevailed over the children of Seir at this time, and the children of Seir were smitten before the children of Esau, and the children of Esau slew from them about two thousand men. [32] And all the mighty men of the children of Seir died in this battle, and there only remained their young children that were left in their cities. [33] And all Midian and the children of the east went themselves to escape from the battle, and they left the children of Seir and fled when they saw that the battle was severe on them, and the children of Esau pursued all the children of the east until they reached their land. [34] And the children of Esau slew yet of them about two hundred and fifty men, and from the people of the children of Esau there fell in that battle about thirty men, but this evil came on them through their brothers turning from them to assist the children of Seir the Horite, and the children of Esau again heard of the evil doings of their brothers, and they again mourned on account of this thing. [35] And it came to pass after the battle, the children of Esau turned back and came home to Seir, and the children of Esau slew those who had remained in the land of the children of Seir; they also slew their wives and little ones; they did not leave a soul alive except fifty young boys and young girls whom they allowed to live, and the children of Esau did not put them to death, and the boys became their slaves, and they took the young girls for wives. ³⁶ And the children of Esau dwelt in Seir in the place of the children of Seir, and they inherited their land and took possession of it. ³⁷ And the children of Esau took all belonging to the children of Seir in the land, also their flocks, their bullocks, and their goods, and the children of Esau took all belonging to the children of Seir, and the children of Esau dwelt in Seir in the place of the children of Seir to this day, and the children of Esau divided the land into divisions to the five sons of Esau, according to their families. ³⁸ And it came to pass in those days that the children of Esau resolved to crown a king over them in the land of which they possessed. And they said to each other, "Not so, for he will reign over us in our land, and we will be under his counsel and he will fight our battles against our enemies," and they did so. ³⁹ And all the children of Esau swore, saying that none of their brothers should ever reign over them, but a strange man who is not of their brothers, for the souls of all the children of Esau were embittered—every man against his son, brother, and friend—on account of the evil they sustained from their brothers when they fought with the children of Seir. ⁴⁰ Therefore the sons of Esau swore, saying from that day forward they would not choose a king from their brothers, but one from a strange land to this day. ⁴¹ And there was a man there from the people of Angeas king of Dinhabah; his name was Bela the son of Beor, who was a very valiant man, beautiful, and handsome, and wise in all wisdom, and a man of sense and counsel; and there was none of the people of Angeas like to him. ⁴² And all the children of Esau took him and anointed him, and they crowned him for a king, and they bowed down to him, and they said to him, "May the king live, may the king live!" ⁴³ And they spread out the sheet, and they brought him, each man, earrings of gold and silver or rings or bracelets, and they made him very rich in silver and in gold, in onyx stones and bdellium, and they made him a royal throne, and they placed a regal crown on his head, and they built a palace for him and he dwelt therein, and he became king over all the children of Esau. ⁴⁴ And the people of Angeas took their hire for their battle from the children of Esau, and they went and returned at that time to their master in Dinhabah. ⁴⁵ And Bela reigned over the children of Esau thirty years, and the children of Esau dwelt in the land instead of the children of Seir, and they dwelt securely in their stead to this day.

CHAPTER 58

¹ And it came to pass in the thirty-second year of the Israelites going down to Egypt, that is in the seventy-first year of the life of Joseph, in that year Pharaoh king of Egypt died, and his son Magron reigned in his stead. ² And before his death Pharaoh commanded Joseph to be a father to his son Magron, and that

Magron should be under the care of Joseph and under his counsel. ³ And all Egypt consented to this thing that Joseph should be king over them, for all the Egyptians loved Joseph as before now, only Magron the son of Pharaoh sat on his father's throne, and he became king in those days in his father's stead. ⁴ Magron was forty-one years old when he began to reign, and he reigned [for] forty years in Egypt, and all Egypt called his name Pharaoh after the name of his father as it was their custom to do in Egypt to every king that reigned over them. ⁵ And it came to pass when Pharaoh reigned in his father's stead, he placed the laws of Egypt and all the affairs of government in the hand of Joseph as his father had commanded him. ⁶ And Joseph became king over Egypt, for he superintended over all Egypt, and all Egypt was under his care and under his counsel, for all Egypt inclined to Joseph after the death of Pharaoh, and they loved him exceedingly to reign over them. ⁷ But there were some people among them who did not like him, saying, "No stranger will reign over us"; still the whole government of Egypt devolved in those days on Joseph, after the death of Pharaoh, he being the regulator, doing as he liked throughout the land without anyone interfering. ⁸ And all Egypt was under the care of Joseph, and Joseph made war with all his surrounding enemies, and he subdued them; Joseph also subdued all the land and all the Philistines to the borders of Canaan, and they were all under his power and they gave a yearly tax to Joseph. ⁹ And Pharaoh king of Egypt sat on his throne in his father's stead, but he was under the control and counsel of Joseph as he was at first under the control of his father. ¹⁰ Neither did he reign but in the land of Egypt alone, [but only] under the counsel of Joseph, but Joseph reigned over the whole country at that time, from Egypt to the great river Perath. ¹¹ And Joseph was successful in all his ways, and the LORD was with him, and the LORD gave Joseph additional wisdom, and honor, and glory, and love toward him in the hearts of the Egyptians and throughout the land, and Joseph reigned over the whole country [for] forty years. ¹² And all the countries of the Philistines, and Canaan, and Zidon, and on the other side of Jordan brought presents to Joseph all his days, and the whole country was in the hand of Joseph, and they brought a yearly tribute to him as it was regulated, for Joseph had fought against all his surrounding enemies and subdued them, and the whole country was in the hand of Joseph, and Joseph sat securely on his throne in Egypt. ¹³ And all his brothers, the sons of Jacob, also dwelt securely in the land all the days of Joseph, and they were fruitful and multiplied exceedingly in the land, and they served the LORD all their days as their father Jacob had commanded them. ¹⁴ And it came to pass at the end of many days and years when the children of Esau were dwelling quietly in their land with Bela, their king, that the children of Esau were fruitful and multiplied in the land, and they resolved to go and fight with the sons of Jacob and all Egypt, and to deliver their brother Zepho, the son of Eliphaz, and his men, for they were still slaves to Joseph in those days. ¹⁵ And the children of Esau sent to all the children of the east, and they made peace with them, and all the children of the east came to them to go with the children of Esau to Egypt to battle. ¹⁶ And there also came to them [those] of the people of Angeas, king of Dinhabah, and they also sent to the children of Ishmael and they also came to them. ¹⁷ And all this people assembled and came to Seir to assist the children of Esau in their battle, and this camp was very large and heavy with people, numerous as the sand of the sea, about eight hundred thousand men, infantry and cavalry, and all these troops went down to Egypt to fight with the sons of Jacob, and they encamped by Rameses. ¹⁸ And Joseph went out with his brothers with the mighty men of Egypt, about six hundred men, and they fought with them in the land of Rameses; and the sons of Jacob again fought with the children of Esau at that time, in the fiftieth year of the sons of Jacob going down to Egypt, that is the thirtieth year of the reign of Bela over the children of Esau in Seir. ¹⁹ And the LORD gave all the mighty men of Esau and the children of the east into the hand of Joseph and his brothers, and the people of the children of Esau and the children of the east were smitten before Joseph. ²⁰ And of the people of Esau and the children of the east that were slain, there fell before the sons of Jacob about two hundred thousand men, and their king, Bela the son of Beor, fell with them in the battle, and when the children of Esau saw that their king had fallen in battle and was dead, their hands became weak in the combat. ²¹ And Joseph, and his brothers, and all Egypt were still striking the people of the house of Esau, and all Esau's people were afraid of the sons of Jacob and fled from before them. ²² And Joseph, and his brothers, and all Egypt pursued them a day's journey, and they slew yet from them about three hundred men, continuing to strike them in the road; and afterward they turned back from them. ²³ And Joseph and all his brothers returned to Egypt; not one man was missing from them, but of the Egyptians there fell twelve men. ²⁴ And when Joseph returned to Egypt he ordered Zepho and his men to be additionally bound, and they bound them in irons and they increased their grief. ²⁵ And all the people of the children of Esau and the children of the east each returned in shame to his city, for all the mighty men that were with them had fallen in battle. ²⁶ And when the children of Esau saw that their king had died in battle, they hastened and took a man from the people of the children of the east; his name was Jobab the son of Zarach, from the land of Botzrah, and they caused him to reign over them instead of Bela, their king. ²⁷ And Jobab sat on the throne of Bela as king in his stead, and Jobab reigned in Edom over all the children of Esau ten years, and the children of Esau no longer went to fight with the sons of Jacob from that day forward, for the sons of Esau knew the valor of the sons of Jacob, and they were greatly afraid of them. ²⁸ But from that day forward the children of Esau hated the sons of Jacob, and the hatred and enmity were very strong between them all the days, to this day. ²⁹ And it came to pass after this, at the end of ten years, Jobab, the son of Zarach, from Botzrah, died, and the children of Esau took a man whose name was Chusham, from the land of Teman, and they made him king over them instead of Jobab, and Chusham reigned in Edom over all the children of Esau for twenty years. ³⁰ And Joseph, king of Egypt, and his brothers, and all the sons of Israel dwelt securely in Egypt in those days, together with all the children of Joseph and his brothers, having no hindrance or evil accident and the land of Egypt was at that time at rest from war in the days of Joseph and his brothers.

CHAPTER 59

¹ And these are the names of the sons of Israel who dwelt in Egypt who had come with Jacob (all the sons of Jacob came to Egypt, every man with his household). ² The children of Leah were Reuben, Simeon, Levi, Judah, Issachar, and Zebulun, and their sister Dinah. ³ And the sons of Rachel were Joseph and Benjamin. ⁴ And the sons of Zilpah, the handmaid of Leah, were Gad and Asher. ⁵ And the sons of Bilhah, the handmaid of Rachel, were Dan and Naphtali. ⁶ And these were their offspring that were born to them in the land of Canaan before they came to Egypt with their father Jacob. ⁷ The sons of Reuben were Chanoch, Pallu, Chetzron, and Carmi. ⁸ And the sons of Simeon were Jemuel, Jamin, Ohad, Jachin, Zochar, and Saul, the son of the Canaanite woman. ⁹ And the children of Levi were Gershon, Kehas, and Merari, and their sister Jochebed who was born to them in their going down to Egypt. ¹⁰ And the sons of Judah were Er, Onan, Shelah, Perez, and Zarach. ¹¹ And Er and Onan died in the land of Canaan; and the sons of Perez were Chezron and Chamul. ¹² And the sons of Issachar were Tola, Puvah, Job, and Shomron. ¹³ And the sons of Zebulun were Sered, Elon, and Jachleel. And the son of Dan was Chushim. ¹⁴ And the sons of Naphtali were Jachzeel, Guni, Jetzer, and Shilam. ¹⁵ And the sons of Gad were Ziphion, Chaggi, Shuni, Ezbon, Eri, Arodi, and Areli. ¹⁶ And the children of Asher were Jimnah, Jishvah, Jishvi, Beriah, and their sister Serach; and the sons of Beriah were Cheber and Malchiel. ¹⁷ And the sons of Benjamin were Bela, Becher, Ashbel, Gera, Naaman, Achi, Rosh, Mupim, Chupim, and Ord. ¹⁸ And the sons of Joseph that were born to him in Egypt were Manasseh and Ephraim. ¹⁹ And all the souls that went out from the loins of Jacob were seventy souls; these

are they who came to Egypt with their father Jacob to dwell there: and Joseph and all his brothers dwelt securely in Egypt, and they ate of the best of Egypt all the days of the life of Joseph. [20] And Joseph lived in the land of Egypt [for] ninety-three years, and Joseph reigned over all Egypt [for] eighty years. [21] And when the days of Joseph drew near that he should die, he sent and called for his brothers and all his father's household, and they all came together and sat before him. [22] And Joseph said to his brothers and to the whole of his father's household, "Behold, I die, and God will surely visit you and bring you up from this land to the land which He swore to your fathers to give to them. [23] And it will be when God will visit you to bring you up from here to the land of your fathers, then bring up my bones with you from here." [24] And Joseph made the sons of Israel to swear for their seed after them, saying, "God will surely visit you and you will bring up my bones with you from here." [25] And it came to pass after this that Joseph died in that year, the seventy-first year of the Israelites going down to Egypt. [26] And Joseph was one hundred and ten years old when he died in the land of Egypt, and all his brothers and all his servants rose up and embalmed Joseph as was their custom, and his brothers and all Egypt mourned over him for seventy days. [27] And they put Joseph in a coffin filled with spices and all sorts of perfume, and they buried him by the side of the river, that is Sihor, and his sons, and all his brothers, and the whole of his father's household made a seven days' mourning for him. [28] And it came to pass after the death of Joseph, all the Egyptians began to rule over the sons of Israel in those days, and Pharaoh, king of Egypt, who reigned in his father's stead, took all the laws of Egypt and conducted the whole government of Egypt under his counsel, and he reigned securely over his people.

CHAPTER 60

[1] And when the year came round, being the seventy-second year from the Israelites going down to Egypt, after the death of Joseph, Zepho, the son of Eliphaz, the son of Esau, fled from Egypt, he and his men, and they went away. [2] And he came to Africa, which is Dinhabah, to Angeas king of Africa, and Angeas received them with great honor, and he made Zepho the captain of his host. [3] And Zepho found favor in the sight of Angeas and in the sight of his people, and Zepho was captain of the host to Angeas king of Africa for many days. [4] And Zepho enticed Angeas king of Africa to collect all his army to go and fight with the Egyptians and with the sons of Jacob, and to avenge of them the cause of his brothers. [5] But Angeas would not listen to Zepho to do this thing, for Angeas knew the strength of the sons of Jacob and what they had done to his army in their warfare with the children of Esau. [6] And Zepho was very great in those days in the sight of Angeas and in the sight of all his people, and he continually enticed them to make war against Egypt, but they would not. [7] And it came to pass in those days there was in the land of Chittim a man in the city of Puzimna whose name was Uzu, and he became degenerately deified by the children of Chittim, and the man died and had no son, only one daughter whose name was Jania. [8] And the young woman was exceedingly attractive, beautiful and intelligent, there was none seen like to her for beauty and wisdom throughout the land. [9] And the people of Angeas king of Africa saw her and they came and praised her to him, and Angeas sent to the children of Chittim, and he requested to take her to himself for a wife, and the people of Chittim consented to give her to him for a wife. [10] And when the messengers of Angeas were going out from the land of Chittim to take their journey, behold, the messengers of Turnus king of Bibentu came to Chittim, for Turnus king of Bibentu also sent his messengers to request Jania for him, to take to himself for a wife, for all his men had also praised her to him, therefore he sent all his servants to her. [11] And the servants of Turnus came to Chittim, and they asked for Jania to be taken to Turnus, their king, for a wife. [12] And the people of Chittim said to them, "We cannot give her, because Angeas king of Africa desired her to take her to himself for a wife before you came, and that we should give her to him, and now therefore, we cannot do this thing to deprive Angeas of the young woman in order to give her to Turnus. [13] For we are greatly afraid of Angeas lest he come in battle against us and destroy us, and your master Turnus will not be able to deliver us from his hand." [14] And when the messengers of Turnus heard all the words of the children of Chittim, they turned back to their master and told him all the words of the children of Chittim. [15] And the children of Chittim sent a memorial to Angeas, saying, "Behold, Turnus has sent for Jania to take her to himself for a wife, and thus we have answered him; and we heard that he has collected his whole army to go to war against you, and he intends to pass by the road of Sardunia to fight against your brother Lucus, and after that he will come to fight against you." [16] And Angeas heard the words of the children of Chittim which they sent to him in the record, and his anger was kindled, and he rose up and assembled his whole army, and he came through the islands of the sea, the road to Sardunia, to his brother Lucus king of Sardunia. [17] And Niblos, the son of Lucus, heard that his uncle Angeas was coming, and he went out to meet him with a heavy army, and he kissed him and embraced him, and Niblos said to Angeas, "When you ask my father after his welfare, when I will go with you to fight with Turnus, ask of him to make me captain of his host," and Angeas did so, and he came to his brother and his brother came to meet him, and he asked him after his welfare. [18] And Angeas asked his brother Lucus after his

welfare, and to make his son Niblos captain of his host, and Lucus did so, and Angeas and his brother Lucus rose up and they went toward Turnus to battle, and there was with them a great army and a heavy people. ¹⁹ And he came in ships, and they came into the province of Ashtorash, and behold, Turnus came toward them, for he went out to Sardunia, and intended to destroy it and afterward to pass on from there to Angeas to fight with him. ²⁰ And Angeas and his brother Lucus met Turnus in the Valley of Canopia, and the battle was strong and mighty between them in that place. ²¹ And the battle was severe on Lucus king of Sardunia, and all his army fell, and his son Niblos also fell in that battle. ²² And his uncle Angeas commanded his servants, and they made a golden coffin for Niblos, and they put him into it, and Angeas again waged battle toward Turnus, and Angeas was stronger than he, and he slew him, and he struck all his people with the edge of the sword, and Angeas avenged the cause of his brother's son Niblos and the cause of the army of his brother Lucus. ²³ And when Turnus died, the hands of those that survived the battle became weak, and they fled from before Angeas and his brother Lucus. ²⁴ And Angeas and his brother Lucus pursued them to the high road, which is between Alphanu and Romah, and they slew the whole army of Turnus with the edge of the sword. ²⁵ And Lucus king of Sardunia commanded his servants that they should make a coffin of brass, and that they should place therein the body of his son Niblos, and they buried him in that place. ²⁶ And they built a high tower on it there on the high road, and they called its name after the name of Niblos to this day, and they also buried Turnus king of Bibentu there in that place with Niblos. ²⁷ And behold, on the high road between Alphanu and Romah the grave of Niblos is on one side and the grave of Turnus on the other, and [there is] a pavement between them to this day. ²⁸ And when Niblos was buried, his father Lucus returned with his army to his land, Sardunia, and his brother Angeas, king of Africa, went with his people to the city of Bibentu, that is the city of Turnus. ²⁹ And the inhabitants of Bibentu heard of his fame, and they were greatly afraid of him, and they went out to meet him with weeping and supplication, and the inhabitants of Bibentu entreated of Angeas not to slay them nor destroy their city; and he did so, for Bibentu was reckoned as one of the cities of the children of Chittim in those days; therefore he did not destroy the city. ³⁰ But from that day forward the troops of the king of Africa would go to Chittim to spoil and plunder it, and whenever they went, Zepho the captain of the host of Angeas would go with them. ³¹ And it was after this that Angeas turned with his army and they came to the city of Puzimna, and Angeas took Jania the daughter of Uzu from there for a wife and brought her to his city, to Africa.

CHAPTER 61

¹ And it came to pass at that time, Pharaoh king of Egypt commanded all his people to make a strong palace in Egypt for him. ² And he also commanded the sons of Jacob to assist the Egyptians in the building, and the Egyptians made a beautiful and elegant palace for a royal habitation, and he dwelt therein, and he renewed his government and reigned securely. ³ And Zebulun the son of Jacob died in that year, that is the seventy-second year of the going down of the Israelites to Egypt, and Zebulun died one hundred and fourteen years old, and was put into a coffin and given into the hands of his children. ⁴ And in the seventy-fifth year his brother Simeon died; he was one hundred and twenty years old at his death, and he was also put into a coffin and given into the hands of his children. ⁵ And Zepho the son of Eliphaz, the son of Esau, captain of the host to Angeas king of Dinhabah, was still daily enticing Angeas to prepare for battle to fight with the sons of Jacob in Egypt, and Angeas was unwilling to do this thing, for his servants had related to him all the might of the sons of Jacob, what they had done to them in their battle with the children of Esau. ⁶ And Zepho was enticing Angeas daily in those days to fight with the sons of Jacob in those days. ⁷ And after some time Angeas listened to the words of Zepho and consented to him to fight with the sons of Jacob in Egypt, and Angeas got all his people in order, a people [as] numerous as the sand which is on the seashore, and he formed his resolution to go to Egypt to battle. ⁸ And among the servants of Angeas was a youth fifteen years old, Balaam the son of Beor was his name, and the youth was very wise and understood the art of witchcraft. ⁹ And Angeas said to Balaam, "Please conjure for us with the witchcraft that we may know who will prevail in this battle to which we are now proceeding." ¹⁰ And Balaam ordered that they should bring him wax, and he made thereof the likeness of chariots and horsemen representing the army of Angeas and the army of Egypt, and he put them in the cunningly prepared waters that he had for that purpose, and he took the boughs of myrtle trees in his hand, and he exercised his cunning, and he joined them over the water, and there appeared to him in the water the resembling images of the hosts of Angeas falling before the resembling images of the Egyptians and the sons of Jacob. ¹¹ And Balaam told this thing to Angeas, and Angeas despaired and did not arm himself to go down to Egypt to battle, and he remained in his city. ¹² And when Zepho the son of Eliphaz saw that Angeas despaired of going out to battle with the Egyptians, Zepho fled from Angeas from Africa, and he went and came to Chittim. ¹³ And all the people of Chittim received him with great honor, and they hired him to fight their battles all the days, and Zepho became exceedingly rich in those days, and the troops of the king of Africa still spread themselves in those days,

and the children of Chittim assembled and went to Mount Cuptizia on account of the troops of Angeas, king of Africa, who were advancing on them. [14] And it was one day that Zepho lost a young heifer, and he went to seek it, and he heard it lowing around the mountain. [15] And Zepho went, and he saw, and behold, there was a large cave at the bottom of the mountain, and there was a great stone there at the entrance of the cave, and Zepho split the stone, and he came into the cave, and he looked, and behold, a large animal was devouring the ox; from the middle upward it resembled a man, and from the middle downward it resembled an animal, and Zepho rose up against the animal and slew it with his swords. [16] And the inhabitants of Chittim heard of this thing, and they rejoiced exceedingly, and they said, "What will we do to this man who has slain this animal that devoured our cattle?" [17] And they all assembled to consecrate one day in the year to him, and they called the name thereof Zepho after his name, and they brought drink offerings to him year after year on that day, and they brought gifts to him. [18] At that time Jania the daughter of Uzu, wife of King Angeas, became sick, and her sickness was heavily felt by Angeas and his officers, and Angeas said to his wise men, "What will I do to Jania and how will I heal her from her sickness?" And his wise men said to him, "Because the air of our country is not like the air of the land of Chittim, and our water is not like their water, therefore the queen has become sick from this. [19] For through the change of air and water she became sick, and also because in her country she only drank the water which came from Purmah, which her ancestors had brought up with bridges." [20] And Angeas commanded his servants, and they brought to him in vessels of the waters of Purmah belonging to Chittim, and they weighed those waters with all the waters of the land of Africa, and they found those waters lighter than the waters of Africa. [21] And Angeas saw this thing, and he commanded all his officers to assemble the hewers of stone in thousands and tens of thousands, and they hewed stone without number, and the builders came and they built an exceedingly strong bridge, and they transported the spring of water from the land of Chittim to Africa, and those waters were for Jania the queen and for all her concerns, to drink from and to bake, wash and bathe with [them], and also to water with [them] all seed from which food can be obtained, and all fruit of the ground. [22] And the king commanded that they should bring of the soil of Chittim in large ships, and they also brought stones to build with, and the builders built palaces for Jania the queen, and the queen became healed of her sickness. [23] And at the revolution of the year the troops of Africa continued coming to the land of Chittim to plunder as usual, and Zepho son of Eliphaz heard their report, and he gave orders concerning them, and he fought with them, and they fled before him, and he delivered the land of Chittim from them. [24] And the children of Chittim saw the valor of Zepho, and the children of Chittim resolved and they made Zepho king over them, and he became king over them, and while he reigned, they went to subdue the children of Tubal, and all the surrounding islands. [25] And their king, Zepho, went at their head, and they made war with Tubal and the islands and subdued them, and when they returned from the battle they renewed his government for him, and they built a very large palace for him for his royal habitation and seat, and they made a large throne for him, and Zepho reigned over the whole land of Chittim and over the land of Italia [for] fifty years.

CHAPTER 62

[1] In that year, being the seventy-ninth year of the Israelites going down to Egypt, Reuben the son of Jacob died in the land of Egypt; Reuben was one hundred and twenty-five years old when he died, and they put him into a coffin, and he was given into the hands of his children. [2] And in the eightieth year his brother Dan died; he was one hundred and twenty years [old] at his death, and he was also put into a coffin and given into the hands of his children. [3] And in that year Chusham king of Edom died, and Hadad the son of Bedad reigned after him for thirty-five years; and in the eighty-first year Issachar the son of Jacob died in Egypt, and Issachar was one hundred and twenty-two years old at his death, and he was put into a coffin in Egypt and given into the hands of his children. [4] And in the eighty-second year his brother Asher died; he was one hundred and twenty-three years old at his death, and he was placed in a coffin in Egypt and given into the hands of his children. [5] And in the eighty-third year Gad died; he was one hundred and twenty-five years old at his death, and he was put into a coffin in Egypt, and given into the hands of his children. [6] And it came to pass in the eighty-fourth year, that is the fiftieth year of the reign of Hadad son of Bedad, king of Edom, that Hadad assembled all the children of Esau, and he got his whole army in readiness, about four hundred thousand men, and he directed his way to the land of Moab, and he went to fight with Moab and to make them tributary to him. [7] And the children of Moab heard this thing, and they were very much afraid, and they sent to the children of Midian to assist them in fighting with Hadad son of Bedad, king of Edom. [8] And Hadad came to the land of Moab, and Moab and the children of Midian went out to meet him, and they placed themselves in battle array against him in the field of Moab. [9] And Hadad fought with Moab, and there fell of the children of Moab and the children of Midian many slain ones, about two hundred thousand men. [10] And the battle was very severe on Moab, and when the children of Moab saw that the battle was severe on them, they weakened their hands, and

turned their backs, and left the children of Midian to carry on the battle. [11] And the children of Midian did not know the intentions of Moab, but they strengthened themselves in battle and fought with Hadad and all his host, and all Midian fell before him. [12] And Hadad struck all Midian with a heavy striking, and he slew them with the edge of the sword; he left none remaining of those who came to assist Moab. [13] And when all the children of Midian had perished in battle and the children at Moab had escaped, Hadad made all Moab tributary to him at that time, and they came under his hand, and they gave a yearly tax as it was ordered, and Hadad turned and went back to his land. [14] And at the revolution of the year, when the rest of the people of Midian that were in the land heard that all their brothers had fallen in battle with Hadad for the sake of Moab, because the children of Moab had turned their backs in battle and left Midian to fight, then five of the princes of Midian resolved with the rest of their brothers who remained in their land to fight with Moab to avenge the cause of their brothers. [15] And the children of Midian sent to all their brothers, the children of the east, and all their brothers; all the children of Keturah came to assist Midian to fight with Moab. [16] And the children of Moab heard this thing, and they were greatly afraid that all the children of the east had assembled together against them for battle, and they, the children of Moab, sent a memorial to the land of Edom to Hadad the son of Bedad, saying, [17] "Come to us now, and assist us, and we will strike Midian, for they all assembled together and have come against us with all their brothers, the children of the east, to battle, to avenge the cause of Midian that fell in battle." [18] And Hadad son of Bedad, king of Edom, went out with his whole army and went to the land of Moab to fight with Midian, and Midian and the children of the east fought with Moab in the field of Moab, and the battle was very fierce between them. [19] And Hadad struck all the children of Midian and the children of the east with the edge of the sword, and at that time Hadad delivered Moab from the hand of Midian, and those that remained of Midian and of the children of the east fled before Hadad and his army, and Hadad pursued them to their land, and struck them with a very heavy slaughter, and the slain fell in the road. [20] And Hadad delivered Moab from the hand of Midian, for all the children of Midian had fallen by the edge of the sword, and Hadad turned and went back to his land. [21] And from that day forward the children of Midian hated the children of Moab, because they had fallen in battle for their sake, and there was a great and mighty enmity between them all the days. [22] And all that were found of Midian in the road of the land of Moab perished by the sword of Moab, and all that were found of Moab in the road of the land of Midian perished by the sword of Midian; thus Midian did to Moab and Moab to Midian for many days. [23] And it came to pass at that time that Judah the son of Jacob died in Egypt, in the eighty-sixth year of Jacob's going down to Egypt, and Judah was one hundred and twenty-nine years old at his death, and they embalmed him and put him into a coffin, and he was given into the hands of his children. [24] And in the eighty-ninth year Naphtali died; he was one hundred and thirty-two years old, and he was put into a coffin, and given into the hands of his children. [25] And it came to pass in the ninety-first year of the Israelites going down to Egypt, that is in the thirtieth year of the reign of Zepho the son of Eliphaz, the son of Esau, over the children of Chittim, the children of Africa came on the children of Chittim to plunder them as usual, but they had not come on them for these thirteen years. [26] And they came to them in that year, and Zepho the son of Eliphaz went out to them with some of his men and struck them desperately, and the troops of Africa fled from before Zepho and the slain fell before him, and Zepho and his men pursued them, going on and striking them until they were near to Africa. [27] And Angeas king of Africa heard the thing which Zepho had done, and it vexed him exceedingly, and Angeas was afraid of Zepho all the days.

CHAPTER 63

[1] And in the ninety-third year Levi the son of Jacob died in Egypt, and Levi was one hundred and thirty-seven years old when he died, and they put him into a coffin, and he was given into the hands of his children. [2] And it came to pass after the death of Levi, when all Egypt saw that the sons of Jacob, the brothers of Joseph, were dead, all the Egyptians began to afflict the children of Jacob, and to embitter their lives from that day to the day of their going out from Egypt, and they took from their hands all the vineyards and fields which Joseph had given to them, and all the elegant houses in which the people of Israel lived, and all the fat of Egypt; the Egyptians took everything from the sons of Jacob in those days. [3] And the hand of all Egypt became more grievous in those days against the sons of Israel, and the Egyptians injured the Israelites until the sons of Israel were wearied of their lives on account of the Egyptians. [4] And it came to pass in those days, in the one hundred and second year of Israel's going down to Egypt, that Pharaoh king of Egypt died, and his son Melol reigned in his stead, and all the mighty men of Egypt and all that generation which knew Joseph and his brothers died in those days. [5] And another generation rose up in their stead, which had not known the sons of Jacob, and all the good which they had done to them, and all their might in Egypt. [6] Therefore all Egypt began from that day out to embitter the lives of the sons of Jacob and to afflict them with all manner of hard labor, because they had not known their ancestors who had delivered them in the days of the famine. [7] And this was also from the

LORD, for the sons of Israel, to benefit them in their latter days, in order that all the sons of Israel might know the LORD their God, [8] and in order to know the signs and mighty wonders which the LORD would do in Egypt on account of His people Israel, in order that the sons of Israel might fear the LORD God of their ancestors and walk in all His ways—they and their seed after them [for] all the days. [9] Melol was twenty years old when he began to reign, and he reigned ninety-four years, and all Egypt called his name Pharaoh after the name of his father as it was their custom to do to every king who reigned over them in Egypt. [10] At that time all the troops of Angeas king of Africa went out to spread along the land of Chittim as usual for plunder. [11] And Zepho the son of Eliphaz, the son of Esau, heard their report, and he went out to meet them with his army, and he fought them there in the road. [12] And Zepho struck the troops of the king of Africa with the edge of the sword and left none remaining of them, and not even one returned to his master in Africa. [13] And Angeas heard of this which Zepho the son of Eliphaz had done to all his troops, that he had destroyed them, and Angeas assembled all his troops, all the men of the land of Africa, a people numerous like the sand by the seashore. [14] And Angeas sent to his brother Lucus, saying, "Come to me with all your men and help me to strike Zepho and all the children of Chittim who have destroyed my men," and Lucus came with his whole army, a very great force, to assist his brother Angeas to fight with Zepho and the children of Chittim. [15] And Zepho and the children of Chittim heard this thing, and they were greatly afraid, and a great terror fell on their hearts. [16] And Zepho also sent a letter to the land of Edom to Hadad the son of Bedad king of Edom and to all the children of Esau, saying, [17] "I have heard that Angeas king of Africa is coming to us with his brother for battle against us, and we are greatly afraid of him, for his army is very great, particularly as he comes against us with his brother and his army likewise. [18] Now therefore, come up with me also and help me, and we will fight together against Angeas and his brother Lucus, and you will save us out of their hands, but if not, know that we will all die." [19] And the children of Esau sent a letter to the children of Chittim and to Zepho their king, saying, "We cannot fight against Angeas and his people for a covenant of peace has been between us these many years, from the days of Bela the first king, and from the days of Joseph the son of Jacob, king of Egypt, with whom we fought on the other side of the Jordan when he buried his father." [20] And when Zepho heard the words of his brothers, the children of Esau, he refrained from them, and Zepho was greatly afraid of Angeas. [21] And Angeas and his brother Lucus arrayed all their forces, about eight hundred thousand men, against the children of Chittim. [22] And all the children of Chittim said to Zepho, "Pray for us to the God of your ancestors; perhaps He may deliver us from the hand of Angeas and his army, for we have heard that He is a great God and that He delivers all who trust in Him." [23] And Zepho heard their words, and Zepho sought the LORD, and he said, [24] "O LORD God of my ancestors Abraham and Isaac, this day I know that you are a true God, and all the gods of the nations are vain and useless. [25] Now this day remember for me Your covenant with our father Abraham, which our ancestors related to us, and do graciously with me this day for the sake of our fathers Abraham and Isaac, and save me and the children of Chittim from the hand of the king of Africa who comes against us for battle." [26] And the LORD listened to the voice of Zepho, and He had regard for him on account of Abraham and Isaac, and the LORD delivered Zepho and the children of Chittim from the hand of Angeas and his people. [27] And Zepho fought Angeas king of Africa and all his people on that day, and the LORD gave all the people of Angeas into the hands of the children of Chittim. [28] And the battle was severe on Angeas, and Zepho struck all the men of Angeas and his brother Lucus with the edge of the sword, and there fell from them to the evening of that day about four hundred thousand men. [29] And when Angeas saw that all his men perished, he sent a letter to all the inhabitants of Africa to come to him, to assist him in the battle, and he wrote in the letter, saying, "Let all who are found in Africa come to me from ten years old and upward; let them all come to me, and behold, if he does not come, he will die, and the king will take all that he has, with his whole household." [30] And all the rest of the inhabitants of Africa were terrified at the words of Angeas, and there went out of the city about three hundred thousand men and boys, from ten years upward, and they came to Angeas. [31] And at the end of ten days Angeas renewed the battle against Zepho and the children of Chittim, and the battle was very great and strong between them. [32] And from the army of Angeas and Lucus, Zepho sent many of the wounded to his hand, about two thousand men, and Sosiphtar, the captain of the host of Angeas, fell in that battle. [33] And when Sosiphtar had fallen, the African troops turned their backs to flee, and they fled, and Angeas and his brother Lucus were with them. [34] And Zepho and the children of Chittim pursued them, and they struck them still heavily on the road, about two hundred men, and they pursued Azdrubal the son of Angeas who had fled with his father, and they struck twenty of his men in the road, and Azdrubal escaped from the children of Chittim, and they did not slay him. [35] And Angeas and his brother Lucus fled with the rest of their men, and they escaped and came into Africa with terror and consternation, and Angeas feared all the days lest Zepho the son of Eliphaz should go to war with him.

JASHER

CHAPTER 64

¹ And at that time Balaam the son of Beor was with Angeas in the battle, and when he saw that Zepho prevailed over Angeas, he fled from there and came to Chittim. ² And Zepho and the children of Chittim received him with great honor, for Zepho knew Balaam's wisdom, and Zepho gave many gifts to Balaam and he remained with him. ³ And when Zepho had returned from the war, he commanded all the children of Chittim to be numbered who had gone into battle with him, and behold, not one was missed. ⁴ And Zepho rejoiced at this thing, and he renewed his kingdom, and he made a feast to all his subjects. ⁵ But Zepho did not remember the LORD and did not consider that the LORD had helped him in battle and that He had delivered him and his people from the hand of the king of Africa, but still walked in the ways of the children of Chittim and the wicked children of Esau to serve other gods which his brothers, the children of Esau, had taught him; it is therefore said, "From the wicked goes out wickedness." ⁶ And Zepho reigned over all the children of Chittim securely, but did not know the LORD who had delivered him and all his people from the hand of the king of Africa; and the troops of Africa no longer came to Chittim to plunder as usual, for they knew of the power of Zepho who had smitten them all at the edge of the sword, so Angeas was afraid of Zepho the son of Eliphaz and of the children of Chittim [for] all the days. ⁷ At that time, when Zepho had returned from the war, and when Zepho had seen how he prevailed over all the people of Africa and had smitten them in battle at the edge of the sword, then Zepho advised with the children of Chittim to go to Egypt to fight with the sons of Jacob and with Pharaoh king of Egypt, ⁸ for Zepho heard that the mighty men of Egypt were dead, and that Joseph and his brothers, the sons at Jacob, were dead, and that all their children, the sons of Israel, remained in Egypt. ⁹ And Zepho considered to go to fight against them and all Egypt, to avenge the cause of his brothers, the children of Esau, whom Joseph with his brothers and all Egypt had smitten in the land of Canaan when they went up to bury Jacob in Hebron. ¹⁰ And Zepho sent messengers to Hadad son of Bedad, king of Edom, and to all his brothers, the children of Esau, saying, ¹¹ "Did you not say that you would not fight against the king of Africa, for he is a member of your covenant? Behold, I fought with him and struck him and all his people. ¹² Now therefore, I have resolved to fight against Egypt and the children of Jacob who are there, and I will be revenged of them for what Joseph, his brothers, and [his] ancestors did to us in the land of Canaan when they went up to bury their father in Hebron. ¹³ Now then, if you are willing to come to me to assist me in fighting against them and Egypt, then we will avenge the cause of our brothers." ¹⁴ And the children of Esau listened to the words of Zepho, and the children of

Esau gathered themselves together, a very great people, and they went to assist Zepho and the children of Chittim in battle. ¹⁵ And Zepho sent to all the children of the east and to all the children of Ishmael with words like to these, and they gathered themselves and came to the assistance of Zepho and the children of Chittim in the war on Egypt. ¹⁶ And all these kings, the king of Edom, and the children of the east, and all the children of Ishmael, and Zepho the king of Chittim went out and arrayed all their hosts in Hebron. ¹⁷ And the camp was very heavy, extending in length a distance of three days' journey, a people [as] numerous as the sand on the seashore which cannot be counted. ¹⁸ And all these kings and their hosts went down, and came against all Egypt in battle, and encamped together in the Valley of Pathros. ¹⁹ And all Egypt heard their report, and they also gathered themselves together, all the people of the land of Egypt, and of all the cities belonging to Egypt, about three hundred thousand men. ²⁰ And the men of Egypt also sent to the sons of Israel who were in the land of Goshen in those days to come to them in order to go and fight with these kings. ²¹ And the men of Israel assembled and were about one hundred and fifty men, and they went into battle to assist the Egyptians. ²² And the men of Israel and of Egypt went out, about three hundred thousand men and one hundred and fifty men, and they went toward these kings to battle, and they placed themselves from outside the land of Goshen opposite Pathros. ²³ And the Egyptians did not believe in Israel to go with them in their camps together for battle, for all the Egyptians said, "Perhaps the sons of Israel will deliver us into the hand of the children of Esau and Ishmael, for they are their brothers." ²⁴ And all the Egyptians said to the sons of Israel, "Remain together here in your position and we will go and fight against the children of Esau and Ishmael, and if these kings should prevail over us, then come altogether on them and assist us," and the sons of Israel did so. ²⁵ And Zepho the son of Eliphaz, the son of Esau, king of Chittim, and Hadad the son of Bedad, king of Edom, and all their camps, and all the children of the east, and children of Ishmael, a people [as] numerous as sand, encamped together in the Valley of Pathros opposite Tachpanches. ²⁶ And Balaam the son of Beor, the Syrian, was there in the camp of Zepho, for he came with the children of Chittim to the battle, and Balaam was a man highly honored in the eyes of Zepho and his men. ²⁷ And Zepho said to Balaam, "Try by divination for us that we may know who will prevail in the battle—we or the Egyptians." ²⁸ And Balaam rose up and tried the art of divination, and he was skillful in the knowledge of it, but he was confused and the work was destroyed in his hand. ²⁹ And he tried it again, but it did not succeed, and Balaam despaired of it, and left it, and did not complete it, for this was from the LORD in order to cause Zepho and

~ 422 ~

his people to fall into the hand of the sons of Israel who had trusted in the LORD, the God of their ancestors, in their war. ³⁰ And Zepho and Hadad put their forces in battle array, and all the Egyptians went alone against them, about three hundred thousand men, and not one man of Israel was with them. ³¹ And all the Egyptians fought with these kings opposite Pathros and Tachpanches, and the battle was severe against the Egyptians. ³² And the kings were stronger than the Egyptians in that battle, and about one hundred and eighty men of Egypt fell on that day, and about thirty men of the forces of the kings, and all the men of Egypt fled from before the kings, so the children of Esau and Ishmael pursued the Egyptians, continuing to strike them to the place where the camp of the sons of Israel was. ³³ And all the Egyptians cried to the sons of Israel, saying, "Hasten to us, and assist us, and save us from the hand of Esau, Ishmael, and the children of Chittim." ³⁴ And the one hundred and fifty men of the sons of Israel ran from their station to the camps of these kings, and the sons of Israel cried to the LORD their God to deliver them. ³⁵ And the LORD listened to Israel, and the LORD gave all the men of the kings into their hand, and the sons of Israel fought against these kings, and the sons of Israel struck about four thousand of the kings' men. ³⁶ And the LORD threw a great consternation in the camp of the kings, so that the fear of the sons of Israel fell on them. ³⁷ And all the hosts of the kings fled from before the sons of Israel, and the sons of Israel pursued them, continuing to strike them to the borders of the land of Cush. ³⁸ And the sons of Israel slew of them in the road yet two thousand [more] men, and not one of the sons of Israel fell. ³⁹ And when the Egyptians saw that the sons of Israel had fought with the kings with such few men, and that the battle was so very severe against them, ⁴⁰ all the Egyptians were greatly afraid for their lives on account of the strong battle, and all Egypt fled, every man hiding himself from the arrayed forces, and they hid themselves in the road, and they left the Israelites to fight. ⁴¹ And the sons of Israel inflicted a terrible blow on the kings' men, and they returned from them after they had driven them to the border of the land of Cush. ⁴² And all Israel knew the thing which the men of Egypt had done to them, that they had fled from them in battle and had left them to fight alone, ⁴³ so the sons of Israel also acted with cunning, and as the sons of Israel returned from battle, they found some of the Egyptians in the road and struck them there. ⁴⁴ And while they slew them, they said to them these words: ⁴⁵ "Why did you go from us and leave us, being a few people, to fight against these kings who had a great people to strike us, that you might thereby deliver your own souls?" ⁴⁶ And of some which the Israelites met on the road, they, the sons of Israel, spoke to each other, saying, "Strike, strike, for he is an Ishmaelite, or an Edomite, or from the children of Chittim!" And they stood over

him and slew him, and they knew that he was an Egyptian. ⁴⁷ And the sons of Israel did these things cunningly against the Egyptians, because they had deserted them in battle and had fled from them. ⁴⁸ And the sons of Israel slew of the men of Egypt in the road in this manner about two hundred men. ⁴⁹ And all the men of Egypt saw the evil which the sons of Israel had done to them, so all Egypt feared the sons of Israel greatly, for they had seen their great power and that not one man of them had fallen. ⁵⁰ So all the sons of Israel returned with joy on their road to Goshen, and the rest of Egypt returned—each man to his place.

CHAPTER 65

¹ And it came to pass after these things that all the counselors of Pharaoh, king of Egypt, and all the elders of Egypt assembled, and came before the king, and bowed down to the ground, and they sat before him. ² And the counselors and elders of Egypt spoke to the king, saying, ³ "Behold, the people of the sons of Israel are greater and mightier than we are, and you know all the evil which they did to us in the road when we returned from battle. ⁴ And you have also seen their strong power, for this power is to them from their fathers, for but a few men stood up against a people [as] numerous as the sand and struck them at the edge of the sword, and not one of them has fallen, so that if they had been numerous, they would then have utterly destroyed them. ⁵ Now therefore, give us counsel [regarding] what to do with them until we gradually destroy them from among us, lest they become too numerous for us in the land. ⁶ For if the sons of Israel should increase in the land, they will become an obstacle to us, and if any war should happen to take place, they will join our enemy against us with their great strength and fight against us, destroy us from the land, and go away from it." ⁷ So the king answered the elders of Egypt and said to them, "This is the plan advised against Israel, from which we will not depart: ⁸ behold, Pithom and Rameses are in the land, cities unfortified against battle; it is necessary for you and us to build them and to fortify them. ⁹ Now therefore, go also, and act cunningly toward them, and proclaim a voice in Egypt and in Goshen at the command of the king, saying, ¹⁰ All you men of Egypt, Goshen, Pathros, and all their inhabitants: the king has commanded us to build Pithom and Rameses and to fortify them for battle; who among you of all Egypt, of the sons of Israel and of all the inhabitants of the cities, are willing to build with us, will each have his wages given to him daily at the king's order; so first go and do cunningly, and gather yourselves, and come to Pithom and Rameses to build. ¹¹ And while you are building, cause a proclamation of this kind to be made throughout Egypt every day at the command of the king. ¹² And when some of the sons of Israel will come to build with you, you will give them their wages

daily for a few days. [13] And after they will have built with you for their daily hire, drag yourselves away from them daily one by one in secret, and then you will rise up and become their taskmasters and officers, and afterward you will leave them to build without wages, and should they refuse, then force them with all your might to build. [14] And if you do this, it will be well with us to strengthen our land against the sons of Israel, for on account of the fatigue of the building and the work, the sons of Israel will decrease, because you will deprive them from their wives day by day." [15] And all the elders of Egypt heard the counsel of the king, and the counsel seemed good in their eyes, and in the eyes of the servants of Pharaoh, and in the eyes of all Egypt, and they did according to the word of the king. [16] And all the servants went away from the king, and they caused a proclamation to be made in all Egypt, in Tachpanches, and in Goshen, and in all the cities which surrounded Egypt, saying, [17] "You have seen what the children of Esau and Ishmael did to us, who came to war against us and wished to destroy us. [18] Now therefore, the king commanded us to fortify the land, to build the cities [of] Pithom and Rameses, and to fortify them for battle if they should come against us again. [19] Whoever of you from all Egypt and from the sons of Israel will come to build with us, he will have his daily wages given by the king as his command is to us." [20] And when Egypt and all the sons of Israel heard all that the servants of Pharaoh had spoken, [many] came from the Egyptians and the sons of Israel to build Pithom and Rameses with the servants of Pharaoh, but none of the children of Levi came with their brothers to build. [21] And all the servants of Pharaoh and his princes came at first with deceit to build with all Israel as daily hired laborers, and they gave to Israel their daily hire at the beginning. [22] And the servants of Pharaoh built with all Israel and were employed in that work with Israel for a month. [23] And at the end of the month, all the servants of Pharaoh began to withdraw secretly from the people of Israel daily. [24] And Israel went on with the work at that time, but they received their daily hire then, because some of the men of Egypt were yet carrying on the work with Israel at that time; therefore, the Egyptians gave Israel their hire in those days in order that they, the Egyptians, their fellow-workmen, might also take the pay for their labor. [25] And at the end of a year and four months all the Egyptians had withdrawn from the sons of Israel, so that the sons of Israel were left alone engaged in the work. [26] And after all the Egyptians had withdrawn from the sons of Israel they returned and became oppressors and officers over them, and some of them stood over the sons of Israel as taskmasters to receive from them all that they gave them for the pay of their labor. [27] And the Egyptians did in this manner to the sons of Israel day by day in order to afflict [them] in their work. [28] And all the sons of Israel were engaged in the labor alone, and the Egyptians refrained from giving any pay to the sons of Israel from that time forward. [29] And when some of the men of Israel refused to work on account of the wages not being given to them, then the exactors and the servants of Pharaoh oppressed them, and struck them with heavy blows, and made them return by force to labor with their brothers; thus all the Egyptians did to the sons of Israel all the days. [30] And all the sons of Israel were greatly afraid of the Egyptians in this matter, and all the sons of Israel returned and worked alone without pay. [31] And the sons of Israel built Pithom and Rameses, and all the sons of Israel did the work, some making bricks and some building, and the sons of Israel built and fortified all the land of Egypt and its walls, and the sons of Israel were engaged in work for many years until the time came when the LORD remembered them and brought them out of Egypt. [32] But the children of Levi were not employed in the work with their brothers of Israel from the beginning to the day of their going out from Egypt. [33] For all the children of Levi knew that the Egyptians had spoken all these words with deceit to the Israelites, therefore the children of Levi refrained from approaching to the work with their brothers. [34] And the Egyptians did not direct their attention to make the children of Levi work afterward since they had not been with their brothers at the beginning; therefore the Egyptians left them alone. [35] And the hands of the men of Egypt were directed with continued severity against the sons of Israel in that work, and the Egyptians made the sons of Israel work with rigor. [36] And the Egyptians embittered the lives of the sons of Israel with hard work in mortar and bricks, and also in all manner of work in the field. [37] And the sons of Israel called Melol, the king of Egypt, "Meror, king of Egypt," because in his days the Egyptians had embittered their lives with all manner of work. [38] And all the work wherein the Egyptians made the sons of Israel labor, they exacted with rigor in order to afflict the sons of Israel, but the more they afflicted them, the more they increased and grew, and the Egyptians were grieved because of the sons of Israel.

CHAPTER 66

[1] At that time Hadad the son of Bedad, king of Edom, died, and Samlah from Mesrekah, from the country of the children of the east, reigned in his place. [2] In the thirteenth year of the reign of Pharaoh king of Egypt, which was the one hundred and twenty-fifth year of the Israelites going down into Egypt, Samlah had reigned over Edom eighteen years. [3] And when he reigned, he drew out his hosts to go and fight against Zepho the son of Eliphaz and the children of Chittim, because they had made war against Angeas king of Africa and had destroyed his whole army. [4] But he did not engage with him, for the children of Esau

prevented him, saying, "He was their brother," so Samlah listened to the voice of the children of Esau, and turned back with all his forces to the land of Edom, and did not proceed to fight against Zepho the son of Eliphaz. [5] And Pharaoh king of Egypt heard this thing, saying, "Samlah king of Edom has resolved to fight the children of Chittim, and afterward he will come to fight against Egypt." [6] And when the Egyptians heard this matter, they increased the labor on the sons of Israel, lest the Israelites should do to them as they did to them in their war with the children of Esau in the days of Hadad. [7] So the Egyptians said to the sons of Israel, "Hasten and do your work, and finish your task, and strengthen the land, lest the children of Esau, your brothers, should come to fight against us, for they will come against us on your account." [8] And the sons of Israel did the work of the men of Egypt day by day, and the Egyptians afflicted the sons of Israel in order to lessen them in the land. [9] But as the Egyptians increased the labor on the sons of Israel, so the sons of Israel increased and multiplied, and all Egypt was filled with the sons of Israel. [10] And in the one hundred and twenty-fifth year of Israel's going down into Egypt, all the Egyptians saw that their counsel did not succeed against Israel, but that they increased and grew, and the land of Egypt and the land of Goshen were filled with the sons of Israel. [11] So all the elders of Egypt and its wise men came before the king, and bowed down to him, and sat before him. [12] And all the elders of Egypt and the wise men thereof said to the king, "May the king live forever; you counseled us the counsel against the sons of Israel, and we did to them according to the word of the king. [13] But in proportion to the increase of the labor so do they increase and grow in the land, and behold, the whole country is filled with them. [14] Now therefore, our lord and king, the eyes of all Egypt are on you to give them advice with your wisdom, by which they may prevail over Israel to destroy them or to diminish them from the land"; and the king answered them, saying, "Give counsel in this matter that we may know what to do to them." [15] And an officer, one of the king's counselors, whose name was Job, from Mesopotamia, in the land of Uz, answered the king, saying, [16] "If it pleases the king, let him hear the counsel of his servant"; and the king said to him, "Speak." [17] And Job spoke before the king, the princes, and before all the elders of Egypt, saying, [18] "Behold, the counsel of the king which he advised formerly respecting the labor of the sons of Israel is very good, and you must not ever remove that labor from them. [19] But this is the advice counseled by which you may lessen them if it seems good to the king to afflict them: [20] behold, we have feared war for a long time, and we said, When Israel becomes fruitful in the land, they will drive us from the land if a war should take place. [21] If it pleases the king, let a royal decree go out and let it be written

in the laws of Egypt, which will not be revoked, that every male child born to the Israelites, his blood will be spilled on the ground. [22] And by your doing this, when all the male sons of Israel will have died, the evil of their wars will cease; let the king do so, and send for all the Hebrew midwives and order them to execute it in this matter"; so the thing pleased the king and the princes, and the king did according to the word of Job. [23] And the king sent for the Hebrew midwives to be called, of which the name of one was Shephrah, and the name of the other Puah. [24] And the midwives came before the king and stood in his presence. [25] And the king said to them, "When you do the office of a midwife to the Hebrew women and see them on the stools, if it is a son, then you will kill him, but if it is a daughter, then she will live. [26] But if you will not do this thing, then I will burn you and all your houses up with fire." [27] But the midwives feared God and did not listen to the king of Egypt nor to his words, and when the Hebrew women brought out a son or daughter to the midwife, then the midwife did all that was necessary for the child and let it live; thus the midwives did all the days. [28] And this thing was told to the king, and he sent and called for the midwives, and he said to them, "Why have you done this thing and have saved the children alive?" [29] And the midwives answered and spoke together before the king, saying, [30] "Do not let the king think that the Hebrew women are as the Egyptian women, for all the sons of Israel are vigorous, and before the midwife comes to them they are delivered, and as for us, your handmaids, for many days no Hebrew woman has brought out on us, for all the Hebrew women are their own midwives, because they are vigorous." [31] And Pharaoh heard their words and believed them in this matter, and the midwives went away from the king, and God dealt well with them, and the people multiplied and waxed exceedingly.

CHAPTER 67

[1] There was a man in the land of Egypt of the seed of Levi, whose name was Amram the son of Kehas, the son of Levi, the son of Israel. [2] And this man went and took a wife, namely Jochebed the daughter of Levi, his father's sister, and she was one hundred and twenty-six years old, and he came to her. [3] And the woman conceived and bore a daughter, and she called her name Miriam, because in those days the Egyptians had embittered the lives of the sons of Israel. [4] And she conceived again, and bore a son, and she called his name Aaron, for in the days of her conception, Pharaoh began to spill the blood of the male sons of Israel. [5] In those days Zepho the son of Eliphaz, son of Esau, king of Chittim, died, and Janeas reigned in his stead. [6] And the time that Zepho reigned over the children of Chittim was fifty years, and he died and was buried in the city of Nabna in the land of Chittim. [7] And Janeas, one of the mighty men

of the children of Chittim, reigned after him and he reigned fifty years. ⁸ And it was after the death of the king of Chittim that Balaam the son of Beor fled from the land of Chittim, and he went and came to Egypt, to Pharaoh king of Egypt. ⁹ And Pharaoh received him with great honor, for he had heard of his wisdom, and he gave him presents, and made him for a counselor, and aggrandized him. ¹⁰ And Balaam dwelt in Egypt, in honor with all the nobles of the king, and the nobles exalted him, because they all coveted to learn his wisdom. ¹¹ And in the one hundred and thirtieth year of Israel's going down to Egypt, Pharaoh dreamed that he was sitting on his kingly throne, and he lifted up his eyes and saw an old man standing before him, and there were scales in the hands of the old man, such scales as are used by merchants. ¹² And the old man took the scales and hung them before Pharaoh. ¹³ And the old man took all the elders of Egypt and all its nobles and great men, and he tied them together and put them in one scale. ¹⁴ And he took a milk kid and put it into the other scale, and the kid exceeded over all. ¹⁵ And Pharaoh was astonished at this dreadful vision, why the kid should exceed over all, and Pharaoh awoke, and behold, it was a dream. ¹⁶ And Pharaoh rose up early in the morning, and called all his servants, and related the dream to them, and the men were greatly afraid. ¹⁷ And the king said to all his wise men, "Now interpret the dream which I dreamed [so] that I may know it." ¹⁸ And Balaam the son of Beor answered the king and said to him, "This means nothing else but [that] a great calamity that will spring up against Egypt in the latter days. ¹⁹ For a son will be born to Israel who will destroy all Egypt and its inhabitants and bring out the Israelites from Egypt with a mighty hand. ²⁰ Now therefore, O king, take counsel on this matter that you may destroy the hope of the sons of Israel and their expectation before this calamity arises against Egypt." ²¹ And the king said to Balaam, "And what will we do to Israel? Surely after a certain manner we at first counseled against them and could not prevail over them. ²² Now therefore, also give advice against them by which we may prevail over them." ²³ And Balaam answered the king, saying, "Send now and call your two counselors, and we will see what their advice is on this matter and afterward your servant will speak." ²⁴ And the king sent for and called his two counselors Reuel the Midianite and Job the Uzite, and they came and sat before the king. ²⁵ And the king said to them, "Behold, you have both heard the dream which I have dreamed and the interpretation thereof; now therefore, give counsel, and know, and see what is to be done to the sons of Israel whereby we may prevail over them before their evil will spring up against us." ²⁶ And Reuel the Midianite answered the king and said, "May the king live, may the king live forever. ²⁷ If it seems good to the king, let him desist from the Hebrews and leave them, and do not let him stretch out his hand against them. ²⁸ For these are they whom the LORD chose in days of old, and took as the lot of His inheritance from among all the nations of the earth and the kings of the earth; and who is there that stretched his hand against them with impunity, of whom their God was not avenged? ²⁹ Surely you know that when Abraham went down to Egypt, Pharaoh, the former king of Egypt, saw his wife Sarah and took her for a wife, because Abraham said, She is my sister, for he was afraid, lest the men of Egypt should slay him on account of his wife. ³⁰ And when the king of Egypt had taken Sarah, then God struck him and his household with heavy plagues until he restored to Abraham his wife Sarah—then he was healed. ³¹ And Abimelech the Gerarite, king of the Philistines, God punished on account of Sarah, [the] wife of Abraham, in stopping up every womb from man to beast ³² when their God came to Abimelech in the dream of night and terrified him in order that He might restore to Abraham Sarah whom he had taken, and afterward all the people of Gerar were punished on account of Sarah, and Abraham prayed to his God for them, and He was entreated by him, and He healed them. ³³ And Abimelech feared all this evil that came on him and his people, and he returned to Abraham his wife Sarah, and gave him many gifts with her. ³⁴ He also did so to Isaac when he had driven him from Gerar, and God had done wonderful things to him, that all the water courses of Gerar were dried up, and their productive trees did not bring out ³⁵ until Abimelech of Gerar, and Ahuzzath, one of his friends, and Pichol, the captain of his host, went to him, and bent, and bowed down to the ground before him. ³⁶ And they requested of him to supplicate for them, and he prayed to the LORD for them, and the LORD was entreated by him, and He healed them. ³⁷ Jacob also, the plain man, was delivered through his integrity from the hand of his brother Esau, and the hand of Laban the Syrian, his mother's brother, who had sought his life, [and] likewise from the hand of all the kings of Canaan who had come together against him and his children to destroy them, and the LORD delivered them out of their hands, that they turned on them and struck them, for who had ever stretched out his hand against them with impunity? ³⁸ Surely the former Pharaoh, your father's father, raised Joseph the son of Jacob above all the princes of the land of Egypt when he saw his wisdom, for through his wisdom he rescued all the inhabitants of the land from the famine, ³⁹ after which he ordered Jacob and his children to come down to Egypt in order that through their virtue the land of Egypt and the land of Goshen might be delivered from the famine. ⁴⁰ Now therefore, if it seems good in your eyes, cease from destroying the sons of Israel, but if it is not your will that they will dwell in Egypt, send them out from here [so] that they may go to the land of Canaan, the land where their ancestors sojourned." ⁴¹ And when Pharaoh heard the words of Jethro, he was very angry with him, so that he rose from the king's presence with shame, and went to Midian, his land, and took Joseph's stick with him. ⁴² And the king said to Job the Uzite, "What do you say, Job? And what is your advice respecting the Hebrews?" ⁴³ So Job said to the king, "Behold, all the inhabitants of the land are in your power: let the king do as it seems good in his eyes." ⁴⁴ And the king said to Balaam, "What do you say, Balaam? Speak your word [so] that we may hear it." ⁴⁵ And Balaam said to the king, "Of all that the king has counseled against the Hebrews they will be delivered, and the king will not be able to prevail over them with any counsel. ⁴⁶ For if you think to lessen them by the flaming fire, you cannot prevail over them, for surely their God delivered their father Abraham from Ur of the Chaldeans; and if you think to destroy them with a sword, surely their father Isaac was delivered from it, and a ram was placed in his stead. ⁴⁷ And if you think to lessen them with hard and rigorous labor, you will not prevail even in this, for their father Jacob served Laban in all manner of hard work and prospered. ⁴⁸ Now therefore, O king, hear my words, for this is the counsel which is counseled against them, by which you will prevail over them, and from which you should not depart: ⁴⁹ if it pleases the king, let him order all their children which will be born from this day forward to be thrown into the water, for by this you can wipe away their name, for none of them, nor of their fathers, were tried in this manner." ⁵⁰ And the king heard the words of Balaam, and the thing pleased the king and the princes, and the king did according to the word of Balaam. ⁵¹ And the king ordered a proclamation to be issued and a law to be made throughout the land of Egypt, saying, "Every male child born to the Hebrews from this day forward will be thrown into the water." ⁵² And Pharaoh called to all his servants, saying, "Go now, and seek throughout the land of Goshen where the sons of Israel are, and see that every son born to the Hebrews will be cast into the river, but you will let every daughter live." ⁵³ And when the sons of Israel heard this thing which Pharaoh had commanded, to cast their male children into the river, some of the people separated from their wives and others adhered to them. ⁵⁴ And from that day forward, when the time of delivery arrived for those women of Israel who had remained with their husbands, they went to the field to deliver, and brought out in the field, and left their children on the field, and returned home. ⁵⁵ And the LORD who had sworn to their ancestors to multiply them sent one of His ministering messengers which are in Heaven to wash each child in water, to anoint and swathe it, and to put two smooth stones into its hands from one of which it sucked milk and from the other honey, and He caused its hair to grow to its knees, by which it might cover itself to comfort it and to cleave to it, through His compassion for it. ⁵⁶ And

when God had compassion over them and had desired to multiply them on the face of the land, He ordered His earth to receive them to be preserved therein until the time of their growing up, after which the earth opened its mouth, and vomited them out, and they sprouted out from the city like the herb of the earth and the grass of the forest, and they each returned to his family and to his father's house, and they remained with them. ⁵⁷ And the babies of the sons of Israel were on the earth like the herb of the field through God's grace to them. ⁵⁸ And when all the Egyptians saw this thing, they went out, each to his field with his yoke of oxen and his plowshare, and they plowed it up as one plows the earth at seed-time. ⁵⁹ And when they plowed, they were unable to hurt the infants of the sons of Israel, so the people increased and waxed exceedingly. ⁶⁰ And Pharaoh ordered his officers to go to Goshen daily to seek for the babies of the sons of Israel. ⁶¹ And when they had sought and found one, they took it from its mother's bosom by force and threw it into the river, but they left the female child with its mother; thus the Egyptians did to the Israelites all the days.

CHAPTER 68

¹ And it was at that time the Spirit of God was on Miriam the daughter of Amram, the sister of Aaron, and she went out and prophesied about the house, saying, "Behold, [at] this time a son will be born to us from my father and mother, and he will save Israel from the hands of Egypt." ² And when Amram heard the words of his daughter, he went and took his wife back to the house after he had driven her away at the time when Pharaoh ordered every male child of the house of Jacob to be thrown into the water. ³ So Amram took his wife Jochebed three years after he had driven her away, and he came to her, and she conceived. ⁴ And at the end of seven months from her conception she brought out a son, and the whole house was filled with great light as of the light of the sun and moon at the time of their shining. ⁵ And when the woman saw that the child was good and pleasing to the sight, she hid it for three months in an inner room. ⁶ In those days the Egyptians conspired to destroy all the Hebrews there. ⁷ And the Egyptian women went to Goshen where the sons of Israel were, and they carried their young ones on their shoulders, their babies who could not yet speak. ⁸ And in those days, when the women of the sons of Israel brought out, each woman had hidden her son from before the Egyptians, [so] that the Egyptians might not know of their bringing out and might not destroy them from the land. ⁹ And the Egyptian women came to Goshen and their children who could not speak were on their shoulders, and when an Egyptian woman came into the house of a Hebrew woman her baby began to cry. ¹⁰ And when it cried, the child that was in the inner room answered it, so the Egyptian women went and

told it at the house of Pharaoh. ¹¹ And Pharaoh sent his officers to take the children and slay them; thus the Egyptians did to the Hebrew women all the days. ¹² And it was at that time, about three months from Jochebed's concealment of her son, that the thing was known in Pharaoh's house. ¹³ And the woman hastened to take her son away before the officers came, and she took an ark of bulrushes for him, and daubed it with slime and with pitch, and put the child therein, and she laid it in the flags by the river's brink. ¹⁴ And his sister Miriam stood far off to know what would be done to him and what would become of her words. ¹⁵ And God sent out a terrible heat in the land of Egypt at that time, which burned up the flesh of man like the sun in his circuit, and it greatly oppressed the Egyptians. ¹⁶ And all the Egyptians went down to bathe in the river on account of the consuming heat which burned up their flesh. ¹⁷ And Bathia, the daughter of Pharaoh, also went to bathe in the river, owing to the consuming heat, and her maidens walked at the riverside, and all the women of Egypt as well. ¹⁸ And Bathia lifted up her eyes to the river, and she saw the ark on the water, and sent her maid to fetch it. ¹⁹ And she opened it and saw the child, and behold, the baby wept, and she had compassion on him, and she said, "This is one of the Hebrew children." ²⁰ And all the women of Egypt walking on the riverside desired to give him suck, but he would not suck, for this thing was from the LORD in order to restore him to his mother's breast. ²¹ And at that time his sister Miriam was among the Egyptian women at the riverside, and she saw this thing, and she said to Pharaoh's daughter, "Will I go and fetch a nurse of the Hebrew women that she may nurse the child for you?" ²² And Pharaoh's daughter said to her, "Go," and the young woman went and called the child's mother. ²³ And Pharaoh's daughter said to Jochebed, "Take this child away and suckle it for me, and I will pay you your wages, two bits of silver daily"; and the woman took the child and nursed it. ²⁴ And at the end of two years, when the child grew up, she brought him to the daughter of Pharaoh, and he was as a son to her, and she called his name Moses, for she said, "Because I drew him out of the water." ²⁵ And his father Amram called his name Chabar, for he said, "It was for him that he associated with his wife whom he had turned away." ²⁶ And his mother Jochebed called his name Jekuthiel, because, she said, "I have hoped for him to the Almighty, and God restored him to me." ²⁷ And his sister Miriam called him Jered, for she descended after him to the river to know what his end would be. ²⁸ And his brother Aaron called his name Abi Zanuch, saying, "My father left my mother and returned to her on his account." ²⁹ And Kehas, the father of Amram, called his name Abigdor, because on his account God repaired the breach of the house of Jacob, [so] that they could no longer throw their male children into the water. ³⁰ And their nurse called him Abi Socho,

saying, "He was hidden in his dwelling place for three months on account of the children of Ham." ³¹ And all Israel called his name Shemaiah, son of Nethanel, for they said, "In his days God has heard their cries and rescued them from their oppressors." ³² And Moses was in Pharaoh's house, and was to Bathia, Pharaoh's daughter, as a son, and Moses grew up among the king's children.

CHAPTER 69

¹ And the king of Edom died in those days, in the eighteenth year of his reign, and was buried in his temple which he had built for himself as his royal residence in the land of Edom. ² And the children of Esau sent to Pethor, which is on the river, and they fetched a young man of beautiful eyes and handsome aspect from there whose name was Saul, and they made him king over them in the place of Samlah. ³ And Saul reigned over all the children of Esau in the land of Edom for forty years. ⁴ And when Pharaoh king of Egypt saw that the counsel which Balaam had advised respecting the sons of Israel did not succeed, but that they were still fruitful, multiplied, and increased throughout the land of Egypt, ⁵ then Pharaoh commanded in those days that a proclamation should be issued throughout Egypt to the sons of Israel, saying, "No man will diminish anything of his daily labor. ⁶ And the man who will be found deficient in his labor which he performs daily, whether in mortar or in bricks, then his youngest son will be put in their place." ⁷ And the labor of Egypt strengthened on the sons of Israel in those days, and behold, if one brick was deficient in any man's daily labor, the Egyptians took his youngest boy by force from his mother and put him into the building in the place of the brick which his father had left wanting. ⁸ And the men of Egypt did so to all the sons of Israel day by day, all the days for a long period. ⁹ But at that time the tribe of Levi did not work with the Israelites, their brothers, from the beginning, for the children of Levi knew the cunning of the Egyptians which they exercised at first toward the Israelites.

CHAPTER 70

¹ And in the third year from the birth of Moses, Pharaoh was sitting at a banquet when Alparanith the queen was sitting at his right and Bathia at his left, and the youth Moses was lying on her bosom, and Balaam the son of Beor with his two sons, and all the princes of the kingdom were sitting at [the] table in the king's presence. ² And the youth stretched out his hand on the king's head, and took the crown from the king's head, and placed it on his own head. ³ And when the king and princes saw the work which the boy had done, the king and princes were terrified, and one man expressed astonishment to his neighbor. ⁴ And the king said to the princes who were before him at the table, "What do you speak and what do you

say, O you princes, in this matter, and what is to be the judgment against the boy on account of this act?" ⁵ And Balaam the son of Beor, the magician, answered before the king and princes, and he said, "Remember now, O my lord and king, the dream which you dreamed many days since, and that which your servant interpreted to you. ⁶ Now therefore, this is a child from the Hebrew children, in whom is the Spirit of God, and do not let my lord the king imagine that this youngster did this thing without knowledge. ⁷ For he is a Hebrew boy, and wisdom and understanding are with him although he is still a child, and with wisdom he has done this and chosen the kingdom of Egypt for himself. ⁸ For this is the manner of all the Hebrews to deceive kings and their nobles, to do all these things cunningly in order to make the kings of the earth and their men tremble. ⁹ Surely you know that their father Abraham acted thus, who deceived the army of Nimrod king of Babel and Abimelech king of Gerar, and that he possessed the land of the children of Heth for himself and all the kingdoms of Canaan, ¹⁰ and that he descended into Egypt and said of his wife Sarah, She is my sister, in order to mislead Egypt and her king. ¹¹ His son Isaac also did so when he went to Gerar and dwelt there, and his strength prevailed over the army of Abimelech king of the Philistines. ¹² He also thought of making the kingdom of the Philistines stumble in saying that his wife Rebekah was his sister. ¹³ Jacob also dealt treacherously with his brother and took his birthright and his blessing from his hand. ¹⁴ Then he went to Padan-Aram to the house of Laban, his mother's brother, and cunningly obtained from him his daughter, his cattle, and all belonging to him, and fled away and returned to the land of Canaan to his father. ¹⁵ His sons sold their brother Joseph, who went down into Egypt, and became a slave, and was placed in the prison-house for twelve years ¹⁶ until the former Pharaoh dreamed dreams, and withdrew him from the prison-house, and magnified him above all the princes in Egypt on account of his interpreting his dreams to him. ¹⁷ And when God caused a famine throughout the land, he sent for and brought his father, and all his brothers, and the whole of his father's household, and supported them without price or reward, and bought the Egyptians for slaves. ¹⁸ Now therefore, my lord king, behold, this child has risen up in their stead in Egypt to do according to their deeds and to trifle with every king, prince, and judge. ¹⁹ If it pleases the king, let us now spill his blood on the ground, lest he grow up and take away the government from your hand, and the hope of Egypt perish after he will have reigned." ²⁰ And Balaam said to the king, "Let us moreover call for all the judges of Egypt and the wise men thereof, and let us know if the judgment of death is due to this boy as you said, and then we will slay him." ²¹ And Pharaoh sent and called for all the wise men of Egypt and they came

before the king, and a messenger of the LORD came among them, and he was like one of the wise men of Egypt. ²² And the king said to the wise men, "Surely you have heard what this Hebrew boy who is in the house has done, and thus Balaam has judged in the matter. ²³ Now you also judge and see what is due to the boy for the act he has committed." ²⁴ And the messenger, who seemed like one of the wise men of Pharaoh, answered and said as follows before all the wise men of Egypt and before the king and the princes: ²⁵ "If it pleases the king, let the king send for men who will bring an onyx stone and a coal of fire before him, and place them before the child, and if the child will stretch out his hand and take the onyx stone, then we will know that the youth has done all that he has done with wisdom, and we must slay him. ²⁶ But if he stretches out his hand on the coal, then we will know that it was not with knowledge that he did this thing, and he will live." ²⁷ And the thing seemed good in the eyes of the king and the princes, so the king did according to the word of the messenger of the LORD. ²⁸ And the king ordered the onyx stone and coal to be brought and placed before Moses. ²⁹ And they placed the boy before them, and the youth endeavored to stretch out his hand to the onyx stone, but the messenger of the LORD took his hand and placed it on the coal, and the coal became extinguished in his hand, and he lifted it up, and put it into his mouth, and burned part of his lips and part of his tongue, and he became heavy in mouth and tongue. ³⁰ And when the king and princes saw this, they knew that Moses had not acted with wisdom in taking off the crown from the king's head. ³¹ So the king and princes refrained from slaying the child, so Moses remained in Pharaoh's house, growing up, and the LORD was with him. ³² And while the boy was in the king's house, he was robed in purple and he grew among the children of the king. ³³ And when Moses grew up in the king's house, Bathia the daughter of Pharaoh considered him as a son, and all the household of Pharaoh honored him, and all the men of Egypt were afraid of him. ³⁴ And daily he went out and came into the land of Goshen where his brothers, the sons of Israel, were, and Moses saw them daily in shortness of breath and hard labor. ³⁵ And Moses asked them, saying, "Why is this labor meted out to you day by day?" ³⁶ And they told him all that had befallen them, and all the injunctions which Pharaoh had put on them before his birth. ³⁷ And they told him all the counsels which Balaam the son of Beor had counseled against them, and what he had also counseled against him in order to slay him when he had taken the king's crown from off his head. ³⁸ And when Moses heard these things, his anger was kindled against Balaam, and he sought to kill him, and he was in ambush for him day by day. ³⁹ And Balaam was afraid of Moses, and he and his two sons rose up and went out from Egypt, and they fled and delivered their souls, and they went to the land of Cush, to Kikianus, king of Cush. [40] And Moses was in the king's house, going out and coming in; the LORD gave him favor in the eyes of Pharaoh, and in the eyes of all his servants, and in the eyes of all the people of Egypt, and they loved Moses exceedingly. [41] And the day arrived when Moses went to Goshen to see his brothers, and he saw the sons of Israel in their burdens and hard labor, and Moses was grieved on their account. [42] And Moses returned to Egypt, and came to the house of Pharaoh, and came before the king, and Moses bowed down before the king. [43] And Moses said to Pharaoh, "Please my lord, I have come to seek a small request from you: do not turn my face away empty"; and Pharaoh said to him, "Speak." [44] And Moses said to Pharaoh, "Let there be given to your servants, the sons of Israel who are in Goshen, one day to rest therein from their labor." [45] And the king answered Moses and said, "Behold, I have lifted up your face in this thing to grant your request." [46] And Pharaoh ordered a proclamation to be issued throughout Egypt and Goshen, saying, [47] "To you, all the sons of Israel, thus says the king: for six days you will do your work and labor, but on the seventh day you will rest and will not perform any work; thus you will do all the days as the king and Moses the son of Bathia have commanded." [48] And Moses rejoiced at this thing which the king had granted to him, and all the sons of Israel did as Moses ordered them, [49] for this thing was from the LORD to the sons of Israel, for the LORD had begun to remember the sons of Israel to save them for the sake of their fathers. [50] And the LORD was with Moses and his fame went throughout Egypt. [51] And Moses became great in the eyes of all the Egyptians, and in the eyes of all the sons of Israel [because of his] seeking good for his people Israel and speaking words of peace regarding them to the king.

CHAPTER 71

[1] And when Moses was eighteen years old, he desired to see his father and mother and he went to them, to Goshen, and when Moses had come near Goshen, he came to the place where the sons of Israel were engaged in work, and he observed their burdens, and he saw an Egyptian striking one of his Hebrew brothers. [2] And when the man who was beaten saw Moses, he ran to him for help, for the man Moses was greatly respected in the house of Pharaoh, and he said to him, "My lord, attend to me! This Egyptian came to my house in the night, bound me, and came to my wife in my presence, and now he seeks to take my life away." [3] And when Moses heard this wicked thing, his anger was kindled against the Egyptian, and he turned this way and the other, and when he saw there was no man there, he struck the Egyptian, and hid him in the sand, and delivered the Hebrew from the hand of him that struck him. [4] And the Hebrew went to his house, and Moses returned to his home, and went out and came back to the king's house. [5] And when the

man had returned home, he thought of repudiating his wife, for it was not right in the house of Jacob for any man to come to his wife after she had been defiled. [6] And the woman went and told her brothers, and the woman's brothers sought to slay him, and he fled to his house and escaped. [7] And on the second day Moses went out to his brothers, and saw, and behold, two men were quarreling, and he said to the wicked one, "Why do you strike your neighbor?" [8] And he answered him and said to him, "Who has set you for a prince and judge over us? Do you think to slay me as you slew the Egyptian?" And Moses was afraid, and he said, "Surely the thing is known?" [9] And Pharaoh heard of this affair and he ordered Moses to be slain, so God sent His messenger and he appeared to Pharaoh in the likeness of a captain of the guard. [10] And the messenger of the LORD took the sword from the hand of the captain of the guard, and took his head off with it, for the likeness of the captain of the guard was turned into the likeness of Moses. [11] And the messenger of the LORD took hold of the right hand of Moses, and brought him out from Egypt, and placed him from outside the borders of Egypt, a distance of forty days' journey. [12] And only his brother Aaron remained in the land of Egypt, and he prophesied to the sons of Israel, saying, [13] "Thus says the LORD God of your ancestors: Throw away, each man, the abominations of his eyes, and do not defile yourselves with the idols of Egypt." [14] And the sons of Israel rebelled and would not listen to Aaron at that time. [15] And the LORD thought to destroy them were it not that the LORD remembered the covenant which He had made with Abraham, Isaac, and Jacob. [16] In those days the hand of Pharaoh continued to be severe against the sons of Israel, and he crushed and oppressed them until the time when God sent out His word and took notice of them.

CHAPTER 72

[1] And it was in those days that there was a great war between the children of Cush and the children of the east and Aram, and they rebelled against the king of Cush in whose hands they were. [2] So Kikianus king of Cush went out with all the children of Cush, a people [as] numerous as the sand, and he went to fight against Aram and the children of the east, to bring them under subjection. [3] And when Kikianus went out, he left Balaam the magician, with his two sons, to guard the city, and the lowest sort of the people of the land. [4] So Kikianus went out to Aram and the children of the east, and he fought against them and struck them, and they all fell down wounded before Kikianus and his people. [5] And he took many of them [as] captives, and he brought them under subjection as at first, and he encamped on their land to take tribute from them as usual. [6] And Balaam the son of Beor, when the king of Cush had left him to guard the city and the poor of the city, he rose up and advised

with the people of the land to rebel against King Kikianus, not to let him enter the city when he should come home. [7] And the people of the land listened to him, and they swore to him, and they made him king over them and his two sons for captains of the army. [8] So they rose up and raised the walls of the city at the two corners, and they built an exceedingly strong building. [9] And at the third corner they dug ditches without number between the city and the river which surrounded the whole land of Cush, and they made the waters of the river burst out there. [10] At the fourth corner they collected numerous serpents by their incantations and enchantments, and they fortified the city and dwelt therein, and no one went out or in before them. [11] And Kikianus fought against Aram and the children of the east and he subdued them as before, and they gave him their usual tribute, and he went and returned to his land. [12] And when Kikianus the king of Cush approached his city and all the captains of the forces with him, they lifted up their eyes and saw that the walls of the city were built up and greatly elevated, so the men were astonished at this. [13] And they said to one another, "It is because they saw that we were delayed in battle, and were greatly afraid of us, therefore they have done this thing, and raised the city walls, and fortified them so that the kings of Canaan might not come in battle against them." [14] So the king and the troops approached the city door, and they looked up, and behold, all the gates of the city were closed, and they called out to the sentinels, saying, "Open to us [so] that we may enter the city." [15] But the sentinels refused to open to them by the order of Balaam the magician, their king; they did not permit them to enter their city. [16] So they raised a battle with them opposite the city gate, and one hundred and thirty men of the army of Kikianus fell on that day. [17] And on the next day they continued to fight, and they fought at the side of the river; they endeavored to pass but were not able, so some of them sank in the pits and died. [18] So the king ordered them to cut down trees to make rafts on which they might pass to them, and they did so. [19] And when they came to the place of the ditches, the waters revolved by mills, and two hundred men on ten rafts were drowned. [20] And on the third day they came to fight at the side where the serpents were, but they could not approach there, for the serpents slew one hundred and seventy of their men, and they ceased fighting against Cush, and they besieged Cush for nine years—no person came out or in. [21] At the time that the war and the siege were against Cush, Moses fled from Egypt from Pharaoh who sought to kill him for having slain the Egyptian. [22] And Moses was eighteen years old when he fled from Egypt from the presence of Pharaoh, and he fled and escaped to the camp of Kikianus, which at that time was besieging Cush. [23] And Moses was nine years in the camp of Kikianus king of Cush, all the time that they were besieging Cush, and Moses went out and came in with them. [24] And the king, and princes, and all the fighting men loved Moses, for he was great and worthy; his stature was like a noble lion, his face was like the sun, and his strength was like that of a lion, and he was a counselor to the king. [25] And at the end of nine years, Kikianus was seized with a mortal disease, and his sickness prevailed over him, and he died on the seventh day. [26] So his servants embalmed him, and carried him, and buried him opposite the city gate to the north of the land of Egypt. [27] And they built an elegant, strong, and high building over him, and they placed great stones below. [28] And the king's scribes engraved on those stones all the might of their King Kikianus and all his battles which he had fought; behold, they are written there at this day. [29] Now after the death of Kikianus king of Cush it grieved his men and troops greatly on account of the war, [30] so they said to one another, "Give us counsel [regarding] what we are to do at this time, as we have resided in the wilderness away from our homes [for] nine years. [31] If we say we will fight against the city, many of us will fall wounded or killed, and if we remain here in the siege we will also die. [32] For now all the kings of Aram and of the children of the east will hear that our king is dead, and they will suddenly attack us in a hostile manner, and will fight against us, and leave no remnant of us. [33] Now therefore, let us go and make a king over us, and let us remain in the siege until the city is delivered up to us." [34] And on that day they wished to choose a man for king from the army of Kikianus, and they found no object of their choice comparable to Moses to reign over them. [35] And they hastened, and stripped off each man's garments, and cast them on the ground, and they made a great heap and placed Moses thereon. [36] And they rose up, and blew with trumpets, and called out before him, and said, "May the king live, may the king live!" [37] And all the people and nobles swore to him to give him Adoniah the queen, the Cushite, wife of Kikianus, for a wife, and they made Moses king over them on that day. [38] And all the people of Cush issued a proclamation on that day, saying, "Every man must give something to Moses of what is in his possession." [39] And they spread out a sheet on the heap and every man cast something into it of what he had: one gold earring and the other a coin. [40] The children of Cush also cast onyx stones, bdellium, pearls, and marble on the heap for Moses—also silver and gold in great abundance. [41] And Moses took all the silver and gold, all the vessels, and the bdellium and onyx stones, which all the children of Cush had given to him, and he placed them among his treasures. [42] And on that day Moses reigned over the children of Cush in the place of Kikianus king of Cush.

CHAPTER 73

¹ In the fifty-fifth year of the reign of Pharaoh king of Egypt, that is in the one hundred and fifty-seventh year of the Israelites going down into Egypt, Moses reigned in Cush. ² Moses was twenty-seven years old when he began to reign over Cush, and he reigned forty years. ³ And the LORD granted Moses favor and grace in the eyes of all the children of Cush, and the children of Cush loved him exceedingly, so Moses was favored by the LORD and by men. ⁴ And in the seventh day of his reign, all the children of Cush assembled, and came before Moses, and bowed down to him to the ground. ⁵ And all the children spoke together in the presence of the king, saying, "Give us counsel that we may see what is to be done to this city. ⁶ For it is now nine years that we have been besieging around the city and have not seen our children and our wives." ⁷ So the king answered them, saying, "If you will listen to my voice in all that I will command you, then the LORD will give the city into our hands and we will subdue it. ⁸ For if we fight with them as in the former battle which we had with them before the death of Kikianus, many of us will fall down wounded as before. ⁹ Now therefore, behold, here is counsel for you in this matter: if you will listen to my voice, then the city will be delivered into our hands." ¹⁰ So all the forces answered the king, saying, "All that our lord will command—that we will do." ¹¹ And Moses said to them, "Pass through and proclaim a voice in the whole camp to all the people, saying, ¹² Thus says the king, Go into the forest and bring with you of the young ones of the stork—each man [must have] a young one in his hand. ¹³ And any person transgressing the word of the king, who will not bring his young one, he will die, and the king will take all belonging to him. ¹⁴ And when you will bring them, they will be in your keeping; you will rear them until they grow up, and you will teach them to dart on, as is the way of the young ones of the hawk." ¹⁵ So all the children of Cush heard the words of Moses, and they rose up and caused a proclamation to be issued throughout the camp, saying, ¹⁶ "To you—all the children of Cush: the king's order is that you all go to the forest together and catch the young storks there; each man [must have] his young one in his hand, and you will bring them home. ¹⁷ And any person violating the order of the king will die, and the king will take all that belongs to him." ¹⁸ And all the people did so, and they went out to the wood, and climbed the fir trees, and caught—each man [with] a young one in his hand—all the young of the storks, and they brought them into the desert, and reared them by order of the king, and taught them to dart on, similar to the young hawks. ¹⁹ And after the young storks were reared, the king ordered them to be starved for three days, and all the people did so. ²⁰ And on the third day, the king said to them, "Strengthen yourselves and become valiant men, and each man

put on his armor, and gird his sword on him, and each man ride his horse, and each take his young stork in his hand. ²¹ And we will rise up and fight against the city at the place where the serpents are"; and all the people did as the king had ordered. ²² And each man took his young one in his hand, and they went away, and when they came to the place of the serpents, the king said to them, "Each man send out his young stork on the serpents." ²³ And each man sent out his young stork at the king's order, and the young storks ran on the serpents, and devoured them all, and destroyed them out of that place. ²⁴ And when the king and people had seen that all the serpents were destroyed in that place, all the people set up a great shout. ²⁵ And they approached, and fought against the city, and took it, and subdued it, and they entered the city. ²⁶ And there died on that day one thousand and one hundred men of the people of the city—all that inhabited the city—but of the people besieging, not [even] one died. ²⁷ So all the children of Cush each went to his home, to his wife and children, and to all belonging to him. ²⁸ And Balaam the magician, when he saw that the city was taken, he opened the gate and he and his two sons and eight brothers fled and returned to Egypt, to Pharaoh king of Egypt. ²⁹ They are the sorcerers and magicians who are mentioned in the Scroll of the Law, standing against Moses when the LORD brought the plagues on Egypt. ³⁰ So Moses took the city by his wisdom, and the children of Cush placed him on the throne instead of Kikianus king of Cush. ³¹ And they placed the royal crown on his head, and they gave him Adoniah the Cushite queen, wife of Kikianus, for a wife. ³² And Moses feared the LORD God of his fathers, so that he did not come to her, nor did he turn his eyes to her, ³³ for Moses remembered how Abraham had made his servant Eliezer swear, saying to him, "You will not take a woman from the daughters of Canaan for my son Isaac." ³⁴ Also what Isaac did when Jacob had fled from his brother, when he commanded him, saying, "You will not take a wife from the daughters of Canaan, nor make alliance with any of the children of Ham. ³⁵ For the LORD our God gave Ham, the son of Noah, and his children, and all his seed, as slaves to the children of Shem, and to the children of Japheth, and to their seed after them for slaves—agelong." ³⁶ Therefore Moses did not turn his heart nor his eyes to the wife of Kikianus all the days that he reigned over Cush. ³⁷ And Moses feared the LORD his God all his life, and Moses walked before the LORD in truth, with all his heart and soul; he did not turn from the right way all the days of his life; he did not decline from the way, either to the right or to the left, in which Abraham, Isaac, and Jacob had walked. ³⁸ And Moses strengthened himself in the kingdom of the children of Cush, and he guided the children of Cush with his usual wisdom, and Moses prospered in his kingdom. ³⁹ And at that time Aram and the children of the east heard that Kikianus king of Cush had died, so Aram and the children of the east rebelled against Cush in those days. ⁴⁰ And Moses gathered all the children of Cush, a people very mighty, about thirty thousand men, and he went out to fight with Aram and the children of the east. ⁴¹ And they went at first to the children of the east, and when the children of the east heard their report, they went to meet them, and engaged in battle with them. ⁴² And the war was severe against the children of the east, so the LORD gave all the children of the east into the hand of Moses, and about three hundred men fell down slain. ⁴³ And all the children of the east turned back and retreated, so Moses and the children of Cush followed them, and subdued them, and put a tax on them, as was their custom. ⁴⁴ So Moses and all the people with him passed from there to the land of Aram for battle. ⁴⁵ And the people of Aram also went to meet them, and they fought against them, and the LORD delivered them into the hand of Moses, and many of the men of Aram fell down wounded. ⁴⁶ And Aram was also subdued by Moses and the people of Cush, and also gave their usual tax. ⁴⁷ And Moses brought Aram and the children of the east under subjection to the children of Cush; and Moses and all the people who were with him turned to the land of Cush. ⁴⁸ And Moses strengthened himself in the kingdom of the children of Cush, and the LORD was with him, and all the children of Cush were afraid of him.

CHAPTER 74

¹ In the end of years Saul king of Edom died, and Ba'al Chanan the son of Achbor reigned in his place. ² In the sixteenth year of the reign of Moses over Cush, Ba'al Chanan the son of Achbor reigned in the land of Edom over all the children of Edom for thirty-eight years. ³ In his days Moab rebelled against the power of Edom, having been under Edom since the days of Hadad the son of Bedad who struck them and Midian and brought Moab under subjection to Edom. ⁴ And when Ba'al Chanan the son of Achbor reigned over Edom, all the children of Moab withdrew their allegiance from Edom. ⁵ And Angeas king of Africa died in those days, and his son Azdrubal reigned in his stead. ⁶ And in those days Janeas king of the children of Chittim died, and they buried him in his temple which he had built for a residence for himself in the plain of Canopia, and Latinus reigned in his stead. ⁷ In the twenty-second year of the reign of Moses over the children of Cush, Latinus reigned over the children of Chittim forty-five years. ⁸ And he also built a great and mighty tower for himself, and he built an elegant temple for his residence therein, to conduct his government, as was the custom. ⁹ In the third year of his reign he caused a proclamation to be made to all his skillful men who made many ships for him. ¹⁰ And Latinus assembled all his forces, and they came in ships, and went therein to fight with Azdrubal

son of Angeas, king of Africa, and they came to Africa and engaged in battle with Azdrubal and his army. ¹¹ And Latinus prevailed over Azdrubal, and Latinus took from Azdrubal the aqueduct which his father had brought from the children of Chittim when he took Janiah the daughter of Uzi for a wife, so Latinus overthrew the bridge of the aqueduct, and struck the whole army of Azdrubal [with] a severe blow. ¹² And the remaining strong men of Azdrubal strengthened themselves, and their hearts were filled with envy, and they courted death, and again engaged in battle with Latinus king of Chittim. ¹³ And the battle was severe on all the men of Africa, and they all fell wounded before Latinus and his people, and Azdrubal the king also fell in that battle. ¹⁴ And King Azdrubal had a very beautiful daughter whose name was Ushpezena, and all the men of Africa embroidered her likeness on their garments on account of her great beauty and attractive appearance. ¹⁵ And the men of Latinus saw Ushpezena, the daughter of Azdrubal, and praised her to Latinus, their king. ¹⁶ And Latinus ordered her to be brought to him, and Latinus took Ushpezena for a wife, and he turned back on his way to Chittim. ¹⁷ And it was after the death of Azdrubal son of Angeas, when Latinus had turned back to his land from the battle, that all the inhabitants of Africa rose up and took Anibal the son of Angeas, the younger brother of Azdrubal, and made him king over the whole land of Africa instead of his brother. ¹⁸ And when he reigned, he resolved to go to Chittim to fight with the children of Chittim, to avenge the cause of his brother Azdrubal and the cause of the inhabitants of Africa, and he did so. ¹⁹ And he made many ships, and he came therein with his whole army, and he went to Chittim. ²⁰ So Anibal fought with the children of Chittim, and the children of Chittim fell wounded before Anibal and his army, and Anibal avenged his brother's cause. ²¹ And Anibal continued the war for eighteen years with the children of Chittim, and Anibal dwelt in the land of Chittim and encamped there for a long time. ²² And Anibal struck the children of Chittim very severely, and he slew their great men and princes, and he struck about eighty thousand men of the rest of the people. ²³ And at the end of days and years, Anibal returned to his land of Africa, and he reigned securely in the place of his brother Azdrubal.

CHAPTER 75

¹ At that time, in the one hundred and eightieth year of the Israelites going down into Egypt, there went out from Egypt valiant men, thirty thousand on foot, from the sons of Israel, who were all of the tribe of Joseph, of the children of Ephraim the son of Joseph. ² For they said the period was completed which the LORD had appointed to the sons of Israel in the times of old, which he had spoken to Abraham. ³ And these men girded themselves, and each man put his sword

at his side, and every man [put] his armor on him, and they trusted in their strength, and they went out together from Egypt with a mighty hand. ⁴But they brought no provision for the road, only silver and gold; they did not even bring bread for that day in their hands, for they thought of getting their provision for pay from the Philistines, and if not, they would take it by force. ⁵And these men were very mighty and valiant men: one man could pursue one thousand and two could rout ten thousand, so they trusted in their strength and went together as they were. ⁶And they directed their course toward the land of Gath, and they went down and found the shepherds of Gath feeding the cattle of the children of Gath. ⁷And they said to the shepherds, "Give us some of the sheep for pay [so] that we may eat, for we are hungry, for we have eaten no bread this day." ⁸And the shepherds said, "Are they our sheep or cattle that we should give them to you even for pay?" So the children of Ephraim approached to take them by force. ⁹And the shepherds of Gath shouted over them that their cry was heard at a distance, so all the children of Gath went out to them. ¹⁰And when the children of Gath saw the evil doings of the children of Ephraim, they returned and assembled the men of Gath, and each man put on his armor and came out to the children of Ephraim for battle. ¹¹And they engaged with them in the Valley of Gath, and the battle was severe, and they struck from each other a great many on that day. ¹²And on the second day the children of Gath sent to all the cities of the Philistines [so] that they should come to their aid, saying, ¹³"Come up to us and help us [so] that we may strike the children of Ephraim who have come out from Egypt to take our cattle and to fight against us without cause." ¹⁴Now the souls of the children of Ephraim were exhausted with hunger and thirst, for they had eaten no bread for three days. And forty thousand men went out from the cities of the Philistines to the assistance of the men of Gath. ¹⁵And these men were engaged in battle with the children of Ephraim, and the LORD delivered the children of Ephraim into thc hands of thc Philistines. ¹⁶And they struck all the children of Ephraim—all who had gone out from Egypt; none were remaining except ten men who had run away from the engagement. ¹⁷For this calamity was from the LORD against the children of Ephraim, for they transgressed the word of the LORD in going out from Egypt before the period had arrived which the LORD in the days of old had appointed to Israel. ¹⁸And there also fell a great many of the Philistines, about twenty thousand men, and their brothers carried them and buried them in their cities. ¹⁹And the slain of the children of Ephraim remained forsaken in the Valley of Gath for many days and years, and were not brought to burial, and the valley was filled with men's bones. ²⁰And the men who had escaped from the battle came to Egypt and told all the sons of Israel all that had befallen

them. ²¹And their father Ephraim mourned over them for many days, and his brothers came to console him. ²²And he came to his wife and she bore a son, and he called his name Beriah, for she was unfortunate in his house.

CHAPTER 76

¹And Moses the son of Amram was still king in the land of Cush in those days, and he prospered in his kingdom, and he conducted the government of the children of Cush in justice, in righteousness, and [in] integrity. ²And all the children of Cush loved Moses all the days that he reigned over them, and all the inhabitants of the land of Cush were greatly afraid of him. ³And in the fortieth year of the reign of Moses over Cush, Moses was sitting on the royal throne while Adoniah the queen was before him, and all the nobles were sitting around him. ⁴And Adoniah the queen said before the king and the princes, "What is this thing which you, the children of Cush, have done for this long time? ⁵Surely you know that for forty years that this man has reigned over Cush he has not approached me, nor has he served the gods of the children of Cush. ⁶Now therefore, hear, O you children of Cush, and let this man no longer reign over you as he is not of our flesh. ⁷Behold, my son Menacrus is grown up: let him reign over you, for it is better for you to serve the son of your lord, than to serve a stranger, a slave of the king of Egypt." ⁸And all the people and nobles of the children of Cush heard the words which Adoniah the queen had spoken in their ears. ⁹And all the people were preparing until the evening, and in the morning, they rose up early and made Menacrus, son of Kikianus, king over them. ¹⁰And all the children of Cush were afraid to stretch out their hand against Moses, for the LORD was with Moses, and the children of Cush remembered the oath which they swore to Moses; therefore, they did no harm to him. ¹¹But the children of Cush gave many presents to Moses and sent him from them with great honor. ¹²So Moses went out from the land of Cush, and went home and ceased to reign over Cush, and Moses was sixty-six years old when he went out of the land of Cush, for the thing was from the LORD, for the period had arrived which He had appointed in the days of old, to bring out Israel from the affliction of the children of Ham. ¹³So Moses went to Midian, for he was afraid to return to Egypt on account of Pharaoh, and he went and sat at a well of water in Midian. ¹⁴And the seven daughters of Reuel the Midianite went out to feed their father's flock. ¹⁵And they came to the well and drew water to water their father's flock. ¹⁶So the shepherds of Midian came and drove them away, and Moses rose up, and helped them, and watered the flock. ¹⁷And they came home to their father Reuel and told him what Moses did for them. ¹⁸And they said, "An Egyptian man has delivered us from the hands of the shepherds; he drew

up water for us and watered the flock." ¹⁹ And Reuel said to his daughters, "And where is he? Why have you left the man?" ²⁰ And Reuel sent for him, and fetched him, and brought him home, and he ate bread with him. ²¹ And Moses related to Reuel that he had fled from Egypt, and that he reigned over Cush [for] forty years, and that afterward they had taken the government from him and had sent him away in peace with honor and with presents. ²² And when Reuel had heard the words of Moses, Reuel said within himself, "I will put this man into the prison-house, whereby I will conciliate the children of Cush, for he has fled from them." ²³ And they took and put him into the prison-house, and Moses was in prison [for] ten years, and while Moses was in the prison-house, Zipporah the daughter of Reuel took pity over him, and supported him with bread and water all the time. ²⁴ And all the sons of Israel were yet in the land of Egypt serving the Egyptians in all manner of hard work, and the hand of Egypt continued in severity over the sons of Israel in those days. ²⁵ At that time the LORD struck Pharaoh king of Egypt, and he was afflicted with the plague of leprosy from the sole of his foot to the crown of his head; this plague was from the LORD on Pharaoh king of Egypt at that time, owing to the cruel treatment of the sons of Israel. ²⁶ For the LORD had listened to the prayer of His people, the sons of Israel, and their cry reached Him on account of their hard work. ²⁷ Still His anger did not turn from them, and the hand of Pharaoh was still stretched out against the sons of Israel, and Pharaoh hardened his neck before the LORD, and increased his yoke over the sons of Israel, and embittered their lives with all manner of hard work. ²⁸ And when the LORD had inflicted the plague on Pharaoh king of Egypt, he asked his wise men and sorcerers to cure him. ²⁹ And his wise men and sorcerers said to him that if the blood of little children were put into the wounds he would be healed. ³⁰ And Pharaoh listened to them and sent his ministers to Goshen to the sons of Israel to take their little children. ³¹ And Pharaoh's ministers went and took the infants of the sons of Israel from the bosoms of their mothers by force, and they brought them to Pharaoh daily, a child each day, and the physicians killed them and applied them to the plague; thus they did all the days. ³² And the number of the children which Pharaoh slew was three hundred and seventy-five. ³³ But the LORD did not listen to the physicians of the king of Egypt, and the plague went on increasing mightily. ³⁴ And Pharaoh was afflicted with that plague [for] ten years, yet the heart of Pharaoh was [still] more hardened against the sons of Israel. ³⁵ And at the end of ten years the LORD continued to afflict Pharaoh with destructive plagues. ³⁶ And the LORD struck him with a bad tumor and sickness of the stomach, and that plague turned to a severe boil. ³⁷ At that time the two ministers of Pharaoh came from the land of Goshen where all the

sons of Israel were, and went to the house of Pharaoh, and said to him, "We have seen the sons of Israel slackened in their work and negligent in their labor." ³⁸ And when Pharaoh heard the words of his ministers, his anger was kindled against the sons of Israel exceedingly, for he was greatly grieved at his bodily pain. ³⁹ And he answered and said, "Now that the sons of Israel know that I am sick, they turn and scoff at us; now therefore, harness my chariot for me, and I will go to Goshen myself and will see the scoff of the sons of Israel with which they are deriding me"; so his servants harnessed the chariot for him. ⁴⁰ And they took him and made him ride on a horse, for he was not able to ride by himself; ⁴¹ And he took ten horsemen and ten footmen with him and went to the sons of Israel, to Goshen. ⁴² And when they had come to the border of Egypt, the king's horse passed into a narrow place, elevated in the hollow part of the vineyard, fenced on both sides, the low, plain country being on the other side. ⁴³ And the horses ran rapidly in that place and pressed each other, and the other horses pressed the king's horse. ⁴⁴ And the king's horse fell into the low plain while the king was riding on it, and when he fell, the chariot turned over the king's face and the horse lay on the king, and the king cried out, for his flesh was very sore. ⁴⁵ And the flesh of the king was torn from him, and his bones were broken, and he could not ride, for this thing was from the LORD to him, for the LORD had heard the cries of His people, the sons of Israel, and their affliction. ⁴⁶ And his servants carried him on their shoulders, a little at a time, and they brought him back to Egypt, and the horsemen who were with him also came back to Egypt. ⁴⁷ And they placed him in his bed, and the king knew that his end had come to die, so Aparanith the queen, his wife, came and cried before the king, and the king wept a great weeping with her. ⁴⁸ And all his nobles and servants came on that day, and saw the king in that affliction, and wept a great weeping with him. ⁴⁹ And the princes of the king and all his counselors advised the king to cause one to reign in his stead in the land, whomsoever he should choose from his sons. ⁵⁰ And the king had three sons and two daughters which Aparanith the queen, his wife, had borne to him besides the king's children of concubines. ⁵¹ And these were their names: the firstborn Othri, the second Adikam, and the third Morion, and their sisters, the name of the elder Bathia and of the other Acuzi. ⁵² And Othri, the firstborn of the king, was an idiot, precipitate and hurried in his words. ⁵³ But Adikam was a cunning and wise man and knowing in all the wisdom of Egypt, but of unseemly aspect, thick in flesh, and very short in stature; his height was one cubit. ⁵⁴ And when the king saw his son Adikam intelligent and wise in all things, the king resolved that he should be king in his stead after his death. ⁵⁵ And he took a wife for him, Gedudah daughter of Abilot, and he was ten years old, and she bore four sons to him. ⁵⁶ And afterward he went and took three wives and begot eight sons and three daughters. ⁵⁷ And the disorder greatly prevailed over the king, and his flesh stank like the flesh of a carcass cast on the field in summertime, during the heat of the sun. ⁵⁸ And when the king saw that his sickness had greatly strengthened itself over him, he ordered his son Adikam to be brought to him, and they made him king over the land in his place. ⁵⁹ And at the end of three years, the king died in shame, disgrace, and disgust, and his servants carried him and buried him in the tomb of the kings of Egypt in Zoan Mizraim. ⁶⁰ But they did not embalm him as was usual with kings, for his flesh was putrid, and they could not approach to embalm him on account of the stench, so they buried him in haste. ⁶¹ For this calamity was from the LORD to him, for the LORD had paid him back evil for the evil which he had done to Israel in his days. ⁶² And he died with terror and with shame, and his son Adikam reigned in his place.

CHAPTER 77

¹ Adikam was twenty years old when he reigned over Egypt; he reigned four years. ² In the two hundred and sixth year of Israel's going down to Egypt Adikam reigned over Egypt, but he did not continue as long in his reign over Egypt as his fathers had continued their reigns. ³ For his father Melol reigned ninety-four years in Egypt, but he was sick [for] ten years and died, for he had been wicked before the LORD. ⁴ And all the Egyptians called the name of Adikam Pharaoh like the name of his fathers, as was their custom to do in Egypt. ⁵ And all the wise men of Pharaoh called the name of Adikam Ahuz ([he] is called Ahuz for short in the Egyptian language). ⁶ And Adikam was exceedingly ugly, and he was a cubit and a span, and he had a great beard which reached to the soles of his feet. ⁷ And Pharaoh sat on his father's throne to reign over Egypt, and he conducted the government of Egypt in his wisdom. ⁸ And while he reigned, he exceeded his father and all the preceding kings in wickedness, and he increased his yoke over the sons of Israel. ⁹ And he went with his servants to Goshen, to the sons of Israel, and he strengthened the labor over them and he said to them, "Complete your work—each day's task—and do not let your hands slacken from our work from this day forward as you did in the days of my father." ¹⁰ And he placed officers over them from among the sons of Israel, and over these officers he placed taskmasters from among his servants. ¹¹ And he placed over them a measure of bricks for them to do according to that number, day by day, and he turned back and went to Egypt. ¹² At that time the taskmasters of Pharaoh ordered the officers of the sons of Israel according to the command of Pharaoh, saying, ¹³ "Thus says Pharaoh: Do your work each day, and finish your task, and observe the daily measure of bricks; do not diminish

anything. ¹⁴ And it will come to pass that if you are deficient in your daily bricks, I will put your young children in their place." ¹⁵ And the taskmasters of Egypt did so in those days as Pharaoh had ordered them. ¹⁶ And whenever any deficiency was found in the sons of Israel's measure of their daily bricks, the taskmasters of Pharaoh would go to the wives of the sons of Israel and take infants of the sons of Israel according to the number of deficient bricks; they would take them by force from their mother's laps and put them in the building instead of the bricks ¹⁷ while their fathers and mothers were crying over them and weeping when they heard the weeping voices of their infants in the wall of the building. ¹⁸ And the taskmasters prevailed over Israel [so] that the Israelites should place their [own] children in the building, so that a man placed his son in the wall and put mortar over him while his eyes wept over him and his tears ran down on his child. ¹⁹ And the taskmasters of Egypt did so to the babies of Israel for many days, and no one pitied or had compassion over the babies of the sons of Israel. ²⁰ And the number of all the children killed in the building was two hundred and seventy, some whom they had built on instead of the bricks which had been left deficient by their fathers, and some whom they had drawn out dead from the building. ²¹ And the labor imposed on the sons of Israel in the days of Adikam exceeded in hardship that which they performed in the days of his father. ²² And the sons of Israel sighed every day on account of their heavy work, for they had said to themselves, "Behold, when Pharaoh will die, his son will rise up and lighten our work!" ²³ But they increased the latter work more than the former, and the sons of Israel sighed at this and their cry ascended to God on account of their labor. ²⁴ And in those days God heard the voice of the sons of Israel and their cry, and God remembered His covenant with them which He had made with Abraham, Isaac, and Jacob. ²⁵ And God saw the burden of the sons of Israel and their heavy work in those days, and He determined to deliver them. ²⁶ And Moses the son of Amram was still confined in the dungeon in those days, in the house of Reuel the Midianite, and Zipporah the daughter of Reuel secretly supported him with food day by day. ²⁷ And Moses was confined in the dungeon in the house of Reuel for ten years. ²⁸ And at the end of ten years, which was the first year of the reign of Pharaoh over Egypt in the place of his father, ²⁹ Zipporah said to her father Reuel, "No person inquires or seeks after the Hebrew man whom you bound in prison now ten years. ³⁰ Now therefore, if it seems good in your sight, let us send and see whether he is living or dead," but her father did not know that she had supported him. ³¹ And her father Reuel answered and said to her, "Has such a thing ever happened that a man should be shut up in a prison without food for ten years, and that he should live?" ³² And Zipporah answered her father, saying, "Surely you have heard that the God of the Hebrews is great and awful, and does wonders for them at all times. [33] It was He who delivered Abraham from Ur of the Chaldeans, and Isaac from the sword of his father, and Jacob from the Messenger of the LORD who wrestled with him at the ford of Jabbuk. [34] He has also done many things with this man: He delivered him from the river in Egypt, and from the sword of Pharaoh, and from the children of Cush—so He can also deliver him from famine and make him live." [35] And the thing seemed good in the sight of Reuel, so he did according to the word of his daughter and sent to the dungeon to ascertain what became of Moses. [36] And he saw, and behold, the man Moses was living in the dungeon, standing on his feet, praising and praying to the God of his ancestors. [37] And Reuel commanded Moses to be brought out of the dungeon, so they shaved him, and he changed his prison garments and ate bread. [38] And afterward Moses went into the garden of Reuel which was behind the house, and there he prayed to the LORD his God who had done mighty wonders for him. [39] And it was that while he prayed, he looked opposite to him, and behold, a sapphire stick was placed in the ground, which was planted in the midst of the garden. [40] And he approached the stick and looked, and behold, the Name of the LORD God of Hosts was engraved thereon, written and developed on the stick. [41] And he read it, and stretched out his hand, and plucked it like a forest tree from the thicket, and the stick was in his hand. [42] And this is the stick with which all the works of our God were performed after He had created the heavens and earth, and all the host of them, seas, rivers, and all their fishes. [43] And when God had driven Adam from the garden of Eden, he took the stick in his hand and went and tilled the ground from which he was taken. [44] And the stick came down to Noah and was given to Shem and his descendants until it came into the hand of Abraham the Hebrew. [45] And when Abraham had given all he had to his son Isaac, he also gave this stick to him. [46] And when Jacob had fled to Padan-Aram, he took it into his hand, and when he returned to his father, he had not left it behind him. [47] Also when he went down to Egypt, he took it into his hand and gave it to Joseph, one portion above his brothers, for Jacob had taken it by force from his brother Esau. [48] And after the death of Joseph, the nobles of Egypt came into the house of Joseph, and the stick came into the hand of Reuel the Midianite, and when he went out of Egypt, he took it in his hand and planted it in his garden. [49] And all the mighty men of the Kinites tried to pluck it when they endeavored to get his daughter Zipporah, but they were unsuccessful. [50] So that stick remained planted in the garden of Reuel until he came who had a right to it and took it. [51] And when Reuel saw the stick in the hand of Moses, he wondered at it, and he gave him his daughter Zipporah for a wife.

CHAPTER 78

[1] At that time Ba'al Channan son of Achbor, king of Edom, died, and he was buried in his house in the land of Edom. [2] And after his death the children of Esau sent to the land of Edom and took a man from there who was in Edom, whose name was Hadad, and they made him king over them in the place of Ba'al Channan, their king. [3] And Hadad reigned over the children of Edom [for] forty-eight years. [4] And when he reigned, he resolved to fight against the children of Moab, to bring them under the power of the children of Esau as they were before, but he was not able, because the children of Moab heard this thing, and they rose up and hastened to choose a king over them from among their brothers. [5] And afterward they gathered a great people together and sent to their brothers, the children of Ammon, for help to fight against Hadad king of Edom. [6] And Hadad heard the thing which the children of Moab had done, and was greatly afraid of them, and refrained from fighting against them. [7] In those days Moses the son of Amram took Zipporah the daughter of Reuel, the Midianite, for a wife in Midian. [8] And Zipporah walked in the ways of the daughters of Jacob; she was nothing short of the righteousness of Sarah, Rebekah, Rachel, and Leah. [9] And Zipporah conceived and bore a son and he called his name Gershom, for he said, "I was a stranger in a foreign land"; but he did not circumcise his foreskin at the command of his father-in-law Reuel. [10] And she conceived again and bore a son, but circumcised his foreskin, and he called his name Eliezer, for Moses said, "Because the God of my fathers was my help and delivered me from the sword of Pharaoh." [11] And Pharaoh king of Egypt greatly increased the labor of the sons of Israel in those days and continued to make his yoke heavier on the sons of Israel. [12] And he ordered a proclamation to be made in Egypt, saying, "No longer give straw to the people to make bricks with; let them go and gather straw themselves as they can find it. [13] Also, let them give the number of bricks which they must make each day, and diminish nothing from them, for they are idle in their work." [14] And the sons of Israel heard this, and they mourned and sighed, and they cried to the LORD on account of the bitterness of their souls. [15] And the LORD heard the cries of the sons of Israel and saw the oppression with which the Egyptians oppressed them. [16] And the LORD was jealous for His people and His inheritance, and heard their voice, and resolved to take them out of the affliction of Egypt, to give them the land of Canaan for a possession.

CHAPTER 79

[1] And in those days Moses was feeding the flock of Reuel the Midianite, his father-in-law, beyond the wilderness of Sin, and the stick which he took from his father-in-law was in his hand. [2] And it came to pass one day that a kid of goats strayed from the flock,

and Moses pursued it, and it came to the mountain of God, to Horeb. ³ And when he came to Horeb, the LORD appeared there to him in the bush, and he found the bush burning with fire, but the fire had no power over the bush to consume it. ⁴ And Moses was greatly astonished at this sight, why the bush was not consumed, and he approached to see this mighty thing, and the LORD called to Moses out of the fire and commanded him to go down to Egypt, to Pharaoh king of Egypt, to send the sons of Israel from his service. ⁵ And the LORD said to Moses, "Go; return to Egypt, for all those men who sought your life are dead, and you will speak to Pharaoh to send out the sons of Israel from his land." ⁶ And the LORD commanded him to do signs and wonders in Egypt before the eyes of Pharaoh and the eyes of his subjects in order that they might believe that the LORD had sent him. ⁷ And Moses listened to all that the LORD had commanded him, and he returned to his father-in-law and told him the thing, and Reuel said to him, "Go in peace." ⁸ And Moses rose up to go to Egypt, and he took his wife and sons with him, and he was at an inn in the road, and a messenger of God came down and sought an occasion against him. ⁹ And he wished to kill him on account of his firstborn son, because he had not circumcised him, and had transgressed the covenant which the LORD had made with Abraham. ¹⁰ For Moses had listened to the words of his father-in-law which he had spoken to him, [so as] not to circumcise his firstborn son, therefore he did not circumcise him. ¹¹ And Zipporah saw the messenger of the LORD seeking an occasion against Moses, and she knew that this thing was owing to his not having circumcised her son Gershom. ¹² And Zipporah hastened and took of the sharp rock stones that were there, and she circumcised her son, and delivered her husband and her son from the hand of the messenger of the LORD. ¹³ And Aaron the son of Amram, the brother of Moses, was in Egypt walking at the riverside on that day. ¹⁴ And the LORD appeared to him in that place, and He said to him, "Go now toward Moses in the wilderness," and he went and met him in the mountain of God, and he kissed him. ¹⁵ And Aaron lifted up his eyes and saw Zipporah the wife of Moses and her children, and he said to Moses, "Who are these to you?" ¹⁶ And Moses said to him, "They are my wife and sons, which God gave to me in Midian"; and the thing grieved Aaron on account of the woman and her children. ¹⁷ And Aaron said to Moses, "Send the woman and her children away that they may go to her father's house," and Moses listened to the words of Aaron, and did so. ¹⁸ And Zipporah returned with her children, and they went to the house of Reuel, and remained there until the time arrived when the LORD had visited His people and brought them out from Egypt from the hand of Pharaoh. ¹⁹ And Moses and Aaron came to Egypt to the community of the sons of Israel, and they spoke to them all the words of the LORD, and the people rejoiced an exceedingly great rejoicing. ²⁰ And Moses and Aaron rose up early on the next day, and they went to the house of Pharaoh, and they took the stick of God in their hands. ²¹ And when they came to the king's gate, two young lions were confined there with iron instruments, and no person went out or came in from before them, unless those whom the king ordered to come, when the conjurers came and withdrew the lions by their incantations, and this brought them to the king. ²² And Moses hastened and lifted up the stick on the lions, and he loosed them, and Moses and Aaron came into the king's house. ²³ The lions also came with them in joy, and they followed them and rejoiced as a dog rejoices over his master when he comes from the field. ²⁴ And when Pharaoh saw this thing, he was astonished at it, and he was greatly terrified at the report, for their appearance was like the appearance of the children of God. ²⁵ And Pharaoh said to Moses, "What do you require?" And they answered him, saying, "The LORD God of the Hebrews has sent us to you, to say, Send out My people that they may serve Me." ²⁶ And when Pharaoh heard their words he was greatly terrified before them, and he said to them, "Go today and come back to me tomorrow," and they did according to the word of the king. ²⁷ And when they had gone, Pharaoh sent for Balaam the magician, and to his sons Jannes and Jambres, and to all the magicians, and conjurers, and counselors which belonged to the king, and they all came and sat before the king. ²⁸ And the king told them all the words which Moses and his brother Aaron had spoken to him, and the magicians said to the king, "But how did the men come to you with the lions which were confined at the gate?" ²⁹ And the king said, "Because they lifted up their rod against the lions and loosed them, and came to me, and the lions also rejoiced at them as a dog rejoices to meet his master." ³⁰ And Balaam the son of Beor, the magician, answered the king, saying, "These are nothing other than magicians like ourselves. ³¹ Now therefore, send for them, and let them come, and we will try them," and the king did so. ³² And in the morning Pharaoh sent for Moses and Aaron to come before the king, and they took the rod of God, and came to the king, and spoke to him, saying, ³³ "Thus said the LORD God of the Hebrews: Send My people that they may serve Me." ³⁴ And the king said to them, "But who will believe you that you are the messengers of God and that you come to me by His order? ³⁵ Now therefore, give a wonder or sign in this matter, and then the words which you speak will be believed." ³⁶ And Aaron hastened and threw the rod out of his hand before Pharaoh and before his servants, and the rod turned into a serpent. ³⁷ And the sorcerers saw this, and each man cast his rod on the ground and they became serpents. ³⁸ And the serpent of Aaron's rod lifted up its head and opened its mouth to swallow the rods of the magicians. ³⁹ And Balaam the magician answered and said, "This thing has been from the days of old, that a serpent should swallow its fellow, and that living things devour each other. ⁴⁰ Now therefore, restore it to a rod as it was at first, and we will also restore our rods as they were at first, and if your rod will swallow our rods, then we will know that the Spirit of God is in you, and if not, you are only a craftsman like ourselves." ⁴¹ And Aaron hastened, and stretched out his hand, and caught hold of the serpent's tail, and it became a rod in his hand, and the sorcerers did the same with their rods, and each man took hold of the tail of his serpent, and they became rods as at first. ⁴² And when they were restored to rods, the rod of Aaron swallowed up their rods. ⁴³ And when the king saw this thing, he ordered the scroll of records that related to the kings of Egypt to be brought, and they brought the scroll of records, the chronicles of the kings of Egypt, in which all the idols of Egypt were inscribed, for they thought of finding the Name of the LORD therein, but they did not find it. ⁴⁴ And Pharaoh said to Moses and Aaron, "Behold, I have not found the Name of your God written in this scroll, and I do not recognize His Name." ⁴⁵ And the counselors and wise men answered the king, "We have heard that the God of the Hebrews is a son of the wise, the son of ancient kings." ⁴⁶ And Pharaoh turned to Moses and Aaron and said to them, "I do not know the LORD whom you have declared; neither will I send His people." ⁴⁷ And they answered and said to the king, "The LORD God of gods is His Name, and He proclaimed His Name over us from the days of our ancestors, and sent us, saying, Go to Pharaoh and say to him, Send My people that they may serve Me. ⁴⁸ Now therefore, send us [so] that we may take a journey for three days in the wilderness, and may sacrifice to Him there, for from the days of our going down to Egypt, He has not taken from our hands either burnt-offering, oblation, or sacrifice, and if you will not send us, His anger will be kindled against you, and He will strike Egypt either with the plague or with the sword." ⁴⁹ And Pharaoh said to them, "Tell me now of His power and His might"; and they said to him, "He created the heavens and the earth, the seas and all their fishes; He formed the light, created the darkness, caused rain on the earth and watered it, and made the herbage and grass to sprout; He created man, and beast, and the animals of the forest, the birds of the air, and the fish of the sea, and by His mouth they live and die. ⁵⁰ He surely created you in your mother's womb, and put into you the breath of life, and reared you, and placed you on the royal throne of Egypt, and He will take your breath and soul from you, and return you to the ground from where you were taken." ⁵¹ And the anger of the king was kindled at their words, and he said to them, "But who among all the gods of the nations can do this? My river is my own, and I have made it for myself." ⁵² And he drove them from him, and he ordered the labor on Israel to be more severe than it was yesterday and before. ⁵³ And Moses and Aaron went out from the king's presence, and they saw the sons of Israel in an evil condition, for the taskmasters had made their labor exceedingly heavy. ⁵⁴ And Moses returned to the LORD and said, "Why have you mistreated Your people? For since I came to speak to Pharaoh—the reason You sent me—he has exceedingly mistreated the sons of Israel." ⁵⁵ And the LORD said to Moses, "Behold, you will see that with an outstretched hand and heavy plagues, Pharaoh will send the sons of Israel from his land." ⁵⁶ And Moses and Aaron dwelt in Egypt among their brothers, the sons of Israel. ⁵⁷ And as for the sons of Israel: the Egyptians embittered their lives with the heavy work which they imposed on them.

CHAPTER 80

¹ And at the end of two years, the LORD sent Moses to Pharaoh again to bring out the sons of Israel, and to send them out of the land of Egypt. ² And Moses went and came to the house of Pharaoh, and he spoke to him the words of the LORD who had sent him, but Pharaoh would not listen to the voice of the LORD, and God roused His might in Egypt on Pharaoh and his subjects, and God struck Pharaoh and his people with very great and severe plagues. ³ And the LORD sent by the hand of Aaron and turned all the waters of Egypt into blood, with all their streams and rivers. ⁴ And when an Egyptian came to drink and draw water, he looked into his pitcher, and behold, all the water was turned into blood; and when he came to drink from his cup, the water in the cup became blood. ⁵ And when a woman kneaded her dough and cooked her victuals, their appearance was turned to that of blood. ⁶ And the LORD sent again and caused all their waters to bring out frogs, and all the frogs came into the houses of the Egyptians. ⁷ And when the Egyptians drank, their bellies were filled with frogs and they danced in their bellies as they dance when in the river. ⁸ And all their drinking water and cooking water turned to frogs; also, when they lay in their beds their perspiration bred frogs. ⁹ Notwithstanding all this, the anger of the LORD did not turn from them, and His hand was stretched out against all the Egyptians to strike them with every heavy plague. ¹⁰ And He sent and struck their dust to lice, and the lice became in Egypt to the height of two cubits on the earth. ¹¹ The lice were also very numerous in the flesh of man and beast in all the inhabitants of Egypt; the LORD also sent the lice on the king and queen, and it grieved Egypt exceedingly on account of the lice. ¹² Notwithstanding this, the anger of the LORD did not turn away, and His hand was still stretched out over Egypt. ¹³ And the LORD sent all kinds of beasts of the field into Egypt, and they came and destroyed all Egypt—man, and beast, and trees, and all things that

were in Egypt. [14] And the LORD sent fiery serpents, scorpions, mice, weasels, toads, together with others creeping in dust— [15] flies, hornets, fleas, bugs, and gnats, each swarm according to its kind. [16] And all reptiles and winged animals according to their kind came to Egypt and grieved the Egyptians exceedingly. [17] And the fleas and flies came into the eyes and ears of the Egyptians. [18] And the hornet came on them and drove them away, and they removed from it into their inner rooms, and it pursued them. [19] And when the Egyptians hid themselves on account of the swarm of animals, they locked their doors after them, and God ordered the Sulanuth, which was in the sea, to come up and go into Egypt. [20] And she had long arms—ten cubits in length of the cubit of a man. [21] And she went on the roofs and uncovered the raftering and flooring, and cut them, and stretched out her arm into the house, and removed the lock and the bolt, and opened the houses of Egypt. [22] Afterward, the swarm of animals came into the houses of Egypt, and the swarm of animals destroyed the Egyptians, and it grieved them exceedingly. [23] Notwithstanding this, the anger of the LORD did not turn away from the Egyptians, and His hand was yet stretched out against them. [24] And God sent the pestilence, and the pestilence pervaded Egypt, in the horses and donkeys, and in the camels, in herds of oxen and sheep, and in man. [25] And when the Egyptians rose up early in the morning to take their cattle to pasture, they found all their cattle dead. [26] And there remained of the cattle of the Egyptians only one in ten, and of the cattle belonging to Israel in Goshen not one died. [27] And God sent a burning inflammation in the flesh of the Egyptians, which burst their skins, and it became a severe itch in all the Egyptians from the soles of their feet to the crowns of their heads. [28] And many boils were in their flesh [so] that their flesh wasted away until they became rotten and putrid. [29] Notwithstanding this, the anger of the LORD did not turn away, and His hand was still stretched out over all Egypt. [30] And the LORD sent a very heavy hail, which struck their vines, and broke their fruit trees, and dried them up that they fell on them. [31] Also every green herb became dry and perished, for a mingling fire descended amidst the hail; therefore, the hail and the fire consumed all things. [32] Also men and beasts that were found abroad perished by the flames of fire and of the hail, and all the young lions were exhausted. [33] And the LORD sent and brought numerous locusts into Egypt: the Chasel, Salom, Chargol, and Chagole—locusts each after its kind, which devoured all that the hail had left remaining. [34] Then the Egyptians rejoiced at the locusts, although they consumed the produce of the field, and they caught them in abundance and salted them for food. [35] And the LORD turned a mighty wind of the sea which took away all the locusts, even those that were salted, and thrust them into the Red Sea; not one locust remained within the boundaries of Egypt. [36] And God sent darkness over Egypt [so] that the whole land of Egypt and Pathros became dark for three days, so that a man could not see his hand when he lifted it to his mouth. [37] At that time many of the people of Israel died who had rebelled against the LORD, and who would not listen to Moses and Aaron, and did not believe in them, that God had sent them, [38] and who had said, "We will not go out from Egypt lest we perish with hunger in a desolate wilderness," and who would not listen to the voice of Moses. [39] And the LORD plagued them in the three days of darkness, and the Israelites buried them in those days without the Egyptians knowing of them or rejoicing over them. [40] And the darkness was very great in Egypt for three days, and any person who was standing when the darkness came remained standing in his place, and he that was sitting remained sitting, and he that was lying continued lying in the same state, and he that was walking remained sitting on the ground in the same spot; and this thing happened to all the Egyptians until the darkness had passed away. [41] And the days of darkness passed away, and the LORD sent Moses and Aaron to the sons of Israel, saying, "Celebrate your feast and make your Passover, for behold, I come in the midst of the night among all the Egyptians, and I will strike all their firstborn, from the firstborn of a man to the firstborn of a beast, and when I see your Passover, I will pass over you." [42] And the sons of Israel did according to all that the LORD had commanded Moses and Aaron—thus they did in that night. [43] And it came to pass in the middle of the night that the LORD went out in the midst of Egypt and struck all the firstborn of the Egyptians, from the firstborn of man to the firstborn of beast. [44] And Pharaoh rose up in the night, he, and all his servants, and all the Egyptians, and there was a great cry throughout Egypt in that night, for there was not a house in which there was not a corpse. [45] Also the likenesses of the firstborn of Egypt, which were carved in the walls of their houses, were destroyed and fell to the ground. [46] Even the bones of their firstborn, who had died before this and whom they had buried in their houses, were raked up by the dogs of Egypt on that night, and dragged before the Egyptians, and cast before them. [47] And all the Egyptians saw this evil which had suddenly come on them, and all the Egyptians cried out with a loud voice. [48] And all the families of Egypt wept on that night, each man for his son and each man for his daughter, being the firstborn, and the tumult of Egypt was heard at a distance on that night. [49] And Bathia the daughter of Pharaoh went out with the king on that night to seek Moses and Aaron in their houses, and they found them in their houses eating, and drinking, and rejoicing with all Israel. [50] And Bathia said to Moses, "Is this the reward for the good which I have done to you, who have reared you and stretched you out, and you have brought this calamity on me and my father's house?" ⁵¹ And Moses said to her, "Surely the LORD brought ten plagues on Egypt; did any evil accrue to you from any of them? Did one of them affect you?" And she said, "No." ⁵² And Moses said to her, "Although you are the firstborn to your mother, you will not die, and no calamity will reach you in the midst of Egypt." ⁵³ And she said, "What advantage is it to me when I see the king, my brother, and all his household and subjects in this calamity, whose firstborn perish with all the firstborn of Egypt?" ⁵⁴ And Moses said to her, "Surely your brother and his household and subjects, the families of Egypt, would not listen to the words of the LORD, therefore this calamity came on them." ⁵⁵ And Pharaoh king of Egypt approached Moses, and Aaron, and some of the sons of Israel who were with them in that place, and he prayed to them, saying, ⁵⁶ "Rise up and take your brothers, all the sons of Israel who are in the land, with their sheep and oxen, and all belonging to them—they will leave nothing remaining; only pray for me to the LORD your God." ⁵⁷ And Moses said to Pharaoh, "Behold, though you are your mother's firstborn, yet do not fear, for you will not die, for the LORD has commanded that you will live in order to show you His great might and strong outstretched arm." ⁵⁸ And Pharaoh ordered the sons of Israel to be sent away, and all the Egyptians strengthened themselves to send them, for they said, "We are all perishing." ⁵⁹ And all the Egyptians sent the Israelites out with great riches—sheep, and oxen, and precious things—according to the oath of the LORD between him and our Father Abraham. ⁶⁰ And the sons of Israel delayed going out at night, and when the Egyptians came to them to bring them out, they said to them, "Are we thieves that we should go out at night?" ⁶¹ And the sons of Israel asked of the Egyptians vessels of silver, and vessels of gold, and garments, and the sons of Israel stripped the Egyptians. ⁶² And Moses hastened, and rose up, and went to the river of Egypt, and brought up the coffin of Joseph from there, and took it with him. ⁶³ Each man [of] the sons of Israel also brought up his father's coffin with him, and each man [brought up] the coffins of his tribe.

CHAPTER 81

¹ And the sons of Israel journeyed from Rameses to Succoth, about six hundred thousand men on foot, besides the little ones and their wives. ² Also a mixed multitude went up with them, and flocks and herds, even many cattle. ³ And the sojourning of the sons of Israel, who dwelt in the land of Egypt in hard labor, was two hundred and ten years. ⁴ And at the end of two hundred and ten years, the LORD brought out the sons of Israel from Egypt with a strong hand. ⁵ And the sons of Israel traveled from Egypt, and from Goshen, and from Rameses, and encamped in Succoth on the fifteenth day of the first month. ⁶ And

the Egyptians buried all their firstborn whom the LORD had smitten, and all the Egyptians buried their slain for three days. ⁷ And the sons of Israel traveled from Succoth and encamped in Ethom, at the end of the wilderness. ⁸ And on the third day after the Egyptians had buried their firstborn, many men rose up from Egypt and went after Israel to make them return to Egypt, for they regretted that they had sent the Israelites away from their servitude. ⁹ And one man said to his neighbor, "Surely Moses and Aaron spoke to Pharaoh, saying, We will go a three days' journey in the wilderness and sacrifice to the LORD our God. ¹⁰ Now therefore, let us rise up early in the morning and cause them to return, and it will be that if they return with us to Egypt to their masters, then we will know that there is faith in them, but if they will not return, then we will fight with them and make them come back with great power and a strong hand." ¹¹ And all the nobles of Pharaoh rose up in the morning, and with them about seven hundred thousand men, and they went out from Egypt on that day and came to the place where the sons of Israel were. ¹² And all the Egyptians saw, and behold, Moses, and Aaron, and all the sons of Israel were sitting before Pi-Hahiroth, eating, and drinking, and celebrating the celebration of the LORD. ¹³ And all the Egyptians said to the sons of Israel, "Surely you said, We will go on a journey for three days in the wilderness, and sacrifice to our God, and return. ¹⁴ Now therefore, this day makes five days since you went, why do you not return to your masters?" ¹⁵ And Moses and Aaron answered them, saying, "Because the LORD our God has testified to us, saying, You will never return to Egypt; but we will journey ourselves to a land flowing with milk and honey as the LORD our God had sworn to our ancestors to give to us." ¹⁶ And when the nobles of Egypt saw that the sons of Israel did not listen to them to return to Egypt, they girded themselves to fight with Israel. ¹⁷ And the LORD strengthened the hearts of the sons of Israel over the Egyptians [so] that they gave them a severe beating, and the battle was severe on the Egyptians, and all the Egyptians fled from before the sons of Israel, for many of them perished by the hand of Israel. ¹⁸ And the nobles of Pharaoh went to Egypt and told Pharaoh, saying, "The sons of Israel have fled and will no longer return to Egypt, and Moses and Aaron spoke to us in this manner." ¹⁹ And Pharaoh heard this thing, and his heart and the hearts of all his subjects were turned against Israel, and they regretted that they had sent Israel; and all the Egyptians advised Pharaoh to pursue the sons of Israel to make them come back to their burdens. ²⁰ And each man said to his brother, "What is this which we have done, that we have sent Israel from our servitude?" ²¹ And the LORD strengthened the hearts of all the Egyptians to pursue the Israelites, for the LORD desired to overthrow the Egyptians in the Red Sea. ²² And

Pharaoh rose up and harnessed his chariot, and he ordered all the Egyptians to assemble; not one man was left except the little ones and the women. ²³ And all the Egyptians went out with Pharaoh to pursue the sons of Israel, and the camp of Egypt was an exceedingly large and heavy camp, about one million men. ²⁴ And the whole of this camp went and pursued the sons of Israel to bring them back to Egypt, and they reached them encamping by the Red Sea. ²⁵ And the sons of Israel lifted up their eyes and beheld all the Egyptians pursuing them, and the sons of Israel were greatly terrified at them, and the sons of Israel cried to the LORD. ²⁶ And on account of the Egyptians, the sons of Israel divided themselves into four divisions, and they were divided in their opinions, for they were afraid of the Egyptians, and Moses spoke to each of them. ²⁷ The first division was of the children of Reuben, Simeon, and Issachar, and they resolved to cast themselves into the sea, for they were exceedingly afraid of the Egyptians. ²⁸ And Moses said to them, "Do not fear, stand still and see the salvation of the LORD which He will effect this day for you." ²⁹ The second division was of the children of Zebulun, Benjamin, and Naphtali, and they resolved to go back to Egypt with the Egyptians. ³⁰ And Moses said to them, "Do not fear, for as you have seen the Egyptians this day, so you will see them no more forever." ³¹ The third division was of the children of Judah and Joseph, and they resolved to go to meet the Egyptians to fight with them. ³² And Moses said to them, "Stand in your places, for the LORD will fight for you, and you will remain silent." ³³ And the fourth division was of the children of Levi, Gad, and Asher, and they resolved to go into the midst of the Egyptians to confound them, and Moses said to them, "Remain in your stations and do not fear, only call to the LORD that He may save you out of their hands." ³⁴ After this, Moses rose up from amidst the people, and he prayed to the LORD and said, ³⁵ "O LORD God of the whole earth, save Your people now whom You brought out from Egypt, and do not let the Egyptians boast that power and might are theirs." ³⁶ So the LORD said to Moses, "Why do you cry to Me? Speak to the sons of Israel that they will proceed, and you will stretch out your rod on the sea and divide it, and the sons of Israel will pass through it." ³⁷ And Moses did so, and he lifted up his rod on the sea and divided it. ³⁸ And the waters of the sea were divided into twelve parts, and the sons of Israel passed through on foot, with shoes, as a man would pass through a prepared road. ³⁹ And the LORD manifested His wonders to the sons of Israel in Egypt and in the sea by the hand of Moses and Aaron. ⁴⁰ And when the sons of Israel had entered the sea, the Egyptians came after them, and the waters of the sea resumed on them, and they all sank in the water, and not one man was left except Pharaoh, who gave thanks to the LORD and believed in Him; therefore, the LORD did not cause him to perish at that time with the Egyptians. ⁴¹ And the LORD ordered a messenger to take him from among the Egyptians, who cast him on the land of Ninevah and he reigned over it for a long time. ⁴² And on that day the LORD saved Israel from the hand of Egypt, and all the sons of Israel saw that the Egyptians had perished, and they beheld the great hand of the LORD, in what He had performed in Egypt and in the sea. ⁴³ Then Moses and the sons of Israel sang this song to the LORD on the day when the LORD caused the Egyptians to fall before them. ⁴⁴ And all Israel sang in concert, saying, "I will sing to the LORD for He is greatly exalted, ‖ The horse and his rider He has cast into the sea; Behold, it is written in the Scroll of the Law of God." ⁴⁵ After this the sons of Israel proceeded on their journey and encamped in Marah, and the LORD gave to the sons of Israel statutes and judgments in that place in Marah, and the LORD commanded the sons of Israel to walk in all His ways and to serve Him. ⁴⁶ And they journeyed from Marah and came to Elim, and there were twelve springs of water and seventy date trees in Elim, and the children encamped there by the waters. ⁴⁷ And they journeyed from Elim and came to the wilderness of Sin on the fifteenth day of the second month after their departure from Egypt. ⁴⁸ At that time the LORD gave the manna to the sons of Israel to eat, and the LORD caused food to rain from Heaven for the sons of Israel day by day. ⁴⁹ And the sons of Israel ate the manna for forty years, all the days that they were in the wilderness, until they came to the land of Canaan to possess it. ⁵⁰ And they proceeded from the wilderness of Sin and encamped in Alush. ⁵¹ And they proceeded from Alush and encamped in Rephidim. ⁵² And when the sons of Israel were in Rephidim, Amalek the son of Eliphaz, the son of Esau, the brother of Zepho, came to fight with Israel. ⁵³ And he brought with him eight hundred and one thousand men, magicians and conjurers, and he prepared for battle with Israel in Rephidim. ⁵⁴ And they carried on a great and severe battle against Israel, and the LORD delivered Amalek and his people into the hands of Moses and the sons of Israel, and into the hand of Joshua the son of Nun, the Ephrathite, the servant of Moses. ⁵⁵ And the sons of Israel struck Amalek and his people at the edge of the sword, but the battle was very severe on the sons of Israel. ⁵⁶ And the LORD said to Moses, "Write this thing as a memorial for you in a scroll, and place it in the hand of Joshua the son of Nun, your servant, and you will command the sons of Israel, saying, When you will come to the land of Canaan, you will utterly efface the remembrance of Amalek from under Heaven." ⁵⁷ And Moses did so, and he took the scroll and wrote on it these words, saying, ⁵⁸ "Remember what Amalek has done to you in the road when you went out from Egypt, ⁵⁹ who met you in the road and struck your rear, even those that were feeble behind you when you were faint and weary. ⁶⁰ Therefore, it will be when the

LORD your God will have given you rest from all your surrounding enemies in the land which the LORD your God gives you for an inheritance to possess it, that you will blot out the remembrance of Amalek from under Heaven—you will not forget it. 61 And the king who will have pity on Amalek, or on his memory, or on his seed, behold, I will require it of him, and I will cut him off from among his people." 62 And Moses wrote all these things in a scroll, and he commanded the sons of Israel respecting all these matters.

CHAPTER 82

1 And the sons of Israel proceeded from Rephidim, and they encamped in the wilderness of Sinai in the third month from their going out from Egypt. 2 At that time Reuel the Midianite, the father-in-law of Moses, came with his daughter Zipporah and her two sons, for he had heard of the wonders of the LORD which He had done to Israel, that He had delivered them from the hand of Egypt. 3 And Reuel came to Moses, to the wilderness where he was encamped, where the mountain of God was. 4 And Moses went out to meet his father-in-law with great honor, and all Israel was with him. 5 And Reuel and his children remained among the Israelites for many days, and Reuel knew the LORD from that day forward. 6 And in the third month from the sons of Israel's departure from Egypt, on the sixth day thereof, the LORD gave to Israel the Ten Commandments on Mount Sinai. 7 And all Israel heard all these commands, and all Israel rejoiced exceedingly in the LORD on that day. 8 And the glory of the LORD rested on Mount Sinai, and He called to Moses, and Moses came in the midst of a cloud and ascended the mountain. 9 And Moses was on the mount [for] forty days and forty nights; he ate no bread and drank no water, and the LORD instructed him in the statutes and judgments in order to teach the sons of Israel. 10 And the LORD wrote the Ten Commandments which He had commanded the sons of Israel on two tablets of stone, which He gave to Moses to command the sons of Israel. 11 And at the end of forty days and forty nights, when the LORD had finished speaking to Moses on Mount Sinai, then the LORD gave the tablets of stone to Moses, written with the finger of God. 12 And when the sons of Israel saw that Moses tarried to come down from the mount, they gathered around Aaron, and said, "As for this man Moses, we do not know what has become of him. 13 Now therefore, rise up; make a god for us who will go before us, so that you will not die." 14 And Aaron was greatly afraid of the people, and he ordered them to bring him gold, and he made it into a molten calf for the people. 15 And the LORD said to Moses before he had come down from the mount, "Get down, for your people whom you brought out from Egypt have corrupted themselves. 16 They have made a molten calf for themselves and have bowed down to it; now therefore, leave Me [so] that I may consume them

from off the earth, for they are a stiff-necked people." 17 And Moses implored the countenance of the LORD, and he prayed to the LORD for the people on account of the calf which they had made, and afterward he descended from the mount and in his hands were the two tablets of stone which God had given him to command the Israelites. 18 And when Moses approached the camp and saw the calf which the people had made, the anger of Moses was kindled, and he broke the tablets under the mount. 19 And Moses came to the camp, and he took the calf and burned it with fire, and he ground it until it became fine dust, and scattered it on the water, and gave it to the Israelites to drink. 20 And there died of the people by the swords of each other about three thousand men who had made the calf. 21 And the next day Moses said to the people, "I will go up to the LORD; perhaps I may make atonement for your sins which you have sinned to the LORD." 22 And Moses went up to the LORD again, and he remained with the LORD [for] forty days and forty nights. 23 And during the forty days Moses entreated the LORD in behalf of the sons of Israel, and the LORD listened to the prayer of Moses, and the LORD was entreated of him on behalf of Israel. 24 Then the LORD spoke to Moses to hew two [new] stone tablets and to bring them up to the LORD, who would write on them the Ten Commandments. 25 Now Moses did so, and he came down, and hewed the two tablets, and went up to Mount Sinai to the LORD, and the LORD wrote the Ten Commandments on the tablets. 26 And Moses remained with the LORD yet forty days and forty nights, and the LORD instructed him in statutes and judgments to impart to Israel. 27 And the LORD commanded him respecting the sons of Israel that they should make a sanctuary for the LORD, that His Name might rest therein, and the LORD showed him the likeness of the sanctuary and the likeness of all its vessels. 28 And at the end of the forty days, Moses came down from the mount and the two tablets were in his hand. 29 And Moses came to the sons of Israel and spoke to them all the words of the LORD, and he taught them laws, statutes, and judgments which the LORD had taught him. 30 And Moses told the sons of Israel the word of the LORD, that a sanctuary should be made for Him to dwell among the sons of Israel. 31 And the people rejoiced greatly at all the good which the LORD had spoken to them through Moses, and they said, "We will do all that the LORD has spoken to you." 32 And the people rose up like one man, and they made generous offerings to the sanctuary of the LORD, and each man brought the offering of the LORD for the work of the sanctuary, and for all its service. 33 And all the sons of Israel—each man—brought of all that was found in his possession for the work of the sanctuary of the LORD: gold, silver, and brass, and everything that was serviceable for the sanctuary. 34 And all the wise men who were experienced in work came and made the sanctuary of the LORD according to all that the LORD had commanded, every man in the work in which he had been experienced; and all the wise men in heart made the sanctuary, and its furniture, and all the vessels for the holy service as the LORD had commanded Moses. ³⁵ And the work of the sanctuary of the Dwelling Place was completed at the end of five months, and the sons of Israel did all that the LORD had commanded Moses. ³⁶ And they brought the sanctuary and all its furniture to Moses; like to the representation which the LORD had shown to Moses, so the sons of Israel did. ³⁷ And Moses saw the work, and behold, they did it as the LORD had commanded him, so Moses blessed them.

CHAPTER 83

¹ And in the twelfth month, in the twenty-third day of the month, Moses took Aaron and his sons, and he dressed them in their garments, and anointed them, and did to them as the LORD had commanded him, and Moses brought up all the offerings which the LORD had on that day commanded him. ² Afterward Moses took Aaron and his sons and said to them, "For seven days you will remain at the door of the Dwelling Place, for thus I am commanded." ³ And Aaron and his sons did all that the LORD had commanded them through Moses, and they remained for seven days at the door of the Dwelling Place. ⁴ And on the eighth day, being the first day of the first month, in the second year from the Israelites' departure from Egypt, Moses erected the sanctuary, and Moses put up all the furniture of the Dwelling Place and all the furniture of the sanctuary, and he did all that the LORD had commanded him. ⁵ And Moses called to Aaron and his sons, and they brought the burnt-offering and the sin offering for themselves and the sons of Israel as the LORD had commanded Moses. ⁶ On that day the two sons of Aaron, Nadab and Abihu, took strange fire and brought it before the LORD who had not commanded them, and a fire went out from before the LORD and consumed them, and they died before the LORD on that day. ⁷ Then on the day when Moses had completed to erect the sanctuary, the princes of the sons of Israel began to bring their offerings before the LORD for the dedication of the altar. ⁸ And each prince brought up their offerings for one day, a prince each day for twelve days. ⁹ And all the offerings which they brought, each man in his day: one silver charger weighing one hundred and thirty shekels, one silver bowl of seventy shekels after the shekel of the sanctuary, both of them full of fine flour, mingled with oil for a meat offering, ¹⁰ one spoon weighing ten shekels of gold, full of incense, ¹¹ one young bullock, one ram, one lamb of the first year for a burnt-offering, ¹² and one kid of the goats for a sin offering. ¹³ And for a sacrifice of a peace offering: two oxen, five rams, five male goats, five lambs of a year old.

¹⁴ Thus the twelve princes of Israel did day by day, each man in his day. ¹⁵ And it was after this, in the thirteenth day of the month, that Moses commanded the sons of Israel to observe the Passover. ¹⁶ And the sons of Israel kept the Passover in its season in the fourteenth day of the month; as the LORD had commanded Moses, so the sons of Israel did. ¹⁷ And in the second month, on the first day thereof, the LORD spoke to Moses, saying, ¹⁸ "Number the heads of all the males of the sons of Israel from twenty years old and upward, you, and your brother Aaron, and the twelve princes of Israel." ¹⁹ And Moses did so, and Aaron came with the twelve princes of Israel, and they numbered the sons of Israel in the wilderness of Sinai. ²⁰ And the numbers of the sons of Israel by the houses of their fathers, from twenty years old and upward, were six hundred and three thousand, five hundred and fifty. ²¹ But the children of Levi were not numbered among their brothers, the sons of Israel. ²² And the number of all the males of the sons of Israel from one month old and upward was twenty-two thousand, two hundred and seventy-three. ²³ And the number of the children of Levi from one month old and above was twenty-two thousand. ²⁴ And Moses placed the priests and the Levites, each man to his service and to his burden, to serve the sanctuary of the Dwelling Place as the LORD had commanded Moses. ²⁵ And on the twentieth day of the month, the cloud was taken away from the Dwelling Place of testimony. ²⁶ At that time the sons of Israel continued their journey from the wilderness of Sinai, and they took a journey of three days, and the cloud rested on the wilderness of Paran; there the anger of the LORD was kindled against Israel, for they had provoked the LORD in asking Him for meat that they might eat. ²⁷ And the LORD listened to their voice and gave them meat which they ate for one month. ²⁸ But after this the anger of the LORD was kindled against them, and He struck them with a great slaughter, and they were buried there in that place. ²⁹ And the sons of Israel called that place Kebroth Hattaavah, because there they buried the people that lusted after flesh. ³⁰ And they departed from Kebroth Hattaavah and pitched [their tents] in Hazeroth, which is in the wilderness of Paran. ³¹ And while the sons of Israel were in Hazeroth, the anger of the LORD was kindled against Miriam on account of Moses, and she became leprous—white as snow. ³² And she was confined outside the camp for seven days until she had been received again after her leprosy. ³³ Afterward the sons of Israel departed from Hazeroth and pitched in the end of the wilderness of Paran. ³⁴ At that time, the LORD spoke to Moses to send twelve men from the sons of Israel, one man to a tribe, to go and explore the land of Canaan. ³⁵ And Moses sent the twelve men, and they came to the land of Canaan to search and examine it, and they explored the whole land from the wilderness of Sin to Rechob as you come to Chamoth.

36 And at the end of forty days they came to Moses and Aaron, and they brought him word as it was in their hearts, and ten of the men brought up an evil report to the sons of Israel regarding the land which they had explored, saying, "It is better for us to return to Egypt than to go to this land, a land that consumes its inhabitants." 37 But Joshua the son of Nun, and Caleb the son of Jephuneh, who were of those that explored the land, said, "The land is exceedingly good. 38 If the LORD delight in us, then He will bring us to this land and give it to us, for it is a land flowing with milk and honey." 39 But the sons of Israel would not listen to them, and they listened to the words of the ten men who had brought up an evil report of the land. 40 And the LORD heard the murmurings of the sons of Israel, and He was angry and swore, saying, 41 "Surely not [even] one man of this wicked generation will see the land from twenty years old and upward except Caleb the son of Jephuneh and Joshua the son of Nun. 42 But surely this wicked generation will perish in this wilderness, and their children will come to the land and they will possess it"; so the anger of the LORD was kindled against Israel, and He made them wander in the wilderness for forty years until the end of that wicked generation, because they did not follow the LORD. 43 And the people dwelt in the wilderness of Paran a long time, and afterward they proceeded to the wilderness by the way of the Red Sea.

CHAPTER 84

1 At that time Korah the son of Jetzer, the son of Kehas, the son of Levi, took many men of the sons of Israel, and they rose up and quarreled with Moses, and Aaron, and the whole congregation. 2 And the LORD was angry with them, and the earth opened its mouth and swallowed them up with their houses, and all belonging to them, and all the men belonging to Korah. 3 And after this, God made the people go around by the way of Mount Seir for a long time. 4 At that time the LORD said to Moses, "Do not provoke a war against the children of Esau, for I will not give to you of anything belonging to them, as much as the sole of the foot could tread on, for I have given Mount Seir for an inheritance to Esau." 5 Therefore the children of Esau fought against the children of Seir in former times, and the LORD had delivered the children of Seir into the hands of the children of Esau and destroyed them from before them, and the children of Esau dwelt in their place to this day. 6 Therefore the LORD said to the sons of Israel, "Do not fight against the children of Esau, your brothers, for nothing in their land belongs to you, but you may buy food from them for money and eat it, and you may buy water from them for money and drink it." 7 And the sons of Israel did according to the word of the LORD. 8 And the sons of Israel went around the wilderness, going around by the way of Mount Sinai for a long time, and did not touch the children of Esau, and they continued in that district for nineteen years. 9 At that time Latinus king of the children of Chittim died in the forty-fifth year of his reign, which is the fourteenth year of the sons of Israel's departure from Egypt. 10 And they buried him in his place which he had built for himself in the land of Chittim, and Abimnas reigned in his place for thirty-eight years. 11 And the sons of Israel passed the boundary of the children of Esau in those days, at the end of nineteen years, and they came and passed the road of the wilderness of Moab. 12 And the LORD said to Moses, "Do not besiege Moab, and do not fight against them, for I will give you nothing of their land." 13 And the sons of Israel passed the road of the wilderness of Moab for nineteen years, and they did not fight against them. 14 And in the thirty-sixth year of the sons of Israel's departing from Egypt, the LORD struck the heart of Sihon, king of the Amorites, and he waged war, and went out to fight against the children of Moab. 15 And Sihon sent messengers to Beor the son of Janeas, the son of Balaam, counselor to the king of Egypt, and to his son Balaam, to curse Moab, in order that it might be delivered into the hand of Sihon. 16 And the messengers went and brought Beor the son of Janeas and his son Balaam from Pethor in Mesopotamia, so Beor and his son Balaam came to the city of Sihon and they cursed Moab and their king in the presence of Sihon king of the Amorites. 17 So Sihon went out with his whole army, and he went to Moab and fought against them, and he subdued them, and the LORD delivered them into his hands, and Sihon slew the king of Moab. 18 And Sihon took all the cities of Moab in the battle; he also took Heshbon from them, for Heshbon was one of the cities of Moab, and Sihon placed his princes and his nobles in Heshbon, and Heshbon belonged to Sihon in those days. 19 Therefore the allegory speakers Beor and his son Balaam uttered these words, saying, "Come to Heshbon; the city of Sihon will be built and established. 20 Woe to you Moab! You are lost, O people of Kemosh! Behold, it is written on the Scroll of the Law of God." 21 And when Sihon had conquered Moab, he placed guards in the cities which he had taken from Moab, and a considerable number of the children of Moab fell in battle into the hand of Sihon, and he made a great capture of them—sons and daughters—and he slew their king; so Sihon turned back to his own land. 22 And Sihon gave numerous presents of silver and gold to Beor and his son Balaam, and he dismissed them, and they went to Mesopotamia to their home and country. 23 At that time all the sons of Israel passed from the road of the wilderness of Moab, and returned, and surrounded the wilderness of Edom. 24 So the whole congregation came to the wilderness of Sin in the first month of the fortieth year from their departure from Egypt, and the sons of Israel dwelt there in Kadesh, of the wilderness of Sin, and Miriam died there, and she was buried

there. ²⁵ At that time Moses sent messengers to Hadad king of Edom, saying, "Thus says your brother Israel: Please let me pass through your land; we will not pass through field or vineyard; we will not drink the water of the well; we will walk in the king's road." ²⁶ And Edom said to him, "You will not pass through my country," and Edom went out to meet the sons of Israel with a mighty people. ²⁷ And the children of Esau refused to let the sons of Israel pass through their land, so the Israelites removed from them and did not fight against them. ²⁸ For before this, the LORD had commanded the sons of Israel, saying, "You will not fight against the children of Esau," therefore the Israelites removed from them and did not fight against them. ²⁹ So the sons of Israel departed from Kadesh, and all the people came to Mount Hor. ³⁰ At that time the LORD said to Moses, "Tell your brother Aaron that he will die there, for he will not come to the land which I have given to the sons of Israel." ³¹ And Aaron went up to Mount Hor at the command of the LORD in the fortieth year, in the fifth month, in the first day of the month. ³² And Aaron was one hundred and twenty-three years old when he died in Mount Hor.

CHAPTER 85

¹ And King Arad the Canaanite, who dwelt in the south, heard that the Israelites had come by the way of the spies, and he arranged his forces to fight against the Israelites. ² And the sons of Israel were greatly afraid of him, for he had a great and heavy army, so the sons of Israel resolved to return to Egypt. ³ And the sons of Israel turned back about the distance of three days' journey to Maserath Beni Jaakon, for they were greatly afraid on account of King Arad. ⁴ And the sons of Israel would not get back to their places, so they remained in Beni Jaakon for thirty days. ⁵ And when the children of Levi saw that the sons of Israel would not turn back, they were jealous for the sake of the LORD, and they rose up and fought against the Israelites, their brothers, and slew a great body of them, and forced them to turn back to their place, Mount Hor. ⁶ And when they returned, King Arad was still arranging his host for battle against the Israelites. ⁷ And Israel vowed a vow, saying, "If You will deliver this people into my hand, then I will utterly destroy their cities." ⁸ And the LORD listened to the voice of Israel, and He delivered the Canaanites into their hand, and He utterly destroyed them and their cities, and [Israel] called the name of the place Hormah. ⁹ And the sons of Israel journeyed from Mount Hor and pitched [their tents] in Oboth, and they journeyed from Oboth and they pitched at Ije-abarim in the border of Moab. ¹⁰ And the sons of Israel sent to Moab, saying, "Let us now pass through your land into our place," but the children of Moab would not permit the sons of Israel to pass through their land, for the children of Moab were greatly afraid lest the sons of Israel should do to them as Sihon king of the Amorites had done to them, who had taken their land and had slain many of them. ¹¹ Therefore Moab would not permit the Israelites to pass through his land, and the LORD commanded the sons of Israel, saying that they should not fight against Moab, so the Israelites removed from Moab. ¹² And the sons of Israel journeyed from the border of Moab, and they came to the other side of Arnon, the border of Moab, between Moab and the Amorites, and they pitched in the border of Sihon, king of the Amorites, in the wilderness of Kedemoth. ¹³ And the sons of Israel sent messengers to Sihon, king of the Amorites, saying, ¹⁴ "Let us pass through your land; we will not turn into the fields or into the vineyards; we will go along by the king's highway until we will have passed your border," but Sihon would not permit the Israelites to pass. ¹⁵ So Sihon collected all the people of the Amorites and went out into the wilderness to meet the sons of Israel, and he fought against Israel in Jahaz. ¹⁶ And the LORD delivered Sihon king of the Amorites into the hand of the sons of Israel, and Israel struck all the people of Sihon with the edge of the sword and avenged the cause of Moab. ¹⁷ And the sons of Israel took possession of the land of Sihon, from Aram to Jabuk, to the children of Ammon, and they took all the spoil of the cities. ¹⁸ And Israel took all these cities, and Israel dwelt in all the cities of the Amorites. ¹⁹ And all the sons of Israel resolved to fight against the children of Ammon, to take their land also. ²⁰ So the LORD said to the sons of Israel, "Do not besiege the children of Ammon, nor stir up battle against them, for I will give nothing to you of their land," and the sons of Israel listened to the word of the LORD and did not fight against the children of Ammon. ²¹ And the sons of Israel turned and went up by the way of Bashan to the land of Og, king of Bashan, and Og the king of Bashan went out to meet the Israelites in battle, and he had many valiant men with him, and a very strong force from the people of the Amorites. ²² And Og king of Bashan was a very powerful man, but his son Naaron was exceedingly powerful, even stronger than he was. ²³ And Og said in his heart, "Behold, now the whole camp of Israel takes up a space of seven miles; now I will strike them at once, without sword or spear." ²⁴ And Og went up Mount Jahaz and took one large stone from there, the length of which was seven miles, and he placed it on his head, and resolved to throw it on the camp of the sons of Israel, to strike all the Israelites with that stone. ²⁵ And the Messenger of the LORD came and pierced the stone on the head of Og, and the stone fell on the neck of Og [so] that Og fell to the earth on account of the weight of the stone on his neck. ²⁶ At that time the LORD said to the sons of Israel, "Do not be afraid of him, for I have given him, and all his people, and all his land into your hand, and you will do to him as you did to Sihon." ²⁷ And Moses went

down to him with a small number of the sons of Israel, and Moses struck Og with a stick at the ankles of his feet and slew him. ²⁸ Afterward the sons of Israel pursued the children of Og and all his people, and they beat and destroyed them until there was no remnant left of them. ²⁹ Afterward Moses sent some of the sons of Israel to spy out Jaazer, for Jaazer was a very famous city. ³⁰ And the spies went to Jaazer and explored it, and the spies trusted in the LORD, and they fought against the men of Jaazer. ³¹ And these men took Jaazer and its villages, and the LORD delivered them into their hand, and they drove out the Amorites who had been there. ³² And the sons of Israel took the land of the two kings of the Amorites, sixty cities which were on the other side of [the] Jordan, from the Brook of Arnon to Mount Hermon. ³³ And the sons of Israel journeyed and came into the plain of Moab, which is on this side of [the] Jordan, by Jericho. ³⁴ And the children of Moab heard all the evil which the sons of Israel had done to the two kings of the Amorites, to Sihon and Og, so all the men of Moab were greatly afraid of the Israelites. ³⁵ And the elders of Moab said, "Behold, the two kings of the Amorites, Sihon and Og, who were more powerful than all the kings of the earth, could not stand against the sons of Israel; how then can we stand before them? ³⁶ Surely they sent us a message before now to pass through our land on their way, and we would not permit them, now they will turn on us with their heavy swords and destroy us"; and Moab was distressed on account of the sons of Israel, and they were greatly afraid of them, and they counseled together what was to be done to the sons of Israel. ³⁷ And the elders of Moab resolved and took one of their men, Balak the son of Zippor, the Moabite, and made him king over them at that time, and Balak was a very wise man. ³⁸ And the elders of Moab rose up and sent to the children of Midian to make peace with them, for a great battle and enmity had existed between Moab and Midian in those days, from the days of Hadad the son of Bedad, king of Edom, who struck Midian in the field of Moab, to these days. ³⁹ And the children of Moab sent to the children of Midian, and they made peace with them, and the elders of Midian came to the land of Moab to make peace in behalf of the children of Midian. ⁴⁰ And the elders of Moab counseled with the elders of Midian what to do in order to save their lives from Israel. ⁴¹ And all the children of Moab said to the elders of Midian, "Now therefore, the sons of Israel lick up all that are around us as the ox licks up the grass of the field, for thus they did to the two kings of the Amorites who are stronger than we are." ⁴² And the elders of Midian said to Moab, "We have heard that at the time when Sihon king of the Amorites fought against you, when he prevailed over you and took your land, he had sent to Beor the son of Janeas and to his son Balaam from Mesopotamia, and they came and cursed you; therefore the hand of Sihon

prevailed over you [so] that he took your land. ⁴³ Now therefore, send to his son Balaam also, for he still remains in his land, and give him his hire [so] that he may come and curse all the people of whom you are afraid"; so the elders of Moab heard this thing, and it pleased them to send to Balaam the son of Beor. ⁴⁴ So Balak the son of Zippor, king of Moab, sent messengers to Balaam, saying, ⁴⁵ "Behold, there is a people having come out from Egypt: behold, they cover the face of the earth, and they abide near me. ⁴⁶ Now therefore, come and curse this people for me, for they are too mighty for me; perhaps [then] I will prevail to fight against them and drive them out, for I heard that he whom you bless is blessed, and whom you curse is cursed." ⁴⁷ So the messengers of Balak went to Balaam and brought Balaam to curse the people to fight against Moab. ⁴⁸ And Balaam came to Balak to curse Israel, and the LORD said to Balaam, "Do not curse this people for it is blessed." ⁴⁹ And Balak urged Balaam to curse Israel day by day, but Balaam did not listen to Balak on account of the word of the LORD which He had spoken to Balaam. ⁵⁰ And when Balak saw that Balaam would not accede to his wish, he rose up and went home, and Balaam also returned to his land, and he went from there to Midian. ⁵¹ And the sons of Israel journeyed from the plain of Moab and pitched by the Jordan from Beth-Jesimoth even to Abel-Shittim, at the end of the plains of Moab. ⁵² And when the sons of Israel dwelt in the plain of Shittim, they began to commit whoredom with the daughters of Moab. ⁵³ And the sons of Israel approached Moab, and the children of Moab pitched their tents opposite to the camp of the sons of Israel. ⁵⁴ And the children of Moab were afraid of the sons of Israel, and the children of Moab took all their daughters and their wives of beautiful aspect and attractive appearance and dressed them in gold, and silver, and costly garments. ⁵⁵ And the children of Moab seated those women at the door of their tents in order that the sons of Israel might see them and turn to them, and not fight against Moab. ⁵⁶ And all the children of Moab did this thing to the sons of Israel, and every man placed his wife and daughter at the door of his tent, and all the sons of Israel saw the act of the children of Moab, and the sons of Israel turned to the daughters of Moab and coveted them, and they went to them. ⁵⁷ And it came to pass that when a Hebrew came to the door of the tent of Moab, and saw a daughter of Moab, and desired her in his heart, and spoke with her at the door of the tent that he desired, while they were speaking together the men of the tent would come out and speak to the Hebrew like to these words: ⁵⁸ "Surely you know that we are brothers: we are all the descendants of Lot and the descendants of his brother Abraham; why then will you not remain with us, and why will you not eat our bread and our sacrifice?" ⁵⁹ And when the children of Moab had thus overwhelmed him with their speeches, and enticed him by their flattering words, they seated him in the tent, and cooked and sacrificed for him, and he ate of their sacrifice and of their bread. [60] Then they gave him wine, and he drank and became intoxicated, and they placed a beautiful young woman before him, and he did with her as he liked, for he did not know what he was doing since he had drunk of wine abundantly. [61] Thus the children of Moab did to Israel in that place, in the plain of Shittim, and the anger of the LORD was kindled against Israel on account of this matter, and He sent a pestilence among them, and there died of the Israelites twenty-four thousand men. [62] Now there was a man of the children of Simeon whose name was Zimri, the son of Salu, who connected himself with the Midianite Cosbi, the daughter of Zur, king of Midian, in the sight of all the sons of Israel. [63] And Phinehas the son of Eleazar, the son of Aaron the priest, saw this wicked thing which Zimri had done, and he took a spear, and rose up, and went after them, and pierced them both, and slew them, and the pestilence ceased from the sons of Israel.

CHAPTER 86

[1] At that time after the pestilence, the LORD spoke to Moses, and to Eleazar the son of Aaron the priest, saying, [2] "Number the heads of the whole community of the sons of Israel, from twenty years old and upward, all that went out in the army." [3] And Moses and Eleazar numbered the sons of Israel after their families, and the number of all Israel was seven hundred thousand, seven hundred and thirty. [4] And the number of the children of Levi, from one month old and upward, was twenty-three thousand, and among these there was not a man of those numbered by Moses and Aaron in the wilderness of Sinai. [5] For the LORD had told them that they would die in the wilderness, so they all died, and not one had been left of them except Caleb the son of Jephuneh, and Joshua the son of Nun. [6] And it was after this that the LORD said to Moses, "Say to the sons of Israel to avenge on Midian the cause of their brothers, the sons of Israel." [7] And Moses did so, and the sons of Israel chose from among them twelve thousand men, being one thousand to a tribe, and they went to Midian. [8] And the sons of Israel warred against Midian, and they slew every male, also the five princes of Midian, and they slew Balaam the son of Beor with the sword. [9] And the sons of Israel took the wives of Midian captive, with their little ones, and their cattle, and all belonging to them. [10] And they took all the spoil and all the prey, and they brought it to Moses and to Eleazar in the plains of Moab. [11] And Moses, and Eleazar, and all the princes of the congregation went out to meet them with joy. [12] And they divided all the spoil of Midian, and the sons of Israel had been avenged on Midian for the cause of their brothers, the sons of Israel.

CHAPTER 87

[1] At that time the LORD said to Moses, "Behold, your days are approaching to an end; now take Joshua the son of Nun, your servant, and place him in the Dwelling Place, and I will command him," and Moses did so. [2] And the LORD appeared in the Dwelling Place in a pillar of cloud, and the pillar of cloud stood at the entrance of the Dwelling Place. [3] And the LORD commanded Joshua the son of Nun and said to him, "Be strong and courageous, for you will bring the sons of Israel to the land which I swore to give them, and I will be with you." [4] And Moses said to Joshua, "Be strong and courageous, for you will make the sons of Israel inherit the land, and the LORD will be with you; He will not leave you nor forsake you; do not be afraid nor disheartened." [5] And Moses called to all the sons of Israel and said to them, "You have seen all the good which the LORD your God has done for you in the wilderness. [6] Now therefore, observe all the words of this law and walk in the way of the LORD your God; do not turn from the way which the LORD has commanded you, either to the right or to the left." [7] And Moses taught the sons of Israel statutes, and judgments, and laws to do in the land as the LORD had commanded him. [8] And he taught them the way of the LORD and His laws; behold, they are written on the Scroll of the Law of God which He gave to the sons of Israel by the hand of Moses. [9] And Moses finished commanding the sons of Israel, and the LORD spoke to him, saying, "Go up to Mount Abarim and die there, and be gathered to your people as your brother Aaron was gathered." [10] And Moses went up as the LORD had commanded him, and he died there in the land of Moab by the order of the LORD, in the fortieth year from the Israelites going out from the land of Egypt. [11] And the sons of Israel wept for Moses in the plains of Moab for thirty days, and the days of weeping and mourning for Moses were completed.

CHAPTER 88

[1] And it was after the death of Moses that the LORD spoke to Joshua the son of Nun, saying, [2] "Rise up and pass the Jordan to the land which I have given to the sons of Israel, and you will make the sons of Israel inherit the land. [3] Every place on which the sole of your feet will tread will belong to you, from the wilderness of Lebanon to the great river; the river of Perath will be your boundary. [4] No man will stand up against you all the days of your life; as I was with Moses, so I will be with you; only be strong and of good courage to observe all the Law which Moses commanded you; do not turn from the way, either to the right or to the left, in order that you may prosper in all that you do." [5] And Joshua commanded the officers of Israel, saying, "Pass through the camp and command the people, saying, Prepare provisions for yourselves, for in three more days you will pass the Jordan to possess the land." [6] And the officers of the

sons of Israel did so, and they commanded the people and they did all that Joshua had commanded. [7] And Joshua sent two men to spy out the land of Jericho, and the men went and spied out Jericho. [8] And at the end of seven days they came to Joshua in the camp and said to him, "The LORD has delivered the whole land into our hands, and the inhabitants thereof have melted with fear because of us." [9] And it came to pass after that, that Joshua rose up in the morning and all Israel with him, and they journeyed from Shittim, and Joshua and all Israel with him passed the Jordan; and Joshua was eighty-two years old when he passed the Jordan with Israel. [10] And the people went up from Jordan on the tenth day of the first month, and they encamped in Gilgal at the eastern corner of Jericho. [11] And the sons of Israel kept the Passover in Gilgal, in the plains of Jericho, on the fourteenth day of the month as it is written in the Law of Moses. [12] And the manna ceased at that time on the next day of the Passover, and there was no more manna for the sons of Israel, and they ate of the produce of the land of Canaan. [13] And Jericho was entirely closed against the sons of Israel—no one came out or went in. [14] And it was in the second month, on the first day of the month, that the LORD said to Joshua, "Rise up; behold, I have given Jericho into your hand with all the people thereof; and all your fighting men will go around the city once each day: thus you will do for six days. [15] And the priests will blow on trumpets, and when you will hear the sound of the trumpet, all the people will give a great shouting [so] that the walls of the city will fall down; all the people will go up—every man against his opponent." [16] And Joshua did so according to all that the LORD had commanded him. [17] And on the seventh day they went around the city seven times, and the priests blew on trumpets. [18] And at the seventh round, Joshua said to the people, "Shout! For the LORD has delivered the whole city into our hands. [19] Only the city and all that it contains will be accursed to the LORD, and keep yourselves from the accursed thing, lest you make the camp of Israel accursed and trouble it. [20] But all the silver, and gold, and brass, and iron will be consecrated to the LORD; they will come into the treasury of the LORD." [21] And the people blew on trumpets and made a great shouting, and the walls of Jericho fell down, and all the people went up, every man straight before him, and they took the city and utterly destroyed all that was in it, both man and woman, young and old, ox, and sheep, and donkey, with the edge of the sword. [22] And they burned the whole city with fire; only the vessels of silver and gold, and brass and iron, they put into the treasury of the LORD. [23] And Joshua swore at that time, saying, "Cursed be the man who builds Jericho; he will lay the foundation thereof in his firstborn, and in his youngest son he will set up the gates thereof." [24] And Achan the son of Carmi, the son of Zabdi, the son of Zerah, son of Judah, dealt treacherously in the accursed thing, and he took of the accursed thing and hid it in the tent, and the anger of the LORD was kindled against Israel. [25] And it was after this when the sons of Israel had returned from burning Jericho, Joshua also sent men to spy out Ai and to fight against it. [26] And the men went up and spied out Ai, and they returned and said, "Do not let all the people go up with you to Ai; only let about three thousand men go up and strike the city, for the men thereof are but few." [27] And Joshua did so, and there went up with him of the sons of Israel about three thousand men, and they fought against the men of Ai. [28] And the battle was severe against Israel, and the men of Ai struck thirty-six men of Israel, and the sons of Israel fled from before the men of Ai. [29] And when Joshua saw this thing, he tore his garments and fell on his face to the ground before the LORD, he, with the elders of Israel, and they put dust on their heads. [30] And Joshua said, "Why, O LORD, did You bring this people over the Jordan? What will I say after the Israelites have turned their backs against their enemies? [31] Now therefore, all the Canaanites, inhabitants of the land, will hear this thing, and surround us and cut off our name." [32] And the LORD said to Joshua, "Why do you fall on your face? Rise, get up, for the Israelites have sinned and taken of the accursed thing; I will no longer be with them unless they destroy the accursed thing from among them." [33] And Joshua rose up, and assembled the people, and brought the Lights by the order of the LORD, and the tribe of Judah was taken, and Achan the son of Carmi was taken. [34] And Joshua said to Achan, "Tell me, my son, what have you done?" And Achan said, "I saw among the spoil a fancy garment of Shinar, and two hundred shekels of silver, and a wedge of gold of fifty shekels weight; I coveted them and took them, and behold, they are all hid in the earth in the midst of the tent." [35] And Joshua sent men who went and took them from the tent of Achan, and they brought them to Joshua. [36] And Joshua took Achan and these utensils, and his sons and daughters, and all belonging to him, and they brought them into the Valley of Achor. [37] And Joshua burned them there with fire, and all the Israelites stoned Achan with stones, and they raised a heap of stones over him; therefore, he called that place the Valley of Achor, so the LORD's anger was appeased, and afterward Joshua came to the city and fought against it. [38] And the LORD said to Joshua, "Do not fear, neither be dismayed: behold, I have given Ai, her king, and her people into your hand, and you will do to them as you did to Jericho and her king—only the spoil thereof and the cattle thereof you will take for a prey for yourselves; lay an ambush for the city behind it." [39] So Joshua did according to the word of the LORD, and he chose thirty thousand valiant men from among the sons of war, and he sent them, and they lay in ambush for the city. [40] And he commanded them, saying, "When you will see us, we will flee before them with cunning, and they will pursue us, you will then rise out of the ambush and take the city," and they did so. ⁴¹ And Joshua fought, and the men of the city went out toward Israel not knowing that they were lying in ambush for them behind the city. ⁴² And Joshua and all the Israelites pretended themselves [to be] wearied out before them, and they fled by the way of the wilderness with cunning. ⁴³ And the men of Ai gathered all the people who were in the city to pursue the Israelites, and they went out and were drawn away from the city—not one remained; and they left the city open and pursued the Israelites. ⁴⁴ And those who were lying in ambush rose up out of their places, and hastened to come to the city, and took it, and set it on fire, and the men of Ai turned back, and behold, the smoke of the city ascended to the skies, and they had no means of retreating either one way or the other. ⁴⁵ And all the men of Ai were in the midst of Israel, some on this side and some on that side, and they struck them so that not one of them remained. ⁴⁶ And the sons of Israel took Melosh king of Ai alive, and they brought him to Joshua, and Joshua hanged him on a tree, and he died. ⁴⁷ And the sons of Israel returned to the city after having burned it, and they struck all those that were in it with the edge of the sword. ⁴⁸ And the number of those that had fallen of the men of Ai, both man and woman, was twelve thousand; only the cattle and the spoil of the city they took to themselves, according to the word of the LORD to Joshua. ⁴⁹ And all the kings on this side Jordan, all the kings of Canaan, heard of the evil which the sons of Israel had done to Jericho and to Ai, and they gathered themselves together to fight against Israel. ⁵⁰ Only the inhabitants of Gibeon were greatly afraid of fighting against the Israelites lest they should perish, so they acted cunningly, and they came to Joshua and to all Israel, and said to them, "We have come from a distant land; now therefore, make a covenant with us." ⁵¹ And the inhabitants of Gibeon outwitted the sons of Israel, and the sons of Israel made a covenant with them, and they made peace with them, and the princes of the congregation swore to them, but afterward the sons of Israel knew that they were neighbors to them and were dwelling among them. ⁵² But the sons of Israel did not slay them, for they had sworn to them by the LORD, and they became hewers of wood and drawers of water. ⁵³ And Joshua said to them, "Why did you deceive me, to do this thing to us?" And they answered him, saying, "Because it was told to your servants all that you had done to all the kings of the Amorites, and we were greatly afraid for our lives, and we did this thing." ⁵⁴ And Joshua appointed them on that day to hew wood and to draw water, and he divided them for slaves to all the tribes of Israel. ⁵⁵ And when Adonizedek king of Jerusalem heard all that the sons of Israel had done to Jericho and to Ai, he sent to Hoham king of Hebron, and to

Piram king at Jarmuth, and to Japhia king of Lachish, and to Deber king of Eglon, saying, ⁵⁶ "Come up to me and help me [so] that we may strike the sons of Israel and the inhabitants of Gibeon who have made peace with the sons of Israel." ⁵⁷ And they gathered themselves together, and the five kings of the Amorites went up with all their camps—a mighty people [as] numerous as the sand of the seashore. ⁵⁸ And all these kings came and encamped before Gibeon, and they began to fight against the inhabitants of Gibeon, and all the men of Gibeon sent to Joshua, saying, "Come up quickly to us and help us, for all the kings of the Amorites have gathered together to fight against us." ⁵⁹ And Joshua and all the fighting people went up from Gilgal, and Joshua came suddenly to them, and struck these five kings with a great slaughter. ⁶⁰ And the LORD confounded them before the sons of Israel, who struck them with a terrible slaughter in Gibeon, and pursued them along the way that goes up to Beth-Horon to Makkedah, and they fled from before the sons of Israel. ⁶¹ And while they were fleeing, the LORD sent hailstones on them from Heaven, and more of them died by the hailstones than by the slaughter of the sons of Israel. ⁶² And the sons of Israel pursued them, and they still struck them in the road, going on and striking them. ⁶³ And when they were striking, the day was declining toward evening, and Joshua said in the sight of all the people, "Sun, stand still on Gibeon, and moon, in the Valley of Ajalon, until the nation will have avenged itself on its enemies." ⁶⁴ And the LORD listened to the voice of Joshua, and the sun stood still in the midst of the heavens, and it stood still thirty-six moments, and the moon also stood still and did not hasten to go down [for] a whole day. ⁶⁵ And there was no day like that, before it or after it, [in] that the LORD listened to the voice of a man, for the LORD fought for Israel.

CHAPTER 89

¹ Then Joshua spoke this song on the day that the LORD had given the Amorites into the hand of Joshua and the sons of Israel, and he said in the sight of all Israel, ² "You have done mighty things, O LORD, ‖ You have performed great deeds; Who is like You? My lips will sing to Your Name— ³ My goodness and my fortress, my high tower, ‖ I will sing a new song to You, ‖ I will sing to You with thanksgiving; You are the strength of my salvation. ⁴ All the kings of the earth will praise You, ‖ The princes of the world will sing to You, ‖ The sons of Israel will rejoice in Your salvation, ‖ They will sing and praise Your power. ⁵ To You, O LORD, we confided; We said You are our God, ‖ For You were our shelter and strong tower against our enemies. ⁶ To You we cried and were not ashamed; In You we trusted and were delivered; When we cried to You, You heard our voice, ‖ You delivered our souls from the sword, ‖ You showed

Your grace to us, ‖ You gave Your salvation to us, ‖ You made our hearts rejoice with Your strength. ⁷You went out for our salvation, ‖ With Your arm You redeemed Your people; You answered us from the heavens of Your holiness, ‖ You saved us from tens of thousands of people. ⁸The sun and moon stood still in [the] heavens, ‖ And You stood in Your wrath against our oppressors ‖ And commanded Your judgments over them. ⁹All the princes of the earth stood up, ‖ The kings of the nations had gathered themselves together; They were not moved at Your presence, ‖ They desired Your battles. ¹⁰You rose against them in Your anger ‖ And brought down Your wrath on them; You destroyed them in Your anger ‖ And cut them off in Your heart. ¹¹Nations have been consumed with Your fury, ‖ Kingdoms have declined because of Your wrath, ‖ You wounded kings in the day of Your anger. ¹²You poured out Your fury on them—Your wrathful anger took hold of them; You turned their iniquity on them ‖ And cut them off in their wickedness. ¹³They spread a trap, they fell therein, ‖ In the net they hid, their foot was caught. ¹⁴Your hand was ready for all Your enemies who said, ‖ Through their sword they possessed the land, ‖ Through their arm they dwelt in the city; You filled their faces with shame, ‖ You brought their horns down to the ground, ‖ You terrified them in Your wrath, ‖ And destroyed them in Your anger. ¹⁵The earth trembled and shook at the sound of Your storm over them, ‖ You did not withhold their souls from death, ‖ And brought down their lives to the grave. ¹⁶You pursued them in Your storm, ‖ You consumed them in Your whirlwind, ‖ You turned their rain into hail; They fell into deep pits so that they could not rise. ¹⁷Their carcasses were like rubbish cast out in the middle of the streets. ¹⁸They were consumed and destroyed in Your anger, ‖ You saved your people with Your might. ¹⁹Therefore our hearts rejoice in You, ‖ Our souls exalt in Your salvation. ²⁰Our tongues will relate Your might, ‖ We will sing and praise Your wondrous works. ²¹For You saved us from our enemies, ‖ You delivered us from those who rose up against us, ‖ You destroyed them from before us ‖ And depressed them beneath our feet. ²²Thus all Your enemies will perish O Lord, ‖ And the wicked will be like chaff driven by the wind, ‖ And Your beloved will be like trees planted by the waters." ²³So Joshua and all Israel with him returned to the camp in Gilgal after having smitten all the kings, so that not [even] a remnant was left of them. ²⁴And the five kings fled alone on foot from battle, and hid themselves in a cave, and Joshua sought for them in the field of battle and did not find them. ²⁵And afterward it was told to Joshua, saying, "The kings have been found, and behold, they are hidden in a cave." ²⁶And Joshua said, "Appoint men to be at the mouth of the cave to guard them, lest they escape"; and the sons of Israel did so. ²⁷And Joshua called to

all Israel and said to the officers of battle, "Place your feet on the necks of these kings," and Joshua said, "So the Lord will do to all your enemies." ²⁸And afterward Joshua commanded that they should slay the kings, and cast them into the cave, and to put great stones at the mouth of the cave. ²⁹And afterward Joshua went to Makkedah with all the people that were with him on that day, and he struck it with the edge of the sword. ³⁰And he utterly destroyed the souls and all belonging to the city, and he did to the king and people thereof as he had done to Jericho. ³¹And he passed from there to Libnah, and he fought against it, and the Lord delivered it into his hand, and Joshua struck it with the edge of the sword, and all the souls thereof, and he did to it and to the king thereof as he had done to Jericho. ³²And from there he passed on to Lachish to fight against it, and Horam king of Gaza went up to assist the men of Lachish, and Joshua struck him and his people until there was none left to him. ³³And Joshua took Lachish and all the people thereof, and he did to it as he had done to Libnah. ³⁴And Joshua passed from there to Eglon, and he took that also, and he struck it and all the people thereof with the edge of the sword. ³⁵And from there he passed to Hebron, and fought against it, and took it, and utterly destroyed it, and he returned from there with all Israel to Debir, and he fought against it and struck it with the edge of the sword. ³⁶And he destroyed every soul in it—he left none remaining; and he did to it and the king thereof as he had done to Jericho. ³⁷And Joshua struck all the kings of the Amorites from Kadesh-Barnea to Azah, and he took their country at once, for the Lord had fought for Israel. ³⁸And Joshua came to the camp with all Israel, to Gilgal. ³⁹When at that time Jabin king of Chazor heard all that Joshua had done to the kings of the Amorites, Jabin sent to Jobat king of Midian, and to Laban king of Shimron, to Jephal king of Achshaph, and to all the kings of the Amorites, saying, ⁴⁰"Come quickly to us and help us [so] that we may strike the sons of Israel before they come on us and do to us as they have done to the other kings of the Amorites." ⁴¹And all these kings listened to the words of Jabin, king of Chazor, and they went out with all their camps, seventeen kings, and their people were as numerous as the sand on the seashore, together with horses and innumerable chariots, and they came and pitched [their tents] together at the waters of Merom, and they were gathered together to fight against Israel. ⁴²And the Lord said to Joshua, "Do not fear them, for about this time tomorrow I will deliver them all up slain before you: you will hamstring their horses and burn their chariots with fire." ⁴³And Joshua with all the men of war came suddenly on them and struck them, and they fell into their hands, for the Lord had delivered them into the hands of the sons of Israel. ⁴⁴So the sons of Israel pursued all these kings with their camps and struck them until there was none left of them, and Joshua did to them as the LORD had spoken to him. ⁴⁵ And Joshua returned at that time to Chazor, and struck it with the sword, and destroyed every soul in it, and burned it with fire; and Joshua passed from Chazor to Shimron, and struck it, and utterly destroyed it. ⁴⁶ From there he passed to Achshaph and he did to it as he had done to Shimron. ⁴⁷ From there he passed to Adulam and he struck all the people in it, and he did to Adulam as he had done to Achshaph and to Shimron. ⁴⁸ And he passed from them to all the cities of the kings which he had smitten, and he struck all the people that were left of them and utterly destroyed them. ⁴⁹ Only their plunder and cattle the Israelites took to themselves as a prey, but every human being they struck; they did not permit a soul to live. ⁵⁰ As the LORD had commanded Moses, so Joshua and all Israel did; they did not fail in anything. ⁵¹ So Joshua and all the sons of Israel struck the whole land of Canaan as the LORD had commanded them, and struck all their kings, being thirty-one kings, and the sons of Israel took their whole country, ⁵² besides the kingdoms of Sihon and Og, which are on the other side Jordan, of which Moses had smitten many cities, and Moses gave them to the Reubenites, and the Gadites, and to half the tribe of Manasseh. ⁵³ And Joshua struck all the kings that were on this side of the Jordan to the west, and he gave them for an inheritance to the nine tribes and to the half tribe of Israel. ⁵⁴ For five years Joshua carried on the war with these kings, and he gave their cities to the Israelites, and the land became tranquil from battle throughout the cities of the Amorites and the Canaanites.

CHAPTER 90

¹ At that time, in the fifth year after the sons of Israel had passed over [the] Jordan, after the sons of Israel had rested from their war with the Canaanites, at that time great and severe battles arose between Edom and the children of Chittim, and the children of Chittim fought against Edom. ² And Abianus king of Chittim went out in that year, that is in the thirty-first year of his reign, and a great force with him of the mighty men of the children of Chittim, and he went to Seir to fight against the children of Esau. ³ And Hadad the king of Edom heard of his report, and he went out to meet him with a heavy people and a strong force, and he engaged in battle with him in the field of Edom. ⁴ And the hand of Chittim prevailed over the children of Esau, and the children of Chittim slew twenty-two thousand men of the children of Esau, and all the children of Esau fled from before them. ⁵ And the children of Chittim pursued them, and they reached Hadad king of Edom who was running before them, and they caught him alive and brought him to Abianus king of Chittim. ⁶ And Abianus ordered him to be slain, and Hadad king of Edom died in the forty-eighth year of his reign. ⁷ And the children of Chittim

continued their pursuit of Edom, and they struck them with a great slaughter, and Edom became subject to the children of Chittim. ⁸ And the children of Chittim ruled over Edom, and Edom came under the hand of the children of Chittim and became one kingdom from that day. ⁹ And from that time on they could no longer lift up their heads, and their kingdom became one with the children of Chittim. ¹⁰ And Abianus placed officers in Edom, and all the children of Edom became subject and tributary to Abianus, and Abianus turned back to his own land, Chittim. ¹¹ And when he returned, he renewed his government, and built for himself a spacious and fortified palace for a royal residence, and reigned securely over the children of Chittim and over Edom. ¹² In those days, after the sons of Israel had driven away all the Canaanites and the Amorites, Joshua was old and advanced in years, ¹³ and the LORD said to Joshua, "You are old, advanced in life, and a great part of the land remains to be possessed. ¹⁴ Now therefore, divide this land for an inheritance to the nine tribes and to the half tribe of Manasseh," and Joshua rose up and did as the LORD had spoken to him. ¹⁵ And he divided the whole land to the tribes of Israel as an inheritance according to their divisions. ¹⁶ But to the tribe at Levi he gave no inheritance—the offerings of the LORD are their inheritance as the LORD had spoken of them by the hand of Moses. ¹⁷ And Joshua gave Mount Hebron to Caleb the son of Jephuneh, one portion above his brothers, as the LORD had spoken through Moses. ¹⁸ Therefore Hebron became an inheritance to Caleb and his children to this day. ¹⁹ And Joshua divided the whole land by lots to all Israel for an inheritance as the LORD had commanded him. ²⁰ And the sons of Israel gave cities to the Levites from their own inheritance, and suburbs for their cattle and property; as the LORD had commanded Moses, so the sons of Israel did, and they divided the land by lot whether great or small. ²¹ And they went to inherit the land according to their boundaries, and the sons of Israel gave to Joshua the son of Nun an inheritance among them. ²² By the word of the LORD they gave to him the city which he required, Timnath-Serah in Mount Ephraim, and he built the city and dwelt therein. ²³ These are the inheritances which Eleazar the priest, and Joshua the son of Nun, and the heads of the fathers of the tribes portioned out to the sons of Israel by lot in Shiloh, before the LORD, at the door of the Dwelling Place, and they ceased dividing the land. ²⁴ And the LORD gave the land to the Israelites, and they possessed it as the LORD had spoken to them and as the LORD had sworn to their ancestors. ²⁵ And the LORD gave to the Israelites rest from all their enemies around them, and no man stood up against them, and the LORD delivered all their enemies into their hands, and not one thing failed of all the good which the LORD had spoken to the sons of Israel—the LORD performed everything. ²⁶ And Joshua called to all the sons of Israel, and he blessed them and commanded them to serve the LORD, and afterward he sent them away, and each man went to his city, and each man to his inheritance. [27] And the sons of Israel served the LORD all the days of Joshua, and the LORD gave them rest from all around them, and they dwelt securely in their cities. [28] And it came to pass in those days that Abianus king of Chittim died in the thirty-eighth year of his reign, that is the seventh year of his reign over Edom, and they buried him in his place which he had built for himself, and Latinus reigned in his stead [for] fifty years. [29] And during his reign, he brought out an army, and he went and fought against the inhabitants of Britannia and Kernania, the children of Elisha son of Javan, and he prevailed over them and made them tributary. [30] He then heard that Edom had revolted from under the hand of Chittim, and Latinus went to them, and struck them, and subdued them, and placed them under the hand of the children of Chittim, and Edom became one kingdom with the children of Chittim all the days. [31] And for many years there was no king in Edom, and their government was with the children of Chittim and their king. [32] And it was in the twenty-sixth year after the sons of Israel had passed the Jordan, that is the sixty-sixth year after the sons of Israel had departed from Egypt, that Joshua was old, advanced in years, being one hundred and eight years old in those days. [33] And Joshua called to all Israel, to their elders, their judges and officers, after the LORD had given to all the Israelites rest from all their surrounding enemies, and Joshua said to the elders of Israel, and to their judges, "Behold, I am old, advanced in years, and you have seen what the LORD has done to all the nations whom He has driven away from before you, for it is the LORD who has fought for you. [34] Now therefore, strengthen yourselves to keep and to do all the words of the Law of Moses, not to deviate from it to the right or to the left, and not to come among those nations who are left in the land; neither will you make mention of the name of their gods, but you will cleave to the LORD your God as you have done to this day." [35] And Joshua greatly exhorted the sons of Israel to serve the LORD all their days. [36] And all the Israelites said, "We will serve the LORD our God all our days—we, and our children, and our children's children, and our seed forever." [37] And Joshua made a covenant with the people on that day, and he sent the sons of Israel away, and each man went to his inheritance and to his city. [38] And it was in those days, when the sons of Israel were dwelling securely in their cities, that they buried the coffins of the tribes of their ancestors, which they had brought up from Egypt—each man in the inheritance of his children; the sons of Israel buried the twelve sons of Jacob—each man in the possession of his children. [39] And these are the names of the cities wherein they buried the twelve sons of Jacob, whom the sons of Israel had brought up from Egypt. [40] And they buried Reuben and Gad on this side of the Jordan, in Romia, which Moses had given to their children. [41] And they buried Simeon and Levi in the city [of] Mauda, which he had given to the children of Simeon, and the suburb of the city was for the children of Levi. [42] And they buried Judah in the city of Benjamin opposite Beth-Lehem. [43] And they buried the bones of Issachar and Zebulun in Zidon, in the portion which fell to their children. [44] And Dan was buried in the city of his children, in Eshtael. And they buried Naphtali and Asher in Kadesh-Naphtali, each man in his place which he had given to his children. [45] And they buried the bones of Joseph in Shechem, in the part of the field which Jacob had purchased from Hamor, and which became an inheritance for Joseph. [46] And they buried Benjamin in Jerusalem opposite the Jebusite, which was given to the children of Benjamin; the sons of Israel buried their fathers—each man in the city of his children. [47] And at the end of two years, Joshua the son of Nun died, [being] one hundred and ten years old, and the time which Joshua judged Israel was twenty-eight years, and Israel served the LORD all the days of his life. [48] And the other affairs of Joshua, and his battles, and his reproofs with which he reproved Israel, and all which he had commanded them, and the names of the cities which the sons of Israel possessed in his days, behold, they are written in the scroll of the words of Joshua to the sons of Israel, and in the scroll of the Wars of the LORD, which Moses, and Joshua, and the sons of Israel had written. [49] And the sons of Israel buried Joshua in the border of his inheritance, in Timnath-Serah, which was given to him in Mount Ephraim. [50] And Eleazar the son of Aaron died in those days, and they buried him in a hill belonging to his son Phinehas, which was given [to] him in Mount Ephraim.

CHAPTER 91

[1] At that time, after the death of Joshua, the children of the Canaanites were still in the land, and the Israelites resolved to drive them out. [2] And the sons of Israel asked of the LORD, saying, "Who will first go up for us to the Canaanites to fight against them?" And the LORD said, "Judah will go up." [3] And the children of Judah said to Simeon, "Go up with us into our lot, and we will fight against the Canaanites, and we will likewise go up with you in your lot," so the children of Simeon went with the children of Judah. [4] And the children of Judah went up and fought against the Canaanites, so the LORD delivered the Canaanites into the hands of the children of Judah, and they struck them in Bezek—ten thousand men. [5] And they fought with Adonibezek in Bezek, and he fled from before them, and they pursued him and caught him, and they took hold of him and cut off his thumbs and great toes. [6] And Adonibezek said, "Seventy kings having their thumbs and great toes cut off gathered their meat under my table; as I have

done, so God has paid me back," and they brought him to Jerusalem and he died there. ⁷ And the children of Simeon went with the children of Judah, and they struck the Canaanites with the edge of the sword. ⁸ And the LORD was with the children of Judah, and they possessed the mountain, and the children of Joseph went up to Bethel, the same is Luz, and the LORD was with them. ⁹ And the children of Joseph spied out Bethel, and the watchmen saw a man going out from the city, and they caught him and said to him, "Show us the entrance of the city now and we will show kindness to you." ¹⁰ And that man showed them the entrance of the city, and the children of Joseph came and struck the city with the edge of the sword. ¹¹ And they sent the man away with his family, and he went to the Hittites and built a city, and he called the name thereof Luz, so all the Israelites dwelt in their cities, and the children of Israel dwelt in their cities, and the sons of Israel served the LORD all the days of Joshua, and all the days of the elders, who had lengthened their days after Joshua, and saw the great work of the LORD which He had performed for Israel. ¹² And the elders judged Israel after the death of Joshua for seventeen years. ¹³ And all the elders also fought the battles of Israel against the Canaanites, and the LORD drove the Canaanites from before the sons of Israel in order to place the Israelites in their land. ¹⁴ And He accomplished all the words which He had spoken to Abraham, Isaac, and Jacob, and the oath which He had sworn, to give the land of the Canaanites to them and to their children. ¹⁵ And the LORD gave the whole land of Canaan to the sons of Israel as He had sworn to their ancestors, and the LORD gave them rest from those around them, and the sons of Israel dwelt securely in their cities. ¹⁶ Blessed is the LORD forever—amen and amen! ¹⁷ Strengthen yourselves and let the hearts of all you that trust in the LORD be of good courage.

LIFE OF ADAM AND EVE

The Life of Adam and Eve, also known in its Greek version as the Apocalypse of Moses, is a Jewish apocryphal group of writings. It recounts the lives of Adam and Eve from after their expulsion from the Garden of Eden to their deaths. It provides more detail about the Fall of Man, including Eve's version of the story. Satan explains that he rebelled when God commanded him to bow down to Adam. After Adam dies, he and all his descendants are promised a resurrection. The extant version comes from the first to fifth centuries AD, but there is widespread consensus the original work was composed in the 1st century or earlier.

CHAPTER 1

[1] This is the story of Adam and Eve after they had gone out of Paradise. [2] And Adam knew his wife Eve and went upwards to the sun-rising and abode there eighteen years and two months. [3] And Eve conceived and bore two sons: Adiaphotos, who is called Cain, and Amilabes, who is called Abel.

CHAPTER 2

[1] And after this, Adam and Eve were with one another and while they were sleeping, Eve said to Adam her lord, "My lord, Adam, behold, [2] I have seen in a dream this night the blood of my son Amilabes, who is styled Abel, being poured into the mouth of his brother Cain, and he went on drinking it without pity. But he begged him to leave him a little of it. [3] Yet he did not listen to him, but gulped down the whole; nor did it stay in his stomach, but came out of his mouth." [4] And Adam said, "Let us arise and go and see what has happened to them. [I fear] lest the adversary may be assailing them somewhere."

CHAPTER 3

[1] And they both went and found Abel murdered by the hand of his brother Cain. [2] And God says to the chief-messenger Michael, "Say to Adam: Do not reveal the secret that you know to Cain your son, for he is a son of wrath. But do not grieve, for I will give you another son in his stead; he will show [to you] all that you will do. Do not tell him anything." Thus spoke the chief-messenger to Adam. [3] But he kept the word in his heart, and with him also Eve, though they grieved concerning their son Abel.

CHAPTER 4

[1] And after this, Adam knew his wife Eve, and she conceived and bore Seth. [2] And Adam said to Eve, "See! We have begotten a son in place of Abel, whom Cain slew, let us give glory and sacrifice to God."

CHAPTER 5

[1] And Adam begot thirty sons and thirty daughters and Adam lived nine hundred and thirty years; [2] and he fell sick and cried with a loud voice and said, "Let all my sons come to me that I may see them before I die." [3] And all assembled, for the earth was divided into three parts. And his son Seth said to him, [4] "Father Adam, what is your complaint?" [5] And he says, "My children, I am crushed by the burden of trouble." And they say to him, "What is trouble?"

CHAPTER 6

[1] And Seth answered and said to him, "Have you called to mind, father, the fruit of paradise of which you used to eat, and have been grieved in yearning for it? [2] If this be so, tell me—I will go and bring you fruit from paradise. For I will set dung on my head and will weep and pray that the LORD will listen to me and send His messenger (and bring me a plant from paradise), and I will bring it to you that your trouble may cease from you." [3] Adam says to him, "No, my son Seth, but I have [much] sickness and trouble!" Seth says to him, "And how has this come on you?"

CHAPTER 7

[1] And Adam said to him, "When God made us, me and your mother, through whom also I die, He gave us power to eat of every tree which is in paradise, but, concerning that one only, He charged us not to eat of it, and through this one we are to die. [2] And the hour drew near for the messengers who were guarding your mother to go up and worship the LORD, and I was far from her, and the enemy knew that she was alone and gave to her, and she ate of the tree of which she had been told not to eat. [3] Then she also gave to me to eat."

CHAPTER 8

[1] "And God was angry with us, and the LORD came into paradise and called me in a terrible voice and said, Adam, where are you and why do you hide from My face? Will the house be able to hide itself from its builder? And He says to me, Since you have abandoned My covenant, I have brought on your body seventy-two strokes; the trouble of the first stroke is a pain of the eyes, the second stroke an affection of the hearing, and likewise in turn all the strokes will befall you."

CHAPTER 9

[1] As he said this to his sons, Adam groaned sore and said, "What will I do? I am in great distress." [2] And Eve wept and said, "My lord Adam, rise up and give me half of your trouble and I will endure it; for it is

on my account that this has happened to you, on my account you are beset with toils and troubles." ³ But Adam said to Eve, "Arise and go with my son Seth near to paradise, and put earth on your heads and weep and pray [to] God to have mercy on me and [to] send His messenger to paradise, and give me of the tree out of which the oil flows, and bring it me, and I will anoint myself and will have rest from my complaint."

CHAPTER 10

¹ Then Seth and Eve went toward paradise, and Eve saw her son, and a wild beast assailing him, and Eve wept and said, ² "Woe is me! If I come to the day of the resurrection, all those who have sinned will curse me, saying, Eve has not kept the commandment of God." ³ And she spoke to the beast: "You wicked beast, do you not fear to fight with the image of God? How was your mouth opened? How were your teeth made strong? How did you not call to mind your subjection? For long ago you were made subject to the image of God." ⁴ Then the beast cried out and said:

CHAPTER 11

¹ "It is not our concern, Eve, your greed and your wailing, but your own; for [it is] from you that the rule of the beasts has arisen. ² How was your mouth opened to eat of the tree concerning which God enjoined you not to eat of it? On this account, our nature has also been transformed. ³ Now therefore, you cannot endure it if I begin to reprove you."

CHAPTER 12

¹ Then Seth speaks to the beast, "Close your mouth and be silent and stand off from the image of God until the Day of Judgment." ² Then the beast says to Seth: "Behold, I stand off from the image of God." And he went to his lair.

CHAPTER 13

¹ And Seth went with Eve near paradise, and they wept there, and prayed [to] God to send His messenger and give them the oil of mercy. ² And God sent the chief-messenger Michael and he spoke to Seth: "Seth, man of God, do not weary yourself with prayers and entreaties concerning the tree which flows with oil to anoint your father Adam. For it will not be yours now, but in the end of the times. ³ Then will all flesh be raised up from Adam until that great day—all that will be of the holy people. ⁴ Then the delights of paradise will be given to them and God will be in their midst. ⁵ And they will no longer sin before His face, for the evil heart will be taken from them and there will be given them a heart understanding the good and to serve God only. ⁶ But you go back to your father. For the term of his life has been fulfilled and he will live three days from today

and will die. ⁷ But when his soul is departing, you will behold the awful [scene of] his passing."

CHAPTER 14

¹ Thus spoke the messenger and departed from them. And Seth and Eve came to the hut where Adam was laid. ² And Adam says to Eve, "Eve, what have you worked in us? You have brought on us great wrath, which is death, [[lording it over all our race]]." ³ And he says to her, "Call all our children and our children's children and tell them the manner of our transgression."

CHAPTER 15

¹ Then Eve says to them, "Hear, all my children and children's children, and I will relate to you how the enemy deceived us. ² It befell that we were guarding paradise—each of us the portion allotted to us from God. ³ Now I guarded in my lot, the west and the south. But the Devil went to Adam's lot, where the male creatures were. [[For God divided the creatures; all the males he gave to your father and all the females he gave to me.]]"

CHAPTER 16

¹ "And the Devil spoke to the serpent, saying, ² Rise up, come to me, and I will tell you a word whereby you may have profit. And he arose and came to him. And the Devil says to him, ³ I hear that you are wiser than all the beasts, and I have come to counsel you. Why do you eat of Adam's tares and not of paradise? ⁴ Rise up and we will cause him to be cast out of paradise, even as we were cast out through him. The serpent says to him, I fear lest the LORD be angry with me. ⁵ The Devil says to him, Do not fear, only be my vessel and I will speak through your mouth words to deceive him."

CHAPTER 17

¹ "And instantly he hung himself from the wall of paradise, and when the messengers ascended to worship God, then Satan appeared in the form of a messenger and sang hymns like the messengers. ² And I bent over the wall and saw him, like a messenger. But he says to me, Are you Eve? ³ And I said to him, I am. [He said,] What are you doing in paradise? And I said to him, God set us to guard and to eat of it. ⁴ The Devil answered through the mouth of the serpent: You do well, but you do not eat of every plant. ⁵ And I said, Yes, we eat of all, save one only, which is in the midst of paradise, concerning which, God charged us not to eat of it; for, He said to us, On the day on which you eat of it, you will die the death."

CHAPTER 18

¹ "Then the serpent says to me, May God live! But I am grieved on your account, for I would not have you ignorant. ² But arise, [come] here, listen to me and eat

and mind the value of that tree. ³But I said to him, I fear lest God be angry with me as He told us. And he says to me, Do not fear, for as soon as you eat of it, you too will be as God, in that you will know good and evil. ⁴But God perceived this that you would be like Him, so he envied you and said, You will not eat of it. ⁵No, give heed to the plant and you will see its great glory. ⁶Yet I feared to take of the fruit. And he says to me, Come here, and I will give it you. Follow me."

CHAPTER 19

¹"And I opened to him and he walked a little way, then turned and said to me, ²I have changed my mind and I will not give you to eat until you swear to me to give also to your husband. [And] I said, What sort of oath will I swear to you? Yet what I know, I say to you: ³By the throne of the Master, and by the cherubim and the Tree of Life! I will also give to my husband to eat. ⁴And when he had received the oath from me, he went and poured on the fruit the poison of his wickedness, which is lust, the root and beginning of every sin, and he bent the branch on the earth, and I took of the fruit and I ate."

CHAPTER 20

¹"And in that very hour my eyes were opened, ²and immediately I knew that I was bare of the righteousness with which I had been clothed [on], and I wept and said to him, ³Why have you done this to me in that you have deprived me of the glory with which I was clothed? But I also wept about the oath, which I had sworn. But he descended from the tree and vanished. ⁴And I began to seek, in my nakedness, in my part for leaves to hide my shame, but I found none, for, as soon as I had eaten, the leaves showered down from all the trees in my part, except the fig tree only. ⁵But I took leaves from it and made for myself a girdle and it was from the very same plant of which I had eaten."

CHAPTER 21

¹"And I cried out in that very hour, Adam, Adam! Where are you? ²Rise up, come to me and I will show you a great secret. ³But when your father came, I spoke to him words of transgression [[which have brought us down from our great glory]]. For, when he came, I opened my mouth and the Devil was speaking, and I began to exhort him and said, ⁴Come here, my lord Adam, listen to me and eat of the fruit of the tree of which God told us not to eat of it, and you will be as a God. And your father answered and said, I fear lest God be angry with me. ⁵And I said to him, Do not fear, for as soon as you have eaten you will know good and evil. And speedily I persuaded him, and he ate and immediately his eyes were opened, and he too knew his nakedness. ⁶And to me

he says, O wicked woman! What have I done to you that you have deprived me of the glory of God?"

CHAPTER 22

¹"And in that same hour, we heard the chief-messenger Michael blowing with his trumpet and calling to the messengers, and saying, ²Thus says the LORD: Come with me to Paradise and hear the judgment with which I will judge Adam. ³And when God appeared in paradise, mounted on the chariot of His cherubim with the messengers proceeding before Him and singing hymns of praises, all the plants of paradise, both of your father's lot and mine, broke out into flowers. ⁴And the throne of God was fixed where the Tree of Life was."

CHAPTER 23

¹"And God called Adam, saying, Adam, where are you? Can the house be hidden from the presence of its builder? ²Then your father answered, It is not because we do not think to be found by you, LORD, that we hide, but I was afraid, because I am naked, and I was ashamed before Your might, [my] Master. ³God says to him, Who showed you that you are naked, unless you have forsaken My commandment, which I delivered you to keep? ⁴Then Adam called to mind the word which I spoke to him, [saying,] I will make you secure before God. And he turned and said to me, Why have you done this? And I said, The serpent deceived me."

CHAPTER 24

¹"God says to Adam, Since you have disregarded My commandment and have listened to your wife, cursed is the earth in your labors. ²You will work it and it will not give its strength: thorns and thistles will spring up for you, and in the sweat of your face you will eat your bread. [[You will be in manifold toils; you will be crushed by bitterness, but you will not taste of sweetness.]] ³You will be weary and will not rest; you will be tired by heat; you will be straightened by cold: you will busy yourself abundantly, but you will not be rich; and you will grow fat, but come to no end. ⁴The beasts, over whom you ruled, will rise up in rebellion against you, for you have not kept My commandment."

CHAPTER 25

¹"And the LORD turned to me and said, Since you have listened to the serpent, and turned a deaf ear to My commandment, ²you will be in throes of travail and intolerable agonies; you will bear children in much trembling and in one hour you will come to the birth, and lose your life, ³from your sore trouble and anguish. But you will confess and say: ⁴LORD, LORD, save me, and I will no longer turn to the sin of the flesh. And on this account, from your own words I

will judge you, by reason of the enmity which the enemy has planted in you."

CHAPTER 26

[1] "But He turned to the serpent and said, Since you have done this, and become a thankless vessel until you have deceived the innocent hearts, cursed are you among all beasts. [2] You will be deprived of the victual of which you ate and will feed on dust all the days of your life: [3] on your breast and your belly you will walk and be robbed of hands and feet. [4] There will not be left [to] you ear nor wing, nor one limb of all that with which you ensnared them in your malice and caused them to be cast out of paradise; [5] and I will put enmity between you and his Seed: He will bruise your head and you will bruise His heel until the Day of Judgment."

CHAPTER 27

[1] "Thus He spoke and commanded the messengers have us cast out of paradise: and as we were being driven out amid our loud lamentations, your father Adam implored the messengers and said, [2] Leave me a little [space] that I may entreat the LORD that He have compassion on me and pity me, for I only have sinned. [3] And they left off driving him and Adam cried aloud and wept, saying, Pardon me, O LORD, my deed. [4] Then the LORD says to the messengers, Why have you ceased from driving Adam from paradise? Why do you not cast him out? Is it I who have done wrong? [5] Or is My judgment badly judged? [6] Then the messengers fell down on the ground and worshiped the LORD, saying, You are just, O LORD, and You judge righteous judgment."

CHAPTER 28

[1] "But the LORD turned to Adam and said, I will not permit you henceforward to be in paradise. [2] And Adam answered and said, Grant me, O LORD, of the Tree of Life that I may eat of it, before I be cast out. [3] Then the LORD spoke to Adam, You will not take of it now, for I have commanded the cherubim with the flaming sword that turns [every way] to guard it from you that you do not taste of it; [4] but you have the war which the adversary has put into you, yet when you are gone out of paradise, if you should keep yourself from all evil, as one about to die, when again the resurrection has come to pass, I will raise you up and then there will be given to you the Tree of Life."

CHAPTER 29

[1] "Thus spoke the LORD and ordered us to be cast out of paradise. [2] But your father Adam wept before the messengers opposite paradise and the messengers say to him, What would you have us to do, Adam? [3] And your father says to them, Behold, you cast me out. Please, allow me to take away fragrant herbs from paradise, so that I may offer an offering to God after

I have gone out of paradise that he [may] hear me." [4] And the messengers approached God and said, YAH'EL, Perpetual King, command, my Lord, that there be given to Adam incense of sweet fragrance from paradise and seeds for his food. [5] And God commanded Adam go in and take sweet spices and fragrant herbs from paradise and seeds for his food. [6] And the messengers let him go and he took four kinds: crocus, and nard, and calamus, and cinnamon, and the other seeds for his food; [7] and, after taking these, he went out of paradise. And we were on the earth."

CHAPTER 30

[1] "Now then, my children, I have shown you the way in which we were deceived; and you [must] guard yourselves from transgressing against the good."

CHAPTER 31

[1] And when Eve had said this in the midst of her sons, while Adam was lying sick and bound to die after a single day from the sickness which had fastened on him, she says to him, [2] "How is it that you die and I live or how long have I to live after you are dead? Tell me." [3] And Adam says to her, "Do not pay heed to this, for you do not tarry after me, but even both of us are to die together. And she will lie in my place. [4] But when I die, anoint me and let no man touch me until the messenger of the LORD will speak somewhat concerning me. [5] For God will not forget me, but will seek His own creature; and now arise rather, and pray to God until I give up my spirit into His hands who gave it me. [6] For we do not know how we are to meet our Maker, whether He is angry with us, or is merciful and intends to pity and receive us."

CHAPTER 32

[1] And Eve rose up and went outside and fell on the ground and began to say: "I have sinned, O God, I have sinned, O God of All, I have sinned against You. [2] I have sinned against the chosen messengers. I have sinned against the cherubim. I have sinned against Your fearful and unshakable Throne. I have sinned before You and all sin has begun through my doing in the creation." [3] Even thus prayed Eve on her knees; [and] behold, the messenger of humanity came to her, and raised her up and said, [4] "Rise up, Eve, for behold, your husband Adam has gone out of his body. Rise up and behold his spirit borne aloft to his Maker."

CHAPTER 33

[1] And Eve rose up and wiped off her tears with her hand, and the messenger says to her, [2] "Lift yourself up from the earth." And she gazed steadfastly into Heaven, and beheld a chariot of light, borne by four bright eagles, [and] it was impossible for any man born of woman to tell the glory of them or behold their face— [3] and messengers going before the

chariot—and when they came to the place where your father Adam was, the chariot halted and the seraphim. ⁴ And I beheld golden censers, between your father and the chariot, and all the messengers with censers and frankincense came in haste to the incense-offering and blew on it and the smoke of the incense veiled the expanses. ⁵ And the messengers fell down and worshiped God, crying aloud, and saying, "YAH'EL, Holy One, have pardon, for he is Your image, and the work of Your holy hands."

CHAPTER 34

¹ And I, Eve, beheld two great and fearful wonders standing in the presence of God and I wept for fear, ² and I cried aloud to my son Seth and said, "Rise up, Seth, from the body of your father Adam and come to me, and you will see a spectacle which no man's eye has yet beheld."

CHAPTER 35

¹ Then Seth arose and came to his mother and to her he says, "What is your trouble? Why do you weep?" [And] she says to him, ² "Look up and see with your eyes the seven heavens opened, and see how the soul of your father lies on its face and all the holy messengers are praying on his behalf, and saying, Pardon him, Father of All, for he is Your image. ³ Pray, my child Seth, what will this mean? And will he one day be delivered into the hands of the Invisible Father, even our God? ⁴ But who are the two dark ones who stand by at the prayers for your father Adam?"

CHAPTER 36

¹ And Seth tells his mother that, "They are the sun and moon, and they fall down and pray on behalf of my father Adam." ² Eve says to him, "And where is their light and why have they taken on such a black appearance?" ³ And Seth answers her, "The light has not left them, but they cannot shine before the Light of the Universe, the Father of Light; and on this account their light has been hidden from them."

CHAPTER 37

¹ Now while Seth was saying this to his mother, behold, a messenger blew the trumpet, and there stood up all the messengers, [and they were] lying on their faces, and they cried aloud in an awful voice and said, ² "Blessed [is] the glory of the LORD from the works of His making, for He has pitied Adam, the creature of His hands." ³ But when the messengers had said these words, behold, there came one of the seraphim with six wings and snatched up Adam and carried him off to the Acherusian lake, and washed him three times, in the presence of God.

CHAPTER 38

¹ And God says to him, "Adam, what have you done? If you had kept My commandment, there would now be no rejoicing among those who are bringing you down to this place. ² Yet, I tell you that I will turn their joy to grief, and I will turn your grief to joy, and I will transform you to your former glory and set you on the throne of your deceiver. ³ But he will be cast into this place to see you sitting above him, then he will be condemned and they that heard him, and he will be sorely grieved when he sees you sitting on his honorable throne."

CHAPTER 39

¹ And he stayed there three hours, lying down, and thereafter the Father of all, sitting on His holy throne, stretched out His hand, and took Adam and handed him over to the chief-messenger Michael, saying, ² "Lift him up into Paradise to the third heaven, and leave him there until that fearful day of My reckoning, which I will make in the world." ³ Then Michael took Adam and left him where God told him.

CHAPTER 40

¹ But after all this, the chief-messenger asked concerning the laying out of the remains. ² And God commanded that all the messengers should assemble in His presence, each in his order, and all the messengers assembled, some having censers in their hands, and others trumpets. ³ And behold, the LORD of Hosts came on and four winds drew Him, and cherubim mounted on the winds and the messengers from Heaven [were] escorting Him, and they came on the earth where the body of Adam was. ⁴ And they came to paradise and all the leaves of paradise were stirred so that all men begotten of Adam slept from the fragrance save Seth alone, because he was born according to the appointment of God. ⁵ Then Adam's body lay there in paradise on the earth and Seth grieved exceedingly over him.

CHAPTER 41

¹ Then God spoke to the chief-messenger[[s]] Michael, [[Gabriel, Uriel, and Raphael]]: ² "Go away to Paradise in the third heaven, and spread linen clothes and cover the body of Adam, and bring oil of the oil of fragrance and pour it over him." ³ And they acted thus—the three great messengers—and they prepared him for burial. And God said, "Let the body of Abel also be brought." ⁴ And they brought other linen clothes and prepared his [body] also. For he was unburied since the day when his brother Cain slew him; for wicked Cain took great pains to conceal [him] but could not, for the earth would not receive him for the body sprang up from the earth and a voice went out of the earth, saying, ⁵ "I will not receive a companion body, until the earth which was taken and fashioned in me comes to me." At that time, the messengers took it and placed it on a rock, until his father Adam was buried. ⁶ And both were buried, according to the commandment of God, in the spot

where God found the dust, and He caused the place to be dug for two. ⁷And God sent seven messengers to paradise and they brought many fragrant spices and placed them in the earth, and they took the two bodies and placed them in the spot which they had dug and built.

CHAPTER 42

¹And God called and said, "Adam, Adam." And the body answered from the earth and said, "Here I am, Lord." ²And God says to him, "I told you [that] you are earth and to earth you will return. ³Again I promise to you the resurrection; I will raise you up in the resurrection with every man who is of your seed."

CHAPTER 43

¹After these words, God made a seal and sealed the tomb, that no one might do anything to him for six days until his rib should return to him. Then the LORD and His messengers went to their place. ²And Eve also, when the six days were fulfilled, fell asleep. ³But while she was living, she wept bitterly about Adam's falling on sleep, for she did not know where he was laid. For when the LORD came to paradise to bury Adam, she was asleep, and her sons too, except Seth, until He commanded Adam be prepared for burial; and no man knew on earth, except her son Seth. ⁴And Eve prayed in the hour of her death that she might be buried in the place where her husband Adam was. And after she had finished her prayer, she says, ⁵"LORD, Master, God of all rule, do not estrange me, Your handmaid, from the body of Adam, for from his members You made me. ⁶But deem me worthy, even me, unworthy that I am, and a sinner, to enter into his dwelling place, even as I was with him in paradise, both without separation from each other; just as in our transgression, we were led astray, and transgressed Your command, but were not separated. ⁷Even so, Lord, do not separate us now." But after she had prayed, she gazed heavenwards and groaned aloud and struck her breast and said, ⁸"God of all, receive my spirit," and immediately she delivered up her spirit to God.

CHAPTER 44

¹And Michael came and taught Seth how to prepare Eve for burial. And there came three messengers and they buried her [body] where Adam's body was and Abel's. ²And thereafter Michael spoke to Seth and says, "Lay out in this way every man that dies until the day of the resurrection." ³And after giving him this rule he says to him, "Do not mourn beyond six days, but on the seventh day, rest and rejoice on it, because on that very day, God rejoices, and we messengers, with the righteous soul, who has passed away from the earth." ⁴Even thus spoke the messenger, and ascended into Heaven, glorifying [God], and saying, "Hallelujah! ⁵[[HOLY, HOLY, HOLY is the LORD, in the glory of God the Father, for to Him it is appropriate to give glory, honor and worship, with the continuous life-giving Spirit now, and always, and forever. Amen. HOLY, HOLY, HOLY is the LORD of Hosts. To whom be glory and power forever and forever. Amen." ⁶Then the chief-messenger Joel glorified God, saying, "HOLY, HOLY, HOLY Lord, the heavens and earth are full of Your glory."]]

BOOK OF CREATION

Otherwise known as Sefer Yetzirah

The Sefer Yetzirah ("Book of Formation" or "Book of Creation") is the title of the earliest extant book on Jewish mysticism, although some early commentators treated it as a treatise on mathematical and linguistic theory as opposed to Kabbalah. The book is traditionally ascribed to the patriarch Abraham, although others attribute its writing to Rabbi Akiva. Modern scholars have not reached a consensus on the question of its origins and tend to date it between the 2nd century BC and 2nd century AD.

CHAPTER 1

¹ In thirty-two mysterious paths of wisdom YAH—the LORD of Hosts, the God of Israel, the living God, the King of ages, the merciful and gracious God, the Exalted One, the Dweller in eternity, Most High and holy—engraved His Name by the three Sepharim: numbers, letters, and sounds. ² Ten are the ineffable Sephiroth. Twenty-two are the letters, the foundation of all things; there are three mothers, seven double, and twelve simple letters. ³ The ineffable Sephiroth are ten, as are the numbers; and as there are in man five fingers over against five, so over them is established a covenant of strength, by word of mouth, and by the circumcision of the flesh. ⁴ Ten is the number of the ineffable Sephiroth—ten and not nine, ten and not eleven. Understand this wisdom and be wise by the perception. Search out concerning it, restore the word to its creator, and pass from Him who formed it on His throne. ⁵ The ten ineffable Sephiroth have ten vast regions bound to them—boundless in origin and having no ending; an abyss of good and of ill; measureless height and depth; boundless to the east and the west; boundless to the north and south; and the LORD, the only God, the faithful King, rules all these from His holy seat, forever and ever. ⁶ The ten ineffable Sephiroth have the appearance of the lightning flash, their origin is unseen, and no end is perceived. The Word is in them as they rush forth and as they return, they speak as from the whirlwind, and returning fall prostrate in adoration before the Throne. ⁷ The ten ineffable Sephiroth, whose ending is even as their origin, are like as a flame arising from a burning coal. For God is superlative in his unity; there is none equal to Him: what number can you place before one? ⁸ Ten are the ineffable Sephiroth; seal up your lips lest you speak of them, and guard your heart as you consider them; and if your mind escapes from you, bring it back to your control; even as it was said, "running and returning"—[(the living creatures ran and returned)]—and hence was the Covenant made. ⁹ The ineffable Sephiroth give forth the ten numbers. First, the Spirit of the God of the living; blessed and more than blessed is the living God of ages. The Voice, the Spirit, and the Utterance—these are the Holy Spirit. ¹⁰ Second, from the Spirit He produced air, and formed in it twenty-two sounds—the letters; three are mothers, seven are double, and twelve are simple; but the Spirit is first and above these. Third, from the air He formed the waters, and from the formless and void He made mire and clay, and designed surfaces on them, and hewed recesses in them, and formed the strong material foundation. Fourth, from the water He formed fire and made for Himself a throne of glory with auphanim, seraphim, and kerubim, as His ministering messengers; and with these three He completed His dwelling, as it is written: "Who makes His messengers spirits and His ministers a flaming fire." ¹¹ He selected three letters from among the simple ones and sealed them and formed them into a great Name: Y-H-W; and with this He sealed the universe in six directions. ¹² Fifth, He looked above, and sealed the height with Y-H-W. ¹³ Sixth, He looked below, and sealed the depth with Y-W-H. ¹⁴ Seventh, He looked forward, and sealed the east with H-Y-W. ¹⁵ Eighth, He looked backward, and sealed the west with H-W-Y. ¹⁶ Ninth, He looked to the right, and sealed the south with W-Y-H. ¹⁷ Tenth, He looked to the left, and sealed the north with W-H-Y. ¹⁸ Behold! From the ten ineffable Sephiroth proceed the one Spirit of the living God, air, water, fire, and also height, depth, east, west, south, and north.

CHAPTER 2

¹ The twenty-two sounds and letters are the foundation of all things. Three mothers, seven doubles, and twelve simples. The three mothers are Aleph, Mem, and Shin; they are air, water, and fire. Water is silent, fire is sibilant, and air derived from the Spirit is as the tongue of a balance standing between these contraries which are in equilibrium, reconciling and mediating between them. ² He has formed, weighed, and composed with these twenty-two letters every created thing, and the form of everything which will hereafter be. ³ These twenty-two sounds or letters are formed by the voice, impressed on the air, and audibly modified in five places: in the throat, in the mouth, by the tongue, through the teeth, and by the lips. ⁴ These twenty-two letters, which are the foundation of all things, He arranged as on a sphere with two hundred and thirty-one gates, and the sphere may be rotated forward or backward, whether for good or for evil; from the good

comes true pleasure, from evil nothing but torment. [5] For He showed the combination of these letters, each with the other: Aleph with all, and all with Aleph; Beth with all, and all with Beth. Thus, in combining all together in pairs, the two hundred and thirty-one gates of knowledge are produced. [6] And from the non-existent He made something, and all forms of speech and everything that has been produced; from the empty void He made the material world, and from the inert earth He brought forth everything that has life. [7] He hewed, as it were, vast columns out of the intangible air, and by the power of His Name made every creature and everything that is; and the production of all things from the twenty-two letters is the proof that they are all but parts of one living body.

CHAPTER 3

[1] The foundation of all the other sounds and letters is provided by the three mothers: Aleph, Mem, and Shin; they resemble a balance, on the one hand the guilty, on the other hand the purified, and Aleph—the air—is like the tongue of a balance standing between them. [2] The three mothers, Aleph, Mem, and Shin, are a great Mystery, very admirable and most recondite, and sealed as with six rings; and from them proceed air, fire, and water, which divide into active and passive forces. The three mothers, Aleph, Mem, and Shin, are the foundation, from them spring three fathers, and from these have proceeded all things that are in the world. [3] The three mothers in the world are Aleph, Mem, and Shin: the heavens were produced from fire; the earth from the eater; and the air from the Spirit is as a reconciler between the fire and the water. [4] The three mothers, Aleph, Mem, and Shin—fire, water, and air—are shown in the year: from the fire came heat, from the waters came cold, and from the air was produced the temperate state, again a mediator between them. The three mothers, Aleph, Mem, and Shin—fire, water, and air—are found in man: from the fire was formed the head, from the water the belly, and from the air was formed the chest, again placed as a mediator between the others. [5] He produced and designed these three mothers and combined them; and He sealed them as the three mothers in the universe, in the year and in man—both male and female. [6] He caused the letter Aleph to reign in air and crowned it, and combining it with the others He sealed it, as air in the world, as the temperate [climate] of the year, and as the breath in the chest in man: the male with Aleph, Mem, Shin, the female with Shin, Mem, Aleph. [7] He caused the letter Mem to reign in water, crowned it, and combining it with the others, formed the earth in the world, cold in the year, and the belly in man, male and female, the former with Mem, Aleph, Shin, the latter with Mem, Shin, Aleph. [8] He caused Shin to reign in fire, and crowned it, and combining it with the others, sealed

with it the heavens in the universe, heat in the year, and the head in man, male and female.

CHAPTER 4

[1] The seven double letters, Beth, Gimel, Daleth, Kaph, Pe, Resh, and Taw, each have two sounds associated with them. They are referred to [as] life, peace, wisdom, riches, grace, fertility, and power. The two sounds of each letter are the hard and the soft—the aspirated and the softened. They are called double, because each letter presents a contrast or permutation; thus, life and death, peace and war, wisdom and folly, riches and poverty, grace and indignation, fertility and solitude, power and servitude. [2] These seven double letters point out seven localities: above, below, east, west, north, south, and the palace of holiness in the midst of them sustaining all things. [3] He designed, produced, and combined these seven double letters, and formed with them the planets of this world, the days of the week, and the gates of the soul [(the orifices of perception)] in man. From these seven He has produced the seven heavens, the seven earths, the seven Sabbaths; for this reason, He has loved and blessed the number seven more than all things under Heaven. [4] Two letters produce two houses; three form six; four form twenty-four; five form one hundred and twenty; six form seven hundred and twenty; seven form five thousand and forty; and beyond this their numbers increase so that the mouth can hardly utter them, nor the ear hear the number of them. [5] So now, behold the stars of our world, the planets which are seven: the Sun, Venus, Mercury, Moon, Saturn, Jupiter, and Mars. The seven are also the seven days of creation and the seven gateways of the soul of man—the two eyes, the two ears, the mouth, and the two nostrils. So with the seven are formed the seven heavens, the seven earths, and the seven periods of time; and so has He preferred the number seven above all things under His Heaven. [[6] He produced Beth, and connected it to wisdom; He crowned it, combined and formed with it the Moon in the universe, the first day of the week, and the right eye of man. [7] He produced Gimel, and connected it to health; He crowned it, combined and joined with it Mars in the universe, the second day of the week, and the right ear of man. [8] He produced Daleth, and connected it to fertility; He crowned it, combined and formed with it the Sun in the universe, the third day of the week, and the right nostril of man. [9] He produced Kaph, and connected it to life; He crowned it, combined and formed with it Venus in the universe, the fourth day of the week, and the left eye of man. [10] He produced Pe, and connected it to power; He crowned it, combined and formed with it Mercury in the universe, the fifth day of the week, and the left ear of man. [11] He produced Resh, and connected it to peace; He crowned it, combined and formed with it Saturn in the universe, the sixth day of the week, and

the left nostril of man. [12] He produced Taw, and connected it to beauty; He crowned it, combined and formed with it Jupiter in the universe, the seventh day of the week, and the mouth of man. [13] By these seven letters were also made seven worlds, seven heavens, seven earths, seven seas, seven rivers, seven deserts, seven days, seven weeks from Passover to Pentecost, and every seventh year a Jubilee.]]

CHAPTER 5

[1] The twelve simple letters are He, Waw, Zayin, Heth, Teth, Yod, Lamed, Nun, Samekh, Ayin, Tsade, and Qof; they are the foundations of these twelve properties: sight, hearing, smell, speech, taste, sexual love, work, movement, anger, mirth, imagination, and sleep. [2] These twelve are also allotted to the directions in space: northeast, southeast, the east above, the east below, the north above, the north below, the southwest, the northwest, the west above, the west below, the south above, and the south below; these diverge to infinity, and are as the arms of the universe. [3] He designed and combined these twelve simple letters, and formed with them the twelve celestial constellations—the twelve signs. [4] The twelve are also the months of the year: Nisan, Iyar, Sivan, Tammuz, Av, Elul, Tishri, Cheshvan, Kislev, Tevet, Shevat, and Adar. [5] The twelve are also the twelve organs of living creatures: the two hands, the two feet, the two kidneys, the spleen, the liver, the gall, private parts, stomach, and intestines. [6] He made these, as it were provinces, and arranged them as in order of battle for warfare. And God also made one from the region of the other. [7] Three mothers and three fathers; and from there issue fire, air, and water. Three mothers, seven doubles, and twelve simple letters and sounds. [8] Behold, now these are the twenty-two letters from which YAH—the LORD of Hosts, the living God, the God of Israel, exalted and sublime, the Dweller in eternity—formed and established all things; high and holy is His Name. [[[9] God produced He predominant in speech, crowned it, combined and formed with it Aries in the universe, Nisan in the year, and the right foot of man. [10] He produced Waw, predominant in mind, crowned it, combined and formed with it Taurus in the universe, Iyar in the year, and the right kidney of man. [11] He produced Zayin, predominant in movement, crowned it, combined and formed with it Gemini in the universe, Sivan in the year, and the left foot of man. [12] He produced Heth, predominant in sight, crowned it, combined and formed with it Cancer in the universe, Tammuz in the year, and the right hand of man. [13] He produced Teth, predominant in hearing, crowned it, combined and formed with it Leo in the universe, Av in the year, and the left kidney in man. [14] He produced Yod, predominant in work, crowned it, combined and formed with it Virgo in the universe, Elul in the year, and the left hand of man. [15] He produced Lamed, predominant in sexual desire,

crowned it, combined and formed with it Libra in the universe, Tishri in the year, and the private parts of man. [16] He produced Nun, predominant in smell, crowned it, combined and formed with it Scorpio in the universe, Cheshvan in the year, and the intestines of man. [17] He produced Samekh, predominant in sleep, crowned it, combined and formed with it Sagittarius in the universe, Kislev in the year, and the stomach of man. [18] He produced Ayin, predominant in anger, crowned it, combined and formed with it Capricornus in the universe, Tevet in the year, and the liver of man. [19] He produced Tsade, predominant in taste, crowned it, combined and formed with it Aquarius in the year, and the gullet in man. [20] He produced Qof, predominant in mirth, crowned it, combined and formed with it Pisces in the universe, Adar in the year, and the spleen of man.]]

CHAPTER 6

[1] Three fathers and their generations, seven conquerors and their armies, and twelve bounds of the universe. See now, of these words, the faithful witnesses are the universe, the year, and man. The dodecad, the heptad, and the triad with their provinces; above is the Celestial Dragon, T-L-Y, and below is the world, and lastly the heart of man. The three are water, air, and fire—fire above, water below, and air conciliating between them; and the sign of these things is that the fire sustains the waters; Mem is mute, Shin is sibilant, and Aleph is the mediator and as it were a friend placed between them. [2] The Celestial Dragon, T-L-Y, is placed over the universe like a king on the throne; the revolution of the year is as a king over his dominion; the heart of man is as a king in warfare. Moreover, He made all things, one from the other; and God set good over against evil, and made good things from good, and evil things from evil: with the good He tested the evil, and with the evil He tried the good. Happiness is reserved for the good, and misery is kept for the wicked. [3] The three are one, and that one stands above. The seven are divided: three are over against three, and one stands between the triads. The twelve stand as in warfare: three are friends, three are enemies, three are life givers, [and] three are destroyers. The three friends are the heart, the ears, and the mouth; the three enemies are the liver, the gall, and the tongue; while God the faithful King rules over all. One above three, three above seven, and seven above twelve: and all are connected—the one with the other. [4] And after that our father Abraham had perceived and understood, and had taken down and engraved all these things, the LORD Most High revealed Himself, and called him His beloved, and made a covenant with him and his seed; and Abraham believed on Him and it was imputed to him for righteousness. And He made this Covenant as between the ten toes of the feet—this is that of circumcision; and as between the

ten fingers of the hands and this is that of the tongue. And He formed the twenty-two letters into speech and showed him all the mysteries of them. He drew them through the waters; He burned them in the fire; He vibrated them in the air; seven planets in the heavens, and twelve celestial constellations of the stars of the twelve signs.

TESTAMENT OF ABRAHAM

The Testament of Abraham was probably composed sometime in the 1st or 2nd century AD and is extant in Greek in two recensions (one long, the other short). The long recension is included here. The Testament of Abraham is often humorous in tone, indicating the text might actually be an entertaining fiction extrapolating on the life of the patriarch—even in the first verse we see Abraham's enormously exaggerated age. Though not necessarily composed by the same author, the *Testaments* (of Abraham, Isaac, and Jacob, *respectively*) are closely related works and are often grouped together.

CHAPTER 1

[1] Abraham lived the measure of his life, nine hundred and ninety-five years, and having lived all the years of his life in quietness, gentleness, and righteousness, the righteous one was exceedingly hospitable; [2] for, pitching his tent in the crossways at the oak of Mamre, he received everyone, both rich and poor, kings and rulers, the maimed and the helpless, friends and strangers, neighbors and travelers, all alike did the devout, all-holy, righteous, and hospitable Abraham entertain. [3] Even on him, however, there came the common, inexorable, bitter lot of death, and the uncertain end of life. [4] Therefore the LORD God, summoning His chief-messenger Michael, said to him, "Go down, chief-captain Michael, to Abraham and speak to him concerning his death, that he may set his affairs in order, [5] for I have blessed him as the stars of the heavens, and as the sand by the seashore, and he is in abundance of long life and many possessions, and is becoming exceedingly rich. [6] Beyond all men, moreover, he is righteous in every goodness, hospitable and loving to the end of his life; [7] but you, chief-messenger Michael, go to Abraham, my beloved friend, and announce to him his death and assure him thus: You will at this time depart from this vain world, and will quit the body, and go to your own Lord among the good."

CHAPTER 2

[1] And the chief-captain departed from before the face of God, and went down to Abraham to the oak of Mamre, and found the righteous Abraham in the field close by, sitting beside yokes of oxen for plowing, together with the sons of Masek and other servants, to the number of twelve. [2] And behold, the chief-captain came to him, and Abraham, seeing the chief-captain Michael coming from afar, like to a very handsome warrior, arose and met him as was his custom, meeting and entertaining all strangers. [3] And the chief-captain saluted him and said, "Greetings, most honored father, righteous soul chosen of God, true son of the heavenly one." [4] Abraham said to the chief-captain: "Greetings, most honored warrior, bright as the sun and most beautiful above all the sons of men; you are welcome; therefore, I implore your presence, tell me from where the youth of your age has come; teach me, your suppliant, from where and from what army and from what journey your beauty has come here." [5] The chief-captain said, "I, O righteous Abraham, come from the great city. I have been sent by the great King to take the place of a good friend of His, for the King has summoned him." [6] And Abraham said, "Come, my Lord, go with me as far as my field." The chief-captain said, "I come"; and going into the field of the plowing, they sat down beside the company. [7] And Abraham said to his servants, the sons of Masek, "Go to the herd of horses, and bring two horses, quiet, and gentle, and tame, so that I and this stranger may sit thereon." [8] But the chief-captain said, "No, my Lord Abraham, let them not bring horses, for I abstain from ever sitting on any four-footed beast. Is my king not rich in much merchandise, having power over both men and all kinds of cattle? [9] But I abstain from ever sitting on any four-footed beast. Let us go, then, O righteous soul, walking lightly until we reach your house." [10] And Abraham said, "Amen, be it so."

CHAPTER 3

[1] And as they went on from the field toward his house, beside that way there stood a cypress tree, and by the command of the LORD the tree cried out with a human voice, saying, "HOLY, HOLY, HOLY is the LORD God that calls Himself to those that love Him"; but Abraham hid the mystery, thinking that the chief-captain had not heard the voice of the tree. [2] And coming near to the house they sat down in the court, and Isaac, seeing the face of the messenger, said to his mother Sarah, "My lady mother, behold, the man sitting with my father Abraham is not a son of the race of those that dwell on the earth." [3] And Isaac ran, and saluted him, and fell at the feet of the incorporeal, and the incorporeal blessed him and said, "The LORD God will grant you His promise that He made to your father Abraham and to his seed, and will also grant you the precious prayer of your father and your mother." [4] Abraham said to his son Isaac, "My son Isaac, draw water from the well, and bring it me in the vessel, that we may wash the feet of this stranger, for he is tired, having come to us from off a long journey." [5] And Isaac ran to the well and drew water in the vessel and brought it to them, and Abraham went up and washed the feet of the chief captain Michael, and the heart of Abraham was moved, and

he wept over the stranger. ⁶ And Isaac, seeing his father weeping, wept also, and the chief captain, seeing them weeping, also wept with them, and the tears of the chief captain fell on the vessel into the water of the basin and became precious stones. ⁷ And Abraham seeing the marvel, and being astonished, took the stones secretly, and hid the mystery, keeping it by himself in his heart.

CHAPTER 4

¹ And Abraham said to his son Isaac, "Go, my beloved son, into the inner chamber of the house and beautify it. Spread two couches for us there—one for me and one for this man that is guest with us this day. ² Prepare a seat, and a candlestick, and a table for us there with abundance of every good thing. ³ Beautify the chamber, my son, and spread under us linen and purple and fine linen. Burn every precious and excellent incense there, and bring sweet-smelling plants from the garden and fill our house with them. ⁴ Kindle seven lamps full of oil, so that we may rejoice, for this man that is our guest this day is more glorious than kings or rulers, and his appearance surpasses all the sons of men." ⁵ And Isaac prepared all things well, and Abraham taking the chief-messenger Michael, went into the chamber, and they both sat down on the couches, and between them he placed a table with abundance of every good thing. ⁶ Then the chief-captain arose and went out, as if by constraint of his belly to make issue of water, and ascended to Heaven in the twinkling of an eye, and stood before the LORD, and said to Him: "LORD and Master, let Your power know that I am unable to remind that righteous man of his death, for I have not seen on the earth a man like him, pitiful, hospitable, righteous, truthful, devout, refraining from every evil deed. ⁷ And now know, Lord, that I cannot remind him of his death." ⁸ And the LORD said, "Go down, chief-captain Michael, to my friend Abraham, and whatever he says to you, that do also, and whatever he eats, eat also with him. ⁹ And I will send My Holy Spirit on his son Isaac, and will put the remembrance of his death into the heart of Isaac, so that even he in a dream may see the death of his father, and Isaac will relate the dream, and you will interpret it, and he himself will know his end." ¹⁰ And the chief-captain said, "Lord, all the heavenly spirits are incorporeal, and neither eat nor drink, and this man has set before me a table with abundance of all good things earthly and corruptible. ¹¹ Now, Lord, what will I do? How will I escape him, sitting at one table with him?" ¹² The LORD said, "Go down to him, and take no thought for this, for when you sit down with him, I will send on you a devouring spirit, and it will consume out of your hands and through your mouth all that is on the table. ¹³ Rejoice together with him in everything, only you will interpret well the things of the vision, that Abraham may know the sickle of

death and the uncertain end of life, and may make disposal of all his possessions, for I have blessed him above the sand of the sea and as the stars of the heavens."

CHAPTER 5

¹ Then the chief captain went down to the house of Abraham, and sat down with him at the table, and Isaac served them. ² And when the supper was ended, Abraham prayed after his custom, and the chief-captain prayed together with him, and each lay down to sleep on his couch. ³ And Isaac said to his father, "Father, I too would fain sleep with you in this chamber, that I also may hear your discourse, for I love to hear the excellence of the conversation of this virtuous man." ⁴ Abraham said, "No, my son, but go to your own chamber and sleep on your own couch, lest we be troublesome to this man." ⁵ Then Isaac, having received the prayer from them, and having blessed them, went to his own chamber and lay down on his couch. ⁶ But the LORD cast the thought of death into the heart of Isaac as in a dream, and about the third hour of the night Isaac awoke and rose up from his couch, and came running to the chamber where his father was sleeping together with the chief-messenger. ⁷ Isaac, therefore, on reaching the door cried out, saying, "My father Abraham, arise and open to me quickly, that I may enter and hang on your neck, and embrace you before they take you away from me." ⁸ Abraham therefore arose and opened to him, and Isaac entered and hung on his neck, and began to weep with a loud voice. ⁹ Abraham therefore being moved at heart, also wept with a loud voice, and the chief-captain, seeing them weeping, wept also. ¹⁰ Sarah being in her room, heard their weeping, and came running to them, and found them embracing and weeping. ¹¹ And Sarah said with weeping, "My Lord Abraham, what is this that you weep? Tell me, my Lord, has this brother that has been entertained by us this day brought you tidings of Lot, your brother's son, that he is dead? Is it for this that you grieve thus?" ¹² The chief-captain answered and said to her, "No, my sister Sarah, it is not as you say, but your son Isaac, it seems to me, beheld a dream, and came to us weeping, and we, seeing him, were moved in our hearts and wept."

CHAPTER 6

¹ Then Sarah, hearing the excellence of the conversation of the chief-captain, immediately knew that it was a messenger of the LORD that spoke. ² Sarah therefore signified to Abraham to come out toward the door, and said to him, "My Lord Abraham, do you know who this man is?" ³ Abraham said, "I do not know." Sarah said, "You know, my Lord, the three men from Heaven that were entertained by us in our tent beside the oak of Mamre, when you killed the kid without blemish, and set a table before them. ⁴ After

the flesh had been eaten, the kid rose again, and sucked its mother with great joy. Do you not know, my Lord Abraham, that by promise they gave to us Isaac as the fruit of the womb? This is one of these three holy men." ⁵Abraham said, "O Sarah, in this you speak the truth. Glory and praise from our God and the Father. ⁶For late in the evening when I washed his feet in the basin I said in my heart, These are the feet of one of the three men that I washed then; and his tears that fell into the basin then became precious stones." ⁷And shaking them out from his lap he gave them to Sarah, saying, "If you do not believe me, look now at these." ⁸And Sarah receiving them, bowed down and saluted, and said, "Glory be to God that shows us wonderful things. ⁹And now know, my Lord Abraham, that there is among us the revelation of something, whether it be evil or good!"

CHAPTER 7

¹And Abraham left Sarah, and went into the chamber, and said to Isaac, "Come here, my beloved son, tell me the truth, what it was you saw and what befell you that you came so hastily to us." ²And Isaac answering began to say, "I saw, my Lord, in this night the sun and the moon above my head, surrounding me with its rays and giving me light. ³As I gazed at this and rejoiced, I saw the Heaven opened, and a man bearing light descend from it, shining more than seven suns. ⁴And this man like the sun came and took away the sun from my head, and went up into the heavens from where he came, but I was greatly grieved that he took away the sun from me. ⁵After a little while, as I was still sorrowing and sorely troubled, I saw this man come forth from Heaven a second time, and he also took away the moon from me, from off my head, ⁶and I wept greatly and called on that man of light, and said, Do not, my Lord, take away my glory from me; pity me and hear me, and if you take away the sun from me, then leave the moon to me. ⁷He said, Permit them to be taken up to the King above, for He wishes them there. And he took them away from me, but he left the rays on me." ⁸The chief-captain said, "Hear, O righteous Abraham; the sun which your son saw is you his father, and the moon likewise is Sarah his mother. ⁹The man bearing light who descended from Heaven, this is the one sent from God who is to take your righteous soul from you. ¹⁰And now know, O most honored Abraham, that at this time you will leave this worldly life, and remove to God." ¹¹Abraham said to the chief captain, "O strangest of marvels! And now are you he that will take my soul from me?" ¹²The chief-captain said to him, "I am the chief-captain Michael, that stands before the LORD, and I was sent to you to remind you of your death, and then I will depart to Him as I was commanded." ¹³Abraham said, "Now I know that you are a messenger of the LORD, and were sent to take my

soul, but I will not go with you; but do whatever you are commanded."

CHAPTER 8

¹The chief-captain, hearing these words, immediately vanished, and ascending into Heaven stood before God, and told all that he had seen in the house of Abraham; ²and the chief-captain said this also to his Lord, "Thus says Your friend Abraham, I will not go with you, but do whatever you are commanded; and now, O LORD Almighty, does Your glory and immortal kingdom order anything?" ³God said to the chief-captain Michael, "Go to My friend Abraham yet once again, and speak to him thus, Thus says the LORD your God, He that brought you into the land of promise, that blessed you above the sand of the sea and above the stars of the heavens, that opened the womb of barrenness of Sarah, and granted you Isaac as the fruit of the womb in old age: ⁴Truly I say to you that blessing I will bless you, and multiplying I will multiply your seed, and I will give you all that you will ask from Me, for I am the LORD your God, and besides Me there is no other. ⁵Tell me why you have rebelled against Me, and why there is grief in you, and why you rebelled against My chief-messenger Michael? ⁶Do you not know that all who have come from Adam and Eve have died, and that none of the prophets has escaped death? ⁷None of those that rule as kings is immortal; none of your forefathers has escaped the mystery of death. ⁸They have all died, they have all departed into Hades, they are all gathered by the sickle of death. But on you I have not sent death, I have not suffered any deadly disease to come on you, I have not permitted the sickle of death to meet you, I have not allowed the nets of Hades to enfold you, I have never wished you to meet with any evil. ⁹But for good comfort I have sent my chief-captain Michael to you, that you may know your departure from the world, and set your house in order, and all that belongs to you, and bless your beloved son Isaac. ¹⁰And now know that I have done this not wishing to grieve you. ¹¹Why then have you said to my chief-captain, I will not go with you? Why have you spoken thus? ¹²Do you not know that if I give leave to death and he comes on you, then I should see whether you would come or not?"

CHAPTER 9

¹And the chief-captain, receiving the exhortations of the LORD, went down to Abraham, and seeing him the righteous one, fell on his face to the ground as one dead, and the chief-captain told him all that he had heard from the Most High. ²Then the holy and just Abraham, rising with many tears, fell at the feet of the incorporeal, and implored him, saying, "I implore you, chief-captain of the hosts above, since you have wholly deigned to come yourself to me a sinner and in all things your unworthy servant, I implore you

even now, O chief-captain, to carry my word yet again to the Most High, and you will say to Him: [3] Thus says your servant Abraham, Lord, Lord, in every work and word which I have asked of You You have heard me, and have fulfilled all my counsel. [4] Now, Lord, I do not resist Your power, for I too know that I am not immortal but mortal. [5] Since, therefore, all things yield to Your command, and fear and tremble at the face of Your power, I also fear, but I ask one request of You, and now, Lord and Master, hear my prayer, for while still in this body I desire to see all the inhabited earth, and all the creations which You established by one word, and when I see these, then if I will depart from life I will be without sorrow." [6] So the chief-captain went back again, and stood before God, and told him all, saying, "Thus says Your friend Abraham, I desired to behold all the earth in my lifetime before I died. [7] And the Most High hearing this, again commanded the chief-captain Michael, and said to him, Take a cloud of light, and the messengers that have power over the chariots, and go down, take the righteous Abraham on a chariot of the cherubim, and exalt him into the air of Heaven that he may behold all the earth."

CHAPTER 10

[1] And the chief-messenger Michael went down and took Abraham on a chariot of the cherubim, and exalted him into the air of Heaven, and led him on the cloud together with sixty messengers, and Abraham ascended on the chariot over all the earth. [2] And Abraham saw the world as it was in that day, some plowing, others driving wagons, in one place men herding flocks, and in another watching them by night, and dancing and playing and harping, in another place men striving and contending at law, elsewhere men weeping and having the dead in remembrance. [3] He also saw the newly-wedded received with honor, and in a word he saw all things that are done in the world, both good and bad. [4] Abraham therefore, passing over them, saw men bearing swords, wielding in their hands sharpened swords, and Abraham asked the chief-captain, "Who are these?" [5] The chief-captain said, "These are thieves, who intend to commit murder, and to steal, and burn, and destroy." [6] Abraham said, "Lord, Lord, hear my voice, and command that wild beasts may come out of the wood and devour them." [7] And even as he spoke there came wild beasts out of the wood and devoured them. [8] And he saw in another place a man with a woman committing fornication with each other, and said, "Lord, Lord, command that the earth may open and swallow them," and immediately the earth was cleft and swallowed them. [9] And he saw in another place men digging through a house, and carrying away other men's possessions, and he said, "Lord, Lord, command that fire may come down from Heaven and consume them." [10] And even as he spoke,

fire came down from Heaven and consumed them. [11] And immediately there came a voice from Heaven to the chief-captain, saying thus, "O chief-captain Michael, command the chariot to stop, and turn Abraham away that he may not see all the earth, for if he beholds all that live in wickedness, he will destroy all creation. [12] For behold, Abraham has not sinned, and has no pity on sinners, but I have made the world, and do not desire to destroy any one of them, but wait for the death of the sinner, until he [may] be converted and live. [13] But take Abraham up to the first gate of Heaven, that he may see there the judgments and repayments, and regret the souls of the sinners that he has destroyed."

CHAPTER 11

[1] So Michael turned the chariot and brought Abraham to the east, to the first gate of Heaven; and Abraham saw two ways, the one narrow and contracted, the other broad and spacious, and there he saw two gates, the one broad on the broad way, and the other narrow on the narrow way. [2] And outside the two gates there he saw a man sitting on a gilded throne, and the appearance of that man was terrible, as of the LORD. And they saw many souls driven by messengers and led in through the broad gate, and other souls, few in number, that were taken by the messengers through the narrow gate. [3] And when the wonderful one who sat on the golden throne saw few entering through the narrow gate, and many entering through the broad one, immediately that wonderful one tore the hairs of his head and the sides of his beard, and threw himself on the ground from his throne, weeping and lamenting. [4] But when he saw many souls entering through the narrow gate, then he arose from the ground and sat on his throne in great joy, rejoicing and exulting. [5] And Abraham asked the chief-captain, "My Lord chief-captain, who is this most marvelous man, adorned with such glory, and sometimes he weeps and laments, and sometimes he rejoices and exults?" [6] The incorporeal one said, "This is the first-created Adam who is in such glory, and he looks on the world because all are born from him, and when he sees many souls going through the narrow gate, then he arises and sits on his throne rejoicing and exulting in joy, because this narrow gate is that of the just that leads to life, and they that enter through it go into Paradise. For this, then, the first-created Adam rejoices, because he sees the souls being saved. [7] But when he sees many souls entering through the broad gate, then he pulls out the hairs of his head, and casts himself on the ground weeping and lamenting bitterly, for the broad gate is that of sinners, which leads to destruction and continuous punishment. [8] And for this the first-formed Adam falls from his throne weeping and lamenting for the destruction of sinners, for they are many that are lost, and they are few that are saved, for in seven thousand there is

scarcely found one soul saved, being righteous and undefiled."

CHAPTER 12

[1] While he was yet saying these things to me, behold two messengers, fiery in aspect, and pitiless in mind, and severe in look, and they drove on thousands of souls, pitilessly lashing them with fiery thongs. [2] The messenger laid hold of one soul, and they drove all the souls in at the broad gate to destruction. [3] So we also went along with the messengers, and came within that broad gate, and between the two gates stood a throne terrible of aspect, of terrible crystal, gleaming as fire, and on it sat a wondrous man bright as the sun, like to the Son of God. [4] Before him stood a table like crystal, all of gold and fine linen, and on the table there was lying a scroll, the thickness of it six cubits, and the breadth of it ten cubits, and on the right and left of it stood two messengers holding paper, and ink, and pen. [5] Before the table sat a messenger of light, holding in his hand a balance, and on his left sat a messenger all fiery, pitiless, and severe, holding in his hand a trumpet, having within it all-consuming fire with which to try the sinners. [6] The wondrous man who sat on the throne himself judged and sentenced the souls, and the two messengers on the right and on the left wrote down, the one on the right the righteousness and the one on the left the wickedness. [7] The one before the table, who held the balance, weighed the souls, and the fiery messenger, who held the fire, tried the souls. [8] And Abraham asked the chief-captain Michael, "What is this that we behold?" [9] And the chief-captain said, "These things that you see, holy Abraham, are the judgment and repayment." [10] And behold, the messenger holding the soul in his hand, and he brought it before the judge, and the judge said to one of the messengers that served him, "Open this scroll, and find me the sins of this soul." [11] And opening the scroll he found its sins and its righteousness equally balanced, and he neither gave it to the tormentors, nor to those that were saved, but set it in the midst.

CHAPTER 13

[1] And Abraham said, "My Lord chief-captain, who is this most wondrous judge? And who are the messengers that write down? And who is the messenger like the sun, holding the balance? And who is the fiery messenger holding the fire?" [2] The chief-captain said, "Do you see, most holy Abraham, the terrible man sitting on the throne? [3] This is the son of the first-created Adam, who is called Abel, whom the wicked Cain killed, and he sits thus to judge all creation, and examines righteous men and sinners. [4] For God has said, I will not judge you, but every man born of man will be judged. [5] Therefore He has given to him judgment, to judge the world until His great and glorious coming, and then, O righteous Abraham,

is the perfect judgment and repayment, continuous and unchangeable, which no one can alter. [6] For every man has come from the first-created, and therefore they are first judged here by his son, and at the second coming they will be judged by the twelve tribes of Israel, every breath and every creature. [7] But the third time they will be judged by the LORD God of all, and then, indeed, the end of that judgment is near, and the sentence terrible, and there is none to deliver. [8] And now by three tribunals the judgment of the world and the repayment is made, and for this reason a matter is not finally confirmed by one or two witnesses, but by three witnesses will everything be established. [9] The two messengers on the right hand and on the left, these are they that write down the sins and the righteousness, the one on the right hand writes down the righteousness, and the one on the left the sins. [10] The messenger like the sun, holding the balance in his hand, is the chief-messenger Dokiel, the just weigher, and he weighs the righteousnesses and sins with the righteousness of God. [11] The fiery and pitiless messenger, holding the fire in his hand, is the chief-messenger Puruel, who has power over fire, and tries the works of men through fire, and if the fire consumes the work of any man, the messenger of judgment immediately seizes him, and carries him away to the place of sinners, a most bitter place of punishment. [12] But if the fire approves the work of anyone, and does not seize on it, that man is justified, and the messenger of righteousness takes him and carries him up to be saved in the lot of the just. [13] And thus, most righteous Abraham, all things in all men are tried by fire and the balance."

CHAPTER 14

[1] And Abraham said to the chief-captain, "My Lord the chief-captain, the soul which the messenger held in his hand, why was it adjudged to be set in the midst?" [2] The chief-captain said, "Listen, righteous Abraham: because the judge found its sins and its righteousnesses equal, he neither committed it to judgment nor to be saved, until the Judge of all will come." [3] Abraham said to the chief-captain, "And what yet is wanting for the soul to be saved?" [4] The chief-captain said, "If it obtains one righteousness above its sins, it enters into salvation." [5] Abraham said to the chief-captain, "Come here, chief-captain Michael, let us make prayer for this soul, and see whether God will hear us." [6] The chief-captain said, "Amen, be it so"; and they made prayer and entreaty for the soul, and God heard them, and when they rose up from their prayer they did not see the soul standing there. [7] And Abraham said to the messenger, "Where is the soul that you held in the midst?" [8] And the messenger answered, "It has been saved by your righteous prayer, and behold a messenger of light has taken it and carried it up into Paradise." Abraham said, "I glorify the Name of God, the Most High, and

His immeasurable mercy." ⁹ And Abraham said to the chief-captain, "I implore you, chief-messenger, listen to my prayer, and let us yet call on the LORD, and supplicate His compassion, and entreat His mercy for the souls of the sinners whom I formerly, in my anger, cursed and destroyed, whom the earth devoured, and the wild beasts tore in pieces, and the fire consumed through my words. ¹⁰ Now I know that I have sinned before the LORD our God. Come then, O Michael, chief-captain of the hosts above, come, let us call on God with tears that He may forgive me my sin, and grant them to me." ¹¹ And the chief-captain heard him, and they made entreaty before the LORD, and when they had called on Him for a long space, ¹² there came a voice from Heaven, saying, "Abraham, Abraham, I have listened to your voice and your prayer, and forgive you your sin, and those whom you think that I destroyed I have called up and brought them into life by My exceeding kindness, because for a season I have repaid them in judgment, and those whom I destroy living on earth, I will not repay in death."

CHAPTER 15

¹ And the voice of the LORD also said to the chief-captain Michael, "Michael, My servant, turn Abraham back to his house, for behold his end has come near, and the measure of his life is fulfilled, that he may set all things in order, and then take him and bring him to Me." ² So the chief-captain, turning the chariot and the cloud, brought Abraham to his house, and going into his chamber he sat on his couch. ³ And his wife Sarah came and embraced the feet of the incorporeal, and spoke humbly, saying, "I give you thanks, my Lord, that you have brought my Lord Abraham, for behold, we thought he had been taken up from us." ⁴ And his son Isaac also came and fell on his neck, and in the same way all his menservants and maidservants surrounded Abraham and embraced him, glorifying God. ⁵ And the incorporeal one said to them, "Listen, righteous Abraham. Behold your wife Sarah, behold also your beloved son Isaac, behold also all your menservants and maidservants around you. ⁶ Make disposition of all that you have, for the day has come near in which you will depart from the body and go to the LORD once for all." ⁷ Abraham said, "Has the LORD said it, or do you say this of yourself?" The chief-captain answered, "Listen, righteous Abraham. ⁸ The LORD has commanded, and I tell it to you." Abraham said, "I will not go with you." ⁹ The chief-captain, hearing these words, immediately went forth from the presence of Abraham, and went up into the heavens, and stood before God the Most High, and said, "LORD Almighty, behold I have listened to Your friend Abraham in all he has said to You, and have fulfilled his requests. ¹⁰ I have shown to him Your power, and all the earth and sea that is under Heaven. I have shown to him judgment and repayment by means of

cloud and chariots, and again he says, I will not go with you." ¹¹ And the Most High said to the messenger, "Does My friend Abraham say thus again, I will not go with you?" ¹² The chief-messenger said, "LORD Almighty, he says thus, and I refrain from laying hands on him, because from the beginning he is Your friend, and has done all things pleasing in Your sight. ¹³ There is no man like him on earth, not even Job the wondrous man, and therefore I refrain from laying hands on him. Command, therefore, Immortal King, what will be done."

CHAPTER 16

¹ Then the Most High said, "Call to me here Death that is called the shameless countenance and the pitiless look." ² And Michael the incorporeal went and said to Death, "Come here; the Lord of creation, the immortal King, calls you." ³ And Death, hearing this, shivered and trembled, being possessed with great terror, and coming with great fear it stood before the invisible Father, shivering, groaning, and trembling, awaiting the command of the LORD. ⁴ Therefore the invisible God said to Death, "Come here, you bitter and fierce name of the world, hide your fierceness, cover your corruption, and cast away your bitterness from you, and put on your beauty and all your glory, and go down to My friend Abraham, and take him and bring him to Me. ⁵ But now also I tell you not to terrify him, but bring him with fair speech, for he is My own friend." ⁶ Having heard this, Death went out from the presence of the Most High, and put on a robe of great brightness, and made his appearance like the sun, and became fair and beautiful above the sons of men, assuming the form of a chief-messenger, having his cheeks flaming with fire, and he departed to Abraham. ⁷ Now the righteous Abraham went out of his chamber, and sat under the trees of Mamre, holding his chin in his hand, and awaiting the coming of the chief-messenger Michael. ⁸ And behold, a smell of sweet fragrance came to him, and a flashing of light, and Abraham turned and saw Death coming toward him in great glory and beauty. ⁹ And Abraham arose and went to meet him, thinking that it was the chief-captain of God, and Death beholding him saluted him, saying, "Rejoice, precious Abraham, righteous soul, true friend of the Most High God, and companion of the holy messengers." ¹⁰ Abraham said to Death, "Greetings you of appearance and form like the sun, most glorious helper, bringer of light, wondrous man, from where does your glory come to us, and who are you, and from where do you come?" ¹¹ Then Death said, "Most righteous Abraham, behold, I tell you the truth: I am the bitter lot of death." ¹² Abraham said to him, "No, but you are the comeliness of the world, you are the glory and beauty of messengers and men, you are fairer in form than every other, and you say, I am the bitter lot of death, and not rather, I am fairer than every good thing."

[13] Death said, "I tell you the truth. What the LORD has named me, that also I tell you." [14] Abraham said, "Why have you come here?" Death said, "I have come for your holy soul." [15] Then Abraham said, "I know what you mean, but I will not go with you"; and Death was silent and did not answer him a word.

CHAPTER 17

[1] Then Abraham arose, and went into his house, and Death also accompanied him there. And Abraham went up into his chamber, and Death went up with him. [2] And Abraham lay down on his couch, and Death came and sat by his feet. Then Abraham said, "Depart, depart from me, for I desire to rest on my couch." Death said, "I will not depart until I take your spirit from you." [3] Abraham said to him, "By the immortal God I charge you to tell me the truth. Are you death?" Death said to him, "I am Death. I am the destroyer of the world." [4] Abraham said, "I implore you, since you are Death, tell me if you come thus to all in such fairness, and glory, and beauty?" [5] Death said, "No, my Lord Abraham, for your righteousnesses, and the boundless sea of your hospitality, and the greatness of your love toward God has become a crown on my head, and in beauty and great peace and gentleness I approach the righteous, but to sinners I come in great corruption, and fierceness, and the greatest bitterness, and with fierce and pitiless look." [6] Abraham said, "I implore you, listen to me, and show me your fierceness and all your corruption and bitterness." [7] And Death said, "You cannot behold my fierceness, most righteous Abraham." [8] Abraham said, "Yes, I will be able to behold all your fierceness by means of the Name of the living God, for the might of my God that is in Heaven is with me." [9] Then Death put off all his comeliness and beauty, and all his glory and the form like the sun with which he was clothed, and put on himself a tyrant's robe, and made his appearance gloomy and fiercer than all kind of wild beasts, and more unclean than all uncleanness. [10] And he showed to Abraham seven fiery heads of serpents and fourteen faces, [one] of flaming fire and of great fierceness, and a face of darkness, and a most gloomy face of a viper, and a face of a most terrible precipice, and a face fiercer than an asp, and a face of a terrible lion, and a face of a cerastes and basilisk. [11] He showed him also a face of a fiery scimitar, and a sword-bearing face, and a face of lightning, lightening terribly, and a noise of dreadful thunder. [12] He also showed him another face of a fierce stormy sea, and a fierce rushing river, and a terrible three-headed serpent, and a cup mingled with poisons, and in short, he showed to him great fierceness and unendurable bitterness, and every mortal disease as of the odor of death. [13] And from the great bitterness and fierceness there died servants and maidservants in number about seven thousand, and the righteous Abraham came into indifference of death so that his spirit failed him.

CHAPTER 18

[1] And the all-holy Abraham, seeing these things thus, said to Death, "I implore you, all-destroying Death, hide your fierceness, and put on your beauty and the shape which you had before." [2] And immediately Death hid his fierceness, and put on his beauty which he had before. [3] And Abraham said to Death, "Why have you done this, that you have slain all my servants and maidservants? Has God sent you here for this end this day?" [4] Death said, "No, my Lord Abraham, it is not as you say, but on your account I was sent here." [5] Abraham said to Death, "How then have these died? Has the LORD not spoken it?" Death said, "Believe, most righteous Abraham, that this is also wonderful, that you also were not taken away with them. [6] Nevertheless I tell you the truth, for if the right hand of God had not been with you at that time, you also would have had to depart from this life." [7] The righteous Abraham said, "Now I know that I have come into indifference of death, so that my spirit fails, but I implore you, all-destroying Death, since my servants have died before their time, come, let us pray to the LORD our God that He may hear us and raise up those who died by your fierceness before their time." [8] And Death said, "Amen, be it so." [9] Therefore Abraham arose and fell on the face of the ground in prayer, and Death together with him, and the LORD sent a spirit of life on those that were dead and they were made alive again. [10] Then the righteous Abraham gave glory to God.

CHAPTER 19

[1] And going up into his chamber he lay down, and Death came and stood before him. And Abraham said to him, "Depart from me, for I desire to rest, because my spirit is in indifference." Death said, "I will not depart from you until I take your soul." [2] And Abraham, with an austere countenance and angry look, said to Death, "Who has ordered you to say this? [3] You say these words of yourself boastfully, and I will not go with you until the chief-captain Michael comes to me, and I will go with him. [4] But this I also tell you, if you desire that I will accompany you, explain to me all your changes, the seven fiery heads of serpents and what the face of the precipice is, and what the sharp sword, and what the loud-roaring river, and what the tempestuous sea that rages so fiercely. [5] Teach me also the unendurable thunder, and the terrible lightning, and the evil-smelling cup mingled with poisons. Teach me concerning all these." [6] And Death answered, "Listen, righteous Abraham. For seven ages I destroy the world and lead all down to Hades, kings and rulers, rich and poor, slaves and free men, I convoy to the bottom of Hades, and for this I showed you the seven heads of serpents.

⁷ The face of fire I showed you because many die consumed by fire, and behold death through a face of fire. ⁸ The face of the precipice I showed you, because many men die descending from the tops of trees or terrible precipices and losing their life, and see death in the shape of a terrible precipice. ⁹ The face of the sword I showed you because many are slain in wars by the sword, and see death as a sword. ¹⁰ The face of the great rushing river I showed you because many are drowned and perish snatched away by the crossing of many waters and carried off by great rivers, and see death before their time. ¹¹ The face of the angry raging sea I showed you because many in the sea falling into great surges and becoming shipwrecked are swallowed up and behold death as the sea. ¹² The unendurable thunder and the terrible lightning I showed you because many men in the moment of anger meet with unendurable thunder and terrible lightning coming to seize on men, and see death thus. ¹³ I showed you also the poisonous wild beasts, asps and basilisks, leopards and lions and lions' whelps, bears and vipers, and in short, the face of every wild beast I showed you, most righteous one, because many men are destroyed by wild beasts, and others by poisonous snakes—serpents, and asps, and cerastes, and basilisks, and vipers—breathe out their life and die. ¹⁴ I also showed you the destroying cups mingled with poison, because many men, being given poison to drink by other men, immediately depart unexpectedly."

CHAPTER 20

¹ Abraham said, "I implore you, is there also an unexpected death? Tell me." ² Death said, "Truly, truly, I tell you in the truth of God that there are seventy-two deaths. One is the just death, buying its fixed time, and many men in one hour enter into death being given over to the grave. ³ Behold, I have told you all that you have asked, now I tell you, most righteous Abraham, to dismiss all counsel, and cease from asking anything once for all, and come, go with me, as the God and judge of all has commanded me."

⁴ Abraham said to Death, "Depart from me yet a little while, that I may rest on my couch, for I am very faint at heart, for since I have seen you with my eyes my strength has failed me, all the limbs of my flesh seem to me a weight as of lead, and my spirit is exceedingly distressed. ⁵ Depart for a little while; for I have said I cannot bear to see your shape." ⁶ Then his son Isaac came and fell on his breast weeping, and his wife Sarah came and embraced his feet, lamenting bitterly. ⁷ There also came his menservants and maidservants and they surrounded his couch, lamenting greatly. ⁸ And Abraham came into indifference of death, and Death said to Abraham, "Come, take my right hand, and may cheerfulness, and life, and strength come to you." ⁹ For Death deceived Abraham, and he took his right hand, and immediately his soul adhered to the hand of Death. ¹⁰ And immediately the chief-messenger Michael came with a multitude of messengers and took up his precious soul in his hands in a divinely woven linen cloth, ¹¹ and they tended the body of the just Abraham with divine ointments and perfumes until the third day after his death, and buried him in the land of promise, the oak of Mamre, but the messengers received his precious soul, and ascended into Heaven, singing the hymn of "Thrice Holy" to the Lord, the God of all, and they set it there to worship the God and Father. ¹² And after great praise and glory had been given to the Lord, and Abraham bowed down to worship, there came the undefiled voice of the God and Father, saying thus: "Take, therefore, My friend Abraham into Paradise, where the dwelling places of my righteous ones are, and the abodes of my saints Isaac and Jacob in his bosom, where there is no trouble, nor grief, nor sighing, ¹³ but peace, and rejoicing, and life unending." [[¹³ And let us, too, my beloved brothers, imitate the hospitality of the patriarch Abraham, and attain to his virtuous way of life, that we may be thought worthy of the continuous life, glorifying the Father, Son, and Holy Spirit—to whom be glory and power forever. Amen.]]

TESTAMENT OF ISAAC

The Testament of Isaac begins with Isaac being told of his impending death by an angel, and his message to his son in response. Isaac is portrayed as foretelling both the Twelve Tribes of Israel and Jesus—the latter thought by some to be a later Christian addition to an older, perhaps second-century AD Jewish text.

THIS IS THE GOING FORTH FROM THE BODY OF ISAAC THE PATRIARCH. HE DIED ON THE TWENTY-FOURTH OF MESORE IN THE PEACE OF GOD. AMEN.

CHAPTER 1

¹ Now the patriarch Isaac writes his testament and addresses his words of instruction to his son Jacob and to all those gathered around him. ² The blessings of the patriarch will be on those who come after us, even those who listen to these words, to these words of instruction and these medicines of life, so that the grace of God may be with all those who believe. ³ This is the end of obedience, as it is written: You have heard a word, let it abide with you—which means that a man should strive patiently with what he hears. ⁴ God gives grace to those who believe; he who believes the words of God and of His saints will be an inheritor of the Kingdom of God. ⁵ God has been with the generations gone by, which have passed away, because of their innocence and their faith toward God. He will also be with the generations to come.

CHAPTER 2

¹ Now it came to pass, when the time had come for the Patriarch Isaac to go forth from the body, God sent to him the messenger of his father Abraham at dawn on the twenty-second of Mesore. ² He said to him, "Greetings, son of promise!" Now it was the daily custom of the righteous old man Isaac to converse with the messengers. ³ He lifted his face up to the face of the messenger: he saw him assuming the likeness of his father Abraham; and he opened his mouth and raised his voice and cried out in great joy, "I have seen your face like someone who has seen the face of God." ⁴ The messenger said to him, "Listen, my beloved Isaac: I have been sent for you by God to take you to the heavens and set you beside your father Abraham, so that you can see all the saints; for your father is expecting you and is coming for you himself. ⁵ Behold, a throne has been set up for you close to your father Abraham, and your lot and your beloved son Jacob's lot will surpass that of all others in the whole of God's creation; that is why you have been given forevermore the name of Patriarch and Father of the World." ⁶ But the God-loving old man Isaac said to the messenger, "I am astonished by you, for

you are my father." ⁷ The messenger answered, "My beloved Isaac, I am the messenger that ministers to your father Abraham. But rejoice now, for I am to take you out of sorrow into gladness, out of suffering to rest forever. ⁸ I am to transport you from prison to a place where you can range at will—to a place of joy and gladness; I am to take you to where there is light, and merriment, and rejoicing, and abundance that never fails. ⁹ So then, draw up your testament and a statement for your household, for I am to translate you to rest for all eternity. ¹⁰ Blessed is your father who begot you; blessed are you also; blessed is your son Jacob; and blessed are your descendants that will come after you."

CHAPTER 3

¹ Now Jacob heard them talking together, but he said nothing. Our father Isaac said to the messenger with a heavy heart, "What will I do about the light of my eyes, my beloved son Jacob? ² For I am afraid of what Esau might do to him—you know the situation." ³ The messenger said to him, "My beloved Isaac, if all the nations on earth were gathered together, they would not be able to bring these blessings pronounced over Jacob to nothing. ⁴ When you blessed him, the Father, and the Son, and the Holy Spirit blessed him; and Michael, and Gabriel, and all the messengers, and all the heavenly ones, and the spirits of all the righteous, and your father Abraham all answered, Amen. ⁵ Therefore, the sword will not touch his body, but he will be held in high honor and grow great and spread far and wide, and twelve thrones will spring from him." ⁶ Our father Isaac said to the messenger, "You have given me much comfort, but do not let Jacob know in case he is distressed." ⁷ The messenger said to him, "My beloved Isaac, blessed is every righteous man who goes forth from the body; blessed are they when they meet with God. ⁸ Woe, woe, woe—three times woe—to the sinner, because he has been born into this world; great sufferings will come to him. ⁹ Isaac, beloved of God, give these instructions, therefore, to your sons, and the instructions your father has given you. ¹⁰ Hide nothing from Jacob, so that he can write them as instructions for the generations that will come after you, and those who love God may live their lives in accordance with them. ¹¹ And take care that I am able to fetch you with joy, without delay. The peace of my Lord that He has given me, I give to you, as I go to Him who sent me."

CHAPTER 4

¹ And when the messenger had said this, he rose from the bed on which Isaac was sleeping. He went back to the worlds on high while our father Isaac watched him

go, astonished at the vision he had seen. ² And he said, "I will not see daylight before I am sent for." And while he was thinking this, behold, Jacob got up and came to the door of the room. ³ The messenger had cast a sleep over him so that he should not hear them; and he got up and ran to where his father slept and said to him, "My father, whom have you been talking to?" ⁴ Our father Isaac said to him, "You have heard, my son: your aged father has been sent for to be taken from you," and Jacob put his arms around his father's neck and wept, saying, "Ah me! My strength has left me! Today you have made me an orphan, my father." ⁵ Our father Isaac embraced his son Jacob and wept; and both wept together until they could weep no more. ⁶ And Jacob said, "Take me with you, father Isaac." But Isaac replied, "I would not have it so, my son; wait until you are sent for, my loved one. I remember on the day when the whole earth was shaken from end to end talking to my lord and father Abraham, and I had no strength to do anything. ⁷ What God has ordained, He has ordained for each one by sure authority; His ordinances are immutable. ⁸ But I know, and I am glad that I am to go to God, and I am strengthened by a guiding spirit; for this is a way that no one can escape. ⁹ Listen, my son. Where is the first creation of the hands of God—our father Adam and our mother Eve? Where is Abel, and after him Mahalalel, and Jared, and our father Enoch, and Methuselah, and our father Noah, and his sons Shem, Ham, and Japheth? ¹⁰ After these Arphaxad, and Cainan, and Shelah, and Eber, and Reu, and Serug, and Nahor, and Terah, and my blessed father Abraham, and his brother Lot? ¹¹ All these experienced death except the perfect one, our father Enoch. ¹² After these, forty-two generations more will pass until Christ comes, born of a pure virgin called Mary. ¹³ He will spend thirty years preaching in the world. At the end of all this, He will choose twelve men and reveal to them His mysteries and teach them about the archetype of His body and His true blood by means of bread and wine: ¹⁴ and the bread will become the body of God and the wine will become the blood of God. ¹⁵ And then He will ascend the tree of the Cross and die for the whole creation, and rise on the third day and despoil Hades, and deliver all mankind from the enemy. ¹⁶ The generations to come will be saved by His body and by His blood until the end of time. ¹⁷ The sacrifices of Christians will not cease until the end of time, whether offered secretly or openly; ¹⁸ and the Antichrist will not appear so long as they offer up their sacrifice. ¹⁹ Blessed is every man who performs that service and believes in it, because the archetypal service is in the heavens; and they will celebrate with the Son of God in His kingdom."

CHAPTER 5

¹ While the God-loving old man, our father Isaac, was saying this, all his household gathered around him and wept. ² His son told all his relations, and they came to him in tears. ³ Now our father Isaac had made for himself a bedroom in his house; and when his sight began to fail, he withdrew into it and remained there for one hundred years, fasting daily until evening, and offering for himself and his household a young animal for their soul. ⁴ And he spent half the night in prayer and praise of God. ⁵ Thus he lived an ascetic life for one hundred years. And he kept three periods of forty days as fasts each year, neither drinking wine nor eating fruit nor sleeping on his bed. ⁶ And he prayed and gave thanks to God continually.

CHAPTER 6

¹ Now when it became generally known that the man of God had regained his sight, people gathered to him from everywhere, listening to his words of life; for they realized that [the] Holy Spirit of God was speaking in him. ² The great ones who came said to him, "You can now see clearly enough: how come it [is] that after your sight had failed you have now regained it?" ³ The God-loving old man smiled and said to them, "My sons and brothers, the God of my father Abraham has brought this about to comfort me in my old age." ⁴ But the priest of God said to him, "Tell me what I ought to do, my father Isaac." ⁵ Our father Isaac said to him, "Keep your body holy, for the temple of God is set in it. Do not engage in controversy with other men in case an angry word escapes your mouth. Be on your guard against evil-speaking, against vainglory, and against uttering any thoughtless word; and see that your hands do not reach out after what is not yours. ⁶ Do not offer a sacrifice with a blemish in it; and wash yourself with water when you approach the altar. Do not mix the thoughts of the world with the thoughts of God when you stand before Him. ⁷ Do your utmost to be at peace with everyone. When you stand before God and offer your sacrifice—when you come to offer it on the altar— ⁸ you should recite privately one hundred prayers to God and make this confession to God, saying, Oh God, the incomprehensible, the unfathomable, the unattainable, the pure treasure, purify me in love, for I am flesh and blood and I run defiled to You, that You may purify me. ⁹ I come burdened, and I ask that You may lighten my burden. A fire will burn wood, and Your mercy will take away my iniquities. Forgive me—I that am a sinner; I forgive the whole creation that You have made, I have no complaint against anyone: ¹⁰ I am at peace with all that is made in Your image. ¹¹ I am unmoved by all the evil reasonings that have been brought before me. I am Your servant and the son of Your maidservant: I am the one who sins, You are the one who forgives. ¹² Forgive me and enable me to stand in Your holy place. Let my sacrifice be acceptable before You. ¹³ Do not reject me because of my sins, but receive me to You, in spite of my many sins, like a sheep that has

gone astray. [14] God who has been with our father Adam, and Abel, and Noah, and our father Abraham, and his son Isaac, who has been with Jacob, be with me also, and receive my sacrifice from my hand. [15] As you recite all this, take your sacrifice and offer it; and strive heavenwards because of the sacrifice of God, so that you do not displease Him. For the work of the priest is no small thing."

CHAPTER 7

[1] Every priest today, and until the end of time, must be temperate as regards his food, and drink, and sleep; neither should he talk about events connected with this world, nor listen to anyone who is talking about them. [2] Rather should he spend his whole life occupied with prayer, and vigils, and recitation until our God sends for him in peace. [3] Every man on earth, be he priest or monk—for after a long time they will love the life of holy retreat—must renounce the world and all its evil cares and join in the holy service the messengers render in purity to God. [4] And they will be honored before God and His messengers because of their holy sacrifices and their angelic service, which is like the archetype that is rendered in the heavens. [5] And the messengers will be their friends, because of their perfect faith and their purity; and great is their honor before God. [6] In a word, whether great or small, sinlessness is required of us. [7] The chief sins worthy of conversion are these: You will not kill with the sword; You will not kill with the tongue either; [8] You will not commit fornication with your body; You will not commit fornication with your thoughts; You will not go in to the young to defile them; [9] You will not be envious; You will not be angry until the sun has set; [10] You will not be proud in disposition; You will not rejoice over your neighbour's fall; You will not slander; [11] You will not look at a woman with a lustful eye; and, Do not readily listen to slander. [12] We need to beware of these things, and of others like them, until each one of us is secure from the wrath that will be revealed from Heaven."

CHAPTER 8

[1] Now when the people gathered about him heard him, they cried out aloud, saying, "This is appropriate and right. Amen." But the God-loving old man was silent: he drew up his blanket [and] he covered his face. [2] And the people and the priest were silent, so that he could rest himself a little while. [3] But the messenger of his father Abraham came to him and took him up into the heavens. He saw terrors and tumults spread abroad on this side and on that; and it was a terror and a tumult fearful to behold. [4] Some had the face of a camel, others had the face of a lion; some had the face of a dog, others had but one eye and had tongs in their hands, three ells long, all of iron. [5] I looked, and behold, a man was brought, and those who brought

him went with him. When they reached the beasts, those who went with him withdrew to one side. The lion advanced toward him, tore him apart into little pieces, and swallowed him; [6] it then vomited him up, and he became like himself again; and the next beast treated him in just the same way. [7] In short, they passed him on from one to the other; each one would tear him into pieces, swallow him, and then vomit him up; and he would become like himself again. [8] I said to the messenger, "What sin has this man committed, my lord, that all this is done to him?" The messenger said to me, "This man you are looking at now had a quarrel with his neighbour, and he died without their being reconciled. [9] See, he has been handed over to five chief tormentors: they spend a year tormenting him for every hour he spent quarreling with his neighbour." [10] The messenger also said to me, "My beloved Isaac, do you think these are the only ones? Believe me Isaac, beloved of God, there are six hundred thousand tormentors. [11] They spend a year tormenting a man for every hour that he spends sinning—if he did not convert, that is, before he went forth from the body."

CHAPTER 9

[1] He led me on and brought me to a fiery river, the waters of which were an ell high, and its noise like the noise of Heaven's thunder. [2] And I saw a host of souls submerged in it; and those who were in that river cried out and wept aloud, and there was a great commotion and much groaning. [3] But it is a discerning fire that does not touch the righteous, yet burns up sinners and boils them in the stench that surrounds them. [4] I also saw the pit of the abyss, the smoke of which went up in clouds; I saw men sunk in it grinding their teeth, crying out and wailing, and each one was groaning. [5] The messenger said to me, "Look and see these others too." And when I had looked at them the messenger said to me, "These are those who have committed the sin of Sodom; these are indeed in great distress." I also saw pits full of worms that do not sleep; I saw Abdemerouchos who is in charge of the punishments, made all of fire, threatening the tormentors in Gehenna, and saying, "Beat them until they know that God is." I saw a house built of fiery stone, and there were grown men underneath it, crying out and wailing. The messenger said to me, "Look with your eyes and contemplate the punishments." I said to the messenger, "My eyes could not endure it; for how long must these punishments go on?" He said to me, "Until the merciful God has pity."

CHAPTER 10

[1] After this the messenger took me up into the heavens; I saw my father Abraham, and I made obeisance to him. [2] He saluted me, with all the saints, and the saints honored me because of my father; they

walked with me and took me to my [heavenly] Father—I worshiped Him with all the saints. [3] Songs of praise rang out: "YOU ARE HOLY, YOU ARE HOLY, YOU ARE HOLY. King, LORD of Hosts, the heavens and the earth are full of Your holy glory." [4] The LORD said to my father from the holy place, "[It] is good that you have come, Abraham, you righteous root and faithful saint: it is good that you have come to our city. Whatever you may want to ask now, make your requests in the name of your beloved son Isaac, and they will be yours indeed." [5] My father Abraham said, "Yours is the power, O LORD Almighty." The LORD said to Abraham, "As for all those who are given the name of my beloved Isaac, let each one of them copy out his testament and honor it, and feed a poor man with bread in the name of my beloved Isaac on the day of his holy commemoration; I will grant them to you as sons in My kingdom." [6] Abraham said, "My almighty Lord, if a man cannot copy out his testament, can You not in Your mercy accept him, for You are merciful and compassionate?" [7] The LORD said to Abraham, "Let him feed a poor man with bread, and I will give him to you as a gift and as a son in My Kingdom, and he will come with you to the first hour of the thousand years." [8] Abraham said, "Suppose he is poor and has no means of getting bread?" [9] The LORD said, "Let him spend the night of my beloved Isaac's commemoration without sleep, and I will give him to you as a gift and an inheritor in My Kingdom." [10] My father Abraham said, "Suppose he is weak and has no strength, can You not in Your mercy accept him in love?" [11] The LORD said to him, "Let him offer up a little incense in the name of your beloved son Isaac, and I will give him to you as a son in My Kingdom. [12] If he has no means of getting incense, let him seek out a copy of his testament and read it on my beloved Isaac's day. [13] If he cannot read it, let him go and listen to others who can. If he is unable to do any of these things, let him go into his house and say one hundred prayers, and I will give him to you as a son in My Kingdom. [14] But the most essential thing of all is that he should offer a sacrifice in my beloved Isaac's name, for his body was offered as a sacrifice. [15] Yet not only will I give you everyone called by my beloved Isaac's name as a son in My Kingdom, [but] I will also give you everyone who does one of the things I have mentioned. [16] And I will give you everyone who concerns himself about Isaac's life and his testament, or does any compassionate act, such as giving someone a cup of water to drink, or who copies out his testament with his own hand, and those who read it with all their heart in faith, believing everything that I have said. [17] My power and the power of My beloved Son and the Holy Spirit will be with them, and I will give them to you as sons in My Kingdom. Peace to all of you, all My saints."

CHAPTER 11

[1] Now when He had said this, songs of praise rang out: "YOU ARE HOLY, YOU ARE HOLY, YOU ARE HOLY. King, LORD of Hosts, the heavens and the earth are full of Your holy glory." [2] The Father said to Michael from the holy place, "Michael, My steward, go quickly and gather together the messengers and all the saints, so that they may come and meet My beloved Isaac." [3] And Michael sounded the trumpet at once. All the saints gathered with the messengers and came to the couch of our father Isaac. [4] The LORD mounted His chariot, and the seraphim were in front of Him with the messengers. And when they came to our father Isaac's couch, our father Isaac beheld our Lord's face immediately turned toward him full of joy. [5] He cried out, "It is good that You have come, my Lord, and Your great chief-messenger Michael! It is good that you have come, my father Abraham, and all the saints."

CHAPTER 12

[1] Now when he had said this, Jacob embraced his father; he kissed his mouth and wept. Our father Isaac fixed his eyes on him and motioned to him to be silent. [2] Our father Isaac said to the LORD, "Remember my beloved Jacob." The LORD said to him, "My power will be with him; and when the time comes and I become man and die and rise from the dead on the third day, I will put your name in everyone's mind, and they will invoke you as their father." [3] Isaac said to Jacob, "My beloved son, this is the last commandment I give you today: keep a sharp eye on yourself; do not dishonor the image of God; for what you do to the image of man, you do to the image of God, and God will do it to you, too, in the place where you will meet Him. This is the beginning and the end." [4] Now when he had said this, our Lord brought his soul out of his body, and it was white as snow. [5] He greeted it [and] set it on the chariot with Him; He took it up into the heavens, with the seraphim making music before Him, and all the messengers and the saints. [6] He freely granted him the good things of His Kingdom forever, and all the requests our father Abraham had asked of the LORD He freely granted him as a covenant forever.

CHAPTER 13

[1] This is the going forth from the body of our father Isaac, the patriarch, on the twenty-fourth of the month Mesore. [2] And the day on which his father Abraham offered him as a sacrifice is the eighteenth of Mechir. [3] The heavens and the earth were full of the soothing fragrance of our father Isaac, like choice silver: this is the sacrifice of our father Isaac the patriarch. [4] When Abraham offered him as a sacrifice to God, the soothing fragrance of Isaac's sacrifice went up into the heavens. [5] Blessed is every man who performs an act of mercy in the name of these patriarchs, for they

will be their sons in the kingdom of the heavens. [6] For our Lord has made a covenant with them forever, that everyone who performs an act of mercy on the day of their commemoration will be given to them as a son in the kingdom of the heavens forever. [7] And they will come to the first hour of the thousand years, in accordance with the promise of our Lord, even our God and our Savior Jesus Christ, [8] through whom every glory is due to Him, and His good Father, and the Holy Spirit, the giver of life to all creation and one in being with the Father and the Son, now and always, forever and ever. Amen.

TESTAMENT OF JACOB

The Testament of Jacob is the tale of Jacob's visitation by the archangel Michael who tells him of his impending death. Jacob is then taken on a visit to Heaven, where he sees the torment of the sinful dead, and then meets his deceased grandfather Abraham. In this Testament it is the angels that Jacob meets who deliver most of the sermonizing material. It was probably written in the 2nd or 3rd century AD.

CHAPTER 1

¹ In the Name of the Father, the Son, and the Holy Spirit—the one God. ² We begin, with the help of God Most High and through His intercession, to write the account of the life of our father, the patriarch Jacob, son of the patriarch Isaac, on the twenty-eighth day of the month of Mesore. ³ May the blessing of his prayer guard and protect us from the temptations of the unyielding adversary. Amen! Amen! Amen! ⁴ He said, "Come, listen, my beloved ones and my brothers who love the LORD, to what has been received." ⁵ Now when the time of our father Jacob, father of fathers, son of Isaac, son of Abraham, approached and drew near for him to go forth from his body, this faithful one was advanced in years and distinction. ⁶ So the LORD sent Michael to him, the chief of the messengers, who said to him, "O Israel, my beloved, of noble lineage, write down your spoken legacy and your instruction for your household and give them a covenant; also concern yourself with the proper ordering of your household, for the time has drawn near for you to go to your fathers to rejoice with them forever." ⁷ So when our father Jacob, the faithful one, heard this from the messenger, he answered and said, as was his custom every day to speak in this manner with the messengers, ⁸ "Let the will of the LORD be done." And God pronounced a blessing on our father Jacob. ⁹ Jacob had a secluded place which he would enter to offer his prayers before the LORD in the night and in the day. ¹⁰ The messengers would visit him and guard him and strengthen him in all things. ¹¹ God blessed him and multiplied his people in the land of Egypt at the time when he went down to the land of Egypt to meet his son Joseph. ¹² His eyes had become dull from weeping, but when he went down to Egypt he saw clearly when he beheld his son. ¹³ So Jacob-Israel bowed with his face to the ground, then fell on the neck of his son Joseph and kissed him, while weeping and saying, "I can die now, my son, because I have seen your face once more in my lifetime; O my beloved son."

CHAPTER 2

¹ Joseph continued to rule over all Egypt, while Jacob stayed in the land of Goshen for seventeen years and became very old, so that his lifespan was completed. ² He continually kept all the commandments and feared the LORD. ³ His eyes grew dim and his lifetime was so nearly finished that he could not see a single person because of his advanced age and decline. ⁴ Then he lifted his eyes toward the light of Isaac, but he was afraid and became disturbed. ⁵ So the messenger said to him, "Do not fear, O Jacob; ⁶ I am the messenger who has been walking with you and guarding you from your infancy. ⁷ I announced that you would receive the blessing of your father and of Rebekah, your mother. ⁸ I am the one who is with you, O Israel, in all your acts and in everything which you have witnessed. ⁹ I saved you from Laban when he was endangering you and pursuing you. ¹⁰ At that time I gave you all his possessions and blessed you, your wives, your children, and your flocks. ¹¹ I am the one who saved you from the hand of Esau. ¹² I am the one who accompanied you to the land of Egypt, O Israel, and a very great people was given to you. ¹³ Blessed is your father Abraham, for he has become the friend of God—may He be exalted—because of his generosity and love of strangers. ¹⁴ Blessed is your father Isaac who begot you, for he was a perfect sacrifice, acceptable to God. ¹⁵ Blessed are you also, O Jacob, for you have seen God face to face. ¹⁶ You saw the messenger of God—may He be exalted—and you saw the ladder standing firm on the ground with its top in the heavens. ¹⁷ Then you beheld the LORD sitting at its top with a power which no one could describe. ¹⁸ You spoke out and said, This is the house of God and this is the gate of Heaven. ¹⁹ Blessed are you, for you have come near to God and He is strong among mankind, so now do not be troubled, O chosen one of God. ²⁰ Blessed are you, O Israel, and blessed is all your progeny. ²¹ For all of you will be called The Patriarchs to the end of the age and of the epochs; you are the people and the lineage of the servants of God. ²² Blessed is the nation which will strive for your purity and will see your good works. Blessed is the man who will remember you on the day of your noble festival. ²³ Blessed is the one who will perform acts of mercy in honor of your several names, and will give someone a cup of water to drink, or will come with an offering to the sanctuary, or will take in strangers, or visit the sick and console their children, or will clothe a naked one in honor of your several names. ²⁴ Such a one will neither lack any of the good things of this world, nor life everlasting in the world to come. ²⁵ Moreover, whoever will have caused the stories of your several lives and sufferings to be written at his

own expense, or will have written them by his own hand, or will have read them soberly, or will hear them in faith, or will remember your deeds—such persons will have their sins forgiven and their trespasses pardoned, and they will go on account of you and your progeny into the kingdom of the heavens. [26] And now rise up, Jacob, for you will be translated from hardship and pain of heart to continuous rest, and you will enter into the repose which will not pass away, into mercy, continuous light, and spiritual joy. [27] So now make your statement to your household, and peace be on you, for I am about to go to Him who sent me."

CHAPTER 3

[1] So when the messenger had made this statement to our father Jacob, he ascended from him into Heaven, as Jacob bid him farewell. [2] Those who were around Jacob heard him as he thanked God and glorified Him with praise. [3] And all the members of his household, great and small, gathered around him, weeping over him, deeply grieving and saying, "You are going away and leaving us as orphans." [4] And they kept on saying to him, "O our beloved father, what will we do, for we are in a strange land?" [5] So Jacob said to them, "Do not fear; God Himself appeared to me in Upper Mesopotamia and said to me: I am the God of your fathers; do not fear, for I am with you forever and with your descendants who will come after you. [6] This land in which you are I am about to give to you and to your descendants after you forever. [7] And do not be afraid to go down to Egypt. [8] I will make a great people for you and your descendants will increase and multiply forever. [9] Joseph will put his hand on your eyes and your people will multiply in the land of Egypt. [10] Afterward they will come to this place and will be without care. I will do good to them for your sake, though for the time being they will be displaced from here."

CHAPTER 4

[1] After this, the time for Jacob-Israel to leave his body had arrived. [2] So he summoned Joseph and said to him, "If indeed you have found grace, place your blessed hand under my side and swear an oath before the LORD that you will place my body in the tomb of my fathers." [3] Then Joseph said to him, "I will do exactly what you command me, O beloved of God." [4] But he said to Joseph, "I want you to swear to me." [5] So Joseph swore to Jacob, his father, to the effect that he would carry his body to the tomb of his fathers, and Jacob accepted the oath of his son. [6] Afterward, this report reached Joseph: "Your father has become uneasy." [7] So he took his two sons, Ephraim and Manasseh, and went before his father Jacob. [8] Joseph said to him, "These are my sons whom God has given me in the land of Egypt to come after me." [9] Israel said, "Bring them closer to me here."

[10] For the eyes of Israel had become dim from his advanced age so that he could not see. [11] So Joseph brought his sons closer and Jacob kissed them. Then Joseph commanded them, namely Ephraim and Manasseh, to bow down before Jacob to the ground. [12] Joseph took Manasseh and put him at Israel's right hand and Ephraim at his left hand. [13] But Israel reversed his hands and let his right hand rest on the head of Ephraim and his left hand on the head of Manasseh. [14] He blessed them and gave them back to their father and said, "May the God under whose authority my fathers, Abraham and Isaac, served in reverence, the God who has strengthened me from my youth up to the present time when the messenger has saved me from all my afflictions, may he bless these boys, Manasseh and Ephraim. [15] May my name be on them, also the names of my holy fathers, Abraham and Isaac." [16] After this, Israel said to Joseph, "I will die, and all of you will return to the land of your fathers and God will be with you. [17] And you have personally received a mighty favor, greater than that of your brothers, for I have taken this arrow with my bow and my sword from the Amorites."

CHAPTER 5

[1] Then Jacob sent for all his children and said to them, "Gather around me that I may inform you of everything which will come on you and what will overtake each one of you in the last days." [2] So they gathered around Israel from the eldest to the youngest of them. [3] Then Jacob-Israel spoke up and said to his sons, "Listen, O sons of Jacob, listen to your father Israel, from Reuben my firstborn to Benjamin." [4] Then he told them what would come on the twelve children, calling each one of them and his tribe by name; [5] and he blessed them with the celestial blessing. [6] After this they were silent for a short time in order that he might rest. So the heavens rejoiced that he could observe the places of repose. [7] And behold, there approached numerous tormentors differing in their aspects. They were prepared to torment the sinners, who are these: adulterers, male and female; those lusting after males; the vicious who degrade the semen given by God; [8] the astrologers and the sorcerers; the evildoers and the worshipers of idols who hold onto abominations; and the slanderers who pass judgment with two tongues. [9] And as to all these sinners, their punishment is the fire which will not be extinguished and the outer darkness where there is weeping and gnashing of teeth.

CHAPTER 6

[1] And when the days of their mourning were finished, Pharaoh was still weeping over Jacob because of his regard for Joseph. [2] Then Joseph addressed the nobles of Pharaoh and said to them, "Since I have found favor with you, will you speak on my behalf to Pharaoh the king, and say to him that Jacob made me

take an oath that when he went out from his body I would bury his body in the tomb of my fathers in the land of Canaan, in that very place?" [3] So Pharaoh said to Joseph, "Go in peace and bury your father in accordance with the oath which he required of you. [4] And take chariots and horses with you, the best of my kingdom and from my own household as you desire." [5] So Joseph worshiped God in the presence of Pharaoh, went forth from him, and set out to bury his father. [6] And there set out with him the slaves of Pharaoh, the elders of Egypt, all the household of Joseph, and his brothers and all Israel. [7] They all went up with him into the chariots, and the entourage moved along like a great army. [8] They descended into the land of Canaan to the riverbank across the Jordan and they mourned for him in that place with very great grief indeed. [9] They maintained that great grief for him for seven days. [10] So when the inhabitants of Dan heard about the mourning in their land, they said, "This great mourning is that of the Egyptians." [11] To this day [[they call that place "the Mourning of the Egyptians"]]. [12] Then Israel was carried forward and was buried in the land of Canaan in the second tomb. [13] This is the one which Abraham had bought with authorization for burials from Ephron opposite Mature. [14] After that, Joseph returned to the land of Egypt with his brothers and all the entourage of Pharaoh. [15] And Joseph lived after the death of his father many years. [16] He continued to rule over Egypt, though Jacob had died and was left behind with his own people.

CHAPTER 7

[1] This is what we have transmitted: We have described the demise of and the mourning for the father of fathers, Jacob-Israel, to the extent of our ability to do this; [2] also as it is written in the spiritual scrolls of God and as we have found it in the ancient treasury of knowledge of our fathers, the holy, pure apostles. [3] And if you wish to know the life history and get new knowledge of the father of fathers, Jacob, then take a father who is attested in the Old Testament. [4] Moses is the one who wrote it, the first of the prophets, the author of the Law. Read from it and enlighten your insights. [5] You will find this and more in it, written for your sake. [6] You will find that God and His messengers were their friends while they were in their bodies, and that God kept on speaking to them many times in various passages from the Scroll. [7] Also He says in many passages with regard to the patriarch Jacob, the father of fathers, in the Scroll, thus, "My son, I will bless your descendants like the stars of the heavens." [8] And our father Jacob would speak to his son Joseph and say to him, "My God appeared to me in the land of Canaan at Luz and blessed me and said to me, I will bless you and multiply you and make you a mighty people. [9] They will go out [to war] like the other nations of this earth

and your descendants will increase forever." [10] This is what we have heard, O my brothers and my loved ones, from our fathers, the patriarchs. [11] And it is incumbent on us that we have zeal for their deeds, their purity, their faith, their love of mankind, and their acceptance of strangers; [12] in order that we may lay claim to be their sons in the kingdom of the heavens, so that they will intercede for us before God that we may be saved from the torture of Gehenna. [13] These are the ones whom the Arabs have designated as the holy fathers. [14] Jacob instructed his sons with regard to punishment, and he would call them the sword of the LORD, which is the river of fire, prepared with its waves to engulf the evildoers and the impure. [15] These are the things the power of which the father of fathers, Jacob, expounded and taught to all his sons that the wise ones might hear and pursue righteousness in mutual love with mercy and compassion. [16] For mercy saves people from penalties and mercy overcomes a multitude of wrongs. Truly, one who shows mercy to the poor, that one makes a loan to God. [17] So now, my beloved sons, do not slacken from prayer and fasting ever at any time, and by the life of the religion you will drive away the demons. [18] O my dear son, avoid the evil ways of the world, which are anger and depravity and all vicious deeds. [19] And beware of injustice and blasphemy and abduction. [20] For the unjust will not inherit the Kingdom of God, nor will the adulterers, nor the accursed, nor those who commit outrages and have sexual intercourse with males, nor the gluttons, nor the worshipers of idols, nor those who utter imprecations, nor those who pollute themselves outside of pure marriage; and others whom we have not presented or even mentioned will not come near the Kingdom of God. [21] O my sons, honor the saints, for they are the ones who will intercede for you. [22] O my sons, be generous to strangers and you will be given exactly what was given to the great Abraham, the father of fathers, and to our father Isaac, his son. [23] O my sons, do for the poor what will increase compassion for them here and now, so that God will give you the bread of life forever in the Kingdom of God. [24] For to the one who has given a poor person bread in this world God will give a portion from the Tree of Life. [25] Clothe the poor person who is naked on the earth, so that God may clothe you with the apparel of glory in the kingdom of the heavens, and you will be the sons of our holy fathers, Abraham, Isaac, and Jacob in Heaven forever. [26] Be concerned with the reading of the word of God in His scrolls here below, and remember the saints who have written of their lives, their sufferings, and their prostrations in prayer. [27] In the future, it will not be prevented that they should be inscribed in the Scroll of Life in the kingdom of the heavens. [28] And you will be counted among the saints, those who pleased God in their lifetime and will rejoice with the messengers in the land of continuous life.

CHAPTER 8

[1] You will honor the memory of our fathers, the patriarchs, at this time each year and on this same day, which is the twenty-eighth of the month of Mesore. [2] This is what we have found written in the ancient documents of our fathers, the saints who were pleasing to God. [3] Because of their intercession and their prayer, we will have all things, namely a share and a place in the kingdom of the heavens which belongs to our Lord and our God and our Master and our Savior, Jesus the Messiah. [4] He is the one whom we ask to forgive us for our mistakes and our errors and to overlook our misdeeds. [5] May He be kind to us on the day of His judgment and let us hear the voice filled with joy, kindness, and gladness, saying, "Come to Me, O blessed ones of My Father, inherit the kingdom which was yours from before the creation of the world." [6] And may we be worthy to receive His divine secrets, which are the means to the pardon of our sins. [7] May He help us toward the salvation of our souls, and may He ward off from us the blows of the wicked enemy. [8] May He let us stand at His right hand on the great and terrible day for the intercession of the mistress of intercessions, the source of purity, generosity, and blessings, the mother of salvation, and for the intercession of all the martyrs, saints, doers of pleasing deeds, and everyone who has pleased the LORD with his pious deeds and his good will. [9] Amen! Amen! Amen! And praise to God always, forever, [and] perpetually.

LADDER OF JACOB

The Ladder of Jacob, composed in the 1st or 2nd century AD at the latest, has been preserved only in Slavonic, which is itself clearly a translation from a now lost Greek version. The book is an expansion of the biblical account of Jacob's dream found in Genesis 28:11–19. Chapter 7 (7–8 here) is thought by some to be a later Christian development of the text.

CHAPTER 1

[[¹ Now Jacob went to his uncle Laban, and he found a place and fell asleep there, laying his head on a stone, for the sun was set: and there he saw a vision.]] ² And behold, a ladder was set up on the earth, whose top reached to Heaven. ³ And the top of the ladder was a face as of a man, hewn out of fire. ⁴ Now it had twelve steps up to the top of the ladder, and on each step up to the top were two human faces on the right and on the left—twenty-four faces seen to their breast, on the ladder. ⁵ But the middle face was higher than them all, which I saw made of fire, to the shoulder and the arm, very terribly, more than the twenty-four faces. ⁶ And as I looked, behold, the messengers of God ascending and descending thereon, but the LORD was set above it, ⁷ and He called me, saying, "Jacob, Jacob." And I said, "Here I am, Lord"; ⁸ And He said to me, "The land whereon you sleep I will give to you and to your seed after you: and I will multiply your seed as the stars of the heavens and as the sand of the sea; through your seed all the earth will be blessed, and they that dwell thereon, to the last times, the years of the end. ⁹ My blessing with which I have blessed you will pour out from you to the last generation. All in the east and the west will be full of your seed."

CHAPTER 2

¹ And when I heard it from above, fear and trembling fell on me, and I rose up from my dream. ² And while the Voice of God was yet in my ears, I said, "How dreadful is this place! This is none other than the house of God, and this is the gate of Heaven." ³ And I set up the stone that was under my head for a pillar, and poured oil on the top of it, and I called the name of that place the house of God. ⁴ [[And I prayed to God and said,]] "LORD God of Adam—Yours—and LORD God of Abraham and my father Isaac, and of all whose ways are right before You, You that sit mighty on the cherubim and on the throne of the majesty, of fire and full of eyes, as I saw in my dream; ⁵ that holds the cherubim with four faces, that bears the seraphim full of eyes, that bears the whole world under His arm, and is borne of none. ⁶ You have established the Heaven for the glory of Your Name. You have spread out on the clouds of the heavens the heaven that flies [[or rests]] under You, that under it You may move the sun and hide it in the night, lest it be held for God. ⁷ You have ordained the way for the moon and the stars, and You make her to wax and wane, but for the stars, You have commanded them to pass over, lest these also should be supposed gods. ⁸ Before the face of Your majesty the six-winged seraphim fear, and hide their feet and their face with their wings, and with the others they fly, and sing . . . ⁹ . . . Highest, with twelve faces, many-named, fiery, lightning-formed, Holy One! HOLY, HOLY, HOLY, YAH THE LORD, YAH'EL, SABAKDOS, CHABOD, SABAOTH, OMLELECH, ELABER, AME, S'ME BARECH, PERPETUAL KING, [who is] strong, mighty, very great, long-suffering. ¹⁰ [The] Blessed One that fills the heavens, and earth, and the sea, and the abyss, and all ages with Your glory. ¹¹ Hear my song with which I have praised You, and grant me my petition for which I pray to You, and show me the interpretation of my dream. ¹² For You are strong, and mighty, and glorious, a holy God, the Lord of me and my fathers."

CHAPTER 3

¹ And while I yet spoke my prayer, there appeared a voice before my face, saying, "Sarekl, prince of them that rejoice, you that are over visions, go make Jacob to understand the interpretation of the dream which he saw, and show him all things, whatever he saw, but first bless him." ² And the chief-messenger Sarekl came to me, and I saw: it was a face . . . terrible. ³ But I did not fear before his look, for the face which I had seen in my dream . . . was more than this, and I did not fear the face of a messenger. ⁴ And the messenger said to me, "What is your name?" And I said, "Jacob." [He said to me,] "Your name will no longer be called Jacob, but your name will be like my name, Israel." ⁵ And when I came from Fandana, in Syria, to meet my brother Esau, he came to me and blessed me, and called my name Israel, and did not tell me his name until I adjured him, and then he told me: "Because you were . . ."

CHAPTER 4

¹ But this he said to me: "The ladder which you saw, which had twelve steps having two human faces which changed their appearance—now this ladder is this age, and the twelve steps are the times of this age, and the twenty-four faces are the kings of the lawless heathen of this age. ² Under these kings [[your children's children and the line]] of your sons will be tried: they will rise up against the lawlessness of your descendants and will lay this place waste through four descents [because] of the sins of your descendants,

[3] and of the substance of the forefathers this palace will be built in the temple of the Name of your God and your fathers; [4] but through the wrath of your descendants it will be desolate until the fourth descent of this age; for you saw four visions [[*or* faces]]."

CHAPTER 5

[1] "The first that stumbles on the steps . . . messengers ascending and descending and faces in the midst of the steps: [2] the Most High will raise up an heir of the descendants of your brother Esau, and all the lords of the nations of the earth will accept it, who have done evil against your seed, and will be given into his hand, and he will be hardly borne by them. [3] But he begins to rule them with violence and to reign over them, and they cannot resist him, until the day when his decree goes forth against them to serve the idols . . . [4] . . . and to all them that appear in such a cause, and so many [[to the Most High out of your race, and]] so many to Thalkonagargael."

CHAPTER 6

[1] "And know, O Jacob, that your seed will be strangers in a strange land, and men will mistreat them with bondage and lay blows on them daily, but the LORD will judge the people whom they serve. [2] When a king arises and fights, then there will be to that place . . . then your seed, even Israel, will go forth out of the bondage of the heathen who ruled over them with violence, and will be set free from all reproach of their enemies. [3] For this king is the head of every revenge and retribution of them that make attacks on you, Israel. [4] And [at] the end of the age—for the miserable will rise and cry, and the LORD hears them, and will be softened, and the mighty lets Himself pity their sufferings, because the messengers and chief-messengers pour out their prayers for the saving of your race. [5] Then their women will bear much fruit, and then the LORD will fight for your race."

CHAPTER 7

[[[1] "But whereas you saw messengers descending and ascending on the ladder, in the last times there will be a Man from the Most High, and He will desire to join the upper with the lower. [2] Before His coming, your sons and your daughters will prophesy of Him, and your young men will see visions of Him. [3] For there will be such signs as these at the time of His coming: a tree felled by the axe will drop blood; boys of three months old will speak rationally; a child in its mother's womb will proclaim His way; a young man will be as an old man. [4] And then comes the Expected One, whose path will be perceived by no man. [5] Then the earth will rejoice, because it has received the glory of Heaven. That which was above will be below. [6] And a royal Root of your seed will grow up; and He will increase and destroy the power of the evil one, but He Himself will be a Savior of the heathen, and the rest of them that are weary, and a cloud which shades the whole world from the heat, [7] for otherwise that which is disordered could not be put in order, if He did not come: otherwise, that which is below could not be joined to that which is above."

CHAPTER 8

[1] "Now at His coming images of brass, and stone, and all graven things will utter their voice for three days long. [2] And they announce to the wise men and let them know what will befall on earth, and by the star they will know the way to Him, when they see Him on earth whom the messengers do not see above. [3] Then the Almighty will be found in a body on the earth, and encompassed by the arms of a mortal, and He renews the state of man and restores [Adam and] Eve that died through the fruit of the tree. [4] Then the deceit of the godless one will be overcome, and all idols fall on their faces, for they will be put to shame by one who is adorned with honor, because they made lying inventions. [5] From then on, they will not have power to rule or to give prophecies, for their honor will be taken from them, and they will remain without glory. [6] For He that has come takes the power and might from them and repays to Abraham the truth [[*or* righteousness]] which He promised him. [7] Then He rounds off all that is sharp, and He makes every rough thing smooth, and He casts all unrighteousness into the depths of the sea: and He does wonders in Heaven and on the earth. [8] And He will be wounded in the midst of the house of the beloved. But when He is wounded, then also the saving and the end of all corruption draws near. [9] For they that have wounded Him will themselves receive a wound which will not be healed for them forever. [10] But all creatures will worship the Wounded One, and many will hope on Him, and everywhere, and among all the nations, He will be known. But they that have known His Name will not be put to shame. And His own might and His years will not fail forever."]]

JOSEPH AND ASENATH

Joseph and Asenath is an embellished account of Joseph's relationship with Asenath, the daughter of the Egyptian priest of Heliopolis. Joseph's marriage to Asenath, given only a brief mention in Genesis 41:45–50 and 46:20, is herein turned into a sweeping narrative describing Asenath's conversion to faith in YHWH, her subsequent marriage to Joseph, the birth of Ephraim and Manasseh, and a fanciful plot by Pharaoh's son, along with Dan and Gad, to kill Joseph. The story is thought to have been written sometime between 200 BC and 200 AD, either as a Jewish midrash with later Christian interpolations, or as a Judeo-Christian work from the onset.

CHAPTER 1

[1] In the first year of plenty, in the second month, on the fifth of the month, Pharaoh sent Joseph to go around all the land of Egypt; and in the fourth month of the first year, on the eighteenth of the month, Joseph came to the borders of Heliopolis, and he was gathering the corn of that country as the sand of the sea. [2] And there was a certain man in that city, Pentephres by name, who was a priest of Heliopolis and a satrap of Pharaoh, and chief of all Pharaoh's satraps and princes; and this man was exceedingly rich and very sage and gentle, and he was also a counselor of Pharaoh, because he was prudent beyond all Pharaoh's princes. [3] And he had a virgin daughter, by name Asenath, of eighteen years, tall and lovely, and exceedingly beautiful to behold—beyond every virgin on the earth. [4] Now Asenath herself bore no likeness to the daughters of the Egyptians, but was in all things like the daughters of the Hebrews, being tall as Sarah, and lovely as Rebecca, and beautiful as Rachel; [5] and the fame of her beauty spread abroad into all that land and to the ends of the world, so that by reason of this all the sons of the princes and the satraps desired to woo her, moreover, and the sons of the kings also—all young men and mighty—and there was great strife among them because of her, and they strove to fight against one another. [6] And Pharaoh's firstborn son also heard about her, and he continued entreating his father to give her to him to be [his] wife and saying to him: "Give me, father, Asenath, the daughter of Pentephres, the first man of Heliopolis, to be [my] wife." [7] And his father Pharaoh said to him, "Therefore, do you on your part seek a wife lower than yourself when you are king of all this land? [8] But rather, behold, the daughter of Joacim, the king of Moab, is betrothed to you, and she herself is a queen and exceedingly beautiful to behold. Take this one then to yourself to be [your] wife."

CHAPTER 2

[1] But Asenath set at nothing and scorned every man, being boastful and haughty, and a man had never seen her, inasmuch as Pentephres had in his house an adjoining tower, great and exceedingly high, and above the tower was a loft containing ten chambers. [2] And the first chamber was great, and very lovely, and paved with purple stones, and the walls thereof were faced with precious and multicolored stones, and also the roof of that chamber was of gold. [3] And within that chamber gods of the Egyptians, whereof was no number, gold and silver, were fixed, and Asenath worshiped all of those, and she feared them, and she performed sacrifices to them every day. [4] And the second chamber also contained all of Asenath's adornments and chests, and there was gold in it, and much silver and limitless gold-woven raiment, and choice stones of great price, and fine garments of linen, and all the adornment of her virginity was there. [5] And the third chamber was Asenath's storehouse, containing all the good things of the earth. [6] And the remaining seven chambers the seven virgins who ministered to Asenath occupied, each one having one chamber, for they were of the same age, born on the same night with Asenath, and she loved them much; [7] and they were also exceedingly beautiful as the stars of heaven, and a man or male child never conversed with them. [8] Now Asenath's great chamber where her virginity was fostered had three windows; and the first window was very large, looking over the court to the east; [9] and the second looked toward the south, and the third looked over the street. [10] And a golden bedstead stood in the chamber looking toward the east; and the bed was laid with purple stuff interwoven with gold, the bed being woven of scarlet and crimson stuff and fine linen. [11] On this bed Asenath slept alone, and never had man or other woman sat thereon. [12] And there was also a great court adjoining the house all round, and an exceedingly high wall around the court built of great rectangular stones; and there were also four gates in the court overlaid with iron, and these were each kept by eighteen strong young men, armed; [13] and there were also planted along the wall fair trees of all kinds and all bearing fruit, their fruit being ripe, for it was the season of harvest; [14] and there was also a rich fountain of water springing from the right of the same court; and beneath the fountain was a great cistern receiving the water of that fountain, from where there went, as it were, a stream through the midst of the court and it watered all the trees of that court.

JOSEPH AND ASENATH

CHAPTER 3

¹ And it came to pass in the first year of the seven years of plenty, in the fourth month, on the twenty-eighth of the month, that Joseph came to the borders of Heliopolis collecting the corn of that district. ² And when Joseph drew near to that city, he sent twelve men before him to Pentephres, the priest of Heliopolis, saying, "I will come in to you today, because it is the time of noon and of the midday meal, and there is great heat of the sun, and that I may cool myself under the roof of your house." ³ And Pentephres, when he heard these things, rejoiced with exceedingly great joy, and said, "Blessed be the LORD God of Joseph, because my lord Joseph has thought me worthy." ⁴ And Pentephres called the overseer of his house and said to him, "Hurry and make my house ready, and prepare a great dinner, because Joseph, the mighty one of God, comes to us today." ⁵ And when Asenath heard that her father and mother had come from the possession of their inheritance, she rejoiced greatly and said, "I will go and see my father and mother, because they have come from the possession of our inheritance." (For it was the season of harvest). ⁶ And Asenath hastened into her chamber where her robes lay, and put on a fine linen robe made of crimson stuff and interwoven with gold, and girded herself with a golden girdle, and [placed] bracelets around her hands; ⁷ and around her feet she put golden buskins, and around her neck she cast an ornament of great price and precious stones, which were embellished on all sides, also having the names of the gods of the Egyptians everywhere engraved on them, both on the bracelets and the stones; ⁸ and she also put a tiara on her head, and bound a diadem around her temples, and covered her head with a mantle.

CHAPTER 4

¹ And thereon she hurried and went down the stairs from her loft, and came to her father and mother, and kissed them. ² And Pentephres and his wife rejoiced over their daughter Asenath with exceedingly great joy, for they beheld her adorned and embellished as the bride of God; ³ and they brought forth all the good things which they had brought from the possession of their inheritance and gave them to their daughter; ⁴ and Asenath rejoiced over all the good things, over the late summer fruit, and the grapes, and the dates, and over the doves, and over the mulberries and the figs, because they were all fair and pleasant to taste. ⁵ And Pentephres said to his daughter Asenath, "Child." And she said, "Here I am, my lord." ⁶ And he said to her, "Sit down between us, and I will speak my words to you." ⁷ She sat down between her father and her mother, and her father Pentephres took hold of her right hand with his right hand, and kissed it tenderly, and said, "Dearest child." ⁸ And she said to him, "Here I am, my lord father." And Pentephres said to her, "Behold, Joseph, the mighty one of God,

comes to us today, and this man is ruler of all the land of Egypt; ⁹ and King Pharaoh appointed him ruler of all our land and king, and he himself gives corn to all this country, and saves it from the coming famine; ¹⁰ and this Joseph is a man that worships God, and [is as] discreet and a virgin as you are today, and a man mighty in wisdom and knowledge, and the Spirit of God is on him, and the grace of the LORD is in him. ¹¹ Come, dearest child, and I will give you over to him to be [his] wife, and you will be to him for a bride, and he himself will be your bridegroom forever." ¹² And when Asenath heard these words from her father, a great sweat was poured out on her over her face, and she grew angry with great anger, and she looked suspiciously with her eyes at her father, ¹³ and said, "Therefore, my lord father, [why] do you speak these words? Do you wish to give me over as a captive to an alien, and a fugitive, and one that has been sold? Is this not the son of the shepherd from the land of Canaan? And he himself has been left behind by him. ¹⁴ Is this not he who lay with his mistress, and his lord cast him into the prison of darkness, and Pharaoh brought him out from the prison inasmuch as he interpreted his dream, as the older women of the Egyptians also interpret? ¹⁵ But rather, I will be married to the king's firstborn son, because he himself is king of all the land." ¹⁶ When he heard these things Pentephres was ashamed to speak further to his daughter Asenath about Joseph, for she answered him with boastfulness and anger.

CHAPTER 5

¹ And behold, a young man of Pentephres' servants sprang in, and he says to him, "Behold, Joseph stands before the doors of our court." ² And when Asenath heard these words, she fled from the face of her father and mother, and went up into the loft, and she came into her chamber, and stood at the great window looking east to see Joseph coming into her father's house. ³ And Pentephres came out with his wife, and all their relatives, and their servants, to meet Joseph; ⁴ and when the gates of the court that looked east were opened, Joseph came in, seated in the second chariot of Pharaoh; ⁵ and there were yoked four horses white like snow with golden bits, and the chariot was fashioned entirely of pure gold. ⁶ And Joseph was clad in a tunic white and rare, and the robe that was thrown around him was purple, made of fine linen interwoven with gold, and a golden wreath was on his head, and around his wreath were twelve choice stones, and above the stones twelve golden rays, and in his right hand a royal staff, which had an olive branch outstretched, and there was abundance of fruit thereon. ⁷ When, then, Joseph had come into the court and the doors thereof had been shut, and every strange man and woman remained outside the court, for the guards of the gates drew to and closed the doors, Pentephres came with his wife and all their relatives,

except their daughter Asenath, and they paid homage to Joseph on their faces on the earth; [8] and Joseph descended from his chariot and greeted them with his hand.

CHAPTER 6

[1] And when Asenath saw Joseph she was sorely struck in the soul, and her heart was crushed, and her knees were loosed, and her whole body trembled, and she feared with great fear, [2] and then she groaned and said in her heart: "Oh miserable me! Where now will I, the wretched one, go away? Or where will I be hidden from his face? Or how will Joseph, the son of God, see me, for on my part I have spoken evil things about him? Oh miserable me! [3] Where will I go away and be hidden, because he himself sees every hiding place, and knows all things, and no hidden thing escapes him by reason of the great light that is in him? [4] And now may the God of Joseph be gracious to me because in ignorance I have spoken wicked words against him. [5] What now will I, the wretched one, follow? Have I not said, Joseph comes, the son of the shepherd, from the land of Canaan? [6] Now he has therefore come to us in his chariot as the sun from heaven, and he entered our house today, and he shines into it like light on the earth. [7] But I am foolish and bold, because I scorned him, and spoke evil words about him, and did not know that Joseph is a son of God. [8] For who among men will ever beget such beauty, or what womb of woman will give birth to such light? [9] I am wretched and foolish, because I have spoken evil words to my father. [10] Now therefore, let my father give me to Joseph for a handmaid and a bondwoman rather, and I will be in bondage to him forever."

CHAPTER 7

[1] And Joseph came into the house of Pentephres and sat on a chair. [2] And they washed his feet, and set a table before him separately, for Joseph did not eat with the Egyptians, since this was an abomination to him. [3] And Joseph looked up and saw Asenath peeping out, and he says to Pentephres: "Who is that woman who is standing in the loft by the window? Let her go away from this house." [4] For Joseph feared, saying, "Lest she herself also annoy me," for all the wives and daughters of the princes and the satraps of all the land of Egypt used to annoy him in order that they might lie with him; [5] but many wives and daughters of the Egyptians also, as many as beheld Joseph, were distressed on account of his beauty; [6] and the envoys whom the women sent to him with gold, and silver, and precious gifts Joseph sent back with threatening and insult, saying, "I will not sin in the sight of the LORD God and the face of my father Israel." [7] For Joseph always had God before his eyes and always remembered the injunctions of his father; [8] for Jacob often spoke and admonished his son

Joseph and all his sons: "Keep yourselves, children, securely from a strange woman so as not to have fellowship with her, for fellowship with her is ruin and destruction." [9] Therefore Joseph said, "Let that woman depart from this house." [10] And Pentephres said to him, "My lord, that woman whom you have seen standing in the loft is not a stranger, but is our daughter, one who hates every man, and no other man has ever seen her except you only today; [11] and if you wish, lord, she will come and speak to you, for that daughter of ours is as your sister." [12] And Joseph rejoiced with exceedingly great joy, for Pentephres said, "She is a virgin hating every man." [13] And Joseph said to Pentephres and his wife, "If she is your daughter, and is a virgin, let her come, for she is my sister, and I love her from today as my sister."

CHAPTER 8

[1] Then her mother went up into the loft and brought Asenath to Joseph, and Pentephres said to her, "Kiss your brother, because he is also a virgin even as you [are] today and hates every strange woman even as you hate every strange man." [2] And Asenath said to Joseph, "Greetings, lord, blessed of God Most High." [3] And Joseph said to her, "God who quickens all things will bless you, girl." [4] Then Pentephres says to his daughter Asenath, "Come and kiss your brother." [4] When Asenath then came up to kiss Joseph, Joseph stretched forth his right hand, and laid it on her chest between her two breasts (for her breasts were already standing forth like lovely apples), [5] and Joseph said, "It is not fitting for a man that worships God, who blesses the living God with his mouth, and eats the blessed bread of life, and drinks the blessed cup of immortality, and is anointed with the blessed unction of incorruption, to kiss a strange woman who blesses dead and deaf idols with her mouth, and eats the bread of strangling from their table, and drinks the cup of deceit from their libation, and is anointed with the unction of destruction; [6] but the man that worships God will kiss his mother, and the sister who is born of his mother, and the sister who is born of his tribe, and the wife who shares his couch, who bless the living God with their mouth. [7] Likewise also, it is not fitting for a woman that worships God to kiss a strange man, for this is an abomination in the sight of the LORD God." [8] And when Asenath heard these words from Joseph, she was sorely distressed and groaned; [9] and as she was looking steadfastly at Joseph with her eyes open, they were filled with tears. [10] And Joseph, when he saw her weeping, pitied her exceedingly, for he was mild, and merciful, and one who feared the LORD. [11] Then he lifted up his right hand above her head and said, "LORD God of my father Israel, the Most High and the mighty God, who quickened all things and called from the darkness to the light, and from error to truth, and from death to life, [12] bless this virgin also, and quicken her, and

renew her with Your Holy Spirit, and let her eat the bread of Your life and drink the cup of Your blessing, and number her with Your people whom You chose before all things were made, [13] and let her enter into Your rest which You prepared for Your elect, and let her live in Your continuous life forever."

CHAPTER 9

[1] And Asenath rejoiced over the blessing of Joseph with exceedingly great joy. [2] Then she hurried and came up into her loft by herself, and fell on her bed in infirmity, for there was in her joy, and sorrow, and great fear; [3] and a continuous sweat was poured over her when she heard these words from Joseph, and when he spoke to her in the Name of God Most High. [4] Then she wept with a great and bitter weeping, and she turned in penitence from her gods whom she was accustomed to worship, and the idols which she spurned, and waited for evening to come. [5] But Joseph ate and drank; and he told his menservants to yoke the horses to their chariots, and to go around all the land. [6] And Pentephres said to Joseph, "Let my lord lodge here today, and in the morning you will go your way." [7] And Joseph said, "But rather, I will go away today, for this is the day on which God began to make all His created things, and on the eighth day I also return to you and will lodge here."

CHAPTER 10

[1] And when Joseph had left the house, Pentephres also and all his relatives departed to their inheritance, and Asenath was left alone with the seven virgins, listless and weeping until the sun set; and she neither ate bread nor drank water, but while all slept, she herself alone was awake, and weeping, and frequently beating her breast with her hand. [2] And after these things Asenath rose from her bed, and quietly went down the stairs from the loft, and on coming to the gateway, found the doorkeeper sleeping with her children; [3] and she hurried and took down from the door the leather cover of the curtain, and filled it with cinders, and carried it up to the loft, and laid it on the floor. [4] And thereon she shut the door securely, and fastened it with the iron bolt from the side, and groaned with great groaning together with much and very great weeping. [5] But the virgin whom Asenath loved above all the virgins, having heard her groaning, hurried and came to the door after also awaking the other virgins and found it shut. [6] And when she had listened to the groaning and the weeping of Asenath, she said to her [while] standing outside, "What is it, my mistress? And are you therefore sad? And what is it that troubles you? Open to us and let us see you." [7] And Asenath said to her, being shut inside, "Great and grievous pain has attacked my head, and I am resting in my bed, and I am not able to rise and open to you, for I am weak in all my limbs. [8] Therefore, each of you go to her

chamber and sleep, and let me be still." [9] And when the virgins had departed, each to her own chamber, Asenath rose, and opened the door of her bedroom quietly, and went away into her second chamber where the chests of her adornment were, and she opened her coffer, and took a black and somber tunic which she had put on and mourned in when her firstborn brother died. [10] Having taken, then, this tunic, she carried it into her chamber, and again shut the door securely, and put the bolt through from the side. [11] Then, therefore, Asenath took off her royal robe, and put on the mourning tunic, and loosed her golden girdle, and girded herself with a rope, and put off the tiara, that is the turban, from her head, likewise also the diadem, and the chains from her hands and her feet were also all laid on the floor. [12] Then she takes her choice robe, and the golden girdle, and the turban, and her diadem, and she cast them through the window that looked toward the north, to the poor. [13] And thereon she took all her gods that were in her chamber, the gods of gold and of silver whereof there was no number, and broke them up into fragments, and cast them through the window to poor men and beggars. [14] And again Asenath took her royal dinner, and the fatlings, and the fish, and heifer's flesh, and all the sacrifices of her gods, and the vessels of the wine of libation, and cast all of them through the window that looked north as food for the dogs. [15] And after these things she took the leather cover containing the cinders and poured them on the floor; and thereon she took sackcloth and girded her loins; and she also loosed the net of the hair of her head and sprinkled ashes over her head. [16] And she also strewed cinders on the floor, and fell on the cinders, and kept beating her breast constantly with her hands and weeping all night with groaning until the morning. [17] And when Asenath arose in the morning and saw, and behold, the cinders were beneath her as clay from her tears, she again fell on her face on the cinders until the sun set. [18] Thus Asenath did for seven days, not tasting anything whatsoever.

CHAPTER 11

[1] And on the eighth day, when the dawn came, and the birds were already chirping, and the dogs barking at the passers by, Asenath lifted up her head a little from the floor and the cinders whereon she was seated, for she was exceedingly weary and had lost the power of her limbs from her great humiliation; [2] for Asenath had grown weary and faint and her strength was failing, and thereon she turned toward the wall, sitting under the window that looked east; [3] and she laid her head on her bosom, wrapping the fingers of her hands over her right knee; [4] and her mouth was shut, and she did not open it during the seven days and during the seven nights of her humiliation. [5] And she said in her heart, not opening her mouth: "What will I do—I, the lowly one—or where will I go? And with whom again

will I find refuge hereafter? Or to whom will I speak—the virgin that is an orphan, and desolate, and abandoned by all, and hated? ⁶Everyone has now come to hate me, and among these even my father and my mother, for I spurned the gods with loathing, and made away with them, and have given them to the poor to be destroyed by men. ⁷For my father and my mother said, Asenath is not our daughter, but all my relatives have also come to hate me, and all men, for I have given their gods to destruction. ⁸And I have hated every man and all who wooed me, and now in this humiliation of mine I have been hated by all and they rejoice over my tribulation. ⁹But the Lord and God of the mighty Joseph hates all who worship the idols, for He is a zealous God and terrible, as I have heard, against all who worship strange gods; ¹⁰from which He has hated me also, because I worshiped dead and deaf idols and blessed them. ¹¹But now I have shunned their sacrifice, and my mouth has become estranged from their table, and I have no courage to call on the LORD God of Heaven—the Most High and powerful one of the mighty Joseph—for my mouth is polluted from the sacrifices of the idols. ¹²But I have heard many saying that the God of the Hebrews is a true God, and a living God, and a merciful God, and compassionate, and long-suffering, and full of mercy, and gentle, and one who does not reckon the sin of a man who is humble, and especially of one who sins in ignorance, and does not convict of lawlessnesses in the time of the affliction of a man that is afflicted; ¹³accordingly, I also, the humble one, will be bold, and will turn to Him, and seek refuge with Him, and confess all my sins to Him, and pour out my petition before Him, and He will have mercy on my misery. ¹⁴For who knows if He will see this humiliation of mine and the desolation of my soul and pity me, and will also see the orphanhood of my wretchedness and [my] virginity and defend me. ¹⁵For, as I hear, He is Himself a Father of orphans, and a consolation of the afflicted, and a helper of the persecuted. ¹⁶But in any case, I also, the humble one, will be bold and will cry to Him." ¹⁷Then Asenath rose up from the wall where she was sitting, and raised herself on her knees toward the east, and directed her eyes toward Heaven, and opened her mouth, and said to God:

CHAPTER 12

¹"LORD God of the righteous, ‖ Who created the ages and gives life to all things, ‖ Who gave the breath of life to all Your creation, ‖ Who brought the invisible things out into the light, ²Who made all things and made manifest things that did not appear, ‖ Who lifted up the heaven and founded the earth on the waters, ‖ Who fixed the great stones on the abyss of the water, ‖ Which will not be submerged but are to the end doing Your will, ³For You, LORD, said the word and all things came into being, ‖ And Your word, LORD,

is the life of all Your creatures— ⁴To You I flee for refuge, O LORD my God; From henceforth I will cry to You, LORD, ‖ And to You I will confess my sins; ⁵To you I will pour out my petition, Master, ‖ And to You I will reveal my lawlessnesses. ⁶Spare me, LORD, spare, ‖ For I committed many sins against You, ‖ I did lawlessness and ungodliness, ‖ I have spoken things not to be uttered, ‖ And wicked in Your sight; ⁷My mouth, LORD, has been polluted from the sacrifices of the idols of the Egyptians, ‖ And from the table of their gods: ⁸I sinned, LORD, I sinned in Your sight, ‖ Both in knowledge and in ignorance I did ungodliness ‖ In that I worshiped dead and deaf idols, ‖ And I am not worthy to open my mouth to You, LORD— ⁹I, the miserable Asenath, daughter of Pentephres the priest, ‖ The virgin and queen who was once proud and haughty ‖ And one that prospered in my father's riches above all men, ¹⁰But now an orphan, and desolate, and abandoned by all men. ¹¹To You I flee, LORD, ‖ And to You I offer my petition, ‖ And to You I will cry. Deliver me from them that pursue me, Master, ‖ Before I am taken by them; ¹²For as an infant in fear of some one flees to his father and mother, ‖ And his father stretches out his hands and catches him up against his breast, ‖ So you, LORD, stretch out Your undefiled and terrible hands on me ‖ Like a child-loving father, ‖ And catch me out of the hand of the transcendent enemy. ¹³For behold, the ancient, and savage, and cruel lion pursues me, ‖ For he is father of the gods of the Egyptians, ‖ And the gods of the idol-maniacs are his children, ‖ And I have come to hate them, ‖ And I made away with them, ‖ Because they are a lion's children; ¹⁴And I cast all the gods of the Egyptians from me ‖ And did away [with] them, ‖ And the lion, or their father the Devil, ‖ In wrath against me is trying to swallow me up. ¹⁵But You, LORD, deliver me from his hands, ‖ And I will be rescued from his mouth, ‖ Lest he tears me apart ‖ And casts me into the flame of fire, ‖ And the fire casts me into a storm, ‖ And the storm prevails over me in darkness ‖ And casts me into the depth of the sea, ‖ And the great beast who is from everlasting swallows me up, ‖ And I perish forever. ¹⁶Deliver me, LORD, before all these things come on me; Deliver me, Master, the desolate and defenseless, ‖ For my father and my mother have denied me ‖ And said, Asenath is not our daughter, ‖ Because I broke their gods in pieces and made away with them, ‖ As having wholly hated them. ¹⁷And now I am an orphan and desolate, ‖ And I have no other hope except You, LORD, ‖ Nor another refuge except Your mercy—You friend of men, ¹⁸Because You alone are Father of the orphans, ‖ And champion of the persecuted, ‖ And helper of the afflicted. ¹⁹Have mercy on me, LORD, ‖ And keep me pure and virgin, the forsaken and orphan, ‖ For You alone, LORD, ‖ Are a sweet, and good, and gentle Father. ²⁰For what father is [as] sweet and good as You,

LORD? ²¹ For behold, all the houses of my father Pentephres, ‖ Which he has given to me for an inheritance, ‖ Are for a moment and [are] vanishing; But the houses of Your inheritance, LORD, ‖ Are incorruptible and perpetual."

CHAPTER 13

¹ "Visit, LORD, my humiliation, ‖ And have mercy on my orphanhood, ‖ And pity me, the afflicted. ² For behold, I, Master, fled from all ‖ And sought refuge with You, ‖ The only friend of men. ³ Behold, I left all the good things of the earth ‖ And sought refuge with You. LORD—in sackcloth and ashes, naked and solitary. ⁴ Behold, now I put off my royal robe of fine linen ‖ And of crimson stuff interwoven with gold ‖ And have put on a black tunic of mourning. ⁵ Behold, I have loosed my golden girdle, ‖ And cast it from me, ‖ And girded myself with rope and sackcloth. ⁶ Behold, I have cast my diadem and my turban from my head ‖ And I have sprinkled myself with cinders. ⁷ Behold, the floor of my chamber that was paved with multicolored and purple stones, ‖ Which was formerly moistened with ointments ‖ And was dried with bright linen cloths, ‖ Is now moistened with my tears ‖ And has been dishonored in that it is strewn with ashes. ⁸ Behold, my Lord, from the cinders and my tears ‖ Much clay has been formed in my chamber as on a broad road. ⁹ Behold, my Lord, my royal dinner ‖ And the meats I have given to the dogs. ¹⁰ Behold, I have also, Master, been fasting seven days and seven nights ‖ And neither ate bread nor drank water, ¹¹ And my mouth is [as] dry as a wheel ‖ And my tongue [is] as a horn, ‖ And my lips [are] as a potsherd, ‖ And my face has shrunk, ‖ And my eyes have failed from shedding tears. ¹² But You, LORD my God, deliver me from my many ignorances, ‖ And forgive me for that, being a virgin and unknowing, ‖ I have gone astray. ¹³ Behold, now all the gods whom I worshiped before in ignorance ‖ I have now known to have been deaf and dead idols, ‖ And I broke them in pieces ‖ And gave them to be trampled on by all men, ‖ And the thieves spoiled them, ‖ Who were [only] gold and silver; ¹⁴ And with You I sought refuge, LORD God, ‖ The only compassionate one and friend of men. ¹⁵ Forgive me, LORD, for I committed many sins against You in ignorance, ‖ And have spoken blasphemous words against my lord Joseph, ‖ And did not know—I, the miserable—That he is Your son. ¹⁶ LORD, since the wicked men urged by envy said to me, ‖ Joseph is a son of a shepherd from the land of Canaan, ‖ Therefore I, the miserable one, have believed them and gone astray, ‖ And I set him at nothing, ‖ And have spoken wicked things about him, ‖ Not knowing that he is Your son. ¹⁷ For who among men begot or will ever beget such beauty? Or who else is such as he, wise and mighty, as the all-beautiful Joseph? ¹⁸ But to You, LORD, I commit him, ‖ Because for my part I love him more than my soul.

¹⁹ Keep him safe in the wisdom of Your grace, ‖ And commit me to him for a handmaid and a bondwoman, ‖ That I may wash his feet, and make his bed, ‖ And minister to him, and serve him, ²⁰ And I will be a bondwoman to him for [all] the times of my life."

CHAPTER 14

¹ And when Asenath had ceased making confession to the LORD, behold, the morning star also arose out of the heaven in the east; ² and Asenath saw it, and rejoiced, and said, "Has the LORD God then heard my prayer? For this star is a messenger and herald of the light of the great day." ³ And behold, close by the morning star the heaven was rent and a great and ineffable light appeared. ⁴ And when she saw it Asenath fell on her face on the cinders, and immediately there came to her a man from Heaven, sending forth rays of light, and stood above her head. ⁵ And as she lay on her face, the divine messenger said to her, "Asenath, stand up." ⁶ And she said, "Who is he that called me, for the door of my chamber is shut and the tower is high, and how then has he come into my chamber? ⁷ And he called her again a second time, saying, "Asenath, Asenath." And she said, "Here I am, lord, tell me who you are." ⁸ And he said, "I am the chief captain of the LORD God and commander of all the host of the Most High: stand up and stand on your feet, that I may speak my words to you." ⁹ And she lifted up her face and saw, and behold, a man in all things like to Joseph, in robe, and wreath, and royal staff, except that his face was as lightning, and his eyes as the light of the sun, and the hairs of his head as the flame of fire of a burning torch, and his hands and his feet like iron shining from fire, for sparks, as it were, proceeded both from his hands and from his feet. ¹⁰ Seeing these things, Asenath feared and fell on her face, unable even to stand on her feet, for she became greatly afraid and all her limbs trembled. ¹¹ And the man said to her, "Be of good cheer, Asenath, and do not fear; but stand up and stand on your feet, that I may speak my words to you." ¹² Then Asenath stood up and stood on her feet, and the messenger said to her, "Go without impediment into your second chamber, and lay aside the black tunic wherein you are clad, and cast off the sackcloth from your loins, and shake out the cinders from your head, and wash your face and your hands with pure water, and put on a white untouched robe, and gird your loins with the bright girdle of virginity—the double one—and come to me again, and I will speak to you the words that are sent to you from the LORD." ¹³ Then Asenath hurried and went into her second chamber wherein were the chests of her adorning, and opened her coffer, and took a white, fine, untouched robe, and put it on, having first put off the black robe, and also ungirded the rope and the sackcloth from her loins, and girded herself in a bright, double girdle of her virginity—one girdle

around her loins and another girdle around her breast. [14] And she also shook out the cinders from her head, and washed her hands and face with pure water, and she took a most beautiful and fine mantle and veiled her head.

CHAPTER 15

[1] And thereon she came to the divine chief captain and stood before him, and the messenger of the LORD says to her, "Now take the mantle from your head, for you are a pure virgin today, and your head is as of a young man." [2] And Asenath took it from her head. [3] And again the divine messenger says to her, "Be of good cheer, Asenath, the virgin and pure, for behold, the LORD God heard all the words of your confession and your prayer, [4] and He has also seen the humiliation and affliction of the seven days of your abstinence, for from your tears much clay has been formed before your face on these cinders. [5] Accordingly, be of good cheer, Asenath, the virgin and pure, for behold, your name has been written in the Scroll of Life and will not be blotted out forever; [6] but from this day [forward] you will be renewed, and refashioned, and re-quickened, [7] and you will eat the blessed bread of life, and drink a cup filled with immortality, and be anointed with the blessed unction of incorruption. [8] Be of good cheer, Asenath, the virgin and pure, behold, the LORD God has given you to Joseph for a bride today, and he himself will be your bridegroom forever. [9] And henceforth you will no longer be called Asenath, but your name will be City of Refuge, for in you many nations will seek refuge and they will lodge under your wings, and many nations will find shelter by your means, and on your walls they who cleave to God Most High through penitence will be kept secure; [10] for Penitence is a daughter of the Most High, and she herself entreats God Most High for you every hour and for all that convert, since He is father of Penitence, and she herself is the completion and overseer of all virgins, loving you exceedingly and imploring the Most High for you every hour, [11] and for all who convert she will provide a place of rest in the heavens, and she renews everyone who has converted. [12] And Penitence is exceedingly lovely, a virgin pure, and gentle, and mild; and therefore God Most High loves her, and all the messengers revere her, and I love her exceedingly, for she herself is also my sister, and as she loves you virgins, I also love you. [13] And behold, for my part I go to Joseph and will speak to him all these words concerning you, and he will come to you today, and see you, and rejoice over you, and love you, and be your bridegroom, and you will be his beloved bride forever. [14] Accordingly, hear me, Asenath, and put on a wedding robe, the ancient and first robe that is yet laid up in your chamber from of old, and also put all your choice adornments around you, and adorn yourself as a good bride and make yourself ready to meet him; [15] for behold, he

himself comes to you today and will see you and rejoice." [16] And when the messenger of the LORD, in the shape of a man, had finished speaking these words to Asenath, she rejoiced with great joy over all the things that were spoken by him, and fell on her face on the earth, and paid homage before his feet, [17] and said to him, "Blessed is the LORD your God who sent you to deliver me from the darkness and to bring me from the foundations of the abyss itself into the light, and blessed is your name forever. [18] If I have found grace, my lord, in your sight, and will know that you will perform all the words which you have said to me so that they are accomplished, let your handmaid speak to you." [19] And the messenger says to her, "Speak on." [20] And she said, "Please, lord, sit down on this bed [for] a little while, because this bed is pure and undefiled, for another man or other woman never sat on it, [21] and I will set a table and bread before you, and you will eat, and I will also bring you wine, aged and good, the aroma of it will reach to heaven, and you will drink thereof and afterward will depart on your way." [22] And he says to her, "Hurry and bring it quickly."

CHAPTER 16

[1] And Asenath hurried and set an empty table before him; and as she was starting to fetch bread, the divine messenger says to her, "Bring me a honeycomb also." [2] And she stood still, and was perplexed, and grieved because she did not have a bee's comb in her storehouse. [3] And the divine messenger says to her, "You therefore stand still?" [4] And she said, "My lord, I will send a boy to the suburb, because the possession of our inheritance is near, and he will come and bring one quickly from there, and I will set it before you." [5] The divine messenger says to her, "Enter your storehouse and you will find a bee's comb lying on the table; take it up and bring it here." [6] And she said, "Lord, there is no bee's comb in my storehouse." And he said, "Go and you will find [one]." [7] And Asenath entered her storehouse and found a honeycomb lying on the table; and the comb was great and white like snow and full of honey, and that honey was as the dew of heaven, and the aroma of it [was] as the aroma of life. [8] Then Asenath wondered and said in herself: "Is this comb from the mouth of this man himself?" And Asenath took that comb, and brought it, and set it forth on the table, [9] and the messenger said to her, "Why is it that you said, There is no honeycomb in my house, and behold, you have brought it to me?" [10] And she said, "Lord, I have never put a honeycomb in my house, but as you said so, it has been made. Did this come forth from your mouth? For the aroma of it is as the aroma of ointment." [11] And the man smiled at the woman's understanding. [12] Then he calls her to himself, and when she came, he stretched out his right hand and took hold of her head, and when he shook her head with his right hand, Asenath feared the

messenger's hand greatly, for sparks proceeded from his hands after the manner of red-hot iron, and accordingly, she was gazing with much fear and trembling at the messenger's hand the whole time. [13] And he smiled and said, "Blessed are you, Asenath, because the ineffable mysteries of God have been revealed to you; and blessed are all who cleave to the LORD God in penitence, because they will eat of this comb, [14] for this comb is the Spirit of life, and the bees of the paradise of delight have made this from the dew of the roses of life that are in the paradise of God and [from] every flower, [15] and the messengers, and all the elect of God, and all the sons of the Most High eat of it, and whosoever will eat of it will not die forever." [16] Then the divine messenger stretched out his right hand and took a small piece from the comb and ate, and with his own hand placed what was left in Asenath's mouth and said to her, "Eat," and she ate. [17] And the messenger says to her, "Behold, now you have eaten the bread of life, and have drunk the cup of immortality, and been anointed with the unction of incorruption; [18] behold, now today your flesh produces flowers of life from the fountain of the Most High, and your bones will be made fat like the cedars of the paradise of delight of God, and unwearying powers will maintain you; [19] accordingly, your youth will not see old age, nor will your beauty fail forever, but you will be as a walled mother-city of all." [20] And the messenger incited the comb, and many bees arose from the cells of that comb, and the cells were numberless—myriads of myriads and thousands of thousands. [21] And the bees were also white like snow, and their wings as purple and crimson stuff and as scarlet; and they also had sharp stings and injured no man. [22] Then all those bees encircled Asenath from feet to head, and other great bees like their queens arose from the cells, and they circled around on her face and on her lips, and made a comb on her mouth and on her lips like the comb that lay before the messenger; [23] and all those bees ate from the comb that was on Asenath's mouth. And the messenger said to the bees, "Go now to your place." [24] Then all the bees rose, and flew, and departed to Heaven; but as many as wished to injure Asenath all fell on the earth and died. [25] And thereon the messenger stretched his staff over the dead bees and said to them, "Rise and depart, you also, into your place." [26] Then all the dead bees rose, and departed into the court that adjoined Asenath's house, and took up their lodging on the fruit-bearing trees.

CHAPTER 17

[1] And the messenger saith to Asenath, "Have you seen this thing?" And she said, "Yes, my lord, I have seen all these things." [2] The divine messenger says to her, "So all my words will be, as many as I have spoken to you today." [3] Then the messenger of the LORD stretched forth his right hand for the third time and touched the side of the comb, and immediately fire came up from the table and devoured the comb, but it did not injure the table a bit. [4] And when much fragrance had come forth from the burning of the comb and filled the chamber, Asenath said to the divine messenger, "Lord, I have seven virgins who were brought up with me from my youth and were born on one night with me, who wait on me, and I love all of them as my sisters. I will call them, and you will bless them too, even as you blessed me." [5] And the messenger said to her, "Call them." Then Asenath called the seven virgins and set them before the messenger, [6] and the messenger said to them, "The LORD God Most High will bless you, and you will be [pillars] of refuge of seven cities, and all the elect of that city who dwell together will [rest on you] forever." [7] And after these things the divine messenger says to Asenath, "Take away this table." [8] And when Asenath turned to remove the table, he immediately departed from her eyes, and Asenath saw as it were a chariot with four horses that were going eastward to Heaven, [9] and the chariot was as a flame of fire, and the horses as lightning, and the messenger was standing above that chariot. [10] Then Asenath said, "Silly and foolish am I, the lowly one, for I have spoken as that a man came into my chamber from Heaven! [11] I did not know that God came into it; and behold, now he goes back to Heaven, to his place." [12] And she said in herself: "Be gracious, LORD, to Your bondmaid, and spare your handmaid, because, for my part, I have spoken rash things before You in ignorance."

CHAPTER 18

[1] And while Asenath was yet speaking these words to herself, behold, a young man, one of the servants of Joseph, came, saying, "Joseph, the mighty man of God, comes to you today." [2] And immediately Asenath called the overseer of her house and said to him, "Hurry and prepare my house and make a good dinner ready, for Joseph, the mighty man of God, comes to us today." [3] And when the overseer of the house saw her (for her face had shrunk from the seven days' affliction, and weeping, and abstinence) he sorrowed and wept; [4] and he took hold of her right hand, and kissed it tenderly, and said, "What afflicts you, my lady, that your face is thus shrunken?" [5] And she said, "I have had great pain about my head, and sleep departed from my eyes." [6] Then the overseer of the house went away and prepared the house and the dinner. [7] And Asenath remembered the messenger's words and his injunctions, and hurried and entered her second chamber where the chests of her adornments were, and opened her great coffer, and brought out her first robe, like lightning to behold, and put it on; [8] and she also girded herself with a bright and royal girdle that was of gold and precious stones, and on her hands she put golden bracelets, and

on her feet golden buskins, and a precious ornament around her neck, and she put a golden wreath around her head; [9] and on the wreath as on its front was a great sapphire stone, and around the great stone [were] six stones of great price, and with a very marvelous mantle she veiled her head. [10] And when Asenath remembered the words of the overseer of her house, for he said to her that her face had shrunk, she sorrowed exceedingly, and groaned, and said, "Woe is me, the lowly one, since my face is shrunken. [11] Joseph will see me thus and I will be set at nothing by him." [12] And she says to her handmaid, "Bring me pure water from the fountain." [13] And when she had brought it, she poured it out into the basin, and bending down to wash her face, she sees her own face shining like the sun, and her eyes as the morning star when it rises, and her cheeks as a star of heaven, and her lips as red roses; [14] the hairs of her head were as the vine that blooms among his fruits in the paradise of God, her neck as an all-variegated cypress. [15] And Asenath, when she saw these things, marveled in herself at the sight, and rejoiced with exceedingly great joy, and did not wash her face, for she said, "Lest I wash off this great and attractive beauty." [16] The overseer of her house then came back to tell her, "All things are done that you commanded"; [17] and when he beheld her, he feared greatly and was seized with trembling for a long time, and he fell at her feet and began to say, "What is this, my mistress? What is this beauty that surrounds you that is great and marvelous? [18] Has the LORD God of Heaven chosen you as a bride for His son Joseph?"

CHAPTER 19

[1] And while they were yet speaking these things, a boy came, saying to Asenath, "Behold, Joseph stands before the doors of our court." [2] Then Asenath hurried and went down the stairs from her loft with the seven virgins to meet Joseph and stood in the porch of her house. [3] And Joseph, having come into the court, the gates were shut, and all strangers remained outside. [4] And Asenath came out from the porch to meet Joseph, and when he saw her, he marveled at her beauty, and said to her, "Who are you, girl? Tell me quickly." [5] And she says to him, "I, lord, am your handmaid Asenath; I have cast all the idols away from me and they perished. [6] And a man came to me today from Heaven and has given me bread of life and I ate, and I drank a blessed cup, [7] and he said to me, I have given you for a bride to Joseph, and he himself will be your bridegroom forever; [8] and your name will not be called Asenath, but it will be called City of Refuge, and the LORD God will reign over many nations, and through you they will seek refuge with God Most High. [9] And the man said, I will also go to Joseph that I may speak into his ears these words concerning you. And now you know, lord, if that man has come to you and if he has spoken to you concerning me." [10] Then

Joseph says to Asenath, "Blessed are you, woman, of God Most High, and blessed is your name forever, for the LORD God has laid the foundations of your walls, and the sons of the living God will dwell in your city of refuge, and the LORD God will reign over them forever. [11] For that man came from Heaven to me today and said these words to me concerning you. [12] And now come here to me, you virgin and pure— and [why] do you therefore stand far off?" [13] Then Joseph stretched out his hands and embraced Asenath, and Asenath Joseph, and they kissed one another for a long time, and both lived again in their spirit. [14] And Joseph kissed Asenath and gave her the Spirit of life, then the second time he gave her the Spirit of wisdom, and the third time he kissed her tenderly and gave her the Spirit of truth.

CHAPTER 20

[1] And when they had embraced around one another for a long time and intertwined the chains of their hands, Asenath said to Joseph, "Come here, lord, and enter our house, for on my part I have prepared our house and a great dinner." [2] And she took hold of his right hand, and led him into her house, and seated him on the chair of her father Pentephres; and she brought water to wash his feet. [3] And Joseph said, "Let one of the virgins come and wash my feet." [4] And Asenath said to him, "No, lord, for henceforth you are my lord and I am your handmaid. [5] And do you therefore seek this—that another virgin should wash your feet? [6] For your feet are my feet, and your hands my hands, and your soul my soul, and another will not wash your feet." [7] And she constrained him and washed his feet. [8] Then Joseph took hold of her right hand and kissed her tenderly and Asenath kissed his head tenderly, and thereon he seated her at his right hand. [9] Her father, and mother, and all her relatives then came from the possession of their inheritance, and they saw her sitting with Joseph and clad in a wedding garment. [10] And they marveled at her beauty and rejoiced and glorified God who quickens the dead. [11] And after these things they ate and drank; and all having made cheer, Pentephres said to Joseph, "Tomorrow I will call all the princes and satraps of all the land of Egypt, and will make a wedding for you, and you will take my daughter Asenath to be [your] wife." [12] But Joseph said, "Tomorrow I go to Pharaoh the king, for he himself is my father and appointed me ruler over all this land, and I will speak to him concerning Asenath, and he will give her to me to be [my] wife." [13] And Pentephres said to him, "Go in peace."

CHAPTER 21

[1] And Joseph stayed with Pentephres that day, and he did not go in to Asenath, for he was accustomed to say: "It is not fitting for a man who worships God to sleep with his wife before his marriage." [2] And Joseph

rose early, and departed to Pharaoh, and said to him, "Give me Asenath, daughter of Pentephres, priest of Heliopolis, to be [my] wife." ³ And Pharaoh rejoiced with great joy, and he says to Joseph, "Behold, has this one not been betrothed to you to be [your] wife from eternity? ⁴ Accordingly, let her be your wife henceforth and to time continuous." ⁴ Then Pharaoh sent and called Pentephres, and Pentephres brought Asenath and set her before Pharaoh; ⁵ and when Pharaoh saw her he marveled at her beauty and said, "The LORD God of Joseph will bless you, child, and this beauty of yours will remain forever, for the LORD God of Joseph chose you as a bride for him, for Joseph is as the son of the Most High, and you will be called his bride henceforth and forever." ⁶ And after these things Pharaoh took Joseph and Asenath and set golden wreaths on their heads, which were in his house from of old and from ancient times, and Pharaoh set Asenath at Joseph's right hand. ⁷ And Pharaoh put his hands on their heads and said, "The LORD God Most High will bless you and will multiply, and magnify, and glorify you to time continuous." ⁸ Then Pharaoh turned them around to face one another and brought them mouth to mouth, and they kissed one another. ⁹ And Pharaoh made a wedding for Joseph, and a great dinner, and much drinking during seven days, ¹⁰ and he called together all the rulers of Egypt and all the kings of the nations, having made proclamation in the land of Egypt, saying, "Every man who will do work during the seven days of the wedding of Joseph and Asenath will surely die." ¹¹ And while the wedding was going on, and when the dinner was ended, Joseph went in to Asenath, and Asenath conceived by Joseph and bore Manasseh and his brother Ephraim in Joseph's house.

CHAPTER 22

¹ And when the seven years of plenty had passed, the seven years of famine began to come. ² And when Jacob heard about his son Joseph, he came into Egypt with all his relatives in the second year of the famine, in the second month, on the twenty-first of the month, and settled in Goshen. ³ And Asenath said to Joseph, "I will go and see your father, for your father Israel is as my father and God." ⁴ And Joseph said to her, "You will go with me and see my father." ⁵ And Joseph and Asenath came to Jacob in the land of Goshen, and Joseph's brothers met them and paid homage to them on their faces on the earth. ⁶ Then both went in to Jacob; and Jacob was sitting on his bed, and he himself was an old man in a robust old age. ⁷ And when Asenath saw him, she marveled at his beauty, for Jacob was exceedingly beautiful to behold and his old age as the youth of a handsome man, ⁸ and all his head was white like snow, and the hairs of his head were all close and exceedingly thick, and his beard [was] white, reaching to his breast, his eyes cheerful and glittering, his sinews, and his shoulders, and his

arms as of a messenger, his thighs, and his calves, and his feet as of a giant. ⁹ Then Asenath, when she saw him thus, marveled, and fell down, and paid homage on her face on the earth. ¹⁰ And Jacob said to Joseph, "Is this my daughter-in-law, your wife? She will be blessed of God Most High." ¹¹ Then Jacob called Asenath to himself, and blessed her, and kissed her tenderly; ¹² and Asenath stretched out her hands, and took hold of Jacob's neck, and hung on to his neck, and kissed him tenderly. ¹³ And after these things they ate and drank. ¹⁴ And thereon both Joseph and Asenath went to their house; and Simeon and Levi, the sons of Leah, alone conducted them forth, but the sons of Bilhah and Zilpah, the handmaids of Leah and Rachel, did not join in conducting them forth, for they envied and detested them. ¹⁵ And Levi was at Asenath's right and Simeon at her left. ¹⁶ And Asenath took hold of Levi's hand, for she loved him exceedingly above all of Joseph's brothers and as a prophet, and a worshiper of God, and one who feared the LORD. ¹⁷ For he was an understanding man and a prophet of the Most High, and he himself saw letters written in Heaven, and read them, and revealed them to Asenath in secret; ¹⁸ for Levi himself also loved Asenath much and saw the place of her rest in the highest.

CHAPTER 23

¹ And it came to pass as Joseph and Asenath were passing by, when they were going to Jacob, Pharaoh's firstborn son saw them from the wall, and when he saw Asenath, he became crazed with her by reason of her surpassing beauty. ² Then Pharaoh's son sent messengers, and called Simeon and Levi to himself; ³ and when they came and stood before him, Pharaoh's firstborn son says to them, "I for my part know that you are today mighty men above all men on the earth, and with these right hands of yours the city of the Shechemites was overthrown, and with your two swords thirty thousand warriors were cut down. ⁴ And I today will take you to myself as companions and give you much gold, and silver, and menservants, and handmaids, and houses, and great inheritances, and you contend on my side and do me kindness; ⁵ for I received great injury from your brother Joseph, since he himself took Asenath to be [his] wife, and this woman was betrothed to me from of old. ⁶ And now come with me, and I will fight against Joseph to slay him with my sword, and I will take Asenath to be [my] wife, and you will be to me as brothers and faithful friends. ⁷ But if you will not listen to my words, I will slay you with my sword." ⁸ And when he had said these things, he drew out his sword and showed it to them. ⁹ And Simeon was a bold and daring man, and he thought to lay his right hand on the hilt of his sword, and draw it from the sheath thereof, and smite Pharaoh's son, for he had spoken hard words to them. ¹⁰ Levi then saw the

thought of his heart, because he was a prophet, and he trod with his foot on Simeon's right foot and pressed it, signaling to him to cease from his wrath. ¹¹ And Levi was quietly saying to Simeon, "Are you therefore angry against this man? We are men who worship God, and it is not fitting for us to render evil for evil." ¹² Then Levi said to Pharaoh's son openly, with mildness of heart, "Does our lord therefore speak these words? We are men who worship God, and our father is a friend of God Most High, and our brother is as a son of God. ¹³ And how will we do this wicked thing, to sin in the sight of our God and of our father Israel and in the sight ot our brother Joseph? ¹⁴ And now hear my words: it is not fitting for a man who worships God to harm any man in any way; and if anyone wishes to harm a man who worships God, that man who worships God does not avenge himself on him, for there is no sword in his hands. ¹⁵ And you must beware of speaking anymore of these words about our brother Joseph. ¹⁶ But if you continue in your evil counsel, behold, our swords are drawn against you." ¹⁷ Then Simeon and Levi drew their swords from their sheaths and said, "Do you now see these swords? ¹⁸ With these two swords the LORD punished the injury of the Shechemites, by which they did injury to the sons of Israel through our sister Dinah, whom Shechem the son of Hamor defiled." ¹⁹ And Pharaoh's son, when he saw the swords drawn, feared exceedingly and trembled all over his body, for they glittered like a flame of fire, and his eyes became dim, and he fell on his face on the earth beneath their feet. ²⁰ Then Levi stretched out his right hand and took hold of him, saying, "Stand up and do not fear, only beware of speaking any evil word anymore concerning our brother Joseph." ²¹ And so both Simeon and Levi went out from before his face.

CHAPTER 24

¹ Pharaoh's son then continued to be full of fear and grief for he feared Joseph's brothers, and again he was exceedingly crazed by reason of Asenath's beauty, and he grieved greatly. ² Then his menservants say in his ear: "Behold, the sons of Bilhah and the sons of Zilpah, the handmaids of Leah and Rachel, Jacob's wives, are at great enmity against Joseph and Asenath and hate them; these will be to you in all things according to your will." ³ Therefore Pharaoh's son immediately sent messengers and called them, and they came to him at the first hour of the night, and they stood in his presence, ⁴ and he says to them, "I have learned from many that you are mighty men." ⁵ And Dan and Gad, the elder brothers, said to him, "Let my lord now speak to his menservants what he wishes [so] that your menservants may hear and we may do according to your will." ⁶ Then Pharaoh's son rejoiced with exceedingly great joy and said to his menservants, "Withdraw now for a short space from me, for I have

secret speech to hold with these men." And they all withdrew. ⁷ Then Pharaoh's son lied, and he says to them, "Behold, now blessing and death are before your faces: you therefore take the blessing rather than the death, because you are mighty men and will not die as women; but be brave and avenge yourselves on your enemies. ⁸ For I have heard your brother Joseph saying to Pharaoh, my father: "Dan, and Gad, and Naphtali, and Asher are not my brothers, but children of my father's handmaids: I therefore wait for my father's death and will blot them out from the earth and all their issue, lest they should inherit with us, because they are children of handmaids. ⁹ For these also sold me to the Ishmaelites, and I will render to them again according to their injury which they wickedly committed against me; only my father will die. ¹⁰ And my father Pharaoh commended him for these things and said to him, "You have spoken well, child. ¹¹ Accordingly, take mighty men from me and proceed against them according to what they worked against you, and I will be a helper to you." ¹² And when Dan and Gad heard these things from Pharaoh's son they were very troubled, and exceedingly grieved, ¹³ and they said to him, "Please, lord, help us; for henceforth we are your slaves and bondmen and will die with you." ¹⁴ And Pharaoh's son said, "I will be a helper to you if you will also listen to my words." ¹⁵ And they said to him, "Command us what you wish and we will do according to your will." ¹⁶ And Pharaoh's son says to them, "I will slay my father Pharaoh this night, for Pharaoh is as Joseph's father and said to him that he would help against you; ¹⁷ and you slay Joseph, and I will take Asenath to myself to be [my] wife, and you will be my brothers and fellow-heirs of all my possessions. Only do this thing." ¹⁸ And Dan and Gad said to him, "We are your menservants today and will do all [the] things that you have commanded us. ¹⁹ And we have heard Joseph saying to Asenath, Go tomorrow to the possession of our inheritance, for it is the season of the vintage; and he sent six hundred mighty men to war with her and fifty forerunners. ²⁰ Now therefore, hear us and we will speak to our lord." And they spoke to him all their secret words. ²¹ Then Pharaoh's son gave the four brothers five hundred men each and appointed them their chiefs and leaders. ²² And Dan and Gad said to him, "We are your menservants today and will do all the things that you have commanded us, and we will set forth by night, and lie in wait in the ravine, and hide ourselves in the thicket of the reeds; ²³ and you take with yourself fifty bowmen on horses and go a long way before us, and Asenath will come and fall into our hands, and we will cut down the men that are with her, and she herself will flee before [us] with her chariot and fall into your hands, and you will do to her as your soul desires; ²⁴ and after these things we will also slay Joseph while he is grieving for Asenath; ²⁵ we will also likewise slay his children before his eyes." [26] Pharaoh's firstborn son then, when he heard these things, rejoiced exceedingly, and he sent them forth and two thousand fighting men with them. [27] And when they came to the ravine, they hid themselves in the thicket of the reeds, and they divided into four companies, and took up their station on the far side of the ravine as in the front part—five hundred men on this side of the road and on that; [28] and on the near side of the ravine likewise the rest remained, and they themselves also took up their station in the thicket ot the reeds—five hundred men on this side and on that of the road; and between them was a broad and wide road.

CHAPTER 25

[1] Then Pharaoh's son rose up the same night and came to his father's bed-chamber to slay him with the sword. [2] His father's guards thereon hindered him from coming in to his father and said to him, "What do you command, lord?" [3] And Pharaoh's son said to them, "I wish to see my father, for I am going to gather the vintage of my newly planted vineyard." [4] And the guards said to him, "Your father suffers pain, and lies awake the whole night, and now rests, and he said to us that no one was to come in to him, Not even if it is my firstborn son." [5] And he on hearing these things went away in wrath and immediately took mounted bowmen, fifty in number, and went away before them as Dan and Gad had said to him. [6] And the younger brothers, Naphtali and Asher, spoke to their elder brothers Dan and Gad, saying, "Therefore do you on your part again work wickedness against your father Israel and against your brother Joseph? [7] And God preserves him as the apple of an eye. Behold, did you not once sell Joseph? And he is king today of all the land of Egypt and food-giver. [8] Now therefore, if you again wish to work wickedness against him, he will cry to the Most High, and He will send fire from Heaven and it will devour you, and the messengers of God will fight against you." [9] Then the elder brothers were moved to anger against them and said, "And will we die as women? Far be it." [10] And they went out to meet Joseph and Asenath.

CHAPTER 26

[1] And Asenath rose in the morning and said to Joseph, "I am going to the possession of our inheritance as you have said; but my soul exceedingly fears for you are parting from me." [2] And Joseph said to her, "Be of good cheer and do not be afraid, but rather go away rejoicing, in dread of no man whatsoever, for the LORD is with you and He Himself will preserve you as the apple of an eye from every evil. [3] And I will set forth for my giving of food and will give to all the men in the city, and no man will perish of hunger in the land of Egypt." [4] Then Asenath departed on her way, and Joseph for his giving of food. [5] And when

Asenath reached the place of the ravine with the six hundred men, suddenly they who were with Pharaoh's son came forth from their ambush and joined battle with those who were with Asenath, and cut them all down with their swords, and all her forerunners they slew, but Asenath fled with her chariot. [6] Then Levi, the son of Leah, knew all these things by the Spirit as a prophet and told his brothers of Asenath's danger, and immediately each of them took his sword on his thigh, and their shields on their arms, and the spears in their right hands, and pursued after Asenath with great speed. [7] And as Asenath was fleeing before, behold, Pharaoh's son met her and fifty horsemen with him: [8] and Asenath, when she saw him, was seized with very great fear and was trembling, and she called on the Name of the LORD her God.

CHAPTER 27

[1] And Benjamin was sitting with her on the chariot on the right side; and Benjamin was a strong young man of about nineteen years, and on him was ineffable beauty and might as of a lion's whelp, and he was also one who feared God exceedingly. [2] Then Benjamin leapt down from the chariot, and took a round stone from the ravine, and filled his hand, and hurled [it] at Pharaoh's son, and struck his left temple, and wounded him with a grievous wound, and he fell from his horse on the earth half-dead. [3] And thereon Benjamin, having run up onto a rock, says to Asenath's charioteer: "Give me stones from the ravine." [4] And he gave him fifty stones. And Benjamin hurled the stones and slew the fifty men who were with Pharaoh's son, all the stones sinking in through their temples. [5] Then the sons of Leah, Reuben and Simeon, Levi and Judah, Issachar and Zebulun, pursued after the men who had lain in wait against Asenath, and fell on them stealthily, and cut them all down; and the six men slew two thousand and seventy-six men. [6] And the sons of Bilhah and Zilpah fled from their face and said, "We have perished at the hands of our brothers, and Pharaoh's son has also died by the hand of the young man Benjamin, and all who were with him perished by the hand of the boy Benjamin. [7] Accordingly, therefore, come let us slay Asenath and Benjamin and flee to the thicket of these reeds." [8] And they came against Asenath, holding their swords drawn, covered with blood. [9] And when Asenath saw them, she feared greatly and said, "LORD God, who quickened me and delivered me from the idols and the corruption of death, even as You said to me that my soul will live forever, now also deliver me from these wicked men." [10] And the LORD God heard Asenath's voice, and immediately the swords of the adversaries fell from their hands on the earth and were turned into ashes.

JOSEPH AND ASENATH

CHAPTER 28

[1] And the sons of Bilhah and Zilpah, when they saw the strange miracle that had been worked, feared and said, "The LORD fights against us on Asenath's behalf." [2] Then they fell on their faces on the earth, and paid homage to Asenath, and said, "Have mercy on us, your bondmen, for you are our mistress and queen. [3] We wickedly committed evil deeds against you and against our brother Joseph, but the LORD repaid us according to our works. [4] Therefore we your bondmen beg you: have mercy on us, the lowly and miserable, and deliver us from the hands of our brothers, for they will make themselves avengers of the injury done to you and their swords are against us. [5] Accordingly, be gracious to your bondmen, mistress, before them." [6] And Asenath said to them, "Be of good cheer and do not be afraid of your brothers, for they themselves are men who worship God and fear the LORD; [7] but go into the thicket of these reeds until I will appease them on your behalf and stay their wrath on account of the great crimes which you on your part have dared to commit against them. [8] But may the LORD see and judge between me and you." [9] Then Dan and Gad fled into the thicket of the reeds; and their brothers, Leah's sons, came running like stags with great haste against them. [10] And Asenath stepped down from the chariot that was her cover and gave them her right hand with tears, [11] and they themselves fell down and paid homage to her on the earth and wept with a loud voice; [12] and they continued asking for their brothers, the sons of the handmaids, to put them to death. [13] And Asenath said to them, "Please spare your brothers, and do not render to them evil for evil. [14] For the LORD saved me from them and shattered their daggers and swords from out of their hands, and behold, they have melted and were burned to ashes on the earth like wax from before fire, and this is sufficient for us that the LORD fights for us against them. [15] Accordingly, spare your brothers, for they are your brothers and the blood of your father Israel." [16] And Simeon said to her, "Does our mistress therefore speak good words on behalf of her enemies? [17] No, but rather we will cut them down limb from limb with our swords, for they devised evil things concerning our brother Joseph and our father Israel and against you, our mistress, today." [18] Then Asenath stretched out her right hand, and touched Simeon's beard, and kissed him tenderly, and said, "In no way, brother, render evil for evil to your neighbor, for the LORD will avenge this injury. [19] They themselves, you know, are your brothers and the offspring of your father Israel, and they fled far from your face. Accordingly, grant them pardon." [20] Then Levi came up to her and kissed her right hand tenderly, for he knew that she was pleased to save the men from their brothers' anger that they should not slay them. [21] And they themselves were near at hand in the thicket of the reed-bed: and their brother Levi, knowing this, did not declare it to his brothers, for he feared lest in their anger they should cut their brothers down.

CHAPTER 29

[1] And Pharaoh's son rose from the earth, and sat up, and spat blood from his mouth, for the blood was running down from his temple into his mouth. [2] And Benjamin ran up to him, and took his sword, and drew it from Pharaoh's son's sheath (for Benjamin was not wearing a sword on his thigh), and wished to strike Pharaoh's son on the breast. [3] Then Levi ran up to him, and took hold of his hand, and said, "In no way, brother, do [this], for it is not fitting for a man who worships God to render evil for evil, nor to trample on one who has fallen, nor utterly to crush his enemy even to death. [4] And now put back the sword into his place, and come and help me, and let us heal him of this wound; and if he lives, he will be our friend and his father Pharaoh will be our father." [5] Then Levi raised Pharaoh's son from the earth, and washed away the blood from his face, and tied a bandage over his wound, and set him on his horse, and led him to his father Pharaoh, relating to him all the things that had happened and befallen. [6] And Pharaoh arose from his throne, and paid homage to Levi on the earth, and blessed him. [7] Then when the third day had passed, Pharaoh's son died from the stone with which he was wounded by Benjamin. [8] And Pharaoh mourned for his firstborn son exceedingly, from which grief Pharaoh fell sick and died at one hundred and nine years, and he left his diadem to the all-beautiful Joseph. [9] And Joseph reigned alone in Egypt forty-eight years; and after these things Joseph gave back the diadem to Pharaoh's younger child, who was at the breast when the old man Pharaoh died. [10] And Joseph was then on as father of Pharaoh's younger child in Egypt until his death, glorifying and praising God.

TESTAMENT OF JOB

The Testament of Job is a book likely written in the 1st century BC or the 1st century AD (thus part of a tradition often called "intertestamental literature" by Christian scholars). The earliest surviving manuscript is in Coptic of the 5th century; other early surviving manuscripts are in Greek and Old Slavonic. Similar to other apocryphal testaments, it is an account of the last events and words of the protagonist (here, Job).

CHAPTER 1

¹ On the day he became sick and knew that he would have to leave his bodily abode, he called his seven sons and his three daughters together and spoke to them as follows: ² Form a circle around me, children, and hear, and I will relate to you what the LORD did for me and all that happened to me. ³ For I am your father Job. ⁴ Know then, my children, that you are the generation of a chosen one and take heed of your noble birth. ⁵ For I am of the sons of Esau. My brother is Nahor, and your mother is Dinah. I have become your father by her. ⁶ For my first wife died with my other ten children in bitter death. ⁷ Hear now, children, and I will reveal to you what happened to me. ⁸ I was a very rich man living in the east, in the land of Uz, and before the LORD had named me Job, I was called Jobab. ⁹ The beginning of my trial was thus: near my house there was the idol of one worshiped by the people; and I saw burnt-offerings constantly brought to him as a god. ¹⁰ Then I pondered and said to myself, "Is this he who made the heavens and earth, the sea, and all of us? How will I know the truth?" ¹¹ And in that night as I lay asleep, a voice came and called: "Jobab! Jobab! Rise up, and I will tell you who is the One whom you wish to know. ¹² This, however, to whom the people bring burnt-offerings and libations, is not God, but this is the power and work of the Seducer by which he deceives the people." ¹³ And when I heard this, I fell on the earth and I prostrated myself, saying, ¹⁴ "O my Lord, who speaks for the salvation of my soul—please, if this is the idol of Satan, please, let me go on and destroy it and purify this spot. ¹⁵ For there is none that can forbid me doing this, as I am the king of this land, so that those that live in it will no longer be led astray." ¹⁶ And the voice that spoke out of the flame answered to me: "You can purify this spot. ¹⁷ But behold, I announce to you what the LORD ordered me to tell you, for I am the chief-messenger of the God." ¹⁸ And I said, "Whatever will be told to His servant, I will hear." ¹⁹ And the chief-messenger said to me, "Thus speaks the LORD: If you undertake to destroy and take away the image of Satan, he will set himself with wrath to wage war against you, and he will display all his malice against you. ²¹ He will bring on you many severe plagues and take from you all that you have. ²¹ He will take away your children and will inflict many calamities on you. ²² Then you must wrestle like an athlete and resist pain, [being] sure of your reward, [and] overcome trials and afflictions. ²³ But when you endure, I will make your name renowned throughout all generations of the earth until the [very] end of the world. ²⁴ And I will restore you to all that you had, and the double part of what you will lose will be given to you in order that you may know that God does not consider the person but gives to each who deserves the good. ²⁵ And also to you will it be given, and you will put on a crown of amaranth. ²⁶ And at the resurrection you will awaken for continuous life. Then you will know that the LORD is just, and true, and mighty." ²⁷ Immediately, my children, I replied: "I will from love of God endure all that will come on me until death, and I will not shrink back." ²⁸ Then the messenger put his seal on me and left me.

CHAPTER 2

¹ After this I rose up in the night and took fifty slaves and went to the temple of the idol and destroyed it to the ground. ² And so I went back to my house and gave orders that the door should be firmly locked, saying to my doorkeepers: ³ "If somebody will ask for me, bring no report to me, but tell him: He investigates urgent affairs. He is inside." ⁴ Then Satan disguised himself as a beggar and knocked heavily at the door, saying to the doorkeeper: ⁵ "Report to Job and say that I desire to meet him," ⁶ and the doorkeeper came in and told me that, but heard from me that I was studying. ⁷ The evil one, having failed in this, went away and took on his shoulder an old, torn basket and went in and spoke to the doorkeeper, saying, "Tell Job: Give me bread from your hands that I may eat." ⁸ And when I heard this, I gave her burnt bread to give it to him, and I made known to him: "Do not expect to eat of my bread, for it is forbidden to you." ⁹ But the doorkeeper, being ashamed to hand him the burnt and ashy bread, as she did not know that it was Satan, took of her own fine bread and gave it to him. ¹⁰ But he took it, and knowing what occurred, said to the maiden, "Go on, bad servant, and bring me the bread that was given you to hand to me." ¹¹ And the servant cried and spoke in grief: "You speak the truth, saying that I am a bad servant, because I have not done as I was instructed by my master." ¹² And he turned back and brought him the burnt bread and said to him, "Thus says my lord: You will not eat of my bread anymore, for it is forbidden to you. ¹³ And he gave me this in order that the charge may not be brought against me that I did

not give to the enemy who asked." ¹⁴ And when Satan heard this, he sent the servant back to me, saying, "As you see this bread all burnt, so I will soon burn your body to make it like this." ¹⁵ And I replied, "Do what you desire to do and accomplish whatever you plot. For I am ready to endure whatever you bring on me." ¹⁶ And when the Devil heard this, he left me, and walking up to under the [highest] Heaven, he took from the LORD the oath that he might have power over all my possessions. ¹⁷ And after having taken the power, he went and instantly took away all my wealth.

CHAPTER 3

¹ For I had one hundred and thirty thousand sheep, and of these I separated seven thousand for the clothing of orphans, and widows, and of needy and sick ones. ² I had a herd of eight hundred dogs who watched my sheep, and besides these two hundred to watch my house. ³ And I had nine mills working for the whole city and ships to carry goods, and I sent them into every city, and into the villages to the feeble, and sick, and to those that were unfortunate. ⁴ And I had three hundred and forty thousand nomadic donkeys, and of these I set aside five hundred, and the offspring of these I order to be sold and the proceeds to be given to the poor and the needy. ⁵ For from all the lands the poor came to meet me. ⁶ For the four doors of my house were opened, each, being in charge of a watchman who had to see whether there were any people coming, asking [for] alms, and whether they would see me sitting at one of the doors so that they could leave through the other and take whatever they needed. ⁷ I also had thirty immovable tables set at all hours for the strangers alone, and I also had twelve tables spread for the widows. ⁸ And if anyone came asking for alms, he found food on my table to take all he needed, and I turned nobody away to leave my door with an empty stomach. ⁹ I also had three thousand five hundred yokes of oxen, and I selected of these five hundred and had them tend to the plowing. ¹⁰ And with these I had done all the work in each field by those who would take it in charge, and I laid aside the income of their crops for the poor on their table. ¹¹ I also had fifty bakeries from which I sent [the bread] to the table for the poor. ¹² And I had slaves selected for their service. ¹³ There were also some strangers who saw my good will; they wished to serve as waiters themselves. ¹⁴ Others, being in distress and unable to obtain a living, came with the request, saying, ¹⁵ "Please, since we can also fill this office of servants and have no possession, have pity on us and advance money to us in order that we may go into the great cities and sell merchandise. ¹⁶ And the surplus of our profit we may give as help to the poor, and then we will return to you your own [money]." ¹⁷ And when I heard this, I was glad that they should take this altogether from me for the farming of charity for the poor. ¹⁸ And I gave them what they wanted with a willing heart, and I accepted their written bond, but would not take any other security from them except the written document. ¹⁹ And they went abroad and gave to the poor as far as they were successful. ²⁰ Frequently, however, some of their goods were lost on the road or on the sea, or they would be robbed of them. ²¹ Then they would come and say, "Please act generously toward us in order that we may see how we can restore to you your own." ²² And when I heard this, I had sympathy with them, and handed their bond to them, and often, having read it before them, tore it up and released them of their debt, saying to them, ²³ "What I have consecrated for the benefit of the poor, I will not take from you." ²⁴ And so I accepted nothing from my debtor. ²⁵ And when a man with cheerful heart came to me, saying, "I am not in need to be compelled to be a paid worker for the poor, ²⁶ but I wish to serve the needy at your table," and he consented to work, and he ate his share, ²⁷ so I gave him his wages nevertheless, and I went home rejoicing. ²⁸ And when he did not wish to take it, I forced him to do so, saying, "I know that you are a laboring man who looks for and waits for his wages, and you must take it." ²⁹ I never deferred paying the wages of the hireling or any other, nor kept back in my house for a single evening his hire that was due to him. ³⁰ Those that milked the cows and the ewes signaled to the passers by that they should take their share. ³¹ For the milk flowed in such plenty that it curdled into butter on the hills and by the roadside; and by the rocks and the hills the cattle lay which had given birth to their offspring. ³² For my servants grew weary keeping the meat of the widows and the poor and dividing it into small pieces. ³³ For they would curse and say, "Oh that we had of his flesh that we could be satisfied," although I was very kind to them. ³⁴ I also had six harps, [and six slaves to play the harps,] and also a cithara, [and] a decachord, and I struck it during the day. ³⁵ And I took the cithara, and the widows responded after their meals. ³⁶ And with the musical instrument I reminded them of God, that they should give praise to the LORD. ³⁷ And when my maidservants would murmur, then I took the musical instruments and played as much as they would have done for their wages, and gave them respite from their labor and sighs.

CHAPTER 4

¹ And my children, after having taken charge of the service, took their meals each day along with their three sisters beginning with the older brother, and made a feast. ² And I rose in the morning and offered fifty rams and nineteen sheep as a sin-offering for them, and what remained as a residue was consecrated to the poor. ³ And I said to them, "Take these as residue and pray for my children. ⁴ Perhaps

my sons have sinned before the LORD, speaking in haughtiness of spirit: We are children of this rich man. All these goods are ours; why should we be servants of the poor? [5] And speaking thus in a haughty spirit they may have provoked the anger of God, for overbearing pride is an abomination before the LORD." [6] So I brought oxen as offerings to the priest at the altar, saying, "May my children never think evil toward God in their hearts." [7] While I lived in this manner, the Seducer could not bear to see the good [I did], and he demanded the warfare of God against me. [8] And he came on me cruelly. [9] First he burned up the large number of sheep, then the camels, then he burned up the cattle and all my herds; or they were captured not only by enemies but also by such as had received benefits from me. [10] And the shepherds came and announced that to me. [11] But when I heard it, I gave praise to God and did not blaspheme. [12] And when the Seducer learned of my fortitude, he plotted new things against me. [13] He disguised himself as [the] king of Persia and besieged my city, and after he had led off all that were therein, he spoke to them in malice, saying in boastful language, [14] "This man Job, who has obtained all the goods of the earth and left nothing for others, has destroyed and torn down the temple of god. [15] Therefore I will repay to him what he has done to the house of the great god. [16] Now come with me and we will pillage all that is left in his house." [17] And they answered and said to him: "He has seven sons and three daughters. [18] Take heed lest they flee into other lands and they may become our tyrants and then come over us with force and kill us." [19] And he said, "Do not be afraid at all. I have destroyed his flocks and his wealth by fire, and I have captured the rest, and behold, I will kill his children." [20] And having spoken thus, he went and threw the house on my children and killed them. [21] And my fellow-citizens, seeing that what was said by him had become true, came and pursued me, and robbed me of all that was in my house. [22] And I saw with mine own eyes the pillage of my house, and men without culture and without honor sat at my table and on my couches, and I could not remonstrate against them. [23] For I was exhausted like a woman with her loins let loose from multitude of pains, remembering chiefly that this warfare had been predicted to me by the LORD through His messenger. [24] And I became like one who, when seeing the rough sea and the adverse winds, while the lading of the vessel in mid-ocean is too heavy, casts the burden into the sea, saying, [25] "I wish to destroy all this only in order to come safely into the city so that I may take as profit the rescued ship and the best of my things." [26] Thus I managed my own affairs. [27] But there came another messenger and announced to me the ruin of my own children, and I was shaken with terror. [28] And I tore my clothes and said, "The LORD has given, the LORD has taken. As it has deemed best to the LORD, thus it has come to be. May the Name of the LORD be blessed."

CHAPTER 5

[1] And when Satan saw that he could put me to despair, he went and asked of the LORD [for] my body in order to inflict plague on me, for the evil one could not bear my patience. [2] Then the LORD delivered me into his hands to use my body as he wanted, but He gave him no power over my soul. [3] And he came to me as I was sitting on my throne, still mourning over my children. [4] And he resembled a great hurricane and turned over my throne and threw me on the ground. [5] And I continued lying on the floor for three hours, and he struck me with a hard plague from the top of my head to the toes of my feet. [6] And I left the city in great terror and woe and sat down on a dunghill, my body being worm-eaten. [7] And I wet the earth with the moistness of my sore body, for matter flowed off my body, and many worms covered it. [8] And when a single worm crept off my body, I put it back, saying, "Remain on the spot where you have been placed until He who has sent you will order you elsewhere." [9] Thus I endured for several years, sitting on a dunghill outside of the city while being plague-stricken. [10] And I saw with my own eyes my longed-for children [carried by messengers to Heaven], [11] and my humbled wife who had been brought to her bridal chamber in such great luxuriousness and with spearmen as bodyguards. I saw her do a water-carrier's work like a slave in the house of a common man in order to win some bread and bring it to me. [12] And in my sore affliction I said, "Oh that these braggart city rulers whom I should not have thought to be equal with my shepherd dogs should now employ my wife as servant!" [13] And after this I took courage again. [14] Yet afterward they withheld even the bread that she should only have her own nourishment. [15] But she took it and divided it between herself and me, saying woefully, "Woe to me! Very soon he may no longer have bread to eat, and he cannot go to the market to ask [for] bread from the bread-sellers in order to bring it to me that he may eat." [16] And when Satan learned this, he took the guise of a bread-seller, and it was as if by chance that my wife met him and asked him for bread thinking that it was that sort of man. [17] But Satan said to her, "Give me the value, and then take what you wish." [18] Immediately she answered, saying, "Where will I get money? Do you not know what misfortune happened to me? If you have pity, show it to me; if not, you will see." [19] And he replied, saying, "If you did not deserve this misfortune, you would not have suffered all this. [20] Now, if there is no silver piece in your hand, give me the hair of your head and take three loaves of bread for it, so that you may live on these for three days." [21] Then she said to herself: "What is the hair of my head in comparison with my starving husband?"

²² And so after having pondered over the matter, she said to him, "Rise and cut off my hair." ³ Then he took a pair of scissors and took off the hair of her head in the presence of all, and gave her three loaves of bread. ²⁴ Then she took them and brought them to me. And Satan went behind her on the road, hiding himself as he walked and troubling her heart greatly.

CHAPTER 6

¹ And immediately my wife came near me, and crying aloud and weeping she said, "Job! Job! How long will you sit on the dunghill outside of the city, still pondering for a while and expecting to obtain your hoped-for salvation? ² And I have been wandering from place to place, roaming around as a hired servant; behold, the memory has already died away from earth. ³ And my sons and the daughters that I carried on my bosom and the labors and pains that I sustained have been for nothing. ⁴ And you sit in the fetid state of soreness and worms, passing the nights in the cold air. ⁵ And I have undergone all trials, and troubles, and pains day and night, until I succeeded in bringing bread to you. ⁶ For your surplus of bread is no longer allowed to me; and as I can scarcely take my own food and divide it between us, I pondered in my heart that it was not right that you should be in pain and hunger for bread. ⁷ And so I ventured to go to the market without bashfulness, and when the bread-seller told me: Give me money, and you will have bread; I disclosed to him our state of distress. ⁸ Then I heard him say: If you have no money, hand me the hair of your head, and take three loaves of bread in order that you may live on these for three days. ⁹ And I yielded to the wrong and said to him: Rise and cut off my hair! And he rose and in disgrace cut off with the scissors the hair of my head on the marketplace while the crowd stood by and wondered. ¹⁰ Who would then not be astonished, saying, Is this Sitis, the wife of Job, who had fourteen curtains to cover her inner sitting room, and doors within doors so that he was greatly honored who would be brought near her? And now behold, she barters off her hair for bread! ¹¹ Who had camels laden with goods, and they were brought into remote lands to the poor, and now she sells her hair for bread! ¹² Behold her who had seven tables immovably set in her house at which each poor man and each stranger ate, and now she sells her hair for bread! ¹³ Behold her who had the basin with which to wash her feet made of gold and silver, and now she walks on the ground and [[sells her hair for bread!]] ¹⁴ Behold her who had her garments made of byssus interwoven with gold, and now she exchanges her hair for bread! ¹⁵ Behold her who had couches of gold and of silver, and now she sells her hair for bread! ¹⁶ In short then, Job, after the many things that have been said to me, I now say in one word to you: ¹⁷ since the feebleness of my heart has crushed my bones, rise then and take these loaves of bread and enjoy them, and then speak some word against the LORD and die! ¹⁸ For I too would exchange the torpor of death for the sustenance of my body." ¹⁹ But I replied to her, "Behold, I have been plague-stricken for these seven years, and I have withstood the worms of my body, and I was not weighed down in my soul by all these pains. ²⁰ And as to the word which you say: Speak some word against God and die; together with you I will sustain the evil which you see, and let us endure the ruin of all that we have. ²¹ Yet you desire that we should say some word against God and that He should be exchanged for the great Pluto. ²² Why do you not remember those great goods which we possessed? If these goods come from the lands of the LORD, should we not also endure evils and be high-minded in everything until the LORD will have mercy again and show pity to us? ²³ Do you not see the Seducer stand behind you and confound your thoughts in order that you should deceive me?" ²⁴ And he turned to Satan and said, "Why do you not come openly to me? Stop hiding yourself you wretched one! ²⁵ Does the lion show his strength in the weasel cage? Or does the bird fly in the basket? I now tell you: go away and wage your war against me." ²⁶ Then he went off from behind my wife and placed himself before me, crying, and he said, "Behold, Job, I yield and give way to you who are but flesh while I am a spirit. ²⁷ You are plague-stricken, but I am in great trouble. ²⁸ For I am like a wrestler contesting with a wrestler who has, in single-handed combat, torn down his antagonist and covered him with dust and broken every limb of his, whereas the other one who lies beneath, having displayed his bravery, gives forth sounds of triumph testifying to his own superior excellence. ²⁹ Thus you, O Job, are beneath and stricken with plague and pain, and yet you have carried the victory in the wrestling-match with me, and behold, I yield to you." Then he left me embarrassed. ³⁰ Now my children, you must also show a firm heart in all the evil that happens to you, for firmness of heart is greater than all things.

CHAPTER 7

¹ At this time the kings heard what had happened to me and they rose and came to me—each from his land—to visit me and to comfort me. ² And when they came near me, they cried with a loud voice and each tore his clothes. ³ And after they had prostrated themselves, touching the earth with their heads, they sat down next to me for seven days and seven nights, and none spoke a word. ⁴ They were four in number: Eliphaz, the king of Teman, and Bildad, and Zophar, and Elihu. ⁵ And when they had taken their seat, they conversed about what had happened to me. ⁶ Now when they had come to me for the first time and I had shown them my precious stones, they were astonished and said, ⁷ "If of us three kings all our possessions would be brought together into one, it would not

come up to the precious stones of Jobab's kingdom. For you are of greater nobility than all the people of the east." ⁸ And when, therefore, they now came to the land of Uz to visit me, they asked in the city: "Where is Jobab, the ruler of this whole land?" ⁹ And they told them concerning me: "He sits on the dunghill outside of the city, for he has not entered the city for seven years." ¹⁰ And then they again inquired concerning my possessions, and there was revealed to them all what happened to me. ¹¹ And when they had learned this, they went out of the city with the inhabitants, and my fellow-citizens pointed me out to them. ¹² But these remonstrated and said, "Surely this is not Jobab." ¹³ And while they hesitated, Eliphaz, the King of Teman, said, "Come, let us step near and see." ¹⁴ And when they came near, I remembered them, and I wept very much when I learned the purpose of their journey. ¹⁵ And I threw earth on my head, and while shaking my head I revealed to them that I was [Job]. ¹⁶ And when they saw me shake my head, they threw themselves down on the ground, all overcome with emotion. ¹⁷ And while their hosts were standing around, I saw the three kings lie on the ground for three hours like dead. ¹⁸ Then they rose and said to each other, "We cannot believe that this is Jobab." ¹⁹ And finally, after they had inquired after everything concerning me and searched for my flocks and other possessions for seven days, they said, ²⁰ "Do we not know how many goods were sent by him to the cities and the villages around to be given to the poor, aside from all that was given away by him within his own house? How then could he have fallen into such a state of perdition and misery?" ²¹ And after the seven days Elihu said to the kings, "Come, let us step near and examine him accurately, whether he is truly Jobab or not." ²² And they, being not four stadia distant from his fetid body, rose and stepped near, carrying perfume in their hands, while their soldiers went with them and threw fragrant incense around them so that they could come near me. ²³ And after they had thus passed three hours, covering the way with aroma, they drew near. ²⁴ And Eliphaz began and said, "Are you, indeed, Job, our fellow-king? Are you the one who owned the great glory? ²⁵ Are you he who once shone like the sun of day on the whole earth? Are you he who once resembled the moon and the stars, radiant throughout the night?" ²⁶ And I answered him and said, "I am," and thereon all wept and lamented, and they sang a royal song of lamentation, their whole army joining them in a chorus. ²⁷ And again Eliphaz said to me, "Are you he who had ordered seven thousand sheep to be given for the clothing of the poor? Where then has the glory of your throne gone? ²⁸ Are you he who had ordered three thousand cattle to do the plowing of the field for the poor? Where then has your glory gone? ²⁹ Are you he who had golden couches, and now you sit on a dunghill? [[Where then has your glory gone?]] ³⁰ Are you he who had sixty tables set for the poor? Are you he who had censers for the fine perfume made of precious stones, and now you are in a fetid state? Where then has your glory gone? ³¹ Are you he who had golden candelabras set on silver stands, and now must you long for the natural gleam of the moon? [[Where then has your glory gone?]] ³² Are you the one who had ointment made of the spices of frankincense, and now you are in a state of repulsiveness? [[Where then has your glory gone?]] ³³ Are you he who laughed the wrongdoers and sinners to scorn and now you have become a laughingstock to all? [[Where then has your glory gone?]]" ³⁴ And when Eliphaz had cried and lamented for a long time, while all the others joined him, so that the commotion was very great, I said to them, ³⁵ "Be silent and I will show you my throne, and the glory of its splendor: my glory will be everlasting. ³⁶ The whole world will perish, and its glory will vanish, and all those who hold fast to it will remain beneath, but my throne is in the upper world and its glory and splendor will be to the right of the Savior in the heavens. ³⁷ My throne exists in the life of the holy ones and its glory in the imperishable world. ³⁸ For rivers will be dried up and their arrogance will go down to the depth of the abyss, but the streams of my land in which my throne is erected will not dry up but will remain unbroken in strength. ³⁹ The kings perish, and the rulers vanish, and their glory and pride are as the shadow in a looking-glass, but my kingdom lasts forever and ever, and its glory and beauty are in the chariot of my Father."

CHAPTER 8

¹ When I spoke thus to them, Eliphaz became angry and said to the other friends, "For what purpose is it that we have come here with our hosts to comfort him? ⁹ Behold, he scolds us. Therefore, let us return to our countries. ² This man sits here in misery, worm-eaten amidst an unbearable state of putrefaction, and yet he challenges its saving: Kingdoms will perish and their rulers, but my kingdom, he says, will last forever." ³ Eliphaz then rose in great commotion, and turning away from them in great fury, said, "I go on. We have indeed come to comfort him, but he declares war to us in view of our armies." ⁴ But then Bildad seized him by the hand and said, "One ought not to speak thus to an afflicted man, and especially to one stricken down with so many plagues. ⁵ Behold, we, being in good health, dared not approach him on account of the offensive odor, except with the help of plenty of fragrant aroma. But you, Eliphaz, are forgetful of all this. ⁶ Let me speak plainly. Let us be magnanimous and learn what the cause is. Must he, in remembering his former days of happiness, not become mad in his mind? ⁷ Who should not be altogether perplexed seeing himself thus lapse into misfortune and plagues? But let me step near him that

TESTAMENT OF JOB

I may find by what cause he is thus." ⁹And Bildad rose and approached me, saying, "Are you Job?" And he said, "Is your heart still in good keeping?" ⁹And I said, "I did not hold fast to the earthly things, since the earth, with all that inhabit it, is unstable. But my heart holds fast to Heaven, because there is no trouble in Heaven." ¹⁰Then Bildad rejoined and said, "We know that the earth is unstable, for it changes according to season. At times it is in a state of peace, and at times it is in a state of war. But of Heaven we hear that it is perfectly steady. ¹¹But are you truly in a state of calmness? Therefore let me ask and speak, and when you answer me to my first word, I will have a second question to ask, and if again you answer in well-set words, it will be manifest that your heart has not been unbalanced." ¹²And he said, "On what do you set your hope?" And I said, "On the living God." ¹³And he said to me, "Who deprived you of all you possessed, and who inflicted you with these plagues?" And I said, "God." ¹⁴And he said, "If you still place your hope on God, how can He do wrong in judgment, having brought on you these plagues and misfortunes, and having taken from you all your possessions? ¹⁵And since He has taken these, it is clear that He has given you nothing. No king will disgrace his soldier who has served him well as bodyguard." ¹⁶[[And I answered, saying,]] "Who understands the depths of the Lᴏʀᴅ and of His wisdom to be able to accuse God of injustice?" ¹⁷[And Bildad said,] "Answer me, O Job, to this. Again, I say to you: if you are in a state of calm reason, teach me if you have wisdom: ¹⁸why do we see the sun rise in the east and set in the west? And again, when rising in the morning we find him rise in the east. Tell me your thought about this." ¹⁹Then I said, "Why will I betray the mighty mysteries of God? And should my mouth stumble in revealing things belonging to the Master? Never! ²⁰Who are we that we should pry into matters concerning the upper world while we are only of flesh, no, earth and ashes! ²¹In order that you know that my heart is sound, hear what I ask you: ²²through the stomach comes food, and water you drink through the mouth, and then it flows through the same throat, and when the two go down to become excrement, they again part; who effects this separation?" ²³And Bildad said, "I do not know." And I rejoined and said to him, "If you do not even understand the exits of the body, how can you understand the celestial circuits?" ²⁴Then Zophar rejoined and said, "We do not inquire after our own affairs, but we desire to know whether you are in a sound state, and behold, we see that your reason has not been shaken. ²⁵What now do you wish that we should do for you? Behold, we have come here and brought the physicians of three kings, and if you wish, you may be cured by them." ²⁶But I answered and said, "My cure and my restoration come from God, the Maker of physicians."

CHAPTER 9

¹And when I spoke thus to them, behold, there my wife Sitis came running, dressed in rags from the service of the master by whom she was employed as slave though she had been forbidden to leave, lest the kings, on seeing her, might take her as captive. ²And when she came, she threw herself prostrate to their feet, crying and saying, "Remember, Eliphaz and you other friends, what I once was with you, and how I have changed, how I am now dressed to meet you." ³Then the kings broke forth in great weeping and, being in double perplexity, they kept silent. But Eliphaz took his purple mantle and cast it around her to wrap her up with it. ⁴But she asked him, saying, "I ask as a favor of you, my lords, that you order your soldiers that they should dig among the ruins of our house which fell on my children, so that their bones could be brought in a perfect state to the tombs. ⁵For as we have, owing to our misfortune, no power at all, and so we may at least see their bones. ⁶For I have, like a brute, the motherly feeling of wild beasts that my ten children should have perished on one day and I could not give a decent burial to one of them." ⁷And the kings gave order that the ruins of my house should be dug up. But I prohibited it, saying, ⁸"Do not go to the trouble in vain; for my children will not he found, for they are in the keeping of their Maker and Ruler." ⁹And the kings answered and said, "Who will deny that he is out of his mind and raves? ¹⁰For while we desire to bring the bones of his children back, he forbids us to do so, saying, They have been taken and placed [in] the keeping of their Maker. Therefore, prove the truth to us." ¹¹But I said to them, "Raise me that I may stand up," and they lifted me, holding up my arms from both sides. ¹²And I stood upright, and first pronounced the praise of God and after the prayer I said to them: "Look with your eyes to the east." ¹³And they looked and saw my children with crowns near the glory of the King, the Ruler of Heaven. ¹⁴And when my wife Sitis saw this, she fell to the ground and prostrated [herself] before God, saying, "Now I know that my memory remains with the Lᴏʀᴅ." ¹⁵And after she had spoken this, and the evening came, she went to the city, back to the master whom she served as slave, and lay herself down at the manger of the cattle and died there from exhaustion. ¹⁶And when her despotic master searched for her and did not find her, he came to the fold of his herds, and there he saw her stretched out on the manger dead, while all the animals around were crying about her. ¹⁷And all who saw her wept and lamented, and the cry extended throughout the whole city. ¹⁸And the people brought her down and wrapped her up and buried her by the house which had fallen on her children. ¹⁹And the poor of the city made a great mourning for her and said, "Behold this Sitis whose like in nobility and in glory is not found in any woman. Aah! She was not

found worthy of a proper tomb!" [20] The dirge for her you will find in the record.

CHAPTER 10

[1] But Eliphaz and those that were with him were astonished at these things, and they sat down with me and replying to me, spoke in boastful words concerning me for twenty-seven days. [2] They repeated it again and again that I suffered deservedly thus for having committed many sins, and that there was no hope left for me, but I retorted to these men in zest of contention myself. [3] And they rose in anger, ready to part in wrathful spirit. But Elihu conjured them to stay yet a little while until he would have shown them what it was. [4] "For," he said, "you passed so many days allowing Job to boast that he is just. But I will no longer permit it. [5] For from the beginning I continued crying over him, remembering his former happiness. But now he speaks boastfully, and in overbearing pride he says that he has his throne in the heavens. [6] Therefore, hear me, and I will tell you what the cause of his destiny is." [7] Then, imbued with the spirit of Satan, Elihu spoke hard words which are written down in the records left of Elihu. [8] And after he had ended, God appeared to me in a storm and in clouds, and spoke, blaming Elihu and showing me that he who had spoken was not a man, but a wild beast. [9] And when God had finished speaking to me, the LORD spoke to Eliphaz: "You and your friends have sinned in that you have not spoken the truth concerning My servant Job. [10] Therefore rise up and make him bring a sin-offering for you in order that your sins may be forgiven; for were it not for him, I would have destroyed you." [11] And so they brought to me all that belonged to a sacrifice, and I took it and brought a sin-offering for them, and the LORD received it favorably and forgave them their wrong. [12] Then when Eliphaz, Bildad, and Zophar saw that God had graciously pardoned their sin through His servant Job, but that He did not stoop to pardon Elihu, then Eliphaz began to sing a hymn while the others responded, their soldiers also joining while standing by the altar. [13] And Eliphaz spoke thus: "The sin is removed, and our injustice gone, [14] But Elihu, the evil one, will have no remembrance among the living; His luminary is extinguished and has lost its light. [15] The glory of his lamp will announce itself for him, || For he is the son of darkness, and not of light. [16] The doorkeepers of the place of darkness || Will give him their glory and beauty as share. His kingdom has vanished, his throne has decayed, || And the honor of his stature is in Hades. [17] For he has loved the beauty of the serpent and the scales of the dragon—His gall and his venom belong to the Northern One. [18] For he did not own himself to the LORD nor did he fear Him, || But he hated those whom He has chosen. [19] Thus God forgot him, and the holy ones forsook him, || His wrath and anger will be to him desolation, || And he

will have no mercy in his heart nor peace, || Because he had the venom of an adder on his tongue. [20] The LORD is righteous, and His judgments are true. With Him there is no preference of person, || For He judges all alike. [21] Behold, the LORD comes! Behold, the holy ones have been prepared! The crowns and the prizes of the victors precede them! [22] Let the saints rejoice, and let their hearts exult in gladness, || For they will receive the glory which is in store for them. Chorus: [23] Our sins are forgiven, our injustice has been cleansed, || But Elihu has no remembrance among the living." [24] After Eliphaz had finished the hymn, we rose and went back to the city, each to the house where they lived. [25] And the people made a feast for me in gratitude and delight of God, and all my friends came back to me. [26] And all those who had seen me in my former state of happiness, asked me, saying, "What are those three ones among us here?"

CHAPTER 11

[1] But I, being desirous to take up my work of benevolence for the poor again, asked them, saying, [2] "Give me each a lamb for the clothing of the poor in their state of nakedness, and four drachmas of silver or gold." [3] Then the LORD blessed all that was left to me, and after a few days I became rich again in merchandise, in flocks and all things which I had lost, and I received all in double number again. [4] Then I also took your mother as wife and became the father of you ten in place of the ten children that had died. [5] And now, my children, let me admonish you: "Behold, I die. You will take my place. [6] Only do not forsake the LORD. Be charitable toward the poor; Do not disregard the feeble. Do not take wives from strangers to yourselves. [7] Behold, my children, I will divide what I possess among you, so that each may have control over his own and have full power to do good with his share." [8] And after he had spoken thus, he brought all his goods and divided them among his seven sons, but he gave nothing of his goods to his daughters. [9] Then they said to their father, "Our lord and father! Are we not also your children? Why, then, do you not also give us a share of your possessions?" [10] Then Job said to his daughters, "Do not become angry my daughters. I have not forgotten you. Behold, I have preserved for you a possession better than that which your brothers have taken." [11] And he called his daughter, whose name was Day, and said to her, "Take this double ring used as a key, and go to the treasure-house, and bring me the golden casket, that I may give you your possession." [12] And she went and brought it to him, and he opened it and took out three-stringed girdles about the appearance of which no man can speak. [13] For they were not earthly work, but celestial sparks of light flashed through them like the rays of the sun. [14] And he gave one string to each of his daughters and said, "Put these as girdles around you in order that all the days of your life they may

encircle you and endow you with every good thing."
[15] And the other daughter, whose name was Kassiah, said, "Is this the possession of which you say it is better than that of our brothers? Now how can we live on this?" [16] And their father said to them, "Not only do you have here [what is] sufficient to live on, but these bring you into a better world to live in—in the heavens. [17] Or do you not know, my children, the value of these things here? Hear then! When the LORD had deemed me worthy to have compassion on me and to take the plagues and the worms off my body, He called me and handed these three strings to me. [18] And He said to me, Rise and gird up your loins like a man. I will demand of you and you will declare it to Me. [19] And I took them and girt them around my loins, and immediately the worms left my body, and likewise the plagues, and my whole body took new strength through the LORD, and thus I passed on, as though I had never suffered. [20] But I also forgot the pains in my heart. Then the LORD spoke to me in His great power and showed to me all that was and will be. [21] Now then, my children, in keeping these, you will not have the enemy plotting against you nor [evil] intentions in your mind because this is a charm from the LORD. [22] Rise then and gird these around you before I die in order that you may see the messengers come at my parting so that you may behold, with wonder, the powers of God." [23] Then the one whose name was Day rose and girt herself; and immediately she departed her body as her father had said, and she put on another heart, as if she never cared for earthly things. [24] And she sang angelic hymns in the voice of messengers, and she chanted forth the angelic praise of God while dancing. [25] Then the other daughter, Kassia by name, put on the girdle, and her heart was transformed, so that she no longer wished for worldly things. [26] And her mouth assumed the dialect of the heavenly rulers and she sang the doxology of the work of the High Place, and if anyone wishes to know the work of the heavens, he may take an insight into the hymns of Kassia. [27] Then the other daughter, by the name of Amalthea's Horn, girt herself and her mouth spoke in the language of those on high; for her heart was transformed, being lifted above the worldly things. [28] She spoke in the dialect of the cherubim, singing the praise of the Ruler of the cosmic powers and extolling their [[or His]] glory. [29] And he who desires to follow the vestiges of the "Glory of the Father" will find them written down in the Prayers of Amalthea's Horn.

CHAPTER 12

[1] After these three had finished singing hymns, I, Nahor, brother of Job, sat down next to him as he lay down. [2] And I heard the marvelous things of the three daughters of my brother, one always succeeding the other amidst awful silence. [3] And I wrote down this scroll containing the hymns, except the hymns and signs of the [holy] word, for these were the great things of God. [4] And Job lay down from sickness on his couch, yet without pain and suffering, because his pain did not take strong hold of him on account of the charm of the girdle which he had wound around himself. [5] But after three days Job saw the holy messengers come for his soul, and instantly he rose and took the cithara and gave it to his daughter Day, [6] and he gave a censer to Kassia, and he gave a timbrel to Amalthea's Horn in order that they might bless the holy messengers who came for his soul. [7] And they took these, and sang, and played on the psaltery, and praised and glorified God in the holy dialect. [8] And after this He came—He who sits on the great chariot—and kissed Job, while his three daughters looked on, but the others did not see it. [9] And He took the soul of Job and He soared upward, taking her [(the soul)] by the arm and carrying her on the chariot, and He went toward the east. [10] His body, however, was brought to the grave while the three daughters marched ahead, having put on their girdles and singing hymns in praise of God. [11] Then Nahor, his brother, and his seven sons, with the rest of the people and the poor, the orphans and the feeble ones, held a great mourning over him, saying, [12] "Woe to us! For today the strength of the feeble, the light of the blind, the father of the orphans has been taken from us! [13] The receiver of strangers has been taken—the leader of the erring, the cover of the naked, the shield of the widows. Who should not mourn for the man of God?" [14] And as they were mourning in this and in that form, they would not permit him to be put into the grave. [15] After three days, however, he was finally put into the grave, like one in sweet slumber, and he received the name of the beautiful who will remain renowned throughout all generations of the world. [16] He left seven sons and three daughters, and there were no daughters found on earth as fair as the daughters of Job. [17] The name of Job was formerly Jobab, and he was called Job by the LORD. [18] He had lived eighty-five years before his plague, and after the plague he took the double share of all; hence he also doubled his years, which were one hundred seventy years. Thus, he lived two hundred fifty-five years altogether, [19] and he saw sons of his sons to the fourth generation. It is written that he will rise up with those whom the LORD will reawaken. To our Lord be glory. Amen.

TESTAMENT OF MOSES

Otherwise known as the Assumption of Moses

The Testament of Moses, also called the Assumption of Moses, is thought to have been composed in the 1st century BC or 1st century AD, in Hebrew or a similar Semitic language, and then translated into Koine. The surviving manuscript is actually a 6th century Latin translation of the Greek. There is speculation that a missing portion of the work includes the dispute between Michael and Satan over the body of Moses, which is also found in Jude 1:9. The book is backward and forward-looking, and apocalyptic in nature, dealing with Moses' handoff to Joshua prior to death.

CHAPTER 1

¹ And it came to pass in the one hundred and twentieth year of the life of Moses, ² that is, the two thousand five hundredth year from the creation of the world, ⁶ that he called Joshua the son of Nun to himself, a man approved of the LORD, ⁷ that he might be the minister of the people and of the Dwelling Place of the testimony with all its holy things, ⁸ and that he might bring the people into the land given to their fathers, ⁹ that it should be given to them according to the covenant and the oath, which he spoke in the Dwelling Place to give [it] by Joshua, saying these words to Joshua: ¹⁰ "Be strong and of good courage, according to your might so as to do what has been commanded that you may be blameless to God"— ¹¹ so says the Lord of the world. ¹² For He has created the world on behalf of His people. ¹³ But He was not pleased to manifest this purpose of creation from the foundation of the world, in order that the nations might thereby be convicted, indeed, [that] by [their] arguments they might convict one another to their own humiliation. ¹⁴ Accordingly, He designed and devised me, and He prepared me before the foundation of the world, that I should be the mediator of His covenant. ¹⁵ And now I declare to you that the time of the years of my life is fulfilled and I am passing away to sleep with my fathers even in the presence of all the people. ¹⁶ Now receive this writing that you may know how to preserve the scrolls which I will deliver to you, ¹⁷ and you will set these in order, and anoint them with oil of cedar, and put them away in earthen vessels in the place which He made from the beginning of the creation of the world, ¹⁸ that His Name should be called on until the day of conversion in the visitation with which the LORD will visit them in the consummation of the end of the days.

CHAPTER 2

¹ And now they will go by means of you into the land which He determined and promised to give to their fathers, ² in which you will bless, and give to them individually, and confirm to them their inheritance in me, and establish the kingdom for them, and appoint prefectures for them according to the good pleasure of their Lord, in judgment and righteousness. ³ And in the sixth year after they enter into the land, that thereafter they will be ruled by chiefs and kings for eighteen years, and for nineteen years the ten tribes will be apostates. ⁴ And the twelve tribes will go down and transfer the Dwelling Place of the testimony. Then the God of Heaven will make the court of His Dwelling Place and the tower of His sanctuary, and the two holy tribes will be established [there], ⁵ but the ten tribes will establish kingdoms for themselves according to their own ordinances. ⁶ And they will offer sacrifices throughout twenty years, ⁷ and seven will entrench the walls, and I will protect nine, but [four] will transgress the covenant of the LORD and profane the oath which the LORD made with them. ⁸ And they will sacrifice their sons to strange gods, and they will set up idols in the sanctuary, to worship them. ⁹ And in the house of the LORD they will work impiety and engrave every [form] of beast—many abominations.

CHAPTER 3

¹ And in those days a king from the east will come against them and cover their land with [his] cavalry. ² And he will burn their colony with fire, together with the holy temple of the LORD, and he will carry away all the holy vessels. ³ And he will cast forth all the people, and he will take them to the land of his nativity, yes, he will take the two tribes with him. ⁴ Then the two tribes will call on the ten tribes and will be indignant as a lioness on the dusty plains, being hungry and thirsty. ⁵ And they will cry aloud: "Righteous and holy is the LORD, for, inasmuch as you have sinned, we too, in like manner, have been carried away with you, together with our children." ⁶ Then the ten tribes will mourn on hearing the reproaches of the two tribes, ⁷ and they will say, "What have we done to you, brothers? Surely this tribulation has not come on all the house of Israel?" ⁸ And all the tribes will mourn, crying to Heaven and saying, ⁹ "God of Abraham, God of Isaac, and God of Jacob, remember Your covenant which You made with them, and the oath which You swore to them by Yourself, that their seed should never fail in the land which You have given them." ¹⁰ Then they will remember me, saying, in that day, tribe to tribe and each man to his neighbour: ¹¹ "Is this not that which Moses declared to us then in prophecies, who suffered many things in Egypt, and in the Red Sea,

TESTAMENT OF MOSES

and in the wilderness for forty years, ¹² and assuredly called the heavens and earth to witness against us, that we should not transgress His commandments, in the which he was a mediator to us? ¹³ Behold these things have befallen us after his death according to his words and according to his declaration, as he declared to us at that time—yes, behold, these have taken place even to our being carried away captive into the country of the east, ¹⁴ who will also be in bondage for about seventy-seven years."

CHAPTER 4

¹ Then there will enter one who is over them, and he will spread forth his hands, and kneel on his knees, and pray on their behalf, saying, ² "Lord of all, King on the lofty throne, who rules the world, and willed that this people should be Your chosen people: then You willed that You should be called their God, according to the covenant which You made with their fathers, ³ and yet they have gone into captivity with their wives and their children into another land, and around the gates of strange peoples, and where there is great vanity. ⁴ Regard and have compassion on them, O Lord of Heaven." ⁵ Then God will remember them on account of the covenant which He made with their fathers, and He will also manifest His compassion in those times. ⁶ And He will put it into the mind of a king to have compassion on them, and he will send them off to their land and country. ⁷ Then some portions of the tribes will go up, and they will come to their appointed place, and they will entrench the place, restoring [it]. ⁸ And the two tribes will continue in their prescribed faith, sad and lamenting because they will not be able to offer sacrifices to the Lord of their fathers. ⁹ And the ten tribes will increase and multiply among the nations during the time of their captivity.

CHAPTER 5

¹ And when the times of discipline draw near and vengeance arises through the kings who share in their guilt and punish them, ² they themselves will also be divided as to the truth. ³ For what reason it has come to pass: "They will turn aside from righteousness and approach iniquity, and they will defile the house of their worship with pollutions," and "they will go whoring after strange gods." ⁴ For they will not follow the truth of God, but some will pollute the altar with the very gifts which they offer to the LORD, who are not priests but slaves, sons of slaves. ⁵ And many will respect rich persons in those times, and will receive gifts, and wrest judgment [on receiving presents]. ⁶ And on this account the colony and the borders of their habitation will be filled with lawless deeds and iniquities: they will forsake the LORD; they will be impious judges; they will be ready to judge for money as each may wish.

CHAPTER 6

¹ Then kings will be raised up to them bearing rule, and they will call themselves high priests of God; they will assuredly work iniquity in the Holy of Holies. ² And an insolent king will succeed them who will not be of the race of the priests, a man bold and shameless, and he will judge them as they will deserve. ³ And he will cut off their chief men with the sword, and will destroy [them] in secret places, so that no one may know where their bodies are. ⁴ He will slay the old and the young, and he will not spare. ⁵ Then the fear of him will be bitter to them in their land. ⁶ And he will execute judgments on them as the Egyptians executed on them for thirty-four years, and he will punish them. ⁷ And he will beget children, who succeeding him will rule for shorter periods. ⁸ Into their parts cohorts and a powerful king of the west will come, who will conquer them; ⁹ and he will take them captive, and burn a part of their temple with fire, [and] will crucify some around their colony.

CHAPTER 7

¹ And when this is done the times will be ended, in a moment the [second] course will be [ended], the four hours will come. ² They will be forced . . . ³ And, in the time of these, scornful and impious men will rule, saying that they are just. ⁴ And these will conceal the wrath of their minds, being treacherous men, self-pleasers, impostors in all their own affairs, and lovers of banquets at every hour of the day, gluttons, gourmands . . . ⁵ . . . ⁶ devourers of the goods of the poor, saying that they do so on the ground of their justice, but [in reality] to destroy them, complainers, deceitful, concealing themselves lest they should be recognized, impious, filled with lawlessness and iniquity from sunrise to sunset, ⁸ saying, "We will have feastings and luxury, eating and drinking, yes, we will drink our fill, we will be as princes." ⁹ And though their hands and their minds touch unclean things, yet their mouth will speak great things, and they will furthermore say, ¹⁰ "Do not touch me lest you should pollute me in the place where I stand."

CHAPTER 8

¹ And there will come on them a second visitation and wrath, such as has not befallen them from the beginning until that time, in which He will stir up against them a king of the kings of the earth and one that rules with great power, who will crucify those who confess to their circumcision: ² and he will torture those who conceal [it] and deliver them up to be bound and led into prison. ³ And their wives will be given to the gods among the nations, and their young sons will be operated on by the physicians in order to bring forward their foreskin. ⁴ And others among them will be punished by tortures, and fire, and sword, and they will be forced to bear their idols in public, [which are as] polluted as the [shrines] that

contain them. ⁵ And they will likewise be forced by those who torture them to enter their inmost sanctuary, and they will be forced by goads to blaspheme the Name with insolence, [and] finally, after these things, the laws and what they had above their altar [as well].

CHAPTER 9

¹ Then in that day there will be a man of the tribe of Levi, whose name will be Taxo, who having seven sons will speak to them exhorting [them]: ² "Observe, my sons; behold, a second ruthless [and] unclean visitation has come on the people, and a punishment merciless and far exceeding the first. ³ For what nation, or what region, or what people of those who are impious toward the LORD, who have done many abominations, have suffered calamities as great as have befallen us? ⁴ Now therefore, my sons, hear me; for observe and know that neither [our] fathers nor their forefathers tempted God, so as to transgress His commands. ⁵ And you know that this is our strength, and thus we will do. ⁶ Let us fast for the space of three days, and on the fourth let us go into a cave which is in the field, and let us die rather than transgress the commands of the Lord of lords, the God of our fathers. ⁷ For if we do this and die, our blood will be avenged before the LORD."

CHAPTER 10

¹ And then His kingdom will appear throughout all His creation, ‖ And then Satan will no longer be, ‖ And sorrow will depart with him. ² Then the hands of the messenger will be filled, ‖ And he will be appointed chief, ‖ And he will immediately avenge them of their enemies. ³ For the heavenly One will arise from His royal throne, ‖ And He will go forth from His holy habitation, ‖ And His wrath will burn on account of His sons. ⁴ And the earth will tremble: It will be shaken to its confines, ‖ And the high mountains will be made low, ‖ And the hills will be shaken and fall. ⁵ And the horns of the sun will be broken, ‖ And he will be turned into darkness; And the moon will not give her light, ‖ And will be turned wholly into blood; And the circle of the stars will be disturbed. ⁶ And the sea will retire into the abyss, ‖ And the fountains of waters will fail, ‖ And the rivers will dry up. ⁷ For the Most High will arise, the Perpetual God alone, ‖ And He will appear to punish the nations, ‖ And He will destroy all their idols. ⁸ Then you, O Israel, will be happy, ‖ And you will mount up on the neck [and wings] of the eagle, ‖ And [the days of your mourning] will be ended. ⁹ And God will exalt you, ‖ And He will cause you to approach to the heaven of the stars, ‖ And He will establish your habitation among them. ¹⁰ And you will look from on high and will see your enemies in Gehenna, ‖ And you will recognize them and rejoice, ‖ And you will give thanks and confess your Creator. ¹¹ And you,

Joshua [the son of] Nun, must keep these words and this scroll, ¹² for from my death—[my] assumption—until His advent there will be two hundred fifty times. ¹³ And this is their course which they will pursue until they are consummated. ¹⁴ And I will go to sleep with my fathers. ¹⁵ For what reason, Joshua—you, [son of] Nun—be of good courage; God has chosen [you] to be my successor in the same covenant.

CHAPTER 11

¹ And when Joshua had heard the words of Moses that were written in his writing, as well as all that he had previously said, he tore his clothes and cast himself at Moses' feet. ² And Moses comforted him and wept with him. ³ And Joshua answered him and said, ⁴ "Why do you comfort me, lord Moses? And how will I be comforted in regard to that which you have spoken—the bitter word which has gone forth from your mouth, which is full of tears and lamentation, in that you depart from this people? ⁵ And now what place will receive you? ⁶ Or what will be the sign that marks [your] grave? ⁷ Or who will dare to move your body from there as a man from place to place? ⁸ For when they die, all men have their graves on earth according to their age, but your grave is from the rising to the setting sun, and from the south to the confines of the north: all the world is your grave. ⁹ My lord, you are departing, and who will feed this people? ¹⁰ Or who is there that will have compassion on them, and who will be their guide by the way? ¹¹ Or who will pray for them, not omitting a single day, in order that I may lead them into the land of [their] forefathers? ¹² Therefore, how am I to control this people as a father [his] only son, or as a mistress [her] virgin daughter, who is being prepared to be handed over to the husband she will revere, while she guards her person from the sun, and [takes care] that her feet are not unshod for running on the ground? ¹³ And how will I supply them with food and drink according to the pleasure of their will? ¹⁴ For of them there will be six hundred thousand men, for these have multiplied to this degree through your prayers, [my] lord Moses. ¹⁵ And what wisdom or understanding do I have that I should judge or answer by word in the house of the LORD? ¹⁶ And the kings of the Amorites will also be emboldened to attack us then; [and] believing that there is no longer among them the sacred spirit who was worthy of the LORD, manifold and incomprehensible, the lord of the word, who was faithful in all things, God's chief prophet throughout the earth, the most perfect teacher in the world, that he is no longer among them, they will say, Let us go against them. ¹⁷ If the enemy has but once worked impiously against their Lord, they have no advocate to offer prayers on their behalf to the LORD, as Moses the great messenger did, who every hour day and night had his knees fixed to the earth, praying to and looking for help from Him that rules all the world

with compassion and righteousness, calling to mind the covenant of the fathers, and propitiating the LORD with the oath. [18] For they will say, He is not with them; therefore, let us go and destroy them from off the face of the earth. [19] What then will become of this people, my lord Moses?"

CHAPTER 12

[1] And when Joshua had finished [these] words, he again cast himself at the feet of Moses. [2] And Moses took his hand and raised him into the seat before him, and answered and said to him, [3] "Joshua, do not despise yourself, but set your mind at ease, and listen to my words. [4] All the nations which are in the earth God has created as He has us; He has foreseen [both] them and us from the beginning of the creation of the earth to the end of the age, and nothing has been neglected by Him even to the least thing, but He has foreseen all things and caused all to come forth. [5] All things which are to be in this earth the LORD has foreseen, and behold, they are brought forward [into the light] . . . [6] . . . [[The LORD]] has appointed me on their behalf to pray for their sins and make intercession for them. [7] For [it was] not because of any virtue or strength of mine, but in His compassion and longsuffering was He pleased to call me. [8] For I say to you, Joshua: it is not on account of the godliness of this people that you will root out the nations. [9] The lights of the heavens [and] the foundations of the earth have been made and approved by God and are under the signet ring of His right hand. [10] Therefore, those who do and fulfill the commandments of God will increase and be prospered, [11] but those who sin and set the commandments at nothing will be without the blessings previously mentioned, and they will be punished by the nations with many torments. [12] But to wholly root out and destroy them is not permitted. [13] For God, who has foreseen all things forever, will go forth; and His covenant has been established and the oath which . . ."

TESTAMENT OF SOLOMON

The Testament of Solomon is the account of his receiving a ring of great power from the archangel Michael that enables him to systematically overcome and enslave a series of demons. He then forces these demons to help build the First Temple in Jerusalem. It is thought by most that the text was developed and organized in the medieval period, but at least some of the core material likely dates from the 1st century AD or earlier because of early citations and even an early reference to the title.

[THE] TESTAMENT OF SOLOMON, SON OF DAVID, WHO WAS KING IN JERUSALEM, AND [WHO] MASTERED AND CONTROLLED ALL SPIRITS OF THE AIR, ON THE EARTH, AND UNDER THE EARTH. BY MEANS OF THEM HE ALSO WORKED ALL THE TRANSCENDENT WORKS OF THE TEMPLE, ALSO TELLING OF THE AUTHORITIES THEY WIELD AGAINST MEN, AND BY WHAT MESSENGERS THESE DEMONS ARE BROUGHT TO NOTHING. OF THE SAGE SOLOMON. BLESSED ARE YOU, O LORD GOD, WHO GAVE SOLOMON SUCH AUTHORITY. GLORY TO YOU AND MIGHT TO THE AGES! AMEN.

CHAPTER 1

[1] And behold, when the temple of the city of Jerusalem was being built and the craftsmen were working there, the demon Ornias came among them toward sunset; [2] and he took away half of the pay of the chief-deviser's little boy, as well as half his food. He also continued to suck the thumb of his right hand every day. [3] And the child grew thin, although he was very much loved by the king. [4] So King Solomon called the boy one day, and questioned him, saying, "Do I not love you more than all the artisans who are working in the temple of God? [5] Do I not give you double wages and a double supply of food? How is it that day by day and hour by hour you grow thinner?" [6] But the child said to the king, "Please, O king. Listen to what has befallen all that your child has. After we are all released from our work on the temple of God, after sunset, when I lie down to rest, one of the evil demons comes and takes away from me one half of my pay and one half of my food. [7] Then he also takes hold of my right hand and sucks my thumb. And behold, my soul is oppressed, and so my body waxes thinner every day."

CHAPTER 2

[1] Now when I, Solomon, heard this, I entered the temple of God, and prayed with all my soul, night and day, that the demon might be delivered into my hands, and that I might gain authority over him. [2] And it came about through my prayer that grace was given to me from the LORD of Hosts by His chief-messenger Michael. [3] [He brought me] a little ring, having a seal consisting of an engraved stone, and said to me, "Take, O Solomon—king, son of David—the gift which the LORD God, the Highest of Hosts, has sent you. With it you will lock up all demons of the earth, [both] male and female; and with their help you will build up Jerusalem. [4] [But] you [must] wear this seal of God. And this engraving of the seal of the ring sent to you is a Pentalpha." [5] And I, Solomon, was overjoyed, and praised and glorified the God of the heavens and earth. And on the next day I called the boy, and gave him the ring, [6] and said to him, "take this, and at the hour in which the demon will come to you, throw this ring at the chest of the demon, and say to him: In the Name of God, King Solomon calls you here. [7] And then come running to me, without having any misgivings or fear in respect of anything you may hear on the part of the demon."

CHAPTER 3

[1] So the child took the ring and went off; and behold, at the customary hour Ornias, the fierce demon, came like a burning fire to take the pay from the child. [2] But the child, according to the instructions received from the king, threw the ring at the chest of the demon, and said, "King Solomon calls you here." [3] And then he went off running to the king. But the demon cried out aloud, saying, "Child, why have you done this to me? Take the ring off me, and I will render the gold of the earth to you. Only take this off me, and refrain from leading me away to Solomon." [4] But the child said to the demon, "As the LORD God of Israel lives, I will not allow you [this], so come here." [5] And the child came running, rejoicing, to the king, and said, "I have brought the demon, O king, as you commanded me, O my master. [6] And behold, he stands before the gates of the court of your palace, crying out, and supplicating with a loud voice, offering me the silver and gold of the earth if I will only bring him to you."

CHAPTER 4

[1] And when Solomon heard this, he rose up from his throne, and went outside into the vestibule of the court of his palace; [2] and there he saw the demon, shuddering and trembling. [3] And he said to him, "Who are you?" And the demon answered: "I am called Ornias." [4] And Solomon said to him, "Tell me, O demon, to which of the twelve signs you are subject." And he answered: "To the Water-pourer [[or Aquarius]]. And those who are consumed with desire for the noble virgins on earth . . . these I strangle. [5] But in case there is no disposition to sleep, I am changed into three forms. Whenever men come to be

enamored with women, I transform myself into a beautiful female; and I take hold of the men in their sleep and play with them. ⁶ And after a while I take to my wings again and hasten to the heavenly regions. ⁷ I also appear as a lion, and I am commanded by all the demons. I am an offspring of the chief-messenger Uriel, the power of God."

CHAPTER 5

¹ I, Solomon, having heard the name of the chief-messenger, prayed and glorified God, the Lord of the heavens and earth. ² And I sealed the demon and set him to work at stone-cutting, so that he might cut the stones in the temple, which, lying along the shore, had been brought by the Sea of Arabia. ³ But he, fearful of the iron, continued and said to me, "Please, King Solomon, let me go free, and I will bring you all the demons." ⁴ And as he was not willing to be subject to me, I pleaded [with] the chief-messenger Uriel to come and assist me; and I immediately beheld the chief-messenger Uriel coming down to me from the heavens.

CHAPTER 6

¹ And the messenger commanded the whales of the sea to come out of the abyss. And he cast his destiny on the ground, and that [destiny] made the great demon subject [to him]. ² And he commanded the great demon and bold Ornias to cut stones at the temple. ³ And accordingly I, Solomon, glorified the God of Heaven and Maker of the earth. ⁴ And he commanded Ornias to come with his destiny, and gave him the seal, saying, "Away with you, and bring the prince of all the demons here to me."

CHAPTER 7

¹ So Ornias took the finger-ring, and went off to Beelzebul, who has kingship over the demons. He said to him, "Here! Solomon calls you." ² But Beelzebul, having heard, said to him, "Tell me, who is this Solomon of whom you speak to me?" Then Ornias threw the ring at the chest of Beelzebul, saying, "Solomon the king calls you." ³ But Beelzebul cried aloud with a mighty voice, and shot out a great burning flame of fire; and he arose, and followed Ornias, and came to Solomon. ⁴ And when I saw the prince of demons, I glorified the LORD God, Maker of the heavens and earth, and I said, "Blessed are You, LORD God Almighty, who has given wisdom to Your servant Solomon, the assessor of the wise, and has subjected all the power of the Devil to me." ⁵ And I questioned him, and said, "Who are you?" The demon replied: "I am Beelzebul, the exarch of the demons. And all the demons have their chief seats close to me. ⁶ And it is I who make the apparition of each demon manifest." ⁷ And he promised to bring all the unclean spirits to me in bonds. And I again glorified the God

of the heavens and earth, as I always give thanks to Him.

CHAPTER 8

¹ I then asked of the demon if there were females among them. And when he told me that there were, I said that I desired to see them. ² So Beelzebul went off at high speed, and brought to me Onoskelis, who had a very pretty shape, and the skin of a lovely woman; and she tossed her head. ³ And when she had come, I said to her, "Tell me, who are you?" But she said to me, "I am called Onoskelis, a spirit worked . . . lurking on the earth. ⁴ There is a golden cave where I lie. But I have a place that always shifts. At one time I strangle men with a noose; at another, I creep up from the nature to the arms. ⁵ But my most frequent dwelling-places are the precipices, caves, [and] ravines. Oftentimes, however, I consort with men in the semblance of a woman, and above all with those of a dark skin. ⁶ For they share my star with me, since it is they who privily or openly worship my star, without knowing that they harm themselves, and but whet my appetite for further mischief. ⁷ For they wish to provide money by means of memory, but I supply a little to those who worship me fairly." ⁸ And I, Solomon, questioned her about her birth, and she replied: "I was born of an untimely voice, the so-called echo of a man's filth dropped in a wood." ⁹ And I said to her, "Under what star do you pass?" And she answered me: "Under the star of the full moon, for the reason that the moon travels over most things." ¹⁰ Then I said to her, "And what messenger is it that frustrates you?" And she said to me, "He that in you [[or through you]] is reigning." ¹¹ And I thought that she mocked me, and I commanded a soldier to strike her, but she cried aloud and said, "I am [subjected] to you, O king, by the wisdom of God given to you, and by the messenger Joel." ¹² So I commanded her to spin the hemp for the ropes used in the building of the house of God; and accordingly, when I had sealed and bound her, she was so overcome and brought to nothing as to stand night and day spinning the hemp.

CHAPTER 9

¹ And I immediately commanded another demon to be led to me; and instantly the demon Asmodeus approached me, bound, and I asked him, "Who are you?" ² But he shot a glance of anger and rage at me, and said, "And who are you?" And I said to him, "Thus punished as you are, [this is how] you answer me?" ³ But he, with rage, said to me, "But how will I answer you, for you are a son of man, whereas I was born of a messenger's seed by a daughter of man, so that no word of our heavenly kind addressed to the earth-born can be overconfident. ⁴ For what reason also my star is bright in the sky, and some men call it the Wagon [[or Ursa Major]], and some the Dragon's Child. I keep near to this star. ⁵ So do not ask me many

things; for your kingdom also after a short time is to be disrupted, and your glory is but for a season. [6] And your tyranny over us will be short; and then we will have free range over mankind again, so as that they will revere us as if we were gods, not knowing, men that they are, the names of the messengers set over us." [7] And I, Solomon, on hearing this, bound him more carefully, and ordered him to be flogged with thongs of ox-hide, and to humbly tell me what was his name and what [was] his business. [8] And he answered me thus: "I am called Asmodeus among mortals, and my business is to plot against the newly wedded, so that they may not know one another. [9] And I utterly sever them by many calamities, and I waste away the beauty of virgin women, and estrange their hearts." And I said to him, "Is this your only business?" [10] And he answered me: "I transport men into fits of madness and desire, when they have wives of their own, so that they leave them, and go off by night and day to others that belong to other men, with the result that they commit sin, and fall into murderous deeds." [11] And I adjured him by the Name of the LORD of Hosts, saying, "Fear God, Asmodeus, and tell me by what messenger you are frustrated." [12] But he said, "By Raphael, the chief-messenger that stands before the throne of God. But the liver and gall of a fish put me to flight, when smoked over ashes of the tamarisk." [13] I asked him again, and said, "Do not hide anything from me. For I am Solomon, son of David, King of Israel. Tell me the name of the fish which you revere." [14] And he answered: "It is the Glanos by name, and is found in the rivers of Assyria, for what reason it is that I roam around in those parts." [15] And I said to him, "Do you have nothing else [to say] concerning yourself, Asmodeus?" [16] And he answered: "The power of God knows, which has bound me with the indissoluble bonds of that one's seal, that whatever I have told you is true. Please, King Solomon, do not condemn me to [go into] water." [17] But I smiled, and said to him, "As the LORD God of my fathers lives, I will lay iron on you to wear. But you will also make the clay for the entire construction of the temple, treading it down with your feet." [18] And I ordered them to give him ten water-jars to carry water in. And the demon groaned terribly and did the work I ordered him to do. [19] And I did this because that fierce demon Asmodeus even knew the future. And I, Solomon, glorified God, who gave wisdom to me, His servant Solomon. [20] And I hung the liver of the fish and its gall on the spike of a reed and burned it over Asmodeus because of his being so strong, and his unbearable malice was thus frustrated.

CHAPTER 10

[1] And I summoned Beelzebul, the prince of demons, to stand before me again, and I sat him down on a raised seat of honor and said to him, "Why are you alone, prince of the demons?" [2] And he said to me, "Because I alone am left of the messengers of Heaven that came down. For I was first messenger in the first heaven being entitled Beelzebul. And now I control all those who are bound in Tartarus. [3] But I too have a child, and he haunts the Red Sea. And on any suitable occasion he comes up to me again, being subject to me, and reveals to me what he has done, and I support him." [4] I, Solomon, said to him, "Beelzebul, what is your employment?" [5] And he answered me: "I destroy kings. I ally myself with foreign tyrants. And my own demons I set on to men, in order that the latter may believe in them and be lost. [6] And the chosen servants of God, priests and faithful men, I excite to desires for wicked sins, and evil heresies, and lawless deeds; and they obey me, and I bear them on to destruction. [7] And I inspire men with envy, and murder, and for wars, and sodomy, and other evil things. And I will destroy the world." [8] So I said to him, "Bring to me your child, who is, as you say, in the Red Sea." [9] But he said to me, "I will not bring him to you, but another demon called Ephippas will come to me. I will bind him, and he will bring him up to me from the deep." [10] And I said to him, "How does your son come to be in the depth of the sea, and what is his name?" [11] And he answered me: "Do not ask me, for you cannot learn from me. However, he will come to you by any command, and will tell you openly." [12] I said to him, "Tell me by what messenger you are frustrated." [13] And he answered: "By the holy and precious Name of the Almighty God, called by the Hebrews by a row of numbers, of which the sum is six hundred forty-four, and among the Greeks it is Emmanuel. And if one of the Romans adjures me by the great name of the power Eleéth, I disappear at once." [14] I, Solomon, was astounded when I heard this; and I ordered him to saw up Theban marbles. And when he began to saw the marbles, the other demons cried out with a loud voice, howling because of their king, Beelzebul. [15] But I, Solomon, questioned him, saying, "If you would gain a respite, discourse to me about the things in Heaven." [16] And Beelzebul said, "Hear, O king, if you burn gum, and incense, and bulb of the sea, with nard and saffron, and light seven lamps in an earthquake, you will firmly fix your house. [17] And if, being pure, you light them at dawn in the sun gleaming, then you will see the heavenly dragons, how they wind themselves along and drag the chariot of the sun." [18] And I, Solomon, having heard this, rebuked him, and said, "Silence for this moment, and continue to saw the marbles as I commanded you."

CHAPTER 11

[1] And I, Solomon, praised God, and commanded another demon to present himself to me, [2] and one came before me who carried his face high up in the air, but the rest of the spirit curled away like a snail. [3] And it broke through the few soldiers, and also raised a terrible dust on the ground, and carried it

upwards, and then hurled it back again to frighten us, and asked what questions I could ask as a rule. ⁴ And I stood up, and spat on the ground in that spot, and sealed [it] with the ring of God. And immediately the dust-wind stopped. ⁵ Then I asked him, saying, "Who are you, O wind?" Then he once more shook up a dust, and answered me: "What would you have [of me], King Solomon?" ⁶ I answered him: "Tell me what you are called, and I would will to ask you a question. But so far I give thanks to God who has made me wise to answer their evil plots." ⁷ But [the demon] answered me: "I am the spirit of the ashes (Tephras)." ⁸ And I said to him, "What is your pursuit?" And he said, "I bring darkness on men, and set fire to fields, and I bring homesteads to nothing. But I am most busy in summer. ⁹ However, when I get an opportunity, I creep into corners of the wall, by night and day. For I am offspring of the great one, and nothing less." ¹⁰ Accordingly I said to him, "Under what star do you lie?" And he answered: "In the very tip of the moon's horn, when it is found in the south. My star is there. ¹¹ For I have been commanded to restrain the convulsions of the tertian fever; and this is why many men pray for the tertian fever using these three names: Bultala, Thallal, Melchal. And I heal them." ¹² And I said to him, "I am Solomon; when therefore you would do harm, by whose aid do you do it?" But he said to me, "By the messenger's, by whom also the third day's fever is lulled to rest." ¹³ So I questioned him, and said, "And by what name?" And he answered: "That of the chief-messenger Azael." ¹⁴ And I summoned the chief-messenger Azael, and set a seal on the demon, and commanded him to seize great stones and toss them up to the workmen on the higher parts of the temple. ¹⁵ And, being compelled, the demon began to do what he was commanded to do.

CHAPTER 12

¹ And I again glorified God who gave me this authority and ordered another demon to come before me, ² and seven spirits came, females, bound and woven together—lovely in appearance and beautiful. ³ And I, Solomon, seeing them, questioned them and said, "Who are you?" ⁴ But they, with one accord, said with one voice: "We are of the thirty-three elements of the cosmic ruler of the darkness." ⁵ And the first said, "I am Deception." The second said, "I am Strife." The third: "I am Klothod, which is Battle." The fourth: "I am Jealousy." The fifth: "I am Power." The sixth: "I am Error." ⁶ The seventh: "I am the worst of all, and our stars are in Heaven. Seven stars humble in sheen, and all together. And we are called, as it were, goddesses. ⁷ We change our place—all and together, and together we live, sometimes in Lydia, sometimes in Olympus, sometimes in a great mountain." ⁸ So I, Solomon, questioned them one by one, beginning with the first, and going down to the seventh. ⁹ The first said, "I am Deception, I deceive and weave snares here and there. I whet and excite heresies. But I have a messenger who frustrates me, Lamechalal." ¹⁰ Likewise also the second said, "I am Strife, strife of strifes. I bring timbers, stones, hangers—my weapons on the spot. But I have a messenger who frustrates me, Baruchiachel." ¹¹ Likewise also the third said, "I am called Klothod, which is Battle, and I cause the well-behaved to scatter and fall foul of one another. And why do I say so much? I have a messenger that frustrates me: Marmarath." ¹² Likewise also the fourth said, "I cause men to forget their sobriety and moderation. I part them and split them into parties; for Strife follows me hand in hand. I tear the husband from the sharer of his bed, and children from parents, and brothers from sisters. But why tell so much to my disdain? I have a messenger that frustrates me, the great Balthial." ¹³ Likewise also the fifth said, "I am Power. By power I raise up tyrants and tear down kings. I furnish power to all rebels. I have a messenger that frustrates me, Asteraôth." ¹⁴ Likewise also the sixth said, "I am Error, O King Solomon. And I will make you to err, as I have before made you to err, when I caused you to slay your own brother. I will lead you into error, so as to pry into graves, and teach them that dig; and I lead errant souls away from all piety, and many other evil traits are mine. But I have a messenger that frustrates me, Uriel." ¹⁵ Likewise also the seventh said, "I am the worst, and I make you worse off than you were, because I will impose the bonds of Artemis. But the locust will set me free, for by means thereof it is fated that you will achieve my desire . . . For if one were wise, he would not turn his steps toward me." ¹⁶ So I, Solomon, having heard and wondered, sealed them with my ring; and since they were so considerable, I commanded them to dig the foundations of the temple of God. ¹⁷ For the length of it was two hundred fifty cubits. And I commanded them to be industrious, and with one murmur of joint protest they began to perform the tasks enjoined.

CHAPTER 13

¹ But I, Solomon, glorified the LORD, and commanded another demon to come before me, ² and a demon having all the limbs of a man was brought to me, but without a head. ³ And I, seeing him, said to him, "Tell me, who are you?" And he answered: "I am a demon." So I said to him, "Which?" ⁴ And he answered me: "I am called Envy. For I delight to devour heads, being desirous to secure a head for myself, but I do not eat enough, but am anxious to have such a head as you have." ⁵ I, Solomon, on hearing this, sealed him, stretching out my hand against his chest, ⁶ whereon the demon leapt up, and threw himself down, and gave a groan, saying, "Woe is me! Where have I come to? O traitor Ornias, I cannot see!" ⁷ So I said to him, "I am Solomon. Tell

me then how you manage to see." [8] And he answered me: "By means of my feelings." [9] I then, Solomon, having heard his voice come up to me, asked him how he managed to speak. And he answered me: "I, O King Solomon, am wholly voice, for I have inherited the voices of many men. For in the case of all men who are called dumb, it is I who smashed their heads when they were children and had reached their eighth day. [10] Then when a child is crying in the night, I become a spirit, and glide by means of his voice . . . [11] In the crossways I also have many services to render, and my encounter is fraught with harm. [12] For in an instant I grasp a man's head, and with my hands, as with a sword, I cut it off, and put it on myself. [13] And in this way, by means of the fire which is in me, it is swallowed up through my neck. It is I that send grave and incurable mutilations on men's feet, and inflict sores." [14] And I, Solomon, on hearing this, said to him, "Tell me how you discharge forth the fire? Out of what sources do you emit it?" [15] And the spirit said to me, "From the Daystar. For here that Elburion, to whom men offer prayers and kindle lights, has not yet been found. And his name is invoked by the seven demons before me. And he cherishes them." [16] But I said to him, "Tell me his name." But he answered: "I cannot tell you. For if I tell his name, I render myself incurable. But he will come in response to his name." [17] And on hearing this, I, Solomon, said to him, "Tell me then by what messenger you are frustrated." [18] And he answered: "By the fiery flash of lightning." [19] And I bowed myself before the LORD God of Israel, and commanded him to remain in the keeping of Beelzebul until I should come.

CHAPTER 14

[1] Then I ordered another demon to come before me, and a hound came into my presence having a very large shape, and it spoke with a loud voice, and said, "Greetings, lord, King Solomon!" [2] And I, Solomon, was astounded. I said to it, "Who are you, O hound?" And it answered: "I do indeed seem to be a hound to you, but before you were, O King Solomon, I was a man that worked many unholy deeds on earth. [3] I was surpassingly educated in letters, and was so mighty that I could hold the stars of the heavens back. [4] And I prepared many divine works. For I do harm to men who follow after our star and turn them . . . [5] And I seize the frenzied men by the larynx, and so destroy them." [6] And I, Solomon, said to him, "What is your name?" And he answered: "Staff" (Rabdos). [7] And I said to him, "What is your employment? And what results can you achieve?" [8] And he replied, "Give me your man, and I will lead him away into a mountainous spot, and will show him a green stone tossed to and fro, with which you may adorn the temple of the LORD God." [9] And I, Solomon, on hearing this, ordered my servant to set off with him,

and to take the finger-ring bearing the seal of God with him. [10] And I said to him, "Whoever will show you the green stone, seal him with this finger-ring, and mark the spot with care, and bring me the demon here." [11] And the demon showed him the green stone, and he sealed it, and brought the demon to me. [12] And I, Solomon, decided to confine with my seal on my right hand the two—the headless demon [and] likewise the hound that was so huge; he should be bound as well. [13] And I commanded the hound to keep the fiery spirit safe so that lamps, as it were, might cast their light through its maw on the artisans at work by day and night. [14] And I, Solomon, took from the mine of that stone two hundred shekels for the supports of the table of incense, which was similar in appearance. [15] And I, Solomon, glorified the LORD God, and then closed around the treasure of that stone. [16] And again I ordered the demons to cut marble for the construction of the house of God. [17] And I, Solomon, prayed to the LORD, and asked the hound, saying, "By what messenger are you frustrated?" And the demon replied, "By the great Brieus."

CHAPTER 15

[1] And I praised the LORD God of the heavens and earth and commanded another demon to come forward to me, and one in the form of a roaring lion came before me. [2] And he stood and answered me, saying, "O king, in the form which I have, I am a spirit quite incapable of being perceived. [3] I leap on all men who lie prostrate with sickness, coming stealthily along; and I render the man weak, so that his habit of body is enfeebled. But I also have another glory, O king: [4] I cast out demons, and I have legions under my control. And I am capable of being received in my dwelling-places, along with all the demons belonging to the legions under me." [5] But I, Solomon, on hearing this, asked him: "What is your name?" But he answered: "Lion-bearer, Rath in kind." [6] And I said to him, "How are you to be frustrated along with your legions? What messenger is it that frustrates you?" [7] And he answered: "If I tell you my name, I do not only bind myself, but also the legions of demons under me." [8] So I said to him, "I adjure you in the Name of the God of Hosts to tell me by what name you are frustrated along with your host." [9] And the spirit answered me: "THE GREAT AMONG MEN, who is to suffer many things at the hands of men, whose name is the figure six hundred forty-four, which is Emmanuel; it is He who has bound us, and who will then come and plunge us from the steep under water. He is spread abroad in the three letters which bring Him down." [10] And I, Solomon, on hearing this, glorified God, and condemned his legion to carry wood from the thicket. [11] And I condemned the lion-shaped one himself to saw up the wood small with his teeth, for burning in the unquenchable furnace for the temple of God.

CHAPTER 16

[1] And I worshiped the LORD God of Israel and commanded another demon to come forward, and a dragon came before me, three-headed, of fearful aspect. [2] And I questioned him: "Who are you?" And he answered me: "I am a caltrop-like spirit, whose activity [is] in three lines. [3] But I blind children in women's wombs and twirl their ears around. And I make them deaf and mute. [4] And I have again in my third head means of slipping in. And I strike men in the limbless part of the body, and cause them to fall down, and foam, and grind their teeth. [5] But I have my own way of being frustrated, Jerusalem being signified in writing, to the place called [PLACE] OF [THE] SKULL." [6] For there is appointed beforehand the Messenger of the great counsel, and now He will openly dwell on the Cross. He frustrates me, and I am subject to Him. [7] But in the place where you sit, O King Solomon, stands a column in the air, of purple . . . The demon called Ephippas has brought [it] up from the Red Sea, from inner Arabia. [8] It is he that will be shut up in a skin-bottle and brought before you. [9] But at the entrance of the temple, which you have begun to build, O King Solomon, lies much stored gold, which you can dig up and carry off." [10] And I, Solomon, sent my servant, and found it to be as the demon told me. And I sealed him with my ring and praised the LORD God." [11] So I said to him, "What are you called?" And the demon said, "I am the crest of dragons." And I commanded him to make bricks in the temple. He had human hands.

CHAPTER 17

[1] And I adored the LORD God of Israel and commanded another demon to present himself, and a spirit in woman's form came before me that had a head without any limbs, and her hair was dishevelled. [2] And I said to her, "Who are you?" But she answered: "No, who are you? And why do you want to hear concerning me? But, as you would learn, here I stand bound before your face. [3] Go then into your royal storehouses and wash your hands. Then sit down again before your tribunal, and ask me questions, and you will learn, O king, who I am." [4] And I, Solomon, did as she enjoined me, and restrained myself because of the wisdom dwelling in me, in order that I might hear of her deeds, and reprehend them, and manifest them to men. [5] And I sat down, and said to the demon, "What are you?" And she said, "I am called Obizuth among men; and I do not sleep by night, but go my rounds over all the world, and visit women in childbirth. [6] And divining the hour, I take my stand; and if I am lucky, I strangle the child. But if not, I retire to another place. For I cannot retire unsuccessfully for a single night. [7] For I am a fierce spirit, of myriad names and many shapes. And now here, now there I roam. And to westward parts I go my rounds. [8] But as it now is, though you have sealed me around with the ring of God, you have done nothing. I am not standing before you, and you will not be able to command me. [9] For I have no work other than the destruction of children, and the making their ears to be deaf, and the working of evil to their eyes, and the binding their mouths with a bond, and the ruin of their minds, and paining of their bodies." [10] When I, Solomon, heard this, I marveled at her appearance, for I beheld all her body to be in darkness. [11] But her glance was altogether bright and greenish, and her hair was tossed wildly like a dragon's; and the whole of her limbs were invisible. [12] And her voice was very clear as it came to me. And I cunningly said, "Tell me by what messenger you are frustrated, O evil spirit?" [13] But she answered me: "By the messenger of God called Afarôt, which is interpreted Raphael, by whom I am frustrated now and for all time. [14] His name, if any man knows it, and writes the same on a woman in childbirth, then I will not be able to enter her. Of this name the number is six thousand four hundred and one." [15] And I, Solomon, having heard this, and having glorified the LORD, ordered her hair to be bound, and that she should be hung up in front of the temple of God, that all the sons of Israel, as they passed, might see it, and glorify the LORD God of Israel, who had given me this authority, with wisdom and power from God, by means of this signet.

CHAPTER 18

[1] And I again ordered another demon to come before me, and this came, rolling itself along—one in appearance like to a dragon, but having the face and hands of a man. [2] And all its limbs, except the feet, were those of a dragon; and it had wings on its back. [3] And when I beheld it, I was astonished, and said, "Who are you, demon, and what are you called? And from where have you come? Tell me." [4] And the spirit answered and said, "This is the first time I have stood before you, O King Solomon. I am a spirit made into a god among men, but now brought to nothing by the ring and wisdom given to you by God. [5] Now I am the so-called winged dragon, and I do not chamber with many women, but only with a few that are of fair shape, which possess the name of Xuli, of this star. [6] And I pair with them in the guise of a spirit winged in form, committing sodomy. [7] And she on whom I have leapt goes heavy with child, and that which is born of her becomes desire. [8] But since such offspring cannot be carried by men, the woman in question breaks wind. Such is my role. [9] Suppose then that I alone am satisfied, and all the other demons molested and disturbed by you will speak the whole truth. [10] But those composed of fire will cause the material of the logs which is to be collected by them for the building in the temple to be burned up by fire." [11] And as the demon said this, I saw the spirit going forth from his mouth, and it consumed the wood of the

frankincense-tree, and it burned up all the logs which we had placed in the temple of God. ¹²And I, Solomon, saw what the spirit had done, and I marveled. ¹³And, having glorified God, I asked the dragon-shaped demon, and said, "Tell me, by what messenger are you frustrated?" ¹⁴And he answered: "By the great messenger who has his seat in the second heaven, which is called in Hebrew Bazazeth." And I, Solomon, having heard this, and having invoked his messenger, condemned him to saw up marbles for the building of the temple of God.

CHAPTER 19

¹And I praised God and commanded another demon to come before me, ²and another spirit came before my face, as it were a woman in the form she had. But on her shoulders she had two other heads with hands. ³And I asked her, and said, "Tell me, who are you?" And she said to me, "I am Enêpsigos, who also have a myriad of names." ⁴And I said to her, "By what messenger are you frustrated?" But she said to me, "What do you seek, what do you ask? I undergo changes, I am called like the goddess. And I change again, and pass into possession of another shape. ⁵And do not be desirous, therefore, to know all that concerns me. But since you are before me for this much, listen. I have my abode in the moon, and for that reason I possess three forms. ⁶At times I am magically invoked by the wise as Kronos. ⁷At other times, in connection with those who bring me down, I come down and appear in another shape. ⁸The measure of the element is inexplicable and undefinable, and not to be frustrated. I then, changing into these three forms, come down and become such as you see me; but I am frustrated by the messenger Rathanael, who sits in the third heaven. ⁹This then is why I speak to you. That temple cannot contain me." ¹⁰Therefore I, Solomon, prayed to my God, and I invoked the messenger of whom Enêpsigos spoke to me, and used my seal. ¹¹And I sealed her with a triple chain, and [placed] the fastening of the chain beneath her. ¹²I used the seal of God, and the spirit prophesied to me, saying, "This is what you, King Solomon, do to us. But after a time, your kingdom will be broken, and again in season this temple will be split apart; and all Jerusalem will be undone by the King of the Persians, and Medes, and Chaldaeans. ¹³And the vessels of this temple, which you make, will be put to servile uses of the gods; and along with them all the jars, in which you shut us up, will be broken by the hands of men. ¹⁴And then we will go forth in great power here and there, and be disseminated all over the world. ¹⁵And we will lead the inhabited world astray for a long season, until the Son of God is stretched on the Cross. ¹⁶For never before does a king arise like Him—one frustrating us all, whose mother will not have contact with man. ¹⁷Who else can receive such authority over spirits, except He, whom the first Devil will seek to tempt, but will not prevail over? The number of His Name is six thousand four hundred forty-two, which is Emmanuel. ¹⁸For what reason, O King Solomon, your time is evil, and your years short and evil, and your kingdom will be given to your servant." ¹⁹And I, Solomon, having heard this, glorified God. And though I marveled at the apology of the demons, I did not credit it until it came true. ²⁰And I did not believe their words, but when they were realized, then I understood, and at my death I wrote this Testament to the sons of Israel, and gave it to them, so that they might know the powers of the demons and their shapes, and the names of their messengers, by which these messengers are frustrated. ²¹And I glorified the LORD God of Israel and commanded the spirits to be bound with indissoluble bonds.

CHAPTER 20

¹And having praised God, I commanded another spirit to come before me, and another demon came before my face, having the shape of a horse in front, but [that] of a fish in back. ²And he had a mighty voice, and said to me, "O King Solomon, I am a fierce spirit of the sea, and I am greedy for gold and silver. ³I am such a spirit as rounds itself and comes over the expanses of the water of the sea, and I trip up the men who sail thereon. ⁴For I round myself into a wave, and transform myself, and then throw myself on ships and come right in on them. ⁵And that is my business, and my way of getting hold of money and men. For I take the men, and whirl them around with myself, and hurl the men out of the sea. ⁶For I am not covetous of men's bodies, but cast them up out of the sea so far. ⁷But since Beelzebul, ruler of the spirits of air and of those under the earth, and lord of earthly ones, has a joint kingship with us in respect of the deeds of each one of us, I therefore went up from the sea, to get a certain outlook in his company. ⁸But I also have another character and role. I transform myself into waves and come up from the sea. ⁹And I show myself to men, so that those on earth call me Kunopaston, because I assume the human form. ¹⁰And my name is a true one. For by my passage up into men, I send forth a certain nausea. ¹¹I came then to take counsel with the prince Beelzebul, and he bound me and delivered me into your hands. ¹²And I am here before you because of this seal, and you now torment me. ¹³Behold now, in two or three days the spirit that [now] converses with you will fail, because I will have no water." ¹⁴And I said to him, "Tell me by what messenger you are frustrated." And he answered: "By Lameth." And I glorified God. ¹⁵I commanded the spirit to be thrown into a vial along with ten jugs of seawater of two measures each. ¹⁶And I sealed them around, above the marbles, and asphalt, and pitch in the mouth of the vessel. And having sealed it with my ring, I ordered it to be deposited in the temple of God.

TESTAMENT OF SOLOMON

CHAPTER 21

[1] And I ordered another spirit to come before me, [2] and another enslaved spirit came before my face, having the obscure form of a man, with gleaming eyes, and bearing a blade in his hand. [3] And I asked: "Who are you?" But he answered: "I am a lascivious spirit, engendered of a giant man who dies in the massacre in the time of the giants." [4] I said to him, "Tell me what you are employed in on earth, and where you have your dwelling." [5] And he said, "My dwelling is in fruitful places, but my procedure is this: I seat myself beside the men who pass along among the tombs, and in untimely season I assume the form of the dead; [6] and if I catch anyone, I immediately destroy him with my sword. But if I cannot destroy him, I cause him to be possessed with a demon, and to devour his own flesh, and the hair to fall off his chin." [7] But I said to him, "Be then in fear of the God of Heaven and of earth, and tell me by which messenger you are frustrated." [8] And he answered: "He destroys me who is to become Savior, a Man whose figure, if anyone will write it on his forehead, he will defeat me, and I will quickly retreat in fear. [9] And, indeed, if anyone writes this sign on him, I will be in fear." And I, Solomon, on hearing this, and having glorified the LORD God, shut this demon up like the rest.

CHAPTER 22

[1] And I commanded another demon to come before me, and thirty-six spirits came before my face, their heads shapeless like dogs, but in themselves they were human in form, with faces of donkeys, faces of oxen, and faces of birds. [2] And I, Solomon, on hearing and seeing them, wondered, and I asked them and said, "Who are you?" [3] But they, of one accord with one voice, said, "We are the thirty-six elements, the world-rulers of this darkness. [4] But, O King Solomon, you will not wrong us nor imprison us, nor lay command on us; but since the LORD God has given you authority over every spirit, in the air, and on the earth, and under the earth, therefore we also present ourselves before you like the other spirits, from ram and bull, from both twin and crab, lion and virgin, scales and scorpion, archer, goat-horned, water-pourer, and fish." [5] Then I, Solomon, invoked the Name of the LORD of Hosts, and questioned each in turn as to what was its character. [6] And I commanded each one to come forward and tell of its actions. [7] Then the first one came forward, and said, "I am the first decan of the ecliptic, and I am called the ram, and with me are these two." [8] So I put the question to them: "Who are you called?" The first said, "I, O lord, am called Ruax, and I cause the heads of men to be idle, and I pillage their brows. But let me only hear the words, Michael, imprison Ruax, and I immediately retreat." [9] And the second said, "I am called Barsafael, and I cause those who are subject to my hour to feel the pain of migraine. If only I hear the words, Gabriel, imprison Barsafael, I immediately retreat." [10] The third said, "I am called Arôtosael. I do harm to eyes, and grievously injure them. Only let me hear the words, Uriel, imprison Arôtosael, I immediately retreat." [11] The fifth said, "I am called Iudal, and I bring about a block in the ears and deafness of hearing. If I hear, Uruel Iudal, I immediately retreat." [12] The sixth said, "I am called Sphendonaêl. I cause tumors of the parotid gland, and inflammations of the tonsils, and tetanic recurvation. If I hear, Sabrael, imprison Sphendonaêl, I immediately retreat." [13] And the seventh said, "I am called Sphandôr, and I weaken the strength of the shoulders, and cause them to tremble; and I paralyze the nerves of the hands, and I break and bruise the bones of the neck. And I suck out the marrow. But if I hear the words, Araêl, imprison Sphandôr, I immediately retreat." [14] And the eighth said, "I am called Belbel. I distort the hearts and minds of men. If I hear the words, Araêl, imprison Belbel, I immediately retreat." [15] And the ninth said, "I am called Kurtaêl. I send colics in the bowels. I induce pains. If I hear the words, Iaôth, imprison Kurtaêl, I immediately retreat." [16] The tenth said, "I am called Metathiax. I cause the reins to ache. If I hear the words, Adônaêl, imprison Metathiax, I immediately retreat." [17] The eleventh said, "I am called Katanikotaêl. I create strife and wrongs in men's homes and send on them hard temper. If anyone would be at peace in his home, let him write on seven leaves of laurel the name of the messenger that frustrates me, along with these names: Iae, Ieô, sons of hosts, in the Name of the great God let him shut up Katanikotaêl. Then let him wash the laurel-leaves in water, and sprinkle his house with the water, from within to the outside. And I immediately retreat." [18] The twelfth said, "I am called Saphathoraél, and I inspire partisanship in men, and delight in causing them to stumble. If anyone will write on paper these names of messengers, Iacô, Iealô, Iôelet, Sabaôth, Ithoth, Bae, and having folded it up, wear it around his neck or against his ear, I immediately retreat and dissipate the drunken fit." [19] The thirteenth said, "I am called Bobêl, and I cause nervous sickness by my assaults. If I hear the name of the great Adonaêl, imprison Bothothêl, I immediately retreat." [20] The fourteenth said, "I am called Kumeatêl, and I inflict shivering fits and torpor. If only I hear the words: Zôrôêl, imprison Kumentaêl, I immediately retreat." [21] The fifteenth said, "I am called Roêlêd. I cause cold, and frost, and pain in the stomach. Let me only hear the words: Lax, do not remain, do not be warmed, for Solomon is fairer than eleven fathers, I [immediately] retreat." [22] The sixteenth said, "I am called Atrax. I inflict on men fevers, irremediable and harmful. If you would imprison me, chop up coriander and smear it on the lips, reciting the following charm: The fever

which is from dirt—I exorcise you by the throne of the Most High God, retreat from dirt and retreat from the creature fashioned by God. And I immediately retreat." [23] The seventeenth said, "I am called Ieropaêl. On the stomach of men I sit, and cause convulsions in the bath and in the road; and wherever I am found, or find a man, I throw him down. But if anyone will say to the afflicted, into their ear, these names three times over, into the right ear: Ludarizê, Sabunê, Denôê, I immediately retreat." [24] The eighteenth said, "I am called Buldumêch. I separate wife from husband and bring about a grudge between them. If anyone writes down the names of your sires, Solomon, on paper and places it in the ante-chamber of his house, I retreat there. And the legend written will be as follows: The God of Abram, and the God of Isaac, and the God of Jacob commands you—retreat from this house in peace. And I immediately retreat." [25] The nineteenth said, "I am called Naôth, and I take my seat on the knees of men. If anyone writes on paper: Phnunoboêol, depart Nathath, and you do not touch the neck, I immediately retreat." [26] The twentieth said, "I am called Marderô. I send on men incurable fever. If anyone writes on the page of a scroll: Sphênêr, Raphael, retreat, do not drag me around, do not flay me, and ties it around his neck, I immediately retreat." [27] The twenty-first said, "I am called Alath, and I cause coughing and hard-breathing in children. If anyone writes on paper: Rorêx, pursue Alath, and fastens it around his neck, I immediately retreat." [28] The twenty-third said, "I am called Nefthada. I cause the reins to ache, and I bring about dysuria. If anyone writes on a plate of tin the words: Lathôth, Uruêl, Nephthada, and fastens it around the loins, I immediately retreat." [29] The twenty-fourth said, "I am called Akton. I cause ribs and lumbar muscles to ache. If one engraves on copper material, taken from a ship which has missed its anchorage, this: Marmaraôth, Sabaôth, pursue Akton, and fastens it round the loin, I immediately retreat." [30] The twenty-fifth said, "I am called Anatreth, and I tear burnings and fevers into the entrails. But if I hear: Arara, Charara, I immediately retreat." [31] The twenty-sixth said, "I am called Enenuth. I steal away men's minds, and change their hearts, and make a man toothless. If one writes: Allazoôl, pursue Enenuth, and ties the paper around him, I immediately retreat." [32] The twenty-seventh said, "I am called Phêth. I make men consumptive and cause hemorrhaging. If one exorcises me in wine, sweet-smelling and unmixed by the eleventh age, and says: I exorcise you by the eleventh age to stop, I demand, Phêth (Axiôphêth), then gives it to the patient to drink, I then immediately retreat." [33] The twenty-eighth said, "I am called Harpax, and I send sleeplessness on men. If one writes Kokphnêdismos, and binds it around the temples, I immediately retreat." [34] The twenty-ninth said, "I am called Anostêr. I engender uterine mania and pains in the bladder. If one powders into pure oil three seeds of laurel and smears it on, saying, I exorcise you, Anostêr, stop by Marmaraô, I immediately retreat." [35] The thirtieth said, "I am called Alleborith. If in eating fish one has swallowed a bone, then he must take a bone from the fish and cough, and I immediately retreat." [36] The thirty-first said, "I am called Hephesimireth, and cause lingering disease. If you throw salt, rubbed in the hand, into oil and smear it on the patient, saying, Seraphim, cherubim, help me! I immediately retreat." [37] The thirty-second said, "I am called Ichthion. I paralyze muscles and contuse them. If I hear Adonaêth, help! I immediately retreat." [38] The thirty-third said, "I am called Agchoniôn. I lie among swaddling-clothes and in the precipice. And if anyone writes on fig-leaves Lycurgos, taking away one letter at a time, and writes it reversing the letters, I immediately retreat—Lycurgos, ycurgos, curgos, urgos, gos, os." [39] The thirty-fourth said, "I am called Autothith. I cause grudges and fighting. Therefore, I am frustrated by Alpha and Omega, if written down." [40] The thirty-fifth said, "I am called Phthenoth. I cast an evil eye on every man. Therefore, the eye, much suffering, if it is drawn, frustrates me." [41] The thirty-sixth said, "I am called Bianakith. I have a grudge against the body. I lay waste houses, I cause flesh to decay, and all else that is similar. If a man writes on the front-door of his house: Mêltô, Ardu, Anaath, I flee from that place."

CHAPTER 23

[1] And I, Solomon, when I heard this, glorified the God of the heavens and earth. And I commanded them to fetch water in the temple of God. [2] And I furthermore prayed to the LORD God to cause the demons outside, that hamper humanity, to be bound and made to approach the temple of God. [3] I condemned some of these demons to do the heavy work of the construction of the temple of God. [4] Others I shut up in prisons. Others I ordered to wrestle with fire in [the making of] gold and silver, sitting down by lead and spoon, [5] and to make places ready for the other demons in which they should be confined. [6] And I, Solomon, had much quiet in all the earth, and spent my life in profound peace, honored by all men and by all under Heaven. [7] And I built the entire temple of the LORD God. And my kingdom was prosperous, and my army was with me. [8] And for the rest, the city of Jerusalem had repose, rejoicing and delighted. [8] And all the kings of the earth came to me from the ends of the earth to behold the temple which I built to the LORD God. [9] And having heard of the wisdom given to me, they paid homage to me in the temple, bringing gold, and silver, and many and various precious stones, and bronze, and iron, and lead, and cedar logs. [10] And woods did not decay [that] they brought me for the equipment of the temple of God. [11] And among them the queen of the south, being a witch, also came

in great concern and bowed low to the earth before me. [12] And having heard my wisdom, she glorified the God of Israel, and she made formal trial of all my wisdom, of all love in which I instructed her, according to the wisdom imparted to me. And all the sons of Israel glorified God.

CHAPTER 24

[1] And behold, in those days one of the workmen of ripe old age threw himself down before me, and said, "King Solomon, pity me, because I am old." [2] So I commanded him to stand up, and said, "Tell me, old man, all you will." [3] And he answered: "I implore you king, I have an only-born son, and he insults and beats me openly, and plucks out the hair of my head, and threatens me with a painful death. Therefore, I implore you: avenge me." [4] And I, Solomon, on hearing this, felt compunction as I looked at his old age; and I commanded the child to be brought to me. [5] And when he was brought, I questioned him whether it was true. And the youth said, "I was not so filled with madness as to strike my father with my hand. Be kind to me, O king. [6] For I have not dared to commit such impiety, poor wretch that I am." [7] But I, Solomon, on hearing this from the youth, exhorted the old man to reflect on the matter, and accept his son's apology. [8] However, he would not, but said he would rather let him die. And as the old man would not yield, I was about to pronounce sentence on the youth, when I saw the demon Ornias laughing. [9] I was very angry at the demon's laughing in my presence; and I ordered my men to remove the other parties and bring Ornias forward before my tribunal. [10] And when he was brought before me, I said to him, "Accursed one, why did you look at me and laugh?" [11] And the demon answered: "Please, king, it was not because of you I laughed, but because of this ill-fated old man and the wretched youth—his son. [12] For after three days his son will die untimely; and behold, the old man desires to unfairly make away with him." [13] But I, Solomon, having heard this, said to the demon, "Is that which you speak true?" And he answered: "It is true, O king." [14] And I, on hearing that, commanded them to remove the demon, and that they should bring the old man with his son before me again. [15] I commanded them to make friends with one another again, and I supplied them with food. [16] And then I told the old man after three days to bring his son to me again here; "and," I said, "I will attend to him." And they saluted me and went their way. [17] And when they were gone, I ordered Ornias to be brought forward, and said to him, "Tell me how you know this"; and he answered: "We demons ascend into the expanse of Heaven, and fly around among the stars. [18] And we hear the sentences which go forth on the souls of men, and immediately we come, and whether by force of influence, or by fire, or by sword, or by some accident, we veil our act of destruction; [19] and if a man

does not die by some untimely disaster or by violence, then we demons transform ourselves in such a way as to appear to men and be worshiped in our human nature." [20] I therefore, having heard this, glorified the LORD God, and I questioned the demon again, saying, "Tell me how you can ascend into Heaven, being demons, and intermingle amidst the stars and holy messengers." [21] And he answered: "Just as things are fulfilled in Heaven, so also on earth the types of all of them. [22] For there are principalities, authorities, world-rulers, and we demons fly around in the air; and we hear the voices of the heavenly beings, and survey all the powers. [23] And as having no ground on which to descend and rest, we lose strength and fall off like leaves from trees. [24] And men seeing us imagine that the stars are falling from [the] sky. [25] But it is not really so, O king; but we fall because of our weakness, and because we have nothing anywhere to lay hold of; and so we suddenly fall down like lightnings in the depth of night. [26] And we set cities in flames and the fields [on] fire. For the stars have firm foundations in the heavens like the sun and the moon." [27] And I, Solomon, having heard this, ordered the demon to be guarded for five days. [28] And after the five days I recalled the old man and was about to question him, but he came to me in grief and with dark countenance. [29] And I said to him, "Tell me, old man, where is your son? And what does this [gloomy] appearance mean?" [30] And he answered: "Behold, I have become childless and sit by my son's grave in despair. For it is already two days that he is dead." But I, Solomon, on hearing that, and knowing that the demon Ornias had told me the truth, glorified the God of Israel.

CHAPTER 25

[1] And the queen of the south saw all this, and marveled, glorifying the God of Israel; and she beheld the temple of the LORD being built. [2] And she gave a siklos of gold and one hundred myriads of silver and choice bronze, and she went into the temple. [3] And [she beheld] the altar of incense and the brazen supports of this altar, and the gems of the lamps flashing forth of different colors, and of the lampstand of stone, and of emerald, and hyacinth, and sapphire; [4] and she beheld the vessels of gold, and silver, and bronze, and wood, and the folds of skins dyed red with madder. [5] And she saw the bases of the pillars of the temple of the LORD. All were of one gold . . . [6] . . . apart from the demons whom I condemned to labor. And there was peace in the circle of my kingdom and over all the earth.

CHAPTER 26

[1] And it came to pass, when I was in my kingdom, the king of the Arabians, Adares, sent me a letter, and the writing of the letter was written as follows: [2] "To King Solomon, greetings! Behold, we have heard, and it

has been heard to all the ends of the earth, concerning the wisdom given in you, and that you are a man merciful from the LORD. ³ And understanding has been granted to you over all the spirits of the air, and on earth, and under the earth. ⁴ Now indeed, there is present in the land of Arabia a spirit of the following kind: at early dawn there begins to blow a certain wind until the third hour. ⁵ And its blast is harsh and terrible, and it slays man and beast. And no spirit can live on earth against this demon. ⁶ Please then, forasmuch as the spirit is a wind, contrive something according to the wisdom given in you by the LORD your God, and deign to send a man [who is] able to capture it. ⁷ And behold, King Solomon, I, and my people, and all my land will serve you to death. ⁸ And all Arabia will be at peace with you, if you will perform this act of righteousness for us. ⁹ For what reason, please do not despise our humble prayer, and do not permit the territory subordinated to your authority to be utterly brought to nothing. ¹⁰ Because we are suppliants—both I, and my people, and all my land. ¹¹ Farewell to my lord. All health [be to you]!"

¹² And I, Solomon, read this letter; and I folded it up and gave it to my people, and said to them, "After seven days you will remind me of this letter." ¹³ And Jerusalem was built, and the temple was being completed. And there was a stone, the end stone of the corner lying there—great, chosen out, one which I desired to lay in the head of the corner of the completion of the temple. ¹⁴ And all the workmen, and all the demons helping them, came to the same place to bring up the stone and lay it on the pinnacle of the holy temple, and were not strong enough to stir it and lay it on the corner allotted to it. ¹⁵ For that stone was exceedingly great and useful for the corner of the temple. ¹⁶ And after seven days, being reminded of the letter of Adares, king of Arabia, I called my servant and said to him, "Order your camel and take a leather flask for yourself, and also take this seal. ¹⁷ And go away into Arabia to the place in which the evil spirit blows; and take the flask there, and the signet-ring in front of the mouth of the flask, and [hold them] toward the blast of the spirit. ¹⁸ And when the flask is blown out, you will understand that the demon is [in it]. ¹⁹ Then quickly tie up the mouth of the flask, and seal it securely with the seal-ring, and lay it carefully on the camel, and bring it to me here. ²⁰ And if on the way it offers you gold, or silver, or treasure in return for letting it go, see that you are not persuaded. But arrange [it] without using an oath to release it. ²¹ And then if it points out to the places where gold or silver are, mark the places and seal them with this seal. And bring the demon to me. And now depart, and farewell." ²² Then the youth did as was commanded him. And he ordered his camel, and laid a flask on it, and set off into Arabia. ²³ And the men of that region would not believe that he would be able to catch the evil spirit. ²⁴ And when it was dawn, the servant stood before the spirit's blast, and laid the flask on the ground, and the finger-ring on the mouth of the flask. ²⁵ And the demon blew through the middle of the finger-ring into the mouth of the flask, and going in, blew out the flask. ²⁶ But the man promptly stood up to it and drew the mouth of the flask tight with his hand in the Name of the LORD God of Hosts. ²⁷ And the demon remained within the flask. And after that, the youth remained in that land three days to make trial. ²⁸ And the spirit no longer blew against that city. And all the Arabs knew that he had safely shut the spirit in. ²⁹ Then the youth fastened the flask on the camel, and the Arabs sent him forth on his way with much honor and precious gifts, praising and magnifying the God of Israel. ³⁰ But the youth brought in the bag and laid it in the middle of the temple. And on the next day, I, King Solomon, went into the temple of God and sat in deep distress regarding the stone of the end of the corner. ³¹ And when I entered the temple, the flask stood up and walked around some seven steps and then fell on its mouth and paid homage to me. ³² And I marveled that even along with the bottle the demon still had power and could walk around; and I commanded it to stand up. ³³ And the flask stood up and stood on its feet all blown out. And I questioned him, saying, "Tell me, who are you?" ³⁴ And the spirit within said, "I am the demon called Ephippas, that is in Arabia." ³⁵ And I said to him, "Is this your name?" And he answered: "Yes; wheresoever I will, I descend, and set fire, and do [it] to death." ³⁶ And I said to him, "By what messenger are you frustrated?" And he answered: "By the only-ruling God that even has authority over me to be heard— ³⁷ He that is to be born of a virgin and crucified by the Jews on a cross, whom the messengers and chief-messengers worship. ³⁸ He frustrates me and weakens me of my great strength, which has been given to me by my father the Devil." ³⁹ And I said to him, "What can you do?" And he answered: "I am able to remove mountains, to overthrow the oaths of kings. I wither trees and make their leaves to fall off." ⁴⁰ And I said to him, "Can you raise this stone, and lay it for the beginning of this corner which exists in the fair plan of the temple?" ⁴¹ And he said, "Not only raise this, O king, but also, with the help of the demon who presides over the Red Sea, I will bring up the pillar of air, and will stand it where you will in Jerusalem." ⁴² Saying this, I laid stress on him, and the flask became as if depleted of air. And I placed it under the stone, and [the spirit] girded himself up, and lifted it up [to the] top of the flask. ⁴³ And the flask went up the steps, carrying the stone, and laid it down at the end of the entrance of the temple. ⁴⁴ And I, Solomon, beholding the stone raised aloft and placed on a foundation, said, "Truly the Writing is fulfilled, which says: The stone which the builders rejected on trial, that same has become the head of the corner. ⁴⁵ For this is not mine to grant,

TESTAMENT OF SOLOMON

but God's, that the demon should be strong enough to lift up such a great stone and deposit it in the place I wished." ⁴⁶ And Ephippas led the demon of the Red Sea with the column. And they both took the column and raised it aloft from the earth. ⁴⁷ And I outwitted these two spirits, so that they could not shake the entire earth in a moment of time. ⁴⁸ And then I sealed around on this side and that with my ring, and said, "Watch." ⁴⁹ And the spirits have remained upholding it until this day, for proof of the wisdom given to me. And there the pillar was hanging of enormous size, in midair, supported by the winds. ⁵⁰ And thus the spirits appeared underneath, like air, supporting it. And if one looks fixedly, the pillar is a little oblique, being supported by the spirits; and it is so today.

CHAPTER 27

¹ And I, Solomon, questioned the other spirit which came up with the pillar from the depth of the Red Sea. ² And I said to him, "Who are you, and what calls you? And what is your business? For I hear many things about you." ³ And the demon answered: "I, O King Solomon, am called Abezithibod. I am a descendant of the chief-messenger. ⁴ When once I sat in the first heaven, of which the name is Ameleouth, I was then a fierce and winged spirit, and with a single wing I was plotting against every spirit under Heaven. ⁵ I was present when Moses went in before Pharaoh, king of Egypt, and I hardened his heart. ⁶ I am he whom Jannes and Jambres invoked, striving with Moses in Egypt. I am he who fought against Moses with wonders with signs." ⁷ I therefore said to him, "How were you found in the Red Sea?" ⁸ And he answered: "In the exodus of the sons of Israel I hardened the heart of Pharaoh. ⁹ And I excited his heart and that of his ministers. And I caused them to pursue after the sons of Israel. ¹⁰ And Pharaoh followed with [me] and all the Egyptians. Then I was present there, and we followed together. ¹¹ And we all came up on the Red Sea. And it came to pass when the sons of Israel had crossed over, the water returned and hid all the host of the Egyptians and all their might. ¹² And I remained in the sea, being kept under this pillar. But when Ephippas came, being sent by you, shut up in the vessel of a flask, he fetched me up

to you." ¹³ I, therefore, Solomon, having heard this, glorified God and adjured the demons not to disobey me, but to remain supporting the pillar. ¹⁴ And they both swore, saying, "[As] the LORD your God lives, we will not let go of this pillar until the world's end. But on whatever day this stone falls, then will be the end of the world."

CHAPTER 28

¹ And I, Solomon, glorified God, and adorned the temple of the LORD with all pleasant appearance. ² And I was glad in spirit in my kingdom, and there was peace in my days. And I took wives of my own from every land, who were numberless. ³ And I marched against the Jebusites, and there I saw a Jebusite man's daughter, and fell violently in love with her, and desired to take her to be [my] wife along with my other wives. ⁴ And I said to their priests, "Give me the Shunammite to be [my] wife." ⁵ But the priests of Moloch said to me, "If you love this maiden, go in and worship our gods, the great god Remphan and the god called Moloch." ⁶ I, therefore, was in fear of the glory of God, and did not follow to worship. ⁷ And I said to them, "I will not worship a strange god. What is this proposal, that you compel me to do so much?" But they said, ". . . by our fathers." ⁸ And when I answered that I would on no account worship strange gods, they told the maiden not to sleep with me until I complied and sacrificed to the gods. ⁹ I then was moved, but crafty Eros brought and laid by her five grasshoppers for me, saying, "Take these grasshoppers, and crush them together in the name of the god Moloch; and then I will sleep with you." ¹⁰ And I actually did this. And at once the Spirit of God departed from me, and I became weak as well as foolish in my words. ¹¹ And after that I was obliged by her to build a temple of idols to Ba'al, and to Rapha, and to Moloch, and to the other idols. ¹² I then, wretch that I am, followed her advice, and the glory of God yet departed from me, and my spirit was darkened, and I became the sport of idols and demons. ¹³ For this reason I wrote out this Testament, that you who get possession of it may pity, and attend to the last things, and not to the first, ¹⁴ so that you may find grace forever and ever. Amen.

PSALMS OF SOLOMON

The apocryphal psalms attributed to Solomon were likely written in the 1st or 2nd centuries BC. While they do not belong to any current canon, they have been found in copies of the Peshitta and Septuagint.

PSALM 1

[1] I cried to the LORD when I was in distress, || To God when sinners assailed. [2] Suddenly the alarm of war was heard before me; [I said], "He will listen to me, for I am full of righteousness." [3] I thought in my heart that I was full of righteousness, || Because I was well off and had become rich in children. [4] Their wealth spread to the whole earth, || And their glory to the end of the earth. [5] They were exalted to the stars; They said they would never fall. [6] But they became insolent in their prosperity, || And they were without understanding, [7] Their sins were in secret, || And even I had no knowledge [of them]. [8] Their transgressions [went] beyond those of the heathen before them; They utterly polluted the holy things of the LORD.

PSALM 2

[1] A PSALM OF SOLOMON. CONCERNING JERUSALEM. When the sinner waxed proud, with a battering-ram he cast down fortified walls, || And You did not restrain [him]. [2] Alien nations ascended Your altar, || They trampled [it] proudly with their sandals, [3] Because the sons of Jerusalem had defiled the holy things of the LORD, || [And] had profaned with iniquities the offerings of God. [4] Therefore He said, "Cast them far from Me"; [5] It was set at nothing before God, || It was utterly dishonored; [6] The sons and the daughters were in grievous captivity, || Their neck [was] sealed, [it was] branded among the nations. [7] He has done to them according to their sins, || For He has left them in the hands of them that prevailed. [8] He has turned His face away from pitying them—Young, and old, and their children together; [9] For they had done evil, one and all, in not listening. [10] And the heavens were angry, || And the earth abhorred them; [11] For no man on it had done what they did, [12] And the earth recognized all Your righteous judgments, O God. [13] They set the sons of Jerusalem to be mocked at in return for [the] harlots in her; Every wayfarer entered in in the full light of day. [14] They made a mockery with their transgressions, as they themselves were frequent to do; In the full light of day they revealed their iniquities. [15] And the daughters of Jerusalem were defiled in accordance with Your judgment, || Because they had defiled themselves with unnatural intercourse. I am pained in my bowels and my inward parts for these things. [16] And yet, I will justify You, O God, in uprightness of heart, || For in Your judgments is Your righteousness [displayed], O God. [17] For You have rendered to the sinners according to their deeds, || Yes, according to their sins, which were very wicked. [18] You have uncovered their sins, that Your judgment might be manifest; [19] You have wiped out their memorial from the earth. God is a righteous judge, || And He is no respecter of persons. [20] For the nations reproached Jerusalem, trampling it down; Her beauty was dragged down from the throne of glory. [21] She girded on sackcloth instead of beautiful raiment, || A rope [was] around her head instead of a crown. [22] She put off the glorious diadem which God had set on her, || In dishonor her beauty was cast on the ground. [23] And I saw and entreated the LORD and said, || "Long enough, O LORD, has Your hand been heavy on Israel in bringing the nations on [them]. [24] For they have made sport unsparingly in wrath and fierce anger; [25] And they will make an utter end, unless You, O LORD, rebuke them in Your wrath. [26] For they have not done it in zeal, but in lust of soul, || Pouring out their wrath on us with a view to plunder. [27] Do not delay, O God, to repay them on [their] heads, || To turn the pride of the dragon into dishonor." [28] And I did not have long to wait before God showed me the insolent one || Slain on the mountains of Egypt, || Esteemed of less account than the least on land and sea; [29] His body, [too,] borne here and there on the billows with much insolence, || With none to bury [him], because He had rejected him with dishonor. [30] He did not consider that he was man, || And did not consider the latter end; [31] He said, "I will be lord of land and sea"; And he did not recognize that it is God who is great, || Mighty in His great strength. [32] He is King over the heavens, || And judges kings and kingdoms, [33] Who sets me up in glory, || And brings down the proud to continuous destruction in dishonor, || Because they did not know Him. [34] And now behold, you princes of the earth, || The judgment of the LORD, || For [He is] a great and righteous King, || Judging [all] that is under Heaven. [35] Bless God, you that fear the LORD with wisdom, || For the mercy of the LORD will be on them that fear Him, in the Judgment, [36] So that He will distinguish between the righteous and the sinner, || [And] repay the sinners forever according to their deeds, [37] And have mercy on the righteous, [delivering him] from the affliction of the sinner, || And repaying the sinner for what he has done to the righteous. [38] For the LORD is good to them that call on Him in patience, || Doing according to His mercy to His pious ones, || Establishing [them] at all times before Him in strength. [39] Blessed is the LORD forever before His servants.

PSALMS OF SOLOMON

PSALM 3

[1] A PSALM OF SOLOMON. CONCERNING THE RIGHTEOUS. Why do you sleep, O my soul, || And do not bless the LORD? [2] Sing a new song, || To God who is worthy to be praised. Sing and be wakeful against His awaking, || For a psalm [sung] to God from a glad heart is good. [3] The righteous remember the LORD at all times, || With thanksgiving and declaration of the righteousness of the LORD's judgments. [4] The righteous does not despise the disciplining of the LORD; His will is always before the LORD. [5] The righteous stumbles and holds the LORD righteous: He falls and looks out for what God will do to him; [6] He seeks out from where his deliverance will come. [7] The steadfastness of the righteous is from God their deliverer; There does not lodge in the house of the righteous sin on sin. [8] The righteous continually searches his house, || To utterly remove [all] iniquity [done] by him in error. [9] He makes atonement for [sins of] ignorance by fasting and afflicting his soul, || [10] And the LORD counts guiltless every pious man and his house. [11] The sinner stumbles and curses his life, || The day when he was begotten, and his mother's travail. [12] He adds sins to sins, while he lives; He falls—truly grievous is his fall—and rises no longer. [13] The destruction of the sinner is forever, || And he will not be remembered when the righteous is visited. [14] This is the portion of sinners forever. [15] But they that fear the LORD will rise to continuous life, || And their life [will be] in the light of the LORD, and will come to an end no more.

PSALM 4

[1] A CONVERSATION OF SOLOMON WITH THE MEN-PLEASERS. Why do you sit, O profane [man], in the council of the pious, || Seeing that your heart is far removed from the LORD, || Provoking the God of Israel with transgressions? [2] Extravagant in speech, extravagant in outward seeming beyond all [men], || Is he that is severe of speech in condemning sinners in judgment. [3] And his hand is first on him as [though he acted] in zeal, || And [yet] he is himself guilty in respect of manifold sins and of wantonness. [4] His eyes are on every woman without distinction; His tongue lies when he makes contract with an oath. [5] By night and in secret he sins as though unseen, || With his eyes he talks to every woman of evil compacts. [6] He is swift to enter every house with cheerfulness as though guileless. [7] Let God remove those that live in hypocrisy in the company of the pious, || [Even] the life of such a one with corruption of his flesh and destitution. [8] Let God reveal the deeds of the men-pleasers, || The deeds of such a one with laughter and derision; [9] That the pious may count righteous the judgment of their God, || When sinners are removed from before the righteous, [10] [Even the] man-pleaser who utters law guilefully. [11] And their eyes [are fixed] on any man's house that is [still] secure, || That they

may, like [the] Serpent, destroy the wisdom of . . . with words of transgressors, [12] His words are deceitful that [he] may accomplish [his] wicked desire. [13] He never ceases from scattering [families] as though [they were] orphans, || Yes, he lays waste a house on account of [his] lawless desire. [14] He deceives with words, [saying,] "There is none that sees, or judges." [15] He fills one [house] with lawlessness, || And [then] his eyes [are fixed] on the next house, || To destroy it with words that give wing to [desire]. [Yet] with all these his soul, like Sheol, is not satisfied. [16] Let his portion, O LORD, be dishonored before You; Let him go forth groaning and come home cursed. [17] Let his life be [spent] in anguish, and destitution, and want, O LORD; Let his sleep be [beset] with pains and his awaking with perplexities. [18] Let sleep be withdrawn from his eyelids at night; Let him fail dishonorably in every work of his hands. [19] Let him come home empty-handed to his house, || And his house be void of everything with which he could satisfy his appetite. [20] [Let] his old age [be spent] in childless loneliness until his removal. [21] Let the flesh of the men-pleasers be torn by wild beasts, || And [let] the bones of the lawless [lie] dishonored in the sight of the sun. [22] Let ravens peck out the eyes of the hypocrites. [23] For they have laid waste many houses of men, in dishonor, || And scattered [them] in [their] lust; [24] And they have not remembered God, || Nor feared God in all these things; [25] But they have provoked God's anger and vexed Him. May He remove them from off the earth, || Because with deceit they deceived the souls of the flawless. [26] Blessed are they that fear the LORD in their flawlessness; [27] The LORD will deliver them from guileful men and sinners, || And deliver us from every stumbling-block of the lawless [men]. [28] Let God destroy them that insolently work all unrighteousness, || For a great and mighty judge is the LORD our God in righteousness. [29] Let Your mercy, O LORD, be on all them that love You.

PSALM 5

[1] A PSALM OF SOLOMON. O LORD God, I will praise Your Name with joy, || In the midst of them that know Your righteous judgments. [2] For You are good and merciful, the refuge of the poor; [3] When I cry to You, do not silently disregard me. [4] For no man takes spoil from a mighty man. [5] Who, then, can take anything of all that You have made, except You Yourself give? [6] For man and his portion [lie] before You in the balance; He cannot add to, so as to enlarge, what has been prescribed by You. [7] O God, when we are in distress, we call on You for help, || And You do not turn back our petition, for You are our God. [8] Do not cause Your hand to be heavy on us, || Lest through necessity we sin. [9] Even though You do not restore us, we will not keep away; But we will come to You. [10] For if I hunger, I will cry to You, O God; And You will give to me. [11] You nourish birds and fish, || In that

You give rain to the plains that green grass may spring up, || To prepare fodder in the plain for every living thing; ¹²And if they hunger, they lift up their face to You. ¹³You nourish kings, and rulers, and peoples, O God; And who is the help of the poor and needy, if not You, O LORD? ¹⁴And You will listen— for who is good and gentle but You— Making glad the soul of the humble by opening Your hand in mercy. ¹⁵Man's goodness is [bestowed] grudgingly and . . . And if he repeats [it] without murmuring, even that is marvelous. ¹⁶But Your gift is great in goodness and wealth, || And he whose hope is [set] on You will have no lack of gifts. ¹⁷Your mercy is on the whole earth, O LORD, in goodness. ¹⁸Happy is he whom God remembers in [granting to him] a due sufficiency; ¹⁹If a man abounds over much, he sins. ²⁰Sufficient are moderate means with righteousness, || And hereby the blessing of the LORD [becomes] abundance with righteousness. ²¹They that fear the LORD rejoice in good [gifts], || And Your goodness is on Israel in Your kingdom. Blessed is the glory of the LORD, for He is our King.

PSALM 6

¹IN HOPE. OF SOLOMON. Happy is the man whose heart is fixed to call on the Name of the LORD; ²When he remembers the Name of the LORD, he will be saved. ³His ways are made even by the LORD, || And the works of his hands are preserved by the LORD his God. ⁴At what he sees in his bad dreams, his soul will not be troubled; ⁵When he passes through rivers and the tossing of the seas, he will not be dismayed. ⁶He arises from his sleep, and blesses the Name of the LORD: ⁷When his heart is at peace, he sings to the Name of his God, || And he entreats the LORD for all his house. ⁸And the LORD hears the prayer of everyone that fears God, || And the LORD accomplishes every request of the soul that hopes for Him. ⁹Blessed is the LORD, who shows mercy to those who love Him in sincerity.

PSALM 7

¹OF SOLOMON. OF TURNING. Do not make Your dwelling far from us, O God; Lest they assail us that hate us without cause. ²For You have rejected them, O God; Do not let their foot trample on Your holy inheritance. ³Discipline us Yourself in Your good pleasure; But do not give [us] up to the nations; ⁴For, if You send pestilence, || You Yourself give it charge concerning us; For You are merciful, || And will not be angry to the point of consuming us. ⁵While Your Name dwells in our midst, we will find mercy; ⁶And the nations will not prevail against us. For You are our shield, || ⁷And when we call on You, You listen to us; ⁸For You will pity the seed of Israel forever || And You will not reject [them], || But we [will be] under Your yoke forever, || And [under] the rod of Your disciplining. ⁹You will establish us in the time

that You help us, || Showing mercy to the house of Jacob on the day wherein You promised [to help them].

PSALM 8

¹OF SOLOMON. OF THE CHIEF MUSICIAN. My ear has heard distress and the sound of war; The sound of a trumpet announcing slaughter and calamity, ²The sound of many people as of an exceedingly high wind, || As a tempest with mighty fire sweeping through the Negeb. ³And I said in my heart, "Surely God judges us"; ⁴I hear a sound [moving] toward Jerusalem, the holy city. ⁵My loins were broken at what I heard, my knees tottered: ⁶My heart was afraid, my bones were dismayed like flax. ⁷I said, "They establish their ways in righteousness." I thought on the judgments of God since the creation of the heavens and earth; I held God righteous in His judgments which have been from of old. ⁸God laid bare their sins in the full light of day; All the earth came to know the righteous judgments of God. ⁹In secret places underground their iniquities [were committed] to provoke [Him] to anger; ¹⁰They worked confusion, son with mother and father with daughter; ¹¹They committed adultery, every man with his neighbor's wife. They concluded covenants with one another with an oath touching these things; ¹²They plundered the sanctuary of God, as though there was no avenger. ¹³They trod the altar of the LORD, [coming straight] from all manner of uncleanness; And with menstrual blood they defiled the sacrifices, as [though these were] common flesh. ¹⁴They left no sin undone, wherein they did not surpass the heathen. ¹⁵Therefore God mingled for them a spirit of wandering; And gave them a cup of undiluted wine to drink, that they might become drunken. ¹⁶He brought him that is from the end of the earth, that strikes mightily; ¹⁷He decreed war against Jerusalem, and against her land. ¹⁸The princes of the land went to meet him with joy; They said to him, "Blessed is your way! Come, enter in with peace." ¹⁹They made the rough ways even, before his entering in; They opened the gates to Jerusalem, they crowned its walls. ²⁰As a father [enters] the house of his sons, [so] he entered [Jerusalem] in peace; He established his feet [there] in great safety. ²¹He captured her fortresses and the wall of Jerusalem; ²²For God Himself led him in safety, while they wandered. ²³He destroyed their princes and everyone wise in counsel; He poured out the blood of the inhabitants of Jerusalem like the water of uncleanness. ²⁴He led away their sons and daughters, whom they had begotten in defilement. ²⁵They did according to their uncleanness, even as their fathers [had done]: ²⁶They defiled Jerusalem and the things that had been hallowed to the Name of God. ²⁷[But] God has shown Himself righteous in His judgments on the nations of the earth; ²⁸And the pious [servants] of God are like

innocent lambs in their midst. ²⁹Worthy to be praised is the LORD that judges the whole earth in His righteousness. ³⁰Behold, now, O God, You have shown us Your judgment in Your righteousness; ³¹Our eyes have seen Your judgments, O God. We have justified Your Name that is honored forever; ³²For You are the God of righteousness, judging Israel with disciplining. ³³Turn, O God, Your mercy on us, and have pity on us; ³⁴Gather together the dispersed of Israel, with mercy and goodness; ³⁵For Your faithfulness is with us. And [though] we have stiffened our neck, yet You are our chastener; ³⁶Do not overlook us, O our God, lest the nations swallow us up, as though there were none to deliver. ³⁷But You are our God from the beginning, || And on You is our hope [set], O LORD; ³⁸And we will not depart from You, || For Your judgments on us are good. ³⁹Ours and our children's be Your good pleasure forever; O LORD our Savior, we will never more be moved. ⁴⁰The LORD is worthy to be praised for His judgments with the mouth of His pious ones; And blessed is Israel of the LORD forever.

PSALM 9

¹OF SOLOMON. FOR REBUKE. When Israel was led away captive into a strange land, || When they fell away from the LORD who redeemed them, ²They were cast away from the inheritance, which the LORD had given them. Among every nation [were] the dispersed of Israel according to the word of God, ³That You might be justified, O God, in Your righteousness by reason of our transgressions: ⁴For You are a just judge over all the peoples of the earth. ⁵For from Your knowledge none that does unjustly is hidden, ⁶And the righteous deeds of Your pious ones [are] before You, O LORD, || Where, then, can a man hide himself from Your knowledge, O God? ⁷Our works are subject to our own choice and power || To do right or wrong in the works of our hands; ⁸And in Your righteousness You visitest the sons of men. ⁹He that does righteousness lays up life for himself with the LORD; And he that does wrongly forfeits his life to destruction; ¹⁰For the judgments of the LORD are [given] in righteousness to [every] man and [his] house. To whom are You good, O God, except to them that call on the LORD? ¹²He cleanses a soul from sins when it makes confession, when it makes acknowledgement; ¹³For shame is on us and on our faces on account of all these things. ¹⁴And to whom does He forgive sins, except to them that have sinned? ¹⁵You bless the righteous, and do not reprove them for the sins that they have committed; And Your goodness is on them that sin, when they convert. ¹⁶And now, You are our God, and we the people whom You have loved: Behold and show pity, O God of Israel, for we are Yours; And do not remove Your mercy from us, lest they assail us. ¹⁷For You chose the seed of Abraham before all the nations, || And set Your Name on us, O LORD, ¹⁸And You will not reject [us] forever. You made a covenant with our fathers concerning us; ¹⁹And we hope in You, when our soul turns [to You]. May the mercy of the LORD be on the house of Israel forever and ever.

PSALM 10

¹A HYMN OF SOLOMON. Happy is the man whom the LORD remembers with reproving, || And whom He restrains from the way of evil with strokes, || That he may be cleansed from sin, that it may not be multiplied. ²He that makes his back ready for strokes will be cleansed, || For the LORD is good to them that endure disciplining. ³For He makes straight the ways of the righteous, || And does not pervert [them] by His disciplining. ⁴And the mercy of the LORD [is] on them that love Him in truth, || And the LORD remembers His servants in mercy. ⁵For the testimony [is] in the law of the perpetual covenant, || The testimony of the LORD [is] on the ways of men in [His] visitation. ⁶Just and kind is our LORD in His judgments forever, || And Israel will praise the Name of the LORD in gladness. ⁷And the pious will give thanks in the assembly of the people; And God will have mercy on the poor in the gladness of Israel; ⁸For God is good and merciful forever, || And the assemblies of Israel will glorify the Name of the LORD. May the salvation of the LORD be on the house of Israel to everlasting gladness!

PSALM 11

¹OF SOLOMON. TO EXPECTATION. Blow on the trumpet in Zion to summon [the] saints, ²Cause the voice of him that brings good tidings to be heard in Jerusalem; For God has had pity on Israel in visiting them. ³Stand on the height, O Jerusalem, and behold your children, || From the East and the West, gathered together by the LORD; ⁴From the North they come in the gladness of their God, || From the isles far off God has gathered them. ⁵He has abased high mountains into a plain for them; ⁶The hills fled at their entrance. The woods gave them shelter as they passed by; ⁷Every sweet-smelling tree God caused to spring up for them, || That Israel might pass by in the visitation of the glory of their God. ⁸Put on, O Jerusalem, your glorious garments; Make your holy robe ready; For God has spoken good concerning Israel, forever and ever. ⁹Let the LORD do what He has spoken concerning Israel and Jerusalem; Let the LORD raise up Israel by His glorious Name. May the mercy of the LORD be on Israel forever and ever.

PSALM 12

¹OF SOLOMON. AGAINST THE TONGUE OF TRANSGRESSORS. O LORD, deliver my soul from [the] lawless and wicked man, || From the tongue that is lawless and slanderous, and speaks lies and deceit. ²Manifoldly twisted are the words of the tongue of the wicked man, || Even as among a people a fire that

burns up their beauty. [3]So he delights to fill houses with a lying tongue, || To cut down the trees of gladness which sets transgressors on fire, [4]To involve households in warfare by means of slanderous lips. May God remove far from the innocent the lips of transgressors by [bringing them to] want || And may the bones of slanderers be scattered [far] away from them that fear the LORD! [5]In flaming fire, make the slanderous tongue perish [far] away from the pious! [6]May the LORD preserve the quiet soul that hates the unrighteous; And may the LORD establish the man that follows peace at home. [7]May the salvation of the LORD be on His servant Israel forever; And let the sinners perish together at the presence of the LORD; But let the LORD's pious ones inherit the promises of the LORD.

PSALM 13

[1]A PSALM OF SOLOMON. Comfort for the righteous. The right hand of the LORD has covered me; The right hand of the LORD has spared us. [2]The arm of the LORD has saved us from the sword that passed through, || From famine and the death of sinners. [3]Ghastly beasts ran on them: They tore their flesh with their teeth, || And crushed their bones with their molars, || But the LORD delivered us from all these things. [4]The righteous was troubled on account of his errors, || Lest he should be taken away along with the sinners; [5]For the overthrow of the sinner is terrible; But not one of all these things touches the righteous. For not alike are the disciplining of the righteous [for sins done] in ignorance, || And the overthrow of the sinners. [7]The righteous is disciplined secretly, || Lest the sinner rejoice over the righteous. [8]For He corrects the righteous as a beloved son, || And his discipline is as that of a firstborn. [9]For the LORD spares His pious ones, || And blots out their errors by His disciplining. For the life of the righteous will be forever, [10]But sinners will be taken away into destruction, || And their memorial will be found no longer. [11]But the mercy of the LORD is on the pious, || And His mercy on them that fear Him.

PSALM 14

[1]A HYMN OF SOLOMON. Faithful is the LORD to them that love Him in truth, || To them that endure His disciplining, || To them that walk in the righteousness of His commandments, || In the law which He commanded us that we might live. [2]The pious of the LORD will live by it forever; The Paradise of the LORD, the trees of life, are His pious ones. [3]Their planting is rooted forever; They will not be plucked up all the days of Heaven. For the portion and the inheritance of God is Israel. [4]But not so are the sinners and transgressors, || Who love [the brief] day [spent] in companionship with their sin; Their delight is in fleeting corruption, [5]And they do not remember God. For the ways of men are known before Him at

all times, || And He knows the secrets of the heart before they come to pass. [6]Therefore their inheritance is Sheol and darkness and destruction, || And they will not be found in the day when the righteous obtain mercy; [7]But the pious of the LORD will inherit life in gladness.

PSALM 15

[1]A PSALM OF SOLOMON. WITH A SONG. When I was in distress, I called on the Name of the LORD, || I hoped for the help of the God of Jacob and was saved; [2]For the hope and refuge of the poor are You, O God. [3]For who, O God, is strong except to give thanks to You in truth? [4]And wherein is a man powerful except in giving thanks to Your Name [5]A new psalm with song in gladness of heart, || The fruit of the lips with the well-tuned instrument of the tongue, || The first-fruits of the lips from a pious and righteous heart— [6]He that offers these things will never be shaken by evil; The flame of fire and the wrath against the unrighteous will not touch him [7]When it goes forth from the face of the LORD against sinners, || To destroy all the substance of sinners, [8]For the mark of God is on the righteous that they may be saved. Famine, and sword, and pestilence [will be] far from the righteous, [9]For they will flee away from the pious as men pursued in war; But they will pursue sinners and overtake [them], || And they that do lawlessness will not escape the judgment of God; As by enemies experienced [in war], they will be overtaken, [10]For the mark of destruction is on their forehead. [11]And the inheritance of sinners is destruction and darkness, || And their iniquities will pursue them to Sheol beneath. [12]Their inheritance will not be found of their children, [13]For sins will lay waste the houses of sinners. And sinners will perish forever in the day of the LORD's judgment [14]When God visits the earth with His judgment. [15]But they that fear the LORD will find mercy therein, || And will live by the compassion of their God; But sinners will perish forever.

PSALM 16

[1]A HYMN OF SOLOMON. FOR HELP TO THE PIOUS. When my soul slumbered, [being far] from the LORD, || I had all but slipped down to the pit || When [I was] far from God; [2]My soul had been well nearly poured out to death—Near to the gates of Sheol with the sinner [3]When my soul departed from the LORD God of Israel—Had the LORD not helped me with His everlasting mercy. [4]He pricked me as a horse is pricked, that I might serve Him; My Savior and helper at all times saved me. [5]I will give thanks to You, O God, for You have helped me to [my] salvation, || And have not counted me with sinners to [my] destruction. [6]Do not remove Your mercy from me, O God, || Nor Your memorial from my heart until I die. [7]Rule me, O God, [keeping me back] from wicked sin, || And from every wicked woman that causes the simple to

stumble. [8] And do not let the beauty of a lawless woman deceive me, || Nor anyone that is subject to unprofitable sin. [9] Establish the works of my hands before You, || And preserve my goings in the remembrance of You. [10] Protect my tongue and my lips with words of truth; Put anger and unreasoning wrath far from me. [11] Remove murmuring and impatience in affliction far from me || When, if I sin, You discipline me that I may return [to You]. [12] But support my soul with goodwill and cheerfulness; When You strengthen my soul, what is given [to me] will be sufficient for me. [13] For if You do not give strength, || Who can endure discipline with poverty? [14] When a man is rebuked by means of his corruption, || Your testing [of him] is in his flesh and in the affliction of poverty. [15] If the righteous endures in all these [trials], he will receive mercy from the LORD.

PSALM 17

[1] A PSALM OF SOLOMON. WITH SONG. OF THE KING. O LORD, You are our King forever and ever, || For our soul glories in You, O God. [2] How long are the days of man's life on the earth? As are his days, so is the hope [set] on him. [3] But we hope in God, our deliverer; For the might of our God is forever with mercy, [4] And the kingdom of our God is forever over the nations in judgment. [5] You, O LORD, chose David [to be] king over Israel, || And swore to him touching his seed that never should his kingdom fail before You. [6] But, for our sins, sinners rose up against us; They assailed us and thrust us out; What You had not promised to them, they took away [from us] with violence. [7] They did not glorify Your honorable Name at all; They set a [worldly] monarchy in place of [that which was] their excellency; [8] They laid waste the throne of David in tumultuous arrogance. But You, O God, cast them down and removed their seed from the earth, [9] In that there rose up against them a man that was alien to our race. [10] According to their sins You repaid them, O God, || So that it befell them according to their deeds. [11] God showed them no pity; He sought out their seed and does not let one of them go free. [12] Faithful is the LORD in all His judgments || Which He does on the earth. [13] The lawless one laid waste our land so that none inhabited it, || They destroyed young and old and their children together. [14] In the heat of His anger He sent them away, even to the west, || And [He exposed] the rulers of the land unsparingly to derision. [15] Being an alien the enemy acted proudly, || And his heart was alien from our God. [16] And all things, [whatever he did in] Jerusalem, || As also the nations [in the cities to their gods]. [17] And the children of the covenant in the midst of the mingled peoples [surpassed them in evil]. There was not among them one that worked in the midst of Jerusalem mercy and truth. [18] They that loved the synagogues of the pious fled from them, || As sparrows that fly from their nest. [19] They wandered in deserts that their lives might be saved from harm, || And precious in the eyes of them that lived abroad was any that escaped alive from them. [20] They were scattered over the whole earth by lawless [men]. [21] For the heavens withheld the rain from dropping on the earth, || Springs were stopped perennially out of the deeps [that ran down] from lofty mountains; For there was none among them that worked righteousness and justice; From the chief of them to the least [of them]—all were sinful; [22] The king was a transgressor, and the judge disobedient, and the people sinful. [23] Behold, O LORD, and raise up to them their king, the Son of David, || At the time in which You see, O God, that He may reign over Your servant Israel; [24] And gird Him with strength, that He may shatter unrighteous rulers, [25] And that He may purge Jerusalem from nations that trample [her] down to destruction. [26] Wisely, righteously, He will thrust out sinners from [the] inheritance, || [And] will destroy the pride of the sinner as a potter's vessel. With a rod of iron, He will break in pieces all their substance; [27] He will destroy the godless nations with the word of His mouth; At His rebuke nations will flee before Him, || And He will reprove sinners for the thoughts of their heart. [28] And He will gather together a holy people, whom He will lead in righteousness, || And He will judge the tribes of the people that has been sanctified by the LORD His God. [29] And He will not permit unrighteousness to lodge any more in their midst, || Nor will there dwell with them any man that knows wickedness, [30] For He will know them, that they are all sons of their God. And He shall divide them according to their tribes on the land, [31] And neither sojourner nor alien will sojourn with them any more. He will judge peoples and nations in the wisdom of His righteousness. Selah. [32] And He will have the heathen nations to serve Him under His yoke; And He will glorify the LORD in a place to be seen of all the earth; [33] And He will purge Jerusalem, making it holy as of old: [34] So that nations will come from the ends of the earth to see His glory, || Bringing as gifts her sons who had fainted, [35] And to see the glory of the LORD, with which God has glorified her. And He [will be] a righteous King, taught of God, over them, [36] And there will be no unrighteousness in His days in their midst, || For all will be holy and their King the anointed of the LORD. [37] For He will not put His trust in horse, and rider, and bow, || Nor will He multiply for Himself gold and silver for war, || Nor will He gather confidence from a multitude for the day of battle. [38] The LORD Himself is His King, the hope of him that is mighty through [his] hope in God. All nations [will be] in fear before Him, [39] For He will strike the earth with the word of His mouth forever. [40] He will bless the people of the LORD with wisdom and gladness, [41] And He Himself [will be] pure from sin, so that He may rule a great people. He will rebuke rulers and remove sinners by the might of His word; [42] And [relying] on His God, throughout His days He

will not stumble; For God will make Him mighty by means of [His] Holy Spirit, || And wise by means of the spirit of understanding, with strength and righteousness. [43] And the blessing of the LORD [will be] with Him; He will be strong and not stumble; [44] His hope [will be] in the LORD: who then can prevail against Him? [He will be] mighty in His works, and strong in the fear of God; [45] [He will be] shepherding the flock of the LORD faithfully and righteously, || And will permit none among them to stumble in their pasture. [46] He will lead them all correctly, || And there will be no pride among them that any among them should be oppressed. [47] This [will be] the majesty of the King of Israel whom God knows; He will raise Him up over the house of Israel to correct him. [48] His words [will be] more refined than costly gold, the choicest; In the assemblies He will judge the peoples, the tribes of the sanctified. [49] His words [will be] like the words of the holy ones in the midst of sanctified peoples. [50] Blessed are they that will be in those days, || In that they will see the good fortune of Israel which God will bring to pass in the gathering together of the tribes. [51] May the LORD hasten His mercy on Israel! May He deliver us from the uncleanness of unholy enemies! The LORD Himself is our King forever and ever.

PSALM 18

[1] A PSALM OF SOLOMON. AGAIN OF THE ANOINTED OF THE LORD. LORD, Your mercy is over the works of Your hands forever; Your goodness is over Israel with a rich gift. [2] Your eyes look on them, so that none of them suffers want; [3] Your ears listen to the hopeful prayer of the poor. Your judgments [are executed] on the whole earth in mercy; [4] And Your love [is] toward the seed of Abraham, the sons of Israel. Your discipline is on us as [on] a firstborn, only-begotten son, [5] To turn back the obedient soul from folly [that is worked] in ignorance. [6] May God cleanse Israel against the day of mercy and blessing, || Against the day of choice when He brings back His anointed. [7] Blessed will they be that will be in those days, || In that they will see the goodness of the LORD which He will perform for the generation that is to come, [8] Under the rod of disciplining of the LORD's anointed in the fear of his God, || In the spirit of wisdom and righteousness and strength; [9] That he may direct [every} man in the works of righteousness by the fear of God, || That he may establish them all before the LORD— [10] A good generation [living] in the fear of God in the days of mercy. Selah. [11] Great is our God and glorious, dwelling in the highest, [12] Who has established the lights [of Heaven] in [their] courses for determining seasons from year to year, || And they have not turned aside from the way which He appointed them; [13] In the fear of God [they pursue] their path every day, || From the day God created them and forevermore. [14] And they have not erred since the day He created them. Since the generations of old they have not withdrawn from their path, || Unless God commanded them [to do so] by the command of His servants.

LIVES OF THE PROPHETS

Lives of the Prophets is a record of the lives and deaths of the significant Old Testament-era prophets. At least some of the material is very ancient, from the 1st century AD or earlier. The Apostle Paul may have been familiar with some of these accounts as reflected in the Pauline epistles.

THE NAMES OF THE PROPHETS, AND FROM WHERE THEY WERE, WHERE THEY DIED, AND HOW AND WHERE THEY WERE BURIED.

ISAIAH

[1] He was of Jerusalem. He met his death at the hands of Manasseh, sawn in two, and was buried below the fountain of Rogel, hard by the conduit of the waters which Hezekiah spoiled [for the enemy] by blocking their course. [2] For the prophet's sake God worked the miracle of Siloah; for before his death, in fainting condition he prayed for water, and it was sent to him from this source. Hence it was called Siloah, which means "sent." [3] Also in the time of Hezekiah, before the king made the pools and the reservoirs, at the prayer of Isaiah a little water came forth here, lest the city, at that time besieged by the nations, should be destroyed through lack of water. [4] For the enemies were seeking a drinking place, and as they surrounded the city, they encamped near Siloah. If then the Hebrews came to the pool, water flowed forth; if the nations came, there was none. Hence even to the present day the water issues suddenly, to keep the miracle in mind. [5] Because this was worked through the prayer of Isaiah, the people in remembrance buried his body near the spot, with care and high honor, in order that through his prayers, even after his death, they might continue to have the benefit of the water. Indeed, a revelation had been given to them concerning him. [6] His tomb, however, is near the Tomb of the Kings, behind the Tomb of the Priests on the side toward the south. [7] Solomon constructed the tombs, which had been designed by David, on the east of Zion, where there is an entering road from Gibeon—the town twenty stadia distant from the city. He made a winding construction, its location unsuspected; even to the present day it is unknown to most of the priests, and wholly unknown to the people. [8] There the king kept the gold and the spices from Ethiopia. [9] When Hezekiah showed to the nations the secret of David and Solomon, and defiled the bones of his ancestors, therefore God laid on him the curse, that his descendants should be in servitude to their enemies; and God made him to be childless, from that day.

JEREMIAH

[1] He was of Anathoth, and he died in Taphnes in Egypt, stoned to death by the Jews. [2] He is buried in the place where Pharaoh's palace stood; for the Egyptians held him in honor, because of the benefit which they had received through him. [3] For at his prayer, the serpents which the Egyptians call "ephoth" departed from them; [4] and even at the present day the faithful servants of God pray on that spot, and taking of the dust of the place they heal the bites of serpents. [5] We have been told by the children of Antigonus and Ptolemy, aged men, that Alexander the Macedonian, when he stood at the place where the prophet was buried, and learned of the wonders which he had worked, carried away his bones to Alexandria, placing them around with due ceremony; [6] immediately the whole race of poisonous serpents was driven out of the land. With like purpose he had introduced into Egypt the so-called "serpent fighters." [7] Jeremiah also gave a sign to the priests of Egypt, that their idols would be shaken and their gods made with hands would all collapse, when there should arrive in Egypt a virgin bearing a Child of divine appearance. [8] For what reason even to the present time they honor a virgin mother, and placing a baby in a manger they bow down to it. When Ptolemy the king sought the reason for this, they said to him, "It is a mystery handed down from our fathers, a sign delivered to them by a holy prophet, and we are awaiting its fulfiment." [9] This prophet, before the destruction of the temple, took possession of the Ark of the Law and the things within it, and caused them to be swallowed up in a rocky cliff, and he said to those who were present, [10] "The LORD departed from Sinai into Heaven, and He will again come with might; and this will be for you the sign of His appearance: when all the nations worship a piece of wood." [11] He also said, "No one will bring forth this Ark but Aaron, and the tablets within it no one of the priests or prophets will unfold but Moses the chosen one of God." [12] And in the resurrection the Ark will rise first, and come forth from the rock, and will be placed on Mount Sinai; and all the saints will be assembled to it there, awaiting the LORD and fleeing from the enemy wishing to destroy them. [13] He sealed in the rock with his finger the Name of God, and the writing was as though carved with iron. A cloud then covered the Name; and no one knows the place, nor can the writing be read, to the present day and even to the end. [14] The rock is in the wilderness where the Ark was at first, between the two mountains on which Moses and Aaron are buried, and by night there is a cloud as it were of fire, according to the primal ordinance that the glory of God should never cease

from His law. [15] And God gave the favor of completing this wonder to Jeremiah, so that he might be the associate of Moses, and they are together to this day.

EZEKIEL

[1] He was from the district of Sarira, of the priests; and he died in the land of Chaldea, in the time of the captivity, after uttering many prophecies to those who were in Judea. [2] He was slain by the leader of the Israelite exiles, who had been rebuked by him for his worship of idols; [3] and they buried him in the field of Nahor, in the tomb of Shem and Arphaxad, the ancestors of Abraham. [4] The tomb is a double cave, according to whose plan Abraham also made the tomb of Sarah in Hebron. [5] It is called "double" because it has a winding [stairway] and there is an upper chamber hidden from the main floor, hung in the rock above the ground-level. [6] This prophet gave a sign to the people, that they should pay attention to the River Chebar; [7] when its waters should fail, they were to expect "the sickle of desolation to the ends of the earth"; when it should overflow, the return to Jerusalem. [8] While the saint was dwelling there, many kept coming to him; [9] and on one occasion, when a throng had assembled to him, the Chaldeans feared an uprising and came on them to destroy them. [10] He made the water cease its flow, so that they could flee to the other side, but when the enemy ventured to pursue, they were drowned. [11] Through his prayer he provided for them ample sustenance in fish which came of their own accord to be caught. Many who were at the point of death he cheered with the news of life coming to them from God. [12] When the people were being destroyed by the enemy, he went to the hostile captains and so terrified them with marvels which he worked that they ceased. [13] It was then that he said to the people, "Are we indeed perishing? Is our hope at an end?" And by the vision of the dry bones he persuaded them that there is hope for Israel both now and in the time to come. [14] While he was there, he showed to the people of Israel what was being done in Jerusalem and in the temple. [15] He himself was borne away there, and came to Jerusalem, for a rebuke to the faithless. [16] Also after the manner of Moses he foresaw the fashion of the temple, with its walls and its broad surroundings, as Daniel also declared that it should be built. [17] He pronounced judgment in Babylon on the tribes of Dan and Gad, because they dealt wickedly against the LORD, [18] persecuting those who were keeping the law; and he worked on them this grievous wonder, that their children and all their cattle should be killed by serpents. [19] He also foretold, that because of their sin Israel would not return to its land but would remain in Media, until the end of this evildoing. [20] One of their number was the man who slew Ezekiel, for they opposed him all the days of his life.

DANIEL

[1] He was of the tribe of Judah, of a prominent family in the service of the king; but in his childhood he was carried away from Judea to the land of Chaldea. [2] He was born in Upper Beth-Horon. In his manhood he was chaste, so that the Jews thought he [was] a eunuch. [3] He mourned greatly over the city, and in fasting abstained from every sort of delicious food. He was lean and haggard in the eyes of men, but beautiful in the grace of the Most High. [4] He made great supplication in behalf of Nebuchadnezzar, whose son Belshazzar implored him for aid at the time when the king became a beast of the field, lest he should perish. [5] For his head and foreparts were those of an ox, his legs and hinder parts those of a lion. [6] The meaning of this marvel was revealed to the prophet: the king became a beast because of his self-indulgence and his stubbornness. [7] It is the manner of tyrants that in their youth they come under the yoke of Satan; in their latter years they become wild beasts, snatching, destroying, striking, and slaying. [8] The prophet knew by divine revelation that the king was eating grass like an ox, and that it became for him the food of a human being. [9] Therefore it was that Nebuchadnezzar himself, recovering human reason when digestion was completed, used to weep and implore the LORD, praying forty times each day and night. [10] Then the mind of a dumb animal would [again] take possession of him and he would forget that he had been a human being. [11] His tongue had lost the power of speech; when he understood his condition he wept, and his eyes were like raw flesh from his weeping. [12] There were many who went out from the city to see him; Daniel alone had no wish to see him, but during all the time of his transformation he was in prayer for him. [13] He declared that the king would be restored to human form, but they did not believe him. [14] Daniel caused the seven years to become seven months. [15] The mystery of the seven times was fulfilled on the king, for in seven months he was restored, and in the [remaining] six years and five months he was doing penance to the LORD and confessing his wickedness. When his sin had been forgiven, the kingdom was given back to him. [16] He ate neither bread nor flesh in the time of his conversion, for Daniel had bid him to eat pulse and greens while appeasing the LORD. [17] The king named the prophet Belshazzar because he wished to make him a joint heir with his children, [18] but the holy man said, "Far be it from me to forsake the heritage of my fathers and join in the inheritances of the uncircumcised." [19] He also did for the other Persian kings many wonderful things which were not written down. [20] He died there, and was buried with great honor, by himself, in the royal grave. [21] He appointed a sign in the mountains which are above Babylon: WHEN THE MOUNTAIN ON THE NORTH WILL SMOKE, THE END OF BABYLON WILL COME; WHEN IT WILL BURN AS

WITH FIRE, THE END OF ALL THE EARTH WILL BE AT HAND. IF THE MOUNTAIN ON THE SOUTH WILL FLOW WITH WATER, ISRAEL WILL RETURN TO ITS LAND; IF IT WILL RUN BLOOD, IT PORTENDS A SLAUGHTER BROUGHT BY SATAN ON ALL THE EARTH. ²² And the holy prophet slept in peace.

HOSEA
¹ He was from Belemoth, of the tribe of Issachar, and he was buried in peace, in his own land. ² He gave a sign that the LORD would come to the earth when the oak tree which is in Shiloh should of its own accord be divided and become twelve oaks.

MICAH
¹ He was of the tribe of Ephraim. Having given much trouble to King Ahab, he was killed, thrown from a cliff, by Ahab's son Joram, because he rebuked him for the wickedness of his fathers. ² He was given solitary burial in his own land, near the burying place of the giants.

AMOS
¹ He was from Tekoa. Amaziah [the priest of Bethel] had often beaten him, and at last Amaziah's son killed him with a cudgel, striking him on the temple. ² While still living he made his way to his land, and after some days died and was buried there.

JOEL
¹ He was from the territory of Reuben, of the field of Beth-Meon. He died in peace and was buried there.

OBADIAH
¹ He was from the region of Shechem, of the field of Beth-Hakkerem. ² He was a pupil of Elijah, and having done much in his service he was saved from death by him. ³ He was that third captain of fifty whom Elijah spared, and went down with him to Ahaziah. ⁴ Afterward, leaving the service of the king he became a prophet, and on his death he was buried with his fathers.

JONAH
¹ He was from the district of Kiriath-Maon, near the nation city of Azotus on the sea. ² After he had been cast on shore by the whale and had made his journey to Nineveh, on his return he did not stay in his own land, but took his mother and settled in Tyre, a country of foreign peoples. ³ For he said, "In this way I will take away my reproach, that I prophesied falsely against the great city Nineveh." ⁴ Elijah was at that time rebuking the house of Ahab, and having called a famine on the land he fled. Coming to the region of Tyre he found the widow and her son, for he himself could not lodge with the uncircumcised. ⁵ He brought her a blessing; and when her child died, God raised him from the dead through Elijah, for he wished to show him that it is not possible to flee from God. ⁶ After the famine was over, Jonah came into the land of Judea. On the way there his mother died, and he buried her beside the oak of Deborah. ⁷ Thereafter having settled in the land of Seir, he died there and was buried in the tomb of the Kenizzite, the first who became judge in the days when there was no king. ⁸ He gave a sign to Jerusalem and to all the land: When they should see a stone crying aloud in distress, the end would be at hand; and when they should see all the nations gathered in Jerusalem, the city would be razed to its foundations.

NAHUM
¹ He was of Elkosh, on the other side of the mountains toward Beth-Gabrin, of the tribe of Simeon. ² This prophet after the time of Jonah gave a sign to Nineveh, that it would be destroyed by fresh waters and by underground fire; and indeed, this came to pass. ³ For the lake which surrounded the city overwhelmed it in an earthquake, and fire coming from the desert burned its upper portion. ⁴ He died in peace and was buried in his land.

HABAKKUK
¹ He was from the tribe of Simeon, of the field of Beth-Zechariah. ² Before the captivity he had a vision of the destruction of Jerusalem, and he grieved exceedingly. ³ When Nebuchadnezzar came against Jerusalem, he fled to Ostracina [in Egypt], and then sojourned in the land of Ishmael. ⁴ When the Chaldeans returned [to their country], and all those who were left in Jerusalem went down to Egypt, he settled again in his own land. ⁵ He was accustomed to carry food to the reapers of the harvest in his field; ⁶ and one day, as he received the food, he announced to his family: "I am off for a far country, but will return immediately; if I should delay, carry out the food to the reapers." ⁷ Finding himself immediately in Babylon, and having given Daniel his meal, he stood by the reapers as they ate; and he told no one what had happened. ⁸ He had knowledge that the people would soon come back from Babylon. ⁹ Two years before the return he died and was buried alone in his own field. ¹⁰ He gave a sign to the people in Judea, that they would see in the temple a light shining, and thus they would know the glory of the sanctuary. ¹¹ Concerning the end of the temple, he foretold that it would be brought to pass by a western nation. ¹² Then, he said, the veil of the inner sanctuary will be torn to pieces, and the capitals of the two pillars will be taken away, ¹³ and no one will know where they are; but they will be carried away by messengers into the wilderness where in the beginning the Tent of Witness was pitched. ¹⁴ In the end, the presence of the LORD will be made known by

them, for they will give light to those who are pursued by the Serpent in darkness as at the beginning.

ZEPHANIAH

[1] He was of the tribe of Simeon, of the field of Sabaratha. [2] He prophesied concerning the city, also concerning the end of the nations and the confounding of the wicked. [3] When he died, he was buried in his own field.

HAGGAI

[1] Probably as a youth he came from Babylon to Jerusalem, and he had prophesied publicly in regard to the return of the people. [2] He witnessed the building of the temple in part. On his death he was buried near the tomb of the priests, honored as though one of their number.

ZECHARIAH SON OF IDDO

[1] He came from Chaldea when already advanced in age. While there, he often prophesied to the people, and did wonders in proof of his authority. [2] He foretold to Jozadak that he would beget a son who would serve as priest in Jerusalem; [3] he also congratulated Shealtiel on the birth of a son and gave him the name Zerubbabel. [4] In the time of Cyrus he gave the king a sign of victory and foretold the service which he was destined to perform for Jerusalem, and he praised him greatly. [5] His prophecies uttered in Jerusalem had to do with the end of the nations, with Israel and the temple, with the laziness of prophets and priests, and with a double judgment. [6] After reaching great age he was taken sick, and dying, was buried beside Haggai.

MALACHI

[1] He was born in Sopha, after the return from the exile. [2] Even in his boyhood he lived a blameless life, and since all the people paid him honor for his piety and his mildness, they called him "Malachi"; he was also fair to look on. [3] Moreover, whatever things he uttered in prophecy were repeated on that same day by a messenger of God who appeared, as had happened in the days when there was no king in Israel, as is written in the scroll of Judges. [4] While yet in his youth, he was joined to his fathers in his own field.

NATHAN

[1] He, David's prophet, was from Gibeon, of a Hivite clan, and it was he who taught the king the Law of the LORD. [2] He foresaw David's sin with Bathsheba, and set out in haste to warn him, but Belial thwarted his attempt. He found the naked body of a man who had been slain lying by the road; [3] and while he was detained by this duty, he knew that in that night the king had committed the sin; [4] so he turned back to Gibeon in sorrow. Then when David caused the death of Bathsheba's husband, the LORD sent Nathan to convict him. [5] He lived to an advanced old age, and when he died, he was buried in his own land.

AHIJAH

[1] He was from Shiloh, the city of Eli, where the Dwelling Place stood in days of old. [2] He declared of Solomon that he would provoke the LORD to anger. [3] He also rebuked Jeroboam, because he dealt treacherously with the LORD, and he had a vision of two bullocks trampling on the people and charging on the priests. [4] He foretold to Solomon that his wives would bring disgrace on him and all his house. [5] On his death he was buried beside the oak of Shiloh.

JOED

[1] He was of the district of Samarim. He was that prophet whom the lion attacked and slew, when he had rebuked Jeroboam concerning the bullocks— [2] he who was buried in Bethel beside the false prophet who led him astray.

AZARIAH

[1] He was from Subatha, the prophet who turned away from Judah the captivity that befell Israel. [2] His burial was in his own field.

ZECHARIAH SON OF JEHOIADA

[1] He was of Jerusalem, the son of Jehoiada the priest, the prophet whom Joash king of Judah slew beside the altar, whose blood the house of David shed within the sanctuary, in the court. The priests buried him beside his father. [2] From that time on there were portentous appearances in the temple, and the priests could see no vision of messengers of God, nor give forth oracles from the inner sanctuary; nor were they able to inquire with the ephod, nor to give answer to the people by Lights and Perfections, as in former time.

ELIJAH

[1] He was a Tishbite, from the land of the Arabs, of the family of Aaron, residing in Gilead because Tishbi had been assigned to the priests. [2] At the time of his birth his father, Shobach, saw how certain men of shining white appearance addressed the baby, and that they wrapped him in swaddling clothes of fire and gave him a flame of fire to eat. [3] When he went and reported this in Jerusalem, the oracle gave answer: "Do not fear; for his dwelling will be light, and his word revelation, and he will judge Israel with sword and with fire."

ELISHA

[1] He was from Abel-Meholah, of the territory of Reuben. [2] When he was born in Gilgal, a marvelous thing happened: the golden calf bellowed so loudly that the shrill sound was heard in Jerusalem; [3] and the

priest announced by Lights and Perfections that a prophet had been born to Israel who should destroy their graven and molten idols. [4]On his death he was buried in Samaria.

WORDS OF GAD THE SEER

The Words of Gad the Seer is a record missing from the biblical canon but mentioned in 1 Chronicles 29:29. Gad was a prophet who operated contemporaneously with King David and the prophet Nathan (1 Sam. 22:5). The translation here provided is from a likely pseudepigraphic book by the same title, extant in the form of a manuscript from the Cochin Jews of India. While the extant manuscript shows features of medieval Kabbalistic thought, recent scholarship suggests the work, in its primal form, originated in the 1st or 2nd century AD, perhaps based on even older material; and the work is clearly Messianic in nature, pointing to the person and work of Christ, even His substitutionary sacrifice and reign (Ch. 1). Chapter 2 is an excoriating rebuke of the replacement theology and self-righteousness of Rome. The rest of the book is a collection of narratives involving King David and his son Solomon. There are also several psalms.

CHAPTER 1

[1] In the thirty-first year of King David's reign in Jerusalem, which is the thirty-eighth year of David's reign, the word of the LORD came to Gad the Seer in the month of Iyar, near the stream of the Kidron Valley, saying, [2] "Thus says the LORD: Go, be courageous, and stand in the midst of the stream, and cry with a great voice: Tarry and hasten, tarry and hasten, tarry and hasten! For there is still a vision for the son of Jesse. [3] And during the cry, face the Eastern Gate on the east side of the city, and stretch forth your hands toward heaven." [4] And I did exactly what I had been commanded to do. [5] And it came to pass when I finished crying out, I opened my eyes and saw a yoke of oxen, led by a donkey and a camel, coming up from the Brook of Kidron, the donkey on the right side of the yoke and the camel on the left. [6] And a great voice like the roll of thunder was following them, crying with a bitter voice: [7] "Seer, seer, seer! These are four mixtures that confuse the people of the LORD. [8] For the impure and the pure have been mixed, and then impurity took control over purity; a mixture from Seir [(Edom)] to rule over them, [9] to increase power over, and betray, a righteous doer, [10] to destroy holiness, to crown wickedness, to set up impure matters in the guise of purity." [11] And after the voice, a great shaking occurred that shook over the impurity and blew the donkey and the camel into the moon with a stormy wind. [12] And the moon was opened and looked like a bow, a semicircle, and both her points reached toward the ground. [13] And behold, the sun came out of heaven in the shape of a man, with a crown on his head, carrying a Lamb over his right shoulder, despised and rejected. [14] And on the crown on his head three shepherds are seen, shackled with twelve shackles, [15] and these shackles were of gold, plated with silver. And the voice of the Lamb was heard, great and dreadful like the voice of a lion roaring over his prey: "Woe to Me! Woe to Me! Woe to Me! My image has been diminished, || My refuge has been lost, || My lot and destiny has turned Me over to My spoilers, || And I was defiled until evening by the touch of impurity." [16] And it came to pass when the voice of the Lamb ceased speaking, behold, a Man dressed in linen came with three vine-branches and twelve palms in His hand. [17] And He took the Lamb from the hand of the sun and put the crown on His head, and the vine-branches and palms on His heart. [18] And the Man, dressed in linen, cried like a ram's horn, saying, "What are you doing here, impurity, and how did you get here, impurity, [19] that you have carved yourself a place to combine impurity with My covenant that I have set with the vine-branches and palms?" [20] And I heard the Lamb's Shepherd saying, "There is a place with Me for the pure, but not for the impure, for I am a holy God, and I do not want the impure, I only want the pure; [21] even though I created them both, and My eyes are equally on them both. [22] But there is an advantage to the abundance of purity over the abundance of impurity, just like there is an advantage of a man over a shadow. [23] For the shadow does not exist without man, and only by the man's existence is the shadow given to the tired and exhausted; this applies in the same way to the pure and impure. [24] For all gates of intelligence are turned around since the death of the eight branches of the vine. [25] As is found in words of righteousness in the true scroll, but because of the wanderings of the sheep, their rest, and divisions, [26] intelligence is stopped up until I do greatly in keeping grace." [27] I saw that impurity was driven from the moon and was given over to a consuming wrath, ground into fine dust, and blown away by the daily wind. [28] And the day burns as a furnace to remove impurity and to erase the transgressions. [29] And the Lamb was put on the moon forever and ever. [30] And the Lamb took from the pure the impurity that had been mixed with them and brought it as a peace-offering sacrifice on the altar before God Almighty, zealous LORD of Hosts. [31] And I heard those singing the song of the Lamb, saying, [32] "I will give thanks to You, O LORD, || For though You were angry with me, You forgave. [33] For the LORD is my strength and song, || And He has become my Redeemer. [34] I will sing to the LORD, || For He is highly exalted; He had thrown the horse and his rider into the Sea of Reeds. [35] Arise, intelligence; Arise, power; Arise, kingship; [36] Arise, majesty and glory;

Arise help of the LORD. [37] For God has saved one who had taken away || And obliterated the impurity from the earth. [38] He fought my fight || And brought into the light my righteousness by His help. [39] My help comes from the Lord || Who made heaven and earth. [40] Truly, who is like You, || Glorious in holiness, but not in impurity? [41] For You are great over all; Raised over all; You spoke and acted. [42] For You declared the end from the beginning, || And You sealed everything by Your words || And turned my heart and convicted me. [43] For Your seal is on me, my Lord, || And these are three vine-branches and twelve palms that are on my heart. [44] You glorified me, || You erased the vanity of fearing man, || And You gave me a pure heart forever. [45] For that I will praise You at all times, || And thank You among the nations, || For You have greatly redeemed me for my king || And showed favor to the Chosen One, David's seed, || Forever and ever." [46] And I heard a voice crying from Heaven, saying, [47] "You are My Son, You are My firstborn, You are My first-fruits. [48] Have I not brought You up from the Brook of Egypt wholeheartedly to be My daily delight? [49] But You have given My gifts and dressed up the impure with the pure, and that is why all these things have happened to You. [50] And who is like to You among all the creatures on earth? For they lived in Your shadow and by Your wounds they were healed. [51] For consider well that which is before You. [52] Because You have fulfilled the words of the Shepherd all the days You have been in the sun and You did not leave them; therefore, all this honor will be Yours." [53] And I, Gad, son of Ahimelech of the Jabez family, of the tribe of Judah, son of Israel, was amazed by the vision and could not settle my spirit. [54] And the One dressed in linen came down to me and touched me, saying, "Write these words and seal them with the seal of truth, for YHWH is My Name, and with My Name you will bless the whole house of Israel, for they are of a true seed. [55] In a little while you will go, and be quietly gathered to your fathers, but at the end of days you will see with your own eyes all these things, not as a vision, but in reality. [56] For in those days they will not be called Jacob, but Israel; for no iniquity will be found in their remnant, for they will entirely belong to the LORD. [57] And these words will restore your life and spirit. And this will be the sign to you: when you enter the town, you will find My servant David while he is reading these words from the Scroll of [the] Covenant: [58] And yet for all that, when they are in the land of their enemies, I will not reject them, neither will I abhor them, to utterly destroy them, and to break My covenant with them; for I am the LORD their God. [59] And you will tell him about the scene you have just seen; and when he sees you, he will be glad in his heart." [60] And it came to pass, when I came to the house of David, the man of God, I found him as the One dressed in linen had said, and I told him of all my visions. [61] Then David spoke the words of this song to the LORD, saying, "I love You, O LORD, my strength." [62] And to me he said, "The LORD has blessed you and has not removed His covenant from you, for He is true, and His word is true, and His seal is true."

CHAPTER 2

[1] After these true things, I had a vision from God, saying, [2] "Set your face eastward, northward, southward, and westward. [3] And whistle with your mouth as a bird whistles to its young, and say, Four corners of the earth, listen to the word of the LORD! [4] Thus says the LORD, who sits and dwells over the cherubim: Give, give, give, take out, take out, take out My seed that I have sown in you, for the time for the seed has come. [5] For yet a little while I will collect My seed on My threshing-floor. [6] And the threshing-floor will be holy; an impure seed will not be found there. [7] Prior to those days My seed was mixed with lentils, and barley, and fitches, beans, and gourds. [8] And in the end of days the sower will be true, and the seed will be true, and from the seed all the land will be blessed. [9] Be joyful and glad, remnant of Judah and rejected of Israel, for salvation is with the LORD. [10] As you will be a curse and blasphemy to all the families of the earth, so you will be a blessing and grace forever. [11] At that time no cursed or unholy people will be found among you, [12] for everyone will join you in the covenant, the Law, testimonies, statutes, and ordinances. [13] And you and they will have one God, one covenant, one law, one language, for all will speak in the language of Hebrew, the holy language. [14] Blessed are you, O Israel, who is like to you? A people saved by the LORD, for He will go before you to fight your wars with your enemies. [15] Woe to you, O Edom, that sits in the land of Kittim in the north of the sea. [16] For your destroyers will emerge from a terrible nation. They will not even leave you a remnant. [17] For you have said: I sit on high, and I alone have a covenant with the God of gods, for the LORD chose me instead of His holy people, for He abhorred them. [18] And His former people, despised and rejected, did not truly know the LORD because they did not know His image [(the Son)]. [19] We are truly wise and intelligent; we know the LORD and His law, we know His image and presence. [20] But thus says the LORD: Because you rose up in pride to brag about the God of gods, know that you will perish in your conceitedness. [21] For why would you put confidence in man, whose life is like a vapor, which begins in the morning, and is gone by noon-day, placing him to sit beside God. [22] For it is not you whom I knew formerly, and where is the bill of divorce of My people, that you said would be a prey; show it to Me! [23] Your corpses will fall among My people. [24] O zealous LORD, come out; come out of Your place and smite Edom; consume them. [25] Come to Zerephath, come to Sepharad, come to Ashkenaz, come to Garmania;

they will come and fall in the lowest pit, in destruction, and in the shadow of death, for your mouth will fail you, and no one will help you. [26] At the end of days Michael the great prince will stand up in war like a whirlwind against Samael the prince of this world to put him under his feet, in the wind of the LORD, and it will be eaten up; for the LORD has spoken it. [27] At the end of days the robbed will overcome the robber, and the weak, the strong, truly and in righteousness. [28] Your God is your Savior, O Israel; with Him you will be saved, for He is a merciful God. He will not abandon you, [29] for you will keep on doing all that I commanded you in the Law of My servant Moses."

CHAPTER 3

[1] When the feast of Passover came, on the fifteenth of the first month, a Moabite shepherd came to David and talked with him, saying, "My lord the king, you have known that I, your servant, have been loyal to Israel from my youth, and now take me away from dwelling among uncircumcised people and circumcise the flesh of my foreskin to take away my reproach, so that I can sit among your people." [2] And David said, "The LORD does not want your people, and He commanded: An Ammonite or a Moabite will not enter into the assembly of the LORD forever. And we cannot seek your peace nor your prosperity, but how can I help you today?" [3] The servant answered, "Is it not true that Ruth was of our people, and you are one of her children and descendants, and the LORD has chosen you and your descendants forever?" [4] Then he said, "You have given a convincing argument. Stand here with me to ask from the mouth of my Lord." [5] And David asked the LORD about the statement of the Moabite servant. [6] And David said, "O LORD, LORD of Hosts, teach me wondrous things out of Your law so that I may know how to rule for this servant, and what should be done with him." [7] And the LORD said to Nathan the prophet, "Go to My servant David and tell him the message that I tell you." [8] And Nathan went to David, to his chambers, saying, "This is what the LORD of Hosts says: I have heard your prayer, so tell the Moabite: You are a Moabite man, not a Moabite woman, for I never said, a Moabite woman, and, an Ammonite woman, because their women and daughters belong to the LORD; however, you are cursed by the LORD, and forbidden to enter the LORD's assembly." [9] When the Moabite heard the message of the LORD, he cried out and exclaimed: "I am forbidden from entering the assembly of the LORD!" [10] And the king took him and appointed him a shepherd among David's shepherds, and he was there until the third year of the reign of King Solomon, then he died. [11] And he had a daughter whose name was Sephirah; she had a beautiful form and was very fair to look on. King Solomon took her to be his concubine, and she found grace and favor in his sight more than all the other concubines, and she became the chief of the concubines' residence. [12] And this became the statute in Israel forever.

CHAPTER 4

[1] In those days a man from Bethlehem, the city of David, went to Jerusalem to pay the vow which he had vowed to the LORD. His name was Zabad the Parhi, and he was of the family of the Perezites. [2] Zabad's father was very sick, even to the point of death, so Zabad vowed: "When the LORD heals my father of his sickness, I will weigh out two talents of silver and give them to the House of the LORD, into the hand of King David." [3] And it came to pass, when he was at the house of the shepherds along the way, he lost the pouch with the money in it and he was upset. [4] He came to the city of Jerusalem, into the inner city, and he wrote on all the gates these words: [5] "ANYONE WHO FINDS A LOST POUCH WITH TWO TALENTS OF SILVER AND BRINGS IT TO ME I WILL GIVE HIM A TALENT OF SILVER AS A REWARD." [6] After a while, a man from the tribe of Dan came and had in his hand the pouch with the silver talents that he found along the way and he gave it to the owner of the pouch. [7] And the Danite said to Zabad, "Give me the talent of silver as you promised." [8] And Zabad said, "No, there were actually three talents in my pouch, and you have already stolen one talent; I mistakenly wrote down the wrong number." [9] So both of them came and stood before the king. [10] And the king said to Zabad, "Swear to me by the LORD that you truly had three talents of silver in your pouch." And Zabad swore to him by the LORD. [11] And the king continued, saying to the Danite, "Swear to me by the LORD that you only found two talents of silver in the pouch." And he swore to him by the LORD. [12] And David said to Zabad, "Give the pouch with the talents back to the Danite, because this is his money that the LORD has given to him by chance. [13] Now, go and write on the city gates: WHOEVER FINDS THE POUCH WITH THREE TALENTS SHOULD BRING IT TO ME, because this is not your pouch." [14] And David took the pouch with the talents of silver from the hand of Zabad and gave it to the Danite. [15] And the Danite bowed his head, and prostrated himself to the earth, and said, "Long live my lord, King David, forever." [16] And all Israel heard of this judgment, and they marveled over David and were overjoyed, because they saw that he was full of the wisdom of God.

CHAPTER 5

[1] All the Philistines assembled themselves together to fight against Israel. There were so many multitudes of Philistines that they could not be numbered. [2] And David was greatly distressed because he was afraid of the Philistines. [3] And the LORD said to Gad, "Go and tell My servant David: Do not be worried about these uncircumcised Philistines, because tomorrow I will

give them, and those other oppressors with them, into your hand." [4] And David said to Gad, "I am not worthy of all the mercies that the LORD has shown to me, but blessed be the Name of the LORD forever and ever." [5] That night a fire-messenger came from Heaven with his drawn sword in his hand [6] and he attacked the camp of the uncircumcised. It was such a great slaughter that none of them were left alive. [7] And it came to pass the next morning, they came to David, saying, "Behold, all the Philistines have been killed by someone who rose up against them; not a single one of them was left alive." [8] And David raised his voice and said, "Now I know that nothing can hinder the LORD. He can save us from many or few, and His salvation can be in a blink of an eye." [9] And he said, "Blessed are You, O LORD, who has been taking revenge for us on our enemies." [10] And he set up a pillar and called it the "Pillar of Revenge" to this day.

CHAPTER 6

[1] The LORD said to Gad, "Go tell My servant David, [2] Thus says the LORD: Do not let the mighty man glory in his might. [3] But let him that glories glory in this, that My help is with him. [4] Then you should go and not fear, for the LORD is with you." [5] And Gad came and told David what the LORD had said. [6] And David said to Gad, "I have known the help of the LORD from my youth. [7] For who struck down the lion and the bear? Who destroyed the Philistines? Who destroyed my enemies? Was it not by the help of God?" [8] And when the LORD heard that, He was very pleased with David's heart. [9] And He said, "Because David has acknowledged My help instead of his own glory, My help will dwell in the house of David forever." [10] And Gad told David what the LORD said. [11] And David bowed down before the LORD and said, "Blessed be the LORD, for I have found favor in His eyes."

CHAPTER 7

[1] And again the anger of the LORD was kindled against Israel [2] and He moved Satan against David, saying, "Go, number Israel and Judah," to bring them the evil He spoke through Samuel the seer. [3] And the king said to Joab the captain and to the princes of the people: "Go now through all the tribes of Israel, from Dan even to Beersheba, and number the people, and bring me word [so] that I may know the sum of them." [4] And Joab said to the king, "May the LORD add to the people howsoever many they may be, a hundredfold, and may the eyes of the LORD our God watch over them; but, my lord the king, are they not all my lord's servants? Why does my lord require this thing? And why should it be a cause of trespass to Israel? For the LORD has said: Which cannot be numbered for the multitude." [5] Notwithstanding, the king's word prevailed against Joab and against the captains of the host. And Joab and the captains of the host went from the presence of the king to number the people of Israel. [6] And they passed over the Jordan, and camped in Aroer, south of the town in the middle of the river of Gad, and toward Jazer. [7] And they came to Gilead, and then to the land of the Hittites, to Kadesh, and they came to Dan and Enan, and around to Zidon. [8] And they came to the stronghold of Tyre, and to all the cities of the Hivites and the Canaanites. And they went out to the south of Judah, to Beersheba. [9] So when they had gone through all the land, they came to Jerusalem at the end of nine months and twenty days. But Joab did not number Levi and Benjamin, for the king's word was abominable to Joab. [10] And Joab gave up the sum of the number of the people to David. And all they of Israel were eight hundred thousand valiant men and three hundred thousand men that drew a sword, and in Judah there were four hundred and seventy thousand valiant men and thirty thousand men that drew a sword. [11] And the LORD God was displeased with this act of Israel, and He sent Gad the seer to David, saying, [12] "Thus said the LORD: I am the King of Israel, and I am their Portion; I am their Avenger, I am their Fortress and Might; and you know that it is not with a sword or a spear that I will save, and not with a man of valiance that draws a sword, for this is the portion of the heathens that stand on their might and many warriors. [13] But you are not like that, for I am a lone warrior and there is no one with Me. Why would you do this evil to number your people? For that, I will strike Israel, so that you will know that I am the LORD in the midst of the earth." [14] And David's heart was grieved after that. And David said to the LORD, "I have sinned greatly in what I have done; but now, O LORD, I beg You, take away the iniquity of Your servant, for I have acted very foolishly." [15] And David rose up in the morning, and the word of the LORD had already come to Gad the prophet, David's seer, saying, [16] "Go and say to David: Thus says the LORD: I offer you three things—choose one of them [so] that I may do it to you." [17] So Gad came to David and told him, and said to him, "Will four years of famine come to the land of Israel and three years in the land of Judah? Or will you flee three months before your adversaries while they pursue you, while the sword of your enemies overtakes you? Or will there be three days of the sword of the LORD, which is pestilence, in your land, and the messenger of the LORD destroying throughout all the land of Israel? Now advise yourself, and decide what answer I will return to Him who sent me." [18] And David said to Gad, "I am in a great strait; let me fall, and let us fall now, into the hand of the LORD, for His mercies are great; and let me not fall into the hand of man." [19] So the LORD sent a pestilence on Israel, from the morning even to the time appointed; and there died of the people from Dan even to Beersheba seventy thousand men. [20] And God sent a messenger to Jerusalem to destroy it; and as he was destroying

it, the LORD beheld, and He relented Himself of the calamity, and said to the messenger that was destroying the people: "It is enough; now stay your hand." And the messenger of the LORD was standing by the threshing-floor of Ornan the Jebusite. ²¹ And David lifted up his eyes and saw the messenger of the LORD standing between the heaven and the earth, having a drawn sword in his hand stretched out over Jerusalem. And David and the elders, who were clothed in sackcloth, fell on their faces. ²² And David said to God, "Is it not I that commanded the people to be numbered? Even I it is that have sinned and acted wickedly; but these sheep, what have they done? O LORD my God, let Your hand be against me and against my father's house, but not against Your people, that they should be plagued. Will not the Judge of all the earth do justice?" ²³ And the LORD said, "They incited Satan against you to number them, saying thus: We will be like all the nations; but I am a God of justice; may I return their high heart into their own bosoms. ²⁴ For a broken or a contrite heart I will not despise forever." ²⁵ And the messenger of the LORD told Gad to tell David that David should go up and rear an altar to the LORD on the threshing-floor of Ornan the Jebusite. ²⁶ And David went up according to the words of Gad which he spoke in the Name of the LORD. ²⁷ And Ornan was looking, and he saw the king and his four sons with him. Now Ornan was threshing wheat. ²⁸ And Ornan looked and saw David, and he went out of the threshing-floor, and bowed down to David with his face to the ground. ²⁹ Then David said to Ornan, "Sell me the place of this threshing-floor, that I may build an altar therein to the LORD; you will sell it to me for the full price, that the plague may be stayed from the people." ³⁰ And Ornan said to David, "Take it, and let my lord the king do that which is good in his eyes; behold, I also give the oxen for burnt-offering, and the threshing instruments for wood, and the wheat for the meal-offering; I give it all." ³¹ And King David said to Ornan, "No, but I will truly buy it for the full price; for I will not take that which is yours for the LORD, nor offer a burnt-offering without paying for it." ³² So David gave Ornan six hundred shekels of gold for the place, and for the cattle fifty shekels of silver, by weight. ³³ And David built an altar there to the LORD, and offered burnt-offerings and peace-offerings, and called on the LORD; and He answered him from Heaven by fire on the altar of burnt-offering. ³⁴ And the LORD commanded the messenger, and he put his sword back into the sheath thereof, and the plague was stayed from Israel. ³⁵ At that time, when David saw that the LORD had answered him in the threshing-floor of Ornan the Jebusite, and He did not despise him, then he sacrificed there to the LORD for the rest of his life. ³⁶ For David would no longer go and sacrifice to the LORD in the high place at Gibeon, where there was an altar to the LORD and [the]

Dwelling Place which Moses made, for he was terrified and weakened because of the sword of the messenger of the LORD that he had seen.

CHAPTER 8

¹ The LORD appeared to David when he was old and said to him, "Behold, I am with you, and I am your God, and behold, My covenant is with you; do not be afraid, nor discouraged, because your God is your helper." ² And David bowed down to the LORD and rejoiced in his heart. ³ And the LORD said, "Speak these words in My Name to the people and make sure they understand and obey so that they will live. If they do, I will no longer be angry with them." ⁴ And the LORD put His words in his mouth. ⁵ Then David assembled all Israel in Jerusalem, and he made a pulpit of wood for himself, and he stood on it and addressed all the people. He opened his mouth and said, ⁶ "Hear, O Israel, your God and my God is one, the only one, and unique; there is no one like His individuality. He is hidden from everyone. He always has been and always will be. He fills His creation, but His creation does not fill Him. He sees everything, but is not seen. He knows the future and reveals it to mankind, for He is the everlasting God, and there is no end to His presence, power, and truth—whole worlds are full of His glory. ⁷ He gave each person free choice: if one person wants to do good, he will be helped, but if a person wants to do evil, he will find a way. ⁸ As for us, we will worship our God who is our King, our Lord, and our Savior, with love and awe. For your wisdom begins with the fear of the LORD, and if you truly understand Him, you will depart from evil. ⁹ Remember and obey the Law of Moses, the man of God, so that you will live a blessed life all of your days. ¹⁰ Ask your fathers, and they will teach you; ask your elders, and they will instruct you. ¹¹ Do not just listen to the Law, but be strong and valiant to obey all of it. ¹² Hearing is like the seed, but a deed shows that the seed has taken root in you. It then becomes a tree of belief which produces the fruit of true righteousness. ¹³ What becomes of a smelly rotten seed if no root will come out of it? ¹⁴ So hurry; be quick to hear and act. For if you are a true seed, if you have belief and righteousness, then the LORD will bless you all with peace. ¹⁵ Live in peace with each other. Love the deeds and those created in the image of the LORD like your own selves, ¹⁶ because it is a sign that you love the Creator if you love His creation. ¹⁷ You cannot take hold of the one but withdraw your hand from the other. Love the LORD and also man so that it will be well with you all the days of your life." ¹⁸ David raised his voice, and lifted his hands toward Heaven, and said, "LORD, O God, the God of the spirits of all flesh, God, merciful and gracious, guard Israel forever. ¹⁹ Save Your people, and bless Your inheritance, and tend to them, and uphold them forever." ²⁰ And all the people called out: "Amen!

Amen!" [21] And David sent the people away and they went home peacefully.

CHAPTER 9

[1] Hiram king of Tyre sent messengers to David, saying, [2] "I know that the LORD your God is the one true God, so now deal with me as a true brother and teach me the Law of your God, for I will worship Him all the days of my life." [3] Then the messengers came to David with an offering in their hands for the LORD and for David. They told him everything that Hiram had said and presented him with the offerings. [4] And David replied to Hiram, [5] "Go and tell my brother Hiram: This is what your brother David says: Reverence the LORD, creator of heaven and fire, the sea and the earth, the wet and the dry, the heat and the cold, the mineral and the vegetation, the living and the speaking, [6] the planets, the Pleiades and Orion, the sun and the moon, the substantial and the spiritual, the wandering stars, the senses, and everything. [7] These were all created without a blemish by God Almighty, whose Name is YHWH. [8] If you do this and observe the commandments that were ordered to the children of your father Noah, then God will bless you all the days of your life. [9] We are both His allies; but we are different from you by the Law of truth, sealed by the seal of [the] Almighty, called children of the true God. [10] We must therefore obey the whole Law that the Name commands of us, saying, And you will be to Me a kingdom of priests, and a holy nation. These are the words which you will speak to the children of Israel. [11] But He has not dealt the same way with any other nation as He has with us. He did not choose us for any other reason than the great love that He has for us." [12] The messengers then returned to Hiram, their king, and told him everything that King David had told them. [13] And Hiram rejoiced with all his heart, and called all his princes and servants, and said to them, [14] "Tyrians and Sidonians, listen carefully to what I am about to tell you: [15] have reverence and respect for God Almighty, who is the God of Israel. He made everything by speaking and by the breath of His mouth; and who will tell Him what He can do? For He is one. [16] Repeat after me: Blessed is the LORD God of Israel who chooses His people, and blessed is His servant David, king of His people, and blessed is Israel whom the LORD has chosen to be His inheritance. [17] We would be blessed to simply be the servants of the children of Israel who are called children of the LORD their God." [18] And all his princes and his servants replied: "Amen! May it be so." [19] And Hiram lifted up his voice and said, "I have seen, but not now, || I have beheld, but not near: There will step forth a sun from David, || And a moon will rise out of the house of Judah, || And He will smite all the children of Ham || And break down all the children of Japheth || And He will possess all the kingdoms of the world. And who is like the LORD, God above all gods? [20] And who is like Israel, a people above the nations? May our end be like theirs." [21] When the LORD heard what Hiram had said, He was very pleased with him. [22] And the LORD said to Gad, the seer of David, [23] "Go to My servant and tell him the message that I gave you." [24] And Gad, the one in whose hand was the word of the LORD, came to David, and said, "Thus says the LORD God of Hosts: I have heard what Hiram, king of Tyre, has said and what his princes and servants have said, and I am very pleased. [25] Therefore I will give him and his people a heart of wisdom and understanding to prepare My house where I will put My Name, and that will cause his kingdom to grow, for I have chosen them and will not reject them." [26] And David said to Gad, "Now I know that the LORD our God rewards all His creatures and all the works He has created with goodness, because He is a God of mercy who dwells on high and looks after the lowly, and whoever is banished will not remain an outcast from Him. Blessed be the LORD forever. Amen and amen! [27] For as the heaven is high above the earth, so great is His mercy toward them that fear Him and toward His works. [28] Bless the LORD, all you His works, in all His places of His dominion. Bless the LORD, O my soul. Hallelujah!"

CHAPTER 10

[1] At that time David wrote this psalm of praise: "I will exalt You, my God, O King; And I will bless Your Name forever and ever. [2] Every day I will bless You, || And I will praise Your Name forever and ever. [3] Great is the LORD, and greatly to be praised; And His greatness is unsearchable. [4] Generation after generation will praise Your works, || And will declare Your mighty acts. [5] The glorious splendor of Your majesty, || And Your wondrous works I will declare. [6] And men will speak of the might of Your awesome works; And I will declare Your greatness. [7] They will abundantly express the memory of Your goodness, || And they will sing of Your righteousness. [8] The LORD is gracious and full of compassion, || Slow to anger, and great in mercy. [9] The LORD is good to all, || And His tender mercies are over all His works. [10] All Your works will thank You, O LORD; And Your saints bless You. [11] They will speak of the glory of Your kingdom, || And talk of Your power, [12] To make known to the sons of men His mighty acts, || And the glorious majesty of His kingdom. [13] Your kingdom is an everlasting kingdom, || And Your dominion endures through all generations. [[or All Your enemies have fallen, O LORD, || And all of their might has come to nothing.]] [14] The LORD sustains all those who fall, || And raises up all those who are bowed down. [15] The eyes of all wait on You; And You give them their food in due season. [16] You open Your hands, || And satisfy the desire of every living thing with favor. [17] The LORD is righteous in all His ways, || And holy in all His works. [18] The LORD is near to all who call on Him,

|| To all that call on Him in truth. [19] He will grant the desire of them that fear Him, || And He will also hear their prayer and save them. [20] The LORD preserves all of them that love Him, || But all the wicked He will destroy. [21] My mouth will speak the praise of the LORD, || And let all flesh bless His holy Name forever and ever."

CHAPTER 11

[1] THE PSALM OF DAVID PRAISING THE LORD ON THE DAY WHEN ELHANAN THE SON OF JAIR SLEW LAHMI THE BROTHER OF GOLIATH THE GITTITE, AND JONATHAN THE SON OF SHIMEA KILLED A MAN OF GREAT STATURE, saying, "Blessed be the LORD my rock, || Who instructs my hands for war, || And my fingers for battle. [2] My mercy and my fortress; My high tower and my deliverer; My protector and He in whom I take refuge, || Who subdues peoples under me. [3] LORD, what is man, that You take knowledge of him? Or the son of man, that You make account of him? [4] Man is like to a breath: His days are as a shadow that passes away. [5] O LORD, bow Your heavens and come down: Touch the mountains so that they smoke. [6] Send lightning, and scatter them: Shoot out Your arrows, and destroy them. [7] Send forth Your hand from above—deliver me, || And deliver me out of many waters, || Out of the hand of foreigners [8] Whose mouths speak falsehood, || And whose right hand is a right hand of lying. [9] O God, I will sing to You a new song: I will sing praise to You on a psaltery of ten strings, [10] Who gives salvation to kings, || Who rescues Your servant David from an evil sword. [11] Rescue me and deliver me from the hand of foreigners || Whose mouths speak lies, || And whose right hand is a right hand of falsehood; [12] May our children be as plants grown up in their youth; May our daughters be cornerstones hewn like the form of the temple. [13] May our garners be full, affording all manner of store; May our sheep increase by thousands || And myriads in our markets. [14] May our oxen be strong to labor; No breaking in, nor going out, || Nor complaining in our streets. [15] Happy is the people that is in such a case. Happy is the people whose God is the LORD. [16] Happy is he who waits until there will be good to all Israel forever."

CHAPTER 12

[1] David addressed the LORD and all of Israel shortly before his death. David said, [2] "Our blessed God, who is great, the only one, guileless, just, [3] avenger and benefactor of the miserable, beloved, our Father, God Almighty. [4] Holy One, have mercy on the vine, Your good inheritance. [5] Answer us this very day as we call on You. [6] My Lord, hear my prayer and supplication, for You hear prayers of all people; [7] listen and accept the cry of Your people, [8] for they are Your flock and Your inheritance. [9] Send Your light and truth to help them. [10] Give them one heart to worship You, one

shoulder [to serve] as one body, so they will be one in Your hand. [11] And do not lose any of them, for Your Name is to be one, as our fathers and mothers are one. [12] For, hear, O Israel, the LORD is our God, the LORD is one. [13] Do not turn to the idols, for they are false and will completely pass away. [14] Cling only to your God, for only He can be your avenger and fortress; [15] only He can defeat your spiritual enemies and physical enemies and put them under your feet; [16] only He can bring you into the New Jerusalem of the future, [17] where you will see Him face to face, and be in the presence of the living God that is seen face to face. And you are one people; if you grow in belief, you will be filled with gates of intelligence. [18] Blessed is the eye that has seen all these things. [19] But if you grow in unbelief, you will reach gates of impurity. [20] So then cleanse and purify yourself before the LORD, your King, and it will be well with you all the days of your life." [21] And David died in the afternoon on the Sabbath day, in the fortieth year of his reign over Judah and Israel. [22] He was seventy years old when he died, and he was buried with great honor in the City of David. [23] And the rest of the deeds of King David, during his mighty reign and the events that befell him, Israel, and all the kingdoms of the countries, behold, they are written in the Scroll of Samuel the Seer and in the Scroll of Nathan the Prophet.

CHAPTER 13

[1] Solomon was able to strengthen his kingdom, because the LORD his God was with him, and greatly magnified him. [2] Later, David's daughter, Tamar, sister of Absalom, fled to the house of the king of Geshur, and she spent a year and eight months in her mother's home, which is in the king's palace. [3] And King Solomon did not know that she left, because she went secretly, and she concealed her going not only from the king, but all the people as well. [4] And King Solomon said, "I will pay a reward of royal clothes plus fifty shekels of gold to whoever finds Tamar, the sister of my father, and brings her to me." [5] And the king's servants searched for her throughout all the land of Israel, but they could not find her. [6] And she was hiding at her mother's home in Geshur, at her grandfather's palace. [7] And there was a friend of the king, whose name was Pirshaz, and he lusted after the young woman very much, for she was very beautiful and attractive to look on. [8] In those days the king of Geshur went to see King Solomon, as all the kings of the land are required to do. [9] King Solomon asked him, saying, "Is it well with you?" And he said, "It is well." [10] And he said, "Is it well with Maachah [(Tamar's mother)] in your house?" And he said, "It is well." And then King Solomon cunningly asked, "Is it well with my sister Tamar?" And he lied to him, saying, "I do not know, for I have never met her." [11] And it came to pass when the king of Geshur was in

Jerusalem, his friend, Pirshaz, came to Tamar's room, saying to her, "Lie with me." [12] But Tamar refused him, saying, "Let us not, my lord; do not do this indecent thing to me, because I am a king's daughter." [13] However, he would not listen to her, because he was burning with lust. [14] And Tamar knew she was no match for this man, so she cunningly said, "My lord, listen to the words of your maidservant. [15] Behold, I play the harp beautifully. First, lie down at my knees and listen to my song. [16] And after I play the song of my heart, then I will do all your heart's desire." And Pirshaz listened to Tamar, and he lay in her bosom. [17] And as Tamar took the harp and began to play beautifully, she said in her heart: "LORD, King of my father David, Your servant, [18] send Your light and truth to hold me, and do not allow this wicked, uncircumcised, impure man to have his way with me. [19] For You know what is in my heart, so do not let this daughter of Your servant David sin. [20] My Father, my Father, my Father, remember the disgrace of Your servant David, my father, and your daughter's disgrace. [21] I go before God Almighty's throne of glory, and ask mercy for myself, to the God of Hosts, to help me by His help. [22] For He does not want wicked men to triumph, and His desire is to help those who have been robbed to overcome the strong. [23] I implore You, O LORD, save me now. I implore You, O LORD, let me prosper. [24] I call on You this day because I am frightened; please answer me, and do not let this impure man cause me to lose holy seed by this impure act, for You are a holy God, and I trust You." [25] And the LORD heard the voice of David's daughter, and God caused Pirshaz to fall into a deep sleep. He fell asleep on her bosom while she was playing the relaxing sounds of the harp. [26] And when Tamar saw that he had fallen asleep, she unsheathed the sword that was girded around his waist. [27] And she said, "LORD of Hosts, remember my father David, and sustain me with Your strength like You did my father. [28] Help me as You helped [Jael], the wife of Heber the Kenite, to rid sins and sinners from the earth, so all will know that You are the only LORD." [29] And she took the sword and ran it through Pirshaz's heart, and Pirshaz fell to the ground dead. [30] And Tamar saw that Pirshaz was dead, and she cried with a loud voice: "May all Your enemies and the enemies of Your people perish this way, O LORD. [31] And now I have seen that You have heard my voice because of my father. You have intervened to not allow his daughter to be disgraced by this impure man. [32] Blessed are You from everlasting to everlasting. Amen." [33] At the time of the noon meal, Pirshaz's servants came to call their master to the king's table. [34] When they came to the inner-chamber, they found Tamar with his bloody sword in her hand standing over the dead body of their master Pirshaz. [35] And they turned trembling to one another, saying, "What happened?" And they took Tamar into custody and brought her to the king's ministers. [36] And the king's servants said to Tamar, "What have you done? You have killed the king's friend. You know that our master, the king, will consider this a disgrace." [37] And Tamar said, "Should one deal with a king's daughter like a harlot? His blood is on his own head, and I will be seen as guiltless and pure in the king's eyes." [38] And they took Tamar and put her in the hands of the warden of the prison. [39] And they sent a letter to their king who was still in Jerusalem, by the hands of the couriers, that Tamar, the king's granddaughter, had killed his friend Pirshaz, and that Tamar was sent to prison until the time the king returned. [40] And the couriers came to Jerusalem and King Solomon's guards stopped them. And he asked them, "Where are you from?" [41] And they said, "We come from Geshur to bring letters to our master the king." [42] And the guards seized them and brought them to King Solomon. [43] And King Solomon said, "You came here to spy out the land. Give me your king's letters and I will see if you are sinning against me or not." [44] And King Solomon took the letters and gave them to the sons of Shisha, the king's scribes, to read. [45] And they read through them and found where Tamar had killed Pirshaz and that she was in prison. [46] And King Solomon called Ahishar, who was head of the household, and said, "Put these uncircumcised men in jail and bring the king of Geshur to me." [47] And he did exactly as he had been commanded. And the king of Geshur was brought before King Solomon and he bowed his head toward the ground. [48] And King Solomon said, "Why have you deceived me, lying, while my sister Tamar was with you? You told me that you had never met her in your entire life. [49] As the LORD lives, who has redeemed my father David out of all evil, you will die this very day." [50] And King Solomon called Benaiah, the son of Jehoiada, and said to him, "Go, and execute the king of Geshur and his couriers." And he executed them, and they all died, because they had lied to King Solomon. [51] And they buried them in a cave right before the Fish Gate. [52] This is why the name of the cave right before the Fish Gate is called Cave of the Uncircumcised Ones to this day. [53] And Solomon sent Benaiah, the son of Jehoiada, and ten thousand valiant men of Judah with him, and he said to them, [54] "Go to Geshur and bring back Tamar, my father's daughter, with you, and destroy the royal palace, but be careful not to harm Tamar's mother, for she was King David's wife." [55] And they went and did all that King Solomon had commanded, and they brought Tamar before King Solomon. [56] And Tamar bowed down to the ground, before the king, and said, "Let my lord the king, my brother, live forever." [57] And King Solomon asked her: "Why did you flee to Geshur?" [58] And she answered, "I was living in my brother Absalom's home, disgraced because of what my brother Amnon had done to me, and I decided to go to my mother's house so I would not be disgraced in the eyes of the princes there. [59] And King Solomon asked her: "Why did you kill Pirshaz?" And she answered, "This is what that uncircumcised one did to me, and this is what I did to him in revenge." [60] And King Solomon said, "The LORD has truly blessed you with discretion. You were wise, and acted, and you were victorious." [61] Then King Solomon spoke openly to all of his servants, saying, "Has anyone found such a charming and heroic woman?" And he said, "Daughter, God is gracious to you. [62] From this day forward you will not be called my sister, but my daughter, because you were extremely wise." [63] And King Solomon gave his daughter Tamar to Abinadab's son to be his wife, and she found grace in her husband's eyes, and he loved her very much. [64] He was an officer over all the region of Dor. [65] And King Solomon renamed his daughter Tamar Taphath, for stacte, the first of the incense, and this was her name the rest of her life.

CHAPTER 14

[1] And it came to pass on the first day of the seventh month, at the beginning of the year, in the four hundred and seventy-eighth year after the children of Israel came out of the land of Egypt, in the second year of King Solomon's reign over Israel, I had a vision from the LORD when I was on the Spring of Gihon. [2] And I raised my eyes, and behold, the heavens rolled back like a scroll, and I saw the glory of the LORD sitting on an extremely high throne. [3] And here is the appearance of the throne: twelve stairs led up to the throne—six of gold and six of silver—and there was a square back to the throne, like a sapphire stone. [4] And at its right side were three chairs and at its left side were four chairs near the throne, like the seven that see the King's face, covered with gold, and silver, and precious stones. [5] And the glory of the LORD had the appearance like that of the rainbow, His

covenant. [6] And the host of Heaven were standing before Him on His right hand and on His left, and Satan was standing by them, but behind them. [7] And then a Man dressed in linen brought before the glory of the LORD three scrolls that contained the records of every man. [8] And He read the first scroll and it contained the just deeds of His people, and the LORD said, "These are granted continuous life." [9] And Satan said, "Who are these guilty people?" And the Man dressed in linen cried to Satan like a ram's horn, saying, "Silence! This day is holy to our Lord." [10] And He read the second scroll, and it contained the unintentional sins of His people, and the LORD said, "Put that scroll aside, but save it until one-third of the month passes by, to see what they will do." [11] And He read the third scroll, and it contained the wicked deeds of His people. [12] And the LORD said to Satan, "These are your share. Take them and do what you want with them." [13] And Satan took the wicked to a wasteland to destroy them there. [14] And the Man dressed in linen cried like a ram's horn, saying, [15] "Blessed are the people who know the joyful shout, O LORD, who walk in the light of Your countenance." [16] And I heard the voice of the host of Heaven rejoicing and saying, "Master of Justice, the LORD of Hosts, the whole heaven and earth is full of Your glory." [17] And I was shocked by the vision since I did not know what the LORD had done for me. [18] Then one of the cherubs flew up to me and he put an olive leaf on my mouth, and said, "Behold, this has touched your mouth, and your iniquity is taken away, and your sin forgiven. [19] And this law that you have seen is a statute for Israel, and a law to the God of Abraham, and peace to your father Isaac. [20] And the LORD will bless your people in the trial with everlasting peace." [21] And I said, "Amen. May the LORD our God do this for us forever and ever." [22] And the messenger answered, "Amen and Amen."

ASCENSION OF ISAIAH

The Ascension of Isaiah was probably composed sometime in the 1st or 2nd centuries AD and consists of three key parts: "The Martyrdom of Isaiah" (chs. 1–5), "The Testament of Hezekiah" (an insertion in chs. 3–4), and "The Vision of Isaiah" (chs. 6–11). The text revolves around an account of Isaiah's martyrdom in which he was sawn in two. It also includes prophetic material and a "vision" in which Isaiah is transported through the seven dimensions (or *levels*) of the heavens.

CHAPTER 1

¹ And it came to pass in the twenty-sixth year of the reign of Hezekiah, king of Judah, that he called his son Manasseh. Now he was his only one. ² And he called him into the presence of Isaiah, the son of the prophet Amoz, and into the presence of Josab, the son of Isaiah, in order to deliver the words of righteousness to him which the king himself had seen, ³ and of the continuous judgments and torments of Gehenna, and of the prince of this world, and of his messengers, and his authorities and his powers. ⁴ And the words of the faith of the Beloved which he himself had seen in the fifteenth year of his reign during his sickness. ⁵ And he delivered the written words to him which Samnas the scribe had written, and also those which Isaiah, the son of Amoz, had given to him, and also to the prophets, that they might write and store up with him what he himself had seen in the king's house regarding the judgment of the messengers, and the destruction of this world, and regarding the garments of the saints and their going forth, and regarding their transformation and the persecution and ascension of the Beloved. ⁶ In the twentieth year of the reign of Hezekiah, Isaiah had seen the words of this prophecy and had delivered them to his son Josab. And while he gave commands, Josab, the son of Isaiah, [was] standing by. ⁷ Isaiah said to Hezekiah the king—but not only in the presence of Manasseh did he say to him—"As the LORD lives, and the Spirit which speaks in me lives, all these commands and these words will be made of no effect by your son Manasseh, and through the agency of his hands I will depart amid the torture of my body. ⁸ And Sammael Malchira will serve Manasseh, and execute all his desire, and he will become a follower of Belial rather than of me: ⁹ and he will cause many in Jerusalem and in Judea to abandon the true faith, and Belial will dwell in Manasseh, and by his hands I will be sawn apart." ¹⁰ And when Hezekiah heard these words he wept very bitterly, and tore his garments, and placed earth on his head, and fell on his face. ¹¹ And Isaiah said to him, "The counsel of Sammael against

Manasseh is consummated: nothing will avail you." ¹² And on that day, Hezekiah resolved in his heart to slay his son Manasseh. ¹³ And Isaiah said to Hezekiah, "The Beloved has made your design of no effect, and the purpose of your heart will not be accomplished, for with this calling I have been called and I will inherit the heritage of the Beloved."

CHAPTER 2

¹ And it came to pass after that Hezekiah died and Manasseh became king, [and] that he did not remember the commands of his father Hezekiah, but forgot them, and Sammael abode in Manasseh and clung fast to him. ² And Manasseh forsook the service of the God of his father, and he served Satan, and his messengers, and his powers. ³ And he turned aside the house of his father, which had been before the face of Hezekiah [from] the words of wisdom and from the service of God. ⁴ And Manasseh turned aside his heart to serve Belial; for the messenger of lawlessness, who is the ruler of this world, is Belial, whose name is Mantanbuchus, and he delighted in Jerusalem because of Manasseh, and he made him strong in apostatizing [Israel] and in the lawlessness which were spread abroad in Jerusalem. ⁵ And witchcraft and magic increased, and divination, and portending, and fornication, [[and adultery]], and the persecution of the righteous by Manasseh, [and Belchira,] and Tobia the Canaanite, and John of Anathoth, and by [Zadok] the chief of the works. ⁶ And the rest of the acts, behold they are written in the scroll of the Kings of Judah and Israel. ⁷ And when Isaiah, the son of Amoz, saw the lawlessness which was being perpetrated in Jerusalem and the worship of Satan and his wantonness, he withdrew from Jerusalem and settled in Beth-Lehem of Judah. ⁸ And there also there was much lawlessness; and withdrawing from Beth-Lehem, he settled on a mountain in a desert place. ⁹ And Micaiah the prophet, and the aged Ananias, and Joel and Habakkuk, and his son Josab, and many of the faithful who believed in the ascension into Heaven, withdrew and settled on the mountain. ¹⁰ They were all clothed with garments of hair, and they were all prophets. And they had nothing with them but were naked, and they all lamented with a great lamentation because of the going astray of Israel. ¹¹ And these eat nothing save wild herbs which they gathered on the mountains, and having cooked them, they lived thereon together with the prophet Isaiah. And they spent two years of days on the mountains and hills. ¹² And after this, while they were in the desert, there was a certain man in Samaria named Belchira, of the family of Zedekiah, the son of Chenaan, a false prophet, whose dwelling was in

ASCENSION OF ISAIAH

Beth-Lehem. Now Hezekiah the son of Chanani, who was the brother of his father, and in the days of Ahab, king of Israel, had been the teacher of the four hundred prophets of Ba'al, had himself smitten and reproved Micaiah, the son of Amada the prophet. 13 And he, Micaiah, had been reproved by Ahab and cast into prison. [And he was] with Zedekiah the prophet: they were with Ahaziah, the son of Ahab, king in Samaria. 14 And Elijah the prophet of Tebon of Gilead was reproving Ahaziah and Samaria, and prophesied regarding Ahaziah that he should die on his bed of sickness, and that Samaria should be delivered into the hand of Leba Nasr because he had slain the prophets of God. 15 And [this was] when the false prophets, who were with Ahaziah, the son of Ahab, and their teacher Jalerjas of Mount Joel, had heard. 16 Now he was a brother of Zedekiah when they persuaded Ahaziah, the king of Aguaron, and [slew] Micaiah.

CHAPTER 3

1 And Belchira recognized and saw the place of Isaiah and the prophets who were with him, for he dwelt in the region of Beth-Lehem and was an adherent of Manasseh. And he prophesied falsely in Jerusalem, and many belonging to Jerusalem were confederate with him, and he was a Samaritan. 2 And it came to pass when Alagar Zagar, king of Assyria, had come and [made them] captive, and led them away to the mountains of the Medes and the rivers of Tazon; 3 This [Belchira], while still a youth, had escaped and come to Jerusalem in the days of Hezekiah king of Judah, but he did not walk in the ways of his father of Samaria; for he feared Hezekiah. 4 And he was found in the days of Hezekiah speaking words of lawlessness in Jerusalem. 5 And the servants of Hezekiah accused him, and he made his escape to the region of Beth-Lehem. And they persuaded . . . 6 And Belchira accused Isaiah and the prophets who were with him, saying, "Isaiah and those who are with him prophesy against Jerusalem and against the cities of Judah that they will be laid waste, and [[against the children of Judah, and]] Benjamin also, that they will go into captivity, and also against you, O lord the king, that you will go [bound] with hooks and iron chains, 7 but they prophesy falsely against Israel and Judah. 8 And Isaiah himself has said, I see more than Moses the prophet. 9 But Moses said, No man can see God and live; and Isaiah has said, I have seen God and behold I live. 10 Know, therefore, O king, that he is lying. And he has also called Jerusalem Sodom, and he has declared the princes of Judah and Jerusalem to be the people of Gomorrah." And he brought many accusations against Isaiah and the prophets before Manasseh. 11 But Belial dwelt in the heart of Manasseh, and in the heart of the princes of Judah and Benjamin, and of the eunuchs, and of the counselors of the king. 12 And the words of Belchira pleased him,

and he sent for and seized Isaiah. 13 For Belial was in great wrath against Isaiah by reason of the vision, and because of the exposure with which he had exposed Sammael, and because through him the going forth of the Beloved from the seventh heaven had been made known, and His transformation and His descent and the likeness into which He should be transformed— the likeness of man, and the persecution with which He should be persecuted, and the torturers with which the sons of Israel should torture Him, and the coming of His twelve disciples, and the teaching, and that He should before the Sabbath be crucified on the tree, and should be crucified together with wicked men, and that He should be buried in the grave, 14 and the twelve who were with Him should be offended because of Him, and the watch of those who watched the grave, 15 and the descent of the messenger of the Christian Assembly, which is in the heavens, whom He will summon in the last days. 16 And that [Gabriel], the messenger of the Holy Spirit, and Michael, the chief of the holy messengers, on the third day will open the grave: 17 and the Beloved sitting on their shoulders will come forth and send out His twelve disciples; 18 and they will teach all the nations and every tongue of the resurrection of the Beloved, and those who believe in His cross will be saved, and in His ascension into the seventh heaven from where He came, 19 and that many who believe in Him will speak through the Holy Spirit, 20 and many signs and wonders will be worked in those days. 21 And afterward, on the eve of His approach, His disciples will forsake the teachings of the Twelve Apostles, and their faith, and their love, and their purity. 22 And there will be much contention on the eve of [His advent and] His approach. 23 And in those days, many will love office, though devoid of wisdom. 24 And there will be many lawless elders, and shepherds dealing wrongly by their own sheep, and they will ravage [them], owing to their not having holy shepherds. 25 And many will change the honor of the garments of the saints for the garments of the covetous, and there will be much respect of persons in those days and lovers of the honor of this world. 26 And there will be much slander and vainglory at the approach of the LORD, and the Holy Spirit will withdraw from [the] many. 27 And there will not be in those days many prophets, nor those who speak trustworthy words, save one here and there in various places, 28 on account of the spirit of error, and fornication, and of vainglory, and of covetousness, which will be in those who will be called servants of that One and in those who will receive that One. 29 And there will be great hatred in the shepherds and elders toward each other. 30 For there will be great jealousy in the last days; for everyone will say what is pleasing in his own eyes. 31 And they will make of no effect the prophecy of the prophets which were before me, and they will also make these visions of mine of no effect, in order to speak after the impulse of their own hearts.

CHAPTER 4

[1] And now Hezekiah and my son Josab, these are the days of the completion of the world. [2] After it is consummated, the great ruler Belial, the king of this world, will descend, who has ruled it since it came into being; yes, he will descend from his expanse in the likeness of a man, a lawless king, the slayer of his mother: who himself [is even] this king. [3] He will persecute the plant which the Twelve Apostles of the Beloved have planted. Of the Twelve, one will be delivered into his hands. [4] This ruler, in the form of that king, will come, and there will come with him all the powers of this world, and they will listen to him in all that he desires. [5] And at his word the sun will rise at night and he will make the moon to appear at the sixth hour. [6] And all that he has desired he will do in the world: he will do and speak like the Beloved and he will say, "I am God and before me there has been none." [7] And all the people in the world will believe in him. [8] And they will sacrifice to him and they will serve him, saying, "This is God and besides Him there is no other." [9] And the greater number of those who will have been associated together in order to receive the Beloved, he will turn aside after him. [10] And there will be the power of his miracles in every city and region. [11] And he will set up his image before him in every city. [12] And he will bear sway three years and seven months and twenty-seven days. [13] And many believers and saints will have seen Him for whom they were hoping, who was crucified—the Lord Jesus Christ. [[After that, I, Isaiah, had seen Him who was crucified and ascended,]] and those also who were believers in Him—of these few in those days will be left as His servants, while they flee from desert to desert, awaiting the coming of the Beloved. [14] And after [one thousand] three hundred and thirty-two days the Lord will come with His messengers and with the armies of the holy ones from the seventh heaven with the glory of the seventh heaven, and He will drag Belial into Gehenna and also his armies. [15] And He will give rest of the godly whom He will find in the body in this world—[[and the sun wil be ashamed]]— [16] and to all who because of [their] faith in Him have execrated Belial and his kings. But the saints will come with the Lord with their garments which are [now] stored up on high in the seventh heaven: they will come with the Lord, whose spirits are clothed, they will descend and be present in the world, and He will strengthen those who have been found in the body, together with the saints, in the garments of the saints, and the Lord will minister to those who have kept watch in this world. [17] And afterward they will turn themselves upward in their garments, and their body will be left in the world. [18] Then the voice of the Beloved will in wrath rebuke the things of Heaven, and the things of earth, and the mountains, and the hills, and the cities, and the desert, and the forests, and the messenger of the sun and that of the moon, and all things wherein Belial manifested himself and acted openly in this world, and there will be [[a resurrection and]] a judgment in their midst in those days, and the Beloved will cause fire to go forth from Him, and it will consume all the godless, and they will be as though they had not been created. [19] And the rest of the words of the vision is written in the vision of Babylon. [20] And the rest of the vision regarding the Lord, behold, it is written in three parables according to my words which are written in the scroll which I publicly prophesied. [21] And the descent of the Beloved into Sheol, behold, it is written in the section, where the Lord says, "Behold, My Son will understand." And all these things, behold, they are written in the parables [[or Psalms]] of David, the son of Jesse, and in the Proverbs of his son Solomon, and in the words of Korah, and Ethan the Israelite, and in the words of Asaph, and also in the rest of the Psalms which the messenger of the Spirit inspired— [22] [namely,] in those which do not have the name written, and in the words of my father Amoz, and of Hosea the prophet, and of Micah, and Joel, and Nahum, and Jonah, and Obadiah, and Habakkuk, and Haggai, and Malachi, and in the words of Joseph the Just, and in the words of Daniel.

CHAPTER 5

[1] On account of these visions, therefore, Belial was angry with Isaiah, and he dwelt in the heart of Manasseh, and he sawed him apart with a wooden saw. [2] And when Isaiah was being sawn apart, Belchira stood up, accusing him, and all the false prophets stood up, laughing and rejoicing because of Isaiah. [3] And Belchira, with the aid of Mechembechus, stood up before Isaiah, [laughing] deriding; [4] and Belchira said to Isaiah, "Say, I have lied in all that I have spoken, and likewise the ways of Manasseh are good and right. [5] And the ways also of Belchira and of his associates are good." [6] And this he said to him when he began to be sawn apart. [7] But Isaiah was [entranced] in a vision of the Lord, and though his eyes were open, he [did not] see them. [8] And Belchira spoke thus to Isaiah: "Say what I say to you and I will turn their hearts, and I will compel Manasseh, and the princes of Judah, and the people, and all Jerusalem to give reverence to you." [9] And Isaiah answered and said, "So far as I have utterance: Damned and accursed are you, and all your powers, and all your house. [10] For you cannot take [from me] anything except the skin of my body." [11] And they seized and sawed apart Isaiah, the son of Amoz, with a wooden saw. [12] And Manasseh, and Belchira, and the false prophets, and the princes, and the people all stood looking on. [13] And to the prophets who were with him he said before he had been sawn apart, "Go

to the region of Tyre and Sidon; for God has only mingled the cup for me." [14] And when Isaiah was being sawn apart, he neither cried aloud nor wept, but his lips spoke with the Holy Spirit until he was sawn in half. [15] Belial did this to Isaiah through Belchira and Manasseh; for Sammael was very wrathful against Isaiah from the days of Hezekiah, king of Judah, on account of the things which he had seen regarding the Beloved. [16] And on account of the destruction of Sammael, which he had seen through the LORD while his father Hezekiah was still king. And he did according to the will of Satan.

CHAPTER 6

[1] THE VISION WHICH ISAIAH THE SON OF AMOZ SAW: In the twentieth year of the reign of Hezekiah, king of Judah, Isaiah the son of Amoz, and Josab the son of Isaiah, came to Hezekiah to Jerusalem from Galgala. [2] And [having entered,] he sat down on the couch of the king, and they brought him a seat, but he would not sit [thereon]. [3] And when Isaiah began to speak the words of faith and truth with King Hezekiah, all the princes of Israel were seated—and the eunuchs and the counselors of the king. And there were forty prophets and sons of the prophets there: they had come from the villages and from the mountains and the plains when they had heard that Isaiah was coming from Galgala to Hezekiah. [4] And they had come to salute him and to hear his words, [5] and that he might place his hands on them, and that they might prophesy and that he might hear their prophecy: and they were all before Isaiah. [6] And when Isaiah was speaking the words of truth and faith to Hezekiah, they all heard a door which one had opened and the voice of the Holy Spirit. [7] And the king summoned all the prophets and all the people who were found there, and they came, and Macaiah, and the aged Ananias, and Joel, and Josab sat on his right hand [[and on the left]]. [8] And it came to pass when they had all heard the voice of the Holy Spirit, they all worshiped on their knees, and glorified the God of truth, the Most High who is in the upper world and who sits on high—the Holy One—and who rests among His holy ones. [9] And they gave glory to Him who had thus bestowed a door in an alien world [and] had bestowed [it] on a man. [10] And as he was speaking in the Holy Spirit in the hearing of all, he became silent, and his mind was taken up from him and he did not see the men that stood before him, [11] though his eyes were indeed open. Moreover, his lips were silent and the mind in his body was taken up from him. [12] But his breath was in him, for he was seeing a vision. [13] And the messenger who was sent to make him see was not of this expanse, nor was he of the messengers of glory of this world, but he had come from the seventh heaven. [14] And the people who stood near did [not] think, but the circle of the prophets [did], that the holy Isaiah had been taken up. [15] And the vision which the holy Isaiah saw was not from this world, but from the world which is hidden from the flesh. [16] And after Isaiah had seen this vision, he narrated it to Hezekiah, and to his son Josab, and to the other prophets who had come. [17] But the leaders, and the eunuchs, and the people did not hear, but only Samna the scribe, and Ijoaqem, and Asaph the recorder; for these were also doers of righteousness, and the sweet smell of the Spirit was on them. But the people had not heard, for Micaiah and his son Josab had caused them to go forth when the wisdom of this world had been taken from him and he became as one dead.

CHAPTER 7

[1] And the vision which Isaiah saw, he told to Hezekiah, and his son Josab, and Micaiah, and the rest of the prophets, [and] said: [2] At this moment, when I prophesied according to the [words] heard which you heard, I saw a glorious messenger not like to the glory of the messengers which I used to always see, but possessing such glory and position that I cannot describe the glory of that messenger. [3] And having seized me by my hand he raised me on high, and I said to him, "Who are you, and what is your name, and to where are you raising me on high?" For strength was given me to speak with him. [4] And he said to me, "When I have raised you on high and made you see the vision, on account of which I have been sent, then you will understand who I am, but you do not know my name, [5] because you will return into this body of yours; but to where I am raising you on high, you will see; for this purpose I have been sent." [6] And I rejoiced because he spoke courteously to me. [7] And he said to me, "Have you rejoiced because I have spoken courteously to you?" And he said, "And you will see how [one] greater than I am will also speak courteously and peaceably with you. [8] And His Father who is greater you will also see; for this purpose I have been sent from the seventh heaven in order to explain all these things to you." [9] And we ascended to the expanse, he and I, and there I saw Sammael and his hosts, and there was great fighting therein and the messengers of Satan were envying one another. [10] And as above so on the earth also; for the likeness of that which is in the expanse is here on the earth. [11] And I said to the messenger [who was with me], "[[What is this war and]] what is this envying?" [12] And he said to me, "So has it been since this world was made until now, and this war [will continue] until He, whom you will see will come and destroy him." [13] And afterward he caused me to ascend [to that which is] above the expanse, which is the [first] heaven. [14] And there I saw a throne in the midst, and on his right and on his left were messengers. [15] And [those on the left were] not like to the messengers who stood on the right, but those who stood on the right had the greater glory, and they all praised with one voice, and there was a throne in the midst; and

those who were on the left gave praise after them, but their voice was not such as the voice of those on the right, nor their praise like the praise of those. ¹⁶ And I asked the messenger who conducted me, and I said to him, "To whom is this praise sent?" ¹⁷ And he said to me, "[It is sent] to the praise of [Him who sits in] the seventh heaven: to Him who rests in the holy world, and to His Beloved, from where I have been sent to you." ¹⁸ And again, he made me to ascend to the second heaven. Now the height of that heaven is the same as from the heaven to the earth. ¹⁹ And [I saw there, as] in the first heaven, messengers on the right and on the left, and a throne in the midst, and the praise of the messengers in the second heaven; and he who sat on the throne in the second heaven was more glorious than all [the rest]. ²⁰ And there was great glory in the second heaven, and the praise also was not like the praise of those who were in the first heaven. ²¹ And I fell on my face to worship him, but the messenger who conducted me did not permit me, but said to me, "Worship neither throne nor messenger which belongs to the six heavens—for this reason I was sent to conduct you until I tell you in the seventh heaven. ²² For above all the heavens and their messengers your throne has been placed, and your garments and your crown which you will see." ²³ And I rejoiced with great joy, that those who love the Most High and His Beloved will afterward ascend there by the messenger of the Holy Spirit. ²⁴ And he raised me to the third heaven, and in like manner I saw those on the right and on the left, and there was a throne there in the midst; but the memorial of this world is there unheard of. ²⁵ And I said to the messenger who was with me—for the glory of my appearance was undergoing transformation as I ascended to each heaven in turn—"Nothing of the vanity of that world is here named." ²⁶ And he answered me, and said to me, "Nothing is named on account of its weakness, and nothing is hidden there of what is done." ²⁷ And I wished to learn how it is known, and he answered me, saying, "When I have raised you to the seventh heaven from where I was sent, to that which is above these, then you will know that there is nothing hidden from the thrones and from those who dwell in the heavens and from the messengers." And the praise with which they praised and [the] glory of him who sat on the throne was great, and the glory of the messengers on the right hand and on the left was beyond that of the heaven which was below them. ²⁸ And again he raised me to the fourth heaven, and the height from the third to the height from the third to the fourth heaven was greater than from the earth to the expanse. ²⁹ And there I again saw those who were on the right hand and those who were on the left, and him who sat on the throne was in the midst, and there also they were praising. ³⁰ And the praise and glory of the messengers on the right was greater than that of those on the left. ³¹ And again the glory of him who sat on the throne was greater than that of the messengers on the right, and their glory was beyond that of those who were below. ³² And he raised me to the fifth heaven. ³³ And again I saw those on the right hand and on the left, and him who sat on the throne possessing greater glory that those of the fourth heaven. ³⁴ And the glory of those on the right hand was greater than that of those on the left [from the third to the fourth]. ³⁵ And the glory of him who was on the throne was greater than that of the messengers on the right hand. ³⁶ And their praise was more glorious than that of the fourth heaven. ³⁷ And I praised Him who is not named, and the Only-begotten who dwells in the heavens, whose Name is not known to any flesh, who has bestowed such glory on the several heavens, and who makes great the glory of the messengers, and more excellent the glory of Him who sits on the throne.

CHAPTER 8

¹ And again he raised me into the air of the sixth heaven, and I saw such glory as I had not seen in the five heavens. ² For I saw messengers possessing great glory. ³ And the praise there was holy and wonderful. ⁴ And I said to the messenger who conducted me, "What is this which I see, my Lord?" ⁵ And he said, "I am not your lord, but your fellow servant." ⁶ And again I asked him, and I said to him, "Why are there not angelic fellow servants [on the left]?" ⁷ And he said, "From the sixth heaven there are no longer messengers on the left, nor a throne set in the midst, but [they are directed] by the power of the seventh heaven, where dwells He that is not named and the Chosen One, whose Name has not been made known, and none of the heavens can learn His Name, ⁸ for it is He alone to whose voice all the heavens and thrones give answer. I have therefore been empowered and sent to raise you here that you may see this glory, ⁹ and that you may see the Lord of all those heavens and these thrones, ¹⁰ undergoing [successive] transformation until He resembles your form and likeness. ¹¹ I indeed say to you, Isaiah, no man about to return into a body of that world has ascended or seen what you see or perceived what you have perceived and what you will see. ¹² For it has been permitted to you in the lot of the LORD to come here. [[And from there comes the power of the sixth heaven and of the air]]." ¹³ And I magnified my Lord with praise, in that through His lot I should come here. ¹⁴ And he said, "Hear, furthermore, therefore, this also from your fellow servant: when from the body by the will of God you have ascended here, then you will receive the garment which you see, and likewise other numbered garments laid up you will see. ¹⁵ And then you will become equal to the messengers of the seventh heaven." ¹⁶ And he raised me up into the sixth heaven, and there were no [messengers] on the left, nor a throne in the midst, but all had one appearance

and their [power of] praise was equal. ¹⁷ And [power] was given to me also, and I also praised along with them and that messenger also, and our praise was like theirs. ¹⁸ And there they all named the primal Father and His Beloved, the Christ, and the Holy Spirit, all with one voice. ¹⁹ And [their voice] was not like the voice of the messengers in the five heavens, ²⁰ but the voice was different there, and there was much light there. ²¹ And then, when I was in the sixth heaven, I thought the light which I had seen in the five heavens to be but darkness. ²² And I rejoiced and praised Him who has bestowed such lights on those who wait for His promise. ²³ And I implored the messenger who conducted me that I should no longer return to the carnal world. ²⁴ I indeed say to you, Hezekiah, and my son Josab, and Micaiah, that there is much darkness here. ²⁵ And the messenger who conducted me discovered what I thought and said, "If you rejoice in this light, how much more will you rejoice when you see the light in the seventh heaven where the LORD and His Beloved are, [[from where I have been sent, who is to be called Son in this world. ²⁶ It has not been manifested [when] He will be in the corruptible world]] and the garments, and the thrones, and the crowns which are laid up for the righteous, for those who trust in that Lord who will descend in your form. For the light which is there is great and wonderful. ²⁷ And as concerning your not returning into the body, your days are not yet fulfilled for coming here." ²⁸ And when I heard, I was troubled, and he said, "Do not be troubled."

CHAPTER 9

¹ And he took me into the air of the seventh heaven, and moreover I heard a voice, saying, "How far will he ascend that dwells in the flesh?" And I feared and trembled. ² And when I trembled, behold, I heard from there another voice being sent forth, and saying, "It is permitted to the holy Isaiah to ascend here; for here is his garment." ³ And I asked the messenger who was with me and said, "Who is he who forbade me and who is he who permitted me to ascend?" ⁴ And he said to me, "He who forbade you is he who is over the praise-giving of the sixth heaven. ⁵ And He who permitted you, this is your LORD God, the Lord Christ, who will be called Jesus in the world, but His Name you cannot hear until you have ascended out of your body." ⁶ And he raised me up into the seventh heaven, and I saw there a wonderful light and innumerable messengers. ⁷ And there I saw the holy Abel and all the righteous. ⁸ And there I saw Enoch and all who were with him, stripped of the garments of the flesh, ⁹ and I saw them in their garments of the upper world, and they were like messengers, standing there in great glory. ¹⁰ But they did not sit on their thrones, nor were their crowns of glory on them. ¹¹ And I asked the messenger who was with me: "How is it that they have received the garments, but do not

have the thrones and the crowns?" ¹² And he said to me, "They do not receive crowns and thrones of glory until the Beloved will descend in the form in which you will see Him descend into the world in the last days—the LORD, who will be called Christ. ¹³ Nevertheless, they see and know whose thrones will be, and whose the crowns when He has descended and been made in your form, and they will think that He is flesh and is a man. ¹⁴ And the god of that world will stretch forth his hand against the Son, and they will crucify Him on a tree, and will slay Him not knowing who He is. ¹⁵ And thus His descent, as you will see, will be hidden even from the heavens, so that it will not be known who He is. ¹⁶ And when He has plundered the messenger of death, He will ascend on the third day. ¹⁷ And then many of the righteous will ascend with Him, whose spirits do not receive their garments until the Lord Christ ascends and they ascend with Him. ¹⁸ Then they will indeed receive their [garments, and] thrones, and crowns when He has ascended into the seventh heaven." ¹⁹ And I said to him that which I had asked him in the third heaven: ²⁰ "Show me how everything which is done in that world is made known here." ²¹ And while I was still speaking with him, behold, one of the messengers who stood near, more glorious than the glory of that messenger who had raised me up from the world, ²² showed me a scroll, and he opened it, and the scroll was written, but not as a scroll of this world. And he gave [it] to me and I read it, and behold, the deeds of the sons of Israel were written therein, and the deeds of those whom I [do not] know, my son Josab. ²³ And I said, "In truth, there is nothing hidden in the seventh heaven, which is done in this world." ²⁴ And I saw there many garments laid up, and many thrones and many crowns. ²⁵ And I said to the messenger, "Whose are these garments, and thrones, and crowns?" ²⁶ And he said to me, "Many from that world will receive these garments, believing in the words of that One who will be named as I told you, and they will observe those things, and believe in them, and believe in His Cross; these are laid up for them." ²⁷ And I saw a certain One standing, whose glory surpassed that of all, and His glory was great and wonderful. ²⁸ And after I had seen Him, all the righteous whom I had seen and also the messengers whom I had seen came to Him. And Adam, and Abel, and Seth, and all the righteous first drew near and worshiped Him, and they all praised Him with one voice, and I myself also gave praise with them, and my giving of praise was as theirs. ²⁹ And then all the messengers drew near and worshiped and gave praise. ³⁰ And I was transformed and became like a messenger. ³¹ And thereon the messenger who conducted me said to me, "Worship this One," and I worshiped and praised. ³² And the messenger said to me, "This is the Lord of all the praise-givings which you have seen." ³³ And while he was still speaking, I saw another glorious One who was like Him, and the righteous drew near and worshiped and praised, and I praised together with them. But my glory was not transformed into accordance with their form. ³⁴ And thereon the messengers drew near and worshiped Him. ³⁵ And I saw the LORD and the second messenger, and they were standing. ³⁶ And the second whom I saw was on the left of my Lord. And I asked, "Who is this?" and he said to me, "Worship Him, for He is the Messenger—the Holy Spirit, who speaks in you and the rest of the righteous." ³⁷ And I saw the great glory, the eyes of my spirit being open, and I could not thereon see, nor yet could the messenger who was with me, nor all the messengers whom I had seen worshiping my Lord. ³⁸ But I saw the righteous beholding with great power the glory of that One. ³⁹ And my Lord drew near to me and the Messenger— the Spirit—and He said, "See how it is given to you to see God, and on your account, power is given to the messenger who is with you." ⁴⁰ And I saw how my Lord and the Messenger—the Spirit—worshiped, and they both together praised God. ⁴¹ And thereon all the righteous drew near and worshiped. ⁴² And the messengers drew near and worshiped, and all the messengers praised.

CHAPTER 10

¹ And thereon I heard the voices and the giving of praise, which I had heard in each of the six heavens, ascending and being heard there: ² and all were being sent up to that glorious One whose glory I could not behold. ³ And I myself was hearing and beholding the praise [which was given] to Him. ⁴ And the LORD and the Messenger—the Spirit—were beholding all and hearing all. ⁵ And all the praises which are sent up from the six heavens are not only heard, but seen. ⁶ And I heard the messenger who conducted me and he said, "This is the Most High of the high ones, dwelling in the holy world, and resting in His holy ones, who will be called by the Holy Spirit through the lips of the righteous the Father of the Lord." ⁷ And I heard the voice of the Most High, the Father of my Lord, saying to my Lord Christ who will be called Jesus: ⁸ "Go forth and descend through all the heavens, and You will descend to the expanse and that world; You will descend to the messenger in Sheol, but You will not go to Haguel. ⁹ And You will become like to the likeness of all who are in the five heavens. ¹⁰ And You will be careful to become like the form of the messengers of the expanse [[and the messengers who are also in Sheol]]. ¹¹ And none of the messengers of that world will know that You are with Me of the seven heavens and of their messengers. ¹² And they will not know that You are with Me, until I have called with a loud voice [to] the heavens, and their messengers and their lights—to the sixth heaven, in order that You may judge and destroy the princes, and messengers, and gods of that world,

and the world that is dominated by them, ¹³ for they have denied Me and said, We are alone and there is none besides us. ¹⁴ And afterward from the messengers of death You will ascend to Your place. And You will not be transformed in each Heaven, but You will ascend in glory and sit on My right hand. ¹⁵ And thereon the princes and powers of that world will worship You." ¹⁶ I heard the Great Glory giving these commands to my Lord. ¹⁷ And so I saw my Lord go forth from the seventh heaven into the sixth heaven. ¹⁸ And the messenger who conducted me said to me, "Understand, Isaiah, and see [how] the transformation and descent of the LORD will appear." ¹⁹ And I saw, and when the messengers saw Him, thereon those in the sixth heaven praised and lauded Him; for He had not been transformed after the shape of the messengers there, and they praised Him, and I also praised with them. ²⁰ And I saw when He descended into the fifth heaven, that in the fifth heaven He made Himself like to the form of the messengers there, and they did not praise Him [nor worship Him], for His form was like to theirs. ²¹ And then He descended into the fourth heaven and made Himself like to the form of the messengers there. ²² And when they saw Him, they did not praise or laud Him, for His form was like to their form. ²³ And again I saw when He descended into the third heaven, and He made Himself like to the form of the messengers in the third heaven. ²⁴ And those who kept the gate of the [third] heaven demanded the password, and the LORD gave [it] to them in order that He should not be recognized. And when they saw Him, they did not praise or laud Him, for His form was like to their form. ²⁵ And again I saw when He descended into the second heaven, and again He gave the password there; and those who kept the gate proceeded to demand the LORD to give [it]. ²⁶ And I saw when He made Himself like to the form of the messengers in the second heaven, and they saw Him, and they did not praise Him, for His form was like to their form. ²⁷ And again I saw when He descended into the first heaven, and there also He gave the password to those who kept the gate, and He made Himself like to the form of the messengers who were on the left of that throne, and they neither praised nor lauded Him, for His form was like to their form. ²⁸ But as for me, no one asked me on account of the messenger who conducted me. ²⁹ And again He descended into the expanse where the ruler of this world dwells, and He gave the password to those on the left, and His form was like theirs, and they did not praise Him there; but they were envying one another and fighting, for here there is a power of evil and envying about trifles. ³⁰ And I saw when He descended and made Himself like to the messengers of the air, and He was like one of them. ³¹ And He gave no password, for one was plundering and doing violence to another.

ASCENSION OF ISAIAH

CHAPTER 11

¹ After this I saw, and the messenger who spoke with me, who conducted me, said to me, "Understand, Isaiah, son of Amoz, for I have been sent from God for this purpose." ² And I indeed saw a woman of the family of the prophet David, named Mary, and Virgin, and she was espoused to a man named Joseph, a carpenter, and he was also of the seed and family of the righteous David of Beth-Lehem [in] Judah. ³ And he came into his lot. And when she was espoused, she was found with child, and Joseph the carpenter was desirous to put her away. ⁴ But the messenger of the Spirit appeared in this world, and after that Joseph did not put her away, but kept Mary and did not reveal this matter to anyone. ⁵ And he did not approach Mary, but kept her as a holy virgin, though with child. ⁶ And he did not live with her for two months. ⁷ And after two months of days while Joseph was in his house, and Mary his wife, but both alone, ⁸ it came to pass that when they were alone that Mary immediately looked with her eyes and saw a small baby, and she was astonished. ⁹ And after she had been astonished, her womb was found as formerly before she had conceived. ¹⁰ And when her husband Joseph said to her, "What has astonished you?" his eyes were opened and he saw the Infant and praised God, because God had come into his portion. ¹¹ And a voice came to them: "Tell this vision to no one." ¹² And the story regarding the Infant was spread widely in Beth-Lehem. ¹³ Some said, "The Virgin Mary has borne a child before she was married two months." ¹⁴ And many said, "She has not borne a child, nor has a midwife gone up [to her], nor have we heard the cries of [labor] pains." And they were all blinded respecting Him and they all knew regarding Him, though they did not know where He was from. ¹⁵ And they took Him and went to Nazareth in Galilee. ¹⁶ And I saw, O Hezekiah and my son Josab, and I declare to the other prophets who are also standing by, that [this] has escaped all the heavens, and all the princes, and all the gods of this world. ¹⁷ And I saw: in Nazareth He sucked the breast as a baby and as is customary in order that He might not be recognized. ¹⁸ And when He had grown up, He worked great signs and wonders in the land of Israel and of Jerusalem. ¹⁹ And after this the adversary envied Him and roused the sons of Israel against Him, not knowing who He was, and they delivered Him to the king, and crucified Him, and He descended to the messenger [of Sheol]. ²⁰ I indeed saw Him being crucified on a tree in Jerusalem: ²¹ and likewise after the third day rise again and remain [forty] days. ²² And the messenger who conducted me said, "Understand, Isaiah": and I saw when He sent out the Twelve Apostles and ascended. ²³ And I saw Him, and He was in the expanse, but He had not changed Himself into their form, and all the messengers of the expanse and the adversaries saw Him, and they worshiped. ²⁴ And there was much sorrow there, while they said, "How did our Lord descend in our midst, and we did not perceive the glory which we see has been on Him from the sixth heaven?" ²⁵ And He ascended into the second heaven, and He did not transform Himself, but all the messengers who were on the right, and on the left, and the throne in the midst ²⁶ both worshiped Him and praised Him and said, "How did our Lord escape us while descending, and we did not perceive [it]?" ²⁷ And in like manner He ascended into the third heaven, and they praised and said in like manner. ²⁸ And in the fourth heaven and also in the fifth they said precisely after the same manner. ²⁹ But there was one glory, and from it He did not change Himself. ³⁰ And I saw when He ascended into the sixth heaven, and they worshiped and glorified Him. ³¹ But in all the heavens the praise increased. ³² And I saw how He ascended into the seventh heaven, and all the righteous and all the messengers praised Him. And then I saw Him sit down on the right hand of that Great Glory whose glory I told you that I could not behold. ³³ And also the Messenger—the Holy Spirit—I saw sitting on the left hand. ³⁴ And this messenger said to me, "Isaiah, son of Amoz, it is enough for you; for you have seen what no child of flesh has seen. ³⁵ And you will return into your garment [of flesh] until your days are completed. Then you will come here." ³⁶ Isaiah saw these things and told [it] to all that stood before him, and they praised. And he spoke to Hezekiah the king and said, "I have spoken these things; ³⁷ both the end of this world ³⁸ and all this vision will be consummated in the last generations." ³⁹ And Isaiah made him swear that he would not tell [it] to the people of Israel, nor give these words to any man to transcribe. ⁴⁰ . . . such things you will read. And watch in the Holy Spirit in order they you may receive your garments, and thrones, and crowns of glory, which are laid up in the seventh heaven. ⁴¹ On account of these visions and prophecies Sammael, Satan, sawed apart Isaiah the son of Amoz, the prophet, by the hand of Manasseh. ⁴² And Hezekiah delivered all these things to Manasseh in the twenty-sixth year. ⁴³ But Manasseh did not remember them nor place these things in his heart, but becoming the servant of Satan, he was destroyed. HERE ENDS THE VISION OF ISAIAH THE PROPHET WITH HIS ASCENSION.

2 BARUCH

2 Baruch is a Jewish text, likely pseudepigraphical, thought to have been written in the 1st or 2nd century AD. It is also known as the Syriac Apocalypse of Baruch (used to distinguish it from the Greek Apocalypse of Baruch—3 Baruch). The Apocalypse proper occupies the first 77 chapters of the book. Chapters 78–87 are usually referred to as the "Letter of Baruch to the Nine and a Half Tribes."

CHAPTER 1

¹ And it came to pass in the twenty-fifth year of Jehoiachin, king of Judah, that the word of the LORD came to Baruch, the son of Neriah, and said to him: ² "Have you seen all that this people are doing to Me, that the evils which these two tribes which remained have done are greater than [those of] the ten tribes which were carried away captive? ³ For the former tribes were forced by their kings to commit sin, but these two of themselves have been forcing and compelling their kings to commit sin. ⁴ For this reason, behold, I bring calamity on this city and on its inhabitants, and it will be removed from before Me for a time, and I will scatter this people among the nations that they may do good to the nations. And My people will be disciplined, and the time will come when they will seek for the prosperity of their times."

CHAPTER 2

¹ "For I have said these things to you that you may bid Jeremiah, and all those that are like you, to retire from this city. ² For your works are to this city as a firm pillar, || And your prayers as a strong wall."

CHAPTER 3

¹ And I said, "O LORD, my Lord, have I come into the world for this purpose that I might see the calamities of my mother? No, my Lord. ² If I have found grace in Your sight, first take my spirit that I may go to my fathers and not behold the destruction of my mother. For two things vehemently constrain me: for I cannot resist You, and my soul, moreover, cannot behold the calamities of my mother. ⁴ But one thing I will say in Your presence, O LORD. ⁵ What, therefore, will there be after these things? For if You destroy Your city, and deliver up Your land to those that hate us, how will the name of Israel be remembered again? ⁶ Or how will one speak of Your praises? Or to whom will that which is in Your law be explained? Or will the world return to its nature of former times, and the age revert to primeval silence? And will the multitude of souls be taken away, and the nature of man not again be named? And where is all that which You said regarding us?"

CHAPTER 4

¹ And the LORD said to me: "This city will be delivered up for a time, || And the people will be disciplined during a time, || And the world will not be given over to oblivion." [[² "Do you think that this is that city of which I said, On the palms of My hands I have graven you? ³ This building now built in your midst is not that which is revealed with Me, that which [was] prepared beforehand here from the time when I took counsel to make Paradise, and showed Adam before he sinned, but when he transgressed the commandment it was removed from him, as also Paradise. ⁴ And after these things I showed it to My servant Abraham by night among the portions of the victims. ⁵ And again I also showed it to Moses on Mount Sinai when I showed to the likeness of the Dwelling Place and all its vessels. ⁶ And now, behold, it is preserved with Me, as Paradise. ⁷ Go, therefore, and do as I command you."]]

CHAPTER 5

¹ And I answered and said, "So then I am destined to grieve for Zion, || For Your enemies will come to this place and pollute Your sanctuary, || And lead Your inheritance into captivity, || And make themselves masters of those whom You have loved, || And they will depart again to the place of their idols, || And will boast before them: And what will You do for Your great Name?" ² And the LORD said to me: "My Name and My glory are to all eternity; And My judgment will maintain its right in its own time. ³ And you will see with your eyes || That the enemy will not overthrow Zion, || Nor will they burn Jerusalem, || But be the ministers of the Judge for the time. ⁴ But you go and do whatever I have said to you." ⁵ And I went and took Jeremiah, and Adu, and Seriah, and Jabish, and Gedaliah, and all the honorable men of the people, and I led them to the Valley of Kidron, and I narrated to them all that had been said to me. ⁶ And they lifted up their voice, and they all wept. ⁷ And we sat there and fasted until the evening.

CHAPTER 6

¹ And it came to pass on the next day that, behold, the army of the Chaldees surrounded the city, and at the time of the evening, I, Baruch, left the people, and I went forth and stood by the oak. ² And I was grieving over Zion and lamenting over the captivity which had come on the people. ³ And behold, suddenly a strong spirit raised me, and bore me aloft over the wall of Jerusalem. ⁴ And I beheld, and behold, four messengers standing at the four corners of the city, each of them holding a torch of fire in his hands. ⁵ And another messenger began to descend from Heaven,

and said to them, "Hold your lamps, and do not light them until I tell you. ⁶For I am first sent to speak a word to the earth, and to place in it what the LORD the Most High has commanded me." ⁷And I saw him descend into the Holy of Holies, and take from there the veil, and holy Ark, and the propitiatory covering, and the two tablets, and the holy raiment of the priests, and the altar of incense, and the forty-eight precious stones with which the priest was adorned, and all the holy vessels of the Dwelling Place. ⁸And he spoke to the earth with a loud voice: "Earth, earth, earth! Hear the word of the mighty God, || And receive what I commit to you, || And guard them until the last times, || So that, when you are ordered, you may restore them, || So that strangers may not get possession of them. ⁹For the time comes when Jerusalem will also be delivered for a time, || Until it is said that it is again restored forever." ¹⁰And the earth opened its mouth and swallowed them up.

CHAPTER 7

¹And after these things I heard that messenger saying to those messengers who held the lamps: "Destroy, therefore, and overthrow its wall to its foundations, lest the enemy should boast and say, || We have overthrown the wall of Zion, || And we have burned the place of the mighty God." ²And they have seized the place where I had been standing before.

CHAPTER 8

¹Now the messengers did as he had commanded them, and when they had broken up the corners of the walls, a voice was heard from the interior of the temple, after the wall had fallen, saying, ²"Enter, you enemies, || And come, you adversaries; For He who kept the house has forsaken [it]." ³And I, Baruch, departed. ⁴And it came to pass after these things that the army of the Chaldees entered and seized the house, and all that was around it. And they led the people away captive and slew some of them, and bound Zedekiah the king, and sent him to the king of Babylon.

CHAPTER 9

¹And I, Baruch, came, and Jeremiah, whose heart was found pure from sins, who had not been captured in the seizure of the city. ²And we tore our garments, we wept, and mourned, and fasted seven days.

CHAPTER 10

¹And it came to pass after seven days, that the word of God came to me, and said to me: ²"Tell Jeremiah to go and support the captivity of the people to Babylon. ³But remain here amid the desolation of Zion, and I will show to you after these days what will befall at the end of days." ⁴And I spoke to Jeremiah as the LORD commanded me. ⁵And he, indeed, departed with the people, but I, Baruch, returned and sat before the gates of the temple, and I lamented with the following lamentation over Zion and said, ⁶"Blessed is he who was not born, || Or he, who having been born, has died. ⁷But as for us who live, woe to us, || Because we see the afflictions of Zion, || And what has befallen Jerusalem. ⁸I will call the Sirens from the sea, || And you Lilin, come from the desert, || And you Shedim and dragons from the forests: Awake and gird up your loins to mourning, || And take up the dirges with me, || And make lamentation with me. ⁹You farmers, do not sow again; And, O earth, why do you give your harvest fruits? Keep within you the sweets of your sustenance. ¹⁰And you, vine, why further do you give your wine? For an offering will not be made again from there in Zion, || Nor will first-fruits be offered again. ¹¹And you, O heavens, withhold your dew, || And do not open the treasuries of rain; ¹²And you, O sun, withhold the light of your rays; And you, O moon, extinguish the multitude of your light. For why should light rise again || Where the light of Zion is darkened? ¹³And you—you bridegrooms—do not enter in, || And do not let the brides adorn themselves with garlands; And, you women, do not pray that you may bear. ¹⁴For the barren will above all rejoice, || And those who have no sons will be glad, || And those who have sons will have anguish. ¹⁵For why should they bear in pain, || Only to bury in grief? ¹⁶Or why, again, should mankind have sons? Or why should the seed of their kind be named again, || Where this mother is desolate, || And her sons are led into captivity? ¹⁷From this time forward, do not speak of beauty, || And do not discourse of gracefulness. ¹⁸Moreover, you priests, take the keys of the sanctuary, || And cast them into the height of Heaven, || And give them to the LORD and say, || Guard Your house Yourself, || For behold, we are found false stewards. ¹⁹And you—you virgins who weave fine linen || And silk with gold of Ophir—Take all [these] things with haste || And cast [them] into the fire, || That it may bear them to Him who made them, || And the flame send them to Him who created them, || Lest the enemy get possession of them."

CHAPTER 11

¹Moreover, I, Baruch, say this against you, Babylon: "If you had prospered, || And Zion had dwelt in her glory, || Yet the grief to us had been great || That you should be equal to Zion. ²But now, behold, the grief is infinite, || And the lamentation measureless, || For behold, you are prospered || And Zion desolate. ³Who will be judge regarding these things? Or to whom will we complain regarding that which has befallen us? O LORD, how have You borne [it]? ⁴Our fathers went to rest without grief, || And behold, the righteous sleep in the earth in tranquility; ⁵For they did not know this anguish, || Nor yet had they heard of that which had befallen us. ⁶Would that you had ears, O earth, || And

that you had a heart, O dust, ‖ That you might go and announce in Sheol, ‖ And say to the dead: ⁷Blessed are you more than we who live."

CHAPTER 12

¹ "But I will say this as I think, ‖ And speak against you—the land that is prospering. ² The noonday does not always burn, ‖ Nor do the rays of the sun constantly give light. ³ And do not expect to rejoice, ‖ Nor condemn greatly. ⁴ For assuredly in its season the [divine] wrath will be awakened against you, ‖ Which is now restrained by long-suffering as it were by a rein." ⁵ And when I had said these things, I fasted seven days.

CHAPTER 13

¹ And it came to pass after these things that I, Baruch, was standing on Mount Zion, and behold, a voice came forth from the height and said to me: ² "Stand on your feet, Baruch, and hear the word of the mighty God. ³ Because you have been astonished at what has befallen Zion, you will therefore be assuredly preserved to the consummation of the times, that you may be for a testimony. ⁴ So that, if ever those prosperous cities say: ⁵ Why has the mighty God brought this retribution on us? Say to them, You and those like you will have seen this evil and retribution which is coming on you and on your people in its [appointed] time that the nations may be thoroughly smitten. ⁶ And then they will be in anguish. ⁷ And if they say at that time: ⁸ For how long? You will say to them: You who have drunk the strained wine, ‖ Drink also of its dregs—The judgment of the Lofty One ‖ Who has no respect of persons; ⁹ On this account He formerly had no mercy on His own sons, ‖ But afflicted them as His enemies, because they sinned, ¹⁰ Then, therefore, they were disciplined ‖ That they might be sanctified. ¹¹ But now, you peoples and nations, you are guilty ‖ Because you have always trodden down the earth, ‖ And used the creation unrighteously. ¹² For I have always benefited you. And you have always been ungrateful for the beneficence."

CHAPTER 14

¹ And I answered and said, "Behold, You have shown me the methods of the times, and that which will be. And You have said to me that the retribution which was spoken of by You will be endured by the nations. ² And now I know that those who have sinned are many, and they have lived . . . and departed from the world, but that few nations will be left in those times to whom . . . the words [which] You said. ³ And what advantage [is there] in this or what worse than [these?] ⁴ But I will again speak in Your presence: ⁵ What have they profited who had knowledge before You and have not walked in vanity as the rest of the nations, and have not said to the dead, Give us life,

but always feared You, and have not left Your ways? ⁶ And behold, they have been carried off, nor on their account have You had mercy on Zion. ⁷ And if others did evil, it was due to Zion that on account of the works of those who worked good works she should be forgiven and should not be overwhelmed on account of the works of those who worked unrighteousness. ⁸ But who, O LORD, my Lord, will comprehend Your judgment, ‖ Or who will search out the profoundness of Your way? Or who will think out the weight of Your path? ⁹ Or who will be able to think out Your incomprehensible counsel? Or who of those that are born has ever found ‖ The beginning or end of Your wisdom? ¹⁰ For we have all been made like a breath. ¹¹ For as the breath ascends involuntarily, and again dies, so it is with the nature of men, who do not depart according to their own will, and do not know what will befall them in the end. ¹² For the righteous justly hope for the end, and without fear depart from this habitation, because they have with You a store of works preserved in treasuries. ¹³ On this account also, these without fear leave this world, and trusting with joy they hope to receive the world which You have promised them. ¹⁴ But as for us—woe to us, who are also now shamefully entreated, and at that time look forward [only] to calamities. ¹⁵ But You know accurately what You have done by means of Your servants; for we are not able to understand that which is good as You are, our Creator. ¹⁶ But again I will speak in Your presence, O LORD, my Lord. ¹⁷ When of old there was no world with its inhabitants, You devised and spoke with a word, and immediately the works of creation stood before You. ¹⁸ And You said that You would make for Your world man as the administrator of Your works, that it might be known that he was by no means made on account of the world, but the world on account of him. ¹⁹ And now I see that as for the world which was made on account of us, behold, it abides; but we, on account of whom it was made, depart."

CHAPTER 15

¹ And the LORD answered and said to me: "You are rightly astonished regarding the departure of man, but you have not judged well regarding the calamities which befall those who sin. ² And as regards what you have said, that the righteous are carried off and the impious are prospered, ³ and as regards what you have said, Man does not know Your judgment—on this account hear, and I will speak to you, and listen, and I will cause you to hear My words. ⁵ Man would not rightly have understood My judgment, unless he had accepted the law, and I had instructed him in understanding. ⁶ But now, because he transgressed willfully, yes, just on this ground that he knows, he will be tormented. ⁷ And as regards what you said touching the righteous, that on account of them this

world has come, so also again, that which is to come will come on their account. [8] For this world is to them a strife and a labor with much trouble; and that accordingly which is to come—a crown with great glory."

CHAPTER 16

[1] And I answered and said, [2] "LORD, my Lord, behold, the years of this time are few and evil, and who is able in his short time to acquire that which is measureless?"

CHAPTER 17

[1] And the LORD answered and said to me: "With the Most High account is not taken of time nor of a few years. [2] For what did it profit Adam that he lived nine hundred and thirty years and transgressed that which he was commanded? Therefore, the multitude of time that he lived did not profit him, but brought death and cut off the years of those who were born from him, wherein Moses suffered loss in that he lived only one hundred and twenty years, and inasmuch he was subject to Him who formed him, brought the law to the seed of Jacob, and lighted a lamp for the nation of Israel?"

CHAPTER 18

[1] And I answered and said, "He that lighted has taken from the light, and there are but few that have imitated him. [2] But those many whom he has lighted have taken from the darkness of Adam and have not rejoiced in the light of the lamp."

CHAPTER 19

[1] And He answered and said to me: "For what reason at that time he appointed for them a covenant and said, Behold, I have placed before you life and death, || And he called the heavens and earth to witness against them. [2] For he knew that his time was but short, || But that the heavens and earth always endure. [3] But after his death they sinned and transgressed, || Though they knew that they had the law reproving [them], || And the light in which nothing could err, || Also the spheres which testify, and Me. [4] Now regarding everything that is, it is I that judge, but do not take counsel in your soul regarding these things, nor afflict yourself because of those which have been. [5] For now it is the consummation of time that should be considered, whether of business, or of prosperity, or of shame, and not the beginning thereof. [6] Because if a man is prospered in his beginnings and shamefully entreated in his old age, he forgets all the prosperity that he had. [7] And again, if a man is shamefully entreated in his beginnings, and at his end is prospered, he does not remember again his evil entreatment. [8] And again listen: though each one were prospered all that time—all the time from the day on which death was decreed against those who

transgress—and in his end was destroyed, everything would have been in vain."

CHAPTER 20

[1] "Therefore, behold! The days come, || And the times will hasten more than the former, || And the seasons will speed by more than those that are past, || And the years will pass more quickly than the present [years]. [2] Therefore I have now taken Zion away, || That I may the more speedily visit the world in its season. [3] Now therefore, hold fast in your heart everything that I command you, || And seal it in the recesses of your mind. [4] And then I will show you the judgment of My might, || And My ways which are unsearchable. [5] Go therefore and sanctify yourself seven days, and eat no bread, nor drink water, nor speak to anyone. [6] And afterward come to that place and I will reveal Myself to you, and speak true things with you, and I will give you commandment regarding the method of the times; for they are coming and do not tarry."

CHAPTER 21

[1] And I went there and sat in the Valley of Kidron in a cave of the earth, and I sanctified my soul there, and I ate no bread, yet I was not hungry, and I drank no water, yet I did not thirst, and I was there until the seventh day, as He had commanded me. [2] And afterward I came to that place where He had spoken with me. [3] And it came to pass at sunset that my soul took much thought, and I began to speak in the presence of the Mighty One, and said, [4] "O You that have made the earth, hear me, that have fixed the expanse by the word, and have made firm the height of the Heaven by the Spirit, that have called from the beginning of the world that which did not yet exist, and they obey You. [5] You that have commanded the air by Your nod and have seen those things which are to be as those things which You are doing. [6] You that rule with great thought the hosts that stand before You; also the countless holy beings, which You made from the beginning, of flame and fire, which stand around Your throne, You rule with indignation. [7] To You only does this belong that You should immediately do whatever You wish. [8] [You] who cause the drops of rain to rain by number on the earth, and alone knows the consummation of the times before they come, have respect to my prayer. [9] For You alone are able to sustain all who are, and those who have passed away, and those who are to be, those who sin, and those who are righteous (as living and being past finding out). [10] For You alone live [as] immortal and past finding out, and know the number of mankind. [11] And if in time many have sinned, yet others—not a few—have been righteous. [12] You know where You preserve the end of those who have sinned, or the consummation of those who have been righteous. [13] For if there were this life only, which belongs to all men, nothing could be more bitter than

this. [14] For of what profit is strength that turns to sickness, || Or fullness of food that turns to famine, || Or beauty that turns to ugliness. [15] For the nature of man is always changeable. [16] For what we were formerly now we no longer are and what we now are we will not afterward remain. [16] For if a consummation had not been prepared for all, in vain would have been their beginning. But regarding everything that comes from You, You inform me, and regarding everything about which I ask You, You enlighten me. [19] How long will that which is corruptible remain, and how long will the time of mortals be prospered, and until what time will those who transgress in the world be polluted with much wickedness? [20] Therefore command in mercy and accomplish all that You said You would bring, that Your might may be made known to those who think that Your long-suffering is weakness. [21] And show to those who do not know, that everything that has befallen us and our city until now has been according to the long-suffering of Your power, because on account of Your Name You have called us a beloved people. [22] Therefore, henceforth, bring mortality to an end. [23] And reprove the messenger of death accordingly, and let Your glory appear, and let the might of Your beauty be known, and let Sheol be sealed so that from this time forward it may not receive the dead, and let the treasuries of souls restore those which are enclosed in them. [24] For there have been many years like those that are desolate from the days of Abraham, and Isaac, and Jacob, and of all those who are like them, who sleep in the earth, on whose account You said that You had created the world. [25] And now quickly show Your glory, and do not defer what has been promised by You." [26] And [when] I had completed the words of this prayer I was greatly weakened.

CHAPTER 22

[1] And it came to pass after these things that, behold, the heavens were opened, and I saw, and power was given to me, and a voice was heard from on high, and it said to me: [2] "Baruch, Baruch, why are you troubled? [3] He who travels by a road but does not complete it, or who departs by sea but does not arrive at the port, can he be comforted? [4] Or he who promises to give a present to another, but does not fulfill it, is it not robbery? [5] Or he who sows the earth, but does not reap its fruit in its season, does he not lose everything? [6] Or he who plants a plant unless it grows until the time suitable to it, does he who planted it expect to receive fruit from it? [7] Or a woman who has conceived, if she brings forth untimely, does she not assuredly slay her infant? [8] Or he who builds a house, if he does not roof it and complete it, can it be called a house? Tell Me that first."

CHAPTER 23

[1] And I answered and said, "Not so, O LORD, my Lord." [2] And He answered and said to me, "Why are you therefore troubled about that which you do not know, and why are you ill at ease about things in which you are ignorant? [3] For as you have not forgotten the people who now are and those who have passed away, so I remember those who are appointed to come. [4] Because when Adam sinned and death was decreed against those who should be born, then the multitude of those who should be born was numbered, and for that number a place was prepared where the living might dwell and the dead might be guarded. Therefore, before the number previously mentioned is fulfilled, the creature will not live again [[for My Spirit is the creator of life]], and Sheol will receive the dead. [6] And again it is given to you to hear what things are to come after these times. [7] For My redemption has truly drawn near and is not far distant as before."

CHAPTER 24

[1] "For behold! The days come and the scrolls will be opened in which are written the sins of all those who have sinned, and again also the treasuries in which the righteousness of all those who have been righteous in creation is gathered. [2] For it will come to pass at that time that you will see—and the many that are with you—the long-suffering of the Most High, which has been throughout all generations, who has been long-suffering toward all who are born, [both] those who sin and [those who] are righteous." [3] And I answered and said, "But, behold! O LORD, no one knows the number of those things which have passed nor yet of those things which are to come. [4] For I indeed know that which has befallen us, but I do not know what will happen to our enemies, and when You will visit Your works."

CHAPTER 25

[1] And He answered and said to me: "You, too, will be preserved until that time until that sign which the Most High will work for the inhabitants of the earth in the end of days. [2] This will therefore be the sign: [3] when a stupor will seize the inhabitants of the earth, and they will fall into many tribulations, and again when they will fall into great torments. And it will come to pass when they say in their thoughts by reason of their much tribulation: The Mighty One no longer remembers the earth—yes, it will come to pass when they abandon hope, that the time will then awake."

CHAPTER 26

[1] And I answered and said, "Will that tribulation which is to come continue [for] a long time, and will that necessarily comprise many years?"

CHAPTER 27

[1] And He answered and said to me: "That time is divided into twelve parts, and each one of them is reserved for that which is appointed for it. [2] In the first part there will be the beginning of commotions. [3] And in the second part [there will be] slayings of the great ones. [4] And in the third part the fall of many by death. [5] And in the fourth part the sending of the sword. [6] And in the fifth part famine and the withholding of rain. [7] And in the sixth part earthquakes and terrors. [8] [And in the seventh part] ... [9] And in the eighth part a multitude of specters and attacks of the Shedim. [10] And in the ninth part the fall of fire. [11] And in the tenth part plunder and much oppression. [12] And in the eleventh part wickedness and unchastity. [13] And in the twelfth part confusion from the mingling together of all those things previously mentioned. [14] For these parts of that time are reserved and will be mingled with one another and minister to one another. [15] For some will leave out some of their own, and receive [in its stead] from others, and some complete their own and that of others, so that those may not understand who are on the earth in those days that this is the consummation of the times."

CHAPTER 28

[1] "Nevertheless, whoever understands will then be wise. [2] For the measure and reckoning of that time are two parts a week of seven weeks." [3] And I answered and said, "It is good for a man to come and behold, but it is better that he should not come lest he fall. [4] [[But I will say this also: [5] Will He who is incorruptible despise those things which are corruptible, and whatever befalls in the case of those things which are corruptible, so that He might look only to those things which are not corruptible?]] [6] But if, O LORD, those things will assuredly come to pass which You have foretold to me, so also show this to me if indeed I have found grace in Your sight. [7] Is it in one place or in one of the parts of the earth that those things have come to pass, or will the whole earth experience [them]?"

CHAPTER 29

[1] And He answered and said to me: "Whatever will then befall [will befall] the whole earth; therefore, all who live will experience [them]. [2] For at that time I will only protect those who are found in those same days in this land. [3] And it will come to pass when all is accomplished that was to come to pass in those parts, that the Messiah will then begin to be revealed. [4] And Behemoth will be revealed from his place and Leviathan will ascend from the sea—those two great monsters which I created on the fifth day of creation, and will have kept until that time; and then they will be for food for all that are left. [5] The earth will also yield its fruit ten-thousandfold, and on each vine there will be one thousand branches, and each branch will produce one thousand clusters, and each cluster produce one thousand grapes, and each grape produce a cor of wine. [6] And those who have hungered will rejoice: moreover also, they will behold marvels every day. [7] For winds will go forth from before Me to bring every morning the fragrance of aromatic fruits, and at the close of the day clouds distilling the dew of health. [8] And it will come to pass at that same time that the treasury of manna will again descend from on high, and they will eat of it in those years, because these are they who have come to the consummation of time."

CHAPTER 30

[1] "And it will come to pass after these things, when the time of the advent of the Messiah is fulfilled, that He will return in glory. [2] Then all who have fallen asleep in hope of Him will rise again. And it will come to pass at that time that the treasuries will be opened in which is preserved the number of the souls of the righteous, and they will come forth, and a multitude of souls will be seen together in one assemblage of one thought, and the first will rejoice and the last will not be grieved. [3] For they know that the time has come of which it is said that it is the consummation of the times. [4] But the souls of the wicked, when they behold all these things, will then waste away more. [5] For they will know that their torment has come, and their perdition has arrived."

CHAPTER 31

[1] And it came to pass after these things that I went to the people and said to them: "Assemble to me all your elders and I will speak words to them." [2] And they all assembled in the Valley of the Kidron. [3] And I answered and said to them: "Hear, O Israel, and I will speak to you, || And give ear, O seed of Jacob, and I will instruct you. [4] Do not forget Zion, || But hold in remembrance the anguish of Jerusalem. [5] For behold, the days come || When everything that is will become the prey of corruption || And be as though it had not been."

CHAPTER 32

[1] "But as for you, if you prepare your hearts so as to sow in them the fruits of the law, it will protect you in that time in which the Mighty One is to shake the whole creation. [2] [[Because after a short time the building of Zion will be shaken in order that it may be built again. But that building will not remain, but will again after a time be rooted out, and will remain desolate until the time. [4] And afterward it must be renewed in glory and perfected forevermore.]] [5] Therefore we should not be distressed so much over the calamity which has now come as over that which is still to be. [6] For there will be a greater trial than these two tribulations when the Mighty One will renew His creation. [7] And now do not draw near to me

for a few days, nor seek me until I come to you." ⁸ And it came to pass when I had spoken all these words to them, that I, Baruch, went my way, and when the people saw me setting out, they lifted up their voice and lamented and said, ⁹ "To where are you departing from us, Baruch, and are you forsaking us as a father who forsakes his orphan children, and departs from them?"

CHAPTER 33

¹ "Are these the commands which your companion, Jeremiah the prophet, commanded you, and said to you: Look to this people until I go and make ready the rest of the brothers in Babylon against whom has gone forth the sentence that they should be led into captivity? And now if you also forsake us, it were good for us all to die before you, then that you should withdraw from us."

CHAPTER 34

¹ And I answered and said to the people: "Far be it from me to forsake you or to withdraw from you, ² but I will only go to the Holy of Holies to inquire of the Mighty One concerning you and concerning Zion, if in some respect I should receive more illumination: and after these things I will return to you."

CHAPTER 35

¹ And I, Baruch, went to the holy place, and sat down on the ruins and wept, and said, ² "O that my eyes were springs, ‖ And my eyelids a fount of tears. ³ For how will I lament for Zion, ‖ And how will I mourn for Jerusalem? ⁴ Because in that place where I am now prostrate, ‖ Of old the high priest offered holy sacrifices, ‖ And placed an incense of fragrant odors thereon. ⁵ But now our glorying has been made into dust, ‖ And the desire of our soul into sand."

CHAPTER 36

¹ And when I had said these things, I fell asleep there, and I saw a vision in the night. ² And behold, a forest of trees planted on the plain, and lofty and rugged rocky mountains surrounded it, and that forest occupied much space. ³ And behold, over against it arose a vine, and from under it there went forth a fountain peacefully. ⁴ Now that fountain came to the forest and was [stirred] into great waves, and those waves submerged that forest, and suddenly they rooted out the greater part of that forest and overthrew all the mountains which were around it. ⁵ And the height of the forest began to be made low, and the top of the mountains was made low, and that fountain prevailed greatly, so that it left nothing of that great forest save one cedar only. ⁶ Also, when it had cast it down and had destroyed and rooted out the greater part of that forest, so that nothing was left of it, nor could its place be recognized, then that vine began to come with the fountain in peace and great tranquility,

and it came to a place which was not far from that cedar, and they brought the cedar which had been cast down to it. ⁷ And I beheld, and behold, that vine opened its mouth and spoke and said to that cedar: "Are you not that cedar which was left of the forest of wickedness, and by whose means wickedness persisted, and was worked all those years, and never for good? ⁸ And you kept conquering that which was not yours, and to that which was yours you never showed compassion, and you kept extending your power over those who were far from you, and those who drew near you, you held fast in the toils of your wickedness, and you always uplifted yourself as one that could not be rooted out! ⁹ But now your time has sped, and your hour has come. ¹⁰ Do you also therefore depart, O cedar, after the forest, which departed before you, and become dust with it, and let your ashes be mingled together? ¹¹ And now recline in anguish and rest in torment until your last time comes, in which you will come again, and be tormented still more."

CHAPTER 37

¹ And after these things I saw that cedar burning, and the vine growing, itself and all around it, the plain full of unfading flowers. ² And I indeed awoke and arose.

CHAPTER 38

¹ And I prayed and said, "O LORD, my Lord, You always enlighten those who are led by understanding. ² Your law is life, and Your wisdom is right guidance. ³ Therefore make known to me the interpretation of this vision. ⁴ For You know that my soul has always walked in Your law, and from my [earliest] days I did not depart from Your wisdom."

CHAPTER 39

¹ And He answered and said to me: "Baruch, this is the interpretation of the vision which you have seen. ² As you have seen the great forest, which lofty and rugged mountains surrounded, this is the word. ³ Behold! The days come, and this kingdom will be destroyed which once destroyed Zion, and it will be subjected to that which comes after it. ⁴ Moreover, that also again after a time will be destroyed, and another, a third, will arise, and that also will have dominion for its time, and will be destroyed. ⁵ And after these things a fourth kingdom will arise, whose power will be harsh and evil far beyond those which were before it, and it will rule many times as the forests on the plain, and it will hold fast for times, and will exalt itself more than the cedars of Lebanon. ⁶ And by it the truth will be hidden, and all those who are polluted with iniquity will flee to it, as evil beasts flee and creep into the forest. ⁷ And it will come to pass when the time of its consummation—that it should fall—has approached, then the principate of My Messiah will be revealed, which is like the

fountain and the vine, and when it is revealed it will root out the multitude of its host. ⁸ And as touching that which you have seen, the lofty cedar, which was left of that forest, and the fact that the vine spoke those words with it which you heard, this is the word."

CHAPTER 40

¹ "The last leader of that time will be left alive, when the multitude of his hosts will be put to the sword, and he will be bound, and they will take him up to Mount Zion, and My Messiah will convict him of all his impieties, and will gather and set before him all the works of his hosts. ² And afterward he will put him to death, and protect the rest of My people which will be found in the place which I have chosen. ³ And His principate will stand forever, until the world of corruption is at an end, and until the times previously mentioned are fulfilled. ⁴ This is your vision, and this is its interpretation."

CHAPTER 41

¹ And I answered and said, "For whom and for how many will these things be? Or who will be worthy to live at that time? ² For I will speak before You everything that I think, and I will ask of You regarding those things which I meditate. ³ For behold, I see many of Your people who have withdrawn from Your covenant, and cast from themselves the yoke of Your law. ⁴ But others again I have seen who have forsaken their vanity, and fled for refuge beneath Your wings. ⁵ What therefore will be to them? Or how will the last time receive them? ⁶ Or perhaps the time of these will assuredly be weighed, and as the beam inclines will they be judged accordingly?"

CHAPTER 42

¹ And He answered and said to me: "I will also show these things to you. ² As for what you said—To whom will these things be, and how many [will they be]? To those who have believed there will be the good which was spoken of formerly, and to those who despise there will be the contrary of these things. ³ And as for what you said regarding those who have drawn near and those who have withdrawn this in the word. ⁴ As for those who were before subject, and afterward withdrew and mingled themselves with the seed of mingled peoples, the time of these was the former, and was accounted as something exalted. ⁵ And as for those who before did not know but afterward knew life, and mingled [only] with the seed of the people which had separated itself, the time of these [is] the latter, and is accounted as something exalted. ⁶ And time will succeed to time and season to season, and one will receive from another, and then with a view to the consummation, everything will be compared according to the measure of the times and the hours of the seasons. ⁷ For corruption will take those that

belong to it, and life those that belong to it. ⁸ And the dust will be called, and there will be said to it: Give back that which is not yours and raise up all that you have kept until its time."

CHAPTER 43

¹ "But you, Baruch, direct your heart to that which has been said to you, || And understand those things which have been shown to you; For there are many continuous consolations for you. ² For you will depart from this place, || And you will pass from the regions which are now seen by you, || And you will forget whatever is corruptible, || And will not again recall those things which happen among mortals. ³ Therefore go and command your people, and come to this place, and afterward fast seven days, and then I will come to you and speak with you."

CHAPTER 44

¹ And I, Baruch, went from there, and came to my people, and I called my firstborn son and [the Gedaliahs] my friends, and seven of the elders of the people, and I said to them: "Behold, I go to my fathers || According to the way of all the earth. ³ But do not withdraw from the way of the law, || But guard and admonish the people which remain, || Lest they withdraw from the commandments of the Mighty One. ⁴ For you see that He whom we serve is just, || And our Creator is no respecter of persons. ⁵ And see what has befallen Zion, || And what has happened to Jerusalem. ⁶ For the judgment of the Mighty One will [thereby] be made known, || And His ways, which, though past finding out, are right. ⁷ For if you endure and persevere in His fear, || And do not forget His law, || The times will change over you for good, || And you will see the consolation of Zion. ⁸ Because whatever is now is nothing, || But that which will be is very great. ⁹ For everything that is corruptible will pass away, || And everything that dies will depart, || And all the present time will be forgotten, || Nor will there be any remembrance of the present time, which is defiled with evils. ¹⁰ For that which runs now runs to vanity, || And that which prospers will quickly fall and be humiliated. ¹¹ For that which is to be will be the object of desire, || And for that which comes afterward will we hope; For it is a time that does not pass away, ¹² And the hour comes which abides forever. And the new world [comes] which does not turn to corruption those who depart to its blessedness, || And has no mercy on those who depart to torment, || And does not lead to perdition those who live in it. ¹³ For these are they who will inherit that time which has been spoken of, || And theirs is the inheritance of the promised time. ¹⁴ These are they who have acquired for themselves treasures of wisdom, || And with them are found stores of understanding, || And they have not withdrawn from mercy, || And they have preserved the truth of the law. ¹⁵ For the world to come will be

given to them, || But the dwelling of the rest, who are many, will be in the fire."

CHAPTER 45

[1] "Therefore, so far as you are able, instruct the people, for that labor is ours. [2] For if you teach them, you will restore them."

CHAPTER 46

[1] And my son and the elders of the people answered and said to me: "Has the Mighty One humiliated us to such a degree || As to take you from us quickly? [2] And we will truly be in darkness, || And there will be no light to the people who are left, [3] For where again will we seek the law, || Or who will distinguish between death and life for us?" [4] And I said to them, "I cannot resist the throne of the Mighty One; Nevertheless, there will not be wanting to Israel a wise man || Nor a son of the law to the race of Jacob. [5] But only prepare your hearts, that you may obey the law, || And be subject to those who in fear are wise and understanding; And prepare your souls that you may not depart from them. [6] For if you do these things, || Good tidings will come to you, [[|| Which I before told you of; Nor will you fall into the torment, of which I testified to you before." [7] (But with regard to the word that I was to have taken, I did not make [it] known to them or to my son.)]]

CHAPTER 47

[1] And when I had gone forth and dismissed them, I went there and said to them: "Behold! I go to Hebron; for the Mighty One has sent me there." [2] And I came to that place where the word had been spoken to me, and I sat there, and fasted seven days.

CHAPTER 48

[1] And it came to pass after the seventh day, that I prayed before the Mighty One and said, [2] "O my Lord, You summon the advent of the times, || And they stand before You; You cause the power of the ages to pass away, || And they do not resist You; You arrange the method of the seasons, || And they obey You. [3] You alone know the duration of the generations, || And You do not reveal Your mysteries to many. [4] You make known the multitude of the fire, || And You weigh the lightness of the wind. [5] You explore the limit of the heights, || And You scrutinize the depths of the darkness. [6] You care for the number which pass away that they may be preserved, || And You prepare an abode for those that are to be. [7] You remember the beginning which You have made, || And the destruction that is to be, You do not forget. [8] With nods of fear and indignation You command the flames, || And they change into spirits, || And with a word You give life to that which was not, || And with mighty power You hold that which has not yet come. [9] You instruct created things in Your understanding, ||

And You make wise the spheres so as to minister in their orders. [10] Innumerable armies stand before You || And minister in their orders quietly at Your nod. [11] Hear Your servant || And give ear to my petition. [12] For in a short time are we born, || And in a short time we return. [13] But with You hours are as an age, || And days as generations. [14] Therefore, do not be angry with man, for he is nothing; [15] And do not take account of our works; For what are we? For behold, by Your gift we come into the world, || And we do not depart of our own will. [16] For we did not say to our parents, Beget us, || Nor did we send to Sheol and say, Receive us. [17] What therefore is our strength that we should bear Your wrath, || Or what are we that we should endure Your judgment? [18] Protect us in Your compassions, || And help us in Your mercy. [19] Behold the little ones that are subject to You, || And save all that draw near to You: And do not destroy the hope of our people, || And do not cut short the times of our aid. [20] For this is the nation which You have chosen, || And these are the people to whom You find no equal. [21] But now I will speak before You, || And I will say as my heart thinks. [22] We trust in You, for behold, Your law is with us, || And we know that we will not fall so long as we keep Your statutes. [23] [[We are blessed for all time at all events in this—That we have not mingled with the nations.]] [24] For we are all one celebrated people, || Who have received one law from One: And the law which is among us will aid us, || And the surpassing wisdom which is in us will help us." [25] And when I had prayed and said these things, I was greatly weakened. [26] And He answered and said to me: "You have prayed simply, O Baruch, || And all your words have been heard. [27] But My judgment exacts its own || And My law exacts its rights. [28] For from your words I will answer you, || And from your prayer I will speak to you. [29] For this is as follows: he that is corrupted is not at all; he has both worked iniquity so far as deceit could do anything, and has not remembered My goodness, nor accepted My long-suffering. [30] Therefore, you will surely be taken up, as I before told you. [31] For that time will arise which brings affliction; for it will come and pass by with quick vehemence, and it will be turbulent, coming in the heat of indignation. [32] And it will come to pass in those days that all the inhabitants of the earth will be moved against one another, because they do not know that My judgment has drawn near. [33] For there will not be found many wise at that time, || And the intelligent will be but a few: Moreover, even those who know will most of all be silent. [34] And there will be many rumors and tidings—not a few, || And the doing of illusions will be manifest, || And promises—not a few—will be recounted, || Some of them [will prove] idle, || And some of them will be confirmed. [35] And honor will be turned into shame, || And strength humiliated into contempt, || And integrity destroyed, || And beauty will become ugliness. [36] And many will say to many at that time: Where has the multitude of intelligence hidden itself, || And to where has the multitude of wisdom removed itself? ³⁷ And while they are meditating on these things, || Then envy will arise in those who had not thought anything of themselves || And passion will seize him that is peaceful, || And many will be stirred up in anger to injure many, || And they will rouse up armies in order to shed blood, || And in the end they will perish together with them. ³⁸ And it will come to pass at the same time, || That a change of times will manifestly appeal to every man, || Because in all those times they polluted themselves || And they practiced oppression, || And every man walked in his own works, || And did not remember the Law of the Mighty One. ³⁹ Therefore a fire will consume their thoughts, || And in flame the meditations of their reins will be tried; For the Judge will come and will not tarry. ⁴⁰ Because each of the inhabitants of the earth knew when he was transgressing. But they did not know My Law by reason of their pride. ⁴¹ But many will then assuredly weep, || Yes, over the living more than over the dead." ⁴² And I answered and said, "O Adam, what have you done to all those who are born from you? And what will be said to the first Eve who listened to the serpent? ⁴³ For all this multitude are going to corruption, || Nor is there any numbering of those whom the fire devours. ⁴⁴ But again I will speak in Your presence. ⁴⁵ You, O LORD, my Lord, know what is in Your creature. ⁴⁶ For You commanded the ancient dust to produce Adam, and You know the number of those who are born from him, and how far they have sinned before You, who have existed and not confessed You as their Creator. ⁴⁷ And as regards all these their end will convict them, and Your law which they have transgressed will repay them on Your day." ⁴⁸ [["But now let us dismiss the wicked and inquire about the righteous. ⁴⁹ And I will recount their blessedness and not be silent in celebrating their glory, which is reserved for them. ⁵⁰ For assuredly as in a short time in this transitory world in which you live you have endured much labor, so in that world to which there is no end, you will receive great light."]]

CHAPTER 49

¹ "Nevertheless, I will again ask from You, O Mighty One, yes, I will ask You who made all things. ² In what shape will those live who live in Your day? Or how will the splendor of those who [are] after that time continue? ³ Will they then resume this form of the present, || And put on these entangling members, || Which are now involved in evils, || And in which evils are consummated, || Or will You perhaps change these things which have been in the world || As also the world?"

CHAPTER 50

¹ And He answered and said to me: "Hear, Baruch, this word, and write in the remembrance of your heart all that you will learn. ² For the earth will then assuredly restore the dead, [[which it now receives, in order to preserve them.]] It will make no change in their form, but as it has received, so will it restore them, and as I delivered them to it, so also will it raise them. ³ For then it will be necessary to show the living that the dead have come to life again, and that those who had departed have returned [again]. ⁴ And it will come to pass, when they have individually recognized those whom they now know, then judgment will grow strong, and those things which before were spoken of will come."

CHAPTER 51

¹ "And it will come to pass, when that appointed day has gone by, that then will the aspect of those who are condemned be afterward changed, and the glory of those who are justified. ² For the aspect of those who now act wickedly will become worse than it is, as they will suffer torment. ³ Also, the glory of those who have now been justified in My law, who have had understanding in their life, and who have planted in their heart the root of wisdom, then their splendor will be glorified in changes, and the form of their face will be turned into the light of their beauty, that they may be able to acquire and receive the world which does not die, which is then promised to them. ⁴ For over this, above all, those who come will then lament that they rejected My law and stopped their ears that they might not hear wisdom or receive understanding. ⁵ When, therefore, they see those over whom they are now exalted, [but] who will then be exalted and glorified more than they, they will respectively be transformed, the latter into the splendor of messengers, and the former will yet more waste away in wonder at the visions and in the beholding of the forms. ⁶ For they will first behold and afterward depart to be tormented. ⁷ But those who have been saved by their works, || And to whom the law has now been a hope, || And understanding an expectation, || And wisdom a confidence, || Will wondrously appear in their time. ⁸ For they will behold the world which is now invisible to them, || And they will behold the time which is now hidden from them: ⁹ And time will no longer age them. ¹⁰ For they will dwell in the heights of that world, || And they will be made like to the messengers, || And be made equal to the stars, || And they will be changed into every form they desire, || From beauty into loveliness, || And from light into the splendor of glory. ¹¹ For there will be spread before them the extents of Paradise, || And there will be shown to them the beauty of the majesty of the living creatures which are beneath the throne, || And all the armies of the messengers, who are now held fast by My word, || Lest they should appear, and are

held fast by a command, that they may stand in their places until their advent comes. ¹²Moreover, there will then be excellency in the righteous surpassing that in the messengers. ¹³For the first will receive the last, those whom they were expecting, ‖ And the last, those of whom they used to hear that they had passed away. ¹⁴For they have been delivered from this world of tribulation, ‖ And laid down the burden of anguish. ¹⁵For what then have men lost their life, ‖ And for what have those who were on the earth exchanged their soul? ¹⁶For then they did not choose for themselves this time, ‖ Which, beyond the reach of anguish, could not pass away, ‖ But they chose for themselves that time, ‖ Whose issues are full of lamentations and evils, ‖ And they denied the world which does not age those who come to it, ‖ And they rejected the time of glory, ‖ So that they will not come to the honor of which I told you before."

CHAPTER 52

¹And I answered and said, "How can we forget those for whom woe is then reserved? ²And why therefore do we again mourn for those who die? Or why do we weep for those who depart to Sheol? ³Let lamentations be reserved for the beginning of that coming torment, ‖ And let tears be laid up for the advent of the destruction of that time. ⁴[[But even in the face of these things I will speak. ⁵And as for the righteous, what will they do now? ⁶Rejoice in the suffering which you now suffer; For why do you look for the decline of your enemies? ⁷Make ready your soul for that which is reserved for you, ‖ And prepare your souls for the reward which is laid up for you."]]

CHAPTER 53

¹And when I had said these things, I fell asleep there, and I saw a vision, and behold, a cloud was ascending from a very great sea, and I kept gazing on it, and behold, it was full of white and black waters, and there were many colors in those same waters, and as it were the likeness of great lightning was seen at its summit. ²And I saw the cloud passing swiftly in quick courses, and it covered all the earth. ³And it came to pass after these things that that cloud began to pour on the earth the waters that were in it. ⁴And I saw that there was not one and the same likeness in the waters which descended from it. ⁵For in the first beginning they were black and many, and afterward I saw that the waters became bright, but they were not many, and after these things again I saw black [waters], and after these things again bright, and again black and again bright. ⁶Now this was done twelve times, but the black were always more numerous than the bright. ⁷And it came to pass at the end of the cloud, that behold, it rained black waters, and they were darker than had been all those waters that were before, and fire was mingled with them, and where those waters descended, they worked devastation and destruction.

⁸And after these things I saw how that lightning which I had seen on the summit of the cloud, seized hold of it and hurled it to the earth. ⁹Now that lightning shone exceedingly, so as to illuminate the whole earth, and it healed those regions where the last waters had descended and worked devastation. ¹⁰And it took hold of the whole earth and had dominion over it. ¹¹And I saw after these things, and behold, twelve rivers were ascending from the sea, and they began to surround that lightning and to become subject to it. ¹²And by reason of my fear I awoke.

CHAPTER 54

¹And I implored the Mighty One, and said, "You alone, O LORD, know of the former times—the deep things of the world, ‖ And the things which befall in their times You bring about by Your word, ‖ And against the works of the inhabitants of the earth You hasten the beginnings of the times, ‖ And You alone know the end of the seasons. ²[You] for whom nothing is too hard, ‖ But who does everything easily by a nod: ³[You] to whom the depths come as the heights, ‖ And whose word the beginnings of the ages serve: ⁴[You] who reveal to those who fear You what is prepared for them, ‖ That from then on they may be comforted. ⁵You show great acts to those who do not know; You break up the enclosure of those who are ignorant, ‖ And light up what is dark, ‖ And reveal what is hidden to the pure, ‖ [[Who in faith have submitted themselves to You and Your law.]] ⁶You have shown this vision to Your servant; Also reveal its interpretation to me. ⁷For I know that as regards those things wherein I implored You, I have received a response, ‖ And as regards what I implored, You revealed to me with what voice I should praise You, ‖ And from what members I should cause praises and hallelujahs to ascend to You. ⁸For if my members were mouths, ‖ And the hairs of my head voices, ‖ Even so I could not give You the reward of praise, ‖ Nor laud You as is befitting, ‖ Nor could I recount Your praise, ‖ Nor tell the glory of Your beauty. ⁹For what am I among men, ‖ Or why am I reckoned among those who are more excellent than I, ‖ That I have heard all these marvelous things from the Most High, ‖ And numberless promises from Him who created me? ¹⁰Blessed is my mother among those that bear, ‖ And praised among women is she that bore me. ¹¹For I will not be silent in praising the Mighty One, ‖ And with the voice of praise I will recount His marvelous deeds. ¹²For who does like to Your marvelous deeds, O God, ‖ Or who comprehends Your deep thought of life? ¹³For with Your counsel You govern all the creatures which Your right hand has created, ‖ And You have established every fountain of light beside You, ‖ And You have prepared the treasures of wisdom beneath Your throne. ¹⁴And justly do they perish who have not loved Your law, ‖ And the torment of judgment will

await those who have not submitted themselves to Your power. ¹⁵ For though Adam first sinned ‖ And brought untimely death on all, ‖ Yet of those who were born from him ‖ Each one of them has prepared for his own soul torment to come, ‖ And again each one of them has chosen for himself glories to come. ¹⁶ [[For assuredly he who believes will receive reward. ¹⁷ But now, as for you, you wicked that now are, ‖ Turn to destruction, because you will be speedily visited, in that formerly you rejected the understanding of the Most High. ¹⁸ For His works have not taught you, ‖ Nor has the skill of His creation—which is at all times—persuaded you.]] ¹⁹ Adam is therefore not the cause, save only of his own soul, ‖ But each of us has been the Adam of his own soul. ²⁰ But You, O LORD, expound to me regarding those things which You have revealed to me, ‖ And inform me regarding that which I implored You. ²¹ For at the consummation of the world vengeance will be taken on those who have done wickedness according to their wickedness, ‖ And You will glorify the faithful according to their faithfulness. ²² For those who are among Your own You rule, ‖ And those who sin You blot out from among Your own."

CHAPTER 55

¹ And it came to pass when I had finished speaking the words of this prayer, that I sat there under a tree, that I might rest in the shade of the branches. ² And I wondered and was astonished, and pondered in my thoughts regarding the multitude of goodness which sinners who are on the earth have rejected, and regarding the great torment which they have despised, though they knew that they should be tormented because of the sin they had committed. And when I was pondering on these things and the like, behold, the messenger Ramiel who presides over true visions was sent to me, and he said to me: ⁴ "Why does your heart trouble you, Baruch, ‖ And why does your thought disturb you? ⁵ For if owing to the report which you have only heard of judgment you are so moved, ‖ What [will you be] when you will see it manifestly with your eyes? ⁶ And if with the expectation with which you do expect the day of the Mighty One you are so overcome, ‖ What [will you be] when you will come to its advent? ⁷ And, if at the word of the announcement of the torment of those who have done foolishly you are so wholly distraught, ‖ How much more when the event will reveal marvelous things? ⁸ And if you have heard tidings of the good and evil things which are then coming and are grieved, ‖ What—when you will behold what the majesty will reveal, ‖ Which will convict these and cause those to rejoice?"

CHAPTER 56

¹ "Nevertheless, because you have implored the Most High to reveal to you the interpretation of the vision which you have seen, I have been sent to tell you. ² And the Mighty One has assuredly made known to you the methods of the times that have passed, and of those that are destined to pass in His world from the beginning of its creation even to its consummation, of those things which [are] deceit and of those which [are] in truth. ³ For as you saw a great cloud which ascended from the sea, and went and covered the earth, this is the duration of the age which the Mighty One made when he took counsel to make the world. ⁴ And it came to pass when the word had gone forth from His presence, that the duration of the world had come into being in a small degree, and was established according to the multitude of the intelligence of Him who sent it. ⁵ And as you previously saw on the summit of the cloud black waters which descended previously on the earth, this is the transgression with which Adam the first man transgressed. ⁶ For [since] when he transgressed ‖ Untimely death came into being, ‖ Grief was named ‖ And anguish was prepared, ‖ And pain was created, ‖ And trouble consummated, ‖ And disease began to be established, ‖ And Sheol kept demanding that it should be renewed in blood, ‖ And the begetting of children was brought about, ‖ And the passion of parents produced, ‖ And the greatness of humanity was humiliated, ‖ And goodness languished. ⁷ What therefore can be blacker or darker than these things? ⁸ This is the beginning of the black waters which you have seen. ⁹ And from these black [waters] again were black derived, and the darkness of darkness was produced. ¹⁰ For he became a danger to his own soul: even to the messengers. ¹¹ For moreover, at that time when he was created, they enjoyed liberty. ¹² And he became a danger; some of them descended and mingled with the women. ¹³ And then those who did so were tormented in chains. ¹⁴ But the rest of the multitude of the messengers, of which there is [no] number, restrained themselves. ¹⁵ And those who dwelt on the earth perished together [with them] through the waters of the deluge. ¹⁶ These are the black first waters."

CHAPTER 57

¹ "And after these [waters] you saw bright waters: this is the fount of Abraham, also his generations and advent of his son, and of his son's son, and of those like them. ² Because at that time the unwritten law was named among them, ‖ And the works of the commandments were then fulfilled, ‖ And belief in the coming judgment was then generated, ‖ And hope of the world that was to be renewed was then built up, ‖ And the promise of the life that should come hereafter was implanted. ³ These are the bright waters, which you have seen."

2 BARUCH

CHAPTER 58

¹ "And the black third waters which you have seen, these are the mingling of all sins, which the nations afterward worked after the death of those righteous men, and the wickedness of the land of Egypt, wherein they did wickedly in the service with which they made their sons to serve. ² Nevertheless, these also perished at last."

CHAPTER 59

¹ "And the bright fourth waters which you have seen are the advent of Moses, and Aaron, and Miriam, and Joshua the son of Nun, and Caleb, and of all those like them. ² For at that time the lamp of the perpetual law shone on all those who sat in darkness, which announced to them that believe the promise of their reward, and to them that deny, the torment of fire which is reserved for them. ³ But also the heavens at that time were shaken from their place, and those who were under the throne of the Mighty One were perturbed, when He was taking Moses to Himself. ⁴ For He showed him many admonitions together with the principles of the law and the consummation of the times, as also to you, and likewise the pattern of Zion and its measures, in the pattern of which the sanctuary of the present time was to be made. ⁵ But then He also showed to him the measures of the fire, also the depths of the abyss, and the weight of the winds, and the number of the drops of rain; ⁶ and the suppression of anger, and the multitude of long-suffering, and the truth of judgment; ⁷ and the root of wisdom, and the riches of understanding, and the fount of knowledge; ⁸ and the height of the air, and the greatness of Paradise, and the consummation of the ages, and the beginning of the Day of Judgment; ⁹ and the number of the offerings, and the earths which have not yet come; ¹⁰ and the mouth of Gehenna, and the station of vengeance, and the place of faith, and the region of hope; ¹¹ and the likeness of future torment, and the multitude of innumerable messengers, and the flaming hosts, and the splendor of the lightnings, and the voice of the thunders, and the orders of the chiefs of the messengers, and the treasuries of light, and the changes of the times, and the investigations of the law. ¹² These are the bright fourth waters which you have seen."

CHAPTER 60

¹ "And the black fifth waters which you have seen raining are the works which the Amorites worked, and the spells of their incantations which they worked, and the wickedness of their mysteries, and the mingling of their pollution. ² But even Israel was then polluted by sins in the days of the judges, though they saw many signs which were from Him who made them."

CHAPTER 61

¹ "And the bright sixth waters which you saw, this is the time in which David and Solomon were born. ² And there was at that time the building of Zion, ‖ And the dedication of the sanctuary, ‖ And the shedding of much blood of the nations that sinned then, ‖ And many offerings which were offered then in the dedication of the sanctuary. ³ And peace and tranquility existed at that time, ‖ ⁴ And wisdom was heard in the assembly; And the riches of understanding were magnified in the congregations, ‖ ⁵ And the holy festivals were fulfilled in blessedness and in much joy. ⁶ And the judgment of the rulers was then seen to be without guile, ‖ And the righteousness of the precepts of the Mighty One was accomplished with truth. ⁷ And the land [which] was then beloved by the LORD, ‖ And because its inhabitants did not sin, it was glorified beyond all lands, ‖ And the city Zion ruled then over all lands and regions. ⁸ These are the bright waters which you have seen."

CHAPTER 62

¹ "And the black seventh waters which you have seen, this is the perversion [brought about] by the counsel of Jeroboam, who took counsel to make two calves of gold; ² and all the iniquities which kings who were after him iniquitously worked. ³ And the curse of Jezebel and the worship of idols which Israel practiced at that time. ⁴ And the withholding of rain, and the famines which occurred until women ate the fruit of their wombs. ⁵ And the time of their captivity which came on the nine and a half tribes, because they were in many sins. ⁶ And Shalmanezzar king of Assyria came and led them away captive. ⁷ But regarding the nations, it is tedious to tell how they always worked impiety and wickedness, and never worked righteousness. ⁸ These are the black seventh waters which you have seen."

CHAPTER 63

¹ "And the bright eighth waters which you have seen, this is the rectitude and uprightness of Hezekiah king of Judah, and the grace [of God] which came on him ² when Sennacherib was stirred up in order that he might perish, and his wrath troubled him in order that he might thereby perish, for the multitude also of the nations which were with him. ³ When, moreover, Hezekiah the king heard those things which the king of Assyria was devising, to come and seize him and destroy his people—the two and a half tribes which remained—moreover, that he wished to overthrow Zion also, Hezekiah then trusted in his works, and had hope in his righteousness, and spoke with the Mighty One and said, ⁴ For behold, Sennacherib is prepared to destroy us, and he will be boastful and uplifted when he has destroyed Zion." ⁵ And the Mighty One heard him, for Hezekiah was wise, and He had respect to his prayer, because he was righteous. ⁶ And thereon

the Mighty One commanded His messenger Ramiel who speaks with you. [7] And I went forth and destroyed their multitude, the number of whose chiefs alone was one hundred and eighty-five thousand, and each one of them had an equal number [at his command]. [8] And at that time I burned their bodies within, but their raiment and arms I preserved outwardly, in order that the still more wonderful deeds of the Mighty One might appear, and that His Name might thereby be spoken of throughout the whole earth. [9] And Zion was saved and Jerusalem delivered: Israel was also freed from tribulation. [10] And all those who were in the holy land rejoiced, and the Name of the Mighty One was glorified so that it was spoken of. [11] These are the bright waters which you have seen."

CHAPTER 64

[1] "And the black ninth waters which you have seen, this is all the wickedness which was in the days of Manasseh the son of Hezekiah. [2] For he worked much impiety, and he slew the righteous, and he wrested judgment, and he shed the blood of the innocent, and he violently polluted wedded women, and he overturned the altars, and destroyed their offerings, and drove forth their priests lest they should minister in the sanctuary. [3] And he made an image with five faces: four of them looked to the four winds, and the fifth on the summit of the image as an adversary of the zeal of the Mighty One. [4] And then wrath went forth from the presence of the Mighty One to the intent that Zion should be rooted out, as also it befell in your days. But also, against the two and a half tribes went forth a decree that they should also be led away captive, as you have now seen. [5] And the impiety of Manasseh increased to such a degree that it removed the praise of the Most High from the sanctuary. [7] On this account Manasseh was at that time named the impious, and finally his abode was in the fire. [8] For though his prayer was heard with the Most High, finally, when he was cast into the brazen horse and the brazen horse was melted, it served as a sign to him for the hour. [9] For he had not lived perfectly, for he was not worthy—but that from then on he might know by whom finally he should be tormented. [10] For he who is able to benefit is also able to torment."

CHAPTER 65

[1] "Thus, moreover, Manasseh acted impiously, and thought that in his time the Mighty One would not inquire into these things. [2] These are the black ninth waters which you have seen."

CHAPTER 66

[1] "And the bright tenth waters which you have seen: this is the purity of the generations of Josiah king of Judah, who was the only one at the time who submitted himself to the Mighty One with all his heart and with all his soul. [2] And he cleansed the land from idols, and hallowed all the vessels which had been polluted, and restored the offerings to the altar, and raised the horn of the holy, and exalted the righteous, and honored all that were wise in understanding, and brought back the priests to their ministry, and destroyed and removed the magicians, and enchanters, and necromancers from the land. [3] And not only did he slay the impious that were living, but they also took from the graves the bones of the dead and burned them with fire. [4] [[And the festivals and the Sabbaths he established in their sanctity]], and their polluted ones he burned in the fire, and the lying prophets which deceived the people, these he also burned in the fire, and the people who listened to them when they were living, he cast them into the Brook of Kidron, and heaped stones on them. [5] And he was zealous with zeal for the Mighty One with all his soul, and he alone was firm in the law at that time, so that he left none that was uncircumcised, or that worked impiety in all the land, all the days of his life. [6] Therefore he will receive a continuous reward, and he will be glorified with the Mighty One beyond many at a later time. [7] For on his account and on account of those who are like him were the honorable glories, of which you were told before, created and prepared. These are the bright waters which you have seen."

CHAPTER 67

[1] "And the black eleventh waters which you have seen: this is the calamity which is now befalling Zion. [2] Do you think that there is no anguish to the messengers in the presence of the Mighty One, that Zion was so delivered up, and that, behold, the nations boast in their hearts, and assemble before their idols and say, She is trodden down who oftentimes trod down, and she has been reduced to servitude who reduced [other nations to servitude]? [3] Do you think that in these things the Most High rejoices, or that His Name is glorified? [4] [[But how will it serve toward His righteous judgment?]] [5] Yet after these things the dispersed among the nations will be taken hold of by tribulation, and in shame they will dwell in every place. [6] Because so far as Zion is delivered up and Jerusalem laid waste, idols will prosper in the cities of the nations, and the vapor of the smoke of the incense of the righteousness which is by the law is extinguished in Zion; and in the region of Zion in every place, behold, there is the smoke of impiety. [7] But the king of Babylon will arise who has now destroyed Zion, and he will boast over the people, and he will speak great things in his heart in the presence of the Most High. [8] But he will also fall at last. These are the black waters."

2 BARUCH

CHAPTER 68

[1] "And the bright twelfth waters which you have seen: this is the word. For after these things, a time will come when your people will fall into distress, so that they will all run the risk of perishing together. [3] Nevertheless, they will be saved, and their enemies will fall in their presence. [4] And they will have in [due] time much joy. [5] And at that time, after a short interval, Zion will again be rebuilt, and its offerings will again be restored, and the priests will return to their ministry, and also the nations will come to glorify it. [6] Nevertheless, not fully as in the beginning. [7] But it will come to pass after these things that there will be the fall of many nations. [8] These are the bright waters which you have seen."

CHAPTER 69

[1] "For the last waters which you have seen which were darker than all that were before them, those which were after the twelfth number, which were collected together, belong to the whole world. [2] For the Most High made division from the beginning, because He alone knows what will befall. [3] For as to the enormities and the impieties which should be worked before Him, He foresaw six kinds of them. [4] And of the good works of the righteous which should be accomplished before Him, He foresaw six kinds of them, beyond those which He should work at the consummation of the age. [5] On his account there were not black waters with black, nor bright with bright; for it is the consummation."

CHAPTER 70

[1] "Therefore hear the interpretation of the last black waters which are to come: this [is] the word. [2] Behold! The days come, and it will be when the time of the age has ripened, || And the harvest of its evil and good seeds has come, || That the Mighty One will bring on the earth and its inhabitants and on its rulers || Perturbation of spirit and stupor of heart. [3] And they will hate one another, || And provoke one another to fight, || And the mean will rule over the honorable, || And those of low degree will be extolled above the famous. [4] And the many will be delivered into the hands of the few, || And those who were nothing will rule over the strong, || And the poor will have abundance beyond the rich, || And the impious will exalt themselves above the heroic. [5] And the wise will be silent, || And the foolish will speak, || Neither will the thought of men be then confirmed, || Nor the counsel of the mighty, || Nor will the hope of those who hope be confirmed. [6] And when those things which were predicted have come to pass, || Then confusion will fall on all men, || And some of them will fall in battle, || And some of them will perish in anguish, || [7] And some of them will be destroyed by their own. Then the peoples of the Most High, whom He has prepared before, || Will come and make war

with the leaders that will then be left. [8] And it will come to pass that whoever gets safe out of the war will die in the earthquake, || And whoever gets safe out of the earthquake will be burned by the fire, || And whoever gets safe out of the fire will be destroyed by famine. [9] [[And it will come to pass that whoever of the victors and the vanquished gets safe out of and escapes all these things previously mentioned will be delivered into the hands of My servant Messiah.]] [10] For all the earth will devour its inhabitants."

CHAPTER 71

[1] "And the holy land will have mercy on its own, and it will protect its inhabitants at that time. [2] This is the vision which you have seen, and this is the interpretation. [3] For I have come to tell you these things, because your prayer has been heard with the Most High."

CHAPTER 72

[1] "Now also hear regarding the bright lightning which is to come at the consummation after these black [waters]: this is the word. [2] After the signs have come of which you were told before, when the nations become turbulent, and the time of My Messiah is come, He will both summon all the nations, and some of them He will spare, and some of them He will slay. [3] Therefore these things will come on the nations which are to be spared by Him. [4] Every nation which does not know Israel and has not trodden down the seed of Jacob, will indeed be spared. [5] And this because some out of every nation will be subjected to your people. [6] But all those who have ruled over you, or have known you, will be given up to the sword."

CHAPTER 73

[1] "And it will come to pass, when He has brought low everything that is in the world, || And has sat down in peace for the age on the throne of His kingdom, || That joy will then be revealed, || And rest will appear. [2] And then healing will descend in dew, || And disease will withdraw, || And anxiety, and anguish, and lamentation will pass from among men, || And gladness will proceed through the whole earth. [3] And no one will die untimely again, || Nor will any adversity suddenly befall. [4] And judgments, and abusive talk, and contentions, and revenges, || And blood, and passions, and envy, and hatred, || And whatever things are like these will go into condemnation when they are removed. [5] For it is these very things which have filled this world with evils, || And on account of these the life of man has been greatly troubled. [6] And wild beasts will come from the forest and minister to men || And asps and dragons will come forth from their holes to submit themselves to a little child. [7] And women will no longer then have pain when they bear, || Nor will they suffer torment when they yield the fruit of the womb."

2 BARUCH

CHAPTER 74

[1] "And it will come to pass in those days that the reapers will not grow weary, || Nor those that build be toil-worn; For the works will of themselves speedily advance || Together with those who do them in much tranquility. [2] For that time is the consummation of that which is corruptible, || And the beginning of that which is not corruptible. [3] Therefore those things which were predicted will belong to it: Therefore, it is far away from evils, and near to those things which do not die. [4] This is the bright lightning which came after the last dark waters."

CHAPTER 75

[1] And I answered and said, "Who can understand, O LORD, Your goodness? For it is incomprehensible. [2] Or who can search into Your compassions, || Which are infinite? [3] Or who can comprehend Your intelligence? [4] Or who is able to recount the thoughts of Your mind? [5] Or who of those who are born can hope to come to those things, || Unless he is one to whom You are merciful and gracious? [6] Because, assuredly, if You did not have compassion on man, || Those who are under Your right hand, || They could not come to those things, || But those who are in the numbers named can be called. [7] But if, indeed, we who exist know why we have come, || And submit ourselves to Him who brought us out of Egypt, || We will come again and remember those things which have passed, || And will rejoice regarding that which has been. [8] But if now we do not know why we have come, || And do not recognize the principate of Him who brought us up out of Egypt, || We will come again and seek after those things which have been now, || And be grieved with pain because of those things which have befallen."

CHAPTER 76

[1] And He answered and said to me: "[[Inasmuch as the revelation of this vision has been interpreted to you as you requested]], hear the word of the Most High that you may know what is to befall you after these things. [2] For you will surely depart from this earth, nevertheless not to death, but you will be preserved to the consummation of the times. [3] Therefore go up to the top of that mountain, and there will pass before you all the regions of that land, and the figure of the inhabited world, and the top of the mountains, and the depth of the valleys, and the depths of the seas, and the number of the rivers, that you may see what you are leaving, and to where you are going. [4] Now this will befall after forty days. Therefore, go now during these days and instruct the people so far as you are able, that they may learn so as not to die at the last time, but may learn in order that they may live at the last times."

CHAPTER 77

[1] And I, Baruch, went there and came to the people, and assembled them together from the greatest to the least, and said to them: [2] "Hear, you sons of Israel, behold how many you are who remain of the twelve tribes of Israel. [3] For to you and to your fathers the LORD gave a law more excellent than to all peoples. [4] And because your brothers transgressed the commandments of the Most High, || He brought vengeance on you and on them, || And He did not spare the former, || And the latter He also gave into captivity: And He did not leave a residue of them, [5] But behold! You are here with me. [6] If, therefore, you direct your ways correctly, || You also will not depart as your brothers departed, || But they will come to you. [7] For He is merciful whom you worship, || And He is gracious in whom you hope, || And He is true, so that He will do good and not evil. [8] Have you not seen here what has befallen Zion? [9] Or do you perhaps think that the place had sinned, || And that on this account it was overthrown? Or that the land had worked foolishness, || And that therefore it was delivered up? [10] And do you not know that on account of you who sinned, || That which did not sin was overthrown, || And, on account of those who worked wickedly, || That which did not work foolishness was delivered up to enemies?" [11] And the whole people answered and said to me: "So far as we can recall the good things which the Mighty One has done to us, we do recall them; and those things which we do not remember He in His mercy knows. [12] Nevertheless, do this for us your people: also write to our brothers in Babylon a letter of doctrine and a scroll of hope, that you may confirm them also before you depart from us. [13] For the shepherds of Israel have perished, || And the lamps which gave light are extinguished, || And the fountains have withheld their stream from which we used to drink. [14] And we are left in the darkness, || And amid the trees of the forest, || And the thirst of the wilderness." [15] And I answered and said to them: "Shepherds, and lamps, and fountains come from the law: And though we depart, yet the law abides. [16] If, therefore, you have respect to the law, || And are intent on wisdom, || A lamp will not be wanting, || And a shepherd will not fail, || And a fountain will not dry up. [17] Nevertheless, as you said to me, I will also write to your brothers in Babylon, and I will send by means of men, and I will write in like manner to the nine and a half tribes, and send by means of a bird." [18] And it came to pass on the twenty-first day in the eighth month that I, Baruch, came and sat down under the oak under the shadow of the branches, and no man was with me, but I was alone. [19] And I wrote these two letters: one I sent by an eagle to the nine and a half tribes; and the other I sent to those that were at Babylon by means of three men. [20] And I called the eagle and spoke these words to it: [21] "The Most High has made you that you should be higher than all birds.

²² And now go and do not tarry in [any] place, nor enter a nest, nor settle on any tree, until you have passed over the breadth of the many waters of the Euphrates River, and have gone to the people that dwell there, and cast down this letter to them. ²³ Remember, moreover, that, at the time of the deluge, Noah received from a dove the fruit of the olive, when he sent it forth from the Ark. ²⁴ Yes, also the ravens ministered to Elijah, bearing him food, as they had been commanded. ²⁵ Solomon also, in the time of his kingdom, wherever he wished to send or seek for anything, commanded a bird, and it obeyed him as he commanded it. ²⁶ And now, do not let it weary you, and do not turn to the right hand nor the left, but fly and go by a direct way, that you may preserve the command of the Mighty One, according as I spoke to you."

THE EPISTLE OF BARUCH, THE SON OF NERIAH, WHICH HE WROTE TO THE NINE AND A HALF TRIBES

CHAPTER 78

¹ These are the words of that letter which Baruch the son of Neriah sent to the nine and a half tribes, which were across the River Euphrates, in which these things were written. ² Thus says Baruch the son of Neriah to the brothers carried into captivity: "Mercy and peace." I bear in mind, my brothers, the love of Him who created us, who loved us from of old, and never hated us, but above all educated us. ³ And truly I know, that behold, all of us—the twelve tribes—are bound by one bond, inasmuch as we are born from one father. ⁴ For what reason I have been more careful to leave you the words of this letter before I die, that you may be comforted regarding the calamities which have come on you, and that you may also be grieved regarding the evil that has befallen your brothers; and again, also, that you may justify His judgment which ⁵ He has decreed against you that you should be carried away captive—for what you have suffered is disproportioned to what you have done—in order that, at the last times, you may be found worthy of your fathers. ⁶ Therefore, if you consider that you have now suffered those things for your good, that you may not finally be condemned and tormented, then you will receive continuous hope; if above all you destroy from your heart vain error, on account of which you departed hence. ⁷ For if you so do these things, He will continually remember you, He who always promised on our behalf to those who were more excellent than we, that He will never forget or forsake us, but with much mercy will again gather together those who were dispersed.

CHAPTER 79

¹ Now, my brothers, first learn what befell Zion: how that Nebuchadnezzar king of Babylon came up against us. ² For we have sinned against Him who made us, and we have not kept the commandments which He commanded us, yet He has not disciplined us as we deserved. ³ For what befell you we also suffer in a preeminent degree, for it befell us also.

CHAPTER 80

¹ And now, my brothers, I make known to you that when the enemy had surrounded the city, the messengers of the Most High were sent, and they overthrew the fortifications of the strong wall, and they destroyed the firm iron corners, which could not be rooted out. ² Nevertheless, they hid all the vessels of the sanctuary, lest the enemy should get possession of them. ³ And when they had done these things, they delivered thereon to the enemy the overthrown wall, and the plundered house, and the burnt temple, and the people who were overcome because they were delivered up, lest the enemy should boast and say: "Thus by force we have been able to lay waste even the house of the Most High in war." They have also bound your brothers and led [them] away to Babylon, and have caused them to dwell there. ⁵ But we have been left here, being very few. ⁶ This is the tribulation about which I wrote to you. ⁷ For assuredly I know that [the consolation of] the inhabitants of Zion consoles you; so far as you knew that it was prospered, [your consolation] was greater than the tribulation which you endured in having to depart from it.

CHAPTER 81

¹ But regarding consolation, hear the word. ² For I was mourning regarding Zion, and I prayed for mercy from the Most High, and I said, ³ "How long will these things endure for us? And will these calamities always come on us?" ⁴ And the Mighty One did according to the multitude of His mercies, ‖ And the Most High according to the greatness of His compassion, ‖ And He revealed to me the word, that I might receive consolation, ‖ And He showed me visions that I should not again endure anguish, ‖ And He made known to me the mystery of the times, ‖ And He showed me the advent of the hours.

CHAPTER 82

¹ Therefore, my brothers, I have written to you that you may comfort yourselves regarding the multitude of your tribulations. ² For know that our Maker will assuredly avenge us on all our enemies, according to all that they have done to us, also that the consummation which the Most High will make is very near, and His mercy that is coming, and the consummation of His judgment, is by no means far off. ³ For behold, we see now the multitude of the prosperity of the nations, ‖ Though they act impiously, ‖ But they will be like a vapor: ⁴ And we behold the multitude of their power, ‖ Though they do

wickedly, || But they will be made like to a drop: ⁵ And we see the firmness of their might, || Though they resist the Mighty One every hour, || But they will be accounted as spittle. ⁶ And we consider the glory of their greatness, || Though they do not keep the statutes of the Most High, || But they will pass away as smoke. ⁷ And we meditate on the beauty of their gracefulness, || Though they have to do with pollutions, || But as grass that withers, they will fade away. ⁸ And we consider the strength of their cruelty, || Though they do not remember the end, || But as a wave that passes, they will be broken. ⁹ And we remark [regarding] the boastfulness of their might, || Though they deny the beneficence of God, who gave [it] to them, || But they will pass away as a passing cloud.

CHAPTER 83

¹ For the Most High will assuredly hasten His times, || And He will assuredly bring on His hours. ² And He will assuredly judge those who are in His world, || And will visit in truth all things by means of all their hidden works. ³ And He will assuredly examine the secret thoughts, || And that which is laid up in the secret chambers of all the members of mail, || And will make manifest in the presence of all with reproof. ⁴ Let none therefore of these present things ascend into your hearts, but above all let us be expectant, because that which is promised to us will come. ⁵ And let us not now look to the delights of the nations in the present, but let us remember what has been promised to us in the end. ⁶ For the ends of the times, and of the seasons, and whatever is with them will assuredly pass by together. ⁷ Moreover, the consummation of the age will then show the great might of its ruler, when all things come to judgment. ⁸ Therefore, prepare your hearts for that which before you believed, lest you come to be in bondage in both worlds, so that you be led away captive here and be tormented there. ⁹ For that which exists now, or which has passed away, or which is to come, in all these things, neither is the evil fully evil, nor again the good fully good. ¹⁰ For all healthinesses of this time are turning into diseases, ¹¹ And all might of this time is turning into weakness, || And all the force of this time is turning into impotence, ¹² And every energy of youth is turning into old age and consummation. And every beauty of gracefulness of this time is turning faded and hateful, ¹³ And every proud dominion of the present is turning into humiliation and shame, ¹⁴ And every praise of the glory of this time is turning into the shame of silence, || And every vain splendor and insolence of this time is turning into voiceless ruin. ¹⁵ And every delight and joy of this time is turning to worms and corruption, ¹⁶ And every clamor of the pride of this time is turning into dust and stillness. ¹⁷ And every possession of riches of this time is being turned into Sheol alone, ¹⁸ And all the plunder of passion of this time is turning into involuntary death,

|| And every passion of the lusts of this time is turning into a judgment of torment. ¹⁹ And every artifice and craftiness of this time is turning into a proof of the truth, || ²⁰ And every sweetness of ointments of this time is turning into judgment and condemnation, ²¹ And every love of lying is turning to insult through truth. [[²² Since therefore all these things are done now, does anyone think that they will not be avenged? But the consummation of all things will come to the truth.]]

CHAPTER 84

¹ Behold! I have therefore made known to you [these things] while I live, for I have said [it] that you should learn the things that are excellent; for the Mighty One has commanded me to instruct you: and I will set before you some of the commandments of His judgment before I die. ² Remember that formerly Moses assuredly called the heavens and earth to witness against you and said, "If you transgress the law you will be dispersed, but if you keep it you will be kept." ³ And other things he also used to say to you when you, the twelve tribes, were together in the desert. ⁴ And after his death you cast them away from you. On this account there came on you what had been predicted. ⁵ And now Moses used to tell you before they befell you, and behold, they have befallen you, for you have forsaken the law. ⁶ Behold, I also say to you after you have suffered, that if you obey those things which have been said to you, you will receive from the Mighty One whatever has been laid up and reserved for you. ⁷ Moreover, let this letter be for a testimony between me and you, that you may remember the commandments of the Mighty One, and that there may also be a defense for me in the presence of Him who sent me. ⁸ And remember the law and Zion, and the holy land and your brothers, and the covenant of your fathers, and do not forget the festivals and the Sabbaths. And deliver this letter and the traditions of the law to your sons after you, as your fathers also delivered [them] to you. ¹⁰ And at all times make request perseveringly and pray diligently with your whole heart that the Mighty One may be reconciled to you, and that He may not reckon the multitude of your sins, but remember the rectitude of your fathers. ¹¹ For if He does not judge us according to the multitude of His mercies, woe to all of us who are born.

CHAPTER 85

¹ Know, moreover, that in former times and in the generations of old our fathers had helpers, righteous men and holy prophets, [but] no longer. ² We were in our own land, [[and they helped us when we sinned]], and they prayed for us to Him who made us, because they trusted in their works, and the Mighty One heard their prayer and was gracious to us. ³ But now the righteous have been gathered and the prophets have

fallen asleep, and we have also gone forth from the land, and Zion has been taken from us, and we have nothing now except the Mighty One and His law. [4] If, therefore, we direct and dispose our hearts, we will receive everything that we lost, and much better things than we lost by many times. [5] For what we have lost was to corruption, and what we will receive will not be corruptible. [[[6] Moreover, I also have written thus to our brothers to Babylon, that I also may attest to them those very things.]] [7] And let all those things previously mentioned always be before your eyes, because we are still in the spirit and the power of our liberty. [8] Again, moreover, the Most High is also long-suffering toward us here, and He has shown to us that which is to be, and has not concealed from us what will befall in the end. [9] Therefore, before judgment exacts its own, and truth that which is its due, let us prepare our soul that we may enter into possession of, and not be taken possession of, and that we may hope and not be put to shame, and that we may rest with our fathers and not be tormented with our enemies. [10] And the strength of the creation is already exhausted, and the advent of the times is very short, yes, they have passed by; and the pitcher is near to the cistern, and the ship to the port, and the course of the journey to the city, and life to consummation. [11] And again prepare your souls, so that when you sail and ascend from the ship you may have rest and not be condemned when you depart. [12] For behold, when the Most High will bring to pass all these things, there will not again be there an opportunity for returning, nor a limit to the times, nor adjournment to the hours, nor change of ways, nor place for prayer, nor sending of petitions, nor receiving of knowledge, nor giving of love, nor place of conversion, nor supplication for offenses, nor intercession of the fathers, nor prayer of the prophets, nor help of the righteous. [13] There, there, is the sentence of corruption, the way of fire, and the path which brings to Gehenna. [14] On this account there is one law by one, one age and an end for all who are in it. [15] Then He will preserve those to whom He finds He may be gracious, and at the same time destroy those who are polluted with sins.

CHAPTER 86

[1] When you therefore receive this—my letter—read it in your congregations with care. [2] And meditate thereon, above all on the days of your fasts. [3] And bear me in mind by means of this letter, as I also bear you in mind in it, and always farewell.

CHAPTER 87

[1] And it came to pass when I had ended all the words of this letter, and had written it sedulously to its close, [2] that I folded it, and sealed it carefully, and bound it to the neck of the eagle, and dismissed and sent it. Here ends the Scroll of Baruch, the son of Neriah.

3 BARUCH

3 Baruch, also called the Greek Apocalypse of Baruch, is a visionary, probably pseudepigraphic text thought by most to have been written some time between the fall of Jerusalem in 70 AD and the 3rd century AD. Scholars disagree on whether it was written by a Jew or a Christian, or whether a clear distinction can be made in this era. It is self-attributed to the scribe of Jeremiah, Baruch ben Neriah, and does not form part of the biblical canon of either Jews or Christians. It is extant in certain Greek and Old Slavonic manuscripts.

A NARRATIVE AND REVELATION OF BARUCH, CONCERNING THOSE INEFFABLE THINGS WHICH HE SAW BY COMMAND OF GOD. BLESS YOU, O LORD. A REVELATION OF BARUCH, WHO STOOD ON THE RIVER GEL WEEPING OVER THE CAPTIVITY OF JERUSALEM, WHEN ABIMELECH WAS ALSO PRESERVED BY THE HAND OF GOD, AT THE FARM OF AGRIPPA. AND HE WAS SITTING THUS AT THE BEAUTIFUL GATES, WHERE THE HOLY OF HOLIES LAY.

CHAPTER 1

¹ Truly I, Baruch, was weeping in my mind and sorrowing on account of the people, and that Nebuchadnezzar the king was permitted by God to destroy His city, saying, ² "Lord, why did You set Your vineyard on fire, and lay it waste? Why did You do this? And why, Lord, did You not repay us with another discipline, but delivered us to nations such as these, so that they reproach us and say, Where is their God?" ³ And behold, as I was weeping and saying such things, I saw a messenger of the LORD coming and saying to me, "Understand, O man, greatly beloved, and do not trouble yourself so greatly concerning the salvation of Jerusalem, for thus says the LORD God, the Almighty. ⁴ For He sent me before you, to make known and to show to you all [the things] of God. ⁵ For your prayer was heard before Him, and entered into the ears of the LORD God." ⁶ And when he had said these things to me, I was silent. ⁷ And the messenger said to me, "Cease to provoke God, and I will show you other mysteries, greater than these." And I Baruch said, "As the LORD God lives, if you will show me, and I hear a word of yours, I will not continue to speak any longer. ⁸ God will add to my judgment in the Day of Judgment, if I speak hereafter." And the messenger of the powers said to me, "Come, and I will show you the mysteries of God."

CHAPTER 2

¹ And he took me and led me where the expanse has been set fast, and where there was a river which no one can cross, nor any strange breeze of all those which God created. ² And he took me and led me to the first heaven and showed me a door of great size. ³ And he said to me, "Let us enter through it," and we entered as though borne on wings, a distance of about thirty days' journey. And he showed me a plain within the heaven; and there were men dwelling thereon, with the faces of oxen, and the horns of stags, and the feet of goats, and the haunches of lambs. ⁴ And I, Baruch, asked the messenger, "Make known to me, please, what is the thickness of the heaven in which we journeyed, or what is its extent, or what is the plain, in order that I may also tell the sons of men?" ⁵ And the messenger whose name is Phamael said to me, "This door which you see is the door of Heaven, and as great as is the distance from earth to Heaven, so great also is its thickness; and again as great as is the distance [[from north to south, so great]] is the length of the plain which you saw." ⁶ And again the messenger of the powers said to me, "Come, and I will show you greater mysteries." ⁷ But I said, "Please show me what these men are." And he said to me, "These are they who built the tower of strife against God, and the LORD banished them."

CHAPTER 3

¹ And the messenger of the LORD took me and led me to [the] second heaven. ² And he also showed me a door there like the first and said, "Let us enter through it." ³ And we entered, being borne on wings a distance of about sixty days' journey. ⁴ And he also showed me a plain there, and it was full of men, whose appearance was like that of dogs, and whose feet were like those of stags. ⁵ And I asked the messenger: "Please, Lord, tell me who these are." ⁶ And he said, "These are they who gave counsel to build the tower, for they whom you see drove forth multitudes of both men and women to make bricks; among whom, a woman making bricks was not allowed to be released in the hour of child-birth, but brought forth while she was making bricks, and carried her child in her apron, and continued to make bricks. ⁷ And the LORD appeared to them and confused their speech, when they had built the tower to the height of four hundred and sixty-three cubits. ⁸ And they took a gimlet, and sought to pierce the heaven, saying, Let us see [whether] the heaven is made of clay, or of brass, or of iron. ⁹ When God saw this, He did not permit them, but struck them with blindness and confusion of speech, and rendered them as you see."

CHAPTER 4

¹ And I, Baruch, said, "Behold, Lord, you showed me great and wonderful things; and now show me all things for the sake of the LORD." ² And the messenger said to me, "Come, let us proceed." ³ [And I proceeded] with the messenger from that place about one hundred and eighty-five days' journey. ⁴ And he showed me a plain and a serpent, which appeared to be two hundred plethra in length. And he showed me Hades, and its appearance was dark and abominable. ⁵ And I said, "Who is this dragon, and who is this monster around him?" ⁶ And the messenger said, "The dragon is he who eats the bodies of those who spend their life wickedly, and he is nourished by them. And this is Hades, which itself also closely resembles him, in that it also drinks about a cubit from the sea, which does not sink at all." ⁷ Baruch said, "And how?" And the messenger said, "Listen, the LORD God made three hundred and sixty rivers, of which the chief of all are Alphias, Abyrus, and the Gericus; and because of these the sea does not sink." ⁸ And I said, "Please show me which is the tree which led Adam astray." And the messenger said to me, "It is the vine, which the messenger Sammael planted, at which the LORD God was angry, and He cursed him and his plant, while also on this account He did not permit Adam to touch it, and therefore the Devil being envious deceived him through his vine." [[⁹ And I, Baruch, said, "Since also the vine has been the cause of such great evil, and is under judgment of the curse of God, and was the destruction of the first created, how is it now so useful?" And the messenger said, "You ask correctly. ¹⁰ When God caused the deluge on earth, and destroyed all flesh, and four hundred and nine thousand giants, and the water rose fifteen cubits above the highest mountains, then the water entered into Paradise and destroyed every flower; but it wholly removed the shoot of the vine outside the bounds and cast it outside. ¹¹ And when the earth appeared out of the water, and Noah came out of the Ark, he began to plant of the plants which he found. But he also found the shoot of the vine; and he took it, and was reasoning in himself, What then is it? ¹² And I came and spoke to him the things concerning it. And he said, Will I plant it, or what will I do? ¹³ Since Adam was destroyed because of it, let me not also meet with the anger of God because of it. ¹⁴ And saying these things he prayed that God would reveal to him what he should do concerning it. ¹⁵ And when he had completed the prayer which lasted forty days, and having implored many things and wept, he said, Lord, I entreat You to reveal to me what I will do concerning this plant. But God sent His messenger Sarasael, and said to him, Arise, Noah, and plant the shoot of the vine, for thus says the LORD: Its bitterness will be changed into sweetness, and its curse will become a blessing, and that which is produced from it will become the blood of God; and as through it the human race obtained condemnation, so again through Jesus Christ, the Immanuel, they will receive in Him the upward calling, and the entry into Paradise.]] ¹⁶ Know therefore, O Baruch, that as Adam through this very tree obtained condemnation, and was divested of the glory of God, so also the men who now drink insatiably the wine which is begotten of it, transgress worse than Adam, and are far from the glory of God, and are surrendering themselves to the continuous fire. ¹⁷ For [no] good comes through it. For those who drink it to excess do these things: neither does a brother pity his brother, nor a father his son, nor children their parents, but from the drinking of wine come all evils, such as murders, adulteries, fornications, perjuries, thefts, and such like. And nothing good is established by it."

CHAPTER 5

¹ And I, Baruch, said to the messenger, "Let me ask you one thing, Lord. ² Since you said to me that the dragon drinks one cubit out of the sea, say to me also, how great is his belly?" ³ And the messenger said, "His belly is Hades; and as far as a plummet is thrown [by] three hundred men, so great is his belly. Come, then, that I may show you also greater works than these."

CHAPTER 6

¹ And he took me and led me where the sun goes forth; ² and he showed me a chariot and four, under which burned a fire, and in the chariot was sitting a man, wearing a crown of fire, [and] the chariot [was] drawn by forty messengers. ³ And behold, a bird circling before the sun, about nine cubits away. ⁴ And I said to the messenger, "What is this bird?" And he said to me, "This is the guardian of the earth." ⁵ And I said, "Lord, how is he the guardian of the earth? Teach me." ⁶ And the messenger said to me, "This bird flies alongside of the sun, and expanding his wings, receives its fiery rays. For if he were not receiving them, the human race would not be preserved, nor any other living creature. ⁷ But God appointed this bird to that." And he expanded his wings, and I saw on his right wing very large letters, as large as the space of a threshing-floor, the size of about four thousand modii; and the letters were of gold. ⁸ And the messenger said to me, "Read them." ⁹ And I read, and they ran thus: NEITHER EARTH NOR HEAVEN BRING ME FORTH, BUT WINGS OF FIRE BRING ME FORTH. ¹⁰ And I said, "Lord, what is this bird, and what is his name?" ¹¹ And the messenger said to me, "His name is called Phoenix." [And I said,] "And what does he eat?" And he said to me, "The manna of Heaven and the dew of earth." ¹² And I said, "Does the bird excrete?" And he said to me, "He excretes a worm, and the excrement of the worm is cinnamon, which kings and princes use. ¹³ But wait and you will see the glory of God." And while he was conversing with me, there was as a

thunderclap, and the place was shaken on which we were standing. ¹⁴ And I asked the messenger, "My Lord, what is this sound?" And the messenger said to me, "Even now the messengers are opening the three hundred and sixty-five gates of Heaven, and the light is being separated from the darkness." ¹⁵ And a voice came which said, "Light giver, give to the world radiance." ¹⁶ And when I heard the noise of the bird, I said, "Lord, what is this noise?" ¹⁷ And he said, "This is the bird who awakens from slumber the cocks on earth. For as men do through the mouth, so also does the cock signify to those in the world, in his own speech. For the sun is made ready by the messengers, and the cock crows."

CHAPTER 7

¹ And I said, "And where does the sun begin its labors, after the cock crows?" ² And the messenger said to me, "Listen, Baruch: all things, whatever I showed you, are in the first and second heaven, and in the third heaven the sun passes through and gives light to the world. But wait, and you will see the glory of God." ³ And while I was conversing with him, I saw the bird, and he appeared in front, and grew less and less, and at length returned to his full size. ⁴ And behind him I saw the shining sun, and the messengers which draw it, and a crown on its head, the sight of which we were not able to gaze on and behold. ⁵ And as soon as the sun shone, the phoenix also stretched out his wings. ⁶ But I, when I beheld such great glory, was brought low with great fear, and I fled and hid in the wings of the messenger. ⁷ And the messenger said to me, "Do not fear, Baruch, but wait and you will also see their setting."

CHAPTER 8

¹ And he took me and led me toward the west; and when the time of the setting came, I again saw the bird coming before it, and as soon as it came, I saw the messengers, and they lifted the crown from its head. ² But the bird stood exhausted and with wings contracted. ³ And beholding these things, I said, "Lord, why did they lift the crown from the head of the sun, and why is the bird so exhausted?" ⁴ And the messenger said to me, "The crown of the sun, when it has run through the day, four messengers take it, and bear it up to Heaven, and renew it, because it and its rays have been defiled on earth; moreover, it is so renewed each day." ⁵ And I Baruch said, "Lord, and why are its beams defiled on earth?" ⁶ And the messenger said to me, "Because it beholds the lawlessness and unrighteousness of men, namely fornications, adulteries, thefts, extortions, idolatries, drunkenness, murders, strife, jealousies, evil-speakings, murmurings, whisperings, divinations, and such like [these], which are not well-pleasing to God. On account of these things is it defiled, and therefore is it renewed. ⁷ But you ask concerning the

bird, how it is exhausted: because by restraining the rays of the sun through the fire and burning heat of the whole day, it is exhausted thereby. ⁸ For, as we said before, unless his wings were screening the rays of the sun, no living creature would be preserved."

CHAPTER 9

¹ And they having retired, the night also fell, and at the same time the chariot of the moon came, along with the stars. ² And I, Baruch, said, "Lord, show me it also, I implore of you, how it goes forth, where it departs, and in what form it moves along." ³ And the messenger said, "Wait and you will also see it shortly." And on the next day I also saw it in the form of a woman, and [she was] sitting on a wheeled chariot. And before it there were oxen and lambs in the chariot, and a multitude of messengers in like manner. ⁴ And I said, "Lord, what are the oxen and the lambs?" ⁵ And he said to me, "They are also messengers." And again I asked, "Why is it that it at one time increases, but at another time decreases?" ⁶ And [he said to me], "Listen, O Baruch: this which you see had been written by God beautiful as no other. ⁷ And at the transgression of the first Adam, it was near to Sammael when he took the serpent as a garment. ⁸ And it did not hide itself but increased, and God was angry with it, and afflicted it, and shortened its days." ⁹ And I said, "And how does it not also shine always, but only in the night?" ¹⁰ And the messenger said, "Listen: as in the presence of a king, the courtiers cannot speak freely, so the moon and the stars cannot shine in the presence of the sun; for the stars are always suspended, but they are screened by the sun, and the moon, although it is uninjured, is consumed by the heat of the sun."

CHAPTER 10

¹ And when I had learned all these things from the chief-messenger, he took [me] and led me into [the] fourth heaven. ² And I saw a monotonous plain, and in the middle of it a pool of water. ³ And there were multitudes of birds in it of all kinds, but not like those here on earth. ⁴ But I saw a crane as great as great oxen; and all the birds were great beyond those in the world. ⁵ And I asked the messenger, "What is the plain, and what the pool, and what the multitudes of birds around it?" ⁶ And the messenger said, "Listen, Baruch: the plain which contains the pool in it and other wonders is the place where the souls of the righteous come, when they hold converse, living together in choirs. ⁷ But the water is that which the clouds receive, and rain on the earth, and the fruits increase." ⁸ And I said again to the messenger of the LORD, "But [what] are these birds?" And he said to me, "They are those which continually sing praise to the LORD." ⁹ And I said, "Lord, and how do men say that the water which descends in rain is from the sea?" ¹⁰ And the messenger said, "The water which

descends in rain—this is also from the sea, and from the waters on earth; but that which stimulates the fruits is [only] from the latter source. ¹¹Know therefore, henceforth, that from this source is what is called the dew of Heaven."

CHAPTER 11

¹And the messenger took me and led me from there to [the] fifth heaven. And the gate was closed. ²And I said, "Lord, is this gateway not open that we may enter?" And the messenger said to me, "We cannot enter until Michael comes, who holds the keys of the Kingdom of Heaven; but wait and you will see the glory of God." ³And there was a great sound, as thunder. And I said, "Lord, what is this sound?" ⁴And he said to me, "Even now Michael, the commander of the messengers, comes down to receive the prayers of men." ⁵And behold a voice came, "Let the gates be opened." ⁶And they opened them, and there was a roar as of thunder. ⁷And Michael came, and the messenger who was with me came face to face with him and said, "Greetings, my commander, and that of all our order." ⁸And the commander Michael said, "Greetings you also, our brother, and the interpreter of the revelations to those who pass through life virtuously." And having saluted one another thus, they stood still. ⁹And I saw the commander Michael say, "Greetings you also, our brother, and the interpreter of the revelations to those who pass through life virtuously." ¹⁰And having saluted one another thus, they stood still. And I saw the commander Michael, holding an exceedingly great vessel; its depth was as great as the distance from Heaven to earth, and its breadth as great as the distance from north to south. ¹¹And I said, "Lord, what is that which Michael the chief-messenger is holding?" ¹²And he said to me, "This is where the merits of the righteous enter, and such good works as they do, which are escorted before the heavenly God."

CHAPTER 12

¹And as I was conversing with them, behold, messengers came bearing baskets full of flowers. ²And they gave them to Michael. And I asked the messenger, "Lord, who are these, and what are the things brought here from beside them?" ³And he said to me, "These are messengers [who] are over the righteous." ⁴And the chief-messenger took the baskets and cast them into the vessel. ⁵And the messenger said to me, "These flowers are the merits of the righteous." ⁶And I saw other messengers bearing baskets which were [neither] empty nor full. ⁷And they began to lament, and did not venture to draw near, because they did not have the prizes complete. ⁸And Michael cried and said, "Come here, also, you messengers; bring what you have brought." And Michael was exceedingly grieved, and the

messenger who was with me, because they did not fill the vessel.

CHAPTER 13

¹And then other messengers came in like manner, weeping and lamenting, and saying with fear, "Behold, how we are over-clouded, O Lord, for we were delivered to evil men, and we wish to depart from them." ²And Michael said, "You cannot depart from them, in order that the enemy may not prevail to the end; but say to me what you ask." ³And they said, "Please, Michael our commander, transfer us from them, for we cannot abide with wicked and foolish men, for there is nothing good in them, but every kind of unrighteousness and greed. ⁴For we do not behold them entering [[into [the] assembly at all, nor among spiritual fathers, nor]] into any good work. ⁵But where there is murder, there also are they in the midst, and where are fornications, adulteries, thefts, slanders, perjuries, jealousies, drunkenness, strife, envy, murmurings, whispering, idolatry, divination, and such like [these], then are they workers of such works, and of others worse. ⁶For what reason we entreat that we may depart from them." ⁷And Michael said to the messengers, "Wait until I learn from the LORD what will come to pass."

CHAPTER 14

¹And in that very hour Michael departed, and the doors were closed. ²And there was a sound like thunder. And I asked the messenger, "What is the sound?" ³And he said to me, "Michael is even now presenting the merits of men to God."

CHAPTER 15

¹And in that very hour Michael descended, and the gate was opened; and he brought oil. ²And as for the messengers which brought the baskets which were full, he filled them with oil, saying, "Take it away, reward our friends a hundredfold, and those who have laboriously worked good works. For those who sowed virtuously, also reap virtuously." ³And he also said to those bringing the half-empty baskets, "Come here you also; take away the reward according as you brought, and deliver it to the sons of men." [[⁴Then he also said to those who brought the full and to those who brought the half-empty baskets: "Go and bless our friends, and say to them that thus says the LORD, You are faithful over a few things, I will set you over many things; enter into the joy of your Lord."]]

CHAPTER 16

¹And turning, he also said to those who brought nothing: "Thus says the LORD, Do not be sad of countenance, and do not weep, nor leave the sons of men alone. ²But since they angered Me in their works, go and make them envious and angry and provoked against a people that is no people, a people

that has no understanding. [3] Further, besides these, send forth the caterpillar and the unwinged locust, and the mildew, and the common locust, [and] hail with lightnings and anger, and punish them severely with the sword and with death, and their children with demons. [4] For they did not listen to My voice, nor did they observe My commandments, nor do them, but were despisers of My commandments, and insolent toward the priests who proclaimed My words to them."

CHAPTER 17

[1] And while he yet spoke, the door was closed, and we withdrew. [2] And the messenger took me and restored me to the place where I was at the beginning. [3] And having come to myself, I gave glory to God, who counted me worthy of such honor. [4] For what reason you also, brothers, who obtained such a revelation, yourselves also glorify God, so that He also may glorify you, now and ever, and to all eternity. Amen.

4 BARUCH

4 Baruch, also called the Paralipomena of Jeremiah (meaning "things left out of Jeremiah"), appears as the title in several Ancient Greek manuscripts of the work. It is part of a larger Ethiopian Orthodox book that includes Lamentations and additions to Lamentations. 4 Baruch is usually dated to the first half of the 2nd century AD.

CHAPTER 1

[1] It came to pass whenever the sons of Israel were taken captive by the king of the Chaldeans, that God spoke to Jeremiah, saying, "Jeremiah, my chosen one, arise and depart from this city, you and Baruch, since I am going to destroy it because of the multitude of the sins of those who dwell in it. [2] For your prayers are like a solid pillar in its midst, and like an impenetrable wall surrounding it. [3] Now then, arise and depart before the host of the Chaldeans surrounds it." [4] And Jeremiah answered, saying, "I implore You, Lord, permit me, Your servant, to speak in Your presence." [5] And the LORD said to him: "Speak, My chosen one Jeremiah." [6] And Jeremiah spoke, saying, "LORD Almighty, would You deliver the chosen city into the hands of the Chaldeans, so that the king with the multitude of his people might boast and say: I have prevailed over the holy city of God? [7] No, my Lord, but if it is Your will, let it be destroyed by Your hands." [9] "For neither the king nor his host will be able to enter it unless I first open its gates. [10] Arise, then, and go to Baruch, and tell him these words. [11] And when you have arisen at the sixth hour of the night, go out on the city walls and I will show you that unless I first destroy the city, they cannot enter it." [12] When the LORD had said this, He departed from Jeremiah.

CHAPTER 2

[1] And Jeremiah ran and told these things to Baruch; and as they went into the temple of God, Jeremiah tore his garments and put dust on his head and entered the holy place of God. [2] And when Baruch saw him with dust sprinkled on his head and his garments torn, he cried out in a loud voice, saying, "Father Jeremiah, what are you doing? What sin has the people committed?" [3] For whenever the people sinned, Jeremiah would sprinkle dust on his head and would pray for the people until their sin was forgiven. [4] So Baruch asked him, saying, "Father, what is this?" [5] And Jeremiah said to him: "Refrain from rending your garments—rather, let us tear our hearts! And let us not draw water for the trough, but let us weep and fill them with tears! For the LORD will not have mercy on this people." [6] And Baruch said, "Father Jeremiah,

what has happened?" [7] And Jeremiah said, "God is delivering the city into the hands of the king of the Chaldeans, to take the people captive into Babylon." [8] And when Baruch heard these things, he also tore his garments and said, "Father Jeremiah, who has made this known to you?" [9] And Jeremiah said to him: "Stay with me awhile, until the sixth hour of the night, so that you may know that this word is true." [10] Therefore they both remained near the altar, weeping, and their garments were torn.

CHAPTER 3

[1] And when the hour of the night arrived, as the LORD had told Jeremiah they came up together on the walls of the city, Jeremiah and Baruch. [2] And behold, there came a sound of trumpets; and messengers emerged from Heaven holding torches in their hands, and they set them on the walls of the city. [3] And when Jeremiah and Baruch saw them, they wept, saying, "Now we know that the word is true!" [4] And Jeremiah implored the messengers, saying, "I implore you, do not destroy the city yet, until I say something to the LORD." [5] And the LORD spoke to the messengers, saying, "Do not destroy the city until I speak to My chosen one, Jeremiah." [6] Then Jeremiah spoke, saying, "I beg You, Lord, bid me to speak in Your presence." [7] And the LORD said, "Speak, My chosen one Jeremiah." [8] And Jeremiah said, "Behold, Lord, now we know that You are delivering the city into the hands of its enemies, and they will take the people away to Babylon. What do You want me to do with the holy vessels of the temple service?" [10] And the LORD said to him: "Take them and consign them to the earth, saying, Hear, Earth, the voice of Your Creator who formed you in the abundance of waters, who sealed you with seven seals for seven epochs, and after this you will receive your ornaments— [11] guard the vessels of the temple service until the gathering of the beloved!" [12] And Jeremiah spoke, saying, "I implore You, Lord, show me what I should do for Abimelech the Ethiopian, for he has done many kindnesses to Your servant Jeremiah. [13] For he pulled me out of the miry pit; and I do not wish that he should see the destruction and desolation of this city, but that You should be merciful to him and that he should not be grieved." [14] And the LORD said to Jeremiah: "Send him to the vineyard of Agrippa, and I will hide him in the shadow of the mountain until I cause the people to return to the city. [15] And you, Jeremiah, go with your people into Babylon and stay with them, preaching to them, until I cause them to return to the city. [16] But leave Baruch here until I speak with him." [17] When He had said these things, the LORD ascended from Jeremiah into Heaven. [18] But

Jeremiah and Baruch entered the holy place, and taking the vessels of the temple service, they consigned them to the earth as the LORD had told them. ¹⁹ And immediately the earth swallowed them. ²⁰ And they both sat down and wept. ²¹ And when morning came, Jeremiah sent Abimelech, saying, "Take a basket and go to the estate of Agrippa by the mountain road, and bring back some figs to give to the sick among the people; for the favor of the LORD is on you and His glory is on your head." ²² And when he had said this, Jeremiah sent him away; and Abimelech went as he told him.

CHAPTER 4

¹ And when morning came, behold, the host of the Chaldeans surrounded the city. ² And the great messenger trumpeted, saying, "Enter the city, host of the Chaldeans; for behold, the gate is opened for you. ³ Therefore let the king enter, with his multitudes, and let him take all the people captive." ⁴ But taking the keys of the temple, Jeremiah went outside the city and threw them away in the presence of the sun, saying, "I say to you, Sun, take the keys of the temple of God and guard them until the day in which the LORD asks you for them. ⁵ For we have not been found worthy to keep them, for we have become unfaithful guardians." ⁶ While Jeremiah was still weeping for the people, they brought him out with the people and dragged them into Babylon. ⁷ But Baruch put dust on his head and sat and wailed this lamentation, saying, "Why has Jerusalem been devastated? Because of the sins of the beloved people ‖ She was delivered into the hands of enemies ‖ Because of our sins and those of the people. ⁸ But do not let the lawless ones boast and say: We were strong enough to take the city of God by our might; But it was delivered to you because of our sins. ⁹ And God will pity us and cause us ‖ To return to our city, ‖ But you will not survive! ¹⁰ Blessed are our fathers, Abraham, Isaac and Jacob, ‖ For they departed from this world ‖ And did not see the destruction of this city." ¹¹ When he had said this, Baruch departed from the city, weeping and saying, "Grieving because of you, Jerusalem, I went out from you." ¹² And he remained sitting in a tomb, while the messengers came to him and explained to him everything that the LORD revealed to him through them.

CHAPTER 5

¹ But Abimelech took the figs in the burning heat; and coming on a tree, he sat under its shade to rest a bit. ² And leaning his head on the basket of figs, he fell asleep and slept for sixty-six years; and he was not awakened from his slumber. ³ And afterward, when he awoke from his sleep, he said, "I slept sweetly for a little while, but my head is heavy because I did not get enough sleep." ⁴ Then he uncovered the basket of figs and found them dripping milk. ⁵ And he said, "I would like to sleep a little longer, because my head is heavy. But I am afraid that I might fall asleep and be late in awakening and my father Jeremiah would think badly of me; for if he were not in a hurry, he would not have sent me today at daybreak. ⁶ So I will get up, and proceed in the burning heat; for isn't there heat, isn't there toil every day?" ⁷ So he got up and took the basket of figs and placed it on his shoulders, and he entered into Jerusalem and did not recognize it—neither his own house, nor the place—nor did he find his own family or any of his acquaintances. ⁸ And he said, "The LORD be blessed, for a great trance has come over me today! ⁹ This is not the city Jerusalem—and I have lost my way because I came by the mountain road when I arose from my sleep; and since my head was heavy because I did not get enough sleep, I lost my way. ¹⁰ It will seem incredible to Jeremiah that I lost my way!" ¹¹ And he departed from the city; and as he searched he saw the landmarks of the city, and he said, "Indeed, this is the city; I lost my way." ¹² And again he returned to the city and searched, and found no one of his own people; and he said, "The LORD be blessed, for a great trance has come over me!" ¹³ And again he departed from the city, and he stayed there grieving, not knowing where he should go. ¹⁴ And he put down the basket, saying, "I will sit here until the LORD takes this trance from me." ¹⁵ And as he sat, he saw an old man coming from the field; and Abimelech said to him: "I say to you, old man, what city is this?" ¹⁶ And he said to him: "It is Jerusalem." ¹⁷ And Abimelech said to him: "Where is Jeremiah the priest, and Baruch the secretary, and all the people of this city, for I could not find them?" ¹⁸ And the old man said to him: "Are you not from this city, seeing that you remember Jeremiah today, because you are asking about him after such a long time? ¹⁹ For Jeremiah is in Babylon with the people; for they were taken captive by King Nebuchadnezzar, and Jeremiah is with them to preach the good news to them and to teach them the word." ²⁰ As soon as Abimelech heard this from the old man, he said, "If you were not an old man, and if it were not for the fact that it is not lawful for a man to scold one older than himself, I would laugh at you and say that you are out of your mind—since you say that the people have been taken captive into Babylon. ²¹ Even if the heavenly torrents had descended on them, there has not yet been time for them to go into Babylon! ²² For how much time has passed since my father Jeremiah sent me to the estate of Agrippa to bring a few figs, so that I might give them to the sick among the people? ²³ And I went and got them, and when I came to a certain tree in the burning heat, I sat to rest a little; and I leaned my head on the basket and fell asleep. ²⁴ And when I awoke, I uncovered the basket of figs, supposing that I was late; and I found the figs dripping milk, just as I had collected them. ²⁵ But you claim that the people have been taken

captive into Babylon. ²⁶ But that you might know, take the figs and see!" ²⁷ And he uncovered the basket of figs for the old man, and he saw them dripping milk. ²⁸ And when the old man saw them, he said, "O my son, you are a righteous man, and God did not want you to see the desolation of the city, so He brought this trance on you. ²⁹ For behold it is sixty-six years today since the people were taken captive into Babylon. ³⁰ But that you might learn, my son, that what I tell you is true—look into the field and see that the ripening of the crops has not appeared. ³¹ And notice that the figs are not in season, and be enlightened." ³² Then Abimelech cried out in a loud voice, saying, "I bless You, God of the heavens and earth, the Rest of the souls of the righteous in every place!" ³³ Then he said to the old man: "What month is this?" ³⁴ And he said, "Nisan," which is Abib. ³⁵ And taking some of [the] figs, he gave them to the old man and said to him: "May God illuminate your way to the city above—Jerusalem."

CHAPTER 6

¹ After this, Abimelech went out of the city and prayed to the LORD. ² And behold, a messenger of the LORD came and took him by the right hand and brought him back to where Baruch was sitting, and he found him in a tomb. ³ And when they saw each other, they both wept and kissed each other. ⁴ But when Baruch looked up, he saw with his own eyes the figs that were covered in Abimelech's basket. ⁵ And lifting his eyes to Heaven, he prayed, saying, ⁶ "You are the God who gives a reward to those who love You. Prepare yourself, my heart, and rejoice and be glad while you are in your dwelling place, saying to your fleshly house, Your grief has been changed to joy; for the Sufficient One is coming and will deliver you in your dwelling place—for there is no sin in you. ⁷ Revive in your dwelling place, in your virginal faith, and believe that you will live! ⁸ Look at this basket of figs—for behold, they are sixty-six years old and have not become shrivelled or rotten, but they are dripping milk. ⁹ So it will be with you, my flesh, if you do what is commanded of you by the messenger of righteousness. ¹⁰ He who preserved the basket of figs, the same will again preserve you by his power." ¹¹ When Baruch had said this, he said to Abimelech: "Stand up and let us pray that the LORD may make known to us how we will be able to send to Jeremiah in Babylon the report about the shelter provided for you on the way." ¹² And Baruch prayed, saying, "LORD God, our strength is the chosen light which comes forth from Your mouth. ¹³ We implore and beg of Your goodness—You whose great Name no one is able to know—hear the voice of Your servants and let knowledge come into our hearts. ¹⁴ What will we do, and how will we send this report to Jeremiah in Babylon?" ¹⁵ And while Baruch was still praying, behold a messenger of the LORD came and said all

these words to Baruch: "Agent of the light, do not be anxious about how you will send to Jeremiah; for an eagle is coming to you at the hour of light tomorrow, and you will direct him to Jeremiah. ¹⁶ Therefore, write in a letter: Say to the sons of Israel: Let the stranger who comes among you be set apart and let fifteen days go by; and after this I will lead you into your city, says the LORD. ¹⁷ He who is not separated from Babylon will not enter into the city; and I will punish them by keeping them from being received back by the Babylonians, says the LORD." ¹⁸ And when the messenger had said this, he departed from Baruch. ¹⁹ And Baruch sent to the market of the nations and got papyrus and ink and wrote a letter as follows: Baruch, the servant of God, writes to Jeremiah in the captivity of Babylon: ²⁰ Greetings! Rejoice, for God has not allowed us to depart from this body grieving for the city which was laid waste and outraged. ²¹ For what reason the LORD has had compassion on our tears, and has remembered the covenant which He established with our fathers Abraham, Isaac, and Jacob. ²² And he sent His messenger to me, and he told me these words which I send to you. ²³ These, then, are the words which the LORD, the God of Israel, spoke, who led us out of Egypt, out of the great furnace: Because you did not keep My ordinances, but your heart was lifted up, and you were haughty before Me, in anger and wrath I delivered you to the furnace in Babylon. ²⁴ If, therefore, says the LORD, you listen to My voice, from the mouth of Jeremiah My servant, I will bring the one who listens up from Babylon; but the one who does not listen will become a stranger to Jerusalem and to Babylon. ²⁵ And you will test them by means of the water of the Jordan; whoever does not listen will be exposed—this is the sign of the great seal.

CHAPTER 7

¹ And Baruch got up and departed from the tomb and found the eagle sitting outside the tomb. ² And the eagle said to him in a human voice: "Greetings, Baruch, steward of the faith." ³ And Baruch said to him: "You who speak are chosen from among all the birds of Heaven, for this is clear from the gleam of your eyes; tell me, then, what are you doing here?" ⁴ And the eagle said to him: "I was sent here so that you might send whatever message you want through me." ⁵ And Baruch said to him: "Can you carry this message to Jeremiah in Babylon?" ⁶ And the eagle said to him: "Indeed, it was for this reason I was sent." ⁷ And Baruch took the letter, and fifteen figs from Abimelech's basket, and tied them to the eagle's neck and said to him: "I say to you, king of the birds, go in peace with good health and carry the message for me. ⁸ Do not be like the raven which Noah sent out and which never came back to him in the Ark; but be like the dove which, the third time, brought a report to the righteous one. ⁹ So you also, take this good message

to Jeremiah and to those in bondage with him, that it may be well with you. Take this papyrus to the people and to the chosen one of God. [10] Even if all the birds of Heaven surround you and want to fight with you, struggle—the LORD will give you strength. [11] And do not turn aside to the right or to the left, but straight as a speeding arrow, go in the power of God, and the glory of the LORD will be with you the entire way." [12] Then the eagle took flight and went away to Babylon, having the letter tied to his neck; and when he arrived, he rested on a post outside the city in a desert place. [13] And he kept silent until Jeremiah came along, for he and some of the people were coming out to bury a corpse outside the city. [14] For Jeremiah had petitioned King Nebuchadnezzar, saying, "Give me a place where I may bury those of my people who have died"; and the king gave it to him. [15] And as they were coming out with the body, and weeping, they came to where the eagle was. [16] And the eagle cried out in a loud voice, saying, "I say to you, Jeremiah the chosen one of God, go and gather together the people and come here so that they may hear a letter which I have brought to you from Baruch and Abimelech." [17] And when Jeremiah heard this, he glorified God; and he went and gathered together the people along with their wives and children, and he came to where the eagle was. [18] And the eagle came down on the corpse, and it revived. [19] Now this took place so that they might believe. [20] And all the people were astounded at what had happened, and said, "This is the God who appeared to our fathers in the wilderness through Moses, and now he has appeared to us through the eagle." [21] And the eagle said, "I say to you, Jeremiah, come, untie this letter and read it to the people"—so he untied the letter and read it to the people. [22] And when the people heard it, they wept and put dust on their heads, and they said to Jeremiah: "Deliver us and tell us what to do that we may once again enter our city." [23] And Jeremiah answered and said to them: "Do whatever you heard from the letter, and the LORD will lead us into our city." [24] And Jeremiah wrote a letter to Baruch, saying thus: My beloved son, do not be negligent in your prayers, imploring God on our behalf, that He might direct our way until we come out of the jurisdiction of this lawless king. [25] For you have been found righteous before God, and He did not let you come here, lest you see the affliction which has come on the people at the hands of the Babylonians. [26] For it is like a father with an only son, who is given over for punishment; and those who see his father and console him cover his face, lest he see how his son is being punished, and be even more ravaged by grief. [27] For thus God took pity on you and did not let you enter Babylon lest you see the affliction of the people. [28] For since we came here, grief has not left us, for sixty-six years today. [29] For many times when I went out I found some of the people hung up by King Nebuchadnezzar, crying and

saying, "Have mercy on us, God-Zar!" [30] When I heard this, I grieved and cried with double mourning, not only because they were hung up, but because they were calling on a foreign god, saying, "Have mercy on us." [31] But I remembered days of festivity which we celebrated in Jerusalem before our captivity; and when I remembered, I groaned, and returned to my house wailing and weeping. [32] Now, then, pray in the place where you are—you and Abimelech—for this people, that they may listen to my voice and to the decrees of my mouth, so that we may depart from here. [33] For I tell you that the entire time that we have spent here they have kept us in subjection, saying, "Recite for us a song from the songs of Zion—the song of your God." [34] And we reply to them: "How will we sing for you since we are in a foreign land?" [35] And after this, Jeremiah tied the letter to the eagle's neck, saying, "Go in peace, and may the LORD watch over both of us." [36] And the eagle took flight and came to Jerusalem and gave the letter to Baruch; and when he had untied it he read it and kissed it and wept when he heard about the distresses and afflictions of the people. [37] But Jeremiah took the figs and distributed them to the sick among the people, and he kept teaching them to abstain from the pollutions of the nations of Babylon.

CHAPTER 8

[1] And the day came in which the LORD brought the people out of Babylon. [2] And the LORD said to Jeremiah: "Rise up—you and the people—and come to the Jordan and say to the people: Let anyone who desires the LORD forsake the works of Babylon. [3] As for the men who took wives from them and the women who took husbands from them—those who listen to you will cross over, and you take them into Jerusalem; but those who do not listen to you, do not lead them there." [4] And Jeremiah spoke these words to the people, and they arose and came to the Jordan to cross over. [5] As he told them the words that the LORD had spoken to him, half of those who had taken spouses from them did not wish to listen to Jeremiah, but said to him: "We will never forsake our wives, but we will bring them back with us into our city." [6] So they crossed the Jordan and came to Jerusalem. [7] And Jeremiah and Baruch and Abimelech stood up and said, "No man joined with Babylonians will enter this city!" [8] And they said to one another: "Let us arise and return to Babylon—to our place." And they departed. [9] But while they were coming to Babylon, the Babylonians came out to meet them, saying, "You will not enter our city, for you hated us and you left us secretly; therefore you cannot come in with us. [10] For we have taken a solemn oath together in the name of our god to receive neither you nor your children, since you left us secretly." [11] And when they heard this, they returned and came to a desert place some distance from Jerusalem and built a city for

themselves and named it Samaria. ¹²And Jeremiah sent to them, saying, "Convert, for the messenger of righteousness is coming and will lead you to your exalted place."

CHAPTER 9

¹Now those who were with Jeremiah were rejoicing and offering sacrifices on behalf of the people for nine days. ²But on the tenth, Jeremiah alone offered sacrifice. ³And he prayed a prayer, saying, "HOLY, HOLY, HOLY, Fragrant Aroma of the living trees, True Light that enlightens me until I ascend to You; ⁴For Your mercy, I beg You—for the sweet voice of the two seraphim, I beg—for another fragrant aroma. ⁵And may Michael, chief-messenger of righteousness, who opens the gates to the righteous, be my guardian until he causes the righteous to enter. ⁶I beg You, almighty Lord of all creation, unbegotten and incomprehensible, in whom all judgment was hidden before these things came into existence." ⁷When Jeremiah had said this, and while he was standing near the altar with Baruch and Abimelech, he became as one whose soul had departed. ⁸And Baruch and Abimelech were weeping and crying out in a loud voice: "Woe to us! For our father Jeremiah has left us—the priest of God has departed!" ⁹And all the people heard their weeping, and they all ran to them and saw Jeremiah lying on the ground as if dead. ¹⁰And they tore their garments and put dust on their heads and wept bitterly. ¹¹And after this they prepared to bury him. ¹²And behold, there came a voice, saying, "Do not bury the one who yet lives, for his soul is returning to his body!" ¹³And when they heard the voice they did not bury him, but stayed around his dwelling place for three days, saying, "When will he arise?" ¹⁴And after three days his soul came back into his body and he raised his voice in the midst of them all and said, "Glorify God with one voice! All of you glorify God and the Son of God who awakens us—Messiah Jesus—the Light of all the ages, the inextinguishable Lamp, the Life of faith. ¹⁵But after these times there will be four hundred seventy-seven years more, and He comes to earth. ¹⁶And the Tree of Life planted in the midst of paradise will cause all the unfruitful trees to bear fruit, and will grow and sprout forth. ¹⁷And the trees that had sprouted and became

haughty, and said, We have supplied our power to the air, He will cause them to wither, with the grandeur of their branches, and He will cause them to be judged—that firmly rooted tree! ¹⁸And what is crimson will become white as wool—the snow will be blackened—the sweet waters will become salty, and the salty sweet, in the intense light of the joy of God. ¹⁹And He will bless the isles so that they become fruitful by the word of the mouth of His Messiah. ²⁰For He will come, and He will go out and choose for Himself twelve apostles to proclaim the news among the nations—He whom I have seen adorned by His Father and coming into the world on the Mount of Olives—and He will fill the hungry souls." ²¹When Jeremiah was saying this concerning the Son of God—that He is coming into the world—the people became very angry and said, "This is a repetition of the words spoken by Isaiah son of Amos, when he said, I saw God and the Son of God. ²²Come, then, and let us not kill him by the same sort of death with which we killed Isaiah, but let us stone him with stones." ²³And Baruch and Abimelech were greatly grieved because they wanted to hear in full the mysteries that he had seen. ²⁴But Jeremiah said to them: "Be silent and do not weep, for they cannot kill me until I describe for you everything I saw." ²⁵And he said to them: "Bring a stone here to me." ²⁶And he set it up and said, "Light of the ages, make this stone to become like me in appearance, until I have described to Baruch and Abimelech everything I saw." ²⁷Then the stone, by God's command, took on the appearance of Jeremiah. ²⁸And they were stoning the stone, supposing that it was Jeremiah! ²⁹But Jeremiah delivered to Baruch and to Abimelech all the mysteries he had seen, and immediately he stood in the midst of the people desiring to complete his ministry. ³⁰Then the stone cried out, saying, "O foolish sons of Israel, why do you stone me, supposing that I am Jeremiah? Behold, Jeremiah is standing in your midst!" ³¹And when they saw him, immediately they rushed on him with many stones, and his ministry was fulfilled. ³²And when Baruch and Abimelech came, they buried him, and taking the stone they placed it on his tomb and inscribed it thus: This is the stone that was the ally of Jeremiah.

REVELATION OF ABRAHAM

The Apocalypse of Abraham, called the Revelation of Abraham in the LSV—"apocalypse" meaning a "revelation," "unveiling," or, even more literally, "an uncovering"—was written fairly early in the current era, possibly between 70 and 150 AD. The narrative includes a history of Abraham in his father's house and his conversion to monotheism. That section is followed by a prophetic vision and an account of his journey through the heavens.

THE SCROLL OF THE REVELATION OF ABRAHAM, THE SON OF TERAH, THE SON OF NAHOR, THE SON OF SERUG, THE SON OF REU, THE SON OF ARPHAXAD, THE SON OF SHEM, THE SON OF NOAH, THE SON OF LAMECH, THE SON OF METHUSELAH, THE SON OF ENOCH, THE SON OF JARED.

CHAPTER 1

[1] On the day when I planed the gods of my father Terah and the gods of his brother Nahor, when I was searching as to who the Mighty God in truth is—I, Abraham, at the time when it fell to my lot, when I fulfilled the sacrifices of my father Terah to his gods of wood and stone, gold and silver, brass and iron; having entered into their temple for service, I found the god whose name was Merumath [which was] hewn out of stone, fallen forward at the feet of the iron god Nahon. [2] And it came to pass, when I saw it, my heart was perplexed, and I considered in my mind that I should not be able to bring him back to his place, I, Abraham, alone, because he was heavy, being of a large stone, and I went forth and made it known to my father. [3] And he entered in with me, and when both of us moved him forward, so that we might bring him back to his place, his head fell from him while I was still holding him by the head. [4] And it came to pass, when my father saw that the head of Merumath had fallen from him, he said to me: "Abraham!" And I said, "Here I am." [5] And he said to me: "Bring me an axe, of the small ones, from the house." And I brought it to him. [6] And he correctly hewed another Merumath out of another stone, without head, and the head which had been thrown down from Merumath he placed on it, and the rest of Merumath he shattered.

CHAPTER 2

[1] And he made five other gods, and gave them to me [and] commanded me to sell them outside in the street of the town. [2] And I saddled my father's donkey, and placed them on it, and went toward the inn to sell them. And behold, merchants from Fandana in Syria were traveling with camels going to Egypt, to trade.

And I spoke with them. [3] And one of their camels uttered a groan, and the donkey took fright and sprang away and upset the gods; and three of them were smashed, and two were preserved. [4] And it came to pass, when the Syrians saw that I had gods, they said to me: "Why did you not tell us [[that you had gods? Then we would have bought them]] before the donkey heard the sound of the camel, and they would not have been lost. [5] Give us, at any rate, the gods that remain, and we will give you the proper price for the broken gods, also for the gods that have been preserved." [6] For I was concerned in my heart as to how I could bring to my father the purchase-price; and the three broken ones I cast into the water of the River Gur, which was at that place, and they sank into the depths, and there was nothing more of them.

CHAPTER 3

[1] When I was still going on the way, my heart was perplexed within me, and my mind was distracted. [2] And I said in my heart: [["What evil deed is this that my father is doing? Is he not, rather, the god of his gods, since they come into existence through his chisels and lathes, and his wisdom, and is it not rather fitting that they should worship my father, since they are his work? What is this delusion of my father in his works?]] [3] Behold, Merumath fell and could not rise in his own temple, nor could I, by myself, move him until my father came, and the two of us moved him; and as we were thus too weak, his head fell from him, and he set it on another stone of another god, which he had made without head. [4] And the other five gods were broken in pieces down from the donkey, which were able neither to help themselves, nor to hurt the donkey, because it had broken them to pieces; nor did their broken fragments come up out of the river." [5] And I said in my heart: "If this be so, how can Merumath, my father's god, having the head of another stone, and himself being made of another stone, rescue a man, or hear a man's prayer and reward him?"

CHAPTER 4

[1] And while I meditated thus, I reached my father's house; and having watered the donkey, and set out hay for it, I brought the silver and gave it into the hand of my father Terah. [2] When he saw it, he was glad, [and] he said, "Blessed are you, Abraham, of my gods, because you have brought the price of the gods, so that my work was not in vain." [3] And I answered and said to him: "Hear, O my father Terah! Blessed are the gods of you, for you are their god, since you have made them; for their blessing is ruination, and their power is vain; they who did not help themselves,

how will they, then, help you or bless me? [4] I have been kind to you in this affair, because by [using] my intelligence, I have brought you the money for the broken gods." [5] And when he heard my word, he became furiously angry with me, because I had spoken hard words against his gods.

CHAPTER 5

[1] I, however, having thought over my father's anger, went out; [[and after I had gone out]] my father cried, saying, "Abraham!" [2] And I said, "Here I am." And he said, "Take and collect the splinters of the wood out of which I made gods of pinewood before you came; and make ready for me the food of the midday meal." [3] And it came to pass, when I collected the splinters of wood, I found under them a little god which had been lying among the brushwood on my left, and on his forehead was written: GOD BARISAT. [4] And I did not inform my father that I had found the wooden god Barisat under the chips. [5] And it came to pass, when I had laid the splinters in the fire, in order that I might make food ready for my father—on going out to ask a question regarding the food, I placed Barisat before the kindled fire, [6] saying threateningly to him: "Pay careful attention, Barisat, [that] the fire does not die down until I come; if, however, it dies down, blow on it that it may burn up again." [7] And I went out and accomplished my purpose. And on returning I found Barisat fallen backwards, and his feet surrounded by fire and horribly burnt. [8] I burst into a fit of laughter, and I said to myself, "Truly, O Barisat, you can kindle the fire and cook food!" [9] And it came to pass, while I spoke [thus] in my laughter he was gradually burned up by the fire and reduced to ashes. And I brought the food to my father, and he ate. [10] And I gave him wine and milk, and he was gladdened and blessed his god Merumath. And I said to him, "O father Terah, do not bless your god Merumath, and do not praise him, but rather praise your god Barisat because, loving you more, he has cast himself into the fire to cook your food!" [11] And he said to me, "And where is he now?" [And I said,] "He is burned to ashes in the violence of the fire and is reduced to dust." [12] And he said, "Great is the power of Barisat! I make another today, and tomorrow he will prepare my food."

CHAPTER 6

[1] However, when I, Abraham, heard such words from my father, I laughed in my mind and sighed in the grief and in the anger of my soul, and said, "How then can that which is made by him—manufactured statues—be a helper of my father? [2] Or will the body then be subject to its soul, and the soul to the spirit, and the spirit to folly and ignorance?" [3] And I said, "It is fitting to once endure evil, so I will direct my mind to what is pure and lay my thoughts open before him." [4] [And] I answered and said, "O father Terah,

whichever of these you praise as a god, you are foolish in your mind. Behold the gods of your brother Ora, which stand in the holy temple, are more worthy of honor than [these of] yours. [5] For behold, Zucheus, the god of your brother Oron, is more worthy of honor than your god Merumath, because he is made of gold which is highly valued by people, and when he grows old in years he will be remodeled; [6] but if your god Merumath is changed or broken, he will not be renewed, because he is a stone; the which is also the case with the god Joavon [[who stands with Zucheus over the other gods—how much more worthy of honor is he than the god Barisat, who is made of wood, while he is forged of silver! [7] How is he made, by adaptation of man, valuable to outward appearance! But your god Barisat, while he still was, before he had been prepared, rooted up on the earth and was great and wonderful with the glory of branches and blossom, you hewed out with the axe, and by means of your axe he has been made into a god. [8] And behold, his fatness is already withered and perished, he is fallen from the height to the ground, he has come from great estate to littleness, and the appearance of his countenance has vanished, and he,]] [9] Barisat himself, is burned up by fire and reduced to ashes and is no more; and you say: Today I will make another which tomorrow will make my food ready! He has perished to utter destruction!"

CHAPTER 7

[1] "Behold, the fire is more worthy of honor than all things formed because even that which is not subjected is subjected to it, and things easily perishable are mocked by its flames. [2] But even more worthy of honor is the water, because it conquers the fire and satisfies the earth. But even it I do not call god, because it is subjected to the earth under which the water inclines. But I call the earth much more worthy of honor, because it overpowers the nature of the water. [3] Even it, however, I do not call god—it, too, is dried up by the sun, [and] is apportioned to man to be tilled. [4] [[I call the sun more worthy of honor than the earth,]] because it with its rays illuminates the whole world and the different atmospheres. [5] [But] even it I do not call god, because at night and by clouds its course is obscured. [6] Nor, again, do I call the moon or the stars god, because they also in their season obscure [their] light at night. [7] [But] hear [this], my father Terah; for I will make known to you the God who has made everything, not these we consider as gods. [8] Who then is He, ‖ Or what is He, who has crimsoned the heavens, and made the sun golden, ‖ And the moon lustrous, and with it the stars; And has made the earth dry in the midst of many waters, [9] And set you in . . . [[and tested me in the confusion of my thoughts]]. Yet may God reveal Himself to us through Himself!"

CHAPTER 8

[1] And it came to pass while I spoke thus to my father Terah in the court of my house, there comes down the voice of a Mighty One from Heaven in a fiery rainstorm, saying and crying: "Abraham, Abraham!" [2] And I said, "Here I am." And He said, "You are seeking in the understanding of Your heart the God of gods and the Creator; I am He: Go out from your father Terah, and get out from the house, that you also are not slain in the sins of your father's house." [3] And I went out. And it came to pass when I went out, that before I succeeded in getting out in front of the door of the court, there came a sound of a [great] thunder and [fire] burned him, and his house, and everything, whatever was in his house, down to the ground—forty cubits.

CHAPTER 9

[1] Then a voice came to me speaking twice: "Abraham, Abraham!" And I said, "Here I am!" [2] And He said, "Behold, it is I; do not fear, for I am before the worlds, and a mighty God who has created the light of the world. I am a shield over you, and I am your helper. [3] Go, bring Me a young heifer of three years old, and a female goat of three years old, and a ram of three years old, and a turtledove and a pigeon, and bring Me a pure sacrifice. [4] And in this sacrifice, I will lay before you the ages [to come], and make known to you what is reserved, and you will see great things which you have not seen [until now], because you have loved to search Me out, and I have named you My friend. [5] But abstain from every form of food that proceeds out of the fire, and from the drinking of wine, and from anointing [yourself] with oil, forty days, and then set forth for Me the sacrifice which I have commanded you, in the place which I will show you on a high mountain, [6] and there I will show you the ages which have been created and established, made and renewed, by My Word, and I will make known to you what will come to pass in them on those who have done evil and [practiced] righteousness in the generation of men."

CHAPTER 10

[1] And it came to pass, when I heard the voice of Him who spoke such words to me, [and] I looked here and there, and behold, there was no breath of a man, and my spirit was frightened, and my soul fled from me, and I became like a stone, and fell down on the earth, for I had no more strength to stand on the earth. [2] And while I was still lying with my face on the earth, I heard the voice of the Holy One speaking: "Go, Yahoel, and by means of My ineffable Name raise that man for Me, and strengthen him [so that he recovers] from his trembling." [3] And the messenger came, whom He had sent to me, in the likeness of a man, and grasped me by my right hand, and set me up on my feet, and said to me: "Stand up, friend of God who loves you; do not let the trembling of man seize you! [4] For behold, I have been sent to you to strengthen you and bless you in the Name of God—who loves you—the Creator of the celestial and terrestrial. Be fearless and hasten to Him. [5] I am called Yahoel by Him who moves that which exists with me on the seventh heaven on the expanse, a power in virtue of the ineffable Name that is dwelling in me. [6] I am the one who has been given to restrain, according to His commandment, the threatening attack of the living creatures of the cherubim against one another, and teach those who carry Him the song of the seventh hour of the night of man. [7] I am ordained to restrain the Leviathan, for to me are subject the attack and menace of every single reptile. [[I am he who has been commissioned to loosen Hades, to destroy him who stares at the dead.]] [8] I am the one who was commissioned to set on fire your father's house together with him, because he displayed reverence for dead [idols]. [9] I have been sent to bless you now, and the land which the Perpetual One, whom you have invoked, has prepared for you, and for your sake I have journeyed my way on the earth. [10] Stand up, Abraham! Go without fear; be rightly glad and rejoice; and I am with you! For continuous honor has been prepared for you by the Perpetual One. [11] Go, fulfill the sacrifices commanded. For behold, I have been appointed to be with you and with the generation prepared [to spring] from you; and with me Michael blesses you forever. Be of good cheer, go!"

CHAPTER 11

[1] And I rose up and saw him who had grasped me by my right hand and set me up on my feet: [2] and the appearance of his body was like sapphire, and the look of his countenance like chrysolite, and the hair of his head like snow, and the turban on his head like the appearance of the rainbow, and the clothing of his garments like purple; and a golden scepter was in his right hand. [3] And he said to me, "Abraham!" And I said, "Here I am, your servant." [4] And he said, "Do not let my look frighten you, nor my speech, that your soul is not perturbed. [5] Come with me and I will go with you, until the sacrifice, visible, but after the sacrifice, invisible forever. Be of good cheer, and come!"

CHAPTER 12

[1] And we went, the two of us together, forty days and nights, and I ate no bread, and drank no water, because my food was to see the messenger who was with me, and his speech—that was my drink. [2] And we came to the Mount of God, the glorious Horeb. And I said to the messenger: "Singer of the Perpetual One! Behold, I have no sacrifice with me, nor am I aware of a place of an altar on the mountain; how can I bring a sacrifice?" [3] And he said to me, "Look around!" And I looked around, and behold, there were

following us all the prescribed sacrificial [animals]—the young heifer, and the female goat, and the ram, and the turtle-dove, and the pigeon. [4] And the messenger said to me, "Abraham!" I said, "Here I am." And he said to me, "Slaughter all of these, and divide the animals into halves, one against the other, but do not sever the birds; and give to the men, whom I will show you, standing by you, for these are the altar on the mountain, to offer a sacrifice to the Perpetual; [5] but give the turtledove and the pigeon to me, for I will ascend on the wings of the bird, in order to show you in Heaven, and on the earth, and in the sea, and in the abyss, and in the underworld, and in the Garden of Eden, and in its rivers and in the fullness of the whole world and its circle—you will gaze in [them] all."

CHAPTER 13

[1] And I did everything according to the commandment of the messenger, and gave the messengers, who had come to us, the divided animals, but the messenger took the birds. [2] And I waited for the evening sacrifice. And there flew an unclean bird down on the carcasses, and I drove it away. [3] And the unclean bird spoke to me, and said, "What are you doing, Abraham, on the holy heights, where no man eats or drinks, neither is there on them food of man, but these consume everything with fire, and burn you up? [4] Forsake the man who is with you and flee; for if you ascend to the heights, they will make an end of you." [5] And it came to pass, when I saw the bird speak, I said to the messenger, "What is this, my lord?" And he said, "This is ungodliness, this is Azazel." [6] And he said to it: "Disgrace on you, Azazel! For Abraham's lot is in Heaven, but yours on the earth, because you have chosen and loved this for the dwelling-[place] of your uncleanness, therefore the perpetual mighty LORD made you a dweller on the earth and through you every evil spirit of lies, and through you wrath and trials for the generations of ungodly men; [7] for God, the Perpetual, Mighty One, has not permitted that the bodies of the righteous should be in your hand, in order that thereby the life of the righteous and the destruction of the unclean may be assured. [8] Hear, friend, go away from me with shame. For it has not been given to you to play the tempter in regard to all the righteous. [9] Depart from this man! You cannot lead him astray, because he is an enemy to you, and of those who follow you and love what you will. [10] For behold, the vesture which in Heaven was formerly yours has been set aside for him, and the mortality which was his has been transferred to you."

CHAPTER 14

[1] The messenger said to me, [["Abraham!" And I said, "Here I am, your servant." [2] And he said, "Know from now on that the Perpetual One has chosen you, [He] whom you love; be of good courage and use this authority, so far as I bid you, against him who slanders truth; [3] should I not be able to put him to shame who has scattered over the earth the secrets of Heaven and has rebelled against the Mighty One?]] [4] Say to him: Be the burning coal of the furnace of the earth; go, Azazel, into the inaccessible parts of the earth; [[for your heritage is over those existing with you being born with the stars and clouds, with the men whose portion you are, and through your being exist; and your enmity is justification. [5] On this account, by your perdition disappear from me." And I uttered the words which the messenger had taught me. And he said, "Abraham!" [6] And I said, "Here I am, your servant."]] [7] And the messenger said to me: "Do not answer him; for God has given him will over those who answer him." [[[8] And the messenger spoke to me a second time and said, "Now rather, however much he speaks to you, do not answer him, that his will may have no free course in you, because the Perpetual and Mighty One has given him weight and will; do not answer him." I did what was commanded me by the messenger;]] [9] and however much he spoke to me, I answered him nothing at all.

CHAPTER 15

[1] And it came to pass when the sun went down, that behold, [there was] a smoke as of a furnace. And the messengers who had the portions of the sacrifice ascended from the top of the smoking furnace. [2] And the messenger took me with the right hand and set me on the right wing of the pigeon, and set himself on the left wing of the turtle-dove, which [birds] had neither been slaughtered nor divided. [3] And he bore me to the borders of the flaming fire [[and we ascended as with many winds to the Heaven which was fixed on the surface. And I saw on the air]] on the height, to which we ascended a strong light, which it was impossible to describe, [4] and behold, in this light a fiercely burning fire for people, many people of male appearance, all [constantly] changing in aspect and form, running and being transformed, and worshiping and crying with a sound of words which I did not know.

CHAPTER 16

[1] And I said to the messenger, "Why have you brought me up here now, because now I cannot see, for I have already grown weak, and my spirit departs from me?" [2] And he said to me, "Remain by me; do not fear! And He whom you see come straight toward us with great voice of holiness —that is the Perpetual One who loves you; but Himself you cannot see. [3] But do not let your spirit grow faint [[on account of the loud crying]], for I am with you, strengthening you."

CHAPTER 17

[1] And while he yet spoke, behold, fire came against us [all] around, and a voice was in the fire like a voice

of many waters, like the sound of the sea in its uproar. [2] And the messenger bent his head with me and worshiped. And I desired to fall down on the earth, and the high place, on which we stood, [[at one moment rose upright,]] but at another rolled downwards. [3] And he said, "Only worship, Abraham, and utter the song which I have taught you"; because there was no earth to fall on. [4] And I only worshiped and uttered the song which he had taught me. And he said, "Recite without ceasing." [5] And I recited, and he also himself recited the song with me: "Perpetual, mighty, Holy, El, God alone—Supreme! [6] You who are self-existent, incorruptible, spotless, || Uncreated, immaculate, immortal, || Self-complete, self-illuminating; [7] Without father, without mother, unbegotten, || Exalted, fiery One! Lover of men, benevolent, bountiful, jealous over me and very compassionate; [8] Eli, that is, || My God—Perpetual, mighty Holy [One] of Hosts, very glorious El, El, El, El, YAH'EL! [9] You are He whom my soul has loved! Perpetual Protector, shining like fire, || Whose voice is like the thunder, || Whose look is like the lightning—all-seeing, || Who receives the prayers of such as honor You, [[[10] And turns away from the requests of such as embarrass with the embarrassment of their provocations, || Who dissolves the confusions of the world which arise from the ungodly and righteous in the corruptible age, renewing the age of the righteous!]] [11] You, O Light, shine before the light of the morning on Your creatures, || And in Your heavenly dwelling places there is no need of any other light than [that] of the unspeakable splendor from the lights of Your countenance. [12] Accept my prayer [[and be well-pleased with it]], likewise also the sacrifice which You have prepared through me who sought You! Accept me favorably, and show me, and teach me, || And make known to Your servant as You have promised me!"

CHAPTER 18

[1] And while I still recited the song, the mouth of the fire which was on the surface rose up on high. And I heard a voice like the roaring of the sea; nor did it cease on account of the rich abundance of the fire. [2] And as the fire raised itself up, ascending into the height, I saw a throne of fire under the fire, and all-seeing ones around it, reciting the song, and under the throne four fiery living creatures singing, and their appearance was one, each one of them with four faces. [3] And such was the appearance of their countenances: of a lion, of a man, of an ox, of an eagle; four heads [[were on their bodies so that the four creatures had sixteen faces]]; and each had six wings; from their shoulders, [[and their sides,]] and their loins. [4] And with the [two] wings from their shoulders they covered their faces, and with the [two] wings which [sprang] from their loins they covered their feet, while the [two] middle wings they spread

out for flying straightforward. [5] And when they had ended the singing, they looked at one another and threatened one another. [6] And it came to pass when the messenger who was with me saw that they were threatening each other, he left me and went running to them, and turned the countenance of each living creature from the countenance immediately confronting him, in order that they might not see their countenances threatening each other. [7] And he taught them the song of peace which has its origin [[in the Perpetual One]]. [8] And as I stood alone and looked, I saw behind the living creatures a chariot with fiery wheels, each wheel full of eyes [all] around; and over the wheels was a throne, which I saw, and this was covered with fire, and fire encircled it around, and behold, an indescribable fire enclosed a fiery host. [9] And I heard its holy voice like the voice of a man.

CHAPTER 19

[1] And a voice came to me out of the midst of the fire, saying, "Abraham, Abraham!" I said, "Here I am!" [2] And He said, "Consider the expanses which are under the expanse on which you are placed, and see how on no single expanse is there any other but He whom you have sought, or who has loved you." [3] And while He was yet speaking [and], behold, the expanses opened, and beneath me the heavens. [4] And I saw on the seventh heaven on which I stood a fire widely extended, and light, and dew, and a multitude of messengers, and a power of invisible glory over the living creatures which I saw; but I saw no other being there. [5] And I looked from the mountain in which I stood [[downwards]] to the sixth heaven, and saw a multitude of messengers there, of [pure] spirit, without bodies, who carried out the commands of the fiery messengers who were on the eighth heaven, as I was standing suspended over them. [6] And behold, on this expanse there were no other powers of [any] other form, but only messengers of [pure] spirit, like the power which I saw on the seventh heaven. [7] And He commanded that the sixth heaven should be taken away. [8] And I saw there, on the fifth heaven, the powers of the stars which carry out the commands laid on them, and the elements of the earth obeyed them.

CHAPTER 20

[1] And the Perpetual Mighty One said to me, "Abraham, Abraham!" And I said, "Here I am." [[And He said,]] "Consider from above the stars which are beneath you, and number them [[for Me]], and make known [[to Me]] their number." [2] And I said, "When can I? For I am but a man [[of dust and ashes]]." [3] And He said to me, "As the number of the stars and their power, [so will] I make your seed a nation and a people, set apart for Me in My heritage with Azazel." [4] And I said, "O Perpetual, Mighty One! Let Your servant speak before You, and do not let

Your anger kindle against Your chosen one! ⁵Behold, before You led me up, Azazel raged against me. How, then, while he is not now before You, have You constituted Yourself with him?"

CHAPTER 21

¹And He said to me, "Now look beneath your feet at the heavens and understand the creation foreshadowed in this expanse, the creatures existing on it, and the age prepared according to it." ²And I saw beneath [[the surfaces of the feet, and I saw beneath]] the sixth heaven and what was therein, and then the earth and its fruits, and what moved on it and its animate beings; and the power of its men, and the ungodliness of their souls, and their righteous deeds, [[and the beginnings of their works]], and the lower regions and the perdition therein, the abyss and its torments. ³I saw there the sea and its islands, and its monsters and its fishes, and Leviathan and his dominion, and his camping-ground, and his caves, and the world which lay on him, and his movements, and the destructions of the world on his account. ⁴I saw streams there and the rising of their waters, and their windings. ⁵And I saw there the Garden of Eden and its fruits, the source of the stream issuing from it, and its trees and their bloom, and those who behaved righteously. ⁶And I saw therein their foods and blessedness. ⁷And I saw there a great multitude— men, and women, and children—[[half of them on the right side of the picture]] and half of them on the left side of the picture.

CHAPTER 22

¹And I said, "O Perpetual, Mighty One! What is this picture of the creatures?" And He said to me, "This is My will with regard to those who exist in the [divine] world-counsel, and it seemed well-pleasing before My sight, and then afterward I gave commandment to them through My Word. ²And it came to pass, whatever I had determined to be, was already planned beforehand in this [picture], and it stood before Me before it was created, as you have seen." ³And I said, "O LORD, mighty and perpetual! Who are the people in this picture on this side and on that?" ⁴And He said to me, "These which are on the left side are the multitude of the peoples which have formerly been in existence and which are destined after you, some for judgment and restoration, and others for vengeance and destruction at the end of the world. ⁵But these which are on the right side of the picture—they are the people set apart for me of the peoples with Azazel. ⁶These are they whom I have ordained to be born of you and to be called My people."

CHAPTER 23

¹"Now look again in the picture, who it is who seduced Eve and what is the fruit of the tree, [[and]] you will know what there will be, and how it will be

to your seed among the people at the end of the days of the age, and so far as you cannot understand I will make known to you, for you are well-pleasing in My sight, and I will tell you what is kept in My heart." ²And I looked into the picture, and my eyes ran to the side of the Garden of Eden. ³And I saw there a man very great in height and fearful in breadth, incomparable in aspect, embracing a woman, who likewise approximated to the aspect and shape of the man. ⁴And they were standing under a tree of Eden, and the fruit of this tree was like the appearance of a bunch of grapes of the vine, and behind the tree was standing as it were a serpent in form, having hands and feet like a man's, and wings on its shoulders—six on the right side and six on the left, and they were holding the grapes of the tree in their hands, and both were eating it whom I had seen embracing. ⁵And I said, "Who are these mutually embracing, or who is this who is between them, or what is the fruit which they are eating, O Mighty Perpetual One?" ⁶And He said, "This is the human world, this is Adam, and this is their desire on the earth, [and] this is Eve; but he who is between them represents ungodliness, their beginning [on the way] to perdition, even Azazel." ⁷And I said, "O Perpetual, Mighty One! Why have You given such power to destroy the generation of men in their works on the earth?" ⁸And He said to me, "They who will [to do] evil—and how much I hated [it] in those who do it—over them I gave him power, and to be beloved of them." ⁹And I answered and said, "O Perpetual, Mighty One! Why have You willed to effect that evil should be desired in the hearts of men, since You indeed are angered over that which was willed by You, at him who is doing what is unprofitable in Your counsel?"

CHAPTER 24

¹And He said to me, "Being angered at the nations on your account, and on account of the people of your family who are [to be] separated after you, as you see in the picture the burden [of destiny] that [is laid] on them—and I will tell you what will be, and how much will be, in the last days. Now look at everything in the picture." ²And I looked and saw there what was before me in creation; I saw Adam, and Eve existing with him, and with them the cunning Adversary, ³and Cain who acted lawlessly through the Adversary, and the slaughtered Abel, [and] the destruction brought and caused on him through the lawless one. ⁴I also saw impurity there, and those who lust after it, and its pollution, and their jealousy, and the fire of their corruption in the lowest parts of the earth. ⁵I saw theft there, and those who hasten after it, and the arrangement [[of their retribution, the judgment of the Great Court]]. ⁶I saw naked men there, the foreheads against each other, and their disgrace, and their passion which [they had] against each other, and their retribution. ⁷I saw desire there, and in her hand the

head of every kind of lawlessness, [[and her scorn, and her waste assigned to perdition]].

CHAPTER 25

¹ I saw the likeness of the idol of jealousy there, having the likeness of woodwork such as my father was accustomed to make, and its statue was of glittering bronze; and before it a man, and he worshiped it; ² and in front of him an altar, and on it a boy slain in the presence of the idol. ³ But I said to Him, "What is this idol, or what is the altar, or who are they that are sacrificed, or who is the sacrificer? ⁴ Or what is the temple which I see that is beautiful in art, and its beauty [being like] the glory that lies beneath Your throne?" ⁵ And He said, "Hear, Abraham. This which you see, the temple, and altar, and beauty, is My idea of the priesthood of My glorious Name, in which dwells every single prayer of man, and the rise of kings and prophets, and whatever sacrifice I ordain to be offered to Me among My people who are to come out of your generation. ⁶ But the statue which you saw is My anger with which the people anger Me who are to proceed for Me from you. ⁷ But the man whom you saw slaughtering—that is he who incites murderous sacrifices, of which are a witness to Me of the final judgment, even at the beginning of creation."

CHAPTER 26

¹ And I said, "O Perpetual, Mighty One! Why have You established that it should be so, and then proclaim the knowledge thereof?" ² And He said to me, "Hear, Abraham; understand what I say to you, and answer Me as I question you. Why did your father Terah not listen to your voice, and [why] did he not cease from the devilish idolatry until he perished [[and]] his whole household with him?" ³ And I said, "O Perpetual, [[Mighty One]]! [It was] entirely because he did not choose to listen to me; but I, too, did not follow his works." ⁴ And He said [[to me]]: "Hear, Abraham. As the counsel of your father is in him, and as your counsel is in you, so also is the counsel of My will in Me ready for the coming days, before you have knowledge of these, or [can] see with your eyes what is future in them. How those of your seed will be, look in the picture."

CHAPTER 27

¹ And I looked and saw: behold, the picture swayed and on its left side a heathen people emerged, and they pillaged those who were on the right side—men, and women, and children; [[some they slaughtered,]] others they retained with themselves. ² Behold, I saw them run toward them through four entrances, and they burned the temple with fire, and the holy things that were therein they plundered. ³ And I said, "O Perpetual One! Behold, the people [that spring] from me, whom You have accepted, the hordes of the heathen plunder, and some they kill, while others they hold fast as aliens, and they have burned the temple with fire, and they rob the beautiful things therein. ⁴ O Perpetual, Mighty One! If this be so, why have You now lacerated my heart, and why should this be so?" ⁵ And He said to me, "Hear, Abraham. What you have seen will happen on account of your seed who anger Me by reason of the statue which you saw, and on account of the human slaughter in the picture, through zeal in the temple; and as you saw so will it be." ⁶ And I said, "O Perpetual, Mighty One! May the works of evil [worked] in ungodliness now pass by, but [show me] rather those who fulfilled the commandments, even the works of his righteousness, ⁷ for You can do this." And He said to me, "The time of the righteous meets [them] first through the holiness from kings and righteous-dealing rulers whom I at first created in order from such to rule among them. ⁸ But from these issue men who care for their interests, as I have made known to you and you have seen."

CHAPTER 28

¹ And I answered and said, "O Mighty, [[Perpetual One]], hallowed by Your power! Be favorable to my petition, [[for this have You brought me up here—and show me]]. ² As You have brought me up to Your height, so make [this] known to me, Your beloved one, as much as I ask—whether what I saw will happen to them for long?" ³ And He showed me a multitude of His people, and said to me: "On their account through four issues, as you saw, I will be provoked by them, and in these My retribution for their deeds will be [accomplished]. ⁴ But in the fourth outgoing of one hundred years and one hour of the age—the same is one hundred years—it will be in misfortune among the heathen, [[but one hour in mercy and insult, as among the heathen]]."

CHAPTER 29

¹ And I said, "O Perpetual, [[Mighty One]]! And how long a time is an hour of the age?" ² And He said, "I have ordained twelve years of this ungodly age to rule among the heathen and in your seed; and until the end of the times it will be as you saw. ³ And reckon, and understand, and look into the picture." ⁴ And I [[looked and]] saw a Man going out from the left side of the heathen; and there went out men, and women, and children from the side of the heathen, many hosts, and worshiped Him. ⁵ And while I still looked there came out from the right side [many], and some insulted that Man, while some struck Him; others, however, worshiped Him. ⁶ [And] I saw how these worshiped Him, and Azazel ran and worshiped Him, and having kissed His face he turned and stood behind Him. ⁷ And I said, "O Perpetual, Mighty One! Who is the Man insulted and beaten, who is worshiped by the heathen with Azazel?" ⁸ And He answered and said, "Hear, Abraham! The Man whom you saw insulted

and beaten and again worshiped—that is the relief [granted] by the heathen to the people who proceed from you, in the last days, in this twelfth hour of the age of ungodliness. ⁹But in the twelfth year of My final age, I will set up this Man from your generation, whom you saw from My people; all will follow this one, and such as are called by Me [will] join, [even] those who change in their counsels. ¹⁰And those whom you saw emerge from the left side of the picture—the meaning is [this]: there will be many from the heathen who set their hopes on Him; and as for those whom you saw from your seed on the right side, some insulting and striking, others worshiping Him—many of them will be offended at Him. ¹¹He, however, is testing those who have worshiped Him of your seed, in that twelfth hour of the end, with a view to shortening the age of ungodliness. ¹²Before the age of the righteous begins to grow, My judgment will come on the lawless heathen through the people of your seed who have been separated for Me. ¹³In those days I will bring on all creatures of the earth ten plagues, through misfortune and disease and sighing of the grief of their soul. ¹⁴Thus much will I bring on the generations of men that be on it on account of the provocation and the corruption of its creatures, whereby they provoke Me. ¹⁵And then will righteous men of your seed be left in the number which is kept secret by Me, hastening in the glory of My Name to the place prepared beforehand for them, which you saw devastated in the picture; ¹⁶and they will live and be established through sacrifices and gifts of righteousness and truth in the age of the righteous, and will rejoice in Me continually; ¹⁷and they will destroy those who have destroyed them, and will insult those who have insulted them; and of those who defamed them they will spit in the face, scorned by Me, while they will behold Me full of joy, rejoicing with My people, and receiving those who return to Me [[in conversion]]. ¹⁸See, Abraham, what you have seen, and [hear] what you have heard, and [[take full knowledge of]] what you have come to know. Go to your heritage, and behold, I am with you forever."

CHAPTER 30

¹But while He was still speaking, I found myself on the earth. And I said, "O Perpetual, [[Mighty One]], I am no longer in the glory in which I was [while] on high, and what my soul longed to understand in my heart I do not understand." ²And He said to me,

"What is desired in your heart I will tell you, because you have sought to see the ten plagues which I have prepared for the heathen, and have prepared beforehand at the passing over of the twelfth hour of the earth. ³Hear what I divulge to you, so will it come to pass: the first [is] pain of great distress; the second, conflagration of many cities; ⁴the third, destruction and pestilence of animals; the fourth, hunger of the whole world and of its people; ⁵the fifth by destruction among its rulers, destruction by earthquake and the sword; ⁶the sixth, multiplication of hail and snow; the seventh, the wild beasts will be their grave; ⁷the eighth, hunger and pestilence will alternate with their destruction; the ninth, punishment by the sword and flight in distress; ⁸the tenth, thunder, and voices, and destructive earthquake."

CHAPTER 31

¹"And then I will sound the trumpet out of the air, and will send My Chosen One, having in Him all My power—one measure; ²and this one will summon My despised people from the nations, and I will burn with fire those who have insulted them and who have ruled among them in [this] age. ³And I will give those who have covered Me with mockery to the scorn of the coming age; and I have prepared them to be food for the fire of Hades and for ceaseless flight to and fro through the air in the underworld beneath the earth— [[the body filled with worms. ⁴For on them will they see the righteousness of the Creator—those, namely, who have chosen to do My will, and those who have openly kept My commandments, [and] they will rejoice with joy over the downfall of the men who still remain, who have followed the idols and their murders. ⁵For they will decay in the body of the evil worm Azazel, and be burned with the fire of Azazel's tongue; ⁶for I hoped that they would come to Me, and not have loved and praised the strange [god], and not have adhered to him for whom they were not allotted, but [instead] they have forsaken the mighty Lord."

CHAPTER 32

¹"Therefore hear, O Abraham, and see; behold, your seventh generation [will] go with you, and they will go out into a strange land, and they will enslave them, ²and mistreat them as it were an hour of the age of ungodliness, but the nation whom they will serve I will judge."]]

REVELATION OF ELIJAH

The Revelation of Elijah, commonly called the Apocalypse of Elijah or Apocalypse of Elias, may have been written in the 1st or 2nd century AD, and some speculate Paul briefly quoted from the work in 1 Corinthians 2:9 and Ephesians 5:14, although the Ephesians reference is unlikely and the 1 Corinthians 2:9 reference would require the Revelation of Elijah to be pre-Pauline, which may also be unlikely. The text may, however, have a more primordial core of material, with other parts added in later, including an account of the Antichrist and the two witnesses (identified in the book as Elijah and Enoch).

CHAPTER 1

[1] The word of the LORD came to me, saying, "Son of man, say to this people, Why do you add sins to your sins, and anger the LORD God who created you?" [2] Don't love the world or the things which are in the world, for the boasting of the world and its destruction belong to the Devil. [3] Remember that the Lord of glory, who created everything, had mercy on you so that He might save us from the captivity of this age. [4] For many times the Devil desired not to let the sun rise above the earth and not to let the earth yield fruit, since he desires to consume men like a fire which rages in stubble, and he desires to swallow them like water. [5] Therefore, on account of this, the God of glory had mercy on us, and He sent His Son to the world so that He might save us from the captivity. [6] He did not inform a messenger or a chief-messenger or any principality when He was about to come to us, but He changed Himself to be like a man when He was about to come to us so that He might save us . . . [7] Therefore, become sons to Him since He is a father to you. [8] Remember that He has prepared thrones and crowns for you in Heaven, saying, "Everyone who will obey Me will receive thrones and crowns among those who are Mine." [9] The LORD said, "I will write My Name on their forehead and I will seal their right hand, and they will not hunger or thirst. [10] Neither will the son of lawlessness prevail over them, nor will the thrones hinder them, but they will walk with the messengers up to My city." [11] Now as for the sinners, they will be shamed and they will not pass by the thrones, but the thrones of death will seize them and rule over them because the messengers will not agree with them. [12] They have alienated themselves from His dwellings. [13] Hear, O wise men of the land, concerning the deceivers who will multiply in the last times so that they will set down for themselves doctrines which do not belong to God, setting aside the Law of God, those who have made their belly their God, saying, "The fast does not exist, nor did God create it," making themselves strangers to the covenant of God and robbing themselves of the glorious promises. [14] Now these are not ever correctly established in the firm faith. Therefore, don't let those people lead you astray. [15] Remember that from the time when He created the heavens, the LORD created the fast for a benefit to men on account of the passions and desires which fight against you so that the evil will not inflame you. [16] "But it is a pure fast which I have created," said the LORD. [17] The one who fasts continually will not sin although jealousy and strife are within him. [18] Let the pure one fast, but whenever the one who fasts is not pure, he has angered the LORD and also the messengers. [19] And he has grieved his soul, gathering up wrath for himself for the day of wrath. [20] But a pure fast is what I created, with a pure heart and pure hands. [21] It releases sin. It heals diseases. It casts out demons. [22] It is effective up to the throne of God for an ointment and for a release from sin by means of a pure prayer. [23] Who among you, if he is honored in his craft, will go forth to the field without a tool in his hand? Or who will go forth to the battle to fight without a breastplate on? [24] If he is found, will he not be killed because he despised the service of the king? [25] Likewise, no one is able to enter the holy place if he is double-minded. [26] The one who is double-minded in his prayer is darkness to himself. And even the messengers do not trust him. [27] Therefore be single-minded in the LORD at all times so that you might know every moment.

CHAPTER 2

[1] Furthermore, concerning the kings of Assyria and the dissolution of the Heaven and the earth and the things beneath the earth. [2] "Now therefore, they will not be overcome," says the LORD, "nor will they fear in the battle." [3] When they see [one] who rises in the north, "the king of Assyria," this king of injustice [will increase] his battles and his disturbances against Egypt. [4] The land will groan together because your children will be seized. [5] Many will desire death in those days, but death will flee from them. [6] And a king who will be called "the king of peace" will rise up in the west. [7] He will run on the sea like a roaring lion. [8] He will kill the king of injustice, and he will take vengeance on Egypt with battles and much bloodshed. [9] It will come to pass in those days that he will command [peace] and a gift in Egypt. [10] [He will give] peace to these who are holy, [saying], "The Name of [God] is one." [11] [He will] give honors to the [saints and] an exalting to the places of the saints. [12] He will give vain gifts to the house of God. [13] He will wander around in the cities of Egypt with guile,

without their knowing. [14] He will take count of the holy places. He will weigh the idols of the heathen. He will take count of their wealth. He will establish priests for them. [15] He will command that the wise men and the great ones of the people be seized, and they will be brought to the metropolis which is by the sea, saying, "There is but one language." [16] But when you hear, "Peace and joy exist," I will . . . [17] Now I will tell you his signs so that you might know him. [18] For he has two sons: one on his right and one on his left. [19] The one on his right will receive a demonic face, [and] he will fight against the Name of God. [20] Now four kings will descend from that king. [21] In his thirtieth year he will come up to Memphis, [and] he will build a temple in Memphis. [22] On that day his own son will rise up against him and kill him. [23] The whole land will be disturbed. [24] On that day he will issue an order over the whole land so that the priests of the land and all of the saints will be seized, saying, "You will repay doubly every gift and all of the good things which my father gave to you." [25] He will shut up the holy places. He will take their houses. He will take their sons prisoner. [26] He will give command, and sacrifices and abominations and bitter evils will be done in the land. [27] He will appear before the sun and the moon. [28] On that day the priests of the land will tear their clothes. [29] Woe to you , O rulers of Egypt, in those days because your day has passed. [30] The violence [being done to] the poor will turn against you, and your children will be seized as plunder. [31] In those days the cities of Egypt will groan for the voice of the one who sells and the one who buys will not be heard. The markets of the cities of Egypt will become dusty. [32] Those who are in Egypt will weep together. They will desire death, [but] death will flee and leave them. [33] In those days, they will run up to the rocks and leap off, saying, "Fall on us." And still they will not die. [34] A double affliction will multiply on the whole land. [35] In those days, the king will command, and all the nursing women will be seized and brought to him bound. They will suckle serpents. And their blood will be drawn from their breasts, and it will be applied as poison to the arrows. [36] On account of their distress of the cities, he will command again, and all the young boys from twelve years and under will be seized and presented in order to teach them to shoot arrows. [37] The midwife who is on the earth will grieve. The woman who has given birth will lift her eyes to Heaven, saying, "Why did I sit on the birthstool, to bring forth a son to the earth?" [38] The barren woman and the virgin will rejoice, saying, "It is our time to rejoice, because we have no child on the earth, but our children are in Heaven." [39] In those days, three kings will arise among the Persians, and they will take captive the Jews who are in Egypt. They will bring them to Jerusalem, and they will inhabit it and dwell there. [40] Then when you hear that there is security in Jerusalem, tear you garments, O priests of the land,

because the son of perdition will soon come. [41] In those days, the lawless one will appear in the holy places— [42] In [those] days the kings of the Persians will hasten, and they will stand to fight with the kings of Assyria. Four kings will fight with three. [43] They will spend three years in that place until they carry off the wealth of the temple which is in that place. [44] In those days, blood will flow from Kos to Memphis. The river of Egypt will become blood, and they will not be able to drink from it for three days. [45] Woe to Egypt and those who are in it. [46] In those days a king will arise in the city which is called "The City of the Sun," and the whole land will be disturbed. He will flee to Memphis. [47] In the sixth year, the Persian kings will plot an ambush in Memphis. They will kill the Assyrian king. [48] The Persians will take vengeance on the land, and they will command to kill all the heathen and the lawless ones. They will command to build the temples of the saints. [49] They will give double gifts to the house of God. They will say, "The Name of God is one." [50] The whole land will greet the Persians. [51] Even the remnant, who did not die under the afflictions, will say, "The LORD has sent us a righteous king so that the land will not become a desert" [52] He will command that no royal matter be presented for three years and six months. The land will be full of good in an abundant well-being. [53] Those who are alive will go to those who are dead, saying, "Rise up and be with us in this rest."

CHAPTER 3

[1] In the fourth year of that king, the son of lawlessness will appear, saying, "I am the Christ," although he is not. Don't believe him! [2] When the Christ comes, He will come in the manner of a covey of doves with the crown of doves surrounding Him. He will walk on the vaults of Heaven with the sign of the Cross leading Him. [3] The whole world will behold Him like the sun which shines from the eastern horizon to the western. [4] This is how He will come, with all His messengers surrounding Him. [5] But the son of lawlessness will begin to stand again in the holy places. [6] He will say to the sun, "Fall," and it will fall. He will say, "Shine," and it will do it. He will say, "Darken," and it will do it. [7] He will say to the moon, "Become bloody," and it will do it. [8] He will go forth with them from the sky. He will walk on the sea and the rivers as on dry land. [9] He will cause the lame to walk. He will cause the deaf to hear. He will cause the dumb to speak. He will cause the blind to see. [10] The lepers he will cleanse. The sick he will heal. The demons he will cast out. [11] He will multiply his signs and his wonders in the presence of everyone. [12] He will do the works which the Christ did, except for raising the dead alone. [13] In this you will know that he is the son of lawlessness, because he is unable to give life. [14] For behold I will tell you his signs so that you might know him. [15] He is a . . . of a skinny-legged young man,

having a tuft of gray hair at the front of his bald head. His eyebrows will reach to his ears. There is a leprous bare spot on the front of his hands. [16] He will transform himself in the presence of those who see him. He will become a young child. He will become old. [17] He will transform himself in every sign. But the signs of his head will not be able to change. [18] Therein you will know that he is the son of lawlessness.

CHAPTER 4

[1] The virgin, whose name is Tabitha, will hear that the shameless one has revealed himself in the holy places. And she will put on her garment of fine linen. [2] And she will pursue him up to Judea, scolding him up to Jerusalem, saying, "O shameless one, O son of lawlessness, O you who have been hostile to all the saints." [3] Then the shameless one will be angry at the virgin. He will pursue her up to the regions of the sunset. He will suck her blood in the evening. [4] And he will cast her on the temple, and she will become a healing for the people. [5] She will rise up at dawn. And she will live and scold him, saying, "O shameless one, you have no power against my soul or my body, because I live in the LORD always. [6] And also my blood which you have cast on the temple has become a healing for the people." [7] Then when Elijah and Enoch hear that the shameless one has revealed himself in the holy place, they will come down and fight with him, saying, [8] "Are you indeed not ashamed? When you attach yourself to the saints, because you are always estranged. [9] You have been hostile to those who belong to Heaven. You have acted against those belonging to the earth. [10] You have been hostile to the thrones. You have acted against the messengers. You are always a stranger. [11] You have fallen from Heaven like the morning stars. You were changed, and your tribe became dark for you. [12] But you are not ashamed, when you stand firmly against God you are a devil." [13] The shameless one will hear and he will be angry, and he will fight with them in the marketplace of the great city. And he will spend seven days fighting with them. [14] And they will spend three and one half days in the marketplace dead, while all the people see them. [15] But on the fourth day they will rise up and they will scold him saying. "O shameless one, O son of lawlessness. Are you indeed not ashamed of yourself since you are leading astray the people of God for whom you did not suffer? Do you not know that we live in the LORD?" [16] As the words were spoken, they prevailed over him, saying, "Furthermore, we will lay down before the flesh for the spirit, and we will kill you since you are unable to speak on that day because we are always strong in the LORD. But you are always hostile to God." [17] The shameless one will hear, and he will be angry and fight them. [18] And the whole city will surround them. [19] On that day they will shout up to Heaven as they shine while all the people and all

the world see them. [20] The son of lawlessness will not prevail over them. He will be angry at the land, and he will seek to sin against the people. [21] He will pursue all of the saints. They and the priests of the land will be brought back bound. [22] He will kill them and destroy them . . . them. And their eyes will be removed with iron spikes. [23] He will remove their skin from their heads. He will remove their nails one by one. He will command that vinegar and lime be put in their nose. [24] Now those who are unable to bear up under the tortures of that king will take gold and flee over the fords to the desert places. They will lie down as one who sleeps. [25] The LORD will receive their spirits and their souls to Himself. [26] Their flesh will petrify. No wild animals will eat them until the last Day of the Great Judgment. [27] And they will rise up and find a place of rest, but they will not be in the kingdom of the Christ as those who have endured because the LORD said, "I will grant to them that they sit on My right hand." [28] They will receive favor over others, and they will triumph over the son of lawlessness. And they will witness the dissolution of the heavens and earth. [29] They will receive the thrones of glory and the crowns. [30] The sixty righteous ones who are prepared for this hour will hear. [31] And they will gird on the breastplate of the LORD, and they will run to Jerusalem and fight with the shameless one, saying, "All powers which the prophets have done from the beginning you have done. But you were unable to raise the dead because you have no power to give life. Therein we have known that you are the son of lawlessness." [32] He will hear, and he will be angry and command to kindle altars. [33] And the righteous ones will be bound. They will be lifted up and burned.

CHAPTER 5

[1] And on that day the heart of many will harden and they will flee from him, saying, "This is not the Christ. The Christ does not kill the righteous. He does not pursue men so that He might seek them, but He persuades them with signs and wonders." [2] On that day the Christ will pity those who are His own. And He will send from Heaven his sixty-four thousand messengers, each of whom has six wings. [3] The sound will move the heavens and earth when they give praise and glory. [4] Now those on whose forehead the Name of Christ is written and on whose hand is the seal—both the small and the great—will be taken up on their wings and lifted up before His wrath. [5] Then Gabriel and Uriel will become a pillar of light leading them into the holy land. [6] It will be granted to them to eat from the Tree of Life. They will wear white garments . . . and messengers will watch over them. They will not thirst, nor will the son of lawlessness be able to prevail over them. [7] And on that day the earth will be disturbed, and the sun will darken, and peace will be removed from the earth. [8] The birds will fall

on the earth, dead. ⁹ The earth will be dry. The waters of the sea will dry up. ¹⁰ The sinners will groan on the earth, saying, "What have you done to us, O son of lawlessness, saying, I am the Christ, when you are the Devil? ¹¹ You are unable to save yourself so that you might save us. You produced signs in our presence until you alienated us from the Christ who created us. Woe to us because we listened to you. ¹² Behold, now we will die in a famine. Where indeed is now the trace of a righteous one and we will worship him, or where indeed is the one who will teach us, and we will appeal to him. ¹³ Now indeed we will be wrathfully destroyed because we disobeyed the LORD. ¹⁴ We went to the deep places of the sea, and we did not find water. We dug in the rivers and papyrus reeds, and we did not find water." ¹⁵ Then on that day, the shameless one will speak, saying, "Woe to me because my time has passed by for me while I was saying that my time would not pass by for me. ¹⁶ My years became months and my days have passed away as dust passes away. Now therefore I will perish together with you. ¹⁷ Now therefore run forth to the desert. Seize the robbers and kill them. ¹⁸ Bring up the saints. For because of them, the earth yields fruit. For because of them the sun shines on the earth. For because of them the dew will come on the earth." ¹⁹ The sinners will weep, saying, "You made us hostile to the LORD. If you are able, rise up and pursue them." ²⁰ Then he will take his fiery wings and fly out after the saints. He will fight with them again. ²¹ The messengers will hear and come down. They will fight with him a battle of many swords. ²² It will come to pass on that day that the LORD will hear and command the Heaven and the earth with great wrath. And they will send for fire. ²³ And the fire will prevail over the earth seventy-two cubits. It will consume the sinners and the devils like stubble. ²⁴ A true judgment will occur. ²⁵ On that day, the mountains and the earth will utter speech. The byways will speak with one another, saying, "Have you heard today the voice of a man who walks who has not come to the judgment of the Son of the LORD?" ²⁶ The sins of each one will stand against him in the place where they were committed, whether those of the day or of the night. ²⁷ Those who belong to the righteous and . . . will see the sinners and those who persecuted them and those who handed them over to death in their torments. ²⁸ Then the sinners will see the place of the righteous. ²⁹ And thus grace will occur. In those days, that which the righteous will ask for many times will be given to them. ³⁰ On that day, the LORD will judge the Heaven and the earth. He will judge those who transgressed in Heaven, and those who did so on earth. ³¹ He will judge the shepherds of the people. He will ask about the flock of sheep, and they will be given to Him, without any deadly guile existing in them. ³² After these things, Elijah and Enoch will come down. They will lay down the flesh of the world, and they will receive their spiritual flesh. They will pursue the son of lawlessness and kill him since he is not able to speak. ³³ On that day, he will dissolve in their presence like ice which was dissolved by a fire. He will perish like a serpent which has no breath in it. ³⁴ They will say to him, "Your time has passed by for you. Now, therefore, those who believe you will perish." ³⁵ They will be cast into the bottom of the abyss and it will be closed for them. ³⁶ On that day, the Christ, the King and all His saints will come forth from Heaven. ³⁷ He will burn the earth. He will spend one thousand years on it. ³⁸ Because the sinners prevailed over it, He will create a new Heaven and a new earth. No deadly devil will exist in them. ³⁹ He will rule with His saints, ascending and descending, while they are always with the messengers and they are with the Christ for one thousand years.

REVELATION OF ZEPHANIAH

The Apocalypse of Zephaniah (Revelation of Zephaniah in the LSV), purporting to be additional words from the Old Testament prophet, was likely written between 100 BC and the late 2nd century AD, probably in the late 1st century AD. Fragment 1 is a quotation of the text made by Clement of Alexandria. Fragment 2 is from a Coptic manuscript from the 5th century. Fragment 3, the longest, and also Coptic, was found on papyri from the 4th century.

FRAGMENT 1

[1] And a spirit took me and brought me up into the fifth heaven. And I saw messengers who are called "lords." [2] And the crown was set on them in the Holy Spirit, and the throne of each of them was seven times brighter than the light of the rising sun. [3] And they were dwelling in the temples of salvation and singing hymns to the indescribable God.

FRAGMENT 2

[1] I saw a soul which five thousand messengers punished and guarded. [2] They took it to the east, and they brought it to the west. They beat its ... they gave it one hundred ... lashes for each one daily. [3] I was afraid, and I cast myself on my face so that my joints dissolved. [4] The messenger helped me. He said to me, "Be strong, O one who will triumph, and prevail so that you will triumph over the accuser and you will come up from Hades." [5] And after I arose, I said, "Who is this whom they are punishing?" [6] He said to me, "This is a soul which was found in its lawlessness." And before it attained to converting, it was visited and taken out of its body. [7] Truly, I, Zephaniah, saw these things in my vision. [8] And the messenger of the LORD went with me. I saw a great broad place, thousands of thousands surrounded it on its left side and myriads of myriads on its right side. The form of each one was different. [9] Their hair was loose like that belonging to women. Their teeth were like the teeth of . . .

FRAGMENT 3

CHAPTER 1

[1] . . . dead. We will bury him like any man. [2] Whenever he dies, we will carry him out playing the lyre before him and chanting psalms and odes over his body.

CHAPTER 2

[1] Now I went with the messenger of the LORD, and he took me over all of my city. There was nothing before my eyes. [2] Then I saw two men walking together on one road. I watched them as they talked. [3] And, moreover, I also saw two women grinding together at a mill. And I watched them as they talked. [4] And I also saw two on a bed, each one of them acting for their [mutual] ... on a bed. [5] And I saw the whole inhabited world hanging like a drop of water which is suspended from a bucket when it comes up from a well. [6] I said to the messenger of the LORD. "Then does darkness or night not exist in this place?" [7] He said to me, "No, because darkness does not exist in that place where the righteous and the saints are, but rather they always exist in the light." [8] And I saw all the souls of men as they existed in punishment. [9] And I cried out to the LORD Almighty, "O God, if You remain with the saints, You [certainly] have compassion on behalf of the world and the souls which are in this punishment."

CHAPTER 3

[1] The messenger of the LORD said to me, "Come, let me show you the place of righteousness." [2] And he took me up on Mount Seir and he showed me three men, as two messengers walked with them rejoicing and exulting over them. [3] I said to the messenger, "Of what sort are these?" [4] He said to me, "These are the three sons of Joatham, the priest, who neither kept the commandment of their father nor observed the ordinances of the LORD." [5] Then I saw two other messengers weeping over the three sons of Joatham, the priest. [6] I said, "O messenger, who are these?" He said, "These are the messengers of the LORD Almighty. They write down all the good deeds of the righteous on their scrolls as they watch at the gate of Heaven. [7] And I take them from their hands and bring them up before the LORD Almighty; He writes their name in the Scroll of the Living. [8] Also the messengers of the accuser who is on the earth, they also write down all the sins of men on their scrolls. [9] They also sit at the gate of Heaven. They tell the accuser and he writes them on his scroll so that he might accuse them when they come out of the world [and go] down there."

CHAPTER 4

[1] Then I walked with the messenger of the LORD. I looked before me and I saw a place there. [2] Thousands of thousands and myriads of myriads of messengers entered through it. [3] Their faces were like a leopard, their tusks being outside their mouth like wild boars. [4] Their eyes were mixed with blood. Their hair was loose like the hair of women, and fiery scourges were in their hands. [5] When I saw them, I was afraid. I said to that messenger who walked with me, "Of what sort are these?" [6] He said to me, "These are the servants of

all creation who come to the souls of ungodly men and bring them and leave them in this place. [7] They spend three days going around with them in the air before they bring them and cast them into their continuous punishment." [8] I said, "I implore you, O Lord, do not give them authority to come to me." [9] The messenger said, "Do not fear. I will not permit them to come to you because you are pure before the LORD. I will not permit them to come to you because the LORD Almighty sent me to you because [you] are pure before Him." [10] Then he beckoned to them, and they withdrew themselves and they ran from me.

CHAPTER 5

[1] But I went with the messenger of the LORD, and I looked in front of me and I saw gates. [2] Then when I approached them, I discovered that they were bronze gates. [3] The messenger touched them, and they opened before him. I entered with him and found its whole square like a beautiful city, and I walked in its midst. [4] Then the messenger of the LORD transformed himself beside me in that place. [5] Now I looked at them, and I discovered that they were bronze gates and bronze bolts and iron bars. [6] Now my mouth was shut therein. I beheld the bronze gates in front of me as fire was being cast forth for about fifty stadia.

CHAPTER 6

[1] Again I turned back and walked, and I saw a great sea. [2] But I thought that it was a sea of water. I discovered that it was entirely a sea of flame like a slime which casts forth much flame and whose waves burn sulfur and bitumen. [3] They began to approach me. [4] Then I thought that the LORD Almighty had come to visit me. [5] Then when I saw, I fell on my face before him in order that I might worship him. [6] I was very much afraid, and I entreated him that he might save me from this distress. [7] I cried out, saying, "Eloi, LORD, Adonai, of Hosts. I implore You to save me from this distress because it has befallen me." [8] In that same instant I stood up, and I saw a great messenger before me. His hair was spread out like that of lionesses'. His teeth were outside his mouth like a bear. His hair was spread out like women's. His body was like the serpent's when he wished to swallow me. [9] And when I saw him, I was afraid of him so that all the parts of my body were loosened, and I fell on my face. [10] I was unable to stand, and I prayed before the LORD Almighty, "You will save me from this distress. You are the one who saved Israel from the hand of Pharaoh, the king of Egypt. You saved Susanna from the hand of the elders of injustice. You saved the three holy men, Shadrach, Meshach, Abednego, from the furnace of burning fire. I beg you to save me from this distress." [11] Then I arose and stood, and I saw a great messenger standing before me with his face shining like the rays of the sun in its glory since his face is like that which is perfected in its glory. [12] And he was girded as if a golden girdle were on his breast. His feet were like bronze which is melted in a fire. [13] And when I saw him, I rejoiced, for I thought that the LORD Almighty had come to visit me. [14] I fell on my face, and I worshiped him. [15] He said to me, "Take heed. Do not worship me. I am not the LORD Almighty, but am the great messenger, Eremiel, who is over the abyss and Hades, the one in which all of the souls are imprisoned from the end of the flood, which came on the earth, until this day." [16] Then I inquired of the messenger, "What is the place to which I have come?" He said to me, "It is Hades." [17] Then I asked him, "Who is the great messenger who stands thus, whom I saw?" He said, "This is the one who accuses men in the presence of the LORD."

CHAPTER 7

[1] Then I looked, and I saw him with a scroll in his hand. He began to unroll it. [2] Now after he had spread it out, I read it in my [own] language. I found that all my sins which I had done were written in it, those which I had done from my youth until this day. [3] They were all written on that scroll of mine without there being a false word in them. [4] If I did not go to visit a sick man or a widow, I found it written down as a shortcoming on my manuscript. [5] If I did not visit an orphan, it was found written down as a shortcoming on my scroll. [6] A day on which I did not fast [or] pray in the time of prayer I found written down as a failing on my scroll. [7] And a day when I did not turn to the sons of Israel—since it is a shortcoming—I found written down on my scroll [8] so that I threw myself on my face and prayed before the LORD Almighty, "May Your mercy reach me and may You wipe out my scroll because Your mercy has come to be in every place and has filled every place." [9] Then I arose and stood, and I saw a great messenger before me, saying to me, "Triumph, prevail because you have prevailed and have triumphed over the accuser, and you have come up from Hades and the abyss. You will now cross over the crossing place." [10] Again he brought another scroll which was written by hand. [11] He began to unroll it, and I read it, and found it written in my [own] language ...

CHAPTER 8

[1] ... They helped me and set me on that boat. [2] Thousands of thousands and myriads of myriads of messengers gave praise before me. [3] I, myself, put on an angelic garment. I saw all of those messengers praying. [4] I, myself, prayed together with them. [5] I knew their language, which they spoke with me. [6] Now, moreover, my sons, this is the trial because it is necessary that the good and the evil be weighed in a balance.

REVELATION OF ZEPHANIAH

CHAPTER 9

[1] Then a great messenger came forth having a golden trumpet in his hand, and he blew it three times over my head, saying, "Be courageous! O one who has triumphed. Prevail! O one who has prevailed. For you have triumphed over the accuser, and you have escaped from the abyss and Hades. [2] You will now cross over the crossing place. For your name is written in the Scroll of the Living." [3] I wanted to embrace him, [but] I was unable to embrace the great messenger because his glory is great. [4] Then he ran to all the righteous ones, namely, Abraham, and Isaac, and Jacob, and Enoch, and Elijah, and David. [5] He spoke with them as friend to friend speaking with one another.

CHAPTER 10

[1] Then the great messenger came to me with the golden trumpet in his hand, and he blew it up to Heaven. [2] Heaven opened from the place where the sun rises to where it sets, from the north to the south. [3] I saw the sea which I had seen at the bottom of Hades. Its waves came up to the clouds. [4] I saw all the souls sinking in it. I saw some whose hands were bound to their neck, with their hands and feet being bound. [5] I said, "Who are these?" He said to me, "These are the ones who were bribed and they were given gold and silver until the souls of men were led astray." [6] And I saw others covered with mats of fire. [7] I said, "Who are these?" He said to me, "These are the ones who give money at interest, and they receive interest for interest." [8] And I also saw some blind ones crying out. And I was amazed when I saw all these works of God. [9] I said, "Who are these?" He said to me, "These are catechumens who heard the word of God, but they were not perfected in the work which they heard." [10] And I said to him, "Then they have no conversion here?" He said, "Yes," [11] I said, "How long?" He said to me, "Until the day when the LORD will judge." [12] And I saw others with their hair on them. [13] I said, "Then there is hair and body in this place?" [14] He said, "Yes, the LORD gives body and hair to them as He desires."

CHAPTER 11

[1] And I also saw multitudes. He brought them forth. [2] As they looked at all of the torments, they called out, praying before the LORD Almighty, saying, "We pray to You on account of those who are in all these torments so that You might have mercy on all of them." [3] And when I saw them, I said to the messenger who spoke with me, [["Who are these?"]] [4] He said, "These who implore the LORD are Abraham, and Isaac, and Jacob. [5] Then at a certain hour daily they come forth with the great messenger. He sounds a trumpet up to Heaven and another sounds on the earth. [6] All the righteous hear the sound. They come running, praying to the LORD Almighty daily on behalf of these who are in all these torments."

CHAPTER 12

[1] And again the great messenger comes forth with the golden trumpet in his hand, blowing over the earth. [2] They hear [it] from the place of the sunrise to the place of the sunset and from the southern regions to the northern regions. [3] And again he blows [it] up to Heaven and its sound is heard. [4] I said, "O Lord, why did you not leave me until I saw them all?" [5] He said to me, "I have no authority to show them to you until the LORD Almighty rises up in His wrath to destroy the earth and the heavens. [6] They will see and be disturbed, and they will all cry out, saying, All flesh which is ascribed to You we will give to You on the Day of the LORD. [7] Who will stand in His presence when He rises in His wrath [to destroy] the earth [and the heavens]? [8] Every tree which grows on the earth will be plucked up with its roots and fall down. And every high tower and the birds which fly will fall . . ."

APOCRYPHON OF EZEKIEL

The Apocryphon of Ezekiel, also called 2 Ezekiel, was likely composed in the 1st century BC or 1st century AD, with later Christian interpolations. It is quoted in a number of early works. Fragment 1 comes from the Dead Sea Scrolls and was quoted in the letter of Bar-Naba and the Revelation of Peter. Fragment 2 is identified from a quotation of the Apocryphon found in 1 Clement chapter 8. Fragment 3 was identified with Ezekiel by Tertullian. Fragment 4 was attributed to Jesus by Justin Martyr, and sourced from the Apocryphon by other early writers. Fragment 5 is found in the writings of Clement of Alexandria, among others. Fragment 6 was attributed to Ezekiel by Epiphanius but is dissimilar to the other fragments.

FRAGMENT 1

[1] THESE ARE THE WORDS OF EZEKIEL. And the word of the LORD came to me, saying, "Son of man, prophesy and say, Behold, the day of the destruction of the nations is coming; [2] . . . Egypt, and there will be anguish in Put, and a sword in Egypt . . . will shake, Cush and Put, and the mighty ones of Arabia, also some of the children of the covenant, and Arabia will fall at the gates of Egypt. [3] And . . . will perish . . . by the sword of Egypt . . . will be devastated . . . you will not die . . . [4] For I am the LORD, who redeems My people, giving the covenant to them." [5] And I said, "O LORD, I have seen many from Israel who have loved Your Name and walked in the ways of righteousness. [6] So, when will these things come to pass? And how will they be rewarded for their piety?" [7] And the LORD said to me, "I will make it manifest . . . the sons of Israel to see, and they will know that I am the LORD." [8] And He said, "Son of man, prophesy over these bones, and speak to the bone, and let them be joined bone to its bone, and joint to its joint." And it was so. [9] And He said a second time, "Prophesy, and let sinews come on them and let skin cover them." And it was so. [10] And He said, "Again, prophesy to the four winds of the heavens, and let them blow on the slain." And it was so. [11] And a great multitude of men came to life. And they blessed the LORD of Hosts who had given life to them. [12] And I said, "O LORD, when will these things be completed?" And the LORD said to me, ". . . and after many days, a piece of wood falls down and rises again [[and when blood drips from a tree]]." [13] . . . and . . . LORD. And all the people arose and stood on their feet to give thanks . . . and to praise the LORD of Hosts. [14] And I also spoke with them . . . And the LORD said to me, "Son of man, say to them . . . in their graves they will lie until . . . from your tombs and from the earth . . . that the yoke of Egypt . . . land, and they will know that I am the LORD."

[15] And He said to me, "Look, son of man, at the land of Israel." And I said, "I have seen, O LORD, and behold it is a wasteland. When will You gather them together?" [16] And the LORD said, "A son of Belial is planning to oppress My people, but I will not permit him. His dominion will not persist; and from the impure, no seed will survive, nor will new wine come from the caper bush, nor will a hornet make honey . . . and I will slay the wicked in Memphis. [17] But I will bring My sons out of Memphis, and I will turn toward their remnant. As they will say, There was peace and quiet, they will say, The land will be as it was in the days of . . . old. Therefore, I will arouse wrath on them from the four winds of the heavens . . . like a devouring fire as . . . and he will show no mercy on the poor, but he will bring them to Babel." [18] And Babel is but a cup in the hand of the LORD, in her time He will cast her away . . . in Babel and it will be . . . a dwelling place for demons . . . desolation and . . . will pasture . . . to Babel . . . instead of my grief make my soul rejoice. [19] And the days will hasten quickly until men say, "Are not the days hastening so that the sons of Israel might take possession?" [20] And the LORD said to me, "I will not turn your face away, Ezekiel. Behold, I am cutting short the days and the years . . . a few, just [as] you said to Me . . . For the mouth of the LORD has spoken these things. [21] . . . And My people will be . . . with a cheerful heart and with a willing soul . . . and hide a little while . . . and from the breaches . . ." [22] . . . the vision which Ezekiel saw . . . the brightness of the chariot, and the four living creatures, a living creature . . . and as they moved they did not turn back. [23] Every living creature moved on two wheels, and its two legs . . . on . . . in one there was breath. [24] And their faces were one beside the other. And the appearance of the faces: one of a lion, one of an eagle, one of a calf, and one of a man. [25] And the hand of a man was joined to the backs of the living creatures and attached to their wings . . . and the wheels . . . wheel joined to wheel when they moved, and from both sides of the wheels were streams of fire, [26] and in the midst of the coals were living creatures like flaming coals . . . and the wheels, the living creatures and the wheels. [27] Now there was . . . over their heads an expanse, like an awesome gleam of crystal. And a voice came from above the expanse . . .

FRAGMENT 2

[1] Convert, house of Israel, from your lawless ways. [2] I say to you—My people—even if the list of your sins stretches from Heaven to earth, and if they are as black as they can be, and you turn to Me, and with all

of your heart say, "Father," I will forgive you, and look on you as holy.

FRAGMENT 3

[1] Look at the cow, she has calved, and yet she is pregnant . . .

FRAGMENT 4

[1] In this manner, our Lord Jesus Christ also said, "It is what I have seen you doing that I will judge you for."

FRAGMENT 5

[1] "And I will bind up the lame persons, and I will heal the sick, and I will bring back the wandering. [2] And I will feed them on My holy mountain, and I will be their Shepherd, and I will be closer to them than a garment is to their skin. [3] They will call Me, and I will say, Behold, here I am. And if they cross, they will not slip," says the LORD.

FRAGMENT 6

[[[1] A certain king had everyone in his kingdom drafted, and had no civilians with an exception of two: one lame and one blind, and each one lived by himself in his own home. [2] And when the king was preparing a wedding feast for his own son, he invited everyone in his kingdom, but he despised the two civilians, the lame man and the blind man. [3] And they were indignant within themselves and resolved to carry out a plot against the king. Now the king had a garden. [4] And the blind man addressed the lame man from a distance, saying, "How much would our crumb of bread have been among the crowds who were invited to the celebration? So come on, let us retaliate [against] him for what he did to us!" "How?" asked the other. [5] And [the blind man] said, "Let us go into his garden, and there, ruin the other things in the garden." But [the lame man] said, "But how can I, for I am lame and unable to crawl?" [6] And the blind man said, "Am I able to do anything myself, since I am unable to see where I am going? But let us use trickery." [7] Plucking the nearby grass and braiding a rope, [the lame man] threw [it] to the blind man, and said, "Grab [it], and come here to me by rope." [8] And he did as he had urged. When he neared, [the lame man] said, "Come here. You be [my] feet and carry me, and I will be your eyes, guiding you from on top to the right and to the left." [9] So by doing this, they went down into the garden. And whether they did any damage or not, nevertheless their footprints were visible in the garden. [10] Now when the celebrants dispersed from the wedding feast, going down into the garden, they were surprised to find the footprints in the garden. [11] So they reported these things to the king, saying, "Everyone in your kingdom is a soldier and no one is a civilian. So why are there civilian footprints in the garden?" [12] And [the king] was astounded. So he summoned the lame man and the blind man. [13] And he asked the blind man, "Did you not come down into the garden?" But [the blind man] replied, "Who—me, lord? You see my handicap, you know that I cannot see where I walk." [14] Then approaching the lame man, [the king] also asked him, "Did you come down into my garden?" [15] And answering, he said, "O lord, do you wish to embitter my soul over my handicap?" [16] And finally the judgment was delayed. What then did the righteous judge do? [17] Realizing in what manner the two had joined together, he put the lame man on the blind man and examined them both under the lash. [18] And they were unable to deny [it]. They each convicted the other. [19] The lame man, on the one hand, said to the blind man, "Did you not pick me up and carry me?" [20] And the blind man said to the lame man, "Did you yourself not become my eyes?"]]

EPISTLE OF ARISTEAS

Otherwise known as the Letter of Aristeas

The Letter of Aristeas to Philocrates, herein called the Epistle of Aristeas, is a Hellenistic work from the 3rd or early 2nd century BC, thought by some biblical scholars to be pseudepigraphical. Josephus ascribes it to Aristeas of Marmora and suggests it was written to a certain Philocrates. The letter describes the Greek translation of the Hebrew Bible by seventy-two interpreters sent into Egypt from Jerusalem at the request of the librarian of Alexandria, resulting in the Septuagint translation (LXX). Some have argued that its story of the creation of the Greek translation of the Hebrew Bible is fictitious, although its ancient date provides an important counterargument. The letter is a vital resource for understanding the Hellenistic Judaism of Jesus' day and is the earliest text to mention the Great Library of Alexandria, which has been lost to history.

CHAPTER 1

[1] Since I have collected material for a memorable history of my visit to Eleazar the chief priest of the Jews, and because you, Philocrates, as you lose no opportunity of reminding me, have set great store on receiving an account of the motives and object of my mission, I have attempted to draw up a clear exposition of the matter for you, for I perceive that you possess a natural love of learning, a quality which is the highest possession of man—to be constantly attempting "to add to his stock of knowledge and acquirements" whether through the study of history or by actually participating in the events themselves. [2] It is by this means, by taking up into itself the noblest elements, that the soul is established in purity, and having fixed its aim on piety, the noblest goal of all, it uses this as its infallible guide and so acquires a definite purpose. [3] It was my devotion to the pursuit of religious knowledge that led me to undertake the embassy to the man I have mentioned, who was held in the highest esteem by his own citizens and by others both for his virtue and his majesty and who had in his possession documents of the highest value to the Jews in his own country and in foreign lands for the interpretation of the Divine Law, for their laws are written on leather parchments in Jewish characters. [4] I then undertook this embassy with enthusiasm, having first of all found an opportunity of pleading with the king on behalf of the Jewish captives who had been transported from Judea to Egypt by the king's father, when he first obtained possession of this city and conquered the land of Egypt. [5] It is worthwhile that I should also tell you this story, since I am convinced that you, with your disposition toward holiness and your sympathy with men who are living in accordance with the holy Law, will all the more readily listen to the account which I purpose to set forth, since you yourself have lately come to us from the island and are anxious to hear everything that tends to build up the soul. [6] On a former occasion I also sent you a record of the facts which I thought [were] worth relating about the Jewish race—the record which I had obtained from the most learned chief priests of the most learned land of Egypt. [7] As you are so eager to acquire the knowledge of those things which can benefit the mind, I feel it incumbent on me to impart to you all the information in my power. I should feel the same duty toward all who possessed the same disposition, but I feel it especially toward you since you have aspirations which are so noble, and since you are not only my brother in character no less than in blood but are one with me as well in the pursuit of goodness. [8] For neither the pleasure derived from gold nor any other of the possessions which are prized by shallow minds confers the same benefit as the pursuit of culture and the study which we expend in securing it. [9] But that I may not weary you by a too lengthy introduction, I will proceed at once to the substance of my narrative.

CHAPTER 2

[1] Demetrius of Phalerum, the president of the king's library, received vast sums of money for the purpose of collecting together, as far as he possibly could, all the scrolls in the world. [2] By means of purchase and transcription, he carried out, to the best of his ability, the purpose of the king. [3] On one occasion when I was present, he was asked, "How many thousand scrolls are there in the library?" [4] And he replied, "More than two hundred thousand, O king, and I will make endeavour in the immediate future to gather together the remainder also, so that the total of five hundred thousand may be reached. I am told that the laws of the Jews are worth transcribing and deserve a place in your library." [5] "What is to prevent you from doing this?" replied the king. "Everything that is necessary has been placed at your disposal." [6] "They need to be translated," answered Demetrius, "for in the country of the Jews they use a peculiar alphabet (just as the Egyptians, too, have a special form of letters) and speak a peculiar dialect. They are supposed to use the Syriac tongue, but this is not the case; their language is quite different." [7] And when the king understood all the facts of the case, he ordered a letter to be written to the Jewish chief priest that his purpose (which has already been described) might be accomplished.

CHAPTER 3

[1] Thinking that the time had come to press the demand which I had often laid before Sosibius of Tarentum and Andreas, the chief of the bodyguard, for the emancipation of the Jews who had been transported from Judea by the king's father— [2] for when by a combination of good fortune and courage he had brought his attack on the whole district of Coele-Syria and Phoenicia to a successful resolution, in the process of terrorizing the country into subjection, he transported some of his adversaries and others he reduced to captivity. [3] The number of those whom he transported from the country of the Jews to Egypt amounted to no less than one hundred thousand. [4] Of these he armed thirty thousand chosen men and settled them in garrisons in the country districts. [5] (And even before this time large numbers of Jews had come into Egypt with the Persian, and in an earlier period still others had been sent to Egypt to help Psammetichus in his campaign against the king of the Ethiopians. But these were nothing like so numerous as the captives whom Ptolemy the son of Lagus transported.) [6] As I have already stated, Ptolemy chose out the best of these, the men who were in the prime of life and distinguished for their courage, and armed them, but the great mass of the others, those who were too old or too young for this purpose, and the women too, he reduced to slavery— not that he wished to do this of his own free will, but he was compelled by his soldiers who claimed them as a reward for the services which they had rendered in war. [7] Having, as has already been stated, obtained an opportunity for securing their emancipation, I addressed the king with the following arguments: [8] "Let us not be so unreasonable as to allow our deeds to give the lie to our words. Since the Law which we wish not only to transcribe but also to translate belongs to the whole Jewish race, what justification will we be able to find for our embassy while such vast numbers of them remain in a state of slavery in your kingdom? [9] In the perfection and wealth of your clemency, release those who are held in such miserable bondage, since as I have been at pains to discover, the God who gave them their law is the God who maintains your kingdom. [10] They worship the same God—the Lord and Creator of the universe, as all other men, as we ourselves, O king, though we call Him by different names, such as Zeus or Dis. [11] This name was very appropriately bestowed on Him by our first ancestors in order to signify that He, through whom all things are endowed with life and come into being, is necessarily the Ruler and Lord of the universe. [12] Set all mankind an example of magnanimity by releasing those who are held in bondage." [13] After a brief interval, while I was offering up an earnest prayer to God that He would so dispose the mind of the king that all the captives might be set at liberty (for the human race, being the creation of God, is swayed and influenced by Him), therefore with many manifold prayers I called on Him who rules the heart that the king might be constrained to grant my request. [14] For I had great hopes with regard to the salvation of the men since I was assured that God would grant a fulfillment of my prayer, for when men from pure motives plan some action in the interest of righteousness and the performance of noble deeds, Almighty God brings their efforts and purposes to a successful issue. [15] The king raised his head, and looking up at me with a cheerful countenance, asked, "How many thousands do you think they will number?" Andreas, who was standing near, replied, "A little more than one hundred thousand." [16] "It is a small boon indeed," said the king, "that Aristeas asks of us!" [17] Then Sosibius and some others who were present said, "Yes, but it will be a fit tribute to your magnanimity for you to offer the liberation of these men as an act of devotion to the supreme God. [18] You have been greatly honored by Almighty God and exalted above all your forefathers in glory and it is only fitting that you should render to Him the greatest thank offering in your power." [19] Extremely pleased with these arguments, he gave orders that an addition should be made to the wages of the soldiers by the amount of the redemption money that twenty drachmas should be paid to the owners for every slave, that a public order should be issued, and that registers of the captives should be attached to it. [20] He showed the greatest enthusiasm in the business, for it was God who had brought our purpose to fulfillment in its entirety and constrained him to redeem not only those who had come into Egypt with the army of his father but any who had come before that time or had been subsequently brought into the kingdom. [21] It was pointed out to him that the ransom money would exceed four hundred talents.

CHAPTER 4

[1] I think it will be useful to insert a copy of the decree, for in this way the magnanimity of the king, who was empowered by God to save such vast multitudes, will be made clearer and more manifest. [2] The decree of the king ran as follows: "All who served in the army of our father in the campaign against Syria and Phoenicia and in the attack on the country of the Jews, and became possessed of Jewish captives, and brought them back to the city of Alexandria and the land of Egypt or sold them to others—and in the same way any captives who were in our land before that time or were brought here afterward—all who possess such captives are required to set them at liberty at once, receiving twenty drachmas per head as ransom money. [3] The soldiers will receive this money as a gift added to their wages, the others from the king's treasury. [4] We think that it was against our father's will and against all propriety that they should

have been made captives and that the devastation of their land and the transportation of the Jews to Egypt was an act of military wantonness. [5] The spoil which fell to the soldiers on the field of battle was all the plunder which they should have claimed. To reduce the people to slavery in addition was an act of absolute injustice. [6] Therefore since it is acknowledged that we are accustomed to render justice to all men and especially to those who are unfairly in a condition of servitude, and since we strive to deal fairly with all men according to the demands of justice and piety, we have decreed, in reference to the persons of the Jews who are in any condition of bondage in any part of our dominion, that those who possess them will receive the stipulated sum of money and set them at liberty and that no man will show any tardiness in discharging his obligations. [7] Within three days after the publication of this decree, they must make lists of slaves for the officers appointed to carry out our will, and immediately produce the persons of the captives. [8] For we consider that it will be advantageous to us and to our affairs that the matter should be brought to a conclusion. [9] Anyone who likes may give information about any who disobey the decree on condition that if the man is proved guilty, he will become his slave; his property, however, will be handed over to the royal treasury."

CHAPTER 5

[1] When the decree was brought to be read over to the king for his approval, it contained all the other provisions except the phrase "any captives who were in the land before that time or were brought here afterward," and in his magnanimity and the largeness of his heart the king inserted this clause and gave orders that the grant of money required for the redemption should be deposited in full with the paymasters of the forces and the royal bankers, and so the matter was decided and the decree ratified within seven days. [2] The grant for the redemption amounted to more than six hundred and sixty talents; for many infants at the breast were emancipated together with their mothers. [3] When the question was raised whether the sum of twenty talents was to be paid for these, the king ordered that it should be done, and thus he carried out his decision in the most comprehensive way. [4] When this had been done, he ordered Demetrius to draw up a memorial with regard to the transcription of the Jewish scrolls, for all affairs of state used to be carried out by means of decrees and with the most painstaking accuracy by these Egyptian kings, and nothing was done in a careless or haphazard fashion. [5] And so I have inserted copies of the memorial and the letters, the number of the presents sent, and the nature of each, since every one of them excelled in magnificence and technical skill. The following is a copy of the memorial:

CHAPTER 6

[1] "Since you have given me instructions, O king, that the scrolls which are needed to complete your library should be collected together, and that those which are defective should be repaired, I have devoted myself with the utmost care to the fulfillment of your wishes, and I now have the following proposal to lay before you: [2] the scrolls of the Law of the Jews (with several others) are absent from the library. They are written in the Hebrew characters and language and have been carelessly interpreted, and do not represent the original text as I am informed by those who know; for they have never had a king's care to protect them. [3] It is necessary that these should be made accurate for your library since the law which they contain, in as much as it is of divine origin, is full of wisdom and free from all blemish. [4] For this reason, literary men, and poets, and the mass of historical writers have held aloof from referring to these scrolls and the men who have lived and are living in accordance with them, because their conception of life is so sacred and religious, as Hecataeus of Abdera says. [5] If it pleases you, O king, a letter will be written to the chief priest in Jerusalem, asking him to send six elders out of every tribe—men who have lived the noblest life and are most skilled in their law—that we may find out the points in which the majority of them are in agreement, and so having obtained an accurate translation, may place it in a conspicuous place in a manner worthy of the work itself and your purpose. [6] May continual prosperity be yours!"

CHAPTER 7

[1] When this memorial had been presented, the king ordered a letter to be written to Eleazar on the matter, giving also an account of the emancipation of the Jewish captives. [2] And he gave fifty talents weight of gold, and seventy talents of silver, and a large quantity of precious stones to make bowls, and vials, and a table, and libation cups. [3] He also gave orders to those who had the custody of his coffers to allow the craftsmen to make a selection of any materials they might require for the purpose, and that one hundred talents in money should be sent to provide sacrifices for the temple and for other needs. [4] I will give you a full account of the workmanship after I have set copies of the letters before you. [5] The letter of the king ran as follows: "King Ptolemy sends greeting and salutation to the chief priest Eleazar. [6] Since there are many Jews settled in our realm who were carried off from Jerusalem by the Persians at the time of their power and many more who came with my father into Egypt as captives, large numbers of these he placed in the army and paid them higher wages than usual, and when he had proved the loyalty of their leaders, he built fortresses and placed them in their charge that the native Egyptians might be intimidated by them. [7] And I, when I ascended the throne, adopted a kindly

attitude toward all my subjects, and more particularly to those who were citizens of yours—I have set at liberty more than one hundred thousand captives, paying their owners the appropriate market price for them, and if ever evil has been done to your people through the passions of the mob, I have made them reparation. [8] The motive which prompted my action has been the desire to act piously and render to the supreme God a thank offering for maintaining my kingdom in peace and great glory in all the world. [9] Moreover, those of your people who were in the prime of life I have drafted into my army, and those who were fit to be attached to my person and worthy of the confidence of the court, I have established in official positions. [10] Now since I am anxious to show my gratitude to these men, and to the Jews throughout the world, and to the generations yet to come, I have determined that your law will be translated from the Hebrew tongue, which is in use among you, into the Greek language, that these scrolls may be added to the other royal scrolls in my library. [11] It will be a kindness on your part and a regard for my zeal if you will select six elders from each of your tribes, men of noble life and skilled in your law and able to interpret it, that in questions of dispute we may be able to discover the verdict in which the majority agree, for the investigation is of the highest possible importance. [12] I hope to win great renown by the accomplishment of this work. [13] I have sent Andreas, the chief of my bodyguard, and Aristeas—men whom I hold in high esteem—to lay the matter before you and present you with one hundred talents of silver, the first-fruits of my offering for the temple and the sacrifices and other religious rites. [14] If you will write to me concerning your wishes in these matters, you will confer a great favor on me and afford me a new pledge of friendship, for all your wishes will be carried out as speedily as possible. Farewell."

CHAPTER 8

[1] To this letter Eleazar replied appropriately as follows: "Eleazar the chief priest sends greetings to King Ptolemy, his true friend. My highest wishes are for your welfare and the welfare of Queen Arsinoe, your sister, and your children. [2] I also am well. I have received your letter and am greatly rejoiced by your purpose and your noble counsel. [3] I summoned together the whole people and read it to them that they might know of your devotion to our God. [4] I also showed them the cups which you sent, twenty of gold and thirty of silver, the five bowls, and the table of dedication, and the one hundred talents of silver for the offering of the sacrifices and providing the things of which the temple stands in need. [5] These gifts were brought to me by Andreas, one of your most honored servants, and by Aristeas, both good men and true, distinguished by their learning, and worthy in every way to be the representatives of your high principles

and righteous purposes. [6] These men imparted your message to me and received an answer from me in agreement with your letter. I will consent to everything which is advantageous to you even though your request is very unusual. [7] For you have bestowed on our citizens great and never to be forgotten benefits in many. [8] Therefore I immediately offered sacrifices on behalf of you, your sister, your children, and your friends, and all the people prayed that your plans might continually prosper, and that Almighty God might preserve your kingdom in peace with honor, and that the translation of the holy Law might prove advantageous to you and be carried out successfully. [9] In the presence of all the people I selected six elders from each tribe, good men and true, and I have sent them to you with a copy of our law. [10] It will be a kindness, O righteous king, if you will give instruction that as soon as the translation of the Law is completed, the men will be restored to us again in safety. Farewell."

CHAPTER 9

[1] The following are the names of the elders. Of the first tribe: Joseph, Hezekiah, Zechariah, John, Hezekiah, Elisha. [2] Of the second tribe: Judas, Simon, Samuel, Adaeus, Mattathias, Eschlemias. [3] Of the third tribe: Nehemiah, Joseph, Theodosius, Baseas, Ornias, Dakis. [4] Of the fourth tribe: Jonathan, Abraeus, Elisha, Ananias, Chabrias. [5] Of the fifth tribe: Isaac, Jacob, Jesus, Sabbataeus, Simon, Levi. [6] Of the sixth tribe: Judas, Joseph, Simon, Zacharias, Samuel, Selemias. [7] Of the seventh tribe: Sabbataeus, Zedekiah, Jacob, Isaac, Jesias, Natthaeus. [8] Of the eighth tribe: Theodosius, Jason, Jesus, Theodotus, John, Jonathan. [9] Of the ninth tribe: Theophilus, Abraham, Arsamos, Jason, Endemias, Daniel. [10] Of the tenth tribe: Jeremiah, Eleazar, Zechariah, Baneas, Elisha, Dathaeus. [11] Of the eleventh tribe: Samuel, Joseph, Judas, Jonathes, Chabu, Dositheus. [12] Of the twelfth tribe: Isaelus, John, Theodosius, Arsamos, Abietes, Ezekiel. [13] They were seventy-two in all. Such was the answer which Eleazar and his friends gave to the king's letter.

CHAPTER 10

[1] I will now proceed to redeem my promise and give a description of the works of art. [2] They were wrought with exceptional skill, for the king spared no expense and personally superintended the workmen individually. [3] They could not therefore skimp any part of the work or finish it off negligently. [4] First of all, I will give you a description of the table. The king was anxious that this piece of work should be of exceptionally large dimensions, and he caused inquiries to be made of the Jews in the locality with regard to the size of the table already in the temple at Jerusalem. [5] And when they described the measurements, he proceeded to ask whether he might

make a larger structure. [6] And some of the priests and the other Jews replied that there was nothing to prevent him. [7] And he said that he was anxious to make it five times the size, but he hesitated lest it should prove useless for the temple services. [8] He was desirous that his gift should not merely be stationed in the temple, for it would afford him much greater pleasure if the men whose duty it was to offer the fitting sacrifices were able to do so appropriately on the table which he had made. [9] He did not suppose that it was owing to lack of gold that the former table had been made of small size, but there seems to have been, he said, some reason why it was made of this dimension. [10] For had the order been given, there would have been no lack of means. Therefore, we must not transgress or go beyond the proper measure. [11] At the same time, he ordered them to press into service all the manifold forms of art, for he was a man of the loftiest conceptions, and nature had endowed him with a keen imagination which enabled him to picture the appearance which would be presented by the finished work. [12] He also gave orders that where there were no instructions laid down in the Jewish Scriptures, everything should be made as beautiful as possible. When such instructions were laid down, they were to be carried out to the letter.

CHAPTER 11

[1] They made the table two cubits long, one cubit broad, one and a half cubits high, fashioning it of pure solid gold. [2] What I am describing was not thin gold laid over another foundation, but the whole structure was of massive gold welded together. [3] And they made a border of a hand's breadth around it. And there was a wreath of wave-work, engraved in relief in the form of ropes marvelously wrought on its three sides. [4] For it was triangular in shape and the style of the work was exactly the same on each of the sides, so that whichever side they were turned, they presented the same appearance. [5] Of the two sides under the border, the one which sloped down to the table was a very beautiful piece of work, but it was the outer side which attracted the gaze of the spectator. [6] Now the upper edge of the two sides, being elevated, was sharp since, as we have said, the rim was three-sided from whatever point of view one approached it. [7] And there were layers of precious stones on it in the midst of the embossed cord-work, and they were interwoven with one another by an inimitable artistic device. [8] For the sake of security they were all fixed by golden needles which were inserted in perforations in the stones. [9] At the sides they were clamped together by fastenings to hold them firm. [10] On the part of the border around the table which slanted upwards and met the eyes, there was wrought a pattern of eggs in precious stones, elaborately engraved by a continuous piece of fluted relief-work, closely connected together around the whole table. [11] And under the stones which had been arranged to represent eggs, the artists made a crown containing all kinds of fruits, having at its top clusters of grapes and ears of corn, dates also and apples, and pomegranates and the like, conspicuously arranged. [12] These fruits were wrought out of precious stones, of the same color as the fruits themselves, and they fastened them edgewise around all the sides of the table with a band of gold. [13] And after the crown of fruit had been put on, underneath there was inserted another pattern of eggs in precious stones, and other fluting and embossed work, that both sides of the table might be used according to the wishes of the owners, and for this reason the wave-work and the border were extended down to the feet of the table. [14] They made and fastened under the whole width of the table a massive plate four fingers thick, that the feet might be inserted into it, and clamped fast with linchpins which fitted into sockets under the border, so that which ever side of the table people preferred might be used. [15] Thus it became manifestly clear that the work was intended to be used either way. [16] On the table itself they engraved Meander, having precious stones standing out in the middle of it—rubies, and emeralds, and an onyx too, and many other kinds of stones which excel in beauty. [17] And next to the Meander there was placed a wonderful piece of network, which made the center of the table appear like a rhomboid in shape, and on it a crystal and amber, as it is called, had been wrought, which produced an incomparable impression on the beholders. [18] They made the feet of the table with heads like lilies, so that they seemed to be like lilies bending down beneath the table, and the parts which were visible represented leaves which stood upright. [19] The basis of the foot on the ground consisted of a ruby and measured a hand's breadth high all around. It had the appearance of a shoe and was eight fingers broad. The whole expanse of the foot rested on it. [20] And they made the foot appear like ivy growing out of the stone, interwoven with akanthus and surrounded with a vine which encircled it with clusters of grapes, which were worked in stones, up to the top of the foot. [21] All the four feet were made in the same style, and everything was wrought and fitted so skillfully, and such remarkable skill and knowledge were expended on making it true to nature, that when the air was stirred by a breath of wind, movement was imparted to the leaves, and everything was fashioned to correspond with the actual reality which it represented. [22] And they made the top of the table in three parts like a triptychon, and they were so fitted and dovetailed together with spigots along the whole breadth of the work, that the meeting of the joints could not be seen or even discovered. [23] The thickness of the table was not less than half a cubit, so that the whole work must have cost many talents. For since the king did not wish to

add to its size, he expended on the details the same sum of money which would have been required if the table could have been of larger dimensions. ²⁴ And everything was completed in accordance with his plan in a most wonderful and remarkable way, with inimitable art and incomparable beauty.

CHAPTER 12

¹ Of the mixing bowls, two were wrought [in gold], and from the base to the middle were engraved with relief work in the pattern of scales, and between the scales precious stones were inserted with great artistic skill. ² Then there was a Meander one cubit in height, with its surface wrought out of precious stones of many colors, displaying great artistic effort and beauty. ³ On this there was a mosaic, worked in the form of a rhombus, having a net-like appearance and reaching right up to the brim. ⁴ In the middle, small shields which were made of different precious stones, placed alternately and varying in kind, not less than four fingers broad, enhanced the beauty of their appearance. ⁵ On the top of the brim there was an ornament of lilies in bloom, and intertwining clusters of grapes were engraven all around. Such then was the construction of the golden bowls, and they held more than two firkins each. ⁶ The silver bowls had a smooth surface and were wonderfully made as if they were intended for looking-glasses, so that everything which was brought near to them was reflected even more clearly than in mirrors. ⁷ But it is impossible to describe the real impression which these works of art produced on the mind when they were finished, for when these vessels had been completed and placed side by side, first a silver bowl, and then a golden, then another silver, and then another golden, the appearance they presented is altogether indescribable, and those who came to see them were not able to tear themselves from the brilliant sight and entrancing spectacle. ⁸ The impressions produced by the spectacle were various in kind. When men looked at the golden vessels, and their minds made a complete survey of each detail of workmanship, their souls were thrilled with wonder. ⁹ Again, when a man wished to direct his gaze to the silver vessels as they stood before him, everything seemed to flash with light around the place where he was standing and afforded a still greater delight to the onlookers, so that it is really impossible to describe the artistic beauty of the works. ¹⁰ The golden vials they engraved in the center with vine wreaths. And around the rims they wove a wreath of ivy, and myrtle, and olive in relief work and inserted precious stones in it. ¹¹ The other parts of the relief work they wrought in different patterns, since they made it a point of honor to complete everything in a way worthy of the majesty of the king. ¹² In a word it may be said that neither in the king's treasury nor in any other were there any works which equalled these in costliness or in artistic

skill, for the king spent no little thought on them, for he loved to gain glory for the excellence of his designs. ¹³ For oftentimes he would neglect his official business and spend his time with the artists in his anxiety that they should complete everything in a manner worthy of the place to which the gifts were to be sent. ¹⁴ So everything was carried out on a grand scale, in a manner worthy of the king who sent the gifts and of the chief priest who was the ruler of the land. ¹⁵ There was no stint of precious stones, for not less than five thousand were used and they were all of large size. ¹⁶ The most exceptional artistic skill was employed, so that the cost of the stones and the workmanship was five times as much as that of gold.

CHAPTER 13

¹ I have given you this description of the presents because I thought it was necessary. ² The next point in the narrative is an account of our journey to Eleazar, but I will first of all give you a description of the whole country. ³ When we arrived in the land of the Jews, we saw the city situated in the middle of the whole of Judea on the top of a mountain of considerable altitude. ⁴ On the summit the temple had been built in all its splendor. It was surrounded by three walls more than seventy cubits high and in length and breadth corresponding to the structure of the edifice. ⁵ All the buildings were characterized by a magnificence and costliness quite unprecedented. It was obvious that no expense had been spared on the door and the fastenings, which connected it with the doorposts, and the stability of the lintel. ⁶ The style of the curtain too was thoroughly in proportion to that of the entrance. ⁷ Its fabric owing to the draught of wind was in perpetual motion, and as this motion was communicated from the bottom and the curtain bulged out to its highest extent, it afforded a pleasant spectacle from which a man could scarcely tear himself away. ⁸ The construction of the altar was in keeping with the place itself and with the burnt-offerings which were consumed by fire on it, and the approach to it was on a similar scale. ⁹ There was a gradual slope up to it, conveniently arranged for the purpose of decency, and the ministering priests were robed in linen garments down to their ankles. ¹⁰ The temple faces the east, and its back is toward the west. ¹¹ The whole of the floor is paved with stones and slopes down to the appointed places, that water may be conveyed to wash away the blood from the sacrifices, for many thousand beasts are sacrificed there on the feast days. ¹² And there is an inexhaustible supply of water, because an abundant natural spring gushes up from within the temple area. ¹³ There are moreover wonderful and indescribable cisterns underground, as they pointed out to me, at a distance of five furlongs all around the site of the temple, and each of them has countless pipes so that the different

streams converge together. ¹⁴And all these were fastened with lead at the bottom and at the sidewalls, and over them a great quantity of plaster had been spread, and every part of the work had been most carefully carried out. ¹⁵There are many openings for water at the base of the altar which are invisible to all except to those who are engaged in the ministration, so that all the blood of the sacrifices which is collected in great quantities is washed away in the twinkling of an eye. ¹⁶Such is my opinion with regard to the character of the reservoirs and I will now show you how it was confirmed. ¹⁷They led me more than four furlongs outside the city and commanded me to peer down toward a certain spot and listen to the noise that was made by the meeting of the waters, so that the great size of the reservoirs became manifest to me, as has already been pointed out.

CHAPTER 14

¹The ministration of the priests is in every way unsurpassed both for its physical endurance and for its orderly and silent service. ²For they all work spontaneously, though it entails much painful exertion, and each one has a special task allotted to him. ³The service is carried on without interruption—some provide the wood, others the oil, others the fine wheat flour, others the spices; others again bring the pieces of flesh for the burnt-offering, exhibiting a wonderful degree of strength. ⁴For they take up the limbs of a calf with both hands, each of them weighing more than two talents, and throw them with each hand in a wonderful way onto the high place of the altar and never miss placing them on the proper spot. ⁵In the same way the pieces of the sheep and also of the goats are wonderful both for their weight and their fatness. ⁶For those whose business it is always select the beasts which are without blemish and especially fat, and thus the sacrifice which I have described is carried out. ⁷There is a special place set apart for them to rest in where those who are relieved from duty sit. When this takes place, those who have already rested and are ready to assume their duties rise up spontaneously since there is no one to give orders with regard to the arrangement of the sacrifices. ⁸The most complete silence reigns so that one might imagine that there was not a single person present, though there are actually seven hundred men engaged in the work, besides the vast number of those who are occupied in bringing up the sacrifices. ⁹Everything is carried out with reverence and in a way worthy of the great God.

CHAPTER 15

¹We were greatly astonished when we saw Eleazar engaged in the ministration, at the mode of his dress and the majesty of his appearance, which was revealed in the robe which he wore and the precious stones on his person. ²There were golden bells on the garment which reached down to his feet, giving forth a peculiar kind of melody, and on both sides of them there were pomegranates with variegated flowers of a wonderful hue. ³He was girded with a girdle of conspicuous beauty, woven in the most beautiful colors. ⁴On his breast he wore the oracle of God, as it is called, on which twelve stones, of different kinds, were inset, fastened together with gold, containing the names of the leaders of the tribes according to their original order, each one flashing forth in an indescribable way its own particular color. ⁵On his head he wore a tiara, as it is called, and on this in the middle of his forehead an inimitable turban, the royal diadem full of glory with the Name of God inscribed in sacred letters on a plate of gold . . . having been judged worthy to wear these emblems in the ministrations. ⁶Their appearance created such awe and confusion of mind as to make one feel that one had come into the presence of a man who belonged to a different world. ⁷I am convinced that anyone who takes part in the spectacle which I have described will be filled with astonishment and indescribable wonder and be profoundly affected in his mind at the thought of the sanctity which is attached to each detail of the service.

CHAPTER 16

¹But in order that we might gain complete information, we ascended to the summit of the neighboring citadel and looked around us. ²It is situated in a very lofty spot, and is fortified with many towers, which have been built up to the very top of immense stones, with the object, as we were informed, of guarding the temple precincts, so that if there were an attack, or an insurrection, or an onslaught of the enemy, no one would be able to force an entrance within the walls that surround the temple. ³On the towers of the citadel engines of war were placed and different kinds of machines, and the position was much higher than the circle of walls which I have mentioned. ⁴The towers were also guarded by most trusty men who had given the utmost proof of their loyalty to their country. ⁵These men were never allowed to leave the citadel, except on feast days and then only in detachments; nor did they permit any stranger to enter it. ⁶They were also very careful when any command came from the chief officer to admit any visitors to inspect the place, as our own experience taught us. ⁷They were very reluctant to admit us—although we were only two unarmed men—to view the offering of the sacrifices. ⁸And they asserted that they were bound by an oath when the trust was committed to them, for they had all sworn and were bound to carry out the oath sacredly to the letter, that although they were five hundred in number, they would not permit more than five men to enter at one time. ⁹The citadel was the special protection of the temple and its founder had

fortified it so strongly that it might efficiently protect it.

CHAPTER 17

[1] The size of the city is of moderate dimensions. It is about forty furlongs in circumference, as far as one could conjecture. It has its towers arranged in the shape of a theater, with thoroughfares leading between them. [2] Now the crossroads of the lower towers are visible, but those of the upper towers are more frequented. For the ground ascends, since the city is built on a mountain. [3] There are also steps which lead up to the crossroads, and some people are always going up, and others down, and they keep as far apart from each other as possible on the road because of those who are bound by the rules of purity, lest they should touch anything which is unlawful. [4] It was not without reason that the original founders of the city built it in due proportions, for they possessed clear insight with regard to what was required. [5] For the country is extensive and beautiful. Some parts of it are level, especially the districts which belong to Samaria, as it is called, and which border on the land of the Idumeans, other parts are mountainous, especially [those which are contiguous to the land of Judea]. [6] The people are therefore bound to devote themselves to agriculture and the cultivation of the soil that by this means they may have a plentiful supply of crops. [7] In this way cultivation of every kind is carried on and an abundant harvest reaped in the whole of the aforementioned land. [8] The cities which are large and enjoy a corresponding prosperity are well-populated, but they neglect the country districts, since all men are inclined to a life of enjoyment, for everyone has a natural tendency toward the pursuit of pleasure. [9] The same thing happened in Alexandria, which excels all cities in size and prosperity. [10] Country people by migrating from the rural districts and settling in the city brought agriculture into disrepute: and so to prevent them from settling in the city, the king issued orders that they should not stay in it for more than twenty days. [11] And in the same way he gave the judges written instructions, that if it was necessary to issue a summons against anyone who lived in the country, the case must be settled within five days. [12] And since he considered the matter one of great importance, he appointed also legal officers for every district with their assistants, that the farmers and their advocates might not in the interests of business empty the granaries of the city—I mean of the produce of husbandry. [13] I have permitted this digression because it was Eleazar who pointed out with great clearness the points which have been mentioned. [14] For great is the energy which they expend on the tillage of the soil. For the land is thickly planted with multitudes of olive trees, with crops of corn and pulse, with vines too, and there is abundance of honey. [15] Other kinds of fruit trees and dates do not count compared with these. [16] There are cattle of all kinds in great quantities and a rich pasturage for them. [17] Therefore, they rightly recognize that the country districts need a large population, and the relations between the city and the villages are properly regulated. [18] A great quantity of spices, and precious stones, and gold is brought into the country by the Arabs. [19] For the country is well adapted not only for agriculture but also for commerce, and the city is rich in the arts and lacks none of the merchandise which is brought across the sea. [20] It also possesses suitable and commodious harbors at Ashkelon, Joppa, and Gaza, as well as at Ptolemais which was founded by the king and holds a central position compared with the other places named, being not far distant from any of them. [21] The country produces everything in abundance, since it is well-watered in all directions and well-protected from storms. [22] The Jordan River, as it is called, which never runs dry, flows through the land. [23] Originally [the country] contained not less than sixty million acres—although afterward the neighboring peoples made incursions against it—and six hundred thousand men were settled on it in farms of a hundred acres each. [24] Like the Nile, the river rises in [the] time of harvest and irrigates a large portion of the land. Near the district belonging to the people of Ptolemais it issues into another river and this flows out into the sea. [25] Other mountain torrents, as they are called, flow down into the plain and encompass the parts around Gaza and the district of Ashdod. [26] The country is encircled by a natural fence and is very difficult to attack and cannot be assailed by large forces, owing to the narrow passes, with their overhanging precipices and deep ravines, and the rugged character of the mountainous regions which surround all the land. [27] We were told that from the neighboring mountains of Arabia copper and iron were formerly obtained. [28] This was stopped, however, at the time of the Persian rule, since the authorities of the time spread abroad a false report that the working of the mines was useless and expensive in order to prevent their country from being destroyed by the mining in these districts and possibly taken away from them owing to the Persian rule, since by the assistance of this false report they found an excuse for entering the district.

CHAPTER 18

[1] I have now, my dear brother Philocrates, given you all the essential information on this subject in brief form. I will describe the work of translation in the sequel. [2] The chief priest selected men of the finest character and the highest culture, such as one would expect from their noble parentage. [3] They were men who had not only acquired proficiency in Jewish literature but had studied most carefully that of the Greeks as well. [4] They were therefore especially qualified for serving on embassies and they

undertook this duty whenever it was necessary. [5] They possessed a great facility for conferences and the discussion of problems connected with the Law. [6] They espoused the middle course—and this is always the best course to pursue. They renounced the rough and uncouth manner, but they were altogether above pride and never assumed an air of superiority over others, and in conversation they were ready to listen and give an appropriate answer to every question. [7] And all of them carefully observed this rule and were anxious above everything else to excel each other in its observance and all of them were worthy of their leader and of his virtue. [8] And one could observe how they loved Eleazar by their unwillingness to be torn away from him and how he loved them. [9] For besides the letter which he wrote to the king concerning their safe return, he also earnestly sought Andreas to work for the same end and urged me, too, to assist to the best of my ability; [10] and although we promised to give our best attention to the matter, he said that he was still greatly distressed, for he knew that the king out of the goodness of his nature considered it his highest privilege, whenever he heard of a man who was superior to his fellows in culture and wisdom, to summon him to his court. [11] For I have heard of a fine saying of his to the effect that by securing just and prudent men around his person he would secure the greatest protection for his kingdom, since such friends would unreservedly give him the most beneficial advice. [12] And the men who were now being sent to him by Eleazar undoubtedly possessed these qualities. [13] And he frequently asserted on oath that he would never let the men go if it were merely some private interest of his own that constituted the impelling motive—but it was for the common advantage of all the citizens that he was sending them. [14] "For," he explained, "the good life consists in the keeping of the enactments of the Law, and this end is achieved much more by hearing than by reading." [15] From this and other similar statements it was clear what his feelings toward them were.

CHAPTER 19

[1] It is worthwhile to briefly mention the information which he gave in reply to our questions. [2] For I suppose that most people feel a curiosity with regard to some of the enactments in the Law, especially those about meats, and drinks, and animals recognized as unclean. [3] When we asked why, since there is but one form of creation, some animals are regarded as unclean for eating, and others unclean even to the touch (for though the Law is scrupulous on most points, it is especially scrupulous on such matters as these) he began his reply as follows: "You observe," he said, "what an effect our modes of life and our associations produce on us; [4] by associating with the bad, men catch their depravities and become miserable throughout their life, but if they live with the wise and prudent, they find the means of escaping from ignorance and amending their lives. [5] Our lawgiver first of all laid down the principles of piety and righteousness and inculcated them point by point, not merely by prohibitions, but [also] by the use of examples as well, demonstrating the injurious effects of sin and the punishments inflicted by God on the guilty. [6] For he proved first of all that there is only one God and that His power is manifested throughout the universe, since every place is filled with His sovereignty and none of the things which are wrought in secret by men on the earth escapes His knowledge. [7] For all that a man does and all that is to come to pass in the future are manifest to Him. [8] Working out these truths carefully and having made them plain he showed that even if a man should think of doing evil—to say nothing of actually effecting it—he would not escape detection, for he made it clear that the power of God pervaded the whole of the Law. [9] Beginning from this starting point he went on to show that all mankind, except ourselves, believe in the existence of many gods, though they themselves are much more powerful than the beings whom they vainly worship. [10] For when they have made statues of stone and wood, they say that they are the images of those who have invented something useful for life and they worship them, although they have clear proof that they possess no feeling. [11] For it would be utterly foolish to suppose that anyone became a god in virtue of his inventions. [12] For the inventors simply took certain objects already created and by combining them together, showed that they possessed a fresh utility: they did not themselves create the substance of the thing, and so it is a vain and foolish thing for people to make gods of men like themselves. [13] For in our times there are many who are much more inventive and much more learned than the men of former days who have been deified, and yet they would never come to worship them. [14] The makers and authors of these myths think that they are the wisest of the Greeks. [15] Why do we need to speak of other infatuated people, Egyptians and the like, who place their reliance on wild beasts, and most kinds of creeping things, and cattle, and worship them, and offer sacrifices to them both while living and when dead?"

CHAPTER 20

[1] "Now our lawgiver, being a wise man and especially endowed by God to understand all things, took a comprehensive view of each particular detail, and fenced us around with impregnable ramparts and walls of iron, that we might not mingle at all with any of the other nations, but remain pure in body and soul, free from all vain imaginations, worshiping the one Almighty God above the whole creation. [2] Hence the leading Egyptian priests, having looked carefully into many matters, and being cognizant with [our] affairs,

call us Men of God. This is a title which does not belong to the rest of mankind but only to those who worship the true God. [3] The rest are men not of God but of meats, and drinks, and clothing, for their whole disposition leads them to find solace in these things. [4] Among our people such things are reckoned of no account, but throughout their whole life their main consideration is the sovereignty of God. [5] Therefore, lest we should be corrupted by any abomination, or our lives be perverted by evil communications, he hedged us around on all sides by rules of purity, affecting alike what we eat, or drink, or touch, or hear, or see. [6] For though, speaking generally, all things are alike in their natural constitution, since they are all governed by one and the same power, yet there is a deep reason in each individual case why we abstain from the use of certain things and enjoy the common use of others. [7] For the sake of illustration I will run over one or two points and explain them to you, for you must not fall into the degrading idea that it was out of regard to mice, and weasels, and other such things that Moses drew up his laws with such exceeding care. [8] All these ordinances were made for the sake of righteousness to aid the quest for virtue and the perfecting of character. [9] For all the birds that we use are tame and distinguished by their cleanliness, feeding on various kinds of grain and pulse, such as for instance pigeons, turtle-doves, locusts, partridges, geese also, and all other birds of this class. [10] But the birds which are forbidden you will find to be wild and carnivorous, tyrannizing over the others by the strength which they possess, and cruelly obtaining food by preying on the tame birds enumerated above, and not only this, but they seize lambs and kids, and also injure human beings, whether dead or alive, [11] and so by naming them unclean, he gave a sign by means of them that those for whom the legislation was ordained must practice righteousness in their hearts and not tyrannize over anyone in reliance on their own strength, nor rob them of anything, but steer their course of life in accordance with justice, just as the tame birds, already mentioned, consume the different kinds of pulse that grow on the earth and do not tyrannize to the destruction of their own kind. [12] Our legislator therefore taught us that it is by such methods as these that indications are given to the wise, that they must be just, and effect nothing by violence, and refrain from tyrannizing over others in reliance on their own strength. [13] For since it is considered unseemly even to touch such unclean animals as have been mentioned, on account of their particular habits, ought we not to take every precaution lest our own characters should be destroyed to the same extent? [14] Therefore, all the rules which he has laid down with regard to what is permitted in the case of these birds and other animals, he has enacted with the object of teaching us a moral lesson. [15] For the division of the hoof and the separation of the claws are intended to teach us that we must discriminate between our individual actions with a view to the practice of virtue. [16] For the strength of our whole body and its activity depend on our shoulders and limbs. Therefore, he compels us to recognize that we must perform all our actions with discrimination according to the standard of righteousness—more especially because we have been distinctly separated from the rest of mankind. [17] For most other men defile themselves by promiscuous intercourse, thereby working great iniquity, and whole countries and cities pride themselves on such vices. [18] For they not only have intercourse with men, but they defile their own mothers and even their daughters. But we have been kept separate from such sins. [19] And the people who have been separated in the aforementioned way are also characterized by the lawgiver as possessing the gift of memory. [20] For all animals which are cloven-footed and chew the cud represent to the initiated the symbol of memory. For the act of chewing the cud is nothing else than the reminiscence of life and existence. [21] For life is accustomed to being sustained by means of food, therefore he also exhorts us in the Scripture in these words: You will surely remember the LORD that wrought in you those great and wonderful things. [22] For when they are properly conceived, they are manifestly great and glorious: first the construction of the body, and the disposition of the food, and the separation of each individual limb, and, far more, the organization of the senses, the operation and invisible movement of the mind, the rapidity of its particular actions, and its discovery of the arts, display an infinite resourcefulness. [23] Therefore, he exhorts us to remember that the aforementioned parts are kept together by the divine power with consummate skill. [24] For he has marked out every time and place that we may continually remember the God who rules and preserves [us]. [25] For in the matter of meats and drinks he commands us first of all [to] offer part as a sacrifice and then forthwith enjoy our meal. [26] Moreover, on our garments he has given us a symbol of remembrance, and in like manner he has ordered us to put the divine oracles on our gates and doors as a remembrance of God. [27] And on our hands, too, he expressly orders the symbol to be fastened, clearly showing that we ought to perform every act in righteousness, remembering [our own creation], and above all, the fear of God. [28] He also commands men, when lying down to sleep and rising up again, to meditate on the works of God, not only in word, but by distinctly observing the change and impression produced on them, when they are going to sleep, and also their waking, how divine and incomprehensible the change from one of these states to the other is. [29] The excellency of the analogy in regard to discrimination and memory has now been pointed out to you, according to our interpretation of the cloven hoof and the chewing of the cud. ³⁰ For our laws have not been drawn up at random or in accordance with the first casual thought that occurred to the mind, but with a view to truth and the indication of right reason. ³¹ For by means of the directions which he gives with regard to meats, and drinks, and particular cases of touching, he commands us neither to do nor listen to anything, thoughtlessly, nor to resort to injustice by the abuse of the power of reason. ³² In the case of the wild animals, too, the same principle may be discovered, for the character of the weasel, and of mice, and such animals as these, which are expressly mentioned, is destructive. ³³ Mice defile and damage everything, not only for their own food but even to the extent of rendering absolutely useless to man whatever it falls in their way to damage. ³⁴ The weasel class, too, is peculiar: for besides what has been said, it has a characteristic which is defiling: it conceives through the ears and brings forth through the mouth. ³⁵ And it is for this reason that a like practice is declared unclean in men. ³⁶ For by embodying in speech all that they receive through the ears, they involve others in evils and work no ordinary impurity, being themselves altogether defiled by the pollution of impiety. ³⁷ And your king, as we are informed, does quite right in destroying such men." ³⁸ Then I said, "I suppose you mean the informers, for he constantly exposes them to tortures and to painful forms of death." ³⁹ "Yes," he replied, "these are the men I mean, for to watch for men's destruction is an unholy thing. And our law forbids us to injure anyone either by word or deed. ⁴⁰ My brief account of these matters ought to have convinced you that all our regulations have been drawn up with a view to righteousness, and that nothing has been enacted in the Scripture thoughtlessly or without due reason, but its purpose is to enable us throughout our whole life and in all our actions to practice righteousness before all men, being mindful of Almighty God. ⁴¹ And so concerning meats and things unclean, creeping things, and wild beasts, the whole system aims at righteousness and righteous relationships between man and man."

CHAPTER 21

¹ He seemed to me to have made a good defense on all the points, for in reference also to the calves, and rams, and goats which are offered, he said that it was necessary to take them from the herds and flocks, and sacrifice tame animals and offer nothing wild, that the offerers of the sacrifices might understand the symbolic meaning of the lawgiver and not be under the influence of an arrogant self-consciousness. ² For he who offers a sacrifice also makes an offering of his own soul in all its moods. ³ I think that these particulars with regard to our discussion are worth narrating, and on account of the sanctity and natural meaning of the Law I have been induced to explain them to you clearly, Philocrates, because of your own devotion to learning.

CHAPTER 22

¹ And Eleazar, after offering the sacrifice, and selecting the envoys, and preparing many gifts for the king, despatched us on our journey in great security. ² And when we reached Alexandria, the king was at once informed of our arrival. On our admission to the palace, Andreas and I warmly greeted the king and handed over to him the letter written by Eleazar. ³ The king was very anxious to meet the envoys and gave orders that all the other officials should be dismissed and the envoys summoned to his presence at once. ⁴ Now this excited general surprise, for it is customary for those who come to seek an audience with the king on matters of importance to be admitted to his presence on the fifth day, while envoys from kings or very important cities with difficulty secure admission to the court in thirty days— ⁵ but he counted these men worthy of greater honor since he held their master in such high esteem, and so he immediately dismissed those whose presence he regarded as superfluous and continued walking around until they came in and he was able to welcome them. ⁶ When they entered with the gifts which had been sent with them and the valuable parchments on which the Law was inscribed in gold in Jewish characters, for the parchment was wonderfully prepared and the connection between the pages had been so effected as to be invisible, the king, as soon as he saw them, began to ask them about the scrolls. ⁷ And when they had taken the rolls out of their coverings and unfolded the pages, the king stood still for a long time and then paying homage seven times, he said: "I thank you, my friends, and I thank him that sent you still more, and most of all God, whose oracles these are." ⁸ And when all the envoys and also the others who were present shouted out at one time and with one voice: "God save the king!" he burst into tears of joy. ⁹ For his exaltation of soul and the sense of the overwhelming honor which had been paid him compelled him to weep over his good fortune. ¹⁰ He commanded them to put the rolls back in their places, and then after saluting the men, said, "It was right, men of God, that I should first of all pay my reverence to the scrolls for the sake of which I summoned you here and then, [and] when I had done that, to extend the right hand of friendship to you. It was for this reason that I did this first. ¹¹ I have decreed that this day on which you arrived will be kept as a great day, and it will be celebrated annually throughout my lifetime. ¹² It so happens that it is the anniversary of my naval victory over Antigonus. Therefore, I will be glad to feast with you today. ¹³ Everything that you may have occasion to use," he said, "will be prepared [for you] in a suitable manner—and for me also with you." ¹⁴ After they had expressed their delight, he gave orders that

the best quarters near the citadel should be assigned to them, and that preparations should be made for the banquet. [15] And Nicanor summoned the lord high steward, Dorotheus, who was the special officer appointed to look after the Jews, and commanded him to make the necessary preparation for each one. [16] For this arrangement had been made by the king and it is an arrangement which you see maintained today. For as many cities [as] have [special] customs in the matter of drinking, eating, and reclining, have special officers appointed to look after their requirements. [17] And whenever they come to visit the kings, preparations are made in accordance with their own customs, in order that there may be no discomfort to disturb the enjoyment of their visit. The same precaution was taken in the case of the Jewish envoys. [18] Now Dorotheus, who was the patron appointed to look after Jewish guests, was a very conscientious man. [19] All the stores which were under his control and set apart for the reception of such guests he brought out for the feast. [20] He arranged the seats in two rows in accordance with the king's instructions, for he had ordered him to make half the men sit at his right hand and the rest behind him in order that he might not withhold from them the highest possible honor. [21] When they had taken their seats, he instructed Dorotheus to carry out everything in accordance with the customs which were in use among his Jewish guests. [22] Therefore, he dispensed with the services of the sacred heralds, and the sacrificing priests, and the others who were accustomed to offer the prayers, and called on one of our number, Eleazar, the oldest of the Jewish priests, to offer prayer instead. [23] And he rose up and made a remarkable prayer: "May Almighty God enrich you, O king, with all the good things which He has made, and may He grant you, and your wife, and your children, and your comrades the continual possession of them as long as you live." [24] At these words a loud and joyous applause broke out which lasted for a considerable time, and then they turned to the enjoyment of the banquet which had been prepared. [25] All the arrangements for service at table were carried out in accordance with the injunction of Dorotheus. [26] Among the attendants were the royal pages and others who held places of honor at the king's court.

CHAPTER 23

[1] Taking an opportunity afforded by a pause in the banquet, the king asked the envoy who sat in the seat of honor (for they were arranged according to seniority) how he could keep his kingdom unimpaired to the end. [2] After pondering for a moment, he replied, "You could best establish its security if you were to imitate the unceasing kindness of God. For if you exhibit clemency and inflict mild punishments on those who deserve them in accordance with their deservings, you will turn them from evil and lead them to conversion." [3] The king praised the answer and then asked the next man how he could do everything for the best in all his actions. [4] And he replied, "If a man maintains a just bearing toward all, he will always act rightly on every occasion, remembering that every thought is known to God. If you take the fear of God as your starting point, you will never miss the goal." [5] The king complimented this man, too, on his answer and asked another how he could have friends like-minded with himself. [6] He replied, "If they see you studying the interests of the multitudes over whom you rule; you will do well to observe how God bestows His benefits on the human race, providing health, and food, and all other things for them in due season." [7] After expressing his agreement with the reply, the king asked the next guest how in giving audiences and passing judgments he could gain the praise even of those who failed to win their suit. [8] And he said, "If you are fair in speech to all alike and never act insolently nor tyrannically in your treatment of offenders. And you will do this if you watch the method by which God acts. [9] The petitions of the worthy are always fulfilled, while those who fail to obtain an answer to their prayers are informed by means of dreams or events of what was harmful in their requests and that God does not strike them according to their sins or the greatness of His strength, but acts with forbearance toward them." [10] The king praised the man warmly for his answer and asked the next in order how he could be invincible in military affairs. [11] And he replied, "If he did not entirely trust in his multitudes or his warlike forces, but continually called on God to bring his enterprises to a successful issue, while he himself discharged all his duties in the spirit of justice." [12] Welcoming this answer, he asked another how he might become an object of dread to his enemies. [13] And he replied, "If while maintaining a vast supply of arms and forces he remembered that these things were powerless to achieve a permanent and conclusive result. [14] For even God instills fear into the minds of men by granting reprieves and making merely a display of the greatness of His power." [15] This man the king praised and then said to the next, "What is the highest good in life?" [16] And he answered, "To know that God is Lord of the universe, and that in our finest achievements it is not we who attain success but God who by His power brings all things to fulfillment and leads us to the goal." [17] The king exclaimed that the man had answered well and then asked the next how he could keep all his possessions intact and finally hand them down to his successors in the same condition. [18] And he answered, "By praying constantly to God that you may be inspired with high motives in all your undertakings and by warning your descendants not to be dazzled by fame or wealth, for it is God who bestows all these gifts, and men never

win the supremacy by themselves." ¹⁹ The king expressed his agreement with the answer and inquired of the next guest how he could bear with composure whatever befell him. ²⁰ And he said, "If you have a firm grasp of the thought that all men are appointed by God to share the greatest evil as well as the greatest good, since it is impossible for one who is a man to be exempt from these. ²¹ But God, to whom we always ought to pray, inspires us with courage to endure." ²² Delighted with the man's reply, the king said that all their answers had been good. "I will put a question to one other," he added, "and then I will stop for the present [so] that we may turn our attention to the enjoyment of the feast and spend a pleasant time." ²³ Thereon he asked the man, "What is the true aim of courage?" And he answered, "If a right plan is carried out in the hour of danger in accordance with the original intention. For all things are accomplished by God to your advantage, O king, since your purpose is good." ²⁴ When all had signified by their applause their agreement with the answer, the king said to the philosophers (for not a few of them were present), "It is my opinion that these men excel in virtue and possess extraordinary knowledge, since on the spur of the moment they have given fitting answers to these questions which I have put to them, and have all made God the starting point of their words." ²⁵ And Menedemus, the philosopher of Eretria, said, "True, O king, for since the universe is managed by providence and since we rightly perceive that man is the creation of God, it follows that all power and beauty of speech proceed from God." ²⁶ When the king had nodded his assent to this sentiment, the speaking ceased and they proceeded to enjoy themselves. When evening came on, the banquet ended.

CHAPTER 24

¹ On the following day they sat down to table again and continued the banquet according to the same arrangements. ² When the king thought that a fitting opportunity had arrived to put inquiries to his guests, he proceeded to ask further questions of the men who sat next in order to those who had given answers on the previous day. ³ He began to open the conversation with the eleventh man, for there were ten who had been asked questions on the former occasion. ⁴ When silence was established, he asked how he could continue to be rich. ⁵ After a brief reflection, the man who had been asked the question replied, "If he did nothing unworthy of his position, never acted licentiously, never lavished expense on empty and vain pursuits, but by acts of benevolence made all his subjects well-disposed toward himself. ⁶ For it is God who is the author of all good things and man needs to obey Him." ⁷ The king bestowed praise on him and then asked another how he could maintain the truth. ⁸ In reply to the question he said, "By recognizing that

a lie brings great disgrace on all men, and more especially on kings. For since they have the power to do whatever they wish, why should they resort to lies? ⁹ In addition to this, you must always remember, O king, that God is a lover of the truth." ¹⁰ The king received the answer with great delight, and looking at another, said, "What is the teaching of wisdom?" ¹¹ And the other replied, "As you wish that no evil should befall you, but to be a partaker of all good things, so you should act on the same principle toward your subjects and offenders, and you should mildly admonish the noble and good, for God draws all men to Himself by His kindness." ¹² The king praised him and asked the next in order how he could be the friend of men. ¹³ And he replied, "By observing that the human race increases and is born with much trouble and great suffering: therefore, you must not lightly punish or inflict torments on them, since you know that the life of men is made up of pains and penalties. ¹⁴ For if you understood everything you would be filled with pity, for God is also pitiful." ¹⁵ The king received the answer with approval and inquired of the next, "What is the most essential qualification for ruling?" ¹⁶ "To keep oneself," he answered, "free from bribery and to practice sobriety during the greater part of one's life, to honor righteousness above all things, and to make friends of men of this type. For God, too, is a lover of justice." ¹⁷ Having signified his approval, the king said to another, "What is the true mark of piety?" ¹⁸ And he replied, "To perceive that God constantly works in the universe and knows all things, and no man who acts unjustly and works wickedness can escape His notice. ¹⁹ As God is the benefactor of the whole world, so you, too, must imitate Him and be void of offense." ²⁰ The king signified his agreement and said to another, "What is the essence of kingship?" ²¹ And he replied, "To rule oneself well and not to be led astray by wealth or fame to unrestrained or unseemly desires; this is the true way of ruling if you reason the matter well out. ²² For all that you really need is yours, and God is free from need and benevolent with all. ²³ Let your thoughts be such as suit a man, and do not desire many things, but only such as are necessary for ruling." ²⁴ The king praised him and asked another man how his deliberations might be for the best. ²⁵ And he replied, "If he constantly set justice before him in everything and thought that injustice was equivalent to deprivation of life, for God always promises the highest blessings to the just." ²⁶ Having praised him, the king asked the next how he could be free from disturbing thoughts in his sleep. ²⁷ And he replied, "You have asked me a question which is very difficult to answer, for we cannot bring our true selves into play during the hours of sleep, but are held fast in these by imaginations that cannot be controlled by reason. ²⁸ For our souls possess the feeling that they actually see the things that enter into our consciousness during sleep, but we make a mistake if we suppose that we are actually sailing on the sea in boats, or flying through the air, or traveling to other regions, or anything else of the kind, and yet we actually do imagine such things to be taking place. ²⁹ So far as it is possible for me to decide, I have reached the following conclusion: you must in every possible way, O king, govern your words and actions by the rule of piety [so] that you may have the consciousness that you are maintaining virtue and that you never choose to gratify yourself at the expense of reason, and never by abusing your power do injury to righteousness. ³⁰ For the mind mostly busies itself in sleep with the same things with which it occupies itself when awake. ³¹ And he who has all his thoughts and actions set toward the noblest ends establishes himself in righteousness both when he is awake and when he is asleep. ³² You must therefore be steadfast in the constant discipline of self." ³³ The king bestowed praise on the man and said to another, "Since you are the tenth to answer, when you have spoken, we will devote ourselves to the banquet." ³⁴ And then he put [forward] the question, "How can I avoid doing anything unworthy of myself?" ³⁵ And he replied, "Always look to your own fame and your own supreme position, that you may speak and think only such things as are consistent with it, knowing that all your subjects think and talk about you. ³⁶ For you must not appear to be worse than the actors, who study the role carefully, which it is necessary for them to play, and shape all their actions in accordance with it. ³⁷ You are not acting a part, but are really a king, since God has bestowed on you a royal authority in keeping with your character." ³⁸ When the king had applauded loud and long in the most gracious way, the guests were urged to seek repose, so when the conversation ceased, they devoted themselves to the next course of the feast.

CHAPTER 25

¹ On the following day, the same arrangement was observed, and when the king found an opportunity of putting questions to the men, he questioned the first of those who had been left over for the next interrogation, "What is the highest form of government?" ² And he replied, "To rule oneself and not to be carried away by impulses. For all men possess a certain natural bent of mind. ³ It is probable that most men have an inclination toward food, and drink, and pleasure, and kings a bent toward the acquisition of territory and great renown, but it is good that there should be moderation in all things. ⁴ What God gives, you may take and keep, but never yearn for things that are beyond your reach." ⁵ Pleased with these words, the king asked the next how he could be free from envy. ⁶ And he, after a brief pause, replied, "If you consider first of all that it is God who bestows on all kings glory and great wealth and no one is king by his own power. All men wish to share this glory but cannot, since it is the gift of God." ⁷ The king praised the man in a long speech and then asked another how he could despise his enemies. ⁸ And he replied, "If you show kindness to all men and win their friendship, you need to fear no one. To be popular with all men is the best of good gifts to receive from God." ⁹ Having praised this answer, the king ordered the next man to reply to the question how he could maintain his great renown. ¹⁰ And he replied that "If you are generous and big-hearted in bestowing kindness and acts of grace on others, you will never lose your renown, but if you wish the aforementioned graces to continue [as] yours, you must continually call on God." ¹¹ The king expressed his approval and asked the next, "To whom ought a man show liberality?" ¹² And he replied, "All men acknowledge that we ought to show liberality to those who are well-disposed toward us, but I think that we ought to show the same keen spirit of generosity to those who are opposed to us that by this means we may win them over to the right and to what is advantageous to ourselves. ¹³ But we must pray to God that this may be accomplished, for He rules the minds of all men." ¹⁴ Having expressed his agreement with the answer, the king asked the sixth to reply to the question, "To whom ought we to exhibit gratitude?" ¹⁵ And he replied, "To our parents continually, for God has given us a most important commandment with regard to the honor due to parents. ¹⁶ In the next place He reckons the attitude of friend toward friend for He speaks of a friend which is as your own soul. You do well in trying to bring all men into friendship with yourself." ¹⁷ The king spoke kindly to him and then asked the next, "What is it that resembles beauty in value?" ¹⁸ And he said, "Piety, for it is the preeminent form of beauty, and its power lies in love, which is the gift of God. This you have already acquired and with it all the blessings of life." ¹⁹ The king applauded the answer in the most gracious way and asked another how, if he were to fail, he could regain his reputation again to the same degree. ²⁰ And he said, "It is not possible for you to fail, for you have sown in all men the seeds of gratitude which produce a harvest of goodwill, and this is mightier than the strongest weapons and guarantees the greatest security. ²¹ But if any man fails, he must never again do those things which caused his failure, but he must form friendships and act justly, for it is the gift of God to be able to do good actions and not the contrary." ²² Delighted with these words, the king asked another how he could be free from grief. ²³ And he replied, "If he never injured anyone, but did good to everybody and followed the pathway of righteousness, for its fruits bring freedom from grief. But we must pray to God that unexpected evils such as death, or disease, or pain, or anything of this kind may not come on us and injure us. ²⁴ But since you are

devoted to piety, no such misfortune will ever come on you." ²⁵ The king bestowed great praise on him and asked the tenth, "What is the highest form of glory?" ²⁶ And he said, "To honor God, and this is done not with gifts and sacrifices but with purity of soul and holy conviction, since all things are fashioned and governed by God in accordance with His will. ²⁷ Of this purpose you are in constant possession as all men can see from your achievements in the past and in the present." ²⁸ With a loud voice the king greeted them all and spoke kindly to them, and all those who were present expressed their approval, especially the philosophers. ²⁹ For they were far superior to them both in conduct and in argument, since they always made God their starting point. ³⁰ After this, the king, to show his good pleasure, proceeded to drink the health of his guests.

CHAPTER 26

¹ On the following day the same arrangements were made for the banquet, and the king, as soon as an opportunity occurred, began to put questions to the men who sat next to those who had already responded, and he said to the first, "Is wisdom capable of being taught?" ² And he said, "The soul is so constituted that it is able by the divine power to receive all the good and reject the contrary." ³ The king expressed approval and asked the next man, "What is it that is most beneficial to health?" ⁴ And he said, "Temperance, and it is not possible to acquire this unless God creates a disposition toward it." ⁵ The king spoke kindly to the man and said to another, "How can a man worthily pay the debt of gratitude to his parents?" ⁶ And he said, "By never causing them pain, and this is not possible unless God disposes the mind to the pursuit of the noblest ends." ⁷ The king expressed agreement and asked the next how he could become an eager listener. ⁸ And he said, "By remembering that all knowledge is useful, because it enables you by the help of God in a time of emergency to select some of the things which you have learned and apply them to the crisis which confronts you. And so the efforts of men are fulfilled by the assistance of God." ⁹ The king praised him and asked the next how he could avoid doing anything contrary to law. ¹⁰ And he said, "If you recognize that it is God who has put the thoughts into the hearts of the lawgivers that the lives of men might be preserved, you will follow them." ¹¹ The king acknowledged the man's answer and said to another, "What is the advantage of kinship?" ¹² And he replied, "If we consider that we ourselves are afflicted by the misfortunes which fall on our relatives and if their sufferings become our own—then the strength of kinship is apparent at once, for it is only when such feeling is shown that we will win honor and esteem in their eyes. ¹³ For help, when it is linked with kindness, is of itself a bond which is altogether

indissoluble. And in the day of their prosperity, we must not crave their possessions, but must pray [for] God to bestow all manner of good on them." ¹⁴ And having accorded to him the same praise as to the rest, the king asked another how he could attain freedom from fear. ¹⁵ And he said, "When the mind is conscious that it has wrought no evil and when God directs it to all noble counsels." ¹⁶ The king expressed his approval and asked another how he could always maintain a right judgment. ¹⁷ And he replied, "If he constantly set the misfortunes which befall men before his eyes and recognized that it is God who takes away prosperity from some and brings others to great honor and glory." ¹⁸ The king gave a kindly reception to the man and asked the next to answer the question how he could avoid a life of ease and pleasure. ¹⁹ And he replied, "If he continually remembered that he was the ruler of a great empire and the lord of vast multitudes, and that his mind should not be occupied with other things, but he should always be considering how he could best promote their welfare. ²⁰ He must also pray to God that no duty might be neglected." ²¹ Having bestowed praise on him, the king asked the tenth how he could recognize those who were dealing treacherously with him. ²² And he replied to the question, "If he observed whether the bearing of those around him was natural and whether they maintained the proper rule of precedence at receptions and councils, and in their general intercourse, never going beyond the bounds of propriety in congratulations or in other matters of conduct. ²³ But God will incline your mind, O king, to all that is noble." ²⁴ When the king had expressed his loud approval and praised them all individually (amid the plaudits of all who were present), they turned to the enjoyment of the feast.

CHAPTER 27

¹ And on the next day, when the opportunity offered, the king asked the next man, "What is the greatest form of neglect?" ² And he replied, "If a man does not care for his children and devote every effort to their education. ³ For we always pray to God not so much for ourselves as for our children that every blessing may be theirs. ⁴ Our desire that our children may possess self-control is only realized by the power of God." ⁵ The king said that he had spoken well and then asked another how he could be patriotic. ⁶ "By keeping before your mind," he replied, "the thought that it is good to live and die in one's own country. Residence abroad brings contempt on the poor and shame on the rich as though they had been banished for a crime. ⁷ If you bestow benefits on all, as you continually do, God will give you favor with all and you will be accounted patriotic." ⁸ After listening to this man, the king asked the next in order how he could live amicably with his wife. ⁹ And he answered, "By recognizing that womankind are by nature

headstrong and energetic in the pursuit of their own desires, and subject to sudden changes of opinion through fallacious reasoning, and their nature is essentially weak. [10] It is necessary to deal wisely with them and not to provoke strife. [11] For the successful conduct of life the pilot must know the goal toward which he ought to direct his course. [12] It is only by calling on the help of God that men can steer a true course of life at all times." [13] The king expressed his agreement and asked the next how he could be free from error. [14] And he replied, "If you always act with deliberation and never give credence to slanders, but prove for yourself the things that are said to you, and decide by your own judgment the requests which are made to you, and carry out everything in the light of your judgment, you will be free from error, O king. [15] But the knowledge and practice of these things is the work of the divine power." [16] Delighted with these words, the king asked another how he could be free from wrath. [17] And he said in reply to the question, "If he recognized that he had power over all even to inflict death on them, if he gave way to wrath, and that it would be useless and pitiful if he, just because he was lord, deprived many of life. [18] What need was there for wrath when all men were in subjection and no one was hostile to him? [19] It is necessary to recognize that God rules the whole world in the spirit of kindness and without wrath at all, and you," he said, "O king, must of necessity copy His example." [20] The king said that he had answered well and then inquired of the next man, "What is good counsel?" [21] "To act well at all times and with due reflection," he explained, "comparing what is advantageous to our own policy with the injurious effects that would result from the adoption of the opposite view, in order that by weighing every point we may be well-advised and our purpose may be accomplished. [22] And most important of all, by the power of God every plan of yours will find fulfillment because you practice piety." [23] The king said that this man had answered well, and asked another, "What is philosophy?" [24] And he explained, "To deliberate well in reference to any question that emerges and never to be carried away by impulses, but to ponder over the injuries that result from the passions, and to act rightly as the circumstances demand, practicing moderation. [25] But we must pray to God to instill into our mind a regard for these things." [26] The king signified his consent and asked another how he could meet with recognition when traveling abroad. [27] "By being fair to all men," he replied, "and by appearing to be inferior rather than superior to those among whom he was traveling. [28] For it is a recognized principle that God by His very nature accepts the humble. And the human race loves those who are willing to be in subjection to them." [29] Having expressed his approval at this reply, the king asked another how he could build in such a way that his structures would endure after him. [30] And he replied to the question, "If his creations were on a great and noble scale, so that the beholders would spare them for their beauty, and if he never dismissed any of those who wrought such works and never compelled others to minister to his needs without wages. [31] For observing how God provides for the human race, granting them health, and mental capacity, and all other gifts, he himself should follow His example by rendering a recompense to men for their arduous toil. [32] For it is the deeds that are wrought in righteousness that abide continually." [32] The king said that this man had also answered well and asked the tenth, "What is the fruit of wisdom?" [33] And he replied, "That a man should be conscious in himself that he has wrought no evil and that he should live his life in the truth, since it is from these, O mighty king, that the greatest joy, and steadfastness of soul, and strong faith in God accrue to you if you rule your realm in piety." [34] And when they heard the answer, they all shouted with loud acclaim, and afterward the king in the fullness of his joy began to drink their healths.

CHAPTER 28

[1] And on the next day the banquet followed the same course as on previous occasions, and when the opportunity presented itself, the king proceeded to put questions to the remaining guests, and he said to the first, "How can a man keep himself from pride?" [2] And he replied, "If he maintains equality and remembers on all occasions that he is a man ruling over men. And God brings the proud to nothing, and exalts the meek and humble." [3] The king spoke kindly to him and asked the next, "Whom should a man select as his counselors?" [4] And he replied, "Those who have been tested in many affairs and maintain unmingled goodwill toward him and partake of his own disposition. [5] And God manifests Himself to those who are worthy that these ends may be attained." [6] The king praised him and asked another, "What is the most necessary possession for a king?" [7] "The friendship and love of his subjects," he replied, "for it is through this that the bond of goodwill is rendered indissoluble. [8] And it is God who ensures that this may come to pass in accordance with your wish." [9] The king praised him and inquired of another, "What is the goal of speech?" [10] And he replied, "To convince your opponent by showing him his mistakes in a well-ordered array of arguments, for in this way you will win your hearer, not by opposing him, but by bestowing praise on him with a view to persuading him. [11] And it is by the power of God that persuasion is accomplished." [12] The king said that he had given a good answer and asked another how he could live amicably with the many different races who formed the population of his kingdom. [13] "By acting the proper part toward each," he replied, "and taking righteousness as your guide, as you are now doing

with the help of the insight which God bestows on you." ¹⁴ The king was delighted by this reply, and asked another, "Under what circumstances should a man suffer grief?" ¹⁵ "In the misfortunes that befall our friends," he replied, "when we see that they are protracted and irremediable. ¹⁶ Reason does not allow us to grieve for those who are dead and set free from evil, but all men do grieve over them because they think only of themselves and their own advantage. ¹⁷ It is by the power of God alone that we can escape all evil." ¹⁸ The king said that he had given a fitting answer, and asked another, "How is reputation lost?" ¹⁹ And he replied, "When pride and unbounded self-confidence hold sway, dishonor and loss of reputation are engendered. ²⁰ For God is the Lord of all reputation and bestows it where He will." ²¹ The king gave his confirmation to the answer, and asked the next man, "To whom should men entrust themselves?" ²² "To those," he replied, "who serve you from goodwill and not from fear or self-interest, thinking only of their own gain. ²³ For the one is the sign of love, the other the mark of ill-will and time-serving. ²⁴ For the man who is always watching for his own gain is a traitor at heart, but you possess the affection of all your subjects by the help of the good counsel which God bestows on you." ²⁵ The king said that he had answered wisely, and asked another, "What is it that keeps a kingdom safe?" ²⁶ And he replied to the question, "Care and forethought that no evil may be wrought by those who are placed in a position of authority over the people, and this you always do by the help of God who inspires you with grave judgment." ²⁷ The king spoke words of encouragement to him, and asked another, "What is it that maintains gratitude and honor?" ²⁸ And he replied, "Virtue, for it is the creator of good deeds, and by it evil is destroyed, even as you exhibit nobility of character toward all by the gift which God bestows on you." ²⁹ The king graciously acknowledged the answer and asked the eleventh (since there were two more than seventy) how he could maintain tranquility of soul in time of war. ³⁰ And he replied, "By remembering that he had done no evil to any of his subjects, and that all would fight for him in return for the benefits which they had received, knowing that even if they lose their lives, you will care for those dependent on them. ³¹ For you never fail to make reparation to any—such is the kindheartedness with which God has inspired you." ³² The king loudly applauded them all, and spoke very kindly to them, and then drank a long draught to the health of each, giving himself up to enjoyment, and lavishing the most generous and joyous friendship on his guests.

CHAPTER 29

¹ On the seventh day much more extensive preparations were made, and many others were present from the different cities (among them a large number of ambassadors). ² When an opportunity occurred, the king asked the first of those who had not yet been questioned how he could avoid being deceived by fallacious reasoning. ³ And he replied, "By carefully noticing the speaker, the thing spoken, and the subject under discussion, and by putting the same questions again after an interval in different forms. ⁴ But to possess an alert mind and to be able to form a sound judgment in every case is one of the good gifts of God, and you possess it, O king." ⁵ The king loudly applauded the answer and asked another, "Why is it that the majority of men never become virtuous?" ⁶ "Because," he replied, "all men are by nature intemperate and inclined to pleasure. Hence, injustice springs up and a flood of avarice. ⁷ The habit of virtue is a hindrance to those who are devoted to a life of pleasure because it enjoins on them the preference of temperance and righteousness. For it is God who is the master of these things." ⁸ The king said that he had answered well, and asked, "What should kings obey?" ⁹ And he said, "The laws, in order that by righteous enactments they may restore the lives of men. ¹⁰ Even as you by such conduct in obedience to the divine command have laid up in store for yourself a perpetual memorial." ¹¹ The king said that this man had also spoken well, and asked the next, "Whom should we appoint as governors?" ¹² And he replied, "All who hate wickedness, and imitating your own conduct, act righteously that they may constantly maintain a good reputation. ¹³ For this is what you do, O mighty king," he said, "and it is God who has bestowed on you the crown of righteousness." ¹⁴ The king loudly acclaimed the answer and then, looking at the next man, said, "Whom should we appoint as officers over the forces?" ¹⁵ And he explained, "Those who excel in courage and righteousness and those who are more anxious about the safety of their men than to gain a victory by risking their lives through rashness. ¹⁶ For as God acts well toward all men, so you also in imitation of Him are the benefactor of all your subjects." ¹⁷ The king said that he had given a good answer and asked another, "What man is worthy of admiration?" ¹⁸ And he replied, "The man who is furnished with reputation, and wealth, and power, and possesses a soul equal to it all. ¹⁹ You yourself show by your actions that you are most worthy of admiration through the help of God who makes you care for these things." ²⁰ The king expressed his approval and said to another, "To what affairs should kings devote most time?" ²¹ And he replied, "To reading and the study of the records of official journeys, which are written in reference to the various kingdoms, with a view to the reformation and preservation of the subjects. ²² And it is by such activity that you have attained to a glory which has never been approached by others, through the help of

God who fulfils all your desires." ²³ The king spoke enthusiastically to the man and asked another how a man should occupy himself during his hours of relaxation and recreation. ²⁴ And he replied, "To watch those plays which can be acted with propriety and to set before one's eyes scenes taken from life and enacted with dignity and decency are profitable and appropriate. ²⁵ For there is some edification to be found even in these amusements, for often some desirable lesson is taught by the most insignificant affairs of life. ²⁶ But by practicing the utmost propriety in all your actions, you have shown that you are a philosopher and are honored by God on account of your virtue." ²⁷ The king, pleased with the words which had just been spoken, said to the ninth man, "How should a man conduct himself at banquets?" ²⁸ And he replied, "You should summon to your side men of learning and those who are able to give you useful hints with regard to the affairs of your kingdom and the lives of your subjects (for you could not find any theme more suitable or more educational than this) since such men are dear to God because they have trained their minds to contemplate the noblest themes—as you indeed are doing yourself, since all your actions are directed by God." ²⁹ Delighted with the reply, the king inquired of the next man, "What is best for the people—that a private citizen should be made king over them or a member of the royal family?" ³⁰ And he replied, "He who is best by nature, for kings who come of royal lineage are often harsh and severe toward their subjects. ³¹ And still more is this the case with some of those who have risen from the ranks of private citizens, who after having experienced evil and borne their share of poverty, when they rule over multitudes turn out to be crueler than the godless tyrants. ³² But, as I have said, a good nature which has been properly trained is capable of ruling, and you are a great king, not so much because you excel in the glory of your rule and your wealth, but rather because you have surpassed all men in clemency and philanthropy, thanks to God who has endowed you with these qualities." ³³ The king spent some time in praising this man and then asked the last of all, "What is the greatest achievement in ruling an empire?" ³⁴ And he replied, "That the subjects should continually dwell in a state of peace, and that justice should be speedily administered in cases of dispute. ³⁵ These results are achieved through the influence of the ruler, when he is a man who hates evil, and loves the good, and devotes his energies to saving the lives of men, just as you consider injustice the worst form of evil and by your just administration have fashioned for yourself an undying reputation, since God bestows on you a mind which is pure and untainted by any evil." ³⁶ And when he ceased, loud and joyful applause broke out for some considerable time. ³⁷ When it stopped, the king took a cup and gave a toast in honor of all his guests and the words which they had uttered. ³⁸ Then in conclusion he said, "I have derived the greatest benefit from your presence. I have profited much by the wise teaching which you have given me in reference to the art of ruling." ³⁹ Then he ordered that three talents of silver should be presented to each of them and appointed one of his slaves to deliver over the money. ⁴⁰ All at once shouted their approval, and the banquet became a scene of joy while the king gave himself up to a continuous round of festivity.

CHAPTER 30

¹ I have written at length and must crave your pardon, Philocrates. ² I was astonished beyond measure at the men and the way in which on the spur of the moment they gave answers which really needed a long time to devise. ³ For though the questioner had given great thought to each particular question, those who replied one after the other had their answers ready at once and so they seemed to me, and to all who were present, and especially to the philosophers, to be worthy of admiration. ⁴ And I suppose that the thing will seem incredible to those who will read my narrative in the future. ⁵ But it is unseemly to misrepresent facts which are recorded in the public archives. And it would not be right for me to transgress in such a matter as this. ⁶ I tell the story just as it happened, conscientiously avoiding any error. ⁷ I was so impressed by the force of their utterances that I made an effort to consult those whose business it was to make a record of all that happened at the royal audiences and banquets. ⁸ For it is the custom, as you know, from the moment the king begins to transact business until the time when he retires to rest, for a record to be taken of all his sayings and doings—a most excellent and useful arrangement. ⁹ For on the following day the minutes of the doings and sayings of the previous day are read over before business commences, and if there has been any irregularity, the matter is at once set right. ¹⁰ I obtained therefore, as has been said, accurate information from the public records, and I have set forth the facts in proper order since I know how eager you are to obtain useful information.

CHAPTER 31

¹ Three days later Demetrius took the men, and passing along the seawall, seven stadia long, to the island, crossed the bridge and made for the northern districts of Pharos. ² There he assembled them in a house which had been built on the seashore, of great beauty and in a secluded situation, and invited them to carry out the work of translation since everything that they needed for the purpose was placed at their disposal. ³ So they set to work comparing their several results and making them agree, and whatever they agreed on was suitably copied out under the direction of Demetrius. ⁴ And the session lasted until the ninth

hour; after this they were set free to minister to their physical needs. ⁵Everything they wanted was furnished for them on a lavish scale. In addition to this, Dorotheus made the same preparations for them daily as were made for the king himself—for thus he had been commanded by the king. ⁶In the early morning they appeared daily at the court, and after saluting the king, went back to their own place. ⁷And as is the custom of all the Jews, they washed their hands in the sea, and prayed to God, and then devoted themselves to reading and translating the particular passage on which they were engaged. ⁸And I put the question to them why it was that they washed their hands before they prayed. ⁹And they explained that it was a token that they had done no evil (for every form of activity is wrought by means of the hands) since in their noble and holy way they regard everything as a symbol of righteousness and truth.

CHAPTER 32

¹As I have already said, they met together daily in the place which was delightful for its quiet and its brightness and applied themselves to their task. ²And it so happened that the work of translation was completed in seventy-two days, just as if this had been arranged of set purpose. ³When the work was completed, Demetrius collected together the Jewish population in the place where the translation had been made and read it over to all in the presence of the translators, who also met with a great reception from the people because of the great benefits which they had conferred on them. ⁴They also bestowed warm praise on Demetrius and urged him to have the whole Law transcribed and present a copy to their leaders. ⁵After the scrolls had been read, the priests, and the elders of the translators, and the Jewish community, and the leaders of the people stood up and said that since so excellent, and sacred, and accurate a translation had been made, it was only right that it should remain as it was, and no alteration should be made in it. ⁶And when the whole company expressed their approval, they commanded them [to] pronounce a curse in accordance with their custom on anyone who should make any alteration either by adding anything or changing in any way any of the words which had been written or making any omission. ⁷This was a very wise precaution to ensure that the scroll might be preserved for all the future time unchanged. ⁸When the matter was reported to the king, he rejoiced greatly, for he felt that the design which he had formed had been safely carried out. ⁹The whole scroll was read over to him and he was greatly astonished at the Spirit of the lawgiver. ¹⁰And he said to Demetrius, "How is it that none of the historians or the poets have ever thought it worth their

while to allude to such a wonderful achievement?" ¹¹And he replied, "Because the Law is sacred and of divine origin. And some of those who formed the intention of dealing with it have been smitten by God and therefore desisted from their purpose." ¹²He said that he had heard from Theopompus that he had been driven out of his mind for more than thirty days because he intended to insert in his history some of the incidents from the earlier and somewhat unreliable translations of the Law. ¹³When he had recovered a little, he sought God to make it clear to him why the misfortune had befallen him. ¹⁴And it was revealed to him in a dream, that from idle curiosity he was wishing to communicate sacred truths to common men, and that if he desisted, he would recover his health. ¹⁵I have heard, too, from the lips of Theodektes, one of the tragic poets, that when he was about to adapt some of the incidents recorded in the scroll for one of his plays, he was affected with a cataract in both his eyes. ¹⁶And when he perceived the reason why the misfortune had befallen him, he prayed to God for many days and was afterward restored. ¹⁷And after the king, as I have already said, had received the explanation of Demetrius on this point, he paid homage, and ordered that great care should be taken of the scrolls, and that they should be sacredly guarded. ¹⁸And he urged the translators to visit him frequently after their return to Judea, for it was only right, he said, that he should now send them home. ¹⁹But when they came back, he would treat them as friends, as was right, and they would receive rich presents from him. ²⁰He ordered preparations to be made for them to return home and treated them most lavishly. ²¹He presented each one of them with three robes of the finest sort, two talents of gold, a sideboard weighing one talent, [and] all the furniture for three couches. ²²And with the escort he sent Eleazar ten couches with silver legs and all the necessary equipment, a sideboard worth thirty talents, ten robes, purple, and a magnificent crown, and one hundred pieces of the finest woven linen, also bowls and dishes, and two golden beakers to be dedicated to God. ²³He also urged him in a letter that if any of the men preferred to come back to him, not to hinder them, for he counted it a great privilege to enjoy the society of such learned men, and he would rather lavish his wealth on them than on vanities. ²⁴And now Philocrates, you have the complete story in accordance with my promise. ²⁵I think that you find greater pleasure in these matters than in the writings of the mythologists, for you are devoted to the study of those things which can benefit the soul and spend much time on it. ²⁶I will attempt to narrate whatever other events are worth recording, that by perusing them you may secure the highest reward for your zeal.

NEW TESTAMENT

DIDACHE

Didache, which means "Teaching," is a very early Christian treatise purporting to have been written by the Twelve Apostles per the opening line. It is thought to have been written between 50 and 150 AD. The document covers basic Christian principles of godly living, conversion, and ritual.

THE LORD'S TEACHING TO THE HEATHEN BY THE TWELVE APOSTLES.

CHAPTER 1

[1] There are two Ways, one of Life and one of Death, and there is a great difference between the two Ways. [2] The Way of Life is this: "First, you will love the God who made you, secondly, your neighbor as yourself; and whatever you would not have done to yourself, do not do to another." [3] Now, the teaching of these words is this: "Bless those that curse you, and pray for your enemies, and fast for those that persecute you. For what credit is it to you if you love those that love you? Do not even the heathen do the same?" But, for your part, "love those that hate you," and you will have no enemy. [4] "Abstain from carnal and bodily lusts." "If any man strikes you on the right cheek, turn to him the other cheek also," and you will be perfect. "If any man impresses you to go with him one mile, go with him two. If any man takes your coat, give him your shirt also. If any man will take from you what is yours, do not refuse it"—not even if you can. [5] Give to everyone that asks you, and do not refuse, for the Father's will is that we give to all from the gifts we have received. Blessed is he that gives according to the mandate; for he is innocent. Woe to him who receives; for if any man receive alms under pressure of need he is innocent; but he who receives it without need will be tried as to why he took and for what, and being in prison, he will be examined as to his deeds, and "he will not come out from there until he pays the last penny." [6] But concerning this it was also said, "Let your alms sweat into your hands until you know to whom you are giving."

CHAPTER 2

[1] But the second command of the teaching is this: [2] "You will not murder; you will not commit adultery"; you will not commit sodomy; you will not commit fornication; you will not steal; you will not use magic; you will not use love potions; you will not procure abortion, nor commit infanticide; "you will not covet your neighbor's goods"; [3] you will not commit perjury, "you will not bear false witness"; you will not speak evil; you will not bear malice. [4] You will not be double-minded nor double-tongued, for to be double-tongued is the snare of death. [5] Your speech will not be false, nor vain, but completed in action. [6] You will not be covetous nor extortionate, nor a hypocrite, nor malignant, nor proud; you will make no evil plan against your neighbor. [7] You will hate no man; but some you will reprove, and for some you will pray, and some you will love more than your own life.

CHAPTER 3

[1] My child, flee from every evil man and from all like him. [2] Do not be proud, for pride leads to murder, nor jealous, nor contentious, nor passionate, for from all these murders are engendered. [3] My child, do not be lustful, for lust leads to fornication, nor a speaker of base words, nor a lifter up of the eyes, for from all these is adultery engendered. [4] My child, do not regard omens, for this leads to idolatry; neither be an enchanter, nor an astrologer, nor a magician, neither wish to see these things, for from them all is idolatry engendered. [5] My child, do not be a liar, for lying leads to theft, nor a lover of money, nor vainglorious, for from all these things are thefts engendered. [6] My child, do not be a grumbler, for this leads to blasphemy, nor stubborn, nor a thinker of evil, for from all these are blasphemies engendered, [7] but be "meek, for the meek will inherit the earth"; [8] be long-suffering, and merciful, and guileless, and quiet, and good, and always fearing the words which you have heard. [9] You will not exalt yourself, nor let your soul be presumptuous. Your soul will not consort with the lofty, but you will walk with righteous and humble men. [10] Receive the accidents that befall you as good, knowing that nothing happens without God.

CHAPTER 4

[1] My child, you will remember, day and night, him who speaks the word of God to you, and you will honor him as the LORD, for where the LORD's nature is spoken of, there He is present. [2] And you will seek daily the presence of the holy ones, that you may find rest in their words. [3] You will not desire a schism, but will reconcile those that strive. You will give righteous judgment; you will favor no man's person in reproving transgression. [4] You will not be of two minds whether it will be or not. [5] Do not be one who stretches out his hands to receive, but shuts them

when it comes to giving. [6] Of whatever you have gained by your hands you will give a ransom for your sins. [7] You will not hesitate to give, nor will you grumble when you give, for you will know who the good Paymaster of the reward is. [8] You will not turn the needy away, but will share everything with your brother, and will not say that it is your own, for if you are sharers in the imperishable, how much more in the things which perish? [9] You will not withhold your hand from your son or from your daughter, but you will teach them the fear of God from their youth up. [10] You will not command in your bitterness your slave or your handmaid, who hope in the same God, lest they cease to fear the God who is over you both; for He does not come to call men with respect of persons, but those whom the Spirit has prepared. [11] But you who are slaves, be subject to your master, as to God's representative, in reverence and fear. [12] You will hate all hypocrisy, and everything that is not pleasing to the LORD. [13] You will not forsake the commands of the LORD, but you will keep what you received, "adding nothing to it and taking nothing away." [14] In the congregation you will confess your transgressions, and you will not go yourself to prayer with an evil conscience. This is the Way of Life.

CHAPTER 5

[1] But the Way of Death is this: first of all, it is wicked and full of cursing, murders, adulteries, lusts, fornications, thefts, idolatries, witchcrafts, charms, robberies, false witness, hypocrisies, a double heart, fraud, pride, malice, stubbornness, covetousness, foul speech, jealousy, impudence, haughtiness, boastfulness. [2] Persecutors of the good, haters of truth, lovers of lies, not knowing the reward of righteousness, not cleaving to the good nor to righteous judgment, spending wakeful nights not for good but for wickedness, from whom meekness and patience is far, lovers of vanity, following after reward, unmerciful to the poor, not working for him who is oppressed with toil, without knowledge of Him who made them, murderers of children, corrupters of God's creatures, turning away the needy, oppressing the distressed, advocates of the rich, unjust judges of the poor, altogether sinful; may you be delivered, my children, from all these.

CHAPTER 6

[1] See "that no one make you to err" from this Way of the teaching, for he teaches you without God. [2] For if you can bear the whole yoke of the LORD, you will be perfect, but if you cannot, do what you can. [3] And concerning food, bear what you can, but keep strictly

from that which is offered to idols, for it is the worship of dead gods.

CHAPTER 7

[1] Concerning immersion, immerse thus: having first rehearsed all these things, "immerse in the Name of the Father, and of the Son, and of the Holy Spirit," in running water; [2] but if you have no running water, immerse in other water, and if you cannot in cold, then in warm. [3] But if you have neither, pour water three times on the head "in the Name of the Father, Son, and Holy Spirit." [4] And before the immersion let the immerser and him who is to be immersed fast, and any others who are able. And you will bid him who is to be immersed to fast one or two days before.

CHAPTER 8

[1] Do not let your fasts be with the hypocrites, for they fast on Mondays and Thursdays, but you fast on Wednesdays and Fridays. [2] And do not pray as the hypocrites, but as the LORD commanded in His good news, pray thus: "Our Father who is in Heaven, hallowed be Your Name, Your Kingdom come, Your will be done, as in Heaven so also on earth; give us today our daily bread, and forgive us our debt as we forgive our debtors, and do not lead us into trial, but deliver us from the evil [one], for Yours is the power and the glory for all time." [3] Pray thus three times a day.

CHAPTER 9

[1] And concerning the Thanksgiving, hold Thanksgiving thus: [2] first concerning the cup: "We give thanks to You, our Father, for the Holy Vine of Your child David, which You made known to us through Your Child Jesus. To You be glory for all time." [3] And concerning the broken bread: "We give You thanks, our Father, for the life and knowledge which You made known to us through Your Child Jesus. To You be glory for all time. [4] As this broken bread was scattered on the mountains, but was brought together and became one, so let Your Assembly be gathered together from the ends of the earth into Your Kingdom, for Yours is the glory and the power through Jesus Christ for all time." [5] But let none eat or drink of Your Thanksgiving except those who have been immersed in the LORD's Name. For concerning this also the LORD said, "Do not give that which is holy to the dogs."

CHAPTER 10

[1] But after you are satisfied with food, thus give thanks: [2] "We give thanks to You, O Holy Father, for Your Holy Name which You made to dwell in our

DIDACHE

hearts, and for the knowledge, and faith, and immortality which You made known to us through Your Child Jesus. To You be glory for all time. ³ You, LORD Almighty, created all things for Your Name's sake, and gave food and drink to men for their enjoyment, that they might give thanks to You, but You have blessed us with spiritual food and drink and continuous light through Your Child. ⁴ Above all we give thanks to You for that You are mighty. To You be glory for all time. ⁵ Remember, LORD, Your Assembly, to deliver it from all evil and to make it perfect in Your love, and gather it together in its holiness from the four winds to Your Kingdom which You have prepared for it. For Yours is the power and the glory for all time. ⁶ Let grace come and let this world pass away. Hosanna to the God of David. If any man is holy, let him come! If any man is not, let him convert: Maranatha! Amen!" ⁷ But permit the prophets to hold Thanksgiving as they will.

CHAPTER 11

¹ Whoever then comes and teaches you all these things previously mentioned, receive him. ² But if the teacher himself is perverted and teaches another doctrine to destroy these things, do not listen to him, but if his teaching is for the increase of righteousness and knowledge of the LORD, receive him as the LORD. ³ And concerning the apostles and prophets, act thus according to the ordinance of the good news. ⁴ Let every apostle who comes to you be received as the LORD, ⁵ but do not let him stay more than one day, or if need be a second as well; but if he stays three days, he is a false prophet. ⁶ And when an apostle goes forth let him accept nothing but bread until he reaches his night's lodging; but if he asks for money, he is a false prophet. ⁷ Do not test or examine any prophet who is speaking in [the] Spirit, "for every sin will be forgiven, but this sin will not be forgiven." ⁸ But not everyone who speaks in a spirit is a prophet, except [if] he has the behavior of the LORD. From his behavior, then, the false prophet and the true prophet will be known. ⁹ And no prophet who orders a meal in [the] Spirit will eat of it: otherwise, he is a false prophet. ¹⁰ And every prophet who teaches the truth, if he does not do what he teaches, is a false prophet. ¹¹ But no prophet who has been tried and is genuine, though he enacts a worldly mystery of the Assembly, if he does not teach others to do what he does himself, will be judged by you; for he has his judgment with God, for so also did the prophets of old. ¹² But whoever will say in a spirit "Give me money, or something else," you will not listen to him; but if he tells you to give on behalf of others in want, let none judge him.

CHAPTER 12

¹ Let everyone who "comes in the Name of the LORD" be received; but when you have tested him you will know him, for you will have understanding of true and false. ² If he who comes is a traveler, help him as much as you can, but he will not remain with you more than two days, or, if need be, three. ³ And if he wishes to settle among you and has a craft, let him work for his bread. ⁴ But if he has no craft provide for him according to your understanding, so that no man will live among you in idleness because he is a Christian. ⁵ But if he will not do so, he is making traffic of Christ; beware of such.

CHAPTER 13

¹ But every true prophet who wishes to settle among you is "worthy of his food." ² Likewise, a true teacher is himself worthy, like the workman, of his food. ³ Therefore you will take the first-fruit of the produce of the winepress and of the threshing-floor, and of oxen and sheep, and will give them as the first-fruits to the prophets, for they are your chief priests. ⁴ But if you do not have a prophet, give to the poor. ⁵ If you make bread, take the first-fruits, and give it according to the command. ⁶ Likewise, when you open a jar of wine or oil, give the first-fruits to the prophets. ⁷ Of money also and clothes, and of all your possessions, take the first-fruits, as it seems best to you, and give according to the command.

CHAPTER 14

¹ On the LORD'S Day come together, break bread, and hold Thanksgiving, after confessing your transgressions that your offering may be pure; ² but let none who has a quarrel with his fellow join in your meeting until they are reconciled, that your sacrifice is not defiled. ³ For this is that which was spoken by the LORD, "In every place and time offer Me a pure sacrifice, for I am a great King," says the LORD, "and My Name is wonderful among the heathen."

CHAPTER 15

¹ Therefore, appoint for yourselves overseers and servants worthy of the LORD—meek men, and not lovers of money, and truthful and approved, for they also minister to you the ministry of the prophets and teachers. ² Therefore do not despise them, for they are your honorable men together with the prophets and teachers. ³ And do not reprove one another in wrath, but in peace as you find in the good news, and let none speak with any who has done a wrong to his neighbor, nor let him hear a word from you until he converts. ⁴ But perform your prayers, and kindness, and all your acts as you find in the good news of our Lord.

CHAPTER 16

[1] "Watch" over your life; do not "let your lamps" be quenched; and do not "let your loins" be ungirded; but be "ready," for you have not known "the hour in which our Lord comes." [2] But be frequently gathered together seeking the things which are profitable for your souls, for the whole time of your faith will not profit you except you be found perfect at the last time; [3] for in the last days the false prophets and the corrupters will be multiplied, and the sheep will be turned into wolves, and love will change to hate; [4] for as lawlessness increases they will hate one another, and persecute, and betray, and then the deceiver of the world will appear as a son of God, and he will do signs and wonders, and the earth will be given over into his hands, and he will commit iniquities which have never been since the world began. [5] Then the creation of mankind will come to the fiery trial and "many will be offended" and be lost, but "they who endure" in their faith "will be saved" by the curse itself. [6] And "then will appear the signs" of the truth. First, the sign spread out in [the] sky, then the sign of the sound of the trumpet, and thirdly the resurrection of the dead: [7] but not of all the dead, but as it was said, "The LORD will come and all His holy ones with Him." [8] Then the world will "see the LORD coming on the clouds of Heaven."

REVELATION OF PETER

Otherwise known as the Apocalypse of Peter

The Revelation of Peter was listed in the Muratorian Canon among the two apocalypses (the other being the Revelation of John). It was also supported by Clement of Alexandria. The translation that follows comes from the Ethiopic text. A Greek fragment discovered at Akhmîm differs considerably (cf. chs. 2, 4), but seems less supported—the Ethiopic thought to be older. Two other small Greek fragments have been found (Bodleian and Rainer).

CHAPTER 1

¹ THE SECOND COMING OF CHRIST AND RESURRECTION OF THE DEAD WHO DIED BECAUSE OF THEIR SINS, FOR THAT THEY DID NOT KEEP THE COMMAND OF GOD THEIR CREATOR. ² And he [(Peter)] pondered thereon, that he might perceive the mystery of the Son of God, the merciful and lover of mercy. ³ And when the LORD was seated on the Mount of Olives, His disciples came to Him. ⁴ And we implored and entreated Him separately and pleaded [to] Him, saying to Him, "Declare to us what are the signs of Your coming and of the end of the world, that we may perceive and mark the time of Your coming and instruct them that come after us, to whom we preach the word of Your good news, and whom we set over Your Assembly, that when they hear it they may take heed to themselves and mark the time of Your coming." ⁵ And our Lord answered us, saying, "Take heed that no man deceive you, and that you not be doubters and serve other gods. Many will come in My Name, saying, I am the Christ. Do not believe them, neither draw near to them. For the coming of the Son of God will not be plain, but as the lightning that shines from the east to the west, so I will come on the clouds of Heaven with a great host in My majesty; I will come in My majesty with My cross going before My face; I will come in My majesty—shining sevenfold more than the sun—with all My holy ones, My messengers. And My Father will set a crown on My head, that I may judge the quick and the dead and reward every man according to his works. ⁶ And you, take the likeness thereof from the fig tree: so soon as the shoot thereof has come forth and the twigs grown, the end of the world will come." ⁷ And I, Peter, answered and said to Him, "Interpret to me concerning the fig tree, whereby we will perceive it; for throughout all its days the fig tree sends forth shoots, and every year it brings forth its fruit for its master. What, then, does the allegory of the fig tree mean? We do not know it."

⁸ And the Master answered and said to me, "Do you not understand that the fig tree is the house of Israel? Even as a man that planted a fig tree in his garden, and it brought forth no fruit. And he sought the fruit thereof many years and when he did not find it, he said to the keeper of his garden: Root up this fig tree [so] that it does not make our ground to be unfruitful. And the gardener said to God: [Allow us] to rid it of weeds and dig the ground around it and water it. If then it does not bear fruit, we will immediately remove its roots out of the garden and plant another in place of it. Have you not understood that the fig tree is the house of Israel? Truly I say to you, when the twigs thereof have sprouted forth in the last days, then pretend Christs will come and awake expectation, saying, I am the Christ that has now come into the world. And when they [(Israel)] will perceive the wickedness of their deeds, they will turn away after them and deny him [whom our fathers praised], even the first Christ whom they crucified and therein sinned a great sin. But this deceiver [(the Antichrist)] is not the Christ. And when they reject him, he will slay with the sword, and there will be many martyrs. Then the twigs of the fig tree—that is, the house of Israel—will shoot forth; many will become martyrs at his hand. Enoch and Elijah will be sent to teach them that this is the deceiver which must come into the world and do signs and wonders to deceive. And therefore, they that die by his hand will be martyrs, and will be reckoned among the good and righteous martyrs who have pleased God in their life." ⁹ And He showed me in His right hand the souls of all men, and on the palm of His right hand the image of that which will be accomplished at the last day: and how the righteous and the sinners will be separated, and how they do that are upright in heart, and how the evildoers will be rooted out throughout all ages. We beheld how the sinners wept in great affliction and sorrow, until all that saw it with their eyes wept, whether righteous or messengers, and He Himself also. ¹⁰ And I asked Him and said to him, "Lord, permit me to speak Your word concerning the sinners: It were better for them if they had not been created." And the Savior answered and said to me, "Peter, why do you speak thus, that it were better for them to not have been created? You resist God. You would not have more compassion than He for His image, for He has created them and brought them forth out of not being. Now because you have seen

~ 621 ~

the lamentation which will come on the sinners in the last days, therefore your heart is troubled; but I will show you their works, whereby they have sinned against the Most High. ¹¹ Now behold what will come on them in the last days, when the Day of God and the Day of the decision of the judgment of God comes. From the east to the west all the children of men will be gathered together before My Father that lives forever. And He will command Hades to open its bars of adamant and give up all that is therein. ¹² And He will command the wild beasts and the birds to restore all the flesh that they have devoured, because He wills that men should appear; for nothing perishes before God, and nothing is impossible with Him, because all things are His. ¹³ For all things come to pass on the day of decision, on the Day of Judgment, at the word of God: and as all things were done when He created the world and commanded all that is therein, and it was done—even so will it be in the last days; for all things are possible with God. And, therefore, He says in the Writing: Son of man, prophesy on the several bones and say to the bones: Bone to bone, in joints, sinew, nerves, flesh, and skin, and hair thereon, [[and soul, and spirit]]. ¹⁴ And the great Uriel will give them soul and spirit at the command of God; for God has set him over the rising again of the dead at the Day of Judgment. ¹⁵ Behold and consider the corns of wheat that are sown in the earth. As things dry and men sow them in the earth without soul, so they live again and bear fruit, and the earth restores them as a pledge entrusted to it. ¹⁶ [[And this that dies, that is sown as seed in the earth, and will become alive and be restored to life, is man.]] ¹⁷ How much more will God raise up on the Day of Decision them that believe in Him and are chosen of Him, for whose sake He made the world? And the earth will restore all things on the Day of Decision, for it will also be judged with them, and the Heaven with it. ¹⁸ And at the Day of Judgment this will come on them that have fallen away from faith in God and that have committed sin: floods of fire will be let loose, and darkness and obscurity will come up and clothe and veil the whole world, and the waters will be changed and turned into coals of fire, and all that is in them will burn, and the sea will become fire. Under the sky will be a sharp fire that cannot be quenched, and [it] flows to fulfill the judgment of wrath. And the stars will fly in pieces by flames of fire, as if they had not been created, and the powers [[or expanses]] of the heavens will pass away for lack of water and will be as though they had not been. And the lightnings of the sky will no longer be, and by their enchantment they will frighten the world [[or The sky will turn to lightning and the lightnings thereof will frighten the world. The spirits of the dead

bodies will also be like to them]] and will become fire at the command of God. ¹⁹ And so soon as the whole creation dissolves, the men that are in the east will flee to the west, [and those in the west] to the east; they that are in the south will flee to the north, and they that are in the [north to the] south. And in all places the wrath of a fearful fire will overtake them, and an unquenchable flame driving them will bring them to the judgment of wrath, to the stream of unquenchable fire that flows, flaming with fire, and when the waves thereof part themselves from one another, burning, there will be a great gnashing of teeth among the children of men. ²⁰ Then they will all behold Me coming on a continuous cloud of brightness—and the messengers of God that are with Me. And I will sit on the throne of My glory at the right hand of My heavenly Father; and He will set a crown on My head. And when the nations behold it, they will weep, every nation apart. ²¹ Then He will command them to enter into the river of fire while the works of each of them will stand before them—to every man according to his deeds. As for the chosen ones that have done good, they will come to Me and not see death by the devouring fire. But the unrighteous, the sinners, and the hypocrites will stand in the depths of darkness that will not pass away, and their discipline is the fire, and messengers bring forward their sins and prepare for them a place wherein they will be punished agelong [[everyone according to his transgression]]. ²² Uriel, the messenger of God, will bring forth the souls of those sinners who perished in the flood, and of all that dwelt in all idols, in every molten image, in every [object of] love, and in pictures, and of those that dwelt on all hills, and in stones, and by the wayside, whom men called gods: they will burn them with them in continuous fire; and after that, all of them—with their dwelling places—are destroyed. They will be punished agelong."

CHAPTER 2

¹ "Then men and women will come to the place prepared for them. By their tongues with which they have blasphemed the way of righteousness they will be hanged up. There is spread under them unquenchable fire, and they do not escape it. ² Behold, another place: therein is a pit, great and full. In it are they that have denied righteousness; and messengers of punishment punish them and there they kindle on them the fire of their torment. ³ And again, behold—women: they hang them up by their neck and by their hair; they will cast them into the pit. These are they which plaited their hair, not for good [[or not to make them beautiful]] but to turn them to fornication, that

they might ensnare the souls of men to perdition. And the men that lay with them in fornication will be hung by their loins in that place of fire; and they will say to one another: We did not know that we should come to continuous punishment. ⁴ And the murderers and them that have made common cause with them they will cast into the fire, in a place full of venomous beasts, and they will be tormented without rest, feeling their pains; and their worms will be as many in number as a dark cloud. And the messenger Azrael will bring forth the souls of them that have been slain, and they will behold the torment of them that slew them, and say to one another: Righteousness and justice is the judgment of God. For we heard, but we did not believe, that we should come into this place of continuous judgment. ⁵ And near by this flame will be a great and very deep pit, and into it flows from above all manner of torment, foulness, and issue. And women are swallowed up therein up to their necks and tormented with great pain. These are they that have caused their children to be born untimely and have corrupted the work of God that created them. Over against them will be another place where their children sit alive, and they cry to God. And lightnings go forth from those children and pierce the eyes of them that for fornication's sake have caused their destruction. ⁶ Other men and women will stand above them, naked; and their children stand over against them in a place of delight, and sigh and cry to God because of their parents, saying, These are they that have despised, and cursed, and transgressed Your commands and delivered us to death: they have cursed the messenger that formed us, and have hanged us up, and withheld from us the light which You have given to all creatures. And the milk of their mothers flowing from their breasts will congeal, and from it will come beasts devouring flesh, which will come forth, and turn, and torment them agelong with their husbands, because they forsook the commands of God and slew their children. As for their children, they will be delivered to the messenger Temlakos. And they that slew them will be tormented continuously, for God wills it so. ⁷ Azrael, the messenger of wrath, will bring men and women—the half of their bodies burning—and cast them into a place of darkness, even the Gehenna of men; and a spirit of wrath will punish them with all manner of torment, and a worm that does not sleep will devour their entrails: and these are the persecutors and betrayers of My righteous ones. ⁸ And beside them that are there, will be other men and women, gnawing their tongues; and they will torment them with red-hot iron and burn their eyes. These are they that slander and doubt of My righteousness. Other men

and women whose works were done in deceitfulness will have their lips cut off, and fire enters into their mouth and their entrails. These are the false witnesses [[or these are they that caused the martyrs to die by their lying]]. ⁹ And beside them, in a place near at hand, on the stone will be a pillar of fire, and the pillar is sharper than swords. And there will be men and women clad in rags and filthy garments, and they will be cast thereon, to suffer the judgment of a torment that does not cease: these are they that trusted in their riches and despised the widows and the woman with fatherless children . . . before God. ¹⁰ And into another place hard by, full of filth, they cast men and women up to the knees. These are they that lent money and took usury. ¹¹ And other men and women cast themselves down from a high place and return again and run, and devils drive them. And they put them to the end of their wits, and they cast themselves down. And thus they do continually, and are tormented continuously. These are they which have cut their flesh as [apostles] of a man: and the women that were with them . . . and these are the men that defiled themselves together as women. ¹² And beside them will be a brazier, and beneath them the messenger Azrael will prepare a place of much fire: and all the idols of gold and silver, all idols, the work of men's hands, and the semblances of images of cats and lions, of creeping things and wild beasts, and the men and women that have prepared the images thereof, will be in chains of fire and will be punished because of their error before the idols, and this is their judgment forever. ¹³ And beside them will be other men and women, burning in the fire of the judgment, and their torment is continuous. These are they that have forsaken the command of God and followed the persuasions of devils."

CHAPTER 3

¹ "And there will be another place—very high. [[There will be a furnace and a brazier wherein fire will burn. The fire that will burn will come from one end of the brazier.]] The men and women whose feet slip will go rolling down into a place where fear is. And again, while the fire that is prepared flows, they mount up, and fall down again, and continue to roll down. Thus they will be tormented continuously. These are they that did not honor their father and mother, and of their own accord withheld themselves from them. Therefore, they will be punished continuously. ² Furthermore, the messenger Azrael will bring children and maidens to show them those that are tormented. They will be punished with pains, with hanging up, and with a multitude of wounds which flesh-devouring birds will inflict on them.

These are they that boast themselves in their sins, and do not obey their parents, and do not follow the instruction of their fathers, and do not honor them that are more aged than they. ³ Beside them will be girls clad in darkness for a garment and they will be severely punished, and their flesh will be torn in pieces. These are they that did not keep their virginity until they were given in marriage, and with these torments they will be punished, and will feel them. ⁴ And again, other men and women, gnawing their tongues without ceasing, and being tormented with continuous fire—these are the servants which were not obedient to their masters; and this then is their continuous judgment. ⁵ And hard by this place of torment will be men and women mute and blind, whose raiment is white. They will crowd on one another and fall on coals of unquenchable fire. These are they that give alms and say, We are righteous before God, whereas they have not sought after righteousness. ⁶ Azrael, the messenger of God, will bring them forth out of this fire and establish a judgment of decision. This then is their judgment: a river of fire will flow and all [those in] judgment will be drawn down into the middle of the river. And Uriel will set them there. ⁷ And there are wheels of fire and men and women hung thereon by the strength of the whirling thereof. And they that are in the pit will burn: now these are the sorcerers and sorceresses. Those wheels will be in a decision by fire without number. ⁸ Thereafter the messengers will bring My chosen ones and righteous which are perfect in all uprightness, and bear them in their hands, and clothe them with the raiment of the life that is above. They will see their desire on them that hated them, when he punishes them, and the torment of everyone will be continuous according to his works. ⁹ And all they that are in torment will say with one voice: Have mercy on us, for now we know the judgment of God, which He declared to us formerly, and we did not believe. And the messenger Tatirokos will come and punish them with yet greater torment, and say to them: Now do you convert, when it is no longer the time for conversion, and nothing of life remains. And they will say: The judgment of God is righteous, for we have heard and perceived that His judgment is good; for we are repaid according to our deeds. ¹⁰ Then I will give to My chosen ones and righteous the immersion and the salvation for which they have implored Me, in the field of Acherusa [[or Elysium]]. They will adorn the portion of the righteous with flowers, and I will go . . . I will rejoice with them. I will cause the peoples to enter into My continuous Kingdom and show them that continuous thing [[or life]] whereon I have made them to set their hope, even I and My Father which is in Heaven. ¹¹ I have spoken this to you, Peter, and declared it to you. Therefore, go forth and go to the land [[or city]] of the west. [[And enter into the vineyard which I will tell you of, in order that by the sufferings of the Son who is without sin the deeds of corruption may be sanctified. As for you, you are chosen according to the promise which I have given you. Therefore, spread My good news throughout all the world in peace. Truly men will rejoice: My words will be the source of hope and of life, and suddenly the world will be ravished.]]"

CHAPTER 4

¹ And my Lord Jesus Christ our King said to me, "Let us go to the holy mountain." And His disciples went with Him, praying. And behold, there were two men there, and we could not look on their faces, for a light came from them, shining more than the sun, and their raiment was also shining, and cannot be described, and nothing is sufficient to be compared to them in this world. And the sweetness of them . . . that no mouth is able to utter the beauty of their appearance, for their aspect was astonishing and wonderful. And the other, great, I say, shines in his aspect above crystal. Like the flower of roses is the appearance of the color of his aspect and of his body. Their head was a marvel. And on his [[or their]] shoulders and on their foreheads was a crown of nard woven of fair flowers. As the rainbow in the water [[or in the time of rain]], so was their hair. And such was the comeliness of their countenance, adorned with all manner of ornament. And when we saw them all of a sudden, we marveled. And I drew near to the Lord Jesus Christ and said to Him, "O my Lord, who are these?" And He said to me, "They are Moses and Elijah." And I said to Him, "[What about] Abraham, and Isaac, and Jacob, and the rest of the righteous fathers?" And He showed us a great garden, open, full of fair trees and blessed fruits, and of the fragrance of perfumes. The fragrance thereof was pleasant and came even to us. And thereof I saw much fruit. And my Lord and God Jesus Christ said to me, "Have you seen the companies of the fathers? ² As is their rest, such also is the honor and the glory of them that are persecuted for My righteousness' sake." And I rejoiced, and believed, and understood that which is written in the scroll of my Lord Jesus Christ. And I said to Him, "O my Lord, will You that I make three shelters here, one for You, and one for Moses, and one for Elijah?" And He said to me in wrath: "Satan makes war against you and has veiled your understanding; and the good things of this world prevail against you. Your eyes, therefore, must be opened and your ears unstopped that [you may

perceive] a dwelling place not made with men's hands, which My heavenly Father has made for Me and for the chosen ones." And we beheld it and were full of gladness. [3] And behold, suddenly there came a voice from Heaven, saying, "This is My beloved Son in whom I am well pleased." And then came a great and exceeding white cloud over our heads and carried away our Lord, and Moses, and Elijah. And I trembled and was afraid: and we looked up and the sky opened, and we beheld men in the flesh, and they came and greeted our Lord, and Moses, and Elijah

and went into another heaven. And the word of the Writing was fulfilled: "This is the generation that seeks Him and seeks the face of the God of Jacob." And great fear and commotion was there in Heaven and the messengers pressed on one another that the word of the Writing might be fulfilled which says: "Open the gates, you princes." [4] Thereafter the sky that had been open was shut. [5] And we prayed and went down from the mountain, glorifying God, who has written the names of the righteous in Heaven in the Scroll of Life.

EPISTLE OF BARNABAS

The Epistle of Barnabas, in reality more a treatise than a letter, is preserved completely in the Codex Sinaiticus, where it is located at the end of the New Testament. It is traditionally thought Barnabas from the Acts of the Apostles penned the document, while others ascribe it to a "Barnabas of Alexandria," or some other unidentified early writer.

CHAPTER 1

[1] Greetings, sons and daughters, in the Name of the LORD who loved us, in peace. [2] Exceedingly and abundantly I rejoice over your blessed and glorious spirit for the greatness and richness of God's ordinances toward you—so innate a grace of the gift of the Spirit you have received. [3] For what reason I congratulate myself the more in my hope of salvation, because I truly see in you that the Spirit has been poured out on you from the LORD, who is rich in His bounty, so that the sight of you, for which I longed, amazed me. [4] Being persuaded then of this, and being conscious that since I spoke among you I have much understanding because the LORD has traveled with me in the way of righteousness, I am above all constrained to this, to love you above my own life, because great faith and love dwell in you in the "hope of His life." [5] I have therefore reckoned that, if I make it my care in your behalf to communicate somewhat of that which I received, it will bring me the reward of having ministered to such spirits, and I hasten to send you a short letter in order that your knowledge may be perfected along with your faith. [6] There are then three doctrines of the LORD: "the hope of life" is the beginning and end of our faith; and righteousness is the beginning and end of judgment; love of joy and of gladness is the testimony of the works of righteousness. [7] For the LORD made known to us through the prophets, things past and things present, and has given us the first-fruits of the taste of things to come; and when we see these things coming to pass one by one, as He said, we should make a richer and deeper offering for fear of Him. [8] But I will show you a few things, not as a teacher but as one of yourselves, in which you will rejoice at this present time.

CHAPTER 2

[1] Seeing then that the days are evil, and that the worker of evil is himself in power, we should give heed to ourselves, and seek out the ordinances of the LORD. [2] Fear then, and patience, are the helpers of our faith, and long-suffering and continence are our allies. [3] While then these things remain in holiness toward the LORD, wisdom, prudence, understanding, and knowledge rejoice with them. [4] For He has made plain to us through all the prophets that He needs neither sacrifices, nor burnt-offerings, nor oblations, saying in one place, [5] "What is the multitude of your sacrifices to Me? Says the LORD. I am full of burnt-offerings, and do not desire the fat of lambs and the blood of bulls and goats, not even when you come to appear before Me. For who has required these things at your hands? From now on you will tread My court no longer. If you bring flour, it is vain. Incense is an abomination to Me. I cannot endure your new moons and Sabbaths." [6] These things, then, He abolished in order that the new law of our Lord Jesus Christ, which is without the yoke of necessity, might have its oblation not made by man. [7] And again He says to them, "Did I command your fathers when they came out of the land of Egypt to offer Me burnt-offerings and sacrifices? [8] No, but rather I commanded them this: Let none of you cherish any evil in his heart against his neighbor, and do not love a false oath." [9] We should then understand, if we are not foolish, the loving intention of our Father, for He speaks to us, wishing that we should not err like them, but seek how we may make our offering to Him. [10] To us then He speaks thus: "Sacrifice for the LORD is a broken heart, a smell of sweet savor to the LORD is a heart that glorifies Him that made it." We should, therefore, brothers, carefully inquire concerning our salvation, in order that the evil one may not achieve a deceitful entry into us and hurl us away from our life.

CHAPTER 3

[1] To them He says then again concerning these things, "Why do you fast for Me—says the LORD—so that your voice is heard this day with a cry? This is not the fast which I chose—says the LORD—not a man humbling his soul; [2] nor though you bend your neck as a hoop, and put on sackcloth, and make your bed of ashes, not even so will you call it an acceptable fast." [3] But to us He says, "Behold this is the fast which I chose," says the LORD, "loose every bond of wickedness, set loose the fastenings of harsh agreements, send away the bruised in forgiveness, and tear up every unjust contract; give your bread to the hungry, and if you see a naked man clothe him; bring the homeless into your house, and if you see a humble man, do not despise him—neither you nor any of the household of your seed. [4] Then your light

will break forth as the dawn, and your robes will rise quickly, and your righteousness will go before you, and the glory of God will surround you." [5] "Then you will cry and God will hear you; while you are still speaking He will say, Behold, I am here; if you put away from you bondage, and violence, and the word of murmuring, and give your bread to the poor with a cheerful heart, and pity the soul that is abased." [6] So then, brothers, the long-suffering One foresaw that the people whom He prepared in His beloved should believe in guilelessness, and made all things plain to us beforehand that we should not be shipwrecked by conversion to their law.

CHAPTER 4

[1] We should, then, inquire earnestly into the things which now are, and to seek out those which are able to deliver us. Let us then utterly flee from all the works of lawlessness, lest the works of lawlessness overcome us, and let us hate the error of this present time, that we may be loved in that which is to come. [2] Let us give no freedom to our souls to have power to walk with sinners and wicked men, lest we be made like to them. [3] The final stumbling block is at hand of which it was written, as Enoch says, "For to this end the LORD has cut short the times and the days, that His beloved should hurry and come to His inheritance." [4] And the prophet also says thus: "Ten kingdoms will reign on the earth and there will rise up after them a little king, who will subdue three of the kings under one." [5] Daniel says likewise concerning the same: "And I beheld the fourth beast, wicked, and powerful, and fiercer than all the beasts of the sea, and that ten horns sprang from it, and out of them a little outgrown horn, and that it subdued under one three of the great horns." [6] You should then understand. And this I also ask you, as being one of yourselves, and especially as loving you all above my own life; take heed to yourselves now, and do not be made like to some, heaping up your sins and saying that the covenant is both theirs and ours. [7] It is ours, but in this way they finally lost it when Moses had just received it, for the Writing says: "And Moses was in the mount fasting forty days and forty nights, and he received the covenant from the LORD, tablets of stone written with the finger of the hand of the LORD." [8] But they turned to idols and lost it. For thus says the LORD: "Moses, Moses, go down quickly, for your people, whom you brought forth out of the land of Egypt, have broken the Law." And Moses understood and cast the two tablets out of his hands, and their covenant was broken, in order that the covenant of Jesus the Beloved should be sealed in our hearts in hope of His faith. [9] (And though I wish to write much, I hasten to write in devotion to you, not as a teacher, but as it suits one who loves to leave out nothing of that which we have.) For what reason let us pay heed in the last days, for the whole time of our life and faith will profit us nothing, unless we resist, as suits the sons of God in this present evil time, against the offenses which are to come, that the dark one may have no opportunity of entry. [10] Let us flee from all vanity; let us utterly hate the deeds of the path of wickedness. Do not, by retiring apart, live alone as if you were already made righteous, but come together and seek out the common good. [11] For the Writing says: "Woe to them who are prudent for themselves and understanding in their own sight." Let us be spiritual; let us be a temple consecrated to God; so far as lies in us, let us "exercise ourselves in the fear" of God, and let us strive to keep His commands in order that we may rejoice in His ordinances. [12] The LORD will judge the world "without respect of persons." Each will receive according to his deeds. If he is good his righteousness will lead him; if he is evil the reward of iniquity is before him. [13] Let us never rest as though we were called, and slumber in our sins, lest the wicked ruler gain power over us and thrust us out from the Kingdom of the LORD. [14] And consider this also, my brothers, when you see that after such great signs and wonders were worked in Israel, they were even then finally abandoned; let us take heed lest, as it was written, we are found [as] "many called but few chosen."

CHAPTER 5

[1] For it was for this reason that the LORD endured to deliver up His flesh to corruption, that we should be sanctified by the forgiveness of sin, that is, by His sprinkled blood. [2] For the Writing concerning Him relates partly to Israel, partly to us, and it speaks thus: "He was wounded for our transgressions and bruised for our iniquities, by His stripes we were healed. He was brought as a sheep to the slaughter, and as a lamb silent before its shearer." [3] Therefore we should give great thanks to the LORD that He has given us knowledge of the past, and wisdom for the present, and that we are not without understanding for the future. [4] And the Writing says, "Not unjustly are the nets spread out for the birds." This means that a man deserves to perish who has a knowledge of the way of righteousness, but turns aside into the way of darkness. [5] Moreover, my brothers, if the LORD endured to suffer for our life, though He is the Lord of all the world, to whom God said before the foundation of the world, "Let us make man in our image and likeness," how, then, did He endure to suffer at the hand of man? [6] Learn [this]: the prophets

who received grace from Him prophesied of Him, and He, in order that He "might destroy death," and show forth the resurrection from the dead, because He must necessarily be made "manifest in the flesh," endured [7] in order to fulfill the promise made to the fathers, and Himself prepare for Himself the new people and show while He was on earth that He Himself will raise the dead and judge the risen. [8] Furthermore, while teaching Israel and doing such great signs and wonders, He preached to them and loved them greatly; [9] but when He chose out His own apostles who were to preach His good news, He chose those who were iniquitous above all sin to show that "He came not to call the righteous but sinners": then He manifested Himself as God's Son. [10] For if He had not come in the flesh, men could in no way have been saved by beholding Him, seeing that they do not have the power when they look at the sun to gaze straight at its rays, though it is destined to perish, and is the work of His hands. [11] So then the Son of God came in the flesh for this reason, that He might complete the total of the sins of those who persecuted His prophets to death. [12] For this reason He endured. For God says of the discipline of His flesh that it is from them: "When they will strike their Shepherd, then the sheep of the flock will be destroyed." [13] And He was willing to suffer thus, for it was necessary that He should suffer on a tree, for the prophet says of Him, "Spare My soul from the sword," and "Nail My flesh, for the synagogues of the wicked have risen against Me." [14] And again he says: "Behold, I have given My back to scourges, and My cheeks to strokes, and I have set My face as a solid rock."

CHAPTER 6

[1] Therefore, when He made the command what does He say? "Who is he that comes into court with Me? Let him oppose Me; or, who is he that seeks justice against Me? Let him draw near to the LORD's servant. [2] Woe to you, for you will all wax old as a garment and the moth will eat you up." And again, the prophet says that He was placed as a strong stone for crushing, "Behold, I will place for the foundations of Zion a precious stone, chosen out, a chief cornerstone, honorable." [3] Then what does he say? "And he that hopes on it will live continuously." Is then our hope on a stone? God forbid. But he means that the LORD placed His flesh in strength. For he says, "And he placed me as a solid rock." [4] And again the prophet says, "The stone which the builders rejected, this has become the head of the corner," and again he says, "This is the great and wonderful day which the LORD made." [5] I write to you more simply that you may understand: I am devoted to your love. [6] What then

does the prophet say again? "The synagogue of the sinners surrounded Me, they surrounded Me as bees around the honeycomb," and "They cast lots for My clothing." [7] Therefore, since He was destined to be manifest and to suffer in the flesh, His passion was foretold. For the prophet says concerning Israel, "Woe to their soul, for they have plotted an evil plot against themselves, saying, Let us bind the Just One, for He is unprofitable to us." [8] What does the other prophet, Moses, say to them? "Behold, thus says the LORD God, enter into the good land which the LORD swore that He would give to Abraham, Isaac, and Jacob, and inherit it, a land flowing with milk and honey." [9] But learn what knowledge says. Hope, it says, on that Jesus who will be manifested to you in the flesh. For man is earth which suffers, for the creation of Adam was from the face of the earth. [10] What then is the meaning of "into the good land, a land flowing with milk and honey"? Blessed is our Lord, brothers, who has placed in us wisdom and understanding of His secrets. For the prophet speaks an allegory of the LORD: "Who will understand except he who is wise, and learned, and a lover of his Lord?" [11] Since then He made us new by the forgiveness of sins, He made us another type, that we should have the soul of children, as though He were creating us afresh. [12] For it is concerning us that the Writing says that He says to the Son, "Let Us make man after Our image and likeness, and let them rule the beasts of the earth, and the birds of the heavens, and the fishes of the sea." And the LORD said, when He saw our fair creation, "Increase, and multiply, and fill the earth"; these things were spoken to the Son. [13] Again I will show you how He speaks to us. In the last days He made a second creation; and the LORD says, "See, I make the last things as the first." To this, then, the prophet referred when he proclaimed, "Enter into a land flowing with milk and honey, and rule over it." [14] See then, we have been created afresh, as He says again in another prophet, "See," says the LORD, "I will take out from them" (that is those whom the Spirit of the LORD foresaw) "the hearts of stone and I will put in hearts of flesh." Because He Himself was going to be manifest in the flesh and to dwell among us. [15] For, my brothers, the habitation of our hearts is a shrine holy to the LORD. [16] For the LORD says again, "And with which will I appear before the LORD My God and be glorified?" He says, "I will confess to You in the assembly of My brothers, and will sing to You in the midst of the assembly of holy ones." We then are they whom He brought into the good land. [17] What then is the milk and the honey? Because a child is first nourished with honey, and afterward with milk. Thus, therefore we also, being nourished on the faith of the promise and by the word, will live and possess the earth. [18] And we have said above, "And let them increase, and multiply, and rule over the fishes." Who then is it who is now able to rule over beasts, or fishes, or the birds of the heavens? For we should understand that to rule implies authority, so that one may give commands and have domination. [19] If, then, this does not happen at present, He has told us the time when it will—when we ourselves have also been made perfect as heirs of the covenant of the LORD.

CHAPTER 7

[1] Therefore understand, children of gladness, that the good Lord made all things plain beforehand to us, that we should know Him to whom we should give thanks and praise for everything. [2] If then the Son of God, though He was the LORD and was "destined to judge the living and the dead," suffered in order that His wounding might make us alive, let us believe that the Son of God could not suffer except for our sakes. [3] But moreover, when He was crucified "He was given vinegar and gall to drink." Listen how the priests of the temple foretold this. The command was written: "Whoever does not keep the fast will die the death," and the LORD commanded this because He Himself was going to offer the vessel of the Spirit as a sacrifice for our sins, in order that the type established in Isaac, who was offered on the altar, might be fulfilled. [4] What then does He say in the Prophet[s]? "And let them eat of the goat which is offered in the fast for all their sins." Attend carefully, "and let all the priests alone eat the entrails unwashed with vinegar." [5] Why? Because you are going "to give to Me gall and vinegar to drink" when I am on the point of offering My flesh for My new people, therefore you alone will eat, while the people fast and mourn in sackcloth and ashes, to show that He must suffer for them. [6] Note what was commanded: "Take two goats, attractive and alike, and offer them, and let the priest take the one as a burnt-offering for sins." [7] But what are they to do with the other? "The other," He says, "is accursed." Notice how the type of Jesus is manifested: [8] "And you all spit on it, and goad it, and bind the scarlet wool around its head, and so let it be cast into the desert." And when it is so done, he who takes the goat into the wilderness drives it forth, and takes away the wool, and puts it on a shrub which is called Rachel, of which we are accustomed to eat the shoots when we find them in the country: thus of Rachel alone is the fruit sweet. [9] What does this mean? Listen: "the first goat is for the altar, but the other is accursed," and note that the one that is accursed is crowned, because then "they will see Him" on that day with the long scarlet robe "down to the feet" on His body, and they will say, "Is this not He whom we once crucified, and rejected, and pierced, and spat on? Of a truth it was He who then said that He was the Son of God." [10] But how is He like to the goat? For this reason: "the goats will be alike, beautiful, and a pair," in order that when they see Him come at that time they may be astonished at the likeness of the goat. See then the type of Jesus destined to suffer. [11] But why is it that they put the wool in the middle of the thorns? It is a type of Jesus placed in the Assembly, because whoever wishes to take away the scarlet wool must suffer much because the thorns are terrible, and he can gain it only through pain. Thus He says, "those who will see Me, and attain to My Kingdom, must lay hold of Me through pain and suffering."

CHAPTER 8

[1] But what do you think that it means, that the commandment has been given to Israel that the men in whom sin is complete offer a heifer, and slay it, and burn it, and that boys then take the ashes, and put them into vessels, and bind scarlet wool on sticks (see again the type of the Cross and the scarlet wool) and hyssop, and that the boys all sprinkle the people thus, one by one, in order that they all be purified from their sins? [2] Observe how plainly He speaks to you: the calf is Jesus; the sinful men offering it are those who brought Him to be slain. Then there are no longer men, no longer the glory of sinners. [3] The boys who sprinkle are they who preached to us the forgiveness of sins, and the purification of the heart, to whom He gave the power of the good news to preach, and there are twelve as a testimony to the tribes, because there are twelve tribes of Israel. [4] But why are there three boys who sprinkle? As a testimony to Abraham, Isaac, and Jacob, for these are great before God. [5] And why was the wool put on the wood? Because the Kingdom of Jesus is on the wood, and because those who hope on Him will live forever. [6] But why are the wool and the hyssop together? Because in His Kingdom there will be evil and foul days, in which we will be saved, for he also who has pain in his flesh is cured by the foulness of the hyssop. [7] And for this reason, the things which were thus done are plain to us, but obscure to them, because they did not hear the voice of [the] LORD.

CHAPTER 9

[1] For He speaks again concerning the ears, how He circumcised our hearts; for the LORD says in the Prophet[s]: "In the hearing of the ear they obey Me." And again He says, "They who are far off will hear

clearly, they will know the things that I have done," and "Circumcise your hearts, says the LORD." [2] And again He says, "Hear, O Israel, thus says the LORD your God," and again the Spirit of the LORD prophesies, "Who is he that will live continuously? Let him hear the voice of My servant." [3] And again He says, "Hear, O Heaven, and give ear, O earth, for the LORD has spoken these things for a testimony." And again He says, "Hear the word of the LORD, you rulers of this people." And again He says, "Hear, O children, a voice of one crying in the wilderness." So then, He circumcised our hearing in order that we should hear the word and believe. [4] But moreover, the circumcision in which they trusted has been abolished. For He declared that circumcision was not of the flesh, but they erred because an evil messenger was misleading them. [5] He says to them, "Thus says the LORD your God" (here I find a command), "Do not sow among thorns; be circumcised to your Lord." And what does He say? "Circumcise the hardness of your heart, and do not stiffen your neck." Receive it again: "Behold, says the LORD, all the heathen are uncircumcised in the foreskin, but this people is uncircumcised in heart." [6] But will you say [that] the people has surely received circumcision as a seal? Yes, but every Syrian, and Arab, and all priests of the idols have been circumcised; are then these also within their covenant? Indeed, even the Egyptians belong to the circumcision. [7] Learn fully then, children of love, concerning all things, for Abraham, who first circumcised, did so looking forward in the Spirit to Jesus, and had received the doctrines of three letters. [8] For it says, "And Abraham circumcised from his household eighteen men and three hundred." What then was the knowledge that was given to him? Notice that he first mentions the eighteen, and after a pause the three hundred. The eighteen is I [(ten)] and H [(eight)]—you have Jesus—and because the Cross was destined to have grace in the T, he says, "and three hundred." So he indicates Jesus in the two letters and the Cross in the other. [9] He knows this who placed the gift of His teaching in our hearts. No one has heard a more excellent lesson from me, but I know that you are worthy.

CHAPTER 10

[1] Now, in that Moses said, "You will not eat swine, nor an eagle, nor a hawk, nor a crow, nor any fish which has no scales on itself," he included three doctrines in his understanding. [2] Moreover, He says to them in Deuteronomy, "And I will make a covenant of My ordinances with this people." So then the ordinance of God is not abstinence from eating, but Moses spoke in the Spirit. [3] He mentioned the swine

for this reason: you will not consort; He means with men who are like swine; that is to say, when they have plenty, they forget the LORD, but when they are in want, they recognize the LORD, just as the swine when it eats does not know its master, but when it is hungry it cries out, and after receiving food is again silent. [4] "Neither will you eat the eagle, nor the hawk, nor the kite, nor the crow." You will not, He means, join yourself or make yourself like to such men, as do not know how to gain their food by their labor and sweat, but plunder other people's property in their iniquity, and lay wait for it, though they seem to walk in innocence, and look around to see whom they may plunder in their covetousness, just as these birds alone provide no food for themselves, but sit idle, and seek how they may devour the flesh of others, and become pernicious in their iniquity. [5] "You will not eat," He says, "the eel, nor the mollusk, nor the cuttlefish." You will not, he means, consort with or become like such men who are utterly ungodly and who are already condemned to death, just as these fish alone are accursed, and float in the deep water, not swimming like the others, but living on the ground at the bottom of the sea. [6] Moreover, "You will not," he says, "eat the hare." Why? "You will not be a corrupter of boys, nor like such." Because the hare multiplies, year by year, the places of its conception; for as many years as it lives so many it has. [7] Moreover, "You will not eat the hyena." He means, "You will not be an adulterer, nor a corrupter, nor be like to them that are such." Why? Because that animal annually changes its sex, and is at one time male, and at another female. [8] Moreover, he has rightly detested the weasel. For he means, "You will not be like to those whom we hear of as committing wickedness with the mouth, on account of their uncleanness; nor will you be joined to those impure women who commit iniquity with the mouth. For this animal conceives by the mouth." [9] Moses received three doctrines concerning food and thus spoke of them in the Spirit; but they received them as really referring to food, owing to the lust of their flesh. [10] But David received knowledge concerning the same three doctrines, and says: "Blessed is the man who has not gone in the counsel of the ungodly" as the fishes go in darkness in the deep waters, "and has not stood in the way of sinners" like those who seem to fear the LORD, but sin like the swine, "and has not sat in the seat of the scorners" like the birds who sit and wait for their prey. Grasp fully the doctrines concerning food. [11] Moses says again, "Eat of every animal that is cloven-hoofed and ruminant." What does he mean? That he who receives food knows Him who feeds him, and rests on Him and seems to rejoice. He spoke well with regard to the command. What then does He mean? Consort with those who fear the LORD, with those who meditate in their heart on the meaning of the word which they have received, with those who speak of and observe the ordinances of the LORD, with those who know that meditation is a work of gladness, and who ruminate on the word of the LORD. But what does "the cloven-hoofed" mean? That the righteous [man] both walks in this world and looks forward to the holy age. See how well Moses legislated. [12] But how was it possible for them to understand or comprehend these things? But we, having a righteous understanding of them, announce the commands as the LORD wished. For this reason, He circumcised our hearing and our hearts that we should comprehend these things.

CHAPTER 11

[1] But let us inquire if the LORD took pains to foretell the water of immersion and the Cross. Concerning the water, it has been written with regard to Israel that they will not receive the immersion that brings the forgiveness of sins, but will build for themselves. [2] For the prophet says, "Be astonished O Heaven, and let the earth tremble the more at this, that this people has committed two evils: they have deserted Me, the spring of life, and they have dug for themselves a cistern of death. [3] Is My holy mountain, Sinai, a desert rock? For you will be as the fledgling birds, fluttering about when they are taken away from the nest." [4] And again the prophet says, "I will go before you and I will make mountains level, and I will break gates of brass, and I will shatter bars of iron, and I will give you treasures of darkness, secret, invisible, that they may know that I am the LORD God." [5] And, "You will dwell in a lofty cave of a strong rock." And, "His water is sure; you will see the King in His glory, and your soul will meditate on the fear of the LORD." [6] And again He says in another prophet, "And he who does these things will be as the tree, which is planted at the partings of the waters, which will give its fruit in its season, and its leaf will not fade, and all things, whatever he does, will prosper. [7] It is not so with the wicked, it is not so; but they are even as the chaff which the wind drives away from the face of the earth. Therefore, the wicked will not rise up in judgment, nor sinners in the counsel of the righteous, for the LORD knows the way of the righteous, and the way of the ungodly will perish." [8] Mark how He described the water and the Cross together. For He means this: blessed are those who hoped on the Cross and descended into the water. For He speaks of their reward "in his season"; "at that time," He says, "I will repay." But now when He says, "Their leaves will not fade," He means that every word which will come forth from your mouth in faith and love, will be for conversion and hope for many. [9] And again another prophet says, "And the land of Jacob was praised above every land." He means to say that He is glorifying the vessel of His Spirit. [10] What does He say next? "And there was a river flowing on the right hand, and beautiful trees grew out of it, and whoever will eat of them will live continuously." [11] He means to say that we go down into the water full of sins and foulness, and we come up bearing the fruit of fear in our hearts, and having hope on Jesus in the Spirit. "And whoever will eat of them will live continuously." He means that whoever hears and believes these things spoken will live continuously.

CHAPTER 12

[1] Similarly, again, He describes the Cross in another prophet, who says, "And when will all these things be accomplished? Says the LORD. When the tree will fall and rise, and when blood will flow from the tree." Here again you have a reference to the Cross, and to Him who should he crucified. [2] And He says again to Moses, when Israel was assailed by strangers, and in order to remind those who were assailed that they were delivered to death by reason of their sins—the Spirit speaks to the heart of Moses to make a representation of the Cross, and of Him who should suffer, because, he says, unless they put their trust in Him, they will suffer war continuously. Therefore, Moses placed one shield on another in the midst of the fight, and standing there, raised above them all, kept stretching out his hands, and so Israel again began to be victorious: then, whenever he let them drop, they began to perish. [3] Why? That they may know that they cannot be saved if they do not hope on Him. [4] And again He says in another prophet, "I stretched out My hands the whole day to a disobedient people and one that refuses My righteous way." [5] Again Moses makes a representation of Jesus, showing that He must suffer, and will Himself give life, though they will believe that He has been put to death, by the sign given when Israel was falling (for the LORD made every serpent bite them, and they were perishing, for the fall took place in Eve through the serpent), in order to convince them that they will be delivered over to the affliction of death because of their transgression. [6] Moreover, though Moses commanded them: "You will have neither graven nor molten image for your God," yet he makes one himself to show a type of Jesus. Therefore, Moses makes a graven serpent, and places it in honor and calls the people by a proclamation. [7] So they came together and implored Moses that he would offer

prayer on their behalf for their healing. But Moses said to them, "Whenever one of you," he said, "is bitten, let him come to the serpent that is placed on the tree, and let him hope, in faith that it, though dead, is able to give life, and he will immediately be saved." And they did so. In this also you have again the glory of Jesus, for all things are in Him and for Him. [8] Again, why does Moses say to Jesus [(Joshua)], the son of Nun, when he gives him, prophet as he is, this name, that the whole people should listen to him alone? Because the Father was revealing everything concerning His Son Jesus. [9] Moses therefore says to Jesus, the son of Nun, after giving him this name, when he sent him to spy out the land, "Take a scroll in your hands and write what the LORD says, that the Son of God will tear up the whole house of Amalek by the roots in the last day." [10] See again Jesus, not as Son of Man, but as Son of God, but manifested in a type in the flesh. Therefore, since they are going to say that the Christ is David's son, David himself prophesies, fearing and understanding the error of the sinners, "The LORD said to my Lord, Sit on My right hand until I make Your enemies Your footstool." [11] And again Isaiah speaks thus, "The LORD said to Christ my Lord, whose right hand I held, that the nations should obey before Him, and I will shatter the strength of kings." See how "David calls Him Lord" and does not say "son."

CHAPTER 13

[1] Now let us see whether this people or the former people is the heir, and whether the covenant is for us or for them. [2] Hear then what the Writing says concerning the people: "And Isaac prayed concerning his wife Rebecca, because she was barren, and she conceived. Then Rebecca went forth to inquire of the LORD and the LORD said to her: Two nations are in your womb, and two peoples in your belly, and one people will overcome a people, and the greater will serve the less." [3] You should understand who Isaac is and who Rebecca is, and of whom He has shown that this people is greater than that people. [4] And in another prophecy, Jacob speaks more plainly to his son Joseph, saying, "Behold, the LORD has not deprived me of your presence; bring me your sons, that I may bless them." [5] And he brought Ephraim and Manasseh, and wished that Manasseh should be blessed, because he was the elder; for Joseph brought him to the right hand of his father Jacob. But Jacob saw in the Spirit a type of the people of the future. And what does He say? "And Jacob crossed his hands and placed his right hand on the head of Ephraim, the second and younger son, and blessed him; and Joseph said to Jacob, Change your right hand to the head of Manasseh, for he is my firstborn son. And Jacob said to Joseph, I know it, my child, I know it; but the greater will serve the less, and this one will indeed be blessed." [6] See who it is of whom He ordained that this people is the first and heir of the covenant. [7] If then, besides this, He also remembered it in the case of Abraham, we reach the perfection of our knowledge. What then does He say to Abraham, when he alone was faithful, and it was counted to him for righteousness? "Behold, I have made you, Abraham, the father of the nations who believe in God in uncircumcision."

CHAPTER 14

[1] So it is. But let us see whether the covenant which He swore to the fathers to give to the people— whether He has given it. He has given it. But they were not worthy to receive it because of their sins. [2] For the prophet says, "And Moses was fasting on Mount Sinai, to receive the covenant of the LORD for the people, forty days and forty nights. And Moses received from the LORD the two tablets, written by the finger of the hand of the LORD in the Spirit"; and Moses took them, and carried them down to give them to the people. [3] And the LORD said to Moses, "Moses, Moses, go down quickly, for your people whom you brought out of the land of Egypt have broken the Law. And Moses perceived that they had again made themselves molten images, and he cast them out of his hands, and the tablets of the covenant of the LORD were broken." [4] Moses received it, but they were not worthy. But learn how we received it. Moses received it when he was a servant, but the LORD Himself gave it to us, as the people of the inheritance, by suffering for our sakes. [5] And it was made manifest both that the tale of their sins should be completed in their sins, and that we through Jesus, the Lord who inherits the covenant, should receive it, for He was prepared for this purpose, that when He appeared He might redeem our hearts from darkness, which were already paid over to death, and given over to the iniquity of error, and by His word might make a covenant with us. [6] For it is written that the Father prescribes on Him that He should redeem us from darkness and prepare a holy people for Himself. [7] The prophet therefore says, "I, the LORD your God, called you in righteousness, and I will hold your hands, and I will give you strength, and I have given you for a covenant of the people, for a light to the nations, to open the eyes of the blind, and to bring forth from their chains those that are bound and those that sit in darkness out of the prison-house." We know then from where we have been redeemed. [8] Again the prophet says, "Behold, I have made you a light for the

nations, to be for salvation to the ends of the earth, thus says the LORD, the God who redeemed you." [9] And again the prophet says, "The Spirit of the LORD is on Me, because He anointed Me to preach the good news of grace to the humble; He sent Me to heal the brokenhearted, to proclaim delivery to the captives, and sight to the blind, to announce a year acceptable to the LORD, and a day of repayment, to comfort all who mourn."

CHAPTER 15

[1] Furthermore, it was written concerning the Sabbath in the ten words which He spoke on Mount Sinai face to face with Moses: "Sanctify also the Sabbath of the LORD with pure hands and a pure heart." [2] And in another place He says, "If My sons keep the Sabbath, then I will bestow My mercy on them." [3] He speaks of the Sabbath at the beginning of the Creation, "And God made in six days the works of His hands and on the seventh day He made an end, and rested in it and sanctified it." [4] Notice, children, what is the meaning of "He made an end in six days"? He means this: that the LORD will make an end of everything in six thousand years, for a day with Him means one thousand years. And He Himself is my witness when He says, "Behold, the Day of the LORD will be as one thousand years." So then, children, in six days (that is, in six thousand years) everything will be completed. [5] "And He rested on the seventh day." This means, when His Son comes, He will destroy the time of the wicked one, and will judge the godless, and will change the sun, and the moon, and the stars, and then He will truly rest on the seventh day. [6] Furthermore He says, "You will sanctify it with clean hands and a pure heart." If, then, anyone has at present the power to keep holy the day which God made holy, by being pure in heart, we are altogether deceived. [7] See that we will indeed keep it holy at that time, when we enjoy true rest, when we will be able to do so because we have been made righteous ourselves and have received the promise, when there is no more sin, but all things have been made new by the LORD: then we will be able to keep it holy because we ourselves have first been made holy. [8] Furthermore He says to them, "Your new moons and the Sabbaths I cannot bear with." Do you see what He means? "The present Sabbaths are not acceptable to Me, but that which I have made, in which I will give rest to all things and make the beginning of an eighth day, that is the beginning of another world." [9] For what reason we also celebrate with gladness the eighth day in which Jesus also rose from the dead, and was made manifest, and ascended into Heaven.

CHAPTER 16

[1] I will also speak with you concerning the temple and show how the wretched men erred by putting their hope on the building, and not on the God who made them, and is the true house of God. [2] For they consecrated him in the temple almost like the heathen. But learn how the LORD speaks, in bringing it to nothing, "Who has measured the Heaven with a span, or the earth with his outstretched hand? Have not I? Says the LORD. Heaven is My throne, and the earth is My footstool, what house will you build for Me, or what is the place of My rest?" You know that their hope was vain. [3] Furthermore, He says again, "Behold, they who destroyed this temple will themselves build it." [4] That is happening now. For owing to the war, it was destroyed by the enemy; at present, even the servants of the enemy will build it up again. [5] Again, it was made manifest that the city, and the temple, and the people of Israel were to be delivered up. For the Writing says: "And it will come to pass in the last days that the LORD will deliver the sheep of His pasture, and the sheepfold, and their tower to destruction." And it took place according to what the LORD said. [6] But let us inquire if a temple of God exists. Yes, it exists, where He Himself said that He makes and perfects it. For it is written: "And it will come to pass when the week is ended that a temple of God will be built gloriously in the Name of the LORD." [7] I find then that a temple exists. Learn then how it will be built in the Name of the LORD. Before we believed in God the habitation of our heart was corrupt and weak, like a temple really built with hands, because it was full of idolatry, and was the house of demons through doing things which were contrary to God. [8] "But it will be built in the Name of the LORD." Now give heed, in order that the temple of the LORD may be built gloriously. Learn in what way. When we received the forgiveness of sins, and put our hope on the Name, we became new, being created again from the beginning; for what reason God truly dwells in us, in the habitation which we are. [9] How? His word of faith, the calling of His promise, the wisdom of the ordinances, the commands of the teaching, Himself prophesying in us, Himself dwelling in us, by opening the door of the temple (that is the mouth) to us, giving conversion to us, and thus He leads us, who have been enslaved to death into the incorruptible temple. [10] For he who desires to be saved does not look at the man, but at Him who dwells and speaks in him, and is amazed at Him, for he has never either heard him speak such words with his mouth, nor has he himself ever desired to hear them. This is a spiritual temple being built for the LORD.

CHAPTER 17

[1] So far as possibility and simplicity allow an explanation to be given to you, my soul hopes that none of the things which are necessary for salvation

EPISTLE OF BARNABAS

have been omitted, according to my desire. ² For if I write to you concerning things present or things to come, you will not understand because they are hid in allegories. This then suffices.

CHAPTER 18

¹ Now let us pass on to another lesson and teaching. There are two ways of teaching and power: one of light and one of darkness. And there is a great difference between the two ways. For light-bringing messengers of God are set over the one, but messengers of Satan over the other. ² And the one is Lord from age and to age, and the other is the ruler of the present time of iniquity.

CHAPTER 19

¹ The way of light is this: if any man desires to journey to the appointed place, let him be zealous in his works. Therefore the knowledge given to us of this kind that we may walk in it is as follows: ² you will love your Maker, you will fear your Creator, you will glorify Him who redeemed you from death, you will be simple in heart, and rich in [the] Spirit; you will not join yourself to those who walk in the way of death, you will hate all that is not pleasing to God, you will hate all hypocrisy; you will not desert the commands of the LORD. ³ You will not exalt yourself, but will be humble-minded in all things; you will not take glory to yourself. You will form no evil plan against your neighbor, you will not let your soul be divisive. ⁴ You will not commit fornication, you will not commit adultery, you will not commit sodomy. You will not let the word of God depart from you among the impurity of any men. You will not respect persons in the reproving of transgression. You will be meek, you will be quiet, you will fear the words which you have heard. You will not bear malice against your brother. ⁵ You will not be in two minds whether it will be or not. "You will not take the Name of the LORD in vain." You will love your neighbor more than your own life. You will not procure abortion, you will not commit infanticide. You will not withhold your hand from your son or from your daughter, but will teach them the fear of God from their youth up. ⁶ You will not covet your neighbor's goods, you will not be greedy. You will not be joined in soul with the haughty, but will converse with humble and righteous men. You will receive the trials that befall you as good, knowing that nothing happens without God. ⁷ You will not be double-minded or talkative. You will obey your masters as a type of God in modesty and fear; you will not command in bitterness your slave or handmaid who hope on the same God, lest they cease to fear the God who is over you both; for He did not come to call men with respect of persons, but those whom the Spirit prepared. ⁸ You will share all things with your neighbor and will not say that they are your own property; for if you are

sharers in that which is incorruptible, how much more in that which is corruptible? You will not be forward to speak, for the mouth is a snare of death. So far as you can, you will keep your soul pure. ⁹ Do not be one who stretches out the hands to take and shuts them when it comes to giving. You will love "as the apple of your eye" all who speak the word of the LORD to you. ¹⁰ You will remember the Day of Judgment day and night, and you will seek each day the society of the holy ones, either laboring by speech, and going out to exhort, and striving to save souls by the word, or working with your hands for the ransom of your sins. ¹¹ You will not hesitate to give, and when you give you will not grumble, but you will know who the good paymaster of the reward is. "You will keep the precepts" which you have received, "adding nothing and taking nothing away." You will utterly hate evil. "You will give righteous judgment." ¹² You will not cause quarrels, but will bring together and reconcile those that strive. You will confess your sins. You will not go yourself to prayer with an evil conscience. This is the way of light.

CHAPTER 20

¹ But the way of the dark one is crooked and full of cursing, for it is the way of continuous death with punishment, and in it are the things that destroy their soul: idolatry, divisiveness, arrogance of power, hypocrisy, double-heartedness, adultery, murder, robbery, pride, transgression, fraud, malice, self-sufficiency, enchantments, magic, covetousness, the lack of the fear of God; ² persecutors of the good, haters of the truth, lovers of lies, not knowing the reward of righteousness, who "do not cleave to the good," nor to righteous judgment, who do not attend to the cause of the widow and orphan, spending wakeful nights not in the fear of God, but in the pursuit of vice, from whom meekness and patience are far and distant, "loving vanity, seeking rewards," without pity for the poor, not working for him who is oppressed with toil, prone to evil speaking, without knowledge of their Maker, murderers of children, corrupters of God's creation, turning away the needy, oppressing the afflicted, advocates of the rich, unjust judges of the poor, altogether sinful.

CHAPTER 21

¹ It is therefore good that he who has learned the ordinances of the LORD—as many as have been written—should walk in them. For he who does these things will be glorified in the Kingdom of God, and he who chooses the others will perish with his works. For this reason, there is a resurrection; for this reason, there is a repayment. ² I implore those who are in high positions: if you will receive any counsel of my goodwill, have among yourselves those to whom you may do good; do not fail. ³ The day is at hand when all things will perish with the evil one; "The LORD

and His reward is at hand." [4] I implore you again and again: be good lawgivers to each other, remain faithful counselors of each other, remove all hypocrisy from yourselves. [5] Now may God, who is the Lord over all the world, give you wisdom, understanding, prudence, knowledge of His ordinances, patience. [6] And be taught of God, seeking out what the LORD requires from you, and see that you be found faithful in the Day of Judgment. [7] If there is any memory of good, meditate on these things and remember me, that my desire and my watchfulness may find some good end. I implore you, asking it of your favor. [8] While the fair vessel is with you, do not fail in any of them, but seek these things diligently, and fulfill every command; for these things are worthy. [9] For what reason I was the more zealous to write to you of my ability, to give you gladness. May you gain salvation, children of love and peace. The Lord of glory and of all grace be with your spirit.

3 CORINTHIANS

The Epistle of the Corinthians to Paul, and his purported response, are here in the LSV referred to as "3 Corinthians." These letters are considered by most to have been written in the 2nd century, probably very early, as a pseudonymous response to the burgeoning Gnostic heresies. The later Acts of Paul included 3 Corinthians. 3 Corinthians was included in Syrian and Armenian canons.

[THEY] PRAYED THAT A MESSENGER BE SENT TO PHILIPPI. FOR THE CORINTHIANS WERE IN GREAT TROUBLE CONCERNING PAUL, THAT HE WOULD DEPART OUT OF THE WORLD BEFORE IT WAS TIME. FOR THERE WERE CERTAIN MEN WHO CAME TO CORINTH, SIMON AND CLEOBIUS, SAYING [THAT] THERE IS NO RESURRECTION OF THE FLESH, BUT THAT OF THE SPIRIT ONLY; AND THAT THE BODY OF MAN IS NOT THE CREATION OF GOD; AND ALSO CONCERNING THE WORLD, THAT GOD DID NOT CREATE IT, AND THAT GOD DOES NOT KNOW THE WORLD, AND THAT JESUS CHRIST WAS NOT CRUCIFIED, BUT IT WAS [ONLY] AN APPEARANCE, AND THAT LIE, [SAYING HE] WAS NOT BORN OF MARY, NOR OF THE SEED OF DAVID. AND IN A WORD, THERE WERE MANY THINGS WHICH THEY HAD TAUGHT IN CORINTH, DECEIVING MANY OTHER MEN, [AND DECEIVING] THEMSELVES. WHEN THEREFORE THE CORINTHIANS HEARD THAT PAUL WAS AT PHILIPPI, THEY SENT A LETTER TO PAUL, TO MACEDONIA, BY THE DEACONS THREPTUS AND EUTYCHUS. AND THE LETTER WAS AFTER THIS MANNER:

CHAPTER 1

¹ Stephanus and the elders that are with him, even Daphnus, and Eubulus, and Theophilus, and Zenon, to Paul their perpetual brother: greetings in the LORD. ² There have come to Corinth two men, Simon and Cleobius, which are overthrowing the faith of many with evil words, ³ which you [must] prove and examine: ⁴ for we have never heard such words from you nor from the other apostles: ⁵ but all that we have received from you or from them, that do we hold fast. ⁶ Since therefore the LORD has had mercy on us, that while you are still in the flesh we may hear these things again from you; ⁷ if it be possible, either come to us or write to us. ⁸ For we believe, according as it has been revealed to Theonoe, that the LORD has delivered you out of the hand of the lawless one. ⁹ Now the things which these men say and teach are these: ¹⁰ They say that we must not use the prophets, ¹¹ and that God is not almighty, ¹² and that there will be no resurrection of the flesh, ¹³ and that man was not made by God, ¹⁴ and that Christ has not come in the flesh, neither was born of Mary, ¹⁵ and that the world is not of God, but of the messengers. ¹⁶ Therefore, brother, please use all diligence to come to us, that the assembly of the Corinthians may remain without offense, and the madness of these men may be made plain. Farewell—always in the LORD.

CHAPTER 2

¹ The deacons Threptus and Eutychus brought the letter to Philippi, ² so that Paul received it, being in bonds because of Stratonice the wife of Apollophanes, and he forgot his bonds, and was severely afflicted, ³ and cried out, saying, "It were better for me to die and to be with the LORD, than to continue in the flesh and to hear such things and the calamities of false doctrine, so that trouble comes on trouble. ⁴ And over and above this so great affliction I am in bonds and behold these evils whereby the devices of Satan are accomplished." ⁵ Paul therefore, in great affliction, wrote a letter, answering thus:

CHAPTER 3

¹ Paul, a prisoner of Jesus Christ, to the brothers which are in Corinth: greetings. ² Being in the midst of many tribulations, I do not marvel if the teachings of the evil one run abroad apace. ³ For my Lord Jesus Christ will hasten His coming and will set at nothing them that falsify His words. ⁴ For I delivered to you in the beginning the things which I received of the holy apostles which were before me, who were at all times with Jesus Christ: ⁵ namely, that our Lord Jesus Christ was born of Mary which is of the seed of David according to the flesh, the Holy Spirit being sent forth from Heaven from the Father to her by the messenger Gabriel, ⁶ that He might come down into this world and redeem all flesh by His flesh, and raise us up from the dead in the flesh, like as He has shown to us in Himself for an example. ⁷ And because man was formed by His Father, ⁸ therefore he was sought when he was lost, that he might be restored by adoption. ⁹ For to this end God Almighty, who made the heavens and earth, first sent the prophets to the Jews, that they might be drawn away from their sins. ¹⁰ For He designed to save the house of Israel: therefore, He conferred a portion of the Spirit of Christ on the prophets and sent them to the Jews first, and they proclaimed the true worship of God for a long space of time. ¹¹ But the prince of iniquity, desiring to be God, laid hands on them and slew them, and bound all flesh by evil lusts [[and the end of the world by judgment drew near]]. ¹² But God Almighty, who is righteous, would not cast away His own creation, but had compassion on them from Heaven, ¹³ and sent His Spirit into Mary in Galilee, [[¹⁴ who believed with all her heart and received the Holy Spirit in her womb,

that Jesus might come into the world,]] [15] that by that flesh whereby that wicked one had brought in death, by the same he should be shown to be overcome. [16] For by His own body Jesus Christ saved all flesh [[and restored it to life]], [17] that He might show forth the temple of righteousness in His body. [18] In whom we are saved [[*or* in whom, if we believe, we are set free]]. [19] Therefore, they are not children of righteousness but children of wrath, who reject the wisdom of God, saying that the heavens and the earth and all that are in them are not the work of God. [20] Therefore, they are children of wrath, for they are cursed, following the teaching of the serpent, [21] whom you drive out from you and flee from their doctrine. [[[22] for you are not children of disobedience, but of the well-beloved Assembly. [23] Therefore is the time of the resurrection proclaimed to all.]] [24] And as for that which they say—that there is no resurrection of the flesh—they indeed will have no resurrection to life, but to judgment, [25] because they do not believe in Him that is risen from the dead, not believing nor understanding, [26] for they do not know, O Corinthians, the seeds of wheat or of other seeds, how they are cast bare into the earth and are corrupted and rise again by the will of God with bodies, and clothed. [27] And not only that [body] which is cast in rises again, but manifold more blessing itself. [28] And if we must not take an example from seeds only, but from more noble bodies, [29] you know how Jonah the son of Amathi, when he would not preach to them of Nineveh, but fled, was swallowed by the sea-monster; [30] and after three days and three nights God heard the prayer of Jonah out of the lowest [part of] Hades, and no part of him was consumed, not even a hair nor an eyelash. [31] How much more, O you of little faith, will He raise up you that have believed in Christ Jesus, like as He Himself arose. [32] Likewise also, a dead man was cast on the bones of the prophet Elisha by the sons of Israel, and he arose—both body, and soul, and bones, and spirit; how much more will you which have been cast on the body, and bones, and Spirit of the LORD [[*or* how much more, O you of little faith, will you which have been cast on Him]] arise again in that day having your flesh whole, even as He arose? [[[33] Likewise also, concerning the prophet Elijah, he raised up the widow's son from death: how much more will the Lord Jesus raise you up from death at the sound of the trumpet, in the twinkling of an eye? For He has showed us an example in His own body.]] [34] If then, you receive any other doctrine, God will be witness against you; and let no man trouble me, [35] for I bear these bonds that I may win Christ, and I therefore bear His marks in my body that I may attain to the resurrection of the dead. [36] And whoever receives the rule which He has received by the blessed prophets and the holy good news, will receive a repayment from the LORD, and when he rises from the dead will obtain continuous life. [37] But whoever transgresses these things, with him is the fire, and with them that walk in like manner [[*or* with them that go before in the same way, who are men without God]], [38] which are a generation of vipers, [39] whom you reject in the power of the LORD, [40] and peace, grace, and love will be with you.

1 CLEMENT

Though the author of the First Epistle of Clement is anonymous, it was thought to have been written by Clement of Rome (possibly consecrated by the Apostle Peter) and is highly regarded, at one point even considered for inclusion in the New Testament canon. Internal evidence places the date of composition around the end of the 1st century, although some even suspect before 70 AD.

THE ASSEMBLY OF GOD WHICH SOJOURNS AT ROME, TO THE ASSEMBLY OF GOD WHICH SOJOURNS AT CORINTH, TO THEM THAT ARE CALLED AND SANCTIFIED IN THE WILL OF GOD THROUGH OUR LORD JESUS CHRIST: GRACE AND PEACE BE MULTIPLIED TO YOU FROM ALMIGHTY GOD THROUGH JESUS CHRIST.

CHAPTER 1

[1] On account of the sudden and repeated calamities and misfortunes, brothers, that have come on us, we suppose that we have the more slowly given heed to the things that are disputed among you, beloved, and to the foul and unholy sedition, alien and foreign to the chosen ones of God, which a few headstrong and self-willed persons have kindled to such a degree of madness, that your venerable and famous name, worthy to be loved of all men, is greatly blasphemed. [2] For who that has tarried among you has not approved your most virtuous and firm faith, has not admired your sober and seemly piety in Christ, has not proclaimed your splendid disposition of hospitality, has not deemed blessed your perfect and unerring knowledge? [3] For you did all things without respect of persons, and walked in the laws of God, submitting yourselves to them that have the rule over you, and giving the due honor to the elders that are among you. Young men you prescribed to think such things as are sober and grave. Women you exhorted to perform all things in a blameless, and honorable, and pure conscience, loving dutifully their own husbands; and you taught them to manage the affairs of their houses with gravity, keeping in the rule of obedience, being temperate in all things.

CHAPTER 2

[1] And you were all humble, boasting of nothing, submitting yourselves rather than subjecting others, more gladly giving than receiving, content with the provision that God had given you; and attending diligently to His words, you received them into your very hearts, and His sufferings were before your eyes.

[2] Thus a deep and rich peace was given to all, and an insatiable longing for doing good, and a plentiful outpouring of the Holy Spirit was on all of you. [3] And you, being filled with a holy desire, with excellent zeal and pious confidence, stretched out your arms to Almighty God, imploring Him to be merciful to you, if you had in anything unwillingly done wrong. [4] You contended day and night for the whole brotherhood, that in His mercy and good pleasure the number of His chosen ones might be saved. [5] You were simple and sincere, without malice toward one another: [6] all sedition and all schism were abominable to you. You grieved over the transgressions of your neighbor, judging his shortcomings your own. [7] You did not relent of any well-doing, "being ready to every good work"; [8] and being adorned with a very virtuous and holy habit of life, you did all things in His fear. The commands and ordinances of the LORD were written on the breadth of your heart.

CHAPTER 3

[1] All honor and enlargement were given to you, and then was fulfilled that which is written: "The beloved ate and drank, and was enlarged and grew fat and kicked." [2] From this came emulation and envy, strife and sedition, persecution and disorder, war and captivity. [3] Thus the mean men were lifted up against the honorable; those of no regard against those of good regard; the foolish against the wise; the young against the elder. [4] Through this, justice and peace are far off, because each of you leaves off the fear of God and is dimsighted in his faith, nor walks in the laws of His commands, nor behaves as becomes a citizen of Christ; but each walks according to his own evil lusts, having taken up unjust and unholy envy, by which death also entered into the world.

CHAPTER 4

[1] For it is thus written: "And it came to pass after certain days, that Cain brought of the fruits of the ground a sacrifice to God, and Abel brought also of the firstlings of the sheep and of their fat. [2] And God had respect to Abel and to his gifts; but to Cain and his gifts he had no regard. [3] And Cain was grieved greatly, and his countenance fell. [4] And God said to Cain, Why are you very sorrowful, and why has your countenance fallen? If you have rightly offered, but have not rightly divided, have you not sinned? [5] Hold your peace; your gift returns to you, and you will be master over it. [6] And Cain said to Abel, Let us pass

over into the field. And it came to pass while they were in the field, Cain rose up against his brother Abel and slew him." [7] You see, brothers, jealousy and envy worked the slaughter of a brother. [8] Through envy our father Jacob fled from the face of his brother Esau. [9] Envy caused Joseph to be persecuted to death, and to enter into bondage. [10] Envy compelled Moses to flee from the face of Pharaoh, king of Egypt, because he heard his countryman say, "Who made you a judge or a decider over us? Will you kill me, as you did the Egyptian yesterday?" [11] Through envy Aaron and Miriam pitched their tents outside the camp. [12] Envy brought down Dathan and Abiram alive to the grave, because they contended against Moses, the servant of God. [13] Through envy David suffered jealousy not only of foreigners, but was also persecuted by Saul, king of Israel.

CHAPTER 5

[1] But let us pass from ancient examples and come to those who have in the times nearest to us wrestled for the faith. [2] Let us take the noble examples of our own generation. Through jealousy and envy the greatest and most just pillars of the Assembly were persecuted, and even came to death. [3] Let us place before our eyes the good apostles. [4] Peter, through unjust envy, endured not one or two but many labors, and at last, having delivered his testimony, departed to the place of glory due to him. [5] Through envy Paul, too, showed by example the prize that is given to patience: [6] seven times was he cast into chains; he was banished; he was stoned; having become a herald, both in the east and in the west, he obtained the noble renown due to his faith; [7] and having preached righteousness to the whole world, and having come to the extremity of the west, and having borne witness before rulers, he departed at length out of the world, and went to the holy place, having become the greatest example of patience.

CHAPTER 6

[1] To these men, who walked in holiness, there was gathered a great multitude of the chosen ones, who, having suffered, through envy, many insults and tortures, became a most excellent example among us. [2] Through envy women were persecuted, even the Danaides and Dircae, who, after enduring dreadful and unholy insults, attained to the sure course of the faith; and they who were weak in body received a noble reward. [3] Envy has estranged the minds of wives from their husbands, and changed the saying of our father Adam: "This is now bone of my bone, and flesh of my flesh." [4] Envy and strife have overthrown mighty cities and rooted out great nations.

CHAPTER 7

[1] These things we urge you, beloved, not only by way of admonition to you, but as also putting ourselves in mind. For we are in the same arena, and the same contest is imposed on us. [2] For what reason, let us leave empty and vain thoughts, and come to the glorious and venerable rule of our holy calling. [3] Let us consider what is good, and pleasing, and acceptable before Him who made us. [4] Let us look steadfastly to the blood of Christ and see how precious in the sight of God His blood is, which, having been poured out for our salvation, brought to the whole world the grace of conversion. [5] Let us go back to all generations and learn that in every generation God has granted a place for conversion to such as wished to return to Him. [6] Noah preached conversion, and as many as listened to him were saved. [7] Jonah prophesied destruction to the Ninevites, and they, converting from their sins, appeased God through prayer, and, though alien from God, obtained salvation.

CHAPTER 8

[1] The ministers of the grace of God spoke by the Holy Spirit concerning conversion; [2] and the Lord of all, Himself spoke concerning conversion with an oath: "As I live, says the LORD, I do not desire the death of a sinner, as I desire his conversion"; adding to that an excellent saying: [3] "Convert, O house of Israel, from your iniquity: Say to the sons of My people, Though your sins reach from earth to Heaven, and though they are redder than scarlet, and blacker than sackcloth, and you turn to Me with your whole heart and say, My Father, I will listen to you as to a holy people." [4] And in another place He speaks in this way: "Wash, and be clean; take away the wickedness from your souls from before My eyes; cease from your evil deeds, learn to do well; seek judgment; deliver him that is oppressed; give judgment for the orphan, and justify the widow; and come and let us reason together," He says, "and though your sins be as purple, I will make them white as snow; and though they are as scarlet, I will make them white as wool. And if you are willing and listen to Me, you will eat the good things of the earth; but if you are not willing, and do not listen, the sword will devour you; for the mouth of the LORD has said this." [5] Desiring, therefore, that all His beloved ones should partake of conversion, He has confirmed it by His almighty will.

CHAPTER 9

[1] For what reason, let us submit ourselves to His excellent and glorious will, and, becoming suppliants of His mercy and goodness, let us fall before Him and

go ourselves to His mercies, having laid aside the vain toil, and the strife, and the jealousy that leads to death. [2] Let us look steadfastly at those that have ministered with perfectness to His excellent glory. [3] Let us take as example Enoch, who, having been found just by reason of obedience, was translated, and his death was not found. [4] Noah, having been found faithful, preached, by his ministry, regeneration to the world, and by him God preserved the animals that entered with one consent into the Ark.

CHAPTER 10

[1] Abraham, who was called the friend, was found faithful, inasmuch as he became obedient to the words of God. [2] This man, by obedience, went out from his land and his countrymen, and the house of his father, that, by leaving a scant land, and weak countrymen, and a small house, he might inherit the promises of God. [3] For He says to him, "Go out from your land, and your countrymen, and the house of your father, to the land that I will show you, and I will make you a great nation, and bless you, and magnify your name, and you will be blessed; and I will bless them that bless you, and curse them that curse you, and in you all the tribes of the earth will be blessed." [4] And again, when he separated from Lot, God said to him, "Lift up your eyes, and look from the place where you are now to the north and to the south, and to the east and to the sea; for all the land which you see, I will give it to you and to your seed for all time, [5] and I will make your seed as the dust of the earth: if any man can number the dust of the earth, your seed will also be numbered." [6] And again He says, "God brought forth Abraham, and said to him: Look up to Heaven and number the stars, if you are able to number them, so will your seed be. And Abraham believed God, and it was counted to him for righteousness." [7] Through faith and hospitality a son was given to him in old age, and through obedience he offered him a sacrifice to God on one of the mountains that he showed him.

CHAPTER 11

[1] By hospitality and goodness Lot was saved out of Sodom when the whole region around was judged with fire and brimstone; the LORD making it manifest that He does not leave them that hope on Him, but appoints to punishment and torment them that turn in another way. [2] For his wife, who went out together with him, being of another mind, and not being in concord with him, was on that account placed as a sign, so that she became a pillar of salt even to this day; that it might be known to all that the double-

minded, and they who doubt concerning the power of God, are for a judgment and a sign to all generations.

CHAPTER 12

[1] Through faith and hospitality the harlot Rahab was saved; [2] for when spies were sent to Jericho by Jesus [(Joshua)], the son of Nun, the king of the land knew that they had come to spy out his country, and sent out men to apprehend them that they might be taken and put to death. [3] But the hospitable Rahab having received them, hid them in an upper story under the stalks of flax. [4] Therefore, when the men from the king came on her, and said, "There came to you men who are spies of this land of ours; bring them out, for the king so commands it"; she answered, "The two men whom you are seeking entered in to me, but they departed quickly and are on their way"; but she did not show the men to them. [5] And she said to the men, "I know for certain that the LORD your God has given over this city to you; for the fear and trembling of you has fallen on them that inhabit it. Therefore, when it has happened to you to take it, save me and the house of my father." [6] And they say to her, "So will it be, even as you have spoken to us. Therefore, when you have perceived that we are coming, you will gather together all your household under your roof, and they will be saved; but as many as will be found outside the house will be destroyed." [7] And they proceeded further to give her a sign, that she should hang scarlet from her house, making it manifest beforehand that through the blood of the LORD there will be redemption to all who believe and hope on God. [8] Behold, beloved, how there was not only faith, but prophecy in the woman.

CHAPTER 13

[1] Let us therefore, brothers, be humble, laying aside all boasting and pride, and folly and wrath, and let us do that which is written; for the Holy Spirit says, "Do not let the wise boast in his wisdom, nor the strong in his strength, nor the rich in his riches; but let him that boasts make his boast in the LORD, even by seeking Him and doing judgment and justice." Let us especially remember the words of our Lord Jesus Christ which He spoke when teaching gentleness and long-suffering, for He spoke thus: [2] "Show mercy, that you may obtain mercy; forgive, that it may be forgiven to you; as you do, so will it be done to you; as you give, so will it be given to you; as you judge, so will you be judged; as you are kindly affectioned, so will kindness be showed to you; with whatsoever measure you measure, with the same will it be measured to you." [3] With this command and with these exhortations let us strengthen ourselves, that we

may walk obedient to His holy words with all humility. For the Holy Writing says, ⁴"On whom will I have respect but on him that is meek and quiet, and that trembles at My words?"

CHAPTER 14

¹ It is therefore appropriate and right, men and brothers, that we should be obedient to God rather than follow them that in pride and disorderliness are leaders of detestable sedition. ² For we will incur no slight harm, but rather a great danger, if we rashly give ourselves up to the wills of men who launch out into strife and sedition so as to estrange us from that which is good. ³ Let us, therefore, show kindness toward them according to the mercy and sweetness of Him that made us. ⁴ For it is written: "The men of kindness will inherit the land. The innocent will be left on it; but they that are lawless will be destroyed out of it." ⁵ And again it says, "I saw the unrighteous man exalted on high and lifted up like the cedars of Lebanon. And I passed by, and behold, he was not; I sought his place and did not find it. Keep innocence, and regard righteousness; for there is a remnant that remains to the man of peace."

CHAPTER 15

¹ Let us therefore cleave to them who live in peace and godliness, not to them who hypocritically profess to desire peace. ² For He says in a certain place, "This people honors Me with their lips, but their heart is far from Me." ³ And again, "They blessed with their mouth, but they cursed with their heart. ⁴ And again it says, "They loved Him with their mouth, and with their tongue they lied against Him. For their heart was not right with Him, nor were they faithful in His covenant. ⁵ Let the crafty lips be put to silence, and may the LORD destroy all the deceitful lips, even the haughty tongue, they who said, Let us magnify our tongue, our lips are our own; who is master over us?" ⁶ "On account of the misery of the poor, and on account of the groaning of the needy, I will now arise, says the LORD; I will set him in safety, I will deal confidently with him."

CHAPTER 16

¹ For Christ belongs to them that are humble, not to them that exalt themselves over His flock. ² Our Lord Jesus Christ, who is the scepter of the majesty of God, did not come in the arrogance of boasting and pride, though He was able to do so; but in humility, even as the Holy Spirit spoke concerning Him. ³ For it says, "LORD, who has believed our report, and to whom has the arm of the LORD been revealed? Like a child we have delivered our message before Him; He is as a root in a thirsty land. There is no form nor glory in Him, and we beheld Him, and He had neither form nor comeliness, but His form was despised, lacking comeliness, beyond the form of the sons of men. He was a man stricken and in toil, knowing how to bear infirmity, for His face was turned away; it was dishonored and held in no reputation. ⁴ He bears our sins and suffers pain on our account, and we esteemed Him as one in toil, stricken, and afflicted. ⁵ He was wounded for our sins, and for our transgressions He suffered infirmity; the discipline of our peace was on Him, and by His stripes we were healed. ⁶ All we, like sheep, have gone astray, everyone has erred in his own way, ⁷ and the LORD has given Him up for our sins; and He, through affliction, does not open His mouth. He was led like a sheep to the slaughter, and as a lamb before its shearers is silent, so He does not open His mouth. ⁸ In His humiliation His judgment was taken away, and who will declare His generation? For His life is taken from the earth; ⁹ for the iniquity of My people He has come to death. ¹⁰ And I will give the wicked in return for His burial, and the rich for His death, for He did not sin, neither was guile found in His mouth: and the LORD wills to purify from Him [with] stripes. ¹¹ If You make an offering for sin Your soul will prolong its days. ¹² And the LORD wills to take away from the travail of His soul, to show Him light and to form Him by knowledge, to justify the righteous man who serves many well; and He will bear their sins Himself. ¹³ For what reason He will receive the inheritance of many, and will divide the spoils of the strong, because His soul was delivered up to death, and He was numbered among the transgressors, ¹⁴ and He bore the sins of many, and was given up for their sins." ¹⁵ And again He says, "I am a worm and no man—a reproach of men and despised of the people; ¹⁶ all they who saw Me mocked Me, they spoke with their lips, they shook the head; He hoped in God, let Him deliver Him, let Him save Him, because He desires Him." ¹⁷ See, beloved, what is the example that has been given to us; for if the LORD so humbled Himself, what will we do who have, through His mercy, come under the yoke of His grace?

CHAPTER 17

¹ Let us also be imitators of them who went around in goatskins and sheepskins, preaching the coming of Christ; we mean Elijah, and Elisha, and Ezekiel the prophets, and beside them those who have obtained a good report. ² Abraham obtained an exceedingly good report, and was called the friend of God, and says, looking steadfastly to the glory of God in humility, "I am but earth and ashes." ³ And, moreover, concerning

Job, it is thus written: "Job was a just man and blameless, truthful, one that feared God and abstained from all evil." [4] But he himself, accusing himself, says, "No one is pure from pollution, though his life is but for one day." [5] Moses was called faithful in all his house, and by his ministry God judged His people Israel by stripes and punishment. But he, though he was greatly glorified, did not speak haughtily, but said, when the oracle was given to him out of the bush, "Who am I that You send me? I am weak of voice and slow of tongue." [6] And again he says, "I am but as the smoke from a pot."

CHAPTER 18

[1] But what will we say of David, who obtained a good report; to whom God said, "I have found a man after My own heart, David, the son of Jesse; I have anointed him with My continuous mercy. [2] But he himself says to God, "Have mercy on me, O God, according to Your great mercy, according to the multitude of Your compassion do away with my iniquity; [3] wash me thoroughly from my iniquity, and cleanse me from my sin. For I know my iniquity, and my sin is ever before me. [4] Against You only have I sinned, and done this evil in Your sight, that You might be justified in Your words, and overcome when You are judged. [5] Behold, I was fashioned in wickedness, and in sin my mother conceived me. [6] Behold, You have loved truth; You have shown me the secret and hidden things of Your wisdom. [7] You will sprinkle me with hyssop, and I will be clean. You will wash me, and I will be whiter than snow. [8] You will make me to hear of joy and gladness; the bones that have been humiliated will rejoice. [9] Turn away Your face from my sins and blot out all my misdeeds. [10] Create in me a new heart, O LORD, and renew a right spirit within me. [11] Do not cast me away from Your presence, and do not take Your Holy Spirit from me. [12] Give me the joy of Your salvation again, and establish me with Your guiding Spirit. [13] I will teach sinners Your ways; the ungodly will be converted to You. [14] Deliver me from blood-guiltiness, O God, You God of my salvation; [15] my tongue will rejoice in Your righteousness. O LORD, You will open my mouth, and my lips will show forth Your praise. [16] For if You had desired sacrifice, I would have given it; in whole burnt-offerings You will not delight. [17] The sacrifice of God is a broken spirit; a broken and a contrite heart God will not despise."

CHAPTER 19

[1] The humility of men so many in number and so great, and who have obtained such a good report, and their subjection through obedience, has made not only us but the generations before us better, namely, those who in fear and truth have received His oracles. [2] Since, therefore, we have become the partakers in many great and glorious actions, let us finally return to that goal of peace that was given us from the beginning; let us look steadfastly to the Father and Creator of the whole world, and let us cleave to the glorious and excellent gifts and benefits of His peace. [3] Let us behold Him in spirit and look with the eyes of the soul to His long-suffering will. Let us consider how gentle He is toward all His creation.

CHAPTER 20

[1] The heavens, being put in motion by His appointment, are subject to Him in peace; [2] night and day they accomplish the course ordered by Him, in nothing hindering one another. [3] The sun, and the moon, and the dances of the stars according to His appointment, in harmony and without any violation of order, roll on the courses appointed to them. [4] The fruitful earth brings forth in due season, according to His will, abundant nourishment for men and beasts; doubting nothing, nor changing in anything from the things that are decreed by Him. [5] The unsearchable things of the abyss, and the secret ordinances of the lower parts of the earth, are held together by the same command. [6] The hollow of the vast sea, gathered together by His hand into its reservoirs, does not transgress the bounds placed around it; but even as He has appointed to it, so it does; [7] for He said, "You will come thus far, and your waves will be broken within you." [8] The ocean, impassable to men, and the worlds that are beyond it, are governed by the same commands of their Master. [9] The seasons of spring and summer, autumn and winter, in peace succeed one another. [10] The fixed stations of the winds, each in their due time, perform their services without offense. The ever-flowing fountains, made for enjoyment and health, offer their breasts without fail to sustain the lives of men. Even the smallest of animals come together in peace and harmony. [11] All these things the great Maker and Master of all things has appointed to be in peace and harmony, doing good to all things, but more especially to us, who have fled for refuge to His mercies, through our Lord Jesus Christ, [12] to whom be glory and majesty forever and ever. Amen.

CHAPTER 21

[1] Beware, beloved, lest His many blessings come to be a condemnation to all of us, unless, walking worthily of Him, we do what is honorable and well pleasing before Him with oneness of mind. [2] For He says in a certain place, "The Spirit of the LORD is a candle, searching out the secret places of the heart."

1 CLEMENT

³ Let us see how near He is at hand, and how none of our thoughts and reasonings escape Him. ⁴ It is right, therefore, that we should not desert from His will. ⁵ Let us offend against men who are foolish, and senseless, and puffed up in the pride of their own speech, rather than against God. ⁶ Let us have respect to our Lord Jesus Christ, whose blood was given for us. Let us revere them that are over us. Let us honor our elders. Let us instruct the young in the discipline of the fear of God. Let us direct our wives to that which is good; ⁷ let them show forth the lovely habit of chastity and exhibit the pure disposition of meekness. Let them make manifest by their conversation the government of their tongues; let them show love, not according to partiality, but equally to all that fear the LORD in holiness. ⁸ Let your children be partakers of the discipline of Christ; let them learn how much humility avails before God; what power a pure love has with God; how His fear is honorable and great, preserving all who, with a pure mind, walk in holiness before Him. ⁹ For He is a searcher out of thoughts and counsels, His breath is in us, and when He wills He will take it away.

CHAPTER 22

¹ The faith which is in Christ assures all these things. For He Himself, through the Holy Spirit, thus calls to us: "Come, you children, listen to Me, I will teach you the fear of the LORD. ² What man is he that wishes for life and would gladly see good days? ³ Keep your tongue from evil, and your lips that they speak no guile. ⁴ Turn away from evil and do good; ⁵ seek peace and pursue it. ⁶ The eyes of the LORD are over the just, and His ears are open to their prayer. But the face of the LORD is against them that do evil, to destroy their memorial out of the land. ⁷ The righteous cried, and the LORD heard him, and delivered him out of all his troubles." ⁸ "Many are the afflictions of the sinner, but they that hope in the LORD, mercy will surround them."

CHAPTER 23

¹ The Father whose mercies are over all things, who loves to do good, has yearnings of compassion for them that fear Him, and with gentleness and kindness bestows His favor on them that come to Him with a pure mind. ² For what reason let us not be double-minded, nor let our hearts form vain imaginations concerning His excellent and glorious gifts. ³ Do not let that Writing be applicable to us which says, "Wretched are the double-minded, even they that doubt in their heart and say, We have heard these things in the time of our fathers; and behold, we have grown old, and none of them has happened to us." ⁴ O

foolish ones! Compare yourselves to a tree. Take, for example, the vine: first it sheds its leaves, then comes the bud, then the leaf, then the flower, after that the unripe grape, then the ripe grape. See how in a short time the fruit of the tree attains to maturity. ⁵ Of a truth, quickly and suddenly will His will be fulfilled; the Writing also bearing witness that He will come quickly, and will not tarry; and the LORD will come suddenly into His temple, even the Holy One, whom you expect.

CHAPTER 24

¹ Let us consider, beloved, how the Master shows to us continually the resurrection that is about to be, of which He has made our Lord Jesus Christ the first-fruit, having raised Him from the dead. ² Let us look, beloved, at the resurrection that is always taking place— ³ day and night show the resurrection to us; the night is lulled to rest, the day arises; the day departs, the night comes on. ⁴ Let us consider the fruits, in what way a grain of corn is sown. ⁵ The sower goes forth and casts it into the ground, and when the seeds are cast into the ground, they that fell into the ground dry and naked are dissolved; then after their dissolution, the mighty power of the providence of the LORD raises them up, and from one seed many grow up and bring forth fruits.

CHAPTER 25

¹ Let us consider the wonderful sign that happens in the region of the east, even about Arabia. ² There is a bird which is called the phoenix. This, being the only one of its kind, lives for five hundred years. And when the time of its death draws near, it makes for itself a nest of frankincense, and myrrh, and the other perfumes, into which, when its time is fulfilled, it enters, and then dies. ³ But as its flesh rots, a certain worm is produced, which being nourished by the moisture of the dead animal, puts forth feathers. Then, when it has become strong, it takes the nest wherein are the bones of its ancestor, and bearing them, it flies from the region of Arabia to that of Egypt, to the city which is called Heliopolis; ⁴ there, in daytime, in the sight of all, it flies up, and places them on the altar of the sun, and having done so, returns back. ⁵ The priests, therefore, look into the registers of the times, and find that it has come at the completion of the five-hundredth year.

CHAPTER 26

¹ Will we then think it great and wonderful, if the Maker of all things will make a resurrection of those who, in the confidence of a good faith, have piously seized Him, when even by means of a bird He shows

the greatness of His promises? ² For He says in a certain place, "And You will raise me up, and I will give thanks to You"; and again: "I slumbered and slept; I rose up because You are with me. ³ And again Job says, "You will raise up this flesh of mine, which has suffered all these things."

CHAPTER 27

¹ In this hope, therefore, let our souls be bound to Him who is faithful in His promises and just in His judgments. ² He who has commanded men not to lie, much more will He not lie, for nothing is impossible with God, except to lie. ³ Let our faith, therefore, be kindled in Him afresh within us, and let us consider that all things are near to Him. ⁴ By the word of His majesty He constituted all things, and by a word He is able to destroy them. ⁵ "Who will say to Him, What have You done? Or who will resist the might of His strength?" He will do all things when He wills and as He wills, and none of the things decreed by Him will pass away. ⁶ All things are before Him, and nothing has escaped His counsel, ⁷ seeing that "the heavens declare the glory of God, and the expanse shows the work of His hands: day to day utters speech, and night to night proclaims knowledge; and there is no speech nor language where their voices are not heard."

CHAPTER 28

¹ Therefore, since all things are seen and heard by Him, let us fear Him and abandon the filthy desires for evil deeds, that we may be sheltered by His mercy from the judgments to come. ² For, to where can any of us fly from His mighty hand, and what world will receive any of them that desert from Him? ³ For the Writing says in a certain place: "To where will I go, and where will I conceal myself from Your face? If I ascend into Heaven, You are there; if I depart into the uttermost parts of the earth, Your right hand is there; if I will make my bed in the abyss, Your Spirit is there." ⁴ To where then will we depart, and where will we fly from Him that embraces all things?

CHAPTER 29

¹ Therefore, let us approach Him with holiness of spirit, lifting pure and undefiled hands to Him; loving the kind and compassionate Father who has made us a part of His chosen ones. ² For it is thus written: "When the Most High divided the nations, when He dispersed the sons of Adam, He settled the boundaries of the nations according to the number of the messengers of God. The portion of the LORD was His people Jacob." ³ Israel was the measurement of His inheritance. And in another place it says, "Behold, the LORD takes to Himself a nation from the midst of the nations, even as a man takes the first-fruits of his threshingfloor; and there will go forth from that nation the Holy of Holies."

CHAPTER 30

¹ Since, therefore, we are a portion of the Holy One, let us do all such things as pertain to holiness, avoiding evil-speaking, foul and impure embraces, drunkenness, disorderliness, abominable desires, detestable adultery, execrable pride; ² "for God," it says, "resists the proud, but gives grace to the humble." ³ Let us cleave, therefore, to them to whom grace has been given from God. Let us clothe ourselves with concord, being humble, temperate, keeping ourselves far from all whispering and evil-speaking, justified by our deeds, and not by our words. ⁴ For it says, "He who says many things will, in return, hear many things. Does he that is eloquent think himself to be just? ⁵ Does he that is born of woman and lives but for a short time think himself to be blessed? Do not be abundant in speech." ⁶ Let our praise be in God, and not for ourselves, for God hates the self-praisers. ⁷ Let the testimony of right actions be given us from others, even as it was given to our fathers who were just. ⁸ Audacity, self-will, and boldness belong to them who are accursed of God; but moderation, humility, and meekness, to them that are blessed of God.

CHAPTER 31

¹ Therefore, let us cleave to His blessing, and let us see what the ways of blessing are. Let us consult the records of the things that happened from the beginning. ² On what account was our father Abraham blessed? Was it not that he worked righteousness and truth through faith? ³ Isaac, with confidence, knowing the future, willingly became a sacrifice. ⁴ Jacob, with humility, flying from his brother, went out from his own land and journeyed to Laban and served as a slave, and there were given to him the twelve tribes of Israel.

CHAPTER 32

¹ If anyone will consider these things with sincerity and one by one, he will recognize the magnificence of the gifts that were given by him. ² For from Jacob came the priests and all the Levites that serve the altar of God. From him came our Lord Jesus Christ according to the flesh; from him came the kings, and rulers, and governors of the tribe of Judah; and the remainder of his tribes are of no small glory, since God has promised, "Your seed will be as the stars of the heavens." ³ Therefore, all these have been glorified and magnified, not through themselves, or

through their works, or through the righteousness that they have done, but through His will. [4] And we who through His will have been called in Christ Jesus are justified, not by ourselves, or through our wisdom, or understanding, or godliness, or the works that we have done in holiness of heart, but by faith, by which all men from the beginning have been justified by Almighty God, to whom be glory through the ages of the ages. Amen.

CHAPTER 33

[1] What, then, will we do, brothers? Will we cease from well-doing, and abandon charity? May the Master never allow that this should happen to us! But let us rather with diligence and zeal hasten to fulfill every good work. [2] For the Maker and Lord of all things rejoices in His works. [3] By His supreme power He founded the heavens, and by His incomprehensible understanding He ordered them. He separated the earth from the water that surrounded it, and fixed it on the firm foundation of His own will. The animals which inhabit therein He commanded to be by His ordinance. Having made beforehand the sea and the animals that are therein, He shut them in by His own power. [4] Man, the most excellent of all animals, infinite in faculty, He moulded with His holy and faultless hands, in the impress of His likeness. [5] For thus says God: "Let Us make man in Our own image, and after Our own likeness. And God made man. He made them male and female." [6] Therefore, when He had finished all things, He praised and blessed them, and said, "Be fruitful, and multiply." [7] Let us see, therefore, how all the just have been adorned with good works. Yes, the LORD Himself rejoiced when He had adorned Himself with His works. [8] Having, therefore, this example, let us come in without shrinking to His will; let us work with all our strength the work of righteousness.

CHAPTER 34

[1] The good workman boldly receives the bread of his labor, but the slothful and remiss does not look his employer in the face. [2] It is therefore right that we should be zealous in well-doing, for from Him are all things; [3] for He tells us beforehand: "Behold, the LORD comes, and His reward is before His face, to give to everyone according to his work." [4] He exhorts us, therefore, with this reward in view, to strive with our whole heart not to be slothful or remiss toward every good work. [5] Let our glorying and our confidence be in Him; let us submit ourselves to His will; let us consider the whole multitude of His messengers, how they stand by and serve His will. [6] For the Writing says, "Ten thousand times ten thousand stood beside Him, and thousands of thousands served Him; and they cried, HOLY, HOLY, HOLY, LORD of Hosts! All creation is full of His glory." [7] And let us, being gathered together in harmony and a good conscience, cry earnestly, as it were with one mouth, to Him, that we may become partakers of His great and glorious promises; [8] for He says, "Eye has not seen, and ear has not heard, neither has there entered into the heart of man, what things He has prepared for them that wait for Him."

CHAPTER 35

[1] Behold, beloved, how blessed and wonderful are the gifts of God— [2] life in immortality, cheerfulness in righteousness, truth in liberty, faith in confidence, temperance in sanctification; and all these things have already come within our cognizance. [3] What therefore are the things that are prepared for them that abide in patience? The Maker and Father of the worlds, the All-Holy One, He knows how many and how beautiful they are. [4] Let us, therefore, strive to be found in the number of them that await Him, that we may partake of the promised gifts. [5] And how will this be, beloved? If our mind is established by faith toward God; if we seek out what is pleasant and acceptable in His sight; if we perform such things as harmonize with His blameless will, and follow in the way of truth, casting from us all unrighteousness and lawlessness, covetousness, strife, malice and fraud, whispering and evil-speaking, hatred of God, pride and insolence, vainglory and intractableness. [6] For they who do these things are hateful to God, and not only they who do them, but also they who have pleasure in them that do them. [7] For the Writing says: "But to the sinner God has said, Why do you speak of My ordinances, and take My covenant in your mouth? [8] But you have hated instruction and have cast My words behind you. When you saw a thief you went with him and have cast in your portion with the adulterers; your mouth has abounded with evil, and your tongue has contrived deceit. You sat and spoke against your brother and have slandered the son of your mother. [9] You have done this, and I kept silence. You thought, O wicked one, that I was like to you; [10] but I will convict you and will set yourself before you. [11] Consider this, you who forget God, lest He seize you as a lion, and there is none to save you. [12] The sacrifice of praise will honor Me; and there is the way by which I will show him the salvation of God."

CHAPTER 36

[1] This is the way, beloved, in which we found our salvation—even Jesus Christ, the Chief Priest of our

oblations, the champion and defender of our weakness. ²Through Him we look steadfastly to the heights of the heavens; through Him we behold, as in a glass, the immaculate and lofty countenance of God the Father; through Him the eyes of our heart were opened; through Him our foolish and darkened understanding springs up again to His marvelous light; through Him the LORD has willed us to taste of immortal knowledge, "who, being the brightness of His glory, is so far better than the messengers, as He has, by inheritance, obtained a more excellent Name than they." ³For it is thus written: "Who makes His messengers spirits, ‖ His ministers a flame of fire." ⁴But of His Son the LORD has thus said, "You are My Son, today have I begotten You. Ask of Me, and I will give You the heathen for Your inheritance, ‖ And the uttermost parts of the world for Your possession." ⁵And, again, He says to Him: "Sit on My right hand ‖ Until I make Your enemies Your footstool." ⁶Who then are the enemies? Even the wicked, and they who resist the will of God.

CHAPTER 37

¹Let us, therefore, men and brothers, carry on our warfare with all earnestness in His faultless ordinances. ²Let us consider those who fight under our rulers, how orderly, and obediently, and submissively they perform what is commanded them. ³All are not prefects, or commanders of thousands, or commanders of hundreds, or commanders of fifties, or such-like; but each in his own rank performs what has been ordered by the king or the commanders. ⁴The great cannot exist without the small, nor the small without the great. There is a certain mixture in all things, and from there arises their use. ⁵Let us take, for example, our body: the head is nothing without the feet, nor the feet without the head. The smallest members of the body are necessary and useful to the whole body, and all unite and work with harmonious obedience for the preservation of the whole body.

CHAPTER 38

¹Therefore, let our whole body be saved in Christ Jesus, and let each be subject to his neighbor according to the gift which he has received. ²Do not let the strong man despise the weak; and let the weak pay regard to the strong. Let him that is rich minister to him that is poor. Let him that is poor praise God that He has given to him one by whom his want may be supplied. Let the wise show his wisdom, not in words, but in good deeds; let him that is humble not bear witness to himself, but leave another to bear witness to him. Let him that is pure in the flesh not boast of it, knowing that it is another that gives him

the power of continence. ³Let us consider, brothers, of what matter we are made, of what sort and who we are that have come into the world, as it were out of the tomb and darkness. He that made and fashioned us has brought us into this world, having prepared beforehand His benefactions, even before we were born. ⁴Therefore, having all these things from Him, we should in all respects give thanks to Him, to whom be glory through the ages of the ages. Amen.

CHAPTER 39

¹The senseless and unwise, the foolish and unruly, make a mockery of us, wishing to exalt themselves in their own imagination. ²For what can a mortal do? Or what strength has he that is born of earth? ³For it is written: "There was no form before my eyes, only I heard a breath and a voice. ⁴For what? Will a mortal be pure before the LORD? Or is a man blameless from his works? Seeing that He puts no trust in His servants, and even beholds iniquity in His messengers; ⁵yes, the Heaven is not pure in His sight. Away, you who dwell in houses of clay, of whom are we also even of the same clay. He has smitten them even as it were a moth, and in a single day they are no more. Because they could not help themselves, they perished: ⁶He blew among them, and they died, because they had no wisdom. ⁷Call, now, and see if there is anyone that will obey you, if you will behold any of the holy messengers. For anger destroys the fool, and envy puts him to death that is gone out of the way. ⁸I have beheld the foolish casting forth roots, but immediately his habitation was eaten up. ⁹Let his sons be far from safety, let them be mocked at the gates of their inferiors, and there will be none to deliver them. For that which had been prepared for them the just will eat, and they will not be delivered out of their troubles."

CHAPTER 40

¹Therefore, since these things have been made manifest before to us, and since we have looked into the depths of the divine knowledge, we should do everything in order, whatever the LORD has commanded us to do at the appointed seasons, and to perform the offerings and services. ²He has not commanded these to be done at random or in disorder, but at fixed times and seasons. ³But when and by whom He wishes them to be fulfilled He Himself has decided by His supreme will, that all things, being done piously, according to His good pleasure, might be acceptable to His will. ⁴Therefore, they who at the appointed seasons make their offerings are acceptable and blessed; for while following the laws of the Master they do not completely sin. ⁵For to the Chief

Priest were assigned special services, and to the priests a special place has been appointed; and on the Levites special duties are imposed. But he that is a layman is bound by the ordinances of laymen.

CHAPTER 41

[1] Let each of you, brothers, in his own order, give thanks to God, continuing in a good conscience, not transgressing the fixed rule of his ministry, with all gravity. [2] Not in every place, brothers, are sacrifices offered continually, either in answer to prayer, or concerning sin and neglect, but in Jerusalem only; and even there the offering is not made in every place, but before the temple in the court of the altar, after that which is offered has been diligently examined by the chief priest and the appointed ministers. [3] They, therefore, who do anything contrary to that which is according to His will have death for their punishment. [4] You see, brothers, by as much as we have been thought worthy of greater knowledge, by so much the more are we exposed to danger.

CHAPTER 42

[1] The apostles received the good news for us from our Lord Jesus Christ; our Lord Jesus Christ received it from God. [2] Christ, therefore, was sent out from God, and the apostles from Christ; and both these things were done in good order, according to the will of God. [3] They, therefore, having received the promises, having been fully persuaded by the resurrection of our Lord Jesus Christ, and having been confirmed by the word of God, with the full persuasion of the Holy Spirit, went forth preaching the good tidings that the Kingdom of God was at hand. [4] Preaching, therefore, through the countries and cities, they appointed their first-fruits to be overseers and servants over such as should believe, after they had proved them in the Spirit. [5] And this they did in no new way, for in truth it had in long past time been written concerning overseers and servants; for the Writing, in a certain place, says in this way: "I will establish their overseers in righteousness, and their servants in faith."

CHAPTER 43

[1] And wherein is it wonderful, if they who, in Christ, were entrusted by God with this work appointed the previously mentioned officers? Since even the blessed Moses, the faithful servant in all his house, signified in the sacred scrolls all the things that were commanded to him, whom also the prophets have followed, bearing witness together to the laws which were appointed by him. [2] For he, when a strife arose concerning the priesthood, and when the tribes contended which of them should be adorned with that glorious name, commanded the twelve chiefs of the tribes to bring to him rods, each inscribed with the name of a tribe; and when he had taken them, he bound them together, and sealed them with the seals of the heads of the tribes, and laid them up on the table of God, in the Dwelling Place of the testimony. [3] And when he had closed the Dwelling Place, he sealed the keys, and likewise the rods, [4] and said to them, "Men and brothers, of whatever tribe the rod will bud, this has God chosen to be His priest, and to serve Him." [5] And when morning had come, he called together all Israel, even six hundred thousand men, and showed to the heads of the tribes the seals, and opened the Dwelling Place of the testimony and brought forth the rods, and the rod of Aaron was found not only to have budded, but also bearing fruit. [6] What do you think, beloved? Did Moses not know beforehand that this was about to happen? Most assuredly he knew it, but, that there might be no disorder in Israel, he did thus that the Name of the true and only God might be glorified, to whom be glory through the ages of the ages. Amen.

CHAPTER 44

[1] Our apostles, too, by the instruction of our Lord Jesus Christ, knew that strife would arise concerning the dignity of an overseer; [2] and on this account, having received perfect foreknowledge, they appointed the above-mentioned as overseers and servants: and then gave a rule of succession, in order that, when they had fallen asleep, other men, who had been approved, might succeed to their ministry. [3] Those who were thus appointed by them, or afterward by other men of good regard, with the consent of the whole Assembly, who have blamelessly ministered to the flock of Christ with humility, quietly, and without illiberality, and who for a long time have obtained a good report from all, these, we think, have been unjustly deposed from the ministry. [4] For it will be no small sin in us if we depose from the office of overseer those who blamelessly and piously have made the offerings. [5] Happy are the elders who finished their course before and died in mature age after they had borne fruit; for they do not fear lest anyone should remove them from the place appointed for them. [6] For we see that you have removed some men of honest conversation from the ministry, which had been blamelessly and honorably performed by them.

CHAPTER 45

[1] You are contentious, brothers, and are zealous concerning things that do not pertain to salvation.

² Look diligently into the Writings, which are the true sayings of the Holy Spirit. ³ You know how that nothing unjust or corrupt has been written in them; for you will not find in them the just expelled by holy men. ⁴ The just were persecuted, but it was by the lawless; they were thrown into prison, but it was by the unholy; they were stoned, but it was by sinners; they were slain, but it was by wicked men, even by those who had taken up an unjust envy against them. ⁵ They, therefore, when they suffered all these things, suffered them with a good report. ⁶ For what will we say, brothers? Was it by those that feared God that Daniel was cast into the den of lions? ⁷ Was it by those who practiced the magnificent and glorious worship of the Most High that Hananiah, Azariah, and Mishael were shut up in the fiery furnace? Let us not suppose that such was the case. Who, then, were the men who did these things? Abominable men and full of all wickedness were inflamed to such a degree of wrath that they cast into tortures those who, with a holy and blameless purpose, served God, not knowing that the Most High is a champion and defender of those who with a pure conscience serve His most excellent Name, to whom be glory through the ages of the ages. Amen. ⁸ But they, abiding steadfastly in their confidence, have inherited honor and glory, and have both been exalted and made beautiful by God, in the memory that is made of them through the ages of the ages. Amen.

CHAPTER 46

¹ We should also cleave to such examples, brothers. ² For it is written: "Cleave to them that are holy, for they that cleave to them will be made holy." ³ And again, in another place it says, "With the guiltless man you will be guiltless, and with the excellent you will be excellent, and with him that is crooked you will be perverse." ⁴ Therefore, let us cleave to the guiltless and the just, for they are the chosen ones of God. ⁵ Why are there strivings, and anger, and division, and war among you? ⁶ Do we not have one God and one Christ? Is the Spirit of grace, which was poured out on us, not one? Is our calling in Christ not one? ⁷ Why do we tear apart and split apart the members of Christ, and make sedition against our body, and come to such a degree of madness that we forget we are members of one another? Remember the words of our Lord Jesus, ⁸ for He said, "Woe to that man; it were good for him if he had never been born, rather than that he should cause one of My chosen ones to offend. It were better for him that a millstone were tied around him, and that he were cast into the sea, rather than that he should cause one of My little ones to offend. ⁹ This schism of yours has perverted many, [and] has cast many into despondency, many into doubt, [and] all of us into grief, and, as yet, your sedition remains.

CHAPTER 47

¹ Take into your hands the letter of the blessed apostle Paul. ² What did he first write to you in the beginning of his good news? ³ Of a truth, he warned you spiritually, in a letter, concerning himself, and concerning Cephas and Apollos, because even then there were factions among you; ⁴ but the faction of that time brought less sin on you; for you inclined to apostles of good regard, and to a man approved among them. ⁵ But now consider who they are that have perverted you and have diminished the glory of your famous brotherly love. ⁶ It is disgraceful, brothers, yes, very disgraceful, and unworthy of the conduct which is in Christ, that it should be reported that the most firm and ancient assembly of the Corinthians has, on account of one or two persons, made sedition against its elders. ⁷ And this report did not only come to us, but also to the nations, who do not go with us, so that you heap blasphemies on the Name of the Lᴏʀᴅ through your folly, and in addition cause danger to yourselves.

CHAPTER 48

¹ Therefore, let us remove this thing as quickly as possible, and let us fall before the feet of the Master, and implore Him with tears, that He will have mercy and be reconciled to us, and restore us again to the grave and pure conversation of brotherly love. ² For this is a gate of righteousness opened to life, as it is written: "Open to me the gates of righteousness; I will go in to them, and give thanks to the Lᴏʀᴅ: ³ this is the gate of the Lᴏʀᴅ; the righteous will enter thereby." ⁴ Now, since many gates have been opened, the gate of righteousness is that which is in Christ. Happy are all they that enter therein, and who keep their path straight in holiness and righteousness, quietly performing all their duties. ⁵ If a man is faithful, if he is mighty to expound knowledge, if he is wise in the interpretation of words, if he is pure in his deeds, ⁶ by so much the more should he be humble, and by as much as he seems to be greater, by so much the more should he seek the common advantage of all, and not of himself alone.

CHAPTER 49

¹ Let him that has the love which is in Christ keep the commands of Christ. ² Who can describe sufficiently the bond of the love of God? ³ Who is sufficient to speak as he should of the excellence of its beauty? ⁴ The height to which love leads up is unspeakable. ⁵ Love joins us to God; love hides a multitude of sins;

love bears all things; is long suffering in all things. In love there is nothing illiberal, nothing haughty. Love has no schism; love does not make sedition; love does all things in harmony; in love all the chosen ones of God have been made perfect. Without love nothing is acceptable to God. [6] In love, our Master has taken us to Himself. Through the love that He has for us, Jesus Christ our Lord has given His blood for us, by the will of God, His flesh for our flesh, His soul for our soul.

CHAPTER 50

[1] You see, brothers, how great and wonderful a thing love is, and how there is no describing its perfection. [2] Who is sufficient to be found in it, except those whom God will have deemed worthy? Therefore, let us pray and ask from His mercy that we may live in love, without human partiality, blameless. [3] All the generations from Adam, even to this day, have gone by, but they who have been made perfect in love according to the grace of God, inhabit the abode of the pious and will be made manifest in the visitation of the Kingdom of Christ. [4] For it is written: "Enter into the secret chambers but a little while, until My anger and wrath have passed, and I will remember the good day, and will raise you up from your tombs." [5] Blessed are we, beloved, if we do the commands of God in the harmony of love, so that through love our sins may be forgiven us. [6] For it is written: "Blessed are they whose iniquities are forgiven, and whose sins are covered. Blessed is the man to whom the LORD does not impute sin, and in whose mouth there is no guile." [7] This blessedness comes to them who are chosen by God, through Jesus Christ our Lord, to whom be glory through the ages of the ages. Amen.

CHAPTER 51

[1] Therefore, whatever errors we have committed through the assaults of the adversary, let us ask pardon for these; and they who have been leaders of the sedition and division should consider the common ground of our hope. [2] For they who have their conversation in fear and love wish that they themselves, rather than their neighbors, should fall into suffering; and would rather that they should undergo condemnation themselves, than that the harmony which has been honorably and justly handed down to us should do so. [3] For it is better that a man should make confession concerning his sins, than that he should harden his heart, even as the heart of them was hardened who made sedition against Moses, the servant of God—[they] whose condemnation was manifest; [4] for they went down alive into Hades, and death swallowed them up. [5] Pharaoh and his army, and all the leaders of Egypt, their chariots and their riders, through no other cause were sunk in the Red Sea, and perished there, than through the hardening of their foolish hearts, after that the signs and wonders happened in Egypt through the hand of Moses, the servant of God.

CHAPTER 52

[1] The Lord of all things, brothers, is in need of nothing; neither does He require anything of anyone, except to confess to Him. [2] For the chosen one, David, says, "I will confess to the LORD, and that will please Him more than a young calf that puts forth horns and hooves. Let the poor behold and rejoice at that." [3] And again he says, "Offer to the LORD the sacrifice of praise: pay your vows to the Most High. And call on Me in the day of your affliction, and I will deliver you, and you will glorify Me. [4] For the sacrifice to God is a broken spirit."

CHAPTER 53

[1] You know, beloved, and know well, the sacred Writings, and have looked into the oracles of God; therefore, call these things to remembrance. [2] For, when Moses had gone up into the mount, and had tarried there forty days and forty nights in fasting and humiliation, the LORD said to Him, "Moses, Moses, come down quickly from here, for your people, whom you brought out of the land of Egypt, have worked iniquity. They have quickly gone astray out of the way that you command them and have made molten images for themselves." [3] And the LORD said to him, "I have spoken to you once and twice, saying, I have beheld this people, and behold, it is a stiff-necked people. Leave Me alone, that I may destroy them, and I will wipe out their name from under Heaven, and make of you a nation great and wonderful, and far more numerous than they." [4] And Moses said, "Be it far from You, O LORD. Forgive this people their sin, or also wipe my name out of the Scroll of the Living." [5] Oh, the great love! Oh, the unsurpassable perfection! The servant is bold toward the LORD: he asks forgiveness for the people or demands otherwise that he himself should be destroyed together with them.

CHAPTER 54

[1] Who among you is noble? Who is compassionate? Who is filled with love? [2] Let him speak in this way: "If through me sedition and strife arise, I will depart, I will go away to wherever you will, and I will do that which is commanded by the majority, only let the flock of Christ be at peace together with the appointed elders." [3] He who does this will gain for himself great glory in the LORD, and every place will receive him, "for the earth is the LORD's, and the fullness thereof."

⁴ These things they have done who are citizens of the Kingdom of God, which does not need to be converted of, and these things they will yet do.

CHAPTER 55

¹ But, to bring forward examples from the nations, also many kings and leaders, when a time of pestilence had arisen, being warned by oracles, gave themselves to death, that they might deliver their citizens by their blood. Many went out from their own cities, that there might no longer be sedition therein. ² We know that many among us gave themselves up to bonds, that they might deliver others. Many have given themselves up to slavery, and, having received their own price, have with that fed others. ³ Many women, waxing strong through the grace of God, have performed many manly deeds. ⁴ The blessed Judith, when the city was besieged, asked of the elders that she should be permitted to go forth into the camp of the aliens. ⁵ She therefore delivered herself to danger and went out through love of her country and of her people, who were besieged. And the LORD delivered Holofernes into the hands of a woman. ⁶ To no smaller danger did Esther, being perfect in faith, expose herself, that she might deliver the twelve tribes of Israel who were about to perish. For by fasting and humiliation she implored the Master, who overlooks all things, the God of Ages, who, seeing the humiliation of her soul, delivered the people for whose sake she put herself in danger.

CHAPTER 56

¹ Therefore, let us pray for those who have fallen into any transgression, that moderation and humility may be given to them, to the end that they should submit themselves, I do not say to us, but to the will of God; for so they will obtain a fruitful and perfect remembrance and compassion before God and His holy ones. ² Let us accept, brothers, that discipline at which no one needs to be offended. The admonition which we make toward one another is exceedingly good and useful, for it joins us to the will of God. ³ For thus speaks the holy word: "The LORD has disciplined me with disciplines, but He has not given me over to death." ⁴ "For whom the LORD loves He disciplines, and scourges every son whom He receives." ⁵ "The righteous will discipline me in pity and will rebuke me, but do not let the oil of sinners anoint my head." ⁶ And again it says: "Blessed is the man whom the LORD has rebuked; do not refuse the admonition of the Almighty, for He makes you to grieve, and again He restores you; ⁷ He has smitten, and His hands have healed you; ⁸ six times will He deliver you from calamity, and the seventh time evil will not touch you.

⁹ In the time of famine He will deliver you from death, in war He will redeem you from the hand of iron. ¹⁰ From the scourge of the tongue He will hide you, and you will not be afraid when evils approach. ¹¹ The unjust and the sinner you will laugh to scorn; ¹² and of the wild beasts you will not be afraid, for the wild beasts will be at peace with you. ¹³ Then you will know that your house will be at peace; the habitation of your dwelling place will not fail. ¹⁴ You will know that your seed is abundant, your children like all the herb of the field. ¹⁵ You will come to your tomb like a ripe ear of corn reaped in due season, like the heap of a threshing-floor that is gathered at its proper time." ¹⁶ You see, beloved, that there is a protection for them that are disciplined by the Master, for God chastens us because He is good, to the end that we should be admonished by His holy discipline.

CHAPTER 57

¹ Therefore, you that have laid the foundation of the sedition: submit yourselves to the elders, and be disciplined to conversion, bending the knees of your hearts. ² Learn to submit yourselves, laying aside the vain and haughty self-will of your tongues; for it is better that you should be small and approved in the flock of Christ, rather than that, seeming to be superior to others, you should be cast out of His hope. ³ For thus says the most excellent Wisdom: "Behold, I will send on you the language of My Spirit; I will teach you My word. ⁴ Since I called and you did not listen, and prolonged My words, and you did not attend [to them], but made My counsels of no effect, and were not obedient to My reproofs, therefore I will laugh at your destruction, I will exult when desolation comes on you; when perturbation has suddenly come on you, and ruin is at hand like a whirlwind, when tribulation and oppression comes on you. ⁵ For the time will come when you will call on Me, and I will not listen to you; the wicked will seek Me, and will not find Me. They hated wisdom and did not choose the fear of the LORD; they were not willing to attend to My counsels, they mocked at My rebukes. ⁶ For what reason they will eat the fruits of their own way; they will be filled with their own unrighteousness. ⁷ For because they wronged the innocent they will be slain, and judgment will destroy the unrighteous; but he who listens to Me will abide, trusting in hope, and will rest securely from all evil."

CHAPTER 58

¹ Let us, therefore, submit to His all-holy and glorious Name, and escape the threats that have been before spoken by Wisdom against the disobedient, that we may abide trusting in the most holy Name of His

greatness. ²Accept this advice of ours, and it will not be regretted by you. For as God lives, and as the Lord Jesus Christ lives, and the Holy Spirit—the confidence and hope of the chosen ones—He who observes in humility with earnest obedience, and not complaining, the ordinances and commands given by God, he will be reckoned and counted in the number of them that are saved by Jesus Christ, through whom is the glory to Him through the ages of the ages. Amen.

CHAPTER 59

¹But if some should be disobedient to the things spoken by Him through us, let them know that they will entangle themselves in no small transgression and danger, ²but that we will be guiltless of this sin; and we will ask, making our prayer and supplication with earnestness, that the Maker of all things may keep uninjured in all the world the number of those that have been numbered as His chosen ones, through His beloved Son, Jesus Christ, through whom He has called us from darkness to light, and from ignorance to a knowledge of the glory of His Name. ³That we may hope in Your Name, which is the first of all things, open the eyes of our heart to know You, who are alone highest among the highest, holy among the holy, who puts down the haughtiness of the proud, who scatters the reasonings of the nations, who exalts the humble on high, and lowers the lofty, who makes rich and makes poor, who kills and makes to live, the only benefactor of spirits, and God of all flesh, who looks into the abysses, who beholds the works of men, who is the helper of those in danger, the Savior of those who have lost hope, who is the maker and overseer of every soul, who makes the nations to multiply on earth, and out of all has chosen those that love You through Your beloved Son Jesus Christ, through whom You have taught us, have sanctified us, have honored us. ⁴We ask You, Lord, to be our helper and assister; save those of us who are in affliction, have compassion on the humble, raise the fallen, appear to those who are in need, heal the sinners, convert those of Your people who are wandering from the way, feed the hungry, ransom our prisoners, raise up the sick, encourage the feeble-hearted, let all the nations know that You are God alone and Jesus Christ Your Son, and that we are Your people and the sheep of Your pasture.

CHAPTER 60

¹You have made manifest the perpetual constitution of the world by the things that happen. You, Lord, who are faithful in all generations, have founded the world. You who are just in Your judgments, who are wonderful in strength and greatness; You who are wise in creating and prudent in establishing the things that are made; You that are good in the things that are seen and faithful among them that trust on You, merciful and compassionate, forgive us our transgressions and unrighteousnesses, our sins and our negligences. ²Do not take into account every sin of Your servants and handmaids, but purify us with the purification of Your truth, and make straight our steps in holiness, and righteousness, and singleness of heart, that we may so walk and do such things as are right and well pleasing before You, and before our rulers. ³Yes, Lord, cause Your face to appear to us in peace to our good, that we may be sheltered by Your mighty hand, and preserved from all sin by Your lofty arm, and deliver us from those that hate us unjustly. ⁴Give unity and peace both to us and to all that dwell on the earth, as You gave to our fathers when they called on You with faith and truth, so that we should become obedient to Your all-powerful and most excellent Name, and to those who rule and govern us on the earth.

CHAPTER 61

¹You, Lord, have given the authority of the Kingdom to them through Your almighty and unspeakable power, so that we, knowing the estimation and honor given to them by You, might submit ourselves to them, in no way opposing Your will; to whom give, O Lord, health, peace, concord, stability, so that they may discharge the rule given to them by You without offense; ²for You, heavenly Lord, perpetual King, give to the sons of men glory, and honor, and authority over the things that are on the earth. You, Lord, direct their counsel according to what is good and pleasing before You, that, fulfilling with peace, and meekness, and piety the authority given to them by You, they may obtain mercy from You. ³You who alone are able to do these and greater good things among us, to You do we give thanks through the Chief Priest and protector of our souls, Jesus Christ, through whom to You be the glory and majesty, now and to all generations, through the ages of the ages. Amen.

CHAPTER 62

¹Concerning the things that pertain to our religion, and the things that are most useful to a virtuous life, for those who are willing to live piously and righteously, we have sufficiently charged you, men and brothers. ²For we have handled every argument concerning faith and conversion, and genuine love and temperance, and moderation and patience, reminding you that you must, by righteousness, and

truth, and long-suffering, approve yourselves with piety to Almighty God, being of one mind, without malice, in love and peace with earnest obedience, even as our fathers, who were previously mentioned, approved themselves with humility both with regard to God the Father and Creator, and to all men. ³ And these things we have so much the more gladly put you in mind of, inasmuch as we knew plainly that we wrote to men who are faithful and of high regard, and who have looked into the oracles of the instruction of God.

CHAPTER 63

¹ It is right, therefore, that those who have attended to so great and so many examples should submit their necks, and fill the place of obedience, so that being at peace from the vain sedition we may attain, without any blame, to the end set before us in truth. ² For you will afford us joy and rejoicing if, becoming obedient to the things that have been written by us, you put an end, by the suggestion of the Holy Spirit, to the unlawful wrath of your discord, according to the supplication which we have made concerning peace and unity in this letter. ³ But we have also sent men to you who are faithful and prudent, who from youth up to old age have behaved blamelessly among us, who also will be witnesses between yourselves and us; ⁴ and this we have done that you may know that our whole thought has been and is this: that you may speedily be at peace among yourselves.

CHAPTER 64

¹ Finally, may my God, who overlooks all things, who is the Master of spirits and Lord of all flesh, who has chosen our Lord Jesus Christ, and us through Him to be a peculiar people, give to every soul that is called after His glorious and holy Name, faith, fear, peace, patience, long-suffering, continence, purity, sobriety, to the well-pleasing of His Name, through our Chief Priest and protector, Jesus Christ, through whom be ascribed to Him glory and greatness, strength and honor, both now and through the ages of the ages. Amen.

CHAPTER 65

¹ See that you quickly send back to us in peace and with joy Claudius Ephebus and Valerius Bito, together also with Fortunatus, who were sent to you from us, that they may the more quickly bring us news of your peace and order, which we pray for and desire, so that we may the sooner have joy concerning your good order. ² The grace of our Lord Jesus Christ be with you, and with all who everywhere are called of God through Him, to whom through Him be glory, honor, might, majesty, and continuous dominion, through the ages of the ages. Amen.

2 CLEMENT

Like 1 Clement, the Second Epistle of Clement has an anonymous author and is ascribed to Clement of Rome by tradition, but unlike 1 Clement, the ascription of 2 Clement to Clement of Rome is more dubious. It was considered for canonization early on and is in fact included in some Coptic Bibles. It was likely written in the late 1st century or early 2nd century.

CHAPTER 1

[1] Brothers, we should so think of our Lord Jesus Christ as of God, as of the Judge of quick and dead, and we should not think lightly concerning our salvation; [2] for if we think little concerning Him, we also expect that we will receive little; and if we listen to it as though it were a small thing, we err, not knowing from where we are called, nor by whom, nor to what place, nor what great things Jesus Christ has endured to suffer on our behalf. [3] What repayment, therefore, will we give to Him, or what fruit worthy of that which He has given to us? How many things that help to holiness has He given to us? [4] For He has given us the light, He has called us sons as though He were our father, He has saved us when we were ready to perish. [5] What praise, therefore, will we give to Him, or what repayment of reward for the things that we have received? [6] For we were maimed in our understanding, worshiping stocks and stones, and gold, and silver, and iron, the work of men, and our whole life was nothing but death. We, therefore, who were surrounded with darkness, and who had our sight filled with such gloom, have recovered our sight, having, according to His will, laid aside the cloud that was around us. [7] For He has had compassion on us, and, pitying us, has saved us, having beheld in us much wandering and destruction, when we had no hope of salvation except that which is from Him. [8] For He has called us when as yet we were not, and has willed us to be when we were nothing.

CHAPTER 2

[1] "Rejoice, you barren that do not bear; break forth and shout, you that do not travail, for the desolate has many more children than she that has a husband." In that He said, "Rejoice, you barren that do not bear," He has spoken of us, for our assembly was barren before that children were given to her. [2] But in that He said, "Shout, you that do not travail," He means that we should offer our prayers to God with simplicity, that we do not faint like women in travail. [3] But in that He said, "The children of the desolate are many more than they of her that has a husband," He means that

our people seemed to be deserted of God, and now, after that we have believed, we have become more in number than they which seemed to have God. [4] And another Writing says, "I did not come to call the righteous but sinners." [5] He means this, that it is necessary to save them that are perishing. [6] For this is great and wonderful—not to establish the things that are standing, but the things that are falling; [7] thus Christ willed to save the things that were perishing, and He saved many, having come and called us who were already perishing.

CHAPTER 3

[1] Therefore, since He has showed such compassion to us—first, that we who live should not sacrifice to gods that are dead, neither worship them, but know through Him the Father of truth—what is this knowledge of Him except the not denying Him through whom we know Him? [2] For He Himself says, "Whoever has confessed Me before men, I will confess Him before My Father." [3] This, therefore, is our reward if we confess Him through whom we have been saved. [4] But whereby will we confess Him? Even by doing what He commands, and not disobeying His commands, and honoring Him not only with our lips but with our whole heart and whole understanding. [5] For He says in Isaiah, "This people honors Me with their lips, but their heart is far from Me."

CHAPTER 4

[1] Therefore, let us not only call Him Lord, for that will not save us. [2] For He says, "It is not everyone that says to Me, Lord, Lord, that will be saved, but he that does righteousness." [3] For what reason, brothers, let us confess Him in our deeds, by loving one another, by not committing adultery, and not speaking ill of each other, neither being envious, but by being continent, compassionate, kind. We should also sympathize with one another, and to abstain from covetousness; it is by these works that we acknowledge Him, and not by the contrary; [4] and we should not fear men but rather God. [5] For what reason, if we do these things, the LORD has said, "Though you have been gathered together with Me in My bosom and do not do My commands, I will cast you from Me, and I will say to you, Depart from Me; I do not know from where you are, you workers of iniquity."

CHAPTER 5

[1] For what reason, brothers, having left our sojourning in this world, let us do the will of Him who called us, and let us not fear to depart from this world. [2] For the LORD says, "You will be as lambs in the midst of wolves." [3] But Peter answered and says to Him,

"What, then, if the wolves tear the sheep?" ⁴ Jesus says to Peter, "Do not let the lambs after that they are dead fear the wolves; and do not fear them that kill you but can do nothing more to you, but fear Him who, after you are dead, has authority over body and soul, even to cast them into the Gehenna of fire." ⁵ And you know, brothers, that the sojourning of our flesh in this world is but short and for a little while, but the promise of Christ is great and wonderful, even the rest of the kingdom which is to come, and of continuous life. ⁶ What, therefore, will we do that we may attain to them, except to lead a holy and just life, and to deem the things of this world to be alien to us, and not to desire them? ⁷ For while we desire to obtain these things, we fall from the right way.

CHAPTER 6

¹ For the LORD says, "No servant can serve two masters." If, therefore, we wish to serve both God and wealth, it is inexpedient for us; ² for what advantage is it if a man gains the whole world, but loses his soul? ³ Now this life and the life to come are two enemies. ⁴ This life preaches adultery, corruption, covetousness, and deceit; but the life that is to come renounces these things. ⁵ We cannot, therefore, be friends to both; it is necessary for us then to renounce the one and to use the other. ⁶ Therefore, let us consider that it is better to hate the things that are here, as being small, and short-lived, and corruptible, but to love the things that are there, as being good and incorruptible. ⁷ If, therefore, we do the will of Christ, we will find rest; but if not, nothing will deliver us from continuous punishment, if we do not obey His commands. ⁸ For the Writing says in Ezekiel: "If Noah, and Job, and Daniel should rise up, they will not deliver their children in the captivity." ⁹ If, therefore, such righteous men as these cannot by their righteousness deliver their children, with what confidence will we, if we do not keep our immersion pure and undefiled, come to the Kingdom of God? Or who will be our advocate unless we are found having the works that are holy and just?

CHAPTER 7

¹ For what reason, my brothers, let us strive, knowing that the contest is at hand. We know, too, that many put in for corruptible contests, but all are not crowned, but they only who have labored much and fought a good fight. ² Therefore, let us contend that we may all be crowned. ³ Let us run in the straight course, in the incorruptible contest; and let us be many that put into it; and let us so contend that we may also be crowned. And if we cannot all be crowned, let us at least come near to the crown. ⁴ It is necessary for us to know that he who contends in a corruptible contest, if he is found acting unfairly is flogged, and taken away, and cast out of the course. ⁵ What do you think? What will he suffer that acts unfairly in an incorruptible contest?

⁶ For of them who have not kept their seal he says, "Their worm will not die, and their fire will not be quenched, and they will be for a spectacle to all flesh."

CHAPTER 8

¹ Therefore, while we are on the earth, let us convert. ² For we are as clay in the hands of the workman. In like manner as the potter, if while he is making a vessel, it turns wrongly in his hands, or is crushed, can mould it again, but if he has once cast it into the fiery furnace he can no longer amend it; so let us, so long as we are in this world, convert with all our hearts of the wickedness that we have committed in the flesh, that we may be saved of the LORD while as yet we have time for conversion. ³ For after we have departed out of this world, we are no longer able there to confess or convert. ⁴ For what reason, brothers, if we have done the will of the Father, and preserved our flesh pure, and kept the commands of the LORD, we will receive continuous life. ⁵ For the LORD says in the Gospel, "If you have not kept that which is little, who will give you that which is great? For I say to you, he that is faithful in that which is least is also faithful in much." ⁶ Does he not, therefore, say this, "Keep your flesh pure and your seal unspotted, that you may inherit continuous life?"

CHAPTER 9

¹ And do not let any one of you say that this flesh of ours is not judged nor raised again. ² Consider this: in what were you saved, in what did you recover your sight, if not in this flesh? ³ We should, therefore, guard our flesh as the temple of God; ⁴ for in the same manner as you were called in the flesh, in the flesh you will also come. ⁵ There is one Christ, our Lord who saved us, who being spirit at the first, was made flesh, and thus called us. So we will also receive the reward in this flesh. ⁶ Therefore, let us love one another, that we may all come to the Kingdom of God. ⁷ While we have opportunity to be healed, let us give ourselves up to God who heals, giving a repayment to Him. ⁸ And of what kind? Conversion from a sincere heart. ⁹ For He foreknows all things and knows the things that are in our hearts. ¹⁰ Therefore, let us give Him praise, not from the mouth alone, but also from the heart, that He may receive us as sons. ¹¹ For of a truth the LORD has said, "My brothers are they who do the will of My Father."

CHAPTER 10

¹ For what reason, my brothers, let us do the will of the Father who has called us, that we may live; and let us rather pursue virtue, and abandon vice which leads us into sins, and let us fly from ungodliness lest evil seize us; for if we are zealous to do good, peace will pursue us. ² For this reason it is not possible that a man should find peace. ³ For they introduce the fear

of men, choosing rather the present enjoyment that is here than the future promise. [4] For they are ignorant of how great a torment the enjoyment of this world brings, and what delight the future promise has. [5] And if they themselves alone did these things, it would be endurable; but now they continue to instruct innocent souls in evil, not knowing that they will have a twofold condemnation—both themselves and they that listen to them.

CHAPTER 11

[1] Therefore, let us serve God with a pure heart, and we will be righteous; but if we do not serve Him, because we do not believe the promise of God, we will be wretched. [2] For the prophetic word says, "Wretched are the double-minded who doubt in their heart, and say, We have heard these things of old, even in the time of our fathers, but we have seen none of them, though we expect them from day to day. [3] You fools, compare yourselves to a tree; take for an example the vine: in the first place it sheds its leaves, then there comes a shoot, after that the unripe grape, then the mature cluster. [4] In like manner My people, in time past, has had disorder and trouble, but afterward it will receive the things that are good." [5] For what reason, my brothers, let us not be double-minded, but let us abide in hope, that we may obtain our reward. [6] Faithful is He that has promised that He will give to each the repayment of his works. [7] If, therefore, we do righteousness before God, we will enter into His Kingdom, and receive the promises which "ear has not heard nor eye seen, neither have entered into the heart of man."

CHAPTER 12

[1] Let us, therefore, in love and righteousness expect the Kingdom of God every hour, since we do not know the day of the appearing of God. [2] For the LORD Himself, when He was asked by a certain man when His Kingdom should come, replied, "When two will be one, and that which is without as that which is within, and the male with the female neither male nor female." [3] Now two are one when we speak the truth to one another, and there is, without hypocrisy, one soul in two bodies. [4] And by that which is without being as that which is within, He means this: He calls the soul that which is within, and the body that which is without; in like manner, therefore, as your body is visible, let your soul be made manifest by good deeds. [5] And by the male with the female neither male nor female, He means this: When a brother seeing a sister does not in any way regard her as a female, nor does she regard him as a male; [6] "when you do these things," He says, "the Kingdom of My Father will come."

CHAPTER 13

[1] My brothers, therefore let us convert immediately; let us be sober and followers of what is good, for we are burdened with much folly and wickedness. Let us wipe out from among us our former sins and convert sincerely and be saved. And let us not be pleasers of men, nor let us wish to please one another alone, but let us also please them that are outside by our righteous conduct, that the Name may not be blasphemed on our account. [2] For the LORD says, "My Name is continually blasphemed among all the nations"; and again, "Why is My Name blasphemed, whereby it is blasphemed? In that you do not do the things that I will." [3] For the nations, when they hear from our mouth the oracles of God, admire them as beautiful and weighty; but afterward perceiving our deeds, that they are not worthy of the words that we say, they turn thereafter to blasphemy, saying that the matter is but fable and deceit. [4] For when they hear from us that God says, "There is no thanks for you if you love them that love you, but there is thanks for you if you love your enemies and them that hate you"; when they hear these things, they wonder at the excess of the goodness. But when they see that we do not only not love those that hate us, but do not even love those that love us, they turn us to ridicule, and the Name is blasphemed.

CHAPTER 14

[1] For what reason, my brothers, by doing the will of our Father, God, we will be of the first, the spiritual Assembly, which was founded before the sun and moon were made; but if we do not do the will of the LORD, we will be of the Writing that says, "My house has become a den of thieves." Therefore, let us choose to be of the Assembly of life that we may be saved. [2] But I do not think that you are ignorant that the living Assembly is the body of Christ. For the Writing says: "God made man, male and female." Now, the male signifies Christ, the female the Assembly. You also know that both the Scrolls and the apostles say that the Assembly is not new, but was from the beginning; for it was of a spiritual kind, as was also our Jesus, but was made manifest in the last days that it might save us. [3] But the Assembly, though spiritual, was manifested in the flesh of Christ, showing to us that if anyone keep it in his flesh, and does not corrupt it, he will receive it in the Holy Spirit; for this flesh is the counterpart of the Spirit; no one, therefore, who corrupts the copy will receive the original in exchange. He therefore means this, my brothers: "Keep the flesh pure, that you may partake of the Spirit." [4] But if we say that the flesh is the Assembly, and the spirit, Christ, he then who does injury to the flesh does injury to the Assembly. Such a one therefore will not partake of the spirit, which is Christ. [5] Such life and immortality is this flesh able to partake of by the union of the Holy Spirit with it. Nor can any

say or declare what the LORD has prepared for His chosen ones.

CHAPTER 15

[1] Now, I do not think that I have given advice of little importance concerning temperance, which, if a man practices, he will not regret it, but will save both himself and me who advise him. For it is no small service to convert a wandering and perishing soul to salvation. [2] For we are able to give this repayment in return to God who created us, if he who speaks and hears both speaks and hears with faith and love. [3] Therefore, let us remain with righteousness and holiness in the things in which we have believed, that we may with boldness ask of God, who says, "While you are still speaking, I will say, Behold, I am here." [4] For this saying is the token of a great promise. For the LORD says of Himself that He is more ready to give than him that asks. [5] Therefore, since we partake in so much goodness, let us not grudge ourselves the attaining of so many good things; for by so much as His words bring pleasure to those who do them, by so much do they bring condemnation to those who disobey them.

CHAPTER 16

[1] For what reason, brothers, since we have received no small opportunity for conversion, let us, while we have time, turn to the God who has called us, while we still have one who will receive us. [2] For if we bid farewell to the luxuries of this world and conquer our soul so that we do not fulfill evil lusts, we will partake of the mercy of Jesus. [3] But know that the Day of Judgment is already coming as a burning furnace, and certain of the heavens will be melted, and the whole earth will be as lead melting on the fire; and then both the secret and open deeds of men will be made manifest. [4] Therefore, kindness is good, as showing conversion from sin; better is fasting than prayer, and kindness than both; for love covers a multitude of sins, and prayer that goes forth from a good conscience saves from death. Happy is everyone who is found full of these things, for kindness becomes a lightening of sin.

CHAPTER 17

[1] Therefore, let us convert with our whole heart lest any of us perish by the way. For if we have received commands and make this our business—to tear men away from idols and instruct them—how much more should a soul not perish that has already come to a knowledge of God? [2] Therefore, let us endeavor to elevate with regard to what is good them that are weak, to the end that we may all be saved; and let us convert one another and reprove one another. [3] And let us not seem to attend and believe now only, while we are being admonished by the elders, but also when we have departed to our homes, let us remember the commands of the LORD; and let us not, on the other hand, be drawn aside by the lusts of the world, but let us endeavor, by coming more frequently, to make progress in the commands of the LORD, to the end that we all being of one mind may be gathered together to life. [4] For the LORD has said, "I come to gather together all the nations, tribes, and tongues." And He says this of the day of His appearing, when He will come and repay each of us according to his works. [5] And the unbelieving will behold His glory and strength, and will be astonished when they see the kingdom of the world in the hands of Jesus, and will say, "Woe to us, for You were and we did not know it, and did not believe, nor did we obey the elders who preached to us concerning our salvation." And their worm will not die, nor their fire be quenched, and they will be for a spectacle to all flesh. [6] He speaks of that Day of Judgment when they will see punished those among us who have lived ungodly and set at nothing the commands of Jesus Christ. [7] But the just, who have done well, and have abided the tests, and have hated the luxuries of the soul, when they behold those who have missed the way and have denied Jesus either by words or deeds, how they are punished with dreadful tortures in unquenchable fire, will give glory to their God, saying that there will be a hope for him who has served God with his whole heart.

CHAPTER 18

[1] Therefore, let us be of those who give thanks, of those who have served God, and not of the ungodly who are judged. [2] For I myself, being in all respects a sinner, and not having yet escaped temptation, but being still in the midst of the snares of the Devil, yet endeavor to follow after righteousness, that I may be able, at any rate, to be near it, fearing the judgment to come.

CHAPTER 19

[1] For what reason, my brothers and sisters, after the reading of the words of the God of truth, I also read an exhortation to you, to the end that you should attend to what has been written, that you may both save yourselves and him who preaches among you; for I ask of you, as my reward, that you should convert with your whole heart, gaining for yourselves salvation and life. For by so doing, we will offer an aim to all the young, who are willing to labor cheerfully for the worship and goodness of God. [2] And do not let those of us who are unlearned be vexed or offended when one exhorts us and turns us from sin to righteousness. For we at times when doing what is wrong, do not know it, from the doubt and unbelief that is in our hearts, and are blinded in our understanding by vain lusts. [3] Therefore, let us practice righteousness, that we may be saved at the last. Blessed are they who obey these commands, for if for a short time they suffer in the world that now is,

they will gather hereafter the immortal fruit of the resurrection. [4] Therefore, do not let the pious man be vexed if he is afflicted in the times that now are—a blessed time awaits him. He will live above again with the fathers and will rejoice without sorrow continuously.

CHAPTER 20

[1] And do not let even that trouble your mind, that we see the unjust prosperous and the servants of God in misery. [2] Let us have faith, my brothers and sisters. We are making trial of the living God and contending in the present life that we may be crowned in the life to come. [3] For none of the just receive a speedy reward, but wait for it. [4] For if God gave speedily the reward of the righteous, we should immediately practice gain and not godliness; for we should seem to be righteous, not on account of what is pious, but on account of what is profitable. And on this account the divine judgment has overtaken a spirit that is not righteous, and has burdened it with chains. [5] Now to the only God, the invisible, the Father of truth, who has sent to us the Savior and leader of immortality, through whom He has made known to us the truth and the heavenly life—to Him be the glory through the ages of the ages. Amen.

SEVEN EPISTLES OF IGNATIUS

Ignatius, the overseer of Antioch, and fellow disciple with Polycarp of John the Apostle, penned seven letters while en route to his martyrdom in Rome. These letters are generally well-attested and are considered part of the Apostolic Fathers. Ignatius is believed to have died in approximately 108 or 140 AD.

TO THE EPHESIANS

IGNATIUS, WHO IS ALSO THEOPHORUS, TO HER WHICH HAS BEEN BLESSED IN GREATNESS THROUGH THE ABUNDANCE OF GOD THE FATHER; WHICH HAS BEEN FOREORDAINED BEFORE THE AGES TO BE FOREVER ABIDING AND UNCHANGEABLE GLORY, UNITED AND CHOSEN IN A TRUE PASSION, BY THE WILL OF THE FATHER AND OF JESUS CHRIST OUR GOD; EVEN TO THE ASSEMBLY WHICH IS IN EPHESUS [OF ASIA], WORTHY OF ALL COMMENDATIONS: ABUNDANT GREETINGS IN CHRIST JESUS AND IN BLAMELESS JOY.

CHAPTER 1

[1] While I welcomed in God [your] well-beloved name, which you bear by natural right by faith and love in Christ Jesus our Savior—being imitators of God, and having your hearts kindled in the blood of God, you have perfectly fulfilled your congenial work— [2] for when you heard that I was on my way from Syria, in bonds for the sake of the common Name and hope, and was hoping through your prayers to succeed in fighting with wild beasts in Rome, that by so succeeding I might have power to be a disciple, you were eager to visit me— [3] seeing then that in God's Name I have received your whole multitude in the person of Onesimus, whose love passes utterance and who is moreover your overseer [in the flesh]— and I pray that you may love him according to Jesus Christ and that you all may be like him; for blessed is He that granted to you according to your deserving to have such an overseer.

CHAPTER 2

[1] But as touching my fellow-servant Burrhus, who by the will of God is your blessed servant in all things, I pray that he may remain with me to the honor of yourselves and of your overseer. Yes, and Crocus also, who is worthy of God and of you, whom I received as an example of the love which you bear me, has relieved me in all ways—even so may the Father of Jesus Christ refresh him—together with Onesimus, and Burrhus, and Euplus, and Fronto; in whom I saw you all with the eyes of love. [2] May I always have your joy, if [it] so be I am worthy of it.

It is therefore appropriate for you in every way to glorify Jesus Christ who glorified you; that being perfectly joined together in one submission, submitting yourselves to your overseer and eldership, you may be sanctified in all things.

CHAPTER 3

[1] I do not command you, as though I were someone. For even though I am in bonds for the Name's sake, I am not yet perfected in Jesus Christ. [For] now I am beginning to be a disciple; and I speak to you as to my schoolmates. For I should be trained by you for the contest in faith, in admonition, in endurance, in long-suffering. [2] But, since love does not permit me to be silent concerning you, therefore I was forward to exhort you, that you run in harmony with the mind of God; for Jesus Christ also, our inseparable life, is the mind of the Father, even as the overseers that are settled in the farthest parts of the earth are in the mind of Jesus Christ.

CHAPTER 4

[1] So then it is appropriate for you to run in harmony with the mind of the overseer; which thing also you do. For your honorable eldership, which is worthy of God, is attuned to the overseer, even as its strings to a lyre. Therefore, in your concord and harmonious love, Jesus Christ is sung. [2] And you, each and all, form yourselves into a chorus, that being harmonious in concord and taking the key note of God you may in unison sing with one voice through Jesus Christ to the Father, that He may both hear you and acknowledge you by your good deeds to be members of His Son. It is therefore profitable for you to be in blameless unity, that you may also be partakers of God always.

CHAPTER 5

[1] For if I in a short time had such converse with your overseer, which was not after the manner of men but in the Spirit, how much more do I congratulate you who are closely joined with him as the Assembly is with Jesus Christ and as Jesus Christ is with the Father, that all things may be harmonious in unity. [2] Let no man be deceived: if anyone is not within the precinct of the altar, he lacks the bread [of God]. For, if the prayer of one and another has such great force, how much more that of the overseer and of the whole Assembly. [3] Therefore, whoever does not come to the congregation thereby shows his pride and has separated himself; for it is written: "God resists the proud." Let us therefore be careful not to resist the overseer, that by our submission we may give ourselves to God.

CHAPTER 6

[1] And in proportion as a man sees that his overseer is silent, let him fear him the more. For everyone whom the Master of the household sends to be steward over His own house, we should so receive as Him that sent him. Therefore, we should plainly regard the overseer as the LORD Himself. [2] Now Onesimus of his own accord highly praises your orderly conduct in God, for that you all live according to truth, and that no heresy has a home among you: no, you do not so much as listen to anyone, if he speaks of anything else save concerning Jesus Christ in truth.

CHAPTER 7

[1] For some are accustomed of malicious guile to carry about the Name, while they do certain other things unworthy of God. You should shun these men as wild beasts, for they are mad dogs, biting by stealth; against whom you should be on your guard, for they are hard to heal. [2] There is only one Physician—of flesh and of spirit, generate and ingenerate, God in man, true Life in death, Son of Mary and Son of God, first passible and then impassible—Jesus Christ our Lord.

CHAPTER 8

[1] Therefore, let no one deceive you, as indeed you are not deceived, seeing that you belong wholly to God. For when no lust is established in you, which has power to torment you, then truly you live after God. I devote myself for you, and I dedicate myself as an offering for the assembly of you Ephesians which is famous to all the ages. [2] They that are of the flesh cannot do the things of the Spirit, neither can they that are of the Spirit do the things of the flesh; even as faith cannot do the things of unfaithfulness, neither unfaithfulness the things of faith. No, even those things which you do after the flesh are spiritual; for you do all things in Jesus Christ.

CHAPTER 9

[1] But I have learned that certain persons passed through you from over there, bringing evil doctrine; whom you did not permit to sow seed in you, for you stopped your ears, so that you might not receive the seed sown by them. For you are stones of a temple, which were prepared beforehand for a building of God the Father, being hoisted up to the heights through the engine of Jesus Christ, which is the Cross, and using the Holy Spirit for a rope, while your faith is your windlass, and love is the way that leads up to God. [2] So then you are all companions in the way, carrying your God and your shrine, your Christ and your holy things, being arrayed from head to foot in the commands of Jesus Christ. And I too, taking part in the festivity, am permitted by letter to bear you company and to rejoice with you, that you do not set your love on anything after the common life of men, but only on God.

CHAPTER 10

[1] And also, pray without ceasing for the rest of mankind (for there is in them a hope of conversion), that they may find God. Therefore, permit them to take lessons at least from your works. [2] Against their outbursts of wrath be meek; against their proud words be humble; against their railings set your prayers; against their errors be steadfast in the faith; against their fierceness be gentle. And do not be zealous to imitate them by requital. [3] Let us show ourselves their brothers by our forbearance; but let us be zealous to be imitators of the LORD, vying with each other who will suffer the greater wrong, who will be defrauded, who will be set at nothing; that no herb of the Devil be found in you, but in all purity and temperance abide in Christ Jesus, with your flesh and with your spirit.

CHAPTER 11

[1] These are the last times. From now on let us have reverence; let us fear the long-suffering of God, lest it turn into a judgment against us. For either let us fear the wrath which is to come or let us love the grace which now is—the one or the other; provided only that we be found in Christ Jesus to true life. [2] Let nothing glitter in your eyes apart from Him, in whom I carry about my bonds, my spiritual pearls in which I would gladly rise again through your prayer, of which may it be my lot to be always a partaker, that I may be found in the company of those Christians of Ephesus who moreover were ever of one mind with the apostles in the power of Jesus Christ.

CHAPTER 12

[1] I know who I am and to whom I write. I am a convict, you have received mercy: I am in peril, you are established. [2] You are the high-road of those that are on their way to die to God. You are associates in the mysteries with Paul, who was sanctified, who obtained a good report, who is worthy of all commendations; in whose footsteps I would gladly be found treading when I will attain to God, who in every letter makes mention of you in Christ Jesus.

CHAPTER 13

[1] Therefore, do your diligence to meet together more frequently for thanksgiving to God and for His glory. For when you meet together frequently, the powers of Satan are cast down; and his mischief comes to nothing in the concord of your faith. [2] There is nothing better than peace, in which all warfare of things in Heaven and things on earth is abolished.

CHAPTER 14

[1] None of these things is hidden from you if you are perfect in your faith and love toward Jesus Christ, for these are the beginning and end of life—faith is the beginning and love is the end—and the two being found in unity are God, while all things else follow in their train to true nobility. [2] No man professing faith sins, and no man possessing love hates. The tree is manifest from its fruit; so they that profess to be Christ's will be seen through their actions. For the work is not a thing of profession now, but is seen then when one is found in the power of faith to the end.

CHAPTER 15

[1] It is better to keep silence and to be, than to talk and not to be. It is a fine thing to teach, if the speaker practices [what he teaches]. Now there is one Teacher who spoke, and it came to pass: yes, and even the things which He has done in silence are worthy of the Father. [2] He that truly possesses the word of Jesus is also able to listen to His silence, that he may be perfect; that through his speech he may act and through his silence he may be known. [3] Nothing is hidden from the LORD, but even our secrets are near to Him. Let us therefore do all things as knowing that He dwells in us, to the end that we may be His temples and He Himself may be in us as our God. This is so, and it will also be made clear in our sight from the love which we rightly bear toward Him.

CHAPTER 16

[1] Do not be deceived, my brothers. Corrupters of houses will not inherit the Kingdom of God. [2] If then they which do these things after the flesh are put to death, how much more if a man through evil doctrine corrupts the faith of God for which Jesus Christ was crucified. Such a man, having defiled himself, will go into the unquenchable fire; and in like manner also will he that listens to him.

CHAPTER 17

[1] For this reason the LORD received ointment on His head, that He might breathe incorruption on the Assembly. Do not be anointed with the ill odor of the teaching of the prince of this world, lest he lead you captive and rob you of the life which is set before you. [2] And for what reason do we not all walk prudently, receiving the knowledge of God, which is Jesus Christ? Why should we perish in our folly, not knowing the gift of grace which the LORD has truly sent?

CHAPTER 18

[1] My spirit is made an outcast for the Cross, which is a stumbling-block to them that are unbelievers, but to us—salvation and continuous life. Where is the wise? Where is the disputer? Where is the boasting of them that are called prudent? [2] For our God, Jesus the Christ, was conceived in the womb by Mary according to a dispensation, of the seed of David but also of the Holy Spirit; and He was born and was immersed that by His passion He might cleanse water.

CHAPTER 19

[1] And hidden from the prince of this world were the virginity of Mary, and her childbearing, and likewise also the death of the LORD—three mysteries to be cried aloud—the which were worked in the silence of God. [2] How then were they made manifest to the ages? A star shone forth in the Heaven [[or sky]] above all the stars; and its light was unutterable, and its strangeness caused amazement; and all the rest of the constellations with the sun and moon formed themselves into a chorus around the star, but the star itself far outshone them all; and there was perplexity to know where this strange appearance came from which was so unlike them. [3] From that time forward every sorcery and every spell was dissolved, the ignorance of wickedness vanished away, [and] the ancient kingdom was pulled down when God appeared in the likeness of man to newness of continuous life; and that which had been perfected in the counsels of God began to take effect. There all things were perturbed, because the abolishing of death was taken in hand.

CHAPTER 20

[1] If Jesus Christ should count me worthy through your prayer, and it should be the Divine will, in my second tract, which I intend to write to you, I will further set before you the dispensation of which I have begun to speak, relating to the new man Jesus Christ, which consists in faith toward Him and in love toward Him, in His passion and resurrection, [2] especially if the LORD should reveal anything to me. Assemble yourselves together in common, each of you separately, man by man, in grace, in one faith and one Jesus Christ, who after the flesh was of David's race, who is Son of Man and Son of God, to the end that you may obey the overseer and eldership without distraction of mind, breaking one bread, which is the medicine of immortality and the antidote that we should not die but live forever in Jesus Christ.

CHAPTER 21

[1] I am devoted to you and to those whom for the honor of God you sent to Smyrna, from where I also write to you with thanksgiving to the LORD, having love for Polycarp as I have for you also. Remember me, even as I would that Jesus Christ may also remember you. [2] Pray for the assembly which is in Syria, from where I am led a prisoner to Rome—I who am the very last of the faithful there, according as I was counted worthy to be found to the honor of God. Farewell in God the Father and in Jesus Christ our common hope.

SEVEN EPISTLES OF IGNATIUS

TO THE MAGNESIANS

IGNATIUS, WHO IS ALSO THEOPHORUS, TO HER WHICH HAS BEEN BLESSED THROUGH THE GRACE OF GOD THE FATHER IN CHRIST JESUS OUR SAVIOR, IN WHOM I SALUTE THE ASSEMBLY WHICH IS IN MAGNESIA ON THE MAEANDER, AND I WISH HER ABUNDANT GREETINGS IN GOD THE FATHER AND IN JESUS CHRIST.

CHAPTER 1

¹ When I learned of the exceeding good order of your love in the ways of God, I was delighted, and I determined to address you in the faith of Jesus Christ. ² For being counted worthy to bear a most godly name, which I carry around in these bonds, I sing the praise of the assemblies; and I pray that there may be in them union of the flesh and of the spirit which are Jesus Christ's, our never-failing life—a union of faith and of love which is preferred before all things, and, what is more than all—a union with Jesus and with the Father, in whom, if we patiently endure all, despite the prince of this world, and escape from that, we will attain to God.

CHAPTER 2

¹ Forasmuch then as I was permitted to see you in the person of Damas, your godly overseer, and your worthy elders Bassus and Apollonius, and my fellow-servant, the servant Zotion, of whom I would gladly have joy, for that he is subject to the overseer as to the grace of God and to the eldership as to the law of Jesus Christ:

CHAPTER 3

¹ Yes, and it is appropriate for you also not to presume on the youth of your overseer, but according to the power of God the Father to render to him all reverence, even as I have learned that the holy elders have also not taken advantage of his outwardly youthful estate, but give place to him as to one prudent in God; yet not to him, but to the Father of Jesus Christ, even to the Overseer of all. ² For the honor, therefore, of Him that desired you, it is suitable that you should be obedient without deception. For a man does not so much deceive this overseer who is seen, as cheat that Other who is invisible; and in such a case he must reckon not with flesh but with God who knows the hidden things.

CHAPTER 4

¹ It is therefore appropriate that we not only be called Christians, but also be such, even as some persons have the overseer's name on their lips, but in everything act apart from him. Such men appear to me not to keep a good conscience, forasmuch as they do not assemble themselves together lawfully according to command.

CHAPTER 5

¹ Seeing, then, that all things have an end, these two are set together before us: life and death; and each man will go to his own place. ² For just as there are two coinages—the one of God and the other of the world, so also each of them has its proper stamp impressed on it—the unbelievers the stamp of this world, but the faithful in love the stamp of God the Father through Jesus Christ, through whom, unless of our own free choice we accept to die into His passion, His life is not in us.

CHAPTER 6

¹ Seeing, then, that in the previously mentioned persons I beheld your whole people in faith and embraced them, I advise you: be zealous to do all things in godly concord—the overseer presiding after the likeness of God and the elders after the likeness of the council of the apostles, with the servants also who are most dear to me, having been entrusted with the office of servant of Jesus Christ, who was with the Father before the worlds and appeared at the end of time. ² Therefore, you should all study conformity to God and pay reverence to one another; and let no man regard his neighbor after the flesh, but always love one another in Jesus Christ. Let there be nothing among you which will have power to divide you, but be united with the overseer and with them that preside over you as an example and a lesson of incorruptibility.

CHAPTER 7

¹ Therefore, as the LORD did nothing without the Father, either by Himself or by the apostles, so neither do you do anything without the overseer and the elders. And do not attempt to think anything right for yourselves apart from others, but let there be one prayer in common, one supplication, one mind, one hope, in love and in joy unblameable, which is Jesus Christ, than whom there is nothing better. ² Hasten for all of you to come together, as to one temple, even God; as to one altar, even to one Jesus Christ, who came forth from One Father and is with One and departed to One.

CHAPTER 8

¹ Do not be seduced by strange doctrines nor by antiquated fables, which are profitless. For if even to this day we live after the manner of Judaism, we avow that we have not received grace: ² for the divine prophets lived after Christ Jesus. For this reason, they were also persecuted, being inspired by His grace to the end that they which are disobedient might be fully persuaded that there is one God who manifested Himself through His Son Jesus Christ, who is His Word that proceeded from silence, who in all things was well-pleasing to Him that sent Him.

SEVEN EPISTLES OF IGNATIUS

CHAPTER 9

[1] If then those who had walked in ancient practices attained to newness of hope, no longer observing Sabbaths but fashioning their lives after the LORD's Day, on which our life also arose through Him and through His death which some men deny—a mystery whereby we attained to belief, and for this reason we endure patiently, that we may be found disciples of Jesus Christ our only teacher— [2] if this be so, how will we be able to live apart from Him? Seeing that even the prophets, being His disciples, were expecting Him as their teacher through the Spirit. And for this reason, He whom they rightly awaited, when He came, raised them from the dead.

CHAPTER 10

[1] Therefore, let us not be insensible to His goodness. For if He should imitate us according to our deeds, we are lost. For this reason, seeing that we have become His disciples, let us learn to live as befits Christianity. For whoever is called by another name besides this, is not of God. [2] Therefore, put away the vile leaven which has waxed stale and sour, and go yourselves to the new leaven, which is Jesus Christ. Be salted in Him, that none among you grow putrid, seeing that by your savor you will be proved. [3] It is monstrous to talk of Jesus Christ and to practice Judaism. For Christianity did not believe in Judaism, but Judaism in Christianity, wherein every tongue believed and was gathered together to God.

CHAPTER 11

[1] Now these things I say, my dearly beloved, not because I have learned that any of you are so minded; but as being less than any of you, I would have you be on your guard early, that you do not fall into the snares of vain doctrine; but be fully persuaded concerning the birth, and the passion, and the resurrection, which took place in the time of the governorship of Pontius Pilate; for these things were truly and certainly done by Jesus Christ our hope; from which hope may it not befall any of you to be turned aside.

CHAPTER 12

[1] Let me have your joy in all things, if I am worthy. For even though I am in bonds, yet I am not comparable to one of you who are at liberty. I know that you are not puffed up; for you have Jesus Christ in yourselves. And, when I praise you, I know that you only feel the more shame; as it is written: "The righteous man is a self-accuser."

CHAPTER 13

[1] Therefore, do your diligence that you may be confirmed in the ordinances of the LORD and of the apostles, that you may prosper in all things—whatever you do in flesh and spirit—by faith and by

love, in the Son, and Father, and in the Spirit, in the beginning and in the end, with your revered overseer, and with the fitly-wreathed spiritual circlet of your eldership, and with the servants who walk after God. [2] Be obedient to the overseer and to one another, as Jesus Christ was to the Father, and as the apostles were to Christ and to the Father, that there may be union both of flesh and of spirit.

CHAPTER 14

[1] Knowing that you are full of God, I have exhorted you briefly. Remember me in your prayers, that I may attain to God; and also remember the assembly which is in Syria, of which I am not worthy to be called a member. For I have need of your united prayer and love in God, that it may be granted to the assembly which is in Syria to be refreshed by the dew of your fervent supplication.

CHAPTER 15

[1] The Ephesians from Smyrna salute you, from where also I write to you. They are here with me for the glory of God, as you also are; and they have comforted me in all things, together with Polycarp, overseer of the Smyrnaeans. Yes, and all the other assemblies salute you in the honor of Jesus Christ. Farewell in godly concord, and may you possess a steadfast spirit, which is Jesus Christ.

TO THE TRALLIANS

IGNATIUS, WHO IS ALSO THEOPHORUS, TO HER THAT IS BELOVED BY GOD THE FATHER OF JESUS CHRIST; TO THE HOLY ASSEMBLY WHICH IS IN TRALLES OF ASIA, CHOSEN AND WORTHY OF GOD, HAVING PEACE IN FLESH AND SPIRIT THROUGH THE PASSION OF JESUS CHRIST, WHO IS OUR HOPE THROUGH OUR RESURRECTION TO HIM; WHICH ASSEMBLY I ALSO SALUTE IN THE DIVINE ABUNDANCE AFTER THE APOSTOLIC FASHION, AND I WISH HER ABUNDANT GREETINGS.

CHAPTER 1

[1] I have learned that you have a mind unblameable and steadfast in patience, not from habit, but by nature, according as your overseer Polybius informed me, who by the will of God and of Jesus Christ visited me in Smyrna; and so greatly did he rejoice with me in my bonds in Christ Jesus, that in him I beheld the whole multitude of you. [2] Having therefore received your godly benevolence at his hands, I gave glory, forasmuch as I had found you to be imitators of God, even as I had learned.

CHAPTER 2

[1] For when you are obedient to the overseer as to Jesus Christ, it is evident to me that you are living not after

men but after Jesus Christ, who died for us, that believing on His death you might escape death. [2] It is therefore necessary, even as your custom is, that you should do nothing without the overseer; but also be obedient to the eldership, as to the apostles of Jesus Christ our hope; for if we live in Him, we will also be found in Him. [3] And those likewise who are servants of the mysteries of Jesus Christ must please all men in all ways. For they are not servants of meats and drinks but servants of the Assembly of God. It is therefore right that they should beware of blame as of fire.

CHAPTER 3

[1] In like manner let all men respect the servants as Jesus Christ, even as they should respect the overseer as being a type of the Father and the elders as the council of God and as the college of apostles. Apart from these there is not even the name of an assembly. [2] And I am persuaded that you are so minded as touching these matters; for I received the example of your love, and I have it with me, in the person of your overseer, whose very demeanor is a great lesson, while his gentleness is power—a man to whom I think even the godless pay reverence. [3] Seeing that I love you I thus spare you, though I might write more sharply on his behalf, but I did not think myself competent for this, that being a convict I should order you as though I were an apostle.

CHAPTER 4

[1] I have many deep thoughts in God, but I take the measure of myself, lest I perish in my boasting. For now I should be the more afraid and not to give heed to those that would puff me up; for they that say these things to me are a scourge to me. [2] For though I desire to suffer, yet I do not know whether I am worthy; for the envy of the Devil is indeed unseen by many, but against me it wages the fiercer war. So then, I crave gentleness, whereby the prince of this world is brought to nothing.

CHAPTER 5

[1] Am I not able to write to you of heavenly things? But I fear lest I should cause you harm, being babies. So bear with me, lest not being able to take them in, you should be choked. [2] For I myself also, although I am in bonds, can comprehend heavenly things, and the arrays of the messengers, and the musterings of the principalities—things visible and things invisible—I myself am not yet by reason of this a disciple. For we lack many things, that God may not be lacking to us.

CHAPTER 6

[1] Therefore I exhort you—yet not I, but the love of Jesus Christ—take only Christian food, and abstain from strange herbage, which is heresy: [2] for these men even mingle poison with Jesus Christ, imposing on others by a show of honesty, like persons administering a deadly drug with honeyed wine, so that one who does not know it, fearing nothing, drinks in death with a destructive delight.

CHAPTER 7

[1] Therefore, be on your guard against such men. And this will surely be, if you are not puffed up and if you are inseparable from Jesus Christ, and from the overseer, and from the ordinances of the apostles. [2] He that is within the sanctuary is clean; but he that is outside the sanctuary is not clean, that is, he that does anything without the overseer, and eldership, and servants; this man is not clean in his conscience.

CHAPTER 8

[1] Indeed, not that I have known of any such thing among you, but I keep watch over you early, as my beloved, for I foresee the snares of the Devil. Therefore, arm yourselves with gentleness and recover yourselves in faith, which is the flesh of the LORD, and in love which is the blood of Jesus Christ. [2] Let none of you bear a grudge against his neighbor. Give no occasion to the nations, lest by reason of a few foolish men the godly multitude is blasphemed; for, "Woe to him through whom My Name is vainly blasphemed before any."

CHAPTER 9

[1] Therefore, be deaf when any man speaks to you apart from Jesus Christ, who was of the race of David, who was the Son of Mary, who was truly born, and ate, and drank, was truly persecuted under Pontius Pilate, [and] was truly crucified and died in the sight of those in Heaven, and those on earth, and those under the earth; [2] who moreover was truly raised from the dead, His Father having raised Him, who in like fashion will so raise us also who believe on Him—His Father, I say, will raise us—in Christ Jesus, apart from whom we do not have true life.

CHAPTER 10

[1] But if it were as certain persons who are godless— that is, unbelievers—say, that He suffered only in semblance, being themselves mere semblance, why am I in bonds? And why do I also desire to fight with wild beasts? So I die in vain. Truly then I lie against the LORD.

SEVEN EPISTLES OF IGNATIUS

CHAPTER 11

[1] Therefore, shun those vile offshoots that gender a deadly fruit, of which if a man taste, immediately he dies. For these men are not the Father's planting, for if they had been, they would have been seen to be branches of the Cross, and their fruit imperishable— the Cross whereby He through His passion invites us, being His members. Now it cannot be that a head should be found without members, seeing that God promises union, and this union is Himself.

CHAPTER 12

[1] I salute you from Smyrna, together with the assemblies of God that are present with me; men who refreshed me in all ways both in flesh and in spirit. [2] My bonds exhort you, which for Jesus Christ's sake I bear about, entreating that I may attain to God; abide in your concord and in prayer with one another. For it is appropriate for you separately, and more especially the elders, to cheer the soul of your overseer to the honor of the Father [and to the honor] of Jesus Christ and of the apostles. [3] I pray that you may listen to me in love, lest I be for a testimony against you by having so written. And also pray for me who has need of your love in the mercy of God, that I may be granted the lot which I am eager to attain, to the end that I am not found reprobate.

CHAPTER 13

[1] The love of the Smyrnaeans and Ephesians salutes you. Remember in your prayers the assembly which is in Syria, of which I am not worthy to be called a member, being the very last of them. [2] Farewell in Jesus Christ, submitting yourselves to the overseer as to the command, and likewise also to the eldership; and each of you separately must love one another with an undivided heart. [3] My spirit is offered up for you, not only now, but also when I will attain to God. For I am still in peril; but the Father is faithful in Jesus Christ to fulfill my petition and yours. May we be found unblameable in Him.

TO THE ROMANS

Ignatius, who is also Theophorus, to her that has found mercy in the bountifulness of the Father Most High and of Jesus Christ His only Son; to the assembly that is beloved and enlightened through the will of Him who willed all things that are, by faith and love toward Jesus Christ our God; even to her that has the presidency in the country of the region of the Romans, being worthy of God, worthy of honor, worthy of commendations, worthy of praise, worthy of success, worthy in purity, and having the presidency of love, walking in the law of Christ and bearing the Father's Name; which assembly I also salute in the Name of Jesus Christ the Son of the Father; to them that in flesh and spirit are united to His every command, being filled with the grace of God without wavering, and filtered clear from every foreign stain; abundant greetings in Jesus Christ our God in blamelessness.

CHAPTER 1

[1] In answer to my prayer to God it has been granted to me to see your godly faces, so that I have obtained even more than I asked; for wearing bonds in Christ Jesus I hope to salute you, if it be the Divine will that I should be counted worthy to reach to the end; [2] for the beginning is truly well ordered, if [it] so be I will attain to the goal, that I may receive my inheritance without hindrance. For I dread your very love, lest it do me an injury; for it is easy for you to do what you will, but for me it is difficult to attain to God, unless you will spare me.

CHAPTER 2

[1] For I would not have you to be men-pleasers but to please God, as indeed you do please Him. For neither will I myself ever find an opportunity such as this to attain to God, nor can you, if you are silent, win the credit of any nobler work. For, if you are silent and leave me alone, I am a word of God; but if you desire my flesh, then I will be again a mere cry. [2] Grant me nothing more than that I am poured out [as] a libation to God, while there is still an altar ready, that forming yourselves into a chorus in love you may sing to the Father in Jesus Christ, for that God has granted that the overseer from Syria should be found in the west, having summoned him from the east. It is good to set from the world to God, that I may rise to Him.

CHAPTER 3

[1] You never grudged anyone; you were the instructors of others. And my desire is that those lessons will hold good which as teachers you prescribe. [2] Only pray that I may have power inwardly and outwardly, so that I may not only say it but also desire it; that I may not only be called a Christian, but also be found one. For if I will be found so, then I can also be called one, and be faithful then, when I am no longer visible to the world. [3] Nothing visible is good. For our God Jesus Christ, being in the Father, is the more plainly visible. The work is not of persuasiveness, but Christianity is a thing of might, whenever it is hated by the world.

CHAPTER 4

[1] I write to all the assemblies, and I bid all men know, that of my own free will I die for God, unless you should hinder me. I exhort you, do not be an

unseasonable kindness to me. Let me be given to the wild beasts, for through them I can attain to God. I am God's wheat, and I am ground by the teeth of wild beasts that I may be found pure bread [of Christ]. [2] Rather entice the wild beasts, that they may become my tomb and may leave no part of my body behind, so that I may not, when I have fallen asleep, be burdensome to anyone. Then I will truly be a disciple of Jesus Christ, when the world will not so much as see my body. Supplicate the LORD for me, that through these instruments I may be found a sacrifice to God. [3] I do not command you, as Peter and Paul did. They were apostles, I am a convict; they were free, but I am a slave to this very hour. Yet if I will suffer, then I am a freedman of Jesus Christ, and I will rise free in Him. Now I am learning in my bonds to put away every desire.

CHAPTER 5

[1] From Syria even to Rome I fight with wild beasts, by land and sea, by night and by day, being bound amidst ten leopards, even a company of soldiers, who only wax worse when they are kindly treated. However, through their wrongdoings I become more completely a disciple; yet am I not hereby justified. [2] May I have joy of the beasts that have been prepared for me; and I pray that I may find them prompt; no, I will entice them that they may devour me promptly, not as they have done to some, refusing to touch them through fear. Yes, though of themselves they should not be willing while I am ready, I myself will force them to it. [3] Bear with me. I know what is expedient for me. Now am I beginning to be a disciple. May nothing of things visible and things invisible envy me, that I may attain to Jesus Christ. Come fire, and cross, and grapplings with wild beasts, wrenching of bones, hacking of limbs, crushings of my whole body, come cruel tortures of the Devil to assail me. Only be it mine to attain to Jesus Christ.

CHAPTER 6

[1] The farthest bounds of the universe will profit me nothing, neither the kingdoms of this world. It is good for me to die for Jesus Christ rather than to reign over the farthest bounds of the earth. I seek Him who died on our behalf; I desire Him who rose again for our sake. The pangs of a new birth are on me. [2] Bear with me, brothers. Do not hinder me from living; do not desire my death. Do not bestow on the world one who desires to be God's, neither allure him with material things. Permit me to receive the pure light. When I have come there, then I will be a man. [3] Permit me to be an imitator of the passion of my God. If any man has Him within himself, let him understand what I desire, and let him have fellow-feeling with me, for he knows the things which constrict me.

CHAPTER 7

[1] The prince of this world would gladly tear me in pieces and corrupt my mind toward God. Therefore, do not let any of you who are near aid him. Rather, stand on my side, that is on God's side. Do not speak of Jesus Christ and in addition desire the world. [2] Do not let envy have a home in you. Even though I myself, when I am with you, should implore you, do not obey me, but rather give credence to these things which I write to you. I write to you in the midst of life yet lusting after death. My lust has been crucified, and there is no fire of material longing in me, but only water living [[and speaking]] in me, saying within me, "Come to the Father." [3] I have no delight in the food of corruption or in the delights of this life. I desire the bread of God, which is the flesh of Christ who was of the seed of David; and I desire His blood for a drink, which is love incorruptible.

CHAPTER 8

[1] I no longer desire to live after the manner of men; and this will be, if you desire it. Desire that you yourselves may also be desired. [2] In a brief letter I implore you; believe me. And Jesus Christ will make these things manifest to you, that I speak the truth— Jesus Christ, the unerring mouth in whom the Father has spoken. [3] Entreat [Him] for me, that I may attain [what I desire]. I do not write to you after the flesh, but after the mind of God. If I will suffer, it was your desire; if I will be rejected, it was your hatred.

CHAPTER 9

[1] Remember in your prayers the assembly which is in Syria, which has God for its shepherd in my stead. Jesus Christ alone will be its overseer—He and your love. [2] But for myself I am ashamed to be called one of them; for neither am I worthy, being the very last of them and an untimely birth, but I have found mercy that I should be someone, if [it] so be [that] I will attain to God. [3] My spirit salutes you, and the love of the assemblies which received me in the Name of Jesus Christ, not as a mere wayfarer; for even those assemblies which did not lie on my route after the flesh went before me from city to city.

CHAPTER 10

[1] Now I write these things to you from Smyrna by the hand of the Ephesians who are worthy of all commendations. And Crocus also, a name very dear to me, is with me, with many others besides. [2] As touching those who went before me from Syria to Rome to the glory of God, I believe that you have received instructions; whom also apprise that I am near; for they are all worthy of God and of you, and it is appropriate for you to refresh them in all things. [3] These things I write to you on the ninth before the Calends of September. Farewell to the end in the patient waiting for Jesus Christ.

SEVEN EPISTLES OF IGNATIUS

TO THE PHILADELPHIANS

IGNATIUS, WHO IS ALSO THEOPHORUS, TO THE ASSEMBLY OF GOD THE FATHER AND OF JESUS CHRIST, WHICH IS IN PHILADELPHIA OF ASIA, WHICH HAS FOUND MERCY AND IS FIRMLY ESTABLISHED IN THE CONCORD OF GOD AND REJOICES IN THE PASSION OF OUR LORD AND IN HIS RESURRECTION WITHOUT WAVERING, BEING FULLY ASSURED IN ALL MERCY; WHICH ASSEMBLY I SALUTE IN THE BLOOD OF JESUS CHRIST, THAT IS CONTINUOUS AND ABIDING JOY; MORE ESPECIALLY IF THEY ARE AT ONE WITH THE OVERSEER AND THE ELDERS WHO ARE WITH HIM, AND WITH THE SERVANTS THAT HAVE BEEN APPOINTED ACCORDING TO THE MIND OF JESUS CHRIST, WHOM AFTER HIS OWN WILL HE CONFIRMED AND ESTABLISHED BY HIS HOLY SPIRIT.

CHAPTER 1

[1] I have found your overseer to hold the ministry which pertains to the common [good], not of himself or through men, nor yet for vain glory, but in the love of God the Father and the Lord Jesus Christ. And I am amazed at his forbearance, whose silence is more powerful than others' speech. [2] For he is attuned in harmony with the commands, as a lyre with its strings. For what reason my soul blesses his godly mind, for I have found that it is virtuous and perfect—even the composed and calm temper which he has, while living in all godly forbearance.

CHAPTER 2

[1] Therefore, as children of the light and truth, shun division and wrong doctrines; and where the shepherd is, follow there as sheep. [2] For many deceptive wolves with destructive delights lead captive the runners in God's race; but, where you are at one, they will find no place.

CHAPTER 3

[1] Abstain from noxious herbs, which are not the farming of Jesus Christ, because they are not the planting of the Father. Not that I have found division among you, but filtering. [2] For as many as are of God and of Jesus Christ, they are with the overseer; and as many as will convert and enter into the unity of the Assembly, these also will be of God, that they may be living after Jesus Christ. [3] Do not be deceived, my brothers. If any man follows one that makes a schism, he does not inherit the Kingdom of God. If any man walks in strange doctrine, he has no fellowship with the passion.

CHAPTER 4

[1] Therefore, be careful to observe one thanksgiving (for there is one flesh of our Lord Jesus Christ and one cup to union in His blood; there is one altar, as there is one overseer, together with the eldership and the servants—my fellow-servants), that whatever you do, you may do it after God.

CHAPTER 5

[1] My brothers, my heart overflows altogether in love toward you; and rejoicing above measure I watch over your safety; yet not I, but Jesus Christ, wearing whose bonds I am the more afraid, because I am not yet perfected. But your prayer will make me perfect [to God], that I may attain to the inheritance wherein I have found mercy, taking refuge in the good news as the flesh of Jesus and in the apostles as the eldership of the Assembly. [2] Yes, and we love the prophets also, because they too pointed to the good news in their preaching and set their hope on Him and awaited Him; in whom also having faith, they were saved in the unity of Jesus Christ, being worthy of all love and admiration as holy men, approved of Jesus Christ and numbered together in the good news of our common hope.

CHAPTER 6

[1] But if anyone presents Judaism to you, do not hear him; for it is better to hear Christianity from a man who is circumcised than Judaism from one uncircumcised. But if either the one or the other does not speak concerning Jesus Christ, I look on them as tombstones and graves of the dead, whereon are inscribed only the names of men. [2] Therefore, shun the wicked arts and plottings of the prince of this world, lest by chance you are crushed by his devices, and grow weak in your love. But assemble all yourselves together with undivided heart. [3] And I give thanks to my God, that I have a good conscience in my dealings with you, and no man can boast, either in secret or openly, that I was burdensome to anyone in small things or in great. Yes, and for all among whom I spoke, it is my prayer that they may not turn it into a testimony against themselves.

CHAPTER 7

[1] For even though certain persons desired to deceive me after the flesh, yet the Spirit is not deceived, being from God; for He knows from where He comes and where He goes, and He searches out the hidden things. I cried out when I was among you; I spoke with a loud voice, with God's own voice, "Give heed to the overseer, and the eldership, and servants." [2] However, there were those who suspected me of saying this, because I knew beforehand of the division of certain persons. But He in whom I am bound is my witness that I did not learn it from flesh of man; it was the preaching of the Spirit who spoke concerning this: "Do nothing without the overseer; keep your flesh as a temple of God; cherish union; shun divisions; be imitators of Jesus Christ, as He Himself also was of His Father."

CHAPTER 8

[1] Therefore, I did my own part, as a man composed to union. But where there is division and anger, there God does not abide. Now the LORD forgives all men when they convert, if converting they return to the unity of God and to the council of the overseer. I have faith in the grace of Jesus Christ, who will strike off every chain from you; [2] and I entreat you to do nothing in a spirit of factiousness, but after the teaching of Christ. For I heard certain persons saying, "If I do not find it in the charters, I do not believe it in the good news." And when I said to them, "It is written," they answered me, "That is the question." But as for me, my charter is Jesus Christ, the inviolable charter is His cross, and His death, and His resurrection, and faith through Him, wherein I desire to be justified through your prayers.

CHAPTER 9

[1] The priests likewise were good, but better is the Chief Priest to whom is committed the Holy of Holies; for to Him alone are committed the hidden things of God, He Himself being the door of the Father, through which Abraham, and Isaac, and Jacob enter in, and the prophets, and the apostles, and the whole Assembly; all these things combine in the unity of God. [2] But the good news has a singular preeminence in the advent of the Savior, even our Lord Jesus Christ, and His passion and resurrection. For the beloved prophets in their preaching pointed to Him; but the good news is the completion of immortality. All things together are good, if you believe through love.

CHAPTER 10

[1] Seeing that in answer to your prayer and to the tender sympathy which you have in Christ Jesus, it has been reported to me that the assembly which is in Antioch of Syria has peace, it is appropriate for you, as an assembly of God, to appoint a servant to go there as God's ambassador, that he may congratulate them when they are assembled together, and may glorify the Name. [2] Blessed in Jesus Christ is he that will be counted worthy of such a service; and you yourselves will be glorified. Now if you desire it, it is not impossible for you to do this for the Name of God, even as the assemblies which are nearest have sent overseers, and others elders and servants.

CHAPTER 11

[1] But as touching Philo the servant from Cilicia, a man of good report, who now also ministers to me in the word of God, together with Rhaius Agathopus, a chosen one who follows me from Syria, having bid farewell to this present life, these also bear witness to you—and I myself thank God on your behalf, because you received them, as I trust the LORD will receive you. But may those who treated them with dishonor

be redeemed through the grace of Jesus Christ. [2] The love of the brothers which are in Troas salutes you; from where I also write to you by the hand of Burrhus, who was sent with me by the Ephesians and Smyrnaeans as a mark of honor. The LORD will honor them, even Jesus Christ, on whom their hope is set in flesh, and soul, and spirit, by faith, by love, by concord. Farewell in Christ Jesus our common hope.

TO THE SMYRNAEANS

IGNATIUS, WHO IS ALSO THEOPHORUS, TO THE ASSEMBLY OF GOD THE FATHER AND OF JESUS CHRIST THE BELOVED, WHICH HAS BEEN MERCIFULLY ENDOWED WITH EVERY GRACE, BEING FILLED WITH FAITH AND LOVE, AND LACKING IN NO GRACE, MOST WORTHY AND BEARING HOLY TREASURES; TO THE ASSEMBLY WHICH IS IN SMYRNA OF ASIA, IN A BLAMELESS SPIRIT AND IN THE WORD OF GOD: ABUNDANT GREETINGS.

CHAPTER 1

[1] I give glory to Jesus Christ, the God who bestowed such wisdom on you; for I have perceived that you are established in immovable faith, being as it were nailed on the Cross of the Lord Jesus Christ, in flesh and in spirit, and firmly grounded in love in the blood of Christ, fully persuaded as touching our Lord that He is truly of the race of David according to the flesh, but Son of God by the Divine will and power, truly born of a virgin and immersed by John that all righteousness might be fulfilled by Him, [2] truly nailed up in the flesh for our sakes under Pontius Pilate and Herod the tetrarch (of which fruit we are—that is, of His most blessed passion), that He might set up an ensign to all the ages through His resurrection, for His holy ones and faithful people, whether among Jews or among nations, in one body of His Assembly.

CHAPTER 2

[1] For He suffered all these things for our sakes, that we might be saved; and He truly suffered, as He also truly raised Himself; not as certain unbelievers say, that He suffered in semblance [only], being themselves mere semblance. And according as their opinions are, so will it happen to them, for they are without body and demon-like.

CHAPTER 3

[1] For I know and believe that He was in the flesh even after the resurrection; [2] and when He came to Peter and his company, He said to them, "Lay hold and handle Me, and see that I am not a bodiless spirit." And immediately they touched Him, and they believed, being joined to His flesh and His blood. For what reason they also despised death, no, they were found superior to death. [3] And after His resurrection, He ate with them and drank with them as one in the

flesh, though spiritually He was united with the Father.

CHAPTER 4

[1] But these things I warn you, dearly beloved, knowing that you yourselves are so minded. However, I watch over you early to protect you from wild beasts in human form—men whom not only you should not receive, but, if it were possible, not so much as meet [them]; only pray for them, if by chance they may convert. This is indeed difficult, but Jesus Christ, our true life, has power over it. [2] For if these things were done by our Lord in semblance, then I am also a prisoner in semblance. And why then have I delivered myself over to death, to fire, to sword, to wild beasts? But near to the sword, near to God; in company with wild beasts, in company with God. Only let it be in the Name of Jesus Christ, so that we may suffer together with Him. I endure all things, seeing that He Himself, who is perfect Man, enables me.

CHAPTER 5

[1] But certain persons ignorantly deny Him, or rather have been denied by Him, being advocates of death rather than of the truth; and they have not been persuaded by the prophecies, nor by the Law of Moses, no, nor even to this very hour by the good news, nor by the sufferings of each of us separately; [2] for they are of the same mind also concerning us. For what profit is it [to me] if a man praises me, but blasphemes my Lord, not confessing that He was a bearer of flesh? Yet he that does not affirm this, does thereby deny Him altogether, being himself a bearer of a corpse. [3] But their names, being unbelievers, I have not thought fit to record in writing; no, far be it from me even to remember them, until they convert and return to the passion, which is our resurrection.

CHAPTER 6

[1] Let no man be deceived. Even the heavenly beings, and the glory of the messengers, and the rulers visible and invisible, if they do not believe in the blood of Christ, judgment awaits them also. He that receives let him receive. Do not let office puff up any man; for faith and love are all in all, and nothing is preferred before them. [2] But mark those who hold strange doctrine touching the grace of Jesus Christ which came to us, how that they are contrary to the mind of God. They have no care for love, none for the widow, none for the orphan, none for the afflicted, none for the prisoner, none for the hungry or thirsty. They abstain from thanksgiving and prayer, because they do not allow that the thanksgiving is the flesh of our Savior Jesus Christ, which flesh suffered for our sins, and which the Father of His goodness raised up.

CHAPTER 7

[1] Therefore, they that deny the good gift of God perish by their questionings. But it would be expedient for them to have love, that they may also rise again. [2] It is therefore appropriate that you should abstain from such, and not speak of them either privately or in public, but should give heed to the prophets, and especially to the good news, wherein the passion is shown to us and the resurrection is accomplished.

CHAPTER 8

[1] [But] shun divisions, as the beginning of evils. All of you must follow your overseer, as Jesus Christ followed the Father, and the eldership as the apostles; and pay respect to the servants, as to God's command. Let no man do anything of things pertaining to the Assembly apart from the overseer. Let that be held a valid thanksgiving which is under the overseer or one to whom he will have committed it. [2] Wherever the overseer will appear, let the people be there, even as where Jesus may be, there is the universal Assembly. It is not lawful apart from the overseer either to immerse or to hold a love-feast; but whatever he will approve, this is also well-pleasing to God, that everything which you do may be sure and valid.

CHAPTER 9

[1] It is reasonable, from now on, that we wake to soberness, while we have time to convert and turn to God. It is good to recognize God and the overseer. He that honors the overseer is honored of God; he that does anything without the knowledge of the overseer renders service to the Devil. [2] Therefore, may all things abound to you in grace, for you are worthy. You refreshed me in all things, and Jesus Christ will refresh you. In my absence and in my presence, you cherished me. May God reward you, for whose sake if you endure all things, you will attain to Him.

CHAPTER 10

[1] Philo and Rhaius Agathopus, who followed me in the cause of God, you did well to receive as ministers of God—who also give thanks to the LORD for you, because you refreshed them in every way. Nothing will be lost to you. [2] My spirit is devoted for you, as are my bonds also, which you did not despise, neither were ashamed of them. Nor will He, who is perfect faithfulness, be ashamed of you, even Jesus Christ.

CHAPTER 11

[1] Your prayer sped forth to the assembly which is in Antioch of Syria, from where, coming [as] a prisoner in most godly bonds, I salute all men, though I am not worthy to belong to it, being the very last of them. By the Divine will this was granted to me—not of my own complicity, but by God's grace, which I pray may be given to me perfectly, that through your prayers I may attain to God. [2] Therefore, that your

work may be perfected both on earth and in Heaven, it is suitable that your assembly should appoint, for the honor of God, an ambassador of God that he may go as far as Syria and congratulate them because they are at peace, and have recovered their proper stature, and their proper bulk has been restored to them. ³It seemed to me, therefore, a fitting thing that you should send one of your own people with a letter, that he might join with them in giving glory for the calm which by God's will had overtaken them, and because they were already reaching a haven through your prayers. Seeing you are perfect, let your counsels also be perfect; for if you desire to do well, God is ready to grant the means.

CHAPTER 12

¹The love of the brothers which are in Troas salutes you, from where I also write to you by the hand of Burrhus, whom you sent with me jointly with the Ephesians, your brothers. He has refreshed me in all ways. And I wish that all imitated him, for he is an example of the ministry of God. The Divine grace will repay him in all things. ²I salute your godly overseer, and your venerable eldership, [and] my fellow-servants the servants, and all of you separately and in a body, in the Name of Jesus Christ, and in His flesh and blood, in His passion and resurrection, which was both carnal and spiritual, in the unity of God and of yourselves. Grace to you, mercy, peace, patience, always.

CHAPTER 13

¹I salute the households of my brothers with their wives and children, and the virgins who are called widows. I bid you farewell in the power of the Father. Philo, who is with me, salutes you. ²I salute the household of Gavia, and I pray that she may be grounded in faith and love, both of flesh and of spirit. I salute Alce, a name very dear to me, and the incomparable Daphnus, and Eutecnus, and all by name. Farewell in the grace of God.

TO POLYCARP

IGNATIUS, WHO IS ALSO THEOPHORUS, TO POLYCARP WHO IS OVERSEER OF THE ASSEMBLY OF THE SMYRNAEANS, OR RATHER, WHO HAS FOR HIS OVERSEER GOD THE FATHER AND JESUS CHRIST: ABUNDANT GREETINGS.

CHAPTER 1

¹Welcoming your godly mind which is grounded as it were on an immovable rock, I give exceeding glory that it has been granted to me to see your blameless face, of which I would gladly have joy in God. ²I exhort you in the grace with which you are clothed to press forward in your course and to exhort all men that they may be saved. Vindicate your office in all

diligence of flesh and of spirit. Have a care for union, more than which there is nothing better. Bear all men, as the LORD also bears you. Permit all men in love, as you do also. ³Give yourself to unceasing prayers. Ask for larger wisdom than you have. Be watchful and keep your spirit from slumbering. Speak to each man separately after the manner of God. Bear the ailments of all, as a perfect athlete. Where there is more toil, there is much gain.

CHAPTER 2

¹If you love good scholars, this is not worthy of thanks in you. Rather, bring the more pernicious to submission by gentleness. All wounds are not healed by the same salve. Lessen sharp pains by poultices. ²Be prudent as the serpent in all things and always guileless as the dove. Therefore, you are made of flesh and spirit, that you may humor the things which appear before your eyes; and as for the invisible things, pray that they may be revealed to you, that you may be lacking in nothing, but may abound in every spiritual gift. ³The season requires you, as pilots require winds or as a storm-tossed mariner a haven, that it may attain to God. Be sober, as God's athlete. The prize is incorruption and continuous life, concerning which you are also persuaded. In all things I am devoted to you—myself and my bonds which you cherished.

CHAPTER 3

¹Do not let those that seem to be plausible and yet teach strange doctrine dismay you. Stand firm, as an anvil when it is smitten. It is the part of a great athlete to receive blows and be victorious. But we must especially endure all things for God's sake, that He may also endure us. ²Be more diligent than you are. Mark the seasons. Await Him that is above every season—the Perpetual, the Invisible, who became visible for our sake; the Impalpable, the Impassible, who suffered for our sake, who endured in all ways for our sake.

CHAPTER 4

¹Do not let widows be neglected. After the LORD, be their protector. Let nothing be done without your consent; neither do anything without the consent of God, as indeed you do not. Be steadfast. ²Let meetings be held more frequently. Seek out all men by name. ³Do not despise slaves, whether men or women. Yet do not let these be puffed up, but rather let them serve the more faithfully to the glory of God, that they may obtain a better freedom from God. Do not let them desire to be set free at the public cost, lest they are found slaves of lust.

CHAPTER 5

¹Flee evil arts, or rather, hold discourse about these. Tell my sisters to love the LORD and to be content

with their husbands in flesh and in spirit. In like manner also, charge my brothers in the Name of Jesus Christ to love their wives, as the LORD loved the Assembly. [2] If anyone is able to abide in chastity to the honor of the flesh of the LORD, let him so abide without boasting. If he boasts, he is lost; and if it is known beyond the overseer, he is polluted. It is appropriate for men and women too, when they marry, to unite themselves with the consent of the overseer, that the marriage may be after the LORD and not after lust. Let all things be done to the honor of God.

CHAPTER 6

[1] Give heed to the overseer, that God may also give heed to you. I am devoted to those who are subject to the overseer, the elders, [and] the servants. May it be granted to me to have my portion with them in the presence of God. Toil together with one another, struggle together, run together, suffer together, lie down together, rise up together, as God's stewards, and assessors, and ministers. [2] Please the Captain in whose army you serve, from whom you will also receive your pay. Let none of you be found a deserter. Let your immersion abide with you as your shield, your faith as your helmet, your love as your spear, your patience as your body armor. Let your works be your deposits, that you may receive your assets due to you. Therefore, be long-suffering with one another in gentleness, as God is with you. May I have your joy always.

CHAPTER 7

[1] Seeing that the assembly which is in Antioch of Syria has peace, as it has been reported to me, through your prayers, I myself have also been the more comforted since God has banished my care, if [it] so be [that] I may attain to God through suffering, that I may be found a disciple through your intercession. [2] It is appropriate for you, most blessed Polycarp, to call together a godly council and to choose some one among you who is very dear to you and zealous also, who will be fit to bear the name of God's courier—to appoint him, I say, that he may go to Syria and glorify your zealous love to the glory of God. [3] A Christian has no authority over himself, but gives his time to God. This is God's work, and yours also, when you will complete it; for I trust in the Divine grace, that you are ready for an act of well-doing which is [to] meet for God. Knowing the fervor of your sincerity, I have exhorted you in a short letter.

CHAPTER 8

[1] Since I have not been able to write to all the assemblies, by reason of my sailing suddenly from Troas to Neapolis, as the Divine will prescribes, you will write to the assemblies in front, as one possessing the mind of God, to the intent that they may also do this same thing—let those who are able send messengers, and the rest letters by the persons who are sent by you, that you may be glorified by an ever memorable deed—for this is worthy of you. [2] I salute all by name, and especially the wife of Epitropus with her whole household and her children's. I salute my beloved Attalus. I salute him that will be appointed to go to Syria. Grace will be with him always, and with Polycarp who sends him. [3] I bid you farewell always in our God Jesus Christ, in whom you abide in the unity and supervision of God. I salute Alce, a name very dear to me. Farewell in the LORD.

EPISTLE OF POLYCARP TO THE PHILIPPIANS

Polycarp, overseer of Smyrna and a disciple of John the Apostle, was martyred for his faith in about 155 AD at the age of 86 or 87. His letter to the Philippians is a central and well-attested document among early Christian writings and forms part of what is popularly called the *Apostolic Fathers*.

POLYCARP AND THE ELDERS WITH HIM TO THE ASSEMBLY OF GOD SOJOURNING IN PHILIPPI; MERCY AND PEACE FROM GOD ALMIGHTY AND JESUS CHRIST OUR SAVIOR BE MULTIPLIED TO YOU.

CHAPTER 1

[1] I greatly rejoice with you in our Lord Jesus Christ that you have followed the pattern of true love, and have helped on their way, as opportunity was given you, those who were bound in chains, which become the holy ones, and are the diadems of those who have been truly chosen by God and our Lord. [2] I also rejoice that your firmly rooted faith, which was famous in past years, still flourishes and bears fruit to our Lord Jesus Christ, who endured for our sins, even to the suffering of death, "whom God raised up, having loosed the pangs of Hades, [3] in whom, though you did not see Him, you believed in unspeakable and glorified joy"—into which joy many desire to come, knowing that "by grace you are saved, not by works" but by the will of God through Jesus Christ.

CHAPTER 2

[1] "For what reason, girding up your loins, serve God in fear" and truth, putting aside empty vanity and vulgar error, "believing on Him who raised up our Lord Jesus Christ from the dead and gave Him glory," and a throne on His right hand, "to whom are subject all things in the heavens and earth," whom all breath serves, who is coming as "the Judge of the living and of the dead," whose blood God will require from them who disobey Him. [2] Now "He who raised Him" from the dead "will also raise us up" if we do His will, and walk in His commands, and love the things which He loved, refraining from all unrighteousness, covetousness, love of money, evil speaking, false witness, "not rendering evil for evil, or railing for railing," or blow for blow, or curse for curse, [3] but remembering what the LORD taught when He said, "Do not judge so that you are not judged, forgive and

it will be forgiven to you, be merciful that you may obtain mercy, with what measure you mete, it will be measured to you again," and "Blessed are the poor, and they who are persecuted for righteousness' sake, for theirs is the Kingdom of God."

CHAPTER 3

[1] These things, brothers, I write to you concerning righteousness, not at my own instance, but because you first invited me. [2] For neither am I, nor is any other like me, able to follow the wisdom of the blessed and glorious Paul, who when he was among you in the presence of the men of that time accurately and steadfastly taught the word of truth, and also when he was absent wrote letters to you, from the study of which you will be able to build yourselves up into the faith given to you, [3] "which is the mother of us all" when faith follows, and love of God, and Christ, and neighbor goes before. For if one is in this company, he has fulfilled the command of righteousness, for he who has love is far from all sin.

CHAPTER 4

[1] "But the beginning of all evils is the love of money." Knowing therefore that "we brought nothing into the world and we can take nothing out of it," let us arm ourselves with the armor of righteousness, and let us first of all teach ourselves to walk in the command of the LORD; [2] next teach our wives to remain in the faith given to them, and in love and purity, tenderly loving their husbands in all truth, and loving all others equally in all chastity, and to educate their children in the fear of God. [3] Let us teach the widows to be discreet in the faith of the LORD, praying ceaselessly for all men, being far from all slander, evil speaking, false witness, love of money, and all evil, knowing that they are the altar of God, and that all offerings are tested, and that nothing escapes Him of reasonings or thoughts, or of "the secret things of the heart."

CHAPTER 5

[1] Knowing then that "God is not mocked," we should walk worthily of His command and glory. [2] Likewise must the servants be blameless before His righteousness, as the servants of God and Christ and not of man, not slanderers, not double-tongued, not

lovers of money, [but] temperate in all things, compassionate, careful, walking according to the truth of the LORD, who was the "servant of all." For if we please Him in this present world, we will receive from Him that which is to come, even as He promised us to raise us from the dead, and that if we are worthy citizens of His community, "we will also reign with Him," if we have but faith. ³Likewise also, let the younger men be blameless in all things, caring, above all, for purity, and curbing themselves from all evil; for it is good to be cut off from the lust of the things in the world, because "every lust wars against the Spirit, and neither fornicators, nor the effeminate, nor sodomites will inherit the Kingdom of God," nor they who do iniquitous things. For what reason it is necessary to refrain from all these things, and to be subject to the elders and servants as to God and Christ. The virgins must walk with a blameless and pure conscience.

CHAPTER 6

¹And let the elders also be compassionate, merciful to all, bringing back those that have wandered, caring for all the weak, neglecting neither widow, nor orphan, nor poor, but "always providing for that which is good before God and man," refraining from all wrath, respect of persons, [and] unjust judgment, [and] being far from all love of money, not quickly believing evil of any, not hasty in judgment, knowing that "we all owe the debt of sin." ²If then we pray to the LORD to forgive us, we also should forgive, for we stand before the eyes of the LORD and of God, and "we must all appear before the judgment seat of Christ, and each must give an account of himself." ³So then "let us serve Him with fear and all reverence," as He Himself commanded us, and as did the apostles, who brought us the good news, and the prophets who foretold the coming of our Lord. Let us be zealous for good, refraining from offense, and from the false brothers, and from those who bear the Name of the LORD in hypocrisy, who deceive empty-minded men.

CHAPTER 7

¹"For everyone who does not confess that Jesus Christ has come in the flesh is an antichrist"; and whoever does not confess the testimony of the Cross is of the Devil; and whoever perverts the oracles of the LORD for his own lusts, and says that there is neither resurrection nor judgment—this man is the firstborn of Satan. ²For what reason, leaving the foolishness of the crowd, and their false teaching, let us turn back to the word which was delivered to us in the beginning, "watching to prayer" and persevering

in fasting, imploring the all-seeing God in our supplications "to lead us not into temptation," even as the LORD said, "The spirit is forward, but the flesh weak."

CHAPTER 8

¹Let us then persevere unceasingly in our hope, and in the pledge of our righteousness, that is in Christ Jesus, "who bore our sins in His own body on the tree, who did no sin, neither was guile found in His mouth," but for our sakes, that we might live in Him, He endured all things. ²Let us then be imitators of His endurance, and if we suffer for His Name's sake, let us glorify Him. For this is the example which He gave us in Himself, and this is what we have believed.

CHAPTER 9

¹Now I implore you all to obey the word of righteousness, and to endure with all the endurance which you also saw before your eyes, not only in the blessed Ignatius, and Zosimus, and Rufus, but also in others among yourselves, and in Paul himself, and in the other apostles; ²being persuaded that all of these "did not run in vain," but in faith and righteousness, and that they are with the LORD in the "place which is their due," with whom they also suffered. For they did not "love this present world" but Him who died on our behalf, and was raised by God for our sakes.

CHAPTER 10

¹Therefore, stand firm in these things and follow the example of the LORD, "firm and unchangeable in faith, loving the brotherhood, affectionate to one another," joined together in the truth, preempting one another in the gentleness of the LORD, despising no man. ²When you can do good, do not defer it, "for kindness sets free from death; let all be subject to one another, having your conversation blameless among the nations," that you may receive praise "for your good works" and that the LORD not be blasphemed in you. ³"But woe to him through whom the Name of the LORD is blasphemed." Therefore, teach sobriety to all and show it forth in your own lives.

CHAPTER 11

¹I am deeply sorry for Valens, who was once made an elder among you, that he so little understands the place which was given to him. I advise, therefore, that you keep from greed, and be pure and truthful. Keep yourselves from all evil. ²For how may he who cannot attain self-control in these matters prescribe it on another? If any man does not abstain from greed he will be defiled by idolatry and will be judged as if he were among the nations who "do not know the

judgment of God." Or do we "not know that the holy ones will judge the world?" as Paul teaches. [3]But I have neither perceived nor heard any such thing among you, among whom the blessed Paul labored, who are praised in the beginning of his Letter. For concerning you he boasts in all the assemblies who then alone had known the LORD, for we had not yet known Him. [4]Therefore, brothers, I am deeply sorry for him [(Valens)] and for his wife, and "may the LORD grant them true conversion." Therefore, be also moderate in this matter yourselves, and "do not regard such men as enemies," but call them back as fallible and straying members, that you may make whole the body of you all. For in doing this you edify yourselves.

CHAPTER 12

[1]For I am confident that you are well versed in the Writings, and from you nothing is hidden; but to me this is not granted. Only, as it is said in these Writings, "Be angry and do not sin," and "Do not let the sun go down on your wrath." Blessed is the man who remembers this, and I believe that it is so with you. [2]Now may God and the Father of our Lord Jesus Christ, and the "perpetual Priest" Himself—Jesus Christ, the Son of God—build you up in faith and truth, and in all gentleness, and without wrath, and in patience, and in long-suffering, and endurance, and purity, and may He give you lot and part with His holy ones, and to us with you, and to all under Heaven who will believe in our Lord and God Jesus Christ

and in His "Father who raised Him from the dead." [3]"Pray for all the holy ones. Pray also for the emperors," and for potentates, and princes, and for "those who persecute you and hate you," and for "the enemies of the Cross" that "your fruit may be manifest among all men, that you may be perfected" in Him.

CHAPTER 13

[1]Both you and Ignatius wrote to me that if anyone was going to Syria he should also take your letters. I will do this if I have a convenient opportunity—either myself or the man whom I am sending as a representative for you and me. [2]We send you, as you asked, the letters of Ignatius, which were sent to us by him, and others which we had by us. These are appended to this letter, and you will be able to benefit greatly from them. For they contain faith, patience, and all the edification which pertains to our LORD. Let us know anything further which you have heard about Ignatius himself and those who are with him.

CHAPTER 14

[1]I have written this to you by Crescens, whom I commended to you when I was present, and now commend again. For he has behaved blamelessly among us, and I believe that he will do the same with you. His sister will be commended to you when she comes to you. Farewell in the Lord Jesus Christ in grace, with all who are yours. Amen.

MARTYRDOM OF POLYCARP

Written as a letter from the church in Smyrna to the church in Philomelium, this is a vivid account of the martyrdom of Polycarp at the hands of the Romans. One of the most famous calls to Christian courage in the face of great persecution is found in this account: "Be strong . . . play the man!" (v. 9:1). An alternative conclusion found in the Moscow Codex (ch. 23) was later added to address the heretical Marcionites, but is not included here.

THE ASSEMBLY OF GOD WHICH SOJOURNS IN SMYRNA, TO THE ASSEMBLY OF GOD WHICH SOJOURNS IN PHILOMELIUM, AND TO ALL THE SOJOURNINGS OF THE HOLY UNIVERSAL ASSEMBLY IN EVERY PLACE. "MERCY, PEACE, AND LOVE" OF GOD THE FATHER AND OUR LORD JESUS CHRIST BE MULTIPLIED.

CHAPTER 1

¹ We write to you, brothers, the story of the martyrs and of the blessed Polycarp, who put an end to the persecution by his martyrdom as though adding the seal. For one might almost say that all that had gone before happened in order that the LORD might show to us from above a martyrdom in accordance with the good news. ² For he waited to be betrayed as also the LORD had done, that we too might become his imitators, "not thinking of ourselves alone, but also of our neighbors." For it is the mark of true and steadfast love not to wish that oneself may be saved alone, but all the brothers also.

CHAPTER 2

¹ Blessed then and noble are all the martyrdoms which took place according to the will of God, for we must be very careful to assign the power over all to God. ² For who would not admire their nobility, and patience, and love of their Master? For some were torn by scourging until the mechanism of their flesh was seen even to the lower veins and arteries, and they endured so that even the bystanders pitied them and mourned. And some even reached such a pitch of nobility that none of them groaned or wailed, showing to all of us that at that hour of their torture the noble martyrs of Christ were absent from the flesh, or rather that the LORD was standing by and talking with them. ³ And paying heed to the grace of Christ they despised worldly tortures, by a single hour purchasing continuous life. And the fire of their cruel torturers had no heat for them, for they set before their eyes an escape from the fire which is continuous and is never quenched, and with the eyes of their heart they looked up to the good things which are preserved for those who have endured, "which neither ear has heard nor eye has seen, nor has it entered into the heart of man," but it was shown by the LORD to them who were no longer men but already messengers. ⁴ And in the same way also, those who were condemned to the beasts endured terrible torment, being stretched on sharp shells and buffeted with other kinds of various torments, that if it were possible, the tyrant might bring them to a denial by continuous torture. For the Devil used many schemes against them.

CHAPTER 3

¹ But thanks be to God, for he had no power over any. For the most noble Germanicus encouraged their fears by the endurance which was in him, and he fought gloriously with the wild beasts. For when the proconsul wished to persuade him and commanded him to have pity on his youth, he violently dragged the beast toward himself, wishing to be released more quickly from their unrighteous and lawless life. ² So after this, all the crowd, wondering at the nobility of the God-loving and God-fearing people of the Christians, cried out: "Away with the atheists! Let Polycarp be searched for."

CHAPTER 4

¹ But one, named Quintus, a Phrygian having lately come from Phrygia, when he saw the wild beasts, played the coward. Now it was he who had forced himself and some others to come forward of their own accord. Him the proconsul persuaded with many entreaties to take the oath and offer sacrifice. For this reason, therefore, brothers, we do not commend those who give themselves up, since the good news does not give this teaching.

CHAPTER 5

¹ But the most wonderful Polycarp, when he first heard it, was not disturbed, but wished to remain in the city; but the majority persuaded him to go away quietly, and he went out quietly to a farm, not far distant from the city, and stayed with a few friends, doing nothing but pray night and day for all, and for the assemblies throughout the world, as was his custom. ² And while he was praying, he fell into a trance three days before he was arrested and saw the pillow under his head burning with fire, and he turned

and said to those who were with him: "I must be burned alive."

CHAPTER 6

[1] And when the searching for him persisted he went to another farm; and those who were searching for him came up at once, and when they did not find him, they arrested young slaves, and one of them confessed under torture. [2] For it was indeed impossible for him to remain hidden, since those who betrayed him were of his own house, and the police captain who had been allotted the very name, being called Herod, hastened to bring him to the arena that he might fulfill his appointed lot by becoming a partaker of Christ, while they who betrayed him should undergo the same punishment as Judas.

CHAPTER 7

[1] Taking the slave then, police and cavalry went out on Friday about dinnertime, with their usual arms, as if they were advancing against a robber. And late in the evening they came up together against him and found him lying in an upper room. And he might have departed to another place, but would not, saying, "May the will of God be done." [2] So when he heard that they had arrived he went down and talked with them, while those who were present wondered at his age and courage, and why there was so much haste for the arrest of an old man of such a kind. Therefore, he ordered food and drink to be set before them at that hour, whatever they should wish, and he asked them to give him an hour to pray without hindrance. [3] To this they assented, and he stood and prayed—thus filled with the grace of God—so that for two hours he could not be silent, and those who listened were astounded, and many regretted that they had come against such a venerable old man.

CHAPTER 8

[1] Now when he had at last finished his prayer, after remembering all who had ever even come his way, both small and great, high and low, and the whole universal Assembly throughout the world, the hour came for departure, and they set him on a donkey, and led him into the city, on a great Sabbath day. [2] And the police captain Herod and his father Niketas met him and removed him into their carriage, and sat by his side trying to persuade him, and saying, "But what harm is it to say, Lord Caesar, and to offer sacrifice, and so forth, and to be saved?" But he at first did not answer them, but when they continued he said, "I am not going to do what you counsel me." [3] And they gave up the attempt to persuade him, and began to speak fiercely to him, and turned him out in such a

hurry that in getting down from the carriage he scraped his shin; and without turning around, as though he had suffered nothing, he walked on promptly and quickly, and was taken to the arena, while the uproar in the arena was so great that no one could even be heard.

CHAPTER 9

[1] Now when Polycarp entered into the arena there came a voice from Heaven: "Be strong, Polycarp, and play the man!" And no one saw the speaker, but our friends who were there heard the voice. And next he was brought forward, and there was a great uproar of those who heard that Polycarp had been arrested. [2] Therefore, when he was brought forward the proconsul asked him if he was Polycarp, and when he admitted it he tried to persuade him to deny [it], saying, "Respect your age," and so forth, as they are accustomed to say: "Swear by the genius of Caesar, convert, say: Away with the Atheists"; but Polycarp, with a stern countenance looked on all the crowd of lawless heathen in the arena, and waving his hand at them, he groaned and looked up to Heaven and said, "Away with the Atheists." [3] But when the proconsul pressed him and said, "Take the oath and I let you go; revile Christ," Polycarp said, "For eighty-six years I have been His servant, and He has done me no wrong, and how can I blaspheme my King who saved me?"

CHAPTER 10

[1] But when he persisted again, and said, "Swear by the genius of Caesar," he answered him: "If you vainly suppose that I will swear by the genius of Caesar, as you say, and pretend that you are ignorant of who I am, listen plainly: I am a Christian. And if you wish to learn the doctrine of Christianity fix a day and listen." [2] The proconsul said, "Persuade the people." And Polycarp said, "I have thought it worthy to give you an account, for we have been taught to render honor [to authorities] as is suitable, if it does not hurt us, to princes and authorities appointed by God. But as for those, I do not count them worthy that a defense should be made to them."

CHAPTER 11

[1] And the proconsul said, "I have wild beasts. I will deliver you to them, unless you convert." And he said, "Call for them, for conversion from better to worse is not allowed us; but it is good to change from evil to righteousness." [2] And again he said to him, "I will cause you to be consumed by fire, if you despise the beasts, unless you convert." But Polycarp said, "You threaten with the fire that burns for a time, and is quickly quenched, for you do not know the fire which

awaits the wicked in the judgment to come and in continuous punishment. But why are you waiting? Come, do what you will."

CHAPTER 12

¹ And with these and many other words he was filled with courage and joy, and his face was full of grace so that it not only did not fall with trouble at the things said to him, but that the proconsul, on the other hand, was astounded and sent his herald into the midst of the arena to announce three times: "Polycarp has confessed that he is a Christian." ² When this had been said by the herald, all the multitude of heathen and Jews living in Smyrna cried out with uncontrollable wrath and a loud shout: "This is the teacher of Asia, the father of the Christians, the destroyer of our gods, who teaches many neither to offer sacrifice nor to worship." And when they said this, they cried out and asked Philip the Asiarch to let loose a lion on Polycarp. But he said he could not legally do this, since he had closed the games. ³ Then they found it good to cry out with one mind that he should burn Polycarp alive, for the vision which had appeared to him on his pillow must be fulfilled, when he saw it burning, while he was praying, and he turned and said prophetically to those of the faithful who were with him, "I must be burned alive."

CHAPTER 13

¹ These things then happened with such great speed— quicker than it takes to tell—and the crowd came together immediately, and prepared wood and bundles from the workshops and baths, and the Jews were extremely zealous, as is their custom, in assisting at this. ² Now when the fire was ready, he took off all his clothes, and loosened his girdle, and also tried to take off his shoes, though he did not do this before, because each of the faithful was always zealous, which of them might the more quickly touch his flesh. For he had been treated with all respect because of his noble life, even before his martyrdom. ³ Therefore, he was immediately fastened to the instruments which had been prepared for the fire, but when they were going to nail him as well, he said, "Leave me thus, for He who gives me power to endure the fire, will grant me to remain in the flames unmoved even without the security you will give by the nails."

CHAPTER 14

¹ So they did not nail him, but bound him, and he put his hands behind him and was bound as a noble ram out of a great flock, for an oblation, a whole burnt-offering made ready and acceptable to God; and he looked up to Heaven and said, "O Lord God Almighty, Father of Your beloved and blessed Child, Jesus Christ, through whom we have received full knowledge of You—the God of Messengers, and powers, and of all creation, and of the whole family of the righteous who live before You— ² I bless You, that You have granted me this day and hour, that I may share, among the number of the martyrs, in the cup of Your Christ, for the resurrection to continuous life, both of soul and body in the immortality of the Holy Spirit. And may I, today, be received among them before You, as a rich and acceptable sacrifice, as You—the God who does not lie and is truth—have prepared beforehand, and shown forth, and fulfilled. ³ For this reason I also praise You for all things, I bless You, I glorify You through the continuous and heavenly Chief Priest, Jesus Christ, Your beloved Child, through whom be glory to You with Him and the Holy Spirit, both now and for the ages that are to come, Amen."

CHAPTER 15

¹ Now when he had uttered his Amen and finished his prayer, the men in charge of the fire lit it, and a great flame blazed up and we, to whom it was given to see, saw a marvel. And we have been preserved to report to others what befell. ² For the fire made the likeness of a room, like the sail of a vessel filled with wind, and surrounded the body of the martyr as with a wall, and he was not within it as burning flesh, but as bread that is being baked, or as gold and silver being refined in a furnace. And we perceived such a fragrant smell as the scent of incense or other costly spices.

CHAPTER 16

¹ At length the lawless men, seeing that his body could not be consumed by the fire, commanded an executioner to go up and pierce him with a dagger, and when he did this, there came out a dove, and [very] much blood, so that the fire was quenched, and all the crowd marveled that there was such a difference between the unbelievers and the chosen ones. ² And of the chosen ones was he indeed one, the wonderful martyr, Polycarp, who in our days was an apostolic and prophetic teacher, overseer of the universal Assembly in Smyrna. For every word which he uttered from his mouth was both fulfilled and will be fulfilled.

CHAPTER 17

¹ But the jealous and envious evil one who resists the family of the righteous, when he saw the greatness of his martyrdom, and his blameless career from the beginning, and that he was crowned with the crown

of immortality, and had carried off the unspeakable prize, took care that not even his poor body should be taken away by us, though many desired to do so, and to have fellowship with his holy flesh. [2] Therefore, he put forward Niketas, the father of Herod, and the brother of Alce, to ask the governor not to give his body, "Lest," he said, "they leave the crucified one and begin to worship this man." And they said this owing to the suggestions and pressure of the Jews, who also watched when we were going to take it from the fire, for they do not know that we will never be able either to abandon Christ, who suffered for the salvation of those who are being saved in the whole world—the innocent in place of sinners—or to worship any other. [3] For we worship Him as the Son of God, but we love the martyrs as disciples and imitators of the LORD; and rightly, because of their unsurpassable affection toward their own King and Teacher. God grant that we too may be their companions and fellow-disciples.

CHAPTER 18

[1] Therefore, when the centurion saw the strife caused by the Jews, he put the body in the midst of the fire and burned it. [2] Thus afterward we took up his bones—more precious than precious stones, and finer than gold—and put them where it was suitable. [3] There the LORD will permit us to come together according to our power in gladness and joy, and celebrate the anniversary of his martyrdom, both in memory of those who have already contested, and for the practice and training of those whose fate it will be.

CHAPTER 19

[1] Such was the lot of the blessed Polycarp, who—though he was, together with those from Philadelphia, the twelfth martyr in Smyrna—is alone especially remembered by all, so that he is spoken of in every place, even by the heathen. He was not only a famous teacher, but also a notable martyr, whose martyrdom all desire to imitate, for it followed the good news of Christ. [2] By his endurance he overcame the unrighteous ruler, and thus gained the crown of immortality, and he is glorifying God and the almighty Father, rejoicing with the apostles and all the righteous, and he is blessing our Lord Jesus Christ, the Savior of our souls, and Governor of our bodies, and the Shepherd of the universal Assembly throughout the world.

CHAPTER 20

[1] You, indeed, asked that the events should be explained to you at length, but we have for the present explained them in summary by our brother Marcion; therefore, when you have heard these things, send the letter to the brothers further on, that they also may glorify the LORD, who takes His chosen ones from His own servants. [2] And to Him who is able to bring us all, in His grace and bounty, to His heavenly Kingdom by His only begotten Child, Jesus Christ, be glory, honor, might, and majesty for all time. Greet all the holy ones. Those who are with us, and Evarestus, who wrote the letter, with his whole house, greet you.

CHAPTER 21

[1] Now the blessed Polycarp was martyred on the second day of the first half of the month of Xanthicus, the seventh day before the Calends of March, a great Sabbath, at the eighth hour. And he was arrested by Herod, when Philip of Tralles was chief priest, when Statius Quadratus was proconsul, but Jesus Christ was reigning for all time, to whom be glory, honor, majesty, and a continuous throne, from generation to generation, Amen.

CHAPTER 22

[1] We bid you farewell, brothers, who walk according to the good news in the word of Jesus Christ (with whom be glory to God and the Father, and the Holy Spirit), for the salvation of the holy chosen ones, even as the blessed Polycarp suffered martyrdom, in whose footsteps may it be granted us to be found in the Kingdom of Jesus Christ. [2] Gaius copied this from the writing of Irenaeus, a disciple of Polycarp, and he lived with Irenaeus, and I, Socrates, wrote it out in Corinth, from the copies of Gaius. Grace be with you all. [3] And I, again, Pionius, wrote it out from the former writings, after searching for it, because the blessed Polycarp showed it to me in a vision, as I will explain in what follows, and I gathered it together when it was almost worn out by age, that the Lord Jesus Christ may also gather me together with His chosen ones into His heavenly Kingdom, to whom be glory with the Father and the Holy Spirit, forever and ever, Amen.

EPISTLE OF MATHETES TO DIOGNETUS

The Epistle to Diognetus is one of the early Christian apologetics and is counted among the works of the Apostolic Fathers. The actual author and recipient are unknown, and it is believed to have been composed as early as 130 AD or as late as 200 AD. Some scholars dispute the inclusion of chapters 11 and 12.

CHAPTER 1

[1] Since I see, most excellent Diognetus, that you are exceedingly anxious to understand the religion of the Christians, and that your inquiries respecting them are distinctly and carefully made, as to what God they trust and how they worship Him, that they all disregard the world and despise death, and take no account of those who are regarded as gods by the Greeks, neither observe the superstition of the Jews, and as to the nature of the affection which they entertain to one another, and of this new development or interest, which has entered into men's lives now and not before: I gladly welcome this zeal in you, and I ask of God, who supplies both the speaking and the hearing to us, that it may be granted to myself to speak in such a way that you may be made better by the hearing, and to you—that you may so listen that I, the speaker, may not be disappointed.

CHAPTER 2

[1] Come then, clear yourself of all the preconceptions which occupy your mind, and throw off the habit which leads you astray, and become a new man, as it were, from the beginning, as one who would listen to a new story, even as you yourself confessed. Do not see with only your eyes, but with your intellect also, of what substance or of what form they happen to be whom you call and regard as gods. [2] Is not one of them stone, like that which we tread under foot, and another bronze, no better than the vessels which are forged for our use, and another wood, which has already become rotten, and another silver, which needs a man to guard it lest it be stolen, and another iron, which is corroded with rust, and another earthenware, not a bit more pleasant than that which is supplied for the most dishonorable service? [3] Are not all these of perishable matter? Are they not forged by iron and fire? Did not the sculptor make one, and the brass-founder another, and the silversmith another, and the potter another? Before they were moulded into this shape by the crafts of these several craftsmen, was it not possible for each one of them to have been changed in form and made to resemble these several utensils? Might

the vessels which are now made out of the same material, if they met with the same craftsmen, not be made like to such as these? [4] Could these things which are now worshiped by you, by human hands, not be made vessels again like the rest? Are they not all deaf and blind, are they not lifeless, senseless, motionless? Do they not all rot and decay? [5] These things you call gods, to these you are slaves, these you worship; and you end by becoming altogether like to them. [6] Therefore, you hate the Christians, because they do not consider these to be gods. [7] For do you yourselves, who now regard and worship them, not much more despise them? Do you not much rather mock and insult them, worshiping those that are of stone and earthenware unguarded, but shutting up those that are of silver and gold by night, and setting guards over them by day, to prevent their being stolen? [8] And as for the honors which you think to offer to them, if they are sensible of them, you rather punish them thereby, whereas, if they are insensible, you reproach them by propitiating them with the blood and fat of victims. [9] Let one of yourselves undergo this treatment; let him submit to these things being done to him. No, not so much as a single individual will willingly submit to such punishment, for he has sensibility and reason; but a stone submits, because it is insensible. Therefore, you convict his sensibility. [10] Well, I could say much more concerning the Christians not being enslaved to such gods as these; but if anyone thinks what has been said insufficient, I hold it redundant to say more.

CHAPTER 3

[1] In the next place, I imagine that you are chiefly anxious to hear about their not practicing their religion in the same way as the Jews. [2] The Jews then, so far as they abstain from the mode of worship described above, do well in claiming to give reverence to one God of the universe and to regard Him as Master; but so far as they offer Him this worship in methods similar to those already mentioned, they are altogether at fault. [3] For whereas the Greeks, by offering these things to senseless and deaf images, make an exhibition of stupidity, the Jews, considering that they are presenting them to God as if He were in need of them, should in all reason count it folly and not religious worship. [4] For He that made the heavens, and the earth, and all things that are therein, and furnishes us all with what we need, cannot Himself need any of these things which He Himself supplies to them that imagine they are

giving them to Him. ⁵ But those who think to perform sacrifices to Him with blood, and fat, and whole burnt-offerings, and to honor Him with such honors, seem to me in no way different from those who show the same respect toward deaf images; for the one class thinks fit to make offerings to things unable to participate in the honor, the other class to One who is in need of nothing.

CHAPTER 4

¹ But again their qualms concerning meats, and their superstition relating to the Sabbath, and the vanity of their circumcision, and the deception of their fasting and new moons—I do [not] suppose you need to learn from me—are ridiculous and unworthy of any consideration. ² For of the things created by God for the use of man to receive some as created well, but to decline others as useless and superfluous, is this not impious? ³ And again to lie against God, as if He forbade us to do any good thing on the Sabbath day, is this not profane? ⁴ Again, to vaunt the mutilation of the flesh as a token of [divine] selection as though for this reason they were particularly beloved by God, is this not ridiculous? ⁵ And to watch the stars and the moon, and to keep the observance of months and of days, and to distinguish the arrangements of God and the changes of the seasons according to their own impulses, making some into festivals and others into times of mourning, who would regard this as an exhibition of godliness and not much more of folly? ⁶ That the Christians are therefore right in holding aloof from the common silliness and error of the Jews and from their excessive fussiness and pride, I consider that you have been sufficiently instructed; but as regards the mystery of their own religion, do not expect that you can be instructed by man.

CHAPTER 5

¹ For Christians are not distinguished from the rest of mankind either in locality, or in speech, or in customs. ² For they do not dwell somewhere in cities of their own, neither do they use some different language, nor practice an extraordinary kind of life. ³ Nor again do they possess any invention discovered by any intelligence or study of ingenious men, nor are they masters of any human dogma as some are. ⁴ But while they dwell in cities of Greeks and barbarians as the lot of each is cast, and follow the native customs in dress, and food, and the other arrangements of life, yet the constitution of their own citizenship, which they set forth, is marvelous, and confessedly contradicts expectation. ⁵ They dwell in their own countries, but only as sojourners; they bear their share in all things as citizens, and they endure all hardships as strangers. Every foreign country is a fatherland to them, and every fatherland is foreign. ⁶ They marry like all other men and they beget children; but they do not cast away their offspring. ⁷ They have their meals in common, but not their wives. ⁸ They find themselves in the flesh, and yet they do not live after the flesh. ⁹ Their existence is on earth, but their citizenship is in Heaven. ¹⁰ They obey the established laws, and they surpass the laws in their own lives. ¹¹ They love all men, and they are persecuted by all. ¹² They are ignored, and yet they are condemned. They are put to death, and yet they are endued with life. ¹³ They are in destitution, and yet they make many rich. They are in want of all things, and yet they abound in all things. ¹⁴ They are dishonored, and yet they are glorified in their dishonor. They are evil spoken of, and yet they are vindicated. ¹⁵ They are reviled, and they bless; they are insulted, and they respect. ¹⁶ Doing good, they are punished as evildoers; being punished they rejoice, as if they were thereby restored by life. ¹⁷ War is waged against them as aliens by the Jews, and persecution is carried on against them by the Greeks, and yet those that hate them cannot tell the reason of their hostility.

CHAPTER 6

¹ In a word, what the soul is in a body, this the Christians are in the world. ² The soul is spread through all the members of the body, and Christians through the various cities of the world. ³ The soul has its abode in the body, and yet it is not of the body. So Christians have their abode in the world, and yet they are not of the world. ⁴ The soul which is invisible is guarded in the body which is visible; so Christians are recognized as being in the world, and yet their religion remains invisible. ⁵ The flesh hates the soul and wages war with it, though it receives no wrong, because it is forbidden to indulge in pleasures; so the world hates Christians, though it receives no wrong from them, because they set themselves against its pleasures. ⁶ The soul loves the flesh which hates it, and the members; so Christians love those that hate them. ⁷ The soul is enclosed in the body, and yet itself holds the body together; so Christians are kept in the world as in a prison-house, and yet they themselves hold the world together. ⁸ The soul, though itself immortal, dwells in a mortal dwelling place; so Christians sojourn amidst perishable things, while they look for the imperishability which is in the heavens. ⁹ The soul, when ill-treated in the matter of meats and drinks, is improved; and so Christians, when punished, increase more and more daily. ¹⁰ So great is the office for which God has appointed them, and which it is not lawful for them to decline.

CHAPTER 7

¹ For it is no earthly discovery, as I said, which was committed to them, neither do they care to guard so carefully any mortal invention, nor have they entrusted to them the dispensation of human mysteries. ² But truly the almighty Creator of the universe, the invisible God Himself, from Heaven

planted among men the truth and the holy teaching which surpasses the perception of man, and fixed it firmly in their hearts, not as any man might imagine, by sending [to mankind] a lieutenant, or messenger, or ruler, or one of those that direct the affairs of earth, or one of those who have been entrusted with the dispensations in Heaven, but the very Craftsman and Creator of the universe Himself, by whom He made the heavens, by whom He enclosed the sea in its proper bounds, whose mysteries all the elements faithfully observe, from whom [the sun] has received even the measure of the courses of the day to keep them, whom the moon obeys as He bids her shine by night, whom the stars obey as they follow the course of the moon, by whom all things are ordered, and bounded, and placed in subjection—the heavens and the things that are in the heavens, the earth and the things that are in the earth, the sea and the things that are in the sea, fire, air, abyss, the things that are in the heights, the things that are in the depths, the things that are between the two. Him He sent to them. ³Do you think He was sent as any man might suppose, to establish a sovereignty, to inspire fear and terror? ⁴Not so. But in gentleness [and] meekness He has sent Him, as a king might send his son who is a king. He sent Him as sending God; He sent Him as [a man] to men; He sent Him as Savior, as using persuasion, not force; for force is no attribute of God. ⁵He sent Him as summoning, not as persecuting; He sent Him as loving, not as judging. ⁶For He will send Him in judgment, and who will endure His presence? ⁷[Do you not see] them thrown to wild beasts so that they may deny the Lᴏʀᴅ, and yet not overcome? ⁸Do you not see that the more of them are punished, just so many others abound? ⁹These do not look like the works of a man; they are the power of God; they are proofs of His presence.

CHAPTER 8

¹For what man at all had any knowledge what God was before He came? ²Or do you accept the empty and nonsensical statements of those pretentious philosophers, of whom some said that God was fire (they call that God, whereto they themselves will go), and others water, and others some other of the elements which were created by God? ³And yet if any of these statements is worthy of acceptance, any one other created thing might just as well be made out to be God. ⁴No, all this is the quackery and deceit of the magicians; ⁵and no man has either seen or recognized Him, but He revealed Himself. ⁶And He revealed [Himself] by faith, whereby alone it is given to see God. ⁷For God, the Master and Creator of the universe, who made all things and arranged them in order, was found to be not only friendly to men, but also long-suffering. ⁸And such indeed He always was, and is, and will be: kind, and good, and dispassionate, and true, and He alone is good. ⁹And

having conceived a great and unutterable plan, He communicated it to His Son alone. ¹⁰For so long as He kept and guarded His wise design as a mystery, He seemed to neglect us and to be careless about us. ¹¹But when He revealed it through His beloved Son and manifested the purpose which He had prepared from the beginning, He gave us all these gifts at once, participation in His benefits, and sight and understanding of [mysteries] which none of us ever would have expected.

CHAPTER 9

¹Having thus already planned everything in His mind with His Son, He permitted us during the former time to be borne along by disorderly impulses as we desired, led astray by pleasures and lusts, not at all because He took delight in our sins, but because He bore with us, not because He approved of the past season of iniquity, but because He was creating the present season of righteousness, that, being convicted in the past time by our own deeds as unworthy of life, we might now be made deserving by the goodness of God, and having made clear our inability to enter into the Kingdom of God of ourselves, might be enabled by the ability of God. ²And when our iniquity had been fully accomplished, and it had been made perfectly manifest that punishment and death were expected as its repayment, and the season came which God had ordained, when from now on He should manifest His goodness and power (O the exceedingly great kindness and love of God), He did not hate us, neither rejected us, nor bore us malice, but was long-suffering and patient, and in pity for us took our sins on Himself, and Himself parted with His own Son as a ransom for us—the holy for the lawless, the guileless for the evil, the just for the unjust, the incorruptible for the corruptible, the immortal for the mortal. ³For what else but His righteousness would have covered our sins? ⁴In whom was it possible for us lawless and ungodly men to have been justified, save only in the Son of God? ⁵O the sweet exchange, O the inscrutable creation, O the unexpected benefits, that the iniquity of many should be concealed in one righteous Man, and the righteousness of [the] One should justify many that are iniquitous! ⁶Having then in the former time demonstrated the inability of our nature to obtain life, and having now revealed a Savior able to save even creatures which have no ability, He willed that for both reasons we should believe in His goodness and should regard Him as nurse, father, teacher, counselor, physician, mind, light, honor, glory, strength, and life.

CHAPTER 10

¹This faith, if you also desire, first apprehend full knowledge of the Father. ²For God loved men for whose sake He made the world, to whom He subjected all things that are in the earth, to whom He

gave reason and mind, whom alone He permitted to look up to Heaven, whom He created after His own image, to whom He sent His only begotten Son, to whom He promised the Kingdom, which is in Heaven, and will give it to those that have loved Him. [3] And when you have attained to this full knowledge, with what joy do you think that you will be filled, or how will you love Him that so loved you before? [4] And loving Him you will be an imitator of His goodness. And do not marvel that a man can be an imitator of God. He can, if God wills it. [5] For happiness does not consist in lordship over one's neighbors, nor in desiring to have more than weaker men, nor in possessing wealth and using force to inferiors; neither can anyone imitate God in these matters; no, these lie outside His greatness. [6] But whoever takes on himself the burden of his neighbor, whoever desires to benefit one that is worse off in that in which he himself is superior, whoever by supplying to those that are in want possessions which he received from God becomes [like] God to those who receive them from him—he is an imitator of God. [7] Then, though you are placed on earth, you will behold that God lives in Heaven; then you will begin to declare the mysteries of God; then you will both love and admire those that are punished because they will not deny God; then you will condemn the deceit and error of the world when you will perceive the true life which is in Heaven, when you will despise the apparent death which is here on earth, when you will fear the real death, which is reserved for those that will be condemned to the continuous fire that will punish those delivered over to it to the end. [8] Then you will admire those who endure for righteousness' sake the fire that is for a season, and will count them blessed when you perceive that fire . . .

CHAPTER 11

[1] Mine are no strange discourses, nor perverse questionings, but having been a disciple of apostles I come forward as a teacher of the nations, ministering worthily to them, as they present themselves disciples of the truth, the lessons which have been handed down. [2] For who that has been rightly taught and has entered into friendship with the Word does not seek to learn distinctly the lessons revealed openly by the Word to the disciples; to whom the Word appeared and declared them, speaking plainly, not perceived by the unbelieving, but relating them to disciples who being reckoned faithful by Him were taught the mysteries of the Father? [3] For this reason He sent forth the Word, that He might appear to the world, who being dishonored by the people, and preached by the apostles, was believed in by the nations. [4] This Word, who was from the beginning, who appeared as new and yet was proved to be old, and is engendered always young in the hearts of holy ones, [5] He, I say, who is continuous, who today was accounted [the]

Son, through whom the Assembly is enriched, and grace is unfolded and multiplied among the holy ones—grace which confers understanding, which reveals secrets, which announces seasons, which rejoices over the faithful, which is bestowed on those who seek her, even those by whom the pledges of faith are not broken, nor the boundaries of the fathers overstepped. [6] After which the fear of the law is sung, and the grace of the prophets is recognized, and the faith of the Gospels is established, and the apostles' tradition is preserved, and the joy of the Assembly exults. [7] If you do not grieve this grace, you will understand the discourses which the Word holds by the mouth of those whom He desires when He wishes. [8] For in all things, that by the will of the commanding Word we were moved to utter with many pains, we become sharers with you, through love of the things revealed to us.

CHAPTER 12

[1] Confronted with these truths and listening to them with attention, you will know how much God bestows on those that love [Him] rightly, who become a paradise of delight, a tree bearing all manner of fruits and flourishing, growing up in themselves and adorned with various fruits. [2] For in this garden a Tree of Knowledge and a Tree of Life have been planted; yet the Tree of Knowledge does not kill, but disobedience kills; [3] for the Writings state clearly how God from the beginning planted a Tree [[of Knowledge and a Tree]] of Life in the midst of Paradise, revealing life through knowledge; and because our first parents did not use it genuinely, they were made naked by the deceit of the serpent. [4] For neither is there life without knowledge, nor sound knowledge without true life; therefore the one [tree] is planted near the other. [5] Discerning the force of this and blaming the knowledge which is exercised apart from the truth of the injunction which leads to life, the apostle says, "Knowledge puffs up, but love builds up." [6] For the man who supposes that he knows anything without the true knowledge, which is testified by the life, is ignorant; he is deceived by the serpent, because he did not love life; whereas he who with fear recognizes and desires life plants in hope, expecting fruit. [7] Let your heart be knowledge, and your life true reason, properly comprehended. [8] Of which, if you bear the tree and pluck the fruit, you will ever gather the harvest which God looks for, which serpent does not touch, nor deceit infect, neither is Eve corrupted, but is believed on as a virgin, [9] and salvation is set forth, and the apostles are filled with understanding, and the Passover of the LORD goes forward, and the congregations are gathered together, and [all things] are arranged in order, and as He teaches the holy ones, the Word is gladdened, through whom the Father is glorified, to whom be glory forever and ever. Amen.

THE SHEPHERD OF HERMAS

This work, composed as early as the late 1st century AD, but more likely in the mid 2nd century, was highly regarded and even considered canonical by some sources such as Irenaeus. It is found in the Codex Sinaiticus and takes its name from a messenger appearing as a shepherd in order to deliver twelve commands to Hermas. It is thought the shepherd may represent Jesus as the Good Shepherd. Those who believe The Shepherd of Hermas was written in the 1st century associate it with the Hermas mentioned in Romans 16:14, while the majority believe the "Hermas" in question is none other than the brother of Pius I, who would have thus written in the mid 2nd century. Besides the possibly late date of composition, also weighing heavily against its canonicity is the message of impossible moral perfectionism outside the mainstream of Christian thought, and the fact it lacks the essential message of Christ's atoning sacrifice besides a passing mention in Similitude 5. It also, while not Gnostic, arguably presents a Christology that differs from that found in the Bible—although this is not entirely clear given the work is largely an allegory. It consists of five *visions*, twelve *commands*, and ten *similitudes*.

SECTION 1:
VISIONS

VISION 1

[1] He who had brought me up, sold me to one Rhode in Rome. Many years after this I recognized her, and I began to love her as a sister. Sometime after, I saw her bathe in the river Tiber; and I gave her my hand and drew her out of the river. [2] The sight of her beauty made me think with myself, "I would be a happy man if I could only get a wife as attractive and good as she is." This was the only thought that passed through me: this and nothing more. [3] A short time after this, as I was walking on my road to the villages, and magnifying the creatures of God, and thinking how magnificent, and beautiful, and powerful they are, I fell asleep. [4] And the Spirit carried me away, and took me through a pathless place, through which a man could not travel, for it was situated in the midst of rocks; it was rugged and impassible on account of water. [5] Having passed over this river, I came to a plain. I then bent down on my knees and began to pray to the LORD and to confess my sins. And as I prayed, the heavens were opened, and I see the woman whom I had desired saluting me from the sky, and saying, "Greetings, Hermas!" [6] And looking up to her, I said, "Lady, what are you doing here?" And she answered me, "I have been taken up here to accuse you of your sins before the LORD." "Lady," I said, "are you to be the subject of my accusation?" [7] "No," she said; "but hear the words which I am going to speak to you. God, who dwells in the heavens, and made out of nothing the things that exist, and multiplied and increased them on account of His holy Assembly, is angry with you for having sinned against me." [8] I answered her, "Lady, have I sinned against you? How? Or when did I speak an unseemly word to you? Did I not always think of you as a lady? Did I not always respect you as a sister? Why do you falsely accuse me of this wickedness and impurity?" [9] With a smile she replied to me, "The desire of wickedness arose within your heart. Is it not your opinion that a righteous man commits sin when an evil desire arises in his heart? There is sin in such a case, and the sin is great," she said; [10] "for the thoughts of a righteous man should be righteous. For by thinking righteously his character is established in the heavens, and he has the LORD merciful to him in every business. But those who entertain wicked thoughts in their minds are bringing on themselves death and captivity; and especially is this the case with those who set their affections on this world, and glory in their riches, and do not look forward to the blessings of the life to come. [11] For their regrets will be many; for they have no hope, but have despaired of themselves and their life. But pray to God, and He will heal your sins, and the sins of your whole house, and of all the holy ones." [12] After she had spoken these words, the heavens were shut. I was overwhelmed with sorrow and fear, and said to myself, "If this sin is assigned to me, how can I be saved, or how will I propitiate God in regard to my sins, which are of the grossest character? With what words will I ask the LORD to be merciful to me? [13] While I was thinking over these things, and discussing them in my mind, I saw opposite to me a chair, white, made of white wool, of great size. And there came up an old woman, arrayed in a splendid robe, and with a scroll in her hand; [14] and she sat down alone, and saluted me, "Greetings, Hermas!" And in sadness and tears I said to her, "Lady, greetings!" [15] And she said to me, "Why are you downcast, Hermas? For you were accustomed to be patient and temperate, and always smiling. Why are you so gloomy, and not cheerful?" [16] I answered her and said, "O Lady, I have been reproached by a very good woman, who says that I sinned against her." [17] And she said, "Far be such a deed from a servant of

God. But perhaps a desire after her has arisen within your heart. Such a wish, in the case of the servants of God, produces sin. For it is a wicked and horrible wish in an all-chaste and already well-tried spirit to desire an evil deed; [18] and especially for Hermas to do so, who keeps himself from all wicked desire, and is full of all simplicity, and of great guilelessness. [19] "But God is not angry with you on account of this, but that you may convert [those of] your house, which have committed iniquity against the Lord, and against you, their parents. And although you love your sons, yet you did not warn your house, but permitted them to be terribly corrupted. [20] On this account the LORD is angry with you, but He will heal all the evils which have been done in your house. For, on account of their sins and iniquities, you have been destroyed by the affairs of this world. [21] But now the mercy of the LORD has taken pity on you and your house, and will strengthen you, and establish you in His glory. Only, do not be easy-minded, but be of good courage and comfort your house. For as a smith hammers out his work, and accomplishes whatever he wishes, so will righteous daily speech overcome all iniquity. [22] Therefore, do not cease to admonish your sons; for I know that, if they will convert with all their heart, they will be enrolled in the scrolls of [the] living with the holy ones." [23] Having ended these words, she said to me, "Do you wish to hear me read?" I say to her, "Lady, I do." "Listen then and give ear to the glories of God." [24] And then I heard from her, magnificently and admirably, things which my memory could not retain. For all the words were terrible, such as man could not endure. [25] The last words, however, I did remember; for they were useful to us, and gentle. [26] "Behold, the God of powers, who by His invisible strong power and great wisdom has created the world, and by His glorious counsel has surrounded His creation with beauty, and by His strong word has fixed the heavens and laid the foundations of the earth on the waters, and by His own wisdom and providence has created His holy Assembly, which He has blessed, [27] behold, He removes the heavens and the mountains, the hills and the seas, and all things become plain to His chosen ones, that He may bestow on them the blessing which He has promised them, with much glory and joy, if only they will keep the commandments of God which they have received in great faith." [28] When she had ended her reading, she rose from the chair, and four young men came and carried off the chair and went away to the east. [29] And she called me to herself and touched my breast, and said to me, "Have you been pleased with my reading?" And I say to her, "Lady, the last words please me, but the first are cruel and harsh." [30] Then she said to me, "The last are for the righteous; the first are for heathens and apostates." [31] And while she spoke to me, two men appeared and raised her on their shoulders, and they went to where the chair was in the east. [32] She departed with joyful countenance; and as she went, she said to me, "Behave like a man, Hermas."

VISION 2

[1] As I was going to the country about the same time as on the previous year, in my walk I recalled to memory the vision of that year. And again, the Spirit carried me away, and took me to the same place where I had been the year before. [2] On coming to that place, I bowed my knees and began to pray to the LORD, and to glorify His Name, because He had deemed me worthy, and had made known to me my former sins. [3] On rising from prayer, I see opposite me that old woman, whom I had seen the year before, walking and reading some scroll. And she says to me, "Can you carry a report of these things to the chosen ones of God?" [4] I say to her, "Lady, so much I cannot retain in my memory, but give me the scroll and I will transcribe it." "Take it," she says, "and you will give it back to me." [5] Thereupon I took it, and going away into a certain part of the country, I transcribed the whole of it letter by letter; but the syllables of it I did not catch. [6] No sooner, however, had I finished the writing of the scroll, than all of a sudden it was snatched from my hands; but who the person was that snatched it, I did not see. Fifteen days after, when I had fasted and prayed much to the Lord, the knowledge of the writing was revealed to me. [7] Now the writing was to this effect: "Your seed, O Hermas, has sinned against God, and they have blasphemed against the LORD, and in their great wickedness they have betrayed their parents. And they passed as traitors of their parents, and by their treachery they did not reap profit. [8] And even now they have added to their sins lusts and iniquitous pollutions, and thus their iniquities have been filled up. [9] But make known these words to all your children, and to your wife, who is to be your sister. For she does not restrain her tongue, with which she commits iniquity; but, on hearing these words, she will control herself, and will obtain mercy. [10] For after you have made known to them these words which my Lord has commanded me to reveal to you, then they will be forgiven all the sins which in former times they committed, and forgiveness will be granted to all the holy ones who have sinned even to the present day, if they convert with all their heart, and drive all doubts from their minds. [11] For the LORD has sworn by His glory, in regard to His chosen ones, that if any one of them sin after a certain day which has been fixed, he will not be saved. For the conversion of the righteous

has limits. Filled up are the days of conversion to all the holy ones; but to the heathen, conversion will be possible even to the last day. [12] You will tell, therefore, those who preside over the Assembly, to direct their ways in righteousness, that they may receive in full the promises with great glory. [13] Stand steadfast, therefore, you who work righteousness, and do not doubt, that your passage may be with the holy messengers. [14] Happy are you who endure the great tribulation that is coming on, and happy are they who will not deny their own life. For the LORD has sworn by His Son, that those who denied their Lord have abandoned their life in despair, for even now these are to deny Him in the days that are coming. To those who denied in earlier times, God became gracious, on account of His exceedingly tender mercy. [15] But as for you, Hermas, do not remember the wrongs done to you by your children, nor neglect your sister, that they may be cleansed from their former sins. For they will be instructed with righteous instruction, if you do not remember the wrongs they have done to you. For the remembrance of wrongs works death. [16] And you, Henna, have endured great personal tribulations on account of the transgressions of your house, because you did not attend to them, but were careless and engaged in your wicked transactions. [17] But you are saved, because you did not depart from the living God, and on account of your simplicity and great self-control. These have saved you, if you remain steadfast. And they will save all who act in the same manner, and walk in guilelessness and simplicity. [18] Those who possess such virtues will wax strong against every form of wickedness, and will abide to continuous life. Blessed are all they who practice righteousness, for they will never be destroyed. [19] Now you will tell Maximus: Behold, tribulation is coming. If it seems good to you, deny again. The LORD is near to them who return to Him, as it is written in Eldad and Medad, who prophesied to the people in the wilderness." [20] Now a revelation was given to me, my brothers, while I slept, by a young man of handsome appearance, who said to me, "Who do you think that old woman is from whom you received the scroll?" [21] And I said, "The Sibyl." "You are mistaken," he says; "it is not the Sibyl." "Who is it then?" I say. And he said, "It is the Assembly." And I said to him, "Why then is she an old woman?" [22] "Because," he said, "she was created first of all. On this account is she old. And for her sake was the world made." [23] After that I saw a vision in my house, and that old woman came and asked me if I had yet given the scroll to the elders. And I said that I had not. [24] And then she said, "You have done well for I have some words to add. But when I finish all the words, all the chosen ones will then become acquainted with them through you. [25] You will therefore write two scrolls, and you will send the one to Clemens and the other to Grapte. And Clemens will send his to foreign countries, for permission has been granted to him to do so. And Grapte will admonish the widows and the orphans. [26] But you will read the words in this city, along with the elders who preside over the Assembly.

VISION 3

[1] The vision which I saw, my brothers, was of the following nature. [2] Having fasted frequently, and having prayed to the LORD that He would show me the revelation which He promised to show me through that old woman, the same night that old woman appeared to me, and said to me, "Since you are so anxious and eager to know all things, go into the part of the country where you tarry; and about the fifth hour I will appear to you, and show you all that you ought to see." [3] I asked her, saying "Lady, into what part of the country am I to go?" And she said, "Into any part you wish." Then I chose a spot which was suitable, and retired. [4] Before, however, I began to speak and to mention the place, she said to me, "I will come where you wish." Accordingly, I went to the country, and counted the hours, and reached the place where I had promised to meet her. [5] And I see an ivory seat already placed, and on it a linen cushion, and above the linen cushion was spread a covering of fine linen. Seeing these laid out, and yet no one in the place, I began to feel awe, and as it were a trembling seized hold of me, and my hair stood on end, and as it were a horror came on me when I saw that I was all alone. [6] But on coming back to myself and calling to mind the glory of God, I took courage, bent my knees, and again confessed my sins to God as I had done before. [7] Immediately the old woman approached, accompanied by six young men whom I had also seen before; and she stood behind me, and listened to me, as I prayed and confessed my sins to the LORD. [8] And touching me she said, "Hermas, cease praying continually for your sins; pray for righteousness, that you may have a portion of it immediately in your house." [9] On this, she took me up by the hand, and brought me to the seat, and said to the young men, "Go and build." [10] When the young men had gone and we were alone, she said to me, "Sit here." I say to her, "Lady, permit my elders to be seated first." "Do what I bid you," she said; "sit down." [11] When I would have sat down on her right, she did not permit me, but with her hand beckoned to me to sit down on the left. [12] While I was thinking about this, and feeling vexed that she did not let me sit on the right, she said, "Are you vexed, Hermas? The place to the right is for others who have already

pleased God and have suffered for His Name's sake; and you have yet much to accomplish before you can sit with them. But abide as you now do in your simplicity, and you will sit with them, and with all who do their deeds and bear what they have borne." [13] "What have they borne?" I said. "Listen," she said: "scourges, prisons, great tribulations, crosses, wild beasts, for God's Name's sake. On this account is assigned to them the division of sanctification on the right hand, and to everyone who will suffer for God's Name: to the rest is assigned the division on the left. [14] But both for those who sit on the right, and those who sit on the left, there are the same gifts and promises; only those sit on the right, and have some glory. [15] You then are eager to sit on the right with them, but your shortcomings are many. But you will be cleansed from your shortcomings; and all who are not given to doubts will be cleansed from all their iniquities up until this day." [16] Saying this, she wished to go away. But falling down at her feet, I begged her by the LORD that she would show me the vision which she had promised to show me. And then she again took hold of me by the hand, and raised me, and made me sit on the seat to the left; [17] and lifting up a splendid rod, she said to me, "Do you see something great?" And I say, "Lady, I see nothing." She said to me, "Behold, do you not see opposite to you a great tower, built on the waters, of splendid square stones?" [18] For the tower was built square by those six young men who had come with her. But myriads of men were carrying stones to it, some dragging them from the depths, others removing them from the land, and they handed them to these six young men. [19] They were taking them and building; and those of the stones that were dragged out of the depths, they placed in the building just as they were: for they were polished and fitted exactly into the other stones and became so united one with another that the lines of juncture could not be perceived. And in this way the building of the tower looked as if it were made out of one stone. [20] Those stones, however, which were taken from the earth suffered a different fate; for the young men rejected some of them, some they fitted into the building, and some they cut down, and cast far away from the tower. [21] Many other stones, however, lay around the tower, and the young men did not use them in building; for some of them were rough, others had cracks in them, others had been made too short, and others were white and round, but did not fit into the building of the tower. [22] Moreover, I saw other stones thrown far away from the tower, and falling into the public road; yet they did not remain on the road, but were rolled into a pathless place. And I saw others falling into the fire and burning, others falling close to the water, and yet not capable of being rolled into the water, though they wished to be rolled down, and to enter the water. [23] On showing me these visions, she wished to retire. I said to her, "What is the use of my having seen all this, while I do not know what it means?" She said to me, "You are a cunning fellow, wishing to know everything that relates to the tower." "Even so, O Lady," I said, "that I may tell it to my brothers, that, hearing this, they may know the LORD in much glory." [24] And she said, "Many will indeed hear, and hearing, some will be glad, and some will weep. But even these, if they hear and convert, will also rejoice. [25] Hear, then, the allegories of the tower; for I will reveal all to you, and give me no more trouble in regard to revelation: for these revelations have an end, for they have been completed. But you will not cease praying for revelations, for you are shameless. [26] The tower which you see building is myself, the Assembly, who has appeared to you now and on the former occasion. Ask, then, whatever you like in regard to the tower, and I will reveal it to you, that you may rejoice with the holy ones." [27] I said to her, "Lady, since you have granted to reveal all to me this once, reveal it." She said to me, "Whatever ought to be revealed, will be revealed; only let your heart be with God, and do not doubt whatever you will see." [28] I asked her, "Why was the tower built on the waters, O Lady?" She answered, "I told you before, and you still inquire carefully: therefore, inquiring, you will find the truth. [29] Hear then why the tower is built on the waters. It is because your life has been, and will be, saved through water. For the tower was founder on the word of the almighty and glorious Name and it is kept together by the invisible power of the LORD." [30] In reply I said to her, "This is magnificent and marvelous. But who are the six young men who are engaged in building?" And she said, "These are the holy messengers of God, who were first created, and to whom the LORD handed over His whole creation, that they might increase, and build up, and rule over the whole creation. By these the building of the tower will be finished." [31] "But who are the other persons who are engaged in carrying the stones?" "These are also holy messengers of the LORD, but the former six are more excellent than these. The building of the tower will be finished, and all will rejoice together around the tower, and they will glorify God, because the tower is finished." [32] I asked her, saying, "Lady, I should like to know what became of the stones, and what was meant by the various kinds of stones?" [33] In reply she said to me, "Not because you are more deserving than all others that this revelation should be made to you—for there are others before you, and better than you, to whom these visions should have been revealed—but

THE SHEPHERD OF HERMAS

that the Name of God may be glorified, has the revelation been made to you, and it will be made on account of the doubtful who ponder in their hearts whether these things will be or not. ³⁴ Tell them that all these things are true, and that none of them is beyond the truth.│All of them are firm and sure, and established on a strong foundation. ³⁵ Hear now with regard to the stones which are in the building. Those square white stones, which fitted exactly into each other, are apostles, overseers, teachers, and servants, who have lived in godly purity, and have acted as overseers, and teachers, and servants chastely and reverently to the chosen ones of God. ³⁶ Some of them have fallen asleep, and some still remain alive. And they have always agreed with each other, and been at peace among themselves, and listened to each other. On account of this, they join exactly into the building of the tower." ³⁷ "But who are the stones that were dragged from the depths, and which were laid into the building and fitted in with the rest of the stones previously placed in the tower?" "They are those who suffered for the LORD's sake." ³⁸ "But I wish to know, O Lady, who are the other stones which were carried from the land." "Those," she said, "which go into the building without being polished, are those whom God has approved of, for they walked in the straight ways of the LORD and practiced His commandments." ³⁹ "But who are those who are in the act of being brought and placed in the building?" "They are those who are young in faith and are faithful. But they are admonished by the messengers to do good, for no iniquity has been found in them." ⁴⁰ "Who then are those whom they rejected and cast away?" "These are they who have sinned and wish to convert. On this account they have not been thrown far from the tower, because they will yet be useful in the building, if they convert. ⁴¹ Those then who are to convert, if they do convert, will be strong in faith, if they now convert while the tower is building. For if the building is finished, there will not be more room for anyone, but he will be rejected. This privilege, however, will belong only to him who has now been placed near the tower. ⁴² As to those who were cut down and thrown far away from the tower, do you wish to know who they are? They are the sons of iniquity, and they believed in hypocrisy, and wickedness did not depart from them. For this reason, they are not saved, since they cannot be used in the building on account of their iniquities. ⁴³ Therefore, they have been cut off and cast far away on account of the anger of the LORD, for they have roused Him to anger. ⁴⁴ But I will explain to you the other stones which you saw lying in great numbers, and not going into the building. Those which are rough are those who have known the truth and not remained

in it, nor have they been joined to the holy ones. On this account they are unfit for use." ⁴⁵ "Who are those that have rents?" "These are they who are at discord in their hearts with one another, and are not at peace among themselves: they indeed keep peace before each other, but when they separate from one another, their wicked thoughts remain in their hearts. These, then, are the rents which are in the stones. ⁴⁶ But those which are shortened are those who have indeed believed, and have the larger share of righteousness; yet they have also a considerable share of iniquity, and therefore they are shortened and not whole." ⁴⁷ "But who are these, Lady, that are white and round, and yet do not fit into the building of the tower?" She answered and said, "How long will you be foolish and stupid, and continue to put every kind of question and understand nothing? These are those who indeed have faith, but they also have the riches of this world. ⁴⁸ Therefore, when tribulation comes, on account of their riches and business they deny the LORD." I answered and said to her, "When, then, will they be useful for the building, Lady?" ⁴⁹ "When the riches that now seduce them have been circumscribed, then they will be of use to God. For as a round stone cannot become square unless portions are cut off and cast away, so also those who are rich in this world cannot be useful to the LORD unless their riches are cut down. ⁵⁰ Learn this first from your own case. When you were rich, you were useless; but now you are useful and fit for life. Be useful to God; for you also will be used as one of these stones. ⁵¹ Now the other stones which you saw cast far away from the tower, and falling on the public road and rolling from it into pathless places, are those who have indeed believed, but through doubt have abandoned the true road. Thinking, then, that they could find a better [way], they wander and become wretched, and enter on pathless places. ⁵² But those which fell into the fire and were burned are those who have departed forever from the living God; nor does the thought of conversion ever come into their hearts, on account of their devotion to their lusts and to the crimes which they committed. ⁵³ Do you wish to know who are the others which fell near the waters, but could not be rolled into them? These are they who have heard the word and wish to be immersed in the Name of the LORD, but when the chastity demanded by the truth comes into their recollection, they draw back, and again walk after their own wicked desires." ⁵⁴ She finished her exposition of the tower. But I, shameless as I yet was, asked her, "Is conversion possible for all those stones which have been cast away and did not fit into the building of the tower, and will they yet have a place in this tower?" ⁵⁵ "Conversion," she said, "is yet possible, but in this tower they cannot find a suitable place. But in another and much inferior place they will be laid, and that, too, only when they have been tortured and completed the days of their sins. [56] And on this account, they will be transferred, because they have partaken of the righteous Word. And only then will they be removed from their punishments when the thought of converting of the evil deeds which they have done has come into their hearts. But if it does not come into their hearts, they will not be saved, on account of the hardness of their heart." [57] When then I ceased asking in regard to all these matters, she said to me, "Do you wish to see anything else?" And as I was extremely eager to see something more, my countenance beamed with joy. [58] She looked toward me with a smile, and said, "Do you see seven women around the tower?" "I do, Lady," I said. [59] "This tower," she said, "is supported by them according to the precept of the LORD. Now listen to their functions. The first of them, who is clasping her hands, is called Faith. Through her the chosen ones of God are saved. [60] Another, who has her garments tucked up and acts with vigor, is called Self-restraint. She is the daughter of Faith. Whoever then follows her will become happy in his life, because he will restrain himself from all evil works, believing that, if he restrains himself from all evil desire, he will inherit continuous life." [61] "But the others," I said, "O Lady, who are they?" And she said to me, "They are daughters of each other. One of them is called Simplicity, another Guilelessness, another Chastity, another Intelligence, another Love. [62] When then you do all the works of their mother, you will be able to live." [63] "I should like to know," I said, "O Lady, what power each one of them possesses." [64] "Hear," she said, "what power they have. Their powers are regulated by each other, and follow each other in the order of their birth. For from Faith arises Self-restraint; from Self-restraint, Simplicity; from Simplicity, Guilelessness; from Guilelessness, Chastity; from Chastity, Intelligence; and from Intelligence, Love. [65] The deeds, then, of these are pure, and chaste, and divine. Whoever devotes himself to these, and is able to hold fast by their works, will have his dwelling in the tower with the holy ones of God." [66] Then I asked her in regard to the ages, if now there is the conclusion. She cried out with a loud voice, "Foolish man! Do you not see the tower yet building? When the tower is finished and built, then comes the end; and I assure you it will soon be finished. [67] Ask me no more questions. Let you and all the holy ones be content with what I have called to your remembrance, and with my renewal of your spirits. But observe that it is not for your own sake only that these revelations have been made to you, but they have

been given you that you may show them to all. [68] For after three days—this you will take care to remember—I command you to speak all the words which I am to say to you into the ears of the holy ones, that hearing them and doing them, they may be cleansed from their iniquities, and you along with them. [69] Give ear to me, O sons: I have brought you up in much simplicity, and guilelessness, and chastity, on account of the mercy of the LORD, who has dropped His righteousness down on you, that you may be made righteous and holy from all your iniquity and depravity; but you do not wish to rest from your iniquity. [70] Now, therefore, listen to me, and be at peace one with another, and visit each other, and bear each other's burdens, and do not partake of God's creatures alone, but give abundantly of them to the needy. [71] For some through the abundance of their food produce weakness in their flesh, and thus corrupt their flesh; while the flesh of others who have no food is corrupted, because they have not sufficient nourishment. And on this account their bodies waste away. [72] This intemperance in eating is thus injurious to you who have abundance and do not distribute among those who are needy. Give heed to the judgment that is to come. [73] You, therefore, who are high in position, seek out the hungry as long as the tower is not yet finished; for after the tower is finished, you will wish to do good, but will find no opportunity. [74] Give heed, therefore, you who glory in your wealth, lest those who are needy should groan, and their groans should ascend to the LORD, and you are shut out with all your goods beyond the gate of the tower. [75] Therefore, I now say to you who preside over the Assembly and love the first seats: do not be like to drug-mixers. For the drug-mixers carry their drugs in boxes, but you carry your drug and poison in your heart. [76] You are hardened, and do not wish to cleanse your hearts, and to add unity of aim to purity of heart, that you may have mercy from the great King. Take heed, therefore, children, that these dissensions of yours do not deprive you of your life. [77] How will you instruct the chosen ones of the LORD if you yourselves have no instruction? Instruct each other therefore, and be at peace among yourselves, that I also, standing joyful before your Father, may give an account of you all to your Lord." [78] On her ceasing to speak to me, those six young men who were engaged in building came and conveyed her to the tower, and another four lifted up the seat and carried it also to the tower. The faces of these last I did not see, for they were turned away from me. [79] And as she was going, I asked her to reveal to me the meaning of the three forms in which she appeared to me. [80] In reply she said to me: "With regard to them, you must ask another to reveal their meaning to you." [81] For she had appeared to me, brothers, in the first vision the previous year under the form of an exceedingly old woman, sitting in a chair. [82] In the second vision her face was youthful, but her skin and hair indicated age, and she stood while she spoke to me. She was also more joyful than on the first occasion. [83] But in the third vision she was entirely youthful and exquisitely beautiful, except only that she had the hair of an old woman; but her face beamed with joy, and she sat on a seat. [84] Now I was exceedingly sad in regard to these appearances, for I longed much to know what the visions meant. Then I see the old woman in a vision of the night saying to me: "Every prayer should be accompanied with humility: fast, therefore, and you will obtain from the LORD what you beg." I therefore fasted for one day. [85] That very night there appeared to me a young man, who said, "Why do you frequently ask revelations in prayer? Take heed lest by asking many things you injure your flesh; be content with these revelations. Will you be able to see greater revelations than those which you have seen?" [86] I answered and said to him, "Lord, one thing only I ask, that in regard to these three forms the revelation may be rendered complete." [87] He answered me, "How long are you senseless? But your doubts make you senseless, because you do not have your hearts turned toward the LORD." [88] But I answered and said to him, "From you, lord, we will learn these things more accurately." [89] "Hear then," he said, "with regard to the three forms, concerning which you are inquiring. Why in the first vision did she appear to you as an old woman seated on a chair? [90] Because your spirit is now old and withered up, and has lost its power in consequence of your infirmities and doubts. For, like elderly men who have no hope of renewing their strength, and expect nothing but their last sleep, so you, weakened by worldly occupations, have given yourselves up to sloth, and have not cast your cares on the LORD. Your spirit is therefore broken, and you have grown old in your sorrows." [91] "I should like then to know, lord, why she sat on a chair?" He answered, "Because every weak person sits on a chair on account of his weakness, that his weakness may be sustained. Behold, you have the form of the first vision. [92] Now in the second vision you saw her standing with a youthful countenance, and more joyful than before; still she had the skin and hair of an aged woman. Hear," he said, "this allegory also. [93] When one becomes somewhat old, he despairs of himself on account of his weakness and poverty, and looks forward to nothing but the last day of his life. [94] Then suddenly an inheritance is left him: and hearing of this, he rises up, and becoming exceedingly joyful, he puts on strength. And now he no longer reclines,

but stands up; and his spirit, already destroyed by his previous actions, is renewed, and he no longer sits, but acts with vigor. [95] So it happened with you on hearing the revelation which God gave you. For the LORD had compassion on you, and renewed your spirit, and you laid aside your infirmities. [96] Vigor arose within you, and you grew strong in faith; and the LORD, seeing your strength, rejoiced. On this account He showed you the building of the tower; and He will show you other things, if you continue at peace with each other with all your heart. [97] Now, in the third vision, you saw her still younger, and she was noble and joyful, and her shape was beautiful. [98] For, just as when some good news comes suddenly to one who is sad, immediately he forgets his former sorrows, and looks for nothing else than the good news which he has heard, and for the future is made strong for good, and his spirit is renewed on account of the joy which he has received; so you also have received the renewal of your spirits by seeing these good things. [99] As to your seeing her sitting on a seat, that means that her position is one of strength, for a seat has four feet and stands firmly. For the world is also kept together by means of four elements. Therefore, those who convert completely and with the whole heart, will become young and firmly established. [100] You now have the revelation completely given to you. Make no further demands for revelations. If anything ought to be revealed, it will be revealed to you."

VISION 4

[1] Twenty days after the former vision I saw another vision, brothers—a representation of the tribulation that is to come. [2] I was going to a country house along the Campanian road. Now the house lay about ten furlongs from the public road. The district is one rarely traversed. [3] And as I walked alone, I prayed [for] the LORD to complete the revelations which He had made to me through His holy Assembly, that He might strengthen me, and give conversion to all His servants who were going astray, that His great and glorious Name might be glorified because He granted to show me His marvels. [4] And while I was glorifying Him and giving Him thanks, a voice, as it were, answered me, "Do not doubt, Hermas;" [5] and I began to think within myself, and to say, "What reason have I to doubt—I who have been established by the LORD, and who have seen such glorious sights?" [6] I advanced a little, brothers, and behold, I see dust rising even to the heavens. I began to say to myself, "Are cattle approaching and raising the dust?" [7] It was about a furlong's distance from me. And behold, I see the dust rising more and more, so that I imagined that it was something sent from God. But the sun now shone out

a little, and behold, I see a mighty beast like a whale, and out of its mouth fiery locusts proceeded. [8]But the size of that beast was about a hundred feet, and it had a head like an urn. I began to weep, and to call on the LORD to rescue me from it. Then I remembered the word which I had heard, "Do not doubt, O Hermas." [9]Clothed, therefore, my brothers, with faith in the LORD, and remembering the great things which He had taught me, I boldly faced the beast. Now that beast came on with such noise and force, that it could itself have destroyed a city. [10]I came near it, and the monstrous beast stretched itself out on the ground, and showed nothing but its tongue, and did not stir at all until I had passed by it. Now the beast had four colors on its head: black, then fiery and bloody, then golden, and lastly white. [11]Now after I had passed by the wild beast, and had moved forward about thirty feet, behold, a virgin meets me, adorned as if she were proceeding from the bridal chamber, clothed entirely in white, and with white sandals, and veiled up to her forehead, and her head was covered by a hood. And she had white hair. [12]I knew from my former visions that this was the Assembly, and I became more joyful. [13]She saluted me, and said, "Greetings, O man!" And I returned her salutation, and said, "Lady, greetings!" [14]And she answered, and said to me, "Has nothing crossed your path?" I say, "I was met by a beast of such size that it could destroy peoples, but through the power of the LORD and His great mercy I escaped from it." [15]"Well did you escape from it," she says, "because you cast your care on God, and opened your heart to the LORD, believing that you can be saved by no other than by His great and glorious Name. [16]On this account the LORD has sent His messenger, who has rule over the beasts, and whose name is Thegri, and has shut up its mouth, so that it cannot tear you. [17]You have escaped from great tribulation on account of your faith, and because you did not doubt in the presence of such a beast. [18]Therefore, go and tell the chosen ones of the LORD His mighty deeds, and say to them that this beast is a type of the great tribulation that is coming. If then you prepare yourselves, and convert with all your heart, and turn to the LORD, it will be possible for you to escape it, if your heart is pure and spotless, and you spend the rest of the days of your life in serving the LORD blamelessly. [19]Cast your cares on the LORD, and He will direct them. Trust the Lord, you who doubt, for He is all-powerful, and can turn His anger away from you, and send scourges on the doubters. [20]Woe to those who hear these words and despise them: it would be better for them not to have been born." [21]I asked her about the four colors which the beast had on his head. And she answered, and said to me, "Again you are inquisitive in regard to such matters." "Yea, Lady," I said, "make known to me what they are." [22]"Listen," she said: "the black is the world in which we dwell, and the fiery and bloody points out that the world must perish through blood and fire, and the golden part are you who have escaped from this world. [23]For as gold is tested by fire, and thus becomes useful, so are you tested who dwell in it. Those, therefore, who continue steadfast, and are put through the fire, will be purified by means of it. For as gold casts away its dross, so also will you cast away all sadness and trouble, and will be made pure so as to fit into the building of the tower. [24]But the white part is the age that is to come, in which the chosen ones of God will dwell, since those selected by God to continuous life will be spotless and pure. [25]Therefore, do not cease speaking these things into the ears of the holy ones. This then is the type of the great tribulation that is to come. If you wish it, it will be nothing. Remember those things which were written down before." [26]And saying this, she departed. But I did not see into what place she retired. There was a noise, however, and I turned around in alarm, thinking that that beast was coming.

VISION 5

[1]After I had been praying at home, and had sat down on my couch, there entered a Man of glorious aspect, dressed like a shepherd, with a white goat's skin, a wallet on his shoulders, and a rod in His hand, and He saluted me. I returned His salutation. [2]And immediately He sat down beside me, and said to me, "I have been sent by a most venerable messenger to dwell with you the remaining days of your life." [3]And I thought that He had come to tempt me, and I said to Him, "Who are You? For I know Him to whom I have been entrusted." He said to me, "Do you not know Me?" "No," I said. "I," he said, "am that Shepherd to whom you have been entrusted." [4]And as He was speaking, His figure was changed; and then I knew that it was He to whom I had been entrusted. And immediately I became confused, and fear took hold of me, and I was overpowered with deep sorrow that I had answered Him so wickedly and foolishly. [5]But He answered, and said to me, "Do not be confounded, but receive strength from the commandments which I am going to give you. For I have been sent," He said, "to show you again all the things which you saw before, especially those of them which are useful to you. [6]First of all, then, write down My commandments and similitudes, and you will write the other things as I will show you. [7]For this purpose," He said, "I command you to write down the commandments and similitudes first, that you may read them easily, and be able to keep them." [8]Accordingly, I wrote down the

commandments and similitudes, exactly as He had ordered me. If then, when you have heard these, you keep them and walk in them, and practice them with pure minds, you will receive from the LORD all that He has promised to you. ⁹But if, after you have heard them, you do not convert, but continue to add to your sins, then you will receive from the LORD the opposite things. ¹⁰All these words did the Shepherd, even the Messenger of conversion, command me to write.

SECTION 2:
COMMANDMENTS

COMMANDMENT 1

¹First of all, believe that there is one God who created and finished all things, and made all things out of nothing. He alone is able to contain the whole, but Himself cannot be contained. ²Therefore, have faith in Him, and fear Him; and fearing Him, exercise self-control. ³Keep these commands, and you will cast away all wickedness from yourself, and put on the strength of righteousness, and live to God, if you keep this commandment.

COMMANDMENT 2

¹He said to me, "Be simple and guileless, and you will be as the children who do not know the wickedness that ruins the life of men. ²First, then, speak evil of no one, nor listen with pleasure to anyone who speaks evil of another. But if you listen, you will partake of the sin of him who speaks evil, if you believe the slander which you hear; for believing it, you will also have something to say against your brother. ³Thus, then, will you be guilty of the sin of him who slanders. For slander is evil and an unsteady demon. It never abides in peace, but always remains in discord. Keep yourself from it, and you will always be at peace with all. ⁴Put on a holiness in which there is no wicked cause of offense, but all deeds that are composed and joyful. ⁵Practice goodness; and from the rewards of your labors, which God gives you, give to all the needy in simplicity, not hesitating as to whom you are to give or not to give. Give to all, for God wishes His gifts to be shared among all. ⁶They who receive, will render an account to God why and for what they have received. For the afflicted who receive will not be condemned, but they who receive on false pretenses will suffer punishment. He, then, who gives is guiltless. ⁷For as he received from the LORD, so has he accomplished his service in simplicity, not hesitating as to whom he should give and to whom he should not give. This service, then, if accomplished in simplicity, is glorious with God. He, therefore, who thus ministers in simplicity, will live to God. ⁸Therefore, keep these

commandments, as I have given them to you, that your conversion and the conversion of your house may be found in simplicity, and your heart may be pure and stainless."

COMMANDMENT 3

¹Again, He said to me, "Love the truth, and let nothing but truth proceed from your mouth, that the spirit which God has placed in your flesh may be found truthful before all men; and the LORD, who dwells in you, will be glorified, because the LORD is truthful in every word, and in Him is no falsehood. ²Therefore, they who lie deny the LORD, and rob Him, not giving back to Him the deposit which they have received. For they received from Him a spirit free from falsehood. If they give Him back this spirit untruthful, they pollute the commandment of the LORD, and become robbers." ³On hearing these words, I wept most violently. When He saw me weeping, He said to me, "Why do you weep?" And I said, "Because, Lord, I do not know if I can be saved." ⁴"Why?" He said. And I said, "Because, Lord, I never spoke a true word in my life, but have ever spoken cunningly to all, and have affirmed a lie for the truth to all; and no one ever contradicted me, but credit was given to my word. How then can I live, since I have acted thus?" ⁵And He said to me, "Your feelings are indeed right and sound, for you ought as a servant of God to have walked in truth, and not to have joined an evil conscience with the spirit of truth, nor to have caused sadness to the holy and true Spirit." ⁶And I said to Him, "Never, Lord, did I listen to these words with so much attention." ⁷And He said to me, "Now you hear them, and keep them, that even the falsehoods which you formerly told in your transactions may come to be believed through the truthfulness of your present statements. For even they can become worthy of credit. ⁸If you keep these precepts, and from this time forward you speak nothing but the truth, it will be possible for you to obtain life. ⁹And whosoever will hear this commandment, and depart from that great wickedness—falsehood, will live to God."

COMMANDMENT 4

¹"I charge you," He said, "to guard your chastity, and let no thought enter your heart of another man's wife, or of fornication, or of similar iniquities; for by doing this you commit a great sin. ²But if you always remember your own wife, you will never sin. For if this thought enters your heart, then you will sin; and if, in like manner, you think other wicked thoughts, you commit sin. ³For this thought is a great sin in a servant of God. But if anyone commits this wicked deed, he works death for himself. ⁴Attend, therefore,

and refrain from this thought; for where purity dwells, there iniquity ought not to enter the heart of a righteous man." [5] I said to Him, "Lord, permit me to ask you a few questions." "Ask on," He said. [6] And I said to Him, "Lord, if anyone has a wife who trusts in the LORD, and if he detects her in adultery, does the man sin if he continues to live with her?" [7] And He said to me, "As long as he remains ignorant of her sin, the husband commits no transgression in living with her. But if the husband knows that his wife has gone astray, and if the woman does not convert, but persists in her fornication, and yet the husband continues to live with her, he is also guilty of her crime, and a sharer in her adultery." [8] And I said to Him, "What then, Lord, is the husband to do, if his wife continues in her vicious practices?" [9] And He said, "The husband should put her away, and remain by himself. But if he puts his wife away and marries another, he also commits adultery." [10] And I said to Him, "What if the woman put away should convert, and wish to return to her husband: will she not be taken back by her husband?" [11] And He said to me, "Assuredly. If the husband does not take her back, he sins, and brings a great sin on himself; for he ought to take back the sinner who has converted. But not frequently. For there is but one conversion to the servants of God. [12] In case, therefore, that the divorced wife may convert, the husband ought to not marry another when his wife has been put away. In this matter man and woman are to be treated exactly in the same way. [13] Moreover, adultery is committed not only by those who pollute their flesh, but by those who imitate the heathen in their actions. Therefore, if anyone persists in such deeds, and does not convert, withdraw from him, and cease to live with him. Otherwise you are a sharer in his sin. [14] Therefore the injunction has been laid on you, that you should remain by yourselves, both man and woman, for in such persons conversion can take place. [15] But I do not," He said, "give opportunity for the doing of these deeds, but that he who has sinned may sin no more. But with regard to his previous transgressions, there is One who is able to provide a cure; for it is He, indeed, who has power over all." [16] I asked Him again, and said, "Since the LORD has granted to always dwell with me, hear me while I utter a few words; for I understand nothing, and my heart has been hardened by my previous mode of life. [17] Give me understanding, for I am exceedingly dull, and I understand absolutely nothing." And He answered and said to me, "I am set over conversion, and I give understanding to all who convert. [18] Do you not think," he said, "that it is great wisdom to convert? For conversion is great wisdom. For he who has sinned understands that he acted wickedly in the sight of the

LORD, and remembers the actions he has done, and he converts, and no longer acts wickedly, but does good liberally, and humbles and torments his soul because he has sinned. You see, therefore, that conversion is great wisdom." [19] And I said to Him, "It is for this reason, Lord, that I inquire carefully into all things, especially because I am a sinner; that I may know what works I should do, that I may live: for my sins are many and various." [20] And He said to me, "You will live if you keep My commandments, and walk in them; and whosoever will hear and keep these commandments, will live to God." [21] And I said to Him, "I should like to continue my questions." "Speak on," He said. And I said, "I heard, Lord, some teachers maintain that there is no other conversion than that which takes place, when we descended into the water and received remission of our former sins." [22] He said to me, "That was sound doctrine which you heard; for that is really the case. For he who has received remission of his sins ought not to sin anymore, but to live in purity. [23] Since, however, you inquire diligently into all things, I will also point this out to you, not as giving occasion for error to those who are to believe, or have lately believed, in the LORD. [24] For those who have now believed, and those who are to believe, have no conversion for their sins; but they have remission of their previous sins. For to those who have been called before these days, the LORD has set conversion. [25] For the LORD, knowing the heart, and foreknowing all things, knew the weakness of men and the manifold wiles of the Devil, that he would inflict some evil on the servants of God, and would act wickedly toward them. [26] The LORD, therefore, being merciful, has had mercy on the work of His hand, and has set conversion for them; and He has entrusted to me power over this conversion. [27] And therefore, I say to you, that if anyone is tempted by the Devil, and sins after that great and holy calling, in which the LORD has called His people to continuous life, he has opportunity to convert but once. [28] But if he should sin frequently after this, and then convert, to such a man his conversion will be of no avail; for he will live with difficulty." [29] And I said, "Lord, I feel that life has come back to me in listening attentively to these commandments; for I know that I will be saved, if in [the] future I sin no more." And He said, "You will be saved, you and all who keep these commandments." [30] And again I asked Him, saying, "Lord, since you have been so patient in listening to me, will you show me this also?" "Speak," He said. And I said, "If a wife or husband dies, and the widower or widow marries, does he or she commit sin?" [31] "There is no sin in marrying again," He said; "but if they remain unmarried, they gain greater honor and glory with the

LORD; but if they marry, they do not sin. Therefore, guard your chastity and purity, and you will live to God. ³²What commandments I now give you, and what I am to give, keep from henceforth, yea, from the very day when you were entrusted to Me, and I will dwell in your house. And your former sins will be forgiven, if you keep My commandments. ³³And all will be forgiven who keep these commandments of Mine and walk in this chastity."

COMMANDMENT 5

¹"Be patient," He said, "and of good understanding, and you will rule over every wicked work, and you will work all righteousness. For if you are patient, the Holy Spirit that dwells in you will be pure. ²He will not be darkened by any evil spirit, but, dwelling in a broad region, He will rejoice and be glad; and with the vessel in which He dwells He will serve God in gladness, having great peace within Himself. ³But if any outburst of anger takes place, immediately the Holy Spirit, who is tender, is troubled, not having a pure place, and He seeks to depart. For He is choked by the vile spirit, and cannot attend on the LORD as He wishes, for anger pollutes Him. ⁴For the LORD dwells in long-suffering, but the Devil in anger. ⁵The two spirits, then, when dwelling in the same habitation, are at discord with each other, and are troublesome to that man in whom they dwell. ⁶For if an exceedingly small piece of wormwood is taken and put into a jar of honey, is the honey not entirely destroyed, and does the exceedingly small piece of wormwood not entirely take away the sweetness of the honey, so that it no longer affords any gratification to its owner, but has become bitter, and lost its use? ⁷But if the wormwood is not put into the honey, then the honey remains sweet, and is of use to its owner. ⁸You see, then, that patience is sweeter than honey, and useful to God, and the LORD dwells in it. But anger is bitter and useless. ⁹Now, if anger is mingled with patience, the patience is polluted, and its prayer is not then useful to God." ¹⁰"I should like, Lord," I said, "to know the power of anger, that I may guard myself against it." ¹¹And He said, "If you do not guard yourself against it, you and your house lose all hope of salvation. Guard yourself, therefore, against it. For I am with you, and all will depart from it who convert with their whole heart. ¹²For I will be with them, and I will save them all. For all are justified by the most holy Messenger. ¹³"Hear now," He said, "how wicked is the action of anger, and in what way it overthrows the servants of God by its action, and turns them from righteousness. But it does not turn away those who are full of faith, nor does it act on them, for the power of the LORD is with them. ¹⁴It is the thoughtless and doubting that it turns away.

For as soon as it sees such men standing steadfast, it throws itself into their hearts, and for nothing at all the man or woman becomes embittered on account of occurrences in their daily life, as for instance on account of their food, or some superfluous word that has been uttered, or on account of some friend, or some gift or debt, or some such senseless affair. ¹⁵For all these things are foolish and empty and unprofitable to the servants of God. ¹⁶But patience is great, and mighty, and strong, and calm in the midst of great enlargement, joyful, rejoicing, free from care, glorifying God at all times, having no bitterness in her, and abiding continually meek and quiet. ¹⁷Now this patience dwells with those who have complete faith. But anger is foolish, and fickle, and senseless. ¹⁸Now, of folly is begotten bitterness, and of bitterness anger, and of anger frenzy. This frenzy, the product of so many evils, ends in great and incurable sin. ¹⁹For when all these spirits dwell in one vessel in which the Holy Spirit also dwells, the vessel cannot contain them, but overflows. The tender Spirit, then, not being accustomed to dwell with the wicked spirit, nor with hardness, withdraws from such a man, and seeks to dwell with meekness and peacefulness. ²⁰Then, when He withdraws from the man in whom He dwelt, the man is emptied of the righteous Spirit; and being henceforward filled with evil spirits, He is in a state of anarchy in every action, being dragged here and there by the evil spirits, and there is a complete darkness in his mind as to everything good. ²¹This, then, is what happens to all the angry. Therefore, depart from that most wicked spirit—anger, and put on patience, and resist anger and bitterness, and you will be found in company with the purity which is loved by the LORD. ²²Take care, then, that you do not neglect by any chance this commandment: for if you obey this commandment, you will be able to keep all the other commandments which I am to give you. ²³Be strong, then, in these commandments, and put on power, and let all put on power, as many as wish to walk in them."

COMMANDMENT 6

¹"I gave you," He said, "directions in the first commandment to attend to faith, and fear, and self-restraint." "Even so, Lord," I said. ²And He said, "Now I wish to show you the powers of these, that you may know what power each possesses. For their powers are double, and have relation alike to the righteous and the unrighteous. ³Therefore, trust the righteous, but put no trust in the unrighteous. For the path of righteousness is straight, but that of unrighteousness is crooked. ⁴But walk in the straight and even way, and do not mind the crooked. For the crooked path has no roads, but has many pathless

places and stumbling-blocks in it, and it is rough and thorny. It is injurious to those who walk therein. [5] But they who walk in the straight road walk evenly without stumbling, because it is neither rough nor thorny. You see, then, that it is better to walk in this road." [6] "I wish to go by this road," I said. "You will go by it," He said; "and whoever turns to the LORD with all his heart will walk in it." [7] "Hear now," He said, "in regard to faith. There are two messengers with a man—one of righteousness, and the other of iniquity." And I said to Him, "How, Lord, am I to know the powers of these, for both messengers dwell with me?" [8] "Hear," He said, "and understand them. The messenger of righteousness is gentle and modest, meek and peaceful. Therefore, when he ascends into your heart, immediately he talks to you of righteousness, purity, chastity, contentment, and of every righteous deed and glorious virtue. [9] When all these ascend into your heart, know that the messenger of righteousness is with you. These are the deeds of the messenger of righteousness. Trust him, then, and his works. [10] Look now at the works of the messenger of iniquity. First, he is wrathful, and bitter, and foolish, and his works are evil, and ruin the servants of God. When, then, he ascends into your heart, know him by his works." [11] And I said to Him, "How, Lord, I will perceive him—I do not know." "Hear and understand" He said. [12] "When anger comes on you, or harshness, know that he is in you; and you will know this to be the case also, when you are attacked by a longing after many transactions, and the richest delicacies, and drunken revels, and various luxuries, and things improper, and by a hankering after women, and by overreaching, and pride, and blustering, and by whatever is like to these. [13] When these ascend into your heart, know that the messenger of iniquity is in you. Now that you know his works, depart from him, and in no respect trust him, because his deeds are evil, and unprofitable to the servants of God. [14] These, then, are the actions of both messengers. Understand them and trust the messenger of righteousness; but depart from the messenger of iniquity, because his instruction is bad in every deed. [15] For though a man be most faithful, and the thought of this messenger ascend into his heart, that man or woman must sin. [16] On the other hand, be a man or woman ever so bad, yet, if the works of the messenger of righteousness ascend into his or her heart, he or she must do something good. [17] You see, therefore, that it is good to follow the messenger of righteousness, but to bid farewell to the messenger of iniquity. [18] This commandment exhibits the deeds of faith, that you may trust the works of the messenger of righteousness, and doing them you may live to God. But believe the works of the messenger of iniquity are hard. If you refuse to do them, you will live to God."

COMMANDMENT 7

[1] "Fear," He said, "the LORD, and keep His commandments. For if you keep the commandments of God, you will be powerful in every action, and every one of your actions will be incomparable. [2] For, fearing the LORD, you will do all things well. This is the fear which you ought to have, that you may be saved. [3] But do not fear the Devil; for, fearing the LORD, you will have dominion over the Devil, for there is no power in him. [4] But he in whom there is no power ought on no account to be an object of fear; but He in whom there is glorious power is truly to be feared. For every one that has power ought to be feared; but he who has no power is despised by all. [5] Therefore, fear the deeds of the Devil, since they are wicked. For, fearing the LORD, you will not do these deeds, but will refrain from them. [6] For fears are of two kinds: for if you do not wish to do that which is evil, fear the LORD, and you will not do it; but, again, if you wish to do that which is good, fear the LORD, and you will do it. Therefore, the fear of the LORD is strong, and great, and glorious. [7] Fear, then, the LORD, and you will live to Him, and as many as fear Him and keep His commandments will live to God." [8] "Why," I said, "Lord, did You say in regard to those that keep His commandments, that they will live to God?" "Because," He says, "all creation fears the LORD, but all creation does not keep His commandments. [9] They only who fear the LORD and keep His commandments have life with God; but as to those who do not keep His commandments, there is no life in them."

COMMANDMENT 8

[1] "I told you," He said, "that the creatures of God are double, for restraint is also double; for in some cases restraint has to be exercised in others [where] there is no need of restraint." [2] "Make known to me, Lord," I say, "in what cases restraint has to be exercised, and in what cases it does not." [3] "Restrain yourself in regard to evil, and do not do it; but exercise no restraint in regard to good, but do it. For if you exercise restraint in the doing of good, you will commit a great sin; but if you exercise restraint, so as not to do that which is evil, you are practicing great righteousness. [4] Restrain yourself, therefore, from all iniquity, and do that which is good." [5] "What, Lord," I say, "are the evil deeds from which we must restrain ourselves?" [6] "Hear," He says: "from adultery and fornication, from unlawful reveling, from wicked luxury, from indulgence in many kinds of food and the extravagance of riches, and from boastfulness, and

haughtiness, and insolence, and lies, and backbiting, and hypocrisy, from the remembrance of wrong, and from all slander. [7] These are the deeds that are most wicked in the life of men. From all these deeds, therefore, the servant of God must restrain himself. [8] For he who does not restrain himself from these, cannot live to God. Listen, then, to the deeds that accompany these." [9] "Are there, Lord," I said, "any other evil deeds?" "There are," He says; "and many of them, too, from which the servant of God must restrain himself—theft, lying, robbery, false witness, overreaching, wicked lust, deceit, vainglory, boastfulness, and all other vices like to these." [10] "Do you not think that these are really wicked?" "Exceedingly wicked in the servants of God. From all of these the servant of God must restrain himself. [11] Restrain yourself, then, from all these, that you may live to God, and you will be enrolled among those who restrain themselves in regard to these matters. These, then, are the things from which you must restrain yourself. [12] But listen," He says, "to the things in regard to which you do not have to exercise self-restraint, but which you ought to do. [13] Do not restrain yourself in regard to that which is good, but do it." "And tell me, Lord," I say, "the nature of the good deeds, that I may walk in them and wait on them, so that doing them I can be saved." [14] "Listen," He says, "to the good deeds which you ought to do, and in regard to which there is no self-restraint requisite. First of all there is faith, then fear of the LORD, love, concord, words of righteousness, truth, patience. [15] Than these, nothing is better in the life of men. If anyone attends to these, and does not restrain himself from them, he is blessed in his life. [16] Then there are the following attendant on these: helping widows, looking after orphans and the needy, rescuing the servants of God from necessities, the being hospitable—for in hospitality doing good finds a field—never opposing anyone, the being quiet, having fewer needs than all men, reverencing the aged, practicing righteousness, watching the brotherhood, bearing insolence, being long-suffering, encouraging those who are sick in soul, not casting those who have fallen into sin from the faith, but turning them back and restoring them to peace of mind, admonishing sinners, not oppressing debtors and the needy, and if there are any other actions like these. [17] Do these seem to you good?" He says. "For what, Lord," I say, "is better than these?" "Walk then in them," He says, "and do not restrain yourself from them, and you will live to God. [18] Therefore, keep this commandment. If you do good, and do not restrain yourself from it, you will live to God. All who act thus will live to God. [19] And, again, if you refuse to do evil, and restrain yourself from it, you will live to God. And all will live to God who keep these commandments and walk in them."

COMMANDMENT 9

[1] He says to me, "Put away doubting from you and do not hesitate to ask of the LORD, saying to yourself, How can I ask of the LORD and receive from Him, seeing I have sinned so much against Him? [2] Do not thus reason with yourself, but with all your heart turn to the LORD and ask of Him without doubting, and you will know the multitude of His tender mercies; that He will never leave you, but fulfill the request of your soul. [3] For He is not like men, who remember evils done against them; but He Himself does not remember evils and has compassion on His own creature. [4] Therefore, cleanse your heart from all the vanities of this world, and from the words already mentioned, and ask of the LORD and you will receive all, and in none of your requests will you be denied which you make to the LORD without doubting. But if you doubt in your heart, you will receive none of your requests. [5] For those who doubt regarding God are double-souled, and do not obtain one of their requests. But those who are perfect in faith ask everything, trusting in the LORD; and they obtain, because they ask nothing doubting, and not being double-souled. [6] For every double-souled man, even if he converts, will be saved with difficulty. Cleanse your heart, therefore, from all doubt, and put on faith, because it is strong, and trust God that you will obtain from Him all that you ask. [7] And if at any time, after you have asked of the LORD, you are slower in obtaining your request [than you expected], do not doubt because you have not soon obtained the request of your soul; for invariably it is on account of some temptation or some sin of which you are ignorant that you are slower in obtaining your request. [8] Therefore, do not cease to make the request of your soul, and you will obtain it. But if you grow weary and waver in your request, blame yourself, and not Him who does not give to you. [9] Consider this doubting state of mind, for it is wicked and senseless, and turns many away entirely from the faith, even though they might be very strong. [10] For this doubting is the daughter of the Devil, and acts exceedingly wickedly to the servants of God. [11] Despise, then, doubting, and gain the mastery over it in everything; clothing yourself with faith, which is strong and powerful. For faith promises all things, perfects all things; but doubt having no thorough faith in itself, fails in every work which it undertakes. [12] You see, then," He says, "that faith is from above—from the LORD—and has great power; but doubt is an earthly spirit, coming from the Devil, and has no power. [13] Serve, then, that which has power, namely faith, and

keep away from doubt, which has no power, and you will live to God. And all will live to God whose minds have been set on these things."

COMMANDMENT 10

[1] "Remove from yourself," He says, "grief; for she is the sister of doubt and anger." "How, Lord," I say, "is she the sister of these? For anger, doubt, and grief seem to be quite different from each other." [2] "You are senseless, O man. Do you not perceive that grief is more wicked than all the spirits, and most terrible to the servants of God, and more than all other spirits destroys man and crushes out the Holy Spirit, and yet, on the other hand, she saves him?" [3] "I am senseless, Lord," I say, "and do not understand these allegories. For how she can crush out, and on the other hand save, I do not perceive." [4] "Listen," He says. "Those who have never searched for the truth, nor investigated the nature of the Divinity, but have simply believed, when they devote themselves to and become mixed up with business, and wealth, and heathen friendships, and many other actions of this world, do not perceive the allegories of Divinity; [5] for their minds are darkened by these actions, and they are corrupted and become dried up. Even as beautiful vines, when they are neglected, are withered up by thorns and various plants, so men who have believed, and have afterward fallen away into many of those actions above mentioned, go astray in their minds, and lose all understanding in regard to righteousness; [6] for if they hear of righteousness, their minds are occupied with their business, and they give no heed at all. [7] Those, on the other hand, who have the fear of God, and search after [the] Godhead and truth, and have their hearts turned to the LORD, quickly perceive and understand what is said to them, because they have the fear of the LORD in them. [8] For where the LORD dwells, there is much understanding. Cleave, then, to the LORD, and you will understand and perceive all things. [9] "Hear, then," He says, "foolish man, how grief crushes out the Holy Spirit, and on the other hand saves. When the doubting man attempts any deed, and fails in it on account of his doubt, this grief enters into the man, and grieves the Holy Spirit, and crushes Him out. [10] Then, on the other hand, when anger attaches itself to a man in regard to any matter, and he is embittered, then grief enters into the heart of the man who was irritated, and he is grieved at the deed which he did, and converts that he has wrought a wicked deed. [11] This grief, then, appears to be accompanied by salvation, because the man, after having done a wicked deed, converted. Both actions grieve the Spirit: doubt, because it did not accomplish its object; and anger grieves the Spirit, because it did what was wicked. [12] Both these are grievous to the Holy Spirit—doubt and anger. Therefore, remove grief from yourself, and do not crush the Holy Spirit which dwells in you, lest He entreat God against you, and He withdraw from you. [13] For the Spirit of God which has been granted to us to dwell in this body does not endure grief nor trouble. [14] Therefore, put on cheerfulness, which is always agreeable and acceptable to God, and rejoice in it. For every cheerful man does what is good, and minds what is good, and despises grief; but the sorrowful man always acts wickedly. [15] First, he acts wickedly because he grieves the Holy Spirit, which was given to man—a cheerful Spirit. [16] Secondly, grieving the Holy Spirit, he works iniquity, neither entreating the LORD nor confessing to Him. For the entreaty of the sorrowful man has no power to ascend to the altar of God." [17] "Why," I say, "does the entreaty of the grieved man not ascend to the altar?" "Because," He says, "grief sits in his heart. Grief, then, mingled with his entreaty, does not permit the entreaty to ascend pure to the altar of God. [18] For as vinegar and wine, when mixed in the same vessel, do not give the same pleasure [as wine alone gives], so grief mixed with the Holy Spirit does not produce the same entreaty [as would be produced by the Holy Spirit alone]. [19] Cleanse yourself from this wicked grief, and you will live to God; and all will live to God who drive away grief from themselves, and put on all cheerfulness."

COMMANDMENT 11

[1] He pointed out to me some men sitting on a seat, and one man sitting on a chair. And He says to me, "Do you see the persons sitting on the seat?" "I do, Lord," I said. "These," He says, "are the faithful, and he who sits on the chair is a false prophet, ruining the minds of the servants of God. It is the doubters, not the faithful, that he ruins. [2] These doubters then go to him as to a soothsayer, and inquire of him what will happen to them; and he, the false prophet, not having the power of a Divine Spirit in him, answers them according to their inquiries, and according to their wicked desires, and fills their souls with expectations, according to their own wishes. [3] For being himself empty, he gives empty answers to empty inquirers; for every answer is made to the emptiness of man. Some true words he does occasionally utter; for the Devil fills him with his own spirit, in the hope that he may be able to overcome some of the righteous. [4] As many, then, as are strong in the faith of the LORD, and are clothed with truth, have no connection with such spirits, but keep away from them; but as many as are of doubtful minds and frequently convert, take themselves to soothsaying, even as the heathen, and

bring greater sin on themselves by their idolatry. [5] For he who inquires of a false prophet in regard to any action is an idolater, and devoid of the truth, and foolish. For no spirit given by God requires to be asked; but such a spirit having the power of Divinity speaks all things of itself, for it proceeds from above from the power of the Divine Spirit. [6] But the spirit which is asked and speaks according to the desires of men is earthly, light, and powerless, and it is altogether silent if it is not questioned." [7] "How then, Lord," I say, "will a man know which of them is the prophet, and which the false prophet?" [8] "I will tell you," He says, "about both the prophets, and then you can try the true and the false prophet according to My directions. [9] Try the man who has the Divine Spirit by his life. First, he who has the Divine Spirit proceeding from above is meek, and peaceable, and humble, and refrains from all iniquity and the vain desire of this world, and contents himself with fewer wants than those of other men, and when asked he makes no reply; [10] nor does he speak privately, nor when man wishes the spirit to speak does the Holy Spirit speak, but it speaks only when God wishes it to speak. [11] When, then, a man having the Divine Spirit comes into an assembly of righteous men who have faith in the Divine Spirit, and this assembly of men offers up prayer to God, then the messenger of the prophetic Spirit, who is destined for him, fills the man; and the man being filled with the Holy Spirit, speaks to the multitude as the Lord wishes. [12] Thus, then, will the Spirit of Divinity become manifest. Whatever power therefore comes from the Spirit of Divinity belongs to the Lord. [13] Hear, then," He says, "in regard to the spirit which is earthly, and empty, and powerless, and foolish. First, the man who seems to have the Spirit, [but does not,] exalts himself, and wishes to have the first seat, and is bold, and impudent, and talkative, and lives in the midst of many luxuries and many other delusions, and takes rewards for his prophecy; and if he does not receive rewards, he does not prophesy. [14] Can, then, the Divine Spirit take rewards and prophesy? It is not possible that the prophet of God should do this, but prophets of this character are possessed by an earthly spirit. [15] Then it never approaches an assembly of righteous men, but shuns them. And it associates with doubters and the vain, and prophesies to them in a corner, and deceives them, speaking to them, according to their desires, mere empty words: for they are empty to whom it gives its answers. [16] For the empty vessel, when placed along with the empty, is not crashed, but they correspond to each other. [17] When, therefore, it comes into an assembly of righteous men who have a Spirit of Divinity, and they offer up prayer, that man is made empty, and the earthly spirit flees from him through fear, and that man is made dumb, and is entirely crashed, being unable to speak. [18] For if you closely pack a storehouse with wine or oil, and put an empty jar in the midst of the vessels of wine or oil, you will find that jar empty as when you placed it, if you should wish to clear the storehouse. [19] So also the empty prophets, when they come to the spirits of the righteous, are found [on leaving] to be such as they were when they came. [20] This, then, is the mode of life of both prophets. Try by his deeds and his life the man who says that he is inspired. [21] But as for you, trust the Spirit which comes from God, and has power; but the spirit which is earthly and empty do not trust at all, for there is no power in it: it comes from the Devil. [22] Hear, then, the allegory which I am to tell you. Take a stone, and throw it to the sky, and see if you can touch it. Or again, take a squirt of water and squirt into the sky, and see if you can penetrate the sky." [23] "How, Lord," I say, "can these things take place? For both of them are impossible." "As these things," He says, "are impossible, so also are the earthly spirits powerless and weak. [24] But look, on the other hand, at the power which comes from above. Hail is of the size of a very small grain, yet when it falls on a man's head how much annoyance it gives him! [25] Or again, take the drop which falls from a pitcher to the ground, and yet it hollows a stone. You see, then, that the smallest things coming from above have great power when they fall on the earth. [26] Thus is the Divine Spirit, which comes from above, also powerful. Trust, then, that Spirit, but have nothing to do with the other."

COMMANDMENT 12

[1] He says to me, "Put away from yourself all wicked desire, and clothe yourself with good and chaste desire; for clothed with this desire you will hate wicked desire, and will rein yourself in even as you wish. [2] For wicked desire is wild and is tamed with difficulty. For it is terrible and consumes men exceedingly by its wildness. Especially is the servant of God terribly consumed by it, if he falls into it and is devoid of understanding. [3] Moreover, it consumes all such as do not have on them the garment of good desire, but are entangled and mixed up with this world. These it delivers up to death." [4] "What then, Lord," I say, "are the deeds of wicked desire which deliver men over to death? Make them known to me, and I will refrain from them." [5] "Listen, then, to the works in which evil desire slays the servants of God." "Foremost of all is the desire after another's wife or husband, and after extravagance, and many useless delicacies and drinks, and many other foolish luxuries; for all luxury is foolish and empty in the servants of

God. [6] These, then, are the evil desires which slay the servants of God. For this evil desire is the daughter of the Devil. You must refrain from evil desires, that by refraining you may live to God. [7] But as many as are mastered by them, and do not resist them, will perish at last, for these desires are fatal. [8] Put on, then, the desire of righteousness; and arming yourself with the fear of the LORD, resist them. For the fear of the LORD dwells in good desire. [9] But if evil desire sees you armed with the fear of God, and resisting it, it will flee far from you, and it will no longer appear to you, for it fears your armor. [10] Go, then, adorned with the crown which you have gained for victory over it, to the desire of righteousness, and, delivering up to it the prize which you have received, serve it even as it wishes. [11] If you serve good desire, and be subject to it, you will gain the mastery over evil desire, and make it subject to you even as you wish." [12] "I should like to [know] how," I say, "in what way I ought to serve good desire." [13] "Hear," He says: "You will practice righteousness and virtue, truth and the fear of the LORD, faith and meekness, and whatever excellencies are like to these. Practicing these, you will be a well-pleasing servant of God, and you will live to Him; and everyone who will serve good desire, will live to God." [14] He concluded the twelve commandments, and said to me, "You now have these commandments. Walk in them and exhort your hearers that their conversion may be pure during the remainder of their life. [15] Carefully fulfill this ministry which I now entrust to you, and you will accomplish much. For you will find favor among those who are to convert, and they will give heed to your words; for I will be with you, and will compel them to obey you." [16] I say to Him, "Lord, these commandments are great, and good, and glorious, and fitted to gladden the heart of the man who can perform them. [17] But I do not know if these commandments can be kept by man, because they are exceedingly hard." [18] He answered and said to me, "If you lay it down as certain that they can be kept, then you will easily keep them, and they will not be hard. But if you come to imagine that they cannot be kept by man, then you will not keep them. [19] Now I say to you, if you do not keep them, but neglect them, you will not be saved, nor your children, nor your house, since you have already determined for yourself that these commandments cannot be kept by man." [20] He said these things to me in tones of the deepest anger, so that I was confounded and exceedingly afraid of Him, for His figure was altered so that a man could not endure His anger. [21] But seeing me altogether agitated and confused, He began to speak to me in more gentle tones; and He said: "O feel, senseless and doubting, do you not perceive how great is the glory of God, and how strong and marvelous, in that He created the world for the sake of man, and subjected all creation to him, and gave him power to rule over everything under heaven? [22] If, then, man is lord of the creatures of God, and rules over all, is he not able to be lord also of these commandments? For," He says, "the man who has the LORD in his heart can also be lord of all, and of every one of these commandments. [23] But to those who have the LORD only on their lips, but their hearts hardened, and who are far from the LORD, the commandments are hard and difficult. [24] Put, therefore—you who are empty and fickle in your faith—the LORD in your heart, and you will know that there is nothing easier or sweeter, or more manageable, than these commandments. [25] Return, you who walk in the commandments of the Devil, in hard, and bitter, and wild licentiousness, and do not fear the Devil; [26] for there is no power in him against you, for I will be with you, the Messenger of conversion, who am Lord over him. The Devil has fear only, but his fear has no strength. Do not fear him, then, and he will flee from you." [27] I say to Him, "Lord, listen to me for a moment." "Say what you wish," He says. "Man, Lord," I say, "is eager to keep the commandments of God, and there is no one who does not ask of the LORD that strength may be given him for these commandments, and that he may be subject to them; but the Devil is hard, and holds sway over them." [28] "He cannot," He says, "hold sway over the servants of God, who with all their heart place their hopes in Him. The Devil can wrestle against these, [but] he cannot overthrow them. [29] If, then, you resist him, he will be conquered, and flee in disgrace from you. As many, therefore," He says, "as are empty, fear the Devil, as possessing power. [30] When a man has filled very suitable jars with good wine, and a few among those jars are left empty, then he comes to the jars, and does not look at the full jars, for he knows that they are full; but he looks at the empty, being afraid lest they have become sour. For empty jars quickly become sour, and the goodness of the wine is gone. [31] So also, the Devil goes to all the servants of God to try them. As many, then, as are full in the faith, resist him strongly, and he withdraws from them, having no way by which he might enter them. He goes, then, to the empty, and finding a way of entrance into them, he produces in them whatever he wishes, and they become his servants. [32] But I, the Messenger of conversion, say to you: do not fear the Devil; for I was sent," He says, "to be with you who convert with all your heart, and to make you strong in faith. [33] Trust God, then, you who on account of your sins have despaired of life, and who add to your sins and weigh down your life; for if you return to the LORD with all

THE SHEPHERD OF HERMAS

your heart, and practice righteousness the rest of your days, and serve Him according to His will, He will heal your former sins, and you will have power to hold sway over the works of the Devil. [34] But as to the threats of the Devil, do not fear them at all, for he is powerless as the sinews of a dead man. [35] Give ear to Me, then, and fear Him who has all power, both to save and destroy, and keep His commandments, and you will live to God." [36] I say to Him, "Lord, I am now made strong in all the ordinances of the LORD, because You are with me; and I know that You will crush all the power of the Devil, and we will have rule over him, and will prevail against all his works. [37] And I hope, Lord, to be able to keep all these commandments which You have enjoined on me, the LORD strengthening me." [38] "You will keep them," He says, "if your heart is pure toward the LORD; and all will keep them who cleanse their hearts from the vain desires of this world, and they will live to God."

SECTION 3:
SIMILITUDES

SIMILITUDE 1

[1] He says to me, "You know that you who are the servants of God dwell in a strange land; for your city is far away from this one. [2] If then," He continues, "you know your city in which you are to dwell, why do you here provide lands, and make expensive preparations, and accumulate dwellings and useless buildings? He who makes such preparations for this city cannot return again to his own. [3] Oh foolish, and unstable, and miserable man! Do you not understand that all these things belong to another, and are under the power of another? [4] For the lord of this city will say, I do not wish you to dwell in my city; but depart from this city, because you do not obey my laws. [5] You, therefore, although having fields and houses, and many other things, when cast out by him, what will you do with your land, and house, and other possessions which you have gathered to yourself? [6] For the lord of this country justly says to you, Either obey my laws or depart from my dominion. What, then, do you intend to do, having a law in your own city, on account of your lands, and the rest of your possessions? [7] You will altogether deny your law, and walk according to the law of this city. See lest it be to your hurt to deny your law; for if you will desire to return to your city, you will not be received, because you have denied the law of your city, but will be excluded from it. [8] Have a care, therefore, as one living in a foreign land: make no further preparations for yourself than such merely as may be sufficient; and be ready, when the master of this city will come to cast you out for disobeying his

law, to leave his city, and to depart to your own, and to obey your own law without being exposed to annoyance, but in great joy. [9] Have a care, then, you who serve the LORD, and have Him in your heart, that you work the works of God, remembering His commandments and promises which He promised, and believe that He will bring them to pass if His commandments are observed. [10] Instead of lands, therefore, buy afflicted souls, according as each one is able, and visit widows and orphans, and do not overlook them; and spend your wealth and all your preparations, which you received from the LORD, on such lands and houses. [11] For to this end the Master made you rich, that you might perform these services to Him; and it is much better to purchase such lands, and possessions, and houses, as you will find in your own city, when you come to reside in it. [12] This is a noble and sacred expenditure, attended neither with sorrow nor fear, but with joy. [13] Do not practice the expenditure of the heathen, for it is injurious to you who are the servants of God; but practice an expenditure of your own, in which you can rejoice; [14] and do not corrupt nor touch what is another's, nor covet it, for it is an evil thing to covet the goods of other men; but work your own work, and you will be saved."

SIMILITUDE 2

[1] As I was walking in the field, and observing an elm and vine, and determining in my own mind respecting them and their fruits, the Shepherd appears to me, and says, "What is it that you are thinking about the elm and vine?" [2] "I am considering," I reply, "that they suit each other exceedingly well." [3] "These two trees," he continues, "are intended as an example for the servants of God." [4] "I would like to know," I said, "the example which these trees You say, are intended to teach." [5] "Do you see," He says, "the elm and the vine?" "I see them Lord," I replied. "This vine," He continued, "produces fruit, and the elm is an unfruitful tree; but unless the vine be trained on the elm, it cannot bear much fruit when extended at length on the ground; and the fruit which it bears is rotten, because the plant is not suspended on the elm. [6] Therefore, when the vine is cast on the elm, it yields fruit both from itself and from the elm. You see, moreover, that the elm also produces much fruit, not less than the vine, but even more; because," He continued, "the vine, when suspended on the elm, yields much fruit, and good; but when thrown on the ground, what it produces is small and rotten. [7] This similitude, therefore, is for the servants of God—for the poor man and for the rich." "How so, Lord?" I said; "explain the matter to me." [8] "Listen," He said: "The rich man has much wealth,

but is poor in matters relating to the LORD, because he is distracted about his riches; and he offers very few confessions and intercessions to the LORD, and those which he offers are small and weak, and have no power above. [9] But when the rich man refreshes the poor, and assists him in his necessities, believing that what he does to the poor man will be able to find its reward with God—because the poor man is rich in intercession and confession, and his intercession has great power with God—then the rich man helps the poor in all things without hesitation; [10] and the poor man, being helped by the rich, intercedes for him, giving thanks to God for him who bestows gifts on him. [11] And he still continues to interest himself zealously for the poor man, that his wants may be constantly supplied. For he knows that the intercession of the poor man is acceptable and influential with God. Both, accordingly, accomplish their work. [12] The poor man makes intercession; a work in which he is rich, which he received from the LORD, and with which he recompenses the master who helps him. [13] And the rich man, in like manner, unhesitatingly bestows on the poor man the riches which he received from the LORD. And this is a great work, and acceptable before God, because he understands the object of his wealth, and has given to the poor of the gifts of the LORD, and rightly discharged his service to Him. [14] Among men, however, the elm does not appear to produce fruit, and they do not know nor understand that if a drought comes, the elm, which contains water, nourishes the vine; and the vine, having an unfailing supply of water, yields double fruit both for itself and for the elm. [15] So also poor men interceding with the LORD on behalf of the rich, increase their riches; and the rich, again, aiding the poor in their necessities, satisfy their souls. Both, therefore, are partners in the righteous work. [16] He who does these things will not be deserted by God, but will be enrolled in the scrolls of the living. [17] Blessed are they who have riches, and who understand that they are from the LORD. [[For they who are of that mind will be able to do some good.]]"

SIMILITUDE 3

[1] He showed me many trees having no leaves, but withered, as it seemed to me; for all were alike. And He said to me, "Do you see those trees?" "I see, Lord," I replied, "that all are alike, and withered." [2] He answered me, and said, "These trees which you see are those who dwell in this world." [3] "Why, then, Lord," I said, "are they withered, as it were, and alike?" "Because," He said, "neither are the righteous manifest in this life, nor sinners, but they are alike; for this life is a winter to the righteous, and they do not manifest themselves, because they dwell with sinners:

[4] for as in winter trees that have cast their leaves are alike, and it is not seen which are dead and which are living, so in this world neither do the righteous show themselves, nor sinners, but all are alike one to another."

SIMILITUDE 4

[1] He showed me again many trees, some budding, and others withered. And He said to me, "Do you see these trees?" "I see, Lord," I replied, "some putting forth buds, and others withered." [2] "Those," He said, "which are budding are the righteous who are to live in the world to come; for the coming world is the summer of the righteous, but the winter of sinners. [3] When, therefore, the mercy of the LORD shines forth, then they will be made manifest who are the servants of God, and all men will be made manifest. [4] For as in summer the fruits of each individual tree appear, and it is ascertained of what sort they are, so also the fruits of the righteous will be manifest, and all who have been fruitful in that world will be made known. [5] But the heathen and sinners, like the withered trees which you saw, will be found to be those who have been withered and unfruitful in that world, and will be burnt as wood, and made manifest, because their actions were evil during their lives. [6] For the sinners will be consumed because they sinned and did not convert, and the heathen will be burned because they did not know Him who created them. [7] Therefore, bear fruit, that in that summer your fruit may be known. [8] And refrain from much business, and you will never sin: for they who are occupied with much business also commit many sins, being distracted with their affairs, and not at all serving their Lord. [9] How, then," He continued, "can such a one ask and obtain anything from the LORD, if he does not serve Him? [10] They who serve Him will obtain their requests, but they who do not serve Him will receive nothing. [11] And in the performance even of a single action a man can serve the LORD; for his mind will not be perverted from the LORD, but he will serve Him, having a pure mind. [12] If, therefore, you do these things, you will be able to bear fruit for the life to come. And everyone who will do these things will bear fruit."

SIMILITUDE 5

[1] While fasting and sitting on a certain mountain, and giving thanks to the LORD for all His dealings with me, I see the Shepherd sitting down beside me, and saying, "Why have you come here early in the morning?" [2] "Because, Lord," I answered, "I have a station." "What is a station?" He asked. "I am fasting, Lord," I replied. "What is this fasting," He continued, "which you are observing?" "As I have been accustomed,

Lord," I reply, "so I fast." [3] "You do not know," He says, "how to fast to the LORD: this useless fasting which you observe to Him is of no value." "Why, Lord," I answered, "do you say this?" [4] "I say to you," He continued, "that the fasting which you think you observe is not a fasting. But I will teach you what is a full and acceptable fasting to the LORD. [5] Listen," He continued: "God does not desire such an empty fasting, for fasting to God in this way you will do nothing for a righteous life; [6] but offer to God a fasting of the following kind: do no evil in your life and serve the LORD with a pure heart; keep His commandments, walking in His precepts, and let no evil desire arise in your heart; and believe in God. [7] If you do these things, and fear Him, and abstain from every evil thing, you will live to God; and if you do these things, you will keep a great fast, and one acceptable before God. [8] Hear the similitude which I am about to narrate to you relative to fasting. [9] A certain man had a field and many slaves, and he planted a certain part of the field with a vineyard, and selecting a faithful, and beloved, and much valued slave, he called him to himself, and said, Take this vineyard which I have planted, and stake it until I come, and do nothing else to the vineyard; and attend to this order of mine, and you will receive your freedom from me. [10] And the master of the slave departed to a foreign country. And when he was gone, the slave took and staked the vineyard; and when he had finished the staking of the vines, he saw that the vineyard was full of weeds. [11] He then reflected, saying, I have kept this order of my master: I will dig up the rest of this vineyard, and it will be more beautiful when dug up; and being free of weeds, it will yield more fruit, not being choked by them. [12] Therefore, he took and dug up the vineyard, and rooted out all the weeds that were in it. And that vineyard became very beautiful and fruitful, having no weeds to choke it. [13] And after a certain time the master of the slave and of the field returned and entered into the vineyard. And seeing that the vines were suitably supported on stakes, and the ground, moreover, dug up, and all the weeds rooted out, and the vines fruitful, he was greatly pleased with the work of his slave. [14] And calling his beloved son who was his heir, and his friends who were his counselors, he told them what orders he had given his slave, and what he had found performed. And they rejoiced along with the slave at the testimony which his master bore to him. [15] And he said to them, I promised this slave freedom if he obeyed the command which I gave him; and he has kept my command, and has also done a good work to the vineyard, and has pleased me exceedingly. [16] In return, therefore, for the work which he has done, I wish to make him co-heir with my son, because,

having good thoughts, he did not neglect them, but carried them out. [17] With this resolution of the master, his son and friends were well pleased. [18] After a few days the master made a feast and sent to his slave many dishes from his table. And the slave receiving the dishes that were sent him from his master, took of them what was sufficient for himself, and distributed the rest among his fellow-slaves. [19] And his fellow-slaves rejoiced to receive the dishes, and began to pray for him, that he might find still greater favor with his master for having so treated them. His master heard all these things that were done and was again greatly pleased with his conduct. [20] And the master again calling together his friends and his son, reported to them the slave's proceeding with regard to the dishes which he had sent him. [21] And they were still more satisfied that the slave should become co-heir with his son." [22] I said to Him, "Lord, I do not see the meaning of these similitudes, nor am I able to comprehend them, unless You explain them to me." [23] "I will explain them all to you," He said, "and whatever I will mention in the course of our conversations I will show you. [24] [[Keep the commandments of the LORD, and you will be approved, and inscribed among the number of those who observe His commands.]] [25] And if you do any good beyond what is commanded by God, you will gain for yourself more abundant glory, and will be more honored by God than you would otherwise be. [26] If, therefore, in keeping the commandments of God, you do, in addition, these services, you will have joy if you observe them according to My command." [27] I said to Him, "Lord, whatever You enjoin on me I will observe, for I know that You are with me." [28] "I will be with you," He replied, "because you have such a desire for doing good; and I will be with all those," He added, "who have such a desire. [29] This fasting," He continued, "is very good, provided the commandments of the LORD are observed. Thus, then, will you observe the fasting which you intend to keep. [30] First of all, be on your guard against every evil word, and every evil desire, and purify your heart from all the vanities of this world. If you guard against these things, your fasting will be perfect. [31] And you will also do as follows: having fulfilled what is written, in the day on which you fast you will taste nothing but bread and water; and having reckoned up the price of the dishes of that day which you intended to have eaten, you will give it to a widow, or an orphan, or to some person in want, and thus you will exhibit humility of mind, so that he who has received benefit from your humility may fill his own soul, and pray for you to the LORD. [32] If you observe fasting, as I have commanded you, your sacrifice will be acceptable to God, and this fasting

THE SHEPHERD OF HERMAS

will be written down; and the service thus performed is noble, and sacred, and acceptable to the LORD. ³³ These things, therefore, you will thus observe with your children, and all your house, and in observing them you will be blessed; and as many as hear these words and observe them will be blessed; and whatever they ask of the LORD they will receive." ³⁴ I pleaded with Him much that he would explain to me the similitude of the field, and of the master of the vineyard, and of the slave who staked the vineyard, and of the sakes, and of the weeds that were plucked out of the vineyard, and of the son, and of the friends who were fellow-counselors, for I knew that all these things were a kind of allegory. ³⁵ And He answered me, and said, "You are exceedingly persistent with your questions. You ought not," He continued, "to ask any questions at all; for if it is needful to explain anything, it will be made known to you." ³⁶ I said to Him "Lord, whatever You show me, and do not explain, I will have seen to no purpose, not understanding its meaning. In like manner also, if You speak allegories to me, and do not unfold them, I will have heard Your words in vain." ³⁷ And He answered me again, saying, "Everyone who is the servant of God, and has his Lord in his heart, asks of Him understanding, and receives it, and opens up every allegory; and the words of the LORD become known to him which are spoken in allegories; ³⁸ but those who are weak and slothful in prayer, hesitate to ask anything from the LORD; but the LORD is full of compassion, and gives without fail to all who ask Him. ³⁹ But you, having been strengthened by the holy Messenger, and having obtained from Him such intercession, and not being slothful, why do you not ask of the LORD understanding, and receive it from Him?" ⁴⁰ I said to Him, "Lord, having You with me, I am necessitated to ask questions of You, for You show me all things, and converse with me; but if I were to see or hear these things without You, I would then ask the LORD to explain them." ⁴¹ "I said to you a little while ago," He answered, "that you were cunning and obstinate in asking explanations of the allegories; but since you are so persistent, I will unfold to you the meaning of the similitudes of the field, and of all the others that follow, that you may make them known to everyone. ⁴² Hear now," He said, "and understand them. The field is this world; and the Lord of the field is He who created, and perfected, and strengthened all things; [[and the son is the Holy Spirit;]] and the slave is the Son of God; ⁴³ and the vines are this people, whom He Himself planted; and the stakes are the holy messengers of the LORD, who keep His people together; and the weeds that were plucked out of the vineyard are the iniquities of God's servants; ⁴⁴ and the dishes which He sent Him from His table are the

commandments which He gave His people through His Son; and the friends and fellow-counselors are the holy messengers who were first created; and the Master's absence from home is the time that remains until His appearing." ⁴⁵ I said to Him, "Lord, all these are great, and marvelous, and glorious things. Could I, therefore," I continued, "understand them? No, nor could any other man, even if exceedingly wise. ⁴⁶ Moreover," I added, "explain to me what I am about to ask you." "Say what you wish," He replied. "Why, Lord," I asked, "is the Son of God in the allegory in the form of a slave?" ⁴⁷ "Hear," He answered: "the Son of God is not in the form of a slave, but in great power and might." "How so, Lord?" I said; "I do not understand." ⁴⁸ "Because," He answered, "God planted the vineyard, that is to say, He created the people, and gave them to His Son; and the Son appointed His messengers over them to keep them; ⁴⁹ and He Himself purged away their sins, having suffered many trials and undergone many labors, for no one is able to dig without labor and toil. ⁵⁰ He Himself, then, having purged away the sins of the people, showed them the paths of life by giving them the law which He received from His Father. ⁵¹ [[You see," He said, "that He is the Lord of the people, having received all authority from His Father.]] And why the LORD took His Son as counselor, and the glorious messengers, regarding the heirship of the slave, listen. ⁵² The holy, pre-existent Spirit, that created every creature, God made to dwell in flesh, which He chose. This flesh, accordingly, in which the Holy Spirit dwelt, was nobly subject to that Spirit, walking religiously and chastely, in no respect defiling the Spirit; ⁵³ and accordingly, after living excellently and purely, and after laboring and cooperating with the Spirit, and having in everything acted vigorously and courageously along with the Holy Spirit, He assumed it as a partner with it. ⁵⁴ For this conduct of the flesh pleased Him, because it was not defiled on the earth while having the Holy Spirit. Therefore, He took as fellow-counselors His Son and the glorious messengers, in order that this flesh, which had been subject to the body without a fault, might have some place of tabernacle, and that it might not appear that the reward [[of its servitude had been lost]], ⁵⁵ for the flesh that has been found without spot or defilement, in which the Holy Spirit dwelt, [[will receive a reward]]. You have now the explanation of this allegory also." ⁵⁶ "I rejoice, Lord," I said, "to hear this explanation." "Hear," again He replied: "Keep this flesh pure and stainless, that the Spirit which inhabits it may bear witness to it, and your flesh may be justified. ⁵⁷ See that the thought never arises in your mind that this flesh of yours is corruptible, and you misuse it by any act of defilement. ⁵⁸ If you defile your flesh, you will also defile the Holy Spirit; and if you defile your flesh [and spirit], you will not live." ⁵⁹ "And if anyone, Lord," I said, "has been ignorant until now, before he heard these words, how can such a man be saved who has defiled his flesh?" ⁶⁰ "Respecting former sins of ignorance," He said, "God alone is able to heal them, for to Him belongs all power. ⁶¹ [[But be on your guard now, and the all-powerful and compassionate God will heal former transgressions]], if for the time to come you do not defile your body nor your spirit; for both are common, and cannot be defiled, the one without the other: therefore, keep both pure, and you will live to God."

SIMILITUDE 6

¹ Sitting in my house, and glorifying the LORD for all that I had seen, and reflecting on the commandments, that they are excellent, and powerful, and glorious, and able to save a man's soul, I said within myself, "I will be blessed if I walk in these commandments, and everyone who walks in them will be blessed." ² While I was saying these words to myself, I suddenly see Him sitting beside me, and hear Him thus speak: "Why are you in doubt about the commandments which I gave you? They are excellent: have no doubt about them at all, but put on faith in the LORD, and you will walk in them, for I will strengthen you in them. ³ These commandments are beneficial to those who intend to convert: for if they do not walk in them, their conversion is in vain. You, therefore, who convert, cast away the wickedness of this world which wears you out; and by putting on all the virtues of a holy life, you will be able to keep these commandments, and will no longer add to the number of your sins. ⁴ Therefore, walk in these commandments of Mine, and you will live to God. All these things have been spoken to you by Me." ⁵ And after He had uttered these words, He said to me, "Let us go into the fields, and I will show you the shepherds of the flocks." "Let us go, Lord," I replied. ⁶ And we came to a certain plain, and He showed me a young man, a shepherd, clothed in a suit of garments of a yellow color: and he was herding very many sheep, and these sheep were feeding luxuriously, as it were, and riotously, and merrily skipping here and there. ⁷ The shepherd himself was merry, because of his flock; and the appearance of the shepherd was joyous, and he was running about among his flock. [[And other sheep I saw rioting and luxuriating in one place, but not, however, leaping about.]] ⁸ And He said to me, "Do you see this shepherd?" "I see him, Lord," I said. "This," He answered, "is the messenger of luxury and deceit: he wears out the souls of the servants of God, and perverts them from the truth, deceiving them with wicked desires, through which they will perish; ⁹ for they forget the commandments of the living God, and walk in deceits and empty luxuries; and they are ruined by the messenger, some being brought to death, others to corruption." ¹⁰ I said to Him, "Lord, I do not know the meaning of these words: To death, and to corruption." ¹¹ "Listen," He said. "The sheep which you saw merry and leaping about, are those which have torn themselves away from God forever, and have delivered themselves over to luxuries and deceits [[of this world. Among them there is no return to life through conversion, because they have added to their other sins, and blasphemed the Name of the LORD. Such men, therefore, are appointed to death. ¹² And the sheep which you saw not leaping, but feeding in one place, are they who have delivered themselves over to luxury and deceit]], but have committed no blasphemy against the LORD. ¹³ These have been perverted from the truth: among them there is the hope of conversion, by which it is possible to live. Corruption, then, has a hope of a kind of renewal, but death has continuous ruin." ¹⁴ Again, I went forward a little way, and He showed me a tall shepherd, somewhat savage in his appearance, clothed in a white goatskin, and having a wallet on his shoulders, and a very hard staff with branches, and a large whip. ¹⁵ And he had a very sour look, so that I was afraid of him, so forbidding was his aspect. This shepherd, accordingly, was receiving the sheep from the young shepherd, those [that were rioting and luxuriating, but not leaping]; ¹⁶ and he cast them into a precipitous place, full of thistles and thorns, so that it was impossible to extricate the sheep from the thorns and thistles; but they were completely entangled among them. ¹⁷ These, accordingly, thus entangled, pastured among the thorns and thistles, and were exceedingly miserable, being beaten by him; and he drove them here and there, and gave them no rest; and, altogether, these sheep were in a wretched plight. ¹⁸ Seeing them, therefore, so beaten and so badly used, I was grieved for them, because they were so tormented, and had no rest at all. And I said to the Shepherd who talked with me, "Lord, who is this shepherd, who is so pitiless and severe, and so completely devoid of compassion for these sheep?" ¹⁹ "This," He replied, "is the messenger of punishment; and he belongs to the just messengers, and is appointed to punish. He accordingly takes those who wander away from God, and who have walked in the desires and deceits of this world, and disciplines them as they deserve with terrible and diverse punishments." ²⁰ "I would know, Lord," I said, "Of what nature are these diverse tortures and punishments?" "Hear," He said, "the various tortures and punishments. ²¹ The tortures are such as occur

during life. For some are punished with losses, others with want, others with sicknesses of various kinds, and others with all kinds of disorder and confusion; others are insulted by unworthy persons, and exposed to suffering in many other ways: ²² for many, becoming unstable in their plans, try many things, and none of them at all succeed, and they say they are not prosperous in their undertakings; and it does not occur to their minds that they have done evil deeds, but they blame the LORD. ²³ Therefore, when they have been afflicted with all kinds of affliction, then they are delivered to Me for good training, and they are made strong in the faith of the LORD; ²⁴ and for the rest of the days of their life they are subject to the LORD with pure hearts, and are successful in all their undertakings, obtaining from the LORD everything they ask; and then they glorify the LORD, that they were delivered to Me, and no longer suffer any evil." ²⁵ I said to Him, "Lord, explain this to me also." "What is it you ask?" He said. "Whether, Lord," I continued, "they who indulge in luxury, and who are deceived, are tortured for the same period of time that they have indulged in luxury and deceit?" ²⁶ He said to me, "They are tortured in the same manner." [["They are tormented much less, Lord," I replied;]] "for those who are so luxurious and who forget God ought to be tortured sevenfold." ²⁷ He said to me, "You are foolish, and do not understand the power of torment." "Why, Lord," I said, "if I had understood it, I would not have asked You to show me." ²⁸ "Hear," He said, "the power of both. The time of luxury and deceit is one hour; but the hour of torment is equivalent to thirty days. ²⁹ If, accordingly, a man indulges in luxury for one day, and is deceived and is tortured for one day, the day of his torture is equivalent to a whole year. For all the days of luxury, therefore, there are as many years of torture to be undergone. ³⁰ You see, then," He continued, "that the time of luxury and deceit is very short, but that of punishment and torture long." ³¹ "Still," I said, "I do not quite understand about the time of deceit, and luxury, and torture; explain it to me more clearly." ³² He answered, and said to me, "Your folly is persistent; and you do not wish to purify your heart and serve God. Have a care," He added, "lest the time be fulfilled, and you are found foolish. ³³ Hear now," He added, "as you desire, that you may understand these things. He who indulges in luxury, and is deceived for one day, and who does what he wishes, is clothed with much foolishness, and does not understand the act which he does until the next day; for he forgets what he did the day before. ³⁴ For luxury and deceit have no memories, on account of the folly with which they are clothed; but when punishment and torture cleave to a man for one day, he is punished and

tortured for a year; for punishment and torture have powerful memories. ³⁵ While tortured and punished, therefore, for a whole year, he remembers at last his luxury and deceit, and knows that on their account he suffers evil. ³⁶ Every man, therefore, who is luxurious and deceived is thus tormented, because, although having life, they have given themselves over to death." ³⁷ "What kinds of luxury, Lord," I asked, "are hurtful?" "Every act of a man which he performs with pleasure," He replied, "is an act of luxury; for the sharp-tempered man, when gratifying his tendency, indulges in luxury; ³⁸ and the adulterer, and the drunkard, and the back-biter, and the liar, and the covetous man, and the thief, and he who does things like these, gratifies his peculiar propensity, and in so doing indulges in luxury. All these acts of luxury are hurtful to the servants of God. ³⁹ On account of these deceits, therefore, do they suffer, who are punished and tortured. And there are also acts of luxury which save men; ⁴⁰ for many who do good indulge in luxury, being carried away by their own pleasure: this luxury, however, is beneficial to the servants of God, and gains life for such a man; ⁴¹ but the injurious acts of luxury before enumerated bring tortures and punishment on them; and if they continue in them and do not convert, they bring death on themselves."

SIMILITUDE 7

¹ After a few days I saw Him in the same plain where I had also seen the shepherds; and He said to me, "What do you wish with Me?" I said to Him, "Lord, that you would order the shepherd who punishes to depart out of my house, because he afflicts me exceedingly." ² "It is necessary," He replied, "that you are afflicted; for thus," He continued, "did the glorious messenger command concerning you, as he wishes you to be tried." "What have I done which is so bad, Lord," I replied, "that I should be delivered over to this messenger?" ³ "Listen," he said: "Your sins are many, but not so great as to require that you are delivered over to this messenger; but your household has committed great iniquities and sins, and the glorious messenger has been incensed at them on account of their deeds; ⁴ and for this reason, he commanded you to be afflicted for a certain time, that they also might convert, and purify themselves from every desire of this world. Therefore, when they convert and are purified, then the messenger of punishment will depart." ⁵ I said to Him, "Lord, if they have done such things as to incense the glorious messenger against them, yet what have I done?" ⁶ He replied, "They cannot be afflicted at all, unless you, the head of the house, are afflicted: for when you are afflicted, of necessity they also suffer affliction; but if you are in

comfort, they can feel no affliction." [7] "Well, Lord," I said, "they have converted with their whole heart." "I know, too," He answered, "that they have converted with their whole heart: do you think, however, that the sins of those who convert are remitted? [8] Not altogether, but he who converts must torture his own soul, and be exceedingly humble in all his conduct, and be afflicted with many kinds of affliction; [9] and if he endures the afflictions that come on him, He who created all things, and endued them with power, will assuredly have compassion, and will heal him; [10] and He will do this when He sees the heart of every penitent pure from every evil thing: and it is profitable for you and for your house to suffer affliction now. [11] But why should I say much to you? You must be afflicted, as that messenger of the LORD commanded who delivered you to Me. [12] And for this give thanks to the LORD, because He has deemed you worthy of showing you beforehand this affliction, that, knowing it before it comes, you may be able to bear it with courage." [13] I said to Him, "Lord, be with me, and I will be able to bear all affliction." "I will be with you," He said, "and I will ask the messenger of punishment to afflict you more lightly; [14] nevertheless, you will be afflicted for a short time, and again you will be re-established in your house. [15] Only, remain humble, and serve the LORD in all purity of heart—you, and your children, and your house—and walk in My commands which I enjoin on you, and your conversion will be deep and pure; [16] and if you observe these things with your household, every affliction will depart from you. And affliction," He added, "will depart from all who walk in these commandments of Mine."

SIMILITUDE 8

[1] He showed me a large willow tree overshadowing plains and mountains, and under the shade of this willow had assembled all those who were called by the Name of the LORD. [2] And a glorious messenger of the LORD, who was very tall, was standing beside the willow, having a large pruning-knife, and he was cutting little twigs from the willow and distributing them among the people that were overshadowed by the willow; and the twigs which he gave them were small, about a cubit, as it were, in length. [3] And after they had all received the twigs, the messenger laid down the pruning-knife, and that tree was sound, as I had seen it at first. [4] And I marveled within myself, saying, "How is the tree sound, after so many branches have been cut off?" And the Shepherd said to me, "Do not be surprised if the tree remains sound after so many branches were lopped off; [but wait,] and when you will have seen everything, then it will be explained to you what it means." [5] The messenger who

had distributed the branches among the people again asked them from them, and in the order in which they had received them were they summoned to him, and each one of them returned his branch. [6] And the messenger of the LORD took and looked at them. From some he received the branches withered and moth-eaten; those who returned branches in that state the messenger of the LORD ordered to stand apart. [7] Others, again, returned them withered, but not moth-eaten; and these he ordered to stand apart. And others returned them half-withered, and these stood apart; and others returned their branches half-withered and having cracks in them, and these stood apart. [8] [[And others returned their branches green and having cracks in them; and these stood apart.]] And others returned their branches, one-half withered and the other green; and these stood apart. And others brought their branches two-thirds green and the remaining third withered; and these stood apart. [9] And others returned them two-thirds withered and one-third green; and these stood apart. And others returned their branches nearly all green, the smallest part only, the top, being withered, but they had cracks in them; and these stood apart. [10] And of others very little was green, but the remaining parts withered; and these stood apart. And others came bringing their branches green, as they had received them from the messenger. [11] And the majority of the crowd returned branches of that kind, and with these the messenger was exceedingly pleased; and these stood apart. [[And others returned their branches green and having offshoots; and these stood apart, and with these the messenger was exceedingly delighted.]] [12] And others returned their branches green and with offshoots, and the offshoots had some fruit, as it were; and those men whose branches were found to be of that kind were exceedingly joyful. [13] And the messenger was exultant because of them; and the Shepherd also rejoiced greatly because of them. [14] And the messenger of the LORD ordered crowns to be brought; and there were brought crowns, formed, as it were, of palms; and he crowned the men who had returned the branches which had offshoots and some fruit, and sent them away into the tower. [15] And he also sent the others into the tower, those, namely, who had returned branches that were green and had offshoots but no fruit, having given them seals. And all who went into the tower had the same clothing—white as snow. [16] And those who returned their branches green, as they had received them, he set free, giving them clothing and seals. [17] Now after the messenger had finished these things, he said to the Shepherd, "I am going away, and you will send these away within the walls, according as each one is worthy to have his dwelling. [18] And examine their branches carefully, and so dismiss them; but examine them with care. See that no one escapes [from] you," he added; "and if any escapes [from] you, I will try them at the altar." [19] Having said these words to the Shepherd, he departed. And after the messenger had departed, the Shepherd said to me, "Let us take the branches of all these and plant them, and see if any of them will live." [20] I said to Him, "Lord, how can these withered branches live?" He answered, and said, "This tree is a willow, and of a kind that is very tenacious of life. If, therefore, the branches are planted, and receive a little moisture, many of them will live. [21] And now let us try and pour waters on them; and if any of them live I will rejoice with them, and if they do not, I at least will not be found neglectful." [22] And the Shepherd ordered me call them as each one was placed. And they came, rank by rank, and gave their branches to the Shepherd. And the Shepherd received the branches and planted them in rows; and after He had planted them, He poured much water on them, so that the branches could not be seen for the water; [23] and after the branches had drunk it in, He said to me, "Let us go, and return after a few days, and inspect all the branches; for He who created this tree wishes all those to live who received branches from it. [24] And I also hope that the greater part of these branches which received moisture and drank of the water will live." [25] I said to Him, "Lord, explain to me what this tree means, for I am perplexed about it, because, after so many branches have been cut off, it continues sound, and nothing appears to have been cut away from it. By this, now, I am perplexed." [26] "Listen," He said: "This great tree that casts its shadow over plains, and mountains, and all the earth, is the law of God that was given to the whole world; and this law is the Son of God, proclaimed to the ends of the earth; and the people who are under its shadow are they who have heard the proclamation, and have believed on Him. [27] And the great and glorious messenger Michael is he who has authority over this people, and governs them; for this is he who gave them the law into the hearts of believers: he accordingly superintends them to whom he gave it, to see if they have kept the same. [28] And you see the branches of each one, for the branches are the law you see, accordingly, many branches that have been rendered useless, and you will know them all—those who have not kept the law; and you will see the dwelling of each one." [29] I said to Him, "Lord, why did he dismiss some into the tower, and leave others to you?" "All," He answered, "who transgressed the law which they received from him, he left under my power for conversion; but all who have satisfied the law, and kept it, he retains under his own authority." [30] "Who, then," I continued, "are they who were crowned, and

who go to the tower?" "These are they who have suffered on account of the law; but the others, and they who returned their branches green, and with offshoots, but without fruit, are they who have been afflicted on account of the law, but who have not suffered nor denied their law; and they who returned their branches green as they had received them, are the venerable, and the just, and they who have walked carefully in a pure heart, and have kept the commandments of the LORD. [31] And the rest you will know when I have examined those branches which have been planted and watered." [32] And after a few days we came to the place, and the Shepherd sat down in the messenger's place, and I stood beside Him. And He said to me, "Gird yourself with pure, undressed linen made of sackcloth;" and seeing me girded, and ready to minister to Him, "Summon," He said, "the men to whom belong the branches that were planted, according to the order in which each one gave them in." [33] So I went away to the plain, and summoned them all, and they all stood in their ranks. He said to them, "Let each one pull out his own branch, and bring it to Me." [34] The first to give in were those who had them withered and cut; and because they were found to be thus withered and cut, He commanded them to stand apart. And next they gave them in who had them withered, but not cut. [35] And some of them gave in their branches green, and some withered and eaten as by a moth. Those that gave them in green, accordingly, He ordered to stand apart; and those who gave them in dry and cut, He ordered to stand along with the first. [36] Next, they gave them in who had them half-withered and cracked; and many of them gave them in green and without crocks; and some green and with offshoots and fruits on the offshoots, such as they had who went, after being crowned, into the tower. [37] And some handed them in withered and eaten, and some withered and uneaten; and some as they were, half-withered and cracked. And He commanded them each one to stand apart, some toward their own rows, and others apart from them. [38] Then they gave in their branches who had them green, but cracked: all these gave them in green, and stood in their own row. [39] And the Shepherd was pleased with these, because they were all changed, and had lost their cracks. And they also gave them in who had them half-green and half-withered: of some, accordingly, the branches were found completely green; of others, half-withered; of others, withered and eaten; of others, green, and having offshoots. [40] All these were sent away, each to his own row. [[Next, they gave in who had them two parts green and one-third withered. Many of them gave them half-withered; and others withered and rotten; and others half-withered and cracked, and a few green. These all stood in their own row.]] ⁴¹ And they gave them in who had them green, but to a very slight extent withered and cracked. Of these, some gave them in green, and others green and with offshoots. And these also went away to their own row. ⁴² Next, they gave them who had a very small part green and the other parts withered. Of these the branches were found for the most part green and having offshoots, and fruit on the offshoots, and others altogether green. ⁴³ With these branches the Shepherd was exceedingly pleased, because they were found in this state. And these went away, each to his own row. ⁴⁴ After the Shepherd had examined the branches of them all, He said to me, "I told you that this tree was tenacious of life. You see," He continued, "how many converted and were saved." ⁴⁵ "I see, Lord," I replied. "That you may behold," He added, "the great mercy of the LORD, that it is great and glorious, and that He has given His Spirit to those who are worthy of conversion." ⁴⁶ "Why then, Lord," I said, "did these not all convert?" He answered, "To them whose heart He saw would become pure, and obedient to Him, He gave power to convert with the whole heart. ⁴⁷ But to them whose deceit and wickedness He perceived, and saw that they intended to convert hypocritically, He did not grant conversion, lest they should again profane His Name." ⁴⁸ I said to Him, "Lord, show me now, with respect to those who gave in the branches, of what sort they are, and their abode, in order that they hearing it who believed, and received the seal, and broke it, and did not keep it whole, may, on coming to a knowledge of their deeds, convert, and receive from You a seal, and may glorify the LORD because He had compassion on them, and sent You to renew their spirits." ⁴⁹ "Listen," He said: "they whose branches were found withered and moth-eaten are the apostates and traitors of the Assembly, who have blasphemed the LORD in their sins, and have, moreover, been ashamed of the Name of the LORD by which they were called. These, therefore, at the end were lost to God. ⁵⁰ And you see that not a single one of them converted, although they heard the words which I spoke to them, which I enjoined on you. ⁵¹ From such life departed, and they who gave them in withered and undecayed, these also were near to them; for they were hypocrites, and introducers of strange doctrines, and subverters of the servants of God, especially of those who had sinned, not allowing them to convert, but persuading them by foolish doctrines. ⁵² These, accordingly, have a hope of conversion. And you see that many of them have also converted since I spoke to them, and they will still convert. ⁵³ But all who will not convert have lost their lives; and as many of them as converted became good, and their dwelling

was appointed within the first walls; and some of them even ascended into the tower. ⁵⁴ You see, then," He said, "that conversion involves life to sinners, but non-conversion death. ⁵⁵ And as many as gave in the branches half-withered and cracked, hear about them also. They whose branches were half-withered to the same extent are the wavering; for they neither live, nor are they dead. And they who have them half-withered and cracked are both waverers and slanderers, [[railing against the absent,]] and never at peace with one another, but always at variance. ⁵⁶ And yet to these also," he continued, "conversion is possible. You see," He said, "that some of them have converted, and there is still remaining in them," he continued, "a hope of conversion. ⁵⁷ And as many of them," He added, "as have converted, will have their dwelling in the tower. And those of them who have been slower in converting will dwell within the walls. ⁵⁸ And as many as do not convert at all, but abide in their deeds, will utterly perish. ⁵⁹ And they who gave in their branches green and cracked were always faithful and good, though emulating each other about the foremost places, and about fame: now all these are foolish, in indulging in such a rivalry. ⁶⁰ Yet they also, being naturally good, on hearing My commandments, purified themselves, and soon converted. Their dwelling, accordingly, was in the tower. But if anyone relapses into strife, he will be cast out of the tower, and will lose his life. ⁶¹ Life is the possession of all who keep the commandments of the LORD; but in the commandments there is no rivalry in regard to the first places, or glory of any kind, but in regard to patience and personal humility. ⁶² Among such persons, then, is the life of the LORD, but among the quarrelsome and transgressors—death. ⁶³ And they who gave in their branches half-green and half-withered, are those who are immersed in business, and do not cleave to the holy ones. For this reason, the one half of them is living, and the other half dead. ⁶⁴ Many, accordingly, who heard My commands converted, and those at least who converted had their dwelling in the tower. But some of them at last fell away: these, accordingly, do not have conversion, for on account of their business they blasphemed the LORD, and denied Him. ⁶⁵ They therefore lost their lives through the wickedness which they committed. And many of them doubted. These still have conversion in their power, if they convert speedily; and their abode will be in the tower. ⁶⁶ But if they are slower in converting, they will dwell within the walls; and if they do not convert, they too have lost their lives. ⁶⁷ And they who gave in their branches two-thirds withered and one-third green, are those who have denied [the LORD] in various ways. Many, however, converted, but some of them hesitated and were in doubt. These, then, have conversion within their reach, if they convert quickly, and do not remain in their pleasures; but if they abide in their deeds, these, too, work to themselves death. ⁶⁸ And they who returned their branches two-thirds withered and one-third green, are those that were indeed faithful; but after acquiring wealth, and becoming distinguished among the heathen, they clothed themselves with great pride, and became lofty-minded, and deserted the truth, and did not cleave to the righteous, but lived with the heathen, and this way of life became more agreeable to them. ⁶⁹ They did not, however, depart from God, but remained in the faith, although not working the works of faith. Many of them accordingly converted, and their dwelling was in the tower. ⁷⁰ And others continuing to live until the end with the heathen, and being corrupted by their vain glories, [[departed from God, serving the works and deeds of the heathen.]] These were reckoned with the heathen. ⁷¹ But others of them hesitated, not hoping to be saved on account of the deeds which they had done; while others were in doubt and caused divisions among themselves. ⁷² To those, therefore, who were in doubt on account of their deeds, conversion is still open; but their conversion ought to be speedy, that their dwelling may be in the tower. ⁷³ And to those who do not convert, but abide in their pleasures, death is near. ⁷⁴ And they who give in their branches green, but having the tips withered and cracked, these were always good, and faithful, and distinguished before God; but they sinned a very little through indulging small desires, and finding little faults with one another. ⁷⁵ But on hearing my words the greater part of them quickly converted, and their dwelling was on the tower. Yet some of them were in doubt; and certain of them who were in doubt wrought greater dissension. ⁷⁶ Among these, therefore, is hope of conversion, because they were always good; and with difficulty will any one of them perish. ⁷⁷ And they who gave up their branches withered, but having a very small part green, are those who believed only, yet continue working the works of iniquity. ⁷⁸ They never, however, departed from God, but gladly bore His Name, and joyfully received His servants into their houses. Having accordingly heard of this conversion, they unhesitatingly converted, and practice all virtue and righteousness; and some of them even [[suffered, being willingly put to death]], knowing their deeds which they had done. Of all these, therefore, the dwelling will be in the tower." ⁷⁹ And after He had finished the explanations of all the branches, He said to me, "Go and tell them to everyone, that they may convert, and they will live to God. ⁸⁰ Because the LORD, having had compassion on all men, has sent Me

to give conversion, although some are not worthy of it on account of their works; but the LORD, being long-suffering, desires those who were called by His Son to be saved." ⁸¹ I said to Him, "Lord, I hope that all who have heard them will convert; for I am persuaded that each one, on coming to a knowledge of his own works, and fearing the LORD, will convert." ⁸² He answered me, and said, "All who with their whole heart will purify themselves from their wickedness before enumerated, and will add no more to their sins, will receive healing from the LORD for their former transgressions, if they do not hesitate at these commandments; and they will live to God. ⁸³ But you: walk in My commandments, and live." Having shown me these things, and spoken all these words, He said to me, "And the rest I will show you after a few days."

SIMILITUDE 9

¹ After I had written down the commandments and similitudes of the Shepherd, the Messenger of conversion, He came to me and said, "I wish to explain to you what the Holy Spirit that spoke with you in the form of the Assembly showed you, for that Spirit is the Son of God. ² For, as you were somewhat weak in the flesh, it was not explained to you by the messenger. ³ When, however, you were strengthened by the Spirit, and your strength was increased, so that you were able to see the messenger also, then accordingly was the building of the tower shown you by the Assembly. ⁴ In a noble and solemn manner you saw everything as if shown you by a virgin; but now you see [them] through the same Spirit as if shown by a messenger. ⁵ You must, however, learn everything from Me with greater accuracy. For I was sent for this purpose by the glorious messenger to dwell in your house, that you might see all things with power, entertaining no fear, even as it was before." ⁶ And He led me away into Arcadia, to a round hill; and He placed me on the top of the hill, and showed me a large plain, and around the plain—twelve mountains, all having different forms. ⁷ The first was black as soot; and the second bare, without grass; and the third full of thorns and thistles; and the fourth with grass half-withered, the upper parts of the plants green, and the parts about the roots withered; and some of the grasses, when the sun scorched them, became withered. ⁸ And the fifth mountain had green grass, and was ragged. And the sixth mountain was quite full of clefts, some small and others large; and the clefts were grassy, but the plants were not very vigorous, but rather, as it were, decayed. ⁹ The seventh mountain, again, had cheerful pastures, and the whole mountain was blooming, and every kind of cattle and birds were feeding on that mountain; and the more the cattle and

the birds ate, the more the grass of that mountain flourished. ¹⁰ And the eighth mountain was full of fountains, and every kind of the LORD's creatures drank of the fountains of that mountain. ¹¹ But the ninth mountain [[had no water at all, and was wholly a desert, and had within it deadly serpents, which destroy men. And the tenth mountain]] had very large trees, and was completely shaded, and under the shadow of the trees sheep lay resting and ruminating. ¹² And the eleventh mountain was very thickly wooded, and those trees were productive, being adorned with various sons of fruits, so that anyone seeing them would desire to eat of their fruits. ¹³ The twelfth mountain, again, was wholly white, and its aspect was cheerful, and the mountain in itself was very beautiful. ¹⁴ And in the middle of the plain He showed me a large white rock that had arisen out of the plain. And the rock was more lofty than the mountains, rectangular in shape, so as to be capable of containing the whole world: ¹⁵ and that rock was old, having a gate cut out of it; and the cutting out of the gate seemed to me as if recently done. And the gate glittered to such a degree under the sunbeams, that I marveled at the splendor of the gate; ¹⁶ and around the gate were standing twelve virgins. The four who stood at the corners seemed to me more distinguished than the others—they were all, however, distinguished— and they were standing at the four parts of the gate; two virgins between each part. ¹⁷ And they were clothed with linen tunics, and gracefully girded, having their right shoulders exposed, as if about to bear some burden. Thus they stood ready; for they were exceedingly cheerful and eager. ¹⁸ After I had seen these things, I marveled in myself, because I was beholding great and glorious sights. And again, I was perplexed about the virgins, because, although so delicate, they were standing courageously, as if about to carry the whole heavens. ¹⁹ And the Shepherd said to me, "Why are you reasoning in yourself, and perplexing your mind, and distressing yourself? For the things which you cannot understand, do not attempt to comprehend, as if you were wise; but ask the LORD, that you may receive understanding and know them. ²⁰ You cannot see what is behind you, but you see what is before. Whatever, then, you cannot see, leave alone, and do not torment yourself about it: but what you see, make yourself master of it, and do not waste your labor about other things; and I will explain to you everything that I show you. Therefore, look on the things that remain." ²¹ I saw six men come, tall, and distinguished, and similar in appearance, and they summoned a multitude of men. ²² And they who came were also tall men, and handsome, and powerful; and the six men commanded them to build a tower

above the rock. ²³ And the noise of those men who came to build the tower was great, as they ran here and there around the gate. ²⁴ And the virgins who stood around the gate told the men to hasten to build the tower. Now the virgins had spread out their hands, as if about to receive something from the men. ²⁵ And the six men commanded stones to ascend out of a certain pit, and to go to the building of the tower. And there went up ten shining rectangular stones, not hewn in a quarry. ²⁶ And the six men called the virgins, and ordered them to carry all the stones that were intended for the building, and to pass through the gate, and give them to the men who were about to build the tower. ²⁷ And the virgins put on each other the ten first stones which had ascended from the pit, and carried them together, each stone by itself. And as they stood together around the gate, those who seemed to be strong carried them, and they stooped down under the corners of the stone; and the others stooped down under the sides of the stones. ²⁸ And in this way they carried all the stones. And they carried them through the gate as they were commanded, and gave them to the men for the tower; and they took the stones and proceeded with the building. ²⁹ Now the tower was built on the great rock, and above the gate. Those ten stones were prepared as the foundation for the building of the tower. And the rock and gate were the support of the whole of the tower. ³⁰ And after the ten stones, twenty[-five] other [stones] came up out of the pit, and these were fired into the building of the tower, being carried by the virgins as before. ³¹ And after these ascended thirty-five. And these in like manner were fitted into the tower. And after these, forty other stones came up; and all these were cast into the building of the tower, [[and there were four rows in the foundation of the tower,]] and they ceased ascending from the pit. And the builders also ceased for a little while. ³² And again, the six men commanded the multitude of the crowd to bear stones from the mountains for the building of the tower. They were accordingly brought from all the mountains of various colors, and being hewn by the men, were given to the virgins; ³³ and the virgins carried them through the gate and gave them for the building of the tower. And when the stones of various colors were placed in the building, they all became white alike, and lost their different colors. ³⁴ And certain stones were given by the men for the building, and these did not become shining; but as they were placed, such also were they found to remain: for they were not given by the virgins, nor carried through the gate. ³⁵ These stones, therefore, were not in keeping with the others in the building of the tower. And the six men, seeing these unsuitable stones in the building, commanded them to be taken away, and to be carried away down to their own place from where they had been taken; [36] [[and being removed one by one, they were laid aside; and]] they say to the men who brought the stones, "Do not bring any stones at all for the building, but lay them down beside the tower, that the virgins may carry them through the gate, and may give them for the building. [37] For unless," they said, "they are carried through the gate by the hands of the virgins, they cannot change their colors: do not toil, therefore," they said, "for no purpose." [38] And on that day the building was finished, but the tower was not completed; for additional building was again about to be added, and there was a cessation in the building. [39] And the six men commanded all the builders to withdraw a little distance, and to rest, but enjoined the virgins not to withdraw from the tower; and it seemed to me that the virgins had been left to guard the tower. [40] Now after all had withdrawn, and were resting themselves, I said to the Shepherd, "What is the reason that the building of the tower was not finished?" [41] "The tower," He answered, "cannot be finished just yet, until the Lord of it comes and examines the building, in order that, if any of the stones are found to be decayed, He may change them: for the tower is built according to His pleasure." [42] "I would like to know, Lord," I said, "what is the meaning of the building of this tower, and what [of] the rock and gate, and the mountains, and [the] meaning of the virgins, and the stones that ascended from the pit, and were not hewn, but came as they were to the building. [43] Why, in the first place, were ten stones placed in the foundation, then twenty-five, then thirty-five, then forty? [44] And I also wish to know about the stones that went to the building, and were again taken out and returned to their own place? On all these points put my mind at rest, Lord, and explain them to me." [45] "If you are not found to be curious about trifles," He replied, "you will know everything. For after a few days [[we will come here, and you will see the other things that happen to this tower, and will know accurately all the similitudes." [46] After a few days]] we came to the place where we sat down. And He said to me, "Let us go to the tower; for the Master of the tower is coming to examine it." [47] And we came to the tower, and there was no one at all near it, save the virgins only. And the Shepherd asked the virgins if perhaps the Master of the tower had come; and they replied that He was about to come to examine the building. [48] And behold, after a little while I see an array of many men coming, and in the midst of them one Man of so remarkable a size as to overtop the tower. [49] And the six men who had worked on the building were with Him, and many other honorable men were around Him. And the virgins who

kept the tower ran forward and kissed Him, and began to walk near Him around the tower. [50] And that Man examined the building carefully, feeling every stone separately; and holding a rod in His hand, He struck every stone in the building three times. [51] And when He struck them, some of them became black as soot, and some appeared as if covered with scabs, and some cracked, and some mutilated, and some neither white nor black, and some rough and not in keeping with the other stones, and some having very many stains: such were the varieties of decayed stones that were found in the building. [52] He ordered all these to be taken out of the tower, and to be laid down beside it, and other stones to be brought and put in their stead. [[And the builders asked Him from what mountain He wished them to be brought and put in their place.]] [53] And He did not command them to be brought from the mountains, [[but He ordered them be brought from a certain plain which was near at hand.]] [54] And the plain was dug up, and shining rectangular stones were found, and some also of a round shape; and all the stones which were in that plain were brought, and carried through the gate by the virgins. [55] And the rectangular stones were hewn and put in place of those that were taken away; but the rounded stones were not put into the building, because they were hard to hew, and appeared to field slowly to the chisel; they were deposited, however, beside the tower, as if intended to be hewn and used in the building, for they were exceedingly brilliant. [56] The glorious Man, the Lord of the whole tower, having accordingly finished these alterations, called the Shepherd to Himself, and delivered to Him all the stones that were lying beside the tower, that had been rejected from the building, and said to Him, "Carefully clean all these stones, and put aside such for the building of the tower as may harmonize with the others; and those that do not, throw [them] far away from the tower." [57] [[Having given these orders to the Shepherd, He departed from the tower]] with all those with whom He had come. [58] Now the virgins were standing around the tower, keeping it. [59] I said again to the Shepherd, "Can these stones return to the building of the tower, after being rejected?" He answered me, and said, "Do you see these stones?" "I see them, Lord," I replied. "The greater part of these stones," He said, "I will hew, and put into the building, and they will harmonize with the others." [60] "How, Lord," I said, "can they, after being cut all over, fill up the same space?" He answered, "Those that will be found small will be thrown into the middle of the building, and those that are larger will be placed on the outside, and they will hold them together." [61] Having spoken these words, He said to me, "Let us go, and after two days let us come and clean these stones, and cast them into the building; for all things around the tower must be cleaned, lest the Master comes suddenly and finds the places around the tower dirty, and is displeased, and these stones are not returned for the building of the tower, and I also will seem to be neglectful toward the Master." 62 And after two days we came to the tower, and He said to me, "Let us examine all the stones, and ascertain those which may return to the building." I said to Him, "Lord, let us examine them!" 63 And beginning, we first examined the black stones: and such as they had been taken out of the building, were they found to remain; and the Shepherd ordered them to be removed out of the tower, and to be placed apart. 64 Next, He examined those that had scabs; and He took and hewed many of these and commanded the virgins to take them up and cast them into the building. And the virgins lifted them up and put them in the middle of the building of the tower. 65 And the rest He ordered to be laid down beside the black ones; for these, too, were found to be black. 66 He next examined those that had cracks; and He hewed many of these, and commanded them to be carried by the virgins to the building: and they were placed on the outside, because they were found to be sounder than the others; but the rest, on account of the multitude of the cracks, could not be hewn, and for this reason, therefore, they were rejected from the building of the tower. 67 He next examined the chipped stones, and many among these were found to be black, and some to have great crocks. And these He also commanded to be laid down along with those which had been rejected. 68 But the remainder, after being cleaned and hewn, He commanded to be placed in the building. And the virgins took them up and fitted them into the middle of the building of the tower, for they were somewhat weak. 69 He next examined those that were half white and half black, and many of them were found to be black. And He commanded these also to be taken away along with those which had been rejected. 70 And the rest were all taken away by the virgins; for, being white, they were fitted by the virgins themselves into the building. 71 And they were placed on the outside, because they were found to be sound, so as to be able to support those which were placed in the middle, for no part of them was chipped at all. 72 He next examined those that were rough and hard; and a few of them were rejected because they could not be hewn, as they were found exceedingly hard. 73 But the rest of them were hewn, and carried by the virgins, and fitted into the middle of the building of the tower; for they were somewhat weak. 74 He next examined those that had stains; and of these a very few were black, and were thrown aside with the others; but the greater part were found to be bright, and these were fitted by the virgins into the building, but on account of their strength were placed on the outside. 75 He next came to examine the white and rounded stones, and said to me, "What are we to do with these stones?" "How do I know, Lord?" I replied. 76 "Have you no intentions regarding them?" "Lord," I answered, "I am not acquainted with this art, neither am I a stone-cutter, nor can I tell." "Do you not see," He said, "that they are exceedingly round? And if I wish to make them rectangular, a large portion of them must be cut away; for some of them must of necessity be put into the building." 77 "If therefore," I said, "they must, why do You torment Yourself, and not at once choose for the building those which you prefer, and fit them into it?" 78 He selected the larger ones among them, and the shining ones, and hewed them; and the virgins carried and fitted them into the outside parts of the building. And the rest which remained over were hauled away, and laid down on the plain from which they were brought. 79 They were not, however, rejected, "because," He said, "there remains yet a little addition to be built to the tower. 80 And the Lord of this tower wishes all the stones to be fitted into the building, because they are exceedingly bright." 81 And twelve women were called, very beautiful in form, clothed in black, and with disheveled hair. And these women seemed to me to be fierce. But the Shepherd commanded them to lift the stones that were rejected from the building, and to carry them away to the mountains from which they had been brought. 82 And they were merry, and hauled away all the stones, and put them in the place from where they had been taken. 83 Now after all the stones were removed, and there was no longer a single one lying around the tower, He said, "Let us go around the tower and see, lest there be any defect in it." 84 So I went around the tower along with Him. And the Shepherd, seeing that the tower was beautifully built, rejoiced exceedingly; for the tower was built in such a way, that, on seeing it, I coveted the building of it, for it was constructed as if built of one stone, without a single joining. 85 And the stone seemed as if hewn out of the rock; having to me the appearance of a monolith. 86 And as I walked along with Him, I was full of joy, beholding so many excellent things. 87 And the Shepherd said to me, "Go and bring unslaked lime and fine-baked clay, that I may fill up the forms of the stones that were taken and thrown into the building; for everything about the tower must be smooth." 88 And I did as He commanded me and brought it to Him. "Assist Me," He said, "and the work will soon be finished." 89 He accordingly filled up the forms of the stones that were returned to the building, and commanded the places around the tower to be swept and to be cleaned; 90 and the virgins took brooms and swept the place, and carried all the dirt out of the tower, and brought water, and the ground around the tower became cheerful and very beautiful. [91] The Shepherd says to me, "Everything has been cleared away; if the Lord of the tower comes to inspect it, He can have no fault to find with us." Having spoken these words, He wished to depart; but I laid hold of Him by the wallet, and began to adjure Him by the LORD that He would explain what He had showed me. [92] He said to me, "I must rest a little, and then I will explain to you everything; wait for Me here until I return." I said to Him, "Lord, what can I do here alone?" "You are not alone," He said, "for these virgins are with you." "Give me in charge to them, then," I replied. [93] The Shepherd called them to him, and said to them, "I entrust him to you until I come," and went away. [94] And I was alone with the virgins; and they were rather merry, but were friendly to me, especially the four more distinguished of them. [95] The virgins said to me, "The Shepherd does not come here today." "What, then," I said, "am I to do?" They replied, "Wait for Him until He comes; and if He comes, He will converse with you, and if He does not come, you will remain here with us until He does come." [96] I said to them, "I will wait for Him until it is late; and if He does not arrive, I will go away into the house, and come back early in the morning." [97] And they answered and said to me, "You were entrusted to us; you cannot go away from us." "Where, then," I said, "am I to remain?" "You will sleep with us," they replied, "as a brother, and not as a husband: for you are our brother, and for the time to come we intend to abide with you, for we love you exceedingly!" [98] But I was ashamed to remain with them. And she who seemed to be the first among them began to kiss me. [And the others seeing her kissing me, began to kiss me also], and to lead me round the tower, and to play with me. [99] And I, too, became like a young man, and began to play with them: for some of them formed a chorus, and others danced, and others sang; and I, keeping silence, walked with them around the tower, and was merry with them. [100] And when it grew late I wished to go into the house; and they would not let me, but detained me. So I remained with them during the night, and slept beside the tower. [101] Now the virgins spread their linen tunics on the ground and made me lie down in the midst of them; and they did nothing at all but pray; and I without ceasing prayed with them, and not less than they. [102] And the virgins rejoiced because I thus prayed. And I remained there with the virgins until the next day at the second hour. [103] Then the Shepherd returned, and said to the virgins, "Did you offer him any insult?" "Ask him," they said. [104] I said to Him, "Lord, I was delighted that I remained

with them." "On what," He asked, "did you dine?" "I dined, Lord," I replied, "on the words of the LORD the whole night." "Did they receive you well?" He inquired. "Yes, Lord," I answered. [105] "Now," He said, "what do you wish to hear first?" "I wish to hear in the order," I said, "in which You showed me from the beginning. I beg of You, Lord, that as I will ask You, so also You will give me the explanation." [106] "As you wish," He replied, "so also will I explain to you, and will conceal nothing at all from you." [107] "First of all, Lord," I said, "explain this to me: what is the meaning of the rock and the gate?" "This rock," He answered, "and this gate are the Son of God." [108] "How, Lord?" I said; "the rock is old, and the gate is new." "Listen," He said, "and understand, O ignorant man. The Son of God is older than all His creatures, so that He was a fellow-counselor with the Father in His work of creation: for this reason He is old." [109] "And why is the gate new, Lord?" I said. "Because," He answered, "He became manifest in the last days of the dispensation: for this reason the gate was made new, that they who are to be saved by it might enter into the Kingdom of God. [110] Did you see," He said, "that those stones which came in through the gate were used for the building of the tower, and that those which did not come, were again thrown back to their own place?" "I saw, Lord," I replied. [111] "In like manner," He continued, "no one will enter into the Kingdom of God unless he receives His holy Name. For if you desire to enter into a city, and that city is surrounded by a wall, and has but one gate, can you enter into that city save through the gate which it has?" [112] "Why, how can it be otherwise, Lord?" I said. "If, then, you cannot enter into the city except through its gate, so, in like manner, a man cannot otherwise enter into the Kingdom of God than by the Name of His beloved Son. [113] You saw," He added, "the multitude who were building the tower?" "I saw them, Lord," I said. "Those," He said, "are all glorious messengers, and by them accordingly is the LORD surrounded. And the gate is the Son of God. This is the one entrance to the LORD. In no other way, then, will anyone enter in to Him except through His Son. [114] Did you see," He continued, "the six men, and the tall and glorious Man in the midst of them, who walked around the tower, and rejected the stones from the building?" "I saw Him, Lord," I answered. [115] "The glorious Man," He said, "is the Son of God, and those six glorious messengers are those who support Him on the right hand and on the left. None of these glorious messengers," He continued, "will enter in to God apart from Him. Whosoever does not receive His Name, will not enter into the Kingdom of God." [116] "And the tower," I asked, "what does it mean?" "This tower," He replied, "is the Assembly." [117] "And these virgins, who are they?" "They are holy spirits, and men cannot otherwise be found in the Kingdom of God unless these have put their clothing on them: for if you receive the Name only, and do not receive from them the clothing, they are of no advantage to you. [118] For these virgins are the powers of the Son of God. If you bear His Name but do not possess His power, it will be in vain that you bear His Name. [119] Those stones," He continued, "which you saw rejected, bore His Name, but did not put on the clothing of the virgins." [120] "Of what nature is their clothing, Lord?" I asked. "Their very names," He said, "are their clothing. Everyone who bears the Name of the Son of God, ought to bear the names of these also; for the Son Himself bears the names of these virgins. [121] As many stones," He continued, "as you saw [come into the building of the tower through the hands] of these virgins, and remaining, have been clothed with their strength. [122] For this reason, you see that the tower became of one stone with the rock. So also, they who have believed on the Lord through His Son, and are clothed with these spirits, will become one spirit, one body, and the color of their garments will be one. And the dwelling of such as bear the names of the virgins is in the tower." [123] "Those stones, Lord, that were rejected," I inquired, "on what account were they rejected? For they passed through the gate, and were placed by the hands of the virgins in the building of the tower." [124] "Since you take an interest in everything," He replied, "and examine minutely, hear about the stones that were rejected. [125] These all," He said, "received the Name of God, and they also received the strength of these virgins. Having received, then, these spirits, they were made strong, and were with the servants of God; and theirs was one spirit, and one body, and one clothing. For they were of the same mind, and wrought righteousness. [126] After a certain time, however, they were persuaded by the women whom you saw clothed in black, and having their shoulders exposed and their hair disheveled, and beautiful in appearance. [127] Having seen these women, they desired to have them, and clothed themselves with their strength, and put off the strength of the virgins. These, accordingly, were rejected from the house of God, and were given over to these women. [128] But they who were not deceived by the beauty of these women remained in the house of God. You have," He said, "the explanation of those who were rejected." [129] "What, then, Lord," I said, "if these men, being such as they are, convert and put away their desires after these women, and again return to the virgins, and walk in their strength and in their works, will they not enter into the house of God?" [130] "They will enter in," He said, "if they put away the works of these women, and put on again the strength of the virgins, and walk in their works. For on this account there was a cessation in the building, in order that, if these convert, they may depart into the building of the tower. [131] But if they do not convert, then others will come in their place, and these at the end will be cast out." For all these things I gave thanks to the Lord, because He had pity on all that call on His Name; and sent the Messenger of conversion to us who sinned against Him and renewed our spirit; and when we were already destroyed, and had no hope of life, He restored us to newness of life. [132] "Now, Lord," I continued, "show me why the tower was not built on the ground, but on the rock and on the gate." [133] "Are you still," He said, "without sense and understanding?" "I must, Lord," I said, "ask you of all things, because I am wholly unable to understand them; for all these things are great and glorious, and difficult for man to understand." [134] "Listen," He said: "the Name of the Son of God is great, and cannot be contained, and supports the whole world. If, then, the whole creation is supported by the Son of God, what do you think of those who are called by Him, and bear the Name of the Son of God, and walk in His commandments? [135] Do you see what kind of persons He supports? Those who bear His Name with their whole heart. He Himself, accordingly, became a foundation to them, and supports them with joy, because they are not ashamed to bear His Name." [136] "Explain to me, Lord," I said, "the names of these virgins, and of those women who were clothed in black raiment." [137] "Hear," He said, "the names of the stronger virgins who stood at the corners. The first is Faith, the second Continence, the third Power, the fourth Patience. [138] And the others standing in the midst of these have the following names: Simplicity, Innocence, Purity, Cheerfulness, Truth, Understanding, Harmony, Love. [138] He who bears these names and that of the Son of God will be able to enter into the Kingdom of God. [139] Hear, also," He continued, "the names of the women who had the black garments; and of these, four are stronger than the rest. The first is Unbelief; the second, Incontinence; the third, Disobedience; the fourth, Deceit. [140] And their followers are called Sorrow, Wickedness, Wantonness, Anger, Falsehood, Folly, Backbiting, Hatred. The servant of God who bears these names will see, indeed, the Kingdom of God, but will not enter into it." [141] "And the stones, Lord," I said, "which were taken out of the pit and fitted into the building: what are they?" [142] "The first—" He said, "the ten, [namely, that were placed as a foundation,] are the first generation, and the twenty-five the second generation, of righteous men; and the thirty-five are the prophets of God and His ministers; and the forty are the apostles and teachers of the preaching of the Son of God." [143] "Why, then, Lord," I asked, "did the virgins also carry these stones through the gate, and give them for the building of the tower?" [144] "Because," He answered, "these were the first who bore these spirits, and they never departed from each other, neither the spirits from the men nor the men from the spirits, but the spirits remained with them until their falling asleep. And unless they had had these spirits with them, they would not have been of use for the building of this tower." [145] "Explain to me a little further, Lord," I said. "What is it that you desire?" He asked. "Why, Lord," I said, "did these stones ascend out of the pit, and be applied to the building of the tower, after having borne these spirits?" [146] "They were obliged," He answered, "to ascend through water in order that they might be made alive; for, unless they laid aside the deadness of their life, they could not in any other way enter into the Kingdom of God. Accordingly, those also who fell asleep received the seal of the Son of God. [147] For," he continued, "before a man bears the Name of the Son of God, he is dead; but when he receives the seal he lays aside his deadness, and obtains life. [148] The seal, then, is the water: they descend into the water dead, and they arise alive. And to them, accordingly, was this seal preached, and they made use of it that they might enter into the Kingdom of God." [149] "Why, Lord," I asked, "did the forty stones also ascend with them out of the pit, having already received the seal?" [150] "Because," He said, "these apostles and teachers who preached the Name of the Son of God, after falling asleep in the power and faith of the Son of God, preached it not only to those who were asleep, but themselves also gave them the seal of the preaching. [151] Accordingly, they descended with them into the water, and again ascended. [[But these descended alive and rose up again alive; whereas they who had previously fallen asleep descended dead, but rose up again alive.]] [152] By these, then, were they quickened and made to know the Name of the Son of God. For this reason, they also ascended with them, and were fitted along with them into the building of the tower, and, untouched by the chisel, were built in along with them. [153] For they slept in righteousness and in great purity, but only—they did not have this seal. Accordingly, you have the explanation of these also." [154] "I understand, Lord," I replied. "Now, Lord," I continued, "explain to me, with respect to the mountains, why their forms are various and diverse." [155] "Listen," He said: "these mountains are the twelve tribes, which inhabit the whole world. The Son of God, accordingly, was preached to them by the apostles." [156] "But why are the mountains of various kinds, some having one form, and others another?

Explain that to me, Lord." [157] "Listen," He answered: "these twelve tribes that inhabit the whole world are twelve nations. And they vary in prudence and understanding. [158] As numerous, then, as are the varieties of the mountains which you saw, are also the diversities of mind and understanding among these nations. And I will explain to you the actions of each one." [159] "First, Lord," I said, "explain this: why, when the mountains are so diverse, their stones, when placed in the building, became one color, also shining like those that had ascended out of the pit." [160] "Because," He said, "all the nations that dwell under Heaven were called by hearing and believing on the Name of the Son of God. [161] Having, therefore, received the seal, they had one understanding and one mind; and their faith became one, and their love one, and with the Name they also bore the spirits of the virgins. [162] On this account the building of the tower became of one color, bright as the sun. But after they had entered into the same place, and became one body, certain of these defiled themselves, and were expelled from the race of the righteous, and again became what they were before, or rather worse." [163] "How, Lord," I said, "did they become worse, after having known God?" "He that does not know God," He answered, "and practices evil, receives a certain discipline for his wickedness; but he that has known God ought to not do evil any longer, but to do good. [164] If, accordingly, when he ought to do good, he does evil, does he not appear to do greater evil than he who does not know God? [165] For this reason, they who have not known God and do evil are condemned to death; but they who have known God, and have seen His mighty works, and still continue in evil, will be punished doubly, and will die forever. [166] In this way, then, the Assembly of God will be purified. For as you saw the stones rejected from the tower, and delivered to the evil spirits, and cast out from there, so [[they will also be cast out, and]] there will be one body of the purified; as the tower also became, as it were, of one stone after its purification. [167] In like manner also, it will be with the Assembly of God, after it has been purified, and has rejected the wicked, and the hypocrites, and the blasphemers, and the waverers, and those who commit wickedness of different kinds. [168] After these have been cast away, the Assembly of God will be one body, of one mind, of one understanding, of one faith, of one love. And then the Son of God will be exceedingly glad, and will rejoice over them, because He has received His people pure." [169] "All these things, Lord," I said, "are great and glorious. "Moreover, Lord," I said, "explain to me the power and the actions of each one of the mountains, that every soul, trusting in the LORD, and hearing it, may glorify His great, and marvelous, and glorious

Name." [170] "Hear," He said, "the diversity of the mountains and of the twelve nations. [171] From the first mountain, which was black, they that believed are the following: apostates and blasphemers against the LORD, and betrayers of the servants of God. [172] To these conversion is not open; but death lies before them, and on this account they are also black, for their race is a lawless one. [173] And from the second mountain, which was bare, they who believed are the following: hypocrites and teachers of wickedness. And these, accordingly, are like the former, not having any fruits of righteousness; for as their mountain was destitute of fruit, so also such men indeed have a name, but are empty of faith, and there is no fruit of truth in them. [174] They indeed have conversion in their power, if they convert quickly; but if they are slow in so doing, they will die along with the former." [175] "Why, Lord," I said, "do these have conversion, but the former do not? For their actions are nearly the same." [176] "On this account," He said, "these have conversion, because they did not blaspheme their Lord, nor become betrayers of the servants of God; but on account of their desire of possessions they became hypocritical, and each one taught according to the desires of men that were sinners. [177] But they will suffer a certain punishment; and conversion is before them, because they were not blasphemers or traitors. [178] And from the third mountain, which had thorns and thistles, they who believed are the following: some of them are rich, and others immersed in much business. The thistles are the rich, and the thorns are they who are immersed in much business. [179] Those cleave to the servants of God, but wander away, being choked by their business transactions; and the rich cleave with difficulty to the servants of God, fearing lest these should ask something of them. [180] Such persons, accordingly, will have difficulty in entering the Kingdom of God. For as it is disagreeable to walk among thistles with naked feet, so also it is hard for such to enter the Kingdom of God. [181] But to all these conversion—and that speedily—is open, in order that what they did not do in former times they may make up for in these days, and do some good, and they will live to God. But if they abide in their deeds, they will be delivered to those women who will put them to death. [182] And from the fourth mountain, which had much grass—the upper parts of the plants green, and the parts about the roots withered, and some also scorched by the sun—they who believed are the following: [183] the doubtful, and they who have the LORD on their lips, but do not have Him in their heart. On this account their foundations are withered and have no strength; and their words alone live, while their works are dead. Such persons are [neither alive nor] dead. [184] They resemble, therefore, the waverers: for the wavering are neither withered nor green, being neither living nor dead. For as their blades, on seeing the sun, were withered, so also the wavering, when they hear of affliction, on account of their fear, worship idols, and are ashamed of the Name of their Lord. [185] Such, then, are neither alive nor dead. But these also may yet live, if they convert quickly; and if they do not convert, they are already delivered to the women, who take away their life. [186] And from the fifth mountain, which had green grass, and was rugged, they who believed are the following: believers, indeed, but slow to learn, and obstinate, and pleasing themselves, wishing to know everything, and knowing nothing at all. [187] On account of this obstinacy of theirs, understanding departed from them, and foolish senselessness entered into them. And they praise themselves as having wisdom, and desire to become teachers, although destitute of sense. [188] On account, therefore, of this loftiness of mind, many became vain, exalting themselves: for self-will and empty confidence is a great demon. Of these, accordingly, many were rejected, but some converted and believed, and subjected themselves to those that had understanding, knowing their own foolishness. [189] And to the rest of this class conversion is open; for they were not wicked, but rather foolish, and without understanding. Therefore, if these convert, they will live to God; but if they do not convert, they will have their dwelling with the women who wrought wickedness among them. [190] And those from the sixth mountain, which had clefts large and small, and decayed grass in the clefts, who believed, were the following: they who occupy the small clefts are those who bring charges against one another, and by reason of their slanders have decayed in the faith. [191] Many of them, however, converted; and the rest will also convert when they hear My commandments, for their slanders are small, and they will quickly convert. [192] But they who occupy the large clefts are persistent in their slanders, and vindictive in their anger against each other. [193] These, therefore, were thrown away from the tower, and rejected from having a part in its building. Such persons, accordingly, will have difficulty in living. [194] If our God and Lord, who rules over all things, and has power over all His creation, does not remember evil against those who confess their sins, but is merciful, [how] does man, who is corruptible and full of sins, remember evil against a fellow-man, as if he were able to destroy or to save him? [195] I, the Messenger of conversion, say to you: as many of you as are of this way of thinking, lay it aside, and convert, and the LORD will heal your former sins if you purify yourselves from this demon; but if not, you will be delivered over to him for death. [196] And those who believed from the seventh mountain, on which the grass was green and flourishing, and the whole of the mountain fertile, and every kind of cattle and the birds of [the] sky were feeding on the grass on this mountain, and the grass on which they pastured became more abundant, were the following: [197] they were always simple, and harmless, and blessed, bringing no charges against one another, but always rejoicing greatly because of the servants of God, and being clothed with the Holy Spirit of these virgins, and always having pity on every man, and giving aid from their own labor to every man, without reproach and without hesitation. [198] The LORD, therefore, seeing their simplicity and all their meekness, multiplied them amid the labors of their hands, and gave them grace in all their doings. [199] And I, the Messenger of conversion, say to you who are such: continue to be such as these, and your seed will never be blotted out; for the LORD has made trial of you, and inscribed you in the number of us, and the whole of your seed will dwell with the Son of God; for you have received of His Spirit. [200] And they who believed from the eighth mountain, where the many fountains were, and where all the creatures of God drank of the fountains, were the following: [201] apostles and teachers who preached to the whole world, and who taught solemnly and purely the word of the LORD, and did not fall into evil desires at all, but always walked in righteousness and truth, according as they had received the Holy Spirit. Therefore, such persons will enter in with the messengers. [202] And they who believed from the ninth mountain, which was deserted, and had in it creeping things and wild beasts which destroy men, were the following: [203] they who had the stains as servants, who discharged their duty ill, and who plundered widows and orphans of their livelihood, and gained possessions for themselves from the ministry, which they had received. [204] Therefore, if they remain under the dominion of the same desire, they are dead, and there is no hope of life for them; but if they convert, and finish their ministry in a holy manner, they will be able to live. [205] And they who were covered with scabs are those who have denied their Lord, and have not returned to Him again; but becoming withered and desert-like, and not cleaving to the servants of God, but living in solitude, they destroy their own souls. [206] For as a vine, when left within an enclosure, and meeting with neglect, is destroyed, and is made desolate by the weeds, and in time grows wild, and is no longer of any use to its master, so also are such men—as have given themselves up and become useless to their Lord—from having contracted savage habits. [207] Therefore, these men have conversion in

their power, unless they are found to have denied from the heart; but if anyone is found to have denied from the heart, I do not know if he may live. [208] And I say this not for these present days, in order that anyone who has denied may obtain conversion, for It is impossible for him to be saved who now intends to deny his Lord; but to those who denied Him long ago, conversion seems to be possible. [209] Therefore, if anyone intends to convert, let him do so quickly, before the tower is completed; for if not, he will be utterly destroyed by the women. [210] And the chipped stones are the deceitful and the slanderers; and the wild beasts, which you saw on the ninth mountain, are the same. [210] For as wild beasts destroy and kill a man by their poison, so also do the words of such men destroy and ruin a man. These, accordingly, are mutilated in their faith, on account of the deeds which they have done in themselves; yet some converted, and were saved. [211] And the rest, who are of such a character, can be saved if they convert; but if they do not convert, they will perish with those women, whose strength they have assumed. [212] And from the tenth mountain, where trees were which overshadowed certain sheep, they who believed were the following: overseers given to hospitality, who always gladly received into their houses the servants of God, without dissimulation. [213] And the overseers never failed to protect, by their service, the widows, and those who were in want, and always maintained a holy conversation. [214] All these, accordingly, will be protected by the LORD forever. They who do these things are honorable before God, and their place is already with the messengers, if they remain serving God to the end. [215] And from the eleventh mountain, where trees were full of fruits, adorned with fruits of various kinds, they who believed were the following: they who suffered for the Name of the Son of God, and who also suffered cheerfully with their whole heart, and laid down their lives." [216] "Why, then, Lord," I said, "do all these trees bear fruit, and some of them—fairer than the rest?" [217] "Listen," He said: "all who once suffered for the Name of the LORD are honorable before God; and of all these the sins were remitted, because they suffered for the Name of the Son of God. And why their fruits are of various kinds, and some of them superior, listen. [218] All," He continued, "who were brought before the authorities and were examined, and did not deny, but suffered cheerfully—these are held in greater honor with God, and of these the fruit is superior; [219] but all who were cowards, and in doubt, and who reasoned in their hearts whether they would deny or confess, and yet suffered, of these the fruit is less, because that suggestion came into their hearts; for that suggestion—that a servant should deny his Lord—is evil. [220] Have a care, therefore, you who are planning such things, lest that suggestion remain in your hearts, and you perish to God. [221] And you who suffer for His Name ought to glorify God, because He deemed you worthy to bear His Name, that all your sins might be healed. [[Therefore, rather deem yourselves happy]], and think that you have done a great thing, if any of you suffer on account of God. [222] The LORD bestows life on you, and you do not understand, for your sins were heavy; but if you had not suffered for the Name of the LORD, you would have died to God on account of your sins. [223] These things I say to you who are hesitating about denying or confessing: acknowledge that you have the LORD, lest, denying Him, you are delivered up to prison. [224] If the heathen punishes their slaves when one of them denies his master, what do you think your Lord will do, who has authority over all men? Put away these counsels out of your hearts, that you may continually live to God. [225] And they who believed from the twelfth mountain, which was white, are the following: they are as infant children, in whose hearts no evil originates; nor did they know what wickedness is, but always remained as children. [226] Such accordingly, without doubt, dwell in the Kingdom of God, because they defiled the commandments of God in nothing; but they remained like children all the days of their life in the same mind. [227] All of you, then, who will remain steadfast, and be as children, without doing evil, will be more honored than all who have been previously mentioned; for all infants are honorable before God, and are the first persons with Him. [228] Blessed, then, are you who put away wickedness from yourselves, and put on innocence. You will live to God as the first of all." [229] After He had finished the similitudes of the mountains, I said to Him, "Lord, now explain to me about the stones that were taken out of the plain, and put into the building instead of the stones that were taken out of the tower; and about the round stones that were put into the building; and those that still remain round." [230] "Hear," He answered, "about all these also. The stones taken out of the plain and put into the building of the tower instead of those that were rejected, are the roots of this white mountain. [231] Therefore, when they who believed from the white mountain were all found guileless, the Lord of the tower commanded those from the roots of this mountain to be cast into the building of the tower; [232] for He knew that if these stones were to go to the building of the tower, they would remain bright, and not one of them would become black. [233] But if He had so resolved with respect to the other mountains, it would have been necessary for Him to visit that tower again, and to cleanse it. [234] Now all these persons were

found white who believed, and who will yet believe, for they are of the same race. This is a happy race, because it is innocent. Hear now, further, about these round and shining stones. [235] All these are also from the white mountain. Hear, moreover, why they were found round: because their riches had obscured and darkened them a little from the truth, although they never departed from God; nor did any evil word proceed out of their mouth, but all justice, virtue, and truth. [236] When the LORD, therefore, saw the mind of these persons, that they were born good, and could be good, He ordered their riches to be cut down, not to be taken away forever, that they might be able to do some good with what was left them; and they will live to God, because they are of a good race. [237] Therefore, they were rounded a little by the chisel, and put in the building of the tower. [238] But the other round stones, which had not yet been adapted to the building of the tower, and had not yet received the seal, were for this reason put back into their place, because they are exceedingly round. [239] Now this age must be cut down in these things, and in the vanities of their riches, and then they will meet in the Kingdom of God; for they must of necessity enter into the Kingdom of God, because the LORD has blessed this innocent race. [240] Of this race, therefore, no one will perish; for although any of them might be tempted by the most wicked devil, and commit sin, he will quickly return to his Lord. [241] I deem you happy, I, who am the Messenger of conversion, whoever of you are innocent as children, because your part is good, and honorable before God. [242] Moreover, I say to you all, who have received the seal of the Son of God, be clothed with simplicity, and do not be mindful of offenses, nor remain in wickedness. [243] Therefore, lay aside the recollection of your offenses and bitternesses, and you will be formed in one spirit. [244] And heal and take away from you those wicked schisms, that if the Lord of the flocks comes, He may rejoice concerning you. And He will rejoice if He finds all things sound, and none of you will perish. [245] But if He finds any one of these sheep strayed, woe to the shepherds! And if the shepherds themselves have strayed, what answer will they give Him for their flocks? [246] Will they perhaps say that they were harassed by their flocks? They will not be believed, for the thing is incredible that a shepherd could suffer from his flock; rather, he will be punished on account of his falsehood. [247] And I myself am a shepherd, and I am under a most stringent necessity of rendering an account of you. [248] Therefore heal yourselves while the tower is still building. The LORD dwells in men that love peace, because He loved peace; but from the contentious and the utterly wicked He is far distant. [249] Restore to Him, therefore, a spirit as sound as you received it. [250] For when you have given a new garment to a fuller, and desire to receive it back whole at the end, if, then, the fuller returns a torn garment to you, will you take it from him, and not rather be angry, and abuse him, saying, I gave you a garment that was whole: why have you rent it, and made it useless, so that it can be of no use on account of the rent which you have made in it? [251] Would you not say all this to the fuller about the rent which you found in your garment? Therefore, if you grieve about your garment, and complain because you have not received it whole, what do you think the LORD will do to you, who gave you a sound spirit, which you have rendered altogether useless, so that it can be of no service to its possessor? [252] For its use began to be unprofitable, seeing it was corrupted by you. Therefore, will the LORD, because of this conduct of yours regarding His Spirit, not act in the same way, and deliver you over to death? [253] Assuredly, I say, He will do the same to all those whom He will find retaining a recollection of offenses. [254] Do not trample His mercy under foot, He says, but rather honor Him, because He is so patient with your sins, and is not as you are. Convert, for it is useful to you. [255] All these things which are written above, I, the Shepherd, the Messenger of conversion, have showed and spoken to the servants of God. [256] Therefore, if you believe, and listen to My words, and walk in them, and amend your ways, you will have it in your power to live: but if you remain in wickedness, and in the recollection of offenses, no sinner of that class will live to God. [257] All these words which I had to say have been spoken to you." The Shepherd said to me, "Have you asked Me everything?" And I replied, "Yes, Lord." [258] "Why did you not ask Me about the shape of the stones that were put into the building, that I might explain to you why we filled up the shapes?" And I said, "I forgot, Lord." [259] "Hear now, then," He said, "about this also. These are they who have now heard My commandments and converted with their whole hearts. [260] And when the LORD saw that their conversion was good and pure, and that they were able to remain in it, He ordered their former sins to be blotted out. For these shapes were their sins, and they were leveled down, that they might not appear."

SIMILITUDE 10

[1] After I had fully written down this scroll, that messenger who had delivered me to the Shepherd came into the house in which I was, and sat down on a couch, and the Shepherd stood on his right hand. [2] He then called me, and spoke to me as follows: "I have delivered you and your house to the Shepherd, that you may be protected by Him." "Yes, Lord," I said.

[3] "If you wish, therefore, to be protected," he said, "from all annoyance, and from all harsh treatment, and to have success in every good work and word, and to possess all the virtues of righteousness, walk in these commandments which He has given you, and you will be able to subdue all wickedness. [4] For if you keep those commandments, every desire and pleasure of the world will be subject to you, and success will attend to you in every good work. [5] Take to yourself His experience and moderation, and say to all that He is in great honor and dignity with God, and that He is a president with great power, and mighty in His office. [6] To Him alone throughout the whole world is the power of conversion assigned. Does He seem to you to be powerful? [7] But you despise His experience, and the moderation which He exercises toward you." [8] I said to him, "Ask Him, lord, whether from the time that He has entered my house I have done anything improper, or have offended Him in any respect." [9] He answered, "I also know that you neither have done nor will do anything improper, and therefore I speak these words to you, that you may persevere. For He had a good report of you to me, and you will say these words to others, that they also who have either converted or will still convert may entertain the same feelings with you, and He may report well of these to me, and I to the LORD." [10] And I said, "Lord, I make known to every man the great works of God: and I hope that all those who love them, and have sinned before, on hearing these words, may convert, and receive life again."

[11] "Therefore, continue in this ministry, and finish it. And all who follow out His commands will have life, and great honor with the LORD. [12] But those who do not keep His commandments, flee from His life, and despise Him. But He has His own honor with the LORD. [13] All, therefore, who will despise Him, and not follow His commands, deliver themselves to death, and every one of them will be guilty of his own blood. [14] But I enjoin you, that you obey His commands, and you will have a cure for your former sins. [15] Moreover, I sent you these virgins, that they may dwell with you. For I saw that they were courteous to you. You will therefore have them as assistants, that you may be the better able to keep His commands: for it is impossible that these commandments can be observed without these virgins. [16] I see, moreover, that they abide with you willingly; but I will also instruct them not to depart at all from your house: only, keep your house pure, as they will delight to dwell in a pure abode. [17] For they are pure, and chaste, and industrious, and have all influence with the LORD. Therefore, if they find your house to be pure, they will remain with you; but if any defilement, even a little, befalls it, they will immediately withdraw from your house. For these

virgins do not like any defilement at all." [18] I said to him, "I hope, lord, that I will please them, so that they may always be willing to inhabit my house. And as He to whom you entrusted me has no complaint against me, so neither will they have." [19] He said to the Shepherd, "I see that the servant of God wishes to live, and to keep these commandments, and will place these virgins in a pure habitation." [20] When he had spoken these words, he again delivered me to the Shepherd, and called those virgins, and said to them, "Since I see that you are willing to dwell in his house, I commend him and his house to You, asking that You do not withdraw from it at all." And the virgins heard these words with pleasure. [21] The messenger then said to me, "Conduct yourself courageously in this service, and make known to everyone the great things of God, and you will have favor in this ministry. [22] Whoever, therefore, will walk in these commandments, will have life, and will be happy in his life; but whosoever will neglect them will not have life, and will be unhappy in this life. Enjoin all, who are able to act rightly, not to cease well-doing; for, to practice good works is useful to them. [23] And I say that every man ought to be saved from inconveniences. For both he who is in want, and he who suffers inconveniences in his daily life, is in great torture and necessity. Whoever, therefore, rescues a soul of this kind from necessity, will gain for himself great joy. [24] For he who is harassed by inconveniences of this kind, suffers equal torture with him who is in chains. [25] Moreover many, on account of calamities of this sort, when they could not endure them, hasten their own deaths. Whoever, then, knows a calamity of this kind afflicting a man, and does not save him, commits a great sin, and becomes guilty of his blood. [26] Therefore, do good works, you who have received good from the LORD, lest, while you delay to do them, the building of the tower is finished, and you are rejected from the edifice: there is now no other tower being built. [27] For on your account the work of building was suspended. Unless, then, you make haste to do rightly, the tower will be completed, and you will be excluded." [28] After he had spoken with me, he rose up from the couch, and taking the Shepherd and the virgins, he departed. But he said to me that he would send the Shepherd and the virgins back to my dwelling. Amen.

ODES OF PEACE

Otherwise known as Odes of Solomon

The Odes of Peace, more commonly known as the Odes of Solomon, are a collection of early Christian poems, in the form of odes, that were likely composed in the late 1st century or early 2nd century. They are known from early citations and various extant copies. The elaborate and beautiful language reflects the deity of Christ and exhibits a primordial Trinitarianism. While later Gnostic works cite the Odes, the Odes themselves are not Gnostic, and reflect, rather, a more orthodox view of the early Christian faith heavily influenced by wisdom literature. Ode 2 is not extant.

ODE 1

[1] The LORD is on my head like a crown, ‖ And I will not be without Him. [2] They wove for me a crown of truth, ‖ And it caused Your branches to bud in me. [3] For it is not like a withered crown which does not bud, ‖ But You live on my head, ‖ And You have blossomed on my head. [4] Your fruits are full-grown and perfect, ‖ They are full of Your salvation.

ODE 3

[1] . . . I put on. [2] And His members are with Him. And I stand on them, ‖ And He loves me: [3] For I should not have known love, ‖ If the LORD had not loved me. [4] For who is able to distinguish love except the one that is loved? [5] I love the Beloved and my soul loves Him: [6] And where His rest is, ‖ There I am also; [7] And I will be no stranger, for with the LORD Most High and Merciful there is no grudging. [8] I have been united to Him, ‖ For the lover has found the Beloved, [9] And because I will love Him that is the Son, ‖ I will become a son; [10] For he that is joined to Him that is immortal, ‖ Will also himself become immortal; [11] And he who has pleasure in the Living One, ‖ Will become living. [12] This is the Spirit of the LORD, ‖ Which does not lie, ‖ Which teaches the sons of men to know His ways. [13] Be wise and understanding and vigilant. Hallelujah!

ODE 4

[1] No man, O my God, changes Your holy place; [2] And it is not [possible] that he should change it and put it in another place, ‖ Because he has no power over it, [3] For You have designed Your sanctuary before You made [other] places: [4] That which is the elder will not be altered by those that are younger than itself. [5] You have given Your heart, O LORD, to Your believers: You will never fail, ‖ Nor be without fruits, [6] For one hour of Your faith is days and years. [7] For who is there [that] put on Your grace, and is hurt? [8] For Your seal is known, ‖ And Your creatures know it, ‖ And Your [heavenly] hosts possess it, ‖ And the chosen chief-messengers are clad with it. [9] You have given us Your fellowship. It was not that You were in need of us, ‖ But that we are in need of You; [10] Distill Your dews on us and open Your rich fountains that pour forth to us milk and honey, [11] For there is no relenting with You that You should relent of anything that You have promised. [12] And the end was revealed before You, ‖ For what You gave, You gave freely, [13] So that You may not draw them back and take them again, [14] For all was revealed before You as God, ‖ And ordered from the beginning before You; And You, O God, have made all things. Hallelujah!

ODE 5

[1] I will give thanks to You, O LORD, ‖ Because I love You; [2] O Most High, You will not forsake me for You are my hope: [3] Freely I have received Your grace, ‖ I will live thereby: [4] My persecutors will come and not see me: [5] A cloud of darkness will fall on their eyes; And an air of thick gloom will darken them: [6] And they will have no light to see; They may not take hold on me. [7] Let their counsel become thick darkness, ‖ And what they have cunningly devised, ‖ Let it return on their own heads, [8] For they have devised a counsel and it did not succeed; [9] For my hope is on the LORD and I will not fear, ‖ And because the LORD is my salvation, ‖ I will not fear; And He is a garland on my head and I will not be moved; Even if everything should be shaken, ‖ I stand firm; [11] And if all things visible should perish, ‖ I will not die, ‖ Because the LORD is with me and I am with Him. Hallelujah!

ODE 6

[1] As the hand moves over the harp, ‖ And the strings speak, [2] So speaks in my members the Spirit of the LORD, ‖ And I speak by His love. [3] For it destroys what is foreign and everything that is bitter: [4] For thus it was from the beginning and will be to the end, ‖ That nothing should be His adversary, ‖ And nothing should stand up against Him. [5] The LORD has multiplied the knowledge of Himself, ‖ And is zealous that these things should be known, ‖ Which by His grace have been given to us. [6] And the praise of His Name He gave us: Our spirits praise His holy Spirit. [7] For there went forth a stream that became a river great and broad; [8] For it flooded and broke up everything and it brought [water] to the temple; [9] And the restrainers of the children of men were not able to restrain it, ‖ Nor the arts of those whose business it is to restrain waters; [10] For it spread over the face of the whole earth, ‖ And filled everything: And all the

ODES OF PEACE

thirsty on earth were given to drink of it; [11] And thirst was relieved and quenched, ‖ For from the Most High the drink was given. [12] Blessed then are the ministers of that drink who are entrusted with that water [13] They have assuaged the dry lips, ‖ And the will that had fainted they have raised up; [14] And souls that were near departing they have caught back from death; [15] And limbs that had fallen they straightened and set up. [16] They gave strength for their feebleness and light to their eyes, [17] For everyone knew them in the Lord, ‖ And they lived by the water of life forever. Hallelujah!

ODE 7

[1] As the impulse of anger against evil, ‖ So is the impulse of joy over what is lovely, ‖ And brings in of its fruits without restraint: [2] My joy is the Lord and my impulse is toward Him; This path of mine is excellent, [3] For I have a helper—the Lord. [4] He has caused me to know Himself, ‖ Without grudging, by His simplicity: His kindness has humbled His greatness. [5] He became like me, ‖ In order that I might receive Him; He was reckoned like myself in order that I might put Him on; [7] And I did not tremble when I saw Him, ‖ Because He was gracious to me. [8] He became like my nature that I might learn Him, ‖ And like my form, that I might not turn back from Him. [9] The Father of knowledge is the word of knowledge: [10] He who created wisdom is wiser than His works; [11] And He who created me when I was yet not knew what I should do when I came into being, [12] For what reason He pitied me in His abundant grace, ‖ And granted me to ask from Him and to receive from His sacrifice, [13] Because it is He that is incorruptible— The fullness of the ages and their Father. [14] He has given Him to be seen of them that are His, ‖ In order that they may recognize Him that made them, ‖ And that they might not suppose that they came of themselves; [15] For He has appointed knowledge as its way, ‖ Has widened it and extended it, ‖ And brought to all perfection, [16] And set over it the traces of His light, ‖ And I walked therein from the beginning even to the end. [17] For by Him it was worked, ‖ And He was resting in the Son, ‖ And for its salvation He will take hold of everything. [18] And the Most High will be known in His holy ones, ‖ To announce to those that have songs of the coming of the Lord: [19] That they may go forth to meet Him, ‖ And may sing to Him with joy and with the harp of many tones. [20] The seers will come before Him and they will be seen before Him, [21] And they will praise the Lord for His love, ‖ Because He is near and beholds. [22] And hatred will be taken from the earth, ‖ And along with jealousy it will be drowned: [23] For ignorance has been destroyed, ‖ Because the knowledge of the Lord has arrived. [24] They who make songs will sing the grace of the Lord Most High; [25] And they will bring their songs, ‖ And their heart will be like the day, ‖ And like the excellent beauty of the Lord their pleasant song; [26] And there will neither be anything that breathes without knowledge nor any that is dumb, [27] For He has given a mouth to His creation, ‖ To open the voice of the mouth toward Him, ‖ To praise Him, [28] Confess His power, ‖ And show forth His grace. Hallelujah!

ODE 8

[1] Open, open your hearts to the exultation of the Lord, [2] And let your love be multiplied from the heart and even to the lips, [3] To bring forth living [and] holy fruit to the Lord, ‖ And to talk with watchfulness in His light. [4] Rise up, and stand erect, ‖ You who once were brought low: [5] Tell forth, you who were in silence, ‖ That your mouth has been opened. [6] You, therefore, that were despised, be lifted up from now on, ‖ Because your righteousness has been exalted. [7] For the right hand of the Lord is with you, ‖ And He is your helper; [8] And peace was prepared for you, ‖ Before your war ever was. [9] Hear the word of truth, ‖ And receive the knowledge of the Most High. [10] Your flesh has not known what I am saying to you: Neither have your hearts known what I am showing to you. [11] Keep My secret, ‖ You who are kept by it. [12] Keep My faith, ‖ You who are kept by it. [13] And understand My knowledge, ‖ You who know Me in truth, [14] Love Me with affection, ‖ You who love! [15] For I do not turn away My face from them that are Mine; [16] For I know them and before they came into being I took knowledge of them, ‖ And on their faces I set My seal, [17] I fashioned their members, ‖ [And] I prepared My own breasts for them, ‖ That they might drink My holy milk and live thereby. [18] I took pleasure in them and am not ashamed of them, [19] For they are My workmanship and the strength of My thoughts. [20] Who then will rise up against My handiwork, ‖ Or who is there that is not subject to them? [21] I willed and fashioned mind and heart: And they are Mine, and by My own right hand I set My chosen ones, [22] And My righteousness goes before them and they will not be deprived of My Name, ‖ For it is with them. [23] Ask, and abound, and abide in the love of the Lord, [24] You beloved ones in the Beloved—Those who are kept in Him that lives, [25] And they that are saved in Him that was saved— [26] And you will be found incorruptible in all ages through the Name of your Father. Hallelujah!

ODE 9

[1] Open your ears and I will speak to you. Give me your souls that I may also give you my soul, [2] The word of the Lord and His good pleasures, ‖ The holy thought which He has devised concerning His Messiah. [3] For in the will of the Lord is your salvation, ‖ And His thought is everlasting life; And your end is immortality. [4] Be enriched in God the Father, ‖ And receive the thought of the Most High. [5] Be strong and be redeemed by His grace. [6] For I announce peace to you, ‖ To you His holy ones, [6] That none of those who

hear may fall in war, || And that those again who have known Him may not perish, || And that those who receive may not be ashamed. [8] Truth is an everlasting crown forever. Blessed are they who set it on their heads: [9] It is a stone of great price; And there have been wars on account of the crown. [10] And righteousness has taken it and has given it to you. [11] Put on the crown in the true covenant of the LORD. [12] And all those who have conquered will be written in His scroll. [13] For their scroll is victory which is yours. And she [(Victory)] sees you before her and wills that you will be saved. Hallelujah!

ODE 10

[1] The LORD has directed My mouth by His word, || And He has opened My heart by His light, || And He has caused His deathless life to dwell in Me, [2] And He gave Me that I might speak the fruit of peace: [3] To convert the souls of them who are willing to come to Him, || And to lead captive a good captivity for freedom. [4] I was strengthened and made mighty and took the world captive; [5] And it became to Me for the praise of the Most High, || And of God My Father. [6] And the nations were gathered together who were scattered abroad. [7] And I was unpolluted by My love for them, || Because they confessed Me in high places: And the traces of the light were set on their heart, [8] And they walked in My life and were saved and became My people forever and ever. Hallelujah!

ODE 11

[1] My heart was split, || And its flower appeared; And grace sprang up in it: And it brought forth fruit to the LORD, [2] For the Most High cleaved my heart by His Holy Spirit and searched my affection toward Him: And filled me with His love. [3] And His opening of me became my salvation; And I ran in His way in His peace even in the way of truth: [4] from the beginning and even to the end I acquired His knowledge, [5] And I was established on the rock of truth, || Where He had set me up; [6] And speaking waters touched my lips from the fountain of the LORD plenteously, [7] And I drank and was inebriated with the living water that does not die; [8] And my inebriation was not one without knowledge, || But I forsook vanity and turned to my God, the Most High, [9] And I was enriched by His bounty, || And I forsook the folly which is diffused over the earth; And I stripped it off and cast it from me: [10] And the LORD renewed me in His raiment, || And possessed me by His light, || And from above He gave me rest in incorruption; [11] And I became like the land which blossoms and rejoices in its fruits: [12] And the LORD was like the sun shining on the face of the land; [13] He lightened my eyes and my face received the dew—The pleasant fragrance of the LORD; [14] And He carried me to His Paradise, || Where the abundance of the pleasure of the LORD is; [15] And I worshiped the LORD on account of His glory; And I

said, "Blessed, O LORD, are they who are planted in Your land, || And those who have a place in Your Paradise; [16] And they grow by the fruits of the trees. And they have changed from darkness to light. [17] Behold! All Your servants are fair, who do good works, || And turn away from wickedness to the pleasantness that is Yours: [18] And they have turned back the bitterness of the trees from them, || When they were planted in Your land; [19] And everything became like a relic of Yourself, || And memorial forever of Your faithful works. [20] For there is abundant room in Your Paradise, || And nothing is useless therein; [21] But everything is filled with fruit; Glory be to You, O God, the Delight of Paradise forever. Hallelujah!"

ODE 12

[1] He has filled me with words of truth, || That I may speak the same; [2] And like the flow of waters flows truth from my mouth, || And my lips show forth His fruit. [3] And He has caused His knowledge to abound in me, || Because the mouth of the LORD is the true Word, || And the door of His light; [4] And the Most High has given Him to His generations, || Which are the interpreters of His own beauty, || And the repeaters of His praise, || And the confessors of His counsel, || And the heralds of His thought, || And the chasteners of His servants. [5] For the swiftness of the Word is inexpressible, || And like His expression is His swiftness and force; [6] And His course knows no limit. He never fails, but He stands sure, || And He does not know descent nor the way of it. [7] For as His work is, so is His end, || For He is light and the dawning of thought; [8] And by Him the worlds talk to one another; And in the Word there were those that were silent; [9] And from Him came love and concord; And they spoke to one another whatever was theirs; And they were penetrated by the Word; [10] And they knew Him who made them, || Because they were in concord; For the mouth of the Most High spoke to them; And His explanation ran by means of Him. [11] For the dwelling-place of the Word is man, || And His truth is love. [12] Blessed are they who by means thereof have understood everything, || And have known the LORD in His truth. Hallelujah!

ODE 13

[1] Behold! The LORD is our mirror: Open the eyes and see them in Him, || And learn the manner of your face, [2] And tell forth praise to His Spirit, || And wipe off the filth from your face, || And love His holiness, || And clothe yourselves with it, [3] And be without stain at all times before Him. Hallelujah!

ODE 14

[1] As the eyes of a son to his father, || So are my eyes, O LORD, at all times toward You. [2] For with You are my consolations and my delight. [3] Do not turn Your

ODES OF PEACE

mercies away from me, O Lord: And do not take Your kindness from me. ⁴Stretch out to me, O Lord, at all times Your right hand, ‖ And be my guide even to the end, ‖ According to Your good pleasure. ⁵Let me be well-pleasing before You, ‖ Because of Your glory and because of Your Name. ⁶Let me be preserved from evil, ‖ And let Your meekness, O Lord, ‖ Abide with me, and the fruits of Your love. ⁷Teach me the psalms of Your truth, ‖ That I may bring forth fruit in You, ⁸And open to me the harp of Your Holy Spirit, ‖ That with all His notes I may praise You, O Lord. ⁹And according to the multitude of Your tender mercies, ‖ So You will give to me; And hasten to grant our petitions; And You are able for all our needs. Hallelujah!

ODE 15

¹As the sun is the joy to them that seek for its daybreak, ‖ So my joy is the Lord, ²Because He is my Sun, and His rays have lifted me up, and His light has dispelled all darkness from my face. In Him I have acquired eyes and have seen His holy day: ⁴Ears have become mine and I have heard His truth. ⁵The thought of knowledge has been mine, ‖ And I have been delighted through Him. ⁶I have left the way of error, ‖ And have walked toward Him, ‖ And have received salvation from Him without grudging. ⁷And according to His bounty He has given to me, ‖ And according to His excellent beauty He has made me. ⁸I have put on incorruption through His Name, ‖ And have put off corruption by His grace. ⁹Death has been destroyed before my face, ‖ And Sheol has been abolished by my word; ¹⁰And there has gone up deathless life in the Lord's land, ¹¹And it has been made known to His faithful ones, ‖ And has been given without limit to all those that trust in Him. Hallelujah!

ODE 16

¹As the work of the farmer is the plowshare, ‖ And the work of the helmsman is the guidance of the ship, ²So also my work, my craft, is the psalm of the Lord, ³Because His love has nourished my heart, ‖ And even to my lips He poured out His fruits. ⁴For my love is the Lord, ‖ And I will therefore sing to Him: ⁵For I am made strong in His praise, ‖ And I have faith in Him. ⁶I will open my mouth and His Spirit will utter in me ‖ The glory of the Lord and His beauty, ‖ The work of His hands and the operation of His fingers, ⁷The multitude of His mercies and the strength of His word. ⁸For the Word of the Lord searches out all things, ‖ Both the invisible and that which reveals His thought, ⁹For the eye sees His works and the ear hears His thought. ¹⁰He spread out the earth and settled the waters in the sea; ¹¹He measured the heavens and fixed the stars; And He established the creation and set it up; ¹²And He rested from His works. ¹³Thus created things run in their courses, ‖ And do their works: ¹⁴And they do not know how to stand and be idle; And His heavenly hosts are subject to His Word. ¹⁵The treasure-chamber of the light is the sun, ‖ And the treasury of the darkness is the night; ¹⁶And He made the sun for the day that it may be bright, ‖ But night brings darkness over the face of the land; ¹⁷And their cycles, one after another, speak the beauty of God. ¹⁸And there is nothing that is without the Lord, For He was before anything came into being, ¹⁹And the worlds were made by His word, ‖ And by the thought of His heart. Glory and honor to His Name. Hallelujah!

ODE 17

¹I was crowned by My God—My crown is living; ²And I was justified in My Lord—My incorruptible salvation is He. ³I was loosed from vanity, ‖ And I was not condemned; ⁴The choking bonds were cut off by her hands. I received the face and the fashion of a new person, ‖ And I walked in it and was delivered. ⁵And the thought of truth led Me on; And I walked after it and did not wander. ⁶And all that have seen Me were amazed: And I was regarded by them as a strange person. ⁷And He who knew and brought Me up is the Most High in all His perfection. And He glorified Me by His kindness, ‖ And raised My thoughts to the height of His truth. ⁸And from there He gave Me the way of His precepts, ‖ And I opened the doors that were closed, ⁹And broke in pieces the bars of iron, ‖ But my iron melted and dissolved before Me; ¹⁰Nothing appeared closed to Me, ‖ Because I was the door of everything. ¹¹And I went over to all My bound ones to loose them, ‖ That I might not leave any man bound or binding. ¹²And I imparted My knowledge without grudging, ‖ And My prayer was in My love; ¹³And I sowed My fruits in hearts, ‖ And transformed them into Myself; And they received My blessing and lived; ¹⁴And they were gathered to Me and were saved, ‖ Because they were to Me as My own members, and I was their Head. Glory to You, our Head, the Lord Messiah. Hallelujah!

ODE 18

¹My heart was lifted up in the love of the Most High and was enlarged, ‖ That I might praise Him for His Name's sake. ²My members were strengthened that they might not fall from His strength. ³Sicknesses departed from my body, ‖ And it stood to the Lord by His will, ‖ For His kingdom is true. ⁴O Lord, for the sake of them that are deficient, do not remove Your word from me! ⁵Neither for the sake of their works do You restrain from me Your perfection! ⁶Do not let the luminary be conquered by the darkness, ‖ Nor let truth flee away from falsehood. ⁷You will appoint me to victory; Your right hand is our salvation. And You will receive men from all quarters. ⁸And You will preserve whosoever is held

in evils: [9] You are my God. Falsehood and death are not in Your mouth, [10] For Your will is perfection, || And You do not know vanity, [11] Nor does it know You. [12] And You do not know error, [13] Neither does it know You. [14] And ignorance appeared like a blind man, || And like the foam of the sea, [15] And they supposed of that vain thing that it was something great; [16] And they, too, came in likeness of it and became vain; And those have understood who have known and meditated; [17] And they have not been corrupt in their imagination, || For such were in the mind of the LORD; [18] And they mocked at them that were walking in error; [19] And they spoke truth from the inspiration which the Most High breathed into them. Praise and great honor to His Name. Hallelujah!

ODE 19

[1] A cup of milk was offered to me, || And I drank it in the sweetness of the delight of the LORD. [2] The Son is the cup and He who was milked is the Father: [3] And the Holy Spirit milked Him, || Because His breasts were full, || And it was necessary for Him that His milk should be sufficiently released; [4] And the Holy Spirit opened His bosom and mingled the milk from the two breasts of the Father and gave the mixture to the world without their knowing: [5] And they who receive in its fullness are the ones on the right hand. [6] The Spirit opened the womb of the virgin and she received conception and brought forth; And the virgin became a mother with many mercies; [7] And she travailed and brought forth a Son without incurring pain; [8] And because she was not sufficiently prepared, || And she had not sought a midwife (for He brought her to bear) she brought forth, || As if she were a man, of her own will; [9] And she brought Him forth openly, || And acquired Him with great dignity, [10] And loved Him in His swaddling clothes and guarded Him kindly, || And showed Him in Majesty. Hallelujah!

ODE 20

[1] I am a priest of the LORD, || And to Him I do priestly service: And to Him I offer the sacrifice of His thought. [2] For His thought is not like the thought of the world nor the thought of the flesh, || Nor like them that serve carnally. [3] The sacrifice of the LORD is righteousness, || And purity of heart and lips. [4] Present your reins before Him blamelessly, || And do not let your heart do violence to heart, || Nor your soul to soul. [5] You will not acquire a stranger by the price of your silver, || Neither will you seek to devour your neighbor, [6] Neither will you deprive him of the covering of his nakedness. [7] But put on the grace of the LORD without limit; And come into His Paradise and make a garland from its tree; [8] And put it on your head and be glad; And recline on His rest, || And glory will go before you, [9] And you will receive of His kindness and of His grace; And you will be

flourishing in truth in the praise of His holiness. Praise and honor be to His Name. Hallelujah!

ODE 21

[1] I lifted up my arms to the Most High, || Even to the grace of the LORD, || Because He had cast off my bonds from me, || And my Helper had lifted me up to His grace and to His salvation. [2] And I put off darkness and clothed myself with light, [3] And my soul acquired a body free from sorrow, or affliction, or pains. [4] And increasingly helpful to me was the thought of the LORD, || And His fellowship in incorruption: [5] And I was lifted up in His light; And I served before Him, [6] And I became near to Him, || Praising and confessing Him; [7] My heart ran over and was found in my mouth, || And it arose on my lips, || And the exultation of the LORD increased on my face, || And His praise likewise. Hallelujah!

ODE 22

[1] He who brought Me down from on high, || Also brought Me up from the regions below; [2] And He who gathers together the things that are in between is He who also cast Me down; [3] He who scattered My enemies and My adversaries had existed from ancient [times]. [4] He who gave Me authority over bonds that I might loose them, [5] He that overthrew the dragon with seven heads by My hands, || And set Me over his roots that I might destroy his seed— [6] You were there and helped Me, || And in every place Your Name was a rampart to Me. [7] Your right hand destroyed his wicked poison; And Your hand leveled the way for those who believe in You. [8] And You chose them from the graves and separated them from the dead. [9] You took dead bones and covered them with bodies. [10] They were motionless, || And You gave them energy for life. [11] Your way and Your face were without corruption; You brought Your world to corruption, || That everything might be dissolved, and then renewed, [12] And that the foundation for everything might be Your rock: And on it You built Your Kingdom; And it became the dwelling-place of the holy ones. Hallelujah!

ODE 23

[1] Joy is of the holy ones! And who will put it on, but they alone? [2] Grace is of the chosen ones! And who will receive it except those who trust in it from the beginning? [3] Love is of the chosen ones! And who will put it on except those who have possessed it from the beginning? [4] Walk in the knowledge of the Most High without grudging: To His exultation and to the perfection of His knowledge. [5] And His thought was like a letter; His will descended from on high, || And it was sent like an arrow which is violently [shot] from the bow: [6] And many hands rushed to the letter to seize it and to take and read it, [7] And it escaped their fingers, and they were frightened at it and at the seal

that was on it, [8] Because it was not permitted to them to loose its seal, || For the power that was over the seal was greater than they. [9] But those who saw it went after the letter that they might know where it would descend, || And who should read it and who should hear it. [10] But a wheel received it and came over it: [11] And there was with it a sign of the Kingdom and of the government, [12] And everything which tried to move the wheel it mowed and cut down. [13] And it gathered the multitude of adversaries, || And bridged the rivers and crossed over, and rooted up many forests and made a broad path. [14] The head went down to the feet, for the wheel ran down to the feet, || And that which was a sign on it. [15] The letter was one of command, || For there were included in it all districts; [16] And there was seen at its head, || The Head which was revealed—even the Son of Truth from the Most High Father, [17] And He inherited and took possession of everything. And the thought of many was brought to nothing. [18] And all the apostates hastened and fled away. And those who persecuted and were enraged became extinct, [19] And the letter was a great volume, || Which was wholly written by the finger of God: [20] And the Name of the Father was on it, and of the Son and of the Holy Spirit, || To rule forever and ever. Hallelujah!

ODE 24

[1] The Dove fluttered over the Messiah, || Because He was her head; And she sang over Him and her voice was heard, [2] And the inhabitants were afraid, and the sojourners were moved, [3] The birds dropped their wings, and all creeping things died in their holes; And the abysses were opened which had been hidden, || And they cried to the LORD like women in travail: [4] And no food was given to them, || Because it did not belong to them; [5] And they sealed up the abysses with the seal of the LORD, || And they perished in the thought [of] those that had existed from ancient times, [6] For they were corrupt from the beginning; And the end of their corruption was life: [7] And each of them that was imperfect perished, || For it was not possible to give them a word that they might remain, [8] And the LORD destroyed the imaginations of all them that did not have the truth with them. [9] For they who were lifted up in their hearts were deficient in wisdom, and so they were rejected, || Because the truth was not with them. [10] For the LORD disclosed His way and spread His grace abroad: And those who understood it know His holiness. Hallelujah!

ODE 25

[1] I was rescued from my bonds and to You, my God, I fled, [2] For You are the right hand of my salvation and my helper. [3] You have restrained those that rise up against me, [4] And I will see him no longer, || Because Your face was with me, || Which saved me by Your grace. [5] But I was despised and rejected in the eyes of many, || And I was like lead in their eyes, [6] And strength was mine from Yourself and [Your] help. [7] You set a lamp at my right hand and at my left, || And in me there will be nothing that is not bright. [8] And I was clothed with the covering of Your Spirit, || And You removed my raiment of skin from me; [9] For Your right hand lifted me up and removed sickness from me, [10] And I became mighty in the truth, || And holy by Your righteousness; And all my adversaries were afraid of me. [11] And I became admirable by the Name of the LORD, || And I was justified by His gentleness, || And His rest is forever and ever. Hallelujah!

ODE 26

[1] I poured out praise to the LORD, for I am His: [2] And I will speak His holy song for my heart is with Him. [3] For His harp is in my hands, || And the odes of His rest will not be silent. [4] I will cry to Him from my whole heart; I will praise and exalt Him with all my members. [5] For from the east and even to the west is His praise; [6] And from the south and even to the north is the confession of Him; [7] And from the top of the hills to their utmost bound is His perfection. [8] Who can write the psalms of the LORD, || Or who read them? [9] Or who can train his soul for life that his soul may be saved? [10] Or who can press on the Most High, || So that with His mouth He may speak? [11] Who is able to interpret the wonders of the LORD? [12] For he who could interpret would be dissolved and would become that which is interpreted. [13] For it suffices to know and to rest, || For in rest the singers stand, [14] Like a river which has an abundant fountain, || And flows to the help of them that seek it. Hallelujah!

ODE 27

[1] I stretched out my hands and sanctified my Lord, [2] For the extension of my hands is His sign: [3] And my expansion is the upright tree [[or cross]].

ODE 28

[1] As the wings of doves over their nestlings, || And the mouth of their nestlings toward their mouths, [2] So are also the wings of the Spirit over my heart. [3] My heart is delighted and exults || Like the baby who exults in the womb of his mother. [4] I believed, therefore I was at rest, || For He in whom I have believed is faithful. [5] He has richly blessed me, and my head is with Him, || And the sword will not divide me from Him, || Nor the scimitar, [6] For I am ready before destruction comes; And I have been set on His immortal pinions. [7] And He showed me His sign: [Poured] forth and given me to drink, || And from that life is the spirit within me and it cannot die, for it lives. [8] They who saw me marveled at me, || Because I was persecuted, || And they supposed that I was swallowed up, || For I seemed to them as one of the lost; [9] And my oppression became my salvation; And I was their

reprobation because there was no seal in me. [10] I was hated because I did good to every man, [11] And they came around me like mad dogs || Who ignorantly attack their masters, [12] For their thought is corrupt and their understanding perverted. [13] But I was carrying water in my right hand and their bitterness I endured by my sweetness: [14] And I did not perish, || For I was not their brother nor was my birth like theirs. [15] And they sought for my death and did not find it, || For I was older than the memorial of them; [16] And vainly did they make attack on me, || And those who, without reward, came after me: [17] They sought to destroy the memorial of Him who was before them. [18] For the thought of the Most High cannot be anticipated; And His heart is superior to all wisdom. Hallelujah!

ODE 29

[1] The LORD is my hope: In Him I will not be confounded. [2] For according to His praise He made me, || And according to His goodness even so He gave to me, [3] And according to His mercies He exalted me, || And according to His excellent beauty He set me on high, [4] And brought me up out of the depths of Sheol, || And from the mouth of death He drew me. [5] And You laid my enemies low, || And He justified me by His grace. [6] For I believed in the LORD's Messiah: And it appeared to me that He is the LORD. [7] And He showed me His sign, || And He led me by His light, || And gave me the rod of His power [8] That I might subdue the imaginations of the peoples, || And the power of the men of might, to bring them low, [9] To make war by His word, || And to take victory by His power. [10] And the LORD overthrew my enemy by His word: And he became like the stubble which the wind carries away; [11] And I gave praise to the Most High because He exalted me—His servant and the son of His handmaid. Hallelujah!

ODE 30

[1] Fill waters for yourselves from the living fountain of the LORD, || For it is opened to you: [2] And come all you thirsty and take the drink; And rest by the fountain of the LORD. [3] For it is fair and pure and gives rest to the soul. Its waters are much more pleasant than honey; [4] And the honeycomb of bees is not to be compared with it. [5] For it flows forth from the lips of the LORD, || And from the heart of the LORD is its name. [6] And it came infinitely and invisibly: And until it was set in the midst, they did not know it. [7] Blessed are they who have drunk from that and have found rest thereby. Hallelujah!

ODE 31

[1] The abysses were dissolved before the LORD, || And darkness was destroyed by His appearance. [2] Error went astray and perished at His hand, || And folly found no path to walk in, || And was submerged by the truth of the LORD. [3] He opened His mouth and spoke grace and joy: And He spoke a new song of praise to His Name. [4] And He lifted up His voice to the Most High, || And offered the sons that were with Him. [5] And His face was justified, || For thus His holy Father had given to Him. [6] Come forth, you that have been afflicted, and receive joy, || And possess your souls by His grace; And take immortal life to yourself. [7] And they made Me a debtor when I rose up—Me who had been a debtor: And they divided My spoil, || Though nothing was due to them. [8] But I endured, and held My peace, and was silent as if not moved by them. [9] But I stood unshaken like a firm rock which is beaten by the waves and endures. [10] And I bore their bitterness for humility's sake, [11] In order that I might redeem My people and inherit it, || And that I might not make void My promises || To the fathers to whom I promised the salvation of their seed. Hallelujah!

ODE 32

[1] To the blessed there is joy from their hearts, || And light from Him that dwells in them, [2] And words from the Truth, who was self-existent; For He is strengthened by the holy power of the Most High: And He is unmoved forever and ever. Hallelujah!

ODE 33

[1] Again Grace ran and renounced the corruptor, || And came down on him to bring him to nothing— [2] And he who caused destruction [and] perdition from before him, || And devastated all his order. [3] And he stood on a lofty summit || And uttered his voice from one end of the earth to the other, [4] And drew to himself all those who obeyed him, || For he did not appear as [the] evil one. [5] But there stood a perfect virgin who was proclaiming, and calling, and saying, [6] "O you sons of men, return! And you daughters of men, come! [7] And forsake the ways of that corruptor and draw near to me, || And I will enter into you, || And will bring you forth from perdition, [8] And make yourself wise in the ways of truth, || That you are not destroyed nor perish. [9] Hear me and be redeemed! For I am telling of the Grace of God among you": And by My means you will be redeemed and become blessed. [10] I am your Judge; And they who have put Me on will not be injured, || But they will possess the new world that is incorruptible. [11] My chosen ones walk in Me, || And I will make known My ways to them that seek Me, || And I will make them trust in My Name. Hallelujah!

ODE 34

[1] No way is hard where there is a simple heart, [2] Nor is there any wound where the thoughts are upright, [3] Nor is there any storm in the depth of the illuminated thought. [4] Where one is surrounded on every side by beauty, || There is nothing that is divided. [5] The likeness of what is below is that which is above, || For

everything is above. What is below is nothing but the imagination of those that are without knowledge. [6] Grace has been revealed for your salvation. Believe, and live, and be saved. Hallelujah!

ODE 35

[1] In quietness He distilled the dew of the LORD on me, [2] And He caused the cloud of peace to rise over my head, || Which guarded me continually; [3] It was to me for salvation: Everything was shaken, and they were frightened; [4] And there came forth from them smoke and judgment; And I was keeping quiet in the order of the LORD. [5] He was more than a shelter to me and more than a foundation. [6] And I was carried like a child by its mother: And He gave me milk, || The dew of the LORD, [7] And I grew great by His bounty, || And rested in His perfection, [8] And I spread out my hands in the lifting up of my soul: And I was made right with the Most High, || And I was redeemed with Him. Hallelujah!

ODE 36

[1] I rested in the Spirit of the LORD, || And the Spirit raised Me on high, [2] And made Me stand on My feet in the height of the LORD, || Before His perfection and His glory, || While I was praising Him by the composition of His songs. [3] The Spirit brought Me forth before the face of the LORD, || And, although [the] Son of Man, || I was [also] named the Illuminate, the Son of God, [4] While I was praised among the praising ones, || And I was great among the mighty ones. [5] For according to the greatness of the Most High, || So He made Me; And like His own newness He renewed Me, || And He anointed Me from His own perfection. [6] And I became one of His neighbors; And My mouth was opened like a cloud of dew, [7] And my heart poured out as it were a gushing stream of righteousness, [8] And my access to Him was in peace. And I was established by the Spirit of His government. Hallelujah!

ODE 37

[1] I stretched out my hands to my Lord, || And to the Most High I raised my voice: [2] And I spoke with the lips of my heart, || And He heard me when my voice reached Him; [3] His answer came to me and gave me the fruits of my labors; [4] And it gave me rest by the grace of the LORD. Hallelujah!

ODE 38

[1] I went up to the light of Truth as if into a chariot: [2] And the Truth took me and led me, || And carried me across pits and ravines; And from the rocks and the waves He preserved me. [3] And He became to me a haven of salvation, || And He set me on the arms of immortal life; [4] And He went with me and made me rest, || And did not permit me to wander because He was and is the Truth. [5] And I ran no risk, || Because I walked with Him; [6] And I did not error in anything because I obeyed the Truth. [7] For error flees away from Him and does not meet Him, || But the Truth proceeds in the right path. [8] And whatever I did not know, He made clear to me, || All the poisons of error, || And the plagues of death which they think to be sweetness. [9] And I saw the destroying of the destroyer, || When the bride who is corrupted is adorned: And the bridegroom who corrupts and is corrupted. [10] And I asked the Truth, "Who are these?" And He said to me, "This is the deceiver and the error: [11] And they are alike in the beloved and in his bride; And they lead astray and corrupt the whole world. [12] And they invite many to the banquet, [13] And give them to drink of the wine of their intoxication, || And remove their wisdom and knowledge, || And so they make them without intelligence; [14] And then they leave them; And then these go about like madmen corrupting: Seeing that they are without heart, || Nor do they seek for it." [15] And I was made wise so as not to fall into the hands of the deceiver; And I congratulated myself because the Truth went with me, [16] And I was established, and lived, and was redeemed, [17] And my foundations were laid on the hand of the LORD, || Because He established me. [18] For He set the root, and watered it, and fixed it, and blessed it; And its fruits are forever. [19] It struck deep, and sprung up, and spread out, and was full and enlarged. [20] And the LORD alone was glorified in His planting and in His farming || By His care and by the blessing of His lips, [21] By the beautiful planting of His right hand, || And by the discovery of His planting, || And by the thought of His mind. Hallelujah!

ODE 39

[1] Great rivers are the power of the LORD: [2] And they carry headlong those who despise Him, || And entangle their paths; [3] And they sweep away their fords, || And catch their bodies, and destroy their lives. [4] For they are swifter than lightning and more rapid, || And those who cross them in faith are not moved; [5] And those who walk on them without blemish will not be afraid. [6] For the sign in them is the LORD; And the sign is the way of those who cross in the Name of the LORD; [7] Therefore put on the Name of the Most High, || And know Him and you will cross without danger, || For the rivers will be subject to you. [8] The LORD has bridged them by His word; And He walked and crossed them on foot: [9] And His footsteps stand firm on the water, || And are not injured; They are as firm as a tree that is truly set up. [10] And the waves were lifted up on this side and on that, || But the footsteps of our Lord Messiah stand firm, and are not obliterated, and are not defaced. [11] And a way has been appointed for those who cross after Him, and for those who adhere to the course of faith in Him and worship His Name. Hallelujah!

ODE 40

[1] As the honey distills from the comb of the bees, [2] And the milk flows from the woman that loves her children; [3] So also is my hope on You, my God. [4] As the fountain gushes out its water, [5] So my heart gushes out the praise of the LORD, and my lips utter praise to Him, || And my tongue His psalms, [6] And my face exults with His gladness, and my spirit exults in His love, and my soul shines in Him. [7] And reverence confides in Him, || And redemption stands assured in Him. [8] And His inheritance is immortal life, || And those who participate in it are incorruptible. Hallelujah!

ODE 41

[1] All the LORD's children will praise Him, || And will collect the truth of His faith. [2] And His children will be known to Him. Therefore, we will sing in His love. [3] We live in the LORD by His grace, || And we receive life in His Messiah. [4] For a great day has shined on us: And marvelous is He who has given us of His glory. [5] Therefore, let all of us unite together in the Name of the LORD, || And let us honor Him in His goodness, [6] And let our faces shine in His light, || And let our hearts meditate in His love by night and by day. [7] Let us exult with the joy of the LORD. [8] All those that see me will be astonished, || For I am from another race; [9] For the Father of truth remembered me—He who possessed me from the beginning. [10] For His bounty begot me, || And the thought of His heart. [11] And His Word is with us in all our ways— [12] The Savior who makes alive and does not reject our souls; [13] The Man who was humbled, || And exalted by His own righteousness. [14] The Son of the Most High appeared in the perfection of His Father, [15] And light dawned from the Word that was before time in Him. [16] The Messiah is truly one; And He was known before the foundation of the world, [17] That He might save souls forever by the truth of His Name: A new song arises from those who love Him. Hallelujah!

ODE 42

[1] I stretched out my hands and approached my Lord, [2] For the stretching of my hands is His sign. [2] My expansion is the outspread tree [[or cross]], which was set up on the way of the Righteous One. [4] And I became of no account to those who did not take hold of Me and I will be with those who love Me. [5] All my persecutors are dead; And they sought after Me who hoped in Me, || Because I was alive. [6] And I rose up and am with them; And I will speak by their mouths, [7] For they have despised those who persecuted them. [8] And I lifted up over them the yoke of My love. [9] Like the arm of the bridegroom over the bride, [10] So was My yoke over those that know Me; [11] And as the couch that is spread in the house of the bridegroom and bride, [12] So is My love over those that believe in Me. [13] And I was not rejected though I was reckoned to be so. [14] I did not perish [forever], || Though they devised it against Me. [15] Sheol saw Me and was made miserable: [16] Death cast Me up and many along with Me. [17] I had gall and bitterness, || And I went down with him to the utmost of his depth: [18] And the feet and the head he let go, || For they were not able to endure My face. [19] And I made a congregation of living men among his dead men, || And I spoke with them by living lips, [20] Because My word will not be void. [21] And those who had died ran toward Me, || And they cried and said, "Son of God, have pity on us, || And do with us according to Your kindness. [22] And bring us out from the bonds of darkness, || And open to us the door by which we will come out to You. [23] For we see that our death has not touched You. [24] Let us also be redeemed with You, || For You are our Redeemer." [25] And I heard their voice, || And I sealed My Name on their heads; [26] For they are free men, and they are Mine. Hallelujah!

APOLOGY OF ARISTIDES

The Apology of Aristides the Philosopher is the earliest complete apologetic still extant. It was written sometime between 117 and 138 AD and set the stage for all Christian apologetics to come. It may have even been the basis for a portion of the Apostles' Creed.

ALL-POWERFUL CAESAR TITUS HADRIANUS ANTONINUS, VENERABLE AND MERCIFUL, FROM MARCIANUS ARISTIDES, AN ATHENIAN PHILOSOPHER:

CHAPTER 1

[1] I, O King, by the grace of God came into this world; [2] and when I had considered the heavens, and the earth, and the seas, and had surveyed the sun and the rest of creation, [3] I marveled at the beauty of the world. [4] And I perceived that the world and all that is therein are moved by the power of another; [5] and I understood that He who moves them is God, who is hidden in them, and veiled by them. [6] And it is manifest that that which causes motion is more powerful than that which is moved. [7] But that I should make search concerning this same Mover of all, as to what is His nature (for it seems to me, He is indeed unsearchable in His nature), [8] and that I should argue as to the constancy of His government, so as to grasp it fully—this is a vain effort for me; [9] for it is not possible that a man should fully comprehend it. [10] I say, however, concerning this Mover of the world, that He is God of all, [11] who made all things for the sake of mankind. [12] And it seems to me that this is reasonable, that one should fear God and should not oppress man. [13] I say, then, that God is not born, not made, an ever-abiding nature without beginning and without end, immortal, perfect, and incomprehensible. [14] Now when I say that He is "perfect," this means that there is not in Him any defect, [15] and He is not in need of anything but all things are in need of Him. [16] And when I say that He is "without beginning," this means that everything which has beginning has also an end, and that which has an end may be brought to an end. [17] He has no name, for everything which has a name is related to things created. [18] He has no form, nor yet any union of members; for whatever possesses these is related to things fashioned. [19] He is neither male nor female. [20] The heavens do not limit Him, but the heavens and all things, visible and invisible, receive their bounds from Him. [21] He has no adversary, for there exists not any stronger than He. [22] Wrath and indignation He does not possess, for there is nothing which is able to stand against Him. [23] Ignorance and forgetfulness are not in His nature, for He is altogether wisdom and understanding; [24] and in Him stands fast all that exists. [25] He requires not sacrifice and libation, nor even one of things visible; [26] He requires not anything from any, but all living creatures stand in need of Him.

CHAPTER 2

[1] Since, then, we have addressed you concerning God, so far as our discourse can bear on Him, [2] let us now come to the race of men, that we may know which of them participate in the truth of which we have spoken, and which of them go astray from it. [3] This is clear to you, O King, that there are four classes of men in this world: Barbarians and Greeks, Jews and Christians. [4] The Barbarians, indeed, trace the origin of their kind of religion from Kronos and from Rhea and their other gods; [5] the Greeks, however, from Helenos, who is said to be sprung from Zeus. [6] And by Helenos there were born Aiolos and Xuthos; [7] and there were others descended from Inachos and Phoroneus, [8] and lastly from the Egyptian Danaos and from Kadmos and from Dionysos. [9] The Jews, again, trace the origin of their race from Abraham, who begot Isaac, of whom was born Jacob. [10] And he begot twelve sons who migrated from Syria to Egypt; [11] and there they were called the nation of the Hebrews, by him who made their laws; [12] and at length they were named Jews. [13] The Christians, then, trace the beginning of their religion from Jesus the Messiah; [14] and He is named the Son of God Most High. [15] And it is said that God came down from Heaven, [16] and from a Hebrew virgin assumed and clothed Himself with flesh; [17] and the Son of God lived in a daughter of man. [18] This is taught in the Gospel, as it is called, which a short time was preached among them; [19] and you also if you will read therein, may perceive the power which belongs to it. [20] This Jesus, then, was born of the race of the Hebrews; [21] and He had twelve disciples in order that the purpose of His incarnation might in time be accomplished. [22] But He Himself was pierced by the Jews, and He died and was buried; [23] and they say that after three days He rose and [later] ascended to Heaven. [24] Thereon these twelve disciples went forth throughout the known parts of the world and kept showing His greatness with all modesty and uprightness. [25] And hence also those of the present day who believe that preaching are called Christians, and they have become famous. [26] So then there are, as I said above, four classes of men: Barbarians and Greeks, Jews and Christians. [27] Moreover the wind is obedient to God, and fire to the messengers; the waters also to the demons and the earth to the sons of men.

CHAPTER 3

[1] Let us begin, then, with the Barbarians, and go on to the rest of the nations one after another, [2] that we may see which of them hold the truth as to God and which of them hold error. [3] The Barbarians, then, as they did not apprehend God, went astray among the elements, [4] and began to worship things created instead of their Creator; [5] and for this end they made images and shut them up in shrines, and behold, they worship them, [6] guarding them the while with much care, lest their gods be stolen by robbers. [7] And the Barbarians did not observe that that which acts as guard is greater than that which is guarded, [8] and that everyone who creates is greater than that which is created. [9] If it be, then, that their gods are too feeble to see to their own safety, how will they take thought for the safety of men? [10] Great then is the error into which the Barbarians wandered in worshiping lifeless images which can do nothing to help them. [11] And I am led to wonder, O King, at their philosophers, how that even they went astray, and gave the name of gods to images which were made in honor of the elements; [12] and that their sages did not perceive that the elements are also dissoluble and perishable. [13] For if a small part of an element is dissolved or destroyed, the whole of it may be dissolved and destroyed. [14] If then the elements themselves are dissolved and destroyed and forced to be subject to another that is more stubborn than they, [15] and if they are not in their nature gods, why, indeed, do they call the images which are made in their honor, God? [16] Great, then, is the error which the philosophers among them have brought on their followers.

CHAPTER 4

[1] Let us turn now, O King, to the elements in themselves, [2] that we may make clear in regard to them, that they are not gods, but a created thing, liable to ruin and change, which is of the same nature as man; [3] whereas God is imperishable and unvarying, and invisible, while yet He sees, and overrules, and transforms all things. [4] Those then who believe concerning the earth that it is a god have until now deceived themselves, [5] since it is furrowed and set with plants and trenched; [6] and it takes in the filthy refuse of men and beasts and cattle. [7] And at times it becomes unfruitful, for if it be burned to ashes it becomes devoid of life, [8] for nothing germinates from an earthen jar. [9] And besides if water be collected on it, it is dissolved together with its products. [10] And behold, it is trodden under foot of men and beast, and receives the blood of the slain; [11] and it is dug open, and filled with the dead, and becomes a tomb for corpses. [12] But it is impossible that a nature, which is holy and worthy and blessed and immortal, should allow of any one of these things. [13] And hence it appears to us that the earth is not a god but a creation of God.

CHAPTER 5

[1] In the same way, again, those erred who believed the waters to be gods. [2] For the waters were created for the use of man, and are put under his rule in many ways. [3] For they suffer change and admit impurity, and are destroyed and lose their nature while they are boiled into many substances. [4] And they take colors which do not belong to them; [5] they are also congealed by frost and are mingled and permeated with the filth of men and beasts, and with the blood of the slain. [6] And being checked by skilled workmen through the restraint of aqueducts, they flow and are diverted against their inclination, [7] and come into gardens and other places in order that they may be collected and issue forth as a means of fertility for man, [8] and that they may cleanse away every impurity and fulfill the service man requires from them. [9] For what reason it is impossible that the waters should be a god, but they are a work of God and a part of the world. [10] In like manner also they who believed that fire is a god erred to no slight extent. [11] For it, too, was created for the service of men, and is subject to them in many ways: in the preparation of meats, and as a means of casting metals, and for other ends of which your Majesty is aware. [12] At the same time it is quenched and extinguished in many ways. [13] Again they also erred who believed the motion of the winds to be a god. [14] For it is well known to us that those winds are under the dominion of another, [15] at times their motion increases, and at times it fails and ceases at the command of Him who controls them. [16] For they were created by God for the sake of men, in order to supply the necessity of trees and fruits and seeds; [17] and to bring over the sea ships which transport for men necessities and goods from places where they are found to places where they are not found; [18] and to govern the quarters of the world. [19] And as for itself, at times it increases and again abates; [20] and in one place brings help and in another causes disaster at the bidding of Him who rules it. [21] And mankind is also able by known means to confine and keep it in check in order that it may fulfill for them the service they require from it. [22] And of itself it does not have any authority at all. [23] And hence it is impossible that the winds should be called gods, but rather a thing made by God.

CHAPTER 6

[1] So also, they erred who believed that the sun is a god. [2] For we see that it is moved by the compulsion of another, and revolves and makes its journey, [3] and proceeds from sign to sign, rising and setting every day, so as to give warmth for the growth of plants and trees, [4] and to bring forth into the air with which it [(sunlight)] is mingled every growing thing which is on the earth. [5] And to it there belongs by comparison a part in common with the rest of the stars in its course; [6] and though it is one in its nature it is

associated with many parts for the supply of the needs of men; [7] and that not according to its own will but rather according to the will of Him who rules it. [8] And hence it is impossible that the sun should be a god, but the work of God; [9] and in like manner also the moon and the stars.

CHAPTER 7

[1] And those who believed of the men of the past, that some of them were gods, they too were much mistaken. [2] For as you yourself allow, O King, man is constituted of the four elements, and of a soul and a spirit (and hence he is called a microcosm), [3] and without any one of these parts he could not consist. [4] He has a beginning and an end, and he is born and dies. [5] But God, as I said, has none of these things in His nature, but is uncreated and imperishable. [6] And hence it is not possible that we should set up man to be of the nature of God— [7] man, to whom at times when he looks for joy, there comes trouble, and when he looks for laughter there comes to him weeping, [8] who is wrathful and covetous and envious, with other defects as well. [9] And he is destroyed in many ways by the elements and also by the animals. [10] And hence, O King, we are bound to recognize the error of the Barbarians, [11] that thereby, since they did not find traces of the true God, they fell aside from the truth, and went after the desire of their imagination, [12] serving the perishable elements and lifeless images, and through their error not apprehending what the true God is.

CHAPTER 8

[1] Let us turn further to the Greeks also, that we may know what opinion they hold as to the true God. [2] The Greeks, then, because they are more subtle than the Barbarians, have gone further astray than the Barbarians; [3] inasmuch as they have introduced many fictitious gods, and have set up some of them as males and some as females; [4] and in that some of their gods were found who were adulterers, and did murder, and were deluded, and envious, and wrathful and passionate, and parricides, and thieves, and robbers. [5] And some of them, they say, were crippled and limped, and some were sorcerers, and some actually went mad, and some played on lyres, and some were given to roaming on the hills, and some even died, and some were struck dead by lightning, and some were made servants even to men, and some escaped by flight, and some were kidnapped by men, and some, indeed, were lamented and deplored by men. [6] And some, they say, went down to Sheol, and some were grievously wounded, and some transformed themselves into the likeness of animals to seduce the race of mortal women, and some polluted themselves by lying with males. [7] And some, they say, were wedded to their mothers and their sisters and their daughters. [8] And they say of their gods that they committed adultery with the daughters of men; [9] and of these there was born a certain race which also was mortal. [10] And they say that some of the females disputed about beauty and appeared before men for judgment. [11] Thus, O King, have the Greeks put forward foulness, and absurdity, and folly about their gods and about themselves, in that they have called those that are of such a nature gods, who are not gods. [12] And hence mankind has received incitements to commit adultery and fornication, and to steal and to practice all that is offensive and hated and abhorred. [13] For if they who are called their gods practiced all these things which are written above, how much more should men practice them— [14] men, who believe that their gods themselves practiced them. [15] And owing to the foulness of this error there have happened to mankind harassing wars, and great famines, and bitter captivity, and complete desolation. [16] And behold, it was by reason of this alone that they suffered and that all these things came on them; [17] and while they endured those things they did not perceive in their mind that for their error those things came on them.

CHAPTER 9

[1] Let us proceed further to their account of their gods that we may carefully demonstrate all that is said above. [2] First of all, the Greeks bring forward as a god Kronos, that is to say Chiun [(Saturn)]. [3] And his worshipers sacrifice their children to him, and they burn some of them alive in his honor. [4] And they say that he took to himself among his wives Rhea, and begot many children by her. [5] By her too he begot Dios, who is called Zeus. [6] And at length he [(Kronos)] went mad, and through fear of an oracle that had been made known to him, he began to devour his sons. [7] And from him Zeus was stolen away without his knowledge; [8] and at length Zeus bound him, and mutilated the signs of his manhood, and flung them into the sea. [9] And hence, as they say in a fable, there was engendered Aphrodite, who is called Astarte. [10] And he [(Zeus)] cast out Kronos bound into darkness. [11] Great then is the error and ignominy which the Greeks have brought forward about the first of their gods, [12] in that they have said all this about him, O King. [13] It is impossible that a god should be bound or mutilated; and if it be otherwise, he is indeed miserable. [14] And after Kronos they bring forward another god Zeus. [15] And they say of him that he assumed the sovereignty and was king over all the gods. [16] And they say that he changed himself into a beast and other shapes in order to seduce mortal women, and to raise up by them children for himself. [17] Once, they say, he changed himself into a bull through love of Europe and Pasiphae. [18] And again he changed himself into the likeness of gold through love of Danae, and to a swan through love of Leda, and to a man through love of Antiope, and to lightning through love of Luna, [19] and so by these he begot

APOLOGY OF ARISTIDES

many children. [20] For by Antiope, they say, that he begot Zethus and Amphion, and by Luna Dionysos, by Alcmena Hercules, [21] and by Leto, Apollo and Artemis, and by Danae Perseus, and by Leda, Castor and Polydeuces, and Helene and Paludus, [22] and by Mnemosyne he begot nine daughters whom they styled the Muses, [23] and by Europe, Minos and Rhadamanthos and Sarpedon. [24] And lastly, he changed himself into the likeness of an eagle through his passion for Ganydemos [(Ganymede)] the shepherd. [25] By reason of these tales, O King, much evil has arisen among men, who to this day are imitators of their gods, [26] and practice adultery and defile themselves with their mothers and their sisters, [27] and by lying with males, [28] and some make bold to slay even their parents. [29] For if he who is said to be the chief and king of their gods does these things, how much more should his worshipers imitate him? [30] And great is the folly which the Greeks have brought forward in their narrative concerning him. [31] For it is impossible that a god should practice adultery or fornication or come near to lie with males or kill his parents; [32] and if it be otherwise, he is much worse than a destructive demon.

CHAPTER 10

[1] Again they bring forward as another god Hephaistos. [2] And they say of him, that he is lame, and a cap is set on his head, and he holds in his hands firetongs and a hammer; [3] and he follows the craft of iron working, that thereby he may procure the necessities of his livelihood. [4] Is then this god so very needy? [5] But it cannot be that a god should be needy or lame, else he is very worthless. [6] And further they bring in another god and call him Hermes. [7] And they say that he is a thief, a lover of wealth, and greedy for gain, and a magician, and mutilated, and an athlete, and an interpreter of language. [8] But it is impossible that a god should be a magician, or greedy, or maimed, or craving for what is not his, or an athlete. [9] And if it be otherwise, he is found to be useless. [10] And after him they bring forward as another god Asclepius. [11] And they say that he is a physician and prepares drugs and plaster that he may supply the necessities of his livelihood. [12] Is then this god in want? [13] And at length he was struck with lightning by Dios on account of Tyndareos of Lacedaemon, and so he died. [14] If then Asclepius were a god, and, when he was struck with lightning, was unable to help himself, how should he be able to give help to others? [15] But that a divine nature should be in want or be destroyed by lightning is impossible. [16] And again they bring forward another as a god, and they call him Ares. [17] And they say that he is a warrior, and jealous, and covets sheep and things which are not his. [18] And he makes gain by his arms. [19] And they say that at length he committed adultery with Aphrodite, and was caught by the little boy Eros and by Hephaistos the husband of

Aphrodite. [20] But it is impossible that a god should be a warrior or bound or an adulterer. [21] And again they say of Dionysos that he, indeed, is a god, who arranges carousals by night, and teaches drunkenness, and carries off women who do not belong to him. [22] And at length, they say, he went mad and dismissed his handmaidens and fled into the desert; and during his madness he ate serpents. [23] And at last he was killed by Titanos. [24] If then Dionysos were a god, and when he was being killed was unable to help himself, how is it possible that he should help others? [25] Herakles next they bring forward and say that he is a god, who hates detestable things, a tyrant, and warrior and a destroyer of plagues. [26] And of him also they say that at length he became mad and killed his own children, and cast himself into a fire and died. [27] If then Herakles is a god, and in all these calamities was unable to rescue himself, how should others ask help from him? [28] But it is impossible that a god should be mad, or drunken, or a slayer of his children, or consumed by fire.

CHAPTER 11

[1] And after him they bring forward another god and call him Apollo. [2] And they say that he is jealous and inconstant, and at times he holds the bow and quiver, and again the lyre and plectron. [3] And he utters oracles for men that he may receive rewards from them. [4] Is then this god in need of rewards? [5] But it is an insult that all these things should be found with a god. [6] And after him they bring forward as a goddess Artemis, the sister of Apollo; [7] and they say that she was a huntress and that she herself used to carry a bow and bolts, and to roam about on the mountains, leading the hounds to hunt stags or wild bears of the field. [8] But it is disgraceful that a virgin maid should roam alone on the hills or hunt in the chase for animals. [9] For what reason it is impossible that Artemis should be a goddess. [10] Again they say of Aphrodite that she indeed is a goddess. [11] And at times she dwells with their gods, but at other times she is a neighbor to men. [12] And once she had Ares as a lover, and again Adonis who is Tammuz. [13] Once also, Aphrodite was wailing and weeping for the death of Tammuz, and they say that she went down to Sheol that she might redeem Adonis from Persephone, who is the daughter of Sheol [(Hades)]. [14] If then Aphrodite is a goddess and was unable to help her lover at his death, how will she find it possible to help others? [15] And this cannot be listened to, that a divine nature should come to weeping and wailing and adultery. [16] And again they say of Tammuz that he is a god. [17] And he is, indeed, a hunter and an adulterer. [18] And they say that he was killed by a wound from a wild boar, without being able to help himself. [19] And if he could not help himself, how can he take thought for the human race? [20] But that a god should be an adulterer or a hunter or should die by violence is impossible. [21] Again they say

of Rhea that she is the mother of their gods. ²² And they say that she had once a lover Atys, and that she used to delight in depraved men. ²³ And at last she raised a lamentation and mourned for Atys her lover. ²⁴ If then the mother of their gods was unable to help her lover and deliver him from death, how can she help others? ²⁵ So it is disgraceful that a goddess should lament and weep and take delight in depraved men. ²⁶ Again they introduce Kore and say that she is a goddess, and she was stolen away by Pluto, and could not help herself. ²⁷ If then she is a goddess and was unable to help herself how will she find means to help others? ²⁸ For a god who is stolen away is very powerless. ²⁹ All this, then, O King, have the Greeks brought forward concerning their gods, ³⁰ and they have invented and declared it concerning them. ³¹ And hence all men received an impulse to work all profanity and all defilements; and hereby the whole earth was corrupted.

CHAPTER 12

¹ The Egyptians, moreover, because they are more base and stupid than every people that is on the earth, have themselves erred more than all. ² For the deities [[or religion]] of the Barbarians and the Greeks did not suffice for them, but they introduced some also of the nature of the animals, and said thereof that they were gods, ³ and likewise of creeping things which are found on the dry land and in the waters. ⁴ And of plants and herbs they said that some of them were gods. ⁵ And they were corrupted by every kind of delusion and defilement more than every people that is on the earth. ⁶ For from ancient times they worshiped Isis, and they say that she is a goddess whose husband was Osiris her brother. ⁷ And when Osiris was killed by Typhon his brother, Isis fled with Horos her son to Byblos in Syria, and was there for a certain time until her son was grown. ⁸ And he contended with Typhon his uncle, and killed him. ⁹ And then Isis returned and went around with Horos her son and sought for the dead body of Osiris her lord, bitterly lamenting his death. ¹⁰ If then Isis be a goddess, and could not help Osiris her brother and lord, how can she help another? ¹¹ But it is impossible that a divine nature should be afraid, and flee for safety, or should weep and wail; or else it is very miserable. ¹² And of Osiris also they say that he is a serviceable god. ¹³ And he was killed by Typhon and was unable to help himself. ¹⁴ But it is well known that this cannot be asserted of divinity. ¹⁵ And further, they say of his brother Typhon that he is a god, who killed his brother and was killed by his brother's son and by his bride, being unable to help himself. ¹⁶ And how, pray, is he a god who does not save himself? ¹⁷ As the Egyptians, then, were more stupid than the rest of the nations, these and such like gods did not suffice for them. ¹⁸ No, but they even apply the name of gods to animals in which there is no soul at all. ¹⁹ For some of

them worship the sheep and others the calf; ²⁰ and some the pig and others the shad fish; ²¹ and some the crocodile, and the hawk, and the fish, and the ibis, and the vulture, and the eagle, and the raven. ²² Some of them worship the cat, and others the turbot-fish, some the dog, some the adder, and some the asp, and others the lion; ²³ and others the garlic, and onions, and thorns, ²⁴ and others the tiger and other such things. ²⁵ And the poor creatures do not see that all these things are nothing, ²⁶ although they daily witness their gods being eaten and consumed by men and also by their fellows; ²⁷ while some of them are cremated, and some die and decay and become dust, without their observing that they perish in many ways. ²⁸ So the Egyptians have not observed that such things which are not equal to their own deliverance, are not gods. ²⁹ And if, indeed, they are weak in the case of their own deliverance, from where have they power to help in the case of deliverance of their worshipers? ³⁰ Great then is the error into which the Egyptians wandered—greater, indeed, than that of any people which is on the face of the earth.

CHAPTER 13

¹ But it is a marvel, O King, with regard to the Greeks, who surpass all other peoples in their manner of life and reasoning, how they have gone astray after dead idols and lifeless images. ² And yet they see their gods in the hands of their craftsmen being sawn out, and planed and docked, and hacked short, and charred, and ornamented, and being altered by them in every kind of way. ³ And when they grow old, and are worn away through lapse of time, and when they are molten and crushed to powder, how, I wonder, did they not perceive concerning them, that they are not gods? ⁴ And as for those who did not find deliverance for themselves, how can they serve the distress of men? ⁵ But even the writers and philosophers among them have wrongly alleged that the gods are such as are made in honor of God Almighty. ⁶ And they err in seeking to liken [them] to God whom man has not at any time seen nor can see to what He is like. ⁷ Herein too [they err] in asserting of deity that any such thing as deficiency can be present to it; ⁸ as when they say that He receives sacrifice and requires burnt-offering and libation and immolations of men, and temples. ⁹ But God is not in need, and none of these things is necessary to Him; ¹⁰ and it is clear that men err in these things they imagine. ¹¹ Further their writers and their philosophers represent and declare that the nature of all their gods is one. ¹² And they have not apprehended God our Lord who while He is one, is in all. They err therefore. ¹³ For if the body of a man while it is many in its parts is not in dread, one member of another, but, since it is a united body, wholly agrees with itself; even so also God is one in His nature. ¹⁴ A single essence is proper to Him, since He is uniform in His nature and His essence; ¹⁵ and He

is not afraid of Himself. [16] If then the nature of the gods is one, it is not proper that a god should either pursue or slay or harm a god. [17] If then gods be pursued and wounded by gods, and some be kidnapped, and some struck dead by lightning, it is obvious that the nature of their gods is not one. [18] And hence it is known, O King, that it is a mistake when they reckon and bring the natures of their gods under a single nature. [19] If then it becomes us to admire a god which is seen and does not see, [20] how much more praiseworthy is it that one should believe in a nature which is invisible and all-seeing? [21] And if further it is fitting that one should approve the handiworks of a craftsman, how much more is it fitting that one should glorify the Creator of the craftsman? [22] For behold, when the Greeks made laws, they did not perceive that by their laws they condemn their gods. [23] For if their laws are righteous, their gods are unrighteous, since they transgressed the law in killing one another, and practicing sorcery, and committing adultery, and in robbing and stealing, and in lying with males, and by their other practices as well. [24] For if their gods were right in doing all these things as they are described, then the laws of the Greeks are unrighteous in not being made according to the will of their gods. [25] And in that case the whole world is gone astray. [26] For the narratives about their gods are some of them myths, and some of them nature-poems, and some of them hymns and elegies. [27] The hymns indeed and elegies are empty words and noise. [28] But these nature-poems, even if they are made as they say, still those are not gods who do such things and suffer and endure such things. [29] And those myths are shallow tales with no depth whatever in them.

CHAPTER 14

[1] Let us come now, O King, to the history of the Jews also, and see what opinion they have as to God. [2] The Jews then say that God is one, the Creator of all, and omnipotent; [3] and that it is not right that any other should be worshiped except this God alone. [4] And herein they appear to approach the truth more than all the nations, especially in that they worship God and not His works. [5] And they imitate God by the philanthropy which prevails among them; [6] for they have compassion on the poor, and they release the captives, and bury the dead, and do such things as these, which are acceptable before God and well-pleasing also to men, [7] which they have received from their forefathers. [8] Nevertheless, they too erred from true knowledge. [9] And in their imagination, they conceive that it is God they serve; [10] whereas by their mode of observance it is to the messengers and not to God that their service is rendered— [11] as when they celebrate Sabbaths and the beginning of the months, and feasts of unleavened bread, and a great fast; [12] and fasting, and circumcision, and the purification of

meats, which things, however, they do not observe perfectly.

CHAPTER 15

[1] But the Christians, O King, while they went around and made search, have found the truth; [2] and as we learned from their writings, they have come nearer to truth and genuine knowledge than the rest of the nations. [3] For they know and trust in God, the Creator of Heaven and of earth, in whom and from whom are all things, to whom there is no other god as companion, [4] from whom they received commands which they engraved on their minds and observe in hope and expectation of the world which is to come. [5] For what reason they do not commit adultery nor fornication, nor bear false witness, nor embezzle what is held in pledge, nor covet what is not theirs. [6] They honor father and mother, and show kindness to those near to them; and whenever they are judges, they judge uprightly. [7] They do not worship idols in the image of man; [8] and whatever they would not that others should do to them, they do not do to others; [9] and of the food which is consecrated to idols they do not eat, for they are pure. [10] And their oppressors they comfort and make them their friends; they do good to their enemies; [11] and their women, O King, are pure as virgins, and their daughters are modest; [12] and their men keep themselves from every unlawful union and from all uncleanness, in the hope of a reward to come in the other world. [13] Further, if one or other of them have bondmen and bondwomen, or children, through love toward them they persuade them to become Christians, [14] and when they have done so, they call them brothers without distinction. [15] They do not worship strange gods, and they go their way in all modesty and cheerfulness. [16] Falsehood is not found among them; and they love one another, and from widows they do not turn away their esteem; [17] and they deliver the orphan from him who treats him harshly. [18] And he who has, gives to him who does not have, without boasting. [19] And when they see a stranger, they take him into their homes and rejoice over him as a very brother; [20] for they do not call them brothers after the flesh, but brothers after the spirit and in God. [21] And whenever one of their poor passes from the world, each one of them according to his ability gives heed to him and carefully sees to his burial. [22] And if they hear that one of their number is imprisoned or afflicted on account of the name of their Messiah, all of them anxiously minister to his necessity, and if it is possible to redeem him they set him free. [23] And if there is among them any that is poor and needy, and if they have no spare food, they fast two or three days in order to supply to the needy their lack of food. [24] They observe the precepts of their Messiah with much care, living justly and soberly as the LORD their God commanded them. [25] Every morning and every hour they give thanks and praise

to God for His loving-kindnesses toward them; [26] and for their food and their drink they offer thanksgiving to Him. [27] And if any righteous man among them passes from the world, they rejoice and offer thanks to God; and they escort his body as if he were setting out from one place to another near. [28] And when a child has been born to one of them, they give thanks to God; [29] and if moreover it happens to die in childhood, they give thanks to God the more, as for one who has passed through the world without sins. [30] And further if they see that any one of them dies in his ungodliness or in his sins, for him they grieve bitterly, and sorrow as for one who goes to meet his doom.

CHAPTER 16

[1] Such, O King, is the command of the law of the Christians, and such is their manner of life. [2] As men who know God, they ask from Him petitions which are fitting for Him to grant and for them to receive. [3] And thus they employ their whole lifetime. [4] And since they know the loving-kindnesses of God toward them, behold, for their sake the glorious things which are in the world flow forth to view. [5] And truly, they are those who found the truth when they went around and made search for it; [6] and from what we considered, we learned that they alone come near to a knowledge of the truth. [7] And they do not proclaim in the ears of the multitude the kind deeds they do, but are careful that no one should notice them; [8] and they conceal their giving just as he who finds a treasure and conceals it. [9] And they strive to be righteous as those who expect to behold their Messiah, and to receive from Him with great glory the promises made concerning them. [10] And as for their words and their precepts, O King, and their glorying in their worship, and the hope of earning according to the work of each one of them their reward which they look for in another world, you may learn about these from their writings. [11] It is enough for us to have shortly informed your Majesty concerning the conduct and the truth of the Christians. [12] For great indeed, and wonderful, is their doctrine to him who will search into it and reflect on it. [13] And truly, this is a new people, and there is a divine admixture in the midst of them. [14] Take, then, their writings, and read therein, and behold, you will find that I have not put forth these things on my own authority, nor spoken thus as their advocate; [15] but since I read in their writings I was fully assured of these things as also of things which are to come. [16] And for this reason I was constrained to declare the truth to such as care for it and seek the world to come. [17] And to me there is no doubt but that the earth abides through the supplication of the Christians. [18] But the rest of the nations err and cause error in wallowing before the elements of the world, since beyond these their mental vision will not pass. [19] And they search about as if in darkness because they will not recognize the truth; [20] and like drunken men they reel and jostle one another and fall.

CHAPTER 17

[1] Thus far, O King, I have spoken; [2] for concerning that which remains, as is said above, there are found in their other writings things which are hard to utter and difficult for one to narrate, [3] which are not only spoken in words but also worked out in deeds. [4] Now the Greeks, O King, as they follow base practices in intercourse with males, and a mother and a sister and a daughter, impute their monstrous impurity in turn to the Christians. [5] But the Christians are just and good, and the truth is set before their eyes, and their spirit is long-suffering; [6] and, therefore, though they know the error of these [(the Greeks)], and are persecuted by them, they bear and endure it; [7] and for the most part they have compassion on them, as men who are destitute of knowledge. [8] And on their side, they offer prayer that these may convert from their error; [9] and when it happens that one of them has converted, he is ashamed before the Christians of the works which were done by him; [10] and he makes confession to God, saying, "I did these things in ignorance." [11] And he purifies his heart, and his sins are forgiven him, [12] because he committed them in ignorance in the former time, when he used to blaspheme and speak evil of the true knowledge of the Christians. [13] And assuredly the race of the Christians is more blessed than all the men who are on the face of the earth. [14] From now on let the tongues of those who utter vanity and harass the Christians be silent; [15] and hereafter let them speak the truth. [16] For it is of serious consequence to them that they should worship the true God rather than worship a senseless sound. [17] And truly whatever is spoken in the mouth of the Christians is of God; and their doctrine is the gateway of light. [18] For what reason let all who are without the knowledge of God draw near to that; [19] and they will receive incorruptible words, which are from all time and forever. [20] So they will appear before the awful judgment which through Jesus the Messiah is destined to come on the whole human race.

· THE END OF THE APOCRYPHA ·

APOCRYPHAL FRAGMENTS

This collection consists of fragments copied from source material thought to have been composed very early (first and second centuries). Heretical, demonstrably Gnostic, or widely-disputed fragments are not included. Section 1 is a translation of what remains of a five-volume work by Papias of Hierapolis, who may have had access to eyewitness disciples and those who knew the Apostles of the Lord. It is thought that these volumes were composed sometime around 100 AD. Irenaeus says of him: "Now testimony is borne to these things in writing by Papias, an ancient man, who was a hearer of John, and a friend of Polycarp, in the fourth of his books; for five books were composed by him." Section 2 is a short fragment remaining from Quadratus, who, like Aristides, addressed Hadrian. Section 3 is a translation of two fragments from an unknown Gospel—called "Egerton"—that was probably composed in the middle of the 2nd century at the latest. Section 4 translates the Oxyrhynchus 840 and 1224 fragments of an ancient Gospel (or Gospels) that were composed as early as the second half of the 1st century. Section 5 is a translation of the Muratorian Fragment, the oldest surviving list of the New Testament canon, which is thought to have been composed around 170 AD. The Muratorian Canon lists all of the current twenty-seven books of the New Testament, minus Hebrews, James, and both Epistles of Peter. The fragment is damaged where Matthew and Mark are listed, but their inclusion is beyond dispute. The Revelation of Peter and Wisdom are included, although Peter's Apocalypse is disputed by the author. Finally, Section 6 is the oldest, extant, primordial form of the Christian creeds, likely predating the Apostles' Creed and Old Roman Symbol. It is taken from the tenth chapter of Irenaeus' first volume of *Against Heresies*, and is dated as early as 174 AD. This Rule of Faith is probably derived from older material.

SECTION 1:
EXPOSITION OF THE ORACLES OF THE LORD

FRAGMENT 1

[1] But I will not be unwilling to put down, along with my interpretations, [2] whatever instructions I received with care at any time from the elders, [3] and stored up with care in my memory, assuring you at the same time of their truth. [4] For I did not, like the multitude, take pleasure in those who spoke much, [5] but in those who taught the truth; [6] nor in those who related strange commands, [7] but in those who rehearsed the commands given by the LORD to faith, and proceeding from truth itself. [8] If then, anyone who had attended on the elders came, [9] I asked minutely after their sayings—what Andrew or Peter said, or what was said by Philip, or by Thomas, or by James, or by John, or by Matthew, or by any other of the LORD's disciples: [10] which things Aristion and the elder John, the disciples of the LORD, say. [11] For I imagined that what was to be gotten from scrolls was not so profitable to me as what came from the living and abiding voice.

FRAGMENT 2

[1] [The early Christians] called those who practiced a godly guilelessness, "children."

FRAGMENT 3

[1] Judas walked about in this world a sad example of impiety; [2] for his body having swollen to such an extent that he could not pass where a chariot could pass easily, [3] he was crushed by the chariot, so that his bowels gushed out.

FRAGMENT 4

[1] [The LORD taught]: "The days will come in which vines will grow, having each ten thousand branches, and in each branch ten thousand twigs, and in each true twig ten thousand shoots, [2] and in each of the shoots ten thousand clusters, and on each of the clusters ten thousand grapes, [3] and every grape when pressed will give twenty-five metretes of wine. [4] And when any one of the holy ones will lay hold of a cluster, another will cry out, I am a better cluster, take me; bless the LORD through me." [5] In like manner, [He said] that "a grain of wheat would produce ten thousand ears, and that every ear would have ten thousand grains, [6] and every grain would yield ten pounds of clear, pure, fine flour; [7] and that apples, and seeds, and grass would produce in similar proportions; [8] and that all animals, feeding then only on the productions of the earth, [9] would become peaceable and harmonious, and be in perfect subjection to man." [10] . . . "Now these things are credible to believers." [11] And Judas the traitor, not believing, and asking, "How will such growths be accomplished by the LORD?" [12] The LORD said, "They will see who will come to them."

FRAGMENT 5

[1] As the elders say, then those who are deemed worthy of an abode in Heaven will go there, [2] others will enjoy the delights of Paradise, [3] and others will possess the splendor of the city; [4] for everywhere the Savior will be seen, according as they will be worthy

APOCRYPHAL FRAGMENTS

who see Him. [5]But that there is this distinction between the habitation of those who produce a hundredfold, and that of those who produce sixty-fold, and that of those who produce thirty-fold; [6]for the first will be taken up into the heavens, the second class will dwell in Paradise, and the last will inhabit the city; [7]and that on this account the LORD said, "In My Father's house are many rooms." [8]For all things belong to God, who supplies all with a suitable dwelling-place, [9]even as His word says, that a share is given to all by the Father, according as each one is or will be worthy. [10]And this is the couch in which they will recline who feast, being invited to the wedding. [11]The elders, the disciples of the apostles, say that this is the gradation and arrangement of those who are saved, [12]and that they advance through steps of this nature; [13]and that, moreover, they ascend through the Spirit to the Son, and through the Son to the Father; [14]and that in due time the Son will yield up His work to the Father, [15]even as it is said by the apostle, "For He must reign until He has put all enemies under His feet. [16]The last enemy that will be destroyed is death." For in the times of the kingdom the just man who is on the earth will forget to die. [17]"But when He says all things are put under Him, it is manifest that He is excepted which did put all things under Him. [18]And when all things will be subdued to Him, then will the Son also Himself be subject to Him that put all things under Him, that God may be all in all."

FRAGMENT 6

[1]And the elder said this. [2]Mark having become the interpreter of Peter, wrote down accurately whatever he remembered. [3]It was not, however, in exact order that he related the sayings or deeds of Christ. [4]For he neither heard the LORD nor accompanied Him. [5]But afterward, as I said, he accompanied Peter, who accommodated his instructions to the necessities [of his hearers], [6]but with no intention of giving a regular narrative of the LORD's sayings. [7]For what reason Mark made no mistake in thus writing some things as he remembered them. [8]For of one thing he took special care, not to omit anything he had heard, and not to put anything fictitious into the statements. [9]. . . Matthew put together the oracles [of the LORD] in the Hebrew language, [10]and each one interpreted them as best he could.

FRAGMENT 7

[1]To some of them [(messengers)] He gave dominion over the arrangement of the world, and He commissioned them to exercise their dominion well, [2]but it happened that their arrangement came to nothing.

SECTION 2:
APOLOGY FOR CHRISTIANITY

FRAGMENT 1

[1]But the works of our Savior were always present, for they were genuine: [2]those that were healed, and those that were raised from the dead, who were seen not only when they were healed and when they were raised, but were also always present; [3]and not merely while the Savior was on earth, but also after His death, they were alive for quite a while, so that some of them lived even to our day.

SECTION 3:
THE UNKNOWN GOSPEL

FRAGMENT 1

[1]. . . [And Jesus said] to the lawyers, "[Punish] every wrongdoer and transgressor, and not Me"; [2]. . . And turning to the rulers of the people He spoke this, saying, [3]"Search the Writings, in which you think that you have life; [4]these are they which bear witness of Me. [5]Do not think that I came to accuse you to My Father; there is one that accuses you, even Moses, on whom you have set your hope." [6]And when they said, "We know well that God spoke to Moses, but as for You, we do not know from where You are," [7]Jesus answered and said to them, "Now is your unbelief accused . . ." [8][They gave counsel to] the multitude to [gather] stones together and stone Him. [9]And the rulers sought to lay their hands on Him that they might take Him and [hand Him over] to the multitude; [10]and they could not take Him, because the hour of His betrayal was not yet come. [11]But He Himself, even the LORD, going out through the midst of them, departed from them. [12]And behold, there comes to Him a leper and says, "Master Jesus, journeying with lepers and eating with them in the inn I myself also became a leper. [13]If, therefore, you will, I am made clean." [14]The LORD then said to him, "I will; be made clean." [15]And immediately the leprosy departed from him. [16][And the LORD said to him], "Go, [show yourself] to the [priests] . . ."

FRAGMENT 2

[1]. . . coming to Him began to tempt Him with a question, saying, "Master Jesus, we know that You have come from God, for the things which You testify above all the prophets. [2]Tell us therefore: Is it lawful [to render] to kings that which pertains to their rule? [3][Will we render to them], or not?" [4]But Jesus, knowing their thought, being moved with indignation, said to them, "Why do you call Me Master with your mouth, when you do not hear what I say? [5]Well did Isaiah prophesy of you, saying, This people honors Me with their lips, but their heart is far from Me. [6]In vain do they worship Me, [teaching as their doctrines the] precepts [of men] . . ." [7]". . . shut

APOCRYPHAL FRAGMENTS

up . . . in . . . place . . . its weight unweighed?" ⁸ And when they were perplexed at His strange question, Jesus, as He walked, stood still on the edge of the River Jordan, ⁹ and stretching forth His right hand, He [filled it with water] and sprinkled it on the . . . ¹⁰ And then . . . water that had been sprinkled . . . before them and sent forth fruit . . .

SECTION 4:
THE OXYRHYNCHUS GOSPELS

FRAGMENT 1

¹ ". . . before he does wrong makes all manner of subtle excuse. ² But give heed lest you also suffer the same things as they; ³ for the evildoers among men do not receive their reward among the living only, ⁴ but also await punishment and much torment." ⁵ And He took them and brought them into the very place of purification, and was walking in the temple. ⁶ And a certain Pharisee, a chief priest, whose name was Levi, met them and said to the Savior, "Who gave You leave to walk in this place of purification and to see these holy vessels, ⁷ when You have not washed nor yet have Your disciples bathed their feet? ⁸ But You have walked in this temple defiled, which is a pure place, ⁹ wherein no other man walks except he has washed himself and changed his garments, neither does he venture to see these holy vessels." ¹⁰ And the Savior immediately stood still with His disciples and answered him, "Are you then, being here in the temple, clean?" ¹¹ He says to Him, "I am clean; for I washed in the pool of David, and having descended by one staircase I ascended by another, ¹² and I put on white and clean garments, and then I came and looked on these holy vessels." ¹³ The Savior answered and said to him, "Woe you blind, who see not. ¹⁴ You have washed in these running waters wherein dogs and swine have been cast night and day, ¹⁵ and have cleansed and wiped the outside skin which also the harlots and flute-girls anoint and wash and wipe and beautify for the lust of men; ¹⁶ but within they are full of scorpions and all wickedness. ¹⁷ But My disciples and I, who you say have not bathed, have been dipped in the waters of continuous life which come from . . . ¹⁸ but woe to the . . ."

FRAGMENT 2

¹ "It weighed me down." ² Then Jesus approached in a vision and said, "Why are you discouraged? For not . . . you, but the . . ." ³ ". . . You said, although You are not answering. ⁴ What then did You renounce? What is the new doctrine that they say You teach, ⁵ or what is the new immersion that You proclaim? ⁶ Answer and . . ." ⁷ When the scribes and Pharisees and priests saw Him, they were angry that He was reclining in the midst of sinners. ⁸ But when Jesus heard, He said, "Those who are healthy have no need of a physician . . ." ⁹ ". . . and pray for your enemies.

For the one who is not against you is for you. ¹⁰ The one who is far away today, tomorrow will be near you and in . . ." ¹¹ ". . . the adversary . . ."

SECTION 5:
THE MURATORIAN CANON

FRAGMENT 1

¹ ". . . at which nevertheless he was present, and so he placed [them in his narrative]. ² The third scroll of the Gospel is that according to Luke. ³ Luke, the well-known physician, after the ascension of Christ, when Paul had taken with him as one zealous for the law, composed it in his own name, according to [the general] belief. ⁴ Yet he himself had not seen the LORD in the flesh; and therefore, as he was able to ascertain events, so indeed he begins to tell the story from the birth of John. ⁵ The fourth of the Gospels is that of John, [one] of the disciples. ⁶ To his fellow disciples and overseers, who had been urging him [to write], he said, "Fast with me from today to three days, and what will be revealed to each one let us tell it to one another." ⁷ In the same night it was revealed to Andrew, [one] of the apostles, that John should write down all things in his own name while all of them should review it. ⁸ And so, though various elements may be taught in the individual scrolls of the Gospels, nevertheless this makes no difference to the faith of believers, ⁹ since by the one sovereign Spirit all things have been declared in all [the Gospels]: ¹⁰ concerning the nativity, concerning the passion, concerning the resurrection, concerning life with His disciples, and concerning His twofold coming; ¹¹ the first in lowliness when He was despised, which has taken place, the second glorious in royal power, which is still in the future. ¹² What marvel is it then, if John so consistently mentions these particular points also in his Epistles, ¹³ saying about himself, "What we have seen with our eyes and heard with our ears and our hands have handled, these things we have written to you"? ¹⁴ For in this way he professes [himself] to be not only an eyewitness and hearer, but also a writer of all the marvelous deeds of the LORD, in their order. ¹⁵ Moreover, the Acts of all the Apostles were written in one scroll. ¹⁶ For "most excellent Theophilus" Luke compiled the individual events that took place in his presence— ¹⁷ as he plainly shows by omitting the martyrdom of Peter as well as the departure of Paul from the city [of Rome] when he journeyed to Spain. ¹⁸ As for the Epistles of Paul, they themselves make clear to those desiring to understand, which ones [they are], from what place, or for what reason they were sent. ¹⁹ First of all, to the Corinthians, prohibiting their heretical schisms; ²⁰ next, to the Galatians, against circumcision; ²¹ then to the Romans he wrote at length, explaining the order [[or plan]] of the Writings, and also that Christ is their principle. ²² It is necessary for us to discuss these one by one,

since the blessed apostle Paul himself, following the example of his predecessor John, writes by name to only seven assemblies in the following sequence: [23] To the Corinthians first, to the Ephesians second, to the Philippians third, to the Colossians fourth, to the Galatians fifth, to the Thessalonians sixth, to the Romans seventh. [24] It is true that he writes once more to the Corinthians and to the Thessalonians for the sake of admonition, [25] yet it is clearly recognizable that there is one Assembly spread throughout the whole extent of the earth. [26] For John also in the Revelation, though he writes to seven assemblies, nevertheless speaks to all. [27] [Paul also wrote] out of affection and love one to Philemon, one to Titus, and two to Timothy; [28] and these are held sacred in the esteem of the Assembly universal for the regulation of ecclesiastical discipline. [29] There is current also [an epistle] to the Laodiceans, [and] another to the Alexandrians, [both] forged in Paul's name to [further] the heresy of Marcion, [30] and several others which cannot be received into the universal Assembly—for it is not fitting that gall be mixed with honey. [31] Moreover, the epistle of Jude and two of the above-mentioned [[or bearing the name of]] John are counted [[or used]] in the universal [Assembly]; [32] and Wisdom, written by the friends of Solomon in his honor. [33] We receive only the revelations of John and Peter, though some of us are not willing that the latter be read in an assembly. [34] But Hermas wrote the Shepherd very recently, in our times, in the city of Rome, while overseer Pius, his brother, was occupying the chair of the assembly of the city of Rome. [35] And therefore it should indeed be read; but it cannot be read publicly to the people in an assembly either among the prophets, whose number is complete, or among the apostles, for it is after [their] time. [36] But we accept nothing whatever of Arsinous or Valentinus or Miltiades, who also composed a new scroll of psalms for Marcion, together with Basilides, the Asian founder of the Cataphrygians . . .

SECTION 6:
THE RULE OF FAITH

FRAGMENT 1

[1] The Assembly, though dispersed throughout the whole world, even to the ends of the earth, has received from the apostles and their disciples this faith [2] in one God, the Father Almighty, Maker of Heaven, and earth, and the sea, and all things that are in them; [3] and in one Christ Jesus, the Son of God, who became incarnate for our salvation; [4] and in the Holy Spirit, who proclaimed through the prophets the dispensations of God, and the advents, [5] and the birth from a virgin, and the passion, and the resurrection from the dead, and the ascension into Heaven in the flesh of the beloved Christ Jesus, our Lord, [6] and His [future] manifestation from Heaven in the glory of the Father "to gather all things in one," and to raise up anew all flesh of the whole human race, [7] in order that to Christ Jesus, our Lord, and God, and Savior, and King, according to the will of the invisible Father, [8] "every knee should bow, of things in Heaven, and things in earth, and things under the earth, and that every tongue should confess" to Him, [9] and that He should execute just judgment toward all; [10] that He may send "spiritual wickednesses," and the messengers who transgressed and became defectors, together with the ungodly, and unrighteous, and wicked, and profane among men, into continuous fire; [11] but may, in the exercise of His grace, confer immortality on the righteous and holy, and those who have kept His commands, and have persevered in His love, [12] some from the beginning, and others from their conversion, [13] and may surround them with continuous glory.

COVENANT OF THE CCC

WE BELIEVE in One God, revealed to the world as YHWH of Israel,
Uncreated, self-existent, eternal, all-powerful, and unchanging.
He knows all things and there is nowhere where He is not.
He is good, His word is inerrant, and His nature is love.

WE BELIEVE God subsists as the mutual indwelling of three persons:
The Father, the Son, and the Holy Spirit, in eternal communion.
God the Son and God the Holy Spirit come from God the Father,
And throughout eternity they have always existed with the Father.

WE BELIEVE God created time, space, matter, and all things,
Accomplishing His initial act of creation in only six days.
On the sixth day God created Man in His own image out of dust,
Adam the first male and Eve the first female.

WE BELIEVE God said the man should be joined to his wife,
And in so doing the two would become one flesh in marriage.
In diversity He created the marital union sacred, monogamous,
And dissoluble only by death or unfaithfulness.

WE BELIEVE God gave Man the choice of obedience or rebellion,
And Adam and Eve willfully rebelled by eating the forbidden fruit,
Which came from the Tree of the Knowledge of Good and Evil.
They suffered spiritual death and passed their sin nature on to us.

WE BELIEVE that God justly judged the world with a flood,
Sparing Noah and his family through whom came the nations.
And from Noah's son Shem came Abraham, Isaac, and Jacob,
And from Jacob the twelve tribes of Israel and the prophets.

WE BELIEVE that in the fullness of time God gave us His Son,
Born under the law to redeem those condemned by the law.
He was born in the town of Bethlehem to a virgin named Mary,
And in accordance with God's command was named Jesus.

WE BELIEVE Jesus was chosen before the creation of the world,
To live a sinless human life in perfect obedience to the Father,
That He might die a substitutionary death in place of sinners,
Giving forgiveness of sins and eternal life to all who trust in Him.

WE BELIEVE Jesus freely gave His life in obedience to the Father,
  And at the order of Pontius Pilate was flogged and crucified.
At the ninth hour He declared His purpose in death was finished,
And He died and was buried in the tomb of Joseph of Arimathea.

  WE BELIEVE that death had no power over God's perfect Son,
  And on the third day He conquered death by rising to life again.
This was literal, physical, and attested to by over 500 witnesses,
  And is the event that gives power and validation to our faith.

WE BELIEVE men are only reconciled to God through Jesus Christ,
  And receive salvation by grace through faith apart from works.
By the Spirit all believers are baptized into one body, the Church.
  Christians baptize, share communion, and love one another.

  WE BELIEVE the Church is a universal priesthood of believers.
  Membership is not obtained by belonging to a denomination,
  But is received by trusting in Jesus for the forgiveness of sins.
The Church awaits Jesus' soon return when He will call us home.

CONVICTIONS OF THE CCC

1. THERE IS ONE GOD WHO IS ETERNAL, SELF-EXISTENT, ALL-POWERFUL, ALL-KNOWING, EVERYWHERE-PRESENT, COMPLETELY GOOD, AND NEVER CHANGING. GOD IS PERFECT IN MORAL CHARACTER AND HIS NATURE IS LOVE. GOD ALONE CAN DECLARE WHETHER CONDUCT IS RIGHT OR WRONG.

Scripture References: Deuteronomy 6:4, Isaiah 44:8, Psalm 90:2, Isaiah 40:28, Exodus 3:14, Revelation 19:6, Psalm 147:5, 1 John 3:20, Psalm 139:7–8, Jeremiah 23:24, Psalm 119:68, James 1:17, Hebrews 13:8, 1 John 4:8, Judges 21:25, Isaiah 45:19

2. GOD SUBSISTS ETERNALLY IN THREE PERSONS: THE FATHER, THE SON, AND THE HOLY SPIRIT. THESE THREE ARE NEITHER PARTS NOR MODES.

Scripture References: Matthew 28:19, Luke 1:35, 3:21–22, John 1:1–2, 10:30, 14:16, 2 Corinthians 13:14, 1 Peter 1:2; see also Genesis 1:26, 3:22, 11:7

3. THE BIBLE IS A COMPILATION OF GOD'S WORDS AND IN ITS ORIGINAL HEBREW, GREEK, AND ARAMAIC FORM IS INERRANT AND SUFFICIENT IN ITSELF FOR TEACHING CHRISTIAN BELIEF AND PRACTICE. IT SHOULD BE INTERPRETED LITERALLY, HISTORICALLY, AND AT FACE VALUE UNLESS THE TEXT ITSELF ALLOWS FOR A DIFFERENT INTERPRETATION IN A SPECIFIC PASSAGE.

Scripture References: Exodus 20:11, Matthew 5:18, 19:4–6, 24:37–39, John 10:35, Acts 1:16, Romans 15:4, 2 Timothy 3:16, 2 Peter 1:20–21, 3:15–16, 2 Thessalonians 2:14–15, Revelation 22:18–19; see also Genesis 41:25–27, Matthew 13:18–23, 13:36–43, Revelation 1:20

4. MANKIND WAS GIVEN THE FREE CHOICE TO OBEY GOD OR REBEL AGAINST HIM IN THE GARDEN OF EDEN AND FREELY CHOSE TO REBEL BY EATING THE FORBIDDEN FRUIT FROM THE TREE OF THE KNOWLEDGE OF GOOD AND EVIL. THIS CHOICE BROUGHT DEATH, SEPARATION FROM GOD, AND A SINFUL NATURE TO THE ENTIRE HUMAN RACE.

Scripture References: Genesis 2:16–17, 3, 6:5, Isaiah 59:1–2, Romans 3:23, 5:12–18, 6:23, 1 Corinthians 15:22

5. GOD PLANNED IN ADVANCE TO SEND HIS SON INTO THE WORLD TO DIE FOR THE SINS OF MANKIND. THIS PLAN INCLUDED THE COVENANT OF BLESSING WITH ABRAHAM AND THE INSTITUTION OF THE NATION OF ISRAEL AND WAS FORESHADOWED BY THE SYSTEM OF ATONING SACRIFICES IN THE LEVITICAL LAW.

Scripture References: Genesis 22:17–18, Isaiah 53, Jeremiah 1:5, Luke 24:27, John 5:39, Acts 8:30–35, Colossians 2:17, Hebrews 10:1–23, Revelation 13:8

6. GOD BECAME MAN IN THE PERSON OF JESUS CHRIST. JESUS LIVED A SINLESS AND MORALLY PERFECT LIFE. HE WAS CRUCIFIED AT THE HANDS OF THE ROMANS AND THROUGH DEATH HE ATONED FOR THE SINS OF MANKIND. HE WAS BURIED AND ON THE THIRD DAY ROSE PHYSICALLY FROM THE DEAD, CONQUERING DEATH AND SIN. SALVATION IS FOUND IN CHRIST ALONE BY GRACE ALONE THROUGH FAITH ALONE AND NOT BY WORKS.

Scripture References: Isaiah 7:14, 9:6, Matthew 1:22–23, Luke 1:35, John 1:14, Philippians 2:6–8, Colossians 1:15, 1 John 4:2, Isaiah 53:9, John 19:4, 2 Corinthians 5:21, 1 Peter 1:18–19, 2:22, Hebrews 4:15, 1 John 3:5, Mark 15:43–47, Matthew 28:1–15, Romans 6:4, 8:11, 1 Corinthians 15:1–32, 1 Peter 1:3, Ephesians 2:8–9

7. JESUS PROMISED THAT IN ACCORDANCE WITH THE SCRIPTURES HE WOULD PHYSICALLY RETURN TO EARTH TO RESCUE HIS CHURCH, PUT AN END TO SIN, AND REIGN AS KING OVER ISRAEL AND THE WHOLE EARTH. BY HIM THE LIVING AND THE DEAD WILL BE JUDGED, SOME INHERITING ETERNAL LIFE AND OTHERS RECEIVING ETERNAL PUNISHMENT. CHRISTIANS MUST BE WATCHFUL AND READY FOR THESE EVENTS.

Scripture References: Psalms 72:8–11, Daniel 2:44, 7:13–14, Ezekiel 33:1–6, Zechariah 14:1–9, Matthew 16:27, 24:37–44, 25:1–13, 25:46, Luke 12:37–40, 17:28–30, 18:8, 21:34–36, John 5:22, 14:3, Romans 2:16, 1 Corinthians 15:52, 1 Thessalonians 4:13–18, Revelation 1:7, 11:15, 20:4–6

POSITIONS OF THE CCC

All believers and associated denominations are strongly exhorted to hold fast to these positions regardless of familial, cultural, or political pressure, recognizing that believing in and practicing biblical morality is strong evidence of one's saving faith.

Abortion is without question the murder of a child made in God's image. It should not be permitted even in the case of rape or incest as the child is innocent of any perpetrator's crime. The commission of the terrible evil of rape or incest can never justify the terrible evil of murder. In exceptional cases a mother's life may be jeopardized by pregnancy and only in this exceptional case does the CCC not take an absolute position. However, the mark of a Christian is love and sacrifice and the exemplary mother will put her child's life before her own, trusting that God will be faithful in the midst of tragic circumstances.

Adultery is intrinsically evil and never permissible under any circumstances, not only the physical act of adultery (Ex. 20:14), but also adulterous thoughts (Mt. 5:27–28).

Alcohol consumption is permissible and is in fact encouraged in some Scriptures (1 Tim. 5:23; Eccl. 9:7), but moderation is necessary. Intoxication and drunkenness are not permissible (Eph. 5:18; 1 Cor. 6:10). The Christian should never drink so much that he or she loses cognitive control and the ability to maintain a Christlike demeanor (Prov. 20:1; Prov. 23:29–35).

Anti-Semitism, a form of racism, should never be found in the thoughts, words, writings, or actions of a believer. Gentile believers have not replaced Jewish believers and in fact salvation has come from the Jews. The Apostle Paul likens the entirety of the people of God to an olive tree, which is Israel. Unbelieving Jews have been cut off from the tree and believing Gentiles have been grafted in (Rom. 11:17–24), but the roots of the tree remain Jewish through Abraham, Isaac, Jacob, and the King of the Jews—Jesus. In fact, the Bible promises that one day the Jews will return to God and all Israel will be saved (Rom. 11:25–28; Isa. 45:17; Jer. 31:1). God gave to the descendants of Abraham through Isaac and Jacob a specific area of land that they still have yet to take full possession of according to the promise. Since God is the ultimate sovereign of the earth and His word is true and the land deed still stands, Christians cannot support efforts such as the two-state solution. The Bible proclaims that judgment will befall those who divide God's covenant land (Jl. 3:1–2).

Contraception is not mentioned in Scripture except in the case of Onan who sinned by preventing his wife from becoming pregnant in order to withhold from her dead husband an heir (Gen. 38:8–10). For this reason only contraception that may result in the death of an embryo or done against the will of one's spouse is forbidden. Christians should be wise about this and research diligently before engaging in intercourse with one's spouse. Drugs such as Plan B are never permissible, but even typical hormonal contraception drugs may result in abortion and their use is thus discouraged. Natural family planning is encouraged and in all cases the husband and wife should be one in heart and mind.

Divorce is inherently evil (Mk. 10:11–12), except in the case of marital unfaithfulness (Mt. 5:32). However, even in the case of adultery it is exemplary and most commendable to extend grace and forgiveness and ultimately reconcile with one's spouse recognizing that Christ died for us while we were yet sinners (Rom. 5:8) and God has reconciled us by the death of His Son (Rom. 5:10).

Embryonic stem cell research is never permissible because the embryos are in fact children in their earliest stage of development and therefore those who destroy embryos are murdering children made in the image of God. The Bible is clear that human life begins in the womb (Job 31:15; Ps. 22:10; 139:13; Jer. 1:5; Ex. 21:22–23) and science is clear that an organism's life begins at conception.

Eugenics in most forms should be understood as evil—especially historic eugenics programs that aimed at eradicating minority populations, killing the mentally handicapped, and murdering the terminally ill. Eugenics continues today in many forms including sex-selective abortions, minority-focused placement of abortion facilities, abortion of babies with trisomy disorders, and many instances of euthanasia. These are all intrinsically evil and Christians should themselves avoid these things while preaching forcefully against them.

Euthanasia, which is the intentional killing of a man or woman by both the perpetrator and the one being killed, is unquestionably murder and must not be committed or advocated by any believer.

Fornication, which is sexual activity outside of marriage, is always sinful (Mt. 15:19; 1 Cor. 6:9). God created sex to be enjoyed within the boundaries of marriage and within those boundaries there is great freedom for husband and wife. God created sex for building unity between husband and wife (Gen. 2:24, Mk. 10:8), for pleasure (1 Cor. 7:3–9; Prov. 5:18–19; Song 4:1–16), and for producing offspring (Gen. 1:28; 9:7; Mal. 2:15) and it is only in the context of marriage that these three purposes find their ultimate fulfillment. Men and women in a romantic relationship should not cohabitate before marriage, so that they avoid fornication and the appearance of evil (1 Thess. 5:22).

Gender roles are biblical and must be upheld in the Christian community. Men and women are equal before God in regard to intrinsic value and salvation (Gen. 1:27; Gal. 3:28), but nevertheless have been given by God specific callings. The man is the head of his family—not as a coercive force, but as a servant leader (1 Cor. 11:3). The man is called by God to protect and manage his family well (1 Tim. 3:4), love his wife, and even lay his life down for her (Eph. 5:25). In regard to church leadership, men are called to exercise authority over the congregation, both in teaching to the collective assembly (1 Cor. 14:34–35) and in shepherding (1 Tim. 2:8–3:13). Women are called to respect their husbands out of willful humility (1 Pet. 3:1) and to help and encourage them (Gen. 2:18). In the Christian community women are uniquely called to teach and disciple other women (Tit. 2:3–5).

Genetic manipulation of plants and animals without combining genes from different species is permissible although the Bible does not appear to speak to this issue. Wisdom should be exercised in regard to this issue. However, the creation of hybrid species is unadvisable since God created plants and animals after their own kind (Gen. 1:11, Gen. 1:24). The creation of human/animal hybrids, three-parent babies, or babies resulting from the genetic material of two men or two women are intrinsically evil acts and Christian geneticists should seriously and prayerfully consider the spiritual implications of these creations.

Homosexuality is repeatedly condemned in the Bible as a sin and an abomination (1 Tim. 1:9–10; 1 Cor. 6:9–10; Lev. 18:22; 20:13), as well as unnatural (Rom. 1:26–28). God created sexuality for the purpose of intimacy and pleasure between a husband and wife and ultimately for bringing children into the world. Christians who struggle with homosexuality should flee temptation by any means necessary and should not define themselves by their struggle (1 Cor. 6:11).

Homosexual marriage is intrinsically evil for two reasons: first, because homosexual acts are sinful and unnatural, and second, because it is diametrically opposed to God's design for marriage, which is repeatedly defined in the Bible as the union of one man and one woman (Gen. 2:24; Mt. 19:5; Mk. 10:7; Eph. 5:31).

In Vitro Fertilization is not permissible for the same reason embryonic stem cell research is not permissible: embryos are necessarily destroyed thus the act of murder is committed.

Marrying unbelievers is not permissible for the committed Christian (2 Cor. 6:14), though having already been married before coming to faith is a common occurrence. In such a case the believer must remain committed to their unbelieving spouse and through love and faithfulness attempt to win them over with the Gospel (1 Cor. 7:12–16; 1 Pet. 3:1).

Media must be monitored and controlled in the Christian life. There is no justification, artistic or otherwise, for Christians to watch or listen to sinful things for the purpose of entertainment. There is much media a believer can enjoy, but that which is full of cursing, wonton violence, or sexuality is never permissible. The martyr Telemachus stands as an eternal symbol of this truth.

Narcotic use for the express purpose of treating an injury or disease is permissible, but narcotic use for the purpose of intoxication is a great and destructive evil to oneself, to one's family, and to one's society. There is evidence that drug intoxication is partly what was intended when the Bible speaks of the sin of sorcery.

Pornography is never permissible in any form as it is a form of adultery, or in the case of the unmarried, fornication. Pornography also promotes the objectification and abuse of women and children, is by some measures more addictive than heroine, causes permanent emotional and physical desensitization, and even induces early puberty in children exposed from a young age.

Racism is not in accord with the character of Christ who has made all believers one (Gal. 3:28; Rom. 3:29) for God does not show partiality (Acts 10:34; Rom. 2:11). Believers must not favor the rich over the poor (Jas. 2:1–9), but must show equal favor to all in regard to wealth, station, fame, or race. However, culture has greatly twisted and abused the word *racism* by extending it to include areas where believers in fact should lovingly discriminate between right and wrong: regarding religion, culture, and sinful behaviors.

Slavery, including and especially sexual slavery and trafficking, is never tolerable. Modern slavery differs greatly from biblical indentured servitude, which in certain times and cultures was lawful, in that modern slavery is illegal, always abusive, and routinely violent and coercive. With more people enslaved today than at any time in history, Christians should advocate zealously for their freedom and protection.

Speech should be Christlike in every way and "seasoned with salt" (Col. 4:6). Lies, curses, crude joking, and malicious gossip should never proceed from the mouth of a believer (Mt. 12:36; Prov. 19:5; Tit. 3:2; Eph. 5:4; 1 Tim. 5:13).

Theft is an obvious and unquestionable sin and is not dependent on circumstance (Ex. 20:15). The poor may not steal from the rich even though the rich have more and the poor have less. Instead, the believer struggling with poverty should work diligently (2 Thess. 3:10), trusting in God to provide (Mt. 6:25–34), and making his or her needs known openly to the Christian community (Acts 2:44–45). Believers should not take anything unlawfully, including intellectual property, music, or media. Believers selling products or services that they know are scams or falsely advertised are committing theft as well as lying and should cease immediately (Prov. 11:1; 20:23), returning the money that was stolen.

Transgenderism is both sinful and a great deceit. Sinful in that it defies God's created order of male and female and deceitful in that it convinces a person that they can be something that they are not nor could ever be. Christians must refer to a man in masculine terms and a female in feminine terms regardless of how that person may define himself—even if this results in physical, emotional, or legal consequences for the believer. Men should strive for masculinity and women for femininity (1 Cor. 6:9; 16:13), fully embracing God's design.

The Covenant Christian Coalition is an international, evangelical, post-denominational coalition of churches still faithful to Christ and the Gospel.

You can learn more at www.ccc.one.

SOLA FIDE · SOLA GRATIA · SOLUS CHRISTUS · SOLA SCRIPTURA · SOLI DEO GLORIA